Cities Ranked & Rated

More Than 400 Metropolitan Areas Evaluated in the U.S. and Canada

1st Edition

Bert Sperling & Peter Sander

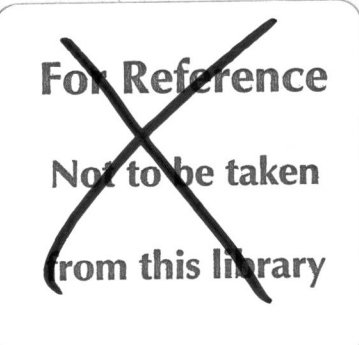

WILEY

Wiley Publishing, Inc.

Acknowledgments

First, I would like to recognize the Wiley team and particularly our editor, Lisa Torrance Duffy, whose wisdom and adroit guidance added incalculably to the success of this project. Others helped along the way, including Gerry King of Atlanta, Georgia; William Brown of the National Climatic Data Center in Asheville, North Carolina; and Paul Bartman of Richmond Hill, Ontario. Of course my family, wife Jennifer and boys Julian and Jonathan, contributed both inspiration and notable patience throughout. Finally, my parents Jerry and Betty Sander must be recognized for dispensing with the Disneyland trips in favor of adventurous land travels, bringing me the rich experience of 38 states before my 18th birthday.

—Peter Sander

My words fail to express all the support and insight that my wife, Gretchen, has provided with grace, understanding, and humor. She has been a steadfast partner in the 30 years of our venture to find the Best Places. Our two sons, Ted and Bertrand, were the perfect companions during our many trips to discover this great country and meet its residents. I've been very lucky to have Bertrand work by my side for the last 2 years, providing invaluable assistance for our studies and this book. Lastly, thanks go out to our team at John Wiley & Sons. Editor Lisa Torrance Duffy and publisher Mike Spring provided a clear vision, firm hand, and not the least, patience, in guiding this book to fruition. An author could not wish for a better publisher.

—Bert Sperling

Published by:

Wiley Publishing, Inc.

111 River St.
Hoboken, NJ 07030-5774

Editor: Lisa Torrance Duffy
Production Editor: Tammy Ahrens
Cartographer: Roberta Stockwell
Photo Editor: Richard Fox
Interior Designer: Marie Kristine Parial-Leonardo
Production by Wiley Indianapolis Composition Services

ISBN 0-7645-2562-X

For information on our other products and services or to obtain technical support, please contact our Customer Care Department within the U.S. at 800/762-2974, outside the U.S. at 317/572-3993 or fax 317/572-4002.

Wiley also publishes its books in a variety of electronic formats. Some content that appears in print may not be available in electronic formats.

Manufactured in the United States of America

5 4 3 2 1

Contents

Tables

Maps

About the Authors

Peter Sander is a professional author, researcher, and consultant in the fields of business and personal finance. He has written eight books including *Value Investing For Dummies*, *The Pocket Idiot's Guide to Living on a Budget*, *Everything Personal Finance*, and *Niche and Grow Rich*. His educational background includes an MBA in Logistics Management from Indiana University and a BA in Urban Affairs and Administration from Miami University of Ohio, and professional training and examination as a Certified Financial Planner (CFP™). His career includes 20 years as a marketing and logistics specialist for a major high-tech firm. Originally from Cincinnati, Ohio, and now living in Granite Bay, California, he has traveled in all 50 U.S. states.

Bert Sperling has been choosing our country's Best Places for 20 years. He created *Money* magazine's original "Best Places to Live" list, and his work continues to appear in the media on a monthly basis. His studies have become part of our national culture, appearing in *The Simpsons*, Jay Leno jokes, and questions on *Jeopardy*. His website, Sperling's BestPlaces (www.bestplaces.net), has become a popular Internet resource, and provides content to other sites such as Yahoo!, MSN, eBay, and the *Wall Street Journal*.

Annually, his "Healthiest Cities for Women" study is featured in *SELF* magazine. Other recent projects include "Best Places to Retire" *(MSN)*, "Best Cities for Women" *(Ladies' Home Journal)*, "Great College Towns" *(Newsweek)*, "This Town Rocks! Best Cities for Teens" *(Seventeen)*, "Best Places to Buy a Second Home" *(Smart Money)*, "Best Places to Raise an Outdoor Family" *(Outdoor Explorer)*, "Hot Dating in Small Towns (MTV), "America's Best City to Live" and "Most Energetic City" *(USA Weekend)* and features in *Men's Health, Men's Journal, Men's Fitness*, and *Kiplinger's*.

Bert currently makes his home in Portland and Depoe Bay, Oregon, after living in Kodiak (Alaska), Carmel Valley (California), Key West (Florida), San Diego (California), Brooklyn, Hempstead, and East Meadow (New York), Norfolk (Virginia), and Oslo, Norway.

An Invitation to the Reader

In this book, we've compiled many facts that provide insights into living and working in different metro areas. But there's much more to know, and we'd like your help. *You* are an expert in your own city or neighborhood. Please take some time to share your observations or experiences to let others know what it's like to live in your hometown. You can enter your information online at the *Cities Ranked & Rated* Web page at www.bestplaces.net/CRAR or at www.frommers.com, or you can write to:

Cities Ranked & Rated, 1st Edition
Wiley Publishing, Inc. • 111 River St. • Hoboken, NJ 07030-5774

Introduction

Whether the grass is greener or otherwise, people are naturally curious about places to live—including their own. Some may want to move if they can find a better place, while others must move and want to know more about what they are getting into. Still others just like to browse, perhaps looking for a city that suits their own long-term plan. Regardless of the reason, the sheer complexity of factors that makes one place better than another makes the evaluation rich and challenging.

Numerous characteristics, good and bad, determine what makes a city the *best* place to live. Living in a dream home in the suburbs of a large city might involve a 1½-hour commute to work or a high cost of living—or both. A more "ideal" place may be a bucolic burgh with tree-lined streets, a short walk to work, and affordable necessities, but the location could be a 1-hour airplane flight from a symphony or surgical hospital or even a good bookstore. Another place may be a beach paradise that comes with the downsides of crowds and standing in line to pay 30% more than the rest of the country for recreational activities. Rumors fly about places with lower taxes—maybe no income or sales tax at all. Real estate flyers show glowing photos of attractive, well-built homes on large, wooded lots in nice neighborhoods at apparent bargain prices. Some places have reputations for great nightlife, restaurants, theater, or activities for children.

But what is the truth in these stories? How do these cities really stack up against one another? And how can people weigh the pros and cons to determine the best fit for their chosen lifestyle and financial means? *Cities Ranked & Rated* is designed to answer these questions and help readers find their ideal place to live.

What Is *Cities Ranked & Rated?*

Put simply, *Cities Ranked & Rated* compares places to live. The book offers a rich set of comparative facts and figures on 403 North American cities—376 in the United States and 27 in Canada. Comparisons start with the facts, which are then blended with a subjective assessment of a place's image, character, and overall quality of life, to determine each city's rank in relation to the others.

This book is useful for the following:

- *Immediate voluntary (or involuntary) relocation.* Many are looking to relocate to somewhere better suited to their immediate needs, tastes, and financial means. Others make career-change or migration decisions based on job opportunities. A move may involve a lifestage change, such as graduation from college, marriage, arrival of children, or retirement. Statistically, by a slim margin, job or career issues are the number one reason cited for relocation. See the sidebar "Moving: The Reasons Why," at the end of this introduction, for more details.

- *Long-term planning.* This book can help to build a career, financial, or retirement plan that eventually results in a move to an ideal place. By studying and comparing places as they are today, readers can track what happens with those places as their plans unfold.

- *Business relocation/site selection.* Entrepreneurs are interested in the business and tax climates of different places, and want to go where other people are going and know why they're going there.

- *Curiosity and reference. Cities Ranked & Rated* provides statistics and analysis in an accessible package not available in one place anywhere else. People wanting to learn more about an area can use it as a reference.

Cities Ranked & Rated is not a "study." Many studies emerge from periodicals, universities, and other sources, usually on a small cross section of the "best places" theme. Examples include "Best Places to Retire" (MSN), "Best Places to Be Single" (forbes.com), and "Most Literate Cities" (University of Wisconsin-Whitewater). While these studies are usually high quality, and many use the same data used in this book, they are limited in scope, covering perhaps 40 or 50 different places, and rely on smaller sets of data. If you share common characteristics or interests with one of these groups, these articles give an interesting if less complete take on the "best place" question.

Cities Ranked & Rated is also not a travel guide. Travel books cover restaurants, lodging, and temporal points of interest and things to do in a place. While one may go out of their way while traveling to see an old Indian burial site or a place where Abraham Lincoln once slept, these features would not influence one's decision to *live* in a place.

What Makes a Best Place Best?

Particularly for those looking to relocate, *Cities Ranked & Rated* is a book about choices. If every U.S. citizen had the same "top city," in mind, there would be 290 million people living there, and it wouldn't be a "top city" any more. What makes the choice intriguing is that everyone has different goals, needs, aspirations, and interests. People are in different lifestages and desire different lifestyles. The choice is not *just* about lifestyle—otherwise most would choose to live in Beverly Hills or the Hamptons in Long Island—it is also about means, the financial considerations and prospects for those who live there.

Most people consider four broad categories when evaluating a place: economy, cost of living, climate, and character. Economy refers to the economic health and commercial character of a place. Cost of living is the relative cost of basic housing and necessities like food, utilities, and transportation as well as local tax burden. It may surprise some, but according to the U.S. Census, climate is far from the primary reason most people decide to relocate. But it probably does play a role in deciding *where* to relocate. Character, the broadest, most nebulous, and most personally unique category, includes an area's look and feel, activities, and services along with such negatives as crime and health problems.

The evaluation process of *Cities Ranked & Rated* relies on the following 10 categories to determine score and rank for each place:

Economy & Jobs	Crime
Cost of Living	Transportation
Climate	Leisure
Education	Arts & Culture
Health & Healthcare	Quality of Life

Chapter 3 includes an in-depth explanation of these categories and their components, and explains how each is built into the ranking process.

Data Sources

The facts used and compared in *Cities Ranked & Rated* come from an assortment of public and private sources widely used in demographic and market research. Much of the information is available for free—the hard part is knowing where to find it and how to assemble it into a practical and usable package.

As an example, the National Climatic Data Center (NCDC), a branch of the National Oceanic and Atmospheric Administration (NOAA) of the U.S. Department of Commerce, publishes vast amounts of climate and weather statistics, all available, and most of it online, for free. However, they include up to 70 years of monthly weather observations for 18,000 weather stations around the United States. *Cities Ranked & Rated* distills this ocean of detail into what's important to know for the 376 U.S. places in this book.

Among the major U.S. data sources are:

- U.S. Census Bureau for population and demographics, commute statistics, and commercial activity
- Bureau of Labor Statistics for economy, employment, and cost of living
- National Climatic Data Center for climate and weather

- Department of Education, National Center for Education Statistics for education
- Centers for Disease Control and Prevention for health
- Claritas, Inc., a private market data services provider

And among those used for Canada:

- Statistics Canada for population, demographics, economic, crime, and education
- Environment Canada for climate data

Additional data comes from published sources and from industry associations and trade groups. In discussing attributes, chapter 3 details specific data sources, which can also be found in Table 5.1.

Data Timeliness

Most of the data in this book is compiled from U.S. government and public agency sources. These agencies collect mountains of data, particularly from the decennial (every 10 years) U.S. Census. Follow-up surveys and projections are developed and posted by these agencies, but they often lag natural time due to the sheer volume of processing required to compile and present the date. While the U.S. Census updated population estimates for 2002 in mid-2003, studies from the 2000 census are still being compiled and published as this book is released. Is this a problem? Normally not. Large numbers don't normally change quickly. *Cities Ranked & Rated* makes every attempt to be as current as possible with information, and only information currently indicative of the attribute being discussed is presented.

Online Research

Bert Sperling, one of the co-creators of this book, has been analyzing livable cities for over 20 years, and is responsible for many of the best-known studies and articles on the subject. His website, Sperling's BestPlaces (www.bestplaces.net), features thousands of city and neighborhood profiles, and tools that allow users to compare places head-to-head and to find their own best place using personal criteria and weightings. The page www.bestplaces.net/CRAR includes additional data not included in *Cities Ranked & Rated* and can be used as a companion tool for the book.

In addition to bestplaces.net, readers may have already discovered numerous other online sources. They may also have discovered that online content can be inconsistent and overly "salesy" at times. That said, the following types of websites can be helpful when researching a place:

- *City website.* Most cities and towns have their own site. These are largely administrative in nature, with information on garbage collection, road closures, and other mostly irrelevant topics, but some of the better ones have sections describing the city, its history, its infrastructure, and awards they may have received in other rating studies. In some cases, better sites are found at the county level.

- *Chamber of Commerce.* Most places we examine have a chamber of commerce with their own website. The goal and orientation of these organizations is to attract business and commerce to an area. Some are loaded with sales hype but few facts, and some concentrate on industrial parks and other potential business locations in the area.

- *Convention and Visitors Bureau.* Most larger cities have a convention and visitors bureau oriented to attracting events and meetings. Many of these sites are filled with information on accommodations, restaurants, and entertainment attractions more suited to a travel guide. The better ones include photos of the area—although to be sure, they only show the "good side."

- *Realtor sites.* Obviously oriented to selling property, these sites may have some information directed toward potential relocation candidates. Most have pictures of homes, which give a good idea not only of home value but also of the character and appearance of local residences.

- *Local evangelists.* Finally, some people love their place so much that they create their own website to share its virtues with the world. Some of these can be quite good, but they aren't found everywhere. A notable example is www.jefflindsay.com/Appleton.html for the tri-cities area of Appleton-Neenah-Oshkosh, Wisconsin.

U.S. Postal Codes

The tables in this book use the two-letter postal codes assigned and used by the U.S. Postal Service. See Table 0.1 for a guide to the abbreviations.

Table 0.1: U.S. States & Postal Codes

As Assigned by the U.S. Postal Service

Alaska	AK	Hawaii	HI	Maine	ME	New Jersey	NJ	South Dakota	SD
Alabama	AL	Iowa	IA	Michigan	MI	New Mexico	NM	Tennessee	TN
Arkansas	AR	Idaho	ID	Minnesota	MN	Nevada	NV	Texas	TX
Arizona	AZ	Illinois	IL	Missouri	MO	New York	NY	Utah	UT
California	CA	Indiana	IN	Mississippi	MS	Ohio	OH	Virginia	VA
Colorado	CO	Kansas	KS	Montana	MT	Oklahoma	OK	Vermont	VT
Connecticut	CT	Kentucky	KY	North Carolina	NC	Oregon	OR	Washington	WA
Delaware	DE	Louisiana	LA	North Dakota	ND	Pennsylvania	PA	Wisconsin	WI
Florida	FL	Massachusetts	MA	Nebraska	NE	Rhode Island	RI	West Virginia	WV
Georgia	GA	Maryland	MD	New Hampshire	NH	South Carolina	SC	Wyoming	WY

MOVING: THE REASONS WHY

Roughly 40 million U.S. citizens contemplate an immediate move each year. On average, about one in seven people move each year. Or put another way, the average U.S. citizen moves once every 7 years. This figure has remained remarkably constant over the years, with a slight peak during the "boom" 1990s and a noticeable falloff in the 2000–2001 period. Table 0.2 shows these numbers and indicates moves within the same county, different county, same state, or different state. Demographers call this "mobility."

In Table 0.2, note the falloff in mobility from a consistent 16% to 14.2% in the 2000–2001 period, while at the same time intercounty moves and particularly inter*state* moves increased as a percentage of total moves. Interpretation: The poor economy brought fewer discretionary moves, which are usually within the same city for better housing or convenience to amenities, in favor of moves owing to job-related necessity. Local, housing-related moves probably picked up again in 2002 and 2003 because of lower interest rates, but the U.S. Census Bureau has not released this data.

The U.S. Census Bureau also tracks the stated reason for moving. The most recent statistics are compiled in Table 0.3. This data shows that jobs, housing, and personal situation (marriage, for example) are the main reasons for moving, both for intercounty and intracounty moves. Interestingly, climate and neighborhood are not primary reasons, although it seems that people talk about them the most frequently. Another notable point is that intercounty moves are more likely to be driven by job and career-related concerns, while intracounty moves are driven by housing-related issues, supporting the conclusions drawn from the moving rates shown in Table 0.2.

Table 0.2: U.S. Population Mobility, 1990-2001

Mobility Period	Total, 1 Year Old and Over	Total Movers	% of Population Moving	Intracounty		Intercounty					
				Total Movers	% of Movers	Total Movers	% of Movers	Same State	% of Movers	Different State	% of Movers
2000-2001	275,611	39,007	14.2%	21,918	56.2%	15,333	39.3%	7,550	19.4%	7,783	20.0%
1999-2000	270,219	43,388	16.1%	24,399	56.2%	17,242	39.7%	8,814	20.3%	8,428	19.4%
1998-1999	267,933	42,636	15.9%	25,268	59.3%	15,939	37.4%	8,423	19.8%	7,516	17.6%
1997-1998	265,209	42,507	16.0%	27,082	63.7%	14,222	33.5%	7,867	18.5%	6,355	15.0%
1996-1997	262,976	43,391	16.5%	27,740	63.9%	14,348	33.1%	7,960	18.3%	6,389	14.7%
1995-1996	260,406	42,537	16.3%	26,696	62.8%	14,480	34.0%	8,009	18.8%	6,471	15.2%
1994-1995	258,248	42,317	16.4%	27,908	65.9%	13,631	32.2%	7,888	18.6%	5,743	13.6%
1993-1994	255,774	42,835	16.7%	26,638	62.2%	14,952	34.9%	8,226	19.2%	6,726	15.7%
1992-1993	252,799	43,099	17.0%	26,932	62.5%	14,772	34.3%	7,855	18.2%	6,916	16.0%
1991-1992	247,380	42,800	17.3%	26,587	62.1%	14,957	34.9%	7,853	18.3%	7,105	16.6%
1990-1991	244,884	41,539	17.0%	25,151	60.5%	15,003	36.1%	7,881	19.0%	7,122	17.1%

Source: U.S. Census Bureau

Table 0.3: Reasons for Moving, 2000-2001

People Moving, in Thousands

Reason	Intercounty		Intracounty	
	Moves	Percentage	Moves	Percentage
Personal or Family	**3,924**	**25.6%**	**6,137**	**28.0%**
Change in marital status	851	5.6%	1,428	6.5%
To Establish Own Household	712	4.6%	2,158	9.8%
Other Family Reason	2,361	15.4%	2,551	11.6%
Job or Career Related	**4,747**	**31.0%**	**999**	**4.6%**
New Job or Job Transfer	3,384	22.1%	258	1.2%
To Find Work/Lost Job	500	3.3%	59	0.3%
To Be Closer to Work/Easier Commute	631	4.1%	578	2.6%
Other Job Related Reason	232	1.5%	104	0.5%
Retirement	**187**	**1.2%**	**34**	**0.2%**
Housing Related	**4,231**	**27.6%**	**12,857**	**58.7%**
Wanted Own Home, Not Rent	1,182	7.7%	2,754	12.6%
Wanted New or Better Home	1,495	9.8%	5,356	24.4%
Wanted Cheaper Housing	541	3.5%	1,587	7.2%
Other Housing Reason	1,013	6.6%	3,160	14.4%
Lifestyle Related	**2,244**	**14.6%**	**1,891**	**8.6%**
Crime	500	3.3%	1,015	4.6%
To Attend or Leave College	758	4.9%	266	1.2%
Change of Climate	205	1.3%	9	0.0%
Health Reasons	292	1.9%	226	1.0%
Other Reasons	489	3.2%	375	1.7%
Total Moves	**15,333**		**21,918**	

Source: U.S. Census Bureau

part I

Finding Your Best Place to Live

The Places

In an ideal world, *Cities Ranked & Rated* would examine *every* place to live in North America, from giant New York City to bucolic burghs like Oxford, Ohio, and Cottage Grove, Oregon. But, of course, that isn't possible. Instead, the selection follows the "80-20" rule, focusing on 20% of the total places that represent 80% of the most popular choices.

Cities Ranked & Rated examines over 400 places to live—376 in the United States and 27 in Canada. The 376 U.S. places are classified as Metropolitan Statistical Areas, or MSAs. They represent, according to the latest census, 83% of the total U.S. population. Canadian cities are larger but similarly defined Census Metropolitan Areas, or CMAs, and cover 65% of the Canadian population.

Metropolitan Statistical Areas (MSAs)

Metropolitan Statistical Areas, or MSAs, are defined by the U.S. Office of Management and Budget (OMB), an arm of the U.S. Executive Branch, for the twin purposes of analysis and budget allocation. Other U.S. government agencies, such as the Census Bureau and Bureau of Labor Statistics, use these definitions in various ways to collect and classify their information. The terms "MSA," "metropolitan area," and "metro area," are used interchangeably throughout this book.

Definition

The definition for a Metropolitan Statistical Area is " . . . [a place] *that has at least one urbanized area of 50,000 or more population, plus adjacent territory that has a high degree of social integration with the core as measured by commuting ties.*" (OMB, 6/03).

MSAs are typically defined as one, and sometimes more than one, urban core and their county or counties. An MSA can cross state lines, and many do. The relationship between urban cores and counties can be one-to-one, one-to-many, many-to-one, or many-to-many, as the following examples illustrate:

- One core to one county (Altoona, Pennsylvania–Blair County; Bakersfield, California–Kern County)

- One core to many counties (Ann Arbor, Michigan–Washtenaw, Livingston, and Lenawee counties)

- Many cores to one county (Fort Collins and Loveland, Colorado–Larimer County; Davis and Woodland, California–Yolo County)

- Many cores to many counties (Appleton-Oshkosh-Neenah, Wisconsin–Outagamie, Winnebago, and Calumet counties)

In all areas except New England, if a county is integrated with an urban core, the *entire* county is included, regardless of size and content. Ordinarily this is logical, but it produces odd situations in the West where large, empty areas are classified as part of an MSA. Examples include the Mojave Desert in San Bernardino County (part of the MSA of Riverside–San Bernardino, California) and much of the Grand Canyon in Cococino County (part of the Flagstaff, Arizona MSA). Aside from perhaps evoking a smile, such situations don't much affect the ranking and evaluation of these places.

2003 Definition Changes

In mid-2003, the OMB announced a series of changes to metropolitan area definitions. These are summarized below in the bulleted list and in the two sections that follow.

- Metropolitan Statistical Areas (MSAs) retain the same definition, but new census analysis added 45 areas to the base of 314. *Cities Ranked & Rated* considers these new MSAs as "emerging."

- For the 11 MSAs with populations exceeding 2.5 million, OMB created a category called Metropolitan Divisions, which clusters certain areas like Manhattan and Brooklyn within New York City. This book does not include this category.

- The OMB introduced a new classification, *Micro*politan Statistical Areas. These are defined like traditional MSAs, but have an urban core or "cluster" between 10,000 and 50,000 inhabitants. (Eventually, a new acronym will probably be supplied to avoid confusion with traditional MSAs.) The 565 places with this designation are not included in this book.

Consolidated Metropolitan Statistical Areas (CMSAs)

Recognizing the immense size and complexity of certain areas, OMB has traditionally defined highly interlocked groupings of MSAs into Consolidated Metropolitan Statistical Areas, or CMSAs. These include places such as New York City, Los Angeles, and other interdependent city complexes. CMSAs are used in *Cities Ranked & Rated* to give certain areas, such as Long Island, a "halo" effect for being close enough and integrated enough with major cities to take advantage of certain amenities. However, in mid-2003 OMB changed the definitions eliminating CMSAs, but *Cities Ranked & Rated* still uses them to group integrated MSAs for purposes of analysis.

OMB now uses the classification Combined Statistical Area, or CSAs, which includes multiple Metropolitan and Micropolitan Statistical Areas. The 116 CSAs are not studied as separate entities in this book.

New England County Metropolitan Areas (NECMAs)

In the six New England states, federal government demographers have long recognized the importance of the "township" and "town" political divisions used in those areas. While townships and towns do appear as political divisions across most of the country, they are more important as governing structures in New England. As a result, OMB defines New England County Metropolitan Areas, or NECMAs, as including one or more core cities and a collection of towns and townships that may or may not include whole counties. The precise definition of individual NECMAs can be very complex, and while this book presents data aligned with 17 NECMAs, *Cities Ranked & Rated* only lists in Table 1.1 the counties that are touched by the NECMA boundary, not the individual town structure.

In 2003 OMB changed the NECMA name to Metropolitan NECTA (New England City and Town Area), but did not materially change the definition or add new areas.

Census Metropolitan Areas (CMAs)

Canadian government officials define Census Metropolitan Areas, or CMAs, as an urban core of 100,000 and surrounding areas "with a high degree of social and economic interaction" with the core areas. Aside from the different population threshold, the Canadian approach differs from the United States in that once an area is designated a CMA, it always remains so, regardless of subsequent population declines. There are 27 CMAs in Canada.

What's Included in *Cities Ranked & Rated*?

The complex and shifting definitions may be frustrating, so for clarity, here is a summary of what's included in *Cities Ranked & Rated*:

- 331 "principal" U.S. Metropolitan Statistical Areas based on 2002 definitions and classifications (Table 1.1). Included are 314 traditional MSAs and 17 traditional NECMAs. These MSAs receive full analysis, ranking, and descriptive treatment in chapter 5.

- 27 Canada Census Metropolitan Areas (Table 1.2). Due to inherent difficulties with comparisons of not quite "apples-to-apples" data, and the relatively few readers considering migration between countries, Canadian CMAs are presented in chapter 6 in an abbreviated fashion similar to emerging MSAs (see Table 1.3 below) and are likewise not included in the principal MSA rankings. Canada CMAs are ranked among themselves, and an estimate is made of where they would rank among U.S. metropolitan areas.

- 45 "emerging" U.S. Metropolitan Statistical Areas (Table 1.3). As these definitions are too new at time of publication to collect complete data and give full analysis, these areas are presented with abbreviated data and narrative. They are not included in the principal MSA scoring and ranking analysis, but are ranked among themselves.

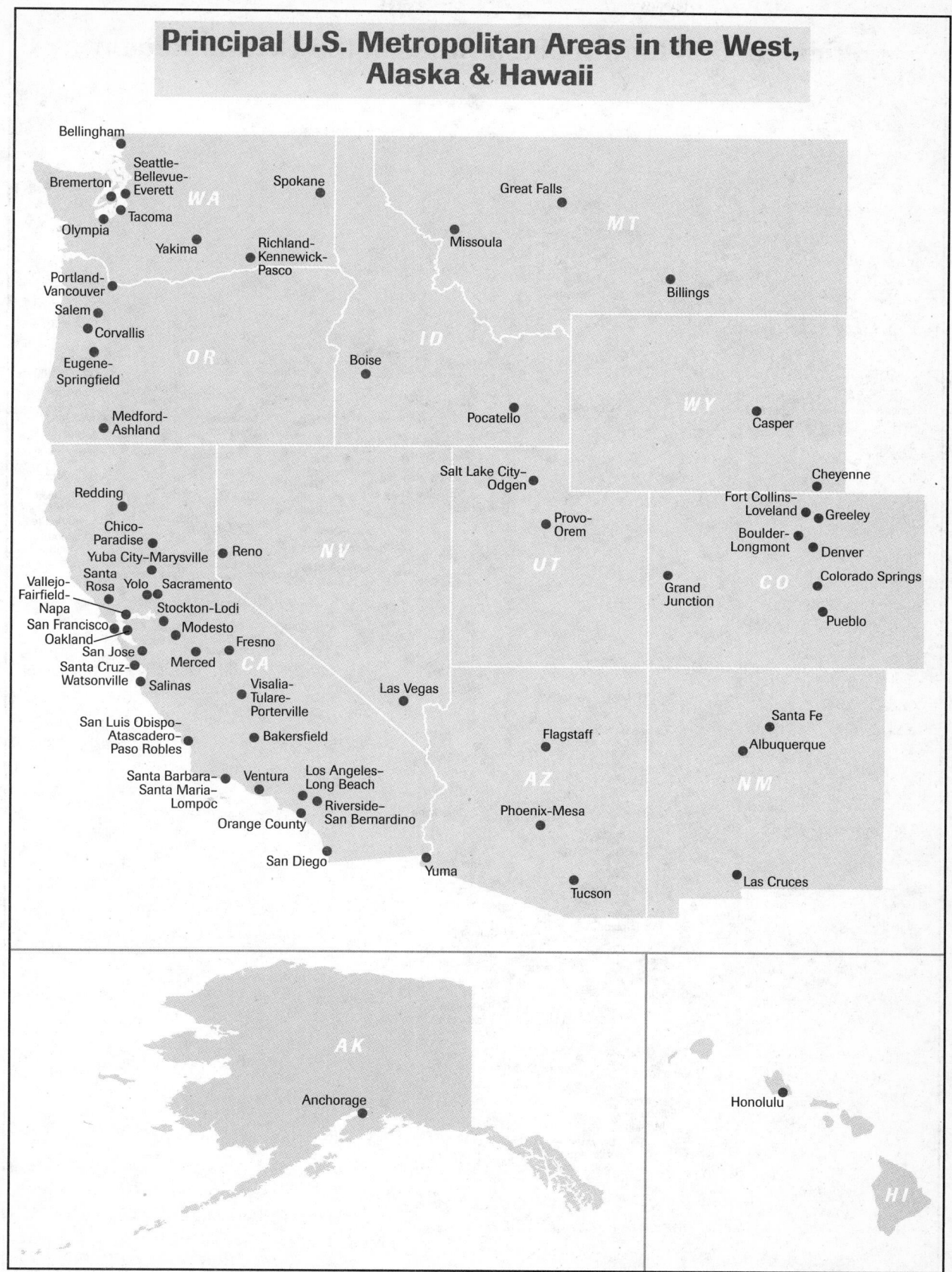

Principal U.S. Metropolitan Areas in the West, Alaska & Hawaii

Bellingham

Seattle-Bellevue-Everett

Bremerton

Spokane

Great Falls

WA

MT

Tacoma

Olympia

Missoula

Yakima

Richland-Kennewick-Pasco

Portland-Vancouver

Billings

Salem

Corvallis

OR

Boise

ID

Eugene-Springfield

WY

Casper

Medford-Ashland

Pocatello

Salt Lake City-Odgen

Cheyenne

Redding

Provo-Orem

Fort Collins-Loveland

Greeley

Chico-Paradise

Boulder-Longmont

Denver

Reno

Yuba City–Marysville

NV

UT

Santa Rosa

Yolo

Sacramento

Grand Junction

CO

Colorado Springs

Vallejo-Fairfield-Napa

Stockton-Lodi

San Francisco

Modesto

Pueblo

Oakland

Fresno

San Jose

Merced

Santa Cruz-Watsonville

Salinas

CA

Visalia-Tulare-Porterville

Las Vegas

San Luis Obispo-Atascadero-Paso Robles

Bakersfield

Santa Fe

Flagstaff

Albuquerque

Santa Barbara-Santa Maria-Lompoc

Ventura

Los Angeles-Long Beach

AZ

NM

Riverside-San Bernardino

Orange County

Phoenix-Mesa

San Diego

Yuma

Las Cruces

Tucson

AK

Anchorage

Honolulu

HI

Principal U.S. Metropolitan Areas in the Central Region

Principal U.S. Metropolitan Areas in the Northeast

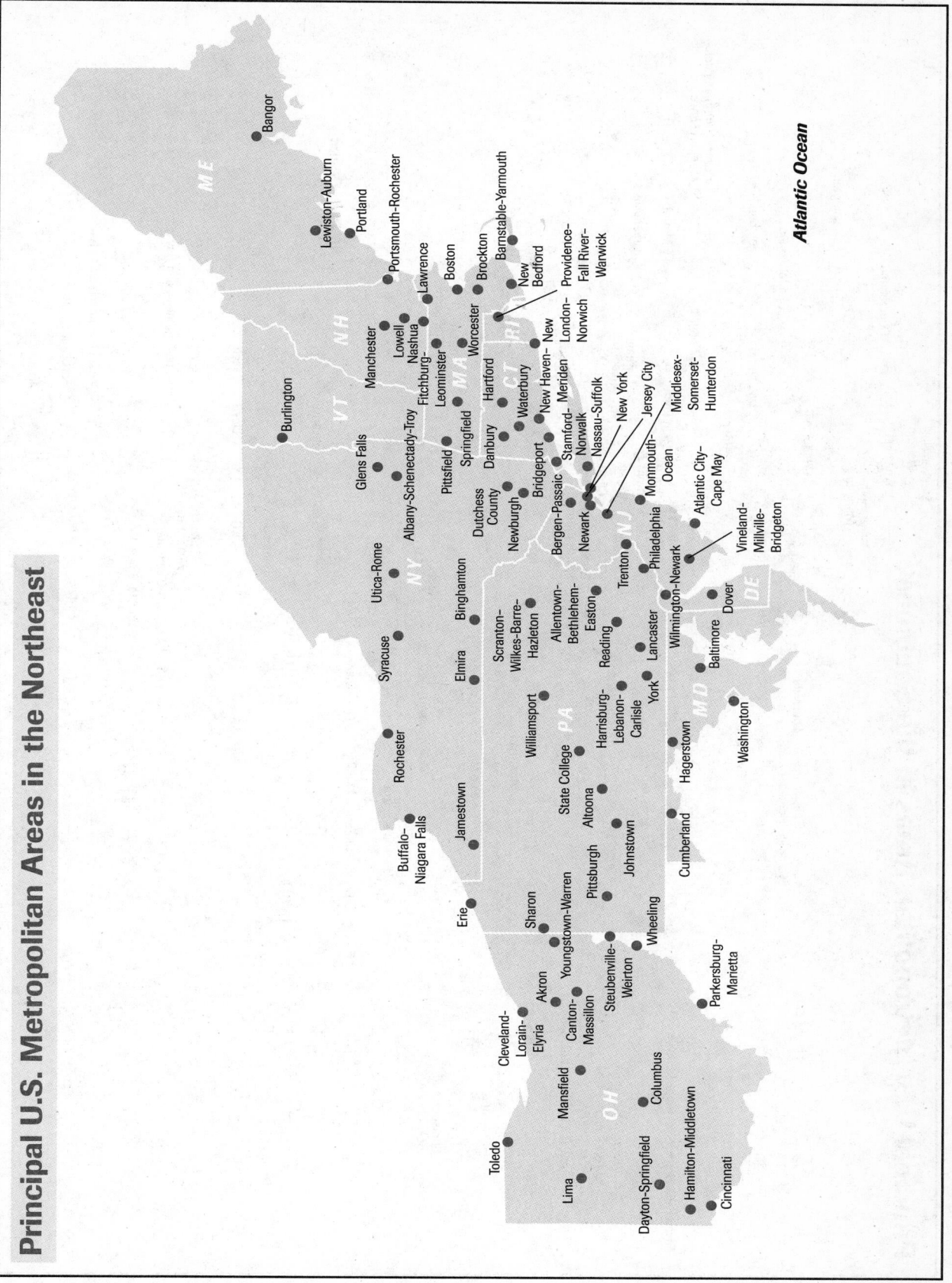

Atlantic Ocean

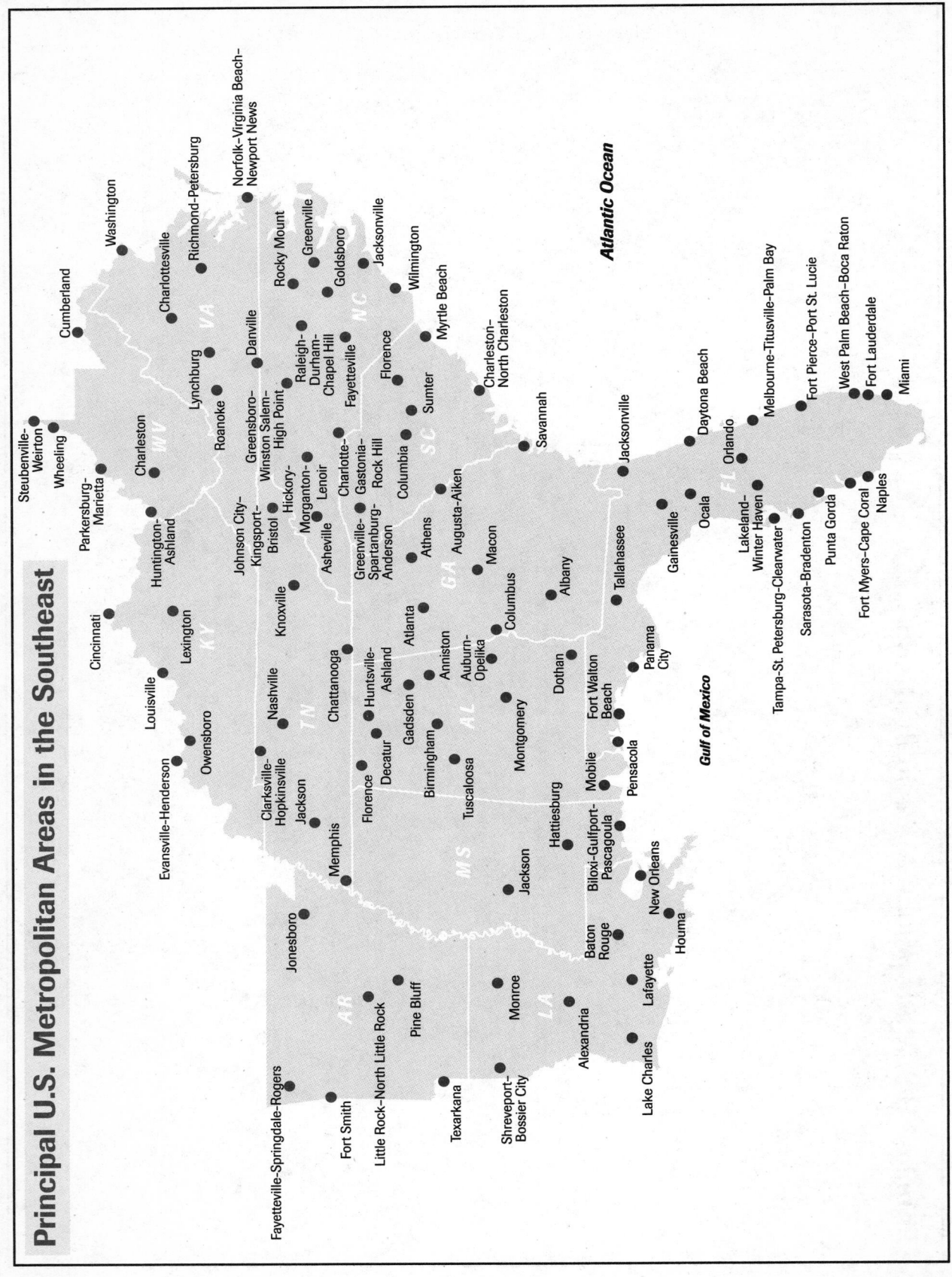

Principal U.S. Metropolitan Areas in the Southeast

Table 1.1: Principal U.S. Metropolitan Statistical Areas

2002 Designation (314 MSAs, 17 NECMAs)

MSA and Included Counties	2002 Population	2000 Population	1990 Population	Change 1990-2002	Percentage Change 1990-2002
Abilene, TX	**125,647**	**126,555**	**119,655**	**5,992**	**5.0%**
Taylor County	125,647	126,555	119,655	5,992	5.0%
Akron, OH	**700,267**	**694,960**	**657,575**	**42,692**	**6.5%**
Summit County	546,381	542,899	514,990	31,391	6.1%
Portage County	153,886	152,061	142,585	11,301	7.9%
Albany, GA	**123,257**	**120,822**	**112,561**	**10,696**	**9.5%**
Dougherty County	95,875	96,065	96,311	-436	-0.5%
Lee County	27,382	24,757	16,250	11,132	68.5%
Albany-Schenectady-Troy, NY	**884,969**	**875,583**	**861,424**	**23,545**	**2.7%**
Albany County	296,173	294,565	292,594	3,579	1.2%
Saratoga County	207,135	200,635	181,276	25,859	14.3%
Rensselaer County	153,299	152,538	154,429	-1,130	-0.7%
Schenectady County	147,120	146,555	149,285	-2,165	-1.5%
Montgomery County	49,387	49,708	51,981	-2,594	-5.0%
Schoharie County	31,855	31,582	31,859	-4	0.0%
Albuquerque, NM	**737,324**	**712,738**	**589,131**	**148,193**	**25.2%**
Bernalillo County	573,675	556,678	480,577	93,098	19.4%
Sandoval County	96,071	89,908	63,319	32,752	51.7%
Valencia County	67,578	66,152	45,235	22,343	49.4%
Alexandria, LA	**126,881**	**126,337**	**131,556**	**-4,675**	**-3.6%**
Rapides Parish	126,881	126,337	131,556	-4,675	-3.6%
Allentown-Bethlehem-Easton, PA	**650,545**	**637,958**	**595,081**	**55,464**	**9.3%**
Lehigh County	317,533	312,090	291,130	26,403	9.1%
Northampton County	273,324	267,066	247,105	26,219	10.6%
Carbon County	59,688	58,802	56,846	2,842	5.0%
Altoona, PA	**127,840**	**129,144**	**130,542**	**-2,702**	**-2.1%**
Blair County	127,840	129,144	130,542	-2,702	-2.1%
Amarillo, TX	**222,915**	**217,858**	**187,547**	**35,368**	**18.9%**
Potter County	116,093	113,546	97,874	18,219	18.6%
Randall County	106,822	104,312	89,673	17,149	19.1%
Anchorage, AK	**268,983**	**260,283**	**226,338**	**42,645**	**18.8%**
Anchorage Municipality	268,983	260,283	226,338	42,645	18.8%
Ann Arbor, MI	**603,358**	**578,736**	**490,058**	**113,300**	**23.1%**
Washtenaw County	334,351	322,895	282,937	51,414	18.2%
Livingston County	168,862	156,951	115,645	53,217	46.0%
Lenawee County	100,145	98,890	91,476	8,669	9.5%
Anniston, AL	**111,616**	**112,249**	**116,034**	**-4,418**	**-3.8%**
Calhoun County	111,616	112,249	116,034	-4,418	-3.8%
Appleton-Oshkosh-Neenah, WI	**366,914**	**358,365**	**315,121**	**51,793**	**16.4%**
Outagamie County	166,148	160,971	140,510	25,638	18.2%
Winnebago County	158,401	156,763	140,320	18,081	12.9%
Calumet County	42,365	40,631	34,291	8,074	23.5%
Asheville, NC	**231,205**	**225,965**	**191,774**	**39,431**	**20.6%**
Buncombe County	211,201	206,330	174,821	36,380	20.8%
Madison County	20,004	19,635	16,953	3,051	18.0%
Athens, GA	**157,862**	**153,444**	**126,262**	**31,600**	**25.0%**
Clarke County	103,881	101,489	87,594	16,287	18.6%
Oconee County	27,264	26,225	17,618	9,646	54.8%
Madison County	26,717	25,730	21,050	5,667	26.9%
Atlanta, GA	**4,386,330**	**4,112,198**	**2,959,950**	**1,426,380**	**48.2%**
Fulton County	825,431	816,006	648,951	176,480	27.2%
DeKalb County	676,996	665,865	545,837	131,159	24.0%
Cobb County	651,485	607,751	447,745	203,740	45.5%
Gwinnett County	650,771	588,448	352,910	297,861	84.4%
Clayton County	252,733	236,517	182,052	70,681	38.8%
Cherokee County	159,295	141,903	90,204	69,091	76.6%
Henry County	139,699	119,341	58,741	80,958	137.8%

continued

Table 1.1: Principal U.S. Metropolitan Statistical Areas *(continued)*

MSA and Included Counties	2002 Population	2000 Population	1990 Population	Change 1990-2002	Percentage Change 1990-2002
Atlanta, GA *(cont.)*					
Forsyth County	116,924	98,407	44,083	72,841	165.2%
Douglas County	98,650	92,174	71,120	27,530	38.7%
Coweta County	97,771	89,215	53,853	43,918	81.6%
Fayette County	96,611	91,263	62,415	34,196	54.8%
Carroll County	94,907	87,268	71,422	23,485	32.9%
Paulding County	94,184	81,678	41,611	52,573	126.3%
Bartow County	82,607	76,019	55,911	26,696	47.7%
Rockdale County	73,558	70,111	54,091	19,467	36.0%
Newton County	71,594	62,001	41,808	29,786	71.2%
Walton County	67,069	60,687	38,586	28,483	73.8%
Spalding County	59,410	58,417	54,457	4,953	9.1%
Barrow County	51,016	46,144	29,721	21,295	71.6%
Pickens County	25,619	22,983	14,432	11,187	77.5%
Atlantic City–Cape May, NJ	**361,436**	**354,878**	**319,416**	**42,020**	**13.2%**
Atlantic County	259,423	252,552	224,327	35,096	15.6%
Cape May County	102,013	102,326	95,089	6,924	7.3%
Auburn-Opelika, AL	**118,123**	**115,092**	**87,146**	**30,977**	**35.5%**
Lee County	118,123	115,092	87,146	30,977	35.5%
Augusta-Aiken, GA-SC	**484,382**	**477,441**	**415,184**	**69,198**	**16.7%**
Richmond County, GA	197,842	199,775	189,719	8,123	4.3%
Aiken County, SC	145,276	142,552	120,940	24,336	20.1%
Columbia County, GA	94,958	89,288	66,031	28,927	43.8%
Edgefield County, SC	24,868	24,595	18,375	6,493	35.3%
McDuffie County, GA	21,438	21,231	20,119	1,319	6.6%
Austin–San Marcos, TX	**1,349,291**	**1,249,763**	**846,227**	**503,064**	**59.4%**
Travis County	850,813	812,280	576,407	274,406	47.6%
Williamson County	289,924	249,967	139,551	150,373	107.8%
Hays County	109,570	97,589	65,614	43,956	67.0%
Bastrop County	63,934	57,733	38,263	25,671	67.1%
Caldwell County	35,050	32,194	26,392	8,658	32.8%
Bakersfield, CA	**694,059**	**661,645**	**543,477**	**150,582**	**27.7%**
Kern County	694,059	661,645	543,477	150,582	27.7%
Baltimore, MD	**2,601,990**	**2,552,994**	**2,382,172**	**219,818**	**9.2%**
Baltimore County	770,298	754,292	692,134	78,164	11.3%
Baltimore city	638,614	651,154	736,014	-97,400	-13.2%
Anne Arundel County	503,388	489,656	427,239	76,149	17.8%
Howard County	260,117	247,842	187,328	72,789	38.9%
Harford County	227,713	218,590	182,132	45,581	25.0%
Carroll County	159,025	150,897	123,372	35,653	28.9%
Queen Anne's County	42,835	40,563	33,953	8,882	26.2%
Bangor, ME	**91,773**	**90,864**	**91,629**	**144**	**0.2%**
Penobscot County (part)	88,114	87,262	88,454	-340	-0.4%
Waldo County (part)	3,659	3,602	3,175	484	15.2%
Barnstable-Yarmouth, MA	**167,117**	**162,582**	**134,954**	**32,163**	**23.8%**
Barnstable County (part)	167,117	162,582	134,954	32,163	23.8%
Baton Rouge, LA	**614,491**	**602,894**	**528,264**	**86,227**	**16.3%**
East Baton Rouge Parish	412,008	412,852	380,105	31,903	8.4%
Livingston Parish	99,066	91,814	70,526	28,540	40.5%
Ascension Parish	81,792	76,627	58,214	23,578	40.5%
West Baton Rouge Parish	21,625	21,601	19,419	2,206	11.4%
Beaumont–Port Arthur, TX	**382,242**	**385,090**	**361,226**	**21,016**	**5.8%**
Jefferson County	248,890	252,051	239,397	9,493	4.0%
Orange County	84,364	84,966	80,509	3,855	4.8%
Hardin County	48,988	48,073	41,320	7,668	18.6%
Bellingham, WA	**174,362**	**166,814**	**127,780**	**46,582**	**36.5%**
Whatcom County	174,362	166,814	127,780	46,582	36.5%
Benton Harbor, MI	**162,285**	**162,453**	**161,378**	**907**	**0.6%**
Berrien County	162,285	162,453	161,378	907	0.6%
Bergen-Passaic, NJ	**1,391,737**	**1,373,167**	**1,278,440**	**113,297**	**8.9%**
Bergen County	895,091	884,118	825,380	69,711	8.4%
Passaic County	496,646	489,049	453,060	43,586	9.6%

MSA and Included Counties	2002 Population	2000 Population	1990 Population	Change 1990-2002	Percentage Change 1990-2002
Billings, MT	**131,622**	**129,352**	**113,419**	**18,203**	**16.0%**
Yellowstone County	131,622	129,352	113,419	18,203	16.0%
Biloxi-Gulfport-Pascagoula, MS	**368,868**	**363,988**	**312,368**	**56,500**	**18.1%**
Harrison County	190,936	189,601	165,365	25,571	15.5%
Jackson County	133,259	131,420	115,243	18,016	15.6%
Hancock County	44,673	42,967	31,760	12,913	40.7%
Binghamton, NY	**252,096**	**252,320**	**264,497**	**-12,401**	**-4.7%**
Broome County	200,324	200,536	212,160	-11,836	-5.6%
Tioga County	51,772	51,784	52,337	-565	-1.1%
Birmingham, AL	**935,168**	**921,106**	**840,140**	**95,028**	**11.3%**
Jefferson County	661,153	662,047	651,525	9,628	1.5%
Shelby County	153,832	143,293	99,358	54,474	54.8%
St. Clair County	67,215	64,742	50,009	17,206	34.4%
Blount County	52,968	51,024	39,248	13,720	35.0%
Bismarck, ND	**96,349**	**94,719**	**83,831**	**12,518**	**14.9%**
Burleigh County	71,080	69,416	60,131	10,949	18.2%
Morton County	25,269	25,303	23,700	1,569	6.6%
Bloomington, IN	**121,229**	**120,563**	**108,978**	**12,251**	**11.2%**
Monroe County	121,229	120,563	108,978	12,251	11.2%
Bloomington-Normal, IL	**154,453**	**150,433**	**129,180**	**25,273**	**19.6%**
McLean County	154,453	150,433	129,180	25,273	19.6%
Boise, ID	**464,670**	**432,345**	**295,851**	**168,819**	**57.1%**
Ada County	319,687	300,904	205,775	113,912	55.4%
Canyon County	144,983	131,441	90,076	54,907	61.0%
Boston, MA-NH	**3,439,372**	**3,406,829**	**3,227,707**	**211,665**	**6.6%**
Middlesex County, MA (part)	1,177,716	1,171,779	1,124,581	53,135	4.7%
Suffolk County, MA	689,925	689,807	663,906	26,019	3.9%
Norfolk County, MA (part)	652,037	645,865	611,529	40,508	6.6%
Essex County, MA (part)	466,582	458,546	430,071	36,511	8.5%
Plymouth County, MA (part)	246,789	239,872	218,832	27,957	12.8%
Bristol County, MA (part)	110,622	108,350	90,533	20,089	22.2%
Worcester County, MA (part)	86,492	83,832	81,012	5,480	6.8%
Rockingham County, NH (part)	9,209	8,778	7,243	1,966	27.1%
Boulder-Longmont, CO	**279,197**	**291,288**	**225,339**	**53,858**	**23.9%**
Boulder County	279,197	291,288	225,339	53,858	23.9%
Brazoria, TX	**257,256**	**241,767**	**191,707**	**65,549**	**34.2%**
Brazoria County	257,256	241,767	191,707	65,549	34.2%
Bremerton, WA	**236,174**	**231,969**	**189,731**	**46,443**	**24.5%**
Kitsap County	236,174	231,969	189,731	46,443	24.5%
Bridgeport, CT	**465,089**	**459,479**	**443,722**	**21,367**	**4.8%**
Fairfield County (part)	348,726	345,708	335,126	13,600	4.1%
New Haven County (part)	116,363	113,771	108,596	7,767	7.2%
Brockton, MA	**261,755**	**255,459**	**236,409**	**25,346**	**10.7%**
Plymouth County (part)	222,332	216,978	202,177	20,155	10.0%
Bristol County (part)	34,974	34,038	29,674	5,300	17.9%
Norfolk County (part)	4,449	4,443	4,558	-109	-2.4%
Brownsville–Harlingen–San Benito, TX	**353,561**	**335,227**	**260,120**	**93,441**	**35.9%**
Cameron County	353,561	335,227	260,120	93,441	35.9%
Bryan–College Station, TX	**156,099**	**152,415**	**121,862**	**34,237**	**28.1%**
Brazos County	156,099	152,415	121,862	34,237	28.1%
Buffalo–Niagara Falls, NY	**1,163,148**	**1,170,111**	**1,189,288**	**-26,140**	**-2.2%**
Erie County	945,049	950,265	968,532	-23,483	-2.4%
Niagara County	218,099	219,846	220,756	-2,657	-1.2%
Burlington, VT	**172,508**	**169,391**	**151,506**	**21,002**	**13.9%**
Chittenden County (part)	140,864	138,661	124,640	16,224	13.0%
Franklin County (part)	27,718	27,079	23,820	3,898	16.4%
Grand Isle County (part)	3,926	3,651	3,046	880	28.9%
Canton-Massillon, OH	**407,106**	**406,934**	**394,106**	**13,000**	**3.3%**
Stark County	377,940	378,098	367,585	10,355	2.8%
Carroll County	29,166	28,836	26,521	2,645	10.0%
Casper, WY	**67,336**	**66,533**	**61,226**	**6,110**	**10.0%**
Natrona County	67,336	66,533	61,226	6,110	10.0%

continued

Table 1.1: Principal U.S. Metropolitan Statistical Areas *(continued)*

MSA and Included Counties	2002 Population	2000 Population	1990 Population	Change 1990-2002	Percentage Change 1990-2002
Cedar Rapids, IA	**194,970**	**191,701**	**168,767**	**26,203**	**15.5%**
Linn County	194,970	191,701	168,767	26,203	15.5%
Champaign-Urbana, IL	**183,159**	**179,669**	**173,025**	**10,134**	**5.9%**
Champaign County	183,159	179,669	173,025	10,134	5.9%
Charleston, WV	**248,020**	**251,662**	**250,454**	**-2,434**	**-1.0%**
Kanawha County	195,790	200,073	207,619	-11,829	-5.7%
Putnam County	52,230	51,589	42,835	9,395	21.9%
Charleston–North Charleston, SC	**562,666**	**549,033**	**506,875**	**55,791**	**11.0%**
Charleston County	316,559	309,969	295,039	21,520	7.3%
Berkeley County	145,274	142,651	128,776	16,498	12.8%
Dorchester County	100,833	96,413	83,060	17,773	21.4%
Charlotte–Gastonia–Rock Hill, NC-SC	**1,584,898**	**1,499,293**	**1,162,093**	**422,805**	**36.4%**
Mecklenburg County, NC	737,950	695,454	511,433	226,517	44.3%
Gaston County, NC	193,443	190,365	175,093	18,350	10.5%
York County, SC	173,755	164,614	131,497	42,258	32.1%
Cabarrus County, NC	140,182	131,063	98,935	41,247	41.7%
Union County, NC	139,611	123,677	84,211	55,400	65.8%
Rowan County, NC	133,359	130,340	110,605	22,754	20.6%
Lincoln County, NC	66,598	63,780	50,319	16,279	32.4%
Charlottesville, VA	**164,197**	**159,576**	**131,107**	**33,090**	**25.2%**
Albemarle County	81,888	79,236	68,040	13,848	20.4%
Charlottesville city	43,833	45,049	40,341	3,492	8.7%
Fluvanna County	22,207	20,047	12,429	9,778	78.7%
Greene County	16,269	15,244	10,297	5,972	58.0%
Chattanooga, TN-GA	**470,880**	**465,161**	**424,347**	**46,533**	**11.0%**
Hamilton County, TN	309,321	307,896	285,536	23,785	8.3%
Walker County, GA	61,949	61,053	58,340	3,609	6.2%
Catoosa County, GA	56,341	53,282	42,464	13,877	32.7%
Marion County, TN	27,654	27,776	24,860	2,794	11.2%
Dade County, GA	15,615	15,154	13,147	2,468	18.8%
Cheyenne, WY	**82,894**	**81,607**	**73,142**	**9,752**	**13.3%**
Laramie County	82,894	81,607	73,142	9,752	13.3%
Chicago, IL	**8,449,180**	**8,272,768**	**7,410,858**	**1,038,322**	**14.0%**
Cook County	5,377,507	5,376,741	5,105,067	272,440	5.3%
DuPage County	924,589	904,161	781,666	142,923	18.3%
Lake County	674,850	644,356	516,418	158,432	30.7%
Will County	559,861	502,266	357,313	202,548	56.7%
Kane County	443,041	404,119	317,471	125,570	39.6%
McHenry County	277,710	260,077	183,241	94,469	51.6%
DeKalb County	91,561	88,969	77,932	13,629	17.5%
Kendall County	61,222	54,544	39,413	21,809	55.3%
Grundy County	38,839	37,535	32,337	6,502	20.1%
Chico-Paradise, CA	**209,203**	**203,171**	**182,120**	**27,083**	**14.9%**
Butte County	209,203	203,171	182,120	27,083	14.9%
Cincinnati, OH-KY-IN	**1,669,136**	**1,646,395**	**1,526,092**	**143,044**	**9.4%**
Hamilton County, OH	833,721	845,303	866,228	-32,507	-3.8%
Clermont County, OH	183,352	177,977	150,187	33,165	22.1%
Warren County, OH	175,133	158,383	113,909	61,224	53.7%
Kenton County, KY	152,164	151,464	142,031	10,133	7.1%
Boone County, KY	93,290	85,991	57,589	35,701	62.0%
Campbell County, KY	88,604	88,616	83,866	4,738	5.6%
Dearborn County, IN	47,333	46,109	38,835	8,498	21.9%
Brown County, OH	43,464	42,285	34,966	8,498	24.3%
Grant County, KY	23,620	22,384	15,737	7,883	50.1%
Pendleton County, KY	14,815	14,390	12,036	2,779	23.1%
Gallatin County, KY	7,836	7,870	5,393	2,443	45.3%
Ohio County, IN	5,804	5,623	5,315	489	9.2%
Clarksville-Hopkinsville, TN-KY	**209,508**	**207,033**	**169,439**	**40,069**	**23.6%**
Montgomery County, TN	138,241	134,768	100,498	37,743	37.6%
Christian County, KY	71,267	72,265	68,941	2,326	3.4%
Cleveland-Lorain-Elyria, OH	**2,250,347**	**2,250,871**	**2,202,069**	**48,278**	**2.2%**
Cuyahoga County	1,379,049	1,393,978	1,412,140	-33,091	-2.3%

MSA and Included Counties	2002 Population	2000 Population	1990 Population	Change 1990-2002	Percentage Change 1990-2002
Cleveland-Lorain-Elyria, OH *(cont.)*					
Lorain County	288,360	284,664	271,126	17,234	6.4%
Lake County	229,004	227,511	215,499	13,505	6.3%
Medina County	158,439	151,095	122,354	36,085	29.5%
Ashtabula County	102,515	102,728	99,821	2,694	2.7%
Geauga County	92,980	90,895	81,129	11,851	14.6%
Colorado Springs, CO	**543,818**	**516,929**	**397,014**	**146,804**	**37.0%**
El Paso County	543,818	516,929	397,014	146,804	37.0%
Columbia, MO	**139,492**	**135,454**	**112,379**	**27,113**	**24.1%**
Boone County	139,492	135,454	112,379	27,113	24.1%
Columbia, SC	**551,983**	**536,691**	**453,331**	**98,652**	**21.8%**
Richland County	329,086	320,677	285,720	43,366	15.2%
Lexington County	222,897	216,014	167,611	55,286	33.0%
Columbus, GA-AL	**275,895**	**274,624**	**260,860**	**15,035**	**5.8%**
Muscogee County, GA	185,948	186,291	179,278	6,670	3.7%
Russell County, AL	49,415	49,756	46,860	2,555	5.5%
Harris County, GA	25,092	23,695	17,788	7,304	41.1%
Chattahoochee County, GA	15,440	14,882	16,934	-1,494	-8.8%
Columbus, OH	**1,583,907**	**1,540,157**	**1,345,450**	**238,457**	**17.7%**
Franklin County	1,086,814	1,068,978	961,437	125,377	13.0%
Licking County	148,731	145,491	128,300	20,431	15.9%
Fairfield County	129,161	122,759	103,461	25,700	24.8%
Delaware County	125,399	109,989	66,929	58,470	87.4%
Pickaway County	53,437	52,727	48,255	5,182	10.7%
Madison County	40,365	40,213	37,068	3,297	8.9%
Corpus Christi, TX	**382,188**	**380,783**	**349,894**	**32,294**	**9.2%**
Nueces County	314,696	313,645	291,145	23,551	8.1%
San Patricio County	67,492	67,138	58,749	8,743	14.9%
Corvallis, OR	**78,618**	**78,153**	**70,811**	**7,807**	**11.0%**
Benton County	78,618	78,153	70,811	7,807	11.0%
Cumberland, MD-WV	**101,290**	**102,008**	**101,643**	**-353**	**-0.3%**
Allegany County, MD	74,203	74,930	74,946	-743	-1.0%
Mineral County, WV	27,087	27,078	26,697	390	1.5%
Dallas, TX	**3,743,254**	**3,519,176**	**2,676,248**	**1,067,006**	**39.9%**
Dallas County	2,283,953	2,218,899	1,852,810	431,143	23.3%
Collin County	566,798	491,675	264,036	302,762	114.7%
Denton County	488,481	432,976	273,525	214,956	78.6%
Ellis County	120,052	111,360	85,167	34,885	41.0%
Hunt County	79,361	76,596	64,343	15,018	23.3%
Kaufman County	77,954	71,313	52,220	25,734	49.3%
Henderson County	75,797	73,277	58,543	17,254	29.5%
Rockwall County	50,858	43,080	25,604	25,254	98.6%
Danbury, CT	**223,580**	**217,980**	**193,597**	**29,983**	**15.5%**
Fairfield County (part)	187,834	183,303	162,584	25,250	15.5%
Litchfield County (part)	35,746	34,677	31,013	4,733	15.3%
Danville, VA	**109,341**	**110,156**	**108,711**	**630**	**0.6%**
Pittsylvania County	61,745	61,745	55,655	6,090	10.9%
Danville city	47,596	48,411	53,056	-5,460	-10.3%
Davenport–Moline–Rock Island, IA-IL	**358,230**	**359,062**	**350,861**	**7,369**	**2.1%**
Scott County, IA	159,445	158,668	150,979	8,466	5.6%
Rock Island County, IL	148,171	149,374	148,723	-552	-0.4%
Henry County, IL	50,614	51,020	51,159	-545	-1.1%
Daytona Beach, FL	**516,812**	**493,175**	**399,413**	**117,399**	**29.4%**
Volusia County	459,435	443,343	370,712	88,723	23.9%
Flagler County	57,377	49,832	28,701	28,676	99.9%
Dayton-Springfield, OH	**947,446**	**950,558**	**951,270**	**-3,824**	**-0.4%**
Montgomery County	554,470	559,062	573,809	-19,339	-3.4%
Greene County	149,964	147,886	136,731	13,233	9.7%
Clark County	143,416	144,742	147,548	-4,132	-2.8%
Miami County	99,596	98,868	93,182	6,414	6.9%
Decatur, AL	**146,380**	**145,867**	**131,556**	**14,824**	**11.3%**
Morgan County	111,725	111,064	100,043	11,682	11.7%

continued

Table 1.1: Principal U.S. Metropolitan Statistical Areas *(continued)*

MSA and Included Counties	2002 Population	2000 Population	1990 Population	Change 1990-2002	Percentage Change 1990-2002
Decatur, AL *(cont.)*					
Lawrence County	34,655	34,803	31,513	3,142	10.0%
Decatur, IL	**112,013**	**114,706**	**117,206**	**-5,193**	**-4.4%**
Macon County	112,013	114,706	117,206	-5,193	-4.4%
Denver, CO	**2,187,464**	**2,109,282**	**1,622,980**	**564,484**	**34.8%**
Denver County	560,415	554,636	467,610	92,805	19.8%
Jefferson County	531,723	527,056	438,430	93,293	21.3%
Arapahoe County	510,136	487,967	391,511	118,625	30.3%
Adams County	374,099	363,857	265,038	109,061	41.1%
Douglas County	211,091	175,766	60,391	150,700	249.5%
Des Moines, IA	**471,436**	**456,022**	**392,928**	**78,508**	**20.0%**
Polk County	385,691	374,601	327,140	58,551	17.9%
Dallas County	44,222	40,750	29,755	14,467	48.6%
Warren County	41,523	40,671	36,033	5,490	15.2%
Detroit, MI	**4,464,531**	**4,441,551**	**4,266,654**	**197,877**	**4.6%**
Wayne County	2,045,540	2,061,162	2,111,687	-66,147	-3.1%
Oakland County	1,202,721	1,194,156	1,083,592	119,129	11.0%
Macomb County	808,529	788,149	717,400	91,129	12.7%
St. Clair County	167,712	164,235	145,607	22,105	15.2%
Monroe County	149,253	145,945	133,600	15,653	11.7%
Lapeer County	90,776	87,904	74,768	16,008	21.4%
Dothan, AL	**139,152**	**137,916**	**130,964**	**8,188**	**6.3%**
Houston County	89,966	88,787	81,331	8,635	10.6%
Dale County	49,186	49,129	49,633	-447	-0.9%
Dover, DE	**131,069**	**126,697**	**110,993**	**20,076**	**18.1%**
Kent County	131,069	126,697	110,993	20,076	18.1%
Dubuque, IA	**89,387**	**89,143**	**86,403**	**2,984**	**3.5%**
Dubuque County	89,387	89,143	86,403	2,984	3.5%
Duluth-Superior, MN-WI	**243,721**	**243,815**	**239,971**	**3,750**	**1.6%**
St. Louis County, MN	199,983	200,528	198,213	1,770	0.9%
Douglas County, WI	43,738	43,287	41,758	1,980	4.7%
Dutchess County, NY	**287,752**	**280,150**	**259,462**	**28,290**	**10.9%**
Dutchess County	287,752	280,150	259,462	28,290	10.9%
Eau Claire, WI	**150,295**	**148,337**	**137,543**	**12,752**	**9.3%**
Eau Claire County	94,219	93,142	85,183	9,036	10.6%
Chippewa County	56,076	55,195	52,360	3,716	7.1%
El Paso, TX	**697,562**	**679,622**	**591,610**	**105,952**	**17.9%**
El Paso County	697,562	679,622	591,610	105,952	17.9%
Elkhart-Goshen, IN	**186,465**	**182,791**	**156,198**	**30,267**	**19.4%**
Elkhart County	186,465	182,791	156,198	30,267	19.4%
Elmira, NY	**90,614**	**91,070**	**95,195**	**-4,581**	**-4.8%**
Chemung County	90,614	91,070	95,195	-4,581	-4.8%
Enid, OK	**57,246**	**57,813**	**56,735**	**511**	**0.9%**
Garfield County	57,246	57,813	56,735	511	0.9%
Erie, PA	**280,370**	**280,843**	**275,572**	**4,798**	**1.7%**
Erie County	280,370	280,843	275,572	4,798	1.7%
Eugene-Springfield, OR	**326,666**	**322,959**	**282,912**	**43,754**	**15.5%**
Lane County	326,666	322,959	282,912	43,754	15.5%
Evansville-Henderson, IN-KY	**297,353**	**296,195**	**278,990**	**18,363**	**6.6%**
Vanderburgh County, IN	171,744	171,922	165,058	6,686	4.1%
Warrick County, IN	53,624	52,383	44,920	8,704	19.4%
Henderson County, KY	44,995	44,829	43,044	1,951	4.5%
Posey County, IN	26,990	27,061	25,968	1,022	3.9%
Fargo-Moorhead, ND-MN	**177,064**	**174,367**	**153,296**	**23,768**	**15.5%**
Cass County, ND	125,117	123,138	102,874	22,243	21.6%
Clay County, MN	51,947	51,229	50,422	1,525	3.0%
Fayetteville, NC	**303,328**	**302,963**	**274,566**	**28,762**	**10.5%**
Cumberland County	303,328	302,963	274,566	28,762	10.5%
Fayetteville-Springdale-Rogers, AR	**332,011**	**311,121**	**210,908**	**121,103**	**57.4%**
Washington County	166,511	157,715	113,409	53,102	46.8%
Benton County	165,500	153,406	97,499	68,001	69.7%

MSA and Included Counties	2002 Population	2000 Population	1990 Population	Change 1990-2002	Percentage Change 1990-2002
Fitchburg-Leominster, MA	**145,233**	**142,284**	**138,165**	**7,068**	**5.1%**
Worcester County (part)	142,329	139,439	135,448	6,881	5.1%
Middlesex County (part)	2,904	2,845	2,717	187	6.9%
Flagstaff, AZ-UT	**126,416**	**122,366**	**101,760**	**24,656**	**24.2%**
Coconino County, AZ	120,295	116,320	96,591	23,704	24.5%
Kane County, UT	6,121	6,046	5,169	952	18.4%
Flint, MI	**441,423**	**436,141**	**430,459**	**10,964**	**2.5%**
Genesee County	441,423	436,141	430,459	10,964	2.5%
Florence, AL	**141,966**	**142,950**	**131,327**	**10,639**	**8.1%**
Lauderdale County	87,116	87,966	79,661	7,455	9.4%
Colbert County	54,850	54,984	51,666	3,184	6.2%
Florence, SC	**127,237**	**125,761**	**114,344**	**12,893**	**11.3%**
Florence County	127,237	125,761	114,344	12,893	11.3%
Fort Collins–Loveland, CO	**264,605**	**251,494**	**186,136**	**78,469**	**42.2%**
Larimer County	264,605	251,494	186,136	78,469	42.2%
Fort Lauderdale, FL	**1,709,118**	**1,623,018**	**1,255,488**	**453,630**	**36.1%**
Broward County	1,709,118	1,623,018	1,255,488	453,630	36.1%
Fort Myers–Cape Coral, FL	**475,639**	**440,888**	**335,113**	**140,526**	**41.9%**
Lee County	475,639	440,888	335,113	140,526	41.9%
Fort Pierce–Port St. Lucie, FL	**337,638**	**319,426**	**251,071**	**86,567**	**34.5%**
St. Lucie County	205,420	192,695	150,171	55,249	36.8%
Martin County	132,218	126,731	100,900	31,318	31.0%
Fort Smith, AR-OK	**212,045**	**207,290**	**175,911**	**36,134**	**20.5%**
Sebastian County, AR	117,220	115,071	99,590	17,630	17.7%
Crawford County, AR	54,973	53,247	42,493	12,480	29.4%
Sequoyah County, OK	39,852	38,972	33,828	6,024	17.8%
Fort Walton Beach, FL	**175,708**	**170,498**	**143,776**	**31,932**	**22.2%**
Okaloosa County	175,708	170,498	143,776	31,932	22.2%
Fort Wayne, IN	**508,915**	**502,141**	**456,281**	**52,634**	**11.5%**
Allen County	337,512	331,849	300,836	36,676	12.2%
DeKalb County	40,525	40,285	35,324	5,201	14.7%
Huntington County	38,243	38,075	35,427	2,816	7.9%
Adams County	33,500	33,625	31,095	2,405	7.7%
Whitley County	31,339	30,707	27,651	3,688	13.3%
Wells County	27,796	27,600	25,948	1,848	7.1%
Fort Worth–Arlington, TX	**1,802,465**	**1,702,625**	**1,361,034**	**441,431**	**32.4%**
Tarrant County	1,527,366	1,446,219	1,170,103	357,263	30.5%
Johnson County	136,332	126,811	97,165	39,167	40.3%
Parker County	94,618	88,495	64,785	29,833	46.0%
Hood County	44,149	41,100	28,981	15,168	52.3%
Fresno, CA	**964,897**	**922,516**	**755,580**	**209,317**	**27.7%**
Fresno County	834,632	799,407	667,490	167,142	25.0%
Madera County	130,265	123,109	88,090	42,175	47.9%
Gadsden, AL	**103,105**	**103,459**	**99,840**	**3,265**	**3.3%**
Etowah County	103,105	103,459	99,840	3,265	3.3%
Gainesville, FL	**222,254**	**217,955**	**181,596**	**40,658**	**22.4%**
Alachua County	222,254	217,955	181,596	40,658	22.4%
Galveston–Texas City, TX	**261,219**	**250,158**	**217,399**	**43,820**	**20.2%**
Galveston County	261,219	250,158	217,399	43,820	20.2%
Gary, IN	**637,419**	**631,362**	**604,526**	**32,893**	**5.4%**
Lake County	487,016	484,564	475,594	11,422	2.4%
Porter County	150,403	146,798	128,932	21,471	16.7%
Glens Falls, NY	**125,101**	**124,345**	**118,539**	**6,562**	**5.5%**
Warren County	63,906	63,303	59,209	4,697	7.9%
Washington County	61,195	61,042	59,330	1,865	3.1%
Goldsboro, NC	**112,954**	**113,329**	**104,666**	**8,288**	**7.9%**
Wayne County	112,954	113,329	104,666	8,288	7.9%
Grand Forks, ND-MN	**96,035**	**97,478**	**103,181**	**-7,146**	**-6.9%**
Grand Forks County, ND	64,920	66,109	70,683	-5,763	-8.2%
Polk County, MN	31,115	31,369	32,498	-1,383	-4.3%
Grand Junction, CO	**121,419**	**116,255**	**93,145**	**28,274**	**30.4%**
Mesa County	121,419	116,255	93,145	28,274	30.4%

continued

Table 1.1: Principal U.S. Metropolitan Statistical Areas *(continued)*

MSA and Included Counties	2002 Population	2000 Population	1990 Population	Change 1990-2002	Percentage Change 1990-2002
Grand Rapids–Muskegon–Holland, MI	**1,114,965**	**1,088,514**	**937,891**	**177,074**	**18.9%**
Kent County	587,951	574,335	500,631	87,320	17.4%
Ottawa County	245,913	238,314	187,768	58,145	31.0%
Muskegon County	171,765	170,200	158,983	12,782	8.0%
Allegan County	109,336	105,665	90,509	18,827	20.8%
Great Falls, MT	**79,389**	**80,357**	**77,691**	**1,698**	**2.2%**
Cascade County	79,389	80,357	77,691	1,698	2.2%
Greeley, CO	**205,014**	**180,936**	**131,821**	**73,193**	**55.5%**
Weld County	205,014	180,936	131,821	73,193	55.5%
Green Bay, WI	**232,185**	**226,778**	**194,594**	**37,591**	**19.3%**
Brown County	232,185	226,778	194,594	37,591	19.3%
Greensboro–Winston-Salem–High Point, NC	**1,286,265**	**1,251,509**	**1,050,304**	**235,961**	**22.5%**
Guilford County	430,937	421,048	347,420	83,517	24.0%
Forsyth County	314,933	306,067	265,878	49,055	18.5%
Davidson County	151,238	147,246	126,677	24,561	19.4%
Alamance County	135,893	130,800	108,213	27,680	25.6%
Randolph County	134,217	130,454	106,546	27,671	26.0%
Stokes County	44,984	44,711	37,223	7,761	20.9%
Yadkin County	37,329	36,348	30,488	6,841	22.4%
Davie County	36,734	34,835	27,859	8,875	31.9%
Greenville, NC	**137,240**	**133,798**	**107,924**	**29,316**	**27.2%**
Pitt County	137,240	133,798	107,924	29,316	27.2%
Greenville-Spartanburg-Anderson, SC	**987,855**	**962,441**	**830,563**	**157,292**	**18.9%**
Greenville County	391,334	379,616	320,167	71,167	22.2%
Spartanburg County	259,322	253,791	226,800	32,522	14.3%
Anderson County	170,578	165,740	145,196	25,382	17.5%
Pickens County	113,097	110,757	93,894	19,203	20.5%
Cherokee County	53,524	52,537	44,506	9,018	20.3%
Hagerstown, MD	**134,246**	**131,923**	**121,393**	**12,853**	**10.6%**
Washington County	134,246	131,923	121,393	12,853	10.6%
Hamilton-Middletown, OH	**340,543**	**332,807**	**291,479**	**49,064**	**16.8%**
Butler County	340,543	332,807	291,479	49,064	16.8%
Harrisburg-Lebanon-Carlisle, PA	**635,751**	**629,401**	**587,986**	**47,765**	**8.1%**
Dauphin County	252,933	251,798	237,813	15,120	6.4%
Cumberland County	217,743	213,674	195,257	22,486	11.5%
Lebanon County	121,199	120,327	113,744	7,455	6.6%
Perry County	43,876	43,602	41,172	2,704	6.6%
Hartford, CT	**1,203,169**	**1,183,110**	**1,157,585**	**45,584**	**3.9%**
Hartford County (part)	865,279	855,171	849,917	15,362	1.8%
Tolland County (part)	140,368	135,671	128,087	12,281	9.6%
Middlesex County (part)	100,753	104,442	96,996	3,757	3.9%
Litchfield County (part)	38,183	37,163	37,712	471	1.2%
Windham County (part)	29,530	29,205	27,852	1,678	6.0%
New London County (part)	22,074	21,458	17,021	5,053	29.7%
Hattiesburg, MS	**114,632**	**111,674**	**98,738**	**15,894**	**16.1%**
Forrest County	73,465	72,604	68,314	5,151	7.5%
Lamar County	41,167	39,070	30,424	10,743	35.3%
Hickory-Morganton-Lenoir, NC	**349,241**	**341,851**	**292,409**	**56,832**	**19.4%**
Catawba County	146,690	141,685	118,412	28,278	23.9%
Burke County	89,638	89,148	75,744	13,894	18.3%
Caldwell County	78,513	77,415	70,709	7,804	11.0%
Alexander County	34,400	33,603	27,544	6,856	24.9%
Honolulu, HI	**896,019**	**876,156**	**836,231**	**59,788**	**7.1%**
Honolulu County	896,019	876,156	836,231	59,788	7.1%
Houma, LA	**196,860**	**194,477**	**182,842**	**14,018**	**7.7%**
Terrebonne Parish	105,638	104,503	96,982	8,656	8.9%
Lafourche Parish	91,222	89,974	85,860	5,362	6.2%
Houston, TX	**4,420,081**	**4,177,646**	**3,322,025**	**1,098,056**	**33.1%**
Harris County	3,557,055	3,400,578	2,818,199	738,856	26.2%
Fort Bend County	399,537	354,452	225,421	174,116	77.2%
Montgomery County	328,449	293,768	182,201	146,248	80.3%
Liberty County	73,739	70,154	52,726	21,013	39.9%

MSA and Included Counties	2002 Population	2000 Population	1990 Population	Change 1990-2002	Percentage Change 1990-2002
Houston, TX *(cont.)*					
Waller County	34,057	32,663	23,390	10,667	45.6%
Chambers County	27,244	26,031	20,088	7,156	35.6%
Huntington-Ashland, WV-KY-OH	**313,239**	**315,538**	**312,529**	**710**	**0.2%**
Cabell County, WV	95,266	96,784	96,827	-1,561	-1.6%
Lawrence County, OH	62,172	62,319	61,834	338	0.5%
Boyd County, KY	49,603	49,752	51,150	-1,547	-3.0%
Wayne County, WV	42,382	42,903	41,636	746	1.8%
Greenup County, KY	36,761	36,891	36,742	19	0.1%
Carter County, KY	27,055	26,889	24,340	2,715	11.2%
Huntsville, AL	**353,742**	**342,376**	**293,047**	**60,695**	**20.7%**
Madison County	285,900	276,700	238,912	46,988	19.7%
Limestone County	67,842	65,676	54,135	13,707	25.3%
Indianapolis, IN	**1,655,097**	**1,607,486**	**1,380,491**	**274,606**	**19.9%**
Marion County	863,429	860,454	797,159	66,270	8.3%
Hamilton County	205,610	182,740	108,936	96,674	88.7%
Madison County	132,068	133,358	130,669	1,399	1.1%
Johnson County	121,604	115,209	88,109	33,495	38.0%
Hendricks County	114,301	104,093	75,717	38,584	51.0%
Morgan County	67,791	66,689	55,920	11,871	21.2%
Hancock County	58,343	55,391	45,527	12,816	28.2%
Boone County	48,277	46,107	38,147	10,130	26.6%
Shelby County	43,674	43,445	40,307	3,367	8.4%
Iowa City, IA	**114,300**	**111,006**	**96,119**	**18,181**	**18.9%**
Johnson County	114,300	111,006	96,119	18,181	18.9%
Jackson, MI	**160,972**	**158,422**	**149,756**	**8,666**	**5.8%**
Jackson County	160,972	158,422	149,756	8,666	5.8%
Jackson, MS	**449,028**	**440,801**	**395,396**	**45,405**	**11.5%**
Hinds County	249,579	250,800	254,441	-3,641	-1.4%
Rankin County	121,577	115,327	87,161	28,166	32.3%
Madison County	77,872	74,674	53,794	20,880	38.8%
Jackson, TN	**109,290**	**107,377**	**90,801**	**16,576**	**18.3%**
Madison County	93,367	91,837	77,982	13,855	17.8%
Chester County	15,923	15,540	12,819	2,721	21.2%
Jacksonville, FL	**1,154,809**	**1,100,491**	**906,727**	**193,764**	**21.4%**
Duval County	806,120	778,879	672,971	105,908	15.7%
Clay County	152,093	140,814	105,986	34,828	32.9%
St. Johns County	136,038	123,135	83,829	39,306	46.9%
Nassau County	60,558	57,663	43,941	13,722	31.2%
Jacksonville, NC	**149,003**	**150,355**	**149,838**	**517**	**0.3%**
Onslow County	149,003	150,355	149,838	517	0.3%
Jamestown, NY	**138,332**	**139,750**	**141,895**	**-2,145**	**-1.5%**
Chautauqua County	138,332	139,750	141,895	-2,145	-1.5%
Janesville-Beloit, WI	**154,092**	**152,307**	**139,510**	**14,582**	**10.5%**
Rock County	154,092	152,307	139,510	14,582	10.5%
Jersey City, NJ	**611,439**	**608,975**	**553,099**	**58,340**	**10.5%**
Hudson County	611,439	608,975	553,099	58,340	10.5%
Johnson City–Kingsport–Bristol, TN-VA	**482,934**	**480,091**	**436,047**	**46,887**	**10.8%**
Sullivan County, TN	153,051	153,048	143,596	9,455	6.6%
Washington County, TN	109,019	107,198	92,315	16,704	18.1%
Carter County, TN	56,746	56,742	51,505	5,241	10.2%
Hawkins County, TN	54,793	53,563	44,565	10,228	23.0%
Washington County, VA	51,331	51,103	45,887	5,444	11.9%
Scott County, VA	23,136	23,403	23,204	-68	-0.3%
Unicoi County, TN	17,740	17,667	16,549	1,191	7.2%
Bristol city, VA	17,118	17,367	18,426	-1,308	-7.1%
Johnstown, PA	**229,908**	**232,621**	**241,247**	**-11,339**	**-4.7%**
Cambria County	150,452	152,598	163,029	-12,577	-7.7%
Somerset County	79,456	80,023	78,218	1,238	1.6%
Jonesboro, AR	**84,074**	**82,148**	**68,956**	**15,118**	**21.9%**
Craighead County	84,074	82,148	68,956	15,118	21.9%

continued

Table 1.1: Principal U.S. Metropolitan Statistical Areas (continued)

MSA and Included Counties	2002 Population	2000 Population	1990 Population	Change 1990-2002	Percentage Change 1990-2002
Joplin, MO	**160,203**	**157,322**	**134,910**	**25,293**	**18.7%**
Jasper County	107,073	104,686	90,465	16,608	18.4%
Newton County	53,130	52,636	44,445	8,685	19.5%
Kalamazoo–Battle Creek, MI	**457,081**	**452,851**	**429,453**	**27,628**	**6.4%**
Kalamazoo County	241,471	238,603	223,411	18,060	8.1%
Calhoun County	138,375	137,985	135,982	2,393	1.8%
Van Buren County	77,235	76,263	70,060	7,175	10.2%
Kankakee, IL	**104,657**	**103,833**	**96,255**	**8,402**	**8.7%**
Kankakee County	104,657	103,833	96,255	8,402	8.7%
Kansas City, MO-KS	**1,828,247**	**1,776,062**	**1,582,875**	**245,372**	**15.5%**
Jackson County, MO	660,773	654,880	633,232	27,541	4.3%
Johnson County, KS	476,536	451,086	355,054	121,482	34.2%
Clay County, MO	191,381	184,006	153,411	37,970	24.8%
Wyandotte County, KS	158,331	157,882	161,993	-3,662	-2.3%
Cass County, MO	87,310	82,092	63,808	23,502	36.8%
Platte County, MO	77,655	73,781	57,867	19,788	34.2%
Leavenworth County, KS	70,789	68,691	64,371	6,418	10.0%
Lafayette County, MO	33,125	32,960	31,107	2,018	6.5%
Miami County, KS	28,904	28,351	23,466	5,438	23.2%
Ray County, MO	23,811	23,354	21,971	1,840	8.4%
Clinton County, MO	19,632	18,979	16,595	3,037	18.3%
Kenosha, WI	**154,433**	**149,577**	**128,181**	**26,252**	**20.5%**
Kenosha County	154,433	149,577	128,181	26,252	20.5%
Killeen-Temple, TX	**319,163**	**312,952**	**255,301**	**63,862**	**25.0%**
Bell County	244,668	237,974	191,088	53,580	28.0%
Coryell County	74,495	74,978	64,213	10,282	16.0%
Knoxville, TN	**704,431**	**687,249**	**585,960**	**118,471**	**20.2%**
Knox County	389,327	382,032	335,749	53,578	16.0%
Blount County	109,849	105,823	85,969	23,880	27.8%
Sevier County	74,456	71,170	51,043	23,413	45.9%
Anderson County	71,627	71,330	68,250	3,377	4.9%
Loudon County	40,631	39,086	31,255	9,376	30.0%
Union County	18,541	17,808	13,694	4,847	35.4%
Kokomo, IN	**101,372**	**101,541**	**96,946**	**4,426**	**4.6%**
Howard County	84,838	84,964	80,827	4,011	5.0%
Tipton County	16,534	16,577	16,119	415	2.6%
La Crosse, WI-MN	**127,994**	**126,838**	**116,401**	**11,593**	**10.0%**
La Crosse County, WI	108,148	107,120	97,904	10,244	10.5%
Houston County, MN	19,846	19,718	18,497	1,349	7.3%
Lafayette, IN	**185,973**	**182,821**	**161,572**	**24,401**	**15.1%**
Tippecanoe County	152,001	148,955	130,598	21,403	16.4%
Clinton County	33,972	33,866	30,974	2,998	9.7%
Lafayette, LA	**389,672**	**385,647**	**344,953**	**44,719**	**13.0%**
Lafayette Parish	192,896	190,503	164,762	28,134	17.1%
St. Landry Parish	88,199	87,700	80,331	7,868	9.8%
Acadia Parish	58,920	58,861	55,882	3,038	5.4%
St. Martin Parish	49,657	48,583	43,978	5,679	12.9%
Lake Charles, LA	**183,344**	**183,577**	**168,134**	**15,210**	**9.0%**
Calcasieu Parish	183,344	183,577	168,134	15,210	9.0%
Lakeland–Winter Haven, FL	**498,721**	**483,924**	**405,382**	**93,339**	**23.0%**
Polk County	498,721	483,924	405,382	93,339	23.0%
Lancaster, PA	**478,561**	**470,658**	**422,822**	**55,739**	**13.2%**
Lancaster County	478,561	470,658	422,822	55,739	13.2%
Lansing–East Lansing, MI	**453,620**	**447,728**	**432,674**	**20,946**	**4.8%**
Ingham County	281,362	279,320	281,912	-550	-0.2%
Eaton County	105,590	103,655	92,879	12,711	13.7%
Clinton County	66,668	64,753	57,883	8,785	15.2%
Laredo, TX	**207,611**	**193,117**	**133,239**	**74,372**	**55.8%**
Webb County	207,611	193,117	133,239	74,372	55.8%
Las Cruces, NM	**178,664**	**174,682**	**135,510**	**43,154**	**31.8%**
Doña Ana County	178,664	174,682	135,510	43,154	31.8%

MSA and Included Counties	2002 Population	2000 Population	1990 Population	Change 1990-2002	Percentage Change 1990-2002
Las Vegas, NV-AZ	**1,722,256**	**1,563,282**	**852,737**	**869,519**	**102.0%**
Clark County, NV	1,522,164	1,375,765	741,459	780,705	105.3%
Mohave County, AZ	165,593	155,032	93,497	72,096	77.1%
Nye County, NV	34,499	32,485	17,781	16,718	94.0%
Lawrence, KS	**102,316**	**99,962**	**81,798**	**20,518**	**25.1%**
Douglas County	102,316	99,962	81,798	20,518	25.1%
Lawrence, MA-NH	**405,419**	**396,230**	**353,232**	**52,187**	**14.8%**
Essex County, MA (part)	269,024	264,873	240,009	29,015	12.1%
Rockingham County, NH (part)	136,395	131,357	113,223	23,172	20.5%
Lawton, OK	**113,414**	**114,996**	**111,486**	**1,928**	**1.7%**
Comanche County	113,414	114,996	111,486	1,928	1.7%
Lewiston-Auburn, ME	**91,220**	**90,830**	**93,679**	**-2,459**	**-2.6%**
Androscoggin County (part)	91,220	90,830	93,679	-2,459	-2.6%
Lexington, KY	**489,717**	**479,198**	**405,936**	**83,781**	**20.6%**
Fayette County	263,618	260,512	225,366	38,252	17.0%
Madison County	73,334	70,872	57,508	15,826	27.5%
Jessamine County	40,740	39,041	30,508	10,232	33.5%
Scott County	35,320	33,061	23,867	11,453	48.0%
Clark County	33,726	33,144	29,496	4,230	14.3%
Woodford County	23,403	23,208	19,955	3,448	17.3%
Bourbon County	19,576	19,360	19,236	340	1.8%
Lima, OH	**154,584**	**155,084**	**154,340**	**244**	**0.2%**
Allen County	108,120	108,473	109,755	-1,635	-1.5%
Auglaize County	46,464	46,611	44,585	1,879	4.2%
Lincoln, NE	**257,513**	**250,291**	**213,641**	**43,872**	**20.5%**
Lancaster County	257,513	250,291	213,641	43,872	20.5%
Little Rock–North Little Rock, AR	**595,563**	**583,845**	**513,117**	**82,446**	**16.1%**
Pulaski County	364,381	361,474	349,660	14,721	4.2%
Faulkner County	89,590	86,014	60,006	29,584	49.3%
Saline County	86,290	83,529	64,183	22,107	34.4%
Lonoke County	55,302	52,828	39,268	16,034	40.8%
Longview-Marshall, TX	**212,288**	**208,780**	**193,801**	**18,487**	**9.5%**
Gregg County	113,255	111,379	104,948	8,307	7.9%
Harrison County	62,534	62,110	57,483	5,051	8.8%
Upshur County	36,499	35,291	31,370	5,129	16.4%
Los Angeles–Long Beach, CA	**9,806,577**	**9,519,338**	**8,863,164**	**943,413**	**10.6%**
Los Angeles County	9,806,577	9,519,338	8,863,164	943,413	10.6%
Louisville, KY-IN	**1,039,599**	**1,025,598**	**948,829**	**90,770**	**9.6%**
Jefferson County, KY	698,080	693,604	664,937	33,143	5.0%
Clark County, IN	98,198	96,472	87,777	10,421	11.9%
Floyd County, IN	71,633	70,823	64,404	7,229	11.2%
Bullitt County, KY	63,800	61,236	47,567	16,233	34.1%
Oldham County, KY	49,310	46,178	33,263	16,047	48.2%
Harrison County, IN	35,244	34,325	29,890	5,354	17.9%
Scott County, IN	23,334	22,960	20,991	2,343	11.2%
Lowell, MA-NH	**305,212**	**301,686**	**280,578**	**24,634**	**8.8%**
Middlesex County, MA (part)	293,540	290,772	271,170	22,370	8.2%
Hillsborough County, NH (part)	11,672	10,914	9,408	2,264	24.1%
Lubbock, TX	**247,574**	**242,628**	**222,636**	**24,938**	**11.2%**
Lubbock County	247,574	242,628	222,636	24,938	11.2%
Lynchburg, VA	**216,163**	**214,911**	**193,928**	**22,235**	**11.5%**
Lynchburg city	64,616	65,269	66,049	-1,433	-2.2%
Bedford County	61,875	60,371	45,656	16,219	35.5%
Campbell County	51,471	51,078	47,572	3,899	8.2%
Amherst County	31,976	31,894	28,578	3,398	11.9%
Bedford city	6,225	6,299	6,073	152	2.5%
Macon, GA	**330,853**	**322,549**	**290,909**	**39,944**	**13.7%**
Bibb County	154,824	153,887	149,967	4,857	3.2%
Houston County	116,768	110,765	89,208	27,560	30.9%
Jones County	24,492	23,639	20,739	3,753	18.1%
Peach County	24,224	23,668	21,189	3,035	14.3%
Twiggs County	10,545	10,590	9,806	739	7.5%

continued

Table 1.1: Principal U.S. Metropolitan Statistical Areas (continued)

MSA and Included Counties	2002 Population	2000 Population	1990 Population	Change 1990-2002	Percentage Change 1990-2002
Madison, WI	**443,110**	**426,526**	**367,085**	**76,025**	**20.7%**
Dane County	443,110	426,526	367,085	76,025	20.7%
Manchester, NH	**204,359**	**198,378**	**173,783**	**30,576**	**17.6%**
Hillsborough County (part)	153,701	149,985	132,944	20,757	15.6%
Rockingham County (part)	33,242	31,829	27,423	5,819	21.2%
Merrimack County (part)	17,416	16,564	13,416	4,000	29.8%
Mansfield, OH	**174,424**	**175,818**	**174,007**	**417**	**0.2%**
Richland County	128,004	128,852	126,137	1,867	1.5%
Crawford County	46,420	46,966	47,870	-1,450	-3.0%
McAllen-Edinburg-Mission, TX	**614,474**	**569,463**	**383,545**	**230,929**	**60.2%**
Hidalgo County	614,474	569,463	383,545	230,929	60.2%
Medford-Ashland, OR	**186,430**	**181,269**	**146,389**	**40,041**	**27.4%**
Jackson County	186,430	181,269	146,389	40,041	27.4%
Melbourne–Titusville–Palm Bay, FL	**495,576**	**476,230**	**398,978**	**96,598**	**24.2%**
Brevard County	495,576	476,230	398,978	96,598	24.2%
Memphis, TN-AR-MS	**1,160,065**	**1,135,614**	**1,007,306**	**152,759**	**15.2%**
Shelby County, TN	905,678	897,472	826,330	79,348	9.6%
DeSoto County, MS	118,458	107,199	67,910	50,548	74.4%
Tipton County, TN	53,436	51,271	37,568	15,868	42.2%
Crittenden County, AR	51,291	50,866	49,939	1,352	2.7%
Fayette County, TN	31,202	28,806	25,559	5,643	22.1%
Merced, CA	**225,398**	**210,554**	**178,403**	**46,995**	**26.3%**
Merced County	225,398	210,554	178,403	46,995	26.3%
Miami, FL	**2,332,599**	**2,253,362**	**1,937,094**	**395,505**	**20.4%**
Miami-Dade County	2,332,599	2,253,362	1,937,094	395,505	20.4%
Middlesex-Somerset-Hunterdon, NJ	**1,211,230**	**1,169,641**	**1,019,835**	**191,395**	**18.8%**
Middlesex County	775,549	750,162	671,780	103,769	15.4%
Somerset County	309,886	297,490	240,279	69,607	29.0%
Hunterdon County	125,795	121,989	107,776	18,019	16.7%
Milwaukee-Waukesha, WI	**1,512,504**	**1,500,741**	**1,432,149**	**80,355**	**5.6%**
Milwaukee County	937,136	940,164	959,275	-22,139	-2.3%
Waukesha County	370,554	360,767	304,715	65,839	21.6%
Washington County	120,899	117,493	95,328	25,571	26.8%
Ozaukee County	83,915	82,317	72,831	11,084	15.2%
Minneapolis–St. Paul, MN-WI	**3,054,637**	**2,968,806**	**2,538,834**	**515,803**	**20.3%**
Hennepin County, MN	1,122,259	1,116,200	1,032,431	89,828	8.7%
Ramsey County, MN	510,568	511,035	485,765	24,803	5.1%
Dakota County, MN	368,972	355,904	275,227	93,745	34.1%
Anoka County, MN	309,790	298,084	243,641	66,149	27.2%
Washington County, MN	210,270	201,130	145,896	64,374	44.1%
Scott County, MN	103,681	89,498	57,846	45,835	79.2%
Wright County, MN	98,083	89,986	68,710	29,373	42.7%
Carver County, MN	75,620	70,205	47,915	27,705	57.8%
Sherburne County, MN	71,471	64,417	41,945	29,526	70.4%
St. Croix County, WI	68,122	63,155	50,251	17,871	35.6%
Chisago County, MN	44,580	41,101	30,521	14,059	46.1%
Pierce County, WI	37,422	36,804	32,765	4,657	14.2%
Isanti County, MN	33,799	31,287	25,921	7,878	30.4%
Missoula, MT	**98,102**	**95,802**	**78,687**	**19,415**	**24.7%**
Missoula County	98,102	95,802	78,687	19,415	24.7%
Mobile, AL	**548,095**	**540,258**	**476,923**	**71,172**	**14.9%**
Mobile County	400,163	399,843	378,643	21,520	5.7%
Baldwin County	147,932	140,415	98,280	49,652	50.5%
Modesto, CA	**482,440**	**446,997**	**370,522**	**111,918**	**30.2%**
Stanislaus County	482,440	446,997	370,522	111,918	30.2%
Monmouth-Ocean, NJ	**1,166,901**	**1,126,217**	**986,327**	**180,574**	**18.3%**
Monmouth County	629,836	615,301	553,124	76,712	13.9%
Ocean County	537,065	510,916	433,203	103,862	24.0%
Monroe, LA	**147,342**	**147,250**	**142,191**	**5,151**	**3.6%**
Ouachita Parish	147,342	147,250	142,191	5,151	3.6%
Montgomery, AL	**337,721**	**333,055**	**292,517**	**45,204**	**15.5%**
Montgomery County	223,346	223,510	209,085	14,261	6.8%

MSA and Included Counties	2002 Population	2000 Population	1990 Population	Change 1990-2002	Percentage Change 1990-2002
Montgomery, AL *(cont.)*					
Elmore County	68,771	65,874	49,210	19,561	39.8%
Autauga County	45,604	43,671	34,222	11,382	33.3%
Muncie, IN	**118,197**	**118,769**	**119,659**	**-1,462**	**-1.2%**
Delaware County	118,197	118,769	119,659	-1,462	-1.2%
Myrtle Beach, SC	**206,039**	**196,629**	**144,053**	**61,986**	**43.0%**
Horry County	206,039	196,629	144,053	61,986	43.0%
Naples, FL	**276,691**	**251,377**	**152,099**	**124,592**	**81.9%**
Collier County	276,691	251,377	152,099	124,592	81.9%
Nashua, NH	**196,910**	**190,949**	**168,233**	**28,677**	**17.0%**
Hillsborough County (part)	196,910	190,949	168,233	28,677	17.0%
Nashville, TN	**1,270,520**	**1,231,311**	**985,026**	**285,494**	**29.0%**
Davidson County	570,785	569,891	510,784	60,001	11.7%
Rutherford County	194,934	182,023	118,570	76,364	64.4%
Williamson County	136,889	126,638	81,021	55,868	69.0%
Sumner County	136,170	130,449	103,281	32,889	31.8%
Wilson County	93,079	88,809	67,675	25,404	37.5%
Robertson County	57,446	54,433	41,494	15,952	38.4%
Dickson County	44,231	43,156	35,061	9,170	26.2%
Cheatham County	36,986	35,912	27,140	9,846	36.3%
Nassau-Suffolk, NY	**2,803,547**	**2,753,913**	**2,609,212**	**194,335**	**7.4%**
Suffolk County	1,458,655	1,419,369	1,321,864	136,791	10.3%
Nassau County	1,344,892	1,334,544	1,287,348	57,544	4.5%
New Bedford, MA	**177,035**	**175,198**	**175,641**	**1,394**	**0.8%**
Bristol County (part)	160,409	159,226	161,374	-965	-0.6%
Plymouth County (part)	16,626	15,972	14,267	2,359	16.5%
New Haven–Meriden, CT	**549,333**	**542,149**	**530,180**	**19,153**	**3.6%**
New Haven County (part)	529,647	523,037	512,599	17,048	3.3%
Middlesex County (part)	19,686	19,112	17,581	2,105	12.0%
New London–Norwich, CT-RI	**297,991**	**293,566**	**290,734**	**7,257**	**2.5%**
New London County, CT (part)	235,977	233,086	233,874	2,103	0.9%
Washington County, RI (part)	31,687	30,802	28,478	3,209	11.3%
Windham County, CT (part)	19,842	19,311	18,830	1,012	5.4%
Middlesex County, CT (part)	10,485	10,367	9,552	933	9.8%
New Orleans, LA	**1,336,603**	**1,337,726**	**1,285,270**	**51,333**	**4.0%**
Orleans Parish	473,681	484,674	496,938	-23,257	-4.7%
Jefferson Parish	452,789	455,466	448,306	4,483	1.0%
St. Tammany Parish	201,462	191,268	144,508	56,954	39.4%
St. Bernard Parish	66,219	67,229	66,631	-412	-0.6%
St. Charles Parish	49,250	48,072	42,437	6,813	16.1%
St. John the Baptist Parish	44,521	43,044	39,996	4,525	11.3%
Plaquemines Parish	27,332	26,757	25,575	1,757	6.9%
St. James Parish	21,349	21,216	20,879	470	2.3%
New York, NY	**9,411,687**	**9,314,235**	**8,546,846**	**864,841**	**10.1%**
Kings County	2,488,194	2,465,326	2,300,664	187,530	8.2%
Queens County	2,237,815	2,229,379	1,951,598	286,217	14.7%
New York County	1,546,856	1,537,195	1,487,536	59,320	4.0%
Bronx County	1,354,068	1,332,650	1,203,789	150,279	12.5%
Westchester County	937,279	923,459	874,866	62,413	7.1%
Richmond County	457,383	443,728	378,977	78,406	20.7%
Rockland County	291,835	286,753	265,475	26,360	9.9%
Putnam County	98,257	95,745	83,941	14,316	17.1%
Newark, NJ	**2,064,011**	**2,032,989**	**1,915,928**	**148,083**	**7.7%**
Essex County	798,301	793,633	778,206	20,095	2.6%
Union County	530,763	522,541	493,819	36,944	7.5%
Morris County	478,730	470,212	421,353	57,377	13.6%
Sussex County	148,680	144,166	130,943	17,737	13.5%
Warren County+A823	107,537	102,437	91,607	15,930	17.4%
Newburgh, NY-PA	**406,868**	**387,669**	**335,613**	**71,255**	**21.2%**
Orange County, NY	356,773	341,367	307,647	49,126	16.0%
Pike County, PA	50,095	46,302	27,966	22,129	79.1%

continued

Table 1.1: Principal U.S. Metropolitan Statistical Areas *(continued)*

MSA and Included Counties	2002 Population	2000 Population	1990 Population	Change 1990-2002	Percentage Change 1990-2002
Norfolk–Virginia Beach–Newport News, VA-NC	**1,605,822**	**1,569,541**	**1,443,244**	**162,578**	**11.3%**
Virginia Beach city, VA	433,934	425,257	393,069	40,865	10.4%
Norfolk city, VA	239,036	234,403	261,229	-22,193	-8.5%
Chesapeake city, VA	206,665	199,184	151,976	54,689	36.0%
Newport News city, VA	180,272	180,150	170,045	10,227	6.0%
Hampton city, VA	145,921	146,437	133,793	12,128	9.1%
Portsmouth city, VA	99,790	100,565	103,907	-4,117	-4.0%
Suffolk city, VA	69,966	63,677	52,141	17,825	34.2%
York County, VA	59,720	56,297	42,422	17,298	40.8%
James City County, VA	51,418	48,102	34,859	16,559	47.5%
Gloucester County, VA	35,755	34,780	30,131	5,624	18.7%
Isle of Wight County, VA	31,085	29,728	25,053	6,032	24.1%
Currituck County, NC	19,623	18,190	13,736	5,887	42.9%
Williamsburg city, VA	11,693	11,998	11,530	163	1.4%
Poquoson city, VA	11,686	11,566	11,005	681	6.2%
Mathews County, VA	9,258	9,207	8,348	910	10.9%
Oakland, CA	**2,464,668**	**2,392,557**	**2,082,914**	**381,754**	**18.3%**
Alameda County	1,472,310	1,443,741	1,279,182	193,128	15.1%
Contra Costa County	992,358	948,816	803,732	188,626	23.5%
Ocala, FL	**272,553**	**258,916**	**194,833**	**77,720**	**39.9%**
Marion County	272,553	258,916	194,833	77,720	39.9%
Odessa-Midland, TX	**239,981**	**237,132**	**225,545**	**14,436**	**6.4%**
Ector County	122,312	121,123	118,934	3,378	2.8%
Midland County	117,669	116,009	106,611	11,058	10.4%
Oklahoma City, OK	**1,109,083**	**1,083,346**	**958,839**	**150,244**	**15.7%**
Oklahoma County	672,487	660,448	599,611	72,876	12.2%
Cleveland County	215,652	208,016	174,253	41,399	23.8%
Canadian County	91,441	87,697	74,409	17,032	22.9%
Pottawatomie County	66,740	65,521	58,760	7,980	13.6%
Logan County	34,527	33,924	29,011	5,516	19.0%
McClain County	28,236	27,740	22,795	5,441	23.9%
Olympia, WA	**217,641**	**207,355**	**161,238**	**56,403**	**35.0%**
Thurston County	217,641	207,355	161,238	56,403	35.0%
Omaha, NE-IA	**734,270**	**716,998**	**639,580**	**94,690**	**14.8%**
Douglas County, NE	472,744	463,585	416,444	56,300	13.5%
Sarpy County, NE	129,319	122,595	102,583	26,736	26.1%
Pottawattamie County, IA	88,157	87,704	82,628	5,529	6.7%
Cass County, NE	24,839	24,334	21,318	3,521	16.5%
Washington County, NE	19,211	18,780	16,607	2,604	15.7%
Orange County, CA	**2,938,507**	**2,846,289**	**2,410,556**	**527,951**	**21.9%**
Orange County	2,938,507	2,846,289	2,410,556	527,951	21.9%
Orlando, FL	**1,752,192**	**1,644,561**	**1,224,852**	**527,340**	**43.1%**
Orange County	946,484	896,344	677,491	268,993	39.7%
Seminole County	381,686	365,196	287,529	94,157	32.7%
Lake County	233,835	210,528	152,104	81,731	53.7%
Osceola County	190,187	172,493	107,728	82,459	76.5%
Owensboro, KY	**91,694**	**91,545**	**87,189**	**4,505**	**5.2%**
Daviess County	91,694	91,545	87,189	4,505	5.2%
Panama City, FL	**151,901**	**148,217**	**126,994**	**24,907**	**19.6%**
Bay County	151,901	148,217	126,994	24,907	19.6%
Parkersburg-Marietta, WV-OH	**149,867**	**151,237**	**149,169**	**698**	**0.5%**
Wood County, WV	87,306	87,986	86,915	391	0.4%
Washington County. OH	62,561	63,251	62,254	307	0.5%
Pensacola, FL	**424,484**	**412,153**	**344,406**	**80,078**	**23.3%**
Escambia County	297,272	294,410	262,798	34,474	13.1%
Santa Rosa County	127,212	117,743	81,608	45,604	55.9%
Peoria-Pekin, IL	**346,569**	**347,387**	**339,172**	**7,397**	**2.2%**
Peoria County	182,362	183,433	182,827	-465	-0.3%
Tazewell County	128,107	128,485	123,692	4,415	3.6%
Woodford County	36,100	35,469	32,653	3,447	10.6%
Philadelphia, PA-NJ	**5,149,098**	**5,100,931**	**4,922,175**	**226,923**	**4.6%**
Philadelphia County, PA	1,492,231	1,517,550	1,585,577	-93,346	-5.9%

MSA and Included Counties	2002 Population	2000 Population	1990 Population	Change 1990-2002	Percentage Change 1990-2002
Philadelphia, PA-NJ (cont.)					
Montgomery County, PA	766,517	750,097	678,111	88,406	13.0%
Bucks County, PA	610,440	597,635	541,174	69,266	12.8%
Delaware County, PA	553,435	550,864	547,651	5,784	1.1%
Camden County, NJ	511,957	508,932	502,824	9,133	1.8%
Chester County, PA	450,160	433,501	376,396	73,764	19.6%
Burlington County, NJ	437,871	423,394	395,066	42,805	10.8%
Gloucester County, NJ	262,049	254,673	230,082	31,967	13.9%
Salem County, NJ	64,438	64,285	65,294	-856	-1.3%
Phoenix-Mesa, AZ	**3,500,151**	**3,251,876**	**2,238,480**	**1,261,671**	**56.4%**
Maricopa County	3,303,876	3,072,149	2,122,101	1,181,775	55.7%
Pinal County	196,275	179,727	116,379	79,896	68.7%
Pine Bluff, AR	**83,374**	**84,278**	**85,487**	**-2,113**	**-2.5%**
Jefferson County	83,374	84,278	85,487	-2,113	-2.5%
Pittsburgh, PA	**2,346,525**	**2,358,695**	**2,394,811**	**-48,286**	**-2.0%**
Allegheny County	1,269,904	1,281,666	1,336,449	-66,545	-5.0%
Westmoreland County	368,428	369,993	370,321	-1,893	-0.5%
Washington County	204,110	202,897	204,584	-474	-0.2%
Beaver County	179,351	181,412	186,093	-6,742	-3.6%
Butler County	178,078	174,083	152,013	26,065	17.1%
Fayette County	146,654	148,644	145,351	1,303	0.9%
Pittsfield, MA	**83,584**	**84,699**	**88,695**	**-5,111**	**-5.8%**
Berkshire County (part)	83,584	84,699	88,695	-5,111	-5.8%
Pocatello, ID	**75,804**	**75,565**	**66,026**	**9,778**	**14.8%**
Bannock County	75,804	75,565	66,026	9,778	14.8%
Portland, ME	**247,395**	**243,537**	**221,095**	**26,300**	**11.9%**
Cumberland County (part)	222,639	219,712	200,443	22,196	11.1%
York County (part)	24,756	23,825	20,652	4,104	19.9%
Portland-Vancouver, OR-WA	**2,006,308**	**1,918,009**	**1,515,452**	**490,856**	**32.4%**
Multnomah County, OR	677,626	660,486	583,887	93,739	16.1%
Washington County, OR	473,263	445,342	311,554	161,709	51.9%
Clark County, WA	370,236	345,238	238,053	132,183	55.5%
Clackamas County, OR	351,815	338,391	278,850	72,965	26.2%
Yamhill County, OR	88,055	84,992	65,551	22,504	34.3%
Columbia County, OR	45,313	43,560	37,557	7,756	20.7%
Portsmouth-Rochester, NH-ME	**249,200**	**240,698**	**223,271**	**25,929**	**11.6%**
Strafford County, NH (part)	108,426	104,947	98,111	10,315	10.5%
Rockingham County, NH (part)	97,383	94,376	88,769	8,614	9.7%
York County, ME (part)	43,391	41,375	36,391	7,000	19.2%
Providence–Fall River–Warwick, RI-MA	**1,213,264**	**1,188,613**	**1,134,350**	**78,914**	**7.0%**
Providence County, RI	634,827	621,602	596,270	38,557	6.5%
Bristol County, MA (part)	237,429	233,064	224,744	12,685	5.6%
Kent County, RI	170,499	167,090	161,135	9,364	5.8%
Washington County, RI (part)	94,406	91,734	80,692	13,714	17.0%
Bristol County, RI	51,287	50,648	48,859	2,428	5.0%
Newport County, RI (part)	24,816	24,475	22,650	2,166	9.6%
Provo-Orem, UT	**387,817**	**368,536**	**263,590**	**124,227**	**47.1%**
Utah County	387,817	368,536	263,590	124,227	47.1%
Pueblo, CO	**146,880**	**141,472**	**123,051**	**23,829**	**19.4%**
Pueblo County	146,880	141,472	123,051	23,829	19.4%
Punta Gorda, FL	**148,678**	**141,627**	**110,975**	**37,703**	**34.0%**
Charlotte County	148,678	141,627	110,975	37,703	34.0%
Racine, WI	**191,012**	**188,831**	**175,034**	**15,978**	**9.1%**
Racine County	191,012	188,831	175,034	15,978	9.1%
Raleigh–Durham–Chapel Hill, NC	**1,267,676**	**1,187,941**	**855,545**	**412,131**	**48.2%**
Wake County	675,518	627,846	423,380	252,138	59.6%
Durham County	234,199	223,314	181,835	52,364	28.8%
Johnston County	133,159	121,965	81,306	51,853	63.8%
Orange County	120,458	118,227	93,851	26,607	28.4%
Chatham County	53,893	49,329	38,759	15,134	39.0%
Franklin County	50,449	47,260	36,414	14,035	38.5%

continued

Table 1.1: Principal U.S. Metropolitan Statistical Areas (continued)

MSA and Included Counties	2002 Population	2000 Population	1990 Population	Change 1990-2002	Percentage Change 1990-2002
Rapid City, SD	**90,856**	**88,565**	**81,343**	**9,513**	**11.7%**
Pennington County	90,856	88,565	81,343	9,513	11.7%
Reading, PA	**382,108**	**373,638**	**336,523**	**45,585**	**13.5%**
Berks County	382,108	373,638	336,523	45,585	13.5%
Redding, CA	**171,799**	**163,256**	**147,036**	**24,763**	**16.8%**
Shasta County	171,799	163,256	147,036	24,763	16.8%
Reno, NV	**362,325**	**339,486**	**254,667**	**107,658**	**42.3%**
Washoe County	362,325	339,486	254,667	107,658	42.3%
Richland-Kennewick-Pasco, WA	**203,111**	**191,822**	**150,033**	**53,078**	**35.4%**
Benton County	150,366	142,475	112,560	37,806	33.6%
Franklin County	52,745	49,347	37,473	15,272	40.8%
Richmond-Petersburg, VA	**1,023,419**	**996,512**	**865,640**	**157,779**	**18.2%**
Chesterfield County	271,142	259,903	209,274	61,868	29.6%
Henrico County	268,270	262,300	217,881	50,389	23.1%
Richmond city	197,456	197,790	203,056	-5,600	-2.8%
Hanover County	92,050	86,320	63,306	28,744	45.4%
Prince George County	34,135	33,047	27,394	6,741	24.6%
Petersburg city	33,115	33,740	38,386	-5,271	-13.7%
Dinwiddie County	24,747	24,533	20,960	3,787	18.1%
Powhatan County	23,997	22,377	15,328	8,669	56.6%
Hopewell city	22,525	22,354	23,101	-576	-2.5%
Goochland County	17,523	16,863	14,163	3,360	23.7%
Colonial Heights city	17,063	16,897	16,064	999	6.2%
New Kent County	14,157	13,462	10,445	3,712	35.5%
Charles City County	7,239	6,926	6,282	957	15.2%
Riverside–San Bernardino, CA	**3,515,184**	**3,254,821**	**2,588,793**	**926,391**	**35.8%**
San Bernardino County	1,816,072	1,709,434	1,418,380	397,692	28.0%
Riverside County	1,699,112	1,545,387	1,170,413	528,699	45.2%
Roanoke, VA	**235,918**	**235,932**	**224,477**	**11,441**	**5.1%**
Roanoke city	93,873	94,911	96,397	-2,524	-2.6%
Roanoke County	85,937	85,778	79,332	6,605	8.3%
Botetourt County	31,272	30,496	24,992	6,280	25.1%
Salem city	24,836	24,747	23,756	1,080	4.5%
Rochester, MN	**128,961**	**124,277**	**106,470**	**22,491**	**21.1%**
Olmsted County	128,961	124,277	106,470	22,491	21.1%
Rochester, NY	**1,102,581**	**1,098,201**	**1,062,470**	**40,111**	**3.8%**
Monroe County	738,422	735,343	713,968	24,454	3.4%
Ontario County	101,567	100,224	95,101	6,466	6.8%
Wayne County	94,078	93,765	89,123	4,955	5.6%
Livingston County	64,824	64,328	62,372	2,452	3.9%
Genesee County	59,799	60,370	60,060	-261	-0.4%
Orleans County	43,891	44,171	41,846	2,045	4.9%
Rockford, IL	**379,376**	**371,236**	**329,676**	**49,700**	**15.1%**
Winnebago County	282,627	278,418	252,913	29,714	11.7%
Ogle County	52,129	51,032	45,957	6,172	13.4%
Boone County	44,620	41,786	30,806	13,814	44.8%
Rocky Mount, NC	**144,293**	**143,026**	**133,235**	**11,058**	**8.3%**
Nash County	89,286	87,420	76,677	12,609	16.4%
Edgecombe County	55,007	55,606	56,558	-1,551	-2.7%
Sacramento, CA	**1,749,335**	**1,628,197**	**1,340,010**	**409,325**	**30.5%**
Sacramento County	1,305,082	1,223,499	1,041,219	263,863	25.3%
Placer County	278,509	248,399	172,796	105,713	61.2%
El Dorado County	165,744	156,299	125,995	39,749	31.5%
Saginaw–Bay City–Midland, MI	**403,878**	**403,070**	**399,320**	**4,558**	**1.1%**
Saginaw County	210,087	210,039	211,946	-1,859	-0.9%
Bay County	109,672	110,157	111,723	-2,051	-1.8%
Midland County	84,119	82,874	75,651	8,468	11.2%
St. Cloud, MN	**172,183**	**167,392**	**148,976**	**23,207**	**15.6%**
Stearns County	135,867	133,166	118,791	17,076	14.4%
Benton County	36,316	34,226	30,185	6,131	20.3%
St. Joseph, MO	**102,064**	**102,490**	**97,715**	**4,349**	**4.5%**
Buchanan County	85,313	85,998	83,083	2,230	2.7%

MSA and Included Counties	2002 Population	2000 Population	1990 Population	Change 1990-2002	Percentage Change 1990-2002
St. Joseph, MO *(cont.)*					
Andrew County	16,751	16,492	14,632	2,119	14.5%
St. Louis, MO-IL	**2,633,925**	**2,603,607**	**2,492,525**	**141,400**	**5.7%**
St. Louis County, MO	1,018,102	1,016,315	993,529	24,573	2.5%
St. Louis city, MO	338,353	348,189	396,685	-58,332	-14.7%
St. Charles County, MO	303,030	283,883	212,907	90,123	42.3%
Madison County, IL	261,409	258,941	249,238	12,171	4.9%
St. Clair County, IL	257,904	256,082	262,852	-4,948	-1.9%
Jefferson County, MO	203,993	198,099	171,380	32,613	19.0%
Franklin County, MO	95,890	93,807	80,603	15,287	19.0%
Lincoln County, MO	42,280	38,944	28,892	13,388	46.3%
Clinton County, IL	35,855	35,535	33,944	1,911	5.6%
Monroe County, IL	29,058	27,619	22,422	6,636	29.6%
Warren County, MO	26,193	24,525	19,534	6,659	34.1%
Jersey County, IL	21,858	21,668	20,539	1,319	6.4%
Salem, OR	**357,812**	**347,214**	**278,024**	**79,788**	**28.7%**
Marion County	293,155	284,834	228,483	64,672	28.3%
Polk County	64,657	62,380	49,541	15,116	30.5%
Salinas, CA	**413,408**	**401,762**	**355,660**	**57,748**	**16.2%**
Monterey County	413,408	401,762	355,660	57,748	16.2%
Salt Lake City–Ogden, UT	**1,372,699**	**1,333,914**	**1,072,227**	**300,472**	**28.0%**
Salt Lake County	919,308	898,387	725,956	193,352	26.6%
Davis County	249,224	238,994	187,941	61,283	32.6%
Weber County	204,167	196,533	158,330	45,837	29.0%
San Angelo, TX	**103,018**	**104,010**	**98,458**	**4,560**	**4.6%**
Tom Green County	103,018	104,010	98,458	4,560	4.6%
San Antonio, TX	**1,660,205**	**1,592,383**	**1,324,749**	**335,456**	**25.3%**
Bexar County	1,446,333	1,392,931	1,185,394	260,939	22.0%
Guadalupe County	94,215	89,023	64,873	29,342	45.2%
Comal County	85,109	78,021	51,832	33,277	64.2%
Wilson County	34,548	32,408	22,650	11,898	52.5%
San Diego, CA	**2,906,660**	**2,813,833**	**2,498,016**	**408,644**	**16.4%**
San Diego County	2,906,660	2,813,833	2,498,016	408,644	16.4%
San Francisco, CA	**1,714,832**	**1,731,183**	**1,603,678**	**111,154**	**6.9%**
San Francisco County	764,049	776,733	723,959	40,090	5.5%
San Mateo County	703,202	707,161	649,623	53,579	8.2%
Marin County	247,581	247,289	230,096	17,485	7.6%
San Jose, CA	**1,683,505**	**1,682,585**	**1,497,577**	**185,928**	**12.4%**
Santa Clara County	1,683,505	1,682,585	1,497,577	185,928	12.4%
San Luis Obispo–Atascadero–Paso Robles, CA	**253,408**	**246,681**	**217,162**	**36,246**	**16.7%**
San Luis Obispo County	253,408	246,681	217,162	36,246	16.7%
Santa Barbara–Santa Maria–Lompoc, CA	**403,084**	**399,347**	**369,608**	**33,476**	**9.1%**
Santa Barbara County	403,084	399,347	369,608	33,476	9.1%
Santa Cruz–Watsonville, CA	**253,814**	**255,602**	**229,734**	**24,080**	**10.5%**
Santa Cruz County	253,814	255,602	229,734	24,080	10.5%
Santa Fe, NM	**152,830**	**147,635**	**117,043**	**35,787**	**30.6%**
Santa Fe County	134,525	129,292	98,928	35,597	36.0%
Los Alamos County	18,305	18,343	18,115	190	1.0%
Santa Rosa, CA	**468,386**	**458,614**	**388,222**	**80,164**	**20.6%**
Sonoma County	468,386	458,614	388,222	80,164	20.6%
Sarasota-Bradenton, FL	**620,136**	**589,959**	**489,483**	**130,653**	**26.7%**
Sarasota County	339,625	325,957	277,776	61,849	22.3%
Manatee County	280,511	264,002	211,707	68,804	32.5%
Savannah, GA	**299,790**	**293,000**	**258,060**	**41,730**	**16.2%**
Chatham County	233,702	232,048	216,935	16,767	7.7%
Effingham County	40,832	37,535	25,687	15,145	59.0%
Bryan County	25,256	23,417	15,438	9,818	63.6%
Scranton–Wilkes-Barre–Hazleton, PA	**617,289**	**624,776**	**638,466**	**-21,177**	**-3.3%**
Luzerne County	314,643	319,250	328,149	-13,506	-4.1%
Lackawanna County	210,711	213,295	219,039	-8,328	-3.8%
Columbia County	64,134	64,151	63,202	932	1.5%
Wyoming County	27,801	28,080	28,076	-275	-1.0%

continued

Table 1.1: Principal U.S. Metropolitan Statistical Areas (continued)

MSA and Included Counties	2002 Population	2000 Population	1990 Population	Change 1990-2002	Percentage Change 1990-2002
Seattle-Bellevue-Everett, WA	**2,468,601**	**2,414,616**	**2,033,156**	**435,445**	**21.4%**
King County	1,759,604	1,737,034	1,507,319	252,285	16.7%
Snohomish County	633,947	606,024	465,642	168,305	36.1%
Island County	75,050	71,558	60,195	14,855	24.7%
Sharon, PA	**119,514**	**120,293**	**121,003**	**-1,489**	**-1.2%**
Mercer County	119,514	120,293	121,003	-1,489	-1.2%
Sheboygan, WI	**112,480**	**112,646**	**103,877**	**8,603**	**8.3%**
Sheboygan County	112,480	112,646	103,877	8,603	8.3%
Sherman-Denison, TX	**113,860**	**110,595**	**95,021**	**18,839**	**19.8%**
Grayson County	113,860	110,595	95,021	18,839	19.8%
Shreveport–Bossier City, LA	**393,390**	**392,302**	**376,330**	**17,060**	**4.5%**
Caddo Parish	251,145	252,161	248,253	2,892	1.2%
Bossier Parish	100,736	98,310	86,088	14,648	17.0%
Webster Parish	41,509	41,831	41,989	-480	-1.1%
Sioux City, IA-NE	**123,670**	**124,130**	**115,018**	**8,652**	**7.5%**
Woodbury County, IA	103,331	103,877	98,276	5,055	5.1%
Dakota County, NE	20,339	20,253	16,742	3,597	21.5%
Sioux Falls, SD	**180,200**	**172,412**	**139,236**	**40,964**	**29.4%**
Minnehaha County	152,545	148,281	123,809	28,736	23.2%
Lincoln County	27,655	24,131	15,427	12,228	79.3%
South Bend, IN	**267,120**	**265,559**	**247,052**	**20,068**	**8.1%**
St. Joseph County	267,120	265,559	247,052	20,068	8.1%
Spokane, WA	**427,506**	**417,939**	**361,364**	**66,142**	**18.3%**
Spokane County	427,506	417,939	361,364	66,142	18.3%
Springfield, IL	**203,201**	**201,437**	**189,550**	**13,651**	**7.2%**
Sangamon County	190,630	188,951	178,386	12,244	6.9%
Menard County	12,571	12,486	11,164	1,407	12.6%
Springfield, MA	**595,495**	**591,932**	**587,884**	**7,611**	**1.3%**
Hampden County (part)	446,869	444,276	445,399	1,470	0.3%
Hampshire County (part)	144,838	143,879	139,086	5,752	4.1%
Franklin County (part)	3,788	3,777	3,399	389	11.4%
Springfield, MO	**335,143**	**325,721**	**264,346**	**70,797**	**26.8%**
Greene County	243,355	240,391	207,949	35,406	17.0%
Christian County	59,117	54,285	32,644	26,473	81.1%
Webster County	32,671	31,045	23,753	8,918	37.5%
Stamford-Norwalk, CT	**359,642**	**353,556**	**329,935**	**29,707**	**9.0%**
Fairfield County (part)	359,642	353,556	329,935	29,707	9.0%
State College, PA	**138,524**	**135,758**	**123,786**	**14,738**	**11.9%**
Centre County	138,524	135,758	123,786	14,738	11.9%
Steubenville-Weirton, OH-WV	**129,663**	**132,008**	**142,523**	**-12,860**	**-9.0%**
Jefferson County, OH	72,402	73,894	80,298	-7,896	-9.8%
Hancock County, WV	32,082	32,667	35,233	-3,151	-8.9%
Brooke County, WV	25,179	25,447	26,992	-1,813	-6.7%
Stockton-Lodi, CA	**614,302**	**563,598**	**480,628**	**133,674**	**27.8%**
San Joaquin County	614,302	563,598	480,628	133,674	27.8%
Sumter, SC	**105,198**	**104,646**	**102,637**	**2,561**	**2.5%**
Sumter County	105,198	104,646	102,637	2,561	2.5%
Syracuse, NY	**735,059**	**732,117**	**742,177**	**-7,118**	**-1.0%**
Onondaga County	460,776	458,336	468,973	-8,197	-1.7%
Oswego County	122,932	122,377	121,771	1,161	1.0%
Cayuga County	81,562	81,963	82,313	-751	-0.9%
Madison County	69,789	69,441	69,120	669	1.0%
Tacoma, WA	**732,282**	**700,820**	**586,203**	**146,079**	**24.9%**
Pierce County	732,282	700,820	586,203	146,079	24.9%
Tallahassee, FL	**289,274**	**284,539**	**233,598**	**55,676**	**23.8%**
Leon County	243,995	239,452	192,493	51,502	26.8%
Gadsden County	45,279	45,087	41,105	4,174	10.2%
Tampa–St. Petersburg–Clearwater, FL	**2,490,295**	**2,395,997**	**2,067,959**	**422,336**	**20.4%**
Hillsborough County	1,053,864	998,948	834,054	219,810	26.4%
Pinellas County	926,716	921,482	851,659	75,057	8.8%
Pasco County	371,245	344,765	281,131	90,114	32.1%
Hernando County	138,470	130,802	101,115	37,355	36.9%

MSA and Included Counties	2002 Population	2000 Population	1990 Population	Change 1990-2002	Percentage Change 1990-2002
Terre Haute, IN	**147,934**	**149,192**	**147,585**	**349**	**0.2%**
Vigo County	105,078	105,848	106,107	-1,029	-1.0%
Clay County	26,357	26,556	24,705	1,652	6.7%
Vermillion County	16,499	16,788	16,773	-274	-1.6%
Texarkana, TX-AR	**131,027**	**129,749**	**120,132**	**10,895**	**9.1%**
Bowie County, TX	89,894	89,306	81,665	8,229	10.1%
Miller County, AR	41,133	40,443	38,467	2,666	6.9%
Toledo, OH	**618,466**	**618,203**	**614,128**	**4,338**	**0.7%**
Lucas County	453,506	455,054	462,361	-8,855	-1.9%
Wood County	122,387	121,065	113,269	9,118	8.0%
Fulton County	42,573	42,084	38,498	4,075	10.6%
Topeka, KS	**170,748**	**169,871**	**160,976**	**9,772**	**6.1%**
Shawnee County	170,748	169,871	160,976	9,772	6.1%
Trenton, NJ	**359,463**	**350,761**	**325,824**	**33,639**	**10.3%**
Mercer County	359,463	350,761	325,824	33,639	10.3%
Tucson, AZ	**881,221**	**843,746**	**666,880**	**214,341**	**32.1%**
Pima County	881,221	843,746	666,880	214,341	32.1%
Tulsa, OK	**821,256**	**803,235**	**708,954**	**112,302**	**15.8%**
Tulsa County	571,348	563,299	503,341	68,007	13.5%
Rogers County	75,567	70,641	55,170	20,397	37.0%
Creek County	68,836	67,367	60,915	7,921	13.0%
Wagoner County	60,339	57,491	47,883	12,456	26.0%
Osage County	45,166	44,437	41,645	3,521	8.5%
Tuscaloosa, AL	**166,512**	**164,875**	**150,522**	**15,990**	**10.6%**
Tuscaloosa County	166,512	164,875	150,522	15,990	10.6%
Tyler, TX	**181,437**	**174,706**	**151,309**	**30,128**	**19.9%**
Smith County	181,437	174,706	151,309	30,128	19.9%
Utica-Rome, NY	**298,707**	**299,896**	**316,633**	**-17,926**	**-5.7%**
Oneida County	234,966	235,469	250,836	-15,870	-6.3%
Herkimer County	63,741	64,427	65,797	-2,056	-3.1%
Vallejo-Napa-Fairfield, CA	**541,340**	**518,821**	**451,186**	**90,154**	**20.0%**
Solano County	411,072	394,542	340,421	70,651	20.8%
Napa County	130,268	124,279	110,765	19,503	17.6%
Ventura, CA	**783,920**	**753,197**	**669,016**	**114,904**	**17.2%**
Ventura County	783,920	753,197	669,016	114,904	17.2%
Victoria, TX	**84,932**	**84,088**	**74,361**	**10,571**	**14.2%**
Victoria County	84,932	84,088	74,361	10,571	14.2%
Vineland-Millville-Bridgeton, NJ	**147,768**	**146,438**	**138,053**	**9,715**	**7.0%**
Cumberland County	147,768	146,438	138,053	9,715	7.0%
Visalia-Tulare-Porterville, CA	**381,772**	**368,021**	**311,921**	**69,851**	**22.4%**
Tulare County	381,772	368,021	311,921	69,851	22.4%
Waco, TX	**217,713**	**213,517**	**189,123**	**28,590**	**15.1%**
McLennan County	217,713	213,517	189,123	28,590	15.1%
Washington, DC-MD-VA-WV	**5,162,029**	**4,923,153**	**4,223,485**	**938,544**	**22.2%**
Fairfax County, VA	997,580	969,749	818,584	178,996	21.9%
Montgomery County, MD	910,156	873,341	757,027	153,129	20.2%
Prince George's County, MD	833,084	801,515	729,268	103,816	14.2%
District of Columbia	570,898	572,059	606,900	-36,002	-5.9%
Prince William County, VA	311,892	280,813	215,686	96,206	44.6%
Frederick County, MD	209,125	195,277	150,208	58,917	39.2%
Loudoun County, VA	204,054	169,599	86,129	117,925	136.9%
Arlington County, VA	189,927	189,453	170,936	18,991	11.1%
Alexandria city, VA	130,804	128,283	111,183	19,621	17.6%
Charles County, MD	129,040	120,546	101,154	27,886	27.6%
Stafford County, VA	104,823	92,446	61,236	43,587	71.2%
Spotsylvania County, VA	102,570	90,395	57,403	45,167	78.7%
Berkeley County, WV	81,262	75,905	59,253	22,009	37.1%
Calvert County, MD	80,906	74,563	51,372	29,534	57.5%
Fauquier County, VA	59,245	55,139	48,741	10,504	21.6%
Jefferson County, WV	44,926	42,190	35,926	9,000	25.1%
Manassas city, VA	37,288	35,135	27,957	9,331	33.4%
Culpeper County, VA	36,893	34,262	27,791	9,102	32.8%

continued

Table 1.1: Principal U.S. Metropolitan Statistical Areas (continued)

MSA and Included Counties	2002 Population	2000 Population	1990 Population	Change 1990-2002	Percentage Change 1990-2002
Washington, DC-MD-VA-WV (cont.)					
Warren County, VA	32,910	31,584	26,142	6,768	25.9%
Fairfax city, VA	22,055	21,498	19,622	2,433	12.4%
Fredericksburg city, VA	20,076	19,279	19,027	1,049	5.5%
King George County, VA	17,657	16,803	13,527	4,130	30.5%
Clarke County, VA	13,290	12,652	12,101	1,189	9.8%
Manassas Park city, VA	10,909	10,290	6,734	4,175	62.0%
Falls Church city, VA	10,659	10,377	9,578	1,081	11.3%
Waterbury, CT	**232,519**	**228,984**	**221,629**	**10,890**	**4.9%**
New Haven County (part)	189,647	187,200	183,024	6,623	3.6%
Litchfield County (part)	42,872	41,784	38,605	4,267	11.1%
Waterloo–Cedar Falls, IA	**127,394**	**128,012**	**123,798**	**3,596**	**2.9%**
Black Hawk County	127,394	128,012	123,798	3,596	2.9%
Wausau, WI	**126,728**	**125,834**	**115,400**	**11,328**	**9.8%**
Marathon County	126,728	125,834	115,400	11,328	9.8%
West Palm Beach–Boca Raton, FL	**1,190,390**	**1,131,184**	**863,518**	**326,872**	**37.9%**
Palm Beach County	1,190,390	1,131,184	863,518	326,872	37.9%
Wheeling, WV-OH	**150,472**	**153,172**	**159,301**	**-8,829**	**-5.5%**
Belmont County, OH	69,448	70,226	71,074	-1,626	-2.3%
Ohio County, WV	46,126	47,427	50,871	-4,745	-9.3%
Marshall County, WV	34,898	35,519	37,356	-2,458	-6.6%
Wichita, KS	**555,846**	**545,220**	**485,270**	**70,576**	**14.5%**
Sedgwick County	461,937	452,869	403,662	58,275	14.4%
Butler County	60,534	59,482	50,580	9,954	19.7%
Harvey County	33,375	32,869	31,028	2,347	7.6%
Wichita Falls, TX	**138,960**	**140,518**	**130,351**	**8,609**	**6.6%**
Wichita County	129,964	131,664	122,378	7,586	6.2%
Archer County	8,996	8,854	7,973	1,023	12.8%
Williamsport, PA	**119,000**	**120,044**	**118,710**	**290**	**0.2%**
Lycoming County	119,000	120,044	118,710	290	0.2%
Wilmington, NC	**244,279**	**233,450**	**171,269**	**73,010**	**42.6%**
New Hanover County	165,712	160,307	120,284	45,428	37.8%
Brunswick County	78,567	73,143	50,985	27,582	54.1%
Wilmington-Newark, DE-MD	**602,705**	**586,216**	**513,293**	**89,412**	**17.4%**
New Castle County, DE	512,370	500,265	441,946	70,424	15.9%
Cecil County, MD	90,335	85,951	71,347	18,988	26.6%
Worcester, MA-CT	**524,714**	**511,389**	**478,384**	**46,330**	**9.7%**
Worcester County, MA (part)	513,210	500,104	467,531	45,679	9.8%
Windham County, CT (part)	9,064	8,878	8,668	396	4.6%
Hampden County, MA (part)	2,440	2,407	2,185	255	11.7%
Yakima, WA	**224,823**	**222,581**	**188,823**	**36,000**	**19.1%**
Yakima County	224,823	222,581	188,823	36,000	19.1%
Yolo, CA	**180,856**	**168,660**	**141,092**	**39,764**	**28.2%**
Yolo County	180,856	168,660	141,092	39,764	28.2%
York, PA	**389,209**	**381,751**	**339,574**	**49,635**	**14.6%**
York County	389,209	381,751	339,574	49,635	14.6%
Youngstown-Warren, OH	**588,632**	**594,746**	**600,895**	**-12,263**	**-2.0%**
Mahoning County	253,308	257,555	264,806	-11,498	-4.3%
Trumbull County	223,518	225,116	227,813	-4,295	-1.9%
Columbiana County	111,806	112,075	108,276	3,530	3.3%
Yuba City–Marysville, CA	**144,919**	**139,149**	**122,643**	**22,276**	**18.2%**
Sutter County	82,580	78,930	64,415	18,165	28.2%
Yuba County	62,339	60,219	58,228	4,111	7.1%
Yuma, AZ	**167,407**	**160,026**	**106,895**	**60,512**	**56.6%**
Yuma County	167,407	160,026	106,895	60,512	56.6%

Note: (part) indicates that only part of the county is in the MSA.

Source: U.S. Census Bureau

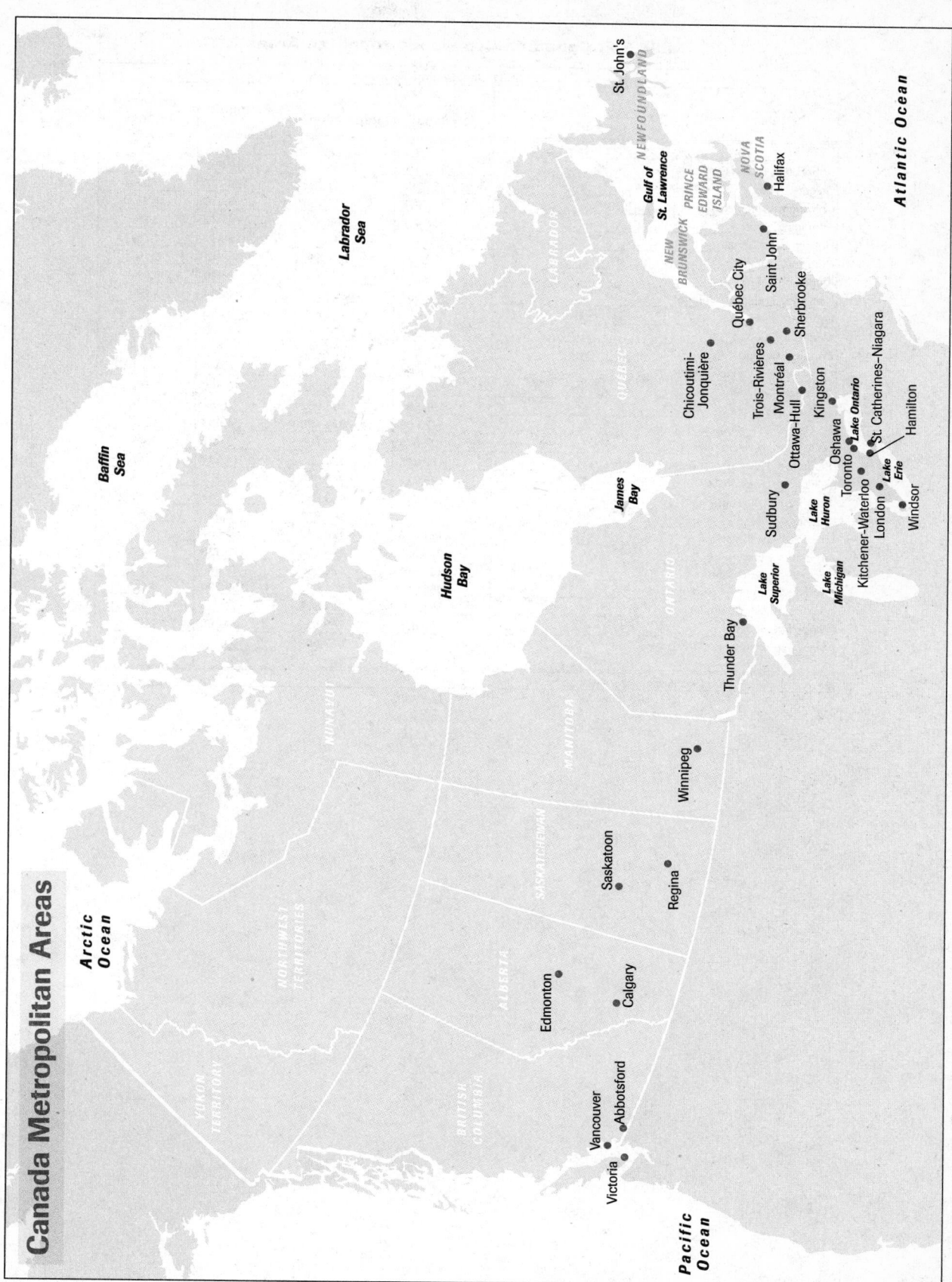

Canada Metropolitan Areas

Table 1.2: Canadian Census Metropolitan Areas

CMA	2001 Population	1996 Population	Change	Percentage Change
	2001 Designation			
Abbotsford, British Columbia	147,370	136,480	10,890	8.0%
Calgary, Alberta	951,395	821,628	129,767	15.8%
Chicoutimi-Jonquière, Québec	154,938	160,454	(5,516)	-3.4%
Edmonton, Alberta	937,845	862,597	75,248	8.7%
Halifax, Nova Scotia	359,183	342,966	16,217	4.7%
Hamilton, Ontario	662,401	624,360	38,041	6.1%
Kingston, Ontario	146,838	144,528	2,310	1.6%
Kitchener-Waterloo, Ontario	414,284	382,940	31,344	8.2%
London, Ontario	432,451	416,546	15,905	3.8%
Montréal, Québec	3,426,350	3,326,447	99,903	3.0%
Oshawa, Ontario	296,298	268,773	27,525	10.2%
Ottawa-Hull, Ontario-Québec	1,063,664	998,718	64,946	6.5%
Québec City, Québec	682,757	671,889	10,868	1.6%
Regina, Saskatchewan	192,800	193,652	(852)	-0.4%
St. Catharines–Niagara, Ontario	377,009	372,406	4,603	1.2%
Saint John, New Brunswick	122,678	125,705	(3,027)	-2.4%
St. John's, Newfoundland and Labrador	172,918	174,051	(1,133)	-0.7%
Saskatoon, Saskatchewan	225,927	219,056	6,871	3.1%
Sherbrooke, Québec	153,811	149,569	4,242	2.8%
Sudbury, Ontario	155,601	165,618	(10,017)	-6.0%
Thunder Bay, Ontario	121,986	126,643	(4,657)	-3.7%
Toronto, Ontario	4,682,897	4,263,759	419,138	9.8%
Trois-Rivières, Québec	137,507	139,956	(2,449)	-1.7%
Vancouver, British Columbia	1,986,965	1,831,665	155,300	8.5%
Victoria, British Columbia	311,902	304,827	7,075	2.3%
Windsor, Ontario	307,877	286,811	21,066	7.3%
Winnepeg, Manitoba	671,274	667,093	4,181	0.6%

Source: Statistics Canada, Canadian Global Almanac 2003

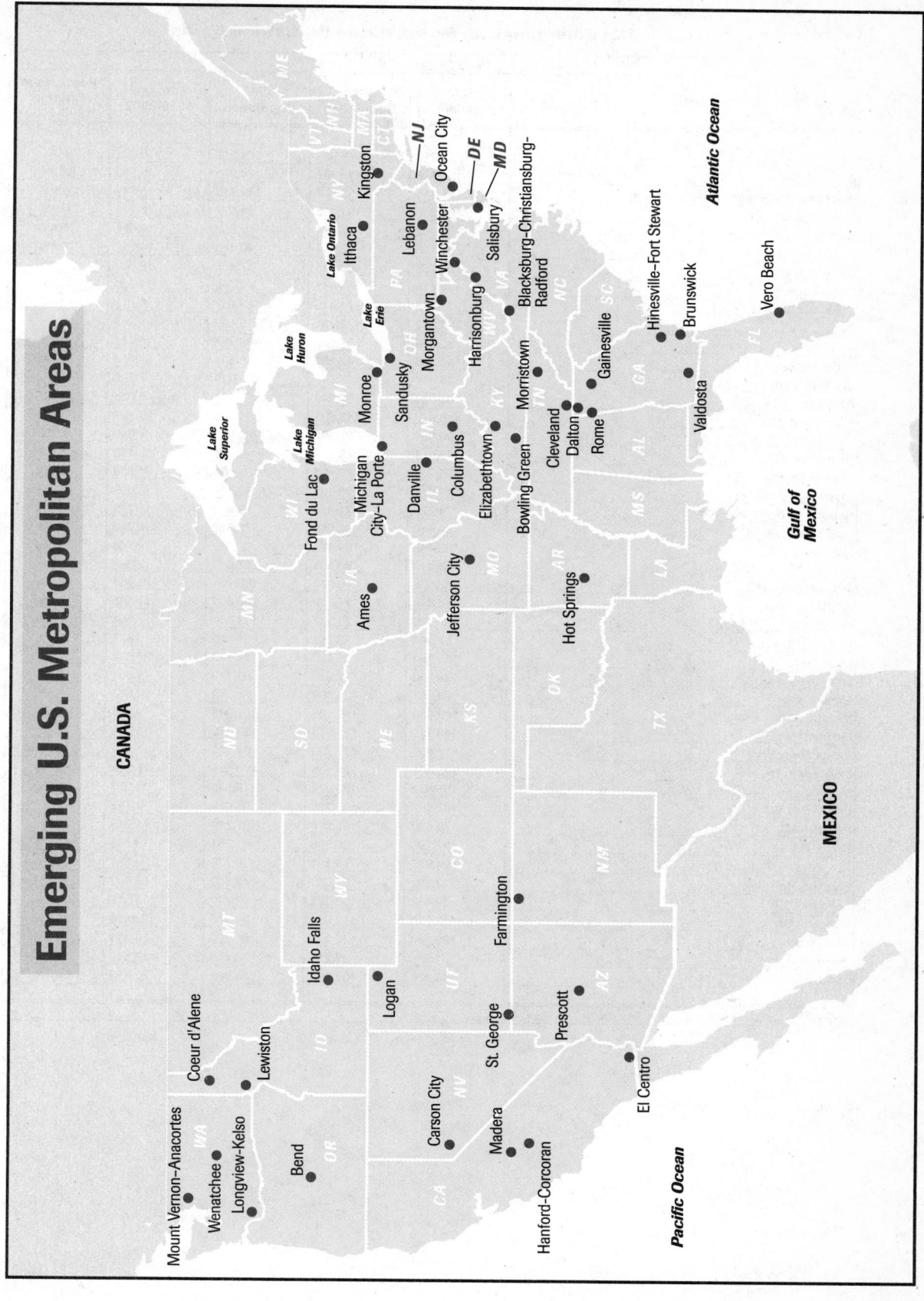

Emerging U.S. Metropolitan Areas

Table 1.3: Emerging U.S. Metropolitan Statistical Areas

MSA	2003 Designation				
	2002 Population	2000 Population	1990 Population	Change 1990-2002	Percentage Change 1990-2002
Ames, IA	80,910	79,981	74,252	6,658	9.0%
Bend, OR	121,506	115,367	74,976	46,530	62.1%
Blacksburg-Christiansburg-Radford, VA	154,456	151,272	140,715	13,741	9.8%
Bowling Green, KY	106,256	104,166	88,077	18,179	20.6%
Brunswick, GA	94,902	93,044	82,207	12,695	15.4%
Carson City, NV	55,155	52,457	40,443	14,712	36.4%
Cleveland, TN	105,857	104,015	87,355	18,502	21.2%
Coeur d'Alene, ID	114,415	108,685	69,795	44,620	63.9%
Columbus, IN	71,906	71,435	63,657	8,249	13.0%
Dalton, GA	123,862	120,031	98,609	25,253	25.6%
Danville, IL	82,529	83,919	88,257	(5,728)	-6.5%
El Centro, CA	146,356	142,361	109,303	37,053	33.9%
Elizabethtown, KY	108,254	107,547	100,919	7,335	7.3%
Fairbanks, AK	83,233	82,840	77,720	5,513	7.1%
Farmington, NM	116,673	113,801	91,605	25,068	27.4%
Fond du Lac, WI	98,082	97,296	90,083	7,999	8.9%
Gainesville, GA	148,913	139,277	95,434	53,479	56.0%
Hanford-Corcoran, CA	136,303	129,461	101,469	34,834	34.3%
Harrisonburg, VA	113,079	108,193	88,189	24,890	28.2%
Hinesville–Fort Stewart, GA	74,225	71,914	58,947	15,278	25.9%
Hot Springs, AR	89,640	88,068	73,397	16,243	22.1%
Idaho Falls, ID	103,498	101,677	88,750	14,748	16.6%
Ithaca, NY	96,493	96,501	94,097	2,396	2.5%
Jefferson City, MO	142,368	140,052	120,704	21,664	17.9%
Kingston, NY	178,649	177,749	165,304	13,345	8.1%
Lebanon, PA	121,328	120,327	113,744	7,584	6.7%
Lewiston, ID-WA	57,987	57,961	51,359	6,628	12.9%
Logan, UT-ID	105,391	102,720	79,415	25,976	32.7%
Longview-Kelso, WA	94,680	92,948	82,119	12,561	15.3%
Madera, CA	128,657	123,109	88,090	40,567	46.1%
Michigan City–LaPorte, IN	109,669	110,106	107,066	2,603	2.4%
Monroe, MI	148,326	145,945	133,600	14,726	11.0%
Morgantown, WV	111,857	111,200	104,546	7,311	7.0%
Morristown, TN	125,882	123,081	100,591	25,291	25.1%
Mount Vernon–Anacortes, WA	105,822	102,979	79,545	26,277	33.0%
Ocean City, NJ	102,842	102,326	95,089	7,753	8.2%
Prescott, AZ	179,030	167,517	107,714	71,316	66.2%
Rome, GA	92,136	90,565	81,251	10,885	13.4%
St. George, UT	94,677	79,551	76,779	17,898	95.0%
Salisbury, MD	112,202	90,354	48,560	63,642	14.8%
Sandusky, OH	79,432	109,391	97,779	(18,347)	3.5%
Valdosta, GA	122,650	119,560	99,244	23,406	23.6%
Vero Beach, FL	120,519	112,947	90,208	30,311	33.6%
Wenatchee, WA	101,967	99,219	78,455	23,512	30.0%
Winchester, VA-WV	106,276	102,997	84,168	22,108	26.3%

Source: U.S. Office of Management & Budget (OMB), U.S. Census Bureau

chapter 2

The Rankings

In chapter 5, *Cities Ranked & Rated* scores each of the 331 principal U.S. metropolitan areas, or MSAs (as defined in chapter 1), and ranks them in sequence from no. 1 (best) through no. 331 (worst). The ranking is based on a composite score of nine sets of statistical attributes and one subjective appraisal, with some adjustments. All categories are weighted according to the expected needs and interests of the typical individual citizen and family and then figured into an area's overall score.

For the rankings of all 331 metropolitan areas, refer to Tables 2.4 and 2.5 at the end of this chapter. For just the highest and lowest ranked cities, see Tables 2.1 and 2.2 below.

Table 2.1: The Top 30 U.S. Metropolitan Areas			
Rank	**Score**	**Metropolitan Area**	**State**
1	100.0	Charlottesville	VA
2	99.3	Santa Fe	NM
3	97.2	San Luis Obispo–Atascadero–Paso Robles	CA
4	95.2	Santa Barbara–Santa Maria–Lompoc	CA
5	91.7	Honolulu	HI
6	91.2	Ann Arbor	MI
7	91.1	Atlanta	GA
8	90.4	Asheville	NC
9	89.3	Reno	NV
10	89.0	Corvallis	OR
11	88.6	Roanoke	VA
12	88.2	Portland-Vancouver	OR-WA
13	87.4	Raleigh–Durham–Chapel Hill	NC
14	86.4	Bryan–College Station	TX
15	86.0	Lynchburg	VA
16	85.9	Olympia	WA
17	85.8	Norfolk–Virginia Beach–Newport News	VA-NC
18	85.8	Colorado Springs	CO
19	85.5	Nassau-Suffolk	NY
20	85.1	Pueblo	CO
21	85.1	Eugene-Springfield	OR
22	84.1	Austin–San Marcos	TX
23	84.0	Lafayette	IN
24	83.9	Minneapolis–St. Paul	MN-WI
25	82.6	Dover	DE
26	82.6	Washington	DC-MD-VA-WV
27	82.5	Fayetteville-Springdale-Rogers	AR
28	82.5	Pittsburgh	PA
29	82.2	Bloomington	IN
30	82.1	Stamford-Norwalk	CT

Table 2.2: The Bottom 30 U.S. Metropolitan Areas			
Rank	**Score**	**Metropolitan Area**	**State**
302	32.9	Macon	GA
303	32.4	Owensboro	KY
304	32.2	Jackson	TN
305	32.0	Wheeling	WV-OH
306	31.0	Joplin	MO
307	30.0	Racine	WI
308	29.6	Sharon	PA
309	29.4	Erie	PA
310	28.2	Dutchess County	NY
311	28.2	Dubuque	IA
312	27.2	Waterbury	CT
313	26.4	Lewiston-Auburn	ME
314	25.5	Brownsville–Harlingen–San Benito	TX
315	25.2	Yuba City–Marysville	CA
316	25.0	Modesto	CA
317	23.8	McAllen-Edinburg-Mission	TX
318	23.6	Jacksonville	NC
319	23.4	New Bedford	MA
320	23.3	Houma	LA
321	22.7	Alexandria	LA
322	21.8	Fort Smith	AR-OK
323	20.8	Anniston	AL
324	20.5	Gadsden	AL
325	20.3	Pine Bluff	AR
326	19.5	Lawrence	MA-NH
327	18.7	Kankakee	IL
328	12.4	Merced	CA
329	9.9	Newburgh	NY-PA
330	0.0	Stockton-Lodi	CA
331	0.0	Laredo	TX

About the *Cities Ranked & Rated* Model

The model produces a score and rank for each of the nine statistical categories and a composite score and rank for the metropolitan area derived from those figures. At its core, the *Cities Ranked & Rated* scoring and ranking model is an adjustable points-based model. It awards points for good things and more points for better things; it awards fewer points or may even deduct points for bad things. The model weighs specific data and entire categories according to how much influence they are believed to have on the everyday life and long-term goals of a typical citizen or family. It also examines the consistency of scoring across the nine categories.

Category Point Scoring

Points are assigned to specific attributes within each of nine statistical ranking categories. Once a point value is calculated the result is weighed by importance and accumulated inside the category. For example, points are assigned for having relatively few days with temperatures below 0°F. Points are also assigned for having relatively few thunderstorms. But since bitter cold weather is less desirable for most people than the occasional occurrence of thunderstorms, the "0°F" factor gets more weight, and consequently more points are assigned.

Points are calculated and assigned for each of the following categories:

1. Economy & Jobs
2. Cost of Living
3. Climate
4. Education
5. Health & Healthcare
6. Crime
7. Transportation
8. Leisure
9. Arts & Culture

A 10th, subjective category, Quality of Life (QOL), considers overall appearance, heritage, and livability.

Scoring Model Results

Once the data is "crunched" inside each category, a point score is accumulated for each of the nine statistical categories and for the subjective Quality of Life rating for a total of 10 category scores for each metropolitan area. Each point total is converted to a 0–100 percentile scale to allow for easier comparison. The 10 category scores are then accumulated to reach the area's composite total score, which is also converted to a 0–100 scale. That score is then used to determine the overall ranking for the metropolitan area.

The model allows different category weightings. *Cities Ranked & Rated* weighs Cost of Living, Climate, and Quality of Life slightly more than the other categories. This decision was based on the notion that these attributes have the most profound effect on daily life and long-term goals. All factors have been set to reflect expected relative importance of different factors to the typical citizen or family.

Obviously, readers desire different lifestyles and have different interests and means. Simulating results tailored to individual preferences can be done on the "Find Your Best Place" page on Sperling's BestPlaces (www.bestplaces. net). While the model on the website isn't as comprehensive as this book, nor does it rank all 331 metropolitan areas side by side, it does provide insight into how individual needs, interests, and tastes can be met.

Consistency Rating

In the *Cities Ranked & Rated* category scores, some individual cities excel in certain categories but score very poorly in others, while other cities sort of plod along, not being "best in class" in anything but being good overall. An example of the former is New York, which consistently rates at the top of the list in the categories of arts and culture, education, and leisure—but scores very low for cost of living and economy and jobs. Similarly, California cities score high for climate, leisure, and arts and culture, but fail miserably on cost of living and transportation (specifically, the commute). Small Texas towns flourish on cost of living, but flounder on arts and culture and sometimes education. Adjusting category weights, as was done with the individual data, doesn't work in these cases because such an adjustment would bias the model result across the board instead of penalizing or rewarding individual cities that excel or fall well below average.

To address this issue, a *consistency* factor is added to the determination of overall score. A city scoring consistently high—above the 60th percentile—in seven of nine data categories receives a bonus, while a city with a particularly poor individual category score—below the 25th percentile—receives a penalty against their total composite score. Therefore, a city like Los Angeles with mostly good scores but a few really poor ones will receive a penalty, just as in real life where the high cost of living or a 40-minute commute might taint an otherwise stellar appraisal of a place. Note that with this approach, one city can receive both a bonus and a penalty. When this happens, they cancel one another, either partially or completely.

Reading the Ranking Report

Tables 2.4 and 2.5 show the overall and category rankings for the 331 U.S. metropolitan areas included in chapter 5. To better understand how to read these tables, which are organized by rank and alphabetically, refer to Table 2.3, which includes seven cities from Table 2.5.

Reading from left to right:

- *Rank* is the position among the principal U.S. metropolitan areas. Billings, Montana, the first city in the sample, is 106th out of 331 cities overall.

- *Score* is a composite of scores from the 10 ranking categories, on a 0–100 scale, weighed according to importance and adjusted by the consistency factor.

- *Metropolitan Area* and *State* are the complete name of the Metropolitan Statistical Area (MSA) and the state or states in which it is located.

- *Category Rankings* show scores in the 10 individual ranking categories on a 0–100 scale.

Billings, Montana, provides an interesting illustration of scoring and the concept of consistency. This city has six categories—Economy & Jobs, Education, Health & Healthcare, Crime, Transportation, and Quality of Life—scoring at 60 or above on the 0–100 scale. As a result, it received a consistency bonus. However, the score for Climate (10) is below 25, so it also received a penalty. These adjustments largely cancel out, and the area retains a mostly favorable score of 65.4 for a rank of 106 among the 331 metropolitan areas. This composite score reflects the weighting of individual categories and consistency adjustments. Had it not been for the climate factor, Billings would have scored and ranked noticeably higher, and had it not been for the consistency factor, it would have scored and ranked noticeably lower.

Table 2.3: Ranking Report Sample

Rank	Score	Metropolitan Area	State	Economy & Jobs	Cost of Living	Climate	Education	Health & Healthcare	Crime	Transportation	Leisure	Arts & Culture	Quality of Life
106	65.4	Billings	MT	100	58	10	63	95	83	81	41	34	90
293	36.0	Biloxi-Gulfport-Pascagoula	MS	6	66	76	44	17	17	12	33	32	50
241	47.7	Binghamton	NY	55	37	7	66	77	87	69	38	56	18
218	50.9	Birmingham	AL	61	36	25	30	65	39	4	31	58	18
195	54.2	Bismarck	ND	41	63	24	79	98	99	76	0	12	42
29	82.2	Bloomington	IN	96	55	50	87	40	82	80	67	84	55
42	78.1	Bloomington-Normal	IL	71	34	37	88	66	84	92	30	55	33

Table 2.4: U.S. Metropolitan Areas by Rank

Rank	Score	Metropolitan Area	State	Category Rankings (0-100 Scale)									
				Economy & Jobs	Cost of Living	Climate	Education	Health & Healthcare	Crime	Transportation	Leisure	Arts & Culture	Quality of Life
1	100.0	Charlottesville	VA	96	42	69	86	97	70	28	34	63	91
2	99.3	Santa Fe	NM	36	11	94	83	69	63	71	63	39	97
3	97.2	San Luis Obispo–Atascadero–Paso Robles	CA	31	5	98	68	39	93	34	83	35	99
4	95.2	Santa Barbara–Santa Maria–Lompoc	CA	20	1	98	54	43	94	76	85	34	99
5	91.7	Honolulu	HI	96	3	98	54	31	41	91	77	90	79
6	91.2	Ann Arbor	MI	93	13	40	89	70	88	84	71	86	99
7	91.1	Atlanta	GA	60	23	72	96	26	46	95	91	91	84
8	90.4	Asheville	NC	30	29	65	73	94	66	29	28	51	98
9	89.3	Reno	NV	34	33	84	46	27	39	90	74	48	47
10	89.0	Corvallis	OR	50	22	66	90	76	83	59	51	74	86
11	88.6	Roanoke	VA	85	74	75	66	99	62	57	29	81	50
12	88.2	Portland–Vancouver	OR–WA	1	20	77	85	72	36	84	82	89	93
13	87.4	Raleigh–Durham–Chapel Hill	NC	30	23	63	96	80	29	21	44	79	92
14	86.4	Bryan–College Station	TX	92	79	67	86	63	40	83	45	46	33
15	86.0	Lynchburg	VA	33	79	69	40	99	92	20	35	25	28
16	85.9	Olympia	WA	62	45	45	81	56	50	60	84	27	98
17	85.8	Norfolk–Virginia Beach–Newport News	VA–NC	66	54	62	71	20	46	35	73	70	79
18	85.8	Colorado Springs	CO	12	26	90	92	66	47	41	73	37	95
19	85.5	Nassau–Suffolk	NY	93	3	75	96	35	99	93	99	86	79
20	85.1	Pueblo	CO	30	58	66	36	98	32	45	68	53	58
21	85.1	Eugene–Springfield	OR	23	49	64	62	48	47	84	80	56	68
22	84.1	Austin–San Marcos	TX	13	50	88	90	23	47	44	50	82	92
23	84.0	Lafayette	IN	49	77	49	56	44	89	80	55	53	81
24	83.9	Minneapolis–St. Paul	MN–WI	42	10	12	97	42	69	85	93	98	95
25	82.6	Dover	DE	51	64	60	28	31	48	45	26	29	64
26	82.6	Washington	DC–MD–VA–WV	85	5	43	99	32	67	74	97	99	97
27	82.5	Fayetteville–Springdale–Rogers	AR	53	75	53	33	80	78	54	30	26	58
28	82.5	Pittsburgh	PA	21	54	29	91	50	78	93	86	97	87
29	82.2	Bloomington	IN	96	55	50	82	40	82	80	67	84	55
30	82.1	Stamford–Norwalk	CT	57	0	74	88	24	96	97	87	82	81
31	81.6	State College	PA	25	63	42	85	93	95	64	14	70	93
32	81.2	Abilene	TX	91	88	90	62	55	70	86	28	59	18
33	80.7	Champaign–Urbana	IL	71	48	39	91	47	64	95	25	66	75
34	80.7	Athens	GA	38	51	53	60	78	33	37	60	61	64
35	80.6	Wichita	KS	94	57	57	44	43	28	65	32	80	28

Rank	Score	Metropolitan Area	State	Economy & Jobs	Cost of Living	Climate	Education	Health & Healthcare	Crime	Transportation	Leisure	Arts & Culture	Quality of Life
36	80.5	Fort Worth–Arlington	TX	44	60	86	61	10	24	94	81	59	81
37	80.2	Madison	WI	98	15	23	98	95	73	85	40	91	99
38	80.0	Bellingham	WA	53	47	81	58	68	38	67	63	19	90
39	80.0	Las Cruces	NM	24	61	91	28	11	30	29	23	71	46
40	79.3	New York	NY	13	2	77	99	25	77	98	100	100	92
41	79.0	Dayton–Springfield	OH	56	36	46	66	46	35	83	73	90	47
42	78.1	Bloomington–Normal	IL	71	34	37	89	66	84	92	30	55	33
43	78.1	Sarasota–Bradenton	FL	11	78	82	48	52	30	30	69	24	84
44	78.0	Bremerton	WA	26	33	80	77	32	54	1	86	20	86
45	77.8	Albuquerque	NM	55	24	85	59	33	0	57	66	80	89
46	77.7	Harrisburg–Lebanon–Carlisle	PA	46	66	34	58	86	89	40	50	58	55
47	77.7	Evansville–Henderson	IN–KY	64	86	38	24	42	75	50	22	56	47
48	77.4	Tampa–St. Petersburg–Clearwater	FL	21	87	81	49	26	11	50	90	83	73
49	77.4	Punta Gorda	FL	24	81	82	22	89	76	10	61	36	60
50	77.2	Columbia	SC	74	52	35	79	67	45	21	33	65	58
51	77.0	Peoria–Pekin	IL	65	57	39	37	64	66	61	27	76	33
52	77.0	Des Moines	IA	35	23	25	83	80	63	77	29	63	81
53	76.1	Naples	FL	70	20	83	64	74	66	5	62	13	93
54	76.0	Los Angeles–Long Beach	CA	63	5	97	93	3	42	97	99	98	57
55	75.9	Richmond–Petersburg	VA	70	49	36	73	78	33	33	53	90	32
56	75.5	Gainesville	FL	6	77	83	91	67	20	51	33	82	33
57	75.5	Fort Lauderdale	FL	18	39	78	27	71	56	30	83	21	60
58	75.5	Ocala	FL	29	93	83	13	35	51	2	32	31	47
59	75.3	Tacoma	WA	12	28	80	60	40	21	69	89	83	47
60	75.2	Denver	CO	43	14	54	90	46	43	96	91	95	95
61	75.0	Mansfield	OH	41	76	23	13	60	75	38	31	29	68
62	74.9	Grand Junction	CO	59	34	69	47	96	62	57	68	4	72
63	74.5	Charleston–North Charleston	SC	64	30	56	47	22	36	14	66	72	95
64	74.4	Melbourne–Titusville–Palm Bay	FL	43	91	76	56	35	20	18	74	28	64
65	74.0	Orange County	CA	39	1	97	58	39	96	10	96	53	58
66	73.7	Daytona Beach	FL	32	90	76	36	27	29	14	69	37	50
67	73.3	New London–Norwich	CT–RI	94	16	74	80	26	73	28	79	81	33
68	73.1	Boise	ID	3	42	57	89	54	67	54	59	66	86
69	72.7	West Palm Beach–Boca Raton	FL	32	43	64	38	61	16	31	88	54	78
70	72.4	Tucson	AZ	12	40	95	55	28	4	42	76	83	87
71	72.3	Boston	MA–NH	28	4	31	100	29	87	95	97	99	93
72	72.1	Medford–Ashland	OR	9	35	57	32	63	84	67	38	66	75
73	71.9	Middlesex–Somerset–Hunterdon	NJ	86	6	58	92	17	98	92	92	95	91
74	71.5	San Diego	CA	15	3	96	79	9	72	70	96	86	95

continued

Table 2.4: U.S. Metropolitan Areas by Rank (continued)

	Score	Metropolitan Area	State	Category Rankings (0-100 Scale)									
				Economy & Jobs	Cost of Living	Climate	Education	Health & Healthcare	Crime	Transportation	Leisure	Arts & Culture	Quality of Life
75	70.7	Barnstable–Yarmouth	MA	29	7	65	94	36	90	44	61	41	42
76	70.6	Philadelphia	PA–NJ	62	12	63	98	15	51	93	95	97	79
77	70.6	Johnson City–Kingsport–Bristol	TN–VA	36	97	56	37	96	26	16	36	33	50
78	69.8	Vallejo–Fairfield–Napa	CA	22	6	95	41	2	70	39	96	38	68
79	69.6	Indianapolis	IN	47	66	49	50	12	59	41	75	88	68
80	69.3	Greenville–Spartanburg–Anderson	SC	65	52	51	55	74	50	19	55	79	58
81	68.9	Greensboro–Winston-Salem–High Point	NC	42	46	58	67	80	30	30	33	57	18
82	68.7	Jacksonville	FL	38	71	52	43	13	41	20	34	23	64
83	68.7	Wilmington–Newark	DE–MD	77	52	59	32	31	25	68	82	40	33
84	68.6	Salt Lake City–Ogden	UT	27	26	30	61	40	53	92	90	83	88
85	68.6	Sacramento	CA	26	10	94	57	3	59	21	90	67	75
86	68.6	Goldsboro	NC	57	69	61	23	89	28	46	23	60	10
87	68.1	Fargo–Moorhead	ND–MN	43	62	36	88	94	84	88	16	61	47
88	68.0	Seattle–Bellevue–Everett	WA	8	11	80	94	51	37	96	98	92	93
89	68.0	Greeley	CO	31	43	54	50	38	60	10	84	50	33
90	67.9	Muncie	IN	52	82	50	39	47	79	66	50	78	18
91	67.9	Lexington	KY	48	40	39	74	83	61	42	18	76	73
92	67.8	Cincinnati	OH–KY–IN	71	32	32	33	13	27	63	80	96	84
93	67.5	San Antonio	TX	52	70	88	43	7	0	50	62	50	90
94	67.4	Columbus	GA–AL	31	35	48	22	45	25	32	5	39	64
95	67.3	Dallas	TX	37	42	86	89	7	13	96	89	93	79
96	67.0	Missoula	MT	81	30	22	78	83	50	83	43	18	90
97	67.0	St. Louis	MO–IL	71	50	36	75	22	14	87	87	89	68
98	66.6	Charlotte–Gastonia–Rock Hill	NC–SC	38	25	44	65	43	7	35	65	70	68
99	66.5	Little Rock–North Little Rock	AR	55	61	44	50	88	18	26	37	33	50
100	66.3	Sioux Falls	SD	38	79	19	69	93	95	84	20	21	76
101	66.2	Kokomo	IN	92	84	49	30	51	45	64	38	25	10
102	65.8	Fort Wayne	IN	92	83	42	26	27	62	46	31	87	18
103	65.7	Knoxville	TN	33	80	37	52	82	43	19	57	70	33
104	65.6	Decatur	IL	70	82	38	13	52	57	77	21	36	32
105	65.5	Galveston–Texas City	TX	46	70	93	53	18	20	72	72	32	10
106	65.4	Billings	MT	100	58	10	60	95	83	81	41	34	90
107	65.3	San Francisco	CA	4	0	99	81	15	69	100	98	99	94
108	65.0	Green Bay	WI	78	31	16	46	82	95	88	47	48	76
109	64.9	Memphis	TN–AR–MS	27	62	47	29	23	0	68	32	72	47
110	64.8	Columbus	OH	56	27	43	87	34	9	49	46	92	33
111	64.7	Tuscaloosa	AL	63	76	22	36	92	16	30	28	29	81
112	64.6	Altoona	PA	20	83	42	10	81	49	53	27	38	28
113	64.6	Waterloo–Cedar Falls	IA	53	45	30	29	91	57	90	13	85	33

Rank	Score	Metropolitan Area	State	Category Rankings (0-100 Scale)									
				Economy & Jobs	Cost of Living	Climate	Education	Health & Healthcare	Crime	Transportation	Leisure	Arts & Culture	Quality of Life
114	64.5	Richland-Kennewick-Pasco	WA	40	65	34	51	34	74	96	40	22	7
115	64.2	La Crosse	WI-MN	68	40	13	66	94	90	78	24	47	81
116	64.0	Fresno	CA	2	26	89	12	1	20	40	70	71	32
117	63.9	Appleton-Oshkosh-Neenah	WI	91	37	16	44	83	90	82	53	21	64
118	63.7	Hamilton-Middletown	OH	67	55	33	41	21	28	48	64	76	33
119	63.3	Springfield	MO	43	65	31	68	96	10	43	26	67	28
120	63.3	Lubbock	TX	98	84	85	52	90	2	86	22	60	17
121	63.1	Corpus Christi	TX	84	78	86	20	16	5	66	46	69	28
122	63.0	Reading	PA	33	50	33	14	62	68	26	57	41	28
123	63.0	Atlantic City-Cape May	NJ	59	23	84	39	19	44	71	58	20	60
124	62.8	Santa Cruz-Watsonville	CA	6	1	99	70	2	71	82	67	41	95
125	62.7	Miami	FL	8	41	79	8	65	2	52	94	85	68
126	62.7	Lakeland-Winter Haven	FL	33	89	77	10	15	32	6	79	30	72
127	62.5	Bangor	ME	80	66	28	65	59	61	44	43	30	33
128	62.4	Fort Collins-Loveland	CO	16	16	54	93	73	85	32	88	56	94
129	62.4	Las Vegas	NV-AZ	1	51	79	18	16	60	86	84	60	46
130	62.3	Kansas City	MO-KS	59	27	21	85	29	3	69	80	96	60
131	62.2	Janesville-Beloit	WI	66	32	24	38	88	58	46	20	16	42
132	62.2	South Bend	IN	60	85	27	37	38	10	62	30	72	33
133	62.0	Tulsa	OK	15	46	78	52	28	19	52	37	74	60
134	61.9	Orlando	FL	14	77	82	57	20	8	47	88	75	32
135	61.8	Eau Claire	WI	37	44	12	63	85	80	70	25	46	64
136	61.8	St. Cloud	MN	23	29	16	43	79	72	62	53	39	50
137	61.1	Jamestown	NY	84	35	11	76	86	98	79	35	49	33
138	61.1	Tyler	TX	94	90	72	47	55	35	13	21	10	42
139	61.0	New Orleans	LA	56	36	70	3	13	23	31	91	80	68
140	60.8	Akron	OH	61	40	19	57	33	42	38	76	76	31
141	60.7	Salem	OR	18	41	66	36	60	30	18	61	45	76
142	60.7	Boulder-Longmont	CO	0	8	55	97	75	52	90	86	60	97
143	60.6	Longview-Marshall	TX	60	98	73	42	29	21	15	16	26	42
144	60.6	Rochester	MN	86	19	12	86	100	77	98	71	97	46
145	60.5	Bridgeport	CT	84	7	73	82	23	60	21	93	81	60
146	60.3	Provo-Orem	UT	10	21	55	84	18	89	53	80	74	84
147	60.0	Ventura	CA	17	4	97	40	32	99	7	81	20	81
148	59.9	Duluth-Superior	MN-WI	53	33	5	74	84	48	67	76	71	86
149	59.8	New Haven-Meriden	CT	90	12	73	84	53	64	47	66	95	10
150	59.8	Davenport-Moline-Rock Island	IA-IL	47	35	17	49	57	36	75	23	28	28
151	59.6	Nashua	NH	70	46	2	76	30	87	56	59	24	86
152	59.4	Fort Walton Beach	FL	57	85	68	75	63	57	26	34	0	10

continued

Table 2.4: U.S. Metropolitan Areas by Rank *(continued)*

Rank	Score	Metropolitan Area	State	Category Rankings (0-100 Scale)									
				Economy & Jobs	Cost of Living	Climate	Education	Health & Healthcare	Crime	Transportation	Leisure	Arts & Culture	Quality of Life
153	59.3	Salinas	CA	4	2	100	10	0	73	36	73	35	50
154	59.1	Killeen–Temple	TX	64	94	67	64	28	51	23	10	64	2
155	59.0	Chicago	IL	45	10	27	99	8	26	99	99	98	92
156	59.0	Savannah	GA	73	48	60	17	30	6	33	41	62	84
157	58.9	Grand Rapids–Muskegon–Holland	MI	57	49	10	48	37	65	51	63	69	33
158	58.9	Houston	TX	58	47	56	65	0	14	61	89	93	75
159	58.8	Lawton	OK	49	78	75	45	10	48	70	23	33	0
160	58.6	Anchorage	AK	99	56	6	71	21	34	91	69	73	68
161	58.5	Oklahoma City	OK	90	53	70	73	16	23	41	36	51	7
162	58.5	Lansing–East Lansing	MI	96	47	8	80	80	54	59	44	86	33
163	58.3	Fort Pierce–Port St. Lucie	FL	21	72	64	25	64	52	3	51	47	33
164	58.2	Augusta-Aiken	GA-SC	73	70	53	32	59	54	8	10	23	68
165	58.0	Oakland	CA	23	0	99	82	1	45	0	98	63	58
166	57.7	Santa Rosa	CA	7	2	95	59	3	90	64	92	45	95
167	57.3	Louisville	KY-IN	45	38	45	26	11	40	65	40	90	81
168	57.1	San Jose	CA	1	0	96	83	4	90	38	95	75	58
169	57.0	Trenton	NJ	86	17	58	73	33	33	80	87	92	28
170	57.0	Riverside–San Bernardino	CA	28	14	96	15	5	63	0	94	69	60
171	57.0	Brazoria	TX	80	73	56	46	10	74	27	56	22	7
172	56.5	Wilmington	NC	3	37	52	67	64	13	23	43	43	68
173	56.5	Providence–Fall River–Warwick	RI-MA	91	9	32	54	19	66	66	86	78	89
174	56.5	Mobile	AL	36	53	60	8	24	10	5	47	45	47
175	56.4	Cumberland	MD-WV	51	73	51	20	87	56	4	51	5	42
176	56.4	Bergen-Passaic	NJ	89	3	47	64	25	91	97	97	68	73
177	56.3	Redding	CA	14	21	96	27	12	80	49	74	33	2
178	56.2	Jackson	MS	89	68	51	53	46	19	17	29	55	50
179	56.2	Baltimore	MD	80	12	43	90	35	15	62	93	94	73
180	55.9	Greenville	NC	3	62	53	49	71	4	27	36	26	57
181	55.8	Danbury	CT	97	4	1	86	25	100	94	75	64	87
182	55.8	Cheyenne	WY	83	94	41	80	49	64	86	2	6	33
183	55.8	Beaumont–Port Arthur	TX	63	91	67	21	30	34	23	45	55	33
184	55.8	Hagerstown	MD	82	46	44	7	68	69	5	53	52	60
185	55.6	Casper	WY	83	100	41	76	72	65	73	2	16	28
186	55.6	Lancaster	PA	75	45	33	4	26	86	55	58	0	76
187	55.5	Johnstown	PA	10	93	41	8	85	78	23	54	40	50
188	55.3	Terre Haute	IN	36	87	50	33	38	40	36	19	41	18
189	54.9	Columbia	MO	11	65	23	95	98	60	73	12	73	67
190	54.8	Spokane	WA	17	69	30	77	67	13	33	49	62	76
191	54.8	Iowa City	IA	45	22	26	98	99	76	89	7	7	55

Rank	Score	Metropolitan Area	State	Economy & Jobs	Cost of Living	Climate	Education	Health & Healthcare	Crime	Transportation	Leisure	Arts & Culture	Quality of Life
192	54.5	Auburn-Opelika	AL	85	74	25	71	85	7	35	6	43	75
193	54.5	Parkersburg-Marietta	WV-OH	28	67	46	34	75	79	31	9	75	2
194	54.3	Lawrence	KS	66	30	31	97	44	58	42	0	1	55
195	54.2	Bismarck	ND	41	63	24	72	98	99	76	0	12	42
196	53.9	Springfield	IL	68	59	38	55	70	41	71	16	78	10
197	53.7	Topeka	KS	99	56	43	43	78	1	79	52	54	18
198	53.6	Milwaukee-Waukesha	WI	50	13	15	63	47	40	74	85	96	79
199	53.6	Sheboygan	WI	98	32	17	22	66	92	93	85	93	55
200	53.2	Yolo	CA	9	9	93	63	4	83	55	60	31	31
201	53.1	Omaha	NE-IA	81	28	18	69	65	16	74	47	84	79
202	53.0	Allentown-Bethlehem-Easton	PA	49	30	32	40	60	61	24	75	63	18
203	52.8	Monmouth-Ocean	NJ	68	6	83	61	6	96	79	96	50	89
204	52.7	Yuma	AZ	0	68	90	2	9	94	94	61	41	42
205	52.7	Buffalo-Niagara Falls	NY	78	18	14	76	50	73	75	83	96	68
206	52.6	Nashville	TN	40	60	21	53	73	7	19	65	73	75
207	52.6	Cedar Rapids	IA	34	27	18	84	86	68	82	16	53	60
208	52.1	Wausau	WI	83	37	17	35	90	82	70	8	49	50
209	52.0	Decatur	AL	95	91	20	23	51	71	6	20	10	33
210	51.9	Chattanooga	TN-GA	46	80	24	19	76	2	14	35	35	72
211	51.8	Visalia-Tulare-Porterville	CA	5	38	89	1	6	32	24	64	12	46
212	51.5	Great Falls	MT	65	63	14	56	96	37	90	46	16	42
213	51.4	St. Joseph	MO	26	85	21	16	56	52	63	6	3	33
214	51.2	Rochester	NY	76	19	13	93	36	81	66	78	84	50
215	51.0	Clarksville-Hopkinsville	TN-KY	25	99	20	40	49	22	13	49	11	33
216	51.0	Williamsport	PA	47	72	13	31	91	93	56	22	6	33
217	50.9	Steubenville-Weirton	OH-WV	76	90	29	18	41	24	11	56	31	2
218	50.9	Birmingham	AL	61	36	25	48	65	39	4	31	58	18
219	50.9	Saginaw-Bay City-Midland	MI	86	68	18	25	59	58	37	42	52	32
220	50.6	Fort Myers-Cape Coral	FL	18	83	81	25	75	26	16	53	13	64
221	50.6	Sherman-Denison	TX	74	92	87	53	57	50	6	18	25	2
222	50.5	Vineland-Millville-Bridgeton	NJ	71	39	84	3	16	31	77	59	15	60
223	50.4	Lincoln	NE	88	23	13	83	69	11	81	38	85	58
224	50.4	Kenosha	WI	50	23	15	34	33	49	99	67	30	18
225	50.4	El Paso	TX	26	73	88	5	13	31	53	37	67	6
226	50.4	Huntsville	AL	86	58	20	70	42	44	28	10	48	10
227	50.1	Waco	TX	75	91	87	44	24	12	50	26	19	10
228	49.9	Huntington-Ashland	WV-KY-OH	48	74	79	19	83	44	9	19	88	18
229	49.9	Amarillo	TX	86	91	86	41	58	6	68	6	46	2
230	49.5	Lowell	MA-NH	20	7	9	92	53	98	52	77	59	68

continued

Table 2.4: U.S. Metropolitan Areas by Rank *(continued)*

Rank	Score	Metropolitan Area	State	Economy & Jobs	Cost of Living	Climate	Education	Health & Healthcare	Crime	Transportation	Leisure	Arts & Culture	Quality of Life
				Category Rankings (0-100 Scale)									
231	49.5	Rockford	IL	50	31	22	16	73	41	26	24	39	10
232	49.4	Burlington	VT	57	18	1	96	92	79	46	48	44	90
233	49.3	Charleston	WV	19	58	80	33	84	25	38	17	68	18
234	49.1	Flint	MI	23	51	26	31	30	23	25	72	77	0
235	48.9	Manchester	NH	93	55	5	80	62	93	2	68	27	67
236	48.7	Portland	ME	66	13	0	95	77	97	41	60	64	88
237	48.5	Kalamazoo–Battle Creek	MI	76	56	11	72	76	16	58	52	56	28
238	48.4	Enid	OK	95	88	70	26	87	43	61	19	2	18
239	47.8	Pensacola	FL	8	88	68	49	50	59	8	52	53	18
240	47.8	Albany-Schenectady-Troy	NY	74	15	4	95	61	86	60	64	93	42
241	47.7	Binghamton	NY	55	37	7	79	77	87	69	38	56	18
242	47.2	Shreveport-Bossier City	LA	61	70	72	28	49	18	37	17	43	10
243	47.2	Pittsfield	MA	75	25	4	69	87	91	72	70	3	42
244	46.9	Flagstaff	AZ-UT	0	18	63	77	22	34	53	40	2	76
245	46.7	Jackson	MI	52	60	9	24	68	22	20	36	20	33
246	46.6	Syracuse	NY	95	26	6	93	46	70	73	64	87	6
247	46.3	Monroe	LA	30	85	73	19	54	1	48	9	43	7
248	46.2	Lake Charles	LA	65	80	65	5	20	24	32	9	38	18
249	46.1	Tallahassee	FL	14	67	60	81	89	9	36	15	50	33
250	46.1	Fayetteville	NC	32	61	62	51	12	27	27	9	19	47
251	46.0	Springfield	MA	72	25	1	78	45	15	81	56	88	50
252	45.9	Panama City	FL	15	87	68	35	56	8	40	40	27	2
253	45.7	Hartford	CT	78	14	2	94	60	76	80	71	89	42
254	45.7	Hickory-Morganton-Lenoir	NC	6	63	59	16	92	65	21	23	4	10
255	45.1	Albany	GA	60	83	61	9	41	45	59	5	32	2
256	45.1	Dothan	AL	80	99	47	14	95	55	34	4	8	18
257	44.9	Jonesboro	AR	77	79	48	26	93	53	54	1	9	18
258	44.6	Montgomery	AL	82	89	55	28	62	5	15	25	51	18
259	44.5	Grand Forks	ND-MN	42	75	36	78	97	80	89	3	3	18
260	43.7	York	PA	37	64	33	38	55	88	9	27	17	55
261	43.5	Newark	NJ	89	6	46	88	21	75	87	93	94	10
262	43.5	Jersey City	NJ	26	8	46	7	6	63	87	90	49	42
263	43.1	Detroit	MI	77	17	40	60	20	33	76	95	91	18
264	42.8	Cleveland-Lorain-Elyria	OH	54	19	15	45	23	55	73	92	94	79
265	42.3	Yakima	WA	4	69	34	4	37	43	58	49	46	18
266	42.1	Myrtle Beach	SC	5	44	52	42	70	3	28	42	52	0
267	41.9	Toledo	OH	24	39	40	30	39	11	60	50	87	17
268	41.9	Florence	SC	75	67	35	6	72	1	99	10	23	10
269	41.8	Florence	AL	2	97	20	13	91	82	9	16	34	33

Rank	Score	Metropolitan Area	State	Economy & Jobs	Cost of Living	Climate	Education	Health & Healthcare	Crime	Transportation	Leisure	Arts & Culture	Quality of Life
270	41.8	Sioux City	IA-NE	18	44	28	15	71	56	77	8	71	18
271	41.6	Scranton–Wilkes-Barre–Hazleton	PA	17	58	19	16	89	94	39	39	37	33
272	41.4	Elkhart-Goshen	IN	99	63	27	5	45	38	64	4	42	10
273	40.8	Phoenix-Mesa	AZ	10	41	90	75	10	19	60	94	18	79
274	40.7	Sumter	SC	28	76	35	15	35	3	91	4	60	0
275	40.6	Gary	IN	40	56	28	23	18	48	98	83	66	0
276	40.3	Lima	OH	72	82	23	20	43	54	58	12	36	2
277	39.8	San Angelo	TX	88	95	93	31	69	10	72	15	6	18
278	39.3	Canton-Massillon	OH	35	57	14	20	53	37	54	70	36	18
279	39.1	Pocatello	ID	93	47	5	63	60	86	77	0	14	72
280	39.0	Brockton	MA	68	9	10	87	5	53	88	78	44	72
281	38.8	Chico-Paradise	CA	13	16	91	38	14	76	34	60	30	17
282	38.7	Bakersfield	CA	5	43	93	3	3	67	21	42	14	2
283	38.4	Odessa-Midland	TX	97	90	87	17	17	53	56	14	11	2
284	38.4	Rapid City	SD	48	93	7	70	66	35	76	3	2	42
285	38.3	Glens Falls	NY	96	34	4	67	58	97	13	55	10	55
286	38.2	Worcester	MA-CT	39	19	3	74	44	88	16	79	58	68
287	37.8	Portsmouth-Rochester	NH-ME	63	28	0	70	19	92	0	70	28	81
288	37.6	Elmira	NY	53	50	7	51	70	79	83	48	18	10
289	37.4	Utica-Rome	NY	88	35	6	62	74	81	56	46	17	10
290	37.4	Victoria	TX	88	95	85	12	34	36	18	17	13	10
291	37.0	Youngstown-Warren	OH	46	54	8	14	48	39	24	63	65	7
292	36.4	Fitchburg-Leominster	MA	72	20	3	56	37	85	12	76	44	28
293	36.0	Biloxi-Gulfport-Pascagoula	MS	6	66	76	24	17	17	12	33	32	50
294	36.0	Wichita Falls	TX	66	96	78	42	58	4	63	6	6	2
295	35.6	Baton Rouge	LA	34	53	71	11	7	9	7	39	80	64
296	35.6	Texarkana	TX-AR	83	98	73	23	79	17	32	7	7	2
297	35.2	Lafayette	LA	53	81	71	0	6	29	3	43	40	18
298	35.1	Danville	VA	42	89	59	30	86	74	15	13	17	33
299	35.0	Benton Harbor	MI	82	33	0	2	59	26	48	43	8	67
300	34.5	Hattiesburg	MS	39	76	61	45	40	85	10	5	0	10
301	34.0	Rocky Mount	NC	3	70	63	10	52	15	40	15	62	18
302	32.9	Macon	GA	79	60	50	17	54	12	13	10	25	33
303	32.4	Owensboro	KY	68	72	40	7	57	68	43	0	7	18
304	32.2	Jackson	TN	10	94	37	33	90	18	50	1	21	18
305	32.0	Wheeling	WV-OH	11	73	30	6	80	81	18	18	79	18
306	31.0	Joplin	MO	7	97	29	21	73	13	45	6	23	10
307	30.0	Racine	WI	86	31	16	18	53	46	63	66	4	18
308	29.6	Sharon	PA	22	86	8	35	93	93	43	11	5	18

continued

Part I: Finding Your Best Place to Live

Table 2.4: U.S. Metropolitan Areas by Rank *(continued)*

Rank	Score	Metropolitan Area	State	Category Rankings (0-100 Scale)									
				Economy & Jobs	Cost of Living	Climate	Education	Health & Healthcare	Crime	Transportation	Leisure	Arts & Culture	Quality of Life
309	29.4	Erie	PA	9	70	11	21	88	86	75	30	77	2
310	28.2	Dutchess County	NY	90	10	3	87	50	96	1	72	12	64
311	28.2	Dubuque	IA	43	40	6	2	76	23	89	8	15	60
312	27.2	Waterbury	CT	56	16	2	59	40	56	17	56	57	50
313	26.4	Lewiston–Auburn	ME	40	29	0	30	79	71	16	2	15	47
314	25.5	Brownsville–Harlingen–San Benito	TX	25	96	91	1	8	5	36	43	7	18
315	25.2	Yuba City–Marysville	CA	0	22	94	9	1	71	3	57	5	0
316	25.0	Modesto	CA	20	17	92	3	2	27	2	54	10	7
317	23.8	McAllen–Edinburg–Mission	TX	2	99	76	0	5	17	25	20	9	33
318	23.6	Jacksonville	NC	18	86	71	46	11	14	11	81	77	10
319	23.4	New Bedford	MA	16	14	66	27	14	76	6	77	43	50
320	23.3	Houma	LA	81	94	70	0	8	22	1	82	16	7
321	22.7	Alexandria	LA	62	98	62	3	82	6	12	14	24	10
322	21.8	Fort Smith	AR-OK	51	81	48	11	63	12	17	13	1	10
323	20.8	Anniston	AL	79	96	26	10	76	6	8	13	14	18
324	20.5	Gadsden	AL	68	96	26	12	84	21	3	12	12	2
325	20.3	Pine Bluff	AR	34	84	45	9	54	0	25	0	1	0
326	19.5	Lawrence	MA-NH	16	7	10	72	14	97	49	78	68	50
327	18.7	Kankakee	IL	21	53	9	6	48	31	7	26	9	10
328	12.4	Merced	CA	16	21	92	1	0	38	4	45	3	2
329	9.9	Newburgh	NY-PA	79	11	3	68	9	83	11	48	11	55
330	0.0	Stockton–Lodi	CA	13	13	92	6	0	8	0	58	65	7
331	0.0	Laredo	TX	6	93	89	0	4	3	47	2	0	10

Table 2.5: U.S. Metropolitan Areas by Alphabetical Sequence with Rank

Rank	Score	Metropolitan Area	State	Category Rankings (0-100 Scale)									
				Economy & Jobs	Cost of Living	Climate	Education	Health & Healthcare	Crime	Transportation	Leisure	Arts & Culture	Quality of Life
32	81.2	Abilene	TX	91	88	90	62	55	70	86	28	59	18
140	60.8	Akron	OH	61	40	19	57	33	42	38	76	76	31
255	45.1	Albany	GA	60	83	61	9	41	45	59	5	32	2
240	47.8	Albany-Schenectady-Troy	NY	74	15	4	95	61	86	60	64	93	42
45	77.8	Albuquerque	NM	55	24	85	59	33	0	57	66	80	89
321	22.7	Alexandria	LA	62	98	62	3	82	6	12	14	24	10
202	53.0	Allentown-Bethlehem-Easton	PA	49	30	32	40	60	61	24	75	63	18
112	64.6	Altoona	PA	20	83	42	10	81	49	53	27	38	28
229	49.9	Amarillo	TX	86	91	86	41	58	6	68	6	46	2
160	58.6	Anchorage	AK	99	56	6	71	21	34	91	69	73	68
6	91.2	Ann Arbor	MI	93	13	40	89	70	88	84	71	86	99
323	20.8	Anniston	AL	79	96	26	10	76	6	8	13	14	18
117	63.9	Appleton-Oshkosh-Neenah	WI	91	37	16	44	83	90	82	53	21	64
8	90.4	Asheville	NC	30	29	65	73	94	66	29	28	51	98
34	80.7	Athens	GA	38	51	53	60	78	33	37	60	61	64
7	91.1	Atlanta	GA	60	23	72	96	26	46	95	91	91	84
123	63.0	Atlantic City-Cape May	NJ	59	23	84	39	19	44	71	58	20	60
192	54.5	Auburn-Opelika	AL	85	74	25	71	85	7	35	6	43	75
164	58.2	Augusta-Aiken	GA-SC	73	70	53	32	59	54	8	10	23	68
22	84.1	Austin-San Marcos	TX	13	50	88	90	23	47	44	50	82	92
282	38.7	Bakersfield	CA	5	43	93	3	3	67	21	42	14	2
179	56.2	Baltimore	MD	80	12	43	90	35	15	62	93	94	73
127	62.5	Bangor	ME	80	66	28	65	59	61	44	43	30	33
75	70.7	Barnstable-Yarmouth	MA	29	7	65	94	36	90	44	61	41	42
295	35.6	Baton Rouge	LA	34	53	71	11	7	9	7	39	80	64
183	55.8	Beaumont-Port Arthur	TX	63	91	67	21	30	34	23	45	55	33
38	80.0	Bellingham	WA	53	47	81	58	68	38	67	63	19	90
299	35.0	Benton Harbor	MI	82	33	0	30	59	26	48	43	8	67
176	56.4	Bergen-Passaic	NJ	89	3	47	64	25	91	97	97	68	73
106	65.4	Billings	MT	100	58	10	60	95	83	81	41	34	90
293	36.0	Biloxi-Gulfport-Pascagoula	MS	6	66	76	24	17	17	12	33	32	50
241	47.7	Binghamton	NY	55	37	7	79	7	87	69	38	56	18
218	50.9	Birmingham	AL	61	36	25	48	65	39	4	31	58	18
195	54.2	Bismarck	ND	41	63	24	72	98	99	76	0	12	42
29	82.2	Bloomington	IN	96	55	50	82	40	82	80	67	84	55

continued

Table 2.5: U.S. Metropolitan Areas by Alphabetical Sequence with Rank *(continued)*

Rank	Score	Metropolitan Area	State	Economy & Jobs	Cost of Living	Climate	Education	Health & Healthcare	Crime	Transportation	Leisure	Arts & Culture	Quality of Life
42	78.1	Bloomington–Normal	IL	71	34	37	89	66	84	92	30	55	33
68	73.1	Boise	ID	3	42	57	89	54	67	54	59	66	86
71	72.3	Boston	MA-NH	28	4	31	100	29	87	95	97	99	93
142	60.7	Boulder–Longmont	CO	0	8	55	97	75	52	90	86	60	97
171	57.0	Brazoria	TX	80	73	56	46	10	74	27	56	22	7
44	78.0	Bremerton	WA	26	33	80	77	32	54	1	86	20	86
145	60.5	Bridgeport	CT	84	7	73	82	23	60	21	93	81	60
280	39.0	Brockton	MA	68	9	10	87	5	53	88	78	44	72
314	25.5	Brownsville–Harlingen–San Benito	TX	25	96	91	1	8	5	36	43	7	18
14	86.4	Bryan–College Station	TX	92	79	67	86	63	40	83	45	46	33
205	52.7	Buffalo–Niagara Falls	NY	78	18	14	76	50	73	75	83	96	68
232	49.4	Burlington	VT	57	18	1	96	92	79	46	48	44	90
278	39.3	Canton–Massillon	OH	35	57	14	20	53	37	54	70	36	18
185	55.6	Casper	WY	83	100	41	76	72	65	73	2	16	28
207	52.6	Cedar Rapids	IA	34	27	18	84	86	68	82	16	53	60
33	80.7	Champaign–Urbana	IL	71	48	39	91	47	64	95	25	66	75
233	49.3	Charleston	WV	19	58	80	33	84	25	38	17	68	18
63	74.5	Charleston–North Charleston	SC	64	30	56	47	22	36	14	66	72	95
98	66.6	Charlotte–Gastonia–Rock Hill	NC-SC	38	25	44	65	43	7	35	65	70	68
1	100.0	Charlottesville	VA	96	42	69	86	97	70	28	34	63	91
210	51.9	Chattanooga	TN-GA	46	80	24	19	76	2	14	35	35	72
182	55.8	Cheyenne	WY	83	94	41	80	49	64	86	2	6	33
155	59.0	Chicago	IL	45	10	27	99	8	26	99	99	98	92
281	38.8	Chico–Paradise	CA	13	16	91	38	14	76	34	60	30	17
92	67.8	Cincinnati	OH-KY-IN	71	32	32	33	13	27	63	80	96	84
215	51.0	Clarksville–Hopkinsville	TN-KY	25	99	20	40	49	22	13	49	11	33
264	42.8	Cleveland–Lorain–Elyria	OH	54	19	15	45	23	55	73	92	94	79
18	85.8	Colorado Springs	CO	12	26	90	92	66	47	41	73	37	95
189	54.9	Columbia	MO	11	65	23	95	98	60	73	12	73	67
50	77.2	Columbia	SC	74	52	35	79	67	45	21	33	65	58
94	67.4	Columbus	GA-AL	31	35	48	22	45	25	32	5	39	64
110	64.8	Columbus	OH	56	27	43	87	34	9	49	46	92	33
121	63.1	Corpus Christi	TX	84	78	86	20	16	5	66	46	69	28
10	89.0	Corvallis	OR	50	22	66	90	76	83	59	51	74	86
175	56.4	Cumberland	MD-WV	51	73	51	20	87	56	4	51	5	42
95	67.3	Dallas	TX	37	42	86	89	7	13	96	89	93	79
181	55.8	Danbury	CT	97	4	1	86	25	100	94	75	64	87
298	35.1	Danville	VA	42	89	59	2	86	74	15	13	17	33
150	59.8	Davenport–Moline–Rock Island	IA-IL	47	35	17	49	57	36	75	23	28	28

Category Rankings (0–100 Scale)

Rank	Score	Metropolitan Area	State	Economy & Jobs	Cost of Living	Climate	Education	Health & Healthcare	Crime	Transportation	Leisure	Arts & Culture	Quality of Life
66	73.7	Daytona Beach	FL	32	90	76	36	27	29	14	69	37	50
41	79.0	Dayton-Springfield	OH	56	36	46	66	46	35	83	73	90	47
209	52.0	Decatur	AL	95	91	20	23	51	71	6	20	10	33
104	65.6	Decatur	IL	70	82	38	13	52	57	77	21	36	32
60	75.2	Denver	CO	43	14	54	90	46	43	96	91	95	95
52	77.0	Des Moines	IA	35	23	25	83	80	63	77	29	63	81
263	43.1	Detroit	MI	77	17	40	60	20	33	76	95	91	18
256	45.1	Dothan	AL	80	99	47	14	95	55	34	4	8	18
25	82.6	Dover	DE	51	64	60	28	31	48	45	26	29	64
311	28.2	Dubuque	IA	43	40	6	2	76	23	89	8	15	60
148	59.9	Duluth-Superior	MN-WI	53	33	5	74	84	48	67	76	71	86
310	28.2	Dutchess County	NY	90	10	3	87	50	96	1	72	12	64
135	61.8	Eau Claire	WI	37	44	12	63	85	80	70	25	46	64
225	50.4	El Paso	TX	26	73	88	5	13	31	53	37	67	6
272	41.4	Elkhart-Goshen	IN	99	63	27	5	45	38	64	4	42	10
288	37.6	Elmira	NY	53	50	7	51	70	79	83	48	18	10
238	48.4	Enid	OK	95	88	70	26	87	43	61	19	2	18
309	29.4	Erie	PA	9	70	11	21	88	86	75	30	77	2
21	85.1	Eugene-Springfield	OR	23	49	64	62	48	47	84	80	56	68
47	77.7	Evansville-Henderson	IN-KY	64	86	38	24	42	75	50	22	56	47
87	68.1	Fargo-Moorhead	ND-MN	43	62	36	88	94	84	88	16	61	47
250	46.1	Fayetteville	NC	32	61	62	51	12	27	27	9	19	47
27	82.5	Fayetteville-Springdale-Rogers	AR	53	75	53	33	80	78	54	30	26	58
292	36.4	Fitchburg-Leominster	MA	72	20	3	56	37	85	12	76	44	28
244	46.9	Flagstaff	AZ-UT	0	18	63	77	22	34	53	40	2	76
234	49.1	Flint	MI	23	51	26	31	30	23	25	72	77	0
269	41.8	Florence	AL	2	97	20	13	91	82	9	16	34	33
268	41.9	Florence	SC	75	67	35	6	72	1	99	10	23	10
128	62.4	Fort Collins-Loveland	CO	16	16	54	93	73	85	32	88	56	94
57	75.5	Fort Lauderdale	FL	18	39	78	27	71	56	30	83	21	60
220	50.6	Fort Myers-Cape Coral	FL	18	83	81	25	75	26	16	53	13	64
163	58.3	Fort Pierce-Port St. Lucie	FL	21	72	64	25	64	52	3	51	47	33
322	21.8	Fort Smith	AR-OK	51	81	48	11	63	12	17	13	1	10
152	59.4	Fort Walton Beach	FL	57	85	68	75	63	57	26	34	0	10
102	65.8	Fort Wayne	IN	92	83	42	26	27	62	46	31	87	18
36	80.5	Fort Worth-Arlington	TX	44	60	86	61	10	24	94	81	59	81
116	64.0	Fresno	CA	2	26	89	12	1	20	40	70	71	32
324	20.5	Gadsden	AL	68	96	26	12	84	21	3	12	12	33
56	75.5	Gainesville	FL	6	77	83	91	67	20	51	33	82	33

continued

Table 2.5: U.S. Metropolitan Areas by Alphabetical Sequence with Rank (continued)

Rank	Score	Metropolitan Area	State	Economy & Jobs	Cost of Living	Climate	Education	Health & Healthcare	Crime	Transportation	Leisure	Arts & Culture	Quality of Life
105	65.5	Galveston–Texas City	TX	46	70	93	53	18	20	72	72	32	10
275	40.6	Gary	IN	40	56	28	23	18	48	98	83	66	0
285	38.3	Glens Falls	NY	96	34	4	67	58	97	13	55	10	55
86	68.6	Goldsboro	NC	57	69	61	23	89	28	46	23	60	10
259	44.5	Grand Forks	ND-MN	42	75	36	78	97	80	89	3	3	18
62	74.9	Grand Junction	CO	59	34	69	47	96	62	57	68	4	72
157	58.9	Grand Rapids–Muskegon–Holland	MI	57	49	10	48	37	65	51	63	69	33
212	51.5	Great Falls	MT	65	63	14	56	96	37	90	46	16	42
89	68.0	Greeley	CO	31	43	54	50	38	60	10	84	50	33
108	65.0	Green Bay	WI	78	31	16	46	82	95	88	47	48	76
81	68.9	Greensboro–Winston-Salem–High Point	NC	42	46	58	67	80	30	30	33	57	18
180	55.9	Greenville	NC	3	62	53	49	71	4	27	36	26	57
80	69.3	Greenville-Spartanburg-Anderson	SC	65	52	51	55	74	50	19	55	79	58
184	55.8	Hagerstown	MD	82	46	44	7	68	69	5	53	52	60
118	63.7	Hamilton-Middletown	OH	67	55	33	41	21	28	48	64	76	33
46	77.7	Harrisburg-Lebanon-Carlisle	PA	46	66	34	58	86	89	40	50	58	55
253	45.7	Hartford	CT	78	14	2	94	60	76	80	71	89	42
300	34.5	Hattiesburg	MS	39	76	61	45	40	85	10	5	0	10
254	45.7	Hickory-Morganton-Lenoir	NC	6	63	59	16	92	65	21	23	4	10
5	91.7	Honolulu	HI	96	3	98	54	31	41	91	77	90	79
320	23.3	Houma	LA	81	94	70	0	8	22	1	82	16	7
158	58.9	Houston	TX	58	47	56	65	0	14	61	89	93	75
228	49.9	Huntington-Ashland	WV-KY-OH	48	74	79	19	83	44	9	19	88	18
226	50.4	Huntsville	AL	86	58	20	70	42	44	28	10	48	10
79	69.6	Indianapolis	IN	47	66	49	50	12	59	41	75	88	68
191	54.8	Iowa City	IA	45	22	26	98	99	76	89	7	7	55
245	46.7	Jackson	MI	52	60	9	24	68	22	20	36	20	33
178	56.2	Jackson	MS	89	68	51	53	46	19	17	29	55	50
304	32.2	Jackson	TN	10	94	37	33	90	18	50	1	21	18
82	68.7	Jacksonville	FL	38	71	52	43	13	41	20	34	23	64
318	23.6	Jacksonville	NC	18	86	71	46	11	14	11	81	77	10
137	61.1	Jamestown	NY	84	35	11	76	86	98	79	35	49	33
131	62.2	Janesville-Beloit	WI	66	32	24	38	88	58	46	20	16	42
262	43.5	Jersey City	NJ	26	8	46	7	6	63	87	90	49	42
77	70.6	Johnson City–Kingsport–Bristol	TN-VA	36	97	56	37	96	26	16	36	33	50
187	55.5	Johnstown	PA	10	93	41	8	85	78	23	54	40	50
257	44.9	Jonesboro	AR	77	79	48	26	93	53	54	1	9	18
306	31.0	Joplin	MO	7	97	29	21	73	13	45	6	23	10
237	48.5	Kalamazoo–Battle Creek	MI	76	56	11	72	76	16	58	52	56	28

Rank	Score	Metropolitan Area	State	Category Rankings (0-100 Scale)									
				Economy & Jobs	Cost of Living	Climate	Education	Health & Healthcare	Crime	Transportation	Leisure	Arts & Culture	Quality of Life
327	18.7	Kankakee	IL	21	53	9	6	48	31	7	26	9	10
130	62.3	Kansas City	MO-KS	59	27	21	85	29	3	69	80	96	60
224	50.4	Kenosha	WI	50	23	15	34	33	49	99	67	30	18
154	59.1	Killeen-Temple	TX	64	94	67	64	28	51	23	10	64	2
103	65.7	Knoxville	TN	33	80	37	52	82	43	19	57	70	33
101	66.2	Kokomo	IN	92	84	49	30	51	45	64	38	25	10
115	64.2	La Crosse	WI-MN	68	40	13	66	94	90	78	24	47	81
23	84.0	Lafayette	IN	49	77	49	56	44	89	80	55	53	81
297	35.2	Lafayette	LA	53	81	71	0	6	29	3	43	40	18
248	46.2	Lake Charles	LA	65	80	65	5	20	24	32	9	38	18
126	62.7	Lakeland-Winter Haven	FL	33	89	77	10	15	32	6	79	30	72
186	55.6	Lancaster	PA	75	45	33	4	26	86	55	58	0	76
162	58.5	Lansing-East Lansing	MI	96	47	8	80	80	54	59	44	86	33
331	0.0	Laredo	TX	6	93	89	0	4	3	47	2	0	10
39	80.0	Las Cruces	NM	24	61	91	28	11	30	29	23	71	46
129	62.4	Las Vegas	NV-AZ	1	51	79	18	16	60	86	84	60	46
194	54.3	Lawrence	KS	66	30	31	97	44	58	42	0	1	55
326	19.5	Lawrence	MA-NH	16	7	10	72	14	97	49	78	68	50
159	58.8	Lawton	OK	49	78	75	45	10	48	70	23	33	0
313	26.4	Lewiston-Auburn	ME	40	29	0	30	79	71	16	2	15	47
91	67.9	Lexington	KY	48	40	39	74	83	61	42	18	76	73
276	40.3	Lima	OH	72	82	23	20	43	54	58	12	36	2
223	50.4	Lincoln	NE	88	23	13	83	69	11	81	38	85	58
99	66.5	Little Rock-North Little Rock	AR	55	61	44	50	88	18	26	37	33	50
143	60.6	Longview-Marshall	TX	60	98	73	42	29	21	15	16	26	42
54	76.0	Los Angeles-Long Beach	CA	63	5	97	93	3	42	97	99	98	57
167	57.3	Louisville	KY-IN	45	38	45	26	11	40	65	40	90	81
230	49.5	Lowell	MA-NH	20	7	9	92	53	98	52	77	59	68
120	63.3	Lubbock	TX	98	84	85	52	90	2	86	22	60	17
15	86.0	Lynchburg	VA	33	79	69	40	99	92	20	35	25	28
302	32.9	Macon	GA	79	60	50	17	54	12	13	10	25	33
37	80.2	Madison	WI	98	15	23	98	95	73	85	40	91	99
235	48.9	Manchester	NH	93	55	5	80	62	93	2	68	27	67
61	75.0	Mansfield	OH	41	76	23	13	60	75	38	31	29	68
317	23.8	McAllen-Edinburg-Mission	TX	2	99	76	0	5	17	25	20	9	33
72	72.1	Medford-Ashland	OR	9	35	57	32	63	84	67	38	66	75
64	74.4	Melbourne-Titusville-Palm Bay	FL	43	91	76	56	35	20	18	74	28	64
109	64.9	Memphis	TN-AR-MS	27	62	47	29	23	0	68	32	72	47
328	12.4	Merced	CA	16	21	92	1	0	38	4	45	3	2

continued

Table 2.5: U.S. Metropolitan Areas by Alphabetical Sequence with Rank *(continued)*

Rank	Score	Metropolitan Area	State	Economy & Jobs	Cost of Living	Climate	Education	Health & Healthcare	Crime	Transportation	Leisure	Arts & Culture	Quality of Life
				— Category Rankings (0-100 Scale)									
125	62.7	Miami	FL	8	41	79	8	65	2	52	94	85	68
73	71.9	Middlesex-Somerset-Hunterdon	NJ	86	6	58	92	17	98	92	92	95	91
198	53.6	Milwaukee-Waukesha	WI	50	13	15	63	47	40	74	85	96	79
24	83.9	Minneapolis-St. Paul	MN-WI	42	10	12	97	42	69	85	93	98	95
96	67.0	Missoula	MT	81	30	22	78	83	50	83	43	18	90
174	56.5	Mobile	AL	36	53	60	8	24	10	5	47	45	47
316	25.0	Modesto	CA	20	17	92	3	2	27	2	54	10	7
203	52.8	Monmouth-Ocean	NJ	68	6	83	61	6	96	79	96	50	89
247	46.3	Monroe	LA	30	85	73	19	54	1	48	9	43	7
258	44.6	Montgomery	AL	82	89	55	28	62	5	15	25	51	18
90	67.9	Muncie	IN	52	82	50	39	47	79	66	50	78	18
266	42.1	Myrtle Beach	SC	5	44	52	42	70	3	28	42	52	0
53	76.1	Naples	FL	70	20	83	64	74	66	5	62	13	93
151	59.6	Nashua	NH	70	46	2	76	30	87	56	59	24	86
206	52.6	Nashville	TN	40	60	21	53	73	7	19	65	73	75
19	85.5	Nassau-Suffolk	NY	93	3	75	96	35	99	93	99	86	79
319	23.4	New Bedford	MA	16	14	66	27	14	76	6	77	43	50
149	59.8	New Haven-Meriden	CT	90	12	73	84	53	64	47	66	95	10
67	73.3	New London-Norwich	CT-RI	94	16	74	80	26	73	28	79	81	33
139	61.0	New Orleans	LA	56	36	70	3	13	23	31	91	80	68
40	79.3	New York	NY	13	2	77	99	25	77	98	100	100	92
261	43.5	Newark	NJ	89	6	46	88	21	75	87	93	94	10
329	9.9	Newburgh	NY-PA	79	11	3	68	9	83	11	48	11	55
17	85.8	Norfolk–Virginia Beach–Newport News	VA-NC	66	54	62	71	20	46	35	73	70	79
165	58.0	Oakland	CA	23	0	99	82	1	45	0	98	63	58
58	75.5	Ocala	FL	29	93	83	13	35	51	2	32	31	47
283	38.4	Odessa-Midland	TX	97	90	87	17	17	53	56	14	11	2
161	58.5	Oklahoma City	OK	90	53	70	73	16	23	41	36	51	7
16	85.9	Olympia	WA	62	45	45	81	56	50	60	84	27	98
201	53.1	Omaha	NE-IA	81	28	18	69	65	16	74	47	84	79
65	74.0	Orange County	CA	39	1	97	58	39	96	10	96	53	58
134	61.9	Orlando	FL	14	77	82	57	20	8	47	88	75	32
303	32.4	Owensboro	KY	68	72	40	7	57	68	43	0	7	18
252	45.9	Panama City	FL	15	87	68	35	56	8	40	40	27	2
193	54.5	Parkersburg-Marietta	WV-OH	28	67	46	34	75	79	31	9	75	2
239	47.8	Pensacola	FL	8	88	68	49	50	59	8	52	53	18
51	77.0	Peoria-Pekin	IL	65	57	39	37	64	66	61	27	76	33
76	70.6	Philadelphia	PA-NJ	62	12	63	98	15	51	93	95	97	79
273	40.8	Phoenix-Mesa	AZ	10	41	90	75	10	19	60	94	18	79

Rank	Score	Metropolitan Area	State	Category Rankings (0-100 Scale)									
				Economy & Jobs	Cost of Living	Climate	Education	Health & Healthcare	Crime	Transportation	Leisure	Arts & Culture	Quality of Life
325	20.3	Pine Bluff	AR	34	84	45	9	54	0	25	0	1	0
28	82.5	Pittsburgh	PA	21	54	29	91	50	78	93	86	97	87
243	47.2	Pittsfield	MA	75	25	4	69	87	91	72	70	3	42
279	39.1	Pocatello	ID	93	47	5	63	60	86	77	0	14	72
236	48.7	Portland	ME	66	13	0	95	77	97	41	60	64	88
12	88.2	Portland–Vancouver	OR-WA	1	20	77	85	72	36	84	82	89	93
287	37.8	Portsmouth–Rochester	NH-ME	63	28	0	70	19	92	0	70	28	81
173	56.5	Providence–Fall River–Warwick	RI-MA	91	9	32	54	19	66	66	86	78	89
146	60.3	Provo–Orem	UT	10	21	55	84	18	89	53	80	74	84
20	85.1	Pueblo	CO	30	58	66	36	98	32	45	68	53	58
49	77.4	Punta Gorda	FL	24	81	82	22	89	76	10	61	36	60
307	30.0	Racine	WI	86	31	16	18	53	46	63	66	4	18
13	87.4	Raleigh–Durham–Chapel Hill	NC	30	23	63	96	80	29	21	44	79	92
284	38.4	Rapid City	SD	48	93	7	70	66	35	76	3	2	42
122	63.0	Reading	PA	33	50	33	14	62	68	26	57	41	28
177	56.3	Redding	CA	14	21	96	27	12	80	49	74	33	2
9	89.3	Reno	NV	34	33	84	46	27	39	90	74	48	47
114	64.5	Richland–Kennewick–Pasco	WA	40	65	34	51	34	74	96	40	22	7
55	75.9	Richmond–Petersburg	VA	70	49	36	73	78	33	33	53	90	32
170	57.0	Riverside–San Bernardino	CA	28	14	96	15	5	63	0	94	69	60
11	88.6	Roanoke	VA	85	74	75	66	99	62	57	29	81	50
144	60.6	Rochester	MN	86	19	12	86	100	77	98	71	97	46
214	51.2	Rochester	NY	76	19	13	93	36	81	66	78	84	50
231	49.5	Rockford	IL	50	31	22	16	73	41	26	24	39	10
301	34.0	Rocky Mount	NC	3	70	63	10	52	15	40	15	62	18
85	68.6	Sacramento	CA	26	10	94	57	3	59	21	90	67	75
219	50.9	Saginaw–Bay City–Midland	MI	86	68	18	25	59	58	37	42	52	32
136	61.8	St. Cloud	MN	23	29	16	43	79	72	62	53	39	50
213	51.4	St. Joseph	MO	26	85	21	16	56	52	63	6	3	33
97	67.0	St. Louis	MO-IL	71	50	36	75	22	14	87	87	89	68
141	60.7	Salem	OR	18	41	66	36	60	30	18	61	45	76
153	59.3	Salinas	CA	4	2	100	10	0	73	36	73	35	50
84	68.6	Salt Lake City–Ogden	UT	27	26	30	61	40	53	92	90	83	88
277	39.8	San Angelo	TX	88	95	93	31	69	10	72	15	6	18
93	67.5	San Antonio	TX	52	70	88	43	7	0	50	62	50	90
74	71.5	San Diego	CA	15	3	96	79	9	72	70	96	86	95
107	65.3	San Francisco	CA	4	0	99	81	15	69	100	98	99	94
168	57.1	San Jose	CA	1	0	96	83	4	90	38	95	75	58
3	97.2	San Luis Obispo–Atascadero–Paso Robles	CA	31	5	98	68	39	93	34	83	35	99

continued

Table 2.5: U.S. Metropolitan Areas by Alphabetical Sequence with Rank *(continued)*

Rank	Score	Metropolitan Area	State	Economy & Jobs	Cost of Living	Climate	Education	Health & Healthcare	Crime	Transportation	Leisure	Arts & Culture	Quality of Life
4	95.2	Santa Barbara–Santa Maria–Lompoc	CA	20	1	98	54	43	94	76	85	34	99
124	62.8	Santa Cruz–Watsonville	CA	6	1	99	70	2	71	82	67	41	95
2	99.3	Santa Fe	NM	36	11	94	83	69	63	71	63	39	97
166	57.7	Santa Rosa	CA	7	2	95	59	3	90	64	92	45	95
43	78.1	Sarasota–Bradenton	FL	11	78	82	48	52	30	30	69	24	84
156	59.0	Savannah	GA	73	48	60	17	30	6	33	41	62	84
271	41.6	Scranton–Wilkes-Barre–Hazleton	PA	17	58	19	16	89	94	39	39	37	33
88	68.0	Seattle–Bellevue–Everett	WA	8	11	80	94	51	37	96	98	92	93
308	29.6	Sharon	PA	22	86	8	35	93	93	43	11	5	18
199	53.6	Sheboygan	WI	98	32	17	22	66	92	93	85	93	55
221	50.6	Sherman–Denison	TX	74	92	87	53	57	50	6	18	25	2
242	47.2	Shreveport–Bossier City	LA	61	70	72	28	49	18	37	17	43	10
270	41.8	Sioux City	IA-NE	18	44	28	15	71	56	77	8	71	18
100	66.3	Sioux Falls	SD	38	79	19	69	93	95	84	20	21	76
132	62.2	South Bend	IN	60	85	27	37	38	10	62	30	72	33
190	54.8	Spokane	WA	17	69	30	77	67	13	33	49	62	76
196	53.9	Springfield	IL	68	59	38	55	70	41	71	16	78	10
251	46.0	Springfield	MA	72	25	1	78	45	15	81	56	88	50
119	63.3	Springfield	MO	43	65	31	68	96	10	43	26	67	28
30	82.1	Stamford–Norwalk	CT	57	0	74	88	24	96	97	87	82	81
31	81.6	State College	PA	25	63	42	85	93	95	64	14	70	93
217	50.9	Steubenville–Weirton	OH-WV	76	90	29	18	41	24	11	56	31	2
330	0.0	Stockton–Lodi	CA	13	13	92	6	0	8	0	58	65	7
274	40.7	Sumter	SC	28	76	35	15	35	3	91	4	60	0
246	46.6	Syracuse	NY	95	26	6	93	46	70	73	64	87	6
59	75.3	Tacoma	WA	12	28	80	60	40	21	69	89	83	47
249	46.1	Tallahassee	FL	14	67	60	81	89	9	36	15	50	33
48	77.4	Tampa–St. Petersburg–Clearwater	FL	21	87	81	49	26	11	50	90	83	73
188	55.3	Terre Haute	IN	36	87	50	33	38	40	36	19	41	18
296	35.6	Texarkana	TX-AR	83	98	73	23	79	17	32	7	7	2
267	41.9	Toledo	OH	24	39	40	30	39	11	60	50	87	17
197	53.7	Topeka	KS	99	56	43	43	78	1	79	52	54	18
169	57.0	Trenton	NJ	86	17	58	73	33	33	80	87	92	28
70	72.4	Tucson	AZ	12	40	95	55	28	4	42	76	83	87
133	62.0	Tulsa	OK	15	46	78	52	28	19	52	37	74	60
111	64.7	Tuscaloosa	AL	63	76	22	36	92	16	30	28	29	81
138	61.1	Tyler	TX	94	90	72	47	55	35	13	21	10	42
289	37.4	Utica–Rome	NY	88	35	6	62	74	81	56	46	17	10
78	69.8	Vallejo–Fairfield–Napa	CA	22	6	95	41	2	70	39	96	38	68

Rank	Score	Metropolitan Area	State	Economy & Jobs	Cost of Living	Climate	Education	Health & Healthcare	Crime	Transportation	Leisure	Arts & Culture	Quality of Life
147	60.0	Ventura	CA	17	4	97	40	32	99	7	81	20	81
290	37.4	Victoria	TX	88	95	85	12	34	36	18	17	13	10
222	50.5	Vineland-Millville-Bridgeton	NJ	71	39	84	3	16	31	77	59	15	60
211	51.8	Visalia-Tulare-Porterville	CA	5	38	89	1	6	32	24	64	12	46
227	50.1	Waco	TX	75	91	87	44	24	12	50	26	19	10
26	82.6	Washington	DC-MD-VA-WV	85	5	43	99	32	67	74	97	99	97
312	27.2	Waterbury	CT	56	16	2	59	40	56	17	56	57	50
113	64.6	Waterloo–Cedar Falls	IA	53	45	30	29	91	57	90	13	85	33
208	52.1	Wausau	WI	83	37	17	35	90	82	70	8	49	50
69	72.7	West Palm Beach–Boca Raton	FL	32	43	64	38	61	16	31	88	54	78
305	32.0	Wheeling	WV-OH	11	73	30	6	80	81	18	18	79	18
35	80.6	Wichita	KS	94	57	57	44	43	28	65	32	80	28
294	36.0	Wichita Falls	TX	66	96	78	42	58	4	63	6	6	2
216	51.0	Williamsport	PA	47	72	13	31	91	93	56	22	6	33
172	56.5	Wilmington	NC	3	37	52	67	64	13	23	43	43	68
83	68.7	Wilmington-Newark	DE-MD	77	52	59	32	31	25	68	82	40	33
286	38.2	Worcester	MA-CT	39	19	3	74	44	88	16	79	58	68
265	42.3	Yakima	WA	4	69	34	4	37	43	58	49	46	18
200	53.2	Yolo	CA	9	9	93	63	4	83	55	60	31	31
260	43.7	York	PA	37	64	33	38	55	88	9	27	17	55
291	37.0	Youngstown-Warren	OH	46	54	8	14	48	39	24	63	65	7
315	25.2	Yuba City-Marysville	CA	0	22	94	9	1	71	3	57	5	0
204	52.7	Yuma	AZ	0	68	90	2	9	94	94	61	41	42

The Categories

The scoring and ranking tables presented in chapter 2 start the journey toward understanding what places are best and why. Charlottesville, Santa Fe, and Atlanta probably are better places to live for most people than Bismarck, Tallahassee, and Benton Harbor. But there's still a lot more to know.

While by itself the ranking helps to build a general impression of an area, comparing specific attributes provides a much richer understanding of a place and its offerings. What is the experience of those living there, and how much does it cost? What are the good and bad features of a place, and how do they trade off? What is the weather like, and how many below-zero nights are there? What about home prices? How do they compare with national averages and other cities? What are the best and worst places for home prices? Cost of living? Education? Healthcare? Commute times? Availability and quality of museums? This chapter helps answer those questions by enriching understanding of the data used in this book to determine the quality of a place and its ranking.

Specifically, this chapter explains the format and content for metropolitan area data tables in chapter 5. Many of the explanations also apply to tables in chapters 6 and 7—the introductions to those chapters address any differences that are not obvious. This chapter clarifies the definition, origin, and significance of individual data items while also pointing out important facts and trends observed in overall categories. The "highlights" summary for each category shows best and worst, most and least, highest and lowest, and other notable extracts. For example, there are listings of cities with the most and fewest cloudy days, highest and lowest cost of living, and highest and lowest job growth.

Reading the Data

Cities Ranked & Rated presents data in different ways depending on what is being explained or compared. An explanation and clarification of terms up front will help avoid confusion.

Means, Medians & Averages

Most figures in the metropolitan area data tables are presented as a statistic for the area, followed by, to its right, a figure representing a U.S. average where such an average is meaningful. Figures are presented either as absolute numbers, percentages, or dollars—whichever makes the most sense for the item and category.

The terms *mean, median,* and *average* occur frequently both in tables and in the discussion that follows in this chapter. Essentially *mean* and *average* are the same thing and are used interchangeably. A mean (or average) is the *arithmetic* average of all data in a set, that is, all figures are added and divided by the total number of figures. An

average population growth of all U.S. metropolitan areas of 1.6% doesn't necessarily mean that half of all metropolitan areas grow more and half grow less. A limited number of cities growing at a much higher rate may raise the average.

A *median,* on the other hand, is a common statistical representation of data designed to balance the effects of unusual pockets of data far removed from an average. A median population growth of all U.S. metropolitan areas of 1.6% would mean that exactly half of the metropolitan areas were higher and half were lower. Such data as home prices is commonly represented as a median; otherwise, a few expensive homes would distort the single representative figure.

Scores, Ratings & Indexes

In presenting metropolitan area data, *Cities Ranked & Rated* makes consistent use of three different presentation formats.

Understanding the nature and differences among the formats will enrich the reader's understanding of the data.

- A *score* is an accumulation of points converted to a 0–100 scale, with 0 being the lowest or worst and 100 being the highest or best. Points are usually accumulated as a sum of several variables. For instance, the air-quality score is compiled from individual measures of particulates, volatile organic compounds, ozone, and other combustion byproducts. The raw score is converted to a 0–100 scale to facilitate comparison among metro areas by indicating where an individual area stacks up against the highest and lowest levels observed for the attribute. An area with an air-quality score of 100 is the best among the 331 metro areas. An area with a 90 is good and, in rough figures, 90% as good as the best area. An area with a score of 20 has relatively dirty air. Air quality, diversity, and pollen/allergy attributes are presented as scores, as are the composite figures for the nine major ranking categories—Economy & Jobs, Cost of Living, Climate, Education, Health & Healthcare, Crime, Transportation, Leisure, and Arts & Culture. An area with a 100 for Arts & Culture is best, a 0 is worst, and so forth. *Note:* SAT and ACT scores, reported in the Education category, represent true test scores, not scores based on a 0–100 scale as used elsewhere in this book.

- A *rating* is a qualitative assessment of an attribute presented on a 1–10 scale, with 1 being the lowest or worst and 10 being the highest or best. In the Leisure and Arts & Culture categories, ratings are used to represent a blend of quantitative and subjective assessments. Ratings incorporate "hard" numbers such as the number, size, and cost of available facilities with "soft" assessments of quality, accessibility, and proximity. Ratings are used to evaluate such attributes as restaurants, professional sports, performing arts, and museums.

- An *index* compares a quantifiable attribute measured against a national average or norm. Using 100 to represent the average or norm, an individual index is less than 100 for area attributes less than the average or norm and greater than 100 for attributes greater than the norm. The actual figure indicates the percentage difference: 140 is 40% higher than the average; 83 is 17% lower than the average. Cost of living figures are among those presented as an index. Indexes are useful in comparing areas with each other. Suppose the Cost of Living Index for Area A is 120 and for Area B is 80. The comparative quotient of 120 over 80 or 1.50 suggests that A is actually 50% more expensive than B. Using real numbers, Chicago has a COL Index of 119.8, meaning it is 19.8% more expensive than the national average. Casper, Wyoming, has an index of 86.7, making it 13.3% cheaper than the national average. Thus, in round numbers Chicago is 38% more expensive than Casper.

To summarize:

- *Scores* are 0–100 and based mainly on quantitative data.

- *Ratings* are 1–10 and are a mix of quantitative and subjective influences.

- *Indexes* are quantitative comparisons with an average or norm represented by 100.

Use of Data for Ranking & Scoring

Not all data presented in this book is used to determine metropolitan area scores and ranks. Some information is shown only to indicate more fully the character of a place. The Population category, for example, doesn't have a score and isn't factored into the overall rank. Because high and low population density can indicate different things, and may be a matter of personal preference rather than a universally accepted element of area quality, this data point is information only. Likewise, personal incomes and population numbers above and below certain income levels are interesting to know, but *Cities Ranked & Rated* doesn't place a comparative value judgment on a place strictly because of these factors.

Only data that is clearly driven by the nature and characteristic of an area and that can be easily qualified as *good* or *bad* is used in the rankings. Employment data, for example, are used for scoring and ranking in the Economy & Jobs category. Employment is one of the purest indicators of a strong economy and whether a job, a better job, or income growth can result for a resident. Even the economic health of those *not* in the job market, such as self-employed and retired people, is ultimately affected by an area's job and job-growth picture. In addition, employment and job growth not only make an area better, they often occur because an area is better. Therefore, this data point is a two-fold indicator of an area's prospects.

Population

The Population category includes the total population of an area along with population density and growth. Additional data shows ethnic composition and the marital and family status of residents.

Overall Population Trends

The most notable trend is the continuing migration of the U.S population toward the South and West, most particularly the South. Table 3.1 shows the total *net* migration (those moving in *less* those moving out) for the 11-year period, 1990–2001.

Table 3.1: Net Gain or Loss in Population by Region

1990-2001			
Northeast	**Midwest**	**South**	**West**
-1,920,000	-181,000	2,029,000	71,000

Source: U.S. Census Bureau

Better climate and the persistently low costs of living and doing business have drawn people and jobs to the South and, aside from the larger California cities, to the West. No factor has greater influence on these population shifts than the continued expansion of air-conditioning and climate-control technology. Without it, places like Phoenix, Houston, Atlanta, Las Vegas, and Sacramento would be largely unbearable in summer, particularly for those in commerce and industry.

Additionally, the population concentration in coastal areas has grown. According to the 2000 U.S. Census, over 148 million people, or 53% of the population, live along the oceans or Gulf of Mexico. Projections call for a 50% growth in coastal populations over the next 12 years. Aside from the obvious recreational opportunities, people are lured by the more moderate climates and—in most cases—physical beauty. Furthermore, new immigrants from other nations, particularly from Asia, tend to settle along the coasts. But persistent increases in cost of living, housing costs, and crime in some of these places may dampen the trend.

Population Attributes

Many *Cities Ranked & Rated* population attributes are based on the 2000 U.S. Census published in 2001. Total population figures have been updated through 2002 by the U.S. Census Annual Population Survey. For estimates and projections of census data as it becomes available, see www.bestplaces.net/CRAR.

Table 3.2 shows the Population table exactly as presented in chapter 5 for Charlottesville, Virginia.

- *Population* is the 2002 U.S. Census estimated Metropolitan Statistical Area (MSA) population, including the urban core and surrounding county or counties. In New England, NECMA (now called NECTA) town areas are included. See chapter 1 for an explanation of these designations.

- *Population density* is the number of people *per square mile* in an area. The average density for a U.S. metropolitan area is 1,254.3 people. This number ranges from under 100 in places with large county areas like Flagstaff, Arizona, and in smaller towns like Huntsville, Alabama, and Pine Bluff, Arkansas, to over 20,000 per square mile in New York City. The size of the county surrounding the core urban area influences reported density. For more on density and crowding, see the "Urban Sprawl" sidebar at the end of this section.

- *Population growth* represents the area's population increase or decrease in the 1990–2002 period as a percentage. The population of Las Vegas, Nevada, has more than doubled, while that of Steubenville-Weirton, Ohio–West Virginia, has declined 9% during the period. The average population growth per metro area is 16.1%.

- *Median age* indicates the median years of age for the area's population. For Charlottesville, the median is 34.7 years, meaning that half the population is younger than 34.7 and half is older. The U.S. median age of 35.5 is evidence that the population of Charlottesville is, on average, slightly younger than the country as a whole.

Table 3.2: Sample Population Data from Charlottesville, Virginia

DEMOGRAPHICS	AREA	U.S. AVG	ETHNIC COMPOSITION	AREA	U.S. AVG	RESIDENT PROFILE	AREA	U.S. AVG
Population	164,197		White	78.2%	75.1%	Single	46.0%	43.6%
Population density per sq. mile	139.5	447.3	Black	19.9%	12.3%	Married	54.0%	56.4%
Population growth	25.2%	16.1%	Asian	1.7%	3.6%	Divorced	6.8%	8.4%
Median age	34.7	35.5	American Indian	.1%	.9%	Separated	3.4%	3.0%
Average family size	2.7	2.7	Hispanic	1.4%	12.5%	Married with children	28.4%	28.7%
			Diversity measure	34.4%	35.2%	Single with children	9.4%	10.1%

POPULATION

URBAN SPRAWL

Urban sprawl—the expansion of a city and its suburbs into rural land at the periphery of the urban area—is a major factor in determining an area's long-term quality of life. Many places have experienced the effects of sprawl. Distances expand from residential areas to the central city and *between* residential areas. Commutes are longer and transportation infrastructure is generally stressed. Air pollution increases. Overall appearance takes on a "grinding sameness" with fast-food joints and strip malls along every roadway. Some states, like New Jersey, Oregon, and Washington, have taken a proactive stance in promoting anti-sprawl measures. Others unwittingly promote sprawl by encouraging retail construction that increases their local tax intake. It is no wonder that states with large local sales tax components, like Colorado, California, Texas, Nevada, Illinois, and Arizona, have problems with urban sprawl. Sprawl is further aggravated in states with liberal annexation policies in which cities and towns are able to annex nearby unincorporated land to build the tax base. The more farsighted states like Virginia and New Jersey have curtailed such practices, albeit after difficult court battles in some cases.

But not all sprawl is bad. Some like the "newness" and convenience of the expanding areas and the avoidance of urban cores with narrow streets designed for 19th-century transportation. Some of the better-planned areas include pedestrian-friendly zones with good public transportation and natural, "green" spaces. Individual states are coming up with their own solutions. New Jersey actively fights sprawl and promotes "Brownfield" programs, in which developers are encouraged—*incentivized*—to build in "infill" areas currently in disuse. California is revisiting the state-local split inherent in the sales tax code, although this may prove to be more directed toward solving fiscal stress than urban sprawl.

Although no-growth proponents and environmentalists can get carried away with their pronouncements on sprawl and development (the population and economy does grow, after all, and some repurposing of land use is necessary and justified), some of their efforts are worth noting. Table 3.3 shows the Sierra Club's 1998 report on the country's most "sprawl-threatened" cities.

The numbers in the chapter 5 tables may indicate sprawl in an MSA. The combination of a relatively modest *Population,* low *Population density,* and a high *Average commute time* (see "Transportation" below) suggest the likelihood of sprawl. If this is the case and more information is needed, a visit to the place or a talk with local suburban residents might be the most revealing sources of information.

Table 3.3: Most Sprawl-Threatened Cities			
Population Over 1 Million	**Population 500K-1 Million**	**Population 200K-500K**	**"Dishonorable Mentions"**
Atlanta, GA	Orlando, FL	McAllen, TX	Los Angeles, CA
St. Louis, MO	Austin, TX	Raleigh, NC	San Diego, CA
Washington, D.C.	Las Vegas, NV	Pensacola, FL	Phoenix, AZ
Cincinnati, OH	West Palm Beach, FL	Daytona Beach, FL	
Kansas City, MO	Akron, OH	Little Rock, AR	
Denver, CO			
Seattle, WA			
Minneapolis–St. Paul, MN			
Fort Lauderdale, FL			
Chicago, IL			
Source: Sierra Club, 1998 Sprawl Report			

- *Average family size* is the average number of persons in a household for a household with more than one member.

- *White, Black, Asian, American Indian, and Hispanic* shows the percentage of these ethnic groups in an area. These figures can add up to more than 100% because groups overlap. The most common overlap occurs between white (a large and inclusive *race*) and Hispanic (an ethnic group with a common cultural or national origin).

- *Diversity measure* is a calculation furnished by Sperling's BestPlaces (www.bestplaces.net). It represents the comparative probability that the next person met "on the street" is of a different ethnic origin than one's own. This is the best measure of overall diversity as "person A" who encounters someone else on the street represents *all* races and ethnic groups, not just the white majority group. A high score indicates a high probability of meeting someone unlike oneself.

Results range from a low of 5.3% in Altoona, Pennsylvania, to a high of 76.2% in Honolulu, Hawaii. The average percentage across U.S. metro areas is 35.2%.

- *Single, Married, Divorced,* and *Separated* show the percentage of individuals in an area with these profiles.

- *Married with children* or *Single with children* show the percentage of families of either marital status with one or more children. A high presence of families with children *may* indicate that an area is well suited for children. In this case, schools may be better, more activities may exist for children, and crime may be lower. The married-with-children statistic is the lowest in Florida where the presence of retirees drives the figure below 20% in most cities; eight of the lowest nine cities are in that state. Conversely, Utah cities and Texas border towns score above 40%. The U.S. average is 28.7%.

Population Highlights, Tables 3.4–3.8

Table 3.4: Largest & Smallest Metropolitan Areas

By Population

Largest MSAs				Smallest MSAs		
Los Angeles–Long Beach	CA	9,806,577	Enid	OK		57,246
New York	NY	9,411,687	Casper	WY		67,336
Chicago	IL	8,449,180	Pocatello	ID		75,804
Washington	DC-MD-VA-WV	5,162,029	Corvallis	OR		78,618
Philadelphia	PA-NJ	5,149,098	Great Falls	MT		79,389
Detroit	MI	4,464,531	Cheyenne	WY		82,894
Houston	TX	4,420,081	Pine Bluff	AR		83,374
Atlanta	GA	4,386,330	Pittsfield	MA		83,584
Dallas	TX	3,743,254	Jonesboro	AR		84,074
Riverside–San Bernardino	CA	3,515,184	Victoria	TX		84,932
Phoenix-Mesa	AZ	3,500,151	Dubuque	IA		89,387
Boston	MA-NH	3,439,372	Elmira	NY		90,614
Minneapolis–St. Paul	MN-WI	3,054,637	Rapid City	SD		90,856
Orange County	CA	2,938,507	Lewiston-Auburn	ME		91,220
San Diego	CA	2,906,660	Owensboro	KY		91,694
Nassau-Suffolk	NY	2,803,547	Bangor	ME		91,773
St. Louis	MO-IL	2,633,925	Grand Forks	ND-MD		96,035
Baltimore	MD	2,601,990	Bismarck	ND		96,349
Tampa–St. Petersburg–Clearwater	FL	2,490,295	Missoula	MT		98,102
Seattle-Bellevue-Everett	WA	2,468,601	Cumberland	MD-WV		101,290
Oakland	CA	2,464,668	Kokomo	IN		101,372
Pittsburgh	PA	2,346,525	St. Joseph	MO		102,064
Miami	FL	2,332,599	Lawrence	KS		102,316
Cleveland-Lorain-Elyria	OH	2,250,347	San Angelo	TX		103,018
Denver	CO	2,187,464	Gadsden	AL		103,105
Newark	NJ	2,064,011	Kankakee	IL		104,657
Portland-Vancouver	OR-WA	2,006,308	Sumter	SC		105,198
Kansas City	MO-KS	1,828,247	Jackson	TN		109,290
Fort Worth–Arlington	TX	1,802,465	Danville	VA		109,341
Orlando	FL	1,752,192	Anniston	AL		111,616

Source: U.S. Census Bureau, 2002 Population Survey

Table 3.5: Fastest Growing Metropolitan Areas

MSA		By Population			
		2002 Population	1990 Population	Change	Percentage Growth
Las Vegas	NZ-AZ	1,722,256	1,563,282	852,737	102.0%
Naples	FL	276,691	251,377	152,099	81.9%
McAllen-Edinburg-Mission	TX	614,474	569,463	383,545	60.2%
Austin–San Marcos	TX	1,349,291	1,249,763	846,227	59.4%
Fayetteville-Springdale-Rogers	AR	332,011	311,121	210,908	57.4%
Boise	ID	464,670	432,345	295,851	57.1%
Yuma	AZ	167,407	160,026	106,895	56.6%
Phoenix-Mesa	AZ	3,500,151	3,251,876	2,238,480	56.4%
Laredo	TX	207,611	193,117	133,239	55.8%
Greeley	CO	205,014	180,936	131,821	55.5%
Atlanta	GA	4,386,330	4,112,198	2,959,950	48.2%
Raleigh–Durham–Chapel Hill	NC	1,267,676	1,187,941	855,545	48.2%
Provo-Orem	UT	387,817	368,536	263,590	47.1%
Orlando	FL	1,752,192	1,644,561	1,224,852	43.1%
Myrtle Beach	SC	206,039	196,629	144,053	43.0%
Wilmington	NC	244,279	233,450	171,269	42.6%
Reno	NV	362,325	339,486	254,667	42.3%
Fort Collins–Loveland	CO	264,605	251,494	186,136	42.2%
Fort Myers–Cape Coral	FL	475,639	440,888	335,113	41.9%
Ocala	FL	272,553	258,916	194,833	39.9%
Dallas	TX	3,743,254	3,519,176	2,676,248	39.9%
West Palm Beach–Boca Raton	FL	1,190,390	1,131,184	863,518	37.9%
Colorado Springs	CO	543,818	516,929	397,014	37.0%
Bellingham	WA	174,362	166,814	127,780	36.5%
Charlotte–Gastonia–Rock Hill	NC-SC	1,584,898	1,499,293	1,162,093	36.4%
Fort Lauderdale	FL	1,709,118	1,623,018	1,255,488	36.1%
Brownsville–Harlingen–San Benito	TX	353,561	335,227	260,120	35.9%
Riverside–San Bernardino	CA	3,515,184	3,254,821	2,588,793	35.8%
Auburn-Opelika	AL	118,123	115,092	87,146	35.5%
Richland-Kennewick-Pasco	WA	203,111	191,822	150,033	35.4%

Source: U.S. Census Bureau, 2002 Population Survey

Table 3.6: Declining & Slowest Growing Metropolitan Areas

MSA		By Population			
		2002 Population	1990 Population	Change	Percentage Growth
Steubenville-Weirton	OH-WV	129,663	132,008	142,523	-9.0%
Grand Forks	ND-MN	96,035	97,478	103,181	-6.9%
Pittsfield	MA	83,584	84,699	88,695	-5.8%
Utica-Rome	NY	298,707	299,896	316,633	-5.7%
Wheeling	WV-OH	150,472	153,172	159,301	-5.5%
Elmira	NY	90,614	91,070	95,195	-4.8%
Johnstown	PA	229,908	232,621	241,247	-4.7%
Binghamton	NY	252,096	252,320	264,497	-4.7%
Decatur	IL	112,013	114,706	117,206	-4.4%
Anniston	AL	111,616	112,249	116,034	-3.8%
Alexandria	LA	126,881	126,337	131,556	-3.6%
Scranton–Wilkes-Barre–Hazleton	PA	617,289	624,776	638,466	-3.3%
Lewiston-Auburn	ME	91,220	90,830	93,679	-2.6%
Jamestown	NY	138,332	139,750	141,895	-2.5%
Pine Bluff	AR	83,374	84,278	85,487	-2.5%
Buffalo–Niagara Falls	NY	1,163,148	1,170,111	1,189,288	-2.2%
Altoona	PA	127,840	129,144	130,542	-2.1%
Youngstown-Warren	OH	588,632	594,746	600,895	-2.0%
Pittsburgh	PA	2,346,525	2,358,695	2,394,811	-2.0%
Sharon	PA	119,514	120,293	121,003	-1.2%
Muncie	IN	118,197	118,769	119,659	-1.2%
Charleston	WV	248,020	251,662	250,454	-1.0%
Syracuse	NY	735,059	732,117	742,177	-1.0%
Jacksonville	NC	149,003	150,355	149,838	-0.6%
Dayton-Springfield	OH	947,446	950,558	951,270	-0.4%
Cumberland	MD-WV	101,290	102,008	101,643	-0.3%
Bangor	ME	91,773	90,864	91,629	0.2%
Lima	OH	154,584	155,084	154,340	0.2%
Huntington-Ashland	WV-KY-OH	313,239	315,538	312,529	0.2%
Terre Haute	IN	147,934	149,192	147,585	0.2%

Source: U.S. Census Bureau, 2002 Population Survey

Table 3.7: Population Density

Per Square Mile

Most Crowded MSAs			Least Crowded MSAs		
New York	NY	24,750.7	Flagstaff	AZ-UT	5.4
Jersey City	NJ	16,235.8	Bismarck	ND	28.5
Los Angeles–Long Beach	CA	8,392.8	Enid	OK	53.3
San Francisco	CA	8,253.0	Pine Bluff	AR	59.6
Miami	FL	6,221.7	Decatur	IL	75.9
Bergen-Passaic	NJ	6,009.7	Jackson	TN	76.1
Orange County	CA	5,700.5	Jonesboro	AR	80.3
Boston	MA-NH-ME	4,871.8	Rapid City	SD	100.0
San Jose	CA	4,834.1	Danville	VA	106.3
Chicago	IL	4,764.3	Sioux Falls	SD	114.8
Oakland	CA	4,669.9	Savannah	GA	115.2
Trenton	NJ	4,507.4	Dothan	AL	115.5
Fort Lauderdale	FL	4,209.1	Texarkana	TX-AR	128.4
Newark	NJ	3,946.2	Alexandria	LA	131.3
Bridgeport	CT	3,920.5	Columbia	MO	132.3
Philadelphia	PA-NJ	3,894.2	Jamestown	NY	138.2
Nassau-Suffolk	NY	3,516.9	Pittsfield	MA	139.6
San Diego	CA	3,455.2	Joplin	MO	139.9
Honolulu	HI	3,439.8	Redding	CA	145.1
Seattle-Bellevue-Everett	TX	3,137.4	Grand Forks	ND-MN	151.2
Stamford-Norwalk	CT	3,103.9	Cumberland	MD-WV	154.4
Tallahassee	FL	3,039.4	Houma	LA	155.8
Denver	CO	3,039.3	Auburn-Opelika	AL	162.8
Lowell	MA-NH	2,818.0	Kokomo	IN	167.0
El Paso	TX	2,767.4	Clarksville-Hopkinsville	TN-KY	167.3
Milwaukee-Waukesha	WI	2,764.6	Glens Falls	NY	169.0
Detroit	MI	2,694.7	Eau Claire	WI	169.8
Washington	DC-MD-VA-WV	2,689.6	Fayetteville-Springdale-Rogers	AR	171.5
Providence–Fall River–Warwick	RI-MA	2,682.8	Lynchburg	VA	172.5
Bloomington	IN	2,656.4	Gadsden	AL	175.1

Source: U.S. Census Bureau, 2002 Population Survey

Table 3.8: Diversity Measure

Probability Next Person Met of Different Ethnic Origin

Most Diverse MSAs			Least Diverse MSAs		
Honolulu	HI	72.6%	Altoona	PA	5.3%
New York	NY	72.0%	Parkersburg-Marietta	WV-OH	6.0%
Jersey City	NJ	70.9%	Bangor	ME	6.7%
Los Angeles–Long Beach	CA	70.8%	Dubuque	IA	6.8%
Miami	FL	68.2%	Lewiston-Auburn	ME	6.9%
Oakland	CA	66.9%	Portsmouth-Rochester	NH-ME	7.1%
San Jose	CA	66.9%	Sheboygan	WI	7.6%
Stockton-Lodi	CA	65.5%	Portland	ME	7.7%
Houston	TX	65.1%	Johnstown	PA	8.0%
Fresno	CA	64.8%	Huntington-Ashland	WV-KY-OH	8.3%
Merced	CA	63.4%	Johnson City–Kingsport–Bristol	TN-VA	8.4%
Salinas	CA	63.4%	Eau Claire	WI	8.5%
San Francisco	CA	63.2%	Wheeling	WV-OH	9.0%
Riverside–San Bernardino	CA	62.6%	Glens Falls	NY	9.1%
Vallejo-Fairfield-Napa	CA	62.4%	Salem	OR	9.1%
Orange County	CA	61.1%	Burlington	VT	9.7%
Bakersfield	CA	60.6%	Bismarck	ND	9.9%
Albuquerque	NM	60.2%	Duluth-Superior	MN-WI	10.6%
San Antonio	TX	59.9%	Barnstable-Yarmouth	MA	10.7%
San Diego	CA	59.7%	Manchester	NH	10.9%
Fayetteville	NC	59.3%	La Crosse	WI-MN	10.9%
Washington	DC-MD-VA-WV	58.8%	Steubenville-Weirton	OH-WV	11.1%
Visalia-Tulare-Porterville	CA	58.5%	Pittsfield	MA	11.4%
Dallas	TX	58.3%	Fargo-Moorhead	ND-MN	11.6%
Killeen-Temple	TX	58.2%	Appleton-Oshkosh-Neenah	WI	12.1%
Vineland-Millville-Bridgeton	NJ	57.9%	Williamsport	PA	12.2%
Chicago	IL	57.2%	St. Joseph	MO	12.4%
Yolo	CA	56.8%	Wausau	WI	12.5%
Fort Lauderdale	FL	56.7%	Cumberland	MD-WV	12.5%
Newark	NJ	56.6%	Owensboro	KY	12.8%

Source: Sperling's BestPlaces

Ethnic Diversity

Legend:
- ● Highest 20%
- ● (light gray)
- ○ Middle 20%
- ● (gray)
- ● Lowest 20%

Ethnic Diversity of Principal MSAs Grouped by Quintiles

Economy & Jobs

The Economy & Jobs category includes specific information on personal and household income, employment, and the largest industries in an area.

Overall Employment Trends

The two notable long-term trends are (1) a transition from manufacturing to service jobs and (2) sustained long-term growth in health and healthcare professions. Other "trends" are more fleeting. In the 2001–2003 recession, an estimated 3 million jobs were lost—2 million of those in manufacturing. While the service sector has picked up some of these workers, service sector job gains have leveled off. Among specific professions, only healthcare has really prospered. The boom in high-tech jobs has waned, while a construction boom driven in large part by low interest rates is probably not sustainable. The employment data presented in this section depicts all economic sectors and professions, white and blue collar.

Economy & Jobs Attributes

The Economy & Jobs category is divided into *Income, Employment,* and *Largest Employing Industry.* Income and employment data come from the U.S. Department of Labor Bureau of Labor Statistics, the U.S. Census Bureau including the U.S. Economic Census, and Claritas, Inc., a large private supplier of market and demographic data. For updated employment data, cost-of-living statistics, sales-tax rates, and income-tax tables, see www.bestplaces.net/CRAR.

Table 3.9 shows the Economy & Jobs table for Santa Fe, New Mexico.

Income

Of the following data points, only *Household income growth* is included in scoring and ranking.

- *Per capita income* is the average annual dollar income for every man, woman, and child in the U.S. population in 2000. Metropolitan area and national averages are shown.

- *Household income* is the average annual 2003 dollar income per U.S. household, defined as a home with more than one member. Household income indicates the true economic status of an average family and standard of living in general. Areas with a relatively large difference between per capita and household income probably have more two-earner households. These figures range from a low of $25,000–$28,000 annually in Texas border towns to over $93,000 in San Jose, California, with a U.S. average of $46,060.

- *Household income < $25K* and *Household income > $75K.* These 2003 figures expressed as percentages of the total population indicate income distribution. Areas with a high percentage below $25K are disadvantaged; likewise, areas with a high percentage above $75K indicate wealth and a higher standard of living. Note that these figures are not absolute indicators of standard of living because cost of living varies widely between areas. (The *Financial Progress Index,* see "Cost of Living" below, does reflect income against cost of living.) The numbers for college towns, where underemployed students mix with academics and administrators with larger incomes, may be misleading.

- *Household income growth* is the percentage change in household incomes over the 1990–2003 period. Figures above national averages tell of a strong economy and an improving job mix, while figures below national averages may indicate economic challenges ahead for the average family. While the U.S. average is just over 57% for the 13-year period, the range is wide, from 22.6% in Merced, California, to just over 114% in Austin–San Marcos, Texas.

Table 3.9: Sample Economy & Jobs Data from Santa Fe, New Mexico

INCOME	AREA	U.S. AVG	EMPLOYMENT	AREA	U.S. AVG	LARGEST EMPLOYING INDUSTRY
Per capita income	$30,013	$23,420	Unemployment rate	3.4%	6.1%	Healthcare and Social Assistance
Household income	$52,824	$46,060	Recent job growth	3.2%	.9%	
Household income < $25K	19.9%	26.4%	Projected future job growth	30.6%	15.1%	
Household income > $75K	32.0%	24.5%	White collar	67.4%	54.5%	
Household income growth	63.4%	57.3%	Blue collar	32.6%	45.5%	

ECONOMY & JOBS
SCORE: 36/RANK: 210

THE U.S. ECONOMIC CENSUS

The U.S. Economic Census tabulates large amounts of information about business and industry, and, conveniently, organizes and presents it by metropolitan area. To learn more, go to www.census.gov/epcd/www/econ97.html. The summary page at www.census.gov/epcd/ec97/us/US000.HTM allows selection of an individual metropolitan area. Users can request a complete breakdown of industries in each area by class and subclass. The most recent data, from a 2002 survey, should be available in mid-2004.

Employment

These attributes represent employment level and mix. Employment level includes unemployment rates and recent and future job growth. Employment mix presents the percentage of those in "white-" and "blue-collar" professions, defined below. Unemployment rate and recent and future job growth figure stongly in scoring.

- *Unemployment rate* is the standard figure, provided by the Bureau of Labor Statistics, that is frequently reported in the media. Representing the percentage of active job seekers without a job, the figure excludes all of those not seeking employment, whether they have gone back to school or given up their search. Because of this, the number may understate the true amount of economic dislocation in an area. It may also be affected by surges of new job seekers, such as college students looking for work at the beginning of summer. Regardless, it is a relevant indicator of the economy in a local area, particularly when examined over time. The figures are from August 2003 when the U.S. average unemployment rate was 6.1%.

- *Recent job growth* shows the percentage growth in total jobs from August 2002 through August 2003. The figure reveals the recent economic health of an area.

- *Projected future job growth*, a projection through 2010 calculated by Sperling's BestPlaces, is based on recent job growth and other economic indicators present in an area. Like any growth projection, it is subject to error depending on the economy as a whole and dynamics within a particular area. The calculation is especially revealing when (1) compared to national averages and (2) compared between metropolitan areas. While the U.S. average is 15.1%, the figure ranges from a low of 2.6% in Elmira, New York, to a sizzling 42% in Las Vegas, Nevada.

- *White collar* represents the percentage of the employment base considered executive, managerial, technical, sales, clerical, administrative, or of such professional specialties as law, medicine, or education. These jobs generally require a college education or specific, academically oriented skills. A comparatively high percentage of white-collar workers indicates higher paying jobs, greater affluence, and a higher educational base for the population, although the inclusion of hourly retail workers in this category slightly weakens that conclusion.

- *Blue collar* represents the percentage in the trades and labor sector, including such professions as production operators, repair technicians, transportation workers, construction trades and laborers, and agricultural workers, to name a few. These professions are less likely to require 4-year college education and are more likely to receive lower compensation than those in white-collar jobs.

Largest Employing Industry

The largest elements of a local economy help determine the quality of a place. A mining town will have a far different flavor than a banking and insurance center. An economy dominated by one or two companies will have different dynamics from one characterized by a number of small businesses or large government entities. The environmental quality and attractiveness of a setting may be tied to the dominating industries. The data presented in chapter 5 doesn't give a complete picture, but it does provide a strong sense of what readers can expect. Data is based on NAICS (North American Industry Classification System) codes from the U.S. Economic Census and represents the largest industry in the area by number of people employed.

Table 3.10: Household Income

Combined Annual Gross Household Incomes

MSAs with Highest Household Incomes			MSAs with Lowest Household Incomes		
San Jose	CA	$93,503	McAllen-Edinburg-Mission	TX	$25,726
Stamford-Norwalk	CT	$86,410	Brownsville–Harlingen–San Benito	TX	$27,679
Danbury	CT	$81,775	Laredo	TX	$29,892
Middlesex-Somerset-Hunterdon	NJ	$79,975	Huntington-Ashland	WV-KY-OH	$29,981
Bridgeport	CT	$79,096	Johnstown	PA	$30,250
Nassau-Suffolk	NY	$78,879	Auburn-Opelika	AL	$30,615
San Francisco	CA	$76,164	Las Cruces	NM	$30,819
Lowell	MA-NH	$75,771	Cumberland	MD-WV	$31,176
Washington	DC-MD-VA-WV	$72,781	Danville	VA	$31,305
Oakland	CA	$71,689	Merced	CA	$31,368
Anchorage	AK	$70,833	Gadsden	AL	$31,460
Bergen-Passaic	NJ	$69,764	Ocala	FL	$31,547
Seattle-Bellevue-Everett	WA	$69,730	Steubenville-Weirton	OH-WV	$31,625
Trenton	NJ	$69,514	Yuma	AZ	$31,911
Santa Cruz–Watsonville	CA	$69,148	El Paso	TX	$31,932
Newark	NJ	$68,961	Anniston	AL	$32,190
Orange County	CA	$68,923	Rocky Mount	NC	$32,401
New Haven–Meriden	CT	$68,472	Hattiesburg	MS	$32,581
Ventura	CA	$67,322	Punta Gorda	FL	$32,633
Boulder-Longmont	CO	$66,602	Lafayette	LA	$32,755
Minneapolis–St. Paul	MN-WI	$65,330	Florence	AL	$32,788
Lawrence	MA-NH	$64,927	Johnson City–Kingsport–Bristol	TN-VA	$32,897
Boston	MA-NH-ME	$63,784	Wheeling	WV-OH	$32,899
Nashua	NH	$63,653	Alexandria	LA	$33,022
Vallejo-Fairfield-Napa	CA	$63,508	Jamestown	NY	$33,311
Chicago	IL	$63,096	Pine Bluff	AR	$33,714
Denver	CO	$62,986	Redding	CA	$33,940
Ann Arbor	MI	$62,119	Chico-Paradise	CA	$34,282
Dutchess County	NY	$62,088	Enid	OK	$34,287
Rochester	MN	$62,051	Greenville	NC	$34,395

Source: Claritas, Inc., 2003

Table 3.11: Household Income Growth

1990-2003

MSAs with Highest Growth			MSAs with Lowest Growth		
Austin–San Marcos	TX	114.2%	Merced	CA	22.6%
Provo-Orem	UT	94.1%	Punta Gorda	FL	26.7%
Greeley	CO	93.4%	Bakersfield	CA	27.3%
Fort Collins–Loveland	CO	92.8%	Steubenville-Weirton	OH-WV	30.7%
Houma	LA	91.5%	Bangor	ME	31.5%
Boulder-Longmont	CO	88.9%	Redding	CA	32.0%
Hattiesburg	MS	88.8%	Binghamton	NY	32.3%
Colorado Springs	CO	88.0%	Rocky Mount	NC	34.1%
San Diego	CA	87.9%	Fresno	CA	34.3%
Santa Barbara–Santa Maria–Lompoc	CA	86.3%	Glens Falls	NY	34.3%
Denver	CO	85.9%	Fort Pierce–Port St. Lucie	FL	34.4%
Springfield	MA	83.2%	Pittsfield	MA	34.4%
Biloxi-Gulfport-Pascagoula	MS	80.7%	Anniston	AL	34.5%
Lafayette	LA	79.6%	Melbourne–Titusville–Palm Bay	FL	34.5%
Laredo	TX	79.0%	Yuma	AZ	34.7%
Salem	OR	78.4%	Danville	VA	35.5%
Santa Cruz–Watsonville	CA	78.3%	Mansfield	OH	35.6%
Killeen-Temple	TX	78.2%	Vineland-Millville-Bridgeton	NJ	35.6%
Jackson	MS	77.8%	Jamestown	NY	37.4%
Corvallis	OR	77.3%	Riverside–San Bernardino	CA	37.5%
Kenosha	WI	76.8%	Lewiston-Auburn	ME	37.8%
Boise City	ID	76.3%	Newburgh	NY-PA	38.7%
Spokane	WA	76.3%	Springfield	MA	39.0%
Clarksville-Hopkinsville	TN-KY	76.2%	Johnstown	PA	40.3%
Fayetteville-Springdale-Rogers	AR	76.2%	Williamsport	PA	40.3%
Pueblo	CO	75.8%	Ocala	FL	40.6%
Raleigh–Durham–Chapel Hill	NC	75.3%	Dover	DE	40.8%
Duluth-Superior	MN-WI	75.2%	Atlantic City–Cape May	NJ	40.8%
San Angelo	TX	74.9%	Las Cruces	NM	40.9%
Eau Claire	WI	74.9%	El Paso	TX	40.9%

Source: Claritas, Inc.

Table 3.12: Unemployment Rate

Percent of Eligible Workforce

MSAs with Highest Unemployment			MSAs with Lowest Unemployment		
Yuma	AZ	34.0%	Sioux Falls	SD	2.3%
McAllen–Edinburg-Mission	TX	13.6%	Fort Walton Beach	FL	2.4%
Visalia-Tulare-Porterville	CA	13.1%	Columbia	MO	2.4%
Merced	CA	11.5%	Gainesville	FL	2.5%
Fresno	CA	11.1%	Portland	ME	2.5%
Yuba City–Marysville	CA	11.0%	Fargo-Moorhead	ND-MN	2.5%
Brownsville–Harlingen–San Benito	TX	10.6%	Rapid City	SD	2.6%
Bakersfield	CA	10.5%	Fayetteville-Springdale-Rogers	AR	2.6%
El Paso	TX	9.8%	Bryan–College Station	TX	2.6%
Beaumont–Port Arthur	TX	9.6%	Bismarck	ND	2.7%
Flint	MI	9.6%	Bloomington-Normal	IL	2.7%
Danville	VA	9.5%	Bangor	ME	2.8%
Modesto	CA	9.3%	Madison	WI	2.9%
Yakima	WA	9.3%	Burlington	VT	3.1%
Stockton-Lodi	CA	9.2%	Enid	OK	3.1%
Brazoria	TX	9.1%	Billings	MT	3.1%
Hickory-Morganton-Lenoir	NC	9.0%	Missoula	MT	3.1%
Galveston–Texas City	TX	8.8%	Stamford-Norwalk	CT	3.2%
Fort Pierce–Port St. Lucie	FL	8.6%	Champaign-Urbana	IL	3.2%
Rocky Mount	NC	8.5%	San Luis Obispo–Atascadero–Paso Robles	CA	3.2%
Racine	WI	8.4%	Knoxville	TN	3.2%
Rockford	IL	8.2%	Bloomington	IN	3.2%
Pine Bluff	AR	8.2%	Athens	GA	3.2%
Vineland-Millville-Bridgeton	NJ	8.1%	Dutchess County	NY	3.3%
Portland-Vancouver	OR-WA	8.1%	State College	PA	3.3%
Lawrence	MA-NH	8.0%	Roanoke	VA	3.3%
Florence	AL	7.9%	Barnstable-Yarmouth	MA	3.3%
Saginaw–Bay City–Midland	MI	7.9%	Washington	DC-MD-VA-WV	3.3%
Jackson	MI	7.9%	Harrisburg-Lebanon-Carlisle	PA	3.4%
Florence	SC	7.9%	Danbury	CT	3.4%

Source: U.S. Bureau of Labor Statistics, August 2003

Table 3.13: Recent Job Growth

August 2002-August 2003

MSAs with Highest Job Growth			MSAs with Lowest Job Growth		
Billings	MT	13.6%	Boulder-Longmont	CO	-11.9%
Anchorage	AK	11.2%	Myrtle Beach	SC	-5.5%
Florence	SC	6.7%	Cedar Rapids	IA	-5.3%
Brownsville–Harlingen–San Benito	TX	6.6%	Florence	AL	-4.7%
Topeka	KS	6.3%	Iowa City	IA	-4.4%
Pocatello	ID	5.7%	San Jose	CA	-4.2%
Merced	CA	5.6%	Yuma	AZ	-4.0%
Elkhart-Goshen	IN	5.5%	Erie	PA	-4.0%
Bellingham	WA	4.7%	Dubuque	IA	-3.8%
Missoula	MT	4.6%	Joplin	MO	-3.6%
Naples	FL	4.5%	Sharon	PA	-3.4%
Bloomington	IN	4.5%	Lowell	MA-NH	-3.4%
Lubbock	TX	4.5%	Boise	ID	-3.3%
Grand Junction	CO	4.5%	Sioux City	IA-NE	-3.2%
Bryan–College Station	TX	4.3%	Jackson	TN	-3.2%
Corpus Christi	TX	4.3%	Hickory-Morganton-Lenoir	NC	-3.0%
Madison	WI	4.1%	Jacksonville	NC	-3.0%
Laredo	TX	4.0%	Des Moines	IA	-2.8%
Olympia	WA	4.0%	Gainesville	FL	-2.7%
Charleston	WV	3.9%	Scranton–Wilkes-Barre–Hazleton	PA	-2.7%
Tyler	TX	3.9%	Pensacola	FL	-2.6%
El Paso	TX	3.9%	New Bedford	MA	-2.4%
Fayetteville-Springdale-Rogers	AR	3.8%	Williamsport	PA	-2.4%
McAllen–Edinburg-Mission	TX	3.7%	Tallahassee	FL	-2.4%
Denver	CO	3.7%	Worcester	MA-CT	-2.4%
Charlottesville	VA	3.6%	Johnstown	PA	-2.3%
Brazoria	TX	3.5%	Waterloo–Cedar Falls	IA	-2.3%
Punta Gorda	FL	3.5%	Reading	PA	-2.2%
Jackson	MI	3.5%	Pittsburgh	PA	-2.2%
Honolulu	HI	3.4%	Miami	FL	-2.1%

Source: U.S. Bureau of Labor Statistics, August 2003

Future Job Growth

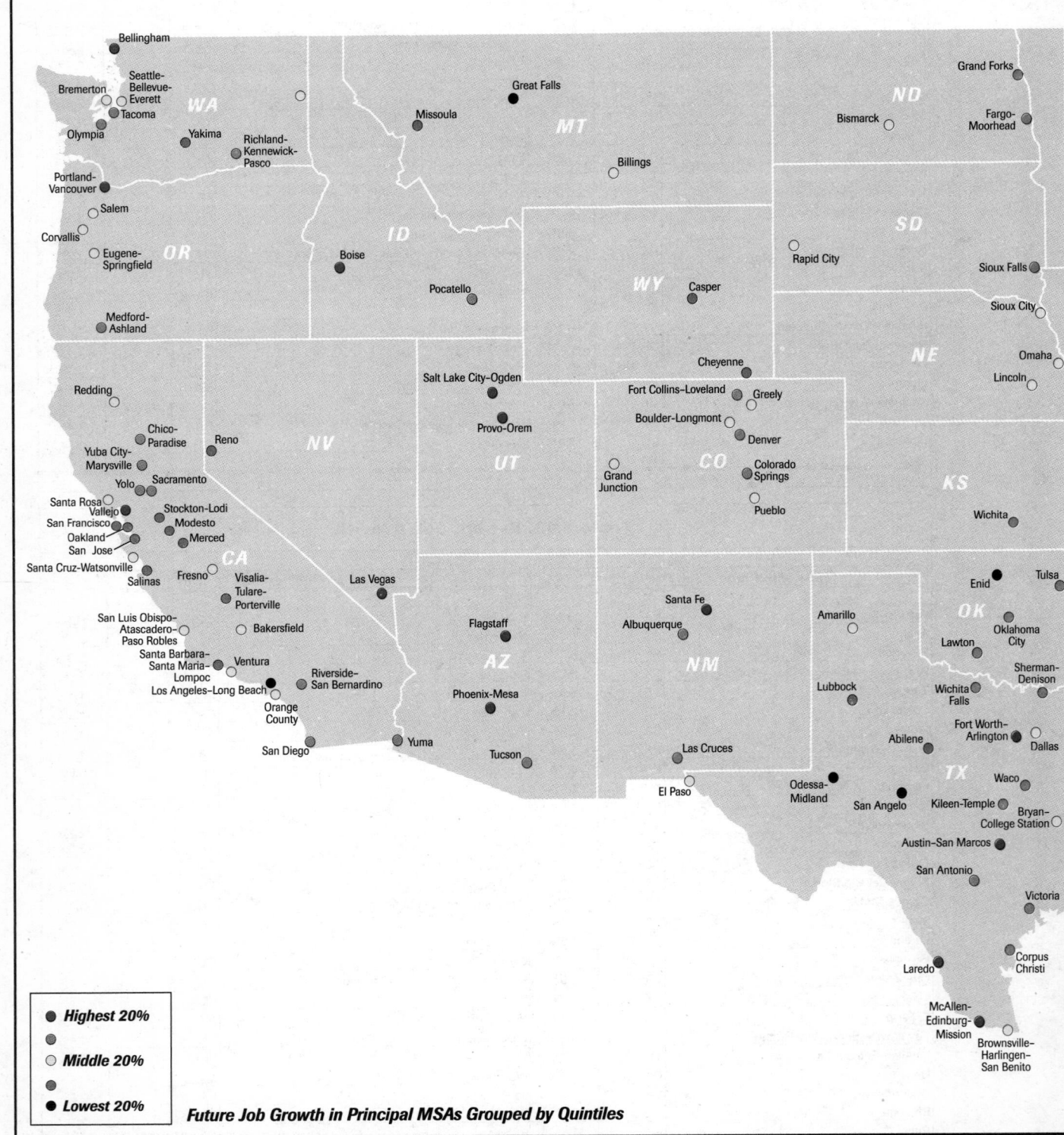

Future Job Growth in Principal MSAs Grouped by Quintiles

Table 3.14: Projected Future Job Growth					
2003–2010					
MSAs with Best Job Outlook			MSAs with Worst Job Outlook		
Las Vegas	NV-AZ	42.0%	Elmira	NY	2.6%
Punta Gorda	FL	34.7%	Decatur	IL	3.7%
Austin–San Marcos	TX	33.2%	Jamestown	NY	3.8%
Provo-Orem	UT	33.1%	Newark	NJ	3.8%
Fayetteville-Springdale-Rogers	AR	31.5%	Steubenville-Weirton	OH-WV	3.8%
Santa Fe	NM	30.6%	Bergen-Passaic	NJ	4.0%
Sarasota-Bradenton	FL	30.5%	New York	NY	4.5%
Laredo	TX	30.3%	Stamford-Norwalk	CT	5.1%
Flagstaff	AZ-UT	29.2%	Bridgeport	CT	5.3%
Wilmington-Newark	DE-MD	28.8%	Pittsfield	MA	5.4%
Salt Lake City–Ogden	UT	28.5%	Danville	VA	5.6%
Myrtle Beach	SC	28.4%	Providence–Fall River–Warwick	RI-MA	5.7%
Phoenix-Mesa	AZ	28.4%	Glens Falls	NY	5.8%
Greenville	NC	27.2%	Springfield	MA	5.8%
Fort Worth–Arlington	TX	27.0%	Williamsport	PA	5.8%
Naples	FL	26.8%	St. Joseph	MO	5.8%
Portland-Vancouver	OR-WA	26.6%	Kokomo	IN	5.9%
Orlando	FL	26.4%	Vineland-Millville-Bridgeton	NJ	6.0%
McAllen-Edinburg-Mission	TX	26.2%	Buffalo–Niagara Falls	NY	6.0%
Vallejo-Fairfield-Napa	CA	25.9%	Los Angeles–Long Beach	CA	6.2%
Bellingham	WA	25.7%	Danbury	CT	6.3%
Boise	ID	25.6%	Scranton–Wilkes-Barre–Hazleton	PA	6.3%
Riverside–San Bernardino	CA	25.3%	Worcester	MA-CT	6.4%
Columbia	MO	25.3%	New Haven–Meriden	CT	6.5%
Raleigh–Durham–Chapel Hill	NC	24.8%	Jersey City	NJ	6.6%
San Antonio	TX	24.6%	Waterbury	CT	6.7%
Fort Collins–Loveland	CO	24.5%	Fitchburg-Leominster	MA	7.1%
Yolo	CA	24.3%	Odessa-Midland	TX	7.3%
Fort Myers–Cape Coral	FL	24.3%	Binghamton	NY	7.3%
Colorado Springs	CO	23.9%	Rochester	MN	7.4%

Source: Sperling's BestPlaces

Cost of Living

The Cost of Living category displays overall cost of living and its key components as compared to U.S. averages and expected income levels. Components include taxes, housing, and necessities, such as food, utilities, transportation, healthcare, and miscellaneous expenses.

For most people, cost of living is one of the most critical elements in determining standard of living and even the lifestyle of an individual or family unit. The cost-of-living range among places is surprisingly high, with areas in the south-central United States running 25% below national averages, while places on the East and West coasts run as much as *twice* the national average. But understanding the factors that drive cost of living is critical to seeing the overall picture. Particularly in big cities and coastal areas, housing costs are the biggest factor, followed by taxes. Housing costs vary considerably within regions, metropolitan areas, and even among the local assortment of housing choices. The impact of taxes varies by area and individual circumstances because each locality taxes income (income

tax), consumption (sales tax), and wealth (property tax) differently. Housing and tax costs thus depend on *where* you are and *who* you are.

Cost of Living Trends

Fortunately, federal government policy and a weak economy have kept inflation tame in the period since 2000. As a result, overall cost of living has remained fairly stable nationally. Through mid-2003, the total Consumer Price Index, or CPI, for all items except housing, rose a total of 7% since 2000, or only 2.3% per year on a compounded basis. This is the good news. The bad news is that low interest rates, continued growth in household formation, favorable tax policy, higher building and land development costs, and redeployment of investment capital away from corporate equities have caused housing costs to rise significantly from 2000 to 2003. The median 3-year home price increase among U.S. metro areas was 17.9%. This is 5.6% per year compounded annually, or more than double the inflation rate. Increases were much stronger in attractive,

Table 3.15: Sample Cost of Living Table from San Luis Obispo–Atascadero–Paso Robles, California

COST OF LIVING SCORE: 5/RANK: 312

INDEXES & TAXES	AREA	U.S. AVG	HOUSING	AREA	U.S. AVG	NECESSITIES	AREA	U.S. AVG
Cost of Living Index	155.1	100.0	Median home price	$380,130	$160,100	Food Index	112.4	100.0
Financial Progress Index	66.5	100.0	Home price appreciation	18.2%	7.1%	Housing Index	236.1	100.0
Income tax rate	6.000%	4.625%	Median rent	$917	$670	Utilities Index	116.6	100.0
Sales tax rate	7.250%	6.474%	Homes owned	52.9%	63.9%	Transportation Index	111.5	100.0
Property tax rate	$11.1	$15.6	Homes rented	33.3%	25.3%	Healthcare Index	112.0	100.0
			Housing affordability	42.0%	54.5%	Miscellaneous Cost Index	103.2	100.0

small California towns and on the East Coast, while remaining tame in the Midwest and in more isolated areas. Obviously, those who already own a home and those who want to buy one experience this trend differently. If planning to move to a "hot" area, look out. Likewise, those sensitive to cost-of-living factors need to keep track of changes in tax policy, and, because of recent upheaval in the energy markets, the Utilities Index.

Cost of Living Attributes

Cost of Living is divided into *Indexes & Taxes, Housing,* and *Necessities.* Table 3.15 shows the Cost of Living table for the metropolitan area of San Luis Obispo–Atascadero–Paso Robles, California.

Indexes & Taxes

■ *Cost of Living Index,* captured in the first quarter of 2003, is a composite of all cost factors, including housing and other necessities, expressed as an index against a national average of 100. The figure, provided by the Bureau of Labor Statistics and frequently quoted in the media, is an important standard and barometer of comparative area performance. Analysis shows that 232 of the 331 metro areas have a COL Index below the national average of 100. The largest group is in the range from 80 to 90, or 10% to 20% below the national average. Table 3.16 shows the COL Index ranges for all MSAs.

Table 3.16: Cost of Living Index Ranges

COL Index	Number of MSAs
> 120	41
110-120	25
100-110	33
90-100	87
80-90	119
70-80	26

■ *Financial Progress Index* (FPI), designed by *Cities Ranked & Rated,* indicates the potential for long-term financial progress in an area. The index compares income to cost of living and assumes that high incomes disappear fast when cost of living is also high. The index is calculated as a ratio of household income to cost of living, presented as an index compared to the national average. Families looking toward long-term financial goals should find places with a high FPI, which indicates a better chance to build net worth over time because incomes are high relative to costs. National results vary widely, with the highest Financial Progress Index at 136.8 (Fort Worth–Arlington, TX) and the lowest at 59.9 (Merced, CA). In general, many areas in Texas and the South have high FPIs, while those in California and on the East Coast are low.

■ *Income tax rate, Sales tax rate,* and *Property tax rate* are compiled by Sperling's BestPlaces from several sources, including the Commerce Clearing House, Federation of Tax Administrators, and the District of Columbia Tax Rates and Tax Burdens study. Because tax rates are more complex than meets the eye—total tax paid depending not only on *rate,* but also on *basis,* the amount to which the rate applies—*Cities Ranked & Rated* shows approximate tax rates at the metropolitan area level for the sake of comparison. To learn more about a particular area, readers should take a close look at local laws. For a more complete look at tax policy and its effects, see "Taxation" in chapter 4.

• *Income tax rate* is the approximate state income tax rate, with local income taxes added in where known. The reported figure represents the highest marginal rate for the area and may not be representative of what a family with average income would pay.

Cheapest & Most Expensive Cities

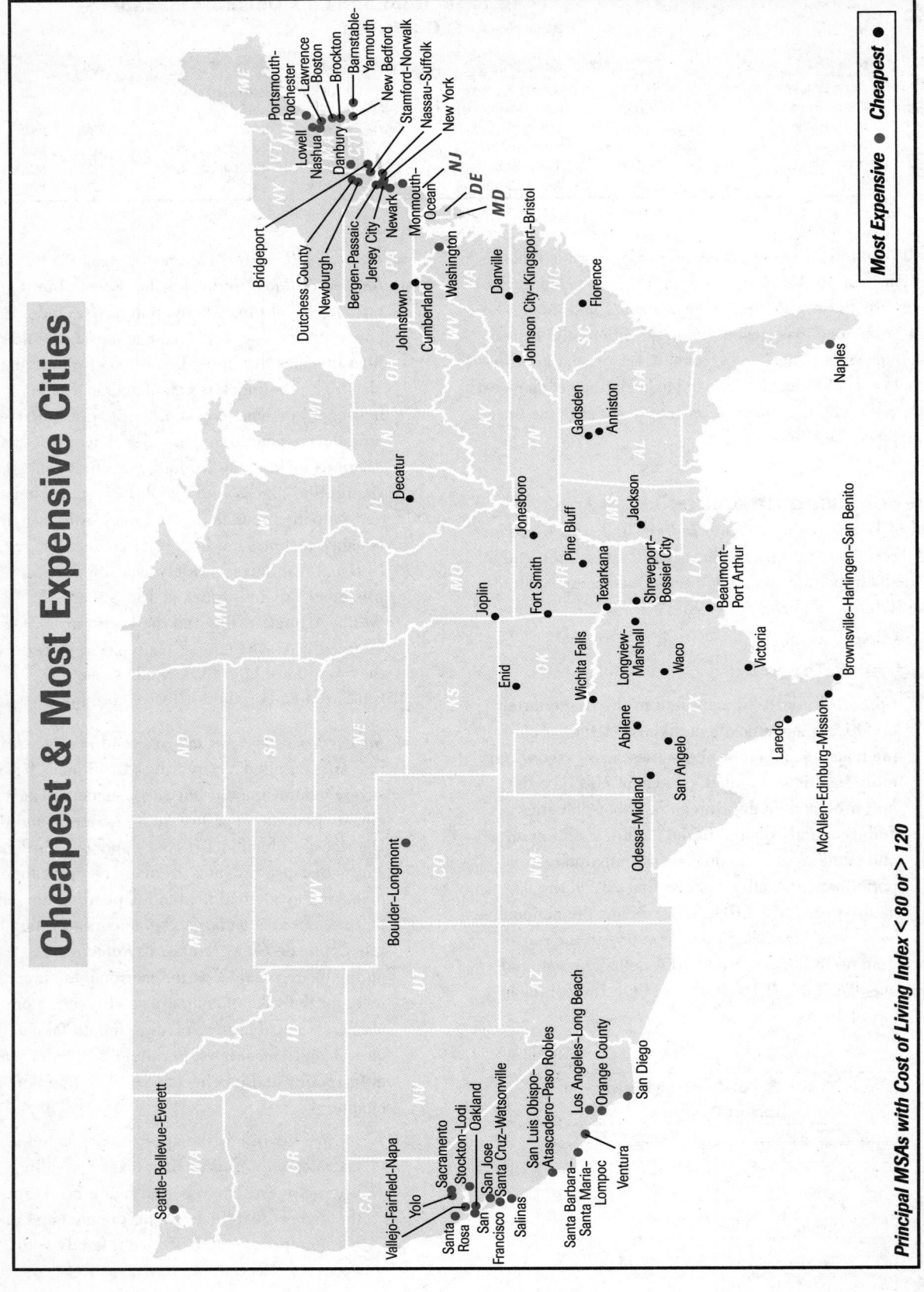

Seattle-Bellevue-Everett

Vallejo-Fairfield-Napa
Yolo
Sacramento
Santa Rosa
Stockton-Lodi
Oakland
San Francisco
San Jose
Santa Cruz-Watsonville
Salinas
San Luis Obispo-Atascadero-Paso Robles
Santa Barbara-Santa Maria-Lompoc
Ventura
Los Angeles-Long Beach
Orange County
San Diego

Boulder-Longmont

Portsmouth-Rochester
Lawrence
Boston
Brockton
Barnstable-Yarmouth
Lowell
Nashua
Danbury
New Bedford
Stamford-Norwalk
Nassau-Suffolk
New York

Bridgeport
Dutchess County
Newburgh
Bergen-Passaic
Jersey City
Newark
Monmouth-Ocean
Washington
Danville
Johnson City-Kingsport-Bristol
Florence
Johnstown
Cumberland

Decatur

Joplin
Enid
Fort Smith
Jonesboro
Pine Bluff
Jackson
Texarkana
Shreveport-Bossier City
Beaumont-Port Arthur
Wichita Falls
Longview-Marshall
Waco
Victoria
Abilene
San Angelo
Odessa-Midland
Laredo
McAllen-Edinburg-Mission
Brownsville-Harlingen-San Benito
Gadsden
Anniston
Naples

Most Expensive ● *Cheapest* ●

Principal MSAs with Cost of Living Index < 80 or > 120

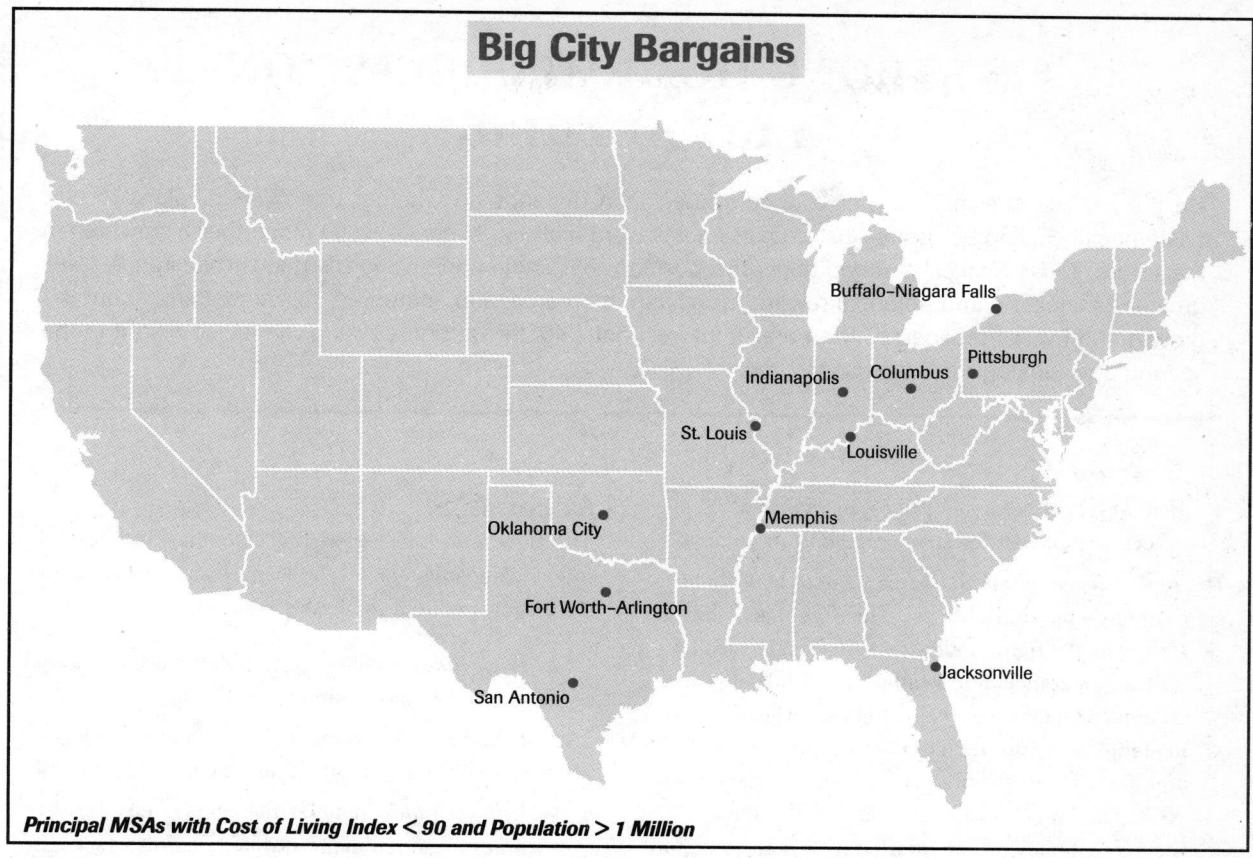

Big City Bargains

Buffalo–Niagara Falls
Pittsburgh
Columbus
Indianapolis
St. Louis
Louisville
Memphis
Oklahoma City
Fort Worth–Arlington
Jacksonville
San Antonio

Principal MSAs with Cost of Living Index < 90 and Population > 1 Million

- *Sales tax rate* shows the state base sales tax rate, with local general sales taxes and special tax surcharges (for schools, transit projects, and so on) added in where known. When an area has multiple sales tax rates, the one paid by the majority of the population is shown.

- *Property tax rate* shows the average dollar amount paid per $1,000 property valuation in an area. Note that both statutory rates and valuations vary widely among and even within areas; these figures are averages.

Housing

Housing price data is compiled by Sperling's BestPlaces from an assortment of sources, including the National Association of Realtors, Freddie Mac, and the U.S. Census Bureau.

- *Median home price* shows the price for an average home in the area based on early 2003 sales. (Recall that median means half the homes sold for more, half for less.) The "average home in the area" can vary considerably from a one-bedroom apartment in Manhattan to a three-bedroom house on a suburban half-acre with a garage and basement. Of course, location, style, quality, uniqueness, and special features will cause a specific home or even a neighborhood to deviate considerably from the averages. The range among metropolitan areas is extremely wide, with median prices well over $400,000 in better California cities and over $500,000 in Santa Barbara and Stamford-Norwalk, Connecticut. In the smaller Texas, Arkansas, and Oklahoma cities, median prices are in the $60,000 to $70,000 range. For updated home prices, see www.bestplaces.net/CRAR.

- *Home price appreciation* shows the growth in median home prices as a compounded annual growth rate over the 2000–2003 period. Because of a recent surge in California real estate prices, 15 of the top 18 metro areas are located in that state, which has an average annual growth rate over 15%. Meanwhile, Springfield, Illinois, brings up the rear at 2.1%. Updated rates are available at www.bestplaces.net/CRAR.

IS STRONG HOME APPRECIATION A GOOD THING?

On the surface, the merit of home price appreciation depends on whether one owns or plans to buy. Sustainability is another issue—just because costs were high for 3 years doesn't mean they'll stay high in the future. *Cities Ranked & Rated* takes the position that *some* appreciation is good. This stance gives greater justification and potential reward for buying in an area, and, moreover, tells something about the growth and overall prospects for an area's future. That said, this attribute was given lower weight in the scoring and ranking for the reasons cited.

- *Median rent.* Like home prices, median rent reflects rental cost for an average unit in an area.

- *Homes owned* shows the percentage of households living in a purchased home. This figure and the *Homes rented* figure below give an idea of the stability, appearance, and availability of housing in an area. The highest levels of home ownership are in stable, small towns like Owensboro, Kentucky, and York, Pennsylvania, with ownership rates over 75%. The lowest levels are in areas like Jersey City, New Jersey, where affordability is an issue, or in military towns with more population transience.

- *Homes rented* shows the percentage of households living in rented homes, apartments, and other residences.

- *Housing affordability* represents the percentage of the local population that can afford the average purchased or rented residence. This information comes from a study prepared by the National Low Income Housing Coalition. Figures range from a low of 33% in New Bedford, Massachusetts, to a high of 68% in Sheboygan, Wisconsin; Fort Walton Beach, Florida; and Victoria, Texas. The national average is 54.5%.

Necessities

The Bureau of Labor Statistics calculates indexes for the following components of the overall Cost of Living Index. Data shown is from the first quarter of 2003.

- *Food Index* includes a standard "basket" of food purchased in the area.

- *Housing Index* measures the cost of acquiring (purchasing or renting) and maintaining a home.

- *Utilities Index* includes the average cost (price times usage) of major utilities, mainly electricity and heating fuels.

- *Transportation Index* includes most costs of driving an automobile, including the vehicle itself, fuel, repairs, insurance, licensing, parking, and public transit.

- *Healthcare Index* includes the cost of physician, clinical, and hospital services, as well as medications and supplies.

- *Miscellaneous Cost Index* includes a variety of items needed to support daily living, including clothing, durable goods, and an assortment of services, such as personal care and financial services.

Cost of Living Highlights, Tables 3.17–3.20

Table 3.17: Cost of Living Index

MSAs with Highest COL Index			MSAs with Lowest COL Index		
Stamford-Norwalk	CT	202.9	Texarkana	TX-AR	73.4
San Francisco	CA	196.4	Joplin	MO	74.2
San Jose	CA	184.1	McAllen-Edinburg-Mission	TX	74.2
Oakland	CA	179.3	Victoria	TX	75.5
Santa Cruz–Watsonville	CA	177.6	Abilene	TX	75.7
Santa Rosa	CA	177.3	Longview-Marshall	TX	76.0
Santa Barbara–Santa Maria–Lompoc	CA	173.6	Odessa-Midland	TX	76.2
Salinas	CA	169.5	Brownsville–Harlingen–San Benito	TX	76.2
Orange County	CA	168.2	Fort Smith	AR-OK	76.4
Boston	MA-NH-ME	162.9	Enid	OK	76.8
New York	NY	161.0	Wichita Falls	TX	76.9
Danbury	CT	160.7	San Angelo	TX	77.3
Nassau-Suffolk	NY	159.6	Laredo	TX	77.3
San Diego	CA	157.6	Decatur	IL	77.4
Bergen-Passaic	NJ	156.5	Jonesboro	AR	77.5
San Luis Obispo–Atascadero–Paso Robles	CA	155.1	Gadsden	AL	77.8
Honolulu	HI	152.7	Danville	VA	78.0
Ventura	CA	149.2	Waco	TX	78.3
Vallejo-Fairfield-Napa	CA	149.1	Shreveport–Bossier City	LA	78.5
Barnstable-Yarmouth	MA	141.7	Cumberland	MD-WV	79.0
Boulder-Longmont	CO	140.8	Anniston	AL	79.1
Newark	NJ	140.5	Pine Bluff	AR	79.1
Los Angeles–Long Beach	CA	139.3	Florence	SC	79.1
Lawrence	MA-NH	138.9	Jackson	MS	79.1
Brockton	MA	138.7	Johnstown	PA	79.7
Monmouth-Ocean	NJ	137.4	Johnson City–Kingsport–Bristol	TN-VA	79.9
Lowell	MA-NH	137.3	Beaumont–Port Arthur	TX	80.0
Middlesex-Somerset-Hunterdon	NJ	137.0	Lubbock	TX	80.2
Yolo	CA	136.9	Corpus Christi	TX	80.3
Bridgeport	CT	136.8	Amarillo	TX	80.3

Note: U.S. average: 100

Source: U.S. Bureau of Labor Statistics, 2003

Table 3.18: Financial Progress Index

Average Household Income / Cost of Living Shown as an Index

MSAs with Highest FP Index			MSAs with Lowest FP Index		
Fort Worth–Arlington	TX	136.8	Merced	CA	59.9
Austin–San Marcos	TX	134.3	Chico-Paradise	CA	62.9
Dallas	TX	132.7	Santa Barbara–Santa Maria–Lompoc	CA	63.0
Atlanta	GA	131.1	San Luis Obispo–Atascadero–Paso Robles	CA	66.5
Trenton	NJ	131.1	Yuba City–Marysville	CA	67.9
Houston	TX	129.2	Redding	CA	68.7
Rochester	MN	128.8	New York	NY	69.3
Indianapolis	IN	128.3	Yolo	CA	71.4
Wilmington-Newark	DE-MD	127.9	Punta Gorda	FL	73.0
Anchorage	AK	127.4	Auburn-Opelika	AL	73.1
Cedar Rapids	IA	127.3	Fresno	CA	73.3
Appleton-Oshkosh-Neenah	WI	126.3	Santa Rosa	CA	73.8
Jackson	MS	126.2	McAllen-Edinburg-Mission	TX	73.9
Des Moines	IA	125.6	San Diego	CA	74.3
New Haven–Meriden	CT	124.8	Salinas	CA	74.5
Middlesex-Somerset-Hunterdon	NJ	124.4	Barnstable-Yarmouth	MA	75.4
Salt Lake City–Ogden	UT	124.1	Jersey City	NJ	76.3
St. Louis	MO-IL	124.0	Medford-Ashland	OR	76.5
Washington	DC-MD-VA-WV	123.7	Yuma	AZ	76.8
Decatur	IL	123.6	Los Angeles–Long Beach	CA	76.8
Bridgeport	CT	123.2	Las Cruces	NM	77.3
Victoria	TX	123.0	Brownsville–Harlingen–San Benito	TX	77.4
Fort Wayne	IN	122.7	Miami	FL	77.6
Bloomington-Normal	IL	122.6	Ocala	FL	78.1
Elkhart-Goshen	IN	122.0	Stockton-Lodi	CA	78.1
Grand Rapids–Muskegon–Holland	MI	121.5	Huntington-Ashland	WV-KY-OH	78.7
Brazoria	TX	121.5	Modesto	CA	79.7
Huntsville	AL	121.4	Steubenville-Weirton	OH-WV	80.4
Minneapolis–St. Paul	MN-WI	121.4	Johnstown	PA	80.9
Sioux Falls	SD	121.3	Rocky Mount	NC	81.0

Note: U.S. average: 100

Source: Calculation based on U.S. Bureau of Labor Statistics data, 2003

Table 3.19: Median Home Prices

For Average Home in Area

MSAs with Most Expensive Homes			MSAs with Least Expensive Homes		
Stamford-Norwalk	CT	$544,340	McAllen-Edinburg-Mission	TX	$61,460
San Francisco	CA	$516,400	Brownsville–Harlingen–San Benito	TX	$61,570
San Jose	CA	$478,000	Pine Bluff	AR	$62,880
Santa Barbara–Santa Maria–Lompoc	CA	$463,740	Odessa-Midland	TX	$66,550
Oakland	CA	$455,630	Wichita Falls	TX	$67,420
Santa Cruz–Watsonville	CA	$447,000	Abilene	TX	$69,140
Orange County	CA	$434,600	Enid	OK	$69,240
Santa Rosa	CA	$432,390	San Angelo	TX	$73,530
Salinas	CA	$431,880	Wheeling	WV-OH	$75,120
Boston	MA-NH-ME	$386,300	Texarkana	TX-AR	$75,530
San Luis Obispo–Atascadero–Paso Robles	CA	$380,130	Decatur	IL	$77,170
San Diego	CA	$379,300	Waco	TX	$77,290
Danbury	CT	$360,330	Johnstown	PA	$77,340
Ventura	CA	$357,850	Jamestown	NY	$78,380
Bergen-Passaic	NJ	$350,200	Terre Haute	IN	$78,730
Honolulu	HI	$350,000	Fort Smith	AR-OK	$78,900
Boulder-Longmont	CO	$334,390	Steubenville-Weirton	OH-WV	$79,360
Nassau-Suffolk	NY	$333,600	Lawton	OK	$79,890
New York	NY	$320,300	Victoria	TX	$80,560
Vallejo-Fairfield-Napa	CA	$317,330	Joplin	MO	$80,570
Los Angeles–Long Beach	CA	$304,600	Longview-Marshall	TX	$80,680
Newark	NJ	$301,900	Lubbock	TX	$80,750
Barnstable-Yarmouth	MA	$299,830	Beaumont–Port Arthur	TX	$81,500
Lawrence	MA-NH	$295,190	Cumberland	MD-WV	$81,790
Lowell	MA-NH	$290,560	Elmira	NY	$83,310
Brockton	MA	$287,040	Huntington-Ashland	WV-KY-OH	$83,670
Middlesex-Somerset-Hunterdon	NJ	$284,300	Altoona	PA	$84,040
Yolo	CA	$275,690	Sherman-Denison	TX	$84,050
Monmouth-Ocean	NJ	$261,700	Sioux City	IA-NE	$84,270
Washington	DC-MD-VA-WV	$258,700	Buffalo–Niagara Falls	NY	$85,400

Median Home Prices by Region

Northeast		$182,500
Midwest		$140,800
South		$157,400
West		$233,300

Notes: 2003 Q2 median U.S. home price: $160,100

Source: National Association of Realtors, 2003

Table 3.20: Home Price Appreciation

By Compound Annual Growth Rate, 2000-2003

MSAs with Highest Appreciation			MSAs with Lowest Appreciation		
Barnstable-Yarmouth	MA	18.8%	Springfield	MO	2.1%
Vallejo-Fairfield-Napa	CA	18.4%	Kankakee	IL	2.6%
San Luis Obispo–Atascadero–Paso Robles	CA	18.2%	Fayetteville	NC	2.7%
Salinas	CA	17.6%	Provo-Orem	UT	2.9%
Yolo	CA	17.5%	Pine Bluff	AR	3.0%
Nassau-Suffolk	NY	16.7%	Salt Lake City–Ogden	UT	3.0%
Santa Rosa	CA	16.5%	Sioux City	IA-NE	3.0%
Santa Barbara–Santa Maria–Lompoc	CA	16.5%	Albuquerque	NM	3.0%
Brockton	MA	16.4%	Lafayette	LA	3.0%
Oakland	CA	16.4%	Wichita Falls	TX	3.1%
San Diego	CA	16.3%	Jackson	MI	3.1%
Santa Cruz–Watsonville	CA	16.2%	Victoria	TX	3.2%
Merced	CA	16.2%	Corvallis	OR	3.2%
Stockton-Lodi	CA	15.5%	Las Cruces	NM	3.2%
Modesto	CA	15.4%	Montgomery	AL	3.3%
Sacramento	CA	15.3%	Eugene-Springfield	OR	3.3%
Manchester	NH	15.3%	Spokane	WA	3.3%
Lawrence	MA-NH	15.1%	Yakima	WA	3.3%
Lowell	MA-NH	14.9%	Decatur	IL	3.4%
New Bedford	MA	14.9%	Bloomington-Normal	IL	3.4%
Dutchess County	NY	14.9%	Grand Forks	ND-MN	3.4%
Nashua	NH	14.9%	Rockford	IL	3.5%
Boston	MA-NH-ME	14.8%	Pocatello	ID	3.5%
Monmouth-Ocean	NJ	14.7%	Rochester	MN	3.5%
Providence–Fall River–Warwick	RI-MA	14.6%	Terre Haute	IN	3.6%
Worcester	MA-CT	14.6%	Columbia	MO	3.6%
Fitchburg-Leominster	MA	14.5%	Decatur	AL	3.6%
Naples	FL	14.5%	Florence	SC	3.6%
New York	NY	14.3%	Charleston–North Charleston	SC	3.7%
Portsmouth-Rochester	NH-ME	14.3%	Lawton	OK	3.7%

Source: Sperling's BestPlaces/National Association of Realtors

Climate

Although most don't cite climate as the primary reason to relocate, it is almost certainly taken into consideration. Climatology—the study of climate—is extremely complex and fairly technical in nature. *Cities Ranked & Rated* presents data on the key components of climate—temperature, precipitation, cloud cover, humidity, and hazards—to provide an image of what a place is like most of the year.

Climate Drivers

Specific factors unique to a place determine the kind of climate present.

- *Latitude* represents the north-south location of a place. In general, places farther south are warmer and have less seasonal effect, while those farther north are colder and have more pronounced seasonal changes. Differences in sun angle mean larger seasonal changes and greater variety in length of day for places farther north. Places in the northern United States and Canada have summer days 15 to 18 hours long and winter days 6 to 9 hours long. Places farther south see much smaller seasonal differences.

- *Altitude,* like latitude, can have a profound effect on climate. Less dense air at higher altitudes allows greater heat loss and less water content (that is, humidity). The general rule: Temperatures average 5°F lower for every 1,000 feet in elevation, although many other factors enter into temperature differences. Aside from temperature and humidity, altitude is also a consideration for those with health problems. Thinner air means less oxygen, increased fatigue, and greater strain on the human circulatory system. Elevation is given in the opening box of each city in chapter 5.

- *Nearby water*—and the size, location, and temperature of that water—can have profound impact on local climates. Water retains heat and provides moisture. Areas near water receive significant temperature moderation. A shoreline city can see

THE DIFFERENCE BETWEEN CLIMATE & WEATHER

The difference between *climate* and *weather* is sometimes confusing. In general, climate is the *cause* and weather is the *effect*. Climate is the result of a set of physical factors, including latitude, altitude, water presence, wind direction, nearby landforms, seasons, and natural atmospheric patterns. Although there can be minor variations in atmospheric patterns and wind direction, most of these factors are fixed, and therefore, climate is fixed. Weather, on the other hand, is the result of the daily interaction of these phenomena, and can vary considerably from 1 day to the next and even 1 minute to the next. Weather describes the events—rain, snow, heat, cold, clouds, sun—that occur, while climate speaks to the permanent physical phenomena that govern daily weather.

winter low temperatures 5°F, 10°F, even 20°F warmer than areas just a few miles inland; likewise, summer highs may be 5°F to 20°F cooler, depending on local wind direction and water temperature. So Baltimore has more moderate temperatures than Hagerstown, Maryland, and Seattle more so than Yakima, Washington. Water moderates no matter the latitude, but the effects are more pronounced when the wind direction is onshore. Places to the lee or downwind from bodies of water receive the effects of its moisture, particularly when dramatic differences between water and air temperature are present. Nowhere is this more true than upstate New York or northern Indiana, where moisture and temperature differences create impressive "lake effect" snows from Lake Erie and Lake Michigan, respectively. Both of these phenomena can work on a smaller scale, as observed in Burlington, Vermont, on Lake Champlain.

■ *Wind direction* significantly effects climate. The prevailing wind direction across the middle latitudes of North America is west to east; however, local variations exist due to landforms, upper air and storm patterns, and water. Prevailing wind direction is the main reason that coastal New England cities do not enjoy the same temperature moderation as those in the Pacific Northwest. A mid-Atlantic/Caribbean phenomenon known as the "Bermuda High" circulates warm, moist Gulf of Mexico air from the southwest to the northeast in the summer, giving high heat and humidity in the southeast and spreading into the central United States and Canada. Cold, dry winds from the

northwest and Canada bring cold spells and strong temperature fluctuations. Prevailing winter winds in much of the central part of the continent are from the northwest.

■ *Landforms*, such as mountains and valleys, often greatly influence local climate. First, where mountain ranges block prevailing winds, a rain shadow occurs, creating drier and less humid climates than places just a few miles upwind. Sheltered by the Cascade Range, Yakima, Washington, for example, is one of the 10 driest metro areas in the United States, with 8 inches of precipitation annually, while Seattle, just 150 miles west, gets five times as much rain with three times as many cloudy days. Effects are less pronounced for cities shadowed by the Appalachians. Second, mountains also shelter places from cold, winter air invading from the north. Valleys can trap warm or cold air, reducing winds and temperature changes, but keep a cold chill or a hot spell firmly in place. Finally, areas downwind from large mountain barriers can experience rapid and prolonged winter warming atypical of the region and latitude when downslope winds compress and become warmer. These chinook winds occur on the Front Range of the Rocky Mountains as far north as Edmonton, Alberta.

■ *Storm tracks* strongly affect the climates of places in their path. Due to the Earth's rotation and the presence of solar energy, rivers of air continuously circulate the planet at high speeds in the upper elevations of the atmosphere. Known as jet streams, these currents cause atmospheric mixing

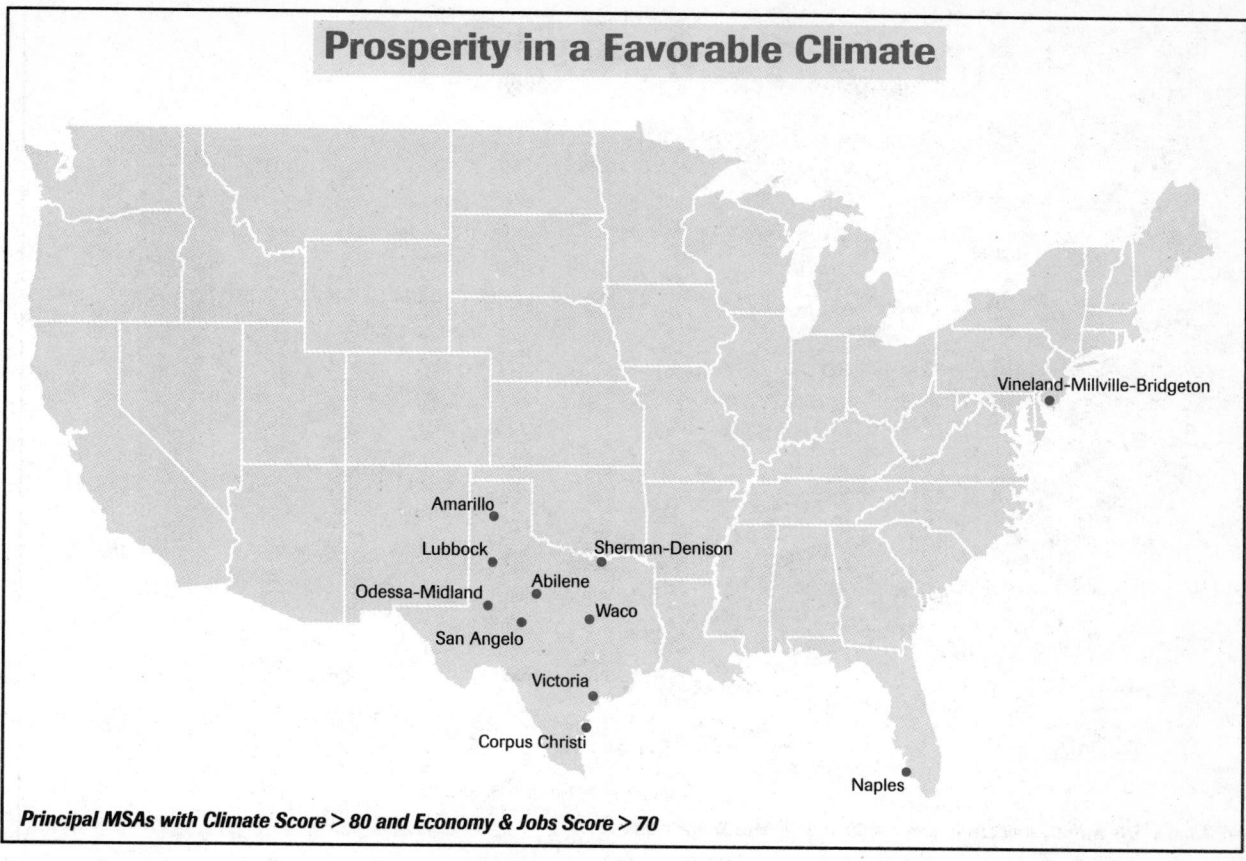

Prosperity in a Favorable Climate

Amarillo
Lubbock
Odessa-Midland
San Angelo
Abilene
Sherman-Denison
Waco
Victoria
Corpus Christi
Naples
Vineland-Millville-Bridgeton

Principal MSAs with Climate Score > 80 and Economy & Jobs Score > 70

and determine the direction and speed of storms. Where these currents flow is a matter of land and water location, seasons, and some cyclical fluctuation. The typical storm track for the continental United States is west to east, entering the continent in the Pacific Northwest, sweeping across the Rockies, and bending south into the southern Great Plains, then swinging back northeast more or less along the Ohio River Valley and into New England. The pattern fluctuates in shape and strength and tends to move farther south in winter and farther north in summer. Areas commonly on or near storm tracks—Oklahoma City, Oklahoma; Evansville, Indiana; Cleveland, Ohio; and Albany, New York—tend to see greater swings in weather and strong storms.

Climate Zones

Climate experts divide land areas into climate zones, each indicative of the prevailing climate type in that area. Zones define seasonal patterns, temperature ranges, and precipitation, among other characteristics. *Subtropical* climates have persistent hot, humid summers and mild winters. *Continental* climates are influenced by vast land areas with little water, and thus have strong seasonal

LONG SUMMER EVENINGS

Those who enjoy long summer evenings to play golf, enjoy a backyard barbeque, or sit at a sidewalk cafe, should look for a place that is (1) farther north (2) at the western edge of a time zone and (3) that practices daylight savings time (most places do, but Hawaii, most of Arizona, and Indiana do *not*). Best bets are Michigan, Minnesota, Montana, Washington, and naturally, Alaska.

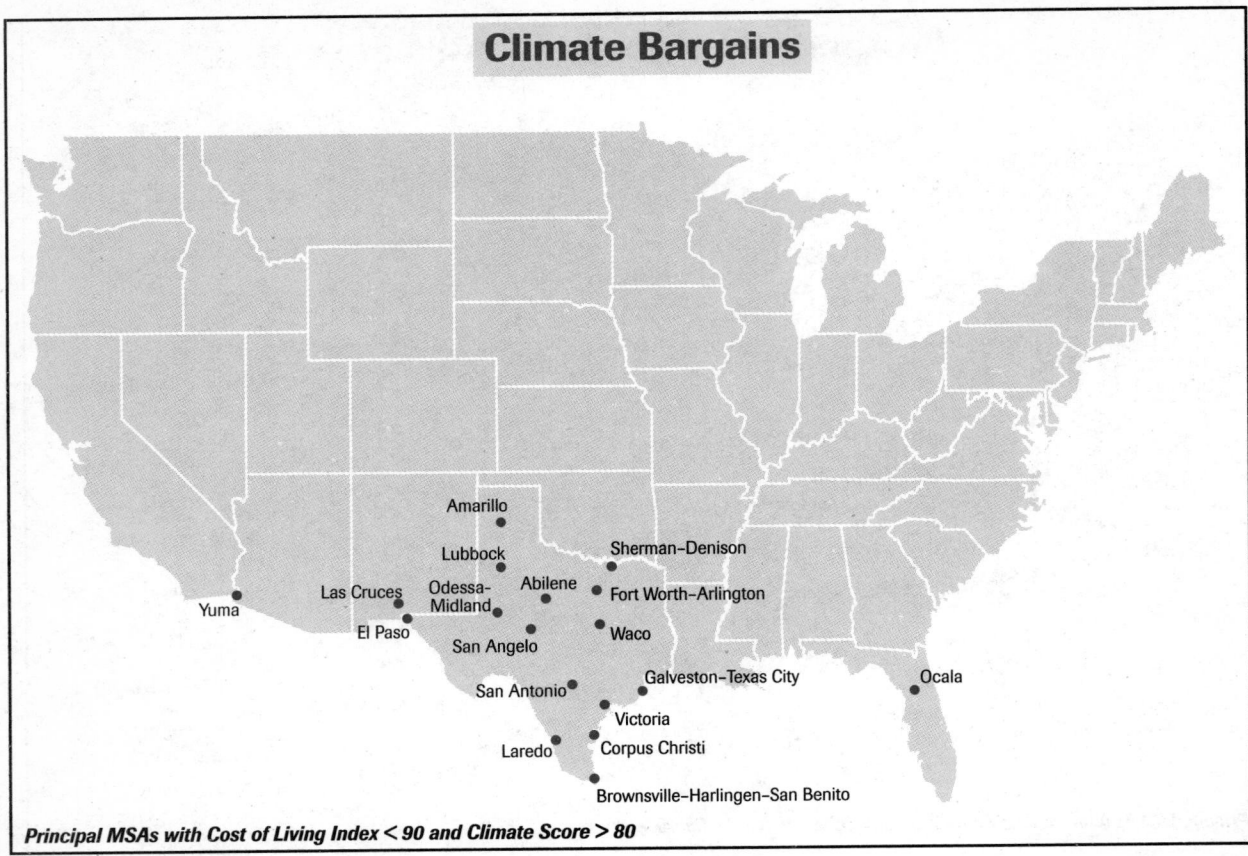

Climate Bargains

Principal MSAs with Cost of Living Index < 90 and Climate Score > 80

patterns, rapid changes, and extreme temperatures. *Steppe* or *semi-arid* climates are higher, drier versions of continental climates, with variable summers, cold winters, and little rain. *Arid* climates are hot and dry, with fewer than 10 inches of precipitation per year. *Marine* climates are found mainly near coastlines, and have less extreme temperatures and are often quite wet. Finally, the *Mediterranean* climate has long, clear, rainless summers and cool, wet winters.

Climate zones are mentioned in the individual metropolitan area descriptions. See Table 4.6 in chapter 4 for more detail on climate zones.

Climate Attributes

The combined attributes of temperature, precipitation, comfort factors, and hazards define a climate. Each of these breaks down into several individual variables. The data source is the U.S. National Climatic Data Center (NCDC) section of the National Oceanic and Atmospheric Administration (NOAA) arm of the Department of Commerce. Most data represents annual averages calculated over as many as 70 years of monthly and daily data observations. For additional climate data, including dew point and wind speed, see www.bestplaces.net/CRAR.

Table 3.21 shows the Climate table for the metropolitan area of Santa Barbara–Santa Maria–Lompoc, California.

THE PROFOUND EFFECT OF ALTITUDE

Altitude has a significant effect on temperature. The metropolitan area with the most days (nights, actually) observed with temperatures below 32°F is not in Minnesota, North Dakota, nor Maine—it is Flagstaff, Arizona! At an altitude of nearly 7,000 feet, Flagstaff experiences temperatures of 32°F or below 210 days a year.

Table 3.21: Sample Climate Table from Santa Barbara–Santa Maria–Lompoc, California

CLIMATE SCORE: 98/RANK: 6

TEMPERATURE	AREA	U.S. AVG	PRECIPITATION	AREA	U.S. AVG	COMFORTS & HAZARDS	AREA	U.S. AVG
January low	38.3°F	26.4°F	Annual inches precipitation	12.0	35.9	July relative humidity	74.0%	68.8%
July high	73.9°F	86.7°F	Annual inches snowfall	0.0	24.2	Annual days mostly sunny	285	212
Annual days > 90°F	6	38	Annual days precipitation	45	111	Annual days with thunderstorms	2	39
Annual days < 32°F	24	88	Annual days rain > 0.5 inches	8	23	Tornado risk score	1	19
Annual days < 0°F	0	6	Annual days snow > 1.5 inches	0	6	Hurricane risk score	0	15

TEMPERATURE

PRECIPITATION

DAYS OF CLOUDS & PRECIPITATION

Temperature

Temperature attributes indicate average temperatures for the periods given.

- *January low* is the average minimum temperature for each day during January. Not surprisingly, average minimums are below zero in North Dakota and parts of Minnesota and in the mid-50s in Florida.

- *July high* is the average maximum temperature for each day during the month of July. These averages range from the mid-60s in Alaska and on the northern California coast to just under 100°F in central Texas and Oklahoma to over 100°F in Phoenix and Yuma, Arizona, and Las Vegas.

- *Annual days > 90°F* is the average number of days per year where the high temperature exceeds 90°F. Places in central California and the desert Southwest top the list with over 100 and up to 164 days, which is almost 1 day in 2.

- *Annual days < 32°F* is the number of days per year with a low temperature below freezing. Topping the list are higher latitude and higher elevation locations such as Flagstaff, Arizona; Reno, Nevada; and Anchorage, Alaska, with as many as 210 days followed by cities in the upper Midwest.

- *Annual days < 0°F* is the number of days (nights, actually) with a low temperature below zero. Bitter cold places include the likely suspects—Grand Forks and Fargo, North Dakota, and Duluth, Minnesota—with 50+ below-zero days per year.

Precipitation

Precipitation attributes indicate the amount and kind of rain and snow.

- *Annual inches precipitation* represents rain and snow combined. Ten inches to 12 inches of snow, on average, equal 1 inch of rain. The U.S. range is 4 inches to 67 inches per year, with Las Vegas the lowest and Gulf Coast cities typically the highest.

- *Annual inches snowfall* is total inches of measurable snowfall each year.

- *Annual days precipitation* is the average number of days per year with at least some measurable rain or snow. Together with *Annual inches precipitation*, this forms a clear climate picture. Cities in the Pacific Northwest, like Bellingham, Washington, and in the eastern Great Lakes, like Erie, Pennsylvania, have high numbers of days with rain, but relatively moderate rainfall totals. This means they receive frequent light rain and drizzle. Cities in the South and Florida have high rainfall totals and relatively moderate days of precipitation, indicating heavy downpours. Annual days precipitation ranges from the 30s in the desert Southwest to the 180s (1 day in 2) in the eastern Great Lakes.

- *Annual days rain > 0.5 inches* shows the number of days with significant rain each year.

- *Annual days snow > 1.5 inches* shows the number of days with significant snowfall accumulation.

Comforts & Hazards

Such factors as presence of sunshine, humidity, and stormy weather combine with temperature to make a place more or less comfortable.

- *July relative humidity* is the moisture content of the air relative to temperature. As air temperature changes, the amount of moisture it can hold also changes. Relative humidity is measured as the amount of moisture present as a percentage of the total amount the air can hold at that temperature. Technical details aside, greater humidity means less comfort. This measure is taken in July when high humidity degrades comfort the most. The most humid places are on the Gulf Coast and up the Atlantic seaboard with 75% to 80% relative humidity, while the desert Southwest and Rocky Mountain areas are driest with 30% to 50% readings.

- *Annual days mostly sunny.* The NCDC tracks the number of days that are sunny or minimally cloudy. Combined with *Annual days precipitation* and *Annual inches precipitation,* a climate picture forms. Because of marine moisture, Pacific Northwest and Great Lakes cities tend to be cloudy, but the rainy day and precipitation totals aren't that high. Michigan cities in particular are extremely cloudy, but not extremely wet. Not surprisingly, desert Southwest and California cities are the sunniest and the driest. Sunny day totals range from the 130s (2 in 3 days are cloudy) in Anchorage, Seattle, and Portland to 300 for Las Vegas.

- *Annual days with thunderstorms* shows the average number of days each year with thunder and lightning present.

- *Tornado risk score* and *Hurricane risk score* reflect the probability and severity of tornados, on a 0–100 scale, based on prevailing meteorological or geophysical patterns and the history of that locality and nearby areas. A place may have a high score even if it has yet to record a damaging tornado or hurricane. Calculations come from Sperling's BestPlaces. For information on such hazards as earthquakes, hail, and wind, see www.bestplaces.net/CRAR.

Charts

Three charts present important climate elements. The first shows average daily temperatures in each month of the year, with average daily minimums and maximums. The second shows annual precipitation, rain and snow, in inches. The third shows annual cloudy days and rainy days.

Climate Rankings

The Climate ranking, which takes all of the category's attributes into consideration, is based on desirable ranges. For example, too much rain or no rain at all is undesirable. *Cities Ranked & Rated* defines a desirable range for rainfall of 20 inches to 30 inches per year. Areas falling within this range receive maximum points. Areas outside the range get reduced points, which are further reduced the farther away the number falls. Table 3.22 shows the desirable ranges used in the rankings.

Table 3.22: Desirable Ranges for Climate Attributes	
Attribute	**Desirable Range**
January low	30°F-60°F
July high	72°F-82°F
Annual days > 90°F	3-10
Annual days < 32°F	0-30
Annual days < 0°F	0
Annual inches precipitation	20-30
Annual inches snowfall	0-24
Annual days precipitation	50-100
July relative humidity	50%-70%
Annual days mostly sunny	250-300

Table 3.23: Winter Temperatures

Average January Lows

MSAs with Warmest Winters			MSAs with Coldest Winters		
Honolulu	HI	65.3°F	Fargo-Moorhead	ND-MN	-3.6°F
Miami	FL	58.7°F	Grand Forks	ND-MN	-3.0°F
Fort Lauderdale	FL	58.7°F	St. Cloud	MN	-1.4°F
Fort Pierce–Port St. Lucie	FL	55.9°F	Bismarck	ND	-1.1°F
West Palm Beach–Boca Raton	FL	55.9°F	Duluth-Superior	MN-WI	-0.6°F
Naples	FL	52.3°F	Wausau	WI	3.1°F
Punta Gorda	FL	52.3°F	Rochester	MN	3.2°F
Fort Myers–Cape Coral	FL	52.3°F	Minneapolis–St. Paul	MN-WI	3.2°F
Lakeland–Winter Haven	FL	51.0°F	La Crosse	WI-MN	3.2°F
Brownsville–Harlingen–San Benito	TX	51.0°F	Eau Claire	WI	3.2°F
Sarasota-Bradenton	FL	50.1°F	Anchorage	AK	3.5°F
Tampa–St. Petersburg–Clearwater	FL	50.1°F	Sioux Falls	SD	3.7°F
Orlando	FL	50.0°F	Iowa City	IA	5.0°F
Gainesville	FL	50.0°F	Green Bay	WI	6.9°F
Ocala	FL	50.0°F	Appleton-Oshkosh-Neenah	WI	6.9°F
Galveston–Texas City	TX	48.3°F	Waterloo–Cedar Falls	IA	6.9°F
Melbourne–Titusville–Palm Bay	FL	47.6°F	Burlington	VT	7.6°F
Daytona Beach	FL	47.6°F	Sioux City	IA-NE	7.7°F
Corpus Christi	TX	46.1°F	Madison	WI	8.2°F
San Diego	CA	45.8°F	Janesville-Beloit	WI	8.2°F
Biloxi-Gulfport-Pascagoula	MS	45.5°F	Dubuque	IA	9.0°F
Los Angeles–Long Beach	CA	45.4°F	Manchester	NH	9.9°F
Orange County	CA	45.4°F	Kankakee	IL	10.0°F
Ventura	CA	45.4°F	Rapid City	SD	10.0°F
Jacksonville	FL	44.5°F	Bangor	ME	10.2°F
Riverside–San Bernardino	CA	44.4°F	Lewiston-Auburn	ME	11.0°F
McAllen-Edinburg-Mission	TX	43.6°F	Great Falls	MT	11.0°F
New Orleans	LA	43.5°F	Des Moines	IA	11.3°F
Houma	LA	43.5°F	Milwaukee-Waukesha	WI	11.4°F
Pensacola	FL	43.0°F	Sheboygan	WI	11.4°F

Source: U.S. National Climatic Data Center

Table 3.24: Summer Temperatures

Average July Highs

MSAs with Hottest Summers			MSAs with Coolest Summers		
Yuma	AZ	104.8°F	Anchorage	AK	65.6°F
Phoenix-Mesa	AZ	104.8°F	Oakland	CA	69.7°F
Las Vegas	NV-AZ	103.9°F	Santa Cruz–Watsonville	CA	73.6°F
Bryan–College Station	TX	99.2°F	San Francisco	CA	73.6°F
Wichita Falls	TX	99.2°F	Salinas	CA	73.6°F
Killeen-Temple	TX	99.2°F	San Luis Obispo–Atascadero–Paso Robles	CA	73.9°F
Bakersfield	CA	99.1°F	Santa Barbara–Santa Maria–Lompoc	CA	73.9°F
Lawton	OK	99.1°F	Bellingham	WA	75.1°F
Tucson	AZ	98.3°F	Bremerton	WA	75.1°F
Fresno	CA	98.2°F	Seattle-Bellevue-Everett	WA	75.1°F
Visalia-Tulare-Porterville	CA	98.2°F	Tacoma	WA	75.1°F
Redding	CA	98.0°F	Los Angeles–Long Beach	CA	75.8°F
Chico-Paradise	CA	96.5°F	Orange County	CA	75.8°F
Waco	TX	96.2°F	Ventura	CA	75.8°F
Sherman-Denison	TX	96.1°F	Duluth-Superior	MN-WI	76.4°F
Dallas	TX	96.1°F	Wausau	WI	77.0°F
San Antonio	TX	95.9°F	San Diego	CA	77.3°F
Laredo	TX	95.9°F	Erie	PA	77.4°F
Austin–San Marcos	TX	95.9°F	Jamestown	NY	77.4°F
Fort Worth–Arlington	TX	95.5°F	Bangor	ME	77.5°F
Abilene	TX	95.3°F	Lewiston-Auburn	ME	78.0°F
Odessa-Midland	TX	95.0°F	Olympia	WA	78.4°F
San Angelo	TX	95.0°F	Binghamton	NY	78.5°F
El Paso	TX	94.9°F	San Jose	CA	78.6°F
Corpus Christi	TX	94.8°F	Portland-Vancouver	OR-WA	79.0°F
Stockton-Lodi	CA	94.7°F	Elmira	NY	79.0°F
Modesto	CA	94.7°F	Portsmouth-Rochester	NH-ME	79.1°F
Merced	CA	94.7°F	Portland	ME	79.1°F
Houston	TX	94.3°F	Nashua	NH	79.4°F
Brazoria	TX	94.3°F	Worcester	MA-CT	79.4°F

Source: U.S. National Climatic Data Center

Table 3.25: Temperature Extremes

Number of Days Per Year with Extreme Temperatures

Days > 90°F

City	State	Days
Yuma	AZ	164
Phoenix-Mesa	AZ	164
Tucson	AZ	139
Las Vegas	NV-AZ	131
San Antonio	TX	111
Laredo	TX	111
Bakersfield	CA	110
San Angelo	TX	109
Fresno	CA	107
Visalia-Tulare-Porterville	CA	107
Bryan-College Station	TX	106
Wichita Falls	TX	106
Killeen-Temple	TX	106
Naples	FL	106
Punta Gorda	FL	106
Fort Myers-Cape Coral	FL	106
Waco	TX	105
Victoria	TX	105
Orlando	FL	104
Gainesville	FL	104
Ocala	FL	104
El Paso	TX	103
Brownsville-Harlingen-San Benito	TX	102
Austin-San Marcos	TX	101
McAllen-Edinburg-Mission	TX	101
Redding	CA	98
Corpus Christi	TX	96
Odessa-Midland	TX	92
Fort Worth-Arlington	TX	92
Chico-Paradise	CA	92

Days < 32°F

City	State	Days
Flagstaff	AZ-UT	210
Anchorage	AK	192
Reno	NV	189
Duluth-Superior	MN-WI	187
Bismarck	ND	186
Casper	WY	183
Cheyenne	WY	181
Fargo-Moorhead	ND-MN	180
Grand Forks	ND-MN	178
St. Cloud	MN	176
Manchester	NH	171
Sioux Falls	SD	170
Wausau	WI	169
Rapid City	SD	167
Missoula	MT	166
Pocatello	ID	164
Madison	WI	164
Janesville-Beloit	WI	163
Boulder-Longmont	CO	163
Denver	CO	163
Fort Collins-Loveland	CO	163
Greeley	CO	163
Green Bay	WI	163
Appleton-Oshkosh-Neenah	WI	162
Burlington	VT	160
Colorado Springs	CO	160
Portsmouth-Rochester	NH-ME	159
Portland	ME	158
Waterloo-Cedar Falls	IA	157
Rochester	MN	156

Days < 0°F

City	State	Days
Bismarck	ND	56
Grand Forks	ND-MN	55
Fargo-Moorhead	ND-MN	54
Duluth-Superior	MN-WI	51
St. Cloud	MN	46
Anchorage	AK	41
Wausau	WI	38
Rochester	MN	34
Minneapolis-St. Paul	MN-WI	34
La Crosse	WI-MN	34
Eau Claire	WI	34
Sioux Falls	SD	33
Rapid City	SD	31
Waterloo-Cedar Falls	IA	31
Green Bay	WI	29
Appleton-Oshkosh-Neenah	WI	29
Iowa City	IA	29
Burlington	VT	28
Great Falls	MT	28
Manchester	NH	26
Madison	WI	25
Janesville-Beloit	WI	25
Missoula	MT	24
Casper	WY	22
Cheyenne	WY	22
Sioux City	IA-NE	22
Billings	MT	18
Dubuque	IA	18
Lewiston-Auburn	ME	18
Dutchess County	NY	17

Source: U.S. National Climatic Data Center

Table 3.26: Annual Inches Precipitation

Average Total Precipitation (Rain and Snowmelt) in Inches

Wettest MSAs			Driest MSAs		
Mobile	AL	67.0	Las Vegas	NV-AZ	4.0
Pensacola	FL	64.2	Bakersfield	CA	6.0
Panama City	FL	64.2	Reno	NV	7.0
Fort Walton Beach	FL	64.2	Yuma	AZ	7.0
Fort Pierce–Port St. Lucie	FL	62.1	Phoenix-Mesa	AZ	7.0
West Palm Beach–Boca Raton	FL	62.1	Las Cruces	NM	8.0
Tallahassee	FL	62.0	Richland-Kennewick-Pasco	WA	8.0
Albany	GA	62.0	Yakima	WA	8.0
Miami	FL	60.0	Albuquerque	NM	8.0
Fort Lauderdale	FL	60.0	El Paso	TX	8.0
Biloxi-Gulfport-Pascagoula	MS	59.0	Grand Junction	CO	9.0
New Orleans	LA	57.0	San Diego	CA	9.0
Houma	LA	57.0	Fresno	CA	10.0
Lake Charles	LA	55.5	Visalia-Tulare-Porterville	CA	10.0
Beaumont–Port Arthur	TX	55.1	Tucson	AZ	11.0
Baton Rouge	LA	54.1	Pueblo	CO	11.9
Lafayette	LA	54.1	Casper	WY	12.0
Auburn-Opelika	AL	54.0	Cheyenne	WY	12.0
Wilmington	NC	54.0	Pocatello	ID	12.0
Greenville	NC	54.0	Boise City	ID	12.0
Myrtle Beach	SC	54.0	San Luis Obispo–Atascadero–Paso Robles	CA	12.0
Jacksonville	NC	54.0	Santa Barbara–Santa Maria–Lompoc	CA	12.0
Alexandria	LA	54.0	Riverside–San Bernardino	CA	12.0
Jacksonville	FL	54.0	Los Angeles–Long Beach	CA	12.0
Naples	FL	54.0	Orange County	CA	12.0
Punta Gorda	FL	54.0	Ventura	CA	12.0
Fort Myers–Cape Coral	FL	54.0	Odessa-Midland	TX	13.5
Anniston	AL	53.0	Anchorage	AK	14.0
Birmingham	AL	53.0	Billings	MT	14.0
Gadsden	AL	53.0	Modesto	CA	14.2

Source: U.S. National Climatic Data Center

Table 3.27: Snowiest Metropolitan Areas

MSAs by Annual Inches Snowfall

Syracuse	NY	109.0
Utica-Rome	NY	109.0
Flagstaff	AZ-UT	99.0
Bangor	ME	95.0
Buffalo–Niagara Falls	NY	90.0
Rochester	NY	88.4
Binghamton	NY	86.0
Erie	PA	83.6
Jamestown	NY	83.6
Elmira	NY	82.0
Casper	WY	81.0
Cheyenne	WY	81.0
Burlington	VT	79.0
Duluth-Superior	MN-WI	78.0
Kalamazoo–Battle Creek	MI	77.0
Grand Rapids–Muskegon–Holland	MI	77.0
Nashua	NH	75.0
Worcester	MA-CT	75.0
Fitchburg-Leominster	MA	75.0
Portsmouth-Rochester	NH-ME	74.0
Portland	ME	74.0
Pittsfield	MA	73.0
Dutchess County	NY	71.0
Newburgh	NY-PA	71.0
Albany-Schenectady-Troy	NY	71.0
Glens Falls	NY	71.0
Lewiston-Auburn	ME	71.0
Anchorage	AK	70.0
Manchester	NH	64.0
Great Falls	MT	63.0

Source: U.S. National Climatic Data Center

Table 3.28: Annual Days of Precipitation

Average Number of Days of Measurable Precipitation Each Year

MSAs with Highest Number of Days			MSAs with Lowest Number of Days		
Erie	PA	188	Las Vegas	NV-AZ	24
Jamestown	NY	188	Yuma	AZ	34
Wausau	WI	185	Phoenix-Mesa	AZ	34
Rochester	NY	182	Riverside–San Bernardino	CA	35
Youngstown-Warren	OH	181	Los Angeles–Long Beach	CA	35
Sharon	PA	181	Ventura	CA	35
Saginaw–Bay City–Midland	MI	181	Santa Fe	NM	36
Syracuse	NY	168	Bakersfield	CA	36
Utica-Rome	NY	168	Orange County	CA	40
Buffalo–Niagara Falls	NY	168	San Diego	CA	41
Canton-Massillon	OH	168	Fresno	CA	44
Tacoma	WA	164	Visalia-Tulare-Porterville	CA	44
Binghamton	NY	163	El Paso	TX	45
Olympia	WA	163	San Luis Obispo–Atascadero–Paso Robles	CA	45
Bellingham	WA	160	Santa Barbara–Santa Maria–Lompoc	CA	45
Bremerton	WA	160	San Jose	CA	47
Seattle-Bellevue-Everett	WA	160	Santa Rosa	CA	47
Elmira	NY	159	Vallejo-Fairfield-Napa	CA	47
Cleveland-Lorain-Elyria	OH	156	Reno	NV	49
Lansing–East Lansing	MI	156	Tucson	AZ	50
Jackson	MI	156	Modesto	CA	52
Williamsport	PA	156	Merced	CA	52
Burlington	VT	153	Stockton-Lodi	CA	52
Scranton–Wilkes-Barre–Hazleton	PA	153	Las Cruces	NM	53
Akron	OH	153	Odessa-Midland	TX	53
Steubenville-Weirton	OH-WV	152	Sacramento	CA	57
Pittsburgh	PA	152	San Angelo	TX	58
Wheeling	WV-OH	152	Albuquerque	NM	59
Mansfield	OH	152	Lubbock	TX	60
Lima	OH	152	Yolo	CA	60

Source: U.S. National Climatic Data Center

Table 3.29: Summer Humidity

Average July Relative Humidity as a Percent

Most Humid MSAs			Least Humid MSAs		
Beaumont–Port Arthur	TX	79%	Las Vegas	NV-AZ	29%
Galveston–Texas City	TX	78%	Flagstaff	AZ-UT	36%
Lake Charles	LA	78%	Yuma	AZ	36%
Daytona Beach	FL	78%	Phoenix-Mesa	AZ	36%
Melbourne–Titusville–Palm Bay	FL	78%	Tucson	AZ	38%
Brazoria	TX	77%	El Paso	TX	39%
Houston	TX	77%	Albuquerque	NM	43%
Asheville	NC	77%	Grand Junction	CO	47%
Alexandria	LA	77%	Cheyenne	WY	49%
Biloxi-Gulfport-Pascagoula	MS	77%	Casper	WY	49%
Corpus Christi	TX	77%	Colorado Springs	CO	49%
New Orleans	LA	77%	Las Cruces	NM	49%
Houma	LA	77%	Reno	NV	50%
Saginaw–Bay City–Midland	MI	76%	Pueblo	CO	50%
New Bedford	MA	76%	Tulsa	OK	52%
Barnstable-Yarmouth	MA	76%	Redding	CA	52%
Charleston–North Charleston	SC	76%	Bakersfield	CA	52%
Tallahassee	FL	76%	Boulder-Longmont	CO	53%
Albany	GA	76%	Denver	CO	53%
Brownsville–Harlingen–San Benito	TX	76%	Fort Collins–Loveland	CO	53%
Oakland	CA	76%	Greeley	CO	53%
Naples	FL	76%	Odessa-Midland	TX	53%
Punta Gorda	FL	76%	Santa Fe	NM	53%
Fort Myers–Cape Coral	FL	76%	Provo-Orem	UT	54%
Elmira	NY	75%	Salt Lake City–Ogden	UT	54%
Jackson	MS	75%	Billings	MT	55%
Hattiesburg	MS	75%	Amarillo	TX	55%
Wilmington	NC	75%	Missoula	MT	56%
Greenville	NC	75%	Lubbock	TX	56%
Myrtle Beach	SC	75%	Boise City	ID	57%

Source: U.S. National Climatic Data Center

Table 3.30: Days of Sunshine

Average Annual Days Mostly Sunny					
Cloudiest MSAs			**Sunniest MSAs**		
Anchorage	AK	131	Las Vegas	NV-AZ	300
Tacoma	WA	136	Yuma	AZ	295
Bellingham	WA	136	Phoenix-Mesa	AZ	295
Bremerton	WA	136	Riverside–San Bernardino	CA	268
Seattle-Bellevue-Everett	WA	136	Los Angeles–Long Beach	CA	258
Olympia	WA	137	Ventura	CA	258
Portland-Vancouver	OR-WA	137	Santa Fe	NM	283
Binghamton	NY	151	Bakersfield	CA	281
Elmira	NY	151	Orange County	CA	258
Corvallis	OR	153	San Diego	CA	267
Eugene-Springfield	OR	158	Fresno	CA	271
Missoula	MT	158	Visalia-Tulare-Porterville	CA	271
Buffalo–Niagara Falls	NY	159	El Paso	TX	294
Salem	OR	159	San Luis Obispo–Atascadero–Paso Robles	CA	285
Erie	PA	161	Santa Barbara–Santa Maria–Lompoc	CA	285
Jamestown	NY	161	San Jose	CA	257
Burlington	VT	161	Santa Rosa	CA	285
Steubenville-Weirton	OH-WV	161	Vallejo-Fairfield-Napa	CA	285
Pittsburgh	PA	161	Reno	NV	255
Wheeling	WV-OH	161	Tucson	AZ	287
Saginaw–Bay City–Midland	MI	163	Modesto	CA	261
Kalamazoo–Battle Creek	MI	163	Merced	CA	261
Grand Rapids–Muskegon–Holland	MI	163	Stockton-Lodi	CA	261
Youngstown-Warren	OH	164	Las Cruces	NM	287
Sharon	PA	164	Odessa-Midland	TX	263
Syracuse	NY	164	Sacramento	CA	265
Utica-Rome	NY	164	San Angelo	TX	254
Charleston	WV	166	Albuquerque	NM	283
Huntington-Ashland	WV-KY-OH	166	Lubbock	TX	267
Cleveland-Lorain-Elyria	OH	168	Yolo	CA	276

Source: U.S. National Climatic Data Center

Education

The Education category encompasses both primary/secondary schooling and post-secondary—college and post-graduate—schooling for young and older adults. The importance of education is obvious for families with school-age children, but the level of educational attainment and the quality of education affects the lifestyle and quality of life of everyone in an area.

Although recent legislation and trends appear to be having a positive effect, large gaps still exist in the quality of public, primary, and secondary education among schools, nationally and locally. Unfortunately, quality of primary and secondary education has traditionally been difficult to assess. School comparisons have generally been based on process measures, such as investment (expenditures), numbers of schools and teachers, and student-teacher ratios, rather than results measures. Recent legislation and trends have led to a greater use of testing, some standardized, to determine student achievement and school performance, but these programs are still in the implementation phase. Primary school testing is not scheduled for completion until the 2005–2006 academic year for basic reading, math, and language arts. Even if testing were fully implemented and successfully executed, many believe that because education involves experiences beyond academics and testing, these newer assessments will never be adequate.

Readers wishing a more complete picture of education may want to go to the U.S. Department of Education National Center for Education Statistics website (www.nces.ed.gov) for a broad array of statistics and studies on both a national and local level. The website www.bestplaces.net/CRAR provides thousands of profiles of public and private schools from the primary through university levels.

Education Trends

No discussion of trends in primary/secondary public education would be complete without an overview of the No Child Left Behind Act passed in January 2002. Born out of frustration over a long history of increased educational spending with little corresponding improvement, and of the indicated success of such programs on a smaller scale in some states, the Bush Administration made this Act a priority. In the words of Rod Paige, Secretary, U.S. Department of Education, the Act calls for sweeping changes, giving " . . . states and school districts unprecedented flexibility in how they spend their education dollars, in return for setting standards for student achievement and holding students and educators accountable for results." In addition, it allows more flexibility for parents of children from disadvantaged backgrounds and an emphasis on teaching methods and teacher education. States are required to do annual assessments of reading and math in the third through eighth grades, and results will be used to direct resources and recognize schools with outstanding performance (the top 10% are known as "Blue Ribbon" schools). Schools that fail will get additional assistance and face restructuring if they can't meet standards. The ramifications of this program are potentially enormous and will eventually result in more meaningful data on the quality of public education, particularly academic achievement. The U.S. Department of Education showcases the Act at its general website (www.ed.gov) and at a separate site (www.nclb.gov). The NCLB National Assessment of Education Progress website (http://nces.ed.gov/nationsreportcard/states) provides more about state and local educational achievement under the Act.

Despite the increased focus on quality and results, the amount of investment per pupil has leveled off or increased only modestly over the past 10 years. Student/teacher ratios have actually declined, although this might be misleading due to the increased numbers of special educators with relatively small numbers of students.

The higher education landscape has experienced more gradual change. One enduring trend is the increased cost of higher education, aggravated recently by persistent and growing state budget deficits. Another trend is increased enrollment, particularly for students just out of high school. While high school graduation rates have increased only from 85% in the early 1970s to 88% in 2001, the percentage of high school students going straight to college has risen from 57% to 67%. Fifty-eight percent of 25- to 29-year-olds have completed some college education, up from 34% in the early '70s. Another trend is the increased presence of women on college campuses, particularly in graduate programs, where women now outnumber men.

Education Attributes

Cities Ranked & Rated presents data in the categories of *Achievement, Public Schools,* and *Higher Education.* All of the attributes except SAT/ACT scores are used in scoring and ranking. Due to varying data validity and influence on the true educational climate, the attributes are weighed differently. *Cities Ranked & Rated* gives the highest weighting to high school, 4-year college, and graduate degree attainment; ratio of public to private schools; number of 4-year colleges; and number of highly ranked institutions. Lower weights are given to expenditures per pupil (because of problems cited below) and 2-year college attainment.

Table 3.31 shows the Education table for the metropolitan area of Honolulu, Hawaii.

Achievement

Achievement represents student learning as reflected in the attainment of various levels of education. Data comes from the U.S. Census Bureau.

- *High school degree* shows the percentage of the population completing high school and earning a diploma. In the United States, the overall high school completion rate is 88% (2001), but large variations exist among metropolitan areas. The percentage range is in the mid-50s to low-60s in the rural south and large inner city areas like Los Angeles and Newark, New Jersey, up to the mid-90s in college towns like Ann Arbor, Michigan, and Iowa City, Iowa.

Table 3.31: Sample Education Table from Honolulu, Hawaii

EDUCATION SCORE: 54/RANK: 151

ACHIEVEMENT	AREA	U.S. AVG	PUBLIC SCHOOLS	AREA	U.S. AVG	HIGHER EDUCATION	AREA	U.S. AVG
High school degree	83.4%	80.2%	Expenditures per pupil	$5,859	$5,894	No. 2-year colleges	6	3
2-year college degree	6.8%	6.2%	Student/teacher ratio	17.3	16.7	No. 4-year colleges/universities	4	4
4-year college degree	18.9%	15.8%	Attending public school	82.3%	90.2%	No. highly ranked universities	1	1
Graduate/professional degree	9.0%	9.6%	State SAT score	1002*	1020			
			State ACT score	21.8	21.0			

- *2-year college degree* attainment ranges from 2.5% to 11% among metropolitan areas. There is no real pattern other than that both high and low figures tend to be in small towns. Figures are probably driven by the relative availability of 2-year and 4-year programs and the local job market.

- *4-year college degree* attainment ranges widely from 5% to 35% among metropolitan areas. The highest percentages tend to be in college towns and wealthier areas like Orange County, California, and Naples, Florida, with lower figures in working-class towns such as Reading, Pennsylvania; Gary, Indiana; and Lima, Ohio.

- *Graduate/professional degree* attainment is similar to 4-year degrees, with 25% to 40% rates in college towns and 2% to 3% in working-class towns.

Public Schools

Data in the first three categories comes from the National Center for Education Statistics in the U.S. Department of Education. SAT and ACT scores come from the College Board, Inc., and the American College Testing Service, Inc.

- *Expenditures per pupil* is widely used, although its meaning has been diluted by numerous changes and inconsistencies in calculation (for instance, does it include administrative costs?) and an increased emphasis on achievement and results. Nevertheless, there are notable differences, ranging from $10,000 to $15,000 per student per year in big eastern cities to $4,000 to $5,000 in small, Midwestern and southern towns with Utah at the bottom. To some degree these figures reflect cost of living through teacher salaries.

- *Student/teacher ratio*, like *Expenditures per pupil*, has seen changes and inconsistencies in calculation; however, it is still a benchmark for school districts and metropolitan areas. Lower figures in large inner cities or small towns can be misleading because the presence of special educators distorts figures by their abundance in inner cities or by the relative lack of students in smaller towns. The higher ratios are from 22 to 30 in Texas (probably a matter of deliberate policy), Southern California, and New Jersey. Lower figures of 10 to 12 occur in smaller towns and some college towns.

- *Attending public school* is the percentage of total elementary and secondary students enrolled in public schools. A lower percentage reflects greater parental apathy about public schools, although there are other significant factors, such as household affluence, strength of religious affiliations, and the availability of parochial and private schools. This statistic ranges from 69% (Dubuque, Iowa) to almost 99% (Decatur, Alabama) with no strong geographic pattern.

- *State SAT score* and *State ACT score* are state averages, with an asterisk (*) denoting the test emphasized in that state. See "Education" in chapter 4 for details on SAT and ACT scores and their correct interpretation.

Higher Education

This data includes the number and quality of colleges and universities in an area. The presence of such facilities tells something of the educational opportunity, climate, and amenities available in an area. Interestingly, higher education facilities are present in all but 3 of the 331 metropolitan areas: San Angelo, Texas; Racine, Wisconsin; and Punta Gorda, Florida. Data in the first two categories comes from the National Center for Education Statistics in the U.S. Department of Education. *No. highly ranked universities* data comes from a Princeton Review study.

- *No. 2-year colleges.* Most cities have at least some 2-year college presence. There are 8 to 15 such colleges, public and private, in medium-size cities and 15 up to 28 in some of the largest urban centers.

- *No. 4-year colleges/universities.* The definition of 4-year colleges and universities is fairly broad and includes branch campuses of larger universities. All but 28 metro areas have at least some 4-year college presence. There is 1 facility in 110 metro areas and 10 or more in 33 areas.

- *No. highly ranked universities.* This measure counts the number of educational institutions judged by the Princeton Review facilities as having selective admissions standards based on test score requirements and percentage of applicants admitted. This statistic is fairly selective: 195 metro areas have no such facilities, 81 have one, and 42 have two or three. Boston, Massachusetts, has by far the most with 15.

Table 3.32: High School Graduation Rate

Percent of Population with High School Degrees

MSAs with Highest Graduation Rate			MSAs with Lowest Graduation Rate		
Iowa City	IA	93.7%	McAllen-Edinburg-Mission	TX	50.4%
Corvallis	OR	93.1%	Laredo	TX	53.0%
Boulder-Longmont	CO	92.8%	Brownsville-Harlingen-San Benito	TX	55.2%
Lawrence	KS	92.4%	Visalia-Tulare-Porterville	CA	61.7%
Fort Collins-Loveland	CO	92.3%	Merced	CA	63.8%
Madison	WI	92.2%	El Paso	TX	65.8%
Barnstable-Yarmouth	MA	91.8%	Yuma	AZ	65.8%
Colorado Springs	CO	91.2%	Houma	LA	66.7%
Rochester	MN	91.1%	Fresno	CA	67.2%
Champaign-Urbana	IL	91.0%	Danville	VA	67.8%
Missoula	MT	91.0%	Miami	FL	67.9%
Provo-Orem	UT	90.9%	Salinas	CA	68.4%
Bremerton	WA	90.8%	Bakersfield	CA	68.5%
Bloomington-Normal	IL	90.7%	Vineland-Millville-Bridgeton	NJ	68.5%
Cedar Rapids	IA	90.6%	Yakima	WA	68.7%
Minneapolis-St. Paul	MN-WI	90.6%	Los Angeles-Long Beach	CA	69.9%
Lincoln	NE	90.5%	Las Cruces	NM	70.0%
Anchorage	AK	90.3%	Hickory-Morganton	NC	70.3%
Portland	ME	90.1%	Modesto	CA	70.4%
Seattle-Bellevue-Everett	WA	90.1%	Jersey City	NJ	70.5%
Ann Arbor	MI	90.0%	Stockton-Lodi	CA	71.2%
Fargo-Moorhead	ND-MN	89.7%	Lafayette	LA	71.3%
Olympia	WA	89.5%	Rocky Mount	NC	71.8%
Columbia	MO	89.2%	Yuba City	CA	72.5%
Cheyenne	WY	89.1%	Florence	SC	73.1%
Spokane	WA	89.1%	Johnson City-Kingsport-Bristol	TN-VA	73.3%
La Crosse	WI-MN	89.0%	Odessa-Midland	TX	73.6%
Des Moines	IA	88.6%	Decatur	AL	73.8%
Lansing-East Lansing	MI	88.6%	Anniston	AL	73.9%
Sioux Falls	SD	88.6%	Corpus Christi	TX	73.9%

Source: U.S. National Center for Education Statistics, 2002

Table 3.33: Combined College & Graduate Degree Attainment

Percent of Population with 4-Year or Graduate Degree as Highest Level of Attainment

MSAs with Most Degrees			MSAs with Fewest Degrees		
Boulder-Longmont	CO	52.4%	Merced	CA	11.0%
Iowa City	IA	47.6%	Danville	VA	11.3%
Corvallis	OR	47.4%	Visalia-Tulare-Porterville	CA	11.5%
San Francisco	CA	43.6%	Vineland-Millville-Bridgeton	NJ	11.8%
Lowell	MA-NH	43.1%	Mansfield	OH	11.8%
Lawrence	KS	42.7%	Yuma	AZ	11.9%
Washington	DC-MD-VA-WV	41.8%	Steubenville-Weirton	OH-WV	12.0%
Columbia	MO	41.8%	Houma	LA	12.3%
Madison	WI	40.6%	Johnstown	PA	12.8%
San Jose	CA	40.4%	McAllen-Edinburg-Mission	TX	12.9%
Charlottesville	VA	40.0%	Yuba City	CA	13.2%
Santa Fe	NM	39.9%	Brownsville-Harlingen-San Benito	TX	13.3%
Stamford-Norwalk	CT	39.8%	Gadsden	AL	13.4%
Bloomington	IN	39.6%	Cumberland	MD-WV	13.4%
Fort Collins-Loveland	CO	39.5%	Bakersfield	CA	13.5%
Raleigh-Durham-Chapel Hill	NC	39.0%	Lima	OH	13.5%
Gainesville	FL	38.7%	Ocala	FL	13.7%
Champaign-Urbana	IL	38.0%	Hickory-Morganton	NC	13.7%
Danbury	CT	37.8%	Fort Smith	AR-OK	13.8%
Middlesex-Somerset-Hunterdon	NJ	37.4%	Laredo	TX	13.9%
Bryan-College Station	TX	37.0%	Rocky Mount	NC	13.9%
Bridgeport	CT	36.9%	Altoona	PA	13.9%
Ann Arbor	MI	36.9%	Modesto	CA	14.0%
Austin-San Marcos	TX	36.7%	Huntington-Ashland	WV-KY-OH	14.4%
Tallahassee	FL	36.7%	Lewiston-Auburn	ME	14.4%
State College	PA	36.3%	Stockton-Lodi	CA	14.6%
Bloomington-Normal	IL	36.2%	Hagerstown	MD	14.6%
Seattle-Bellevue-Everett	WA	35.8%	Wheeling	WV-OH	14.6%
Oakland	CA	35.0%	Beaumont-Port Arthur	TX	14.7%
Burlington	VT	34.9%	Jacksonville	NC	14.7%

Source: U.S. National Center for Education Statistics, 2002

Table 3.34: Public School Investment

Annual Expenditures Per Student

MSAs with Highest Expenditures			MSAs with Lowest Expenditures		
Nassau-Suffolk	NY	$11,562	Provo-Orem	UT	$3,767
Stamford-Norwalk	CT	$10,497	San Diego	CA	$3,863
Bergen-Passaic	NJ	$10,178	Jackson	MI	$4,273
Newark	NJ	$10,159	Joplin	MO	$4,290
Jersey City	NJ	$9,928	Hattiesburg	MS	$4,331
Trenton	NJ	$9,802	Montgomery	AL	$4,443
Vineland-Millville-Bridgeton	NJ	$9,540	Biloxi-Gulfport-Pascagoula	MS	$4,455
Middlesex-Somerset-Hunterdon	NJ	$9,491	Phoenix-Mesa	AZ	$4,500
Monmouth-Ocean	NJ	$8,943	Jonesboro	AR	$4,534
Atlantic City–Cape May	NJ	$8,916	Mobile	AL	$4,542
New London–Norwich	CT-RI	$8,755	Oklahoma City	OK	$4,582
New York	NY	$8,640	Boise	ID	$4,582
Buffalo–Niagara Falls	NY	$8,605	Bismarck	ND	$4,586
Dutchess County	NY	$8,487	Pocatello	ID	$4,588
Hartford	CT	$8,452	Yuma	AZ	$4,595
Rochester	NY	$8,436	St. Joseph	MO	$4,610
New Haven–Meriden	CT	$8,417	Tucson	AZ	$4,632
Albany-Schenectady-Troy	NY	$8,386	Tulsa	OK	$4,635
Bridgeport	CT	$8,319	Enid	OK	$4,651
Utica-Rome	NY	$8,222	Anniston	AL	$4,671
Danbury	CT	$8,149	Fayetteville-Springdale-Rogers	AR	$4,671
Waterbury	CT	$8,141	Lafayette	IN	$4,678
Elmira	NY	$8,130	Rapid City	SD	$4,715
Jamestown	NY	$8,070	Monroe	LA	$4,720
Newburgh	NY-PA	$8,065	Decatur	IL	$4,747
Boston	MA-NH-ME	$8,055	Jacksonville	FL	$4,754
Syracuse	NY	$8,011	Clarksville-Hopkinsville	TN-KY	$4,757
Binghamton	NY	$7,886	Springfield	IL	$4,780
St. Louis	MO-IL	$7,802	Modesto	CA	$4,784
Milwaukee-Waukesha	WI	$7,697	Odessa-Midland	TX	$4,789

Source: U.S. National Center for Education Statistics, 2002

Table 3.35: Student/Teacher Ratios

Average Class Size

MSAs with Best Ratios			MSAs with Worst Ratios		
Burlington	VT	10.4	Provo-Orem	UT	24.0
Jamestown	NY	12.4	San Diego	CA	22.9
Providence–Fall River–Warwick	RI-MA	12.6	Orange County	CA	22.9
Charlottesville	VA	12.7	Anchorage	AK	22.5
Stamford-Norwalk	CT	12.7	Santa Cruz–Watsonville	CA	22.4
Vineland-Millville-Bridgeton	NJ	12.8	Riverside–San Bernardino	CA	22.4
Atlantic City–Cape May	NJ	12.8	Ventura	CA	22.4
New London–Norwich	CT-RI	13.2	Los Angeles–Long Beach	CA	22.1
Abilene	TX	13.3	Sacramento	CA	21.6
Binghamton	NY	13.3	Modesto	CA	21.6
Asheville	NC	13.7	San Luis Obispo–Atascadero–Paso Robles	CA	21.4
Rochester	NY	13.7	San Antonio	TX	21.4
Victoria	TX	13.8	Redding	CA	21.4
Wichita Falls	TX	13.8	Fresno	CA	21.2
Louisville	KY-IN	13.9	Merced	CA	21.1
Roanoke	VA	13.9	Corvallis	OR	21.1
Danbury	CT	13.9	Fort Lauderdale	FL	21.1
Madison	WI	13.9	Vallejo-Fairfield-Napa	CA	21.1
New Haven–Meriden	CT	14.0	Visalia-Tulare-Porterville	CA	20.9
Hartford	CT	14.0	Stockton-Lodi	CA	20.9
Lewiston-Auburn	ME	14.0	Santa Rosa	CA	20.9
Longview-Marshall	TX	14.1	Oakland	CA	20.9
Lincoln	NE	14.1	Bakersfield	CA	20.8
Chattanooga	TN-GA	14.1	Yuma	AZ	20.8
Sioux Falls	SD	14.1	Eugene-Springfield	OR	20.7
Texarkana	TX-AR	14.1	Las Vegas	NV-AZ	20.6
Memphis	TN-AR-MS	14.2	Yuba City–Marysville	CA	20.6
Norfolk–Virginia Beach–Newport News	VA-NC	14.3	Chico-Paradise	CA	20.5
Jackson	TN	14.3	Sherman-Denison	TX	20.4
Lubbock	TX	14.3	Springfield	MO	20.3

Source: U.S. National Center for Education Statistics, 2002

Table 3.36: Public School Utilization

Percentage of Students Attending Public School					
MSAs with Highest % in Public School			MSAs with Lowest % in Public School		
Decatur	AL	98.5%	Dubuque	IA	69.2%
Provo-Orem	UT	98.4%	New Orleans	LA	75.4%
McAllen-Edinburg-Mission	TX	97.8%	San Francisco	CA	77.2%
Naples	FL	97.6%	Wilmington-Newark	DE-MD	78.5%
Yuma	AZ	97.6%	Philadelphia	PA-NJ	78.9%
Lawton	OK	97.5%	Erie	PA	79.7%
Brazoria	TX	97.3%	Louisville	KY-IN	79.8%
Sherman-Denison	TX	97.2%	Cincinnati	OH-KY-IN	80.1%
Glens Falls	NY	97.1%	New York	NY	80.3%
Fresno	CA	97.1%	Milwaukee-Waukesha	WI	80.7%
Brockton	MA	97.1%	Lancaster	PA	81.0%
Abilene	TX	97.0%	Lafayette	LA	81.1%
Hickory-Morganton-Lenoir	NC	97.0%	St. Louis	MO-IL	81.4%
Texarkana	TX-AR	97.0%	Jersey City	NJ	81.8%
Jacksonville	NC	96.8%	Scranton–Wilkes-Barre–Hazleton	PA	82.0%
Las Cruces	NM	96.8%	Honolulu	HI	82.3%
Casper	WY	96.7%	Toledo	OH	82.4%
Killeen-Temple	TX	96.6%	Racine	WI	82.5%
San Angelo	TX	96.3%	Baton Rouge	LA	82.5%
Lawrence	KS	96.2%	Waterloo–Cedar Falls	IA	82.6%
Huntington-Ashland	WV-KY-OH	96.2%	Cleveland-Lorain-Elyria	OH	82.8%
Flagstaff	AZ-UT	96.2%	Bergen-Passaic	NJ	82.8%
Yakima	WA	96.1%	Owensboro	KY	83.0%
Merced	CA	96.1%	La Crosse	WI-MN	83.0%
Pueblo	CO	96.1%	Appleton-Oshkosh-Neenah	WI	83.4%
Greeley	CO	96.1%	Trenton	NJ	83.6%
Visalia-Tulare-Porterville	CA	96.0%	Wheeling	WV-OH	83.6%
Longview-Marshall	TX	95.9%	Baltimore	MD	83.7%
Johnson City–Kingsport–Bristol	TN-VA	95.9%	Mobile	AL	83.8%
Salt Lake City–Ogden	UT	95.9%	Manchester	NH	83.9%

Source: U.S. National Center for Education Statistics, 2002

Health & Healthcare

Health and healthcare have become an important issue for increasing numbers of people. Why? The aging population means more health problems and increased health risks. The cost of healthcare has far outpaced inflation in recent years, a trend that is expected to continue. Plus, expectations for good health are rising, particularly as life expectancy continues to grow and as aging adults pursue active lives.

Much like education, healthcare services can be difficult to evaluate, as it is easier to appraise the quantity than the quality of those services. The number of physicians or hospital beds in an area measures the quantity of healthcare service available, but it doesn't speak to its effectiveness. Nonetheless, knowing that the infrastructure exists can be reassuring.

Health & Healthcare Trends

Health, healthcare, and health consciousness have improved gradually in the United States during the past century. Total life expectancy for the average U.S. citizen has gone from 47.3 years in 1900 to 76.9 years in 2000. Heart disease death rates have dropped by almost half since the 1950s. However, notable changes have occurred in the healthcare system and related costs. New treatments, fancy drugs, and the increasing depth of treatments for complex diseases like cancer have, in part, driven healthcare costs rapidly higher. Skyrocketing costs have led to a dramatic increase in managed care (for example, health maintenance organizations [HMOs]), outpatient treatment, preventative medicine, and alternative treatments. Tables 3.37 through 3.40 show healthcare statistics gathered by the National Center for Health Statistics.

Table 3.37: Average Life Expectancy in Years

All U.S. Citizens					
1900	1920	1840	1960	1980	2000
47.3	54.1	62.7	69.7	73.7	76.9

Source: National Center for Health Statistics

Table 3.38: U.S. Healthcare Expenditures

	1960	1980	2000
Total Expenditures	$26.7B	$245.8B	$1,299.5B
Per Capita Expenditures	$143	$1,067	$4,623

Source: National Center for Health Statistics

Table 3.39: U.S. HMO Enrollment

By Years	Percentage
1980	4%
1990	13.4%
2001	28.3%

By Region	Percentage
Northeast	35.1%
Midwest	21.7%
South	21.0%
West	40.7%

Source: National Center for Health Statistics

Table 3.40: U.S. Hospital Care

	1946	1960	1980	2000
Number of Hospital Beds	1,416,000	1,658,000	1,365,000	994,000
Average Length of Stay in Days	9.1	7.6	7.6	5.9

Note: The annual number of outpatient visits has quadrupled in the period 1960-2000.

Source: National Center for Health Statistics

Table 3.41: Sample Health & Healthcare Table from Ann Arbor, Michigan

HEALTH & HEALTHCARE SCORE: 70/RANK: 96

HAZARDS & ILLNESSES	AREA	U.S. AVG	HEALTHCARE	AREA	U.S. AVG
Air-quality score	6	45	Physicians per capita	500.2	261.1
Water-quality score	12	33	Hospital beds per capita	377.5	432.2
Pollen/allergy score	58	61	No. teaching hospitals	3	4
Stress score	25	50	Cost per doctor visit	$69	$67
Cancer mortality per capita	164.6	169.0	Cost per dental visit	$95	$82
Depression days per month	3.1	2.8	Cost per daily hospital room	$666	$733

Health & Healthcare Attributes

Cities Ranked & Rated takes a two-pronged approach to examining health and healthcare. The first approach looks at hazards that cause health problems. The second examines healthcare services and their costs. All attributes figure into the Health and Healthcare scoring and ranking. Air quality, incidence of disease and allergies, and availability of doctors and hospital beds get the highest weighting.

Table 3.41 shows the Health & Healthcare table for the metropolitan area of Ann Arbor, Michigan.

Hazards & Illnesses

Cities Ranked & Rated presents data on those health hazards that affect the greatest number of people. Sources for this information include the U.S. Environmental Protection Agency and Centers for Disease Control and Prevention (U.S. Department of Health and Human Services), with calculations by Sperling's BestPlaces.

■ *Air-quality score* is a complex measure of several air pollutants, including particulates, ozone, volatile organic compounds, and various combustion byproducts on a 0–100 scale, with 100 being the highest or best. Not surprisingly, Los Angeles, California, receives a 2. But, interestingly, Chicago scores 72; Youngstown-Warren, Ohio, scores 95; and Pittsburgh, Pennsylvania, scores 98. Areas on or near storm tracks and with a high degree of atmospheric circulation and change tend to score better, while areas with greater stagnation tend to score low.

■ *Water-quality score* refers to the quality of runoff and ground water—not necessarily the quality of drinking water. It reflects both natural minerals and man-made pollutants, such as agricultural and mine waste. The score, presented on a 0–100 scale, is much more evenly distributed than air quality. Worst areas include places in west Texas, the Colorado Front Range, and Florida. Better areas are typically in the Midwest and Pacific Northwest.

■ *Pollen/allergy score* is significant to the estimated 38% of all U.S. citizens who suffer from the effects of one or more airborne allergies. The score, on a 0–100 scale, is a composite of multiple allergy types, including grass, tree pollen, and mold allergies.

■ *Stress score* is a composite of eight measures calculated by Sperling's BestPlaces based on a concept originally appearing in *Psychology Today*. The eight factors include divorce rate, commute time, unemployment rate, total crime rate, suicide rate, alcohol-use rate, days feeling depressed, and cloudy days. The score is presented on a 0–100 scale, with 100 being the most stressful and 0 being the least. Places like Tacoma, Washington; Detroit and Flint, Michigan; and Mobile, Alabama, score high because of such factors as challenging climates, unemployment, and crime. Upper Midwest cities like Dubuque, Iowa, and Bismarck, North Dakota, are the least stressful. Sources include the Centers for Disease Control and Prevention, Bureau of Labor Statistics, Federal Bureau of Investigation, National Climatic Data Center, U.S. Census Bureau, and National Vital Statistics Program.

■ *Cancer mortality per capita* shows an age-weighted number of cancer deaths per 100,000 person-years. This unusual but universally accepted measure accounts for both size and age of a population in determining the rate. In other words, areas with a high incidence of cancer among relatively younger people will get a higher (worse) figure than an area with the same incidence among a relatively older population. Ranges are from a low of 114.1 in Provo-Orem, Utah, to 207.1 in Jersey City, New Jersey. Areas with high concentrations of chemical industries are notably higher. Data is from the Centers for Disease Control and Prevention. For cancer rates by types of cancer and gender, see www.bestplaces.net/CRAR.

- *Depression days per month* shows the results of a Centers for Disease Control and Prevention survey based on this question: "Now thinking about your mental health, which includes stress, depression, and problems with emotions, for how many days in the past 30 days was your mental health not good?" There is no discernable pattern to the responses, although college towns and areas with little to do and/or cloudy weather appear to have more depression days. This statistic is included in the *Stress score* explained above.

Healthcare

Physician data comes from the American Medical Association. Information on hospitals comes from the U.S. Department of Health and Human Services. Healthcare costs are from a 2003 survey from the American Chamber of Commerce Research Association.

- *Physicians per capita* refers to the total number of accredited physicians, generalists and specialists, in an area per 100,000 residents. It is important to remember that this attribute does not directly translate into availability of medical services because many of these professionals do not treat patients directly. Because of the presence of the Mayo Clinic, Rochester, Minnesota, has far and away the largest number of physicians per capita (1,814.5 per every 100,000 residents) followed by many college towns with teaching hospitals like

Iowa City, Iowa, and Columbia, Missouri. Most cities—about 180 of the 331 metro areas—fall into the 150 to 250 physicians per 100,000 range. At the low end are south Texas, the California Central Valley, and an assortment of small mostly Southern towns.

- *Hospital beds per capita,* presented as a rate of number of beds per 100,000 residents, is a figure that's declining in importance with the increase in outpatient services. Nevertheless, the number indicates the availability of hospital facilities in a more general sense. Rochester, Minnesota; college towns; and a few military towns make the top of the list, while an assortment of mostly small towns and towns close to other large metropolitan areas are at the bottom. For a complete list of hospitals, see www.bestplaces.net/CRAR.

- *No. teaching hospitals* represents the number of hospitals that are accredited to train physicians, a fact suggesting the breadth and depth of staff, available services, and overall quality. Large cities tend to have the highest number, with New York leading the field with 64, Chicago second with 57, Philadelphia with 51, Los Angeles with 48, and so forth. Only 75 metropolitan areas do not have a teaching hospital.

- *Cost per doctor visit, Cost per dental visit,* and *Cost per daily hospital room* are based on average dollars billed per incident, not including prescription medicine or other services, obtained from the American Chamber of Commerce Research Association in the first quarter of 2003. The range of these costs is striking. Hospital costs in most of California and the larger East coast cities are over $1,200 per day, while 80 areas, mostly in the South and Midwest, are under $400 per day. Dental visits range from $54 in Jackson, Mississippi, to $145 in Anchorage, Alaska, with generally higher costs in the West, while the range of doctor costs is narrower.

Table 3.42: Air Quality

Composite of Particulates, Volatile Organic Compounds, and Ozone, Represented as 0-100 Score

MSAs with Dirtiest Air			MSAs with Cleanest Air		
Philadelphia	PA-NJ	0	Syracuse	NY	100
Houston	TX	0	Bergen-Passaic	NJ	99
Fresno	CA	0	Boston	MA-NH-ME	99
Bakersfield	CA	1	Tucson	AZ	99
Riverside–San Bernardino	CA	1	Hartford	CT	98
Phoenix-Mesa	AZ	2	Nassau-Suffolk	NY	98
Sacramento	CA	2	Pittsburgh	PA	98
Los Angeles–Long Beach	CA	2	Norfolk–Virginia Beach–Newport News	VA-NC	95
Ventura	CA	2	Richmond-Petersburg	VA	95
Texarkana	TX-AR	3	Raleigh–Durham–Chapel Hill	NC	95
Mansfield	OH	3	Charleston–North Charleston	SC	95
Des Moines	IA	3	Youngstown-Warren	OH	95
Monroe	LA	3	Scranton–Wilkes-Barre–Hazleton	PA	95
Las Vegas	NV-AZ	3	Orlando	FL	95
Beaumont–Port Arthur	TX	4	Jacksonville	FL	95
Dallas	TX	4	Tacoma	WA	95
Wichita	KS	4	San Francisco	CA	95
Oakland	CA	4	San Antonio	TX	94
Longview-Marshall	TX	6	Tampa–St. Petersburg–Clearwater	FL	94
Houma	LA	6	San Jose	CA	94
Decatur	AL	6	Providence–Fall River–Warwick	RI-MA	91
Brockton	MA	6	Middlesex-Somerset-Hunterdon	NJ	91
Dubuque	IA	6	Buffalo–Niagara Falls	NY	91
Brownsville–Harlingen–San Benito	TX	6	Akron	OH	91
Lowell	MA-NH	6	Omaha	NE-IA	91
State College	PA	6	Springfield	MA	91
Pine Bluff	AR	6	Milwaukee-Waukesha	WI	91
Fort Smith	AR-OK	6	Dayton-Springfield	OH	91
Alexandria	LA	6	Minneapolis–St. Paul	MN-WI	91
Davenport–Moline–Rock Island	IA-IL	6	Denver	CO	91

Source: Sperling's BestPlaces

Table 3.43: Water Quality

Composite Index of Watershed Quality, Represented as 0-100 Score

MSAs with Dirtiest Water			MSAs with Cleanest Water		
Topeka	KS	0	Richmond-Petersburg	VA	100
Atlantic City–Cape May	NJ	2	Portland	ME	100
Kansas City	MO-KS	2	Boulder-Longmont	CO	100
Lawrence	KS	2	Lewiston-Auburn	ME	100
Vineland-Millville-Bridgeton	NJ	4	Nashua	NH	100
Reno	NV	4	Wichita Falls	TX	100
Canton-Massillon	OH	4	Fort Collins–Loveland	CO	100
Hamilton-Middletown	OH	4	Myrtle Beach	SC	100
Vallejo-Fairfield-Napa	CA	4	Laredo	TX	100
St. Joseph	MO	4	Altoona	PA	100
Galveston–Texas City	TX	4	State College	PA	100
Lima	OH	4	Dothan	AL	100
Sioux Falls	SD	4	Williamsport	PA	100
Dayton-Springfield	OH	5	Austin–San Marcos	TX	96
Spokane	WA	5	Bangor	ME	96
Fort Wayne	IN	5	Sherman-Denison	TX	96
San Luis Obispo–Atascadero–Paso Robles	CA	5	Fitchburg-Leominster	MA	96
Salinas	CA	5	Springfield	MO	96
Jackson	MS	5	Erie	PA	96
Wichita	KS	5	Fayetteville	NC	96
Bakersfield	CA	5	Charlottesville	VA	87
Trenton	NJ	6	Lynchburg	VA	87
Gary	IN	6	Danville	VA	87
Albuquerque	NM	6	Scranton–Wilkes-Barre–Hazleton	PA	82
Monmouth-Ocean	NJ	6	Pueblo	CO	82
Santa Rosa	CA	6	Manchester	NH	82
Corpus Christi	TX	6	Panama City	FL	82
Brockton	MA	6	Grand Junction	CO	82
Brazoria	TX	6	Johnson City–Kingsport–Bristol	TN-VA	77
Melbourne–Titusville–Palm Bay	FL	6	Roanoke	VA	77

Source: Sperling's BestPlaces

Table 3.44: Cancer Mortality Rates

Reported Cases Per 100,000 Person Years (Age Weighted)

MSAs with Highest Rates			MSAs with Lowest Rates		
Jersey City	NJ	207.1	Provo-Orem	UT	114.1
Galveston–Texas City	TX	198.7	McAllen-Edinburg-Mission	TX	119.9
New Orleans	LA	195.6	Brownsville–Harlingen–San Benito	TX	131.8
Baltimore	MD	194.7	San Diego	CA	132.5
Middlesex-Somerset-Hunterdon	NJ	194.3	Fort Collins–Loveland	CO	133.3
Monmouth-Ocean	NJ	192.0	Greeley	CO	134.2
Cincinnati	OH-KY-IN	191.0	Boulder-Longmont	CO	136.5
Buffalo–Niagara Falls	NY	190.8	Laredo	TX	139.3
Newburgh	NY-PA	190.5	Pocatello	ID	141.0
Nassau-Suffolk	NY	190.4	Flagstaff	AZ-UT	141.1
Nashua	NH	190.1	Lawrence	KS	141.5
Las Vegas	NV-AZ	189.9	Pueblo	CO	141.6
Atlantic City–Cape May	NJ	189.7	Savannah	GA	142.9
Houma	LA	189.6	Corvallis	OR	143.4
Jacksonville	NC	188.9	Colorado Springs	CO	144.5
Lafayette	IN	188.6	Bryan–College Station	TX	146.3
Philadelphia	PA-NJ	188.6	Lubbock	TX	148.7
Bergen-Passaic	NJ	188.5	Boise	ID	148.9
Providence–Fall River–Warwick	RI-MA	188.0	Salem	OR	149.1
Wilmington	NC	187.7	Las Cruces	NM	149.3
Lewiston-Auburn	ME	187.3	Grand Junction	CO	149.9
Steubenville-Weirton	OH-WV	187.2	Tuscaloosa	AL	149.9
Newark	NJ	187.0	Yuma	AZ	150.1
Cleveland-Lorain-Elyria	OH	186.8	Killeen-Temple	TX	150.2
Albany	GA	186.7	Fayetteville-Springdale-Rogers	AR	150.2
New York	NY	186.4	Hickory-Morganton-Lenoir	NC	150.2
Trenton	NJ	186.4	Athens	GA	151.1
Portsmouth-Rochester	NH-ME	186.1	San Angelo	TX	151.1
Mobile	AL	186.0	Abilene	TX	151.3
Gary	IN	186.0	Rochester	MN	151.5

Source: Centers for Disease Control and Prevention, 2003

Table 3.45: Physicians Per Capita

Number of Physicians Per 100,000 Residents

MSAs with the Most Physicians			MSAs with the Fewest Physicians		
Rochester	MN	1,814.5	Decatur	AL	19.8
Iowa City	IA	1,096.2	Laredo	TX	97.3
Charlottesville	VA	858.7	Merced	CA	98.5
Columbia	MO	754.9	Lowell	MA-NH	101.2
Gainesville	FL	718.1	McAllen-Edinburg-Mission	TX	105.6
Burlington	VT	582.0	Yuma	AZ	106.3
Greenville	NC	567.6	Visalia-Tulare-Porterville	CA	111.3
Portland	ME	534.8	Jackson	MI	124.2
Bangor	ME	528.5	Brownsville–Harlingen–San Benito	TX	124.4
New Haven–Meriden	CT	525.2	Fitchburg-Leominster	MA	125.3
Pittsfield	MA	524.0	Brockton	MA	129.5
Ann Arbor	MI	500.2	Elkhart-Goshen	IN	130.3
Boston	MA-NH-ME	499.6	Kenosha	WI	132.1
Madison	WI	483.9	Hamilton-Middletown	OH	132.1
San Francisco	CA	482.1	Jacksonville	NC	132.9
Flagstaff	AZ-UT	475.4	Stockton-Lodi	CA	135.1
Galveston–Texas City	TX	456.7	Provo-Orem	UT	135.1
Springfield	IL	432.1	Jamestown	NY	135.2
Raleigh–Durham–Chapel Hill	NC	431.7	Bakersfield	CA	136.3
Nassau-Suffolk	NY	429.0	Houma	LA	137.2
New York	NY	406.8	Rocky Mount	NC	138.6
Shreveport–Bossier City	LA	399.1	Steubenville-Weirton	OH-WV	138.8
Little Rock–North Little Rock	AR	397.8	Sumter	SC	138.8
Roanoke	VA	395.9	Greeley	CO	140.5
Augusta-Aiken	GA-SC	394.3	New Bedford	MA	141.2
Jackson	MS	393.5	Las Cruces	NM	141.6
Charleston–North Charleston	SC	393.1	Mansfield	OH	143.9
New Orleans	LA	390.8	Lakeland–Winter Haven	FL	146.8
Lexington	KY	387.8	Riverside–San Bernardino	CA	147.8
Stamford-Norwalk	CT	387.3	Clarksville-Hopkinsville	TN-KY	148.9

Source: American Medical Association, 2002

Table 3.46: Hospital Beds Per Capita

Number of Hospital Beds Per 100,000 Residents

MSAs with the Most Hospital Beds			MSAs with the Fewest Hospital Beds		
Enid	OK	1,133.0	Yolo	CA	103.8
Lynchburg	VA	1,105.1	Bellingham	WA	128.9
Wheeling	WV-OH	1,029.6	Brazoria	TX	138.6
Lubbock	TX	1,019.3	Bremerton	WA	141.0
Alexandria	LA	1,018.7	Greeley	CO	143.7
Rochester	MN	1,016.3	Jacksonville	FL	156.3
Great Falls	MT	986.8	Santa Cruz–Watsonville	CA	158.4
Columbia	MO	895.5	Santa Fe	NM	170.7
Iowa City	IA	895.4	Salinas	CA	174.5
Monroe	LA	894.4	Boulder-Longmont	CO	175.4
Victoria	TX	880.0	Lawrence	KS	182.1
Goldsboro	NC	878.9	Danbury	CT	185.8
Jackson	MI	833.5	Merced	CA	186.7
Pueblo	CO	807.9	Dover	DE	191.0
Florence	SC	803.9	Yuma	AZ	191.8
San Angelo	TX	799.9	Kenosha	WI	193.2
Elmira	NY	792.8	Colorado Springs	CO	194.2
Wichita Falls	TX	787.8	Barnstable-Yarmouth	MA	196.2
Dothan	AL	763.5	Seattle-Bellevue-Everett	WA	196.4
Bismarck	ND	760.1	New London–Norwich	CT-RI	197.9
Roanoke	VA	748.5	Fort Collins–Loveland	CO	200.4
Grand Forks	ND-MN	745.8	Portland-Vancouver	OR-WA	205.5
Vallejo-Fairfield-Napa	CA	735.7	Corvallis	OR	208.6
Tallahassee	FL	731.7	Waterbury	CT	210.1
Florence	AL	704.4	Eugene-Springfield	OR	210.9
Texarkana	TX-AR	704.4	Stockton-Lodi	CA	213.1
Jonesboro	AR	689.0	Olympia	WA	214.1
Steubenville-Weirton	OH-WV	684.0	Riverside–San Bernardino	CA	217.4
Springfield	MA	683.1	Flagstaff	AZ-UT	219.0
Little Rock–North Little Rock	AR	676.4	Lakeland–Winter Haven	FL	142.0

Source: U.S. Department of Health and Human Services (DHHS), 2002

Table 3.47: Cost Per Daily Hospital Room

Average Cost Per Day

Most Expensive Hospital Rooms			Least Expensive Hospital Rooms		
Trenton	NJ	$3,152	Fort Smith	AR-OK	$298
Jersey City	NJ	$2,971	Mobile	AL	$301
Bergen-Passaic	NJ	$2,812	Jackson	MS	$304
Newark	NJ	$2,801	Greensboro–Winston-Salem–High Point	NC	$315
San Francisco	CA	$2,576	Charleston	WV	$318
Monmouth-Ocean	NJ	$2,537	Nashville	TN	$323
Vineland-Millville-Bridgeton	NJ	$2,392	Wilmington	NC	$343
Middlesex-Somerset-Hunterdon	NJ	$2,363	Jonesboro	AR	$343
San Jose	CA	$2,184	Albany	GA	$355
Atlantic City–Cape May	NJ	$2,184	Jacksonville	NC	$363
Oakland	CA	$1,987	Bismarck	ND	$363
Sacramento	CA	$1,874	Appleton-Oshkosh-Neenah	WI	$366
Santa Rosa	CA	$1,821	York	PA	$370
New York	NY	$1,785	Sumter	SC	$371
Vallejo-Fairfield-Napa	CA	$1,762	Great Falls	MT	$372
Santa Cruz–Watsonville	CA	$1,717	Odessa-Midland	TX	$374
Yuba City–Marysville	CA	$1,710	Little Rock–North Little Rock	AR	$378
Yolo	CA	$1,695	Jackson	TN	$380
Chico-Paradise	CA	$1,661	Goldsboro	NC	$380
Stockton-Lodi	CA	$1,598	Victoria	TX	$381
Modesto	CA	$1,511	Monroe	LA	$386
Philadelphia	PA-NJ	$1,493	Las Cruces	NM	$392
Salinas	CA	$1,439	Augusta-Aiken	GA-SC	$395
Merced	CA	$1,427	Hickory-Morganton-Lenoir	NC	$401
San Diego	CA	$1,399	Pine Bluff	AR	$404
Nassau-Suffolk	NY	$1,370	Roanoke	VA	$404
Redding	CA	$1,327	Youngstown-Warren	OH	$408
Visalia-Tulare-Porterville	CA	$1,300	Amarillo	TX	$410
Orange County	CA	$1,295	Johnson City–Kingsport–Bristol	TN-VA	$411
Riverside–San Bernardino	CA	$1,293	Lawton	OK	$413

Source: American Chamber of Commerce Research Association, 2003

Crime

Particularly for those who have been victims, the incidence of serious crime is a major consideration when examining a place. The Federal Bureau of Investigation (U.S. Department of Justice) keeps close tabs on violent and nonviolent crime rates and efforts toward law enforcement.

Numerous doctorate degrees have been conferred on studies of crime and its causes. True cause and effect will probably never be known, but there are some interesting correlations and geographic relationships. First, crime appears to be influenced by the economy and particularly the job market for fairly obvious reasons. The 1990s saw a dramatic decline in overall crime rates, but the rates began to tick up slightly in 2001 and leveled off in 2002. Second, there is a relationship to climate. Areas with warm—extremely warm—climates tend to have higher crime rates. Miami, Florida; Memphis, Tennessee; and Pine Bluff, Arkansas have the highest murder rates, and total crime rates have been highest in states like Arizona, New Mexico, South Carolina, Texas, and Florida. Reasons are sketchy, but it may have to do with opportunity (more favorable weather to execute crimes), temperament, and stress, or population compositions and the presence of economically disadvantaged groups in these areas. Finally, crime is (as can be expected) reduced by more and better law enforcement. The western portion of the United States has the lowest concentration of law enforcement personnel (2.5 per 1,000 residents) and is seeing the highest growth in crime rates.

Crime Trends

Total crime rates declined significantly through the 1990s. Both violent and nonviolent crime rates dropped nearly 30% for the 10-year period, but started to tick back upward in 2001. In addition to the economy, the increased age and education of the population and improved law enforcement have been credited with the improvement.

Regional trends are significant, showing decreases in the East and large increases in the West. Total crime rates in the East decreased 1.2% in 2001 and 3.3% in 2002. They increased in the West, up 4.9% in 2001 and 2.9% in 2002. In the Midwest, they increased modestly in 2001 (+0.9%) and dropped 2.1% in 2002. In the South, rates increased 1.9% in 2001 and dropped 0.1% in 2002.

There is some evidence that crime is moving to suburbs. In 2002, while U.S.-wide violent crime decreased 1.4% and nonviolent crime decreased 0.8%, crime in the suburbs was up 1.8%. Forcible rape has increased steadily, but this may be due to increased reporting.

On average, there are 3.1 law enforcement personnel per 1,000 residents in the United States, with a fairly wide range. Cities of one million or more have 4.8 per million residents. Cities in the East and South have 3.5 per million residents, with 2.8 in the Midwest and 2.5 in the West. Recent state fiscal problems are likely to hurt, especially in states like California where budget stress is the highest and crime trends are already going in the wrong direction.

Crime Attributes

The data in this section comes from the U.S. Department of Justice Federal Bureau of Investigation Uniform Crime Reports. Statistics are only kept for reported, serious crimes. Routine traffic violations, trespassing, or disorderly conduct don't count. Total nonviolent crimes typically run about 10 times the rate of violent crimes, although the mix can vary in different places. All crime data is used in scoring and ranking. For updated and historical crime rates, see www.bestplaces.net/CRAR.

Table 3.48 shows the Crime table for the metropolitan area of Atlanta, Georgia.

Table 3.48: Sample Crime Table from Atlanta, Georgia

CRIME SCORE: 46/RANK: 176

CRIME	AREA	U.S. AVG
Violent crime rate	570.1	456.0
Change in violent crime rate	-29.4%	-17.2%
Property crime rate	4,255.6	3,950.0
Change in property crime rate	-33.7%	-16.8%

- *Violent crime rate* is the combined incidence of murder, rape, robbery, and assault per 100,000 residents per year.

- *Change in violent crime rate* reflects the percentage growth or decrease in violent crime rates during the period 1996–2001.

- *Property crime rate*, or nonviolent crime rate, is the combined incidence of burglary, theft, and auto theft.

- *Change in property crime* reflects the percentage growth or decrease in property crime rates during the period 1996–2001.

Table 3.49: Violent Crime Rate

Reported Incidents of Murder, Forcible Rape, Robbery, and Assault Per 100,000 Residents

MSAs with Highest Violent Crime Rates			MSAs with Lowest Violent Crime Rates		
Pine Bluff	AR	1,473.2	Bismarck	ND	70.5
Miami	FL	1,151.3	Sioux City	IA-NE	98.7
Memphis	TN-AR-MS	1,104.4	Bangor	ME	104.3
Lubbock	TX	1,058.7	Danbury	CT	107.9
Baltimore	MD	1,026.0	Provo-Orem	UT	108.9
Albuquerque	NM	1,022.1	Appleton-Oshkosh-Neenah	WI	115.0
Tallahassee	FL	989.0	State College	PA	120.0
Nashville	TN	970.9	La Crosse	WI-MN	124.4
Florence	AL	946.1	Eau Claire	WI	129.2
Los Angeles–Long Beach	CA	926.6	Wausau	WI	130.2
Sumter	SC	914.4	Fargo-Moorhead	ND-MN	133.8
Jackson	MI	904.6	Nassau-Suffolk	NY	136.2
Tampa–St. Petersburg–Clearwater	FL	904.1	Green Bay	WI	144.5
St. Louis	MO-IL	902.1	Portsmouth-Rochester	NH-ME	146.0
Stockton-Lodi	CA	901.3	Nashua	NH	147.0
Chicago	IL	893.9	Grand Forks	ND-MN	147.4
Monroe	LA	887.0	Dubuque	IA	148.5
Orlando	FL	878.1	Portland	ME	149.9
Jacksonville	NC	867.2	Burlington	VT	155.3
Gainesville	FL	866.3	Sheboygan	WI	158.2
Kansas City	MO-KS	858.5	Lewiston-Auburn	ME	161.6
Chattanooga	TN-GA	821.4	Mansfield	OH	161.8
Charlotte–Gastonia–Rock Hill	NC-SC	801.9	Manchester	NH	169.2
Myrtle Beach	SC	789.2	Cheyenne	WY	171.3
New Orleans	LA	786.7	Lafayette	IN	173.0
Alexandria	LA	780.3	Shreveport–Bossier City	LA	174.0
Auburn-Opelika	AL	774.4	Bloomington	IN	177.3
New York	NY	773.7	Middlesex-Somerset-Hunterdon	NJ	182.6
Tuscaloosa	AL	773.3	Corvallis	OR	186.6
Melbourne–Titusville–Palm Bay	FL	769.8	Binghamton	NY	187.5

Source: U.S. Department of Justice Federal Bureau of Investigation Uniform Crime Reports, 2001

Table 3.50: Change in Violent Crime Rate

Percentage of Increase or Decrease, 1996-2001

MSAs with Greatest Increase			MSAs with Greatest Decrease		
Dubuque	IA	354%	Mansfield	OH	-78%
Wilmington	NC	83%	Lima	OH	-69%
Kenosha	WI	58%	Bloomington	IN	-66%
Allentown-Bethlehem-Easton	PA	57%	Sioux City	IA-NE	-63%
Wausau	WI	49%	Yuba City–Marysville	CA	-63%
Parkersburg-Marietta	WV-OH	47%	Hattiesburg	MS	-62%
Great Falls	MT	42%	Lawton	OK	-59%
San Jose	CA	40%	Cedar Rapids	IA	-58%
San Antonio	TX	39%	Bismarck	ND	-58%
Owensboro	KY	39%	San Luis Obispo–Atascadero–Paso Robles	CA	-57%
Charlottesville	VA	38%	Medford-Ashland	OR	-56%
Nashua	NH	38%	Yakima	WA	-54%
Joplin	MO	37%	Fitchburg-Leominster	MA	-52%
Fort Smith	AR-OK	37%	Grand Junction	CO	-52%
Huntington-Ashland	WV-KY-OH	35%	Lowell	MA-NH	-51%
St. Joseph	MO	32%	Green Bay	WI	-50%
Altoona	PA	30%	Yolo	CA	-50%
Johnson City–Kingsport–Bristol	TN-VA	29%	Baton Rouge	LA	-50%
Salem	OR	25%	Yuma	AZ	-49%
Jackson	MS	25%	Benton Harbor	MI	-49%
Decatur	AL	23%	Athens	GA	-48%
Portsmouth-Rochester	NH-ME	22%	Birmingham	AL	-48%
Wheeling	WV-OH	22%	Fayetteville	NC	-48%
Appleton-Oshkosh-Neenah	WI	20%	Newark	NJ	-48%
Auburn-Opelika	AL	20%	Enid	OK	-47%
Johnstown	PA	20%	Abilene	TX	-47%
St. Louis	MO-IL	17%	Dutchess County	NY	-46%
Roanoke	VA	16%	Portland-Vancouver	OR-WA	-46%
Lubbock	TX	16%	Lafayette	IN	-46%
Albuquerque	NM	15%	Pueblo	CO	-46%

Source: U.S. Department of Justice Federal Bureau of Investigation Uniform Crime Reports

Table 3.51: Property Crime Rate

Reported Incidents of Burglary, Theft, and Auto Theft Per 100,000 Residents

MSAs with Highest Property Crime Rates			MSAs with Lowest Property Crime Rates		
Tucson	AZ	6,927.4	Danbury	CT	1,558.0
Myrtle Beach	SC	6,784.4	Johnstown	PA	1,656.4
Topeka	KS	6,780.6	Wheeling	WV-OH	1,906.0
Pine Bluff	AR	6,725.8	Pittsfield	MA	1,909.4
Greenville	NC	6,517.0	Nassau-Suffolk	NY	1,909.9
Miami	FL	6,446.9	Sheboygan	WI	1,916.0
San Jose	CA	6,358.0	Ventura	CA	1,957.4
San Antonio	TX	6,358.0	Dubuque	IA	1,972.0
Memphis	TN-AR-MS	6,312.0	Glens Falls	NY	1,994.8
Laredo	TX	6,283.6	Dutchess County	NY	2,029.1
Corpus Christi	TX	6,228.4	Middlesex-Somerset-Hunterdon	NJ	2,030.0
Baton Rouge	LA	6,204.0	Parkersburg-Marietta	WV-OH	2,036.3
Brownsville–Harlingen–San Benito	TX	6,144.1	Portsmouth-Rochester	NH-ME	2,057.4
Monroe	LA	6,126.4	Lowell	MA-NH	2,078.6
Albuquerque	NM	5,992.2	Shreveport–Bossier City	LA	2,107.5
Waco	TX	5,963.9	Nashua	NH	2,121.7
Amarillo	TX	5,937.1	Wausau	WI	2,185.7
Lincoln	NE	5,915.9	Santa Rosa	CA	2,192.4
Springfield	IL	5,872.0	Lynchburg	VA	2,214.2
Macon	GA	5,862.3	Lawrence	KS	2,237.1
Phoenix-Mesa	AZ	5,860.3	State College	PA	2,242.6
Columbus	OH	5,840.7	Worcester	MA-CT	2,244.0
Wilmington-Newark	DE-MD	5,800.2	Monmouth-Ocean	NJ	2,248.7
Mobile	AL	5,741.1	Manchester	NH	2,263.8
Florence	AL	5,733.4	Appleton-Oshkosh-Neenah	WI	2,274.7
Kansas City	MO-KS	5,696.9	Barnstable-Yarmouth	MA	2,280.3
San Angelo	TX	5,666.0	Newburgh	NY-PA	2,296.0
Little Rock–North Little Rock	AR	5,653.8	Binghamton	NY	2,317.8
Biloxi-Gulfport-Pascagoula	MS	5,653.3	Santa Cruz–Watsonville	CA	2,320.3
Springfield	MO	5,650.9	Jamestown	NY	2,338.5

Source: U.S. Department of Justice Federal Bureau of Investigation Uniform Crime Reports, 2001

Table 3.52: Change in Property Crime Rate

Percentage of Increase or Decrease, 1996-2001

MSAs with Greatest Increase			MSAs with Greatest Decrease		
Steubenville-Weirton	OH-WV	86.4%	Yuma	AZ	-59.9%
Bangor	ME	31.9%	Danbury	CT	-51.8%
Johnson City–Kingsport–Bristol	TN-VA	27.1%	Great Falls	MT	-51.6%
Pine Bluff	AR	16.6%	Billings	MT	-49.1%
Chattanooga	TN-GA	16.5%	Fort Lauderdale	FL	-44.4%
San Angelo	TX	15.7%	New York	NY	-43.9%
Altoona	PA	15.2%	Yolo	CA	-41.5%
Montgomery	AL	15.0%	Redding	CA	-41.0%
Cumberland	MD-WV	14.7%	Orange County	CA	-40.8%
Dothan	AL	13.9%	Las Vegas	NV-AZ	-39.0%
Brownsville–Harlingen–San Benito	TX	13.2%	Miami	FL	-38.2%
Joplin	MO	11.5%	Lawrence	MA-NH	-37.6%
Charleston	WV	11.0%	Ventura	CA	-37.6%
Springfield	MO	10.3%	Portland	ME	-37.5%
Laredo	TX	10.2%	Gainesville	FL	-37.4%
Wichita Falls	TX	9.9%	Santa Barbara–Santa Maria–Lompoc	CA	-37.0%
Johnstown	PA	9.1%	Jersey City	NJ	-36.6%
South Bend	IN	7.5%	Lowell	MA-NH	-36.6%
Mobile	AL	6.6%	San Jose	CA	-36.1%
Columbus	OH	6.3%	Flagstaff	AZ-UT	-35.7%
Anniston	AL	5.4%	Ocala	FL	-35.4%
Huntington-Ashland	WV-KY-OH	5.1%	Atlantic City–Cape May	NJ	-35.2%
Cincinnati	OH-KY-IN	5.0%	Corvallis	OR	-35.2%
Omaha	NE-IA	4.9%	Pocatello	ID	-35.2%
Hamilton-Middletown	OH	4.5%	Tuscaloosa	AL	-35.0%
Biloxi-Gulfport-Pascagoula	MS	4.5%	Riverside–San Bernardino	CA	-34.8%
Sumter	SC	4.4%	Newark	NJ	-34.6%
Houma	LA	4.0%	Albany	GA	-34.5%
Kokomo	IN	3.7%	Sacramento	CA	-34.3%
Florence	SC	3.5%	Los Angeles–Long Beach	CA	-34.2%

Source: U.S. Department of Justice Federal Bureau of Investigation Uniform Crime Reports

Table 3.53: Overall Crime Rate

Reported Incidents of Violent and Nonviolent (Property) Crime Per 100,000 Residents

MSAs with Highest Crime Rates			MSAs with Lowest Crime Rates		
Pine Bluff	AR	8,199.0	Danbury	CT	1,665.90
Tucson	AZ	7,599.0	Johnstown	PA	1,892.30
Miami	FL	7,598.2	Nassau-Suffolk	NY	2,046.11
Myrtle Beach	SC	7,573.6	Sheboygan	WI	2,074.21
Topeka	KS	7,487.1	Dubuque	IA	2,120.46
Memphis	TN-AR-MS	7,416.4	Pittsfield	MA	2,140.40
Greenville	NC	7,152.7	Wheeling	WV-OH	2,145.82
San Jose	CA	7,034.3	Portsmouth-Rochester	NH-ME	2,203.40
San Antonio	TX	7,034.3	Middlesex-Somerset-Hunterdon	NJ	2,212.60
Albuquerque	NM	7,014.3	Ventura	CA	2,219.10
Monroe	LA	7,013.4	Glens Falls	NY	2,236.40
Corpus Christi	TX	6,950.2	Dutchess County	NY	2,258.20
Baton Rouge	LA	6,903.7	Nashua	NH	2,268.72
Laredo	TX	6,876.0	Shreveport–Bossier City	LA	2,281.50
Florence	AL	6,679.5	Wausau	WI	2,315.90
Brownsville–Harlingen–San Benito	TX	6,600.6	Parkersburg-Marietta	WV-OH	2,339.96
Amarillo	TX	6,596.9	State College	PA	2,362.60
Kansas City	MO-KS	6,555.4	Appleton-Oshkosh-Neenah	WI	2,389.70
Waco	TX	6,500.6	Lowell	MA-NH	2,422.50
Lincoln	NE	6,442.3	Manchester	NH	2,433.00
Phoenix-Mesa	AZ	6,426.8	Monmouth-Ocean	NJ	2,447.70
Chattanooga	TN-GA	6,372.9	Lynchburg	VA	2,451.10
Sharon	PA	6,368.9	Binghamton	NY	2,505.30
Lubbock	TX	6,365.5	Jamestown	NY	2,529.30
Columbus	OH	6,346.4	Santa Rosa	CA	2,536.10
Springfield	IL	6,329.6	Lawrence	KS	2,541.40
Macon	GA	6,320.6	Newburgh	NY-PA	2,592.40
Sumter	SC	6,311.8	Bismarck	ND	2,592.50
Wilmington-Newark	DE-MD	6,310.3	York	PA	2,599.42
Tallahassee	FL	6,297.8	Lancaster	PA	2,612.30

Source: U.S. Department of Justice Federal Bureau of Investigation Uniform Crime Reports, 2001

Transportation

Transportation is usually where the true impact of crowding or isolation in an area is most felt. Gauging all daily activity around the avoidance of rush hour (even on weekends), having to drive 350 miles to get to the nearest airport with suitable (and affordable) air service, or commuting 2 hours a day by automobile into a crowded urban core (with $30 per day parking) all indicate failures in transportation service that ultimately affect lifestyle. *Cities Ranked & Rated* presents all the factors—commute times, how people commute to work, availability and utilization of public transportation, intercity transport services, and automobile costs—that come into play.

Transportation Trends

Since 1960, the number of motor vehicle registrations and the average driving distance from home to work both *tripled*, while U.S. population increased 60%. There are over 220 million motor vehicles in the United States, and more drivers are spending more time on the road than ever

before. Road infrastructure, on the other hand, has only grown 11% during the 40-year period, while vehicle miles have *quadrupled*. Result: More traffic and traffic jams and longer commute times almost everywhere, both urban and rural. See Table 3.54 for a summary of significant changes over the past 40 years.

Public transportation has also grown, but problems with utilization persist as far-flung suburban infrastructures, nurtured by the automobile, make it less practical as an alternative. As a result, most cities face a transportation crunch. Worse yet, they face a Catch-22 dilemma, where the most expedient solution of building more roads (if even geographically possible) is met with more urban sprawl and, regrettably, an even greater demand for transportation.

Commuting trends are not encouraging. As Table 3.55 shows, despite massive spending and public policy efforts to create facilities and encourage car-pooling, mass transit, and even telecommuting, these practices haven't been widely adopted in most places. The percentage of single occupancy vehicles has actually increased to an all time high of 78.2%, mostly at the expenses of car pools, and to

Table 3.54: U.S. Highway & Air Transport Activity

	1960	1980	2000	Percentage Change 1960-2000
Vehicles Registered	73.9M	155.8M	221.5M	300%
Road Miles in Place	3.46M	3.86M	3.95M	11.4%
Annual Road Miles Driven	719M	1527M	2,750M	382%
Annual Air Revenue Passengers	197M (1975)	439M	639M	324% (from 1975)

Source: Federal Highway Administration, Federal Aviation Administration

Table 3.55: Principal Means of Transportation to Work

	1985	1993	2001
Automobile	86.5%	88.0%	87.8%
Single Occupant	72.4%	76.6%	78.2%
Car Pool	14.1%	11.4%	9.7%
Public Transport (Bus, Subway, Trolley, or Elevated Rail)	5.1%	4.6%	4.7%
Bicycle or Motorcycle	1.0%	0.7%	0.7%
On Foot	4.0%	3.1%	2.8%
Works at Home/Telecommutes	3.0%	3.0%	2.8%
Other (Includes Vans, Ferries, Surface Trains)	0.3%	0.5%	0.9%

Source: U.S. Census Bureau

"SLUGGING" IT TO WORK

In some areas, the commute is simply so awful that people are willing to sacrifice their privacy to spend time with a complete stranger in a desperate attempt to take advantage of HOV (High Occupancy Vehicle, or car pool) lanes. In Washington, D.C., and a few other large urban areas like San Francisco, Houston, and Seattle, "slugs" line up at commuter parking lots to be "snatched" by other drivers heading into employment centers. The slugs may pay tolls, but eligibility to use the HOV lane in exchange for the ride is the base currency. Slug etiquette includes not talking to the driver unless the driver initiates the conversation, and topics cannot include religion, politics, or sex (a challenge in Washington, D.C.). There are 10,000 sluggers in D.C. alone, two websites, and even a book on the topic, and, amazingly, no reports of foul play.

AMERICA'S MOST DRIVABLE CITIES

Is driving a pleasurable and relaxing experience in most cities? Are traffic jams, rough roads, and high costs a perpetual nightmare? In 2003, Sperling's BestPlaces teamed up with the automotive supply retailer Pep Boys to study these issues. They arrived at these conclusions:

- Small Texas cities do well. Corpus Christi, Texas, took top honors among the 70 cities studied, followed closely by Beaumont–Port Arthur and Brownsville. These areas have the lowest gas prices, short travel times, and low traffic flow. Florida cities, such as Fort Myers and Pensacola, also score well.

- Los Angeles, not surprisingly, rates as the least drivable, with the longest travel times in the nation (which include, but are not exclusive to commute times). San Francisco, with congestion and high gas prices, is second worst, followed by Chicago, Denver, and Boston.

- Cities in the Northeast tend to rank poorly. Philadelphia, Hartford, and New York City all rank in the bottom 20.

- The most drivable *large* city is Atlanta.

- The northern California cities of San Francisco, San Jose, and Oakland have the highest gas prices outside of Hawaii.

- Detroit, Michigan, and Fresno and Sacramento in California have the roughest roads.

Some of the least drivable cities, like Chicago, New York, Boston, and San Francisco, have made up for their shortcomings with excellent public transportation facilities. Others like Los Angeles are behind the curve and likely to remain there for some time.

a lesser extent, walking to work. The most probable reasons are far-flung urban infrastructures, flexibility pressures on individuals with children, and the aging population. A particularly disturbing trend is the increased dependence on family vehicles to deliver children to school, encouraged by myopic public policies that charge parents fees for school bus rides. These children will likely never learn to use public transportation.

Some cities have made valiant efforts to redirect people and especially commuters to new transit systems, such as light rail, but such systems are very expensive, and, on the whole, underutilized. Scheduled public transportation seems to work only in (1) cities like New York and San Francisco where geography makes it the only practical alternative, and (2) where it is *highly* integrated—that is, one can easily interchange between such modes as light rail, subways, or buses.

Intercity rail, provided by Amtrak, still struggles in all but a few corridors, mostly on the East and West coasts. New funding models, equipment, and route structures

have created pockets of local success in northern and southern California, the Oregon-Washington "Cascade" corridor, the Chicago area, and parts of Texas. The northeast corridor from Washington, D.C., to Boston has been a consistent success. New, first-class Acela trains, while expensive, continue to keep people off the highways and out of the skies. The success formula seems to be (1) moderate distances from 100 miles to 200 miles, (2) relatively unattractive driving and flying alternatives, (3) low fares, (4) well-coordinated connecting services, and (5) good service. Legislative debates on Amtrak's strategy, operational funding, and capital spending are almost continuous.

Transportation Attributes

Transportation attributes are subdivided into intracity or intercity services and automobile costs. The time spent commuting, the availability of alternatives, and dependence on cars all determine the transportation picture,

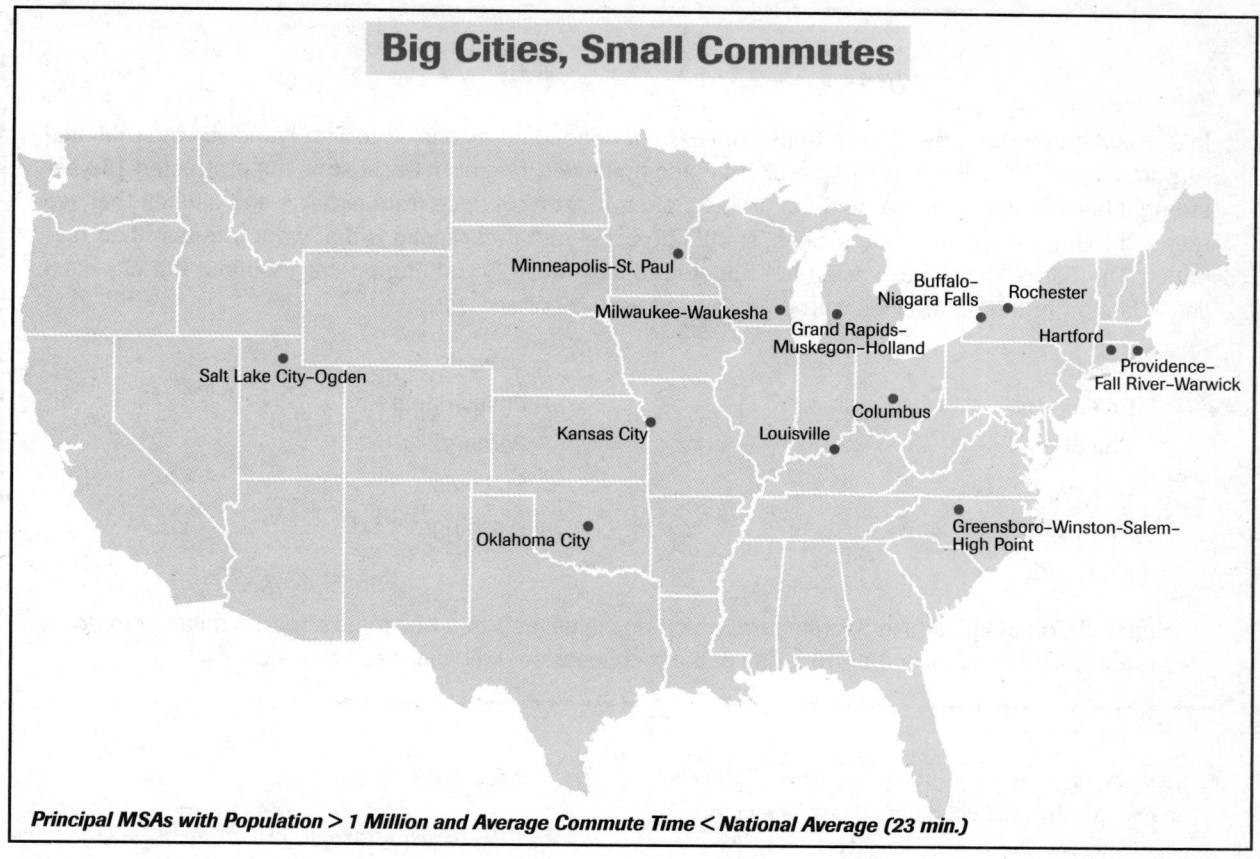

Big Cities, Small Commutes

Minneapolis-St. Paul
Milwaukee-Waukesha
Buffalo–Niagara Falls
Rochester
Grand Rapids–Muskegon-Holland
Hartford
Salt Lake City–Ogden
Providence–Fall River–Warwick
Columbus
Kansas City
Louisville
Oklahoma City
Greensboro–Winston-Salem–High Point

Principal MSAs with Population > 1 Million and Average Commute Time < National Average (23 min.)

particularly in larger cities. Most transportation data comes from the U.S. Department of Transportation and the 2000 U.S. Census. Airport and rail information comes from carriers and local industry associations and is processed by Sperling's BestPlaces. Scoring and ranking uses commute times, available mass transit service, and air and rail departures. Commute times and mass transit get the highest weighting, while air and rail get moderate and light weightings, respectively.

Table 3.56 shows the Transportation table for the metropolitan area of Asheville, North Carolina.

Commute

- *Average commute time* is the average one-way commute in minutes. The worst places tend to be East and West Coast commuter communities around New York, San Francisco, and Los Angeles. Naturally, the best places are smaller towns, such as Cedar Falls–Waterloo, Idaho; Grand Forks, North Dakota; and Rochester, Minnesota. For more detailed information on commuting, see www.bestplaces.net/CRAR.

Table 3.56: Sample Transportation Table from Asheville, North Carolina

TRANSPORTATION SCORE: 29/RANK: 235

COMMUTE	AREA	U.S. AVG	INTERCITY SERVICES	AREA	U.S. AVG	AUTOMOTIVE	AREA	U.S. AVG
Average commute time	21.9 min.	22.6 min.	Miles to nearest major airport	76	46	Insurance, annual premium	$789	$1,011
Commute by auto	92.9%	88.7%	Type of local airport	Small		Gas, cost per gallon	$1.44	$1.50
Commute by mass transit	.8%	1.8%	No. daily airline departures	76	294	Daily vehicle miles per capita	47.5	23.0
Work at home	3.1%	3.9%	Amtrak service	No				
Mass transit miles per capita	3.3	8.0	No. interstate highways	2	1			

"TRAINING" TO FLY

In 2003 when the Bay Area Rapid Transit rail system opened an extension to San Francisco International Airport, a modest 8 miles south of the city, it made headlines, no doubt because of the protracted 15-year struggle leading up to the event. Such projects often meet resistance from airports and airlines that see no need to fund them and from taxicab, shuttle bus, and rental-car factions that want to retain their revenues. The San Francisco extension is estimated to save over 200,000 rental-car trips into the city each year. Hats off to the other cities with direct city-to-airport rail access:

Atlanta	Newark
Baltimore	Philadelphia
Chicago	Portland, OR
Cleveland	St. Louis
Minneapolis–St. Paul	Washington, D.C.
New York	

Hopefully, other cities (like Sacramento, which doesn't even run a bus to its airport 6 miles from downtown, lest they cannibalize the $10 a day parking concession) will join these ranks soon.

- *Commute by auto* shows the percentage of all commutes done by automobile, inclusive of single occupants and car pools. Not surprisingly, New York has the lowest percentage of auto commutes at 51.2% followed by a number of college towns. Small towns in the South tend to have the highest percentages.

- *Commute by mass transit* shows the utilization of scheduled public transport services, including bus, subway, rail, and ferry. This statistic has the most meaning in medium and large cities and in commuter suburbs.

- *Work at home* shows the percentage of those who avoid a commute either as self-employed workers or telecommuters sponsored by their firms. Recognizing the impact on local infrastructure and work productivity, some companies and governmental jurisdictions have implemented progressive telecommute programs, but these are in the early stages. Interestingly, the highest work-at-home percentages tend to be in smaller Upper Midwest cities, many of which exceed 10%, while the lowest tend to be in smaller cities in the South.

- *Mass transit miles per capita* indicates the availability of public transportation in the area. This figure represents the number of vehicle miles traveled by all types of transit vehicles—whether full or empty—per person.

Intercity Services

- *Miles to nearest major airport* represents the driving distance to the nearest airport referred to by the Federal Aviation Administration as a hub.

- *Type of local airport* profiles the airport and air service available in a metropolitan area. "Large" indicates a large airport with multiple terminals serving as service hubs for one or more carriers and connecting hubs for commuter aircraft. "Medium" indicates a medium airport that may have multiple terminals, usually served by four or more carriers, and a connecting hub for commuter aircraft. "Small" indicates a small airport characterized by a single terminal that might be served by two or three carriers, with full-sized jet service usually available.

- *No. daily airline departures* is the average number of passenger aircraft departing the area's airport(s) per day. Leaders, as might be expected, are the larger regional and national hubs like Chicago, New York, Atlanta, and Los Angeles. Data for communities near these hubs is adjusted to reflect the availability of service.

- *Amtrak service* is a yes/no indicator of whether the metro area has intercity Amtrak service. A total of 169 metropolitan areas have no Amtrak service at

IN THE RIGHT FLIGHT PATH

In recent years, low-cost airlines have been able to enter key markets. With respect to both cost structure and customer satisfaction, these carriers *get it.* Customers willing to give up a few conveniences, like assigned seating and travel-agent bookings, can take advantage of lower fares and, occasionally, have a better flying experience. Those living in the carriers' hub cities have greater access to low-cost service, sometimes from major airlines trying to compete. One downside: These carriers don't serve every city. But overall their prospects look good, particularly when compared to those of major carriers. The stock market value of Southwest is greater than all U.S. national carriers combined, and JetBlue looks to be an eastern version of Southwest. Table 3.57 presents an abbreviated guide to the low-cost carriers and the cities they serve.

Table 3.57: Low-Cost Airlines		
Carrier	**Number of Cities Served**	**Hub Cities**
AirTran	43	Atlanta, Baltimore, Orlando, Philadelphia, Tampa
ATA	46	Chicago (Midway), Indianapolis, Los Angeles, St. Petersburg, San Francisco
Frontier	39	Denver
JetBlue	22	Long Beach, New York (JFK)
Song (Delta)	14	Boston, Fort Lauderdale, New York, Orlando
Southwest	58	Baltimore, Chicago (Midway), Houston (Hobby), Las Vegas, Oakland, Phoenix, Portland (OR), San Diego
Spirit	14	Detroit, Fort Lauderdale

Source: *USA Today*

all, while many cities, mostly on the Northeast Corridor, have more than 10 departures per day.

- *No. interstate highways* shows the number of interstate highways in the area, including beltways and connectors.

Automotive

- *Insurance, annual premium* represents the 2002 average annual cost of auto insurance for an average automobile and a clean driving record. The figure indicates the complexity, difficulty, and dependence on driving in an area, as rates are typically higher in cities with higher accident rates. Decidedly higher auto insurance rates occur on the East Coast, with many rates over $1,500 per year per vehicle. Smaller cities and towns in the Midwest are generally the least expensive at $600 to $700 a year.

- *Gas, cost per gallon* is the average cost for a gallon of unleaded gasoline (summer 2003). While gas prices fluctuate considerably, this indicator is useful as a comparative measure between areas.

- *Daily vehicle miles per capita,* an indicator of sprawl, stress, and cost, measures the 2002 average daily vehicular mileage per person in the metropolitan area. Factors include not only driving distances and urban sprawl but also the concentration of retirees in the area and climate (which may facilitate walking), hence the low 5.9 miles per day driven in Santa Barbara–Santa Maria–Lompoc, California, contrasted with a nationwide average of 23 miles, and a high of 54 in Newburgh, New York, a distant suburb of New York City.

Table 3.58: Commute Times

Average One-Way Commute in Minutes

MSAs with Longest Commutes			MSAs with Shortest Commutes		
New York	NY	38.9	Grand Forks	ND-MN	15.1
Newburgh	NY-PA	34.0	Dubuque	IA	15.5
Monmouth-Ocean	NJ	33.8	Waterloo–Cedar Falls	IA	15.7
Nassau-Suffolk	NY	33.0	Great Falls	MT	16.0
Washington	DC-MD-VA-WV	32.8	Bismarck	ND	16.1
Jersey City	NJ	32.6	Fargo-Moorhead	ND-MN	16.2
Bremerton	WA	32.5	Rochester	NY	16.3
Oakland	CA	32.2	Cheyenne	WY	16.3
Chicago	IL	31.5	Abilene	TX	16.4
Middlesex-Somerset-Hunterdon	NJ	31.3	Casper	WY	16.7
Atlanta	GA	31.2	Bryan–College Station	TX	16.7
Riverside–San Bernardino	CA	31.1	Champaign-Urbana	IL	16.8
Newark	NJ	30.8	Sheboygan	WI	16.9
Miami	FL	30.1	Lawton	OK	16.9
Vallejo-Fairfield-Napa	CA	29.9	Bloomington-Normal	IL	17.0
Dutchess County	NY	29.8	Lubbock	TX	17.1
Baltimore	MD	29.8	Pocatello	ID	17.2
San Francisco	CA	29.4	Rapid City	SD	17.3
Los Angeles–Long Beach	CA	29.4	Sioux Falls	SD	17.3
Stockton-Lodi	CA	29.2	Wichita Falls	TX	17.4
Houston	TX	29.0	Green Bay	WI	17.5
Philadelphia	PA-NJ	28.7	Missoula	MT	17.5
Bergen-Passaic	NJ	28.6	Sioux City	IA-NE	17.6
Tacoma	WA	28.4	Enid	OK	17.7
Brazoria	TX	28.0	Iowa City	IA	17.7
Dallas	TX	27.9	Lafayette	LA	17.7
Santa Cruz–Watsonville	CA	27.8	Lincoln	NE	17.8
Boston	MA-NH-ME	27.7	La Crosse	WI-MN	17.8
New Bedford	MA	27.6	Columbia	SC	17.8
Fort Lauderdale	FL	27.4	Cedar Rapids	IA	17.8

Source: U.S. Census Bureau, 2000

Table 3.59: Commutes by Auto

Percentage of Commutes by Auto vs. Other Means

MSAs with Most Auto Commuters			MSA with Fewest Auto Commuters		
Hickory-Morganton-Lenoir	NC	95.6%	New York	NY	51.2%
Brazoria	TX	95.6%	Jersey City	NJ	56.6%
Auburn-Opelika	AL	95.5%	Bismarck	ND	63.4%
Gadsden	AL	95.4%	Santa Barbara–Santa Maria–Lompoc	CA	70.1%
Huntsville	AL	95.3%	Bloomington	IN	73.8%
Jonesboro	AR	95.1%	Dubuque	IA	73.9%
Flint	MI	94.9%	Fargo-Moorhead	ND-MN	74.3%
Punta Gorda	FL	94.8%	Bremerton	WA	74.4%
Victoria	TX	94.6%	Corvallis	OR	75.0%
Monroe	LA	94.6%	Grand Forks	ND-MN	76.8%
Decatur	IL	94.5%	Stamford-Norwalk	CT	77.7%
Birmingham	AL	94.5%	Honolulu	HI	78.4%
Texarkana	TX-AR	94.5%	Salem	OR	78.7%
Jackson	MS	94.3%	Boston	MA-NH-ME	78.8%
Lynchburg	VA	94.2%	Eau Claire	WI	79.7%
Parkersburg-Marietta	WV-OH	94.1%	Flagstaff	AZ-UT	79.7%
Greenville	NC	94.1%	Trenton	NJ	79.8%
Jackson	TN	94.1%	Oakland	CA	80.0%
Fort Smith	AR-OK	94.0%	Rapid City	SD	80.3%
Waco	TX	94.0%	Yuma	AZ	80.4%
Rocky Mount	NC	94.0%	Boulder-Longmont	CO	80.7%
Odessa-Midland	TX	94.0%	Wausau	WI	81.2%
Montgomery	AL	93.9%	Chicago	IL	81.4%
Beaumont–Port Arthur	TX	93.9%	Iowa City	IA	81.5%
Sumter	SC	93.9%	San Luis Obispo–Atascadero–Paso Robles	CA	82.2%
Fort Pierce–Port St. Lucie	FL	93.9%	La Crosse	WI-MN	82.3%
Goldsboro	NC	93.8%	Greeley	CO	82.6%
Pine Bluff	AR	93.8%	San Antonio	TX	82.6%
Johnson City–Kingsport–Bristol	TN-VA	93.8%	State College	PA	82.8%
Fort Walton Beach	FL	93.6%	Madison	WI	82.9%

Source: U.S. Census Bureau, 2000

Table 3.60: Auto Insurance Premiums

Average Annual Cost for an Average Automobile					
MSAs with Highest Premiums			**MSA with Lowest Premiums**		
New York	NY	$2,279	Sioux City	IA-NE	$643
Phoenix-Mesa	AZ	$1,977	Grand Forks	ND-MN	$646
Los Angeles–Long Beach	CA	$1,812	Rapid City	SD	$646
Tucson	AZ	$1,798	Bismarck	ND	$646
New Orleans	LA	$1,733	Fargo-Moorhead	ND-MN	$647
Miami	FL	$1,707	Waterloo–Cedar Falls	IA	$655
Detroit	MI	$1,701	Iowa City	IA	$656
Las Vegas	NV-AZ	$1,647	Cedar Rapids	IA	$657
Newark	NJ	$1,633	Dubuque	IA	$661
Boston	MA-NH-ME	$1,616	Sioux Falls	SD	$663
Seattle-Bellevue-Everett	WA	$1,615	Casper	WY	$672
Nassau-Suffolk	NY	$1,558	Davenport–Moline–Rock Island	IA-IL	$678
Jersey City	NJ	$1,521	Cheyenne	WY	$680
Houston	TX	$1,519	Des Moines	IA	$681
Dallas	TX	$1,499	Pocatello	ID	$682
Tacoma	WA	$1,484	Boise City	ID	$709
Denver	CO	$1,480	Great Falls	MT	$712
Bergen-Passaic	NJ	$1,467	Billings	MT	$714
Fresno	CA	$1,460	Missoula	MT	$716
Middlesex-Somerset-Hunterdon	NJ	$1,457	Bangor	ME	$720
Monmouth-Ocean	NJ	$1,414	Lewiston-Auburn	ME	$728
Oakland	CA	$1,396	Portland	ME	$732
Buffalo–Niagara Falls	NY	$1,385	Lincoln	NE	$737
Riverside–San Bernardino	CA	$1,378	Janesville-Beloit	WI	$749
Atlantic City–Cape May	NJ	$1,373	La Crosse	WI-MN	$750
Albany-Schenectady-Troy	NY	$1,361	Wausau	WI	$750
Rochester	NY	$1,358	Green Bay	WI	$753
San Diego	CA	$1,357	Eau Claire	WI	$758
Worcester	MA-CT	$1,343	Lawrence	KS	$758
Vineland-Millville-Bridgeton	NJ	$1,340	Sheboygan	WI	$758

Source: American Automobile Association, 2003

Table 3.61: Driving Miles

Average Miles Driven Per Person Per Day					
MSAs with Most Miles Driven			**MSA with Least Miles Driven**		
Newburgh	NY-PA	54.0	Santa Barbara–Santa Maria–Lompoc	CA	5.9
Decatur	AL	49.1	Yuma	AZ	11.9
Asheville	NC	47.5	Portland	ME	12.1
Hickory-Morganton-Lenoir	NC	42.5	Racine	WI	12.6
Sherman-Denison	TX	37.8	Greeley	CO	13.3
Gadsden	AL	37.7	Chico-Paradise	CA	13.4
Houston	TX	37.6	Grand Forks	ND-MN	13.5
Binghamton	NY	36.9	Brownsville–Harlingen–San Benito	TX	13.8
Greensboro–Winston-Salem–High Point	NC	36.6	Great Falls	MT	14.2
Auburn-Opelika	AL	35.6	Jacksonville	NC	14.2
Atlanta	GA	35.6	Merced	CA	14.4
Knoxville	TN	34.8	New Orleans	LA	14.4
Birmingham	AL	34.8	Hattiesburg	MS	14.5
Dothan	AL	34.5	Santa Cruz–Watsonville	CA	14.5
Nashville	TN	34.3	Stockton-Lodi	CA	14.5
Indianapolis	IN	33.6	Lawrence	KS	14.6
Anniston	AL	33.3	Fort Smith	AR-OK	14.6
Santa Fe	NM	33.3	Missoula	MT	14.8
Lakeland–Winter Haven	FL	33.1	Erie	PA	14.8
Austin-San Marcos	TX	32.9	Laredo	TX	15.0
Chattanooga	TN-GA	32.7	Yuba City–Marysville	CA	15.1
Hamilton-Middletown	OH	32.3	Billings	MT	15.2
Tyler	TX	31.7	Bismarck	ND	15.3
Beaumont–Port Arthur	TX	31.7	Sheboygan	WI	15.3
Florence	AL	31.6	Fort Walton Beach	FL	15.3
Harrisburg-Lebanon-Carlisle	PA	31.4	Iowa City	IA	15.4
Terre Haute	IN	31.3	Sioux City	IA-NE	15.5
Las Cruces	NM	31.0	Grand Junction	CO	15.5
Raleigh–Durham–Chapel Hill	NC	30.9	Medford-Ashland	OR	15.7
Lexington	KY	30.5	Salem	OR	15.7

Source: U.S. Department of Transportation Federal Highway Administration, 2002

Leisure

With the apparently hectic pace of life experienced by most people, the concept of spare time would seem to be an afterthought. In reality, most of the Western world has more spare time than ever before. The availability of activities therefore plays a significant role in determining an ideal place to live. *Cities Ranked & Rated* addresses this issue in two categories, Leisure and Arts & Culture.

Leisure covers a cross section of shopping, entertainment, and outdoor recreation activities that broadly reflect the mix and amount of leisure assets in an area. The approach assumes that areas strong in a diverse set of activities are more likely to have specific activities of individual interest. For example, attributes like nightlife and fishing can to some extent be inferred from other data. An area with plentiful water is more likely to have good fishing. An area with good restaurants, performing arts (see "Arts & Culture" below), and maybe many Starbucks outlets is more likely to have good nightlife.

Leisure Trends

The infinite variety of leisure forms leads to about as many leisure trends. This section highlights those trends that broadly impact the landscape and quality of life in an area.

Dining

An ongoing dining trend is the diminishing role of the locally owned family restaurant. It is too early to call it a demise, but new restaurant construction is generally for chains like Applebee's, Joe's Crab Shack, P.F. Chang's, or cookie-cutter fast-food joints. Local legends like Kansas City barbecue and Chicago-style pizza and steakhouses continue to flourish, and recent trends toward back-to-basics "comfort foods" have stemmed the tide a bit. *Cities Ranked & Rated* rates restaurants according to travel publications and other industry sources.

Shopping

Shopping has evolved dramatically and hand in hand with urban sprawl. The availability of retail can be a double-edged sword—both too little and too much reduce the quality of life. Forty years ago, shopping started to migrate from downtown areas to shopping malls, many of which led the charge toward the suburbanization of major cities. In the 1960s and 1970s, big malls prevailed, then high rents, traffic, and overdependence on department stores led to the proliferation of strip malls in the 1980s and then to "big box" retailers and warehouse clubs—with super-sized buying and pricing power—in the 1990s. Today, many urban landscapes are dotted with partially vacant, poorly performing malls, while complexes of those big boxes line freeway interchanges and cause massive traffic headaches as people drive from one store to another.

In smaller towns, big discounters, most notably Wal-Mart, opened up superstores on town fringes. With national purchasing power, low labor, and overhead costs, Wal-Mart put a huge dent in traditional retail, sometimes causing the closure of entire downtown shopping areas. The Wal-Mart formula has now been extended into the suburbs of most cities, and many big-box complexes include a Wal-Mart. The result: Consumers enjoy lower prices on most merchandise, but give up individualized service and wide selection. Worse yet, these stores accelerate urban sprawl in many places, contributing to a downward spiral in the quality of life.

Planning can combat these negative effects. Some places insist that retail developments include well-planned street access and parking, and conform to design standards consistent with local architecture. Many cities in the Midwest and South like Houston, Atlanta, and Columbus, Ohio, have such practices, while states in the West like California, Arizona, and Nevada often allow developers to build whatever they please, which often leads to an ugly, formless jumble of nondescript buildings and parking lots.

To once again attract customers, shopping malls are getting bigger and becoming entertainment destinations with contained amusement parks, movie theaters, and entertainment restaurants like the Rainforest Cafe. The massive 400-store Mall of America in Minneapolis–St. Paul leads this trend in the United States. Finally, the advent of the outlet mall continues to shape the shopping environment, particularly in small towns. Often "outlet" stores are no more than a clever way for manufacturers to bypass retailers. Once located far outside urban areas to protect retailers, many of these malls are opening on urban fringes (like Fairfield-Vallejo-Napa, California), which once again leads to sprawl and traffic.

What does this all mean? Areas with the right mix of well-planned shopping, with traditional and modern venues, are desirable. The continued building of large, traffic-choked complexes of big boxes and strip malls—unvarying assortments of New York Stock Exchange companies seeming to sell the same things—while downtown areas sit unused spells trouble for the future. Look for places that restrict and control development, re-use older buildings, and preserve local businesses, which bring variety to the shopping landscape.

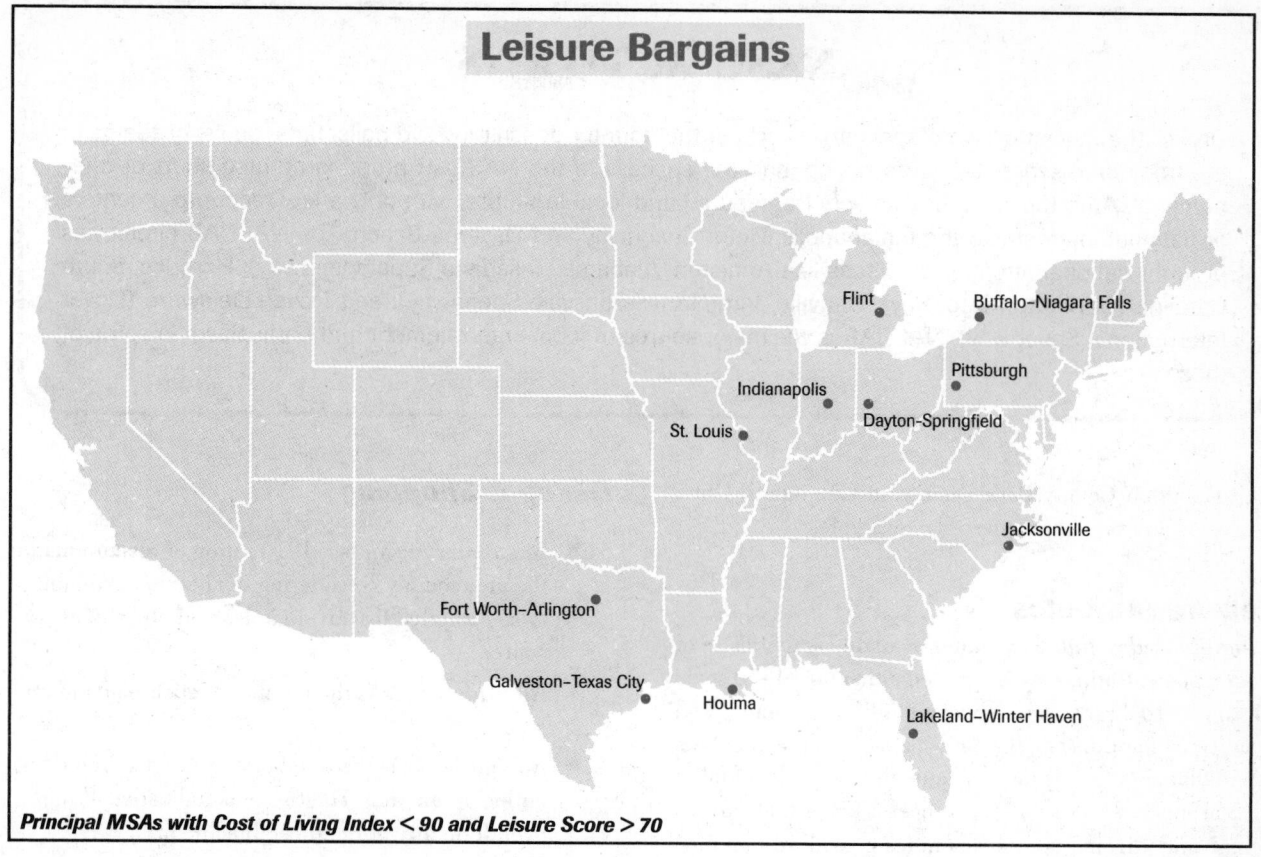

Leisure Bargains

Flint   Buffalo–Niagara Falls

Pittsburgh

Indianapolis   Dayton-Springfield

St. Louis

Jacksonville

Fort Worth–Arlington

Galveston–Texas City   Houma

Lakeland–Winter Haven

Principal MSAs with Cost of Living Index < 90 and Leisure Score > 70

Spectator Sports

Spectator sports continue the boom enjoyed for most of the past 50 years. While major-league sports have become mainstays of big cities, more and more franchises are being created in smaller cities, particularly in the South, like Jacksonville, Florida; Nashville, Tennessee; and Charlotte, North Carolina. Perhaps more interesting is the growth of minor-league sports, particularly baseball and hockey, in places like Fresno, California, and the metropolitan area of Greensboro–Winston-Salem–High Point, North Carolina. The popularity of collegiate sports in college towns is legendary, but the appeal is spreading to wider segments of the population, particularly in states like Alabama and Kentucky, which lack major-league teams.

Outdoor Recreation

After booming in the early 1990s, golf has leveled off, but will probably continue to grow as baby boomers retire. The United States has over 14,000 18-hole equivalent courses, about 85% of which are public. The United States has one full-length equivalent golf course for about every 19,000 residents, better than all but a handful of countries like Canada, New Zealand, and Scotland. Planned golf communities—especially in Florida, Arizona, and Texas—are the biggest growth area in golf today. The Sun Belt, especially Florida, Arizona, and California, is well known for excellent public and private courses, but quality golf facilities exist in or near most metropolitan areas. A good guide to courses can be found on the Web at www.usagolf.com.

Park systems in most places are under strain, both at the national and local level. Improved automobile and transportation infrastructures and increased leisure time have made parks more accessible. Meanwhile, funding continues to suffer as government agencies are forced to cut back. The predictable result is crowding, reduced quality in some cases, and higher entrance fees. National parks in California have been known to close completely to new entrants on holiday weekends, and accommodations, including campsites, must be reserved up to a year in advance. The rule of thumb: Any national park within a weekend drive of a major city is likely to be overcrowded in the high season. As urban sprawl continues, some county and larger city parks once part of the countryside are now becoming true city and suburban treasures, with large areas for recreation, entertainment, water parks, zoos, and preserved history where local funding allows. Of course, New York's Central Park is the original example.

NASCAR TOWNS

One of the fastest growing spectator sports in the country doesn't involve balls, bats, goals, or teams in the traditional sense. It is auto racing, and the success of the NASCAR brand is nothing short of phenomenal. Auto racing was once very fragmented and local in nature, with only a few recognized centers of national interest like the Indianapolis Motor Speedway and Daytona Beach. The NASCAR circuit has brought national attention to places like Anniston, Alabama (Talladega Superspeedway); Florence, South Carolina (Darlington Raceway); Danville, Virginia (Martinsville Speedway); and Dover, Delaware (Dover International Speedway). NASCAR is *the* major source of local entertainment and enthusiasm in some of these areas.

The Hamilton County Park District in Cincinnati, Ohio, serves as an excellent modern-day example.

Leisure Attributes

Cities Ranked & Rated examines available activities in or near a place. Ratings are expressed either on a 1–10 scale (1 worst, 10 best) based on availability, proximity, and quality of facilities in the area or as specific numbers when that approach is more meaningful, as in the number of Starbucks. In the ranking process, areas that have a broad and diverse set of amenities—good restaurants, skiing, and parks—will rate higher than an area located next to a ski resort but nothing else.

These attributes come from a variety of data sources. Dining and shopping information comes from Claritas, Inc., and from individual retailer websites. Sports team information comes from the respective leagues. Golf course data is from Claritas, Inc. and skiing information is from the *White Book of Ski Sites*. National park data and inland water information come from the National Park Service and National Oceanic and Atmospheric Administration, respectively. All information is amended and rated by Sperling's BestPlaces. For lists of specific sports teams, zoos, golf courses, and ski facilities, see www.bestplaces.net/CRAR.

Table 3.62 shows the Leisure table for Reno, Nevada.

Dining & Shopping

- *Restaurant rating* is a 1–10 rating of restaurants in the area mainly considering quality and availability as compiled by travel guides and other industry sources.

- *No. outlet malls* is the number of such malls in an area.

- *No. Starbucks* is the number of Starbucks retail outlets in an area. The figure is indicative of the overall quality of retail establishments.

- *No. warehouse clubs* tallies the number of Costco, Sam's Club, and BJ's stores in an area. The figure is indicative of the availability of large-scale discount shopping.

Entertainment

- *Professional sports rating* is a 1–10 rating for professional baseball, football, basketball, and hockey teams, including major- and minor-league teams. New York leads this category. Its suburban communities share the rating because people will usually travel a commute distance for these events.

Table 3.62: Sample Leisure Table from Reno, Nevada

LEISURE SCORE: 74/RANK: 83

DINING & SHOPPING	AREA	U.S. AVG	ENTERTAINMENT	AREA	U.S. AVG	OUTDOOR ACTIVITIES	AREA	U.S. AVG
Restaurant rating	1	1	Professional sports rating	2	4	Golf-course rating	2	4
No. outlet malls	0	2	College sports rating	4	4	Ski-area rating	10	4
No. Starbucks	11	11	Zoo/aquarium rating	1	3	National Park rating	8	3
No. warehouse clubs	3	4	Amusement park rating	5	3	Sq. miles inland water	10.0	4.0
			Botanical garden/arboretum rating	3	3	Miles of coastline	0.0	11.4

- *College sports rating* rates collegiate sports at all levels on a 1–10 scale. Not surprisingly, college towns and some big cities rate high. Collegiate sports are available in all but 59 metropolitan areas.

- *Zoo/aquarium rating* is a 1–10 rating covering animal parks of all types, including marine parks with a high degree of animal activity. High ratings go to an assortment of big cities and areas near warm water. There are 155 areas with no noted presence.

- *Amusement park rating* covers amusement parks based on number, proximity, and quality of facilities on a 1–10 scale. There are 23 areas rated 9 or 10 and 201 areas with no noted presence.

- *Botanical garden/arboretum rating* represents formal gardens, conservatories, and other botanical facilities on a 1–10 scale. There are 14 areas rated 9 or 10 and 149 areas with no noted presence.

Outdoor Activities

- *Golf-course rating* rates public and private golf courses based on number, quality, and cost on a 1–10 scale. Some of the "leader board" might surprise in this area, including Chicago (no. 1), Detroit, and Philadelphia, along with more expected entrants like Phoenix, Las Vegas, and Tampa–St. Petersburg–Clearwater. Among smaller places, Myrtle Beach, South Carolina, and Jacksonville, Florida, are leaders. Every area has some golf presence, but places like Pine Bluff, Arizona; Pocatello, Idaho; and Laredo, Texas rate poorly.

- *Ski-area rating* takes into account that no metropolitan areas have skiing within their boundaries, so the 1–10 scale rating necessarily considers proximity. No surprises at the top of the list: Denver, Salt Lake City, and Reno. As popularity grows and snowmaking technology improves, even places like Atlanta get a small rating. There are 132 places with no facilities whatsoever, mostly in predictable places in the South and Florida.

- *National Park rating* is a 1–10 scale rating of the availability, proximity, and quality of nearby National Parks and National Forests. The highest ratings occur in western cities at the base of the Sierra Nevada, Rocky, and Cascade mountain ranges and areas in Arizona that border large areas of public land. There are 144 places with no noted national park resources.

- *Square miles inland water* is the measured amount of water in square miles. Inland water refers to completely enclosed bodies of water, not ocean bays or inlets. High on the list are cities in southern Louisiana, northern Minnesota, and Florida. Only 16 areas have no noted inland water.

- *Miles of coastline* represents the number of miles of coastline bordering the entire metropolitan area. Coastline usually refers to ocean coastline, but can also include the Great Lakes. Highest coastline ratings occur on islands: Nassau-Suffolk, New York (Long Island), and Honolulu, Hawaii. There are 247 places with no coastline.

Leisure Highlights, Table 3.63

Table 3.63: MSAs with Highly Rated Recreational Facilities

Rated on a 1-10 Scale

Amusement Parks		Rating	Zoos/Aquariums		Rating	Botanical Gardens/Arboretum		Rating
Atlanta	GA	10	Baltimore	MD	10	Chicago	IL	10
Chicago	IL	10	Chicago	IL	10	Los Angeles–Long Beach	CA	10
Harrisburg–Lebanon–Carlisle	PA	10	Los Angeles–Long Beach	CA	10	Nassau–Suffolk	NY	10
Los Angeles–Long Beach	CA	10	New York	NY	10	New York	NY	10
Minneapolis–St. Paul	MN-WI	10	San Diego	CA	10	Philadelphia	PA-NJ	10
Monmouth–Ocean	NJ	10	Washington	DC-MD-VA	10	San Diego	CA	10
Orange County	CA	10	Atlanta	GA	9	Washington	DC-MD-VA	10
Orlando	FL	10	Minneapolis–St. Paul	MN-WI	9	Atlanta	GA	9
San Jose	CA	10	St. Louis	MO-IL	9	Boston	MA-NH-ME	9
St. Louis	MO-IL	10	Atlantic–Cape May	NJ	8	Harrisburg–Lebanon–Carlisle	PA	9
Akron	OH	9	Boston	MA-NH-ME	8	Miami	FL	9
Cincinnati	OH-KY-IN	9	Bridgeport	CT	8	Minneapolis–St. Paul	MN-WI	9
Fort Worth–Arlington	TX	9	Chattanooga	TN-GA	8	Oklahoma City	OK	9
Houston	TX	9	Cleveland–Lorain–Elyria	OH	8	San Francisco	CA	9
Louisville	KY-IN	9	Detroit	MI	8	Ann Arbor	MI	8
Miami	FL	9	Jacksonville	FL	8	Asheville	NC	8
Norfolk–Virginia Beach–Newport News	VA-NC	9	Miami	FL	8	Atlantic–Cape May	NJ	8
Sacramento	CA	9	New Orleans	LA	8	Cleveland–Lorain–Elyria	OH	8
San Antonio	TX	9	Newark	NJ	8	Dallas	TX	8
San Diego	CA	9	Norfolk–Virginia Beach–Newport News	VA-NC	8	Des Moines	IA	8
Santa Cruz–Watsonville	CA	9	Omaha	NE-IA	8	Fort Worth–Arlington	TX	8
Tampa–St. Petersburg–Clearwater	FL	9	Philadelphia	PA-NJ	8	Honolulu	HI	8
Vallejo–Fairfield–Napa	CA	9	Phoenix–Mesa	AZ	8	Madison	WI	8
Fresno	CA	8	Pittsburgh	PA	8	Orange County	CA	8
Knoxville	TN	8	San Francisco	CA	8	Richmond–Petersburg	VA	8
Portland–Vancouver	OR-WA	8	Seattle–Bellevue–Everett	WA	8	Riverside–San Bernardino	CA	8
Richmond–Petersburg	VA	8	Bergen–Passaic	NJ	7	Seattle–Bellevue–Everett	WA	8
Seattle–Bellevue–Everett	WA	8	Cincinnati	OH-KY-IN	7	Baltimore	MD	7
Allentown–Bethlehem–Easton	PA	7	Columbia	SC	7	Bergen–Passaic	NJ	7
Biloxi–Gulfport–Pascagoula	MS	7	Columbus	OH	7	Charleston–North Charleston	SC	7

Source: Sperling's BestPlaces

Arts & Culture

Arts & Culture encompasses fine art, humanities, science, and history through cultural media, performing arts, and museums. These assets serve the twin purposes of providing intellectually stimulating entertainment and education for families and children. An area with strong cultural assets usually also has good educational ones, a strong sense of tradition and heritage, and finer entertainment options. Furthermore, strong cultural assets tend to attract other assets, thus improving an area's overall quality of life. This fact is not lost on local governments and chambers of commerce, many of which will aggressively pursue such amenities with funding when they can.

Arts & Culture Trends

More than ever, the major issue facing most performing arts is funding. Fiscal health is generally not a problem for the best-known entities, like the New York Philharmonic or the quasi-public Smithsonian Institution. Beyond that, almost every cultural asset faces the same issues: increasing costs, recession-driven declines in contributions and public support, and declining endowments.

Even the Metropolitan Museum of Art in New York reduced its hours of operation recently. Institutions at the fringe in small to medium cities and those dependent on large amounts of unionized talent, like symphony orchestras, are having the hardest time. Most orchestras and many local theaters only cover half of their costs through ticket sales.

Public radio and television are still holding their own, but stations must resort to more creative (and more commercial-like) activities in the face of competition from satellite and cable TV networks and satellite radio. Stations energetically sell program sponsorships to corporations and produce sponsored shows for networks, public and private. Some rent out their studios for income.

Libraries are going through tough budgetary times and "competition" from Internet and other media sources for both educational and entertainment uses. Most libraries have adapted by adding Internet access. Regarding overall library visits, a 2002 research study published by the American Library Association found an even split between those using libraries for educational and entertainment purposes, and that 62% of people surveyed have a library card and a similar number have visited a library

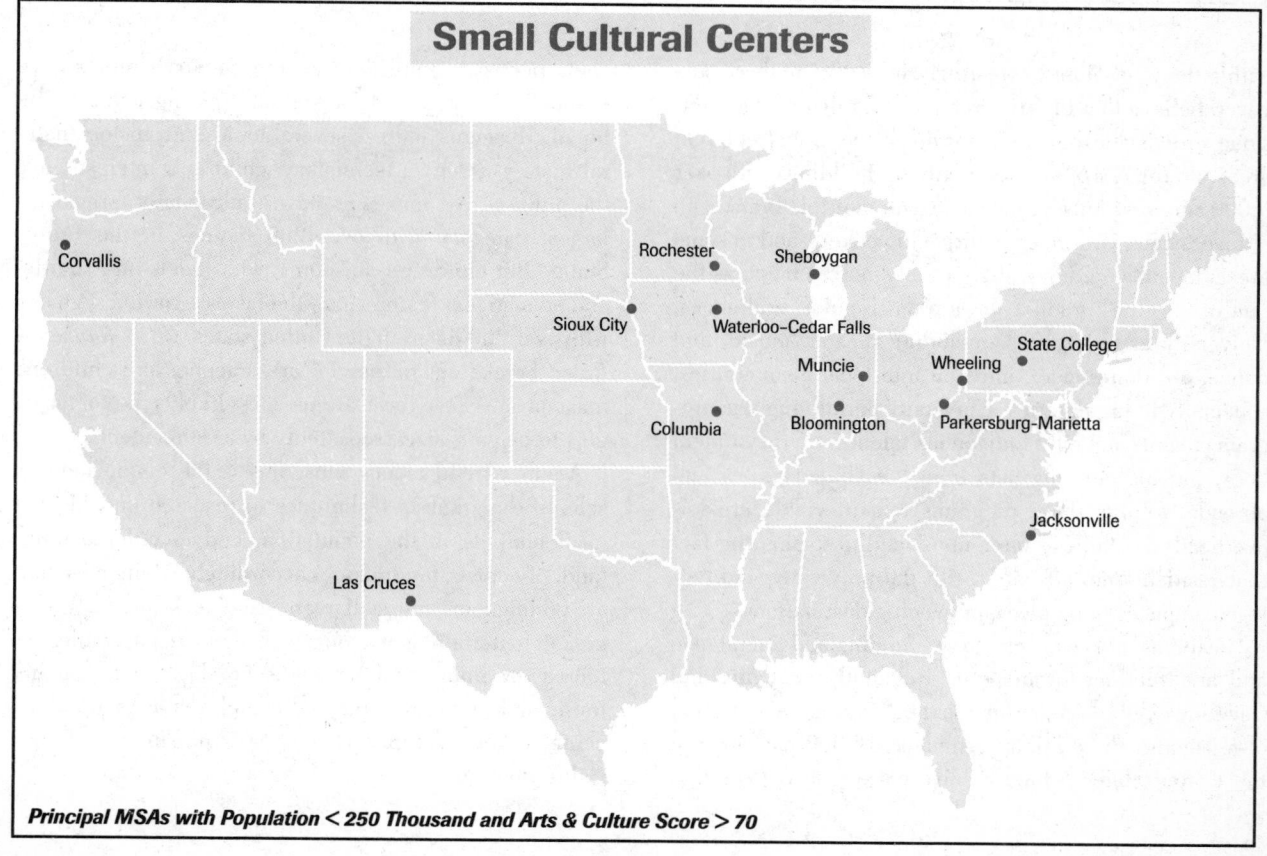

Small Cultural Centers

Principal MSAs with Population < 250 Thousand and Arts & Culture Score > 70

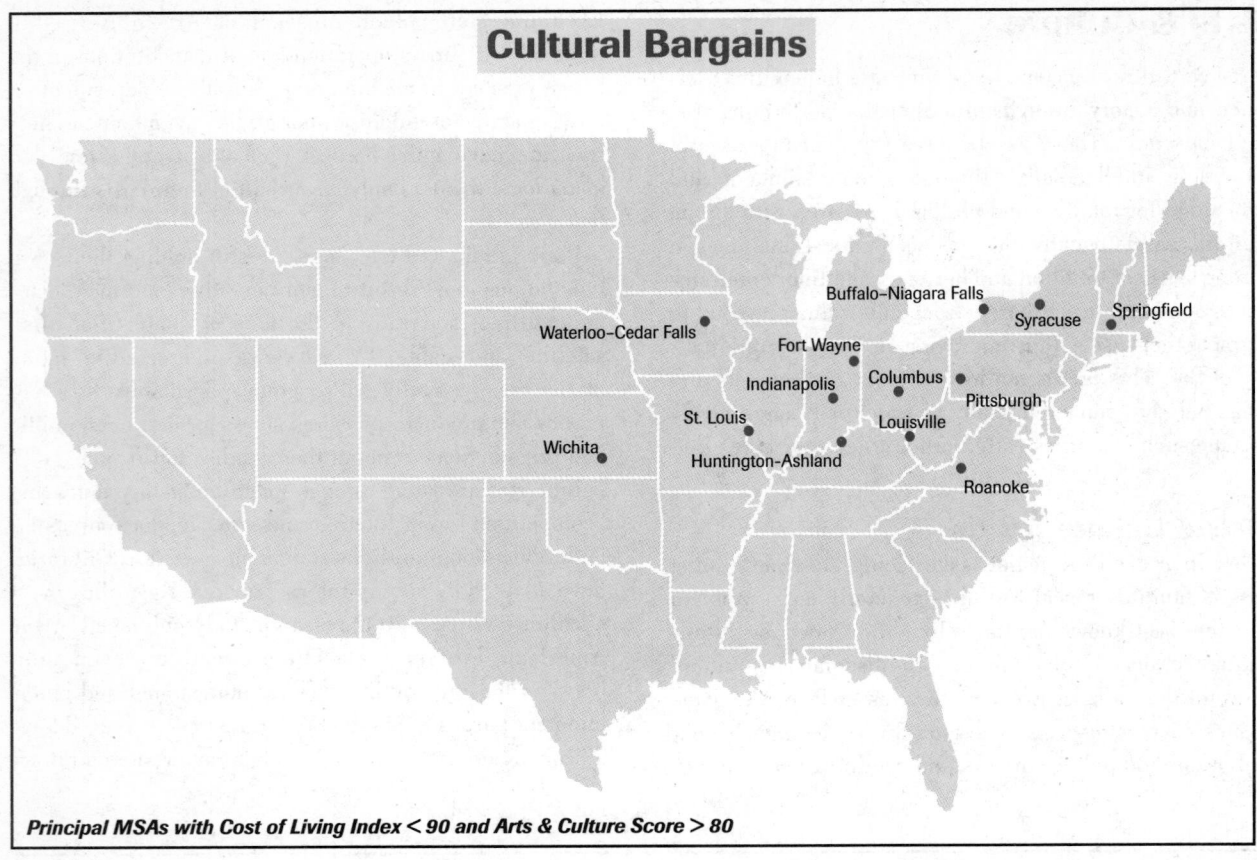

Cultural Bargains

Principal MSAs with Cost of Living Index < 90 and Arts & Culture Score > 80

within the year. More interestingly, over 90% of those surveyed believe that libraries play a vital role and will continue to exist despite the Internet. Among metropolitan areas, there are 16,000 public library buildings with over 9,000 administrative units (some with multiple branches).

Live theater continues to thrive in pockets, and in some areas depends on the quality of the venue as much as the quality of the product to attract regular audiences. University arts programs, including theater, music, and dance, are doing more outreach into local communities, especially in larger cities. University performing arts programs feature not only indigenous talent from the student body, but also touring acts from the United States and abroad. Helping these programs remain viable are low overhead and the use of campus facilities, plus the fact that residents not affiliated with the university find college campuses to be pleasant evening destinations.

Good museums continue to see funding and attendance and are trending toward more frequently changing and traveling exhibits. According to the American Association of Museums, there are an estimated 16,000 museums in the United States, which receive more than 850 million

visits per year, more than all the country's professional baseball, football, and basketball sporting events combined. Museums address several topics: art, history, natural history, science, technology, children's interests, and the military. Art museums have traditionally formed the largest category, with over 200 listings in the United States. But children's museums, with hands-on activities and educational features, are the fastest growing segment, with over 200 listed in the United States. *Cities Ranked & Rated* breaks out ratings for art, science, and children's museums because these are the most likely types of museums to be patronized repeatedly by area residents.

Another trend among museums is the employment of scientific marketing techniques to research and identify local markets in the population, and to tailor exhibits (and, of course, fundraising) accordingly. Many museums are adding more interactive and "fun" exhibits to provide greater entertainment along with educational value. An increasing number of museums are located in smaller towns and museum parks and complexes away from city centers; one example is Balboa Park in San Diego, California.

AMERICA'S MOST LITERATE CITIES

In 2003, the University of Wisconsin at Whitewater released a study and ranking of 64 U.S. cities based on the following variables contributing to literacy: the origination and circulation of local published materials such as periodicals and newspapers, the availability and quality of libraries, the presence of booksellers, and the overall level of educational attainment. A more literate city reads more than—not better than—a less literate city. One interesting trend emerges: Less reading seems to occur in Sun Belt cities.

The top 10 cities, in order:

1. Minneapolis–St. Paul, Minnesota
2. Seattle, Washington
3. Denver, Colorado
4. Atlanta, Georgia
5. San Francisco, California

6. Pittsburgh, Pennsylvania
7. Washington, D.C.
8. Louisville, Kentucky
9. Portland, Oregon
10. Cincinnati, Ohio

And the worst (out of 64 metropolitan areas studied):

54. Los Angeles, California (tie)
55. Toledo, Ohio (tie)
56. Fresno, California
57. Jacksonville, Florida
58. Memphis, Tennessee
59. Santa Ana, California

60. San Antonio, Texas
61. Detroit, Michigan
62. Long Beach, California
63. Corpus Christi, Texas
64. El Paso, Texas

Arts & Culture Attributes

Arts & Culture is divided into three areas: *Media & Libraries, Performing Arts,* and *Museums.* Since most people attend performing arts as a special occasion, rating points are usually given for available amenities up to 100 miles away unless that distance contains a significant geographic or transportation barrier. Most attributes are compiled by Sperling's BestPlaces mainly from cultural association publications. Library and university arts data come from the National Center for Education Statistics, U.S. Department of Education. All values are used in scoring and ranking.

Table 3.64 shows the Arts & Culture table for Corvallis, Oregon.

Media & Libraries

- *Arts radio rating* covers both "listener-supported" stations usually affiliated with National Public Radio (NPR) and private stations broadcasting classical music, jazz, or non-commercial talk formats, all rated on a 1–10 scale. Large cities typically score well, but others like Buffalo, New York; Portland, Oregon; and Columbia, South Carolina, have good ratings. There are 179 places with no noted arts radio presence.

Table 3.64: Sample Arts & Culture Table from Corvallis, Oregon

ARTS & CULTURE SCORE: 74/RANK: 83

MEDIA & LIBRARIES	AREA	U.S. AVG	PERFORMING ARTS	AREA	U.S. AVG	MUSEUMS	AREA	U.S. AVG
Arts radio rating	1	3	Classical music rating	2	4	Overall museum rating	2	6
No. public libraries	4	28	Ballet/dance rating	1	3	Art museum rating	3	5
Library volumes per capita	3.6	2.8	Professional theater rating	1	3	Science museum rating	1	4
			University arts programs rating	4	5	Children's museum rating	1	3

- *No. public libraries* is the total number of library facilities in an area. Fort Wayne, Indiana; Grand Rapids–Muskegon–Holland, Michigan; and Toledo, Ohio, are surprisingly high on the list—Grand Rapids alone has 62 library facilities. Smaller towns with lower incomes and less education dominate the bottom.

- *Library volumes per capita* is the actual number of books available per citizen in the area.

Performing Arts

- *Classical music rating* covers traditional symphony and opera companies in or near an area. The number of musicians, frequency of performances, and overall quality and critical acclaim all figure into the rating on a 1–10 scale. Large cities score well, as do communities in close proximity to large cities or cities with major classical music assets.

- *Ballet/dance rating* covers traditional ballet and dance companies in a manner similar to classical music, rated on a 1–10 scale.

- *Professional theater rating* covers traditional theater companies but not dinner theaters or traveling shows, rated on a 1–10 scale.

- *University arts programs rating* covers classical music, dance, theater, and international programs sponsored by local colleges and universities, all rated on a 1–10 scale.

Museums

- *Overall museum rating* recognizes the number and quality of all museums in the area on a 1–10 scale. Not surprisingly, New York and Washington, D.C., top the list, but Cleveland, Ohio; Detroit, Michigan; and Ann Arbor, Michigan, are up there as well. There are only nine areas with no noted museum presence. The next three attributes single out the types of museums of most interest to long-term residents of an area (in contrast to historical museums, which typically appeal more to the traveler). For a list of 8,000 museums, galleries, and exhibits throughout the United States, see www.bestplaces.net/CRAR.

- *Art museum rating* covers museums designated as art museums by the American Museum Association, rated on a 1–10 scale.

- *Science museum rating* covers museums designated as science museums by the American Museum Association, rated on a 1–10 scale.

- *Children's museum rating* covers museums designated as children's museums by the American Museum Association, rated on a 1–10 scale.

Arts & Culture Highlights, Table 3.65

Table 3.65: MSAs with Highly Rated Museums

Rated on a 1-10 Scale

Art Museums	Rating	Science Museums	Rating	Children's Museums	Rating
Baltimore MD	10	Boston MA-NH-ME	10	Boston MA-NH-ME	10
Boston MA-NH-ME	10	Chicago IL	10	Chicago IL	10
Chicago IL	10	Flagstaff AZ-UT	10	Cincinnati OH-KY-IN	10
Los Angeles–Long Beach CA	10	Los Angeles–Long Beach CA	10	Fort Worth–Arlington TX	10
Minneapolis–St. Paul MN-WI	10	Nassau-Suffolk NY	10	Hartford CT	10
New York NY	10	New York NY	10	Indianapolis IN	10
Philadelphia PA-NJ	10	Norfolk–Virginia Beach–Newport News VA-NC	10	Los Angeles–Long Beach CA	10
Pittsburgh PA	10	Oakland CA	10	New York NY	10
San Francisco CA	10	Riverside–San Bernardino CA	10	Norfolk–Virginia Beach–Newport News VA-NC	10
St. Louis MO-IL	10	San Francisco CA	10	Seattle-Bellevue-Everett WA	10
Washington DC-MD-VA	10	Tucson AZ	10	St. Louis MO-IL	10
Atlanta GA	9	Washington DC-MD-VA	10	Washington DC-MD-VA	10
Buffalo–Niagara Falls NY	9	Albuquerque NM	9	Atlanta GA	9
Cleveland-Lorain-Elyria OH	9	Baltimore MD	9	Baltimore MD	9
Dallas TX	9	Columbus OH	9	Bergen-Passaic NJ	9
Denver CO	9	Hartford CT	9	Kansas City MO-KS	9
Detroit MI	9	Las Vegas NV-AZ	9	Newark NJ	9
Fort Worth–Arlington TX	9	Minneapolis–St. Paul MN-WI	9	Philadelphia PA-NJ	9
Hartford CT	9	Newark NJ	9	San Francisco CA	9
Houston TX	9	Philadelphia PA-NJ	9	San Jose CA	9
Indianapolis IN	9	Phoenix-Mesa AZ	9	West Palm Beach–Boca Raton FL	9
Milwaukee-Waukesha WI	9	Pittsburgh PA	9	Albany-Schenectady-Troy NY	9
Newark NJ	9	San Diego CA	9	Albuquerque NM	8
Norfolk–Virginia Beach–Newport News VA-NC	9	Seattle-Bellevue-Everett WA	9	Birmingham AL	8
Oakland CA	9	Albany-Schenectady-Troy NY	9	Columbus OH	8
Orange County CA	9	Ann Arbor MI	8	Dallas TX	8
Phoenix-Mesa AZ	9	Atlanta GA	8	Greensboro–Winston-Salem–High Point NC	8
Richmond-Petersburg VA	9	Charlotte–Gastonia–Rock Hill NC-SC	8	Houston TX	8
San Diego CA	9	Cleveland-Lorain-Elyria OH	8	Knoxville TN	8
Santa Fe NM	9	Dallas TX	8	Minneapolis–St. Paul MN-WI	8

Source: Sperling's BestPlaces

AWARDS THAT SPEAK VOLUMES

Cities Ranked & Rated recognizes two perennial civic awards given to (usually) smaller towns and cities in recognition of efforts toward preservation and improved quality of life. They are factored into the *Cities Ranked & Rated* Quality of Life score.

- The *Great American Main Street Award* is given annually in association with the National Trust for Historic Preservation " . . . to recognize exceptional accomplishments in revitalizing America's historic downtowns and neighborhood commercial districts." The city of Greenville, South Carolina, won the award in 2003 thanks to a series of improvements to downtown street parking and infrastructure, a luxury convention hotel on main street, and new markets and businesses in older historic buildings, including second floors. Other winners on the *Cities Ranked & Rated* metropolitan area list include:

  2003 Rome, Georgia; Wenatchee, Washington (two emerging MSAs covered in chapter 7)

  2002 La Crosse, Wisconsin

  2001 Enid, Oklahoma; Mansfield, Ohio

  1999 San Luis Obispo, California; Bay City, Michigan; Lafayette, Indiana

- The *All-America City Award* is given by the National Civic League to " . . . communities (including neighborhoods) in which community members, governments, business and nonprofit organizations demonstrate successful resolution of community-critical issues." Winners on the metropolitan area list include:

  2003 New Haven, Connecticut; Des Moines, Iowa; Corpus Christi, Texas; Racine, Wisconsin

  2002 Tuscaloosa, Alabama; Anchorage, Alaska; Buffalo–Niagara Falls, New York; Hampton, Virginia

  2001 South Miami, Florida; Fayetteville, North Carolina; Brownsville, Texas

  2000 Fresno, California; Worcester, Massachusetts; Gastonia, North Carolina; Fargo-Moorhead, North Dakota–Minnesota; Lancaster, Pennsylvania

  1999 Green Bay, Wisconsin; Lowell, Massachusetts; Rocky Mount, North Carolina; Shreveport, Louisiana; Stockton, California; Tallahassee, Florida; Ocala, Florida; Lafayette, Indiana; Louisville, Kentucky; Akron, Ohio

Quality of Life

Coauthors Bert Sperling and Peter Sander determined a combined score for each metropolitan area based on the perceived overall quality of life. The score is included in scoring and ranking, but is not shown in individual city tables. Refer to Tables 2.4 and 2.5 in chapter 2 for the Quality of Life scores for each metropolitan area.

By their very nature, the factors determining this score are difficult to quantify. They are based mainly on perception, personal experience, and anecdotes from others who have spent time in these places. Features considered include:

- *Physical attractiveness.* This includes both the physical setting and overall appearance of the town itself, factors which influence initial impressions and long-term satisfaction in an area. The effects of a pancake-flat, windswept, nondescript landscape with dirty air and little vegetation are far different from that of attractive, well-kept, tree-lined streets with good buildings and a pristine mountain, valley river, or lake-side setting. Cities such as Boulder, Colorado; Corvallis, Oregon; and Burlington, Vermont, do well in this regard, while some larger cities such as Pittsburgh, Pennsylvania, and Chattanooga, Tennessee, are improving.

■ *Heritage.* A city that knows its roots and tries to preserve its physical and cultural heritage is usually more physically attractive as well as genuine in character. These cities are almost invariably better places to live. Metropolitan areas with well-preserved historic districts and public buildings include Charlottesville, Virginia; Boston, Massachusetts; Portland, Maine; and Santa Fe, New Mexico.

■ *Overall ease of living.* The most subjective element in this subjective category, ease of living incorporates crowdedness, attitude and friendliness of people, and simplicity of infrastructure. In essence, it considers the "stress factor." Issues with places like Los Angeles, San Francisco, and New York are obvious, and these cities score poorly, while cities in the South—even the workaholic New South—tend to score high.

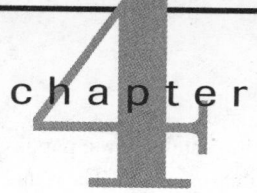
The States

Which states have the most people? The highest growth? The most favorable tax climate? The best educational system? Evaluating information at the state level can shed comparative light on U.S. places. Many state-level attributes and characteristics shape the nature of individual places within the state and identify important structural characteristics common to those places. Some of these facts and figures help to develop a more complete image of the state, while others like tax policy have a direct effect on day-to-day life.

How *Cities Ranked & Rated* Compares States

Cities Ranked & Rated takes a high-level, comparative approach to evaluating states. Complete descriptions of physical environment and most amenities are purposely left out due to space and easy access elsewhere. In addition, many attributes vary considerably within the state and make more sense to examine at a local level. What this chapter does include are comparisons across some of the most interesting aspects of population, physical environment, economics, taxes, politics, law, and education. They offer insight into a state's character and how it might align to an individual's interests. Moreover, many indicate something beyond face value. For example, drunk driving laws say something about the ability—and willingness—of a state legislature to involve itself in ensuring personal safety.

Some statewide attributes may not apply to a particular city under examination. For example, the state of Oregon may be only 44% forested, but someone in Portland might perceive that number to be much higher. Likewise, the political landscape of Georgia may not well describe that of Atlanta, nor does the tax burden in Bridgeport necessarily describe all of Connecticut. Therefore, when examining specific places, it's important not to stop at the state level—this would be like ending a shopping trip at the selection of a store.

Much of this information can be found in an almanac or at U.S. government websites, and some attributes may already be familiar—for instance, that California is no. 1 in population and that Massachusetts tends to vote Democratic. However, *Cities Ranked & Rated* presents this material in such a way as to make easy comparisons and to show *leaders and laggards* among the states for each attribute. Most tables are sorted by *attribute*—not by state—a different approach from most reference resources. There are two columns, one for states that *exceed* the U.S. average for an attribute, and one for states *below* that average. This approach will become clearer with examples that follow.

Overall Rankings

Table 4.1 shows a comparison of the average ranks of the metropolitan areas in chapter 5 by state. The table doesn't rank individual states *per se,* but illustrates which states contain areas with consistently better ratings. When viewing the table, keep in mind that ranks for individual cities in the state may differ widely from the averages, and all states have an assortment of high and low-ranked cities. Note also that these averages are straight arithmetic averages, not weighted by population, so a "good" or "bad" metropolitan area will have equal influence on a state average regardless of size.

Table 4.1: Average MSA Score & Rank by State

	Sort by State			Sort by Rank	
State	Average Score	Average Rank	State	Average Score	Average Rank
AL	45.6	233	NM	85.7	29
AR	49.8	203	OR	79.0	51
AZ	53.2	198	DE	75.6	54
CA	55.8	165	VA	78.6	66
CO	73.2	74	CO	73.2	74
CT	57.8	162	WA	68.6	102
DE	75.6	54	MN	66.5	113
FL	66.0	115	UT	64.5	115
GA	61.7	147	FL	66.0	115
ID	56.1	174	IN	64.8	122
IA	54.1	185	NV	62.4	129
IL	60.3	142	MT	61.3	138
IN	64.8	122	NC	62.6	139
KS	62.9	142	KS	62.9	142
KY	52.6	187	IL	60.3	142
LA	39.7	264	GA	61.7	147
MA	44.2	237	MO	58.7	153
MD	56.1	179	WI	57.9	162
ME	45.9	225	CT	57.8	162
MI	54.6	195	CA	55.8	165
MN	66.5	113	PA	57.1	168
MO	58.7	153	OK	56.9	173
MS	39.1	279	ID	56.1	174
MT	61.3	138	OH	55.5	178
NC	62.6	139	MD	56.1	179
ND	55.6	180	ND	55.6	180
NE	53.1	201	TX	53.7	181
NH	48.7	224	WY	55.7	184
NJ	54.8	186	IA	54.1	185
NM	85.7	29	NJ	54.8	186
NV	62.4	129	TN	53.9	187
NY	41.0	246	KY	52.6	187
OH	55.5	178	SC	53.9	190
OK	56.9	173	SD	52.4	192
OR	79.0	51	MI	54.6	195
PA	57.1	168	AZ	53.2	198
SC	53.9	190	NE	53.1	201
SD	52.4	192	AR	49.8	203
TN	53.9	187	NH	48.7	224
TX	53.7	181	ME	45.9	225
UT	64.5	115	AL	45.6	233
VA	78.6	66	MA	44.2	237
WA	68.6	102	WV	46.4	240
WI	57.9	162	NY	41.0	246
WV	46.4	240	LA	39.7	264
WY	55.7	184	MS	39.1	279

Note: For states with more than one metro area, scores represent an arithmetic average of all metro areas in the state.

Population

With regards to population, state characteristics may fall short of indicating the true nature of a metropolitan area. San Francisco is very different from Bakersfield, California; Detroit from Kalamazoo, Michigan; and Boston from Fitchburg, Massachusetts. Nevertheless, state-level indicators are a valuable place to start.

Tables 4.2, 4.3, and 4.4 present three state views: population, population density, and population growth. The data works together to define the states in terms of crowding (or uncrowding) now and in the future. At the same time, population growth numbers reveal the aggregate decisions of those who've chosen to move from one state to another, although it doesn't reveal the rationale for their choices.

Table 4.2 shows 2001 state population estimates from the U.S. Census Bureau in order from largest to smallest. The population dominance of California, Texas, and New York is no surprise. However, of note is that the top seven states comprise 45% of the U.S. population. The largest group of states—25 in all—has between 2.5 and 9 million people, while the remaining 25 states are relatively less populated.

In terms of crowding, total population figures mean more when looked at against land area, that is, as *population density*, shown in Table 4.3. At first glance, one can take these figures at face value and do no wrong. The smaller East Coast and New England states are generally more dense and crowded, as expected. But most of these states, most notably New Jersey in recent years, have made great strides to plan land use and manage encroaching development. While this may make the populated

Table 4.2: 2001 State Populations

Most Populous		Least Populous	
CA	34,501,130	SC	4,063,011
TX	21,325,018	OR	3,472,867
NY	19,011,376	OK	3,460,097
FL	16,396,515	CT	3,425,074
IL	12,482,301	IA	2,923,179
PA	12,287,150	MS	2,858,029
OH	11,373,541	KS	2,694,641
MI	9,990,817	AR	2,692,090
NJ	8,484,431	UT	2,269,769
GA	8,383,915	NV	2,106,074
NC	8,186,268	NM	1,829,146
VA	7,187,734	WV	1,801,916
MA	6,379,304	NE	1,713,235
IN	6,114,745	ID	1,321,006
WA	5,987,973	ME	1,286,670
TN	5,740,021	NH	1,259,181
MO	5,627,707	HI	1,224,398
WI	5,401,906	RI	1,058,920
MD	5,375,136	MT	904,433
AZ	5,307,331	DE	796,195
MN	4,972,294	SD	756,600
LA	4,465,430	AK	634,892
AL	4,464,356	ND	634,448
CO	4,417,714	VT	613,090
KY	4,065,556	WY	494,423

Notes: Total U.S. population: 284,223,053. District of Columbia (D.C.) not included.

Source: U.S. Census Bureau

Table 4.3: State Population Density

Number of Residents Per Square Mile

Above U.S. Average		Below U.S. Average	
NJ	1,143.9	WV	74.8
RI	1,013.3	VT	66.3
MA	813.7	MN	62.5
CT	706.9	MS	60.9
MD	549.9	IA	52.3
DE	407.5	AR	51.7
NY	402.7	OK	50.4
FL	304.1	AZ	46.7
OH	277.8	CO	42.6
PA	274.2	ME	41.7
IL	224.6	OR	36.2
CA	221.2	KS	32.9
HI	190.6	UT	27.6
VA	181.5	NE	22.3
MI	175.9	NV	19.2
IN	170.5	ID	16.0
NC	168.1	NM	15.1
GA	144.8	SD	10.0
NH	140.4	ND	9.2
TN	139.3	MT	5.2
SC	134.9	WY	5.1
LA	102.5	AK	1.1
KY	102.3		
WI	99.5		
WA	90.0		
AL	88.0		
MO	81.7		
TX	81.5		

Note: U.S. average: 75.0 per square mile
Source: U.S. Census Bureau

Table 4.4: State Population Growth

Estimated, 2000-2001

Above U.S. Average		Below U.S. Average	
NV	5.4%	ME	0.9%
AZ	3.4%	TN	0.9%
CO	2.7%	NJ	0.8%
FL	2.6%	AR	0.7%
GA	2.4%	VT	0.7%
TX	2.3%	WI	0.7%
ID	2.1%	CT	0.6%
CA	1.9%	IN	0.6%
NH	1.9%	KY	0.6%
NC	1.7%	MO	0.6%
DE	1.6%	NM	0.6%
UT	1.6%	IL	0.5%
WA	1.6%	MA	0.5%
MD	1.5%	MI	0.5%
OR	1.5%	MS	0.5%
VA	1.5%	AL	0.4%
AK	1.3%	OK	0.3%
SC	1.3%	KS	0.2%
HI	1.1%	MT	0.2%
MN	1.1%	NY	0.2%
RI	1.0%	OH	0.2%
		SD	0.2%
		NE	0.1%
		WY	0.1%
		PA	0.0%
		IA	-0.1%
		LA	-0.1%
		WV	-0.4%
		ND	-1.2%

Note: U.S. Average: 1.0%
Source: U.S. Census Bureau

areas still *more* dense, the approach creates open space. Likewise, California is shown as no. 12 on the density list. When one realizes that as much as two-thirds of California is made up of uninhabitable desert or mountain areas, the inhabited areas in California become as dense as all but a small handful of states.

Population growth, shown in Table 4.4, is a good indicator of a state's future. Growth has a two-pronged effect: (1) It improves the local economy and (2) it attracts still more people due to the perception of success in the area. But population increases also tend to be a leading indicator of problems—crime, air quality, cost of living—as well as opportunity.

For a host of reasons, including both physical and tax climate, states like Nevada and Arizona have seen exceptional growth in recent years. Infrastructure in those states has become sufficient to support a variety of economic activity, and both areas have become popular retirement spots. Overall, these states have pro-growth attitudes and policies, catering to new business and residential development. Other states, such as Colorado and Florida, grow simply because of location.

Physical Environment

At the state level, the degree of forestation and general climate type tell something of the physical environment.

Forestation

Table 4.5 shows the percentage of state land covered by forest, as reported by the U.S. Forest Service. Although many people like the openness and beauty of agricultural land and even desert, the amount of tree cover is a good indicator of an area's attractiveness and natural state. The table shows that states in the East and South tend to be the most forested. However, in the West, consider that states like Oregon, Washington, and Montana have large areas of dry, "rain shadow" (where mountains block incoming storms) steppes not conducive to forests. So the forested areas of these states are every bit as dense as those in the East. Likewise, a large portion of Wisconsin

is committed to farmland, so the relatively low number may understate the physical attractiveness of the area. Like other facts presented in this chapter, this information helps to form an image, rather than to provide a black-and-white comparison among states.

Climate Type

Climate is most meaningfully discussed at the metropolitan area level because of local variations in topography and proximity to water, two factors that can greatly influence weather conditions. However, climate zones can give an idea of general statewide conditions. Table 4.6 shows the predominant zone in each state where most of the population is located. These zones are not absolute: States like Kansas and Michigan sit across zone boundaries; California, Washington, and Idaho have significant alpine subzones in mountainous areas; and large states such as Texas stretch across multiple zones.

Table 4.5: State Forestation

Percentage of Land Covered by Forest

Above U.S. Average		Below U.S. Average	
NH	83.2%	OR	44.5%
WV	78.2%	LA	41.8%
ME	77.4%	RI	40.6%
VT	73.8%	ID	40.4%
AL	65.5%	FL	39.3%
GA	63.5%	WI	37.0%
SC	59.8%	NJ	36.0%
VA	57.9%	CA	35.6%
PA	57.6%	MD	34.0%
NC	56.0%	CO	32.0%
MS	54.8%	MO	31.4%
NY	53.6%	AK	30.4%
AR	52.5%	MN	30.0%
CT	51.3%	UT	29.9%
TN	50.5%	MI	29.5%
KY	49.2%	OH	27.4%
MA	47.4%	AZ	26.9%
WA	44.9%	HI	26.3%
		DE	25.0%
		MT	23.9%
		NM	19.7%
		IN	19.0%
		OK	16.9%
		WY	15.9%
		NV	12.6%
		IL	11.5%
		TX	11.2%
		IA	5.7%
		SD	3.4%
		KS	2.6%
		NE	1.5%
		ND	1.0%

Note: U.S. average: 44.6%

Source: U.S. Forest Service

Table 4.6: Major U.S. Climate Zones

Climate Type	Description	States
Lower 48 States		
Humid Subtropical (no dry season)	Hot, humid summer days are influenced by Gulf of Mexico moisture. Winters are mild. Precipitation arrives as frequent thunderstorms, steady periods of rain in all seasons, and minimal snow.	AR, AL, DE, FL, GA, KY, LA, MS, OK, NC, SC, TN, TX, VA, WV
Humid Continental (hot summer)	Four definite seasons experience changeable weather, with alternating influence between warm, moist, Gulf of Mexico air and cooler, drier air from the northwest. Hot summer periods, often in the 90s, are intermittently moderated by advancing cold fronts. Winters alternate between below freezing and just above freezing, with occasional colder snaps. Precipitation is variable and occasionally heavy during periods of change.	CT, IA, IL, IN, KS, MD, MO, NE, NJ, OH, PA, RI
Humid Continental (warm summer)	Four definite seasons have changeable weather and normally cool days with occasional periods of warmer weather year-round. Summers temperatures rarely exceed 90°F. Winter typically remains below freezing with occasional bitter cold snaps. Summer precipitation arrives mainly as thundershowers. Winter precipitation is mainly snow, which may remain on the ground all season.	MA, ME, MI, MN, ND, NH, NY, SD, VT, WI
Steppe (semi arid)	Plenty of sunshine and strong diurnal temperature variations characterize this higher altitude climate, typically found at elevations greater than 3,000 feet. Long, warm, summer days have low humidity; cool evenings often require a jacket. Winters are cool and dry. Precipitation arrives mainly as summer thundershowers and winter snow often associated with advancing frontal systems. Snow may be heavy.	CO, ID, MT, NM, NV, UT, WY
Desert (mostly arid)	Precipitation totals less than 10 inches per year. The air and ground are dry at all times. Temperatures are generally hot, with over 100°F common in summer. Winter highs reach the 60s and 70s, sometimes higher. Low humidity means cool, summer evenings and winter nights often below freezing. Precipitation is scarce and often occurs in scattered, heavy downpours.	AZ
Marine West Coast	Strong and persistent flow of moist, marine air from the Pacific governs the climate. Marine influence keeps temperatures in a tight range year-round, with few summer or winter extremes. Persistent moisture flows make clouds and drizzly rain a constant possibility. Occasional stronger storm systems with wind and heavier rain occur. Freezing temperatures and snow are relatively uncommon for the latitude.	OR, WA
Mediterranean	A strong seasonal pattern brings warm, very dry summers followed by cool, wet winters. Virtually all precipitation arrives from November through May, although annual amounts may equal locations in the East or Midwest. Summers are warm near the coast to quite hot inland, with cloudless days and very low humidity the norm. Ocean-borne, rain-free stratus clouds may move in from the Pacific. Winters are the most humid, with frequent cloudy and foggy conditions and drizzle, with an occasional heavier storm.	CA

Economy

This section presents a comparative overview of elements of the private economy (personal income) and public economy (government size). Added in for flavor is state dependence on tourism, a revealing comparison of economic factors.

Per Capita Income

Table 4.7 shows per capita income by state. On a highly averaged basis, this table illustrates what the typical resident earns per year as gross income. There is a surprisingly wide gap between top and bottom, where individuals in Connecticut on average earn twice as much as individuals in Mississippi. The numbers reflect each state's job types, education levels, lifestage mix, and more. The large number of retirees living in Florida brings that state's average down, and states with a mainly rural or farm economy tend to be lower. Interestingly, a large number of

states are below the national average, while a relatively few are above it, but substantially so. Still, one doesn't necessarily become wealthy by living in Connecticut, Massachusetts, or New Jersey. Cost of living and taxes in those states tend to be high. In fact, awareness of the cost of living in those states serves to drive incomes higher, as people are reluctant to live and work there unless they are paid more.

Those considering relocating should note that a high salary in one state is a low salary in another, and vice versa. Earnings should be "stepped up" comparably from one state to another if the latter has a higher cost of living. Likewise, retaining the same income level when moving to a state with a lower cost of living may allow for financial progress. But keep in mind that although taxation tends to level the cost of living picture statewide, differences still exist within a state's borders. For example, in New York, the Cost of Living Index—an area's total cost of living measured against a national average—can range from 82

Table 4.7: 2001 Per Capita Income by State			
Above U.S. Average		Below U.S. Average	
CT	$41,930	WY	$28,807
MA	$38,845	OH	$28,619
NJ	$38,153	NE	$28,564
NY	$35,864	HI	$28,554
MD	$34,950	KS	$28,507
IL	$34,755	FL	$28,493
NH	$33,928	TX	$28,486
CO	$32,957	GA	$28,438
MN	$32,791	MO	$28,029
CA	$32,768	OR	$28,000
VA	$32,295	VT	$27,992
DE	$32,121	IN	$27,532
WA	$31,582	NC	$27,418
AK	$30,997	IA	$27,283
PA	$30,617	TN	$26,758
RI	$29,984	ME	$26,385
NV	$29,860	SD	$26,301
MI	$29,538	ND	$25,538
WI	$28,911	AZ	$25,479
		KY	$25,057
		OK	$24,787
		SC	$24,594
		AL	$24,426
		ID	$24,257
		UT	$24,202
		LA	$24,084
		MT	$23,532
		NM	$23,162
		AR	$22,912
		WV	$22,725
		MS	$21,643

Note: U.S. average: $28,869

Source: U.S. Department of Commerce

(18% below national average, in Elmira) to 161 (61% above national average, in New York City). In California, the COL Index can range from 94 (Visalia-Tulare-Porterville) to 196 (San Francisco).

Size of State Government

Tables 4.8 and 4.9 give a sense of the size of state government, and, reading between the lines, government involvement in income redistribution and daily living in general. Table 4.8 shows total state expenditures, provided by the U.S. Census Bureau and current through 2001. Table 4.9 puts this number into better perspective by showing expenditures per capita, which are calculated by dividing by 2001 U.S. Census population estimates.

The tables illustrate a sizable discrepancy between states on budget size, and, by extension, government size. The numbers give an idea of the sheer size of California's budget, which is larger than the GNP (gross national product) of all but 20 countries in the world. California's

projected 2003–2004 budget gap of $34 billion is larger than the entire budget of all but eight states. However, on a per capita basis, California only ranks 12th. A look at total and per capita expenditures together brings New York to the top of the big government list. Notably, Texas and Florida have the lowest per capita state expenditures. These states have no state income tax, and generally pursue a path of small government and low involvement. Further analysis is needed to understand if this approach affects vital services.

Note: Tables 4.8 and 4.9 reflect expenditures only, not revenues. They do not indicate that state's tax "take," and many of these expenditures are financed by incoming federal funds and directed by federal programs. That is why (besides the small population) Alaska shows such a high per capita figure, having a proportionally large number of federal programs administered by the state. Other states with low populations and large public assets, like Wyoming and Hawaii, similarly reflect large per capita expenditures.

The figures in these tables are from 2001, as most recently collected by the U.S. Census Bureau. In recent years, the soft economy and decline in state revenues have wreaked havoc on state budgets, causing many spending dislocations. Programs are being cut, and at the same time, expenditures for federal-state programs such as unemployment insurance are increasing. Still, the tables reveal the fundamental dynamics of government size and services in each state. But fiscal *health* is as important as fiscal *size*. Large budget deficits eventually result in a combination of higher taxes, reduced services, and reduced economic incentives for industry and commerce—all of which have an effect sooner or later.

Dependence on Tourism

Dependence on tourism, shown in Table 4.10, is the total amount spent on travel and tourism divided by the state's total Gross Domestic Product, or GDP. This indicator shows two things. First, states with a high dependence on tourism experience amplified cycles compared to the economy as a whole. That is, when the U.S. and world economies are strong, tourism increases, and the resulting economic boom is usually stronger than experienced in other neighboring economies. On the flip side, economies of tourism-dependent states may suffer proportionately more during downturns, although in some notable cases like California, tourism has actually reduced the shock.

Second, this piece of information reveals something about the nature and quality of life in an area. As much as a third of Hawaii's economy comes from tourism, and local

Table 4.8: 2001 State Government Expenditures

Total Annual Expenditures in Billions

Above U.S. Average		Below U.S. Average	
CA	$170.5	IN	$21.6
NY	$106.6	MD	$21.5
TX	$64.7	MO	$18.9
PA	$51.5	TN	$18.4
FL	$50.3	CT	$18.2
OH	$47.9	SC	$18.1
MI	$46.7	KY	$17.3
IL	$45.2	AZ	$17.1
NJ	$37.7	AL	$16.7
MA	$32.4	LA	$16.4
NC	$31.6	OR	$16.3
GA	$27.9	CO	$15.7
WA	$27.8	IA	$12.3
VA	$26.8	MS	$11.7
WI	$24.9	OK	$11.4
MN	$24.6	AR	$10.6
		KS	$10.2
		UT	$9.3
		NM	$9.2
		AK	$9.0
		WV	$7.3
		HI	$6.8
		NV	$6.7
		NE	$6.1
		ME	$5.7
		RI	$5.4
		ID	$5.0
		NH	$4.4
		DE	$4.3
		MT	$4.0
		VT	$3.4
		ND	$2.9
		SD	$2.7
		WY	$2.6

Note: U.S. average: $23.7 billion per year
Source: U.S. Census Bureau

Table 4.9: 2001 Per Capita State Expenditures

Above U.S. Average		Below U.S. Average	
AK	$14,250	MS	$4,103
NY	$5,607	UT	$4,077
HI	$5,547	WV	$4,052
VT	$5,498	MD	$3,997
DE	$5,415	AR	$3,936
WY	$5,350	NC	$3,863
CT	$5,311	KS	$3,784
MA	$5,084	ID	$3,748
RI	$5,053	AL	$3,745
NM	$5,015	VA	$3,727
MN	$4,950	LA	$3,675
CA	$4,941	IL	$3,619
OR	$4,700	NE	$3,567
MI	$4,670	SD	$3,556
WA	$4,647	CO	$3,551
WI	$4,602	IN	$3,530
ND	$4,568	NH	$3,503
MT	$4,476	MO	$3,356
ME	$4,460	GA	$3,323
SC	$4,450	OK	$3,299
NJ	$4,439	AZ	$3,230
KY	$4,263	NV	$3,204
OH	$4,210	TN	$3,203
IA	$4,198	FL	$3,066
PA	$4,190	TX	$3,033

Note: U.S. average: $4,166 per person per year
Source: U.S. Census Bureau

Table 4.10: State Dependence on Tourism

Tourist Revenue as Percent of State GDP			
Above U.S. Average		**Below U.S. Average**	
HI	33.5%	MO	5.2%
NV	28.1%	SD	5.2%
FL	11.8%	VA	4.9%
MT	8.7%	GA	4.9%
WY	7.8%	NH	4.8%
VT	7.6%	IL	4.7%
NM	6.4%	IA	4.7%
MS	6.4%	OR	4.6%
SC	6.2%	NE	4.6%
AZ	6.1%	NY	4.5%
ND	6.0%	TX	4.5%
LA	5.9%	KY	4.3%
ME	5.8%	MD	4.3%
UT	5.7%	MA	4.3%
ID	5.7%	AL	4.3%
CO	5.6%	NC	4.2%
TN	5.5%	NJ	4.2%
CA	5.5%	OK	4.0%
AR	5.5%	KS	4.0%
AK	5.4%	WA	3.9%
		RI	3.8%
		WV	3.8%
		MN	3.7%
		WI	3.6%
		PA	3.6%
		MI	3.5%
		OH	3.4%
		CT	3.3%
		IN	3.2%
		DE	3.0%

Note: U.S. average: 5.3% per year

Source: *The World Almanac and Book of Facts, 2003*

residents who aren't serving tourists spend most of their time trying to avoid them. Similarly, high levels of tourists add a crowding factor, particularly in certain seasons. Plus, they may cause the arrival of services and amenities, such as motel strips, souvenir shops, wax museums, and other "tourist sprawl," not particularly attractive to local residents. This is not to say that living in a state depending on tourism is all bad—but it is good to know where a state rates.

Taxation

When comparing states, it is important to look at the complete tax picture, and the tax laws are so different and complex among the states that this becomes quite challenging. Different states tax different things at different rates in different ways, so "apples-to-apples" comparisons can be elusive. As an example, the state of Oregon publishes a 9% marginal (applied to every incremental dollar of earnings) tax rate, which appears high and, in fact, rates the

state as the third highest in this category. But on closer examination, one finds that Oregonians can deduct federal income taxes against adjusted gross income (AGI)—the basis for applying the tax—reducing the effective rate to something less than 7% for most residents. Likewise, many states apply a flat rate to every dollar earned, while others, looking to tax the rich and help the poor, apply higher rates to higher levels of income, a concept known as "progressivity." Sales tax rates not only vary by nominal state rate, but many states allow the addition of local surcharges and differ in terms of what's taxed—some tax groceries and drugs, some do not. Property tax is a patchwork of different rates and rules.

Keep the following in mind when comparing state taxes:

- **Assume states are more similar than they appear.** States need to raise revenue, one way or another. Oregon and Montana are noted for high income tax rates, but have no sales tax. Washington and Texas have no income tax, but have among the highest sales tax rates. California has high income and sales taxes, but relatively low property tax rates—although Californians still pay plenty of property tax due to high basis.

- **Understand that different tax structures affect different lifestyles differently.** Some states aim the bulk of their taxation at income, some at consumption, still others at wealth as represented by property ownership. A self-employed person with healthy income and modest needs may want to live in Washington or Texas; a retired person with modest income might do better in Oregon or Delaware, and might consider both states differently depending on his or her housing situation. A working family might do okay in Connecticut or New Jersey—until they decide to buy an expensive home in a nice neighborhood.

- **Look at total tax burden.** Comparing rates, basis, and progressivity is a good place to start, but to identify the differences—and how a certain lifestyle will be ultimately taxed—examine the total tax burden. See the District of Columbia study, toward the end of this section, for comparative total tax burdens by state.

- **Research further the states under consideration.** Individual state websites provide access to state information. Income tax booklets and other literature can be ordered. For a comprehensive and well-updated web source, the Federation of Tax Administrators, a nonprofit organization, is recommended (www.taxadmin.org).

TAX TALK

When examining any tax, one must understand the underlying components that determine how much tax is actually paid. Understanding the following terms will help avoid erroneous conclusions:

- **Basis** is the base on which the tax is levied. For income tax, the basis is adjusted gross income (AGI), the figure to which the state applies its tax. Basis rules vary—different exemptions for children, deductibility of other taxes, inclusion of Social Security payments are but a few of the defining factors. For sales tax, the basis is purchases, but the taxing of food, groceries, and medications varies by state. Today, sales taxes are applied to goods, but there is a movement afoot (but generally not acted upon so far) to apply sales taxes to services—such as haircuts, construction, and repair labor—as is done by Canada with their national goods and services tax (GST). This practice would increase total sales tax substantially for most people. Finally, there is property tax, where the basis can be the current appraised value, some fraction of that value, or original purchase price of a home. In many cases property tax goes beyond real property into personal property, such as cars and "intangible" investment assets.

- **Rate** is the percentage applied to the basis. For income tax, the *marginal* rate is the rate applied to the last dollar, as in earned income for income tax. The *average* rate is the average of all rates applied in all brackets. It us useful to understand whether the income tax is *progressive*—that is, whether it taxes higher incomes at higher marginal rates. California and New Jersey are highly progressive, while in Michigan and Indiana, everyone pays the same rate. For sales tax, there is a published *state* rate, but there may be surcharges added for local general fund purposes or for such sources as schools and mass transit. Finally, property tax rates vary greatly in some states according to geographic district and the industrial base within that district.

State Income Tax

Table 4.11 is sorted by top marginal rates (the top bracket on an income basis), with states above the 6.4% U.S. average marginal rate (for states that have income tax) on the left, and those below that rate on the right. Also shown are the tax rates at the intermediate basis levels of $50,000 and $100,000. These rates and basis levels are based on "married filing jointly" filing status.

To help interpret the table, consider California as an example. The table shows that California has a 9.3% marginal tax rate on a top marginal bracket of $76,582. That is, every dollar earned above $76,582 is taxed at 9.3%. Each state has a different bracket and rate structure below the top rate—for examples, see the marginal rates at $50,000 and $100,000 income levels. (Amounts on the table are $50,001 and $100,001, because many states draw bracket lines at the round figure.) States listed with a top marginal rate but no top income bracket charge a flat rate for all brackets. The progressive states begin to show (New Jersey, at 2.45% for $50,000 rising to 6.37% at $100,000) as do the less progressive (Kentucky, 6% at all but the lowest levels). Michigan, Indiana, Illinois, and Pennsylvania have flat rates—that is, the same percentage applies regardless of income level or bracket. Even this picture may be incomplete because of additional income basis adjustments and tax credits lurking below the surface.

States with no income tax—Alaska, Florida, Nevada, South Dakota, Texas, Washington, and Wyoming—are particularly noteworthy. Among residents of these states, differences in taxes can be thousands of dollars per year for high-income individuals and families. It is advisable to watch for changes in this status.

State Sales Tax

Table 4.12 shows comparative *base* sales tax rates—the state-legislated tax to which local levies are often added depending on state law. The table also indicates whether food and medication are included in the tax base—an important consideration especially for large families or older individuals. Keep in mind, too, that some states tax the sales of big-ticket items, such as automobiles, while others don't. What is *not* shown are the local add-ons, which can be substantial in some otherwise-favorable

Table 4.11: 2002 State Income Taxes									
Sorted by Top Marginal Rate for Married Filing Jointly									
Above U.S. Average					Below U.S. Average				
State	Top Marginal Rate	Top Income Bracket	Marginal Rate at AGI $50,001	Marginal Rate at AGI $100,001	State	Top Marginal Rate	Top Income Bracket	Marginal Rate at AGI $50,001	Marginal Rate at AGI $100,001
MT	11.00%	$75,400	10.00%	11.00%	NJ	6.37%	$150,000	2.45%	6.37%
CA	9.30%	$76,582	8.00%	9.30%	GA	6.00%	$10,000	6.00%	6.00%
OR	9.00%	$12,500	9.00%	9.00%	KY	6.00%	$8,000	6.00%	6.00%
IA	8.98%	$54,495	7.92%	8.98%	LA	6.00%	$50,000	6.00%	6.00%
ME	8.50%	$33,400	8.50%	8.50%	MO	6.00%	$9,000	6.00%	6.00%
HI	8.25%	$80,000	7.60%	8.25%	DE	5.95%	$60,000	5.55%	5.95%
NC	8.25%	$200,000	7.00%	7.75%	VA	5.75%	$17,000	5.75%	5.75%
NM	8.20%	$100,000	7.10%	8.20%	ND	5.54%	$297,350	3.92%	2.92%
MN	7.85%	$108,660	7.05%	7.05%	MA	5.30%	-	5.30%	5.30%
ID	7.80%	$43,460	7.80%	7.80%	AZ	5.04%	$300,000	3.74%	4.72%
OH	7.50%	$200,000	5.20%	6.90%	AL	5.00%	$6,000	5.00%	5.00%
AR	7.00%	$26,999	7.00%	7.00%	MS	5.00%	$10,000	5.00%	5.00%
OK	7.00%	$10,000	7.00%	7.00%	MD	4.75%	$3,000	4.75%	4.75%
SC	7.00%	$12,500	7.00%	7.00%	CO	4.63%	-	4.63%	4.63%
UT	7.00%	$7,500	7.00%	7.00%	CT	4.50%	$20,000	4.50%	4.50%
NY	6.85%	$40,000	6.85%	6.85%	MI	4.10%	-	4.10%	4.10%
WI	6.75%	$165,000	6.50%	6.50%	IN	3.40%	-	3.40%	3.40%
NE	6.68%	$46,750	5.01%	6.68%	IL	3.00%	-	3.00%	3.00%
WV	6.50%	$30,000	6.50%	6.50%	PA	2.80%	-	2.80%	2.80%
KS	6.45%	$60,000	6.25%	6.45%					

States with Income Tax Tied to Basis Other Than Earned Income		States with No Income Tax
RI	25% of federal income tax	AK, FL, NV, SD, TX, WA, WY
VT	24% of federal income tax	
TN	6% on dividends and interest only	
NH	5% on dividends and interest only	

Notes: U.S. average (among states with income tax) for 2002 is 6.4%. There is fairly wide variation in the base Adjusted Gross Income (AGI) on which the income tax is levied. For example, Oregon allows federal income taxes to be deducted from state AGI, making the effective top marginal rate closer to 7.0%. See local tax documents and websites.

Source: *The World Almanac and Book of Facts, 2003* from the CCH Tax Guide

states such as Colorado. Table 4.13 in the District of Columbia study below sheds some light on this.

The table illustrates that there's no geographic or socioeconomic pattern to who has high rates and who does not. In general, states with higher sales tax have lower income tax (exception: California), and the five states with no sales tax (1) face deep internal struggles to keep it that way, and (2) tend to have higher income tax (exceptions: Alaska and New Hampshire).

District of Columbia Tax Rates & Tax Burdens Study

The list of organizations and individuals interested in the comparative impact of taxation is endless. Conscientious lawmakers and policymakers everywhere want to see what others are doing to determine what is "in line" and

appropriate. The government of the District of Columbia has taken the extra steps to publish the annual *Tax Rates and Tax Burdens In the District of Columbia—A Nationwide Comparison* (known here as the "D.C. study"), a hallmark research piece. The study examines tax burdens for the *largest* city in each of the 50 states. The study estimates basis and applies currently researched rates to that basis, including many of the subtleties of sales tax surcharges, income adjustments, and property valuation. If the study has a weakness, it is that it only calibrates on the largest city—the total burden in New York may exceed that in Binghamton because of different basis, and often, different rates. As a cautionary note, this information is presented as a way to compare *states*. The situation in a particular metropolitan area may be different.

Table 4.12: State Sales Taxes

January 2003 Base Sales Tax Rate, Before Local Surcharges

Above U.S. Average		Basis			Below U.S. Average		Basis		
		Include Food?	Include Rx Drugs?	Include Non-Rx Drugs?			Include Food?	Include Rx Drugs?	Include Non-Rx Drugs?
CA	7.25%	No	No	Yes	AR	5.13%	Yes	No	Yes
MS	7.00%	Yes	No	Yes	IA	5.00%	No	No	Yes
RI	7.00%	No	No	No	ID	5.00%	Yes	No	Yes
TN	7.00%	6.00%	No	Yes	MA	5.00%	No	No	Yes
MN	6.50%	No	No	No	MD	5.00%	No	No	No
NV	6.50%	No	No	No	ME	5.00%	No	No	Yes
WA	6.50%	No	No	Yes	ND	5.00%	No	No	Yes
IL	6.25%	1.00%	1.00%	1.00%	NM	5.00%	Yes	No	Yes
TX	6.25%	No	No	No	OH	5.00%	No	No	Yes
CT	6.00%	No	No	No	SC	5.00%	Yes	No	Yes
FL	6.00%	No	No	No	VT	5.00%	No	No	No
IN	6.00%	No	No	Yes	WI	5.00%	No	No	Yes
KY	6.00%	No	No	Yes	UT	4.75%	Yes	No	Yes
MI	6.00%	No	No	Yes	NC	4.50%	No	No	Yes
NJ	6.00%	No	No	No	OK	4.50%	Yes	No	Yes
PA	6.00%	No	No	No	VA	4.50%	3.50%	No	No
WV	6.00%	Yes	No	Yes	MO	4.23%	1.23%	No	Yes
AZ	5.60%	No	No	Yes	AL	4.00%	Yes	No	Yes
NE	5.50%	No	No	Yes	GA	4.00%	No	No	Yes
KS	5.30%	Yes	No	Yes	HI	4.00%	Yes	No	Yes
					LA	4.00%	Yes	No	Yes
					NY	4.00%	No	No	No
					SD	4.00%	Yes	No	Yes
					WY	4.00%	Yes	No	Yes
					CO	2.90%	No	No	Yes

States with No Sales Tax

AK, DE, MT, NH, OR

Notes: U.S. average (among states with sales tax): 5.25%. For basis, a percentage indicates that item is taxed at the rate shown.

Source: Federation of Tax Administrators

State Sales Tax Detail

Table 4.13 from the D.C. study presents a deeper picture of sales tax beyond Table 4.12 by providing a glimpse of local surcharges to the state general sales tax. This table illuminates states that have chosen to push taxation down to a self-determined local level. Colorado, for example, has a low general tax rate of 2.9%, but an additional 3.5% is added in the Denver area, followed by another 0.8% transit levy, bringing the effective rate to 7.2%. In general, the largest cities in a state are most likely to have supplemental sales, school, and especially transit taxes.

Property Tax

With the exception of a few states, property tax defies a broad, state-level comparison. While basis computation is fairly consistent among states, rates can vary widely. Many states leave rates almost entirely up to local option.

States like Ohio allow localities to determine residential rates based on the industrial base in the locality; that is, residents pay what the industrial base doesn't. As a result, residents in areas with a lot of industry pay relatively little, while residents in areas with little industry might pay a lot. A different system exists in California, where the rate (determined by the historic Proposition 13) is consistent statewide (save for a few minor local district levies voted in), but the *basis* is determined by purchase price and can vary greatly. This means that in an inflating real estate environment, extreme tax variations exist from one parcel of property to another, depending on when it was last sold. As these examples illustrate, determining property tax in a specific area is difficult. The property tax rates given in chapter 5 for the metropolitan areas may also be subject to the same variations as above. These statistics are a "finger in the air" to determine, comparatively, which way the wind blows.

Table 4.13: State & Local General Sales Tax

City	State	Components					Total
		State	City	County	School	Transit	
New Orleans	LA	4.0%	3.5%		1.5%		**9.0%**
Seattle	WA	6.5%	0.9%	0.3%		1.2%	**8.8%**
Chicago	IL	6.3%	1.0%	0.8%		0.8%	**8.8%**
Oklahoma City	OK	4.5%	3.9%				**8.4%**
Los Angeles	CA	6.0%	1.0%	0.3%		1.0%	**8.3%**
New York City	NY	4.0%	4.0%			0.3%	**8.3%**
Memphis	TN	6.0%		2.3%			**8.3%**
Houston	TX	6.3%	1.0%			1.0%	**8.3%**
Birmingham	AL	4.0%	3.0%	1.0%			**8.0%**
Phoenix	AZ	5.6%	1.8%	0.7%			**8.0%**
Las Vegas	NV	2.0%		3.0%	2.3%		**7.5%**
Denver	CO	2.9%	3.5%			0.8%	**7.2%**
Kansas City	MO	4.2%	1.5%	0.9%		0.5%	**7.1%**
Jacksonville	FL	6.0%		0.5%		0.5%	**7.0%**
Atlanta	GA	4.0%		1.0%	1.0%	1.0%	**7.0%**
Minneapolis	MN	6.5%	0.5%				**7.0%**
Jackson	MS	7.0%					**7.0%**
Charlotte	NC	4.5%		2.5%			**7.0%**
Philadelphia	PA	6.0%	1.0%				**7.0%**
Providence	RI	7.0%					**7.0%**
Fargo	ND	5.0%	1.0%	0.5%			**6.5%**
Omaha	NE	5.0%	1.5%				**6.5%**
Salt Lake City	UT	4.8%	1.0%	0.5%		0.3%	**6.5%**
Little Rock	AR	4.6%	0.5%	1.0%			**6.1%**
Bridgeport	CT	6.0%					**6.0%**
Louisville	KY	6.0%					**6.0%**
Detroit	MI	6.0%					**6.0%**
Newark	NJ	6.0%					**6.0%**
Sioux Falls	SD	4.0%	2.0%				**6.0%**
Charleston	WV	6.0%					**6.0%**
Cheyenne	WY	4.0%		2.0%			**6.0%**
Wichita	KS	4.9%		1.0%			**5.9%**
Albuquerque	NM	4.5%	1.1%	0.3%			**5.8%**
Washington	DC	5.8%					**5.8%**
Columbus	OH	5.0%		0.5%		0.3%	**5.8%**
Milwaukee	WI	5.0%		0.6%			**5.6%**
Des Moines	IA	5.0%					**5.0%**
Boise	ID	5.0%					**5.0%**
Indianapolis	IN	5.0%					**5.0%**
Boston	MA	5.0%					**5.0%**
Baltimore	MD	5.0%					**5.0%**
Portland	ME	5.0%					**5.0%**
Columbia	SC	5.0%					**5.0%**
Burlington	VT	5.0%					**5.0%**
Virginia Beach	VA	3.5%	1.0%				**4.5%**
Honolulu	HI	4.0%					**4.0%**
Median							**6.5%**

Source: 2001 D.C. Tax Rates & Tax Burdens Study

TAXES TO DIE FOR

While pondering which state has the best and worst taxes for the living, knowing which to *die* in is becoming increasingly significant. Federal estate tax rules changed substantially with the Economic Growth and Tax Relief Reconciliation Act (EGTRRA) passed in 2001. Until now, most state inheritance tax laws matched federal law, and federal estate tax credits offset the impact of state inheritance taxes. That may be changing. While 5 states had decoupled from federal law before the 2001 act, resulting in greater complexity—and net new "death" taxes in some cases—that list is now up to 18 and growing. It's unclear how this will evolve. For estates greater than $1 million, in-state financial advisors should be contacted for current details on that state.

Table 4.14 from the D.C. study shows tax rates in each of the largest cities, and the "assessment level" factor that may strongly influence the basis. The rate and the basis work together to determine the total tax, and many localities use a fraction—often a small fraction—of a property's appraised value (or transaction value) to determine tax. The evolution of this system is unclear, but the political desire to avoid the impression of a drastic wealth tax, or recognition that most people only "own" a small portion of their residence net of the mortgage, may have played a part. That said, states with a low assessment level, such as Arizona, Oklahoma, or North Dakota, seem to compensate for this with a higher tax rate. The "effective rate"—both factors taken together—is shown at the far right. Again—every state is different, and a true apples-to-apples comparison is challenging.

With the property tax basis and rate parameters in Table 4.14, the D.C. study then estimated how much property was owned, on average, by people of differing income levels. To do this, the study referred to a U.S. Census Bureau study of ratios of average home values to total household income compiled for each state. Table 4.15 shows this ratio and the D.C. study's assumed home values for the largest city in each state. Notable are the differences between states, with residents of California and New York extending themselves to buy houses worth over five times their annual income, while those in Kansas, Pennsylvania, or Iowa are spending less than twice their annual income.

Estimated Total Tax Burden

Tables 4.16, 4.17, and 4.18 pull it all together—sales tax, property tax, and state income tax—for the major cities at three different household income levels: $50,000, $100,000, and $150,000. Each table includes a figure for auto tax, which represents registration, sales taxes at purchase, and property taxes related to the ownership of a car.

From the tables, the relatively high tax burdens for East Coast cities, particularly Bridgeport, Connecticut; Newark, New Jersey; and Providence, Rhode Island, are apparent. Property tax is the category that moves these three to the top. Through these tables one can readily separate the high tax states (Connecticut, Minnesota, and New Jersey) from the low tax states (Florida, South Dakota, and Wyoming). Also interesting is the migration of California (Los Angeles) from 24th place at the $50,000 level to 7th place on the $150,000 income list, reflecting the more progressive nature of the state's tax policy. But keep in mind—in California, a much higher percentage of residents achieve the higher levels of income.

The average state and local tax burden is about 10% of income plus or minus 6% depending on situation. Variations in the type of tax levied by each state are greater than the total tax burden.

Note: The figures presented in Tables 4.13 through 4.18 may not agree with those presented at the metropolitan area level in chapter 5, due to local variation in tax laws and differences in the timing of collection of individual data values.

Table 4.14: Residential Property Tax Rates & Assessment Levels

City	State	Nominal Rate per $100	Assessment Level	Effective Rate per $100
Bridgeport	CT	$6.50	70%	$4.55
Des Moines	IA	$4.44	90%	$4.00
Providence	RI	$3.59	100%	$3.59
Newark	NJ	$26.40	12%	$3.12
Manchester	NH	$3.07	100%	$3.07
Milwaukee	WI	$2.84	93%	$2.65
Philadelphia	PA	$8.26	32%	$2.64
Houston	TX	$2.62	100%	$2.62
Portland	ME	$2.40	100%	$2.40
Baltimore	MD	$2.33	100%	$2.33
Detroit	MI	$6.46	35%	$2.23
Fargo	ND	$49.14	4%	$2.06
Burlington	VT	$2.41	83%	$2.00
Jacksonville	FL	$1.97	100%	$1.97
Omaha	NE	$2.01	95%	$1.91
Chicago	IL	$8.35	22%	$1.86
Phoenix	AZ	$18.20	10%	$1.82
Memphis	TN	$7.02	25%	$1.76
Atlanta	GA	$4.30	40%	$1.72
New Orleans	LA	$17.00	10%	$1.70
Jackson	MS	$16.91	10%	$1.69
Boise City	ID	$1.73	96%	$1.65
Anchorage	AK	$1.80	91%	$1.63
Columbus	OH	$5.19	31%	$1.59
Columbia	SC	$37.93	4%	$1.52
Indianapolis	IN	$10.00	15%	$1.50
Portland	OR	$2.07	72%	$1.50
Sioux Falls	SD	$1.73	85%	$1.47
Billings	MT	$1.83	79%	$1.45
Salt Lake City	UT	$1.46	99%	$1.44
Little Rock	AR	$6.90	20%	$1.38
Wilmington	DE	$2.38	55%	$1.31
Albuquerque	NM	$3.76	33%	$1.25
Minneapolis	MN	$1.37	86%	$1.18
Louisville	KY	$1.17	100%	$1.17
Charlotte	NC	$1.31	88%	$1.15
Kansas City	MO	$6.00	19%	$1.14
Virginia Beach	VA	$1.22	92%	$1.12
Oklahoma City	OK	$10.10	11%	$1.11
Boston	MA	$1.11	100%	$1.11
Los Angeles	CA	$1.07	100%	$1.07
Wichita	KS	$1.17	92%	$1.07
Seattle	WA	$1.19	89%	$1.06
Las Vegas	NV	$3.03	35%	$1.06
Charleston	WV	$1.52	60%	$0.91
Washington	DC	$0.96	90%	$0.86
New York City	NY	$11.18	7%	$0.77
Cheyenne	WY	$7.33	10%	$0.70
Birmingham	AL	$6.95	10%	$0.70
Denver	CO	$5.68	9%	$0.52
Honolulu	HI	$0.37	100%	$0.37
Median		$3.05	71.1%	$1.50

Source: 2001 D.C. Tax Rates & Tax Burdens Study

Table 4.15: Factors Used in Housing Value Assumptions

City	State	Housing to Income Ratio	Assumed Value: $50,000 Income	Assumed Value: $100,000 Income	Assumed Value: $150,000 Income
Honolulu	HI	6.87	$343,361	$652,386	$927,075
Los Angeles	CA	5.55	$277,402	$527,064	$748,986
New York City	NY	5.06	$252,942	$480,591	$682,945
Boston	MA	4.32	$215,850	$410,115	$582,795
Seattle	WA	4.17	$208,698	$396,527	$563,486
Newark	NJ	3.87	$193,301	$367,272	$521,913
Atlanta	GA	3.51	$175,391	$333,244	$473,557
Denver	CO	3.44	$172,010	$326,818	$464,426
Washington	DC	3.40	$169,825	$322,667	$458,527
Salt Lake City	UT	3.40	$169,805	$322,630	$458,474
Providence	RI	3.17	$158,307	$300,783	$427,428
Chicago	IL	3.10	$154,948	$294,401	$418,360
Portland	OR	3.08	$154,065	$292,723	$415,975
Bridgeport	CT	2.97	$148,467	$282,088	$400,862
Burlington	VT	2.85	$142,572	$270,886	$384,943
Albuquerque	NM	2.72	$135,805	$258,030	$366,674
Las Vegas	NV	2.72	$136,035	$258,466	$367,294
New Orleans	LA	2.70	$134,981	$256,463	$364,447
Anchorage	AK	2.52	$126,174	$239,730	$340,669
Portland	ME	2.49	$124,275	$236,122	$335,541
Columbia	SC	2.49	$124,403	$236,366	$335,889
Phoenix	AZ	2.42	$121,161	$230,206	$327,135
Charlotte	NC	2.38	$118,814	$225,746	$320,797
Minneapolis	MN	2.34	$116,765	$221,853	$315,265
Boise City	ID	2.32	$116,026	$220,450	$313,271
Virginia Beach	VA	2.31	$115,698	$219,826	$312,385
Manchester	NH	2.28	$114,211	$217,001	$308,369
Louisville	KY	2.24	$112,138	$213,061	$302,771
Billings	MT	2.22	$110,921	$210,750	$299,487
Wilmington	DE	2.21	$110,708	$210,345	$298,912
Cheyenne	WY	2.19	$109,470	$207,992	$295,568
Columbus	OH	2.14	$106,982	$203,266	$288,852
Milwaukee	WI	2.12	$106,127	$201,642	$286,544
Charleston	WV	2.11	$105,680	$200,792	$285,336
Indianapolis	IN	2.01	$100,553	$191,051	$271,494
Sioux Falls	SD	1.97	$98,707	$187,544	$266,509
Houston	TX	1.96	$98,039	$186,275	$264,706
Birmingham	AL	1.95	$97,485	$185,222	$263,210
Baltimore	MD	1.95	$97,494	$185,239	$263,234
Fargo	ND	1.95	$97,750	$185,725	$263,925
Memphis	TN	1.93	$96,380	$183,123	$260,227
Little Rock	AR	1.88	$94,107	$178,803	$254,089
Detroit	MI	1.88	$93,936	$178,478	$253,626
Oklahoma City	OK	1.88	$94,052	$178,699	$253,941
Jacksonville	FL	1.86	$92,924	$176,555	$250,894
Omaha	NE	1.85	$92,678	$176,089	$250,231
Kansas City	MO	1.83	$91,281	$173,433	$246,457
Jackson	MS	1.79	$89,437	$169,930	$241,480
Des Moines	IA	1.74	$87,036	$165,368	$234,997
Philadelphia	PA	1.61	$80,597	$153,135	$217,613
Wichita	KS	1.60	$80,106	$152,202	$216,287
Median		2.31	$115,698	$219,826	$312,385

Source: 2001 D.C. Tax Rates & Tax Burdens Study

Table 4.16: Estimated Tax Burden, $50,000 Total Household Income

For a Family of Four, 2001

Rank	City	State	Income Tax	Property Tax	Sales Tax	Auto Tax	Total Tax Burden	Percent
1	Bridgeport	CT	$316	$6,755	$752	$636	**$8,459**	16.9%
2	Newark	NJ	$598	$6,022	$618	$142	**$7,380**	14.8%
3	Philadelphia	PA	$3,630	$2,131	$656	$206	**$6,623**	13.2%
4	Providence	RI	$1,470	$3,698	$701	$606	**$6,476**	13.0%
5	Des Moines	IA	$1,780	$3,263	$747	$215	**$6,004**	12.0%
6	Detroit	MI	$2,649	$2,093	$671	$207	**$5,619**	11.2%
7	Minneapolis	MN	$1,648	$2,982	$681	$253	**$5,564**	11.1%
8	Baltimore	MD	$2,412	$2,270	$679	$188	**$5,549**	11.1%
9	Portland	ME	$2,595	$2,304	$0	$172	**$5,071**	10.1%
10	Milwaukee	WI	$1,657	$2,580	$734	$217	**$5,188**	10.4%
11	New York City	NY	$2,634	$1,727	$733	$75	**$5,170**	10.3%
12	Louisville	KY	$3,188	$998	$639	$293	**$5,118**	10.2%
13	Portland	OR	$2,595	$2,304	$0	$172	**$5,071**	10.1%
14	Atlanta	GA	$1,507	$2,373	$920	$249	**$5,049**	10.1%
15	Washington	DC	$2,784	$1,176	$754	$218	**$4,933**	9.9%
16	Chicago	IL	$1,135	$2,500	$1,009	$172	**$4,816**	9.6%
17	Columbus	OH	$2,287	$1,484	$638	$185	**$4,594**	9.2%
18	Salt Lake City	UT	$2,046	$1,349	$922	$264	**$4,581**	9.2%
19	Charlotte	NC	$1,972	$1,368	$809	$299	**$4,449**	8.9%
20	Burlington	VT	$1,049	$2,523	$630	$167	**$4,369**	8.7%
21	Kansas City	MO	$2,068	$1,041	$884	$342	**$4,334**	8.7%
22	Boston	MA	$1,830	$1,917	$382	$199	**$4,328**	8.7%
23	Columbia	SC	$1,707	$1,487	$645	$410	**$4,250**	8.5%
24	Los Angeles	CA	$220	$2,893	$787	$340	**$4,240**	8.5%
25	Omaha	NE	$1,252	$1,773	$816	$349	**$4,190**	8.4%
26	Birmingham	AL	$2,273	$650	$1,035	$228	**$4,185**	8.4%
27	Oklahoma City	OK	$1,874	$944	$1,106	$191	**$4,115**	8.2%
28	Honolulu	HI	$2,223	$1,107	$606	$171	**$4,107**	8.2%
29	Little Rock	AR	$1,618	$1,299	$877	$292	**$4,085**	8.2%
30	Manchester	NH	$0	$3,504	$318	$177	**$3,999**	8.0%
31	Albuquerque	NM	$1,107	$1,698	$943	$153	**$3,901**	7.8%
32	Virginia Beach	VA	$1,795	$1,300	$524	$259	**$3,879**	7.8%
33	Charleston	WV	$1,697	$964	$810	$370	**$3,841**	7.7%
34	Phoenix	AZ	$864	$1,705	$1,116	$151	**$3,837**	7.7%
35	Indianapolis	IN	$1,838	$1,243	$635	$110	**$3,826**	7.7%
36	Jackson	MS	$1,089	$1,212	$947	$548	**$3,797**	7.6%
37	Boise City	ID	$1,736	$1,089	$656	$234	**$3,715**	7.4%
38	Fargo	ND	$633	$2,034	$681	$206	**$3,554**	7.1%
39	New Orleans	LA	$1,235	$1,020	$1,015	$210	**$3,480**	7.0%
40	Seattle	WA	$0	$2,222	$1,058	$180	**$3,460**	6.9%
41	Wilmington	DE	$1,837	$1,446	$0	$170	**$3,453**	6.9%
42	Wichita	KS	$1,330	$642	$814	$437	**$3,224**	6.4%
43	Billings	MT	$1,736	$1,163	$0	$272	**$3,170**	6.3%
44	Memphis	TN	$0	$1,691	$1,149	$203	**$3,044**	6.1%
45	Houston	TX	$0	$1,823	$1,006	$190	**$3,020**	6.0%
46	Denver	CO	$850	$894	$808	$241	**$2,793**	5.6%
47	Sioux Falls	SD	$0	$1,452	$938	$167	**$2,557**	5.1%
48	Las Vegas	NV	$0	$1,443	$684	$277	**$2,404**	4.8%
49	Jacksonville	FL	$0	$1,338	$745	$134	**$2,216**	4.4%
50	Anchorage	AK	$0	$2,063	$0	$124	**$2,187**	4.4%
51	Cheyenne	WY	$0	$762	$868	$152	**$1,782**	3.6%
	Median		$1,618	$1,691	$745	$210	**$4,185**	8.4%

Source: 2001 D.C. Tax Rates & Tax Burdens Study

Table 4.17: Estimated Tax Burden, $100,000 Total Household Income

For a Family of Four, 2001

Rank	City	State	Income Tax	Property Tax	Sales Tax	Auto Tax	Total Tax Burden	Percent
1	Bridgeport	CT	$3,616	$12,835	$1,504	$1,496	**$19,450**	19.5%
2	Newark	NJ	$1,838	$11,441	$1,237	$271	**$14,787**	14.8%
3	Providence	RI	$4,101	$7,027	$1,403	$1,607	**$14,137**	14.1%
4	Des Moines	IA	$4,935	$6,393	$1,493	$426	**$13,247**	13.2%
5	Philadelphia	PA	$7,032	$4,050	$1,312	$380	**$12,773**	12.8%
6	New York City	NY	$7,634	$3,491	$1,467	$142	**$12,734**	12.7%
7	Portland	ME	$5,061	$5,667	$1,184	$544	**$12,456**	12.5%
8	Minneapolis	MN	$4,513	$5,665	$1,363	$617	**$12,158**	12.2%
9	Detroit	MI	$6,330	$3,976	$1,341	$431	**$12,078**	12.1%
10	Baltimore	MD	$5,508	$4,312	$1,357	$348	**$11,526**	11.5%
11	Milwaukee	WI	$4,643	$4,968	$1,467	$403	**$11,481**	11.5%
12	Atlanta	GA	$3,913	$5,089	$1,840	$593	**$11,436**	11.4%
13	Los Angeles	CA	$3,456	$5,565	$1,574	$770	**$11,364**	11.4%
14	Washington	DC	$6,838	$2,494	$1,509	$380	**$11,220**	11.2%
15	Portland	OR	$6,516	$4,378	$0	$314	**$11,209**	11.2%
16	Louisville	KY	$6,813	$2,179	$1,278	$672	**$10,942**	10.9%
17	Columbus	OH	$5,900	$2,820	$1,276	$344	**$10,339**	10.3%
18	Charlotte	NC	$5,323	$2,600	$1,618	$654	**$10,195**	10.2%
19	Burlington	VT	$3,193	$5,412	$1,260	$311	**$10,176**	10.2%
20	Columbia	SC	$4,668	$3,186	$1,290	$971	**$10,116**	10.1%
21	Chicago	IL	$2,506	$5,088	$2,018	$321	**$9,934**	9.9%
22	Salt Lake City	UT	$4,824	$2,563	$1,844	$559	**$9,791**	9.8%
23	Omaha	NE	$4,118	$3,368	$1,632	$577	**$9,694**	9.7%
24	Boise City	ID	$5,042	$2,812	$1,312	$438	**$9,604**	9.6%
25	Albuquerque	NM	$3,894	$3,227	$1,887	$285	**$9,293**	9.3%
26	Little Rock	AR	$4,432	$2,467	$1,755	$635	**$9,289**	9.3%
27	Honolulu	HI	$5,476	$2,235	$1,212	$323	**$9,246**	9.2%
28	Boston	MA	$4,322	$3,642	$803	$408	**$9,175**	9.2%
29	Charleston	WV	$4,857	$1,831	$1,620	$812	**$9,119**	9.1%
30	Kansas City	MO	$4,581	$1,977	$1,767	$754	**$9,079**	9.1%
31	Jackson	MS	$3,268	$2,574	$1,895	$1,316	**$9,052**	9.1%
32	Oklahoma City	OK	$4,719	$1,566	$2,212	$371	**$8,868**	8.9%
33	Phoenix	AZ	$2,256	$3,690	$2,232	$512	**$8,690**	8.7%
34	Billings	MT	$5,569	$2,209	$0	$664	**$8,442**	8.4%
35	Virginia Beach	VA	$4,318	$2,470	$1,049	$552	**$8,389**	8.4%
36	Birmingham	AL	$4,548	$1,259	$2,069	$494	**$8,371**	8.4%
37	New Orleans	LA	$2,705	$3,085	$2,029	$356	**$8,175**	8.2%
38	Wichita	KS	$4,143	$1,413	$1,628	$990	**$8,174**	8.2%
39	Wilmington	DE	$4,795	$2,747	$0	$312	**$7,854**	7.9%
40	Indianapolis	IN	$3,987	$2,385	$1,270	$202	**$7,844**	7.8%
41	Manchester	NH	$0	$6,658	$635	$403	**$7,695**	7.7%
42	Fargo	ND	$1,973	$3,865	$1,362	$367	**$7,567**	7.6%
43	Denver	CO	$3,165	$1,698	$1,616	$487	**$6,967**	7.0%
44	Seattle	WA	$0	$4,222	$2,116	$332	**$6,670**	6.7%
45	Houston	TX	$0	$3,669	$2,012	$356	**$6,038**	6.0%
46	Memphis	TN	$30	$3,214	$2,298	$383	**$5,925**	5.9%
47	Sioux Falls	SD	$0	$2,759	$1,875	$309	**$4,943**	4.9%
48	Jacksonville	FL	$0	$2,986	$1,489	$249	**$4,723**	4.7%
49	Las Vegas	NV	$0	$2,741	$1,368	$509	**$4,619**	4.6%
50	Anchorage	AK	$0	$3,919	$0	$239	**$4,158**	4.2%
51	Cheyenne	WY	$0	$1,448	$1,735	$480	**$3,663**	3.7%
	Median		$4,318	$3,214	$1,489	$426	**$9,289**	9.3%

Source: 2001 D.C. Tax Rates & Tax Burdens Study

Table 4.18: Estimated Tax Burden, $150,000 Total Household Income

For a Family of Four, 2001

Rank	City	State	Income Tax	Property Tax	Sales Tax	Auto Tax	Total Tax Burden	Percent
1	Bridgeport	CT	$6,150	$18,239	$2,256	$2,214	**$28,859**	19.2%
2	Newark	NJ	$4,573	$16,259	$1,855	$267	**$22,954**	15.3%
3	Providence	RI	$6,878	$9,985	$2,104	$2,825	**$21,792**	14.5%
4	Des Moines	IA	$8,468	$9,175	$2,240	$565	**$20,448**	13.6%
5	New York City	NY	$12,937	$5,059	$2,200	$139	**$20,335**	13.6%
6	Portland	ME	$8,671	$8,053	$1,776	$702	**$19,202**	12.8%
7	Los Angeles	CA	$7,357	$7,939	$2,361	$1,083	**$18,740**	12.5%
8	Philadelphia	PA	$10,549	$5,755	$1,968	$370	**$18,642**	12.4%
9	Minneapolis	MN	$7,684	$8,051	$2,044	$826	**$18,605**	12.4%
10	Detroit	MI	$9,805	$5,650	$2,012	$383	**$17,850**	11.9%
11	Atlanta	GA	$6,312	$7,504	$2,760	$890	**$17,466**	11.6%
12	Milwaukee	WI	$7,562	$7,092	$2,201	$393	**$17,247**	11.5%
13	Washington	DC	$10,908	$3,665	$2,263	$380	**$17,215**	11.5%
14	Baltimore	MD	$8,662	$6,128	$2,036	$339	**$17,166**	11.4%
15	Portland	OR	$10,396	$6,222	$0	$305	**$16,923**	11.3%
16	Louisville	KY	$10,496	$3,229	$1,918	$965	**$16,608**	11.1%
17	Columbus	OH	$10,066	$4,007	$1,913	$335	**$16,322**	10.9%
18	Burlington	VT	$5,974	$7,691	$1,890	$304	**$15,859**	10.6%
19	Columbia	SC	$7,662	$4,696	$1,936	$1,454	**$15,748**	10.5%
20	Charlotte	NC	$8,549	$3,694	$2,427	$886	**$15,557**	10.4%
21	Omaha	NE	$7,323	$4,786	$2,447	$921	**$15,477**	10.3%
22	Boise City	ID	$8,335	$4,343	$1,969	$429	**$15,075**	10.1%
23	Albuquerque	NM	$7,109	$4,585	$2,830	$279	**$14,803**	9.9%
24	Chicago	IL	$3,891	$7,389	$3,027	$314	**$14,621**	9.7%
25	Little Rock	AR	$7,443	$3,506	$2,632	$848	**$14,430**	9.6%
26	Honolulu	HI	$8,966	$3,238	$1,817	$317	**$14,338**	9.6%
27	Salt Lake City	UT	$7,462	$3,642	$2,679	$520	**$14,303**	9.5%
28	Charleston	WV	$8,105	$2,602	$2,429	$1,093	**$14,229**	9.5%
29	Jackson	MS	$5,423	$3,783	$2,842	$2,000	**$14,049**	9.4%
30	Billings	MT	$9,978	$3,139	$0	$820	**$13,937**	9.3%
31	Kansas City	MO	$7,409	$2,810	$2,651	$1,068	**$13,937**	9.3%
32	Oklahoma City	OK	$7,497	$2,720	$3,318	$365	**$13,900**	9.3%
33	Boston	MA	$6,950	$5,175	$1,231	$442	**$13,798**	9.2%
34	Phoenix	AZ	$3,823	$5,954	$3,349	$632	**$13,757**	9.2%
35	Wichita	KS	$6,972	$2,098	$2,442	$1,404	**$12,916**	8.6%
36	New Orleans	LA	$4,352	$4,921	$3,044	$546	**$12,862**	8.6%
37	Virginia Beach	VA	$6,835	$3,510	$1,573	$702	**$12,620**	8.4%
38	Birmingham	AL	$6,726	$1,829	$3,104	$655	**$12,314**	8.2%
39	Wilmington	DE	$7,901	$3,903	$0	$304	**$12,108**	8.1%
40	Indianapolis	IN	$6,182	$3,400	$1,905	$196	**$11,683**	7.8%
41	Fargo	ND	$3,610	$5,492	$2,044	$359	**$11,505**	7.7%
42	Manchester	NH	$10	$9,461	$953	$488	**$10,912**	7.3%
43	Denver	CO	$5,047	$2,414	$2,424	$574	**$10,459**	7.0%
44	Seattle	WA	$0	$6,000	$3,173	$324	**$9,497**	6.3%
45	Houston	TX	$0	$5,310	$2,909	$349	**$8,568**	5.7%
46	Memphis	TN	$150	$4,567	$3,448	$375	**$8,540**	5.7%
47	Sioux Falls	SD	$0	$3,921	$2,813	$301	**$7,035**	4.7%
48	Jacksonville	FL	$0	$4,450	$2,234	$243	**$6,927**	4.6%
49	Las Vegas	NV	$0	$3,895	$2,052	$634	**$6,582**	4.4%
50	Anchorage	AK	$0	$5,570	$0	$236	**$5,805**	3.9%
51	Cheyenne	WY	$0	$2,058	$2,603	$660	**$5,321**	3.5%
	Median		$7,109	$4,696	$2,234	$488	**$14,338**	9.6%

Source: 2001 D.C. Tax Rates & Tax Burdens Study

Education

For many, education is a state's first responsibility. Indeed, education is the largest item on the whole in state budgets, running about 40% of expenditures on average. Numerous published studies reference aspects of the education process, such as expenditures, pupil-teacher ratios, class size, square feet of facilities, and library books. Chapter 5 includes data for some of these attributes at the metropolitan area level. The focus of this section is achievement and secondary school testing, a rapidly changing area, particularly since the 2002 No Child Left Behind Act. This information gives a flavor for educational quality—and the focus thereon—evident in each state. There is a great deal of intangible content to the educational process, which varies greatly by locality. This is only a place to start.

SAT Scores

The SAT, or Scholastic Aptitude Test, administered by the College Board, is viewed as a standard bellwether for college admissions aptitude. For many, it reflects the degree of preparation that students receive through their primary and secondary education. However, the College Board itself warns against comparing states by score, as important differences exist in the way tests are used and administered among states. Some state schools require the SAT, while others require its cousin, the ACT (American College Test), which is generally considered to be a less stringent test and is seldom used by more selective schools. For that and other reasons, participation in the SAT can vary greatly by state. In states that depend on the ACT, the SAT is taken mainly by students seeking admission to more selective schools. As a result, states emphasizing the ACT may achieve higher SAT test scores because fewer students take it and those who do tend to be more advanced.

Table 4.20 shows verbal, math, and composite (verbal plus math) scores in 1990 and 2002, and the change in composite scores during this period. Considering the College Board advice, the reader should (1) focus on change in scores and (2) make sure participation is comparable among states. Change in scores is less significant in states with lower participation. States such as North and South Carolina, Georgia, Indiana, and Washington have high participation, while South Dakota, Wisconsin, and Tennessee are low.

State Secondary School Testing

In recent years a strong reform movement has materialized with increased emphasis on educational achievement as the benchmark of educational quality. School funding and programs, even teachers' salaries, have become ever more dependent on demonstrated educational achievement. As a result, many states implemented testing programs at the secondary school level. In 2002, the Bush Administration led the charge to pass the No Child Left Behind Act, a broad series of policies designed to encourage and standardize standards-based education and to help disadvantaged students. For details on the act, see "Education" in chapter 3.

Status of Secondary Testing

Nationally standardized achievement tests are currently administered in the fourth and eighth grades. Many states also give them in the fifth through seventh grades—a practice that the 2002 act will eventually standardize. Because results of these tests are only compiled through 2000, *Cities Ranked & Rated* doesn't include them; to see what's currently available, go to the Department of Education NCES website at nces.ed.gov.

Table 4.19 shows the status of secondary school testing in place today at the state level and planned for 2008 (to avoid confusion, note that *primary* school testing under No Child Left Behind is to be implemented by 2006 except for sciences). According to the nonprofit Center on Educational Policy (www.ctredpol.org), 18 states currently have some form of mandatory testing and may, in some cases, withhold high school diplomas pending successful completion. Another six states are phasing in testing programs but are not withholding diplomas. An additional six states have established plans to implement testing by 2008—this number is expected to increase.

The 18 actively testing states comprise over half of all public school students in the United States. By 2008 that figure will rise to over 70%. Interestingly, testing states tend to have more minorities—and making these tests fair to minorities has been the subject of much debate. Estimates claim that 80% of minority students will be tested by 2008.

Despite widespread adoption of these tests, their effectiveness is disputed. Proponents suggest that tests motivate students and help teachers identify and address needs, while opponents cite the imperfections of the process and argue that tests don't measure what is actually taught.

Table 4.19: State Secondary Educational Testing	
Testing in Place 2002	**Phasing in Testing**
AL, FL, GA, IN, LA, MD, MN, MS, NC, NJ, NM, NV, NY, OH, SC, TN, TX, VA	AK, AZ, CA, MA, UT, WA
Source: Center for Educational Policy	

Table 4.20: SAT Scores by State

Sorted by Percent Change

State	1990			2002			Change 1990-2002	Percent Taking SAT
	Verbal	Math	Composite	Verbal	Math	Composite		
IL	542	547	1089	578	596	1174	7.8%	11%
WI	552	559	1111	583	599	1182	6.4%	7%
MI	529	534	1063	558	572	1130	6.3%	11%
MO	548	541	1089	574	580	1154	6.0%	3%
MN	552	558	1110	581	591	1172	5.6%	10%
NC	478	470	948	493	505	998	5.3%	67%
ND	579	578	1157	597	610	1207	4.3%	4%
SC	475	467	942	488	493	981	4.1%	59%
AL	545	534	1079	560	559	1119	3.7%	9%
AR	545	532	1077	560	556	1116	3.6%	5%
GA	478	473	951	489	491	980	3.0%	65%
IN	486	486	972	498	503	1001	3.0%	62%
LA	551	537	1088	561	559	1120	2.9%	8%
WA	513	511	1024	525	529	1054	2.9%	54%
OK	553	542	1095	565	562	1127	2.9%	8%
AZ	521	520	1041	547	523	1070	2.8%	36%
OR	515	509	1024	524	528	1052	2.7%	56%
MA	503	498	1001	512	516	1028	2.7%	81%
KS	566	563	1129	578	580	1158	2.6%	9%
MS	552	528	1080	559	547	1106	2.4%	4%
OH	526	522	1048	533	540	1073	2.4%	27%
HI	480	505	985	488	520	1008	2.3%	53%
CO	533	534	1067	543	548	1091	2.2%	28%
VT	507	493	1000	512	510	1022	2.2%	69%
RI	498	488	986	504	503	1007	2.1%	73%
AK	514	501	1015	516	519	1035	2.0%	52%
VA	501	496	997	510	506	1016	1.9%	68%
NJ	495	498	993	498	513	1011	1.8%	82%
IA	584	588	1172	591	602	1193	1.8%	5%
CT	506	496	1002	509	509	1018	1.6%	83%
NY	489	496	985	494	506	1000	1.5%	79%
ME	501	490	991	503	502	1005	1.4%	69%
TN	558	544	1102	562	555	1117	1.4%	14%
ID	542	524	1066	539	541	1080	1.3%	18%
TX	490	489	979	491	500	991	1.2%	55%
KY	548	541	1089	550	552	1102	1.2%	12%
MD	506	502	1008	507	513	1020	1.2%	67%
PA	497	490	987	498	500	998	1.1%	72%
CA	494	508	1002	496	517	1013	1.1%	52%
SD	580	570	1150	576	586	1162	1.0%	5%
NH	518	510	1028	519	519	1038	1.0%	73%
NE	559	562	1121	561	570	1131	0.9%	8%
FL	495	493	988	496	499	995	0.7%	57%
WV	520	514	1034	525	515	1040	0.6%	18%
MT	540	542	1082	541	547	1088	0.6%	23%
NV	511	511	1022	509	518	1027	0.5%	34%
UT	566	555	1121	563	559	1122	0.1%	6%
WY	534	538	1072	531	537	1068	-0.4%	11%
DE	510	496	1006	502	500	1002	-0.4%	69%
NM	554	546	1100	551	543	1094	-0.5%	14%
U.S. Average	**500**	**501**	**1001**	**504**	**516**	**1,020**	**1.9%**	**46%**

Note: Average U.S. percent change 1990-2002: + 1.9%

Source: The College Board

Table 4.21: State Secondary Educational Testing by Test Type

	2002		2008
MCE	FL, MD, MN, MS, NC, NV, OH, SC, TN, VA	MCE	AK, MN, UT
SBE	AL, GA, IN, LA, NJ, NM, TX	SBE	AL, AZ, CA, FL, IN, LA, MA, NC, NJ, NM, NV, OH, SC, TN, TX, WA
EOC	NY, TX	EOC	GA, MD, MS, NY, VA

Note: Texans choose between SBE and EOC.
Source: Center for Education Policy

Standardization of Testing

Because of the many different types of tests, standardization is an enduring challenge. Some states administer much harder tests—and show much lower scores—than others. This is expected to change in the future. Table 4.21, compiled in 2003 by the Center on Education Policy, shows state testing according to the following commonly used types:

- **MCE** (Minimum Competency Exam) focuses on basic skills, usually at a lower than high school level.
- **SBE** (Standards Based Exam) tests state standards at a high school level.
- **EOC** (End Of Course) exam is tied to a specific subject. Students may be able to choose among subjects tested, and in Texas, they can choose between SBE and EOC.

Politics

Political party affiliation and voting behavior are among the most outward signs of an area's political character. Table 4.22 displays the party of the state governor and shows voting results by party for the 2000 presidential election and the recent 2002 congressional elections. Independent and third party candidates are omitted from presidential results for simplicity, although independent governors and representatives are counted.

The table divides states into four groups.

- **Democrat/Democrat** states voted Democrat in the 2000 election *and* have a majority or equal Democratic representation in Congress. Whether or not they have a Democratic governor was not considered. Within this category, states are sorted according to the percentage of Democratic presidential vote; that is, Rhode Island had the strongest presidential Democratic majority.
- **Democrat/Republican** represents states that voted for the Democratic presidential candidate, but sent a majority of Republican representatives to Congress.
- **Republican/Democrat** states voted Republican for president but sent an equal or majority number of Democrats to Congress.
- **Republican/Republican** states voted consistently Republican for both president and Congress. Wyoming and Idaho lead this group with the highest percentage presidential Republican vote.

The table shows the strength of a state's party commitment. States such as Rhode Island, Massachusetts, New York, and many southern states approach national- and state-level politics quite differently, consistently electing Democrats to serve at the national level but a Republican to serve in the statehouse—or vice versa. Some states like California and Pennsylvania have an enduring reputation of voting differently at different levels to achieve sort of a "check and balance" in their leadership.

STUMPED IN NEW YORK

A June 2003 *New York Times* story illuminated some of the problems with state secondary school testing when it reported a last-minute scramble to issue diplomas to over 1,000 students, originally denied, in time for graduation. The reason: The state math test was deemed too difficult and thus unfair. Clearly, standardized testing is still evolving.

Table 4.22: State Party Lines

State	2000 Presidential Vote *Percent of total vote*		Representatives in Congress *As of January 2003*			Governor
	Democrat	Republican	Democrat	Republican	Total	Party

Democrat/Democrat
States Voting Democrat in 2000 with Equal or Democratic Majority Representation

State	Democrat	Republican	Democrat	Republican	Total	Party
RI	61.0%	31.9%	2	0	2	R
MA	59.8%	32.5%	10	0	10	R
NY	60.2%	35.2%	19	10	29	R
HI	55.8%	37.5%	2	0	2	D
MD	56.5%	40.3%	6	2	8	D
NJ	56.1%	40.3%	7	6	13	D
CA	53.5%	41.6%	33	20	53	R
VT*	50.6%	40.7%	0	0	1	D
WA	50.2%	44.6%	6	3	9	D
ME	49.1%	44.0%	2	0	2	I
OR	47.0%	46.5%	4	1	5	D
WI	47.8%	47.6%	5	4	9	R

Democrat/Republican
States Voting Democrat in 2000 with Republican Majority Representation

State	Democrat	Republican	Democrat	Republican	Total	Party
CT	55.9%	38.4%	2	3	5	R
DE	55.0%	41.9%	0	1	1	D
IL	54.6%	42.6%	9	10	19	R
MI	51.3%	46.2%	6	9	15	R
PA	50.6%	46.4%	7	12	19	R
IA	48.5%	48.2%	1	4	5	D
NM	47.9%	47.9%	1	2	3	R
MN*	47.9%	45.5%	3	4	8	I

Republican/Democrat
States Voting Republican in 2000 with Democratic Majority Representation

State	Democrat	Republican	Democrat	Republican	Total	Party
ND	33.1%	60.7%	1	0	1	R
WV	45.6%	51.9%	2	1	3	D
AR	45.9%	51.3%	3	1	4	R
TN	47.3%	51.2%	5	4	9	R

Republican/Republican
States Voting Republican in 2000 with Equal or Republican Majority Representation

State	Democrat	Republican	Democrat	Republican	Total	Party
WY	27.7%	67.8%	0	1	1	R
ID	27.6%	67.2%	0	2	2	R
UT	26.3%	66.8%	1	2	3	R
NE	33.3%	62.3%	0	3	3	R
OK	38.4%	60.3%	1	4	5	R
SD	37.6%	60.3%	0	1	1	R
TX	38.0%	59.3%	16	16	32	R
AK	27.7%	58.6%	0	1	1	D
MT	33.4%	58.4%	0	1	1	R
KS	37.2%	58.0%	1	3	4	R
MS	40.7%	57.6%	2	2	4	D
SC	40.9%	56.8%	2	4	6	D
IN	41.0%	56.7%	3	6	9	D
KY	41.4%	56.5%	1	5	6	D
GA	43.0%	56.5%	5	8	13	D
AL	41.6%	56.4%	2	5	7	D
NC	43.2%	56.0%	6	7	13	D
LA	44.9%	52.6%	2	4	6	R
VA	44.4%	52.5%	3	8	11	D
AZ	44.7%	51.0%	2	6	8	R
CO	42.4%	50.7%	2	5	7	R
MO	47.1%	50.4%	4	5	9	D
OH	46.4%	50.0%	6	12	18	R
NV	46.0%	49.5%	1	2	3	R
FL	48.8%	48.9%	7	18	25	R
NH	46.8%	48.1%	0	2	2	D

Note: Asterisk (*) denotes at least one Independent congressional representative.
Source: *The World Almanac and Book of Facts, 2003*

Safety & Safety Consciousness

Out of many possible variables, this section looks at drunk driving laws and highway fatalities, which together give a sense of a state's social, political, and legal environment.

State Drunk Driving Laws

All states have cracked down on drunk drivers, but some have gone farther than others. Table 4.23 presents the Insurance Information Institute's appraisal of more than 25 parameters of state law on drunk driving, from definitions and determinations of drunkenness to legal remedies and special clauses for minors and repeat offenders. The report groups states into four categories, with the accompanying characteristics:

- **Good (G)**—blood alcohol concentration (BAC) limit 0.08%, zero percent BAC for drivers under 21, sobriety checkpoints permitted, license revocation of at least 30 days

- **Acceptable (A)**—BAC limit 0.08%, at least one additional provision from the "Good" category
- **Marginal (M)**—zero percent BAC for drivers under 21, sobriety checkpoints permitted
- **Poor (P)**—one or none of the provisions listed in the "Good" category

Highway Fatalities

Grim as they might be, highway fatality statistics, shown in Table 4.24, can be construed as a result of state law, state spending, infrastructure, and social attitudes about safety. A surprisingly wide variation exists among states. States in the South and West tend to fare poorly. But to be fair, experts suggest that states with a largely rural character and a high percentage of two-lane roads will have greater fatalities because accidents, while similar in number, tend to produce more fatalities. The numbers, while supporting this argument, still suggest room for improvement in some states.

Table 4.23: Ratings of State Drunk Driving Laws

Good	Acceptable	Marginal	Poor
AL	AR	PA	MI
AK	CO	SC	MT
AZ	CT		NJ
CA	DE		RI
FL	ID		
GA	IL		
HI	IN		
KS	IA		
LA	KY		
MO	ME		
NE	MD		
NH	MA		
UT	MN		
VT	MS		
	NV		
	NM		
	NY		
	NC		
	ND		
	OH		
	OK		
	OR		
	SD		
	TN		
	TX		
	VA		
	WA		
	WV		
	WI		
	WY		

Source: Insurance Information Institute (www.iii.org)

Table 4.24: State Highway Fatalities

Above U.S. Average		Below U.S. Average	
WY	37.6	NE	14.36
MS	27.4	WI	14.12
SC	26.1	OR	14.05
MT	25.4	AK	13.39
NM	25.3	MI	13.29
AR	22.7	VA	13.01
SD	22.6	UT	12.86
AL	22.3	PA	12.45
TN	21.8	MD	12.28
LA	21.4	OH	12.12
WV	20.9	CA	11.47
KY	20.8	HI	11.43
AZ	19.7	MN	11.42
ID	19.6	IL	11.33
OK	19.5	NH	11.28
MO	19.5	WA	10.84
GA	19.3	CT	9.11
NC	18.7	NJ	8.80
FL	18.4	NY	8.14
KS	18.3	RI	7.65
TX	17.5	MA	7.48
DE	17.1		
CO	16.7		
ND	16.5		
IA	15.3		
VT	15.0		
ME	14.9		
IN	14.9		
NV	14.9		

Traffic Fatalities Per 100,000 Population

Note: U.S. Average: 14.8 per 100,000 annually
Source: Insurance Information Institute (www.iii.org)

part II

Evaluating the Cities

Principal U.S. Metropolitan Areas

Earlier chapters set the stage for the in-depth look at each of the 331 principal metropolitan areas found in this chapter. *Cities Ranked & Rated* presents each metropolitan area in alphabetical order with a header containing identifying characteristics, scores and ranks for the city as a whole and for each category, a narrative description, and complete data tables. The narrative highlights important facts and trends from the data and gives an overview of the qualities, appearance, and climate of the place. Explanations of attributes shown in the data tables can be found in chapter 3 as well as in Table 5.1: Principal U.S. Metropolitan Areas: Data Descriptions & Sources.

Note: The city names in this chapter correspond with Metropolitan Statistical Area (MSA) designations assigned by the U.S. Office of Management and Budget. Many of these areas cross state borders and contain one or more major cities, creating such names as "Washington, DC-MD-VA-WV." For a more complete explanation of MSAs, see chapter 1.

City Profiles

Cities Ranked & Rated employs a set of simple phrases in each city header to describe the role and general nature of a place. Most of these phrases are standard, like "college town" and "capital city," but a few are unique to a particular area or are a combination of several profiles. The more commonly cited profiles are described below.

National Center

A national center is a large urban area recognized both nationally and internationally as a leading center for government, commerce, industry, education, services, and the arts. Population generally exceeds eight million, with an exception given for Washington, D.C., at five million. Numerous satellite cities, ethnically concentrated neighborhoods, and large areas of suburbs characterize a national center. A vibrant downtown, often containing architectural and historic landmarks, is attractive as a working and tourist destination. The ethnic mix and cost-of-living profile in the city are quite different from surrounding areas. A complete transportation network and services, such as air, rail, and public transport, are available. The airport serves as an international gateway for passengers and freight, and the city is a world center for

entire industries, as Los Angeles is for movies and entertainment and New York is for book publishing. Foreign countries use the city as a base for their U.S. operations. Major universities, world-renowned arts and cultural assets, and extensive restaurants and nightlife round out the available amenities.

> Examples: Chicago, Illinois; Los Angeles, California; New York, New York; Washington, D.C.

Regional Center

This major city, or collection of cities, with a large surrounding area usually has a population greater than two million and serves as a multi-state hub for economic and commercial activity, services, and amenities. A large and vibrant downtown is surrounded by neighborhoods and suburbs, often reflecting the population mix of the region. The cost-of-living profile is usually high compared to surrounding areas. It's generally a business center, providing banking and financial services for the region, with offices for national and multinational companies and an assortment of smaller businesses. Also supporting the region are air and transport services and educational facilities.

The city is a destination for shopping, healthcare needs, and other amenities.

> Examples: Atlanta, Georgia; Dallas, Texas; Denver, Colorado; Miami, Florida; Minneapolis–St. Paul, Minnesota

Large City

A self-sufficient city, with a moderately sized surrounding area, usually consists of an area population greater than one million. Often a state's largest city, it serves its own needs and those of a moderately large, generally in-state area. Typical large cities have a well-developed downtown core, with distinct neighborhoods and suburbs, and often reflect the ethnic mix and cultural flavor of the surrounding area. Commercial activities, education, healthcare, transportation, arts, recreation, and other amenities are available, and residents generally don't feel the need to go elsewhere for them.

> Examples: Buffalo–Niagara Falls, New York; Cincinnati, Ohio; Orlando, Florida; Nashville, Tennessee; Omaha, Nebraska; Portland, Oregon; St. Louis, Missouri

Small/Mid-Size City

This is a distinct city with both a big-city and a small-town feel, usually with a population from 100,000 to one million. It typically serves a few counties outside the immediate area, but the area is always smaller than the state as a whole. Generally the city has a small-scale downtown with multistory commercial buildings and a few distinct neighborhoods, and getting around is easy. Cost of living is typically much lower than in larger cities. Some cities have diverse commercial and industrial bases, while others are subject to the economical vulnerability of a single industry. Typically some large-city amenities, including healthcare, air service, and culture and arts, are available, but some residents consider the quality to be inadequate. Residents *occasionally* go to a nearby "large city" or "regional center" for services and amenities such as air service, shopping, or arts. The city may contain the elements of a "college town" or "capital city."

> Examples: Akron, Ohio; Colorado Springs, Colorado; Fresno, California; Johnstown, Pennsylvania; Louisville, Kentucky; Lynchburg, Virginia; Bloomington-Normal, Illinois

Small Town

Normally with a population less than 100,000, the small town area is laid out around a central business district, usually in a rectangular grid pattern with tree-lined streets and abundant sidewalks. The more attractive small towns have walkable central-business districts with stores, restaurants, and commercial buildings, and on-street parking. Some or all buildings have a historic look and feel. Residential areas generally have well-kept older homes, some with historic or architectural interest, with newer construction farther from the center of town. New developments, including shopping malls, strip centers, and franchise outlets, are usually on the outskirts of town along highway and bypass strips. Most industry is light and located on the outskirts. While most of today's small towns have some modern cookie-cutter development, the better ones repurpose older buildings and keep downtown areas functional.

> Examples: Fort Collins, Colorado; Jonesboro, Arkansas; Muncie, Indiana; Visalia, California

Military Town

This place has a strong military presence with one or more military bases located nearby and a large portion of the town's economy tied to the military. Areas of low-cost and base housing are near commercial districts that support the needs of military personnel and their families. Lower income, low cost of living, few cultural amenities, and shopping oriented toward the lower-income ranges characterize the area. The economy may be steady, although turnover among residents and the percentage of rental housing may be high. Investment and infrastructure may deteriorate in towns vulnerable to base closings, although this is less of a threat than it was in the 1990s. Entertainment and nightlife is often oriented toward young men, although family-entertainment amenities sometimes exist. Some military towns, like Fairfield, California, have been encroached upon by advancing suburbs.

> Examples: Jacksonville, North Carolina; Lawton, Oklahoma; Pensacola, Florida

College Town

One or more colleges or universities dominate the economy and local infrastructure. There is usually a large, parklike campus, with historic buildings and a generally attractive appearance, in or adjacent to the central town area. A mix of relatively young, lower income, transient students; relatively higher income, more educated faculty; and institution employees live here. Cost of living, especially housing costs, tends to be high. Overall educational attainment tends to be high. There may be important healthcare and healthcare-research facilities. If there is any industry, it is usually located on the outskirts of town away from the student areas. The often walkable town areas support the commercial and recreational needs of the students and faculty alike, with nightlife, interesting restaurants, and small stores that sell books, supplies, and other items for the young market. The university provides a number of cultural amenities such as museums and performing arts including traveling acts. College sports provide entertainment and often become a local obsession. Some towns, like Tuscaloosa, Alabama, are "pure" college towns, while others (Austin, Texas) have a significant college-town element mixed into a larger community.

> Examples: Boulder, Colorado; Charlottesville, Virginia; Iowa City, Iowa; Lawrence, Kansas; State College, Pennsylvania

Capital City

Capital cities contain the center of state government. Whether government dominates the local economy and infrastructure depends on the size of the capital city. In smaller capitals such as Olympia, Washington, or Dover, Delaware, the governmental element tends to dominate, whereas it is only a player among many in larger capitals such as Atlanta, Georgia, or Denver, Colorado. State governments generally bring attractive, permanent buildings, often in parklike settings (particularly the Capitol building itself) and stable employment. The stability of the employment base extends from the government payroll itself to other enterprises performing services for the government. The government and its sphere of enterprises are generally industries with high paying, white-collar jobs. Capital cities often have museums and items of historical interest pertaining to the state. A small city that is both state capital and home to a large state university brings especially pleasing infrastructure and amenities; examples include Madison, Wisconsin; Austin, Texas; and Lansing, Michigan.

> Examples: Boston, Massachusetts; Indianapolis, Indiana; Phoenix, Arizona; Salem, Oregon; Tallahassee, Florida

Beach Town

Many towns in coastal areas in the east and south have a typical "beach town" look and feel. There is usually a wide beach, separated from the rest of the city by a wide boulevard running parallel to the coast. On the immediate inland side of the boulevard one often finds high-rise hotels and residential buildings with intermittent clusters of smaller commercial buildings, usually containing locally owned restaurants and shops catering to tourists. There are nice walking areas and even classic boardwalks. The area where local residents live and do business is farther inland and often older and less attractive than the beach area. Some beach towns have the beach and commercial strip on a barrier island. The local economy varies within the town, with wealthier and more expensive enclaves near the beach and lower income areas and less expensive housing inland. Crime is often a problem, perhaps due to income disparities and the abundance of tourists. Because of rugged coastal geography, the typical "beach town" format is less common on the West Coast, although some examples exist near Los Angeles.

> Examples: Atlantic City, New Jersey; Fort Walton Beach, Florida; Galveston, Texas; Myrtle Beach, South Carolina; West Palm Beach, Florida

Commuter Community

The city or area mainly serves as a residential or bedroom community for another larger city or urban area. The character is mainly suburban, predominated by large areas of single- and multifamily housing. There are retail and mostly minor entertainment establishments available as a matter of convenience. These areas are connected to the main city center by a well-developed network of commuting routes, many of which are served by public transit. These areas are close enough to the main city to enjoy many of its services and amenities, such as air transport, professional sports teams, and cultural assets.

> Examples: Brockton, Massachusetts; Dutchess County, New York; Nassau-Suffolk, New York; Monmouth-Ocean, New Jersey; Vallejo-Fairfield-Napa, California

Table 5.1: Principal U.S. Metropolitan Areas: Data Descriptions & Sources

Field Name	Description	Source	Date
Population			
Demographics			
Population	Total residents in metropolitan area	U.S. Census Population Survey	2002
Population density per sq. mile	Total residents per square mile in area	U.S. Census Population Survey	2002
Population growth	Growth in metro area population, 1990-2002	U.S. Census Population Survey	2002
Median age	Median age in years	U.S. Census	2000
Average family size	Size of average household greater than one member	U.S. Census	2000
Ethnic Composition			
White	Percentage of population surveyed as Caucasian	U.S. Census	2000
Black	Percentage of population surveyed as African American	U.S. Census	2000
Asian	Percentage of population surveyed of Asian origin	U.S. Census	2000
American Indian	Percentage of population surveyed of Native American origin	U.S. Census	2000
Hispanic	Percentage of population surveyed of Hispanic origin	U.S. Census	2000
Diversity measure	Probability that next person met is ethnicity other than your own	Sperling's BestPlaces	2003
Resident Profile			
Single	Percentage of population surveyed as single	U.S. Census	2000
Married	Percentage of population surveyed as married	U.S. Census	2000
Divorced	Percentage of population surveyed as divorced	U.S. Census	2000
Separated	Percentage of population surveyed as separated	U.S. Census	2000
Married with children	Percent of population surveyed as married with one or more children	U.S. Census	2000
Single with children	Percentage of population surveyed as single with one or more children	U.S. Census	2000
Economy & Jobs			
Income			
Per capita income	Average annual gross income for every U.S. citizen of all ages	U.S. Census	2000
Household income	Average annual gross income for every U.S. household	Claritas, Inc.	2003
Household income < $25K	Percentage of households with annual gross income less than $25,000	Claritas, Inc.	2003
Household income > $75K	Percentage of households with annual gross income over $75,000	Claritas, Inc.	2003
Household income growth	Percentage of growth in average household income, 1990-2003	Claritas, Inc.	2003
Employment			
Unemployment rate	Percentage of active job seekers without a job, August 2003	Bureau of Labor Statistics	2003
Recent job growth	Percentage of job growth or decline, August 2002-August 2003	Bureau of Labor Statistics	2003
Projected future job growth	Percentage of projected job growth or decline through 2010	Sperling's BestPlaces	2003
White collar	Percentage of workers in executive/managerial/professional/ technical/sales/clerical positions	Bureau of Labor Statistics	2003
Blue collar	Percentage of workers in production/repair/transportation/ construction/labor/agriculture positions	Bureau of Labor Statistics	2003
Largest Employing Industry	Industry with the largest employment base in area	Claritas, Inc.	2003

Field Name	Description	Source	Date
Cost of Living			
Indexes & Taxes			
Cost of Living Index	Total cost of living as an index against national average, first quarter 2003; 100 as average	Bureau of Labor Statistics	2003
Financial Progress Index	Household income divided by Cost of Living Index, versus national average; 100 as average	*Cities Ranked & Rated* calculation	2003
Income tax rate	Highest marginal combined state and local rate	Sperling's BestPlaces	2003
Sales tax rate	Most commonly paid total state and local sales tax rate	Sperling's BestPlaces	2003
Property tax rate	Average dollar amount paid per $1,000 in property	Sperling's BestPlaces	2003
Housing			
Median home price	Median selling price for the average home type in the area, second quarter 2003	National Association of Realtors	2003
Home price appreciation	Compound annualized growth rate in home prices, 2000-2003	National Association of Realtors/Sperling's BestPlaces	2003
Median rent	Median rental price for typical rental unit in the area, first half 2003	U.S. Census	2003
Homes owned	Percentage of households owning home	U.S. Census	2003
Homes rented	Percentage of households renting home	U.S. Census	2003
Housing affordability	Total housing costs as a percentage of gross income	National Low Income Housing Coalition	2003
Necessities			
Food Index	Purchased food (groceries) cost against national average, first quarter 2003; 100 as average	Bureau of Labor Statistics	2003
Housing Index	Purchase/rent and upkeep cost against national average, first quarter 2003; 100 as average	Bureau of Labor Statistics	2003
Utilities Index	Gas and electricity cost against national average, first quarter 2003; 100 as average	Bureau of Labor Statistics	2003
Transportation Index	Automotive and other costs against national average, first quarter 2003; 100 as average	Bureau of Labor Statistics	2003
Healthcare Index	Health and health insurance cost against national average, first quarter 2003; 100 as average	Bureau of Labor Statistics	2003
Miscellaneous Cost Index	Other costs against national average, first quarter 2003; 100 as average	Bureau of Labor Statistics	2003
Climate			
Temperature			
January low	January daily low temperature, 70-year average	NOAA/National Climatic Data Center	2003
July high	July daily high temperature, 70-year average	NOAA/National Climatic Data Center	2003
Annual days > 90°F	Average days per year where temperature exceeds 90°F	NOAA/National Climatic Data Center	2003
Annual days < 32°F	Average days per year where temperature drops below freezing, 32°F	NOAA/National Climatic Data Center	2003
Annual days < 0°F	Average days per year where temperature drops below 0°F	NOAA/National Climatic Data Center	2003
Precipitation			
Annual inches precipitation	Annual total precipitation (snow or rain), equivalent water inches, 70-year average	NOAA/National Climatic Data Center	2003
Annual inches snowfall	Annual snowfall in inches, 70-year average	NOAA/National Climatic Data Center	2003
Annual days precipitation	Average days per year with measurable precipitation	NOAA/National Climatic Data Center	2003
Annual days rain > 0.5 inches	Average days per year recording over 0.5 inches of equivalent precipitation	NOAA/National Climatic Data Center	2003
Annual days snow > 1.5 inches	Average days per year recording 1.5 inches or more of snow	NOAA/National Climatic Data Center	2003

continued

Table 5.1: Principal U.S. Metropolitan Areas: Data Descriptions & Sources *(continued)*

Field Name	Description	Source	Date
Comforts & Hazards			
July relative humidity	Average percentage relative humidity recorded during July	NOAA/National Climatic Data Center	2003
Annual days mostly sunny	Average days per year with mostly sun or partly cloudy	NOAA/National Climatic Data Center	2003
Annual days with thunderstorms	Average days per year with observed thunderstorms	NOAA/National Climatic Data Center	2003
Tornado risk score	Calculated likelihood and severity of tornadoes; 0-100 scale	Sperling's BestPlaces	2003
Hurricane risk score	Calculated likelihood and severity of hurricanes; 0-100 scale	Sperling's BestPlaces	2003
Education			
Achievement			
High school degree	Percentage of population surveyed with high school diploma	U.S. Census	2001
2-year college degree	Percentage of population surveyed with 2-year degree or trade school certificate	U.S. Census	2001
4-year college degree	Percentage of population surveyed with 4-year college/university degree	U.S. Census	2001
Graduate/professional degree	Percentage of population surveyed with graduate or professional degree	U.S. Census	2001
Public Schools			
Expenditures per pupil	Dollars spent for public education divided by number of students	National Center for Education Statistics	2002
Student/teacher ratio	Ratio showing number of students per teacher in public schools	National Center for Education Statistics	2002
Attending public school	Percentage of total students in area attending public school	National Center for Education Statistics	2002
State SAT score	Average state SAT score; asterisk denotes state emphasis over ACT	College Board/American College Testing Service	2002
State ACT score	Average state ACT score; asterisk denotes state emphasis over SAT	College Board/American College Testing Service	2002
Higher Education			
No. 2-year colleges	Number of 2-year colleges and trade schools	National Center for Education Statistics	2002
No. 4-year colleges/universities	Number of 4-year colleges, universities, and branch campuses	National Center for Education Statistics	2002
No. highly ranked universities	Number of colleges and universities with selective admission standards	Princeton Review study	2001
Health & Healthcare			
Hazards & Illnesses			
Air-quality score	Composite of particulates, ozone, and volatile organic compounds; 0-100 scale	Sperling's BestPlaces	2003
Water-quality score	Natural and man-made pollutants in runoff and ground water; 0-100 scale	Sperling's BestPlaces	2003
Pollen/allergy score	Composite of grass, tree, and mold allergens; 0-100 scale	Sperling's BestPlaces	2003
Stress score	Composite of eight stress factors; 0-100 scale	Sperling's BestPlaces	2003
Cancer mortality per capita	Number of deaths per 100,000 attributable to cancer or cancer-related causes	National Centers for Disease Control and Prevention	2003
Depression days per month	Number of reported days with stress or depression	Sperling's BestPlaces	2003
Healthcare			
Physicians per capita	Number of accredited generalists and specialists per 100,000 people	American Medical Association	2003
Hospital beds per capita	Number of hospital beds per 100,000 people	U.S. Department of Health and Human Services	2001
No. teaching hospitals	Number of hospitals accredited to teach or train physicians	U.S. Department of Health and Human Services	2001
Cost per doctor visit	Average dollar cost per doctor visit	American Chamber of Commerce Research Association	2003
Cost per dental visit	Average dollar cost per dentist visit	American Chamber of Commerce Research Association	2003
Cost per daily hospital room	Average dollar cost per daily hospital room	American Chamber of Commerce Research Association	2003

Field Name	Description	Source	Date
Crime			
Violent crime rate	Number of murder, rape, robbery, and assault crimes per 100,000 people	FBI Uniform Crime Reports	2002
Change in violent crime rate	Change in violent crime rate, 1996-2001	FBI Uniform Crime Reports	2002
Property crime rate	Number of burglaries, thefts, and auto thefts per 100,000 people	FBI Uniform Crime Reports	2002
Change in property crime rate	Change in property crime rate, 1996-2001	FBI Uniform Crime Reports	2002
Transportation			
Commute			
Average commute time	Average number of minutes per one-way commute to work	U.S. Census Bureau	2000
Commute by auto	Percentage of workers commuting with no additional passengers	U.S. Census Bureau	2000
Commute by mass transit	Percentage of workers commuting by scheduled public transit	U.S. Census Bureau	2000
Work at home	Percentage of workers working at home	U.S. Census Bureau	2000
Mass transit miles per capita	Number of transit vehicle miles available per person per day	U.S. Census Bureau	2000
Intercity Services			
Miles to nearest major airport	Miles to nearest Federal Aviation Administration "hub" airport	Federal Aviation Administration	2003
Type of local airport	Federal Aviation Administration airport type: large, medium, small hub, or non-hub	Federal Aviation Administration	2003
No. daily airline departures	Average number of passenger aircraft departing per day	Federal Aviation Administration	2003
Amtrak service	YES if Amtrak service, NO if none	Sperling's BestPlaces/Amtrak	2003
No. interstate highways	Number of interstate highways present in area	Rand McNally Road Atlas	2003
Automotive			
Insurance, annual premium	Average insurance premium	National Association of Insurance Commissioners	2002
Gas, cost per gallon	Average cost per gallon of regular unleaded gas, August 2003	American Automobile Association	2003
Daily vehicle miles per capita	Average daily road miles per person per day	Federal Highway Administration	2002
Leisure			
Dining & Shopping			
Restaurant rating	Availability and quality of restaurants; 1-10 scale	Sperling's BestPlaces	2003
No. outlet malls	Number of outlet malls	Claritas, Inc.	
No. Starbucks	Number of Starbucks retail stores	Sperling's BestPlaces/Starbucks, Inc.	2003
No. warehouse clubs	Number of Costco, Sam's Club, and BJ's stores	Sperling's BestPlaces/Warehouse club sources	2003
Entertainment			
Professional sports rating	Availability of professional major- and minor-league spectator sports; 1-10 scale	Sperling's BestPlaces	2003
College sports rating	Availability of college sports teams; 1-10 scale	Sperling's BestPlaces	2003
Zoo/aquarium rating	Availability of zoos, aquariums, and animal parks; 1-10 scale	Sperling's BestPlaces	2003
Amusement park rating	Availability, quality, and proximity of traditional amusement parks; 1-10 scale	Sperling's BestPlaces	2003
Botanical garden/arboretum rating	Availability of botanical gardens, arboretums, and conservatories; 1-10 scale	Sperling's BestPlaces	2003
Outdoor Activities			
Golf-course rating	Availability, quality, and cost of public and private golf courses; 1-10 scale	Sperling's BestPlaces	2003
Ski-area rating	Availability, quality, proximity, and cost of ski areas; 1-10 scale	Sperling's BestPlaces	2003
National Park rating	Availability, quality, and proximity of national parks and forests; 1-10 scale	Sperling's BestPlaces	2003
Sq. miles inland water	Square miles of nearby inland freshwater including lakes and streams	Sperling's BestPlaces	2003
Miles of coastline	Miles of ocean or Great Lakes coastline adjacent to area	Sperling's BestPlaces	2003

continued

Table 5.1: Principal U.S. Metropolitan Areas: Data Descriptions & Sources *(continued)*

Field Name	Description	Source	Date
Arts & Culture			
Cultural Media & Libraries			
Arts radio rating	Availability of radio stations (NPR or private) with classical, jazz, or news format; 1-10 scale	Sperling's BestPlaces	2003
No. public libraries	Number of library facilities including branches	Sperling's BestPlaces/National Center for Education Statistics	2002
Library volumes per capita	Number of volumes per 100,000 residents	Sperling's BestPlaces/National Center for Education Statistics	2002
Performing Arts			
Classical music rating	Availability and quality of symphony, chamber, or opera organizations and venues; 1-10 scale	Sperling's BestPlaces/Symphony Magazine	2003
Ballet/dance rating	Availability and quality of ballet and dance organizations and venues; 1-10 scale	Sperling's BestPlaces/Sterns Ballet/Dance Directory	2003
Professional theater rating	Availability of theater venues registered with Sterns Theater Directory; 1-10 scale	Sperling's BestPlaces/Sterns Theater Directory	2003
University arts programs rating	Availability of arts programs associated with or sponsored by local university; 1-10 scale	Sperling's BestPlaces/National Center for Education Statistics	2002
Museums			
Overall museum rating	Availability and quality of all museums; 1-10 scale	Sperling's BestPlaces/American Association of Museums	2003
Art museum rating	Availability and quality of art museums; 1-10 scale	Sperling's BestPlaces/American Association of Museums	2003
Science museum rating	Availability and quality of science museums; 1-10 scale	Sperling's BestPlaces/American Association of Museums	2003
Children's museum rating	Availability and quality of children's museums; 1-10 scale	Sperling's BestPlaces/American Association of Museums	2003

Abilene, TX

Profile: Small town
Location: North-central Texas, 185 miles west of Dallas
Elevation: 1,790 feet
Time zone: Central Standard Time

Score: 81.2 **Rank:** 32

PRO	CON
Cost of living	Isolation
Small-town atmosphere	Minimal recreation
College-town element	Low job growth

Abilene is a former watering hole and junction where the Chisolm Trail met the railroad. Today the area is largely supported by agriculture but also has some minor manufacturing, three small colleges and universities, and nearby Dyess Air Force Base. The town has a limited set of mostly local amenities, and the downtown area was recently recognized for its use of the arts to preserve and revitalize the historic district. Cost of living at 75.7 is among the lowest in the country, and the summer climate is better than most areas of Texas. Abilene has a good balance of qualities and represents typical, small-town Texas life.

To the north and west lie the southern Great Plains, and to the south is the Texas Hill Country. Cattle, occasional crops, and low hills to the south and west dot the mainly level and treeless landscape. The climate is variable. The area borders a humid subtropical climate to the southeast and the semiarid Great Plains to the north and west. Summers are hot and generally dry, with periods of thunderstorms more likely in late spring and early fall. In winter, northerly cold air battles moist warm air from the south; sudden below-freezing temperatures and wind mix with intermittent periods of mild weather. First freeze is early November, last is late April.

POPULATION

DEMOGRAPHICS	AREA	U.S. AVG	ETHNIC COMPOSITION	AREA	U.S. AVG	RESIDENT PROFILE	AREA	U.S. AVG
Population	125,647		White	82.7%	75.1%	Single	44.5%	43.6%
Population density per sq. mile	137.2	447.3	Black	6.9%	12.3%	Married	55.5%	56.4%
Population growth	5.0%	16.1%	Asian	1.9%	3.6%	Divorced	7.3%	8.4%
Median age	32.4	35.5	American Indian	.5%	.9%	Separated	2.3%	3.0%
Average family size	2.7	2.7	Hispanic	19.2%	12.5%	Married with children	36.3%	28.7%
			Diversity measure	42.8%	35.2%	Single with children	7.9%	10.1%

ECONOMY & JOBS SCORE: 91/RANK: 29

INCOME	AREA	U.S. AVG	EMPLOYMENT	AREA	U.S. AVG	LARGEST EMPLOYING INDUSTRY
Per capita income	$19,992	$23,420	Unemployment rate	4.4%	6.1%	Healthcare and Social Assistance
Household income	$37,944	$46,060	Recent job growth	2.6%	.9%	
Household income < $25K	30.9%	26.4%	Projected future job growth	11.5%	15.1%	
Household income > $75K	17.1%	24.5%	White collar	54.7%	54.5%	
Household income growth	53.0%	57.3%	Blue collar	45.3%	45.5%	

COST OF LIVING SCORE: 88/RANK: 38

INDEXES & TAXES	AREA	U.S. AVG	HOUSING	AREA	U.S. AVG	NECESSITIES	AREA	U.S. AVG
Cost of Living Index	75.7	100.0	Median home price	$69,140	$160,100	Food Index	86.2	100.0
Financial Progress Index	106.9	100.0	Home price appreciation	3.9%	7.1%	Housing Index	42.9	100.0
Income tax rate	0.000%	4.625%	Median rent	$517	$670	Utilities Index	98.9	100.0
Sales tax rate	8.250%	6.474%	Homes owned	58.8%	63.9%	Transportation Index	96.4	100.0
Property tax rate	$23.4	$15.6	Homes rented	27.9%	25.3%	Healthcare Index	92.2	100.0
			Housing affordability	61.0%	54.5%	Miscellaneous Cost Index	97.8	100.0

CLIMATE SCORE: 90/RANK: 32

TEMPERATURE	AREA	U.S. AVG	PRECIPITATION	AREA	U.S. AVG	COMFORTS & HAZARDS	AREA	U.S. AVG
January low	31.7°F	26.4°F	Annual inches precipitation	24.0	35.9	July relative humidity	59.0%	68.8%
July high	95.3°F	86.7°F	Annual inches snowfall	5.0	24.2	Annual days mostly sunny	246	212
Annual days > 90°F	89	38	Annual days precipitation	65	111	Annual days with thunderstorms	42	39
Annual days < 32°F	56	88	Annual days rain > 0.5 inches	16	23	Tornado risk score	42	19
Annual days < 0°F	0	6	Annual days snow > 1.5 inches	2	6	Hurricane risk score	2	15

TEMPERATURE

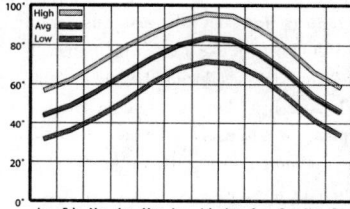

PRECIPITATION

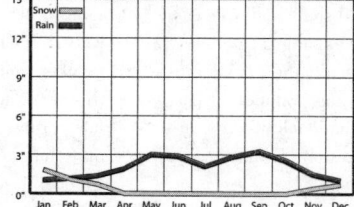

DAYS OF CLOUDS & PRECIPITATION

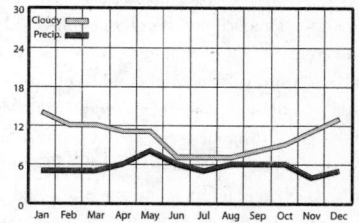

EDUCATION SCORE: 62/RANK: 125

ACHIEVEMENT	AREA	U.S. AVG	PUBLIC SCHOOLS	AREA	U.S. AVG	HIGHER EDUCATION	AREA	U.S. AVG
High school degree	81.2%	80.2%	Expenditures per pupil	$5,370	$5,894	No. 2-year colleges	0	3
2-year college degree	5.5%	6.2%	Student/teacher ratio	13.3	16.7	No. 4-year colleges/universities	3	4
4-year college degree	14.4%	15.8%	Attending public school	97.0%	90.2%	No. highly ranked universities	0	1
Graduate/professional degree	7.6%	9.6%	State SAT score	993*	1020			
			State ACT score	20.1	21.0			

HEALTH & HEALTHCARE SCORE: 55/RANK: 147

CRIME SCORE: 70/RANK: 98

HAZARDS & ILLNESSES	AREA	U.S. AVG	HEALTHCARE	AREA	U.S. AVG	CRIME	AREA	U.S. AVG
Air-quality score	24	45	Physicians per capita	223.6	261.1	Violent crime rate	314.5	456.0
Water-quality score	63	33	Hospital beds per capita	492.3	432.2	Change in violent crime rate	-46.9%	-17.2%
Pollen/allergy score	78	61	No. teaching hospitals	0	4	Property crime rate	3,745.0	3,950.0
Stress score	7	50	Cost per doctor visit	$63	$67	Change in property crime rate	-17.6%	-16.8%
Cancer mortality per capita	151.3	169.0	Cost per dental visit	$71	$82			
Depression days per month	2.1	2.8	Cost per daily hospital room	$516	$733			

TRANSPORTATION SCORE: 86/RANK: 43

COMMUTE	AREA	U.S. AVG	INTERCITY SERVICES	AREA	U.S. AVG	AUTOMOTIVE	AREA	U.S. AVG
Average commute time	16.4 min.	22.6 min.	Miles to nearest major airport	146	46	Insurance, annual premium	$926	$1,011
Commute by auto	87.0%	88.7%	Type of local airport	Small		Gas, cost per gallon	$1.41	$1.50
Commute by mass transit	.2%	1.8%	No. daily airline departures	60	294	Daily vehicle miles per capita	26.3	23.0
Work at home	2.4%	3.9%	Amtrak service	No				
Mass transit miles per capita	5.3	8.0	No. interstate highways	1	1			

LEISURE SCORE: 28/RANK: 237

DINING & SHOPPING	AREA	U.S. AVG	ENTERTAINMENT	AREA	U.S. AVG	OUTDOOR ACTIVITIES	AREA	U.S. AVG
Restaurant rating	1	1	Professional sports rating	2	4	Golf-course rating	2	4
No. outlet malls	0	2	College sports rating	5	4	Ski-area rating	1	4
No. Starbucks	1	11	Zoo/aquarium rating	3	3	National Park rating	1	3
No. warehouse clubs	3	4	Amusement park rating	1	3	Sq. miles inland water	2.0	4.0
			Botanical garden/arboretum rating	4	3	Miles of coastline	0.0	11.4

ARTS & CULTURE SCORE: 59/RANK: 135

MEDIA & LIBRARIES	AREA	U.S. AVG	PERFORMING ARTS	AREA	U.S. AVG	MUSEUMS	AREA	U.S. AVG
Arts radio rating	1	3	Classical music rating	2	4	Overall museum rating	3	6
No. public libraries	3	28	Ballet/dance rating	1	3	Art museum rating	5	5
Library volumes per capita	1.9	2.8	Professional theater rating	1	3	Science museum rating	1	4
			University arts programs rating	7	5	Children's museum rating	4	3

Akron, OH

Score: 60.8   Rank: 140

Profile: Mid-size industrial city
Location: Northeastern Ohio, 40 miles south of Cleveland
Elevation: 1,027 feet
Time zone: Eastern Standard Time

PRO	CON
Revitalizing economy	Industrial atmosphere
Nearby recreation	Entertainment
Proximity to Cleveland	Cloudy, wet climate

Akron is the center of the rubber industry. The area once produced over half the tires made in the United States, in addition to manufacturing other rubber, plastic, and chemical products. Although the majority of the production has shifted south and overseas, Akron remains a corporate center for tire companies, including Goodyear, Uniroyal-Goodrich, and GenCorp. Physically the city is unremarkable, although some of the industrial grime and pollution of past years is gone. Annual local events commanding national attention are the National Soap Box Derby and the PGA at Firestone Country Club. Nearby Cleveland offers many amenities and services.

The rolling to hilly terrain reaches its highest elevation at 1,300 feet. Many small lakes provide water for industry and recreation, and the landscape is a mix of open terrain and wooded areas. Because of the terrain, winter temperatures and snowfall vary considerably over the area, with more snow in the north. Lake Erie, which strongly influences the weather, tempers cold air masses during the late fall and winter and contributes to formations of brief but heavy snow squalls. In between the late springs and pleasant autumns, summers are moderately warm and quite humid. Fog is common, especially in the fall. First freeze is mid-October, last is late April.

POPULATION

DEMOGRAPHICS	AREA	U.S. AVG	ETHNIC COMPOSITION	AREA	U.S. AVG	RESIDENT PROFILE	AREA	U.S. AVG
Population	700,267		White	87.0%	75.1%	Single	48.2%	43.6%
Population density per sq. mile	773.6	447.3	Black	11.2%	12.3%	Married	51.8%	56.4%
Population growth	6.5%	16.1%	Asian	1.5%	3.6%	Divorced	9.5%	8.4%
Median age	37.0	35.5	American Indian	.2%	.9%	Separated	2.4%	3.0%
Average family size	2.5	2.7	Hispanic	.8%	12.5%	Married with children	25.5%	28.7%
			Diversity measure	25.6%	35.2%	Single with children	10.1%	10.1%

ECONOMY & JOBS — SCORE: 61/RANK: 128

INCOME	AREA	U.S. AVG	EMPLOYMENT	AREA	U.S. AVG	LARGEST EMPLOYING INDUSTRY
Per capita income	$24,748	$23,420	Unemployment rate	4.9%	6.1%	Plastics and Rubber Products Manufacturing
Household income	$46,466	$46,060	Recent job growth	2.9%	.9%	
Household income < $25K	25.0%	26.4%	Projected future job growth	18.1%	15.1%	
Household income > $75K	24.8%	24.5%	White collar	55.7%	54.5%	
Household income growth	58.3%	57.3%	Blue collar	44.3%	45.5%	

COST OF LIVING — SCORE: 40/RANK: 197

INDEXES & TAXES	AREA	U.S. AVG	HOUSING	AREA	U.S. AVG	NECESSITIES	AREA	U.S. AVG
Cost of Living Index	93.8	100.0	Median home price	$117,900	$160,100	Food Index	107.4	100.0
Financial Progress Index	105.6	100.0	Home price appreciation	4.8%	7.1%	Housing Index	73.2	100.0
Income tax rate	6.993%	4.625%	Median rent	$658	$670	Utilities Index	124.5	100.0
Sales tax rate	5.750%	6.474%	Homes owned	66.5%	63.9%	Transportation Index	101.4	100.0
Property tax rate	$17.3	$15.6	Homes rented	27.1%	25.3%	Healthcare Index	109.4	100.0
			Housing affordability	54.0%	54.5%	Miscellaneous Cost Index	97.8	100.0

CLIMATE — SCORE: 19/RANK: 267

TEMPERATURE	AREA	U.S. AVG	PRECIPITATION	AREA	U.S. AVG	COMFORTS & HAZARDS	AREA	U.S. AVG
January low	18.6°F	26.4°F	Annual inches precipitation	35.0	35.9	July relative humidity	71.0%	68.8%
July high	82.6°F	86.7°F	Annual inches snowfall	48.0	24.2	Annual days mostly sunny	171	212
Annual days > 90°F	7	38	Annual days precipitation	153	111	Annual days with thunderstorms	40	39
Annual days < 32°F	128	88	Annual days rain > 0.5 inches	21	23	Tornado risk score	13	19
Annual days < 0°F	5	6	Annual days snow > 1.5 inches	10	6	Hurricane risk score	2	15

TEMPERATURE

PRECIPITATION

DAYS OF CLOUDS & PRECIPITATION

EDUCATION — SCORE: 57/RANK: 142

ACHIEVEMENT	AREA	U.S. AVG	PUBLIC SCHOOLS	AREA	U.S. AVG	HIGHER EDUCATION	AREA	U.S. AVG
High school degree	85.7%	80.2%	Expenditures per pupil	$6,127	$5,894	No. 2-year colleges	1	3
2-year college degree	4.8%	6.2%	Student/teacher ratio	15.5	16.7	No. 4-year colleges/universities	3	4
4-year college degree	16.2%	15.8%	Attending public school	88.7%	90.2%	No. highly ranked universities	2	1
Graduate/professional degree	8.1%	9.6%	State SAT score	1077	1020			
			State ACT score	21.4*	21.0			

HEALTH & HEALTHCARE — SCORE: 33/RANK: 220   CRIME — SCORE: 42/RANK: 191

HAZARDS & ILLNESSES	AREA	U.S. AVG	HEALTHCARE	AREA	U.S. AVG	CRIME	AREA	U.S. AVG
Air-quality score	91	45	Physicians per capita	278.2	261.1	Violent crime rate	389.6	456.0
Water-quality score	28	33	Hospital beds per capita	383.2	432.2	Change in violent crime rate	-19.7%	-17.2%
Pollen/allergy score	64	61	No. teaching hospitals	6	4	Property crime rate	3,853.8	3,950.0
Stress score	73	50	Cost per doctor visit	$60	$67	Change in property crime rate	-3.7%	-16.8%
Cancer mortality per capita	176.2	169.0	Cost per dental visit	$73	$82			
Depression days per month	3.3	2.8	Cost per daily hospital room	$712	$733			

TRANSPORTATION — SCORE: 38/RANK: 203

COMMUTE	AREA	U.S. AVG	INTERCITY SERVICES	AREA	U.S. AVG	AUTOMOTIVE	AREA	U.S. AVG
Average commute time	23.0 min.	22.6 min.	Miles to nearest major airport	29	46	Insurance, annual premium	$828	$1,011
Commute by auto	90.3%	88.7%	Type of local airport	Medium		Gas, cost per gallon	$1.46	$1.50
Commute by mass transit	1.8%	1.8%	No. daily airline departures	487	294	Daily vehicle miles per capita	24.3	23.0
Work at home	2.5%	3.9%	Amtrak service	Yes				
Mass transit miles per capita	11.1	8.0	No. interstate highways	2	1			

LEISURE SCORE: 76/RANK: 79

DINING & SHOPPING	AREA	U.S. AVG	ENTERTAINMENT	AREA	U.S. AVG	OUTDOOR ACTIVITIES	AREA	U.S. AVG
Restaurant rating	1	1	Professional sports rating	6	4	Golf-course rating	8	4
No. outlet malls	2	2	College sports rating	5	4	Ski-area rating	2	4
No. Starbucks	5	11	Zoo/aquarium rating	4	3	National Park rating	3	3
No. warehouse clubs	4	4	Amusement park rating	9	3	Sq. miles inland water	3.0	4.0
			Botanical garden/arboretum rating	5	3	Miles of coastline	0.0	11.4

ARTS & CULTURE SCORE: 76/RANK: 75

MEDIA & LIBRARIES	AREA	U.S. AVG	PERFORMING ARTS	AREA	U.S. AVG	MUSEUMS	AREA	U.S. AVG
Arts radio rating	4	3	Classical music rating	6	4	Overall museum rating	6	6
No. public libraries	35	28	Ballet/dance rating	4	3	Art museum rating	6	5
Library volumes per capita	3.8	2.8	Professional theater rating	5	3	Science museum rating	5	4
			University arts programs rating	8	5	Children's museum rating	2	3

Albany, GA

Score: 45.1   Rank: 255

Profile: Small agricultural town
Location: Southwest Georgia in a mostly agricultural region, about 80 miles north of Tallahassee, Florida
Elevation: 200 feet
Time zone: Eastern Standard Time

PRO	CON
Cost of living	Summer heat
Small-town atmosphere	Arts and culture
Mild winters	Isolation

Albany is a commercial center for the pecan and peanut farming area of southwest Georgia. A fairly robust economy and the availability of services make this clean, quiet town livable, if not intellectually stimulating. Downsides include persistent summer heat and limited arts and culture and higher educational opportunities.

The city sits in a plain at the junction of the Flint River and several smaller rivers. The mostly level terrain contains large peanut farms and plantations and a few stands of trees. Proximity to the Gulf of Mexico influences the four-season climate. Summers are very warm and humid with the inland temperatures more extreme than those in the Florida Panhandle to the south. Afternoon thunderstorms are common, but periods of extended dry heat also occur. In winter the meeting of cool continental air and Gulf air often results in long periods of rain and cloudiness. Because of the flat terrain, local floods are possible. Although temperatures are usually mild, freezing occurs every winter. First freeze is early December, last is mid-February.

POPULATION

DEMOGRAPHICS	AREA	U.S. AVG	ETHNIC COMPOSITION	AREA	U.S. AVG	RESIDENT PROFILE	AREA	U.S. AVG
Population	123,257		White	48.3%	75.1%	Single	54.9%	43.6%
Population density per sq. mile	179.8	447.3	Black	50.8%	12.3%	Married	45.1%	56.4%
Population growth	9.5%	16.1%	Asian	.5%	3.6%	Divorced	9.5%	8.4%
Median age	32.6	35.5	American Indian	.2%	.9%	Separated	6.4%	3.0%
Average family size	2.8	2.7	Hispanic	1.7%	12.5%	Married with children	25.5%	28.7%
			Diversity measure	52.7%	35.2%	Single with children	21.5%	10.1%

ECONOMY & JOBS SCORE: 60/RANK: 133

INCOME	AREA	U.S. AVG	EMPLOYMENT	AREA	U.S. AVG	LARGEST EMPLOYING INDUSTRY
Per capita income	$19,449	$23,420	Unemployment rate	4.8%	6.1%	Paper Manufacturing
Household income	$39,954	$46,060	Recent job growth	2.5%	.9%	
Household income < $25K	30.7%	26.4%	Projected future job growth	18.8%	15.1%	
Household income > $75K	20.1%	24.5%	White collar	52.8%	54.5%	
Household income growth	61.9%	57.3%	Blue collar	47.2%	45.5%	

COST OF LIVING SCORE: 83/RANK: 56

INDEXES & TAXES	AREA	U.S. AVG	HOUSING	AREA	U.S. AVG	NECESSITIES	AREA	U.S. AVG
Cost of Living Index	81.9	100.0	Median home price	$92,870	$160,100	Food Index	96.8	100.0
Financial Progress Index	104.0	100.0	Home price appreciation	4.8%	7.1%	Housing Index	57.7	100.0
Income tax rate	6.000%	4.625%	Median rent	$466	$670	Utilities Index	96.4	100.0
Sales tax rate	7.000%	6.474%	Homes owned	57.2%	63.9%	Transportation Index	93.1	100.0
Property tax rate	$13.6	$15.6	Homes rented	33.7%	25.3%	Healthcare Index	88.9	100.0
			Housing affordability	60.0%	54.5%	Miscellaneous Cost Index	97.0	100.0

CLIMATE
SCORE: 61/RANK: 128

TEMPERATURE	AREA	U.S. AVG	PRECIPITATION	AREA	U.S. AVG	COMFORTS & HAZARDS	AREA	U.S. AVG
January low	41.0°F	26.4°F	Annual inches precipitation	62.0	35.9	July relative humidity	76.0%	68.8%
July high	90.6°F	86.7°F	Annual inches snowfall	0.0	24.2	Annual days mostly sunny	233	212
Annual days > 90°F	87	38	Annual days precipitation	119	111	Annual days with thunderstorms	86	39
Annual days < 32°F	36	88	Annual days rain > 0.5 inches	38	23	Tornado risk score	24	19
Annual days < 0°F	0	6	Annual days snow > 1.5 inches	0	6	Hurricane risk score	38	15

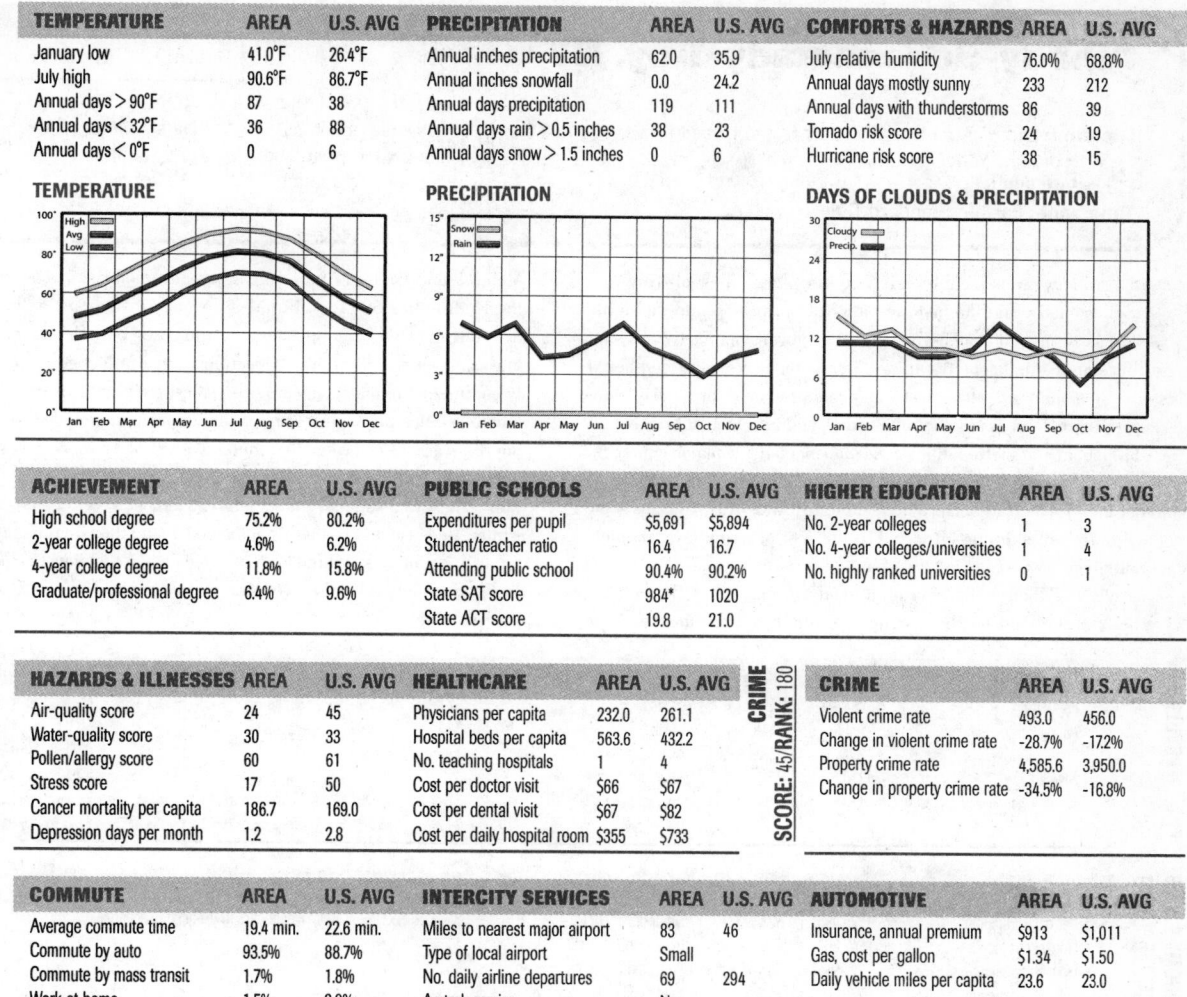

TEMPERATURE

PRECIPITATION

DAYS OF CLOUDS & PRECIPITATION

EDUCATION
SCORE: 9/RANK: 299

ACHIEVEMENT	AREA	U.S. AVG	PUBLIC SCHOOLS	AREA	U.S. AVG	HIGHER EDUCATION	AREA	U.S. AVG
High school degree	75.2%	80.2%	Expenditures per pupil	$5,691	$5,894	No. 2-year colleges	1	3
2-year college degree	4.6%	6.2%	Student/teacher ratio	16.4	16.7	No. 4-year colleges/universities	1	4
4-year college degree	11.8%	15.8%	Attending public school	90.4%	90.2%	No. highly ranked universities	0	1
Graduate/professional degree	6.4%	9.6%	State SAT score	984*	1020			
			State ACT score	19.8	21.0			

HEALTH & HEALTHCARE
SCORE: 41/RANK: 194

CRIME
SCORE: 45/RANK: 180

HAZARDS & ILLNESSES	AREA	U.S. AVG	HEALTHCARE	AREA	U.S. AVG	CRIME	AREA	U.S. AVG
Air-quality score	24	45	Physicians per capita	232.0	261.1	Violent crime rate	493.0	456.0
Water-quality score	30	33	Hospital beds per capita	563.6	432.2	Change in violent crime rate	-28.7%	-17.2%
Pollen/allergy score	60	61	No. teaching hospitals	1	4	Property crime rate	4,585.6	3,950.0
Stress score	17	50	Cost per doctor visit	$66	$67	Change in property crime rate	-34.5%	-16.8%
Cancer mortality per capita	186.7	169.0	Cost per dental visit	$67	$82			
Depression days per month	1.2	2.8	Cost per daily hospital room	$355	$733			

TRANSPORTATION
SCORE: 59/RANK: 134

COMMUTE	AREA	U.S. AVG	INTERCITY SERVICES	AREA	U.S. AVG	AUTOMOTIVE	AREA	U.S. AVG
Average commute time	19.4 min.	22.6 min.	Miles to nearest major airport	83	46	Insurance, annual premium	$913	$1,011
Commute by auto	93.5%	88.7%	Type of local airport	Small		Gas, cost per gallon	$1.34	$1.50
Commute by mass transit	1.7%	1.8%	No. daily airline departures	69	294	Daily vehicle miles per capita	23.6	23.0
Work at home	1.5%	3.9%	Amtrak service	No				
Mass transit miles per capita	5.4	8.0	No. interstate highways	0	1			

LEISURE
SCORE: 5/RANK: 314

DINING & SHOPPING	AREA	U.S. AVG	ENTERTAINMENT	AREA	U.S. AVG	OUTDOOR ACTIVITIES	AREA	U.S. AVG
Restaurant rating	1	1	Professional sports rating	2	4	Golf-course rating	1	4
No. outlet malls	0	2	College sports rating	4	4	Ski-area rating	1	4
No. Starbucks	0	11	Zoo/aquarium rating	1	3	National Park rating	1	3
No. warehouse clubs	3	4	Amusement park rating	1	3	Sq. miles inland water	2.0	4.0
			Botanical garden/arboretum rating	1	3	Miles of coastline	0.0	11.4

ARTS & CULTURE
SCORE: 32/RANK: 223

MEDIA & LIBRARIES	AREA	U.S. AVG	PERFORMING ARTS	AREA	U.S. AVG	MUSEUMS	AREA	U.S. AVG
Arts radio rating	1	3	Classical music rating	3	4	Overall museum rating	3	6
No. public libraries	7	28	Ballet/dance rating	1	3	Art museum rating	3	5
Library volumes per capita	3.1	2.8	Professional theater rating	1	3	Science museum rating	1	4
			University arts programs rating	3	5	Children's museum rating	1	3

Albany-Schenectady-Troy, NY

Score: 47.8 **Rank:** 240

Profile: Capital city
Location: East-central New York, along the Hudson River 160 miles north of New York City
Elevation: 292 feet
Time zone: Eastern Standard Time

PRO	CON
Diverse economy	Harsh winters
Educated population	Entertainment
Nearby recreation	Cost of living

The Albany area includes six counties, the cities of Troy and Schenectady, and the historic Saratoga Springs area to the north. An assortment of commercial and state government activities support this state capital. The downtown area is modern with a number of historic sites and an attractive waterfront. Suburbs are fairly nondescript. There is an assortment of mostly small arts and culture amenities throughout the metropolitan area. Schenectady, a major center for the General Electric Company, is undergoing a renewal but is otherwise unremarkable. The Rensselaer Polytechnic Institute in Troy brings some college-town flavor to that city. At 110 the cost of living is moderately high, although not as high as the urban areas to the south.

The city of Albany is located on a gently rolling valley floor on the west bank of the Hudson River, 8 miles south of the confluence of the Mohawk and Hudson rivers. The area's elevation rises from sea level at the Hudson to 1,500 feet, 11 miles west of Albany. East of the Hudson, the terrain rises more sharply into the Berkshires of western Massachusetts. The Atlantic Ocean has some influence on the primarily continental climate. In warmer seasons, temperatures rise sharply by day, but fall rapidly after sunset; nights are relatively cool. Periods of oppressive heat occasionally extend a week or more. Winters are cold and sometimes severe with lows frequently below 10°F. Most precipitation comes from summer thunderstorms; almost 6 feet of snow falls each winter. Because it is farther from the ocean and the Great Lakes, Albany tends to get more sunshine than other places in the state. First freeze is end of September, last is early May.

POPULATION

DEMOGRAPHICS	AREA	U.S. AVG	ETHNIC COMPOSITION	AREA	U.S. AVG	RESIDENT PROFILE	AREA	U.S. AVG
Population	884,969		White	92.3%	75.1%	Single	44.9%	43.6%
Population density per sq. mile	274.6	447.3	Black	5.4%	12.3%	Married	55.1%	56.4%
Population growth	2.7%	16.1%	Asian	1.4%	3.6%	Divorced	6.8%	8.4%
Median age	37.8	35.5	American Indian	.2%	.9%	Separated	4.2%	3.0%
Average family size	2.5	2.7	Hispanic	2.5%	12.5%	Married with children	27.1%	28.7%
			Diversity measure	22.2%	35.2%	Single with children	9.3%	10.1%

ECONOMY & JOBS SCORE: 74/RANK: 84

INCOME	AREA	U.S. AVG	EMPLOYMENT	AREA	U.S. AVG	LARGEST EMPLOYING INDUSTRY
Per capita income	$25,085	$23,420	Unemployment rate	3.6%	6.1%	Healthcare and Social Assistance
Household income	$48,861	$46,060	Recent job growth	1.2%	.9%	
Household income < $25K	22.9%	26.4%	Projected future job growth	10.2%	15.1%	
Household income > $75K	27.2%	24.5%	White collar	63.4%	54.5%	
Household income growth	50.6%	57.3%	Blue collar	36.6%	45.5%	

COST OF LIVING SCORE: 15/RANK: 279

INDEXES & TAXES	AREA	U.S. AVG	HOUSING	AREA	U.S. AVG	NECESSITIES	AREA	U.S. AVG
Cost of Living Index	110.0	100.0	Median home price	$139,600	$160,100	Food Index	117.2	100.0
Financial Progress Index	94.6	100.0	Home price appreciation	6.5%	7.1%	Housing Index	86.7	100.0
Income tax rate	7.125%	4.625%	Median rent	$634	$670	Utilities Index	151.0	100.0
Sales tax rate	8.000%	6.474%	Homes owned	64.3%	63.9%	Transportation Index	113.8	100.0
Property tax rate	$27.8	$15.6	Homes rented	22.3%	25.3%	Healthcare Index	136.3	100.0
			Housing affordability	57.0%	54.5%	Miscellaneous Cost Index	118.8	100.0

CLIMATE SCORE: 4/RANK: 315

TEMPERATURE	AREA	U.S. AVG	PRECIPITATION	AREA	U.S. AVG	COMFORTS & HAZARDS	AREA	U.S. AVG
January low	12.5°F	26.4°F	Annual inches precipitation	33.0	35.9	July relative humidity	71.0%	68.8%
July high	83.9°F	86.7°F	Annual inches snowfall	71.0	24.2	Annual days mostly sunny	182	212
Annual days > 90°F	8	38	Annual days precipitation	135	111	Annual days with thunderstorms	28	39
Annual days < 32°F	155	88	Annual days rain > 0.5 inches	23	23	Tornado risk score	6	19
Annual days < 0°F	17	6	Annual days snow > 1.5 inches	13	6	Hurricane risk score	7	15

TEMPERATURE

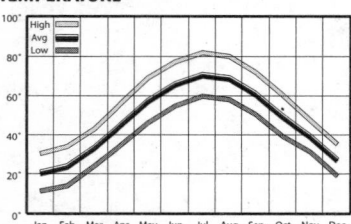

PRECIPITATION

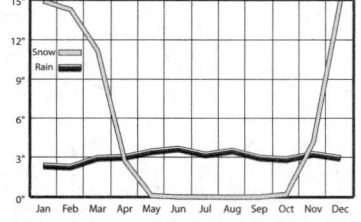

DAYS OF CLOUDS & PRECIPITATION

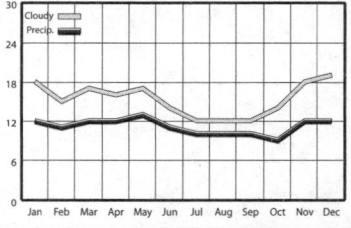

EDUCATION SCORE: 95/RANK: 17

ACHIEVEMENT	AREA	U.S. AVG	PUBLIC SCHOOLS	AREA	U.S. AVG	HIGHER EDUCATION	AREA	U.S. AVG
High school degree	85.6%	80.2%	Expenditures per pupil	$8,386	$5,894	No. 2-year colleges	7	3
2-year college degree	10.0%	6.2%	Student/teacher ratio	14.7	16.7	No. 4-year colleges/universities	9	4
4-year college degree	15.7%	15.8%	Attending public school	89.4%	90.2%	No. highly ranked universities	3	1
Graduate/professional degree	12.6%	9.6%	State SAT score	1006*	1020			
			State ACT score	22.3	21.0			

HEALTH & HEALTHCARE SCORE: 61/RANK: 126

CRIME SCORE: 86/RANK: 47

HAZARDS & ILLNESSES	AREA	U.S. AVG	HEALTHCARE	AREA	U.S. AVG	CRIME	AREA	U.S. AVG
Air-quality score	74	45	Physicians per capita	298.5	261.1	Violent crime rate	289.7	456.0
Water-quality score	43	33	Hospital beds per capita	401.3	432.2	Change in violent crime rate	-25.8%	-17.2%
Pollen/allergy score	42	61	No. teaching hospitals	7	4	Property crime rate	2,737.2	3,950.0
Stress score	26	50	Cost per doctor visit	$64	$67	Change in property crime rate	-24.2%	-16.8%
Cancer mortality per capita	185.6	169.0	Cost per dental visit	$106	$82			
Depression days per month	3.2	2.8	Cost per daily hospital room	$1,195	$733			

TRANSPORTATION SCORE: 60/RANK: 128

COMMUTE	AREA	U.S. AVG	INTERCITY SERVICES	AREA	U.S. AVG	AUTOMOTIVE	AREA	U.S. AVG
Average commute time	22.7 min.	22.6 min.	Miles to nearest major airport	22	46	Insurance, annual premium	$1,361	$1,011
Commute by auto	89.1%	88.7%	Type of local airport	Small		Gas, cost per gallon	$1.55	$1.50
Commute by mass transit	2.8%	1.8%	No. daily airline departures	131	294	Daily vehicle miles per capita	27.5	23.0
Work at home	3.3%	3.9%	Amtrak service	Yes				
Mass transit miles per capita	8.2	8.0	No. interstate highways	3	1			

LEISURE SCORE: 64/RANK: 116

DINING & SHOPPING	AREA	U.S. AVG	ENTERTAINMENT	AREA	U.S. AVG	OUTDOOR ACTIVITIES	AREA	U.S. AVG
Restaurant rating	1	1	Professional sports rating	3	4	Golf-course rating	7	4
No. outlet malls	2	2	College sports rating	10	4	Ski-area rating	7	4
No. Starbucks	7	11	Zoo/aquarium rating	1	3	National Park rating	2	3
No. warehouse clubs	6	4	Amusement park rating	5	3	Sq. miles inland water	5.0	4.0
			Botanical garden/arboretum rating	2	3	Miles of coastline	0.0	11.4

ARTS & CULTURE SCORE: 93/RANK: 20

MEDIA & LIBRARIES	AREA	U.S. AVG	PERFORMING ARTS	AREA	U.S. AVG	MUSEUMS	AREA	U.S. AVG
Arts radio rating	10	3	Classical music rating	5	4	Overall museum rating	9	6
No. public libraries	66	28	Ballet/dance rating	5	3	Art museum rating	8	5
Library volumes per capita	3.6	2.8	Professional theater rating	6	3	Science museum rating	8	4
			University arts programs rating	6	5	Children's museum rating	8	3

Albuquerque, NM

Score: 77.8 Rank: 45

Profile: Mid-size city/College town
Location: Near the center of New Mexico
Elevation: 5,314 feet
Time zone: Mountain Standard Time

PRO	CON
Year-round climate	Crime rate
Attractive setting	Urban sprawl
Arts and culture	Economic cycles

Albuquerque, located at the crossroads of the state's travel routes, is the largest city in New Mexico. Clear, sunny, dry days; an attractive mountain landscape; and a mostly healthy economy attract new residents from around the country. The tax climate is favorable, and the state's fiscal health is among the best in the country. The area is a center for the high-tech industry, with over 100 mostly small- and medium-size companies; however, this industry is vulnerable to economic cycles. Albuquerque boasts a modern downtown and a historic area with shops, restaurants, and entertainment venues. The town sprawls in all directions from the city core; managing growth, sprawl, congestion, and air quality are among the area's biggest challenges. Amenities include the University of New Mexico and a number of arts organizations, although many consider the cultural offerings in Santa Fe,

60 miles the north, to be superior. Within a day's drive are interesting historic and archaeological sites and mountain areas to the east.

The Albuquerque metropolitan area is largely situated in the Rio Grande Valley and on the mesas and piedmont slopes rising on either side of the valley floor. The Sandia and Manzano mountains rise abruptly from the eastern edge of the city with Tijeras Canyon separating the two ranges. West of the city the land gradually rises to the Continental Divide, some 90 miles away. Natural vegetation is mainly desert scrub, grasses, and small trees, with coniferous forests high in the mountains to the east. The climate is arid continental with abundant sunshine, low humidity, scant precipitation, and a wide yet tolerable range of seasonal temperatures. More than three-fourths of daylight hours have sunshine, even in winter. Average summer temperatures are high, with warm days up to 90°F and cool nights. Winter temperatures usually reach the 50s, but can fail to rise above freezing on a few days. Precipitation is adequate only for native vegetation. Snow in the city is light and infrequent, but the mountains get enough for skiing. Most annual precipitation comes from afternoon summer thundershowers, which peak during August. Winter and spring windstorms may bring dust. First freeze is mid-October, last is early May.

POPULATION

DEMOGRAPHICS	AREA	U.S. AVG	ETHNIC COMPOSITION	AREA	U.S. AVG	RESIDENT PROFILE	AREA	U.S. AVG
Population	737,324		White	73.4%	75.1%	Single	45.4%	43.6%
Population density per sq. mile	124.1	447.3	Black	2.7%	12.3%	Married	54.6%	56.4%
Population growth	25.2%	16.1%	Asian	1.6%	3.6%	Divorced	9.4%	8.4%
Median age	35.2	35.5	American Indian	12.8%	.9%	Separated	2.0%	3.0%
Average family size	2.8	2.7	Hispanic	40.0%	12.5%	Married with children	31.9%	28.7%
			Diversity measure	60.2%	35.2%	Single with children	12.7%	10.1%

ECONOMY & JOBS — SCORE: 55/RANK: 149

INCOME	AREA	U.S. AVG	EMPLOYMENT	AREA	U.S. AVG	LARGEST EMPLOYING INDUSTRY
Per capita income	$23,392	$23,420	Unemployment rate	5.3%	6.1%	Healthcare and Social Assistance
Household income	$45,403	$46,060	Recent job growth	2.8%	.9%	
Household income < $25K	25.1%	26.4%	Projected future job growth	21.4%	15.1%	
Household income > $75K	23.8%	24.5%	White collar	60.0%	54.5%	
Household income growth	66.0%	57.3%	Blue collar	40.0%	45.5%	

COST OF LIVING — SCORE: 24/RANK: 249

INDEXES & TAXES	AREA	U.S. AVG	HOUSING	AREA	U.S. AVG	NECESSITIES	AREA	U.S. AVG
Cost of Living Index	94.6	100.0	Median home price	$134,900	$160,100	Food Index	104.9	100.0
Financial Progress Index	102.2	100.0	Home price appreciation	3.0%	7.1%	Housing Index	83.8	100.0
Income tax rate	7.100%	4.625%	Median rent	$673	$670	Utilities Index	97.0	100.0
Sales tax rate	5.813%	6.474%	Homes owned	63.6%	63.9%	Transportation Index	100.1	100.0
Property tax rate	$15.0	$15.6	Homes rented	25.4%	25.3%	Healthcare Index	108.4	100.0
			Housing affordability	51.0%	54.5%	Miscellaneous Cost Index	97.1	100.0

CLIMATE — SCORE: 85/RANK: 48

TEMPERATURE	AREA	U.S. AVG	PRECIPITATION	AREA	U.S. AVG	COMFORTS & HAZARDS	AREA	U.S. AVG
January low	23.5°F	26.4°F	Annual inches precipitation	8.0	35.9	July relative humidity	43.0%	68.8%
July high	92.2°F	86.7°F	Annual inches snowfall	11.0	24.2	Annual days mostly sunny	283	212
Annual days > 90°F	61	38	Annual days precipitation	59	111	Annual days with thunderstorms	43	39
Annual days < 32°F	123	88	Annual days rain > 0.5 inches	2	23	Tornado risk score	9	19
Annual days < 0°F	1	6	Annual days snow > 1.5 inches	3	6	Hurricane risk score	1	15

TEMPERATURE

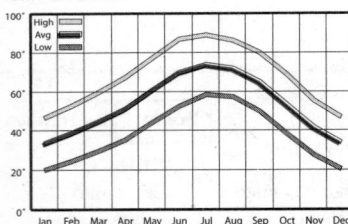

PRECIPITATION

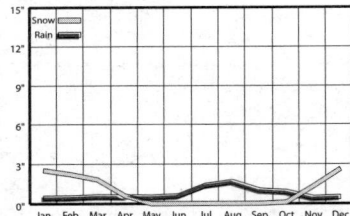

DAYS OF CLOUDS & PRECIPITATION

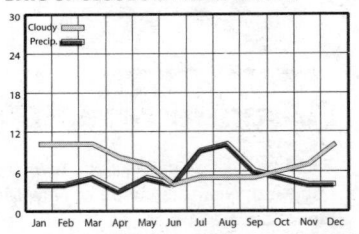

EDUCATION — SCORE: 59/RANK: 134

ACHIEVEMENT	AREA	U.S. AVG	PUBLIC SCHOOLS	AREA	U.S. AVG	HIGHER EDUCATION	AREA	U.S. AVG
High school degree	85.9%	80.2%	Expenditures per pupil	$4,869	$5,894	No. 2-year colleges	3	3
2-year college degree	5.9%	6.2%	Student/teacher ratio	16.1	16.7	No. 4-year colleges/universities	2	4
4-year college degree	18.4%	15.8%	Attending public school	88.3%	90.2%	No. highly ranked universities	1	1
Graduate/professional degree	13.4%	9.6%	State SAT score	1088	1020			
			State ACT score	19.9*	21.0			

HEALTH & HEALTHCARE — SCORE: 33/RANK: 221

HAZARDS & ILLNESSES	AREA	U.S. AVG	HEALTHCARE	AREA	U.S. AVG
Air-quality score	74	45	Physicians per capita	317.4	261.1
Water-quality score	6	33	Hospital beds per capita	316.8	432.2
Pollen/allergy score	74	61	No. teaching hospitals	4	4
Stress score	86	50	Cost per doctor visit	$82	$67
Cancer mortality per capita	153.6	169.0	Cost per dental visit	$96	$82
Depression days per month	2.6	2.8	Cost per daily hospital room	$573	$733

CRIME — SCORE: 0/RANK: 329

CRIME	AREA	U.S. AVG
Violent crime rate	1,022.1	456.0
Change in violent crime rate	16.2%	-17.2%
Property crime rate	5,992.2	3,950.0
Change in property crime rate	-9.8%	-16.8%

TRANSPORTATION SCORE: 57/RANK: 140

COMMUTE	AREA	U.S. AVG	INTERCITY SERVICES	AREA	U.S. AVG	AUTOMOTIVE	AREA	U.S. AVG
Average commute time	22.9 min.	22.6 min.	Miles to nearest major airport	5	46	Insurance, annual premium	$1,255	$1,011
Commute by auto	88.0%	88.7%	Type of local airport	Medium		Gas, cost per gallon	$1.46	$1.50
Commute by mass transit	1.0%	1.8%	No. daily airline departures	184	294	Daily vehicle miles per capita	23.7	23.0
Work at home	4.3%	3.9%	Amtrak service	Yes				
Mass transit miles per capita	8.9	8.0	No. interstate highways	2	1			

LEISURE SCORE: 66/RANK: 112

DINING & SHOPPING	AREA	U.S. AVG	ENTERTAINMENT	AREA	U.S. AVG	OUTDOOR ACTIVITIES	AREA	U.S. AVG
Restaurant rating	1	1	Professional sports rating	3	4	Golf-course rating	3	4
No. outlet malls	0	2	College sports rating	4	4	Ski-area rating	10	4
No. Starbucks	15	11	Zoo/aquarium rating	6	3	National Park rating	5	3
No. warehouse clubs	4	4	Amusement park rating	5	3	Sq. miles inland water	1.0	4.0
			Botanical garden/arboretum rating	1	3	Miles of coastline	0.0	11.4

ARTS & CULTURE SCORE: 80/RANK: 63

MEDIA & LIBRARIES	AREA	U.S. AVG	PERFORMING ARTS	AREA	U.S. AVG	MUSEUMS	AREA	U.S. AVG
Arts radio rating	7	3	Classical music rating	5	4	Overall museum rating	7	6
No. public libraries	33	28	Ballet/dance rating	6	3	Art museum rating	7	5
Library volumes per capita	2.7	2.8	Professional theater rating	1	3	Science museum rating	9	4
			University arts programs rating	5	5	Children's museum rating	8	3

Alexandria, LA

Score: 22.7   Rank: 321

Profile: Small city
Location: Center of Louisiana
Elevation: 118 feet
Time zone: Central Standard Time

PRO	CON
Cost of living	Crime rate
Healthcare	Arts and culture
Air quality	Unattractive downtown

Alexandria, located at the center of the state's major transportation routes, is a nondescript Southern city. During the Civil War, Federal forces wiped out most antebellum buildings, and today the city lacks historic charm. The downtown area, located on the banks of the Red River, with the aptly named Pineville to the northeast, is a mix of decline and modest renewal. The nearby Kisatchie National Forest provides some recreational opportunities. While cost of living is the lowest in the state, the area suffers from high crime, a low high-school graduation rate, and a lack of things to do—hence the low overall rating.

The mainly level terrain supports agriculture beyond the town's sprawl. Pine forests grow in and around the city. The climate is mainly subtropical, although the location is far enough north to receive a continental influence from the north and west. Summer months are still, warm, and humid with a few days above 100°F. Winters are mild with occasional cold snaps. Rain is abundant, with greater amounts in late spring and less in late summer; isolated showers and thunderstorms can persist for days. Winter ice storms and occasional snowfalls occur.

POPULATION

DEMOGRAPHICS	AREA	U.S. AVG	ETHNIC COMPOSITION	AREA	U.S. AVG	RESIDENT PROFILE	AREA	U.S. AVG
Population	126,881		White	72.9%	75.1%	Single	43.0%	43.6%
Population density per sq. mile	95.9	447.3	Black	24.0%	12.3%	Married	57.0%	56.4%
Population growth	-3.6%	16.1%	Asian	.7%	3.6%	Divorced	6.6%	8.4%
Median age	35.7	35.5	American Indian	2.3%	.9%	Separated	4.7%	3.0%
Average family size	2.7	2.7	Hispanic	1.9%	12.5%	Married with children	30.9%	28.7%
			Diversity measure	47.2%	35.2%	Single with children	13.2%	10.1%

ECONOMY & JOBS SCORE: 62/RANK: 126

INCOME	AREA	U.S. AVG	EMPLOYMENT	AREA	U.S. AVG	LARGEST EMPLOYING INDUSTRY
Per capita income	$17,983	$23,420	Unemployment rate	6.9%	6.1%	Healthcare and Social Assistance
Household income	$33,022	$46,060	Recent job growth	-.3%	.9%	
Household income < $25K	38.3%	26.4%	Projected future job growth	11.9%	15.1%	
Household income > $75K	15.0%	24.5%	White collar	52.8%	54.5%	
Household income growth	58.9%	57.3%	Blue collar	47.2%	45.5%	

COST OF LIVING SCORE: 98/RANK: 7

INDEXES & TAXES	AREA	U.S. AVG	HOUSING	AREA	U.S. AVG	NECESSITIES	AREA	U.S. AVG
Cost of Living Index	80.4	100.0	Median home price	$86,770	$160,100	Food Index	89.7	100.0
Financial Progress Index	87.6	100.0	Home price appreciation	5.5%	7.1%	Housing Index	53.9	100.0
Income tax rate	4.000%	4.625%	Median rent	$473	$670	Utilities Index	95.0	100.0
Sales tax rate	7.000%	6.474%	Homes owned	68.9%	63.9%	Transportation Index	100.7	100.0
Property tax rate	$6.9	$15.6	Homes rented	18.5%	25.3%	Healthcare Index	92.4	100.0
			Housing affordability	58.0%	54.5%	Miscellaneous Cost Index	97.7	100.0

CLIMATE SCORE: 62/RANK: 126

TEMPERATURE	AREA	U.S. AVG	PRECIPITATION	AREA	U.S. AVG	COMFORTS & HAZARDS	AREA	U.S. AVG
January low	36.7°F	26.4°F	Annual inches precipitation	54.0	35.9	July relative humidity	77.0%	68.8%
July high	91.8°F	86.7°F	Annual inches snowfall	1.0	24.2	Annual days mostly sunny	219	212
Annual days > 90°F	75	38	Annual days precipitation	106	111	Annual days with thunderstorms	69	39
Annual days < 32°F	43	88	Annual days rain > 0.5 inches	35	23	Tornado risk score	23	19
Annual days < 0°F	0	6	Annual days snow > 1.5 inches	0	6	Hurricane risk score	29	15

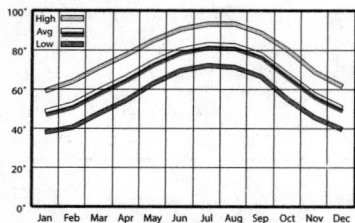

TEMPERATURE

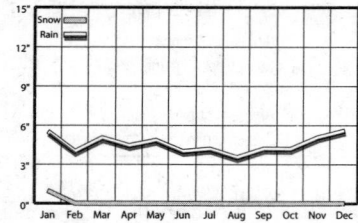

PRECIPITATION

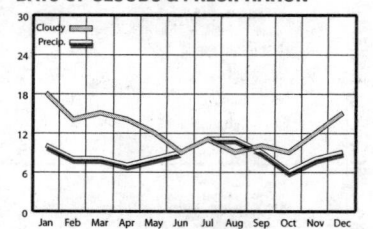

DAYS OF CLOUDS & PRECIPITATION

EDUCATION SCORE: 3/RANK: 321

ACHIEVEMENT	AREA	U.S. AVG	PUBLIC SCHOOLS	AREA	U.S. AVG	HIGHER EDUCATION	AREA	U.S. AVG
High school degree	74.6%	80.2%	Expenditures per pupil	$5,155	$5,894	No. 2-year colleges	1	3
2-year college degree	3.2%	6.2%	Student/teacher ratio	15.7	16.7	No. 4-year colleges/universities	1	4
4-year college degree	11.8%	15.8%	Attending public school	88.5%	90.2%	No. highly ranked universities	0	1
Graduate/professional degree	5.9%	9.6%	State SAT score	1122	1020			
			State ACT score	19.6*	21.0			

HEALTH & HEALTHCARE SCORE: 82/RANK: 58

CRIME SCORE: 6/RANK: 309

HAZARDS & ILLNESSES	AREA	U.S. AVG	HEALTHCARE	AREA	U.S. AVG	CRIME	AREA	U.S. AVG
Air-quality score	6	45	Physicians per capita	285.3	261.1	Violent crime rate	780.3	456.0
Water-quality score	9	33	Hospital beds per capita	1018.7	432.2	Change in violent crime rate	-6.6%	-17.2%
Pollen/allergy score	67	61	No. teaching hospitals	2	4	Property crime rate	5,385.1	3,950.0
Stress score	34	50	Cost per doctor visit	$63	$67	Change in property crime rate	-6.0%	-16.8%
Cancer mortality per capita	167.1	169.0	Cost per dental visit	$73	$82			
Depression days per month	1.2	2.8	Cost per daily hospital room	$450	$733			

TRANSPORTATION SCORE: 12/RANK: 290

COMMUTE	AREA	U.S. AVG	INTERCITY SERVICES	AREA	U.S. AVG	AUTOMOTIVE	AREA	U.S. AVG
Average commute time	23.6 min.	22.6 min.	Miles to nearest major airport	106	46	Insurance, annual premium	$1,119	$1,011
Commute by auto	91.0%	88.7%	Type of local airport	Small		Gas, cost per gallon	$1.43	$1.50
Commute by mass transit	.9%	1.8%	No. daily airline departures	41	294	Daily vehicle miles per capita	20.5	23.0
Work at home	3.7%	3.9%	Amtrak service	No				
Mass transit miles per capita	4.0	8.0	No. interstate highways	0	1			

LEISURE SCORE: 14/RANK: 284

DINING & SHOPPING	AREA	U.S. AVG	ENTERTAINMENT	AREA	U.S. AVG	OUTDOOR ACTIVITIES	AREA	U.S. AVG
Restaurant rating	1	1	Professional sports rating	2	4	Golf-course rating	1	4
No. outlet malls	0	2	College sports rating	1	4	Ski-area rating	1	4
No. Starbucks	0	11	Zoo/aquarium rating	1	3	National Park rating	5	3
No. warehouse clubs	3	4	Amusement park rating	1	3	Sq. miles inland water	2.0	4.0
			Botanical garden/arboretum rating	1	3	Miles of coastline	0.0	11.4

ARTS & CULTURE SCORE: 24/RANK: 250

MEDIA & LIBRARIES	AREA	U.S. AVG	PERFORMING ARTS	AREA	U.S. AVG	MUSEUMS	AREA	U.S. AVG
Arts radio rating	1	3	Classical music rating	3	4	Overall museum rating	3	6
No. public libraries	10	28	Ballet/dance rating	1	3	Art museum rating	4	5
Library volumes per capita	3.1	2.8	Professional theater rating	1	3	Science museum rating	1	4
			University arts programs rating	1	5	Children's museum rating	1	3

Allentown-Bethlehem-Easton, PA

Score: 53.0   Rank: 202

Profile: Mid-size-city complex
Location: East-central Pennsylvania, 20 miles west of the New Jersey border
Elevation: 264 feet
Time zone: Eastern Standard Time

PRO
Historic interest
Nearby recreation
Central location

CON
Economy
Cost of living
Entertainment

The mainly working-class cities of Allentown, Bethlehem, and Easton form a center for truck manufacturing and headquarters for such industrial giants as Bethlehem Steel and Air Products in the chemical industry. The economic challenges of Bethlehem Steel are representative of the area at large—recent and projected job trends are among the worst in the state. Bethlehem, the most interesting of the three, has responded well to the economic dislocations caused by the closure of a steel mill. Notable for its revitalized downtown and interesting historic districts, the city becomes a destination each year at Christmas. Allentown has a larger and more industrial feel. Easton, the easternmost of the three, located along the Delaware River, has the most "small town" feel and is home to Binney & Smith of Crayola Crayon fame. All three cities have a strong European culture, the influence of which can be seen in local architecture, and large areas of older row houses—some attractive, some not. Amenities include several small colleges, including Lehigh University, and a few cultural and entertainment resources. The overall crime rate is low. For what's available locally and considering the faltering economy, the cost of living (99.2) and average home price ($133,680) are high for the region.

Allentown is located in the Lehigh River Valley between mountain ridges running southwest to northeast. The climate is modified continental with moderate temperatures and dependable precipitation. Summers are hot and can be uncomfortably humid. Winters are comparatively mild with the numerous mountain ridges providing some shelter from cold air and winds from the north. Temperatures above 100°F or below 0°F are infrequent. Mountain effects make winters warmer and more comfortable than those of Philadelphia, 50 miles to the south. Summer thunderstorms are often heavy. Snowfall is variable, and cool air trapped in the valley can cause freezing rain. Snowmelt and spring rains create a flood threat. First freeze is mid-October, last is late April.

POPULATION

DEMOGRAPHICS	AREA	U.S. AVG	ETHNIC COMPOSITION	AREA	U.S. AVG	RESIDENT PROFILE	AREA	U.S. AVG
Population	650,545		White	94.9%	75.1%	Single	41.2%	43.6%
Population density per sq. mile	589.7	447.3	Black	2.1%	12.3%	Married	58.8%	56.4%
Population growth	9.3%	16.1%	Asian	1.3%	3.6%	Divorced	6.6%	8.4%
Median age	39.1	35.5	American Indian	.1%	.9%	Separated	2.9%	3.0%
Average family size	2.5	2.7	Hispanic	3.3%	12.5%	Married with children	27.2%	28.7%
			Diversity measure	24.7%	35.2%	Single with children	7.5%	10.1%

ECONOMY & JOBS   SCORE: 49/RANK: 169

INCOME	AREA	U.S. AVG	EMPLOYMENT	AREA	U.S. AVG	LARGEST EMPLOYING INDUSTRY
Per capita income	$24,171	$23,420	Unemployment rate	5.3%	6.1%	Computer and Electronic Product Manufacturing
Household income	$48,157	$46,060	Recent job growth	-1.3%	.9%	
Household income < $25K	22.8%	26.4%	Projected future job growth	7.9%	15.1%	
Household income > $75K	25.2%	24.5%	White collar	54.3%	54.5%	
Household income growth	51.0%	57.3%	Blue collar	45.7%	45.5%	

COST OF LIVING   SCORE: 30/RANK: 229

INDEXES & TAXES	AREA	U.S. AVG	HOUSING	AREA	U.S. AVG	NECESSITIES	AREA	U.S. AVG
Cost of Living Index	99.2	100.0	Median home price	$133,680	$160,100	Food Index	102.9	100.0
Financial Progress Index	103.4	100.0	Home price appreciation	5.7%	7.1%	Housing Index	83.0	100.0
Income tax rate	3.800%	4.625%	Median rent	$647	$670	Utilities Index	117.7	100.0
Sales tax rate	6.000%	6.474%	Homes owned	73.0%	63.9%	Transportation Index	111.2	100.0
Property tax rate	$25.8	$15.6	Homes rented	18.7%	25.3%	Healthcare Index	104.1	100.0
			Housing affordability	57.0%	54.5%	Miscellaneous Cost Index	108.9	100.0

CLIMATE SCORE: 32/RANK: 225

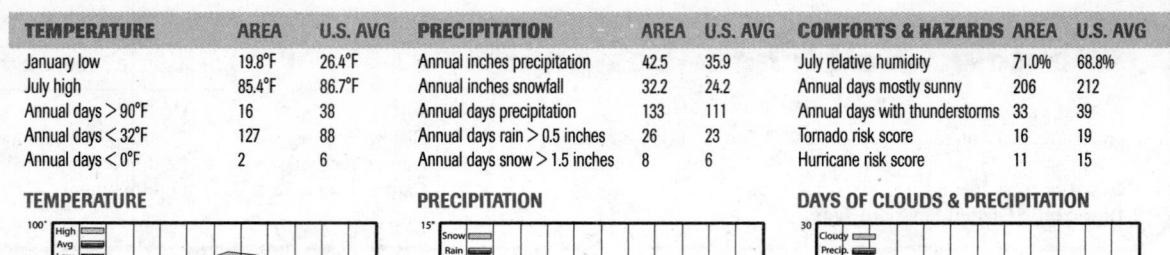

TEMPERATURE	AREA	U.S. AVG	PRECIPITATION	AREA	U.S. AVG	COMFORTS & HAZARDS	AREA	U.S. AVG
January low	19.8°F	26.4°F	Annual inches precipitation	42.5	35.9	July relative humidity	71.0%	68.8%
July high	85.4°F	86.7°F	Annual inches snowfall	32.2	24.2	Annual days mostly sunny	206	212
Annual days > 90°F	16	38	Annual days precipitation	133	111	Annual days with thunderstorms	33	39
Annual days < 32°F	127	88	Annual days rain > 0.5 inches	26	23	Tornado risk score	16	19
Annual days < 0°F	2	6	Annual days snow > 1.5 inches	8	6	Hurricane risk score	11	15

TEMPERATURE

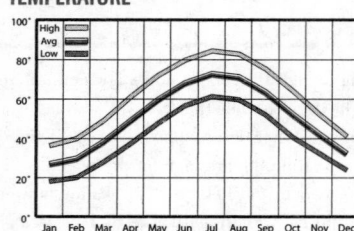

PRECIPITATION

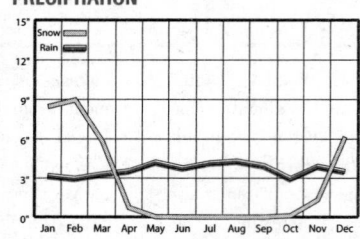

DAYS OF CLOUDS & PRECIPITATION

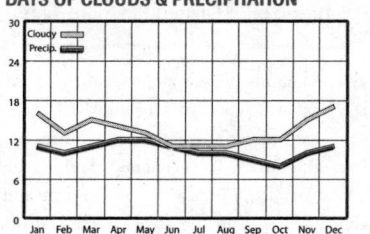

EDUCATION SCORE: 40/RANK: 198

ACHIEVEMENT	AREA	U.S. AVG	PUBLIC SCHOOLS	AREA	U.S. AVG	HIGHER EDUCATION	AREA	U.S. AVG
High school degree	80.8%	80.2%	Expenditures per pupil	$6,369	$5,894	No. 2-year colleges	5	3
2-year college degree	6.8%	6.2%	Student/teacher ratio	17.8	16.7	No. 4-year colleges/universities	7	4
4-year college degree	13.5%	15.8%	Attending public school	85.1%	90.2%	No. highly ranked universities	2	1
Graduate/professional degree	7.8%	9.6%	State SAT score	1002*	1020			
			State ACT score	21.5	21.0			

HEALTH & HEALTHCARE SCORE: 60/RANK: 130

HAZARDS & ILLNESSES	AREA	U.S. AVG	HEALTHCARE	AREA	U.S. AVG
Air-quality score	74	45	Physicians per capita	284.1	261.1
Water-quality score	54	33	Hospital beds per capita	455.2	432.2
Pollen/allergy score	59	61	No. teaching hospitals	6	4
Stress score	20	50	Cost per doctor visit	$58	$67
Cancer mortality per capita	174.9	169.0	Cost per dental visit	$70	$82
Depression days per month	1.5	2.8	Cost per daily hospital room	$790	$733

CRIME SCORE: 61/RANK: 128

CRIME	AREA	U.S. AVG
Violent crime rate	297.8	456.0
Change in violent crime rate	56.8%	-17.2%
Property crime rate	2,674.1	3,950.0
Change in property crime rate	-7.7%	-16.8%

TRANSPORTATION SCORE: 24/RANK: 250

COMMUTE	AREA	U.S. AVG	INTERCITY SERVICES	AREA	U.S. AVG	AUTOMOTIVE	AREA	U.S. AVG
Average commute time	23.6 min.	22.6 min.	Miles to nearest major airport	4	46	Insurance, annual premium	$988	$1,011
Commute by auto	91.4%	88.7%	Type of local airport	Small		Gas, cost per gallon	$1.46	$1.50
Commute by mass transit	1.0%	1.8%	No. daily airline departures	63	294	Daily vehicle miles per capita	21.0	23.0
Work at home	2.8%	3.9%	Amtrak service	Yes				
Mass transit miles per capita	8.0	8.0	No. interstate highways	1	1			

LEISURE SCORE: 75/RANK: 85

DINING & SHOPPING	AREA	U.S. AVG	ENTERTAINMENT	AREA	U.S. AVG	OUTDOOR ACTIVITIES	AREA	U.S. AVG
Restaurant rating	1	1	Professional sports rating	5	4	Golf-course rating	5	4
No. outlet malls	9	2	College sports rating	3	4	Ski-area rating	4	4
No. Starbucks	0	11	Zoo/aquarium rating	1	3	National Park rating	3	3
No. warehouse clubs	4	4	Amusement park rating	7	3	Sq. miles inland water	2.0	4.0
			Botanical garden/arboretum rating	1	3	Miles of coastline	0.0	11.4

ARTS & CULTURE SCORE: 63/RANK: 120

MEDIA & LIBRARIES	AREA	U.S. AVG	PERFORMING ARTS	AREA	U.S. AVG	MUSEUMS	AREA	U.S. AVG
Arts radio rating	5	3	Classical music rating	5	4	Overall museum rating	9	6
No. public libraries	22	28	Ballet/dance rating	3	3	Art museum rating	7	5
Library volumes per capita	2.2	2.8	Professional theater rating	6	3	Science museum rating	6	4
			University arts programs rating	9	5	Children's museum rating	2	3

Altoona, PA

Score: 64.6   Rank: 112

Profile: Small town
Location: South-central Pennsylvania along the main Allegheny Mountain ridge
Elevation: 1,320 feet
Time zone: Eastern Standard Time

PRO	CON
Historic interest	Isolation
Nearby mountains	Weak economy
Small-town atmosphere	Low ethnic diversity

Altoona is a historic railroad town and transportation gateway. Its roots are as a company town for the Pennsylvania Railroad, still a major artery today. But after the railroad ceased to be an independent entity, the town's shops and facilities went into permanent decline. Its role as a transportation gateway likewise declined when the Pennsylvania Turnpike bypassed the area by 50 miles. A modest amount of light industry has taken the railroad's place. Entertainment amenities include a minor-league baseball team and railroad-heritage sights, such as the Altoona Railroader's Memorial Museum and Horseshoe Curve, both destinations for train buffs worldwide. The small but enterprising Altoona Symphony Orchestra was rated a "Leading Small Community Symphony" and has received other national accolades. The area scores relatively consistently across all categories. Although far from big-city amenities and services, the area has a low cost of living (81.4) and a self-sufficient, small-town character. Altoona is also a gateway to the Allegheny Mountain region.

Altoona is located in a narrow valley along the main Allegheny ridge, which runs west of town from southwest to northeast. A series of lower parallel ridges rise to the east. The mountains are heavily forested with mostly deciduous trees and a few rock outcroppings. The climate is humid continental modified only slightly by nearness to the Atlantic seaboard and the Great Lakes. Due to the mountain alignment warm humid air flows in from the southwest generating warm, humid summer days with occasional relief from the northwest. Air-mass collisions can produce significant snow in winter. Weather can change rapidly at all times of the year. First freeze is early October, last is early May.

POPULATION

DEMOGRAPHICS	AREA	U.S. AVG	ETHNIC COMPOSITION	AREA	U.S. AVG	RESIDENT PROFILE	AREA	U.S. AVG
Population	127,840		White	98.2%	75.1%	Single	43.1%	43.6%
Population density per sq. mile	243.1	447.3	Black	1.2%	12.3%	Married	56.9%	56.4%
Population growth	-2.1%	16.1%	Asian	.4%	3.6%	Divorced	6.6%	8.4%
Median age	40.1	35.5	American Indian	.1%	.9%	Separated	3.4%	3.0%
Average family size	2.5	2.7	Hispanic	.5%	12.5%	Married with children	26.5%	28.7%
			Diversity measure	5.3%	35.2%	Single with children	9.6%	10.1%

ECONOMY & JOBS   SCORE: 20/RANK: 265

INCOME	AREA	U.S. AVG	EMPLOYMENT	AREA	U.S. AVG	LARGEST EMPLOYING INDUSTRY
Per capita income	$20,099	$23,420	Unemployment rate	4.1%	6.1%	Paper Manufacturing
Household income	$37,387	$46,060	Recent job growth	-1.0%	.9%	
Household income < $25K	31.8%	26.4%	Projected future job growth	11.3%	15.1%	
Household income > $75K	15.0%	24.5%	White collar	47.6%	54.5%	
Household income growth	60.6%	57.3%	Blue collar	52.4%	45.5%	

COST OF LIVING   SCORE: 83/RANK: 55

INDEXES & TAXES	AREA	U.S. AVG	HOUSING	AREA	U.S. AVG	NECESSITIES	AREA	U.S. AVG
Cost of Living Index	81.4	100.0	Median home price	$84,040	$160,100	Food Index	96.7	100.0
Financial Progress Index	97.9	100.0	Home price appreciation	4.5%	7.1%	Housing Index	52.2	100.0
Income tax rate	2.800%	4.625%	Median rent	$466	$670	Utilities Index	111.2	100.0
Sales tax rate	6.000%	6.474%	Homes owned	71.0%	63.9%	Transportation Index	88.0	100.0
Property tax rate	$21.4	$15.6	Homes rented	21.4%	25.3%	Healthcare Index	93.8	100.0
			Housing affordability	57.0%	54.5%	Miscellaneous Cost Index	99.9	100.0

CLIMATE   SCORE: 42/RANK: 192

TEMPERATURE	AREA	U.S. AVG	PRECIPITATION	AREA	U.S. AVG	COMFORTS & HAZARDS	AREA	U.S. AVG
January low	19.8°F	26.4°F	Annual inches precipitation	37.0	35.9	July relative humidity	67.0%	68.8%
July high	82.6°F	86.7°F	Annual inches snowfall	48.0	24.2	Annual days mostly sunny	180	212
Annual days > 90°F	8	38	Annual days precipitation	122	111	Annual days with thunderstorms	35	39
Annual days < 32°F	132	88	Annual days rain > 0.5 inches	21	23	Tornado risk score	4	19
Annual days < 0°F	4	6	Annual days snow > 1.5 inches	10	6	Hurricane risk score	6	15

TEMPERATURE

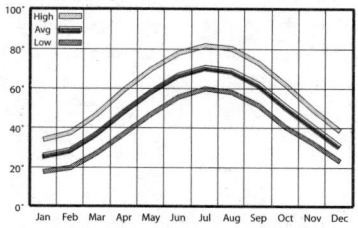

PRECIPITATION

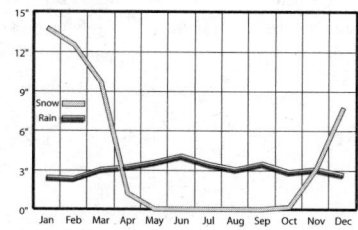

DAYS OF CLOUDS & PRECIPITATION

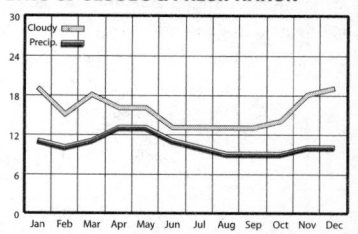

EDUCATION — SCORE: 10/RANK: 294

ACHIEVEMENT	AREA	U.S. AVG	PUBLIC SCHOOLS	AREA	U.S. AVG	HIGHER EDUCATION	AREA	U.S. AVG
High school degree	83.8%	80.2%	Expenditures per pupil	$5,783	$5,894	No. 2-year colleges	1	3
2-year college degree	6.1%	6.2%	Student/teacher ratio	17.1	16.7	No. 4-year colleges/universities	1	4
4-year college degree	9.2%	15.8%	Attending public school	87.7%	90.2%	No. highly ranked universities	0	1
Graduate/professional degree	4.7%	9.6%	State SAT score	1002*	1020			
			State ACT score	21.5	21.0			

HEALTH & HEALTHCARE — SCORE: 81/RANK: 60

CRIME — SCORE: 49/RANK: 167

HAZARDS & ILLNESSES	AREA	U.S. AVG	HEALTHCARE	AREA	U.S. AVG	CRIME	AREA	U.S. AVG
Air-quality score	17	45	Physicians per capita	261.3	261.1	Violent crime rate	264.9	456.0
Water-quality score	100	33	Hospital beds per capita	431.3	432.2	Change in violent crime rate	32.1%	-17.2%
Pollen/allergy score	58	61	No. teaching hospitals	1	4	Property crime rate	2,743.0	3,950.0
Stress score	4	50	Cost per doctor visit	$59	$67	Change in property crime rate	15.2%	-16.8%
Cancer mortality per capita	174.0	169.0	Cost per dental visit	$63	$82			
Depression days per month	1.7	2.8	Cost per daily hospital room	$715	$733			

TRANSPORTATION — SCORE: 53/RANK: 154

COMMUTE	AREA	U.S. AVG	INTERCITY SERVICES	AREA	U.S. AVG	AUTOMOTIVE	AREA	U.S. AVG
Average commute time	20.2 min.	22.6 min.	Miles to nearest major airport	89	46	Insurance, annual premium	$950	$1,011
Commute by auto	90.6%	88.7%	Type of local airport	Small		Gas, cost per gallon	$1.47	$1.50
Commute by mass transit	.4%	1.8%	No. daily airline departures	81	294	Daily vehicle miles per capita	18.6	23.0
Work at home	3.4%	3.9%	Amtrak service	Yes				
Mass transit miles per capita	5.1	8.0	No. interstate highways	0	1			

LEISURE — SCORE: 27/RANK: 241

DINING & SHOPPING	AREA	U.S. AVG	ENTERTAINMENT	AREA	U.S. AVG	OUTDOOR ACTIVITIES	AREA	U.S. AVG
Restaurant rating	1	1	Professional sports rating	2	4	Golf-course rating	2	4
No. outlet malls	0	2	College sports rating	1	4	Ski-area rating	5	4
No. Starbucks	0	11	Zoo/aquarium rating	1	3	National Park rating	2	3
No. warehouse clubs	3	4	Amusement park rating	5	3	Sq. miles inland water	2.0	4.0
			Botanical garden/arboretum rating	1	3	Miles of coastline	0.0	11.4

ARTS & CULTURE — SCORE: 38/RANK: 203

MEDIA & LIBRARIES	AREA	U.S. AVG	PERFORMING ARTS	AREA	U.S. AVG	MUSEUMS	AREA	U.S. AVG
Arts radio rating	1	3	Classical music rating	3	4	Overall museum rating	3	6
No. public libraries	8	28	Ballet/dance rating	3	3	Art museum rating	1	5
Library volumes per capita	3.4	2.8	Professional theater rating	1	3	Science museum rating	1	4
			University arts programs rating	7	5	Children's museum rating	1	3

Amarillo, TX

Score: 49.9   Rank: 229

Profile: Small city
Location: North Texas in center of Texas Panhandle
Elevation: 3,604 feet
Time zone: Central Standard Time

PRO	CON
Cost of living	Isolation
Low unemployment	Unattractive setting
Cool, dry climate	Crime rate

Set in the middle of the rugged plains of the Texas Panhandle, Amarillo is a true "cow town" of cowboys and ranch life, with some color left over from its glory days as a watering hole on legendary Route 66. Today the area is accessible by modern transportation, and modern heating and air-conditioning have tamed the harsh plains environment. These changes have led to population growth and buildup of the downtown area, but other than steakhouses and a few museums and historic sites, cultural amenities are about as scarce as trees. For the region, the area has a relatively pleasant, dry climate; a small-town feel; and low cost of living, but the downside is a wide-open, featureless space.

The Spaniards named Amarillo, which means "yellow" in Spanish, for a dry clay soil in the area. The mostly flat, empty, high plains support scrubby prairie vegetation and irrigated fields. The climate is semiarid continental with dramatic temperature variations and high winds. Summer days are warm to hot with low humidity; evenings are pleasant. Winters are changeable with alternating mild air from the south and cold blasts that can drive temperatures below zero from the northwest. The area is generally sunny and dry with periods of spring and summer thunderstorms and winter snowstorms. Some years when the storm track stays north, droughts occur and dust is a problem. First freeze is early November, last is late April.

POPULATION

DEMOGRAPHICS	AREA	U.S. AVG	ETHNIC COMPOSITION	AREA	U.S. AVG	RESIDENT PROFILE	AREA	U.S. AVG
Population	222,915		White	80.1%	75.1%	Single	45.1%	43.6%
Population density per sq. mile	122.2	447.3	Black	7.4%	12.3%	Married	54.9%	56.4%
Population growth	18.9%	16.1%	Asian	2.1%	3.6%	Divorced	10.3%	8.4%
Median age	33.7	35.5	American Indian	.8%	.9%	Separated	3.5%	3.0%
Average family size	2.6	2.7	Hispanic	23.2%	12.5%	Married with children	29.7%	28.7%
			Diversity measure	44.2%	35.2%	Single with children	10.4%	10.1%

ECONOMY & JOBS SCORE: 86/RANK: 44

INCOME	AREA	U.S. AVG	EMPLOYMENT	AREA	U.S. AVG	LARGEST EMPLOYING INDUSTRY
Per capita income	$21,412	$23,420	Unemployment rate	4.2%	6.1%	Food Manufacturing
Household income	$40,876	$46,060	Recent job growth	2.9%	.9%	
Household income < $25K	29.1%	26.4%	Projected future job growth	14.5%	15.1%	
Household income > $75K	19.2%	24.5%	White collar	53.6%	54.5%	
Household income growth	60.4%	57.3%	Blue collar	46.4%	45.5%	

COST OF LIVING SCORE: 91/RANK: 30

INDEXES & TAXES	AREA	U.S. AVG	HOUSING	AREA	U.S. AVG	NECESSITIES	AREA	U.S. AVG
Cost of Living Index	80.3	100.0	Median home price	$90,900	$160,100	Food Index	90.7	100.0
Financial Progress Index	108.5	100.0	Home price appreciation	5.6%	7.1%	Housing Index	56.5	100.0
Income tax rate	0.000%	4.625%	Median rent	$479	$670	Utilities Index	91.2	100.0
Sales tax rate	8.250%	6.474%	Homes owned	57.5%	63.9%	Transportation Index	98.1	100.0
Property tax rate	$19.6	$15.6	Homes rented	31.5%	25.3%	Healthcare Index	92.6	100.0
			Housing affordability	63.0%	54.5%	Miscellaneous Cost Index	94.8	100.0

CLIMATE SCORE: 86/RANK: 47

TEMPERATURE	AREA	U.S. AVG	PRECIPITATION	AREA	U.S. AVG	COMFORTS & HAZARDS	AREA	U.S. AVG
January low	22.5°F	26.4°F	Annual inches precipitation	20.0	35.9	July relative humidity	55.0%	68.8%
July high	91.4°F	86.7°F	Annual inches snowfall	14.0	24.2	Annual days mostly sunny	265	212
Annual days > 90°F	63	38	Annual days precipitation	67	111	Annual days with thunderstorms	48	39
Annual days < 32°F	108	88	Annual days rain > 0.5 inches	13	23	Tornado risk score	44	19
Annual days < 0°F	2	6	Annual days snow > 1.5 inches	5	6	Hurricane risk score	0	15

TEMPERATURE

PRECIPITATION

DAYS OF CLOUDS & PRECIPITATION

EDUCATION SCORE: 41/RANK: 195

ACHIEVEMENT	AREA	U.S. AVG	PUBLIC SCHOOLS	AREA	U.S. AVG	HIGHER EDUCATION	AREA	U.S. AVG
High school degree	79.3%	80.2%	Expenditures per pupil	$4,864	$5,894	No. 2-year colleges	1	3
2-year college degree	6.5%	6.2%	Student/teacher ratio	15.2	16.7	No. 4-year colleges/universities	1	4
4-year college degree	13.7%	15.8%	Attending public school	94.6%	90.2%	No. highly ranked universities	0	1
Graduate/professional degree	6.8%	9.6%	State SAT score	993*	1020			
			State ACT score	20.1	21.0			

HEALTH & HEALTHCARE SCORE: 58/RANK: 138

HAZARDS & ILLNESSES	AREA	U.S. AVG	HEALTHCARE	AREA	U.S. AVG	CRIME SCORE: 6/RANK: 308	CRIME	AREA	U.S. AVG
Air-quality score	24	45	Physicians per capita	273.2	261.1		Violent crime rate	659.8	456.0
Water-quality score	13	33	Hospital beds per capita	643.5	432.2		Change in violent crime rate	-10.5%	-17.2%
Pollen/allergy score	71	61	No. teaching hospitals	3	4		Property crime rate	5,937.1	3,950.0
Stress score	53	50	Cost per doctor visit	$61	$67		Change in property crime rate	-6.6%	-16.8%
Cancer mortality per capita	159.8	169.0	Cost per dental visit	$68	$82				
Depression days per month	2.9	2.8	Cost per daily hospital room	$410	$733				

TRANSPORTATION SCORE: 68/RANK: 108

COMMUTE	AREA	U.S. AVG	INTERCITY SERVICES	AREA	U.S. AVG	AUTOMOTIVE	AREA	U.S. AVG
Average commute time	18.4 min.	22.6 min.	Miles to nearest major airport	7	46	Insurance, annual premium	$931	$1,011
Commute by auto	91.7%	88.7%	Type of local airport	Small		Gas, cost per gallon	$1.45	$1.50
Commute by mass transit	.9%	1.8%	No. daily airline departures	39	294	Daily vehicle miles per capita	22.8	23.0
Work at home	2.8%	3.9%	Amtrak service	No				
Mass transit miles per capita	4.4	8.0	No. interstate highways	2	1			

LEISURE SCORE: 6/RANK: 308

DINING & SHOPPING	AREA	U.S. AVG	ENTERTAINMENT	AREA	U.S. AVG	OUTDOOR ACTIVITIES	AREA	U.S. AVG
Restaurant rating	1	1	Professional sports rating	3	4	Golf-course rating	2	4
No. outlet malls	0	2	College sports rating	3	4	Ski-area rating	1	4
No. Starbucks	2	11	Zoo/aquarium rating	1	3	National Park rating	4	3
No. warehouse clubs	3	4	Amusement park rating	5	3	Sq. miles inland water	3.0	4.0
			Botanical garden/arboretum rating	1	3	Miles of coastline	0.0	11.4

ARTS & CULTURE SCORE: 46/RANK: 178

MEDIA & LIBRARIES	AREA	U.S. AVG	PERFORMING ARTS	AREA	U.S. AVG	MUSEUMS	AREA	U.S. AVG
Arts radio rating	1	3	Classical music rating	3	4	Overall museum rating	4	6
No. public libraries	5	28	Ballet/dance rating	3	3	Art museum rating	4	5
Library volumes per capita	3.4	2.8	Professional theater rating	1	3	Science museum rating	4	4
			University arts programs rating	1	5	Children's museum rating	5	3

Anchorage, AK

Score: 58.6 Rank: 160

Profile: Regional center
Location: At the head of Cook Inlet in extreme south-central Alaska
Elevation: 132 feet
Time zone: Alaska Standard Time

PRO
Economy
Outdoor recreation
Attractive setting

CON
Cost of living
Dreary winters
Earthquake risk

Anchorage is the largest city and main regional center for the frontier state of Alaska. Most of the state's commercial and industrial activity occurs here. Because of rebuilding after the 1964 earthquake and the recent influx of oil money, the city is quite modern. The area has a strong, growing economy, which is offset by a high cost of living caused by geographic isolation. The climate is moderate, despite the latitude, but cloud cover—Anchorage is one of the cloudiest places in the country, with only 131 annual days of sunshine—combined with short winter days make the area unattractive to many people. When the weather cooperates, beautiful scenery is close at hand and the outdoor recreational opportunities are among the best in the country.

Anchorage is located in a stunning landscape with mountains and abundant water. The city itself is in a valley with terrain rising gradually to the east and marshes interspersed with glacial moraines and small streams. On the far eastern horizon, the Chugach Mountains rise abruptly to elevations of 5,000 feet and 10,000 feet. The much higher Alaskan Range, including Mount McKinley, lies 150 to 200 miles to the north. Snowcapped peaks are visible most of the year.

Anchorage's climate is marine, but the Chugach Mountains block warm, moist air and precipitation from the Gulf of Alaska, but not the clouds. The Alaska Range acts as a barrier against very cold air from the north. Summer high temperatures average 60°F with lows near 50°F. During July and August, 2 out of every 3 days are cloudy and 1 out of 3 has rain. The brief autumn ends in October, with snow becoming more frequent during that month. Winter extends from mid-October through early April, with temperatures dropping below zero on clear days and reaching the 30s on mild, cloudy ones. January highs are near 20°F with lows near 5°F. (Inland temperatures are 50°F to 70°F cooler.) Seventy to 90 inches of snow fall per season. First freeze is early September, last is early June.

POPULATION

DEMOGRAPHICS	AREA	U.S. AVG	ETHNIC COMPOSITION	AREA	U.S. AVG	RESIDENT PROFILE	AREA	U.S. AVG
Population	268,983		White	80.7%	75.1%	Single	45.3%	43.6%
Population density per sq. mile	158.4	447.3	Black	6.9%	12.3%	Married	54.7%	56.4%
Population growth	18.8%	16.1%	Asian	5.8%	3.6%	Divorced	12.5%	8.4%
Median age	32.6	35.5	American Indian	5.3%	.9%	Separated	3.4%	3.0%
Average family size	2.7	2.7	Hispanic	5.0%	12.5%	Married with children	34.3%	28.7%
			Diversity measure	48.8%	35.2%	Single with children	11.3%	10.1%

ECONOMY & JOBS SCORE: 99/RANK: 2

INCOME	AREA	U.S. AVG	EMPLOYMENT	AREA	U.S. AVG	LARGEST EMPLOYING INDUSTRY
Per capita income	$32,532	$23,420	Unemployment rate	5.1%	6.1%	Support Activities for Mining
Household income	$70,833	$46,060	Recent job growth	6.7%	.9%	
Household income < $25K	13.1%	26.4%	Projected future job growth	19.6%	15.1%	
Household income > $75K	46.9%	24.5%	White collar	59.8%	54.5%	
Household income growth	61.1%	57.3%	Blue collar	40.2%	45.5%	

COST OF LIVING SCORE: 56/RANK: 144

INDEXES & TAXES	AREA	U.S. AVG	HOUSING	AREA	U.S. AVG	NECESSITIES	AREA	U.S. AVG
Cost of Living Index	118.5	100.0	Median home price	$186,040	$160,100	Food Index	127.6	100.0
Financial Progress Index	127.4	100.0	Home price appreciation	5.0%	7.1%	Housing Index	115.6	100.0
Income tax rate	0.000%	4.625%	Median rent	$885	$670	Utilities Index	84.0	100.0
Sales tax rate	0.000%	6.474%	Homes owned	45.4%	63.9%	Transportation Index	103.1	100.0
Property tax rate	$16.9	$15.6	Homes rented	41.0%	25.3%	Healthcare Index	157.2	100.0
			Housing affordability	57.0%	54.5%	Miscellaneous Cost Index	125.8	100.0

CLIMATE   SCORE: 6/RANK: 308

TEMPERATURE	AREA	U.S. AVG	PRECIPITATION	AREA	U.S. AVG	COMFORTS & HAZARDS	AREA	U.S. AVG
January low	3.5°F	26.4°F	Annual inches precipitation	14.0	35.9	July relative humidity	71.0%	68.8%
July high	65.6°F	86.7°F	Annual inches snowfall	70.0	24.2	Annual days mostly sunny	131	212
Annual days > 90°F	12	38	Annual days precipitation	113	111	Annual days with thunderstorms	1	39
Annual days < 32°F	192	88	Annual days rain > 0.5 inches	6	23	Tornado risk score	0	19
Annual days < 0°F	41	6	Annual days snow > 1.5 inches	17	6	Hurricane risk score	0	15

TEMPERATURE

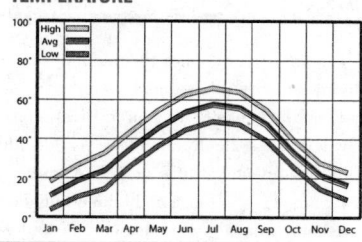

PRECIPITATION

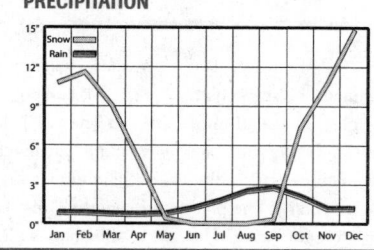

DAYS OF CLOUDS & PRECIPITATION

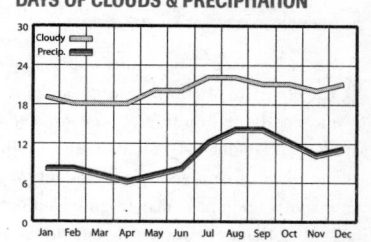

EDUCATION   SCORE: 71/RANK: 96

ACHIEVEMENT	AREA	U.S. AVG	PUBLIC SCHOOLS	AREA	U.S. AVG	HIGHER EDUCATION	AREA	U.S. AVG
High school degree	90.3%	80.2%	Expenditures per pupil	$6,669	$5,894	No. 2-year colleges	0	3
2-year college degree	7.9%	6.2%	Student/teacher ratio	22.5	16.7	No. 4-year colleges/universities	2	4
4-year college degree	18.7%	15.8%	Attending public school	93.0%	90.2%	No. highly ranked universities	0	1
Graduate/professional degree	10.2%	9.6%	State SAT score	1036*	1020			
			State ACT score	21.1	21.0			

HEALTH & HEALTHCARE   SCORE: 21/RANK: 259

CRIME   SCORE: 34/RANK: 218

HAZARDS & ILLNESSES	AREA	U.S. AVG	HEALTHCARE	AREA	U.S. AVG	CRIME	AREA	U.S. AVG
Air-quality score	6	45	Physicians per capita	300.0	261.1	Violent crime rate	663.2	456.0
Water-quality score	26	33	Hospital beds per capita	281.6	432.2	Change in violent crime rate	-33.0%	-17.2%
Pollen/allergy score	57	61	No. teaching hospitals	1	4	Property crime rate	4,350.0	3,950.0
Stress score	97	50	Cost per doctor visit	$93	$67	Change in property crime rate	-30.2%	-16.8%
Cancer mortality per capita	170.2	169.0	Cost per dental visit	$145	$82			
Depression days per month	4.9	2.8	Cost per daily hospital room	$818	$733			

TRANSPORTATION   SCORE: 91/RANK: 28

COMMUTE	AREA	U.S. AVG	INTERCITY SERVICES	AREA	U.S. AVG	AUTOMOTIVE	AREA	U.S. AVG
Average commute time	19.5 min.	22.6 min.	Miles to nearest major airport	28	46	Insurance, annual premium	$1,059	$1,011
Commute by auto	85.1%	88.7%	Type of local airport	Medium		Gas, cost per gallon	$1.63	$1.50
Commute by mass transit	2.3%	1.8%	No. daily airline departures	328	294	Daily vehicle miles per capita	18.4	23.0
Work at home	3.1%	3.9%	Amtrak service	No				
Mass transit miles per capita	13.1	8.0	No. interstate highways	0	1			

LEISURE   SCORE: 69/RANK: 102

DINING & SHOPPING	AREA	U.S. AVG	ENTERTAINMENT	AREA	U.S. AVG	OUTDOOR ACTIVITIES	AREA	U.S. AVG
Restaurant rating	1	1	Professional sports rating	3	4	Golf-course rating	1	4
No. outlet malls	0	2	College sports rating	3	4	Ski-area rating	6	4
No. Starbucks	0	11	Zoo/aquarium rating	3	3	National Park rating	9	3
No. warehouse clubs	5	4	Amusement park rating	1	3	Sq. miles inland water	4.0	4.0
			Botanical garden/arboretum rating	1	3	Miles of coastline	87.6	11.4

ARTS & CULTURE   SCORE: 73/RANK: 89

MEDIA & LIBRARIES	AREA	U.S. AVG	PERFORMING ARTS	AREA	U.S. AVG	MUSEUMS	AREA	U.S. AVG
Arts radio rating	6	3	Classical music rating	4	4	Overall museum rating	5	6
No. public libraries	6	28	Ballet/dance rating	3	3	Art museum rating	7	5
Library volumes per capita	2.4	2.8	Professional theater rating	10	3	Science museum rating	6	4
			University arts programs rating	1	5	Children's museum rating	7	3

Ann Arbor, MI

Score: 91.2   **Rank:** 6

Profile: College town
Location: Southeast Michigan, 40 miles west of Detroit
Elevation: 664 feet
Time zone: Eastern Standard Time

PRO	CON
College-town amenities	Home prices
Attractive downtown	Cost of living
Educated population	Winter climate

Ann Arbor is an important cultural center for Michigan. The University of Michigan and its campus dominate the scene both physically and culturally. The town has a pleasant small-town atmosphere with college-style restaurants, shopping, and entertainment. Coffeehouses and live music are abundant. Many amenities, including spectator sports and museums, are provided by the university. The population's educational attainment is among the top five nationwide. The area has a noted literary tradition, which includes locally headquartered Borders Group. Aside from the university, economic activity is healthy with a mix of industries and research and development activities. Nearby Detroit provides services and transportation not available in the immediate area. Crime rates are the lowest in the state by a large margin. However, home prices are almost double that of the rest of the state, and cost of living is above the national average.

The city is located on the banks of the Huron River on a mostly level plain, surrounded by a mix of agriculture and areas of deciduous woods. The climate is humid continental with a degree of influence from the nearby Great Lakes. Summers are warm and humid but seldom unbearably hot, with occasional rain and thundershowers and mostly cool, pleasant evenings. The winter climate, while consistent with the rest of the state, is unpleasant on a national scale. Winters are a mix of cold, rain, snow, and sleet, although the lakes moderate the worst of the cold. The contrast of lake-effect moisture and cooler temperatures produces cloudy periods in all seasons, particularly fall and winter. First freeze is mid-October, last is late April.

POPULATION

DEMOGRAPHICS	AREA	U.S. AVG	ETHNIC COMPOSITION	AREA	U.S. AVG	RESIDENT PROFILE	AREA	U.S. AVG
Population	603,358		White	92.4%	75.1%	Single	41.8%	43.6%
Population density per sq. mile	297.4	447.3	Black	3.8%	12.3%	Married	58.2%	56.4%
Population growth	23.1%	16.1%	Asian	2.6%	3.6%	Divorced	7.5%	8.4%
Median age	33.8	35.5	American Indian	.4%	.9%	Separated	1.8%	3.0%
Average family size	2.7	2.7	Hispanic	2.7%	12.5%	Married with children	30.7%	28.7%
			Diversity measure	28.4%	35.2%	Single with children	8.8%	10.1%

ECONOMY & JOBS
SCORE: 93/RANK: 21

INCOME	AREA	U.S. AVG	EMPLOYMENT	AREA	U.S. AVG	LARGEST EMPLOYING INDUSTRY
Per capita income	$30,509	$23,420	Unemployment rate	4.0%	6.1%	Transportation Equipment Manufacturing
Household income	$62,119	$46,060	Recent job growth	1.6%	.9%	
Household income < $25K	17.1%	26.4%	Projected future job growth	15.9%	15.1%	
Household income > $75K	40.0%	24.5%	White collar	61.4%	54.5%	
Household income growth	67.1%	57.3%	Blue collar	38.6%	45.5%	

COST OF LIVING
SCORE: 13/RANK: 286

INDEXES & TAXES	AREA	U.S. AVG	HOUSING	AREA	U.S. AVG	NECESSITIES	AREA	U.S. AVG
Cost of Living Index	110.3	100.0	Median home price	$206,900	$160,100	Food Index	103.2	100.0
Financial Progress Index	120.0	100.0	Home price appreciation	7.3%	7.1%	Housing Index	128.5	100.0
Income tax rate	4.400%	4.625%	Median rent	$815	$670	Utilities Index	94.0	100.0
Sales tax rate	6.000%	6.474%	Homes owned	69.1%	63.9%	Transportation Index	100.7	100.0
Property tax rate	$24.7	$15.6	Homes rented	21.6%	25.3%	Healthcare Index	105.0	100.0
			Housing affordability	54.0%	54.5%	Miscellaneous Cost Index	98.1	100.0

CLIMATE
SCORE: 40/RANK: 196

TEMPERATURE	AREA	U.S. AVG	PRECIPITATION	AREA	U.S. AVG	COMFORTS & HAZARDS	AREA	U.S. AVG
January low	17.3°F	26.4°F	Annual inches precipitation	32.0	35.9	July relative humidity	72.0%	68.8%
July high	83.4°F	86.7°F	Annual inches snowfall	39.0	24.2	Annual days mostly sunny	185	212
Annual days > 90°F	11	38	Annual days precipitation	133	111	Annual days with thunderstorms	33	39
Annual days < 32°F	139	88	Annual days rain > 0.5 inches	19	23	Tornado risk score	31	19
Annual days < 0°F	7	6	Annual days snow > 1.5 inches	9	6	Hurricane risk score	3	15

TEMPERATURE

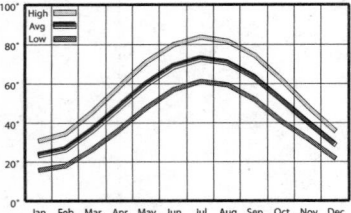

PRECIPITATION

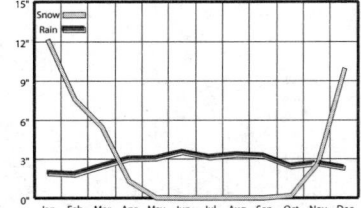

DAYS OF CLOUDS & PRECIPITATION

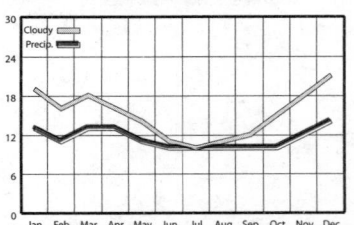

EDUCATION SCORE: 89/RANK: 35

ACHIEVEMENT	AREA	U.S. AVG	PUBLIC SCHOOLS	AREA	U.S. AVG	HIGHER EDUCATION	AREA	U.S. AVG
High school degree	90.0%	80.2%	Expenditures per pupil	$6,484	$5,894	No. 2-year colleges	1	3
2-year college degree	6.8%	6.2%	Student/teacher ratio	19.4	16.7	No. 4-year colleges/universities	6	4
4-year college degree	20.4%	15.8%	Attending public school	92.3%	90.2%	No. highly ranked universities	0	1
Graduate/professional degree	16.5%	9.6%	State SAT score	1140	1020			
			State ACT score	21.3*	21.0			

HEALTH & HEALTHCARE SCORE: 70/RANK: 96

CRIME SCORE: 88/RANK: 38

HAZARDS & ILLNESSES	AREA	U.S. AVG	HEALTHCARE	AREA	U.S. AVG	CRIME	AREA	U.S. AVG
Air-quality score	6	45	Physicians per capita	500.2	261.1	Violent crime rate	269.5	456.0
Water-quality score	12	33	Hospital beds per capita	377.5	432.2	Change in violent crime rate	-26.8%	-17.2%
Pollen/allergy score	58	61	No. teaching hospitals	3	4	Property crime rate	2,739.5	3,950.0
Stress score	25	50	Cost per doctor visit	$69	$67	Change in property crime rate	-25.6%	-16.8%
Cancer mortality per capita	164.6	169.0	Cost per dental visit	$95	$82			
Depression days per month	3.1	2.8	Cost per daily hospital room	$666	$733			

TRANSPORTATION SCORE: 84/RANK: 50

COMMUTE	AREA	U.S. AVG	INTERCITY SERVICES	AREA	U.S. AVG	AUTOMOTIVE	AREA	U.S. AVG
Average commute time	25.0 min.	22.6 min.	Miles to nearest major airport	20	46	Insurance, annual premium	$993	$1,011
Commute by auto	91.1%	88.7%	Type of local airport	Large		Gas, cost per gallon	$1.56	$1.50
Commute by mass transit	.8%	1.8%	No. daily airline departures	781	294	Daily vehicle miles per capita	26.5	23.0
Work at home	3.4%	3.9%	Amtrak service	Yes				
Mass transit miles per capita	7.6	8.0	No. interstate highways	1	1			

LEISURE SCORE: 71/RANK: 96

DINING & SHOPPING	AREA	U.S. AVG	ENTERTAINMENT	AREA	U.S. AVG	OUTDOOR ACTIVITIES	AREA	U.S. AVG
Restaurant rating	1	1	Professional sports rating	8	4	Golf-course rating	7	4
No. outlet malls	3	2	College sports rating	10	4	Ski-area rating	5	4
No. Starbucks	3	11	Zoo/aquarium rating	2	3	National Park rating	1	3
No. warehouse clubs	3	4	Amusement park rating	5	3	Sq. miles inland water	3.0	4.0
			Botanical garden/arboretum rating	8	3	Miles of coastline	0.0	11.4

ARTS & CULTURE SCORE: 86/RANK: 43

MEDIA & LIBRARIES	AREA	U.S. AVG	PERFORMING ARTS	AREA	U.S. AVG	MUSEUMS	AREA	U.S. AVG
Arts radio rating	8	3	Classical music rating	4	4	Overall museum rating	8	6
No. public libraries	30	28	Ballet/dance rating	6	3	Art museum rating	7	5
Library volumes per capita	3.1	2.8	Professional theater rating	1	3	Science museum rating	8	4
			University arts programs rating	8	5	Children's museum rating	7	3

Anniston, AL

Score: 20.8　**Rank:** 323

Profile: Military town
Location: Northeast Alabama between Birmingham and Atlanta, Georgia
Elevation: 630 feet
Time zone: Central Standard Time

PRO	CON
Cost of living	Crime rate
Cost of housing	Arts and culture
Nearby mountains	Entertainment

Anniston is an unremarkable, former textile-company town now known for the Anniston Army Depot and the Talladega Superspeedway, both nearby. The army depot is the mainstay of the economy, and nearby Talladega Mountain provides recreation opportunities. At 79.1, Anniston has a notably low Cost of Living Index, the second lowest in the state and one of the best in the United States, but this is overshadowed in overall ranking and scoring by the relative lack of other features and amenities.

Anniston is located in a tree-lined valley of the Appalachian Foothills just to the west of Talladega Mountain. Cheaha Mountain, about 15 miles south, is the highest point in the state at 2,400 feet. The climate is humid subtropical with an occasional continental influence. Four distinct seasons include long, warm, humid summers and mild winters with occasional cold snaps, ice storms, and snow. First freeze is mid-November, last is mid-March.

POPULATION

DEMOGRAPHICS	AREA	U.S. AVG	ETHNIC COMPOSITION	AREA	U.S. AVG	RESIDENT PROFILE	AREA	U.S. AVG
Population	111,616		White	80.5%	75.1%	Single	42.4%	43.6%
Population density per sq. mile	183.4	447.3	Black	17.2%	12.3%	Married	57.6%	56.4%
Population growth	-3.8%	16.1%	Asian	1.5%	3.6%	Divorced	8.5%	8.4%
Median age	37.8	35.5	American Indian	.3%	.9%	Separated	2.6%	3.0%
Average family size	2.7	2.7	Hispanic	1.8%	12.5%	Married with children	33.4%	28.7%
			Diversity measure	35.3%	35.2%	Single with children	10.4%	10.1%

ECONOMY & JOBS
SCORE: 79/RANK: 68

INCOME	AREA	U.S. AVG	EMPLOYMENT	AREA	U.S. AVG	LARGEST EMPLOYING INDUSTRY
Per capita income	$16,615	$23,420	Unemployment rate	5.4%	6.1%	Fabricated Metal Product Manufacturing
Household income	$32,190	$46,060	Recent job growth	.6%	.9%	
Household income < $25K	38.8%	26.4%	Projected future job growth	8.6%	15.1%	
Household income > $75K	10.0%	24.5%	White collar	44.4%	54.5%	
Household income growth	34.5%	57.3%	Blue collar	55.6%	45.5%	

COST OF LIVING
SCORE: 96/RANK: 12

INDEXES & TAXES	AREA	U.S. AVG	HOUSING	AREA	U.S. AVG	NECESSITIES	AREA	U.S. AVG
Cost of Living Index	79.1	100.0	Median home price	$85,820	$160,100	Food Index	95.5	100.0
Financial Progress Index	86.8	100.0	Home price appreciation	6.2%	7.1%	Housing Index	53.3	100.0
Income tax rate	5.000%	4.625%	Median rent	$413	$670	Utilities Index	96.5	100.0
Sales tax rate	8.000%	6.474%	Homes owned	65.5%	63.9%	Transportation Index	83.9	100.0
Property tax rate	$9.2	$15.6	Homes rented	26.7%	25.3%	Healthcare Index	92.3	100.0
			Housing affordability	59.0%	54.5%	Miscellaneous Cost Index	96.2	100.0

CLIMATE
SCORE: 26/RANK: 244

TEMPERATURE	AREA	U.S. AVG	PRECIPITATION	AREA	U.S. AVG	COMFORTS & HAZARDS	AREA	U.S. AVG
January low	34.0°F	26.4°F	Annual inches precipitation	53.0	35.9	July relative humidity	72.0%	68.8%
July high	90.0°F	86.7°F	Annual inches snowfall	1.0	24.2	Annual days mostly sunny	210	212
Annual days > 90°F	39	38	Annual days precipitation	118	111	Annual days with thunderstorms	58	39
Annual days < 32°F	60	88	Annual days rain > 0.5 inches	37	23	Tornado risk score	24	19
Annual days < 0°F	0	6	Annual days snow > 1.5 inches	1	6	Hurricane risk score	19	15

TEMPERATURE

PRECIPITATION

DAYS OF CLOUDS & PRECIPITATION

EDUCATION
SCORE: 10/RANK: 298

ACHIEVEMENT	AREA	U.S. AVG	PUBLIC SCHOOLS	AREA	U.S. AVG	HIGHER EDUCATION	AREA	U.S. AVG
High school degree	73.7%	80.2%	Expenditures per pupil	$4,671	$5,894	No. 2-year colleges	1	3
2-year college degree	4.8%	6.2%	Student/teacher ratio	16.8	16.7	No. 4-year colleges/universities	1	4
4-year college degree	8.9%	15.8%	Attending public school	94.7%	90.2%	No. highly ranked universities	0	1
Graduate/professional degree	6.3%	9.6%	State SAT score	1111	1020			
			State ACT score	20.1*	21.0			

HEALTH & HEALTHCARE
SCORE: 76/RANK: 75

CRIME
SCORE: 6/RANK: 311

HAZARDS & ILLNESSES	AREA	U.S. AVG	HEALTHCARE	AREA	U.S. AVG	CRIME	AREA	U.S. AVG
Air-quality score	49	45	Physicians per capita	173.8	261.1	Violent crime rate	750.8	456.0
Water-quality score	20	33	Hospital beds per capita	416.9	432.2	Change in violent crime rate	-11.7%	-17.2%
Pollen/allergy score	64	61	No. teaching hospitals	0	4	Property crime rate	5,098.3	3,950.0
Stress score	83	50	Cost per doctor visit	$58	$67	Change in property crime rate	5.4%	-16.8%
Cancer mortality per capita	175.7	169.0	Cost per dental visit	$69	$82			
Depression days per month	4.4	2.8	Cost per daily hospital room	$522	$733			

TRANSPORTATION
SCORE: 8/RANK: 302

COMMUTE	AREA	U.S. AVG	INTERCITY SERVICES	AREA	U.S. AVG	AUTOMOTIVE	AREA	U.S. AVG
Average commute time	23.5 min.	22.6 min.	Miles to nearest major airport	54	46	Insurance, annual premium	$809	$1,011
Commute by auto	91.9%	88.7%	Type of local airport	Small		Gas, cost per gallon	$1.42	$1.50
Commute by mass transit	.9%	1.8%	No. daily airline departures	111	294	Daily vehicle miles per capita	33.3	23.0
Work at home	1.6%	3.9%	Amtrak service	Yes				
Mass transit miles per capita	0.0	8.0	No. interstate highways	1	1			

LEISURE SCORE: 13/RANK: 287

DINING & SHOPPING	AREA	U.S. AVG	ENTERTAINMENT	AREA	U.S. AVG	OUTDOOR ACTIVITIES	AREA	U.S. AVG
Restaurant rating	1	1	Professional sports rating	2	4	Golf-course rating	2	4
No. outlet malls	1	2	College sports rating	2	4	Ski-area rating	1	4
No. Starbucks	0	11	Zoo/aquarium rating	1	3	National Park rating	3	3
No. warehouse clubs	1	4	Amusement park rating	1	3	Sq. miles inland water	2.0	4.0
			Botanical garden/arboretum rating	1	3	Miles of coastline	0.0	11.4

ARTS & CULTURE SCORE: 14/RANK: 283

MEDIA & LIBRARIES	AREA	U.S. AVG	PERFORMING ARTS	AREA	U.S. AVG	MUSEUMS	AREA	U.S. AVG
Arts radio rating	1	3	Classical music rating	3	4	Overall museum rating	2	6
No. public libraries	5	28	Ballet/dance rating	1	3	Art museum rating	1	5
Library volumes per capita	2.0	2.8	Professional theater rating	6	3	Science museum rating	3	4
			University arts programs rating	3	5	Children's museum rating	1	3

Appleton-Oshkosh-Neenah, WI

Score: 63.9 Rank: 117

Profile: Small-city complex
Location: Northeastern Wisconsin along the shore of Lake Winnebago
Elevation: 755 feet
Time zone: Central Standard Time

PRO	CON
Cost of living	Cold winters
Outdoor recreation	Arts and culture
Low crime rate	Low ethnic diversity

Known in a larger sense as the "Fox Cities" for their location in the Fox River Valley, the cities of Appleton, Oshkosh, and Neenah surround Lake Winnebago, the source of the Fox River. Lumber and paper production form the area's economic base, with paper products giant Kimberly-Clark making its headquarters in Neenah. Other industries include clothing (OshKosh B'Gosh) and the usual Wisconsin assortment of dairy products, agriculture, and light manufacturing. The cities have a distinct, clean, small-town feel with lots of trees and historic buildings, and residents have an uncommon pride for the area. Outdoor recreation is abundant, highlighted by watersports in summer and snowmobiling in winter. Lawrence University provides college-town amenities to Appleton. The area has one of the lowest crime rates in the country and the lowest cost of living in Wisconsin. The overall rating would be higher if the winters weren't so harsh.

The Fox Cities sit in a mostly level valley plain surrounded by areas of low rolling and densely wooded hills. The decidedly continental climate receives the full effects of continental air masses, particularly in winter. Summers are pleasantly warm and sometimes humid, with occasional hot spells and cool evenings. Most precipitation arrives as thunderstorms from May through September. Winters are harsh and cold, although the coldest days are often sunny and dry. Most winter precipitation comes as snow with persistent snow cover. First freeze is early October, last is mid-May.

POPULATION

DEMOGRAPHICS	AREA	U.S. AVG	ETHNIC COMPOSITION	AREA	U.S. AVG	RESIDENT PROFILE	AREA	U.S. AVG
Population	366,914		White	96.4%	75.1%	Single	38.0%	43.6%
Population density per sq. mile	262.3	447.3	Black	.8%	12.3%	Married	62.0%	56.4%
Population growth	16.4%	16.1%	Asian	1.2%	3.6%	Divorced	6.0%	8.4%
Median age	35.2	35.5	American Indian	1.3%	.9%	Separated	1.3%	3.0%
Average family size	2.8	2.7	Hispanic	1.1%	12.5%	Married with children	33.2%	28.7%
			Diversity measure	12.1%	35.2%	Single with children	7.1%	10.1%

ECONOMY & JOBS SCORE: 91/RANK: 28

INCOME	AREA	U.S. AVG	EMPLOYMENT	AREA	U.S. AVG	LARGEST EMPLOYING INDUSTRY
Per capita income	$25,149	$23,420	Unemployment rate	4.8%	6.1%	Paper Manufacturing
Household income	$52,817	$46,060	Recent job growth	2.9%	.9%	
Household income < $25K	19.1%	26.4%	Projected future job growth	17.1%	15.1%	
Household income > $75K	27.0%	24.5%	White collar	50.3%	54.5%	
Household income growth	65.2%	57.3%	Blue collar	49.7%	45.5%	

COST OF LIVING SCORE: 37/RANK: 205

INDEXES & TAXES	AREA	U.S. AVG	HOUSING	AREA	U.S. AVG	NECESSITIES	AREA	U.S. AVG
Cost of Living Index	89.1	100.0	Median home price	$111,900	$160,100	Food Index	97.9	100.0
Financial Progress Index	126.3	100.0	Home price appreciation	5.1%	7.1%	Housing Index	69.5	100.0
Income tax rate	6.930%	4.625%	Median rent	$540	$670	Utilities Index	106.4	100.0
Sales tax rate	5.000%	6.474%	Homes owned	75.5%	63.9%	Transportation Index	98.8	100.0
Property tax rate	$25.5	$15.6	Homes rented	19.2%	25.3%	Healthcare Index	101.4	100.0
			Housing affordability	67.0%	54.5%	Miscellaneous Cost Index	99.9	100.0

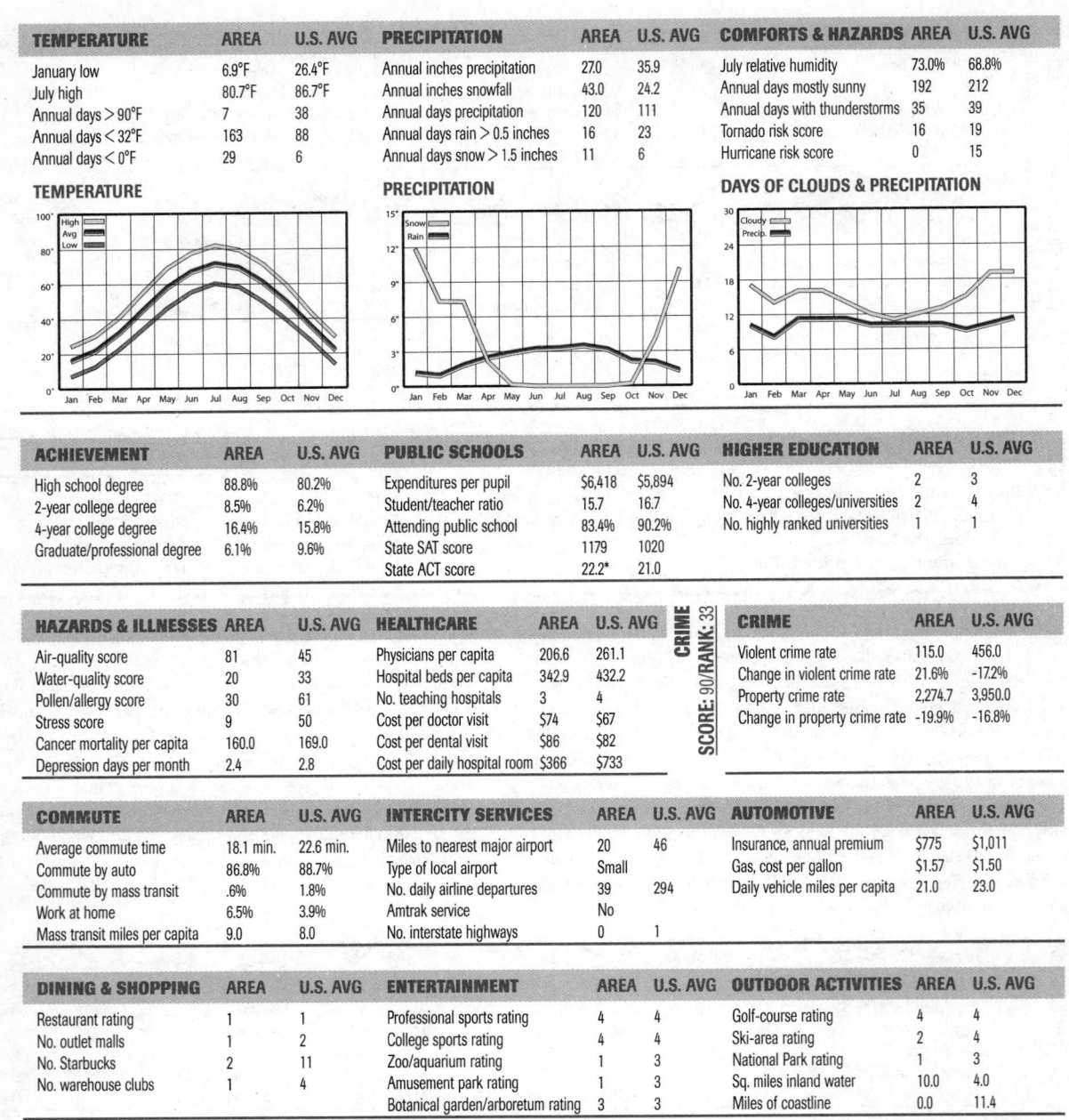

CLIMATE SCORE: 16/RANK: 276

TEMPERATURE	AREA	U.S. AVG	PRECIPITATION	AREA	U.S. AVG	COMFORTS & HAZARDS	AREA	U.S. AVG
January low	6.9°F	26.4°F	Annual inches precipitation	27.0	35.9	July relative humidity	73.0%	68.8%
July high	80.7°F	86.7°F	Annual inches snowfall	43.0	24.2	Annual days mostly sunny	192	212
Annual days > 90°F	7	38	Annual days precipitation	120	111	Annual days with thunderstorms	35	39
Annual days < 32°F	163	88	Annual days rain > 0.5 inches	16	23	Tornado risk score	16	19
Annual days < 0°F	29	6	Annual days snow > 1.5 inches	11	6	Hurricane risk score	0	15

TEMPERATURE

PRECIPITATION

DAYS OF CLOUDS & PRECIPITATION

EDUCATION SCORE: 44/RANK: 184

ACHIEVEMENT	AREA	U.S. AVG	PUBLIC SCHOOLS	AREA	U.S. AVG	HIGHER EDUCATION	AREA	U.S. AVG
High school degree	88.8%	80.2%	Expenditures per pupil	$6,418	$5,894	No. 2-year colleges	2	3
2-year college degree	8.5%	6.2%	Student/teacher ratio	15.7	16.7	No. 4-year colleges/universities	2	4
4-year college degree	16.4%	15.8%	Attending public school	83.4%	90.2%	No. highly ranked universities	1	1
Graduate/professional degree	6.1%	9.6%	State SAT score	1179	1020			
			State ACT score	22.2*	21.0			

HEALTH & HEALTHCARE SCORE: 83/RANK: 53

HAZARDS & ILLNESSES	AREA	U.S. AVG	HEALTHCARE	AREA	U.S. AVG
Air-quality score	81	45	Physicians per capita	206.6	261.1
Water-quality score	20	33	Hospital beds per capita	342.9	432.2
Pollen/allergy score	30	61	No. teaching hospitals	3	4
Stress score	9	50	Cost per doctor visit	$74	$67
Cancer mortality per capita	160.0	169.0	Cost per dental visit	$86	$82
Depression days per month	2.4	2.8	Cost per daily hospital room	$366	$733

CRIME SCORE: 90/RANK: 33

CRIME	AREA	U.S. AVG
Violent crime rate	115.0	456.0
Change in violent crime rate	21.6%	-17.2%
Property crime rate	2,274.7	3,950.0
Change in property crime rate	-19.9%	-16.8%

TRANSPORTATION SCORE: 82/RANK: 58

COMMUTE	AREA	U.S. AVG	INTERCITY SERVICES	AREA	U.S. AVG	AUTOMOTIVE	AREA	U.S. AVG
Average commute time	18.1 min.	22.6 min.	Miles to nearest major airport	20	46	Insurance, annual premium	$775	$1,011
Commute by auto	86.8%	88.7%	Type of local airport	Small		Gas, cost per gallon	$1.57	$1.50
Commute by mass transit	.6%	1.8%	No. daily airline departures	39	294	Daily vehicle miles per capita	21.0	23.0
Work at home	6.5%	3.9%	Amtrak service	No				
Mass transit miles per capita	9.0	8.0	No. interstate highways	0	1			

LEISURE SCORE: 53/RANK: 155

DINING & SHOPPING	AREA	U.S. AVG	ENTERTAINMENT	AREA	U.S. AVG	OUTDOOR ACTIVITIES	AREA	U.S. AVG
Restaurant rating	1	1	Professional sports rating	4	4	Golf-course rating	4	4
No. outlet malls	1	2	College sports rating	4	4	Ski-area rating	2	4
No. Starbucks	2	11	Zoo/aquarium rating	1	3	National Park rating	1	3
No. warehouse clubs	1	4	Amusement park rating	1	3	Sq. miles inland water	10.0	4.0
			Botanical garden/arboretum rating	3	3	Miles of coastline	0.0	11.4

ARTS & CULTURE SCORE: 21/RANK: 261

MEDIA & LIBRARIES	AREA	U.S. AVG	PERFORMING ARTS	AREA	U.S. AVG	MUSEUMS	AREA	U.S. AVG
Arts radio rating	1	3	Classical music rating	2	4	Overall museum rating	7	6
No. public libraries	18	28	Ballet/dance rating	1	3	Art museum rating	5	5
Library volumes per capita	3.6	2.8	Professional theater rating	1	3	Science museum rating	4	4
			University arts programs rating	2	5	Children's museum rating	1	3

Asheville, NC

Score: 90.4   **Rank:** 8

Profile: Small city
Location: Far western North Carolina, 30 miles southeast of Tennessee border, near Great Smoky Mountains National Park
Elevation: 2,207 feet
Time zone: Eastern Standard Time

PRO	CON
Attractive setting	Home prices
Attractive downtown	Air service
Nearby mountains	Winter cold

Asheville lies at the foot of the Great Smoky Mountains, the highest portion of the Appalachian Range. In some ways the town is an eastern equivalent of the many mountain resort towns that dot the American West. Originally settled in the 1850s as a health resort, Asheville has an interesting history—in the late 1800s and especially the 1920s, the area was a popular retreat for wealthy vacationers, including eight presidents and many well-known industrialists. Today the area has an active economy and serves as a getaway from summer heat in the nearby lowlands. The moderately attractive downtown offers a mix of modern and Art Deco buildings and an assortment of trendy restaurants and live-entertainment venues. To the north and west are nice, but not exceptionally attractive, residential sections. The city has controlled urban sprawl better than many of its type. At most times of the year, except winter, tourists can make the area feel crowded. Because of its inland location and higher elevation, the area sees considerably more below-freezing weather than nearby regions.

The city of Asheville sprawls along both banks of the French Broad River, near the center of the French Broad Basin. Mountain ridges to the east and west flank the entire valley with peaks from 2,000 feet to 4,400 feet above the valley floor. At the Carolina-Tennessee border, 25 miles northwest, the relatively high Appalachian/Great Smoky Mountain ridge blocks the northern end of the valley. The Blue Ridge rises about 30 miles south. Mixed vegetation grows in the valley, with densely wooded foothills and mountains surrounding the city, particularly to the north and west. The invigorating climate offers considerable temperature variation from day to day in all seasons. Summers are warm and humid, but the elevation and nearby mountains cause some cooling, particularly in the evenings. The high mountains to the northwest block precipitation and cold fronts in the winter. Precipitation in Asheville, particularly northwest of the immediate city, is the lowest in North Carolina. Significant snowfall is uncommon. Heavy Gulf rains can cause flooding in the river valley. First freeze is late October, last is mid-April.

POPULATION

DEMOGRAPHICS	AREA	U.S. AVG	ETHNIC COMPOSITION	AREA	U.S. AVG	RESIDENT PROFILE	AREA	U.S. AVG
Population	231,205		White	92.6%	75.1%	Single	42.4%	43.6%
Population density per sq. mile	209.1	447.3	Black	6.4%	12.3%	Married	57.6%	56.4%
Population growth	20.6%	16.1%	Asian	.5%	3.6%	Divorced	8.2%	8.4%
Median age	39.4	35.5	American Indian	.3%	.9%	Separated	4.0%	3.0%
Average family size	2.4	2.7	Hispanic	1.2%	12.5%	Married with children	25.0%	28.7%
			Diversity measure	20.9%	35.2%	Single with children	9.1%	10.1%

ECONOMY & JOBS   SCORE: 30/RANK: 230

INCOME	AREA	U.S. AVG	EMPLOYMENT	AREA	U.S. AVG	LARGEST EMPLOYING INDUSTRY
Per capita income	$23,206	$23,420	Unemployment rate	3.6%	6.1%	Textile Mills
Household income	$40,773	$46,060	Recent job growth	1.0%	.9%	
Household income < $25K	29.1%	26.4%	Projected future job growth	16.6%	15.1%	
Household income > $75K	19.0%	24.5%	White collar	51.5%	54.5%	
Household income growth	60.9%	57.3%	Blue collar	48.5%	45.5%	

COST OF LIVING   SCORE: 29/RANK: 235

INDEXES & TAXES	AREA	U.S. AVG	HOUSING	AREA	U.S. AVG	NECESSITIES	AREA	U.S. AVG
Cost of Living Index	94.8	100.0	Median home price	$144,700	$160,100	Food Index	99.2	100.0
Financial Progress Index	91.7	100.0	Home price appreciation	7.1%	7.1%	Housing Index	89.9	100.0
Income tax rate	7.000%	4.625%	Median rent	$582	$670	Utilities Index	89.9	100.0
Sales tax rate	7.000%	6.474%	Homes owned	67.9%	63.9%	Transportation Index	95.3	100.0
Property tax rate	$15.0	$15.6	Homes rented	21.6%	25.3%	Healthcare Index	89.8	100.0
			Housing affordability	57.0%	54.5%	Miscellaneous Cost Index	102.3	100.0

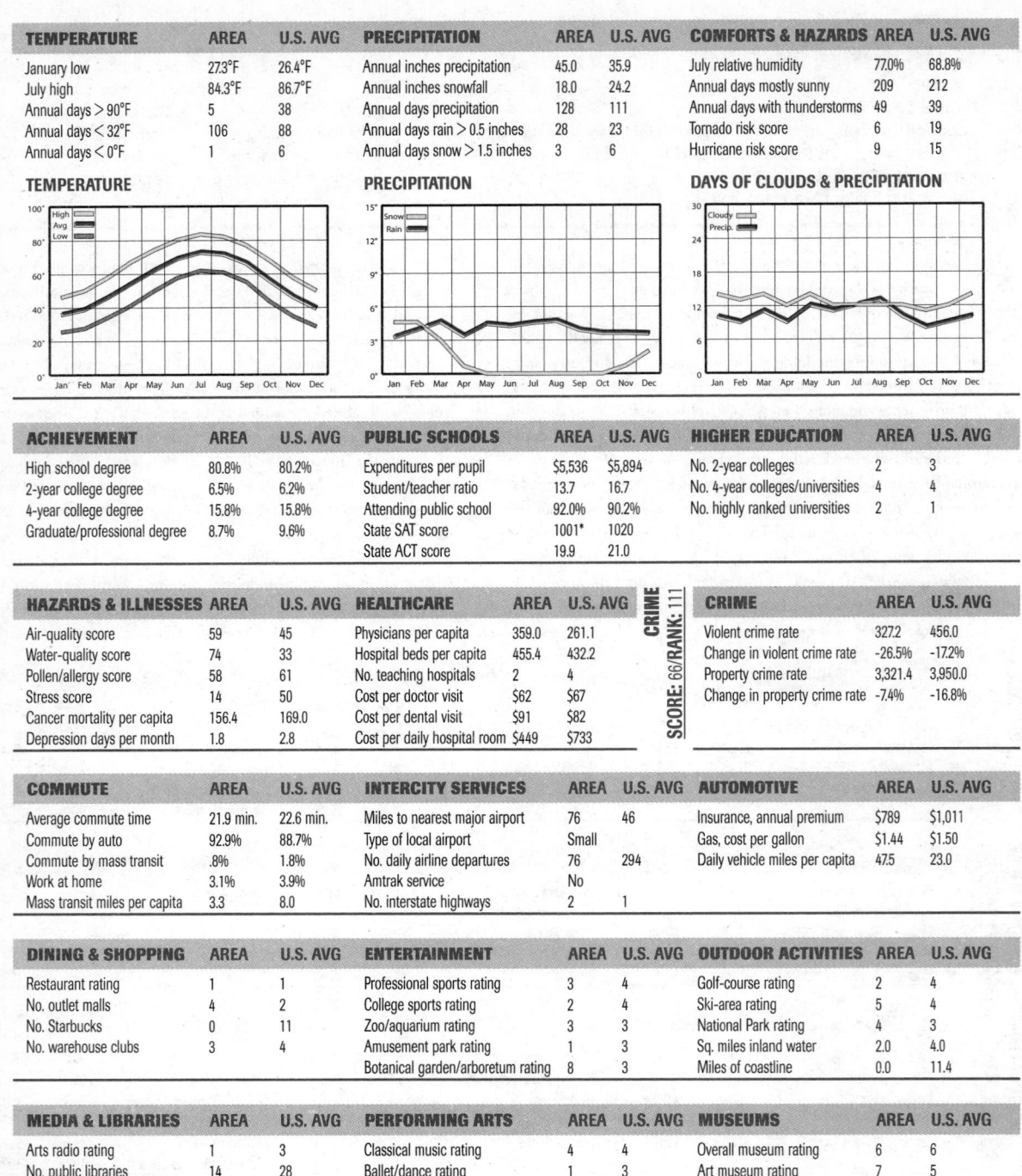

CLIMATE — SCORE: 65/RANK: 114

TEMPERATURE	AREA	U.S. AVG	PRECIPITATION	AREA	U.S. AVG	COMFORTS & HAZARDS	AREA	U.S. AVG
January low	27.3°F	26.4°F	Annual inches precipitation	45.0	35.9	July relative humidity	77.0%	68.8%
July high	84.3°F	86.7°F	Annual inches snowfall	18.0	24.2	Annual days mostly sunny	209	212
Annual days > 90°F	5	38	Annual days precipitation	128	111	Annual days with thunderstorms	49	39
Annual days < 32°F	106	88	Annual days rain > 0.5 inches	28	23	Tornado risk score	6	19
Annual days < 0°F	1	6	Annual days snow > 1.5 inches	3	6	Hurricane risk score	9	15

TEMPERATURE

PRECIPITATION

DAYS OF CLOUDS & PRECIPITATION

EDUCATION — SCORE: 73/RANK: 88

ACHIEVEMENT	AREA	U.S. AVG	PUBLIC SCHOOLS	AREA	U.S. AVG	HIGHER EDUCATION	AREA	U.S. AVG
High school degree	80.8%	80.2%	Expenditures per pupil	$5,536	$5,894	No. 2-year colleges	2	3
2-year college degree	6.5%	6.2%	Student/teacher ratio	13.7	16.7	No. 4-year colleges/universities	4	4
4-year college degree	15.8%	15.8%	Attending public school	92.0%	90.2%	No. highly ranked universities	2	1
Graduate/professional degree	8.7%	9.6%	State SAT score	1001*	1020			
			State ACT score	19.9	21.0			

HEALTH & HEALTHCARE — SCORE: 94/RANK: 19

CRIME — SCORE: 66/RANK: 111

HAZARDS & ILLNESSES	AREA	U.S. AVG	HEALTHCARE	AREA	U.S. AVG	CRIME	AREA	U.S. AVG
Air-quality score	59	45	Physicians per capita	359.0	261.1	Violent crime rate	327.2	456.0
Water-quality score	74	33	Hospital beds per capita	455.4	432.2	Change in violent crime rate	-26.5%	-17.2%
Pollen/allergy score	58	61	No. teaching hospitals	2	4	Property crime rate	3,321.4	3,950.0
Stress score	14	50	Cost per doctor visit	$62	$67	Change in property crime rate	-7.4%	-16.8%
Cancer mortality per capita	156.4	169.0	Cost per dental visit	$91	$82			
Depression days per month	1.8	2.8	Cost per daily hospital room	$449	$733			

TRANSPORTATION — SCORE: 29/RANK: 235

COMMUTE	AREA	U.S. AVG	INTERCITY SERVICES	AREA	U.S. AVG	AUTOMOTIVE	AREA	U.S. AVG
Average commute time	21.9 min.	22.6 min.	Miles to nearest major airport	76	46	Insurance, annual premium	$789	$1,011
Commute by auto	92.9%	88.7%	Type of local airport	Small		Gas, cost per gallon	$1.44	$1.50
Commute by mass transit	.8%	1.8%	No. daily airline departures	76	294	Daily vehicle miles per capita	47.5	23.0
Work at home	3.1%	3.9%	Amtrak service	No				
Mass transit miles per capita	3.3	8.0	No. interstate highways	2	1			

LEISURE — SCORE: 28/RANK: 236

DINING & SHOPPING	AREA	U.S. AVG	ENTERTAINMENT	AREA	U.S. AVG	OUTDOOR ACTIVITIES	AREA	U.S. AVG
Restaurant rating	1	1	Professional sports rating	3	4	Golf-course rating	2	4
No. outlet malls	4	2	College sports rating	2	4	Ski-area rating	5	4
No. Starbucks	0	11	Zoo/aquarium rating	3	3	National Park rating	4	3
No. warehouse clubs	3	4	Amusement park rating	1	3	Sq. miles inland water	2.0	4.0
			Botanical garden/arboretum rating	8	3	Miles of coastline	0.0	11.4

ARTS & CULTURE — SCORE: 51/RANK: 162

MEDIA & LIBRARIES	AREA	U.S. AVG	PERFORMING ARTS	AREA	U.S. AVG	MUSEUMS	AREA	U.S. AVG
Arts radio rating	1	3	Classical music rating	4	4	Overall museum rating	6	6
No. public libraries	14	28	Ballet/dance rating	1	3	Art museum rating	7	5
Library volumes per capita	2.4	2.8	Professional theater rating	1	3	Science museum rating	5	4
			University arts programs rating	5	5	Children's museum rating	5	3

Athens, GA

Score: 80.7   Rank: 34

Profile: College town
Location: Northeast Georgia, about 70 miles east of Atlanta
Elevation: 802 feet
Time zone: Eastern Standard Time

PRO	CON
College-town amenities	Home prices
Nightlife	Property crime
Educated population	Air service

Athens is a clean, attractive town with a distinct Southern flair. The local University of Georgia is the centerpiece of the area's economy. Athens is noted as a center for pop music—REM and the B-52's are from here—and the entertainment scene includes plenty of live music. Other arts and cultural amenities emanate from the university. Home prices are high for a small Georgia town, and air service requires a trip to Atlanta. While not excelling in any category, Athens is consistently good across the board, and an attractive place to live overall.

Athens is located on the Piedmont Plateau. Terrain is rolling to hilly with elevations ranging from 600 feet to 850 feet. The rich red soil is covered with grasses and southern pine forests. The Atlantic, Gulf of Mexico, and southern Appalachians to the north moderate the area's weather. Summers are warm and somewhat humid, but not as hot as other areas in the state. Highs reach 90°F only 19 days a year on average compared to a state average of 60 days. Winters are not severe but have short cold spells. Thunderstorms occur year-round, and spring storms may be severe. Snowfall is infrequent but freezing rain and ice storms occur.

POPULATION

DEMOGRAPHICS	AREA	U.S. AVG	ETHNIC COMPOSITION	AREA	U.S. AVG	RESIDENT PROFILE	AREA	U.S. AVG
Population	157,862		White	77.6%	75.1%	Single	52.8%	43.6%
Population density per sq. mile	267.1	447.3	Black	20.3%	12.3%	Married	47.2%	56.4%
Population growth	25.0%	16.1%	Asian	1.5%	3.6%	Divorced	7.4%	8.4%
Median age	28.2	35.5	American Indian	.2%	.9%	Separated	2.7%	3.0%
Average family size	2.7	2.7	Hispanic	2.1%	12.5%	Married with children	24.5%	28.7%
			Diversity measure	44.2%	35.2%	Single with children	10.7%	10.1%

ECONOMY & JOBS   SCORE: 38/RANK: 205

INCOME	AREA	U.S. AVG	EMPLOYMENT	AREA	U.S. AVG	LARGEST EMPLOYING INDUSTRY
Per capita income	$21,709	$23,420	Unemployment rate	3.2%	6.1%	Fabricated Metal Product Manufacturing
Household income	$37,878	$46,060	Recent job growth	1.6%	.9%	
Household income < $25K	33.9%	26.4%	Projected future job growth	21.4%	15.1%	
Household income > $75K	21.0%	24.5%	White collar	56.0%	54.5%	
Household income growth	64.8%	57.3%	Blue collar	44.0%	45.5%	

COST OF LIVING   SCORE: 51/RANK: 161

INDEXES & TAXES	AREA	U.S. AVG	HOUSING	AREA	U.S. AVG	NECESSITIES	AREA	U.S. AVG
Cost of Living Index	95.4	100.0	Median home price	$141,170	$160,100	Food Index	99.7	100.0
Financial Progress Index	84.6	100.0	Home price appreciation	7.1%	7.1%	Housing Index	87.7	100.0
Income tax rate	6.000%	4.625%	Median rent	$560	$670	Utilities Index	93.8	100.0
Sales tax rate	7.000%	6.474%	Homes owned	60.4%	63.9%	Transportation Index	103.5	100.0
Property tax rate	$13.1	$15.6	Homes rented	32.5%	25.3%	Healthcare Index	106.1	100.0
			Housing affordability	50.0%	54.5%	Miscellaneous Cost Index	98.4	100.0

CLIMATE   SCORE: 53/RANK: 154

TEMPERATURE	AREA	U.S. AVG	PRECIPITATION	AREA	U.S. AVG	COMFORTS & HAZARDS	AREA	U.S. AVG
January low	33.4°F	26.4°F	Annual inches precipitation	50.6	35.9	July relative humidity	72.0%	68.8%
July high	89.5°F	86.7°F	Annual inches snowfall	1.7	24.2	Annual days mostly sunny	218	212
Annual days > 90°F	48	38	Annual days precipitation	112	111	Annual days with thunderstorms	52	39
Annual days < 32°F	54	88	Annual days rain > 0.5 inches	33	23	Tornado risk score	25	19
Annual days < 0°F	0	6	Annual days snow > 1.5 inches	2	6	Hurricane risk score	28	15

TEMPERATURE

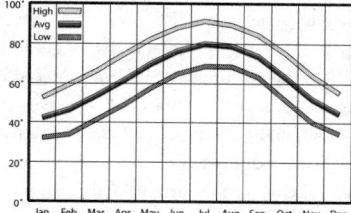

PRECIPITATION

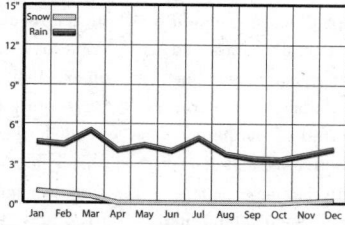

DAYS OF CLOUDS & PRECIPITATION

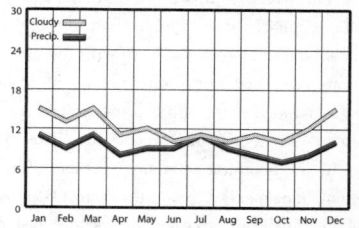

EDUCATION SCORE: 60/RANK: 130

ACHIEVEMENT	AREA	U.S. AVG	PUBLIC SCHOOLS	AREA	U.S. AVG	HIGHER EDUCATION	AREA	U.S. AVG
High school degree	81.0%	80.2%	Expenditures per pupil	$5,788	$5,894	No. 2-year colleges	1	3
2-year college degree	3.8%	6.2%	Student/teacher ratio	16.8	16.7	No. 4-year colleges/universities	1	4
4-year college degree	18.5%	15.8%	Attending public school	91.9%	90.2%	No. highly ranked universities	0	1
Graduate/professional degree	15.6%	9.6%	State SAT score	984*	1020			
			State ACT score	19.8	21.0			

HEALTH & HEALTHCARE SCORE: 78/RANK: 72   **CRIME** SCORE: 33/RANK: 220

HAZARDS & ILLNESSES	AREA	U.S. AVG	HEALTHCARE	AREA	U.S. AVG	CRIME	AREA	U.S. AVG
Air-quality score	24	45	Physicians per capita	224.9	261.1	Violent crime rate	351.9	456.0
Water-quality score	13	33	Hospital beds per capita	469.2	432.2	Change in violent crime rate	-48.4%	-17.2%
Pollen/allergy score	62	61	No. teaching hospitals	0	4	Property crime rate	5,241.6	3,950.0
Stress score	19	50	Cost per doctor visit	$65	$67	Change in property crime rate	-13.5%	-16.8%
Cancer mortality per capita	151.1	169.0	Cost per dental visit	$81	$82			
Depression days per month	3.3	2.8	Cost per daily hospital room	$485	$733			

TRANSPORTATION SCORE: 37/RANK: 207

COMMUTE	AREA	U.S. AVG	INTERCITY SERVICES	AREA	U.S. AVG	AUTOMOTIVE	AREA	U.S. AVG
Average commute time	21.1 min.	22.6 min.	Miles to nearest major airport	62	46	Insurance, annual premium	$927	$1,011
Commute by auto	92.6%	88.7%	Type of local airport	Large		Gas, cost per gallon	$1.36	$1.50
Commute by mass transit	1.0%	1.8%	No. daily airline departures	1,423	294	Daily vehicle miles per capita	27.9	23.0
Work at home	2.6%	3.9%	Amtrak service	No				
Mass transit miles per capita	5.2	8.0	No. interstate highways	0	1			

LEISURE SCORE: 60/RANK: 131

DINING & SHOPPING	AREA	U.S. AVG	ENTERTAINMENT	AREA	U.S. AVG	OUTDOOR ACTIVITIES	AREA	U.S. AVG
Restaurant rating	1	1	Professional sports rating	2	4	Golf-course rating	1	4
No. outlet malls	6	2	College sports rating	8	4	Ski-area rating	1	4
No. Starbucks	1	11	Zoo/aquarium rating	1	3	National Park rating	2	3
No. warehouse clubs	3	4	Amusement park rating	1	3	Sq. miles inland water	1.0	4.0
			Botanical garden/arboretum rating	5	3	Miles of coastline	0.0	11.4

ARTS & CULTURE SCORE: 61/RANK: 129

MEDIA & LIBRARIES	AREA	U.S. AVG	PERFORMING ARTS	AREA	U.S. AVG	MUSEUMS	AREA	U.S. AVG
Arts radio rating	1	3	Classical music rating	6	4	Overall museum rating	6	6
No. public libraries	8	28	Ballet/dance rating	5	3	Art museum rating	5	5
Library volumes per capita	2.0	2.8	Professional theater rating	1	3	Science museum rating	4	4
			University arts programs rating	5	5	Children's museum rating	1	3

Atlanta, GA

Score: 91.1 Rank: 7

Profile: Regional center
Location: North-central Georgia at the southern tip of the Appalachian Mountains
Elevation: 1,034 feet
Time zone: Eastern Standard Time

PRO
Excellent housing
Entertainment
Education

CON
Urban sprawl
Commute time
Summer heat

Cosmopolitan Atlanta, a regional center for the American South, has always been a crossroads. Railroads met here because of the end-of-mountains location, then highways and air traffic. Today, Atlanta originates more flights than any city except Chicago. The old and new South also crossed here with the meeting of agrarian ways and corporate America. The professional middle class and companies like Coca-Cola and Delta Airlines prospered as a result. Today it serves as a crossroads between North and South. The city is full of northerners drawn by the booming economy, pleasant climate, activities, and diversity. Some locals call it the northernmost Southern city, but make no mistake—despite the corporate towers and fast pace, Atlanta retains its Southern roots, which become more apparent the farther you go outside the I-285 beltway.

Atlanta's economy continues to grow as more businesses expand operations in the area and more people move here for employment. The future employment picture looks healthy. For those seeking economic prosperity and a nice home against a lively backdrop, and who can tolerate some summer heat and the side effects of rapid growth, Atlanta is an excellent place. It is the no. 1 *big* city in *Cities Ranked & Rated*.

The city has spread primarily to the north and northeast into the wooded areas of Dekalb and Cherokee counties, where the most desirable residential neighborhoods exist. Most new commercial development is north along I-285. The regions to the east and south are more industrial, while the west is a mix. Some of the more attractive residential areas are inside the beltway around Buckhead, where a satellite city with skyscrapers has emerged adjacent to an area of beautiful historic homes. Outside the beltway are mixed residential and commercial suburbs like Chamblee, Dunwoody, Roswell, and Marietta. Most people commute to somewhere along the beltway, not downtown. The commercial downtown is modern, but not as impressive as Chicago, Seattle, or New York. Some sprawling development has carried development far into Cherokee County, and many commute from there *to* the beltway. Traffic *to and from* the beltway and *on* the beltway has become a major problem. Commuter rail transit has come on line with an airport linkage, but the multidirectional nature of traffic flows is hard to conquer.

Despite traffic, the city is planned with a certain element of common sense. Main arteries such as Peachtree Street, for example, have collector and access roads that aid the flow of traffic. (When Atlantans can't decide on a name for a street or building, they call it "Peachtree.") Homes and new developments are designed to blend with the environment. In fact, housing is one of Atlanta's most attractive features. The city has some of the highest quality residential properties anywhere per dollar spent, particularly for a city of this size. Nice homes are affordable thanks to inexpensive labor, materials, and business costs. Generous, well-built houses on attractive wooded lots are the rule, not the exception. While sprawl is an issue, and excessive strip-mall development has started to creep into some areas, building patterns avoid cookie-cutter development. The area looks nice.

Atlanta is filled with things to do. The "Underground" historic district is the headline nightlife spot and tourist attraction, and the Coca-Cola museum is one of its highlights. But nightlife has also spread into the northern suburbs in Midtown and some ethnic neighborhoods surrounding the city. Atlanta has some of the country's best restaurants, and eateries in general are plentiful and reasonably priced.

Physically, Atlanta is located in a transition zone between forested hills to the north and more level agricultural areas to the south. Nearby mountains and distant water moderate the climate somewhat, resulting in a mix of subtropical and continental types. Summer temperatures are warm but moderated by elevation. There may be prolonged periods of late summer heat. Winters are mild with short cold spells. Active precipitation occurs during spring with thunderstorms, some severe, lasting into July, with frequent dry periods into late summer and fall. Most winter precipitation is rain with occasional snowfall. Ice storms and freezing rain with newsworthy damage and travel disruption occur 2 out of every 3 years. First freeze is mid-November, last is late March.

POPULATION

DEMOGRAPHICS	AREA	U.S. AVG	ETHNIC COMPOSITION	AREA	U.S. AVG	RESIDENT PROFILE	AREA	U.S. AVG
Population	4,386,330		White	72.0%	75.1%	Single	47.2%	43.6%
Population density per sq. mile	716.0	447.3	Black	24.7%	12.3%	Married	52.8%	56.4%
Population growth	48.2%	16.1%	Asian	2.3%	3.6%	Divorced	9.8%	8.4%
Median age	33.1	35.5	American Indian	.2%	.9%	Separated	3.6%	3.0%
Average family size	2.7	2.7	Hispanic	2.9%	12.5%	Married with children	28.5%	28.7%
			Diversity measure	54.1%	35.2%	Single with children	12.1%	10.1%

ECONOMY & JOBS SCORE: 60/RANK: 130

INCOME	AREA	U.S. AVG	EMPLOYMENT	AREA	U.S. AVG	LARGEST EMPLOYING INDUSTRY
Per capita income	$29,037	$23,420	Unemployment rate	4.8%	6.1%	Food Manufacturing
Household income	$59,423	$46,060	Recent job growth	2.4%	.9%	
Household income < $25K	16.9%	26.4%	Projected future job growth	23.2%	15.1%	
Household income > $75K	36.9%	24.5%	White collar	62.1%	54.5%	
Household income growth	66.8%	57.3%	Blue collar	37.9%	45.5%	

COST OF LIVING SCORE: 23/RANK: 252

INDEXES & TAXES	AREA	U.S. AVG	HOUSING	AREA	U.S. AVG	NECESSITIES	AREA	U.S. AVG
Cost of Living Index	96.6	100.0	Median home price	$148,900	$160,100	Food Index	99.5	100.0
Financial Progress Index	131.1	100.0	Home price appreciation	7.5%	7.1%	Housing Index	92.5	100.0
Income tax rate	6.000%	4.625%	Median rent	$944	$670	Utilities Index	91.0	100.0
Sales tax rate	7.000%	6.474%	Homes owned	62.3%	63.9%	Transportation Index	104.8	100.0
Property tax rate	$16.1	$15.6	Homes rented	29.4%	25.3%	Healthcare Index	104.9	100.0
			Housing affordability	52.0%	54.5%	Miscellaneous Cost Index	96.8	100.0

CLIMATE SCORE: 72/RANK: 91

TEMPERATURE	AREA	U.S. AVG	PRECIPITATION	AREA	U.S. AVG	COMFORTS & HAZARDS	AREA	U.S. AVG
January low	33.4°F	26.4°F	Annual inches precipitation	48.0	35.9	July relative humidity	70.0%	68.8%
July high	86.5°F	86.7°F	Annual inches snowfall	2.0	24.2	Annual days mostly sunny	219	212
Annual days > 90°F	19	38	Annual days precipitation	116	111	Annual days with thunderstorms	50	39
Annual days < 32°F	59	88	Annual days rain > 0.5 inches	33	23	Tornado risk score	26	19
Annual days < 0°F	0	6	Annual days snow > 1.5 inches	1	6	Hurricane risk score	19	15

TEMPERATURE
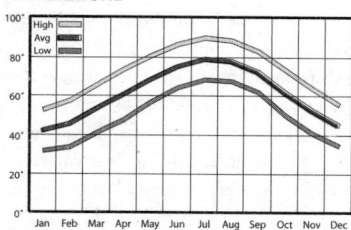

PRECIPITATION
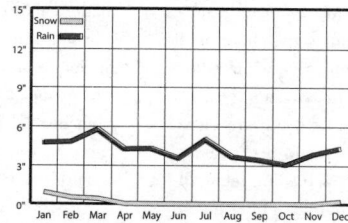

DAYS OF CLOUDS & PRECIPITATION
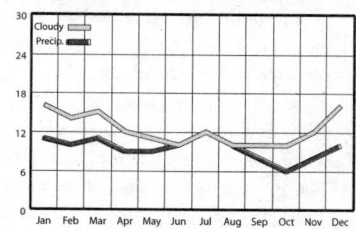

EDUCATION — SCORE: 96/RANK: 11

ACHIEVEMENT	AREA	U.S. AVG	PUBLIC SCHOOLS	AREA	U.S. AVG	HIGHER EDUCATION	AREA	U.S. AVG
High school degree	84.0%	80.2%	Expenditures per pupil	$5,795	$5,894	No. 2-year colleges	9	3
2-year college degree	5.7%	6.2%	Student/teacher ratio	16.2	16.7	No. 4-year colleges/universities	20	4
4-year college degree	21.6%	15.8%	Attending public school	92.4%	90.2%	No. highly ranked universities	4	1
Graduate/professional degree	10.4%	9.6%	State SAT score	984*	1020			
			State ACT score	19.8	21.0			

HEALTH & HEALTHCARE — SCORE: 26/RANK: 244

CRIME — SCORE: 46/RANK: 176

HAZARDS & ILLNESSES	AREA	U.S. AVG	HEALTHCARE	AREA	U.S. AVG	CRIME	AREA	U.S. AVG
Air-quality score	6	45	Physicians per capita	223.8	261.1	Violent crime rate	570.1	456.0
Water-quality score	25	33	Hospital beds per capita	230.4	432.2	Change in violent crime rate	-29.4%	-17.2%
Pollen/allergy score	63	61	No. teaching hospitals	9	4	Property crime rate	4,255.6	3,950.0
Stress score	82	50	Cost per doctor visit	$62	$67	Change in property crime rate	-33.7%	-16.8%
Cancer mortality per capita	166.2	169.0	Cost per dental visit	$81	$82			
Depression days per month	2.8	2.8	Cost per daily hospital room	$497	$733			

TRANSPORTATION — SCORE: 95/RANK: 16

COMMUTE	AREA	U.S. AVG	INTERCITY SERVICES	AREA	U.S. AVG	AUTOMOTIVE	AREA	U.S. AVG
Average commute time	31.2 min.	22.6 min.	Miles to nearest major airport	8	46	Insurance, annual premium	$1,154	$1,011
Commute by auto	90.7%	88.7%	Type of local airport	Large		Gas, cost per gallon	$1.36	$1.50
Commute by mass transit	4.0%	1.8%	No. daily airline departures	1,423	294	Daily vehicle miles per capita	35.6	23.0
Work at home	2.2%	3.9%	Amtrak service	Yes				
Mass transit miles per capita	16.7	8.0	No. interstate highways	3	1			

LEISURE — SCORE: 91/RANK: 28

DINING & SHOPPING	AREA	U.S. AVG	ENTERTAINMENT	AREA	U.S. AVG	OUTDOOR ACTIVITIES	AREA	U.S. AVG
Restaurant rating	8	1	Professional sports rating	7	4	Golf-course rating	9	4
No. outlet malls	5	2	College sports rating	6	4	Ski-area rating	1	4
No. Starbucks	80	11	Zoo/aquarium rating	9	3	National Park rating	2	3
No. warehouse clubs	10	4	Amusement park rating	10	3	Sq. miles inland water	4.0	4.0
			Botanical garden/arboretum rating	9	3	Miles of coastline	0.0	11.4

ARTS & CULTURE — SCORE: 91/RANK: 28

MEDIA & LIBRARIES	AREA	U.S. AVG	PERFORMING ARTS	AREA	U.S. AVG	MUSEUMS	AREA	U.S. AVG
Arts radio rating	9	3	Classical music rating	7	4	Overall museum rating	10	6
No. public libraries	134	28	Ballet/dance rating	9	3	Art museum rating	9	5
Library volumes per capita	1.8	2.8	Professional theater rating	10	3	Science museum rating	8	4
			University arts programs rating	10	5	Children's museum rating	9	3

Atlantic City–Cape May, NJ

Score: 63.0   Rank: 123

Profile: Beach resort–city complex
Location: Southern New Jersey shore
Elevation: 10 feet
Time zone: Eastern Standard Time

PRO	CON
Nearby beaches	Urban decay
Entertainment	Tourist economy
Favorable climate	Arts and culture

Atlantic City lies on a barrier island on the south coast of New Jersey. Once a popular resort area for residents of New York and Philadelphia (the street names in the board game "Monopoly" are from here), the city went into decline after World War II as better travel and transportation services made other destinations accessible. The return to legalized gambling in the late 1970s was a partially successful attempt to revive the earlier prominence. Today the shore area thrives with its renowned Boardwalk and casino properties, while other parts of the city remain run-down. Cost of living and housing are the second lowest in New Jersey. Areas along the coast to the south are more attractive and livable. Beach towns like Ocean City and areas south toward Cape May are more prosperous and retain their historic feel. All of these towns are reasonably priced for the region, but don't offer much beyond beach activities.

Surrounding terrain is mainly flat and composed of tidal marshes and beach sand. Vegetation consists of scrub pine and low underbrush. The climate is principally continental in character. However, the moderating influence of the Atlantic Ocean is apparent throughout the year. As a result, summers are relatively cooler and winters milder than elsewhere at the same latitude. During the warm season, sea breezes in the late morning and afternoon keep temperatures in the 80s. Precipitation is moderate and well distributed through the year. Tropical storms or hurricanes occasionally bring heavy rain. Most winter precipitation comes from coastal storms ("noreasters") and create a rain/snow mix. Large snow accumulations and ice storms are far less common than nearby inland locations. First freeze is late October, last is mid-April.

POPULATION

DEMOGRAPHICS	AREA	U.S. AVG	ETHNIC COMPOSITION	AREA	U.S. AVG	RESIDENT PROFILE	AREA	U.S. AVG
Population	361,436		White	83.8%	75.1%	Single	48.2%	43.6%
Population density per sq. mile	442.7	447.3	Black	11.3%	12.3%	Married	51.8%	56.4%
Population growth	13.2%	16.1%	Asian	1.8%	3.6%	Divorced	8.2%	8.4%
Median age	38.9	35.5	American Indian	.3%	.9%	Separated	4.1%	3.0%
Average family size	2.5	2.7	Hispanic	7.4%	12.5%	Married with children	22.1%	28.7%
			Diversity measure	45.5%	35.2%	Single with children	9.6%	10.1%

ECONOMY & JOBS SCORE: 59/RANK: 136

INCOME	AREA	U.S. AVG	EMPLOYMENT	AREA	U.S. AVG	LARGEST EMPLOYING INDUSTRY		
Per capita income	$23,118	$23,420	Unemployment rate	6.2%	6.1%	Accommodations and Food Services		
Household income	$45,694	$46,060	Recent job growth	2.8%	.9%			
Household income < $25K	24.9%	26.4%	Projected future job growth	13.1%	15.1%			
Household income > $75K	23.9%	24.5%	White collar	50.9%	54.5%			
Household income growth	40.8%	57.3%	Blue collar	49.1%	45.5%			

COST OF LIVING SCORE: 23/RANK: 253

INDEXES & TAXES	AREA	U.S. AVG	HOUSING	AREA	U.S. AVG	NECESSITIES	AREA	U.S. AVG
Cost of Living Index	103.1	100.0	Median home price	$150,800	$160,100	Food Index	106.0	100.0
Financial Progress Index	94.5	100.0	Home price appreciation	12.1%	7.1%	Housing Index	93.7	100.0
Income tax rate	2.450%	4.625%	Median rent	$850	$670	Utilities Index	125.4	100.0
Sales tax rate	6.000%	6.474%	Homes owned	54.6%	63.9%	Transportation Index	106.6	100.0
Property tax rate	$20.2	$15.6	Homes rented	16.3%	25.3%	Healthcare Index	97.9	100.0
			Housing affordability	46.0%	54.5%	Miscellaneous Cost Index	107.6	100.0

CLIMATE SCORE: 84/RANK: 52

TEMPERATURE	AREA	U.S. AVG	PRECIPITATION	AREA	U.S. AVG	COMFORTS & HAZARDS	AREA	U.S. AVG
January low	24.0°F	26.4°F	Annual inches precipitation	46.0	35.9	July relative humidity	73.0%	68.8%
July high	84.7°F	86.7°F	Annual inches snowfall	16.0	24.2	Annual days mostly sunny	204	212
Annual days > 90°F	16	38	Annual days precipitation	112	111	Annual days with thunderstorms	25	39
Annual days < 32°F	15	88	Annual days rain > 0.5 inches	26	23	Tornado risk score	5	19
Annual days < 0°F	1	6	Annual days snow > 1.5 inches	4	6	Hurricane risk score	25	15

TEMPERATURE

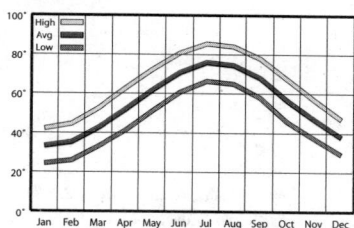

PRECIPITATION

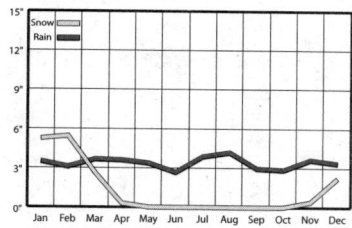

DAYS OF CLOUDS & PRECIPITATION

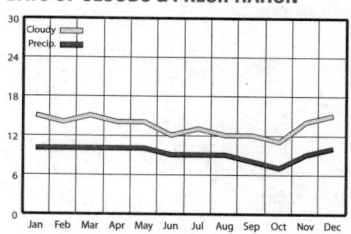

EDUCATION SCORE: 39/RANK: 201

ACHIEVEMENT	AREA	U.S. AVG	PUBLIC SCHOOLS	AREA	U.S. AVG	HIGHER EDUCATION	AREA	U.S. AVG
High school degree	79.3%	80.2%	Expenditures per pupil	$8,916	$5,894	No. 2-year colleges	1	3
2-year college degree	5.4%	6.2%	Student/teacher ratio	12.8	16.7	No. 4-year colleges/universities	1	4
4-year college degree	13.6%	15.8%	Attending public school	89.2%	90.2%	No. highly ranked universities	1	1
Graduate/professional degree	6.0%	9.6%	State SAT score	1016*	1020			
			State ACT score	21.2	21.0			

HEALTH & HEALTHCARE SCORE: 19/RANK: 268

CRIME SCORE: 44/RANK: 183

HAZARDS & ILLNESSES	AREA	U.S. AVG	HEALTHCARE	AREA	U.S. AVG	CRIME	AREA	U.S. AVG
Air-quality score	49	45	Physicians per capita	205.6	261.1	Violent crime rate	481.0	456.0
Water-quality score	2	33	Hospital beds per capita	543.0	432.2	Change in violent crime rate	-30.1%	-17.2%
Pollen/allergy score	60	61	No. teaching hospitals	2	4	Property crime rate	4,764.2	3,950.0
Stress score	55	50	Cost per doctor visit	$75	$67	Change in property crime rate	-35.2%	-16.8%
Cancer mortality per capita	189.7	169.0	Cost per dental visit	$97	$82			
Depression days per month	2.8	2.8	Cost per daily hospital room	$2,184	$733			

TRANSPORTATION SCORE: 71/RANK: 93

COMMUTE	AREA	U.S. AVG	INTERCITY SERVICES	AREA	U.S. AVG	AUTOMOTIVE	AREA	U.S. AVG
Average commute time	23.6 min.	22.6 min.	Miles to nearest major airport	55	46	Insurance, annual premium	$1,373	$1,011
Commute by auto	88.8%	88.7%	Type of local airport	Large		Gas, cost per gallon	$1.46	$1.50
Commute by mass transit	3.3%	1.8%	No. daily airline departures	669	294	Daily vehicle miles per capita	22.6	23.0
Work at home	2.4%	3.9%	Amtrak service	No				
Mass transit miles per capita	24.9	8.0	No. interstate highways	0	1			

DINING & SHOPPING	AREA	U.S. AVG	ENTERTAINMENT	AREA	U.S. AVG	OUTDOOR ACTIVITIES	AREA	U.S. AVG
Restaurant rating	1	1	Professional sports rating	8	4	Golf-course rating	6	4
No. outlet malls	5	2	College sports rating	3	4	Ski-area rating	3	4
No. Starbucks	1	11	Zoo/aquarium rating	8	3	National Park rating	3	3
No. warehouse clubs	4	4	Amusement park rating	6	3	Sq. miles inland water	6.0	4.0
			Botanical garden/arboretum rating	8	3	Miles of coastline	53.2	11.4

MEDIA & LIBRARIES	AREA	U.S. AVG	PERFORMING ARTS	AREA	U.S. AVG	MUSEUMS	AREA	U.S. AVG
Arts radio rating	8	3	Classical music rating	7	4	Overall museum rating	6	6
No. public libraries	24	28	Ballet/dance rating	5	3	Art museum rating	7	5
Library volumes per capita	3.8	2.8	Professional theater rating	5	3	Science museum rating	3	4
			University arts programs rating	3	5	Children's museum rating	2	3

Auburn-Opelika, AL

Score: 54.5 Rank: 192

Profile: College-town complex
Location: East-central Alabama near Georgia border
Elevation: 658 feet
Time zone: Central Standard Time

PRO	CON
College-town amenities	Crime rate
Historic interest	Home prices
Strong economy	Hot, humid summers

Auburn, home to Auburn University, the largest in Alabama, is a typical small college town with an inviting campus and historic buildings. While the Cost of Living Index is a modest 89.2, attractive for a college town, home prices are relatively high for the region. The area is a bit isolated; services and amenities in Atlanta are 110 miles away.

The town sits in an area of gently rolling, wooded hills and a level open plain. The climate is subtropical with warm, still, humid summers with most days in the 90s and frequent thunderstorms. Winters are mild and wet with a few cold periods caused by northerly air masses. First freeze is early November, last is late March.

DEMOGRAPHICS	AREA	U.S. AVG	ETHNIC COMPOSITION	AREA	U.S. AVG	RESIDENT PROFILE	AREA	U.S. AVG
Population	118,123		White	74.3%	75.1%	Single	55.1%	43.6%
Population density per sq. mile	194.0	447.3	Black	23.8%	12.3%	Married	44.9%	56.4%
Population growth	35.5%	16.1%	Asian	1.6%	3.6%	Divorced	7.2%	8.4%
Median age	27.7	35.5	American Indian	.2%	.9%	Separated	2.8%	3.0%
Average family size	2.6	2.7	Hispanic	.7%	12.5%	Married with children	23.3%	28.7%
			Diversity measure	40.9%	35.2%	Single with children	9.7%	10.1%

INCOME	AREA	U.S. AVG	EMPLOYMENT	AREA	U.S. AVG	LARGEST EMPLOYING INDUSTRY
Per capita income	$17,998	$23,420	Unemployment rate	4.3%	6.1%	Transportation Equipment Manufacturing
Household income	$30,615	$46,060	Recent job growth	-1.2%	.9%	
Household income < $25K	42.6%	26.4%	Projected future job growth	12.3%	15.1%	
Household income > $75K	15.1%	24.5%	White collar	54.7%	54.5%	
Household income growth	43.0%	57.3%	Blue collar	45.3%	45.5%	

INDEXES & TAXES	AREA	U.S. AVG	HOUSING	AREA	U.S. AVG	NECESSITIES	AREA	U.S. AVG
Cost of Living Index	89.2	100.0	Median home price	$117,830	$160,100	Food Index	98.8	100.0
Financial Progress Index	73.1	100.0	Home price appreciation	4.2%	7.1%	Housing Index	73.2	100.0
Income tax rate	5.000%	4.625%	Median rent	$499	$670	Utilities Index	98.5	100.0
Sales tax rate	8.500%	6.474%	Homes owned	57.7%	63.9%	Transportation Index	100.7	100.0
Property tax rate	$6.5	$15.6	Homes rented	25.2%	25.3%	Healthcare Index	96.0	100.0
			Housing affordability	36.0%	54.5%	Miscellaneous Cost Index	97.2	100.0

CLIMATE SCORE: 25/RANK: 247

TEMPERATURE	AREA	U.S. AVG	PRECIPITATION	AREA	U.S. AVG	COMFORTS & HAZARDS	AREA	U.S. AVG
January low	33.2°F	26.4°F	Annual inches precipitation	54.0	35.9	July relative humidity	70.0%	68.8%
July high	91.3°F	86.7°F	Annual inches snowfall	.5	24.2	Annual days mostly sunny	214	212
Annual days > 90°F	42	38	Annual days precipitation	117	111	Annual days with thunderstorms	65	39
Annual days < 32°F	65	88	Annual days rain > 0.5 inches	37	23	Tornado risk score	21	19
Annual days < 0°F	0	6	Annual days snow > 1.5 inches	1	6	Hurricane risk score	28	15

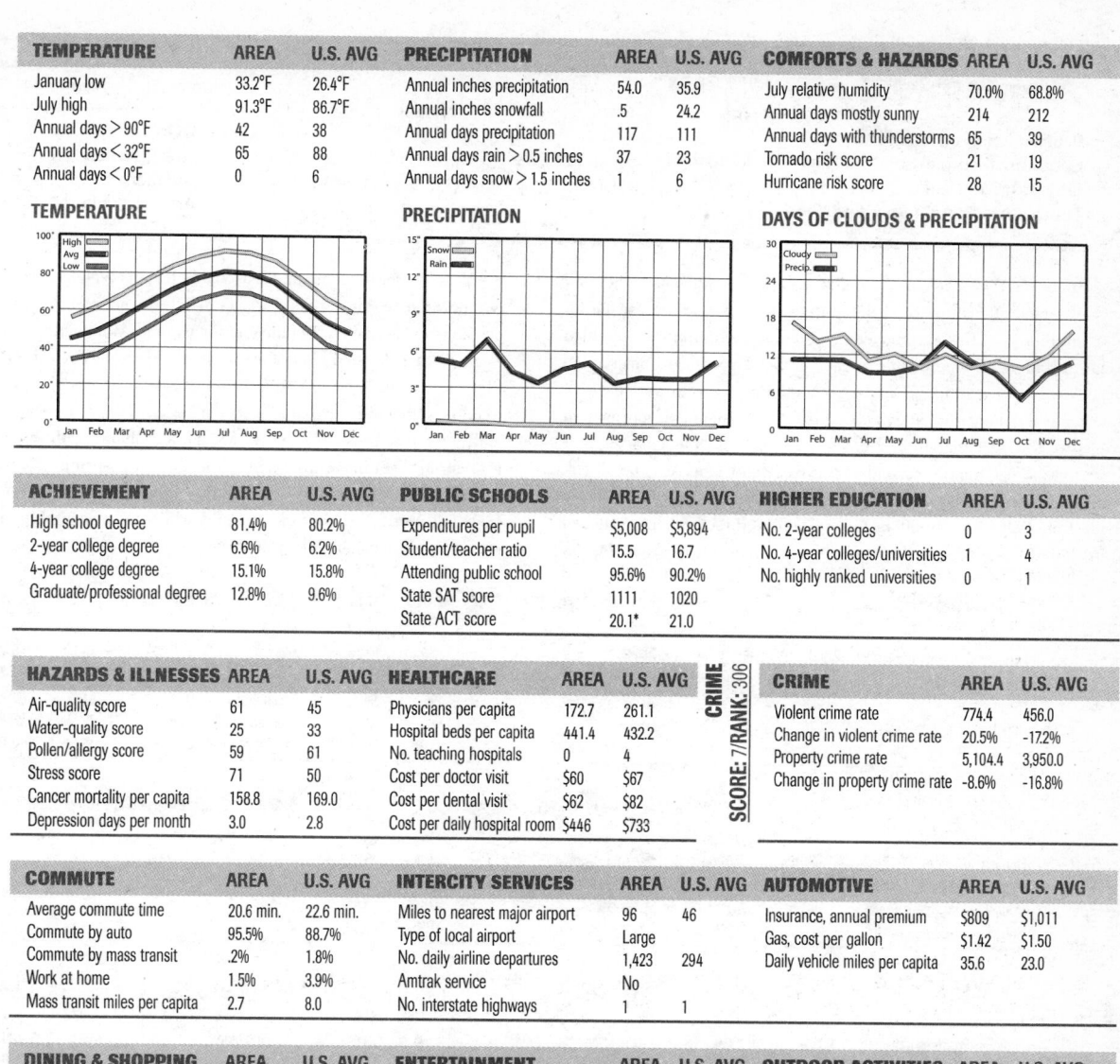

TEMPERATURE

PRECIPITATION

DAYS OF CLOUDS & PRECIPITATION

EDUCATION SCORE: 71/RANK: 97

ACHIEVEMENT	AREA	U.S. AVG	PUBLIC SCHOOLS	AREA	U.S. AVG	HIGHER EDUCATION	AREA	U.S. AVG
High school degree	81.4%	80.2%	Expenditures per pupil	$5,008	$5,894	No. 2-year colleges	0	3
2-year college degree	6.6%	6.2%	Student/teacher ratio	15.5	16.7	No. 4-year colleges/universities	1	4
4-year college degree	15.1%	15.8%	Attending public school	95.6%	90.2%	No. highly ranked universities	0	1
Graduate/professional degree	12.8%	9.6%	State SAT score	1111	1020			
			State ACT score	20.1*	21.0			

HEALTH & HEALTHCARE SCORE: 85/RANK: 47

HAZARDS & ILLNESSES	AREA	U.S. AVG	HEALTHCARE	AREA	U.S. AVG
Air-quality score	61	45	Physicians per capita	172.7	261.1
Water-quality score	25	33	Hospital beds per capita	441.4	432.2
Pollen/allergy score	59	61	No. teaching hospitals	0	4
Stress score	71	50	Cost per doctor visit	$60	$67
Cancer mortality per capita	158.8	169.0	Cost per dental visit	$62	$82
Depression days per month	3.0	2.8	Cost per daily hospital room	$446	$733

CRIME SCORE: 7/RANK: 306

CRIME	AREA	U.S. AVG
Violent crime rate	774.4	456.0
Change in violent crime rate	20.5%	-17.2%
Property crime rate	5,104.4	3,950.0
Change in property crime rate	-8.6%	-16.8%

TRANSPORTATION SCORE: 35/RANK: 213

COMMUTE	AREA	U.S. AVG	INTERCITY SERVICES	AREA	U.S. AVG	AUTOMOTIVE	AREA	U.S. AVG
Average commute time	20.6 min.	22.6 min.	Miles to nearest major airport	96	46	Insurance, annual premium	$809	$1,011
Commute by auto	95.5%	88.7%	Type of local airport	Large		Gas, cost per gallon	$1.42	$1.50
Commute by mass transit	.2%	1.8%	No. daily airline departures	1,423	294	Daily vehicle miles per capita	35.6	23.0
Work at home	1.5%	3.9%	Amtrak service	No				
Mass transit miles per capita	2.7	8.0	No. interstate highways	1	1			

LEISURE SCORE: 6/RANK: 310

DINING & SHOPPING	AREA	U.S. AVG	ENTERTAINMENT	AREA	U.S. AVG	OUTDOOR ACTIVITIES	AREA	U.S. AVG
Restaurant rating	1	1	Professional sports rating	2	4	Golf-course rating	3	4
No. outlet malls	0	2	College sports rating	6	4	Ski-area rating	1	4
No. Starbucks	0	11	Zoo/aquarium rating	1	3	National Park rating	4	3
No. warehouse clubs	1	4	Amusement park rating	1	3	Sq. miles inland water	4.0	4.0
			Botanical garden/arboretum rating	1	3	Miles of coastline	0.0	11.4

ARTS & CULTURE SCORE: 43/RANK: 183

MEDIA & LIBRARIES	AREA	U.S. AVG	PERFORMING ARTS	AREA	U.S. AVG	MUSEUMS	AREA	U.S. AVG
Arts radio rating	1	3	Classical music rating	3	4	Overall museum rating	1	6
No. public libraries	4	28	Ballet/dance rating	1	3	Art museum rating	1	5
Library volumes per capita	1.6	2.8	Professional theater rating	1	3	Science museum rating	2	4
			University arts programs rating	5	5	Children's museum rating	1	3

Augusta-Aiken, GA-SC

Score: 58.2   **Rank:** 164

Profile: Small-city complex
Location: Georgia–South Carolina border along the Savannah River
Elevation: 136 feet
Time zone: Eastern Standard Time

PRO	CON
Historic interest	Low incomes
Cost of living	Isolation
Low crime rate	Arts and culture

Those familiar with professional golf know Augusta. The city emerged after the turn of the 19th century as a winter escape for northerners. Resorts and country clubs, including the heralded Augusta National Country Club, opened at that time. During most of the year, Augusta is a tranquil, mid-size Southern city with varied small industry and commercial activity. In April the Masters golf tournament brings worldwide attention and crowds. People with nicer homes rent them to visiting dignitaries and executives (and receive a tax break thanks to a federal tax loophole seemingly designed for this event). Aside from golf, the city offers history and architectural interest, and even a minor-league ice hockey team. Cost of living (aside from Masters week) is low for the state and reasonable for this type of town. The lack of cultural amenities and air service is offset somewhat by proximity to offerings in Columbia, 70 miles northeast, and Atlanta, 150 miles west.

Augusta is located along the Savannah River between the Piedmont Plateau and the Coastal Plain. The city is in a narrow river plain with wooded rolling hills up to 200 feet on all sides. Lowland is swampy especially to the southeast. Summers are hot and humid with thundershowers; strong storms can occur especially in spring. Because the Appalachian Mountains shield the city from extreme cold and storms from the northwest, winters are mild with rare measurable snow. Ice storms are less common than in Atlanta.

POPULATION

DEMOGRAPHICS	AREA	U.S. AVG	ETHNIC COMPOSITION	AREA	U.S. AVG	RESIDENT PROFILE	AREA	U.S. AVG
Population	484,382		White	65.8%	75.1%	Single	45.9%	43.6%
Population density per sq. mile	221.3	447.3	Black	32.6%	12.3%	Married	54.1%	56.4%
Population growth	16.7%	16.1%	Asian	1.0%	3.6%	Divorced	7.9%	8.4%
Median age	34.8	35.5	American Indian	.2%	.9%	Separated	5.0%	3.0%
Average family size	2.7	2.7	Hispanic	1.8%	12.5%	Married with children	29.5%	28.7%
			Diversity measure	51.6%	35.2%	Single with children	13.4%	10.1%

ECONOMY & JOBS   SCORE: 73/RANK: 87

INCOME	AREA	U.S. AVG	EMPLOYMENT	AREA	U.S. AVG	LARGEST EMPLOYING INDUSTRY
Per capita income	$19,727	$23,420	Unemployment rate	4.9%	6.1%	Chemical Manufacturing
Household income	$40,794	$46,060	Recent job growth	2.6%	.9%	
Household income < $25K	30.1%	26.4%	Projected future job growth	15.7%	15.1%	
Household income > $75K	19.1%	24.5%	White collar	52.1%	54.5%	
Household income growth	42.2%	57.3%	Blue collar	47.9%	45.5%	

COST OF LIVING   SCORE: 70/RANK: 96

INDEXES & TAXES	AREA	U.S. AVG	HOUSING	AREA	U.S. AVG	NECESSITIES	AREA	U.S. AVG
Cost of Living Index	84.7	100.0	Median home price	$99,890	$160,100	Food Index	103.3	100.0
Financial Progress Index	102.7	100.0	Home price appreciation	4.5%	7.1%	Housing Index	62.0	100.0
Income tax rate	6.000%	4.625%	Median rent	$580	$670	Utilities Index	96.2	100.0
Sales tax rate	6.000%	6.474%	Homes owned	63.4%	63.9%	Transportation Index	95.4	100.0
Property tax rate	$13.0	$15.6	Homes rented	24.8%	25.3%	Healthcare Index	93.1	100.0
			Housing affordability	56.0%	54.5%	Miscellaneous Cost Index	95.5	100.0

CLIMATE   SCORE: 53/RANK: 155

TEMPERATURE	AREA	U.S. AVG	PRECIPITATION	AREA	U.S. AVG	COMFORTS & HAZARDS	AREA	U.S. AVG
January low	34.0°F	26.4°F	Annual inches precipitation	43.0	35.9	July relative humidity	72.0%	68.8%
July high	90.8°F	86.7°F	Annual inches snowfall	1.3	24.2	Annual days mostly sunny	217	212
Annual days > 90°F	63	38	Annual days precipitation	107	111	Annual days with thunderstorms	55	39
Annual days < 32°F	59	88	Annual days rain > 0.5 inches	29	23	Tornado risk score	8	19
Annual days < 0°F	0	6	Annual days snow > 1.5 inches	1	6	Hurricane risk score	34	15

TEMPERATURE

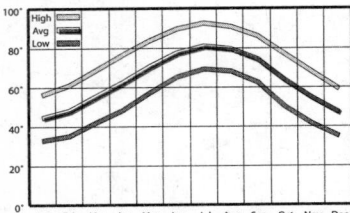

PRECIPITATION

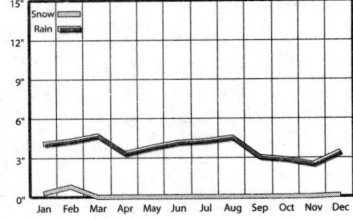

DAYS OF CLOUDS & PRECIPITATION

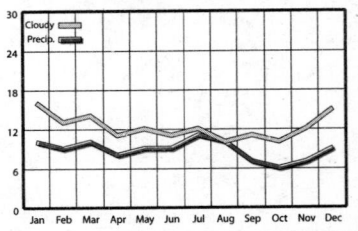

EDUCATION SCORE: 32/RANK: 225

ACHIEVEMENT	AREA	U.S. AVG	PUBLIC SCHOOLS	AREA	U.S. AVG	HIGHER EDUCATION	AREA	U.S. AVG
High school degree	78.1%	80.2%	Expenditures per pupil	$4,998	$5,894	No. 2-year colleges	2	3
2-year college degree	6.5%	6.2%	Student/teacher ratio	17.0	16.7	No. 4-year colleges/universities	3	4
4-year college degree	13.5%	15.8%	Attending public school	92.1%	90.2%	No. highly ranked universities	0	1
Graduate/professional degree	7.4%	9.6%	State SAT score	984*	1020			
			State ACT score	19.8	21.0			

HEALTH & HEALTHCARE SCORE: 59/RANK: 136

HAZARDS & ILLNESSES	AREA	U.S. AVG	HEALTHCARE	AREA	U.S. AVG
Air-quality score	59	45	Physicians per capita	394.3	261.1
Water-quality score	34	33	Hospital beds per capita	433.8	432.2
Pollen/allergy score	62	61	No. teaching hospitals	2	4
Stress score	36	50	Cost per doctor visit	$72	$67
Cancer mortality per capita	181.9	169.0	Cost per dental visit	$74	$82
Depression days per month	2.6	2.8	Cost per daily hospital room	$395	$733

CRIME SCORE: 54/RANK: 150

CRIME	AREA	U.S. AVG
Violent crime rate	342.9	456.0
Change in violent crime rate	-40.2%	-17.2%
Property crime rate	3,913.6	3,950.0
Change in property crime rate	-6.9%	-16.8%

TRANSPORTATION SCORE: 8/RANK: 304

COMMUTE	AREA	U.S. AVG	INTERCITY SERVICES	AREA	U.S. AVG	AUTOMOTIVE	AREA	U.S. AVG
Average commute time	23.9 min.	22.6 min.	Miles to nearest major airport	61	46	Insurance, annual premium	$946	$1,011
Commute by auto	90.0%	88.7%	Type of local airport	Small		Gas, cost per gallon	$1.31	$1.50
Commute by mass transit	1.0%	1.8%	No. daily airline departures	93	294	Daily vehicle miles per capita	22.8	23.0
Work at home	1.5%	3.9%	Amtrak service	No				
Mass transit miles per capita	2.0	8.0	No. interstate highways	1	1			

LEISURE SCORE: 10/RANK: 298

DINING & SHOPPING	AREA	U.S. AVG	ENTERTAINMENT	AREA	U.S. AVG	OUTDOOR ACTIVITIES	AREA	U.S. AVG
Restaurant rating	1	1	Professional sports rating	3	4	Golf-course rating	4	4
No. outlet malls	0	2	College sports rating	2	4	Ski-area rating	1	4
No. Starbucks	0	11	Zoo/aquarium rating	1	3	National Park rating	2	3
No. warehouse clubs	1	4	Amusement park rating	1	3	Sq. miles inland water	3.0	4.0
			Botanical garden/arboretum rating	1	3	Miles of coastline	0.0	11.4

ARTS & CULTURE SCORE: 23/RANK: 252

MEDIA & LIBRARIES	AREA	U.S. AVG	PERFORMING ARTS	AREA	U.S. AVG	MUSEUMS	AREA	U.S. AVG
Arts radio rating	1	3	Classical music rating	3	4	Overall museum rating	6	6
No. public libraries	28	28	Ballet/dance rating	3	3	Art museum rating	4	5
Library volumes per capita	1.4	2.8	Professional theater rating	1	3	Science museum rating	6	4
			University arts programs rating	5	5	Children's museum rating	1	3

Austin–San Marcos, TX

Score: 84.1   Rank: 22

Profile: Capital city/College town
Location: West-central Texas northwest of San Antonio
Elevation: 570 feet
Time zone: Central Standard Time

PRO	CON
Entertainment	Cost of housing
Economy	Summer heat
College-town amenities	Urban sprawl

Austin is often regarded as the best place to live in Texas. Highlights include the University of Texas, an important music scene, and a large high-tech industry, including Dell, Inc. in Round Rock, 20 miles north. The 50,000-student university is located on a large campus north of downtown. The walkable downtown preserves a small-town Texas feel and is packed with nightclubs and music venues, including the famous "Drag" and the Warehouse District. Music is mostly rock 'n' roll, "hard" country, and blues. The high-tech industry is mostly to the east and north, and large areas of new housing have been built among the hills to the west. Cultural amenities are plentiful, as is outdoor recreation on the area's many lakes and in the Hill Country to the south and west. The town is growing and urban sprawl is a threat, but major commute or traffic problems haven't materialized yet and intercity transportation service is available. The cost of living while low on a national scale is the highest in Texas, and home prices are the highest in the state by a wide margin. But incomes are high relative to cost of living, and the area has the third highest expected job-growth rate in the country.

The downtown area sits in a low basin with mostly flat land to the east and hilly areas with limestone outcroppings to the west, separated by a river flowing through town. The landscape is intermittently wooded with deciduous trees. The climate is humid subtropical with occasional continental influence. Summers are hot and moderately humid with most days in the 90s and many evenings in the 70s. Winters are mild with an occasional cold snap. Precipitation is scattered through the year with peaks in late spring and early fall. Moist air and storms from the Gulf can bring heavy rain for days at a time. Winter brings lighter but steady rains. The hills shelter the area from the destructive storms that happen to the north.

POPULATION

DEMOGRAPHICS	AREA	U.S. AVG	ETHNIC COMPOSITION	AREA	U.S. AVG	RESIDENT PROFILE	AREA	U.S. AVG
Population	1,349,291		White	76.7%	75.1%	Single	46.7%	43.6%
Population density per sq. mile	319.3	447.3	Black	10.5%	12.3%	Married	53.3%	56.4%
Population growth	59.4%	16.1%	Asian	2.6%	3.6%	Divorced	9.4%	8.4%
Median age	31.1	35.5	American Indian	.4%	.9%	Separated	3.2%	3.0%
Average family size	2.7	2.7	Hispanic	24.8%	12.5%	Married with children	28.1%	28.7%
			Diversity measure	54.0%	35.2%	Single with children	10.0%	10.1%

ECONOMY & JOBS SCORE: 13/RANK: 286

INCOME	AREA	U.S. AVG	EMPLOYMENT	AREA	U.S. AVG	LARGEST EMPLOYING INDUSTRY
Per capita income	$30,989	$23,420	Unemployment rate	5.6%	6.1%	Computer and Electronic Product Manufacturing
Household income	$60,068	$46,060	Recent job growth	3.1%	.9%	
Household income < $25K	18.9%	26.4%	Projected future job growth	33.2%	15.1%	
Household income > $75K	38.9%	24.5%	White collar	63.9%	54.5%	
Household income growth	114.2%	57.3%	Blue collar	36.1%	45.5%	

COST OF LIVING SCORE: 50/RANK: 165

INDEXES & TAXES	AREA	U.S. AVG	HOUSING	AREA	U.S. AVG	NECESSITIES	AREA	U.S. AVG
Cost of Living Index	95.3	100.0	Median home price	$151,000	$160,100	Food Index	86.9	100.0
Financial Progress Index	134.3	100.0	Home price appreciation	8.8%	7.1%	Housing Index	93.8	100.0
Income tax rate	0.000%	4.625%	Median rent	$914	$670	Utilities Index	91.4	100.0
Sales tax rate	8.250%	6.474%	Homes owned	58.0%	63.9%	Transportation Index	96.9	100.0
Property tax rate	$21.9	$15.6	Homes rented	31.3%	25.3%	Healthcare Index	105.2	100.0
			Housing affordability	50.0%	54.5%	Miscellaneous Cost Index	102.3	100.0

CLIMATE SCORE: 88/RANK: 38

TEMPERATURE	AREA	U.S. AVG	PRECIPITATION	AREA	U.S. AVG	COMFORTS & HAZARDS	AREA	U.S. AVG
January low	39.3°F	26.4°F	Annual inches precipitation	33.0	35.9	July relative humidity	67.0%	68.8%
July high	95.9°F	86.7°F	Annual inches snowfall	1.0	24.2	Annual days mostly sunny	231	212
Annual days > 90°F	101	38	Annual days precipitation	82	111	Annual days with thunderstorms	41	39
Annual days < 32°F	23	88	Annual days rain > 0.5 inches	18	23	Tornado risk score	31	19
Annual days < 0°F	0	6	Annual days snow > 1.5 inches	1	6	Hurricane risk score	17	15

TEMPERATURE

PRECIPITATION

DAYS OF CLOUDS & PRECIPITATION

EDUCATION SCORE: 90/RANK: 32

ACHIEVEMENT	AREA	U.S. AVG	PUBLIC SCHOOLS	AREA	U.S. AVG	HIGHER EDUCATION	AREA	U.S. AVG
High school degree	83.4%	80.2%	Expenditures per pupil	$5,243	$5,894	No. 2-year colleges	3	3
2-year college degree	5.0%	6.2%	Student/teacher ratio	14.8	16.7	No. 4-year colleges/universities	6	4
4-year college degree	25.7%	15.8%	Attending public school	94.3%	90.2%	No. highly ranked universities	1	1
Graduate/professional degree	12.4%	9.6%	State SAT score	993*	1020			
			State ACT score	20.1	21.0			

HEALTH & HEALTHCARE SCORE: 23/RANK: 255

CRIME SCORE: 47/RANK: 174

HAZARDS & ILLNESSES	AREA	U.S. AVG	HEALTHCARE	AREA	U.S. AVG	CRIME	AREA	U.S. AVG
Air-quality score	74	45	Physicians per capita	201.1	261.1	Violent crime rate	364.4	456.0
Water-quality score	96	33	Hospital beds per capita	234.4	432.2	Change in violent crime rate	-37.1%	-17.2%
Pollen/allergy score	76	61	No. teaching hospitals	3	4	Property crime rate	4,478.1	3,950.0
Stress score	56	50	Cost per doctor visit	$76	$67	Change in property crime rate	-18.2%	-16.8%
Cancer mortality per capita	154.0	169.0	Cost per dental visit	$80	$82			
Depression days per month	1.7	2.8	Cost per daily hospital room	$518	$733			

TRANSPORTATION SCORE: 44/RANK: 184

COMMUTE	AREA	U.S. AVG	INTERCITY SERVICES	AREA	U.S. AVG	AUTOMOTIVE	AREA	U.S. AVG
Average commute time	25.5 min.	22.6 min.	Miles to nearest major airport	3	46	Insurance, annual premium	$1,012	$1,011
Commute by auto	89.4%	88.7%	Type of local airport	Medium		Gas, cost per gallon	$1.38	$1.50
Commute by mass transit	2.3%	1.8%	No. daily airline departures	183	294	Daily vehicle miles per capita	32.9	23.0
Work at home	3.8%	3.9%	Amtrak service	Yes				
Mass transit miles per capita	18.1	8.0	No. interstate highways	1	1			

LEISURE SCORE: 50/RANK: 164									
DINING & SHOPPING	**AREA**	**U.S. AVG**	**ENTERTAINMENT**	**AREA**	**U.S. AVG**	**OUTDOOR ACTIVITIES**	**AREA**	**U.S. AVG**
Restaurant rating	1	1	Professional sports rating	3	4	Golf-course rating	4	4
No. outlet malls	3	2	College sports rating	9	4	Ski-area rating	1	4
No. Starbucks	32	11	Zoo/aquarium rating	1	3	National Park rating	1	3
No. warehouse clubs	4	4	Amusement park rating	1	3	Sq. miles inland water	4.0	4.0
			Botanical garden/arboretum rating	6	3	Miles of coastline	0.0	11.4

ARTS & CULTURE SCORE: 82/RANK: 60									
MEDIA & LIBRARIES	**AREA**	**U.S. AVG**	**PERFORMING ARTS**	**AREA**	**U.S. AVG**	**MUSEUMS**	**AREA**	**U.S. AVG**
Arts radio rating	5	3	Classical music rating	4	4	Overall museum rating	8	6
No. public libraries	44	28	Ballet/dance rating	8	3	Art museum rating	8	5
Library volumes per capita	2.4	2.8	Professional theater rating	1	3	Science museum rating	7	4
			University arts programs rating	8	5	Children's museum rating	6	3

Bakersfield, CA

Score: 38.7   Rank: 282

Profile: Small city
Location: South-central California, at the southern end of the Central Valley
Elevation: 492 feet
Time zone: Pacific Standard Time

PRO
Mild winters
Low rainfall
Cost of living

CON
Summer heat
High unemployment
Air quality

Bakersfield is a quiet agricultural and industrial town located in one of the driest inhabited areas of California. Irrigated agriculture, mostly cotton, orchard crops and grapes to the north, and a large oil industry support the region. There isn't much to do, but the metropolitan area is one of two in the state featuring a Cost of Living Index below 100 (the other is Visalia-Tulare-Porterville, just to the north). Summer heat can be relentless with temperatures from 105°F to 110°F frequently observed. Air quality can be a problem in the deep valley. Some recreation is available in the southern Sierra Nevada just to the east and north, and Los Angeles is about 2 hours to the south.

Bakersfield is partially surrounded by a horseshoe-shaped rim of mountains with an open side to the northwest and the crest at an average distance of 40 miles. The valley and surrounding hills are dry grassland with some desert plants; oak-studded grassland becomes more prevalent in the foothills. Climate is Mediterranean semiarid with hot, dry summers and mild winters. Summers are cloudless, with 100°F readings and very low humidity. Winters are mild but fairly humid with frequent fog that usually burns off but can last for weeks.

POPULATION								
DEMOGRAPHICS	**AREA**	**U.S. AVG**	**ETHNIC COMPOSITION**	**AREA**	**U.S. AVG**	**RESIDENT PROFILE**	**AREA**	**U.S. AVG**
Population	694,059		White	73.2%	75.1%	Single	41.3%	43.6%
Population density per sq. mile	85.2	447.3	Black	3.9%	12.3%	Married	58.7%	56.4%
Population growth	27.7%	16.1%	Asian	3.4%	3.6%	Divorced	9.4%	8.4%
Median age	30.8	35.5	American Indian	1.5%	.9%	Separated	4.2%	3.0%
Average family size	3.0	2.7	Hispanic	31.3%	12.5%	Married with children	29.4%	28.7%
			Diversity measure	60.6%	35.2%	Single with children	12.5%	10.1%

ECONOMY & JOBS SCORE: 5/RANK: 314						
INCOME	**AREA**	**U.S. AVG**	**EMPLOYMENT**	**AREA**	**U.S. AVG**	**LARGEST EMPLOYING INDUSTRY**
Per capita income	$15,901	$23,420	Unemployment rate	10.5%	6.1%	Healthcare and Social Assistance
Household income	$36,457	$46,060	Recent job growth	2.5%	.9%	
Household income < $25K	33.0%	26.4%	Projected future job growth	19.7%	15.1%	
Household income > $75K	15.1%	24.5%	White collar	48.1%	54.5%	
Household income growth	27.3%	57.3%	Blue collar	51.9%	45.5%	

COST OF LIVING SCORE: 43/RANK: 186								
INDEXES & TAXES	**AREA**	**U.S. AVG**	**HOUSING**	**AREA**	**U.S. AVG**	**NECESSITIES**	**AREA**	**U.S. AVG**
Cost of Living Index	95.0	100.0	Median home price	$116,330	$160,100	Food Index	112.0	100.0
Financial Progress Index	81.8	100.0	Home price appreciation	7.6%	7.1%	Housing Index	72.3	100.0
Income tax rate	6.000%	4.625%	Median rent	$595	$670	Utilities Index	111.3	100.0
Sales tax rate	7.250%	6.474%	Homes owned	53.9%	63.9%	Transportation Index	107.7	100.0
Property tax rate	$11.1	$15.6	Homes rented	29.8%	25.3%	Healthcare Index	115.3	100.0
			Housing affordability	52.0%	54.5%	Miscellaneous Cost Index	101.2	100.0

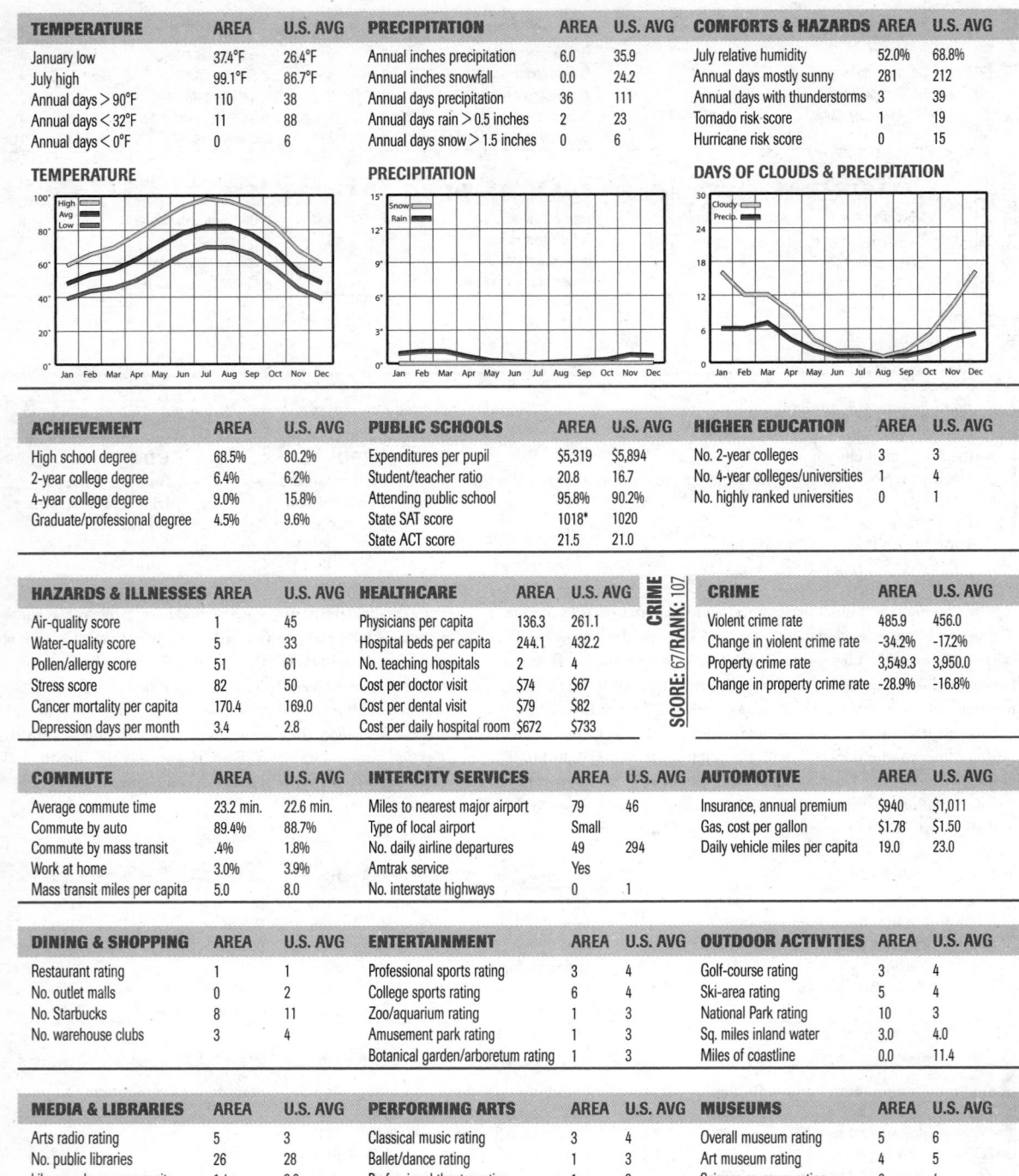

CLIMATE SCORE: 93/RANK: 24

TEMPERATURE	AREA	U.S. AVG
January low	37.4°F	26.4°F
July high	99.1°F	86.7°F
Annual days > 90°F	110	38
Annual days < 32°F	11	88
Annual days < 0°F	0	6

PRECIPITATION	AREA	U.S. AVG
Annual inches precipitation	6.0	35.9
Annual inches snowfall	0.0	24.2
Annual days precipitation	36	111
Annual days rain > 0.5 inches	2	23
Annual days snow > 1.5 inches	0	6

COMFORTS & HAZARDS	AREA	U.S. AVG
July relative humidity	52.0%	68.8%
Annual days mostly sunny	281	212
Annual days with thunderstorms	3	39
Tornado risk score	1	19
Hurricane risk score	0	15

TEMPERATURE

PRECIPITATION

DAYS OF CLOUDS & PRECIPITATION

EDUCATION SCORE: 3/RANK: 319

ACHIEVEMENT	AREA	U.S. AVG
High school degree	68.5%	80.2%
2-year college degree	6.4%	6.2%
4-year college degree	9.0%	15.8%
Graduate/professional degree	4.5%	9.6%

PUBLIC SCHOOLS	AREA	U.S. AVG
Expenditures per pupil	$5,319	$5,894
Student/teacher ratio	20.8	16.7
Attending public school	95.8%	90.2%
State SAT score	1018*	1020
State ACT score	21.5	21.0

HIGHER EDUCATION	AREA	U.S. AVG
No. 2-year colleges	3	3
No. 4-year colleges/universities	1	4
No. highly ranked universities	0	1

HEALTH & HEALTHCARE SCORE: 3/RANK: 321

HAZARDS & ILLNESSES	AREA	U.S. AVG
Air-quality score	1	45
Water-quality score	5	33
Pollen/allergy score	51	61
Stress score	82	50
Cancer mortality per capita	170.4	169.0
Depression days per month	3.4	2.8

HEALTHCARE	AREA	U.S. AVG
Physicians per capita	136.3	261.1
Hospital beds per capita	244.1	432.2
No. teaching hospitals	2	4
Cost per doctor visit	$74	$67
Cost per dental visit	$79	$82
Cost per daily hospital room	$672	$733

CRIME SCORE: 67/RANK: 107

CRIME	AREA	U.S. AVG
Violent crime rate	485.9	456.0
Change in violent crime rate	-34.2%	-17.2%
Property crime rate	3,549.3	3,950.0
Change in property crime rate	-28.9%	-16.8%

TRANSPORTATION SCORE: 21/RANK: 260

COMMUTE	AREA	U.S. AVG
Average commute time	23.2 min.	22.6 min.
Commute by auto	89.4%	88.7%
Commute by mass transit	.4%	1.8%
Work at home	3.0%	3.9%
Mass transit miles per capita	5.0	8.0

INTERCITY SERVICES	AREA	U.S. AVG
Miles to nearest major airport	79	46
Type of local airport	Small	
No. daily airline departures	49	294
Amtrak service	Yes	
No. interstate highways	0	1

AUTOMOTIVE	AREA	U.S. AVG
Insurance, annual premium	$940	$1,011
Gas, cost per gallon	$1.78	$1.50
Daily vehicle miles per capita	19.0	23.0

LEISURE SCORE: 42/RANK: 194

DINING & SHOPPING	AREA	U.S. AVG
Restaurant rating	1	1
No. outlet malls	0	2
No. Starbucks	8	11
No. warehouse clubs	3	4

ENTERTAINMENT	AREA	U.S. AVG
Professional sports rating	3	4
College sports rating	6	4
Zoo/aquarium rating	1	3
Amusement park rating	1	3
Botanical garden/arboretum rating	1	3

OUTDOOR ACTIVITIES	AREA	U.S. AVG
Golf-course rating	3	4
Ski-area rating	5	4
National Park rating	10	3
Sq. miles inland water	3.0	4.0
Miles of coastline	0.0	11.4

ARTS & CULTURE SCORE: 14/RANK: 284

MEDIA & LIBRARIES	AREA	U.S. AVG
Arts radio rating	5	3
No. public libraries	26	28
Library volumes per capita	1.4	2.8

PERFORMING ARTS	AREA	U.S. AVG
Classical music rating	3	4
Ballet/dance rating	1	3
Professional theater rating	1	3
University arts programs rating	1	5

MUSEUMS	AREA	U.S. AVG
Overall museum rating	5	6
Art museum rating	4	5
Science museum rating	6	4
Children's museum rating	7	3

Baltimore, MD

Score: 56.2   Rank: 179

Profile: Large city
Location: East-central Maryland along Chesapeake Bay, 40 miles northeast of Washington, D.C.
Elevation: 32 feet
Time zone: Eastern Standard Time

PRO	CON
Attractive downtown	Crime rate
Historic interest and preservation	Urban sprawl
Arts and culture	Air quality

Baltimore is a well-rounded, East Coast city—sometimes treated as the less attractive sister of Washington, D.C. It surrounds a major inland port on the upper portion of the Chesapeake Bay, and the shipping, transportation, and manufacturing industries are prospering. The city, particularly the downtown, has experienced a vast renewal with a strong orientation toward historic preservation. The restored waterfront is now a commercial and leisure destination, while renewed urban neighborhoods have become attractive and functional places to live.

Transportation has always been one of the city's strengths. Baltimore is one of the few East Coast destinations of discount carrier Southwest Airlines. Train service and interstate highways make Washington D.C., New York, and other cities along the Northeast Corridor easily accessible. Cost of living and housing, while high by U.S. standards, are moderate for the region at large. Leisure activities are plentiful, and the town is big on sports, particularly the Baltimore Orioles baseball and Baltimore Ravens football teams. Camden Yards (next to the historic Baltimore and Ohio Railroad freight station just past the right field wall), exemplifies Baltimore's tradition and vitality, and has become an urban sports icon that other major-league cities have attempted to imitate. However, the city has its downsides. The population is very socioeconomically diverse, run-down neighborhoods still exist, and unattractive sprawl mars the I-695 beltway. The crime rate, particularly for violent crime, is among the nation's highest.

The area is situated on the Chesapeake Bay in a largely level, open plain where several rivers converge to form the Patapsco Bay. The Appalachians rise about 50 miles to the west, beyond areas of modest hills and farmland. Baltimore sits between rigorous northern climates, mild southern ones, and moderating influences from the ocean to the east and the mountains to the west. The climate is changeable, but more moderate than inland locations at the same latitude. Summer brings warm, humid days. Winters are cold but tempered by the ocean and mountains. Snow does occur, but snowfall is generally light except during large spring storms. Some freezing rain and sleet occur each year. Summer precipitation is mainly showers and thunderstorms, and late season Atlantic hurricanes can bring heavy rains. First freeze is late October, last is mid-April.

POPULATION

DEMOGRAPHICS	AREA	U.S. AVG	ETHNIC COMPOSITION	AREA	U.S. AVG	RESIDENT PROFILE	AREA	U.S. AVG
Population	2,601,990		White	77.1%	75.1%	Single	46.7%	43.6%
Population density per sq. mile	997.2	447.3	Black	20.1%	12.3%	Married	53.3%	56.4%
Population growth	9.2%	16.1%	Asian	2.2%	3.6%	Divorced	7.0%	8.4%
Median age	36.6	35.5	American Indian	.3%	.9%	Separated	5.2%	3.0%
Average family size	2.7	2.7	Hispanic	1.9%	12.5%	Married with children	28.3%	28.7%
			Diversity measure	48.0%	35.2%	Single with children	10.3%	10.1%

ECONOMY & JOBS   SCORE: 80/RANK: 65

INCOME	AREA	U.S. AVG	EMPLOYMENT	AREA	U.S. AVG	LARGEST EMPLOYING INDUSTRY
Per capita income	$27,731	$23,420	Unemployment rate	4.9%	6.1%	Healthcare and Social Assistance
Household income	$55,897	$46,060	Recent job growth	.5%	.9%	
Household income < $25K	19.0%	26.4%	Projected future job growth	15.1%	15.1%	
Household income > $75K	32.9%	24.5%	White collar	61.5%	54.5%	
Household income growth	52.8%	57.3%	Blue collar	38.5%	45.5%	

COST OF LIVING   SCORE: 12/RANK: 291

INDEXES & TAXES	AREA	U.S. AVG	HOUSING	AREA	U.S. AVG	NECESSITIES	AREA	U.S. AVG
Cost of Living Index	106.9	100.0	Median home price	$189,500	$160,100	Food Index	94.4	100.0
Financial Progress Index	111.4	100.0	Home price appreciation	9.3%	7.1%	Housing Index	117.7	100.0
Income tax rate	7.450%	4.625%	Median rent	$888	$670	Utilities Index	114.7	100.0
Sales tax rate	5.000%	6.474%	Homes owned	67.9%	63.9%	Transportation Index	102.5	100.0
Property tax rate	$21.4	$15.6	Homes rented	25.2%	25.3%	Healthcare Index	97.5	100.0
			Housing affordability	48.0%	54.5%	Miscellaneous Cost Index	100.8	100.0

CLIMATE — SCORE: 43/RANK: 188

TEMPERATURE	AREA	U.S. AVG	PRECIPITATION	AREA	U.S. AVG	COMFORTS & HAZARDS	AREA	U.S. AVG
January low	24.9°F	26.4°F	Annual inches precipitation	40.0	35.9	July relative humidity	67.0%	68.8%
July high	86.7°F	86.7°F	Annual inches snowfall	22.0	24.2	Annual days mostly sunny	205	212
Annual days > 90°F	31	38	Annual days precipitation	112	111	Annual days with thunderstorms	26	39
Annual days < 32°F	100	88	Annual days rain > 0.5 inches	25	23	Tornado risk score	14	19
Annual days < 0°F	0	6	Annual days snow > 1.5 inches	4	6	Hurricane risk score	14	15

TEMPERATURE
PRECIPITATION
DAYS OF CLOUDS & PRECIPITATION

EDUCATION — SCORE: 90/RANK: 34

ACHIEVEMENT	AREA	U.S. AVG	PUBLIC SCHOOLS	AREA	U.S. AVG	HIGHER EDUCATION	AREA	U.S. AVG
High school degree	81.9%	80.2%	Expenditures per pupil	$6,846	$5,894	No. 2-year colleges	8	3
2-year college degree	5.4%	6.2%	Student/teacher ratio	16.8	16.7	No. 4-year colleges/universities	19	4
4-year college degree	17.3%	15.8%	Attending public school	83.7%	90.2%	No. highly ranked universities	7	1
Graduate/professional degree	11.9%	9.6%	State SAT score	1024*	1020			
			State ACT score	20.7	21.0			

HEALTH & HEALTHCARE — SCORE: 35/RANK: 212 / CRIME — SCORE: 15/RANK: 280

HAZARDS & ILLNESSES	AREA	U.S. AVG	HEALTHCARE	AREA	U.S. AVG	CRIME	AREA	U.S. AVG
Air-quality score	81	45	Physicians per capita	383.0	261.1	Violent crime rate	1,026.0	456.0
Water-quality score	52	33	Hospital beds per capita	503.3	432.2	Change in violent crime rate	-23.2%	-17.2%
Pollen/allergy score	65	61	No. teaching hospitals	18	4	Property crime rate	4,438.7	3,950.0
Stress score	71	50	Cost per doctor visit	$62	$67	Change in property crime rate	-27.4%	-16.8%
Cancer mortality per capita	194.7	169.0	Cost per dental visit	$71	$82			
Depression days per month	2.8	2.8	Cost per daily hospital room	$624	$733			

TRANSPORTATION — SCORE: 62/RANK: 125

COMMUTE	AREA	U.S. AVG	INTERCITY SERVICES	AREA	U.S. AVG	AUTOMOTIVE	AREA	U.S. AVG
Average commute time	29.8 min.	22.6 min.	Miles to nearest major airport	9	46	Insurance, annual premium	$1,100	$1,011
Commute by auto	86.5%	88.7%	Type of local airport	Large		Gas, cost per gallon	$1.46	$1.50
Commute by mass transit	4.4%	1.8%	No. daily airline departures	431	294	Daily vehicle miles per capita	21.0	23.0
Work at home	3.1%	3.9%	Amtrak service	Yes				
Mass transit miles per capita	17.2	8.0	No. interstate highways	4	1			

LEISURE — SCORE: 93/RANK: 20

DINING & SHOPPING	AREA	U.S. AVG	ENTERTAINMENT	AREA	U.S. AVG	OUTDOOR ACTIVITIES	AREA	U.S. AVG
Restaurant rating	3	1	Professional sports rating	9	4	Golf-course rating	8	4
No. outlet malls	8	2	College sports rating	5	4	Ski-area rating	2	4
No. Starbucks	23	11	Zoo/aquarium rating	10	3	National Park rating	3	3
No. warehouse clubs	9	4	Amusement park rating	5	3	Sq. miles inland water	9.0	4.0
			Botanical garden/arboretum rating	7	3	Miles of coastline	94.0	11.4

ARTS & CULTURE — SCORE: 94/RANK: 19

MEDIA & LIBRARIES	AREA	U.S. AVG	PERFORMING ARTS	AREA	U.S. AVG	MUSEUMS	AREA	U.S. AVG
Arts radio rating	8	3	Classical music rating	9	4	Overall museum rating	10	6
No. public libraries	82	28	Ballet/dance rating	7	3	Art museum rating	10	5
Library volumes per capita	3.6	2.8	Professional theater rating	10	3	Science museum rating	9	4
			University arts programs rating	10	5	Children's museum rating	9	3

Bangor, ME

Score: 62.5 **Rank:** 127

Profile: Small town
Location: Central Maine along the Penobscot River, about 30 miles north of the Atlantic Ocean
Elevation: 110 feet
Time zone: Eastern Standard Time

PRO	CON
Attractive setting	Harsh winters
Outdoor recreation	Arts and culture
Nearby university	Low future job growth

Bangor is the gateway to the "north country" and a fairly prosperous lumber, paper, and shipping center and the navigable terminus of the Penobscot River in east-central Maine. The areas to the north are wooded wilderness. The rugged shore area is 30 miles to the south, and the "Down East" coast to the northeast is a vast, unpopulated area of classic New England coastline with fishing and other recreational sites. Acadia National Park is on an island 40 miles to the south. Old Town, on a river island 10 miles north, is home to the University of Maine and the Old Town Canoe Company, a business befitting to the area. Bangor is isolated from many city amenities and services—some residents travel to Canadian cities such as Saint John, New Brunswick, Québec City, or Montreal. For those who can find employment and tolerate the long, hard winter, Bangor is an attractive place.

Bangor lies in a river valley near sea level. The surrounding area is hilly and wooded with a mix of deciduous and coniferous forests. To the largely unpopulated north, the hills get steeper and the forests more dense with a maze of glacial lakes. The climate is continental with a marine influence and four very distinct seasons. Summers are warm and pleasant, normally not uncomfortably hot, and feature cool evenings. Winters are cold, often brutally, and windy when cold air masses descend from the northwest. Below zero temperatures and snow cover are common. Spring comes slowly with frequent freezes. Precipitation is moderate and spread throughout the year, although fall tends to be the driest and most pleasant. First freeze is early October, last is early May.

POPULATION

DEMOGRAPHICS	AREA	U.S. AVG	ETHNIC COMPOSITION	AREA	U.S. AVG	RESIDENT PROFILE	AREA	U.S. AVG
Population	91,773		White	98.6%	75.1%	Single	40.7%	43.6%
Population density per sq. mile	230.9	447.3	Black	.2%	12.3%	Married	59.3%	56.4%
Population growth	.2%	16.1%	Asian	.6%	3.6%	Divorced	8.7%	8.4%
Median age	37.6	35.5	American Indian	.6%	.9%	Separated	1.8%	3.0%
Average family size	2.7	2.7	Hispanic	.4%	12.5%	Married with children	29.9%	28.7%
			Diversity measure	6.7%	35.2%	Single with children	10.0%	10.1%

ECONOMY & JOBS SCORE: 80/RANK: 67

INCOME	AREA	U.S. AVG	EMPLOYMENT	AREA	U.S. AVG	LARGEST EMPLOYING INDUSTRY
Per capita income	$19,666	$23,420	Unemployment rate	2.8%	6.1%	Healthcare and Social Assistance
Household income	$36,147	$46,060	Recent job growth	3.4%	.9%	
Household income < $25K	33.1%	26.4%	Projected future job growth	7.7%	15.1%	
Household income > $75K	13.9%	24.5%	White collar	57.5%	54.5%	
Household income growth	31.5%	57.3%	Blue collar	42.5%	45.5%	

COST OF LIVING SCORE: 66/RANK: 111

INDEXES & TAXES	AREA	U.S. AVG	HOUSING	AREA	U.S. AVG	NECESSITIES	AREA	U.S. AVG
Cost of Living Index	94.4	100.0	Median home price	$104,420	$160,100	Food Index	102.2	100.0
Financial Progress Index	81.6	100.0	Home price appreciation	8.2%	7.1%	Housing Index	64.9	100.0
Income tax rate	8.500%	4.625%	Median rent	$598	$670	Utilities Index	149.2	100.0
Sales tax rate	5.000%	6.474%	Homes owned	66.2%	63.9%	Transportation Index	105.1	100.0
Property tax rate	$19.5	$15.6	Homes rented	15.7%	25.3%	Healthcare Index	112.2	100.0
			Housing affordability	46.0%	54.5%	Miscellaneous Cost Index	106.6	100.0

CLIMATE SCORE: 28/RANK: 236

TEMPERATURE	AREA	U.S. AVG	PRECIPITATION	AREA	U.S. AVG	COMFORTS & HAZARDS	AREA	U.S. AVG
January low	10.2°F	26.4°F	Annual inches precipitation	43.0	35.9	July relative humidity	72.0%	68.8%
July high	77.5°F	86.7°F	Annual inches snowfall	95.0	24.2	Annual days mostly sunny	205	212
Annual days > 90°F	4	38	Annual days precipitation	135	111	Annual days with thunderstorms	18	39
Annual days < 32°F	155	88	Annual days rain > 0.5 inches	28	23	Tornado risk score	0	19
Annual days < 0°F	16	6	Annual days snow > 1.5 inches	17	6	Hurricane risk score	13	15

TEMPERATURE

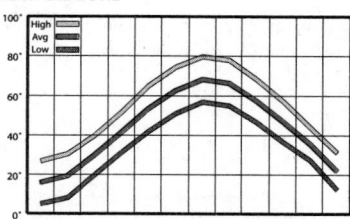

PRECIPITATION

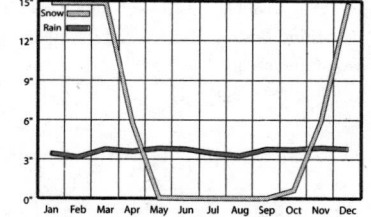

DAYS OF CLOUDS & PRECIPITATION

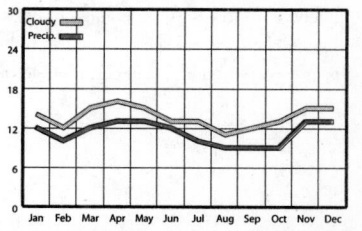

EDUCATION SCORE: 65/RANK: 115

ACHIEVEMENT	AREA	U.S. AVG	PUBLIC SCHOOLS	AREA	U.S. AVG	HIGHER EDUCATION	AREA	U.S. AVG
High school degree	87.0%	80.2%	Expenditures per pupil	$6,225	$5,894	No. 2-year colleges	2	3
2-year college degree	9.0%	6.2%	Student/teacher ratio	14.6	16.7	No. 4-year colleges/universities	2	4
4-year college degree	12.9%	15.8%	Attending public school	93.5%	90.2%	No. highly ranked universities	0	1
Graduate/professional degree	7.4%	9.6%	State SAT score	1004*	1020			
			State ACT score	22.5	21.0			

HEALTH & HEALTHCARE SCORE: 59/RANK: 135

CRIME SCORE: 61/RANK: 129

HAZARDS & ILLNESSES	AREA	U.S. AVG	HEALTHCARE	AREA	U.S. AVG	CRIME	AREA	U.S. AVG
Air-quality score	49	45	Physicians per capita	528.5	261.1	Violent crime rate	104.3	456.0
Water-quality score	96	33	Hospital beds per capita	661.4	432.2	Change in violent crime rate	6.1%	-17.2%
Pollen/allergy score	34	61	No. teaching hospitals	1	4	Property crime rate	4,336.6	3,950.0
Stress score	13	50	Cost per doctor visit	$68	$67	Change in property crime rate	31.9%	-16.8%
Cancer mortality per capita	179.6	169.0	Cost per dental visit	$0	$82			
Depression days per month	2.6	2.8	Cost per daily hospital room	$690	$733			

TRANSPORTATION SCORE: 44/RANK: 183

COMMUTE	AREA	U.S. AVG	INTERCITY SERVICES	AREA	U.S. AVG	AUTOMOTIVE	AREA	U.S. AVG
Average commute time	20.7 min.	22.6 min.	Miles to nearest major airport	111	46	Insurance, annual premium	$720	$1,011
Commute by auto	87.8%	88.7%	Type of local airport	Small		Gas, cost per gallon	$1.53	$1.50
Commute by mass transit	.5%	1.8%	No. daily airline departures	73	294	Daily vehicle miles per capita	23.9	23.0
Work at home	4.9%	3.9%	Amtrak service	No				
Mass transit miles per capita	5.3	8.0	No. interstate highways	1	1			

LEISURE SCORE: 43/RANK: 188

DINING & SHOPPING	AREA	U.S. AVG	ENTERTAINMENT	AREA	U.S. AVG	OUTDOOR ACTIVITIES	AREA	U.S. AVG
Restaurant rating	1	1	Professional sports rating	2	4	Golf-course rating	2	4
No. outlet malls	0	2	College sports rating	3	4	Ski-area rating	7	4
No. Starbucks	0	11	Zoo/aquarium rating	1	3	National Park rating	1	3
No. warehouse clubs	3	4	Amusement park rating	1	3	Sq. miles inland water	3.0	4.0
			Botanical garden/arboretum rating	2	3	Miles of coastline	0.0	11.4

ARTS & CULTURE SCORE: 30/RANK: 232

MEDIA & LIBRARIES	AREA	U.S. AVG	PERFORMING ARTS	AREA	U.S. AVG	MUSEUMS	AREA	U.S. AVG
Arts radio rating	5	3	Classical music rating	3	4	Overall museum rating	6	6
No. public libraries	25	28	Ballet/dance rating	1	3	Art museum rating	2	5
Library volumes per capita	7.1	2.8	Professional theater rating	1	3	Science museum rating	3	4
			University arts programs rating	5	5	Children's museum rating	1	3

Barnstable-Yarmouth, MA

Score: 70.7   Rank: 75

Profile: Resort-town complex
Location: Central portion of Cape Cod
Elevation: 60 feet
Time zone: Eastern Standard Time

PRO	CON
Nearby coastline	Cost of living
Educated population	Tourist impact
Entertainment	Low ethnic diversity

Barnstable-Yarmouth is the commercial center for Cape Cod and is the second highest ranked city in Massachusetts behind Boston. The towns are typical New England coastal towns with attractive commercial and residential areas and seaside wharves. The considerable fishing industry and tourist market support an attractive assortment of restaurants and local entertainment. Surrounding Cape Cod is an outdoor recreation and entertainment paradise. Educational attainment at all levels is the highest in the state. Not surprisingly, cost of living and housing are second highest in the state behind Boston. The area is crowded with tourists at certain times of the year, but escape from the crowds is possible. Those who can handle the high cost and the damp marine climate will probably like the area.

Barnstable-Yarmouth is located on the mostly flat coastal plain of Cape Cod with beaches to the north. Climate is marine continental with a strong water-borne moderating influence year-round. Summers are warm but not hot with more prevalent sunshine than the rest of the state. Other seasons are highly variable with frequent fog, rain, and snow. The area has far fewer rainy days and far less snow than the rest of the state. First freeze is end of October, last is mid-April.

POPULATION

DEMOGRAPHICS	AREA	U.S. AVG	ETHNIC COMPOSITION	AREA	U.S. AVG	RESIDENT PROFILE	AREA	U.S. AVG
Population	167,117		White	96.5%	75.1%	Single	43.3%	43.6%
Population density per sq. mile	642.6	447.3	Black	1.8%	12.3%	Married	56.7%	56.4%
Population growth	23.8%	16.1%	Asian	1.0%	3.6%	Divorced	8.3%	8.4%
Median age	45.2	35.5	American Indian	.6%	.9%	Separated	2.5%	3.0%
Average family size	2.3	2.7	Hispanic	1.7%	12.5%	Married with children	20.2%	28.7%
			Diversity measure	10.7%	35.2%	Single with children	7.4%	10.1%

ECONOMY & JOBS — SCORE: 29/RANK: 233

INCOME	AREA	U.S. AVG	EMPLOYMENT	AREA	U.S. AVG	LARGEST EMPLOYING INDUSTRY
Per capita income	$28,147	$23,420	Unemployment rate	3.3%	6.1%	Healthcare and Social Assistance
Household income	$50,114	$46,060	Recent job growth	.8%	.9%	
Household income < $25K	22.1%	26.4%	Projected future job growth	16.3%	15.1%	
Household income > $75K	28.9%	24.5%	White collar	59.2%	54.5%	
Household income growth	57.7%	57.3%	Blue collar	40.8%	45.5%	

COST OF LIVING — SCORE: 7/RANK: 306

INDEXES & TAXES	AREA	U.S. AVG	HOUSING	AREA	U.S. AVG	NECESSITIES	AREA	U.S. AVG
Cost of Living Index	141.7	100.0	Median home price	$299,830	$160,100	Food Index	112.5	100.0
Financial Progress Index	75.4	100.0	Home price appreciation	18.8%	7.1%	Housing Index	186.2	100.0
Income tax rate	5.950%	4.625%	Median rent	$967	$670	Utilities Index	128.0	100.0
Sales tax rate	5.000%	6.474%	Homes owned	43.4%	63.9%	Transportation Index	116.3	100.0
Property tax rate	$16.8	$15.6	Homes rented	14.8%	25.3%	Healthcare Index	129.8	100.0
			Housing affordability	41.0%	54.5%	Miscellaneous Cost Index	112.3	100.0

CLIMATE — SCORE: 65/RANK: 115

TEMPERATURE	AREA	U.S. AVG	PRECIPITATION	AREA	U.S. AVG	COMFORTS & HAZARDS	AREA	U.S. AVG
January low	21.6°F	26.4°F	Annual inches precipitation	45.0	35.9	July relative humidity	76.0%	68.8%
July high	81.7°F	86.7°F	Annual inches snowfall	36.0	24.2	Annual days mostly sunny	211	212
Annual days > 90°F	5	38	Annual days precipitation	79	111	Annual days with thunderstorms	14	39
Annual days < 32°F	110	88	Annual days rain > 0.5 inches	30	23	Tornado risk score	8	19
Annual days < 0°F	0	6	Annual days snow > 1.5 inches	16	6	Hurricane risk score	21	15

TEMPERATURE

PRECIPITATION

DAYS OF CLOUDS & PRECIPITATION

EDUCATION — SCORE: 94/RANK: 18

ACHIEVEMENT	AREA	U.S. AVG	PUBLIC SCHOOLS	AREA	U.S. AVG	HIGHER EDUCATION	AREA	U.S. AVG
High school degree	91.8%	80.2%	Expenditures per pupil	$6,956	$5,894	No. 2-year colleges	1	3
2-year college degree	9.2%	6.2%	Student/teacher ratio	15.5	16.7	No. 4-year colleges/universities	1	4
4-year college degree	20.3%	15.8%	Attending public school	93.7%	90.2%	No. highly ranked universities	0	1
Graduate/professional degree	13.0%	9.6%	State SAT score	1038*	1020			
			State ACT score	22.3	21.0			

HEALTH & HEALTHCARE — SCORE: 36/RANK: 210

HAZARDS & ILLNESSES	AREA	U.S. AVG	HEALTHCARE	AREA	U.S. AVG
Air-quality score	24	45	Physicians per capita	330.9	261.1
Water-quality score	13	33	Hospital beds per capita	196.2	432.2
Pollen/allergy score	62	61	No. teaching hospitals	1	4
Stress score	42	50	Cost per doctor visit	$71	$67
Cancer mortality per capita	179.7	169.0	Cost per dental visit	$108	$82
Depression days per month	2.3	2.8	Cost per daily hospital room	$737	$733

CRIME — SCORE: 90/RANK: 32

CRIME	AREA	U.S. AVG
Violent crime rate	471.2	456.0
Change in violent crime rate	-40.4%	-17.2%
Property crime rate	2,280.3	3,950.0
Change in property crime rate	-32.2%	-16.8%

TRANSPORTATION — SCORE: 44/RANK: 185

COMMUTE	AREA	U.S. AVG	INTERCITY SERVICES	AREA	U.S. AVG	AUTOMOTIVE	AREA	U.S. AVG
Average commute time	24.1 min.	22.6 min.	Miles to nearest major airport	59	46	Insurance, annual premium	$1,298	$1,011
Commute by auto	89.0%	88.7%	Type of local airport	Small		Gas, cost per gallon	$1.58	$1.50
Commute by mass transit	.9%	1.8%	No. daily airline departures	156	294	Daily vehicle miles per capita	17.5	23.0
Work at home	4.9%	3.9%	Amtrak service	No				
Mass transit miles per capita	15.8	8.0	No. interstate highways	1	1			

LEISURE SCORE: 61/RANK: 127

DINING & SHOPPING	AREA	U.S. AVG	ENTERTAINMENT	AREA	U.S. AVG	OUTDOOR ACTIVITIES	AREA	U.S. AVG
Restaurant rating	3	1	Professional sports rating	5	4	Golf-course rating	1	4
No. outlet malls	1	2	College sports rating	1	4	Ski-area rating	6	4
No. Starbucks	2	11	Zoo/aquarium rating	4	3	National Park rating	1	3
No. warehouse clubs	1	4	Amusement park rating	1	3	Sq. miles inland water	3.0	4.0
			Botanical garden/arboretum rating	4	3	Miles of coastline	25.2	11.4

ARTS & CULTURE SCORE: 41/RANK: 194

MEDIA & LIBRARIES	AREA	U.S. AVG	PERFORMING ARTS	AREA	U.S. AVG	MUSEUMS	AREA	U.S. AVG
Arts radio rating	1	3	Classical music rating	4	4	Overall museum rating	9	6
No. public libraries	33	28	Ballet/dance rating	1	3	Art museum rating	7	5
Library volumes per capita	5.5	2.8	Professional theater rating	1	3	Science museum rating	7	4
			University arts programs rating	2	5	Children's museum rating	1	3

Baton Rouge, LA

Score: 35.6   Rank: 295

Profile: Mid-size capital city/College town
Location: Southeast Louisiana along the Mississippi River north of the Mississippi Delta
Elevation: 64 feet
Time zone: Central Standard Time

PRO	CON
College-town amenities	Hot, humid summers
Historic interest	Crime rate
Future job growth	Traffic and sprawl

Baton Rouge is a busy town with a diverse base as state capital, petrochemical industry center, and college town. The city is about 30 miles up the Mississippi River from New Orleans and 65 miles from the coast. It is the home of Louisiana State University and Southern University. A rich past as an ocean port, center for antebellum commerce, and Louisiana's colorful political history adds spice to the local character. There are many points of interest along the shady streets with their gracious old homes. There is plenty to do: The university brings an assortment of cultural amenities and the active Mississippi waterfront area is tastefully developed with restaurants, theaters, and historic buildings. Downsides include hot summer weather, poor air quality, the high crime rate typical of most of the state, and urban sprawl in areas to the east. Looking past these issues, the area may be a little better than the no. 295 ranking suggests.

The area is near the first evident relief north of the broad, flat delta plain extending to the south. Elevations rise from 25 feet to more than 100 feet above sea level. Yet the landscape is generally level in character, and the soil is wet. Lush wet forests of evergreen, live oak, and magnolia trees grow in the area. Especially to the west lie areas of mixed agricultural use, sugar plantations, and marshland, with areas of woodland and pine forest to the north. The climate is humid subtropical, with some polar influence during winter. Summer months are muggy with clouds, light winds, and abundant rainfall, but seldom exceed 100°F. Showers occur every 1 in 2 days during summer. Winter months are normally mild with a few cold spells, lengthy periods of rain, and a few nights with below-freezing temperatures. It rarely stays below freezing during the day.

POPULATION

DEMOGRAPHICS	AREA	U.S. AVG	ETHNIC COMPOSITION	AREA	U.S. AVG	RESIDENT PROFILE	AREA	U.S. AVG
Population	614,491		White	68.8%	75.1%	Single	47.1%	43.6%
Population density per sq. mile	474.5	447.3	Black	29.6%	12.3%	Married	52.9%	56.4%
Population growth	16.3%	16.1%	Asian	1.1%	3.6%	Divorced	7.7%	8.4%
Median age	32.2	35.5	American Indian	.2%	.9%	Separated	4.5%	3.0%
Average family size	2.8	2.7	Hispanic	1.7%	12.5%	Married with children	30.7%	28.7%
			Diversity measure	48.5%	35.2%	Single with children	14.0%	10.1%

ECONOMY & JOBS SCORE: 34/RANK: 218

INCOME	AREA	U.S. AVG	EMPLOYMENT	AREA	U.S. AVG	LARGEST EMPLOYING INDUSTRY
Per capita income	$21,790	$23,420	Unemployment rate	7.0%	6.1%	Construction
Household income	$42,753	$46,060	Recent job growth	1.3%	.9%	
Household income < $25K	30.2%	26.4%	Projected future job growth	22.9%	15.1%	
Household income > $75K	24.9%	24.5%	White collar	60.2%	54.5%	
Household income growth	58.5%	57.3%	Blue collar	39.8%	45.5%	

COST OF LIVING SCORE: 53/RANK: 156

INDEXES & TAXES	AREA	U.S. AVG	HOUSING	AREA	U.S. AVG	NECESSITIES	AREA	U.S. AVG
Cost of Living Index	95.0	100.0	Median home price	$118,600	$160,100	Food Index	107.0	100.0
Financial Progress Index	95.9	100.0	Home price appreciation	4.5%	7.1%	Housing Index	73.7	100.0
Income tax rate	4.000%	4.625%	Median rent	$535	$670	Utilities Index	121.5	100.0
Sales tax rate	9.000%	6.474%	Homes owned	65.8%	63.9%	Transportation Index	106.9	100.0
Property tax rate	$5.0	$15.6	Homes rented	23.6%	25.3%	Healthcare Index	96.9	100.0
			Housing affordability	59.0%	54.5%	Miscellaneous Cost Index	104.4	100.0

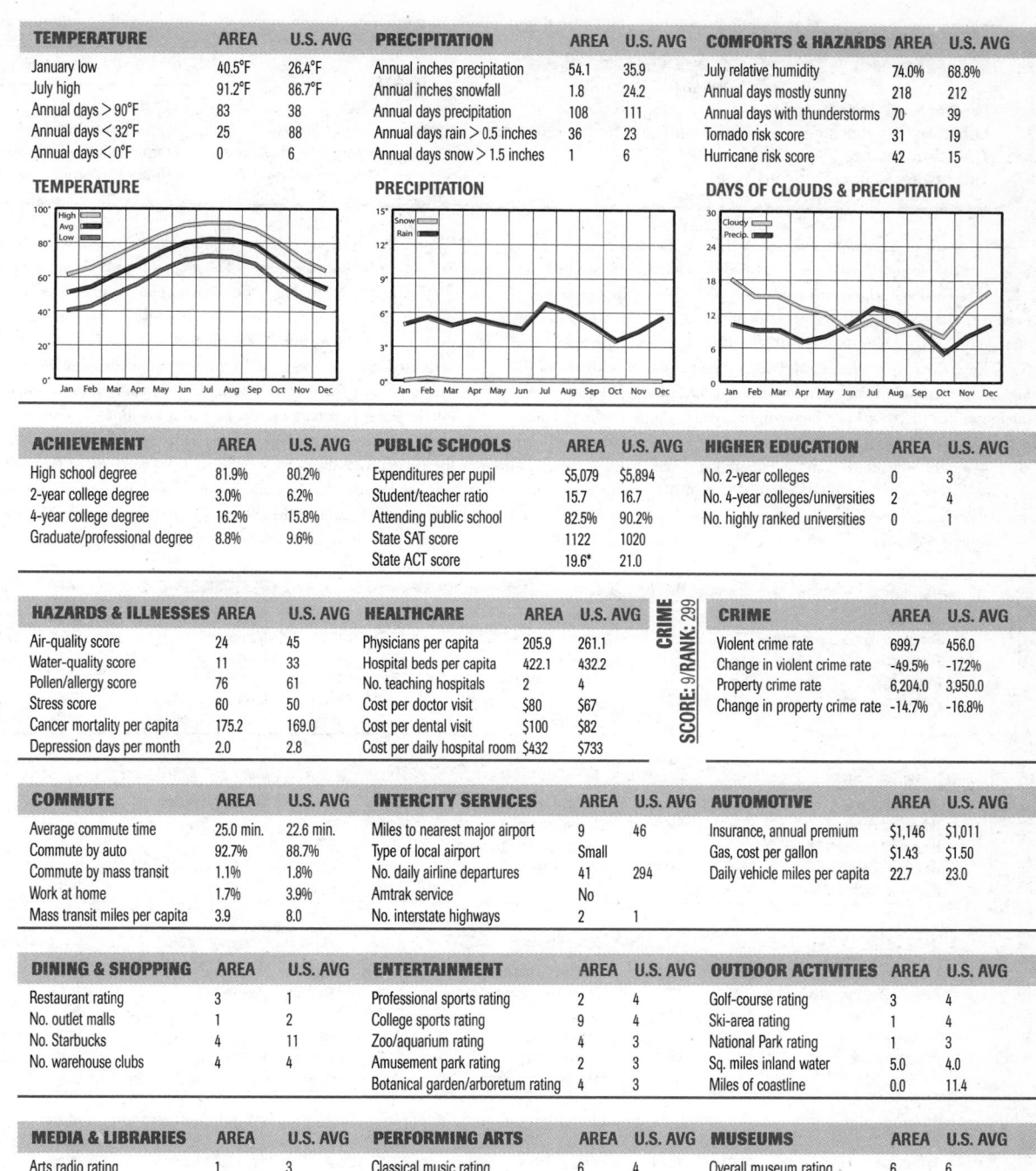

CLIMATE SCORE: 71/RANK: 95

TEMPERATURE	AREA	U.S. AVG	PRECIPITATION	AREA	U.S. AVG	COMFORTS & HAZARDS	AREA	U.S. AVG
January low	40.5°F	26.4°F	Annual inches precipitation	54.1	35.9	July relative humidity	74.0%	68.8%
July high	91.2°F	86.7°F	Annual inches snowfall	1.8	24.2	Annual days mostly sunny	218	212
Annual days > 90°F	83	38	Annual days precipitation	108	111	Annual days with thunderstorms	70	39
Annual days < 32°F	25	88	Annual days rain > 0.5 inches	36	23	Tornado risk score	31	19
Annual days < 0°F	0	6	Annual days snow > 1.5 inches	1	6	Hurricane risk score	42	15

TEMPERATURE

PRECIPITATION

DAYS OF CLOUDS & PRECIPITATION

EDUCATION SCORE: 11/RANK: 292

ACHIEVEMENT	AREA	U.S. AVG	PUBLIC SCHOOLS	AREA	U.S. AVG	HIGHER EDUCATION	AREA	U.S. AVG
High school degree	81.9%	80.2%	Expenditures per pupil	$5,079	$5,894	No. 2-year colleges	0	3
2-year college degree	3.0%	6.2%	Student/teacher ratio	15.7	16.7	No. 4-year colleges/universities	2	4
4-year college degree	16.2%	15.8%	Attending public school	82.5%	90.2%	No. highly ranked universities	0	1
Graduate/professional degree	8.8%	9.6%	State SAT score	1122	1020			
			State ACT score	19.6*	21.0			

HEALTH & HEALTHCARE SCORE: 7/RANK: 307

HAZARDS & ILLNESSES	AREA	U.S. AVG	HEALTHCARE	AREA	U.S. AVG
Air-quality score	24	45	Physicians per capita	205.9	261.1
Water-quality score	11	33	Hospital beds per capita	422.1	432.2
Pollen/allergy score	76	61	No. teaching hospitals	2	4
Stress score	60	50	Cost per doctor visit	$80	$67
Cancer mortality per capita	175.2	169.0	Cost per dental visit	$100	$82
Depression days per month	2.0	2.8	Cost per daily hospital room	$432	$733

CRIME SCORE: 9/RANK: 299

CRIME	AREA	U.S. AVG
Violent crime rate	699.7	456.0
Change in violent crime rate	-49.5%	-17.2%
Property crime rate	6,204.0	3,950.0
Change in property crime rate	-14.7%	-16.8%

TRANSPORTATION SCORE: 7/RANK: 307

COMMUTE	AREA	U.S. AVG	INTERCITY SERVICES	AREA	U.S. AVG	AUTOMOTIVE	AREA	U.S. AVG
Average commute time	25.0 min.	22.6 min.	Miles to nearest major airport	9	46	Insurance, annual premium	$1,146	$1,011
Commute by auto	92.7%	88.7%	Type of local airport	Small		Gas, cost per gallon	$1.43	$1.50
Commute by mass transit	1.1%	1.8%	No. daily airline departures	41	294	Daily vehicle miles per capita	22.7	23.0
Work at home	1.7%	3.9%	Amtrak service	No				
Mass transit miles per capita	3.9	8.0	No. interstate highways	2	1			

LEISURE SCORE: 39/RANK: 200

DINING & SHOPPING	AREA	U.S. AVG	ENTERTAINMENT	AREA	U.S. AVG	OUTDOOR ACTIVITIES	AREA	U.S. AVG
Restaurant rating	3	1	Professional sports rating	2	4	Golf-course rating	3	4
No. outlet malls	1	2	College sports rating	9	4	Ski-area rating	1	4
No. Starbucks	4	11	Zoo/aquarium rating	4	3	National Park rating	1	3
No. warehouse clubs	4	4	Amusement park rating	2	3	Sq. miles inland water	5.0	4.0
			Botanical garden/arboretum rating	4	3	Miles of coastline	0.0	11.4

ARTS & CULTURE SCORE: 80/RANK: 69

MEDIA & LIBRARIES	AREA	U.S. AVG	PERFORMING ARTS	AREA	U.S. AVG	MUSEUMS	AREA	U.S. AVG
Arts radio rating	1	3	Classical music rating	6	4	Overall museum rating	6	6
No. public libraries	25	28	Ballet/dance rating	3	3	Art museum rating	5	5
Library volumes per capita	2.9	2.8	Professional theater rating	1	3	Science museum rating	6	4
			University arts programs rating	8	5	Children's museum rating	4	3

Beaumont–Port Arthur, TX

Score: 55.8 **Rank:** 183

Profile: Small-town complex
Location: Extreme southeast Texas near Gulf Coast and Louisiana border
Elevation: 16 feet
Time zone: Central Standard Time

PRO
Cost of living
Revitalized downtown
Outdoor recreation

CON
Hot, humid summers
Industrial landscape
Recent unemployment

The towns of Beaumont and Port Arthur are located 20 miles apart in extreme southeast Texas. Port Arthur is located on Sabine Lake, a body of water deep enough to support ocean shipping and connected to the Gulf by a canal. Beaumont is inland. The area's destiny changed in 1901 when the first oil well blew in the nearby Spindletop field. Ever since, it has been a thriving oil and gas area, with one of the largest concentrations of oil refineries, oil, and petrochemical-related businesses in the state. The heavy industry and gentle decline of some of that industry took its toll on the city and its environs, but recent focus on renewal of downtown and neighborhood areas helped Beaumont achieve All-America City finalist status in 2002. There are a few museums, although Sabine Lake and surrounding areas are noted for fishing and outdoor recreation opportunities. The area preserves a small-town

life and cost environment while being close enough to Houston to benefit from its big-city amenities. The main downside is summer humidity.

The area is located on a flat coastal plain with mostly treeless areas near the coast giving way to large pine forests moving inland. The climate is a modified humid subtropical suitable for year-round outdoor activities. Sea breezes usually prevent summer temperature extremes. The area lies far enough south that cold air masses are moderated, although freezing temperatures occur a few times a year. The Gulf and evenly distributed rainfall give the area the highest relative humidity in the nation. Cloudy, rainy weather is most common in the winter. Heavy rainfall occurs during thunderstorms and infrequent tropical storms. Slower moving storms bring longer periods of rain in spring and fall. Fog occurs especially in winter and spring.

POPULATION

DEMOGRAPHICS	AREA	U.S. AVG	ETHNIC COMPOSITION	AREA	U.S. AVG	RESIDENT PROFILE	AREA	U.S. AVG
Population	382,242		White	73.3%	75.1%	Single	43.7%	43.6%
Population density per sq. mile	177.4	447.3	Black	20.3%	12.3%	Married	56.3%	56.4%
Population growth	5.8%	16.1%	Asian	2.2%	3.6%	Divorced	9.8%	8.4%
Median age	35.8	35.5	American Indian	.3%	.9%	Separated	3.7%	3.0%
Average family size	2.6	2.7	Hispanic	12.1%	12.5%	Married with children	27.9%	28.7%
			Diversity measure	50.8%	35.2%	Single with children	12.1%	10.1%

ECONOMY & JOBS SCORE: 63/RANK: 122

INCOME	AREA	U.S. AVG	EMPLOYMENT	AREA	U.S. AVG	LARGEST EMPLOYING INDUSTRY
Per capita income	$19,788	$23,420	Unemployment rate	9.6%	6.1%	Chemical Manufacturing
Household income	$38,803	$46,060	Recent job growth	3.4%	.9%	
Household income < $25K	33.3%	26.4%	Projected future job growth	11.6%	15.1%	
Household income > $75K	20.1%	24.5%	White collar	50.0%	54.5%	
Household income growth	51.9%	57.3%	Blue collar	50.0%	45.5%	

COST OF LIVING SCORE: 91/RANK: 27

INDEXES & TAXES	AREA	U.S. AVG	HOUSING	AREA	U.S. AVG	NECESSITIES	AREA	U.S. AVG
Cost of Living Index	80.0	100.0	Median home price	$81,500	$160,100	Food Index	90.5	100.0
Financial Progress Index	103.3	100.0	Home price appreciation	4.4%	7.1%	Housing Index	50.6	100.0
Income tax rate	0.000%	4.625%	Median rent	$512	$670	Utilities Index	95.9	100.0
Sales tax rate	8.250%	6.474%	Homes owned	65.4%	63.9%	Transportation Index	98.2	100.0
Property tax rate	$18.7	$15.6	Homes rented	23.5%	25.3%	Healthcare Index	100.3	100.0
			Housing affordability	57.0%	54.5%	Miscellaneous Cost Index	99.8	100.0

CLIMATE SCORE: 67/RANK: 109

TEMPERATURE	AREA	U.S. AVG	PRECIPITATION	AREA	U.S. AVG	COMFORTS & HAZARDS	AREA	U.S. AVG
January low	42.4°F	26.4°F	Annual inches precipitation	55.1	35.9	July relative humidity	79.0%	68.8%
July high	92.0°F	86.7°F	Annual inches snowfall	.5	24.2	Annual days mostly sunny	217	212
Annual days > 90°F	84	38	Annual days precipitation	104	111	Annual days with thunderstorms	64	39
Annual days < 32°F	18	88	Annual days rain > 0.5 inches	32	23	Tornado risk score	64	19
Annual days < 0°F	0	6	Annual days snow > 1.5 inches	0	6	Hurricane risk score	55	15

TEMPERATURE

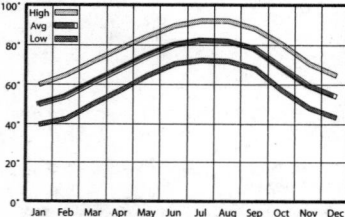

PRECIPITATION

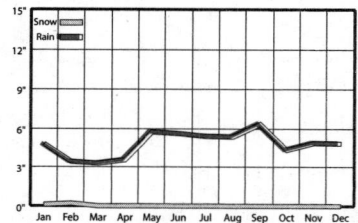

DAYS OF CLOUDS & PRECIPITATION

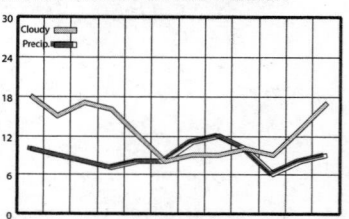

EDUCATION SCORE: 21/RANK: 259

ACHIEVEMENT	AREA	U.S. AVG	PUBLIC SCHOOLS	AREA	U.S. AVG	HIGHER EDUCATION	AREA	U.S. AVG
High school degree	80.6%	80.2%	Expenditures per pupil	$5,535	$5,894	No. 2-year colleges	2	3
2-year college degree	5.1%	6.2%	Student/teacher ratio	14.3	16.7	No. 4-year colleges/universities	1	4
4-year college degree	10.5%	15.8%	Attending public school	94.2%	90.2%	No. highly ranked universities	0	1
Graduate/professional degree	4.2%	9.6%	State SAT score	993*	1020			
			State ACT score	20.1	21.0			

HEALTH & HEALTHCARE SCORE: 30/RANK: 231

HAZARDS & ILLNESSES	AREA	U.S. AVG	HEALTHCARE	AREA	U.S. AVG	CRIME SCORE: 34/RANK: 216 / CRIME	AREA	U.S. AVG
Air-quality score	4	45	Physicians per capita	159.6	261.1	Violent crime rate	540.1	456.0
Water-quality score	43	33	Hospital beds per capita	516.0	432.2	Change in violent crime rate	-21.9%	-17.2%
Pollen/allergy score	71	61	No. teaching hospitals	3	4	Property crime rate	4,375.8	3,950.0
Stress score	94	50	Cost per doctor visit	$66	$67	Change in property crime rate	-20.7%	-16.8%
Cancer mortality per capita	181.7	169.0	Cost per dental visit	$79	$82			
Depression days per month	3.0	2.8	Cost per daily hospital room	$488	$733			

TRANSPORTATION SCORE: 23/RANK: 255

COMMUTE	AREA	U.S. AVG	INTERCITY SERVICES	AREA	U.S. AVG	AUTOMOTIVE	AREA	U.S. AVG
Average commute time	22.0 min.	22.6 min.	Miles to nearest major airport	73	46	Insurance, annual premium	$935	$1,011
Commute by auto	93.9%	88.7%	Type of local airport	Large		Gas, cost per gallon	$1.39	$1.50
Commute by mass transit	.7%	1.8%	No. daily airline departures	729	294	Daily vehicle miles per capita	31.7	23.0
Work at home	1.5%	3.9%	Amtrak service	Yes				
Mass transit miles per capita	2.8	8.0	No. interstate highways	1	1			

LEISURE SCORE: 45/RANK: 181

DINING & SHOPPING	AREA	U.S. AVG	ENTERTAINMENT	AREA	U.S. AVG	OUTDOOR ACTIVITIES	AREA	U.S. AVG
Restaurant rating	1	1	Professional sports rating	3	4	Golf-course rating	3	4
No. outlet malls	0	2	College sports rating	2	4	Ski-area rating	1	4
No. Starbucks	1	11	Zoo/aquarium rating	1	3	National Park rating	5	3
No. warehouse clubs	3	4	Amusement park rating	1	3	Sq. miles inland water	6.0	4.0
			Botanical garden/arboretum rating	6	3	Miles of coastline	31.9	11.4

ARTS & CULTURE SCORE: 55/RANK: 152

MEDIA & LIBRARIES	AREA	U.S. AVG	PERFORMING ARTS	AREA	U.S. AVG	MUSEUMS	AREA	U.S. AVG
Arts radio rating	1	3	Classical music rating	4	4	Overall museum rating	7	6
No. public libraries	21	28	Ballet/dance rating	3	3	Art museum rating	5	5
Library volumes per capita	2.8	2.8	Professional theater rating	1	3	Science museum rating	5	4
			University arts programs rating	4	5	Children's museum rating	1	3

Bellingham, WA

Score: 80.0   Rank: 38

Profile: Small city
Location: East shore of Puget Sound in extreme northwest Washington, 25 miles south of Canadian border
Elevation: 68 feet
Time zone: Pacific Standard Time

PRO	CON
Attractive setting	Clouds and rain
Pleasant summers	Economic cycles
Nearby recreation	Home prices

Bellingham is a lush, green, and revitalizing city 80 miles north of Seattle. A thriving lumber and paper-mill town and seaport for outbound forest products, the city is now becoming an important passenger gateway to Alaska and the San Juan Islands to the west. Some of the mills—notably a major Georgia-Pacific mill in town—have closed. Despite that, projections for future economic growth are healthy. The Fairhaven area south of town is a revitalized Victorian historic district. Lush wooded residential areas farther south along "Chuckanut Drive" have great views of the San Juan Islands to the west and have become a favorite retirement destination. Other parts of town have a more working-class flavor. Big-city amenities are available to the south in Seattle and to the north in Vancouver, British Columbia. Home prices

are high on a state and national scale. While summers are very pleasant, other periods are among the cloudiest and rainiest in the United States. For those tolerant of these negatives and looking for a historic small town in a beautiful setting, Bellingham is a good option.

Bellingham sits in a narrow and mainly level coastal plain along the Puget Sound. To the east and north the land rises sharply to low plateaus with mixed coniferous forests and cleared land. To the south the area is hilly with dense coniferous forests. The San Juan Islands rise up from the Puget Sound to the west, and the 11,000-foot Mount Baker punctuates the sky 25 miles east. The climate is decidedly marine. The orientation of the city towards the Sound and the hills and mountains to the east allow cool, moist marine air to dominate. The pleasantly cool summers are the sunniest, driest time of year, albeit with some clouds and rain. The rest of the year is cloudy more often than not, with periods of mostly light rain. The good news: The rains are seldom torrential and they seldom turn to snow. Winters are damp and chilly but not cold; unlike most areas at this latitude, there are no days below zero and days below 20°F are rare. First freeze is early October, last is May 1.

POPULATION

DEMOGRAPHICS	AREA	U.S. AVG	ETHNIC COMPOSITION	AREA	U.S. AVG	RESIDENT PROFILE	AREA	U.S. AVG
Population	174,362		White	93.8%	75.1%	Single	40.3%	43.6%
Population density per sq. mile	82.2	447.3	Black	.6%	12.3%	Married	59.7%	56.4%
Population growth	36.5%	16.1%	Asian	1.8%	3.6%	Divorced	9.4%	8.4%
Median age	34.5	35.5	American Indian	2.7%	.9%	Separated	2.4%	3.0%
Average family size	2.6	2.7	Hispanic	4.1%	12.5%	Married with children	28.2%	28.7%
			Diversity measure	24.7%	35.2%	Single with children	8.4%	10.1%

ECONOMY & JOBS SCORE: 53/RANK: 153

INCOME	AREA	U.S. AVG	EMPLOYMENT	AREA	U.S. AVG	LARGEST EMPLOYING INDUSTRY
Per capita income	$22,202	$23,420	Unemployment rate	5.8%	6.1%	Food Manufacturing
Household income	$41,931	$46,060	Recent job growth	1.8%	.9%	
Household income < $25K	26.1%	26.4%	Projected future job growth	25.7%	15.1%	
Household income > $75K	20.0%	24.5%	White collar	51.9%	54.5%	
Household income growth	47.5%	57.3%	Blue collar	48.1%	45.5%	

COST OF LIVING SCORE: 47/RANK: 174

INDEXES & TAXES	AREA	U.S. AVG	HOUSING	AREA	U.S. AVG	NECESSITIES	AREA	U.S. AVG
Cost of Living Index	106.6	100.0	Median home price	$183,660	$160,100	Food Index	103.0	100.0
Financial Progress Index	83.8	100.0	Home price appreciation	5.7%	7.1%	Housing Index	114.1	100.0
Income tax rate	0.000%	4.625%	Median rent	$747	$670	Utilities Index	68.6	100.0
Sales tax rate	8.200%	6.474%	Homes owned	59.6%	63.9%	Transportation Index	110.7	100.0
Property tax rate	$8.9	$15.6	Homes rented	20.8%	25.3%	Healthcare Index	119.0	100.0
			Housing affordability	48.0%	54.5%	Miscellaneous Cost Index	105.6	100.0

CLIMATE SCORE: 81/RANK: 61

TEMPERATURE	AREA	U.S. AVG	PRECIPITATION	AREA	U.S. AVG	COMFORTS & HAZARDS	AREA	U.S. AVG
January low	33.0°F	26.4°F	Annual inches precipitation	39.0	35.9	July relative humidity	74.0%	68.8%
July high	75.1°F	86.7°F	Annual inches snowfall	15.0	24.2	Annual days mostly sunny	136	212
Annual days > 90°F	3	38	Annual days precipitation	160	111	Annual days with thunderstorms	7	39
Annual days < 32°F	32	88	Annual days rain > 0.5 inches	24	23	Tornado risk score	0	19
Annual days < 0°F	0	6	Annual days snow > 1.5 inches	2	6	Hurricane risk score	0	15

TEMPERATURE

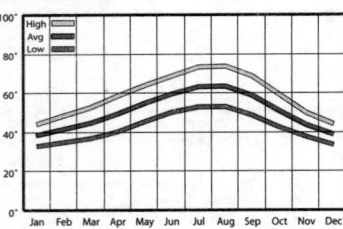

PRECIPITATION

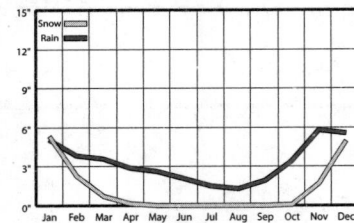

DAYS OF CLOUDS & PRECIPITATION

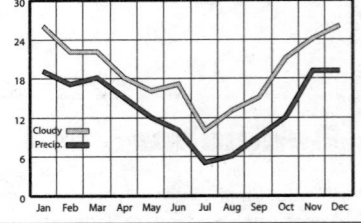

EDUCATION SCORE: 58/RANK: 137

ACHIEVEMENT	AREA	U.S. AVG	PUBLIC SCHOOLS	AREA	U.S. AVG	HIGHER EDUCATION	AREA	U.S. AVG
High school degree	88.5%	80.2%	Expenditures per pupil	$5,593	$5,894	No. 2-year colleges	2	3
2-year college degree	8.5%	6.2%	Student/teacher ratio	19.7	16.7	No. 4-year colleges/universities	1	4
4-year college degree	18.3%	15.8%	Attending public school	91.2%	90.2%	No. highly ranked universities	0	1
Graduate/professional degree	8.9%	9.6%	State SAT score	1062*	1020			
			State ACT score	22.5	21.0			

HEALTH & HEALTHCARE SCORE: 68/RANK: 104

HAZARDS & ILLNESSES	AREA	U.S. AVG	HEALTHCARE	AREA	U.S. AVG
Air-quality score	49	45	Physicians per capita	226.5	261.1
Water-quality score	13	33	Hospital beds per capita	128.9	432.2
Pollen/allergy score	48	61	No. teaching hospitals	0	4
Stress score	83	50	Cost per doctor visit	$72	$67
Cancer mortality per capita	153.2	169.0	Cost per dental visit	$113	$82
Depression days per month	4.1	2.8	Cost per daily hospital room	$516	$733

CRIME SCORE: 38/RANK: 204

CRIME	AREA	U.S. AVG
Violent crime rate	230.1	456.0
Change in violent crime rate	-30.7%	-17.2%
Property crime rate	4,928.9	3,950.0
Change in property crime rate	-8.4%	-16.8%

TRANSPORTATION SCORE: 67/RANK: 107

COMMUTE	AREA	U.S. AVG	INTERCITY SERVICES	AREA	U.S. AVG	AUTOMOTIVE	AREA	U.S. AVG
Average commute time	20.8 min.	22.6 min.	Miles to nearest major airport	90	46	Insurance, annual premium	$979	$1,011
Commute by auto	86.1%	88.7%	Type of local airport	Large		Gas, cost per gallon	$1.62	$1.50
Commute by mass transit	.8%	1.8%	No. daily airline departures	698	294	Daily vehicle miles per capita	19.2	23.0
Work at home	7.1%	3.9%	Amtrak service	Yes				
Mass transit miles per capita	14.4	8.0	No. interstate highways	1	1			

LEISURE SCORE: 63/RANK: 124

DINING & SHOPPING	AREA	U.S. AVG	ENTERTAINMENT	AREA	U.S. AVG	OUTDOOR ACTIVITIES	AREA	U.S. AVG
Restaurant rating	1	1	Professional sports rating	2	4	Golf-course rating	1	4
No. outlet malls	1	2	College sports rating	5	4	Ski-area rating	8	4
No. Starbucks	8	11	Zoo/aquarium rating	1	3	National Park rating	10	3
No. warehouse clubs	3	4	Amusement park rating	1	3	Sq. miles inland water	5.0	4.0
			Botanical garden/arboretum rating	1	3	Miles of coastline	0.0	11.4

ARTS & CULTURE SCORE: 19/RANK: 266

MEDIA & LIBRARIES	AREA	U.S. AVG	PERFORMING ARTS	AREA	U.S. AVG	MUSEUMS	AREA	U.S. AVG
Arts radio rating	5	3	Classical music rating	3	4	Overall museum rating	5	6
No. public libraries	11	28	Ballet/dance rating	3	3	Art museum rating	5	5
Library volumes per capita	3.3	2.8	Professional theater rating	1	3	Science museum rating	3	4
			University arts programs rating	4	5	Children's museum rating	5	3

Benton Harbor, MI

Score: 35.0   Rank: 299

Profile: Small city
Location: Southwestern Michigan on the shore of Lake Michigan
Elevation: 623 feet
Time zone: Eastern Standard Time

PRO	CON
Nearby beaches and water	Recent events
Cost of living	Low educational attainment
Healthcare	Arts and culture

Benton Harbor, and twin city St. Joseph, originally served as an agricultural port for the area. Areas around Benton Harbor are known around the Midwest for almost southern-California-like beaches and summer recreation. Driven in part by tourism, the economy is on the rebound, and cost of living is reasonable. What isn't captured by the numbers—and has made headlines recently—is the urban divide between Benton Harbor and St. Joseph to the south. The racial and economic profiles are diametrically opposed, with Benton Harbor largely African American and impoverished, and St. Joseph mostly Caucasian and relatively prosperous. These differences led to racial tension and economic gridlock in 2003, events that have negatively affected the *Cities Ranked & Rated* ranking.

The area contains mostly level to gently rolling terrain inland with areas of deciduous forest. The climate is mostly continental with moderation from Lake Michigan including fewer temperature extremes, later and cooler springs, and longer and warmer falls than much of the rest of the state. Summer days are pleasantly warm, with lake breezes and a few weeks of hot, humid weather. Most summer nights are comfortable. Winters are cloudy with strong northwesterly winds and occasional heavy lake-effect snows. Prolonged cold waves are infrequent but below-zero temperatures are fairly common. First freeze is early October, last is late April.

POPULATION

DEMOGRAPHICS	AREA	U.S. AVG	ETHNIC COMPOSITION	AREA	U.S. AVG	RESIDENT PROFILE	AREA	U.S. AVG
Population	162,285		White	87.8%	75.1%	Single	44.1%	43.6%
Population density per sq. mile	284.2	447.3	Black	9.5%	12.3%	Married	55.9%	56.4%
Population growth	.6%	16.1%	Asian	1.7%	3.6%	Divorced	8.5%	8.4%
Median age	37.9	35.5	American Indian	.5%	.9%	Separated	2.3%	3.0%
Average family size	2.5	2.7	Hispanic	2.4%	12.5%	Married with children	25.2%	28.7%
			Diversity measure	35.8%	35.2%	Single with children	10.5%	10.1%

ECONOMY & JOBS SCORE: 82/RANK: 58

INCOME	AREA	U.S. AVG	EMPLOYMENT	AREA	U.S. AVG	LARGEST EMPLOYING INDUSTRY
Per capita income	$22,825	$23,420	Unemployment rate	7.2%	6.1%	Machinery Manufacturing
Household income	$44,120	$46,060	Recent job growth	.9%	.9%	
Household income < $25K	28.0%	26.4%	Projected future job growth	7.7%	15.1%	
Household income > $75K	21.8%	24.5%	White collar	51.0%	54.5%	
Household income growth	61.6%	57.3%	Blue collar	49.0%	45.5%	

COST OF LIVING — SCORE: 33/RANK: 222

INDEXES & TAXES	AREA	U.S. AVG	HOUSING	AREA	U.S. AVG	NECESSITIES	AREA	U.S. AVG
Cost of Living Index	84.9	100.0	Median home price	$113,710	$160,100	Food Index	89.6	100.0
Financial Progress Index	110.7	100.0	Home price appreciation	6.3%	7.1%	Housing Index	70.6	100.0
Income tax rate	4.400%	4.625%	Median rent	$542	$670	Utilities Index	90.5	100.0
Sales tax rate	6.000%	6.474%	Homes owned	57.1%	63.9%	Transportation Index	98.6	100.0
Property tax rate	$14.0	$15.6	Homes rented	19.7%	25.3%	Healthcare Index	91.1	100.0
			Housing affordability	57.0%	54.5%	Miscellaneous Cost Index	94.3	100.0

CLIMATE — SCORE: 0/RANK: 330

TEMPERATURE	AREA	U.S. AVG	PRECIPITATION	AREA	U.S. AVG	COMFORTS & HAZARDS	AREA	U.S. AVG
January low	17.0°F	26.4°F	Annual inches precipitation	34.0	35.9	July relative humidity	67.0%	68.8%
July high	84.4°F	86.7°F	Annual inches snowfall	40.0	24.2	Annual days mostly sunny	197	212
Annual days > 90°F	21	38	Annual days precipitation	123	111	Annual days with thunderstorms	40	39
Annual days < 32°F	119	88	Annual days rain > 0.5 inches	20	23	Tornado risk score	28	19
Annual days < 0°F	7	6	Annual days snow > 1.5 inches	9	6	Hurricane risk score	2	15

TEMPERATURE

PRECIPITATION

DAYS OF CLOUDS & PRECIPITATION

EDUCATION — SCORE: 30/RANK: 231

ACHIEVEMENT	AREA	U.S. AVG	PUBLIC SCHOOLS	AREA	U.S. AVG	HIGHER EDUCATION	AREA	U.S. AVG
High school degree	81.9%	80.2%	Expenditures per pupil	$6,347	$5,894	No. 2-year colleges	1	3
2-year college degree	7.7%	6.2%	Student/teacher ratio	17.0	16.7	No. 4-year colleges/universities	1	4
4-year college degree	12.2%	15.8%	Attending public school	88.1%	90.2%	No. highly ranked universities	0	1
Graduate/professional degree	7.4%	9.6%	State SAT score	1140	1020			
			State ACT score	21.3*	21.0			

HEALTH & HEALTHCARE — SCORE: 59/RANK: 134

HAZARDS & ILLNESSES	AREA	U.S. AVG	HEALTHCARE	AREA	U.S. AVG
Air-quality score	24	45	Physicians per capita	165.1	261.1
Water-quality score	19	33	Hospital beds per capita	647.6	432.2
Pollen/allergy score	55	61	No. teaching hospitals	0	4
Stress score	70	50	Cost per doctor visit	$64	$67
Cancer mortality per capita	174.7	169.0	Cost per dental visit	$82	$82
Depression days per month	4.2	2.8	Cost per daily hospital room	$583	$733

CRIME — SCORE: 26/RANK: 245

CRIME	AREA	U.S. AVG
Violent crime rate	501.5	456.0
Change in violent crime rate	-49.0%	-17.2%
Property crime rate	3,880.4	3,950.0
Change in property crime rate	-26.7%	-16.8%

TRANSPORTATION — SCORE: 48/RANK: 171

COMMUTE	AREA	U.S. AVG	INTERCITY SERVICES	AREA	U.S. AVG	AUTOMOTIVE	AREA	U.S. AVG
Average commute time	20.0 min.	22.6 min.	Miles to nearest major airport	30	46	Insurance, annual premium	$960	$1,011
Commute by auto	88.9%	88.7%	Type of local airport	Small		Gas, cost per gallon	$1.52	$1.50
Commute by mass transit	.5%	1.8%	No. daily airline departures	54	294	Daily vehicle miles per capita	29.8	23.0
Work at home	3.7%	3.9%	Amtrak service	Yes				
Mass transit miles per capita	2.5	8.0	No. interstate highways	2	1			

LEISURE — SCORE: 43/RANK: 189

DINING & SHOPPING	AREA	U.S. AVG	ENTERTAINMENT	AREA	U.S. AVG	OUTDOOR ACTIVITIES	AREA	U.S. AVG
Restaurant rating	1	1	Professional sports rating	2	4	Golf-course rating	3	4
No. outlet malls	2	2	College sports rating	1	4	Ski-area rating	5	4
No. Starbucks	0	11	Zoo/aquarium rating	1	3	National Park rating	1	3
No. warehouse clubs	1	4	Amusement park rating	1	3	Sq. miles inland water	2.0	4.0
			Botanical garden/arboretum rating	4	3	Miles of coastline	44.2	11.4

ARTS & CULTURE — SCORE: 8/RANK: 302

MEDIA & LIBRARIES	AREA	U.S. AVG	PERFORMING ARTS	AREA	U.S. AVG	MUSEUMS	AREA	U.S. AVG
Arts radio rating	1	3	Classical music rating	1	4	Overall museum rating	5	6
No. public libraries	14	28	Ballet/dance rating	1	3	Art museum rating	3	5
Library volumes per capita	4.9	2.8	Professional theater rating	1	3	Science museum rating	2	4
			University arts programs rating	2	5	Children's museum rating	4	3

Bergen-Passaic, NJ

Score: 56.4   **Rank:** 176

Profile: Commuter community
Location: Northeastern corner of New Jersey, adjacent to New York State and across the lower Hudson from New York City
Elevation: 72 feet
Time zone: Eastern Standard Time

PRO	CON
Close to New York City	Cost of living
Attractive residential areas	Commute time
Low crime rate	Low employment growth

The Bergen-Passaic area is a complex patchwork of commercial and residential activity, with over 100 villages and towns. Many of these small towns have an upscale, rural character surprising for the proximity to New York City. Only four of these communities— Teaneck, Paramus, Bergenfield, and Paterson—have populations exceeding 25,000. The northern part of Bergen County is particularly pleasant, with mature, wooded residential areas and small-town centers. There is good rail service to New York and good recreational opportunities to the north. Moving south towards Paramus and Passaic, the area has a more middle-class feel, with suburbs, shopping malls, and a variety of commercial/industrial establishments. There are areas of poverty and urban decay around Paterson and other larger, older settlements. Several corporations, such as Union Camp, Toys "R" Us, and Becton, Dickinson and Company, have their headquarters here. It's also a favorite location for U.S. subsidiaries of European companies. The cost of living and housing are the highest in New Jersey and among the highest in the nation.

The area starts at the east with high, densely wooded bluffs overlooking the Hudson River across from Upper Manhattan, the Bronx, and Yonkers. Most of the area is rolling to hilly and heavily wooded, with a few flat and heavily developed areas and a series of straight valleys serving as transportation corridors. The climate is predominantly continental with four distinct seasons. The area is warm and humid in the summer; afternoon thundershowers are common. Winters are cool and wet, receiving both snow and rain. Heavy snows do occur, particularly with coastal "noreaster" storms, and freezing rain once or twice a winter is common. Below-zero temperatures are not common. Spring is variable and wet, while fall is pleasant usually with at least one period of Indian summer. First freeze is mid-October, last is late April.

POPULATION

DEMOGRAPHICS	AREA	U.S. AVG	ETHNIC COMPOSITION	AREA	U.S. AVG	RESIDENT PROFILE	AREA	U.S. AVG
Population	1,391,737		White	80.2%	75.1%	Single	45.0%	43.6%
Population density per sq. mile	3,319.6	447.3	Black	7.3%	12.3%	Married	55.0%	56.4%
Population growth	8.9%	16.1%	Asian	8.6%	3.6%	Divorced	5.9%	8.4%
Median age	38.0	35.5	American Indian	.2%	.9%	Separated	3.0%	3.0%
Average family size	2.7	2.7	Hispanic	12.9%	12.5%	Married with children	26.7%	28.7%
			Diversity measure	51.9%	35.2%	Single with children	7.4%	10.1%

ECONOMY & JOBS SCORE: 89/RANK: 36

INCOME	AREA	U.S. AVG	EMPLOYMENT	AREA	U.S. AVG	LARGEST EMPLOYING INDUSTRY
Per capita income	$34,078	$23,420	Unemployment rate	6.1%	6.1%	Computer and Electronic Product Manufacturing
Household income	$69,764	$46,060	Recent job growth	1.1%	.9%	
Household income < $25K	14.9%	26.4%	Projected future job growth	4.0%	15.1%	
Household income > $75K	45.6%	24.5%	White collar	65.7%	54.5%	
Household income growth	54.6%	57.3%	Blue collar	34.3%	45.5%	

COST OF LIVING SCORE: 3/RANK: 319

INDEXES & TAXES	AREA	U.S. AVG	HOUSING	AREA	U.S. AVG	NECESSITIES	AREA	U.S. AVG
Cost of Living Index	156.5	100.0	Median home price	$350,200	$160,100	Food Index	118.7	100.0
Financial Progress Index	95.0	100.0	Home price appreciation	12.5%	7.1%	Housing Index	217.5	100.0
Income tax rate	2.450%	4.625%	Median rent	$1,133	$670	Utilities Index	133.6	100.0
Sales tax rate	6.000%	6.474%	Homes owned	67.0%	63.9%	Transportation Index	119.7	100.0
Property tax rate	$24.9	$15.6	Homes rented	28.1%	25.3%	Healthcare Index	141.6	100.0
			Housing affordability	47.0%	54.5%	Miscellaneous Cost Index	116.9	100.0

CLIMATE SCORE: 47/RANK: 174

TEMPERATURE	AREA	U.S. AVG	PRECIPITATION	AREA	U.S. AVG	COMFORTS & HAZARDS	AREA	U.S. AVG
January low	24.3°F	26.4°F	Annual inches precipitation	41.5	35.9	July relative humidity	65.0%	68.8%
July high	85.6°F	86.7°F	Annual inches snowfall	28.4	24.2	Annual days mostly sunny	207	212
Annual days > 90°F	20	38	Annual days precipitation	129	111	Annual days with thunderstorms	25	39
Annual days < 32°F	87	88	Annual days rain > 0.5 inches	26	23	Tornado risk score	12	19
Annual days < 0°F	0	6	Annual days snow > 1.5 inches	5	6	Hurricane risk score	16	15

TEMPERATURE

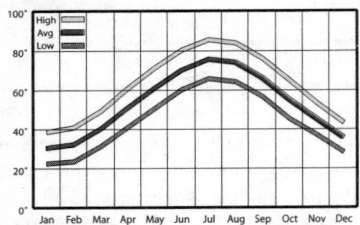

PRECIPITATION

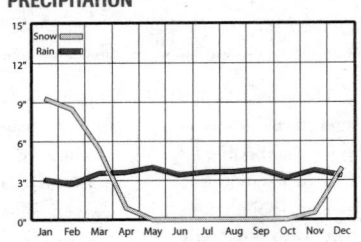

DAYS OF CLOUDS & PRECIPITATION

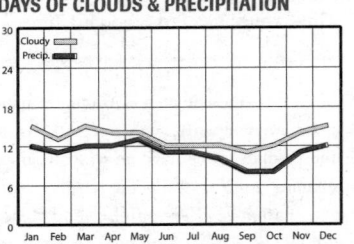

EDUCATION SCORE: 64/RANK: 119

ACHIEVEMENT	AREA	U.S. AVG	PUBLIC SCHOOLS	AREA	U.S. AVG	HIGHER EDUCATION	AREA	U.S. AVG
High school degree	82.1%	80.2%	Expenditures per pupil	$10,178	$5,894	No. 2-year colleges	3	3
2-year college degree	4.8%	6.2%	Student/teacher ratio	14.5	16.7	No. 4-year colleges/universities	4	4
4-year college degree	20.7%	15.8%	Attending public school	82.8%	90.2%	No. highly ranked universities	1	1
Graduate/professional degree	11.8%	9.6%	State SAT score	1016*	1020			
			State ACT score	21.2	21.0			

HEALTH & HEALTHCARE SCORE: 25/RANK: 247

CRIME SCORE: 91/RANK: 28

HAZARDS & ILLNESSES	AREA	U.S. AVG	HEALTHCARE	AREA	U.S. AVG	CRIME	AREA	U.S. AVG
Air-quality score	99	45	Physicians per capita	372.8	261.1	Violent crime rate	280.7	456.0
Water-quality score	13	33	Hospital beds per capita	387.7	432.2	Change in violent crime rate	-14.2%	-17.2%
Pollen/allergy score	62	61	No. teaching hospitals	4	4	Property crime rate	2,340.1	3,950.0
Stress score	13	50	Cost per doctor visit	$70	$67	Change in property crime rate	-27.5%	-16.8%
Cancer mortality per capita	188.5	169.0	Cost per dental visit	$121	$82			
Depression days per month	2.6	2.8	Cost per daily hospital room	$2,812	$733			

TRANSPORTATION SCORE: 97/RANK: 9

COMMUTE	AREA	U.S. AVG	INTERCITY SERVICES	AREA	U.S. AVG	AUTOMOTIVE	AREA	U.S. AVG
Average commute time	28.6 min.	22.6 min.	Miles to nearest major airport	15	46	Insurance, annual premium	$1,467	$1,011
Commute by auto	84.7%	88.7%	Type of local airport	Large		Gas, cost per gallon	$1.46	$1.50
Commute by mass transit	8.6%	1.8%	No. daily airline departures	694	294	Daily vehicle miles per capita	22.8	23.0
Work at home	2.2%	3.9%	Amtrak service	No				
Mass transit miles per capita	24.9	8.0	No. interstate highways	1	1			

LEISURE SCORE: 97/RANK: 12

DINING & SHOPPING	AREA	U.S. AVG	ENTERTAINMENT	AREA	U.S. AVG	OUTDOOR ACTIVITIES	AREA	U.S. AVG
Restaurant rating	1	1	Professional sports rating	10	4	Golf-course rating	9	4
No. outlet malls	10	2	College sports rating	10	4	Ski-area rating	5	4
No. Starbucks	19	11	Zoo/aquarium rating	7	3	National Park rating	3	3
No. warehouse clubs	6	4	Amusement park rating	5	3	Sq. miles inland water	6.0	4.0
			Botanical garden/arboretum rating	7	3	Miles of coastline	0.0	11.4

ARTS & CULTURE SCORE: 68/RANK: 104

MEDIA & LIBRARIES	AREA	U.S. AVG	PERFORMING ARTS	AREA	U.S. AVG	MUSEUMS	AREA	U.S. AVG
Arts radio rating	4	3	Classical music rating	7	4	Overall museum rating	8	6
No. public libraries	84	28	Ballet/dance rating	8	3	Art museum rating	8	5
Library volumes per capita	4.2	2.8	Professional theater rating	8	3	Science museum rating	7	4
			University arts programs rating	10	5	Children's museum rating	9	3

Billings, MT

Profile: Small city
Location: South-central Montana along the Yellowstone River
Elevation: 3,570 feet
Time zone: Mountain Standard Time

| **Score: 65.4** | **Rank: 106** |

PRO	CON
Nearby mountains	Harsh winters
Water recreation	Isolation
Pleasant summers	Low ethnic diversity

Montana's largest city, Billings is a cultural, business, and historic center. Since the days of Lewis and Clark, it has also served as a transportation gateway between the plains to the east and the mountain areas to the west. Advantages include a small-town feel and a few big-city amenities. The area is characterized by the dramatic landscape to the west, pleasant summer weather, and an overall western style. The historic Little Bighorn Battlefield National Monument area is to the southeast. Downsides include winter cold and the 500-plus mile trip to the nearest big city, Denver.

The area is situated in the Yellowstone River valley between the Great Plains and the Rocky Mountains. The Yellowstone River, a world-class fly-fishing stream, bisects the city, and the surrounding countryside is mainly rolling plains and irrigated farmland. To the west, the land rises and becomes more rugged towards the Absaroka Range with peaks exceeding 11,000 feet. The climate is semiarid continental with features of both the northern plains and nearby mountains. The summer season is warm with abundant sunshine and low humidity. Nights are cool from altitude and cool mountain breezes. Afternoon thunderstorms are common but don't bring much rain. Winters are cold and sometimes windy but with mild periods. Spring brings wide fluctuations with periods of cool, cloudy, rainy days. Falls vary in length; some last into December, others end in September. May and June are the wettest months, while winter is driest. Heavy snows occur in fall and spring but do not accumulate. First freeze averages late September but can be late August, last freeze is mid-May but can be as late as the end of June.

POPULATION

DEMOGRAPHICS	AREA	U.S. AVG	ETHNIC COMPOSITION	AREA	U.S. AVG	RESIDENT PROFILE	AREA	U.S. AVG
Population	131,622		White	96.8%	75.1%	Single	35.4%	43.6%
Population density per sq. mile	49.9	447.3	Black	.2%	12.3%	Married	64.6%	56.4%
Population growth	16.0%	16.1%	Asian	.4%	3.6%	Divorced	8.1%	8.4%
Median age	37.1	35.5	American Indian	1.8%	.9%	Separated	1.9%	3.0%
Average family size	2.6	2.7	Hispanic	2.5%	12.5%	Married with children	31.2%	28.7%
			Diversity measure	17.3%	35.2%	Single with children	7.5%	10.1%

ECONOMY & JOBS
SCORE: 100/RANK: 1

INCOME	AREA	U.S. AVG	EMPLOYMENT	AREA	U.S. AVG	LARGEST EMPLOYING INDUSTRY
Per capita income	$21,715	$23,420	Unemployment rate	3.1%	6.1%	Healthcare and Social Assistance
Household income	$41,554	$46,060	Recent job growth	11.2%	.9%	
Household income < $25K	28.1%	26.4%	Projected future job growth	15.7%	15.1%	
Household income > $75K	20.0%	24.5%	White collar	57.2%	54.5%	
Household income growth	59.8%	57.3%	Blue collar	42.8%	45.5%	

COST OF LIVING
SCORE: 58/RANK: 136

INDEXES & TAXES	AREA	U.S. AVG	HOUSING	AREA	U.S. AVG	NECESSITIES	AREA	U.S. AVG
Cost of Living Index	90.3	100.0	Median home price	$119,690	$160,100	Food Index	97.4	100.0
Financial Progress Index	98.0	100.0	Home price appreciation	5.5%	7.1%	Housing Index	74.3	100.0
Income tax rate	11.000%	4.625%	Median rent	$563	$670	Utilities Index	103.3	100.0
Sales tax rate	0.000%	6.474%	Homes owned	65.3%	63.9%	Transportation Index	100.4	100.0
Property tax rate	$15.8	$15.6	Homes rented	20.6%	25.3%	Healthcare Index	102.6	100.0
			Housing affordability	52.0%	54.5%	Miscellaneous Cost Index	98.0	100.0

CLIMATE
SCORE: 10/RANK: 295

TEMPERATURE	AREA	U.S. AVG	PRECIPITATION	AREA	U.S. AVG	COMFORTS & HAZARDS	AREA	U.S. AVG
January low	12.5°F	26.4°F	Annual inches precipitation	14.0	35.9	July relative humidity	55.0%	68.8%
July high	85.6°F	86.7°F	Annual inches snowfall	56.0	24.2	Annual days mostly sunny	206	212
Annual days > 90°F	28	38	Annual days precipitation	95	111	Annual days with thunderstorms	29	39
Annual days < 32°F	152	88	Annual days rain > 0.5 inches	8	23	Tornado risk score	7	19
Annual days < 0°F	18	6	Annual days snow > 1.5 inches	15	6	Hurricane risk score	0	15

TEMPERATURE

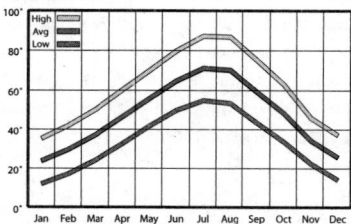

PRECIPITATION

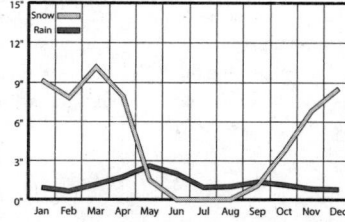

DAYS OF CLOUDS & PRECIPITATION

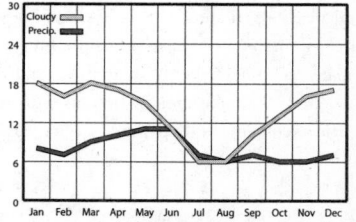

EDUCATION SCORE: 60/RANK: 132

ACHIEVEMENT	AREA	U.S. AVG	PUBLIC SCHOOLS	AREA	U.S. AVG	HIGHER EDUCATION	AREA	U.S. AVG
High school degree	88.7%	80.2%	Expenditures per pupil	$5,149	$5,894	No. 2-year colleges	1	3
2-year college degree	5.1%	6.2%	Student/teacher ratio	17.0	16.7	No. 4-year colleges/universities	2	4
4-year college degree	20.4%	15.8%	Attending public school	92.5%	90.2%	No. highly ranked universities	0	1
Graduate/professional degree	8.2%	9.6%	State SAT score	1081	1020			
			State ACT score	21.7*	21.0			

HEALTH & HEALTHCARE SCORE: 95/RANK: 14

CRIME SCORE: 83/RANK: 56

HAZARDS & ILLNESSES	AREA	U.S. AVG	HEALTHCARE	AREA	U.S. AVG	CRIME	AREA	U.S. AVG
Air-quality score	81	45	Physicians per capita	327.5	261.1	Violent crime rate	193.6	456.0
Water-quality score	30	33	Hospital beds per capita	419.8	432.2	Change in violent crime rate	-3.7%	-17.2%
Pollen/allergy score	27	61	No. teaching hospitals	2	4	Property crime rate	3,894.8	3,950.0
Stress score	6	50	Cost per doctor visit	$73	$67	Change in property crime rate	-49.1%	-16.8%
Cancer mortality per capita	161.4	169.0	Cost per dental visit	$88	$82			
Depression days per month	1.3	2.8	Cost per daily hospital room	$507	$733			

TRANSPORTATION SCORE: 81/RANK: 65

COMMUTE	AREA	U.S. AVG	INTERCITY SERVICES	AREA	U.S. AVG	AUTOMOTIVE	AREA	U.S. AVG
Average commute time	17.9 min.	22.6 min.	Miles to nearest major airport	1	46	Insurance, annual premium	$714	$1,011
Commute by auto	83.2%	88.7%	Type of local airport	Small		Gas, cost per gallon	$1.58	$1.50
Commute by mass transit	.3%	1.8%	No. daily airline departures	80	294	Daily vehicle miles per capita	15.2	23.0
Work at home	6.8%	3.9%	Amtrak service	No				
Mass transit miles per capita	6.8	8.0	No. interstate highways	2	1			

LEISURE SCORE: 41/RANK: 195

DINING & SHOPPING	AREA	U.S. AVG	ENTERTAINMENT	AREA	U.S. AVG	OUTDOOR ACTIVITIES	AREA	U.S. AVG
Restaurant rating	1	1	Professional sports rating	2	4	Golf-course rating	2	4
No. outlet malls	0	2	College sports rating	2	4	Ski-area rating	7	4
No. Starbucks	0	11	Zoo/aquarium rating	1	3	National Park rating	1	3
No. warehouse clubs	3	4	Amusement park rating	1	3	Sq. miles inland water	3.0	4.0
			Botanical garden/arboretum rating	1	3	Miles of coastline	0.0	11.4

ARTS & CULTURE SCORE: 34/RANK: 217

MEDIA & LIBRARIES	AREA	U.S. AVG	PERFORMING ARTS	AREA	U.S. AVG	MUSEUMS	AREA	U.S. AVG
Arts radio rating	1	3	Classical music rating	3	4	Overall museum rating	5	6
No. public libraries	2	28	Ballet/dance rating	1	3	Art museum rating	4	5
Library volumes per capita	2.3	2.8	Professional theater rating	1	3	Science museum rating	2	4
			University arts programs rating	5	5	Children's museum rating	1	3

Biloxi-Gulfport-Pascagoula, MS

Score: 36.0 **Rank:** 293

Profile: Coastal-city complex/Beach-town complex
Location: Mississippi Gulf Coast
Elevation: 15 feet
Time zone: Central Standard Time

PRO	CON
Beaches	Property crime
Winter climate	Tourist sprawl
Entertainment	Arts and culture

The cities of Biloxi, Gulfport, and Pascagoula lie at the base of the narrow Gulf extension of the state of Mississippi. Biloxi is more commercial, Gulfport is more of a residential beach community, and Pascagoula is more industrial with shipyards and other heavier industries. The entire coast developed as a second-class beach resort for locals and others looking for an alternative to Florida. There are some quality developments but more typical are the miles of commercial strips and new casinos, neither of which add to the physical attractiveness of the area. Biloxi is a center for the shrimping and fishing industries and has many good restaurants, activities, and museums related to the seafood trade. But the area is becoming more dependent on tourism, while the economy beyond that is relatively weak. There are a few historic attractions in Biloxi and cost of living is low on a national scale, but property crime is high and intellectual stimulation is noticeably absent.

The surrounding area is a flat coastal plain with barrier islands and peninsulas, and pine forests beginning north of town. The area is considerably influenced by the Gulf of Mexico. Summers are warm and humid but less so than inland. Sea breezes usually keep temperatures reasonable, particularly in late afternoon and evening. There may be a few cold snaps, but they seldom persist and freezes are infrequent. Summer thundershowers are frequent. Given the location and local topography, Biloxi is vulnerable to occasional hurricanes from the Gulf, and was wrecked by Hurricane Camille in 1969.

POPULATION

DEMOGRAPHICS	AREA	U.S. AVG	ETHNIC COMPOSITION	AREA	U.S. AVG	RESIDENT PROFILE	AREA	U.S. AVG
Population	368,868		White	75.7%	75.1%	Single	46.3%	43.6%
Population density per sq. mile	206.7	447.3	Black	21.1%	12.3%	Married	53.7%	56.4%
Population growth	18.1%	16.1%	Asian	2.7%	3.6%	Divorced	10.0%	8.4%
Median age	35.0	35.5	American Indian	.3%	.9%	Separated	3.5%	3.0%
Average family size	2.7	2.7	Hispanic	1.4%	12.5%	Married with children	29.2%	28.7%
			Diversity measure	40.0%	35.2%	Single with children	13.9%	10.1%

ECONOMY & JOBS SCORE: 6/RANK: 310

INCOME	AREA	U.S. AVG	EMPLOYMENT	AREA	U.S. AVG	LARGEST EMPLOYING INDUSTRY
Per capita income	$20,977	$23,420	Unemployment rate	4.6%	6.1%	Ship and Boat Building
Household income	$41,357	$46,060	Recent job growth	.9%	.9%	
Household income < $25K	30.1%	26.4%	Projected future job growth	19.5%	15.1%	
Household income > $75K	20.8%	24.5%	White collar	50.1%	54.5%	
Household income growth	74.9%	57.3%	Blue collar	49.9%	45.5%	

COST OF LIVING SCORE: 66/RANK: 113

INDEXES & TAXES	AREA	U.S. AVG	HOUSING	AREA	U.S. AVG	NECESSITIES	AREA	U.S. AVG
Cost of Living Index	84.5	100.0	Median home price	$100,400	$160,100	Food Index	94.1	100.0
Financial Progress Index	104.3	100.0	Home price appreciation	5.1%	7.1%	Housing Index	62.4	100.0
Income tax rate	5.000%	4.625%	Median rent	$573	$670	Utilities Index	107.4	100.0
Sales tax rate	7.000%	6.474%	Homes owned	58.7%	63.9%	Transportation Index	98.4	100.0
Property tax rate	$9.0	$15.6	Homes rented	27.1%	25.3%	Healthcare Index	91.7	100.0
			Housing affordability	59.0%	54.5%	Miscellaneous Cost Index	96.2	100.0

CLIMATE SCORE: 76/RANK: 79

TEMPERATURE	AREA	U.S. AVG	PRECIPITATION	AREA	U.S. AVG	COMFORTS & HAZARDS	AREA	U.S. AVG
January low	45.5°F	26.4°F	Annual inches precipitation	59.0	35.9	July relative humidity	77.0%	68.8%
July high	89.6°F	86.7°F	Annual inches snowfall	0.0	24.2	Annual days mostly sunny	219	212
Annual days > 90°F	52	38	Annual days precipitation	75	111	Annual days with thunderstorms	94	39
Annual days < 32°F	11	88	Annual days rain > 0.5 inches	37	23	Tornado risk score	30	19
Annual days < 0°F	0	6	Annual days snow > 1.5 inches	0	6	Hurricane risk score	57	15

TEMPERATURE

PRECIPITATION

DAYS OF CLOUDS & PRECIPITATION

EDUCATION SCORE: 24/RANK: 251

ACHIEVEMENT	AREA	U.S. AVG	PUBLIC SCHOOLS	AREA	U.S. AVG	HIGHER EDUCATION	AREA	U.S. AVG
High school degree	80.2%	80.2%	Expenditures per pupil	$4,455	$5,894	No. 2-year colleges	2	3
2-year college degree	8.8%	6.2%	Student/teacher ratio	17.1	16.7	No. 4-year colleges/universities	0	4
4-year college degree	12.0%	15.8%	Attending public school	91.1%	90.2%	No. highly ranked universities	0	1
Graduate/professional degree	6.3%	9.6%	State SAT score	1116	1020			
			State ACT score	18.7*	21.0			

HEALTH & HEALTHCARE SCORE: 17/RANK: 274

CRIME SCORE: 17/RANK: 272

HAZARDS & ILLNESSES	AREA	U.S. AVG	HEALTHCARE	AREA	U.S. AVG	CRIME	AREA	U.S. AVG
Air-quality score	49	45	Physicians per capita	235.9	261.1	Violent crime rate	371.3	456.0
Water-quality score	35	33	Hospital beds per capita	422.8	432.2	Change in violent crime rate	-28.5%	-17.2%
Pollen/allergy score	77	61	No. teaching hospitals	0	4	Property crime rate	5,653.3	3,950.0
Stress score	84	50	Cost per doctor visit	$69	$67	Change in property crime rate	4.5%	-16.8%
Cancer mortality per capita	182.1	169.0	Cost per dental visit	$77	$82			
Depression days per month	1.9	2.8	Cost per daily hospital room	$420	$733			

TRANSPORTATION SCORE: 12/RANK: 291

COMMUTE	AREA	U.S. AVG	INTERCITY SERVICES	AREA	U.S. AVG	AUTOMOTIVE	AREA	U.S. AVG
Average commute time	23.6 min.	22.6 min.	Miles to nearest major airport	45	46	Insurance, annual premium	$917	$1,011
Commute by auto	93.1%	88.7%	Type of local airport	Small		Gas, cost per gallon	$1.42	$1.50
Commute by mass transit	.5%	1.8%	No. daily airline departures	29	294	Daily vehicle miles per capita	24.4	23.0
Work at home	1.9%	3.9%	Amtrak service	Yes				
Mass transit miles per capita	4.4	8.0	No. interstate highways	1	1			

LEISURE SCORE: 33/RANK: 223

DINING & SHOPPING	AREA	U.S. AVG	ENTERTAINMENT	AREA	U.S. AVG	OUTDOOR ACTIVITIES	AREA	U.S. AVG
Restaurant rating	1	1	Professional sports rating	3	4	Golf-course rating	3	4
No. outlet malls	1	2	College sports rating	1	4	Ski-area rating	1	4
No. Starbucks	0	11	Zoo/aquarium rating	2	3	National Park rating	5	3
No. warehouse clubs	3	4	Amusement park rating	7	3	Sq. miles inland water	3.0	4.0
			Botanical garden/arboretum rating	1	3	Miles of coastline	30.3	11.4

ARTS & CULTURE SCORE: 32/RANK: 225

MEDIA & LIBRARIES	AREA	U.S. AVG	PERFORMING ARTS	AREA	U.S. AVG	MUSEUMS	AREA	U.S. AVG
Arts radio rating	5	3	Classical music rating	1	4	Overall museum rating	6	6
No. public libraries	22	28	Ballet/dance rating	1	3	Art museum rating	4	5
Library volumes per capita	1.8	2.8	Professional theater rating	1	3	Science museum rating	1	4
			University arts programs rating	1	5	Children's museum rating	1	3

Binghamton, NY

Score: 47.7   Rank: 241

Profile: Small city
Location: South-central New York, 10 miles north of Pennsylvania border
Elevation: 1,590 feet
Time zone: Eastern Standard Time

PRO
Cost of living
Central location
Low crime rate

CON
Climate
Entertainment
Economy

Binghamton is a diversified manufacturing center and transportation gateway. Manufacturers are varied and led today by IBM. The town itself is quiet and unremarkable, and offers little to do. However, the central location is near several areas of interest: the Finger Lakes and Ithaca to the northwest, where Cornell University provide cultural amenities; New York City to the southeast; and the Adirondacks to the northeast. The climate can be depressing, as Binghamton has the greatest number of cloudy days (214) per year of any city outside the Pacific Northwest, and ranks 14th highest in the U.S. for days of precipitation. Cost of living is reasonable but recent economic performance is mixed.

Binghamton is in a comparatively narrow valley at the confluence of the Susquehanna and Chenango rivers. Within a 5-mile radius hills rise to an elevation of 1,600 feet. The climate is humid continental. Located adjacent to the so-called St. Lawrence Valley storm track, the area has frequent and rapid weather changes. Summers are warm, but temperatures and humidity seldom become oppressing. Daytime temperatures rise rapidly, but hit up to 90°F only a few days each month. Summer evenings are typically cool. Winters are cold but not severe with daytime highs in the 20s and 30s and lows in the mid-teens to 20s. A few sub-zero readings occur each winter. Snowfall is moderate and much higher in the surrounding hills. The cloudiness and valley fogs arise from proximity to Lake Ontario and nearby landforms combined with the storm track location. First freeze is early October, last is early May.

POPULATION

DEMOGRAPHICS	AREA	U.S. AVG	ETHNIC COMPOSITION	AREA	U.S. AVG	RESIDENT PROFILE	AREA	U.S. AVG
Population	252,096		White	95.7%	75.1%	Single	41.4%	43.6%
Population density per sq. mile	205.7	447.3	Black	2.2%	12.3%	Married	58.6%	56.4%
Population growth	-4.7%	16.1%	Asian	1.4%	3.6%	Divorced	7.7%	8.4%
Median age	38.5	35.5	American Indian	.3%	.9%	Separated	3.6%	3.0%
Average family size	2.6	2.7	Hispanic	1.5%	12.5%	Married with children	30.2%	28.7%
			Diversity measure	15.7%	35.2%	Single with children	10.1%	10.1%

ECONOMY & JOBS SCORE: 55/RANK: 148

INCOME	AREA	U.S. AVG	EMPLOYMENT	AREA	U.S. AVG	LARGEST EMPLOYING INDUSTRY
Per capita income	$20,226	$23,420	Unemployment rate	5.1%	6.1%	Computer and Electronic Product Manufacturing
Household income	$38,750	$46,060	Recent job growth	-2.1%	.9%	
Household income < $25K	30.8%	26.4%	Projected future job growth	7.3%	15.1%	
Household income > $75K	17.1%	24.5%	White collar	58.0%	54.5%	
Household income growth	32.3%	57.3%	Blue collar	42.0%	45.5%	

COST OF LIVING SCORE: 37/RANK: 206

INDEXES & TAXES	AREA	U.S. AVG	HOUSING	AREA	U.S. AVG	NECESSITIES	AREA	U.S. AVG
Cost of Living Index	84.7	100.0	Median home price	$86,750	$160,100	Food Index	98.6	100.0
Financial Progress Index	97.5	100.0	Home price appreciation	4.5%	7.1%	Housing Index	53.9	100.0
Income tax rate	7.125%	4.625%	Median rent	$527	$670	Utilities Index	127.4	100.0
Sales tax rate	8.000%	6.474%	Homes owned	71.1%	63.9%	Transportation Index	98.8	100.0
Property tax rate	$32.5	$15.6	Homes rented	18.6%	25.3%	Healthcare Index	89.8	100.0
			Housing affordability	54.0%	54.5%	Miscellaneous Cost Index	100.3	100.0

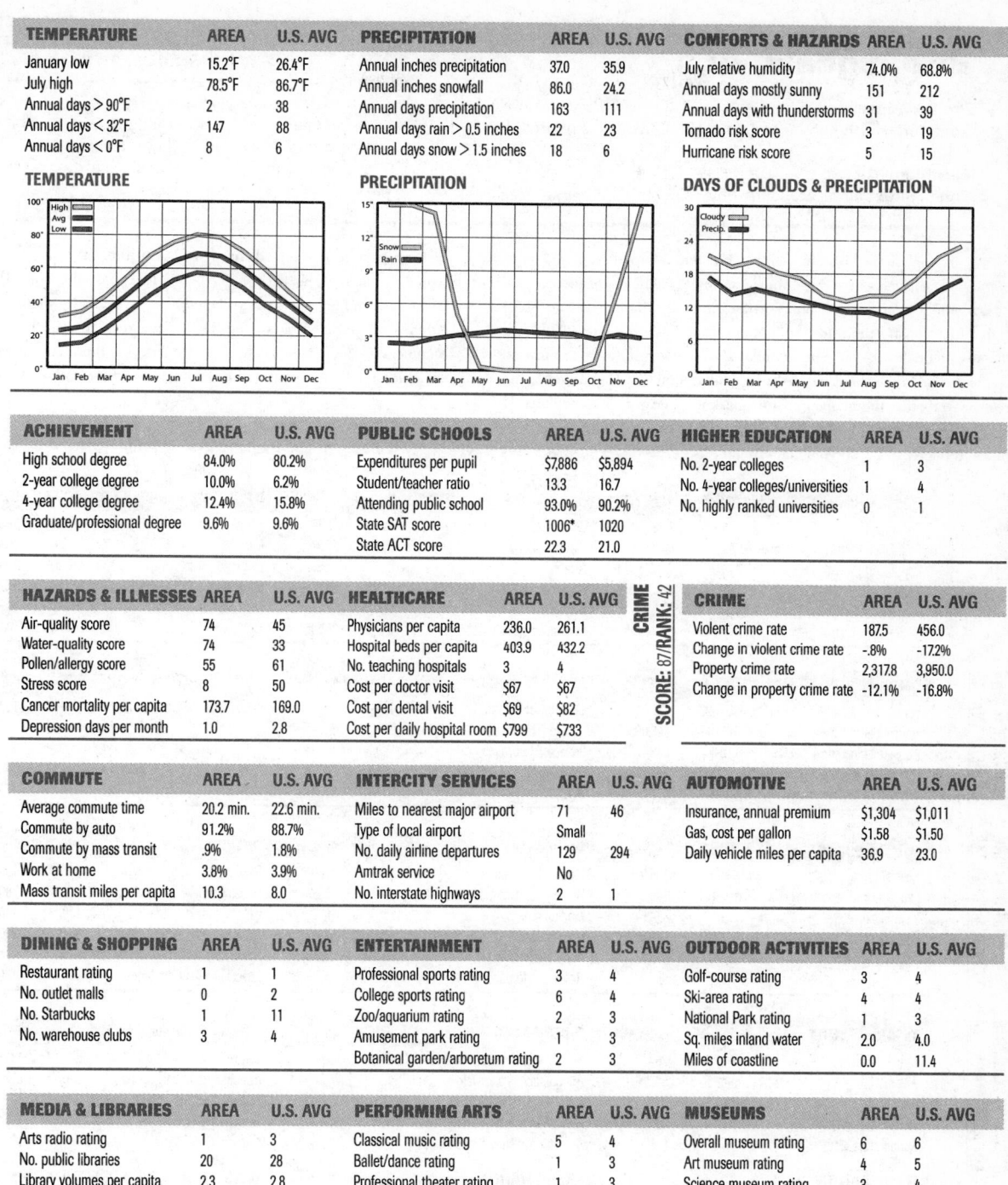

CLIMATE SCORE: 7/RANK: 305

TEMPERATURE	AREA	U.S. AVG	PRECIPITATION	AREA	U.S. AVG	COMFORTS & HAZARDS	AREA	U.S. AVG
January low	15.2°F	26.4°F	Annual inches precipitation	37.0	35.9	July relative humidity	74.0%	68.8%
July high	78.5°F	86.7°F	Annual inches snowfall	86.0	24.2	Annual days mostly sunny	151	212
Annual days > 90°F	2	38	Annual days precipitation	163	111	Annual days with thunderstorms	31	39
Annual days < 32°F	147	88	Annual days rain > 0.5 inches	22	23	Tornado risk score	3	19
Annual days < 0°F	8	6	Annual days snow > 1.5 inches	18	6	Hurricane risk score	5	15

TEMPERATURE

PRECIPITATION

DAYS OF CLOUDS & PRECIPITATION

EDUCATION SCORE: 79/RANK: 71

ACHIEVEMENT	AREA	U.S. AVG	PUBLIC SCHOOLS	AREA	U.S. AVG	HIGHER EDUCATION	AREA	U.S. AVG
High school degree	84.0%	80.2%	Expenditures per pupil	$7,886	$5,894	No. 2-year colleges	1	3
2-year college degree	10.0%	6.2%	Student/teacher ratio	13.3	16.7	No. 4-year colleges/universities	1	4
4-year college degree	12.4%	15.8%	Attending public school	93.0%	90.2%	No. highly ranked universities	0	1
Graduate/professional degree	9.6%	9.6%	State SAT score	1006*	1020			
			State ACT score	22.3	21.0			

HEALTH & HEALTHCARE SCORE: 77/RANK: 74

HAZARDS & ILLNESSES	AREA	U.S. AVG	HEALTHCARE	AREA	U.S. AVG	CRIME	AREA	U.S. AVG
Air-quality score	74	45	Physicians per capita	236.0	261.1	Violent crime rate	187.5	456.0
Water-quality score	74	33	Hospital beds per capita	403.9	432.2	Change in violent crime rate	-.8%	-17.2%
Pollen/allergy score	55	61	No. teaching hospitals	3	4	Property crime rate	2,317.8	3,950.0
Stress score	8	50	Cost per doctor visit	$67	$67	Change in property crime rate	-12.1%	-16.8%
Cancer mortality per capita	173.7	169.0	Cost per dental visit	$69	$82			
Depression days per month	1.0	2.8	Cost per daily hospital room	$799	$733			

CRIME SCORE: 87/RANK: 42

TRANSPORTATION SCORE: 69/RANK: 103

COMMUTE	AREA	U.S. AVG	INTERCITY SERVICES	AREA	U.S. AVG	AUTOMOTIVE	AREA	U.S. AVG
Average commute time	20.2 min.	22.6 min.	Miles to nearest major airport	71	46	Insurance, annual premium	$1,304	$1,011
Commute by auto	91.2%	88.7%	Type of local airport	Small		Gas, cost per gallon	$1.58	$1.50
Commute by mass transit	.9%	1.8%	No. daily airline departures	129	294	Daily vehicle miles per capita	36.9	23.0
Work at home	3.8%	3.9%	Amtrak service	No				
Mass transit miles per capita	10.3	8.0	No. interstate highways	2	1			

LEISURE SCORE: 38/RANK: 204

DINING & SHOPPING	AREA	U.S. AVG	ENTERTAINMENT	AREA	U.S. AVG	OUTDOOR ACTIVITIES	AREA	U.S. AVG
Restaurant rating	1	1	Professional sports rating	3	4	Golf-course rating	3	4
No. outlet malls	0	2	College sports rating	6	4	Ski-area rating	4	4
No. Starbucks	1	11	Zoo/aquarium rating	2	3	National Park rating	1	3
No. warehouse clubs	3	4	Amusement park rating	1	3	Sq. miles inland water	2.0	4.0
			Botanical garden/arboretum rating	2	3	Miles of coastline	0.0	11.4

ARTS & CULTURE SCORE: 56/RANK: 141

MEDIA & LIBRARIES	AREA	U.S. AVG	PERFORMING ARTS	AREA	U.S. AVG	MUSEUMS	AREA	U.S. AVG
Arts radio rating	1	3	Classical music rating	5	4	Overall museum rating	6	6
No. public libraries	20	28	Ballet/dance rating	1	3	Art museum rating	4	5
Library volumes per capita	2.3	2.8	Professional theater rating	1	3	Science museum rating	3	4
			University arts programs rating	4	5	Children's museum rating	4	3

Birmingham, AL

Score: 50.9   **Rank:** 218

Profile: Mid-size city
Location: North-central Alabama, about 300 miles north of the Gulf of Mexico
Elevation: 618 feet
Time zone: Central Standard Time

PRO	CON
Historic feel	Summer heat/humidity
Revitalizing economy	Entertainment
Arts and culture	Air service

Birmingham is Alabama's largest city and a former steel and manufacturing center once known as the "Pittsburgh of the South." Many historic sites observe the city's rich industrial and civil-rights history, and there are a number of antebellum homes. Although the steel industry is still evident, today's economy is in transition toward research, medicine, banking, finance, and technology. Compared to the rest of Alabama, the economy is strong but home prices are relatively high. The city scores relatively well in healthcare, arts, and the economy, and poorly in air service and climate.

Birmingham is located in a valley within a hilly area in the Appalachian foothills. Ridges rise to 600 feet above the valley floor, with a mix of open land and forest. The climate is decidedly southern, humid subtropical with a modifying influence from the Gulf of Mexico. Summers are long, hot, and humid with frequent thunderstorms. Winters are mild. Total annual rainfall is among the highest in the United States.

POPULATION

DEMOGRAPHICS	AREA	U.S. AVG	ETHNIC COMPOSITION	AREA	U.S. AVG	RESIDENT PROFILE	AREA	U.S. AVG
Population	935,168		White	74.5%	75.1%	Single	44.4%	43.6%
Population density per sq. mile	293.4	447.3	Black	24.3%	12.3%	Married	55.6%	56.4%
Population growth	11.3%	16.1%	Asian	.8%	3.6%	Divorced	9.1%	8.4%
Median age	36.2	35.5	American Indian	.3%	.9%	Separated	3.1%	3.0%
Average family size	2.6	2.7	Hispanic	.5%	12.5%	Married with children	27.9%	28.7%
			Diversity measure	46.5%	35.2%	Single with children	11.5%	10.1%

ECONOMY & JOBS — SCORE: 61/RANK: 129

INCOME	AREA	U.S. AVG	EMPLOYMENT	AREA	U.S. AVG	LARGEST EMPLOYING INDUSTRY
Per capita income	$24,526	$23,420	Unemployment rate	4.5%	6.1%	Food Manufacturing
Household income	$45,047	$46,060	Recent job growth	2.6%	.9%	
Household income < $25K	27.8%	26.4%	Projected future job growth	16.7%	15.1%	
Household income > $75K	25.9%	24.5%	White collar	59.4%	54.5%	
Household income growth	69.0%	57.3%	Blue collar	40.6%	45.5%	

COST OF LIVING — SCORE: 36/RANK: 209

INDEXES & TAXES	AREA	U.S. AVG	HOUSING	AREA	U.S. AVG	NECESSITIES	AREA	U.S. AVG
Cost of Living Index	94.0	100.0	Median home price	$140,300	$160,100	Food Index	94.0	100.0
Financial Progress Index	102.1	100.0	Home price appreciation	5.2%	7.1%	Housing Index	87.1	100.0
Income tax rate	6.000%	4.625%	Median rent	$559	$670	Utilities Index	100.1	100.0
Sales tax rate	8.000%	6.474%	Homes owned	68.5%	63.9%	Transportation Index	95.2	100.0
Property tax rate	$7.1	$15.6	Homes rented	22.0%	25.3%	Healthcare Index	92.4	100.0
			Housing affordability	59.0%	54.5%	Miscellaneous Cost Index	102.9	100.0

CLIMATE — SCORE: 25/RANK: 248

TEMPERATURE	AREA	U.S. AVG	PRECIPITATION	AREA	U.S. AVG	COMFORTS & HAZARDS	AREA	U.S. AVG
January low	34.1°F	26.4°F	Annual inches precipitation	53.0	35.9	July relative humidity	72.0%	68.8%
July high	90.3°F	86.7°F	Annual inches snowfall	1.0	24.2	Annual days mostly sunny	210	212
Annual days > 90°F	39	38	Annual days precipitation	118	111	Annual days with thunderstorms	58	39
Annual days < 32°F	60	88	Annual days rain > 0.5 inches	36	23	Tornado risk score	72	19
Annual days < 0°F	0	6	Annual days snow > 1.5 inches	2	6	Hurricane risk score	18	15

TEMPERATURE

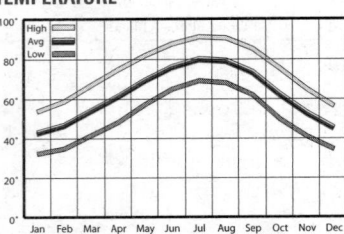

PRECIPITATION

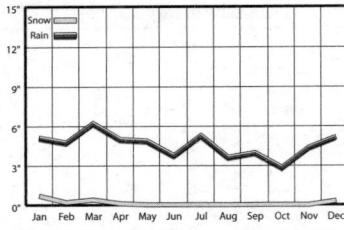

DAYS OF CLOUDS & PRECIPITATION

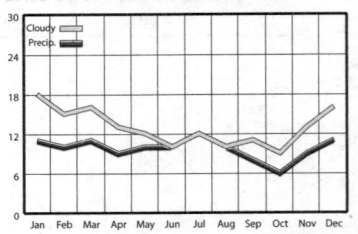

EDUCATION — SCORE: 48/RANK: 172

ACHIEVEMENT	AREA	U.S. AVG	PUBLIC SCHOOLS	AREA	U.S. AVG	HIGHER EDUCATION	AREA	U.S. AVG
High school degree	80.6%	80.2%	Expenditures per pupil	$5,135	$5,894	No. 2-year colleges	4	3
2-year college degree	5.7%	6.2%	Student/teacher ratio	16.1	16.7	No. 4-year colleges/universities	6	4
4-year college degree	16.2%	15.8%	Attending public school	89.9%	90.2%	No. highly ranked universities	1	1
Graduate/professional degree	8.5%	9.6%	State SAT score	1111	1020			
			State ACT score	20.1*	21.0			

HEALTH & HEALTHCARE — SCORE: 65/RANK: 114   CRIME — SCORE: 39/RANK: 201

HAZARDS & ILLNESSES	AREA	U.S. AVG	HEALTHCARE	AREA	U.S. AVG	CRIME	AREA	U.S. AVG
Air-quality score	74	45	Physicians per capita	364.7	261.1	Violent crime rate	556.1	456.0
Water-quality score	30	33	Hospital beds per capita	581.3	432.2	Change in violent crime rate	-48.1%	-17.2%
Pollen/allergy score	68	61	No. teaching hospitals	10	4	Property crime rate	4,300.1	3,950.0
Stress score	51	50	Cost per doctor visit	$59	$67	Change in property crime rate	-20.7%	-16.8%
Cancer mortality per capita	175.1	169.0	Cost per dental visit	$65	$82			
Depression days per month	2.8	2.8	Cost per daily hospital room	$559	$733			

TRANSPORTATION — SCORE: 4/RANK: 316

COMMUTE	AREA	U.S. AVG	INTERCITY SERVICES	AREA	U.S. AVG	AUTOMOTIVE	AREA	U.S. AVG
Average commute time	26.2 min.	22.6 min.	Miles to nearest major airport	4	46	Insurance, annual premium	$865	$1,011
Commute by auto	94.5%	88.7%	Type of local airport	Small		Gas, cost per gallon	$1.41	$1.50
Commute by mass transit	1.2%	1.8%	No. daily airline departures	111	294	Daily vehicle miles per capita	34.8	23.0
Work at home	1.6%	3.9%	Amtrak service	Yes				
Mass transit miles per capita	2.8	8.0	No. interstate highways	3	1			

LEISURE — SCORE: 31/RANK: 228

DINING & SHOPPING	AREA	U.S. AVG	ENTERTAINMENT	AREA	U.S. AVG	OUTDOOR ACTIVITIES	AREA	U.S. AVG
Restaurant rating	1	1	Professional sports rating	2	4	Golf-course rating	6	4
No. outlet malls	1	2	College sports rating	4	4	Ski-area rating	1	4
No. Starbucks	5	11	Zoo/aquarium rating	6	3	National Park rating	2	3
No. warehouse clubs	3	4	Amusement park rating	1	3	Sq. miles inland water	3.0	4.0
			Botanical garden/arboretum rating	5	3	Miles of coastline	0.0	11.4

ARTS & CULTURE — SCORE: 58/RANK: 137

MEDIA & LIBRARIES	AREA	U.S. AVG	PERFORMING ARTS	AREA	U.S. AVG	MUSEUMS	AREA	U.S. AVG
Arts radio rating	6	3	Classical music rating	3	4	Overall museum rating	7	6
No. public libraries	60	28	Ballet/dance rating	3	3	Art museum rating	6	5
Library volumes per capita	2.5	2.8	Professional theater rating	1	3	Science museum rating	5	4
			University arts programs rating	8	5	Children's museum rating	8	3

Bismarck, ND

Score: 54.2   Rank: 195

Profile: Capital city
Location: Central North Dakota
Elevation: 1,697 feet
Time zone: Central Standard Time

PRO	CON
Capital-city amenities	Cold winters
Small-town atmosphere	Entertainment
Cost of living	Low ethnic diversity

The name Bismarck comes from an attempt to attract German capital to build railroads during the late 19th century. Located along the Missouri River near where Lewis and Clark made their famous winter camp, this capital is an agriculture and transportation center for the state. The downtown and the area along the Missouri River are clean and pleasant. The suburbs spread east from the Missouri River. Bismarck has among the lowest cost of living and crime rates for a capital city.

Bismarck is on the east bank of the Missouri River in a shallow basin, 7 miles wide and 11 miles long, surrounded by low-lying hills. The primary vegetation is grassland with areas of trees. The climate is semiarid and strongly continental. Seasonal temperature ranges are extreme and typical of the northern Great Plains. Summers are warm with few hot, humid days. Most annual precipitation falls in the summer as thunderstorms. Winters tend to be long and very cold but with plenty of mild days. Snow has been reported in all months except July and August. Because of low moisture, snowfalls are usually modest; however, the combination of strong winds and low temperatures can produce severe blizzards. Blowing and drifting snow is a frequent hazard. Sunshine is abundant, both summer and winter. First freeze is late September, last is mid-May.

POPULATION

DEMOGRAPHICS	AREA	U.S. AVG	ETHNIC COMPOSITION	AREA	U.S. AVG	RESIDENT PROFILE	AREA	U.S. AVG
Population	96,349		White	98.8%	75.1%	Single	35.1%	43.6%
Population density per sq. mile	27.1	447.3	Black	.1%	12.3%	Married	64.9%	56.4%
Population growth	14.9%	16.1%	Asian	.2%	3.6%	Divorced	4.9%	8.4%
Median age	36.4	35.5	American Indian	.9%	.9%	Separated	.8%	3.0%
Average family size	2.6	2.7	Hispanic	.2%	12.5%	Married with children	31.2%	28.7%
			Diversity measure	9.9%	35.2%	Single with children	4.6%	10.1%

ECONOMY & JOBS — SCORE: 41/RANK: 193

INCOME	AREA	U.S. AVG	EMPLOYMENT	AREA	U.S. AVG	LARGEST EMPLOYING INDUSTRY
Per capita income	$22,852	$23,420	Unemployment rate	2.7%	6.1%	Healthcare and Social Assistance
Household income	$43,662	$46,060	Recent job growth	.4%	.9%	
Household income < $25K	25.2%	26.4%	Projected future job growth	17.6%	15.1%	
Household income > $75K	21.9%	24.5%	White collar	58.7%	54.5%	
Household income growth	61.9%	57.3%	Blue collar	41.3%	45.5%	

COST OF LIVING — SCORE: 63/RANK: 119

INDEXES & TAXES	AREA	U.S. AVG	HOUSING	AREA	U.S. AVG	NECESSITIES	AREA	U.S. AVG
Cost of Living Index	88.8	100.0	Median home price	$107,960	$160,100	Food Index	99.7	100.0
Financial Progress Index	104.8	100.0	Home price appreciation	5.0%	7.1%	Housing Index	67.1	100.0
Income tax rate	3.920%	4.625%	Median rent	$565	$670	Utilities Index	111.1	100.0
Sales tax rate	5.000%	6.474%	Homes owned	67.4%	63.9%	Transportation Index	102.0	100.0
Property tax rate	$17.6	$15.6	Homes rented	14.1%	25.3%	Healthcare Index	88.3	100.0
			Housing affordability	59.0%	54.5%	Miscellaneous Cost Index	101.3	100.0

CLIMATE — SCORE: 24/RANK: 250

TEMPERATURE	AREA	U.S. AVG	PRECIPITATION	AREA	U.S. AVG	COMFORTS & HAZARDS	AREA	U.S. AVG
January low	-1.1°F	26.4°F	Annual inches precipitation	17.0	35.9	July relative humidity	64.0%	68.8%
July high	83.9°F	86.7°F	Annual inches snowfall	39.0	24.2	Annual days mostly sunny	199	212
Annual days > 90°F	20	38	Annual days precipitation	101	111	Annual days with thunderstorms	17	39
Annual days < 32°F	186	88	Annual days rain > 0.5 inches	9	23	Tornado risk score	9	19
Annual days < 0°F	56	6	Annual days snow > 1.5 inches	9	6	Hurricane risk score	0	15

TEMPERATURE

PRECIPITATION

DAYS OF CLOUDS & PRECIPITATION

EDUCATION — SCORE: 72/RANK: 92

ACHIEVEMENT	AREA	U.S. AVG	PUBLIC SCHOOLS	AREA	U.S. AVG	HIGHER EDUCATION	AREA	U.S. AVG
High school degree	85.8%	80.2%	Expenditures per pupil	$4,586	$5,894	No. 2-year colleges	2	3
2-year college degree	11.3%	6.2%	Student/teacher ratio	16.2	16.7	No. 4-year colleges/universities	1	4
4-year college degree	19.3%	15.8%	Attending public school	89.0%	90.2%	No. highly ranked universities	0	1
Graduate/professional degree	6.2%	9.6%	State SAT score	1215	1020			
			State ACT score	21.3*	21.0			

HEALTH & HEALTHCARE — SCORE: 98/RANK: 5

HAZARDS & ILLNESSES	AREA	U.S. AVG	HEALTHCARE	AREA	U.S. AVG
Air-quality score	49	45	Physicians per capita	291.6	261.1
Water-quality score	73	33	Hospital beds per capita	760.1	432.2
Pollen/allergy score	43	61	No. teaching hospitals	2	4
Stress score	1	50	Cost per doctor visit	$59	$67
Cancer mortality per capita	158.6	169.0	Cost per dental visit	$70	$82
Depression days per month	2.7	2.8	Cost per daily hospital room	$363	$733

CRIME — SCORE: 99/RANK: 4

CRIME	AREA	U.S. AVG
Violent crime rate	70.5	456.0
Change in violent crime rate	-57.5%	-17.2%
Property crime rate	2,522.0	3,950.0
Change in property crime rate	-22.8%	-16.8%

TRANSPORTATION — SCORE: 76/RANK: 80

COMMUTE	AREA	U.S. AVG	INTERCITY SERVICES	AREA	U.S. AVG	AUTOMOTIVE	AREA	U.S. AVG
Average commute time	16.1 min.	22.6 min.	Miles to nearest major airport	297	46	Insurance, annual premium	$646	$1,011
Commute by auto	63.4%	88.7%	Type of local airport	Small		Gas, cost per gallon	$1.57	$1.50
Commute by mass transit	.3%	1.8%	No. daily airline departures	65	294	Daily vehicle miles per capita	15.3	23.0
Work at home	21.7%	3.9%	Amtrak service	No				
Mass transit miles per capita	0.0	8.0	No. interstate highways	1	1			

LEISURE SCORE: 0/RANK: 328

DINING & SHOPPING	AREA	U.S. AVG	ENTERTAINMENT	AREA	U.S. AVG	OUTDOOR ACTIVITIES	AREA	U.S. AVG
Restaurant rating	1	1	Professional sports rating	2	4	Golf-course rating	2	4
No. outlet malls	0	2	College sports rating	1	4	Ski-area rating	1	4
No. Starbucks	3	11	Zoo/aquarium rating	2	3	National Park rating	3	3
No. warehouse clubs	1	4	Amusement park rating	1	3	Sq. miles inland water	6.0	4.0
			Botanical garden/arboretum rating	1	3	Miles of coastline	0.0	11.4

ARTS & CULTURE SCORE: 12/RANK: 287

MEDIA & LIBRARIES	AREA	U.S. AVG	PERFORMING ARTS	AREA	U.S. AVG	MUSEUMS	AREA	U.S. AVG
Arts radio rating	1	3	Classical music rating	3	4	Overall museum rating	5	6
No. public libraries	5	28	Ballet/dance rating	1	3	Art museum rating	1	5
Library volumes per capita	2.9	2.8	Professional theater rating	1	3	Science museum rating	2	4
			University arts programs rating	2	5	Children's museum rating	1	3

Bloomington, IN

Score: 82.2   Rank: 29

Profile: College town
Location: South-central Indiana, 45 miles south of Indianapolis
Elevation: 928 feet
Time zone: Eastern Standard Time (no daylight savings time)

PRO	CON
College-town atmosphere	Housing cost
Attractive setting	Undiversified economy
Nearby recreation	Low ethnic diversity

Bloomington is a true college town, with a large and attractive campus to the northeast of downtown; an area of shops, restaurants, and nightlife serving the student community; and a typically Midwestern town square with a courthouse at the center. Indiana University, founded in 1820 and currently serving some 35,000 students, provides a variety of culture and entertainment and is the dominant factor in the local economy and character. Sports, particularly basketball, are a local obsession. The university is also home to one of the top music schools in the nation. Educational attainment here is the highest in the state, crime is low, and the economy is steady. Nearby Lake Monroe, the Hoosier National Forest, and Nashville's Brown County

State Park provide good outdoor recreation; the adventurous can swim in abandoned limestone quarries.

The area is mostly deciduous wooded hills crisscrossed by creek drainages. The climate is continental with changeable weather. Summers are warm and humid with frequent thundershowers, but with diminished severity compared to areas to the north. The city is on the borderline between cold air from the north and warm, moist Gulf air from the south, creating periods of wet, unstable weather. The area is far enough south of Lake Michigan to avoid much of its snows and bitter cold. First freeze is mid-October, last is late April.

POPULATION

DEMOGRAPHICS	AREA	U.S. AVG	ETHNIC COMPOSITION	AREA	U.S. AVG	RESIDENT PROFILE	AREA	U.S. AVG
Population	121,229		White	91.5%	75.1%	Single	60.4%	43.6%
Population density per sq. mile	307.4	447.3	Black	3.4%	12.3%	Married	39.6%	56.4%
Population growth	11.2%	16.1%	Asian	4.6%	3.6%	Divorced	7.2%	8.4%
Median age	27.7	35.5	American Indian	.2%	.9%	Separated	1.1%	3.0%
Average family size	2.3	2.7	Hispanic	1.8%	12.5%	Married with children	22.0%	28.7%
			Diversity measure	18.5%	35.2%	Single with children	7.9%	10.1%

ECONOMY & JOBS SCORE: 96/RANK: 10

INCOME	AREA	U.S. AVG	EMPLOYMENT	AREA	U.S. AVG	LARGEST EMPLOYING INDUSTRY
Per capita income	$22,095	$23,420	Unemployment rate	3.2%	6.1%	Machinery Manufacturing
Household income	$39,395	$46,060	Recent job growth	.1%	.9%	
Household income < $25K	32.2%	26.4%	Projected future job growth	14.7%	15.1%	
Household income > $75K	20.1%	24.5%	White collar	61.1%	54.5%	
Household income growth	58.2%	57.3%	Blue collar	38.9%	45.5%	

COST OF LIVING SCORE: 55/RANK: 148

INDEXES & TAXES	AREA	U.S. AVG	HOUSING	AREA	U.S. AVG	NECESSITIES	AREA	U.S. AVG
Cost of Living Index	94.9	100.0	Median home price	$127,370	$160,100	Food Index	106.6	100.0
Financial Progress Index	88.5	100.0	Home price appreciation	4.0%	7.1%	Housing Index	79.1	100.0
Income tax rate	4.100%	4.625%	Median rent	$684	$670	Utilities Index	93.3	100.0
Sales tax rate	6.000%	6.474%	Homes owned	45.9%	63.9%	Transportation Index	97.3	100.0
Property tax rate	$13.6	$15.6	Homes rented	46.0%	25.3%	Healthcare Index	100.7	100.0
			Housing affordability	40.0%	54.5%	Miscellaneous Cost Index	109.4	100.0

CLIMATE SCORE: 50/RANK: 163

TEMPERATURE	AREA	U.S. AVG	PRECIPITATION	AREA	U.S. AVG	COMFORTS & HAZARDS	AREA	U.S. AVG
January low	19.7°F	26.4°F	Annual inches precipitation	39.0	35.9	July relative humidity	73.0%	68.8%
July high	85.4°F	86.7°F	Annual inches snowfall	21.0	24.2	Annual days mostly sunny	191	212
Annual days > 90°F	15	38	Annual days precipitation	122	111	Annual days with thunderstorms	45	39
Annual days < 32°F	122	88	Annual days rain > 0.5 inches	25	23	Tornado risk score	15	19
Annual days < 0°F	7	6	Annual days snow > 1.5 inches	6	6	Hurricane risk score	4	15

TEMPERATURE

PRECIPITATION

DAYS OF CLOUDS & PRECIPITATION

EDUCATION SCORE: 82/RANK: 59

ACHIEVEMENT	AREA	U.S. AVG	PUBLIC SCHOOLS	AREA	U.S. AVG	HIGHER EDUCATION	AREA	U.S. AVG
High school degree	88.5%	80.2%	Expenditures per pupil	$5,884	$5,894	No. 2-year colleges	0	3
2-year college degree	4.1%	6.2%	Student/teacher ratio	17.6	16.7	No. 4-year colleges/universities	1	4
4-year college degree	20.0%	15.8%	Attending public school	89.8%	90.2%	No. highly ranked universities	0	1
Graduate/professional degree	19.6%	9.6%	State SAT score	1004*	1020			
			State ACT score	21.6	21.0			

HEALTH & HEALTHCARE SCORE: 40/RANK: 195

CRIME SCORE: 82/RANK: 58

HAZARDS & ILLNESSES	AREA	U.S. AVG	HEALTHCARE	AREA	U.S. AVG	CRIME	AREA	U.S. AVG
Air-quality score	24	45	Physicians per capita	254.9	261.1	Violent crime rate	177.3	456.0
Water-quality score	18	33	Hospital beds per capita	373.2	432.2	Change in violent crime rate	-65.7%	-17.2%
Pollen/allergy score	73	61	No. teaching hospitals	0	4	Property crime rate	3,210.1	3,950.0
Stress score	32	50	Cost per doctor visit	$66	$67	Change in property crime rate	-5.0%	-16.8%
Cancer mortality per capita	164.5	169.0	Cost per dental visit	$74	$82			
Depression days per month	5.1	2.8	Cost per daily hospital room	$589	$733			

TRANSPORTATION SCORE: 80/RANK: 62

COMMUTE	AREA	U.S. AVG	INTERCITY SERVICES	AREA	U.S. AVG	AUTOMOTIVE	AREA	U.S. AVG
Average commute time	18.2 min.	22.6 min.	Miles to nearest major airport	42	46	Insurance, annual premium	$774	$1,011
Commute by auto	73.8%	88.7%	Type of local airport	Medium		Gas, cost per gallon	$1.48	$1.50
Commute by mass transit	2.3%	1.8%	No. daily airline departures	319	294	Daily vehicle miles per capita	19.5	23.0
Work at home	3.7%	3.9%	Amtrak service	No				
Mass transit miles per capita	0.0	8.0	No. interstate highways	4	1			

LEISURE SCORE: 67/RANK: 106

DINING & SHOPPING	AREA	U.S. AVG	ENTERTAINMENT	AREA	U.S. AVG	OUTDOOR ACTIVITIES	AREA	U.S. AVG
Restaurant rating	1	1	Professional sports rating	2	4	Golf-course rating	7	4
No. outlet malls	1	2	College sports rating	6	4	Ski-area rating	4	4
No. Starbucks	2	11	Zoo/aquarium rating	1	3	National Park rating	1	3
No. warehouse clubs	3	4	Amusement park rating	1	3	Sq. miles inland water	3.0	4.0
			Botanical garden/arboretum rating	2	3	Miles of coastline	0.0	11.4

ARTS & CULTURE SCORE: 84/RANK: 50

MEDIA & LIBRARIES	AREA	U.S. AVG	PERFORMING ARTS	AREA	U.S. AVG	MUSEUMS	AREA	U.S. AVG
Arts radio rating	1	3	Classical music rating	3	4	Overall museum rating	5	6
No. public libraries	2	28	Ballet/dance rating	1	3	Art museum rating	6	5
Library volumes per capita	3.6	2.8	Professional theater rating	1	3	Science museum rating	4	4
			University arts programs rating	5	5	Children's museum rating	2	3

Bloomington-Normal, IL

| Score: 78.1 | Rank: 42 |

Profile: Mid-size-city complex
Location: North-central Illinois, 100 miles southwest of Chicago
Elevation: 662 feet
Time zone: Central Standard Time

PRO	CON
Small-town atmosphere	Entertainment
Stable economy	Air service
Educational attainment	Low job growth

Bloomington and sister city Normal are a typical Illinois "prairie" town pair near the center of the state. However, the campuses of the Illinois State University and Illinois Wesleyan University, with their college-town flavor, add a unique element. Commercial activity is diversified and centered on agriculture, but the largest employer is the Bloomington-headquartered State Farm Insurance. The city is clean and quiet, with an educated population, a few college-town amenities, and a steady employment base. Living is simple and stress-free. Commutes are among the shortest in the country, crime rates are low, and air quality is excellent. But there is little to do either in town or nearby.

The terrain is a typically flat, agricultural Illinois prairie with few topographic features. The climate is continental with changeable weather and a wide range of temperature extremes. Summers are warm and humid with pleasant weather in June and September. Most precipitation falls as thunderstorms in the summer, and drops off in the winter with a mix of rain and snow. First freeze is late October, last is late April.

POPULATION

DEMOGRAPHICS	AREA	U.S. AVG	ETHNIC COMPOSITION	AREA	U.S. AVG	RESIDENT PROFILE	AREA	U.S. AVG
Population	154,453		White	96.3%	75.1%	Single	36.9%	43.6%
Population density per sq. mile	130.5	447.3	Black	2.2%	12.3%	Married	63.1%	56.4%
Population growth	19.6%	16.1%	Asian	1.0%	3.6%	Divorced	7.1%	8.4%
Median age	30.7	35.5	American Indian	.1%	.9%	Separated	1.3%	3.0%
Average family size	2.6	2.7	Hispanic	1.2%	12.5%	Married with children	31.2%	28.7%
			Diversity measure	21.9%	35.2%	Single with children	7.8%	10.1%

ECONOMY & JOBS
SCORE: 71/RANK: 93

INCOME	AREA	U.S. AVG	EMPLOYMENT	AREA	U.S. AVG	LARGEST EMPLOYING INDUSTRY
Per capita income	$26,850	$23,420	Unemployment rate	2.7%	6.1%	Insurance Carriers and Related Activities
Household income	$54,304	$46,060	Recent job growth	1.9%	.9%	
Household income < $25K	20.0%	26.4%	Projected future job growth	15.4%	15.1%	
Household income > $75K	32.1%	24.5%	White collar	60.7%	54.5%	
Household income growth	71.9%	57.3%	Blue collar	39.3%	45.5%	

COST OF LIVING
SCORE: 34/RANK: 217

INDEXES & TAXES	AREA	U.S. AVG	HOUSING	AREA	U.S. AVG	NECESSITIES	AREA	U.S. AVG
Cost of Living Index	94.4	100.0	Median home price	$126,950	$160,100	Food Index	97.3	100.0
Financial Progress Index	122.6	100.0	Home price appreciation	3.4%	7.1%	Housing Index	78.9	100.0
Income tax rate	3.000%	4.625%	Median rent	$598	$670	Utilities Index	106.3	100.0
Sales tax rate	6.250%	6.474%	Homes owned	69.1%	63.9%	Transportation Index	101.3	100.0
Property tax rate	$27.4	$15.6	Homes rented	24.6%	25.3%	Healthcare Index	96.1	100.0
			Housing affordability	60.0%	54.5%	Miscellaneous Cost Index	109.3	100.0

CLIMATE
SCORE: 37/RANK: 206

TEMPERATURE	AREA	U.S. AVG	PRECIPITATION	AREA	U.S. AVG	COMFORTS & HAZARDS	AREA	U.S. AVG
January low	15.7°F	26.4°F	Annual inches precipitation	35.0	35.9	July relative humidity	72.0%	68.8%
July high	85.5°F	86.7°F	Annual inches snowfall	23.0	24.2	Annual days mostly sunny	197	212
Annual days > 90°F	17	38	Annual days precipitation	111	111	Annual days with thunderstorms	49	39
Annual days < 32°F	132	88	Annual days rain > 0.5 inches	24	23	Tornado risk score	39	19
Annual days < 0°F	11	6	Annual days snow > 1.5 inches	6	6	Hurricane risk score	2	15

TEMPERATURE

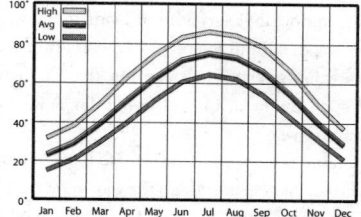

PRECIPITATION

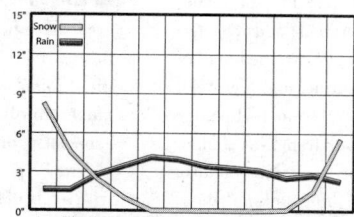

DAYS OF CLOUDS & PRECIPITATION

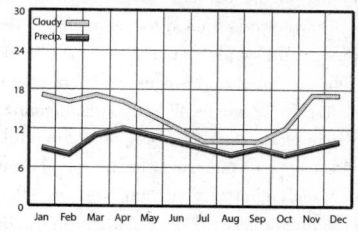

EDUCATION SCORE: 89/RANK: 36

ACHIEVEMENT	AREA	U.S. AVG	PUBLIC SCHOOLS	AREA	U.S. AVG	HIGHER EDUCATION	AREA	U.S. AVG
High school degree	89.8%	80.2%	Expenditures per pupil	$5,368	$5,894	No. 2-year colleges	0	3
2-year college degree	6.1%	6.2%	Student/teacher ratio	15.5	16.7	No. 4-year colleges/universities	2	4
4-year college degree	28.0%	15.8%	Attending public school	93.3%	90.2%	No. highly ranked universities	0	1
Graduate/professional degree	11.8%	9.6%	State SAT score	1179	1020			
			State ACT score	20.2*	21.0			

HEALTH & HEALTHCARE SCORE: 66/RANK: 110

HAZARDS & ILLNESSES	AREA	U.S. AVG	HEALTHCARE	AREA	U.S. AVG
Air-quality score	24	45	Physicians per capita	187.8	261.1
Water-quality score	30	33	Hospital beds per capita	388.2	432.2
Pollen/allergy score	49	61	No. teaching hospitals	0	4
Stress score	12	50	Cost per doctor visit	$68	$67
Cancer mortality per capita	161.6	169.0	Cost per dental visit	$76	$82
Depression days per month	3.2	2.8	Cost per daily hospital room	$652	$733

CRIME SCORE: 84/RANK: 52

CRIME	AREA	U.S. AVG
Violent crime rate	242.0	456.0
Change in violent crime rate	-29.6%	-17.2%
Property crime rate	2,972.0	3,950.0
Change in property crime rate	-22.1%	-16.8%

TRANSPORTATION SCORE: 92/RANK: 27

COMMUTE	AREA	U.S. AVG	INTERCITY SERVICES	AREA	U.S. AVG	AUTOMOTIVE	AREA	U.S. AVG
Average commute time	17.0 min.	22.6 min.	Miles to nearest major airport	110	46	Insurance, annual premium	$892	$1,011
Commute by auto	88.3%	88.7%	Type of local airport	Medium		Gas, cost per gallon	$1.49	$1.50
Commute by mass transit	.2%	1.8%	No. daily airline departures	356	294	Daily vehicle miles per capita	25.1	23.0
Work at home	7.3%	3.9%	Amtrak service	Yes				
Mass transit miles per capita	11.2	8.0	No. interstate highways	2	1			

LEISURE SCORE: 30/RANK: 230

DINING & SHOPPING	AREA	U.S. AVG	ENTERTAINMENT	AREA	U.S. AVG	OUTDOOR ACTIVITIES	AREA	U.S. AVG
Restaurant rating	1	1	Professional sports rating	2	4	Golf-course rating	2	4
No. outlet malls	1	2	College sports rating	4	4	Ski-area rating	2	4
No. Starbucks	0	11	Zoo/aquarium rating	3	3	National Park rating	1	3
No. warehouse clubs	1	4	Amusement park rating	1	3	Sq. miles inland water	2.0	4.0
			Botanical garden/arboretum rating	1	3	Miles of coastline	0.0	11.4

ARTS & CULTURE SCORE: 55/RANK: 148

MEDIA & LIBRARIES	AREA	U.S. AVG	PERFORMING ARTS	AREA	U.S. AVG	MUSEUMS	AREA	U.S. AVG
Arts radio rating	1	3	Classical music rating	6	4	Overall museum rating	5	6
No. public libraries	14	28	Ballet/dance rating	1	3	Art museum rating	2	5
Library volumes per capita	3.9	2.8	Professional theater rating	1	3	Science museum rating	1	4
			University arts programs rating	8	5	Children's museum rating	3	3

Boise, ID

Score: 73.1   Rank: 68

Profile: Mid-size capital city
Location: Southwestern Idaho, on a river plain at the base of the Boise Mountains
Elevation: 2,868 feet
Time zone: Mountain Standard Time

PRO
Attractive setting
Outdoor recreation
Mild climate

CON
Cyclical economy
Urban sprawl
Entertainment

Boise is the capital, largest city, and cultural center of Idaho. Downtown is framed by mountains to the northeast and irrigated agricultural plains to the west. The economy is a diverse blend of agriculture, agricultural processing, light manufacturing, and high-tech industries. For example, the city is headquarters to Micron Technology (semiconductors) and J.R. Simplot (agriculture and french-fry fame). The presence of state government rounds out the economic picture. Outdoor recreation is abundant, with excellent fishing, hiking, bicycling, and other activities, particularly in the Boise National Forest just to the northeast. Bogus Basin offers an after-work ski opportunity 20 miles away. The city has its share of museums and attractions. The North End is a successful, tree-shaded, urban restoration for mixed residential and commercial use. Boise State University adds some college life, but entertainment and nightlife are not the city's strong suits. Residential areas have begun to sprawl into agricultural lands to the west, resulting in unattractive development and concerns about traffic and water supply. Projected future job growth is strong, but there is a risk that too much growth will spoil the area. Cost of living, for now, is reasonable, especially for an attractive capital city.

The Boise Mountains, which rise 5,000 feet to 8,000 feet, are covered with a mix of sagebrush and chaparral, giving way to ridges of fir, spruce, and pine at the summits. To the south and west, the land is generally level with benches defined by former flows of the Boise and Snake rivers. Most of this land is used for irrigated agriculture. The climate is dry and seasonal with sufficient variation. Summer has a typical continental upland climate, with low humidity and generally pleasant days, punctuated by an occasional thunderstorm or heat wave from the south. Temperatures over 100°F occur nearly every year. Winters are mostly mild with periods of clouds and brisk, stormy weather. There is little wind, and occasional cold spells drop temperatures to 10°F or lower with

occasional snow and periods of fog. Most precipitation occurs in the winter. Fall is ideal and spring is pleasant but marked with change. First freeze is early October, last is early May.

POPULATION

DEMOGRAPHICS	AREA	U.S. AVG	ETHNIC COMPOSITION	AREA	U.S. AVG	RESIDENT PROFILE	AREA	U.S. AVG
Population	464,670		White	92.1%	75.1%	Single	41.1%	43.6%
Population density per sq. mile	282.5	447.3	Black	.4%	12.3%	Married	58.9%	56.4%
Population growth	57.1%	16.1%	Asian	1.8%	3.6%	Divorced	10.2%	8.4%
Median age	32.5	35.5	American Indian	.9%	.9%	Separated	2.3%	3.0%
Average family size	2.7	2.7	Hispanic	10.9%	12.5%	Married with children	30.5%	28.7%
			Diversity measure	23.4%	35.2%	Single with children	10.0%	10.1%

ECONOMY & JOBS — SCORE: 3/RANK: 318

INCOME	AREA	U.S. AVG	EMPLOYMENT	AREA	U.S. AVG	LARGEST EMPLOYING INDUSTRY
Per capita income	$23,107	$23,420	Unemployment rate	5.1%	6.1%	Computer and Electronic Product Manufacturing
Household income	$46,322	$46,060	Recent job growth	-3.3%	.9%	
Household income < $25K	22.8%	26.4%	Projected future job growth	25.6%	15.1%	
Household income > $75K	24.8%	24.5%	White collar	56.3%	54.5%	
Household income growth	66.5%	57.3%	Blue collar	43.7%	45.5%	

COST OF LIVING — SCORE: 42/RANK: 190

INDEXES & TAXES	AREA	U.S. AVG	HOUSING	AREA	U.S. AVG	NECESSITIES	AREA	U.S. AVG
Cost of Living Index	91.5	100.0	Median home price	$135,750	$160,100	Food Index	94.4	100.0
Financial Progress Index	107.9	100.0	Home price appreciation	4.8%	7.1%	Housing Index	84.3	100.0
Income tax rate	8.200%	4.625%	Median rent	$593	$670	Utilities Index	76.8	100.0
Sales tax rate	5.000%	6.474%	Homes owned	67.7%	63.9%	Transportation Index	99.3	100.0
Property tax rate	$11.0	$15.6	Homes rented	28.5%	25.3%	Healthcare Index	110.1	100.0
			Housing affordability	59.0%	54.5%	Miscellaneous Cost Index	97.3	100.0

CLIMATE — SCORE: 57/RANK: 141

TEMPERATURE	AREA	U.S. AVG	PRECIPITATION	AREA	U.S. AVG	COMFORTS & HAZARDS	AREA	U.S. AVG
January low	21.4°F	26.4°F	Annual inches precipitation	12.0	35.9	July relative humidity	57.0%	68.8%
July high	90.5°F	86.7°F	Annual inches snowfall	21.0	24.2	Annual days mostly sunny	214	212
Annual days > 90°F	43	38	Annual days precipitation	91	111	Annual days with thunderstorms	15	39
Annual days < 32°F	124	88	Annual days rain > 0.5 inches	3	23	Tornado risk score	4	19
Annual days < 0°F	2	6	Annual days snow > 1.5 inches	5	6	Hurricane risk score	0	15

TEMPERATURE

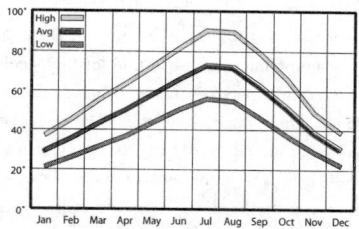

PRECIPITATION

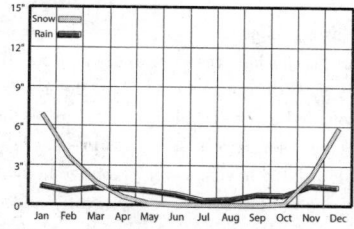

DAYS OF CLOUDS & PRECIPITATION

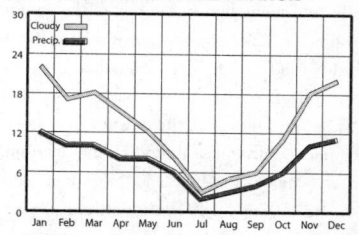

EDUCATION — SCORE: 89/RANK: 37

ACHIEVEMENT	AREA	U.S. AVG	PUBLIC SCHOOLS	AREA	U.S. AVG	HIGHER EDUCATION	AREA	U.S. AVG
High school degree	86.5%	80.2%	Expenditures per pupil	$4,582	$5,894	No. 2-year colleges	0	3
2-year college degree	7.2%	6.2%	Student/teacher ratio	19.1	16.7	No. 4-year colleges/universities	4	4
4-year college degree	18.4%	15.8%	Attending public school	93.4%	90.2%	No. highly ranked universities	1	1
Graduate/professional degree	8.1%	9.6%	State SAT score	1080	1020			
			State ACT score	21.2*	21.0			

HEALTH & HEALTHCARE — SCORE: 54/RANK: 152 ; CRIME — SCORE: 67/RANK: 108

HAZARDS & ILLNESSES	AREA	U.S. AVG	HEALTHCARE	AREA	U.S. AVG	CRIME	AREA	U.S. AVG
Air-quality score	49	45	Physicians per capita	219.5	261.1	Violent crime rate	303.8	456.0
Water-quality score	7	33	Hospital beds per capita	260.2	432.2	Change in violent crime rate	-17.1%	-17.2%
Pollen/allergy score	45	61	No. teaching hospitals	3	4	Property crime rate	3,757.5	3,950.0
Stress score	53	50	Cost per doctor visit	$71	$67	Change in property crime rate	-21.7%	-16.8%
Cancer mortality per capita	148.9	169.0	Cost per dental visit	$94	$82			
Depression days per month	3.3	2.8	Cost per daily hospital room	$592	$733			

TRANSPORTATION SCORE: 54/RANK: 151

COMMUTE	AREA	U.S. AVG	INTERCITY SERVICES	AREA	U.S. AVG	AUTOMOTIVE	AREA	U.S. AVG
Average commute time	20.2 min.	22.6 min.	Miles to nearest major airport	3	46	Insurance, annual premium	$709	$1,011
Commute by auto	89.2%	88.7%	Type of local airport	Small		Gas, cost per gallon	$1.59	$1.50
Commute by mass transit	.4%	1.8%	No. daily airline departures	112	294	Daily vehicle miles per capita	26.8	23.0
Work at home	5.0%	3.9%	Amtrak service	No				
Mass transit miles per capita	3.4	8.0	No. interstate highways	1	1			

LEISURE SCORE: 59/RANK: 135

DINING & SHOPPING	AREA	U.S. AVG	ENTERTAINMENT	AREA	U.S. AVG	OUTDOOR ACTIVITIES	AREA	U.S. AVG
Restaurant rating	1	1	Professional sports rating	3	4	Golf-course rating	2	4
No. outlet malls	0	2	College sports rating	4	4	Ski-area rating	10	4
No. Starbucks	9	11	Zoo/aquarium rating	1	3	National Park rating	2	3
No. warehouse clubs	3	4	Amusement park rating	1	3	Sq. miles inland water	2.0	4.0
			Botanical garden/arboretum rating	1	3	Miles of coastline	0.0	11.4

ARTS & CULTURE SCORE: 66/RANK: 112

MEDIA & LIBRARIES	AREA	U.S. AVG	PERFORMING ARTS	AREA	U.S. AVG	MUSEUMS	AREA	U.S. AVG
Arts radio rating	8	3	Classical music rating	3	4	Overall museum rating	5	6
No. public libraries	15	28	Ballet/dance rating	3	3	Art museum rating	4	5
Library volumes per capita	2.2	2.8	Professional theater rating	1	3	Science museum rating	5	4
			University arts programs rating	5	5	Children's museum rating	1	3

Boston, MA

Score: 72.3   Rank: 71

Profile: Regional center/Capital city
Location: Central Massachusetts coast at the head of Boston Bay
Elevation: 29 feet
Time zone: Eastern Standard Time

PRO	CON
Historic interest	Cost of living
Arts and culture	Traffic and sprawl
Higher education	Economic cycles

Boston is widely viewed as the intellectual and historic capital of the United States. It is a cosmopolitan city with a complete set of services, a broad range of amenities, and a rich tradition and culture almost unmatched in the rest of the country.

Boston has a modern downtown area dotted with historic sites such as the Old North Church—where Paul Revere hung his famous lanterns—and several other sites dating back to revolutionary days. In a manner similar to San Francisco, the downtown area is surrounded by water and tightly packed around a financial and government core. Downtown is a bustling commercial area and tourist attraction flowing with visitors year-round. Streets, which are not laid out on a grid, are crowded and tight. Getting around the city always involves a certain amount of confusion and congestion. Areas near the water, including the restored Faneuil Hall, and around the state house and Boston Common offer excellent dining opportunities and some shopping. As a general rule, arts and culture amenities are exceptional, and most, like the Boston Pops and the Museum of Fine Arts, are well known beyond the city limits. Boston's affinity for professional sports hardly needs mention, and Fenway Park well illustrates the area's devotion to tradition.

Thankfully, most residents don't work in downtown because the auto commute is horrible, and water barriers and antiquated freeways make getting around very difficult at all times. Good public transportation does exist—in fact, the city ranks no. 8 among U.S. cities for the availability of public transportation. New freeway projects, including the "Big Dig"—a massive underground roadway currently under construction—will improve traffic flow and the urban landscape, which is currently marked with unattractive double-decker freeways. Commuting into

Boston from outlying areas, particularly southern New Hampshire, is difficult on a good day. For those who can afford the high costs, living within the city limits, particularly in posh enclaves like Beacon Hill, makes the commute manageable.

The city has two beltways. I-95, the inner beltway better known locally as Route 128, became famous as a location for high-tech companies in the 1980s. The tradition persists today, although the industry now centers on biotech and emerging technologies. The employment picture in recent years has been mixed, partly due to rollover in startup firms and to high business costs. The latter seems to affect businesses such as textiles and shipbuilding the hardest. There are still several industrial areas, but industry and manufacturing do not define the future. Businesses with a stronger research and development component are more likely to prosper.

The greater Boston area is a patchwork of suburbs and old towns, like the famous Lexington and Concord, which have been swallowed by the expanding city. There are several older working-class neighborhoods closer in, and across the Charles River from downtown is the educational mecca of Cambridge, home to Harvard University and the Massachusetts Institute of Technology. In total, Boston has the largest number of highly ranked universities in the country.

For the most part suburban areas are very attractive with numerous trees, spacious homes, and old-town centers displaying character and architectural interest. More so than many other U.S. residents, Bostonians like to preserve appearances and traditions. However, this leads to the challenge of living in this area. The median home price is $386,300, the 10th highest in the country and second highest in the East (behind Stamford-Norwalk, Connecticut). The Cost of Living Index is also the 10th highest in the country. The combination of high cost of living, a hardy climate, and congestion holds the area back from being considered a top place to live.

Boston is located in a basin where the Charles River enters the Boston Bay and Atlantic Ocean. It is relatively level with land rising in all directions. Terrain becomes rolling to hilly to the west and north with relatively more level land to the south. Most areas are covered with dense, deciduous forest. The climate is complex. Storm tracks, latitude, and the coastal location work together to guarantee changing weather patterns and significant precipitation. Hot summer afternoons are frequently relieved by locally celebrated sea breezes, particularly close to shore. Winter cold is moderated by the relatively warm ocean. Summer precipitation comes mainly as intermittent showers and thunderstorms. Passing storms, particularly coastal "noreasters," produce heavy rain and snow especially in winter. Snow on the ground is prevalent with occasional thaws. Fog can be expected all times of year. First freeze is early November, last is early April—but add a month to each end in inland suburban locations.

POPULATION

DEMOGRAPHICS	AREA	U.S. AVG	ETHNIC COMPOSITION	AREA	U.S. AVG	RESIDENT PROFILE	AREA	U.S. AVG
Population	3,439,372		White	87.1%	75.1%	Single	50.4%	43.6%
Population density per sq. mile	1,703.3	447.3	Black	6.0%	12.3%	Married	49.6%	56.4%
Population growth	6.6%	16.1%	Asian	4.9%	3.6%	Divorced	6.8%	8.4%
Median age	36.5	35.5	American Indian	.2%	.9%	Separated	2.8%	3.0%
Average family size	2.5	2.7	Hispanic	4.6%	12.5%	Married with children	24.5%	28.7%
			Diversity measure	31.1%	35.2%	Single with children	7.7%	10.1%

ECONOMY & JOBS SCORE: 28/RANK: 235

INCOME	AREA	U.S. AVG	EMPLOYMENT	AREA	U.S. AVG	LARGEST EMPLOYING INDUSTRY
Per capita income	$31,549	$23,420	Unemployment rate	5.2%	6.1%	Computer and Electronic Product Manufacturing
Household income	$63,784	$46,060	Recent job growth	-1.5%	.9%	
Household income < $25K	19.0%	26.4%	Projected future job growth	8.6%	15.1%	
Household income > $75K	40.7%	24.5%	White collar	67.6%	54.5%	
Household income growth	58.5%	57.3%	Blue collar	32.4%	45.5%	

COST OF LIVING SCORE: 4/RANK: 317

INDEXES & TAXES	AREA	U.S. AVG	HOUSING	AREA	U.S. AVG	NECESSITIES	AREA	U.S. AVG
Cost of Living Index	162.9	100.0	Median home price	$386,300	$160,100	Food Index	108.7	100.0
Financial Progress Index	83.5	100.0	Home price appreciation	14.8%	7.1%	Housing Index	249.9	100.0
Income tax rate	5.950%	4.625%	Median rent	$1,419	$670	Utilities Index	127.2	100.0
Sales tax rate	5.000%	6.474%	Homes owned	61.0%	63.9%	Transportation Index	113.9	100.0
Property tax rate	$13.3	$15.6	Homes rented	32.2%	25.3%	Healthcare Index	128.0	100.0
			Housing affordability	36.0%	54.5%	Miscellaneous Cost Index	109.2	100.0

CLIMATE SCORE: 31/RANK: 226

TEMPERATURE	AREA	U.S. AVG	PRECIPITATION	AREA	U.S. AVG	COMFORTS & HAZARDS	AREA	U.S. AVG
January low	22.5°F	26.4°F	Annual inches precipitation	43.0	35.9	July relative humidity	67.0%	68.8%
July high	81.4°F	86.7°F	Annual inches snowfall	42.0	24.2	Annual days mostly sunny	205	212
Annual days > 90°F	12	38	Annual days precipitation	128	111	Annual days with thunderstorms	19	39
Annual days < 32°F	99	88	Annual days rain > 0.5 inches	38	23	Tornado risk score	10	19
Annual days < 0°F	1	6	Annual days snow > 1.5 inches	14	6	Hurricane risk score	19	15

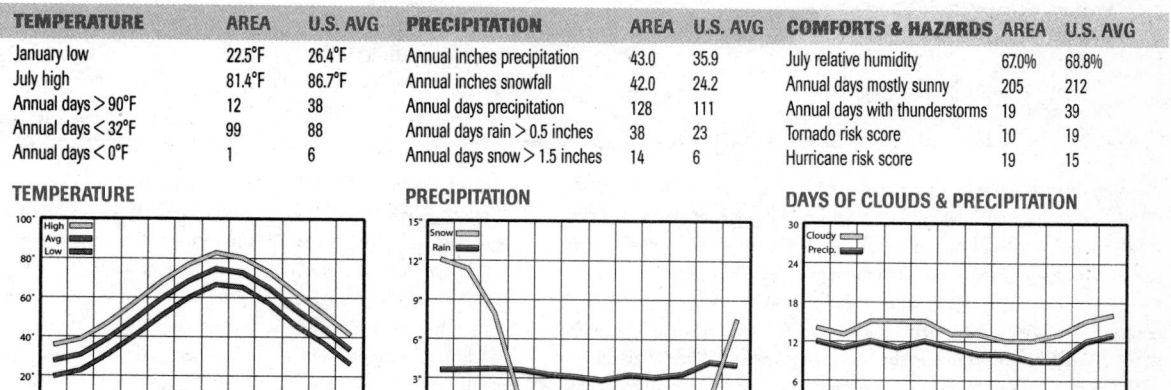

TEMPERATURE   PRECIPITATION   DAYS OF CLOUDS & PRECIPITATION

EDUCATION SCORE: 100/RANK: 1

ACHIEVEMENT	AREA	U.S. AVG	PUBLIC SCHOOLS	AREA	U.S. AVG	HIGHER EDUCATION	AREA	U.S. AVG
High school degree	85.1%	80.2%	Expenditures per pupil	$8,055	$5,894	No. 2-year colleges	16	3
2-year college degree	7.3%	6.2%	Student/teacher ratio	16.3	16.7	No. 4-year colleges/universities	41	4
4-year college degree	20.2%	15.8%	Attending public school	87.3%	90.2%	No. highly ranked universities	14	1
Graduate/professional degree	13.6%	9.6%	State SAT score	1038*	1020			
			State ACT score	22.3	21.0			

HEALTH & HEALTHCARE SCORE: 29/RANK: 235

HAZARDS & ILLNESSES	AREA	U.S. AVG	HEALTHCARE	AREA	U.S. AVG
Air-quality score	99	45	Physicians per capita	499.6	261.1
Water-quality score	27	33	Hospital beds per capita	419.2	432.2
Pollen/allergy score	67	61	No. teaching hospitals	32	4
Stress score	36	50	Cost per doctor visit	$86	$67
Cancer mortality per capita	184.1	169.0	Cost per dental visit	$106	$82
Depression days per month	2.5	2.8	Cost per daily hospital room	$787	$733

CRIME SCORE: 87/RANK: 41

CRIME	AREA	U.S. AVG
Violent crime rate	418.3	456.0
Change in violent crime rate	-35.1%	-17.2%
Property crime rate	2,546.8	3,950.0
Change in property crime rate	-30.8%	-16.8%

TRANSPORTATION SCORE: 95/RANK: 14

COMMUTE	AREA	U.S. AVG	INTERCITY SERVICES	AREA	U.S. AVG	AUTOMOTIVE	AREA	U.S. AVG
Average commute time	27.7 min.	22.6 min.	Miles to nearest major airport	2	46	Insurance, annual premium	$1,616	$1,011
Commute by auto	78.8%	88.7%	Type of local airport	Large		Gas, cost per gallon	$1.53	$1.50
Commute by mass transit	10.2%	1.8%	No. daily airline departures	746	294	Daily vehicle miles per capita	19.8	23.0
Work at home	3.2%	3.9%	Amtrak service	Yes				
Mass transit miles per capita	27.4	8.0	No. interstate highways	3	1			

LEISURE SCORE: 97/RANK: 9

DINING & SHOPPING	AREA	U.S. AVG	ENTERTAINMENT	AREA	U.S. AVG	OUTDOOR ACTIVITIES	AREA	U.S. AVG
Restaurant rating	6	1	Professional sports rating	9	4	Golf-course rating	9	4
No. outlet malls	5	2	College sports rating	10	4	Ski-area rating	7	4
No. Starbucks	91	11	Zoo/aquarium rating	8	3	National Park rating	2	3
No. warehouse clubs	10	4	Amusement park rating	7	3	Sq. miles inland water	7.0	4.0
			Botanical garden/arboretum rating	9	3	Miles of coastline	39.8	11.4

ARTS & CULTURE SCORE: 99/RANK: 4

MEDIA & LIBRARIES	AREA	U.S. AVG	PERFORMING ARTS	AREA	U.S. AVG	MUSEUMS	AREA	U.S. AVG
Arts radio rating	10	3	Classical music rating	10	4	Overall museum rating	10	6
No. public libraries	203	28	Ballet/dance rating	8	3	Art museum rating	10	5
Library volumes per capita	6.0	2.8	Professional theater rating	10	3	Science museum rating	10	4
			University arts programs rating	10	5	Children's museum rating	10	3

Boulder-Longmont, CO

Score: 60.7   Rank: 142

Profile: College town/Small town
Location: 25 miles northwest of Denver at the base of the Rocky Mountain Front Range
Elevation: 5,332 feet
Time zone: Mountain Standard Time

PRO
College-town atmosphere
Attractive downtown
High educational attainment

CON
Cost of living
Urban sprawl
Economy

Boulder, home to the University of Colorado, is a lively archetypical college town, with liberal politics, alternative social lifestyles and attitudes, and an assortment of trendy small businesses, restaurants, galleries, and entertainment venues. There is plenty to do in this bicycle-friendly town, which has a pedestrian mall downtown and outdoor recreation in the nearby mountains. The area has the highest 4-year-college-attainment rate in the nation, and the fifth highest graduate-level attainment. Longmont is an agricultural town to the northeast, and the suburban Denver communities of Lafayette and Louisville round out the area. Boulder would get a much higher ranking if it weren't for the Cost of Living Index of 140.8—by far the highest in Colorado. Housing prices follow suit. Employment took a significant dip recently because of high-tech job losses. Louisville and Lafayette provide more attractively

priced suburban alternatives, but as typical sprawling suburbs one may find anywhere, they lack Boulder charm. Those willing to sacrifice on housing and cost of living will find Boulder an attractive place.

The area is high prairie just at the foot of the Rockies, with gently rolling grassland, lakes, and reservoirs. The climate is typical of the Front Range, with warm sunny summer days with low humidity and occasional thunderstorms, and cool to cold winters with periodic mild spells. The brunt of cold spells tend to miss the area, and the mountains provide some shielding from the worst and windiest cold weather. Summer thunderstorms can be occasionally heavy. Periods of extreme temperatures are short. Large or persistent snow accumulations are uncommon, but occasional heavy snows, particularly in fall and spring, can disrupt transportation. First freeze is early October, last is late April.

POPULATION

DEMOGRAPHICS	AREA	U.S. AVG	ETHNIC COMPOSITION	AREA	U.S. AVG	RESIDENT PROFILE	AREA	U.S. AVG
Population	279,197		White	92.3%	75.1%	Single	49.3%	43.6%
Population density per sq. mile	376.0	447.3	Black	1.6%	12.3%	Married	50.7%	56.4%
Population growth	23.9%	16.1%	Asian	3.3%	3.6%	Divorced	10.7%	8.4%
Median age	33.7	35.5	American Indian	.9%	.9%	Separated	2.1%	3.0%
Average family size	2.4	2.7	Hispanic	7.5%	12.5%	Married with children	24.3%	28.7%
			Diversity measure	28.4%	35.2%	Single with children	8.8%	10.1%

ECONOMY & JOBS SCORE: 0/RANK: 328

INCOME	AREA	U.S. AVG	EMPLOYMENT	AREA	U.S. AVG	LARGEST EMPLOYING INDUSTRY
Per capita income	$34,158	$23,420	Unemployment rate	5.2%	6.1%	Computer Systems Design and Related Services
Household income	$66,602	$46,060	Recent job growth	-11.9%	.9%	
Household income < $25K	16.1%	26.4%	Projected future job growth	16.9%	15.1%	
Household income > $75K	43.8%	24.5%	White collar	70.2%	54.5%	
Household income growth	88.8%	57.3%	Blue collar	29.8%	45.5%	

COST OF LIVING SCORE: 8/RANK: 303

INDEXES & TAXES	AREA	U.S. AVG	HOUSING	AREA	U.S. AVG	NECESSITIES	AREA	U.S. AVG
Cost of Living Index	140.8	100.0	Median home price	$334,390	$160,100	Food Index	113.6	100.0
Financial Progress Index	100.8	100.0	Home price appreciation	11.4%	7.1%	Housing Index	207.7	100.0
Income tax rate	5.000%	4.625%	Median rent	$983	$670	Utilities Index	85.0	100.0
Sales tax rate	8.310%	6.474%	Homes owned	51.4%	63.9%	Transportation Index	104.4	100.0
Property tax rate	$9.1	$15.6	Homes rented	30.4%	25.3%	Healthcare Index	116.6	100.0
			Housing affordability	50.0%	54.5%	Miscellaneous Cost Index	97.5	100.0

CLIMATE SCORE: 55/RANK: 147

TEMPERATURE	AREA	U.S. AVG	PRECIPITATION	AREA	U.S. AVG	COMFORTS & HAZARDS	AREA	U.S. AVG
January low	16.2°F	26.4°F	Annual inches precipitation	16.0	35.9	July relative humidity	53.0%	68.8%
July high	87.4°F	86.7°F	Annual inches snowfall	60.0	24.2	Annual days mostly sunny	246	212
Annual days > 90°F	32	38	Annual days precipitation	88	111	Annual days with thunderstorms	35	39
Annual days < 32°F	163	88	Annual days rain > 0.5 inches	8	23	Tornado risk score	27	19
Annual days < 0°F	10	6	Annual days snow > 1.5 inches	14	6	Hurricane risk score	0	15

TEMPERATURE

PRECIPITATION

DAYS OF CLOUDS & PRECIPITATION

EDUCATION SCORE: 97/RANK: 9

ACHIEVEMENT	AREA	U.S. AVG	PUBLIC SCHOOLS	AREA	U.S. AVG	HIGHER EDUCATION	AREA	U.S. AVG
High school degree	92.8%	80.2%	Expenditures per pupil	$4,981	$5,894	No. 2-year colleges	0	3
2-year college degree	5.7%	6.2%	Student/teacher ratio	18.4	16.7	No. 4-year colleges/universities	2	4
4-year college degree	31.2%	15.8%	Attending public school	86.7%	90.2%	No. highly ranked universities	1	1
Graduate/professional degree	21.2%	9.6%	State SAT score	1104	1020			
			State ACT score	20.1*	21.0			

HEALTH & HEALTHCARE SCORE: 75/RANK: 82

HAZARDS & ILLNESSES	AREA	U.S. AVG	HEALTHCARE	AREA	U.S. AVG
Air-quality score	81	45	Physicians per capita	309.8	261.1
Water-quality score	100	33	Hospital beds per capita	175.4	432.2
Pollen/allergy score	83	61	No. teaching hospitals	1	4
Stress score	48	50	Cost per doctor visit	$73	$67
Cancer mortality per capita	136.5	169.0	Cost per dental visit	$88	$82
Depression days per month	2.0	2.8	Cost per daily hospital room	$758	$733

CRIME SCORE: 52/RANK: 158

CRIME	AREA	U.S. AVG
Violent crime rate	279.4	456.0
Change in violent crime rate	12.9%	-17.2%
Property crime rate	4,087.7	3,950.0
Change in property crime rate	-19.5%	-16.8%

TRANSPORTATION SCORE: 90/RANK: 31

COMMUTE	AREA	U.S. AVG	INTERCITY SERVICES	AREA	U.S. AVG	AUTOMOTIVE	AREA	U.S. AVG
Average commute time	22.4 min.	22.6 min.	Miles to nearest major airport	28	46	Insurance, annual premium	$1,040	$1,011
Commute by auto	80.7%	88.7%	Type of local airport	Large		Gas, cost per gallon	$1.51	$1.50
Commute by mass transit	2.7%	1.8%	No. daily airline departures	812	294	Daily vehicle miles per capita	18.8	23.0
Work at home	6.6%	3.9%	Amtrak service	No				
Mass transit miles per capita	0.0	8.0	No. interstate highways	1	1			

LEISURE SCORE: 86/RANK: 45

DINING & SHOPPING	AREA	U.S. AVG	ENTERTAINMENT	AREA	U.S. AVG	OUTDOOR ACTIVITIES	AREA	U.S. AVG
Restaurant rating	3	1	Professional sports rating	8	4	Golf-course rating	3	4
No. outlet malls	5	2	College sports rating	5	4	Ski-area rating	10	4
No. Starbucks	9	11	Zoo/aquarium rating	2	3	National Park rating	7	3
No. warehouse clubs	1	4	Amusement park rating	2	3	Sq. miles inland water	3.0	4.0
			Botanical garden/arboretum rating	2	3	Miles of coastline	0.0	11.4

ARTS & CULTURE SCORE: 60/RANK: 131

MEDIA & LIBRARIES	AREA	U.S. AVG	PERFORMING ARTS	AREA	U.S. AVG	MUSEUMS	AREA	U.S. AVG
Arts radio rating	4	3	Classical music rating	5	4	Overall museum rating	6	6
No. public libraries	9	28	Ballet/dance rating	6	3	Art museum rating	6	5
Library volumes per capita	3.8	2.8	Professional theater rating	3	3	Science museum rating	5	4
			University arts programs rating	6	5	Children's museum rating	4	3

Brazoria, TX

Score: 57.0   Rank: 171

Profile: Small industrial town
Location: Texas Gulf Coast directly south of Houston area
Elevation: 20 feet
Time zone: Central Standard Time

PRO	CON
Cost of living	Entertainment
Low crime rate	Industrial landscape
Close to Houston	Hot, humid summers

Brazoria is more of a county than a city area and contains Freeport, Lake Jackson, and an assortment of smaller rural towns. Locals call the area the "Real Texas Gulf Coast." The beaches are uninhabited save for an assortment of beach cottages built on stilts to avoid hurricane storm surges. The economy is driven by Dow Chemical and Freeport-McMoRan's gigantic chemical complexes, and the businesses aligned to those industries. The inland small towns seem to run together as an endless four-lane strip marked by recurring donut shops. There are a few museums and seafood restaurants, but most amenities require a trip to Houston. Some residents commute to Houston and its outer suburbs from northern parts of the area.

Brazoria County sits in a level coastal plain with grassy marshy areas defined by the Gulf and drainage of the Brazos River. Long barrier islands extend northeast towards Galveston and southwest all the way to Corpus Christi. Inland areas are level with agriculture and grassland and a few areas of deciduous trees. The climate is Gulf Coast marine humid subtropical. Summers are persistently warm and humid, often cooled by coastal breezes especially at the coast. Hotter periods can result when winds shift from the drier, hotter west-Texas region. Precipitation comes mainly as spring and summer thunderstorms and persistent fall and winter rains. Cold fronts from the north can bring an occasional chill and periods with below-freezing nighttime temperatures, but most winter days are in the 60s and 70s.

POPULATION

DEMOGRAPHICS	AREA	U.S. AVG	ETHNIC COMPOSITION	AREA	U.S. AVG	RESIDENT PROFILE	AREA	U.S. AVG
Population	257,256		White	78.9%	75.1%	Single	39.6%	43.6%
Population density per sq. mile	185.5	447.3	Black	10.0%	12.3%	Married	60.4%	56.4%
Population growth	34.2%	16.1%	Asian	1.7%	3.6%	Divorced	9.0%	8.4%
Median age	34.0	35.5	American Indian	.5%	.9%	Separated	3.8%	3.0%
Average family size	2.9	2.7	Hispanic	23.1%	12.5%	Married with children	35.2%	28.7%
			Diversity measure	49.6%	35.2%	Single with children	10.3%	10.1%

ECONOMY & JOBS SCORE: 80/RANK: 64

INCOME	AREA	U.S. AVG	EMPLOYMENT	AREA	U.S. AVG	LARGEST EMPLOYING INDUSTRY
Per capita income	$21,486	$23,420	Unemployment rate	9.1%	6.1%	Chemical Manufacturing
Household income	$49,908	$46,060	Recent job growth	3.7%	.9%	
Household income < $25K	20.9%	26.4%	Projected future job growth	15.6%	15.1%	
Household income > $75K	26.9%	24.5%	White collar	51.4%	54.5%	
Household income growth	44.7%	57.3%	Blue collar	48.6%	45.5%	

COST OF LIVING SCORE: 73/RANK: 87

INDEXES & TAXES	AREA	U.S. AVG	HOUSING	AREA	U.S. AVG	NECESSITIES	AREA	U.S. AVG
Cost of Living Index	87.5	100.0	Median home price	$106,340	$160,100	Food Index	95.5	100.0
Financial Progress Index	121.5	100.0	Home price appreciation	6.3%	7.1%	Housing Index	66.0	100.0
Income tax rate	0.000%	4.625%	Median rent	$730	$670	Utilities Index	103.6	100.0
Sales tax rate	8.250%	6.474%	Homes owned	62.8%	63.9%	Transportation Index	102.5	100.0
Property tax rate	$24.7	$15.6	Homes rented	21.3%	25.3%	Healthcare Index	110.9	100.0
			Housing affordability	56.0%	54.5%	Miscellaneous Cost Index	96.8	100.0

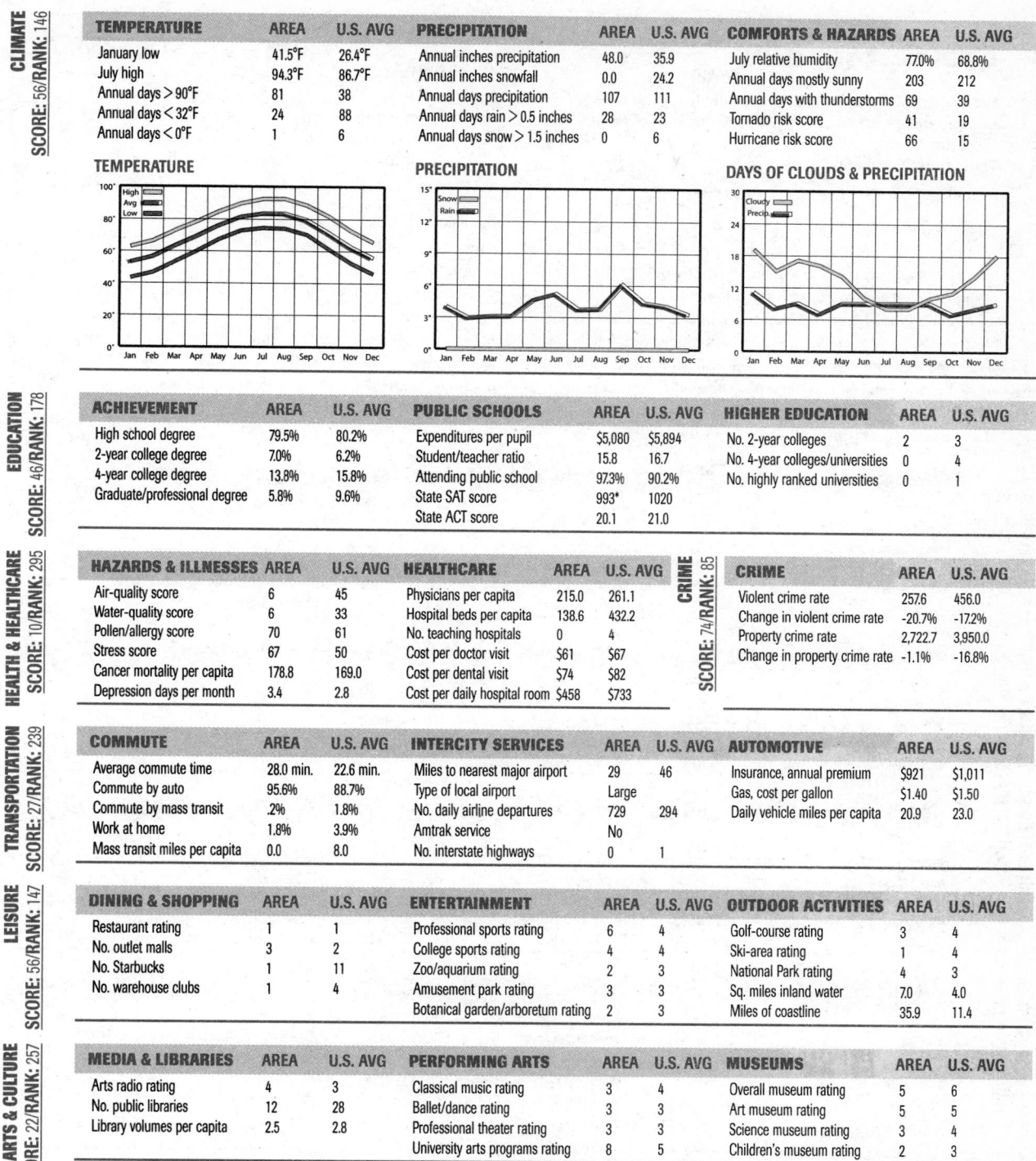

CLIMATE SCORE: 56/RANK: 146

TEMPERATURE	AREA	U.S. AVG	PRECIPITATION	AREA	U.S. AVG	COMFORTS & HAZARDS	AREA	U.S. AVG
January low	41.5°F	26.4°F	Annual inches precipitation	48.0	35.9	July relative humidity	77.0%	68.8%
July high	94.3°F	86.7°F	Annual inches snowfall	0.0	24.2	Annual days mostly sunny	203	212
Annual days > 90°F	81	38	Annual days precipitation	107	111	Annual days with thunderstorms	69	39
Annual days < 32°F	24	88	Annual days rain > 0.5 inches	28	23	Tornado risk score	41	19
Annual days < 0°F	1	6	Annual days snow > 1.5 inches	0	6	Hurricane risk score	66	15

TEMPERATURE

PRECIPITATION

DAYS OF CLOUDS & PRECIPITATION

EDUCATION SCORE: 46/RANK: 178

ACHIEVEMENT	AREA	U.S. AVG	PUBLIC SCHOOLS	AREA	U.S. AVG	HIGHER EDUCATION	AREA	U.S. AVG
High school degree	79.5%	80.2%	Expenditures per pupil	$5,080	$5,894	No. 2-year colleges	2	3
2-year college degree	7.0%	6.2%	Student/teacher ratio	15.8	16.7	No. 4-year colleges/universities	0	4
4-year college degree	13.8%	15.8%	Attending public school	97.3%	90.2%	No. highly ranked universities	0	1
Graduate/professional degree	5.8%	9.6%	State SAT score	993*	1020			
			State ACT score	20.1	21.0			

HEALTH & HEALTHCARE SCORE: 10/RANK: 295

CRIME SCORE: 74/RANK: 85

HAZARDS & ILLNESSES	AREA	U.S. AVG	HEALTHCARE	AREA	U.S. AVG	CRIME	AREA	U.S. AVG
Air-quality score	6	45	Physicians per capita	215.0	261.1	Violent crime rate	257.6	456.0
Water-quality score	6	33	Hospital beds per capita	138.6	432.2	Change in violent crime rate	-20.7%	-17.2%
Pollen/allergy score	70	61	No. teaching hospitals	0	4	Property crime rate	2,722.7	3,950.0
Stress score	67	50	Cost per doctor visit	$61	$67	Change in property crime rate	-1.1%	-16.8%
Cancer mortality per capita	178.8	169.0	Cost per dental visit	$74	$82			
Depression days per month	3.4	2.8	Cost per daily hospital room	$458	$733			

TRANSPORTATION SCORE: 27/RANK: 239

COMMUTE	AREA	U.S. AVG	INTERCITY SERVICES	AREA	U.S. AVG	AUTOMOTIVE	AREA	U.S. AVG
Average commute time	28.0 min.	22.6 min.	Miles to nearest major airport	29	46	Insurance, annual premium	$921	$1,011
Commute by auto	95.6%	88.7%	Type of local airport	Large		Gas, cost per gallon	$1.40	$1.50
Commute by mass transit	.2%	1.8%	No. daily airline departures	729	294	Daily vehicle miles per capita	20.9	23.0
Work at home	1.8%	3.9%	Amtrak service	No				
Mass transit miles per capita	0.0	8.0	No. interstate highways	0	1			

LEISURE SCORE: 56/RANK: 147

DINING & SHOPPING	AREA	U.S. AVG	ENTERTAINMENT	AREA	U.S. AVG	OUTDOOR ACTIVITIES	AREA	U.S. AVG
Restaurant rating	1	1	Professional sports rating	6	4	Golf-course rating	3	4
No. outlet malls	3	2	College sports rating	4	4	Ski-area rating	1	4
No. Starbucks	1	11	Zoo/aquarium rating	2	3	National Park rating	4	3
No. warehouse clubs	1	4	Amusement park rating	3	3	Sq. miles inland water	7.0	4.0
			Botanical garden/arboretum rating	2	3	Miles of coastline	35.9	11.4

ARTS & CULTURE SCORE: 22/RANK: 257

MEDIA & LIBRARIES	AREA	U.S. AVG	PERFORMING ARTS	AREA	U.S. AVG	MUSEUMS	AREA	U.S. AVG
Arts radio rating	4	3	Classical music rating	3	4	Overall museum rating	5	6
No. public libraries	12	28	Ballet/dance rating	3	3	Art museum rating	5	5
Library volumes per capita	2.5	2.8	Professional theater rating	3	3	Science museum rating	3	4
			University arts programs rating	8	5	Children's museum rating	2	3

Bremerton, WA

Score: 78.0   **Rank:** 44

Profile: Small town/Commuter community
Location: West shore of Puget Sound opposite of Seattle
Elevation: 125 feet
Time zone: Pacific Standard Time

PRO	CON
Attractive setting	Clouds and rain
Nearby recreation	Cost of living
Close to Seattle	Arts and culture

The Bremerton metropolitan area represents a group of island communities across Puget Sound's main channel. Bremerton is the largest city with seaport and shipbuilding activities, but the character of the area is mainly rural, with small towns and commuter communities on Bainbridge Island and Vashon Island, among others. There is ample ferry service connecting these areas to the city of Seattle for pedestrians and cars alike, although a recent budget-driven decision to discontinue the faster and more popular passenger-only ferries may raise commute times in the area. Most communities have attractive housing in wooded settings. Residents make the trip to Seattle or Olympia to the south for amenities lacking in the immediate area. Most of the region has a livable small-town atmosphere with excellent outdoor recreation and a pleasant—if wet—climate.

The area is a series of level to slightly hilly islands and inlets with dense coniferous forest. The climate is marine, with a moderate sheltering effect from the Olympic Mountains to the west. Summers are cool and mainly dry. The rest of the year is a mix of clouds, light rain, and an occasional snow, although the water-level location makes snow uncommon. First freeze is early October, last is end of April.

POPULATION

DEMOGRAPHICS	AREA	U.S. AVG	ETHNIC COMPOSITION	AREA	U.S. AVG	RESIDENT PROFILE	AREA	U.S. AVG
Population	236,174		White	88.0%	75.1%	Single	40.8%	43.6%
Population density per sq. mile	596.4	447.3	Black	3.1%	12.3%	Married	59.2%	56.4%
Population growth	24.5%	16.1%	Asian	5.5%	3.6%	Divorced	10.6%	8.4%
Median age	36.0	35.5	American Indian	2.5%	.9%	Separated	3.0%	3.0%
Average family size	2.8	2.7	Hispanic	5.3%	12.5%	Married with children	30.7%	28.7%
			Diversity measure	31.3%	35.2%	Single with children	10.2%	10.1%

ECONOMY & JOBS   SCORE: 26/RANK: 241

INCOME	AREA	U.S. AVG	EMPLOYMENT	AREA	U.S. AVG	LARGEST EMPLOYING INDUSTRY
Per capita income	$22,453	$23,420	Unemployment rate	5.8%	6.1%	Healthcare and Social Assistance
Household income	$47,689	$46,060	Recent job growth	.3%	.9%	
Household income < $25K	20.8%	26.4%	Projected future job growth	17.7%	15.1%	
Household income > $75K	22.8%	24.5%	White collar	52.7%	54.5%	
Household income growth	49.0%	57.3%	Blue collar	47.3%	45.5%	

COST OF LIVING   SCORE: 33/RANK: 219

INDEXES & TAXES	AREA	U.S. AVG	HOUSING	AREA	U.S. AVG	NECESSITIES	AREA	U.S. AVG
Cost of Living Index	108.1	100.0	Median home price	$185,870	$160,100	Food Index	105.8	100.0
Financial Progress Index	94.0	100.0	Home price appreciation	6.9%	7.1%	Housing Index	115.4	100.0
Income tax rate	0.000%	4.625%	Median rent	$781	$670	Utilities Index	86.3	100.0
Sales tax rate	8.500%	6.474%	Homes owned	59.1%	63.9%	Transportation Index	111.3	100.0
Property tax rate	$13.0	$15.6	Homes rented	32.7%	25.3%	Healthcare Index	129.1	100.0
			Housing affordability	56.0%	54.5%	Miscellaneous Cost Index	98.6	100.0

CLIMATE   SCORE: 80/RANK: 64

TEMPERATURE	AREA	U.S. AVG	PRECIPITATION	AREA	U.S. AVG	COMFORTS & HAZARDS	AREA	U.S. AVG
January low	33.0°F	26.4°F	Annual inches precipitation	39.0	35.9	July relative humidity	74.0%	68.8%
July high	75.1°F	86.7°F	Annual inches snowfall	15.0	24.2	Annual days mostly sunny	136	212
Annual days > 90°F	3	38	Annual days precipitation	160	111	Annual days with thunderstorms	7	39
Annual days < 32°F	32	88	Annual days rain > 0.5 inches	26	23	Tornado risk score	0	19
Annual days < 0°F	0	6	Annual days snow > 1.5 inches	2	6	Hurricane risk score	0	15

TEMPERATURE

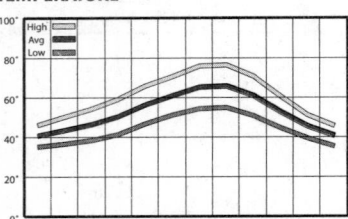

PRECIPITATION

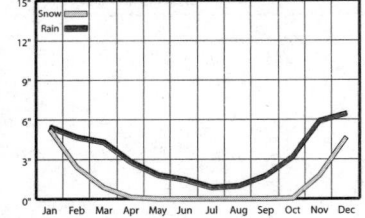

DAYS OF CLOUDS & PRECIPITATION

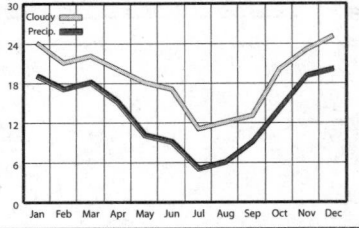

EDUCATION SCORE: 77/RANK: 75

ACHIEVEMENT	AREA	U.S. AVG	PUBLIC SCHOOLS	AREA	U.S. AVG	HIGHER EDUCATION	AREA	U.S. AVG
High school degree	90.8%	80.2%	Expenditures per pupil	$5,555	$5,894	No. 2-year colleges	1	3
2-year college degree	9.1%	6.2%	Student/teacher ratio	19.8	16.7	No. 4-year colleges/universities	1	4
4-year college degree	17.0%	15.8%	Attending public school	94.6%	90.2%	No. highly ranked universities	0	1
Graduate/professional degree	8.3%	9.6%	State SAT score	1062*	1020			
			State ACT score	22.5	21.0			

HEALTH & HEALTHCARE SCORE: 32/RANK: 224

HAZARDS & ILLNESSES	AREA	U.S. AVG	HEALTHCARE	AREA	U.S. AVG
Air-quality score	24	45	Physicians per capita	207.1	261.1
Water-quality score	8	33	Hospital beds per capita	141.0	432.2
Pollen/allergy score	48	61	No. teaching hospitals	0	4
Stress score	97	50	Cost per doctor visit	$68	$67
Cancer mortality per capita	165.9	169.0	Cost per dental visit	$129	$82
Depression days per month	2.9	2.8	Cost per daily hospital room	$775	$733

CRIME SCORE: 54/RANK: 149

CRIME	AREA	U.S. AVG
Violent crime rate	404.4	456.0
Change in violent crime rate	-2.3%	-17.2%
Property crime rate	3,482.9	3,950.0
Change in property crime rate	-14.4%	-16.8%

TRANSPORTATION SCORE: 1/RANK: 326

COMMUTE	AREA	U.S. AVG	INTERCITY SERVICES	AREA	U.S. AVG	AUTOMOTIVE	AREA	U.S. AVG
Average commute time	32.5 min.	22.6 min.	Miles to nearest major airport	20	46	Insurance, annual premium	$998	$1,011
Commute by auto	74.4%	88.7%	Type of local airport	Large		Gas, cost per gallon	$1.58	$1.50
Commute by mass transit	6.8%	1.8%	No. daily airline departures	698	294	Daily vehicle miles per capita	19.8	23.0
Work at home	11.3%	3.9%	Amtrak service	No				
Mass transit miles per capita	23.2	8.0	No. interstate highways	0	1			

LEISURE SCORE: 86/RANK: 48

DINING & SHOPPING	AREA	U.S. AVG	ENTERTAINMENT	AREA	U.S. AVG	OUTDOOR ACTIVITIES	AREA	U.S. AVG
Restaurant rating	1	1	Professional sports rating	7	4	Golf-course rating	3	4
No. outlet malls	3	2	College sports rating	2	4	Ski-area rating	10	4
No. Starbucks	4	11	Zoo/aquarium rating	2	3	National Park rating	7	3
No. warehouse clubs	3	4	Amusement park rating	3	3	Sq. miles inland water	7.0	4.0
			Botanical garden/arboretum rating	2	3	Miles of coastline	30.8	11.4

ARTS & CULTURE SCORE: 20/RANK: 265

MEDIA & LIBRARIES	AREA	U.S. AVG	PERFORMING ARTS	AREA	U.S. AVG	MUSEUMS	AREA	U.S. AVG
Arts radio rating	3	3	Classical music rating	3	4	Overall museum rating	5	6
No. public libraries	9	28	Ballet/dance rating	5	3	Art museum rating	2	5
Library volumes per capita	2.0	2.8	Professional theater rating	3	3	Science museum rating	3	4
			University arts programs rating	2	5	Children's museum rating	3	3

Bridgeport, CT

Score: 60.5   Rank: 145

Profile: Large city
Location: Southwestern Connecticut along Long Island Sound, 50 miles northeast of New York City
Elevation: 7 feet
Time zone: Eastern Standard Time

PRO
Water recreation
Close to New York City
Good climate for region

CON
Cost of living
Industrial areas
Future job growth

Formerly a whaling port, today's Bridgeport is an industrial center on the Long Island Sound, within commuting distance of New York City. Bridgeport and the surrounding communities of Fairfield, Stratford, and Trumbull provide a variety of suburban living environments. Parts of the area are very affluent and the combination of property values and high-property tax rates is among the highest in the nation, although other taxes are relatively modest for the region. (See "Taxation" in chapter 4 for more detail.) Many sectors are industrial and working class.

Sea breezes and the proximity of the Long Island Sound tend to moderate temperatures both in summer and winter, and also to reduce winter snows. Summer temperatures may be 5°F to 10°F lower than nearby inland locations, and winter snowfalls average 10 inches less. Summers are warm and humid, while winters are variable and may be punctuated with heavy "noreaster" snowstorms. Short periods of bitter cold can occur, but are usually shorter in duration than their counterparts in more northerly, inland locations. High tides and large coastal Atlantic storms can create flooding in low-lying areas. First freeze is end of October, last is mid-April.

POPULATION

DEMOGRAPHICS	AREA	U.S. AVG	ETHNIC COMPOSITION	AREA	U.S. AVG	RESIDENT PROFILE	AREA	U.S. AVG
Population	465,089		White	80.3%	75.1%	Single	48.3%	43.6%
Population density per sq. mile	1,776.2	447.3	Black	12.7%	12.3%	Married	51.7%	56.4%
Population growth	4.8%	16.1%	Asian	2.4%	3.6%	Divorced	7.6%	8.4%
Median age	37.6	35.5	American Indian	.2%	.9%	Separated	3.1%	3.0%
Average family size	2.6	2.7	Hispanic	12.6%	12.5%	Married with children	24.4%	28.7%
			Diversity measure	41.7%	35.2%	Single with children	10.8%	10.1%

ECONOMY & JOBS SCORE: 84/RANK: 53

INCOME	AREA	U.S. AVG	EMPLOYMENT	AREA	U.S. AVG	LARGEST EMPLOYING INDUSTRY
Per capita income	$42,349	$23,420	Unemployment rate	6.2%	6.1%	Machinery Manufacturing
Household income	$79,096	$46,060	Recent job growth	.8%	.9%	
Household income < $25K	14.0%	26.4%	Projected future job growth	5.3%	15.1%	
Household income > $75K	51.2%	24.5%	White collar	60.7%	54.5%	
Household income growth	93.4%	57.3%	Blue collar	39.3%	45.5%	

COST OF LIVING SCORE: 7/RANK: 307

INDEXES & TAXES	AREA	U.S. AVG	HOUSING	AREA	U.S. AVG	NECESSITIES	AREA	U.S. AVG
Cost of Living Index	136.8	100.0	Median home price	$258,000	$160,100	Food Index	122.2	100.0
Financial Progress Index	123.2	100.0	Home price appreciation	12.2%	7.1%	Housing Index	160.2	100.0
Income tax rate	4.500%	4.625%	Median rent	$900	$670	Utilities Index	144.6	100.0
Sales tax rate	6.000%	6.474%	Homes owned	66.6%	63.9%	Transportation Index	111.2	100.0
Property tax rate	$19.6	$15.6	Homes rented	26.7%	25.3%	Healthcare Index	142.3	100.0
			Housing affordability	51.0%	54.5%	Miscellaneous Cost Index	118.3	100.0

CLIMATE SCORE: 73/RANK: 87

TEMPERATURE	AREA	U.S. AVG	PRECIPITATION	AREA	U.S. AVG	COMFORTS & HAZARDS	AREA	U.S. AVG
January low	23.4°F	26.4°F	Annual inches precipitation	38.6	35.9	July relative humidity	70.0%	68.8%
July high	81.5°F	86.7°F	Annual inches snowfall	27.7	24.2	Annual days mostly sunny	208	212
Annual days > 90°F	6	38	Annual days precipitation	126	111	Annual days with thunderstorms	21	39
Annual days < 32°F	102	88	Annual days rain > 0.5 inches	24	23	Tornado risk score	7	19
Annual days < 0°F	0	6	Annual days snow > 1.5 inches	5	6	Hurricane risk score	19	15

TEMPERATURE

PRECIPITATION

DAYS OF CLOUDS & PRECIPITATION

EDUCATION SCORE: 82/RANK: 60

ACHIEVEMENT	AREA	U.S. AVG	PUBLIC SCHOOLS	AREA	U.S. AVG	HIGHER EDUCATION	AREA	U.S. AVG
High school degree	84.0%	80.2%	Expenditures per pupil	$8,319	$5,894	No. 2-year colleges	1	3
2-year college degree	5.8%	6.2%	Student/teacher ratio	14.5	16.7	No. 4-year colleges/universities	3	4
4-year college degree	21.2%	15.8%	Attending public school	85.6%	90.2%	No. highly ranked universities	1	1
Graduate/professional degree	15.7%	9.6%	State SAT score	1026*	1020			
			State ACT score	22.1	21.0			

HEALTH & HEALTHCARE SCORE: 23/RANK: 252 / **CRIME** SCORE: 60/RANK: 131

HAZARDS & ILLNESSES	AREA	U.S. AVG	HEALTHCARE	AREA	U.S. AVG	CRIME	AREA	U.S. AVG
Air-quality score	74	45	Physicians per capita	250.5	261.1	Violent crime rate	517.3	456.0
Water-quality score	30	33	Hospital beds per capita	220.0	432.2	Change in violent crime rate	13.9%	-17.2%
Pollen/allergy score	55	61	No. teaching hospitals	3	4	Property crime rate	3,024.9	3,950.0
Stress score	46	50	Cost per doctor visit	$80	$67	Change in property crime rate	-24.9%	-16.8%
Cancer mortality per capita	181.7	169.0	Cost per dental visit	$131	$82			
Depression days per month	2.9	2.8	Cost per daily hospital room	$1,040	$733			

TRANSPORTATION SCORE: 21/RANK: 256

COMMUTE	AREA	U.S. AVG	INTERCITY SERVICES	AREA	U.S. AVG	AUTOMOTIVE	AREA	U.S. AVG
Average commute time	24.2 min.	22.6 min.	Miles to nearest major airport	28	46	Insurance, annual premium	$1,308	$1,011
Commute by auto	89.5%	88.7%	Type of local airport	Small		Gas, cost per gallon	$1.67	$1.50
Commute by mass transit	4.5%	1.8%	No. daily airline departures	98	294	Daily vehicle miles per capita	20.2	23.0
Work at home	2.5%	3.9%	Amtrak service	Yes				
Mass transit miles per capita	6.7	8.0	No. interstate highways	1	1			

LEISURE SCORE: 93/RANK: 25

DINING & SHOPPING	AREA	U.S. AVG	ENTERTAINMENT	AREA	U.S. AVG	OUTDOOR ACTIVITIES	AREA	U.S. AVG
Restaurant rating	1	1	Professional sports rating	10	4	Golf-course rating	8	4
No. outlet malls	10	2	College sports rating	5	4	Ski-area rating	6	4
No. Starbucks	3	11	Zoo/aquarium rating	8	3	National Park rating	3	3
No. warehouse clubs	4	4	Amusement park rating	5	3	Sq. miles inland water	6.0	4.0
			Botanical garden/arboretum rating	4	3	Miles of coastline	16.7	11.4

ARTS & CULTURE SCORE: 81/RANK: 66

MEDIA & LIBRARIES	AREA	U.S. AVG	PERFORMING ARTS	AREA	U.S. AVG	MUSEUMS	AREA	U.S. AVG
Arts radio rating	4	3	Classical music rating	7	4	Overall museum rating	6	6
No. public libraries	21	28	Ballet/dance rating	6	3	Art museum rating	8	5
Library volumes per capita	3.4	2.8	Professional theater rating	8	3	Science museum rating	7	4
			University arts programs rating	8	5	Children's museum rating	5	3

Brockton, MA

Score: 39.0   Rank: 280

Profile: Small town/Commuter community
Location: About 25 miles south of Boston
Elevation: 180
Time zone: Eastern Standard Time

PRO	CON
Proximity to Boston	Cost of living
Attractive setting	Climate
Nearby ocean	Cost of housing

Brockton is a typical New England town about 11 miles south of Boston's inner beltway and about 15 miles west of the coast. It achieved 19th-century fame as the shoe capital of the country, although this industry is largely irrelevant today. Now the town has a diverse industrial and manufacturing base. Residential areas mainly serve those working on the south or west sides of Boston. Proximity to that large city has driven up home prices and the cost of living. Brockton has more than its share of downsides: Commute and climate can be rough, and the violent-crime rate is high.

The terrain is gently rolling with small creek valleys and thick, deciduous woods. Although the Brockton area itself does not lie along the water, the Atlantic and Cape Cod Bay to the east and the Narragansett Bay to the south provide considerable marine influence. Summers are warm and humid but may be refreshed by sea breezes from either direction. Winters are variable and generally cold, with cold snaps arriving from the northwest and snow and rain/snow mixes arriving from the east and south. Bitter cold may be moderated by water depending on wind direction. The location near major storm tracks and water guarantees a large number of cloudy and wet days. First freeze is mid-October, last is late April.

POPULATION

DEMOGRAPHICS	AREA	U.S. AVG	ETHNIC COMPOSITION	AREA	U.S. AVG	RESIDENT PROFILE	AREA	U.S. AVG
Population	261,755		White	94.3%	75.1%	Single	48.2%	43.6%
Population density per sq. mile	880.4	447.3	Black	3.9%	12.3%	Married	51.8%	56.4%
Population growth	10.7%	16.1%	Asian	1.2%	3.6%	Divorced	7.0%	8.4%
Median age	37.2	35.5	American Indian	.2%	.9%	Separated	2.5%	3.0%
Average family size	2.8	2.7	Hispanic	2.7%	12.5%	Married with children	31.6%	28.7%
			Diversity measure	19.6%	35.2%	Single with children	8.6%	10.1%

ECONOMY & JOBS SCORE: 68/RANK: 103

INCOME	AREA	U.S. AVG	EMPLOYMENT	AREA	U.S. AVG	LARGEST EMPLOYING INDUSTRY
Per capita income	$27,465	$23,420	Unemployment rate	6.2%	6.1%	Computer and Electronic Product Manufacturing
Household income	$60,911	$46,060	Recent job growth	.5%	.9%	
Household income < $25K	19.2%	26.4%	Projected future job growth	10.4%	15.1%	
Household income > $75K	38.4%	24.5%	White collar	57.2%	54.5%	
Household income growth	57.9%	57.3%	Blue collar	42.8%	45.5%	

COST OF LIVING SCORE: 9/RANK: 301

INDEXES & TAXES	AREA	U.S. AVG	HOUSING	AREA	U.S. AVG	NECESSITIES	AREA	U.S. AVG
Cost of Living Index	138.7	100.0	Median home price	$287,040	$160,100	Food Index	112.0	100.0
Financial Progress Index	93.6	100.0	Home price appreciation	16.4%	7.1%	Housing Index	178.3	100.0
Income tax rate	5.950%	4.625%	Median rent	$1,046	$670	Utilities Index	131.8	100.0
Sales tax rate	5.000%	6.474%	Homes owned	70.8%	63.9%	Transportation Index	113.7	100.0
Property tax rate	$12.9	$15.6	Homes rented	24.1%	25.3%	Healthcare Index	128.5	100.0
			Housing affordability	39.0%	54.5%	Miscellaneous Cost Index	112.2	100.0

CLIMATE SCORE: 10/RANK: 297

TEMPERATURE	AREA	U.S. AVG	PRECIPITATION	AREA	U.S. AVG	COMFORTS & HAZARDS	AREA	U.S. AVG
January low	18.2°F	26.4°F	Annual inches precipitation	45.2	35.9	July relative humidity	68.0%	68.8%
July high	83.4°F	86.7°F	Annual inches snowfall	50.0	24.2	Annual days mostly sunny	197	212
Annual days > 90°F	16	38	Annual days precipitation	135	111	Annual days with thunderstorms	19	39
Annual days < 32°F	125	88	Annual days rain > 0.5 inches	29	23	Tornado risk score	7	19
Annual days < 0°F	5	6	Annual days snow > 1.5 inches	15	6	Hurricane risk score	21	15

TEMPERATURE

PRECIPITATION

DAYS OF CLOUDS & PRECIPITATION

EDUCATION SCORE: 87/RANK: 43

ACHIEVEMENT	AREA	U.S. AVG	PUBLIC SCHOOLS	AREA	U.S. AVG	HIGHER EDUCATION	AREA	U.S. AVG
High school degree	85.9%	80.2%	Expenditures per pupil	$7,069	$5,894	No. 2-year colleges	1	3
2-year college degree	8.5%	6.2%	Student/teacher ratio	15.3	16.7	No. 4-year colleges/universities	2	4
4-year college degree	18.2%	15.8%	Attending public school	97.1%	90.2%	No. highly ranked universities	0	1
Graduate/professional degree	8.9%	9.6%	State SAT score	1038*	1020			
			State ACT score	22.3	21.0			

HEALTH & HEALTHCARE SCORE: 5/RANK: 312

CRIME SCORE: 53/RANK: 156

HAZARDS & ILLNESSES	AREA	U.S. AVG	HEALTHCARE	AREA	U.S. AVG	CRIME	AREA	U.S. AVG
Air-quality score	6	45	Physicians per capita	129.5	261.1	Violent crime rate	592.6	456.0
Water-quality score	6	33	Hospital beds per capita	26.6	432.2	Change in violent crime rate	-9.2%	-17.2%
Pollen/allergy score	67	61	No. teaching hospitals	0	4	Property crime rate	2,842.9	3,950.0
Stress score	40	50	Cost per doctor visit	$74	$67	Change in property crime rate	-13.9%	-16.8%
Cancer mortality per capita	182.3	169.0	Cost per dental visit	$108	$82			
Depression days per month	2.6	2.8	Cost per daily hospital room	$730	$733			

TRANSPORTATION SCORE: 88/RANK: 38

COMMUTE	AREA	U.S. AVG	INTERCITY SERVICES	AREA	U.S. AVG	AUTOMOTIVE	AREA	U.S. AVG
Average commute time	24.0 min.	22.6 min.	Miles to nearest major airport	20	46	Insurance, annual premium	$1,287	$1,011
Commute by auto	90.7%	88.7%	Type of local airport	Large		Gas, cost per gallon	$1.55	$1.50
Commute by mass transit	1.9%	1.8%	No. daily airline departures	746	294	Daily vehicle miles per capita	20.5	23.0
Work at home	2.4%	3.9%	Amtrak service	No				
Mass transit miles per capita	9.4	8.0	No. interstate highways	1	1			

LEISURE SCORE: 78/RANK: 73

DINING & SHOPPING	AREA	U.S. AVG	ENTERTAINMENT	AREA	U.S. AVG	OUTDOOR ACTIVITIES	AREA	U.S. AVG
Restaurant rating	1	1	Professional sports rating	8	4	Golf-course rating	5	4
No. outlet malls	3	2	College sports rating	5	4	Ski-area rating	7	4
No. Starbucks	1	11	Zoo/aquarium rating	2	3	National Park rating	2	3
No. warehouse clubs	6	4	Amusement park rating	5	3	Sq. miles inland water	4.0	4.0
			Botanical garden/arboretum rating	3	3	Miles of coastline	0.0	11.4

ARTS & CULTURE SCORE: 44/RANK: 184

MEDIA & LIBRARIES	AREA	U.S. AVG	PERFORMING ARTS	AREA	U.S. AVG	MUSEUMS	AREA	U.S. AVG
Arts radio rating	4	3	Classical music rating	5	4	Overall museum rating	5	6
No. public libraries	16	28	Ballet/dance rating	5	3	Art museum rating	7	5
Library volumes per capita	3.0	2.8	Professional theater rating	5	3	Science museum rating	4	4
			University arts programs rating	8	5	Children's museum rating	5	3

Brownsville–Harlingen–San Benito, TX

Score: 25.5   **Rank:** 314

Profile: Small–border city complex
Location: Extreme south Texas along the Rio Grande and Mexican border, 20 miles from the Gulf of Mexico
Elevation: 20 feet
Time zone: Central Standard Time

PRO	CON
Cost of living	Property crime
Nearby water recreation	Low educational attainment
Pleasant winters	Heat and humidity

ocated at the extreme southern tip of Texas and the continental U.S., Brownsville is a thriving border town and minor resort area mainly serving wintering Texans. It is a major trading center and "maquiladora" (border zone) manufacturing center for U.S. companies and an international seaport. There are Gulf Coast beach areas about 20 miles east of town at the mouth of the Rio Grande, notably South Padre Island, a favorite spring-break destination. Recent economic statistics are mixed with high unemployment but strong job growth. In recent decades, the region has undergone rapid growth as industries have located to take advantage of inexpensive labor, the North American Free Trade Agreement (NAFTA), and ocean shipping. Industry is diverse with everything from food processing to petrochemicals to paper bags and hats. The city has a large Hispanic population and a sizable Hispanic middle class. The University of Texas at Brownsville, a consolidation of previous higher education institutions, has 10,000 students. There are few cultural or recreational amenities outside of watersports and cross-border shopping, and though it has the second-lowest median home prices in the nation, parts of the city have problems with traffic, unemployment, and substandard housing. Still, the area managed to win a 2001 National Civic League All-America City Award.

The surrounding country is mainly level agricultural land with marshy coastal areas to the east. The Gulf of Mexico is the dominant climate influence. Prevailing southeast Gulf breezes provide a humid but generally mild tropical-like climate. Winds are frequently strong and gusty in the spring. October through April temperatures are mild with highs in the 70s and 80s. For the remainder of the year, highs are in the 90s with lows in the 70s. Hot, dry winds out of Mexico can yield temperatures of 100°F. Cold weather is infrequent and of short duration. The heaviest rains occur in late spring and again in early fall with some extended periods of cool rainy weather in winter. Torrential rains may accompany tropical storms or hurricanes that occasionally move over the area in summer or fall.

POPULATION

DEMOGRAPHICS	AREA	U.S. AVG	ETHNIC COMPOSITION	AREA	U.S. AVG	RESIDENT PROFILE	AREA	U.S. AVG
Population	353,561		White	86.3%	75.1%	Single	43.5%	43.6%
Population density per sq. mile	390.4	447.3	Black	.8%	12.3%	Married	56.5%	56.4%
Population growth	35.9%	16.1%	Asian	.4%	3.6%	Divorced	6.2%	8.4%
Median age	29.2	35.5	American Indian	.2%	.9%	Separated	4.0%	3.0%
Average family size	3.2	2.7	Hispanic	81.0%	12.5%	Married with children	35.2%	28.7%
			Diversity measure	29.5%	35.2%	Single with children	13.6%	10.1%

ECONOMY & JOBS SCORE: 25/RANK: 248

INCOME	AREA	U.S. AVG	EMPLOYMENT	AREA	U.S. AVG	LARGEST EMPLOYING INDUSTRY
Per capita income	$12,068	$23,420	Unemployment rate	10.6%	6.1%	Healthcare and Social Assistance
Household income	$27,679	$46,060	Recent job growth	2.8%	.9%	
Household income < $25K	45.4%	26.4%	Projected future job growth	19.6%	15.1%	
Household income > $75K	11.9%	24.5%	White collar	47.8%	54.5%	
Household income growth	59.8%	57.3%	Blue collar	52.2%	45.5%	

COST OF LIVING SCORE: 96/RANK: 13

INDEXES & TAXES	AREA	U.S. AVG	HOUSING	AREA	U.S. AVG	NECESSITIES	AREA	U.S. AVG
Cost of Living Index	76.2	100.0	Median home price	$61,570	$160,100	Food Index	88.1	100.0
Financial Progress Index	77.4	100.0	Home price appreciation	5.1%	7.1%	Housing Index	38.2	100.0
Income tax rate	0.000%	4.625%	Median rent	$503	$670	Utilities Index	103.0	100.0
Sales tax rate	8.250%	6.474%	Homes owned	56.3%	63.9%	Transportation Index	98.2	100.0
Property tax rate	$25.1	$15.6	Homes rented	23.2%	25.3%	Healthcare Index	104.3	100.0
			Housing affordability	46.0%	54.5%	Miscellaneous Cost Index	101.0	100.0

CLIMATE — SCORE: 91/RANK: 30

TEMPERATURE	AREA	U.S. AVG	PRECIPITATION	AREA	U.S. AVG	COMFORTS & HAZARDS	AREA	U.S. AVG
January low	51.0°F	26.4°F	Annual inches precipitation	25.0	35.9	July relative humidity	76.0%	68.8%
July high	93.0°F	86.7°F	Annual inches snowfall	0.0	24.2	Annual days mostly sunny	234	212
Annual days > 90°F	102	38	Annual days precipitation	73	111	Annual days with thunderstorms	24	39
Annual days < 32°F	2	88	Annual days rain > 0.5 inches	16	23	Tornado risk score	17	19
Annual days < 0°F	0	6	Annual days snow > 1.5 inches	0	6	Hurricane risk score	46	15

TEMPERATURE

PRECIPITATION

DAYS OF CLOUDS & PRECIPITATION

EDUCATION — SCORE: 1/RANK: 326

ACHIEVEMENT	AREA	U.S. AVG	PUBLIC SCHOOLS	AREA	U.S. AVG	HIGHER EDUCATION	AREA	U.S. AVG
High school degree	55.2%	80.2%	Expenditures per pupil	$5,682	$5,894	No. 2-year colleges	2	3
2-year college degree	4.3%	6.2%	Student/teacher ratio	15.3	16.7	No. 4-year colleges/universities	0	4
4-year college degree	8.3%	15.8%	Attending public school	95.5%	90.2%	No. highly ranked universities	0	1
Graduate/professional degree	5.1%	9.6%	State SAT score	993*	1020			
			State ACT score	20.1	21.0			

HEALTH & HEALTHCARE — SCORE: 8/RANK: 304

CRIME — SCORE: 5/RANK: 312

HAZARDS & ILLNESSES	AREA	U.S. AVG	HEALTHCARE	AREA	U.S. AVG	CRIME	AREA	U.S. AVG
Air-quality score	6	45	Physicians per capita	124.4	261.1	Violent crime rate	456.5	456.0
Water-quality score	13	33	Hospital beds per capita	287.3	432.2	Change in violent crime rate	-12.8%	-17.2%
Pollen/allergy score	81	61	No. teaching hospitals	1	4	Property crime rate	6,144.1	3,950.0
Stress score	44	50	Cost per doctor visit	$82	$67	Change in property crime rate	13.2%	-16.8%
Cancer mortality per capita	131.8	169.0	Cost per dental visit	$70	$82			
Depression days per month	3.6	2.8	Cost per daily hospital room	$553	$733			

TRANSPORTATION — SCORE: 36/RANK: 210

COMMUTE	AREA	U.S. AVG	INTERCITY SERVICES	AREA	U.S. AVG	AUTOMOTIVE	AREA	U.S. AVG
Average commute time	20.7 min.	22.6 min.	Miles to nearest major airport	24	46	Insurance, annual premium	$936	$1,011
Commute by auto	90.3%	88.7%	Type of local airport	Small		Gas, cost per gallon	$1.39	$1.50
Commute by mass transit	.7%	1.8%	No. daily airline departures	28	294	Daily vehicle miles per capita	13.8	23.0
Work at home	3.4%	3.9%	Amtrak service	No				
Mass transit miles per capita	2.4	8.0	No. interstate highways	0	1			

LEISURE — SCORE: 43/RANK: 192

DINING & SHOPPING	AREA	U.S. AVG	ENTERTAINMENT	AREA	U.S. AVG	OUTDOOR ACTIVITIES	AREA	U.S. AVG
Restaurant rating	1	1	Professional sports rating	2	4	Golf-course rating	2	4
No. outlet malls	0	2	College sports rating	1	4	Ski-area rating	1	4
No. Starbucks	0	11	Zoo/aquarium rating	5	3	National Park rating	4	3
No. warehouse clubs	3	4	Amusement park rating	1	3	Sq. miles inland water	10.0	4.0
			Botanical garden/arboretum rating	5	3	Miles of coastline	30.6	11.4

ARTS & CULTURE — SCORE: 7/RANK: 305

MEDIA & LIBRARIES	AREA	U.S. AVG	PERFORMING ARTS	AREA	U.S. AVG	MUSEUMS	AREA	U.S. AVG
Arts radio rating	1	3	Classical music rating	1	4	Overall museum rating	3	6
No. public libraries	8	28	Ballet/dance rating	1	3	Art museum rating	2	5
Library volumes per capita	1.3	2.8	Professional theater rating	1	3	Science museum rating	5	4
			University arts programs rating	1	5	Children's museum rating	4	3

Bryan–College Station, TX

Score: 86.4   Rank: 14

Profile: College town/Small town
Location: Southeast Texas half way between Dallas and Houston
Elevation: 387 feet
Time zone: Central Standard Time

PRO	CON
College-town amenities	Summer heat
Educated population	Isolation
Cost of living	Arts and culture

Bryan, a center for agriculture and light industry, is an unremarkable mid-size town about 60 miles east of Austin. Bryan has grown together with the more notable College Station, home to Texas A&M University, the fourth largest university in the country with 45,000 students. As an A&M university, the school doesn't bring the assortment of arts and cultural amenities one finds in some college towns, but the sports teams are popular and there is an active entertainment scene. Cultural and service amenities can be found in Austin, although it is a difficult drive. The town has a few historic districts, a more attractive setting, and more outdoor recreation opportunities than most Texas towns. Educational attainment at all levels is among the nation's highest. The area has a good balance of features, with a low cost of living, strong economy, a pleasant small-town feel, and plenty to do. The average July temperature of 99.2°F is the major downside.

The area contains level to gently rolling land with mixed agriculture and wooded areas. The Sam Houston National Forest begins about 30 miles east. The climate is lowland humid subtropical, with warm to very hot summers, high humidity, and generally warm evenings. Winters are mild, but cold spells can drop temperatures below freezing at night. Most precipitation falls as rain and thunderstorms mainly in spring and early fall. Infrequent snowfall does occur.

POPULATION

DEMOGRAPHICS	AREA	U.S. AVG	ETHNIC COMPOSITION	AREA	U.S. AVG	RESIDENT PROFILE	AREA	U.S. AVG
Population	156,099		White	76.0%	75.1%	Single	53.4%	43.6%
Population density per sq. mile	266.5	447.3	Black	13.0%	12.3%	Married	46.6%	56.4%
Population growth	28.1%	16.1%	Asian	3.0%	3.6%	Divorced	7.7%	8.4%
Median age	24.0	35.5	American Indian	.3%	.9%	Separated	2.9%	3.0%
Average family size	2.5	2.7	Hispanic	19.8%	12.5%	Married with children	24.3%	28.7%
			Diversity measure	49.7%	35.2%	Single with children	9.3%	10.1%

ECONOMY & JOBS   SCORE: 92/RANK: 25

INCOME	AREA	U.S. AVG	EMPLOYMENT	AREA	U.S. AVG	LARGEST EMPLOYING INDUSTRY
Per capita income	$21,134	$23,420	Unemployment rate	2.6%	6.1%	Healthcare and Social Assistance
Household income	$35,928	$46,060	Recent job growth	5.5%	.9%	
Household income < $25K	37.1%	26.4%	Projected future job growth	17.4%	15.1%	
Household income > $75K	22.0%	24.5%	White collar	62.5%	54.5%	
Household income growth	75.2%	57.3%	Blue collar	37.5%	45.5%	

COST OF LIVING   SCORE: 79/RANK: 70

INDEXES & TAXES	AREA	U.S. AVG	HOUSING	AREA	U.S. AVG	NECESSITIES	AREA	U.S. AVG
Cost of Living Index	82.1	100.0	Median home price	$111,910	$160,100	Food Index	83.5	100.0
Financial Progress Index	93.3	100.0	Home price appreciation	5.2%	7.1%	Housing Index	69.5	100.0
Income tax rate	0.000%	4.625%	Median rent	$596	$670	Utilities Index	85.6	100.0
Sales tax rate	8.250%	6.474%	Homes owned	48.0%	63.9%	Transportation Index	95.2	100.0
Property tax rate	$25.8	$15.6	Homes rented	41.1%	25.3%	Healthcare Index	91.8	100.0
			Housing affordability	39.0%	54.5%	Miscellaneous Cost Index	91.0	100.0

CLIMATE   SCORE: 67/RANK: 107

TEMPERATURE	AREA	U.S. AVG	PRECIPITATION	AREA	U.S. AVG	COMFORTS & HAZARDS	AREA	U.S. AVG
January low	29.4°F	26.4°F	Annual inches precipitation	25.0	35.9	July relative humidity	67.0%	68.8%
July high	99.2°F	86.7°F	Annual inches snowfall	1.5	24.2	Annual days mostly sunny	231	212
Annual days > 90°F	106	38	Annual days precipitation	78	111	Annual days with thunderstorms	49	39
Annual days < 32°F	70	88	Annual days rain > 0.5 inches	16	23	Tornado risk score	9	19
Annual days < 0°F	0	6	Annual days snow > 1.5 inches	1	6	Hurricane risk score	34	15

TEMPERATURE

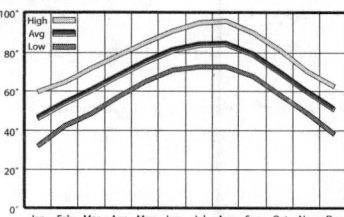

PRECIPITATION

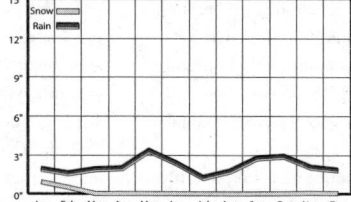

DAYS OF CLOUDS & PRECIPITATION

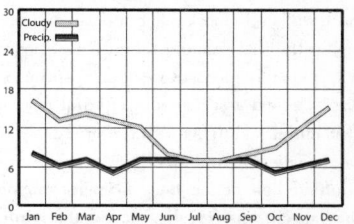

EDUCATION SCORE: 86/RANK: 46

ACHIEVEMENT	AREA	U.S. AVG	PUBLIC SCHOOLS	AREA	U.S. AVG	HIGHER EDUCATION	AREA	U.S. AVG
High school degree	81.3%	80.2%	Expenditures per pupil	$5,340	$5,894	No. 2-year colleges	0	3
2-year college degree	5.0%	6.2%	Student/teacher ratio	14.6	16.7	No. 4-year colleges/universities	1	4
4-year college degree	19.7%	15.8%	Attending public school	95.2%	90.2%	No. highly ranked universities	1	1
Graduate/professional degree	17.3%	9.6%	State SAT score	993*	1020			
			State ACT score	20.1	21.0			

HEALTH & HEALTHCARE SCORE: 63/RANK: 119

HAZARDS & ILLNESSES	AREA	U.S. AVG	HEALTHCARE	AREA	U.S. AVG
Air-quality score	24	45	Physicians per capita	241.5	261.1
Water-quality score	63	33	Hospital beds per capita	310.3	432.2
Pollen/allergy score	74	61	No. teaching hospitals	2	4
Stress score	6	50	Cost per doctor visit	$64	$67
Cancer mortality per capita	146.3	169.0	Cost per dental visit	$71	$82
Depression days per month	3.4	2.8	Cost per daily hospital room	$497	$733

CRIME SCORE: 40/RANK: 196

CRIME	AREA	U.S. AVG
Violent crime rate	401.6	456.0
Change in violent crime rate	-20.1%	-17.2%
Property crime rate	4,438.8	3,950.0
Change in property crime rate	-19.7%	-16.8%

TRANSPORTATION SCORE: 83/RANK: 54

COMMUTE	AREA	U.S. AVG	INTERCITY SERVICES	AREA	U.S. AVG	AUTOMOTIVE	AREA	U.S. AVG
Average commute time	16.7 min.	22.6 min.	Miles to nearest major airport	72	46	Insurance, annual premium	$929	$1,011
Commute by auto	88.4%	88.7%	Type of local airport	Large		Gas, cost per gallon	$1.41	$1.50
Commute by mass transit	1.7%	1.8%	No. daily airline departures	729	294	Daily vehicle miles per capita	26.8	23.0
Work at home	3.2%	3.9%	Amtrak service	No				
Mass transit miles per capita	5.3	8.0	No. interstate highways	0	1			

LEISURE SCORE: 45/RANK: 180

DINING & SHOPPING	AREA	U.S. AVG	ENTERTAINMENT	AREA	U.S. AVG	OUTDOOR ACTIVITIES	AREA	U.S. AVG
Restaurant rating	1	1	Professional sports rating	2	4	Golf-course rating	1	4
No. outlet malls	1	2	College sports rating	6	4	Ski-area rating	1	4
No. Starbucks	1	11	Zoo/aquarium rating	1	3	National Park rating	1	3
No. warehouse clubs	3	4	Amusement park rating	1	3	Sq. miles inland water	2.0	4.0
			Botanical garden/arboretum rating	1	3	Miles of coastline	0.0	11.4

ARTS & CULTURE SCORE: 46/RANK: 179

MEDIA & LIBRARIES	AREA	U.S. AVG	PERFORMING ARTS	AREA	U.S. AVG	MUSEUMS	AREA	U.S. AVG
Arts radio rating	1	3	Classical music rating	3	4	Overall museum rating	4	6
No. public libraries	5	28	Ballet/dance rating	1	3	Art museum rating	4	5
Library volumes per capita	1.4	2.8	Professional theater rating	1	3	Science museum rating	3	4
			University arts programs rating	5	5	Children's museum rating	3	3

Buffalo–Niagara Falls, NY

Score: 52.7 Rank: 205

Profile: Large-city complex
Location: Western New York at eastern end of Lake Erie
Elevation: 706 feet
Time zone: Eastern Standard Time

PRO	CON
Nearby recreation	Winter snow
Arts and culture	Urban decay
Pleasant summers	Economy

Buffalo's image is maligned by weather, urban decay, rabid sports fans, and a strong working-class element. New York's second largest city is a major port and "rust belt" manufacturing center, although its industries are in various stages of decline. Heavy lake-effect snows make Buffalo the fifth snowiest metropolitan area in the country. Downtown is unremarkable but clean and improving, although there are many gritty areas around the city. But positive qualities do exist: The city has notably pleasant weather in spring, summer, and early fall, and there is a good assortment of cultural amenities, historic districts, and architectural highlights with few crowds. The area won a 2002 National Civic League All-America City Award.

Buffalo has better than average shopping supported in part by Canadian citizens traveling across the border to avoid local taxes and high prices—although this comes and goes with fluctuations in the dollar. The city is fanatical about major-league sports, with the Buffalo Bills, Sabres, and a few minor-league teams as focal points. Niagara Falls is a special attraction, and there is a large wine-growing area to the east and west. For a real cosmopolitan getaway, Toronto is 100 miles away. Bottom line: Buffalo is a city of trade-offs; for those able to take the winters and economic malaise it offers numerous amenities at a reasonable cost.

Buffalo is located on the coastal plain of Lake Erie, where the Niagara River connects north to Lake Ontario. The climate is continental with a definite Great-Lakes marine effect. The reputation for bad weather comes from heavy localized lake-effect snows, but summers are among the sunniest, driest, and most pleasant in the Northeast. Winters are generally cloudy, cold, snowy, and changeable with frequent thaws and rain. Snow covers the ground more often than not from Christmas into early March. Lake-effect snows taper off when the lake freezes in January. The lakes modify extreme cold, minimizing below-zero temperatures.

Because of the water, Buffalo warms more slowly in the spring, but the lake also inhibits spring and early summer thunderstorms. Temperatures seldom reach 90°F. First freeze is late September, last is May, but inland conditions are more extreme.

POPULATION

DEMOGRAPHICS	AREA	U.S. AVG	ETHNIC COMPOSITION	AREA	U.S. AVG	RESIDENT PROFILE	AREA	U.S. AVG
Population	1,163,148		White	85.5%	75.1%	Single	48.2%	43.6%
Population density per sq. mile	742.0	447.3	Black	10.7%	12.3%	Married	51.8%	56.4%
Population growth	-2.2%	16.1%	Asian	1.7%	3.6%	Divorced	7.1%	8.4%
Median age	38.5	35.5	American Indian	1.1%	.9%	Separated	3.3%	3.0%
Average family size	2.4	2.7	Hispanic	2.9%	12.5%	Married with children	24.2%	28.7%
			Diversity measure	30.3%	35.2%	Single with children	10.0%	10.1%

ECONOMY & JOBS SCORE: 78/RANK: 71

INCOME	AREA	U.S. AVG	EMPLOYMENT	AREA	U.S. AVG	LARGEST EMPLOYING INDUSTRY
Per capita income	$23,029	$23,420	Unemployment rate	6.2%	6.1%	Motor Vehicle Parts Manufacturing
Household income	$43,785	$46,060	Recent job growth	1.1%	.9%	
Household income < $25K	28.0%	26.4%	Projected future job growth	6.0%	15.1%	
Household income > $75K	23.0%	24.5%	White collar	55.9%	54.5%	
Household income growth	55.6%	57.3%	Blue collar	44.1%	45.5%	

COST OF LIVING SCORE: 18/RANK: 270

INDEXES & TAXES	AREA	U.S. AVG	HOUSING	AREA	U.S. AVG	NECESSITIES	AREA	U.S. AVG
Cost of Living Index	87.6	100.0	Median home price	$85,400	$160,100	Food Index	113.6	100.0
Financial Progress Index	106.5	100.0	Home price appreciation	4.2%	7.1%	Housing Index	53.0	100.0
Income tax rate	7.125%	4.625%	Median rent	$624	$670	Utilities Index	121.3	100.0
Sales tax rate	8.000%	6.474%	Homes owned	64.5%	63.9%	Transportation Index	106.2	100.0
Property tax rate	$35.0	$15.6	Homes rented	26.4%	25.3%	Healthcare Index	103.5	100.0
			Housing affordability	46.0%	54.5%	Miscellaneous Cost Index	98.3	100.0

CLIMATE SCORE: 14/RANK: 282

TEMPERATURE	AREA	U.S. AVG	PRECIPITATION	AREA	U.S. AVG	COMFORTS & HAZARDS	AREA	U.S. AVG
January low	17.6°F	26.4°F	Annual inches precipitation	36.0	35.9	July relative humidity	73.0%	68.8%
July high	79.5°F	86.7°F	Annual inches snowfall	90.0	24.2	Annual days mostly sunny	159	212
Annual days > 90°F	2	38	Annual days precipitation	168	111	Annual days with thunderstorms	31	39
Annual days < 32°F	137	88	Annual days rain > 0.5 inches	22	23	Tornado risk score	8	19
Annual days < 0°F	5	6	Annual days snow > 1.5 inches	19	6	Hurricane risk score	4	15

TEMPERATURE

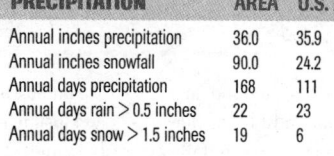

PRECIPITATION

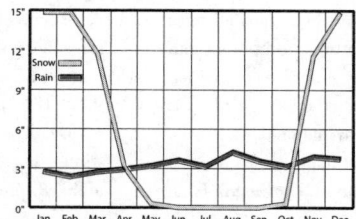

DAYS OF CLOUDS & PRECIPITATION

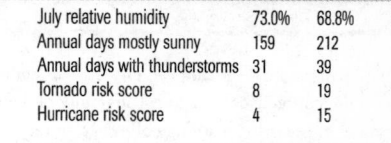
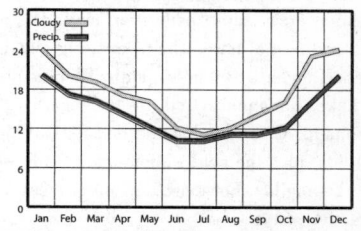

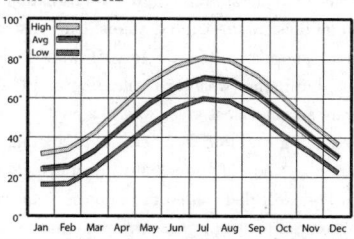

EDUCATION SCORE: 76/RANK: 81

ACHIEVEMENT	AREA	U.S. AVG	PUBLIC SCHOOLS	AREA	U.S. AVG	HIGHER EDUCATION	AREA	U.S. AVG
High school degree	83.0%	80.2%	Expenditures per pupil	$8,605	$5,894	No. 2-year colleges	8	3
2-year college degree	9.6%	6.2%	Student/teacher ratio	14.5	16.7	No. 4-year colleges/universities	8	4
4-year college degree	13.7%	15.8%	Attending public school	84.5%	90.2%	No. highly ranked universities	1	1
Graduate/professional degree	9.5%	9.6%	State SAT score	1006*	1020			
			State ACT score	22.3	21.0			

HEALTH & HEALTHCARE SCORE: 50/RANK: 164

HAZARDS & ILLNESSES	AREA	U.S. AVG	HEALTHCARE	AREA	U.S. AVG
Air-quality score	91	45	Physicians per capita	296.3	261.1
Water-quality score	30	33	Hospital beds per capita	669.3	432.2
Pollen/allergy score	57	61	No. teaching hospitals	10	4
Stress score	28	50	Cost per doctor visit	$55	$67
Cancer mortality per capita	190.8	169.0	Cost per dental visit	$90	$82
Depression days per month	1.9	2.8	Cost per daily hospital room	$686	$733

CRIME SCORE: 73/RANK: 90

CRIME	AREA	U.S. AVG
Violent crime rate	450.8	456.0
Change in violent crime rate	-40.8%	-17.2%
Property crime rate	3,150.4	3,950.0
Change in property crime rate	-25.6%	-16.8%

COMMUTE	AREA	U.S. AVG	INTERCITY SERVICES	AREA	U.S. AVG	AUTOMOTIVE	AREA	U.S. AVG
Average commute time	21.1 min.	22.6 min.	Miles to nearest major airport	7	46	Insurance, annual premium	$1,385	$1,011
Commute by auto	86.7%	88.7%	Type of local airport	Medium		Gas, cost per gallon	$1.59	$1.50
Commute by mass transit	4.4%	1.8%	No. daily airline departures	155	294	Daily vehicle miles per capita	19.4	23.0
Work at home	2.5%	3.9%	Amtrak service	Yes				
Mass transit miles per capita	8.9	8.0	No. interstate highways	1	1			

DINING & SHOPPING	AREA	U.S. AVG	ENTERTAINMENT	AREA	U.S. AVG	OUTDOOR ACTIVITIES	AREA	U.S. AVG
Restaurant rating	1	1	Professional sports rating	6	4	Golf-course rating	6	4
No. outlet malls	1	2	College sports rating	4	4	Ski-area rating	5	4
No. Starbucks	12	11	Zoo/aquarium rating	5	3	National Park rating	1	3
No. warehouse clubs	5	4	Amusement park rating	1	3	Sq. miles inland water	2.0	4.0
			Botanical garden/arboretum rating	4	3	Miles of coastline	29.5	11.4

MEDIA & LIBRARIES	AREA	U.S. AVG	PERFORMING ARTS	AREA	U.S. AVG	MUSEUMS	AREA	U.S. AVG
Arts radio rating	1	3	Classical music rating	7	4	Overall museum rating	8	6
No. public libraries	64	28	Ballet/dance rating	1	3	Art museum rating	9	5
Library volumes per capita	2.7	2.8	Professional theater rating	10	3	Science museum rating	5	4
			University arts programs rating	9	5	Children's museum rating	2	3

Burlington, VT

Score: 49.4   Rank: 232

Profile: College town
Location: Northwest Vermont along east shore of Lake Champlain
Elevation: 200 feet
Time zone: Eastern Standard Time

PRO	CON
College-town amenities	Harsh winters
Attractive downtown	Clouds and rain
Outdoor recreation	Cost of living

Burlington is the largest city in Vermont and its cultural and educational center. The University of Vermont and two smaller colleges bring a strong college-town feel, with culture, entertainment, and a youthful ambience. Downtown is pleasant, with historic lakefront areas and a pedestrian mall. The university is located on a bluff just east of town. The nearest big-city amenities are in Montreal, Québec, under a 100 miles north. There is plenty of outdoor recreation at Lake Champlain and in the nearby Adirondacks and Green Mountains. Cost of living and housing are high by national standards, and that, plus the cold winters and cloudy wet climate, keeps scoring and ranking low. For those tolerant of these negatives, Burlington is an attractive place.

The town is located at the widest part of Lake Champlain. The highest Adirondacks lie 35 miles west while the foothills of the Green Mountains begin 10 miles to the east and southeast. The area is green and lush in summer and is known for beautiful fall seasons. The northerly latitude assures the variety and vigor of a true New England climate, while the lake serves to moderate rapid and severe weather changes. The city is one of the cloudiest in the United States. During winter, temperatures along the lake's shore are often 5°F to 10°F warmer than at the airport 3½ miles inland. Summer weather is pleasant and few days exceed 90°F. This moderate summer heat gives way to a cooler but pleasant fall period, usually extending well into October. Cold Canadian air arrives in winter, but extended periods of bitter cold are unusual. Precipitation, although plentiful and well distributed through the year, is less than in other areas of Vermont due to mountain barriers to the east and west. The heaviest rainfall usually occurs during summer thunderstorms. There is occasional fog. First freeze is early October, last is mid-May.

DEMOGRAPHICS	AREA	U.S. AVG	ETHNIC COMPOSITION	AREA	U.S. AVG	RESIDENT PROFILE	AREA	U.S. AVG
Population	172,508		White	98.0%	75.1%	Single	41.2%	43.6%
Population density per sq. mile	307.0	447.3	Black	.4%	12.3%	Married	58.8%	56.4%
Population growth	13.9%	16.1%	Asian	.9%	3.6%	Divorced	8.0%	8.4%
Median age	35.2	35.5	American Indian	.7%	.9%	Separated	2.2%	3.0%
Average family size	2.7	2.7	Hispanic	.6%	12.5%	Married with children	32.3%	28.7%
			Diversity measure	9.7%	35.2%	Single with children	9.9%	10.1%

INCOME	AREA	U.S. AVG	EMPLOYMENT	AREA	U.S. AVG	LARGEST EMPLOYING INDUSTRY
Per capita income	$25,240	$23,420	Unemployment rate	3.1%	6.1%	Semiconductor and Other Electronic Component
Household income	$52,027	$46,060	Recent job growth	.4%	.9%	Manufacturing
Household income < $25K	21.1%	26.4%	Projected future job growth	14.4%	15.1%	
Household income > $75K	28.9%	24.5%	White collar	63.2%	54.5%	
Household income growth	45.6%	57.3%	Blue collar	36.8%	45.5%	

COST OF LIVING — SCORE: 18/RANK: 269

INDEXES & TAXES	AREA	U.S. AVG	HOUSING	AREA	U.S. AVG	NECESSITIES	AREA	U.S. AVG
Cost of Living Index	109.2	100.0	Median home price	$170,410	$160,100	Food Index	107.3	100.0
Financial Progress Index	101.6	100.0	Home price appreciation	9.3%	7.1%	Housing Index	105.8	100.0
Income tax rate	7.000%	4.625%	Median rent	$850	$670	Utilities Index	144.7	100.0
Sales tax rate	5.000%	6.474%	Homes owned	64.0%	63.9%	Transportation Index	104.1	100.0
Property tax rate	$20.7	$15.6	Homes rented	18.3%	25.3%	Healthcare Index	104.4	100.0
			Housing affordability	48.0%	54.5%	Miscellaneous Cost Index	107.0	100.0

CLIMATE — SCORE: 1/RANK: 326

TEMPERATURE	AREA	U.S. AVG	PRECIPITATION	AREA	U.S. AVG	COMFORTS & HAZARDS	AREA	U.S. AVG
January low	7.6°F	26.4°F	Annual inches precipitation	33.0	35.9	July relative humidity	71.0%	68.8%
July high	81.0°F	86.7°F	Annual inches snowfall	79.0	24.2	Annual days mostly sunny	161	212
Annual days > 90°F	5	38	Annual days precipitation	153	111	Annual days with thunderstorms	25	39
Annual days < 32°F	163	88	Annual days rain > 0.5 inches	21	23	Tornado risk score	0	19
Annual days < 0°F	28	6	Annual days snow > 1.5 inches	17	6	Hurricane risk score	5	15

TEMPERATURE

PRECIPITATION

DAYS OF CLOUDS & PRECIPITATION

EDUCATION — SCORE: 96/RANK: 14

ACHIEVEMENT	AREA	U.S. AVG	PUBLIC SCHOOLS	AREA	U.S. AVG	HIGHER EDUCATION	AREA	U.S. AVG
High school degree	88.5%	80.2%	Expenditures per pupil	$7,433	$5,894	No. 2-year colleges	0	3
2-year college degree	8.9%	6.2%	Student/teacher ratio	10.4	16.7	No. 4-year colleges/universities	5	4
4-year college degree	21.7%	15.8%	Attending public school	87.8%	90.2%	No. highly ranked universities	1	1
Graduate/professional degree	13.2%	9.6%	State SAT score	1027*	1020			
			State ACT score	22.5	21.0			

HEALTH & HEALTHCARE — SCORE: 92/RANK: 25

CRIME — SCORE: 79/RANK: 70

HAZARDS & ILLNESSES	AREA	U.S. AVG	HEALTHCARE	AREA	U.S. AVG	CRIME	AREA	U.S. AVG
Air-quality score	59	45	Physicians per capita	582.0	261.1	Violent crime rate	155.3	456.0
Water-quality score	38	33	Hospital beds per capita	331.8	432.2	Change in violent crime rate	-.4%	-17.2%
Pollen/allergy score	44	61	No. teaching hospitals	1	4	Property crime rate	3,692.4	3,950.0
Stress score	44	50	Cost per doctor visit	$68	$67	Change in property crime rate	-32.9%	-16.8%
Cancer mortality per capita	180.4	169.0	Cost per dental visit	$89	$82			
Depression days per month	2.4	2.8	Cost per daily hospital room	$695	$733			

TRANSPORTATION — SCORE: 46/RANK: 179

COMMUTE	AREA	U.S. AVG	INTERCITY SERVICES	AREA	U.S. AVG	AUTOMOTIVE	AREA	U.S. AVG
Average commute time	21.4 min.	22.6 min.	Miles to nearest major airport	4	46	Insurance, annual premium	$770	$1,011
Commute by auto	86.2%	88.7%	Type of local airport	Small		Gas, cost per gallon	$1.51	$1.50
Commute by mass transit	.6%	1.8%	No. daily airline departures	69	294	Daily vehicle miles per capita	29.8	23.0
Work at home	7.3%	3.9%	Amtrak service	Yes				
Mass transit miles per capita	5.8	8.0	No. interstate highways	1	1			

LEISURE — SCORE: 48/RANK: 170

DINING & SHOPPING	AREA	U.S. AVG	ENTERTAINMENT	AREA	U.S. AVG	OUTDOOR ACTIVITIES	AREA	U.S. AVG
Restaurant rating	1	1	Professional sports rating	2	4	Golf-course rating	1	4
No. outlet malls	0	2	College sports rating	4	4	Ski-area rating	8	4
No. Starbucks	2	11	Zoo/aquarium rating	2	3	National Park rating	1	3
No. warehouse clubs	3	4	Amusement park rating	1	3	Sq. miles inland water	8.0	4.0
			Botanical garden/arboretum rating	1	3	Miles of coastline	0.0	11.4

ARTS & CULTURE — SCORE: 44/RANK: 182

MEDIA & LIBRARIES	AREA	U.S. AVG	PERFORMING ARTS	AREA	U.S. AVG	MUSEUMS	AREA	U.S. AVG
Arts radio rating	1	3	Classical music rating	3	4	Overall museum rating	6	6
No. public libraries	32	28	Ballet/dance rating	1	3	Art museum rating	2	5
Library volumes per capita	3.5	2.8	Professional theater rating	1	3	Science museum rating	4	4
			University arts programs rating	8	5	Children's museum rating	3	3

Canton-Massillon, OH

Score: 39.3   **Rank:** 278

Profile: Small-city complex
Location: Northeast Ohio, 60 miles south of Cleveland and 20 miles south of Akron
Elevation: 1,208 feet
Time zone: Eastern Standard Time

PRO	CON
Cost of living	Industrial feel
Nearby recreation	Low educational attainment
Nearby city amenities	Cloudy, wet climate

Canton is the southernmost city in the industrial corridor stretching south from Cleveland in northeast Ohio. Massillon is almost a twin city just to the west. The area is a center of diverse manufacturing and a gateway to the large Appalachian foothills to the south and east. Cities and residential areas are unremarkable. The Pro Football Hall of Fame in Canton is one local attraction, and areas in the foothills yield recreation and some interesting historic industrial and agricultural areas, including the glassblowing and brick-making areas around Dover and New Philadelphia. Residents drive north to Cleveland for cultural amenities and shopping.

The area has rolling to hilly terrain, which becomes more hilly moving south from the city. Valleys are open and agricultural, and the hills are mostly deciduous woods. The climate is similar to Akron and other cities that face Lake Erie to the north. The lake has considerable influence on area weather, tempering cold air masses during the late fall and winter and contributing to the formation of brief but heavy snowfalls. Lake-related temperature and moisture contrasts produce cloudy days 1 out of every 2 days. Summers are moderately warm and quite humid, with late springs and pleasant fall periods. Temperature and snowfall vary considerably over the area, with more snow in the north. First freeze is mid-October, last is late April.

POPULATION

DEMOGRAPHICS	AREA	U.S. AVG	ETHNIC COMPOSITION	AREA	U.S. AVG	RESIDENT PROFILE	AREA	U.S. AVG
Population	407,106		White	91.6%	75.1%	Single	42.7%	43.6%
Population density per sq. mile	419.3	447.3	Black	7.5%	12.3%	Married	57.3%	56.4%
Population growth	3.3%	16.1%	Asian	.5%	3.6%	Divorced	9.4%	8.4%
Median age	38.7	35.5	American Indian	.3%	.9%	Separated	2.2%	3.0%
Average family size	2.5	2.7	Hispanic	.8%	12.5%	Married with children	27.5%	28.7%
			Diversity measure	17.8%	35.2%	Single with children	9.8%	10.1%

ECONOMY & JOBS   SCORE: 35/RANK: 214

INCOME	AREA	U.S. AVG	EMPLOYMENT	AREA	U.S. AVG	LARGEST EMPLOYING INDUSTRY
Per capita income	$21,508	$23,420	Unemployment rate	6.0%	6.1%	Primary Metal Manufacturing
Household income	$41,834	$46,060	Recent job growth	1.6%	.9%	
Household income < $25K	28.0%	26.4%	Projected future job growth	11.6%	15.1%	
Household income > $75K	18.9%	24.5%	White collar	51.7%	54.5%	
Household income growth	51.0%	57.3%	Blue collar	48.3%	45.5%	

COST OF LIVING   SCORE: 57/RANK: 141

INDEXES & TAXES	AREA	U.S. AVG	HOUSING	AREA	U.S. AVG	NECESSITIES	AREA	U.S. AVG
Cost of Living Index	90.9	100.0	Median home price	$116,330	$160,100	Food Index	103.6	100.0
Financial Progress Index	98.1	100.0	Home price appreciation	5.3%	7.1%	Housing Index	72.3	100.0
Income tax rate	4.993%	4.625%	Median rent	$512	$670	Utilities Index	119.7	100.0
Sales tax rate	5.250%	6.474%	Homes owned	68.3%	63.9%	Transportation Index	93.5	100.0
Property tax rate	$14.6	$15.6	Homes rented	23.8%	25.3%	Healthcare Index	98.8	100.0
			Housing affordability	63.0%	54.5%	Miscellaneous Cost Index	97.7	100.0

CLIMATE   SCORE: 14/RANK: 284

TEMPERATURE	AREA	U.S. AVG	PRECIPITATION	AREA	U.S. AVG	COMFORTS & HAZARDS	AREA	U.S. AVG
January low	18.6°F	26.4°F	Annual inches precipitation	35.1	35.9	July relative humidity	71.0%	68.8%
July high	82.6°F	86.7°F	Annual inches snowfall	48.2	24.2	Annual days mostly sunny	171	212
Annual days > 90°F	7	38	Annual days precipitation	168	111	Annual days with thunderstorms	40	39
Annual days < 32°F	128	88	Annual days rain > 0.5 inches	23	23	Tornado risk score	8	19
Annual days < 0°F	6	6	Annual days snow > 1.5 inches	11	6	Hurricane risk score	3	15

TEMPERATURE

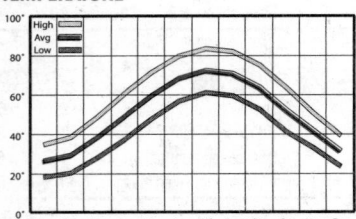

PRECIPITATION

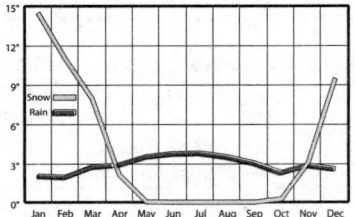

DAYS OF CLOUDS & PRECIPITATION

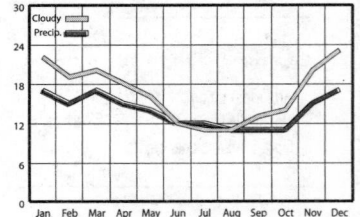

EDUCATION SCORE: 20/RANK: 265

ACHIEVEMENT	AREA	U.S. AVG	PUBLIC SCHOOLS	AREA	U.S. AVG	HIGHER EDUCATION	AREA	U.S. AVG
High school degree	83.2%	80.2%	Expenditures per pupil	$5,656	$5,894	No. 2-year colleges	1	3
2-year college degree	4.1%	6.2%	Student/teacher ratio	17.1	16.7	No. 4-year colleges/universities	4	4
4-year college degree	11.5%	15.8%	Attending public school	89.7%	90.2%	No. highly ranked universities	0	1
Graduate/professional degree	5.8%	9.6%	State SAT score	1077	1020			
			State ACT score	21.4*	21.0			

HEALTH & HEALTHCARE SCORE: 53/RANK: 155

CRIME SCORE: 37/RANK: 208

HAZARDS & ILLNESSES	AREA	U.S. AVG	HEALTHCARE	AREA	U.S. AVG	CRIME	AREA	U.S. AVG
Air-quality score	74	45	Physicians per capita	212.2	261.1	Violent crime rate	370.1	456.0
Water-quality score	4	33	Hospital beds per capita	586.6	432.2	Change in violent crime rate	-27.0%	-17.2%
Pollen/allergy score	63	61	No. teaching hospitals	4	4	Property crime rate	4,205.9	3,950.0
Stress score	52	50	Cost per doctor visit	$62	$67	Change in property crime rate	-2.3%	-16.8%
Cancer mortality per capita	171.1	169.0	Cost per dental visit	$77	$82			
Depression days per month	2.7	2.8	Cost per daily hospital room	$629	$733			

TRANSPORTATION SCORE: 54/RANK: 152

COMMUTE	AREA	U.S. AVG	INTERCITY SERVICES	AREA	U.S. AVG	AUTOMOTIVE	AREA	U.S. AVG
Average commute time	21.7 min.	22.6 min.	Miles to nearest major airport	49	46	Insurance, annual premium	$822	$1,011
Commute by auto	91.6%	88.7%	Type of local airport	Medium		Gas, cost per gallon	$1.44	$1.50
Commute by mass transit	1.0%	1.8%	No. daily airline departures	487	294	Daily vehicle miles per capita	20.6	23.0
Work at home	2.8%	3.9%	Amtrak service	Yes				
Mass transit miles per capita	9.9	8.0	No. interstate highways	1				

LEISURE SCORE: 70/RANK: 99

DINING & SHOPPING	AREA	U.S. AVG	ENTERTAINMENT	AREA	U.S. AVG	OUTDOOR ACTIVITIES	AREA	U.S. AVG
Restaurant rating	1	1	Professional sports rating	3	4	Golf-course rating	5	4
No. outlet malls	2	2	College sports rating	2	4	Ski-area rating	2	4
No. Starbucks	3	11	Zoo/aquarium rating	1	3	National Park rating	1	3
No. warehouse clubs	4	4	Amusement park rating	1	3	Sq. miles inland water	3.0	4.0
			Botanical garden/arboretum rating	1	3	Miles of coastline	0.0	11.4

ARTS & CULTURE SCORE: 36/RANK: 210

MEDIA & LIBRARIES	AREA	U.S. AVG	PERFORMING ARTS	AREA	U.S. AVG	MUSEUMS	AREA	U.S. AVG
Arts radio rating	1	3	Classical music rating	4	4	Overall museum rating	6	6
No. public libraries	23	28	Ballet/dance rating	3	3	Art museum rating	5	5
Library volumes per capita	4.0	2.8	Professional theater rating	1	3	Science museum rating	4	4
			University arts programs rating	5	5	Children's museum rating	7	3

Casper, WY

Score: 55.6   Rank: 185

Profile: Small town
Location: East-central Wyoming on the eastern slope of the Rockies
Elevation: 5,237 feet
Time zone: Mountain Standard Time

PRO	CON
Small-town atmosphere	Wind and cold
Outdoor recreation	Isolation
Cost of living	Low ethnic diversity

Casper is a somewhat remote town supported mainly by the oil and gas industries (exploration, production, and refinement), and more recently by low-sulfur coal in the Powder River Basin to the north and east. Ranching and agriculture are also present. The city has a distinctly Western, almost boom-town feel, with a traditional downtown and suburban development encroaching upon the grasslands. The area is noted for its wide-open spaces and friendliness.

Casper is located in the North Platte River Valley. The immediately surrounding country is mostly rolling and hilly grassland with flat prairies in each direction except toward the south, where Casper Mountain rises 3,500 feet above the valley floor. With a semiarid climate, Casper experiences large diurnal (daily) and annual temperature ranges due to low humidity and high elevation. Summer days are warm, dry, and pleasant with cool evenings. Winters are variable with occasional outbreaks of windy cold. About 70% of annual precipitation occurs during late spring and summer mostly as thunderstorms. Monthly snowfall amounts are unusually uniform from November through February, a bit heavier in March and April. Snow has occurred as early as September and as late as early June. Wind is significant especially in winter and spring. First freeze is late September, last is late May.

POPULATION

DEMOGRAPHICS	AREA	U.S. AVG	ETHNIC COMPOSITION	AREA	U.S. AVG	RESIDENT PROFILE	AREA	U.S. AVG
Population	67,336		White	97.9%	75.1%	Single	41.3%	43.6%
Population density per sq. mile	12.6	447.3	Black	.5%	12.3%	Married	58.7%	56.4%
Population growth	10.0%	16.1%	Asian	.4%	3.6%	Divorced	12.4%	8.4%
Median age	36.7	35.5	American Indian	.6%	.9%	Separated	1.4%	3.0%
Average family size	2.4	2.7	Hispanic	3.0%	12.5%	Married with children	28.0%	28.7%
			Diversity measure	15.5%	35.2%	Single with children	10.2%	10.1%

ECONOMY & JOBS SCORE: 83/RANK: 55

INCOME	AREA	U.S. AVG	EMPLOYMENT	AREA	U.S. AVG	LARGEST EMPLOYING INDUSTRY		
Per capita income	$23,618	$23,420	Unemployment rate	4.2%	6.1%	Construction		
Household income	$45,555	$46,060	Recent job growth	3.5%	.9%			
Household income < $25K	25.9%	26.4%	Projected future job growth	13.1%	15.1%			
Household income > $75K	22.1%	24.5%	White collar	56.7%	54.5%			
Household income growth	64.4%	57.3%	Blue collar	43.3%	45.5%			

COST OF LIVING SCORE: 100/RANK: 1

INDEXES & TAXES	AREA	U.S. AVG	HOUSING	AREA	U.S. AVG	NECESSITIES	AREA	U.S. AVG
Cost of Living Index	86.7	100.0	Median home price	$100,400	$160,100	Food Index	105.0	100.0
Financial Progress Index	111.9	100.0	Home price appreciation	5.9%	7.1%	Housing Index	62.4	100.0
Income tax rate	0.000%	4.625%	Median rent	$527	$670	Utilities Index	106.8	100.0
Sales tax rate	5.000%	6.474%	Homes owned	53.1%	63.9%	Transportation Index	92.5	100.0
Property tax rate	$8.1	$15.6	Homes rented	21.9%	25.3%	Healthcare Index	94.2	100.0
			Housing affordability	61.0%	54.5%	Miscellaneous Cost Index	100.2	100.0

CLIMATE SCORE: 41/RANK: 194

TEMPERATURE	AREA	U.S. AVG	PRECIPITATION	AREA	U.S. AVG	COMFORTS & HAZARDS	AREA	U.S. AVG
January low	12.8°F	26.4°F	Annual inches precipitation	12.0	35.9	July relative humidity	49.0%	68.8%
July high	87.5°F	86.7°F	Annual inches snowfall	81.0	24.2	Annual days mostly sunny	219	212
Annual days > 90°F	26	38	Annual days precipitation	95	111	Annual days with thunderstorms	34	39
Annual days < 32°F	183	88	Annual days rain > 0.5 inches	5	23	Tornado risk score	7	19
Annual days < 0°F	22	6	Annual days snow > 1.5 inches	17	6	Hurricane risk score	0	15

TEMPERATURE

PRECIPITATION

DAYS OF CLOUDS & PRECIPITATION

EDUCATION SCORE: 76/RANK: 80

ACHIEVEMENT	AREA	U.S. AVG	PUBLIC SCHOOLS	AREA	U.S. AVG	HIGHER EDUCATION	AREA	U.S. AVG
High school degree	89.1%	80.2%	Expenditures per pupil	$5,608	$5,894	No. 2-year colleges	1	3
2-year college degree	9.1%	6.2%	Student/teacher ratio	15.6	16.7	No. 4-year colleges/universities	0	4
4-year college degree	14.8%	15.8%	Attending public school	96.7%	90.2%	No. highly ranked universities	0	1
Graduate/professional degree	7.3%	9.6%	State SAT score	1097	1020			
			State ACT score	21.4*	21.0			

HEALTH & HEALTHCARE SCORE: 72/RANK: 90

HAZARDS & ILLNESSES	AREA	U.S. AVG	HEALTHCARE	AREA	U.S. AVG
Air-quality score	24	45	Physicians per capita	215.3	261.1
Water-quality score	10	33	Hospital beds per capita	330.7	432.2
Pollen/allergy score	55	61	No. teaching hospitals	1	4
Stress score	21	50	Cost per doctor visit	$53	$67
Cancer mortality per capita	158.1	169.0	Cost per dental visit	$80	$82
Depression days per month	2.3	2.8	Cost per daily hospital room	$697	$733

CRIME SCORE: 65/RANK: 115

CRIME	AREA	U.S. AVG
Violent crime rate	297.2	456.0
Change in violent crime rate	-11.8%	-17.2%
Property crime rate	4,153.5	3,950.0
Change in property crime rate	-30.8%	-16.8%

TRANSPORTATION SCORE: 73/RANK: 92

COMMUTE	AREA	U.S. AVG	INTERCITY SERVICES	AREA	U.S. AVG	AUTOMOTIVE	AREA	U.S. AVG
Average commute time	16.7 min.	22.6 min.	Miles to nearest major airport	226	46	Insurance, annual premium	$672	$1,011
Commute by auto	86.0%	88.7%	Type of local airport	Large		Gas, cost per gallon	$1.47	$1.50
Commute by mass transit	.1%	1.8%	No. daily airline departures	812	294	Daily vehicle miles per capita	23.6	23.0
Work at home	3.1%	3.9%	Amtrak service	No				
Mass transit miles per capita	0.0	8.0	No. interstate highways	1	1			

LEISURE SCORE: 2/RANK: 321

DINING & SHOPPING	AREA	U.S. AVG	ENTERTAINMENT	AREA	U.S. AVG	OUTDOOR ACTIVITIES	AREA	U.S. AVG
Restaurant rating	1	1	Professional sports rating	2	4	Golf-course rating	1	4
No. outlet malls	0	2	College sports rating	1	4	Ski-area rating	1	4
No. Starbucks	0	11	Zoo/aquarium rating	1	3	National Park rating	2	3
No. warehouse clubs	3	4	Amusement park rating	1	3	Sq. miles inland water	3.0	4.0
			Botanical garden/arboretum rating	1	3	Miles of coastline	0.0	11.4

ARTS & CULTURE SCORE: 16/RANK: 275

MEDIA & LIBRARIES	AREA	U.S. AVG	PERFORMING ARTS	AREA	U.S. AVG	MUSEUMS	AREA	U.S. AVG
Arts radio rating	1	3	Classical music rating	3	4	Overall museum rating	4	6
No. public libraries	3	28	Ballet/dance rating	1	3	Art museum rating	3	5
Library volumes per capita	3.2	2.8	Professional theater rating	1	3	Science museum rating	2	4
			University arts programs rating	1	5	Children's museum rating	1	3

Cedar Rapids, IA

Score: 52.6   Rank: 207

Profile: Small city
Location: East-central Iowa, along Cedar River
Elevation: 594 feet
Time zone: Central Standard Time

PRO	CON
Attractive downtown	Harsh winters
Arts and culture	Recent job declines
Cost of living	Entertainment

Cedar Rapids is a modern city and industrial center built on an island at the "rapids" of the Cedar River. Downtown is modern in appearance, with many attractive parks. Arts and culture amenities are better than average for a small city, with a symphony and an art museum that holds the largest collection of works by native son Grant Wood. The Czech Village provides an interesting slice of cultural diversity. Nightlife and entertainment are somewhat lacking, but can be found in Iowa City, 20 miles south, and the recent employment picture is weak. Overall cost of living is attractive, but home prices are relatively high on an Iowa scale.

The area around Cedar Rapids is mainly agricultural, with areas of wooded hills to the south. The climate is humid continental with four distinct seasons and wide variations in temperature and precipitation. Summers are warm and fairly humid, with showers and thundershowers. Most precipitation falls during the summer months. Winters are cold and dry with brief snowstorms and occasional periods of extreme cold. First freeze is early October, last is late April.

POPULATION

DEMOGRAPHICS	AREA	U.S. AVG	ETHNIC COMPOSITION	AREA	U.S. AVG	RESIDENT PROFILE	AREA	U.S. AVG
Population	194,970		White	96.4%	75.1%	Single	39.8%	43.6%
Population density per sq. mile	271.7	447.3	Black	2.3%	12.3%	Married	60.2%	56.4%
Population growth	15.5%	16.1%	Asian	.9%	3.6%	Divorced	8.1%	8.4%
Median age	35.5	35.5	American Indian	.2%	.9%	Separated	1.6%	3.0%
Average family size	2.6	2.7	Hispanic	1.1%	12.5%	Married with children	29.8%	28.7%
			Diversity measure	13.1%	35.2%	Single with children	7.9%	10.1%

ECONOMY & JOBS SCORE: 34/RANK: 215

INCOME	AREA	U.S. AVG	EMPLOYMENT	AREA	U.S. AVG	LARGEST EMPLOYING INDUSTRY
Per capita income	$27,656	$23,420	Unemployment rate	4.3%	6.1%	Computer and Electronic Product Manufacturing
Household income	$54,695	$46,060	Recent job growth	-5.3%	.9%	
Household income < $25K	18.8%	26.4%	Projected future job growth	14.1%	15.1%	
Household income > $75K	30.8%	24.5%	White collar	58.0%	54.5%	
Household income growth	70.0%	57.3%	Blue collar	42.0%	45.5%	

COST OF LIVING SCORE: 27/RANK: 239

INDEXES & TAXES	AREA	U.S. AVG	HOUSING	AREA	U.S. AVG	NECESSITIES	AREA	U.S. AVG
Cost of Living Index	91.6	100.0	Median home price	$118,400	$160,100	Food Index	89.1	100.0
Financial Progress Index	127.3	100.0	Home price appreciation	4.2%	7.1%	Housing Index	73.5	100.0
Income tax rate	8.920%	4.625%	Median rent	$536	$670	Utilities Index	146.6	100.0
Sales tax rate	6.000%	6.474%	Homes owned	72.2%	63.9%	Transportation Index	98.1	100.0
Property tax rate	$18.0	$15.6	Homes rented	21.7%	25.3%	Healthcare Index	91.9	100.0
			Housing affordability	66.0%	54.5%	Miscellaneous Cost Index	99.6	100.0

CLIMATE — SCORE: 18 / RANK: 270

TEMPERATURE	AREA	U.S. AVG	PRECIPITATION	AREA	U.S. AVG	COMFORTS & HAZARDS	AREA	U.S. AVG
January low	13.0°F	26.4°F	Annual inches precipitation	36.0	35.9	July relative humidity	70.0%	68.8%
July high	85.2°F	86.7°F	Annual inches snowfall	30.0	24.2	Annual days mostly sunny	202	212
Annual days > 90°F	22	38	Annual days precipitation	112	111	Annual days with thunderstorms	47	39
Annual days < 32°F	136	88	Annual days rain > 0.5 inches	25	23	Tornado risk score	15	19
Annual days < 0°F	16	6	Annual days snow > 1.5 inches	9	6	Hurricane risk score	0	15

TEMPERATURE

PRECIPITATION

DAYS OF CLOUDS & PRECIPITATION

EDUCATION — SCORE: 84 / RANK: 54

ACHIEVEMENT	AREA	U.S. AVG	PUBLIC SCHOOLS	AREA	U.S. AVG	HIGHER EDUCATION	AREA	U.S. AVG
High school degree	90.1%	80.2%	Expenditures per pupil	$5,509	$5,894	No. 2-year colleges	1	3
2-year college degree	8.6%	6.2%	Student/teacher ratio	16.2	16.7	No. 4-year colleges/universities	3	4
4-year college degree	21.0%	15.8%	Attending public school	88.9%	90.2%	No. highly ranked universities	2	1
Graduate/professional degree	7.4%	9.6%	State SAT score	1183	1020			
			State ACT score	22.0*	21.0			

HEALTH & HEALTHCARE — SCORE: 86 / RANK: 46   CRIME — SCORE: 68 / RANK: 106

HAZARDS & ILLNESSES	AREA	U.S. AVG	HEALTHCARE	AREA	U.S. AVG	CRIME	AREA	U.S. AVG
Air-quality score	74	45	Physicians per capita	196.4	261.1	Violent crime rate	236.0	456.0
Water-quality score	38	33	Hospital beds per capita	424.6	432.2	Change in violent crime rate	-57.9%	-17.2%
Pollen/allergy score	45	61	No. teaching hospitals	2	4	Property crime rate	4,350.0	3,950.0
Stress score	10	50	Cost per doctor visit	$65	$67	Change in property crime rate	-17.6%	-16.8%
Cancer mortality per capita	167.9	169.0	Cost per dental visit	$79	$82			
Depression days per month	2.0	2.8	Cost per daily hospital room	$439	$733			

TRANSPORTATION — SCORE: 82 / RANK: 60

COMMUTE	AREA	U.S. AVG	INTERCITY SERVICES	AREA	U.S. AVG	AUTOMOTIVE	AREA	U.S. AVG
Average commute time	17.8 min.	22.6 min.	Miles to nearest major airport	6	46	Insurance, annual premium	$657	$1,011
Commute by auto	88.0%	88.7%	Type of local airport	Small		Gas, cost per gallon	$1.46	$1.50
Commute by mass transit	.9%	1.8%	No. daily airline departures	58	294	Daily vehicle miles per capita	21.1	23.0
Work at home	5.6%	3.9%	Amtrak service	No				
Mass transit miles per capita	6.8	8.0	No. interstate highways	1	1			

LEISURE — SCORE: 16 / RANK: 275

DINING & SHOPPING	AREA	U.S. AVG	ENTERTAINMENT	AREA	U.S. AVG	OUTDOOR ACTIVITIES	AREA	U.S. AVG
Restaurant rating	1	1	Professional sports rating	3	4	Golf-course rating	2	4
No. outlet malls	1	2	College sports rating	3	4	Ski-area rating	2	4
No. Starbucks	0	11	Zoo/aquarium rating	1	3	National Park rating	1	3
No. warehouse clubs	3	4	Amusement park rating	1	3	Sq. miles inland water	2.0	4.0
			Botanical garden/arboretum rating	1	3	Miles of coastline	0.0	11.4

ARTS & CULTURE — SCORE: 53 / RANK: 153

MEDIA & LIBRARIES	AREA	U.S. AVG	PERFORMING ARTS	AREA	U.S. AVG	MUSEUMS	AREA	U.S. AVG
Arts radio rating	1	3	Classical music rating	4	4	Overall museum rating	5	6
No. public libraries	11	28	Ballet/dance rating	1	3	Art museum rating	4	5
Library volumes per capita	3.1	2.8	Professional theater rating	1	3	Science museum rating	3	4
			University arts programs rating	6	5	Children's museum rating	5	3

Champaign–Urbana, IL

Profile: College-town complex
Location: East-central Illinois, 110 miles south of Chicago
Elevation: 662 feet
Time zone: Central Standard Time

Score: 80.7   **Rank:** 33

PRO	CON
College-town atmosphere	Isolation
Cost of living	Harsh winters
Educated population	Little outdoor recreation

Champaign-Urbana is an agricultural center as well as home to the University of Illinois. It is a clean agricultural town well rounded by its college presence. The cities offer what one would expect from a large Big Ten university town: entertainment, top sporting events, good museums, and a mix of restaurants. Cost of living is reasonable for a major college town, and the area features stable employment and low commute times. While entertainment and arts amenities are strong, there isn't much outdoor recreation. It gets a high ranking because of a lack of any strong negatives.

The area is mainly level prairie surrounded by farmland. To the east the terrain starts to undulate, particularly near the Wabash River valley just east of the Indiana border. The climate is continental with variety, including warm, humid, intermittently wet summers, and variable winters. Summer thunderstorms are common and winter changes bring alternating periods of mildness and cold with snow cover. First freeze is late October, last is late April.

POPULATION

DEMOGRAPHICS	AREA	U.S. AVG	ETHNIC COMPOSITION	AREA	U.S. AVG	RESIDENT PROFILE	AREA	U.S. AVG
Population	183,159		White	90.5%	75.1%	Single	40.3%	43.6%
Population density per sq. mile	183.7	447.3	Black	5.1%	12.3%	Married	59.7%	56.4%
Population growth	5.9%	16.1%	Asian	3.7%	3.6%	Divorced	7.4%	8.4%
Median age	28.6	35.5	American Indian	.1%	.9%	Separated	1.4%	3.0%
Average family size	2.5	2.7	Hispanic	1.6%	12.5%	Married with children	28.6%	28.7%
			Diversity measure	37.5%	35.2%	Single with children	8.8%	10.1%

ECONOMY & JOBS SCORE: 71/RANK: 92

INCOME	AREA	U.S. AVG	EMPLOYMENT	AREA	U.S. AVG	LARGEST EMPLOYING INDUSTRY
Per capita income	$22,753	$23,420	Unemployment rate	3.2%	6.1%	Healthcare and Social Assistance
Household income	$40,856	$46,060	Recent job growth	2.0%	.9%	
Household income < $25K	28.7%	26.4%	Projected future job growth	13.2%	15.1%	
Household income > $75K	21.2%	24.5%	White collar	62.3%	54.5%	
Household income growth	53.6%	57.3%	Blue collar	37.7%	45.5%	

COST OF LIVING SCORE: 48/RANK: 170

INDEXES & TAXES	AREA	U.S. AVG	HOUSING	AREA	U.S. AVG	NECESSITIES	AREA	U.S. AVG
Cost of Living Index	92.1	100.0	Median home price	$114,900	$160,100	Food Index	98.5	100.0
Financial Progress Index	94.5	100.0	Home price appreciation	5.0%	7.1%	Housing Index	71.4	100.0
Income tax rate	3.000%	4.625%	Median rent	$640	$670	Utilities Index	118.1	100.0
Sales tax rate	6.500%	6.474%	Homes owned	67.2%	63.9%	Transportation Index	106.6	100.0
Property tax rate	$26.6	$15.6	Homes rented	25.6%	25.3%	Healthcare Index	96.4	100.0
			Housing affordability	47.0%	54.5%	Miscellaneous Cost Index	103.3	100.0

CLIMATE SCORE: 39/RANK: 200

TEMPERATURE	AREA	U.S. AVG	PRECIPITATION	AREA	U.S. AVG	COMFORTS & HAZARDS	AREA	U.S. AVG
January low	15.7°F	26.4°F	Annual inches precipitation	35.0	35.9	July relative humidity	72.0%	68.8%
July high	85.5°F	86.7°F	Annual inches snowfall	23.0	24.2	Annual days mostly sunny	197	212
Annual days > 90°F	17	38	Annual days precipitation	111	111	Annual days with thunderstorms	49	39
Annual days < 32°F	132	88	Annual days rain > 0.5 inches	24	23	Tornado risk score	22	19
Annual days < 0°F	11	6	Annual days snow > 1.5 inches	5	6	Hurricane risk score	3	15

TEMPERATURE

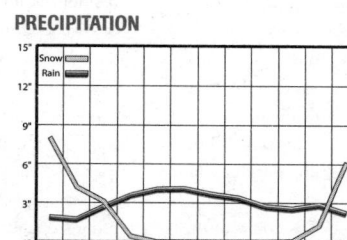

PRECIPITATION

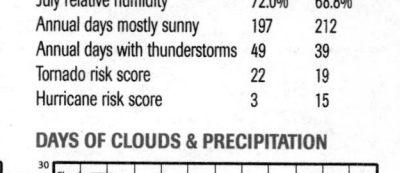

DAYS OF CLOUDS & PRECIPITATION

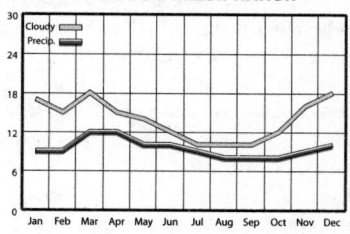

EDUCATION — SCORE: 91/RANK: 29

ACHIEVEMENT	AREA	U.S. AVG	PUBLIC SCHOOLS	AREA	U.S. AVG	HIGHER EDUCATION	AREA	U.S. AVG
High school degree	91.6%	80.2%	Expenditures per pupil	$5,594	$5,894	No. 2-year colleges	1	3
2-year college degree	6.9%	6.2%	Student/teacher ratio	14.5	16.7	No. 4-year colleges/universities	1	4
4-year college degree	18.6%	15.8%	Attending public school	89.2%	90.2%	No. highly ranked universities	0	1
Graduate/professional degree	19.4%	9.6%	State SAT score	1179	1020			
			State ACT score	20.2*	21.0			

HEALTH & HEALTHCARE — SCORE: 47/RANK: 173

CRIME — SCORE: 64/RANK: 119

HAZARDS & ILLNESSES	AREA	U.S. AVG	HEALTHCARE	AREA	U.S. AVG	CRIME	AREA	U.S. AVG
Air-quality score	59	45	Physicians per capita	275.7	261.1	Violent crime rate	397.7	456.0
Water-quality score	30	33	Hospital beds per capita	315.6	432.2	Change in violent crime rate	-30.7%	-17.2%
Pollen/allergy score	54	61	No. teaching hospitals	2	4	Property crime rate	3,737.1	3,950.0
Stress score	5	50	Cost per doctor visit	$67	$67	Change in property crime rate	-22.3%	-16.8%
Cancer mortality per capita	156.8	169.0	Cost per dental visit	$81	$82			
Depression days per month	1.7	2.8	Cost per daily hospital room	$663	$733			

TRANSPORTATION — SCORE: 95/RANK: 18

COMMUTE	AREA	U.S. AVG	INTERCITY SERVICES	AREA	U.S. AVG	AUTOMOTIVE	AREA	U.S. AVG
Average commute time	16.8 min.	22.6 min.	Miles to nearest major airport	109	46	Insurance, annual premium	$896	$1,011
Commute by auto	88.0%	88.7%	Type of local airport	Medium		Gas, cost per gallon	$1.48	$1.50
Commute by mass transit	1.5%	1.8%	No. daily airline departures	319	294	Daily vehicle miles per capita	17.7	23.0
Work at home	5.4%	3.9%	Amtrak service	Yes				
Mass transit miles per capita	16.3	8.0	No. interstate highways	3	1			

LEISURE — SCORE: 25/RANK: 247

DINING & SHOPPING	AREA	U.S. AVG	ENTERTAINMENT	AREA	U.S. AVG	OUTDOOR ACTIVITIES	AREA	U.S. AVG
Restaurant rating	1	1	Professional sports rating	2	4	Golf-course rating	2	4
No. outlet malls	1	2	College sports rating	6	4	Ski-area rating	2	4
No. Starbucks	0	11	Zoo/aquarium rating	1	3	National Park rating	1	3
No. warehouse clubs	3	4	Amusement park rating	1	3	Sq. miles inland water	1.0	4.0
			Botanical garden/arboretum rating	1	3	Miles of coastline	0.0	11.4

ARTS & CULTURE — SCORE: 66/RANK: 111

MEDIA & LIBRARIES	AREA	U.S. AVG	PERFORMING ARTS	AREA	U.S. AVG	MUSEUMS	AREA	U.S. AVG
Arts radio rating	8	3	Classical music rating	3	4	Overall museum rating	5	6
No. public libraries	12	28	Ballet/dance rating	1	3	Art museum rating	6	5
Library volumes per capita	4.4	2.8	Professional theater rating	1	3	Science museum rating	6	4
			University arts programs rating	5	5	Children's museum rating	1	3

Charleston, WV

Score: 49.3   Rank: 233

Profile: Capital city
Location: West-central West Virginia along Kanawha River
Elevation: 827 feet
Time zone: Eastern Standard Time

PRO	CON
Capital-city amenities	Heavy industry
Cost of living	Entertainment
Nearby water recreation	Isolation

Charleston is the state capital and government and commercial center of West Virginia. The city is also an industrial center mainly for chemical-related industries, which stretch up the Kanawha Valley to the east. There are some modest cultural amenities downtown. White-water rafting on the Gawley and New rivers is the most prominent recreational feature. While the economy is cyclical, current job growth prospects are the best in the state. But the city is isolated, and air-service options are among the worst in the country for capital cities.

Charleston lies at the junction of the Kanawha and Elk rivers in the western foothills of the Appalachian Mountains. The main urban and business areas have developed along the two river valleys, while some residential areas are in nearby valleys and on the surrounding deciduous-wooded hills. The climate is highly variable, particularly from mid-autumn through spring. Winters can vary greatly from one season to the next. Summer and early fall are more consistent, with warm temperatures and hazy humidity and an occasional hot spell. Summer precipitation falls mainly as thundershowers. Most winters have two or three extended cold spells where temperatures stay below freezing. Snow falls, but only lingers on hilltops. Cool air may get trapped in the valley, creating fog and occasional smog. First freeze is mid-October, last is late April.

POPULATION

DEMOGRAPHICS	AREA	U.S. AVG	ETHNIC COMPOSITION	AREA	U.S. AVG	RESIDENT PROFILE	AREA	U.S. AVG
Population	248,020		White	95.3%	75.1%	Single	42.1%	43.6%
Population density per sq. mile	198.5	447.3	Black	3.9%	12.3%	Married	57.9%	56.4%
Population growth	-1.0%	16.1%	Asian	.6%	3.6%	Divorced	8.7%	8.4%
Median age	40.3	35.5	American Indian	.1%	.9%	Separated	2.0%	3.0%
Average family size	2.5	2.7	Hispanic	.3%	12.5%	Married with children	28.1%	28.7%
			Diversity measure	15.5%	35.2%	Single with children	9.4%	10.1%

ECONOMY & JOBS — SCORE: 64/RANK: 118

INCOME	AREA	U.S. AVG	EMPLOYMENT	AREA	U.S. AVG	LARGEST EMPLOYING INDUSTRY
Per capita income	$22,893	$23,420	Unemployment rate	5.0%	6.1%	Healthcare and Social Assistance
Household income	$38,723	$46,060	Recent job growth	-.1%	.9%	
Household income < $25K	32.0%	26.4%	Projected future job growth	15.0%	15.1%	
Household income > $75K	20.1%	24.5%	White collar	59.9%	54.5%	
Household income growth	57.2%	57.3%	Blue collar	40.1%	45.5%	

COST OF LIVING — SCORE: 30/RANK: 232

INDEXES & TAXES	AREA	U.S. AVG	HOUSING	AREA	U.S. AVG	NECESSITIES	AREA	U.S. AVG
Cost of Living Index	84.9	100.0	Median home price	$106,400	$160,100	Food Index	99.5	100.0
Financial Progress Index	97.2	100.0	Home price appreciation	3.7%	7.1%	Housing Index	66.1	100.0
Income tax rate	6.000%	4.625%	Median rent	$531	$670	Utilities Index	77.4	100.0
Sales tax rate	6.000%	6.474%	Homes owned	69.0%	63.9%	Transportation Index	104.6	100.0
Property tax rate	$8.2	$15.6	Homes rented	21.3%	25.3%	Healthcare Index	89.4	100.0
			Housing affordability	58.0%	54.5%	Miscellaneous Cost Index	95.9	100.0

CLIMATE — SCORE: 56/RANK: 143

TEMPERATURE	AREA	U.S. AVG	PRECIPITATION	AREA	U.S. AVG	COMFORTS & HAZARDS	AREA	U.S. AVG
January low	25.6°F	26.4°F	Annual inches precipitation	38.9	35.9	July relative humidity	71.0%	68.8%
July high	85.7°F	86.7°F	Annual inches snowfall	25.6	24.2	Annual days mostly sunny	166	212
Annual days > 90°F	17	38	Annual days precipitation	139	111	Annual days with thunderstorms	44	39
Annual days < 32°F	23	88	Annual days rain > 0.5 inches	27	23	Tornado risk score	0	19
Annual days < 0°F	2	6	Annual days snow > 1.5 inches	7	6	Hurricane risk score	5	15

TEMPERATURE

PRECIPITATION

DAYS OF CLOUDS & PRECIPITATION

EDUCATION — SCORE: 47/RANK: 174

ACHIEVEMENT	AREA	U.S. AVG	PUBLIC SCHOOLS	AREA	U.S. AVG	HIGHER EDUCATION	AREA	U.S. AVG
High school degree	80.8%	80.2%	Expenditures per pupil	$6,100	$5,894	No. 2-year colleges	1	3
2-year college degree	4.5%	6.2%	Student/teacher ratio	16.0	16.7	No. 4-year colleges/universities	2	4
4-year college degree	12.5%	15.8%	Attending public school	92.8%	90.2%	No. highly ranked universities	0	1
Graduate/professional degree	7.9%	9.6%	State SAT score	1032	1020			
			State ACT score	20.3*	21.0			

HEALTH & HEALTHCARE — SCORE: 22/RANK: 257 | CRIME — SCORE: 36/RANK: 211

HAZARDS & ILLNESSES	AREA	U.S. AVG	HEALTHCARE	AREA	U.S. AVG	CRIME	AREA	U.S. AVG
Air-quality score	59	45	Physicians per capita	360.1	261.1	Violent crime rate	423.4	456.0
Water-quality score	13	33	Hospital beds per capita	561.9	432.2	Change in violent crime rate	9.4%	-17.2%
Pollen/allergy score	60	61	No. teaching hospitals	1	4	Property crime rate	4,080.4	3,950.0
Stress score	57	50	Cost per doctor visit	$70	$67	Change in property crime rate	11.0%	-16.8%
Cancer mortality per capita	179.6	169.0	Cost per dental visit	$73	$82			
Depression days per month	3.8	2.8	Cost per daily hospital room	$318	$733			

TRANSPORTATION — SCORE: 14/RANK: 282

COMMUTE	AREA	U.S. AVG	INTERCITY SERVICES	AREA	U.S. AVG	AUTOMOTIVE	AREA	U.S. AVG
Average commute time	23.0 min.	22.6 min.	Miles to nearest major airport	116	46	Insurance, annual premium	$942	$1,011
Commute by auto	92.0%	88.7%	Type of local airport	Small		Gas, cost per gallon	$1.49	$1.50
Commute by mass transit	2.1%	1.8%	No. daily airline departures	64	294	Daily vehicle miles per capita	29.1	23.0
Work at home	1.9%	3.9%	Amtrak service	Yes				
Mass transit miles per capita	11.0	8.0	No. interstate highways	1	1			

LEISURE SCORE: 66/RANK: 111

DINING & SHOPPING	AREA	U.S. AVG	ENTERTAINMENT	AREA	U.S. AVG	OUTDOOR ACTIVITIES	AREA	U.S. AVG
Restaurant rating	1	1	Professional sports rating	3	4	Golf-course rating	3	4
No. outlet malls	1	2	College sports rating	2	4	Ski-area rating	1	4
No. Starbucks	0	11	Zoo/aquarium rating	1	3	National Park rating	1	3
No. warehouse clubs	3	4	Amusement park rating	1	3	Sq. miles inland water	3.0	4.0
			Botanical garden/arboretum rating	1	3	Miles of coastline	0.0	11.4

ARTS & CULTURE SCORE: 72/RANK: 90

MEDIA & LIBRARIES	AREA	U.S. AVG	PERFORMING ARTS	AREA	U.S. AVG	MUSEUMS	AREA	U.S. AVG
Arts radio rating	1	3	Classical music rating	4	4	Overall museum rating	4	6
No. public libraries	17	28	Ballet/dance rating	3	3	Art museum rating	6	5
Library volumes per capita	2.8	2.8	Professional theater rating	1	3	Science museum rating	5	4
			University arts programs rating	5	5	Children's museum rating	3	3

Charleston–North Charleston, SC

Score: 74.5   Rank: 63

Profile: Mid-size–coastal-city complex
Location: Southeastern South Carolina on the Atlantic Coast
Elevation: 48 feet
Time zone: Eastern Standard Time

PRO
Historic interest
Arts and culture
Pleasant winters

CON
Air service
Tourist impact
Hot, humid summers

Charleston is a unique, 300-year-old city with a historic tradition as an 18th-century seaport and business center, as well as the location of the initial moments of the Civil War. History has left its imprint, particularly on the city center, where an enormous and beautifully preserved historic district is popular with local residents and tourists. Today there is some small industry, but the major industry and seaport are gone. To the northwest are the characteristics of a typical southern city, with areas of magnolia-lined streets, older homes, and commercial buildings, although there are some less attractive and impoverished areas as well. Farther from the coast and to the west are old plantation homes in varying conditions. Besides historic sites, the city has some minor cultural amenities and good seafood and southern-style restaurants. The lifestyle is slow paced, pleasant, and dignified, but the city is relatively isolated from other big cities. There are a number of recreational opportunities and excellent golf courses, especially in the island areas to the south. Overall cost of living is low for what is available, but there is a big difference in cost between the historic center and outlying areas.

Charleston is a peninsula city bounded by two rivers, opening onto a spacious harbor. The terrain is generally level with gradual increases in elevation toward inland areas. Abundant coniferous forests occur inland. The climate is humid subtropical, modified considerably by the ocean. Winter low temperatures may be 10°F to 15°F higher on the peninsula than inland. Summer is warm and humid, but temperatures exceeding 100°F are infrequent and sea breezes keep coastal temperatures lower. Fall is pleasant with sun, rare temperature extremes, and long Indian summers. The December to February winter is mild with periods of steady rain and chances of snow flurries, but accumulation is rare. Most winters have one cold spell, but temperatures below 20°F are unusual. Spring thunderstorms, some severe, and the occasional Atlantic hurricane, punctuate precipitation patterns.

POPULATION

DEMOGRAPHICS	AREA	U.S. AVG	ETHNIC COMPOSITION	AREA	U.S. AVG	RESIDENT PROFILE	AREA	U.S. AVG
Population	562,666		White	54.9%	75.1%	Single	48.4%	43.6%
Population density per sq. mile	217.1	447.3	Black	43.6%	12.3%	Married	51.6%	56.4%
Population growth	11.0%	16.1%	Asian	1.0%	3.6%	Divorced	6.4%	8.4%
Median age	34.2	35.5	American Indian	.3%	.9%	Separated	5.6%	3.0%
Average family size	2.9	2.7	Hispanic	1.4%	12.5%	Married with children	30.2%	28.7%
			Diversity measure	49.1%	35.2%	Single with children	14.4%	10.1%

ECONOMY & JOBS SCORE: 19/RANK: 266

INCOME	AREA	U.S. AVG	EMPLOYMENT	AREA	U.S. AVG	LARGEST EMPLOYING INDUSTRY
Per capita income	$22,679	$23,420	Unemployment rate	4.6%	6.1%	Motor Vehicle Parts Manufacturing
Household income	$42,473	$46,060	Recent job growth	4.5%	.9%	
Household income < $25K	26.2%	26.4%	Projected future job growth	22.0%	15.1%	
Household income > $75K	22.0%	24.5%	White collar	50.2%	54.5%	
Household income growth	51.1%	57.3%	Blue collar	49.8%	45.5%	

COST OF LIVING SCORE: 58/RANK: 139

INDEXES & TAXES	AREA	U.S. AVG	HOUSING	AREA	U.S. AVG	NECESSITIES	AREA	U.S. AVG
Cost of Living Index	100.0	100.0	Median home price	$162,700	$160,100	Food Index	102.8	100.0
Financial Progress Index	90.5	100.0	Home price appreciation	9.3%	7.1%	Housing Index	101.1	100.0
Income tax rate	7.000%	4.625%	Median rent	$578	$670	Utilities Index	92.4	100.0
Sales tax rate	6.000%	6.474%	Homes owned	64.9%	63.9%	Transportation Index	97.8	100.0
Property tax rate	$10.2	$15.6	Homes rented	21.4%	25.3%	Healthcare Index	96.8	100.0
			Housing affordability	63.0%	54.5%	Miscellaneous Cost Index	100.6	100.0

CLIMATE SCORE: 80/RANK: 67

TEMPERATURE	AREA	U.S. AVG	PRECIPITATION	AREA	U.S. AVG	COMFORTS & HAZARDS	AREA	U.S. AVG
January low	37.3°F	26.4°F	Annual inches precipitation	52.0	35.9	July relative humidity	76.0%	68.8%
July high	89.1°F	86.7°F	Annual inches snowfall	.5	24.2	Annual days mostly sunny	214	212
Annual days > 90°F	47	38	Annual days precipitation	115	111	Annual days with thunderstorms	56	39
Annual days < 32°F	36	88	Annual days rain > 0.5 inches	32	23	Tornado risk score	14	19
Annual days < 0°F	0	6	Annual days snow > 1.5 inches	1	6	Hurricane risk score	60	15

TEMPERATURE

PRECIPITATION

DAYS OF CLOUDS & PRECIPITATION

EDUCATION SCORE: 33/RANK: 221

ACHIEVEMENT	AREA	U.S. AVG	PUBLIC SCHOOLS	AREA	U.S. AVG	HIGHER EDUCATION	AREA	U.S. AVG
High school degree	81.3%	80.2%	Expenditures per pupil	$5,032	$5,894	No. 2-year colleges	2	3
2-year college degree	6.4%	6.2%	Student/teacher ratio	15.5	16.7	No. 4-year colleges/universities	3	4
4-year college degree	16.3%	15.8%	Attending public school	88.0%	90.2%	No. highly ranked universities	1	1
Graduate/professional degree	8.7%	9.6%	State SAT score	989*	1020			
			State ACT score	19.2	21.0			

HEALTH & HEALTHCARE SCORE: 84/RANK: 52

CRIME SCORE: 25/RANK: 246

HAZARDS & ILLNESSES	AREA	U.S. AVG	HEALTHCARE	AREA	U.S. AVG	CRIME	AREA	U.S. AVG
Air-quality score	95	45	Physicians per capita	393.1	261.1	Violent crime rate	613.3	456.0
Water-quality score	26	33	Hospital beds per capita	381.8	432.2	Change in violent crime rate	-35.5%	-17.2%
Pollen/allergy score	70	61	No. teaching hospitals	3	4	Property crime rate	4,392.9	3,950.0
Stress score	56	50	Cost per doctor visit	$75	$67	Change in property crime rate	-26.8%	-16.8%
Cancer mortality per capita	183.8	169.0	Cost per dental visit	$84	$82			
Depression days per month	2.4	2.8	Cost per daily hospital room	$587	$733			

TRANSPORTATION SCORE: 38/RANK: 204

COMMUTE	AREA	U.S. AVG	INTERCITY SERVICES	AREA	U.S. AVG	AUTOMOTIVE	AREA	U.S. AVG
Average commute time	24.6 min.	22.6 min.	Miles to nearest major airport	8	46	Insurance, annual premium	$1,078	$1,011
Commute by auto	90.2%	88.7%	Type of local airport	Small		Gas, cost per gallon	$1.34	$1.50
Commute by mass transit	1.6%	1.8%	No. daily airline departures	65	294	Daily vehicle miles per capita	21.2	23.0
Work at home	2.9%	3.9%	Amtrak service	Yes				
Mass transit miles per capita	5.3	8.0	No. interstate highways	1	1			

LEISURE SCORE: 17/RANK: 273

DINING & SHOPPING	AREA	U.S. AVG	ENTERTAINMENT	AREA	U.S. AVG	OUTDOOR ACTIVITIES	AREA	U.S. AVG
Restaurant rating	3	1	Professional sports rating	3	4	Golf-course rating	4	4
No. outlet malls	0	2	College sports rating	4	4	Ski-area rating	1	4
No. Starbucks	7	11	Zoo/aquarium rating	3	3	National Park rating	9	3
No. warehouse clubs	4	4	Amusement park rating	1	3	Sq. miles inland water	10.0	4.0
			Botanical garden/arboretum rating	7	3	Miles of coastline	72.9	11.4

ARTS & CULTURE SCORE: 68/RANK: 105

MEDIA & LIBRARIES	AREA	U.S. AVG	PERFORMING ARTS	AREA	U.S. AVG	MUSEUMS	AREA	U.S. AVG
Arts radio rating	1	3	Classical music rating	4	4	Overall museum rating	8	6
No. public libraries	22	28	Ballet/dance rating	5	3	Art museum rating	7	5
Library volumes per capita	2.4	2.8	Professional theater rating	1	3	Science museum rating	3	4
			University arts programs rating	8	5	Children's museum rating	1	3

Charlotte–Gastonia–Rock Hill, NC-SC

Score: 66.6   **Rank: 98**

Profile: Mid-size-city complex
Location: Southwest North Carolina along Catawba River near South
    Carolina border
Elevation: 769 feet
Time zone: Eastern Standard Time

PRO	CON
Diverse economy	Crime rate
Educated population	Urban sprawl
Attractive housing	Healthcare

Charlotte is a modern city with agricultural and regional banking roots. Today the city is reputedly the headquarters for more banks than any city outside New York, and is the home to such financial heavyweights as BankAmerica and First Union. A diverse commercial and industrial economy has developed around the financial industry. Downtown is a mix of contemporary skyscrapers and 19th-century neighborhoods. Attractive historic neighborhoods lie to the immediate south, followed by a large area of appealing suburban development and golf courses. Traffic is an issue; the freeways are congested, but well-planned surface streets mitigate some problems. It's not a world-class entertainment center, but the city has a good collection of museums, shopping options, and sports teams. Charlotte is home to the Carolina Panthers NFL team, but is still adjusting to the loss of the Charlotte Hornets NBA team. There is an active NASCAR racing circuit in the area. The city has modern transportation amenities and even a few direct flights to Europe. A $3-billion mass-transit system including five light-rail lines is planned. While it has its share of "New South workaholics," the Charlotte area is an attractive blend of the faster-paced New South and older Southern gentility. Gastonia to the west won a 2001 National Civic League All-America City Award, but it is still in a rebuilding phase and is relatively unattractive.

This city complex sits in the Carolina Piedmont, a transitional area of rolling country between the mountains to the west and the Coastal Plain to the east. The mountains to the northwest moderate winter temperatures by blocking and warming cold northwest winds. The ocean is too far away to cool summer temperatures but does supply some warmth in winter. Summers are warm, with days over 90°F, while winters are cool. Temperatures fall as low as freezing about 1 in 2 winter days. Winter weather is changeable, with occasional cold periods, but extreme cold is rare. Snow and snow accumulation are infrequent. Late summer and fall hurricanes can produce substantial rainfall but seldom damaging winds.

POPULATION

DEMOGRAPHICS	AREA	U.S. AVG	ETHNIC COMPOSITION	AREA	U.S. AVG	RESIDENT PROFILE	AREA	U.S. AVG
Population	1,584,898		White	79.3%	75.1%	Single	45.4%	43.6%
Population density per sq. mile	469.1	447.3	Black	19.0%	12.3%	Married	54.6%	56.4%
Population growth	36.4%	16.1%	Asian	1.1%	3.6%	Divorced	7.5%	8.4%
Median age	34.5	35.5	American Indian	.4%	.9%	Separated	4.8%	3.0%
Average family size	2.6	2.7	Hispanic	1.4%	12.5%	Married with children	27.4%	28.7%
			Diversity measure	43.8%	35.2%	Single with children	10.6%	10.1%

ECONOMY & JOBS SCORE: 38/RANK: 202

INCOME	AREA	U.S. AVG	EMPLOYMENT	AREA	U.S. AVG	LARGEST EMPLOYING INDUSTRY
Per capita income	$26,691	$23,420	Unemployment rate	7.0%	6.1%	Textile Mills
Household income	$51,559	$46,060	Recent job growth	.7%	.9%	
Household income < $25K	21.0%	26.4%	Projected future job growth	18.7%	15.1%	
Household income > $75K	29.7%	24.5%	White collar	54.1%	54.5%	
Household income growth	65.6%	57.3%	Blue collar	45.9%	45.5%	

COST OF LIVING SCORE: 25/RANK: 248

INDEXES & TAXES	AREA	U.S. AVG	HOUSING	AREA	U.S. AVG	NECESSITIES	AREA	U.S. AVG
Cost of Living Index	95.7	100.0	Median home price	$150,000	$160,100	Food Index	98.3	100.0
Financial Progress Index	114.8	100.0	Home price appreciation	4.6%	7.1%	Housing Index	93.2	100.0
Income tax rate	7.000%	4.625%	Median rent	$697	$670	Utilities Index	94.5	100.0
Sales tax rate	7.500%	6.474%	Homes owned	68.1%	63.9%	Transportation Index	96.0	100.0
Property tax rate	$13.2	$15.6	Homes rented	25.9%	25.3%	Healthcare Index	102.6	100.0
			Housing affordability	60.0%	54.5%	Miscellaneous Cost Index	96.4	100.0

CLIMATE SCORE: 44/RANK: 183

TEMPERATURE	AREA	U.S. AVG	PRECIPITATION	AREA	U.S. AVG	COMFORTS & HAZARDS	AREA	U.S. AVG
January low	32.1°F	26.4°F	Annual inches precipitation	43.0	35.9	July relative humidity	69.0%	68.8%
July high	88.3°F	86.7°F	Annual inches snowfall	6.0	24.2	Annual days mostly sunny	214	212
Annual days > 90°F	31	38	Annual days precipitation	111	111	Annual days with thunderstorms	42	39
Annual days < 32°F	71	88	Annual days rain > 0.5 inches	28	23	Tornado risk score	14	19
Annual days < 0°F	0	6	Annual days snow > 1.5 inches	2	6	Hurricane risk score	24	15

TEMPERATURE

PRECIPITATION

DAYS OF CLOUDS & PRECIPITATION

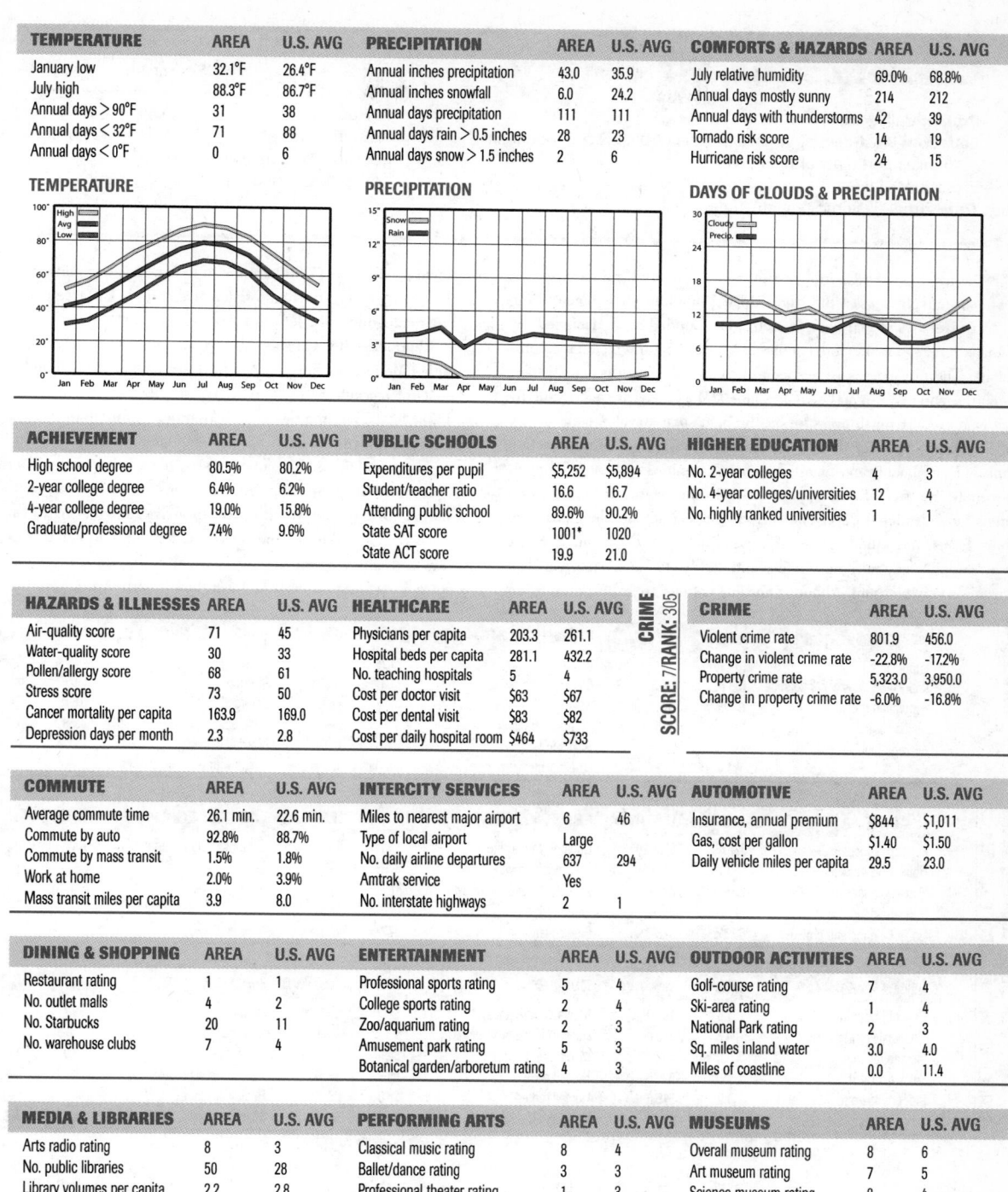

EDUCATION SCORE: 65/RANK: 114

ACHIEVEMENT	AREA	U.S. AVG	PUBLIC SCHOOLS	AREA	U.S. AVG	HIGHER EDUCATION	AREA	U.S. AVG
High school degree	80.5%	80.2%	Expenditures per pupil	$5,252	$5,894	No. 2-year colleges	4	3
2-year college degree	6.4%	6.2%	Student/teacher ratio	16.6	16.7	No. 4-year colleges/universities	12	4
4-year college degree	19.0%	15.8%	Attending public school	89.6%	90.2%	No. highly ranked universities	1	1
Graduate/professional degree	7.4%	9.6%	State SAT score	1001*	1020			
			State ACT score	19.9	21.0			

HEALTH & HEALTHCARE SCORE: 43/RANK: 188

HAZARDS & ILLNESSES	AREA	U.S. AVG	HEALTHCARE	AREA	U.S. AVG
Air-quality score	71	45	Physicians per capita	203.3	261.1
Water-quality score	30	33	Hospital beds per capita	281.1	432.2
Pollen/allergy score	68	61	No. teaching hospitals	5	4
Stress score	73	50	Cost per doctor visit	$63	$67
Cancer mortality per capita	163.9	169.0	Cost per dental visit	$83	$82
Depression days per month	2.3	2.8	Cost per daily hospital room	$464	$733

CRIME SCORE: 7/RANK: 305

CRIME	AREA	U.S. AVG
Violent crime rate	801.9	456.0
Change in violent crime rate	-22.8%	-17.2%
Property crime rate	5,323.0	3,950.0
Change in property crime rate	-6.0%	-16.8%

TRANSPORTATION SCORE: 35/RANK: 214

COMMUTE	AREA	U.S. AVG	INTERCITY SERVICES	AREA	U.S. AVG	AUTOMOTIVE	AREA	U.S. AVG
Average commute time	26.1 min.	22.6 min.	Miles to nearest major airport	6	46	Insurance, annual premium	$844	$1,011
Commute by auto	92.8%	88.7%	Type of local airport	Large		Gas, cost per gallon	$1.40	$1.50
Commute by mass transit	1.5%	1.8%	No. daily airline departures	637	294	Daily vehicle miles per capita	29.5	23.0
Work at home	2.0%	3.9%	Amtrak service	Yes				
Mass transit miles per capita	3.9	8.0	No. interstate highways	2	1			

LEISURE SCORE: 65/RANK: 114

DINING & SHOPPING	AREA	U.S. AVG	ENTERTAINMENT	AREA	U.S. AVG	OUTDOOR ACTIVITIES	AREA	U.S. AVG
Restaurant rating	1	1	Professional sports rating	5	4	Golf-course rating	7	4
No. outlet malls	4	2	College sports rating	2	4	Ski-area rating	1	4
No. Starbucks	20	11	Zoo/aquarium rating	2	3	National Park rating	2	3
No. warehouse clubs	7	4	Amusement park rating	5	3	Sq. miles inland water	3.0	4.0
			Botanical garden/arboretum rating	4	3	Miles of coastline	0.0	11.4

ARTS & CULTURE SCORE: 70/RANK: 98

MEDIA & LIBRARIES	AREA	U.S. AVG	PERFORMING ARTS	AREA	U.S. AVG	MUSEUMS	AREA	U.S. AVG
Arts radio rating	8	3	Classical music rating	8	4	Overall museum rating	8	6
No. public libraries	50	28	Ballet/dance rating	3	3	Art museum rating	7	5
Library volumes per capita	2.2	2.8	Professional theater rating	1	3	Science museum rating	8	4
			University arts programs rating	8	5	Children's museum rating	4	3

Charlottesville, VA

Score: 100.0   Rank: 1

Profile: College town
Location: West-central Virginia at base of Blue Ridge Mountains,
75 miles northeast of Richmond
Elevation: 480 feet
Time zone: Eastern Standard Time

PRO
Historic interest
College-town amenities
Attractive setting

CON
High home prices
Air service
Rapid growth

The no. 1 ranked Charlottesville is one of many Virginia cities set attractively against the Blue Ridge Mountains. It is home to the University of Virginia, which was founded and designed by Thomas Jefferson in the 18th century as an architectural model for a university. The city possesses a special mix of college-town and historic amenities and is clean and heavily shaded. Most areas are accessible by foot or bicycle. Growth pressure has brought some development mainly to the north, but so far the city has resisted most forms of unattractive sprawl. The school brings an assortment of amenities and entertainment, and there are recreational opportunities in the nearby mountains and Shenandoah National Park. The surrounding countryside has attractive horse farms and other agriculture. Washington, D.C., about 2 hours away, supplies any missing services and adds to the area's interest. The climate is very pleasant. Although housing options are excellent, median home prices of $177,000 are the only real negative and directly reflect the quality of the area and resistance to sprawl. The area does well in all other categories. Mr. Jefferson would be proud.

Charlottesville is located on a wooded plateau at the base of the Blue Ridge Mountains. Surrounding hills are mostly wooded and steep with areas of agriculture in the valleys. To the west the mountains rise to 3,200 feet. The area has a mid-Atlantic, modified continental climate influenced by the ocean to the east and mountains to the west. Summers are warm and humid but not excessively hot. Winters are generally mild with mountain shelter from severe storms and cold. Most of the heavier storms travel up the Atlantic coast or arrive from the southwest bringing periods of unstable weather and thunderstorms in summer and mixed rain and snow in winter. Fall is usually dry and warm with beautiful color. First freeze is early October, last is early April.

POPULATION

DEMOGRAPHICS	AREA	U.S. AVG	ETHNIC COMPOSITION	AREA	U.S. AVG	RESIDENT PROFILE	AREA	U.S. AVG
Population	164,197		White	78.2%	75.1%	Single	46.0%	43.6%
Population density per sq. mile	139.5	447.3	Black	19.9%	12.3%	Married	54.0%	56.4%
Population growth	25.2%	16.1%	Asian	1.7%	3.6%	Divorced	6.8%	8.4%
Median age	34.7	35.5	American Indian	.1%	.9%	Separated	3.4%	3.0%
Average family size	2.7	2.7	Hispanic	1.4%	12.5%	Married with children	28.4%	28.7%
			Diversity measure	34.4%	35.2%	Single with children	9.4%	10.1%

ECONOMY & JOBS   SCORE: 96/RANK: 12

INCOME	AREA	U.S. AVG	EMPLOYMENT	AREA	U.S. AVG	LARGEST EMPLOYING INDUSTRY
Per capita income	$27,780	$23,420	Unemployment rate	3.5%	6.1%	Computer and Electronic Product Manufacturing
Household income	$50,130	$46,060	Recent job growth	3.5%	.9%	
Household income < $25K	22.8%	26.4%	Projected future job growth	15.3%	15.1%	
Household income > $75K	27.7%	24.5%	White collar	62.3%	54.5%	
Household income growth	59.3%	57.3%	Blue collar	37.7%	45.5%	

COST OF LIVING   SCORE: 42/RANK: 189

INDEXES & TAXES	AREA	U.S. AVG	HOUSING	AREA	U.S. AVG	NECESSITIES	AREA	U.S. AVG
Cost of Living Index	102.5	100.0	Median home price	$177,840	$160,100	Food Index	99.2	100.0
Financial Progress Index	104.3	100.0	Home price appreciation	9.3%	7.1%	Housing Index	110.5	100.0
Income tax rate	5.750%	4.625%	Median rent	$698	$670	Utilities Index	88.9	100.0
Sales tax rate	4.500%	6.474%	Homes owned	65.9%	63.9%	Transportation Index	104.7	100.0
Property tax rate	$11.9	$15.6	Homes rented	26.8%	25.3%	Healthcare Index	98.5	100.0
			Housing affordability	56.0%	54.5%	Miscellaneous Cost Index	96.8	100.0

CLIMATE
SCORE: 69/RANK: 101

TEMPERATURE	AREA	U.S. AVG
January low	27.3°F	26.4°F
July high	86.1°F	86.7°F
Annual days > 90°F	19	38
Annual days < 32°F	94	88
Annual days < 0°F	1	6

PRECIPITATION	AREA	U.S. AVG
Annual inches precipitation	38.3	35.9
Annual inches snowfall	18.2	24.2
Annual days precipitation	125	111
Annual days rain > 0.5 inches	28	23
Annual days snow > 1.5 inches	3	6

COMFORTS & HAZARDS	AREA	U.S. AVG
July relative humidity	69.0%	68.8%
Annual days mostly sunny	218	212
Annual days with thunderstorms	41	39
Tornado risk score	13	19
Hurricane risk score	15	15

TEMPERATURE   PRECIPITATION   DAYS OF CLOUDS & PRECIPITATION

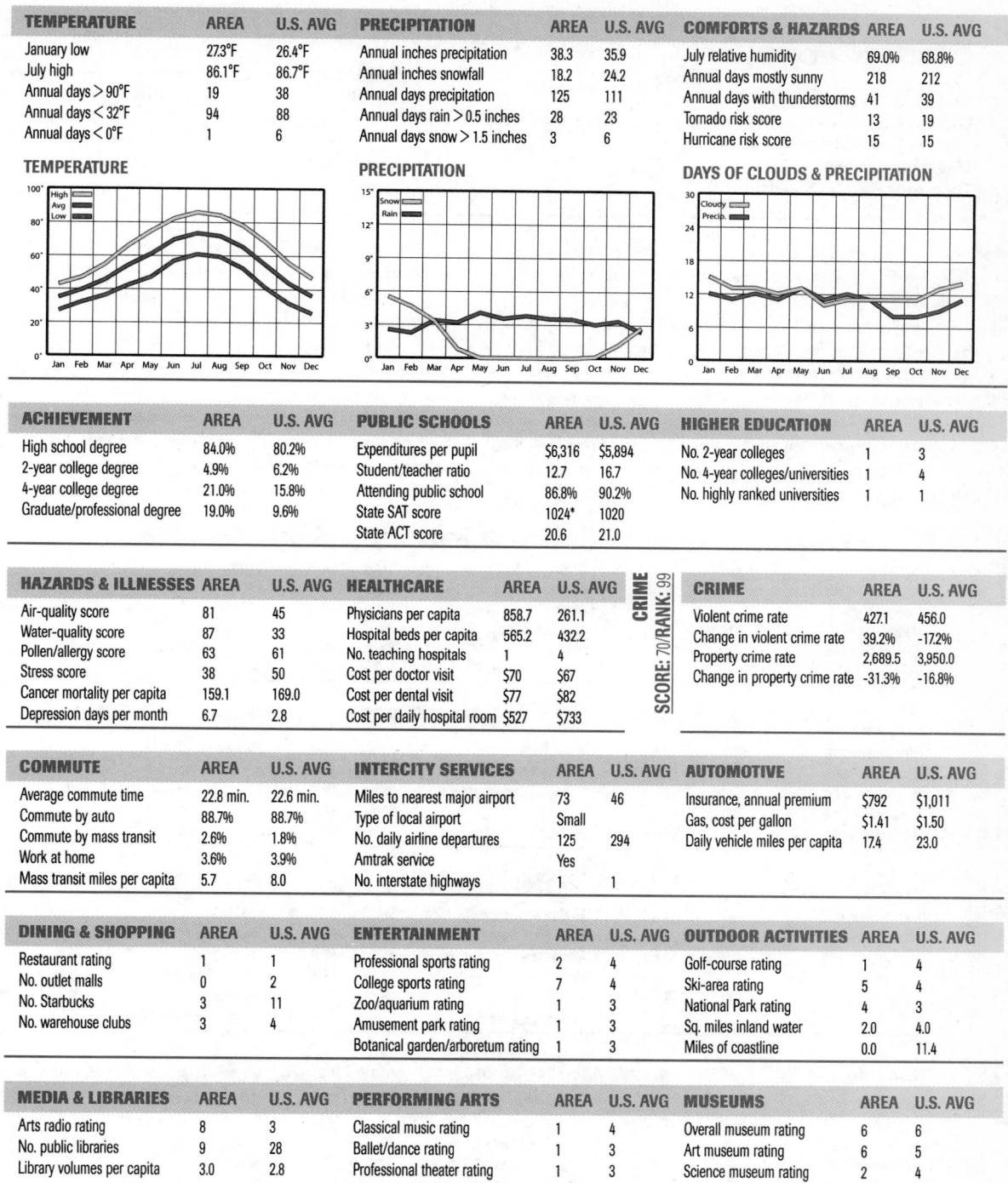

EDUCATION
SCORE: 86/RANK: 45

ACHIEVEMENT	AREA	U.S. AVG
High school degree	84.0%	80.2%
2-year college degree	4.9%	6.2%
4-year college degree	21.0%	15.8%
Graduate/professional degree	19.0%	9.6%

PUBLIC SCHOOLS	AREA	U.S. AVG
Expenditures per pupil	$6,316	$5,894
Student/teacher ratio	12.7	16.7
Attending public school	86.8%	90.2%
State SAT score	1024*	1020
State ACT score	20.6	21.0

HIGHER EDUCATION	AREA	U.S. AVG
No. 2-year colleges	1	3
No. 4-year colleges/universities	1	4
No. highly ranked universities	1	1

HEALTH & HEALTHCARE
SCORE: 97/RANK: 8

HAZARDS & ILLNESSES	AREA	U.S. AVG
Air-quality score	81	45
Water-quality score	87	33
Pollen/allergy score	63	61
Stress score	38	50
Cancer mortality per capita	159.1	169.0
Depression days per month	6.7	2.8

HEALTHCARE	AREA	U.S. AVG
Physicians per capita	858.7	261.1
Hospital beds per capita	565.2	432.2
No. teaching hospitals	1	4
Cost per doctor visit	$70	$67
Cost per dental visit	$77	$82
Cost per daily hospital room	$527	$733

CRIME
SCORE: 70/RANK: 99

CRIME	AREA	U.S. AVG
Violent crime rate	427.1	456.0
Change in violent crime rate	39.2%	-17.2%
Property crime rate	2,689.5	3,950.0
Change in property crime rate	-31.3%	-16.8%

TRANSPORTATION
SCORE: 28/RANK: 237

COMMUTE	AREA	U.S. AVG
Average commute time	22.8 min.	22.6 min.
Commute by auto	88.7%	88.7%
Commute by mass transit	2.6%	1.8%
Work at home	3.6%	3.9%
Mass transit miles per capita	5.7	8.0

INTERCITY SERVICES	AREA	U.S. AVG
Miles to nearest major airport	73	46
Type of local airport	Small	
No. daily airline departures	125	294
Amtrak service	Yes	
No. interstate highways	1	1

AUTOMOTIVE	AREA	U.S. AVG
Insurance, annual premium	$792	$1,011
Gas, cost per gallon	$1.41	$1.50
Daily vehicle miles per capita	17.4	23.0

LEISURE
SCORE: 34/RANK: 218

DINING & SHOPPING	AREA	U.S. AVG
Restaurant rating	1	1
No. outlet malls	0	2
No. Starbucks	3	11
No. warehouse clubs	3	4

ENTERTAINMENT	AREA	U.S. AVG
Professional sports rating	2	4
College sports rating	7	4
Zoo/aquarium rating	1	3
Amusement park rating	1	3
Botanical garden/arboretum rating	1	3

OUTDOOR ACTIVITIES	AREA	U.S. AVG
Golf-course rating	1	4
Ski-area rating	5	4
National Park rating	4	3
Sq. miles inland water	2.0	4.0
Miles of coastline	0.0	11.4

ARTS & CULTURE
SCORE: 63/RANK: 119

MEDIA & LIBRARIES	AREA	U.S. AVG
Arts radio rating	8	3
No. public libraries	9	28
Library volumes per capita	3.0	2.8

PERFORMING ARTS	AREA	U.S. AVG
Classical music rating	1	4
Ballet/dance rating	1	3
Professional theater rating	1	3
University arts programs rating	4	5

MUSEUMS	AREA	U.S. AVG
Overall museum rating	6	6
Art museum rating	6	5
Science museum rating	2	4
Children's museum rating	6	3

Chattanooga, TN

Score: 51.9   Rank: 210

Profile: Mid-size city
Location: Extreme southeast Tennessee along the Tennessee River
at the Georgia border
Elevation: 665 feet
Time zone: Eastern Standard Time

PRO
Revitalized downtown
Cost of living
Entertainment

CON
Crime rate
Arts and culture
Hot, humid summers

The colorfully named Chattanooga is a transportation gateway to the Deep South. It was a zone of contention in the latter stages of the Civil War, and history plays a big role in the city's conscience. Past urban decay and environmental problems have been cleaned up, and the city now has 22 miles of riverfront park and a variety of progressive development. The livable downtown is a popular weekend destination with entertaining museums. Nearby Lookout Mountain rises sharply over the city offering excellent views and nice residential areas with some tourist destinations mixed in. While there is a lot to do in the vicinity, the area is weak on performing arts and many services, but Atlanta is 115 miles south.

Chattanooga and the Tennessee Valley are located between the Cumberland Mountains to the west and the Appalachian Mountains to the east. Local topography is complex with a number of minor valleys and ridges rising as much as 500 feet in the city and 1,200 feet to the north and southwest. The climate is moderate, characterized by cool winters and very warm summers. The topography causes weather variations within short distances. The Cumberland Mountains retard the flow of cold air from the north and west, moderating winter temperatures and precipitation. Winter weather is changeable with highly variable snowfall and occasional freezing rain. Spring and fall weather are particularly pleasant. First freeze is early November, last is late March.

POPULATION

DEMOGRAPHICS	AREA	U.S. AVG	ETHNIC COMPOSITION	AREA	U.S. AVG	RESIDENT PROFILE	AREA	U.S. AVG
Population	470,880		White	80.2%	75.1%	Single	46.7%	43.6%
Population density per sq. mile	258.0	447.3	Black	18.6%	12.3%	Married	53.3%	56.4%
Population growth	11.0%	16.1%	Asian	.8%	3.6%	Divorced	10.8%	8.4%
Median age	37.7	35.5	American Indian	.2%	.9%	Separated	3.2%	3.0%
Average family size	2.5	2.7	Hispanic	.8%	12.5%	Married with children	25.1%	28.7%
			Diversity measure	30.3%	35.2%	Single with children	12.0%	10.1%

ECONOMY & JOBS   SCORE: 46/RANK: 177

INCOME	AREA	U.S. AVG	EMPLOYMENT	AREA	U.S. AVG	LARGEST EMPLOYING INDUSTRY
Per capita income	$23,171	$23,420	Unemployment rate	3.7%	6.1%	Food Manufacturing
Household income	$41,671	$46,060	Recent job growth	-1.1%	.9%	
Household income < $25K	28.8%	26.4%	Projected future job growth	15.0%	15.1%	
Household income > $75K	21.8%	24.5%	White collar	52.4%	54.5%	
Household income growth	62.4%	57.3%	Blue collar	47.6%	45.5%	

COST OF LIVING   SCORE: 80/RANK: 66

INDEXES & TAXES	AREA	U.S. AVG	HOUSING	AREA	U.S. AVG	NECESSITIES	AREA	U.S. AVG
Cost of Living Index	87.1	100.0	Median home price	$112,100	$160,100	Food Index	101.0	100.0
Financial Progress Index	101.9	100.0	Home price appreciation	5.3%	7.1%	Housing Index	69.6	100.0
Income tax rate	0.000%	4.625%	Median rent	$552	$670	Utilities Index	88.3	100.0
Sales tax rate	9.250%	6.474%	Homes owned	63.5%	63.9%	Transportation Index	93.4	100.0
Property tax rate	$13.1	$15.6	Homes rented	26.9%	25.3%	Healthcare Index	88.7	100.0
			Housing affordability	57.0%	54.5%	Miscellaneous Cost Index	101.1	100.0

CLIMATE   SCORE: 24/RANK: 251

TEMPERATURE	AREA	U.S. AVG	PRECIPITATION	AREA	U.S. AVG	COMFORTS & HAZARDS	AREA	U.S. AVG
January low	30.5°F	26.4°F	Annual inches precipitation	52.0	35.9	July relative humidity	72.0%	68.8%
July high	89.5°F	86.7°F	Annual inches snowfall	4.2	24.2	Annual days mostly sunny	213	212
Annual days > 90°F	49	38	Annual days precipitation	121	111	Annual days with thunderstorms	56	39
Annual days < 32°F	75	88	Annual days rain > 0.5 inches	37	23	Tornado risk score	10	19
Annual days < 0°F	0	6	Annual days snow > 1.5 inches	2	6	Hurricane risk score	11	15

TEMPERATURE

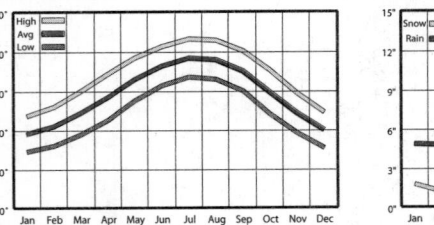

PRECIPITATION

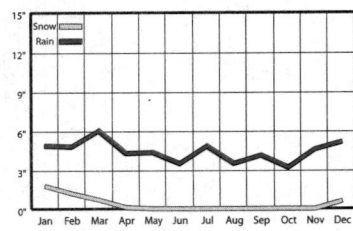

DAYS OF CLOUDS & PRECIPITATION

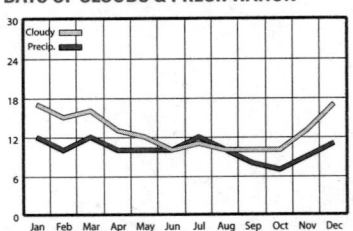

EDUCATION SCORE: 19/RANK: 266

ACHIEVEMENT	AREA	U.S. AVG	PUBLIC SCHOOLS	AREA	U.S. AVG	HIGHER EDUCATION	AREA	U.S. AVG
High school degree	77.6%	80.2%	Expenditures per pupil	$5,075	$5,894	No. 2-year colleges	2	3
2-year college degree	5.6%	6.2%	Student/teacher ratio	14.1	16.7	No. 4-year colleges/universities	4	4
4-year college degree	14.0%	15.8%	Attending public school	85.0%	90.2%	No. highly ranked universities	1	1
Graduate/professional degree	6.6%	9.6%	State SAT score	1128	1020			
			State ACT score	20.4*	21.0			

HEALTH & HEALTHCARE SCORE: 76/RANK: 78

CRIME SCORE: 2/RANK: 324

HAZARDS & ILLNESSES	AREA	U.S. AVG	HEALTHCARE	AREA	U.S. AVG	CRIME	AREA	U.S. AVG
Air-quality score	59	45	Physicians per capita	258.0	261.1	Violent crime rate	821.4	456.0
Water-quality score	50	33	Hospital beds per capita	610.8	432.2	Change in violent crime rate	-2.2%	-17.2%
Pollen/allergy score	64	61	No. teaching hospitals	3	4	Property crime rate	5,551.5	3,950.0
Stress score	62	50	Cost per doctor visit	$84	$67	Change in property crime rate	16.5%	-16.8%
Cancer mortality per capita	171.7	169.0	Cost per dental visit	$76	$82			
Depression days per month	3.1	2.8	Cost per daily hospital room	$626	$733			

TRANSPORTATION SCORE: 14/RANK: 284

COMMUTE	AREA	U.S. AVG	INTERCITY SERVICES	AREA	U.S. AVG	AUTOMOTIVE	AREA	U.S. AVG
Average commute time	23.7 min.	22.6 min.	Miles to nearest major airport	88	46	Insurance, annual premium	$1,046	$1,011
Commute by auto	91.4%	88.7%	Type of local airport	Small		Gas, cost per gallon	$1.43	$1.50
Commute by mass transit	2.6%	1.8%	No. daily airline departures	89	294	Daily vehicle miles per capita	32.7	23.0
Work at home	2.1%	3.9%	Amtrak service	No				
Mass transit miles per capita	5.0	8.0	No. interstate highways	2	1			

LEISURE SCORE: 35/RANK: 213

DINING & SHOPPING	AREA	U.S. AVG	ENTERTAINMENT	AREA	U.S. AVG	OUTDOOR ACTIVITIES	AREA	U.S. AVG
Restaurant rating	1	1	Professional sports rating	2	4	Golf-course rating	3	4
No. outlet malls	2	2	College sports rating	3	4	Ski-area rating	1	4
No. Starbucks	0	11	Zoo/aquarium rating	8	3	National Park rating	2	3
No. warehouse clubs	3	4	Amusement park rating	5	3	Sq. miles inland water	4.0	4.0
			Botanical garden/arboretum rating	1	3	Miles of coastline	0.0	11.4

ARTS & CULTURE SCORE: 35/RANK: 215

MEDIA & LIBRARIES	AREA	U.S. AVG	PERFORMING ARTS	AREA	U.S. AVG	MUSEUMS	AREA	U.S. AVG
Arts radio rating	5	3	Classical music rating	5	4	Overall museum rating	7	6
No. public libraries	14	28	Ballet/dance rating	3	3	Art museum rating	5	5
Library volumes per capita	3.4	2.8	Professional theater rating	1	3	Science museum rating	1	4
			University arts programs rating	8	5	Children's museum rating	6	3

Cheyenne, WY

Score: 55.8   Rank: 182

Profile: Capital city
Location: Southeast corner of Wyoming
Elevation: 6,115 feet
Time zone: Mountain Standard Time

PRO	CON
Small-town atmosphere	Arts and culture
Nearby mountains	Air service
Close to Denver	Winter cold

Cheyenne is the capital city and commercial center of Wyoming. As the gateway from the Great Plains from the advent of the transcontinental railroad, it still serves as a major ground transportation and agricultural center. Despite the invasion of national chains and cookie-cutter businesses, Cheyenne still retains a Western flavor and a pleasant, small-town character. There are a few museums, but the typical cultural amenities of a capital city are lacking. Laramie, 50 miles west, is home to the University of Wyoming and more of a cultural and entertainment center. A greater assortment of services and amenities are in Denver, 100 miles south. Cheyenne has a low cost of living and a friendly quality.

The city is located on a broad plateau between the North and South Platte rivers. The surrounding country is mostly rolling prairie used primarily for grazing. The ground level rises rapidly to a north-south Rocky Mountain ridge approximately 9,000 feet in elevation about 30 miles west of the city. The climate is semiarid, with large diurnal and annual temperature ranges due to conflicting air masses, elevation, and low humidity. The Laramie Mountains block some cold air from the north, and winds from the northwest are "downslope" and produce a marked chinook, or warming effect, which is especially noticeable during the winter months. Winds from the north through east to south are upslope and may cause fog or low stratus clouds throughout the year. The terrain variation and wind direction play an important role in controlling the local temperature and weather. First freeze is mid-October, last is late April.

POPULATION

DEMOGRAPHICS	AREA	U.S. AVG	ETHNIC COMPOSITION	AREA	U.S. AVG	RESIDENT PROFILE	AREA	U.S. AVG
Population	82,894		White	92.5%	75.1%	Single	36.8%	43.6%
Population density per sq. mile	30.9	447.3	Black	2.7%	12.3%	Married	63.2%	56.4%
Population growth	13.3%	16.1%	Asian	1.7%	3.6%	Divorced	8.3%	8.4%
Median age	35.6	35.5	American Indian	.7%	.9%	Separated	1.5%	3.0%
Average family size	2.7	2.7	Hispanic	7.9%	12.5%	Married with children	37.4%	28.7%
			Diversity measure	29.5%	35.2%	Single with children	8.3%	10.1%

ECONOMY & JOBS SCORE: 83/RANK: 54

INCOME	AREA	U.S. AVG	EMPLOYMENT	AREA	U.S. AVG	LARGEST EMPLOYING INDUSTRY
Per capita income	$23,334	$23,420	Unemployment rate	3.6%	6.1%	Insurance Carriers and Related Activities
Household income	$45,478	$46,060	Recent job growth	3.9%	.9%	
Household income < $25K	23.9%	26.4%	Projected future job growth	9.7%	15.1%	
Household income > $75K	22.8%	24.5%	White collar	54.1%	54.5%	
Household income growth	64.6%	57.3%	Blue collar	45.9%	45.5%	

COST OF LIVING SCORE: 94/RANK: 17

INDEXES & TAXES	AREA	U.S. AVG	HOUSING	AREA	U.S. AVG	NECESSITIES	AREA	U.S. AVG
Cost of Living Index	92.5	100.0	Median home price	$127,130	$160,100	Food Index	107.0	100.0
Financial Progress Index	104.7	100.0	Home price appreciation	6.1%	7.1%	Housing Index	79.0	100.0
Income tax rate	0.000%	4.625%	Median rent	$673	$670	Utilities Index	104.0	100.0
Sales tax rate	6.000%	6.474%	Homes owned	57.2%	63.9%	Transportation Index	94.5	100.0
Property tax rate	$8.2	$15.6	Homes rented	31.9%	25.3%	Healthcare Index	101.2	100.0
			Housing affordability	52.0%	54.5%	Miscellaneous Cost Index	96.0	100.0

CLIMATE SCORE: 41/RANK: 193

TEMPERATURE	AREA	U.S. AVG	PRECIPITATION	AREA	U.S. AVG	COMFORTS & HAZARDS	AREA	U.S. AVG
January low	15.6°F	26.4°F	Annual inches precipitation	12.0	35.9	July relative humidity	49.0%	68.8%
July high	82.4°F	86.7°F	Annual inches snowfall	81.0	24.2	Annual days mostly sunny	217	212
Annual days > 90°F	10	38	Annual days precipitation	95	111	Annual days with thunderstorms	34	39
Annual days < 32°F	175	88	Annual days rain > 0.5 inches	6	23	Tornado risk score	16	19
Annual days < 0°F	12	6	Annual days snow > 1.5 inches	17	6	Hurricane risk score	0	15

TEMPERATURE

PRECIPITATION

DAYS OF CLOUDS & PRECIPITATION

EDUCATION SCORE: 80/RANK: 67

ACHIEVEMENT	AREA	U.S. AVG	PUBLIC SCHOOLS	AREA	U.S. AVG	HIGHER EDUCATION	AREA	U.S. AVG
High school degree	89.0%	80.2%	Expenditures per pupil	$5,549	$5,894	No. 2-year colleges	1	3
2-year college degree	9.0%	6.2%	Student/teacher ratio	15.2	16.7	No. 4-year colleges/universities	0	4
4-year college degree	16.0%	15.8%	Attending public school	95.5%	90.2%	No. highly ranked universities	0	1
Graduate/professional degree	8.5%	9.6%	State SAT score	1097	1020			
			State ACT score	21.4*	21.0			

HEALTH & HEALTHCARE SCORE: 49/RANK: 167

CRIME SCORE: 64/RANK: 118

HAZARDS & ILLNESSES	AREA	U.S. AVG	HEALTHCARE	AREA	U.S. AVG	CRIME	AREA	U.S. AVG
Air-quality score	24	45	Physicians per capita	278.7	261.1	Violent crime rate	171.3	456.0
Water-quality score	23	33	Hospital beds per capita	235.3	432.2	Change in violent crime rate	2.9%	-17.2%
Pollen/allergy score	69	61	No. teaching hospitals	1	4	Property crime rate	3,617.5	3,950.0
Stress score	14	50	Cost per doctor visit	$54	$67	Change in property crime rate	-8.0%	-16.8%
Cancer mortality per capita	155.6	169.0	Cost per dental visit	$84	$82			
Depression days per month	2.4	2.8	Cost per daily hospital room	$730	$733			

TRANSPORTATION SCORE: 86/RANK: 48

COMMUTE	AREA	U.S. AVG	INTERCITY SERVICES	AREA	U.S. AVG	AUTOMOTIVE	AREA	U.S. AVG
Average commute time	16.3 min.	22.6 min.	Miles to nearest major airport	96	46	Insurance, annual premium	$680	$1,011
Commute by auto	86.8%	88.7%	Type of local airport	Large		Gas, cost per gallon	$1.43	$1.50
Commute by mass transit	.2%	1.8%	No. daily airline departures	812	294	Daily vehicle miles per capita	21.6	23.0
Work at home	6.1%	3.9%	Amtrak service	No				
Mass transit miles per capita	5.0	8.0	No. interstate highways	2	1			

LEISURE SCORE: 2/RANK: 322	DINING & SHOPPING	AREA	U.S. AVG	ENTERTAINMENT	AREA	U.S. AVG	OUTDOOR ACTIVITIES	AREA	U.S. AVG
	Restaurant rating	1	1	Professional sports rating	2	4	Golf-course rating	1	4
	No. outlet malls	1	2	College sports rating	1	4	Ski-area rating	1	4
	No. Starbucks	1	11	Zoo/aquarium rating	1	3	National Park rating	1	3
	No. warehouse clubs	3	4	Amusement park rating	1	3	Sq. miles inland water	2.0	4.0
				Botanical garden/arboretum rating	3	3	Miles of coastline	0.0	11.4

ARTS & CULTURE SCORE: 6/RANK: 311	MEDIA & LIBRARIES	AREA	U.S. AVG	PERFORMING ARTS	AREA	U.S. AVG	MUSEUMS	AREA	U.S. AVG
	Arts radio rating	1	3	Classical music rating	3	4	Overall museum rating	5	6
	No. public libraries	3	28	Ballet/dance rating	1	3	Art museum rating	5	5
	Library volumes per capita	3.5	2.8	Professional theater rating	1	3	Science museum rating	1	4
				University arts programs rating	1	5	Children's museum rating	1	3

Chicago, IL

Score: 59.0   Rank: 155

Profile: National center
Location: Northeastern Illinois along Lake Michigan
Elevation: 623 feet
Time zone: Central Standard Time

PRO	CON
Variety and diversity	Harsh climate
Arts and culture	Cost of living
Historic interest and preservation	Violent crime

A world-class commercial, industrial, and cultural city, Chicago is a national center and the regional center for America's heartland. It originally emerged as a transport center for cargo headed west and agricultural products headed east. Although transportation technology has changed, the role has not. The city is the most important passenger and freight transport hub in the country with the largest number of air departures and the most rail traffic in the nation. The commercial and manufacturing economy stands out both for its size and diversity. Over 30 Fortune 500 companies in an assortment of industries have headquarters here. Factories and warehouses extend for miles from the downtown area. Chicago is also a major center for small manufacturing and business. There is probably no more diverse an economy in the country.

The city grew up in America's Gilded Age, and the prosperity spilled over into some of the finest neighborhoods and architectural statements in the country. Oak Park, where architect Frank Lloyd Wright started his original studio, is a museum of residential architecture. It is an attractive, typically Midwestern commuter enclave of square city blocks, stately homes with shaded streets, and a shopping area next to the rail station, which still functions as an important commuter terminal. This story is repeated frequently; Riverside to the south is similar but with flowing curved streets and a parklike setting designed by Frederick Law Olmstead of Central Park fame. The city has an extraordinary sense of history and historic preservation. Many architectural styles, both commercial and residential, were invented and first used in Chicago, and the city goes out of its way to preserve them. The old 1880s elevated rail line continues to operate around the "Loop," the city's main business district. The former Navy Pier on Lake Michigan has been restored into a popular entertainment complex. The waterfront Soldier Field was recently remodeled at great expense rather than replaced by a larger stadium with modern amenities. In short: The city is a living museum and monument to American urban history.

Chicago is also a city of neighborhoods. North side, west side, south side—each provides a set of neighborhoods to suit any taste and (mostly) any budget. Areas of older homes and "two-flats" have been restored into viable neighborhoods on major arteries near the central business district. Along the lake and to the north are wealthier areas and the community of Evanston, home of Northwestern University. Areas become more typically middle class (but still with variety) to the northwest, west, and southwest. Like many large cities, Chicago has problems with urban sprawl, which moves west into areas like Naperville and Schaumberg. The city has an excellent urban transportation network with an assortment of rail and bus services; nonetheless, traffic and long commuting times are a problem. A less typical urban problem is that Chicago's downtown and nearby neighborhoods have become so livable—and so many businesses have located on the urban fringe—that rush hour traffic affects people commuting *out* of the city.

Chicago offers numerous amenities. Museums, notably The Art Institute of Chicago, and the performing arts are top quality. Sports are legendary—whether the teams win or lose—and Wrigley Field is another of those American urban icons. Few cities have more or better restaurants. Plus, the area has some of the best higher education in the country, and quality education is available at all levels.

Climate and the "C" factors typical of large city living—cost of living, crowdedness, crime, and commute—are the main negatives. Chicago's climate can be pleasant but downright miserable at times. The lakeside location, facing into the teeth of the storm track, and continental climate from the northwest produce cold, snow, wind, storms, humid heat, and weather changes invigorating for some but intolerable for others. Cost of living varies by neighborhood and lifestyle, but is accelerating after years as a relative bargain for a big city. The violent crime rate was well known even before the television show *ER* and is a problem in some neighborhoods. There are still some grubby, run-down areas that would make some people think twice. These facts hurt the statistical appraisal of Chicago. But for those wanting variety, culture, history, and civic pride at their fingertips—and who are willing to wear gloves at times to deal with the unpleasant side of urban living—Chicago is one of America's great places to live.

Chicago is located on a level coastal plain generally less than 100 feet above the lake. Most land is open and almost completely flat with occasional areas of deciduous woods. The climate is continental with frequently changing weather and is invigorating to say the least. Although lake winds can be strong and channeled by downtown office buildings, the nickname "Windy City" is a bit of a misnomer as average wind through the year is not exceptional. That said, winter wind-chill factors can reach extreme proportions. Summers can be warm and breezy to hot and humid. Lake breezes may moderate downtown temperatures 10°F to 15°F but will only occasionally extend several miles inland. Summer precipitation comes mainly from thunderstorms and can be heavy. Winter precipitation may arrive as frontal systems from the west or heavy squalls off the lake. Fall and spring are changeable, and along with winter, can have long periods of precipitation. Half the summers have temperatures over 96°F, half the winters have temperatures as low as −15°F. First freeze is mid-October, last is late April.

POPULATION

DEMOGRAPHICS	AREA	U.S. AVG	ETHNIC COMPOSITION	AREA	U.S. AVG	RESIDENT PROFILE	AREA	U.S. AVG
Population	8,449,180		White	77.4%	75.1%	Single	46.8%	43.6%
Population density per sq. mile	1,668.2	447.3	Black	14.3%	12.3%	Married	53.2%	56.4%
Population growth	14.0%	16.1%	Asian	4.1%	3.6%	Divorced	7.9%	8.4%
Median age	34.0	35.5	American Indian	.2%	.9%	Separated	2.8%	3.0%
Average family size	2.7	2.7	Hispanic	10.5%	12.5%	Married with children	27.9%	28.7%
			Diversity measure	57.2%	35.2%	Single with children	9.9%	10.1%

ECONOMY & JOBS SCORE: 45/RANK: 181

INCOME	AREA	U.S. AVG	EMPLOYMENT	AREA	U.S. AVG	LARGEST EMPLOYING INDUSTRY
Per capita income	$29,824	$23,420	Unemployment rate	6.8%	6.1%	Fabricated Metal Product Manufacturing
Household income	$63,096	$46,060	Recent job growth	1.1%	.9%	
Household income < $25K	16.9%	26.4%	Projected future job growth	11.1%	15.1%	
Household income > $75K	40.4%	24.5%	White collar	61.2%	54.5%	
Household income growth	73.7%	57.3%	Blue collar	38.8%	45.5%	

COST OF LIVING SCORE: 10/RANK: 298

INDEXES & TAXES	AREA	U.S. AVG	HOUSING	AREA	U.S. AVG	NECESSITIES	AREA	U.S. AVG
Cost of Living Index	119.8	100.0	Median home price	$223,300	$160,100	Food Index	105.9	100.0
Financial Progress Index	112.2	100.0	Home price appreciation	8.2%	7.1%	Housing Index	138.7	100.0
Income tax rate	3.000%	4.625%	Median rent	$951	$670	Utilities Index	108.5	100.0
Sales tax rate	8.750%	6.474%	Homes owned	65.8%	63.9%	Transportation Index	119.0	100.0
Property tax rate	$15.1	$15.6	Homes rented	28.2%	25.3%	Healthcare Index	114.7	100.0
			Housing affordability	48.0%	54.5%	Miscellaneous Cost Index	105.5	100.0

CLIMATE SCORE: 27/RANK: 240

TEMPERATURE	AREA	U.S. AVG	PRECIPITATION	AREA	U.S. AVG	COMFORTS & HAZARDS	AREA	U.S. AVG
January low	17.0°F	26.4°F	Annual inches precipitation	34.0	35.9	July relative humidity	67.0%	68.8%
July high	84.4°F	86.7°F	Annual inches snowfall	40.0	24.2	Annual days mostly sunny	197	212
Annual days > 90°F	21	38	Annual days precipitation	123	111	Annual days with thunderstorms	40	39
Annual days < 32°F	119	88	Annual days rain > 0.5 inches	22	23	Tornado risk score	40	19
Annual days < 0°F	7	6	Annual days snow > 1.5 inches	9	6	Hurricane risk score	2	15

TEMPERATURE

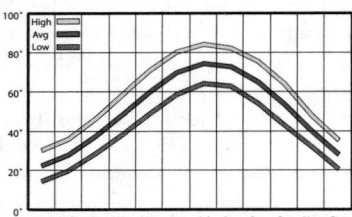

PRECIPITATION

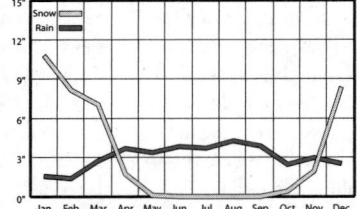

DAYS OF CLOUDS & PRECIPITATION

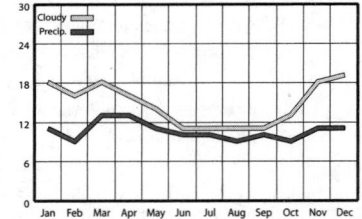

EDUCATION SCORE: 99/RANK: 4

ACHIEVEMENT	AREA	U.S. AVG	PUBLIC SCHOOLS	AREA	U.S. AVG	HIGHER EDUCATION	AREA	U.S. AVG
High school degree	81.0%	80.2%	Expenditures per pupil	$6,567	$5,894	No. 2-year colleges	28	3
2-year college degree	5.6%	6.2%	Student/teacher ratio	17.6	16.7	No. 4-year colleges/universities	46	4
4-year college degree	19.0%	15.8%	Attending public school	84.6%	90.2%	No. highly ranked universities	5	1
Graduate/professional degree	11.1%	9.6%	State SAT score	1179	1020			
			State ACT score	20.2*	21.0			

HEALTH & HEALTHCARE SCORE: 8/RANK: 303

HAZARDS & ILLNESSES	AREA	U.S. AVG	HEALTHCARE	AREA	U.S. AVG
Air-quality score	72	45	Physicians per capita	295.3	261.1
Water-quality score	21	33	Hospital beds per capita	335.7	432.2
Pollen/allergy score	58	61	No. teaching hospitals	57	4
Stress score	77	50	Cost per doctor visit	$74	$67
Cancer mortality per capita	183.4	169.0	Cost per dental visit	$92	$82
Depression days per month	2.5	2.8	Cost per daily hospital room	$864	$733

CRIME SCORE: 26/RANK: 244

CRIME	AREA	U.S. AVG
Violent crime rate	893.9	456.0
Change in violent crime rate	-32.2%	-17.2%
Property crime rate	3,869.9	3,950.0
Change in property crime rate	-22.3%	-16.8%

TRANSPORTATION SCORE: 99/RANK: 2

COMMUTE	AREA	U.S. AVG	INTERCITY SERVICES	AREA	U.S. AVG	AUTOMOTIVE	AREA	U.S. AVG
Average commute time	31.5 min.	22.6 min.	Miles to nearest major airport	15	46	Insurance, annual premium	$1,090	$1,011
Commute by auto	81.4%	88.7%	Type of local airport	Large		Gas, cost per gallon	$1.61	$1.50
Commute by mass transit	9.7%	1.8%	No. daily airline departures	1,388	294	Daily vehicle miles per capita	20.9	23.0
Work at home	3.2%	3.9%	Amtrak service	Yes				
Mass transit miles per capita	26.5	8.0	No. interstate highways	5	1			

LEISURE SCORE: 99/RANK: 2

DINING & SHOPPING	AREA	U.S. AVG	ENTERTAINMENT	AREA	U.S. AVG	OUTDOOR ACTIVITIES	AREA	U.S. AVG
Restaurant rating	9	1	Professional sports rating	9	4	Golf-course rating	10	4
No. outlet malls	6	2	College sports rating	9	4	Ski-area rating	4	4
No. Starbucks	197	11	Zoo/aquarium rating	10	3	National Park rating	2	3
No. warehouse clubs	10	4	Amusement park rating	10	3	Sq. miles inland water	3.0	4.0
			Botanical garden/arboretum rating	10	3	Miles of coastline	32.6	11.4

ARTS & CULTURE SCORE: 98/RANK: 6

MEDIA & LIBRARIES	AREA	U.S. AVG	PERFORMING ARTS	AREA	U.S. AVG	MUSEUMS	AREA	U.S. AVG
Arts radio rating	8	3	Classical music rating	10	4	Overall museum rating	10	6
No. public libraries	291	28	Ballet/dance rating	10	3	Art museum rating	10	5
Library volumes per capita	3.8	2.8	Professional theater rating	10	3	Science museum rating	10	4
			University arts programs rating	10	5	Children's museum rating	10	3

Chico-Paradise, CA

Score: 38.8 Rank: 281

Profile: Small town/College town
Location: Northern California, northeastern portion of the Central Valley at the foot of the Sierra range
Elevation: 230 feet
Time zone: Pacific Standard Time

PRO	CON
Some college-town amenities	Isolation
Mild winters	High unemployment
Nearby mountains	Cost of living

Chico is home to California State University and a variety of agricultural activities. Paradise, located a short distance into the foothills, is a favored retirement community. Nearby mountains, Lassen Volcanic National Park, and Lake Almanor offer outdoor recreation. "Chico State" as the school is known locally brings a few college amenities to the area, but it falls short of description as a classic college town. While summers can be unbearably hot and dry, winters are pleasant and many outdoor activities can be pursued throughout the year. The decline of the forest-products industry has led to unemployment, and the poor air service and 2½-hour drive to Sacramento are negatives. On a California scale, housing, cost of living, and crime are all reasonable, but rankings are done on a national scale.

The immediate terrain is flat to gently rolling and agricultural. Immediately to the east, grassland, oak-studded foothills begin to rise. Mt. Lassen, an 11,000-foot dormant volcano, dominates the skyline to the northeast. Nearby are numerous steep canyons, notably the Feather River Canyon. Climate is typical Central Valley Mediterranean, with long, hot, dry summers and mild, moist winters. Summer days are usually cloudless and in the 90s or low 100s. Evenings may be cooled by mountain air or by "delta" breezes from the San Francisco Bay.

POPULATION

DEMOGRAPHICS	AREA	U.S. AVG	ETHNIC COMPOSITION	AREA	U.S. AVG	RESIDENT PROFILE	AREA	U.S. AVG
Population	209,203		White	87.3%	75.1%	Single	42.7%	43.6%
Population density per sq. mile	127.6	447.3	Black	1.5%	12.3%	Married	57.3%	56.4%
Population growth	14.9%	16.1%	Asian	3.9%	3.6%	Divorced	9.9%	8.4%
Median age	36.3	35.5	American Indian	2.2%	.9%	Separated	3.8%	3.0%
Average family size	2.6	2.7	Hispanic	14.7%	12.5%	Married with children	22.7%	28.7%
			Diversity measure	33.6%	35.2%	Single with children	10.5%	10.1%

ECONOMY & JOBS SCORE: 13/RANK: 287

INCOME	AREA	U.S. AVG	EMPLOYMENT	AREA	U.S. AVG	LARGEST EMPLOYING INDUSTRY
Per capita income	$19,289	$23,420	Unemployment rate	7.0%	6.1%	Healthcare and Social Assistance
Household income	$34,282	$46,060	Recent job growth	3.2%	.9%	
Household income < $25K	35.1%	26.4%	Projected future job growth	21.2%	15.1%	
Household income > $75K	14.9%	24.5%	White collar	52.9%	54.5%	
Household income growth	49.9%	57.3%	Blue collar	47.1%	45.5%	

COST OF LIVING — SCORE: 16/RANK: 276

INDEXES & TAXES	AREA	U.S. AVG	HOUSING	AREA	U.S. AVG	NECESSITIES	AREA	U.S. AVG
Cost of Living Index	116.1	100.0	Median home price	$192,140	$160,100	Food Index	119.8	100.0
Financial Progress Index	62.9	100.0	Home price appreciation	14.0%	7.1%	Housing Index	119.3	100.0
Income tax rate	6.000%	4.625%	Median rent	$660	$670	Utilities Index	108.1	100.0
Sales tax rate	7.250%	6.474%	Homes owned	62.4%	63.9%	Transportation Index	113.0	100.0
Property tax rate	$11.2	$15.6	Homes rented	26.2%	25.3%	Healthcare Index	150.4	100.0
			Housing affordability	42.0%	54.5%	Miscellaneous Cost Index	103.1	100.0

CLIMATE — SCORE: 91/RANK: 29

TEMPERATURE	AREA	U.S. AVG	PRECIPITATION	AREA	U.S. AVG	COMFORTS & HAZARDS	AREA	U.S. AVG
January low	35.7°F	26.4°F	Annual inches precipitation	26.0	35.9	July relative humidity	68.0%	68.8%
July high	96.5°F	86.7°F	Annual inches snowfall	.6	24.2	Annual days mostly sunny	276	212
Annual days > 90°F	92	38	Annual days precipitation	62	111	Annual days with thunderstorms	7	39
Annual days < 32°F	36	88	Annual days rain > 0.5 inches	21	23	Tornado risk score	4	19
Annual days < 0°F	0	6	Annual days snow > 1.5 inches	0	6	Hurricane risk score	0	15

TEMPERATURE

PRECIPITATION

DAYS OF CLOUDS & PRECIPITATION

EDUCATION — SCORE: 38/RANK: 205

ACHIEVEMENT	AREA	U.S. AVG	PUBLIC SCHOOLS	AREA	U.S. AVG	HIGHER EDUCATION	AREA	U.S. AVG
High school degree	82.3%	80.2%	Expenditures per pupil	$5,128	$5,894	No. 2-year colleges	1	3
2-year college degree	7.7%	6.2%	Student/teacher ratio	20.5	16.7	No. 4-year colleges/universities	1	4
4-year college degree	14.8%	15.8%	Attending public school	93.8%	90.2%	No. highly ranked universities	0	1
Graduate/professional degree	7.0%	9.6%	State SAT score	1018*	1020			
			State ACT score	21.5	21.0			

HEALTH & HEALTHCARE — SCORE: 14/RANK: 284

CRIME — SCORE: 76/RANK: 76

HAZARDS & ILLNESSES	AREA	U.S. AVG	HEALTHCARE	AREA	U.S. AVG	CRIME	AREA	U.S. AVG
Air-quality score	59	45	Physicians per capita	191.2	261.1	Violent crime rate	303.9	456.0
Water-quality score	30	33	Hospital beds per capita	360.8	432.2	Change in violent crime rate	-20.0%	-17.2%
Pollen/allergy score	73	61	No. teaching hospitals	0	4	Property crime rate	3,351.6	3,950.0
Stress score	24	50	Cost per doctor visit	$71	$67	Change in property crime rate	-28.1%	-16.8%
Cancer mortality per capita	169.7	169.0	Cost per dental visit	$103	$82			
Depression days per month	.8	2.8	Cost per daily hospital room	$1,661	$733			

TRANSPORTATION — SCORE: 34/RANK: 218

COMMUTE	AREA	U.S. AVG	INTERCITY SERVICES	AREA	U.S. AVG	AUTOMOTIVE	AREA	U.S. AVG
Average commute time	20.9 min.	22.6 min.	Miles to nearest major airport	73	46	Insurance, annual premium	$901	$1,011
Commute by auto	86.1%	88.7%	Type of local airport	Medium		Gas, cost per gallon	$1.69	$1.50
Commute by mass transit	.6%	1.8%	No. daily airline departures	144	294	Daily vehicle miles per capita	13.4	23.0
Work at home	6.8%	3.9%	Amtrak service	Yes				
Mass transit miles per capita	2.4	8.0	No. interstate highways	0	1			

LEISURE — SCORE: 60/RANK: 133

DINING & SHOPPING	AREA	U.S. AVG	ENTERTAINMENT	AREA	U.S. AVG	OUTDOOR ACTIVITIES	AREA	U.S. AVG
Restaurant rating	1	1	Professional sports rating	2	4	Golf-course rating	1	4
No. outlet malls	0	2	College sports rating	5	4	Ski-area rating	10	4
No. Starbucks	3	11	Zoo/aquarium rating	1	3	National Park rating	6	3
No. warehouse clubs	3	4	Amusement park rating	1	3	Sq. miles inland water	2.0	4.0
			Botanical garden/arboretum rating	1	3	Miles of coastline	0.0	11.4

ARTS & CULTURE — SCORE: 30/RANK: 230

MEDIA & LIBRARIES	AREA	U.S. AVG	PERFORMING ARTS	AREA	U.S. AVG	MUSEUMS	AREA	U.S. AVG
Arts radio rating	1	3	Classical music rating	3	4	Overall museum rating	5	6
No. public libraries	6	28	Ballet/dance rating	1	3	Art museum rating	2	5
Library volumes per capita	1.3	2.8	Professional theater rating	1	3	Science museum rating	3	4
			University arts programs rating	4	5	Children's museum rating	3	3

Cincinnati-Covington, OH-KY

Score: 67.8   Rank: 92

Profile: Large city/Mid-size city
Location: Southwestern Ohio along the Ohio River and
  Kentucky/Indiana borders
Elevation: 550 feet
Time zone: Eastern Standard Time

PRO	CON
Arts and culture	Urban sprawl
Entertainment	Recent civil rights issues
Cost of living	Declining downtown

Cincinnati is a livable city at the crossroads—literally and figuratively—of north and south, east and west, and Old World and New World. Called by some the "northernmost Southern city," it is a transportation and cultural gateway between the industrial North and rural South dating back to the days of the underground railroad. The area's largest industry and employer is Procter & Gamble, with a history that dates back to the city's early stockyards when soap was made from animal byproducts. Other companies make soap and cosmetic products, while machine tools are another important industry. German and Italian immigrants brought a distinctly European architectural and cultural flair still evident in certain areas. There are few tourist attractions, but the city is a patchwork of interesting historic neighborhoods, including Mount Adams, an area overlooking the Ohio River with nightlife, restaurants, and cultural amenities. Also present are plain and unremarkable subdivisions and industrial areas. The city has increasing problems with urban sprawl with an unusually wide beltway and surrounding counties vying for new growth. Northern Kentucky areas surrounding Covington are growing rapidly thanks to new highway access.

For a Midwestern city, Cincinnati has excellent and widely recognized cultural amenities, including the well-known Cincinnati Symphony Orchestra and Cincinnati Pops. On the downside, racial tensions and landmark battles between conservative and progressive elements over arts and pornography have made national headlines. The city has a long major-league sports tradition that is more accessible and less expensive—even when the teams are winning—than most cities. Beyond the city, Hamilton County has an excellent park system. Until recently the city had a more substantial cost of living advantage. The downtown area, once a hallmark of urban vitality, is starting to fall victim to excessive suburbanization. Nonetheless, the city scores consistently well in all categories.

The city itself is located in the narrow, relatively steep-sided valley of the Ohio River. The Mill Creek, Licking River, and Miami River valleys join the Ohio with broad tributary valleys giving way to hills and plateaus on both sides of the Ohio. Vegetation is mixed farmland and deciduous woods. The climate is continental with a wide range of temperatures from winter to summer. Often near the dividing line between cooler northern air and moist Gulf air, temperature and precipitation changes are frequent. Summers are warm and humid, in the high 80s and 90s but seldom reach 100°F. Winters are moderately cold with periods of extensive cloudiness. Passing storms can create heavy spring and summer thunderstorms and winter snowfalls. Slow moving systems can cause long rainy periods during all seasons. Heavy snow is fairly uncommon and tends to melt within a few days, although snow can remain on the ground for several weeks during some winters. First freeze is late October, last is mid-April.

POPULATION

DEMOGRAPHICS	AREA	U.S. AVG	ETHNIC COMPOSITION	AREA	U.S. AVG	RESIDENT PROFILE	AREA	U.S. AVG
Population	1,669,136		White	87.7%	75.1%	Single	45.3%	43.6%
Population density per sq. mile	499.4	447.3	Black	11.1%	12.3%	Married	54.7%	56.4%
Population growth	9.4%	16.1%	Asian	1.0%	3.6%	Divorced	9.3%	8.4%
Median age	35.4	35.5	American Indian	.2%	.9%	Separated	2.7%	3.0%
Average family size	2.6	2.7	Hispanic	.6%	12.5%	Married with children	28.3%	28.7%
			Diversity measure	28.2%	35.2%	Single with children	11.4%	10.1%

ECONOMY & JOBS   SCORE: 71/RANK: 95

INCOME	AREA	U.S. AVG	EMPLOYMENT	AREA	U.S. AVG	LARGEST EMPLOYING INDUSTRY
Per capita income	$26,260	$23,420	Unemployment rate	4.6%	6.1%	Transportation Equipment Manufacturing
Household income	$50,023	$46,060	Recent job growth	1.5%	.9%	
Household income < $25K	22.9%	26.4%	Projected future job growth	14.7%	15.1%	
Household income > $75K	29.0%	24.5%	White collar	58.6%	54.5%	
Household income growth	64.4%	57.3%	Blue collar	41.4%	45.5%	

COST OF LIVING   SCORE: 32/RANK: 225

INDEXES & TAXES	AREA	U.S. AVG	HOUSING	AREA	U.S. AVG	NECESSITIES	AREA	U.S. AVG
Cost of Living Index	93.0	100.0	Median home price	$133,600	$160,100	Food Index	100.5	100.0
Financial Progress Index	114.6	100.0	Home price appreciation	5.4%	7.1%	Housing Index	83.0	100.0
Income tax rate	7.093%	4.625%	Median rent	$672	$670	Utilities Index	97.5	100.0
Sales tax rate	6.000%	6.474%	Homes owned	65.3%	63.9%	Transportation Index	95.5	100.0
Property tax rate	$15.2	$15.6	Homes rented	28.0%	25.3%	Healthcare Index	95.5	100.0
			Housing affordability	56.0%	54.5%	Miscellaneous Cost Index	100.0	100.0

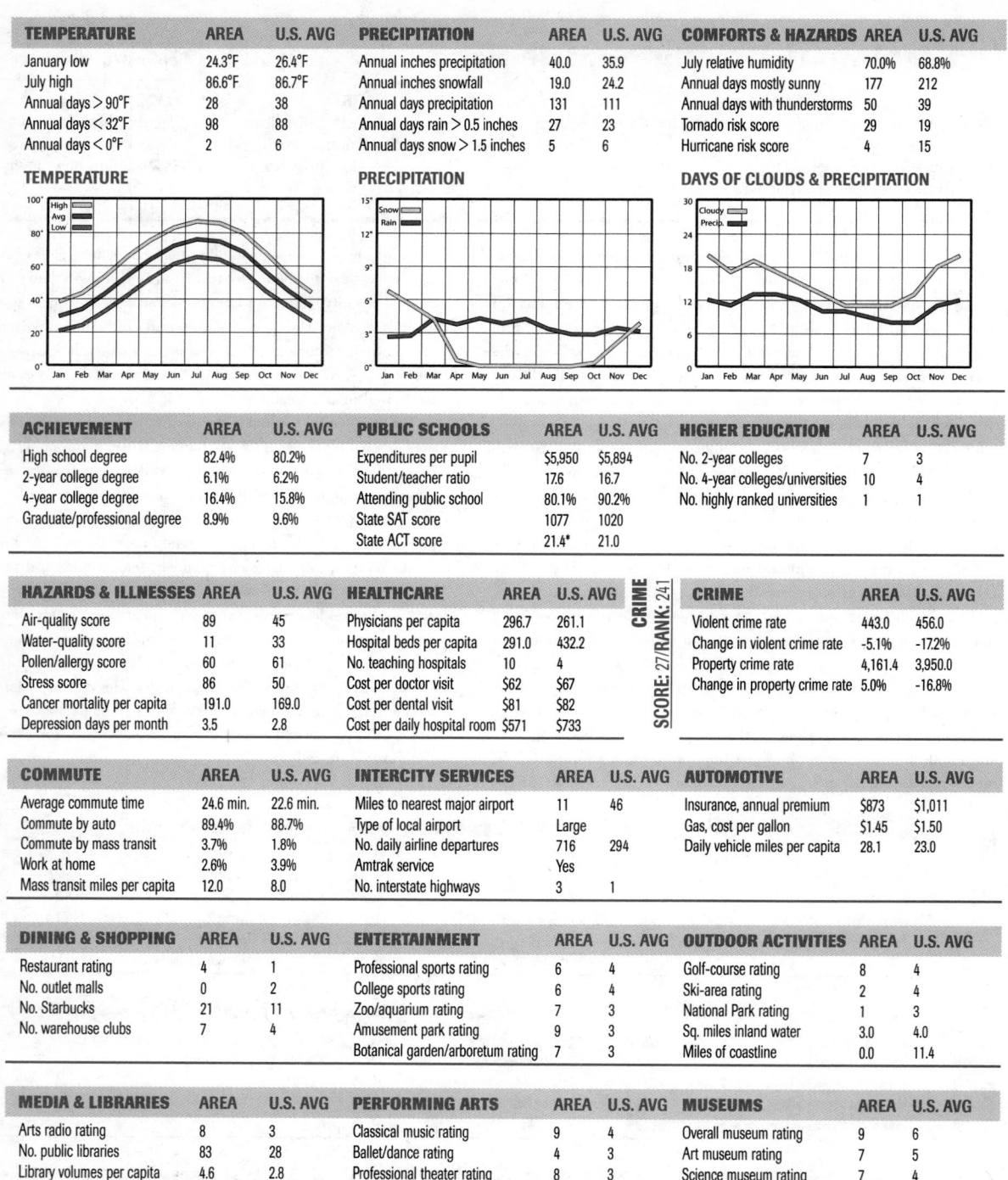

TEMPERATURE

TEMPERATURE	AREA	U.S. AVG	PRECIPITATION	AREA	U.S. AVG	COMFORTS & HAZARDS	AREA	U.S. AVG
January low	24.3°F	26.4°F	Annual inches precipitation	40.0	35.9	July relative humidity	70.0%	68.8%
July high	86.6°F	86.7°F	Annual inches snowfall	19.0	24.2	Annual days mostly sunny	177	212
Annual days > 90°F	28	38	Annual days precipitation	131	111	Annual days with thunderstorms	50	39
Annual days < 32°F	98	88	Annual days rain > 0.5 inches	27	23	Tornado risk score	29	19
Annual days < 0°F	2	6	Annual days snow > 1.5 inches	5	6	Hurricane risk score	4	15

TEMPERATURE   PRECIPITATION   DAYS OF CLOUDS & PRECIPITATION

ACHIEVEMENT	AREA	U.S. AVG	PUBLIC SCHOOLS	AREA	U.S. AVG	HIGHER EDUCATION	AREA	U.S. AVG
High school degree	82.4%	80.2%	Expenditures per pupil	$5,950	$5,894	No. 2-year colleges	7	3
2-year college degree	6.1%	6.2%	Student/teacher ratio	17.6	16.7	No. 4-year colleges/universities	10	4
4-year college degree	16.4%	15.8%	Attending public school	80.1%	90.2%	No. highly ranked universities	1	1
Graduate/professional degree	8.9%	9.6%	State SAT score	1077	1020			
			State ACT score	21.4*	21.0			

HAZARDS & ILLNESSES	AREA	U.S. AVG	HEALTHCARE	AREA	U.S. AVG	CRIME	AREA	U.S. AVG
Air-quality score	89	45	Physicians per capita	296.7	261.1	Violent crime rate	443.0	456.0
Water-quality score	11	33	Hospital beds per capita	291.0	432.2	Change in violent crime rate	-5.1%	-17.2%
Pollen/allergy score	60	61	No. teaching hospitals	10	4	Property crime rate	4,161.4	3,950.0
Stress score	86	50	Cost per doctor visit	$62	$67	Change in property crime rate	5.0%	-16.8%
Cancer mortality per capita	191.0	169.0	Cost per dental visit	$81	$82			
Depression days per month	3.5	2.8	Cost per daily hospital room	$571	$733			

COMMUTE	AREA	U.S. AVG	INTERCITY SERVICES	AREA	U.S. AVG	AUTOMOTIVE	AREA	U.S. AVG
Average commute time	24.6 min.	22.6 min.	Miles to nearest major airport	11	46	Insurance, annual premium	$873	$1,011
Commute by auto	89.4%	88.7%	Type of local airport	Large		Gas, cost per gallon	$1.45	$1.50
Commute by mass transit	3.7%	1.8%	No. daily airline departures	716	294	Daily vehicle miles per capita	28.1	23.0
Work at home	2.6%	3.9%	Amtrak service	Yes				
Mass transit miles per capita	12.0	8.0	No. interstate highways	3	1			

DINING & SHOPPING	AREA	U.S. AVG	ENTERTAINMENT	AREA	U.S. AVG	OUTDOOR ACTIVITIES	AREA	U.S. AVG
Restaurant rating	4	1	Professional sports rating	6	4	Golf-course rating	8	4
No. outlet malls	0	2	College sports rating	6	4	Ski-area rating	2	4
No. Starbucks	21	11	Zoo/aquarium rating	7	3	National Park rating	1	3
No. warehouse clubs	7	4	Amusement park rating	9	3	Sq. miles inland water	3.0	4.0
			Botanical garden/arboretum rating	7	3	Miles of coastline	0.0	11.4

MEDIA & LIBRARIES	AREA	U.S. AVG	PERFORMING ARTS	AREA	U.S. AVG	MUSEUMS	AREA	U.S. AVG
Arts radio rating	8	3	Classical music rating	9	4	Overall museum rating	9	6
No. public libraries	83	28	Ballet/dance rating	4	3	Art museum rating	7	5
Library volumes per capita	4.6	2.8	Professional theater rating	8	3	Science museum rating	7	4
			University arts programs rating	9	5	Children's museum rating	10	3

Clarksville-Hopkinsville, TN-KY

Score: 51.0   Rank: 215

Profile: Military town
Location: Extreme northern Tennessee along Cumberland River at Kentucky border
Elevation: 605 feet
Time zone: Central Standard Time

PRO	CON
Cost of living	Crime rate
Attractive downtown	Entertainment
Close to Nashville	Hot, humid summers

This multi-county area includes parts of Tennessee and Kentucky. Clarksville, 50 miles from Nashville, is a growing city with a well-preserved small-town feel. The nearby Fort Campbell Military Reservation is an economic mainstay, and there is a smattering of other business activity. The downtown area is quaint and attractive although a 1999 tornado caused significant damage. Austin Peay State University supplies most of the cultural amenities. Cost of living at 80.9 is the second lowest in Tennessee and median home prices of $93,450 are the lowest in the state. The city claims to be the third fastest growing city in the state behind Nashville and Memphis.

The city lies in an area of gently rolling hills mostly in agricultural use with some areas of dense deciduous forest. The climate is a mix of continental and subtropical. Summers are long, warm, and humid with frequent thunderstorms. Winters and springs are variable with frequent shifts between cold and mild conditions with periods of rain and storms. Severe cold seldom occurs but snow is not uncommon and can be heavy. Likewise, spring storms can be severe. The first freeze is late October, last is in mid-April.

POPULATION

DEMOGRAPHICS	AREA	U.S. AVG	ETHNIC COMPOSITION	AREA	U.S. AVG	RESIDENT PROFILE	AREA	U.S. AVG
Population	209,508		White	81.7%	75.1%	Single	37.4%	43.6%
Population density per sq. mile	166.2	447.3	Black	15.3%	12.3%	Married	62.6%	56.4%
Population growth	23.6%	16.1%	Asian	1.6%	3.6%	Divorced	7.3%	8.4%
Median age	29.3	35.5	American Indian	.4%	.9%	Separated	2.7%	3.0%
Average family size	2.7	2.7	Hispanic	2.4%	12.5%	Married with children	33.4%	28.7%
			Diversity measure	46.0%	35.2%	Single with children	9.1%	10.1%

ECONOMY & JOBS SCORE: 25/RANK: 247

INCOME	AREA	U.S. AVG	EMPLOYMENT	AREA	U.S. AVG	LARGEST EMPLOYING INDUSTRY
Per capita income	$17,916	$23,420	Unemployment rate	4.9%	6.1%	Ventilation, Heating, Air-Conditioning, and
Household income	$38,331	$46,060	Recent job growth	.3%	.9%	Commercial Refrigeration Equipment
Household income < $25K	28.1%	26.4%	Projected future job growth	19.3%	15.1%	Manufacturing
Household income > $75K	14.9%	24.5%	White collar	40.7%	54.5%	
Household income growth	61.4%	57.3%	Blue collar	59.3%	45.5%	

COST OF LIVING SCORE: 99/RANK: 3

INDEXES & TAXES	AREA	U.S. AVG	HOUSING	AREA	U.S. AVG	NECESSITIES	AREA	U.S. AVG
Cost of Living Index	80.9	100.0	Median home price	$93,450	$160,100	Food Index	93.4	100.0
Financial Progress Index	100.9	100.0	Home price appreciation	4.3%	7.1%	Housing Index	58.0	100.0
Income tax rate	0.000%	4.625%	Median rent	$481	$670	Utilities Index	87.1	100.0
Sales tax rate	9.500%	6.474%	Homes owned	62.2%	63.9%	Transportation Index	95.6	100.0
Property tax rate	$10.9	$15.6	Homes rented	29.4%	25.3%	Healthcare Index	88.3	100.0
			Housing affordability	67.0%	54.5%	Miscellaneous Cost Index	97.2	100.0

CLIMATE SCORE: 20/RANK: 263

TEMPERATURE	AREA	U.S. AVG	PRECIPITATION	AREA	U.S. AVG	COMFORTS & HAZARDS	AREA	U.S. AVG
January low	29.0°F	26.4°F	Annual inches precipitation	46.0	35.9	July relative humidity	71.0%	68.8%
July high	90.2°F	86.7°F	Annual inches snowfall	10.7	24.2	Annual days mostly sunny	210	212
Annual days > 90°F	37	38	Annual days precipitation	119	111	Annual days with thunderstorms	55	39
Annual days < 32°F	75	88	Annual days rain > 0.5 inches	32	23	Tornado risk score	7	19
Annual days < 0°F	1	6	Annual days snow > 1.5 inches	2	6	Hurricane risk score	6	15

TEMPERATURE

PRECIPITATION

DAYS OF CLOUDS & PRECIPITATION

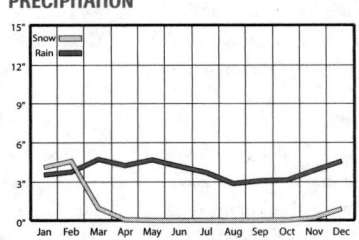

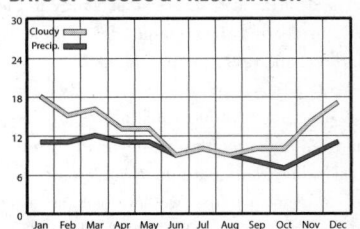

EDUCATION — SCORE: 40/RANK: 199

ACHIEVEMENT	AREA	U.S. AVG	PUBLIC SCHOOLS	AREA	U.S. AVG	HIGHER EDUCATION	AREA	U.S. AVG
High school degree	82.0%	80.2%	Expenditures per pupil	$4,757	$5,894	No. 2-year colleges	2	3
2-year college degree	7.6%	6.2%	Student/teacher ratio	14.8	16.7	No. 4-year colleges/universities	1	4
4-year college degree	11.0%	15.8%	Attending public school	94.1%	90.2%	No. highly ranked universities	0	1
Graduate/professional degree	6.0%	9.6%	State SAT score	1128	1020			
			State ACT score	20.4*	21.0			

HEALTH & HEALTHCARE — SCORE: 49/RANK: 169

HAZARDS & ILLNESSES	AREA	U.S. AVG	HEALTHCARE	AREA	U.S. AVG
Air-quality score	49	45	Physicians per capita	148.9	261.1
Water-quality score	30	33	Hospital beds per capita	411.0	432.2
Pollen/allergy score	68	61	No. teaching hospitals	0	4
Stress score	40	50	Cost per doctor visit	$63	$67
Cancer mortality per capita	155.6	169.0	Cost per dental visit	$78	$82
Depression days per month	2.8	2.8	Cost per daily hospital room	$432	$733

CRIME — SCORE: 22/RANK: 257

CRIME	AREA	U.S. AVG
Violent crime rate	624.6	456.0
Change in violent crime rate	-2.6%	-17.2%
Property crime rate	4,156.3	3,950.0
Change in property crime rate	-1.8%	-16.8%

TRANSPORTATION — SCORE: 13/RANK: 286

COMMUTE	AREA	U.S. AVG	INTERCITY SERVICES	AREA	U.S. AVG	AUTOMOTIVE	AREA	U.S. AVG
Average commute time	23.0 min.	22.6 min.	Miles to nearest major airport	48	46	Insurance, annual premium	$815	$1,011
Commute by auto	91.3%	88.7%	Type of local airport	Medium		Gas, cost per gallon	$1.41	$1.50
Commute by mass transit	.8%	1.8%	No. daily airline departures	264	294	Daily vehicle miles per capita	16.9	23.0
Work at home	3.3%	3.9%	Amtrak service	No				
Mass transit miles per capita	3.1	8.0	No. interstate highways	1	1			

LEISURE — SCORE: 49/RANK: 167

DINING & SHOPPING	AREA	U.S. AVG	ENTERTAINMENT	AREA	U.S. AVG	OUTDOOR ACTIVITIES	AREA	U.S. AVG
Restaurant rating	1	1	Professional sports rating	2	4	Golf-course rating	2	4
No. outlet malls	2	2	College sports rating	1	4	Ski-area rating	1	4
No. Starbucks	0	11	Zoo/aquarium rating	1	3	National Park rating	7	3
No. warehouse clubs	3	4	Amusement park rating	1	3	Sq. miles inland water	2.0	4.0
			Botanical garden/arboretum rating	1	3	Miles of coastline	0.0	11.4

ARTS & CULTURE — SCORE: 11/RANK: 292

MEDIA & LIBRARIES	AREA	U.S. AVG	PERFORMING ARTS	AREA	U.S. AVG	MUSEUMS	AREA	U.S. AVG
Arts radio rating	1	3	Classical music rating	4	4	Overall museum rating	5	6
No. public libraries	2	28	Ballet/dance rating	1	3	Art museum rating	2	5
Library volumes per capita	1.2	2.8	Professional theater rating	1	3	Science museum rating	1	4
			University arts programs rating	3	5	Children's museum rating	1	3

Cleveland-Lorain-Elyria, OH

Score: 42.8 Rank: 264

Profile: Large-city complex
Location: Northeast Ohio along Lake Erie
Elevation: 806 feet
Time zone: Eastern Standard Time

PRO	CON
Revitalized downtown	Industrial areas
Arts and culture	Economic cycles
Attractive neighborhoods	Cloudy, wet climate

Cleveland is a major industrial city and gateway with a storied past and an improving future. The city's industrial heritage is notable, with steel mills and shipping facilities along the waterfront and in the Cuyahoga River valley to the south. A number of factors—the decline of core industries in the '60s and '70s, the decay of the inner city, and pollution problems that culminated in the ignition of the river into a fiery inferno—gave the city a black eye from which it is still recovering, and the local nickname "mistake on the Lake." A massive urban renewal program has cleaned up the industry and restored the "Flats" waterfront area into a viable entertainment and restaurant zone. The spruced-up downtown has become a more attractive commercial center, although it's not one of the best. The I. M. Pei–designed Rock and Roll Hall of Fame and Museum draws visitors and new sports stadiums host well-supported major-league teams. The Cleveland Symphony

Orchestra is world-class. Like many large cities in the "rust belt," Cleveland is a city of neighborhoods, with plain, working-class neighborhoods to the south and west and a mix of more affluent areas to the east and southeast, notably Shaker Heights, University Heights, and Chagrin Falls. The University Circle area around the Case Western Reserve University just east of town is noted for museums and cultural amenities. Some of these better residential areas offer fine homes on large, wooded lots for reasonable prices. Industrial Elyria and Lorain are located along the lakeshore to the west. The bottom line: The city's grimy past and rough winters trade off against numerous entertainment options and a well-kept secret of excellent housing for the dollar. For those willing to deal with the negatives and take a chance on an area with promise, the ranking may understate reality.

Cleveland has 31 miles of Lake Erie frontage. The surrounding terrain is generally level except for an abrupt ridge on the eastern edge of the city rising some 500 feet above the shore. The Cuyahoga River, which flows through a rather deep but narrow north-south valley, bisects the city. Areas around the city, particularly to the south and southeast, have heavy deciduous tree cover. The climate is continental with a strong Lake Erie influence. West to northerly winds blowing off the lake moderate the summer and winter temperatures. Summers are warm and humid with occasional days above 90°F. Winters are cold and cloudy with an average of 5 days below 0°F. Weather changes are common with passing cold fronts from the north. Clouds and precipitation are abundant in all seasons; more than 1 in 2 days are cloudy year-round. Lake snow squalls can drop significant snowfall particularly in the eastern half of the city. First freeze is early October, last is late April.

POPULATION

DEMOGRAPHICS	AREA	U.S. AVG	ETHNIC COMPOSITION	AREA	U.S. AVG	RESIDENT PROFILE	AREA	U.S. AVG
Population	2,250,347		White	84.1%	75.1%	Single	45.9%	43.6%
Population density per sq. mile	831.2	447.3	Black	13.4%	12.3%	Married	54.1%	56.4%
Population growth	2.2%	16.1%	Asian	1.5%	3.6%	Divorced	8.9%	8.4%
Median age	37.8	35.5	American Indian	.2%	.9%	Separated	2.5%	3.0%
Average family size	2.6	2.7	Hispanic	2.2%	12.5%	Married with children	26.6%	28.7%
			Diversity measure	38.9%	35.2%	Single with children	10.4%	10.1%

ECONOMY & JOBS — SCORE: 54/RANK: 150

INCOME	AREA	U.S. AVG	EMPLOYMENT	AREA	U.S. AVG	LARGEST EMPLOYING INDUSTRY
Per capita income	$24,707	$23,420	Unemployment rate	5.9%	6.1%	Fabricated Metal Product Manufacturing
Household income	$46,630	$46,060	Recent job growth	.5%	.9%	
Household income < $25K	24.8%	26.4%	Projected future job growth	9.2%	15.1%	
Household income > $75K	24.9%	24.5%	White collar	57.1%	54.5%	
Household income growth	53.5%	57.3%	Blue collar	42.9%	45.5%	

COST OF LIVING — SCORE: 19/RANK: 268

INDEXES & TAXES	AREA	U.S. AVG	HOUSING	AREA	U.S. AVG	NECESSITIES	AREA	U.S. AVG
Cost of Living Index	99.6	100.0	Median home price	$138,400	$160,100	Food Index	107.6	100.0
Financial Progress Index	99.7	100.0	Home price appreciation	5.0%	7.1%	Housing Index	86.0	100.0
Income tax rate	6.993%	4.625%	Median rent	$752	$670	Utilities Index	126.4	100.0
Sales tax rate	7.000%	6.474%	Homes owned	68.9%	63.9%	Transportation Index	103.5	100.0
Property tax rate	$17.0	$15.6	Homes rented	24.2%	25.3%	Healthcare Index	108.0	100.0
			Housing affordability	48.0%	54.5%	Miscellaneous Cost Index	101.9	100.0

CLIMATE — SCORE: 15/RANK: 281

TEMPERATURE	AREA	U.S. AVG	PRECIPITATION	AREA	U.S. AVG	COMFORTS & HAZARDS	AREA	U.S. AVG
January low	20.3°F	26.4°F	Annual inches precipitation	35.0	35.9	July relative humidity	72.0%	68.8%
July high	81.6°F	86.7°F	Annual inches snowfall	52.0	24.2	Annual days mostly sunny	168	212
Annual days > 90°F	8	38	Annual days precipitation	156	111	Annual days with thunderstorms	36	39
Annual days < 32°F	125	88	Annual days rain > 0.5 inches	21	23	Tornado risk score	14	19
Annual days < 0°F	5	6	Annual days snow > 1.5 inches	13	6	Hurricane risk score	2	15

TEMPERATURE

PRECIPITATION

DAYS OF CLOUDS & PRECIPITATION

EDUCATION — SCORE: 45/RANK: 181

ACHIEVEMENT	AREA	U.S. AVG	PUBLIC SCHOOLS	AREA	U.S. AVG	HIGHER EDUCATION	AREA	U.S. AVG
High school degree	82.8%	80.2%	Expenditures per pupil	$6,750	$5,894	No. 2-year colleges	13	3
2-year college degree	5.7%	6.2%	Student/teacher ratio	15.8	16.7	No. 4-year colleges/universities	13	4
4-year college degree	14.9%	15.8%	Attending public school	82.8%	90.2%	No. highly ranked universities	0	1
Graduate/professional degree	8.4%	9.6%	State SAT score	1077	1020			
			State ACT score	21.4*	21.0			

HEALTH & HEALTHCARE — SCORE: 23/RANK: 253

HAZARDS & ILLNESSES	AREA	U.S. AVG	HEALTHCARE	AREA	U.S. AVG
Air-quality score	49	45	Physicians per capita	350.1	261.1
Water-quality score	16	33	Hospital beds per capita	462.3	432.2
Pollen/allergy score	65	61	No. teaching hospitals	18	4
Stress score	77	50	Cost per doctor visit	$72	$67
Cancer mortality per capita	186.8	169.0	Cost per dental visit	$80	$82
Depression days per month	3.0	2.8	Cost per daily hospital room	$884	$733

CRIME — SCORE: 55/RANK: 148

CRIME	AREA	U.S. AVG
Violent crime rate	378.8	456.0
Change in violent crime rate	-24.6%	-17.2%
Property crime rate	3,433.0	3,950.0
Change in property crime rate	-3.2%	-16.8%

TRANSPORTATION SCORE: 73/RANK: 88									
COMMUTE	**AREA**	**U.S. AVG**	**INTERCITY SERVICES**	**AREA**	**U.S. AVG**	**AUTOMOTIVE**	**AREA**	**U.S. AVG**	
Average commute time	24.3 min.	22.6 min.	Miles to nearest major airport	11	46	Insurance, annual premium	$1,111	$1,011	
Commute by auto	88.4%	88.7%	Type of local airport	Medium		Gas, cost per gallon	$1.50	$1.50	
Commute by mass transit	4.5%	1.8%	No. daily airline departures	487	294	Daily vehicle miles per capita	20.5	23.0	
Work at home	2.6%	3.9%	Amtrak service	Yes					
Mass transit miles per capita	16.4	8.0	No. interstate highways	3	1				

LEISURE SCORE: 92/RANK: 26								
DINING & SHOPPING	**AREA**	**U.S. AVG**	**ENTERTAINMENT**	**AREA**	**U.S. AVG**	**OUTDOOR ACTIVITIES**	**AREA**	**U.S. AVG**
Restaurant rating	3	1	Professional sports rating	8	4	Golf-course rating	10	4
No. outlet malls	2	2	College sports rating	3	4	Ski-area rating	3	4
No. Starbucks	26	11	Zoo/aquarium rating	8	3	National Park rating	2	3
No. warehouse clubs	8	4	Amusement park rating	7	3	Sq. miles inland water	2.0	4.0
			Botanical garden/arboretum rating	8	3	Miles of coastline	56.5	11.4

ARTS & CULTURE SCORE: 94/RANK: 17								
MEDIA & LIBRARIES	**AREA**	**U.S. AVG**	**PERFORMING ARTS**	**AREA**	**U.S. AVG**	**MUSEUMS**	**AREA**	**U.S. AVG**
Arts radio rating	8	3	Classical music rating	10	4	Overall museum rating	10	6
No. public libraries	119	28	Ballet/dance rating	8	3	Art museum rating	9	5
Library volumes per capita	5.9	2.8	Professional theater rating	10	3	Science museum rating	8	4
			University arts programs rating	9	5	Children's museum rating	5	3

Colorado Springs, CO

Score: 85.8 Rank: 18

Profile: Mid-size city
Location: Central Colorado at the base of the Front Range, 65 miles south of Denver
Elevation: 6,170 feet
Time zone: Mountain Standard Time

PRO	CON
Attractive setting	Urban sprawl
Summer climate	Economy
High educational attainment	Arts and culture

The Springs, once known as a resort city, has a strong military presence and a growing commercial economy led by the high-tech industry. Several military installations, including the U.S. Air Force Academy and the Space Command are located within or near the city. The surrounding prairie provides grazing land for cattle and sheep. Summer weather is notably pleasant and dry, with only 15 days above 90°F. The Rockies to the west and Denver to the north provide a broad range of outdoor recreation and other entertainment. The area has seen much growth, some of it unattractive. However, employment growth has slowed, in part due to the downturn in the high-tech industry.

Nevertheless, the city is an attractive place to live overall with no major negatives, hence the rank of 18.

Colorado Springs is located in relatively flat semiarid country on the eastern slope of the Rocky Mountains. Immediately to the west the mountains rise abruptly to heights ranging from 10,000 feet to 14,000 feet. Rolling prairie lies to the east. The climate is high-altitude continental with mild temperatures for the altitude. Uncomfortable extremes in summer and winter are rare and of short duration. Precipitation is relatively sparse, with over 80% falling between April and September mostly as thunderstorms. Humidity is low and it can be windy. First freeze is October 1, last is early May.

POPULATION								
DEMOGRAPHICS	**AREA**	**U.S. AVG**	**ETHNIC COMPOSITION**	**AREA**	**U.S. AVG**	**RESIDENT PROFILE**	**AREA**	**U.S. AVG**
Population	543,818		White	88.5%	75.1%	Single	41.5%	43.6%
Population density per sq. mile	255.7	447.3	Black	5.6%	12.3%	Married	58.5%	56.4%
Population growth	37.0%	16.1%	Asian	2.6%	3.6%	Divorced	9.8%	8.4%
Median age	33.2	35.5	American Indian	.9%	.9%	Separated	3.0%	3.0%
Average family size	2.7	2.7	Hispanic	10.1%	12.5%	Married with children	33.2%	28.7%
			Diversity measure	39.7%	35.2%	Single with children	10.2%	10.1%

ECONOMY & JOBS SCORE: 12/RANK: 289						
INCOME	**AREA**	**U.S. AVG**	**EMPLOYMENT**	**AREA**	**U.S. AVG**	**LARGEST EMPLOYING INDUSTRY**
Per capita income	$25,360	$23,420	Unemployment rate	5.8%	6.1%	Computer and Electronic Product Manufacturing
Household income	$52,276	$46,060	Recent job growth	.2%	.9%	
Household income < $25K	19.0%	26.4%	Projected future job growth	23.9%	15.1%	
Household income > $75K	30.1%	24.5%	White collar	55.7%	54.5%	
Household income growth	76.2%	57.3%	Blue collar	44.3%	45.5%	

COST OF LIVING
SCORE: 26/RANK: 244

INDEXES & TAXES	AREA	U.S. AVG	HOUSING	AREA	U.S. AVG	NECESSITIES	AREA	U.S. AVG
Cost of Living Index	103.1	100.0	Median home price	$179,300	$160,100	Food Index	107.1	100.0
Financial Progress Index	108.0	100.0	Home price appreciation	8.0%	7.1%	Housing Index	111.4	100.0
Income tax rate	5.000%	4.625%	Median rent	$701	$670	Utilities Index	84.8	100.0
Sales tax rate	6.400%	6.474%	Homes owned	58.6%	63.9%	Transportation Index	96.4	100.0
Property tax rate	$6.8	$15.6	Homes rented	31.4%	25.3%	Healthcare Index	109.9	100.0
			Housing affordability	59.0%	54.5%	Miscellaneous Cost Index	94.6	100.0

CLIMATE
SCORE: 90/RANK: 31

TEMPERATURE	AREA	U.S. AVG	PRECIPITATION	AREA	U.S. AVG	COMFORTS & HAZARDS	AREA	U.S. AVG
January low	16.1°F	26.4°F	Annual inches precipitation	16.0	35.9	July relative humidity	49.0%	68.8%
July high	84.4°F	86.7°F	Annual inches snowfall	40.0	24.2	Annual days mostly sunny	249	212
Annual days > 90°F	15	38	Annual days precipitation	87	111	Annual days with thunderstorms	59	39
Annual days < 32°F	162	88	Annual days rain > 0.5 inches	8	23	Tornado risk score	18	19
Annual days < 0°F	7	6	Annual days snow > 1.5 inches	9	6	Hurricane risk score	0	15

TEMPERATURE

PRECIPITATION

DAYS OF CLOUDS & PRECIPITATION

EDUCATION
SCORE: 92/RANK: 26

ACHIEVEMENT	AREA	U.S. AVG	PUBLIC SCHOOLS	AREA	U.S. AVG	HIGHER EDUCATION	AREA	U.S. AVG
High school degree	90.9%	80.2%	Expenditures per pupil	$5,316	$5,894	No. 2-year colleges	3	3
2-year college degree	9.0%	6.2%	Student/teacher ratio	18.1	16.7	No. 4-year colleges/universities	5	4
4-year college degree	21.3%	15.8%	Attending public school	92.8%	90.2%	No. highly ranked universities	1	1
Graduate/professional degree	12.2%	9.6%	State SAT score	1104	1020			
			State ACT score	20.1*	21.0			

HEALTH & HEALTHCARE
SCORE: 92/RANK: 25

CRIME
SCORE: 47/RANK: 173

HAZARDS & ILLNESSES	AREA	U.S. AVG	HEALTHCARE	AREA	U.S. AVG	CRIME	AREA	U.S. AVG
Air-quality score	59	45	Physicians per capita	202.1	261.1	Violent crime rate	439.8	456.0
Water-quality score	74	33	Hospital beds per capita	194.2	432.2	Change in violent crime rate	5.6%	-17.2%
Pollen/allergy score	64	61	No. teaching hospitals	1	4	Property crime rate	3,930.1	3,950.0
Stress score	84	50	Cost per doctor visit	$75	$67	Change in property crime rate	-23.6%	-16.8%
Cancer mortality per capita	144.4	169.0	Cost per dental visit	$83	$82			
Depression days per month	4.0	2.8	Cost per daily hospital room	$696	$733			

TRANSPORTATION
SCORE: 41/RANK: 194

COMMUTE	AREA	U.S. AVG	INTERCITY SERVICES	AREA	U.S. AVG	AUTOMOTIVE	AREA	U.S. AVG
Average commute time	22.3 min.	22.6 min.	Miles to nearest major airport	4	46	Insurance, annual premium	$1,078	$1,011
Commute by auto	86.4%	88.7%	Type of local airport	Medium		Gas, cost per gallon	$1.47	$1.50
Commute by mass transit	.8%	1.8%	No. daily airline departures	75	294	Daily vehicle miles per capita	18.5	23.0
Work at home	5.9%	3.9%	Amtrak service	No				
Mass transit miles per capita	8.4	8.0	No. interstate highways	1	1			

LEISURE
SCORE: 73/RANK: 89

DINING & SHOPPING	AREA	U.S. AVG	ENTERTAINMENT	AREA	U.S. AVG	OUTDOOR ACTIVITIES	AREA	U.S. AVG
Restaurant rating	1	1	Professional sports rating	3	4	Golf-course rating	3	4
No. outlet malls	3	2	College sports rating	4	4	Ski-area rating	10	4
No. Starbucks	14	11	Zoo/aquarium rating	5	3	National Park rating	5	3
No. warehouse clubs	3	4	Amusement park rating	1	3	Sq. miles inland water	2.0	4.0
			Botanical garden/arboretum rating	3	3	Miles of coastline	0.0	11.4

ARTS & CULTURE
SCORE: 37/RANK: 208

MEDIA & LIBRARIES	AREA	U.S. AVG	PERFORMING ARTS	AREA	U.S. AVG	MUSEUMS	AREA	U.S. AVG
Arts radio rating	5	3	Classical music rating	6	4	Overall museum rating	7	6
No. public libraries	13	28	Ballet/dance rating	1	3	Art museum rating	6	5
Library volumes per capita	1.9	2.8	Professional theater rating	1	3	Science museum rating	3	4
			University arts programs rating	8	5	Children's museum rating	1	3

Columbia, MO

Score: 54.9   Rank: 189

Profile: College town
Location: North-central Missouri midway between St. Louis and Kansas City
Elevation: 887 feet
Time zone: Central Standard Time

PRO	CON
College-town amenities	Isolation
Strong economy	Entertainment
Outdoor recreation	Low ethnic diversity

Columbia contains the University of Missouri and two smaller colleges. The area has a distinct college-town feel and most of the amenities that you would expect in a college town. Columbia also has an economic base in the insurance and medical industry. For a town with this profile, there's a low cost of living, but a fairly high crime rate and low diversity. There are plenty of recreational opportunities on and off campus.

The area consists of gently rolling and partially wooded plains at the edge of the broad Missouri River Valley. The climate is continental with moderately cold winters and hot, often humid summers. Summer temperatures generally reach 100°F. Early summer rain is frequent and sometimes heavy tapering off to warm, clear, humid days with less rain toward summer's end. Winter temperatures and conditions are variable, with occasional cold spells alternating with mild days with temperatures rising into the 60s. Temperatures below 0°F occur, but not every winter. Snow falls every winter but snow cover rarely persists more than 3 weeks. First freeze is mid-October, last is mid-April.

POPULATION

DEMOGRAPHICS	AREA	U.S. AVG	ETHNIC COMPOSITION	AREA	U.S. AVG	RESIDENT PROFILE	AREA	U.S. AVG
Population	139,492		White	88.6%	75.1%	Single	50.2%	43.6%
Population density per sq. mile	203.5	447.3	Black	7.6%	12.3%	Married	49.8%	56.4%
Population growth	24.1%	16.1%	Asian	3.2%	3.6%	Divorced	8.5%	8.4%
Median age	29.6	35.5	American Indian	.3%	.9%	Separated	2.0%	3.0%
Average family size	2.4	2.7	Hispanic	1.1%	12.5%	Married with children	24.6%	28.7%
			Diversity measure	27.3%	35.2%	Single with children	10.0%	10.1%

ECONOMY & JOBS   SCORE: 74/RANK: 85

INCOME	AREA	U.S. AVG	EMPLOYMENT	AREA	U.S. AVG	LARGEST EMPLOYING INDUSTRY
Per capita income	$23,941	$23,420	Unemployment rate	2.4%	6.1%	Healthcare and Social Assistance
Household income	$44,112	$46,060	Recent job growth	-1.8%	.9%	
Household income < $25K	27.0%	26.4%	Projected future job growth	25.3%	15.1%	
Household income > $75K	24.9%	24.5%	White collar	65.4%	54.5%	
Household income growth	70.6%	57.3%	Blue collar	34.6%	45.5%	

COST OF LIVING   SCORE: 52/RANK: 158

INDEXES & TAXES	AREA	U.S. AVG	HOUSING	AREA	U.S. AVG	NECESSITIES	AREA	U.S. AVG
Cost of Living Index	89.5	100.0	Median home price	$119,480	$160,100	Food Index	95.9	100.0
Financial Progress Index	105.1	100.0	Home price appreciation	3.6%	7.1%	Housing Index	74.2	100.0
Income tax rate	6.000%	4.625%	Median rent	$514	$670	Utilities Index	94.7	100.0
Sales tax rate	7.350%	6.474%	Homes owned	60.6%	63.9%	Transportation Index	106.1	100.0
Property tax rate	$10.1	$15.6	Homes rented	32.9%	25.3%	Healthcare Index	93.8	100.0
			Housing affordability	60.0%	54.5%	Miscellaneous Cost Index	98.0	100.0

CLIMATE   SCORE: 35/RANK: 213

TEMPERATURE	AREA	U.S. AVG	PRECIPITATION	AREA	U.S. AVG	COMFORTS & HAZARDS	AREA	U.S. AVG
January low	20.6°F	26.4°F	Annual inches precipitation	37.0	35.9	July relative humidity	69.0%	68.8%
July high	87.4°F	86.7°F	Annual inches snowfall	24.0	24.2	Annual days mostly sunny	191	212
Annual days > 90°F	39	38	Annual days precipitation	109	111	Annual days with thunderstorms	51	39
Annual days < 32°F	108	88	Annual days rain > 0.5 inches	26	23	Tornado risk score	22	19
Annual days < 0°F	8	6	Annual days snow > 1.5 inches	6	6	Hurricane risk score	1	15

TEMPERATURE

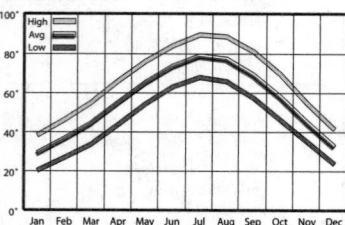

PRECIPITATION

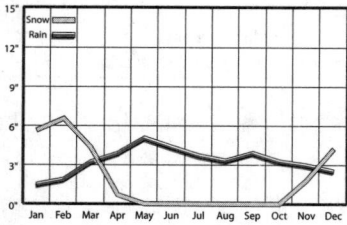

DAYS OF CLOUDS & PRECIPITATION

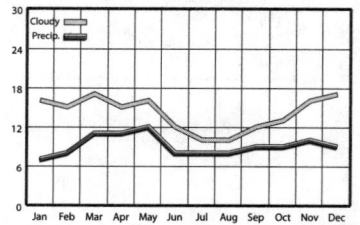

EDUCATION SCORE: 95/RANK: 15

ACHIEVEMENT	AREA	U.S. AVG	PUBLIC SCHOOLS	AREA	U.S. AVG	HIGHER EDUCATION	AREA	U.S. AVG
High school degree	89.2%	80.2%	Expenditures per pupil	$5,234	$5,894	No. 2-year colleges	0	3
2-year college degree	4.3%	6.2%	Student/teacher ratio	14.5	16.7	No. 4-year colleges/universities	3	4
4-year college degree	23.2%	15.8%	Attending public school	92.8%	90.2%	No. highly ranked universities	1	1
Graduate/professional degree	18.6%	9.6%	State SAT score	1165	1020			
			State ACT score	21.4*	21.0			

HEALTH & HEALTHCARE SCORE: 67/RANK: 106

HAZARDS & ILLNESSES	AREA	U.S. AVG	HEALTHCARE	AREA	U.S. AVG
Air-quality score	24	45	Physicians per capita	754.9	261.1
Water-quality score	30	33	Hospital beds per capita	895.5	432.2
Pollen/allergy score	55	61	No. teaching hospitals	2	4
Stress score	18	50	Cost per doctor visit	$57	$67
Cancer mortality per capita	154.4	169.0	Cost per dental visit	$83	$82
Depression days per month	2.2	2.8	Cost per daily hospital room	$630	$733

CRIME SCORE: 45/RANK: 182

CRIME	AREA	U.S. AVG
Violent crime rate	416.0	456.0
Change in violent crime rate	-8.8%	-17.2%
Property crime rate	3,608.5	3,950.0
Change in property crime rate	-22.5%	-16.8%

TRANSPORTATION SCORE: 21/RANK: 261

COMMUTE	AREA	U.S. AVG	INTERCITY SERVICES	AREA	U.S. AVG	AUTOMOTIVE	AREA	U.S. AVG
Average commute time	17.8 min.	22.6 min.	Miles to nearest major airport	106	46	Insurance, annual premium	$836	$1,011
Commute by auto	83.5%	88.7%	Type of local airport	Large		Gas, cost per gallon	$1.45	$1.50
Commute by mass transit	.9%	1.8%	No. daily airline departures	731	294	Daily vehicle miles per capita	21.8	23.0
Work at home	4.2%	3.9%	Amtrak service	No				
Mass transit miles per capita	5.0	8.0	No. interstate highways	1	1			

LEISURE SCORE: 33/RANK: 220

DINING & SHOPPING	AREA	U.S. AVG	ENTERTAINMENT	AREA	U.S. AVG	OUTDOOR ACTIVITIES	AREA	U.S. AVG
Restaurant rating	1	1	Professional sports rating	2	4	Golf-course rating	2	4
No. outlet malls	2	2	College sports rating	5	4	Ski-area rating	1	4
No. Starbucks	0	11	Zoo/aquarium rating	1	3	National Park rating	1	3
No. warehouse clubs	3	4	Amusement park rating	1	3	Sq. miles inland water	2.0	4.0
			Botanical garden/arboretum rating	1	3	Miles of coastline	0.0	11.4

ARTS & CULTURE SCORE: 65/RANK: 113

MEDIA & LIBRARIES	AREA	U.S. AVG	PERFORMING ARTS	AREA	U.S. AVG	MUSEUMS	AREA	U.S. AVG
Arts radio rating	7	3	Classical music rating	3	4	Overall museum rating	4	6
No. public libraries	4	28	Ballet/dance rating	1	3	Art museum rating	3	5
Library volumes per capita	2.7	2.8	Professional theater rating	1	3	Science museum rating	4	4
			University arts programs rating	8	5	Children's museum rating	1	3

Columbia, SC

Score: 77.2   Rank: 50

Profile: College town/Capital city
Location: Central South Carolina
Elevation: 225 feet
Time zone: Eastern Standard Time

PRO	CON
College-town amenities	Hot, humid summers
Historic interest	Air service
Cost of living	Urban sprawl

Columbia is the capital, the largest city, and the commercial, industrial, and educational hub for the state. The city is laid out in a traditional grid along the Congaree River and has a number of historic buildings, although many of the oldest buildings were lost in General Sherman's famous march through the South. Today's downtown is clean and mostly modern with some attractive restoration near the riverfront and a large area of shady streets and historic homes to the east. The city spreads in all directions with some unattractive sprawl at the outskirts. Columbia is home to the University of South Carolina, whose attractive and historic campus in the south part of the downtown area adds a dose of college town feel, a few amenities, and sports-related entertainment to the area. The economy, while losing jobs recently, is stable with relatively low unemployment and a good future outlook. Cost of living at 89.5 is attractive for what is available.

Columbia is located at a river confluence. Surrounding terrain is rolling and wooded and slopes gently from north to south. The climate is humid subtropical. The Appalachian ridge 150 miles to the northwest frequently retards the approach of cold weather in the winter but offers little moderating effect on the summer heat. Long summers are prevalent with persistent warm and humid weather. The mountains and the "Bermuda High" summer high pressure system block cold fronts from the north and west. Typically there are about 6 days over 100°F and midsummer thunderstorms are frequent. Fall is the most pleasant time of year with relatively less rainfall and plenty of sun. Winters are mild with occasional short cold outbreaks. Spring is variable, with occasional storms and cold snaps.

POPULATION

DEMOGRAPHICS	AREA	U.S. AVG	ETHNIC COMPOSITION	AREA	U.S. AVG	RESIDENT PROFILE	AREA	U.S. AVG
Population	551,983		White	68.5%	75.1%	Single	49.0%	43.6%
Population density per sq. mile	378.8	447.3	Black	29.3%	12.3%	Married	51.0%	56.4%
Population growth	21.8%	16.1%	Asian	1.6%	3.6%	Divorced	7.6%	8.4%
Median age	34.2	35.5	American Indian	.2%	.9%	Separated	4.7%	3.0%
Average family size	2.7	2.7	Hispanic	1.4%	12.5%	Married with children	29.0%	28.7%
			Diversity measure	49.8%	35.2%	Single with children	12.5%	10.1%

ECONOMY & JOBS — SCORE: 11/RANK: 292

INCOME	AREA	U.S. AVG	EMPLOYMENT	AREA	U.S. AVG	LARGEST EMPLOYING INDUSTRY
Per capita income	$24,374	$23,420	Unemployment rate	3.9%	6.1%	Healthcare and Social Assistance
Household income	$48,503	$46,060	Recent job growth	2.4%	.9%	
Household income < $25K	22.2%	26.4%	Projected future job growth	21.5%	15.1%	
Household income > $75K	26.2%	24.5%	White collar	60.3%	54.5%	
Household income growth	58.9%	57.3%	Blue collar	39.7%	45.5%	

COST OF LIVING — SCORE: 65/RANK: 115

INDEXES & TAXES	AREA	U.S. AVG	HOUSING	AREA	U.S. AVG	NECESSITIES	AREA	U.S. AVG
Cost of Living Index	89.5	100.0	Median home price	$121,600	$160,100	Food Index	103.3	100.0
Financial Progress Index	115.5	100.0	Home price appreciation	5.4%	7.1%	Housing Index	75.5	100.0
Income tax rate	7.000%	4.625%	Median rent	$588	$670	Utilities Index	96.8	100.0
Sales tax rate	5.000%	6.474%	Homes owned	66.4%	63.9%	Transportation Index	90.9	100.0
Property tax rate	$12.7	$15.6	Homes rented	25.5%	25.3%	Healthcare Index	93.2	100.0
			Housing affordability	63.0%	54.5%	Miscellaneous Cost Index	97.3	100.0

CLIMATE — SCORE: 23/RANK: 254

TEMPERATURE	AREA	U.S. AVG	PRECIPITATION	AREA	U.S. AVG	COMFORTS & HAZARDS	AREA	U.S. AVG
January low	33.9°F	26.4°F	Annual inches precipitation	46.0	35.9	July relative humidity	73.0%	68.8%
July high	92.0°F	86.7°F	Annual inches snowfall	2.0	24.2	Annual days mostly sunny	223	212
Annual days > 90°F	64	38	Annual days precipitation	111	111	Annual days with thunderstorms	54	39
Annual days < 32°F	60	88	Annual days rain > 0.5 inches	31	23	Tornado risk score	24	19
Annual days < 0°F	0	6	Annual days snow > 1.5 inches	1	6	Hurricane risk score	34	15

TEMPERATURE

PRECIPITATION

DAYS OF CLOUDS & PRECIPITATION

EDUCATION — SCORE: 79/RANK: 69

ACHIEVEMENT	AREA	U.S. AVG	PUBLIC SCHOOLS	AREA	U.S. AVG	HIGHER EDUCATION	AREA	U.S. AVG
High school degree	84.3%	80.2%	Expenditures per pupil	$5,817	$5,894	No. 2-year colleges	2	3
2-year college degree	7.8%	6.2%	Student/teacher ratio	16.2	16.7	No. 4-year colleges/universities	5	4
4-year college degree	19.1%	15.8%	Attending public school	92.8%	90.2%	No. highly ranked universities	0	1
Graduate/professional degree	10.1%	9.6%	State SAT score	989*	1020			
			State ACT score	19.2	21.0			

HEALTH & HEALTHCARE — SCORE: 98/RANK: 7

HAZARDS & ILLNESSES	AREA	U.S. AVG	HEALTHCARE	AREA	U.S. AVG
Air-quality score	74	45	Physicians per capita	295.5	261.1
Water-quality score	19	33	Hospital beds per capita	484.3	432.2
Pollen/allergy score	65	61	No. teaching hospitals	2	4
Stress score	50	50	Cost per doctor visit	$57	$67
Cancer mortality per capita	166.7	169.0	Cost per dental visit	$89	$82
Depression days per month	3.0	2.8	Cost per daily hospital room	$448	$733

CRIME — SCORE: 60/RANK: 133

CRIME	AREA	U.S. AVG
Violent crime rate	575.2	456.0
Change in violent crime rate	-42.2%	-17.2%
Property crime rate	4,150.3	3,950.0
Change in property crime rate	-26.9%	-16.8%

TRANSPORTATION — SCORE: 73/RANK: 89

COMMUTE	AREA	U.S. AVG	INTERCITY SERVICES	AREA	U.S. AVG	AUTOMOTIVE	AREA	U.S. AVG
Average commute time	23.5 min.	22.6 min.	Miles to nearest major airport	15	46	Insurance, annual premium	$856	$1,011
Commute by auto	91.0%	88.7%	Type of local airport	Small		Gas, cost per gallon	$1.34	$1.50
Commute by mass transit	1.4%	1.8%	No. daily airline departures	93	294	Daily vehicle miles per capita	23.5	23.0
Work at home	1.8%	3.9%	Amtrak service	Yes				
Mass transit miles per capita	4.6	8.0	No. interstate highways	3	1			

LEISURE SCORE: 12/RANK: 291

DINING & SHOPPING	AREA	U.S. AVG	ENTERTAINMENT	AREA	U.S. AVG	OUTDOOR ACTIVITIES	AREA	U.S. AVG
Restaurant rating	1	1	Professional sports rating	3	4	Golf-course rating	3	4
No. outlet malls	0	2	College sports rating	6	4	Ski-area rating	1	4
No. Starbucks	2	11	Zoo/aquarium rating	7	3	National Park rating	3	3
No. warehouse clubs	4	4	Amusement park rating	1	3	Sq. miles inland water	5.0	4.0
			Botanical garden/arboretum rating	7	3	Miles of coastline	0.0	11.4

ARTS & CULTURE SCORE: 73/RANK: 88

MEDIA & LIBRARIES	AREA	U.S. AVG	PERFORMING ARTS	AREA	U.S. AVG	MUSEUMS	AREA	U.S. AVG
Arts radio rating	1	3	Classical music rating	3	4	Overall museum rating	7	6
No. public libraries	19	28	Ballet/dance rating	3	3	Art museum rating	6	5
Library volumes per capita	3.1	2.8	Professional theater rating	1	3	Science museum rating	6	4
			University arts programs rating	8	5	Children's museum rating	5	3

Columbus, GA

Score: 67.4   Rank: 94

Profile: Small city/Military town
Location: West-central Georgia on Georgia-Alabama border along Chattahoochee River
Elevation: 445 feet
Time zone: Eastern Standard Time

PRO	CON
Cost of living	Summer heat
Water recreation	Performing arts
Small-town atmosphere	Entertainment

Columbus, the third largest city in Georgia, has a diverse industrial base and supports nearby Fort Benning army base. The area has a number of museums, mostly of a military theme. Other services and amenities are available in Atlanta, 100 miles away. Cost of living is the second lowest in the state and the economy is relatively stable. Summers are hot and muggy, but weather the rest of the year is pleasant.

The area is a mix of gently rolling, wooded hills and a level, open plain. Ground elevations range from 200 feet to 500 feet. The climate is typical of the humid southeast, with pronounced maritime and continental effects. Summers are warm and humid with most days in the 90s, a few into the 100s, and frequent thunderstorms. Occasional heavy rains originate from hurricanes in the Gulf of Mexico. Winters are mild with temperatures seldom below 20°F. Snow is rare. First freeze is early November, last is late March.

POPULATION

DEMOGRAPHICS	AREA	U.S. AVG	ETHNIC COMPOSITION	AREA	U.S. AVG	RESIDENT PROFILE	AREA	U.S. AVG
Population	275,895		White	59.2%	75.1%	Single	48.2%	43.6%
Population density per sq. mile	175.1	447.3	Black	38.7%	12.3%	Married	51.8%	56.4%
Population growth	5.8%	16.1%	Asian	1.0%	3.6%	Divorced	8.8%	8.4%
Median age	33.0	35.5	American Indian	.3%	.9%	Separated	5.0%	3.0%
Average family size	2.6	2.7	Hispanic	2.7%	12.5%	Married with children	26.7%	28.7%
			Diversity measure	55.5%	35.2%	Single with children	13.8%	10.1%

ECONOMY & JOBS SCORE: 31/RANK: 228

INCOME	AREA	U.S. AVG	EMPLOYMENT	AREA	U.S. AVG	LARGEST EMPLOYING INDUSTRY
Per capita income	$20,219	$23,420	Unemployment rate	6.1%	6.1%	Textile Mills
Household income	$37,565	$46,060	Recent job growth	.5%	.9%	
Household income < $25K	32.9%	26.4%	Projected future job growth	15.0%	15.1%	
Household income > $75K	17.9%	24.5%	White collar	45.3%	54.5%	
Household income growth	59.1%	57.3%	Blue collar	54.7%	45.5%	

COST OF LIVING SCORE: 73/RANK: 90

INDEXES & TAXES	AREA	U.S. AVG	HOUSING	AREA	U.S. AVG	NECESSITIES	AREA	U.S. AVG
Cost of Living Index	83.2	100.0	Median home price	$95,550	$160,100	Food Index	98.7	100.0
Financial Progress Index	96.3	100.0	Home price appreciation	4.4%	7.1%	Housing Index	59.3	100.0
Income tax rate	6.000%	4.625%	Median rent	$503	$670	Utilities Index	89.0	100.0
Sales tax rate	6.000%	6.474%	Homes owned	60.5%	63.9%	Transportation Index	98.7	100.0
Property tax rate	$13.3	$15.6	Homes rented	27.6%	25.3%	Healthcare Index	94.5	100.0
			Housing affordability	63.0%	54.5%	Miscellaneous Cost Index	97.2	100.0

CLIMATE SCORE: 48/RANK: 170

TEMPERATURE	AREA	U.S. AVG	PRECIPITATION	AREA	U.S. AVG	COMFORTS & HAZARDS	AREA	U.S. AVG
January low	35.9°F	26.4°F	Annual inches precipitation	51.0	35.9	July relative humidity	73.0%	68.8%
July high	90.8°F	86.7°F	Annual inches snowfall	.5	24.2	Annual days mostly sunny	216	212
Annual days > 90°F	74	38	Annual days precipitation	111	111	Annual days with thunderstorms	58	39
Annual days < 32°F	46	88	Annual days rain > 0.5 inches	32	23	Tornado risk score	21	19
Annual days < 0°F	0	6	Annual days snow > 1.5 inches	0	6	Hurricane risk score	28	15

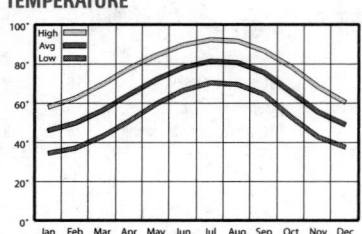

TEMPERATURE

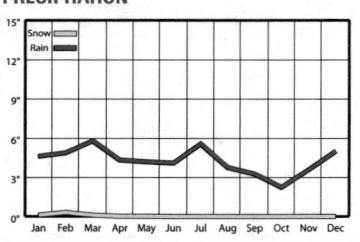

PRECIPITATION

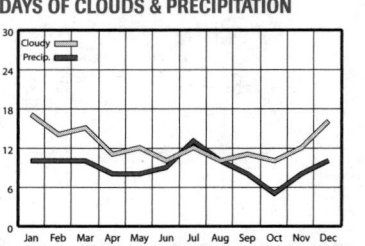

DAYS OF CLOUDS & PRECIPITATION

EDUCATION SCORE: 22/RANK: 257

ACHIEVEMENT	AREA	U.S. AVG	PUBLIC SCHOOLS	AREA	U.S. AVG	HIGHER EDUCATION	AREA	U.S. AVG
High school degree	76.9%	80.2%	Expenditures per pupil	$5,463	$5,894	No. 2-year colleges	2	3
2-year college degree	6.4%	6.2%	Student/teacher ratio	17.0	16.7	No. 4-year colleges/universities	1	4
4-year college degree	11.6%	15.8%	Attending public school	92.6%	90.2%	No. highly ranked universities	0	1
Graduate/professional degree	7.0%	9.6%	State SAT score	984*	1020			
			State ACT score	19.8	21.0			

HEALTH & HEALTHCARE SCORE: 45/RANK: 182

CRIME SCORE: 25/RANK: 248

HAZARDS & ILLNESSES	AREA	U.S. AVG	HEALTHCARE	AREA	U.S. AVG	CRIME	AREA	U.S. AVG
Air-quality score	6	45	Physicians per-capita	215.3	261.1	Violent crime rate	440.0	456.0
Water-quality score	38	33	Hospital beds per capita	611.4	432.2	Change in violent crime rate	-3.3%	-17.2%
Pollen/allergy score	61	61	No. teaching hospitals	1	4	Property crime rate	4,689.2	3,950.0
Stress score	66	50	Cost per doctor visit	$64	$67	Change in property crime rate	-1.7%	-16.8%
Cancer mortality per capita	182.8	169.0	Cost per dental visit	$72	$82			
Depression days per month	4.0	2.8	Cost per daily hospital room	$430	$733			

TRANSPORTATION SCORE: 32/RANK: 225

COMMUTE	AREA	U.S. AVG	INTERCITY SERVICES	AREA	U.S. AVG	AUTOMOTIVE	AREA	U.S. AVG
Average commute time	21.3 min.	22.6 min.	Miles to nearest major airport	83	46	Insurance, annual premium	$937	$1,011
Commute by auto	92.5%	88.7%	Type of local airport	Large		Gas, cost per gallon	$1.35	$1.50
Commute by mass transit	.8%	1.8%	No. daily airline departures	1,423	294	Daily vehicle miles per capita	23.6	23.0
Work at home	1.6%	3.9%	Amtrak service	No				
Mass transit miles per capita	3.8	8.0	No. interstate highways	1	1			

LEISURE SCORE: 5/RANK: 312

DINING & SHOPPING	AREA	U.S. AVG	ENTERTAINMENT	AREA	U.S. AVG	OUTDOOR ACTIVITIES	AREA	U.S. AVG
Restaurant rating	1	1	Professional sports rating	3	4	Golf-course rating	2	4
No. outlet malls	0	2	College sports rating	5	4	Ski-area rating	1	4
No. Starbucks	0	11	Zoo/aquarium rating	1	3	National Park rating	1	3
No. warehouse clubs	3	4	Amusement park rating	1	3	Sq. miles inland water	2.0	4.0
			Botanical garden/arboretum rating	7	3	Miles of coastline	0.0	11.4

ARTS & CULTURE SCORE: 39/RANK: 201

MEDIA & LIBRARIES	AREA	U.S. AVG	PERFORMING ARTS	AREA	U.S. AVG	MUSEUMS	AREA	U.S. AVG
Arts radio rating	1	3	Classical music rating	4	4	Overall museum rating	4	6
No. public libraries	11	28	Ballet/dance rating	1	3	Art museum rating	6	5
Library volumes per capita	2.2	2.8	Professional theater rating	1	3	Science museum rating	1	4
			University arts programs rating	1	5	Children's museum rating	1	3

Columbus, OH

Score: 64.8   **Rank:** 110

Profile: Capital city
Location: Geographic center of Ohio along Scioto River
Elevation: 833 feet
Time zone: Eastern Standard Time

PRO	CON
Diverse economy	Areas of urban decay
Urban revitalization	Urban sprawl
Educated population	Crime rate

Columbus, the capital of Ohio, is a well-blended mixture of government, industry, and the enormous Ohio State University. Sections of downtown are run-down but efforts are underway to revive them. The university brings a strong intellectual and cultural base to the city. Many businesses, particularly in suburbs to the north, find Columbus attractive because of its central location and educated population. Sprawling but attractive residential suburbs have emerged, especially to the northwest. Throughout the area housing value per dollar spent is notably high, but some of the transportation and air-quality effects of sprawl are starting to show. Many growing areas are more spacious and physically attractive than their counterparts in other cities. The city has not graduated to the level of major-league sports but has a number of quality minor-league teams as well as the locally popular Ohio State University football team. Professional sports and stronger

cultural amenities are available in Cleveland to the north and Cincinnati to the south. Columbus is one of a few cities used extensively for test marketing because of its statistically average American population.

The area is flat with four north-south stream valleys forming relatively deep, wooded gorges. Surrounding areas are mostly level plateaus of mixed open land and woods. Columbus has changeable weather. Cold Canadian air masses frequently invade the region, while moist air from the Gulf of Mexico often reaches central Ohio during the summer and to a lesser extent in the fall and winter. Summers are warm and humid with little wind and occasional thundershowers. Winters are typical of the area and latitude with cold temperatures, rain, and snow. Occasionally Atlantic winter storms will affect the area. Precipitation is distributed throughout the year with a little less in fall. Fog is common, especially in the valleys. First freeze is late October, last is mid-April.

POPULATION

DEMOGRAPHICS	AREA	U.S. AVG	ETHNIC COMPOSITION	AREA	U.S. AVG	RESIDENT PROFILE	AREA	U.S. AVG
Population	1,583,907		White	87.5%	75.1%	Single	44.6%	43.6%
Population density per sq. mile	504.1	447.3	Black	10.2%	12.3%	Married	55.4%	56.4%
Population growth	17.7%	16.1%	Asian	1.8%	3.6%	Divorced	9.5%	8.4%
Median age	33.8	35.5	American Indian	.2%	.9%	Separated	2.6%	3.0%
Average family size	2.6	2.7	Hispanic	.9%	12.5%	Married with children	28.4%	28.7%
			Diversity measure	33.0%	35.2%	Single with children	10.5%	10.1%

ECONOMY & JOBS   SCORE: 56/RANK: 143

INCOME	AREA	U.S. AVG	EMPLOYMENT	AREA	U.S. AVG	LARGEST EMPLOYING INDUSTRY
Per capita income	$26,402	$23,420	Unemployment rate	4.5%	6.1%	Fabricated Metal Product Manufacturing
Household income	$50,334	$46,060	Recent job growth	.9%	.9%	
Household income < $25K	22.0%	26.4%	Projected future job growth	15.3%	15.1%	
Household income > $75K	27.8%	24.5%	White collar	61.7%	54.5%	
Household income growth	64.1%	57.3%	Blue collar	38.3%	45.5%	

COST OF LIVING   SCORE: 27/RANK: 240

INDEXES & TAXES	AREA	U.S. AVG	HOUSING	AREA	U.S. AVG	NECESSITIES	AREA	U.S. AVG
Cost of Living Index	95.8	100.0	Median home price	$135,700	$160,100	Food Index	102.2	100.0
Financial Progress Index	112.0	100.0	Home price appreciation	5.3%	7.1%	Housing Index	84.3	100.0
Income tax rate	6.993%	4.625%	Median rent	$640	$670	Utilities Index	110.2	100.0
Sales tax rate	5.750%	6.474%	Homes owned	64.2%	63.9%	Transportation Index	102.9	100.0
Property tax rate	$19.5	$15.6	Homes rented	29.6%	25.3%	Healthcare Index	97.4	100.0
			Housing affordability	61.0%	54.5%	Miscellaneous Cost Index	100.3	100.0

CLIMATE   SCORE: 43/RANK: 187

TEMPERATURE	AREA	U.S. AVG	PRECIPITATION	AREA	U.S. AVG	COMFORTS & HAZARDS	AREA	U.S. AVG
January low	20.4°F	26.4°F	Annual inches precipitation	37.0	35.9	July relative humidity	70.0%	68.8%
July high	84.8°F	86.7°F	Annual inches snowfall	28.0	24.2	Annual days mostly sunny	181	212
Annual days > 90°F	15	38	Annual days precipitation	136	111	Annual days with thunderstorms	42	39
Annual days < 32°F	122	88	Annual days rain > 0.5 inches	25	23	Tornado risk score	19	19
Annual days < 0°F	4	6	Annual days snow > 1.5 inches	6	6	Hurricane risk score	3	15

TEMPERATURE

PRECIPITATION

DAYS OF CLOUDS & PRECIPITATION

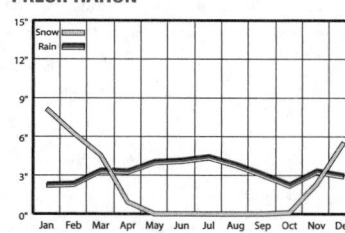

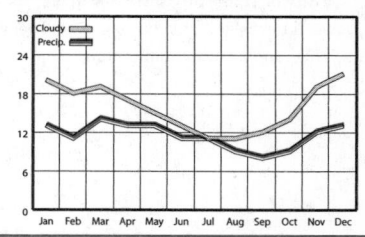

EDUCATION — SCORE: 87/RANK: 42

ACHIEVEMENT	AREA	U.S. AVG	PUBLIC SCHOOLS	AREA	U.S. AVG	HIGHER EDUCATION	AREA	U.S. AVG
High school degree	85.8%	80.2%	Expenditures per pupil	$6,272	$5,894	No. 2-year colleges	5	3
2-year college degree	5.6%	6.2%	Student/teacher ratio	17.6	16.7	No. 4-year colleges/universities	11	4
4-year college degree	19.9%	15.8%	Attending public school	89.7%	90.2%	No. highly ranked universities	4	1
Graduate/professional degree	9.2%	9.6%	State SAT score	1077	1020			
			State ACT score	21.4*	21.0			

HEALTH & HEALTHCARE — SCORE: 34/RANK: 217   CRIME — SCORE: 9/RANK: 301

HAZARDS & ILLNESSES	AREA	U.S. AVG	HEALTHCARE	AREA	U.S. AVG	CRIME	AREA	U.S. AVG
Air-quality score	89	45	Physicians per capita	294.1	261.1	Violent crime rate	505.7	456.0
Water-quality score	15	33	Hospital beds per capita	330.8	432.2	Change in violent crime rate	-24.7%	-17.2%
Pollen/allergy score	57	61	No. teaching hospitals	10	4	Property crime rate	5,840.7	3,950.0
Stress score	65	50	Cost per doctor visit	$65	$67	Change in property crime rate	6.3%	-16.8%
Cancer mortality per capita	180.7	169.0	Cost per dental visit	$76	$82			
Depression days per month	2.0	2.8	Cost per daily hospital room	$618	$733			

TRANSPORTATION — SCORE: 49/RANK: 167

COMMUTE	AREA	U.S. AVG	INTERCITY SERVICES	AREA	U.S. AVG	AUTOMOTIVE	AREA	U.S. AVG
Average commute time	23.2 min.	22.6 min.	Miles to nearest major airport	6	46	Insurance, annual premium	$1,059	$1,011
Commute by auto	90.4%	88.7%	Type of local airport	Medium		Gas, cost per gallon	$1.43	$1.50
Commute by mass transit	2.3%	1.8%	No. daily airline departures	270	294	Daily vehicle miles per capita	27.7	23.0
Work at home	3.0%	3.9%	Amtrak service	No				
Mass transit miles per capita	9.0	8.0	No. interstate highways	2	1			

LEISURE — SCORE: 46/RANK: 179

DINING & SHOPPING	AREA	U.S. AVG	ENTERTAINMENT	AREA	U.S. AVG	OUTDOOR ACTIVITIES	AREA	U.S. AVG
Restaurant rating	1	1	Professional sports rating	5	4	Golf-course rating	8	4
No. outlet malls	2	2	College sports rating	7	4	Ski-area rating	2	4
No. Starbucks	25	11	Zoo/aquarium rating	7	3	National Park rating	1	3
No. warehouse clubs	5	4	Amusement park rating	4	3	Sq. miles inland water	3.0	4.0
			Botanical garden/arboretum rating	5	3	Miles of coastline	0.0	11.4

ARTS & CULTURE — SCORE: 92/RANK: 26

MEDIA & LIBRARIES	AREA	U.S. AVG	PERFORMING ARTS	AREA	U.S. AVG	MUSEUMS	AREA	U.S. AVG
Arts radio rating	7	3	Classical music rating	7	4	Overall museum rating	9	6
No. public libraries	57	28	Ballet/dance rating	7	3	Art museum rating	8	5
Library volumes per capita	4.2	2.8	Professional theater rating	1	3	Science museum rating	9	4
			University arts programs rating	10	5	Children's museum rating	8	3

Corpus Christi, TX

Score: 63.1   Rank: 121

Profile: Mid-size city
Location: South Texas Gulf Coast, 140 miles southeast of San Antonio
Elevation: 44 feet
Time zone: Central Standard Time

PRO
Cost of living
Nearby water recreation
Pleasant winters

CON
Crime rate
Isolation
Industrial landscape

Corpus Christi is a prosperous port town about 160 miles north of the Mexican border. It is a center for the petroleum and petrochemical industry, and a major shipping gateway because of the bay and Intracoastal Waterway. There is a military presence with two naval air stations in the vicinity, and a Texas A&M campus in town. The series of long barrier islands, particularly South Padre Island to the south, provide excellent beach and boating opportunities for tourists and residents alike. There are some local cultural amenities. Like many Texas coastal towns, the area has a good economy, low housing costs and cost of living, and a warm humid climate.

Corpus Christi is located on Corpus Christi Bay, an inlet off the Gulf of Mexico. The climatic conditions vary between the humid subtropical region to the northeast along the Texas coast and the semiarid region to the west and southwest. Summer days are consistent with highs ranging from the mid-80s to the mid-90s with moderating Gulf breezes late in the afternoon. Summer evenings and mornings are warm with lows seldom below 70°F. 100°F temperatures are rare at the coast but common a few miles inland. Winter months have the least rainfall and are quite mild with just a few days below freezing. Severe tropical storms occur about once every 10 years, with lesser storms once every 5 years. Snow falls an average of once every 2 years.

POPULATION

DEMOGRAPHICS	AREA	U.S. AVG	ETHNIC COMPOSITION	AREA	U.S. AVG	RESIDENT PROFILE	AREA	U.S. AVG
Population	382,188		White	75.3%	75.1%	Single	47.0%	43.6%
Population density per sq. mile	250.2	447.3	Black	6.3%	12.3%	Married	53.0%	56.4%
Population growth	9.2%	16.1%	Asian	1.2%	3.6%	Divorced	10.0%	8.4%
Median age	33.3	35.5	American Indian	.5%	.9%	Separated	5.0%	3.0%
Average family size	2.9	2.7	Hispanic	57.9%	12.5%	Married with children	31.0%	28.7%
			Diversity measure	56.4%	35.2%	Single with children	14.2%	10.1%

ECONOMY & JOBS
SCORE: 84/RANK: 52

INCOME	AREA	U.S. AVG	EMPLOYMENT	AREA	U.S. AVG	LARGEST EMPLOYING INDUSTRY
Per capita income	$19,190	$23,420	Unemployment rate	6.8%	6.1%	Healthcare and Social Assistance
Household income	$39,789	$46,060	Recent job growth	4.1%	.9%	
Household income < $25K	32.1%	26.4%	Projected future job growth	13.8%	15.1%	
Household income > $75K	19.9%	24.5%	White collar	50.0%	54.5%	
Household income growth	59.5%	57.3%	Blue collar	50.0%	45.5%	

COST OF LIVING
SCORE: 78/RANK: 73

INDEXES & TAXES	AREA	U.S. AVG	HOUSING	AREA	U.S. AVG	NECESSITIES	AREA	U.S. AVG
Cost of Living Index	80.3	100.0	Median home price	$98,100	$160,100	Food Index	77.8	100.0
Financial Progress Index	105.5	100.0	Home price appreciation	4.5%	7.1%	Housing Index	60.9	100.0
Income tax rate	0.000%	4.625%	Median rent	$595	$670	Utilities Index	101.8	100.0
Sales tax rate	8.125%	6.474%	Homes owned	52.9%	63.9%	Transportation Index	95.1	100.0
Property tax rate	$25.2	$15.6	Homes rented	30.0%	25.3%	Healthcare Index	93.4	100.0
			Housing affordability	57.0%	54.5%	Miscellaneous Cost Index	95.4	100.0

CLIMATE
SCORE: 86/RANK: 46

TEMPERATURE	AREA	U.S. AVG	PRECIPITATION	AREA	U.S. AVG	COMFORTS & HAZARDS	AREA	U.S. AVG
January low	46.1°F	26.4°F	Annual inches precipitation	29.0	35.9	July relative humidity	77.0%	68.8%
July high	94.8°F	86.7°F	Annual inches snowfall	0.0	24.2	Annual days mostly sunny	222	212
Annual days > 90°F	96	38	Annual days precipitation	77	111	Annual days with thunderstorms	31	39
Annual days < 32°F	7	88	Annual days rain > 0.5 inches	18	23	Tornado risk score	43	19
Annual days < 0°F	0	6	Annual days snow > 1.5 inches	0	6	Hurricane risk score	39	15

TEMPERATURE

PRECIPITATION

DAYS OF CLOUDS & PRECIPITATION

EDUCATION
SCORE: 20/RANK: 262

ACHIEVEMENT	AREA	U.S. AVG	PUBLIC SCHOOLS	AREA	U.S. AVG	HIGHER EDUCATION	AREA	U.S. AVG
High school degree	73.9%	80.2%	Expenditures per pupil	$5,349	$5,894	No. 2-year colleges	1	3
2-year college degree	5.9%	6.2%	Student/teacher ratio	15.3	16.7	No. 4-year colleges/universities	1	4
4-year college degree	11.5%	15.8%	Attending public school	94.3%	90.2%	No. highly ranked universities	0	1
Graduate/professional degree	6.3%	9.6%	State SAT score	993*	1020			
			State ACT score	20.1	21.0			

HEALTH & HEALTHCARE
SCORE: 16/RANK: 276

CRIME
SCORE: 5/RANK: 313

HAZARDS & ILLNESSES	AREA	U.S. AVG	HEALTHCARE	AREA	U.S. AVG	CRIME	AREA	U.S. AVG
Air-quality score	17	45	Physicians per capita	229.2	261.1	Violent crime rate	721.8	456.0
Water-quality score	6	33	Hospital beds per capita	625.3	432.2	Change in violent crime rate	-8.8%	-17.2%
Pollen/allergy score	83	61	No. teaching hospitals	3	4	Property crime rate	6,228.4	3,950.0
Stress score	68	50	Cost per doctor visit	$63	$67	Change in property crime rate	-19.3%	-16.8%
Cancer mortality per capita	174.0	169.0	Cost per dental visit	$72	$82			
Depression days per month	1.7	2.8	Cost per daily hospital room	$458	$733			

TRANSPORTATION
SCORE: 66/RANK: 115

COMMUTE	AREA	U.S. AVG	INTERCITY SERVICES	AREA	U.S. AVG	AUTOMOTIVE	AREA	U.S. AVG
Average commute time	20.7 min.	22.6 min.	Miles to nearest major airport	13	46	Insurance, annual premium	$940	$1,011
Commute by auto	90.4%	88.7%	Type of local airport	Small		Gas, cost per gallon	$1.39	$1.50
Commute by mass transit	1.8%	1.8%	No. daily airline departures	42	294	Daily vehicle miles per capita	25.7	23.0
Work at home	3.0%	3.9%	Amtrak service	No				
Mass transit miles per capita	12.0	8.0	No. interstate highways	1	1			

LEISURE SCORE: 46/RANK: 178

DINING & SHOPPING	AREA	U.S. AVG	ENTERTAINMENT	AREA	U.S. AVG	OUTDOOR ACTIVITIES	AREA	U.S. AVG
Restaurant rating	1	1	Professional sports rating	3	4	Golf-course rating	2	4
No. outlet malls	0	2	College sports rating	2	4	Ski-area rating	1	4
No. Starbucks	1	11	Zoo/aquarium rating	1	3	National Park rating	1	3
No. warehouse clubs	3	4	Amusement park rating	1	3	Sq. miles inland water	10.0	4.0
			Botanical garden/arboretum rating	1	3	Miles of coastline	25.0	11.4

ARTS & CULTURE SCORE: 69/RANK: 101

MEDIA & LIBRARIES	AREA	U.S. AVG	PERFORMING ARTS	AREA	U.S. AVG	MUSEUMS	AREA	U.S. AVG
Arts radio rating	5	3	Classical music rating	3	4	Overall museum rating	5	6
No. public libraries	13	28	Ballet/dance rating	3	3	Art museum rating	2	5
Library volumes per capita	1.6	2.8	Professional theater rating	1	3	Science museum rating	2	4
			University arts programs rating	3	5	Children's museum rating	1	3

Corvallis, OR

Score: 89.0 Rank: 10

Profile: College town
Location: North-central Oregon in Willamette Valley, 80 miles south of Portland
Elevation: 282 feet
Time zone: Pacific Standard Time

PRO
Educated population
Nearby recreation
College-town amenities

CON
Cost of living
Clouds and rain
Quality of housing

The Corvallis area includes the cities of Corvallis and Albany, 12 miles apart in the central part of the Willamette Valley. Corvallis is the home of Oregon State University, although the college-town influence is not as strong and of a lesser quality than places with similarly sized schools. The largest employer is Hewlett-Packard, which has a large complex. Educational attainment and resources are notably strong. College sports provide entertainment, and nearby recreation in the mountains and coastal areas is excellent. Albany is mainly working class with employers in the timber, paper, and chemical industries. Although mostly run-down, it has experienced some resurgence and contains a historic downtown district. Corvallis is a "green" city in both senses; it has lush, green countryside and rigidly enforced no-growth policies. On the upside, this curbs urban sprawl and preserves the surrounding area—but it also brings a residential supply-and-demand imbalance and high home prices. Overall, the area has a true small-town flavor with access to a wide and balanced set of amenities and a fairly pleasant climate devoid of extremes.

The level Willamette Valley is mainly agricultural. Large forested hills of the Coast Range rise just to the west of Corvallis, with smaller rolling hills covered by oaks and grassland north of Albany. The climate, like most of Oregon west of the Cascades, is marine with significant winter precipitation and clouds. Summers are usually warm, dry, and pleasant, with temperatures in the 70s or low 80s; one annual hot spell usually raises temperatures to about 100°F. Summer rains are infrequent. Fall, winter, and spring are marked with sequential periods of rain but there is little snow and few freezes. Although mountains to the west block the heaviest precipitation and winds, clouds and rain can last for days.

POPULATION

DEMOGRAPHICS	AREA	U.S. AVG	ETHNIC COMPOSITION	AREA	U.S. AVG	RESIDENT PROFILE	AREA	U.S. AVG
Population	78,618		White	90.7%	75.1%	Single	50.5%	43.6%
Population density per sq. mile	116.3	447.3	Black	.8%	12.3%	Married	49.5%	56.4%
Population growth	11.0%	16.1%	Asian	6.0%	3.6%	Divorced	7.9%	8.4%
Median age	31.7	35.5	American Indian	1.7%	.9%	Separated	2.1%	3.0%
Average family size	2.4	2.7	Hispanic	4.0%	12.5%	Married with children	25.0%	28.7%
			Diversity measure	23.5%	35.2%	Single with children	8.4%	10.1%

ECONOMY & JOBS SCORE: 50/RANK: 163

INCOME	AREA	U.S. AVG	EMPLOYMENT	AREA	U.S. AVG	LARGEST EMPLOYING INDUSTRY
Per capita income	$25,237	$23,420	Unemployment rate	4.0%	6.1%	Computer and Electronic Product Manufacturing
Household income	$48,602	$46,060	Recent job growth	2.6%	.9%	
Household income < $25K	26.1%	26.4%	Projected future job growth	19.2%	15.1%	
Household income > $75K	30.1%	24.5%	White collar	61.2%	54.5%	
Household income growth	78.2%	57.3%	Blue collar	38.8%	45.5%	

COST OF LIVING SCORE: 22/RANK: 256

INDEXES & TAXES	AREA	U.S. AVG	HOUSING	AREA	U.S. AVG	NECESSITIES	AREA	U.S. AVG
Cost of Living Index	109.0	100.0	Median home price	$186,620	$160,100	Food Index	101.3	100.0
Financial Progress Index	95.1	100.0	Home price appreciation	3.2%	7.1%	Housing Index	115.9	100.0
Income tax rate	9.000%	4.625%	Median rent	$710	$670	Utilities Index	93.5	100.0
Sales tax rate	0.000%	6.474%	Homes owned	57.1%	63.9%	Transportation Index	107.2	100.0
Property tax rate	$14.5	$15.6	Homes rented	37.6%	25.3%	Healthcare Index	125.4	100.0
			Housing affordability	47.0%	54.5%	Miscellaneous Cost Index	105.5	100.0

CLIMATE — SCORE: 66/RANK: 110

TEMPERATURE	AREA	U.S. AVG	PRECIPITATION	AREA	U.S. AVG	COMFORTS & HAZARDS	AREA	U.S. AVG
January low	33.0°F	26.4°F	Annual inches precipitation	42.0	35.9	July relative humidity	73.0%	68.8%
July high	81.6°F	86.7°F	Annual inches snowfall	6.0	24.2	Annual days mostly sunny	153	212
Annual days > 90°F	9	38	Annual days precipitation	145	111	Annual days with thunderstorms	5	39
Annual days < 32°F	50	88	Annual days rain > 0.5 inches	25	23	Tornado risk score	2	19
Annual days < 0°F	0	6	Annual days snow > 1.5 inches	1	6	Hurricane risk score	0	15

TEMPERATURE · **PRECIPITATION**

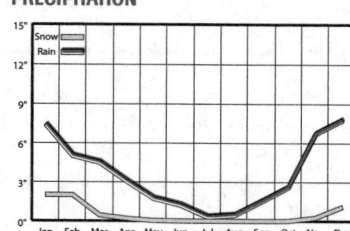

DAYS OF CLOUDS & PRECIPITATION

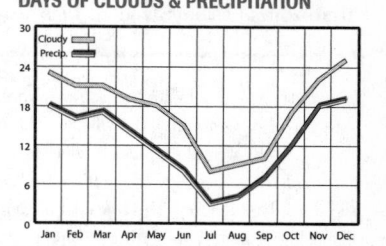

EDUCATION — SCORE: 90/RANK: 31

ACHIEVEMENT	AREA	U.S. AVG	PUBLIC SCHOOLS	AREA	U.S. AVG	HIGHER EDUCATION	AREA	U.S. AVG
High school degree	93.0%	80.2%	Expenditures per pupil	$6,466	$5,894	No. 2-year colleges	0	3
2-year college degree	6.9%	6.2%	Student/teacher ratio	21.1	16.7	No. 4-year colleges/universities	1	4
4-year college degree	26.2%	15.8%	Attending public school	84.8%	90.2%	No. highly ranked universities	0	1
Graduate/professional degree	21.2%	9.6%	State SAT score	1053*	1020			
			State ACT score	22.6	21.0			

HEALTH & HEALTHCARE — SCORE: 76/RANK: 77 · CRIME — SCORE: 83/RANK: 55

HAZARDS & ILLNESSES	AREA	U.S. AVG	HEALTHCARE	AREA	U.S. AVG	CRIME	AREA	U.S. AVG
Air-quality score	64	45	Physicians per capita	283.7	261.1	Violent crime rate	186.6	456.0
Water-quality score	36	33	Hospital beds per capita	208.6	432.2	Change in violent crime rate	-30.1%	-17.2%
Pollen/allergy score	60	61	No. teaching hospitals	0	4	Property crime rate	3,771.6	3,950.0
Stress score	6	50	Cost per doctor visit	$82	$67	Change in property crime rate	-35.2%	-16.8%
Cancer mortality per capita	143.4	169.0	Cost per dental visit	$118	$82			
Depression days per month	2.0	2.8	Cost per daily hospital room	$701	$733			

TRANSPORTATION — SCORE: 59/RANK: 135

COMMUTE	AREA	U.S. AVG	INTERCITY SERVICES	AREA	U.S. AVG	AUTOMOTIVE	AREA	U.S. AVG
Average commute time	17.8 min.	22.6 min.	Miles to nearest major airport	32	46	Insurance, annual premium	$847	$1,011
Commute by auto	75.0%	88.7%	Type of local airport	Small		Gas, cost per gallon	$1.60	$1.50
Commute by mass transit	.4%	1.8%	No. daily airline departures	51	294	Daily vehicle miles per capita	16.4	23.0
Work at home	7.4%	3.9%	Amtrak service	No				
Mass transit miles per capita	0.0	8.0	No. interstate highways	0	1			

LEISURE — SCORE: 51/RANK: 162

DINING & SHOPPING	AREA	U.S. AVG	ENTERTAINMENT	AREA	U.S. AVG	OUTDOOR ACTIVITIES	AREA	U.S. AVG
Restaurant rating	1	1	Professional sports rating	2	4	Golf-course rating	1	4
No. outlet malls	2	2	College sports rating	5	4	Ski-area rating	8	4
No. Starbucks	3	11	Zoo/aquarium rating	1	3	National Park rating	2	3
No. warehouse clubs	1	4	Amusement park rating	1	3	Sq. miles inland water	2.0	4.0
			Botanical garden/arboretum rating	1	3	Miles of coastline	0.0	11.4

ARTS & CULTURE — SCORE: 74/RANK: 83

MEDIA & LIBRARIES	AREA	U.S. AVG	PERFORMING ARTS	AREA	U.S. AVG	MUSEUMS	AREA	U.S. AVG
Arts radio rating	1	3	Classical music rating	2	4	Overall museum rating	2	6
No. public libraries	4	28	Ballet/dance rating	1	3	Art museum rating	3	5
Library volumes per capita	3.6	2.8	Professional theater rating	1	3	Science museum rating	1	4
			University arts programs rating	4	5	Children's museum rating	1	3

Cumberland, MD

Score: 56.4   **Rank:** 175

Profile: Small town
Location: Western Maryland in the western portion of the panhandle, between Pennsylvania and West Virginia
Elevation: 1,233 feet
Time zone: Eastern Standard Time

PRO
Cost of living
Attractive setting
Nearby mountains

CON
Isolation
Arts and culture
Low ethnic diversity

Cumberland has a history as a transportation center and gateway to the west. Originally, the Chesapeake and Ohio Canal met toll roads to the west there. Later came the railroads and the historic National Road—now U.S. 40. Today the town has a small manufacturing base and a tourist economy. The low cost of living relative to the northeast region, quiet mountain setting with abundant outdoor recreational opportunities, and beautiful fall seasons are the area's main draws.

Cumberland is in a small valley, at a bend in the Potomac River, surrounded by deciduous forest and the 3,000 feet-high Appalachian Mountains. Summers are calm, warm, and humid with occasional thundershowers. The mountains moderate winter storms, but periods of cold and snow with occasional freezing rain occur annually. Warm moist southerly air frequently meets cooler, drier northern air, creating periods of extended precipitation. First freeze is late October, last is early April.

POPULATION

DEMOGRAPHICS	AREA	U.S. AVG	ETHNIC COMPOSITION	AREA	U.S. AVG	RESIDENT PROFILE	AREA	U.S. AVG
Population	101,290		White	95.6%	75.1%	Single	41.1%	43.6%
Population density per sq. mile	134.5	447.3	Black	3.8%	12.3%	Married	58.9%	56.4%
Population growth	-.3%	16.1%	Asian	.4%	3.6%	Divorced	6.4%	8.4%
Median age	39.5	35.5	American Indian	.1%	.9%	Separated	2.7%	3.0%
Average family size	2.5	2.7	Hispanic	.5%	12.5%	Married with children	27.1%	28.7%
			Diversity measure	12.5%	35.2%	Single with children	8.2%	10.1%

ECONOMY & JOBS
SCORE: 51/RANK: 162

INCOME	AREA	U.S. AVG	EMPLOYMENT	AREA	U.S. AVG	LARGEST EMPLOYING INDUSTRY
Per capita income	$17,378	$23,420	Unemployment rate	6.1%	6.1%	Paper Manufacturing
Household income	$31,176	$46,060	Recent job growth	.2%	.9%	
Household income < $25K	40.0%	26.4%	Projected future job growth	8.4%	15.1%	
Household income > $75K	11.1%	24.5%	White collar	46.6%	54.5%	
Household income growth	43.3%	57.3%	Blue collar	53.4%	45.5%	

COST OF LIVING
SCORE: 73/RANK: 88

INDEXES & TAXES	AREA	U.S. AVG	HOUSING	AREA	U.S. AVG	NECESSITIES	AREA	U.S. AVG
Cost of Living Index	79.0	100.0	Median home price	$81,790	$160,100	Food Index	89.5	100.0
Financial Progress Index	84.1	100.0	Home price appreciation	4.4%	7.1%	Housing Index	50.8	100.0
Income tax rate	7.450%	4.625%	Median rent	$539	$670	Utilities Index	102.3	100.0
Sales tax rate	5.000%	6.474%	Homes owned	69.3%	63.9%	Transportation Index	89.0	100.0
Property tax rate	$14.8	$15.6	Homes rented	17.5%	25.3%	Healthcare Index	88.1	100.0
			Housing affordability	46.0%	54.5%	Miscellaneous Cost Index	101.3	100.0

CLIMATE
SCORE: 51/RANK: 161

TEMPERATURE	AREA	U.S. AVG	PRECIPITATION	AREA	U.S. AVG	COMFORTS & HAZARDS	AREA	U.S. AVG
January low	40.5°F	26.4°F	Annual inches precipitation	36.0	35.9	July relative humidity	72.0%	68.8%
July high	87.1°F	86.7°F	Annual inches snowfall	35.0	24.2	Annual days mostly sunny	215	212
Annual days > 90°F	28	38	Annual days precipitation	124	111	Annual days with thunderstorms	35	39
Annual days < 32°F	115	88	Annual days rain > 0.5 inches	24	23	Tornado risk score	1	19
Annual days < 0°F	1	6	Annual days snow > 1.5 inches	7	6	Hurricane risk score	9	15

TEMPERATURE

PRECIPITATION

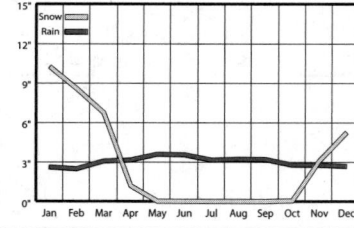

DAYS OF CLOUDS & PRECIPITATION

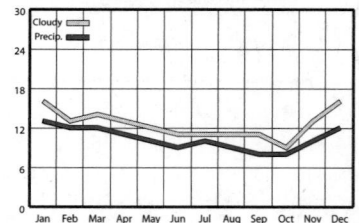

EDUCATION SCORE: 20/RANK: 263

ACHIEVEMENT	AREA	U.S. AVG	PUBLIC SCHOOLS	AREA	U.S. AVG	HIGHER EDUCATION	AREA	U.S. AVG
High school degree	79.3%	80.2%	Expenditures per pupil	$6,545	$5,894	No. 2-year colleges	2	3
2-year college degree	7.8%	6.2%	Student/teacher ratio	16.0	16.7	No. 4-year colleges/universities	1	4
4-year college degree	7.8%	15.8%	Attending public school	91.0%	90.2%	No. highly ranked universities	0	1
Graduate/professional degree	6.2%	9.6%	State SAT score	1024*	1020			
			State ACT score	20.7	21.0			

HEALTH & HEALTHCARE SCORE: 87/RANK: 42 — CRIME SCORE: 56/RANK: 144

HAZARDS & ILLNESSES	AREA	U.S. AVG	HEALTHCARE	AREA	U.S. AVG	CRIME	AREA	U.S. AVG
Air-quality score	81	45	Physicians per capita	191.5	261.1	Violent crime rate	362.0	456.0
Water-quality score	49	33	Hospital beds per capita	658.8	432.2	Change in violent crime rate	-15.3%	-17.2%
Pollen/allergy score	63	61	No. teaching hospitals	0	4	Property crime rate	2,661.5	3,950.0
Stress score	26	50	Cost per doctor visit	$55	$67	Change in property crime rate	14.7%	-16.8%
Cancer mortality per capita	174.0	169.0	Cost per dental visit	$68	$82			
Depression days per month	3.0	2.8	Cost per daily hospital room	$595	$733			

TRANSPORTATION SCORE: 4/RANK: 317

COMMUTE	AREA	U.S. AVG	INTERCITY SERVICES	AREA	U.S. AVG	AUTOMOTIVE	AREA	U.S. AVG
Average commute time	24.5 min.	22.6 min.	Miles to nearest major airport	85	46	Insurance, annual premium	$1,032	$1,011
Commute by auto	91.8%	88.7%	Type of local airport	Medium		Gas, cost per gallon	$1.48	$1.50
Commute by mass transit	.7%	1.8%	No. daily airline departures	675	294	Daily vehicle miles per capita	19.2	23.0
Work at home	2.9%	3.9%	Amtrak service	Yes				
Mass transit miles per capita	0.0	8.0	No. interstate highways	0	1			

LEISURE SCORE: 51/RANK: 160

DINING & SHOPPING	AREA	U.S. AVG	ENTERTAINMENT	AREA	U.S. AVG	OUTDOOR ACTIVITIES	AREA	U.S. AVG
Restaurant rating	1	1	Professional sports rating	2	4	Golf-course rating	1	4
No. outlet malls	2	2	College sports rating	1	4	Ski-area rating	5	4
No. Starbucks	0	11	Zoo/aquarium rating	1	3	National Park rating	2	3
No. warehouse clubs	1	4	Amusement park rating	1	3	Sq. miles inland water	2.0	4.0
			Botanical garden/arboretum rating	1	3	Miles of coastline	0.0	11.4

ARTS & CULTURE SCORE: 5/RANK: 312

MEDIA & LIBRARIES	AREA	U.S. AVG	PERFORMING ARTS	AREA	U.S. AVG	MUSEUMS	AREA	U.S. AVG
Arts radio rating	1	3	Classical music rating	1	4	Overall museum rating	3	6
No. public libraries	9	28	Ballet/dance rating	3	3	Art museum rating	1	5
Library volumes per capita	2.3	2.8	Professional theater rating	1	3	Science museum rating	1	4
			University arts programs rating	3	5	Children's museum rating	1	3

Dallas, TX

Score: 67.3 Rank: 95

Profile: Regional center
Location: Northeast Texas
Elevation: 596 feet
Time zone: Central Standard Time

PRO	CON
Entertainment	Urban sprawl
Arts and culture	Unattractive setting
Diverse economy	Summer heat

Dallas is the eastern, larger half of the Dallas–Fort Worth "Metroplex." Dallas is what most people think of when they first think of Texas—big, busy, growing, cosmopolitan, rich, glitzy, and self-confident. Located topographically in the middle of nowhere, dozens of gleaming downtown skyscrapers tower above the level plains, while an assortment of neighborhoods sprawl in all directions around the city center. It has largely outgrown its first beltway and is working on its second. Long commutes are common, thanks to the large population, growth rate, and urban sprawl, but the city has a rapidly developing rail-transit program. It is a popular convention site and corporate headquarters—largely because of its central location vis-à-vis the rest of the United States, the favorable business climate, the availability of educated workers, and the unspoken notion of being in the center of all things big. Dallas's growth began with the east Texas oil boom. Although there is little produced in the immediate area, oil continues to be a large factor in the local economy.

The strong economy and wealthy population have endowed the city with a collection of arts, cultural assets, and parks. The many cultural landmarks include theaters, the Dallas Museum of Art, the Meyerson Symphony Center, and the Frank Lloyd Wright–inspired Dallas Theater Center. Filling out the roster of major-league teams are the NFL Cowboys, MLB Rangers, NBA Mavericks, and NHL Stars, all drawing a strong local and national following. A few lakes exist to the north and east, but outdoor recreational opportunities in the surrounding flat plains are limited. Nonetheless, as the center of the nation's air-transport networks, and the hub for American and Southwest airlines, Dallas provides numerous getaway opportunities; the city lags only behind Chicago, Los Angeles, and Atlanta in the number of available airline flights.

The city's most notable features are the pace and influence of the business community, high incomes with a low cost of living, the strong arts and cultural presence, and a reputation for having more retail stores and restaurants per capita than any other place in the country. Downsides are urban sprawl, long commutes, and a featureless physical environment.

The Dallas–Fort Worth Metroplex is approximately 250 miles north of the Gulf of Mexico. Terrain is flat to rolling and largely devoid of natural trees. The climate combines humid subtropical and continental elements with hot summers and a wide annual temperature range. Annual precipitation also varies considerably, ranging from less than 20 to more than 50 inches. Summer hot spells are broken into 3- to 5-day periods by thunderstorm activity. Summer daytime temperatures frequently exceed 100°F with occasional nights above 80°F. Winters are mild but north winds bring sudden temperature drops. Occasional periods of extreme cold are short-lived. There are periods of rainy weather and thunderstorm activity with occasional heavy downpours especially in spring. Snowfall is rare. First freeze is late November, last is mid-March.

POPULATION

DEMOGRAPHICS	AREA	U.S. AVG	ETHNIC COMPOSITION	AREA	U.S. AVG	RESIDENT PROFILE	AREA	U.S. AVG
Population	3,743,254		White	74.4%	75.1%	Single	43.9%	43.6%
Population density per sq. mile	605.1	447.3	Black	14.6%	12.3%	Married	56.1%	56.4%
Population growth	39.9%	16.1%	Asian	2.7%	3.6%	Divorced	9.7%	8.4%
Median age	32.0	35.5	American Indian	.5%	.9%	Separated	4.0%	3.0%
Average family size	2.8	2.7	Hispanic	19.2%	12.5%	Married with children	30.2%	28.7%
			Diversity measure	58.3%	35.2%	Single with children	10.9%	10.1%

ECONOMY & JOBS SCORE: 37/RANK: 207

INCOME	AREA	U.S. AVG	EMPLOYMENT	AREA	U.S. AVG	LARGEST EMPLOYING INDUSTRY
Per capita income	$29,970	$23,420	Unemployment rate	7.1%	6.1%	Computer and Electronic Product Manufacturing
Household income	$59,153	$46,060	Recent job growth	.8%	.9%	
Household income < $25K	17.8%	26.4%	Projected future job growth	19.7%	15.1%	
Household income > $75K	36.7%	24.5%	White collar	62.5%	54.5%	
Household income growth	80.7%	57.3%	Blue collar	37.5%	45.5%	

COST OF LIVING SCORE: 42/RANK: 191

INDEXES & TAXES	AREA	U.S. AVG	HOUSING	AREA	U.S. AVG	NECESSITIES	AREA	U.S. AVG
Cost of Living Index	95.0	100.0	Median home price	$134,600	$160,100	Food Index	100.1	100.0
Financial Progress Index	132.7	100.0	Home price appreciation	6.4%	7.1%	Housing Index	83.6	100.0
Income tax rate	0.000%	4.625%	Median rent	$871	$670	Utilities Index	93.9	100.0
Sales tax rate	8.250%	6.474%	Homes owned	59.7%	63.9%	Transportation Index	106.5	100.0
Property tax rate	$23.7	$15.6	Homes rented	29.6%	25.3%	Healthcare Index	109.0	100.0
			Housing affordability	56.0%	54.5%	Miscellaneous Cost Index	100.5	100.0

CLIMATE SCORE: 86/RANK: 45

TEMPERATURE	AREA	U.S. AVG	PRECIPITATION	AREA	U.S. AVG	COMFORTS & HAZARDS	AREA	U.S. AVG
January low	33.9°F	26.4°F	Annual inches precipitation	32.0	35.9	July relative humidity	67.0%	68.8%
July high	96.1°F	86.7°F	Annual inches snowfall	3.0	24.2	Annual days mostly sunny	233	212
Annual days > 90°F	88	38	Annual days precipitation	79	111	Annual days with thunderstorms	46	39
Annual days < 32°F	39	88	Annual days rain > 0.5 inches	20	23	Tornado risk score	44	19
Annual days < 0°F	0	6	Annual days snow > 1.5 inches	1	6	Hurricane risk score	11	15

TEMPERATURE

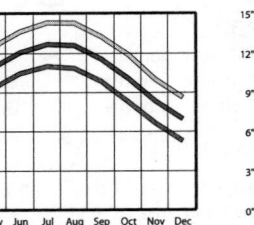

PRECIPITATION

DAYS OF CLOUDS & PRECIPITATION

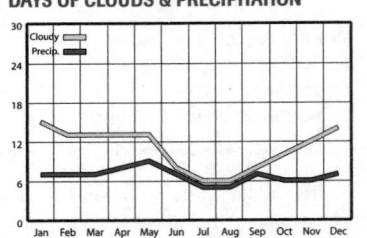

EDUCATION SCORE: 89/RANK: 38

ACHIEVEMENT	AREA	U.S. AVG	PUBLIC SCHOOLS	AREA	U.S. AVG	HIGHER EDUCATION	AREA	U.S. AVG
High school degree	79.4%	80.2%	Expenditures per pupil	$5,162	$5,894	No. 2-year colleges	12	3
2-year college degree	5.4%	6.2%	Student/teacher ratio	15.2	16.7	No. 4-year colleges/universities	14	4
4-year college degree	20.5%	15.8%	Attending public school	92.3%	90.2%	No. highly ranked universities	3	1
Graduate/professional degree	9.6%	9.6%	State SAT score	993*	1020			
			State ACT score	20.1	21.0			

HEALTH & HEALTHCARE — SCORE: 7/RANK: 306

HAZARDS & ILLNESSES	AREA	U.S. AVG	HEALTHCARE	AREA	U.S. AVG
Air-quality score	4	45	Physicians per capita	220.3	261.1
Water-quality score	69	33	Hospital beds per capita	285.8	432.2
Pollen/allergy score	87	61	No. teaching hospitals	17	4
Stress score	94	50	Cost per doctor visit	$73	$67
Cancer mortality per capita	166.4	169.0	Cost per dental visit	$83	$82
Depression days per month	2.5	2.8	Cost per daily hospital room	$628	$733

CRIME — SCORE: 13/RANK: 285

CRIME	AREA	U.S. AVG
Violent crime rate	697.3	456.0
Change in violent crime rate	-14.9%	-17.2%
Property crime rate	5,128.1	3,950.0
Change in property crime rate	-10.9%	-16.8%

TRANSPORTATION — SCORE: 96/RANK: 11

COMMUTE	AREA	U.S. AVG	INTERCITY SERVICES	AREA	U.S. AVG	AUTOMOTIVE	AREA	U.S. AVG
Average commute time	27.9 min.	22.6 min.	Miles to nearest major airport	17	46	Insurance, annual premium	$1,499	$1,011
Commute by auto	91.2%	88.7%	Type of local airport	Large		Gas, cost per gallon	$1.44	$1.50
Commute by mass transit	2.6%	1.8%	No. daily airline departures	1,310	294	Daily vehicle miles per capita	28.3	23.0
Work at home	2.6%	3.9%	Amtrak service	Yes				
Mass transit miles per capita	16.2	8.0	No. interstate highways	4	1			

LEISURE — SCORE: 89/RANK: 35

DINING & SHOPPING	AREA	U.S. AVG	ENTERTAINMENT	AREA	U.S. AVG	OUTDOOR ACTIVITIES	AREA	U.S. AVG
Restaurant rating	5	1	Professional sports rating	9	4	Golf-course rating	8	4
No. outlet malls	6	2	College sports rating	6	4	Ski-area rating	1	4
No. Starbucks	87	11	Zoo/aquarium rating	6	3	National Park rating	1	3
No. warehouse clubs	8	4	Amusement park rating	5	3	Sq. miles inland water	7.0	4.0
			Botanical garden/arboretum rating	8	3	Miles of coastline	0.0	11.4

ARTS & CULTURE — SCORE: 93/RANK: 23

MEDIA & LIBRARIES	AREA	U.S. AVG	PERFORMING ARTS	AREA	U.S. AVG	MUSEUMS	AREA	U.S. AVG
Arts radio rating	8	3	Classical music rating	10	4	Overall museum rating	9	6
No. public libraries	101	28	Ballet/dance rating	8	3	Art museum rating	9	5
Library volumes per capita	2.2	2.8	Professional theater rating	10	3	Science museum rating	8	4
			University arts programs rating	8	5	Children's museum rating	8	3

Danbury, CT

Score: 55.8   Rank: 181

Profile: Small city
Location: Southwestern Connecticut, 5 miles from the New York state border
Elevation: 510 feet
Time zone: Eastern Standard Time

PRO	CON
Attractive setting	Cost of living
Low crime rate	Long commutes
Educated population	Harsh winters

Danbury is a typical southern New England city, with little in the way of urban sprawl and a variety of small businesses and manufacturing industries. The commute to New York City is long, but several important commercial suburbs, such as White Plains, are easily accessible. To the north, Lake Candlewood and nearby state parks provide recreation. Highlights include a clean setting, the lowest crime rate in the United States, and a well-educated community, with 38% of the population holding 4-year and graduate degrees. Downsides are the high cost of living and housing prices—both typical of nicer communities near New York City.

Danbury is located in the flat, fertile, and narrow valley of the Still River. Hills reach 850 feet to the south and 1,000 feet to 1,100 feet to the north. Cover is a mix of deciduous woods and open land. The climate is temperate with a stronger continental influence than most coastal Connecticut locations. Warm, humid days are the summer norm with occasional thundershowers and stronger storms approaching from the west and southwest. In winter, Danbury receives both cold air from the north and warmer, moist air from the south and nearby water areas. Rain-snow mixes are common; snow may fall there when New York City is getting rain. Cool air trapped in the valley produces fog and freezing rain. Spring and fall are quite pleasant, with beautiful crisp fall days and fine fall color. First freeze is early October, last is May 1.

POPULATION

DEMOGRAPHICS	AREA	U.S. AVG	ETHNIC COMPOSITION	AREA	U.S. AVG	RESIDENT PROFILE	AREA	U.S. AVG
Population	223,580		White	93.7%	75.1%	Single	40.0%	43.6%
Population density per sq. mile	577.8	447.3	Black	2.8%	12.3%	Married	60.0%	56.4%
Population growth	15.5%	16.1%	Asian	2.6%	3.6%	Divorced	7.5%	8.4%
Median age	38.1	35.5	American Indian	.2%	.9%	Separated	1.6%	3.0%
Average family size	2.7	2.7	Hispanic	4.6%	12.5%	Married with children	30.7%	28.7%
			Diversity measure	37.9%	35.2%	Single with children	6.0%	10.1%

ECONOMY & JOBS — SCORE: 97/RANK: 8

INCOME	AREA	U.S. AVG	EMPLOYMENT	AREA	U.S. AVG	LARGEST EMPLOYING INDUSTRY
Per capita income	$44,084	$23,420	Unemployment rate	3.4%	6.1%	Machinery Manufacturing
Household income	$81,775	$46,060	Recent job growth	2.7%	.9%	
Household income < $25K	12.8%	26.4%	Projected future job growth	6.3%	15.1%	
Household income > $75K	52.7%	24.5%	White collar	68.6%	54.5%	
Household income growth	52.9%	57.3%	Blue collar	31.4%	45.5%	

COST OF LIVING — SCORE: 4/RANK: 315

INDEXES & TAXES	AREA	U.S. AVG	HOUSING	AREA	U.S. AVG	NECESSITIES	AREA	U.S. AVG
Cost of Living Index	160.7	100.0	Median home price	$360,330	$160,100	Food Index	122.7	100.0
Financial Progress Index	108.5	100.0	Home price appreciation	11.2%	7.1%	Housing Index	223.8	100.0
Income tax rate	4.500%	4.625%	Median rent	$1,084	$670	Utilities Index	143.0	100.0
Sales tax rate	6.000%	6.474%	Homes owned	73.1%	63.9%	Transportation Index	110.8	100.0
Property tax rate	$14.1	$15.6	Homes rented	15.7%	25.3%	Healthcare Index	149.9	100.0
			Housing affordability	56.0%	54.5%	Miscellaneous Cost Index	121.0	100.0

CLIMATE — SCORE: 1/RANK: 325

TEMPERATURE	AREA	U.S. AVG	PRECIPITATION	AREA	U.S. AVG	COMFORTS & HAZARDS	AREA	U.S. AVG
January low	16.1°F	26.4°F	Annual inches precipitation	43.0	35.9	July relative humidity	68.0%	68.8%
July high	84.1°F	86.7°F	Annual inches snowfall	53.0	24.2	Annual days mostly sunny	188	212
Annual days > 90°F	20	38	Annual days precipitation	128	111	Annual days with thunderstorms	22	39
Annual days < 32°F	137	88	Annual days rain > 0.5 inches	26	23	Tornado risk score	6	19
Annual days < 0°F	6	6	Annual days snow > 1.5 inches	9	6	Hurricane risk score	19	15

TEMPERATURE

PRECIPITATION

DAYS OF CLOUDS & PRECIPITATION

EDUCATION — SCORE: 86/RANK: 48

ACHIEVEMENT	AREA	U.S. AVG	PUBLIC SCHOOLS	AREA	U.S. AVG	HIGHER EDUCATION	AREA	U.S. AVG
High school degree	84.5%	80.2%	Expenditures per pupil	$8,149	$5,894	No. 2-year colleges	0	3
2-year college degree	6.0%	6.2%	Student/teacher ratio	13.9	16.7	No. 4-year colleges/universities	1	4
4-year college degree	21.9%	15.8%	Attending public school	89.2%	90.2%	No. highly ranked universities	0	1
Graduate/professional degree	15.9%	9.6%	State SAT score	1026*	1020			
			State ACT score	22.1	21.0			

HEALTH & HEALTHCARE — SCORE: 25/RANK: 246

HAZARDS & ILLNESSES	AREA	U.S. AVG	HEALTHCARE	AREA	U.S. AVG
Air-quality score	59	45	Physicians per capita	284.5	261.1
Water-quality score	38	33	Hospital beds per capita	185.8	432.2
Pollen/allergy score	55	61	No. teaching hospitals	1	4
Stress score	7	50	Cost per doctor visit	$77	$67
Cancer mortality per capita	177.1	169.0	Cost per dental visit	$133	$82
Depression days per month	1.9	2.8	Cost per daily hospital room	$1,203	$733

CRIME — SCORE: 100/RANK: 1

CRIME	AREA	U.S. AVG
Violent crime rate	107.9	456.0
Change in violent crime rate	-14.6%	-17.2%
Property crime rate	1,558.0	3,950.0
Change in property crime rate	-51.8%	-16.8%

TRANSPORTATION — SCORE: 94/RANK: 17

COMMUTE	AREA	U.S. AVG	INTERCITY SERVICES	AREA	U.S. AVG	AUTOMOTIVE	AREA	U.S. AVG
Average commute time	25.1 min.	22.6 min.	Miles to nearest major airport	29	46	Insurance, annual premium	$1,215	$1,011
Commute by auto	89.8%	88.7%	Type of local airport	Medium		Gas, cost per gallon	$1.62	$1.50
Commute by mass transit	2.3%	1.8%	No. daily airline departures	209	294	Daily vehicle miles per capita	25.9	23.0
Work at home	4.9%	3.9%	Amtrak service	No				
Mass transit miles per capita	5.7	8.0	No. interstate highways	1	1			

LEISURE — SCORE: 75/RANK: 81

DINING & SHOPPING	AREA	U.S. AVG	ENTERTAINMENT	AREA	U.S. AVG	OUTDOOR ACTIVITIES	AREA	U.S. AVG
Restaurant rating	1	1	Professional sports rating	10	4	Golf-course rating	8	4
No. outlet malls	6	2	College sports rating	10	4	Ski-area rating	6	4
No. Starbucks	4	11	Zoo/aquarium rating	4	3	National Park rating	3	3
No. warehouse clubs	4	4	Amusement park rating	5	3	Sq. miles inland water	6.0	4.0
			Botanical garden/arboretum rating	6	3	Miles of coastline	0.0	11.4

ARTS & CULTURE
SCORE: 64/RANK: 122

MEDIA & LIBRARIES	AREA	U.S. AVG	PERFORMING ARTS	AREA	U.S. AVG	MUSEUMS	AREA	U.S. AVG
Arts radio rating	4	3	Classical music rating	7	4	Overall museum rating	5	6
No. public libraries	13	28	Ballet/dance rating	7	3	Art museum rating	8	5
Library volumes per capita	4.0	2.8	Professional theater rating	8	3	Science museum rating	7	4
			University arts programs rating	1	5	Children's museum rating	3	3

Danville, VA

Score: 35.1   Rank: 298

Profile: Small town
Location: Extreme south-central Virginia at North Carolina border
Elevation: 500 feet
Time zone: Eastern Standard Time

PRO	CON
Cost of living	Declining economy
Attractive setting	Low educational attainment
Historic interest	Entertainment

Danville, located in what is referred to as the "southside" part of the state, is a center for the tobacco and textile industries. Textile giant Dan River Corporation makes its home there, and the atmosphere is generally business-friendly. However, the current employment and job-prospect figures reflect the poor economic state of the dominant industries. Physically, the city is a mix of historic and small-scale, modern buildings. The Millionaire's Row section of Main Street is listed on the National Register of Historic Places and there are a few minor cultural assets. The city has the lowest home prices and cost of living among Virginia's metropolitan areas, but the declining economy and lack of intellectual stimulation gives the area a notably low rank for the state.

The Dan River bisects the city on a rolling and wooded plain. Hilly, mostly wooded areas surround the city. Danville enjoys four distinct seasons with warm summers and crisp but moderate winters. The nearby hills and mountains to the northwest block extreme cold and strong storms. Precipitation is spread evenly through the year, occurring mainly as summer thunderstorms and periods of fall and winter rain, with occasional snow and freezing rain. First freeze is mid-October, last is late April.

POPULATION

DEMOGRAPHICS	AREA	U.S. AVG	ETHNIC COMPOSITION	AREA	U.S. AVG	RESIDENT PROFILE	AREA	U.S. AVG
Population	109,341		White	66.3%	75.1%	Single	42.8%	43.6%
Population density per sq. mile	107.8	447.3	Black	33.2%	12.3%	Married	57.2%	56.4%
Population growth	.6%	16.1%	Asian	.2%	3.6%	Divorced	6.3%	8.4%
Median age	40.6	35.5	American Indian	.1%	.9%	Separated	4.9%	3.0%
Average family size	2.6	2.7	Hispanic	1.3%	12.5%	Married with children	27.2%	28.7%
			Diversity measure	46.8%	35.2%	Single with children	10.4%	10.1%

ECONOMY & JOBS
SCORE: 42/RANK: 192

INCOME	AREA	U.S. AVG	EMPLOYMENT	AREA	U.S. AVG	LARGEST EMPLOYING INDUSTRY
Per capita income	$17,638	$23,420	Unemployment rate	9.5%	6.1%	Textile Mills
Household income	$31,305	$46,060	Recent job growth	2.2%	.9%	
Household income < $25K	39.7%	26.4%	Projected future job growth	5.6%	15.1%	
Household income > $75K	11.1%	24.5%	White collar	40.1%	54.5%	
Household income growth	35.5%	57.3%	Blue collar	59.9%	45.5%	

COST OF LIVING
SCORE: 89/RANK: 35

INDEXES & TAXES	AREA	U.S. AVG	HOUSING	AREA	U.S. AVG	NECESSITIES	AREA	U.S. AVG
Cost of Living Index	78.0	100.0	Median home price	$87,470	$160,100	Food Index	93.7	100.0
Financial Progress Index	85.5	100.0	Home price appreciation	4.6%	7.1%	Housing Index	54.3	100.0
Income tax rate	5.750%	4.625%	Median rent	$466	$670	Utilities Index	81.6	100.0
Sales tax rate	4.500%	6.474%	Homes owned	65.2%	63.9%	Transportation Index	86.5	100.0
Property tax rate	$11.0	$15.6	Homes rented	18.3%	25.3%	Healthcare Index	94.7	100.0
			Housing affordability	56.0%	54.5%	Miscellaneous Cost Index	94.6	100.0

CLIMATE — SCORE: 59/RANK: 136

TEMPERATURE	AREA	U.S. AVG	PRECIPITATION	AREA	U.S. AVG	COMFORTS & HAZARDS	AREA	U.S. AVG
January low	28.5°F	26.4°F	Annual inches precipitation	41.4	35.9	July relative humidity	72.0%	68.8%
July high	87.5°F	86.7°F	Annual inches snowfall	8.7	24.2	Annual days mostly sunny	217	212
Annual days > 90°F	28	38	Annual days precipitation	121	111	Annual days with thunderstorms	46	39
Annual days < 32°F	85	88	Annual days rain > 0.5 inches	27	23	Tornado risk score	2	19
Annual days < 0°F	0	6	Annual days snow > 1.5 inches	2	6	Hurricane risk score	19	15

TEMPERATURE

PRECIPITATION

DAYS OF CLOUDS & PRECIPITATION

EDUCATION — SCORE: 2/RANK: 323

ACHIEVEMENT	AREA	U.S. AVG	PUBLIC SCHOOLS	AREA	U.S. AVG	HIGHER EDUCATION	AREA	U.S. AVG
High school degree	68.5%	80.2%	Expenditures per pupil	$5,018	$5,894	No. 2-year colleges	1	3
2-year college degree	4.8%	6.2%	Student/teacher ratio	14.8	16.7	No. 4-year colleges/universities	1	4
4-year college degree	8.6%	15.8%	Attending public school	89.2%	90.2%	No. highly ranked universities	0	1
Graduate/professional degree	5.3%	9.6%	State SAT score	1024*	1020			
			State ACT score	20.6	21.0			

HEALTH & HEALTHCARE — SCORE: 86/RANK: 45 — **CRIME** — SCORE: 74/RANK: 84

HAZARDS & ILLNESSES	AREA	U.S. AVG	HEALTHCARE	AREA	U.S. AVG	CRIME	AREA	U.S. AVG
Air-quality score	24	45	Physicians per capita	160.0	261.1	Violent crime rate	261.0	456.0
Water-quality score	87	33	Hospital beds per capita	376.7	432.2	Change in violent crime rate	-6.8%	-17.2%
Pollen/allergy score	61	61	No. teaching hospitals	0	4	Property crime rate	2,586.9	3,950.0
Stress score	16	50	Cost per doctor visit	$69	$67	Change in property crime rate	-2.7%	-16.8%
Cancer mortality per capita	161.9	169.0	Cost per dental visit	$75	$82			
Depression days per month	2.7	2.8	Cost per daily hospital room	$532	$733			

TRANSPORTATION — SCORE: 15/RANK: 280

COMMUTE	AREA	U.S. AVG	INTERCITY SERVICES	AREA	U.S. AVG	AUTOMOTIVE	AREA	U.S. AVG
Average commute time	22.9 min.	22.6 min.	Miles to nearest major airport	46	46	Insurance, annual premium	$792	$1,011
Commute by auto	92.6%	88.7%	Type of local airport	Small		Gas, cost per gallon	$1.37	$1.50
Commute by mass transit	.7%	1.8%	No. daily airline departures	109	294	Daily vehicle miles per capita	22.2	23.0
Work at home	2.8%	3.9%	Amtrak service	Yes				
Mass transit miles per capita	3.1	8.0	No. interstate highways	0	1			

LEISURE — SCORE: 13/RANK: 288

DINING & SHOPPING	AREA	U.S. AVG	ENTERTAINMENT	AREA	U.S. AVG	OUTDOOR ACTIVITIES	AREA	U.S. AVG
Restaurant rating	1	1	Professional sports rating	2	4	Golf-course rating	2	4
No. outlet malls	1	2	College sports rating	1	4	Ski-area rating	2	4
No. Starbucks	0	11	Zoo/aquarium rating	1	3	National Park rating	1	3
No. warehouse clubs	1	4	Amusement park rating	1	3	Sq. miles inland water	2.0	4.0
			Botanical garden/arboretum rating	1	3	Miles of coastline	0.0	11.4

ARTS & CULTURE — SCORE: 17/RANK: 273

MEDIA & LIBRARIES	AREA	U.S. AVG	PERFORMING ARTS	AREA	U.S. AVG	MUSEUMS	AREA	U.S. AVG
Arts radio rating	1	3	Classical music rating	6	4	Overall museum rating	3	6
No. public libraries	6	28	Ballet/dance rating	1	3	Art museum rating	3	5
Library volumes per capita	2.1	2.8	Professional theater rating	1	3	Science museum rating	4	4
			University arts programs rating	2	5	Children's museum rating	1	3

Davenport–Moline–Rock Island, IA–IL

Score: 59.8   **Rank:** 150

Profile: Agricultural/industrial-city complex
Location: Northwest Illinois straddling Mississippi River at Iowa border, 175 miles west of Chicago
Elevation: 594 feet
Time zone: Central Standard Time

PRO
Small-town atmosphere
Cost of living
Air service

CON
Crime rate
Economic cycles
Arts and culture

The "Quad Cities" span the Mississippi River and the Illinois-Iowa border. Davenport and Bettendorf form the Iowa component, and Moline and Rock Island are on the Illinois side. The area, also called the "Breadbasket of America," is a center for agriculture, particularly known as the headquarters of machinery manufacturer John Deere, and the heart of the Corn Belt. Highlights include an attractive setting in the Mississippi Valley, a slow pace, and friendly people. Cost of living is well below Iowa and Illinois averages, but violent crime rates are surprisingly high and the economy is strongly connected to the farming industry. While regional air service is better than many similar towns, the location is far from city amenities.

The river-valley setting is distinct with low bluffs rising on both sides. Rolling prairie and occasional wooded areas lie beyond the bluffs. The climate is continental with a wide temperature range throughout the year. Periods of intense summer heat and humidity and sub-zero winter temperatures are common. There may be 50 to 60 days over 90°F each summer. Precipitation is well distributed annually, with most arriving in summer. Significant weather changes are likely every 3 to 4 days. The low flood plain location and the confluence of the Rock and Mississippi rivers can produce flooding, most recently in 1993. First freeze is late September, last is late May.

POPULATION

DEMOGRAPHICS	AREA	U.S. AVG	ETHNIC COMPOSITION	AREA	U.S. AVG	RESIDENT PROFILE	AREA	U.S. AVG
Population	358,230		White	94.6%	75.1%	Single	39.7%	43.6%
Population density per sq. mile	209.7	447.3	Black	3.4%	12.3%	Married	60.3%	56.4%
Population growth	2.1%	16.1%	Asian	.8%	3.6%	Divorced	8.6%	8.4%
Median age	37.3	35.5	American Indian	.2%	.9%	Separated	1.8%	3.0%
Average family size	2.6	2.7	Hispanic	3.6%	12.5%	Married with children	28.9%	28.7%
			Diversity measure	25.5%	35.2%	Single with children	9.3%	10.1%

ECONOMY & JOBS
SCORE: 47/RANK: 173

INCOME	AREA	U.S. AVG	EMPLOYMENT	AREA	U.S. AVG	LARGEST EMPLOYING INDUSTRY
Per capita income	$22,222	$23,420	Unemployment rate	5.2%	6.1%	Machinery Manufacturing
Household income	$42,924	$46,060	Recent job growth	-.6%	.9%	
Household income < $25K	26.8%	26.4%	Projected future job growth	10.8%	15.1%	
Household income > $75K	21.8%	24.5%	White collar	52.5%	54.5%	
Household income growth	53.2%	57.3%	Blue collar	47.5%	45.5%	

COST OF LIVING
SCORE: 35/RANK: 215

INDEXES & TAXES	AREA	U.S. AVG	HOUSING	AREA	U.S. AVG	NECESSITIES	AREA	U.S. AVG
Cost of Living Index	87.5	100.0	Median home price	$98,800	$160,100	Food Index	99.3	100.0
Financial Progress Index	104.6	100.0	Home price appreciation	5.3%	7.1%	Housing Index	61.4	100.0
Income tax rate	8.920%	4.625%	Median rent	$515	$670	Utilities Index	123.5	100.0
Sales tax rate	6.250%	6.474%	Homes owned	68.9%	63.9%	Transportation Index	103.1	100.0
Property tax rate	$20.6	$15.6	Homes rented	24.4%	25.3%	Healthcare Index	101.2	100.0
			Housing affordability	60.0%	54.5%	Miscellaneous Cost Index	96.4	100.0

CLIMATE
SCORE: 17/RANK: 272

TEMPERATURE	AREA	U.S. AVG	PRECIPITATION	AREA	U.S. AVG	COMFORTS & HAZARDS	AREA	U.S. AVG
January low	13.0°F	26.4°F	Annual inches precipitation	36.0	35.9	July relative humidity	70.0%	68.8%
July high	85.2°F	86.7°F	Annual inches snowfall	30.0	24.2	Annual days mostly sunny	202	212
Annual days > 90°F	22	38	Annual days precipitation	112	111	Annual days with thunderstorms	47	39
Annual days < 32°F	136	88	Annual days rain > 0.5 inches	25	23	Tornado risk score	32	19
Annual days < 0°F	16	6	Annual days snow > 1.5 inches	9	6	Hurricane risk score	0	15

TEMPERATURE

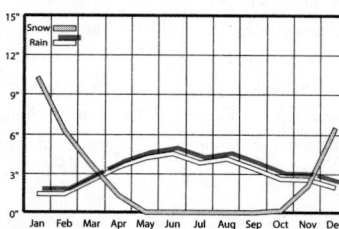

PRECIPITATION

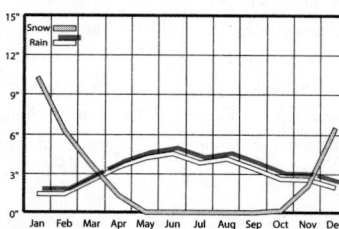

DAYS OF CLOUDS & PRECIPITATION

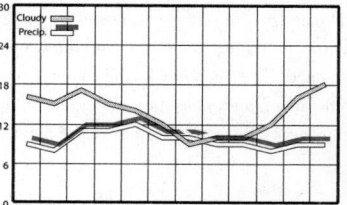

EDUCATION — SCORE: 49/RANK: 167

ACHIEVEMENT	AREA	U.S. AVG	PUBLIC SCHOOLS	AREA	U.S. AVG	HIGHER EDUCATION	AREA	U.S. AVG
High school degree	83.4%	80.2%	Expenditures per pupil	$5,481	$5,894	No. 2-year colleges	4	3
2-year college degree	7.2%	6.2%	Student/teacher ratio	15.8	16.7	No. 4-year colleges/universities	3	4
4-year college degree	14.4%	15.8%	Attending public school	89.5%	90.2%	No. highly ranked universities	1	1
Graduate/professional degree	7.1%	9.6%	State SAT score	1183	1020			
			State ACT score	22.0*	21.0			

HEALTH & HEALTHCARE — SCORE: 57/RANK: 142

HAZARDS & ILLNESSES	AREA	U.S. AVG	HEALTHCARE	AREA	U.S. AVG
Air-quality score	6	45	Physicians per capita	185.9	261.1
Water-quality score	22	33	Hospital beds per capita	410.0	432.2
Pollen/allergy score	48	61	No. teaching hospitals	4	4
Stress score	30	50	Cost per doctor visit	$66	$67
Cancer mortality per capita	174.9	169.0	Cost per dental visit	$78	$82
Depression days per month	2.3	2.8	Cost per daily hospital room	$461	$733

CRIME — SCORE: 36/RANK: 212

CRIME	AREA	U.S. AVG
Violent crime rate	610.0	456.0
Change in violent crime rate	-24.9%	-17.2%
Property crime rate	3,955.5	3,950.0
Change in property crime rate	-19.2%	-16.8%

TRANSPORTATION — SCORE: 75/RANK: 85

COMMUTE	AREA	U.S. AVG	INTERCITY SERVICES	AREA	U.S. AVG	AUTOMOTIVE	AREA	U.S. AVG
Average commute time	19.0 min.	22.6 min.	Miles to nearest major airport	61	46	Insurance, annual premium	$678	$1,011
Commute by auto	88.6%	88.7%	Type of local airport	Small		Gas, cost per gallon	$1.48	$1.50
Commute by mass transit	.5%	1.8%	No. daily airline departures	58	294	Daily vehicle miles per capita	20.6	23.0
Work at home	5.6%	3.9%	Amtrak service	Yes				
Mass transit miles per capita	8.6	8.0	No. interstate highways	2	1			

LEISURE — SCORE: 23/RANK: 254

DINING & SHOPPING	AREA	U.S. AVG	ENTERTAINMENT	AREA	U.S. AVG	OUTDOOR ACTIVITIES	AREA	U.S. AVG
Restaurant rating	1	1	Professional sports rating	3	4	Golf-course rating	4	4
No. outlet malls	0	2	College sports rating	2	4	Ski-area rating	2	4
No. Starbucks	0	11	Zoo/aquarium rating	2	3	National Park rating	2	3
No. warehouse clubs	3	4	Amusement park rating	1	3	Sq. miles inland water	4.0	4.0
			Botanical garden/arboretum rating	1	3	Miles of coastline	0.0	11.4

ARTS & CULTURE — SCORE: 28/RANK: 238

MEDIA & LIBRARIES	AREA	U.S. AVG	PERFORMING ARTS	AREA	U.S. AVG	MUSEUMS	AREA	U.S. AVG
Arts radio rating	1	3	Classical music rating	4	4	Overall museum rating	7	6
No. public libraries	34	28	Ballet/dance rating	1	3	Art museum rating	6	5
Library volumes per capita	4.0	2.8	Professional theater rating	1	3	Science museum rating	6	4
			University arts programs rating	6	5	Children's museum rating	6	3

Daytona Beach, FL

Score: 73.7   Rank: 66

Profile: Beach city
Location: Atlantic coast, 90 miles south of Jacksonville
Elevation: 31 feet
Time zone: Eastern Standard Time

PRO	CON
Auto racing	Low educational attainment
Water recreation	Arts and culture
Cost of living	Violent crime rate

On the map, Daytona Beach is a typical Florida East Coast city with a barrier island, wide beaches, and an inland town and residential area. But as a major center for auto racing and motor sports, and the home of the world-famous Daytona International Speedway, Daytona has distinguished itself as the "birthplace of speed." Upholding a long tradition, one can still drive on the beach where land speed records were once set—however, speed limits are now in effect. Good arts and culture amenities and the usual assortment of watersports are on hand. The economy is the major detraction—Daytona has high unemployment and poor projected future job growth among Florida beach towns. Significant portions of the population commute 50 miles to Orlando or to other southern cities. Educational attainment is the second lowest in the state. On the flip side, cost of living and housing costs are attractive for a beach city on the Atlantic coast.

Wide, white sandy beaches dominate the coastline. Coastal vegetation is low scrub and palm trees with evergreen, live oak, and magnolia forests inland. Summer temperatures, while reaching 90°F or above during the late morning or early afternoon, tend to diminish in the afternoon with sea breezes and frequent afternoon thundershowers, both lowering temperatures into the 80s. Winters are mild with a few cold-air invasions. Long periods of cloudiness and rain are infrequent. While hurricanes do occur, they are not considered a great threat at this latitude.

POPULATION

DEMOGRAPHICS	AREA	U.S. AVG	ETHNIC COMPOSITION	AREA	U.S. AVG	RESIDENT PROFILE	AREA	U.S. AVG
Population	516,812		White	85.9%	75.1%	Single	42.6%	43.6%
Population density per sq. mile	324.9	447.3	Black	9.9%	12.3%	Married	57.4%	56.4%
Population growth	29.4%	16.1%	Asian	1.0%	3.6%	Divorced	9.8%	8.4%
Median age	43.8	35.5	American Indian	.3%	.9%	Separated	3.0%	3.0%
Average family size	2.4	2.7	Hispanic	8.3%	12.5%	Married with children	19.2%	28.7%
			Diversity measure	30.7%	35.2%	Single with children	8.9%	10.1%

ECONOMY & JOBS
SCORE: 56/RANK: 144

INCOME	AREA	U.S. AVG	EMPLOYMENT	AREA	U.S. AVG	LARGEST EMPLOYING INDUSTRY
Per capita income	$20,275	$23,420	Unemployment rate	5.2%	6.1%	Healthcare and Social Assistance
Household income	$35,521	$46,060	Recent job growth	.3%	.9%	
Household income < $25K	32.8%	26.4%	Projected future job growth	16.7%	15.1%	
Household income > $75K	14.1%	24.5%	White collar	54.6%	54.5%	
Household income growth	41.1%	57.3%	Blue collar	45.4%	45.5%	

COST OF LIVING
SCORE: 36/RANK: 210

INDEXES & TAXES	AREA	U.S. AVG	HOUSING	AREA	U.S. AVG	NECESSITIES	AREA	U.S. AVG
Cost of Living Index	86.5	100.0	Median home price	$100,600	$160,100	Food Index	101.0	100.0
Financial Progress Index	87.5	100.0	Home price appreciation	9.8%	7.1%	Housing Index	62.5	100.0
Income tax rate	0.000%	4.625%	Median rent	$628	$670	Utilities Index	100.4	100.0
Sales tax rate	6.500%	6.474%	Homes owned	66.1%	63.9%	Transportation Index	103.5	100.0
Property tax rate	$23.5	$15.6	Homes rented	19.5%	25.3%	Healthcare Index	106.3	100.0
			Housing affordability	56.0%	54.5%	Miscellaneous Cost Index	95.6	100.0

CLIMATE
SCORE: 46/RANK: 176

TEMPERATURE	AREA	U.S. AVG	PRECIPITATION	AREA	U.S. AVG	COMFORTS & HAZARDS	AREA	U.S. AVG
January low	47.6°F	26.4°F	Annual inches precipitation	50.2	35.9	July relative humidity	78.0%	68.8%
July high	89.6°F	86.7°F	Annual inches snowfall	.1	24.2	Annual days mostly sunny	229	212
Annual days > 90°F	54	38	Annual days precipitation	115	111	Annual days with thunderstorms	79	39
Annual days < 32°F	5	88	Annual days rain > 0.5 inches	30	23	Tornado risk score	26	19
Annual days < 0°F	0	6	Annual days snow > 1.5 inches	0	6	Hurricane risk score	75	15

TEMPERATURE

PRECIPITATION

DAYS OF CLOUDS & PRECIPITATION

EDUCATION
SCORE: 36/RANK: 210

ACHIEVEMENT	AREA	U.S. AVG	PUBLIC SCHOOLS	AREA	U.S. AVG	HIGHER EDUCATION	AREA	U.S. AVG
High school degree	82.4%	80.2%	Expenditures per pupil	$5,228	$5,894	No. 2-year colleges	1	3
2-year college degree	7.6%	6.2%	Student/teacher ratio	16.5	16.7	No. 4-year colleges/universities	3	4
4-year college degree	12.6%	15.8%	Attending public school	91.2%	90.2%	No. highly ranked universities	0	1
Graduate/professional degree	6.2%	9.6%	State SAT score	996*	1020			
			State ACT score	20.5	21.0			

HEALTH & HEALTHCARE
SCORE: 46/RANK: 178

CRIME
SCORE: 35/RANK: 214

HAZARDS & ILLNESSES	AREA	U.S. AVG	HEALTHCARE	AREA	U.S. AVG	CRIME	AREA	U.S. AVG
Air-quality score	24	45	Physicians per capita	170.9	261.1	Violent crime rate	670.4	456.0
Water-quality score	8	33	Hospital beds per capita	328.7	432.2	Change in violent crime rate	-4.3%	-17.2%
Pollen/allergy score	77	61	No. teaching hospitals	2	4	Property crime rate	3,841.9	3,950.0
Stress score	95	50	Cost per doctor visit	$63	$67	Change in property crime rate	-15.2%	-16.8%
Cancer mortality per capita	169.2	169.0	Cost per dental visit	$82	$82			
Depression days per month	3.6	2.8	Cost per daily hospital room	$676	$733			

TRANSPORTATION
SCORE: 83/RANK: 55

COMMUTE	AREA	U.S. AVG	INTERCITY SERVICES	AREA	U.S. AVG	AUTOMOTIVE	AREA	U.S. AVG
Average commute time	25.4 min.	22.6 min.	Miles to nearest major airport	1	46	Insurance, annual premium	$1,041	$1,011
Commute by auto	92.1%	88.7%	Type of local airport	Small		Gas, cost per gallon	$1.54	$1.50
Commute by mass transit	.7%	1.8%	No. daily airline departures	11	294	Daily vehicle miles per capita	22.8	23.0
Work at home	2.9%	3.9%	Amtrak service	No				
Mass transit miles per capita	11.9	8.0	No. interstate highways	2	1			

LEISURE SCORE: 73/RANK: 88

DINING & SHOPPING	AREA	U.S. AVG	ENTERTAINMENT	AREA	U.S. AVG	OUTDOOR ACTIVITIES	AREA	U.S. AVG
Restaurant rating	1	1	Professional sports rating	2	4	Golf-course rating	3	4
No. outlet malls	6	2	College sports rating	4	4	Ski-area rating	1	4
No. Starbucks	3	11	Zoo/aquarium rating	1	3	National Park rating	4	3
No. warehouse clubs	4	4	Amusement park rating	1	3	Sq. miles inland water	8.0	4.0
			Botanical garden/arboretum rating	3	3	Miles of coastline	50.3	11.4

ARTS & CULTURE SCORE: 90/RANK: 32

MEDIA & LIBRARIES	AREA	U.S. AVG	PERFORMING ARTS	AREA	U.S. AVG	MUSEUMS	AREA	U.S. AVG
Arts radio rating	1	3	Classical music rating	1	4	Overall museum rating	6	6
No. public libraries	16	28	Ballet/dance rating	1	3	Art museum rating	7	5
Library volumes per capita	1.8	2.8	Professional theater rating	1	3	Science museum rating	6	4
			University arts programs rating	6	5	Children's museum rating	1	3

Dayton-Springfield, OH

Score: 79.0   Rank: 41

Profile: Mid-size-city complex
Location: West-central Ohio at crossroads of north-south I-75 and east-west I-70
Elevation: 905 feet
Time zone: Eastern Standard Time

PRO	CON
Diverse economy	Low job growth
Nearby cities	Entertainment
Arts and culture	Unattractive downtown

Dayton, at the crossroads of southwestern Ohio's major transportation routes, has a distinct industrial heritage. Local NCR Corporation, formerly the National Cash Register Corporation, is a leader in retail information technology and ATM machines. An assortment of other manufacturing and service activities, including the auto industry, round out the area's diverse economy. The more attractive residential areas are in the wooded hills to the southeast. There isn't much to do in the downtown area, but cultural amenities and entertainment can be found in Cincinnati, 50 miles to the south. Springfield, 30 miles east, is a pleasant and diverse mid-size city, manufacturing center, and college town. The Wright-Patterson Air Force Base brings a military presence, economic influence, and first-class aviation museum. The area has notably good air service.

Dayton is located near the center of the Miami River Valley, a nearly flat plain, 50 feet to 200 feet below the general elevation of the adjacent rolling country. Three Miami River tributaries converge to join the main stream within the city limits. Land to the north is open and slopes gradually upward to Indian Lake, near the highest point in the state at 1,500 feet. To the south is a mix of rolling farmland and deciduous wooded hills, sloping generally downward towards the Ohio River. The continental climate is typical of the region. Summers are warm, calm, and humid. Winters are cold and changeable with below-zero temperatures every 4 in 5 years. Frequent air-mass collisions produce precipitation throughout the year, mostly as spring and summer showers and thunderstorms, with periods of winter rain. Snowfall is light to moderate, with frequent winter snow flurries caused by cold polar air flowing over the Great Lakes. First freeze is late October, last is mid-April.

POPULATION

DEMOGRAPHICS	AREA	U.S. AVG	ETHNIC COMPOSITION	AREA	U.S. AVG	RESIDENT PROFILE	AREA	U.S. AVG
Population	947,446		White	84.5%	75.1%	Single	44.2%	43.6%
Population density per sq. mile	562.7	447.3	Black	13.8%	12.3%	Married	55.8%	56.4%
Population growth	-.4%	16.1%	Asian	1.3%	3.6%	Divorced	9.8%	8.4%
Median age	37.0	35.5	American Indian	.2%	.9%	Separated	2.4%	3.0%
Average family size	2.6	2.7	Hispanic	.9%	12.5%	Married with children	27.1%	28.7%
			Diversity measure	31.0%	35.2%	Single with children	11.0%	10.1%

ECONOMY & JOBS SCORE: 32/RANK: 225

INCOME	AREA	U.S. AVG	EMPLOYMENT	AREA	U.S. AVG	LARGEST EMPLOYING INDUSTRY
Per capita income	$23,680	$23,420	Unemployment rate	5.7%	6.1%	Transportation Equipment Manufacturing
Household income	$45,798	$46,060	Recent job growth	.4%	.9%	
Household income < $25K	24.9%	26.4%	Projected future job growth	9.7%	15.1%	
Household income > $75K	23.1%	24.5%	White collar	56.6%	54.5%	
Household income growth	50.1%	57.3%	Blue collar	43.4%	45.5%	

COST OF LIVING — SCORE: 90/RANK: 33

INDEXES & TAXES	AREA	U.S. AVG	HOUSING	AREA	U.S. AVG	NECESSITIES	AREA	U.S. AVG
Cost of Living Index	87.7	100.0	Median home price	$110,900	$160,100	Food Index	95.5	100.0
Financial Progress Index	111.2	100.0	Home price appreciation	3.9%	7.1%	Housing Index	68.9	100.0
Income tax rate	7.243%	4.625%	Median rent	$589	$670	Utilities Index	99.6	100.0
Sales tax rate	6.500%	6.474%	Homes owned	66.4%	63.9%	Transportation Index	101.7	100.0
Property tax rate	$20.1	$15.6	Homes rented	28.0%	25.3%	Healthcare Index	96.6	100.0
			Housing affordability	59.0%	54.5%	Miscellaneous Cost Index	98.9	100.0

CLIMATE — SCORE: 76/RANK: 78

TEMPERATURE	AREA	U.S. AVG	PRECIPITATION	AREA	U.S. AVG	COMFORTS & HAZARDS	AREA	U.S. AVG
January low	20.4°F	26.4°F	Annual inches precipitation	34.4	35.9	July relative humidity	70.0%	68.8%
July high	84.7°F	86.7°F	Annual inches snowfall	28.6	24.2	Annual days mostly sunny	182	212
Annual days > 90°F	17	38	Annual days precipitation	130	111	Annual days with thunderstorms	40	39
Annual days < 32°F	117	88	Annual days rain > 0.5 inches	22	23	Tornado risk score	43	19
Annual days < 0°F	6	6	Annual days snow > 1.5 inches	6	6	Hurricane risk score	4	15

TEMPERATURE

PRECIPITATION

DAYS OF CLOUDS & PRECIPITATION

EDUCATION — SCORE: 66/RANK: 112

ACHIEVEMENT	AREA	U.S. AVG	PUBLIC SCHOOLS	AREA	U.S. AVG	HIGHER EDUCATION	AREA	U.S. AVG
High school degree	83.7%	80.2%	Expenditures per pupil	$5,939	$5,894	No. 2-year colleges	9	3
2-year college degree	6.3%	6.2%	Student/teacher ratio	17.3	16.7	No. 4-year colleges/universities	7	4
4-year college degree	13.7%	15.8%	Attending public school	87.3%	90.2%	No. highly ranked universities	3	1
Graduate/professional degree	8.5%	9.6%	State SAT score	1077	1020			
			State ACT score	21.4*	21.0			

HEALTH & HEALTHCARE — SCORE: 27/RANK: 241

CRIME — SCORE: 29/RANK: 233

HAZARDS & ILLNESSES	AREA	U.S. AVG	HEALTHCARE	AREA	U.S. AVG	CRIME	AREA	U.S. AVG
Air-quality score	91	45	Physicians per capita	268.0	261.1	Violent crime rate	360.4	456.0
Water-quality score	5	33	Hospital beds per capita	425.5	432.2	Change in violent crime rate	-32.1%	-17.2%
Pollen/allergy score	60	61	No. teaching hospitals	8	4	Property crime rate	4,532.8	3,950.0
Stress score	93	50	Cost per doctor visit	$59	$67	Change in property crime rate	-4.4%	-16.8%
Cancer mortality per capita	174.0	169.0	Cost per dental visit	$77	$82			
Depression days per month	3.2	2.8	Cost per daily hospital room	$695	$733			

TRANSPORTATION — SCORE: 14/RANK: 283

COMMUTE	AREA	U.S. AVG	INTERCITY SERVICES	AREA	U.S. AVG	AUTOMOTIVE	AREA	U.S. AVG
Average commute time	21.0 min.	22.6 min.	Miles to nearest major airport	8	46	Insurance, annual premium	$1,122	$1,011
Commute by auto	91.2%	88.7%	Type of local airport	Small		Gas, cost per gallon	$1.46	$1.50
Commute by mass transit	2.1%	1.8%	No. daily airline departures	161	294	Daily vehicle miles per capita	27.1	23.0
Work at home	2.7%	3.9%	Amtrak service	No				
Mass transit miles per capita	11.3	8.0	No. interstate highways	2	1			

LEISURE — SCORE: 69/RANK: 101

DINING & SHOPPING	AREA	U.S. AVG	ENTERTAINMENT	AREA	U.S. AVG	OUTDOOR ACTIVITIES	AREA	U.S. AVG
Restaurant rating	3	1	Professional sports rating	4	4	Golf-course rating	6	4
No. outlet malls	2	2	College sports rating	3	4	Ski-area rating	2	4
No. Starbucks	4	11	Zoo/aquarium rating	4	3	National Park rating	1	3
No. warehouse clubs	4	4	Amusement park rating	1	3	Sq. miles inland water	2.0	4.0
			Botanical garden/arboretum rating	6	3	Miles of coastline	0.0	11.4

ARTS & CULTURE — SCORE: 37/RANK: 206

MEDIA & LIBRARIES	AREA	U.S. AVG	PERFORMING ARTS	AREA	U.S. AVG	MUSEUMS	AREA	U.S. AVG
Arts radio rating	8	3	Classical music rating	6	4	Overall museum rating	8	6
No. public libraries	46	28	Ballet/dance rating	7	3	Art museum rating	8	5
Library volumes per capita	5.0	2.8	Professional theater rating	1	3	Science museum rating	7	4
			University arts programs rating	7	5	Children's museum rating	6	3

Decatur, AL

Score: 52.0   **Rank:** 209

Profile: Small industrial city
Location: Extreme northern Alabama along the Tennessee River
Elevation: 590 feet
Time zone: Central Standard Time

PRO	CON
Cost of living	Summer heat and humidity
Recent job growth	Arts and culture
Low crime rate	Low ethnic diversity

Decatur in northern Alabama is a transportation hub and manufacturing center for a variety of goods and chemicals. Northern industrial interests following the Civil War left the city with some fine older homes and parks. The Cost of Living Index of 82.1 is in the lowest 10% nationwide, and the total crime rate is far below the state average. The Tennessee River provides some recreational opportunities, but the area has few other leisure or arts amenities.

The town lies on a river plain on the southwest bank of the dammed-up Tennessee River. Land rises gently to the southwest into the William Bankhead National Forest, with hills to 1,100 feet. The climate is a humid subtropical and continental mix, with long, hot, muggy summers, and variable, wet winters with occasional snow.

POPULATION

DEMOGRAPHICS	AREA	U.S. AVG	ETHNIC COMPOSITION	AREA	U.S. AVG	RESIDENT PROFILE	AREA	U.S. AVG
Population	146,380		White	81.9%	75.1%	Single	37.8%	43.6%
Population density per sq. mile	114.7	447.3	Black	14.1%	12.3%	Married	62.2%	56.4%
Population growth	11.3%	16.1%	Asian	.2%	3.6%	Divorced	7.7%	8.4%
Median age	36.8	35.5	American Indian	3.8%	.9%	Separated	2.2%	3.0%
Average family size	2.7	2.7	Hispanic	.4%	12.5%	Married with children	32.6%	28.7%
			Diversity measure	31.1%	35.2%	Single with children	9.6%	10.1%

ECONOMY & JOBS
SCORE: 70/RANK: 100

INCOME	AREA	U.S. AVG	EMPLOYMENT	AREA	U.S. AVG	LARGEST EMPLOYING INDUSTRY
Per capita income	$20,472	$23,420	Unemployment rate	6.8%	6.1%	Chemical Manufacturing
Household income	$40,227	$46,060	Recent job growth	4.0%	.9%	
Household income < $25K	32.0%	26.4%	Projected future job growth	9.3%	15.1%	
Household income > $75K	20.2%	24.5%	White collar	45.5%	54.5%	
Household income growth	50.7%	57.3%	Blue collar	54.5%	45.5%	

COST OF LIVING
SCORE: 82/RANK: 59

INDEXES & TAXES	AREA	U.S. AVG	HOUSING	AREA	U.S. AVG	NECESSITIES	AREA	U.S. AVG
Cost of Living Index	82.1	100.0	Median home price	$95,590	$160,100	Food Index	94.8	100.0
Financial Progress Index	104.4	100.0	Home price appreciation	3.6%	7.1%	Housing Index	59.4	100.0
Income tax rate	5.000%	4.625%	Median rent	$471	$670	Utilities Index	84.8	100.0
Sales tax rate	8.000%	6.474%	Homes owned	78.4%	63.9%	Transportation Index	99.0	100.0
Property tax rate	$4.0	$15.6	Homes rented	15.3%	25.3%	Healthcare Index	89.3	100.0
			Housing affordability	59.0%	54.5%	Miscellaneous Cost Index	98.0	100.0

CLIMATE
SCORE: 38/RANK: 204

TEMPERATURE	AREA	U.S. AVG	PRECIPITATION	AREA	U.S. AVG	COMFORTS & HAZARDS	AREA	U.S. AVG
January low	31.3°F	26.4°F	Annual inches precipitation	52.0	35.9	July relative humidity	73.0%	68.8%
July high	90.2°F	86.7°F	Annual inches snowfall	3.0	24.2	Annual days mostly sunny	207	212
Annual days > 90°F	38	38	Annual days precipitation	121	111	Annual days with thunderstorms	58	39
Annual days < 32°F	65	88	Annual days rain > 0.5 inches	36	23	Tornado risk score	51	19
Annual days < 0°F	0	6	Annual days snow > 1.5 inches	2	6	Hurricane risk score	13	15

TEMPERATURE

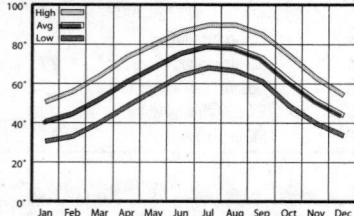

PRECIPITATION

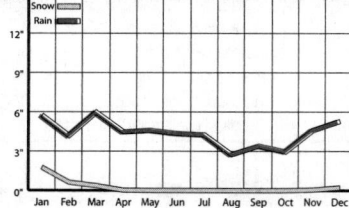

DAYS OF CLOUDS & PRECIPITATION

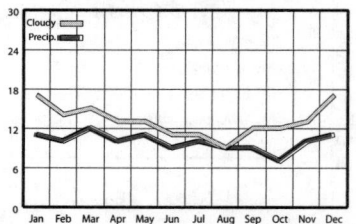

EDUCATION SCORE: 23/RANK: 253

ACHIEVEMENT	AREA	U.S. AVG	PUBLIC SCHOOLS	AREA	U.S. AVG	HIGHER EDUCATION	AREA	U.S. AVG
High school degree	73.8%	80.2%	Expenditures per pupil	$5,344	$5,894	No. 2-year colleges	1	3
2-year college degree	5.9%	6.2%	Student/teacher ratio	15.1	16.7	No. 4-year colleges/universities	0	4
4-year college degree	10.9%	15.8%	Attending public school	98.5%	90.2%	No. highly ranked universities	0	1
Graduate/professional degree	5.0%	9.6%	State SAT score	1111	1020			
			State ACT score	20.1*	21.0			

HEALTH & HEALTHCARE SCORE: 52/RANK: 157

CRIME SCORE: 57/RANK: 141

HAZARDS & ILLNESSES	AREA	U.S. AVG	HEALTHCARE	AREA	U.S. AVG	CRIME	AREA	U.S. AVG
Air-quality score	6	45	Physicians per capita	19.8	261.1	Violent crime rate	217.4	456.0
Water-quality score	43	33	Hospital beds per capita	496.3	432.2	Change in violent crime rate	24.9%	-17.2%
Pollen/allergy score	67	61	No. teaching hospitals	0	4	Property crime rate	2,865.1	3,950.0
Stress score	33	50	Cost per doctor visit	$57	$67	Change in property crime rate	-9.6%	-16.8%
Cancer mortality per capita	159.1	169.0	Cost per dental visit	$74	$82			
Depression days per month	3.0	2.8	Cost per daily hospital room	$518	$733			

TRANSPORTATION SCORE: 77/RANK: 74

COMMUTE	AREA	U.S. AVG	INTERCITY SERVICES	AREA	U.S. AVG	AUTOMOTIVE	AREA	U.S. AVG
Average commute time	24.2 min.	22.6 min.	Miles to nearest major airport	14	46	Insurance, annual premium	$813	$1,011
Commute by auto	94.5%	88.7%	Type of local airport	Small		Gas, cost per gallon	$1.46	$1.50
Commute by mass transit	.4%	1.8%	No. daily airline departures	41	294	Daily vehicle miles per capita	49.1	23.0
Work at home	2.7%	3.9%	Amtrak service	No				
Mass transit miles per capita	0.0	8.0	No. interstate highways	1	1			

LEISURE SCORE: 21/RANK: 261

DINING & SHOPPING	AREA	U.S. AVG	ENTERTAINMENT	AREA	U.S. AVG	OUTDOOR ACTIVITIES	AREA	U.S. AVG
Restaurant rating	1	1	Professional sports rating	2	4	Golf-course rating	2	4
No. outlet malls	1	2	College sports rating	3	4	Ski-area rating	1	4
No. Starbucks	0	11	Zoo/aquarium rating	1	3	National Park rating	5	3
No. warehouse clubs	1	4	Amusement park rating	1	3	Sq. miles inland water	4.0	4.0
			Botanical garden/arboretum rating	1	3	Miles of coastline	0.0	11.4

ARTS & CULTURE SCORE: 36/RANK: 212

MEDIA & LIBRARIES	AREA	U.S. AVG	PERFORMING ARTS	AREA	U.S. AVG	MUSEUMS	AREA	U.S. AVG
Arts radio rating	1	3	Classical music rating	3	4	Overall museum rating	1	6
No. public libraries	5	28	Ballet/dance rating	1	3	Art museum rating	1	5
Library volumes per capita	1.5	2.8	Professional theater rating	1	3	Science museum rating	1	4
			University arts programs rating	1	5	Children's museum rating	1	3

Decatur, IL

Score: 65.6   Rank: 104

Profile: Small agricultural town
Location: East-central Illinois, 30 miles east of Springfield
Elevation: 613 feet
Time zone: Central Standard Time

PRO	CON
Small-town atmosphere	Entertainment
Cost of living	Arts and culture
Stable employment	Low future job growth

Decatur forms the bottom point of a 90-mile wide, 40-mile-tall diamond formed by Springfield to the west, Bloomington-Normal to the north, and Champaign-Urbana to the east. Common to the area, agriculture dominates the commercial activity and the local landscape. Agricultural processing giant Archer Daniels Midland has its headquarters in Decatur. ADM provides a stable employment base, although employment- and income-growth projections are the lowest in the state. On the flip side, cost of living and home prices are by far the lowest in Illinois and among the lowest in the country. The area doesn't offer much in terms of entertainment or arts and culture amenities, but it does have a historic district with a mix of older homes, including some

designed by Frank Lloyd Wright, along with Abraham Lincoln and Civil War sites.

The terrain is level and agricultural. Climate is typical continental with warm summers, fairly cold winters, and sharp seasonal changes. Considerable variation takes place within seasons. Summers are typically warm and humid with periods of mainly afternoon showers and thundershowers, and a few cooler, drier spells. Precipitation is more or less evenly distributed through the year. Spring and fall are typical for the region, with windy, changeable springs and relatively calm autumns with periods of warm, dry Indian summers. First freeze is mid-October, last is mid-April.

POPULATION

DEMOGRAPHICS	AREA	U.S. AVG	ETHNIC COMPOSITION	AREA	U.S. AVG	RESIDENT PROFILE	AREA	U.S. AVG
Population	112,013		White	91.5%	75.1%	Single	37.4%	43.6%
Population density per sq. mile	192.9	447.3	Black	7.5%	12.3%	Married	62.6%	56.4%
Population growth	-4.4%	16.1%	Asian	.7%	3.6%	Divorced	8.0%	8.4%
Median age	38.4	35.5	American Indian	.1%	.9%	Separated	2.1%	3.0%
Average family size	2.5	2.7	Hispanic	1.1%	12.5%	Married with children	30.0%	28.7%
			Diversity measure	29.1%	35.2%	Single with children	8.4%	10.1%

ECONOMY & JOBS   SCORE: 95/RANK: 16

INCOME	AREA	U.S. AVG	EMPLOYMENT	AREA	U.S. AVG	LARGEST EMPLOYING INDUSTRY		
Per capita income	$23,820	$23,420	Unemployment rate	7.7%	6.1%	Food Manufacturing		
Household income	$44,896	$46,060	Recent job growth	.2%	.9%			
Household income < $25K	27.1%	26.4%	Projected future job growth	3.7%	15.1%			
Household income > $75K	23.8%	24.5%	White collar	50.9%	54.5%			
Household income growth	56.7%	57.3%	Blue collar	49.1%	45.5%			

COST OF LIVING   SCORE: 91/RANK: 26

INDEXES & TAXES	AREA	U.S. AVG	HOUSING	AREA	U.S. AVG	NECESSITIES	AREA	U.S. AVG
Cost of Living Index	77.4	100.0	Median home price	$77,170	$160,100	Food Index	92.8	100.0
Financial Progress Index	123.6	100.0	Home price appreciation	3.4%	7.1%	Housing Index	47.9	100.0
Income tax rate	3.000%	4.625%	Median rent	$485	$670	Utilities Index	92.3	100.0
Sales tax rate	6.250%	6.474%	Homes owned	70.5%	63.9%	Transportation Index	100.4	100.0
Property tax rate	$21.9	$15.6	Homes rented	21.6%	25.3%	Healthcare Index	84.4	100.0
			Housing affordability	58.0%	54.5%	Miscellaneous Cost Index	95.0	100.0

CLIMATE   SCORE: 20/RANK: 262

TEMPERATURE	AREA	U.S. AVG	PRECIPITATION	AREA	U.S. AVG	COMFORTS & HAZARDS	AREA	U.S. AVG
January low	18.6°F	26.4°F	Annual inches precipitation	35.0	35.9	July relative humidity	71.0%	68.8%
July high	86.6°F	86.7°F	Annual inches snowfall	22.0	24.2	Annual days mostly sunny	200	212
Annual days > 90°F	28	38	Annual days precipitation	112	111	Annual days with thunderstorms	50	39
Annual days < 32°F	119	88	Annual days rain > 0.5 inches	22	23	Tornado risk score	28	19
Annual days < 0°F	8	6	Annual days snow > 1.5 inches	5	6	Hurricane risk score	3	15

TEMPERATURE

PRECIPITATION

DAYS OF CLOUDS & PRECIPITATION

EDUCATION   SCORE: 13/RANK: 287

ACHIEVEMENT	AREA	U.S. AVG	PUBLIC SCHOOLS	AREA	U.S. AVG	HIGHER EDUCATION	AREA	U.S. AVG
High school degree	83.2%	80.2%	Expenditures per pupil	$4,747	$5,894	No. 2-year colleges	1	3
2-year college degree	5.2%	6.2%	Student/teacher ratio	18.6	16.7	No. 4-year colleges/universities	1	4
4-year college degree	11.3%	15.8%	Attending public school	89.2%	90.2%	No. highly ranked universities	0	1
Graduate/professional degree	5.7%	9.6%	State SAT score	1179	1020			
			State ACT score	20.2*	21.0			

HEALTH & HEALTHCARE   SCORE: 51/RANK: 160

HAZARDS & ILLNESSES	AREA	U.S. AVG	HEALTHCARE	AREA	U.S. AVG
Air-quality score	74	45	Physicians per capita	198.2	261.1
Water-quality score	20	33	Hospital beds per capita	447.2	432.2
Pollen/allergy score	49	61	No. teaching hospitals	2	4
Stress score	81	50	Cost per doctor visit	$65	$67
Cancer mortality per capita	171.3	169.0	Cost per dental visit	$63	$82
Depression days per month	3.8	2.8	Cost per daily hospital room	$567	$733

CRIME   SCORE: 71/RANK: 95

CRIME	AREA	U.S. AVG
Violent crime rate	489.4	456.0
Change in violent crime rate	-30.8%	-17.2%
Property crime rate	3,678.6	3,950.0
Change in property crime rate	-22.6%	-16.8%

TRANSPORTATION   SCORE: 6/RANK: 309

COMMUTE	AREA	U.S. AVG	INTERCITY SERVICES	AREA	U.S. AVG	AUTOMOTIVE	AREA	U.S. AVG
Average commute time	18.2 min.	22.6 min.	Miles to nearest major airport	108	46	Insurance, annual premium	$892	$1,011
Commute by auto	92.4%	88.7%	Type of local airport	Large		Gas, cost per gallon	$1.46	$1.50
Commute by mass transit	.6%	1.8%	No. daily airline departures	731	294	Daily vehicle miles per capita	18.7	23.0
Work at home	3.4%	3.9%	Amtrak service	No				
Mass transit miles per capita	7.9	8.0	No. interstate highways	1	1			

LEISURE SCORE: 20/RANK: 263

DINING & SHOPPING	AREA	U.S. AVG	ENTERTAINMENT	AREA	U.S. AVG	OUTDOOR ACTIVITIES	AREA	U.S. AVG
Restaurant rating	1	1	Professional sports rating	2	4	Golf-course rating	2	4
No. outlet malls	1	2	College sports rating	3	4	Ski-area rating	1	4
No. Starbucks	0	11	Zoo/aquarium rating	1	3	National Park rating	1	3
No. warehouse clubs	3	4	Amusement park rating	1	3	Sq. miles inland water	2.0	4.0
			Botanical garden/arboretum rating	1	3	Miles of coastline	0.0	11.4

ARTS & CULTURE SCORE: 10/RANK: 295

MEDIA & LIBRARIES	AREA	U.S. AVG	PERFORMING ARTS	AREA	U.S. AVG	MUSEUMS	AREA	U.S. AVG
Arts radio rating	1	3	Classical music rating	2	4	Overall museum rating	3	6
No. public libraries	9	28	Ballet/dance rating	1	3	Art museum rating	3	5
Library volumes per capita	3.8	2.8	Professional theater rating	1	3	Science museum rating	1	4
			University arts programs rating	3	5	Children's museum rating	1	3

Denver, CO

Score: 75.2 **Rank:** 60

Profile: Regional center/Capital city
Location: North central Colorado at the base of the Rocky Mountain Front Range
Elevation: 5,280 feet
Time zone: Mountain Standard Time

PRO
Attractive downtown
Arts and culture
Nearby mountains

CON
Urban sprawl
Commute times
Cold winters

Denver is the commercial, financial, industrial, and government center for Colorado and a seven-state region of Rocky Mountain and western Plains states. The downtown features an attractive area of renovated commercial buildings along the South Platte River, near the Denver Union Station rail terminal. This area's successful redevelopment, one of the finest urban-core restorations in the country, created a vital district with many small businesses and entertainment and nightlife venues. The crown jewel is the industrial revival–style Coors Field ballpark. Beyond downtown is a patchwork of older neighborhoods with early-20th-century housing. There is a series of sprawl-ridden suburbs like Aurora to the east and Littleton to the south.

All services and amenities are of the first order. Air service at the new Denver International Airport, the hub of discount carrier Frontier Airlines, is plentiful, although the facility is not conveniently located. The Rockies to the west offer unlimited recreational opportunities, including skiing, hiking, fishing, and watersports. A unique "Snow Train" service takes skiers to Winter Park and other resorts. Museums, performing arts, libraries, bookstores, and professional sports are abundant and more accessible than in comparable places. The historical heritage of the city and region is interesting and well preserved. New gambling venues have revived such mining ghost towns to the west as Central City and Blackhawk; whether this is a tasteful use of historic sites brings different opinions.

Denver's many attractions continue to lure new residents. Population grew 35% from 1990 to 2002 and is showing no signs of slowing. That figure even understates the growth of the entire area, including metro areas to the north. The impact is starting to show in cost of living, now at a borderline high of 118.9. Despite persistent efforts to keep the downtown attractive, urban sprawl has generated traffic, long commute times, and smog, particularly in the summer months. The economy and employment picture are still favorable and the area is attractive overall, but not without risk for the future.

The city lies at the western edge of the undulating high prairie that extends east towards Kansas. The front wall of the Rockies rises abruptly west of town with numerous stream valleys and canyons converging in the South Platte River. The invigorating continental climate, typical of the Rocky Mountain region, brings frequent changes, but only short durations of extremely warm or cold weather. Situated a long distance from any moisture source and separated from the Pacific Ocean by several high mountain barriers, Denver enjoys low relative humidity, light precipitation, and abundant sunshine. Summer days are warm with occasional thundershowers and cool evenings. Severe weather is usually confined to areas farther east. The mountains shelter the area from the strongest winter storms and cold air blasts, but fall and spring usually bring at least one snowstorm. Spring is the cloudiest and wettest season. First freeze is early October, last is late May.

POPULATION

DEMOGRAPHICS	AREA	U.S. AVG	ETHNIC COMPOSITION	AREA	U.S. AVG	RESIDENT PROFILE	AREA	U.S. AVG
Population	2,187,464		White	86.3%	75.1%	Single	46.5%	43.6%
Population density per sq. mile	581.6	447.3	Black	6.3%	12.3%	Married	53.5%	56.4%
Population growth	34.8%	16.1%	Asian	2.9%	3.6%	Divorced	11.7%	8.4%
Median age	34.3	35.5	American Indian	.9%	.9%	Separated	3.3%	3.0%
Average family size	2.6	2.7	Hispanic	14.3%	12.5%	Married with children	26.5%	28.7%
			Diversity measure	45.6%	35.2%	Single with children	10.2%	10.1%

ECONOMY & JOBS — SCORE: 43/RANK: 185

INCOME	AREA	U.S. AVG	EMPLOYMENT	AREA	U.S. AVG	LARGEST EMPLOYING INDUSTRY
Per capita income	$31,801	$23,420	Unemployment rate	5.8%	6.1%	Architectural, Engineering, and Related Services
Household income	$62,986	$46,060	Recent job growth	3.1%	.9%	
Household income < $25K	15.9%	26.4%	Projected future job growth	22.8%	15.1%	
Household income > $75K	39.9%	24.5%	White collar	65.7%	54.5%	
Household income growth	91.5%	57.3%	Blue collar	34.3%	45.5%	

COST OF LIVING — SCORE: 14/RANK: 284

INDEXES & TAXES	AREA	U.S. AVG	HOUSING	AREA	U.S. AVG	NECESSITIES	AREA	U.S. AVG
Cost of Living Index	118.9	100.0	Median home price	$227,900	$160,100	Food Index	113.1	100.0
Financial Progress Index	112.8	100.0	Home price appreciation	11.1%	7.1%	Housing Index	141.6	100.0
Income tax rate	5.000%	4.625%	Median rent	$964	$670	Utilities Index	99.0	100.0
Sales tax rate	8.000%	6.474%	Homes owned	61.3%	63.9%	Transportation Index	109.1	100.0
Property tax rate	$8.2	$15.6	Homes rented	30.0%	25.3%	Healthcare Index	125.8	100.0
			Housing affordability	47.0%	54.5%	Miscellaneous Cost Index	96.7	100.0

CLIMATE — SCORE: 54/RANK: 150

TEMPERATURE	AREA	U.S. AVG	PRECIPITATION	AREA	U.S. AVG	COMFORTS & HAZARDS	AREA	U.S. AVG
January low	16.2°F	26.4°F	Annual inches precipitation	16.0	35.9	July relative humidity	53.0%	68.8%
July high	87.4°F	86.7°F	Annual inches snowfall	60.0	24.2	Annual days mostly sunny	246	212
Annual days > 90°F	32	38	Annual days precipitation	88	111	Annual days with thunderstorms	41	39
Annual days < 32°F	163	88	Annual days rain > 0.5 inches	7	23	Tornado risk score	52	19
Annual days < 0°F	10	6	Annual days snow > 1.5 inches	14	6	Hurricane risk score	0	15

TEMPERATURE

PRECIPITATION

DAYS OF CLOUDS & PRECIPITATION

EDUCATION — SCORE: 90/RANK: 33

ACHIEVEMENT	AREA	U.S. AVG	PUBLIC SCHOOLS	AREA	U.S. AVG	HIGHER EDUCATION	AREA	U.S. AVG
High school degree	86.4%	80.2%	Expenditures per pupil	$5,796	$5,894	No. 2-year colleges	8	3
2-year college degree	6.6%	6.2%	Student/teacher ratio	19.3	16.7	No. 4-year colleges/universities	13	4
4-year college degree	22.1%	15.8%	Attending public school	90.6%	90.2%	No. highly ranked universities	2	1
Graduate/professional degree	12.4%	9.6%	State SAT score	1104	1020			
			State ACT score	20.1*	21.0			

HEALTH & HEALTHCARE — SCORE: 46/RANK: 179

HAZARDS & ILLNESSES	AREA	U.S. AVG	HEALTHCARE	AREA	U.S. AVG	CRIME — SCORE: 43/RANK: 187	AREA	U.S. AVG
Air-quality score	91	45	Physicians per capita	279.5	261.1	Violent crime rate	394.8	456.0
Water-quality score	70	33	Hospital beds per capita	263.1	432.2	Change in violent crime rate	-23.1%	-17.2%
Pollen/allergy score	85	61	No. teaching hospitals	18	4	Property crime rate	4,297.7	3,950.0
Stress score	70	50	Cost per doctor visit	$76	$67	Change in property crime rate	-15.4%	-16.8%
Cancer mortality per capita	152.8	169.0	Cost per dental visit	$108	$82			
Depression days per month	2.4	2.8	Cost per daily hospital room	$820	$733			

TRANSPORTATION — SCORE: 96/RANK: 10

COMMUTE	AREA	U.S. AVG	INTERCITY SERVICES	AREA	U.S. AVG	AUTOMOTIVE	AREA	U.S. AVG
Average commute time	26.5 min.	22.6 min.	Miles to nearest major airport	1	46	Insurance, annual premium	$1,480	$1,011
Commute by auto	86.4%	88.7%	Type of local airport	Large		Gas, cost per gallon	$1.52	$1.50
Commute by mass transit	4.1%	1.8%	No. daily airline departures	812	294	Daily vehicle miles per capita	22.6	23.0
Work at home	4.1%	3.9%	Amtrak service	Yes				
Mass transit miles per capita	24.3	8.0	No. interstate highways	3	1			

LEISURE — SCORE: 91/RANK: 29

DINING & SHOPPING	AREA	U.S. AVG	ENTERTAINMENT	AREA	U.S. AVG	OUTDOOR ACTIVITIES	AREA	U.S. AVG
Restaurant rating	3	1	Professional sports rating	9	4	Golf-course rating	7	4
No. outlet malls	4	2	College sports rating	5	4	Ski-area rating	10	4
No. Starbucks	70	11	Zoo/aquarium rating	7	3	National Park rating	3	3
No. warehouse clubs	5	4	Amusement park rating	7	3	Sq. miles inland water	3.0	4.0
			Botanical garden/arboretum rating	5	3	Miles of coastline	0.0	11.4

ARTS & CULTURE SCORE: 95/RANK: 16

MEDIA & LIBRARIES	AREA	U.S. AVG	PERFORMING ARTS	AREA	U.S. AVG	MUSEUMS	AREA	U.S. AVG
Arts radio rating	9	3	Classical music rating	9	4	Overall museum rating	9	6
No. public libraries	63	28	Ballet/dance rating	9	3	Art museum rating	9	5
Library volumes per capita	2.6	2.8	Professional theater rating	10	3	Science museum rating	7	4
			University arts programs rating	9	5	Children's museum rating	7	3

Des Moines, IA

Score: 77.0   Rank: 52

Profile: Capital city
Location: Just south of geographic center of Iowa
Elevation: 963 feet
Time zone: Central Standard Time

PRO	CON
Attractive downtown	Entertainment
Capital city amenities	Air service
Stable economy	Low ethnic diversity

Des Moines is the cultural and economic heart of Iowa. It is headquarters to nearly 60 companies and a notable center for the insurance industry. Many characterize it as a "gentle" big city, retaining a small-town feel with larger-city amenities, but some also complain of a lack of entertainment and nightlife. It is quintessentially Midwestern with a strong agricultural presence and rectangular tree-lined streets. The wealthier suburbs and most of the museums and parks lie on the west side of town while the east is more industrial. The area contains about 400 factories, many processing food or manufacturing farming products. The city has an assortment of parks, museums, zoos, gardens, and historic attractions. Des Moines is large enough to have a good symphony and ballet and a large, concert venue. With a 140-year-tradition, the Iowa State Fair matches most people's image of a classic American fair. For a larger capital city, air service is relatively lacking and ethnic diversity is low, but cost of living is reasonable.

The gently rolling terrain sits in the shallow valley of the Des Moines River and its tributaries. The climate is continental with a marked seasonal contrast in both temperature and precipitation. The summer season is warm and humid with prevailing southerly winds and precipitation falling mainly as showers and thunderstorms, some heavy. Autumn is characteristically sunny with diminishing precipitation. Winter brings cold dry air, sometimes below 0°F, interrupted by occasional, short show storms. Extensive drifting snow can impede transportation. First freeze is early October, last is early May.

POPULATION

DEMOGRAPHICS	AREA	U.S. AVG	ETHNIC COMPOSITION	AREA	U.S. AVG	RESIDENT PROFILE	AREA	U.S. AVG
Population	471,436		White	94.9%	75.1%	Single	39.4%	43.6%
Population density per sq. mile	272.9	447.3	Black	2.7%	12.3%	Married	60.6%	56.4%
Population growth	20.0%	16.1%	Asian	1.8%	3.6%	Divorced	8.6%	8.4%
Median age	34.9	35.5	American Indian	.3%	.9%	Separated	1.9%	3.0%
Average family size	2.6	2.7	Hispanic	1.9%	12.5%	Married with children	30.5%	28.7%
			Diversity measure	21.6%	35.2%	Single with children	8.6%	10.1%

ECONOMY & JOBS SCORE: 35/RANK: 213

INCOME	AREA	U.S. AVG	EMPLOYMENT	AREA	U.S. AVG	LARGEST EMPLOYING INDUSTRY
Per capita income	$27,998	$23,420	Unemployment rate	3.5%	6.1%	Insurance Carriers and Related Activities
Household income	$55,547	$46,060	Recent job growth	-2.8%	.9%	
Household income < $25K	18.9%	26.4%	Projected future job growth	16.0%	15.1%	
Household income > $75K	31.8%	24.5%	White collar	63.6%	54.5%	
Household income growth	77.8%	57.3%	Blue collar	36.4%	45.5%	

COST OF LIVING SCORE: 23/RANK: 250

INDEXES & TAXES	AREA	U.S. AVG	HOUSING	AREA	U.S. AVG	NECESSITIES	AREA	U.S. AVG
Cost of Living Index	94.2	100.0	Median home price	$132,000	$160,100	Food Index	90.0	100.0
Financial Progress Index	125.6	100.0	Home price appreciation	5.3%	7.1%	Housing Index	82.0	100.0
Income tax rate	8.920%	4.625%	Median rent	$655	$670	Utilities Index	132.4	100.0
Sales tax rate	6.000%	6.474%	Homes owned	71.6%	63.9%	Transportation Index	96.8	100.0
Property tax rate	$17.9	$15.6	Homes rented	23.6%	25.3%	Healthcare Index	105.0	100.0
			Housing affordability	59.0%	54.5%	Miscellaneous Cost Index	99.3	100.0

CLIMATE — SCORE: 25/RANK: 246

TEMPERATURE	AREA	U.S. AVG	PRECIPITATION	AREA	U.S. AVG	COMFORTS & HAZARDS	AREA	U.S. AVG
January low	11.3°F	26.4°F	Annual inches precipitation	31.0	35.9	July relative humidity	69.0%	68.8%
July high	84.9°F	86.7°F	Annual inches snowfall	33.0	24.2	Annual days mostly sunny	199	212
Annual days > 90°F	21	38	Annual days precipitation	106	111	Annual days with thunderstorms	50	39
Annual days < 32°F	137	88	Annual days rain > 0.5 inches	21	23	Tornado risk score	36	19
Annual days < 0°F	16	6	Annual days snow > 1.5 inches	10	6	Hurricane risk score	1	15

TEMPERATURE

PRECIPITATION

DAYS OF CLOUDS & PRECIPITATION

EDUCATION — SCORE: 83/RANK: 56

ACHIEVEMENT	AREA	U.S. AVG	PUBLIC SCHOOLS	AREA	U.S. AVG	HIGHER EDUCATION	AREA	U.S. AVG
High school degree	88.6%	80.2%	Expenditures per pupil	$5,807	$5,894	No. 2-year colleges	2	3
2-year college degree	7.4%	6.2%	Student/teacher ratio	15.5	16.7	No. 4-year colleges/universities	4	4
4-year college degree	20.4%	15.8%	Attending public school	92.0%	90.2%	No. highly ranked universities	1	1
Graduate/professional degree	8.3%	9.6%	State SAT score	1183	1020			
			State ACT score	22.0*	21.0			

HEALTH & HEALTHCARE — SCORE: 80/RANK: 64

HAZARDS & ILLNESSES	AREA	U.S. AVG	HEALTHCARE	AREA	U.S. AVG
Air-quality score	3	45	Physicians per capita	259.2	261.1
Water-quality score	30	33	Hospital beds per capita	408.1	432.2
Pollen/allergy score	40	61	No. teaching hospitals	5	4
Stress score	25	50	Cost per doctor visit	$64	$67
Cancer mortality per capita	172.6	169.0	Cost per dental visit	$80	$82
Depression days per month	2.6	2.8	Cost per daily hospital room	$623	$733

CRIME — SCORE: 63/RANK: 123

CRIME	AREA	U.S. AVG
Violent crime rate	251.1	456.0
Change in violent crime rate	-28.2%	-17.2%
Property crime rate	4,305.5	3,950.0
Change in property crime rate	-22.8%	-16.8%

TRANSPORTATION — SCORE: 77/RANK: 73

COMMUTE	AREA	U.S. AVG	INTERCITY SERVICES	AREA	U.S. AVG	AUTOMOTIVE	AREA	U.S. AVG
Average commute time	19.3 min.	22.6 min.	Miles to nearest major airport	3	46	Insurance, annual premium	$681	$1,011
Commute by auto	89.0%	88.7%	Type of local airport	Small		Gas, cost per gallon	$1.44	$1.50
Commute by mass transit	1.3%	1.8%	No. daily airline departures	106	294	Daily vehicle miles per capita	20.8	23.0
Work at home	5.8%	3.9%	Amtrak service	No				
Mass transit miles per capita	9.4	8.0	No. interstate highways	2	1			

LEISURE — SCORE: 29/RANK: 233

DINING & SHOPPING	AREA	U.S. AVG	ENTERTAINMENT	AREA	U.S. AVG	OUTDOOR ACTIVITIES	AREA	U.S. AVG
Restaurant rating	1	1	Professional sports rating	3	4	Golf-course rating	4	4
No. outlet malls	0	2	College sports rating	3	4	Ski-area rating	4	4
No. Starbucks	2	11	Zoo/aquarium rating	3	3	National Park rating	1	3
No. warehouse clubs	1	4	Amusement park rating	1	3	Sq. miles inland water	2.0	4.0
			Botanical garden/arboretum rating	8	3	Miles of coastline	0.0	11.4

ARTS & CULTURE — SCORE: 63/RANK: 121

MEDIA & LIBRARIES	AREA	U.S. AVG	PERFORMING ARTS	AREA	U.S. AVG	MUSEUMS	AREA	U.S. AVG
Arts radio rating	1	3	Classical music rating	6	4	Overall museum rating	6	6
No. public libraries	35	28	Ballet/dance rating	1	3	Art museum rating	7	5
Library volumes per capita	3.3	2.8	Professional theater rating	1	3	Science museum rating	6	4
			University arts programs rating	6	5	Children's museum rating	6	3

Detroit, MI

Score: 43.1 **Rank:** 263

Profile: Large city
Location: Southeast Michigan, along the Detroit River, across the border from Windsor, Ontario, Canada
Elevation: 664 feet
Time zone: Eastern Standard Time

PRO	CON
Arts and culture	Urban decay
Entertainment	Violent crime
Nearby water	Urban sprawl

Detroit is a lesson in the evolution of urban America. Originally a Great Lakes transportation center, it rapidly became an industrial center thanks to its location between ore resources to the north and energy resources to the south. The transportation industry, the origin of the nickname "motor city," began with carriages, bicycles, and other steel products, and blossomed with Henry Ford and his auto manufacturing empire. The industrial base continued to evolve through World War II with the production of military equipment and other manufactured goods. The large number of unskilled jobs attracted immigrants and U.S. migrants, particularly from the South, creating an ethnically mixed, working-class population. The industrial and commercial activity generated a great deal of wealth as well. Today Detroit retains a diverse socioeconomic character and a variety of neighborhoods, but also has a mixed economic outlook.

Detroit became one of the first cities to experience suburban flight and urban sprawl. The urban area deteriorated quickly with the advent of automobile transportation, and today's downtown area is still trying to rebuild with only modest success. Areas immediately surrounding downtown are still in considerable disrepair and an estimated 14,000 buildings are slated for destruction. Where did everybody go? To the suburbs, mainly west and north. The Detroit metropolitan area is a quilt of perfectly rectangular suburbs of varying socioeconomic status, separated by a grid of roads with names like Seven Mile, Eight Mile, and Ten Mile. Suburbs along the north shore and a few inland areas are more upscale, but, in general, suburbs are middle class. The adverse effects of urban sprawl include traffic, poor air-quality, and unattractive development—characteristics that have long defined the city. Many Detroiters haven't been to the central city in years.

But the area is not a total write-off by any means. There is enough local wealth and civic pride to attract an excellent set of arts and culture amenities, spearheaded by museums and performing arts. Sports are a local obsession, and everybody either watches or plays them. There are excellent recreational areas, and those wishing a getaway can head in several directions including north or to Ann Arbor or Lake Huron. Intercity transportation services are excellent. But as a place to live, Detroit is a gamble. Whether it can recover from its longstanding urban problems is yet unknown. Several good qualities accompany the bad, and for those with patience, the city could eventually pay off.

Detroit and its immediate suburbs occupy a large area approximately 25 miles in radius. Nearly flat land slopes up gently from the water's edge for about 10 miles to the northwest, giving way to increasingly rolling terrain. On the Canadian side, land is relatively level and agricultural. The climate is continental and rigorous, influenced by location on storm tracks and lakes Huron and Erie. Winter storms can bring combinations of rain, snow, freezing rain, and sleet with the possibility of heavy snowfall. In summer, most storms pass to the north allowing for intervals of warm, humid, sunny skies, and occasional thunderstorms followed by days of mild, dry, and fair weather. Lake breezes cool some parts the city. Summer temperatures reach 90°F or higher. Winter lake effects produce considerable cloudiness but also moderate cold temperatures. First freeze is late October, last is late April.

POPULATION

DEMOGRAPHICS	AREA	U.S. AVG	ETHNIC COMPOSITION	AREA	U.S. AVG	RESIDENT PROFILE	AREA	U.S. AVG
Population	4,464,531		White	81.7%	75.1%	Single	47.2%	43.6%
Population density per sq. mile	1,145.6	447.3	Black	15.4%	12.3%	Married	52.8%	56.4%
Population growth	4.6%	16.1%	Asian	1.8%	3.6%	Divorced	9.4%	8.4%
Median age	35.8	35.5	American Indian	.5%	.9%	Separated	2.8%	3.0%
Average family size	2.6	2.7	Hispanic	2.5%	12.5%	Married with children	27.2%	28.7%
			Diversity measure	44.7%	35.2%	Single with children	11.5%	10.1%

ECONOMY & JOBS
SCORE: 77/RANK: 75

INCOME	AREA	U.S. AVG	EMPLOYMENT	AREA	U.S. AVG	LARGEST EMPLOYING INDUSTRY
Per capita income	$28,017	$23,420	Unemployment rate	7.1%	6.1%	Transportation Equipment Manufacturing
Household income	$55,418	$46,060	Recent job growth	2.5%	.9%	
Household income < $25K	22.1%	26.4%	Projected future job growth	9.2%	15.1%	
Household income > $75K	34.2%	24.5%	White collar	56.1%	54.5%	
Household income growth	61.3%	57.3%	Blue collar	43.9%	45.5%	

COST OF LIVING
SCORE: 17/RANK: 273

INDEXES & TAXES	AREA	U.S. AVG	HOUSING	AREA	U.S. AVG	NECESSITIES	AREA	U.S. AVG
Cost of Living Index	101.5	100.0	Median home price	$162,010	$160,100	Food Index	107.4	100.0
Financial Progress Index	116.3	100.0	Home price appreciation	6.9%	7.1%	Housing Index	100.6	100.0
Income tax rate	7.400%	4.625%	Median rent	$801	$670	Utilities Index	94.9	100.0
Sales tax rate	6.000%	6.474%	Homes owned	72.0%	63.9%	Transportation Index	104.7	100.0
Property tax rate	$14.2	$15.6	Homes rented	22.0%	25.3%	Healthcare Index	114.3	100.0
			Housing affordability	50.0%	54.5%	Miscellaneous Cost Index	95.9	100.0

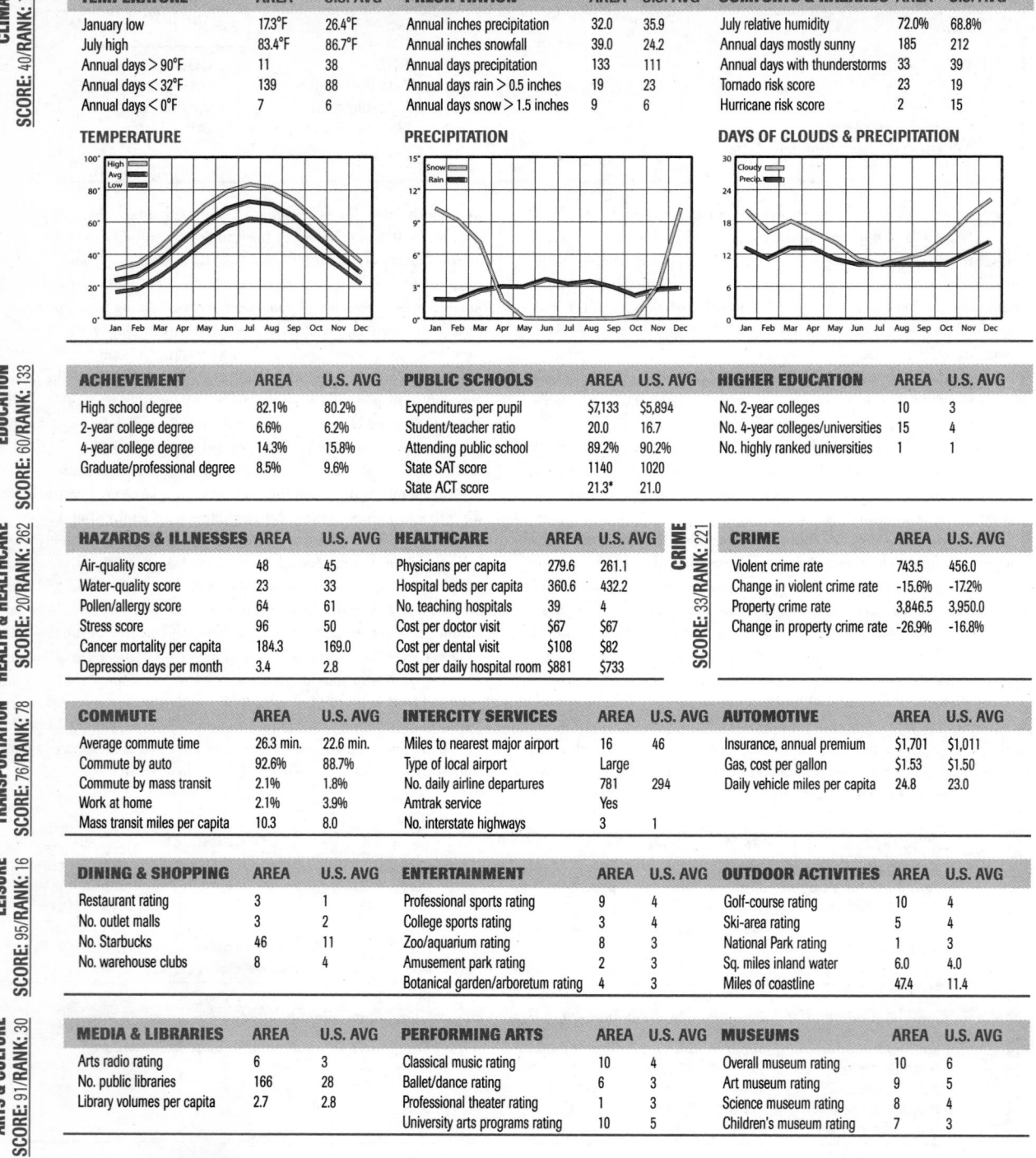

CLIMATE — SCORE: 40/RANK: 197

TEMPERATURE	AREA	U.S. AVG	PRECIPITATION	AREA	U.S. AVG	COMFORTS & HAZARDS	AREA	U.S. AVG
January low	17.3°F	26.4°F	Annual inches precipitation	32.0	35.9	July relative humidity	72.0%	68.8%
July high	83.4°F	86.7°F	Annual inches snowfall	39.0	24.2	Annual days mostly sunny	185	212
Annual days > 90°F	11	38	Annual days precipitation	133	111	Annual days with thunderstorms	33	39
Annual days < 32°F	139	88	Annual days rain > 0.5 inches	19	23	Tornado risk score	23	19
Annual days < 0°F	7	6	Annual days snow > 1.5 inches	9	6	Hurricane risk score	2	15

TEMPERATURE

PRECIPITATION

DAYS OF CLOUDS & PRECIPITATION

EDUCATION — SCORE: 60/RANK: 133

ACHIEVEMENT	AREA	U.S. AVG	PUBLIC SCHOOLS	AREA	U.S. AVG	HIGHER EDUCATION	AREA	U.S. AVG
High school degree	82.1%	80.2%	Expenditures per pupil	$7,133	$5,894	No. 2-year colleges	10	3
2-year college degree	6.6%	6.2%	Student/teacher ratio	20.0	16.7	No. 4-year colleges/universities	15	4
4-year college degree	14.3%	15.8%	Attending public school	89.2%	90.2%	No. highly ranked universities	1	1
Graduate/professional degree	8.5%	9.6%	State SAT score	1140	1020			
			State ACT score	21.3*	21.0			

HEALTH & HEALTHCARE — SCORE: 20/RANK: 262

HAZARDS & ILLNESSES	AREA	U.S. AVG	HEALTHCARE	AREA	U.S. AVG	CRIME	AREA	U.S. AVG
Air-quality score	48	45	Physicians per capita	279.6	261.1	Violent crime rate	743.5	456.0
Water-quality score	23	33	Hospital beds per capita	360.6	432.2	Change in violent crime rate	-15.6%	-17.2%
Pollen/allergy score	64	61	No. teaching hospitals	39	4	Property crime rate	3,846.5	3,950.0
Stress score	96	50	Cost per doctor visit	$67	$67	Change in property crime rate	-26.9%	-16.8%
Cancer mortality per capita	184.3	169.0	Cost per dental visit	$108	$82			
Depression days per month	3.4	2.8	Cost per daily hospital room	$881	$733			

CRIME — SCORE: 33/RANK: 221

TRANSPORTATION — SCORE: 76/RANK: 78

COMMUTE	AREA	U.S. AVG	INTERCITY SERVICES	AREA	U.S. AVG	AUTOMOTIVE	AREA	U.S. AVG
Average commute time	26.3 min.	22.6 min.	Miles to nearest major airport	16	46	Insurance, annual premium	$1,701	$1,011
Commute by auto	92.6%	88.7%	Type of local airport	Large		Gas, cost per gallon	$1.53	$1.50
Commute by mass transit	2.1%	1.8%	No. daily airline departures	781	294	Daily vehicle miles per capita	24.8	23.0
Work at home	2.1%	3.9%	Amtrak service	Yes				
Mass transit miles per capita	10.3	8.0	No. interstate highways	3	1			

LEISURE — SCORE: 95/RANK: 16

DINING & SHOPPING	AREA	U.S. AVG	ENTERTAINMENT	AREA	U.S. AVG	OUTDOOR ACTIVITIES	AREA	U.S. AVG
Restaurant rating	3	1	Professional sports rating	9	4	Golf-course rating	10	4
No. outlet malls	3	2	College sports rating	3	4	Ski-area rating	5	4
No. Starbucks	46	11	Zoo/aquarium rating	8	3	National Park rating	1	3
No. warehouse clubs	8	4	Amusement park rating	2	3	Sq. miles inland water	6.0	4.0
			Botanical garden/arboretum rating	4	3	Miles of coastline	47.4	11.4

ARTS & CULTURE — SCORE: 91/RANK: 30

MEDIA & LIBRARIES	AREA	U.S. AVG	PERFORMING ARTS	AREA	U.S. AVG	MUSEUMS	AREA	U.S. AVG
Arts radio rating	6	3	Classical music rating	10	4	Overall museum rating	10	6
No. public libraries	166	28	Ballet/dance rating	6	3	Art museum rating	9	5
Library volumes per capita	2.7	2.8	Professional theater rating	1	3	Science museum rating	8	4
			University arts programs rating	10	5	Children's museum rating	7	3

Dothan, AL

Score: 45.1   **Rank:** 256

Profile: Small agricultural town
Location: Extreme southeast Alabama near the Florida and Georgia borders
Elevation: 370 feet
Time zone: Central Standard Time

PRO	CON
Small-town atmosphere	Summer heat and humidity
Healthcare	Isolation
Cost of living	Entertainment

Dothan is a quiet but prosperous town serving a large agricultural area. Major industries include food processing and agricultural markets. The city has a low cost of living and not a lot to do. With over 74 90°F-plus days each year, Dothan is the hottest place in Alabama by far. For a Southern city, Dothan is relatively far away from big cities and big-city amenities, but it does have low healthcare costs and good hospital service per capita.

The surrounding flat to gently rolling land supports agriculture, mostly. The climate is decidedly humid subtropical with a strong Gulf influence; however, the town is too far from the Gulf for cooling breezes. Summers are long and hot, while winters are mild and wet and only subject to occasional freezes.

POPULATION

DEMOGRAPHICS	AREA	U.S. AVG	ETHNIC COMPOSITION	AREA	U.S. AVG	RESIDENT PROFILE	AREA	U.S. AVG
Population	139,152		White	76.8%	75.1%	Single	40.9%	43.6%
Population density per sq. mile	121.9	447.3	Black	21.4%	12.3%	Married	59.1%	56.4%
Population growth	6.3%	16.1%	Asian	1.0%	3.6%	Divorced	8.3%	8.4%
Median age	36.3	35.5	American Indian	.5%	.9%	Separated	2.9%	3.0%
Average family size	2.7	2.7	Hispanic	1.3%	12.5%	Married with children	30.2%	28.7%
			Diversity measure	41.7%	35.2%	Single with children	10.5%	10.1%

ECONOMY & JOBS
SCORE: 80/**RANK:** 66

INCOME	AREA	U.S. AVG	EMPLOYMENT	AREA	U.S. AVG	LARGEST EMPLOYING INDUSTRY
Per capita income	$18,995	$23,420	Unemployment rate	4.7%	6.1%	Food Manufacturing
Household income	$35,089	$46,060	Recent job growth	1.1%	.9%	
Household income < $25K	34.9%	26.4%	Projected future job growth	14.3%	15.1%	
Household income > $75K	14.0%	24.5%	White collar	48.4%	54.5%	
Household income growth	43.4%	57.3%	Blue collar	51.6%	45.5%	

COST OF LIVING
SCORE: 99/**RANK:** 2

INDEXES & TAXES	AREA	U.S. AVG	HOUSING	AREA	U.S. AVG	NECESSITIES	AREA	U.S. AVG
Cost of Living Index	80.6	100.0	Median home price	$87,390	$160,100	Food Index	100.4	100.0
Financial Progress Index	92.7	100.0	Home price appreciation	4.1%	7.1%	Housing Index	54.3	100.0
Income tax rate	5.000%	4.625%	Median rent	$426	$670	Utilities Index	77.7	100.0
Sales tax rate	8.000%	6.474%	Homes owned	65.8%	63.9%	Transportation Index	90.4	100.0
Property tax rate	$2.0	$15.6	Homes rented	23.9%	25.3%	Healthcare Index	87.0	100.0
			Housing affordability	64.0%	54.5%	Miscellaneous Cost Index	102.9	100.0

CLIMATE
SCORE: 47/**RANK:** 175

TEMPERATURE	AREA	U.S. AVG	PRECIPITATION	AREA	U.S. AVG	COMFORTS & HAZARDS	AREA	U.S. AVG
January low	35.9°F	26.4°F	Annual inches precipitation	51.0	35.9	July relative humidity	73.0%	68.8%
July high	90.8°F	86.7°F	Annual inches snowfall	.5	24.2	Annual days mostly sunny	216	212
Annual days > 90°F	74	38	Annual days precipitation	111	111	Annual days with thunderstorms	58	39
Annual days < 32°F	46	88	Annual days rain > 0.5 inches	37	23	Tornado risk score	25	19
Annual days < 0°F	0	6	Annual days snow > 1.5 inches	1	6	Hurricane risk score	41	15

TEMPERATURE

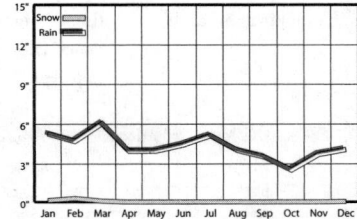

PRECIPITATION

DAYS OF CLOUDS & PRECIPITATION

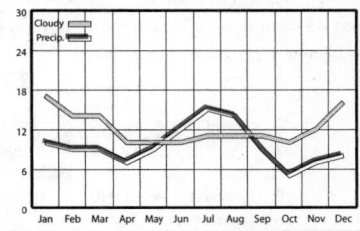

EDUCATION
SCORE: 14/**RANK:** 283

ACHIEVEMENT	AREA	U.S. AVG	PUBLIC SCHOOLS	AREA	U.S. AVG	HIGHER EDUCATION	AREA	U.S. AVG
High school degree	78.5%	80.2%	Expenditures per pupil	$4,924	$5,894	No. 2-year colleges	1	3
2-year college degree	6.5%	6.2%	Student/teacher ratio	15.8	16.7	No. 4-year colleges/universities	1	4
4-year college degree	11.2%	15.8%	Attending public school	89.0%	90.2%	No. highly ranked universities	0	1
Graduate/professional degree	5.6%	9.6%	State SAT score	1111	1020			
			State ACT score	20.1*	21.0			

HEALTH & HEALTHCARE SCORE: 95/RANK: 16

HAZARDS & ILLNESSES	AREA	U.S. AVG	HEALTHCARE	AREA	U.S. AVG
Air-quality score	6	45	Physicians per capita	233.6	261.1
Water-quality score	100	33	Hospital beds per capita	763.5	432.2
Pollen/allergy score	59	61	No. teaching hospitals	0	4
Stress score	13	50	Cost per doctor visit	$56	$67
Cancer mortality per capita	154.4	169.0	Cost per dental visit	$59	$82
Depression days per month	3.4	2.8	Cost per daily hospital room	$523	$733

CRIME SCORE: 55/RANK: 147

CRIME	AREA	U.S. AVG
Violent crime rate	266.5	456.0
Change in violent crime rate	-37.1%	-17.2%
Property crime rate	3,378.8	3,950.0
Change in property crime rate	13.9%	-16.8%

TRANSPORTATION SCORE: 34/RANK: 216

COMMUTE	AREA	U.S. AVG	INTERCITY SERVICES	AREA	U.S. AVG	AUTOMOTIVE	AREA	U.S. AVG
Average commute time	20.2 min.	22.6 min.	Miles to nearest major airport	85	46	Insurance, annual premium	$821	$1,011
Commute by auto	93.2%	88.7%	Type of local airport	Small		Gas, cost per gallon	$1.42	$1.50
Commute by mass transit	.7%	1.8%	No. daily airline departures	69	294	Daily vehicle miles per capita	34.5	23.0
Work at home	2.4%	3.9%	Amtrak service	No				
Mass transit miles per capita	0.0	8.0	No. interstate highways	0	1			

LEISURE SCORE: 4/RANK: 318

DINING & SHOPPING	AREA	U.S. AVG	ENTERTAINMENT	AREA	U.S. AVG	OUTDOOR ACTIVITIES	AREA	U.S. AVG
Restaurant rating	1	1	Professional sports rating	2	4	Golf-course rating	1	4
No. outlet malls	0	2	College sports rating	2	4	Ski-area rating	1	4
No. Starbucks	0	11	Zoo/aquarium rating	1	3	National Park rating	1	3
No. warehouse clubs	3	4	Amusement park rating	1	3	Sq. miles inland water	2.0	4.0
			Botanical garden/arboretum rating	1	3	Miles of coastline	0.0	11.4

ARTS & CULTURE SCORE: 8/RANK: 303

MEDIA & LIBRARIES	AREA	U.S. AVG	PERFORMING ARTS	AREA	U.S. AVG	MUSEUMS	AREA	U.S. AVG
Arts radio rating	1	3	Classical music rating	1	4	Overall museum rating	3	6
No. public libraries	8	28	Ballet/dance rating	3	3	Art museum rating	3	5
Library volumes per capita	2.2	2.8	Professional theater rating	1	3	Science museum rating	5	4
			University arts programs rating	1	5	Children's museum rating	1	3

Dover, DE

Score: 82.6   Rank: 25

Profile: Small capital city
Location: Central Delaware, 5 miles inland from the Delaware Bay
Elevation: 74 feet
Time zone: Eastern Standard Time

PRO	CON
Small-town atmosphere	Violent crime
Capital-city amenities	Recent job declines
Nearby recreation	Healthcare

Dover is one of those pleasant "small city" capitals, with a stable economic base and a rich history. The setting in a flat, mostly agricultural area is idyllic without being too far removed from larger northeastern cities. The nearby Delaware Bay and its beaches and wildlife areas provide ample recreational opportunities. The Dover International Speedway (NASCAR) and the Dover Downs harness racecourse add to entertainment options. Aside from the state government, Dover Air Force Base is a major employer. Reducing the city's ranking are a high violent crime rate and a recent decline in employment. There are no standout categories, but Dover does well in the rankings because of consistency across all categories.

Dover lies in a flat plain separated from the Delaware Bay but has areas of level marshland. To the west and south are areas of level to gently rolling terrain used mostly for agriculture and dairy farming. The influence of the Atlantic and Chesapeake Bay create a climate that's mild for the region. Summers are warm and humid but with maximum temperatures seldom exceeding 80°F. Clouds are common, and humidity and moist Delaware Bay winds can cause fog year-round. Winters are usually mild, with temperatures seldom dropping to 0°F. Most winter precipitation occurs as rain or a mix of rain, sleet, and snow. Summer thunderstorms are common; occasional downpours from Atlantic hurricanes can cause lowland flooding. First freeze is late October, last is mid-April.

POPULATION

DEMOGRAPHICS	AREA	U.S. AVG	ETHNIC COMPOSITION	AREA	U.S. AVG	RESIDENT PROFILE	AREA	U.S. AVG
Population	131,069		White	81.1%	75.1%	Single	42.3%	43.6%
Population density per sq. mile	221.9	447.3	Black	16.0%	12.3%	Married	57.7%	56.4%
Population growth	18.1%	16.1%	Asian	1.5%	3.6%	Divorced	8.9%	8.4%
Median age	34.7	35.5	American Indian	.5%	.9%	Separated	3.8%	3.0%
Average family size	2.8	2.7	Hispanic	3.3%	12.5%	Married with children	33.4%	28.7%
			Diversity measure	43.3%	35.2%	Single with children	11.9%	10.1%

ECONOMY & JOBS — SCORE: 51/RANK: 160

INCOME	AREA	U.S. AVG	EMPLOYMENT	AREA	U.S. AVG	LARGEST EMPLOYING INDUSTRY
Per capita income	$20,031	$23,420	Unemployment rate	4.7%	6.1%	Food Manufacturing
Household income	$41,631	$46,060	Recent job growth	.2%	.9%	
Household income < $25K	27.0%	26.4%	Projected future job growth	14.5%	15.1%	
Household income > $75K	18.0%	24.5%	White collar	49.4%	54.5%	
Household income growth	40.8%	57.3%	Blue collar	50.6%	45.5%	

COST OF LIVING — SCORE: 64/RANK: 118

INDEXES & TAXES	AREA	U.S. AVG	HOUSING	AREA	U.S. AVG	NECESSITIES	AREA	U.S. AVG
Cost of Living Index	96.0	100.0	Median home price	$135,350	$160,100	Food Index	106.7	100.0
Financial Progress Index	92.4	100.0	Home price appreciation	5.9%	7.1%	Housing Index	84.1	100.0
Income tax rate	8.150%	4.625%	Median rent	$663	$670	Utilities Index	117.6	100.0
Sales tax rate	0.000%	6.474%	Homes owned	70.5%	63.9%	Transportation Index	96.4	100.0
Property tax rate	$8.9	$15.6	Homes rented	24.5%	25.3%	Healthcare Index	94.9	100.0
			Housing affordability	56.0%	54.5%	Miscellaneous Cost Index	99.4	100.0

CLIMATE — SCORE: 60/RANK: 130

TEMPERATURE	AREA	U.S. AVG	PRECIPITATION	AREA	U.S. AVG	COMFORTS & HAZARDS	AREA	U.S. AVG
January low	23.8°F	26.4°F	Annual inches precipitation	40.3	35.9	July relative humidity	70.0%	68.8%
July high	85.5°F	86.7°F	Annual inches snowfall	20.8	24.2	Annual days mostly sunny	201	212
Annual days > 90°F	18	38	Annual days precipitation	123	111	Annual days with thunderstorms	31	39
Annual days < 32°F	102	88	Annual days rain > 0.5 inches	26	23	Tornado risk score	13	19
Annual days < 0°F	0	6	Annual days snow > 1.5 inches	5	6	Hurricane risk score	15	15

TEMPERATURE

PRECIPITATION

DAYS OF CLOUDS & PRECIPITATION

EDUCATION — SCORE: 28/RANK: 235

ACHIEVEMENT	AREA	U.S. AVG	PUBLIC SCHOOLS	AREA	U.S. AVG	HIGHER EDUCATION	AREA	U.S. AVG
High school degree	79.4%	80.2%	Expenditures per pupil	$6,858	$5,894	No. 2-year colleges	1	3
2-year college degree	6.7%	6.2%	Student/teacher ratio	17.2	16.7	No. 4-year colleges/universities	2	4
4-year college degree	11.6%	15.8%	Attending public school	91.8%	90.2%	No. highly ranked universities	0	1
Graduate/professional degree	7.0%	9.6%	State SAT score	1002*	1020			
			State ACT score	20.8	21.0			

HEALTH & HEALTHCARE — SCORE: 31/RANK: 228

HAZARDS & ILLNESSES	AREA	U.S. AVG	HEALTHCARE	AREA	U.S. AVG	CRIME — SCORE: 48/RANK: 170	AREA	U.S. AVG
Air-quality score	6	45	Physicians per capita	164.8	261.1	Violent crime rate	656.4	456.0
Water-quality score	25	33	Hospital beds per capita	191.0	432.2	Change in violent crime rate	-4.6%	-17.2%
Pollen/allergy score	51	61	No. teaching hospitals	0	4	Property crime rate	3,283.6	3,950.0
Stress score	63	50	Cost per doctor visit	$75	$67	Change in property crime rate	-27.3%	-16.8%
Cancer mortality per capita	167.8	169.0	Cost per dental visit	$119	$82			
Depression days per month	3.0	2.8	Cost per daily hospital room	$654	$733			

TRANSPORTATION — SCORE: 45/RANK: 180

COMMUTE	AREA	U.S. AVG	INTERCITY SERVICES	AREA	U.S. AVG	AUTOMOTIVE	AREA	U.S. AVG
Average commute time	22.7 min.	22.6 min.	Miles to nearest major airport	52	46	Insurance, annual premium	$1,138	$1,011
Commute by auto	91.9%	88.7%	Type of local airport	Large		Gas, cost per gallon	$1.47	$1.50
Commute by mass transit	.7%	1.8%	No. daily airline departures	669	294	Daily vehicle miles per capita	20.3	23.0
Work at home	3.4%	3.9%	Amtrak service	No				
Mass transit miles per capita	0.0	8.0	No. interstate highways	1	1			

LEISURE — SCORE: 26/RANK: 242

DINING & SHOPPING	AREA	U.S. AVG	ENTERTAINMENT	AREA	U.S. AVG	OUTDOOR ACTIVITIES	AREA	U.S. AVG
Restaurant rating	1	1	Professional sports rating	4	4	Golf-course rating	4	4
No. outlet malls	6	2	College sports rating	2	4	Ski-area rating	3	4
No. Starbucks	0	11	Zoo/aquarium rating	1	3	National Park rating	2	3
No. warehouse clubs	3	4	Amusement park rating	1	3	Sq. miles inland water	5.0	4.0
			Botanical garden/arboretum rating	1	3	Miles of coastline	0.0	11.4

ARTS & CULTURE SCORE: 29/RANK: 233

MEDIA & LIBRARIES	AREA	U.S. AVG	PERFORMING ARTS	AREA	U.S. AVG	MUSEUMS	AREA	U.S. AVG
Arts radio rating	1	3	Classical music rating	4	4	Overall museum rating	5	6
No. public libraries	4	28	Ballet/dance rating	1	3	Art museum rating	2	5
Library volumes per capita	1.2	2.8	Professional theater rating	6	3	Science museum rating	3	4
			University arts programs rating	5	5	Children's museum rating	1	3

Dubuque, IA

Score: 28.2   Rank: 311

Profile: Small industrial town
Location: Extreme eastern Iowa along Mississippi River at Illinois border
Elevation: 798 feet
Time zone: Central Standard Time

PRO	CON
Historic interest	Economy
Small-town atmosphere	Harsh climate
Low crime rate	Low ethnic diversity

Dubuque is an upper Mississippi River town and old industrial center. The city retains a rich historic core with old Victorian brick buildings rising gradually away from the Mississippi waterfront. The town has frequently served as a movie set. Although rated low statistically on a national scale, Dubuque has a few culture and entertainment amenities good for a town of its size including a symphony and theater company. The crime rate is low although with a large percentage step up in reported violent crime, and the economic base shows some signs of decline. The area has extremely low ethnic diversity and is geographically isolated from many big city amenities, but is probably a better place to live than the numbers indicate.

The Mississippi River is shallow and about ¼-mile wide at Dubuque. The surrounding terrain varies from gently rolling to the south and west to steep hills and bluffs around the city and along the Mississippi. The principal climate feature is variety. Summers have frequent change between hot, humid days with thunderstorms and cool, comfortable northerly air. Winters are quite variable with cold snaps driving temperatures well below zero. Historic temperatures range from −32°F to 110°F. Most precipitation occurs during spring and fall seasons, with snow falling as late as May and as early as September. First freeze is early October, last is late April.

POPULATION

DEMOGRAPHICS	AREA	U.S. AVG	ETHNIC COMPOSITION	AREA	U.S. AVG	RESIDENT PROFILE	AREA	U.S. AVG
Population	89,387		White	99.2%	75.1%	Single	36.9%	43.6%
Population density per sq. mile	147.0	447.3	Black	.1%	12.3%	Married	63.1%	56.4%
Population growth	3.5%	16.1%	Asian	.5%	3.6%	Divorced	3.6%	8.4%
Median age	36.8	35.5	American Indian	.0%	.9%	Separated	.8%	3.0%
Average family size	3.0	2.7	Hispanic	.4%	12.5%	Married with children	38.4%	28.7%
			Diversity measure	6.8%	35.2%	Single with children	5.2%	10.1%

ECONOMY & JOBS SCORE: 43/RANK: 188

INCOME	AREA	U.S. AVG	EMPLOYMENT	AREA	U.S. AVG	LARGEST EMPLOYING INDUSTRY
Per capita income	$21,924	$23,420	Unemployment rate	3.4%	6.1%	Machinery Manufacturing
Household income	$44,603	$46,060	Recent job growth	-3.8%	.9%	
Household income < $25K	25.2%	26.4%	Projected future job growth	9.3%	15.1%	
Household income > $75K	21.2%	24.5%	White collar	49.2%	54.5%	
Household income growth	57.1%	57.3%	Blue collar	50.8%	45.5%	

COST OF LIVING SCORE: 40/RANK: 198

INDEXES & TAXES	AREA	U.S. AVG	HOUSING	AREA	U.S. AVG	NECESSITIES	AREA	U.S. AVG
Cost of Living Index	88.8	100.0	Median home price	$107,300	$160,100	Food Index	92.5	100.0
Financial Progress Index	107.0	100.0	Home price appreciation	4.8%	7.1%	Housing Index	66.6	100.0
Income tax rate	7.920%	4.625%	Median rent	$493	$670	Utilities Index	137.0	100.0
Sales tax rate	6.000%	6.474%	Homes owned	75.1%	63.9%	Transportation Index	98.8	100.0
Property tax rate	$19.2	$15.6	Homes rented	18.2%	25.3%	Healthcare Index	95.5	100.0
			Housing affordability	63.0%	54.5%	Miscellaneous Cost Index	97.9	100.0

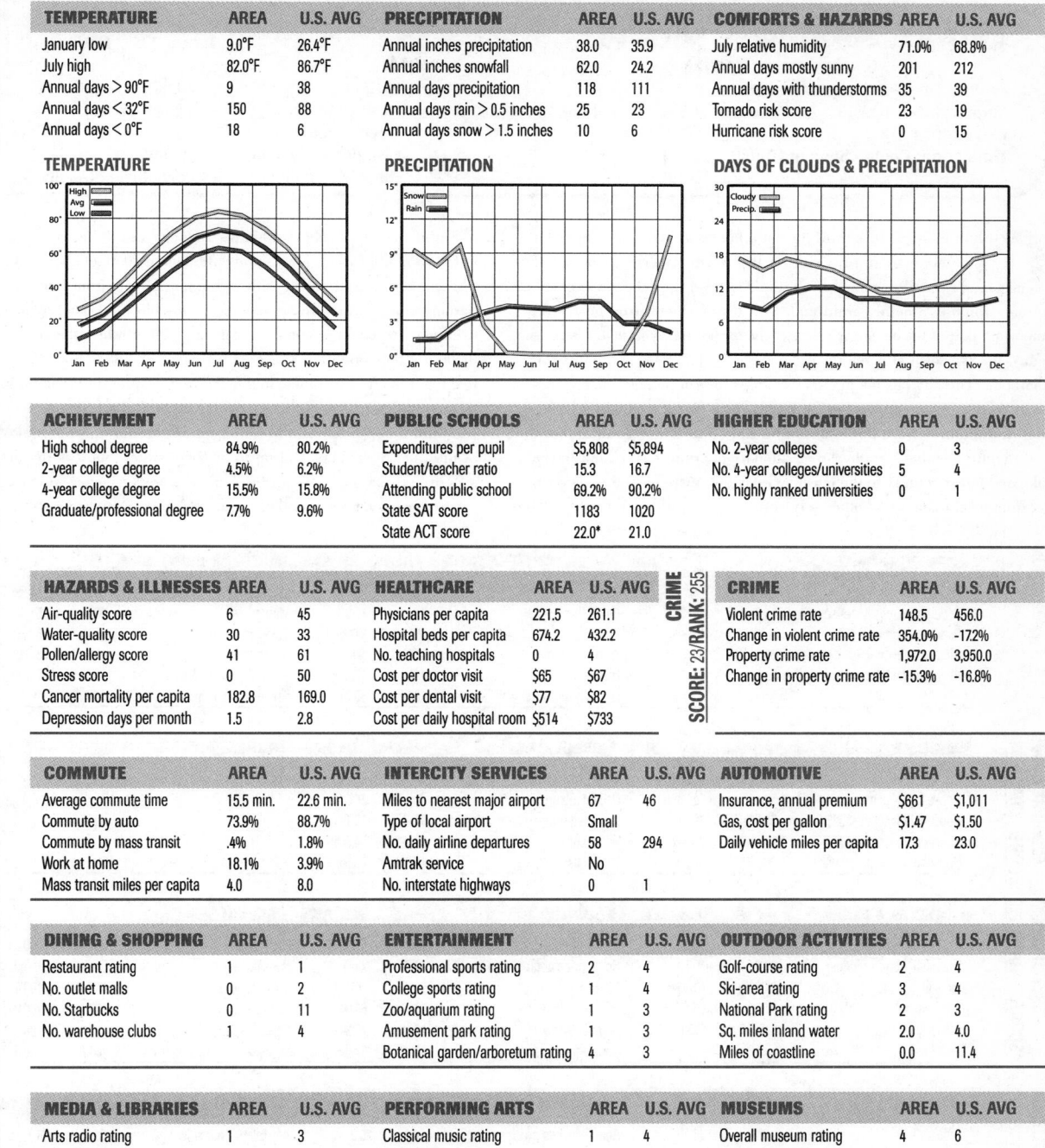

CLIMATE SCORE: 6/RANK: 311

TEMPERATURE	AREA	U.S. AVG
January low	9.0°F	26.4°F
July high	82.0°F	86.7°F
Annual days > 90°F	9	38
Annual days < 32°F	150	88
Annual days < 0°F	18	6

PRECIPITATION	AREA	U.S. AVG
Annual inches precipitation	38.0	35.9
Annual inches snowfall	62.0	24.2
Annual days precipitation	118	111
Annual days rain > 0.5 inches	25	23
Annual days snow > 1.5 inches	10	6

COMFORTS & HAZARDS	AREA	U.S. AVG
July relative humidity	71.0%	68.8%
Annual days mostly sunny	201	212
Annual days with thunderstorms	35	39
Tornado risk score	23	19
Hurricane risk score	0	15

TEMPERATURE

PRECIPITATION

DAYS OF CLOUDS & PRECIPITATION

EDUCATION SCORE: 2/RANK: 324

ACHIEVEMENT	AREA	U.S. AVG
High school degree	84.9%	80.2%
2-year college degree	4.5%	6.2%
4-year college degree	15.5%	15.8%
Graduate/professional degree	7.7%	9.6%

PUBLIC SCHOOLS	AREA	U.S. AVG
Expenditures per pupil	$5,808	$5,894
Student/teacher ratio	15.3	16.7
Attending public school	69.2%	90.2%
State SAT score	1183	1020
State ACT score	22.0*	21.0

HIGHER EDUCATION	AREA	U.S. AVG
No. 2-year colleges	0	3
No. 4-year colleges/universities	5	4
No. highly ranked universities	0	1

HEALTH & HEALTHCARE SCORE: 76/RANK: 79

HAZARDS & ILLNESSES	AREA	U.S. AVG
Air-quality score	6	45
Water-quality score	30	33
Pollen/allergy score	41	61
Stress score	0	50
Cancer mortality per capita	182.8	169.0
Depression days per month	1.5	2.8

HEALTHCARE	AREA	U.S. AVG
Physicians per capita	221.5	261.1
Hospital beds per capita	674.2	432.2
No. teaching hospitals	0	4
Cost per doctor visit	$65	$67
Cost per dental visit	$77	$82
Cost per daily hospital room	$514	$733

CRIME SCORE: 23/RANK: 255

CRIME	AREA	U.S. AVG
Violent crime rate	148.5	456.0
Change in violent crime rate	354.0%	-17.2%
Property crime rate	1,972.0	3,950.0
Change in property crime rate	-15.3%	-16.8%

TRANSPORTATION SCORE: 89/RANK: 35

COMMUTE	AREA	U.S. AVG
Average commute time	15.5 min.	22.6 min.
Commute by auto	73.9%	88.7%
Commute by mass transit	.4%	1.8%
Work at home	18.1%	3.9%
Mass transit miles per capita	4.0	8.0

INTERCITY SERVICES	AREA	U.S. AVG
Miles to nearest major airport	67	46
Type of local airport	Small	
No. daily airline departures	58	294
Amtrak service	No	
No. interstate highways	0	1

AUTOMOTIVE	AREA	U.S. AVG
Insurance, annual premium	$661	$1,011
Gas, cost per gallon	$1.47	$1.50
Daily vehicle miles per capita	17.3	23.0

LEISURE SCORE: 8/RANK: 306

DINING & SHOPPING	AREA	U.S. AVG
Restaurant rating	1	1
No. outlet malls	0	2
No. Starbucks	0	11
No. warehouse clubs	1	4

ENTERTAINMENT	AREA	U.S. AVG
Professional sports rating	2	4
College sports rating	1	4
Zoo/aquarium rating	1	3
Amusement park rating	1	3
Botanical garden/arboretum rating	4	3

OUTDOOR ACTIVITIES	AREA	U.S. AVG
Golf-course rating	2	4
Ski-area rating	3	4
National Park rating	2	3
Sq. miles inland water	2.0	4.0
Miles of coastline	0.0	11.4

ARTS & CULTURE SCORE: 15/RANK: 279

MEDIA & LIBRARIES	AREA	U.S. AVG
Arts radio rating	1	3
No. public libraries	5	28
Library volumes per capita	3.9	2.8

PERFORMING ARTS	AREA	U.S. AVG
Classical music rating	1	4
Ballet/dance rating	1	3
Professional theater rating	1	3
University arts programs rating	3	5

MUSEUMS	AREA	U.S. AVG
Overall museum rating	4	6
Art museum rating	2	5
Science museum rating	1	4
Children's museum rating	1	3

Duluth-Superior, MN-WI

Score: 59.9   **Rank:** 148

Profile: Small-port-city complex
Location: Northeastern Minnesota at western end of Lake Superior
Elevation: 1,417 feet
Time zone: Central Standard Time

PRO	CON
Nearby outdoor recreation	Winter climate
Historic preservation	Isolation
Attractive setting	Low ethnic diversity

Duluth is the world's third largest inland port located about as far as possible from an ocean on the North American continent. Superior, Wisconsin, sits to the south on the other side of the harbor. Shipping, mainly grain and, to a lesser extent, iron ore, is an important part of the economy. Some of the former heavy industry is gone today, but the town still retains a decidedly commercial and industrial character. The city has taken effective steps to turn potential decay into an attractive preservation of its heritage. Many classic industrial buildings and features have been renovated and some house entertainment and nightlife venues. Outdoor recreational opportunities abound in the lake and forest country to the north. Winters are extreme and the area is far from air transport and other services.

Duluth in total is about 20 miles long and lies at the base of a range of hills and bluffs that rise abruptly 600 feet to 800 feet above lake level. The climate is continental with significant effects from Lake Superior. Summer days are warm, sometimes with clouds from the lake, and evenings are cool. Winters are cold and bitter when the lake doesn't moderate temperatures. The area averages 51 below-zero days a year, making it the fourth coldest in the nation. Low-pressure systems passing to the south cause easterly winds across the lake bringing significant snowfall. Easterly winds, the major weather modifier, occur almost 50% of the time in summer and up to 25% in winter. Snow is dry and persistent and ice may form in the harbor from November through April. First freeze is late September, last is mid-May.

POPULATION

DEMOGRAPHICS	AREA	U.S. AVG	ETHNIC COMPOSITION	AREA	U.S. AVG	RESIDENT PROFILE	AREA	U.S. AVG
Population	243,721		White	96.1%	75.1%	Single	41.6%	43.6%
Population density per sq. mile	32.3	447.3	Black	.5%	12.3%	Married	58.4%	56.4%
Population growth	1.6%	16.1%	Asian	.7%	3.6%	Divorced	8.4%	8.4%
Median age	39.3	35.5	American Indian	2.5%	.9%	Separated	1.6%	3.0%
Average family size	2.4	2.7	Hispanic	.6%	12.5%	Married with children	25.0%	28.7%
			Diversity measure	10.6%	35.2%	Single with children	8.4%	10.1%

ECONOMY & JOBS
SCORE: 53/RANK: 151

INCOME	AREA	U.S. AVG	EMPLOYMENT	AREA	U.S. AVG	LARGEST EMPLOYING INDUSTRY
Per capita income	$22,273	$23,420	Unemployment rate	4.7%	6.1%	Healthcare and Social Assistance
Household income	$39,939	$46,060	Recent job growth	.1%	.9%	
Household income < $25K	30.8%	26.4%	Projected future job growth	9.5%	15.1%	
Household income > $75K	19.8%	24.5%	White collar	51.9%	54.5%	
Household income growth	68.2%	57.3%	Blue collar	48.1%	45.5%	

COST OF LIVING
SCORE: 33/RANK: 220

INDEXES & TAXES	AREA	U.S. AVG	HOUSING	AREA	U.S. AVG	NECESSITIES	AREA	U.S. AVG
Cost of Living Index	91.5	100.0	Median home price	$99,290	$160,100	Food Index	98.2	100.0
Financial Progress Index	93.0	100.0	Home price appreciation	10.2%	7.1%	Housing Index	61.7	100.0
Income tax rate	8.000%	4.625%	Median rent	$499	$670	Utilities Index	142.6	100.0
Sales tax rate	6.500%	6.474%	Homes owned	53.1%	63.9%	Transportation Index	107.6	100.0
Property tax rate	$18.2	$15.6	Homes rented	13.4%	25.3%	Healthcare Index	117.1	100.0
			Housing affordability	51.0%	54.5%	Miscellaneous Cost Index	101.6	100.0

CLIMATE
SCORE: 5/RANK: 312

TEMPERATURE	AREA	U.S. AVG	PRECIPITATION	AREA	U.S. AVG	COMFORTS & HAZARDS	AREA	U.S. AVG
January low	-.6°F	26.4°F	Annual inches precipitation	30.0	35.9	July relative humidity	71.0%	68.8%
July high	76.4°F	86.7°F	Annual inches snowfall	78.0	24.2	Annual days mostly sunny	180	212
Annual days > 90°F	2	38	Annual days precipitation	135	111	Annual days with thunderstorms	35	39
Annual days < 32°F	187	88	Annual days rain > 0.5 inches	18	23	Tornado risk score	3	19
Annual days < 0°F	51	6	Annual days snow > 1.5 inches	15	6	Hurricane risk score	0	15

TEMPERATURE

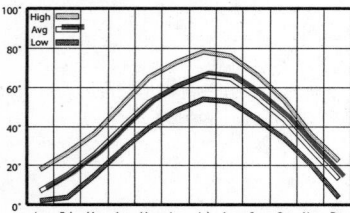

PRECIPITATION

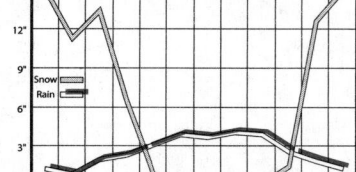

DAYS OF CLOUDS & PRECIPITATION

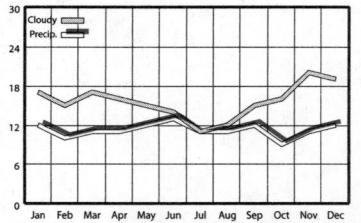

EDUCATION — SCORE: 74/RANK: 86

ACHIEVEMENT	AREA	U.S. AVG	PUBLIC SCHOOLS	AREA	U.S. AVG	HIGHER EDUCATION	AREA	U.S. AVG
High school degree	87.7%	80.2%	Expenditures per pupil	$6,316	$5,894	No. 2-year colleges	4	3
2-year college degree	8.3%	6.2%	Student/teacher ratio	16.9	16.7	No. 4-year colleges/universities	3	4
4-year college degree	14.8%	15.8%	Attending public school	93.9%	90.2%	No. highly ranked universities	1	1
Graduate/professional degree	6.4%	9.6%	State SAT score	1173	1020			
			State ACT score	22.0*	21.0			

HEALTH & HEALTHCARE — SCORE: 84/RANK: 51   CRIME — SCORE: 48/RANK: 172

HAZARDS & ILLNESSES	AREA	U.S. AVG	HEALTHCARE	AREA	U.S. AVG	CRIME	AREA	U.S. AVG
Air-quality score	59	45	Physicians per capita	265.1	261.1	Violent crime rate	229.0	456.0
Water-quality score	38	33	Hospital beds per capita	586.1	432.2	Change in violent crime rate	-9.0%	-17.2%
Pollen/allergy score	44	61	No. teaching hospitals	2	4	Property crime rate	3,937.4	3,950.0
Stress score	56	50	Cost per doctor visit	$72	$67	Change in property crime rate	.5%	-16.8%
Cancer mortality per capita	177.0	169.0	Cost per dental visit	$82	$82			
Depression days per month	2.9	2.8	Cost per daily hospital room	$630	$733			

TRANSPORTATION — SCORE: 67/RANK: 106

COMMUTE	AREA	U.S. AVG	INTERCITY SERVICES	AREA	U.S. AVG	AUTOMOTIVE	AREA	U.S. AVG
Average commute time	19.7 min.	22.6 min.	Miles to nearest major airport	141	46	Insurance, annual premium	$958	$1,011
Commute by auto	87.2%	88.7%	Type of local airport	Large		Gas, cost per gallon	$1.52	$1.50
Commute by mass transit	1.5%	1.8%	No. daily airline departures	624	294	Daily vehicle miles per capita	18.0	23.0
Work at home	5.2%	3.9%	Amtrak service	No				
Mass transit miles per capita	9.4	8.0	No. interstate highways	1	1			

LEISURE — SCORE: 76/RANK: 75

DINING & SHOPPING	AREA	U.S. AVG	ENTERTAINMENT	AREA	U.S. AVG	OUTDOOR ACTIVITIES	AREA	U.S. AVG
Restaurant rating	1	1	Professional sports rating	2	4	Golf-course rating	2	4
No. outlet malls	0	2	College sports rating	4	4	Ski-area rating	4	4
No. Starbucks	0	11	Zoo/aquarium rating	3	3	National Park rating	10	3
No. warehouse clubs	3	4	Amusement park rating	1	3	Sq. miles inland water	10.0	4.0
			Botanical garden/arboretum rating	1	3	Miles of coastline	36.0	11.4

ARTS & CULTURE — SCORE: 71/RANK: 94

MEDIA & LIBRARIES	AREA	U.S. AVG	PERFORMING ARTS	AREA	U.S. AVG	MUSEUMS	AREA	U.S. AVG
Arts radio rating	1	3	Classical music rating	3	4	Overall museum rating	6	6
No. public libraries	19	28	Ballet/dance rating	3	3	Art museum rating	6	5
Library volumes per capita	2.2	2.8	Professional theater rating	1	3	Science museum rating	2	4
			University arts programs rating	5	5	Children's museum rating	5	3

Dutchess County, NY

Score: 28.2   Rank: 310

Profile: Commuter community/College town
Location: Southern New York, along Hudson River, 80 miles north of New York City
Elevation: 292 feet
Time zone: Eastern Standard Time

PRO	CON
Proximity to New York City	Cost of living
College-town amenities	Harsh winters
Future job growth	Long commute

Dutchess County sits between Newburgh to the south and Albany to the north, along the Hudson River about 80 miles north of New York City. The major city is Poughkeepsie, a diverse town on the east bank of the river. Vassar College, a former women's college now admitting both genders, gives Poughkeepsie a college-town element with some good restaurants and entertainment. There is some skiing and recreation in the nearby Catskills. Lying along this section of the Hudson are some of the most extravagant mansions of New York's Gilded Age, notably the Vanderbilt home and the Roosevelt's famous Hyde Park. However, there are also some older, less attractive industrial areas.

The commute to New York City is possible, but lengthy. At 130.2, the Cost of Living Index is the third highest in New York, but future job-growth projections are good. Winters can be hard and unpredictable. Despite the downsides, the area is probably better than the numbers indicate.

High, wooded bluffs and hills surround the narrow Hudson Valley. Poughkeepsie is on a plateau about 250 feet above the river. The climate is continental with warm, humid summers, cool evenings, occasional breezes, and afternoon thundershowers. Winters are rigorous and cold, with frequent snow. First freeze is mid-September, last is late April.

POPULATION

DEMOGRAPHICS	AREA	U.S. AVG	ETHNIC COMPOSITION	AREA	U.S. AVG	RESIDENT PROFILE	AREA	U.S. AVG
Population	287,752		White	89.3%	75.1%	Single	46.6%	43.6%
Population density per sq. mile	358.9	447.3	Black	6.9%	12.3%	Married	53.4%	56.4%
Population growth	10.9%	16.1%	Asian	2.9%	3.6%	Divorced	6.1%	8.4%
Median age	37.1	35.5	American Indian	.2%	.9%	Separated	3.0%	3.0%
Average family size	2.6	2.7	Hispanic	4.0%	12.5%	Married with children	30.2%	28.7%
			Diversity measure	33.9%	35.2%	Single with children	7.8%	10.1%

ECONOMY & JOBS — SCORE: 90/RANK: 32

INCOME	AREA	U.S. AVG	EMPLOYMENT	AREA	U.S. AVG	LARGEST EMPLOYING INDUSTRY
Per capita income	$27,419	$23,420	Unemployment rate	3.3%	6.1%	Computer and Electronic Product Manufacturing
Household income	$62,088	$46,060	Recent job growth	1.7%	.9%	
Household income < $25K	16.1%	26.4%	Projected future job growth	13.4%	15.1%	
Household income > $75K	38.2%	24.5%	White collar	62.5%	54.5%	
Household income growth	46.7%	57.3%	Blue collar	37.5%	45.5%	

COST OF LIVING — SCORE: 10/RANK: 295

INDEXES & TAXES	AREA	U.S. AVG	HOUSING	AREA	U.S. AVG	NECESSITIES	AREA	U.S. AVG
Cost of Living Index	130.2	100.0	Median home price	$233,820	$160,100	Food Index	119.8	100.0
Financial Progress Index	101.6	100.0	Home price appreciation	14.9%	7.1%	Housing Index	145.2	100.0
Income tax rate	7.125%	4.625%	Median rent	$1,054	$670	Utilities Index	141.1	100.0
Sales tax rate	7.250%	6.474%	Homes owned	65.0%	63.9%	Transportation Index	110.6	100.0
Property tax rate	$22.4	$15.6	Homes rented	23.4%	25.3%	Healthcare Index	136.0	100.0
			Housing affordability	39.0%	54.5%	Miscellaneous Cost Index	118.1	100.0

CLIMATE — SCORE: 3/RANK: 320

TEMPERATURE	AREA	U.S. AVG	PRECIPITATION	AREA	U.S. AVG	COMFORTS & HAZARDS	AREA	U.S. AVG
January low	12.5°F	26.4°F	Annual inches precipitation	33.0	35.9	July relative humidity	71.0%	68.8%
July high	83.9°F	86.7°F	Annual inches snowfall	71.0	24.2	Annual days mostly sunny	182	212
Annual days > 90°F	8	38	Annual days precipitation	135	111	Annual days with thunderstorms	28	39
Annual days < 32°F	155	88	Annual days rain > 0.5 inches	23	23	Tornado risk score	11	19
Annual days < 0°F	17	6	Annual days snow > 1.5 inches	13	6	Hurricane risk score	12	15

TEMPERATURE

PRECIPITATION

DAYS OF CLOUDS & PRECIPITATION

EDUCATION — SCORE: 87/RANK: 44

ACHIEVEMENT	AREA	U.S. AVG	PUBLIC SCHOOLS	AREA	U.S. AVG	HIGHER EDUCATION	AREA	U.S. AVG
High school degree	84.0%	80.2%	Expenditures per pupil	$8,487	$5,894	No. 2-year colleges	1	3
2-year college degree	9.2%	6.2%	Student/teacher ratio	15.5	16.7	No. 4-year colleges/universities	4	4
4-year college degree	15.7%	15.8%	Attending public school	88.1%	90.2%	No. highly ranked universities	3	1
Graduate/professional degree	11.9%	9.6%	State SAT score	1006*	1020			
			State ACT score	22.3	21.0			

HEALTH & HEALTHCARE — SCORE: 50/RANK: 163

HAZARDS & ILLNESSES	AREA	U.S. AVG	HEALTHCARE	AREA	U.S. AVG
Air-quality score	24	45	Physicians per capita	231.8	261.1
Water-quality score	30	33	Hospital beds per capita	421.9	432.2
Pollen/allergy score	52	61	No. teaching hospitals	1	4
Stress score	10	50	Cost per doctor visit	$75	$67
Cancer mortality per capita	170.1	169.0	Cost per dental visit	$88	$82
Depression days per month	2.8	2.8	Cost per daily hospital room	$897	$733

CRIME — SCORE: 96/RANK: 14

CRIME	AREA	U.S. AVG
Violent crime rate	229.1	456.0
Change in violent crime rate	-46.5%	-17.2%
Property crime rate	2,029.1	3,950.0
Change in property crime rate	-20.8%	-16.8%

TRANSPORTATION — SCORE: 1/RANK: 327

COMMUTE	AREA	U.S. AVG	INTERCITY SERVICES	AREA	U.S. AVG	AUTOMOTIVE	AREA	U.S. AVG
Average commute time	29.8 min.	22.6 min.	Miles to nearest major airport	45	46	Insurance, annual premium	$1,290	$1,011
Commute by auto	86.5%	88.7%	Type of local airport	Small		Gas, cost per gallon	$1.65	$1.50
Commute by mass transit	2.7%	1.8%	No. daily airline departures	98	294	Daily vehicle miles per capita	27.7	23.0
Work at home	3.1%	3.9%	Amtrak service	Yes				
Mass transit miles per capita	7.2	8.0	No. interstate highways	1	1			

LEISURE SCORE: 72/RANK: 94

DINING & SHOPPING	AREA	U.S. AVG	ENTERTAINMENT	AREA	U.S. AVG	OUTDOOR ACTIVITIES	AREA	U.S. AVG
Restaurant rating	3	1	Professional sports rating	10	4	Golf-course rating	9	4
No. outlet malls	4	2	College sports rating	2	4	Ski-area rating	5	4
No. Starbucks	1	11	Zoo/aquarium rating	6	3	National Park rating	3	3
No. warehouse clubs	4	4	Amusement park rating	5	3	Sq. miles inland water	8.0	4.0
			Botanical garden/arboretum rating	5	3	Miles of coastline	0.0	11.4

ARTS & CULTURE SCORE: 12/RANK: 291

MEDIA & LIBRARIES	AREA	U.S. AVG	PERFORMING ARTS	AREA	U.S. AVG	MUSEUMS	AREA	U.S. AVG
Arts radio rating	4	3	Classical music rating	8	4	Overall museum rating	7	6
No. public libraries	23	28	Ballet/dance rating	6	3	Art museum rating	8	5
Library volumes per capita	2.8	2.8	Professional theater rating	8	3	Science museum rating	7	4
			University arts programs rating	8	5	Children's museum rating	6	3

Eau Claire, WI

Score: 61.8   Rank: 135

Profile: Small town
Location: North-central Wisconsin
Elevation: 838 feet
Time zone: Central Standard Time

PRO
Attractive downtown
Strong economy
Outdoor recreation

CON
Cold winters
Entertainment
Low ethnic diversity

Eau Claire lies in northwest Wisconsin, along I-94 about 80 miles east of the Mississippi River and Minneapolis-St. Paul. A former logging town with a diversified industry today, Eau Claire is a gateway to wilderness and recreation areas to the north and northeast. The attractive town has older buildings and shady streets along a graceful bend in the Chippewa River. Typical of a small Wisconsin town are the low cost of living and crime, and clean, attractive surroundings. The small-town atmosphere so near to Minneapolis–St. Paul is also a plus, but Eau Claire itself offers little to do and winters are harsh.

Eau Claire sits in the scenic Chippewa Valley at the convergence of the Chippewa and Eau Claire rivers. The immediate terrain is level with wooded hills rising in all directions from town. The landscape flattens to the west toward the Mississippi River and many lakes are to the north. The continental climate and location near major storm tracks bring wide fluctuations in temperature and precipitation. Summers are warm with moderate humidity and periods of warmer weather. Winters are cold with varying humidity and outbreaks of bitter cold following storm systems arriving from the west. Summer precipitation occurs mainly as thunderstorms, while snowfall and snow cover persists all winter. The valley location can result in fog on cool nights. The city's position to the west of the Great Lakes means more sunny days than other Wisconsin cities. First freeze is late September, last is mid-May.

POPULATION

DEMOGRAPHICS	AREA	U.S. AVG	ETHNIC COMPOSITION	AREA	U.S. AVG	RESIDENT PROFILE	AREA	U.S. AVG
Population	150,295		White	97.1%	75.1%	Single	40.5%	43.6%
Population density per sq. mile	91.2	447.3	Black	.9%	12.3%	Married	59.5%	56.4%
Population growth	9.3%	16.1%	Asian	1.3%	3.6%	Divorced	6.9%	8.4%
Median age	34.9	35.5	American Indian	.5%	.9%	Separated	1.5%	3.0%
Average family size	2.6	2.7	Hispanic	.6%	12.5%	Married with children	30.2%	28.7%
			Diversity measure	8.5%	35.2%	Single with children	8.2%	10.1%

ECONOMY & JOBS SCORE: 37/RANK: 206

INCOME	AREA	U.S. AVG	EMPLOYMENT	AREA	U.S. AVG	LARGEST EMPLOYING INDUSTRY
Per capita income	$22,183	$23,420	Unemployment rate	4.7%	6.1%	Computer and Electronic Product Manufacturing
Household income	$43,031	$46,060	Recent job growth	1.2%	.9%	
Household income < $25K	27.0%	26.4%	Projected future job growth	22.6%	15.1%	
Household income > $75K	21.1%	24.5%	White collar	48.7%	54.5%	
Household income growth	65.9%	57.3%	Blue collar	51.3%	45.5%	

COST OF LIVING SCORE: 44/RANK: 183

INDEXES & TAXES	AREA	U.S. AVG	HOUSING	AREA	U.S. AVG	NECESSITIES	AREA	U.S. AVG
Cost of Living Index	92.1	100.0	Median home price	$113,190	$160,100	Food Index	99.6	100.0
Financial Progress Index	99.6	100.0	Home price appreciation	6.7%	7.1%	Housing Index	70.3	100.0
Income tax rate	6.930%	4.625%	Median rent	$530	$670	Utilities Index	135.0	100.0
Sales tax rate	5.500%	6.474%	Homes owned	65.6%	63.9%	Transportation Index	101.4	100.0
Property tax rate	$23.1	$15.6	Homes rented	19.2%	25.3%	Healthcare Index	107.3	100.0
			Housing affordability	61.0%	54.5%	Miscellaneous Cost Index	97.6	100.0

CLIMATE SCORE: 12/RANK: 290

TEMPERATURE	AREA	U.S. AVG	PRECIPITATION	AREA	U.S. AVG	COMFORTS & HAZARDS	AREA	U.S. AVG
January low	3.2°F	26.4°F	Annual inches precipitation	26.0	35.9	July relative humidity	69.0%	68.8%
July high	82.4°F	86.7°F	Annual inches snowfall	46.0	24.2	Annual days mostly sunny	200	212
Annual days > 90°F	15	38	Annual days precipitation	113	111	Annual days with thunderstorms	36	39
Annual days < 32°F	158	88	Annual days rain > 0.5 inches	15	23	Tornado risk score	24	19
Annual days < 0°F	34	6	Annual days snow > 1.5 inches	11	6	Hurricane risk score	0	15

TEMPERATURE

PRECIPITATION

DAYS OF CLOUDS & PRECIPITATION

EDUCATION SCORE: 63/RANK: 120

ACHIEVEMENT	AREA	U.S. AVG	PUBLIC SCHOOLS	AREA	U.S. AVG	HIGHER EDUCATION	AREA	U.S. AVG
High school degree	87.1%	80.2%	Expenditures per pupil	$6,917	$5,894	No. 2-year colleges	1	3
2-year college degree	9.4%	6.2%	Student/teacher ratio	14.9	16.7	No. 4-year colleges/universities	1	4
4-year college degree	15.2%	15.8%	Attending public school	87.6%	90.2%	No. highly ranked universities	0	1
Graduate/professional degree	7.0%	9.6%	State SAT score	1179	1020			
			State ACT score	22.2*	21.0			

HEALTH & HEALTHCARE SCORE: 85/RANK: 48

CRIME SCORE: 80/RANK: 66

HAZARDS & ILLNESSES	AREA	U.S. AVG	HEALTHCARE	AREA	U.S. AVG	CRIME	AREA	U.S. AVG
Air-quality score	24	45	Physicians per capita	282.8	261.1	Violent crime rate	129.2	456.0
Water-quality score	74	33	Hospital beds per capita	529.2	432.2	Change in violent crime rate	-16.8%	-17.2%
Pollen/allergy score	44	61	No. teaching hospitals	2	4	Property crime rate	3,079.1	3,950.0
Stress score	12	50	Cost per doctor visit	$92	$67	Change in property crime rate	-8.9%	-16.8%
Cancer mortality per capita	158.0	169.0	Cost per dental visit	$86	$82			
Depression days per month	3.3	2.8	Cost per daily hospital room	$413	$733			

TRANSPORTATION SCORE: 70/RANK: 99

COMMUTE	AREA	U.S. AVG	INTERCITY SERVICES	AREA	U.S. AVG	AUTOMOTIVE	AREA	U.S. AVG
Average commute time	18.7 min.	22.6 min.	Miles to nearest major airport	85	46	Insurance, annual premium	$758	$1,011
Commute by auto	79.7%	88.7%	Type of local airport	Large		Gas, cost per gallon	$1.61	$1.50
Commute by mass transit	.6%	1.8%	No. daily airline departures	624	294	Daily vehicle miles per capita	25.0	23.0
Work at home	12.2%	3.9%	Amtrak service	No				
Mass transit miles per capita	7.0	8.0	No. interstate highways	1	1			

LEISURE SCORE: 25/RANK: 250

DINING & SHOPPING	AREA	U.S. AVG	ENTERTAINMENT	AREA	U.S. AVG	OUTDOOR ACTIVITIES	AREA	U.S. AVG
Restaurant rating	1	1	Professional sports rating	2	4	Golf-course rating	1	4
No. outlet malls	0	2	College sports rating	5	4	Ski-area rating	2	4
No. Starbucks	0	11	Zoo/aquarium rating	1	3	National Park rating	1	3
No. warehouse clubs	3	4	Amusement park rating	1	3	Sq. miles inland water	4.0	4.0
			Botanical garden/arboretum rating	1	3	Miles of coastline	0.0	11.4

ARTS & CULTURE SCORE: 46/RANK: 173

MEDIA & LIBRARIES	AREA	U.S. AVG	PERFORMING ARTS	AREA	U.S. AVG	MUSEUMS	AREA	U.S. AVG
Arts radio rating	1	3	Classical music rating	3	4	Overall museum rating	3	6
No. public libraries	10	28	Ballet/dance rating	1	3	Art museum rating	2	5
Library volumes per capita	3.7	2.8	Professional theater rating	1	3	Science museum rating	1	4
			University arts programs rating	4	5	Children's museum rating	1	3

El Paso, TX

Score: 50.4   Rank: 225

Profile: Mid-size city
Location: Extreme west Texas on the Rio Grande at the
  Mexico–New Mexico border
Elevation: 3,700 feet
Time zone: Mountain Standard Time

PRO
Cost of living
Dry climate
Mild winters

CON
Isolation
Violent crime
Economy

El Paso is a unique American city rather like an island in the sea. Self-sufficient and surprisingly large, the city has a modern downtown, with a commercial district and low skyscrapers, and development spreading mostly to the north and east. Because of its isolation, large industry has never taken root, but the area does have some agriculture, ranching, mining, oil, and "maquiladora" industry powered by low-cost labor from Mexico. Fort Bliss brings a military presence to the economic and social base. There is an assortment of small museums mostly commemorating the history of the area, and the University of Texas at El Paso adds 16,000 students, a nice campus, and some sports amenities. Nearby geologic areas and the Franklin Mountains State Park offer some outdoor recreational opportunities. The climate, low cost of living, and the "get-away-from-it-all" isolation have made it a popular retirement location. The area is hundreds of miles from a city of any size, but the independent spirit and the availability of low-cost airline flights make the area less isolated than geography may imply.

The city is located in a flat valley among dry hills. The Rio Grande flows along the southwest border of the city. The Franklin Mountains begin within the city limits and extend northward with peaks up to 7,200 feet. The climate is characterized by an abundance of sunshine throughout the year, high daytime summer temperatures, very low humidity, scant rainfall, and a relatively mild winter season. Daytime summer temperatures are frequently above 90°F, and occasionally above 100°F, but nights are usually comfortable. Winter daytime temperatures are mild with freezing night temperatures common during mid-winter. Rainfall throughout the year is light and insufficient for any growth except desert vegetation. Dry periods lasting several months are not unusual. Most precipitation occurs July through September from brief but often heavy thunderstorms. Small amounts of snow fall nearly every winter but seldom remain on the ground for more than a few hours. Spring dust storms and sandstorms can occur.

POPULATION

DEMOGRAPHICS	AREA	U.S. AVG	ETHNIC COMPOSITION	AREA	U.S. AVG	RESIDENT PROFILE	AREA	U.S. AVG
Population	697,562		White	76.9%	75.1%	Single	46.3%	43.6%
Population density per sq. mile	688.5	447.3	Black	6.3%	12.3%	Married	53.7%	56.4%
Population growth	17.9%	16.1%	Asian	1.8%	3.6%	Divorced	7.6%	8.4%
Median age	30.1	35.5	American Indian	.5%	.9%	Separated	4.3%	3.0%
Average family size	3.3	2.7	Hispanic	72.6%	12.5%	Married with children	41.3%	28.7%
			Diversity measure	42.0%	35.2%	Single with children	15.1%	10.1%

ECONOMY & JOBS
SCORE: 26/RANK: 244

INCOME	AREA	U.S. AVG	EMPLOYMENT	AREA	U.S. AVG	LARGEST EMPLOYING INDUSTRY
Per capita income	$13,867	$23,420	Unemployment rate	9.8%	6.1%	Apparel Manufacturing
Household income	$31,932	$46,060	Recent job growth	4.3%	.9%	
Household income < $25K	37.7%	26.4%	Projected future job growth	19.6%	15.1%	
Household income > $75K	13.0%	24.5%	White collar	49.9%	54.5%	
Household income growth	40.9%	57.3%	Blue collar	50.1%	45.5%	

COST OF LIVING
SCORE: 73/RANK: 89

INDEXES & TAXES	AREA	U.S. AVG	HOUSING	AREA	U.S. AVG	NECESSITIES	AREA	U.S. AVG
Cost of Living Index	83.1	100.0	Median home price	$92,100	$160,100	Food Index	102.0	100.0
Financial Progress Index	81.9	100.0	Home price appreciation	4.3%	7.1%	Housing Index	57.2	100.0
Income tax rate	0.000%	4.625%	Median rent	$569	$670	Utilities Index	97.3	100.0
Sales tax rate	8.250%	6.474%	Homes owned	52.6%	63.9%	Transportation Index	103.6	100.0
Property tax rate	$24.9	$15.6	Homes rented	42.8%	25.3%	Healthcare Index	94.9	100.0
			Housing affordability	50.0%	54.5%	Miscellaneous Cost Index	92.3	100.0

CLIMATE SCORE: 88/RANK: 40

TEMPERATURE	AREA	U.S. AVG	PRECIPITATION	AREA	U.S. AVG	COMFORTS & HAZARDS	AREA	U.S. AVG
January low	30.2°F	26.4°F	Annual inches precipitation	8.0	35.9	July relative humidity	39.0%	68.8%
July high	94.9°F	86.7°F	Annual inches snowfall	5.0	24.2	Annual days mostly sunny	294	212
Annual days > 90°F	103	38	Annual days precipitation	45	111	Annual days with thunderstorms	36	39
Annual days < 32°F	64	88	Annual days rain > 0.5 inches	6	23	Tornado risk score	3	19
Annual days < 0°F	0	6	Annual days snow > 1.5 inches	2	6	Hurricane risk score	2	15

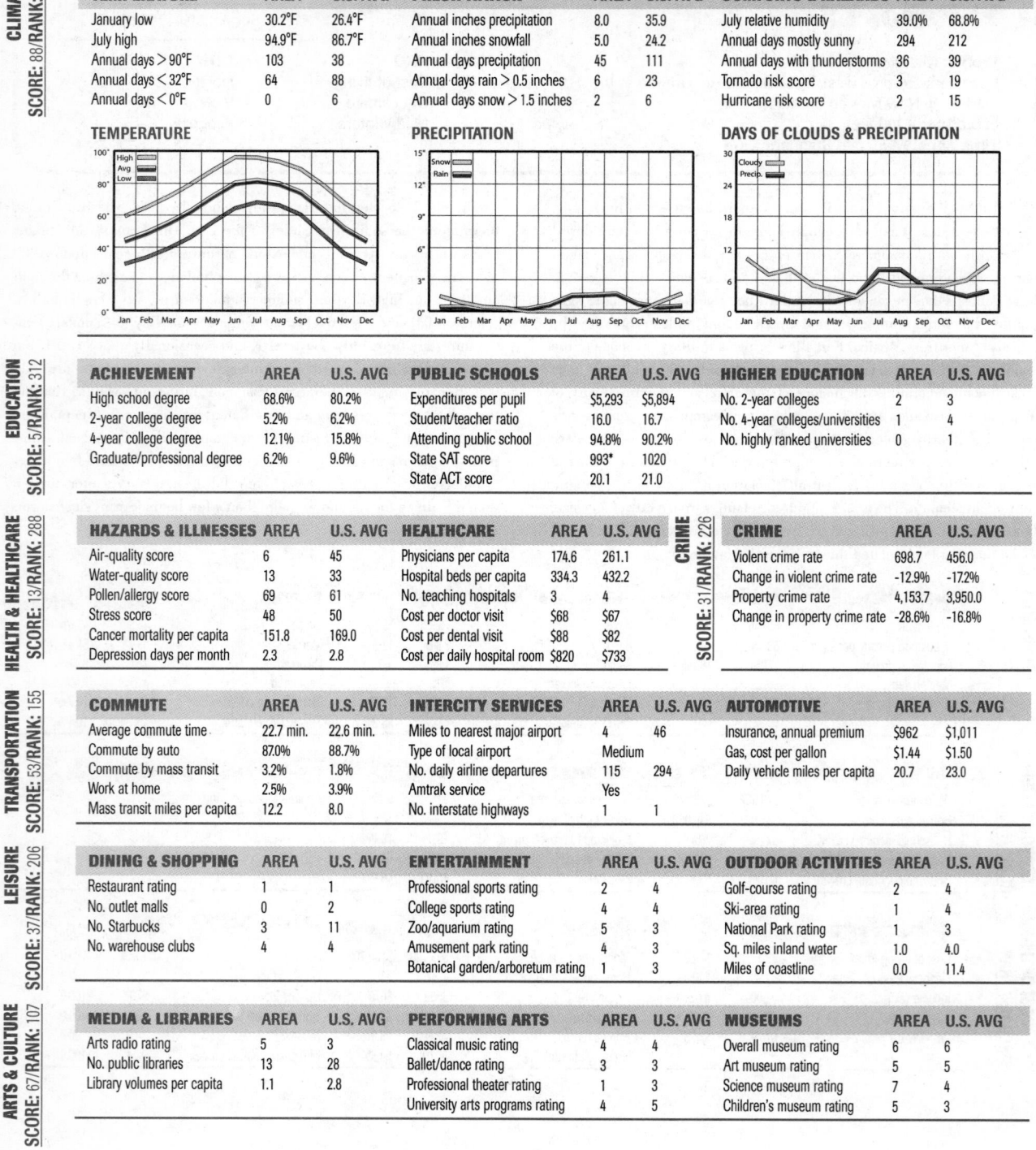

TEMPERATURE — High / Avg / Low

PRECIPITATION — Snow / Rain

DAYS OF CLOUDS & PRECIPITATION — Cloudy / Precip.

EDUCATION SCORE: 5/RANK: 312

ACHIEVEMENT	AREA	U.S. AVG	PUBLIC SCHOOLS	AREA	U.S. AVG	HIGHER EDUCATION	AREA	U.S. AVG
High school degree	68.6%	80.2%	Expenditures per pupil	$5,293	$5,894	No. 2-year colleges	2	3
2-year college degree	5.2%	6.2%	Student/teacher ratio	16.0	16.7	No. 4-year colleges/universities	1	4
4-year college degree	12.1%	15.8%	Attending public school	94.8%	90.2%	No. highly ranked universities	0	1
Graduate/professional degree	6.2%	9.6%	State SAT score	993*	1020			
			State ACT score	20.1	21.0			

HEALTH & HEALTHCARE SCORE: 13/RANK: 288

CRIME SCORE: 31/RANK: 226

HAZARDS & ILLNESSES	AREA	U.S. AVG	HEALTHCARE	AREA	U.S. AVG	CRIME	AREA	U.S. AVG
Air-quality score	6	45	Physicians per capita	174.6	261.1	Violent crime rate	698.7	456.0
Water-quality score	13	33	Hospital beds per capita	334.3	432.2	Change in violent crime rate	-12.9%	-17.2%
Pollen/allergy score	69	61	No. teaching hospitals	3	4	Property crime rate	4,153.7	3,950.0
Stress score	48	50	Cost per doctor visit	$68	$67	Change in property crime rate	-28.6%	-16.8%
Cancer mortality per capita	151.8	169.0	Cost per dental visit	$88	$82			
Depression days per month	2.3	2.8	Cost per daily hospital room	$820	$733			

TRANSPORTATION SCORE: 53/RANK: 155

COMMUTE	AREA	U.S. AVG	INTERCITY SERVICES	AREA	U.S. AVG	AUTOMOTIVE	AREA	U.S. AVG
Average commute time	22.7 min.	22.6 min.	Miles to nearest major airport	4	46	Insurance, annual premium	$962	$1,011
Commute by auto	87.0%	88.7%	Type of local airport	Medium		Gas, cost per gallon	$1.44	$1.50
Commute by mass transit	3.2%	1.8%	No. daily airline departures	115	294	Daily vehicle miles per capita	20.7	23.0
Work at home	2.5%	3.9%	Amtrak service	Yes				
Mass transit miles per capita	12.2	8.0	No. interstate highways	1	1			

LEISURE SCORE: 37/RANK: 206

DINING & SHOPPING	AREA	U.S. AVG	ENTERTAINMENT	AREA	U.S. AVG	OUTDOOR ACTIVITIES	AREA	U.S. AVG
Restaurant rating	1	1	Professional sports rating	2	4	Golf-course rating	2	4
No. outlet malls	0	2	College sports rating	4	4	Ski-area rating	1	4
No. Starbucks	3	11	Zoo/aquarium rating	5	3	National Park rating	1	3
No. warehouse clubs	4	4	Amusement park rating	4	3	Sq. miles inland water	1.0	4.0
			Botanical garden/arboretum rating	1	3	Miles of coastline	0.0	11.4

ARTS & CULTURE SCORE: 67/RANK: 107

MEDIA & LIBRARIES	AREA	U.S. AVG	PERFORMING ARTS	AREA	U.S. AVG	MUSEUMS	AREA	U.S. AVG
Arts radio rating	5	3	Classical music rating	4	4	Overall museum rating	6	6
No. public libraries	13	28	Ballet/dance rating	3	3	Art museum rating	5	5
Library volumes per capita	1.1	2.8	Professional theater rating	1	3	Science museum rating	7	4
			University arts programs rating	4	5	Children's museum rating	5	3

Elkhart-Goshen, IN

Score: 41.4   **Rank:** 272

Profile: Small-manufacturing-town complex
Location: Extreme northern Indiana at Michigan border, 15 miles east of South Bend
Elevation: 700 feet
Time zone: Eastern Standard Time (no daylight savings time)

PRO	CON
Small-town atmosphere	Harsh winters
Nearby recreation	Economic cycles
Nearby college town	Low educational attainment

Elkhart, a small industrial town, has a diversified manufacturing base. A typical small Midwestern town, Goshen, to the southeast, has an agricultural base, an extension of some Elkhart manufacturing, and Goshen College. The industrial base has some unique components. Elkhart is the U.S. center for the manufacture of recreational vehicles, marching band instruments, and firefighting equipment. Among other areas with this profile, Elkhart and Goshen have a better-than-average set of museums. There is also a large Amish and Mennonite community east of Goshen. Even with the economic diversity, the area is vulnerable to economic cycles, particularly in the RV industry. Educational attainment is low and crime rates are relatively high for a small town.

Most of the area is a level glacial plain with mixed agriculture and wooded areas. Downwind Lake-Michigan effects govern weather in all seasons. Summers are warm and humid but subject to cooling lake breezes. The lake moderates temperatures somewhat but creates high humidity, frequent cloudiness, and heavy winter snows. First freeze is early October, last is early May.

POPULATION

DEMOGRAPHICS	AREA	U.S. AVG	ETHNIC COMPOSITION	AREA	U.S. AVG	RESIDENT PROFILE	AREA	U.S. AVG
Population	186,465		White	94.7%	75.1%	Single	38.3%	43.6%
Population density per sq. mile	402.0	447.3	Black	3.6%	12.3%	Married	61.7%	56.4%
Population growth	19.4%	16.1%	Asian	.9%	3.6%	Divorced	8.2%	8.4%
Median age	33.3	35.5	American Indian	.3%	.9%	Separated	1.8%	3.0%
Average family size	2.8	2.7	Hispanic	2.2%	12.5%	Married with children	33.0%	28.7%
			Diversity measure	28.6%	35.2%	Single with children	9.4%	10.1%

ECONOMY & JOBS — SCORE: 99/RANK: 4

INCOME	AREA	U.S. AVG	EMPLOYMENT	AREA	U.S. AVG	LARGEST EMPLOYING INDUSTRY
Per capita income	$23,033	$23,420	Unemployment rate	4.4%	6.1%	Transportation Equipment Manufacturing
Household income	$49,970	$46,060	Recent job growth	6.3%	.9%	
Household income < $25K	19.2%	26.4%	Projected future job growth	11.0%	15.1%	
Household income > $75K	24.0%	24.5%	White collar	47.0%	54.5%	
Household income growth	61.3%	57.3%	Blue collar	53.0%	45.5%	

COST OF LIVING — SCORE: 63/RANK: 122

INDEXES & TAXES	AREA	U.S. AVG	HOUSING	AREA	U.S. AVG	NECESSITIES	AREA	U.S. AVG
Cost of Living Index	87.3	100.0	Median home price	$110,150	$160,100	Food Index	95.8	100.0
Financial Progress Index	122.0	100.0	Home price appreciation	3.9%	7.1%	Housing Index	68.4	100.0
Income tax rate	4.650%	4.625%	Median rent	$579	$670	Utilities Index	111.0	100.0
Sales tax rate	6.000%	6.474%	Homes owned	73.4%	63.9%	Transportation Index	97.1	100.0
Property tax rate	$15.3	$15.6	Homes rented	21.6%	25.3%	Healthcare Index	97.3	100.0
			Housing affordability	65.0%	54.5%	Miscellaneous Cost Index	95.4	100.0

CLIMATE — SCORE: 27/RANK: 241

TEMPERATURE	AREA	U.S. AVG	PRECIPITATION	AREA	U.S. AVG	COMFORTS & HAZARDS	AREA	U.S. AVG
January low	17.5°F	26.4°F	Annual inches precipitation	35.0	35.9	July relative humidity	72.0%	68.8%
July high	84.0°F	86.7°F	Annual inches snowfall	35.0	24.2	Annual days mostly sunny	182	212
Annual days > 90°F	14	38	Annual days precipitation	131	111	Annual days with thunderstorms	41	39
Annual days < 32°F	134	88	Annual days rain > 0.5 inches	22	23	Tornado risk score	100	19
Annual days < 0°F	10	6	Annual days snow > 1.5 inches	12	6	Hurricane risk score	2	15

TEMPERATURE

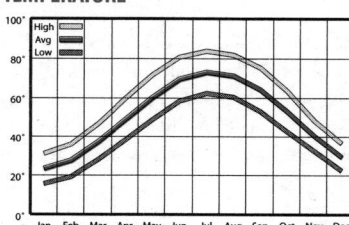

PRECIPITATION

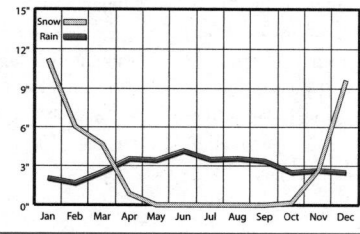

DAYS OF CLOUDS & PRECIPITATION

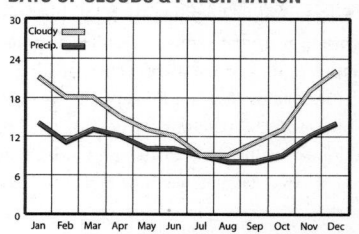

EDUCATION SCORE: 5/RANK: 314

ACHIEVEMENT	AREA	U.S. AVG	PUBLIC SCHOOLS	AREA	U.S. AVG	HIGHER EDUCATION	AREA	U.S. AVG
High school degree	75.7%	80.2%	Expenditures per pupil	$6,232	$5,894	No. 2-year colleges	0	3
2-year college degree	4.1%	6.2%	Student/teacher ratio	18.0	16.7	No. 4-year colleges/universities	1	4
4-year college degree	10.0%	15.8%	Attending public school	90.5%	90.2%	No. highly ranked universities	0	1
Graduate/professional degree	5.6%	9.6%	State SAT score	1004*	1020			
			State ACT score	21.6	21.0			

HEALTH & HEALTHCARE SCORE: 45/RANK: 180

HAZARDS & ILLNESSES	AREA	U.S. AVG	HEALTHCARE	AREA	U.S. AVG
Air-quality score	24	45	Physicians per capita	130.3	261.1
Water-quality score	30	33	Hospital beds per capita	273.5	432.2
Pollen/allergy score	56	61	No. teaching hospitals	0	4
Stress score	22	50	Cost per doctor visit	$64	$67
Cancer mortality per capita	156.5	169.0	Cost per dental visit	$73	$82
Depression days per month	2.0	2.8	Cost per daily hospital room	$567	$733

CRIME SCORE: 38/RANK: 205

CRIME	AREA	U.S. AVG
Violent crime rate	339.5	456.0
Change in violent crime rate	-37.2%	-17.2%
Property crime rate	4,416.3	3,950.0
Change in property crime rate	-1.4%	-16.8%

TRANSPORTATION SCORE: 64/RANK: 122

COMMUTE	AREA	U.S. AVG	INTERCITY SERVICES	AREA	U.S. AVG	AUTOMOTIVE	AREA	U.S. AVG
Average commute time	18.4 min.	22.6 min.	Miles to nearest major airport	18	46	Insurance, annual premium	$771	$1,011
Commute by auto	90.1%	88.7%	Type of local airport	Small		Gas, cost per gallon	$1.44	$1.50
Commute by mass transit	.4%	1.8%	No. daily airline departures	54	294	Daily vehicle miles per capita	29.4	23.0
Work at home	4.8%	3.9%	Amtrak service	Yes				
Mass transit miles per capita	3.4	8.0	No. interstate highways	1	1			

LEISURE SCORE: 4/RANK: 316

DINING & SHOPPING	AREA	U.S. AVG	ENTERTAINMENT	AREA	U.S. AVG	OUTDOOR ACTIVITIES	AREA	U.S. AVG
Restaurant rating	1	1	Professional sports rating	2	4	Golf-course rating	2	4
No. outlet malls	2	2	College sports rating	2	4	Ski-area rating	1	4
No. Starbucks	0	11	Zoo/aquarium rating	1	3	National Park rating	1	3
No. warehouse clubs	3	4	Amusement park rating	1	3	Sq. miles inland water	2.0	4.0
			Botanical garden/arboretum rating	1	3	Miles of coastline	0.0	11.4

ARTS & CULTURE SCORE: 42/RANK: 192

MEDIA & LIBRARIES	AREA	U.S. AVG	PERFORMING ARTS	AREA	U.S. AVG	MUSEUMS	AREA	U.S. AVG
Arts radio rating	1	3	Classical music rating	4	4	Overall museum rating	5	6
No. public libraries	9	28	Ballet/dance rating	1	3	Art museum rating	3	5
Library volumes per capita	4.7	2.8	Professional theater rating	1	3	Science museum rating	1	4
			University arts programs rating	8	5	Children's museum rating	1	3

Elmira, NY

Score: 37.6   Rank: 288

Profile: Small town
Location: Western New York along Pennsylvania border south of the Finger Lakes region
Elevation: 903 feet
Time zone: Eastern Standard Time

PRO	CON
Cost of living	Winter climate
Nearby recreation	Economy
Low crime rate	Arts and culture

Elmira is a quiet, nondescript town in the hills of southwestern New York. The economic base is fairly diverse, with the nearby Corning Glass Works benefiting from the fiber-optics boom in the 1990s. The downturn in that industry resulted in some local job losses. There isn't much to do and the area is somewhat geographically isolated from other cities, but the popular Finger Lakes region and well-known Watkins Glen International Speedway are nearby. The Cost of Living Index at 81.8 is the lowest in the state. Although the location is far enough south to escape the worst lake effects in winter, that season is still harsh.

The city sits in a creek valley surrounded by hills with hardwood forests. The climate is continental with some lake effect that moderates temperatures and produces clouds and precipitation year-round. Summer temperatures are pleasant with only a few days above 90°F, but humidity is high and the valleys trap both warm and cold air. Winters are cold and variable with periods of clouds, rain, snow squalls, and heavier snows. While wind and snowfall are slightly less than areas near the Great Lakes, below-zero temperatures are common. First freeze is October 1, last is early May.

POPULATION

DEMOGRAPHICS	AREA	U.S. AVG	ETHNIC COMPOSITION	AREA	U.S. AVG	RESIDENT PROFILE	AREA	U.S. AVG
Population	90,614		White	92.8%	75.1%	Single	41.6%	43.6%
Population density per sq. mile	222.0	447.3	Black	4.9%	12.3%	Married	58.4%	56.4%
Population growth	-4.8%	16.1%	Asian	1.3%	3.6%	Divorced	7.3%	8.4%
Median age	38.4	35.5	American Indian	.3%	.9%	Separated	3.7%	3.0%
Average family size	2.6	2.7	Hispanic	2.4%	12.5%	Married with children	29.0%	28.7%
			Diversity measure	18.4%	35.2%	Single with children	10.1%	10.1%

ECONOMY & JOBS
SCORE: 53/RANK: 154

INCOME	AREA	U.S. AVG	EMPLOYMENT	AREA	U.S. AVG	LARGEST EMPLOYING INDUSTRY
Per capita income	$19,726	$23,420	Unemployment rate	6.0%	6.1%	Computer and Electronic Product Manufacturing
Household income	$38,514	$46,060	Recent job growth	-.7%	.9%	
Household income < $25K	31.0%	26.4%	Projected future job growth	2.6%	15.1%	
Household income > $75K	16.8%	24.5%	White collar	52.2%	54.5%	
Household income growth	47.2%	57.3%	Blue collar	47.8%	45.5%	

COST OF LIVING
SCORE: 50/RANK: 163

INDEXES & TAXES	AREA	U.S. AVG	HOUSING	AREA	U.S. AVG	NECESSITIES	AREA	U.S. AVG
Cost of Living Index	81.8	100.0	Median home price	$83,310	$160,100	Food Index	96.0	100.0
Financial Progress Index	100.4	100.0	Home price appreciation	7.4%	7.1%	Housing Index	51.7	100.0
Income tax rate	7.125%	4.625%	Median rent	$518	$670	Utilities Index	116.3	100.0
Sales tax rate	8.000%	6.474%	Homes owned	74.8%	63.9%	Transportation Index	96.4	100.0
Property tax rate	$32.5	$15.6	Homes rented	18.2%	25.3%	Healthcare Index	89.0	100.0
			Housing affordability	56.0%	54.5%	Miscellaneous Cost Index	98.2	100.0

CLIMATE
SCORE: 7/RANK: 307

TEMPERATURE	AREA	U.S. AVG	PRECIPITATION	AREA	U.S. AVG	COMFORTS & HAZARDS	AREA	U.S. AVG
January low	15.0°F	26.4°F	Annual inches precipitation	37.0	35.9	July relative humidity	75.0%	68.8%
July high	79.0°F	86.7°F	Annual inches snowfall	82.0	24.2	Annual days mostly sunny	151	212
Annual days > 90°F	3	38	Annual days precipitation	159	111	Annual days with thunderstorms	29	39
Annual days < 32°F	145	88	Annual days rain > 0.5 inches	22	23	Tornado risk score	2	19
Annual days < 0°F	8	6	Annual days snow > 1.5 inches	15	6	Hurricane risk score	5	15

TEMPERATURE

PRECIPITATION

DAYS OF CLOUDS & PRECIPITATION

EDUCATION
SCORE: 51/RANK: 162

ACHIEVEMENT	AREA	U.S. AVG	PUBLIC SCHOOLS	AREA	U.S. AVG	HIGHER EDUCATION	AREA	U.S. AVG
High school degree	82.1%	80.2%	Expenditures per pupil	$8,130	$5,894	No. 2-year colleges	0	3
2-year college degree	8.8%	6.2%	Student/teacher ratio	14.3	16.7	No. 4-year colleges/universities	1	4
4-year college degree	10.4%	15.8%	Attending public school	88.3%	90.2%	No. highly ranked universities	1	1
Graduate/professional degree	8.1%	9.6%	State SAT score	1006*	1020			
			State ACT score	22.3	21.0			

HEALTH & HEALTHCARE
SCORE: 70/RANK: 98

CRIME
SCORE: 79/RANK: 69

HAZARDS & ILLNESSES	AREA	U.S. AVG	HEALTHCARE	AREA	U.S. AVG	CRIME	AREA	U.S. AVG
Air-quality score	59	45	Physicians per capita	251.6	261.1	Violent crime rate	257.3	456.0
Water-quality score	49	33	Hospital beds per capita	792.8	432.2	Change in violent crime rate	5.5%	-17.2%
Pollen/allergy score	57	61	No. teaching hospitals	0	4	Property crime rate	2,788.7	3,950.0
Stress score	30	50	Cost per doctor visit	$68	$67	Change in property crime rate	-21.5%	-16.8%
Cancer mortality per capita	185.0	169.0	Cost per dental visit	$68	$82			
Depression days per month	2.2	2.8	Cost per daily hospital room	$781	$733			

TRANSPORTATION
SCORE: 83/RANK: 53

COMMUTE	AREA	U.S. AVG	INTERCITY SERVICES	AREA	U.S. AVG	AUTOMOTIVE	AREA	U.S. AVG
Average commute time	19.3 min.	22.6 min.	Miles to nearest major airport	79	46	Insurance, annual premium	$1,266	$1,011
Commute by auto	92.5%	88.7%	Type of local airport	Small		Gas, cost per gallon	$1.57	$1.50
Commute by mass transit	1.0%	1.8%	No. daily airline departures	129	294	Daily vehicle miles per capita	25.9	23.0
Work at home	2.5%	3.9%	Amtrak service	No				
Mass transit miles per capita	14.6	8.0	No. interstate highways	1	1			

LEISURE SCORE: 48/RANK: 171

DINING & SHOPPING	AREA	U.S. AVG	ENTERTAINMENT	AREA	U.S. AVG	OUTDOOR ACTIVITIES	AREA	U.S. AVG
Restaurant rating	1	1	Professional sports rating	3	4	Golf-course rating	2	4
No. outlet malls	1	2	College sports rating	1	4	Ski-area rating	1	4
No. Starbucks	0	11	Zoo/aquarium rating	1	3	National Park rating	1	3
No. warehouse clubs	3	4	Amusement park rating	1	3	Sq. miles inland water	1.0	4.0
			Botanical garden/arboretum rating	1	3	Miles of coastline	0.0	11.4

ARTS & CULTURE SCORE: 18/RANK: 270

MEDIA & LIBRARIES	AREA	U.S. AVG	PERFORMING ARTS	AREA	U.S. AVG	MUSEUMS	AREA	U.S. AVG
Arts radio rating	1	3	Classical music rating	1	4	Overall museum rating	5	6
No. public libraries	7	28	Ballet/dance rating	1	3	Art museum rating	2	5
Library volumes per capita	3.2	2.8	Professional theater rating	1	3	Science museum rating	6	4
			University arts programs rating	2	5	Children's museum rating	3	3

Enid, OK

Score: 48.4   **Rank:** 238

Profile: Military town
Location: North-central Oklahoma, 50 miles south of Kansas border
Elevation: 994 feet
Time zone: Central Standard Time

PRO	CON
Cost of living	Entertainment
Small-town atmosphere	Arts and culture
Stable economy	Isolation

A small oil town, Enid is home to Vance Air Force Base. This fairly plain town holds a few surprises. The main attraction is a low cost of living (COL Index 76.8) and housing (median home price $69,240, 7th lowest in the U.S.). The area has a stable employment base and good healthcare mainly resulting from the military presence. In 2001, the town won a National Trust for Historic Preservation Great American Main Street Award. But it offers few cultural, recreational, and service amenities and is somewhat isolated with Oklahoma City 100 miles to the south.

The terrain is mainly flat, grassland plain. The climate is Great Plains continental with some Gulf of Mexico influence. Summers are hot with frequent readings over 100°F, and periods of humidity bring discomfort. Winters fluctuate between the cold, dry winters of the north and more mild winters of the Gulf region. The area is vulnerable to severe weather when Gulf moisture and cooler, drier northern air collide. Winter brings a mix of rain, sleet, and snow with frequent changes. First freeze is early November, last is early April.

POPULATION

DEMOGRAPHICS	AREA	U.S. AVG	ETHNIC COMPOSITION	AREA	U.S. AVG	RESIDENT PROFILE	AREA	U.S. AVG
Population	57,246		White	94.6%	75.1%	Single	34.0%	43.6%
Population density per sq. mile	54.1	447.3	Black	1.7%	12.3%	Married	66.0%	56.4%
Population growth	.9%	16.1%	Asian	.7%	3.6%	Divorced	7.5%	8.4%
Median age	38.0	35.5	American Indian	2.3%	.9%	Separated	1.3%	3.0%
Average family size	2.5	2.7	Hispanic	2.4%	12.5%	Married with children	29.6%	28.7%
			Diversity measure	23.6%	35.2%	Single with children	7.6%	10.1%

ECONOMY & JOBS SCORE: 95/RANK: 17

INCOME	AREA	U.S. AVG	EMPLOYMENT	AREA	U.S. AVG	LARGEST EMPLOYING INDUSTRY
Per capita income	$18,039	$23,420	Unemployment rate	3.1%	6.1%	Healthcare and Social Assistance
Household income	$34,287	$46,060	Recent job growth	6.6%	.9%	
Household income < $25K	35.0%	26.4%	Projected future job growth	7.9%	15.1%	
Household income > $75K	11.9%	24.5%	White collar	49.8%	54.5%	
Household income growth	46.8%	57.3%	Blue collar	50.2%	45.5%	

COST OF LIVING SCORE: 88/RANK: 40

INDEXES & TAXES	AREA	U.S. AVG	HOUSING	AREA	U.S. AVG	NECESSITIES	AREA	U.S. AVG
Cost of Living Index	76.8	100.0	Median home price	$69,240	$160,100	Food Index	92.9	100.0
Financial Progress Index	95.1	100.0	Home price appreciation	5.6%	7.1%	Housing Index	43.0	100.0
Income tax rate	7.000%	4.625%	Median rent	$429	$670	Utilities Index	98.1	100.0
Sales tax rate	7.600%	6.474%	Homes owned	70.4%	63.9%	Transportation Index	91.5	100.0
Property tax rate	$11.1	$15.6	Homes rented	15.4%	25.3%	Healthcare Index	94.4	100.0
			Housing affordability	67.0%	54.5%	Miscellaneous Cost Index	99.9	100.0

CLIMATE   SCORE: 70/RANK: 99

TEMPERATURE	AREA	U.S. AVG	PRECIPITATION	AREA	U.S. AVG	COMFORTS & HAZARDS	AREA	U.S. AVG
January low	26.0°F	26.4°F	Annual inches precipitation	33.0	35.9	July relative humidity	65.0%	68.8%
July high	92.6°F	86.7°F	Annual inches snowfall	9.0	24.2	Annual days mostly sunny	237	212
Annual days > 90°F	64	38	Annual days precipitation	81	111	Annual days with thunderstorms	50	39
Annual days < 32°F	80	88	Annual days rain > 0.5 inches	23	23	Tornado risk score	32	19
Annual days < 0°F	0	6	Annual days snow > 1.5 inches	3	6	Hurricane risk score	2	15

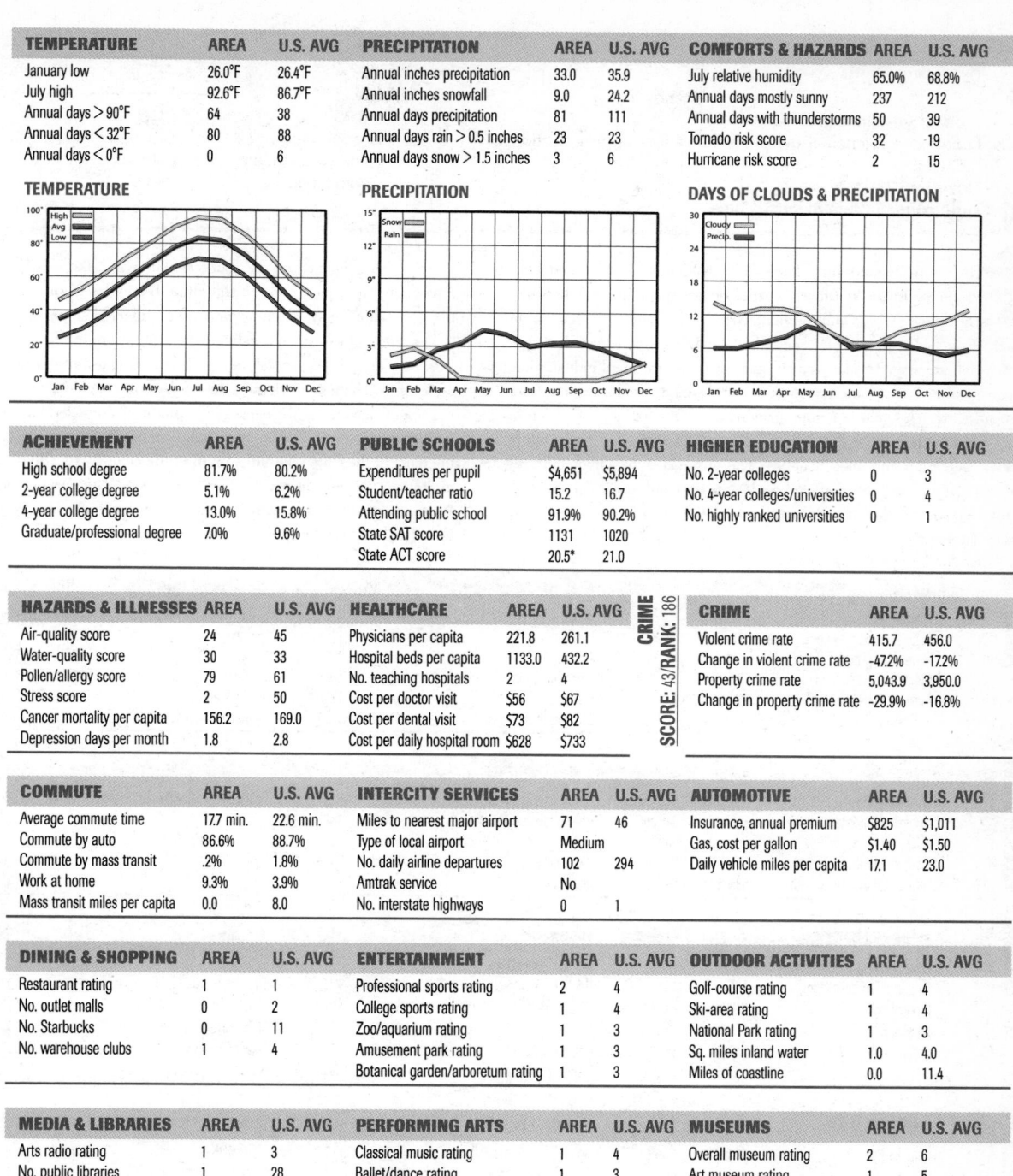

TEMPERATURE   PRECIPITATION   DAYS OF CLOUDS & PRECIPITATION

EDUCATION   SCORE: 26/RANK: 244

ACHIEVEMENT	AREA	U.S. AVG	PUBLIC SCHOOLS	AREA	U.S. AVG	HIGHER EDUCATION	AREA	U.S. AVG
High school degree	81.7%	80.2%	Expenditures per pupil	$4,651	$5,894	No. 2-year colleges	0	3
2-year college degree	5.1%	6.2%	Student/teacher ratio	15.2	16.7	No. 4-year colleges/universities	0	4
4-year college degree	13.0%	15.8%	Attending public school	91.9%	90.2%	No. highly ranked universities	0	1
Graduate/professional degree	7.0%	9.6%	State SAT score	1131	1020			
			State ACT score	20.5*	21.0			

HEALTH & HEALTHCARE   SCORE: 87/RANK: 40   CRIME   SCORE: 43/RANK: 186

HAZARDS & ILLNESSES	AREA	U.S. AVG	HEALTHCARE	AREA	U.S. AVG	CRIME	AREA	U.S. AVG
Air-quality score	24	45	Physicians per capita	221.8	261.1	Violent crime rate	415.7	456.0
Water-quality score	30	33	Hospital beds per capita	1133.0	432.2	Change in violent crime rate	-47.2%	-17.2%
Pollen/allergy score	79	61	No. teaching hospitals	2	4	Property crime rate	5,043.9	3,950.0
Stress score	2	50	Cost per doctor visit	$56	$67	Change in property crime rate	-29.9%	-16.8%
Cancer mortality per capita	156.2	169.0	Cost per dental visit	$73	$82			
Depression days per month	1.8	2.8	Cost per daily hospital room	$628	$733			

TRANSPORTATION   SCORE: 61/RANK: 130

COMMUTE	AREA	U.S. AVG	INTERCITY SERVICES	AREA	U.S. AVG	AUTOMOTIVE	AREA	U.S. AVG
Average commute time	17.7 min.	22.6 min.	Miles to nearest major airport	71	46	Insurance, annual premium	$825	$1,011
Commute by auto	86.6%	88.7%	Type of local airport	Medium		Gas, cost per gallon	$1.40	$1.50
Commute by mass transit	.2%	1.8%	No. daily airline departures	102	294	Daily vehicle miles per capita	17.1	23.0
Work at home	9.3%	3.9%	Amtrak service	No				
Mass transit miles per capita	0.0	8.0	No. interstate highways	0	1			

LEISURE   SCORE: 19/RANK: 268

DINING & SHOPPING	AREA	U.S. AVG	ENTERTAINMENT	AREA	U.S. AVG	OUTDOOR ACTIVITIES	AREA	U.S. AVG
Restaurant rating	1	1	Professional sports rating	2	4	Golf-course rating	1	4
No. outlet malls	0	2	College sports rating	1	4	Ski-area rating	1	4
No. Starbucks	0	11	Zoo/aquarium rating	1	3	National Park rating	1	3
No. warehouse clubs	1	4	Amusement park rating	1	3	Sq. miles inland water	1.0	4.0
			Botanical garden/arboretum rating	1	3	Miles of coastline	0.0	11.4

ARTS & CULTURE   SCORE: 2/RANK: 324

MEDIA & LIBRARIES	AREA	U.S. AVG	PERFORMING ARTS	AREA	U.S. AVG	MUSEUMS	AREA	U.S. AVG
Arts radio rating	1	3	Classical music rating	1	4	Overall museum rating	2	6
No. public libraries	1	28	Ballet/dance rating	1	3	Art museum rating	1	5
Library volumes per capita	1.7	2.8	Professional theater rating	1	3	Science museum rating	1	4
			University arts programs rating	1	5	Children's museum rating	1	3

Erie, PA

Score: 29.4 Rank: 309

Profile: Small industrial city
Location: Extreme northwest Pennsylvania along south shore of Lake Erie
Elevation: 731 feet
Time zone: Eastern Standard Time

PRO
Cost of living
Nearby recreation
Central location

CON
Economy
Entertainment
Wet climate

Erie, Pennsylvania's third-largest city, is a major port and industrial center in the northwest corner of the state. Located between Cleveland, Ohio, and Buffalo, New York, about 75 miles from each, Erie has a pleasant if somewhat declining small-town feel and many historic sites. Its role as a shipping point for the steel industry has been declining for years, and overall employment trends are far from encouraging. The lake is a popular destination for fishing and boating, and Presque Isle State Park, Pennsylvania's largest state park, offers water recreation and good beaches. The city has some minor cultural amenities and museums and a minor-league baseball team. The location with respect to Lake Erie makes it one of the cloudiest, rainiest, and snowiest places in the country.

The area is located on the southeast shore of Lake Erie. The terrain rises gradually away from the shoreline in a series of ridges. Cool lake breezes, which may reach several miles inland, temper summer heat waves, and days with temperatures above 90°F are infrequent. Autumn, with long dry periods and abundant sunshine, is usually the most pleasant season. The lake moderates the temperature of cold air masses arriving from Canada, but the same effect produces considerable cloudiness and frequent snowfall. The area's 83.6 inches of annual snow is by far the most in the state and ranks ninth in the country. Its 188 days of precipitation, the same as nearby Jamestown, New York, are the most in the United States. Spring weather is variable but usually cloudy and cool. First freeze is mid-October, last is early May.

POPULATION

DEMOGRAPHICS	AREA	U.S. AVG	ETHNIC COMPOSITION	AREA	U.S. AVG	RESIDENT PROFILE	AREA	U.S. AVG
Population	280,370		White	93.8%	75.1%	Single	48.0%	43.6%
Population density per sq. mile	349.6	447.3	Black	4.9%	12.3%	Married	52.0%	56.4%
Population growth	1.7%	16.1%	Asian	.7%	3.6%	Divorced	7.6%	8.4%
Median age	36.6	35.5	American Indian	.2%	.9%	Separated	3.8%	3.0%
Average family size	2.6	2.7	Hispanic	1.4%	12.5%	Married with children	26.6%	28.7%
			Diversity measure	18.8%	35.2%	Single with children	10.3%	10.1%

ECONOMY & JOBS SCORE: 9/RANK: 301

INCOME	AREA	U.S. AVG	EMPLOYMENT	AREA	U.S. AVG	LARGEST EMPLOYING INDUSTRY
Per capita income	$20,724	$23,420	Unemployment rate	6.3%	6.1%	Fabricated Metal Product Manufacturing
Household income	$40,948	$46,060	Recent job growth	-4.0%	.9%	
Household income < $25K	29.2%	26.4%	Projected future job growth	8.5%	15.1%	
Household income > $75K	18.0%	24.5%	White collar	50.6%	54.5%	
Household income growth	53.6%	57.3%	Blue collar	49.4%	45.5%	

COST OF LIVING SCORE: 70/RANK: 95

INDEXES & TAXES	AREA	U.S. AVG	HOUSING	AREA	U.S. AVG	NECESSITIES	AREA	U.S. AVG
Cost of Living Index	85.9	100.0	Median home price	$96,890	$160,100	Food Index	107.4	100.0
Financial Progress Index	101.6	100.0	Home price appreciation	4.3%	7.1%	Housing Index	60.2	100.0
Income tax rate	3.800%	4.625%	Median rent	$477	$670	Utilities Index	123.3	100.0
Sales tax rate	6.000%	6.474%	Homes owned	65.3%	63.9%	Transportation Index	91.6	100.0
Property tax rate	$15.1	$15.6	Homes rented	26.1%	25.3%	Healthcare Index	92.1	100.0
			Housing affordability	60.0%	54.5%	Miscellaneous Cost Index	93.1	100.0

CLIMATE SCORE: 11/RANK: 294

TEMPERATURE	AREA	U.S. AVG	PRECIPITATION	AREA	U.S. AVG	COMFORTS & HAZARDS	AREA	U.S. AVG
January low	18.5°F	26.4°F	Annual inches precipitation	38.2	35.9	July relative humidity	74.0%	68.8%
July high	77.4°F	86.7°F	Annual inches snowfall	83.6	24.2	Annual days mostly sunny	161	212
Annual days > 90°F	1	38	Annual days precipitation	188	111	Annual days with thunderstorms	38	39
Annual days < 32°F	134	88	Annual days rain > 0.5 inches	23	23	Tornado risk score	4	19
Annual days < 0°F	5	6	Annual days snow > 1.5 inches	17	6	Hurricane risk score	3	15

TEMPERATURE

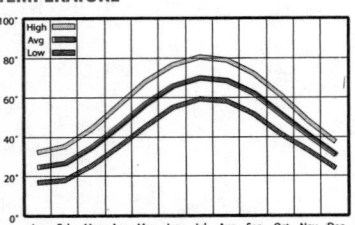

PRECIPITATION

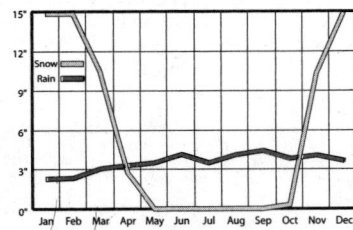

DAYS OF CLOUDS & PRECIPITATION

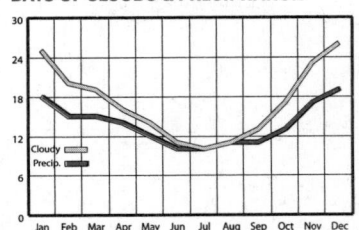

EDUCATION
SCORE: 21/RANK: 261

ACHIEVEMENT	AREA	U.S. AVG	PUBLIC SCHOOLS	AREA	U.S. AVG	HIGHER EDUCATION	AREA	U.S. AVG
High school degree	84.6%	80.2%	Expenditures per pupil	$6,103	$5,894	No. 2-year colleges	4	3
2-year college degree	5.4%	6.2%	Student/teacher ratio	17.1	16.7	No. 4-year colleges/universities	4	4
4-year college degree	13.2%	15.8%	Attending public school	79.7%	90.2%	No. highly ranked universities	2	1
Graduate/professional degree	7.6%	9.6%	State SAT score	1002*	1020			
			State ACT score	21.5	21.0			

HEALTH & HEALTHCARE
SCORE: 88/RANK: 39

CRIME
SCORE: 86/RANK: 45

HAZARDS & ILLNESSES	AREA	U.S. AVG	HEALTHCARE	AREA	U.S. AVG	CRIME	AREA	U.S. AVG
Air-quality score	17	45	Physicians per capita	242.5	261.1	Violent crime rate	250.9	456.0
Water-quality score	96	33	Hospital beds per capita	537.7	432.2	Change in violent crime rate	-31.1%	-17.2%
Pollen/allergy score	32	61	No. teaching hospitals	4	4	Property crime rate	2,663.9	3,950.0
Stress score	55	50	Cost per doctor visit	$58	$67	Change in property crime rate	-15.4%	-16.8%
Cancer mortality per capita	181.8	169.0	Cost per dental visit	$62	$82			
Depression days per month	2.9	2.8	Cost per daily hospital room	$695	$733			

TRANSPORTATION
SCORE: 75/RANK: 81

COMMUTE	AREA	U.S. AVG	INTERCITY SERVICES	AREA	U.S. AVG	AUTOMOTIVE	AREA	U.S. AVG
Average commute time	18.5 min.	22.6 min.	Miles to nearest major airport	89	46	Insurance, annual premium	$971	$1,011
Commute by auto	87.0%	88.7%	Type of local airport	Medium		Gas, cost per gallon	$1.55	$1.50
Commute by mass transit	1.3%	1.8%	No. daily airline departures	155	294	Daily vehicle miles per capita	14.8	23.0
Work at home	3.2%	3.9%	Amtrak service	Yes				
Mass transit miles per capita	7.7	8.0	No. interstate highways	2	1			

LEISURE
SCORE: 30/RANK: 229

DINING & SHOPPING	AREA	U.S. AVG	ENTERTAINMENT	AREA	U.S. AVG	OUTDOOR ACTIVITIES	AREA	U.S. AVG
Restaurant rating	1	1	Professional sports rating	2	4	Golf-course rating	3	4
No. outlet malls	0	2	College sports rating	5	4	Ski-area rating	3	4
No. Starbucks	1	11	Zoo/aquarium rating	4	3	National Park rating	1	3
No. warehouse clubs	3	4	Amusement park rating	4	3	Sq. miles inland water	2.0	4.0
			Botanical garden/arboretum rating	5	3	Miles of coastline	0.0	11.4

ARTS & CULTURE
SCORE: 77/RANK: 74

MEDIA & LIBRARIES	AREA	U.S. AVG	PERFORMING ARTS	AREA	U.S. AVG	MUSEUMS	AREA	U.S. AVG
Arts radio rating	5	3	Classical music rating	3	4	Overall museum rating	6	6
No. public libraries	14	28	Ballet/dance rating	1	3	Art museum rating	4	5
Library volumes per capita	2.3	2.8	Professional theater rating	1	3	Science museum rating	4	4
			University arts programs rating	8	5	Children's museum rating	3	3

Eugene-Springfield, OR

Score: 85.1   Rank: 21

Profile: College-town complex
Location: West-central Oregon at the south end of Willamette River Valley
Elevation: 373 feet
Time zone: Pacific Standard Time

PRO
College-town feel
Attractive downtown
Nearby mountains

CON
Recent unemployment
Wet winters
Low ethnic diversity

Eugene and Springfield sit across from one another on the Willamette River. Home to the University of Oregon, the area has a large timber industry and is a transportation hub for routes south into California. Clean and prosperous downtown Eugene has the kind of shops and restaurants one would expect in a college town. The university and its attendees leave a distinctly liberal, folksy imprint on the otherwise conservative region. The slowing timber industry has created high unemployment, which is projected to improve over time as other businesses locate there. The area has a good mix of setting, climate, and small-town feel and a low cost of living by Oregon standards.

Eugene is located at the southern end of the fertile Willamette Valley. The Cascade Mountains to the east, Coast Range to the west, and low hills to the south surround the valley, while the level valley floor broadens to the north. Foothills to the east obscure the snow-covered Cascade peaks, some 75 miles away. The Pacific coast is 50 miles west. Forested areas lie in every direction except north. The climate is controlled by marine air from the Pacific and the Cascades block all but the strongest continental air masses. Summers are dry and warm with an occasional hot spell up to 95°F and cool evenings. Winter days are cool and damp with highs in the 50s, lows in the 30s, and occasional dips into the 20s. Rain is highly seasonal, starting in September and lasting through May. Although a little south of the main storm track, winter rains are sometimes heavy. Snow is rare and usually melts on contact. The valley location and nearby water cause occasional fog. First freeze is late October, last is late April.

POPULATION

DEMOGRAPHICS	AREA	U.S. AVG	ETHNIC COMPOSITION	AREA	U.S. AVG	RESIDENT PROFILE	AREA	U.S. AVG
Population	326,666		White	95.7%	75.1%	Single	41.4%	43.6%
Population density per sq. mile	71.7	447.3	Black	.5%	12.3%	Married	58.6%	56.4%
Population growth	15.5%	16.1%	Asian	1.8%	3.6%	Divorced	10.7%	8.4%
Median age	37.0	35.5	American Indian	1.6%	.9%	Separated	2.8%	3.0%
Average family size	2.5	2.7	Hispanic	3.6%	12.5%	Married with children	26.1%	28.7%
			Diversity measure	20.7%	35.2%	Single with children	10.4%	10.1%

ECONOMY & JOBS SCORE: 23/RANK: 252

INCOME	AREA	U.S. AVG	EMPLOYMENT	AREA	U.S. AVG	LARGEST EMPLOYING INDUSTRY
Per capita income	$21,420	$23,420	Unemployment rate	7.4%	6.1%	Wood Product Manufacturing
Household income	$39,250	$46,060	Recent job growth	1.3%	.9%	
Household income < $25K	30.3%	26.4%	Projected future job growth	15.1%	15.1%	
Household income > $75K	17.9%	24.5%	White collar	52.1%	54.5%	
Household income growth	55.1%	57.3%	Blue collar	47.9%	45.5%	

COST OF LIVING SCORE: 49/RANK: 168

INDEXES & TAXES	AREA	U.S. AVG	HOUSING	AREA	U.S. AVG	NECESSITIES	AREA	U.S. AVG
Cost of Living Index	99.0	100.0	Median home price	$143,500	$160,100	Food Index	106.4	100.0
Financial Progress Index	84.5	100.0	Home price appreciation	3.3%	7.1%	Housing Index	89.1	100.0
Income tax rate	9.000%	4.625%	Median rent	$675	$670	Utilities Index	79.8	100.0
Sales tax rate	0.000%	6.474%	Homes owned	65.7%	63.9%	Transportation Index	104.8	100.0
Property tax rate	$14.6	$15.6	Homes rented	24.5%	25.3%	Healthcare Index	121.2	100.0
			Housing affordability	49.0%	54.5%	Miscellaneous Cost Index	107.3	100.0

CLIMATE SCORE: 64/RANK: 117

TEMPERATURE	AREA	U.S. AVG	PRECIPITATION	AREA	U.S. AVG	COMFORTS & HAZARDS	AREA	U.S. AVG
January low	33.1°F	26.4°F	Annual inches precipitation	43.0	35.9	July relative humidity	72.0%	68.8%
July high	82.6°F	86.7°F	Annual inches snowfall	7.0	24.2	Annual days mostly sunny	158	212
Annual days > 90°F	15	38	Annual days precipitation	137	111	Annual days with thunderstorms	5	39
Annual days < 32°F	54	88	Annual days rain > 0.5 inches	30	23	Tornado risk score	2	19
Annual days < 0°F	0	6	Annual days snow > 1.5 inches	1	6	Hurricane risk score	0	15

TEMPERATURE

PRECIPITATION

DAYS OF CLOUDS & PRECIPITATION

EDUCATION SCORE: 62/RANK: 124

ACHIEVEMENT	AREA	U.S. AVG	PUBLIC SCHOOLS	AREA	U.S. AVG	HIGHER EDUCATION	AREA	U.S. AVG
High school degree	87.5%	80.2%	Expenditures per pupil	$5,941	$5,894	No. 2-year colleges	1	3
2-year college degree	7.2%	6.2%	Student/teacher ratio	20.7	16.7	No. 4-year colleges/universities	3	4
4-year college degree	15.6%	15.8%	Attending public school	93.7%	90.2%	No. highly ranked universities	0	1
Graduate/professional degree	9.9%	9.6%	State SAT score	1053*	1020			
			State ACT score	22.6	21.0			

HEALTH & HEALTHCARE SCORE: 48/RANK: 171   **CRIME** SCORE: 47/RANK: 175

HAZARDS & ILLNESSES	AREA	U.S. AVG	HEALTHCARE	AREA	U.S. AVG	CRIME	AREA	U.S. AVG
Air-quality score	59	45	Physicians per capita	220.7	261.1	Violent crime rate	305.0	456.0
Water-quality score	30	33	Hospital beds per capita	210.9	432.2	Change in violent crime rate	-24.5%	-17.2%
Pollen/allergy score	64	61	No. teaching hospitals	0	4	Property crime rate	4,957.6	3,950.0
Stress score	98	50	Cost per doctor visit	$81	$67	Change in property crime rate	-27.4%	-16.8%
Cancer mortality per capita	160.2	169.0	Cost per dental visit	$115	$82			
Depression days per month	3.9	2.8	Cost per daily hospital room	$647	$733			

TRANSPORTATION SCORE: 84/RANK: 52

COMMUTE	AREA	U.S. AVG	INTERCITY SERVICES	AREA	U.S. AVG	AUTOMOTIVE	AREA	U.S. AVG
Average commute time	19.9 min.	22.6 min.	Miles to nearest major airport	7	46	Insurance, annual premium	$867	$1,011
Commute by auto	87.1%	88.7%	Type of local airport	Small		Gas, cost per gallon	$1.66	$1.50
Commute by mass transit	1.0%	1.8%	No. daily airline departures	51	294	Daily vehicle miles per capita	17.6	23.0
Work at home	5.6%	3.9%	Amtrak service	Yes				
Mass transit miles per capita	15.5	8.0	No. interstate highways	1	1			

LEISURE SCORE: 80/RANK: 69

DINING & SHOPPING	AREA	U.S. AVG	ENTERTAINMENT	AREA	U.S. AVG	OUTDOOR ACTIVITIES	AREA	U.S. AVG
Restaurant rating	1	1	Professional sports rating	2	4	Golf-course rating	2	4
No. outlet malls	0	2	College sports rating	6	4	Ski-area rating	8	4
No. Starbucks	6	11	Zoo/aquarium rating	1	3	National Park rating	8	3
No. warehouse clubs	3	4	Amusement park rating	1	3	Sq. miles inland water	4.0	4.0
			Botanical garden/arboretum rating	5	3	Miles of coastline	30.4	11.4

ARTS & CULTURE SCORE: 56/RANK: 144

MEDIA & LIBRARIES	AREA	U.S. AVG	PERFORMING ARTS	AREA	U.S. AVG	MUSEUMS	AREA	U.S. AVG
Arts radio rating	1	3	Classical music rating	4	4	Overall museum rating	6	6
No. public libraries	8	28	Ballet/dance rating	6	3	Art museum rating	5	5
Library volumes per capita	2.6	2.8	Professional theater rating	1	3	Science museum rating	6	4
			University arts programs rating	6	5	Children's museum rating	1	3

Evansville-Henderson, IN-KY

Score: 77.7　Rank: 47

Profile: Small-city complex
Location: Southwestern Indiana along the Ohio River on the Kentucky border
Elevation: 388 feet
Time zone: Eastern Standard Time (no daylight savings time)

PRO
Cost of living
Low crime rate
Healthcare

CON
Isolation
Entertainment
Summer heat

Evansville is located in the far southwest portion of the state. This Ohio River port is the commercial and cultural hub of southwest Indiana and the nearby regions of Illinois and Kentucky. Near the waterfront, the city has a pedestrian mall and retains much of its historical significance, while level lowlands to the north and east contain a fair amount of sprawl. The clean and quiet town is pleasant overall, with a low crime rate and the lowest cost of living in Indiana. Downsides include isolation (Louisville is 100 miles east) and lack of things to do.

Located along the Ohio River, the terrain ranges from level to areas of rolling land and low hills near the river. The city itself is located on a flat valley sloping gently down to the river. Evansville lies in the path of moisture-bearing storm systems moving in from the western Gulf region northeastward up the Mississippi and Ohio valleys. Both temperature and precipitation are closely related to the air masses pulled by these storms. Summers are hot and humid as the storm track becomes less active. Both summer and winter are highly variable. Storms and weather transitions bring high winds in all seasons and strong thunderstorms in summer. Snow does occur but Evansville is far enough south to make heavy accumulations uncommon. First freeze is late October, last is early April.

POPULATION

DEMOGRAPHICS	AREA	U.S. AVG	ETHNIC COMPOSITION	AREA	U.S. AVG	RESIDENT PROFILE	AREA	U.S. AVG
Population	297,353		White	94.3%	75.1%	Single	40.5%	43.6%
Population density per sq. mile	202.6	447.3	Black	5.0%	12.3%	Married	59.5%	56.4%
Population growth	6.6%	16.1%	Asian	.4%	3.6%	Divorced	10.1%	8.4%
Median age	37.5	35.5	American Indian	.2%	.9%	Separated	1.5%	3.0%
Average family size	2.5	2.7	Hispanic	.6%	12.5%	Married with children	29.6%	28.7%
			Diversity measure	16.1%	35.2%	Single with children	8.8%	10.1%

ECONOMY & JOBS SCORE: 64/RANK: 119

INCOME	AREA	U.S. AVG	EMPLOYMENT	AREA	U.S. AVG	LARGEST EMPLOYING INDUSTRY
Per capita income	$23,431	$23,420	Unemployment rate	4.2%	6.1%	Plastics and Rubber Products Manufacturing
Household income	$43,944	$46,060	Recent job growth	.7%	.9%	
Household income < $25K	27.2%	26.4%	Projected future job growth	11.1%	15.1%	
Household income > $75K	22.8%	24.5%	White collar	52.0%	54.5%	
Household income growth	61.3%	57.3%	Blue collar	48.0%	45.5%	

COST OF LIVING SCORE: 86/RANK: 45

INDEXES & TAXES	AREA	U.S. AVG	HOUSING	AREA	U.S. AVG	NECESSITIES	AREA	U.S. AVG
Cost of Living Index	81.1	100.0	Median home price	$96,660	$160,100	Food Index	92.3	100.0
Financial Progress Index	115.4	100.0	Home price appreciation	3.9%	7.1%	Housing Index	60.0	100.0
Income tax rate	3.400%	4.625%	Median rent	$532	$670	Utilities Index	84.1	100.0
Sales tax rate	6.000%	6.474%	Homes owned	67.8%	63.9%	Transportation Index	95.1	100.0
Property tax rate	$14.1	$15.6	Homes rented	22.0%	25.3%	Healthcare Index	92.4	100.0
			Housing affordability	57.0%	54.5%	Miscellaneous Cost Index	96.0	100.0

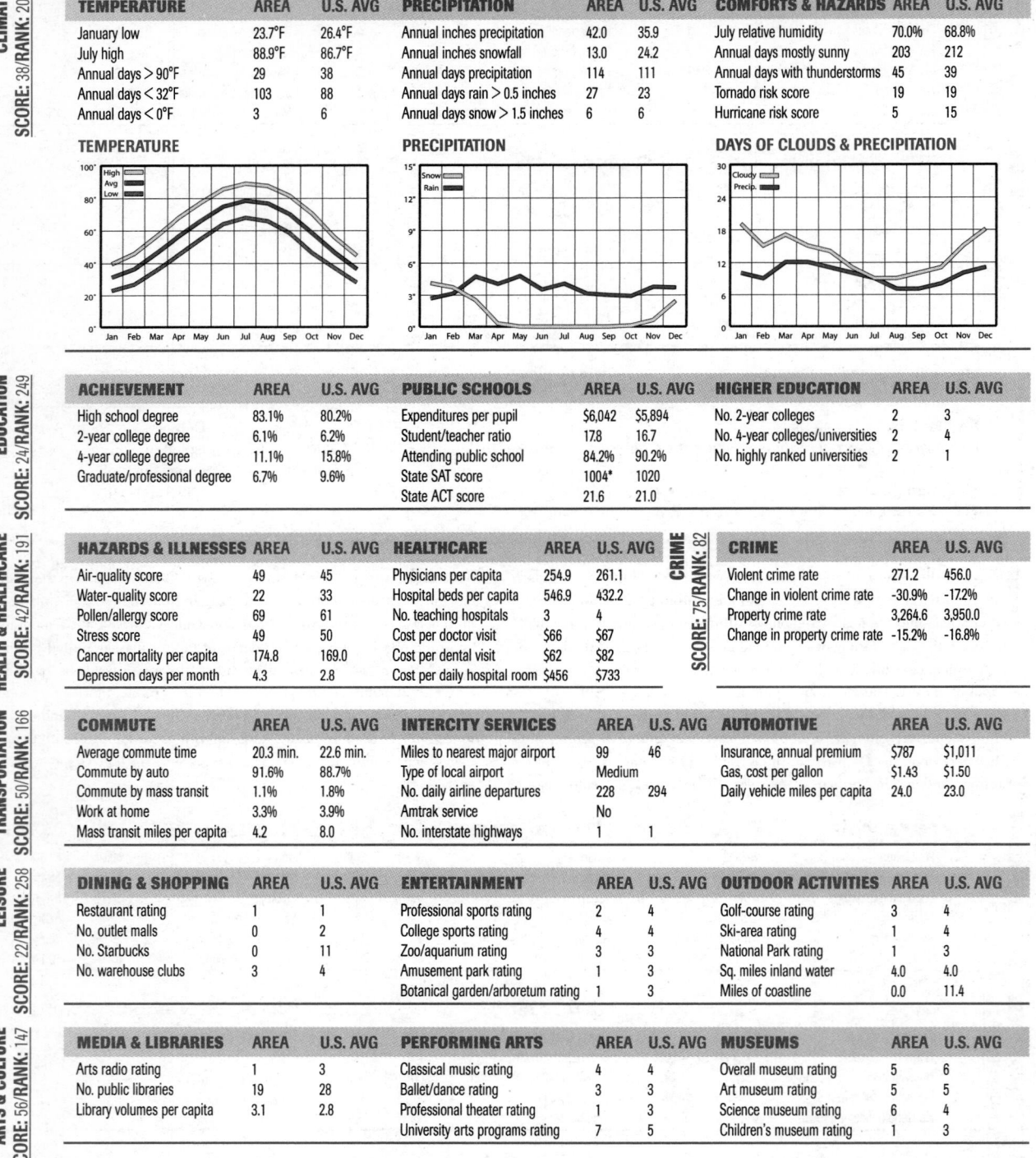

CLIMATE SCORE: 38/RANK: 203

TEMPERATURE	AREA	U.S. AVG	PRECIPITATION	AREA	U.S. AVG	COMFORTS & HAZARDS	AREA	U.S. AVG
January low	23.7°F	26.4°F	Annual inches precipitation	42.0	35.9	July relative humidity	70.0%	68.8%
July high	88.9°F	86.7°F	Annual inches snowfall	13.0	24.2	Annual days mostly sunny	203	212
Annual days > 90°F	29	38	Annual days precipitation	114	111	Annual days with thunderstorms	45	39
Annual days < 32°F	103	88	Annual days rain > 0.5 inches	27	23	Tornado risk score	19	19
Annual days < 0°F	3	6	Annual days snow > 1.5 inches	6	6	Hurricane risk score	5	15

TEMPERATURE

PRECIPITATION

DAYS OF CLOUDS & PRECIPITATION

EDUCATION SCORE: 24/RANK: 249

ACHIEVEMENT	AREA	U.S. AVG	PUBLIC SCHOOLS	AREA	U.S. AVG	HIGHER EDUCATION	AREA	U.S. AVG
High school degree	83.1%	80.2%	Expenditures per pupil	$6,042	$5,894	No. 2-year colleges	2	3
2-year college degree	6.1%	6.2%	Student/teacher ratio	17.8	16.7	No. 4-year colleges/universities	2	4
4-year college degree	11.1%	15.8%	Attending public school	84.2%	90.2%	No. highly ranked universities	2	1
Graduate/professional degree	6.7%	9.6%	State SAT score	1004*	1020			
			State ACT score	21.6	21.0			

HEALTH & HEALTHCARE SCORE: 42/RANK: 191

HAZARDS & ILLNESSES	AREA	U.S. AVG	HEALTHCARE	AREA	U.S. AVG
Air-quality score	49	45	Physicians per capita	254.9	261.1
Water-quality score	22	33	Hospital beds per capita	546.9	432.2
Pollen/allergy score	69	61	No. teaching hospitals	3	4
Stress score	49	50	Cost per doctor visit	$66	$67
Cancer mortality per capita	174.8	169.0	Cost per dental visit	$62	$82
Depression days per month	4.3	2.8	Cost per daily hospital room	$456	$733

CRIME SCORE: 75/RANK: 82

CRIME	AREA	U.S. AVG
Violent crime rate	271.2	456.0
Change in violent crime rate	-30.9%	-17.2%
Property crime rate	3,264.6	3,950.0
Change in property crime rate	-15.2%	-16.8%

TRANSPORTATION SCORE: 50/RANK: 166

COMMUTE	AREA	U.S. AVG	INTERCITY SERVICES	AREA	U.S. AVG	AUTOMOTIVE	AREA	U.S. AVG
Average commute time	20.3 min.	22.6 min.	Miles to nearest major airport	99	46	Insurance, annual premium	$787	$1,011
Commute by auto	91.6%	88.7%	Type of local airport	Medium		Gas, cost per gallon	$1.43	$1.50
Commute by mass transit	1.1%	1.8%	No. daily airline departures	228	294	Daily vehicle miles per capita	24.0	23.0
Work at home	3.3%	3.9%	Amtrak service	No				
Mass transit miles per capita	4.2	8.0	No. interstate highways	1	1			

LEISURE SCORE: 22/RANK: 258

DINING & SHOPPING	AREA	U.S. AVG	ENTERTAINMENT	AREA	U.S. AVG	OUTDOOR ACTIVITIES	AREA	U.S. AVG
Restaurant rating	1	1	Professional sports rating	2	4	Golf-course rating	3	4
No. outlet malls	0	2	College sports rating	4	4	Ski-area rating	1	4
No. Starbucks	0	11	Zoo/aquarium rating	3	3	National Park rating	1	3
No. warehouse clubs	3	4	Amusement park rating	1	3	Sq. miles inland water	4.0	4.0
			Botanical garden/arboretum rating	1	3	Miles of coastline	0.0	11.4

ARTS & CULTURE SCORE: 56/RANK: 147

MEDIA & LIBRARIES	AREA	U.S. AVG	PERFORMING ARTS	AREA	U.S. AVG	MUSEUMS	AREA	U.S. AVG
Arts radio rating	1	3	Classical music rating	4	4	Overall museum rating	5	6
No. public libraries	19	28	Ballet/dance rating	3	3	Art museum rating	5	5
Library volumes per capita	3.1	2.8	Professional theater rating	1	3	Science museum rating	6	4
			University arts programs rating	7	5	Children's museum rating	1	3

Fargo-Moorhead, ND-MN

Score: 68.1   Rank: 87

Profile: Small-city complex
Location: Extreme eastern North Dakota at the Minnesota border
Elevation: 899 feet
Time zone: Central Standard Time

PRO	CON
College-town element	Cold winters
Cool summers	Isolation
Educated population	Low ethnic diversity

Fargo, the largest city in North Dakota, lies alongside the Red River in the southeast part of the state near the Minnesota border. Located along east-west I-94, it is an agricultural, commercial, and transportation center with the strongest economic statistics in the state. The Red River Valley is wheat-growing country called by some the "breadbasket of the world." Fargo is home to North Dakota State University, while Moorhead, Minnesota, across the river, has Moorhead State and Concordia College, bringing some college-town amenities to the area. The well-preserved downtown district is classic mid-America, although Fujifilm Ltd. recently called Fargo "the most unphotogenic in the U.S." On the other hand, Fargo won a 2001 National Civic League All-America City Award.

The Red River flows northward between the two cities (one of few northbound rivers), and is a part of the Hudson Bay drainage area. The surrounding terrain is flat and open prairie. The climate is Great Plains continental with significant temperature change from summer to winter. Summers are generally comfortable with few hot, humid days and cool, comfortable nights. Winters are cold and dry with daytime temperatures rising above freezing only 6 days per month on average with lows dipping below 0°F half the time. Three-quarters of precipitation occurs from April to September, often as thunderstorms, some heavy. Heavy winter snowfall is the exception rather than the rule. But low terrain and high winds lead to the legendary Dakota blizzards and even light snow can drift; however, clear, cold days are the norm. Northerly winds blowing up the valley cause low clouds and fog, and melting snow has recently brought spring floods. First freeze is late September, last is mid-May.

POPULATION

DEMOGRAPHICS	AREA	U.S. AVG	ETHNIC COMPOSITION	AREA	U.S. AVG	RESIDENT PROFILE	AREA	U.S. AVG
Population	177,064		White	98.0%	75.1%	Single	39.0%	43.6%
Population density per sq. mile	63.0	447.3	Black	.2%	12.3%	Married	61.0%	56.4%
Population growth	15.5%	16.1%	Asian	.8%	3.6%	Divorced	4.6%	8.4%
Median age	31.8	35.5	American Indian	.6%	.9%	Separated	.9%	3.0%
Average family size	2.6	2.7	Hispanic	1.2%	12.5%	Married with children	30.9%	28.7%
			Diversity measure	11.6%	35.2%	Single with children	5.5%	10.1%

ECONOMY & JOBS SCORE: 43/RANK: 184

INCOME	AREA	U.S. AVG	EMPLOYMENT	AREA	U.S. AVG	LARGEST EMPLOYING INDUSTRY
Per capita income	$24,415	$23,420	Unemployment rate	2.5%	6.1%	Food Manufacturing
Household income	$45,362	$46,060	Recent job growth	.2%	.9%	
Household income < $25K	25.9%	26.4%	Projected future job growth	21.6%	15.1%	
Household income > $75K	24.2%	24.5%	White collar	58.4%	54.5%	
Household income growth	69.9%	57.3%	Blue collar	41.6%	45.5%	

COST OF LIVING SCORE: 62/RANK: 124

INDEXES & TAXES	AREA	U.S. AVG	HOUSING	AREA	U.S. AVG	NECESSITIES	AREA	U.S. AVG
Cost of Living Index	88.1	100.0	Median home price	$110,600	$160,100	Food Index	100.0	100.0
Financial Progress Index	109.7	100.0	Home price appreciation	5.5%	7.1%	Housing Index	68.7	100.0
Income tax rate	3.920%	4.625%	Median rent	$619	$670	Utilities Index	96.2	100.0
Sales tax rate	6.500%	6.474%	Homes owned	71.9%	63.9%	Transportation Index	98.5	100.0
Property tax rate	$22.0	$15.6	Homes rented	19.6%	25.3%	Healthcare Index	100.3	100.0
			Housing affordability	54.0%	54.5%	Miscellaneous Cost Index	99.4	100.0

CLIMATE SCORE: 36/RANK: 210

TEMPERATURE	AREA	U.S. AVG	PRECIPITATION	AREA	U.S. AVG	COMFORTS & HAZARDS	AREA	U.S. AVG
January low	-3.6°F	26.4°F	Annual inches precipitation	20.0	35.9	July relative humidity	71.0%	68.8%
July high	82.8°F	86.7°F	Annual inches snowfall	35.0	24.2	Annual days mostly sunny	199	212
Annual days > 90°F	12	38	Annual days precipitation	102	111	Annual days with thunderstorms	33	39
Annual days < 32°F	181	88	Annual days rain > 0.5 inches	11	23	Tornado risk score	31	19
Annual days < 0°F	54	6	Annual days snow > 1.5 inches	8	6	Hurricane risk score	0	15

TEMPERATURE

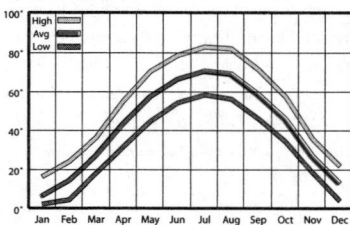

PRECIPITATION

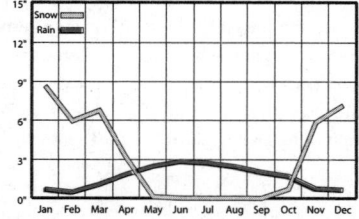

DAYS OF CLOUDS & PRECIPITATION

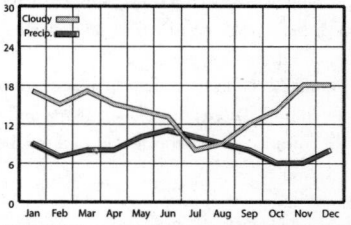

EDUCATION SCORE: 88/RANK: 40

ACHIEVEMENT	AREA	U.S. AVG	PUBLIC SCHOOLS	AREA	U.S. AVG	HIGHER EDUCATION	AREA	U.S. AVG
High school degree	89.7%	80.2%	Expenditures per pupil	$5,194	$5,894	No. 2-year colleges	0	3
2-year college degree	9.2%	6.2%	Student/teacher ratio	16.5	16.7	No. 4-year colleges/universities	3	4
4-year college degree	21.4%	15.8%	Attending public school	92.6%	90.2%	No. highly ranked universities	1	1
Graduate/professional degree	8.0%	9.6%	State SAT score	1215	1020			
			State ACT score	21.3*	21.0			

HEALTH & HEALTHCARE SCORE: 94/RANK: 18

CRIME SCORE: 84/RANK: 53

HAZARDS & ILLNESSES	AREA	U.S. AVG	HEALTHCARE	AREA	U.S. AVG	CRIME	AREA	U.S. AVG
Air-quality score	6	45	Physicians per capita	279.6	261.1	Violent crime rate	133.8	456.0
Water-quality score	20	33	Hospital beds per capita	327.5	432.2	Change in violent crime rate	5.4%	-17.2%
Pollen/allergy score	30	61	No. teaching hospitals	2	4	Property crime rate	2,906.1	3,950.0
Stress score	0	50	Cost per doctor visit	$65	$67	Change in property crime rate	-21.2%	-16.8%
Cancer mortality per capita	158.1	169.0	Cost per dental visit	$76	$82			
Depression days per month	2.1	2.8	Cost per daily hospital room	$512	$733			

TRANSPORTATION SCORE: 88/RANK: 42

COMMUTE	AREA	U.S. AVG	INTERCITY SERVICES	AREA	U.S. AVG	AUTOMOTIVE	AREA	U.S. AVG
Average commute time	16.2 min.	22.6 min.	Miles to nearest major airport	221	46	Insurance, annual premium	$647	$1,011
Commute by auto	74.3%	88.7%	Type of local airport	Large		Gas, cost per gallon	$1.48	$1.50
Commute by mass transit	.2%	1.8%	No. daily airline departures	624	294	Daily vehicle miles per capita	15.9	23.0
Work at home	11.7%	3.9%	Amtrak service	Yes				
Mass transit miles per capita	5.0	8.0	No. interstate highways	1	1			

LEISURE SCORE: 16/RANK: 278

DINING & SHOPPING	AREA	U.S. AVG	ENTERTAINMENT	AREA	U.S. AVG	OUTDOOR ACTIVITIES	AREA	U.S. AVG
Restaurant rating	1	1	Professional sports rating	2	4	Golf-course rating	2	4
No. outlet malls	0	2	College sports rating	8	4	Ski-area rating	1	4
No. Starbucks	0	11	Zoo/aquarium rating	1	3	National Park rating	1	3
No. warehouse clubs	3	4	Amusement park rating	1	3	Sq. miles inland water	2.0	4.0
			Botanical garden/arboretum rating	1	3	Miles of coastline	0.0	11.4

ARTS & CULTURE SCORE: 61/RANK: 127

MEDIA & LIBRARIES	AREA	U.S. AVG	PERFORMING ARTS	AREA	U.S. AVG	MUSEUMS	AREA	U.S. AVG
Arts radio rating	1	3	Classical music rating	3	4	Overall museum rating	5	6
No. public libraries	17	28	Ballet/dance rating	1	3	Art museum rating	4	5
Library volumes per capita	2.5	2.8	Professional theater rating	1	3	Science museum rating	1	4
			University arts programs rating	8	5	Children's museum rating	3	3

Fayetteville, NC

Score: 46.1   Rank: 250

Profile: Military town
Location: South-central North Carolina, along Cape Fear River, 90 miles south of Raleigh-Durham
Elevation: 96 feet
Time zone: Eastern Standard Time

PRO	CON
Attractive downtown	Entertainment
Low home prices	Dependence on military
Falling crime rates	Hot, humid summers

Once an important inland port on the Cape Fear River, Fayetteville houses two large military installations, Fort Bragg and Pope Air Force Base. The two facilities provide the city's main economic base, and the area is highly dependent on them. The clean and attractive downtown contains numerous historic buildings and reflects the results of an extensive revitalization program. These improvements merited a 2001 National Civic League All-America City Award. Median home prices of just over $96,000 are the lowest in the state, and there are appealing new areas of attractive homes and several golf courses. The city is well planned for the most part and sprawl is under control. There are some local arts and culture amenities, but overall the town is quiet. Scoring and ranking data don't reflect many of the area's qualities, particularly recent changes. Fayetteville may be a pleasant surprise to some.

The area at the edge of the Coastal Plain begins to rise into the Carolina Piedmont Plateau. Surrounding terrain is level to gently rolling with agricultural land and mixed forests of pine and hardwood. The climate is mainly humid subtropical with occasional periods of continental influence. Tropical air brings heat and humidity during most of the summer. Afternoon temperatures frequently reach the 90s, with frequent afternoon thundershowers. Coastal storms produce rain year-round. The area is sheltered from extreme cold by mountains to the northwest and the warming effects of the Atlantic. Low temperatures are seldom below 20°F. There may be some snow and sleet, but most winter precipitation is rain.

POPULATION

DEMOGRAPHICS	AREA	U.S. AVG	ETHNIC COMPOSITION	AREA	U.S. AVG	RESIDENT PROFILE	AREA	U.S. AVG
Population	303,328		White	63.9%	75.1%	Single	42.7%	43.6%
Population density per sq. mile	464.4	447.3	Black	29.8%	12.3%	Married	57.3%	56.4%
Population growth	10.5%	16.1%	Asian	2.8%	3.6%	Divorced	7.6%	8.4%
Median age	29.7	35.5	American Indian	1.7%	.9%	Separated	6.1%	3.0%
Average family size	4.0	2.7	Hispanic	5.5%	12.5%	Married with children	38.2%	28.7%
			Diversity measure	59.3%	35.2%	Single with children	12.3%	10.1%

ECONOMY & JOBS   SCORE: 32/RANK: 224

INCOME	AREA	U.S. AVG	EMPLOYMENT	AREA	U.S. AVG	LARGEST EMPLOYING INDUSTRY
Per capita income	$20,256	$23,420	Unemployment rate	5.4%	6.1%	Tire Manufacturing
Household income	$42,175	$46,060	Recent job growth	-1.0%	.9%	
Household income < $25K	24.8%	26.4%	Projected future job growth	14.4%	15.1%	
Household income > $75K	20.0%	24.5%	White collar	41.6%	54.5%	
Household income growth	65.6%	57.3%	Blue collar	58.4%	45.5%	

COST OF LIVING   SCORE: 61/RANK: 128

INDEXES & TAXES	AREA	U.S. AVG	HOUSING	AREA	U.S. AVG	NECESSITIES	AREA	U.S. AVG
Cost of Living Index	87.4	100.0	Median home price	$96,200	$160,100	Food Index	104.1	100.0
Financial Progress Index	102.9	100.0	Home price appreciation	2.7%	7.1%	Housing Index	59.8	100.0
Income tax rate	7.000%	4.625%	Median rent	$515	$670	Utilities Index	97.1	100.0
Sales tax rate	7.000%	6.474%	Homes owned	51.2%	63.9%	Transportation Index	97.9	100.0
Property tax rate	$11.9	$15.6	Homes rented	40.1%	25.3%	Healthcare Index	98.5	100.0
			Housing affordability	67.0%	54.5%	Miscellaneous Cost Index	107.7	100.0

CLIMATE   SCORE: 62/RANK: 125

TEMPERATURE	AREA	U.S. AVG	PRECIPITATION	AREA	U.S. AVG	COMFORTS & HAZARDS	AREA	U.S. AVG
January low	30.0°F	26.4°F	Annual inches precipitation	43.0	35.9	July relative humidity	71.0%	68.8%
July high	87.7°F	86.7°F	Annual inches snowfall	7.0	24.2	Annual days mostly sunny	220	212
Annual days > 90°F	25	38	Annual days precipitation	112	111	Annual days with thunderstorms	46	39
Annual days < 32°F	82	88	Annual days rain > 0.5 inches	28	23	Tornado risk score	26	19
Annual days < 0°F	0	6	Annual days snow > 1.5 inches	2	6	Hurricane risk score	41	15

TEMPERATURE

PRECIPITATION

DAYS OF CLOUDS & PRECIPITATION

EDUCATION   SCORE: 51/RANK: 161

ACHIEVEMENT	AREA	U.S. AVG	PUBLIC SCHOOLS	AREA	U.S. AVG	HIGHER EDUCATION	AREA	U.S. AVG
High school degree	84.8%	80.2%	Expenditures per pupil	$4,841	$5,894	No. 2-year colleges	1	3
2-year college degree	8.9%	6.2%	Student/teacher ratio	18.7	16.7	No. 4-year colleges/universities	2	4
4-year college degree	13.2%	15.8%	Attending public school	94.0%	90.2%	No. highly ranked universities	0	1
Graduate/professional degree	6.0%	9.6%	State SAT score	1001*	1020			
			State ACT score	19.9	21.0			

HEALTH & HEALTHCARE   SCORE: 12/RANK: 290

CRIME   SCORE: 27/RANK: 240

HAZARDS & ILLNESSES	AREA	U.S. AVG	HEALTHCARE	AREA	U.S. AVG
Air-quality score	17	45	Physicians per capita	213.3	261.1
Water-quality score	96	33	Hospital beds per capita	253.5	432.2
Pollen/allergy score	65	61	No. teaching hospitals	1	4
Stress score	28	50	Cost per doctor visit	$65	$67
Cancer mortality per capita	176.9	169.0	Cost per dental visit	$77	$82
Depression days per month	1.2	2.8	Cost per daily hospital room	$523	$733

CRIME	AREA	U.S. AVG
Violent crime rate	495.9	456.0
Change in violent crime rate	-48.1%	-17.2%
Property crime rate	5,487.8	3,950.0
Change in property crime rate	-22.4%	-16.8%

TRANSPORTATION   SCORE: 27/RANK: 241

COMMUTE	AREA	U.S. AVG	INTERCITY SERVICES	AREA	U.S. AVG	AUTOMOTIVE	AREA	U.S. AVG
Average commute time	21.9 min.	22.6 min.	Miles to nearest major airport	55	46	Insurance, annual premium	$784	$1,011
Commute by auto	88.4%	88.7%	Type of local airport	Medium		Gas, cost per gallon	$1.40	$1.50
Commute by mass transit	.6%	1.8%	No. daily airline departures	352	294	Daily vehicle miles per capita	21.4	23.0
Work at home	2.0%	3.9%	Amtrak service	Yes				
Mass transit miles per capita	2.6	8.0	No. interstate highways	1	1			

LEISURE SCORE: 9/RANK: 303

DINING & SHOPPING	AREA	U.S. AVG	ENTERTAINMENT	AREA	U.S. AVG	OUTDOOR ACTIVITIES	AREA	U.S. AVG
Restaurant rating	1	1	Professional sports rating	2	4	Golf-course rating	2	4
No. outlet malls	2	2	College sports rating	3	4	Ski-area rating	1	4
No. Starbucks	0	11	Zoo/aquarium rating	1	3	National Park rating	1	3
No. warehouse clubs	3	4	Amusement park rating	2	3	Sq. miles inland water	2.0	4.0
			Botanical garden/arboretum rating	1	3	Miles of coastline	0.0	11.4

ARTS & CULTURE SCORE: 19/RANK: 268

MEDIA & LIBRARIES	AREA	U.S. AVG	PERFORMING ARTS	AREA	U.S. AVG	MUSEUMS	AREA	U.S. AVG
Arts radio rating	1	3	Classical music rating	2	4	Overall museum rating	5	6
No. public libraries	7	28	Ballet/dance rating	1	3	Art museum rating	6	5
Library volumes per capita	2.4	2.8	Professional theater rating	1	3	Science museum rating	1	4
			University arts programs rating	5	5	Children's museum rating	1	3

Fayetteville-Springdale-Rogers, AR

Score: 82.5   Rank: 27

Profile: Small-city complex/College town
Location: Extreme northwest Arkansas in Ozark foothills
Elevation: 1,263 feet
Time zone: Central Standard Time

PRO	CON
Projected job growth	Isolation
College-town atmosphere	Home prices
Cost of living	Low ethnic diversity

Rogers, Springdale, and Fayetteville are located in a north-south line roughly 10 miles apart. Fayetteville is home to the University of Arkansas and has an attractive campus, historic buildings, and the usual college-town amenities. The area has a low Cost of Living Index (82.0) for an area with this profile and economic picture. It has become attractive for light manufacturing, and Bentonville just north of Rogers is the headquarters for retail giant Wal-Mart, attracting a lot of business to the area. Projected 10-year employment growth of 31.6% is the best in the state and fifth highest in the nation. On the downside, the area is isolated from big-city services, including air transportation, but has enough local amenities to get by. Median home prices are the highest in Arkansas but are still low by national standards. There are no strong negatives, and consistency across most categories drives the high ranking.

The area contains a mix of farmland, nearby lakes, and rolling, wooded hills. Climate is continental and typical of the region, with a strong Gulf influence particularly in summer. However, the elevation and nearby mountains keep temperatures a few degrees cooler than many other parts of the state. Winters are generally mild, with occasional cold spells.

POPULATION

DEMOGRAPHICS	AREA	U.S. AVG	ETHNIC COMPOSITION	AREA	U.S. AVG	RESIDENT PROFILE	AREA	U.S. AVG
Population	332,011		White	95.1%	75.1%	Single	34.9%	43.6%
Population density per sq. mile	185.1	447.3	Black	1.9%	12.3%	Married	65.1%	56.4%
Population growth	57.4%	16.1%	Asian	.7%	3.6%	Divorced	8.0%	8.4%
Median age	33.4	35.5	American Indian	2.0%	.9%	Separated	2.0%	3.0%
Average family size	2.7	2.7	Hispanic	2.5%	12.5%	Married with children	30.6%	28.7%
			Diversity measure	25.5%	35.2%	Single with children	8.0%	10.1%

ECONOMY & JOBS SCORE: 53/RANK: 152

INCOME	AREA	U.S. AVG	EMPLOYMENT	AREA	U.S. AVG	LARGEST EMPLOYING INDUSTRY
Per capita income	$20,961	$23,420	Unemployment rate	2.6%	6.1%	Food Manufacturing
Household income	$40,370	$46,060	Recent job growth	3.4%	.9%	
Household income < $25K	28.0%	26.4%	Projected future job growth	31.5%	15.1%	
Household income > $75K	18.2%	24.5%	White collar	50.1%	54.5%	
Household income growth	64.9%	57.3%	Blue collar	49.9%	45.5%	

COST OF LIVING SCORE: 75/RANK: 82

INDEXES & TAXES	AREA	U.S. AVG	HOUSING	AREA	U.S. AVG	NECESSITIES	AREA	U.S. AVG
Cost of Living Index	82.0	100.0	Median home price	$107,640	$160,100	Food Index	89.0	100.0
Financial Progress Index	104.9	100.0	Home price appreciation	5.1%	7.1%	Housing Index	66.9	100.0
Income tax rate	7.000%	4.625%	Median rent	$547	$670	Utilities Index	81.0	100.0
Sales tax rate	7.125%	6.474%	Homes owned	69.9%	63.9%	Transportation Index	91.4	100.0
Property tax rate	$9.0	$15.6	Homes rented	21.5%	25.3%	Healthcare Index	92.6	100.0
			Housing affordability	63.0%	54.5%	Miscellaneous Cost Index	94.1	100.0

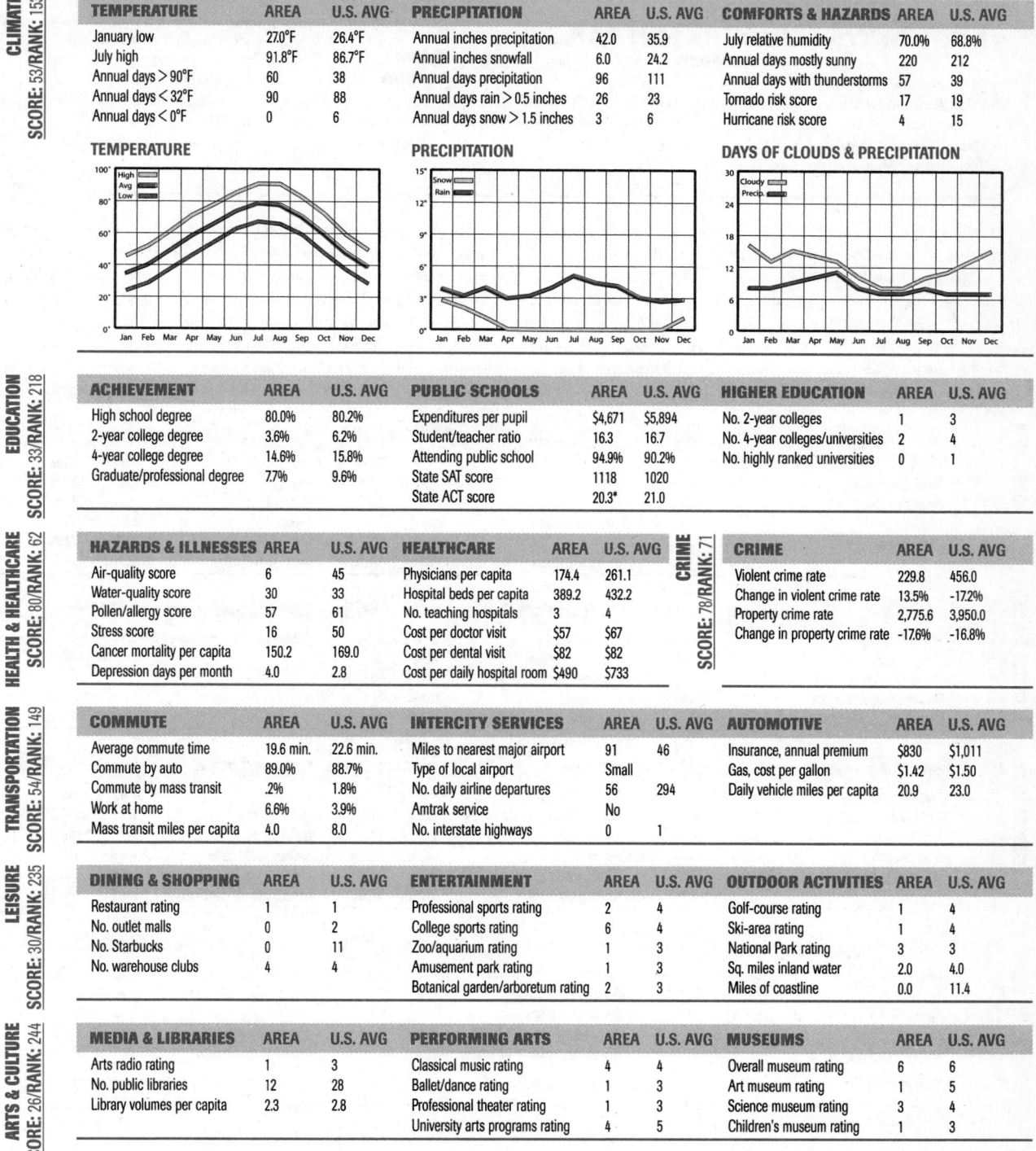

CLIMATE SCORE: 53/RANK: 153

TEMPERATURE	AREA	U.S. AVG	PRECIPITATION	AREA	U.S. AVG	COMFORTS & HAZARDS	AREA	U.S. AVG
January low	27.0°F	26.4°F	Annual inches precipitation	42.0	35.9	July relative humidity	70.0%	68.8%
July high	91.8°F	86.7°F	Annual inches snowfall	6.0	24.2	Annual days mostly sunny	220	212
Annual days > 90°F	60	38	Annual days precipitation	96	111	Annual days with thunderstorms	57	39
Annual days < 32°F	90	88	Annual days rain > 0.5 inches	26	23	Tornado risk score	17	19
Annual days < 0°F	0	6	Annual days snow > 1.5 inches	3	6	Hurricane risk score	4	15

TEMPERATURE

PRECIPITATION

DAYS OF CLOUDS & PRECIPITATION

EDUCATION SCORE: 33/RANK: 218

ACHIEVEMENT	AREA	U.S. AVG	PUBLIC SCHOOLS	AREA	U.S. AVG	HIGHER EDUCATION	AREA	U.S. AVG
High school degree	80.0%	80.2%	Expenditures per pupil	$4,671	$5,894	No. 2-year colleges	1	3
2-year college degree	3.6%	6.2%	Student/teacher ratio	16.3	16.7	No. 4-year colleges/universities	2	4
4-year college degree	14.6%	15.8%	Attending public school	94.9%	90.2%	No. highly ranked universities	0	1
Graduate/professional degree	7.7%	9.6%	State SAT score	1118	1020			
			State ACT score	20.3*	21.0			

HEALTH & HEALTHCARE SCORE: 80/RANK: 62

CRIME SCORE: 78/RANK: 71

HAZARDS & ILLNESSES	AREA	U.S. AVG	HEALTHCARE	AREA	U.S. AVG	CRIME	AREA	U.S. AVG
Air-quality score	6	45	Physicians per capita	174.4	261.1	Violent crime rate	229.8	456.0
Water-quality score	30	33	Hospital beds per capita	389.2	432.2	Change in violent crime rate	13.5%	-17.2%
Pollen/allergy score	57	61	No. teaching hospitals	3	4	Property crime rate	2,775.6	3,950.0
Stress score	16	50	Cost per doctor visit	$57	$67	Change in property crime rate	-17.6%	-16.8%
Cancer mortality per capita	150.2	169.0	Cost per dental visit	$82	$82			
Depression days per month	4.0	2.8	Cost per daily hospital room	$490	$733			

TRANSPORTATION SCORE: 54/RANK: 149

COMMUTE	AREA	U.S. AVG	INTERCITY SERVICES	AREA	U.S. AVG	AUTOMOTIVE	AREA	U.S. AVG
Average commute time	19.6 min.	22.6 min.	Miles to nearest major airport	91	46	Insurance, annual premium	$830	$1,011
Commute by auto	89.0%	88.7%	Type of local airport	Small		Gas, cost per gallon	$1.42	$1.50
Commute by mass transit	.2%	1.8%	No. daily airline departures	56	294	Daily vehicle miles per capita	20.9	23.0
Work at home	6.6%	3.9%	Amtrak service	No				
Mass transit miles per capita	4.0	8.0	No. interstate highways	0	1			

LEISURE SCORE: 30/RANK: 235

DINING & SHOPPING	AREA	U.S. AVG	ENTERTAINMENT	AREA	U.S. AVG	OUTDOOR ACTIVITIES	AREA	U.S. AVG
Restaurant rating	1	1	Professional sports rating	2	4	Golf-course rating	1	4
No. outlet malls	0	2	College sports rating	6	4	Ski-area rating	1	4
No. Starbucks	0	11	Zoo/aquarium rating	1	3	National Park rating	3	3
No. warehouse clubs	4	4	Amusement park rating	1	3	Sq. miles inland water	2.0	4.0
			Botanical garden/arboretum rating	2	3	Miles of coastline	0.0	11.4

ARTS & CULTURE SCORE: 26/RANK: 244

MEDIA & LIBRARIES	AREA	U.S. AVG	PERFORMING ARTS	AREA	U.S. AVG	MUSEUMS	AREA	U.S. AVG
Arts radio rating	1	3	Classical music rating	4	4	Overall museum rating	6	6
No. public libraries	12	28	Ballet/dance rating	1	3	Art museum rating	1	5
Library volumes per capita	2.3	2.8	Professional theater rating	1	3	Science museum rating	3	4
			University arts programs rating	4	5	Children's museum rating	1	3

Fitchburg-Leominster, MA

Score: 36.4   Rank: 292

Profile: Small-city pair
Location: North-central Massachusetts, 20 miles south of New Hampshire border
Elevation: 400 feet
Time zone: Eastern Standard Time

PRO	CON
Nearby recreation	Cost of living
Diverse economy	Unemployment
Attractive setting	Long commutes

Fitchburg has a typical New England flavor and minor cultural assets. Once a mill town and then a paper town, the city has diversified economically to include machine tool and pharmaceutical manufacturers. Leominster in particular is a center of the plastics industry, and a few biotech firms have moved into the area. While the diverse economy looks good on paper, unemployment is high, future job-growth projections are weak, and commute times are long. For the type of area, costs of living and housing appear high.

The twin towns are located in the narrow valley of the Nashua River among hills and dense deciduous forests. The mainly continental climate is influenced by proximity to the Atlantic Ocean, the Long Island Sound, and the Berkshire Hills. Summers are moderately warm and humid with summer thunderstorms developing over the mountains. Winters are moderate for the latitude but have frequent snow and cold snaps. Rapid weather changes occur when storms move northward up the Atlantic Coast. First freeze is mid-October, last is late April.

POPULATION

DEMOGRAPHICS	AREA	U.S. AVG	ETHNIC COMPOSITION	AREA	U.S. AVG	RESIDENT PROFILE	AREA	U.S. AVG
Population	145,233		White	94.5%	75.1%	Single	44.0%	43.6%
Population density per sq. mile	521.4	447.3	Black	1.8%	12.3%	Married	56.0%	56.4%
Population growth	5.1%	16.1%	Asian	1.7%	3.6%	Divorced	7.5%	8.4%
Median age	36.7	35.5	American Indian	.2%	.9%	Separated	2.5%	3.0%
Average family size	2.7	2.7	Hispanic	4.0%	12.5%	Married with children	29.2%	28.7%
			Diversity measure	26.8%	35.2%	Single with children	9.2%	10.1%

ECONOMY & JOBS   SCORE: 72/RANK: 90

INCOME	AREA	U.S. AVG	EMPLOYMENT	AREA	U.S. AVG	LARGEST EMPLOYING INDUSTRY
Per capita income	$26,284	$23,420	Unemployment rate	7.9%	6.1%	Plastics and Rubber Products Manufacturing
Household income	$54,973	$46,060	Recent job growth	1.2%	.9%	
Household income < $25K	21.8%	26.4%	Projected future job growth	7.1%	15.1%	
Household income > $75K	32.2%	24.5%	White collar	55.6%	54.5%	
Household income growth	66.4%	57.3%	Blue collar	44.4%	45.5%	

COST OF LIVING   SCORE: 20/RANK: 262

INDEXES & TAXES	AREA	U.S. AVG	HOUSING	AREA	U.S. AVG	NECESSITIES	AREA	U.S. AVG
Cost of Living Index	114.8	100.0	Median home price	$193,270	$160,100	Food Index	114.2	100.0
Financial Progress Index	102.1	100.0	Home price appreciation	14.5%	7.1%	Housing Index	120.0	100.0
Income tax rate	5.950%	4.625%	Median rent	$805	$670	Utilities Index	107.8	100.0
Sales tax rate	5.000%	6.474%	Homes owned	66.0%	63.9%	Transportation Index	110.5	100.0
Property tax rate	$14.9	$15.6	Homes rented	25.5%	25.3%	Healthcare Index	125.8	100.0
			Housing affordability	50.0%	54.5%	Miscellaneous Cost Index	108.3	100.0

CLIMATE   SCORE: 3/RANK: 319

TEMPERATURE	AREA	U.S. AVG	PRECIPITATION	AREA	U.S. AVG	COMFORTS & HAZARDS	AREA	U.S. AVG
January low	16.2°F	26.4°F	Annual inches precipitation	45.2	35.9	July relative humidity	68.0%	68.8%
July high	79.4°F	86.7°F	Annual inches snowfall	75.0	24.2	Annual days mostly sunny	197	212
Annual days > 90°F	2	38	Annual days precipitation	147	111	Annual days with thunderstorms	21	39
Annual days < 32°F	147	88	Annual days rain > 0.5 inches	31	23	Tornado risk score	13	19
Annual days < 0°F	7	6	Annual days snow > 1.5 inches	22	6	Hurricane risk score	19	15

TEMPERATURE

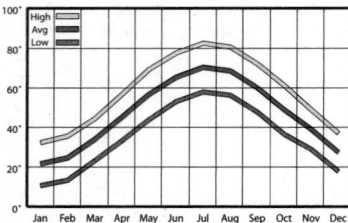

PRECIPITATION

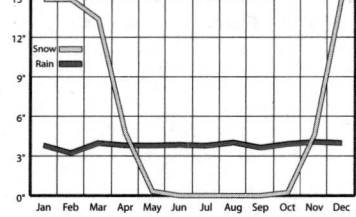

DAYS OF CLOUDS & PRECIPITATION

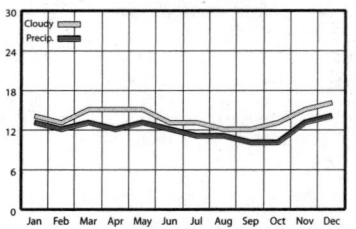

EDUCATION SCORE: 56/RANK: 146

ACHIEVEMENT	AREA	U.S. AVG	PUBLIC SCHOOLS	AREA	U.S. AVG	HIGHER EDUCATION	AREA	U.S. AVG
High school degree	83.6%	80.2%	Expenditures per pupil	$6,522	$5,894	No. 2-year colleges	1	3
2-year college degree	7.1%	6.2%	Student/teacher ratio	15.3	16.7	No. 4-year colleges/universities	1	4
4-year college degree	16.8%	15.8%	Attending public school	86.4%	90.2%	No. highly ranked universities	0	1
Graduate/professional degree	10.5%	9.6%	State SAT score	1038*	1020			
			State ACT score	22.3	21.0			

HEALTH & HEALTHCARE SCORE: 37/RANK: 206

CRIME SCORE: 85/RANK: 50

HAZARDS & ILLNESSES	AREA	U.S. AVG	HEALTHCARE	AREA	U.S. AVG	CRIME	AREA	U.S. AVG
Air-quality score	24	45	Physicians per capita	125.3	261.1	Violent crime rate	363.0	456.0
Water-quality score	96	33	Hospital beds per capita	345.1	432.2	Change in violent crime rate	-51.7%	-17.2%
Pollen/allergy score	54	61	No. teaching hospitals	2	4	Property crime rate	2,749.0	3,950.0
Stress score	64	50	Cost per doctor visit	$94	$67	Change in property crime rate	-21.9%	-16.8%
Cancer mortality per capita	179.6	169.0	Cost per dental visit	$105	$82			
Depression days per month	3.1	2.8	Cost per daily hospital room	$645	$733			

TRANSPORTATION SCORE: 12/RANK: 289

COMMUTE	AREA	U.S. AVG	INTERCITY SERVICES	AREA	U.S. AVG	AUTOMOTIVE	AREA	U.S. AVG
Average commute time	26.1 min.	22.6 min.	Miles to nearest major airport	31	46	Insurance, annual premium	$1,293	$1,011
Commute by auto	92.6%	88.7%	Type of local airport	Small		Gas, cost per gallon	$1.55	$1.50
Commute by mass transit	.9%	1.8%	No. daily airline departures	94	294	Daily vehicle miles per capita	17.8	23.0
Work at home	2.8%	3.9%	Amtrak service	No				
Mass transit miles per capita	13.2	8.0	No. interstate highways	1	1			

LEISURE SCORE: 76/RANK: 80

DINING & SHOPPING	AREA	U.S. AVG	ENTERTAINMENT	AREA	U.S. AVG	OUTDOOR ACTIVITIES	AREA	U.S. AVG
Restaurant rating	1	1	Professional sports rating	8	4	Golf-course rating	5	4
No. outlet malls	3	2	College sports rating	5	4	Ski-area rating	7	4
No. Starbucks	0	11	Zoo/aquarium rating	2	3	National Park rating	2	3
No. warehouse clubs	5	4	Amusement park rating	6	3	Sq. miles inland water	4.0	4.0
			Botanical garden/arboretum rating	3	3	Miles of coastline	0.0	11.4

ARTS & CULTURE SCORE: 44/RANK: 185

MEDIA & LIBRARIES	AREA	U.S. AVG	PERFORMING ARTS	AREA	U.S. AVG	MUSEUMS	AREA	U.S. AVG
Arts radio rating	4	3	Classical music rating	5	4	Overall museum rating	7	6
No. public libraries	8	28	Ballet/dance rating	5	3	Art museum rating	5	5
Library volumes per capita	4.2	2.8	Professional theater rating	8	3	Science museum rating	3	4
			University arts programs rating	6	5	Children's museum rating	3	3

Flagstaff, AZ

Score: 46.9   Rank: 244

Profile: Small mountain city
Location: North-central Arizona, 50 miles south of Grand Canyon National Park
Elevation: 6,993 feet
Time zone: Mountain Standard Time (no daylight savings time)

PRO	CON
Nearby mountains	Economy and jobs
Low heat and humidity	Cost of living
Outdoor recreation	Urban sprawl

Flagstaff is an old Route 66 railroad town, located in the high plateau of the San Francisco Mountains. The city has the second highest altitude of the established metropolitan cities, and thus escapes the desert heat associated with much of Arizona. Serving as a gateway for Grand Canyon National Park, as well as an oasis and junction on east-west I-40, the predominant industry is tourism, supported by relatively unattractive motel and restaurant strips. Downsides include an economy that is not diverse, negative job growth, and high unemployment. However, Northern Arizona University adds a college-town flavor, the population is the best educated in the state, and there's an overall youthful spirit. The 102.9 Cost of Living Index and $168,950 median home price work against the area. A stronger economy and arts and culture presence would improve the area's ranking.

The highest mountains in Arizona surround Flagstaff. Local vegetation is mainly desert scrub, grasses, and small trees, with coniferous forests in the nearby mountains. The landscape is generally attractive but a bit sparse in the immediate city area. The climate is decidedly high-altitude semiarid. Cold nights prevail year-round—at 210 days per year, Flagstaff drops below freezing more often than any other metropolitan area. Summers are mild and pleasantly cool with moderate humidity and a considerable diurnal temperature range. Temperatures often rise above 80°F and may reach 95°F. Winters bring snow cover, clear skies, and below-zero temperatures. Two distinct precipitation seasons occur in winter and late summer. First freeze is late September, last is mid-June.

POPULATION

DEMOGRAPHICS	AREA	U.S. AVG	ETHNIC COMPOSITION	AREA	U.S. AVG	RESIDENT PROFILE	AREA	U.S. AVG
Population	126,416		White	69.8%	75.1%	Single	41.4%	43.6%
Population density per sq. mile	5.6	447.3	Black	.7%	12.3%	Married	58.6%	56.4%
Population growth	24.2%	16.1%	Asian	.6%	3.6%	Divorced	6.9%	8.4%
Median age	30.0	35.5	American Indian	26.8%	.9%	Separated	1.9%	3.0%
Average family size	3.1	2.7	Hispanic	8.1%	12.5%	Married with children	32.0%	28.7%
			Diversity measure	55.0%	35.2%	Single with children	11.2%	10.1%

ECONOMY & JOBS — SCORE: 0/RANK: 329

INCOME	AREA	U.S. AVG	EMPLOYMENT	AREA	U.S. AVG	LARGEST EMPLOYING INDUSTRY
Per capita income	$19,198	$23,420	Unemployment rate	6.6%	6.1%	Accommodations and Food Services
Household income	$40,572	$46,060	Recent job growth	.2%	.9%	
Household income < $25K	29.9%	26.4%	Projected future job growth	29.2%	15.1%	
Household income > $75K	21.2%	24.5%	White collar	53.6%	54.5%	
Household income growth	55.5%	57.3%	Blue collar	46.4%	45.5%	

COST OF LIVING — SCORE: 18/RANK: 271

INDEXES & TAXES	AREA	U.S. AVG	HOUSING	AREA	U.S. AVG	NECESSITIES	AREA	U.S. AVG
Cost of Living Index	102.9	100.0	Median home price	$168,950	$160,100	Food Index	110.0	100.0
Financial Progress Index	84.0	100.0	Home price appreciation	6.4%	7.1%	Housing Index	104.9	100.0
Income tax rate	3.900%	4.625%	Median rent	$887	$670	Utilities Index	83.8	100.0
Sales tax rate	6.300%	6.474%	Homes owned	44.1%	63.9%	Transportation Index	107.8	100.0
Property tax rate	$6.8	$15.6	Homes rented	16.1%	25.3%	Healthcare Index	105.1	100.0
			Housing affordability	42.0%	54.5%	Miscellaneous Cost Index	98.0	100.0

CLIMATE — SCORE: 63/RANK: 122

TEMPERATURE	AREA	U.S. AVG	PRECIPITATION	AREA	U.S. AVG	COMFORTS & HAZARDS	AREA	U.S. AVG
January low	15.0°F	26.4°F	Annual inches precipitation	21.6	35.9	July relative humidity	36.0%	68.8%
July high	82.0°F	86.7°F	Annual inches snowfall	99.0	24.2	Annual days mostly sunny	290	212
Annual days > 90°F	3	38	Annual days precipitation	140	111	Annual days with thunderstorms	62	39
Annual days < 32°F	210	88	Annual days rain > 0.5 inches	11	23	Tornado risk score	1	19
Annual days < 0°F	13	6	Annual days snow > 1.5 inches	18	6	Hurricane risk score	0	15

TEMPERATURE

PRECIPITATION

DAYS OF CLOUDS & PRECIPITATION

EDUCATION — SCORE: 77/RANK: 77

ACHIEVEMENT	AREA	U.S. AVG	PUBLIC SCHOOLS	AREA	U.S. AVG	HIGHER EDUCATION	AREA	U.S. AVG
High school degree	83.9%	80.2%	Expenditures per pupil	$5,135	$5,894	No. 2-year colleges	1	3
2-year college degree	5.9%	6.2%	Student/teacher ratio	16.6	16.7	No. 4-year colleges/universities	3	4
4-year college degree	18.4%	15.8%	Attending public school	96.2%	90.2%	No. highly ranked universities	0	1
Graduate/professional degree	11.0%	9.6%	State SAT score	1049*	1020			
			State ACT score	21.4	21.0			

HEALTH & HEALTHCARE — SCORE: 22/RANK: 258

HAZARDS & ILLNESSES	AREA	U.S. AVG	HEALTHCARE	AREA	U.S. AVG
Air-quality score	24	45	Physicians per capita	475.4	261.1
Water-quality score	24	33	Hospital beds per capita	219.0	432.2
Pollen/allergy score	70	61	No. teaching hospitals	0	4
Stress score	66	50	Cost per doctor visit	$57	$67
Cancer mortality per capita	141.1	169.0	Cost per dental visit	$102	$82
Depression days per month	3.0	2.8	Cost per daily hospital room	$922	$733

CRIME — SCORE: 34/RANK: 217

CRIME	AREA	U.S. AVG
Violent crime rate	509.2	456.0
Change in violent crime rate	-33.8%	-17.2%
Property crime rate	5,183.8	3,950.0
Change in property crime rate	-35.7%	-16.8%

TRANSPORTATION — SCORE: 53/RANK: 156

COMMUTE	AREA	U.S. AVG	INTERCITY SERVICES	AREA	U.S. AVG	AUTOMOTIVE	AREA	U.S. AVG
Average commute time	19.0 min.	22.6 min.	Miles to nearest major airport	60	46	Insurance, annual premium	$1,079	$1,011
Commute by auto	79.7%	88.7%	Type of local airport	Small		Gas, cost per gallon	$1.66	$1.50
Commute by mass transit	.4%	1.8%	No. daily airline departures	168	294	Daily vehicle miles per capita	18.3	23.0
Work at home	3.9%	3.9%	Amtrak service	Yes				
Mass transit miles per capita	0.0	8.0	No. interstate highways	1	1			

LEISURE SCORE: 40/RANK: 202

DINING & SHOPPING	AREA	U.S. AVG	ENTERTAINMENT	AREA	U.S. AVG	OUTDOOR ACTIVITIES	AREA	U.S. AVG
Restaurant rating	1	1	Professional sports rating	2	4	Golf-course rating	6	4
No. outlet malls	0	2	College sports rating	5	4	Ski-area rating	4	4
No. Starbucks	2	11	Zoo/aquarium rating	1	3	National Park rating	10	3
No. warehouse clubs	1	4	Amusement park rating	1	3	Sq. miles inland water	2.0	4.0
			Botanical garden/arboretum rating	3	3	Miles of coastline	0.0	11.4

ARTS & CULTURE SCORE: 2/RANK: 323

MEDIA & LIBRARIES	AREA	U.S. AVG	PERFORMING ARTS	AREA	U.S. AVG	MUSEUMS	AREA	U.S. AVG
Arts radio rating	1	3	Classical music rating	3	4	Overall museum rating	8	6
No. public libraries	27	28	Ballet/dance rating	1	3	Art museum rating	6	5
Library volumes per capita	3.0	2.8	Professional theater rating	1	3	Science museum rating	10	4
			University arts programs rating	4	5	Children's museum rating	1	3

Flint, MI

Score: 49.1   Rank: 234

Profile: Mid-size industrial city
Location: Eastern Michigan, 65 miles northwest of Detroit
Elevation: 771 feet
Time zone: Eastern Standard Time

PRO
Cost of living
Urban revitalization
Arts and culture

CON
Economic cycles
Industrial flavor
Crime rate

Flint is the birthplace of General Motors and is second only to Detroit in auto production. It has seen its fortunes rise and fall with the auto industry. The city's lowest point, in the 1980s, was the focus of a documentary film *Roger & Me*, which depicted the effects of 30,000 lost jobs on the local economy and social fabric. Today, Flint is rebounding to a degree and working to build a broader economic base. There is a small but proud base of cultural attractions including an orchestra and other performing arts, plus a few quality museums. Flint is a case study in city rebirth after an economic disaster; whether it works out is still to be determined. If so, low cost of living, local attractions, and access to Detroit and recreation areas to the north should make Flint a better bet for the future.

The city is located in the Flint River Valley in the center of Genesee County. The surrounding terrain is generally level with some hills 15 miles southeast of the city. Climate is continental with a Great Lakes influence that cools summer days, slightly warms the winter, and prolongs warmer autumn weather—a combination providing favorable conditions for orchards and small fruit. The wettest periods normally occur in the late spring, early summer, and early fall. Winter is normally the driest season. Although snowfall is occasionally heavy, most occurs as frequent light flurries. Winter months are marked by considerable cloudiness and high humidity, while summer humidity is usually not excessive and sunshine is plentiful. Weather changes are frequent. First freeze is early October, last is early May.

POPULATION

DEMOGRAPHICS	AREA	U.S. AVG	ETHNIC COMPOSITION	AREA	U.S. AVG	RESIDENT PROFILE	AREA	U.S. AVG
Population	441,423		White	81.4%	75.1%	Single	48.1%	43.6%
Population density per sq. mile	690.1	447.3	Black	16.2%	12.3%	Married	51.9%	56.4%
Population growth	2.5%	16.1%	Asian	.9%	3.6%	Divorced	10.5%	8.4%
Median age	35.4	35.5	American Indian	.9%	.9%	Separated	3.5%	3.0%
Average family size	2.6	2.7	Hispanic	2.3%	12.5%	Married with children	26.2%	28.7%
			Diversity measure	40.3%	35.2%	Single with children	15.7%	10.1%

ECONOMY & JOBS SCORE: 23/RANK: 255

INCOME	AREA	U.S. AVG	EMPLOYMENT	AREA	U.S. AVG	LARGEST EMPLOYING INDUSTRY
Per capita income	$23,440	$23,420	Unemployment rate	9.6%	6.1%	Motor Vehicle Parts Manufacturing
Household income	$48,069	$46,060	Recent job growth	2.3%	.9%	
Household income < $25K	27.9%	26.4%	Projected future job growth	8.0%	15.1%	
Household income > $75K	27.0%	24.5%	White collar	47.0%	54.5%	
Household income growth	54.9%	57.3%	Blue collar	53.0%	45.5%	

COST OF LIVING SCORE: 51/RANK: 162

INDEXES & TAXES	AREA	U.S. AVG	HOUSING	AREA	U.S. AVG	NECESSITIES	AREA	U.S. AVG
Cost of Living Index	88.5	100.0	Median home price	$112,970	$160,100	Food Index	105.2	100.0
Financial Progress Index	115.8	100.0	Home price appreciation	5.9%	7.1%	Housing Index	70.2	100.0
Income tax rate	5.400%	4.625%	Median rent	$607	$670	Utilities Index	81.3	100.0
Sales tax rate	6.000%	6.474%	Homes owned	71.0%	63.9%	Transportation Index	102.3	100.0
Property tax rate	$15.6	$15.6	Homes rented	23.2%	25.3%	Healthcare Index	102.9	100.0
			Housing affordability	52.0%	54.5%	Miscellaneous Cost Index	97.2	100.0

CLIMATE SCORE: 26/RANK: 243

TEMPERATURE	AREA	U.S. AVG	PRECIPITATION	AREA	U.S. AVG	COMFORTS & HAZARDS	AREA	U.S. AVG
January low	14.6°F	26.4°F	Annual inches precipitation	29.8	35.9	July relative humidity	71.0%	68.8%
July high	81.2°F	86.7°F	Annual inches snowfall	45.4	24.2	Annual days mostly sunny	174	212
Annual days > 90°F	5	38	Annual days precipitation	132	111	Annual days with thunderstorms	33	39
Annual days < 32°F	139	88	Annual days rain > 0.5 inches	17	23	Tornado risk score	24	19
Annual days < 0°F	10	6	Annual days snow > 1.5 inches	10	6	Hurricane risk score	3	15

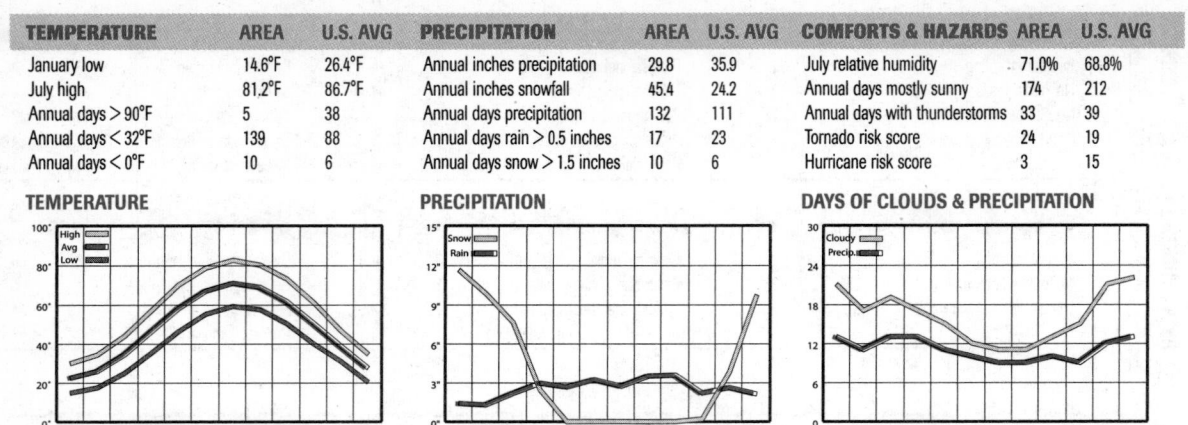

TEMPERATURE PRECIPITATION DAYS OF CLOUDS & PRECIPITATION

EDUCATION SCORE: 31/RANK: 227

ACHIEVEMENT	AREA	U.S. AVG	PUBLIC SCHOOLS	AREA	U.S. AVG	HIGHER EDUCATION	AREA	U.S. AVG
High school degree	83.1%	80.2%	Expenditures per pupil	$6,486	$5,894	No. 2-year colleges	1	3
2-year college degree	8.0%	6.2%	Student/teacher ratio	19.2	16.7	No. 4-year colleges/universities	2	4
4-year college degree	10.5%	15.8%	Attending public school	92.6%	90.2%	No. highly ranked universities	0	1
Graduate/professional degree	5.7%	9.6%	State SAT score	1140	1020			
			State ACT score	21.3*	21.0			

HEALTH & HEALTHCARE SCORE: 30/RANK: 232   **CRIME** SCORE: 23/RANK: 254

HAZARDS & ILLNESSES	AREA	U.S. AVG	HEALTHCARE	AREA	U.S. AVG	CRIME	AREA	U.S. AVG
Air-quality score	6	45	Physicians per capita	238.8	261.1	Violent crime rate	704.5	456.0
Water-quality score	30	33	Hospital beds per capita	390.9	432.2	Change in violent crime rate	-40.0%	-17.2%
Pollen/allergy score	54	61	No. teaching hospitals	5	4	Property crime rate	4,861.3	3,950.0
Stress score	99	50	Cost per doctor visit	$66	$67	Change in property crime rate	-17.5%	-16.8%
Cancer mortality per capita	178.9	169.0	Cost per dental visit	$94	$82			
Depression days per month	4.3	2.8	Cost per daily hospital room	$655	$733			

TRANSPORTATION SCORE: 25/RANK: 248

COMMUTE	AREA	U.S. AVG	INTERCITY SERVICES	AREA	U.S. AVG	AUTOMOTIVE	AREA	U.S. AVG
Average commute time	25.6 min.	22.6 min.	Miles to nearest major airport	49	46	Insurance, annual premium	$1,291	$1,011
Commute by auto	94.9%	88.7%	Type of local airport	Small		Gas, cost per gallon	$1.54	$1.50
Commute by mass transit	.7%	1.8%	No. daily airline departures	65	294	Daily vehicle miles per capita	28.7	23.0
Work at home	1.6%	3.9%	Amtrak service	Yes				
Mass transit miles per capita	15.1	8.0	No. interstate highways	2	1			

LEISURE SCORE: 72/RANK: 91

DINING & SHOPPING	AREA	U.S. AVG	ENTERTAINMENT	AREA	U.S. AVG	OUTDOOR ACTIVITIES	AREA	U.S. AVG
Restaurant rating	1	1	Professional sports rating	8	4	Golf-course rating	7	4
No. outlet malls	5	2	College sports rating	6	4	Ski-area rating	4	4
No. Starbucks	1	11	Zoo/aquarium rating	2	3	National Park rating	1	3
No. warehouse clubs	3	4	Amusement park rating	2	3	Sq. miles inland water	3.0	4.0
			Botanical garden/arboretum rating	2	3	Miles of coastline	0.0	11.4

ARTS & CULTURE SCORE: 77/RANK: 77

MEDIA & LIBRARIES	AREA	U.S. AVG	PERFORMING ARTS	AREA	U.S. AVG	MUSEUMS	AREA	U.S. AVG
Arts radio rating	4	3	Classical music rating	4	4	Overall museum rating	6	6
No. public libraries	23	28	Ballet/dance rating	4	3	Art museum rating	5	5
Library volumes per capita	2.7	2.8	Professional theater rating	1	3	Science museum rating	7	4
			University arts programs rating	6	5	Children's museum rating	3	3

Florence, AL

| Score: 41.8 | Rank: 269 |

Profile: Small city
Location: Extreme northwest Alabama along the Tennessee River
Elevation: 540 feet
Time zone: Central Standard Time

PRO
Cost of living
Low crime rate
Entertainment
 (mainly music)

CON
Isolated
Declining employment
High home prices

Florence is the center of the shoals area of the Tennessee Valley. It includes the more well-known and colorfully named town of Muscle Shoals. Located here are several manufacturing industries, including aluminum, rubber, and steel, but the job base has declined 4%, resulting in the state's highest unemployment rate of 7.9%. The Cost of Living Index is favorable at 79.1. The entertainment scene is bolstered by its blues roots, brought to life by the W. C. Handy Blues Festival and several recording studios in Muscle Shoals.

The town straddles the Tennessee River in a broad river valley, with low hills to the north and south. The climate is a mix of humid subtropical and continental types, with four seasons; long, warm humid summers; and mild but variable winters.

POPULATION

DEMOGRAPHICS	AREA	U.S. AVG	ETHNIC COMPOSITION	AREA	U.S. AVG	RESIDENT PROFILE	AREA	U.S. AVG
Population	141,966		White	85.6%	75.1%	Single	41.3%	43.6%
Population density per sq. mile	112.3	447.3	Black	13.7%	12.3%	Married	58.7%	56.4%
Population growth	8.1%	16.1%	Asian	.3%	3.6%	Divorced	7.6%	8.4%
Median age	38.6	35.5	American Indian	.3%	.9%	Separated	1.7%	3.0%
Average family size	2.5	2.7	Hispanic	.5%	12.5%	Married with children	28.6%	28.7%
			Diversity measure	25.8%	35.2%	Single with children	7.8%	10.1%

ECONOMY & JOBS SCORE: 75/RANK: 82

INCOME	AREA	U.S. AVG	EMPLOYMENT	AREA	U.S. AVG	LARGEST EMPLOYING INDUSTRY
Per capita income	$19,142	$23,420	Unemployment rate	7.9%	6.1%	Apparel Manufacturing
Household income	$32,788	$46,060	Recent job growth	-4.7%	.9%	
Household income < $25K	38.1%	26.4%	Projected future job growth	12.6%	15.1%	
Household income > $75K	14.1%	24.5%	White collar	45.7%	54.5%	
Household income growth	41.6%	57.3%	Blue collar	54.3%	45.5%	

COST OF LIVING SCORE: 67/RANK: 109

INDEXES & TAXES	AREA	U.S. AVG	HOUSING	AREA	U.S. AVG	NECESSITIES	AREA	U.S. AVG
Cost of Living Index	79.1	100.0	Median home price	$88,830	$160,100	Food Index	90.7	100.0
Financial Progress Index	88.3	100.0	Home price appreciation	3.6%	7.1%	Housing Index	55.2	100.0
Income tax rate	5.000%	4.625%	Median rent	$464	$670	Utilities Index	85.0	100.0
Sales tax rate	8.000%	6.474%	Homes owned	69.2%	63.9%	Transportation Index	93.0	100.0
Property tax rate	$3.9	$15.6	Homes rented	21.3%	25.3%	Healthcare Index	88.4	100.0
			Housing affordability	51.0%	54.5%	Miscellaneous Cost Index	97.6	100.0

CLIMATE SCORE: 35/RANK: 214

TEMPERATURE	AREA	U.S. AVG	PRECIPITATION	AREA	U.S. AVG	COMFORTS & HAZARDS	AREA	U.S. AVG
January low	31.3°F	26.4°F	Annual inches precipitation	52.0	35.9	July relative humidity	73.0%	68.8%
July high	90.2°F	86.7°F	Annual inches snowfall	3.0	24.2	Annual days mostly sunny	207	212
Annual days > 90°F	38	38	Annual days precipitation	121	111	Annual days with thunderstorms	58	39
Annual days < 32°F	65	88	Annual days rain > 0.5 inches	36	23	Tornado risk score	19	19
Annual days < 0°F	0	6	Annual days snow > 1.5 inches	2	6	Hurricane risk score	12	15

TEMPERATURE

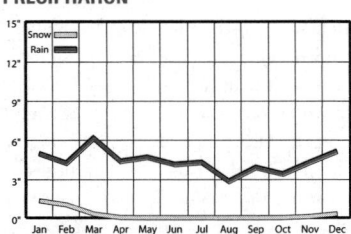

PRECIPITATION

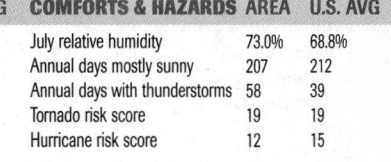

DAYS OF CLOUDS & PRECIPITATION

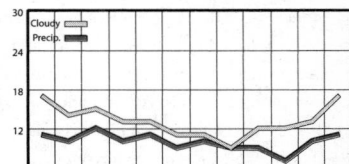

EDUCATION SCORE: 13/RANK: 288

ACHIEVEMENT	AREA	U.S. AVG	PUBLIC SCHOOLS	AREA	U.S. AVG	HIGHER EDUCATION	AREA	U.S. AVG
High school degree	75.2%	80.2%	Expenditures per pupil	$5,428	$5,894	No. 2-year colleges	1	3
2-year college degree	4.7%	6.2%	Student/teacher ratio	15.5	16.7	No. 4-year colleges/universities	2	4
4-year college degree	10.7%	15.8%	Attending public school	91.6%	90.2%	No. highly ranked universities	0	1
Graduate/professional degree	6.1%	9.6%	State SAT score	1111	1020			
			State ACT score	20.1*	21.0			

HEALTH & HEALTHCARE SCORE: 72/RANK: 91

HAZARDS & ILLNESSES	AREA	U.S. AVG	HEALTHCARE	AREA	U.S. AVG
Air-quality score	59	45	Physicians per capita	174.7	261.1
Water-quality score	36	33	Hospital beds per capita	704.4	432.2
Pollen/allergy score	67	61	No. teaching hospitals	0	4
Stress score	33	50	Cost per doctor visit	$57	$67
Cancer mortality per capita	160.1	169.0	Cost per dental visit	$69	$82
Depression days per month	.9	2.8	Cost per daily hospital room	$478	$733

CRIME SCORE: 1/RANK: 327

CRIME	AREA	U.S. AVG
Violent crime rate	187.5	456.0
Change in violent crime rate	-29.0%	-17.2%
Property crime rate	2,766.5	3,950.0
Change in property crime rate	-7.7%	-16.8%

TRANSPORTATION SCORE: 99/RANK: 3

COMMUTE	AREA	U.S. AVG	INTERCITY SERVICES	AREA	U.S. AVG	AUTOMOTIVE	AREA	U.S. AVG
Average commute time	23.7 min.	22.6 min.	Miles to nearest major airport	52	46	Insurance, annual premium	$822	$1,011
Commute by auto	93.2%	88.7%	Type of local airport	Small		Gas, cost per gallon	$1.46	$1.50
Commute by mass transit	.3%	1.8%	No. daily airline departures	41	294	Daily vehicle miles per capita	31.6	23.0
Work at home	2.0%	3.9%	Amtrak service	No				
Mass transit miles per capita	3.2	8.0	No. interstate highways	0	1			

LEISURE SCORE: 10/RANK: 295

DINING & SHOPPING	AREA	U.S. AVG	ENTERTAINMENT	AREA	U.S. AVG	OUTDOOR ACTIVITIES	AREA	U.S. AVG
Restaurant rating	1	1	Professional sports rating	2	4	Golf-course rating	2	4
No. outlet malls	0	2	College sports rating	3	4	Ski-area rating	1	4
No. Starbucks	0	11	Zoo/aquarium rating	1	3	National Park rating	2	3
No. warehouse clubs	3	4	Amusement park rating	1	3	Sq. miles inland water	6.0	4.0
			Botanical garden/arboretum rating	1	3	Miles of coastline	0.0	11.4

ARTS & CULTURE SCORE: 23/RANK: 255

MEDIA & LIBRARIES	AREA	U.S. AVG	PERFORMING ARTS	AREA	U.S. AVG	MUSEUMS	AREA	U.S. AVG
Arts radio rating	1	3	Classical music rating	1	4	Overall museum rating	5	6
No. public libraries	9	28	Ballet/dance rating	1	3	Art museum rating	3	5
Library volumes per capita	2.0	2.8	Professional theater rating	1	3	Science museum rating	1	4
			University arts programs rating	4	5	Children's museum rating	1	3

Florence, SC

Score: 41.9   Rank: 268

Profile: Small town
Location: Northeast South Carolina, 50 miles from the North Carolina border
Elevation: 225 feet
Time zone: Eastern Standard Time

PRO
Cost of living
Diverse economy
Healthcare

CON
Crime rate
Entertainment
Hot, humid summers

Florence has a thriving economy as a transportation and distribution center with manufacturing and agriculture added to the mix. The main transportation routes from the north and east split at this point, continuing inland to Atlanta and down the coast to Savannah and into Florida. Manufacturers include Honda, GE, Maytag, DuPont, and Southeastern Steel. Florence is a typical Southern town with a slow pace. There are shady streets and a historic but fairly nondescript business district. While it's far from big-city services and amenities, the town does have a modest set of local arts assets. The city has an excellent new hospital and medical complex. Darlington Raceway is an active NASCAR track, 5 miles north, and a series of state parks offer some recreation in the piney hills to the northwest. The area is strong financially with an attractive Cost of Living Index of 84.0 and strong recent job growth.

Florence is at the edge of the Coastal Plain where the land begins to rise to a wooded, rolling terrain. Predominant vegetation is pine forest with sections cleared for agriculture. The temperate climate is influenced by mountains to the northwest and the Atlantic 50 miles to the southeast. Warm, moist air and low elevation keep summers hot, sticky, and wet. Winter weather is typically cool and damp but not excessively cold, although nighttime lows frequently drop below freezing.

POPULATION

DEMOGRAPHICS	AREA	U.S. AVG	ETHNIC COMPOSITION	AREA	U.S. AVG	RESIDENT PROFILE	AREA	U.S. AVG
Population	127,237		White	59.9%	75.1%	Single	49.0%	43.6%
Population density per sq. mile	159.2	447.3	Black	39.7%	12.3%	Married	51.0%	56.4%
Population growth	11.3%	16.1%	Asian	.2%	3.6%	Divorced	6.2%	8.4%
Median age	35.8	35.5	American Indian	.1%	.9%	Separated	6.6%	3.0%
Average family size	2.8	2.7	Hispanic	.8%	12.5%	Married with children	28.7%	28.7%
			Diversity measure	50.6%	35.2%	Single with children	16.1%	10.1%

ECONOMY & JOBS
SCORE: 2/RANK: 323

INCOME	AREA	U.S. AVG	EMPLOYMENT	AREA	U.S. AVG	LARGEST EMPLOYING INDUSTRY
Per capita income	$20,539	$23,420	Unemployment rate	7.9%	6.1%	Chemical Manufacturing
Household income	$39,026	$46,060	Recent job growth	4.3%	.9%	
Household income < $25K	33.0%	26.4%	Projected future job growth	19.1%	15.1%	
Household income > $75K	20.1%	24.5%	White collar	49.4%	54.5%	
Household income growth	60.2%	57.3%	Blue collar	50.6%	45.5%	

COST OF LIVING
SCORE: 97/RANK: 8

INDEXES & TAXES	AREA	U.S. AVG	HOUSING	AREA	U.S. AVG	NECESSITIES	AREA	U.S. AVG
Cost of Living Index	84.0	100.0	Median home price	$97,200	$160,100	Food Index	100.7	100.0
Financial Progress Index	99.0	100.0	Home price appreciation	4.5%	7.1%	Housing Index	60.4	100.0
Income tax rate	7.000%	4.625%	Median rent	$509	$670	Utilities Index	90.4	100.0
Sales tax rate	6.000%	6.474%	Homes owned	72.1%	63.9%	Transportation Index	95.2	100.0
Property tax rate	$9.2	$15.6	Homes rented	20.8%	25.3%	Healthcare Index	96.4	100.0
			Housing affordability	59.0%	54.5%	Miscellaneous Cost Index	98.3	100.0

CLIMATE
SCORE: 20/RANK: 265

TEMPERATURE	AREA	U.S. AVG	PRECIPITATION	AREA	U.S. AVG	COMFORTS & HAZARDS	AREA	U.S. AVG
January low	33.9°F	26.4°F	Annual inches precipitation	46.0	35.9	July relative humidity	73.0%	68.8%
July high	92.0°F	86.7°F	Annual inches snowfall	2.0	24.2	Annual days mostly sunny	223	212
Annual days > 90°F	64	38	Annual days precipitation	111	111	Annual days with thunderstorms	54	39
Annual days < 32°F	60	88	Annual days rain > 0.5 inches	31	23	Tornado risk score	15	19
Annual days < 0°F	0	6	Annual days snow > 1.5 inches	1	6	Hurricane risk score	42	15

TEMPERATURE

PRECIPITATION

DAYS OF CLOUDS & PRECIPITATION

EDUCATION
SCORE: 6/RANK: 308

ACHIEVEMENT	AREA	U.S. AVG	PUBLIC SCHOOLS	AREA	U.S. AVG	HIGHER EDUCATION	AREA	U.S. AVG
High school degree	73.1%	80.2%	Expenditures per pupil	$5,005	$5,894	No. 2-year colleges	1	3
2-year college degree	6.6%	6.2%	Student/teacher ratio	15.1	16.7	No. 4-year colleges/universities	1	4
4-year college degree	12.5%	15.8%	Attending public school	86.6%	90.2%	No. highly ranked universities	0	1
Graduate/professional degree	6.2%	9.6%	State SAT score	989*	1020			
			State ACT score	19.2	21.0			

HEALTH & HEALTHCARE
SCORE: 91/RANK: 29

HAZARDS & ILLNESSES	AREA	U.S. AVG	HEALTHCARE	AREA	U.S. AVG
Air-quality score	24	45	Physicians per capita	287.7	261.1
Water-quality score	49	33	Hospital beds per capita	803.9	432.2
Pollen/allergy score	67	61	No. teaching hospitals	1	4
Stress score	62	50	Cost per doctor visit	$67	$67
Cancer mortality per capita	174.2	169.0	Cost per dental visit	$79	$82
Depression days per month	2.0	2.8	Cost per daily hospital room	$501	$733

CRIME
SCORE: 82/RANK: 59

CRIME	AREA	U.S. AVG
Violent crime rate	946.1	456.0
Change in violent crime rate	-6.3%	-17.2%
Property crime rate	5,733.4	3,950.0
Change in property crime rate	3.5%	-16.8%

TRANSPORTATION
SCORE: 9/RANK: 299

COMMUTE	AREA	U.S. AVG	INTERCITY SERVICES	AREA	U.S. AVG	AUTOMOTIVE	AREA	U.S. AVG
Average commute time	24.0 min.	22.6 min.	Miles to nearest major airport	60	46	Insurance, annual premium	$833	$1,011
Commute by auto	93.4%	88.7%	Type of local airport	Small		Gas, cost per gallon	$1.37	$1.50
Commute by mass transit	1.0%	1.8%	No. daily airline departures	51	294	Daily vehicle miles per capita	19.0	23.0
Work at home	1.8%	3.9%	Amtrak service	Yes				
Mass transit miles per capita	61.0	8.0	No. interstate highways	2	1			

DINING & SHOPPING	AREA	U.S. AVG	ENTERTAINMENT	AREA	U.S. AVG	OUTDOOR ACTIVITIES	AREA	U.S. AVG
Restaurant rating	1	1	Professional sports rating	3	4	Golf-course rating	2	4
No. outlet malls	3	2	College sports rating	3	4	Ski-area rating	1	4
No. Starbucks	0	11	Zoo/aquarium rating	1	3	National Park rating	1	3
No. warehouse clubs	3	4	Amusement park rating	1	3	Sq. miles inland water	1.0	4.0
			Botanical garden/arboretum rating	1	3	Miles of coastline	0.0	11.4

MEDIA & LIBRARIES	AREA	U.S. AVG	PERFORMING ARTS	AREA	U.S. AVG	MUSEUMS	AREA	U.S. AVG
Arts radio rating	1	3	Classical music rating	3	4	Overall museum rating	1	6
No. public libraries	6	28	Ballet/dance rating	1	3	Art museum rating	3	5
Library volumes per capita	1.8	2.8	Professional theater rating	1	3	Science museum rating	3	4
			University arts programs rating	1	5	Children's museum rating	1	3

Fort Collins–Loveland, CO

Score: 62.4   Rank: 128

Profile: Small-town complex/College town
Location: Northern Colorado along the Front Range, 25 miles south of the Wyoming border
Elevation: 5,004 feet
Time zone: Mountain Standard Time

PRO
Attractive downtown
Nearby mountains
Low crime rate

CON
Home prices
Economic cycles
Cold winters

Fort Collins is an agricultural and high-tech center on the Front Range. Colorado State University, a diversified university with an agricultural base, provides some amenities and ethnic diversity, but overall the town is more conservative than nearby Boulder. The downtown is attractive and clean with tree-lined streets. Loveland to the south also contains agriculture and high-tech companies, but many large employers in these industries have gone through difficult times. Rocky Mountain National Park and Estes Park (a town, not a park) just to the west provide ample recreational opportunities. Home prices are the second highest among Colorado's metropolitan areas.

Fort Collins is at the western edge of the high prairie grassland just against the base of the Front Range of the Rockies. The western horizon is spectacular with steep creek and river valleys descending into the area. The climate is continental with four well-defined, typically dry seasons. Summer days are warm and evenings are cool thanks to the mountain elevation. Southwest winds can bring periods of hot weather. Occasional thunderstorms produce downpours, but these are more likely to the east. Winters can be quite cold, with temperatures well below zero with strong inflows of Canadian air; wind makes the air seem colder. First freeze is early October, last is late May.

DEMOGRAPHICS	AREA	U.S. AVG	ETHNIC COMPOSITION	AREA	U.S. AVG	RESIDENT PROFILE	AREA	U.S. AVG
Population	264,605		White	94.2%	75.1%	Single	42.7%	43.6%
Population density per sq. mile	101.7	447.3	Black	1.4%	12.3%	Married	57.3%	56.4%
Population growth	42.2%	16.1%	Asian	1.6%	3.6%	Divorced	8.7%	8.4%
Median age	33.6	35.5	American Indian	.7%	.9%	Separated	1.9%	3.0%
Average family size	2.5	2.7	Hispanic	8.5%	12.5%	Married with children	25.2%	28.7%
			Diversity measure	22.6%	35.2%	Single with children	7.6%	10.1%

INCOME	AREA	U.S. AVG	EMPLOYMENT	AREA	U.S. AVG	LARGEST EMPLOYING INDUSTRY
Per capita income	$27,159	$23,420	Unemployment rate	5.0%	6.1%	Computer and Electronic Product Manufacturing
Household income	$52,465	$46,060	Recent job growth	1.5%	.9%	
Household income < $25K	21.2%	26.4%	Projected future job growth	24.5%	15.1%	
Household income > $75K	32.2%	24.5%	White collar	61.8%	54.5%	
Household income growth	76.2%	57.3%	Blue collar	38.2%	45.5%	

INDEXES & TAXES	AREA	U.S. AVG	HOUSING	AREA	U.S. AVG	NECESSITIES	AREA	U.S. AVG
Cost of Living Index	116.3	100.0	Median home price	$228,870	$160,100	Food Index	111.0	100.0
Financial Progress Index	96.1	100.0	Home price appreciation	10.0%	7.1%	Housing Index	142.2	100.0
Income tax rate	5.000%	4.625%	Median rent	$739	$670	Utilities Index	94.0	100.0
Sales tax rate	6.700%	6.474%	Homes owned	54.2%	63.9%	Transportation Index	98.7	100.0
Property tax rate	$7.2	$15.6	Homes rented	28.6%	25.3%	Healthcare Index	105.9	100.0
			Housing affordability	56.0%	54.5%	Miscellaneous Cost Index	97.9	100.0

CLIMATE SCORE: 54/RANK: 152

TEMPERATURE	AREA	U.S. AVG	PRECIPITATION	AREA	U.S. AVG	COMFORTS & HAZARDS	AREA	U.S. AVG
January low	16.2°F	26.4°F	Annual inches precipitation	16.0	35.9	July relative humidity	53.0%	68.8%
July high	87.4°F	86.7°F	Annual inches snowfall	60.0	24.2	Annual days mostly sunny	246	212
Annual days > 90°F	32	38	Annual days precipitation	88	111	Annual days with thunderstorms	41	39
Annual days < 32°F	163	88	Annual days rain > 0.5 inches	7	23	Tornado risk score	25	19
Annual days < 0°F	10	6	Annual days snow > 1.5 inches	13	6	Hurricane risk score	0	15

TEMPERATURE   PRECIPITATION   DAYS OF CLOUDS & PRECIPITATION

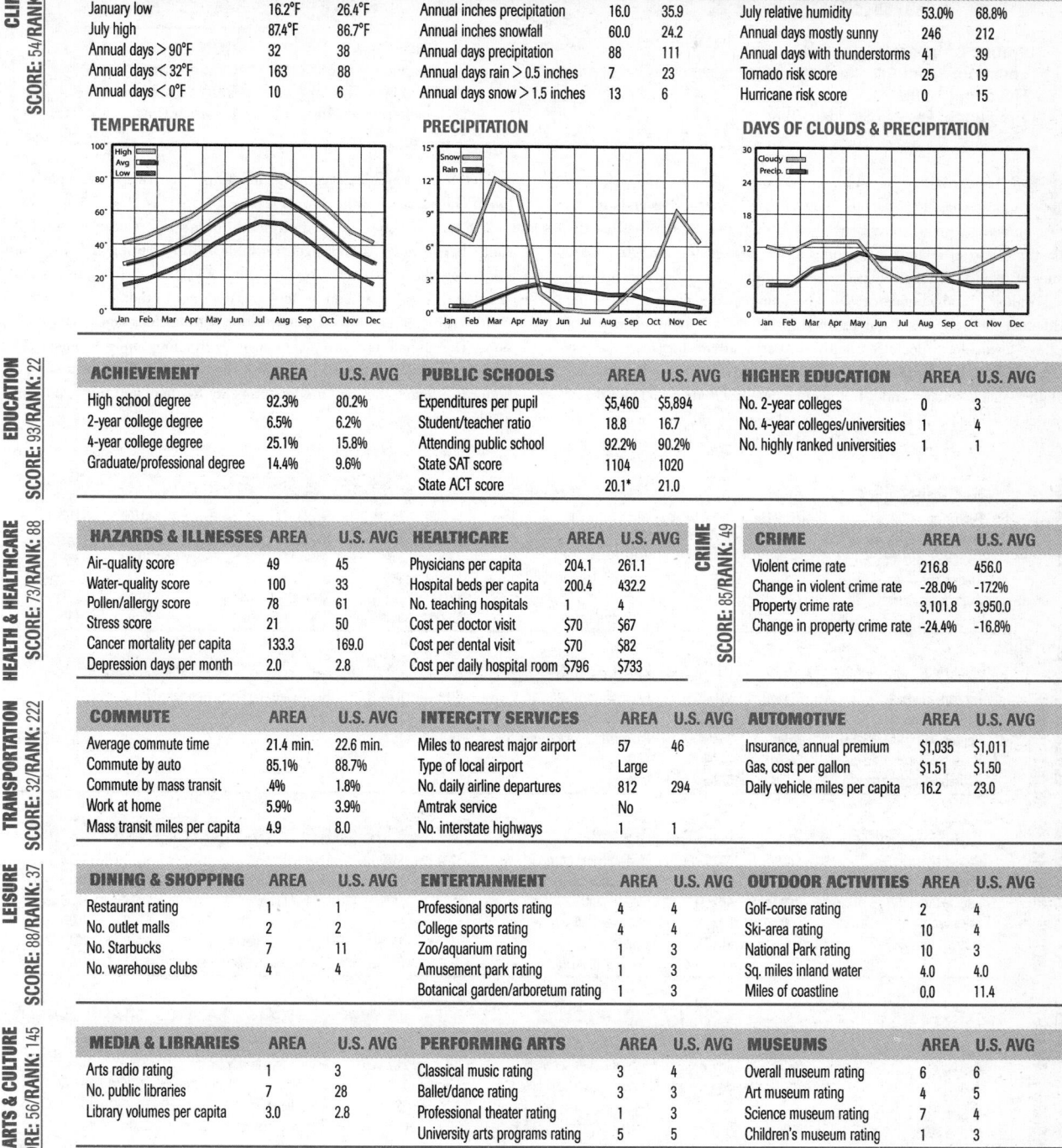

EDUCATION SCORE: 93/RANK: 22

ACHIEVEMENT	AREA	U.S. AVG	PUBLIC SCHOOLS	AREA	U.S. AVG	HIGHER EDUCATION	AREA	U.S. AVG
High school degree	92.3%	80.2%	Expenditures per pupil	$5,460	$5,894	No. 2-year colleges	0	3
2-year college degree	6.5%	6.2%	Student/teacher ratio	18.8	16.7	No. 4-year colleges/universities	1	4
4-year college degree	25.1%	15.8%	Attending public school	92.2%	90.2%	No. highly ranked universities	1	1
Graduate/professional degree	14.4%	9.6%	State SAT score	1104	1020			
			State ACT score	20.1*	21.0			

HEALTH & HEALTHCARE SCORE: 73/RANK: 88

HAZARDS & ILLNESSES	AREA	U.S. AVG	HEALTHCARE	AREA	U.S. AVG
Air-quality score	49	45	Physicians per capita	204.1	261.1
Water-quality score	100	33	Hospital beds per capita	200.4	432.2
Pollen/allergy score	78	61	No. teaching hospitals	1	4
Stress score	21	50	Cost per doctor visit	$70	$67
Cancer mortality per capita	133.3	169.0	Cost per dental visit	$70	$82
Depression days per month	2.0	2.8	Cost per daily hospital room	$796	$733

CRIME SCORE: 85/RANK: 49

CRIME	AREA	U.S. AVG
Violent crime rate	216.8	456.0
Change in violent crime rate	-28.0%	-17.2%
Property crime rate	3,101.8	3,950.0
Change in property crime rate	-24.4%	-16.8%

TRANSPORTATION SCORE: 32/RANK: 222

COMMUTE	AREA	U.S. AVG	INTERCITY SERVICES	AREA	U.S. AVG	AUTOMOTIVE	AREA	U.S. AVG
Average commute time	21.4 min.	22.6 min.	Miles to nearest major airport	57	46	Insurance, annual premium	$1,035	$1,011
Commute by auto	85.1%	88.7%	Type of local airport	Large		Gas, cost per gallon	$1.51	$1.50
Commute by mass transit	.4%	1.8%	No. daily airline departures	812	294	Daily vehicle miles per capita	16.2	23.0
Work at home	5.9%	3.9%	Amtrak service	No				
Mass transit miles per capita	4.9	8.0	No. interstate highways	1	1			

LEISURE SCORE: 88/RANK: 37

DINING & SHOPPING	AREA	U.S. AVG	ENTERTAINMENT	AREA	U.S. AVG	OUTDOOR ACTIVITIES	AREA	U.S. AVG
Restaurant rating	1	1	Professional sports rating	4	4	Golf-course rating	2	4
No. outlet malls	2	2	College sports rating	4	4	Ski-area rating	10	4
No. Starbucks	7	11	Zoo/aquarium rating	1	3	National Park rating	10	3
No. warehouse clubs	4	4	Amusement park rating	1	3	Sq. miles inland water	4.0	4.0
			Botanical garden/arboretum rating	1	3	Miles of coastline	0.0	11.4

ARTS & CULTURE SCORE: 56/RANK: 145

MEDIA & LIBRARIES	AREA	U.S. AVG	PERFORMING ARTS	AREA	U.S. AVG	MUSEUMS	AREA	U.S. AVG
Arts radio rating	1	3	Classical music rating	3	4	Overall museum rating	6	6
No. public libraries	7	28	Ballet/dance rating	3	3	Art museum rating	4	5
Library volumes per capita	3.0	2.8	Professional theater rating	1	3	Science museum rating	7	4
			University arts programs rating	5	5	Children's museum rating	1	3

Fort Lauderdale, FL

Profile: Large city
Location: South Atlantic coast of Florida, 25 miles north of Miami
Elevation: 12 feet
Time zone: Eastern Standard Time

Score: 75.5   **Rank:** 57

PRO	CON
Beaches	Cost of living
Entertainment	Tourist impact
Diverse economy	Urban sprawl

Fort Lauderdale is a large, cosmopolitan city on the southern Atlantic coast long famous as a destination for tourists and college students. Broad sandy beaches and high-rise complexes line the coast and barrier islands. Stretching to the edge of the Everglades are miles of inland sections containing residential areas mixed with diversified industry and commerce. The economy is diverse for the state. Although there are no major universities, there are many elements of college-town life, especially nightlife. Nearby Miami has more amenities, but Fort Lauderdale has a few of its own including the Florida Panthers hockey team and a full-scale commercial airport. The Cost of Living Index of 113.9 is over the national average and the second highest in the state. Urban sprawl has consumed most of the available land

and led to such problems as traffic and air quality. This is a fun place to live if one can accept the downsides.

The terrain is typical for a city on Florida's East Coast: Broad, flat, sandy barrier islands and level terrain give way to tropical forests and inland marshes. Palm trees are abundant. A system of rivers, inlets, and small bays—more inland waterways than any other Florida city—divides the area and provides interesting settings for homes and attractions. The climate is subtropical marine with a long, warm summer and abundant rainfall followed by a mild, dry winter. Inland locations are hotter in summer. Strong thunderstorms are frequent and hurricanes are a significant risk.

POPULATION

DEMOGRAPHICS	AREA	U.S. AVG	ETHNIC COMPOSITION	AREA	U.S. AVG	RESIDENT PROFILE	AREA	U.S. AVG
Population	1,709,118		White	84.0%	75.1%	Single	47.5%	43.6%
Population density per sq. mile	1,413.8	447.3	Black	12.9%	12.3%	Married	52.5%	56.4%
Population growth	36.1%	16.1%	Asian	1.9%	3.6%	Divorced	10.7%	8.4%
Median age	38.2	35.5	American Indian	.2%	.9%	Separated	3.3%	3.0%
Average family size	2.4	2.7	Hispanic	12.0%	12.5%	Married with children	19.9%	28.7%
			Diversity measure	56.7%	35.2%	Single with children	8.5%	10.1%

ECONOMY & JOBS SCORE: 18/RANK: 270

INCOME	AREA	U.S. AVG	EMPLOYMENT	AREA	U.S. AVG	LARGEST EMPLOYING INDUSTRY
Per capita income	$24,329	$23,420	Unemployment rate	5.9%	6.1%	Healthcare and Social Assistance
Household income	$44,247	$46,060	Recent job growth	-.7%	.9%	
Household income < $25K	25.9%	26.4%	Projected future job growth	18.8%	15.1%	
Household income > $75K	24.0%	24.5%	White collar	60.5%	54.5%	
Household income growth	44.7%	57.3%	Blue collar	39.5%	45.5%	

COST OF LIVING SCORE: 39/RANK: 200

INDEXES & TAXES	AREA	U.S. AVG	HOUSING	AREA	U.S. AVG	NECESSITIES	AREA	U.S. AVG
Cost of Living Index	113.9	100.0	Median home price	$204,800	$160,100	Food Index	105.8	100.0
Financial Progress Index	82.8	100.0	Home price appreciation	13.8%	7.1%	Housing Index	127.2	100.0
Income tax rate	0.000%	4.625%	Median rent	$827	$670	Utilities Index	100.2	100.0
Sales tax rate	6.000%	6.474%	Homes owned	63.0%	63.9%	Transportation Index	111.2	100.0
Property tax rate	$16.1	$15.6	Homes rented	24.0%	25.3%	Healthcare Index	116.5	100.0
			Housing affordability	51.0%	54.5%	Miscellaneous Cost Index	104.1	100.0

CLIMATE SCORE: 78/RANK: 71

TEMPERATURE	AREA	U.S. AVG	PRECIPITATION	AREA	U.S. AVG	COMFORTS & HAZARDS	AREA	U.S. AVG
January low	58.7°F	26.4°F	Annual inches precipitation	60.0	35.9	July relative humidity	75.0%	68.8%
July high	89.9°F	86.7°F	Annual inches snowfall	0.0	24.2	Annual days mostly sunny	248	212
Annual days > 90°F	30	38	Annual days precipitation	129	111	Annual days with thunderstorms	75	39
Annual days < 32°F	0	88	Annual days rain > 0.5 inches	32	23	Tornado risk score	61	19
Annual days < 0°F	0	6	Annual days snow > 1.5 inches	0	6	Hurricane risk score	100	15

TEMPERATURE

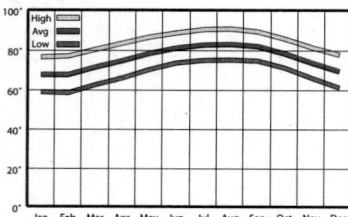

PRECIPITATION

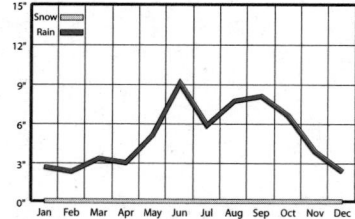

DAYS OF CLOUDS & PRECIPITATION

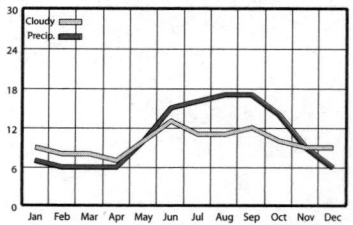

EDUCATION   SCORE: 27/RANK: 239

ACHIEVEMENT	AREA	U.S. AVG	PUBLIC SCHOOLS	AREA	U.S. AVG	HIGHER EDUCATION	AREA	U.S. AVG
High school degree	2.0%	80.2%	Expenditures per pupil	$5,453	$5,894	No. 2-year colleges	3	3
2-year college degree	7.5%	6.2%	Student/teacher ratio	21.1	16.7	No. 4-year colleges/universities	3	4
4-year college degree	15.8%	15.8%	Attending public school	86.6%	90.2%	No. highly ranked universities	0	1
Graduate/professional degree	8.7%	9.6%	State SAT score	996*	1020			
			State ACT score	20.5	21.0			

HEALTH & HEALTHCARE   SCORE: 71/RANK: 93

HAZARDS & ILLNESSES	AREA	U.S. AVG	HEALTHCARE	AREA	U.S. AVG
Air-quality score	48	45	Physicians per capita	226.8	261.1
Water-quality score	20	33	Hospital beds per capita	451.5	432.2
Pollen/allergy score	49	61	No. teaching hospitals	7	4
Stress score	83	50	Cost per doctor visit	$65	$67
Cancer mortality per capita	163.9	169.0	Cost per dental visit	$111	$82
Depression days per month	3.1	2.8	Cost per daily hospital room	$740	$733

CRIME   SCORE: 56/RANK: 143

CRIME	AREA	U.S. AVG
Violent crime rate	605.0	456.0
Change in violent crime rate	-28.6%	-17.2%
Property crime rate	4,054.3	3,950.0
Change in property crime rate	-44.4%	-16.8%

TRANSPORTATION   SCORE: 30/RANK: 232

COMMUTE	AREA	U.S. AVG	INTERCITY SERVICES	AREA	U.S. AVG	AUTOMOTIVE	AREA	U.S. AVG
Average commute time	27.4 min.	22.6 min.	Miles to nearest major airport	24	46	Insurance, annual premium	$1,099	$1,011
Commute by auto	93.0%	88.7%	Type of local airport	Large		Gas, cost per gallon	$1.54	$1.50
Commute by mass transit	1.7%	1.8%	No. daily airline departures	698	294	Daily vehicle miles per capita	23.8	23.0
Work at home	2.2%	3.9%	Amtrak service	Yes				
Mass transit miles per capita	15.5	8.0	No. interstate highways	1	1			

LEISURE   SCORE: 83/RANK: 59

DINING & SHOPPING	AREA	U.S. AVG	ENTERTAINMENT	AREA	U.S. AVG	OUTDOOR ACTIVITIES	AREA	U.S. AVG
Restaurant rating	1	1	Professional sports rating	8	4	Golf-course rating	8	4
No. outlet malls	3	2	College sports rating	3	4	Ski-area rating	1	4
No. Starbucks	22	11	Zoo/aquarium rating	2	3	National Park rating	5	3
No. warehouse clubs	8	4	Amusement park rating	3	3	Sq. miles inland water	3.0	4.0
			Botanical garden/arboretum rating	2	3	Miles of coastline	24.8	11.4

ARTS & CULTURE   SCORE: 21/RANK: 259

MEDIA & LIBRARIES	AREA	U.S. AVG	PERFORMING ARTS	AREA	U.S. AVG	MUSEUMS	AREA	U.S. AVG
Arts radio rating	3	3	Classical music rating	6	4	Overall museum rating	6	6
No. public libraries	41	28	Ballet/dance rating	3	3	Art museum rating	6	5
Library volumes per capita	1.6	2.8	Professional theater rating	3	3	Science museum rating	6	4
			University arts programs rating	6	5	Children's museum rating	5	3

Fort Myers–Cape Coral, FL

Score: 50.6   **Rank: 220**

Profile: Mid-size-city complex
Location: Gulf coast, 130 miles south of Tampa–St. Petersburg
Elevation: 31 feet
Time zone: Eastern Standard Time

PRO	CON
Winter climate	Arts and culture
Baseball spring training	Air service
Attractive downtown	Crime rate

Fort Myers, on the southern Florida Gulf Coast, is a quiet city with palm-tree-lined streets. Not a typical beach town, it nonetheless maintains a tropical flavor, attracts some tourists, and is home to several baseball spring-training camps. Offshore islands Sanibel and Captiva are more touristy, although both are restrained in development compared to other areas in the state. Cape Coral, just to the southwest, is a planned community on the waterfront that's popular with retirees. The Florida climate is generally pleasant, but the southerly and slightly inland location of Fort Myers provides particularly nice and dry winter weather. But on the downside, the area is far from big-city amenities such as arts and culture, entertainment, and air service, and jobs and employment appear to be going to other parts of the state.

Fort Myers is located on the south bank of the Caloosahatchee River about 15 miles inland from the Gulf of Mexico. The terrain is level and low with a mix of coastal plain and wet oak, magnolia, and evergreen forests. The climate is subtropical with a strong Gulf influence. High temperatures generally range from the low 60s in winter to the low 80s in summer. Winters are mild with many bright, warm days and moderately cool nights. Occasional cold snaps drop temperatures to the 30s, but rarely to the 20s. About two-thirds of annual precipitation occurs June through September, mostly as cooling late afternoon thunderstorms 2 out of every 3 days. There are frequent long dry periods in winter. Late summer and fall tropical storms and hurricanes cause occasional torrential downpours, delivering perhaps 6 to 10 inches in 24 hours.

POPULATION

DEMOGRAPHICS	AREA	U.S. AVG	ETHNIC COMPOSITION	AREA	U.S. AVG	RESIDENT PROFILE	AREA	U.S. AVG
Population	475,639		White	90.8%	75.1%	Single	37.3%	43.6%
Population density per sq. mile	591.9	447.3	Black	7.0%	12.3%	Married	62.7%	56.4%
Population growth	41.9%	16.1%	Asian	.7%	3.6%	Divorced	10.1%	8.4%
Median age	45.8	35.5	American Indian	.2%	.9%	Separated	2.3%	3.0%
Average family size	2.4	2.7	Hispanic	6.6%	12.5%	Married with children	19.2%	28.7%
			Diversity measure	30.9%	35.2%	Single with children	8.0%	10.1%

ECONOMY & JOBS SCORE: 18/RANK: 268

INCOME	AREA	U.S. AVG	EMPLOYMENT	AREA	U.S. AVG	LARGEST EMPLOYING INDUSTRY
Per capita income	$26,022	$23,420	Unemployment rate	4.3%	6.1%	Construction
Household income	$41,929	$46,060	Recent job growth	.7%	.9%	
Household income < $25K	24.2%	26.4%	Projected future job growth	24.3%	15.1%	
Household income > $75K	19.0%	24.5%	White collar	55.8%	54.5%	
Household income growth	47.1%	57.3%	Blue collar	44.2%	45.5%	

COST OF LIVING SCORE: 83/RANK: 57

INDEXES & TAXES	AREA	U.S. AVG	HOUSING	AREA	U.S. AVG	NECESSITIES	AREA	U.S. AVG
Cost of Living Index	94.0	100.0	Median home price	$136,400	$160,100	Food Index	99.8	100.0
Financial Progress Index	95.0	100.0	Home price appreciation	12.0%	7.1%	Housing Index	84.7	100.0
Income tax rate	0.000%	4.625%	Median rent	$625	$670	Utilities Index	99.5	100.0
Sales tax rate	6.000%	6.474%	Homes owned	57.8%	63.9%	Transportation Index	107.6	100.0
Property tax rate	$17.5	$15.6	Homes rented	18.8%	25.3%	Healthcare Index	96.5	100.0
			Housing affordability	61.0%	54.5%	Miscellaneous Cost Index	95.3	100.0

CLIMATE SCORE: 81/RANK: 63

TEMPERATURE	AREA	U.S. AVG	PRECIPITATION	AREA	U.S. AVG	COMFORTS & HAZARDS	AREA	U.S. AVG
January low	52.3°F	26.4°F	Annual inches precipitation	54.0	35.9	July relative humidity	76.0%	68.8%
July high	91.5°F	86.7°F	Annual inches snowfall	0.0	24.2	Annual days mostly sunny	264	212
Annual days > 90°F	106	38	Annual days precipitation	112	111	Annual days with thunderstorms	93	39
Annual days < 32°F	1	88	Annual days rain > 0.5 inches	32	23	Tornado risk score	52	19
Annual days < 0°F	0	6	Annual days snow > 1.5 inches	0	6	Hurricane risk score	80	15

TEMPERATURE

PRECIPITATION

DAYS OF CLOUDS & PRECIPITATION

EDUCATION SCORE: 25/RANK: 248

ACHIEVEMENT	AREA	U.S. AVG	PUBLIC SCHOOLS	AREA	U.S. AVG	HIGHER EDUCATION	AREA	U.S. AVG
High school degree	82.3%	80.2%	Expenditures per pupil	$5,746	$5,894	No. 2-year colleges	1	3
2-year college degree	6.0%	6.2%	Student/teacher ratio	19.5	16.7	No. 4-year colleges/universities	1	4
4-year college degree	13.5%	15.8%	Attending public school	90.8%	90.2%	No. highly ranked universities	0	1
Graduate/professional degree	7.6%	9.6%	State SAT score	996*	1020			
			State ACT score	20.5	21.0			

HEALTH & HEALTHCARE SCORE: 75/RANK: 81

HAZARDS & ILLNESSES	AREA	U.S. AVG	HEALTHCARE	AREA	U.S. AVG
Air-quality score	6	45	Physicians per capita	203.3	261.1
Water-quality score	30	33	Hospital beds per capita	416.7	432.2
Pollen/allergy score	72	61	No. teaching hospitals	0	4
Stress score	59	50	Cost per doctor visit	$85	$67
Cancer mortality per capita	158.9	169.0	Cost per dental visit	$90	$82
Depression days per month	2.2	2.8	Cost per daily hospital room	$583	$733

CRIME SCORE: 26/RANK: 242

CRIME	AREA	U.S. AVG
Violent crime rate	650.7	456.0
Change in violent crime rate	-.1%	-17.2%
Property crime rate	4,147.1	3,950.0
Change in property crime rate	-13.9%	-16.8%

TRANSPORTATION SCORE: 16/RANK: 278

COMMUTE	AREA	U.S. AVG	INTERCITY SERVICES	AREA	U.S. AVG	AUTOMOTIVE	AREA	U.S. AVG
Average commute time	25.0 min.	22.6 min.	Miles to nearest major airport	13	46	Insurance, annual premium	$1,068	$1,011
Commute by auto	89.4%	88.7%	Type of local airport	Medium		Gas, cost per gallon	$1.52	$1.50
Commute by mass transit	1.0%	1.8%	No. daily airline departures	92	294	Daily vehicle miles per capita	22.0	23.0
Work at home	2.7%	3.9%	Amtrak service	No				
Mass transit miles per capita	8.3	8.0	No. interstate highways	1	1			

LEISURE
SCORE: 53/RANK: 154

DINING & SHOPPING	AREA	U.S. AVG	ENTERTAINMENT	AREA	U.S. AVG	OUTDOOR ACTIVITIES	AREA	U.S. AVG
Restaurant rating	1	1	Professional sports rating	3	4	Golf-course rating	4	4
No. outlet malls	3	2	College sports rating	1	4	Ski-area rating	1	4
No. Starbucks	1	11	Zoo/aquarium rating	3	3	National Park rating	2	3
No. warehouse clubs	1	4	Amusement park rating	4	3	Sq. miles inland water	10.0	4.0
			Botanical garden/arboretum rating	7	3	Miles of coastline	38.0	11.4

ARTS & CULTURE
SCORE: 13/RANK: 285

MEDIA & LIBRARIES	AREA	U.S. AVG	PERFORMING ARTS	AREA	U.S. AVG	MUSEUMS	AREA	U.S. AVG
Arts radio rating	1	3	Classical music rating	4	4	Overall museum rating	5	6
No. public libraries	14	28	Ballet/dance rating	1	3	Art museum rating	2	5
Library volumes per capita	2.3	2.8	Professional theater rating	1	3	Science museum rating	7	4
			University arts programs rating	2	5	Children's museum rating	7	3

Fort Pierce–Port St. Lucie, FL

Score: 58.3   Rank: 163

Profile: Beach-city complex
Location: Central Atlantic coast between Melbourne and West Palm Beach, 125 miles north of Miami
Elevation: 11 feet
Time zone: Eastern Standard Time

PRO
Attractive setting

Air quality
Water recreation

CON
Low educational attainment
Economy
Isolation

Compared to larger cities and resort areas to the south, Fort Pierce is a small, comfortable, laid-back residential community. Port St. Lucie is a small, business-friendly, but nondescript community just inland from Fort Pierce. Entertainment is provided by baseball spring-training camps and the study and viewing of wildlife. The area is less crowded and affected by sprawl problems than those areas to the south, but it's also far from services such as healthcare and air transportation. The long commute times reflect distances from jobs rather than congestion. The employment picture is somewhat weak and educational attainment is low.

The landscape consists of a barrier island and coastal plain—topography typical of Florida's coastal cities. There is extensive agriculture, tropical trees, and vegetation inland. Lake Okeechobee is 40 miles to the southwest. The subtropical coastal climate is pleasant year-round. Summer temperatures are tempered by ocean breezes and by the frequent formation of afternoon cumulus clouds and showers. Temperatures of 90°F have occurred in all months but seldom reach 100°F. There is some hurricane risk, but the area is north of the major hurricane tracks.

POPULATION

DEMOGRAPHICS	AREA	U.S. AVG	ETHNIC COMPOSITION	AREA	U.S. AVG	RESIDENT PROFILE	AREA	U.S. AVG
Population	337,638		White	82.3%	75.1%	Single	39.7%	43.6%
Population density per sq. mile	299.3	447.3	Black	14.6%	12.3%	Married	60.3%	56.4%
Population growth	34.5%	16.1%	Asian	1.0%	3.6%	Divorced	9.0%	8.4%
Median age	44.6	35.5	American Indian	.2%	.9%	Separated	3.4%	3.0%
Average family size	2.6	2.7	Hispanic	7.3%	12.5%	Married with children	21.8%	28.7%
			Diversity measure	35.3%	35.2%	Single with children	9.8%	10.1%

ECONOMY & JOBS
SCORE: 21/RANK: 260

INCOME	AREA	U.S. AVG	EMPLOYMENT	AREA	U.S. AVG	LARGEST EMPLOYING INDUSTRY
Per capita income	$24,715	$23,420	Unemployment rate	8.6%	6.1%	Retail trade
Household income	$39,650	$46,060	Recent job growth	-1.1%	.9%	
Household income < $25K	29.2%	26.4%	Projected future job growth	17.8%	15.1%	
Household income > $75K	18.1%	24.5%	White collar	53.1%	54.5%	
Household income growth	34.4%	57.3%	Blue collar	46.9%	45.5%	

COST OF LIVING
SCORE: 72/RANK: 93

INDEXES & TAXES	AREA	U.S. AVG	HOUSING	AREA	U.S. AVG	NECESSITIES	AREA	U.S. AVG
Cost of Living Index	96.9	100.0	Median home price	$134,010	$160,100	Food Index	103.2	100.0
Financial Progress Index	87.2	100.0	Home price appreciation	10.5%	7.1%	Housing Index	83.2	100.0
Income tax rate	0.000%	4.625%	Median rent	$711	$670	Utilities Index	97.2	100.0
Sales tax rate	6.500%	6.474%	Homes owned	59.5%	63.9%	Transportation Index	108.9	100.0
Property tax rate	$18.4	$15.6	Homes rented	21.3%	25.3%	Healthcare Index	99.4	100.0
			Housing affordability	51.0%	54.5%	Miscellaneous Cost Index	107.6	100.0

CLIMATE SCORE: 64/RANK: 119

TEMPERATURE	AREA	U.S. AVG	PRECIPITATION	AREA	U.S. AVG	COMFORTS & HAZARDS	AREA	U.S. AVG
January low	55.9°F	26.4°F	Annual inches precipitation	62.1	35.9	July relative humidity	73.0%	68.8%
July high	89.6°F	86.7°F	Annual inches snowfall	0.0	24.2	Annual days mostly sunny	228	212
Annual days > 90°F	55	38	Annual days precipitation	131	111	Annual days with thunderstorms	79	39
Annual days < 32°F	1	88	Annual days rain > 0.5 inches	37	23	Tornado risk score	25	19
Annual days < 0°F	0	6	Annual days snow > 1.5 inches	0	6	Hurricane risk score	87	15

TEMPERATURE

PRECIPITATION

DAYS OF CLOUDS & PRECIPITATION

EDUCATION SCORE: 25/RANK: 246

ACHIEVEMENT	AREA	U.S. AVG	PUBLIC SCHOOLS	AREA	U.S. AVG	HIGHER EDUCATION	AREA	U.S. AVG
High school degree	80.8%	80.2%	Expenditures per pupil	$5,455	$5,894	No. 2-year colleges	1	3
2-year college degree	6.7%	6.2%	Student/teacher ratio	18.6	16.7	No. 4-year colleges/universities	1	4
4-year college degree	13.0%	15.8%	Attending public school	91.1%	90.2%	No. highly ranked universities	0	1
Graduate/professional degree	6.7%	9.6%	State SAT score	996*	1020			
			State ACT score	20.5	21.0			

HEALTH & HEALTHCARE SCORE: 64/RANK: 117

HAZARDS & ILLNESSES	AREA	U.S. AVG	HEALTHCARE	AREA	U.S. AVG
Air-quality score	24	45	Physicians per capita	186.3	261.1
Water-quality score	19	33	Hospital beds per capita	299.3	432.2
Pollen/allergy score	63	61	No. teaching hospitals	0	4
Stress score	92	50	Cost per doctor visit	$61	$67
Cancer mortality per capita	165.7	169.0	Cost per dental visit	$760	$82
Depression days per month	4.0	2.8	Cost per daily hospital room	$640	$733

CRIME SCORE: 52/RANK: 157

CRIME	AREA	U.S. AVG
Violent crime rate	626.2	456.0
Change in violent crime rate	-22.8%	-17.2%
Property crime rate	3,532.8	3,950.0
Change in property crime rate	-28.3%	-16.8%

TRANSPORTATION SCORE: 3/RANK: 319

COMMUTE	AREA	U.S. AVG	INTERCITY SERVICES	AREA	U.S. AVG	AUTOMOTIVE	AREA	U.S. AVG
Average commute time	25.8 min.	22.6 min.	Miles to nearest major airport	44	46	Insurance, annual premium	$1,035	$1,011
Commute by auto	93.9%	88.7%	Type of local airport	Medium		Gas, cost per gallon	$1.58	$1.50
Commute by mass transit	.6%	1.8%	No. daily airline departures	146	294	Daily vehicle miles per capita	28.7	23.0
Work at home	2.6%	3.9%	Amtrak service	No				
Mass transit miles per capita	2.8	8.0	No. interstate highways	1	1			

LEISURE SCORE: 51/RANK: 161

DINING & SHOPPING	AREA	U.S. AVG	ENTERTAINMENT	AREA	U.S. AVG	OUTDOOR ACTIVITIES	AREA	U.S. AVG
Restaurant rating	1	1	Professional sports rating	2	4	Golf-course rating	4	4
No. outlet malls	1	2	College sports rating	1	4	Ski-area rating	1	4
No. Starbucks	0	11	Zoo/aquarium rating	1	3	National Park rating	2	3
No. warehouse clubs	3	4	Amusement park rating	1	3	Sq. miles inland water	5.0	4.0
			Botanical garden/arboretum rating	3	3	Miles of coastline	45.1	11.4

ARTS & CULTURE SCORE: 47/RANK: 174

MEDIA & LIBRARIES	AREA	U.S. AVG	PERFORMING ARTS	AREA	U.S. AVG	MUSEUMS	AREA	U.S. AVG
Arts radio rating	5	3	Classical music rating	1	4	Overall museum rating	5	6
No. public libraries	12	28	Ballet/dance rating	1	3	Art museum rating	3	5
Library volumes per capita	1.8	2.8	Professional theater rating	1	3	Science museum rating	4	4
			University arts programs rating	1	5	Children's museum rating	3	3

Fort Smith, AR-OK

Score: 21.8   **Rank:** 322

Profile: Small city
Location: Extreme western Arkansas at Oklahoma border in Arkansas River Valley
Elevation: 463 feet
Time zone: Central Standard Time

PRO	CON
Cost of living	Isolation
Nearby mountains	Arts and culture
Air quality	Recreation

Fort Smith is a small town with Old West flavor located in a flat valley along the Arkansas River. Major industries include light manufacturing and natural gas. The economy is steady with slightly above average job-growth prospects, and the Cost of Living Index (76.4) and median home price ($78,900) are among the lowest in the state and country. However, there isn't much to do. Aside from outdoor recreation in the Ozarks just to the north, most amenities are in Tulsa, 120 miles to the west.

Local terrain is hilly with flat, fertile rivers and creek bottoms. The Ozarks rise to 1,500 feet in the north and 3,000 feet in the south with areas of national forest and mountain lakes. The climate is continental with four seasons. The warm summers are suitable for growing fruit and wine grapes. Winters are mild with average daytime temperatures above freezing.

POPULATION

DEMOGRAPHICS	AREA	U.S. AVG	ETHNIC COMPOSITION	AREA	U.S. AVG	RESIDENT PROFILE	AREA	U.S. AVG
Population	212,045		White	88.1%	75.1%	Single	36.7%	43.6%
Population density per sq. mile	117.4	447.3	Black	3.6%	12.3%	Married	63.3%	56.4%
Population growth	20.5%	16.1%	Asian	2.1%	3.6%	Divorced	9.0%	8.4%
Median age	35.9	35.5	American Indian	5.9%	.9%	Separated	2.4%	3.0%
Average family size	2.6	2.7	Hispanic	2.2%	12.5%	Married with children	32.0%	28.7%
			Diversity measure	33.9%	35.2%	Single with children	9.7%	10.1%

ECONOMY & JOBS — SCORE: 51/RANK: 161

INCOME	AREA	U.S. AVG	EMPLOYMENT	AREA	U.S. AVG	LARGEST EMPLOYING INDUSTRY
Per capita income	$20,116	$23,420	Unemployment rate	4.5%	6.1%	Food Manufacturing
Household income	$37,488	$46,060	Recent job growth	2.8%	.9%	
Household income < $25K	32.1%	26.4%	Projected future job growth	18.0%	15.1%	
Household income > $75K	16.9%	24.5%	White collar	45.4%	54.5%	
Household income growth	67.2%	57.3%	Blue collar	54.6%	45.5%	

COST OF LIVING — SCORE: 81/RANK: 63

INDEXES & TAXES	AREA	U.S. AVG	HOUSING	AREA	U.S. AVG	NECESSITIES	AREA	U.S. AVG
Cost of Living Index	76.4	100.0	Median home price	$78,900	$160,100	Food Index	90.2	100.0
Financial Progress Index	104.6	100.0	Home price appreciation	4.0%	7.1%	Housing Index	49.0	100.0
Income tax rate	7.000%	4.625%	Median rent	$479	$670	Utilities Index	85.8	100.0
Sales tax rate	8.375%	6.474%	Homes owned	70.1%	63.9%	Transportation Index	94.3	100.0
Property tax rate	$12.0	$15.6	Homes rented	19.2%	25.3%	Healthcare Index	87.7	100.0
			Housing affordability	61.0%	54.5%	Miscellaneous Cost Index	94.9	100.0

CLIMATE — SCORE: 48/RANK: 172

TEMPERATURE	AREA	U.S. AVG	PRECIPITATION	AREA	U.S. AVG	COMFORTS & HAZARDS	AREA	U.S. AVG
January low	28.0°F	26.4°F	Annual inches precipitation	42.0	35.9	July relative humidity	68.0%	68.8%
July high	93.8°F	86.7°F	Annual inches snowfall	6.0	24.2	Annual days mostly sunny	220	212
Annual days > 90°F	65	38	Annual days precipitation	96	111	Annual days with thunderstorms	57	39
Annual days < 32°F	80	88	Annual days rain > 0.5 inches	26	23	Tornado risk score	33	19
Annual days < 0°F	0	6	Annual days snow > 1.5 inches	3	6	Hurricane risk score	5	15

TEMPERATURE

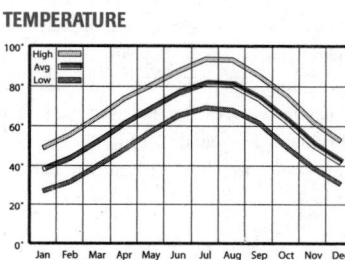

PRECIPITATION

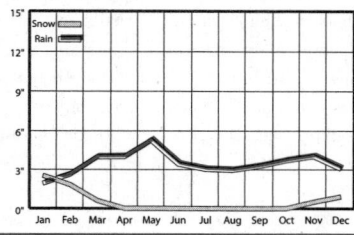

DAYS OF CLOUDS & PRECIPITATION

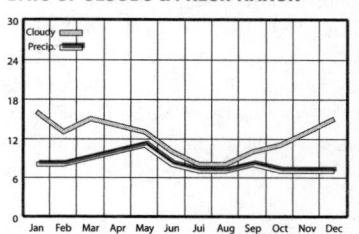

EDUCATION — SCORE: 11/RANK: 293

ACHIEVEMENT	AREA	U.S. AVG	PUBLIC SCHOOLS	AREA	U.S. AVG	HIGHER EDUCATION	AREA	U.S. AVG
High school degree	75.7%	80.2%	Expenditures per pupil	$4,841	$5,894	No. 2-year colleges	1	3
2-year college degree	6.6%	6.2%	Student/teacher ratio	15.6	16.7	No. 4-year colleges/universities	0	4
4-year college degree	8.9%	15.8%	Attending public school	94.1%	90.2%	No. highly ranked universities	0	1
Graduate/professional degree	4.9%	9.6%	State SAT score	1118	1020			
			State ACT score	20.3*	21.0			

HEALTH & HEALTHCARE — SCORE: 63/RANK: 121 | CRIME — SCORE: 12/RANK: 291

HAZARDS & ILLNESSES	AREA	U.S. AVG	HEALTHCARE	AREA	U.S. AVG	CRIME	AREA	U.S. AVG
Air-quality score	6	45	Physicians per capita	213.6	261.1	Violent crime rate	569.1	456.0
Water-quality score	33	33	Hospital beds per capita	538.4	432.2	Change in violent crime rate	37.0%	-17.2%
Pollen/allergy score	64	61	No. teaching hospitals	1	4	Property crime rate	4,661.2	3,950.0
Stress score	44	50	Cost per doctor visit	$65	$67	Change in property crime rate	1.1%	-16.8%
Cancer mortality per capita	166.4	169.0	Cost per dental visit	$83	$82			
Depression days per month	2.2	2.8	Cost per daily hospital room	$298	$733			

TRANSPORTATION — SCORE: 17/RANK: 272

COMMUTE	AREA	U.S. AVG	INTERCITY SERVICES	AREA	U.S. AVG	AUTOMOTIVE	AREA	U.S. AVG
Average commute time	21.8 min.	22.6 min.	Miles to nearest major airport	103	46	Insurance, annual premium	$835	$1,011
Commute by auto	94.0%	88.7%	Type of local airport	Medium		Gas, cost per gallon	$1.39	$1.50
Commute by mass transit	.2%	1.8%	No. daily airline departures	104	294	Daily vehicle miles per capita	14.6	23.0
Work at home	2.9%	3.9%	Amtrak service	No				
Mass transit miles per capita	0.0	8.0	No. interstate highways	1	1			

LEISURE — SCORE: 13/RANK: 289

DINING & SHOPPING	AREA	U.S. AVG	ENTERTAINMENT	AREA	U.S. AVG	OUTDOOR ACTIVITIES	AREA	U.S. AVG
Restaurant rating	1	1	Professional sports rating	2	4	Golf-course rating	2	4
No. outlet malls	0	2	College sports rating	1	4	Ski-area rating	1	4
No. Starbucks	0	11	Zoo/aquarium rating	1	3	National Park rating	5	3
No. warehouse clubs	3	4	Amusement park rating	1	3	Sq. miles inland water	4.0	4.0
			Botanical garden/arboretum rating	1	3	Miles of coastline	0.0	11.4

ARTS & CULTURE — SCORE: 1/RANK: 326

MEDIA & LIBRARIES	AREA	U.S. AVG	PERFORMING ARTS	AREA	U.S. AVG	MUSEUMS	AREA	U.S. AVG
Arts radio rating		3	Classical music rating		4	Overall museum rating		6
No. public libraries		28	Ballet/dance rating		3	Art museum rating		5
Library volumes per capita		2.8	Professional theater rating		3	Science museum rating		4
			University arts programs rating		5	Children's museum rating		3

Fort Walton Beach, FL

Score: 59.4 Rank: 152

Profile: Beach city/Military town
Location: Florida Panhandle, on the Gulf Coast, 40 miles east of Pensacola
Elevation: 112 feet
Time zone: Eastern Standard Time

PRO	CON
Beaches	Arts and culture
Water recreation	Tourist sprawl
Healthy economy	Air service

Fort Walton Beach is located at the head of the Choctawhatchee Bay. The city itself is primarily a tourist center with a long, built-up strip of beachside high-rise hotels. The resort community of Destin, on the barrier island sheltering the bay, has become a major destination for travelers, especially from neighboring southeastern states. Nearby Eglin Air Force Base rounds out the economic picture. Fort Walton Beach is only one of five Florida metro areas exhibiting recent job growth. Downsides include the lack of arts and culture and air service, and few leisure amenities except watersports.

Sandy coastal areas rise slightly inland, where forests of pine and live oak begin, but the area is mostly open and level. The Gulf of Mexico moderates winter cold and creates cool, refreshing daytime breezes in summer. Summer temperatures are in the 80s and 90s; temperatures may rise if sea breezes diminish. Winter highs are usually in the 50s. There may be freezing temperatures, but extended cold waves are infrequent. Although distributed year-round, most rainfall occurs in July and August. Gulf hurricanes are a risk from early July to mid-October.

POPULATION

DEMOGRAPHICS	AREA	U.S. AVG	ETHNIC COMPOSITION	AREA	U.S. AVG	RESIDENT PROFILE	AREA	U.S. AVG
Population	175,708		White	85.4%	75.1%	Single	37.2%	43.6%
Population density per sq. mile	187.8	447.3	Black	9.6%	12.3%	Married	62.8%	56.4%
Population growth	22.2%	16.1%	Asian	3.4%	3.6%	Divorced	9.4%	8.4%
Median age	36.3	35.5	American Indian	.6%	.9%	Separated	2.8%	3.0%
Average family size	2.7	2.7	Hispanic	4.7%	12.5%	Married with children	33.9%	28.7%
			Diversity measure	32.8%	35.2%	Single with children	9.6%	10.1%

ECONOMY & JOBS
SCORE: 57/RANK: 140

INCOME	AREA	U.S. AVG	EMPLOYMENT	AREA	U.S. AVG	LARGEST EMPLOYING INDUSTRY
Per capita income	$22,401	$23,420	Unemployment rate	2.4%	6.1%	Retail trade
Household income	$41,400	$46,060	Recent job growth	-.6%	.9%	
Household income < $25K	24.1%	26.4%	Projected future job growth	22.6%	15.1%	
Household income > $75K	19.1%	24.5%	White collar	50.7%	54.5%	
Household income growth	48.5%	57.3%	Blue collar	49.3%	45.5%	

COST OF LIVING
SCORE: 85/RANK: 47

INDEXES & TAXES	AREA	U.S. AVG	HOUSING	AREA	U.S. AVG	NECESSITIES	AREA	U.S. AVG
Cost of Living Index	88.6	100.0	Median home price	$119,250	$160,100	Food Index	92.3	100.0
Financial Progress Index	99.6	100.0	Home price appreciation	5.6%	7.1%	Housing Index	74.1	100.0
Income tax rate	0.000%	4.625%	Median rent	$542	$670	Utilities Index	83.0	100.0
Sales tax rate	6.000%	6.474%	Homes owned	54.4%	63.9%	Transportation Index	100.8	100.0
Property tax rate	$16.8	$15.6	Homes rented	31.4%	25.3%	Healthcare Index	104.0	100.0
			Housing affordability	68.0%	54.5%	Miscellaneous Cost Index	101.0	100.0

CLIMATE
SCORE: 68/RANK: 104

TEMPERATURE	AREA	U.S. AVG	PRECIPITATION	AREA	U.S. AVG	COMFORTS & HAZARDS	AREA	U.S. AVG
January low	43.0°F	26.4°F	Annual inches precipitation	64.2	35.9	July relative humidity	74.0%	68.8%
July high	89.7°F	86.7°F	Annual inches snowfall	.3	24.2	Annual days mostly sunny	220	212
Annual days > 90°F	55	38	Annual days precipitation	114	111	Annual days with thunderstorms	75	39
Annual days < 32°F	16	88	Annual days rain > 0.5 inches	37	23	Tornado risk score	38	19
Annual days < 0°F	0	6	Annual days snow > 1.5 inches	0	6	Hurricane risk score	58	15

TEMPERATURE

PRECIPITATION

DAYS OF CLOUDS & PRECIPITATION

EDUCATION
SCORE: 75/RANK: 83

ACHIEVEMENT	AREA	U.S. AVG	PUBLIC SCHOOLS	AREA	U.S. AVG	HIGHER EDUCATION	AREA	U.S. AVG
High school degree	89.0%	80.2%	Expenditures per pupil	$4,982	$5,894	No. 2-year colleges	1	3
2-year college degree	8.3%	6.2%	Student/teacher ratio	18.0	16.7	No. 4-year colleges/universities	0	4
4-year college degree	15.0%	15.8%	Attending public school	95.3%	90.2%	No. highly ranked universities	0	1
Graduate/professional degree	9.3%	9.6%	State SAT score	996*	1020			
			State ACT score	20.5	21.0			

HEALTH & HEALTHCARE
SCORE: 63/RANK: 120

HAZARDS & ILLNESSES	AREA	U.S. AVG	HEALTHCARE	AREA	U.S. AVG	CRIME	AREA	U.S. AVG
Air-quality score	24	45	Physicians per capita	229.4	261.1	Violent crime rate	368.7	456.0
Water-quality score	52	33	Hospital beds per capita	305.6	432.2	Change in violent crime rate	10.1%	-17.2%
Pollen/allergy score	63	61	No. teaching hospitals	0	4	Property crime rate	2,954.0	3,950.0
Stress score	40	50	Cost per doctor visit	$58	$67	Change in property crime rate	-4.0%	-16.8%
Cancer mortality per capita	174.6	169.0	Cost per dental visit	$67	$82			
Depression days per month	3.0	2.8	Cost per daily hospital room	$726	$733			

CRIME
SCORE: 57/RANK: 140

TRANSPORTATION
SCORE: 26/RANK: 242

COMMUTE	AREA	U.S. AVG	INTERCITY SERVICES	AREA	U.S. AVG	AUTOMOTIVE	AREA	U.S. AVG
Average commute time	21.9 min.	22.6 min.	Miles to nearest major airport	34	46	Insurance, annual premium	$1,017	$1,011
Commute by auto	93.6%	88.7%	Type of local airport	Small		Gas, cost per gallon	$1.46	$1.50
Commute by mass transit	.4%	1.8%	No. daily airline departures	53	294	Daily vehicle miles per capita	15.3	23.0
Work at home	2.4%	3.9%	Amtrak service	Yes				
Mass transit miles per capita	3.9	8.0	No. interstate highways	1	1			

LEISURE SCORE: 34/RANK: 219

DINING & SHOPPING	AREA	U.S. AVG	ENTERTAINMENT	AREA	U.S. AVG	OUTDOOR ACTIVITIES	AREA	U.S. AVG
Restaurant rating	1	1	Professional sports rating	2	4	Golf-course rating	3	4
No. outlet malls	2	2	College sports rating	1	4	Ski-area rating	1	4
No. Starbucks	0	11	Zoo/aquarium rating	1	3	National Park rating	3	3
No. warehouse clubs	1	4	Amusement park rating	1	3	Sq. miles inland water	5.0	4.0
			Botanical garden/arboretum rating	1	3	Miles of coastline	24.4	11.4

ARTS & CULTURE SCORE: 0/RANK: 328

MEDIA & LIBRARIES	AREA	U.S. AVG	PERFORMING ARTS	AREA	U.S. AVG	MUSEUMS	AREA	U.S. AVG
Arts radio rating	1	3	Classical music rating	4	4	Overall museum rating	4	6
No. public libraries	6	28	Ballet/dance rating	3	3	Art museum rating	1	5
Library volumes per capita	1.2	2.8	Professional theater rating	1	3	Science museum rating	1	4
			University arts programs rating	1	5	Children's museum rating	1	3

Fort Wayne, IN

Score: 65.8   Rank: 102

Profile: Small city
Location: Northeastern Indiana, 15 miles from Ohio border
Elevation: 828 feet
Time zone: Eastern Standard Time (no daylight savings time)

PRO	CON
Diversified economy	Entertainment
Cost of living	Winter climate
Small-town atmosphere	Healthcare

Fort Wayne is a business center and the second largest city in Indiana. Located in the northeast corner of the state at the confluence of three rivers, it is a diverse industrial and commercial center with an attractive downtown and a friendly, small-town feel for a city its size. Its industrial base includes electronics manufacturer Motorola and other high-tech and automotive suppliers, as well as the headquarters of Fortune-500 member Lincoln National Life Insurance. Despite the vulnerability of these industries, employment has held steady thanks to the area's economic diversity. The Cost of Living Index is low at 83.6. The area has a good collection of small-scale arts-and-culture amenities and some recreation in surrounding areas, but there isn't a lot to do.

The surrounding area is generally level south and east of the city, rolling to the southwest, and quite hilly to the north and northwest. While the climate is influenced somewhat by the nearby Great Lakes, it does not differ greatly from that of other Midwestern cities of the same latitude. Summers are warm and humid. Winters are cool and cloudy, and occasionally very cold and windy. Annual precipitation is well distributed with somewhat larger amounts falling in late spring and early summer. Snow squalls and winter-snow cover are common, but blizzards are infrequent. Summer thunderstorms are common and occasionally severe. The river confluence and low elevation has produced some severe floods. First freeze is mid-October, last is late April.

POPULATION

DEMOGRAPHICS	AREA	U.S. AVG	ETHNIC COMPOSITION	AREA	U.S. AVG	RESIDENT PROFILE	AREA	U.S. AVG
Population	508,915		White	94.0%	75.1%	Single	38.9%	43.6%
Population density per sq. mile	207.9	447.3	Black	4.5%	12.3%	Married	61.1%	56.4%
Population growth	11.5%	16.1%	Asian	.7%	3.6%	Divorced	8.0%	8.4%
Median age	34.9	35.5	American Indian	.3%	.9%	Separated	1.7%	3.0%
Average family size	2.7	2.7	Hispanic	1.8%	12.5%	Married with children	32.4%	28.7%
			Diversity measure	23.9%	35.2%	Single with children	8.9%	10.1%

ECONOMY & JOBS SCORE: 92/RANK: 26

INCOME	AREA	U.S. AVG	EMPLOYMENT	AREA	U.S. AVG	LARGEST EMPLOYING INDUSTRY
Per capita income	$23,481	$23,420	Unemployment rate	5.3%	6.1%	Transportation Equipment Manufacturing
Household income	$48,099	$46,060	Recent job growth	2.5%	.9%	
Household income < $25K	21.1%	26.4%	Projected future job growth	10.5%	15.1%	
Household income > $75K	24.0%	24.5%	White collar	51.7%	54.5%	
Household income growth	53.6%	57.3%	Blue collar	48.3%	45.5%	

COST OF LIVING SCORE: 83/RANK: 54

INDEXES & TAXES	AREA	U.S. AVG	HOUSING	AREA	U.S. AVG	NECESSITIES	AREA	U.S. AVG
Cost of Living Index	83.6	100.0	Median home price	$93,100	$160,100	Food Index	95.5	100.0
Financial Progress Index	122.7	100.0	Home price appreciation	4.1%	7.1%	Housing Index	57.8	100.0
Income tax rate	4.400%	4.625%	Median rent	$546	$670	Utilities Index	105.1	100.0
Sales tax rate	6.000%	6.474%	Homes owned	75.5%	63.9%	Transportation Index	100.2	100.0
Property tax rate	$12.8	$15.6	Homes rented	17.8%	25.3%	Healthcare Index	96.3	100.0
			Housing affordability	64.0%	54.5%	Miscellaneous Cost Index	96.9	100.0

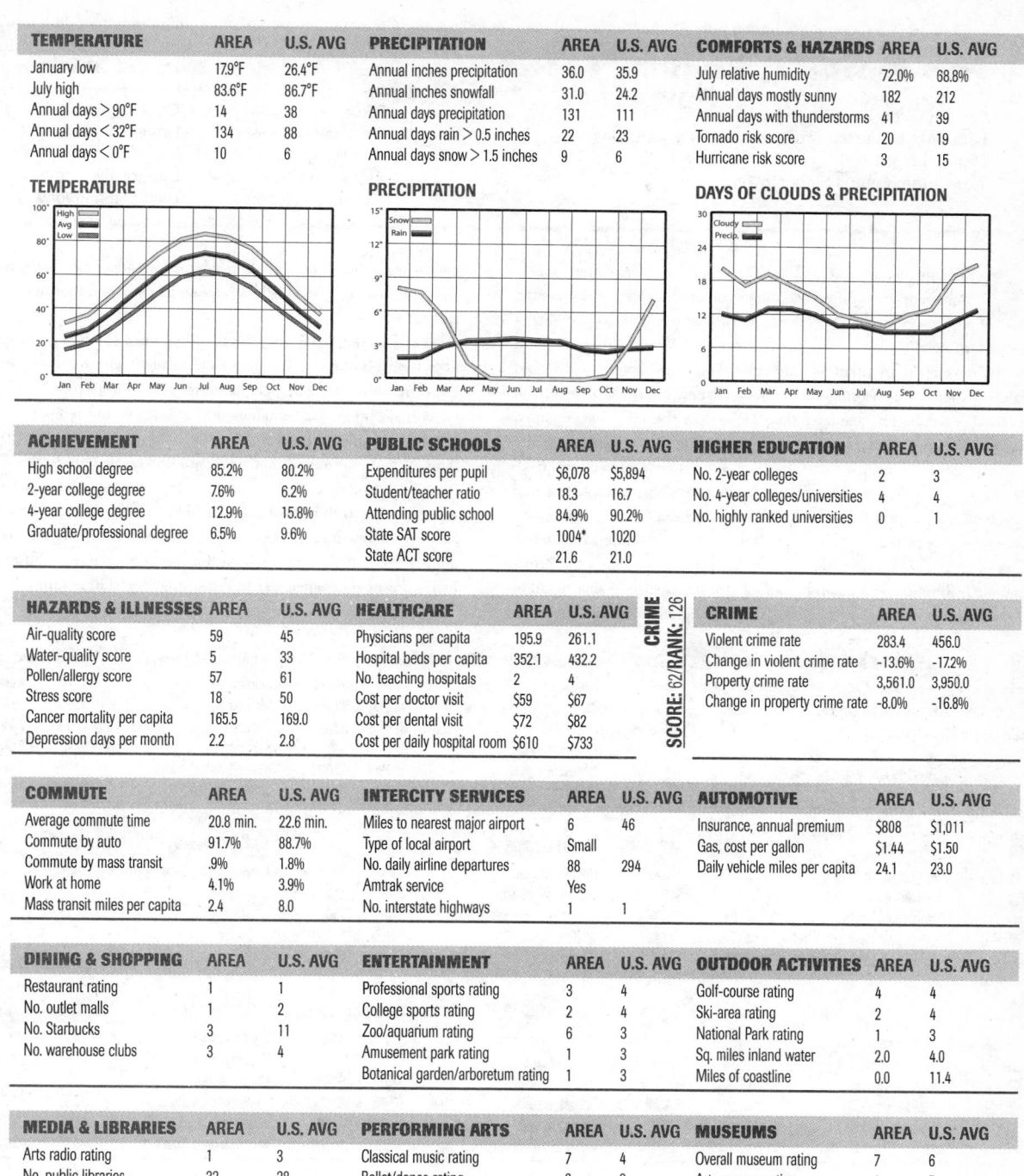

CLIMATE SCORE: 42/RANK: 191

TEMPERATURE	AREA	U.S. AVG
January low	17.9°F	26.4°F
July high	83.6°F	86.7°F
Annual days > 90°F	14	38
Annual days < 32°F	134	88
Annual days < 0°F	10	6

PRECIPITATION	AREA	U.S. AVG
Annual inches precipitation	36.0	35.9
Annual inches snowfall	31.0	24.2
Annual days precipitation	131	111
Annual days rain > 0.5 inches	22	23
Annual days snow > 1.5 inches	9	6

COMFORTS & HAZARDS	AREA	U.S. AVG
July relative humidity	72.0%	68.8%
Annual days mostly sunny	182	212
Annual days with thunderstorms	41	39
Tornado risk score	20	19
Hurricane risk score	3	15

TEMPERATURE (graph: High, Avg, Low)

PRECIPITATION (graph: Snow, Rain)

DAYS OF CLOUDS & PRECIPITATION (graph: Cloudy, Precip.)

EDUCATION SCORE: 26/RANK: 242

ACHIEVEMENT	AREA	U.S. AVG
High school degree	85.2%	80.2%
2-year college degree	7.6%	6.2%
4-year college degree	12.9%	15.8%
Graduate/professional degree	6.5%	9.6%

PUBLIC SCHOOLS	AREA	U.S. AVG
Expenditures per pupil	$6,078	$5,894
Student/teacher ratio	18.3	16.7
Attending public school	84.9%	90.2%
State SAT score	1004*	1020
State ACT score	21.6	21.0

HIGHER EDUCATION	AREA	U.S. AVG
No. 2-year colleges	2	3
No. 4-year colleges/universities	4	4
No. highly ranked universities	0	1

HEALTH & HEALTHCARE SCORE: 27/RANK: 239

HAZARDS & ILLNESSES	AREA	U.S. AVG
Air-quality score	59	45
Water-quality score	5	33
Pollen/allergy score	57	61
Stress score	18	50
Cancer mortality per capita	165.5	169.0
Depression days per month	2.2	2.8

HEALTHCARE	AREA	U.S. AVG
Physicians per capita	195.9	261.1
Hospital beds per capita	352.1	432.2
No. teaching hospitals	2	4
Cost per doctor visit	$59	$67
Cost per dental visit	$72	$82
Cost per daily hospital room	$610	$733

CRIME SCORE: 62/RANK: 126

CRIME	AREA	U.S. AVG
Violent crime rate	283.4	456.0
Change in violent crime rate	-13.6%	-17.2%
Property crime rate	3,561.0	3,950.0
Change in property crime rate	-8.0%	-16.8%

TRANSPORTATION SCORE: 46/RANK: 178

COMMUTE	AREA	U.S. AVG
Average commute time	20.8 min.	22.6 min.
Commute by auto	91.7%	88.7%
Commute by mass transit	.9%	1.8%
Work at home	4.1%	3.9%
Mass transit miles per capita	2.4	8.0

INTERCITY SERVICES	AREA	U.S. AVG
Miles to nearest major airport	6	46
Type of local airport	Small	
No. daily airline departures	88	294
Amtrak service	Yes	
No. interstate highways	1	1

AUTOMOTIVE	AREA	U.S. AVG
Insurance, annual premium	$808	$1,011
Gas, cost per gallon	$1.44	$1.50
Daily vehicle miles per capita	24.1	23.0

LEISURE SCORE: 31/RANK: 227

DINING & SHOPPING	AREA	U.S. AVG
Restaurant rating	1	1
No. outlet malls	1	2
No. Starbucks	3	11
No. warehouse clubs	3	4

ENTERTAINMENT	AREA	U.S. AVG
Professional sports rating	3	4
College sports rating	2	4
Zoo/aquarium rating	6	3
Amusement park rating	1	3
Botanical garden/arboretum rating	1	3

OUTDOOR ACTIVITIES	AREA	U.S. AVG
Golf-course rating	4	4
Ski-area rating	2	4
National Park rating	1	3
Sq. miles inland water	2.0	4.0
Miles of coastline	0.0	11.4

ARTS & CULTURE SCORE: 87/RANK: 44

MEDIA & LIBRARIES	AREA	U.S. AVG
Arts radio rating	1	3
No. public libraries	32	28
Library volumes per capita	7.1	2.8

PERFORMING ARTS	AREA	U.S. AVG
Classical music rating	7	4
Ballet/dance rating	3	3
Professional theater rating	1	3
University arts programs rating	8	5

MUSEUMS	AREA	U.S. AVG
Overall museum rating	7	6
Art museum rating	4	5
Science museum rating	2	4
Children's museum rating	1	3

Fort Worth–Arlington, TX

Score: 80.5 Rank: 36

Profile: Large-city complex
Location: Northeast Texas, 30 miles west of Dallas
Elevation: 551 feet
Time zone: Central Standard Time

PRO	CON
Economy and cost of living	Urban sprawl
Arts and culture	Unattractive setting
Proximity to Dallas	Heat and humidity

Although just west of Dallas, the origins and character of Fort Worth are quite different. The city started as a livestock center, and has grown into a modern city without the glamour and glitz of its eastern neighbor. Arlington sits between Fort Worth and Dallas, in a mostly developed area that also includes Grapevine, Irving, and Grand Prairie. Today, Fort Worth is a commercial and industrial center with more of a small-city character than Dallas. In the mid–20th century, money from the emerging oil industry created an assortment of quality cultural assets, such as museums and interesting architecture. Lake Worth, a large reservoir within the city limits, offers a parklike setting and excellent watersports for beating the summer heat. The city compares very favorably to Dallas: Fort Worth has half the population, 10% lower cost of living, 20% lower median housing prices, two-thirds the crime and air pollution, and a much higher job-growth rate while sharing all of the amenities—air transport, sports, shopping, and entertainment—of its nearby neighbor. Fort Worth residents consider the distinction from Dallas important, and bristle at an outsider's notion that they are "from Dallas."

The area contains mostly flat to rolling hills which begin to rise higher to the west of town. Tree cover is prevalent within the city but not in the surrounding area. The combination humid subtropical and continental climate brings hot summers and a wide annual temperature range. Precipitation also varies considerably, ranging from less than 20 to more than 50 inches. Summer hot spells are broken by thunderstorm activity into 3- to 5-day periods. Summer daytime temperatures frequently exceed 100°F with occasional nights above 80°F. Winters are mild with sudden temperature changes and short periods of extreme cold. Most annual precipitation comes from thunderstorm activity with occasional heavy downpours especially in the spring. Snowfall is rare.

POPULATION

DEMOGRAPHICS	AREA	U.S. AVG	ETHNIC COMPOSITION	AREA	U.S. AVG	RESIDENT PROFILE	AREA	U.S. AVG
Population	1,802,465		White	79.0%	75.1%	Single	43.3%	43.6%
Population density per sq. mile	617.9	447.3	Black	10.8%	12.3%	Married	56.7%	56.4%
Population growth	32.4%	16.1%	Asian	3.0%	3.6%	Divorced	10.0%	8.4%
Median age	33.1	35.5	American Indian	.5%	.9%	Separated	3.9%	3.0%
Average family size	2.7	2.7	Hispanic	17.9%	12.5%	Married with children	30.8%	28.7%
			Diversity measure	50.2%	35.2%	Single with children	10.6%	10.1%

ECONOMY & JOBS SCORE: 44/RANK: 183

INCOME	AREA	U.S. AVG	EMPLOYMENT	AREA	U.S. AVG	LARGEST EMPLOYING INDUSTRY
Per capita income	$26,392	$23,420	Unemployment rate	6.4%	6.1%	Transportation Equipment Manufacturing
Household income	$55,157	$46,060	Recent job growth	2.0%	.9%	
Household income < $25K	19.0%	26.4%	Projected future job growth	27.0%	15.1%	
Household income > $75K	33.3%	24.5%	White collar	58.8%	54.5%	
Household income growth	71.5%	57.3%	Blue collar	41.2%	45.5%	

COST OF LIVING SCORE: 60/RANK: 130

INDEXES & TAXES	AREA	U.S. AVG	HOUSING	AREA	U.S. AVG	NECESSITIES	AREA	U.S. AVG
Cost of Living Index	85.9	100.0	Median home price	$107,500	$160,100	Food Index	94.2	100.0
Financial Progress Index	136.8	100.0	Home price appreciation	6.0%	7.1%	Housing Index	66.8	100.0
Income tax rate	0.000%	4.625%	Median rent	$757	$670	Utilities Index	92.7	100.0
Sales tax rate	8.250%	6.474%	Homes owned	60.8%	63.9%	Transportation Index	95.3	100.0
Property tax rate	$22.3	$15.6	Homes rented	28.7%	25.3%	Healthcare Index	100.0	100.0
			Housing affordability	57.0%	54.5%	Miscellaneous Cost Index	99.7	100.0

CLIMATE — SCORE: 86/RANK: 44

TEMPERATURE	AREA	U.S. AVG	PRECIPITATION	AREA	U.S. AVG	COMFORTS & HAZARDS	AREA	U.S. AVG
January low	33.9°F	26.4°F	Annual inches precipitation	32.3	35.9	July relative humidity	67.0%	68.8%
July high	95.5°F	86.7°F	Annual inches snowfall	3.5	24.2	Annual days mostly sunny	234	212
Annual days > 90°F	92	38	Annual days precipitation	79	111	Annual days with thunderstorms	45	39
Annual days < 32°F	41	88	Annual days rain > 0.5 inches	20	23	Tornado risk score	48	19
Annual days < 0°F	0	6	Annual days snow > 1.5 inches	2	6	Hurricane risk score	10	15

TEMPERATURE **PRECIPITATION** **DAYS OF CLOUDS & PRECIPITATION**

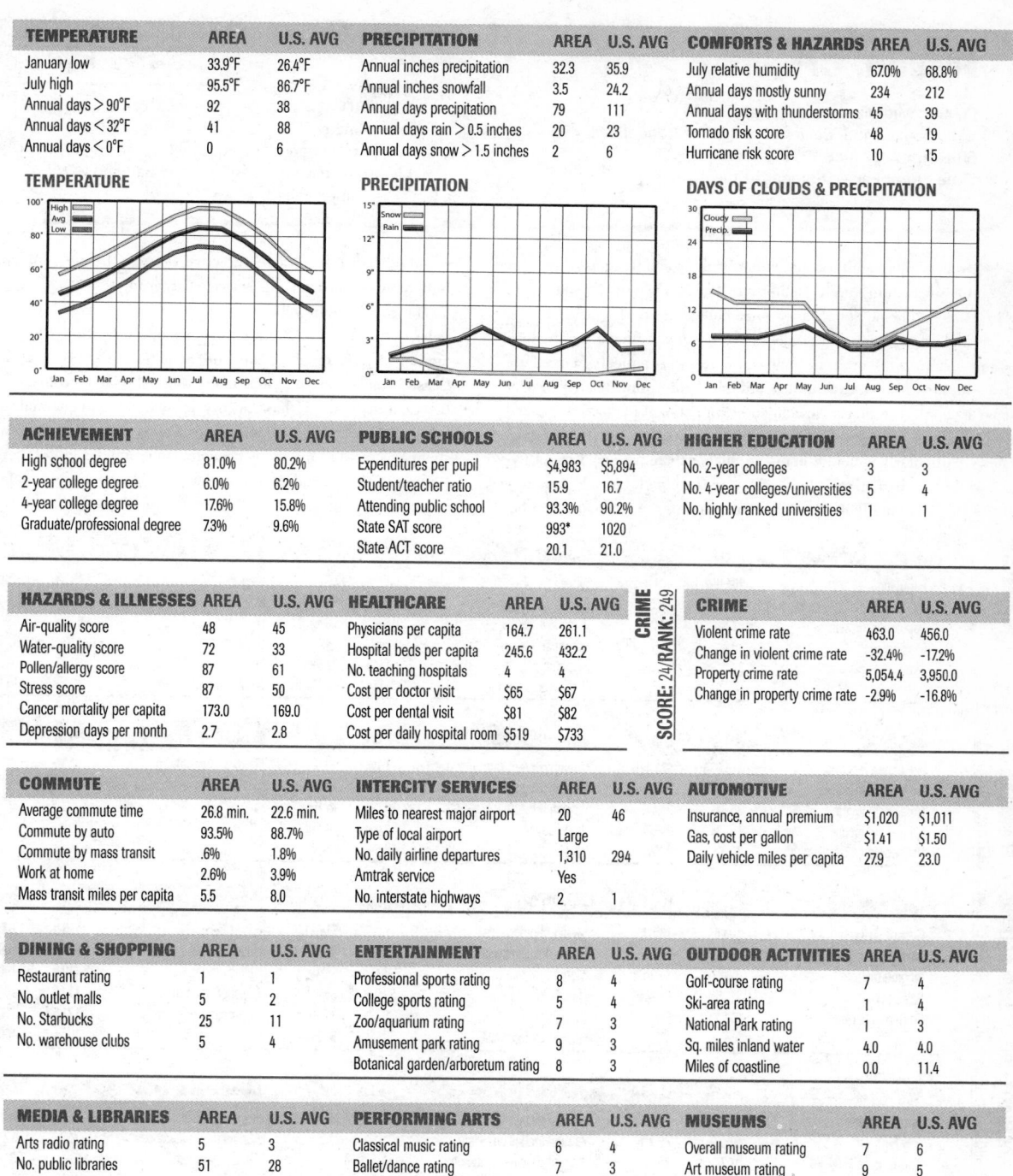

EDUCATION — SCORE: 61/RANK: 127

ACHIEVEMENT	AREA	U.S. AVG	PUBLIC SCHOOLS	AREA	U.S. AVG	HIGHER EDUCATION	AREA	U.S. AVG
High school degree	81.0%	80.2%	Expenditures per pupil	$4,983	$5,894	No. 2-year colleges	3	3
2-year college degree	6.0%	6.2%	Student/teacher ratio	15.9	16.7	No. 4-year colleges/universities	5	4
4-year college degree	17.6%	15.8%	Attending public school	93.3%	90.2%	No. highly ranked universities	1	1
Graduate/professional degree	7.3%	9.6%	State SAT score	993*	1020			
			State ACT score	20.1	21.0			

HEALTH & HEALTHCARE — SCORE: 10/RANK: 297 / CRIME — SCORE: 24/RANK: 249

HAZARDS & ILLNESSES	AREA	U.S. AVG	HEALTHCARE	AREA	U.S. AVG	CRIME	AREA	U.S. AVG
Air-quality score	48	45	Physicians per capita	164.7	261.1	Violent crime rate	463.0	456.0
Water-quality score	72	33	Hospital beds per capita	245.6	432.2	Change in violent crime rate	-32.4%	-17.2%
Pollen/allergy score	87	61	No. teaching hospitals	4	4	Property crime rate	5,054.4	3,950.0
Stress score	87	50	Cost per doctor visit	$65	$67	Change in property crime rate	-2.9%	-16.8%
Cancer mortality per capita	173.0	169.0	Cost per dental visit	$81	$82			
Depression days per month	2.7	2.8	Cost per daily hospital room	$519	$733			

TRANSPORTATION — SCORE: 94/RANK: 19

COMMUTE	AREA	U.S. AVG	INTERCITY SERVICES	AREA	U.S. AVG	AUTOMOTIVE	AREA	U.S. AVG
Average commute time	26.8 min.	22.6 min.	Miles to nearest major airport	20	46	Insurance, annual premium	$1,020	$1,011
Commute by auto	93.5%	88.7%	Type of local airport	Large		Gas, cost per gallon	$1.41	$1.50
Commute by mass transit	.6%	1.8%	No. daily airline departures	1,310	294	Daily vehicle miles per capita	27.9	23.0
Work at home	2.6%	3.9%	Amtrak service	Yes				
Mass transit miles per capita	5.5	8.0	No. interstate highways	2	1			

LEISURE — SCORE: 81/RANK: 65

DINING & SHOPPING	AREA	U.S. AVG	ENTERTAINMENT	AREA	U.S. AVG	OUTDOOR ACTIVITIES	AREA	U.S. AVG
Restaurant rating	1	1	Professional sports rating	8	4	Golf-course rating	7	4
No. outlet malls	5	2	College sports rating	5	4	Ski-area rating	1	4
No. Starbucks	25	11	Zoo/aquarium rating	7	3	National Park rating	1	3
No. warehouse clubs	5	4	Amusement park rating	9	3	Sq. miles inland water	4.0	4.0
			Botanical garden/arboretum rating	8	3	Miles of coastline	0.0	11.4

ARTS & CULTURE — SCORE: 59/RANK: 134

MEDIA & LIBRARIES	AREA	U.S. AVG	PERFORMING ARTS	AREA	U.S. AVG	MUSEUMS	AREA	U.S. AVG
Arts radio rating	5	3	Classical music rating	6	4	Overall museum rating	7	6
No. public libraries	51	28	Ballet/dance rating	7	3	Art museum rating	9	5
Library volumes per capita	2.2	2.8	Professional theater rating	9	3	Science museum rating	7	4
			University arts programs rating	8	5	Children's museum rating	10	3

Fresno, CA

Score: 64.0   **Rank:** 116

Profile: Mid-size city
Location: Central California, center of Central Valley
Elevation: 327 feet
Time zone: Pacific Standard Time

PRO	CON
Climate	Summer heat
Nearby national parks	High unemployment
Some college-town amenities	Urban sprawl

Fresno is an agricultural and minor banking and financial center for the surrounding area. California State University Fresno, nicknamed "Fresno State," adds some college-town benefits including sports and arts activities, but it doesn't have much influence on the look or atmosphere of the town. In some ways, Fresno is typical of large farm towns in the Midwest, except the California-type sprawl has taken over some sections. The Sierra Nevada and twin national parks Sequoia and Kings Canyon provide abundant outdoor recreation activities. Crime rates—particularly violent crime—are higher than average. Cost of living, while high by national standards, is reasonable for a California city of this size. Air quality is poor and often obscures the mountains in what would otherwise be a more attractive setting. The area did win a 2001 National Civic League All-America City Award.

The San Joaquin Valley is generally flat and agricultural. About 15 miles east of Fresno, the terrain slopes upward with the foothills of the Sierra Nevada, rapidly rising to more than 14,000 feet. The lower Coastal Range rises 45 miles to the west. The Mediterranean climate of the Central Valley is hot and dry in summer, with normally pleasant evenings, and mild in winter. Temperatures may reach the low 100s in summer but 90s are more common and rain is almost nonexistent. Winters are moist and heavy fogs may persist. Almost all rainfall occurs in winter.

POPULATION

DEMOGRAPHICS	AREA	U.S. AVG	ETHNIC COMPOSITION	AREA	U.S. AVG	RESIDENT PROFILE	AREA	U.S. AVG
Population	964,897		White	66.1%	75.1%	Single	44.3%	43.6%
Population density per sq. mile	119.1	447.3	Black	3.1%	12.3%	Married	55.7%	56.4%
Population growth	27.7%	16.1%	Asian	6.6%	3.6%	Divorced	8.0%	8.4%
Median age	30.4	35.5	American Indian	1.5%	.9%	Separated	4.0%	3.0%
Average family size	3.2	2.7	Hispanic	44.6%	12.5%	Married with children	30.4%	28.7%
			Diversity measure	64.8%	35.2%	Single with children	13.6%	10.1%

ECONOMY & JOBS   SCORE: 2/RANK: 322

INCOME	AREA	U.S. AVG	EMPLOYMENT	AREA	U.S. AVG	LARGEST EMPLOYING INDUSTRY
Per capita income	$15,898	$23,420	Unemployment rate	11.1%	6.1%	Food Manufacturing
Household income	$35,635	$46,060	Recent job growth	1.4%	.9%	
Household income < $25K	35.3%	26.4%	Projected future job growth	18.4%	15.1%	
Household income > $75K	16.1%	24.5%	White collar	50.4%	54.5%	
Household income growth	34.3%	57.3%	Blue collar	49.6%	45.5%	

COST OF LIVING   SCORE: 26/RANK: 245

INDEXES & TAXES	AREA	U.S. AVG	HOUSING	AREA	U.S. AVG	NECESSITIES	AREA	U.S. AVG
Cost of Living Index	103.6	100.0	Median home price	$142,850	$160,100	Food Index	113.0	100.0
Financial Progress Index	73.3	100.0	Home price appreciation	10.2%	7.1%	Housing Index	88.7	100.0
Income tax rate	6.000%	4.625%	Median rent	$603	$670	Utilities Index	119.5	100.0
Sales tax rate	7.875%	6.474%	Homes owned	52.9%	63.9%	Transportation Index	112.9	100.0
Property tax rate	$11.1	$15.6	Homes rented	36.8%	25.3%	Healthcare Index	121.5	100.0
			Housing affordability	50.0%	54.5%	Miscellaneous Cost Index	105.4	100.0

CLIMATE   SCORE: 89/RANK: 35

TEMPERATURE	AREA	U.S. AVG	PRECIPITATION	AREA	U.S. AVG	COMFORTS & HAZARDS	AREA	U.S. AVG
January low	35.8°F	26.4°F	Annual inches precipitation	10.0	35.9	July relative humidity	61.0%	68.8%
July high	98.2°F	86.7°F	Annual inches snowfall	0.0	24.2	Annual days mostly sunny	271	212
Annual days > 90°F	107	38	Annual days precipitation	44	111	Annual days with thunderstorms	6	39
Annual days < 32°F	29	88	Annual days rain > 0.5 inches	6	23	Tornado risk score	8	19
Annual days < 0°F	0	6	Annual days snow > 1.5 inches	0	6	Hurricane risk score	0	15

TEMPERATURE

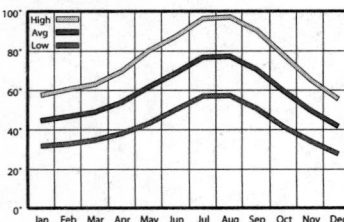

PRECIPITATION

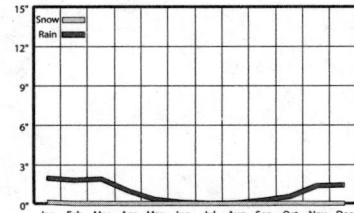

DAYS OF CLOUDS & PRECIPITATION

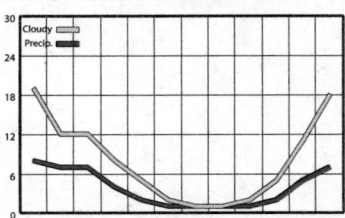

EDUCATION — SCORE: 12/RANK: 289

ACHIEVEMENT	AREA	U.S. AVG	PUBLIC SCHOOLS	AREA	U.S. AVG	HIGHER EDUCATION	AREA	U.S. AVG
High school degree	67.2%	80.2%	Expenditures per pupil	$5,328	$5,894	No. 2-year colleges	4	3
2-year college degree	6.4%	6.2%	Student/teacher ratio	21.2	16.7	No. 4-year colleges/universities	2	4
4-year college degree	11.5%	15.8%	Attending public school	97.1%	90.2%	No. highly ranked universities	1	1
Graduate/professional degree	5.7%	9.6%	State SAT score	1018*	1020			
			State ACT score	21.5	21.0			

HEALTH & HEALTHCARE — SCORE: 1/RANK: 326　　CRIME — SCORE: 20/RANK: 263

HAZARDS & ILLNESSES	AREA	U.S. AVG	HEALTHCARE	AREA	U.S. AVG	CRIME	AREA	U.S. AVG
Air-quality score	0	45	Physicians per capita	169.7	261.1	Violent crime rate	750.1	456.0
Water-quality score	14	33	Hospital beds per capita	224.7	432.2	Change in violent crime rate	-36.9%	-17.2%
Pollen/allergy score	60	61	No. teaching hospitals	3	4	Property crime rate	5,221.6	3,950.0
Stress score	46	50	Cost per doctor visit	$66	$67	Change in property crime rate	-29.2%	-16.8%
Cancer mortality per capita	161.5	169.0	Cost per dental visit	$95	$82			
Depression days per month	1.3	2.8	Cost per daily hospital room	$717	$733			

TRANSPORTATION — SCORE: 40/RANK: 198

COMMUTE	AREA	U.S. AVG	INTERCITY SERVICES	AREA	U.S. AVG	AUTOMOTIVE	AREA	U.S. AVG
Average commute time	22.7 min.	22.6 min.	Miles to nearest major airport	39	46	Insurance, annual premium	$1,460	$1,011
Commute by auto	88.5%	88.7%	Type of local airport	Small		Gas, cost per gallon	$1.69	$1.50
Commute by mass transit	1.2%	1.8%	No. daily airline departures	75	294	Daily vehicle miles per capita	20.1	23.0
Work at home	3.9%	3.9%	Amtrak service	Yes				
Mass transit miles per capita	4.6	8.0	No. interstate highways	0	1			

LEISURE — SCORE: 70/RANK: 97

DINING & SHOPPING	AREA	U.S. AVG	ENTERTAINMENT	AREA	U.S. AVG	OUTDOOR ACTIVITIES	AREA	U.S. AVG
Restaurant rating	3	1	Professional sports rating	3	4	Golf-course rating	3	4
No. outlet malls	0	2	College sports rating	5	4	Ski-area rating	5	4
No. Starbucks	16	11	Zoo/aquarium rating	5	3	National Park rating	10	3
No. warehouse clubs	4	4	Amusement park rating	8	3	Sq. miles inland water	4.0	4.0
			Botanical garden/arboretum rating	1	3	Miles of coastline	0.0	11.4

ARTS & CULTURE — SCORE: 71/RANK: 96

MEDIA & LIBRARIES	AREA	U.S. AVG	PERFORMING ARTS	AREA	U.S. AVG	MUSEUMS	AREA	U.S. AVG
Arts radio rating	5	3	Classical music rating	4	4	Overall museum rating	5	6
No. public libraries	40	28	Ballet/dance rating	3	3	Art museum rating	5	5
Library volumes per capita	1.1	2.8	Professional theater rating	1	3	Science museum rating	3	4
			University arts programs rating	1	5	Children's museum rating	3	3

Gadsden, AL

Score: 20.5　Rank: 324

Profile: Small industrial town
Location: Northeast Alabama, between Birmingham and Chattanooga, Tennessee
Elevation: 624 feet
Time zone: Central Standard Time

PRO	CON
Cost of living	Violent crime
Housing costs	Arts and culture
Nearby water recreation	Low educational attainment

Gadsden is one of the state's largest industrial centers, producing steel, rubber, fabricated metal, and electronic equipment. The nearby dammed-up portions of the Coosa River and a large high-end outlet mall provide some entertainment. The Cost of Living Index at 77.8 and median home price of $85,540 are the best in the state and among the best in the country, but the area doesn't have much else going for it. The 4-year educational attainment of 8% is the lowest in the state and among the lowest in the country.

Gadsden, along the Coosa River in hilly terrain with mixed forest, is located at the south end of the long mountain ridge known as Lookout Mountain. The climate is humid subtropical with a continental influence. There are four seasons with long, hot humid summers and mild winters. The orientation of nearby ridges blocks some cold air from the north but funnels in humid air from the southwest.

POPULATION

DEMOGRAPHICS	AREA	U.S. AVG	ETHNIC COMPOSITION	AREA	U.S. AVG	RESIDENT PROFILE	AREA	U.S. AVG
Population	103,105		White	89.5%	75.1%	Single	39.3%	43.6%
Population density per sq. mile	192.8	447.3	Black	9.2%	12.3%	Married	60.7%	56.4%
Population growth	3.3%	16.1%	Asian	.5%	3.6%	Divorced	8.4%	8.4%
Median age	38.8	35.5	American Indian	.4%	.9%	Separated	2.2%	3.0%
Average family size	2.5	2.7	Hispanic	1.0%	12.5%	Married with children	29.7%	28.7%
			Diversity measure	30.2%	35.2%	Single with children	8.8%	10.1%

ECONOMY & JOBS SCORE: 68/RANK: 104

INCOME	AREA	U.S. AVG	EMPLOYMENT	AREA	U.S. AVG	LARGEST EMPLOYING INDUSTRY
Per capita income	$17,142	$23,420	Unemployment rate	5.9%	6.1%	Food Manufacturing
Household income	$31,460	$46,060	Recent job growth	1.4%	.9%	
Household income < $25K	40.3%	26.4%	Projected future job growth	8.7%	15.1%	
Household income > $75K	11.1%	24.5%	White collar	44.5%	54.5%	
Household income growth	41.1%	57.3%	Blue collar	55.5%	45.5%	

COST OF LIVING SCORE: 96/RANK: 11

INDEXES & TAXES	AREA	U.S. AVG	HOUSING	AREA	U.S. AVG	NECESSITIES	AREA	U.S. AVG
Cost of Living Index	77.8	100.0	Median home price	$85,540	$160,100	Food Index	93.9	100.0
Financial Progress Index	86.1	100.0	Home price appreciation	6.3%	7.1%	Housing Index	53.1	100.0
Income tax rate	5.000%	4.625%	Median rent	$393	$670	Utilities Index	88.9	100.0
Sales tax rate	8.000%	6.474%	Homes owned	72.8%	63.9%	Transportation Index	83.8	100.0
Property tax rate	$6.9	$15.6	Homes rented	19.9%	25.3%	Healthcare Index	83.8	100.0
			Housing affordability	60.0%	54.5%	Miscellaneous Cost Index	97.3	100.0

CLIMATE SCORE: 26/RANK: 245

TEMPERATURE	AREA	U.S. AVG	PRECIPITATION	AREA	U.S. AVG	COMFORTS & HAZARDS	AREA	U.S. AVG
January low	34.1°F	26.4°F	Annual inches precipitation	53.0	35.9	July relative humidity	72.0%	68.8%
July high	90.3°F	86.7°F	Annual inches snowfall	1.0	24.2	Annual days mostly sunny	210	212
Annual days > 90°F	39	38	Annual days precipitation	118	111	Annual days with thunderstorms	58	39
Annual days < 32°F	60	88	Annual days rain > 0.5 inches	36	23	Tornado risk score	23	19
Annual days < 0°F	0	6	Annual days snow > 1.5 inches	2	6	Hurricane risk score	18	15

TEMPERATURE

PRECIPITATION

DAYS OF CLOUDS & PRECIPITATION

EDUCATION SCORE: 12/RANK: 291

ACHIEVEMENT	AREA	U.S. AVG	PUBLIC SCHOOLS	AREA	U.S. AVG	HIGHER EDUCATION	AREA	U.S. AVG
High school degree	74.1%	80.2%	Expenditures per pupil	$4,943	$5,894	No. 2-year colleges	2	3
2-year college degree	6.7%	6.2%	Student/teacher ratio	16.2	16.7	No. 4-year colleges/universities	0	4
4-year college degree	8.1%	15.8%	Attending public school	93.4%	90.2%	No. highly ranked universities	0	1
Graduate/professional degree	5.3%	9.6%	State SAT score	1111	1020			
			State ACT score	20.1*	21.0			

HEALTH & HEALTHCARE SCORE: 84/RANK: 50

CRIME SCORE: 21/RANK: 261

HAZARDS & ILLNESSES	AREA	U.S. AVG	HEALTHCARE	AREA	U.S. AVG	CRIME	AREA	U.S. AVG
Air-quality score	49	45	Physicians per capita	200.8	261.1	Violent crime rate	742.1	456.0
Water-quality score	25	33	Hospital beds per capita	345.1	432.2	Change in violent crime rate	-12.2%	-17.2%
Pollen/allergy score	66	61	No. teaching hospitals	0	4	Property crime rate	4,577.5	3,950.0
Stress score	85	50	Cost per doctor visit	$60	$67	Change in property crime rate	-20.5%	-16.8%
Cancer mortality per capita	168.6	169.0	Cost per dental visit	$63	$82			
Depression days per month	4.7	2.8	Cost per daily hospital room	$599	$733			

TRANSPORTATION SCORE: 3/RANK: 321

COMMUTE	AREA	U.S. AVG	INTERCITY SERVICES	AREA	U.S. AVG	AUTOMOTIVE	AREA	U.S. AVG
Average commute time	24.5 min.	22.6 min.	Miles to nearest major airport	52	46	Insurance, annual premium	$804	$1,011
Commute by auto	95.4%	88.7%	Type of local airport	Small		Gas, cost per gallon	$1.43	$1.50
Commute by mass transit	.1%	1.8%	No. daily airline departures	111	294	Daily vehicle miles per capita	37.7	23.0
Work at home	2.3%	3.9%	Amtrak service	No				
Mass transit miles per capita	0.0	8.0	No. interstate highways	1	1			

LEISURE SCORE: 12/RANK: 292

DINING & SHOPPING	AREA	U.S. AVG	ENTERTAINMENT	AREA	U.S. AVG	OUTDOOR ACTIVITIES	AREA	U.S. AVG
Restaurant rating	1	1	Professional sports rating	2	4	Golf-course rating	1	4
No. outlet malls	1	2	College sports rating	1	4	Ski-area rating	1	4
No. Starbucks	0	11	Zoo/aquarium rating	1	3	National Park rating	1	3
No. warehouse clubs	1	4	Amusement park rating	1	3	Sq. miles inland water	2.0	4.0
			Botanical garden/arboretum rating	1	3	Miles of coastline	0.0	11.4

ARTS & CULTURE SCORE: 12/RANK: 289

MEDIA & LIBRARIES	AREA	U.S. AVG	PERFORMING ARTS	AREA	U.S. AVG	MUSEUMS	AREA	U.S. AVG
Arts radio rating	1	3	Classical music rating	1	4	Overall museum rating	3	6
No. public libraries	9	28	Ballet/dance rating	1	3	Art museum rating	6	5
Library volumes per capita	3.1	2.8	Professional theater rating	1	3	Science museum rating	4	4
			University arts programs rating	1	5	Children's museum rating	5	3

Gainesville, FL

Score: 75.5   Rank: 56

Profile: College town
Location: North-central Florida, 60 miles south of Georgia border
Elevation: 96 feet
Time zone: Eastern Standard Time

PRO	CON
College-town amenities	Summer heat
Performing arts	Crime rate
Healthcare	Declining employment

Gainesville is an agricultural center and home to the University of Florida. The university is the area's largest employer. The economic picture is mixed with one of the largest recent job declines in the state and one of the lowest overall unemployment figures. Located away from the coast, the area is one of the least touristy and most livable in the state. In part because of the university, Gainesville has become a center for the arts, particularly the performing arts, and has excellent venues. The area is also important as a nature and wildlife-viewing center, and natural springs offer some recreational opportunities. A high crime rate and long, hot, sticky summers with over 100 days over 90°F round out the negatives.

The terrain is fairly level with forests of live oak and southern pine within the city and nearby. There are several nearby lakes to the east and south. The central location away from water causes more persistent heat. Winters are mild, with minimum temperatures averaging 44°F. Freezing does occur 18 days per year with record lows in the teens. Rainfall is appreciable in every month but is most abundant from summer showers and thunderstorms. August, which averages 8 inches of rainfall, is the wettest month. Because of its inland location, Gainesville does not have serious problems with hurricanes.

POPULATION

DEMOGRAPHICS	AREA	U.S. AVG	ETHNIC COMPOSITION	AREA	U.S. AVG	RESIDENT PROFILE	AREA	U.S. AVG
Population	222,254		White	75.7%	75.1%	Single	54.5%	43.6%
Population density per sq. mile	254.2	447.3	Black	20.2%	12.3%	Married	45.5%	56.4%
Population growth	22.4%	16.1%	Asian	3.2%	3.6%	Divorced	9.4%	8.4%
Median age	29.1	35.5	American Indian	.2%	.9%	Separated	3.1%	3.0%
Average family size	2.4	2.7	Hispanic	4.7%	12.5%	Married with children	22.0%	28.7%
			Diversity measure	46.0%	35.2%	Single with children	11.8%	10.1%

ECONOMY & JOBS SCORE: 6/RANK: 307

INCOME	AREA	U.S. AVG	EMPLOYMENT	AREA	U.S. AVG	LARGEST EMPLOYING INDUSTRY
Per capita income	$21,510	$23,420	Unemployment rate	2.5%	6.1%	Healthcare and Social Assistance
Household income	$34,900	$46,060	Recent job growth	-2.7%	.9%	
Household income < $25K	35.7%	26.4%	Projected future job growth	20.0%	15.1%	
Household income > $75K	19.2%	24.5%	White collar	66.3%	54.5%	
Household income growth	57.8%	57.3%	Blue collar	33.7%	45.5%	

COST OF LIVING SCORE: 77/RANK: 75

INDEXES & TAXES	AREA	U.S. AVG	HOUSING	AREA	U.S. AVG	NECESSITIES	AREA	U.S. AVG
Cost of Living Index	91.1	100.0	Median home price	$130,800	$160,100	Food Index	99.7	100.0
Financial Progress Index	81.6	100.0	Home price appreciation	7.2%	7.1%	Housing Index	81.2	100.0
Income tax rate	0.000%	4.625%	Median rent	$580	$670	Utilities Index	88.5	100.0
Sales tax rate	6.000%	6.474%	Homes owned	56.8%	63.9%	Transportation Index	97.9	100.0
Property tax rate	$19.6	$15.6	Homes rented	32.9%	25.3%	Healthcare Index	90.2	100.0
			Housing affordability	43.0%	54.5%	Miscellaneous Cost Index	98.6	100.0

CLIMATE SCORE: 83/RANK: 55

TEMPERATURE	AREA	U.S. AVG
January low	50.0°F	26.4°F
July high	90.0°F	86.7°F
Annual days > 90°F	104	38
Annual days < 32°F	2	88
Annual days < 0°F	0	6

PRECIPITATION	AREA	U.S. AVG
Annual inches precipitation	51.0	35.9
Annual inches snowfall	0.0	24.2
Annual days precipitation	116	111
Annual days rain > 0.5 inches	32	23
Annual days snow > 1.5 inches	0	6

COMFORTS & HAZARDS	AREA	U.S. AVG
July relative humidity	74.0%	68.8%
Annual days mostly sunny	242	212
Annual days with thunderstorms	81	39
Tornado risk score	21	19
Hurricane risk score	63	15

TEMPERATURE

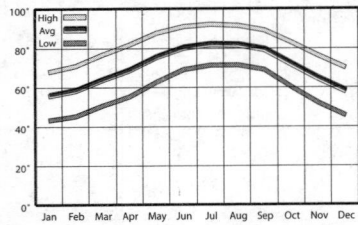

PRECIPITATION

DAYS OF CLOUDS & PRECIPITATION

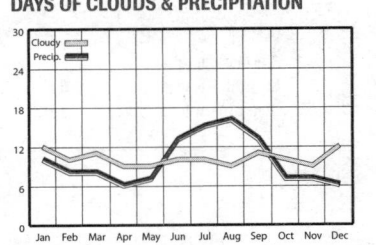

EDUCATION SCORE: 91/RANK: 30

ACHIEVEMENT	AREA	U.S. AVG
High school degree	87.8%	80.2%
2-year college degree	9.4%	6.2%
4-year college degree	20.6%	15.8%
Graduate/professional degree	19.0%	9.6%

PUBLIC SCHOOLS	AREA	U.S. AVG
Expenditures per pupil	$5,183	$5,894
Student/teacher ratio	17.7	16.7
Attending public school	90.3%	90.2%
State SAT score	996*	1020
State ACT score	20.5	21.0

HIGHER EDUCATION	AREA	U.S. AVG
No. 2-year colleges	1	3
No. 4-year colleges/universities	1	4
No. highly ranked universities	0	1

HEALTH & HEALTHCARE SCORE: 67/RANK: 108

HAZARDS & ILLNESSES	AREA	U.S. AVG
Air-quality score	24	45
Water-quality score	20	33
Pollen/allergy score	68	61
Stress score	61	50
Cancer mortality per capita	175.6	169.0
Depression days per month	2.5	2.8

HEALTHCARE	AREA	U.S. AVG
Physicians per capita	718.1	261.1
Hospital beds per capita	602.4	432.2
No. teaching hospitals	2	4
Cost per doctor visit	$65	$67
Cost per dental visit	$70	$82
Cost per daily hospital room	$572	$733

CRIME SCORE: 20/RANK: 264

CRIME	AREA	U.S. AVG
Violent crime rate	866.3	456.0
Change in violent crime rate	-38.9%	-17.2%
Property crime rate	5,225.8	3,950.0
Change in property crime rate	-37.4%	-16.8%

TRANSPORTATION SCORE: 51/RANK: 161

COMMUTE	AREA	U.S. AVG
Average commute time	21.1 min.	22.6 min.
Commute by auto	85.2%	88.7%
Commute by mass transit	1.5%	1.8%
Work at home	3.4%	3.9%
Mass transit miles per capita	9.0	8.0

INTERCITY SERVICES	AREA	U.S. AVG
Miles to nearest major airport	70	46
Type of local airport	Medium	
No. daily airline departures	145	294
Amtrak service	Yes	
No. interstate highways	1	1

AUTOMOTIVE	AREA	U.S. AVG
Insurance, annual premium	$1,019	$1,011
Gas, cost per gallon	$1.54	$1.50
Daily vehicle miles per capita	26.3	23.0

LEISURE SCORE: 33/RANK: 221

DINING & SHOPPING	AREA	U.S. AVG
Restaurant rating	1	1
No. outlet malls	0	2
No. Starbucks	6	11
No. warehouse clubs	3	4

ENTERTAINMENT	AREA	U.S. AVG
Professional sports rating	2	4
College sports rating	9	4
Zoo/aquarium rating	2	3
Amusement park rating	1	3
Botanical garden/arboretum rating	2	3

OUTDOOR ACTIVITIES	AREA	U.S. AVG
Golf-course rating	1	4
Ski-area rating	1	4
National Park rating	1	3
Sq. miles inland water	5.0	4.0
Miles of coastline	0.0	11.4

ARTS & CULTURE SCORE: 82/RANK: 57

MEDIA & LIBRARIES	AREA	U.S. AVG
Arts radio rating	5	3
No. public libraries	11	28
Library volumes per capita	3.7	2.8

PERFORMING ARTS	AREA	U.S. AVG
Classical music rating	4	4
Ballet/dance rating	1	3
Professional theater rating	6	3
University arts programs rating	5	5

MUSEUMS	AREA	U.S. AVG
Overall museum rating	5	6
Art museum rating	5	5
Science museum rating	4	4
Children's museum rating	6	3

Galveston–Texas City, TX

Score: 65.5   Rank: 105

Profile: Small-city complex/Beach-town complex
Location: Southeast Texas coast on Galveston Island, 50 miles southeast of Houston
Elevation: 7 feet
Time zone: Central Standard Time

PRO	CON
Historic interest	Industrial areas
Entertainment	Tourist impact
Water recreation	Storm risk

Galveston, located on a barrier island, is an old seaport town and minor resort community. Texas City on the mainland is a major industrial center dominated by shipping and petrochemicals. Area highlights include a 32-mile-long beach on the south side of the barrier island. The center of Galveston is on the north, or mainland, side of the island. The downtown area is rich in history from antebellum cotton-trading days, the Civil War, and more recent maritime commerce. The downtown historic district contains 19th-century iron-front buildings and well-maintained older homes reminiscent of New Orleans. The area, which can be crowded at times, has become a minor tourist destination and weekend getaway for Houstonians. Quiet beaches, golf courses, and other recreational amenities are nearby. Aside from these and the town's historic sites and museums, tourist attractions, and an assortment of interesting seafood restaurants, residents must travel to Houston for other amenities. The area has a low cost of living overall, but is more expensive in the Galveston historic areas and beachfront.

Galveston Island is 2¾ miles across at the widest point and 29 miles long. Texas City is located at the south edge of the flat, treeless, coastal plain extending down from Houston to the north. The climate is predominantly marine with periods of modified continental influence during the colder months when cold fronts reach the coast. Cold is never severe and freezing temperatures rarely occur. Summers are warm, usually in the 90s and high humidity prevails throughout the year. Precipitation can vary greatly month to month. Summer rainfall comes mostly from thunderstorms while winter precipitation comes as light, steady rain. The island has been subject to tropical storms and hurricanes with the most deadly in U.S. history occurring in 1900.

POPULATION

DEMOGRAPHICS	AREA	U.S. AVG	ETHNIC COMPOSITION	AREA	U.S. AVG	RESIDENT PROFILE	AREA	U.S. AVG
Population	261,219		White	75.3%	75.1%	Single	45.6%	43.6%
Population density per sq. mile	655.2	447.3	Black	16.4%	12.3%	Married	54.4%	56.4%
Population growth	20.2%	16.1%	Asian	2.2%	3.6%	Divorced	11.8%	8.4%
Median age	36.2	35.5	American Indian	.4%	.9%	Separated	4.1%	3.0%
Average family size	2.6	2.7	Hispanic	19.1%	12.5%	Married with children	25.8%	28.7%
			Diversity measure	52.4%	35.2%	Single with children	12.4%	10.1%

ECONOMY & JOBS SCORE: 46/RANK: 176

INCOME	AREA	U.S. AVG	EMPLOYMENT	AREA	U.S. AVG	LARGEST EMPLOYING INDUSTRY
Per capita income	$22,581	$23,420	Unemployment rate	8.8%	6.1%	Healthcare and Social Assistance
Household income	$43,613	$46,060	Recent job growth	2.4%	.9%	
Household income < $25K	28.7%	26.4%	Projected future job growth	16.6%	15.1%	
Household income > $75K	25.1%	24.5%	White collar	55.8%	54.5%	
Household income growth	47.8%	57.3%	Blue collar	44.2%	45.5%	

COST OF LIVING SCORE: 70/RANK: 97

INDEXES & TAXES	AREA	U.S. AVG	HOUSING	AREA	U.S. AVG	NECESSITIES	AREA	U.S. AVG
Cost of Living Index	86.4	100.0	Median home price	$103,390	$160,100	Food Index	91.6	100.0
Financial Progress Index	107.6	100.0	Home price appreciation	6.7%	7.1%	Housing Index	64.2	100.0
Income tax rate	0.000%	4.625%	Median rent	$662	$670	Utilities Index	103.6	100.0
Sales tax rate	8.250%	6.474%	Homes owned	54.9%	63.9%	Transportation Index	101.1	100.0
Property tax rate	$29.6	$15.6	Homes rented	26.9%	25.3%	Healthcare Index	107.3	100.0
			Housing affordability	54.0%	54.5%	Miscellaneous Cost Index	99.2	100.0

CLIMATE SCORE: 93/RANK: 21

TEMPERATURE	AREA	U.S. AVG	PRECIPITATION	AREA	U.S. AVG	COMFORTS & HAZARDS	AREA	U.S. AVG
January low	48.3°F	26.4°F	Annual inches precipitation	42.0	35.9	July relative humidity	78.0%	68.8%
July high	87.6°F	86.7°F	Annual inches snowfall	0.0	24.2	Annual days mostly sunny	203	212
Annual days > 90°F	11	38	Annual days precipitation	96	111	Annual days with thunderstorms	70	39
Annual days < 32°F	4	88	Annual days rain > 0.5 inches	24	23	Tornado risk score	78	19
Annual days < 0°F	0	6	Annual days snow > 1.5 inches	0	6	Hurricane risk score	71	15

TEMPERATURE

PRECIPITATION

DAYS OF CLOUDS & PRECIPITATION

EDUCATION SCORE: 53/RANK: 153

ACHIEVEMENT	AREA	U.S. AVG	PUBLIC SCHOOLS	AREA	U.S. AVG	HIGHER EDUCATION	AREA	U.S. AVG
High school degree	80.9%	80.2%	Expenditures per pupil	$5,087	$5,894	No. 2-year colleges	2	3
2-year college degree	6.3%	6.2%	Student/teacher ratio	15.5	16.7	No. 4-year colleges/universities	1	4
4-year college degree	14.7%	15.8%	Attending public school	93.2%	90.2%	No. highly ranked universities	1	1
Graduate/professional degree	8.0%	9.6%	State SAT score	993*	1020			
			State ACT score	20.1	21.0			

HEALTH & HEALTHCARE SCORE: 18/RANK: 269

CRIME SCORE: 20/RANK: 262

HAZARDS & ILLNESSES	AREA	U.S. AVG	HEALTHCARE	AREA	U.S. AVG	CRIME	AREA	U.S. AVG
Air-quality score	17	45	Physicians per capita	456.7	261.1	Violent crime rate	566.5	456.0
Water-quality score	4	33	Hospital beds per capita	588.8	432.2	Change in violent crime rate	-43.9%	-17.2%
Pollen/allergy score	71	61	No. teaching hospitals	2	4	Property crime rate	5,448.8	3,950.0
Stress score	100	50	Cost per doctor visit	$68	$67	Change in property crime rate	-11.4%	-16.8%
Cancer mortality per capita	198.7	169.0	Cost per dental visit	$82	$82			
Depression days per month	5.3	2.8	Cost per daily hospital room	$605	$733			

TRANSPORTATION SCORE: 72/RANK: 91

COMMUTE	AREA	U.S. AVG	INTERCITY SERVICES	AREA	U.S. AVG	AUTOMOTIVE	AREA	U.S. AVG
Average commute time	26.0 min.	22.6 min.	Miles to nearest major airport	37	46	Insurance, annual premium	$940	$1,011
Commute by auto	92.5%	88.7%	Type of local airport	Medium		Gas, cost per gallon	$1.41	$1.50
Commute by mass transit	1.1%	1.8%	No. daily airline departures	234	294	Daily vehicle miles per capita	19.3	23.0
Work at home	2.2%	3.9%	Amtrak service	No				
Mass transit miles per capita	8.2	8.0	No. interstate highways	1	1			

LEISURE SCORE: 72/RANK: 90

DINING & SHOPPING	AREA	U.S. AVG	ENTERTAINMENT	AREA	U.S. AVG	OUTDOOR ACTIVITIES	AREA	U.S. AVG
Restaurant rating	1	1	Professional sports rating	6	4	Golf-course rating	4	4
No. outlet malls	0	2	College sports rating	5	4	Ski-area rating	1	4
No. Starbucks	4	11	Zoo/aquarium rating	2	3	National Park rating	3	3
No. warehouse clubs	3	4	Amusement park rating	3	3	Sq. miles inland water	9.0	4.0
			Botanical garden/arboretum rating	2	3	Miles of coastline	25.6	11.4

ARTS & CULTURE SCORE: 32/RANK: 224

MEDIA & LIBRARIES	AREA	U.S. AVG	PERFORMING ARTS	AREA	U.S. AVG	MUSEUMS	AREA	U.S. AVG
Arts radio rating	4	3	Classical music rating	3	4	Overall museum rating	6	6
No. public libraries	8	28	Ballet/dance rating	3	3	Art museum rating	5	5
Library volumes per capita	3.0	2.8	Professional theater rating	3	3	Science museum rating	4	4
			University arts programs rating	2	5	Children's museum rating	2	3

Gary, IN

Score: 40.6   Rank: 275

Profile: Industrial city
Location: Extreme northwest Indiana at Illinois border along Lake Michigan, 25 miles southeast of Chicago
Elevation: 623 feet
Time zone: Central Standard Time

PRO	CON
Proximity to Chicago	Industrial setting
Nearby beach areas	Economic cycles
Declining crime rate	Low educational attainment

Gary became a steel center because of its location midway between deposits of iron ore in the upper Great Lakes and coal and limestone resources to the south. Although the steel industry has declined, the city's heavy industrial character remains. Chicago to the northwest and the Indiana Dunes National Lakeshore and Michigan Dunes areas to the east provide recreation to those willing to travel short distances.

Gary lies on a level plain spreading south from the Lake Michigan shore. The landscape is highly industrial with areas of trees and agriculture to the south and southeast. Like Chicago, weather is highly variable. The continental-type climate brings warm, humid summers and blustery, variable winters. However, Gary is downwind from northerly lake winds, so the area gets stronger lake-effect winds and snows compared to Chicago. That said, the lake does moderate temperatures more than comparable inland locations. First freeze is mid-October, last is late April.

POPULATION

DEMOGRAPHICS	AREA	U.S. AVG	ETHNIC COMPOSITION	AREA	U.S. AVG	RESIDENT PROFILE	AREA	U.S. AVG
Population	637,419		White	72.1%	75.1%	Single	48.5%	43.6%
Population density per sq. mile	696.4	447.3	Black	23.5%	12.3%	Married	51.5%	56.4%
Population growth	5.4%	16.1%	Asian	.9%	3.6%	Divorced	9.8%	8.4%
Median age	36.4	35.5	American Indian	.2%	.9%	Separated	3.0%	3.0%
Average family size	2.7	2.7	Hispanic	10.2%	12.5%	Married with children	26.9%	28.7%
			Diversity measure	47.4%	35.2%	Single with children	14.5%	10.1%

ECONOMY & JOBS   SCORE: 40/RANK: 198

INCOME	AREA	U.S. AVG	EMPLOYMENT	AREA	U.S. AVG	LARGEST EMPLOYING INDUSTRY
Per capita income	$22,230	$23,420	Unemployment rate	6.0%	6.1%	Primary Metal Manufacturing
Household income	$47,700	$46,060	Recent job growth	-.1%	.9%	
Household income < $25K	25.2%	26.4%	Projected future job growth	11.4%	15.1%	
Household income > $75K	24.8%	24.5%	White collar	50.9%	54.5%	
Household income growth	50.6%	57.3%	Blue collar	49.1%	45.5%	

COST OF LIVING   SCORE: 56/RANK: 143

INDEXES & TAXES	AREA	U.S. AVG	HOUSING	AREA	U.S. AVG	NECESSITIES	AREA	U.S. AVG
Cost of Living Index	97.6	100.0	Median home price	$117,000	$160,100	Food Index	106.3	100.0
Financial Progress Index	104.1	100.0	Home price appreciation	4.3%	7.1%	Housing Index	72.7	100.0
Income tax rate	3.400%	4.625%	Median rent	$732	$670	Utilities Index	106.6	100.0
Sales tax rate	6.000%	6.474%	Homes owned	66.4%	63.9%	Transportation Index	125.1	100.0
Property tax rate	$14.1	$15.6	Homes rented	26.4%	25.3%	Healthcare Index	120.2	100.0
			Housing affordability	51.0%	54.5%	Miscellaneous Cost Index	108.5	100.0

CLIMATE   SCORE: 28/RANK: 238

TEMPERATURE	AREA	U.S. AVG	PRECIPITATION	AREA	U.S. AVG	COMFORTS & HAZARDS	AREA	U.S. AVG
January low	17.0°F	26.4°F	Annual inches precipitation	34.0	35.9	July relative humidity	67.0%	68.8%
July high	84.4°F	86.7°F	Annual inches snowfall	40.0	24.2	Annual days mostly sunny	197	212
Annual days > 90°F	21	38	Annual days precipitation	123	111	Annual days with thunderstorms	40	39
Annual days < 32°F	119	88	Annual days rain > 0.5 inches	23	23	Tornado risk score	24	19
Annual days < 0°F	7	6	Annual days snow > 1.5 inches	18	6	Hurricane risk score	2	15

TEMPERATURE

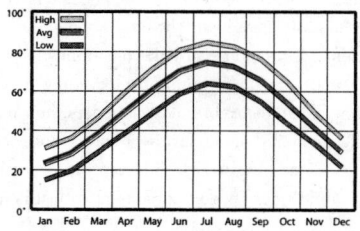

PRECIPITATION

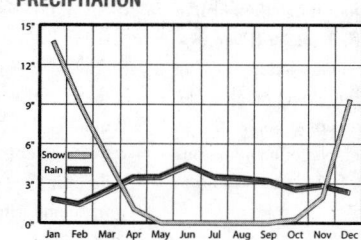

DAYS OF CLOUDS & PRECIPITATION

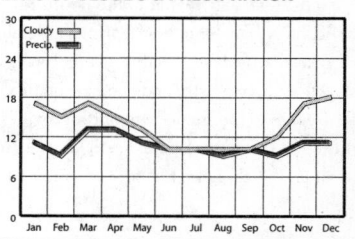

EDUCATION — SCORE: 23/RANK: 254

ACHIEVEMENT	AREA	U.S. AVG	PUBLIC SCHOOLS	AREA	U.S. AVG	HIGHER EDUCATION	AREA	U.S. AVG
High school degree	82.5%	80.2%	Expenditures per pupil	$6,428	$5,894	No. 2-year colleges	3	3
2-year college degree	5.1%	6.2%	Student/teacher ratio	19.1	16.7	No. 4-year colleges/universities	4	4
4-year college degree	11.4%	15.8%	Attending public school	89.2%	90.2%	No. highly ranked universities	1	1
Graduate/professional degree	6.3%	9.6%	State SAT score	1004*	1020			
			State ACT score	21.6	21.0			

HEALTH & HEALTHCARE — SCORE: 18/RANK: 270 | CRIME — SCORE: 48/RANK: 171

HAZARDS & ILLNESSES	AREA	U.S. AVG	HEALTHCARE	AREA	U.S. AVG	CRIME	AREA	U.S. AVG
Air-quality score	80	45	Physicians per capita	183.1	261.1	Violent crime rate	538.3	456.0
Water-quality score	6	33	Hospital beds per capita	445.5	432.2	Change in violent crime rate	-38.4%	-17.2%
Pollen/allergy score	57	61	No. teaching hospitals	4	4	Property crime rate	3,874.4	3,950.0
Stress score	89	50	Cost per doctor visit	$62	$67	Change in property crime rate	-19.6%	-16.8%
Cancer mortality per capita	186.0	169.0	Cost per dental visit	$90	$82			
Depression days per month	3.3	2.8	Cost per daily hospital room	$691	$733			

TRANSPORTATION — SCORE: 98/RANK: 6

COMMUTE	AREA	U.S. AVG	INTERCITY SERVICES	AREA	U.S. AVG	AUTOMOTIVE	AREA	U.S. AVG
Average commute time	26.8 min.	22.6 min.	Miles to nearest major airport	25	46	Insurance, annual premium	$997	$1,011
Commute by auto	91.3%	88.7%	Type of local airport	Medium		Gas, cost per gallon	$1.47	$1.50
Commute by mass transit	3.4%	1.8%	No. daily airline departures	356	294	Daily vehicle miles per capita	23.3	23.0
Work at home	1.7%	3.9%	Amtrak service	Yes				
Mass transit miles per capita	3.4	8.0	No. interstate highways	4	1			

LEISURE — SCORE: 83/RANK: 53

DINING & SHOPPING	AREA	U.S. AVG	ENTERTAINMENT	AREA	U.S. AVG	OUTDOOR ACTIVITIES	AREA	U.S. AVG
Restaurant rating	1	1	Professional sports rating	8	4	Golf-course rating	7	4
No. outlet malls	2	2	College sports rating	2	4	Ski-area rating	4	4
No. Starbucks	3	11	Zoo/aquarium rating	2	3	National Park rating	3	3
No. warehouse clubs	3	4	Amusement park rating	3	3	Sq. miles inland water	2.0	4.0
			Botanical garden/arboretum rating	3	3	Miles of coastline	32.9	11.4

ARTS & CULTURE — SCORE: 66/RANK: 115

MEDIA & LIBRARIES	AREA	U.S. AVG	PERFORMING ARTS	AREA	U.S. AVG	MUSEUMS	AREA	U.S. AVG
Arts radio rating	4	3	Classical music rating	5	4	Overall museum rating	6	6
No. public libraries	40	28	Ballet/dance rating	4	3	Art museum rating	4	5
Library volumes per capita	5.8	2.8	Professional theater rating	5	3	Science museum rating	3	4
			University arts programs rating	8	5	Children's museum rating	3	3

Glens Falls, NY

Score: 38.3   Rank: 285

Profile: Small town
Location: East-central New York at southeast edge of Adirondacks, 60 miles north of Albany
Elevation: 292 feet
Time zone: Eastern Standard Time

PRO	CON
Nearby mountains	Isolation
Nearby recreation	Arts and culture
Small-town atmosphere	Harsh winters

Glens Falls is a minor industrial center and gateway to the Adirondack Region to the north. It is located just to the north of the Albany–Saratoga Springs area along the Hudson River. The town boasts a pleasant small-town feel with low crime, moderate living costs, strong job growth, and good air quality, but there isn't much to do. Lake George to the immediate north provides recreational opportunities and the Lake George Opera Festival. The Adirondacks offer numerous outdoor activities. Lake Placid—of winter Olympic fame—is 85 miles to the north.

The town is located in a small valley at a sharp bend in the Hudson River. It is surrounded by wooded hills, which become larger to the north, rising eventually to 5,300 feet in the heavily wooded Adirondacks. The climate is continental but modified by the mountains. Summer days are warm and sunny and sometimes humid, but evening temperatures fall quickly. Hot, sticky weather occurs most summers, and most precipitation comes from summer thunderstorms. Winters are cold, frequently dropping below 10°F and even 0°F, with heavy and persistent snow during many winters. First freeze is end of September, last is mid-May.

POPULATION

DEMOGRAPHICS	AREA	U.S. AVG	ETHNIC COMPOSITION	AREA	U.S. AVG	RESIDENT PROFILE	AREA	U.S. AVG
Population	125,101		White	96.5%	75.1%	Single	42.1%	43.6%
Population density per sq. mile	73.4	447.3	Black	2.1%	12.3%	Married	57.9%	56.4%
Population growth	5.5%	16.1%	Asian	.7%	3.6%	Divorced	6.4%	8.4%
Median age	38.8	35.5	American Indian	.2%	.9%	Separated	3.7%	3.0%
Average family size	2.6	2.7	Hispanic	2.0%	12.5%	Married with children	29.1%	28.7%
			Diversity measure	9.1%	35.2%	Single with children	8.8%	10.1%

ECONOMY & JOBS SCORE: 96/RANK: 11

INCOME	AREA	U.S. AVG	EMPLOYMENT	AREA	U.S. AVG	LARGEST EMPLOYING INDUSTRY
Per capita income	$20,561	$23,420	Unemployment rate	3.7%	6.1%	Medical Equipment and Supplies Manufacturing
Household income	$39,879	$46,060	Recent job growth	3.7%	.9%	
Household income < $25K	30.0%	26.4%	Projected future job growth	5.8%	15.1%	
Household income > $75K	14.9%	24.5%	White collar	47.8%	54.5%	
Household income growth	34.3%	57.3%	Blue collar	52.2%	45.5%	

COST OF LIVING SCORE: 34/RANK: 216

INDEXES & TAXES	AREA	U.S. AVG	HOUSING	AREA	U.S. AVG	NECESSITIES	AREA	U.S. AVG
Cost of Living Index	95.6	100.0	Median home price	$108,340	$160,100	Food Index	107.9	100.0
Financial Progress Index	88.9	100.0	Home price appreciation	7.3%	7.1%	Housing Index	67.3	100.0
Income tax rate	7.125%	4.625%	Median rent	$596	$670	Utilities Index	142.9	100.0
Sales tax rate	7.000%	6.474%	Homes owned	52.7%	63.9%	Transportation Index	106.0	100.0
Property tax rate	$22.7	$15.6	Homes rented	13.7%	25.3%	Healthcare Index	101.2	100.0
			Housing affordability	56.0%	54.5%	Miscellaneous Cost Index	108.4	100.0

CLIMATE SCORE: 4/RANK: 317

TEMPERATURE	AREA	U.S. AVG	PRECIPITATION	AREA	U.S. AVG	COMFORTS & HAZARDS	AREA	U.S. AVG
January low	12.5°F	26.4°F	Annual inches precipitation	33.0	35.9	July relative humidity	71.0%	68.8%
July high	83.9°F	86.7°F	Annual inches snowfall	71.0	24.2	Annual days mostly sunny	182	212
Annual days > 90°F	8	38	Annual days precipitation	135	111	Annual days with thunderstorms	28	39
Annual days < 32°F	155	88	Annual days rain > 0.5 inches	23	23	Tornado risk score	4	19
Annual days < 0°F	17	6	Annual days snow > 1.5 inches	13	6	Hurricane risk score	6	15

TEMPERATURE

PRECIPITATION

DAYS OF CLOUDS & PRECIPITATION

EDUCATION SCORE: 67/RANK: 110

ACHIEVEMENT	AREA	U.S. AVG	PUBLIC SCHOOLS	AREA	U.S. AVG	HIGHER EDUCATION	AREA	U.S. AVG
High school degree	81.8%	80.2%	Expenditures per pupil	$7,263	$5,894	No. 2-year colleges	1	3
2-year college degree	9.4%	6.2%	Student/teacher ratio	15.2	16.7	No. 4-year colleges/universities	0	4
4-year college degree	11.1%	15.8%	Attending public school	97.1%	90.2%	No. highly ranked universities	0	1
Graduate/professional degree	7.1%	9.6%	State SAT score	1006*	1020			
			State ACT score	22.3	21.0			

HEALTH & HEALTHCARE SCORE: 58/RANK: 137

HAZARDS & ILLNESSES	AREA	U.S. AVG	HEALTHCARE	AREA	U.S. AVG
Air-quality score	81	45	Physicians per capita	189.4	261.1
Water-quality score	36	33	Hospital beds per capita	461.6	432.2
Pollen/allergy score	44	61	No. teaching hospitals	0	4
Stress score	20	50	Cost per doctor visit	$73	$67
Cancer mortality per capita	182.6	169.0	Cost per dental visit	$88	$82
Depression days per month	6.0	2.8	Cost per daily hospital room	$724	$733

CRIME SCORE: 97/RANK: 9

CRIME	AREA	U.S. AVG
Violent crime rate	241.6	456.0
Change in violent crime rate	-33.5%	-17.2%
Property crime rate	1,994.8	3,950.0
Change in property crime rate	-26.6%	-16.8%

TRANSPORTATION SCORE: 13/RANK: 285

COMMUTE	AREA	U.S. AVG	INTERCITY SERVICES	AREA	U.S. AVG	AUTOMOTIVE	AREA	U.S. AVG
Average commute time	22.8 min.	22.6 min.	Miles to nearest major airport	40	46	Insurance, annual premium	$1,282	$1,011
Commute by auto	89.0%	88.7%	Type of local airport	Small		Gas, cost per gallon	$1.54	$1.50
Commute by mass transit	.8%	1.8%	No. daily airline departures	131	294	Daily vehicle miles per capita	28.7	23.0
Work at home	4.8%	3.9%	Amtrak service	Yes				
Mass transit miles per capita	2.7	8.0	No. interstate highways	1	1			

LEISURE SCORE: 55/RANK: 152

DINING & SHOPPING	AREA	U.S. AVG	ENTERTAINMENT	AREA	U.S. AVG	OUTDOOR ACTIVITIES	AREA	U.S. AVG
Restaurant rating	1	1	Professional sports rating	3	4	Golf-course rating	2	4
No. outlet malls	2	2	College sports rating	2	4	Ski-area rating	8	4
No. Starbucks	0	11	Zoo/aquarium rating	1	3	National Park rating	1	3
No. warehouse clubs	1	4	Amusement park rating	4	3	Sq. miles inland water	5.0	4.0
			Botanical garden/arboretum rating	1	3	Miles of coastline	0.0	11.4

ARTS & CULTURE SCORE: 10/RANK: 297

MEDIA & LIBRARIES	AREA	U.S. AVG	PERFORMING ARTS	AREA	U.S. AVG	MUSEUMS	AREA	U.S. AVG
Arts radio rating	1	3	Classical music rating	3	4	Overall museum rating	5	6
No. public libraries	20	28	Ballet/dance rating	1	3	Art museum rating	4	5
Library volumes per capita	5.2	2.8	Professional theater rating	1	3	Science museum rating	6	4
			University arts programs rating	1	5	Children's museum rating	1	3

Goldsboro, NC

Score: 68.6 Rank: 86

Profile: Small town
Location: East-central North Carolina, 40 miles southeast of Raleigh-Durham
Elevation: 121 feet
Time zone: Eastern Standard Time

PRO	CON
Cost of living	Low educational attainment
Proximity to Raleigh-Durham	Unattractive downtown
Diverse economy	Hot, humid summers

Goldsboro is a Southern town with a diversified economy consisting of several small manufacturers, which make everything from roofing and mechanical pumps to slippers, and larger facilities such as a Georgia-Pacific plywood mill. There is some agriculture and a major poultry processing plant. Most industry, as well as Seymour Johnson Air Force Base, are outside of town. The downtown area, once a bright spot, has deteriorated considerably and reflects neglect and some economic malaise. There isn't much to do. However, the cost of living is the best in the state, and the town is close enough to Raleigh-Durham and the coast to take advantage of amenities there. But proximity to that area

has affected scores and ranks, and most will find the area less attractive than the numbers indicate.

Goldsboro is located in a mostly level coastal plain with deciduous wooded areas. The climate is humid subtropical with some marine and mountain influence. Tropical air makes for hot, muggy summers with occasional thundershowers and steady rains from storms moving up the coast. Mountain protection and the coastal influence make winters fairly mild, with most precipitation as rain, although an occasional dusting of snow or sleet occurs.

POPULATION

DEMOGRAPHICS	AREA	U.S. AVG	ETHNIC COMPOSITION	AREA	U.S. AVG	RESIDENT PROFILE	AREA	U.S. AVG
Population	112,954		White	69.2%	75.1%	Single	43.1%	43.6%
Population density per sq. mile	204.4	447.3	Black	28.1%	12.3%	Married	56.9%	56.4%
Population growth	7.9%	16.1%	Asian	1.0%	3.6%	Divorced	6.6%	8.4%
Median age	35.0	35.5	American Indian	.3%	.9%	Separated	5.8%	3.0%
Average family size	2.7	2.7	Hispanic	3.5%	12.5%	Married with children	33.2%	28.7%
			Diversity measure	52.5%	35.2%	Single with children	12.4%	10.1%

ECONOMY & JOBS SCORE: 57/RANK: 142

INCOME	AREA	U.S. AVG	EMPLOYMENT	AREA	U.S. AVG	LARGEST EMPLOYING INDUSTRY
Per capita income	$17,920	$23,420	Unemployment rate	5.6%	6.1%	Food Manufacturing
Household income	$35,942	$46,060	Recent job growth	.5%	.9%	
Household income < $25K	32.8%	26.4%	Projected future job growth	10.2%	15.1%	
Household income > $75K	14.0%	24.5%	White collar	42.0%	54.5%	
Household income growth	52.2%	57.3%	Blue collar	58.0%	45.5%	

COST OF LIVING SCORE: 69/RANK: 102

INDEXES & TAXES	AREA	U.S. AVG	HOUSING	AREA	U.S. AVG	NECESSITIES	AREA	U.S. AVG
Cost of Living Index	81.8	100.0	Median home price	$98,210	$160,100	Food Index	92.5	100.0
Financial Progress Index	93.6	100.0	Home price appreciation	3.9%	7.1%	Housing Index	61.0	100.0
Income tax rate	7.000%	4.625%	Median rent	$513	$670	Utilities Index	91.8	100.0
Sales tax rate	7.000%	6.474%	Homes owned	58.6%	63.9%	Transportation Index	90.3	100.0
Property tax rate	$12.9	$15.6	Homes rented	34.4%	25.3%	Healthcare Index	88.9	100.0
			Housing affordability	60.0%	54.5%	Miscellaneous Cost Index	97.7	100.0

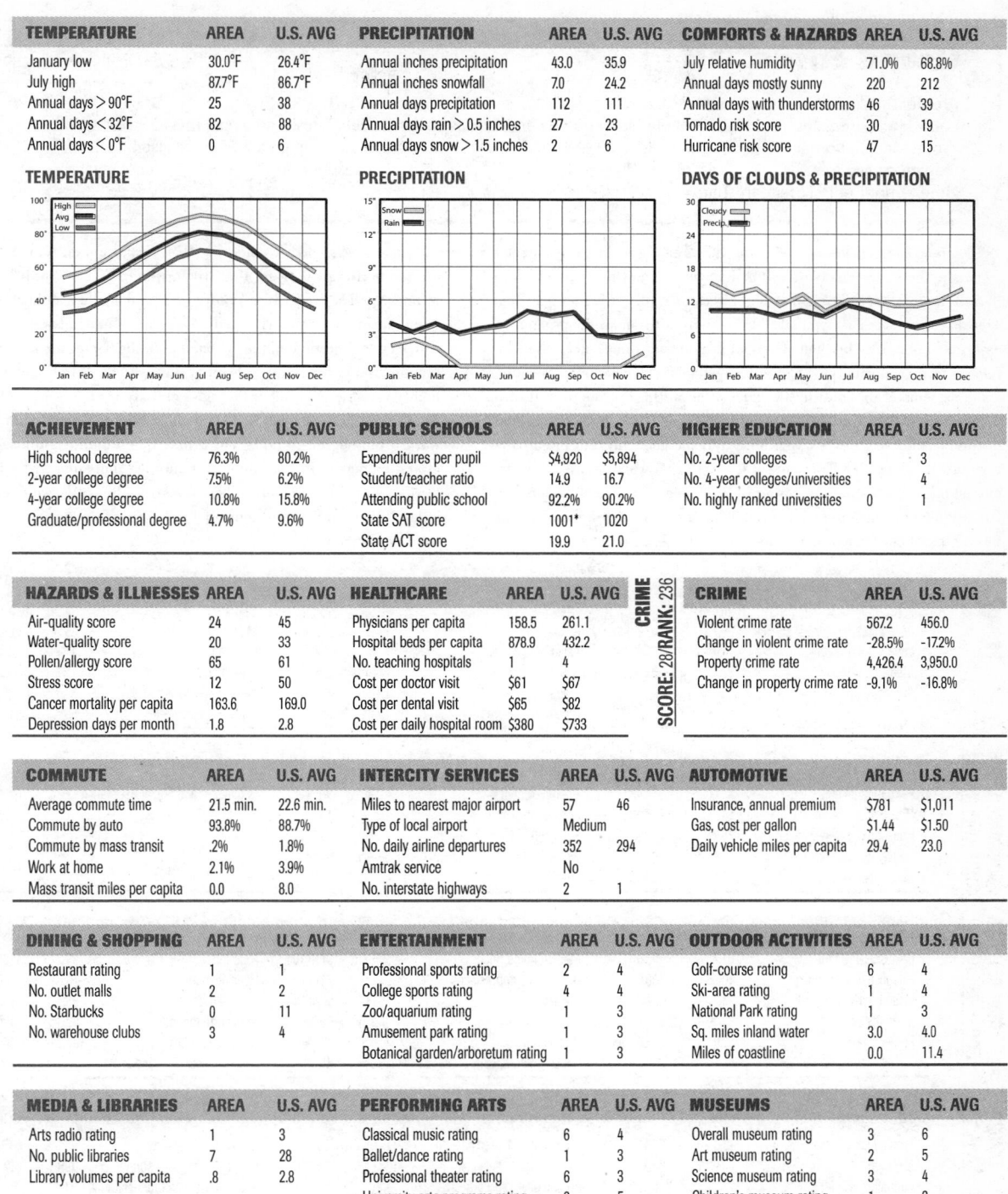

CLIMATE SCORE: 61/RANK: 127

TEMPERATURE	AREA	U.S. AVG	PRECIPITATION	AREA	U.S. AVG	COMFORTS & HAZARDS	AREA	U.S. AVG
January low	30.0°F	26.4°F	Annual inches precipitation	43.0	35.9	July relative humidity	71.0%	68.8%
July high	87.7°F	86.7°F	Annual inches snowfall	7.0	24.2	Annual days mostly sunny	220	212
Annual days > 90°F	25	38	Annual days precipitation	112	111	Annual days with thunderstorms	46	39
Annual days < 32°F	82	88	Annual days rain > 0.5 inches	27	23	Tornado risk score	30	19
Annual days < 0°F	0	6	Annual days snow > 1.5 inches	2	6	Hurricane risk score	47	15

TEMPERATURE

PRECIPITATION

DAYS OF CLOUDS & PRECIPITATION

EDUCATION SCORE: 23/RANK: 252

ACHIEVEMENT	AREA	U.S. AVG	PUBLIC SCHOOLS	AREA	U.S. AVG	HIGHER EDUCATION	AREA	U.S. AVG
High school degree	76.3%	80.2%	Expenditures per pupil	$4,920	$5,894	No. 2-year colleges	1	3
2-year college degree	7.5%	6.2%	Student/teacher ratio	14.9	16.7	No. 4-year colleges/universities	1	4
4-year college degree	10.8%	15.8%	Attending public school	92.2%	90.2%	No. highly ranked universities	0	1
Graduate/professional degree	4.7%	9.6%	State SAT score	1001*	1020			
			State ACT score	19.9	21.0			

HEALTH & HEALTHCARE SCORE: 89/RANK: 33

CRIME SCORE: 28/RANK: 236

HAZARDS & ILLNESSES	AREA	U.S. AVG	HEALTHCARE	AREA	U.S. AVG	CRIME	AREA	U.S. AVG
Air-quality score	24	45	Physicians per capita	158.5	261.1	Violent crime rate	567.2	456.0
Water-quality score	20	33	Hospital beds per capita	878.9	432.2	Change in violent crime rate	-28.5%	-17.2%
Pollen/allergy score	65	61	No. teaching hospitals	1	4	Property crime rate	4,426.4	3,950.0
Stress score	12	50	Cost per doctor visit	$61	$67	Change in property crime rate	-9.1%	-16.8%
Cancer mortality per capita	163.6	169.0	Cost per dental visit	$65	$82			
Depression days per month	1.8	2.8	Cost per daily hospital room	$380	$733			

TRANSPORTATION SCORE: 46/RANK: 176

COMMUTE	AREA	U.S. AVG	INTERCITY SERVICES	AREA	U.S. AVG	AUTOMOTIVE	AREA	U.S. AVG
Average commute time	21.5 min.	22.6 min.	Miles to nearest major airport	57	46	Insurance, annual premium	$781	$1,011
Commute by auto	93.8%	88.7%	Type of local airport	Medium		Gas, cost per gallon	$1.44	$1.50
Commute by mass transit	.2%	1.8%	No. daily airline departures	352	294	Daily vehicle miles per capita	29.4	23.0
Work at home	2.1%	3.9%	Amtrak service	No				
Mass transit miles per capita	0.0	8.0	No. interstate highways	2	1			

LEISURE SCORE: 23/RANK: 255

DINING & SHOPPING	AREA	U.S. AVG	ENTERTAINMENT	AREA	U.S. AVG	OUTDOOR ACTIVITIES	AREA	U.S. AVG
Restaurant rating	1	1	Professional sports rating	2	4	Golf-course rating	6	4
No. outlet malls	2	2	College sports rating	4	4	Ski-area rating	1	4
No. Starbucks	0	11	Zoo/aquarium rating	1	3	National Park rating	1	3
No. warehouse clubs	3	4	Amusement park rating	1	3	Sq. miles inland water	3.0	4.0
			Botanical garden/arboretum rating	1	3	Miles of coastline	0.0	11.4

ARTS & CULTURE SCORE: 60/RANK: 132

MEDIA & LIBRARIES	AREA	U.S. AVG	PERFORMING ARTS	AREA	U.S. AVG	MUSEUMS	AREA	U.S. AVG
Arts radio rating	1	3	Classical music rating	6	4	Overall museum rating	3	6
No. public libraries	7	28	Ballet/dance rating	1	3	Art museum rating	2	5
Library volumes per capita	.8	2.8	Professional theater rating	6	3	Science museum rating	3	4
			University arts programs rating	2	5	Children's museum rating	1	3

Grand Forks, ND

Score: 44.5 Rank: 259

Profile: Small town/College town
Location: Extreme eastern North Dakota along Red River, 60 miles south of Canadian border
Elevation: 840 feet
Time zone: Central Standard Time

PRO	CON
Small-town atmosphere	Cold winters
Cool summers	Isolation
Cost of living	Economy

Grand Forks is located along the U.S. 2 east-west highway corridor at the Minnesota border. It is the home of the University of North Dakota, the state's oldest and largest institute of higher learning. The downtown area is typically Midwestern with small shops and an assortment of mostly brick commercial buildings. Primary industries are related to the university or agriculture—the Red River Valley location contains some of the most fertile land in the world. But the overall economic picture is mixed. A devastating flood in 1997 and the gradual decline of the region as a whole have hurt the economy, but the area is revitalizing effectively. There are a few college-town amenities, but the closest big city is across the border in Winnipeg. Because of its northern Great Plains location and lack of moderating land features, Grand Forks has 55 days below zero—the nation's second highest number.

Grand Forks and its sister city East Grand Forks, Minnesota, straddle the northward-flowing Red River, which divides North Dakota and Minnesota. The Red River Valley is flat and shallow and subject to frequent spring flooding. The Red River Valley is windswept year-round, with frequent arctic outbreaks common in the winter months. Snow covers the ground from mid-December through late March, yet winters are highly variable. November through February is cloudy 75% of the time. Average winter snowfall is 38.0 inches. Summer months are typically warm—but not hot—and humid with frequent thunderstorms. Most precipitation occurs in the late spring through mid-summer thunderstorm season. Annual temperature variations are dramatic, with record lows below −40°F and record highs of 110°F. First freeze is late September, last is early May.

POPULATION

DEMOGRAPHICS	AREA	U.S. AVG	ETHNIC COMPOSITION	AREA	U.S. AVG	RESIDENT PROFILE	AREA	U.S. AVG
Population	96,035		White	96.0%	75.1%	Single	34.8%	43.6%
Population density per sq. mile	28.2	447.3	Black	1.4%	12.3%	Married	65.2%	56.4%
Population growth	-6.9%	16.1%	Asian	1.1%	3.6%	Divorced	4.8%	8.4%
Median age	32.1	35.5	American Indian	1.0%	.9%	Separated	1.0%	3.0%
Average family size	2.6	2.7	Hispanic	2.4%	12.5%	Married with children	32.6%	28.7%
			Diversity measure	15.1%	35.2%	Single with children	5.7%	10.1%

ECONOMY & JOBS SCORE: 42/RANK: 191

INCOME	AREA	U.S. AVG	EMPLOYMENT	AREA	U.S. AVG	LARGEST EMPLOYING INDUSTRY
Per capita income	$21,021	$23,420	Unemployment rate	4.0%	6.1%	Healthcare and Social Assistance
Household income	$40,551	$46,060	Recent job growth	1.2%	.9%	
Household income < $25K	28.2%	26.4%	Projected future job growth	12.8%	15.1%	
Household income > $75K	18.8%	24.5%	White collar	50.7%	54.5%	
Household income growth	66.4%	57.3%	Blue collar	49.3%	45.5%	

COST OF LIVING SCORE: 75/RANK: 81

INDEXES & TAXES	AREA	U.S. AVG	HOUSING	AREA	U.S. AVG	NECESSITIES	AREA	U.S. AVG
Cost of Living Index	81.8	100.0	Median home price	$96,210	$160,100	Food Index	94.2	100.0
Financial Progress Index	105.6	100.0	Home price appreciation	3.4%	7.1%	Housing Index	59.8	100.0
Income tax rate	3.920%	4.625%	Median rent	$603	$670	Utilities Index	88.0	100.0
Sales tax rate	6.500%	6.474%	Homes owned	59.1%	63.9%	Transportation Index	92.3	100.0
Property tax rate	$21.1	$15.6	Homes rented	20.6%	25.3%	Healthcare Index	98.1	100.0
			Housing affordability	56.0%	54.5%	Miscellaneous Cost Index	96.3	100.0

CLIMATE SCORE: 36/RANK: 212

TEMPERATURE	AREA	U.S. AVG	PRECIPITATION	AREA	U.S. AVG	COMFORTS & HAZARDS	AREA	U.S. AVG
January low	-3.0°F	26.4°F	Annual inches precipitation	19.0	35.9	July relative humidity	70.0%	68.8%
July high	83.0°F	86.7°F	Annual inches snowfall	38.0	24.2	Annual days mostly sunny	198	212
Annual days > 90°F	13	38	Annual days precipitation	100	111	Annual days with thunderstorms	31	39
Annual days < 32°F	180	88	Annual days rain > 0.5 inches	10	23	Tornado risk score	9	19
Annual days < 0°F	55	6	Annual days snow > 1.5 inches	8	6	Hurricane risk score	0	15

TEMPERATURE

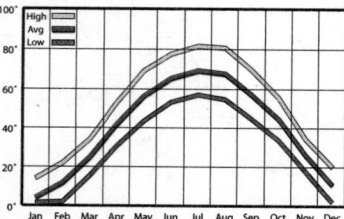

PRECIPITATION

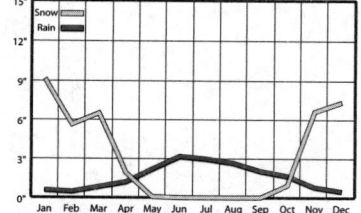

DAYS OF CLOUDS & PRECIPITATION

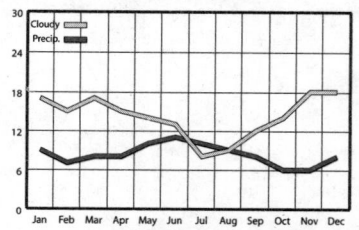

EDUCATION — SCORE: 78/RANK: 74

ACHIEVEMENT	AREA	U.S. AVG	PUBLIC SCHOOLS	AREA	U.S. AVG	HIGHER EDUCATION	AREA	U.S. AVG
High school degree	86.6%	80.2%	Expenditures per pupil	$5,039	$5,894	No. 2-year colleges	0	3
2-year college degree	9.1%	6.2%	Student/teacher ratio	14.9	16.7	No. 4-year colleges/universities	2	4
4-year college degree	16.5%	15.8%	Attending public school	93.6%	90.2%	No. highly ranked universities	0	1
Graduate/professional degree	7.8%	9.6%	State SAT score	1215	1020			
			State ACT score	21.3*	21.0			

HEALTH & HEALTHCARE — SCORE: 97/RANK: 9   CRIME — SCORE: 80/RANK: 65

HAZARDS & ILLNESSES	AREA	U.S. AVG	HEALTHCARE	AREA	U.S. AVG	CRIME	AREA	U.S. AVG
Air-quality score	81	45	Physicians per capita	260.3	261.1	Violent crime rate	147.4	456.0
Water-quality score	21	33	Hospital beds per capita	745.8	432.2	Change in violent crime rate	-.9%	-17.2%
Pollen/allergy score	31	61	No. teaching hospitals	1	4	Property crime rate	3,364.4	3,950.0
Stress score	2	50	Cost per doctor visit	$80	$67	Change in property crime rate	-24.1%	-16.8%
Cancer mortality per capita	151.6	169.0	Cost per dental visit	$73	$82			
Depression days per month	1.7	2.8	Cost per daily hospital room	$621	$733			

TRANSPORTATION — SCORE: 89/RANK: 39

COMMUTE	AREA	U.S. AVG	INTERCITY SERVICES	AREA	U.S. AVG	AUTOMOTIVE	AREA	U.S. AVG
Average commute time	15.1 min.	22.6 min.	Miles to nearest major airport	279	46	Insurance, annual premium	$646	$1,011
Commute by auto	76.8%	88.7%	Type of local airport	Large		Gas, cost per gallon	$1.53	$1.50
Commute by mass transit	.3%	1.8%	No. daily airline departures	624	294	Daily vehicle miles per capita	13.5	23.0
Work at home	15.7%	3.9%	Amtrak service	Yes				
Mass transit miles per capita	2.9	8.0	No. interstate highways	1	1			

LEISURE — SCORE: 3/RANK: 319

DINING & SHOPPING	AREA	U.S. AVG	ENTERTAINMENT	AREA	U.S. AVG	OUTDOOR ACTIVITIES	AREA	U.S. AVG
Restaurant rating	1	1	Professional sports rating	2	4	Golf-course rating	2	4
No. outlet malls	0	2	College sports rating	6	4	Ski-area rating	1	4
No. Starbucks	1	11	Zoo/aquarium rating	1	3	National Park rating	2	3
No. warehouse clubs	3	4	Amusement park rating	1	3	Sq. miles inland water	1.0	4.0
			Botanical garden/arboretum rating	1	3	Miles of coastline	0.0	11.4

ARTS & CULTURE — SCORE: 3/RANK: 318

MEDIA & LIBRARIES	AREA	U.S. AVG	PERFORMING ARTS	AREA	U.S. AVG	MUSEUMS	AREA	U.S. AVG
Arts radio rating	1	3	Classical music rating	3	4	Overall museum rating	4	6
No. public libraries	3	28	Ballet/dance rating	1	3	Art museum rating	4	5
Library volumes per capita	4.2	2.8	Professional theater rating	1	3	Science museum rating	4	4
			University arts programs rating	4	5	Children's museum rating	1	3

Grand Junction, CO

Score: 74.9   Rank: 62

Profile: Small town
Location: Western edge of Colorado, 25 miles from Utah
Elevation: 4,899 feet
Time zone: Mountain Standard Time

PRO	CON
Attractive downtown	Isolation
Year-round climate	Arts and culture
Healthcare	Low ethnic diversity

Grand Junction, a small town on the western desert slopes of the Rockies, has become a pleasant alternative to the Front Range hustle and bustle, particularly for retirees. The climate is sunnier, drier, and generally more pleasant than other Colorado metropolitan areas and it has a well-preserved, western-town flavor. The air-quality score is the best in the state and good on a national scale. Healthcare and especially hospital services are above average. The economy and cost of living are favorable on a Colorado scale. The main downside is isolation—good air service or cultural amenities are located 250 miles east in Denver or 280 miles west in Salt Lake City, Utah. Like other small towns, Grand Junction does not excel in any category but does consistently well in all of them, hence the favorable rank.

The town is located at the junction of the Colorado and Gunnison rivers in a large mountain valley on the west slope of the Rockies. Mountains on all sides reach heights of 9,000 feet to 12,000 feet from the valley floor. Dry conditions lead to desert-fringe vegetation and an arid landscape. The area has a semiarid climate marked by the wide seasonal range typical of interior localities at this latitude. The surrounding mountains block severe weather changes. Summer days are warm, usually in the 90s, but with very low humidity and an occasional thundershower. Long periods of winter cold can occur when cold air gets trapped in the valley. Sudden winter storms are infrequent and winter snows are light. First freeze is mid-September, last is late May.

POPULATION

DEMOGRAPHICS	AREA	U.S. AVG	ETHNIC COMPOSITION	AREA	U.S. AVG	RESIDENT PROFILE	AREA	U.S. AVG
Population	121,419		White	95.0%	75.1%	Single	40.0%	43.6%
Population density per sq. mile	36.5	447.3	Black	1.0%	12.3%	Married	60.0%	56.4%
Population growth	30.4%	16.1%	Asian	.9%	3.6%	Divorced	11.0%	8.4%
Median age	38.5	35.5	American Indian	1.0%	.9%	Separated	2.5%	3.0%
Average family size	2.6	2.7	Hispanic	9.5%	12.5%	Married with children	27.0%	28.7%
			Diversity measure	23.6%	35.2%	Single with children	10.0%	10.1%

ECONOMY & JOBS
SCORE: 59/RANK: 135

INCOME	AREA	U.S. AVG	EMPLOYMENT	AREA	U.S. AVG	LARGEST EMPLOYING INDUSTRY
Per capita income	$21,165	$23,420	Unemployment rate	5.1%	6.1%	Construction
Household income	$39,565	$46,060	Recent job growth	5.7%	.9%	
Household income < $25K	30.2%	26.4%	Projected future job growth	18.8%	15.1%	
Household income > $75K	17.9%	24.5%	White collar	54.8%	54.5%	
Household income growth	67.0%	57.3%	Blue collar	45.2%	45.5%	

COST OF LIVING
SCORE: 34/RANK: 218

INDEXES & TAXES	AREA	U.S. AVG	HOUSING	AREA	U.S. AVG	NECESSITIES	AREA	U.S. AVG
Cost of Living Index	99.3	100.0	Median home price	$144,620	$160,100	Food Index	103.9	100.0
Financial Progress Index	84.9	100.0	Home price appreciation	6.7%	7.1%	Housing Index	89.8	100.0
Income tax rate	5.000%	4.625%	Median rent	$579	$670	Utilities Index	103.0	100.0
Sales tax rate	4.900%	6.474%	Homes owned	60.6%	63.9%	Transportation Index	111.8	100.0
Property tax rate	$6.9	$15.6	Homes rented	25.9%	25.3%	Healthcare Index	115.4	100.0
			Housing affordability	51.0%	54.5%	Miscellaneous Cost Index	99.1	100.0

CLIMATE
SCORE: 69/RANK: 103

TEMPERATURE	AREA	U.S. AVG	PRECIPITATION	AREA	U.S. AVG	COMFORTS & HAZARDS	AREA	U.S. AVG
January low	16.0°F	26.4°F	Annual inches precipitation	9.0	35.9	July relative humidity	47.0%	68.8%
July high	93.0°F	86.7°F	Annual inches snowfall	26.0	24.2	Annual days mostly sunny	260	212
Annual days > 90°F	62	38	Annual days precipitation	70	111	Annual days with thunderstorms	36	39
Annual days < 32°F	134	88	Annual days rain > 0.5 inches	4	23	Tornado risk score	0	19
Annual days < 0°F	4	6	Annual days snow > 1.5 inches	7	6	Hurricane risk score	0	15

TEMPERATURE

PRECIPITATION

DAYS OF CLOUDS & PRECIPITATION

EDUCATION
SCORE: 47/RANK: 173

ACHIEVEMENT	AREA	U.S. AVG	PUBLIC SCHOOLS	AREA	U.S. AVG	HIGHER EDUCATION	AREA	U.S. AVG
High school degree	84.9%	80.2%	Expenditures per pupil	$4,903	$5,894	No. 2-year colleges	1	3
2-year college degree	7.1%	6.2%	Student/teacher ratio	18.5	16.7	No. 4-year colleges/universities	1	4
4-year college degree	14.6%	15.8%	Attending public school	95.0%	90.2%	No. highly ranked universities	0	1
Graduate/professional degree	7.3%	9.6%	State SAT score	1104	1020			
			State ACT score	20.1*	21.0			

HEALTH & HEALTHCARE
SCORE: 96/RANK: 11

CRIME
SCORE: 62/RANK: 125

HAZARDS & ILLNESSES	AREA	U.S. AVG	HEALTHCARE	AREA	U.S. AVG	CRIME	AREA	U.S. AVG
Air-quality score	24	45	Physicians per capita	272.6	261.1	Violent crime rate	229.5	456.0
Water-quality score	82	33	Hospital beds per capita	652.9	432.2	Change in violent crime rate	-51.6%	-17.2%
Pollen/allergy score	60	61	No. teaching hospitals	2	4	Property crime rate	4,358.3	3,950.0
Stress score	41	50	Cost per doctor visit	$67	$67	Change in property crime rate	-13.1%	-16.8%
Cancer mortality per capita	149.9	169.0	Cost per dental visit	$91	$82			
Depression days per month	2.4	2.8	Cost per daily hospital room	$740	$733			

TRANSPORTATION
SCORE: 57/RANK: 142

COMMUTE	AREA	U.S. AVG	INTERCITY SERVICES	AREA	U.S. AVG	AUTOMOTIVE	AREA	U.S. AVG
Average commute time	18.5 min.	22.6 min.	Miles to nearest major airport	202	46	Insurance, annual premium	$1,029	$1,011
Commute by auto	86.1%	88.7%	Type of local airport	Large		Gas, cost per gallon	$1.57	$1.50
Commute by mass transit	.2%	1.8%	No. daily airline departures	812	294	Daily vehicle miles per capita	15.5	23.0
Work at home	8.2%	3.9%	Amtrak service	Yes				
Mass transit miles per capita	1.5	8.0	No. interstate highways	0	1			

LEISURE SCORE: 68/RANK: 108

DINING & SHOPPING	AREA	U.S. AVG	ENTERTAINMENT	AREA	U.S. AVG	OUTDOOR ACTIVITIES	AREA	U.S. AVG
Restaurant rating	1	1	Professional sports rating	2	4	Golf-course rating	1	4
No. outlet malls	0	2	College sports rating	3	4	Ski-area rating	10	4
No. Starbucks	0	11	Zoo/aquarium rating	1	3	National Park rating	3	3
No. warehouse clubs	1	4	Amusement park rating	1	3	Sq. miles inland water	4.0	4.0
			Botanical garden/arboretum rating	1	3	Miles of coastline	0.0	11.4

ARTS & CULTURE SCORE: 4/RANK: 317

MEDIA & LIBRARIES	AREA	U.S. AVG	PERFORMING ARTS	AREA	U.S. AVG	MUSEUMS	AREA	U.S. AVG
Arts radio rating	1	3	Classical music rating	1	4	Overall museum rating	4	6
No. public libraries	9	28	Ballet/dance rating	1	3	Art museum rating	4	5
Library volumes per capita	2.3	2.8	Professional theater rating	1	3	Science museum rating	5	4
			University arts programs rating	3	5	Children's museum rating	3	3

Grand Rapids–Muskegon–Holland, MI

Score: 58.9   Rank: 157

Profile: Mid-size-city complex
Location: West-central Michigan, 25 miles inland from Lake Michigan
Elevation: 803 feet
Time zone: Eastern Standard Time

PRO	CON
Strong economy	Economic cycles
Cultural amenities	Cold cloudy winters
Attractive areas nearby	Isolation

Grand Rapids is the primary cultural and business hub of western Michigan. Nearby hardwood forests made the city a notable furniture-producing center in the 19th and early 20th centuries. That industry continues today but now includes high-tech office furniture. The tempering effect of Lake Michigan promotes a variety of agriculture including berries and such fruit trees as apple, peach, and cherry. Cultural and recreational amenities are above average with a strong performing arts component and abundant outdoor activities, including nearby beaches. Holland, a Dutch settlement, and (not surprisingly) a tulip-growing region, is a short drive to the southwest. The area has experienced some economic cycles, although its relatively lesser dependence on the auto industry has kept employment levels more consistent. At 150 miles from Detroit and 175 miles from Chicago, the location is relatively isolated from big-city amenities and services.

Grand Rapids is located in the Grand River Valley, with high hills rising on either side to 1,020 feet. Lake Michigan moderates the continental climate. In comparison to other Midwestern locations, springs are cooler and later while falls are longer and warmer. Summer days are pleasantly warm with about 3 weeks of hot, humid weather. Most summer nights are comfortable. Hardwood trees make for a colorful fall. Winters are very cloudy, with numerous snow flurries and strong westerly winds. Prolonged cold waves are infrequent, but below-zero temperatures and continuous snow cover are common. First freeze is early October, last is May 1.

POPULATION

DEMOGRAPHICS	AREA	U.S. AVG	ETHNIC COMPOSITION	AREA	U.S. AVG	RESIDENT PROFILE	AREA	U.S. AVG
Population	1,114,965		White	91.3%	75.1%	Single	41.1%	43.6%
Population density per sq. mile	404.2	447.3	Black	5.8%	12.3%	Married	58.9%	56.4%
Population growth	18.9%	16.1%	Asian	1.1%	3.6%	Divorced	8.3%	8.4%
Median age	33.4	35.5	American Indian	.7%	.9%	Separated	2.1%	3.0%
Average family size	2.8	2.7	Hispanic	3.0%	12.5%	Married with children	32.2%	28.7%
			Diversity measure	29.7%	35.2%	Single with children	10.1%	10.1%

ECONOMY & JOBS SCORE: 57/RANK: 141

INCOME	AREA	U.S. AVG	EMPLOYMENT	AREA	U.S. AVG	LARGEST EMPLOYING INDUSTRY
Per capita income	$24,949	$23,420	Unemployment rate	7.4%	6.1%	Transportation Equipment Manufacturing
Household income	$53,279	$46,060	Recent job growth	1.8%	.9%	
Household income < $25K	20.0%	26.4%	Projected future job growth	17.5%	15.1%	
Household income > $75K	30.0%	24.5%	White collar	52.1%	54.5%	
Household income growth	67.5%	57.3%	Blue collar	47.9%	45.5%	

COST OF LIVING SCORE: 49/RANK: 167

INDEXES & TAXES	AREA	U.S. AVG	HOUSING	AREA	U.S. AVG	NECESSITIES	AREA	U.S. AVG
Cost of Living Index	93.5	100.0	Median home price	$126,100	$160,100	Food Index	104.3	100.0
Financial Progress Index	121.5	100.0	Home price appreciation	5.9%	7.1%	Housing Index	78.3	100.0
Income tax rate	5.400%	4.625%	Median rent	$636	$670	Utilities Index	85.4	100.0
Sales tax rate	6.000%	6.474%	Homes owned	73.4%	63.9%	Transportation Index	112.6	100.0
Property tax rate	$12.8	$15.6	Homes rented	18.9%	25.3%	Healthcare Index	96.4	100.0
			Housing affordability	59.0%	54.5%	Miscellaneous Cost Index	102.6	100.0

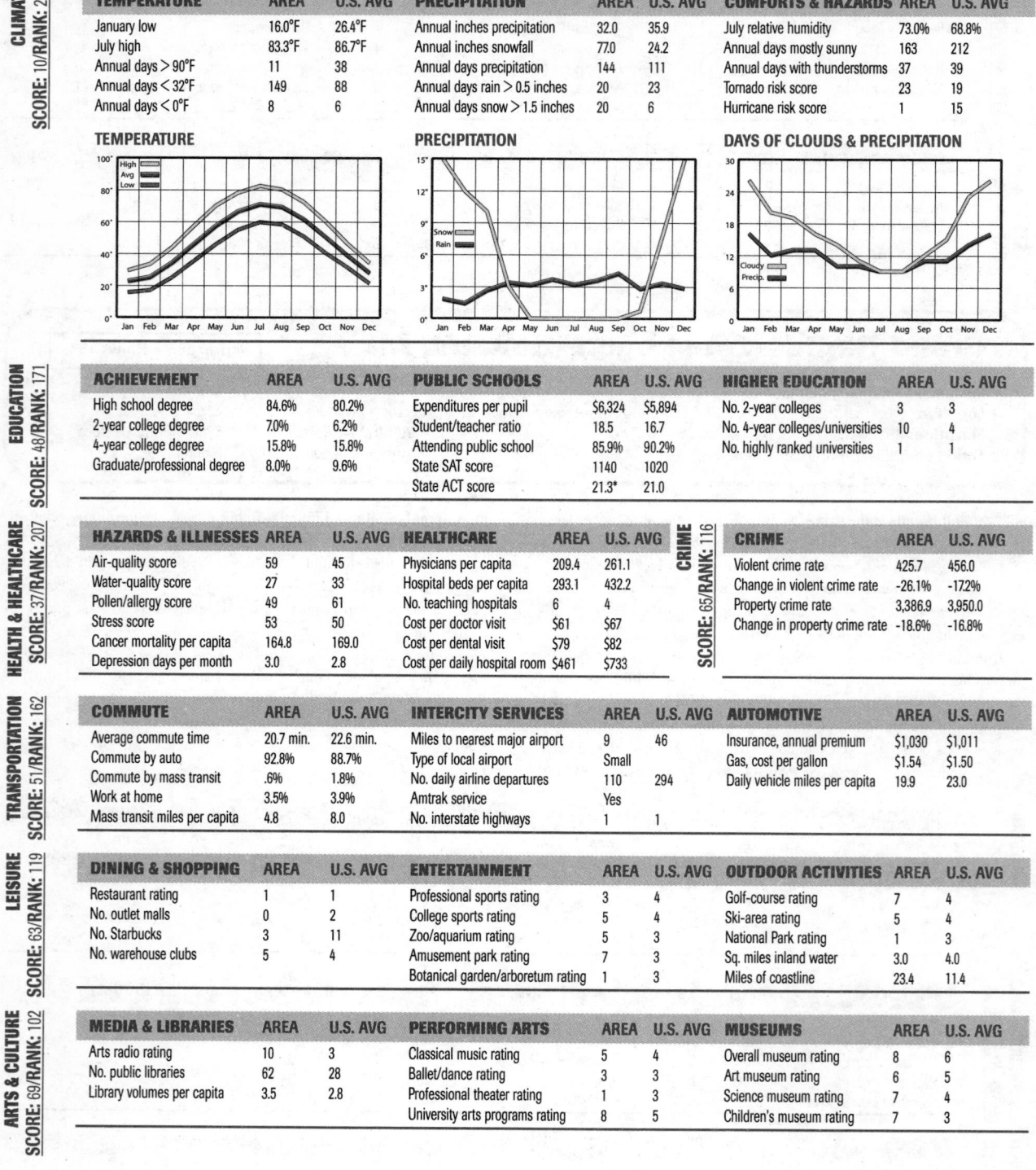

CLIMATE SCORE: 10/RANK: 296

TEMPERATURE	AREA	U.S. AVG
January low	16.0°F	26.4°F
July high	83.3°F	86.7°F
Annual days > 90°F	11	38
Annual days < 32°F	149	88
Annual days < 0°F	8	6

PRECIPITATION	AREA	U.S. AVG
Annual inches precipitation	32.0	35.9
Annual inches snowfall	77.0	24.2
Annual days precipitation	144	111
Annual days rain > 0.5 inches	20	23
Annual days snow > 1.5 inches	20	6

COMFORTS & HAZARDS	AREA	U.S. AVG
July relative humidity	73.0%	68.8%
Annual days mostly sunny	163	212
Annual days with thunderstorms	37	39
Tornado risk score	23	19
Hurricane risk score	1	15

TEMPERATURE

PRECIPITATION

DAYS OF CLOUDS & PRECIPITATION

EDUCATION SCORE: 48/RANK: 171

ACHIEVEMENT	AREA	U.S. AVG
High school degree	84.6%	80.2%
2-year college degree	7.0%	6.2%
4-year college degree	15.8%	15.8%
Graduate/professional degree	8.0%	9.6%

PUBLIC SCHOOLS	AREA	U.S. AVG
Expenditures per pupil	$6,324	$5,894
Student/teacher ratio	18.5	16.7
Attending public school	85.9%	90.2%
State SAT score	1140	1020
State ACT score	21.3*	21.0

HIGHER EDUCATION	AREA	U.S. AVG
No. 2-year colleges	3	3
No. 4-year colleges/universities	10	4
No. highly ranked universities	1	1

HEALTH & HEALTHCARE SCORE: 37/RANK: 207

HAZARDS & ILLNESSES	AREA	U.S. AVG
Air-quality score	59	45
Water-quality score	27	33
Pollen/allergy score	49	61
Stress score	53	50
Cancer mortality per capita	164.8	169.0
Depression days per month	3.0	2.8

HEALTHCARE	AREA	U.S. AVG
Physicians per capita	209.4	261.1
Hospital beds per capita	293.1	432.2
No. teaching hospitals	6	4
Cost per doctor visit	$61	$67
Cost per dental visit	$79	$82
Cost per daily hospital room	$461	$733

CRIME SCORE: 65/RANK: 116

CRIME	AREA	U.S. AVG
Violent crime rate	425.7	456.0
Change in violent crime rate	-26.1%	-17.2%
Property crime rate	3,386.9	3,950.0
Change in property crime rate	-18.6%	-16.8%

TRANSPORTATION SCORE: 51/RANK: 162

COMMUTE	AREA	U.S. AVG
Average commute time	20.7 min.	22.6 min.
Commute by auto	92.8%	88.7%
Commute by mass transit	.6%	1.8%
Work at home	3.5%	3.9%
Mass transit miles per capita	4.8	8.0

INTERCITY SERVICES	AREA	U.S. AVG
Miles to nearest major airport	9	46
Type of local airport	Small	
No. daily airline departures	110	294
Amtrak service	Yes	
No. interstate highways	1	1

AUTOMOTIVE	AREA	U.S. AVG
Insurance, annual premium	$1,030	$1,011
Gas, cost per gallon	$1.54	$1.50
Daily vehicle miles per capita	19.9	23.0

LEISURE SCORE: 63/RANK: 119

DINING & SHOPPING	AREA	U.S. AVG
Restaurant rating	1	1
No. outlet malls	0	2
No. Starbucks	3	11
No. warehouse clubs	5	4

ENTERTAINMENT	AREA	U.S. AVG
Professional sports rating	3	4
College sports rating	5	4
Zoo/aquarium rating	5	3
Amusement park rating	7	3
Botanical garden/arboretum rating	1	3

OUTDOOR ACTIVITIES	AREA	U.S. AVG
Golf-course rating	7	4
Ski-area rating	5	4
National Park rating	1	3
Sq. miles inland water	3.0	4.0
Miles of coastline	23.4	11.4

ARTS & CULTURE SCORE: 69/RANK: 102

MEDIA & LIBRARIES	AREA	U.S. AVG
Arts radio rating	10	3
No. public libraries	62	28
Library volumes per capita	3.5	2.8

PERFORMING ARTS	AREA	U.S. AVG
Classical music rating	5	4
Ballet/dance rating	3	3
Professional theater rating	1	3
University arts programs rating	8	5

MUSEUMS	AREA	U.S. AVG
Overall museum rating	8	6
Art museum rating	6	5
Science museum rating	7	4
Children's museum rating	7	3

Great Falls, MT

Score: 51.5   **Rank:** 212

Profile: Small town
Location: North-central Montana along the upper Missouri River
Elevation: 3,670 feet
Time zone: Mountain Standard Time

PRO	CON
Nearby mountains	Harsh winters
Pleasant summers	Isolation
Small-town atmosphere	Economy

Great Falls is an agricultural and commercial center located at the foot of the Rockies and the western terminus of the Great Plains. The wilderness of the Lewis and Clark National Forest to the west and Glacier National Park to the northwest provides excellent recreational opportunities. Helena, the state capital, lies 90 miles to the south. The area is quiet and attractive, but is isolated geographically and doesn't benefit from the tourism that bolsters the economy of other Montana cities, resulting in poor employment and income statistics. However, fans of Lewis and Clark and Montana in general are starting to discover it.

The city is located along the main stem of the Missouri River at its confluence with the Sun River in a valley surrounded by plateaus and hills. Except to the north and northeast, it is encircled by mountain ranges. The climate is semiarid continental with significant topographic effects. Summertime is pleasant, with cool nights; moderately warm, sunny days; and little hot, humid weather. Winters are not as cold as might be expected for the location because of warming, downslope winds from the mountains, which can raise temperatures by 40°F in 24 hours. While sub-zero weather is common, the coldest weather seldom lasts more than a few days, and snow rarely lingers. Cold polar air also invades quickly causing sharp temperature drops. Late spring and early summer are the wettest with a few summer thunderstorms. Freezing temperatures normally occur any time of year except July and August.

POPULATION

DEMOGRAPHICS	AREA	U.S. AVG	ETHNIC COMPOSITION	AREA	U.S. AVG	RESIDENT PROFILE	AREA	U.S. AVG
Population	79,389		White	95.1%	75.1%	Single	39.3%	43.6%
Population density per sq. mile	29.4	447.3	Black	.5%	12.3%	Married	60.7%	56.4%
Population growth	2.2%	16.1%	Asian	.6%	3.6%	Divorced	9.9%	8.4%
Median age	37.1	35.5	American Indian	3.6%	.9%	Separated	1.7%	3.0%
Average family size	2.4	2.7	Hispanic	1.3%	12.5%	Married with children	25.4%	28.7%
			Diversity measure	19.9%	35.2%	Single with children	8.8%	10.1%

ECONOMY & JOBS   SCORE: 65/RANK: 114

INCOME	AREA	U.S. AVG	EMPLOYMENT	AREA	U.S. AVG	LARGEST EMPLOYING INDUSTRY
Per capita income	$20,138	$23,420	Unemployment rate	3.9%	6.1%	Finance and Insurance
Household income	$36,389	$46,060	Recent job growth	-.7%	.9%	
Household income < $25K	32.1%	26.4%	Projected future job growth	7.6%	15.1%	
Household income > $75K	14.9%	24.5%	White collar	49.6%	54.5%	
Household income growth	53.2%	57.3%	Blue collar	50.4%	45.5%	

COST OF LIVING   SCORE: 63/RANK: 123

INDEXES & TAXES	AREA	U.S. AVG	HOUSING	AREA	U.S. AVG	NECESSITIES	AREA	U.S. AVG
Cost of Living Index	86.3	100.0	Median home price	$104,310	$160,100	Food Index	104.0	100.0
Financial Progress Index	89.8	100.0	Home price appreciation	4.1%	7.1%	Housing Index	64.8	100.0
Income tax rate	11.000%	4.625%	Median rent	$553	$670	Utilities Index	89.7	100.0
Sales tax rate	0.000%	6.474%	Homes owned	55.6%	63.9%	Transportation Index	95.5	100.0
Property tax rate	$18.0	$15.6	Homes rented	18.1%	25.3%	Healthcare Index	96.8	100.0
			Housing affordability	51.0%	54.5%	Miscellaneous Cost Index	99.3	100.0

CLIMATE   SCORE: 14/RANK: 283

TEMPERATURE	AREA	U.S. AVG	PRECIPITATION	AREA	U.S. AVG	COMFORTS & HAZARDS	AREA	U.S. AVG
January low	11.0°F	26.4°F	Annual inches precipitation	15.0	35.9	July relative humidity	58.0%	68.8%
July high	83.0°F	86.7°F	Annual inches snowfall	63.0	24.2	Annual days mostly sunny	187	212
Annual days > 90°F	18	38	Annual days precipitation	103	111	Annual days with thunderstorms	25	39
Annual days < 32°F	155	88	Annual days rain > 0.5 inches	9	23	Tornado risk score	7	19
Annual days < 0°F	28	6	Annual days snow > 1.5 inches	15	6	Hurricane risk score	0	15

TEMPERATURE

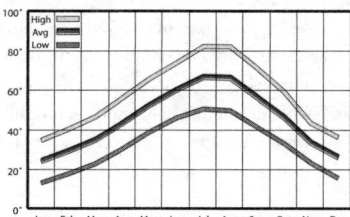

PRECIPITATION

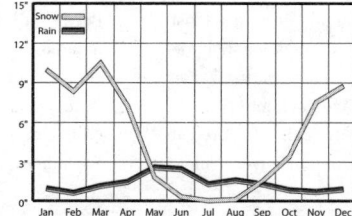

DAYS OF CLOUDS & PRECIPITATION

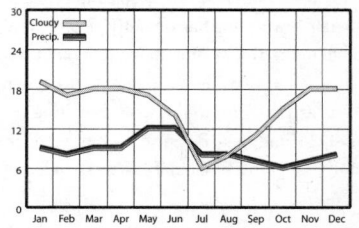

EDUCATION SCORE: 56/RANK: 145

ACHIEVEMENT	AREA	U.S. AVG	PUBLIC SCHOOLS	AREA	U.S. AVG	HIGHER EDUCATION	AREA	U.S. AVG
High school degree	87.2%	80.2%	Expenditures per pupil	$4,947	$5,894	No. 2-year colleges	1	3
2-year college degree	6.8%	6.2%	Student/teacher ratio	16.1	16.7	No. 4-year colleges/universities	1	4
4-year college degree	15.3%	15.8%	Attending public school	94.3%	90.2%	No. highly ranked universities	0	1
Graduate/professional degree	7.1%	9.6%	State SAT score	1081	1020			
			State ACT score	21.7*	21.0			

HEALTH & HEALTHCARE SCORE: 96/RANK: 10

HAZARDS & ILLNESSES	AREA	U.S. AVG	HEALTHCARE	AREA	U.S. AVG	CRIME	AREA	U.S. AVG
Air-quality score	49	45	Physicians per capita	262.0	261.1	Violent crime rate	382.3	456.0
Water-quality score	54	33	Hospital beds per capita	986.8	432.2	Change in violent crime rate	42.5%	-17.2%
Pollen/allergy score	38	61	No. teaching hospitals	0	4	Property crime rate	5,134.3	3,950.0
Stress score	30	50	Cost per doctor visit	$64	$67	Change in property crime rate	-51.6%	-16.8%
Cancer mortality per capita	168.6	169.0	Cost per dental visit	$74	$82			
Depression days per month	2.0	2.8	Cost per daily hospital room	$372	$733			

CRIME SCORE: 37/RANK: 207

TRANSPORTATION SCORE: 90/RANK: 33

COMMUTE	AREA	U.S. AVG	INTERCITY SERVICES	AREA	U.S. AVG	AUTOMOTIVE	AREA	U.S. AVG
Average commute time	16.0 min.	22.6 min.	Miles to nearest major airport	176	46	Insurance, annual premium	$712	$1,011
Commute by auto	83.7%	88.7%	Type of local airport	Small		Gas, cost per gallon	$1.55	$1.50
Commute by mass transit	.4%	1.8%	No. daily airline departures	80	294	Daily vehicle miles per capita	14.2	23.0
Work at home	6.6%	3.9%	Amtrak service	No				
Mass transit miles per capita	6.2	8.0	No. interstate highways	1	1			

LEISURE SCORE: 46/RANK: 177

DINING & SHOPPING	AREA	U.S. AVG	ENTERTAINMENT	AREA	U.S. AVG	OUTDOOR ACTIVITIES	AREA	U.S. AVG
Restaurant rating	1	1	Professional sports rating	2	4	Golf-course rating	1	4
No. outlet malls	0	2	College sports rating	1	4	Ski-area rating	7	4
No. Starbucks	0	11	Zoo/aquarium rating	1	3	National Park rating	8	3
No. warehouse clubs	3	4	Amusement park rating	1	3	Sq. miles inland water	3.0	4.0
			Botanical garden/arboretum rating	1	3	Miles of coastline	0.0	11.4

ARTS & CULTURE SCORE: 16/RANK: 276

MEDIA & LIBRARIES	AREA	U.S. AVG	PERFORMING ARTS	AREA	U.S. AVG	MUSEUMS	AREA	U.S. AVG
Arts radio rating	1	3	Classical music rating	3	4	Overall museum rating	4	6
No. public libraries	3	28	Ballet/dance rating	1	3	Art museum rating	6	5
Library volumes per capita	1.9	2.8	Professional theater rating	1	3	Science museum rating	1	4
			University arts programs rating	2	5	Children's museum rating	1	3

Greeley, CO

Score: 68.0   Rank: 89

Profile: Small agricultural town
Location: North-central Colorado, 55 miles north of Denver
Elevation: 4,715 feet
Time zone: Mountain Standard Time

PRO	CON
Small-town atmosphere	Isolation
Nearby mountains	Economy
High incomes	Long commutes

Greeley is largely agricultural in character—livestock, meatpacking, and sugar beets are especially important. Local feedlots can bring strong agricultural "fragrances," largely imperceptible to long-time residents. The University of Northern Colorado adds a light college-town accent, and some high-tech industry exists, although downsizing has recently occurred in this area. The area is close enough to the Rocky Mountains to benefit from their recreational opportunities. Many residents commute to the more commercialized Fort Collins or Loveland to the west, resulting in average commute times of almost 24 minutes. Because incomes are relatively high compared to cost of living, the Financial Progress Index is favorable. Denver is close

enough to share some of its amenities. Although it doesn't excel in any category, Greeley scores consistently well in most, resulting in a high rank.

The town is located among rolling grassland plains in a shallow valley at the confluence of the Cache La Poudre and South Platte rivers. Locals call the area the "Kansas part of Colorado," accurately depicting both landscape and climate, which is continental. Warm, dry spring and summer days are punctuated by occasional heavy thunderstorms. Winters are variable with alternating cold spells and mild periods. Wind chill can make all winter weather more severe. First freeze end of September, last is mid-May.

POPULATION

DEMOGRAPHICS	AREA	U.S. AVG	ETHNIC COMPOSITION	AREA	U.S. AVG	RESIDENT PROFILE	AREA	U.S. AVG
Population	205,014		White	93.0%	75.1%	Single	39.1%	43.6%
Population density per sq. mile	51.3	447.3	Black	.7%	12.3%	Married	60.9%	56.4%
Population growth	55.5%	16.1%	Asian	1.1%	3.6%	Divorced	7.9%	8.4%
Median age	31.2	35.5	American Indian	.6%	.9%	Separated	2.0%	3.0%
Average family size	2.9	2.7	Hispanic	18.8%	12.5%	Married with children	31.0%	28.7%
			Diversity measure	44.1%	35.2%	Single with children	8.4%	10.1%

ECONOMY & JOBS
SCORE: 31/RANK: 227

INCOME	AREA	U.S. AVG	EMPLOYMENT	AREA	U.S. AVG	LARGEST EMPLOYING INDUSTRY
Per capita income	$19,696	$23,420	Unemployment rate	6.1%	6.1%	Food Manufacturing
Household income	$42,835	$46,060	Recent job growth	3.9%	.9%	
Household income < $25K	27.0%	26.4%	Projected future job growth	16.4%	15.1%	
Household income > $75K	21.1%	24.5%	White collar	48.6%	54.5%	
Household income growth	66.7%	57.3%	Blue collar	51.4%	45.5%	

COST OF LIVING
SCORE: 43/RANK: 187

INDEXES & TAXES	AREA	U.S. AVG	HOUSING	AREA	U.S. AVG	NECESSITIES	AREA	U.S. AVG
Cost of Living Index	106.2	100.0	Median home price	$181,040	$160,100	Food Index	112.9	100.0
Financial Progress Index	86.0	100.0	Home price appreciation	8.8%	7.1%	Housing Index	112.4	100.0
Income tax rate	5.000%	4.625%	Median rent	$745	$670	Utilities Index	93.9	100.0
Sales tax rate	2.900%	6.474%	Homes owned	59.6%	63.9%	Transportation Index	99.8	100.0
Property tax rate	$10.0	$15.6	Homes rented	29.6%	25.3%	Healthcare Index	116.7	100.0
			Housing affordability	46.0%	54.5%	Miscellaneous Cost Index	95.5	100.0

CLIMATE
SCORE: 54/RANK: 151

TEMPERATURE	AREA	U.S. AVG	PRECIPITATION	AREA	U.S. AVG	COMFORTS & HAZARDS	AREA	U.S. AVG
January low	16.2°F	26.4°F	Annual inches precipitation	16.0	35.9	July relative humidity	53.0%	68.8%
July high	87.4°F	86.7°F	Annual inches snowfall	60.0	24.2	Annual days mostly sunny	246	212
Annual days > 90°F	32	38	Annual days precipitation	88	111	Annual days with thunderstorms	41	39
Annual days < 32°F	163	88	Annual days rain > 0.5 inches	7	23	Tornado risk score	49	19
Annual days < 0°F	10	6	Annual days snow > 1.5 inches	13	6	Hurricane risk score	0	15

TEMPERATURE

PRECIPITATION

DAYS OF CLOUDS & PRECIPITATION

EDUCATION
SCORE: 50/RANK: 164

ACHIEVEMENT	AREA	U.S. AVG	PUBLIC SCHOOLS	AREA	U.S. AVG	HIGHER EDUCATION	AREA	U.S. AVG
High school degree	79.3%	80.2%	Expenditures per pupil	$5,311	$5,894	No. 2-year colleges	1	3
2-year college degree	7.0%	6.2%	Student/teacher ratio	16.5	16.7	No. 4-year colleges/universities	1	4
4-year college degree	14.6%	15.8%	Attending public school	96.1%	90.2%	No. highly ranked universities	0	1
Graduate/professional degree	7.1%	9.6%	State SAT score	1104	1020			
			State ACT score	20.1*	21.0			

HEALTH & HEALTHCARE
SCORE: 38/RANK: 205

HAZARDS & ILLNESSES	AREA	U.S. AVG	HEALTHCARE	AREA	U.S. AVG
Air-quality score	59	45	Physicians per capita	140.5	261.1
Water-quality score	63	33	Hospital beds per capita	143.7	432.2
Pollen/allergy score	81	61	No. teaching hospitals	1	4
Stress score	27	50	Cost per doctor visit	$74	$67
Cancer mortality per capita	134.2	169.0	Cost per dental visit	$91	$82
Depression days per month	2.3	2.8	Cost per daily hospital room	$842	$733

CRIME
SCORE: 60/RANK: 132

CRIME	AREA	U.S. AVG
Violent crime rate	354.1	456.0
Change in violent crime rate	11.6%	-17.2%
Property crime rate	3,815.2	3,950.0
Change in property crime rate	-29.1%	-16.8%

TRANSPORTATION
SCORE: 10/RANK: 296

COMMUTE	AREA	U.S. AVG	INTERCITY SERVICES	AREA	U.S. AVG	AUTOMOTIVE	AREA	U.S. AVG
Average commute time	23.7 min.	22.6 min.	Miles to nearest major airport	47	46	Insurance, annual premium	$1,031	$1,011
Commute by auto	82.6%	88.7%	Type of local airport	Large		Gas, cost per gallon	$1.49	$1.50
Commute by mass transit	.4%	1.8%	No. daily airline departures	812	294	Daily vehicle miles per capita	13.3	23.0
Work at home	8.9%	3.9%	Amtrak service	No				
Mass transit miles per capita	3.5	8.0	No. interstate highways	0	1			

LEISURE SCORE: 84/RANK: 50

DINING & SHOPPING	AREA	U.S. AVG	ENTERTAINMENT	AREA	U.S. AVG	OUTDOOR ACTIVITIES	AREA	U.S. AVG
Restaurant rating	1	1	Professional sports rating	8	4	Golf-course rating	3	4
No. outlet malls	2	2	College sports rating	3	4	Ski-area rating	10	4
No. Starbucks	3	11	Zoo/aquarium rating	2	3	National Park rating	3	3
No. warehouse clubs	1	4	Amusement park rating	2	3	Sq. miles inland water	4.0	4.0
			Botanical garden/arboretum rating	2	3	Miles of coastline	0.0	11.4

ARTS & CULTURE SCORE: 50/RANK: 164

MEDIA & LIBRARIES	AREA	U.S. AVG	PERFORMING ARTS	AREA	U.S. AVG	MUSEUMS	AREA	U.S. AVG
Arts radio rating	4	3	Classical music rating	4	4	Overall museum rating	5	6
No. public libraries	11	28	Ballet/dance rating	4	3	Art museum rating	3	5
Library volumes per capita	2.5	2.8	Professional theater rating	3	3	Science museum rating	3	4
			University arts programs rating	4	5	Children's museum rating	2	3

Green Bay, WI

Score: 65.0   Rank: 108

Profile: Small city
Location: Northeastern Wisconsin, at the head of Green Bay
Elevation: 702 feet
Time zone: Central Standard Time

PRO	CON
Small-town atmosphere	Winter climate
Professional football	Isolation
Outdoor recreation	Arts and culture

Green Bay is a quiet paper, agriculture, and dairy town—except during the fall when the legendary NFL Green Bay Packers become a local obsession. The duration and success of the Packers in such a small, out-of-the-way market is unequaled in all professional sports. Aside from football, Green Bay residents enjoy a traditional small-town way of life with ample nearby recreation, including the offerings of the Door Peninsula (the "thumb" of Wisconsin), a New England–like area of farms, small towns, and islands. The area has a complement of local museums, but access to other amenities and services means a long trek to Milwaukee or Chicago. Cost of living is moderate and employment prospects are good.

The city is in the Fox River Valley, where the river empties into the bay, surrounded by slightly higher ground and mostly wooded terrain. The Fox River is one of the largest northward flowing rivers in the United States. The climate is continental, modified by surrounding topography—the bay, nearby Lake Michigan and Lake Superior, and hills. Skies are frequently cloudy, causing further temperature moderation. Most precipitation normally falls from May through September as thunderstorms. Winter snowfall is less than in nearby communities where the ground is slightly higher. Bitter cold periods occur, but they are shorter than those of other inland areas at this latitude because of the water influence. First freeze is early October, last is mid-May.

POPULATION

DEMOGRAPHICS	AREA	U.S. AVG	ETHNIC COMPOSITION	AREA	U.S. AVG	RESIDENT PROFILE	AREA	U.S. AVG
Population	232,185		White	95.0%	75.1%	Single	41.3%	43.6%
Population density per sq. mile	439.3	447.3	Black	1.2%	12.3%	Married	58.8%	56.4%
Population growth	19.3%	16.1%	Asian	1.6%	3.6%	Divorced	6.5%	8.4%
Median age	34.4	35.5	American Indian	1.8%	.9%	Separated	1.5%	3.0%
Average family size	2.8	2.7	Hispanic	1.1%	12.5%	Married with children	32.9%	28.7%
			Diversity measure	19.5%	35.2%	Single with children	7.9%	10.1%

ECONOMY & JOBS SCORE: 78/RANK: 72

INCOME	AREA	U.S. AVG	EMPLOYMENT	AREA	U.S. AVG	LARGEST EMPLOYING INDUSTRY
Per capita income	$26,170	$23,420	Unemployment rate	4.8%	6.1%	Paper Manufacturing
Household income	$52,905	$46,060	Recent job growth	4.5%	.9%	
Household income < $25K	21.2%	26.4%	Projected future job growth	18.0%	15.1%	
Household income > $75K	29.1%	24.5%	White collar	53.6%	54.5%	
Household income growth	68.7%	57.3%	Blue collar	46.4%	45.5%	

COST OF LIVING SCORE: 31/RANK: 226

INDEXES & TAXES	AREA	U.S. AVG	HOUSING	AREA	U.S. AVG	NECESSITIES	AREA	U.S. AVG
Cost of Living Index	93.7	100.0	Median home price	$132,800	$160,100	Food Index	96.0	100.0
Financial Progress Index	120.3	100.0	Home price appreciation	5.0%	7.1%	Housing Index	82.5	100.0
Income tax rate	6.930%	4.625%	Median rent	$576	$670	Utilities Index	111.7	100.0
Sales tax rate	5.500%	6.474%	Homes owned	72.2%	63.9%	Transportation Index	99.8	100.0
Property tax rate	$21.5	$15.6	Homes rented	23.5%	25.3%	Healthcare Index	102.8	100.0
			Housing affordability	63.0%	54.5%	Miscellaneous Cost Index	98.1	100.0

CLIMATE SCORE: 16/RANK: 275

TEMPERATURE	AREA	U.S. AVG	PRECIPITATION	AREA	U.S. AVG	COMFORTS & HAZARDS	AREA	U.S. AVG
January low	6.9°F	26.4°F	Annual inches precipitation	27.0	35.9	July relative humidity	73.0%	68.8%
July high	80.7°F	86.7°F	Annual inches snowfall	43.0	24.2	Annual days mostly sunny	192	212
Annual days > 90°F	7	38	Annual days precipitation	120	111	Annual days with thunderstorms	35	39
Annual days < 32°F	163	88	Annual days rain > 0.5 inches	16	23	Tornado risk score	14	19
Annual days < 0°F	29	6	Annual days snow > 1.5 inches	10	6	Hurricane risk score	0	15

TEMPERATURE

PRECIPITATION

DAYS OF CLOUDS & PRECIPITATION

EDUCATION SCORE: 46/RANK: 17

ACHIEVEMENT	AREA	U.S. AVG	PUBLIC SCHOOLS	AREA	U.S. AVG	HIGHER EDUCATION	AREA	U.S. AVG
High school degree	86.3%	80.2%	Expenditures per pupil	$6,626	$5,894	No. 2-year colleges	1	3
2-year college degree	8.0%	6.2%	Student/teacher ratio	15.5	16.7	No. 4-year colleges/universities	3	4
4-year college degree	16.6%	15.8%	Attending public school	84.7%	90.2%	No. highly ranked universities	0	1
Graduate/professional degree	5.9%	9.6%	State SAT score	1179	1020			
			State ACT score	22.2*	21.0			

HEALTH & HEALTHCARE SCORE: 82/RANK: 57

HAZARDS & ILLNESSES	AREA	U.S. AVG	HEALTHCARE	AREA	U.S. AVG
Air-quality score	81	45	Physicians per capita	219.2	261.1
Water-quality score	17	33	Hospital beds per capita	433.0	432.2
Pollen/allergy score	28	61	No. teaching hospitals	2	4
Stress score	27	50	Cost per doctor visit	$77	$67
Cancer mortality per capita	162.3	169.0	Cost per dental visit	$87	$82
Depression days per month	2.9	2.8	Cost per daily hospital room	$607	$733

CRIME SCORE: 95/RANK: 17

CRIME	AREA	U.S. AVG
Violent crime rate	144.5	456.0
Change in violent crime rate	-50.3%	-17.2%
Property crime rate	2,751.4	3,950.0
Change in property crime rate	-24.6%	-16.8%

TRANSPORTATION SCORE: 88/RANK: 37

COMMUTE	AREA	U.S. AVG	INTERCITY SERVICES	AREA	U.S. AVG	AUTOMOTIVE	AREA	U.S. AVG
Average commute time	17.5 min.	22.6 min.	Miles to nearest major airport	8	46	Insurance, annual premium	$753	$1,011
Commute by auto	88.1%	88.7%	Type of local airport	Small		Gas, cost per gallon	$1.56	$1.50
Commute by mass transit	.9%	1.8%	No. daily airline departures	39	294	Daily vehicle miles per capita	25.8	23.0
Work at home	6.1%	3.9%	Amtrak service	No				
Mass transit miles per capita	9.8	8.0	No. interstate highways	1	1			

LEISURE SCORE: 47/RANK: 174

DINING & SHOPPING	AREA	U.S. AVG	ENTERTAINMENT	AREA	U.S. AVG	OUTDOOR ACTIVITIES	AREA	U.S. AVG
Restaurant rating	1	1	Professional sports rating	6	4	Golf-course rating	2	4
No. outlet malls	1	2	College sports rating	3	4	Ski-area rating	2	4
No. Starbucks	1	11	Zoo/aquarium rating	1	3	National Park rating	1	3
No. warehouse clubs	3	4	Amusement park rating	1	3	Sq. miles inland water	2.0	4.0
			Botanical garden/arboretum rating	1	3	Miles of coastline	17.9	11.4

ARTS & CULTURE SCORE: 48/RANK: 170

MEDIA & LIBRARIES	AREA	U.S. AVG	PERFORMING ARTS	AREA	U.S. AVG	MUSEUMS	AREA	U.S. AVG
Arts radio rating	1	3	Classical music rating	2	4	Overall museum rating	5	6
No. public libraries	9	28	Ballet/dance rating	3	3	Art museum rating	1	5
Library volumes per capita	1.9	2.8	Professional theater rating	1	3	Science museum rating	1	4
			University arts programs rating	6	5	Children's museum rating	3	3

Greensboro–Winston-Salem–High Point, NC

Score: 68.9 Rank: 81

Profile: Mid-size-city complex
Location: Northwest-central North Carolina, 30 miles south of the Virginia border
Elevation: 897 feet
Time zone: Eastern Standard Time

PRO	CON
Cost of living	Declining industries
Attractive downtown areas	Economic cycles
Proximity to Raleigh-Durham	Urban sprawl

The Greensboro–Winston-Salem–High Point complex occupies two counties and is sometimes called the Piedmont Triad. In comparison to the state's better-known triad of Raleigh–Durham–Chapel Hill, the economy and lifestyle is more industrial and working-class, although there is a strong university presence and a high level of educational attainment. Both Greensboro and Winston-Salem have modern downtown areas with glass skyscrapers. The economic situation is mixed, with declining and emerging industries, some in the high-tech sector, but employment has been relatively stable. The area, as the name Winston-Salem implies, is a center for the tobacco industry. (The cigarettes are named after the town, not vice versa.) Winston-Salem is also the home of Wake Forest University. High Point is the center of the state's large furniture-manufacturing industry with a remarkable concentration of facilities; unfortunately, the dislocation of that industry offshore, particularly to China, is starting to have an impact. Greensboro is the triad's financial center and contains some light manufacturing and a large campus of the University of North Carolina. The Cost of Living Index, at just over 91, is attractive for what the triad offers. The amenities of the Raleigh-Durham area, 80 miles east, are close enough for residents to benefit from them.

The city complex is located in northern Piedmont in an area of transition between the eastern coastal plain and mountains to the west. The immediate landscape is slightly rolling with woodlands and open country. The climate is a mix of continental and humid subtropical. Winter temperatures and rainfall are modified somewhat by the mountain barrier. The combination of coastal moisture and northern cold air produce more frequent sleet and ice storms than in most of North Carolina. Snow flurries may occur. Summers are generally mild to warm and humid, with varying temperatures. Most summer precipitation occurs as localized thunderstorms. Late summer and fall hurricanes bring heavy rain. First freeze is late October, last is mid-April.

POPULATION

DEMOGRAPHICS	AREA	U.S. AVG	ETHNIC COMPOSITION	AREA	U.S. AVG	RESIDENT PROFILE	AREA	U.S. AVG
Population	1,286,265		White	82.9%	75.1%	Single	42.9%	43.6%
Population density per sq. mile	331.3	447.3	Black	15.7%	12.3%	Married	57.1%	56.4%
Population growth	22.5%	16.1%	Asian	.7%	3.6%	Divorced	7.4%	8.4%
Median age	36.3	35.5	American Indian	.3%	.9%	Separated	4.3%	3.0%
Average family size	2.5	2.7	Hispanic	1.4%	12.5%	Married with children	26.7%	28.7%
			Diversity measure	42.6%	35.2%	Single with children	9.5%	10.1%

ECONOMY & JOBS SCORE: 42/RANK: 190

INCOME	AREA	U.S. AVG	EMPLOYMENT	AREA	U.S. AVG	LARGEST EMPLOYING INDUSTRY
Per capita income	$24,997	$23,420	Unemployment rate	6.3%	6.1%	Household and Institutional Furniture and Kitchen
Household income	$46,430	$46,060	Recent job growth	.3%	.9%	Cabinet Manufacturing
Household income < $25K	23.8%	26.4%	Projected future job growth	15.5%	15.1%	
Household income > $75K	25.1%	24.5%	White collar	51.1%	54.5%	
Household income growth	59.7%	57.3%	Blue collar	48.9%	45.5%	

COST OF LIVING SCORE: 46/RANK: 178

INDEXES & TAXES	AREA	U.S. AVG	HOUSING	AREA	U.S. AVG	NECESSITIES	AREA	U.S. AVG
Cost of Living Index	91.6	100.0	Median home price	$136,600	$160,100	Food Index	95.4	100.0
Financial Progress Index	108.0	100.0	Home price appreciation	4.6%	7.1%	Housing Index	84.8	100.0
Income tax rate	7.000%	4.625%	Median rent	$595	$670	Utilities Index	92.1	100.0
Sales tax rate	7.000%	6.474%	Homes owned	71.4%	63.9%	Transportation Index	92.7	100.0
Property tax rate	$13.3	$15.6	Homes rented	22.5%	25.3%	Healthcare Index	96.5	100.0
			Housing affordability	60.0%	54.5%	Miscellaneous Cost Index	97.6	100.0

CLIMATE SCORE: 58/RANK: 138

TEMPERATURE	AREA	U.S. AVG	PRECIPITATION	AREA	U.S. AVG	COMFORTS & HAZARDS	AREA	U.S. AVG
January low	28.5°F	26.4°F	Annual inches precipitation	41.4	35.9	July relative humidity	72.0%	68.8%
July high	87.5°F	86.7°F	Annual inches snowfall	8.7	24.2	Annual days mostly sunny	217	212
Annual days > 90°F	28	38	Annual days precipitation	121	111	Annual days with thunderstorms	46	39
Annual days < 32°F	85	88	Annual days rain > 0.5 inches	29	23	Tornado risk score	11	19
Annual days < 0°F	0	6	Annual days snow > 1.5 inches	3	6	Hurricane risk score	21	15

TEMPERATURE
PRECIPITATION
DAYS OF CLOUDS & PRECIPITATION

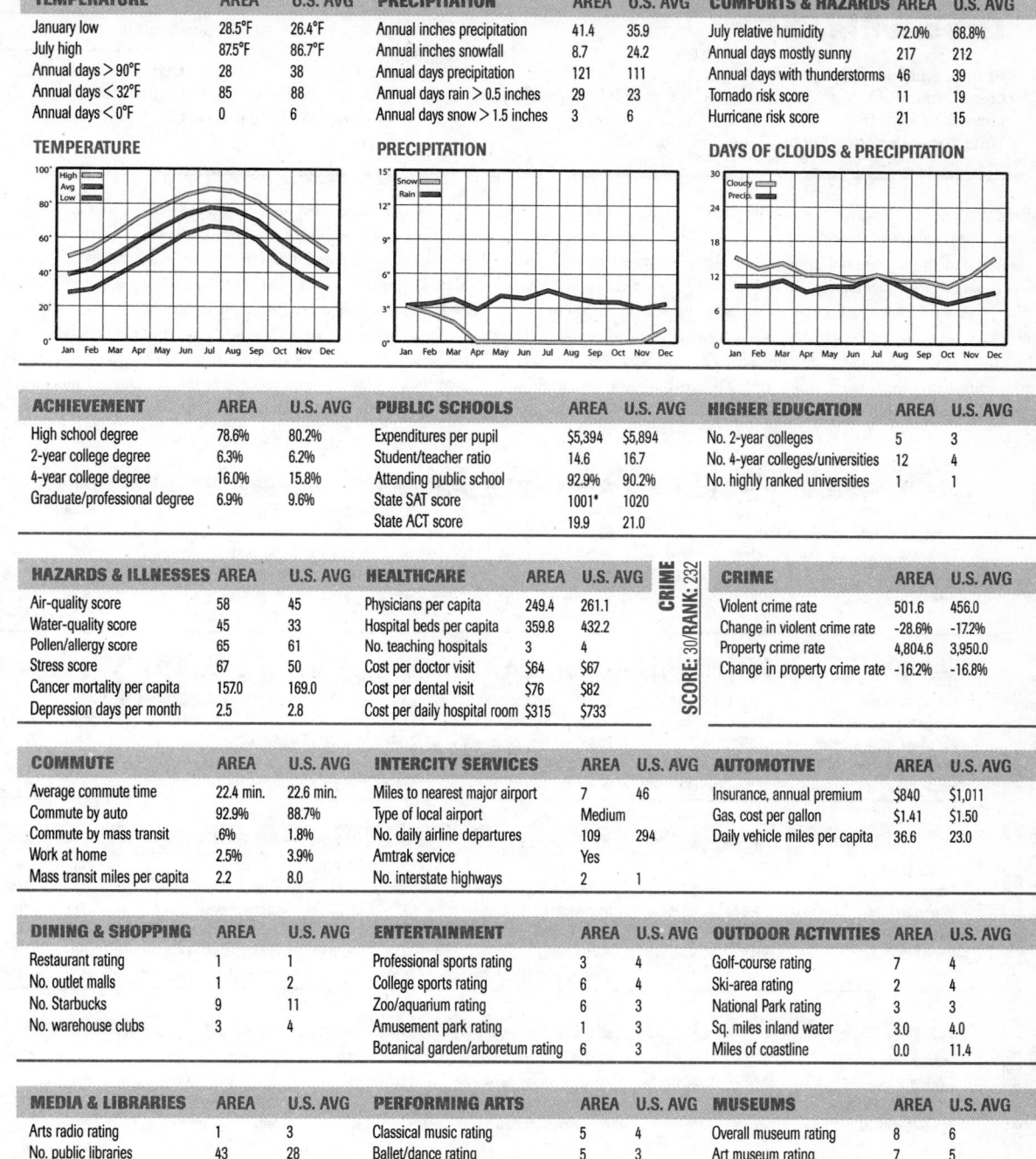

EDUCATION SCORE: 67/RANK: 108

ACHIEVEMENT	AREA	U.S. AVG	PUBLIC SCHOOLS	AREA	U.S. AVG	HIGHER EDUCATION	AREA	U.S. AVG
High school degree	78.6%	80.2%	Expenditures per pupil	$5,394	$5,894	No. 2-year colleges	5	3
2-year college degree	6.3%	6.2%	Student/teacher ratio	14.6	16.7	No. 4-year colleges/universities	12	4
4-year college degree	16.0%	15.8%	Attending public school	92.9%	90.2%	No. highly ranked universities	1	1
Graduate/professional degree	6.9%	9.6%	State SAT score	1001*	1020			
			State ACT score	19.9	21.0			

HEALTH & HEALTHCARE SCORE: 80/RANK: 63

HAZARDS & ILLNESSES	AREA	U.S. AVG	HEALTHCARE	AREA	U.S. AVG
Air-quality score	58	45	Physicians per capita	249.4	261.1
Water-quality score	45	33	Hospital beds per capita	359.8	432.2
Pollen/allergy score	65	61	No. teaching hospitals	3	4
Stress score	67	50	Cost per doctor visit	$64	$67
Cancer mortality per capita	157.0	169.0	Cost per dental visit	$76	$82
Depression days per month	2.5	2.8	Cost per daily hospital room	$315	$733

CRIME SCORE: 30/RANK: 232

CRIME	AREA	U.S. AVG
Violent crime rate	501.6	456.0
Change in violent crime rate	-28.6%	-17.2%
Property crime rate	4,804.6	3,950.0
Change in property crime rate	-16.2%	-16.8%

TRANSPORTATION SCORE: 30/RANK: 231

COMMUTE	AREA	U.S. AVG	INTERCITY SERVICES	AREA	U.S. AVG	AUTOMOTIVE	AREA	U.S. AVG
Average commute time	22.4 min.	22.6 min.	Miles to nearest major airport	7	46	Insurance, annual premium	$840	$1,011
Commute by auto	92.9%	88.7%	Type of local airport	Medium		Gas, cost per gallon	$1.41	$1.50
Commute by mass transit	.6%	1.8%	No. daily airline departures	109	294	Daily vehicle miles per capita	36.6	23.0
Work at home	2.5%	3.9%	Amtrak service	Yes				
Mass transit miles per capita	2.2	8.0	No. interstate highways	2	1			

LEISURE SCORE: 33/RANK: 222

DINING & SHOPPING	AREA	U.S. AVG	ENTERTAINMENT	AREA	U.S. AVG	OUTDOOR ACTIVITIES	AREA	U.S. AVG
Restaurant rating	1	1	Professional sports rating	3	4	Golf-course rating	7	4
No. outlet malls	1	2	College sports rating	6	4	Ski-area rating	2	4
No. Starbucks	9	11	Zoo/aquarium rating	6	3	National Park rating	3	3
No. warehouse clubs	3	4	Amusement park rating	1	3	Sq. miles inland water	3.0	4.0
			Botanical garden/arboretum rating	6	3	Miles of coastline	0.0	11.4

ARTS & CULTURE SCORE: 57/RANK: 142

MEDIA & LIBRARIES	AREA	U.S. AVG	PERFORMING ARTS	AREA	U.S. AVG	MUSEUMS	AREA	U.S. AVG
Arts radio rating	1	3	Classical music rating	5	4	Overall museum rating	8	6
No. public libraries	43	28	Ballet/dance rating	5	3	Art museum rating	7	5
Library volumes per capita	2.0	2.8	Professional theater rating	6	3	Science museum rating	7	4
			University arts programs rating	9	5	Children's museum rating	8	3

Greenville, NC

Score: 55.9   **Rank:** 180

Profile: Small town
Location: Eastern North Carolina, 80 miles east of Raleigh-Durham
Elevation: 40 feet
Time zone: Eastern Standard Time

PRO	CON
Nearby coastline	Crime rate
Cost of living	Hot, humid summers
Economic turnaround	Isolation

Greenville is mainly an agricultural and trading center with a strong tobacco presence. Some employment categories have declined, partially due to cutbacks in the tobacco industry, but the economy is in transition and future job-growth projections at 27% are the highest in the state. Other manufacturing is also in the area. While East Carolina University provides a regional medical center and raises the level of educational attainment, most cultural amenities and services are found in Raleigh to the west. The area is a gateway to the coastal areas of the Outer Banks and Cape Hatteras, 100-plus miles to the east.

Greenville is located just above sea level on a flat coastal plain along the banks of the Tar River. Surrounding areas are agricultural with deciduous woods and tidewater marshes to the east. The climate is humid subtropical with a slight marine influence. Summer is sunny, hot, and humid, with more 90°F-plus days than most towns in North Carolina. Winters are cool and fairly wet, but the area is close enough to the ocean and sheltered enough by the Appalachians to escape extreme cold; however, temperatures drop below freezing 45 times each winter. Annual rainfall is high, but snow is rare. First freeze is late October, last is mid-April.

POPULATION

DEMOGRAPHICS	AREA	U.S. AVG	ETHNIC COMPOSITION	AREA	U.S. AVG	RESIDENT PROFILE	AREA	U.S. AVG
Population	137,240		White	61.6%	75.1%	Single	49.8%	43.6%
Population density per sq. mile	210.6	447.3	Black	37.2%	12.3%	Married	50.2%	56.4%
Population growth	27.2%	16.1%	Asian	.4%	3.6%	Divorced	6.5%	8.4%
Median age	30.7	35.5	American Indian	.1%	.9%	Separated	6.2%	3.0%
Average family size	2.6	2.7	Hispanic	1.8%	12.5%	Married with children	24.7%	28.7%
			Diversity measure	50.8%	35.2%	Single with children	13.7%	10.1%

ECONOMY & JOBS SCORE: 3/RANK: 319

INCOME	AREA	U.S. AVG	EMPLOYMENT	AREA	U.S. AVG	LARGEST EMPLOYING INDUSTRY
Per capita income	$19,084	$23,420	Unemployment rate	7.2%	6.1%	Machinery Manufacturing
Household income	$34,395	$46,060	Recent job growth	1.4%	.9%	
Household income < $25K	37.0%	26.4%	Projected future job growth	27.2%	15.1%	
Household income > $75K	16.0%	24.5%	White collar	54.2%	54.5%	
Household income growth	46.8%	57.3%	Blue collar	45.8%	45.5%	

COST OF LIVING SCORE: 62/RANK: 125

INDEXES & TAXES	AREA	U.S. AVG	HOUSING	AREA	U.S. AVG	NECESSITIES	AREA	U.S. AVG
Cost of Living Index	87.0	100.0	Median home price	$108,390	$160,100	Food Index	97.5	100.0
Financial Progress Index	84.3	100.0	Home price appreciation	3.8%	7.1%	Housing Index	67.3	100.0
Income tax rate	7.000%	4.625%	Median rent	$597	$670	Utilities Index	117.9	100.0
Sales tax rate	7.000%	6.474%	Homes owned	63.1%	63.9%	Transportation Index	90.9	100.0
Property tax rate	$11.9	$15.6	Homes rented	30.4%	25.3%	Healthcare Index	96.8	100.0
			Housing affordability	46.0%	54.5%	Miscellaneous Cost Index	95.1	100.0

CLIMATE SCORE: 53/RANK: 156

TEMPERATURE	AREA	U.S. AVG	PRECIPITATION	AREA	U.S. AVG	COMFORTS & HAZARDS	AREA	U.S. AVG
January low	36.2°F	26.4°F	Annual inches precipitation	54.0	35.9	July relative humidity	75.0%	68.8%
July high	88.8°F	86.7°F	Annual inches snowfall	1.8	24.2	Annual days mostly sunny	219	212
Annual days > 90°F	45	38	Annual days precipitation	117	111	Annual days with thunderstorms	46	39
Annual days < 32°F	45	88	Annual days rain > 0.5 inches	32	23	Tornado risk score	28	19
Annual days < 0°F	0	6	Annual days snow > 1.5 inches	1	6	Hurricane risk score	49	15

TEMPERATURE

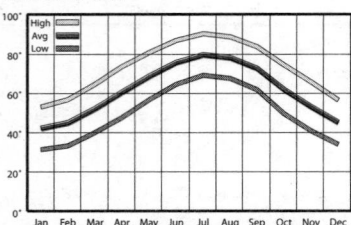

PRECIPITATION

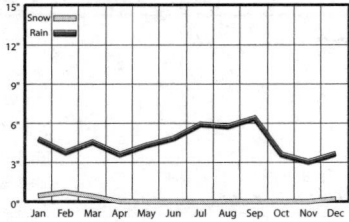

DAYS OF CLOUDS & PRECIPITATION

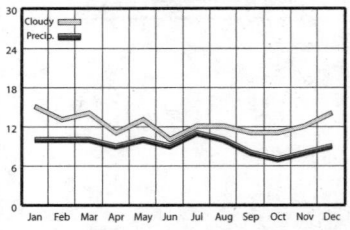

EDUCATION SCORE: 49/RANK: 168

ACHIEVEMENT	AREA	U.S. AVG	PUBLIC SCHOOLS	AREA	U.S. AVG	HIGHER EDUCATION	AREA	U.S. AVG
High school degree	79.9%	80.2%	Expenditures per pupil	$4,965	$5,894	No. 2-year colleges	1	3
2-year college degree	7.7%	6.2%	Student/teacher ratio	15.1	16.7	No. 4-year colleges/universities	1	4
4-year college degree	17.1%	15.8%	Attending public school	89.8%	90.2%	No. highly ranked universities	0	1
Graduate/professional degree	9.2%	9.6%	State SAT score	1001*	1020			
			State ACT score	19.9	21.0			

HEALTH & HEALTHCARE SCORE: 71/RANK: 95

CRIME SCORE: 4/RANK: 317

HAZARDS & ILLNESSES	AREA	U.S. AVG	HEALTHCARE	AREA	U.S. AVG	CRIME	AREA	U.S. AVG
Air-quality score	81	45	Physicians per capita	567.6	261.1	Violent crime rate	635.7	456.0
Water-quality score	25	33	Hospital beds per capita	560.5	432.2	Change in violent crime rate	-21.1%	-17.2%
Pollen/allergy score	66	61	No. teaching hospitals	1	4	Property crime rate	6,517.0	3,950.0
Stress score	43	50	Cost per doctor visit	$65	$67	Change in property crime rate	-4.6%	-16.8%
Cancer mortality per capita	168.6	169.0	Cost per dental visit	$81	$82			
Depression days per month	2.1	2.8	Cost per daily hospital room	$428	$733			

TRANSPORTATION SCORE: 27/RANK: 240

COMMUTE	AREA	U.S. AVG	INTERCITY SERVICES	AREA	U.S. AVG	AUTOMOTIVE	AREA	U.S. AVG
Average commute time	20.7 min.	22.6 min.	Miles to nearest major airport	81	46	Insurance, annual premium	$769	$1,011
Commute by auto	94.1%	88.7%	Type of local airport	Medium		Gas, cost per gallon	$1.42	$1.50
Commute by mass transit	.5%	1.8%	No. daily airline departures	352	294	Daily vehicle miles per capita	22.1	23.0
Work at home	1.7%	3.9%	Amtrak service	No				
Mass transit miles per capita	0.0	8.0	No. interstate highways	0	1			

LEISURE SCORE: 36/RANK: 211

DINING & SHOPPING	AREA	U.S. AVG	ENTERTAINMENT	AREA	U.S. AVG	OUTDOOR ACTIVITIES	AREA	U.S. AVG
Restaurant rating	1	1	Professional sports rating	2	4	Golf-course rating	1	4
No. outlet malls	1	2	College sports rating	3	4	Ski-area rating	1	4
No. Starbucks	1	11	Zoo/aquarium rating	1	3	National Park rating	1	3
No. warehouse clubs	3	4	Amusement park rating	1	3	Sq. miles inland water	3.0	4.0
			Botanical garden/arboretum rating	2	3	Miles of coastline	29.4	11.4

ARTS & CULTURE SCORE: 26/RANK: 245

MEDIA & LIBRARIES	AREA	U.S. AVG	PERFORMING ARTS	AREA	U.S. AVG	MUSEUMS	AREA	U.S. AVG
Arts radio rating	1	3	Classical music rating	3	4	Overall museum rating	2	6
No. public libraries	6	28	Ballet/dance rating	1	3	Art museum rating	3	5
Library volumes per capita	2.1	2.8	Professional theater rating	1	3	Science museum rating	1	4
			University arts programs rating	4	5	Children's museum rating	1	3

Greenville-Spartanburg-Anderson, SC

Score: 69.3   Rank: 80

Profile: Mid-size-city complex
Location: Northwest South Carolina near North Carolina border, 40 miles southwest of Charlotte, North Carolina
Elevation: 971 feet
Time zone: Eastern Standard Time

PRO	CON
Nearby recreation	Hot, humid summers
Strong economy	Violent crime
Historic preservation	Arts and culture

Greenville-Spartanburg-Anderson is a textile and agricultural area located in the mountainous northwest part of the state. Agriculture includes a variety of fruit trees, notably peaches. Automaker BMW recently opened a plant, building the employment base and giving the area greater stature in the U.S. industrial landscape. The population is relatively well educated for the region, driven in part by nearby Clemson University. Greenville, the largest of the three cities, is attractive and includes a small assortment of local cultural amenities. It recently won a 2003 Great American Main Street Award from the National Trust for Historic Preservation—those who see the outstanding city center will understand why. Anderson and Spartanburg are more industrial and considerably less attractive. Outdoor activities are plentiful, particularly in the Blue Ridge Mountains to the north.

Located on the eastern slope of the Southern Appalachian Mountains, Greenville is in rolling country about 20 miles from the first mountain ridge and 55 miles northwest of the main ridge. The climate is a mix of subtropical and continental. The mountains usually protect the area from the full force of northern cold air. Summers are warm and humid with thunderstorms. The elevation provides relatively cool nights during the summer months. Winters are pleasant, with below-freezing daytime temperatures only a few times a year. Rainfall is abundant and spread throughout the year. There are usually two to three small snowstorms and one to two episodes of freezing rain in winter.

POPULATION

DEMOGRAPHICS	AREA	U.S. AVG	ETHNIC COMPOSITION	AREA	U.S. AVG	RESIDENT PROFILE	AREA	U.S. AVG
Population	987,855		White	81.9%	75.1%	Single	45.3%	43.6%
Population density per sq. mile	307.7	447.3	Black	17.1%	12.3%	Married	54.7%	56.4%
Population growth	18.9%	16.1%	Asian	.7%	3.6%	Divorced	7.8%	8.4%
Median age	36.0	35.5	American Indian	.1%	.9%	Separated	4.1%	3.0%
Average family size	2.6	2.7	Hispanic	.8%	12.5%	Married with children	26.9%	28.7%
			Diversity measure	36.0%	35.2%	Single with children	10.6%	10.1%

ECONOMY & JOBS SCORE: 65/RANK: 113

INCOME	AREA	U.S. AVG	EMPLOYMENT	AREA	U.S. AVG	LARGEST EMPLOYING INDUSTRY
Per capita income	$22,412	$23,420	Unemployment rate	6.2%	6.1%	Textile Mills
Household income	$42,630	$46,060	Recent job growth	3.1%	.9%	
Household income < $25K	27.9%	26.4%	Projected future job growth	16.0%	15.1%	
Household income > $75K	21.9%	24.5%	White collar	49.7%	54.5%	
Household income growth	56.1%	57.3%	Blue collar	50.3%	45.5%	

COST OF LIVING SCORE: 52/RANK: 157

INDEXES & TAXES	AREA	U.S. AVG	HOUSING	AREA	U.S. AVG	NECESSITIES	AREA	U.S. AVG
Cost of Living Index	89.4	100.0	Median home price	$128,000	$160,100	Food Index	98.7	100.0
Financial Progress Index	101.6	100.0	Home price appreciation	4.7%	7.1%	Housing Index	79.5	100.0
Income tax rate	7.000%	4.625%	Median rent	$571	$670	Utilities Index	84.0	100.0
Sales tax rate	5.000%	6.474%	Homes owned	69.0%	63.9%	Transportation Index	95.6	100.0
Property tax rate	$11.0	$15.6	Homes rented	23.7%	25.3%	Healthcare Index	96.5	100.0
			Housing affordability	60.0%	54.5%	Miscellaneous Cost Index	95.5	100.0

CLIMATE SCORE: 51/RANK: 160

TEMPERATURE	AREA	U.S. AVG	PRECIPITATION	AREA	U.S. AVG	COMFORTS & HAZARDS	AREA	U.S. AVG
January low	33.0°F	26.4°F	Annual inches precipitation	48.0	35.9	July relative humidity	70.0%	68.8%
July high	87.6°F	86.7°F	Annual inches snowfall	6.0	24.2	Annual days mostly sunny	221	212
Annual days > 90°F	29	38	Annual days precipitation	119	111	Annual days with thunderstorms	44	39
Annual days < 32°F	68	88	Annual days rain > 0.5 inches	37	23	Tornado risk score	18	19
Annual days < 0°F	0	6	Annual days snow > 1.5 inches	2	6	Hurricane risk score	17	15

TEMPERATURE

PRECIPITATION

DAYS OF CLOUDS & PRECIPITATION

EDUCATION SCORE: 55/RANK: 148

ACHIEVEMENT	AREA	U.S. AVG	PUBLIC SCHOOLS	AREA	U.S. AVG	HIGHER EDUCATION	AREA	U.S. AVG
High school degree	75.4%	80.2%	Expenditures per pupil	$5,108	$5,894	No. 2-year colleges	6	3
2-year college degree	6.8%	6.2%	Student/teacher ratio	16.4	16.7	No. 4-year colleges/universities	9	4
4-year college degree	13.9%	15.8%	Attending public school	91.1%	90.2%	No. highly ranked universities	3	1
Graduate/professional degree	6.9%	9.6%	State SAT score	989*	1020			
			State ACT score	19.2	21.0			

HEALTH & HEALTHCARE SCORE: 74/RANK: 85

CRIME SCORE: 50/RANK: 164

HAZARDS & ILLNESSES	AREA	U.S. AVG	HEALTHCARE	AREA	U.S. AVG	CRIME	AREA	U.S. AVG
Air-quality score	89	45	Physicians per capita	219.8	261.1	Violent crime rate	645.6	456.0
Water-quality score	20	33	Hospital beds per capita	323.4	432.2	Change in violent crime rate	-37.4%	-17.2%
Pollen/allergy score	56	61	No. teaching hospitals	3	4	Property crime rate	3,639.8	3,950.0
Stress score	66	50	Cost per doctor visit	$62	$67	Change in property crime rate	-26.6%	-16.8%
Cancer mortality per capita	161.7	169.0	Cost per dental visit	$78	$82			
Depression days per month	3.2	2.8	Cost per daily hospital room	$533	$733			

TRANSPORTATION SCORE: 19/RANK: 267

COMMUTE	AREA	U.S. AVG	INTERCITY SERVICES	AREA	U.S. AVG	AUTOMOTIVE	AREA	U.S. AVG
Average commute time	22.5 min.	22.6 min.	Miles to nearest major airport	24	46	Insurance, annual premium	$894	$1,011
Commute by auto	92.8%	88.7%	Type of local airport	Small		Gas, cost per gallon	$1.33	$1.50
Commute by mass transit	.5%	1.8%	No. daily airline departures	76	294	Daily vehicle miles per capita	17.9	23.0
Work at home	1.5%	3.9%	Amtrak service	Yes				
Mass transit miles per capita	1.9	8.0	No. interstate highways	1	1			

LEISURE SCORE: 55/RANK: 148

DINING & SHOPPING	AREA	U.S. AVG	ENTERTAINMENT	AREA	U.S. AVG	OUTDOOR ACTIVITIES	AREA	U.S. AVG
Restaurant rating	1	1	Professional sports rating	3	4	Golf-course rating	5	4
No. outlet malls	1	2	College sports rating	5	4	Ski-area rating	1	4
No. Starbucks	0	11	Zoo/aquarium rating	3	3	National Park rating	1	3
No. warehouse clubs	5	4	Amusement park rating	1	3	Sq. miles inland water	2.0	4.0
			Botanical garden/arboretum rating	7	3	Miles of coastline	0.0	11.4

ARTS & CULTURE SCORE: 79/RANK: 71

MEDIA & LIBRARIES	AREA	U.S. AVG	PERFORMING ARTS	AREA	U.S. AVG	MUSEUMS	AREA	U.S. AVG
Arts radio rating	1	3	Classical music rating	6	4	Overall museum rating	8	6
No. public libraries	37	28	Ballet/dance rating	3	3	Art museum rating	6	5
Library volumes per capita	2.4	2.8	Professional theater rating	1	3	Science museum rating	7	4
			University arts programs rating	3	5	Children's museum rating	1	3

Hagerstown, MD

Score: 55.8   Rank: 184

Profile: Small city
Location: North-central Maryland near the Pennsylvania border
Elevation: 547 feet
Time zone: Eastern Standard Time

PRO
Small-town atmosphere
Historic interest
Attractive setting

CON
Arts and culture
Low educational attainment
Air service

Hagerstown lies at the gateway to the Western Maryland region. Historically, it was an important transportation center because of its location along north-south routes and near a passage west through the Cumberland Gap. Today, Hagerstown is a pleasant mix of old and new with a notable downtown historic area and an unusually large concentration of pre–Civil War row homes not unlike nearby Baltimore. Entertainment includes minor-league baseball, the Hagerstown Speedway, and the nation's oldest farmer's market. The area is a bit isolated from other East Coast cities, and educational attainment is low.

The area is located in a broad, flat agricultural extension of Virginia's famed Shenandoah Valley. The surroundings, particularly to the northwest and southeast, are hilly and wooded with deciduous trees. Hagerstown has a continental climate influenced by the nearby Atlantic and milder climates to the south and mountains to the west. Summers are warm, calm, and humid, with occasional thunderstorms. Winters are cold but severe effects are moderated by the mountains, which block many heavy storms and cold-air blasts. Occasional heavy snow occurs when storms originating on the Atlantic or from the southwest hit the area. Spring and fall are pleasant. First freeze is late October, last is mid-April.

POPULATION

DEMOGRAPHICS	AREA	U.S. AVG	ETHNIC COMPOSITION	AREA	U.S. AVG	RESIDENT PROFILE	AREA	U.S. AVG
Population	134,246		White	88.6%	75.1%	Single	42.1%	43.6%
Population density per sq. mile	293.0	447.3	Black	9.9%	12.3%	Married	57.9%	56.4%
Population growth	10.6%	16.1%	Asian	.9%	3.6%	Divorced	6.6%	8.4%
Median age	37.8	35.5	American Indian	.2%	.9%	Separated	3.8%	3.0%
Average family size	2.7	2.7	Hispanic	1.3%	12.5%	Married with children	31.0%	28.7%
			Diversity measure	19.9%	35.2%	Single with children	7.6%	10.1%

ECONOMY & JOBS SCORE: 82/RANK: 60

INCOME	AREA	U.S. AVG	EMPLOYMENT	AREA	U.S. AVG	LARGEST EMPLOYING INDUSTRY
Per capita income	$20,754	$23,420	Unemployment rate	3.7%	6.1%	Printing and Related Support Activities
Household income	$42,490	$46,060	Recent job growth	-.1%	.9%	
Household income < $25K	27.1%	26.4%	Projected future job growth	12.2%	15.1%	
Household income > $75K	17.9%	24.5%	White collar	47.6%	54.5%	
Household income growth	43.2%	57.3%	Blue collar	52.4%	45.5%	

COST OF LIVING SCORE: 46/RANK: 177

INDEXES & TAXES	AREA	U.S. AVG	HOUSING	AREA	U.S. AVG	NECESSITIES	AREA	U.S. AVG
Cost of Living Index	91.5	100.0	Median home price	$141,630	$160,100	Food Index	89.2	100.0
Financial Progress Index	98.9	100.0	Home price appreciation	7.2%	7.1%	Housing Index	88.0	100.0
Income tax rate	7.450%	4.625%	Median rent	$602	$670	Utilities Index	103.0	100.0
Sales tax rate	5.000%	6.474%	Homes owned	69.6%	63.9%	Transportation Index	89.8	100.0
Property tax rate	$14.1	$15.6	Homes rented	24.7%	25.3%	Healthcare Index	90.9	100.0
			Housing affordability	59.0%	54.5%	Miscellaneous Cost Index	95.9	100.0

CLIMATE — SCORE: 44/RANK: 185

TEMPERATURE	AREA	U.S. AVG	PRECIPITATION	AREA	U.S. AVG	COMFORTS & HAZARDS	AREA	U.S. AVG
January low	24.9°F	26.4°F	Annual inches precipitation	40.0	35.9	July relative humidity	67.0%	68.8%
July high	86.7°F	86.7°F	Annual inches snowfall	22.0	24.2	Annual days mostly sunny	205	212
Annual days > 90°F	31	38	Annual days precipitation	112	111	Annual days with thunderstorms	26	39
Annual days < 32°F	100	88	Annual days rain > 0.5 inches	25	23	Tornado risk score	6	19
Annual days < 0°F	0	6	Annual days snow > 1.5 inches	4	6	Hurricane risk score	10	15

TEMPERATURE

PRECIPITATION

DAYS OF CLOUDS & PRECIPITATION

EDUCATION — SCORE: 7/RANK: 305

ACHIEVEMENT	AREA	U.S. AVG	PUBLIC SCHOOLS	AREA	U.S. AVG	HIGHER EDUCATION	AREA	U.S. AVG
High school degree	77.8%	80.2%	Expenditures per pupil	$6,094	$5,894	No. 2-year colleges	2	3
2-year college degree	5.2%	6.2%	Student/teacher ratio	15.7	16.7	No. 4-year colleges/universities	0	4
4-year college degree	8.8%	15.8%	Attending public school	87.7%	90.2%	No. highly ranked universities	0	1
Graduate/professional degree	5.8%	9.6%	State SAT score	1024*	1020			
			State ACT score	20.7	21.0			

HEALTH & HEALTHCARE — SCORE: 68/RANK: 103   CRIME — SCORE: 69/RANK: 102

HAZARDS & ILLNESSES	AREA	U.S. AVG	HEALTHCARE	AREA	U.S. AVG
Air-quality score	24	45	Physicians per capita	189.9	261.1
Water-quality score	35	33	Hospital beds per capita	384.3	432.2
Pollen/allergy score	60	61	No. teaching hospitals	0	4
Stress score	16	50	Cost per doctor visit	$62	$67
Cancer mortality per capita	168.9	169.0	Cost per dental visit	$70	$82
Depression days per month	2.7	2.8	Cost per daily hospital room	$614	$733

CRIME	AREA	U.S. AVG
Violent crime rate	380.9	456.0
Change in violent crime rate	-2.3%	-17.2%
Property crime rate	2,343.9	3,950.0
Change in property crime rate	-.6%	-16.8%

TRANSPORTATION — SCORE: 5/RANK: 312

COMMUTE	AREA	U.S. AVG	INTERCITY SERVICES	AREA	U.S. AVG	AUTOMOTIVE	AREA	U.S. AVG
Average commute time	25.1 min.	22.6 min.	Miles to nearest major airport	50	46	Insurance, annual premium	$1,025	$1,011
Commute by auto	91.3%	88.7%	Type of local airport	Medium		Gas, cost per gallon	$1.47	$1.50
Commute by mass transit	1.2%	1.8%	No. daily airline departures	675	294	Daily vehicle miles per capita	22.8	23.0
Work at home	4.2%	3.9%	Amtrak service	No				
Mass transit miles per capita	3.4	8.0	No. interstate highways	2	1			

LEISURE — SCORE: 53/RANK: 153

DINING & SHOPPING	AREA	U.S. AVG	ENTERTAINMENT	AREA	U.S. AVG	OUTDOOR ACTIVITIES	AREA	U.S. AVG
Restaurant rating	1	1	Professional sports rating	8	4	Golf-course rating	5	4
No. outlet malls	4	2	College sports rating	6	4	Ski-area rating	5	4
No. Starbucks	0	11	Zoo/aquarium rating	2	3	National Park rating	3	3
No. warehouse clubs	1	4	Amusement park rating	2	3	Sq. miles inland water	5.0	4.0
			Botanical garden/arboretum rating	3	3	Miles of coastline	0.0	11.4

ARTS & CULTURE — SCORE: 52/RANK: 157

MEDIA & LIBRARIES	AREA	U.S. AVG	PERFORMING ARTS	AREA	U.S. AVG	MUSEUMS	AREA	U.S. AVG
Arts radio rating	5	3	Classical music rating	4	4	Overall museum rating	5	6
No. public libraries	7	28	Ballet/dance rating	4	3	Art museum rating	6	5
Library volumes per capita	2.6	2.8	Professional theater rating	5	3	Science museum rating	4	4
			University arts programs rating	1	5	Children's museum rating	3	3

Hamilton-Middletown, OH

Score: 63.7	**Rank: 118**

Profile: Small-city complex
Location: Southwestern Ohio, 30 miles north of Cincinnati
Elevation: 869 feet
Time zone: Eastern Standard Time

PRO	**CON**
Nearby city amenities	High home prices
Economy	Healthcare
Small-town feel	Low ethnic diversity

Hamilton and nearby Middletown sit on a canal that once served as the major transportation artery to the Ohio River to the north. In the 20th century, the area evolved as a diverse agricultural and industrial center. The AK Steel mill in Middletown is the area's largest industry, and Hamilton has other diversified industry and commercial activity. Statistically, the area is on a rebound after years of decline in the steel industry. Some suburban sprawl has emerged mainly to the south toward Cincinnati, and commutes to the northern suburbs of that city are possible despite congested routes. Hamilton has a historic downtown area. Cultural and service amenities are available in both the nearby Cincinnati and Dayton areas. Oxford, home to Miami University, is a model college town to the west.

Hamilton sits in the broad, flat Great Miami River Valley. The town is surrounded by areas of level to gently rolling hills mainly used for agriculture and expanding residential suburbs. The climate is a highly variable battleground between northwesterly, cool air influenced by the Great Lakes, and warm Gulf air from the south. In summer hot, muggy days with frequent changes, showers, and thunderstorms are common. Winters are also variable, with frequent freezes and thaws. Because of the more northern location and flatter terrain, Hamilton receives more snow and severe weather than Cincinnati. First freeze is mid-October, last is late April.

POPULATION

DEMOGRAPHICS	AREA	U.S. AVG	ETHNIC COMPOSITION	AREA	U.S. AVG	RESIDENT PROFILE	AREA	U.S. AVG
Population	340,543		White	95.0%	75.1%	Single	41.2%	43.6%
Population density per sq. mile	728.7	447.3	Black	3.8%	12.3%	Married	58.8%	56.4%
Population growth	16.8%	16.1%	Asian	1.0%	3.6%	Divorced	9.0%	8.4%
Median age	34.4	35.5	American Indian	.1%	.9%	Separated	1.6%	3.0%
Average family size	2.7	2.7	Hispanic	.5%	12.5%	Married with children	31.3%	28.7%
			Diversity measure	17.6%	35.2%	Single with children	9.2%	10.1%

ECONOMY & JOBS
SCORE: 67/RANK: 107

INCOME	AREA	U.S. AVG	EMPLOYMENT	AREA	U.S. AVG	LARGEST EMPLOYING INDUSTRY
Per capita income	$25,077	$23,420	Unemployment rate	4.1%	6.1%	Paper Manufacturing
Household income	$53,254	$46,060	Recent job growth	1.9%	.9%	
Household income < $25K	21.1%	26.4%	Projected future job growth	19.2%	15.1%	
Household income > $75K	30.9%	24.5%	White collar	57.3%	54.5%	
Household income growth	64.1%	57.3%	Blue collar	42.7%	45.5%	

COST OF LIVING
SCORE: 55/RANK: 149

INDEXES & TAXES	AREA	U.S. AVG	HOUSING	AREA	U.S. AVG	NECESSITIES	AREA	U.S. AVG
Cost of Living Index	95.4	100.0	Median home price	$142,270	$160,100	Food Index	96.0	100.0
Financial Progress Index	119.0	100.0	Home price appreciation	4.9%	7.1%	Housing Index	88.4	100.0
Income tax rate	4.993%	4.625%	Median rent	$647	$670	Utilities Index	102.4	100.0
Sales tax rate	5.500%	6.474%	Homes owned	70.2%	63.9%	Transportation Index	98.5	100.0
Property tax rate	$9.1	$15.6	Homes rented	24.7%	25.3%	Healthcare Index	96.2	100.0
			Housing affordability	59.0%	54.5%	Miscellaneous Cost Index	102.0	100.0

CLIMATE
SCORE: 33/RANK: 219

TEMPERATURE	AREA	U.S. AVG	PRECIPITATION	AREA	U.S. AVG	COMFORTS & HAZARDS	AREA	U.S. AVG
January low	24.3°F	26.4°F	Annual inches precipitation	40.0	35.9	July relative humidity	70.0%	68.8%
July high	86.6°F	86.7°F	Annual inches snowfall	19.0	24.2	Annual days mostly sunny	177	212
Annual days > 90°F	28	38	Annual days precipitation	131	111	Annual days with thunderstorms	50	39
Annual days < 32°F	98	88	Annual days rain > 0.5 inches	25	23	Tornado risk score	25	19
Annual days < 0°F	2	6	Annual days snow > 1.5 inches	5	6	Hurricane risk score	4	15

TEMPERATURE

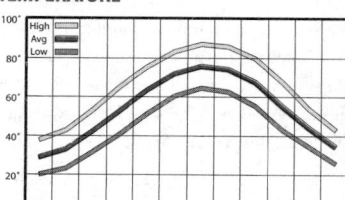

PRECIPITATION

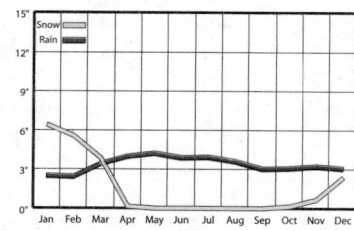

DAYS OF CLOUDS & PRECIPITATION

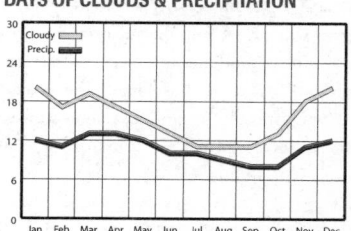

EDUCATION — SCORE: 41/RANK: 194

ACHIEVEMENT	AREA	U.S. AVG	PUBLIC SCHOOLS	AREA	U.S. AVG	HIGHER EDUCATION	AREA	U.S. AVG
High school degree	83.2%	80.2%	Expenditures per pupil	$5,181	$5,894	No. 2-year colleges	2	3
2-year college degree	6.2%	6.2%	Student/teacher ratio	17.7	16.7	No. 4-year colleges/universities	1	4
4-year college degree	15.4%	15.8%	Attending public school	91.9%	90.2%	No. highly ranked universities	0	1
Graduate/professional degree	8.1%	9.6%	State SAT score	1077	1020			
			State ACT score	21.4*	21.0			

HEALTH & HEALTHCARE — SCORE: 21/RANK: 261 / CRIME — SCORE: 28/RANK: 238

HAZARDS & ILLNESSES	AREA	U.S. AVG	HEALTHCARE	AREA	U.S. AVG	CRIME	AREA	U.S. AVG
Air-quality score	59	45	Physicians per capita	132.1	261.1	Violent crime rate	373.4	456.0
Water-quality score	4	33	Hospital beds per capita	283.6	432.2	Change in violent crime rate	-21.4%	-17.2%
Pollen/allergy score	60	61	No. teaching hospitals	0	4	Property crime rate	4,571.0	3,950.0
Stress score	89	50	Cost per doctor visit	$63	$67	Change in property crime rate	4.5%	-16.8%
Cancer mortality per capita	175.9	169.0	Cost per dental visit	$74	$82			
Depression days per month	4.7	2.8	Cost per daily hospital room	$612	$733			

TRANSPORTATION — SCORE: 48/RANK: 170

COMMUTE	AREA	U.S. AVG	INTERCITY SERVICES	AREA	U.S. AVG	AUTOMOTIVE	AREA	U.S. AVG
Average commute time	23.0 min.	22.6 min.	Miles to nearest major airport	24	46	Insurance, annual premium	$796	$1,011
Commute by auto	92.4%	88.7%	Type of local airport	Large		Gas, cost per gallon	$1.45	$1.50
Commute by mass transit	.5%	1.8%	No. daily airline departures	716	294	Daily vehicle miles per capita	32.3	23.0
Work at home	2.6%	3.9%	Amtrak service	Yes				
Mass transit miles per capita	.7	8.0	No. interstate highways	1	1			

LEISURE — SCORE: 64/RANK: 118

DINING & SHOPPING	AREA	U.S. AVG	ENTERTAINMENT	AREA	U.S. AVG	OUTDOOR ACTIVITIES	AREA	U.S. AVG
Restaurant rating	1	1	Professional sports rating	5	4	Golf-course rating	5	4
No. outlet malls	2	2	College sports rating	2	4	Ski-area rating	3	4
No. Starbucks	1	11	Zoo/aquarium rating	2	3	National Park rating	1	3
No. warehouse clubs	1	4	Amusement park rating	3	3	Sq. miles inland water	2.0	4.0
			Botanical garden/arboretum rating	5	3	Miles of coastline	0.0	11.4

ARTS & CULTURE — SCORE: 76/RANK: 80

MEDIA & LIBRARIES	AREA	U.S. AVG	PERFORMING ARTS	AREA	U.S. AVG	MUSEUMS	AREA	U.S. AVG
Arts radio rating	4	3	Classical music rating	4	4	Overall museum rating	5	6
No. public libraries	7	28	Ballet/dance rating	4	3	Art museum rating	6	5
Library volumes per capita	2.7	2.8	Professional theater rating	3	3	Science museum rating	2	4
			University arts programs rating	5	5	Children's museum rating	2	3

Harrisburg-Lebanon-Carlisle, PA

Score: 77.7   Rank: 46

Profile: Capital-city complex
Location: Southeast-central Pennsylvania along the Susquehanna River
Elevation: 351 feet
Time zone: Eastern Standard Time

PRO	CON
Capital-city amenities	Entertainment
Economic potential	Air service
Nearby mountains	Low income levels

Harrisburg, Pennsylvania's state capital, features a nondescript, fairly unattractive downtown for a capital city. A couple of pluses include an assortment of historic museums and a nice waterfront strip along the Susquehanna River. Beyond downtown, residential and industrial areas spread across the river into Camp Hill and Mechanicsburg to the west. The economy has declined recently, but has strong growth projections because of the area's relatively low cost of doing business and the strategic central location within the eastern United States. The city has some minor-league sports and other recreational amenities, but overall is quieter with less to do than many capital cities of its size. The Cost of Living Index at 91.1 is low for a capital city, especially in this region.

Harrisburg is in the Great Valley of the eastern foothills of the Allegheny Mountains. The landscape rises rapidly to the west into the main Allegheny ridge and becomes rolling to more level to the east. Thick deciduous forests cover the mountains with agricultural areas to the east and south. The Blue Mountain ridge serves as a barrier to modify the severe winter climate experienced 50 to 100 miles to the north and west. Summers are warm and humid as landforms allow warm, moist air to invade from the southwest. The city receives substantial precipitation. Occasional late summer and fall hurricanes produce downpours, notably the 15 inches dropped in 3 days by Hurricane Agnes in 1992. First freeze is late October, last is late April.

POPULATION

DEMOGRAPHICS	AREA	U.S. AVG	ETHNIC COMPOSITION	AREA	U.S. AVG	RESIDENT PROFILE	AREA	U.S. AVG
Population	635,751		White	92.1%	75.1%	Single	43.2%	43.6%
Population density per sq. mile	319.3	447.3	Black	6.1%	12.3%	Married	56.8%	56.4%
Population growth	8.1%	16.1%	Asian	1.1%	3.6%	Divorced	7.3%	8.4%
Median age	38.6	35.5	American Indian	.1%	.9%	Separated	3.1%	3.0%
Average family size	2.5	2.7	Hispanic	1.7%	12.5%	Married with children	26.9%	28.7%
			Diversity measure	24.6%	35.2%	Single with children	8.8%	10.1%

ECONOMY & JOBS SCORE: 46/RANK: 178

INCOME	AREA	U.S. AVG	EMPLOYMENT	AREA	U.S. AVG	LARGEST EMPLOYING INDUSTRY
Per capita income	$24,287	$23,420	Unemployment rate	3.4%	6.1%	Food Manufacturing
Household income	$48,289	$46,060	Recent job growth	-.3%	.9%	
Household income < $25K	21.1%	26.4%	Projected future job growth	16.6%	15.1%	
Household income > $75K	23.8%	24.5%	White collar	56.3%	54.5%	
Household income growth	52.4%	57.3%	Blue collar	43.7%	45.5%	

COST OF LIVING SCORE: 66/RANK: 110

INDEXES & TAXES	AREA	U.S. AVG	HOUSING	AREA	U.S. AVG	NECESSITIES	AREA	U.S. AVG
Cost of Living Index	91.1	100.0	Median home price	$121,320	$160,100	Food Index	91.5	100.0
Financial Progress Index	113.0	100.0	Home price appreciation	4.1%	7.1%	Housing Index	75.4	100.0
Income tax rate	2.800%	4.625%	Median rent	$604	$670	Utilities Index	108.6	100.0
Sales tax rate	6.000%	6.474%	Homes owned	67.1%	63.9%	Transportation Index	105.3	100.0
Property tax rate	$14.1	$15.6	Homes rented	23.2%	25.3%	Healthcare Index	91.3	100.0
			Housing affordability	61.0%	54.5%	Miscellaneous Cost Index	102.9	100.0

CLIMATE SCORE: 34/RANK: 216

TEMPERATURE	AREA	U.S. AVG	PRECIPITATION	AREA	U.S. AVG	COMFORTS & HAZARDS	AREA	U.S. AVG
January low	22.5°F	26.4°F	Annual inches precipitation	36.0	35.9	July relative humidity	67.0%	68.8%
July high	86.8°F	86.7°F	Annual inches snowfall	35.0	24.2	Annual days mostly sunny	193	212
Annual days > 90°F	24	38	Annual days precipitation	125	111	Annual days with thunderstorms	33	39
Annual days < 32°F	107	88	Annual days rain > 0.5 inches	25	23	Tornado risk score	13	19
Annual days < 0°F	1	6	Annual days snow > 1.5 inches	7	6	Hurricane risk score	10	15

TEMPERATURE

PRECIPITATION

DAYS OF CLOUDS & PRECIPITATION

EDUCATION SCORE: 58/RANK: 138

ACHIEVEMENT	AREA	U.S. AVG	PUBLIC SCHOOLS	AREA	U.S. AVG	HIGHER EDUCATION	AREA	U.S. AVG
High school degree	83.1%	80.2%	Expenditures per pupil	$6,189	$5,894	No. 2-year colleges	4	3
2-year college degree	5.1%	6.2%	Student/teacher ratio	15.9	16.7	No. 4-year colleges/universities	4	4
4-year college degree	14.4%	15.8%	Attending public school	88.1%	90.2%	No. highly ranked universities	3	1
Graduate/professional degree	8.2%	9.6%	State SAT score	1002*	1020			
			State ACT score	21.5	21.0			

HEALTH & HEALTHCARE SCORE: 86/RANK: 44

CRIME SCORE: 89/RANK: 37

HAZARDS & ILLNESSES	AREA	U.S. AVG	HEALTHCARE	AREA	U.S. AVG	CRIME	AREA	U.S. AVG
Air-quality score	71	45	Physicians per capita	322.9	261.1	Violent crime rate	319.2	456.0
Water-quality score	49	33	Hospital beds per capita	425.5	432.2	Change in violent crime rate	-20.9%	-17.2%
Pollen/allergy score	45	61	No. teaching hospitals	6	4	Property crime rate	2,383.6	3,950.0
Stress score	32	50	Cost per doctor visit	$56	$67	Change in property crime rate	-23.8%	-16.8%
Cancer mortality per capita	170.2	169.0	Cost per dental visit	$61	$82			
Depression days per month	3.1	2.8	Cost per daily hospital room	$693	$733			

TRANSPORTATION SCORE: 40/RANK: 199

COMMUTE	AREA	U.S. AVG	INTERCITY SERVICES	AREA	U.S. AVG	AUTOMOTIVE	AREA	U.S. AVG
Average commute time	22.0 min.	22.6 min.	Miles to nearest major airport	8	46	Insurance, annual premium	$1,001	$1,011
Commute by auto	88.6%	88.7%	Type of local airport	Small		Gas, cost per gallon	$1.48	$1.50
Commute by mass transit	1.6%	1.8%	No. daily airline departures	81	294	Daily vehicle miles per capita	31.4	23.0
Work at home	4.0%	3.9%	Amtrak service	Yes				
Mass transit miles per capita	3.4	8.0	No. interstate highways	3	1			

LEISURE SCORE: 50/RANK: 163

DINING & SHOPPING	AREA	U.S. AVG	ENTERTAINMENT	AREA	U.S. AVG	OUTDOOR ACTIVITIES	AREA	U.S. AVG
Restaurant rating	1	1	Professional sports rating	3	4	Golf-course rating	5	4
No. outlet malls	6	2	College sports rating	5	4	Ski-area rating	4	4
No. Starbucks	0	11	Zoo/aquarium rating	6	3	National Park rating	2	3
No. warehouse clubs	4	4	Amusement park rating	10	3	Sq. miles inland water	4.0	4.0
			Botanical garden/arboretum rating	9	3	Miles of coastline	0.0	11.4

ARTS & CULTURE SCORE: 58/RANK: 138

MEDIA & LIBRARIES	AREA	U.S. AVG	PERFORMING ARTS	AREA	U.S. AVG	MUSEUMS	AREA	U.S. AVG
Arts radio rating	8	3	Classical music rating	3	4	Overall museum rating	7	6
No. public libraries	29	28	Ballet/dance rating	3	3	Art museum rating	6	5
Library volumes per capita	1.8	2.8	Professional theater rating	1	3	Science museum rating	7	4
			University arts programs rating	3	5	Children's museum rating	1	3

Hartford, CT

Score: 45.7   Rank: 253

Profile: Capital city
Location: North-central Connecticut along the Connecticut River, 40 miles from the Long Island Sound
Elevation: 179 feet
Time zone: Eastern Standard Time

PRO	CON
Stable economy	Cost of living
Arts and culture	Air service
Ethnic diversity	Harsh winters

As a state capital and center for the insurance industry, Hartford has a long and colorful history as a colonial center and prosperous industrial-era city. The first insurance company was established here in the late 1700s, and The Hartford Steam Boiler Inspection and Insurance Company, established in 1866, charted the course for industrial safety. Today Hartford is home to 35 insurance companies, which provide stable employment. By the 1870s, Hartford was home to many of the country's leading philanthropists and literary figures, including Mark Twain and Harriet Beecher Stowe. The old city center is located on the Connecticut River with suburbs spreading into the wooded areas in the west. The philanthropic heritage leaves the city well stocked with museums, activities, and special events. In recent years, Hartford has become more ethnically diverse—the city has the greatest percentage of Hispanic residents north of Florida and east of the Mississippi, and the mayor is Hispanic. The large industrial and working-class base results in fairly low educational attainment for a capital city.

Hartford is located in the broad Connecticut River Valley with low north-south mountain ranges on both sides of the city. The climate is New England continental. Prevailing winds bring most weather systems into the area from the west. In winter, Hartford receives polar air masses from the north and moist, tropical air from the south, resulting in variable weather and strong winter storms. Cold air trapped in the river valley can produce freezing rain and ice storms. In summer, the climate is usually warm and pleasant with occasional thunderstorms. First freeze is early October, last is late April.

POPULATION

DEMOGRAPHICS	AREA	U.S. AVG	ETHNIC COMPOSITION	AREA	U.S. AVG	RESIDENT PROFILE	AREA	U.S. AVG
Population	1,203,169		White	89.4%	75.1%	Single	44.5%	43.6%
Population density per sq. mile	717.3	447.3	Black	6.3%	12.3%	Married	55.5%	56.4%
Population growth	3.9%	16.1%	Asian	2.1%	3.6%	Divorced	7.9%	8.4%
Median age	38.0	35.5	American Indian	.2%	.9%	Separated	2.1%	3.0%
Average family size	2.6	2.7	Hispanic	5.8%	12.5%	Married with children	27.5%	28.7%
			Diversity measure	33.1%	35.2%	Single with children	8.1%	10.1%

ECONOMY & JOBS SCORE: 78/RANK: 73

INCOME	AREA	U.S. AVG	EMPLOYMENT	AREA	U.S. AVG	LARGEST EMPLOYING INDUSTRY
Per capita income	$29,707	$23,420	Unemployment rate	5.4%	6.1%	Fabricated Metal Product Manufacturing
Household income	$59,970	$46,060	Recent job growth	-.4%	.9%	
Household income < $25K	16.9%	26.4%	Projected future job growth	9.2%	15.1%	
Household income > $75K	37.3%	24.5%	White collar	63.3%	54.5%	
Household income growth	45.4%	57.3%	Blue collar	36.7%	45.5%	

COST OF LIVING SCORE: 14/RANK: 282

INDEXES & TAXES	AREA	U.S. AVG	HOUSING	AREA	U.S. AVG	NECESSITIES	AREA	U.S. AVG
Cost of Living Index	113.1	100.0	Median home price	$183,500	$160,100	Food Index	117.0	100.0
Financial Progress Index	113.0	100.0	Home price appreciation	9.5%	7.1%	Housing Index	114.0	100.0
Income tax rate	4.500%	4.625%	Median rent	$827	$670	Utilities Index	121.4	100.0
Sales tax rate	6.000%	6.474%	Homes owned	70.2%	63.9%	Transportation Index	109.1	100.0
Property tax rate	$23.1	$15.6	Homes rented	23.6%	25.3%	Healthcare Index	113.8	100.0
			Housing affordability	54.0%	54.5%	Miscellaneous Cost Index	107.5	100.0

CLIMATE
SCORE: 2/RANK: 323

TEMPERATURE	AREA	U.S. AVG	PRECIPITATION	AREA	U.S. AVG	COMFORTS & HAZARDS	AREA	U.S. AVG
January low	16.1°F	26.4°F	Annual inches precipitation	43.0	35.9	July relative humidity	68.0%	68.8%
July high	84.1°F	86.7°F	Annual inches snowfall	53.0	24.2	Annual days mostly sunny	188	212
Annual days > 90°F	20	38	Annual days precipitation	128	111	Annual days with thunderstorms	22	39
Annual days < 32°F	137	88	Annual days rain > 0.5 inches	26	23	Tornado risk score	9	19
Annual days < 0°F	6	6	Annual days snow > 1.5 inches	9	6	Hurricane risk score	19	15

TEMPERATURE

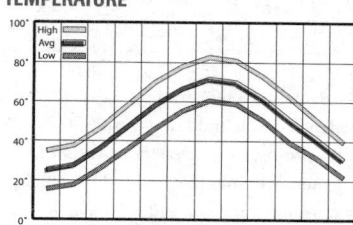

PRECIPITATION

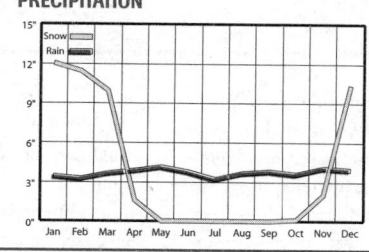

DAYS OF CLOUDS & PRECIPITATION

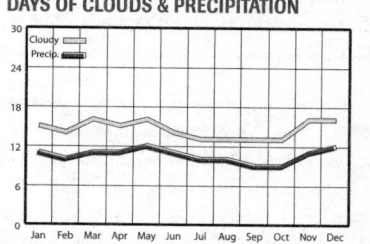

EDUCATION
SCORE: 94/RANK: 20

ACHIEVEMENT	AREA	U.S. AVG	PUBLIC SCHOOLS	AREA	U.S. AVG	HIGHER EDUCATION	AREA	U.S. AVG
High school degree	84.0%	80.2%	Expenditures per pupil	$8,452	$5,894	No. 2-year colleges	7	3
2-year college degree	7.0%	6.2%	Student/teacher ratio	14.0	16.7	No. 4-year colleges/universities	9	4
4-year college degree	18.0%	15.8%	Attending public school	90.1%	90.2%	No. highly ranked universities	3	1
Graduate/professional degree	12.5%	9.6%	State SAT score	1026*	1020			
			State ACT score	22.1	21.0			

HEALTH & HEALTHCARE
SCORE: 60/RANK: 129

CRIME
SCORE: 76/RANK: 80

HAZARDS & ILLNESSES	AREA	U.S. AVG	HEALTHCARE	AREA	U.S. AVG	CRIME	AREA	U.S. AVG
Air-quality score	98	45	Physicians per capita	304.6	261.1	Violent crime rate	342.5	456.0
Water-quality score	53	33	Hospital beds per capita	405.2	432.2	Change in violent crime rate	-29.0%	-17.2%
Pollen/allergy score	53	61	No. teaching hospitals	6	4	Property crime rate	3,192.6	3,950.0
Stress score	37	50	Cost per doctor visit	$80	$67	Change in property crime rate	-25.2%	-16.8%
Cancer mortality per capita	177.1	169.0	Cost per dental visit	$88	$82			
Depression days per month	2.7	2.8	Cost per daily hospital room	$850	$733			

TRANSPORTATION
SCORE: 80/RANK: 63

COMMUTE	AREA	U.S. AVG	INTERCITY SERVICES	AREA	U.S. AVG	AUTOMOTIVE	AREA	U.S. AVG
Average commute time	22.7 min.	22.6 min.	Miles to nearest major airport	12	46	Insurance, annual premium	$1,291	$1,011
Commute by auto	90.9%	88.7%	Type of local airport	Medium		Gas, cost per gallon	$1.62	$1.50
Commute by mass transit	2.6%	1.8%	No. daily airline departures	209	294	Daily vehicle miles per capita	26.8	23.0
Work at home	2.4%	3.9%	Amtrak service	Yes				
Mass transit miles per capita	13.7	8.0	No. interstate highways	3	1			

LEISURE
SCORE: 71/RANK: 93

DINING & SHOPPING	AREA	U.S. AVG	ENTERTAINMENT	AREA	U.S. AVG	OUTDOOR ACTIVITIES	AREA	U.S. AVG
Restaurant rating	1	1	Professional sports rating	3	4	Golf-course rating	6	4
No. outlet malls	6	2	College sports rating	6	4	Ski-area rating	6	4
No. Starbucks	15	11	Zoo/aquarium rating	2	3	National Park rating	1	3
No. warehouse clubs	6	4	Amusement park rating	1	3	Sq. miles inland water	3.0	4.0
			Botanical garden/arboretum rating	4	3	Miles of coastline	0.0	11.4

ARTS & CULTURE
SCORE: 89/RANK: 34

MEDIA & LIBRARIES	AREA	U.S. AVG	PERFORMING ARTS	AREA	U.S. AVG	MUSEUMS	AREA	U.S. AVG
Arts radio rating	5	3	Classical music rating	10	4	Overall museum rating	10	6
No. public libraries	94	28	Ballet/dance rating	5	3	Art museum rating	9	5
Library volumes per capita	3.9	2.8	Professional theater rating	8	3	Science museum rating	9	4
			University arts programs rating	9	5	Children's museum rating	10	3

Hattiesburg, MS

Score: 34.5 **Rank:** 300

Profile: Small city
Location: Southeast Mississippi, about half way between Jackson and the Gulf Coast
Elevation: 150 feet
Time zone: Central Standard Time

PRO
Historic feel
Cost of living
Low crime rate

CON
Arts and culture
Entertainment
Air service

Hattiesburg, the state's second largest city, is definitely Old South, with well-preserved historic homes and a typical Southern town core with shaded streets. The economy is tied to the forest-products industry, although it has diversified somewhat from that base. The University of Southern Mississippi and William Carey College lend some college-town flavor. The cost of living and home prices are low. Many big-city amenities and services are absent, but those who don't mind this shortcoming and who can tolerate the steamy summers will find Hattiesburg a better place than the ranking indicates.

The area mainly contains gently rolling and heavily wooded hills. Summers are consistently warm and humid, with 90°F days prevailing and frequent cooling afternoon thunderstorms. Winters are short and mild but some days can warm into the 80s. Cold spells bring temperatures briefly below freezing, but snow and hard freezes are uncommon. Sub-zero temperatures rarely occur. Fall is warm and relatively dry; spring is variable with more severe storms.

POPULATION

DEMOGRAPHICS	AREA	U.S. AVG	ETHNIC COMPOSITION	AREA	U.S. AVG	RESIDENT PROFILE	AREA	U.S. AVG
Population	114,632		White	77.4%	75.1%	Single	50.6%	43.6%
Population density per sq. mile	118.9	447.3	Black	21.2%	12.3%	Married	49.4%	56.4%
Population growth	16.1%	16.1%	Asian	1.1%	3.6%	Divorced	7.3%	8.4%
Median age	31.1	35.5	American Indian	.2%	.9%	Separated	2.7%	3.0%
Average family size	2.6	2.7	Hispanic	.6%	12.5%	Married with children	27.8%	28.7%
			Diversity measure	42.4%	35.2%	Single with children	11.8%	10.1%

ECONOMY & JOBS SCORE: 39/RANK: 200

INCOME	AREA	U.S. AVG	EMPLOYMENT	AREA	U.S. AVG	LARGEST EMPLOYING INDUSTRY
Per capita income	$18,395	$23,420	Unemployment rate	4.4%	6.1%	Food Manufacturing
Household income	$32,581	$46,060	Recent job growth	2.4%	.9%	
Household income < $25K	38.9%	26.4%	Projected future job growth	14.1%	15.1%	
Household income > $75K	16.8%	24.5%	White collar	55.8%	54.5%	
Household income growth	66.4%	57.3%	Blue collar	44.2%	45.5%	

COST OF LIVING SCORE: 76/RANK: 77

INDEXES & TAXES	AREA	U.S. AVG	HOUSING	AREA	U.S. AVG	NECESSITIES	AREA	U.S. AVG
Cost of Living Index	80.9	100.0	Median home price	$87,750	$160,100	Food Index	89.6	100.0
Financial Progress Index	85.8	100.0	Home price appreciation	3.7%	7.1%	Housing Index	54.5	100.0
Income tax rate	5.000%	4.625%	Median rent	$480	$670	Utilities Index	110.2	100.0
Sales tax rate	7.000%	6.474%	Homes owned	62.2%	63.9%	Transportation Index	91.4	100.0
Property tax rate	$7.0	$15.6	Homes rented	29.7%	25.3%	Healthcare Index	88.6	100.0
			Housing affordability	54.0%	54.5%	Miscellaneous Cost Index	99.3	100.0

CLIMATE SCORE: 61/RANK: 129

TEMPERATURE	AREA	U.S. AVG	PRECIPITATION	AREA	U.S. AVG	COMFORTS & HAZARDS	AREA	U.S. AVG
January low	35.0°F	26.4°F	Annual inches precipitation	49.0	35.9	July relative humidity	75.0%	68.8%
July high	90.0°F	86.7°F	Annual inches snowfall	1.0	24.2	Annual days mostly sunny	217	212
Annual days > 90°F	70	38	Annual days precipitation	100	111	Annual days with thunderstorms	70	39
Annual days < 32°F	40	88	Annual days rain > 0.5 inches	36	23	Tornado risk score	26	19
Annual days < 0°F	0	6	Annual days snow > 1.5 inches	0	6	Hurricane risk score	41	15

TEMPERATURE

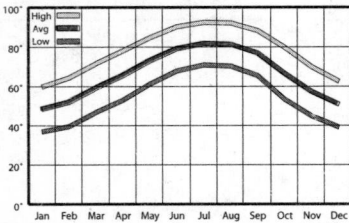

PRECIPITATION

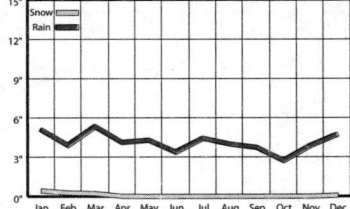

DAYS OF CLOUDS & PRECIPITATION

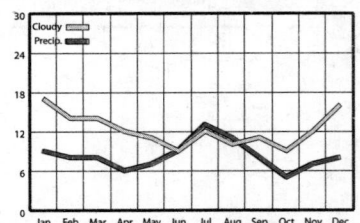

EDUCATION SCORE: 45/RANK: 182

ACHIEVEMENT	AREA	U.S. AVG	PUBLIC SCHOOLS	AREA	U.S. AVG	HIGHER EDUCATION	AREA	U.S. AVG
High school degree	79.1%	80.2%	Expenditures per pupil	$4,331	$5,894	No. 2-year colleges	0	3
2-year college degree	5.2%	6.2%	Student/teacher ratio	15.0	16.7	No. 4-year colleges/universities	2	4
4-year college degree	15.5%	15.8%	Attending public school	93.0%	90.2%	No. highly ranked universities	0	1
Graduate/professional degree	8.8%	9.6%	State SAT score	1116	1020			
			State ACT score	18.7*	21.0			

HEALTH & HEALTHCARE SCORE: 40/RANK: 197   **CRIME** SCORE: 85/RANK: 48

HAZARDS & ILLNESSES	AREA	U.S. AVG	HEALTHCARE	AREA	U.S. AVG	CRIME	AREA	U.S. AVG
Air-quality score	24	45	Physicians per capita	307.9	261.1	Violent crime rate	195.2	456.0
Water-quality score	22	33	Hospital beds per capita	669.8	432.2	Change in violent crime rate	-62.4%	-17.2%
Pollen/allergy score	73	61	No. teaching hospitals	0	4	Property crime rate	3,810.2	3,950.0
Stress score	9	50	Cost per doctor visit	$56	$67	Change in property crime rate	-29.6%	-16.8%
Cancer mortality per capita	173.5	169.0	Cost per dental visit	$83	$82			
Depression days per month	3.4	2.8	Cost per daily hospital room	$451	$733			

TRANSPORTATION SCORE: 10/RANK: 298

COMMUTE	AREA	U.S. AVG	INTERCITY SERVICES	AREA	U.S. AVG	AUTOMOTIVE	AREA	U.S. AVG
Average commute time	22.9 min.	22.6 min.	Miles to nearest major airport	75	46	Insurance, annual premium	$878	$1,011
Commute by auto	90.7%	88.7%	Type of local airport	Small		Gas, cost per gallon	$1.39	$1.50
Commute by mass transit	.4%	1.8%	No. daily airline departures	59	294	Daily vehicle miles per capita	14.5	23.0
Work at home	2.0%	3.9%	Amtrak service	Yes				
Mass transit miles per capita	0.0	8.0	No. interstate highways	1	1			

LEISURE SCORE: 5/RANK: 317

DINING & SHOPPING	AREA	U.S. AVG	ENTERTAINMENT	AREA	U.S. AVG	OUTDOOR ACTIVITIES	AREA	U.S. AVG
Restaurant rating	1	1	Professional sports rating	2	4	Golf-course rating	2	4
No. outlet malls	0	2	College sports rating	1	4	Ski-area rating	1	4
No. Starbucks	0	11	Zoo/aquarium rating	1	3	National Park rating	3	3
No. warehouse clubs	3	4	Amusement park rating	1	3	Sq. miles inland water	3.0	4.0
			Botanical garden/arboretum rating	1	3	Miles of coastline	0.0	11.4

ARTS & CULTURE SCORE: 0/RANK: 330

MEDIA & LIBRARIES	AREA	U.S. AVG	PERFORMING ARTS	AREA	U.S. AVG	MUSEUMS	AREA	U.S. AVG
Arts radio rating	1	3	Classical music rating	1	4	Overall museum rating	1	6
No. public libraries	5	28	Ballet/dance rating	1	3	Art museum rating	2	5
Library volumes per capita	1.6	2.8	Professional theater rating	1	3	Science museum rating	1	4
			University arts programs rating	6	5	Children's museum rating	1	3

Hickory-Morganton-Lenoir, NC

Score: 45.7   Rank: 254

Profile: Small-town complex
Location: Western North Carolina half way between Winston-Salem and Asheville
Elevation: 897 feet
Time zone: Eastern Standard Time

PRO
Nearby mountains
Cost of living
Small-town feel

CON
Economy
Arts and culture
Low ethnic diversity

This tri-city area is located at the eastern base of the Blue Ridge Mountains. As the name "Hickory" implies, this is an area of hardwood forests, the original resource for Hickory's active furniture-making industry. According to local sources, 60% of the furniture made in the United States is made within 200 miles of Hickory. Furniture factory outlets draw people from miles around. The downtown areas of Morganton and Hickory are small but well kept and surprisingly attractive. There are some recreational opportunities in the nearby mountains to the west and large Lake Norman to the southeast. Cost of living is low and crime is the lowest in the state. However, there isn't much to do and little intellectual stimulation.

The terrain is mostly hilly and wooded. The Catawba River runs through the area and turns south into Lake Norman at the east edge of the county, where the land begins to flatten out into the Carolina Piedmont. The climate is typical of the region. The mountains to the northwest block and warm cold northwest winds. The ocean is too far away to affect summer temperatures but can moderate winter cold. Summers are warm with frequent 90°F days and thundershowers. Winters are cool but not excessively so. Winter temperatures frequently touch freezing, but seldom go far below. Snow and snow accumulations are rare. Rainfall is evenly distributed through the year, with fall being the driest.

POPULATION

DEMOGRAPHICS	AREA	U.S. AVG	ETHNIC COMPOSITION	AREA	U.S. AVG	RESIDENT PROFILE	AREA	U.S. AVG
Population	349,241		White	92.7%	75.1%	Single	40.2%	43.6%
Population density per sq. mile	213.1	447.3	Black	6.2%	12.3%	Married	59.8%	56.4%
Population growth	19.4%	16.1%	Asian	.6%	3.6%	Divorced	8.1%	8.4%
Median age	37.1	35.5	American Indian	.2%	.9%	Separated	4.7%	3.0%
Average family size	2.6	2.7	Hispanic	1.2%	12.5%	Married with children	28.1%	28.7%
			Diversity measure	25.5%	35.2%	Single with children	9.6%	10.1%

ECONOMY & JOBS SCORE: 6/RANK: 309

INCOME	AREA	U.S. AVG	EMPLOYMENT	AREA	U.S. AVG	LARGEST EMPLOYING INDUSTRY
Per capita income	$21,075	$23,420	Unemployment rate	9.0%	6.1%	Furniture and Related Product Manufacturing
Household income	$41,734	$46,060	Recent job growth	-3.0%	.9%	
Household income < $25K	27.1%	26.4%	Projected future job growth	12.1%	15.1%	
Household income > $75K	16.9%	24.5%	White collar	39.3%	54.5%	
Household income growth	53.4%	57.3%	Blue collar	60.7%	45.5%	

COST OF LIVING SCORE: 63/RANK: 121

INDEXES & TAXES	AREA	U.S. AVG	HOUSING	AREA	U.S. AVG	NECESSITIES	AREA	U.S. AVG
Cost of Living Index	85.9	100.0	Median home price	$110,710	$160,100	Food Index	98.4	100.0
Financial Progress Index	103.5	100.0	Home price appreciation	5.8%	7.1%	Housing Index	68.8	100.0
Income tax rate	7.000%	4.625%	Median rent	$529	$670	Utilities Index	91.6	100.0
Sales tax rate	7.000%	6.474%	Homes owned	70.0%	63.9%	Transportation Index	91.9	100.0
Property tax rate	$13.0	$15.6	Homes rented	18.3%	25.3%	Healthcare Index	89.6	100.0
			Housing affordability	64.0%	54.5%	Miscellaneous Cost Index	98.1	100.0

CLIMATE SCORE: 59/RANK: 135

TEMPERATURE	AREA	U.S. AVG	PRECIPITATION	AREA	U.S. AVG	COMFORTS & HAZARDS	AREA	U.S. AVG
January low	28.5°F	26.4°F	Annual inches precipitation	41.4	35.9	July relative humidity	72.0%	68.8%
July high	87.5°F	86.7°F	Annual inches snowfall	8.7	24.2	Annual days mostly sunny	217	212
Annual days > 90°F	28	38	Annual days precipitation	121	111	Annual days with thunderstorms	46	39
Annual days < 32°F	85	88	Annual days rain > 0.5 inches	29	23	Tornado risk score	10	19
Annual days < 0°F	0	6	Annual days snow > 1.5 inches	3	6	Hurricane risk score	14	15

TEMPERATURE

PRECIPITATION

DAYS OF CLOUDS & PRECIPITATION

EDUCATION SCORE: 16/RANK: 277

ACHIEVEMENT	AREA	U.S. AVG	PUBLIC SCHOOLS	AREA	U.S. AVG	HIGHER EDUCATION	AREA	U.S. AVG
High school degree	70.3%	80.2%	Expenditures per pupil	$5,030	$5,894	No. 2-year colleges	3	3
2-year college degree	6.5%	6.2%	Student/teacher ratio	15.2	16.7	No. 4-year colleges/universities	1	4
4-year college degree	9.7%	15.8%	Attending public school	97.0%	90.2%	No. highly ranked universities	0	1
Graduate/professional degree	4.0%	9.6%	State SAT score	1001*	1020			
			State ACT score	19.9	21.0			

HEALTH & HEALTHCARE SCORE: 92/RANK: 26

CRIME SCORE: 65/RANK: 114

HAZARDS & ILLNESSES	AREA	U.S. AVG	HEALTHCARE	AREA	U.S. AVG	CRIME	AREA	U.S. AVG
Air-quality score	24	45	Physicians per capita	174.7	261.1	Violent crime rate	259.4	456.0
Water-quality score	49	33	Hospital beds per capita	607.3	432.2	Change in violent crime rate	-28.8%	-17.2%
Pollen/allergy score	65	61	No. teaching hospitals	1	4	Property crime rate	3,628.7	3,950.0
Stress score	35	50	Cost per doctor visit	$64	$67	Change in property crime rate	-7.2%	-16.8%
Cancer mortality per capita	150.2	169.0	Cost per dental visit	$74	$82			
Depression days per month	2.1	2.8	Cost per daily hospital room	$401	$733			

TRANSPORTATION SCORE: 21/RANK: 259

COMMUTE	AREA	U.S. AVG	INTERCITY SERVICES	AREA	U.S. AVG	AUTOMOTIVE	AREA	U.S. AVG
Average commute time	21.2 min.	22.6 min.	Miles to nearest major airport	42	46	Insurance, annual premium	$791	$1,011
Commute by auto	95.6%	88.7%	Type of local airport	Large		Gas, cost per gallon	$1.40	$1.50
Commute by mass transit	.1%	1.8%	No. daily airline departures	637	294	Daily vehicle miles per capita	42.5	23.0
Work at home	1.9%	3.9%	Amtrak service	No				
Mass transit miles per capita	0.0	8.0	No. interstate highways	1	1			

LEISURE SCORE: 23/RANK: 256

DINING & SHOPPING	AREA	U.S. AVG	ENTERTAINMENT	AREA	U.S. AVG	OUTDOOR ACTIVITIES	AREA	U.S. AVG
Restaurant rating	1	1	Professional sports rating	4	4	Golf-course rating	3	4
No. outlet malls	4	2	College sports rating	1	4	Ski-area rating	2	4
No. Starbucks	0	11	Zoo/aquarium rating	1	3	National Park rating	1	3
No. warehouse clubs	3	4	Amusement park rating	1	3	Sq. miles inland water	3.0	4.0
			Botanical garden/arboretum rating	1	3	Miles of coastline	0.0	11.4

ARTS & CULTURE SCORE: 4/RANK: 315

MEDIA & LIBRARIES	AREA	U.S. AVG	PERFORMING ARTS	AREA	U.S. AVG	MUSEUMS	AREA	U.S. AVG
Arts radio rating	1	3	Classical music rating	2	4	Overall museum rating	5	6
No. public libraries	15	28	Ballet/dance rating	1	3	Art museum rating	4	5
Library volumes per capita	1.9	2.8	Professional theater rating	1	3	Science museum rating	4	4
			University arts programs rating	2	5	Children's museum rating	1	3

Honolulu, HI

Score: 91.7   Rank: 5

Profile: Large capital city/Resort city
Location: Southern coast, Island of Oahu
Elevation: 15 feet
Time zone: Hawaii Standard Time

PRO
Year-round climate
Attractive setting
Recreation

CON
Cost of living
Traffic and sprawl
Tourist impact

Often called the "Crossroads of the Pacific," Honolulu is the capital of the multi-island state and port of entry for most of the state's millions of visitors. The city is a diverse commercial, industrial, and economic center for the entire Pacific and a center for tourism and recreation. The Waikiki beachfront area bustles with shopping, nightlife, and active sports. The rest of the city is a mix of residential, commercial, and industrial activity. Most of the city was built in the 1960s. There are large areas of plain and unattractive concrete structures, and there is less historic preservation than one might expect in such a destination.

Honolulu has full-scale shopping centers and commercial strips—and many traffic problems. While the city boasts the only interstate highways in Hawaii, there is considerable congestion, especially at rush hour. Public-transportation facilities are well developed. The nicer residential areas are found in the hills northeast of the central city, but there isn't much land available for building. Several pleasant communities also exist along the highway to the north, within commuting distance. As a rule, although most tourist activity is centered in the Waikiki area, avoiding tourists and their impact is difficult. The city has a strong military presence.

The climate is one of the best in the world. The economy is robust although vulnerable to tourism-driven cycles and the state of the Asian—and particularly the Japanese—economy. The big negative is cost of living. The high Cost of Living Index of 152.7 is driven in a large

part by housing—average home prices are among the country's highest. Because of the isolation from national markets for staples such as food and energy, prices for these items are high. Aside from cost, isolation from the mainland may reduce the appeal for some residents, although most urban amenities are available in abundance.

Honolulu is located on a broad coastal plain of Oahu, the third largest of the Hawaiian Islands. The Koolau Range, at an average elevation of 2,000 feet, parallels the northeastern coast. The Waianae Mountains, somewhat higher in elevation, parallel the west coast. Most of the eastern half of the coastal plain is built up. The Hawaiian climate is unusually pleasant for the tropics. Outstanding features are the persistent northeasterly trade winds, remarkable variance in rainfall over short distances, sunny leeward lowlands with persistent cloudiness over nearby mountain crests, equable temperature, and infrequency of severe storms. The city sits mostly in the lee (downwind) direction of the Koolau Range, which blocks heavier rains at most times of the year. The mountain range is low enough that clouds spill over it, allowing for occasional light rain and drizzle even as the overhead sun shines—an effect known locally as "liquid sunshine." Trade winds—and associated showers—are more prevalent in summer. Temperatures and humidity are generally comfortable, less than 90°F and more than 50°F. But when trade winds subside and tropical "Kona" weather emerges, hot, humid periods can occur. There may be more intense winter storms and heavy downpours associated with nearby tropical storms, but few of them strike directly.

POPULATION

DEMOGRAPHICS	AREA	U.S. AVG	ETHNIC COMPOSITION	AREA	U.S. AVG	RESIDENT PROFILE	AREA	U.S. AVG
Population	896,019		White	34.0%	75.1%	Single	46.1%	43.6%
Population density per sq. mile	1,492.9	447.3	Black	3.5%	12.3%	Married	53.9%	56.4%
Population growth	7.1%	16.1%	Asian	61.3%	3.6%	Divorced	7.9%	8.4%
Median age	36.1	35.5	American Indian	.5%	.9%	Separated	2.5%	3.0%
Average family size	3.0	2.7	Hispanic	8.1%	12.5%	Married with children	34.5%	28.7%
			Diversity measure	72.6%	35.2%	Single with children	10.1%	10.1%

ECONOMY & JOBS — SCORE: 96/RANK: 14

INCOME	AREA	U.S. AVG	EMPLOYMENT	AREA	U.S. AVG	LARGEST EMPLOYING INDUSTRY
Per capita income	$26,047	$23,420	Unemployment rate	4.0%	6.1%	Accommodations and Food Services
Household income	$60,112	$46,060	Recent job growth	4.5%	.9%	
Household income < $25K	16.0%	26.4%	Projected future job growth	10.3%	15.1%	
Household income > $75K	37.9%	24.5%	White collar	55.5%	54.5%	
Household income growth	48.0%	57.3%	Blue collar	44.5%	45.5%	

COST OF LIVING — SCORE: 3/RANK: 321

INDEXES & TAXES	AREA	U.S. AVG	HOUSING	AREA	U.S. AVG	NECESSITIES	AREA	U.S. AVG
Cost of Living Index	152.7	100.0	Median home price	$350,000	$160,100	Food Index	123.5	100.0
Financial Progress Index	83.9	100.0	Home price appreciation	5.8%	7.1%	Housing Index	217.4	100.0
Income tax rate	10.000%	4.625%	Median rent	$858	$670	Utilities Index	83.4	100.0
Sales tax rate	4.000%	6.474%	Homes owned	47.2%	63.9%	Transportation Index	120.2	100.0
Property tax rate	$4.1	$15.6	Homes rented	46.2%	25.3%	Healthcare Index	122.2	100.0
			Housing affordability	56.0%	54.5%	Miscellaneous Cost Index	119.3	100.0

CLIMATE — SCORE: 98/RANK: 7

TEMPERATURE	AREA	U.S. AVG	PRECIPITATION	AREA	U.S. AVG	COMFORTS & HAZARDS	AREA	U.S. AVG
January low	65.3°F	26.4°F	Annual inches precipitation	23.0	35.9	July relative humidity	67.0%	68.8%
July high	87.4°F	86.7°F	Annual inches snowfall	0.0	24.2	Annual days mostly sunny	264	212
Annual days > 90°F	9	38	Annual days precipitation	102	111	Annual days with thunderstorms	7	39
Annual days < 32°F	0	88	Annual days rain > 0.5 inches	12	23	Tornado risk score	0	19
Annual days < 0°F	0	6	Annual days snow > 1.5 inches	0	6	Hurricane risk score	3	15

TEMPERATURE

PRECIPITATION

DAYS OF CLOUDS & PRECIPITATION

EDUCATION — SCORE: 54/RANK: 151

ACHIEVEMENT	AREA	U.S. AVG	PUBLIC SCHOOLS	AREA	U.S. AVG	HIGHER EDUCATION	AREA	U.S. AVG
High school degree	83.4%	80.2%	Expenditures per pupil	$5,859	$5,894	No. 2-year colleges	6	3
2-year college degree	6.8%	6.2%	Student/teacher ratio	17.3	16.7	No. 4-year colleges/universities	4	4
4-year college degree	18.9%	15.8%	Attending public school	82.3%	90.2%	No. highly ranked universities	1	1
Graduate/professional degree	9.0%	9.6%	State SAT score	1002*	1020			
			State ACT score	21.8	21.0			

HEALTH & HEALTHCARE — SCORE: 31/RANK: 226   **CRIME** — SCORE: 41/RANK: 192

HAZARDS & ILLNESSES	AREA	U.S. AVG	HEALTHCARE	AREA	U.S. AVG	CRIME	AREA	U.S. AVG
Air-quality score	74	45	Physicians per capita	323.9	261.1	Violent crime rate	277.0	456.0
Water-quality score	26	33	Hospital beds per capita	340.9	432.2	Change in violent crime rate	-15.4%	-17.2%
Pollen/allergy score	62	61	No. teaching hospitals	7	4	Property crime rate	5,192.9	3,950.0
Stress score	14	50	Cost per doctor visit	$73	$67	Change in property crime rate	-28.9%	-16.8%
Cancer mortality per capita	162.6	169.0	Cost per dental visit	$95	$82			
Depression days per month	1.0	2.8	Cost per daily hospital room	$835	$733			

TRANSPORTATION — SCORE: 91/RANK: 29

COMMUTE	AREA	U.S. AVG	INTERCITY SERVICES	AREA	U.S. AVG	AUTOMOTIVE	AREA	U.S. AVG
Average commute time	27.3 min.	22.6 min.	Miles to nearest major airport	9	46	Insurance, annual premium	$1,275	$1,011
Commute by auto	78.4%	88.7%	Type of local airport	Large		Gas, cost per gallon	$1.81	$1.50
Commute by mass transit	8.4%	1.8%	No. daily airline departures	326	294	Daily vehicle miles per capita	16.8	23.0
Work at home	2.6%	3.9%	Amtrak service	No				
Mass transit miles per capita	32.0	8.0	No. interstate highways	1	1			

LEISURE — SCORE: 77/RANK: 74

DINING & SHOPPING	AREA	U.S. AVG	ENTERTAINMENT	AREA	U.S. AVG	OUTDOOR ACTIVITIES	AREA	U.S. AVG
Restaurant rating	1	1	Professional sports rating	2	4	Golf-course rating	5	4
No. outlet malls	1	2	College sports rating	5	4	Ski-area rating	1	4
No. Starbucks	0	11	Zoo/aquarium rating	6	3	National Park rating	2	3
No. warehouse clubs	4	4	Amusement park rating	1	3	Sq. miles inland water	3.0	4.0
			Botanical garden/arboretum rating	8	3	Miles of coastline	137.8	11.4

ARTS & CULTURE SCORE: 90/RANK: 33

MEDIA & LIBRARIES	AREA	U.S. AVG	PERFORMING ARTS	AREA	U.S. AVG	MUSEUMS	AREA	U.S. AVG
Arts radio rating	7	3	Classical music rating	7	4	Overall museum rating	8	6
No. public libraries	50	28	Ballet/dance rating	6	3	Art museum rating	7	5
Library volumes per capita	2.9	2.8	Professional theater rating	8	3	Science museum rating	8	4
			University arts programs rating	8	5	Children's museum rating	2	3

Houma, LA

Score: 23.3   Rank: 320

Profile: Small town
Location: Southeast Louisiana on the Mississippi Delta, 35 miles south of New Orleans
Elevation: 30 feet
Time zone: Central Standard Time

PRO
Water recreation
Wildlife viewing
Cajun culture

CON
Heat and humidity
Crime rate
Low educational attainment

Houma is deep in the marshlands of the southern Mississippi Delta just a few miles from the Gulf of Mexico. The swampy lowlands create the Venice-like canals and bayous for which the area is known. The area is rich in Cajun culture. Coastal and marshland wildlife is a major attraction, but interesting features pretty much stop there. There is limited industry and port activity along the Intracoastal Waterway, but the area is hardly a transportation or commercial center. Crime is high for a small town, and on the rise. Educational attainment is the lowest in the state. Some hardier souls commute north to the New Orleans area, resulting in an average commute time of 25 minutes. Statistics don't reflect much in the way of amenities.

The terrain is completely flat with wet marshland, slow-moving creeks (called bayous), and some wooded areas. The climate is humid subtropical and governed by the Gulf of Mexico. Summers are wet, hot, and humid. Winters are cool but not cold and fairly wet.

POPULATION

DEMOGRAPHICS	AREA	U.S. AVG	ETHNIC COMPOSITION	AREA	U.S. AVG	RESIDENT PROFILE	AREA	U.S. AVG
Population	196,860		White	77.4%	75.1%	Single	40.6%	43.6%
Population density per sq. mile	84.1	447.3	Black	14.7%	12.3%	Married	59.4%	56.4%
Population growth	7.7%	16.1%	Asian	.8%	3.6%	Divorced	6.2%	8.4%
Median age	33.7	35.5	American Indian	6.9%	.9%	Separated	3.8%	3.0%
Average family size	3.0	2.7	Hispanic	1.8%	12.5%	Married with children	37.7%	28.7%
			Diversity measure	37.2%	35.2%	Single with children	12.3%	10.1%

ECONOMY & JOBS SCORE: 81/RANK: 63

INCOME	AREA	U.S. AVG	EMPLOYMENT	AREA	U.S. AVG	LARGEST EMPLOYING INDUSTRY
Per capita income	$18,155	$23,420	Unemployment rate	4.1%	6.1%	Ship and Boat Building
Household income	$37,128	$46,060	Recent job growth	.7%	.9%	
Household income < $25K	35.3%	26.4%	Projected future job growth	11.2%	15.1%	
Household income > $75K	18.1%	24.5%	White collar	45.1%	54.5%	
Household income growth	71.4%	57.3%	Blue collar	54.9%	45.5%	

COST OF LIVING SCORE: 94/RANK: 19

INDEXES & TAXES	AREA	U.S. AVG	HOUSING	AREA	U.S. AVG	NECESSITIES	AREA	U.S. AVG
Cost of Living Index	88.3	100.0	Median home price	$94,650	$160,100	Food Index	103.9	100.0
Financial Progress Index	89.6	100.0	Home price appreciation	5.9%	7.1%	Housing Index	58.8	100.0
Income tax rate	4.000%	4.625%	Median rent	$446	$670	Utilities Index	114.6	100.0
Sales tax rate	8.500%	6.474%	Homes owned	71.5%	63.9%	Transportation Index	106.5	100.0
Property tax rate	$5.0	$15.6	Homes rented	17.4%	25.3%	Healthcare Index	101.1	100.0
			Housing affordability	67.0%	54.5%	Miscellaneous Cost Index	102.4	100.0

CLIMATE SCORE: 70/RANK: 100

TEMPERATURE	AREA	U.S. AVG	PRECIPITATION	AREA	U.S. AVG	COMFORTS & HAZARDS	AREA	U.S. AVG
January low	43.5°F	26.4°F	Annual inches precipitation	57.0	35.9	July relative humidity	77.0%	68.8%
July high	90.6°F	86.7°F	Annual inches snowfall	.2	24.2	Annual days mostly sunny	229	212
Annual days > 90°F	67	38	Annual days precipitation	113	111	Annual days with thunderstorms	68	39
Annual days < 32°F	13	88	Annual days rain > 0.5 inches	37	23	Tornado risk score	20	19
Annual days < 0°F	0	6	Annual days snow > 1.5 inches	1	6	Hurricane risk score	67	15

TEMPERATURE

PRECIPITATION

DAYS OF CLOUDS & PRECIPITATION

EDUCATION SCORE: 0/RANK: 330

ACHIEVEMENT	AREA	U.S. AVG	PUBLIC SCHOOLS	AREA	U.S. AVG	HIGHER EDUCATION	AREA	U.S. AVG
High school degree	66.7%	80.2%	Expenditures per pupil	$5,104	$5,894	No. 2-year colleges	0	3
2-year college degree	2.9%	6.2%	Student/teacher ratio	14.5	16.7	No. 4-year colleges/universities	1	4
4-year college degree	8.6%	15.8%	Attending public school	84.7%	90.2%	No. highly ranked universities	0	1
Graduate/professional degree	3.7%	9.6%	State SAT score	1122	1020			
			State ACT score	19.6*	21.0			

HEALTH & HEALTHCARE SCORE: 8/RANK: 302

HAZARDS & ILLNESSES	AREA	U.S. AVG	HEALTHCARE	AREA	U.S. AVG
Air-quality score	6	45	Physicians per capita	137.2	261.1
Water-quality score	30	33	Hospital beds per capita	454.0	432.2
Pollen/allergy score	79	61	No. teaching hospitals	1	4
Stress score	19	50	Cost per doctor visit	$61	$67
Cancer mortality per capita	189.6	169.0	Cost per dental visit	$80	$82
Depression days per month	1.9	2.8	Cost per daily hospital room	$491	$733

CRIME SCORE: 22/RANK: 256

CRIME	AREA	U.S. AVG
Violent crime rate	566.6	456.0
Change in violent crime rate	3.1%	-17.2%
Property crime rate	4,107.1	3,950.0
Change in property crime rate	4.0%	-16.8%

TRANSPORTATION SCORE: 1/RANK: 325

COMMUTE	AREA	U.S. AVG	INTERCITY SERVICES	AREA	U.S. AVG	AUTOMOTIVE	AREA	U.S. AVG
Average commute time	25.9 min.	22.6 min.	Miles to nearest major airport	39	46	Insurance, annual premium	$1,093	$1,011
Commute by auto	87.5%	88.7%	Type of local airport	Medium		Gas, cost per gallon	$1.41	$1.50
Commute by mass transit	.8%	1.8%	No. daily airline departures	218	294	Daily vehicle miles per capita	18.2	23.0
Work at home	1.9%	3.9%	Amtrak service	Yes				
Mass transit miles per capita	1.2	8.0	No. interstate highways	0	1			

LEISURE SCORE: 82/RANK: 60

DINING & SHOPPING	AREA	U.S. AVG	ENTERTAINMENT	AREA	U.S. AVG	OUTDOOR ACTIVITIES	AREA	U.S. AVG
Restaurant rating	1	1	Professional sports rating	2	4	Golf-course rating	1	4
No. outlet malls	1	2	College sports rating	1	4	Ski-area rating	1	4
No. Starbucks	0	11	Zoo/aquarium rating	1	3	National Park rating	1	3
No. warehouse clubs	1	4	Amusement park rating	1	3	Sq. miles inland water	10.0	4.0
			Botanical garden/arboretum rating	1	3	Miles of coastline	78.8	11.4

ARTS & CULTURE SCORE: 16/RANK: 277

MEDIA & LIBRARIES	AREA	U.S. AVG	PERFORMING ARTS	AREA	U.S. AVG	MUSEUMS	AREA	U.S. AVG
Arts radio rating	1	3	Classical music rating	1	4	Overall museum rating	2	6
No. public libraries	14	28	Ballet/dance rating	1	3	Art museum rating	1	5
Library volumes per capita	2.0	2.8	Professional theater rating	1	3	Science museum rating	1	4
			University arts programs rating	1	5	Children's museum rating	1	3

Houston, TX

Score: 58.9   **Rank:** 158

Profile: Large city
Location: Southeast Texas, 50 miles inland from the Gulf Coast
Elevation: 108 feet
Time zone: Central Standard Time

PRO
Diverse economy
Entertainment
Cost of living

CON
Urban sprawl
Hot, humid summers
Unattractive setting

Houston is an enormous, diverse, and rapidly growing metropolis, and currently ranks as the fourth largest city in the United States behind New York, Los Angeles, and Chicago. While the economy is still heavily influenced by the petroleum and petrochemical industry, Houston has become more of a corporate center; local companies include Continental Airlines, Browning Ferris Industries, Waste Management, MinuteMaid (owned by Coca-Cola), and American General (insurance). Despite the Enron debacle and Hewlett-Packard's acquisition of the local Compaq Computer Corporation, the city remains a favored business location, and the southeastern Houston Ship Channel provides a deep-water port for shipping as well as boating and waterfront amenities.

The city grew in a fairly haphazard manner, with skyscraper complexes downtown and satellite corporate centers on the periphery. To the northwest, the commercial Galleria area contains a gigantic mall with over 300 stores. Together downtown and the Galleria contain 6½ miles of underground tunnels and malls. The entire metropolitan area covers 900 square miles, more than twice the size of Rhode Island, and traffic consistently snarls to a crawl on the two beltways. Urban sprawl is a major problem. Air quality is the second worst in the country.

Cultural amenities include performing arts, museums, and a variety of entertainment options from the sophisticated to the bawdy. With the new NFL team, the Houston Texans, and the University of Houston and Rice University teams, the city offers a full slate of sports entertainment. The Texas Medical Center is a leading-edge facility including 39 centers and employing 50,000 healthcare professionals. While laid out haphazardly in past decades, residential neighborhoods are improving in quality and planning, particularly in areas to the west of town. Although there are some lakes and the Gulf is 50 miles away, the area is notably lacking in outdoor recreational opportunities and the landscape is relatively featureless. Residents trade off the major downsides—congestion, summer heat, and limited outdoor recreation—for a low cost of living, good housing values, career opportunities, and mild winters.

The Houston landscape is a flat, treeless plain crossed by several small streams and rivers. The climate is humid subtropical with a marine influence. Summers are hot and sultry with daytime temperatures in the 90s and occasionally over 100°F. High relative humidity makes these temperatures uncomfortable—air-conditioning is a must. Winters are cloudy and mild with abundant rainfall. Clear dry days are most common in the fall. Heavy thunderstorms and tropical storms occasionally pass through the area.

POPULATION

DEMOGRAPHICS	AREA	U.S. AVG	ETHNIC COMPOSITION	AREA	U.S. AVG	RESIDENT PROFILE	AREA	U.S. AVG
Population	4,420,081		White	66.8%	75.1%	Single	47.0%	43.6%
Population density per sq. mile	746.5	447.3	Black	18.9%	12.3%	Married	53.0%	56.4%
Population growth	33.1%	16.1%	Asian	3.9%	3.6%	Divorced	10.0%	8.4%
Median age	31.9	35.5	American Indian	.4%	.9%	Separated	4.9%	3.0%
Average family size	2.8	2.7	Hispanic	25.5%	12.5%	Married with children	30.3%	28.7%
			Diversity measure	65.1%	35.2%	Single with children	12.8%	10.1%

ECONOMY & JOBS SCORE: 58/RANK: 137

INCOME	AREA	U.S. AVG	EMPLOYMENT	AREA	U.S. AVG	LARGEST EMPLOYING INDUSTRY
Per capita income	$26,815	$23,420	Unemployment rate	6.9%	6.1%	Fabricated Metal Product Manufacturing
Household income	$55,692	$46,060	Recent job growth	2.8%	.9%	
Household income < $25K	19.8%	26.4%	Projected future job growth	17.8%	15.1%	
Household income > $75K	35.2%	24.5%	White collar	59.6%	54.5%	
Household income growth	76.8%	57.3%	Blue collar	40.4%	45.5%	

COST OF LIVING SCORE: 47/RANK: 175

INDEXES & TAXES	AREA	U.S. AVG	HOUSING	AREA	U.S. AVG	NECESSITIES	AREA	U.S. AVG
Cost of Living Index	91.8	100.0	Median home price	$133,900	$160,100	Food Index	94.4	100.0
Financial Progress Index	129.2	100.0	Home price appreciation	7.3%	7.1%	Housing Index	83.2	100.0
Income tax rate	0.000%	4.625%	Median rent	$760	$670	Utilities Index	94.8	100.0
Sales tax rate	8.250%	6.474%	Homes owned	56.5%	63.9%	Transportation Index	101.9	100.0
Property tax rate	$21.9	$15.6	Homes rented	32.5%	25.3%	Healthcare Index	107.1	100.0
			Housing affordability	57.0%	54.5%	Miscellaneous Cost Index	93.7	100.0

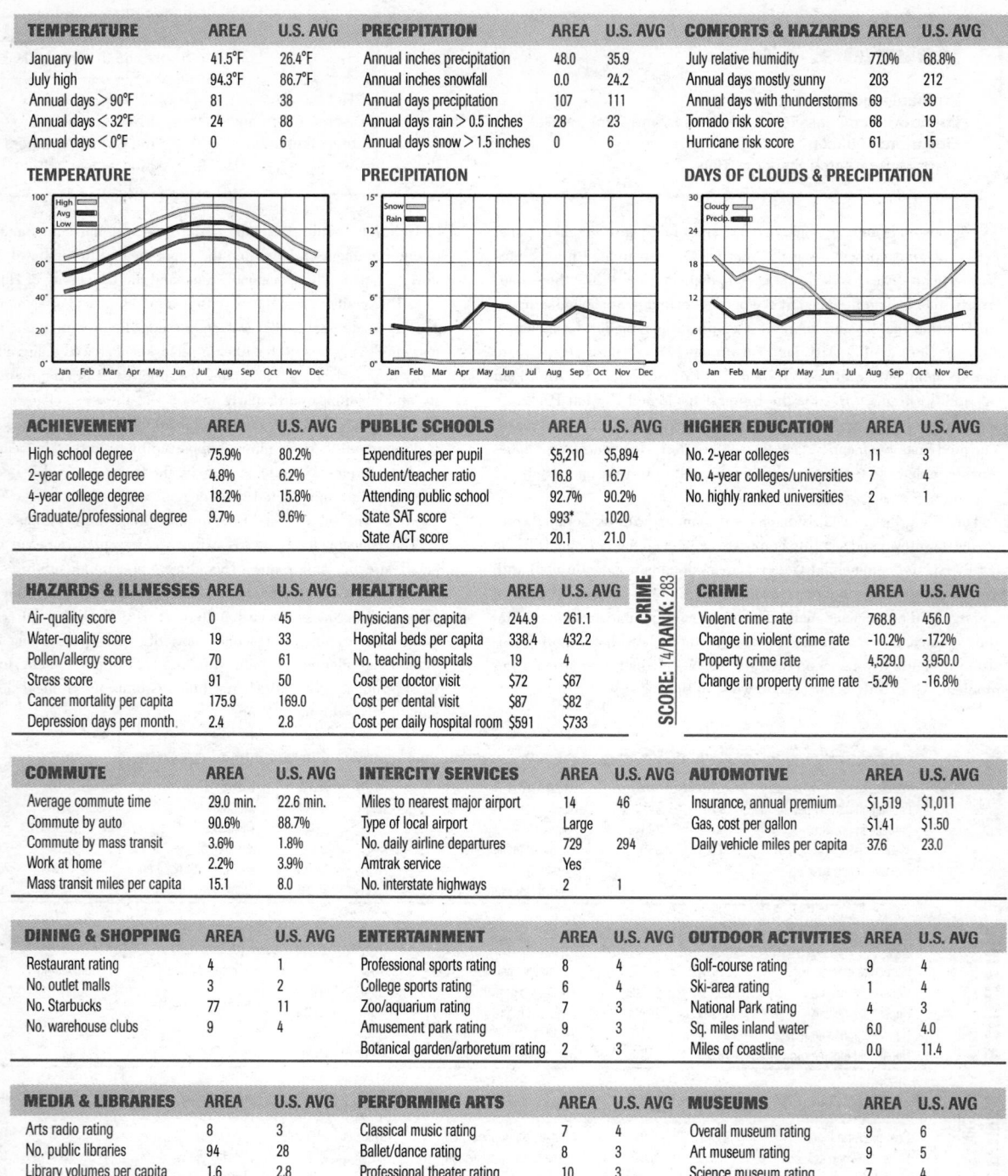

CLIMATE SCORE: 56/RANK: 145

TEMPERATURE	AREA	U.S. AVG	PRECIPITATION	AREA	U.S. AVG	COMFORTS & HAZARDS	AREA	U.S. AVG
January low	41.5°F	26.4°F	Annual inches precipitation	48.0	35.9	July relative humidity	77.0%	68.8%
July high	94.3°F	86.7°F	Annual inches snowfall	0.0	24.2	Annual days mostly sunny	203	212
Annual days > 90°F	81	38	Annual days precipitation	107	111	Annual days with thunderstorms	69	39
Annual days < 32°F	24	88	Annual days rain > 0.5 inches	28	23	Tornado risk score	68	19
Annual days < 0°F	0	6	Annual days snow > 1.5 inches	0	6	Hurricane risk score	61	15

TEMPERATURE

PRECIPITATION

DAYS OF CLOUDS & PRECIPITATION

EDUCATION SCORE: 65/RANK: 116

ACHIEVEMENT	AREA	U.S. AVG	PUBLIC SCHOOLS	AREA	U.S. AVG	HIGHER EDUCATION	AREA	U.S. AVG
High school degree	75.9%	80.2%	Expenditures per pupil	$5,210	$5,894	No. 2-year colleges	11	3
2-year college degree	4.8%	6.2%	Student/teacher ratio	16.8	16.7	No. 4-year colleges/universities	7	4
4-year college degree	18.2%	15.8%	Attending public school	92.7%	90.2%	No. highly ranked universities	2	1
Graduate/professional degree	9.7%	9.6%	State SAT score	993*	1020			
			State ACT score	20.1	21.0			

HEALTH & HEALTHCARE SCORE: 0/RANK: 328

CRIME SCORE: 14/RANK: 283

HAZARDS & ILLNESSES	AREA	U.S. AVG	HEALTHCARE	AREA	U.S. AVG	CRIME	AREA	U.S. AVG
Air-quality score	0	45	Physicians per capita	244.9	261.1	Violent crime rate	768.8	456.0
Water-quality score	19	33	Hospital beds per capita	338.4	432.2	Change in violent crime rate	-10.2%	-17.2%
Pollen/allergy score	70	61	No. teaching hospitals	19	4	Property crime rate	4,529.0	3,950.0
Stress score	91	50	Cost per doctor visit	$72	$67	Change in property crime rate	-5.2%	-16.8%
Cancer mortality per capita	175.9	169.0	Cost per dental visit	$87	$82			
Depression days per month	2.4	2.8	Cost per daily hospital room	$591	$733			

TRANSPORTATION SCORE: 61/RANK: 127

COMMUTE	AREA	U.S. AVG	INTERCITY SERVICES	AREA	U.S. AVG	AUTOMOTIVE	AREA	U.S. AVG
Average commute time	29.0 min.	22.6 min.	Miles to nearest major airport	14	46	Insurance, annual premium	$1,519	$1,011
Commute by auto	90.6%	88.7%	Type of local airport	Large		Gas, cost per gallon	$1.41	$1.50
Commute by mass transit	3.6%	1.8%	No. daily airline departures	729	294	Daily vehicle miles per capita	37.6	23.0
Work at home	2.2%	3.9%	Amtrak service	Yes				
Mass transit miles per capita	15.1	8.0	No. interstate highways	2	1			

LEISURE SCORE: 89/RANK: 34

DINING & SHOPPING	AREA	U.S. AVG	ENTERTAINMENT	AREA	U.S. AVG	OUTDOOR ACTIVITIES	AREA	U.S. AVG
Restaurant rating	4	1	Professional sports rating	8	4	Golf-course rating	9	4
No. outlet malls	3	2	College sports rating	6	4	Ski-area rating	1	4
No. Starbucks	77	11	Zoo/aquarium rating	7	3	National Park rating	4	3
No. warehouse clubs	9	4	Amusement park rating	9	3	Sq. miles inland water	6.0	4.0
			Botanical garden/arboretum rating	2	3	Miles of coastline	0.0	11.4

ARTS & CULTURE SCORE: 93/RANK: 25

MEDIA & LIBRARIES	AREA	U.S. AVG	PERFORMING ARTS	AREA	U.S. AVG	MUSEUMS	AREA	U.S. AVG
Arts radio rating	8	3	Classical music rating	7	4	Overall museum rating	9	6
No. public libraries	94	28	Ballet/dance rating	8	3	Art museum rating	9	5
Library volumes per capita	1.6	2.8	Professional theater rating	10	3	Science museum rating	7	4
			University arts programs rating	9	5	Children's museum rating	8	3

Huntington-Ashland, WV-KY-OH

Score: 49.9 **Rank:** 228

Profile: Small cities
Location: Extreme western West Virginia along the Ohio River
Elevation: 565 feet
Time zone: Eastern Standard Time

PRO	CON
Cost of living	Heavy industry
Small-town atmosphere	Entertainment
Revitalizing downtown	Isolation

Industrial Huntington, located along the Ohio River, is a transport center for traffic between Ohio, the Great Lakes, Kentucky, and points east of the Appalachians. The diverse, industrial base includes chemicals, metal products, and glass and glass products manufacturing. The smaller Ashland, across the river, plays a similar role. The area has a low Cost of Living Index at 81.2 and a low crime rate, and is cleaning up with a new 8-acre revitalization project slated for downtown. Today's ranking is fairly low, but the area may be a good bet for the future for those looking for a small-town climate.

Huntington is at the confluence of the Ohio and Big Sandy rivers across from the southern tip of Ohio. The city is located in a flat valley, with rounded, wooded Appalachian foothills rising on all sides. Summers are moderately warm and humid with valley locations considerably warmer and more humid than the hilltops. Winter months are moderately cold, with an occasional severe cold wave lasting a few days. The four seasons are nearly equal in length and autumn is the most pleasant. The heaviest rainfall occurs in July and August mostly as thunderstorms, and flash floods are common. Winter rainfall occurs mostly with a frontal passage and frequently lasts from 2 to 4 days, possibly causing stream flooding. Snow seldom remains more than 2 days in the valleys, but can linger on hilltops.

POPULATION

DEMOGRAPHICS	AREA	U.S. AVG	ETHNIC COMPOSITION	AREA	U.S. AVG	RESIDENT PROFILE	AREA	U.S. AVG
Population	313,239		White	97.9%	75.1%	Single	40.5%	43.6%
Population density per sq. mile	145.0	447.3	Black	1.5%	12.3%	Married	59.5%	56.4%
Population growth	.2%	16.1%	Asian	.3%	3.6%	Divorced	7.9%	8.4%
Median age	38.6	35.5	American Indian	.2%	.9%	Separated	2.0%	3.0%
Average family size	2.6	2.7	Hispanic	.3%	12.5%	Married with children	30.7%	28.7%
			Diversity measure	8.3%	35.2%	Single with children	9.2%	10.1%

ECONOMY & JOBS — SCORE: 48/RANK: 172

INCOME	AREA	U.S. AVG	EMPLOYMENT	AREA	U.S. AVG	LARGEST EMPLOYING INDUSTRY
Per capita income	$17,397	$23,420	Unemployment rate	6.3%	6.1%	Healthcare and Social Assistance
Household income	$29,981	$46,060	Recent job growth	2.0%	.9%	
Household income < $25K	42.9%	26.4%	Projected future job growth	12.4%	15.1%	
Household income > $75K	11.9%	24.5%	White collar	49.3%	54.5%	
Household income growth	42.2%	57.3%	Blue collar	50.7%	45.5%	

COST OF LIVING — SCORE: 74/RANK: 84

INDEXES & TAXES	AREA	U.S. AVG	HOUSING	AREA	U.S. AVG	NECESSITIES	AREA	U.S. AVG
Cost of Living Index	81.2	100.0	Median home price	$83,670	$160,100	Food Index	104.2	100.0
Financial Progress Index	78.7	100.0	Home price appreciation	5.8%	7.1%	Housing Index	52.0	100.0
Income tax rate	6.000%	4.625%	Median rent	$472	$670	Utilities Index	78.4	100.0
Sales tax rate	6.000%	6.474%	Homes owned	69.3%	63.9%	Transportation Index	101.2	100.0
Property tax rate	$10.1	$15.6	Homes rented	21.1%	25.3%	Healthcare Index	93.2	100.0
			Housing affordability	51.0%	54.5%	Miscellaneous Cost Index	99.0	100.0

CLIMATE — SCORE: 79/RANK: 70

TEMPERATURE	AREA	U.S. AVG	PRECIPITATION	AREA	U.S. AVG	COMFORTS & HAZARDS	AREA	U.S. AVG
January low	25.6°F	26.4°F	Annual inches precipitation	38.9	35.9	July relative humidity	71.0%	68.8%
July high	85.7°F	86.7°F	Annual inches snowfall	25.6	24.2	Annual days mostly sunny	166	212
Annual days > 90°F	17	38	Annual days precipitation	139	111	Annual days with thunderstorms	44	39
Annual days < 32°F	23	88	Annual days rain > 0.5 inches	27	23	Tornado risk score	9	19
Annual days < 0°F	2	6	Annual days snow > 1.5 inches	7	6	Hurricane risk score	5	15

TEMPERATURE

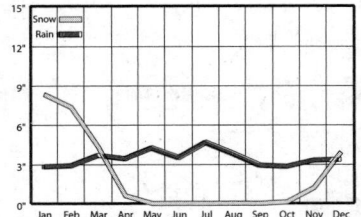

PRECIPITATION

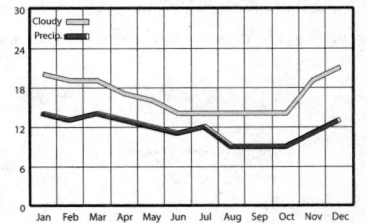

DAYS OF CLOUDS & PRECIPITATION

EDUCATION SCORE: 19/RANK: 267

ACHIEVEMENT	AREA	U.S. AVG	PUBLIC SCHOOLS	AREA	U.S. AVG	HIGHER EDUCATION	AREA	U.S. AVG
High school degree	75.6%	80.2%	Expenditures per pupil	$5,880	$5,894	No. 2-year colleges	2	3
2-year college degree	4.7%	6.2%	Student/teacher ratio	16.5	16.7	No. 4-year colleges/universities	3	4
4-year college degree	8.4%	15.8%	Attending public school	96.2%	90.2%	No. highly ranked universities	0	1
Graduate/professional degree	6.0%	9.6%	State SAT score	1032	1020			
			State ACT score	20.3*	21.0			

HEALTH & HEALTHCARE SCORE: 83/RANK: 56

CRIME SCORE: 44/RANK: 184

HAZARDS & ILLNESSES	AREA	U.S. AVG	HEALTHCARE	AREA	U.S. AVG	CRIME	AREA	U.S. AVG
Air-quality score	59	45	Physicians per capita	273.0	261.1	Violent crime rate	289.0	456.0
Water-quality score	24	33	Hospital beds per capita	603.4	432.2	Change in violent crime rate	36.9%	-17.2%
Pollen/allergy score	60	61	No. teaching hospitals	2	4	Property crime rate	3,147.9	3,950.0
Stress score	59	50	Cost per doctor visit	$68	$67	Change in property crime rate	5.1%	-16.8%
Cancer mortality per capita	176.2	169.0	Cost per dental visit	$70	$82			
Depression days per month	4.5	2.8	Cost per daily hospital room	$568	$733			

TRANSPORTATION SCORE: 9/RANK: 301

COMMUTE	AREA	U.S. AVG	INTERCITY SERVICES	AREA	U.S. AVG	AUTOMOTIVE	AREA	U.S. AVG
Average commute time	24.2 min.	22.6 min.	Miles to nearest major airport	112	46	Insurance, annual premium	$943	$1,011
Commute by auto	91.9%	88.7%	Type of local airport	Medium		Gas, cost per gallon	$1.49	$1.50
Commute by mass transit	.6%	1.8%	No. daily airline departures	270	294	Daily vehicle miles per capita	22.5	23.0
Work at home	2.1%	3.9%	Amtrak service	Yes				
Mass transit miles per capita	3.1	8.0	No. interstate highways	1	1			

LEISURE SCORE: 19/RANK: 266

DINING & SHOPPING	AREA	U.S. AVG	ENTERTAINMENT	AREA	U.S. AVG	OUTDOOR ACTIVITIES	AREA	U.S. AVG
Restaurant rating	1	1	Professional sports rating	2	4	Golf-course rating	3	4
No. outlet malls	0	2	College sports rating	3	4	Ski-area rating	1	4
No. Starbucks	0	11	Zoo/aquarium rating	1	3	National Park rating	1	3
No. warehouse clubs	3	4	Amusement park rating	1	3	Sq. miles inland water	3.0	4.0
			Botanical garden/arboretum rating	3	3	Miles of coastline	0.0	11.4

ARTS & CULTURE SCORE: 88/RANK: 38

MEDIA & LIBRARIES	AREA	U.S. AVG	PERFORMING ARTS	AREA	U.S. AVG	MUSEUMS	AREA	U.S. AVG
Arts radio rating	1	3	Classical music rating	4	4	Overall museum rating	4	6
No. public libraries	22	28	Ballet/dance rating	1	3	Art museum rating	3	5
Library volumes per capita	2.7	2.8	Professional theater rating	1	3	Science museum rating	4	4
			University arts programs rating	4	5	Children's museum rating	3	3

Huntsville, AL

Score: 50.4   Rank: 226

Profile: Mid-size city
Location: Extreme northern Alabama, 15 miles south of Tennessee border
Elevation: 644 feet
Time zone: Central Standard Time

PRO	CON
Growing industry	Entertainment
Low unemployment	Arts and culture
Educated population	Hot, humid summers

Huntsville is an emerging technology and manufacturing center known most for its George C. Marshall Space Flight Center. Both space research and computer and electronics manufacturing have created a stable economy that attracts a well-educated workforce. Its high education attainments are among the best in the state outside of college towns. Other figures are unremarkable on a national or state scale.

Surrounded by Appalachian foothills and 1,200-foot to 1,400-foot mountains, Huntsville is about 7 miles north of the Tennessee River Valley. The climate is humid subtropical with a continental influence mainly in winter. Summers are warm, still, and humid with thunderstorms every 1 in 3 days. Winters are cool with cold snaps alternating with warmer moist periods and occasional snow.

POPULATION

DEMOGRAPHICS	AREA	U.S. AVG	ETHNIC COMPOSITION	AREA	U.S. AVG	RESIDENT PROFILE	AREA	U.S. AVG
Population	353,742		White	79.2%	75.1%	Single	40.1%	43.6%
Population density per sq. mile	257.6	447.3	Black	17.9%	12.3%	Married	59.9%	56.4%
Population growth	20.7%	16.1%	Asian	1.8%	3.6%	Divorced	8.6%	8.4%
Median age	36.0	35.5	American Indian	.7%	.9%	Separated	2.2%	3.0%
Average family size	2.6	2.7	Hispanic	1.4%	12.5%	Married with children	31.3%	28.7%
			Diversity measure	41.5%	35.2%	Single with children	9.0%	10.1%

ECONOMY & JOBS — SCORE: 86/RANK: 42

INCOME	AREA	U.S. AVG	EMPLOYMENT	AREA	U.S. AVG	LARGEST EMPLOYING INDUSTRY
Per capita income	$25,224	$23,420	Unemployment rate	4.6%	6.1%	Computer and Electronic Product Manufacturing
Household income	$49,596	$46,060	Recent job growth	-.9%	.9%	
Household income < $25K	24.0%	26.4%	Projected future job growth	14.6%	15.1%	
Household income > $75K	28.3%	24.5%	White collar	61.8%	54.5%	
Household income growth	55.0%	57.3%	Blue collar	38.2%	45.5%	

COST OF LIVING — SCORE: 58/RANK: 137

INDEXES & TAXES	AREA	U.S. AVG	HOUSING	AREA	U.S. AVG	NECESSITIES	AREA	U.S. AVG
Cost of Living Index	87.1	100.0	Median home price	$113,150	$160,100	Food Index	98.8	100.0
Financial Progress Index	121.4	100.0	Home price appreciation	4.4%	7.1%	Housing Index	70.3	100.0
Income tax rate	5.000%	4.625%	Median rent	$561	$670	Utilities Index	80.1	100.0
Sales tax rate	8.000%	6.474%	Homes owned	67.0%	63.9%	Transportation Index	99.3	100.0
Property tax rate	$4.9	$15.6	Homes rented	27.4%	25.3%	Healthcare Index	91.1	100.0
			Housing affordability	59.0%	54.5%	Miscellaneous Cost Index	100.7	100.0

CLIMATE — SCORE: 20/RANK: 264

TEMPERATURE	AREA	U.S. AVG	PRECIPITATION	AREA	U.S. AVG	COMFORTS & HAZARDS	AREA	U.S. AVG
January low	31.3°F	26.4°F	Annual inches precipitation	52.0	35.9	July relative humidity	73.0%	68.8%
July high	90.2°F	86.7°F	Annual inches snowfall	3.0	24.2	Annual days mostly sunny	207	212
Annual days > 90°F	38	38	Annual days precipitation	121	111	Annual days with thunderstorms	58	39
Annual days < 32°F	65	88	Annual days rain > 0.5 inches	40	23	Tornado risk score	61	19
Annual days < 0°F	0	6	Annual days snow > 1.5 inches	2	6	Hurricane risk score	12	15

TEMPERATURE

PRECIPITATION

DAYS OF CLOUDS & PRECIPITATION

EDUCATION — SCORE: 70/RANK: 99

ACHIEVEMENT	AREA	U.S. AVG	PUBLIC SCHOOLS	AREA	U.S. AVG	HIGHER EDUCATION	AREA	U.S. AVG
High school degree	83.3%	80.2%	Expenditures per pupil	$5,171	$5,894	No. 2-year colleges	1	3
2-year college degree	5.9%	6.2%	Student/teacher ratio	15.9	16.7	No. 4-year colleges/universities	3	4
4-year college degree	20.6%	15.8%	Attending public school	89.9%	90.2%	No. highly ranked universities	1	1
Graduate/professional degree	10.3%	9.6%	State SAT score	1111	1020			
			State ACT score	20.1*	21.0			

HEALTH & HEALTHCARE — SCORE: 42/RANK: 190 | CRIME — SCORE: 44/RANK: 185

HAZARDS & ILLNESSES	AREA	U.S. AVG	HEALTHCARE	AREA	U.S. AVG	CRIME	AREA	U.S. AVG
Air-quality score	59	45	Physicians per capita	255.0	261.1	Violent crime rate	395.4	456.0
Water-quality score	63	33	Hospital beds per capita	321.3	432.2	Change in violent crime rate	-23.9%	-17.2%
Pollen/allergy score	67	61	No. teaching hospitals	1	4	Property crime rate	4,120.1	3,950.0
Stress score	36	50	Cost per doctor visit	$57	$67	Change in property crime rate	-12.1%	-16.8%
Cancer mortality per capita	162.0	169.0	Cost per dental visit	$72	$82			
Depression days per month	3.7	2.8	Cost per daily hospital room	$605	$733			

TRANSPORTATION — SCORE: 28/RANK: 236

COMMUTE	AREA	U.S. AVG	INTERCITY SERVICES	AREA	U.S. AVG	AUTOMOTIVE	AREA	U.S. AVG
Average commute time	21.9 min.	22.6 min.	Miles to nearest major airport	9	46	Insurance, annual premium	$823	$1,011
Commute by auto	95.3%	88.7%	Type of local airport	Small		Gas, cost per gallon	$1.47	$1.50
Commute by mass transit	.2%	1.8%	No. daily airline departures	41	294	Daily vehicle miles per capita	25.9	23.0
Work at home	1.8%	3.9%	Amtrak service	No				
Mass transit miles per capita	3.0	8.0	No. interstate highways	0	1			

LEISURE — SCORE: 10/RANK: 297

DINING & SHOPPING	AREA	U.S. AVG	ENTERTAINMENT	AREA	U.S. AVG	OUTDOOR ACTIVITIES	AREA	U.S. AVG
Restaurant rating	1	1	Professional sports rating	2	4	Golf-course rating	2	4
No. outlet malls	1	2	College sports rating	3	4	Ski-area rating	1	4
No. Starbucks	0	11	Zoo/aquarium rating	1	3	National Park rating	2	3
No. warehouse clubs	3	4	Amusement park rating	2	3	Sq. miles inland water	2.0	4.0
			Botanical garden/arboretum rating	1	3	Miles of coastline	0.0	11.4

MEDIA & LIBRARIES	AREA	U.S. AVG	PERFORMING ARTS	AREA	U.S. AVG	MUSEUMS	AREA	U.S. AVG
Arts radio rating	1	3	Classical music rating	3	4	Overall museum rating	5	6
No. public libraries	16	28	Ballet/dance rating	1	3	Art museum rating	6	5
Library volumes per capita	1.6	2.8	Professional theater rating	1	3	Science museum rating	5	4
			University arts programs rating	3	5	Children's museum rating	1	3

Indianapolis, IN

Score: 69.6   Rank: 79

Profile: Capital city
Location: Geographic center of Indiana
Elevation: 808 feet
Time zone: Eastern Standard Time (no daylight savings time)

PRO	CON
Revitalized downtown	Employment declines
Sports and recreation	Violent crime
Arts and culture	Urban sprawl

Indianapolis, once a poster child for blighted cities, is now a showcase for publicly coordinated and funded urban renewal. The city features a city/county government system, which has worked well for coordinated public efforts. Cost of living is reasonable for this type of city, and its downtown boasts attractive new buildings, pedestrian zones, and a state-of-the-art sports arena. The area has a diverse industrial base of high-tech and agricultural industries, and serves as headquarters to pharmaceutical and research giant Eli Lilly. Spectator sports are a big draw. The venerable Indianapolis Motor Speedway hosts the Indianapolis 500, the Brickyard 400, and other events. Pro and college sports—particularly basketball—also get a lot of attention. The city has NBA, NFL, and minor-league hockey franchises. The NCAA Hall of Fame is located downtown, and the city hosts portions of the NCAA basketball tournament each year. "Indy" also boasts a well-rounded arts and culture scene and the educational opportunities of the nearby Indiana-Purdue joint campus.

Access and transportation around the city are aided by a grid with radiating spokes and a circular beltway. Residential neighborhoods spread out in all directions, with the fashionable and attractive Carmel and Noblesville residential communities to the north. Less desirable developments, characterized by sprawl and traffic problems, are to the northeast. Sections immediately south are more commercial and industrial, while areas farther to the south contain recreational opportunities in the wooded and hilly town of Nashville and Brown County State Park.

The climate is continental with warm, humid summers, but without a dry season and little extreme heat. Precipitation is evenly distributed throughout the year, and winters are cold and variable with intermittent rain and snow. Snowfalls of 3 inches or more occur on average of two to three times each winter. First freeze is mid- to late October, last is late April.

DEMOGRAPHICS	AREA	U.S. AVG	ETHNIC COMPOSITION	AREA	U.S. AVG	RESIDENT PROFILE	AREA	U.S. AVG
Population	1,655,097		White	89.7%	75.1%	Single	41.6%	43.6%
Population density per sq. mile	469.8	447.3	Black	8.9%	12.3%	Married	58.4%	56.4%
Population growth	19.9%	16.1%	Asian	1.0%	3.6%	Divorced	10.0%	8.4%
Median age	34.9	35.5	American Indian	.2%	.9%	Separated	2.0%	3.0%
Average family size	2.6	2.7	Hispanic	1.2%	12.5%	Married with children	30.0%	28.7%
			Diversity measure	32.2%	35.2%	Single with children	10.0%	10.1%

INCOME	AREA	U.S. AVG	EMPLOYMENT	AREA	U.S. AVG	LARGEST EMPLOYING INDUSTRY
Per capita income	$27,330	$23,420	Unemployment rate	4.8%	6.1%	Transportation Equipment Manufacturing
Household income	$52,554	$46,060	Recent job growth	.0%	.9%	
Household income < $25K	20.0%	26.4%	Projected future job growth	15.6%	15.1%	
Household income > $75K	31.0%	24.5%	White collar	59.0%	54.5%	
Household income growth	67.5%	57.3%	Blue collar	41.0%	45.5%	

INDEXES & TAXES	AREA	U.S. AVG	HOUSING	AREA	U.S. AVG	NECESSITIES	AREA	U.S. AVG
Cost of Living Index	87.3	100.0	Median home price	$116,300	$160,100	Food Index	95.9	100.0
Financial Progress Index	128.3	100.0	Home price appreciation	4.7%	7.1%	Housing Index	72.2	100.0
Income tax rate	4.100%	4.625%	Median rent	$592	$670	Utilities Index	96.5	100.0
Sales tax rate	6.000%	6.474%	Homes owned	69.9%	63.9%	Transportation Index	96.2	100.0
Property tax rate	$14.1	$15.6	Homes rented	23.5%	25.3%	Healthcare Index	98.9	100.0
			Housing affordability	63.0%	54.5%	Miscellaneous Cost Index	94.4	100.0

CLIMATE — SCORE: 49/RANK: 168

TEMPERATURE	AREA	U.S. AVG	PRECIPITATION	AREA	U.S. AVG	COMFORTS & HAZARDS	AREA	U.S. AVG
January low	19.7°F	26.4°F	Annual inches precipitation	39.0	35.9	July relative humidity	73.0%	68.8%
July high	85.4°F	86.7°F	Annual inches snowfall	21.0	24.2	Annual days mostly sunny	191	212
Annual days > 90°F	15	38	Annual days precipitation	122	111	Annual days with thunderstorms	45	39
Annual days < 32°F	122	88	Annual days rain > 0.5 inches	27	23	Tornado risk score	33	19
Annual days < 0°F	7	6	Annual days snow > 1.5 inches	6	6	Hurricane risk score	4	15

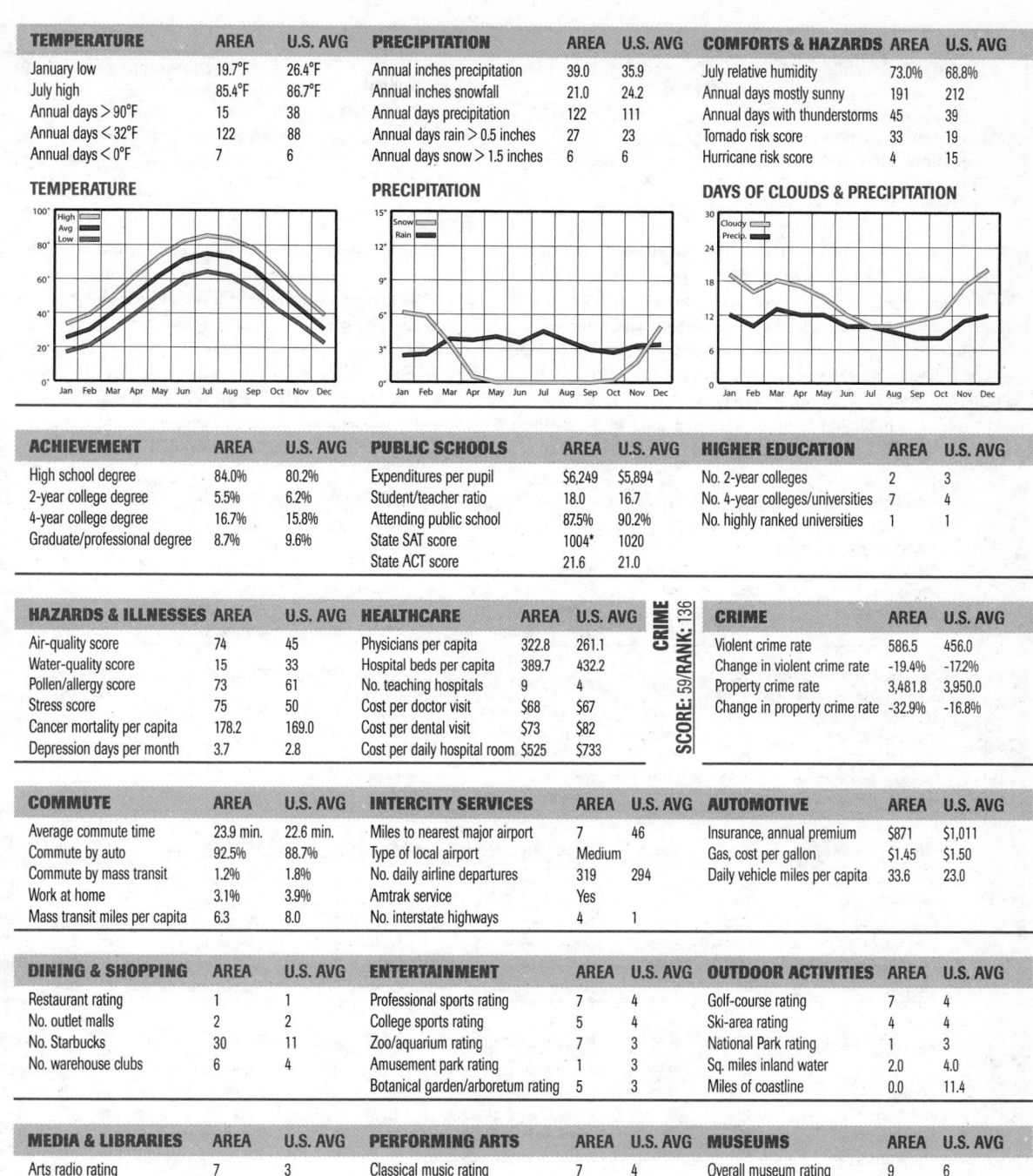

TEMPERATURE — High / Avg / Low

PRECIPITATION — Snow / Rain

DAYS OF CLOUDS & PRECIPITATION — Cloudy / Precip.

EDUCATION — SCORE: 50/RANK: 163

ACHIEVEMENT	AREA	U.S. AVG	PUBLIC SCHOOLS	AREA	U.S. AVG	HIGHER EDUCATION	AREA	U.S. AVG
High school degree	84.0%	80.2%	Expenditures per pupil	$6,249	$5,894	No. 2-year colleges	2	3
2-year college degree	5.5%	6.2%	Student/teacher ratio	18.0	16.7	No. 4-year colleges/universities	7	4
4-year college degree	16.7%	15.8%	Attending public school	87.5%	90.2%	No. highly ranked universities	1	1
Graduate/professional degree	8.7%	9.6%	State SAT score	1004*	1020			
			State ACT score	21.6	21.0			

HEALTH & HEALTHCARE — SCORE: 12/RANK: 289   CRIME — SCORE: 59/RANK: 136

HAZARDS & ILLNESSES	AREA	U.S. AVG	HEALTHCARE	AREA	U.S. AVG	CRIME	AREA	U.S. AVG
Air-quality score	74	45	Physicians per capita	322.8	261.1	Violent crime rate	586.5	456.0
Water-quality score	15	33	Hospital beds per capita	389.7	432.2	Change in violent crime rate	-19.4%	-17.2%
Pollen/allergy score	73	61	No. teaching hospitals	9	4	Property crime rate	3,481.8	3,950.0
Stress score	75	50	Cost per doctor visit	$68	$67	Change in property crime rate	-32.9%	-16.8%
Cancer mortality per capita	178.2	169.0	Cost per dental visit	$73	$82			
Depression days per month	3.7	2.8	Cost per daily hospital room	$525	$733			

TRANSPORTATION — SCORE: 41/RANK: 190

COMMUTE	AREA	U.S. AVG	INTERCITY SERVICES	AREA	U.S. AVG	AUTOMOTIVE	AREA	U.S. AVG
Average commute time	23.9 min.	22.6 min.	Miles to nearest major airport	7	46	Insurance, annual premium	$871	$1,011
Commute by auto	92.5%	88.7%	Type of local airport	Medium		Gas, cost per gallon	$1.45	$1.50
Commute by mass transit	1.2%	1.8%	No. daily airline departures	319	294	Daily vehicle miles per capita	33.6	23.0
Work at home	3.1%	3.9%	Amtrak service	Yes				
Mass transit miles per capita	6.3	8.0	No. interstate highways	4	1			

LEISURE — SCORE: 75/RANK: 82

DINING & SHOPPING	AREA	U.S. AVG	ENTERTAINMENT	AREA	U.S. AVG	OUTDOOR ACTIVITIES	AREA	U.S. AVG
Restaurant rating	1	1	Professional sports rating	7	4	Golf-course rating	7	4
No. outlet malls	2	2	College sports rating	5	4	Ski-area rating	4	4
No. Starbucks	30	11	Zoo/aquarium rating	7	3	National Park rating	1	3
No. warehouse clubs	6	4	Amusement park rating	1	3	Sq. miles inland water	2.0	4.0
			Botanical garden/arboretum rating	5	3	Miles of coastline	0.0	11.4

ARTS & CULTURE — SCORE: 88/RANK: 42

MEDIA & LIBRARIES	AREA	U.S. AVG	PERFORMING ARTS	AREA	U.S. AVG	MUSEUMS	AREA	U.S. AVG
Arts radio rating	7	3	Classical music rating	7	4	Overall museum rating	9	6
No. public libraries	69	28	Ballet/dance rating	6	3	Art museum rating	9	5
Library volumes per capita	3.5	2.8	Professional theater rating	8	3	Science museum rating	8	4
			University arts programs rating	8	5	Children's museum rating	10	3

Iowa City, IA

Score: 54.8   Rank: 191

Profile: College town
Location: Eastern Iowa along I-80
Elevation: 708 feet
Time zone: Central Standard Time

PRO	CON
College-town amenities	Harsh winters
Attractive downtown	Cost of living
Educated population	Outdoor recreation

Once the capital of the state, Iowa City is both home of the University of Iowa and a livable city boasting a diverse cultural environment, attractive tree-lined streets, historic campus buildings, and an assortment of shops, restaurants, and entertainment venues in a lively downtown and riverfront setting. True to a college-town norm, the area has the highest housing costs in the state and one of the highest levels of educational attainment in the country. Although the area is isolated from big-city services (110 miles away in Des Moines),

the overall rating understates the manner in which college-related arts and cultural amenities improve the quality of life.

A scenic mix of flat river valleys and wooded undulating hills dominate the landscape. The climate is continental. Summers are warm and humid, punctuated by frequent thunderstorms, although nearby hills may lessen the severity. Winters are cold and variable, although the hills again shelter the area from some northern fronts. That said, below-zero evening temperatures are fairly common, and blizzards do occur. First freeze is mid-October, last is late April.

POPULATION

DEMOGRAPHICS	AREA	U.S. AVG	ETHNIC COMPOSITION	AREA	U.S. AVG	RESIDENT PROFILE	AREA	U.S. AVG
Population	114,300		White	94.6%	75.1%	Single	45.8%	43.6%
Population density per sq. mile	186.0	447.3	Black	1.4%	12.3%	Married	54.2%	56.4%
Population growth	18.9%	16.1%	Asian	3.6%	3.6%	Divorced	6.9%	8.4%
Median age	28.6	35.5	American Indian	.1%	.9%	Separated	1.2%	3.0%
Average family size	2.5	2.7	Hispanic	1.9%	12.5%	Married with children	28.7%	28.7%
			Diversity measure	20.4%	35.2%	Single with children	6.4%	10.1%

ECONOMY & JOBS   SCORE: 45/RANK: 180

INCOME	AREA	U.S. AVG	EMPLOYMENT	AREA	U.S. AVG	LARGEST EMPLOYING INDUSTRY
Per capita income	$27,299	$23,420	Unemployment rate	3.6%	6.1%	Healthcare and Social Assistance
Household income	$48,432	$46,060	Recent job growth	-4.4%	.9%	
Household income < $25K	25.2%	26.4%	Projected future job growth	16.8%	15.1%	
Household income > $75K	29.2%	24.5%	White collar	64.4%	54.5%	
Household income growth	73.6%	57.3%	Blue collar	35.6%	45.5%	

COST OF LIVING   SCORE: 22/RANK: 257

INDEXES & TAXES	AREA	U.S. AVG	HOUSING	AREA	U.S. AVG	NECESSITIES	AREA	U.S. AVG
Cost of Living Index	97.7	100.0	Median home price	$150,860	$160,100	Food Index	89.8	100.0
Financial Progress Index	105.7	100.0	Home price appreciation	4.7%	7.1%	Housing Index	93.7	100.0
Income tax rate	7.920%	4.625%	Median rent	$615	$670	Utilities Index	135.2	100.0
Sales tax rate	5.000%	6.474%	Homes owned	65.9%	63.9%	Transportation Index	97.7	100.0
Property tax rate	$20.6	$15.6	Homes rented	30.2%	25.3%	Healthcare Index	90.4	100.0
			Housing affordability	52.0%	54.5%	Miscellaneous Cost Index	98.5	100.0

CLIMATE   SCORE: 26/RANK: 242

TEMPERATURE	AREA	U.S. AVG	PRECIPITATION	AREA	U.S. AVG	COMFORTS & HAZARDS	AREA	U.S. AVG
January low	5.0°F	26.4°F	Annual inches precipitation	34.0	35.9	July relative humidity	73.0%	68.8%
July high	84.0°F	86.7°F	Annual inches snowfall	32.0	24.2	Annual days mostly sunny	194	212
Annual days > 90°F	16	38	Annual days precipitation	107	111	Annual days with thunderstorms	41	39
Annual days < 32°F	157	88	Annual days rain > 0.5 inches	24	23	Tornado risk score	22	19
Annual days < 0°F	29	6	Annual days snow > 1.5 inches	9	6	Hurricane risk score	0	15

TEMPERATURE

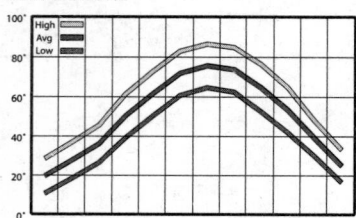

PRECIPITATION

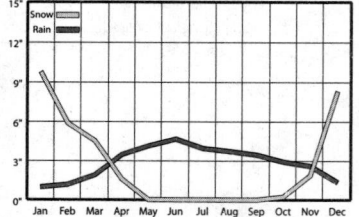

DAYS OF CLOUDS & PRECIPITATION

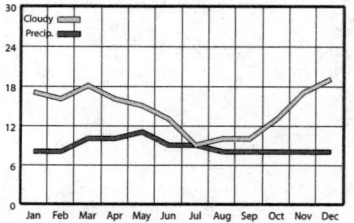

EDUCATION SCORE: 98/RANK: 7

ACHIEVEMENT	AREA	U.S. AVG	PUBLIC SCHOOLS	AREA	U.S. AVG	HIGHER EDUCATION	AREA	U.S. AVG
High school degree	94.8%	80.2%	Expenditures per pupil	$5,599	$5,894	No. 2-year colleges	0	3
2-year college degree	5.8%	6.2%	Student/teacher ratio	17.2	16.7	No. 4-year colleges/universities	1	4
4-year college degree	26.2%	15.8%	Attending public school	89.5%	90.2%	No. highly ranked universities	1	1
Graduate/professional degree	21.4%	9.6%	State SAT score	1183	1020			
			State ACT score	22.0*	21.0			

HEALTH & HEALTHCARE SCORE: 99/RANK: 3

HAZARDS & ILLNESSES	AREA	U.S. AVG	HEALTHCARE	AREA	U.S. AVG
Air-quality score	24	45	Physicians per capita	1096.2	261.1
Water-quality score	30	33	Hospital beds per capita	895.4	432.2
Pollen/allergy score	46	61	No. teaching hospitals	2	4
Stress score	18	50	Cost per doctor visit	$61	$67
Cancer mortality per capita	156.7	169.0	Cost per dental visit	$72	$82
Depression days per month	2.8	2.8	Cost per daily hospital room	$483	$733

CRIME SCORE: 76/RANK: 79

CRIME	AREA	U.S. AVG
Violent crime rate	389.6	456.0
Change in violent crime rate	14.1%	-17.2%
Property crime rate	2,522.4	3,950.0
Change in property crime rate	-26.6%	-16.8%

TRANSPORTATION SCORE: 89/RANK: 34

COMMUTE	AREA	U.S. AVG	INTERCITY SERVICES	AREA	U.S. AVG	AUTOMOTIVE	AREA	U.S. AVG
Average commute time	17.7 min.	22.6 min.	Miles to nearest major airport	18	46	Insurance, annual premium	$656	$1,011
Commute by auto	81.5%	88.7%	Type of local airport	Small		Gas, cost per gallon	$1.47	$1.50
Commute by mass transit	4.0%	1.8%	No. daily airline departures	58	294	Daily vehicle miles per capita	15.4	23.0
Work at home	6.1%	3.9%	Amtrak service	No				
Mass transit miles per capita	13.8	8.0	No. interstate highways	1	1			

LEISURE SCORE: 7/RANK: 307

DINING & SHOPPING	AREA	U.S. AVG	ENTERTAINMENT	AREA	U.S. AVG	OUTDOOR ACTIVITIES	AREA	U.S. AVG
Restaurant rating	1	1	Professional sports rating	2	4	Golf-course rating	2	4
No. outlet malls	1	2	College sports rating	6	4	Ski-area rating	1	4
No. Starbucks	0	11	Zoo/aquarium rating	1	3	National Park rating	1	3
No. warehouse clubs	1	4	Amusement park rating	1	3	Sq. miles inland water	2.0	4.0
			Botanical garden/arboretum rating	1	3	Miles of coastline	0.0	11.4

ARTS & CULTURE SCORE: 7/RANK: 304

MEDIA & LIBRARIES	AREA	U.S. AVG	PERFORMING ARTS	AREA	U.S. AVG	MUSEUMS	AREA	U.S. AVG
Arts radio rating	7	3	Classical music rating	1	4	Overall museum rating	5	6
No. public libraries	5	28	Ballet/dance rating	1	3	Art museum rating	5	5
Library volumes per capita	3.6	2.8	Professional theater rating	1	3	Science museum rating	3	4
			University arts programs rating	5	5	Children's museum rating	1	3

Jackson, MI

Score: 46.7   Rank: 245

Profile: Small town
Location: South-central Michigan, 75 miles west of Detroit
Elevation: 841 feet
Time zone: Eastern Standard Time

PRO
Cost of living
Small-town atmosphere
Central location

CON
Violent crime
Winter climate
Entertainment

Jackson, in the central-southern part of the state, is a diversified commercial and manufacturing center with strong ties to the auto industry. Aside from a high violent crime rate, Jackson scores well as a clean city with a low cost of living. The city benefits from college-town amenities in nearby Ann Arbor and Lansing–East Lansing and is 75 miles west of Detroit. Jackson doesn't stand out in any area but has reasonably good scores across all *Cities Ranked & Rated* categories.

The area sits at the confluence of several creeks into the Kalamazoo River. The surrounding terrain is rolling and wooded with many small lakes nearby. The climate is mainly continental with a Great Lakes influence depending on wind strength. Summers are hot and humid, and winter temperatures are among the coldest in the state. Strong winds and storm fronts bring a variety of clouds, precipitation, and winter wind chill. Snowfall is moderate, and clouds and snow cover are common during winter. First freeze is early October, last is early May.

POPULATION

DEMOGRAPHICS	AREA	U.S. AVG	ETHNIC COMPOSITION	AREA	U.S. AVG	RESIDENT PROFILE	AREA	U.S. AVG
Population	160,972		White	95.3%	75.1%	Single	40.2%	43.6%
Population density per sq. mile	227.8	447.3	Black	3.5%	12.3%	Married	59.8%	56.4%
Population growth	7.5%	16.1%	Asian	.4%	3.6%	Divorced	9.2%	8.4%
Median age	37.0	35.5	American Indian	.5%	.9%	Separated	2.3%	3.0%
Average family size	2.7	2.7	Hispanic	1.4%	12.5%	Married with children	29.8%	28.7%
			Diversity measure	22.6%	35.2%	Single with children	10.5%	10.1%

ECONOMY & JOBS SCORE: 89/RANK: 34

INCOME	AREA	U.S. AVG	EMPLOYMENT	AREA	U.S. AVG	LARGEST EMPLOYING INDUSTRY
Per capita income	$20,773	$23,420	Unemployment rate	7.9%	6.1%	Fabricated Metal Product Manufacturing
Household income	$44,494	$46,060	Recent job growth	1.2%	.9%	
Household income < $25K	26.0%	26.4%	Projected future job growth	11.1%	15.1%	
Household income > $75K	21.9%	24.5%	White collar	50.3%	54.5%	
Household income growth	52.8%	57.3%	Blue collar	49.7%	45.5%	

COST OF LIVING SCORE: 68/RANK: 106

INDEXES & TAXES	AREA	U.S. AVG	HOUSING	AREA	U.S. AVG	NECESSITIES	AREA	U.S. AVG
Cost of Living Index	89.7	100.0	Median home price	$118,910	$160,100	Food Index	99.6	100.0
Financial Progress Index	105.7	100.0	Home price appreciation	7.1%	7.1%	Housing Index	73.9	100.0
Income tax rate	4.400%	4.625%	Median rent	$547	$670	Utilities Index	84.9	100.0
Sales tax rate	6.000%	6.474%	Homes owned	73.9%	63.9%	Transportation Index	101.2	100.0
Property tax rate	$12.3	$15.6	Homes rented	16.8%	25.3%	Healthcare Index	99.3	100.0
			Housing affordability	60.0%	54.5%	Miscellaneous Cost Index	101.5	100.0

CLIMATE SCORE: 51/RANK: 162

TEMPERATURE	AREA	U.S. AVG	PRECIPITATION	AREA	U.S. AVG	COMFORTS & HAZARDS	AREA	U.S. AVG
January low	15.3°F	26.4°F	Annual inches precipitation	30.4	35.9	July relative humidity	74.0%	68.8%
July high	82.6°F	86.7°F	Annual inches snowfall	49.0	24.2	Annual days mostly sunny	179	212
Annual days > 90°F	12	38	Annual days precipitation	156	111	Annual days with thunderstorms	34	39
Annual days < 32°F	151	88	Annual days rain > 0.5 inches	18	23	Tornado risk score	20	19
Annual days < 0°F	13	6	Annual days snow > 1.5 inches	11	6	Hurricane risk score	2	15

TEMPERATURE

PRECIPITATION

DAYS OF CLOUDS & PRECIPITATION

EDUCATION SCORE: 24/RANK: 250

ACHIEVEMENT	AREA	U.S. AVG	PUBLIC SCHOOLS	AREA	U.S. AVG	HIGHER EDUCATION	AREA	U.S. AVG
High school degree	84.2%	80.2%	Expenditures per pupil	$5,868	$5,894	No. 2-year colleges	2	3
2-year college degree	8.0%	6.2%	Student/teacher ratio	18.8	16.7	No. 4-year colleges/universities	1	4
4-year college degree	11.2%	15.8%	Attending public school	89.4%	90.2%	No. highly ranked universities	0	1
Graduate/professional degree	5.1%	9.6%	State SAT score	1140	1020			
			State ACT score	21.3*	21.0			

HEALTH & HEALTHCARE SCORE: 46/RANK: 177

HAZARDS & ILLNESSES	AREA	U.S. AVG	HEALTHCARE	AREA	U.S. AVG
Air-quality score	24	45	Physicians per capita	124.2	261.1
Water-quality score	20	33	Hospital beds per capita	347.8	432.2
Pollen/allergy score	37	61	No. teaching hospitals	0	4
Stress score	87	50	Cost per doctor visit	$63	$67
Cancer mortality per capita	180.8	169.0	Cost per dental visit	$90	$82
Depression days per month	1.8	2.8	Cost per daily hospital room	$628	$733

CRIME SCORE: 19/RANK: 268

CRIME	AREA	U.S. AVG
Violent crime rate	555.1	456.0
Change in violent crime rate	25.4%	-17.2%
Property crime rate	3,891.8	3,950.0
Change in property crime rate	3.4%	-16.8%

TRANSPORTATION SCORE: 17/RANK: 274

COMMUTE	AREA	U.S. AVG	INTERCITY SERVICES	AREA	U.S. AVG	AUTOMOTIVE	AREA	U.S. AVG
Average commute time	23.2 min.	22.6 min.	Miles to nearest major airport	38	46	Insurance, annual premium	$967	$1,011
Commute by auto	94.3%	88.7%	Type of local airport	Small		Gas, cost per gallon	$1.56	$1.50
Commute by mass transit	.2%	1.8%	No. daily airline departures	65	294	Daily vehicle miles per capita	25.0	23.0
Work at home	2.8%	3.9%	Amtrak service	Yes				
Mass transit miles per capita	7.1	8.0	No. interstate highways	1	1			

DINING & SHOPPING	AREA	U.S. AVG	ENTERTAINMENT	AREA	U.S. AVG	OUTDOOR ACTIVITIES	AREA	U.S. AVG
Restaurant rating	1	1	Professional sports rating	2	4	Golf-course rating	3	4
No. outlet malls	2	2	College sports rating	1	4	Ski-area rating	4	4
No. Starbucks	0	11	Zoo/aquarium rating	1	3	National Park rating	1	3
No. warehouse clubs	3	4	Amusement park rating	1	3	Sq. miles inland water	3.0	4.0
			Botanical garden/arboretum rating	1	3	Miles of coastline	0.0	11.4

MEDIA & LIBRARIES	AREA	U.S. AVG	PERFORMING ARTS	AREA	U.S. AVG	MUSEUMS	AREA	U.S. AVG
Arts radio rating	1	3	Classical music rating	4	4	Overall museum rating	2	6
No. public libraries	13	28	Ballet/dance rating	1	3	Art museum rating	3	5
Library volumes per capita	2.9	2.8	Professional theater rating	1	3	Science museum rating	1	4
			University arts programs rating	3	5	Children's museum rating	1	3

Jackson, MS

Score: 56.2   Rank: 178

Profile: Capital city/College town
Location: West-central Mississippi
Elevation: 331 feet
Time zone: Central Standard Time

PRO
Cost of living
Steady economy
College-town amenities

CON
Summer heat
Educational attainment
Air service

Jackson is Mississippi's largest city and a hub of government, commerce, and manufacturing for the state. The city has many attractions highlighting local history and culture. Civil War fires wiped out much of the town's antebellum feel, but there are still several points of historic interest, including the capitol building. The Ross Barnett Reservoir offers water recreation and historic country drives radiate in all directions, notably north on the Natchez Trace to the town of Canton. The University of Mississippi adds college-town features. The area has unusually low educational attainment for a capital city and college town, but at 79.1, the Cost of Living Index is also among the lowest.

The city is located in a wide river plain surrounded by gently rolling terrain and pine forests. The climate is significantly humid most of the year with short mild winters that include frequent cold spells. Summer temperatures reach 90°F or higher every 2 out of 3 days. Extended periods of very hot weather are rare. Rainfall is abundant and well distributed throughout the year. Thunderstorms are common, occurring 1 out of 3 days during summer. Fall is typically the driest season. Winter snow is minimal with 2 of 3 years having no measurable snowfalls. Ice storms occur occasionally.

DEMOGRAPHICS	AREA	U.S. AVG	ETHNIC COMPOSITION	AREA	U.S. AVG	RESIDENT PROFILE	AREA	U.S. AVG
Population	449,028		White	53.6%	75.1%	Single	54.4%	43.6%
Population density per sq. mile	190.0	447.3	Black	45.5%	12.3%	Married	45.6%	56.4%
Population growth	13.6%	16.1%	Asian	.7%	3.6%	Divorced	8.7%	8.4%
Median age	33.3	35.5	American Indian	.1%	.9%	Separated	5.0%	3.0%
Average family size	2.7	2.7	Hispanic	.6%	12.5%	Married with children	24.8%	28.7%
			Diversity measure	52.0%	35.2%	Single with children	16.5%	10.1%

INCOME	AREA	U.S. AVG	EMPLOYMENT	AREA	U.S. AVG	LARGEST EMPLOYING INDUSTRY
Per capita income	$23,889	$23,420	Unemployment rate	4.2%	6.1%	Healthcare and Social Assistance
Household income	$46,856	$46,060	Recent job growth	1.9%	.9%	
Household income < $25K	26.9%	26.4%	Projected future job growth	18.1%	15.1%	
Household income > $75K	27.8%	24.5%	White collar	61.8%	54.5%	
Household income growth	77.3%	57.3%	Blue collar	38.2%	45.5%	

INDEXES & TAXES	AREA	U.S. AVG	HOUSING	AREA	U.S. AVG	NECESSITIES	AREA	U.S. AVG
Cost of Living Index	79.1	100.0	Median home price	$97,430	$160,100	Food Index	87.2	100.0
Financial Progress Index	126.2	100.0	Home price appreciation	4.2%	7.1%	Housing Index	60.5	100.0
Income tax rate	5.000%	4.625%	Median rent	$589	$670	Utilities Index	84.5	100.0
Sales tax rate	7.000%	6.474%	Homes owned	63.0%	63.9%	Transportation Index	97.3	100.0
Property tax rate	$12.9	$15.6	Homes rented	27.9%	25.3%	Healthcare Index	81.9	100.0
			Housing affordability	54.0%	54.5%	Miscellaneous Cost Index	91.4	100.0

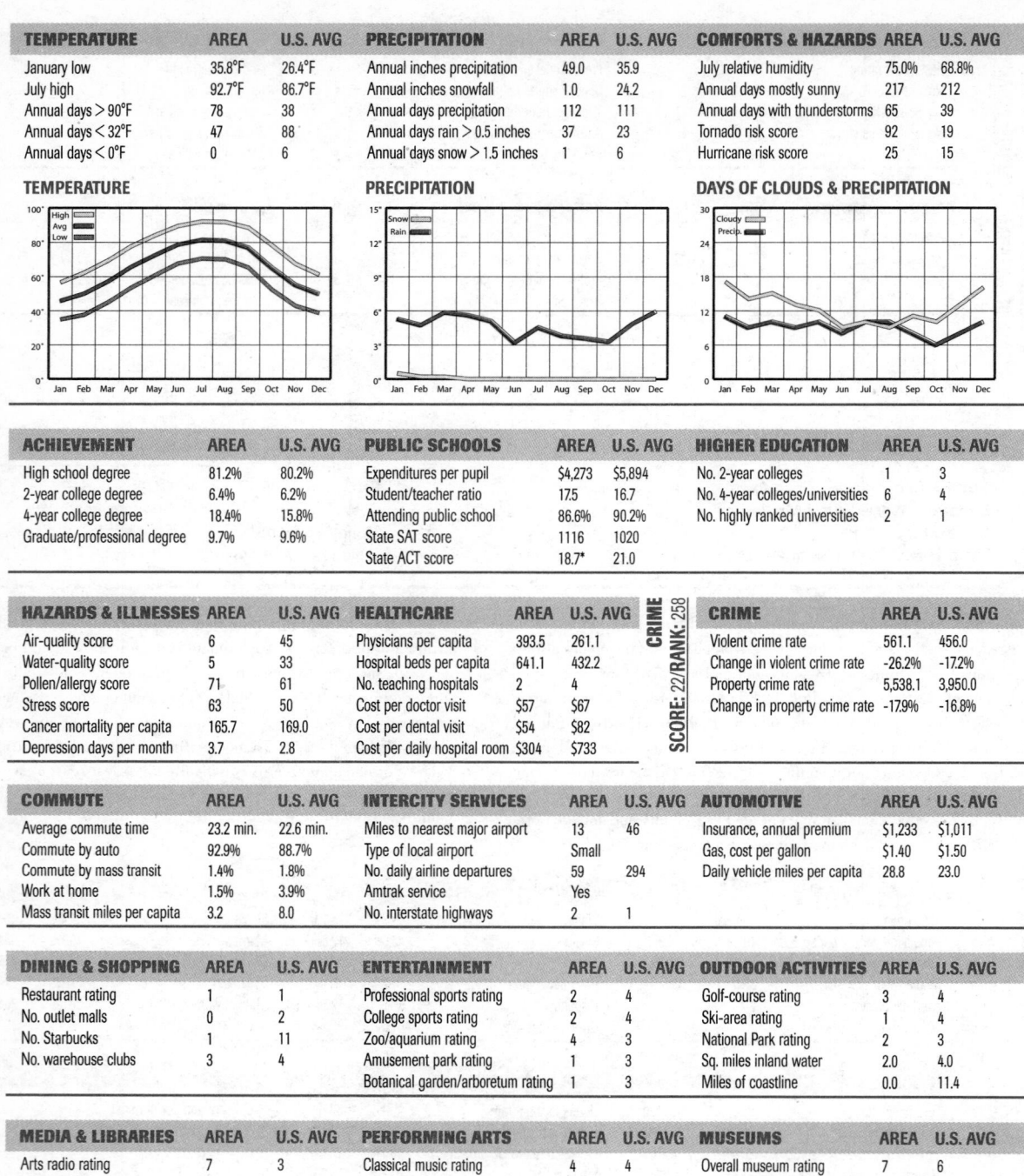

CLIMATE SCORE: 9/RANK: 300

TEMPERATURE	AREA	U.S. AVG
January low	35.8°F	26.4°F
July high	92.7°F	86.7°F
Annual days > 90°F	78	38
Annual days < 32°F	47	88
Annual days < 0°F	0	6

PRECIPITATION	AREA	U.S. AVG
Annual inches precipitation	49.0	35.9
Annual inches snowfall	1.0	24.2
Annual days precipitation	112	111
Annual days rain > 0.5 inches	37	23
Annual days snow > 1.5 inches	1	6

COMFORTS & HAZARDS	AREA	U.S. AVG
July relative humidity	75.0%	68.8%
Annual days mostly sunny	217	212
Annual days with thunderstorms	65	39
Tornado risk score	92	19
Hurricane risk score	25	15

TEMPERATURE

PRECIPITATION

DAYS OF CLOUDS & PRECIPITATION

EDUCATION SCORE: 53/RANK: 154

ACHIEVEMENT	AREA	U.S. AVG
High school degree	81.2%	80.2%
2-year college degree	6.4%	6.2%
4-year college degree	18.4%	15.8%
Graduate/professional degree	9.7%	9.6%

PUBLIC SCHOOLS	AREA	U.S. AVG
Expenditures per pupil	$4,273	$5,894
Student/teacher ratio	17.5	16.7
Attending public school	86.6%	90.2%
State SAT score	1116	1020
State ACT score	18.7*	21.0

HIGHER EDUCATION	AREA	U.S. AVG
No. 2-year colleges	1	3
No. 4-year colleges/universities	6	4
No. highly ranked universities	2	1

HEALTH & HEALTHCARE SCORE: 68/RANK: 105

HAZARDS & ILLNESSES	AREA	U.S. AVG
Air-quality score	6	45
Water-quality score	5	33
Pollen/allergy score	71	61
Stress score	63	50
Cancer mortality per capita	165.7	169.0
Depression days per month	3.7	2.8

HEALTHCARE	AREA	U.S. AVG
Physicians per capita	393.5	261.1
Hospital beds per capita	641.1	432.2
No. teaching hospitals	2	4
Cost per doctor visit	$57	$67
Cost per dental visit	$54	$82
Cost per daily hospital room	$304	$733

CRIME SCORE: 22/RANK: 258

CRIME	AREA	U.S. AVG
Violent crime rate	561.1	456.0
Change in violent crime rate	-26.2%	-17.2%
Property crime rate	5,538.1	3,950.0
Change in property crime rate	-17.9%	-16.8%

TRANSPORTATION SCORE: 20/RANK: 262

COMMUTE	AREA	U.S. AVG
Average commute time	23.2 min.	22.6 min.
Commute by auto	92.9%	88.7%
Commute by mass transit	1.4%	1.8%
Work at home	1.5%	3.9%
Mass transit miles per capita	3.2	8.0

INTERCITY SERVICES	AREA	U.S. AVG
Miles to nearest major airport	13	46
Type of local airport	Small	
No. daily airline departures	59	294
Amtrak service	Yes	
No. interstate highways	2	1

AUTOMOTIVE	AREA	U.S. AVG
Insurance, annual premium	$1,233	$1,011
Gas, cost per gallon	$1.40	$1.50
Daily vehicle miles per capita	28.8	23.0

LEISURE SCORE: 36/RANK: 215

DINING & SHOPPING	AREA	U.S. AVG
Restaurant rating	1	1
No. outlet malls	0	2
No. Starbucks	1	11
No. warehouse clubs	3	4

ENTERTAINMENT	AREA	U.S. AVG
Professional sports rating	2	4
College sports rating	2	4
Zoo/aquarium rating	4	3
Amusement park rating	1	3
Botanical garden/arboretum rating	1	3

OUTDOOR ACTIVITIES	AREA	U.S. AVG
Golf-course rating	3	4
Ski-area rating	1	4
National Park rating	2	3
Sq. miles inland water	2.0	4.0
Miles of coastline	0.0	11.4

ARTS & CULTURE SCORE: 20/RANK: 262

MEDIA & LIBRARIES	AREA	U.S. AVG
Arts radio rating	7	3
No. public libraries	39	28
Library volumes per capita	2.2	2.8

PERFORMING ARTS	AREA	U.S. AVG
Classical music rating	4	4
Ballet/dance rating	3	3
Professional theater rating	6	3
University arts programs rating	8	5

MUSEUMS	AREA	U.S. AVG
Overall museum rating	7	6
Art museum rating	6	5
Science museum rating	7	4
Children's museum rating	1	3

Jackson, TN

Score: 32.2 **Rank:** 304

Profile: Small city
Location: West-central Tennessee
Elevation: 412 feet
Time zone: Central Standard Time

PRO	CON
Small-town feel	Entertainment
Cost of living	Arts and culture
Economic turnaround	Hot, humid summers

Jackson is a transportation center serving the agriculture industry, with cotton being a significant crop. The city is also a diverse manufacturing center for companies such as toolmaker Porter-Cable and Procter & Gamble. The town has a typical Southern-town feel with historic buildings and a vintage 1950s bus station, which is now used as a movie set. There is a low cost of living and a potentially improving job base, although the latter hasn't yet appeared in the numbers. The area has also received recent accolades for the quality of its workforce and growth potential. There isn't much to do nor much cultural interest, but better things may lie in the future.

The surrounding countryside is flat with sections of slightly rolling farmland and deciduous woods. The climate is continental with a subtropical influence. Summers have frequent thundershowers with regular temperatures above 90°F. Winters are changeable with periods of mild weather alternating with cool northerly air. Although temperatures below zero seldom occur, cold snaps and passing storms can deliver significant snowfall. The spring storm-track location brings occasional severe weather such as destructive tornadoes. First freeze is late October, last is April 1.

POPULATION

DEMOGRAPHICS	AREA	U.S. AVG	ETHNIC COMPOSITION	AREA	U.S. AVG	RESIDENT PROFILE	AREA	U.S. AVG
Population	109,290		White	73.9%	75.1%	Single	41.7%	43.6%
Population density per sq. mile	196.2	447.3	Black	25.8%	12.3%	Married	58.3%	56.4%
Population growth	20.4%	16.1%	Asian	.2%	3.6%	Divorced	7.9%	8.4%
Median age	35.0	35.5	American Indian	.1%	.9%	Separated	3.1%	3.0%
Average family size	2.6	2.7	Hispanic	.6%	12.5%	Married with children	28.7%	28.7%
			Diversity measure	47.7%	35.2%	Single with children	10.8%	10.1%

ECONOMY & JOBS SCORE: 10/RANK: 297

INCOME	AREA	U.S. AVG	EMPLOYMENT	AREA	U.S. AVG	LARGEST EMPLOYING INDUSTRY
Per capita income	$22,617	$23,420	Unemployment rate	5.0%	6.1%	Machinery Manufacturing
Household income	$42,715	$46,060	Recent job growth	-3.2%	.9%	
Household income < $25K	28.8%	26.4%	Projected future job growth	18.4%	15.1%	
Household income > $75K	24.1%	24.5%	White collar	53.3%	54.5%	
Household income growth	79.6%	57.3%	Blue collar	46.7%	45.5%	

COST OF LIVING SCORE: 94/RANK: 20

INDEXES & TAXES	AREA	U.S. AVG	HOUSING	AREA	U.S. AVG	NECESSITIES	AREA	U.S. AVG
Cost of Living Index	83.3	100.0	Median home price	$92,720	$160,100	Food Index	104.8	100.0
Financial Progress Index	109.3	100.0	Home price appreciation	3.1%	7.1%	Housing Index	57.6	100.0
Income tax rate	0.000%	4.625%	Median rent	$501	$670	Utilities Index	78.2	100.0
Sales tax rate	9.750%	6.474%	Homes owned	75.1%	63.9%	Transportation Index	97.5	100.0
Property tax rate	$5.8	$15.6	Homes rented	17.8%	25.3%	Healthcare Index	86.9	100.0
			Housing affordability	57.0%	54.5%	Miscellaneous Cost Index	102.6	100.0

CLIMATE SCORE: 37/RANK: 208

TEMPERATURE	AREA	U.S. AVG	PRECIPITATION	AREA	U.S. AVG	COMFORTS & HAZARDS	AREA	U.S. AVG
January low	32.0°F	26.4°F	Annual inches precipitation	47.0	35.9	July relative humidity	70.0%	68.8%
July high	89.0°F	86.7°F	Annual inches snowfall	8.0	24.2	Annual days mostly sunny	209	212
Annual days > 90°F	42	38	Annual days precipitation	111	111	Annual days with thunderstorms	53	39
Annual days < 32°F	65	88	Annual days rain > 0.5 inches	34	23	Tornado risk score	16	19
Annual days < 0°F	0	6	Annual days snow > 1.5 inches	2	6	Hurricane risk score	10	15

TEMPERATURE

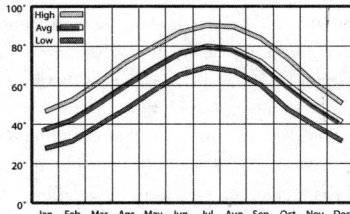

PRECIPITATION

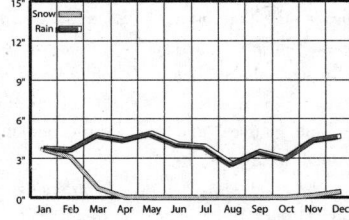

DAYS OF CLOUDS & PRECIPITATION

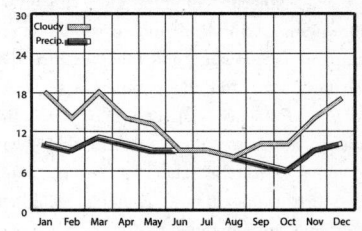

EDUCATION SCORE: 33/RANK: 222

ACHIEVEMENT	AREA	U.S. AVG	PUBLIC SCHOOLS	AREA	U.S. AVG	HIGHER EDUCATION	AREA	U.S. AVG
High school degree	77.7%	80.2%	Expenditures per pupil	$5,241	$5,894	No. 2-year colleges	1	3
2-year college degree	4.7%	6.2%	Student/teacher ratio	14.3	16.7	No. 4-year colleges/universities	4	4
4-year college degree	13.1%	15.8%	Attending public school	90.0%	90.2%	No. highly ranked universities	2	1
Graduate/professional degree	7.0%	9.6%	State SAT score	1128	1020			
			State ACT score	20.4*	21.0			

HEALTH & HEALTHCARE SCORE: 90/RANK: 32

CRIME SCORE: 18/RANK: 271

HAZARDS & ILLNESSES	AREA	U.S. AVG	HEALTHCARE	AREA	U.S. AVG	CRIME	AREA	U.S. AVG
Air-quality score	81	45	Physicians per capita	324.8	261.1	Violent crime rate	904.6	456.0
Water-quality score	30	33	Hospital beds per capita	833.5	432.2	Change in violent crime rate	-27.4%	-17.2%
Pollen/allergy score	66	61	No. teaching hospitals	1	4	Property crime rate	4,679.0	3,950.0
Stress score	33	50	Cost per doctor visit	$65	$67	Change in property crime rate	-26.8%	-16.8%
Cancer mortality per capita	157.6	169.0	Cost per dental visit	$74	$82			
Depression days per month	2.1	2.8	Cost per daily hospital room	$380	$733			

TRANSPORTATION SCORE: 50/RANK: 163

COMMUTE	AREA	U.S. AVG	INTERCITY SERVICES	AREA	U.S. AVG	AUTOMOTIVE	AREA	U.S. AVG
Average commute time	20.0 min.	22.6 min.	Miles to nearest major airport	77	46	Insurance, annual premium	$801	$1,011
Commute by auto	94.1%	88.7%	Type of local airport	Medium		Gas, cost per gallon	$1.40	$1.50
Commute by mass transit	.6%	1.8%	No. daily airline departures	500	294	Daily vehicle miles per capita	28.4	23.0
Work at home	3.3%	3.9%	Amtrak service	No				
Mass transit miles per capita	5.0	8.0	No. interstate highways	1	1			

LEISURE SCORE: 1/RANK: 326

DINING & SHOPPING	AREA	U.S. AVG	ENTERTAINMENT	AREA	U.S. AVG	OUTDOOR ACTIVITIES	AREA	U.S. AVG
Restaurant rating	1	1	Professional sports rating	2	4	Golf-course rating	1	4
No. outlet malls	0	2	College sports rating	1	4	Ski-area rating	1	4
No. Starbucks	1	11	Zoo/aquarium rating	1	3	National Park rating	1	3
No. warehouse clubs	1	4	Amusement park rating	1	3	Sq. miles inland water	1.0	4.0
			Botanical garden/arboretum rating	1	3	Miles of coastline	0.0	11.4

ARTS & CULTURE SCORE: 21/RANK: 260

MEDIA & LIBRARIES	AREA	U.S. AVG	PERFORMING ARTS	AREA	U.S. AVG	MUSEUMS	AREA	U.S. AVG
Arts radio rating	1	3	Classical music rating	3	4	Overall museum rating	3	6
No. public libraries	2	28	Ballet/dance rating	1	3	Art museum rating	1	5
Library volumes per capita	1.5	2.8	Professional theater rating	1	3	Science museum rating	4	4
			University arts programs rating	5	5	Children's museum rating	1	3

Jacksonville, FL

Score: 68.7   Rank: 82

Profile: Large city
Location: Extreme northern Atlantic coast of Florida, slightly inland along the St. Johns River
Elevation: 31 feet
Time zone: Eastern Standard Time

PRO	CON
Cost of living	Low educational attainment
Attractive downtown	Urban sprawl
Arts and culture	Entertainment

Jacksonville is a large commercial and financial center whose qualities are really better than the statistics indicate. The city has the most "northern" feel in the state with skyscrapers in a well-defined downtown area. But the city's essential character is still that of a Southern city. Sprawling and fairly unattractive residential areas surround downtown, and the population has relatively low educational attainment. Category statistics may not reflect nearby recreational amenities, which include the world-class beaches, golf courses, and resort areas of Amelia Island to the east and the historic area of St. Augustine to the southeast. Although healthcare statistics are low in general, they are enhanced by the presence of a Mayo Clinic. The area has a notably low cost of living for a large Sunbelt city and has the highest air-quality score in Florida.

The terrain surrounding Jacksonville is level. The climate is coastal and subtropical. Easterly winds blowing 40% of the time produce a maritime influence modifying summer heat and winter cold. Summers are long, warm, and relatively humid. Winters, although punctuated with periodic invasions of cool to occasionally cold air from the north, are mild. Because of varying distances to the ocean, climatic features across the city differ. Inland summer temperatures frequently exceed 90°F while remaining in the 80s at the beach. Summer thunderstorms are common, occurring 1 day in 2. The area is vulnerable to hurricanes, but is far enough north so that most of them lose strength before reaching the area.

POPULATION

DEMOGRAPHICS	AREA	U.S. AVG	ETHNIC COMPOSITION	AREA	U.S. AVG	RESIDENT PROFILE	AREA	U.S. AVG
Population	1,154,809		White	76.6%	75.1%	Single	46.2%	43.6%
Population density per sq. mile	438.1	447.3	Black	20.5%	12.3%	Married	53.8%	56.4%
Population growth	27.4%	16.1%	Asian	1.9%	3.6%	Divorced	11.0%	8.4%
Median age	35.5	35.5	American Indian	.3%	.9%	Separated	3.9%	3.0%
Average family size	2.7	2.7	Hispanic	4.0%	12.5%	Married with children	28.5%	28.7%
			Diversity measure	44.7%	35.2%	Single with children	12.4%	10.1%

ECONOMY & JOBS
SCORE: 38/RANK: 203

INCOME	AREA	U.S. AVG	EMPLOYMENT	AREA	U.S. AVG	LARGEST EMPLOYING INDUSTRY
Per capita income	$23,821	$23,420	Unemployment rate	5.3%	6.1%	Credit Intermediation and Related Activities
Household income	$45,338	$46,060	Recent job growth	-.8%	.9%	
Household income < $25K	24.0%	26.4%	Projected future job growth	22.4%	15.1%	
Household income > $75K	22.8%	24.5%	White collar	58.1%	54.5%	
Household income growth	53.4%	57.3%	Blue collar	41.9%	45.5%	

COST OF LIVING
SCORE: 71/RANK: 94

INDEXES & TAXES	AREA	U.S. AVG	HOUSING	AREA	U.S. AVG	NECESSITIES	AREA	U.S. AVG
Cost of Living Index	89.0	100.0	Median home price	$121,000	$160,100	Food Index	100.4	100.0
Financial Progress Index	108.5	100.0	Home price appreciation	9.7%	7.1%	Housing Index	75.2	100.0
Income tax rate	0.000%	4.625%	Median rent	$675	$670	Utilities Index	87.9	100.0
Sales tax rate	7.000%	6.474%	Homes owned	61.4%	63.9%	Transportation Index	100.1	100.0
Property tax rate	$17.5	$15.6	Homes rented	29.1%	25.3%	Healthcare Index	87.8	100.0
			Housing affordability	57.0%	54.5%	Miscellaneous Cost Index	98.1	100.0

CLIMATE
SCORE: 52/RANK: 159

TEMPERATURE	AREA	U.S. AVG	PRECIPITATION	AREA	U.S. AVG	COMFORTS & HAZARDS	AREA	U.S. AVG
January low	44.5°F	26.4°F	Annual inches precipitation	54.0	35.9	July relative humidity	75.0%	68.8%
July high	90.0°F	86.7°F	Annual inches snowfall	0.0	24.2	Annual days mostly sunny	226	212
Annual days > 90°F	82	38	Annual days precipitation	116	111	Annual days with thunderstorms	64	39
Annual days < 32°F	12	88	Annual days rain > 0.5 inches	30	23	Tornado risk score	14	19
Annual days < 0°F	0	6	Annual days snow > 1.5 inches	0	6	Hurricane risk score	63	15

TEMPERATURE

PRECIPITATION

DAYS OF CLOUDS & PRECIPITATION

EDUCATION
SCORE: 43/RANK: 186

ACHIEVEMENT	AREA	U.S. AVG	PUBLIC SCHOOLS	AREA	U.S. AVG	HIGHER EDUCATION	AREA	U.S. AVG
High school degree	82.3%	80.2%	Expenditures per pupil	$4,985	$5,894	No. 2-year colleges	1	3
2-year college degree	7.5%	6.2%	Student/teacher ratio	19.2	16.7	No. 4-year colleges/universities	5	4
4-year college degree	14.6%	15.8%	Attending public school	87.1%	90.2%	No. highly ranked universities	2	1
Graduate/professional degree	6.5%	9.6%	State SAT score	996*	1020			
			State ACT score	20.5	21.0			

HEALTH & HEALTHCARE
SCORE: 13/RANK: 287

CRIME
SCORE: 41/RANK: 193

HAZARDS & ILLNESSES	AREA	U.S. AVG	HEALTHCARE	AREA	U.S. AVG	CRIME	AREA	U.S. AVG
Air-quality score	95	45	Physicians per capita	267.0	261.1	Violent crime rate	867.2	456.0
Water-quality score	18	33	Hospital beds per capita	294.0	432.2	Change in violent crime rate	-25.8%	-17.2%
Pollen/allergy score	65	61	No. teaching hospitals	6	4	Property crime rate	4,986.3	3,950.0
Stress score	91	50	Cost per doctor visit	$63	$67	Change in property crime rate	-22.0%	-16.8%
Cancer mortality per capita	188.9	169.0	Cost per dental visit	$64	$82			
Depression days per month	2.6	2.8	Cost per daily hospital room	$467	$733			

TRANSPORTATION
SCORE: 20/RANK: 263

COMMUTE	AREA	U.S. AVG	INTERCITY SERVICES	AREA	U.S. AVG	AUTOMOTIVE	AREA	U.S. AVG
Average commute time	26.6 min.	22.6 min.	Miles to nearest major airport	18	46	Insurance, annual premium	$1,063	$1,011
Commute by auto	89.5%	88.7%	Type of local airport	Medium		Gas, cost per gallon	$1.50	$1.50
Commute by mass transit	2.1%	1.8%	No. daily airline departures	145	294	Daily vehicle miles per capita	27.4	23.0
Work at home	3.1%	3.9%	Amtrak service	Yes				
Mass transit miles per capita	8.6	8.0	No. interstate highways	2	1			

LEISURE SCORE: 34/RANK: 216

DINING & SHOPPING	AREA	U.S. AVG	ENTERTAINMENT	AREA	U.S. AVG	OUTDOOR ACTIVITIES	AREA	U.S. AVG
Restaurant rating	3	1	Professional sports rating	6	4	Golf-course rating	6	4
No. outlet malls	2	2	College sports rating	5	4	Ski-area rating	1	4
No. Starbucks	17	11	Zoo/aquarium rating	8	3	National Park rating	2	3
No. warehouse clubs	6	4	Amusement park rating	1	3	Sq. miles inland water	10.0	4.0
			Botanical garden/arboretum rating	3	3	Miles of coastline	79.9	11.4

ARTS & CULTURE SCORE: 23/RANK: 254

MEDIA & LIBRARIES	AREA	U.S. AVG	PERFORMING ARTS	AREA	U.S. AVG	MUSEUMS	AREA	U.S. AVG
Arts radio rating	1	3	Classical music rating	5	4	Overall museum rating	8	6
No. public libraries	27	28	Ballet/dance rating	1	3	Art museum rating	7	5
Library volumes per capita	2.7	2.8	Professional theater rating	1	3	Science museum rating	5	4
			University arts programs rating	7	5	Children's museum rating	1	3

Jacksonville, NC

Score: 23.6   Rank: 318

Profile: Military town
Location: Southeast North Carolina near coast
Time zone: Eastern Standard Time
Elevation: 30 feet

PRO
Nearby coastal areas
Nearby recreation
Cost of living

CON
Arts and culture
Entertainment
Economy

Jacksonville is located near the Atlantic Coast at the mouth of the New River. The 153,000-acre Camp Lejeune marine base is the mainstay of the local economy and lifestyle. The area is also known for boating and watersports. Cost of living is reasonable and the winter climate is attractive, but the area has few other cultural and service amenities.

Jacksonville is located at the head of a bay formed by the New River, in a mostly level, often marshy coastal plain. The climate is humid subtropical with a marine influence. Summers days are warm and very humid, and are sometimes cooled by marine breezes depending on the prevailing winds. High temperatures of 90°F are reached every 1 in 2 summer days, but 100°F heat is rare. Winters are cool and wet but seldom cold. The area gets significant rain in all seasons, with peaks during summer thunderstorms and coastal storms. Snow is rare.

POPULATION

DEMOGRAPHICS	AREA	U.S. AVG	ETHNIC COMPOSITION	AREA	U.S. AVG	RESIDENT PROFILE	AREA	U.S. AVG
Population	149,003		White	78.0%	75.1%	Single	33.2%	43.6%
Population density per sq. mile	194.3	447.3	Black	15.6%	12.3%	Married	66.8%	56.4%
Population growth	-.6%	16.1%	Asian	3.1%	3.6%	Divorced	6.1%	8.4%
Median age	24.9	35.5	American Indian	.6%	.9%	Separated	3.9%	3.0%
Average family size	2.8	2.7	Hispanic	8.2%	12.5%	Married with children	40.2%	28.7%
			Diversity measure	47.2%	35.2%	Single with children	9.4%	10.1%

ECONOMY & JOBS SCORE: 18/RANK: 269

INCOME	AREA	U.S. AVG	EMPLOYMENT	AREA	U.S. AVG	LARGEST EMPLOYING INDUSTRY
Per capita income	$19,876	$23,420	Unemployment rate	5.2%	6.1%	Healthcare and Social Assistance
Household income	$43,448	$46,060	Recent job growth	-3.0%	.9%	
Household income < $25K	21.0%	26.4%	Projected future job growth	11.6%	15.1%	
Household income > $75K	19.1%	24.5%	White collar	30.8%	54.5%	
Household income growth	85.9%	57.3%	Blue collar	69.2%	45.5%	

COST OF LIVING SCORE: 86/RANK: 46

INDEXES & TAXES	AREA	U.S. AVG	HOUSING	AREA	U.S. AVG	NECESSITIES	AREA	U.S. AVG
Cost of Living Index	83.2	100.0	Median home price	$98,590	$160,100	Food Index	94.3	100.0
Financial Progress Index	111.3	100.0	Home price appreciation	4.7%	7.1%	Housing Index	61.2	100.0
Income tax rate	7.000%	4.625%	Median rent	$499	$670	Utilities Index	108.4	100.0
Sales tax rate	7.000%	6.474%	Homes owned	38.8%	63.9%	Transportation Index	83.8	100.0
Property tax rate	$11.3	$15.6	Homes rented	39.7%	25.3%	Healthcare Index	89.3	100.0
			Housing affordability	67.0%	54.5%	Miscellaneous Cost Index	99.4	100.0

CLIMATE　SCORE: 71/RANK: 94

TEMPERATURE	AREA	U.S. AVG	PRECIPITATION	AREA	U.S. AVG	COMFORTS & HAZARDS	AREA	U.S. AVG
January low	36.2°F	26.4°F	Annual inches precipitation	54.0	35.9	July relative humidity	75.0%	68.8%
July high	88.8°F	86.7°F	Annual inches snowfall	1.8	24.2	Annual days mostly sunny	219	212
Annual days > 90°F	45	38	Annual days precipitation	117	111	Annual days with thunderstorms	46	39
Annual days < 32°F	45	88	Annual days rain > 0.5 inches	33	23	Tornado risk score	18	19
Annual days < 0°F	0	6	Annual days snow > 1.5 inches	1	6	Hurricane risk score	70	15

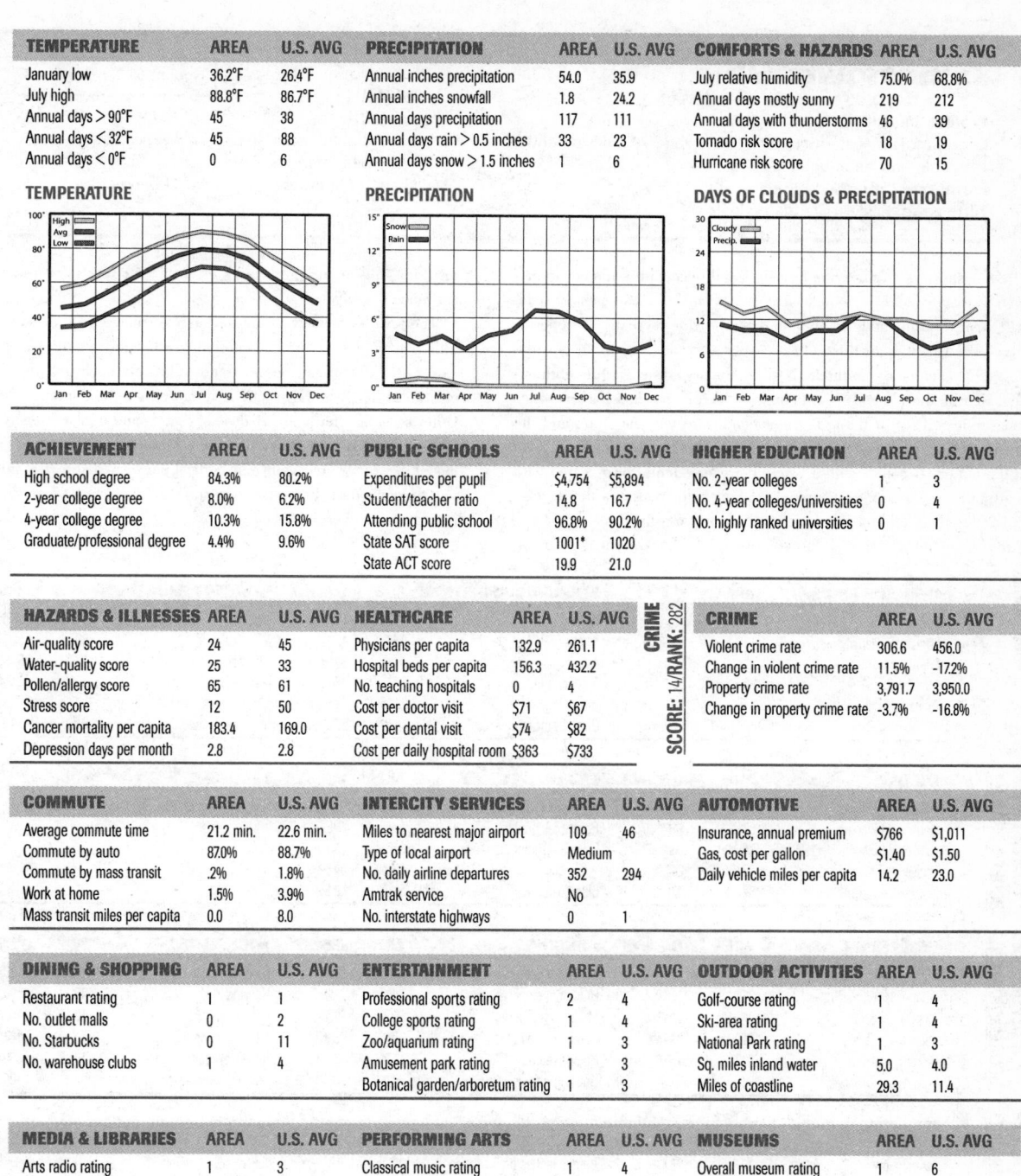

TEMPERATURE

PRECIPITATION

DAYS OF CLOUDS & PRECIPITATION

EDUCATION　SCORE: 46/RANK: 179

ACHIEVEMENT	AREA	U.S. AVG	PUBLIC SCHOOLS	AREA	U.S. AVG	HIGHER EDUCATION	AREA	U.S. AVG
High school degree	84.3%	80.2%	Expenditures per pupil	$4,754	$5,894	No. 2-year colleges	1	3
2-year college degree	8.0%	6.2%	Student/teacher ratio	14.8	16.7	No. 4-year colleges/universities	0	4
4-year college degree	10.3%	15.8%	Attending public school	96.8%	90.2%	No. highly ranked universities	0	1
Graduate/professional degree	4.4%	9.6%	State SAT score	1001*	1020			
			State ACT score	19.9	21.0			

HEALTH & HEALTHCARE　SCORE: 11/RANK: 294

CRIME　SCORE: 14/RANK: 282

HAZARDS & ILLNESSES	AREA	U.S. AVG	HEALTHCARE	AREA	U.S. AVG	CRIME	AREA	U.S. AVG
Air-quality score	24	45	Physicians per capita	132.9	261.1	Violent crime rate	306.6	456.0
Water-quality score	25	33	Hospital beds per capita	156.3	432.2	Change in violent crime rate	11.5%	-17.2%
Pollen/allergy score	65	61	No. teaching hospitals	0	4	Property crime rate	3,791.7	3,950.0
Stress score	12	50	Cost per doctor visit	$71	$67	Change in property crime rate	-3.7%	-16.8%
Cancer mortality per capita	183.4	169.0	Cost per dental visit	$74	$82			
Depression days per month	2.8	2.8	Cost per daily hospital room	$363	$733			

TRANSPORTATION　SCORE: 11/RANK: 292

COMMUTE	AREA	U.S. AVG	INTERCITY SERVICES	AREA	U.S. AVG	AUTOMOTIVE	AREA	U.S. AVG
Average commute time	21.2 min.	22.6 min.	Miles to nearest major airport	109	46	Insurance, annual premium	$766	$1,011
Commute by auto	87.0%	88.7%	Type of local airport	Medium		Gas, cost per gallon	$1.40	$1.50
Commute by mass transit	.2%	1.8%	No. daily airline departures	352	294	Daily vehicle miles per capita	14.2	23.0
Work at home	1.5%	3.9%	Amtrak service	No				
Mass transit miles per capita	0.0	8.0	No. interstate highways	0	1			

LEISURE　SCORE: 81/RANK: 61

DINING & SHOPPING	AREA	U.S. AVG	ENTERTAINMENT	AREA	U.S. AVG	OUTDOOR ACTIVITIES	AREA	U.S. AVG
Restaurant rating	1	1	Professional sports rating	2	4	Golf-course rating	1	4
No. outlet malls	0	2	College sports rating	1	4	Ski-area rating	1	4
No. Starbucks	0	11	Zoo/aquarium rating	1	3	National Park rating	1	3
No. warehouse clubs	1	4	Amusement park rating	1	3	Sq. miles inland water	5.0	4.0
			Botanical garden/arboretum rating	1	3	Miles of coastline	29.3	11.4

ARTS & CULTURE　SCORE: 77/RANK: 76

MEDIA & LIBRARIES	AREA	U.S. AVG	PERFORMING ARTS	AREA	U.S. AVG	MUSEUMS	AREA	U.S. AVG
Arts radio rating	1	3	Classical music rating	1	4	Overall museum rating	1	6
No. public libraries	4	28	Ballet/dance rating	1	3	Art museum rating	1	5
Library volumes per capita	1.0	2.8	Professional theater rating	1	3	Science museum rating	1	4
			University arts programs rating	1	5	Children's museum rating	1	3

Jamestown, NY

Score: 61.1 **Rank:** 137

Profile: Small town
Location: Far western corner of New York, 70 miles southwest of Buffalo on Chautauqua Lake
Elevation: 731 feet
Time zone: Eastern Standard Time

PRO	CON
Attractive setting	Wet climate
Nature centers	Economy
Cost of living	Urban decay

Jamestown is a rather nondescript small town with a lumber-industry history and an industrial economy mixed with some tourism. Nearby skiing and Chautauqua Lake provide recreational opportunities, the Chautauqua Institute presents arts and education, and the Roger Tory Peterson Institute of Natural History attracts nature enthusiasts. Nearby Buffalo and Erie, Pennsylvania, provide missing amenities and services. Cost of living is the second lowest in the state, and the median home price of $78,380 is by far the lowest in New York and 14th in the nation. It comes with a price, however—Jamestown is tied with nearby Erie as the rainiest metropolitan area in the nation, with 188 days of drizzly precipitation each year. The economy has fared poorly, particularly since the demise of the east-west Erie-Lackawanna Railroad,

resulting in some urban decay. Currently state funds are being used to revitalize the city.

The town is located on a level area surrounded by densely wooded hills. The climate is humid continental with significant effects from Lake Erie to the northwest. Summers are relatively cool and pleasant, with only 1 day per year above 90°F and intermittent rain and thunderstorms. Other seasons offer a steady dose of clouds and light rain, with heavier lake-effect snow squalls and frequent larger storms in winter. The lake moderates bitter cold with only 5 days per year below 0°F, but a good portion of winter is below freezing and snow cover is typical. First freeze is early November, last is early April.

POPULATION

DEMOGRAPHICS	AREA	U.S. AVG	ETHNIC COMPOSITION	AREA	U.S. AVG	RESIDENT PROFILE	AREA	U.S. AVG
Population	138,332		White	94.2%	75.1%	Single	41.8%	43.6%
Population density per sq. mile	130.2	447.3	Black	2.5%	12.3%	Married	58.2%	56.4%
Population growth	-2.5%	16.1%	Asian	.7%	3.6%	Divorced	7.8%	8.4%
Median age	38.3	35.5	American Indian	1.5%	.9%	Separated	3.2%	3.0%
Average family size	2.6	2.7	Hispanic	2.2%	12.5%	Married with children	27.7%	28.7%
			Diversity measure	15.3%	35.2%	Single with children	9.5%	10.1%

ECONOMY & JOBS SCORE: 84/RANK: 51

INCOME	AREA	U.S. AVG	EMPLOYMENT	AREA	U.S. AVG	LARGEST EMPLOYING INDUSTRY
Per capita income	$17,206	$23,420	Unemployment rate	5.7%	6.1%	Furniture and Related Product Manufacturing
Household income	$33,311	$46,060	Recent job growth	1.4%	.9%	
Household income < $25K	36.8%	26.4%	Projected future job growth	3.8%	15.1%	
Household income > $75K	12.0%	24.5%	White collar	45.3%	54.5%	
Household income growth	37.4%	57.3%	Blue collar	54.7%	45.5%	

COST OF LIVING SCORE: 35/RANK: 212

INDEXES & TAXES	AREA	U.S. AVG	HOUSING	AREA	U.S. AVG	NECESSITIES	AREA	U.S. AVG
Cost of Living Index	84.6	100.0	Median home price	$78,380	$160,100	Food Index	111.8	100.0
Financial Progress Index	83.9	100.0	Home price appreciation	7.0%	7.1%	Housing Index	48.7	100.0
Income tax rate	8.125%	4.625%	Median rent	$509	$670	Utilities Index	123.7	100.0
Sales tax rate	7.000%	6.474%	Homes owned	60.9%	63.9%	Transportation Index	103.2	100.0
Property tax rate	$32.7	$15.6	Homes rented	18.2%	25.3%	Healthcare Index	101.2	100.0
			Housing affordability	50.0%	54.5%	Miscellaneous Cost Index	94.2	100.0

CLIMATE SCORE: 11/RANK: 292

TEMPERATURE	AREA	U.S. AVG	PRECIPITATION	AREA	U.S. AVG	COMFORTS & HAZARDS	AREA	U.S. AVG
January low	18.5°F	26.4°F	Annual inches precipitation	38.2	35.9	July relative humidity	74.0%	68.8%
July high	77.4°F	86.7°F	Annual inches snowfall	83.6	24.2	Annual days mostly sunny	161	212
Annual days > 90°F	1	38	Annual days precipitation	188	111	Annual days with thunderstorms	38	39
Annual days < 32°F	134	88	Annual days rain > 0.5 inches	24	23	Tornado risk score	9	19
Annual days < 0°F	5	6	Annual days snow > 1.5 inches	18	6	Hurricane risk score	4	15

TEMPERATURE

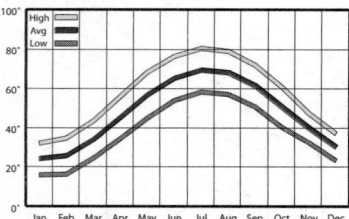

PRECIPITATION

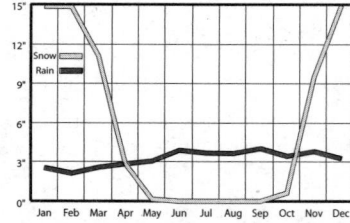

DAYS OF CLOUDS & PRECIPITATION

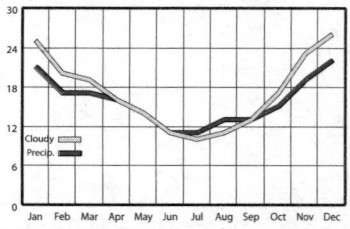

EDUCATION — SCORE: 76/RANK: 78

ACHIEVEMENT	AREA	U.S. AVG	PUBLIC SCHOOLS	AREA	U.S. AVG	HIGHER EDUCATION	AREA	U.S. AVG
High school degree	81.2%	80.2%	Expenditures per pupil	$8,070	$5,894	No. 2-year colleges	2	3
2-year college degree	9.4%	6.2%	Student/teacher ratio	12.4	16.7	No. 4-year colleges/universities	1	4
4-year college degree	9.7%	15.8%	Attending public school	95.1%	90.2%	No. highly ranked universities	1	1
Graduate/professional degree	7.2%	9.6%	State SAT score	1006*	1020			
			State ACT score	22.3	21.0			

HEALTH & HEALTHCARE — SCORE: 86/RANK: 43   CRIME — SCORE: 98/RANK: 6

HAZARDS & ILLNESSES	AREA	U.S. AVG	HEALTHCARE	AREA	U.S. AVG	CRIME	AREA	U.S. AVG
Air-quality score	49	45	Physicians per capita	135.2	261.1	Violent crime rate	190.8	456.0
Water-quality score	74	33	Hospital beds per capita	541.0	432.2	Change in violent crime rate	-31.8%	-17.2%
Pollen/allergy score	40	61	No. teaching hospitals	0	4	Property crime rate	2,338.5	3,950.0
Stress score	24	50	Cost per doctor visit	$65	$67	Change in property crime rate	-32.4%	-16.8%
Cancer mortality per capita	163.8	169.0	Cost per dental visit	$78	$82			
Depression days per month	3.3	2.8	Cost per daily hospital room	$899	$733			

TRANSPORTATION — SCORE: 79/RANK: 71

COMMUTE	AREA	U.S. AVG	INTERCITY SERVICES	AREA	U.S. AVG	AUTOMOTIVE	AREA	U.S. AVG
Average commute time	18.4 min.	22.6 min.	Miles to nearest major airport	63	46	Insurance, annual premium	$1,286	$1,011
Commute by auto	87.6%	88.7%	Type of local airport	Medium		Gas, cost per gallon	$1.60	$1.50
Commute by mass transit	.8%	1.8%	No. daily airline departures	155	294	Daily vehicle miles per capita	26.9	23.0
Work at home	5.1%	3.9%	Amtrak service	No				
Mass transit miles per capita	0.0	8.0	No. interstate highways	1	1			

LEISURE — SCORE: 35/RANK: 214

DINING & SHOPPING	AREA	U.S. AVG	ENTERTAINMENT	AREA	U.S. AVG	OUTDOOR ACTIVITIES	AREA	U.S. AVG
Restaurant rating	1	1	Professional sports rating	2	4	Golf-course rating	3	4
No. outlet malls	0	2	College sports rating	4	4	Ski-area rating	3	4
No. Starbucks	0	11	Zoo/aquarium rating	1	3	National Park rating	1	3
No. warehouse clubs	3	4	Amusement park rating	3	3	Sq. miles inland water	4.0	4.0
			Botanical garden/arboretum rating	1	3	Miles of coastline	0.0	11.4

ARTS & CULTURE — SCORE: 49/RANK: 169

MEDIA & LIBRARIES	AREA	U.S. AVG	PERFORMING ARTS	AREA	U.S. AVG	MUSEUMS	AREA	U.S. AVG
Arts radio rating	1	3	Classical music rating	2	4	Overall museum rating	5	6
No. public libraries	24	28	Ballet/dance rating	3	3	Art museum rating	2	5
Library volumes per capita	6.0	2.8	Professional theater rating	1	3	Science museum rating	3	4
			University arts programs rating	1	5	Children's museum rating	2	3

Janesville-Beloit, WI

Score: 62.2   Rank: 131

Profile: Small-town complex
Location: Extreme south-central Wisconsin at the Illinois border
Elevation: 803 feet
Time zone: Central Standard Time

PRO	CON
Small-town atmosphere	Cold winters
Attractive setting	Economic cycles
Proximity to Chicago	Arts and culture

Janesville and Beloit are located about 15 miles apart in extreme south-central Wisconsin, with Beloit abutting the Illinois border. Both are small industrial towns with a large General Motors plant and Parker Pen in Janesville and a variety of smaller businesses, notably food processing and distribution, in Beloit. Manufacturing and auto industry ties give the area a cyclical economy. Beloit is home to Beloit College, a well-acclaimed small college, as well as historic districts and a few minor cultural assets. Cost of living is reasonable across the entire area.

Both towns are located in the broad, fertile agricultural valley of the Rock River. The continental climate is characterized by hot summers and cold winters. Depending on the wind, Lake Michigan may influence the climate. Summers are warm and humid with occasional hot, muggy spells and frequent afternoon thunderstorms. Winters are generally cold with most precipitation falling as snow and remaining as snow cover. First freeze is mid-October, last is late April.

POPULATION

DEMOGRAPHICS	AREA	U.S. AVG	ETHNIC COMPOSITION	AREA	U.S. AVG	RESIDENT PROFILE	AREA	U.S. AVG
Population	154,092		White	95.4%	75.1%	Single	41.4%	43.6%
Population density per sq. mile	213.9	447.3	Black	3.1%	12.3%	Married	58.7%	56.4%
Population growth	10.5%	16.1%	Asian	.9%	3.6%	Divorced	8.4%	8.4%
Median age	36.2	35.5	American Indian	.3%	.9%	Separated	2.1%	3.0%
Average family size	2.6	2.7	Hispanic	1.6%	12.5%	Married with children	28.9%	28.7%
			Diversity measure	19.7%	35.2%	Single with children	10.3%	10.1%

ECONOMY & JOBS
SCORE: 66/RANK: 111

INCOME	AREA	U.S. AVG	EMPLOYMENT	AREA	U.S. AVG	LARGEST EMPLOYING INDUSTRY
Per capita income	$22,551	$23,420	Unemployment rate	6.5%	6.1%	Transportation Equipment Manufacturing
Household income	$46,791	$46,060	Recent job growth	1.6%	.9%	
Household income < $25K	24.0%	26.4%	Projected future job growth	11.9%	15.1%	
Household income > $75K	21.9%	24.5%	White collar	44.5%	54.5%	
Household income growth	52.6%	57.3%	Blue collar	55.5%	45.5%	

COST OF LIVING
SCORE: 32/RANK: 224

INDEXES & TAXES	AREA	U.S. AVG	HOUSING	AREA	U.S. AVG	NECESSITIES	AREA	U.S. AVG
Cost of Living Index	91.5	100.0	Median home price	$110,470	$160,100	Food Index	101.8	100.0
Financial Progress Index	108.9	100.0	Home price appreciation	4.0%	7.1%	Housing Index	68.6	100.0
Income tax rate	6.930%	4.625%	Median rent	$592	$670	Utilities Index	129.3	100.0
Sales tax rate	5.000%	6.474%	Homes owned	68.5%	63.9%	Transportation Index	103.4	100.0
Property tax rate	$27.1	$15.6	Homes rented	25.9%	25.3%	Healthcare Index	105.1	100.0
			Housing affordability	61.0%	54.5%	Miscellaneous Cost Index	97.8	100.0

CLIMATE
SCORE: 24/RANK: 249

TEMPERATURE	AREA	U.S. AVG	PRECIPITATION	AREA	U.S. AVG	COMFORTS & HAZARDS	AREA	U.S. AVG
January low	8.2°F	26.4°F	Annual inches precipitation	30.0	35.9	July relative humidity	73.0%	68.8%
July high	81.4°F	86.7°F	Annual inches snowfall	39.0	24.2	Annual days mostly sunny	190	212
Annual days > 90°F	12	38	Annual days precipitation	117	111	Annual days with thunderstorms	40	39
Annual days < 32°F	164	88	Annual days rain > 0.5 inches	18	23	Tornado risk score	13	19
Annual days < 0°F	25	6	Annual days snow > 1.5 inches	10	6	Hurricane risk score	1	15

TEMPERATURE

PRECIPITATION

DAYS OF CLOUDS & PRECIPITATION

EDUCATION
SCORE: 38/RANK: 203

ACHIEVEMENT	AREA	U.S. AVG	PUBLIC SCHOOLS	AREA	U.S. AVG	HIGHER EDUCATION	AREA	U.S. AVG
High school degree	83.9%	80.2%	Expenditures per pupil	$7,046	$5,894	No. 2-year colleges	2	3
2-year college degree	6.7%	6.2%	Student/teacher ratio	15.0	16.7	No. 4-year colleges/universities	1	4
4-year college degree	11.3%	15.8%	Attending public school	91.7%	90.2%	No. highly ranked universities	0	1
Graduate/professional degree	5.9%	9.6%	State SAT score	1179	1020			
			State ACT score	22.2*	21.0			

HEALTH & HEALTHCARE
SCORE: 88/RANK: 37

HAZARDS & ILLNESSES	AREA	U.S. AVG	HEALTHCARE	AREA	U.S. AVG
Air-quality score	24	45	Physicians per capita	185.6	261.1
Water-quality score	25	33	Hospital beds per capita	653.3	432.2
Pollen/allergy score	35	61	No. teaching hospitals	1	4
Stress score	47	50	Cost per doctor visit	$83	$67
Cancer mortality per capita	174.5	169.0	Cost per dental visit	$79	$82
Depression days per month	2.4	2.8	Cost per daily hospital room	$645	$733

CRIME
SCORE: 58/RANK: 138

CRIME	AREA	U.S. AVG
Violent crime rate	228.8	456.0
Change in violent crime rate	-16.7%	-17.2%
Property crime rate	3,818.3	3,950.0
Change in property crime rate	-4.3%	-16.8%

TRANSPORTATION
SCORE: 46/RANK: 177

COMMUTE	AREA	U.S. AVG	INTERCITY SERVICES	AREA	U.S. AVG	AUTOMOTIVE	AREA	U.S. AVG
Average commute time	20.3 min.	22.6 min.	Miles to nearest major airport	35	46	Insurance, annual premium	$749	$1,011
Commute by auto	88.8%	88.7%	Type of local airport	Small		Gas, cost per gallon	$1.56	$1.50
Commute by mass transit	.4%	1.8%	No. daily airline departures	49	294	Daily vehicle miles per capita	19.4	23.0
Work at home	5.9%	3.9%	Amtrak service	No				
Mass transit miles per capita	4.9	8.0	No. interstate highways	1	1			

LEISURE SCORE: 20/RANK: 265

DINING & SHOPPING	AREA	U.S. AVG	ENTERTAINMENT	AREA	U.S. AVG	OUTDOOR ACTIVITIES	AREA	U.S. AVG
Restaurant rating	1	1	Professional sports rating	4	4	Golf-course rating	2	4
No. outlet malls	5	2	College sports rating	2	4	Ski-area rating	2	4
No. Starbucks	0	11	Zoo/aquarium rating	1	3	National Park rating	1	3
No. warehouse clubs	1	4	Amusement park rating	1	3	Sq. miles inland water	2.0	4.0
			Botanical garden/arboretum rating	1	3	Miles of coastline	0.0	11.4

ARTS & CULTURE SCORE: 16/RANK: 278

MEDIA & LIBRARIES	AREA	U.S. AVG	PERFORMING ARTS	AREA	U.S. AVG	MUSEUMS	AREA	U.S. AVG
Arts radio rating	1	3	Classical music rating	4	4	Overall museum rating	5	6
No. public libraries	7	28	Ballet/dance rating	1	3	Art museum rating	3	5
Library volumes per capita	3.7	2.8	Professional theater rating	1	3	Science museum rating	1	4
			University arts programs rating	2	5	Children's museum rating	1	3

Jersey City, NJ

Score: 43.5 Rank: 262

Profile: Industrial center/Commuter community
Location: Northeastern New Jersey, across the Hudson River from Manhattan
Elevation: 7 feet
Time zone: Eastern Standard Time

PRO	CON
Proximity to New York City	Cost of living
Revitalized areas	Industrial setting
Educated population	Violent crime

The Jersey City area includes the cities of Bayonne, North Bergen, Secaucus, Union City, and Hoboken in Hudson County. Most of the area lies on a narrow peninsula on the Hudson River between Manhattan and the New Jersey mainland north of Newark. As a long-time transportation gateway between New Jersey and New York City, Hoboken is re-emerging as an area for restaurants, nightlife, working singles, and young couples. The area has the state's highest level of educational attainment, and a few Manhattan companies have relocated their offices here. While Hoboken is going through a bit of a renaissance, the remainder of the area has a highly industrial and working-class character.

The area is level, with a low, mostly built-up coastline and wooded hills in the interior. The climate is predominantly continental with a high degree of variation in temperature, humidity, and precipitation. Summers are hot and humid, but some areas, especially along the Hudson, may receive some cooling effects from late afternoon breezes. There are periods of summer showers and thunderstorms, but few are severe. Winters are cool and wet with a mix of rain, sleet, and snow. A passing "noreaster" coastal storm typically produces 1 to 2 inches of precipitation as rain or snow. Snowfalls of 8 inches or more occur every other year, and snow often lingers on the ground. First freeze is late October, last is mid-April.

POPULATION

DEMOGRAPHICS	AREA	U.S. AVG	ETHNIC COMPOSITION	AREA	U.S. AVG	RESIDENT PROFILE	AREA	U.S. AVG
Population	611,439		White	65.2%	75.1%	Single	58.4%	43.6%
Population density per sq. mile	13,105.8	447.3	Black	15.0%	12.3%	Married	41.5%	56.4%
Population growth	10.5%	16.1%	Asian	10.3%	3.6%	Divorced	7.0%	8.4%
Median age	33.9	35.5	American Indian	.4%	.9%	Separated	6.0%	3.0%
Average family size	2.5	2.7	Hispanic	41.5%	12.5%	Married with children	18.6%	28.7%
			Diversity measure	70.9%	35.2%	Single with children	13.3%	10.1%

ECONOMY & JOBS SCORE: 26/RANK: 245

INCOME	AREA	U.S. AVG	EMPLOYMENT	AREA	U.S. AVG	LARGEST EMPLOYING INDUSTRY
Per capita income	$23,316	$23,420	Unemployment rate	7.8%	6.1%	Securities, Commodity Contracts, and Other
Household income	$47,746	$46,060	Recent job growth	1.3%	.9%	Financial Investments and Related Activities
Household income < $25K	26.2%	26.4%	Projected future job growth	6.6%	15.1%	
Household income > $75K	27.0%	24.5%	White collar	55.0%	54.5%	
Household income growth	54.0%	57.3%	Blue collar	45.0%	45.5%	

COST OF LIVING SCORE: 8/RANK: 302

INDEXES & TAXES	AREA	U.S. AVG	HOUSING	AREA	U.S. AVG	NECESSITIES	AREA	U.S. AVG
Cost of Living Index	133.3	100.0	Median home price	$222,480	$160,100	Food Index	125.0	100.0
Financial Progress Index	76.3	100.0	Home price appreciation	14.0%	7.1%	Housing Index	138.2	100.0
Income tax rate	2.450%	4.625%	Median rent	$1,061	$670	Utilities Index	143.6	100.0
Sales tax rate	6.000%	6.474%	Homes owned	32.4%	63.9%	Transportation Index	120.4	100.0
Property tax rate	$27.1	$15.6	Homes rented	57.3%	25.3%	Healthcare Index	165.7	100.0
			Housing affordability	46.0%	54.5%	Miscellaneous Cost Index	125.7	100.0

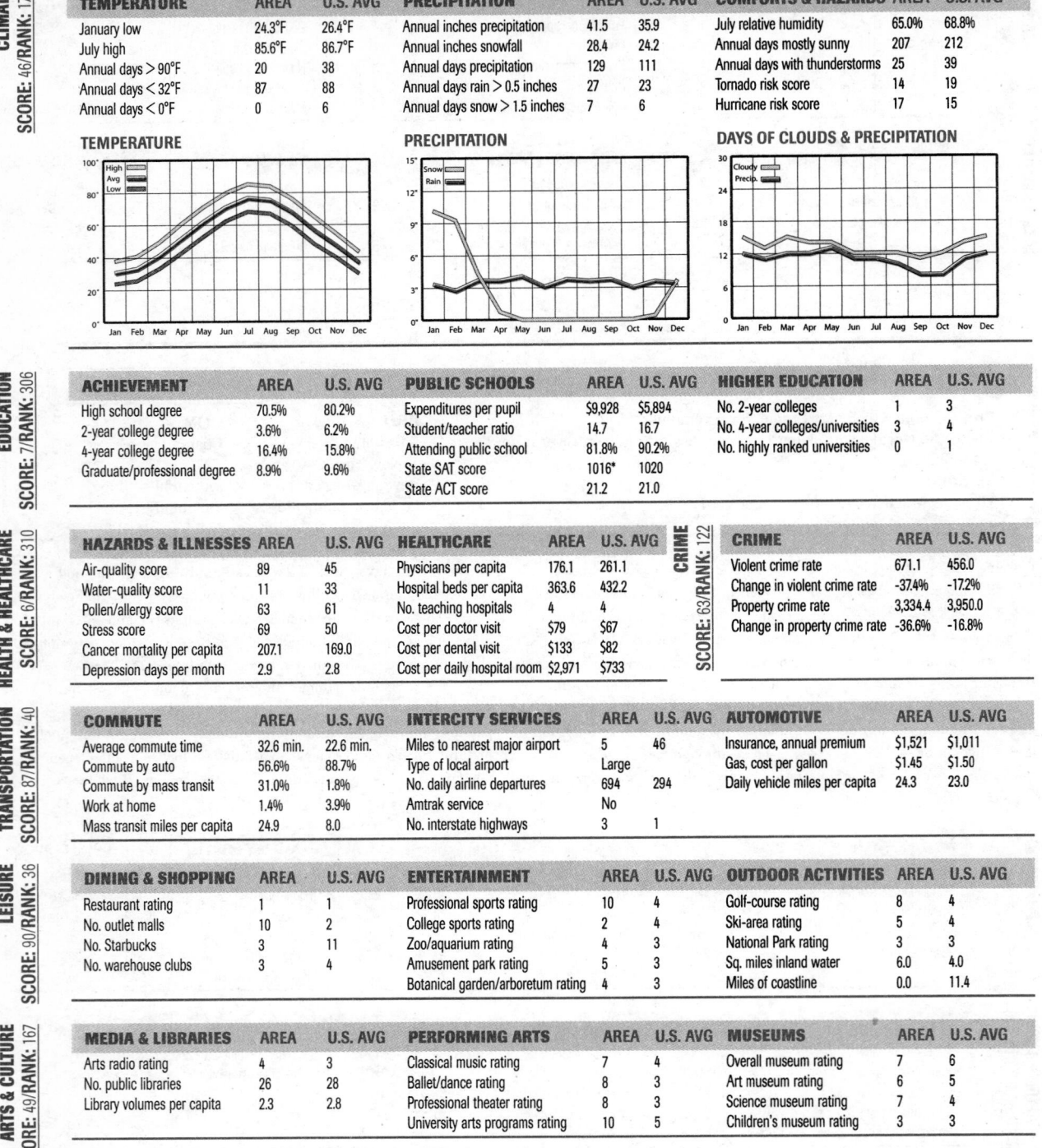

CLIMATE SCORE: 46/RANK: 179

TEMPERATURE	AREA	U.S. AVG
January low	24.3°F	26.4°F
July high	85.6°F	86.7°F
Annual days > 90°F	20	38
Annual days < 32°F	87	88
Annual days < 0°F	0	6

PRECIPITATION	AREA	U.S. AVG
Annual inches precipitation	41.5	35.9
Annual inches snowfall	28.4	24.2
Annual days precipitation	129	111
Annual days rain > 0.5 inches	27	23
Annual days snow > 1.5 inches	7	6

COMFORTS & HAZARDS	AREA	U.S. AVG
July relative humidity	65.0%	68.8%
Annual days mostly sunny	207	212
Annual days with thunderstorms	25	39
Tornado risk score	14	19
Hurricane risk score	17	15

TEMPERATURE

PRECIPITATION

DAYS OF CLOUDS & PRECIPITATION

EDUCATION SCORE: 7/RANK: 306

ACHIEVEMENT	AREA	U.S. AVG
High school degree	70.5%	80.2%
2-year college degree	3.6%	6.2%
4-year college degree	16.4%	15.8%
Graduate/professional degree	8.9%	9.6%

PUBLIC SCHOOLS	AREA	U.S. AVG
Expenditures per pupil	$9,928	$5,894
Student/teacher ratio	14.7	16.7
Attending public school	81.8%	90.2%
State SAT score	1016*	1020
State ACT score	21.2	21.0

HIGHER EDUCATION	AREA	U.S. AVG
No. 2-year colleges	1	3
No. 4-year colleges/universities	3	4
No. highly ranked universities	0	1

HEALTH & HEALTHCARE SCORE: 6/RANK: 310

HAZARDS & ILLNESSES	AREA	U.S. AVG
Air-quality score	89	45
Water-quality score	11	33
Pollen/allergy score	63	61
Stress score	69	50
Cancer mortality per capita	207.1	169.0
Depression days per month	2.9	2.8

HEALTHCARE	AREA	U.S. AVG
Physicians per capita	176.1	261.1
Hospital beds per capita	363.6	432.2
No. teaching hospitals	4	4
Cost per doctor visit	$79	$67
Cost per dental visit	$133	$82
Cost per daily hospital room	$2,971	$733

CRIME SCORE: 63/RANK: 122

CRIME	AREA	U.S. AVG
Violent crime rate	671.1	456.0
Change in violent crime rate	-37.4%	-17.2%
Property crime rate	3,334.4	3,950.0
Change in property crime rate	-36.6%	-16.8%

TRANSPORTATION SCORE: 87/RANK: 40

COMMUTE	AREA	U.S. AVG
Average commute time	32.6 min.	22.6 min.
Commute by auto	56.6%	88.7%
Commute by mass transit	31.0%	1.8%
Work at home	1.4%	3.9%
Mass transit miles per capita	24.9	8.0

INTERCITY SERVICES	AREA	U.S. AVG
Miles to nearest major airport	5	46
Type of local airport	Large	
No. daily airline departures	694	294
Amtrak service	No	
No. interstate highways	3	1

AUTOMOTIVE	AREA	U.S. AVG
Insurance, annual premium	$1,521	$1,011
Gas, cost per gallon	$1.45	$1.50
Daily vehicle miles per capita	24.3	23.0

LEISURE SCORE: 90/RANK: 36

DINING & SHOPPING	AREA	U.S. AVG
Restaurant rating	1	1
No. outlet malls	10	2
No. Starbucks	3	11
No. warehouse clubs	3	4

ENTERTAINMENT	AREA	U.S. AVG
Professional sports rating	10	4
College sports rating	2	4
Zoo/aquarium rating	4	3
Amusement park rating	5	3
Botanical garden/arboretum rating	4	3

OUTDOOR ACTIVITIES	AREA	U.S. AVG
Golf-course rating	8	4
Ski-area rating	5	4
National Park rating	3	3
Sq. miles inland water	6.0	4.0
Miles of coastline	0.0	11.4

ARTS & CULTURE SCORE: 49/RANK: 167

MEDIA & LIBRARIES	AREA	U.S. AVG
Arts radio rating	4	3
No. public libraries	26	28
Library volumes per capita	2.3	2.8

PERFORMING ARTS	AREA	U.S. AVG
Classical music rating	7	4
Ballet/dance rating	8	3
Professional theater rating	8	3
University arts programs rating	10	5

MUSEUMS	AREA	U.S. AVG
Overall museum rating	7	6
Art museum rating	6	5
Science museum rating	7	4
Children's museum rating	3	3

Johnson City–Kingsport–Bristol, TN

Score: 70.6 **Rank:** 77

Profile: Small-city complex
Location: Northeastern tip of Tennessee at the Virginia and North Carolina border
Elevation: 1,525 feet
Time zone: Eastern Standard Time

PRO	CON
Cost of living	Isolation
Nearby recreation	Low ethnic diversity
Diverse economy	Arts and culture

This triad of cities, 20 miles apart, offers Southern small-town character and an assortment of industrial and agricultural activities. Chemicals, forest products, glass, textiles, and metal products are produced in the area. Bristol is a center for small business and industry, and Kingsport holds the largest single industrial employer in the state, Eastman Chemical. As home to East Tennessee State University, Johnson City is more of a college town. Kingsport is a planned city with ample parkland and greenbelts. All the cities have an assortment of arts and recreational activities, as well as access to the nearby Tennessee Valley Authority lakes. The Bristol Motor Speedway is an important NASCAR track. Cost of living is low and the economy is healthy—in fact, the area has received "All American City" and "Most Livable City"

recognition in recent years—but the area is geographically isolated from larger cities. Additional services are usually found in Virginia.

The Tri-Cities Area is located in the upper East Tennessee Valley. The immediate terrain is gently rolling on the east and south to very hilly on the west and north. Mountain ranges rise 4,000 feet to 6,000 feet to the southeast. The variable topography has considerable influence on the weather. Mountains shelter the area from cold and some moisture but open landscape to the southwest allows moist Gulf airflow, causing warm, humid summers. Summer thunderstorms are frequent, with the most rain occurring in July. Atlantic Coast storms can bring heavy winter precipitation. Only the mountains receive snow.

POPULATION

DEMOGRAPHICS	AREA	U.S. AVG	ETHNIC COMPOSITION	AREA	U.S. AVG	RESIDENT PROFILE	AREA	U.S. AVG
Population	482,934		White	97.0%	75.1%	Single	39.2%	43.6%
Population density per sq. mile	168.5	447.3	Black	2.4%	12.3%	Married	60.8%	56.4%
Population growth	10.8%	16.1%	Asian	.3%	3.6%	Divorced	8.3%	8.4%
Median age	39.9	35.5	American Indian	.2%	.9%	Separated	2.2%	3.0%
Average family size	2.5	2.7	Hispanic	.6%	12.5%	Married with children	27.9%	28.7%
			Diversity measure	8.4%	35.2%	Single with children	7.9%	10.1%

ECONOMY & JOBS
SCORE: 36/RANK: 209

INCOME	AREA	U.S. AVG	EMPLOYMENT	AREA	U.S. AVG	LARGEST EMPLOYING INDUSTRY
Per capita income	$19,423	$23,420	Unemployment rate	5.3%	6.1%	Chemical Manufacturing
Household income	$32,897	$46,060	Recent job growth	-.3%	.9%	
Household income < $25K	37.8%	26.4%	Projected future job growth	11.7%	15.1%	
Household income > $75K	14.0%	24.5%	White collar	47.5%	54.5%	
Household income growth	46.8%	57.3%	Blue collar	52.5%	45.5%	

COST OF LIVING
SCORE: 97/RANK: 9

INDEXES & TAXES	AREA	U.S. AVG	HOUSING	AREA	U.S. AVG	NECESSITIES	AREA	U.S. AVG
Cost of Living Index	79.9	100.0	Median home price	$99,820	$160,100	Food Index	90.4	100.0
Financial Progress Index	87.8	100.0	Home price appreciation	5.0%	7.1%	Housing Index	62.0	100.0
Income tax rate	0.000%	4.625%	Median rent	$486	$670	Utilities Index	95.5	100.0
Sales tax rate	4.500%	6.474%	Homes owned	71.4%	63.9%	Transportation Index	87.7	100.0
Property tax rate	$13.3	$15.6	Homes rented	19.2%	25.3%	Healthcare Index	85.4	100.0
			Housing affordability	56.0%	54.5%	Miscellaneous Cost Index	89.8	100.0

CLIMATE
SCORE: 56/RANK: 144

TEMPERATURE	AREA	U.S. AVG	PRECIPITATION	AREA	U.S. AVG	COMFORTS & HAZARDS	AREA	U.S. AVG
January low	26.7°F	26.4°F	Annual inches precipitation	41.0	35.9	July relative humidity	72.0%	68.8%
July high	85.9°F	86.7°F	Annual inches snowfall	16.0	24.2	Annual days mostly sunny	202	212
Annual days > 90°F	13	38	Annual days precipitation	134	111	Annual days with thunderstorms	45	39
Annual days < 32°F	96	88	Annual days rain > 0.5 inches	25	23	Tornado risk score	3	19
Annual days < 0°F	1	6	Annual days snow > 1.5 inches	4	6	Hurricane risk score	7	15

TEMPERATURE

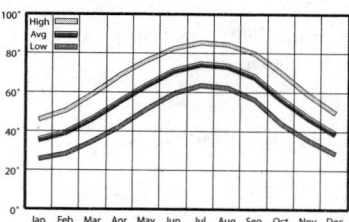

PRECIPITATION

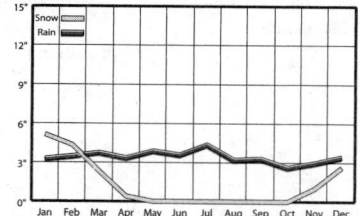

DAYS OF CLOUDS & PRECIPITATION

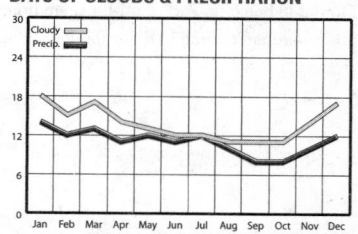

EDUCATION — SCORE: 37/RANK: 207

ACHIEVEMENT	AREA	U.S. AVG	PUBLIC SCHOOLS	AREA	U.S. AVG	HIGHER EDUCATION	AREA	U.S. AVG
High school degree	73.3%	80.2%	Expenditures per pupil	$5,426	$5,894	No. 2-year colleges	2	3
2-year college degree	4.3%	6.2%	Student/teacher ratio	14.5	16.7	No. 4-year colleges/universities	5	4
4-year college degree	10.9%	15.8%	Attending public school	95.9%	90.2%	No. highly ranked universities	2	1
Graduate/professional degree	5.7%	9.6%	State SAT score	1128	1020			
			State ACT score	20.4*	21.0			

HEALTH & HEALTHCARE — SCORE: 96/RANK: 13 | CRIME — SCORE: 26/RANK: 243

HAZARDS & ILLNESSES	AREA	U.S. AVG	HEALTHCARE	AREA	U.S. AVG	CRIME	AREA	U.S. AVG
Air-quality score	59	45	Physicians per capita	304.0	261.1	Violent crime rate	392.6	456.0
Water-quality score	77	33	Hospital beds per capita	453.5	432.2	Change in violent crime rate	30.5%	-17.2%
Pollen/allergy score	60	61	No. teaching hospitals	3	4	Property crime rate	3,204.7	3,950.0
Stress score	36	50	Cost per doctor visit	$68	$67	Change in property crime rate	27.1%	-16.8%
Cancer mortality per capita	158.4	169.0	Cost per dental visit	$63	$82			
Depression days per month	2.4	2.8	Cost per daily hospital room	$411	$733			

TRANSPORTATION — SCORE: 16/RANK: 275

COMMUTE	AREA	U.S. AVG	INTERCITY SERVICES	AREA	U.S. AVG	AUTOMOTIVE	AREA	U.S. AVG
Average commute time	22.4 min.	22.6 min.	Miles to nearest major airport	97	46	Insurance, annual premium	$835	$1,011
Commute by auto	93.8%	88.7%	Type of local airport	Small		Gas, cost per gallon	$1.40	$1.50
Commute by mass transit	.4%	1.8%	No. daily airline departures	89	294	Daily vehicle miles per capita	26.5	23.0
Work at home	2.8%	3.9%	Amtrak service	No				
Mass transit miles per capita	1.3	8.0	No. interstate highways	1	1			

LEISURE — SCORE: 36/RANK: 212

DINING & SHOPPING	AREA	U.S. AVG	ENTERTAINMENT	AREA	U.S. AVG	OUTDOOR ACTIVITIES	AREA	U.S. AVG
Restaurant rating	1	1	Professional sports rating	2	4	Golf-course rating	3	4
No. outlet malls	1	2	College sports rating	3	4	Ski-area rating	2	4
No. Starbucks	1	11	Zoo/aquarium rating	1	3	National Park rating	8	3
No. warehouse clubs	3	4	Amusement park rating	1	3	Sq. miles inland water	4.0	4.0
			Botanical garden/arboretum rating	1	3	Miles of coastline	0.0	11.4

ARTS & CULTURE — SCORE: 33/RANK: 219

MEDIA & LIBRARIES	AREA	U.S. AVG	PERFORMING ARTS	AREA	U.S. AVG	MUSEUMS	AREA	U.S. AVG
Arts radio rating	1	3	Classical music rating	4	4	Overall museum rating	6	6
No. public libraries	25	28	Ballet/dance rating	3	3	Art museum rating	4	5
Library volumes per capita	1.8	2.8	Professional theater rating	8	3	Science museum rating	3	4
			University arts programs rating	6	5	Children's museum rating	6	3

Johnstown, PA

Score: 55.5   Rank: 187

Profile: Small city
Location: West-central Pennsylvania, 70 miles east of Pittsburgh
Elevation: 1,223 feet
Time zone: Eastern Standard Time

PRO	CON
Cost of living	Economy
Low crime rate	Low educational attainment
Small-town atmosphere	Low ethnic diversity

Johnstown is a small city located just west of the main ridge of the Alleghenies. To most outsiders it is associated with four historic, devastating, floods, the most recent in 1977. The city has a mixed and somewhat depressed economy and a slow pace of life. Local amenities focus on museums that commemorate the floods and a historic incline railway. There is good outdoor recreation in the area. The low cost of living, affordable housing, and small-town environment are the main attractions, but there isn't much to do or much intellectual stimulation.

The immediate area around downtown is located on a flat floodplain of the Conemaugh River. Several creeks converge on the plain, with a long, deep gorge to the west and an arrangement of mountains catching moisture flow from the south, creating ideal flood conditions. Steep wooded bluffs and hills surround the town. The climate is humid continental, typical of central Pennsylvania, modified by the mountains and the Great Lakes to the north. Summers are warm and humid, influenced by Gulf air from the south. Winters are cloudy and cool with mixed precipitation but infrequent severe cold.

POPULATION

DEMOGRAPHICS	AREA	U.S. AVG	ETHNIC COMPOSITION	AREA	U.S. AVG	RESIDENT PROFILE	AREA	U.S. AVG
Population	229,908		White	98.0%	75.1%	Single	42.3%	43.6%
Population density per sq. mile	130.4	447.3	Black	1.7%	12.3%	Married	57.7%	56.4%
Population growth	-4.7%	16.1%	Asian	.2%	3.6%	Divorced	5.1%	8.4%
Median age	41.3	35.5	American Indian	.1%	.9%	Separated	2.6%	3.0%
Average family size	2.6	2.7	Hispanic	.5%	12.5%	Married with children	28.3%	28.7%
			Diversity measure	8.0%	35.2%	Single with children	7.2%	10.1%

ECONOMY & JOBS SCORE: 10/RANK: 298

INCOME	AREA	U.S. AVG	EMPLOYMENT	AREA	U.S. AVG	LARGEST EMPLOYING INDUSTRY
Per capita income	$16,484	$23,420	Unemployment rate	6.0%	6.1%	Transportation Equipment Manufacturing
Household income	$30,250	$46,060	Recent job growth	-2.3%	.9%	
Household income < $25K	41.0%	26.4%	Projected future job growth	12.1%	15.1%	
Household income > $75K	9.1%	24.5%	White collar	45.0%	54.5%	
Household income growth	40.3%	57.3%	Blue collar	55.0%	45.5%	

COST OF LIVING SCORE: 93/RANK: 21

INDEXES & TAXES	AREA	U.S. AVG	HOUSING	AREA	U.S. AVG	NECESSITIES	AREA	U.S. AVG
Cost of Living Index	79.7	100.0	Median home price	$77,340	$160,100	Food Index	97.4	100.0
Financial Progress Index	80.9	100.0	Home price appreciation	5.9%	7.1%	Housing Index	48.0	100.0
Income tax rate	2.800%	4.625%	Median rent	$474	$670	Utilities Index	110.9	100.0
Sales tax rate	6.000%	6.474%	Homes owned	71.2%	63.9%	Transportation Index	88.1	100.0
Property tax rate	$15.9	$15.6	Homes rented	15.7%	25.3%	Healthcare Index	91.4	100.0
			Housing affordability	54.0%	54.5%	Miscellaneous Cost Index	99.2	100.0

CLIMATE SCORE: 41/RANK: 195

TEMPERATURE	AREA	U.S. AVG	PRECIPITATION	AREA	U.S. AVG	COMFORTS & HAZARDS	AREA	U.S. AVG
January low	19.8°F	26.4°F	Annual inches precipitation	37.0	35.9	July relative humidity	67.0%	68.8%
July high	82.6°F	86.7°F	Annual inches snowfall	48.0	24.2	Annual days mostly sunny	180	212
Annual days > 90°F	8	38	Annual days precipitation	122	111	Annual days with thunderstorms	35	39
Annual days < 32°F	132	88	Annual days rain > 0.5 inches	20	23	Tornado risk score	6	19
Annual days < 0°F	4	6	Annual days snow > 1.5 inches	10	6	Hurricane risk score	6	15

TEMPERATURE

PRECIPITATION

DAYS OF CLOUDS & PRECIPITATION

EDUCATION SCORE: 8/RANK: 304

ACHIEVEMENT	AREA	U.S. AVG	PUBLIC SCHOOLS	AREA	U.S. AVG	HIGHER EDUCATION	AREA	U.S. AVG
High school degree	79.2%	80.2%	Expenditures per pupil	$6,129	$5,894	No. 2-year colleges	1	3
2-year college degree	5.6%	6.2%	Student/teacher ratio	15.6	16.7	No. 4-year colleges/universities	3	4
4-year college degree	8.4%	15.8%	Attending public school	88.5%	90.2%	No. highly ranked universities	0	1
Graduate/professional degree	4.4%	9.6%	State SAT score	1002*	1020			
			State ACT score	21.5	21.0			

HEALTH & HEALTHCARE SCORE: 85/RANK: 49   **CRIME** SCORE: 78/RANK: 72

HAZARDS & ILLNESSES	AREA	U.S. AVG	HEALTHCARE	AREA	U.S. AVG	CRIME	AREA	U.S. AVG
Air-quality score	59	45	Physicians per capita	207.5	261.1	Violent crime rate	235.9	456.0
Water-quality score	56	33	Hospital beds per capita	546.0	432.2	Change in violent crime rate	20.2%	-17.2%
Pollen/allergy score	67	61	No. teaching hospitals	1	4	Property crime rate	1,656.4	3,950.0
Stress score	27	50	Cost per doctor visit	$55	$67	Change in property crime rate	9.1%	-16.8%
Cancer mortality per capita	164.6	169.0	Cost per dental visit	$54	$82			
Depression days per month	1.5	2.8	Cost per daily hospital room	$518	$733			

TRANSPORTATION SCORE: 23/RANK: 253

COMMUTE	AREA	U.S. AVG	INTERCITY SERVICES	AREA	U.S. AVG	AUTOMOTIVE	AREA	U.S. AVG
Average commute time	22.2 min.	22.6 min.	Miles to nearest major airport	69	46	Insurance, annual premium	$975	$1,011
Commute by auto	90.0%	88.7%	Type of local airport	Large		Gas, cost per gallon	$1.50	$1.50
Commute by mass transit	.6%	1.8%	No. daily airline departures	663	294	Daily vehicle miles per capita	16.6	23.0
Work at home	3.7%	3.9%	Amtrak service	Yes				
Mass transit miles per capita	3.8	8.0	No. interstate highways	0	1			

LEISURE   SCORE: 54/RANK: 151

DINING & SHOPPING	AREA	U.S. AVG	ENTERTAINMENT	AREA	U.S. AVG	OUTDOOR ACTIVITIES	AREA	U.S. AVG
Restaurant rating	1	1	Professional sports rating	5	4	Golf-course rating	3	4
No. outlet malls	0	2	College sports rating	3	4	Ski-area rating	5	4
No. Starbucks	0	11	Zoo/aquarium rating	1	3	National Park rating	2	3
No. warehouse clubs	1	4	Amusement park rating	1	3	Sq. miles inland water	2.0	4.0
			Botanical garden/arboretum rating	1	3	Miles of coastline	0.0	11.4

ARTS & CULTURE   SCORE: 40/RANK: 198

MEDIA & LIBRARIES	AREA	U.S. AVG	PERFORMING ARTS	AREA	U.S. AVG	MUSEUMS	AREA	U.S. AVG
Arts radio rating	1	3	Classical music rating	3	4	Overall museum rating	6	6
No. public libraries	19	28	Ballet/dance rating	1	3	Art museum rating	5	5
Library volumes per capita	2.0	2.8	Professional theater rating	1	3	Science museum rating	1	4
			University arts programs rating	3	5	Children's museum rating	1	3

Jonesboro, AR

Score: 44.9   Rank: 257

Profile: Small town/College town
Location: Northeast Arkansas, about 50 miles northwest of Memphis, Tennessee
Elevation: 333
Time zone: Central Standard Time

PRO	CON
Cost of living	Hot, humid summers
Home prices	Recreation
Healthcare	Low ethnic diversity

Jonesboro, home to Arkansas State University, is a fairly nondescript town with a few college-town amenities. As in nearby places, Jonesboro features a low cost of living (with a COL Index of 77.5), low home prices, and better-than-average healthcare facilities. Arts and culture and recreational amenities are limited except for those associated with the school, but the drive to nearby Memphis fills the gap.

Jonesboro is located in a level area of gently rolling, mostly agricultural land. Climate is mostly continental with a strong subtropical influence from the Gulf of Mexico in summer. Summers are hot and sticky. Winters are mild with occasional cold snaps. Jonesboro gets more snow (8 inches) than any other metropolitan area in Arkansas. First freeze is late October, last is April 1.

POPULATION

DEMOGRAPHICS	AREA	U.S. AVG	ETHNIC COMPOSITION	AREA	U.S. AVG	RESIDENT PROFILE	AREA	U.S. AVG
Population	84,074		White	96.1%	75.1%	Single	37.8%	43.6%
Population density per sq. mile	118.3	447.3	Black	2.9%	12.3%	Married	62.2%	56.4%
Population growth	21.9%	16.1%	Asian	.4%	3.6%	Divorced	8.3%	8.4%
Median age	33.4	35.5	American Indian	.2%	.9%	Separated	2.5%	3.0%
Average family size	2.5	2.7	Hispanic	1.5%	12.5%	Married with children	29.7%	28.7%
			Diversity measure	21.2%	35.2%	Single with children	8.5%	10.1%

ECONOMY & JOBS   SCORE: 77/RANK: 74

INCOME	AREA	U.S. AVG	EMPLOYMENT	AREA	U.S. AVG	LARGEST EMPLOYING INDUSTRY
Per capita income	$20,761	$23,420	Unemployment rate	4.6%	6.1%	Transportation Equipment Manufacturing
Household income	$36,436	$46,060	Recent job growth	4.6%	.9%	
Household income < $25K	34.1%	26.4%	Projected future job growth	16.1%	15.1%	
Household income > $75K	16.0%	24.5%	White collar	50.1%	54.5%	
Household income growth	64.8%	57.3%	Blue collar	49.9%	45.5%	

COST OF LIVING   SCORE: 79/RANK: 69

INDEXES & TAXES	AREA	U.S. AVG	HOUSING	AREA	U.S. AVG	NECESSITIES	AREA	U.S. AVG
Cost of Living Index	77.5	100.0	Median home price	$88,820	$160,100	Food Index	91.6	100.0
Financial Progress Index	100.2	100.0	Home price appreciation	3.9%	7.1%	Housing Index	55.2	100.0
Income tax rate	7.000%	4.625%	Median rent	$498	$670	Utilities Index	79.3	100.0
Sales tax rate	6.125%	6.474%	Homes owned	69.8%	63.9%	Transportation Index	87.4	100.0
Property tax rate	$10.2	$15.6	Homes rented	22.5%	25.3%	Healthcare Index	89.7	100.0
			Housing affordability	56.0%	54.5%	Miscellaneous Cost Index	94.1	100.0

CLIMATE SCORE: 48/RANK: 171

TEMPERATURE	AREA	U.S. AVG	PRECIPITATION	AREA	U.S. AVG	COMFORTS & HAZARDS	AREA	U.S. AVG
January low	31.6°F	26.4°F	Annual inches precipitation	47.0	35.9	July relative humidity	69.0%	68.8%
July high	91.6°F	86.7°F	Annual inches snowfall	8.0	24.2	Annual days mostly sunny	217	212
Annual days > 90°F	63	38	Annual days precipitation	104	111	Annual days with thunderstorms	54	39
Annual days < 32°F	60	88	Annual days rain > 0.5 inches	32	23	Tornado risk score	47	19
Annual days < 0°F	0	6	Annual days snow > 1.5 inches	3	6	Hurricane risk score	8	15

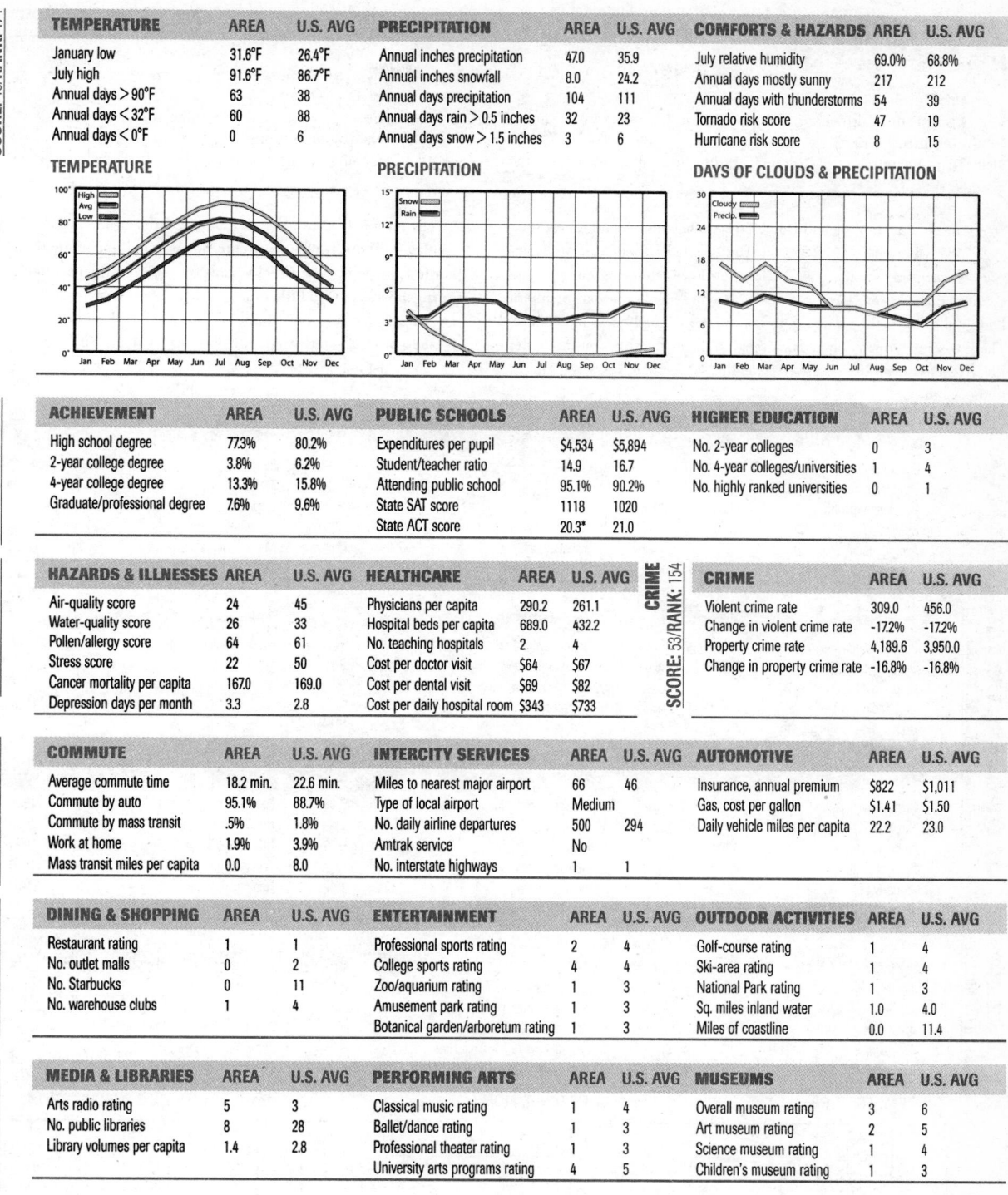

TEMPERATURE

PRECIPITATION

DAYS OF CLOUDS & PRECIPITATION

EDUCATION SCORE: 26/RANK: 245

ACHIEVEMENT	AREA	U.S. AVG	PUBLIC SCHOOLS	AREA	U.S. AVG	HIGHER EDUCATION	AREA	U.S. AVG
High school degree	77.3%	80.2%	Expenditures per pupil	$4,534	$5,894	No. 2-year colleges	0	3
2-year college degree	3.8%	6.2%	Student/teacher ratio	14.9	16.7	No. 4-year colleges/universities	1	4
4-year college degree	13.3%	15.8%	Attending public school	95.1%	90.2%	No. highly ranked universities	0	1
Graduate/professional degree	7.6%	9.6%	State SAT score	1118	1020			
			State ACT score	20.3*	21.0			

HEALTH & HEALTHCARE SCORE: 93/RANK: 20

CRIME SCORE: 53/RANK: 154

HAZARDS & ILLNESSES	AREA	U.S. AVG	HEALTHCARE	AREA	U.S. AVG	CRIME	AREA	U.S. AVG
Air-quality score	24	45	Physicians per capita	290.2	261.1	Violent crime rate	309.0	456.0
Water-quality score	26	33	Hospital beds per capita	689.0	432.2	Change in violent crime rate	-17.2%	-17.2%
Pollen/allergy score	64	61	No. teaching hospitals	2	4	Property crime rate	4,189.6	3,950.0
Stress score	22	50	Cost per doctor visit	$64	$67	Change in property crime rate	-16.8%	-16.8%
Cancer mortality per capita	167.0	169.0	Cost per dental visit	$69	$82			
Depression days per month	3.3	2.8	Cost per daily hospital room	$343	$733			

TRANSPORTATION SCORE: 54/RANK: 150

COMMUTE	AREA	U.S. AVG	INTERCITY SERVICES	AREA	U.S. AVG	AUTOMOTIVE	AREA	U.S. AVG
Average commute time	18.2 min.	22.6 min.	Miles to nearest major airport	66	46	Insurance, annual premium	$822	$1,011
Commute by auto	95.1%	88.7%	Type of local airport	Medium		Gas, cost per gallon	$1.41	$1.50
Commute by mass transit	.5%	1.8%	No. daily airline departures	500	294	Daily vehicle miles per capita	22.2	23.0
Work at home	1.9%	3.9%	Amtrak service	No				
Mass transit miles per capita	0.0	8.0	No. interstate highways	1	1			

LEISURE SCORE: 1/RANK: 325

DINING & SHOPPING	AREA	U.S. AVG	ENTERTAINMENT	AREA	U.S. AVG	OUTDOOR ACTIVITIES	AREA	U.S. AVG
Restaurant rating	1	1	Professional sports rating	2	4	Golf-course rating	1	4
No. outlet malls	0	2	College sports rating	4	4	Ski-area rating	1	4
No. Starbucks	0	11	Zoo/aquarium rating	1	3	National Park rating	1	3
No. warehouse clubs	1	4	Amusement park rating	1	3	Sq. miles inland water	1.0	4.0
			Botanical garden/arboretum rating	1	3	Miles of coastline	0.0	11.4

ARTS & CULTURE SCORE: 9/RANK: 300

MEDIA & LIBRARIES	AREA	U.S. AVG	PERFORMING ARTS	AREA	U.S. AVG	MUSEUMS	AREA	U.S. AVG
Arts radio rating	5	3	Classical music rating	1	4	Overall museum rating	3	6
No. public libraries	8	28	Ballet/dance rating	1	3	Art museum rating	2	5
Library volumes per capita	1.4	2.8	Professional theater rating	1	3	Science museum rating	1	4
			University arts programs rating	4	5	Children's museum rating	1	3

Joplin, MO

Score: 31.0   Rank: 306

Profile: Small town
Location: Southwest corner of Missouri, 6 miles from Kansas border
Elevation: 980 feet
Time zone: Central Standard Time

PRO	CON
Cost of living	Economy
Nearby mountains	Entertainment
Small-town atmosphere	Hot, humid summers

This old zinc mining and Route 66 town has the second lowest Cost of Living Index (74.2) in the United States (tied with McAllen, Texas), and, until recently, had the lowest housing costs in the country. But costs are low for a reason: Besides small Missouri Southern State College and the Ozarks to the south, there simply isn't much here. There is some industry and commerce, but the main attractions are quiet lifestyle and the ability to preserve wealth and income. Tulsa is 90 miles to the southwest.

The town is located near the foothills of the Ozarks, which rise to the southeast. There are large agricultural areas particularly to the west and north. Climate is continental with a strong Gulf influence. Summers are warm and sticky with little relief outside of the occasional thundershower. Winters are cool and variable, with snow and rain-snow mixes and periods of cold alternating with warmer weather. First freeze is mid-October, last is mid-April.

POPULATION

DEMOGRAPHICS	AREA	U.S. AVG	ETHNIC COMPOSITION	AREA	U.S. AVG	RESIDENT PROFILE	AREA	U.S. AVG
Population	160,203		White	95.9%	75.1%	Single	36.8%	43.6%
Population density per sq. mile	126.5	447.3	Black	1.3%	12.3%	Married	63.2%	56.4%
Population growth	18.7%	16.1%	Asian	.6%	3.6%	Divorced	8.2%	8.4%
Median age	36.0	35.5	American Indian	2.0%	.9%	Separated	2.2%	3.0%
Average family size	2.6	2.7	Hispanic	.9%	12.5%	Married with children	29.9%	28.7%
			Diversity measure	15.9%	35.2%	Single with children	8.4%	10.1%

ECONOMY & JOBS
SCORE: 7/RANK: 306

INCOME	AREA	U.S. AVG	EMPLOYMENT	AREA	U.S. AVG	LARGEST EMPLOYING INDUSTRY
Per capita income	$19,541	$23,420	Unemployment rate	5.7%	6.1%	Food Manufacturing
Household income	$36,904	$46,060	Recent job growth	-3.6%	.9%	
Household income < $25K	32.1%	26.4%	Projected future job growth	17.8%	15.1%	
Household income > $75K	16.0%	24.5%	White collar	47.8%	54.5%	
Household income growth	72.4%	57.3%	Blue collar	52.2%	45.5%	

COST OF LIVING
SCORE: 97/RANK: 10

INDEXES & TAXES	AREA	U.S. AVG	HOUSING	AREA	U.S. AVG	NECESSITIES	AREA	U.S. AVG
Cost of Living Index	74.2	100.0	Median home price	$80,570	$160,100	Food Index	89.0	100.0
Financial Progress Index	106.0	100.0	Home price appreciation	5.1%	7.1%	Housing Index	50.0	100.0
Income tax rate	6.000%	4.625%	Median rent	$421	$670	Utilities Index	79.3	100.0
Sales tax rate	4.950%	6.474%	Homes owned	72.1%	63.9%	Transportation Index	78.5	100.0
Property tax rate	$7.1	$15.6	Homes rented	18.7%	25.3%	Healthcare Index	98.0	100.0
			Housing affordability	67.0%	54.5%	Miscellaneous Cost Index	92.0	100.0

CLIMATE
SCORE: 29/RANK: 235

TEMPERATURE	AREA	U.S. AVG	PRECIPITATION	AREA	U.S. AVG	COMFORTS & HAZARDS	AREA	U.S. AVG
January low	22.6°F	26.4°F	Annual inches precipitation	40.0	35.9	July relative humidity	70.0%	68.8%
July high	91.0°F	86.7°F	Annual inches snowfall	15.0	24.2	Annual days mostly sunny	216	212
Annual days > 90°F	40	38	Annual days precipitation	107	111	Annual days with thunderstorms	58	39
Annual days < 32°F	105	88	Annual days rain > 0.5 inches	27	23	Tornado risk score	35	19
Annual days < 0°F	3	6	Annual days snow > 1.5 inches	5	6	Hurricane risk score	3	15

TEMPERATURE

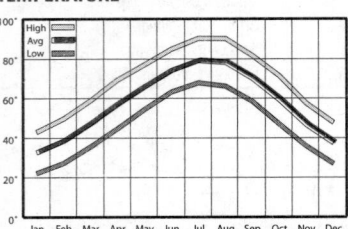

PRECIPITATION

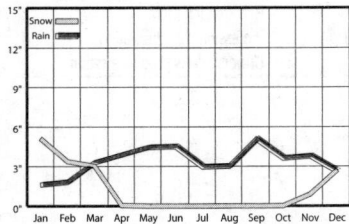

DAYS OF CLOUDS & PRECIPITATION

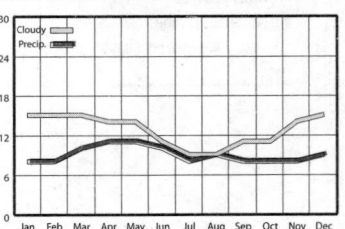

EDUCATION — SCORE: 21/RANK: 260

ACHIEVEMENT	AREA	U.S. AVG	PUBLIC SCHOOLS	AREA	U.S. AVG	HIGHER EDUCATION	AREA	U.S. AVG
High school degree	79.6%	80.2%	Expenditures per pupil	$4,290	$5,894	No. 2-year colleges	1	3
2-year college degree	4.8%	6.2%	Student/teacher ratio	15.3	16.7	No. 4-year colleges/universities	2	4
4-year college degree	11.0%	15.8%	Attending public school	93.8%	90.2%	No. highly ranked universities	0	1
Graduate/professional degree	5.4%	9.6%	State SAT score	1165	1020			
			State ACT score	21.4*	21.0			

HEALTH & HEALTHCARE — SCORE: 73/RANK: 89

HAZARDS & ILLNESSES	AREA	U.S. AVG	HEALTHCARE	AREA	U.S. AVG
Air-quality score	24	45	Physicians per capita	203.5	261.1
Water-quality score	38	33	Hospital beds per capita	516.8	432.2
Pollen/allergy score	56	61	No. teaching hospitals	1	4
Stress score	54	50	Cost per doctor visit	$62	$67
Cancer mortality per capita	171.2	169.0	Cost per dental visit	$79	$82
Depression days per month	2.2	2.8	Cost per daily hospital room	$610	$733

CRIME — SCORE: 13/RANK: 288

CRIME	AREA	U.S. AVG
Violent crime rate	477.6	456.0
Change in violent crime rate	37.7%	-17.2%
Property crime rate	4,592.8	3,950.0
Change in property crime rate	11.5%	-16.8%

TRANSPORTATION — SCORE: 45/RANK: 182

COMMUTE	AREA	U.S. AVG	INTERCITY SERVICES	AREA	U.S. AVG	AUTOMOTIVE	AREA	U.S. AVG
Average commute time	19.1 min.	22.6 min.	Miles to nearest major airport	62	46	Insurance, annual premium	$835	$1,011
Commute by auto	90.0%	88.7%	Type of local airport	Small		Gas, cost per gallon	$1.39	$1.50
Commute by mass transit	.1%	1.8%	No. daily airline departures	56	294	Daily vehicle miles per capita	27.9	23.0
Work at home	6.8%	3.9%	Amtrak service	No				
Mass transit miles per capita	0.0	8.0	No. interstate highways	1	1			

LEISURE — SCORE: 6/RANK: 309

DINING & SHOPPING	AREA	U.S. AVG	ENTERTAINMENT	AREA	U.S. AVG	OUTDOOR ACTIVITIES	AREA	U.S. AVG
Restaurant rating	1	1	Professional sports rating	2	4	Golf-course rating	2	4
No. outlet malls	0	2	College sports rating	4	4	Ski-area rating	1	4
No. Starbucks	0	11	Zoo/aquarium rating	1	3	National Park rating	2	3
No. warehouse clubs	3	4	Amusement park rating	1	3	Sq. miles inland water	1.0	4.0
			Botanical garden/arboretum rating	1	3	Miles of coastline	0.0	11.4

ARTS & CULTURE — SCORE: 23/RANK: 253

MEDIA & LIBRARIES	AREA	U.S. AVG	PERFORMING ARTS	AREA	U.S. AVG	MUSEUMS	AREA	U.S. AVG
Arts radio rating	3	3	Classical music rating	2	4	Overall museum rating	5	6
No. public libraries	6	28	Ballet/dance rating	1	3	Art museum rating	2	5
Library volumes per capita	2.3	2.8	Professional theater rating	1	3	Science museum rating	4	4
			University arts programs rating	4	5	Children's museum rating	1	3

Kalamazoo–Battle Creek, MI

Score: 48.5   Rank: 237

Profile: Mid-size-industrial-city complex
Location: Southwestern Michigan, midway between Detroit and Chicago
Elevation: 803 feet
Time zone: Eastern Standard Time

PRO	CON
Cost of living	Economic cycles
Some college-town amenities	Crime rate
Nearby recreation	Isolation

Kalamazoo and Battle Creek sit about 20 miles apart in Kalamazoo County. Although some discrepancy exists regarding the origin of "Kalamazoo," a colorful name that often appears in poems and children's stories, it is without a doubt Native American. Despite its name, Kalamazoo is a rather plain industrial center with a bit of a college-town flair thanks to Western Michigan University and Kalamazoo College. Put on the map by the breakfast-cereal industry, Battle Creek is home to major cereal manufacturers, including the Kellogg Company. The cereal industry stabilizes the otherwise cyclical economy, and recent statistics reflect reasonable economic health. Neither place is close enough to larger cities to take advantage of their services and amenities regularly; however, the central location among South Bend, Indiana, to the south, Ann Arbor to the east, recreational areas to the north, and beaches to the west is an advantage.

The terrain is flat to gently rolling, with more significant hills (including a ski area) to the northwest. The climate is continental with a strong influence from Lake Michigan. Summers are warm but not too hot and moderately humid. Winters are cold, wet, and snowy with the most extreme cold tempered by the lake and the harshest winds moderated by the hills to the northwest. Still, prevailing winds bring significant cloudiness and precipitation. Warmth from the lake and local hardwood forests create attractive autumns with some periods of clouds and rain. Winter snow cover is common. Freezes are mid-October through late April.

POPULATION

DEMOGRAPHICS	AREA	U.S. AVG	ETHNIC COMPOSITION	AREA	U.S. AVG	RESIDENT PROFILE	AREA	U.S. AVG
Population	457,081		White	88.6%	75.1%	Single	43.3%	43.6%
Population density per sq. mile	242.9	447.3	Black	8.7%	12.3%	Married	56.7%	56.4%
Population growth	6.4%	16.1%	Asian	1.1%	3.6%	Divorced	9.6%	8.4%
Median age	35.0	35.5	American Indian	.7%	.9%	Separated	2.7%	3.0%
Average family size	2.6	2.7	Hispanic	2.7%	12.5%	Married with children	27.1%	28.7%
			Diversity measure	29.0%	35.2%	Single with children	11.8%	10.1%

ECONOMY & JOBS
SCORE: 76/RANK: 77

INCOME	AREA	U.S. AVG	EMPLOYMENT	AREA	U.S. AVG	LARGEST EMPLOYING INDUSTRY
Per capita income	$22,084	$23,420	Unemployment rate	6.4%	6.1%	Transportation Equipment Manufacturing
Household income	$42,578	$46,060	Recent job growth	.1%	.9%	
Household income < $25K	28.1%	26.4%	Projected future job growth	12.7%	15.1%	
Household income > $75K	21.9%	24.5%	White collar	53.4%	54.5%	
Household income growth	46.5%	57.3%	Blue collar	46.6%	45.5%	

COST OF LIVING
SCORE: 56/RANK: 145

INDEXES & TAXES	AREA	U.S. AVG	HOUSING	AREA	U.S. AVG	NECESSITIES	AREA	U.S. AVG
Cost of Living Index	88.5	100.0	Median home price	$116,500	$160,100	Food Index	97.6	100.0
Financial Progress Index	102.5	100.0	Home price appreciation	6.3%	7.1%	Housing Index	72.4	100.0
Income tax rate	4.400%	4.625%	Median rent	$576	$670	Utilities Index	91.9	100.0
Sales tax rate	6.000%	6.474%	Homes owned	68.7%	63.9%	Transportation Index	104.0	100.0
Property tax rate	$16.0	$15.6	Homes rented	20.8%	25.3%	Healthcare Index	93.1	100.0
			Housing affordability	57.0%	54.5%	Miscellaneous Cost Index	97.7	100.0

CLIMATE
SCORE: 11/RANK: 293

TEMPERATURE	AREA	U.S. AVG	PRECIPITATION	AREA	U.S. AVG	COMFORTS & HAZARDS	AREA	U.S. AVG
January low	16.0°F	26.4°F	Annual inches precipitation	32.0	35.9	July relative humidity	73.0%	68.8%
July high	83.3°F	86.7°F	Annual inches snowfall	77.0	24.2	Annual days mostly sunny	163	212
Annual days > 90°F	11	38	Annual days precipitation	144	111	Annual days with thunderstorms	37	39
Annual days < 32°F	149	88	Annual days rain > 0.5 inches	19	23	Tornado risk score	19	19
Annual days < 0°F	8	6	Annual days snow > 1.5 inches	21	6	Hurricane risk score	2	15

TEMPERATURE

PRECIPITATION

DAYS OF CLOUDS & PRECIPITATION

EDUCATION
SCORE: 72/RANK: 93

ACHIEVEMENT	AREA	U.S. AVG	PUBLIC SCHOOLS	AREA	U.S. AVG	HIGHER EDUCATION	AREA	U.S. AVG
High school degree	84.2%	80.2%	Expenditures per pupil	$6,270	$5,894	No. 2-year colleges	2	3
2-year college degree	7.3%	6.2%	Student/teacher ratio	17.2	16.7	No. 4-year colleges/universities	3	4
4-year college degree	14.7%	15.8%	Attending public school	92.0%	90.2%	No. highly ranked universities	2	1
Graduate/professional degree	8.8%	9.6%	State SAT score	1140	1020			
			State ACT score	21.3*	21.0			

HEALTH & HEALTHCARE
SCORE: 76/RANK: 76

CRIME
SCORE: 16/RANK: 278

HAZARDS & ILLNESSES	AREA	U.S. AVG	HEALTHCARE	AREA	U.S. AVG	CRIME	AREA	U.S. AVG
Air-quality score	81	45	Physicians per capita	247.2	261.1	Violent crime rate	636.2	456.0
Water-quality score	20	33	Hospital beds per capita	398.4	432.2	Change in violent crime rate	-12.9%	-17.2%
Pollen/allergy score	49	61	No. teaching hospitals	2	4	Property crime rate	4,832.0	3,950.0
Stress score	82	50	Cost per doctor visit	$62	$67	Change in property crime rate	-4.0%	-16.8%
Cancer mortality per capita	166.4	169.0	Cost per dental visit	$85	$82			
Depression days per month	2.8	2.8	Cost per daily hospital room	$594	$733			

TRANSPORTATION
SCORE: 58/RANK: 138

COMMUTE	AREA	U.S. AVG	INTERCITY SERVICES	AREA	U.S. AVG	AUTOMOTIVE	AREA	U.S. AVG
Average commute time	20.5 min.	22.6 min.	Miles to nearest major airport	42	46	Insurance, annual premium	$1,000	$1,011
Commute by auto	91.5%	88.7%	Type of local airport	Small		Gas, cost per gallon	$1.52	$1.50
Commute by mass transit	.6%	1.8%	No. daily airline departures	110	294	Daily vehicle miles per capita	25.5	23.0
Work at home	3.7%	3.9%	Amtrak service	Yes				
Mass transit miles per capita	5.1	8.0	No. interstate highways	1	1			

LEISURE SCORE: 52/RANK: 159

DINING & SHOPPING	AREA	U.S. AVG	ENTERTAINMENT	AREA	U.S. AVG	OUTDOOR ACTIVITIES	AREA	U.S. AVG
Restaurant rating	1	1	Professional sports rating	3	4	Golf-course rating	3	4
No. outlet malls	1	2	College sports rating	2	4	Ski-area rating	5	4
No. Starbucks	0	11	Zoo/aquarium rating	5	3	National Park rating	1	3
No. warehouse clubs	4	4	Amusement park rating	1	3	Sq. miles inland water	3.0	4.0
			Botanical garden/arboretum rating	7	3	Miles of coastline	0.0	11.4

ARTS & CULTURE SCORE: 56/RANK: 143

MEDIA & LIBRARIES	AREA	U.S. AVG	PERFORMING ARTS	AREA	U.S. AVG	MUSEUMS	AREA	U.S. AVG
Arts radio rating	1	3	Classical music rating	3	4	Overall museum rating	7	6
No. public libraries	32	28	Ballet/dance rating	3	3	Art museum rating	6	5
Library volumes per capita	3.9	2.8	Professional theater rating	1	3	Science museum rating	7	4
			University arts programs rating	7	5	Children's museum rating	2	3

Kankakee, IL

Score: 18.7   Rank: 327

Profile: Small agricultural town
Location: Northeast Illinois, 55 miles south of Chicago
Elevation: 632
Time zone: Central Standard Time

PRO	CON
Small-town atmosphere	Violent crime
Antiques shopping	Low educational attainment
Cost of housing	Cost of living

The Kankakee area is just far enough south of Chicago to miss out on its amenities in the ranking process. This typical Illinois small town has a central-business district with brick buildings, a riverfront park, and abundant agricultural land. Sections of downtown have been turned into a retail antiques center, and there are reputedly 600 antiques shops in the area. Kankakee is closer to Chicago's industrial areas than its attractive ones. Reaching the Chicago's O'Hare International Airport can take 1½ hours or more depending on traffic. Cost of living and crime rates are surprisingly high for a town with Kankakee's profile—the violent crime rate is the second highest in Illinois.

The area sits in a flat agricultural plain, with cornfields spreading across the horizon. Climate is similar to Chicago to the north, but with diminished lake effects with regard to wind, precipitation, and temperature moderation. Summers are variable but mostly warm and humid, with occasional afternoon showers and thundershowers. Winter is cold and variable, with bitter cold snaps and periods of snow accumulation. First freeze is late September, last is early May.

POPULATION

DEMOGRAPHICS	AREA	U.S. AVG	ETHNIC COMPOSITION	AREA	U.S. AVG	RESIDENT PROFILE	AREA	U.S. AVG
Population	104,657		White	88.9%	75.1%	Single	40.6%	43.6%
Population density per sq. mile	154.5	447.3	Black	9.4%	12.3%	Married	59.4%	56.4%
Population growth	8.7%	16.1%	Asian	.6%	3.6%	Divorced	7.4%	8.4%
Median age	35.5	35.5	American Indian	.1%	.9%	Separated	1.9%	3.0%
Average family size	2.7	2.7	Hispanic	2.8%	12.5%	Married with children	31.3%	28.7%
			Diversity measure	35.9%	35.2%	Single with children	9.7%	10.1%

ECONOMY & JOBS SCORE: 21/RANK: 261

INCOME	AREA	U.S. AVG	EMPLOYMENT	AREA	U.S. AVG	LARGEST EMPLOYING INDUSTRY
Per capita income	$20,164	$23,420	Unemployment rate	7.4%	6.1%	Chemical Manufacturing
Household income	$43,233	$46,060	Recent job growth	1.0%	.9%	
Household income < $25K	27.8%	26.4%	Projected future job growth	17.8%	15.1%	
Household income > $75K	20.0%	24.5%	White collar	49.6%	54.5%	
Household income growth	52.0%	57.3%	Blue collar	50.4%	45.5%	

COST OF LIVING SCORE: 53/RANK: 153

INDEXES & TAXES	AREA	U.S. AVG	HOUSING	AREA	U.S. AVG	NECESSITIES	AREA	U.S. AVG
Cost of Living Index	93.7	100.0	Median home price	$107,110	$160,100	Food Index	104.1	100.0
Financial Progress Index	98.4	100.0	Home price appreciation	2.6%	7.1%	Housing Index	66.5	100.0
Income tax rate	3.000%	4.625%	Median rent	$643	$670	Utilities Index	104.9	100.0
Sales tax rate	6.250%	6.474%	Homes owned	69.5%	63.9%	Transportation Index	118.2	100.0
Property tax rate	$20.5	$15.6	Homes rented	24.3%	25.3%	Healthcare Index	115.6	100.0
			Housing affordability	57.0%	54.5%	Miscellaneous Cost Index	107.7	100.0

CLIMATE SCORE: 9/RANK: 301

TEMPERATURE	AREA	U.S. AVG	PRECIPITATION	AREA	U.S. AVG	COMFORTS & HAZARDS	AREA	U.S. AVG
January low	10.0°F	26.4°F	Annual inches precipitation	37.0	35.9	July relative humidity	72.0%	68.8%
July high	84.0°F	86.7°F	Annual inches snowfall	37.0	24.2	Annual days mostly sunny	196	212
Annual days > 90°F	15	38	Annual days precipitation	117	111	Annual days with thunderstorms	43	39
Annual days < 32°F	145	88	Annual days rain > 0.5 inches	23	23	Tornado risk score	20	19
Annual days < 0°F	14	6	Annual days snow > 1.5 inches	12	6	Hurricane risk score	2	15

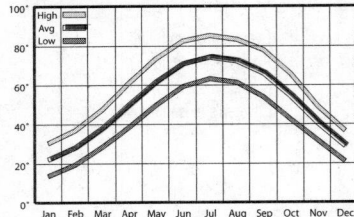

TEMPERATURE

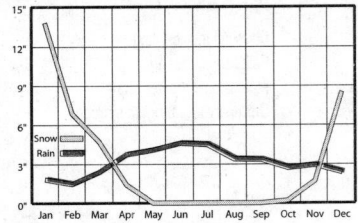

PRECIPITATION

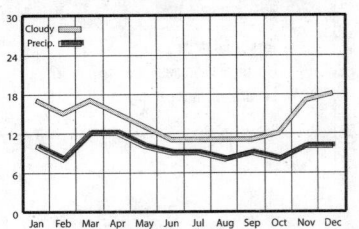

DAYS OF CLOUDS & PRECIPITATION

EDUCATION SCORE: 6/RANK: 310

ACHIEVEMENT	AREA	U.S. AVG	PUBLIC SCHOOLS	AREA	U.S. AVG	HIGHER EDUCATION	AREA	U.S. AVG
High school degree	79.8%	80.2%	Expenditures per pupil	$5,368	$5,894	No. 2-year colleges	1	3
2-year college degree	6.3%	6.2%	Student/teacher ratio	19.4	16.7	No. 4-year colleges/universities	1	4
4-year college degree	9.4%	15.8%	Attending public school	88.9%	90.2%	No. highly ranked universities	0	1
Graduate/professional degree	5.6%	9.6%	State SAT score	1179	1020			
			State ACT score	20.2*	21.0			

HEALTH & HEALTHCARE SCORE: 48/RANK: 172

CRIME SCORE: 31/RANK: 228

HAZARDS & ILLNESSES	AREA	U.S. AVG	HEALTHCARE	AREA	U.S. AVG	CRIME	AREA	U.S. AVG
Air-quality score	24	45	Physicians per capita	149.1	261.1	Violent crime rate	637.1	456.0
Water-quality score	49	33	Hospital beds per capita	475.8	432.2	Change in violent crime rate	-27.9%	-17.2%
Pollen/allergy score	56	61	No. teaching hospitals	0	4	Property crime rate	4,187.3	3,950.0
Stress score	80	50	Cost per doctor visit	$63	$67	Change in property crime rate	-18.3%	-16.8%
Cancer mortality per capita	156.7	169.0	Cost per dental visit	$91	$82			
Depression days per month	1.9	2.8	Cost per daily hospital room	$786	$733			

TRANSPORTATION SCORE: 7/RANK: 305

COMMUTE	AREA	U.S. AVG	INTERCITY SERVICES	AREA	U.S. AVG	AUTOMOTIVE	AREA	U.S. AVG
Average commute time	23.6 min.	22.6 min.	Miles to nearest major airport	46	46	Insurance, annual premium	$886	$1,011
Commute by auto	90.5%	88.7%	Type of local airport	Medium		Gas, cost per gallon	$1.61	$1.50
Commute by mass transit	.7%	1.8%	No. daily airline departures	356	294	Daily vehicle miles per capita	18.5	23.0
Work at home	4.8%	3.9%	Amtrak service	Yes				
Mass transit miles per capita	0.0	8.0	No. interstate highways	1	1			

LEISURE SCORE: 26/RANK: 248

DINING & SHOPPING	AREA	U.S. AVG	ENTERTAINMENT	AREA	U.S. AVG	OUTDOOR ACTIVITIES	AREA	U.S. AVG
Restaurant rating	1	1	Professional sports rating	8	4	Golf-course rating	6	4
No. outlet malls	0	2	College sports rating	4	4	Ski-area rating	1	4
No. Starbucks	0	11	Zoo/aquarium rating	3	3	National Park rating	2	3
No. warehouse clubs	1	4	Amusement park rating	3	3	Sq. miles inland water	2.0	4.0
			Botanical garden/arboretum rating	4	3	Miles of coastline	0.0	11.4

ARTS & CULTURE SCORE: 9/RANK: 301

MEDIA & LIBRARIES	AREA	U.S. AVG	PERFORMING ARTS	AREA	U.S. AVG	MUSEUMS	AREA	U.S. AVG
Arts radio rating	4	3	Classical music rating	4	4	Overall museum rating	5	6
No. public libraries	8	28	Ballet/dance rating	4	3	Art museum rating	2	5
Library volumes per capita	3.5	2.8	Professional theater rating	5	3	Science museum rating	3	4
			University arts programs rating	2	5	Children's museum rating	5	3

Kansas City–Kansas City, MO-KS

Score: 62.3 **Rank:** 130

Profile: Large-city complex
Location: Missouri-Kansas border, on the Missouri River
Elevation: 1,014 feet
Time zone: Central Standard Time

PRO	CON
Diverse economy	Urban sprawl
Entertainment	Home prices
Attractive downtown	Crime rate

Kansas City is a large, self-sufficient city located astride the Missouri River. The downtown area and most of the population are on the older Missouri side, filled with shaded neighborhoods and mixed development. The big growth is on the Kansas side to the southwest in suburbs like Overland Park, Lenexa, and Shawnee. Once grittier and more industrial, the Kansas or "KCK" side is changing its image fast. The combined city grew up as an agricultural center that provided commercial and industrial support to the vast agricultural area to the west. Food processing is still a major industry, but diverse industries such as greeting cards (Hallmark), telecommunications, publishing, and automobile manufacturers have also set up shop. The area is centrally located to all U.S. markets and has an attractive business climate. Although not a boom economy, economic growth projections are solid.

The attractive downtown boasts museums and architectural attractions, including modern buildings and restorations of older sites such as the 1914 Union Station, as well as some notable areas of urban renewal. A mix of migrated workers from the Southeast and local customs led to fame in barbecue ribs and blues music, both available in abundance. Although well known for its restaurants, clubs, and live music, professional sports, particularly the NFL Chiefs and the MLB Royals, are also important. Locals share a strong sense of civic pride and the belief that the area is a well-kept secret.

On the downside, "Westward expansion" takes on a whole new meaning here. One estimate holds that the average person has more "room"— over 85,000 feet—in this metropolitan area than anywhere else in the country. Availability of cheap land, particularly to the west, and few geographic barriers have created a sprawl problem, to the extent that the Sierra Club rated it the fifth most sprawl-threatened city in 1998. A recently completed highway system may have mitigated the effects, but the warning signs are still there. Intercity transport benefits from the presence of discount airlines and the central location. Home prices, the highest in Missouri by far, are commensurate with income-producing opportunities in the area and not high on a national scale.

The area is located on a broad river plain at the confluence of the Missouri and Kansas rivers. Surrounding terrain is gently rolling to hilly with mixed deciduous woods around the city center and open prairie to the west. The climate is continental with no natural topographic obstructions to prevent free weather flow from all directions. Summer has warm days and mild nights with moderate humidity. Winters are not severely cold but occasional cold snaps do occur. Heavy snowfalls are uncommon. Spring is wet with rapid weather fluctuations and autumn is mild and sunny. First freeze is mid-October, last is mid-April.

POPULATION

DEMOGRAPHICS	AREA	U.S. AVG	ETHNIC COMPOSITION	AREA	U.S. AVG	RESIDENT PROFILE	AREA	U.S. AVG
Population	1,828,247		White	87.9%	75.1%	Single	42.3%	43.6%
Population density per sq. mile	338.1	447.3	Black	9.1%	12.3%	Married	57.7%	56.4%
Population growth	15.5%	16.1%	Asian	1.4%	3.6%	Divorced	9.7%	8.4%
Median age	35.4	35.5	American Indian	.6%	.9%	Separated	2.6%	3.0%
Average family size	2.6	2.7	Hispanic	3.3%	12.5%	Married with children	28.8%	28.7%
			Diversity measure	35.8%	35.2%	Single with children	9.9%	10.1%

ECONOMY & JOBS SCORE: 59/RANK: 134

INCOME	AREA	U.S. AVG	EMPLOYMENT	AREA	U.S. AVG	LARGEST EMPLOYING INDUSTRY
Per capita income	$26,636	$23,420	Unemployment rate	5.8%	6.1%	Transportation Equipment Manufacturing
Household income	$52,261	$46,060	Recent job growth	2.1%	.9%	
Household income < $25K	20.9%	26.4%	Projected future job growth	14.2%	15.1%	
Household income > $75K	30.3%	24.5%	White collar	61.2%	54.5%	
Household income growth	65.3%	57.3%	Blue collar	38.8%	45.5%	

COST OF LIVING SCORE: 27/RANK: 241

INDEXES & TAXES	AREA	U.S. AVG	HOUSING	AREA	U.S. AVG	NECESSITIES	AREA	U.S. AVG
Cost of Living Index	95.1	100.0	Median home price	$137,700	$160,100	Food Index	97.0	100.0
Financial Progress Index	117.1	100.0	Home price appreciation	7.1%	7.1%	Housing Index	85.5	100.0
Income tax rate	7.000%	4.625%	Median rent	$713	$670	Utilities Index	101.5	100.0
Sales tax rate	6.975%	6.474%	Homes owned	66.4%	63.9%	Transportation Index	103.0	100.0
Property tax rate	$14.3	$15.6	Homes rented	25.7%	25.3%	Healthcare Index	97.8	100.0
			Housing affordability	59.0%	54.5%	Miscellaneous Cost Index	102.4	100.0

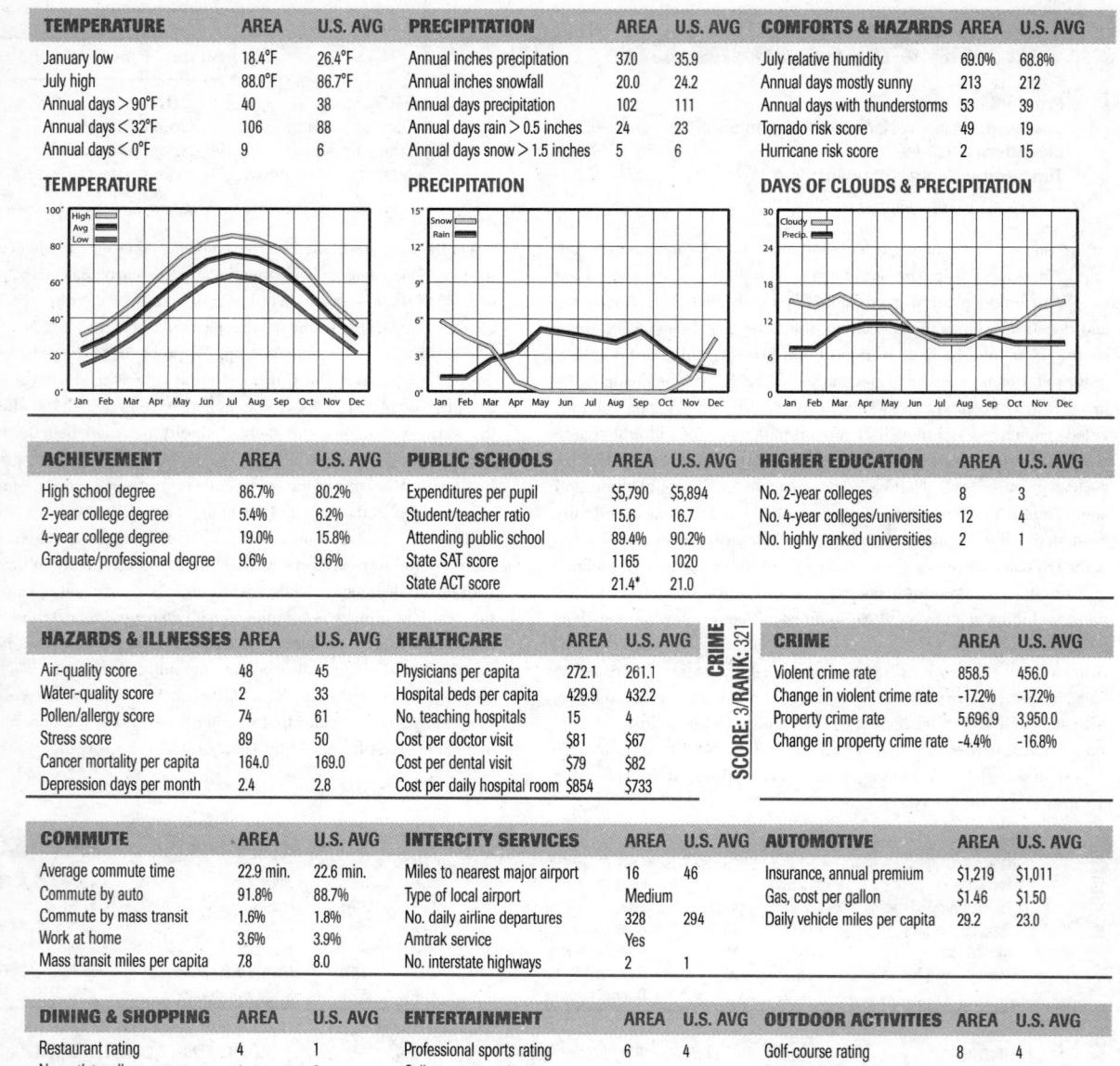

CLIMATE SCORE: 21/RANK: 259

TEMPERATURE	AREA	U.S. AVG	PRECIPITATION	AREA	U.S. AVG	COMFORTS & HAZARDS	AREA	U.S. AVG
January low	18.4°F	26.4°F	Annual inches precipitation	37.0	35.9	July relative humidity	69.0%	68.8%
July high	88.0°F	86.7°F	Annual inches snowfall	20.0	24.2	Annual days mostly sunny	213	212
Annual days > 90°F	40	38	Annual days precipitation	102	111	Annual days with thunderstorms	53	39
Annual days < 32°F	106	88	Annual days rain > 0.5 inches	24	23	Tornado risk score	49	19
Annual days < 0°F	9	6	Annual days snow > 1.5 inches	5	6	Hurricane risk score	2	15

TEMPERATURE

PRECIPITATION

DAYS OF CLOUDS & PRECIPITATION

EDUCATION SCORE: 85/RANK: 51

ACHIEVEMENT	AREA	U.S. AVG	PUBLIC SCHOOLS	AREA	U.S. AVG	HIGHER EDUCATION	AREA	U.S. AVG
High school degree	86.7%	80.2%	Expenditures per pupil	$5,790	$5,894	No. 2-year colleges	8	3
2-year college degree	5.4%	6.2%	Student/teacher ratio	15.6	16.7	No. 4-year colleges/universities	12	4
4-year college degree	19.0%	15.8%	Attending public school	89.4%	90.2%	No. highly ranked universities	2	1
Graduate/professional degree	9.6%	9.6%	State SAT score	1165	1020			
			State ACT score	21.4*	21.0			

HEALTH & HEALTHCARE SCORE: 29/RANK: 234

CRIME SCORE: 3/RANK: 321

HAZARDS & ILLNESSES	AREA	U.S. AVG	HEALTHCARE	AREA	U.S. AVG	CRIME	AREA	U.S. AVG
Air-quality score	48	45	Physicians per capita	272.1	261.1	Violent crime rate	858.5	456.0
Water-quality score	2	33	Hospital beds per capita	429.9	432.2	Change in violent crime rate	-17.2%	-17.2%
Pollen/allergy score	74	61	No. teaching hospitals	15	4	Property crime rate	5,696.9	3,950.0
Stress score	89	50	Cost per doctor visit	$81	$67	Change in property crime rate	-4.4%	-16.8%
Cancer mortality per capita	164.0	169.0	Cost per dental visit	$79	$82			
Depression days per month	2.4	2.8	Cost per daily hospital room	$854	$733			

TRANSPORTATION SCORE: 69/RANK: 101

COMMUTE	AREA	U.S. AVG	INTERCITY SERVICES	AREA	U.S. AVG	AUTOMOTIVE	AREA	U.S. AVG
Average commute time	22.9 min.	22.6 min.	Miles to nearest major airport	16	46	Insurance, annual premium	$1,219	$1,011
Commute by auto	91.8%	88.7%	Type of local airport	Medium		Gas, cost per gallon	$1.46	$1.50
Commute by mass transit	1.6%	1.8%	No. daily airline departures	328	294	Daily vehicle miles per capita	29.2	23.0
Work at home	3.6%	3.9%	Amtrak service	Yes				
Mass transit miles per capita	7.8	8.0	No. interstate highways	2	1			

LEISURE SCORE: 80/RANK: 64

DINING & SHOPPING	AREA	U.S. AVG	ENTERTAINMENT	AREA	U.S. AVG	OUTDOOR ACTIVITIES	AREA	U.S. AVG
Restaurant rating	4	1	Professional sports rating	6	4	Golf-course rating	8	4
No. outlet malls	1	2	College sports rating	2	4	Ski-area rating	2	4
No. Starbucks	19	11	Zoo/aquarium rating	7	3	National Park rating	1	3
No. warehouse clubs	5	4	Amusement park rating	4	3	Sq. miles inland water	4.0	4.0
			Botanical garden/arboretum rating	1	3	Miles of coastline	0.0	11.4

ARTS & CULTURE SCORE: 96/RANK: 11

MEDIA & LIBRARIES	AREA	U.S. AVG	PERFORMING ARTS	AREA	U.S. AVG	MUSEUMS	AREA	U.S. AVG
Arts radio rating	5	3	Classical music rating	9	4	Overall museum rating	9	6
No. public libraries	81	28	Ballet/dance rating	3	3	Art museum rating	8	5
Library volumes per capita	6.9	2.8	Professional theater rating	8	3	Science museum rating	5	4
			University arts programs rating	8	5	Children's museum rating	9	3

Kenosha, WI

Profile: Small industrial town
Location: Southeast Wisconsin along Lake Michigan between Milwaukee and Chicago
Elevation: 693 feet
Time zone: Central Standard Time

PRO	CON
Small-town atmosphere	Winter climate
Nearby skiing	Industrial setting
Close to Chicago	Economic cycles

Kenosha is an industrial center and port located just north of the Wisconsin-Illinois border. Industries vary from auto manufacturing and tools to Jockey International, a manufacturer of undergarments and other textiles. Local plants that had been used by former automaker American Motors Corporation now produce engines for DaimlerChrysler, which bought AMC years ago. The city is pleasant but uninteresting with tree-shaded streets and waterfront areas. Wilmot Mountain ski area is 15 miles west. Chicago provides many services and amenities, and is close enough at 60 miles to influence cost of living and housing.

The town sits on a coastal plain on the western shore of Lake Michigan. Wooded hills rise to the west. The climate is continental with lake influence and changeable weather. The warm summers are influenced both by the lake and the inflow of Gulf moisture from the south. Winter is often humid with frequent snow and cold snaps. Snow can remain on the ground for long periods. Winds off the lake may moderate temperature but add a wind chill. Summer precipitation is mainly thundershowers; spring and fall are variable with alternating pleasant dry days and rainy periods. First freeze is mid-October, last is mid-April.

POPULATION

DEMOGRAPHICS	AREA	U.S. AVG	ETHNIC COMPOSITION	AREA	U.S. AVG	RESIDENT PROFILE	AREA	U.S. AVG
Population	154,433		White	93.3%	75.1%	Single	43.1%	43.6%
Population density per sq. mile	566.1	447.3	Black	4.0%	12.3%	Married	56.9%	56.4%
Population growth	20.5%	16.1%	Asian	.8%	3.6%	Divorced	9.2%	8.4%
Median age	35.1	35.5	American Indian	.4%	.9%	Separated	2.2%	3.0%
Average family size	2.7	2.7	Hispanic	4.2%	12.5%	Married with children	28.1%	28.7%
			Diversity measure	26.2%	35.2%	Single with children	11.0%	10.1%

ECONOMY & JOBS SCORE: 50/RANK: 165

INCOME	AREA	U.S. AVG	EMPLOYMENT	AREA	U.S. AVG	LARGEST EMPLOYING INDUSTRY
Per capita income	$23,559	$23,420	Unemployment rate	5.9%	6.1%	Fabricated Metal Product Manufacturing
Household income	$49,238	$46,060	Recent job growth	2.8%	.9%	
Household income < $25K	21.2%	26.4%	Projected future job growth	17.9%	15.1%	
Household income > $75K	26.0%	24.5%	White collar	48.6%	54.5%	
Household income growth	60.5%	57.3%	Blue collar	51.4%	45.5%	

COST OF LIVING SCORE: 23/RANK: 251

INDEXES & TAXES	AREA	U.S. AVG	HOUSING	AREA	U.S. AVG	NECESSITIES	AREA	U.S. AVG
Cost of Living Index	98.0	100.0	Median home price	$144,640	$160,100	Food Index	99.9	100.0
Financial Progress Index	107.1	100.0	Home price appreciation	6.2%	7.1%	Housing Index	89.8	100.0
Income tax rate	6.930%	4.625%	Median rent	$688	$670	Utilities Index	124.0	100.0
Sales tax rate	5.500%	6.474%	Homes owned	65.5%	63.9%	Transportation Index	104.3	100.0
Property tax rate	$23.6	$15.6	Homes rented	23.0%	25.3%	Healthcare Index	99.1	100.0
			Housing affordability	57.0%	54.5%	Miscellaneous Cost Index	97.1	100.0

CLIMATE SCORE: 15/RANK: 280

TEMPERATURE	AREA	U.S. AVG	PRECIPITATION	AREA	U.S. AVG	COMFORTS & HAZARDS	AREA	U.S. AVG
January low	11.4°F	26.4°F	Annual inches precipitation	29.0	35.9	July relative humidity	69.0%	68.8%
July high	80.4°F	86.7°F	Annual inches snowfall	45.0	24.2	Annual days mostly sunny	195	212
Annual days > 90°F	9	38	Annual days precipitation	122	111	Annual days with thunderstorms	36	39
Annual days < 32°F	146	88	Annual days rain > 0.5 inches	18	23	Tornado risk score	11	19
Annual days < 0°F	16	6	Annual days snow > 1.5 inches	11	6	Hurricane risk score	1	15

TEMPERATURE

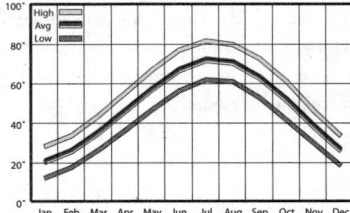

PRECIPITATION

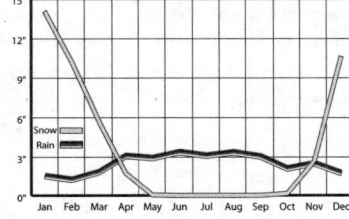

DAYS OF CLOUDS & PRECIPITATION

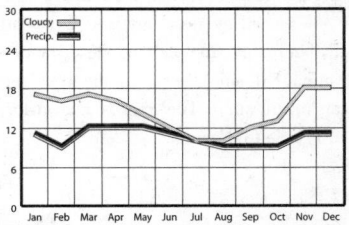

EDUCATION SCORE: 34/RANK: 217

ACHIEVEMENT	AREA	U.S. AVG	PUBLIC SCHOOLS	AREA	U.S. AVG	HIGHER EDUCATION	AREA	U.S. AVG
High school degree	83.5%	80.2%	Expenditures per pupil	$6,522	$5,894	No. 2-year colleges	1	3
2-year college degree	7.8%	6.2%	Student/teacher ratio	16.4	16.7	No. 4-year colleges/universities	2	4
4-year college degree	12.9%	15.8%	Attending public school	88.5%	90.2%	No. highly ranked universities	0	1
Graduate/professional degree	6.4%	9.6%	State SAT score	1179	1020			
			State ACT score	22.2*	21.0			

HEALTH & HEALTHCARE SCORE: 33/RANK: 222

CRIME SCORE: 49/RANK: 168

HAZARDS & ILLNESSES	AREA	U.S. AVG	HEALTHCARE	AREA	U.S. AVG	CRIME	AREA	U.S. AVG
Air-quality score	6	45	Physicians per capita	132.1	261.1	Violent crime rate	440.1	456.0
Water-quality score	10	33	Hospital beds per capita	193.2	432.2	Change in violent crime rate	58.0%	-17.2%
Pollen/allergy score	47	61	No. teaching hospitals	0	4	Property crime rate	2,836.5	3,950.0
Stress score	94	50	Cost per doctor visit	$77	$67	Change in property crime rate	-14.2%	-16.8%
Cancer mortality per capita	177.0	169.0	Cost per dental visit	$78	$82			
Depression days per month	4.3	2.8	Cost per daily hospital room	$461	$733			

TRANSPORTATION SCORE: 99/RANK: 4

COMMUTE	AREA	U.S. AVG	INTERCITY SERVICES	AREA	U.S. AVG	AUTOMOTIVE	AREA	U.S. AVG
Average commute time	25.3 min.	22.6 min.	Miles to nearest major airport	25	46	Insurance, annual premium	$764	$1,011
Commute by auto	92.7%	88.7%	Type of local airport	Medium		Gas, cost per gallon	$1.60	$1.50
Commute by mass transit	1.0%	1.8%	No. daily airline departures	285	294	Daily vehicle miles per capita	16.4	23.0
Work at home	2.7%	3.9%	Amtrak service	No				
Mass transit miles per capita	8.2	8.0	No. interstate highways	1	1			

LEISURE SCORE: 67/RANK: 109

DINING & SHOPPING	AREA	U.S. AVG	ENTERTAINMENT	AREA	U.S. AVG	OUTDOOR ACTIVITIES	AREA	U.S. AVG
Restaurant rating	1	1	Professional sports rating	8	4	Golf-course rating	6	4
No. outlet malls	5	2	College sports rating	4	4	Ski-area rating	3	4
No. Starbucks	1	11	Zoo/aquarium rating	3	3	National Park rating	2	3
No. warehouse clubs	1	4	Amusement park rating	3	3	Sq. miles inland water	2.0	4.0
			Botanical garden/arboretum rating	4	3	Miles of coastline	11.8	11.4

ARTS & CULTURE SCORE: 30/RANK: 229

MEDIA & LIBRARIES	AREA	U.S. AVG	PERFORMING ARTS	AREA	U.S. AVG	MUSEUMS	AREA	U.S. AVG
Arts radio rating	4	3	Classical music rating	4	4	Overall museum rating	4	6
No. public libraries	7	28	Ballet/dance rating	4	3	Art museum rating	5	5
Library volumes per capita	2.5	2.8	Professional theater rating	5	3	Science museum rating	4	4
			University arts programs rating	6	5	Children's museum rating	3	3

Killeen-Temple, TX

Score: 59.1   Rank: 154

Profile: Military town/Small city
Location: East-central Texas along I-35 between Dallas and Austin
Elevation: 833 feet
Time zone: Central Standard Time

PRO
Cost of living
Stable economy
Small-town feel

CON
Entertainment
Arts and culture
Summer heat

Temple is a small Texas town with a transportation heritage starting with the 19th-century Chisholm Trail and continuing today with distribution facilities strategically located to maximize trade with Mexico and proximity to other cities in the state. Headquartered there are McLane Company, Inc., the nation's largest convenience store supplier now owned by Wal-Mart, and Wilsonart International, a maker of plastic laminates. Temple's nondescript downtown is currently under renovation. Killeen, 20 miles to the west, serves the massive Fort Hood military installation. The area is known for spring wildflowers in the Grand Prairie to the west.

Temple and Killeen sit at the border between the Blackland Prairie agricultural area to the east and the Grand Prairie dry hills to the west. The area around both cities is mostly level to gently rolling. The climate is humid subtropical and continental with large variations in temperature. July and August days are particularly hot, with clear skies and relatively low humidity. Spring can be quite wet and stormy, and mild winters are punctuated by windy, cold-air invasions from the north. Winter precipitation may be a mix of snow, rain, sleet, and freezing rain, but snow accumulation is usually minimal.

POPULATION

DEMOGRAPHICS	AREA	U.S. AVG	ETHNIC COMPOSITION	AREA	U.S. AVG	RESIDENT PROFILE	AREA	U.S. AVG
Population	319,163		White	78.7%	75.1%	Single	39.4%	43.6%
Population density per sq. mile	151.2	447.3	Black	11.7%	12.3%	Married	60.6%	56.4%
Population growth	25.0%	16.1%	Asian	2.2%	3.6%	Divorced	7.7%	8.4%
Median age	28.8	35.5	American Indian	.5%	.9%	Separated	3.3%	3.0%
Average family size	2.6	2.7	Hispanic	17.7%	12.5%	Married with children	33.0%	28.7%
			Diversity measure	58.2%	35.2%	Single with children	9.8%	10.1%

ECONOMY & JOBS SCORE: 64/RANK: 117

INCOME	AREA	U.S. AVG	EMPLOYMENT	AREA	U.S. AVG	LARGEST EMPLOYING INDUSTRY
Per capita income	$18,058	$23,420	Unemployment rate	5.5%	6.1%	Healthcare and Social Assistance
Household income	$38,754	$46,060	Recent job growth	2.4%	.9%	
Household income < $25K	27.1%	26.4%	Projected future job growth	13.6%	15.1%	
Household income > $75K	17.2%	24.5%	White collar	41.4%	54.5%	
Household income growth	63.0%	57.3%	Blue collar	58.6%	45.5%	

COST OF LIVING SCORE: 94/RANK: 18

INDEXES & TAXES	AREA	U.S. AVG	HOUSING	AREA	U.S. AVG	NECESSITIES	AREA	U.S. AVG
Cost of Living Index	80.5	100.0	Median home price	$89,940	$160,100	Food Index	84.9	100.0
Financial Progress Index	102.6	100.0	Home price appreciation	5.5%	7.1%	Housing Index	55.9	100.0
Income tax rate	0.000%	4.625%	Median rent	$563	$670	Utilities Index	95.2	100.0
Sales tax rate	8.250%	6.474%	Homes owned	57.7%	63.9%	Transportation Index	96.6	100.0
Property tax rate	$20.4	$15.6	Homes rented	30.3%	25.3%	Healthcare Index	99.0	100.0
			Housing affordability	64.0%	54.5%	Miscellaneous Cost Index	99.0	100.0

CLIMATE SCORE: 67/RANK: 108

TEMPERATURE	AREA	U.S. AVG	PRECIPITATION	AREA	U.S. AVG	COMFORTS & HAZARDS	AREA	U.S. AVG
January low	29.4°F	26.4°F	Annual inches precipitation	31.3	35.9	July relative humidity	67.0%	68.8%
July high	99.2°F	86.7°F	Annual inches snowfall	1.5	24.2	Annual days mostly sunny	231	212
Annual days > 90°F	106	38	Annual days precipitation	78	111	Annual days with thunderstorms	49	39
Annual days < 32°F	70	88	Annual days rain > 0.5 inches	18	23	Tornado risk score	20	19
Annual days < 0°F	0	6	Annual days snow > 1.5 inches	1	6	Hurricane risk score	15	15

TEMPERATURE   PRECIPITATION   DAYS OF CLOUDS & PRECIPITATION

EDUCATION SCORE: 64/RANK: 118

ACHIEVEMENT	AREA	U.S. AVG	PUBLIC SCHOOLS	AREA	U.S. AVG	HIGHER EDUCATION	AREA	U.S. AVG
High school degree	83.8%	80.2%	Expenditures per pupil	$5,186	$5,894	No. 2-year colleges	2	3
2-year college degree	8.6%	6.2%	Student/teacher ratio	14.5	16.7	No. 4-year colleges/universities	1	4
4-year college degree	12.3%	15.8%	Attending public school	96.6%	90.2%	No. highly ranked universities	0	1
Graduate/professional degree	5.8%	9.6%	State SAT score	993*	1020			
			State ACT score	20.1	21.0			

HEALTH & HEALTHCARE SCORE: 28/RANK: 236

HAZARDS & ILLNESSES	AREA	U.S. AVG	HEALTHCARE	AREA	U.S. AVG
Air-quality score	24	45	Physicians per capita	321.2	261.1
Water-quality score	63	33	Hospital beds per capita	281.8	432.2
Pollen/allergy score	78	61	No. teaching hospitals	1	4
Stress score	57	50	Cost per doctor visit	$67	$67
Cancer mortality per capita	150.2	169.0	Cost per dental visit	$77	$82
Depression days per month	4.6	2.8	Cost per daily hospital room	$595	$733

CRIME SCORE: 51/RANK: 161

CRIME	AREA	U.S. AVG
Violent crime rate	362.8	456.0
Change in violent crime rate	-7.7%	-17.2%
Property crime rate	3,643.1	3,950.0
Change in property crime rate	-7.4%	-16.8%

TRANSPORTATION SCORE: 23/RANK: 254

COMMUTE	AREA	U.S. AVG	INTERCITY SERVICES	AREA	U.S. AVG	AUTOMOTIVE	AREA	U.S. AVG
Average commute time	21.1 min.	22.6 min.	Miles to nearest major airport	55	46	Insurance, annual premium	$937	$1,011
Commute by auto	90.9%	88.7%	Type of local airport	Medium		Gas, cost per gallon	$1.38	$1.50
Commute by mass transit	.2%	1.8%	No. daily airline departures	183	294	Daily vehicle miles per capita	18.6	23.0
Work at home	4.1%	3.9%	Amtrak service	Yes				
Mass transit miles per capita	.3	8.0	No. interstate highways	1	1			

LEISURE SCORE: 10/RANK: 293

DINING & SHOPPING	AREA	U.S. AVG	ENTERTAINMENT	AREA	U.S. AVG	OUTDOOR ACTIVITIES	AREA	U.S. AVG
Restaurant rating	1	1	Professional sports rating	2	4	Golf-course rating	2	4
No. outlet malls	0	2	College sports rating	1	4	Ski-area rating	1	4
No. Starbucks	1	11	Zoo/aquarium rating	1	3	National Park rating	1	3
No. warehouse clubs	3	4	Amusement park rating	1	3	Sq. miles inland water	3.0	4.0
			Botanical garden/arboretum rating	1	3	Miles of coastline	0.0	11.4

ARTS & CULTURE SCORE: 64/RANK: 118

MEDIA & LIBRARIES	AREA	U.S. AVG	PERFORMING ARTS	AREA	U.S. AVG	MUSEUMS	AREA	U.S. AVG
Arts radio rating	1	3	Classical music rating	1	4	Overall museum rating	5	6
No. public libraries	9	28	Ballet/dance rating	1	3	Art museum rating	1	5
Library volumes per capita	1.9	2.8	Professional theater rating	1	3	Science museum rating	1	4
			University arts programs rating	3	5	Children's museum rating	1	3

Knoxville, TN

Score: 65.7   Rank: 103

Profile: College town
Location: East-central Tennessee near base of Appalachian range
Elevation: 980 feet
Time zone: Eastern Standard Time

PRO	CON
College-town amenities	Unattractive downtown
Nearby mountains and national park	Violent crime
Economic turnaround	Low ethnic diversity

Knoxville, the largest city in eastern Tennessee and home to the University of Tennessee, serves as a gateway to the tourist and recreation destinations of the Great Smoky Mountain National Park to the southeast. The economic base is a mix of the active university and Tennessee Valley Authority, which has its headquarters here, and declining manufacturing, but future indicators point to a turnaround. The dull downtown area is undergoing a renewal, particularly along the Tennessee River waterfront. The 400-acre university campus with its 26,000 students is located along the waterfront just to the south, and adds a notable college-town element, particularly during football season. For a city its size, Knoxville has a number of quality museums.

Knoxville is located in a broad valley between the Cumberland Mountains northwest and the Great Smoky Mountains to the southeast. The two mountain ranges exercise a marked influence upon the climate. In winter, the Cumberland Mountains slow the flow of cold air from the northwest. In summer, moist, warm air from the south and west prevails. Mountain air keeps summer nights comfortable. Most precipitation occurs in the winter with another peak period in the late spring and summer; frequent afternoon thunderstorms are common in summer. Snow does occur but seldom remains for more than a week. Fall is the driest period. The mountains typically shelter the area from strong winds and severe storms.

POPULATION

DEMOGRAPHICS	AREA	U.S. AVG	ETHNIC COMPOSITION	AREA	U.S. AVG	RESIDENT PROFILE	AREA	U.S. AVG
Population	704,431		White	91.8%	75.1%	Single	42.9%	43.6%
Population density per sq. mile	287.6	447.3	Black	6.8%	12.3%	Married	57.1%	56.4%
Population growth	20.2%	16.1%	Asian	.9%	3.6%	Divorced	10.2%	8.4%
Median age	37.8	35.5	American Indian	.3%	.9%	Separated	2.4%	3.0%
Average family size	2.5	2.7	Hispanic	.7%	12.5%	Married with children	25.7%	28.7%
			Diversity measure	17.2%	35.2%	Single with children	9.0%	10.1%

ECONOMY & JOBS SCORE: 33/RANK: 220

INCOME	AREA	U.S. AVG	EMPLOYMENT	AREA	U.S. AVG	LARGEST EMPLOYING INDUSTRY
Per capita income	$23,163	$23,420	Unemployment rate	3.2%	6.1%	Transportation Equipment Manufacturing
Household income	$40,072	$46,060	Recent job growth	-1.3%	.9%	
Household income < $25K	31.3%	26.4%	Projected future job growth	20.7%	15.1%	
Household income > $75K	21.0%	24.5%	White collar	56.6%	54.5%	
Household income growth	57.1%	57.3%	Blue collar	43.4%	45.5%	

COST OF LIVING SCORE: 80/RANK: 64

INDEXES & TAXES	AREA	U.S. AVG	HOUSING	AREA	U.S. AVG	NECESSITIES	AREA	U.S. AVG
Cost of Living Index	87.2	100.0	Median home price	$119,800	$160,100	Food Index	96.1	100.0
Financial Progress Index	97.9	100.0	Home price appreciation	5.1%	7.1%	Housing Index	74.4	100.0
Income tax rate	0.000%	4.625%	Median rent	$507	$670	Utilities Index	93.7	100.0
Sales tax rate	9.250%	6.474%	Homes owned	64.7%	63.9%	Transportation Index	91.7	100.0
Property tax rate	$7.8	$15.6	Homes rented	25.7%	25.3%	Healthcare Index	88.2	100.0
			Housing affordability	57.0%	54.5%	Miscellaneous Cost Index	96.6	100.0

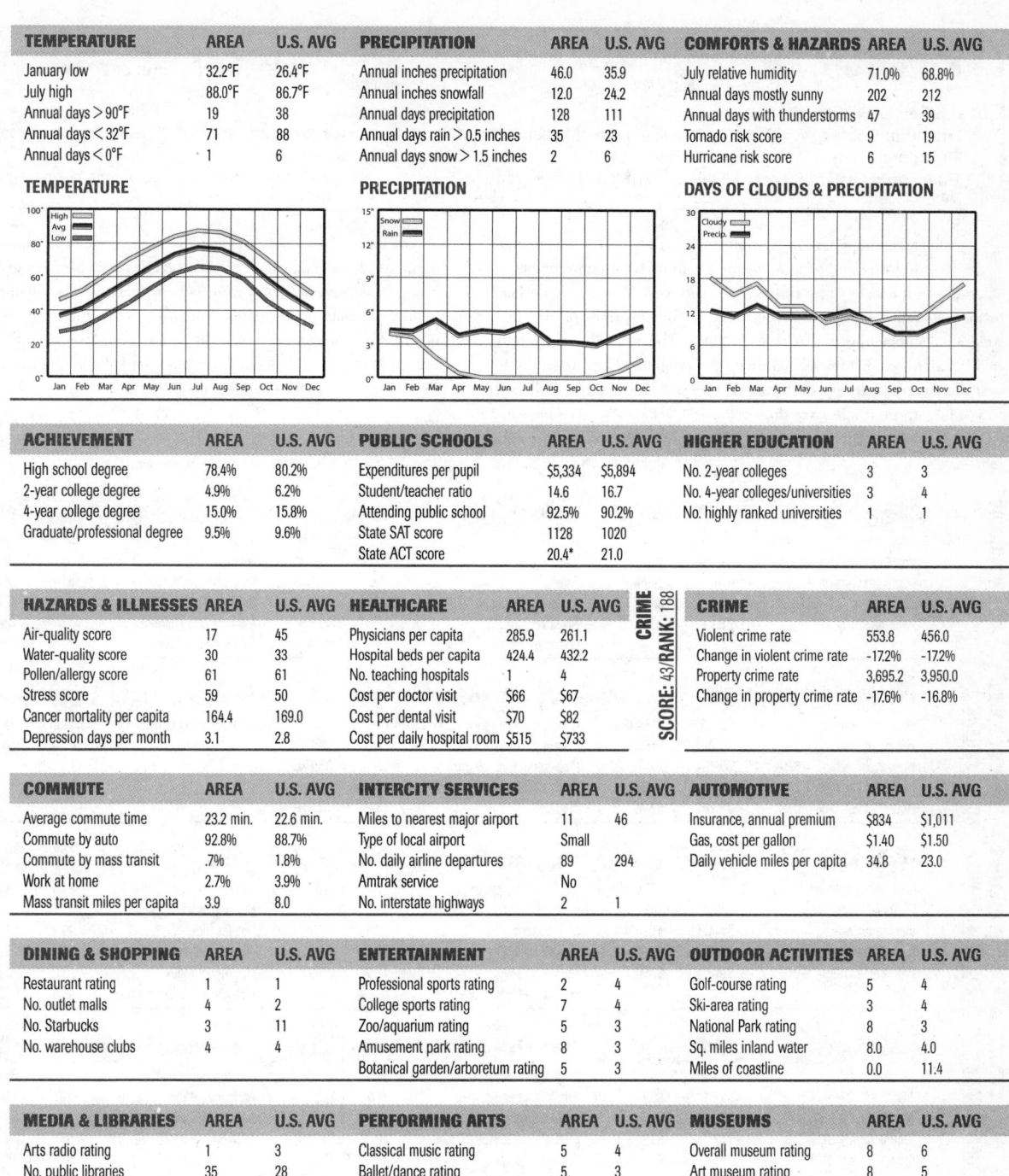

CLIMATE SCORE: 37/RANK: 207

TEMPERATURE	AREA	U.S. AVG	PRECIPITATION	AREA	U.S. AVG	COMFORTS & HAZARDS	AREA	U.S. AVG
January low	32.2°F	26.4°F	Annual inches precipitation	46.0	35.9	July relative humidity	71.0%	68.8%
July high	88.0°F	86.7°F	Annual inches snowfall	12.0	24.2	Annual days mostly sunny	202	212
Annual days > 90°F	19	38	Annual days precipitation	128	111	Annual days with thunderstorms	47	39
Annual days < 32°F	71	88	Annual days rain > 0.5 inches	35	23	Tornado risk score	9	19
Annual days < 0°F	1	6	Annual days snow > 1.5 inches	2	6	Hurricane risk score	6	15

TEMPERATURE

PRECIPITATION

DAYS OF CLOUDS & PRECIPITATION

EDUCATION SCORE: 52/RANK: 157

ACHIEVEMENT	AREA	U.S. AVG	PUBLIC SCHOOLS	AREA	U.S. AVG	HIGHER EDUCATION	AREA	U.S. AVG
High school degree	78.4%	80.2%	Expenditures per pupil	$5,334	$5,894	No. 2-year colleges	3	3
2-year college degree	4.9%	6.2%	Student/teacher ratio	14.6	16.7	No. 4-year colleges/universities	3	4
4-year college degree	15.0%	15.8%	Attending public school	92.5%	90.2%	No. highly ranked universities	1	1
Graduate/professional degree	9.5%	9.6%	State SAT score	1128	1020			
			State ACT score	20.4*	21.0			

HEALTH & HEALTHCARE SCORE: 82/RANK: 59

HAZARDS & ILLNESSES	AREA	U.S. AVG	HEALTHCARE	AREA	U.S. AVG
Air-quality score	17	45	Physicians per capita	285.9	261.1
Water-quality score	30	33	Hospital beds per capita	424.4	432.2
Pollen/allergy score	61	61	No. teaching hospitals	1	4
Stress score	59	50	Cost per doctor visit	$66	$67
Cancer mortality per capita	164.4	169.0	Cost per dental visit	$70	$82
Depression days per month	3.1	2.8	Cost per daily hospital room	$515	$733

CRIME SCORE: 43/RANK: 188

CRIME	AREA	U.S. AVG
Violent crime rate	553.8	456.0
Change in violent crime rate	-17.2%	-17.2%
Property crime rate	3,695.2	3,950.0
Change in property crime rate	-17.6%	-16.8%

TRANSPORTATION SCORE: 19/RANK: 266

COMMUTE	AREA	U.S. AVG	INTERCITY SERVICES	AREA	U.S. AVG	AUTOMOTIVE	AREA	U.S. AVG
Average commute time	23.2 min.	22.6 min.	Miles to nearest major airport	11	46	Insurance, annual premium	$834	$1,011
Commute by auto	92.8%	88.7%	Type of local airport	Small		Gas, cost per gallon	$1.40	$1.50
Commute by mass transit	.7%	1.8%	No. daily airline departures	89	294	Daily vehicle miles per capita	34.8	23.0
Work at home	2.7%	3.9%	Amtrak service	No				
Mass transit miles per capita	3.9	8.0	No. interstate highways	2	1			

LEISURE SCORE: 57/RANK: 142

DINING & SHOPPING	AREA	U.S. AVG	ENTERTAINMENT	AREA	U.S. AVG	OUTDOOR ACTIVITIES	AREA	U.S. AVG
Restaurant rating	1	1	Professional sports rating	2	4	Golf-course rating	5	4
No. outlet malls	4	2	College sports rating	7	4	Ski-area rating	3	4
No. Starbucks	3	11	Zoo/aquarium rating	5	3	National Park rating	8	3
No. warehouse clubs	4	4	Amusement park rating	8	3	Sq. miles inland water	8.0	4.0
			Botanical garden/arboretum rating	5	3	Miles of coastline	0.0	11.4

ARTS & CULTURE SCORE: 70/RANK: 99

MEDIA & LIBRARIES	AREA	U.S. AVG	PERFORMING ARTS	AREA	U.S. AVG	MUSEUMS	AREA	U.S. AVG
Arts radio rating	1	3	Classical music rating	5	4	Overall museum rating	8	6
No. public libraries	35	28	Ballet/dance rating	5	3	Art museum rating	8	5
Library volumes per capita	2.1	2.8	Professional theater rating	1	3	Science museum rating	7	4
			University arts programs rating	8	5	Children's museum rating	8	3

Kokomo, IN

Score: 66.2 **Rank:** 101

Profile: Small industrial town
Location: North-central Indiana, 60 miles north of Indianapolis
Elevation: 808 feet
Time zone: Eastern Standard Time (no daylight savings time)

PRO	CON
Small-town atmosphere	Educational attainment
Cost of living	Crime rate
Proximity to Indianapolis	Economic cycles

Kokomo, an important industrial center mainly tied to the automotive industry, supplies automotive parts for assembly plants in Detroit and to states in the south and west. The city has a long history of auto innovation dating back to the creation of the first American automobile in Kokomo in 1894. The town has a friendly small-town feel with a low cost of living. Mississinewa Lake to the northeast offers recreational opportunities. However, Kokomo is one of the few U.S. cities where crime grew during the last decade. While somewhat economically diversified, the area is still tied to the fortunes of the auto industry.

The town is located on a primarily level, agricultural plain extending north to Lake Michigan. To the northeast lies an area of low wooded hills. The climate is continental with four distinct seasons, including warm, humid summers and variably cold winters. Weather changes are frequent, and winter and summer alike have rainy periods. Winters also bring windy, snowy days partly arising from Lake Michigan to the north. First freeze is mid-October, last is late April.

POPULATION

DEMOGRAPHICS	AREA	U.S. AVG	ETHNIC COMPOSITION	AREA	U.S. AVG	RESIDENT PROFILE	AREA	U.S. AVG
Population	101,372		White	96.8%	75.1%	Single	38.1%	43.6%
Population density per sq. mile	183.2	447.3	Black	2.2%	12.3%	Married	61.9%	56.4%
Population growth	4.6%	16.1%	Asian	.6%	3.6%	Divorced	9.0%	8.4%
Median age	37.8	35.5	American Indian	.3%	.9%	Separated	1.4%	3.0%
Average family size	2.6	2.7	Hispanic	1.2%	12.5%	Married with children	31.1%	28.7%
			Diversity measure	18.0%	35.2%	Single with children	8.7%	10.1%

ECONOMY & JOBS
SCORE: 92/RANK: 27

INCOME	AREA	U.S. AVG	EMPLOYMENT	AREA	U.S. AVG	LARGEST EMPLOYING INDUSTRY
Per capita income	$23,919	$23,420	Unemployment rate	4.9%	6.1%	Transportation Equipment Manufacturing
Household income	$47,020	$46,060	Recent job growth	-1.3%	.9%	
Household income < $25K	26.2%	26.4%	Projected future job growth	5.9%	15.1%	
Household income > $75K	24.1%	24.5%	White collar	46.6%	54.5%	
Household income growth	49.5%	57.3%	Blue collar	53.4%	45.5%	

COST OF LIVING
SCORE: 84/RANK: 51

INDEXES & TAXES	AREA	U.S. AVG	HOUSING	AREA	U.S. AVG	NECESSITIES	AREA	U.S. AVG
Cost of Living Index	83.2	100.0	Median home price	$100,050	$160,100	Food Index	94.0	100.0
Financial Progress Index	120.4	100.0	Home price appreciation	4.0%	7.1%	Housing Index	62.1	100.0
Income tax rate	3.400%	4.625%	Median rent	$571	$670	Utilities Index	99.3	100.0
Sales tax rate	6.000%	6.474%	Homes owned	75.1%	63.9%	Transportation Index	97.7	100.0
Property tax rate	$15.7	$15.6	Homes rented	18.6%	25.3%	Healthcare Index	93.2	100.0
			Housing affordability	59.0%	54.5%	Miscellaneous Cost Index	93.6	100.0

CLIMATE
SCORE: 49/RANK: 169

TEMPERATURE	AREA	U.S. AVG	PRECIPITATION	AREA	U.S. AVG	COMFORTS & HAZARDS	AREA	U.S. AVG
January low	19.7°F	26.4°F	Annual inches precipitation	39.0	35.9	July relative humidity	73.0%	68.8%
July high	85.4°F	86.7°F	Annual inches snowfall	21.0	24.2	Annual days mostly sunny	191	212
Annual days > 90°F	15	38	Annual days precipitation	122	111	Annual days with thunderstorms	45	39
Annual days < 32°F	122	88	Annual days rain > 0.5 inches	26	23	Tornado risk score	35	19
Annual days < 0°F	7	6	Annual days snow > 1.5 inches	7	6	Hurricane risk score	3	15

TEMPERATURE

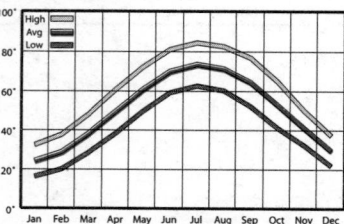

PRECIPITATION

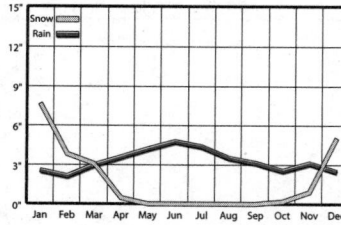

DAYS OF CLOUDS & PRECIPITATION

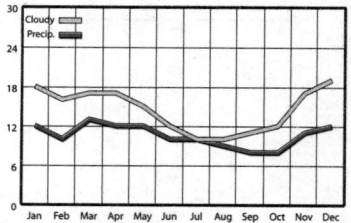

EDUCATION SCORE: 30/RANK: 229

ACHIEVEMENT	AREA	U.S. AVG	PUBLIC SCHOOLS	AREA	U.S. AVG	HIGHER EDUCATION	AREA	U.S. AVG
High school degree	83.4%	80.2%	Expenditures per pupil	$6,566	$5,894	No. 2-year colleges	1	3
2-year college degree	5.0%	6.2%	Student/teacher ratio	16.0	16.7	No. 4-year colleges/universities	1	4
4-year college degree	10.2%	15.8%	Attending public school	91.5%	90.2%	No. highly ranked universities	0	1
Graduate/professional degree	5.6%	9.6%	State SAT score	1004*	1020			
			State ACT score	21.6	21.0			

HEALTH & HEALTHCARE SCORE: 51/RANK: 161

HAZARDS & ILLNESSES	AREA	U.S. AVG	HEALTHCARE	AREA	U.S. AVG
Air-quality score	24	45	Physicians per capita	154.9	261.1
Water-quality score	11	33	Hospital beds per capita	475.7	432.2
Pollen/allergy score	69	61	No. teaching hospitals	0	4
Stress score	34	50	Cost per doctor visit	$65	$67
Cancer mortality per capita	173.5	169.0	Cost per dental visit	$69	$82
Depression days per month	3.4	2.8	Cost per daily hospital room	$541	$733

CRIME SCORE: 45/RANK: 181

CRIME	AREA	U.S. AVG
Violent crime rate	297.7	456.0
Change in violent crime rate	1.8%	-17.2%
Property crime rate	3,600.9	3,950.0
Change in property crime rate	3.7%	-16.8%

TRANSPORTATION SCORE: 64/RANK: 117

COMMUTE	AREA	U.S. AVG	INTERCITY SERVICES	AREA	U.S. AVG	AUTOMOTIVE	AREA	U.S. AVG
Average commute time	18.2 min.	22.6 min.	Miles to nearest major airport	52	46	Insurance, annual premium	$783	$1,011
Commute by auto	93.2%	88.7%	Type of local airport	Medium		Gas, cost per gallon	$1.44	$1.50
Commute by mass transit	.2%	1.8%	No. daily airline departures	319	294	Daily vehicle miles per capita	20.4	23.0
Work at home	3.5%	3.9%	Amtrak service	No				
Mass transit miles per capita	3.5	8.0	No. interstate highways	0	1			

LEISURE SCORE: 38/RANK: 207

DINING & SHOPPING	AREA	U.S. AVG	ENTERTAINMENT	AREA	U.S. AVG	OUTDOOR ACTIVITIES	AREA	U.S. AVG
Restaurant rating	1	1	Professional sports rating	2	4	Golf-course rating	2	4
No. outlet malls	0	2	College sports rating	1	4	Ski-area rating	2	4
No. Starbucks	1	11	Zoo/aquarium rating	1	3	National Park rating	1	3
No. warehouse clubs	3	4	Amusement park rating	1	3	Sq. miles inland water	2.0	4.0
			Botanical garden/arboretum rating	1	3	Miles of coastline	0.0	11.4

ARTS & CULTURE SCORE: 25/RANK: 246

MEDIA & LIBRARIES	AREA	U.S. AVG	PERFORMING ARTS	AREA	U.S. AVG	MUSEUMS	AREA	U.S. AVG
Arts radio rating	1	3	Classical music rating	3	4	Overall museum rating	3	6
No. public libraries	7	28	Ballet/dance rating	1	3	Art museum rating	3	5
Library volumes per capita	4.1	2.8	Professional theater rating	1	3	Science museum rating	1	4
			University arts programs rating	3	5	Children's museum rating	1	3

La Crosse, WI

Score: 64.2   Rank: 115

Profile: Small town
Location: Extreme southwest Wisconsin along Mississippi River and I-90, 60 miles west of Rochester, Minnesota
Elevation: 838 feet
Time zone: Central Standard Time

PRO	CON
Attractive setting	Cold winters
Small-town atmosphere	Air service
Low crime rate	Low ethnic diversity

Eighteenth-century European travelers and trappers founded La Crosse as a crossing point over the Mississippi River. Today's economic base is healthy and diverse with mixed agriculture, orchards, and dairy farms alongside businesses in manufacturing, mail-order, and food distribution. The G. Heilemann Brewery, fronted by a giant six-pack of beer, gives a hint at the good-natured character of the town. The river setting is attractive, with scenic, wooded bluffs on both sides of the river. There are some localized arts and museum amenities, and the town has a number of historic buildings and several pubs. It won a 2002 National Trust for Historic Preservation Great American Main Street Award. Costs of living and housing are reasonable. Rochester, Minnesota, 60 miles to the west, adds some services and amenities not available locally. The area is one of the coldest in Wisconsin and the country.

The city of La Crosse sits on the east bank of the Mississippi River at the confluence of the Mississippi, Black, and La Crosse rivers. Bluffs rise 500 feet above the valley floor. Heavily wooded, steep-sided hills with narrow valleys are characteristic of the region. The invigorating continental climate and storm-track location result in wide and frequent variations in temperature. Summers are warm with moderate humidity and periods of weeklong heat. Summer precipitation arrives as scattered thunderstorms, some severe. Winters are cold and variably humid. Snow is frequent, occasionally heavy, and is the prominent form of winter precipitation. The location west of the Great Lakes results in more sunny days than most Wisconsin cities. First freeze is mid-October, last is late April.

POPULATION

DEMOGRAPHICS	AREA	U.S. AVG	ETHNIC COMPOSITION	AREA	U.S. AVG	RESIDENT PROFILE	AREA	U.S. AVG
Population	127,994		White	97.1%	75.1%	Single	39.9%	43.6%
Population density per sq. mile	126.6	447.3	Black	.6%	12.3%	Married	60.1%	56.4%
Population growth	10.0%	16.1%	Asian	1.8%	3.6%	Divorced	6.4%	8.4%
Median age	34.7	35.5	American Indian	.3%	.9%	Separated	1.5%	3.0%
Average family size	2.6	2.7	Hispanic	.6%	12.5%	Married with children	30.8%	28.7%
			Diversity measure	10.9%	35.2%	Single with children	8.2%	10.1%

ECONOMY & JOBS — SCORE: 68/RANK: 101

INCOME	AREA	U.S. AVG	EMPLOYMENT	AREA	U.S. AVG	LARGEST EMPLOYING INDUSTRY
Per capita income	$21,560	$23,420	Unemployment rate	3.9%	6.1%	Machinery Manufacturing
Household income	$42,400	$46,060	Recent job growth	.8%	.9%	
Household income < $25K	26.8%	26.4%	Projected future job growth	14.8%	15.1%	
Household income > $75K	19.1%	24.5%	White collar	51.8%	54.5%	
Household income growth	58.5%	57.3%	Blue collar	48.2%	45.5%	

COST OF LIVING — SCORE: 40/RANK: 195

INDEXES & TAXES	AREA	U.S. AVG	HOUSING	AREA	U.S. AVG	NECESSITIES	AREA	U.S. AVG
Cost of Living Index	91.7	100.0	Median home price	$112,230	$160,100	Food Index	96.0	100.0
Financial Progress Index	98.5	100.0	Home price appreciation	5.5%	7.1%	Housing Index	69.7	100.0
Income tax rate	6.930%	4.625%	Median rent	$501	$670	Utilities Index	127.4	100.0
Sales tax rate	5.500%	6.474%	Homes owned	72.7%	63.9%	Transportation Index	103.8	100.0
Property tax rate	$25.1	$15.6	Homes rented	21.5%	25.3%	Healthcare Index	110.2	100.0
			Housing affordability	63.0%	54.5%	Miscellaneous Cost Index	100.5	100.0

CLIMATE — SCORE: 13/RANK: 285

TEMPERATURE	AREA	U.S. AVG	PRECIPITATION	AREA	U.S. AVG	COMFORTS & HAZARDS	AREA	U.S. AVG
January low	3.2°F	26.4°F	Annual inches precipitation	26.0	35.9	July relative humidity	69.0%	68.8%
July high	82.4°F	86.7°F	Annual inches snowfall	46.0	24.2	Annual days mostly sunny	200	212
Annual days > 90°F	15	38	Annual days precipitation	113	111	Annual days with thunderstorms	36	39
Annual days < 32°F	158	88	Annual days rain > 0.5 inches	15	23	Tornado risk score	13	19
Annual days < 0°F	34	6	Annual days snow > 1.5 inches	9	6	Hurricane risk score	0	15

TEMPERATURE

PRECIPITATION

DAYS OF CLOUDS & PRECIPITATION

EDUCATION — SCORE: 66/RANK: 113

ACHIEVEMENT	AREA	U.S. AVG	PUBLIC SCHOOLS	AREA	U.S. AVG	HIGHER EDUCATION	AREA	U.S. AVG
High school degree	89.0%	80.2%	Expenditures per pupil	$6,876	$5,894	No. 2-year colleges	1	3
2-year college degree	10.5%	6.2%	Student/teacher ratio	14.8	16.7	No. 4-year colleges/universities	2	4
4-year college degree	15.5%	15.8%	Attending public school	83.0%	90.2%	No. highly ranked universities	0	1
Graduate/professional degree	8.6%	9.6%	State SAT score	1179	1020			
			State ACT score	22.2*	21.0			

HEALTH & HEALTHCARE — SCORE: 94/RANK: 17   CRIME — SCORE: 90/RANK: 34

HAZARDS & ILLNESSES	AREA	U.S. AVG	HEALTHCARE	AREA	U.S. AVG	CRIME	AREA	U.S. AVG
Air-quality score	24	45	Physicians per capita	381.3	261.1	Violent crime rate	124.4	456.0
Water-quality score	19	33	Hospital beds per capita	657.5	432.2	Change in violent crime rate	-19.4%	-17.2%
Pollen/allergy score	41	61	No. teaching hospitals	2	4	Property crime rate	2,830.7	3,950.0
Stress score	3	50	Cost per doctor visit	$77	$67	Change in property crime rate	-21.9%	-16.8%
Cancer mortality per capita	160.0	169.0	Cost per dental visit	$88	$82			
Depression days per month	2.1	2.8	Cost per daily hospital room	$519	$733			

TRANSPORTATION — SCORE: 78/RANK: 72

COMMUTE	AREA	U.S. AVG	INTERCITY SERVICES	AREA	U.S. AVG	AUTOMOTIVE	AREA	U.S. AVG
Average commute time	17.8 min.	22.6 min.	Miles to nearest major airport	107	46	Insurance, annual premium	$750	$1,011
Commute by auto	82.3%	88.7%	Type of local airport	Small		Gas, cost per gallon	$1.56	$1.50
Commute by mass transit	.6%	1.8%	No. daily airline departures	49	294	Daily vehicle miles per capita	21.3	23.0
Work at home	9.7%	3.9%	Amtrak service	Yes				
Mass transit miles per capita	7.4	8.0	No. interstate highways	1	1			

LEISURE SCORE: 24/RANK: 251

DINING & SHOPPING	AREA	U.S. AVG	ENTERTAINMENT	AREA	U.S. AVG	OUTDOOR ACTIVITIES	AREA	U.S. AVG
Restaurant rating	1	1	Professional sports rating	2	4	Golf-course rating	1	4
No. outlet malls	0	2	College sports rating	5	4	Ski-area rating	2	4
No. Starbucks	0	11	Zoo/aquarium rating	1	3	National Park rating	1	3
No. warehouse clubs	3	4	Amusement park rating	1	3	Sq. miles inland water	3.0	4.0
			Botanical garden/arboretum rating	1	3	Miles of coastline	0.0	11.4

ARTS & CULTURE SCORE: 47/RANK: 175

MEDIA & LIBRARIES	AREA	U.S. AVG	PERFORMING ARTS	AREA	U.S. AVG	MUSEUMS	AREA	U.S. AVG
Arts radio rating	1	3	Classical music rating	3	4	Overall museum rating	5	6
No. public libraries	11	28	Ballet/dance rating	1	3	Art museum rating	2	5
Library volumes per capita	3.7	2.8	Professional theater rating	1	3	Science museum rating	4	4
			University arts programs rating	6	5	Children's museum rating	1	3

Lafayette, IN

Score: 84.0   Rank: 23

Profile: College town
Location: Northwest Indiana along I-65 between Indianapolis and Chicago
Elevation: 808 feet
Time zone: Eastern Standard Time (no daylight savings time)

PRO	CON
College-town atmosphere	Urban sprawl
Attractive downtown	Winter climate
Cost of living	Low ethnic diversity

Lafayette is an agricultural and manufacturing center on the Wabash River. The town and area are characteristic of middle America, noted by the National Trust for Historic Preservation with its 1999 Great American Main Street Award. Adding variety and a strong college-town element is Purdue University in West Lafayette. The sports teams of the Purdue "Boilermakers," with a mascot celebrating the area's role as a center of industrial and agricultural technology, are a local obsession. Town highlights include a low cost of living for a major university town, good air quality, and high educational attainment. Downsides are low ethnic diversity for a college town and some sprawl. The northern Indiana climate can be harsh in winter.

The twin cities of Lafayette and West Lafayette are in the shallow valley of the Wabash River. To the north is a flat agricultural plain; to the south is a mix of level, gently rolling terrain. Most of the outlying area is agricultural. The climate is continental with four distinct seasons, including warm humid summers and variably cold winters. Wide temperature fluctuations and rainy periods are frequent. Precipitation is evenly distributed throughout the year, with occasionally heavy, spring and summer thunderstorms. Winters can bring windy, snowy periods partly arising from Lake Michigan to the north. First freeze is mid-October, last is late April.

POPULATION

DEMOGRAPHICS	AREA	U.S. AVG	ETHNIC COMPOSITION	AREA	U.S. AVG	RESIDENT PROFILE	AREA	U.S. AVG
Population	185,973		White	96.8%	75.1%	Single	41.2%	43.6%
Population density per sq. mile	205.5	447.3	Black	1.1%	12.3%	Married	58.8%	56.4%
Population growth	15.1%	16.1%	Asian	1.4%	3.6%	Divorced	8.3%	8.4%
Median age	28.7	35.5	American Indian	.4%	.9%	Separated	1.5%	3.0%
Average family size	2.6	2.7	Hispanic	1.5%	12.5%	Married with children	30.2%	28.7%
			Diversity measure	22.7%	35.2%	Single with children	7.8%	10.1%

ECONOMY & JOBS SCORE: 53/RANK: 156

INCOME	AREA	U.S. AVG	EMPLOYMENT	AREA	U.S. AVG	LARGEST EMPLOYING INDUSTRY
Per capita income	$22,148	$23,420	Unemployment rate	4.3%	6.1%	Transportation Equipment Manufacturing
Household income	$43,472	$46,060	Recent job growth	-1.4%	.9%	
Household income < $25K	26.0%	26.4%	Projected future job growth	14.0%	15.1%	
Household income > $75K	22.9%	24.5%	White collar	55.1%	54.5%	
Household income growth	59.6%	57.3%	Blue collar	44.9%	45.5%	

COST OF LIVING SCORE: 81/RANK: 62

INDEXES & TAXES	AREA	U.S. AVG	HOUSING	AREA	U.S. AVG	NECESSITIES	AREA	U.S. AVG
Cost of Living Index	86.3	100.0	Median home price	$114,250	$160,100	Food Index	91.5	100.0
Financial Progress Index	107.4	100.0	Home price appreciation	3.0%	7.1%	Housing Index	71.0	100.0
Income tax rate	3.400%	4.625%	Median rent	$634	$670	Utilities Index	105.4	100.0
Sales tax rate	6.000%	6.474%	Homes owned	68.9%	63.9%	Transportation Index	95.5	100.0
Property tax rate	$12.0	$15.6	Homes rented	25.5%	25.3%	Healthcare Index	92.7	100.0
			Housing affordability	52.0%	54.5%	Miscellaneous Cost Index	94.0	100.0

CLIMATE — SCORE: 71/RANK: 96

TEMPERATURE	AREA	U.S. AVG	PRECIPITATION	AREA	U.S. AVG	COMFORTS & HAZARDS	AREA	U.S. AVG
January low	19.7°F	26.4°F	Annual inches precipitation	39.0	35.9	July relative humidity	73.0%	68.8%
July high	85.4°F	86.7°F	Annual inches snowfall	21.0	24.2	Annual days mostly sunny	191	212
Annual days > 90°F	15	38	Annual days precipitation	122	111	Annual days with thunderstorms	45	39
Annual days < 32°F	122	88	Annual days rain > 0.5 inches	26	23	Tornado risk score	42	19
Annual days < 0°F	7	6	Annual days snow > 1.5 inches	6	6	Hurricane risk score	3	15

TEMPERATURE

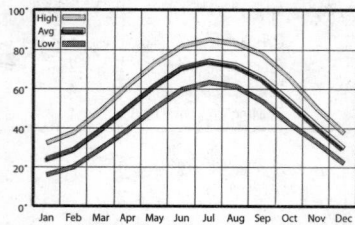

PRECIPITATION

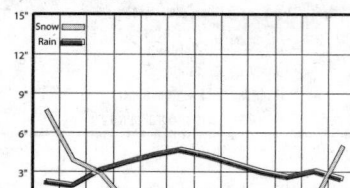

DAYS OF CLOUDS & PRECIPITATION

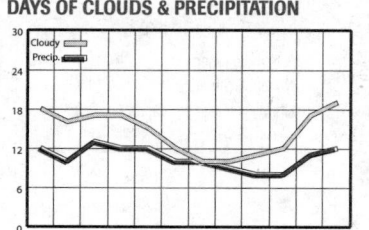

EDUCATION — SCORE: 56/RANK: 143

ACHIEVEMENT	AREA	U.S. AVG	PUBLIC SCHOOLS	AREA	U.S. AVG	HIGHER EDUCATION	AREA	U.S. AVG
High school degree	86.2%	80.2%	Expenditures per pupil	$5,828	$5,894	No. 2-year colleges	1	3
2-year college degree	5.3%	6.2%	Student/teacher ratio	17.3	16.7	No. 4-year colleges/universities	1	4
4-year college degree	15.7%	15.8%	Attending public school	90.4%	90.2%	No. highly ranked universities	0	1
Graduate/professional degree	12.6%	9.6%	State SAT score	1004*	1020			
			State ACT score	21.6	21.0			

HEALTH & HEALTHCARE — SCORE: 6/RANK: 309   CRIME — SCORE: 29/RANK: 234

HAZARDS & ILLNESSES	AREA	U.S. AVG	HEALTHCARE	AREA	U.S. AVG	CRIME	AREA	U.S. AVG
Air-quality score	24	45	Physicians per capita	189.3	261.1	Violent crime rate	173.0	456.0
Water-quality score	17	33	Hospital beds per capita	451.8	432.2	Change in violent crime rate	-46.1%	-17.2%
Pollen/allergy score	66	61	No. teaching hospitals	0	4	Property crime rate	3,255.9	3,950.0
Stress score	10	50	Cost per doctor visit	$61	$67	Change in property crime rate	-23.5%	-16.8%
Cancer mortality per capita	170.9	169.0	Cost per dental visit	$82	$82			
Depression days per month	1.7	2.8	Cost per daily hospital room	$568	$733			

TRANSPORTATION — SCORE: 3/RANK: 320

COMMUTE	AREA	U.S. AVG	INTERCITY SERVICES	AREA	U.S. AVG	AUTOMOTIVE	AREA	U.S. AVG
Average commute time	17.7 min.	22.6 min.	Miles to nearest major airport	57	46	Insurance, annual premium	$782	$1,011
Commute by auto	89.7%	88.7%	Type of local airport	Medium		Gas, cost per gallon	$1.44	$1.50
Commute by mass transit	.8%	1.8%	No. daily airline departures	319	294	Daily vehicle miles per capita	20.7	23.0
Work at home	4.3%	3.9%	Amtrak service	Yes				
Mass transit miles per capita	7.3	8.0	No. interstate highways	1	1			

LEISURE — SCORE: 43/RANK: 186

DINING & SHOPPING	AREA	U.S. AVG	ENTERTAINMENT	AREA	U.S. AVG	OUTDOOR ACTIVITIES	AREA	U.S. AVG
Restaurant rating	1	1	Professional sports rating	2	4	Golf-course rating	2	4
No. outlet malls	0	2	College sports rating	5	4	Ski-area rating	2	4
No. Starbucks	1	11	Zoo/aquarium rating	3	3	National Park rating	1	3
No. warehouse clubs	3	4	Amusement park rating	1	3	Sq. miles inland water	5.0	4.0
			Botanical garden/arboretum rating	2	3	Miles of coastline	0.0	11.4

ARTS & CULTURE — SCORE: 40/RANK: 196

MEDIA & LIBRARIES	AREA	U.S. AVG	PERFORMING ARTS	AREA	U.S. AVG	MUSEUMS	AREA	U.S. AVG
Arts radio rating	1	3	Classical music rating	4	4	Overall museum rating	5	6
No. public libraries	8	28	Ballet/dance rating	1	3	Art museum rating	5	5
Library volumes per capita	3.9	2.8	Professional theater rating	1	3	Science museum rating	2	4
			University arts programs rating	5	5	Children's museum rating	1	3

Lafayette, LA

Score: 35.2   **Rank:** 297

Profile: Small industrial city
Location: South-central Louisiana, 130 miles west of New Orleans
Elevation: 64 feet
Time zone: Central Standard Time

PRO	CON
Cost of living	Hot, humid summers
Economy	Violent crime
Cajun culture	Isolation

Lafayette is a small city in southern Louisiana. Like many Southern towns, it has a modest downtown area with patches of decline and renewal, and a fair amount of sprawl along major arteries. Oil and gas are the main industries. The heart of Cajun country, Lafayette is the center for the flavors, sounds, and history of that colorful culture—a fact earning the place a few recreation and culture points. However, while the area offers some activities and amenities, it is isolated from big-city offerings.

Typical of Louisiana, the level terrain is a mix of open land and wooded areas, with many slow moving creeks called "bayous." The climate is humid subtropical with a modest Gulf influence, which moderates heat extremes but feeds the almost tropical humidity through the summer. Winters are mild with an occasional cold spell. Rainfall is substantial in all seasons, with most precipitation arriving in spring and summer. Severe local storms occur most frequently in spring with hurricanes and tropical rains possible in late summer and fall. Nonetheless, the best seasons are spring and fall, which are mostly mild, dry, and sunny.

POPULATION

DEMOGRAPHICS	AREA	U.S. AVG	ETHNIC COMPOSITION	AREA	U.S. AVG	RESIDENT PROFILE	AREA	U.S. AVG
Population	389,672		White	72.0%	75.1%	Single	44.1%	43.6%
Population density per sq. mile	150.2	447.3	Black	27.1%	12.3%	Married	55.9%	56.4%
Population growth	13.0%	16.1%	Asian	.6%	3.6%	Divorced	6.6%	8.4%
Median age	33.4	35.5	American Indian	.1%	.9%	Separated	4.0%	3.0%
Average family size	2.7	2.7	Hispanic	1.4%	12.5%	Married with children	31.8%	28.7%
			Diversity measure	44.2%	35.2%	Single with children	13.7%	10.1%

ECONOMY & JOBS   SCORE: 49/RANK: 168

INCOME	AREA	U.S. AVG	EMPLOYMENT	AREA	U.S. AVG	LARGEST EMPLOYING INDUSTRY
Per capita income	$18,256	$23,420	Unemployment rate	6.2%	6.1%	Healthcare and Social Assistance
Household income	$32,755	$46,060	Recent job growth	1.0%	.9%	
Household income < $25K	40.0%	26.4%	Projected future job growth	13.9%	15.1%	
Household income > $75K	16.8%	24.5%	White collar	52.7%	54.5%	
Household income growth	63.7%	57.3%	Blue collar	47.3%	45.5%	

COST OF LIVING   SCORE: 77/RANK: 74

INDEXES & TAXES	AREA	U.S. AVG	HOUSING	AREA	U.S. AVG	NECESSITIES	AREA	U.S. AVG
Cost of Living Index	81.4	100.0	Median home price	$94,130	$160,100	Food Index	91.6	100.0
Financial Progress Index	85.7	100.0	Home price appreciation	4.9%	7.1%	Housing Index	58.5	100.0
Income tax rate	4.000%	4.625%	Median rent	$431	$670	Utilities Index	87.9	100.0
Sales tax rate	8.000%	6.474%	Homes owned	65.0%	63.9%	Transportation Index	101.6	100.0
Property tax rate	$4.9	$15.6	Homes rented	22.4%	25.3%	Healthcare Index	92.5	100.0
			Housing affordability	60.0%	54.5%	Miscellaneous Cost Index	95.6	100.0

CLIMATE   SCORE: 49/RANK: 167

TEMPERATURE	AREA	U.S. AVG	PRECIPITATION	AREA	U.S. AVG	COMFORTS & HAZARDS	AREA	U.S. AVG
January low	40.5°F	26.4°F	Annual inches precipitation	54.1	35.9	July relative humidity	74.0%	68.8%
July high	91.2°F	86.7°F	Annual inches snowfall	1.8	24.2	Annual days mostly sunny	218	212
Annual days > 90°F	83	38	Annual days precipitation	108	111	Annual days with thunderstorms	70	39
Annual days < 32°F	25	88	Annual days rain > 0.5 inches	35	23	Tornado risk score	42	19
Annual days < 0°F	0	6	Annual days snow > 1.5 inches	1	6	Hurricane risk score	45	15

TEMPERATURE

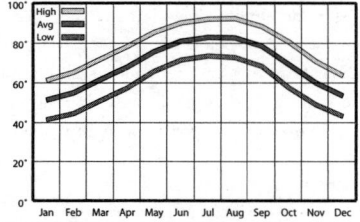

PRECIPITATION

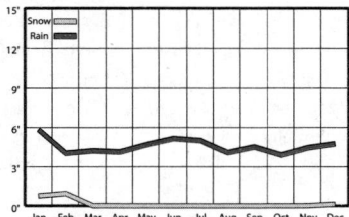

DAYS OF CLOUDS & PRECIPITATION

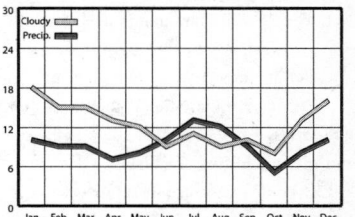

EDUCATION SCORE: 0/RANK: 328

ACHIEVEMENT	AREA	U.S. AVG	PUBLIC SCHOOLS	AREA	U.S. AVG	HIGHER EDUCATION	AREA	U.S. AVG
High school degree	71.3%	80.2%	Expenditures per pupil	$4,678	$5,894	No. 2-year colleges	2	3
2-year college degree	3.7%	6.2%	Student/teacher ratio	15.4	16.7	No. 4-year colleges/universities	1	4
4-year college degree	12.0%	15.8%	Attending public school	81.1%	90.2%	No. highly ranked universities	0	1
Graduate/professional degree	5.5%	9.6%	State SAT score	1122	1020			
			State ACT score	19.6*	21.0			

HEALTH & HEALTHCARE SCORE: 44/RANK: 184

CRIME SCORE: 89/RANK: 36

HAZARDS & ILLNESSES	AREA	U.S. AVG	HEALTHCARE	AREA	U.S. AVG	CRIME	AREA	U.S. AVG
Air-quality score	24	45	Physicians per capita	196.1	261.1	Violent crime rate	607.8	456.0
Water-quality score	10	33	Hospital beds per capita	475.6	432.2	Change in violent crime rate	1.7%	-17.2%
Pollen/allergy score	72	61	No. teaching hospitals	1	4	Property crime rate	3,922.3	3,950.0
Stress score	75	50	Cost per doctor visit	$57	$67	Change in property crime rate	-11.3%	-16.8%
Cancer mortality per capita	188.6	169.0	Cost per dental visit	$75	$82			
Depression days per month	3.1	2.8	Cost per daily hospital room	$503	$733			

TRANSPORTATION SCORE: 80/RANK: 69

COMMUTE	AREA	U.S. AVG	INTERCITY SERVICES	AREA	U.S. AVG	AUTOMOTIVE	AREA	U.S. AVG
Average commute time	26.3 min.	22.6 min.	Miles to nearest major airport	56	46	Insurance, annual premium	$1,119	$1,011
Commute by auto	91.5%	88.7%	Type of local airport	Small		Gas, cost per gallon	$1.43	$1.50
Commute by mass transit	.9%	1.8%	No. daily airline departures	41	294	Daily vehicle miles per capita	28.3	23.0
Work at home	2.9%	3.9%	Amtrak service	Yes				
Mass transit miles per capita	1.9	8.0	No. interstate highways	1	1			

LEISURE SCORE: 55/RANK: 146

DINING & SHOPPING	AREA	U.S. AVG	ENTERTAINMENT	AREA	U.S. AVG	OUTDOOR ACTIVITIES	AREA	U.S. AVG
Restaurant rating	1	1	Professional sports rating	3	4	Golf-course rating	1	4
No. outlet malls	0	2	College sports rating	5	4	Ski-area rating	1	4
No. Starbucks	0	11	Zoo/aquarium rating	1	3	National Park rating	1	3
No. warehouse clubs	3	4	Amusement park rating	1	3	Sq. miles inland water	2.0	4.0
			Botanical garden/arboretum rating	1	3	Miles of coastline	0.0	11.4

ARTS & CULTURE SCORE: 53/RANK: 155

MEDIA & LIBRARIES	AREA	U.S. AVG	PERFORMING ARTS	AREA	U.S. AVG	MUSEUMS	AREA	U.S. AVG
Arts radio rating	1	3	Classical music rating	1	4	Overall museum rating	6	6
No. public libraries	26	28	Ballet/dance rating	1	3	Art museum rating	3	5
Library volumes per capita	2.0	2.8	Professional theater rating	1	3	Science museum rating	3	4
			University arts programs rating	4	5	Children's museum rating	1	3

Lake Charles, LA

Score: 46.2   Rank: 248

Profile: Small industrial city
Location: Southwest Louisiana, 30 miles west of Texas border
Elevation: 9 feet
Time zone: Central Standard Time

PRO	CON
Cost of living	Hot, humid summers
Wildlife viewing	Isolation
Water recreation	Unemployment

Lake Charles is a deepwater port and center for the lumber and petrochemical industries. The city has an industrial small-town feel with some historic areas, including the Victorian-era Charpentier District. The coastal marshlands in the Sabine National and Rockefeller State wildlife refuges to the south offer excellent wildlife viewing. The area is also an important center for Cajun culture. The Cost of Living Index of 80.6 is low by national standards and just misses being the lowest in the state. Unemployment at 7.5 is the state's highest. Major air service and city amenities are distant—Houston, 150 miles west, or Baton Rouge, 130 miles east, are the choices.

The terrain is a flat, level plain. Extensive marshes begin to the south and extend to the coast. Elevations range from near sea level to about 25 feet above sea level. The climate is humid subtropical with a strong marine influence. Winter months are normally mild with brief cold spells. Temperatures of 20°F or below rarely occur. Rainfall is substantial in all seasons, most arriving as brief showers and thundershowers. Spring and fall are mild and pleasant, usually dry and sunny. Severe local storms occur most frequently in spring with hurricanes in late summer and fall.

POPULATION

DEMOGRAPHICS	AREA	U.S. AVG	ETHNIC COMPOSITION	AREA	U.S. AVG	RESIDENT PROFILE	AREA	U.S. AVG
Population	183,344		White	76.8%	75.1%	Single	44.7%	43.6%
Population density per sq. mile	171.2	447.3	Black	22.2%	12.3%	Married	55.3%	56.4%
Population growth	9.0%	16.1%	Asian	.5%	3.6%	Divorced	7.3%	8.4%
Median age	34.9	35.5	American Indian	.3%	.9%	Separated	4.3%	3.0%
Average family size	2.8	2.7	Hispanic	1.5%	12.5%	Married with children	34.2%	28.7%
			Diversity measure	40.9%	35.2%	Single with children	12.1%	10.1%

ECONOMY & JOBS   SCORE: 65/RANK: 116

INCOME	AREA	U.S. AVG	EMPLOYMENT	AREA	U.S. AVG	LARGEST EMPLOYING INDUSTRY
Per capita income	$20,824	$23,420	Unemployment rate	7.5%	6.1%	Chemical Manufacturing
Household income	$40,197	$46,060	Recent job growth	2.6%	.9%	
Household income < $25K	32.3%	26.4%	Projected future job growth	15.0%	15.1%	
Household income > $75K	21.0%	24.5%	White collar	50.0%	54.5%	
Household income growth	64.2%	57.3%	Blue collar	50.0%	45.5%	

COST OF LIVING   SCORE: 80/RANK: 65

INDEXES & TAXES	AREA	U.S. AVG	HOUSING	AREA	U.S. AVG	NECESSITIES	AREA	U.S. AVG
Cost of Living Index	80.6	100.0	Median home price	$90,210	$160,100	Food Index	89.2	100.0
Financial Progress Index	106.3	100.0	Home price appreciation	3.9%	7.1%	Housing Index	56.0	100.0
Income tax rate	4.000%	4.625%	Median rent	$512	$670	Utilities Index	88.7	100.0
Sales tax rate	8.500%	6.474%	Homes owned	65.5%	63.9%	Transportation Index	100.3	100.0
Property tax rate	$7.2	$15.6	Homes rented	26.0%	25.3%	Healthcare Index	98.9	100.0
			Housing affordability	57.0%	54.5%	Miscellaneous Cost Index	96.2	100.0

CLIMATE   SCORE: 65/RANK: 116

TEMPERATURE	AREA	U.S. AVG	PRECIPITATION	AREA	U.S. AVG	COMFORTS & HAZARDS	AREA	U.S. AVG
January low	42.9°F	26.4°F	Annual inches precipitation	55.5	35.9	July relative humidity	78.0%	68.8%
July high	91.2°F	86.7°F	Annual inches snowfall	.3	24.2	Annual days mostly sunny	215	212
Annual days > 90°F	71	38	Annual days precipitation	97	111	Annual days with thunderstorms	76	39
Annual days < 32°F	14	88	Annual days rain > 0.5 inches	32	23	Tornado risk score	33	19
Annual days < 0°F	0	6	Annual days snow > 1.5 inches	1	6	Hurricane risk score	47	15

TEMPERATURE

PRECIPITATION

DAYS OF CLOUDS & PRECIPITATION

EDUCATION   SCORE: 5/RANK: 313

ACHIEVEMENT	AREA	U.S. AVG	PUBLIC SCHOOLS	AREA	U.S. AVG	HIGHER EDUCATION	AREA	U.S. AVG
High school degree	77.0%	80.2%	Expenditures per pupil	$5,083	$5,894	No. 2-year colleges	1	3
2-year college degree	3.8%	6.2%	Student/teacher ratio	15.9	16.7	No. 4-year colleges/universities	1	4
4-year college degree	11.6%	15.8%	Attending public school	88.6%	90.2%	No. highly ranked universities	0	1
Graduate/professional degree	5.3%	9.6%	State SAT score	1122	1020			
			State ACT score	19.6*	21.0			

HEALTH & HEALTHCARE   SCORE: 20/RANK: 264

HAZARDS & ILLNESSES	AREA	U.S. AVG	HEALTHCARE	AREA	U.S. AVG	CRIME SCORE: 24/RANK: 250		
Air-quality score	59	45	Physicians per capita	175.1	261.1	CRIME	AREA	U.S. AVG
Water-quality score	20	33	Hospital beds per capita	627.0	432.2	Violent crime rate	585.0	456.0
Pollen/allergy score	70	61	No. teaching hospitals	2	4	Change in violent crime rate	-40.6%	-17.2%
Stress score	62	50	Cost per doctor visit	$64	$67	Property crime rate	5,383.0	3,950.0
Cancer mortality per capita	184.0	169.0	Cost per dental visit	$75	$82	Change in property crime rate	-21.4%	-16.8%
Depression days per month	2.2	2.8	Cost per daily hospital room	$485	$733			

TRANSPORTATION   SCORE: 32/RANK: 223

COMMUTE	AREA	U.S. AVG	INTERCITY SERVICES	AREA	U.S. AVG	AUTOMOTIVE	AREA	U.S. AVG
Average commute time	20.4 min.	22.6 min.	Miles to nearest major airport	126	46	Insurance, annual premium	$1,113	$1,011
Commute by auto	90.9%	88.7%	Type of local airport	Small		Gas, cost per gallon	$1.39	$1.50
Commute by mass transit	.5%	1.8%	No. daily airline departures	41	294	Daily vehicle miles per capita	22.7	23.0
Work at home	1.9%	3.9%	Amtrak service	Yes				
Mass transit miles per capita	0.0	8.0	No. interstate highways	1	1			

LEISURE SCORE: 9/RANK: 299

DINING & SHOPPING	AREA	U.S. AVG	ENTERTAINMENT	AREA	U.S. AVG	OUTDOOR ACTIVITIES	AREA	U.S. AVG
Restaurant rating	1	1	Professional sports rating	2	4	Golf-course rating	2	4
No. outlet malls	0	2	College sports rating	2	4	Ski-area rating	1	4
No. Starbucks	0	11	Zoo/aquarium rating	1	3	National Park rating	1	3
No. warehouse clubs	3	4	Amusement park rating	1	3	Sq. miles inland water	3.0	4.0
			Botanical garden/arboretum rating	1	3	Miles of coastline	0.0	11.4

ARTS & CULTURE SCORE: 38/RANK: 205

MEDIA & LIBRARIES	AREA	U.S. AVG	PERFORMING ARTS	AREA	U.S. AVG	MUSEUMS	AREA	U.S. AVG
Arts radio rating	1	3	Classical music rating	3	4	Overall museum rating	3	6
No. public libraries	14	28	Ballet/dance rating	3	3	Art museum rating	2	5
Library volumes per capita	2.0	2.8	Professional theater rating	1	3	Science museum rating	1	4
			University arts programs rating	3	5	Children's museum rating	3	3

Lakeland–Winter Haven, FL

Score: 62.7   Rank: 126

Profile: Small city/Resort city
Location: Central Florida, 25 miles inland from the Tampa Bay area
Elevation: 214 feet
Time zone: Eastern Standard Time

PRO
Leisure activities
Attractive setting
Cost of living

CON
Economy
Urban sprawl
Low educational
   attainment

Lakeland is a major agricultural center with citrus growing, processing, and distribution, and a large phosphate mining industry. Winter Haven is a rapidly growing resort area to the east, and both places are becoming retirement destinations. Many lakes provide an assortment of watersports, and the region has a growing number of golf-course communities. Baseball spring training camps round out the entertainment options. Florida Southern University brings a small college-town element and features the largest collection of buildings by Frank Lloyd Wright in one place. Cost of living is reasonable by Florida standards, but downsides include a mixed economic picture, low projected job growth, and areas of overdevelopment. Statistics don't adequately reflect proximity to Tampa Bay and its many amenities—as a result, the ranking may understate the quality of the area.

Lakeland–Winter Haven has a level landscape with a mix of open agricultural, orchard, and wooded areas of stately cypress tress. The humid subtropical climate creates very warm, humid, summer days with highs in the 90s, lows in the upper 60s and 70s, and frequent afternoon showers and thundershowers. Winters are mild with a few days of below freezing temperatures each year, but lingering cold weather seldom occurs. The inland location prevents major damage from hurricanes.

POPULATION

DEMOGRAPHICS	AREA	U.S. AVG	ETHNIC COMPOSITION	AREA	U.S. AVG	RESIDENT PROFILE	AREA	U.S. AVG
Population	498,721		White	82.2%	75.1%	Single	41.6%	43.6%
Population density per sq. mile	266.0	447.3	Black	14.9%	12.3%	Married	58.4%	56.4%
Population growth	23.0%	16.1%	Asian	.9%	3.6%	Divorced	10.0%	8.4%
Median age	39.1	35.5	American Indian	.3%	.9%	Separated	3.6%	3.0%
Average family size	2.5	2.7	Hispanic	6.9%	12.5%	Married with children	23.5%	28.7%
			Diversity measure	40.3%	35.2%	Single with children	11.3%	10.1%

ECONOMY & JOBS SCORE: 33/RANK: 221

INCOME	AREA	U.S. AVG	EMPLOYMENT	AREA	U.S. AVG	LARGEST EMPLOYING INDUSTRY
Per capita income	$19,041	$23,420	Unemployment rate	7.5%	6.1%	Food Manufacturing
Household income	$35,584	$46,060	Recent job growth	-1.7%	.9%	
Household income < $25K	33.0%	26.4%	Projected future job growth	11.4%	15.1%	
Household income > $75K	13.1%	24.5%	White collar	49.0%	54.5%	
Household income growth	41.0%	57.3%	Blue collar	51.0%	45.5%	

COST OF LIVING SCORE: 89/RANK: 36

INDEXES & TAXES	AREA	U.S. AVG	HOUSING	AREA	U.S. AVG	NECESSITIES	AREA	U.S. AVG
Cost of Living Index	87.9	100.0	Median home price	$100,490	$160,100	Food Index	101.5	100.0
Financial Progress Index	86.3	100.0	Home price appreciation	6.5%	7.1%	Housing Index	62.4	100.0
Income tax rate	0.000%	4.625%	Median rent	$518	$670	Utilities Index	100.7	100.0
Sales tax rate	6.000%	6.474%	Homes owned	62.2%	63.9%	Transportation Index	101.4	100.0
Property tax rate	$17.5	$15.6	Homes rented	21.5%	25.3%	Healthcare Index	104.5	100.0
			Housing affordability	63.0%	54.5%	Miscellaneous Cost Index	103.0	100.0

CLIMATE SCORE: 77/RANK: 76

TEMPERATURE	AREA	U.S. AVG	PRECIPITATION	AREA	U.S. AVG	COMFORTS & HAZARDS	AREA	U.S. AVG
January low	51.0°F	26.4°F	Annual inches precipitation	49.4	35.9	July relative humidity	74.0%	68.8%
July high	90.4°F	86.7°F	Annual inches snowfall	.1	24.2	Annual days mostly sunny	259	212
Annual days > 90°F	83	38	Annual days precipitation	120	111	Annual days with thunderstorms	100	39
Annual days < 32°F	2	88	Annual days rain > 0.5 inches	29	23	Tornado risk score	69	19
Annual days < 0°F	0	6	Annual days snow > 1.5 inches	0	6	Hurricane risk score	76	15

TEMPERATURE | **PRECIPITATION** | **DAYS OF CLOUDS & PRECIPITATION**

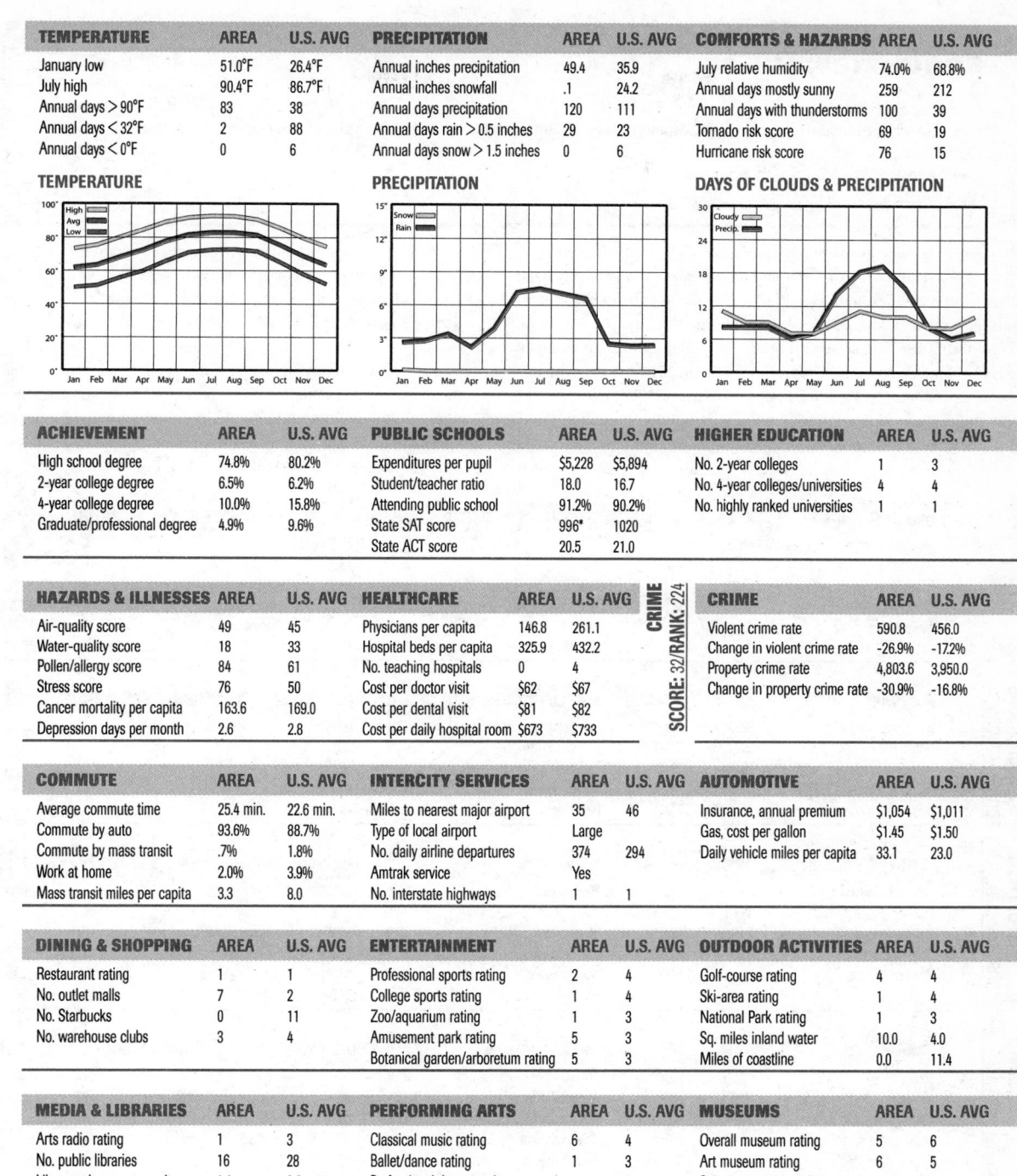

EDUCATION SCORE: 10/RANK: 295

ACHIEVEMENT	AREA	U.S. AVG	PUBLIC SCHOOLS	AREA	U.S. AVG	HIGHER EDUCATION	AREA	U.S. AVG
High school degree	74.8%	80.2%	Expenditures per pupil	$5,228	$5,894	No. 2-year colleges	1	3
2-year college degree	6.5%	6.2%	Student/teacher ratio	18.0	16.7	No. 4-year colleges/universities	4	4
4-year college degree	10.0%	15.8%	Attending public school	91.2%	90.2%	No. highly ranked universities	1	1
Graduate/professional degree	4.9%	9.6%	State SAT score	996*	1020			
			State ACT score	20.5	21.0			

HEALTH & HEALTHCARE SCORE: 15/RANK: 280

HAZARDS & ILLNESSES	AREA	U.S. AVG	HEALTHCARE	AREA	U.S. AVG
Air-quality score	49	45	Physicians per capita	146.8	261.1
Water-quality score	18	33	Hospital beds per capita	325.9	432.2
Pollen/allergy score	84	61	No. teaching hospitals	0	4
Stress score	76	50	Cost per doctor visit	$62	$67
Cancer mortality per capita	163.6	169.0	Cost per dental visit	$81	$82
Depression days per month	2.6	2.8	Cost per daily hospital room	$673	$733

CRIME SCORE: 32/RANK: 224

CRIME	AREA	U.S. AVG
Violent crime rate	590.8	456.0
Change in violent crime rate	-26.9%	-17.2%
Property crime rate	4,803.6	3,950.0
Change in property crime rate	-30.9%	-16.8%

TRANSPORTATION SCORE: 6/RANK: 308

COMMUTE	AREA	U.S. AVG	INTERCITY SERVICES	AREA	U.S. AVG	AUTOMOTIVE	AREA	U.S. AVG
Average commute time	25.4 min.	22.6 min.	Miles to nearest major airport	35	46	Insurance, annual premium	$1,054	$1,011
Commute by auto	93.6%	88.7%	Type of local airport	Large		Gas, cost per gallon	$1.45	$1.50
Commute by mass transit	.7%	1.8%	No. daily airline departures	374	294	Daily vehicle miles per capita	33.1	23.0
Work at home	2.0%	3.9%	Amtrak service	Yes				
Mass transit miles per capita	3.3	8.0	No. interstate highways	1	1			

LEISURE SCORE: 79/RANK: 71

DINING & SHOPPING	AREA	U.S. AVG	ENTERTAINMENT	AREA	U.S. AVG	OUTDOOR ACTIVITIES	AREA	U.S. AVG
Restaurant rating	1	1	Professional sports rating	2	4	Golf-course rating	4	4
No. outlet malls	7	2	College sports rating	1	4	Ski-area rating	1	4
No. Starbucks	0	11	Zoo/aquarium rating	1	3	National Park rating	1	3
No. warehouse clubs	3	4	Amusement park rating	5	3	Sq. miles inland water	10.0	4.0
			Botanical garden/arboretum rating	5	3	Miles of coastline	0.0	11.4

ARTS & CULTURE SCORE: 30/RANK: 231

MEDIA & LIBRARIES	AREA	U.S. AVG	PERFORMING ARTS	AREA	U.S. AVG	MUSEUMS	AREA	U.S. AVG
Arts radio rating	1	3	Classical music rating	6	4	Overall museum rating	5	6
No. public libraries	16	28	Ballet/dance rating	1	3	Art museum rating	6	5
Library volumes per capita	1.4	2.8	Professional theater rating	1	3	Science museum rating	5	4
			University arts programs rating	2	5	Children's museum rating	3	3

Lancaster, PA

Profile: Small city
Location: Southeastern Pennsylvania, 80 miles west of Philadelphia
Elevation: 351 feet
Time zone: Eastern Standard Time

PRO	CON
Historic interest	Arts and culture
Cost of living	Entertainment
Central location	Low educational attainment

Lancaster is the center of Amish country. The surrounding countryside is dotted with old farms and picturesque barns. The city itself is a prosperous and diversified center for light manufacturing of consumer and industrial staples, such as lighting. Its agrarian, Pennsylvania-Dutch heritage supports a sometimes gaudy tourism industry, which adds entertainment value. Amenities lacking in this region are available in Philadelphia, Harrisburg, and Baltimore, all less than 100 miles away. The Amish presence gives a small-town feel while controlling senseless growth and commercialization. As one might expect, crime rates are low, but locally practiced culture also reduces educational attainment, and incomes are low relative to the cost of living. As with other areas of Amish influence, modern agricultural economics challenge the sustainability of small family farms. The area won a 2001 National Civic League All-America City Award.

The area contains mainly level to gentle rolling hills with fertile soil. The climate is humid continental with some influence from mountains to the northwest and water to the southeast. Summers are warm and humid with occasional thunderstorms. Winters are not too rigorous. With the exception of occasional long warm spells in summer and fall, the weather is variable. First freeze is late October, last is mid-April.

POPULATION

DEMOGRAPHICS	AREA	U.S. AVG	ETHNIC COMPOSITION	AREA	U.S. AVG	RESIDENT PROFILE	AREA	U.S. AVG
Population	478,561		White	95.2%	75.1%	Single	38.7%	43.6%
Population density per sq. mile	504.2	447.3	Black	2.0%	12.3%	Married	61.3%	56.4%
Population growth	13.2%	16.1%	Asian	1.4%	3.6%	Divorced	5.6%	8.4%
Median age	36.4	35.5	American Indian	.1%	.9%	Separated	2.7%	3.0%
Average family size	2.8	2.7	Hispanic	2.0%	12.5%	Married with children	32.5%	28.7%
			Diversity measure	20.6%	35.2%	Single with children	7.1%	10.1%

ECONOMY & JOBS SCORE: 75/RANK: 83

INCOME	AREA	U.S. AVG	EMPLOYMENT	AREA	U.S. AVG	LARGEST EMPLOYING INDUSTRY
Per capita income	$23,267	$23,420	Unemployment rate	3.5%	6.1%	Food Manufacturing
Household income	$50,626	$46,060	Recent job growth	-.1%	.9%	
Household income < $25K	18.9%	26.4%	Projected future job growth	10.5%	15.1%	
Household income > $75K	25.0%	24.5%	White collar	47.5%	54.5%	
Household income growth	52.2%	57.3%	Blue collar	52.5%	45.5%	

COST OF LIVING SCORE: 45/RANK: 180

INDEXES & TAXES	AREA	U.S. AVG	HOUSING	AREA	U.S. AVG	NECESSITIES	AREA	U.S. AVG
Cost of Living Index	94.6	100.0	Median home price	$135,900	$160,100	Food Index	93.2	100.0
Financial Progress Index	114.0	100.0	Home price appreciation	4.4%	7.1%	Housing Index	84.4	100.0
Income tax rate	2.800%	4.625%	Median rent	$624	$670	Utilities Index	110.7	100.0
Sales tax rate	6.000%	6.474%	Homes owned	72.4%	63.9%	Transportation Index	105.9	100.0
Property tax rate	$25.6	$15.6	Homes rented	24.1%	25.3%	Healthcare Index	92.6	100.0
			Housing affordability	64.0%	54.5%	Miscellaneous Cost Index	101.5	100.0

CLIMATE SCORE: 33/RANK: 221

TEMPERATURE	AREA	U.S. AVG	PRECIPITATION	AREA	U.S. AVG	COMFORTS & HAZARDS	AREA	U.S. AVG
January low	22.5°F	26.4°F	Annual inches precipitation	36.0	35.9	July relative humidity	67.0%	68.8%
July high	86.8°F	86.7°F	Annual inches snowfall	35.0	24.2	Annual days mostly sunny	193	212
Annual days > 90°F	24	38	Annual days precipitation	125	111	Annual days with thunderstorms	33	39
Annual days < 32°F	107	88	Annual days rain > 0.5 inches	25	23	Tornado risk score	14	19
Annual days < 0°F	1	6	Annual days snow > 1.5 inches	8	6	Hurricane risk score	11	15

TEMPERATURE

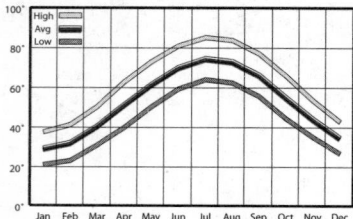

PRECIPITATION

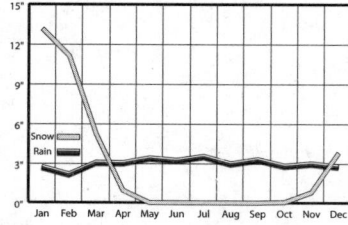

DAYS OF CLOUDS & PRECIPITATION

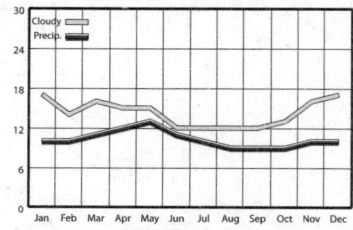

EDUCATION SCORE: 4/RANK: 315

ACHIEVEMENT	AREA	U.S. AVG	PUBLIC SCHOOLS	AREA	U.S. AVG	HIGHER EDUCATION	AREA	U.S. AVG
High school degree	77.4%	80.2%	Expenditures per pupil	$6,075	$5,894	No. 2-year colleges	2	3
2-year college degree	4.5%	6.2%	Student/teacher ratio	16.6	16.7	No. 4-year colleges/universities	4	4
4-year college degree	13.8%	15.8%	Attending public school	81.0%	90.2%	No. highly ranked universities	0	1
Graduate/professional degree	6.7%	9.6%	State SAT score	1002*	1020			
			State ACT score	21.5	21.0			

HEALTH & HEALTHCARE SCORE: 26/RANK: 243

CRIME SCORE: 86/RANK: 44

HAZARDS & ILLNESSES	AREA	U.S. AVG	HEALTHCARE	AREA	U.S. AVG	CRIME	AREA	U.S. AVG
Air-quality score	17	45	Physicians per capita	183.3	261.1	Violent crime rate	235.5	456.0
Water-quality score	25	33	Hospital beds per capita	244.3	432.2	Change in violent crime rate	2.2%	-17.2%
Pollen/allergy score	53	61	No. teaching hospitals	2	4	Property crime rate	2,376.8	3,950.0
Stress score	3	50	Cost per doctor visit	$56	$67	Change in property crime rate	-19.1%	-16.8%
Cancer mortality per capita	160.7	169.0	Cost per dental visit	$62	$82			
Depression days per month	2.0	2.8	Cost per daily hospital room	$704	$733			

TRANSPORTATION SCORE: 55/RANK: 146

COMMUTE	AREA	U.S. AVG	INTERCITY SERVICES	AREA	U.S. AVG	AUTOMOTIVE	AREA	U.S. AVG
Average commute time	21.7 min.	22.6 min.	Miles to nearest major airport	27	46	Insurance, annual premium	$994	$1,011
Commute by auto	86.0%	88.7%	Type of local airport	Small		Gas, cost per gallon	$1.44	$1.50
Commute by mass transit	.6%	1.8%	No. daily airline departures	81	294	Daily vehicle miles per capita	22.2	23.0
Work at home	6.5%	3.9%	Amtrak service	Yes				
Mass transit miles per capita	7.1	8.0	No. interstate highways	0	1			

LEISURE SCORE: 58/RANK: 139

DINING & SHOPPING	AREA	U.S. AVG	ENTERTAINMENT	AREA	U.S. AVG	OUTDOOR ACTIVITIES	AREA	U.S. AVG
Restaurant rating	1	1	Professional sports rating	4	4	Golf-course rating	3	4
No. outlet malls	6	2	College sports rating	5	4	Ski-area rating	4	4
No. Starbucks	1	11	Zoo/aquarium rating	1	3	National Park rating	1	3
No. warehouse clubs	4	4	Amusement park rating	3	3	Sq. miles inland water	3.0	4.0
			Botanical garden/arboretum rating	3	3	Miles of coastline	0.0	11.4

ARTS & CULTURE SCORE: 0/RANK: 331

MEDIA & LIBRARIES	AREA	U.S. AVG	PERFORMING ARTS	AREA	U.S. AVG	MUSEUMS	AREA	U.S. AVG
Arts radio rating	1	3	Classical music rating	1	4	Overall museum rating	7	6
No. public libraries	17	28	Ballet/dance rating	1	3	Art museum rating	4	5
Library volumes per capita	1.6	2.8	Professional theater rating	1	3	Science museum rating	3	4
			University arts programs rating	6	5	Children's museum rating	4	3

Lansing–East Lansing, MI

Score: 58.5   Rank: 162

Profile: Capital city/College town
Location: South-central Michigan halfway between Detroit and Grand Rapids
Elevation: 841 feet
Time zone: Eastern Standard Time

PRO
Capital-city amenities
College-town atmosphere
Stable economy

CON
Economic cycles
Winter climate
Cloudy skies

Lansing is the state capital, and East Lansing contains Michigan State University. Together the two places form the second most-populated area in Michigan. The area economy is a mix of state government and industry. Strong ties to the auto industry previously led to economic downturns in the area, but the presence of government and the university fueled a resurgence. East Lansing, the more attractive of the two places, contains the usual college-town amenities, restaurants, and nightlife. Activities outside the university include a minor-league baseball team called the Lansing Lugnuts. Cost of living is attractive for a capital city and college town.

Terrain is generally a mix of farmland and deciduous forest. The climate alternates between continental and semi-marine, based on the force and direction of the wind and storms. When there is little wind, the weather becomes continental with pronounced fluctuations in temperature. A strong lake wind may temper winter cold and summer heat, albeit with heightened wind chill factors in winter. Precipitation is evenly distributed throughout the year. Snowfall is moderate. There are twice as many cloudy days as clear ones year-round. First freeze is end of September, last is mid-May.

POPULATION

DEMOGRAPHICS	AREA	U.S. AVG	ETHNIC COMPOSITION	AREA	U.S. AVG	RESIDENT PROFILE	AREA	U.S. AVG
Population	453,620		White	89.5%	75.1%	Single	46.9%	43.6%
Population density per sq. mile	265.7	447.3	Black	6.4%	12.3%	Married	53.1%	56.4%
Population growth	4.8%	16.1%	Asian	2.0%	3.6%	Divorced	8.4%	8.4%
Median age	33.1	35.5	American Indian	.6%	.9%	Separated	2.3%	3.0%
Average family size	2.6	2.7	Hispanic	3.6%	12.5%	Married with children	29.2%	28.7%
			Diversity measure	30.9%	35.2%	Single with children	10.8%	10.1%

ECONOMY & JOBS
SCORE: 96/RANK: 13

INCOME	AREA	U.S. AVG	EMPLOYMENT	AREA	U.S. AVG	LARGEST EMPLOYING INDUSTRY
Per capita income	$23,877	$23,420	Unemployment rate	4.6%	6.1%	Transportation Equipment Manufacturing
Household income	$48,810	$46,060	Recent job growth	3.0%	.9%	
Household income < $25K	22.8%	26.4%	Projected future job growth	14.2%	15.1%	
Household income > $75K	27.2%	24.5%	White collar	58.9%	54.5%	
Household income growth	51.5%	57.3%	Blue collar	41.1%	45.5%	

COST OF LIVING
SCORE: 47/RANK: 173

INDEXES & TAXES	AREA	U.S. AVG	HOUSING	AREA	U.S. AVG	NECESSITIES	AREA	U.S. AVG
Cost of Living Index	90.2	100.0	Median home price	$125,400	$160,100	Food Index	101.7	100.0
Financial Progress Index	115.3	100.0	Home price appreciation	6.9%	7.1%	Housing Index	77.9	100.0
Income tax rate	5.400%	4.625%	Median rent	$649	$670	Utilities Index	74.9	100.0
Sales tax rate	6.000%	6.474%	Homes owned	68.5%	63.9%	Transportation Index	98.0	100.0
Property tax rate	$18.0	$15.6	Homes rented	26.8%	25.3%	Healthcare Index	95.3	100.0
			Housing affordability	56.0%	54.5%	Miscellaneous Cost Index	101.8	100.0

CLIMATE
SCORE: 8/RANK: 302

TEMPERATURE	AREA	U.S. AVG	PRECIPITATION	AREA	U.S. AVG	COMFORTS & HAZARDS	AREA	U.S. AVG
January low	15.3°F	26.4°F	Annual inches precipitation	30.4	35.9	July relative humidity	74.0%	68.8%
July high	82.6°F	86.7°F	Annual inches snowfall	49.0	24.2	Annual days mostly sunny	179	212
Annual days > 90°F	12	38	Annual days precipitation	156	111	Annual days with thunderstorms	34	39
Annual days < 32°F	151	88	Annual days rain > 0.5 inches	18	23	Tornado risk score	24	19
Annual days < 0°F	13	6	Annual days snow > 1.5 inches	12	6	Hurricane risk score	2	15

TEMPERATURE

PRECIPITATION

DAYS OF CLOUDS & PRECIPITATION

EDUCATION
SCORE: 80/RANK: 66

ACHIEVEMENT	AREA	U.S. AVG	PUBLIC SCHOOLS	AREA	U.S. AVG	HIGHER EDUCATION	AREA	U.S. AVG
High school degree	88.6%	80.2%	Expenditures per pupil	$6,446	$5,894	No. 2-year colleges	1	3
2-year college degree	7.7%	6.2%	Student/teacher ratio	17.9	16.7	No. 4-year colleges/universities	3	4
4-year college degree	16.9%	15.8%	Attending public school	92.7%	90.2%	No. highly ranked universities	0	1
Graduate/professional degree	11.5%	9.6%	State SAT score	1140	1020			
			State ACT score	21.3*	21.0			

HEALTH & HEALTHCARE
SCORE: 80/RANK: 61

CRIME
SCORE: 54/RANK: 152

HAZARDS & ILLNESSES	AREA	U.S. AVG	HEALTHCARE	AREA	U.S. AVG	CRIME	AREA	U.S. AVG
Air-quality score	81	45	Physicians per capita	262.8	261.1	Violent crime rate	482.6	456.0
Water-quality score	13	33	Hospital beds per capita	262.0	432.2	Change in violent crime rate	-14.8%	-17.2%
Pollen/allergy score	35	61	No. teaching hospitals	3	4	Property crime rate	3,583.3	3,950.0
Stress score	38	50	Cost per doctor visit	$45	$67	Change in property crime rate	-21.1%	-16.8%
Cancer mortality per capita	165.9	169.0	Cost per dental visit	$81	$82			
Depression days per month	2.4	2.8	Cost per daily hospital room	$555	$733			

TRANSPORTATION
SCORE: 59/RANK: 136

COMMUTE	AREA	U.S. AVG	INTERCITY SERVICES	AREA	U.S. AVG	AUTOMOTIVE	AREA	U.S. AVG
Average commute time	21.2 min.	22.6 min.	Miles to nearest major airport	5	46	Insurance, annual premium	$986	$1,011
Commute by auto	86.7%	88.7%	Type of local airport	Small		Gas, cost per gallon	$1.52	$1.50
Commute by mass transit	1.1%	1.8%	No. daily airline departures	65	294	Daily vehicle miles per capita	22.5	23.0
Work at home	3.9%	3.9%	Amtrak service	Yes				
Mass transit miles per capita	9.1	8.0	No. interstate highways	2	1			

LEISURE SCORE: 44/RANK: 185

DINING & SHOPPING	AREA	U.S. AVG	ENTERTAINMENT	AREA	U.S. AVG	OUTDOOR ACTIVITIES	AREA	U.S. AVG
Restaurant rating	1	1	Professional sports rating	3	4	Golf-course rating	5	4
No. outlet malls	3	2	College sports rating	6	4	Ski-area rating	4	4
No. Starbucks	3	11	Zoo/aquarium rating	5	3	National Park rating	1	3
No. warehouse clubs	3	4	Amusement park rating	1	3	Sq. miles inland water	2.0	4.0
			Botanical garden/arboretum rating	4	3	Miles of coastline	0.0	11.4

ARTS & CULTURE SCORE: 86/RANK: 46

MEDIA & LIBRARIES	AREA	U.S. AVG	PERFORMING ARTS	AREA	U.S. AVG	MUSEUMS	AREA	U.S. AVG
Arts radio rating	8	3	Classical music rating	5	4	Overall museum rating	8	6
No. public libraries	29	28	Ballet/dance rating	1	3	Art museum rating	4	5
Library volumes per capita	2.0	2.8	Professional theater rating	6	3	Science museum rating	7	4
			University arts programs rating	5	5	Children's museum rating	1	3

Laredo, TX

Score: 0.0   Rank: 331

Profile: Small border city
Location: South Texas along the Rio Grande and Mexican border, 200 miles inland from the Gulf of Mexico
Elevation: 438 feet
Time zone: Central Standard Time

PRO	CON
Cost of living	Unattractive and industrial areas
Strong job growth	Low educational attainment
Historic core	Hot climate

Once the classic Old West town, modern Laredo is now the largest and most active port of entry to the United States in the Rio Grande Valley. Numerous border-zone manufacturing plants have sprung up since the North American Free Trade Agreement (NAFTA) came about in the early 1990s. The four border-crossing bridges (a fifth is on the way) are busy with truck and container traffic to Nuevo Laredo in Mexico, and rail and air cargo carriers have extensive operations. Laredo has a dominant Hispanic influence with a large middle class and a much larger working class, some living in poverty or near-poverty conditions outside the city. The Spanish-colonial city center has been reinvigorated following a commercial boom but there is still little to do. At 111 days per year above 90°F, the city is one of the hottest in the United States. It also has the second highest population growth rate in the country. The Cost of Living Index is low at 77.3, but the city's constant bustle, lack of intellectual stimulation, poverty, high crime rate, and heat will try most anyone's patience.

Laredo sits far enough west of the Gulf Coastal Plain to be in a zone of dry, rolling hills and plains, supporting scrub vegetation, small cacti, and oak trees. The climate is semiarid. Summers are hot with most days over 90°F, but with humidity lower than areas on the Gulf Coast. Most rain occurs in summer as thundershowers. Winters are mild and dry with many days in the 70s and 80s; evening lows dip below freezing occasionally.

POPULATION

DEMOGRAPHICS	AREA	U.S. AVG	ETHNIC COMPOSITION	AREA	U.S. AVG	RESIDENT PROFILE	AREA	U.S. AVG
Population	207,611		White	74.1%	75.1%	Single	44.0%	43.6%
Population density per sq. mile	61.8	447.3	Black	.8%	12.3%	Married	56.0%	56.4%
Population growth	55.8%	16.1%	Asian	.4%	3.6%	Divorced	5.4%	8.4%
Median age	26.4	35.5	American Indian	.2%	.9%	Separated	3.7%	3.0%
Average family size	3.8	2.7	Hispanic	94.4%	12.5%	Married with children	45.4%	28.7%
			Diversity measure	14.1%	35.2%	Single with children	14.4%	10.1%

ECONOMY & JOBS SCORE: 6/RANK: 311

INCOME	AREA	U.S. AVG	EMPLOYMENT	AREA	U.S. AVG	LARGEST EMPLOYING INDUSTRY
Per capita income	$12,033	$23,420	Unemployment rate	6.8%	6.1%	Transportation and Warehousing
Household income	$29,892	$46,060	Recent job growth	1.9%	.9%	
Household income < $25K	42.3%	26.4%	Projected future job growth	30.3%	15.1%	
Household income > $75K	13.0%	24.5%	White collar	52.4%	54.5%	
Household income growth	64.8%	57.3%	Blue collar	47.6%	45.5%	

COST OF LIVING SCORE: 93/RANK: 24

INDEXES & TAXES	AREA	U.S. AVG	HOUSING	AREA	U.S. AVG	NECESSITIES	AREA	U.S. AVG
Cost of Living Index	77.3	100.0	Median home price	$86,190	$160,100	Food Index	82.2	100.0
Financial Progress Index	82.4	100.0	Home price appreciation	4.9%	7.1%	Housing Index	53.5	100.0
Income tax rate	0.000%	4.625%	Median rent	$523	$670	Utilities Index	86.0	100.0
Sales tax rate	8.250%	6.474%	Homes owned	62.7%	63.9%	Transportation Index	89.3	100.0
Property tax rate	$23.5	$15.6	Homes rented	25.9%	25.3%	Healthcare Index	99.8	100.0
			Housing affordability	49.0%	54.5%	Miscellaneous Cost Index	97.1	100.0

CLIMATE SCORE: 89/RANK: 37

TEMPERATURE	AREA	U.S. AVG	PRECIPITATION	AREA	U.S. AVG	COMFORTS & HAZARDS	AREA	U.S. AVG
January low	39.8°F	26.4°F	Annual inches precipitation	28.0	35.9	July relative humidity	67.0%	68.8%
July high	95.9°F	86.7°F	Annual inches snowfall	.5	24.2	Annual days mostly sunny	227	212
Annual days > 90°F	111	38	Annual days precipitation	81	111	Annual days with thunderstorms	36	39
Annual days < 32°F	22	88	Annual days rain > 0.5 inches	18	23	Tornado risk score	2	19
Annual days < 0°F	0	6	Annual days snow > 1.5 inches	0	6	Hurricane risk score	14	15

TEMPERATURE

PRECIPITATION

DAYS OF CLOUDS & PRECIPITATION

EDUCATION SCORE: 3/RANK: 318

ACHIEVEMENT	AREA	U.S. AVG	PUBLIC SCHOOLS	AREA	U.S. AVG	HIGHER EDUCATION	AREA	U.S. AVG
High school degree	54.8%	80.2%	Expenditures per pupil	$5,201	$5,894	No. 2-year colleges	1	3
2-year college degree	5.4%	6.2%	Student/teacher ratio	17.3	16.7	No. 4-year colleges/universities	1	4
4-year college degree	9.1%	15.8%	Attending public school	95.4%	90.2%	No. highly ranked universities	0	1
Graduate/professional degree	5.6%	9.6%	State SAT score	993*	1020			
			State ACT score	20.1	21.0			

HEALTH & HEALTHCARE SCORE: 0/RANK: 331

HAZARDS & ILLNESSES	AREA	U.S. AVG	HEALTHCARE	AREA	U.S. AVG
Air-quality score	24	45	Physicians per capita	97.3	261.1
Water-quality score	100	33	Hospital beds per capita	234.1	432.2
Pollen/allergy score	87	61	No. teaching hospitals	1	4
Stress score	70	50	Cost per doctor visit	$68	$67
Cancer mortality per capita	139.2	169.0	Cost per dental visit	$79	$82
Depression days per month	2.3	2.8	Cost per daily hospital room	$576	$733

CRIME SCORE: 3/RANK: 318

CRIME	AREA	U.S. AVG
Violent crime rate	592.4	456.0
Change in violent crime rate	-14.3%	-17.2%
Property crime rate	6,283.6	3,950.0
Change in property crime rate	10.2%	-16.8%

TRANSPORTATION SCORE: 47/RANK: 173

COMMUTE	AREA	U.S. AVG	INTERCITY SERVICES	AREA	U.S. AVG	AUTOMOTIVE	AREA	U.S. AVG
Average commute time	21.7 min.	22.6 min.	Miles to nearest major airport	123	46	Insurance, annual premium	$1,074	$1,011
Commute by auto	86.9%	88.7%	Type of local airport	Small		Gas, cost per gallon	$1.39	$1.50
Commute by mass transit	2.2%	1.8%	No. daily airline departures	42	294	Daily vehicle miles per capita	15.0	23.0
Work at home	2.4%	3.9%	Amtrak service	No				
Mass transit miles per capita	10.4	8.0	No. interstate highways	1	1			

LEISURE SCORE: 2/RANK: 323

DINING & SHOPPING	AREA	U.S. AVG	ENTERTAINMENT	AREA	U.S. AVG	OUTDOOR ACTIVITIES	AREA	U.S. AVG
Restaurant rating	1	1	Professional sports rating	3	4	Golf-course rating	1	4
No. outlet malls	0	2	College sports rating	1	4	Ski-area rating	1	4
No. Starbucks	2	11	Zoo/aquarium rating	1	3	National Park rating	1	3
No. warehouse clubs	3	4	Amusement park rating	1	3	Sq. miles inland water	2.0	4.0
			Botanical garden/arboretum rating	1	3	Miles of coastline	0.0	11.4

ARTS & CULTURE SCORE: 0/RANK: 329

MEDIA & LIBRARIES	AREA	U.S. AVG	PERFORMING ARTS	AREA	U.S. AVG	MUSEUMS	AREA	U.S. AVG
Arts radio rating	1	3	Classical music rating	1	4	Overall museum rating	1	6
No. public libraries	4	28	Ballet/dance rating	1	3	Art museum rating	1	5
Library volumes per capita	1.0	2.8	Professional theater rating	1	3	Science museum rating	1	4
			University arts programs rating	1	5	Children's museum rating	2	3

Las Cruces, NM

Score: 80.0   Rank: 39

Profile: Small town/College town
Location: South-central New Mexico along Rio Grande Valley, 45 miles north of El Paso, Texas
Elevation: 3,881 feet
Time zone: Mountain Standard Time

PRO	CON
Pleasant winters	Isolation
Cost of living	Entertainment
Historic interest	Healthcare

Las Cruces is a small agricultural and transportation center, home to 15,000 New Mexico State University students. It is also the gateway to historic, geologic, and recreational sites, including White Sands National Monument to the northeast. The downtown is clean, quiet, and attractively laid out with an Old West feel. At 84.9, the Cost of Living Index is quite low for the region and particularly attractive given the climate. Although the area is reasonably close to El Paso and some air service there, that proximity doesn't relieve the feeling of isolation.

Las Cruces is located in the broad, flat Mesilla Valley, a grazing area with desert hills and mountains on both sides. The alkali desert supports only limited and hardy vegetation and grasses, although there are areas of scrub trees in the hills and mountains. The southerly desert climate allows an abundance of sunshine year-round; hot, dry summer days; and cool evenings. Limited precipitation falls in summer as thundershowers. Winters are mild, sunny, and dry, although below-freezing temperatures happen about once every 3 days. First freeze is mid-December, last is mid-February.

POPULATION

DEMOGRAPHICS	AREA	U.S. AVG	ETHNIC COMPOSITION	AREA	U.S. AVG	RESIDENT PROFILE	AREA	U.S. AVG
Population	178,664		White	93.0%	75.1%	Single	40.7%	43.6%
Population density per sq. mile	46.9	447.3	Black	2.3%	12.3%	Married	59.3%	56.4%
Population growth	31.8%	16.1%	Asian	1.3%	3.6%	Divorced	7.3%	8.4%
Median age	30.4	35.5	American Indian	.4%	.9%	Separated	2.4%	3.0%
Average family size	3.0	2.7	Hispanic	65.8%	12.5%	Married with children	36.9%	28.7%
			Diversity measure	52.4%	35.2%	Single with children	12.1%	10.1%

ECONOMY & JOBS   SCORE: 24/RANK: 249

INCOME	AREA	U.S. AVG	EMPLOYMENT	AREA	U.S. AVG	LARGEST EMPLOYING INDUSTRY
Per capita income	$14,003	$23,420	Unemployment rate	6.4%	6.1%	Support Activities for Transportation
Household income	$30,819	$46,060	Recent job growth	2.1%	.9%	
Household income < $25K	40.6%	26.4%	Projected future job growth	21.4%	15.1%	
Household income > $75K	11.0%	24.5%	White collar	53.4%	54.5%	
Household income growth	40.9%	57.3%	Blue collar	46.6%	45.5%	

COST OF LIVING   SCORE: 61/RANK: 127

INDEXES & TAXES	AREA	U.S. AVG	HOUSING	AREA	U.S. AVG	NECESSITIES	AREA	U.S. AVG
Cost of Living Index	84.9	100.0	Median home price	$100,040	$160,100	Food Index	103.8	100.0
Financial Progress Index	77.3	100.0	Home price appreciation	3.2%	7.1%	Housing Index	62.1	100.0
Income tax rate	7.100%	4.625%	Median rent	$471	$670	Utilities Index	94.4	100.0
Sales tax rate	5.813%	6.474%	Homes owned	63.6%	63.9%	Transportation Index	97.1	100.0
Property tax rate	$8.2	$15.6	Homes rented	27.2%	25.3%	Healthcare Index	95.1	100.0
			Housing affordability	51.0%	54.5%	Miscellaneous Cost Index	95.4	100.0

CLIMATE   SCORE: 91/RANK: 28

TEMPERATURE	AREA	U.S. AVG	PRECIPITATION	AREA	U.S. AVG	COMFORTS & HAZARDS	AREA	U.S. AVG
January low	26.5°F	26.4°F	Annual inches precipitation	8.0	35.9	July relative humidity	49.0%	68.8%
July high	93.5°F	86.7°F	Annual inches snowfall	11.0	24.2	Annual days mostly sunny	287	212
Annual days > 90°F	70	38	Annual days precipitation	53	111	Annual days with thunderstorms	34	39
Annual days < 32°F	15	88	Annual days rain > 0.5 inches	2	23	Tornado risk score	1	19
Annual days < 0°F	6	6	Annual days snow > 1.5 inches	3	6	Hurricane risk score	2	15

TEMPERATURE

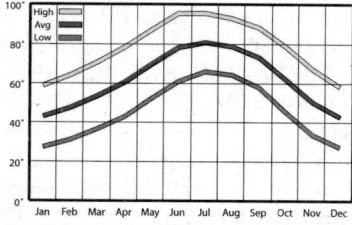

PRECIPITATION

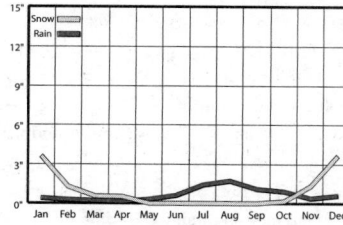

DAYS OF CLOUDS & PRECIPITATION

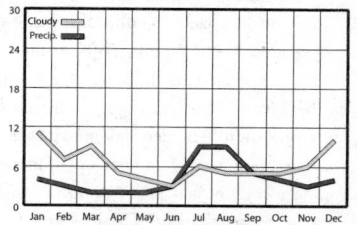

EDUCATION SCORE: 28/RANK: 236

ACHIEVEMENT	AREA	U.S. AVG	PUBLIC SCHOOLS	AREA	U.S. AVG	HIGHER EDUCATION	AREA	U.S. AVG
High school degree	70.0%	80.2%	Expenditures per pupil	$4,911	$5,894	No. 2-year colleges	1	3
2-year college degree	6.5%	6.2%	Student/teacher ratio	16.0	16.7	No. 4-year colleges/universities	1	4
4-year college degree	13.0%	15.8%	Attending public school	96.8%	90.2%	No. highly ranked universities	0	1
Graduate/professional degree	9.2%	9.6%	State SAT score	1088	1020			
			State ACT score	19.9*	21.0			

HEALTH & HEALTHCARE SCORE: 11/RANK: 293

CRIME SCORE: 30/RANK: 229

HAZARDS & ILLNESSES	AREA	U.S. AVG	HEALTHCARE	AREA	U.S. AVG	CRIME	AREA	U.S. AVG
Air-quality score	59	45	Physicians per capita	141.6	261.1	Violent crime rate	469.5	456.0
Water-quality score	10	33	Hospital beds per capita	267.3	432.2	Change in violent crime rate	-17.7%	-17.2%
Pollen/allergy score	69	61	No. teaching hospitals	1	4	Property crime rate	4,537.2	3,950.0
Stress score	47	50	Cost per doctor visit	$55	$67	Change in property crime rate	-11.3%	-16.8%
Cancer mortality per capita	149.3	169.0	Cost per dental visit	$89	$82			
Depression days per month	2.3	2.8	Cost per daily hospital room	$392	$733			

TRANSPORTATION SCORE: 29/RANK: 234

COMMUTE	AREA	U.S. AVG	INTERCITY SERVICES	AREA	U.S. AVG	AUTOMOTIVE	AREA	U.S. AVG
Average commute time	21.3 min.	22.6 min.	Miles to nearest major airport	42	46	Insurance, annual premium	$919	$1,011
Commute by auto	87.9%	88.7%	Type of local airport	Medium		Gas, cost per gallon	$1.44	$1.50
Commute by mass transit	.3%	1.8%	No. daily airline departures	115	294	Daily vehicle miles per capita	31.0	23.0
Work at home	5.1%	3.9%	Amtrak service	No				
Mass transit miles per capita	3.4	8.0	No. interstate highways	2	1			

LEISURE SCORE: 23/RANK: 253

DINING & SHOPPING	AREA	U.S. AVG	ENTERTAINMENT	AREA	U.S. AVG	OUTDOOR ACTIVITIES	AREA	U.S. AVG
Restaurant rating	1	1	Professional sports rating	2	4	Golf-course rating	2	4
No. outlet malls	0	2	College sports rating	3	4	Ski-area rating	3	4
No. Starbucks	0	11	Zoo/aquarium rating	1	3	National Park rating	4	3
No. warehouse clubs	1	4	Amusement park rating	1	3	Sq. miles inland water	1.0	4.0
			Botanical garden/arboretum rating	1	3	Miles of coastline	0.0	11.4

ARTS & CULTURE SCORE: 71/RANK: 93

MEDIA & LIBRARIES	AREA	U.S. AVG	PERFORMING ARTS	AREA	U.S. AVG	MUSEUMS	AREA	U.S. AVG
Arts radio rating	5	3	Classical music rating	3	4	Overall museum rating	5	6
No. public libraries	3	28	Ballet/dance rating	1	3	Art museum rating	5	5
Library volumes per capita	.9	2.8	Professional theater rating	1	3	Science museum rating	6	4
			University arts programs rating	4	5	Children's museum rating	1	3

Las Vegas, NV

Score: 62.4   Rank: 129

Profile: Large resort city
Location: Southern Nevada near Colorado River
Elevation: 2,180 feet
Time zone: Pacific Standard Time

PRO
Desert climate
Entertainment
Air service

CON
Summer heat
Growth and sprawl
Tourist economy

Las Vegas is a "nice place to visit, but would you want to live there?" The answer depends on the kind of lifestyle you want. A truly unique city, Las Vegas is an adult Disneyland developed mainly for playful leisure getaways. In the 1970s, Nevada started to lose its monopoly on legalized gambling, with the emergence of alternative gambling venues in other parts of the country. As a result, Las Vegas casino owners invested in flashier, entertainment-oriented properties, such as the Luxor hotel and casino with its full-scale reproduction of King Tut's tomb. While bigger and more garish, these new "theme park" casinos are actually more family-oriented than their predecessors.

Stripping away tourism and entertainment would reveal a hot, dry, desert town. Las Vegas has the highest growth rate among metropolitan areas, and an accompanying sprawl problem. Sprouting up outside the main strip of casinos are subdivisions and self-contained communities, some filled with residents who avoid the strip altogether. The lack of

income and inheritance taxes attracts large numbers of retirees and affluent residents with assets elsewhere in the country. Local jobs are still tied to the cyclical tourism and entertainment industries, but other businesses are entering the area and the University of Nevada at Las Vegas is a significant employer. The tourist industry guarantees excellent air service to all parts of the country at reasonable prices, and there is continuing talk of high-speed rail service to Los Angeles. The surrounding mountainous terrain offers hiking and rock-climbing opportunities and winter skiing. Downsides include heat, desert monotony, high violent crime rates, and the constant influx of tourists.

Las Vegas is situated near the center of a broad desert valley surrounded by mountains rising 2,000 feet to 10,000 feet. The climate is arid with four distinct seasons. Maximum summer temperatures are in the 100°F range. Mountain proximity contributes to relatively cool (mid-70s) summer nights. About 2 weeks each summer, warm, moist air moves in from the south, causing scattered thunderstorms, occasionally severe, together with higher than average humidity. Winters on the whole are mild and pleasant. Daytime temperatures average near 60°F with mostly clear skies. Spring and fall seasons are generally the most pleasant, although sharp temperature changes can occur during these months. The city is the driest and sunniest in the United States, with cloudy days averaging about 2 per month and rainy days less than 1 per month year-round. Snow rarely falls.

POPULATION

DEMOGRAPHICS	AREA	U.S. AVG	ETHNIC COMPOSITION	AREA	U.S. AVG	RESIDENT PROFILE	AREA	U.S. AVG
Population	1,722,256		White	85.7%	75.1%	Single	43.7%	43.6%
Population density per sq. mile	43.7	447.3	Black	5.2%	12.3%	Married	56.3%	56.4%
Population growth	102.0%	16.1%	Asian	2.7%	3.6%	Divorced	13.7%	8.4%
Median age	35.6	35.5	American Indian	3.2%	.9%	Separated	3.4%	3.4%
Average family size	2.8	2.7	Hispanic	13.7%	12.5%	Married with children	24.1%	28.7%
			Diversity measure	53.0%	35.2%	Single with children	10.3%	10.1%

ECONOMY & JOBS SCORE: 1/RANK: 327

INCOME	AREA	U.S. AVG	EMPLOYMENT	AREA	U.S. AVG	LARGEST EMPLOYING INDUSTRY
Per capita income	$25,013	$23,420	Unemployment rate	5.3%	6.1%	Accommodations and Food Services
Household income	$48,723	$46,060	Recent job growth	-.7%	.9%	
Household income < $25K	22.0%	26.4%	Projected future job growth	42.0%	15.1%	
Household income > $75K	26.2%	24.5%	White collar	48.4%	54.5%	
Household income growth	62.4%	57.3%	Blue collar	51.6%	45.5%	

COST OF LIVING SCORE: 51/RANK: 160

INDEXES & TAXES	AREA	U.S. AVG	HOUSING	AREA	U.S. AVG	NECESSITIES	AREA	U.S. AVG
Cost of Living Index	103.1	100.0	Median home price	$166,100	$160,100	Food Index	108.3	100.0
Financial Progress Index	100.7	100.0	Home price appreciation	6.9%	7.1%	Housing Index	103.2	100.0
Income tax rate	0.000%	4.625%	Median rent	$856	$670	Utilities Index	83.6	100.0
Sales tax rate	7.250%	6.474%	Homes owned	57.5%	63.9%	Transportation Index	107.7	100.0
Property tax rate	$11.0	$15.6	Homes rented	28.9%	25.3%	Healthcare Index	113.2	100.0
			Housing affordability	51.0%	54.5%	Miscellaneous Cost Index	100.9	100.0

CLIMATE SCORE: 79/RANK: 69

TEMPERATURE	AREA	U.S. AVG	PRECIPITATION	AREA	U.S. AVG	COMFORTS & HAZARDS	AREA	U.S. AVG
January low	32.6°F	26.4°F	Annual inches precipitation	4.0	35.9	July relative humidity	29.0%	68.8%
July high	103.9°F	86.7°F	Annual inches snowfall	1.5	24.2	Annual days mostly sunny	300	212
Annual days > 90°F	131	38	Annual days precipitation	24	111	Annual days with thunderstorms	15	39
Annual days < 32°F	41	88	Annual days rain > 0.5 inches	4	23	Tornado risk score	2	19
Annual days < 0°F	0	6	Annual days snow > 1.5 inches	1	6	Hurricane risk score	0	15

TEMPERATURE

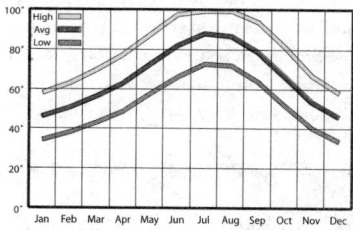

PRECIPITATION

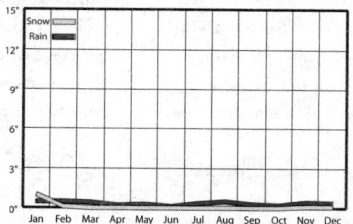

DAYS OF CLOUDS & PRECIPITATION

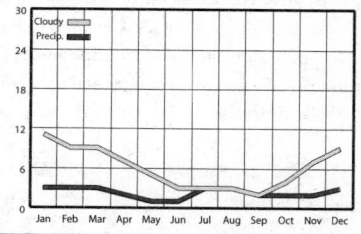

EDUCATION SCORE: 18/RANK: 269

ACHIEVEMENT	AREA	U.S. AVG	PUBLIC SCHOOLS	AREA	U.S. AVG	HIGHER EDUCATION	AREA	U.S. AVG
High school degree	78.5%	80.2%	Expenditures per pupil	$4,948	$5,894	No. 2-year colleges	4	3
2-year college degree	5.7%	6.2%	Student/teacher ratio	20.6	16.7	No. 4-year colleges/universities	1	4
4-year college degree	11.7%	15.8%	Attending public school	95.9%	90.2%	No. highly ranked universities	0	1
Graduate/professional degree	6.5%	9.6%	State SAT score	1027*	1020			
			State ACT score	21.3	21.0			

HEALTH & HEALTHCARE SCORE: 16/RANK: 278

CRIME SCORE: 60/RANK: 130

HAZARDS & ILLNESSES	AREA	U.S. AVG	HEALTHCARE	AREA	U.S. AVG	CRIME	AREA	U.S. AVG
Air-quality score	3	45	Physicians per capita	165.5	261.1	Violent crime rate	616.8	456.0
Water-quality score	11	33	Hospital beds per capita	243.0	432.2	Change in violent crime rate	-43.2%	-17.2%
Pollen/allergy score	71	61	No. teaching hospitals	2	4	Property crime rate	3,858.1	3,950.0
Stress score	94	50	Cost per doctor visit	$80	$67	Change in property crime rate	-39.0%	-16.8%
Cancer mortality per capita	189.9	169.0	Cost per dental visit	$108	$82			
Depression days per month	3.5	2.8	Cost per daily hospital room	$685	$733			

TRANSPORTATION SCORE: 86/RANK: 46

COMMUTE	AREA	U.S. AVG	INTERCITY SERVICES	AREA	U.S. AVG	AUTOMOTIVE	AREA	U.S. AVG
Average commute time	24.1 min.	22.6 min.	Miles to nearest major airport	9	46	Insurance, annual premium	$1,647	$1,011
Commute by auto	89.5%	88.7%	Type of local airport	Large		Gas, cost per gallon	$1.62	$1.50
Commute by mass transit	2.1%	1.8%	No. daily airline departures	545	294	Daily vehicle miles per capita	20.2	23.0
Work at home	1.9%	3.9%	Amtrak service	Yes				
Mass transit miles per capita	15.4	8.0	No. interstate highways	1	1			

LEISURE SCORE: 84/RANK: 52

DINING & SHOPPING	AREA	U.S. AVG	ENTERTAINMENT	AREA	U.S. AVG	OUTDOOR ACTIVITIES	AREA	U.S. AVG
Restaurant rating	1	1	Professional sports rating	3	4	Golf-course rating	3	4
No. outlet malls	5	2	College sports rating	5	4	Ski-area rating	6	4
No. Starbucks	42	11	Zoo/aquarium rating	2	3	National Park rating	10	3
No. warehouse clubs	6	4	Amusement park rating	1	3	Sq. miles inland water	10.0	4.0
			Botanical garden/arboretum rating	3	3	Miles of coastline	0.0	11.4

ARTS & CULTURE SCORE: 60/RANK: 133

MEDIA & LIBRARIES	AREA	U.S. AVG	PERFORMING ARTS	AREA	U.S. AVG	MUSEUMS	AREA	U.S. AVG
Arts radio rating	10	3	Classical music rating	3	4	Overall museum rating	7	6
No. public libraries	48	28	Ballet/dance rating	6	3	Art museum rating	5	5
Library volumes per capita	2.0	2.8	Professional theater rating	1	3	Science museum rating	9	4
			University arts programs rating	4	5	Children's museum rating	7	3

Lawrence, KS

Score: 54.3   Rank: 194

Profile: College town
Location: Northeast Kansas, 40 miles west of Kansas City
Elevation: 939 feet
Time zone: Central Standard Time

PRO
College-town element
Attractive campus and downtown
College sports

CON
Harsh winters
Home prices
Low diversity

Home to the University of Kansas, Lawrence is considered one of the more attractive cities in the state. It has many college-town amenities, including an attractive campus and a handful of interesting museums. The Kansas Jayhawks basketball team, perennially one of the best, provides a great deal of winter and early spring entertainment. To the southwest, man-made Clinton Lake provides recreational opportunities—in fact, recreational and cultural amenities are probably better than the statistics indicate. Home prices and unemployment exceed the state average by far. On the whole, Lawrence's ranking may understate the quality of life in the area.

The land rises into gently rolling prairie, mostly given to agriculture. The climate is variable continental. Summer conditions vary, but may include prolonged periods with temperatures over 100°F. Winters are cold with frequent wind and snow. Spring can be windy and stormy mixed with periods of pleasant weather. Strong storms and severe weather generally happen during spring and summer. First freeze is mid-October, last is late April.

POPULATION

DEMOGRAPHICS	AREA	U.S. AVG	ETHNIC COMPOSITION	AREA	U.S. AVG	RESIDENT PROFILE	AREA	U.S. AVG
Population	102,316		White	90.1%	75.1%	Single	49.1%	43.6%
Population density per sq. mile	223.9	447.3	Black	3.2%	12.3%	Married	50.9%	56.4%
Population growth	25.1%	16.1%	Asian	3.4%	3.6%	Divorced	7.2%	8.4%
Median age	26.9	35.5	American Indian	2.5%	.9%	Separated	1.3%	3.0%
Average family size	2.6	2.7	Hispanic	3.2%	12.5%	Married with children	26.6%	28.7%
			Diversity measure	27.7%	35.2%	Single with children	8.0%	10.1%

ECONOMY & JOBS SCORE: 66/RANK: 108

INCOME	AREA	U.S. AVG	EMPLOYMENT	AREA	U.S. AVG	LARGEST EMPLOYING INDUSTRY
Per capita income	$20,301	$23,420	Unemployment rate	4.1%	6.1%	Computer and Electronic Product Manufacturing
Household income	$39,088	$46,060	Recent job growth	2.1%	.9%	
Household income < $25K	33.7%	26.4%	Projected future job growth	14.2%	15.1%	
Household income > $75K	19.9%	24.5%	White collar	58.6%	54.5%	
Household income growth	55.0%	57.3%	Blue collar	41.4%	45.5%	

COST OF LIVING SCORE: 30/RANK: 230

INDEXES & TAXES	AREA	U.S. AVG	HOUSING	AREA	U.S. AVG	NECESSITIES	AREA	U.S. AVG
Cost of Living Index	95.6	100.0	Median home price	$142,860	$160,100	Food Index	93.8	100.0
Financial Progress Index	87.2	100.0	Home price appreciation	6.6%	7.1%	Housing Index	88.7	100.0
Income tax rate	6.250%	4.625%	Median rent	$585	$670	Utilities Index	113.4	100.0
Sales tax rate	7.300%	6.474%	Homes owned	62.4%	63.9%	Transportation Index	99.8	100.0
Property tax rate	$16.2	$15.6	Homes rented	33.0%	25.3%	Healthcare Index	93.0	100.0
			Housing affordability	54.0%	54.5%	Miscellaneous Cost Index	100.2	100.0

CLIMATE SCORE: 31/RANK: 228

TEMPERATURE	AREA	U.S. AVG
January low	17.0°F	26.4°F
July high	89.0°F	86.7°F
Annual days > 90°F	45	38
Annual days < 32°F	123	88
Annual days < 0°F	5	6

PRECIPITATION	AREA	U.S. AVG
Annual inches precipitation	34.0	35.9
Annual inches snowfall	21.0	24.2
Annual days precipitation	96	111
Annual days rain > 0.5 inches	23	23
Annual days snow > 1.5 inches	5	6

COMFORTS & HAZARDS	AREA	U.S. AVG
July relative humidity	68.0%	68.8%
Annual days mostly sunny	205	212
Annual days with thunderstorms	58	39
Tornado risk score	30	19
Hurricane risk score	2	15

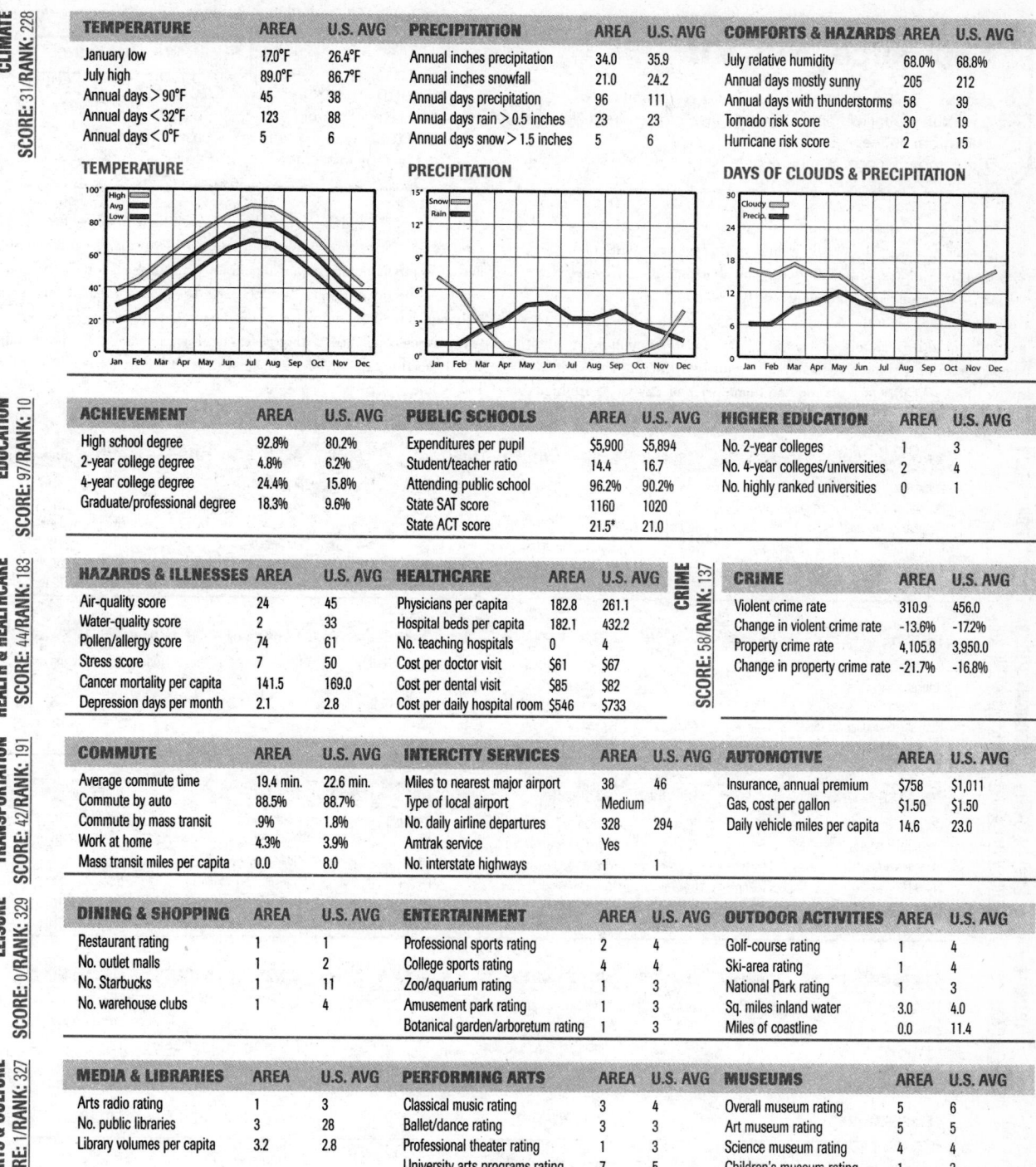

TEMPERATURE · PRECIPITATION · DAYS OF CLOUDS & PRECIPITATION

EDUCATION SCORE: 97/RANK: 10

ACHIEVEMENT	AREA	U.S. AVG
High school degree	92.8%	80.2%
2-year college degree	4.8%	6.2%
4-year college degree	24.4%	15.8%
Graduate/professional degree	18.3%	9.6%

PUBLIC SCHOOLS	AREA	U.S. AVG
Expenditures per pupil	$5,900	$5,894
Student/teacher ratio	14.4	16.7
Attending public school	96.2%	90.2%
State SAT score	1160	1020
State ACT score	21.5*	21.0

HIGHER EDUCATION	AREA	U.S. AVG
No. 2-year colleges	1	3
No. 4-year colleges/universities	2	4
No. highly ranked universities	0	1

HEALTH & HEALTHCARE SCORE: 44/RANK: 183 · **CRIME** SCORE: 58/RANK: 137

HAZARDS & ILLNESSES	AREA	U.S. AVG
Air-quality score	24	45
Water-quality score	2	33
Pollen/allergy score	74	61
Stress score	7	50
Cancer mortality per capita	141.5	169.0
Depression days per month	2.1	2.8

HEALTHCARE	AREA	U.S. AVG
Physicians per capita	182.8	261.1
Hospital beds per capita	182.1	432.2
No. teaching hospitals	0	4
Cost per doctor visit	$61	$67
Cost per dental visit	$85	$82
Cost per daily hospital room	$546	$733

CRIME	AREA	U.S. AVG
Violent crime rate	310.9	456.0
Change in violent crime rate	-13.6%	-17.2%
Property crime rate	4,105.8	3,950.0
Change in property crime rate	-21.7%	-16.8%

TRANSPORTATION SCORE: 42/RANK: 191

COMMUTE	AREA	U.S. AVG
Average commute time	19.4 min.	22.6 min.
Commute by auto	88.5%	88.7%
Commute by mass transit	.9%	1.8%
Work at home	4.3%	3.9%
Mass transit miles per capita	0.0	8.0

INTERCITY SERVICES	AREA	U.S. AVG
Miles to nearest major airport	38	46
Type of local airport	Medium	
No. daily airline departures	328	294
Amtrak service	Yes	
No. interstate highways	1	1

AUTOMOTIVE	AREA	U.S. AVG
Insurance, annual premium	$758	$1,011
Gas, cost per gallon	$1.50	$1.50
Daily vehicle miles per capita	14.6	23.0

LEISURE SCORE: 0/RANK: 329

DINING & SHOPPING	AREA	U.S. AVG
Restaurant rating	1	1
No. outlet malls	1	2
No. Starbucks	1	11
No. warehouse clubs	1	4

ENTERTAINMENT	AREA	U.S. AVG
Professional sports rating	2	4
College sports rating	4	4
Zoo/aquarium rating	1	3
Amusement park rating	1	3
Botanical garden/arboretum rating	1	3

OUTDOOR ACTIVITIES	AREA	U.S. AVG
Golf-course rating	1	4
Ski-area rating	1	4
National Park rating	1	3
Sq. miles inland water	3.0	4.0
Miles of coastline	0.0	11.4

ARTS & CULTURE SCORE: 1/RANK: 327

MEDIA & LIBRARIES	AREA	U.S. AVG
Arts radio rating	1	3
No. public libraries	3	28
Library volumes per capita	3.2	2.8

PERFORMING ARTS	AREA	U.S. AVG
Classical music rating	3	4
Ballet/dance rating	3	3
Professional theater rating	1	3
University arts programs rating	7	5

MUSEUMS	AREA	U.S. AVG
Overall museum rating	5	6
Art museum rating	5	5
Science museum rating	4	4
Children's museum rating	1	3

Lawrence, MA-NH

Score: 19.5   Rank: 326

Profile: Small industrial city/Commuter community
Location: 35 miles north of Boston, just into southern New Hampshire
Elevation: 50 feet
Time zone: Eastern Standard Time

PRO	CON
Historic interest	Cost of living
Proximity to Boston	Cost of housing
Nearby coastline	Economic cycles

Lawrence, a former mill town, has a diverse commercial and manufacturing base. High-tech industry is prevalent, particularly in nearby Andover, although textile and shoe manufacturing are also common. Numerous entertainment and recreational opportunities are available to the east at the Atlantic Coast, to the south in Boston, and to the north in ski areas and along the Maine coast. Commuting to the Boston area is possible, but peak traffic can be difficult. The Cost of Living Index of 138.9 and the median home price of $295,190 are high even for the Greater Boston area.

The terrain is mainly level to low rolling hills with dense forests. The climate is continental with a moderate marine influence and generally active weather. Summers are moderate with an occasional hot, humid spell and thundershowers. Winters have frequent cold snaps and snow, although low temperatures may be moderated somewhat by water and wind. Occasional heavy "noreaster" storms can move up the Atlantic Coast, resulting in considerable snow cover. First freeze is mid-October, last is late April.

POPULATION

DEMOGRAPHICS	AREA	U.S. AVG	ETHNIC COMPOSITION	AREA	U.S. AVG	RESIDENT PROFILE	AREA	U.S. AVG
Population	405,419		White	91.9%	75.1%	Single	41.7%	43.6%
Population density per sq. mile	925.9	447.3	Black	2.2%	12.3%	Married	58.3%	56.4%
Population growth	14.8%	16.1%	Asian	1.6%	3.6%	Divorced	7.3%	8.4%
Median age	37.8	35.5	American Indian	.2%	.9%	Separated	3.1%	3.0%
Average family size	2.8	2.7	Hispanic	7.7%	12.5%	Married with children	32.5%	28.7%
			Diversity measure	25.9%	35.2%	Single with children	8.8%	10.1%

ECONOMY & JOBS — SCORE: 16/RANK: 278

INCOME	AREA	U.S. AVG	EMPLOYMENT	AREA	U.S. AVG	LARGEST EMPLOYING INDUSTRY
Per capita income	$31,417	$23,420	Unemployment rate	8.0%	6.1%	Computer and Electronic Product Manufacturing
Household income	$64,927	$46,060	Recent job growth	-1.8%	.9%	
Household income < $25K	17.8%	26.4%	Projected future job growth	10.0%	15.1%	
Household income > $75K	41.7%	24.5%	White collar	62.1%	54.5%	
Household income growth	61.9%	57.3%	Blue collar	37.9%	45.5%	

COST OF LIVING — SCORE: 7/RANK: 305

INDEXES & TAXES	AREA	U.S. AVG	HOUSING	AREA	U.S. AVG	NECESSITIES	AREA	U.S. AVG
Cost of Living Index	138.9	100.0	Median home price	$295,190	$160,100	Food Index	108.7	100.0
Financial Progress Index	99.6	100.0	Home price appreciation	15.1%	7.1%	Housing Index	183.3	100.0
Income tax rate	5.950%	4.625%	Median rent	$971	$670	Utilities Index	140.2	100.0
Sales tax rate	5.000%	6.474%	Homes owned	69.7%	63.9%	Transportation Index	108.4	100.0
Property tax rate	$13.2	$15.6	Homes rented	23.6%	25.3%	Healthcare Index	118.0	100.0
			Housing affordability	43.0%	54.5%	Miscellaneous Cost Index	110.2	100.0

CLIMATE — SCORE: 10/RANK: 298

TEMPERATURE	AREA	U.S. AVG	PRECIPITATION	AREA	U.S. AVG	COMFORTS & HAZARDS	AREA	U.S. AVG
January low	18.2°F	26.4°F	Annual inches precipitation	45.2	35.9	July relative humidity	68.0%	68.8%
July high	81.4°F	86.7°F	Annual inches snowfall	50.0	24.2	Annual days mostly sunny	197	212
Annual days > 90°F	15	38	Annual days precipitation	137	111	Annual days with thunderstorms	22	39
Annual days < 32°F	120	88	Annual days rain > 0.5 inches	28	23	Tornado risk score	8	19
Annual days < 0°F	5	6	Annual days snow > 1.5 inches	19	6	Hurricane risk score	18	15

TEMPERATURE

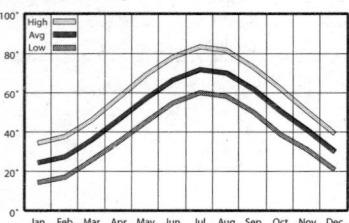

PRECIPITATION

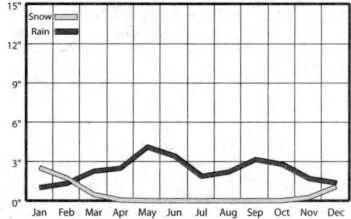

DAYS OF CLOUDS & PRECIPITATION

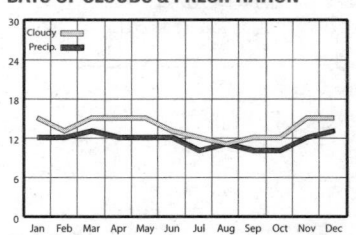

EDUCATION SCORE: 72/RANK: 94

ACHIEVEMENT	AREA	U.S. AVG	PUBLIC SCHOOLS	AREA	U.S. AVG	HIGHER EDUCATION	AREA	U.S. AVG
High school degree	86.6%	80.2%	Expenditures per pupil	$7,131	$5,894	No. 2-year colleges	2	3
2-year college degree	8.2%	6.2%	Student/teacher ratio	15.7	16.7	No. 4-year colleges/universities	2	4
4-year college degree	20.0%	15.8%	Attending public school	84.5%	90.2%	No. highly ranked universities	0	1
Graduate/professional degree	11.3%	9.6%	State SAT score	1038*	1020			
			State ACT score	22.3	21.0			

HEALTH & HEALTHCARE SCORE: 14/RANK: 283

HAZARDS & ILLNESSES	AREA	U.S. AVG	HEALTHCARE	AREA	U.S. AVG
Air-quality score	59	45	Physicians per capita	169.9	261.1
Water-quality score	23	33	Hospital beds per capita	275.6	432.2
Pollen/allergy score	58	61	No. teaching hospitals	2	4
Stress score	45	50	Cost per doctor visit	$84	$67
Cancer mortality per capita	183.2	169.0	Cost per dental visit	$99	$82
Depression days per month	2.7	2.8	Cost per daily hospital room	$659	$733

CRIME SCORE: 97/RANK: 8

CRIME	AREA	U.S. AVG
Violent crime rate	304.3	456.0
Change in violent crime rate	-38.4%	-17.2%
Property crime rate	2,237.1	3,950.0
Change in property crime rate	-37.6%	-16.8%

TRANSPORTATION SCORE: 49/RANK: 168

COMMUTE	AREA	U.S. AVG	INTERCITY SERVICES	AREA	U.S. AVG	AUTOMOTIVE	AREA	U.S. AVG
Average commute time	27.1 min.	22.6 min.	Miles to nearest major airport	24	46	Insurance, annual premium	$1,242	$1,011
Commute by auto	92.0%	88.7%	Type of local airport	Large		Gas, cost per gallon	$1.53	$1.50
Commute by mass transit	1.5%	1.8%	No. daily airline departures	746	294	Daily vehicle miles per capita	27.9	23.0
Work at home	3.1%	3.9%	Amtrak service	No				
Mass transit miles per capita	4.7	8.0	No. interstate highways	1	1			

LEISURE SCORE: 78/RANK: 70

DINING & SHOPPING	AREA	U.S. AVG	ENTERTAINMENT	AREA	U.S. AVG	OUTDOOR ACTIVITIES	AREA	U.S. AVG
Restaurant rating	1	1	Professional sports rating	8	4	Golf-course rating	5	4
No. outlet malls	5	2	College sports rating	4	4	Ski-area rating	7	4
No. Starbucks	3	11	Zoo/aquarium rating	3	3	National Park rating	2	3
No. warehouse clubs	4	4	Amusement park rating	5	3	Sq. miles inland water	5.0	4.0
			Botanical garden/arboretum rating	4	3	Miles of coastline	13.1	11.4

ARTS & CULTURE SCORE: 68/RANK: 108

MEDIA & LIBRARIES	AREA	U.S. AVG	PERFORMING ARTS	AREA	U.S. AVG	MUSEUMS	AREA	U.S. AVG
Arts radio rating	4	3	Classical music rating	5	4	Overall museum rating	6	6
No. public libraries	26	28	Ballet/dance rating	5	3	Art museum rating	6	5
Library volumes per capita	3.7	2.8	Professional theater rating	5	3	Science museum rating	6	4
			University arts programs rating	7	5	Children's museum rating	3	3

Lawton, OK

Score: 58.8   Rank: 159

Profile: Military town
Location: Southwest Oklahoma, 40 miles north of Texas border
Elevation: 994 feet
Time zone: Central Standard Time

PRO	CON
Cost of living	Entertainment
Small-town atmosphere	Isolation
Stable economy	Summer heat

Lawton, a military town at the edge of the southern Great Plains, is neat and clean but fairly nondescript. Fort Sill, the area's main economic base, lies just outside of town. Lawton sits at the edge of the Wichita Mountains, a mostly worn-down series of low hills and bluffs and home to the 60,000-acre Wichita Mountains Wildlife Refuge. Military ties result in the low population, economic growth, and cost of living, including a COL Index of 81.2 and median home prices under $80,000. Oklahoma City is 90 miles northeast and the Dallas and Fort Worth metroplex is 190 miles southeast.

Lawton sits on level, dry grassland typical of the Great Plains. The climate is Great Plains continental, but the area is far enough south to experience summer heat extremes and few cooling breezes. Summers are hot and fairly humid, with average July temperatures of 99°F, placing the city among the top 10 hottest places in the United States. The area gets plenty of sunshine. Winters are generally mild. Spring and summer precipitation is mostly thundershowers and winter receives a mix with mostly rain.

POPULATION

DEMOGRAPHICS	AREA	U.S. AVG	ETHNIC COMPOSITION	AREA	U.S. AVG	RESIDENT PROFILE	AREA	U.S. AVG
Population	113,414		White	73.4%	75.1%	Single	40.8%	43.6%
Population density per sq. mile	106.1	447.3	Black	11.7%	12.3%	Married	59.2%	56.4%
Population growth	1.7%	16.1%	Asian	2.6%	3.6%	Divorced	9.0%	8.4%
Median age	30.0	35.5	American Indian	9.5%	.9%	Separated	2.7%	3.0%
Average family size	2.5	2.7	Hispanic	8.0%	12.5%	Married with children	35.3%	28.7%
			Diversity measure	56.2%	35.2%	Single with children	10.9%	10.1%

ECONOMY & JOBS SCORE: 49/RANK: 167

INCOME	AREA	U.S. AVG	EMPLOYMENT	AREA	U.S. AVG	LARGEST EMPLOYING INDUSTRY
Per capita income	$17,984	$23,420	Unemployment rate	3.4%	6.1%	Plastics and Rubber Products Manufacturing
Household income	$37,990	$46,060	Recent job growth	-1.8%	.9%	
Household income < $25K	28.8%	26.4%	Projected future job growth	11.3%	15.1%	
Household income > $75K	15.1%	24.5%	White collar	45.8%	54.5%	
Household income growth	55.6%	57.3%	Blue collar	54.2%	45.5%	

COST OF LIVING SCORE: 78/RANK: 71

INDEXES & TAXES	AREA	U.S. AVG	HOUSING	AREA	U.S. AVG	NECESSITIES	AREA	U.S. AVG
Cost of Living Index	81.2	100.0	Median home price	$79,890	$160,100	Food Index	95.3	100.0
Financial Progress Index	99.7	100.0	Home price appreciation	3.7%	7.1%	Housing Index	49.6	100.0
Income tax rate	7.000%	4.625%	Median rent	$506	$670	Utilities Index	92.5	100.0
Sales tax rate	8.250%	6.474%	Homes owned	60.1%	63.9%	Transportation Index	102.3	100.0
Property tax rate	$10.7	$15.6	Homes rented	26.9%	25.3%	Healthcare Index	92.4	100.0
			Housing affordability	63.0%	54.5%	Miscellaneous Cost Index	104.4	100.0

CLIMATE SCORE: 75/RANK: 83

TEMPERATURE	AREA	U.S. AVG	PRECIPITATION	AREA	U.S. AVG	COMFORTS & HAZARDS	AREA	U.S. AVG
January low	29.4°F	26.4°F	Annual inches precipitation	27.2	35.9	July relative humidity	66.0%	68.8%
July high	99.1°F	86.7°F	Annual inches snowfall	6.0	24.2	Annual days mostly sunny	241	212
Annual days > 90°F	55	38	Annual days precipitation	71	111	Annual days with thunderstorms	49	39
Annual days < 32°F	70	88	Annual days rain > 0.5 inches	21	23	Tornado risk score	32	19
Annual days < 0°F	0	6	Annual days snow > 1.5 inches	3	6	Hurricane risk score	3	15

TEMPERATURE

PRECIPITATION

DAYS OF CLOUDS & PRECIPITATION

EDUCATION SCORE: 45/RANK: 180

ACHIEVEMENT	AREA	U.S. AVG	PUBLIC SCHOOLS	AREA	U.S. AVG	HIGHER EDUCATION	AREA	U.S. AVG
High school degree	85.4%	80.2%	Expenditures per pupil	$4,900	$5,894	No. 2-year colleges	0	3
2-year college degree	5.8%	6.2%	Student/teacher ratio	17.1	16.7	No. 4-year colleges/universities	1	4
4-year college degree	13.2%	15.8%	Attending public school	97.5%	90.2%	No. highly ranked universities	0	1
Graduate/professional degree	6.1%	9.6%	State SAT score	1131	1020			
			State ACT score	20.5*	21.0			

HEALTH & HEALTHCARE SCORE: 10/RANK: 296　　**CRIME** SCORE: 48/RANK: 169

HAZARDS & ILLNESSES	AREA	U.S. AVG	HEALTHCARE	AREA	U.S. AVG	CRIME	AREA	U.S. AVG
Air-quality score	81	45	Physicians per capita	194.9	261.1	Violent crime rate	552.1	456.0
Water-quality score	30	33	Hospital beds per capita	476.5	432.2	Change in violent crime rate	-58.5%	-17.2%
Pollen/allergy score	87	61	No. teaching hospitals	0	4	Property crime rate	4,305.0	3,950.0
Stress score	17	50	Cost per doctor visit	$63	$67	Change in property crime rate	-26.4%	-16.8%
Cancer mortality per capita	167.0	169.0	Cost per dental visit	$80	$82			
Depression days per month	2.5	2.8	Cost per daily hospital room	$413	$733			

TRANSPORTATION SCORE: 70/RANK: 98

COMMUTE	AREA	U.S. AVG	INTERCITY SERVICES	AREA	U.S. AVG	AUTOMOTIVE	AREA	U.S. AVG
Average commute time	16.9 min.	22.6 min.	Miles to nearest major airport	72	46	Insurance, annual premium	$822	$1,011
Commute by auto	88.5%	88.7%	Type of local airport	Medium		Gas, cost per gallon	$1.39	$1.50
Commute by mass transit	.4%	1.8%	No. daily airline departures	102	294	Daily vehicle miles per capita	17.3	23.0
Work at home	3.0%	3.9%	Amtrak service	No				
Mass transit miles per capita	0.0	8.0	No. interstate highways	0	1			

LEISURE SCORE: 23/RANK: 252 — DINING & SHOPPING	AREA	U.S. AVG	ENTERTAINMENT	AREA	U.S. AVG	OUTDOOR ACTIVITIES	AREA	U.S. AVG
Restaurant rating	1	1	Professional sports rating	2	4	Golf-course rating	1	4
No. outlet malls	0	2	College sports rating	6	4	Ski-area rating	1	4
No. Starbucks	0	11	Zoo/aquarium rating	1	3	National Park rating	4	3
No. warehouse clubs	3	4	Amusement park rating	2	3	Sq. miles inland water	2.0	4.0
			Botanical garden/arboretum rating	1	3	Miles of coastline	0.0	11.4

ARTS & CULTURE SCORE: 33/RANK: 222 — MEDIA & LIBRARIES	AREA	U.S. AVG	PERFORMING ARTS	AREA	U.S. AVG	MUSEUMS	AREA	U.S. AVG
Arts radio rating	5	3	Classical music rating	3	4	Overall museum rating	3	6
No. public libraries	3	28	Ballet/dance rating	3	3	Art museum rating	1	5
Library volumes per capita	1.5	2.8	Professional theater rating	1	3	Science museum rating	1	4
			University arts programs rating	3	5	Children's museum rating	1	3

Lewiston-Auburn, ME

Score: 26.4   Rank: 313

Profile: Small-city complex
Location: Southern Maine, 30 miles north and inland from Portland
Elevation: 340 feet
Time zone: Eastern Standard Time

PRO	CON
Revitalizing economy	Harsh winters
Outdoor recreation	Unemployment
Attractive setting	Low educational attainment

Lewiston, the second largest city in the state, lies across the Androscoggin River from its twin city, Auburn. Once a large textile center, Lewiston and Auburn are currently reinventing themselves as a manufacturing and service center with high-tech businesses, but the transition isn't complete. Employment and future job growth rank low for the state. Educational attainment at all levels is particularly low for New England. The two cites have a small-town feel with a strong French presence, which remains from the 19th century when French Canadians migrated into the area for factory work.

The area is located in the Androscoggin River Valley in an area of forested hills and lakes. It is far enough inland to feel the effects of the variable northeastern continental climate, but close enough to the Atlantic to experience some moderation. Summers are warm and pleasant with cool evenings. Winters are cold with frequent thaws, while springs are wet and variable. Autumn is the most pleasant season. Temperatures well below zero are recorded frequently each winter, and strong winter winds are common. The White Mountains block some snow and cold from the northwest, but snow is common, often arriving with Atlantic Coast "noreaster" storms. First freeze is early October, last is early May.

POPULATION — DEMOGRAPHICS	AREA	U.S. AVG	ETHNIC COMPOSITION	AREA	U.S. AVG	RESIDENT PROFILE	AREA	U.S. AVG
Population	91,220		White	98.2%	75.1%	Single	40.3%	43.6%
Population density per sq. mile	299.5	447.3	Black	.4%	12.3%	Married	59.7%	56.4%
Population growth	-2.6%	16.1%	Asian	.6%	3.6%	Divorced	9.5%	8.4%
Median age	37.6	35.5	American Indian	.3%	.9%	Separated	1.9%	3.0%
Average family size	2.6	2.7	Hispanic	1.2%	12.5%	Married with children	31.8%	28.7%
			Diversity measure	6.9%	35.2%	Single with children	11.0%	10.1%

ECONOMY & JOBS SCORE: 40/RANK: 197 — INCOME	AREA	U.S. AVG	EMPLOYMENT	AREA	U.S. AVG	LARGEST EMPLOYING INDUSTRY
Per capita income	$19,740	$23,420	Unemployment rate	4.0%	6.1%	Plastics and Rubber Products Manufacturing
Household income	$36,956	$46,060	Recent job growth	-.1%	.9%	
Household income < $25K	32.7%	26.4%	Projected future job growth	10.9%	15.1%	
Household income > $75K	12.9%	24.5%	White collar	48.2%	54.5%	
Household income growth	37.8%	57.3%	Blue collar	51.8%	45.5%	

COST OF LIVING SCORE: 29/RANK: 234 — INDEXES & TAXES	AREA	U.S. AVG	HOUSING	AREA	U.S. AVG	NECESSITIES	AREA	U.S. AVG
Cost of Living Index	95.2	100.0	Median home price	$112,920	$160,100	Food Index	99.1	100.0
Financial Progress Index	82.8	100.0	Home price appreciation	7.9%	7.1%	Housing Index	70.1	100.0
Income tax rate	8.500%	4.625%	Median rent	$546	$670	Utilities Index	150.0	100.0
Sales tax rate	5.000%	6.474%	Homes owned	68.3%	63.9%	Transportation Index	104.3	100.0
Property tax rate	$20.1	$15.6	Homes rented	18.9%	25.3%	Healthcare Index	107.2	100.0
			Housing affordability	51.0%	54.5%	Miscellaneous Cost Index	105.4	100.0

CLIMATE
SCORE: 0/RANK: 331

TEMPERATURE	AREA	U.S. AVG	PRECIPITATION	AREA	U.S. AVG	COMFORTS & HAZARDS	AREA	U.S. AVG
January low	11.0°F	26.4°F	Annual inches precipitation	45.1	35.9	July relative humidity	73.0%	68.8%
July high	78.0°F	86.7°F	Annual inches snowfall	71.0	24.2	Annual days mostly sunny	203	212
Annual days > 90°F	3	38	Annual days precipitation	129	111	Annual days with thunderstorms	30	39
Annual days < 32°F	147	88	Annual days rain > 0.5 inches	29	23	Tornado risk score	0	19
Annual days < 0°F	18	6	Annual days snow > 1.5 inches	15	6	Hurricane risk score	15	15

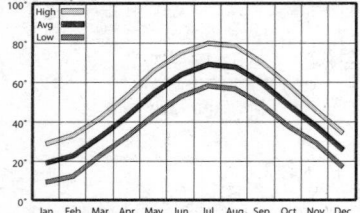

TEMPERATURE

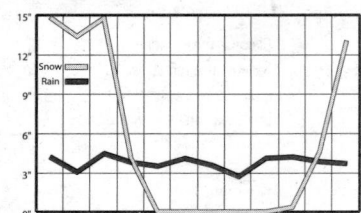

PRECIPITATION

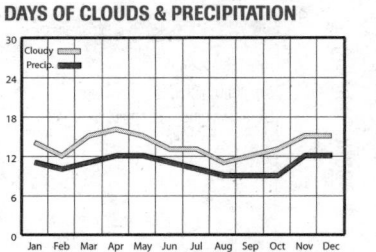

DAYS OF CLOUDS & PRECIPITATION

EDUCATION
SCORE: 30/RANK: 232

ACHIEVEMENT	AREA	U.S. AVG	PUBLIC SCHOOLS	AREA	U.S. AVG	HIGHER EDUCATION	AREA	U.S. AVG
High school degree	79.8%	80.2%	Expenditures per pupil	$6,620	$5,894	No. 2-year colleges	2	3
2-year college degree	5.3%	6.2%	Student/teacher ratio	14.0	16.7	No. 4-year colleges/universities	1	4
4-year college degree	9.9%	15.8%	Attending public school	90.9%	90.2%	No. highly ranked universities	1	1
Graduate/professional degree	4.5%	9.6%	State SAT score	1004*	1020			
			State ACT score	22.5	21.0			

HEALTH & HEALTHCARE
SCORE: 79/RANK: 68

CRIME
SCORE: 71/RANK: 96

HAZARDS & ILLNESSES	AREA	U.S. AVG	HEALTHCARE	AREA	U.S. AVG	CRIME	AREA	U.S. AVG
Air-quality score	59	45	Physicians per capita	267.5	261.1	Violent crime rate	161.6	456.0
Water-quality score	100	33	Hospital beds per capita	561.5	432.2	Change in violent crime rate	-6.6%	-17.2%
Pollen/allergy score	47	61	No. teaching hospitals	1	4	Property crime rate	3,471.2	3,950.0
Stress score	51	50	Cost per doctor visit	$65	$67	Change in property crime rate	-11.7%	-16.8%
Cancer mortality per capita	187.3	169.0	Cost per dental visit	$0	$82			
Depression days per month	3.6	2.8	Cost per daily hospital room	$679	$733			

TRANSPORTATION
SCORE: 16/RANK: 277

COMMUTE	AREA	U.S. AVG	INTERCITY SERVICES	AREA	U.S. AVG	AUTOMOTIVE	AREA	U.S. AVG
Average commute time	23.3 min.	22.6 min.	Miles to nearest major airport	31	46	Insurance, annual premium	$728	$1,011
Commute by auto	91.6%	88.7%	Type of local airport	Small		Gas, cost per gallon	$1.49	$1.50
Commute by mass transit	.6%	1.8%	No. daily airline departures	73	294	Daily vehicle miles per capita	21.3	23.0
Work at home	4.3%	3.9%	Amtrak service	No				
Mass transit miles per capita	6.5	8.0	No. interstate highways	1	1			

LEISURE
SCORE: 2/RANK: 324

DINING & SHOPPING	AREA	U.S. AVG	ENTERTAINMENT	AREA	U.S. AVG	OUTDOOR ACTIVITIES	AREA	U.S. AVG
Restaurant rating	1	1	Professional sports rating	2	4	Golf-course rating	2	4
No. outlet malls	2	2	College sports rating	1	4	Ski-area rating	7	4
No. Starbucks	0	11	Zoo/aquarium rating	1	3	National Park rating	1	3
No. warehouse clubs	3	4	Amusement park rating	1	3	Sq. miles inland water	3.0	4.0
			Botanical garden/arboretum rating	1	3	Miles of coastline	0.0	11.4

ARTS & CULTURE
SCORE: 15/RANK: 281

MEDIA & LIBRARIES	AREA	U.S. AVG	PERFORMING ARTS	AREA	U.S. AVG	MUSEUMS	AREA	U.S. AVG
Arts radio rating	1	3	Classical music rating	1	4	Overall museum rating	3	6
No. public libraries	10	28	Ballet/dance rating	1	3	Art museum rating	3	5
Library volumes per capita	3.2	2.8	Professional theater rating	1	3	Science museum rating	1	4
			University arts programs rating	2	5	Children's museum rating	1	3

Lexington, KY

Profile: Small city/College town
Location: Central Kentucky, 80 miles south of Cincinnati and 75 miles east of Louisville
Elevation: 989 feet
Time zone: Eastern Standard Time

Score: 67.9   **Rank:** 91

PRO	CON
Historic interest	Recreation
College-town amenities	Air service
Attractive countryside	Home prices

Situated in the heart of bluegrass country, Lexington is Kentucky's second-largest city. It is the world capital of the horse industry and a cultural hub of the state. In many ways it's just the right size, not too big to abandon the small-town lifestyle, but large enough to have urban amenities and employment opportunities. Future economic indicators are positive. Tech giant Lexmark and a major Toyota assembly plant in Georgetown are just north of the city. The surrounding countryside with its horse farms and the historic downtown make Lexington visually attractive. The University of Kentucky adds a college-town element and amenities, including basketball. Although some amenities like air service are absent, Lexington is fairly convenient to major cultural and transportation amenities in Cincinnati and Louisville. Daniel Boone National Forest and Lake Cumberland to the south provide outdoor recreation. Home prices, while moderate on a national scale, are high for Kentucky. In the future,

the area may see some negative side effects from growth, such as sprawl to the north near the new industrial development.

Lexington sits on a gently rolling plateau with a mix of open grassland and deciduous wooded forests. The grassland areas typically contain horse farms surrounded by miles of attractive fencing. To the southeast, terrain becomes hillier and more wooded near the foothills of the Appalachian Mountains. The climate is continental with four distinct seasons. Summers are warm and humid, but seldom extremely hot. Winter is typical for the latitude, with alternating mild and cold periods. Below zero temperatures are relatively rare. Precipitation is evenly distributed throughout winter, spring, and summer. Fall is pleasant and somewhat drier. Snowfall amounts are variable and seldom remain for more than a few days. First freeze is late October, last is mid-April.

POPULATION

DEMOGRAPHICS	AREA	U.S. AVG	ETHNIC COMPOSITION	AREA	U.S. AVG	RESIDENT PROFILE	AREA	U.S. AVG
Population	489,717		White	86.6%	75.1%	Single	49.6%	43.6%
Population density per sq. mile	255.1	447.3	Black	10.8%	12.3%	Married	50.4%	56.4%
Population growth	20.6%	16.1%	Asian	2.1%	3.6%	Divorced	9.4%	8.4%
Median age	33.6	35.5	American Indian	.2%	.9%	Separated	2.7%	3.0%
Average family size	2.5	2.7	Hispanic	1.4%	12.5%	Married with children	27.0%	28.7%
			Diversity measure	26.1%	35.2%	Single with children	9.7%	10.1%

ECONOMY & JOBS SCORE: 48/RANK: 170

INCOME	AREA	U.S. AVG	EMPLOYMENT	AREA	U.S. AVG	LARGEST EMPLOYING INDUSTRY
Per capita income	$24,906	$23,420	Unemployment rate	3.8%	6.1%	Transportation Equipment Manufacturing
Household income	$44,066	$46,060	Recent job growth	.9%	.9%	
Household income < $25K	28.2%	26.4%	Projected future job growth	17.9%	15.1%	
Household income > $75K	24.0%	24.5%	White collar	59.2%	54.5%	
Household income growth	63.9%	57.3%	Blue collar	40.8%	45.5%	

COST OF LIVING SCORE: 40/RANK: 196

INDEXES & TAXES	AREA	U.S. AVG	HOUSING	AREA	U.S. AVG	NECESSITIES	AREA	U.S. AVG
Cost of Living Index	92.1	100.0	Median home price	$127,200	$160,100	Food Index	106.0	100.0
Financial Progress Index	102.0	100.0	Home price appreciation	5.5%	7.1%	Housing Index	79.0	100.0
Income tax rate	8.000%	4.625%	Median rent	$565	$670	Utilities Index	99.2	100.0
Sales tax rate	6.000%	6.474%	Homes owned	56.9%	63.9%	Transportation Index	94.8	100.0
Property tax rate	$9.8	$15.6	Homes rented	35.8%	25.3%	Healthcare Index	97.1	100.0
			Housing affordability	59.0%	54.5%	Miscellaneous Cost Index	97.3	100.0

CLIMATE SCORE: 39/RANK: 202

TEMPERATURE	AREA	U.S. AVG	PRECIPITATION	AREA	U.S. AVG	COMFORTS & HAZARDS	AREA	U.S. AVG
January low	24.5°F	26.4°F	Annual inches precipitation	50.0	35.9	July relative humidity	70.0%	68.8%
July high	86.4°F	86.7°F	Annual inches snowfall	16.0	24.2	Annual days mostly sunny	197	212
Annual days > 90°F	16	38	Annual days precipitation	130	111	Annual days with thunderstorms	47	39
Annual days < 32°F	97	88	Annual days rain > 0.5 inches	32	23	Tornado risk score	17	19
Annual days < 0°F	2	6	Annual days snow > 1.5 inches	4	6	Hurricane risk score	6	15

TEMPERATURE

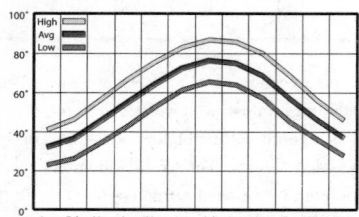

PRECIPITATION

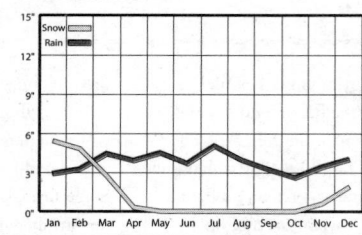

DAYS OF CLOUDS & PRECIPITATION

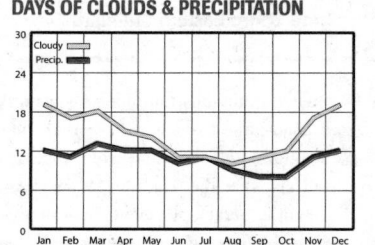

EDUCATION SCORE: 74/RANK: 85

ACHIEVEMENT	AREA	U.S. AVG	PUBLIC SCHOOLS	AREA	U.S. AVG	HIGHER EDUCATION	AREA	U.S. AVG
High school degree	82.1%	80.2%	Expenditures per pupil	$5,478	$5,894	No. 2-year colleges	2	3
2-year college degree	6.4%	6.2%	Student/teacher ratio	19.1	16.7	No. 4-year colleges/universities	7	4
4-year college degree	17.1%	15.8%	Attending public school	87.1%	90.2%	No. highly ranked universities	5	1
Graduate/professional degree	11.6%	9.6%	State SAT score	1106	1020			
			State ACT score	20.2*	21.0			

HEALTH & HEALTHCARE SCORE: 83/RANK: 55

HAZARDS & ILLNESSES	AREA	U.S. AVG	HEALTHCARE	AREA	U.S. AVG	CRIME	AREA	U.S. AVG
Air-quality score	17	45	Physicians per capita	387.8	261.1	Violent crime rate	356.9	456.0
Water-quality score	30	33	Hospital beds per capita	589.3	432.2	Change in violent crime rate	-38.0%	-17.2%
Pollen/allergy score	62	61	No. teaching hospitals	4	4	Property crime rate	3,999.4	3,950.0
Stress score	51	50	Cost per doctor visit	$65	$67	Change in property crime rate	-18.3%	-16.8%
Cancer mortality per capita	169.3	169.0	Cost per dental visit	$77	$82			
Depression days per month	3.9	2.8	Cost per daily hospital room	$558	$733			

CRIME SCORE: 61/RANK: 127

TRANSPORTATION SCORE: 42/RANK: 192

COMMUTE	AREA	U.S. AVG	INTERCITY SERVICES	AREA	U.S. AVG	AUTOMOTIVE	AREA	U.S. AVG
Average commute time	21.2 min.	22.6 min.	Miles to nearest major airport	8	46	Insurance, annual premium	$879	$1,011
Commute by auto	84.8%	88.7%	Type of local airport	Small		Gas, cost per gallon	$1.41	$1.50
Commute by mass transit	.8%	1.8%	No. daily airline departures	52	294	Daily vehicle miles per capita	30.5	23.0
Work at home	3.6%	3.9%	Amtrak service	No				
Mass transit miles per capita	3.9	8.0	No. interstate highways	2	1			

LEISURE SCORE: 18/RANK: 270

DINING & SHOPPING	AREA	U.S. AVG	ENTERTAINMENT	AREA	U.S. AVG	OUTDOOR ACTIVITIES	AREA	U.S. AVG
Restaurant rating	1	1	Professional sports rating	3	4	Golf-course rating	4	4
No. outlet malls	1	2	College sports rating	5	4	Ski-area rating	1	4
No. Starbucks	2	11	Zoo/aquarium rating	1	3	National Park rating	1	3
No. warehouse clubs	3	4	Amusement park rating	1	3	Sq. miles inland water	2.0	4.0
			Botanical garden/arboretum rating	2	3	Miles of coastline	0.0	11.4

ARTS & CULTURE SCORE: 76/RANK: 78

MEDIA & LIBRARIES	AREA	U.S. AVG	PERFORMING ARTS	AREA	U.S. AVG	MUSEUMS	AREA	U.S. AVG
Arts radio rating	8	3	Classical music rating	3	4	Overall museum rating	8	6
No. public libraries	12	28	Ballet/dance rating	3	3	Art museum rating	7	5
Library volumes per capita	2.1	2.8	Professional theater rating	1	3	Science museum rating	5	4
			University arts programs rating	8	5	Children's museum rating	7	3

Lima, OH

Score: 40.3   **Rank:** 276

Profile: Small town
Location: Northwest Ohio along I-75 between Dayton and Toledo
Elevation: 1,295 feet
Time zone: Eastern Standard Time

PRO	CON
Cost of living	Economic decline
Small-town flavor	Low educational attainment
Cost of housing	Entertainment

Lima is at a crossroads geographically between several Midwestern cities as well as metaphorically in its evolution. It has a robust past as a manufacturing center of automotive parts, neon signs, and steam locomotives. The downtown area, which is Midwestern in character, is struggling. However, a strong oil and gas industry tied to local production and reserves does exist. Cost of living and housing are among the lowest in the region, and commutes and general stresses are low. The city knows its problems and is working to resolve them, but the jury is still out on whether revitalization will be successful. The energy industry and central location to many markets may indicate a favorable future.

Lima lies in the level, glaciated plain south of the Lake Erie shore. Most nearby land is agricultural. The climate is continental. Summers are warm and humid with frequent afternoon showers and thunderstorms. Winters are cool and humid with considerable cloudiness and an occasional blast of cold air from the north. Snowfall is generally light to moderate but can be heavy. Alternating freezes and thaws are common, with the first freeze arriving in mid-October and the last occurring in late April.

POPULATION

DEMOGRAPHICS	AREA	U.S. AVG	ETHNIC COMPOSITION	AREA	U.S. AVG	RESIDENT PROFILE	AREA	U.S. AVG
Population	154,584		White	94.0%	75.1%	Single	38.3%	43.6%
Population density per sq. mile	191.9	447.3	Black	5.0%	12.3%	Married	61.7%	56.4%
Population growth	.2%	16.1%	Asian	.6%	3.6%	Divorced	7.1%	8.4%
Median age	36.7	35.5	American Indian	.2%	.9%	Separated	1.5%	3.0%
Average family size	2.7	2.7	Hispanic	.9%	12.5%	Married with children	31.9%	28.7%
			Diversity measure	21.1%	35.2%	Single with children	8.5%	10.1%

ECONOMY & JOBS   SCORE: 72/RANK: 91

INCOME	AREA	U.S. AVG	EMPLOYMENT	AREA	U.S. AVG	LARGEST EMPLOYING INDUSTRY
Per capita income	$19,447	$23,420	Unemployment rate	5.6%	6.1%	Transportation Equipment Manufacturing
Household income	$40,804	$46,060	Recent job growth	.7%	.9%	
Household income < $25K	27.9%	26.4%	Projected future job growth	7.5%	15.1%	
Household income > $75K	17.0%	24.5%	White collar	45.5%	54.5%	
Household income growth	44.8%	57.3%	Blue collar	54.5%	45.5%	

COST OF LIVING   SCORE: 82/RANK: 60

INDEXES & TAXES	AREA	U.S. AVG	HOUSING	AREA	U.S. AVG	NECESSITIES	AREA	U.S. AVG
Cost of Living Index	86.3	100.0	Median home price	$98,730	$160,100	Food Index	100.3	100.0
Financial Progress Index	100.8	100.0	Home price appreciation	5.2%	7.1%	Housing Index	61.3	100.0
Income tax rate	4.993%	4.625%	Median rent	$486	$670	Utilities Index	113.0	100.0
Sales tax rate	6.000%	6.474%	Homes owned	74.2%	63.9%	Transportation Index	99.6	100.0
Property tax rate	$9.8	$15.6	Homes rented	19.3%	25.3%	Healthcare Index	90.6	100.0
			Housing affordability	64.0%	54.5%	Miscellaneous Cost Index	98.8	100.0

CLIMATE   SCORE: 23/RANK: 255

TEMPERATURE	AREA	U.S. AVG	PRECIPITATION	AREA	U.S. AVG	COMFORTS & HAZARDS	AREA	U.S. AVG
January low	20.7°F	26.4°F	Annual inches precipitation	33.7	35.9	July relative humidity	73.0%	68.8%
July high	83.7°F	86.7°F	Annual inches snowfall	42.2	24.2	Annual days mostly sunny	173	212
Annual days > 90°F	7	38	Annual days precipitation	152	111	Annual days with thunderstorms	39	39
Annual days < 32°F	127	88	Annual days rain > 0.5 inches	23	23	Tornado risk score	23	19
Annual days < 0°F	7	6	Annual days snow > 1.5 inches	9	6	Hurricane risk score	3	15

TEMPERATURE

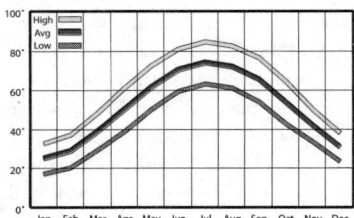

PRECIPITATION

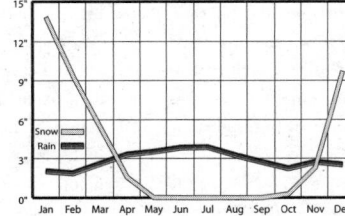

DAYS OF CLOUDS & PRECIPITATION

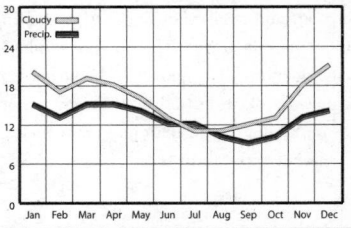

EDUCATION SCORE: 20/RANK: 264

ACHIEVEMENT	AREA	U.S. AVG	PUBLIC SCHOOLS	AREA	U.S. AVG	HIGHER EDUCATION	AREA	U.S. AVG
High school degree	83.5%	80.2%	Expenditures per pupil	$5,031	$5,894	No. 2-year colleges	3	3
2-year college degree	8.0%	6.2%	Student/teacher ratio	18.3	16.7	No. 4-year colleges/universities	1	4
4-year college degree	8.6%	15.8%	Attending public school	88.6%	90.2%	No. highly ranked universities	1	1
Graduate/professional degree	4.9%	9.6%	State SAT score	1077	1020			
			State ACT score	21.4*	21.0			

HEALTH & HEALTHCARE SCORE: 43/RANK: 187

HAZARDS & ILLNESSES	AREA	U.S. AVG	HEALTHCARE	AREA	U.S. AVG
Air-quality score	17	45	Physicians per capita	188.2	261.1
Water-quality score	4	33	Hospital beds per capita	557.1	432.2
Pollen/allergy score	58	61	No. teaching hospitals	1	4
Stress score	48	50	Cost per doctor visit	$61	$67
Cancer mortality per capita	170.8	169.0	Cost per dental visit	$70	$82
Depression days per month	3.5	2.8	Cost per daily hospital room	$489	$733

CRIME SCORE: 54/RANK: 151

CRIME	AREA	U.S. AVG
Violent crime rate	363.7	456.0
Change in violent crime rate	-69.1%	-17.2%
Property crime rate	3,890.2	3,950.0
Change in property crime rate	1.6%	-16.8%

TRANSPORTATION SCORE: 58/RANK: 139

COMMUTE	AREA	U.S. AVG	INTERCITY SERVICES	AREA	U.S. AVG	AUTOMOTIVE	AREA	U.S. AVG
Average commute time	18.3 min.	22.6 min.	Miles to nearest major airport	58	46	Insurance, annual premium	$791	$1,011
Commute by auto	90.6%	88.7%	Type of local airport	Small		Gas, cost per gallon	$1.47	$1.50
Commute by mass transit	.4%	1.8%	No. daily airline departures	161	294	Daily vehicle miles per capita	23.5	23.0
Work at home	3.7%	3.9%	Amtrak service	No				
Mass transit miles per capita	0.0	8.0	No. interstate highways	1	1			

LEISURE SCORE: 12/RANK: 290

DINING & SHOPPING	AREA	U.S. AVG	ENTERTAINMENT	AREA	U.S. AVG	OUTDOOR ACTIVITIES	AREA	U.S. AVG
Restaurant rating	1	1	Professional sports rating	2	4	Golf-course rating	3	4
No. outlet malls	0	2	College sports rating	2	4	Ski-area rating	2	4
No. Starbucks	0	11	Zoo/aquarium rating	1	3	National Park rating	1	3
No. warehouse clubs	3	4	Amusement park rating	1	3	Sq. miles inland water	2.0	4.0
			Botanical garden/arboretum rating	1	3	Miles of coastline	0.0	11.4

ARTS & CULTURE SCORE: 36/RANK: 211

MEDIA & LIBRARIES	AREA	U.S. AVG	PERFORMING ARTS	AREA	U.S. AVG	MUSEUMS	AREA	U.S. AVG
Arts radio rating	5	3	Classical music rating	3	4	Overall museum rating	4	6
No. public libraries	15	28	Ballet/dance rating	1	3	Art museum rating	1	5
Library volumes per capita	4.3	2.8	Professional theater rating	1	3	Science museum rating	3	4
			University arts programs rating	2	5	Children's museum rating	1	3

Lincoln, NE

Score: 50.4   Rank: 223

Profile: Capital city/College town
Location: Southeast Nebraska along I-80, 60 miles southwest of Omaha
Elevation: 1,189 feet
Time zone: Central Standard Time

PRO	CON
Attractive downtown	Harsh climate
College-town amenities	Crime rate
Educational attainment	Low ethnic diversity

As the capital and higher education center of the state, Lincoln is a livable, small city with a diverse economy. The largest employers include state government, the University of Nebraska, Goodyear, and smaller businesses in printing, insurance, and pharmaceutical manufacturing. The university adds college-town amenities and is a major sports draw, particularly during football season. The attractive downtown is clean but fairly ordinary. According to some, the area has more parks per capita than any other metropolitan area, but otherwise recreational opportunities are scarce.

The western edge of the city is in a flat valley. The surrounding area is level to gently rolling open prairie, with deep, rich, fertile soil. The climate is continental with a mix of influences from lower altitudes and the high Plains. Summer brings sunny days and moderate to low humidity. Warm spells can exceed 100°F. Winter cold outbreaks can drive temperatures below zero for consecutive days. High winds add to discomfort in all seasons. Summer thunderstorms, particularly in late spring and early summer, can produce heavy rains and damaging hail, and often occur at night. Most snow is light and melts rapidly, but occasional heavy snows do occur. The first freeze is mid-October, last is mid-April.

POPULATION

DEMOGRAPHICS	AREA	U.S. AVG	ETHNIC COMPOSITION	AREA	U.S. AVG	RESIDENT PROFILE	AREA	U.S. AVG
Population	257,513		White	96.0%	75.1%	Single	42.2%	43.6%
Population density per sq. mile	307.0	447.3	Black	1.5%	12.3%	Married	57.8%	56.4%
Population growth	20.5%	16.1%	Asian	1.5%	3.6%	Divorced	6.8%	8.4%
Median age	32.3	35.5	American Indian	.5%	.9%	Separated	1.3%	3.0%
Average family size	2.5	2.7	Hispanic	2.6%	12.5%	Married with children	29.0%	28.7%
			Diversity measure	20.5%	35.2%	Single with children	6.7%	10.1%

ECONOMY & JOBS SCORE: 88/RANK: 37

INCOME	AREA	U.S. AVG	EMPLOYMENT	AREA	U.S. AVG	LARGEST EMPLOYING INDUSTRY
Per capita income	$26,135	$23,420	Unemployment rate	3.6%	6.1%	Plastics and Rubber Products Manufacturing
Household income	$50,530	$46,060	Recent job growth	1.7%	.9%	
Household income < $25K	22.2%	26.4%	Projected future job growth	17.4%	15.1%	
Household income > $75K	28.0%	24.5%	White collar	60.0%	54.5%	
Household income growth	74.3%	57.3%	Blue collar	40.0%	45.5%	

COST OF LIVING SCORE: 23/RANK: 255

INDEXES & TAXES	AREA	U.S. AVG	HOUSING	AREA	U.S. AVG	NECESSITIES	AREA	U.S. AVG
Cost of Living Index	93.9	100.0	Median home price	$126,300	$160,100	Food Index	98.6	100.0
Financial Progress Index	114.7	100.0	Home price appreciation	3.9%	7.1%	Housing Index	78.4	100.0
Income tax rate	6.680%	4.625%	Median rent	$569	$670	Utilities Index	122.6	100.0
Sales tax rate	7.000%	6.474%	Homes owned	68.9%	63.9%	Transportation Index	98.7	100.0
Property tax rate	$22.6	$15.6	Homes rented	27.1%	25.3%	Healthcare Index	97.7	100.0
			Housing affordability	60.0%	54.5%	Miscellaneous Cost Index	101.7	100.0

CLIMATE SCORE: 13/RANK: 288

TEMPERATURE	AREA	U.S. AVG	PRECIPITATION	AREA	U.S. AVG	COMFORTS & HAZARDS	AREA	U.S. AVG
January low	11.7°F	26.4°F	Annual inches precipitation	29.0	35.9	July relative humidity	68.0%	68.8%
July high	88.9°F	86.7°F	Annual inches snowfall	26.0	24.2	Annual days mostly sunny	212	212
Annual days > 90°F	43	38	Annual days precipitation	88	111	Annual days with thunderstorms	9	39
Annual days < 32°F	146	88	Annual days rain > 0.5 inches	18	23	Tornado risk score	20	19
Annual days < 0°F	17	6	Annual days snow > 1.5 inches	7	6	Hurricane risk score	0	15

TEMPERATURE

PRECIPITATION

DAYS OF CLOUDS & PRECIPITATION

EDUCATION SCORE: 83/RANK: 58

ACHIEVEMENT	AREA	U.S. AVG	PUBLIC SCHOOLS	AREA	U.S. AVG	HIGHER EDUCATION	AREA	U.S. AVG
High school degree	90.2%	80.2%	Expenditures per pupil	$5,949	$5,894	No. 2-year colleges	2	3
2-year college degree	8.4%	6.2%	Student/teacher ratio	14.1	16.7	No. 4-year colleges/universities	3	4
4-year college degree	22.1%	15.8%	Attending public school	85.1%	90.2%	No. highly ranked universities	0	1
Graduate/professional degree	11.2%	9.6%	State SAT score	1151	1020			
			State ACT score	21.7*	21.0			

HEALTH & HEALTHCARE SCORE: 69/RANK: 100 — **CRIME** SCORE: 11/RANK: 294

HAZARDS & ILLNESSES	AREA	U.S. AVG	HEALTHCARE	AREA	U.S. AVG	CRIME	AREA	U.S. AVG
Air-quality score	17	45	Physicians per capita	232.6	261.1	Violent crime rate	526.4	456.0
Water-quality score	30	33	Hospital beds per capita	488.6	432.2	Change in violent crime rate	-12.1%	-17.2%
Pollen/allergy score	50	61	No. teaching hospitals	3	4	Property crime rate	5,915.9	3,950.0
Stress score	19	50	Cost per doctor visit	$71	$67	Change in property crime rate	-6.4%	-16.8%
Cancer mortality per capita	158.6	169.0	Cost per dental visit	$71	$82			
Depression days per month	1.8	2.8	Cost per daily hospital room	$516	$733			

TRANSPORTATION SCORE: 81/RANK: 66

COMMUTE	AREA	U.S. AVG	INTERCITY SERVICES	AREA	U.S. AVG	AUTOMOTIVE	AREA	U.S. AVG
Average commute time	17.8 min.	22.6 min.	Miles to nearest major airport	53	46	Insurance, annual premium	$737	$1,011
Commute by auto	88.2%	88.7%	Type of local airport	Medium		Gas, cost per gallon	$1.49	$1.50
Commute by mass transit	1.3%	1.8%	No. daily airline departures	136	294	Daily vehicle miles per capita	17.2	23.0
Work at home	5.5%	3.9%	Amtrak service	Yes				
Mass transit miles per capita	5.6	8.0	No. interstate highways	1	1			

LEISURE — SCORE: 38/RANK: 203

DINING & SHOPPING	AREA	U.S. AVG	ENTERTAINMENT	AREA	U.S. AVG	OUTDOOR ACTIVITIES	AREA	U.S. AVG
Restaurant rating	1	1	Professional sports rating	2	4	Golf-course rating	2	4
No. outlet malls	1	2	College sports rating	9	4	Ski-area rating	2	4
No. Starbucks	0	11	Zoo/aquarium rating	3	3	National Park rating	1	3
No. warehouse clubs	3	4	Amusement park rating	1	3	Sq. miles inland water	2.0	4.0
			Botanical garden/arboretum rating	5	3	Miles of coastline	0.0	11.4

ARTS & CULTURE — SCORE: 85/RANK: 49

MEDIA & LIBRARIES	AREA	U.S. AVG	PERFORMING ARTS	AREA	U.S. AVG	MUSEUMS	AREA	U.S. AVG
Arts radio rating	1	3	Classical music rating	6	4	Overall museum rating	6	6
No. public libraries	7	28	Ballet/dance rating	1	3	Art museum rating	7	5
Library volumes per capita	3.3	2.8	Professional theater rating	1	3	Science museum rating	4	4
			University arts programs rating	8	5	Children's museum rating	5	3

Little Rock–North Little Rock, AR

Score: 66.5   Rank: 99

Profile: Capital-city complex
Location: Center of the state along the Arkansas River
Elevation: 265 feet
Time zone: Central Standard Time

PRO	CON
Capital-city amenities	Crime rate
Educational attainment	Arts and culture
Healthcare	Air service

Little Rock is the steady but unremarkable capital of Arkansas. Typical of mid-America, the downtown area is laid out on a rectangular grid with mostly average architecture, a sprinkling of older historic structures, and a waterfront park. The city is ranked high because it does modestly well in all categories. Notable attributes include the high level of educational attainment and the availability of healthcare resources. There is a small assortment of cultural assets, mostly local in character. Recreation consists mainly of college sports and nearby watersports. For a capital city, incomes are relatively high for the cost of living, resulting in a favorable Financial Progress Index. Also

in comparison to other capitals, housing costs are particularly low and air service is lacking.

Little Rock is situated between the Ouachita Mountains to the west and the flat Mississippi River Valley lowlands to the east. Hilly residential areas west of the city rise to 600 feet. The climate is continental with an element of humid subtropical, particularly in summer. Winters are mild, but outbreaks of cold air are common. Precipitation is fairly well distributed throughout the year with the majority arriving in summer as thunderstorms. Snow is negligible but occasional ice storms can be severe. First freeze is early November, last is late March.

POPULATION

DEMOGRAPHICS	AREA	U.S. AVG	ETHNIC COMPOSITION	AREA	U.S. AVG	RESIDENT PROFILE	AREA	U.S. AVG
Population	595,563		White	81.1%	75.1%	Single	43.7%	43.6%
Population density per sq. mile	204.8	447.3	Black	17.6%	12.3%	Married	56.3%	56.4%
Population growth	16.1%	16.1%	Asian	.7%	3.6%	Divorced	9.8%	8.4%
Median age	35.0	35.5	American Indian	.4%	.9%	Separated	2.9%	3.0%
Average family size	2.5	2.7	Hispanic	1.7%	12.5%	Married with children	28.1%	28.7%
			Diversity measure	40.7%	35.2%	Single with children	10.7%	10.1%

ECONOMY & JOBS — SCORE: 55/RANK: 147

INCOME	AREA	U.S. AVG	EMPLOYMENT	AREA	U.S. AVG	LARGEST EMPLOYING INDUSTRY
Per capita income	$24,173	$23,420	Unemployment rate	4.4%	6.1%	Transportation Equipment Manufacturing
Household income	$45,421	$46,060	Recent job growth	.3%	.9%	
Household income < $25K	25.0%	26.4%	Projected future job growth	16.4%	15.1%	
Household income > $75K	25.0%	24.5%	White collar	57.6%	54.5%	
Household income growth	70.8%	57.3%	Blue collar	42.4%	45.5%	

COST OF LIVING — SCORE: 61/RANK: 129

INDEXES & TAXES	AREA	U.S. AVG	HOUSING	AREA	U.S. AVG	NECESSITIES	AREA	U.S. AVG
Cost of Living Index	83.4	100.0	Median home price	$98,000	$160,100	Food Index	96.2	100.0
Financial Progress Index	116.1	100.0	Home price appreciation	4.9%	7.1%	Housing Index	60.9	100.0
Income tax rate	7.000%	4.625%	Median rent	$538	$670	Utilities Index	102.5	100.0
Sales tax rate	6.625%	6.474%	Homes owned	64.5%	63.9%	Transportation Index	92.5	100.0
Property tax rate	$12.1	$15.6	Homes rented	26.4%	25.3%	Healthcare Index	94.2	100.0
			Housing affordability	61.0%	54.5%	Miscellaneous Cost Index	95.9	100.0

CLIMATE — SCORE: 44/RANK: 184

TEMPERATURE	AREA	U.S. AVG	PRECIPITATION	AREA	U.S. AVG	COMFORTS & HAZARDS	AREA	U.S. AVG
January low	28.9°F	26.4°F	Annual inches precipitation	49.0	35.9	July relative humidity	70.0%	68.8%
July high	92.6°F	86.7°F	Annual inches snowfall	5.0	24.2	Annual days mostly sunny	220	212
Annual days > 90°F	70	38	Annual days precipitation	104	111	Annual days with thunderstorms	57	39
Annual days < 32°F	63	88	Annual days rain > 0.5 inches	32	23	Tornado risk score	36	19
Annual days < 0°F	0	6	Annual days snow > 1.5 inches	2	6	Hurricane risk score	8	15

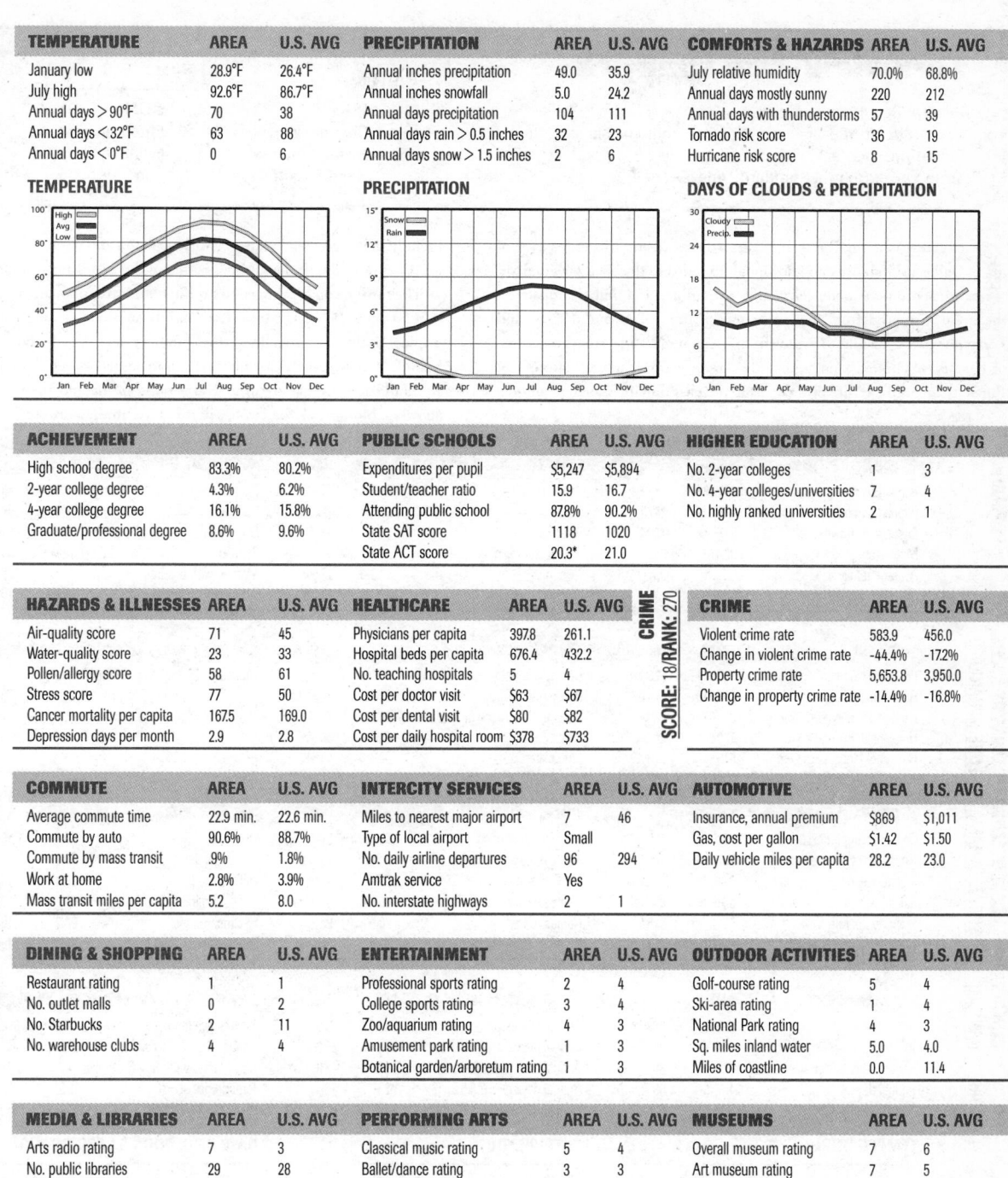

TEMPERATURE — High / Avg / Low

PRECIPITATION — Snow / Rain

DAYS OF CLOUDS & PRECIPITATION — Cloudy / Precip.

EDUCATION — SCORE: 50/RANK: 165

ACHIEVEMENT	AREA	U.S. AVG	PUBLIC SCHOOLS	AREA	U.S. AVG	HIGHER EDUCATION	AREA	U.S. AVG
High school degree	83.3%	80.2%	Expenditures per pupil	$5,247	$5,894	No. 2-year colleges	1	3
2-year college degree	4.3%	6.2%	Student/teacher ratio	15.9	16.7	No. 4-year colleges/universities	7	4
4-year college degree	16.1%	15.8%	Attending public school	87.8%	90.2%	No. highly ranked universities	2	1
Graduate/professional degree	8.6%	9.6%	State SAT score	1118	1020			
			State ACT score	20.3*	21.0			

HEALTH & HEALTHCARE — SCORE: 88/RANK: 38   CRIME — SCORE: 18/RANK: 270

HAZARDS & ILLNESSES	AREA	U.S. AVG	HEALTHCARE	AREA	U.S. AVG	CRIME	AREA	U.S. AVG
Air-quality score	71	45	Physicians per capita	397.8	261.1	Violent crime rate	583.9	456.0
Water-quality score	23	33	Hospital beds per capita	676.4	432.2	Change in violent crime rate	-44.4%	-17.2%
Pollen/allergy score	58	61	No. teaching hospitals	5	4	Property crime rate	5,653.8	3,950.0
Stress score	77	50	Cost per doctor visit	$63	$67	Change in property crime rate	-14.4%	-16.8%
Cancer mortality per capita	167.5	169.0	Cost per dental visit	$80	$82			
Depression days per month	2.9	2.8	Cost per daily hospital room	$378	$733			

TRANSPORTATION — SCORE: 26/RANK: 245

COMMUTE	AREA	U.S. AVG	INTERCITY SERVICES	AREA	U.S. AVG	AUTOMOTIVE	AREA	U.S. AVG
Average commute time	22.9 min.	22.6 min.	Miles to nearest major airport	7	46	Insurance, annual premium	$869	$1,011
Commute by auto	90.6%	88.7%	Type of local airport	Small		Gas, cost per gallon	$1.42	$1.50
Commute by mass transit	.9%	1.8%	No. daily airline departures	96	294	Daily vehicle miles per capita	28.2	23.0
Work at home	2.8%	3.9%	Amtrak service	Yes				
Mass transit miles per capita	5.2	8.0	No. interstate highways	2	1			

LEISURE — SCORE: 37/RANK: 209

DINING & SHOPPING	AREA	U.S. AVG	ENTERTAINMENT	AREA	U.S. AVG	OUTDOOR ACTIVITIES	AREA	U.S. AVG
Restaurant rating	1	1	Professional sports rating	2	4	Golf-course rating	5	4
No. outlet malls	0	2	College sports rating	3	4	Ski-area rating	1	4
No. Starbucks	2	11	Zoo/aquarium rating	4	3	National Park rating	4	3
No. warehouse clubs	4	4	Amusement park rating	1	3	Sq. miles inland water	5.0	4.0
			Botanical garden/arboretum rating	1	3	Miles of coastline	0.0	11.4

ARTS & CULTURE — SCORE: 33/RANK: 221

MEDIA & LIBRARIES	AREA	U.S. AVG	PERFORMING ARTS	AREA	U.S. AVG	MUSEUMS	AREA	U.S. AVG
Arts radio rating	7	3	Classical music rating	5	4	Overall museum rating	7	6
No. public libraries	29	28	Ballet/dance rating	3	3	Art museum rating	7	5
Library volumes per capita	2.2	2.8	Professional theater rating	6	3	Science museum rating	7	4
			University arts programs rating	4	5	Children's museum rating	5	3

Longview-Marshall, TX

Score: 60.6 **Rank:** 143

Profile: Small-city complex
Location: Northeast Texas, 30 miles from Louisiana border
Elevation: 259 feet
Time zone: Central Standard Time

PRO	CON
Cost of living	Entertainment
Historic interest	Isolation
Nearby recreation	Summer heat

Longview is a small city in eastern Texas about 130 miles east of Dallas. Marshall is an additional 35 miles to the east. Originally a transportation center for nearby agriculture and timber industries, the area prospered from the oil booms of the 1920s and 1930s, and Longview has a sizable, downtown, historic area ("One Hundred Acres of History"). The most notable of the area's many lakes is Lake of the Pines to the north. While Shreveport to the east provides some amenities including air service, the area is fairly isolated and offers little to do. The low Cost of Living Index of 76.0 is one of the area's biggest attractions.

The city sits on level to gently rolling land with pine forests and intermittent agriculture. The climate is mainly continental with a strong subtropical influence from the Gulf. Summer months are hot and fairly humid. Winters are mild with a few short periods of cold temperatures. Rainfall occurs as steady winter rains or as spring and summer thundershowers. Storms may be strong, particularly in the spring.

POPULATION

DEMOGRAPHICS	AREA	U.S. AVG	ETHNIC COMPOSITION	AREA	U.S. AVG	RESIDENT PROFILE	AREA	U.S. AVG
Population	212,288		White	74.2%	75.1%	Single	41.6%	43.6%
Population density per sq. mile	120.6	447.3	Black	20.8%	12.3%	Married	58.4%	56.4%
Population growth	9.5%	16.1%	Asian	1.0%	3.6%	Divorced	8.8%	8.4%
Median age	36.1	35.5	American Indian	.4%	.9%	Separated	3.7%	3.0%
Average family size	2.7	2.7	Hispanic	10.3%	12.5%	Married with children	29.4%	28.7%
			Diversity measure	43.2%	35.2%	Single with children	11.1%	10.1%

ECONOMY & JOBS SCORE: 60/RANK: 131

INCOME	AREA	U.S. AVG	EMPLOYMENT	AREA	U.S. AVG	LARGEST EMPLOYING INDUSTRY
Per capita income	$18,931	$23,420	Unemployment rate	6.7%	6.1%	Fabricated Metal Product Manufacturing
Household income	$36,536	$46,060	Recent job growth	2.6%	.9%	
Household income < $25K	34.0%	26.4%	Projected future job growth	15.7%	15.1%	
Household income > $75K	17.0%	24.5%	White collar	47.7%	54.5%	
Household income growth	51.7%	57.3%	Blue collar	52.3%	45.5%	

COST OF LIVING SCORE: 98/RANK: 5

INDEXES & TAXES	AREA	U.S. AVG	HOUSING	AREA	U.S. AVG	NECESSITIES	AREA	U.S. AVG
Cost of Living Index	76.0	100.0	Median home price	$80,680	$160,100	Food Index	89.1	100.0
Financial Progress Index	102.4	100.0	Home price appreciation	4.3%	7.1%	Housing Index	50.1	100.0
Income tax rate	0.000%	4.625%	Median rent	$474	$670	Utilities Index	79.4	100.0
Sales tax rate	8.250%	6.474%	Homes owned	66.8%	63.9%	Transportation Index	87.9	100.0
Property tax rate	$17.7	$15.6	Homes rented	20.6%	25.3%	Healthcare Index	94.2	100.0
			Housing affordability	63.0%	54.5%	Miscellaneous Cost Index	96.2	100.0

CLIMATE SCORE: 73/RANK: 86

TEMPERATURE	AREA	U.S. AVG	PRECIPITATION	AREA	U.S. AVG	COMFORTS & HAZARDS	AREA	U.S. AVG
January low	37.8°F	26.4°F	Annual inches precipitation	45.0	35.9	July relative humidity	71.0%	68.8%
July high	93.8°F	86.7°F	Annual inches snowfall	1.0	24.2	Annual days mostly sunny	217	212
Annual days > 90°F	87	38	Annual days precipitation	97	111	Annual days with thunderstorms	54	39
Annual days < 32°F	1	88	Annual days rain > 0.5 inches	23	23	Tornado risk score	31	19
Annual days < 0°F	0	6	Annual days snow > 1.5 inches	1	6	Hurricane risk score	14	15

TEMPERATURE

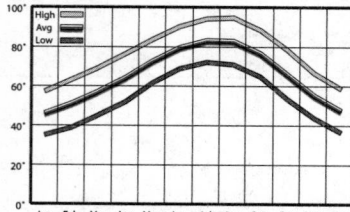

PRECIPITATION

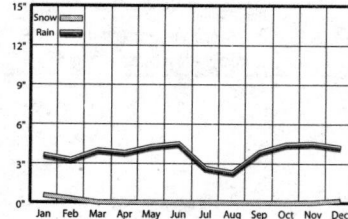

DAYS OF CLOUDS & PRECIPITATION

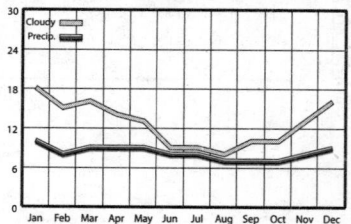

EDUCATION · SCORE: 42/RANK: 190

ACHIEVEMENT	AREA	U.S. AVG	PUBLIC SCHOOLS	AREA	U.S. AVG	HIGHER EDUCATION	AREA	U.S. AVG
High school degree	78.4%	80.2%	Expenditures per pupil	$5,097	$5,894	No. 2-year colleges	1	3
2-year college degree	6.4%	6.2%	Student/teacher ratio	14.1	16.7	No. 4-year colleges/universities	3	4
4-year college degree	11.5%	15.8%	Attending public school	95.9%	90.2%	No. highly ranked universities	1	1
Graduate/professional degree	5.3%	9.6%	State SAT score	993*	1020			
			State ACT score	20.1	21.0			

HEALTH & HEALTHCARE · SCORE: 29/RANK: 233

CRIME · SCORE: 21/RANK: 260

HAZARDS & ILLNESSES	AREA	U.S. AVG	HEALTHCARE	AREA	U.S. AVG	CRIME	AREA	U.S. AVG
Air-quality score	6	45	Physicians per capita	163.5	261.1	Violent crime rate	445.9	456.0
Water-quality score	30	33	Hospital beds per capita	383.7	432.2	Change in violent crime rate	-18.5%	-17.2%
Pollen/allergy score	65	61	No. teaching hospitals	0	4	Property crime rate	4,986.5	3,950.0
Stress score	57	50	Cost per doctor visit	$62	$67	Change in property crime rate	.2%	-16.8%
Cancer mortality per capita	169.5	169.0	Cost per dental visit	$69	$82			
Depression days per month	3.1	2.8	Cost per daily hospital room	$832	$733			

TRANSPORTATION · SCORE: 15/RANK: 279

COMMUTE	AREA	U.S. AVG	INTERCITY SERVICES	AREA	U.S. AVG	AUTOMOTIVE	AREA	U.S. AVG
Average commute time	21.9 min.	22.6 min.	Miles to nearest major airport	55	46	Insurance, annual premium	$928	$1,011
Commute by auto	93.0%	88.7%	Type of local airport	Small		Gas, cost per gallon	$1.40	$1.50
Commute by mass transit	.2%	1.8%	No. daily airline departures	66	294	Daily vehicle miles per capita	23.9	23.0
Work at home	2.4%	3.9%	Amtrak service	Yes				
Mass transit miles per capita	0.0	8.0	No. interstate highways	1	1			

LEISURE · SCORE: 16/RANK: 281

DINING & SHOPPING	AREA	U.S. AVG	ENTERTAINMENT	AREA	U.S. AVG	OUTDOOR ACTIVITIES	AREA	U.S. AVG
Restaurant rating	1	1	Professional sports rating	2	4	Golf-course rating	2	4
No. outlet malls	0	2	College sports rating	2	4	Ski-area rating	1	4
No. Starbucks	1	11	Zoo/aquarium rating	1	3	National Park rating	1	3
No. warehouse clubs	3	4	Amusement park rating	1	3	Sq. miles inland water	2.0	4.0
			Botanical garden/arboretum rating	1	3	Miles of coastline	0.0	11.4

ARTS & CULTURE · SCORE: 26/RANK: 242

MEDIA & LIBRARIES	AREA	U.S. AVG	PERFORMING ARTS	AREA	U.S. AVG	MUSEUMS	AREA	U.S. AVG
Arts radio rating	1	3	Classical music rating	3	4	Overall museum rating	5	6
No. public libraries	6	28	Ballet/dance rating	1	3	Art museum rating	3	5
Library volumes per capita	1.6	2.8	Professional theater rating	1	3	Science museum rating	3	4
			University arts programs rating	3	5	Children's museum rating	1	3

Los Angeles–Long Beach, CA

Score: 76.0   Rank: 54

Profile: National-center complex
Location: Southern California Coast, south of the San Bernardino Mountains
Elevation: 104 feet
Time zone: Pacific Standard Time

PRO
Entertainment
Coastline and beach areas
Big-city amenities

CON
Overcrowding
Air quality
Cost of living

In the mid–20th century, the complex Los Angeles–Long Beach area started as a warm-weather paradise with a strong economic base and the attraction of cosmopolitan adventure. But so many people migrated there from all over the *world* that much of the original attraction has been lost. The area is huge. Because of earthquake risk and the increasing importance of the automobile, the city built outward—into every nook and cranny of available level land for miles—rather than upward. Surrounding a few city centers, the sprawl of low buildings extends 80 miles on a near-perfect grid from the beach at Santa Monica west to San Bernardino. Flying into Los Angeles International for the first time, the view of the sprawling cityscape is stunning—if one can see through the smog.

That isn't to say that everything is the same throughout the area. "L.A." includes some of the nicer places to live in the world, such as Beverly Hills, Malibu, San Marino, and the seemingly endless beach communities that stretch south from Santa Monica toward Long Beach. Pasadena to the northeast has a marvelous "old California" feel, as do areas of Santa Monica and some of the beach communities. But without extensive financial resources, these places are all but inaccessible. Those who cannot afford them feel the full impact of the overcrowded landscape.

The city has some of the best weather in the world. Warm sunny days, cool evenings, low morning clouds and fog, and sea breezes are the norm. Rain only falls in the winter, and seldom at that. Museums, performing arts, professional sports, boating, and beach recreation are among the world's best. All imaginable services—higher education, healthcare, transportation—are available in abundance. As the area is more economically diverse and less dependent on high-tech industry than areas to the north, the economy continues to be relatively strong for California.

The downsides of living in L.A. are legendary. Most are caused by overcrowding and sprawl. Traffic and air-pollution problems are extreme. Commute times are reported as the 13th worst in the nation, but reality could be worse as many of those surveyed are retired or don't commute on a daily basis. Those who do face daily frustration, with freeways seldom moving at full speed at any time of the day. Air quality is the worst in the nation *by far*, to the extent that only two other U.S. cities are within 50% of L.A.'s pollution level. A brown cloud hovers over the city, particularly inland, most months of the year. Violent crime is twice the U.S. average, but property crime is surprisingly moderate. The Cost of Living Index is just over 139, not the state's highest but high enough. The median home price of $304,600 doesn't buy much. A nice home or one in a favorable location for commuting costs *much* more.

Is there hope for L.A.? Maybe not. Recently the area has attempted to reduce dependence on the automobile by introducing light-rail systems. And, the 30-year campaign to reduce auto smog has definitely helped. However, the growing number of cars and miles driven have mitigated these effects. *Cities Ranked & Rated* ranks the L.A. area highly at no. 54 because of the outstanding climate, economy, services, and amenities. For those who can take the bad with the good, or who can afford one of the nicer areas near the beach or in the surrounding hills, L.A. can be a nice place to live. Otherwise, be warned. Those of average means should probably look elsewhere, perhaps to Long Beach or South Pasadena, for a better quality of life at a reasonable price.

Los Angeles proper is located in a level, coastal basin extending eastward from the Pacific Ocean. Downtown is about 10 miles east of the shore, with built up areas extending 60-plus miles east and southeast into San Bernardino and Orange counties. To the north and northwest lie areas of hills and coastal mountains separating the city proper from the flat San Fernando Valley. To the northeast lie the much higher San Bernardino Mountains, rising up to 7,000 feet above the valley floor. Natural vegetation in the foothills is dry grass and brush with a few trees in higher elevations; the valleys are almost entirely built up.

Climate is normally pleasant and mild throughout the year. The Pacific Ocean is the primary moderating influence. Daily temperature ranges are low year-round, varying only 15°F in spring and summer and 20°F in fall and winter. Temperatures above 80°F are observed every month of the year. Like other Pacific Coast areas, rainfall comes in winter, with 85% of precipitation occurring November through March. Rainfall totals increase in foothill areas, and flash floods and mudslides are common in canyon areas. At times, the lack of air movement, combined with a frequent and persistent air inversion (aloft warm, dry, desert air trapping slightly cooler and more moist Pacific air) brings considerable air pollution in the basin, causing health problems for some and reducing or even eliminating visibility of the nearby mountains.

POPULATION

DEMOGRAPHICS	AREA	U.S. AVG	ETHNIC COMPOSITION	AREA	U.S. AVG	RESIDENT PROFILE	AREA	U.S. AVG
Population	9,806,577		White	59.4%	75.1%	Single	54.4%	43.6%
Population density per sq. mile	2,415.4	447.3	Black	10.7%	12.3%	Married	45.6%	56.4%
Population growth	10.6%	16.1%	Asian	13.3%	3.6%	Divorced	9.5%	8.4%
Median age	32.2	35.5	American Indian	.5%	.9%	Separated	4.4%	3.0%
Average family size	2.9	2.7	Hispanic	40.2%	12.5%	Married with children	24.1%	28.7%
			Diversity measure	70.8%	35.2%	Single with children	12.3%	10.1%

ECONOMY & JOBS   SCORE: 63/RANK: 121

INCOME	AREA	U.S. AVG	EMPLOYMENT	AREA	U.S. AVG	LARGEST EMPLOYING INDUSTRY
Per capita income	$23,422	$23,420	Unemployment rate	6.7%	6.1%	Apparel Manufacturing
Household income	$50,203	$46,060	Recent job growth	1.6%	.9%	
Household income < $25K	22.9%	26.4%	Projected future job growth	6.2%	15.1%	
Household income > $75K	30.7%	24.5%	White collar	56.8%	54.5%	
Household income growth	43.4%	57.3%	Blue collar	43.2%	45.5%	

COST OF LIVING   SCORE: 5/RANK: 314

INDEXES & TAXES	AREA	U.S. AVG	HOUSING	AREA	U.S. AVG	NECESSITIES	AREA	U.S. AVG
Cost of Living Index	139.3	100.0	Median home price	$304,600	$160,100	Food Index	111.2	100.0
Financial Progress Index	76.8	100.0	Home price appreciation	11.8%	7.1%	Housing Index	189.2	100.0
Income tax rate	6.000%	4.625%	Median rent	$1,021	$670	Utilities Index	116.3	100.0
Sales tax rate	8.250%	6.474%	Homes owned	49.4%	63.9%	Transportation Index	109.8	100.0
Property tax rate	$11.0	$15.6	Homes rented	43.7%	25.3%	Healthcare Index	121.1	100.0
			Housing affordability	39.0%	54.5%	Miscellaneous Cost Index	107.5	100.0

CLIMATE
SCORE: 97/RANK: 8

TEMPERATURE	AREA	U.S. AVG	PRECIPITATION	AREA	U.S. AVG	COMFORTS & HAZARDS	AREA	U.S. AVG
January low	45.4°F	26.4°F	Annual inches precipitation	12.0	35.9	July relative humidity	71.0%	68.8%
July high	75.8°F	86.7°F	Annual inches snowfall	0.0	24.2	Annual days mostly sunny	258	212
Annual days > 90°F	5	38	Annual days precipitation	35	111	Annual days with thunderstorms	3	39
Annual days < 32°F	0	88	Annual days rain > 0.5 inches	9	23	Tornado risk score	13	19
Annual days < 0°F	0	6	Annual days snow > 1.5 inches	0	6	Hurricane risk score	1	15

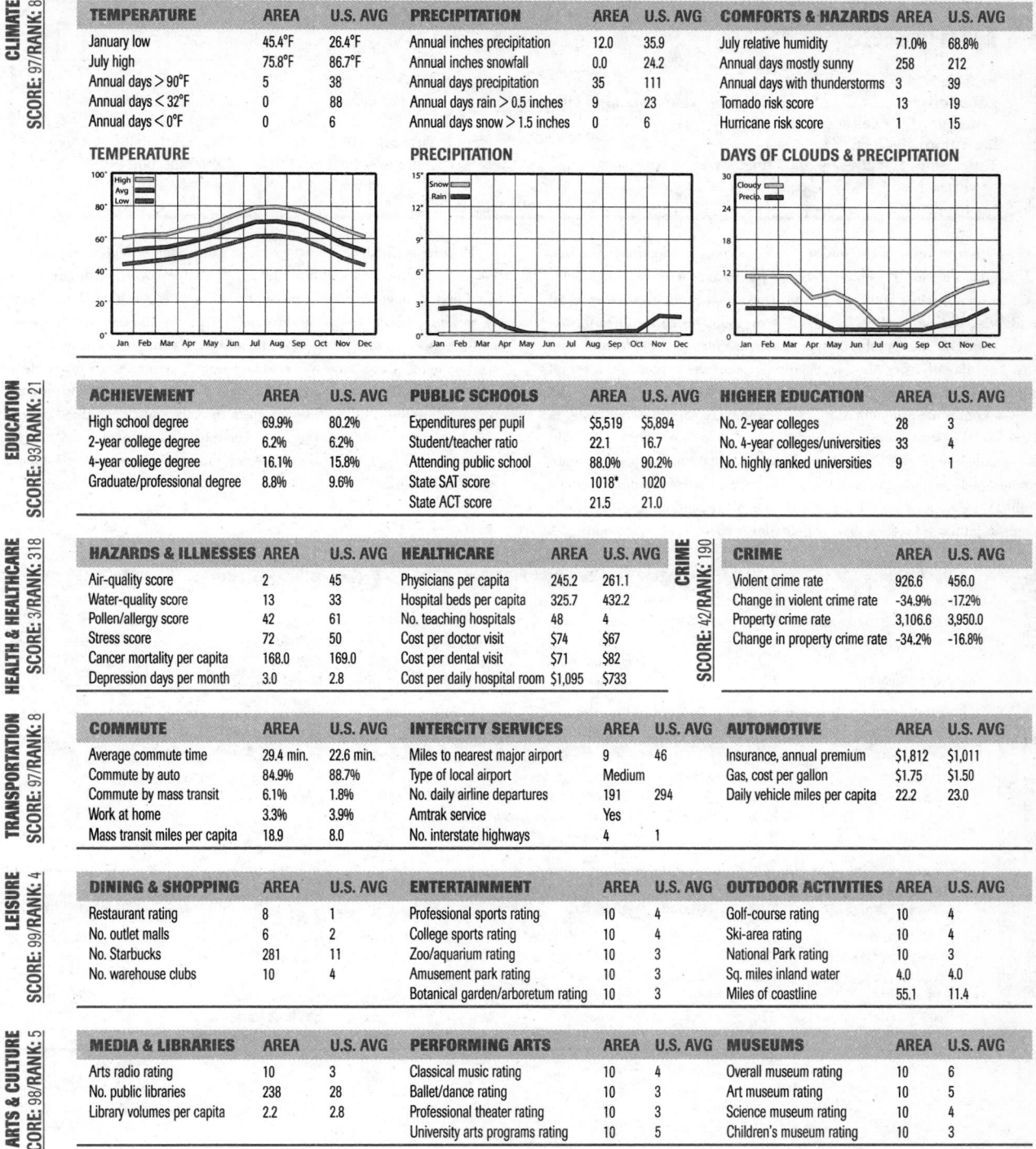

TEMPERATURE — **PRECIPITATION** — **DAYS OF CLOUDS & PRECIPITATION**

EDUCATION
SCORE: 93/RANK: 21

ACHIEVEMENT	AREA	U.S. AVG	PUBLIC SCHOOLS	AREA	U.S. AVG	HIGHER EDUCATION	AREA	U.S. AVG
High school degree	69.9%	80.2%	Expenditures per pupil	$5,519	$5,894	No. 2-year colleges	28	3
2-year college degree	6.2%	6.2%	Student/teacher ratio	22.1	16.7	No. 4-year colleges/universities	33	4
4-year college degree	16.1%	15.8%	Attending public school	88.0%	90.2%	No. highly ranked universities	9	1
Graduate/professional degree	8.8%	9.6%	State SAT score	1018*	1020			
			State ACT score	21.5	21.0			

HEALTH & HEALTHCARE
SCORE: 3/RANK: 318

CRIME
SCORE: 42/RANK: 190

HAZARDS & ILLNESSES	AREA	U.S. AVG	HEALTHCARE	AREA	U.S. AVG	CRIME	AREA	U.S. AVG
Air-quality score	2	45	Physicians per capita	245.2	261.1	Violent crime rate	926.6	456.0
Water-quality score	13	33	Hospital beds per capita	325.7	432.2	Change in violent crime rate	-34.9%	-17.2%
Pollen/allergy score	42	61	No. teaching hospitals	48	4	Property crime rate	3,106.6	3,950.0
Stress score	72	50	Cost per doctor visit	$74	$67	Change in property crime rate	-34.2%	-16.8%
Cancer mortality per capita	168.0	169.0	Cost per dental visit	$71	$82			
Depression days per month	3.0	2.8	Cost per daily hospital room	$1,095	$733			

TRANSPORTATION
SCORE: 97/RANK: 8

COMMUTE	AREA	U.S. AVG	INTERCITY SERVICES	AREA	U.S. AVG	AUTOMOTIVE	AREA	U.S. AVG
Average commute time	29.4 min.	22.6 min.	Miles to nearest major airport	9	46	Insurance, annual premium	$1,812	$1,011
Commute by auto	84.9%	88.7%	Type of local airport	Medium		Gas, cost per gallon	$1.75	$1.50
Commute by mass transit	6.1%	1.8%	No. daily airline departures	191	294	Daily vehicle miles per capita	22.2	23.0
Work at home	3.3%	3.9%	Amtrak service	Yes				
Mass transit miles per capita	18.9	8.0	No. interstate highways	4	1			

LEISURE
SCORE: 99/RANK: 4

DINING & SHOPPING	AREA	U.S. AVG	ENTERTAINMENT	AREA	U.S. AVG	OUTDOOR ACTIVITIES	AREA	U.S. AVG
Restaurant rating	8	1	Professional sports rating	10	4	Golf-course rating	10	4
No. outlet malls	6	2	College sports rating	10	4	Ski-area rating	10	4
No. Starbucks	281	11	Zoo/aquarium rating	10	3	National Park rating	10	3
No. warehouse clubs	10	4	Amusement park rating	10	3	Sq. miles inland water	4.0	4.0
			Botanical garden/arboretum rating	10	3	Miles of coastline	55.1	11.4

ARTS & CULTURE
SCORE: 98/RANK: 5

MEDIA & LIBRARIES	AREA	U.S. AVG	PERFORMING ARTS	AREA	U.S. AVG	MUSEUMS	AREA	U.S. AVG
Arts radio rating	10	3	Classical music rating	10	4	Overall museum rating	10	6
No. public libraries	238	28	Ballet/dance rating	10	3	Art museum rating	10	5
Library volumes per capita	2.2	2.8	Professional theater rating	10	3	Science museum rating	10	4
			University arts programs rating	10	5	Children's museum rating	10	3

Louisville, KY

Score: 57.3 Rank: 167

Profile: Mid-size city
Location: Northern Kentucky along the Ohio River at the Indiana border, 100 miles southwest of Cincinnati
Elevation: 488 feet
Time zone: Eastern Standard Time

PRO	CON
Cost of living	Low public-school utilization
Arts and culture	High pollen/allergy score
Attractive historic districts	Commute time

Louisville (pronounced lou-*ah*-vul locally) is an industrial, shipping, and commercial center. It has a prosperous river-town character with a distinct Southern accent. Downtown contains a few modern buildings, but the skyline is indistinct overall. The shady historic districts with gracious Southern-style homes are far more interesting. The first Saturday of every May, Louisville becomes the center of the sports world with the running of the Kentucky Derby, a major local event. The city is known for production of autos, appliances, and baseball bats; is home to the University of Louisville; and is a busy air cargo hub. Nationally, the city's air service and spectator sports have become more important in recent years. The Ohio River offers some recreational opportunities. Downsides include a low high-school graduation rate, low enrollment in public schools, a high pollen/allergy score, and congestion.

The city is divided into two portions with different topographies. The east is rolling hillsides with mostly residential areas, while the west is a flat flood plain containing industry. The climate is continental and highly variable. Located near storm tracks, it is characterized by frequent shifts between warm moist Gulf air and cooler air from the north and west. Summers are usually warm and humid. Winters are moderately cold though hills to the north in Indiana block polar air. Snow may be observed on those hills while absent in the city and river valley. Spring and summer thunderstorms are common, often producing heavy amounts. Fall is normally the driest season. First freeze is late October, last is mid-April.

POPULATION

DEMOGRAPHICS	AREA	U.S. AVG	ETHNIC COMPOSITION	AREA	U.S. AVG	RESIDENT PROFILE	AREA	U.S. AVG
Population	1,039,599		White	90.1%	75.1%	Single	43.0%	43.6%
Population density per sq. mile	501.7	447.3	Black	8.8%	12.3%	Married	57.0%	56.4%
Population growth	9.6%	16.1%	Asian	.7%	3.6%	Divorced	9.9%	8.4%
Median age	36.9	35.5	American Indian	.2%	.9%	Separated	2.6%	3.0%
Average family size	2.7	2.7	Hispanic	.7%	12.5%	Married with children	30.1%	28.7%
			Diversity measure	30.4%	35.2%	Single with children	10.8%	10.1%

ECONOMY & JOBS   SCORE: 45/RANK: 182

INCOME	AREA	U.S. AVG	EMPLOYMENT	AREA	U.S. AVG	LARGEST EMPLOYING INDUSTRY
Per capita income	$25,300	$23,420	Unemployment rate	4.8%	6.1%	Transportation Equipment Manufacturing
Household income	$46,230	$46,060	Recent job growth	1.6%	.9%	
Household income < $25K	25.9%	26.4%	Projected future job growth	15.7%	15.1%	
Household income > $75K	25.2%	24.5%	White collar	55.5%	54.5%	
Household income growth	68.2%	57.3%	Blue collar	44.5%	45.5%	

COST OF LIVING   SCORE: 38/RANK: 203

INDEXES & TAXES	AREA	U.S. AVG	HOUSING	AREA	U.S. AVG	NECESSITIES	AREA	U.S. AVG
Cost of Living Index	89.5	100.0	Median home price	$119,880	$160,100	Food Index	95.5	100.0
Financial Progress Index	110.0	100.0	Home price appreciation	5.4%	7.1%	Housing Index	74.5	100.0
Income tax rate	8.200%	4.625%	Median rent	$583	$670	Utilities Index	100.5	100.0
Sales tax rate	6.000%	6.474%	Homes owned	71.6%	63.9%	Transportation Index	105.4	100.0
Property tax rate	$12.3	$15.6	Homes rented	21.5%	25.3%	Healthcare Index	88.3	100.0
			Housing affordability	59.0%	54.5%	Miscellaneous Cost Index	98.0	100.0

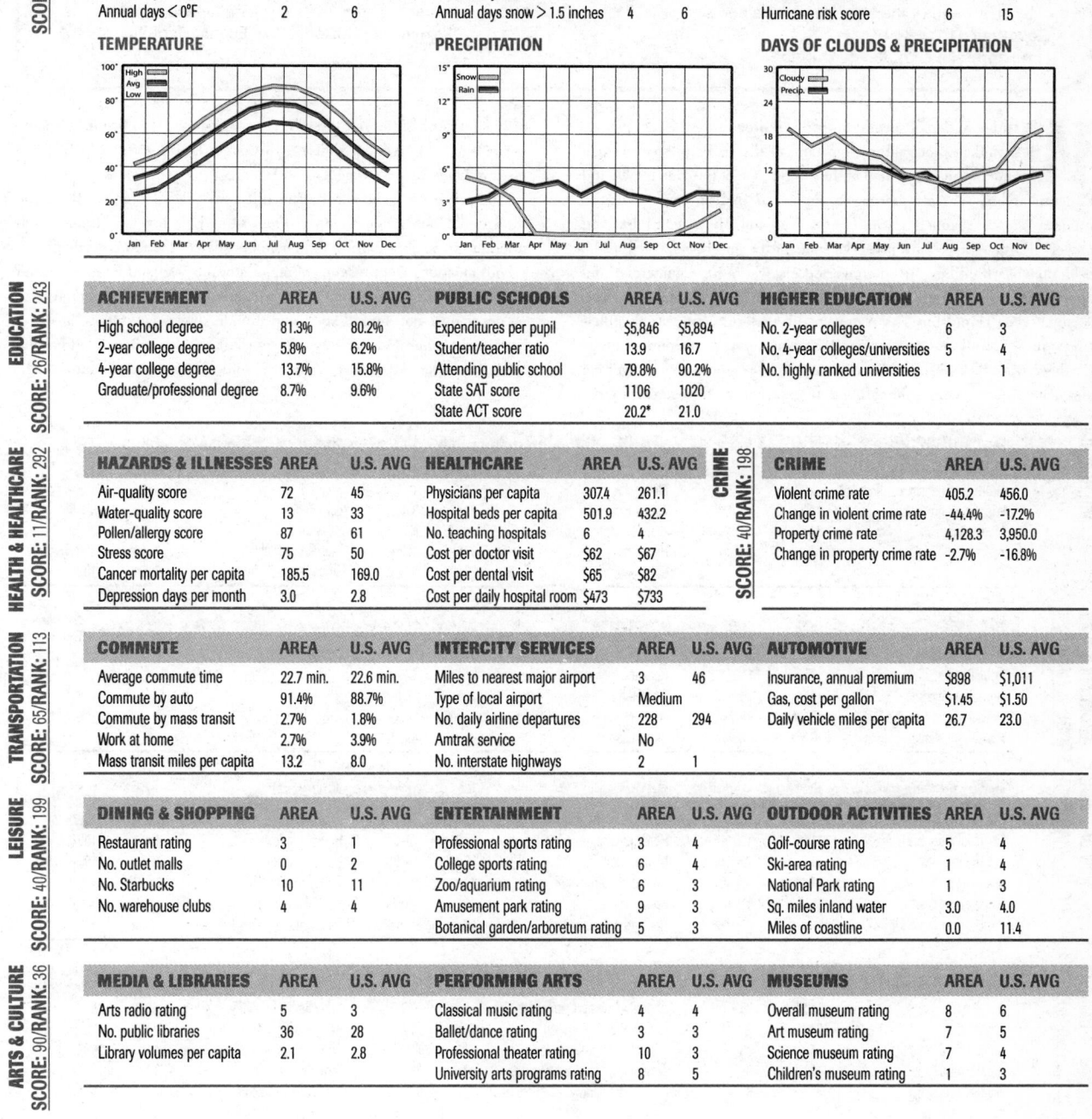

CLIMATE SCORE: 45/RANK: 181

TEMPERATURE	AREA	U.S. AVG	PRECIPITATION	AREA	U.S. AVG	COMFORTS & HAZARDS	AREA	U.S. AVG
January low	24.5°F	26.4°F	Annual inches precipitation	43.0	35.9	July relative humidity	69.0%	68.8%
July high	87.3°F	86.7°F	Annual inches snowfall	17.0	24.2	Annual days mostly sunny	197	212
Annual days > 90°F	24	38	Annual days precipitation	124	111	Annual days with thunderstorms	45	39
Annual days < 32°F	92	88	Annual days rain > 0.5 inches	28	23	Tornado risk score	17	19
Annual days < 0°F	2	6	Annual days snow > 1.5 inches	4	6	Hurricane risk score	6	15

TEMPERATURE

PRECIPITATION

DAYS OF CLOUDS & PRECIPITATION

EDUCATION SCORE: 26/RANK: 243

ACHIEVEMENT	AREA	U.S. AVG	PUBLIC SCHOOLS	AREA	U.S. AVG	HIGHER EDUCATION	AREA	U.S. AVG
High school degree	81.3%	80.2%	Expenditures per pupil	$5,846	$5,894	No. 2-year colleges	6	3
2-year college degree	5.8%	6.2%	Student/teacher ratio	13.9	16.7	No. 4-year colleges/universities	5	4
4-year college degree	13.7%	15.8%	Attending public school	79.8%	90.2%	No. highly ranked universities	1	1
Graduate/professional degree	8.7%	9.6%	State SAT score	1106	1020			
			State ACT score	20.2*	21.0			

HEALTH & HEALTHCARE SCORE: 11/RANK: 292

CRIME SCORE: 40/RANK: 198

HAZARDS & ILLNESSES	AREA	U.S. AVG	HEALTHCARE	AREA	U.S. AVG	CRIME	AREA	U.S. AVG
Air-quality score	72	45	Physicians per capita	307.4	261.1	Violent crime rate	405.2	456.0
Water-quality score	13	33	Hospital beds per capita	501.9	432.2	Change in violent crime rate	-44.4%	-17.2%
Pollen/allergy score	87	61	No. teaching hospitals	6	4	Property crime rate	4,128.3	3,950.0
Stress score	75	50	Cost per doctor visit	$62	$67	Change in property crime rate	-2.7%	-16.8%
Cancer mortality per capita	185.5	169.0	Cost per dental visit	$65	$82			
Depression days per month	3.0	2.8	Cost per daily hospital room	$473	$733			

TRANSPORTATION SCORE: 65/RANK: 113

COMMUTE	AREA	U.S. AVG	INTERCITY SERVICES	AREA	U.S. AVG	AUTOMOTIVE	AREA	U.S. AVG
Average commute time	22.7 min.	22.6 min.	Miles to nearest major airport	3	46	Insurance, annual premium	$898	$1,011
Commute by auto	91.4%	88.7%	Type of local airport	Medium		Gas, cost per gallon	$1.45	$1.50
Commute by mass transit	2.7%	1.8%	No. daily airline departures	228	294	Daily vehicle miles per capita	26.7	23.0
Work at home	2.7%	3.9%	Amtrak service	No				
Mass transit miles per capita	13.2	8.0	No. interstate highways	2	1			

LEISURE SCORE: 40/RANK: 199

DINING & SHOPPING	AREA	U.S. AVG	ENTERTAINMENT	AREA	U.S. AVG	OUTDOOR ACTIVITIES	AREA	U.S. AVG
Restaurant rating	3	1	Professional sports rating	3	4	Golf-course rating	5	4
No. outlet malls	0	2	College sports rating	6	4	Ski-area rating	1	4
No. Starbucks	10	11	Zoo/aquarium rating	6	3	National Park rating	1	3
No. warehouse clubs	4	4	Amusement park rating	9	3	Sq. miles inland water	3.0	4.0
			Botanical garden/arboretum rating	5	3	Miles of coastline	0.0	11.4

ARTS & CULTURE SCORE: 90/RANK: 36

MEDIA & LIBRARIES	AREA	U.S. AVG	PERFORMING ARTS	AREA	U.S. AVG	MUSEUMS	AREA	U.S. AVG
Arts radio rating	5	3	Classical music rating	4	4	Overall museum rating	8	6
No. public libraries	36	28	Ballet/dance rating	3	3	Art museum rating	7	5
Library volumes per capita	2.1	2.8	Professional theater rating	10	3	Science museum rating	7	4
			University arts programs rating	8	5	Children's museum rating	1	3

Lowell, MA

Score: 49.5 **Rank:** 230

Profile: Small industrial city/Commuter community
Location: On outer I-495 Boston beltway, 30 miles north of Boston and 5 miles south of the New Hampshire border
Elevation: 115 feet
Time zone: Eastern Standard Time

PRO	CON
Historic interest	Cost of living
Attractive setting	Traffic and sprawl
Proximity to Boston	Economic cycles

Within a region of several towns extending into New Hampshire, Lowell is practically a museum of the early Industrial Age. The town itself formed at the confluence of the Merrimack and Concord rivers, where waterpower supported a 19th-century textile industry and a planned town. Lowell National Historical Park and Lowell Heritage State Park preserve some of the enormous, brick mills, examples of which have been converted elsewhere for commercial and residential uses. Nearby towns of Chelmsford, Massachusetts, and Nashua, New Hampshire, have developed modern, commercial industries, while Lowell and nearby smaller towns serve as residential areas for those who work in them. Nevertheless, local employment is cyclical and occasionally weak. Commuting to the northern and western suburbs of Boston is possible, but the route is congested. Cost-of-living expenses are similar to Boston, with a high Cost of Living Index of 137.3 and median home prices over $290,560.

The terrain is gently rolling to hilly, with small creek valleys and thick deciduous woods. Compared to Boston, Lowell gets a stronger continental but weaker marine influence because of the more northern and inland location. The presence of major storm tracks and bodies of water makes for rapid changes and active weather. Summers are moderate with an occasional hot, humid spell and thundershowers. Winters have frequent cold snaps and considerable snowfall, with occasional "noreaster" storms from the Atlantic. First freeze is mid-October, last is late April.

POPULATION

DEMOGRAPHICS	AREA	U.S. AVG	ETHNIC COMPOSITION	AREA	U.S. AVG	RESIDENT PROFILE	AREA	U.S. AVG
Population	305,212		White	90.1%	75.1%	Single	45.5%	43.6%
Population density per sq. mile	1,222.2	447.3	Black	1.9%	12.3%	Married	54.5%	56.4%
Population growth	8.8%	16.1%	Asian	6.1%	3.6%	Divorced	6.8%	8.4%
Median age	36.8	35.5	American Indian	.1%	.9%	Separated	2.9%	3.0%
Average family size	2.8	2.7	Hispanic	4.5%	12.5%	Married with children	31.5%	28.7%
			Diversity measure	25.3%	35.2%	Single with children	9.2%	10.1%

ECONOMY & JOBS   SCORE: 20/RANK: 263

INCOME	AREA	U.S. AVG	EMPLOYMENT	AREA	U.S. AVG	LARGEST EMPLOYING INDUSTRY
Per capita income	$37,520	$23,420	Unemployment rate	6.8%	6.1%	Computer and Electronic Product Manufacturing
Household income	$75,771	$46,060	Recent job growth	-3.4%	.9%	
Household income < $25K	14.0%	26.4%	Projected future job growth	7.6%	15.1%	
Household income > $75K	50.2%	24.5%	White collar	61.3%	54.5%	
Household income growth	78.3%	57.3%	Blue collar	38.7%	45.5%	

COST OF LIVING   SCORE: 7/RANK: 304

INDEXES & TAXES	AREA	U.S. AVG	HOUSING	AREA	U.S. AVG	NECESSITIES	AREA	U.S. AVG
Cost of Living Index	137.3	100.0	Median home price	$290,560	$160,100	Food Index	108.2	100.0
Financial Progress Index	117.6	100.0	Home price appreciation	14.9%	7.1%	Housing Index	180.5	100.0
Income tax rate	5.950%	4.625%	Median rent	$1,065	$670	Utilities Index	123.4	100.0
Sales tax rate	5.000%	6.474%	Homes owned	69.9%	63.9%	Transportation Index	113.3	100.0
Property tax rate	$17.0	$15.6	Homes rented	25.0%	25.3%	Healthcare Index	126.9	100.0
			Housing affordability	46.0%	54.5%	Miscellaneous Cost Index	109.0	100.0

CLIMATE   SCORE: 9/RANK: 299

TEMPERATURE	AREA	U.S. AVG	PRECIPITATION	AREA	U.S. AVG	COMFORTS & HAZARDS	AREA	U.S. AVG
January low	18.2°F	26.4°F	Annual inches precipitation	45.2	35.9	July relative humidity	68.0%	68.8%
July high	81.4°F	86.7°F	Annual inches snowfall	50.0	24.2	Annual days mostly sunny	197	212
Annual days > 90°F	15	38	Annual days precipitation	137	111	Annual days with thunderstorms	22	39
Annual days < 32°F	120	88	Annual days rain > 0.5 inches	30	23	Tornado risk score	13	19
Annual days < 0°F	5	6	Annual days snow > 1.5 inches	19	6	Hurricane risk score	18	15

TEMPERATURE

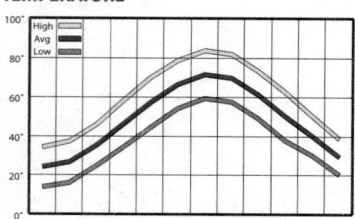

PRECIPITATION

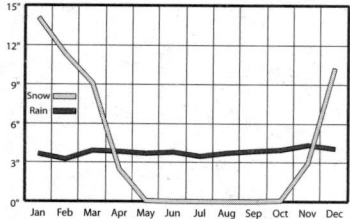

DAYS OF CLOUDS & PRECIPITATION

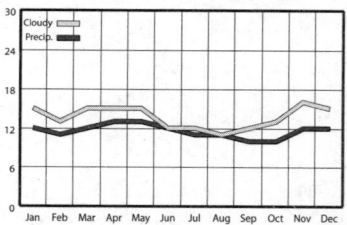

EDUCATION SCORE: 92/RANK: 27

ACHIEVEMENT	AREA	U.S. AVG	PUBLIC SCHOOLS	AREA	U.S. AVG	HIGHER EDUCATION	AREA	U.S. AVG
High school degree	88.4%	80.2%	Expenditures per pupil	$7,033	$5,894	No. 2-year colleges	0	3
2-year college degree	6.4%	6.2%	Student/teacher ratio	15.4	16.7	No. 4-year colleges/universities	1	4
4-year college degree	23.4%	15.8%	Attending public school	88.3%	90.2%	No. highly ranked universities	0	1
Graduate/professional degree	19.7%	9.6%	State SAT score	1038*	1020			
			State ACT score	22.3	21.0			

HEALTH & HEALTHCARE SCORE: 53/RANK: 156

HAZARDS & ILLNESSES	AREA	U.S. AVG	HEALTHCARE	AREA	U.S. AVG
Air-quality score	6	45	Physicians per capita	101.2	261.1
Water-quality score	30	33	Hospital beds per capita	405.7	432.2
Pollen/allergy score	44	61	No. teaching hospitals	0	4
Stress score	46	50	Cost per doctor visit	$82	$67
Cancer mortality per capita	184.6	169.0	Cost per dental visit	$106	$82
Depression days per month	2.8	2.8	Cost per daily hospital room	$720	$733

CRIME SCORE: 98/RANK: 7

CRIME	AREA	U.S. AVG
Violent crime rate	343.9	456.0
Change in violent crime rate	-50.6%	-17.2%
Property crime rate	2,078.6	3,950.0
Change in property crime rate	-36.6%	-16.8%

TRANSPORTATION SCORE: 52/RANK: 157

COMMUTE	AREA	U.S. AVG	INTERCITY SERVICES	AREA	U.S. AVG	AUTOMOTIVE	AREA	U.S. AVG
Average commute time	26.9 min.	22.6 min.	Miles to nearest major airport	4	46	Insurance, annual premium	$1,308	$1,011
Commute by auto	93.0%	88.7%	Type of local airport	Small		Gas, cost per gallon	$1.54	$1.50
Commute by mass transit	1.7%	1.8%	No. daily airline departures	94	294	Daily vehicle miles per capita	25.5	23.0
Work at home	2.2%	3.9%	Amtrak service	No				
Mass transit miles per capita	5.0	8.0	No. interstate highways	1	1			

LEISURE SCORE: 77/RANK: 77

DINING & SHOPPING	AREA	U.S. AVG	ENTERTAINMENT	AREA	U.S. AVG	OUTDOOR ACTIVITIES	AREA	U.S. AVG
Restaurant rating	1	1	Professional sports rating	8	4	Golf-course rating	5	4
No. outlet malls	3	2	College sports rating	6	4	Ski-area rating	7	4
No. Starbucks	1	11	Zoo/aquarium rating	3	3	National Park rating	2	3
No. warehouse clubs	5	4	Amusement park rating	5	3	Sq. miles inland water	4.0	4.0
			Botanical garden/arboretum rating	3	3	Miles of coastline	0.0	11.4

ARTS & CULTURE SCORE: 59/RANK: 136

MEDIA & LIBRARIES	AREA	U.S. AVG	PERFORMING ARTS	AREA	U.S. AVG	MUSEUMS	AREA	U.S. AVG
Arts radio rating	4	3	Classical music rating	4	4	Overall museum rating	6	6
No. public libraries	12	28	Ballet/dance rating	5	3	Art museum rating	6	5
Library volumes per capita	2.8	2.8	Professional theater rating	8	3	Science museum rating	3	4
			University arts programs rating	8	5	Children's museum rating	3	3

Lubbock, TX

Score: 63.3   Rank: 120

Profile: Small city
Location: Southern Texas Panhandle
Elevation: 3,241 feet
Time zone: Central Standard Time

PRO	CON
Cost of living	Crime rate
College influence	Isolation
Healthcare	Recreation

Lubbock is the commercial, educational, and cultural center for the southern part of the Texas Panhandle. The economic base is a mix of industry, agriculture, government, and healthcare. Relatively healthy high-tech firms like Texas Instruments have operations there. The 25,000-student Texas Tech University provides a strong economic and cultural influence, and a college-town element with more than the usual nightlife and live music. The isolated location is 120 miles from the nearest metro area (Amarillo) and 320 miles from the Dallas and Fort Worth metroplex. The recent advent of low-cost air transport has greatly influenced Lubbock's attractiveness.

Lubbock is located in the South Plains region, which is predominately flat but with numerous, small, mostly dry, stream valleys. The climate is semiarid and transitional between desert conditions to the west and humid climates to the east. Summer temperatures are pleasant with low humidity on the hottest days; tropical air invades occasionally bringing heavy afternoon thunderstorms. Winters are variable and can become cold due to altitude and northerly cold-air invasions. Snowfall is generally light and unlikely to remain on the ground beyond a few days. Prolonged, sometimes dusty winds in excess of 25 mph may occur in late winter and spring. First freeze is early November, last is late April.

POPULATION

DEMOGRAPHICS	AREA	U.S. AVG	ETHNIC COMPOSITION	AREA	U.S. AVG	RESIDENT PROFILE	AREA	U.S. AVG
Population	247,574		White	76.0%	75.1%	Single	49.4%	43.6%
Population density per sq. mile	275.2	447.3	Black	9.4%	12.3%	Married	50.6%	56.4%
Population growth	11.2%	16.1%	Asian	1.8%	3.6%	Divorced	8.7%	8.4%
Median age	30.7	35.5	American Indian	.4%	.9%	Separated	3.6%	3.0%
Average family size	3.3	2.7	Hispanic	32.7%	12.5%	Married with children	26.3%	28.7%
			Diversity measure	51.8%	35.2%	Single with children	10.8%	10.1%

ECONOMY & JOBS SCORE: 98/RANK: 6

INCOME	AREA	U.S. AVG	EMPLOYMENT	AREA	U.S. AVG	LARGEST EMPLOYING INDUSTRY
Per capita income	$20,893	$23,420	Unemployment rate	3.9%	6.1%	Healthcare and Social Assistance
Household income	$37,470	$46,060	Recent job growth	2.8%	.9%	
Household income < $25K	33.2%	26.4%	Projected future job growth	13.1%	15.1%	
Household income > $75K	19.1%	24.5%	White collar	56.9%	54.5%	
Household income growth	53.9%	57.3%	Blue collar	43.1%	45.5%	

COST OF LIVING SCORE: 84/RANK: 52

INDEXES & TAXES	AREA	U.S. AVG	HOUSING	AREA	U.S. AVG	NECESSITIES	AREA	U.S. AVG
Cost of Living Index	80.2	100.0	Median home price	$80,750	$160,100	Food Index	91.3	100.0
Financial Progress Index	99.6	100.0	Home price appreciation	5.3%	7.1%	Housing Index	50.2	100.0
Income tax rate	0.000%	4.625%	Median rent	$540	$670	Utilities Index	100.4	100.0
Sales tax rate	7.875%	6.474%	Homes owned	56.9%	63.9%	Transportation Index	100.5	100.0
Property tax rate	$22.2	$15.6	Homes rented	30.7%	25.3%	Healthcare Index	102.9	100.0
			Housing affordability	56.0%	54.5%	Miscellaneous Cost Index	96.9	100.0

CLIMATE SCORE: 85/RANK: 49

TEMPERATURE	AREA	U.S. AVG	PRECIPITATION	AREA	U.S. AVG	COMFORTS & HAZARDS	AREA	U.S. AVG
January low	24.8°F	26.4°F	Annual inches precipitation	18.0	35.9	July relative humidity	56.0%	68.8%
July high	92.4°F	86.7°F	Annual inches snowfall	9.6	24.2	Annual days mostly sunny	267	212
Annual days > 90°F	77	38	Annual days precipitation	60	111	Annual days with thunderstorms	45	39
Annual days < 32°F	98	88	Annual days rain > 0.5 inches	10	23	Tornado risk score	73	19
Annual days < 0°F	0	6	Annual days snow > 1.5 inches	1	6	Hurricane risk score	0	15

TEMPERATURE

PRECIPITATION

DAYS OF CLOUDS & PRECIPITATION

EDUCATION SCORE: 52/RANK: 158

ACHIEVEMENT	AREA	U.S. AVG	PUBLIC SCHOOLS	AREA	U.S. AVG	HIGHER EDUCATION	AREA	U.S. AVG
High school degree	79.5%	80.2%	Expenditures per pupil	$5,478	$5,894	No. 2-year colleges	0	3
2-year college degree	4.6%	6.2%	Student/teacher ratio	14.3	16.7	No. 4-year colleges/universities	2	4
4-year college degree	17.3%	15.8%	Attending public school	94.7%	90.2%	No. highly ranked universities	1	1
Graduate/professional degree	9.3%	9.6%	State SAT score	993*	1020			
			State ACT score	20.1	21.0			

HEALTH & HEALTHCARE SCORE: 90/RANK: 30

HAZARDS & ILLNESSES	AREA	U.S. AVG	HEALTHCARE	AREA	U.S. AVG	CRIME	AREA	U.S. AVG
Air-quality score	49	45	Physicians per capita	382.1	261.1	Violent crime rate	1,058.7	456.0
Water-quality score	30	33	Hospital beds per capita	1019.3	432.2	Change in violent crime rate	16.4%	-17.2%
Pollen/allergy score	69	61	No. teaching hospitals	3	4	Property crime rate	5,306.8	3,950.0
Stress score	48	50	Cost per doctor visit	$70	$67	Change in property crime rate	-7.3%	-16.8%
Cancer mortality per capita	148.7	169.0	Cost per dental visit	$83	$82			
Depression days per month	4.3	2.8	Cost per daily hospital room	$659	$733			

CRIME SCORE: 2/RANK: 322

TRANSPORTATION SCORE: 86/RANK: 45

COMMUTE	AREA	U.S. AVG	INTERCITY SERVICES	AREA	U.S. AVG	AUTOMOTIVE	AREA	U.S. AVG
Average commute time	17.1 min.	22.6 min.	Miles to nearest major airport	6	46	Insurance, annual premium	$930	$1,011
Commute by auto	90.4%	88.7%	Type of local airport	Small		Gas, cost per gallon	$1.45	$1.50
Commute by mass transit	.9%	1.8%	No. daily airline departures	60	294	Daily vehicle miles per capita	20.7	23.0
Work at home	2.7%	3.9%	Amtrak service	No				
Mass transit miles per capita	7.9	8.0	No. interstate highways	1	1			

LEISURE SCORE: 22/RANK: 257

DINING & SHOPPING	AREA	U.S. AVG	ENTERTAINMENT	AREA	U.S. AVG	OUTDOOR ACTIVITIES	AREA	U.S. AVG
Restaurant rating	1	1	Professional sports rating	3	4	Golf-course rating	2	4
No. outlet malls	0	2	College sports rating	4	4	Ski-area rating	1	4
No. Starbucks	1	11	Zoo/aquarium rating	1	3	National Park rating	1	3
No. warehouse clubs	3	4	Amusement park rating	4	3	Sq. miles inland water	2.0	4.0
			Botanical garden/arboretum rating	1	3	Miles of coastline	0.0	11.4

ARTS & CULTURE SCORE: 60/RANK: 130

MEDIA & LIBRARIES	AREA	U.S. AVG	PERFORMING ARTS	AREA	U.S. AVG	MUSEUMS	AREA	U.S. AVG
Arts radio rating	1	3	Classical music rating	4	4	Overall museum rating	3	6
No. public libraries	7	28	Ballet/dance rating	1	3	Art museum rating	1	5
Library volumes per capita	1.6	2.8	Professional theater rating	1	3	Science museum rating	4	4
			University arts programs rating	7	5	Children's museum rating	1	3

Lynchburg, VA

Score: 86.0   Rank: 15

Profile: Small city
Location: West-central Virginia along James River, 50 miles east of Roanoke
Elevation: 648 feet
Time zone: Eastern Standard Time

PRO	CON
Historic interest	Urban sprawl
Cost of living	Air service
Low crime rate	Recent job declines

Lynchburg is a mid-size Virginia town with a Southern feel and views of the Blue Ridge and Appalachian mountains. Downtown is a mix of old and new, and the city is known for the historic districts of refined homes on the surrounding hilltops, five of which are included in the National Register of Historic Districts. Three small colleges provide some college-town amenities. The area has a few good museums and numerous entertainment options. The mountains to the west and Smith Mountain Lake to the south offer outdoor recreation. The Cost of Living Index is a modest 85.3 and home prices are the second lowest among Virginia's metropolitan areas. But the city has had problems with urban sprawl, particularly to the southeast and in the downtown area, to the extent that it became a court battleground for the sprawl-producing practice of annexation. Although on the mend, the downtown area shows signs of neglect even in the historic districts. Because these factors don't show up in statistics, some may find the area less attractive than the numbers indicate.

Lynchburg is situated in the James River Valley at the eastern edge of the Blue Ridge Mountains. Nearby terrain is hilly with deciduous forest and sheltered valleys. The marine-influenced continental climate is usually pleasant. Summers are warm and fairly humid with cool evening breezes and cooler conditions in nearby hills. Rainfall is evenly distributed throughout the year with frequent summer thunderstorms. Fall brings periods of cloudy, cool weather with high humidity and light rain or drizzle. Winter cold fronts bring dry, invigorating air with clear skies. There are snow showers, but the mountains to the west block many storms, high winds, and blasts of bitter cold. First freeze is late October, last is mid-April.

POPULATION

DEMOGRAPHICS	AREA	U.S. AVG	ETHNIC COMPOSITION	AREA	U.S. AVG	RESIDENT PROFILE	AREA	U.S. AVG
Population	216,163		White	80.4%	75.1%	Single	40.4%	43.6%
Population density per sq. mile	120.7	447.3	Black	19.0%	12.3%	Married	59.6%	56.4%
Population growth	11.5%	16.1%	Asian	.4%	3.6%	Divorced	6.7%	8.4%
Median age	38.5	35.5	American Indian	.2%	.9%	Separated	3.7%	3.0%
Average family size	2.6	2.7	Hispanic	.8%	12.5%	Married with children	26.2%	28.7%
			Diversity measure	34.2%	35.2%	Single with children	8.8%	10.1%

ECONOMY & JOBS SCORE: 33/RANK: 219

INCOME	AREA	U.S. AVG	EMPLOYMENT	AREA	U.S. AVG	LARGEST EMPLOYING INDUSTRY
Per capita income	$20,765	$23,420	Unemployment rate	4.7%	6.1%	Computer and Electronic Product Manufacturing
Household income	$38,368	$46,060	Recent job growth	-.1%	.9%	
Household income < $25K	30.7%	26.4%	Projected future job growth	12.2%	15.1%	
Household income > $75K	16.8%	24.5%	White collar	50.5%	54.5%	
Household income growth	43.1%	57.3%	Blue collar	49.5%	45.5%	

COST OF LIVING SCORE: 79/RANK: 68

INDEXES & TAXES	AREA	U.S. AVG	HOUSING	AREA	U.S. AVG	NECESSITIES	AREA	U.S. AVG
Cost of Living Index	85.3	100.0	Median home price	$113,900	$160,100	Food Index	98.4	100.0
Financial Progress Index	95.9	100.0	Home price appreciation	5.2%	7.1%	Housing Index	70.7	100.0
Income tax rate	5.750%	4.625%	Median rent	$476	$670	Utilities Index	73.8	100.0
Sales tax rate	4.500%	6.474%	Homes owned	72.6%	63.9%	Transportation Index	89.4	100.0
Property tax rate	$11.0	$15.6	Homes rented	17.3%	25.3%	Healthcare Index	97.6	100.0
			Housing affordability	63.0%	54.5%	Miscellaneous Cost Index	97.7	100.0

CLIMATE — SCORE: 69/RANK: 102

TEMPERATURE	AREA	U.S. AVG	PRECIPITATION	AREA	U.S. AVG	COMFORTS & HAZARDS	AREA	U.S. AVG
January low	27.3°F	26.4°F	Annual inches precipitation	38.3	35.9	July relative humidity	70.0%	68.8%
July high	86.1°F	86.7°F	Annual inches snowfall	18.2	24.2	Annual days mostly sunny	218	212
Annual days > 90°F	19	38	Annual days precipitation	125	111	Annual days with thunderstorms	41	39
Annual days < 32°F	94	88	Annual days rain > 0.5 inches	28	23	Tornado risk score	2	19
Annual days < 0°F	1	6	Annual days snow > 1.5 inches	4	6	Hurricane risk score	14	15

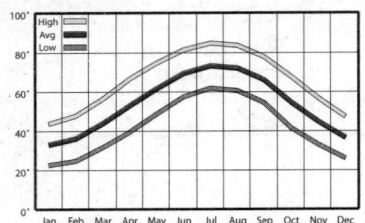

TEMPERATURE

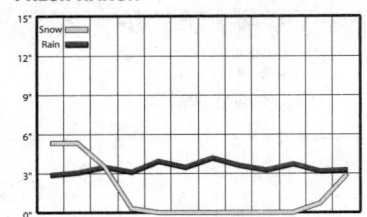

PRECIPITATION

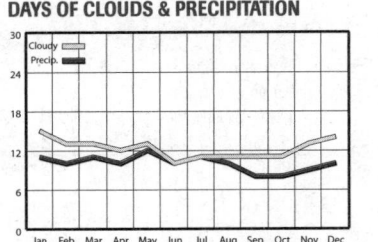

DAYS OF CLOUDS & PRECIPITATION

EDUCATION — SCORE: 40/RANK: 196

ACHIEVEMENT	AREA	U.S. AVG	PUBLIC SCHOOLS	AREA	U.S. AVG	HIGHER EDUCATION	AREA	U.S. AVG
High school degree	78.0%	80.2%	Expenditures per pupil	$4,888	$5,894	No. 2-year colleges	1	3
2-year college degree	5.1%	6.2%	Student/teacher ratio	14.5	16.7	No. 4-year colleges/universities	4	4
4-year college degree	12.6%	15.8%	Attending public school	93.0%	90.2%	No. highly ranked universities	2	1
Graduate/professional degree	6.6%	9.6%	State SAT score	1024*	1020			
			State ACT score	20.6	21.0			

HEALTH & HEALTHCARE — SCORE: 99/RANK: 4   CRIME — SCORE: 92/RANK: 25

HAZARDS & ILLNESSES	AREA	U.S. AVG	HEALTHCARE	AREA	U.S. AVG	CRIME	AREA	U.S. AVG
Air-quality score	49	45	Physicians per capita	182.3	261.1	Violent crime rate	236.9	456.0
Water-quality score	87	33	Hospital beds per capita	1105.1	432.2	Change in violent crime rate	-41.1%	-17.2%
Pollen/allergy score	56	61	No. teaching hospitals	2	4	Property crime rate	2,214.2	3,950.0
Stress score	10	50	Cost per doctor visit	$66	$67	Change in property crime rate	-16.4%	-16.8%
Cancer mortality per capita	156.5	169.0	Cost per dental visit	$68	$82			
Depression days per month	1.5	2.8	Cost per daily hospital room	$679	$733			

TRANSPORTATION — SCORE: 20/RANK: 265

COMMUTE	AREA	U.S. AVG	INTERCITY SERVICES	AREA	U.S. AVG	AUTOMOTIVE	AREA	U.S. AVG
Average commute time	22.8 min.	22.6 min.	Miles to nearest major airport	43	46	Insurance, annual premium	$799	$1,011
Commute by auto	94.2%	88.7%	Type of local airport	Small		Gas, cost per gallon	$1.37	$1.50
Commute by mass transit	.8%	1.8%	No. daily airline departures	64	294	Daily vehicle miles per capita	23.8	23.0
Work at home	2.2%	3.9%	Amtrak service	Yes				
Mass transit miles per capita	4.7	8.0	No. interstate highways	0	1			

LEISURE — SCORE: 35/RANK: 217

DINING & SHOPPING	AREA	U.S. AVG	ENTERTAINMENT	AREA	U.S. AVG	OUTDOOR ACTIVITIES	AREA	U.S. AVG
Restaurant rating	1	1	Professional sports rating	2	4	Golf-course rating	2	4
No. outlet malls	0	2	College sports rating	3	4	Ski-area rating	4	4
No. Starbucks	0	11	Zoo/aquarium rating	1	3	National Park rating	4	3
No. warehouse clubs	3	4	Amusement park rating	1	3	Sq. miles inland water	2.0	4.0
			Botanical garden/arboretum rating	1	3	Miles of coastline	0.0	11.4

ARTS & CULTURE — SCORE: 25/RANK: 243

MEDIA & LIBRARIES	AREA	U.S. AVG	PERFORMING ARTS	AREA	U.S. AVG	MUSEUMS	AREA	U.S. AVG
Arts radio rating	1	3	Classical music rating	2	4	Overall museum rating	7	6
No. public libraries	14	28	Ballet/dance rating	3	3	Art museum rating	3	5
Library volumes per capita	2.7	2.8	Professional theater rating	1	3	Science museum rating	2	4
			University arts programs rating	7	5	Children's museum rating	1	3

Macon, GA

Score: 32.9   Rank: 302

Profile: Small city
Location: Central Georgia, 80 miles southeast of Atlanta
Elevation: 354 feet
Time zone: Eastern Standard Time

PRO
Cost of living
Low unemployment
Historic interest

CON
Summer heat
Property crime
Low educational attainment

Macon is a typical mid-size Southern city in both appearance and feel. The downtown area is nondescript with a large riverfront park. The city has more entries on the National Register of Historic Places than any other city in Georgia. There are a few museums, including the Georgia Music Hall of Fame, highlighting state achievements, and the city is well known for Southern-style food and restaurants. Parts of the city are industrial and run-down. Other downsides include high property crime, low educational attainment, and few activities or entertainment. Some of the town's charm falls outside statistical boundaries, and with Atlanta nearby, it may be a better place than the numbers indicate.

The city is in an area of mainly flat terrain with some hills to the west and a few swampy areas. Most of the surrounding countryside is wooded except for a few farms. At the border of subtropical and continental influences, Macon is well situated to escape climatic extremes. In summer, warm, humid periods are cooled by dry northwesterly winds as well as by showers and thunderstorms. Some storms are severe, with tornadoes observed every year in adjacent counties. The Appalachians block some cold air in the winter. Snow occurs during most winters, but amounts are usually small. First freeze is early November, last is mid-March.

POPULATION

DEMOGRAPHICS	AREA	U.S. AVG	ETHNIC COMPOSITION	AREA	U.S. AVG	RESIDENT PROFILE	AREA	U.S. AVG
Population	330,853		White	62.5%	75.1%	Single	49.1%	43.6%
Population density per sq. mile	216.0	447.3	Black	36.0%	12.3%	Married	50.9%	56.4%
Population growth	13.7%	16.1%	Asian	.9%	3.6%	Divorced	9.0%	8.4%
Median age	34.6	35.5	American Indian	.2%	.9%	Separated	4.5%	3.0%
Average family size	2.7	2.7	Hispanic	2.1%	12.5%	Married with children	28.8%	28.7%
			Diversity measure	51.8%	35.2%	Single with children	14.3%	10.1%

ECONOMY & JOBS SCORE: 79/RANK: 69

INCOME	AREA	U.S. AVG	EMPLOYMENT	AREA	U.S. AVG	LARGEST EMPLOYING INDUSTRY
Per capita income	$21,053	$23,420	Unemployment rate	4.1%	6.1%	Healthcare and Social Assistance
Household income	$42,106	$46,060	Recent job growth	1.1%	.9%	
Household income < $25K	28.9%	26.4%	Projected future job growth	13.8%	15.1%	
Household income > $75K	21.2%	24.5%	White collar	52.4%	54.5%	
Household income growth	50.3%	57.3%	Blue collar	47.6%	45.5%	

COST OF LIVING SCORE: 60/RANK: 132

INDEXES & TAXES	AREA	U.S. AVG	HOUSING	AREA	U.S. AVG	NECESSITIES	AREA	U.S. AVG
Cost of Living Index	85.9	100.0	Median home price	$98,640	$160,100	Food Index	98.8	100.0
Financial Progress Index	104.5	100.0	Home price appreciation	4.6%	7.1%	Housing Index	61.3	100.0
Income tax rate	6.000%	4.625%	Median rent	$546	$670	Utilities Index	103.0	100.0
Sales tax rate	6.000%	6.474%	Homes owned	63.3%	63.9%	Transportation Index	96.7	100.0
Property tax rate	$16.0	$15.6	Homes rented	30.0%	25.3%	Healthcare Index	92.7	100.0
			Housing affordability	58.0%	54.5%	Miscellaneous Cost Index	102.6	100.0

CLIMATE SCORE: 50/RANK: 166

TEMPERATURE	AREA	U.S. AVG	PRECIPITATION	AREA	U.S. AVG	COMFORTS & HAZARDS	AREA	U.S. AVG
January low	36.9°F	26.4°F	Annual inches precipitation	44.5	35.9	July relative humidity	72.0%	68.8%
July high	92.1°F	86.7°F	Annual inches snowfall	.9	24.2	Annual days mostly sunny	217	212
Annual days > 90°F	78	38	Annual days precipitation	111	111	Annual days with thunderstorms	56	39
Annual days < 32°F	51	88	Annual days rain > 0.5 inches	28	23	Tornado risk score	19	19
Annual days < 0°F	0	6	Annual days snow > 1.5 inches	1	6	Hurricane risk score	28	15

TEMPERATURE

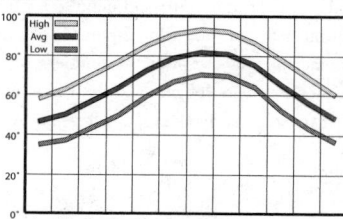

PRECIPITATION

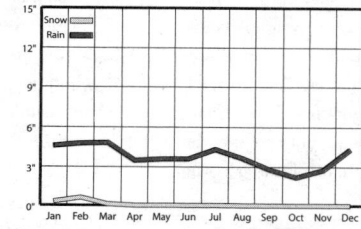

DAYS OF CLOUDS & PRECIPITATION

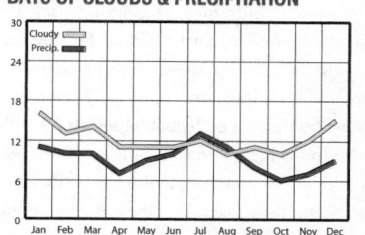

EDUCATION — SCORE: 17/RANK: 274

ACHIEVEMENT	AREA	U.S. AVG	PUBLIC SCHOOLS	AREA	U.S. AVG	HIGHER EDUCATION	AREA	U.S. AVG
High school degree	78.9%	80.2%	Expenditures per pupil	$5,425	$5,894	No. 2-year colleges	0	3
2-year college degree	5.2%	6.2%	Student/teacher ratio	16.6	16.7	No. 4-year colleges/universities	4	4
4-year college degree	12.2%	15.8%	Attending public school	88.6%	90.2%	No. highly ranked universities	0	1
Graduate/professional degree	7.3%	9.6%	State SAT score	984*	1020			
			State ACT score	19.8	21.0			

HEALTH & HEALTHCARE — SCORE: 54/RANK: 149

HAZARDS & ILLNESSES	AREA	U.S. AVG	HEALTHCARE	AREA	U.S. AVG
Air-quality score	24	45	Physicians per capita	260.2	261.1
Water-quality score	22	33	Hospital beds per capita	478.7	432.2
Pollen/allergy score	63	61	No. teaching hospitals	1	4
Stress score	69	50	Cost per doctor visit	$63	$67
Cancer mortality per capita	170.7	169.0	Cost per dental visit	$71	$82
Depression days per month	3.4	2.8	Cost per daily hospital room	$419	$733

CRIME — SCORE: 12/RANK: 290

CRIME	AREA	U.S. AVG
Violent crime rate	458.3	456.0
Change in violent crime rate	-18.5%	-17.2%
Property crime rate	5,862.3	3,950.0
Change in property crime rate	.7%	-16.8%

TRANSPORTATION — SCORE: 13/RANK: 287

COMMUTE	AREA	U.S. AVG	INTERCITY SERVICES	AREA	U.S. AVG	AUTOMOTIVE	AREA	U.S. AVG
Average commute time	22.3 min.	22.6 min.	Miles to nearest major airport	71	46	Insurance, annual premium	$1,202	$1,011
Commute by auto	93.3%	88.7%	Type of local airport	Large		Gas, cost per gallon	$1.33	$1.50
Commute by mass transit	.9%	1.8%	No. daily airline departures	1,423	294	Daily vehicle miles per capita	27.4	23.0
Work at home	1.8%	3.9%	Amtrak service	No				
Mass transit miles per capita	0.0	8.0	No. interstate highways	2	1			

LEISURE — SCORE: 10/RANK: 296

DINING & SHOPPING	AREA	U.S. AVG	ENTERTAINMENT	AREA	U.S. AVG	OUTDOOR ACTIVITIES	AREA	U.S. AVG
Restaurant rating	1	1	Professional sports rating	2	4	Golf-course rating	3	4
No. outlet malls	1	2	College sports rating	2	4	Ski-area rating	1	4
No. Starbucks	0	11	Zoo/aquarium rating	1	3	National Park rating	4	3
No. warehouse clubs	3	4	Amusement park rating	1	3	Sq. miles inland water	2.0	4.0
			Botanical garden/arboretum rating	5	3	Miles of coastline	0.0	11.4

ARTS & CULTURE — SCORE: 25/RANK: 247

MEDIA & LIBRARIES	AREA	U.S. AVG	PERFORMING ARTS	AREA	U.S. AVG	MUSEUMS	AREA	U.S. AVG
Arts radio rating	1	3	Classical music rating	3	4	Overall museum rating	5	6
No. public libraries	20	28	Ballet/dance rating	1	3	Art museum rating	6	5
Library volumes per capita	1.9	2.8	Professional theater rating	1	3	Science museum rating	7	4
			University arts programs rating	7	5	Children's museum rating	1	3

Madison, WI

Score: 80.2 Rank: 37

Profile: Capital city/College town
Location: South-central Wisconsin
Elevation: 863 feet
Time zone: Central Standard Time

PRO	CON
Attractive downtown	Cold winters
College-town amenities	Cost of living
Architectural interest	Low ethnic diversity

If it weren't for the winters and cost of living, Madison would be in serious contention for a top spot in *Cities Ranked & Rated*. The state capital and home to the University of Wisconsin, Madison is clean, attractive, and well planned. The city surrounds a pair of lakes—Lake Mendota and Lake Monona—both of which provide recreation. The area boasts many buildings of architectural interest including several designed by Frank Lloyd Wright. The surrounding countryside is beautiful and includes an assortment of outdoor recreation areas and attractions such as Taliesin, Wright's former home and studio, and the Wisconsin Dells, a collection of touristy, family attractions. Educational attainment is high, and college-town amenities abound, but one pays the price literally in housing and figuratively in winter chill. For those who can accept these negatives, the area is hard to beat.

The downtown sits on a narrow isthmus of land between Lake Mendota and Lake Monona. Madison has a continental climate with an extreme temperature range, historically—from 110°F to –40°F—and frequent temperature changes. Madison lies in the path of frequent storm systems during fall, winter, and spring. Winters are cloudy with occasional outbreaks of cold arctic air, and many days below freezing. Summers are pleasant with only occasional periods of extreme heat or high humidity. Summer months are prone to thunderstorms, and winter precipitation is lighter but lasts longer. Snow cover is common in the winter months. First freeze is early October, last is late April.

POPULATION

DEMOGRAPHICS	AREA	U.S. AVG	ETHNIC COMPOSITION	AREA	U.S. AVG	RESIDENT PROFILE	AREA	U.S. AVG
Population	443,110		White	93.9%	75.1%	Single	46.2%	43.6%
Population density per sq. mile	368.6	447.3	Black	2.6%	12.3%	Married	53.8%	56.4%
Population growth	20.7%	16.1%	Asian	2.6%	3.6%	Divorced	7.6%	8.4%
Median age	33.4	35.5	American Indian	.3%	.9%	Separated	2.0%	3.0%
Average family size	2.5	2.7	Hispanic	1.8%	12.5%	Married with children	27.6%	28.7%
			Diversity measure	22.9%	35.2%	Single with children	7.9%	10.1%

ECONOMY & JOBS SCORE: 98/RANK: 5

INCOME	AREA	U.S. AVG	EMPLOYMENT	AREA	U.S. AVG	LARGEST EMPLOYING INDUSTRY
Per capita income	$28,624	$23,420	Unemployment rate	2.9%	6.1%	Food Manufacturing
Household income	$54,655	$46,060	Recent job growth	4.5%	.9%	
Household income < $25K	19.1%	26.4%	Projected future job growth	15.0%	15.1%	
Household income > $75K	32.1%	24.5%	White collar	66.5%	54.5%	
Household income growth	66.9%	57.3%	Blue collar	33.5%	45.5%	

COST OF LIVING SCORE: 15/RANK: 280

INDEXES & TAXES	AREA	U.S. AVG	HOUSING	AREA	U.S. AVG	NECESSITIES	AREA	U.S. AVG
Cost of Living Index	105.3	100.0	Median home price	$182,000	$160,100	Food Index	100.3	100.0
Financial Progress Index	110.6	100.0	Home price appreciation	6.1%	7.1%	Housing Index	113.0	100.0
Income tax rate	6.930%	4.625%	Median rent	$716	$670	Utilities Index	118.4	100.0
Sales tax rate	5.500%	6.474%	Homes owned	62.6%	63.9%	Transportation Index	101.5	100.0
Property tax rate	$24.1	$15.6	Homes rented	34.2%	25.3%	Healthcare Index	105.6	100.0
			Housing affordability	59.0%	54.5%	Miscellaneous Cost Index	93.8	100.0

CLIMATE SCORE: 23/RANK: 252

TEMPERATURE	AREA	U.S. AVG	PRECIPITATION	AREA	U.S. AVG	COMFORTS & HAZARDS	AREA	U.S. AVG
January low	8.2°F	26.4°F	Annual inches precipitation	30.0	35.9	July relative humidity	73.0%	68.8%
July high	81.4°F	86.7°F	Annual inches snowfall	39.0	24.2	Annual days mostly sunny	190	212
Annual days > 90°F	12	38	Annual days precipitation	117	111	Annual days with thunderstorms	40	39
Annual days < 32°F	164	88	Annual days rain > 0.5 inches	18	23	Tornado risk score	24	19
Annual days < 0°F	25	6	Annual days snow > 1.5 inches	10	6	Hurricane risk score	1	15

TEMPERATURE

PRECIPITATION

DAYS OF CLOUDS & PRECIPITATION

EDUCATION SCORE: 98/RANK: 5

ACHIEVEMENT	AREA	U.S. AVG	PUBLIC SCHOOLS	AREA	U.S. AVG	HIGHER EDUCATION	AREA	U.S. AVG
High school degree	92.4%	80.2%	Expenditures per pupil	$7,553	$5,894	No. 2-year colleges	2	3
2-year college degree	8.9%	6.2%	Student/teacher ratio	13.9	16.7	No. 4-year colleges/universities	2	4
4-year college degree	24.8%	15.8%	Attending public school	91.6%	90.2%	No. highly ranked universities	0	1
Graduate/professional degree	15.8%	9.6%	State SAT score	1179	1020			
			State ACT score	22.2*	21.0			

HEALTH & HEALTHCARE SCORE: 95/RANK: 15   CRIME SCORE: 73/RANK: 89

HAZARDS & ILLNESSES	AREA	U.S. AVG	HEALTHCARE	AREA	U.S. AVG	CRIME	AREA	U.S. AVG
Air-quality score	81	45	Physicians per capita	483.9	261.1	Violent crime rate	236.1	456.0
Water-quality score	26	33	Hospital beds per capita	377.9	432.2	Change in violent crime rate	-8.9%	-17.2%
Pollen/allergy score	34	61	No. teaching hospitals	3	4	Property crime rate	3,207.9	3,950.0
Stress score	23	50	Cost per doctor visit	$74	$67	Change in property crime rate	-13.7%	-16.8%
Cancer mortality per capita	155.1	169.0	Cost per dental visit	$83	$82			
Depression days per month	2.6	2.8	Cost per daily hospital room	$493	$733			

TRANSPORTATION SCORE: 85/RANK: 49

COMMUTE	AREA	U.S. AVG	INTERCITY SERVICES	AREA	U.S. AVG	AUTOMOTIVE	AREA	U.S. AVG
Average commute time	19.9 min.	22.6 min.	Miles to nearest major airport	5	46	Insurance, annual premium	$780	$1,011
Commute by auto	82.9%	88.7%	Type of local airport	Small		Gas, cost per gallon	$1.55	$1.50
Commute by mass transit	2.4%	1.8%	No. daily airline departures	49	294	Daily vehicle miles per capita	22.2	23.0
Work at home	4.9%	3.9%	Amtrak service	No				
Mass transit miles per capita	16.4	8.0	No. interstate highways	2	1			

DINING & SHOPPING	AREA	U.S. AVG	ENTERTAINMENT	AREA	U.S. AVG	OUTDOOR ACTIVITIES	AREA	U.S. AVG
Restaurant rating	1	1	Professional sports rating	2	4	Golf-course rating	3	4
No. outlet malls	1	2	College sports rating	7	4	Ski-area rating	2	4
No. Starbucks	7	11	Zoo/aquarium rating	6	3	National Park rating	1	3
No. warehouse clubs	3	4	Amusement park rating	1	3	Sq. miles inland water	4.0	4.0
			Botanical garden/arboretum rating	8	3	Miles of coastline	0.0	11.4

MEDIA & LIBRARIES	AREA	U.S. AVG	PERFORMING ARTS	AREA	U.S. AVG	MUSEUMS	AREA	U.S. AVG
Arts radio rating	1	3	Classical music rating	4	4	Overall museum rating	7	6
No. public libraries	26	28	Ballet/dance rating	6	3	Art museum rating	7	5
Library volumes per capita	3.8	2.8	Professional theater rating	1	3	Science museum rating	2	4
			University arts programs rating	2	5	Children's museum rating	5	3

Manchester, NH

Score: 48.9　Rank: 235

Profile: Small city
Location: South-central New Hampshire on the Merrimack River
Elevation: 346 feet
Time zone: Eastern Standard Time

PRO
Revitalizing economy
Low crime rate
Historic interest

CON
Harsh winters
Arts and culture
Air service

Located at the Amoskeag Falls of the Merrimack River, Manchester has a long legacy as a mill town and textile-manufacturing center. Local citizens have worked hard to bring other industries and agriculture to the area, and today this industrial metropolis is the state's largest city.

Manchester sits in a river valley, approximately 200 feet above sea level, surrounded by hills to the west and level land with many lakes and ponds to the east. The terrain slopes gently upward from the coast about 40 miles east. The dry, New England continental climate brings cold air during winter and pleasantly cool air in summer. Fall colors are legendary. In winter, 176 days are below freezing (the 10th highest number in the U.S.) and 26 days drop below zero (the 19th highest in the U.S.). Precipitation is relatively consistent throughout the year. Heavier rains and snowfalls come with "noreasters" off the Atlantic. Snow cover normally lasts from mid-December until the end of March, but bare ground is not rare in the winter. First freeze is late September, last is late May.

DEMOGRAPHICS	AREA	U.S. AVG	ETHNIC COMPOSITION	AREA	U.S. AVG	RESIDENT PROFILE	AREA	U.S. AVG
Population	204,359		White	98.0%	75.1%	Single	41.6%	43.6%
Population density per sq. mile	647.3	447.3	Black	.6%	12.3%	Married	58.4%	56.4%
Population growth	17.6%	16.1%	Asian	.9%	3.6%	Divorced	8.4%	8.4%
Median age	37.2	35.5	American Indian	.2%	.9%	Separated	2.2%	3.0%
Average family size	2.7	2.7	Hispanic	1.5%	12.5%	Married with children	30.8%	28.7%
			Diversity measure	10.9%	35.2%	Single with children	8.5%	10.1%

INCOME	AREA	U.S. AVG	EMPLOYMENT	AREA	U.S. AVG	LARGEST EMPLOYING INDUSTRY
Per capita income	$28,647	$23,420	Unemployment rate	4.5%	6.1%	Computer and Electronic Product Manufacturing
Household income	$59,976	$46,060	Recent job growth	1.6%	.9%	
Household income < $25K	16.0%	26.4%	Projected future job growth	14.8%	15.1%	
Household income > $75K	35.3%	24.5%	White collar	62.3%	54.5%	
Household income growth	59.3%	57.3%	Blue collar	37.7%	45.5%	

INDEXES & TAXES	AREA	U.S. AVG	HOUSING	AREA	U.S. AVG	NECESSITIES	AREA	U.S. AVG
Cost of Living Index	115.5	100.0	Median home price	$202,010	$160,100	Food Index	104.2	100.0
Financial Progress Index	110.6	100.0	Home price appreciation	15.3%	7.1%	Housing Index	125.5	100.0
Income tax rate	0.000%	4.625%	Median rent	$888	$670	Utilities Index	138.9	100.0
Sales tax rate	0.000%	6.474%	Homes owned	65.3%	63.9%	Transportation Index	104.3	100.0
Property tax rate	$26.5	$15.6	Homes rented	21.2%	25.3%	Healthcare Index	111.8	100.0
			Housing affordability	51.0%	54.5%	Miscellaneous Cost Index	106.1	100.0

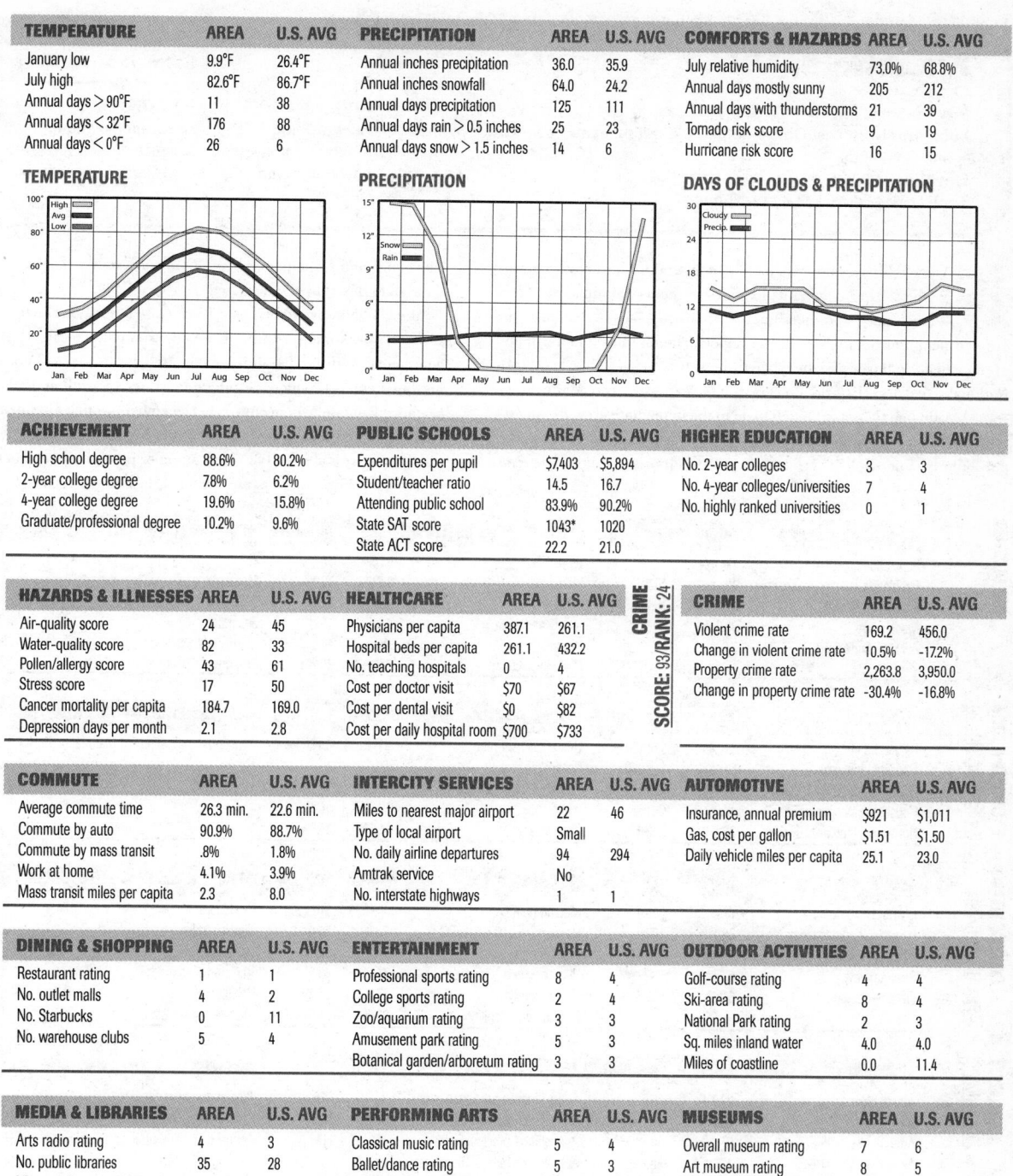

CLIMATE
SCORE: 5/RANK: 313

TEMPERATURE	AREA	U.S. AVG	PRECIPITATION	AREA	U.S. AVG	COMFORTS & HAZARDS	AREA	U.S. AVG
January low	9.9°F	26.4°F	Annual inches precipitation	36.0	35.9	July relative humidity	73.0%	68.8%
July high	82.6°F	86.7°F	Annual inches snowfall	64.0	24.2	Annual days mostly sunny	205	212
Annual days > 90°F	11	38	Annual days precipitation	125	111	Annual days with thunderstorms	21	39
Annual days < 32°F	176	88	Annual days rain > 0.5 inches	25	23	Tornado risk score	9	19
Annual days < 0°F	26	6	Annual days snow > 1.5 inches	14	6	Hurricane risk score	16	15

TEMPERATURE

PRECIPITATION

DAYS OF CLOUDS & PRECIPITATION

EDUCATION
SCORE: 80/RANK: 68

ACHIEVEMENT	AREA	U.S. AVG	PUBLIC SCHOOLS	AREA	U.S. AVG	HIGHER EDUCATION	AREA	U.S. AVG
High school degree	88.6%	80.2%	Expenditures per pupil	$7,403	$5,894	No. 2-year colleges	3	3
2-year college degree	7.8%	6.2%	Student/teacher ratio	14.5	16.7	No. 4-year colleges/universities	7	4
4-year college degree	19.6%	15.8%	Attending public school	83.9%	90.2%	No. highly ranked universities	0	1
Graduate/professional degree	10.2%	9.6%	State SAT score	1043*	1020			
			State ACT score	22.2	21.0			

HEALTH & HEALTHCARE
SCORE: 62/RANK: 123

CRIME
SCORE: 93/RANK: 24

HAZARDS & ILLNESSES	AREA	U.S. AVG	HEALTHCARE	AREA	U.S. AVG	CRIME	AREA	U.S. AVG
Air-quality score	24	45	Physicians per capita	387.1	261.1	Violent crime rate	169.2	456.0
Water-quality score	82	33	Hospital beds per capita	261.1	432.2	Change in violent crime rate	10.5%	-17.2%
Pollen/allergy score	43	61	No. teaching hospitals	0	4	Property crime rate	2,263.8	3,950.0
Stress score	17	50	Cost per doctor visit	$70	$67	Change in property crime rate	-30.4%	-16.8%
Cancer mortality per capita	184.7	169.0	Cost per dental visit	$0	$82			
Depression days per month	2.1	2.8	Cost per daily hospital room	$700	$733			

TRANSPORTATION
SCORE: 2/RANK: 324

COMMUTE	AREA	U.S. AVG	INTERCITY SERVICES	AREA	U.S. AVG	AUTOMOTIVE	AREA	U.S. AVG
Average commute time	26.3 min.	22.6 min.	Miles to nearest major airport	22	46	Insurance, annual premium	$921	$1,011
Commute by auto	90.9%	88.7%	Type of local airport	Small		Gas, cost per gallon	$1.51	$1.50
Commute by mass transit	.8%	1.8%	No. daily airline departures	94	294	Daily vehicle miles per capita	25.1	23.0
Work at home	4.1%	3.9%	Amtrak service	No				
Mass transit miles per capita	2.3	8.0	No. interstate highways	1	1			

LEISURE
SCORE: 68/RANK: 104

DINING & SHOPPING	AREA	U.S. AVG	ENTERTAINMENT	AREA	U.S. AVG	OUTDOOR ACTIVITIES	AREA	U.S. AVG
Restaurant rating	1	1	Professional sports rating	8	4	Golf-course rating	4	4
No. outlet malls	4	2	College sports rating	2	4	Ski-area rating	8	4
No. Starbucks	0	11	Zoo/aquarium rating	3	3	National Park rating	2	3
No. warehouse clubs	5	4	Amusement park rating	5	3	Sq. miles inland water	4.0	4.0
			Botanical garden/arboretum rating	3	3	Miles of coastline	0.0	11.4

ARTS & CULTURE
SCORE: 27/RANK: 239

MEDIA & LIBRARIES	AREA	U.S. AVG	PERFORMING ARTS	AREA	U.S. AVG	MUSEUMS	AREA	U.S. AVG
Arts radio rating	4	3	Classical music rating	5	4	Overall museum rating	7	6
No. public libraries	35	28	Ballet/dance rating	5	3	Art museum rating	8	5
Library volumes per capita	3.5	2.8	Professional theater rating	5	3	Science museum rating	7	4
			University arts programs rating	4	5	Children's museum rating	6	3

Mansfield, OH

Score: 75.0   Rank: 61

Profile: Small town
Location: Northeast Ohio along I-71 about half way between Cleveland and Columbus
Elevation: 1,230 feet
Time zone: Eastern Standard Time

PRO	CON
Cost of living	Unemployment
Small-town flavor	Arts and culture
Low crime rate	Cloudy, wet winters

Mansfield is a mid-size, mostly industrial town in north-central Ohio. The dominant industries—heavy equipment, farm machinery, and metallurgical industries—have declined but are still healthier than others in the region. The city has a better-than-average historic flavor and many sites are well preserved. It won a 2001 National Trust for Historic Preservation Great American Main Street Award. Although there isn't much to do in the immediate area, the small-town environment brings a low cost of living (COL Index of 87.3) and a particularly low violent crime rate. The city is located between Cleveland and Columbus, about 70 miles from each, giving access to their amenities and services.

Mansfield is surrounded by rolling, open farmland. The terrain slopes gently downward toward Lake Erie, 38 miles to the north. The climate is continental with temperatures moderated by the lake. Persistent cold northerly winds produce considerable winter snowfall and cloudy skies. Consistent snow cover occurs from December through March, and spring is short. Lake breezes moderate the hot, humid summers, but temperatures rarely rise above 90°F. Most summer precipitation comes as thundershowers. First freeze is mid-October, last is late April.

POPULATION

DEMOGRAPHICS	AREA	U.S. AVG	ETHNIC COMPOSITION	AREA	U.S. AVG	RESIDENT PROFILE	AREA	U.S. AVG
Population	174,424		White	93.5%	75.1%	Single	40.0%	43.6%
Population density per sq. mile	193.9	447.3	Black	5.6%	12.3%	Married	60.0%	56.4%
Population growth	.2%	16.1%	Asian	.5%	3.6%	Divorced	9.0%	8.4%
Median age	38.3	35.5	American Indian	.2%	.9%	Separated	1.9%	3.0%
Average family size	2.6	2.7	Hispanic	.8%	12.5%	Married with children	29.2%	28.7%
			Diversity measure	17.8%	35.2%	Single with children	9.8%	10.1%

ECONOMY & JOBS   SCORE: 41/RANK: 194

INCOME	AREA	U.S. AVG	EMPLOYMENT	AREA	U.S. AVG	LARGEST EMPLOYING INDUSTRY
Per capita income	$18,458	$23,420	Unemployment rate	7.1%	6.1%	Transportation Equipment Manufacturing
Household income	$36,080	$46,060	Recent job growth	.9%	.9%	
Household income < $25K	31.9%	26.4%	Projected future job growth	12.3%	15.1%	
Household income > $75K	13.0%	24.5%	White collar	43.9%	54.5%	
Household income growth	35.6%	57.3%	Blue collar	56.1%	45.5%	

COST OF LIVING   SCORE: 76/RANK: 78

INDEXES & TAXES	AREA	U.S. AVG	HOUSING	AREA	U.S. AVG	NECESSITIES	AREA	U.S. AVG
Cost of Living Index	87.3	100.0	Median home price	$99,800	$160,100	Food Index	104.9	100.0
Financial Progress Index	88.1	100.0	Home price appreciation	5.3%	7.1%	Housing Index	62.0	100.0
Income tax rate	4.993%	4.625%	Median rent	$471	$670	Utilities Index	126.2	100.0
Sales tax rate	6.250%	6.474%	Homes owned	71.0%	63.9%	Transportation Index	96.6	100.0
Property tax rate	$12.2	$15.6	Homes rented	22.7%	25.3%	Healthcare Index	91.4	100.0
			Housing affordability	65.0%	54.5%	Miscellaneous Cost Index	95.2	100.0

CLIMATE   SCORE: 23/RANK: 253

TEMPERATURE	AREA	U.S. AVG	PRECIPITATION	AREA	U.S. AVG	COMFORTS & HAZARDS	AREA	U.S. AVG
January low	20.7°F	26.4°F	Annual inches precipitation	33.7	35.9	July relative humidity	73.0%	68.8%
July high	83.7°F	86.7°F	Annual inches snowfall	42.2	24.2	Annual days mostly sunny	173	212
Annual days > 90°F	7	38	Annual days precipitation	152	111	Annual days with thunderstorms	39	39
Annual days < 32°F	127	88	Annual days rain > 0.5 inches	23	23	Tornado risk score	22	19
Annual days < 0°F	7	6	Annual days snow > 1.5 inches	8	6	Hurricane risk score	2	15

TEMPERATURE

PRECIPITATION

DAYS OF CLOUDS & PRECIPITATION

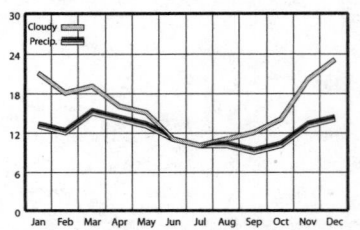

EDUCATION SCORE: 13/RANK: 286

ACHIEVEMENT	AREA	U.S. AVG	PUBLIC SCHOOLS	AREA	U.S. AVG	HIGHER EDUCATION	AREA	U.S. AVG
High school degree	80.2%	80.2%	Expenditures per pupil	$5,990	$5,894	No. 2-year colleges	2	3
2-year college degree	5.8%	6.2%	Student/teacher ratio	14.7	16.7	No. 4-year colleges/universities	0	4
4-year college degree	8.8%	15.8%	Attending public school	91.2%	90.2%	No. highly ranked universities	0	1
Graduate/professional degree	3.7%	9.6%	State SAT score	1077	1020			
			State ACT score	21.4*	21.0			

HEALTH & HEALTHCARE SCORE: 60/RANK: 131

CRIME SCORE: 75/RANK: 83

HAZARDS & ILLNESSES	AREA	U.S. AVG	HEALTHCARE	AREA	U.S. AVG	CRIME	AREA	U.S. AVG
Air-quality score	3	45	Physicians per capita	143.9	261.1	Violent crime rate	161.8	456.0
Water-quality score	9	33	Hospital beds per capita	445.3	432.2	Change in violent crime rate	-77.9%	-17.2%
Pollen/allergy score	58	61	No. teaching hospitals	0	4	Property crime rate	4,007.2	3,950.0
Stress score	78	50	Cost per doctor visit	$62	$67	Change in property crime rate	-7.8%	-16.8%
Cancer mortality per capita	170.3	169.0	Cost per dental visit	$73	$82			
Depression days per month	2.8	2.8	Cost per daily hospital room	$586	$733			

TRANSPORTATION SCORE: 38/RANK: 205

COMMUTE	AREA	U.S. AVG	INTERCITY SERVICES	AREA	U.S. AVG	AUTOMOTIVE	AREA	U.S. AVG
Average commute time	20.2 min.	22.6 min.	Miles to nearest major airport	56	46	Insurance, annual premium	$794	$1,011
Commute by auto	92.1%	88.7%	Type of local airport	Medium		Gas, cost per gallon	$1.45	$1.50
Commute by mass transit	.5%	1.8%	No. daily airline departures	270	294	Daily vehicle miles per capita	15.9	23.0
Work at home	3.5%	3.9%	Amtrak service	No				
Mass transit miles per capita	1.9	8.0	No. interstate highways	1	1			

LEISURE SCORE: 31/RANK: 232

DINING & SHOPPING	AREA	U.S. AVG	ENTERTAINMENT	AREA	U.S. AVG	OUTDOOR ACTIVITIES	AREA	U.S. AVG
Restaurant rating	1	1	Professional sports rating		4	Golf-course rating	2	4
No. outlet malls	1	2	College sports rating	5	4	Ski-area rating	3	4
No. Starbucks	0	11	Zoo/aquarium rating	1	3	National Park rating	1	3
No. warehouse clubs	3	4	Amusement park rating	1	3	Sq. miles inland water	2.0	4.0
			Botanical garden/arboretum rating	5	3	Miles of coastline	0.0	11.4

ARTS & CULTURE SCORE: 29/RANK: 234

MEDIA & LIBRARIES	AREA	U.S. AVG	PERFORMING ARTS	AREA	U.S. AVG	MUSEUMS	AREA	U.S. AVG
Arts radio rating	5	3	Classical music rating	3	4	Overall museum rating	5	6
No. public libraries	14	28	Ballet/dance rating	1	3	Art museum rating	2	5
Library volumes per capita	4.4	2.8	Professional theater rating	1	3	Science museum rating	1	4
			University arts programs rating	3	5	Children's museum rating	1	3

McAllen-Edinburgh-Mission, TX

Score: 23.8   Rank: 317

Profile: Mid-size–border-city complex
Location: Extreme south Texas along the Rio Grande and Mexican border, 80 miles inland from the Gulf of Mexico
Elevation: 104 feet
Time zone: Central Standard Time

PRO	CON
Cost of living	Urban sprawl
Strong projected job growth	Low educational attainment
Pleasant winters	Heat and humidity

McAllen is dominated by local agriculture, border-zone factories, and commerce related to the port of entry at Reynosa into Mexico. Like other border towns, it has a dominant Hispanic heritage, high growth rate, and a low cost of living. The city, which has a reputation for being quieter than the border towns of Brownsville and Laredo, has a nice downtown area and is nicknamed "City of Palms." The area serves the needs of wealthy Mexican residents from northern Mexico as far south as Monterrey. There are many new businesses run by Mexicans. Median home prices are just over $61,000—the lowest in the country. But the general economic picture, particularly current unemployment, is bleak, and there are poor residential areas around the city. Cultural and recreational amenities are minor and locally focused.

For a metropolitan area of its size, it tops the Sierra Club's list of places most threatened by urban sprawl.

The Rio Grande Valley around McAllen is flat and agricultural, giving way to low hills and desert sage and chaparral vegetation to the northwest. The climate is subtropical, influenced by the Gulf of Mexico to the east and the Chihuahuan Desert and mountains to the west. Summers are hot with periods of rain and stronger storms—most days are over 90°F. Although not quite as humid year-round as Texas cities to the east, summers are humid and uncomfortable. Winters are mild, with maybe one or two below-freezing spells, and the very occasional dusting of snow, usually in January.

POPULATION

DEMOGRAPHICS	AREA	U.S. AVG	ETHNIC COMPOSITION	AREA	U.S. AVG	RESIDENT PROFILE	AREA	U.S. AVG
Population	614,474		White	79.1%	75.1%	Single	44.5%	43.6%
Population density per sq. mile	391.6	447.3	Black	.9%	12.3%	Married	55.5%	56.4%
Population growth	60.2%	16.1%	Asian	.4%	3.6%	Divorced	4.6%	8.4%
Median age	27.2	35.5	American Indian	.2%	.9%	Separated	4.2%	3.0%
Average family size	3.8	2.7	Hispanic	89.7%	12.5%	Married with children	42.2%	28.7%
			Diversity measure	23.8%	35.2%	Single with children	15.1%	10.1%

ECONOMY & JOBS
SCORE: 2/RANK: 324

INCOME	AREA	U.S. AVG	EMPLOYMENT	AREA	U.S. AVG	LARGEST EMPLOYING INDUSTRY
Per capita income	$10,661	$23,420	Unemployment rate	13.6%	6.1%	Healthcare and Social Assistance
Household income	$25,726	$46,060	Recent job growth	5.6%	.9%	
Household income < $25K	48.9%	26.4%	Projected future job growth	26.2%	15.1%	
Household income > $75K	10.1%	24.5%	White collar	46.8%	54.5%	
Household income growth	53.6%	57.3%	Blue collar	53.2%	45.5%	

COST OF LIVING
SCORE: 99/RANK: 4

INDEXES & TAXES	AREA	U.S. AVG	HOUSING	AREA	U.S. AVG	NECESSITIES	AREA	U.S. AVG
Cost of Living Index	74.2	100.0	Median home price	$61,460	$160,100	Food Index	80.2	100.0
Financial Progress Index	73.9	100.0	Home price appreciation	5.5%	7.1%	Housing Index	38.2	100.0
Income tax rate	0.000%	4.625%	Median rent	$451	$670	Utilities Index	97.1	100.0
Sales tax rate	8.250%	6.474%	Homes owned	61.6%	63.9%	Transportation Index	96.9	100.0
Property tax rate	$23.5	$15.6	Homes rented	23.3%	25.3%	Healthcare Index	106.5	100.0
			Housing affordability	48.0%	54.5%	Miscellaneous Cost Index	100.0	100.0

CLIMATE
SCORE: 76/RANK: 80

TEMPERATURE	AREA	U.S. AVG	PRECIPITATION	AREA	U.S. AVG	COMFORTS & HAZARDS	AREA	U.S. AVG
January low	43.6°F	26.4°F	Annual inches precipitation	34.3	35.9	July relative humidity	74.0%	68.8%
July high	93.4°F	86.7°F	Annual inches snowfall	.2	24.2	Annual days mostly sunny	204	212
Annual days > 90°F	101	38	Annual days precipitation	88	111	Annual days with thunderstorms	48	39
Annual days < 32°F	12	88	Annual days rain > 0.5 inches	19	23	Tornado risk score	14	19
Annual days < 0°F	0	6	Annual days snow > 1.5 inches	0	6	Hurricane risk score	37	15

TEMPERATURE

PRECIPITATION

DAYS OF CLOUDS & PRECIPITATION

EDUCATION
SCORE: 0/RANK: 329

ACHIEVEMENT	AREA	U.S. AVG	PUBLIC SCHOOLS	AREA	U.S. AVG	HIGHER EDUCATION	AREA	U.S. AVG
High school degree	50.4%	80.2%	Expenditures per pupil	$5,679	$5,894	No. 2-year colleges	0	3
2-year college degree	3.1%	6.2%	Student/teacher ratio	15.6	16.7	No. 4-year colleges/universities	1	4
4-year college degree	8.4%	15.8%	Attending public school	97.8%	90.2%	No. highly ranked universities	0	1
Graduate/professional degree	4.5%	9.6%	State SAT score	993*	1020			
			State ACT score	20.1	21.0			

HEALTH & HEALTHCARE
SCORE: 5/RANK: 314

HAZARDS & ILLNESSES	AREA	U.S. AVG	HEALTHCARE	AREA	U.S. AVG
Air-quality score	24	45	Physicians per capita	105.6	261.1
Water-quality score	13	33	Hospital beds per capita	237.6	432.2
Pollen/allergy score	83	61	No. teaching hospitals	1	4
Stress score	37	50	Cost per doctor visit	$60	$67
Cancer mortality per capita	119.9	169.0	Cost per dental visit	$68	$82
Depression days per month	1.7	2.8	Cost per daily hospital room	$716	$733

CRIME
SCORE: 17/RANK: 273

CRIME	AREA	U.S. AVG
Violent crime rate	546.5	456.0
Change in violent crime rate	-.6%	-17.2%
Property crime rate	5,304.0	3,950.0
Change in property crime rate	-14.4%	-16.8%

TRANSPORTATION
SCORE: 25/RANK: 247

COMMUTE	AREA	U.S. AVG	INTERCITY SERVICES	AREA	U.S. AVG	AUTOMOTIVE	AREA	U.S. AVG
Average commute time	20.9 min.	22.6 min.	Miles to nearest major airport	41	46	Insurance, annual premium	$962	$1,011
Commute by auto	90.1%	88.7%	Type of local airport	Small		Gas, cost per gallon	$1.38	$1.50
Commute by mass transit	.9%	1.8%	No. daily airline departures	28	294	Daily vehicle miles per capita	22.0	23.0
Work at home	3.6%	3.9%	Amtrak service	No				
Mass transit miles per capita	0.0	8.0	No. interstate highways	0	1			

LEISURE SCORE: 20/RANK: 264	DINING & SHOPPING	AREA	U.S. AVG	ENTERTAINMENT	AREA	U.S. AVG	OUTDOOR ACTIVITIES	AREA	U.S. AVG
	Restaurant rating	1	1	Professional sports rating	2	4	Golf-course rating	2	4
	No. outlet malls	0	2	College sports rating	3	4	Ski-area rating	1	4
	No. Starbucks	0	11	Zoo/aquarium rating	1	3	National Park rating	2	3
	No. warehouse clubs	3	4	Amusement park rating	1	3	Sq. miles inland water	3.0	4.0
				Botanical garden/arboretum rating	2	3	Miles of coastline	0.0	11.4

ARTS & CULTURE SCORE: 9/RANK: 299	MEDIA & LIBRARIES	AREA	U.S. AVG	PERFORMING ARTS	AREA	U.S. AVG	MUSEUMS	AREA	U.S. AVG
	Arts radio rating	1	3	Classical music rating	3	4	Overall museum rating	5	6
	No. public libraries	12	28	Ballet/dance rating	1	3	Art museum rating	5	5
	Library volumes per capita	1.5	2.8	Professional theater rating	1	3	Science museum rating	5	4
				University arts programs rating	4	5	Children's museum rating	1	3

Medford-Ashland, OR

Score: 72.1 Rank: 72

Profile: Small-town complex
Location: Southern Oregon along I-5, 30 miles north of the California border
Elevation: 1,298 feet
Time zone: Pacific Standard Time

PRO
Nearby recreation
Attractive setting
College-town element

CON
Recent unemployment
Air quality
Low ethnic diversity

Medford is an agricultural and timber processing center known for fruit growing—particularly pears. The city itself is fairly nondescript but has a full complement of shopping and retail establishments popular with locals and Californians passing through to avoid sales tax. The timber industry is active but in long-term decline. Skiing, watersports, mountain biking, rafting, and hiking opportunities are abundant in the nearby mountains and Rogue River Valley. Ashland, 10 miles south, is a college town and arts community with a renowned annual Shakespeare festival. Proximity to California and local amenities, especially in Ashland, have driven costs and home prices to relatively high levels for this type of community, but on a West Coast scale the area is still attractive.

The Medford area is located in a mountain valley formed by the Rogue River and one of its tributaries. The valley is mainly farmland with tree-covered foothills and mountains. Ashland is located along the ascent toward Siskiyou Summit to the south. The climate is moderate with marked seasonal characteristics. Late fall, winter, and early spring are damp, cloudy, and cool under a marine influence. The rest of the year is sunny, warm, and dry. Summer high temperatures are around 90°F with low humidity and nights cooled by mountain air. There are occasional hot spells with dry heat in the 100s. The Siskiyou and Coast Range rain shadows result in relatively light annual and mostly winter rainfall. Heavy winter snowfall in the surrounding mountains provides excellent skiing, but there is little snowfall in the valley. The valley tends to fill with fog.

POPULATION	DEMOGRAPHICS	AREA	U.S. AVG	ETHNIC COMPOSITION	AREA	U.S. AVG	RESIDENT PROFILE	AREA	U.S. AVG
	Population	186,430		White	95.5%	75.1%	Single	39.4%	43.6%
	Population density per sq. mile	66.9	447.3	Black	.3%	12.3%	Married	60.6%	56.4%
	Population growth	27.4%	16.1%	Asian	1.1%	3.6%	Divorced	11.6%	8.4%
	Median age	39.8	35.5	American Indian	1.8%	.9%	Separated	2.9%	3.0%
	Average family size	2.5	2.7	Hispanic	5.9%	12.5%	Married with children	24.5%	28.7%
				Diversity measure	20.5%	35.2%	Single with children	10.6%	10.1%

ECONOMY & JOBS SCORE: 9/RANK: 300	INCOME	AREA	U.S. AVG	EMPLOYMENT	AREA	U.S. AVG	LARGEST EMPLOYING INDUSTRY
	Per capita income	$20,447	$23,420	Unemployment rate	6.8%	6.1%	Wood Product Manufacturing
	Household income	$38,067	$46,060	Recent job growth	2.2%	.9%	
	Household income < $25K	30.9%	26.4%	Projected future job growth	22.3%	15.1%	
	Household income > $75K	15.9%	24.5%	White collar	48.5%	54.5%	
	Household income growth	51.7%	57.3%	Blue collar	51.5%	45.5%	

COST OF LIVING SCORE: 35/RANK: 213	INDEXES & TAXES	AREA	U.S. AVG	HOUSING	AREA	U.S. AVG	NECESSITIES	AREA	U.S. AVG
	Cost of Living Index	106.0	100.0	Median home price	$181,420	$160,100	Food Index	109.0	100.0
	Financial Progress Index	76.5	100.0	Home price appreciation	9.0%	7.1%	Housing Index	112.7	100.0
	Income tax rate	9.000%	4.625%	Median rent	$659	$670	Utilities Index	74.5	100.0
	Sales tax rate	0.000%	6.474%	Homes owned	67.9%	63.9%	Transportation Index	103.8	100.0
	Property tax rate	$14.9	$15.6	Homes rented	25.7%	25.3%	Healthcare Index	110.3	100.0
				Housing affordability	52.0%	54.5%	Miscellaneous Cost Index	104.1	100.0

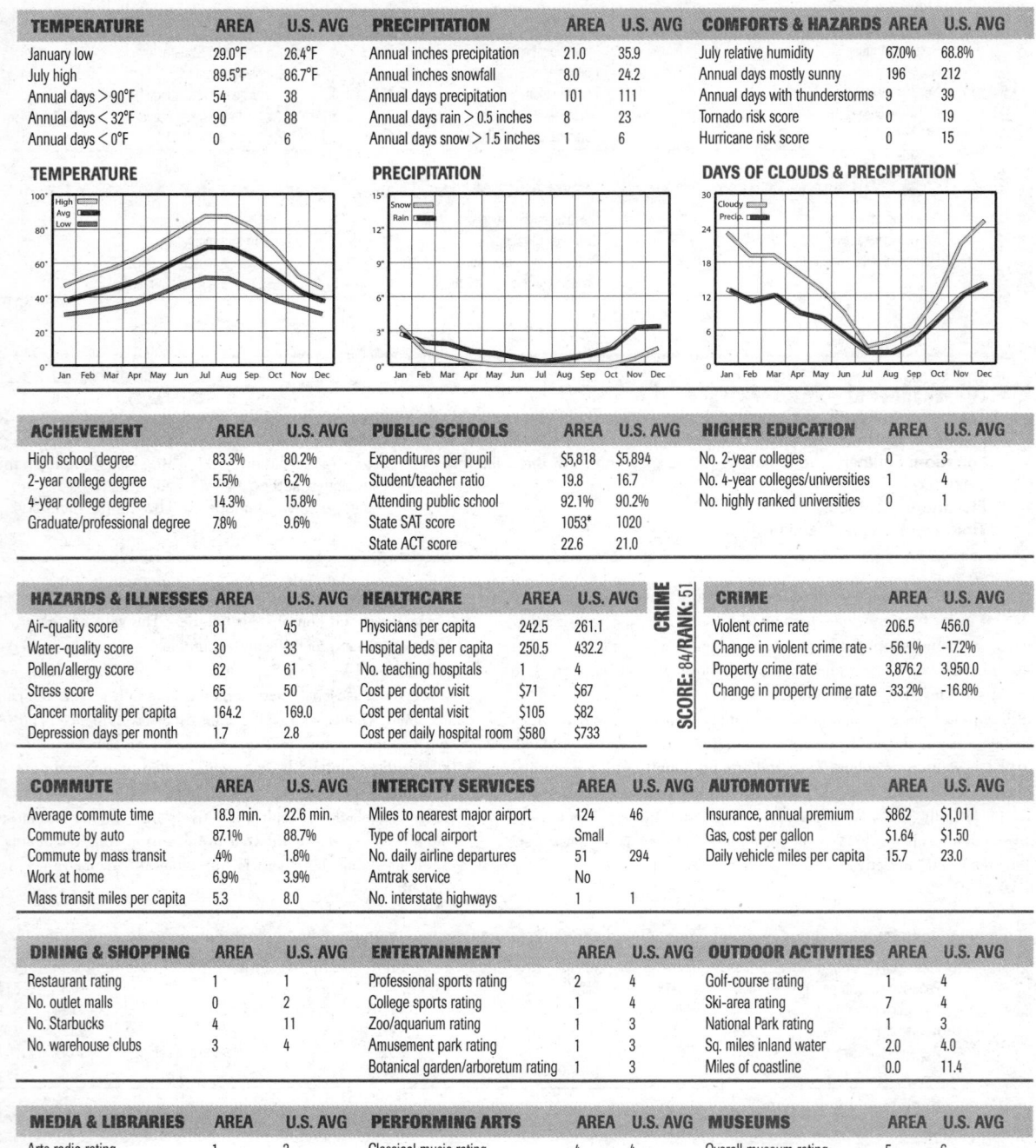

CLIMATE SCORE: 57/RANK: 142

TEMPERATURE	AREA	U.S. AVG	PRECIPITATION	AREA	U.S. AVG	COMFORTS & HAZARDS	AREA	U.S. AVG
January low	29.0°F	26.4°F	Annual inches precipitation	21.0	35.9	July relative humidity	67.0%	68.8%
July high	89.5°F	86.7°F	Annual inches snowfall	8.0	24.2	Annual days mostly sunny	196	212
Annual days > 90°F	54	38	Annual days precipitation	101	111	Annual days with thunderstorms	9	39
Annual days < 32°F	90	88	Annual days rain > 0.5 inches	8	23	Tornado risk score	0	19
Annual days < 0°F	0	6	Annual days snow > 1.5 inches	1	6	Hurricane risk score	0	15

TEMPERATURE PRECIPITATION DAYS OF CLOUDS & PRECIPITATION

EDUCATION SCORE: 32/RANK: 223

ACHIEVEMENT	AREA	U.S. AVG	PUBLIC SCHOOLS	AREA	U.S. AVG	HIGHER EDUCATION	AREA	U.S. AVG
High school degree	83.3%	80.2%	Expenditures per pupil	$5,818	$5,894	No. 2-year colleges	0	3
2-year college degree	5.5%	6.2%	Student/teacher ratio	19.8	16.7	No. 4-year colleges/universities	1	4
4-year college degree	14.3%	15.8%	Attending public school	92.1%	90.2%	No. highly ranked universities	0	1
Graduate/professional degree	7.8%	9.6%	State SAT score	1053*	1020			
			State ACT score	22.6	21.0			

HEALTH & HEALTHCARE SCORE: 63/RANK: 122

CRIME SCORE: 84/RANK: 51

HAZARDS & ILLNESSES	AREA	U.S. AVG	HEALTHCARE	AREA	U.S. AVG	CRIME	AREA	U.S. AVG
Air-quality score	81	45	Physicians per capita	242.5	261.1	Violent crime rate	206.5	456.0
Water-quality score	30	33	Hospital beds per capita	250.5	432.2	Change in violent crime rate	-56.1%	-17.2%
Pollen/allergy score	62	61	No. teaching hospitals	1	4	Property crime rate	3,876.2	3,950.0
Stress score	65	50	Cost per doctor visit	$71	$67	Change in property crime rate	-33.2%	-16.8%
Cancer mortality per capita	164.2	169.0	Cost per dental visit	$105	$82			
Depression days per month	1.7	2.8	Cost per daily hospital room	$580	$733			

TRANSPORTATION SCORE: 67/RANK: 109

COMMUTE	AREA	U.S. AVG	INTERCITY SERVICES	AREA	U.S. AVG	AUTOMOTIVE	AREA	U.S. AVG
Average commute time	18.9 min.	22.6 min.	Miles to nearest major airport	124	46	Insurance, annual premium	$862	$1,011
Commute by auto	87.1%	88.7%	Type of local airport	Small		Gas, cost per gallon	$1.64	$1.50
Commute by mass transit	.4%	1.8%	No. daily airline departures	51	294	Daily vehicle miles per capita	15.7	23.0
Work at home	6.9%	3.9%	Amtrak service	No				
Mass transit miles per capita	5.3	8.0	No. interstate highways	1	1			

LEISURE SCORE: 38/RANK: 205

DINING & SHOPPING	AREA	U.S. AVG	ENTERTAINMENT	AREA	U.S. AVG	OUTDOOR ACTIVITIES	AREA	U.S. AVG
Restaurant rating	1	1	Professional sports rating	2	4	Golf-course rating	1	4
No. outlet malls	0	2	College sports rating	1	4	Ski-area rating	7	4
No. Starbucks	4	11	Zoo/aquarium rating	1	3	National Park rating	1	3
No. warehouse clubs	3	4	Amusement park rating	1	3	Sq. miles inland water	2.0	4.0
			Botanical garden/arboretum rating	1	3	Miles of coastline	0.0	11.4

ARTS & CULTURE SCORE: 66/RANK: 110

MEDIA & LIBRARIES	AREA	U.S. AVG	PERFORMING ARTS	AREA	U.S. AVG	MUSEUMS	AREA	U.S. AVG
Arts radio rating	1	3	Classical music rating	4	4	Overall museum rating	5	6
No. public libraries	15	28	Ballet/dance rating	3	3	Art museum rating	2	5
Library volumes per capita	2.8	2.8	Professional theater rating	10	3	Science museum rating	2	4
			University arts programs rating	1	5	Children's museum rating	6	3

Melbourne–Titusville–Palm Bay, FL

Score: 74.4   Rank: 64

Profile: Beach-city complex
Location: Central Atlantic coast, 50 miles east/southeast of Orlando
Elevation: 31 feet
Time zone: Eastern Standard Time

PRO	CON
Climate	Violent crime
Water recreation	Low income growth
Cost of living	Arts and culture

Melbourne, together with the cities of Titusville, Cocoa Beach, and Palm Bay, comprise an area known as the "Space Coast." Cape Canaveral and the John F. Kennedy Space Center are located on the large barrier islands off the coast, adding interest and economic benefits to the area. There are fine beaches on the barrier islands, while the inland cities tend to carry most of the commercial, residential, and agricultural activity and are considerably less attractive. The cost of living and housing are reasonable, but income growth projections are among the lowest in Florida. Some arts and culture amenities are absent.

The area ranks high because of climate, recreation, cost of living, and overall quality of life and the lack of strong negatives.

The narrow barrier islands are mainly sand and palm trees, becoming wider towards Cape Canaveral. Inland is a mix of agriculture and marshland with a few inland lakes. Climate is typical for the Florida coast. Summer temperatures, while reaching 90°F or above during the late morning or early afternoon, tend to diminish in the afternoon due to sea breezes and frequent afternoon thundershowers. Winters are relatively mild. Summer is the rainy season with thunderstorms, many quite heavy.

POPULATION

DEMOGRAPHICS	AREA	U.S. AVG	ETHNIC COMPOSITION	AREA	U.S. AVG	RESIDENT PROFILE	AREA	U.S. AVG
Population	495,576		White	88.7%	75.1%	Single	40.6%	43.6%
Population density per sq. mile	486.6	447.3	Black	8.3%	12.3%	Married	59.4%	56.4%
Population growth	24.2%	16.1%	Asian	1.9%	3.6%	Divorced	10.3%	8.4%
Median age	42.1	35.5	American Indian	.4%	.9%	Separated	2.9%	3.0%
Average family size	2.4	2.7	Hispanic	5.2%	12.5%	Married with children	22.3%	28.7%
			Diversity measure	28.4%	35.2%	Single with children	8.8%	10.1%

ECONOMY & JOBS   SCORE: 43/RANK: 187

INCOME	AREA	U.S. AVG	EMPLOYMENT	AREA	U.S. AVG	LARGEST EMPLOYING INDUSTRY
Per capita income	$22,658	$23,420	Unemployment rate	4.9%	6.1%	Computer and Electronic Product Manufacturing
Household income	$41,183	$46,060	Recent job growth	-1.8%	.9%	
Household income < $25K	27.0%	26.4%	Projected future job growth	13.3%	15.1%	
Household income > $75K	18.8%	24.5%	White collar	59.4%	54.5%	
Household income growth	34.5%	57.3%	Blue collar	40.6%	45.5%	

COST OF LIVING   SCORE: 91/RANK: 28

INDEXES & TAXES	AREA	U.S. AVG	HOUSING	AREA	U.S. AVG	NECESSITIES	AREA	U.S. AVG
Cost of Living Index	90.4	100.0	Median home price	$115,600	$160,100	Food Index	99.6	100.0
Financial Progress Index	97.0	100.0	Home price appreciation	9.7%	7.1%	Housing Index	71.8	100.0
Income tax rate	0.000%	4.625%	Median rent	$613	$670	Utilities Index	98.4	100.0
Sales tax rate	6.000%	6.474%	Homes owned	63.2%	63.9%	Transportation Index	103.4	100.0
Property tax rate	$14.6	$15.6	Homes rented	25.2%	25.3%	Healthcare Index	102.5	100.0
			Housing affordability	59.0%	54.5%	Miscellaneous Cost Index	101.2	100.0

CLIMATE   SCORE: 76/RANK: 77

TEMPERATURE	AREA	U.S. AVG	PRECIPITATION	AREA	U.S. AVG	COMFORTS & HAZARDS	AREA	U.S. AVG
January low	47.6°F	26.4°F	Annual inches precipitation	50.2	35.9	July relative humidity	78.0%	68.8%
July high	89.6°F	86.7°F	Annual inches snowfall	0.0	24.2	Annual days mostly sunny	229	212
Annual days > 90°F	54	38	Annual days precipitation	115	111	Annual days with thunderstorms	79	39
Annual days < 32°F	5	88	Annual days rain > 0.5 inches	31	23	Tornado risk score	30	19
Annual days < 0°F	0	6	Annual days snow > 1.5 inches	0	6	Hurricane risk score	79	15

TEMPERATURE

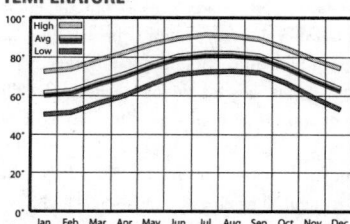

PRECIPITATION

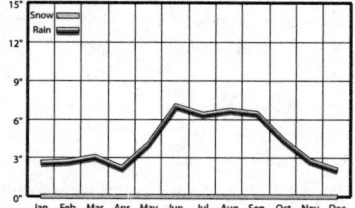

DAYS OF CLOUDS & PRECIPITATION

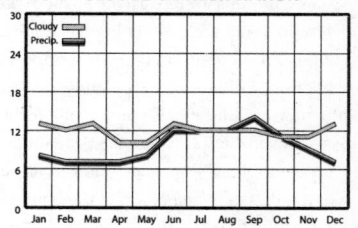

EDUCATION — SCORE: 56/RANK: 144

ACHIEVEMENT	AREA	U.S. AVG	PUBLIC SCHOOLS	AREA	U.S. AVG	HIGHER EDUCATION	AREA	U.S. AVG
High school degree	85.3%	80.2%	Expenditures per pupil	$4,817	$5,894	No. 2-year colleges	1	3
2-year college degree	9.2%	6.2%	Student/teacher ratio	17.7	16.7	No. 4-year colleges/universities	1	4
4-year college degree	15.2%	15.8%	Attending public school	88.4%	90.2%	No. highly ranked universities	1	1
Graduate/professional degree	8.4%	9.6%	State SAT score	996*	1020			
			State ACT score	20.5	21.0			

HEALTH & HEALTHCARE — SCORE: 35/RANK: 213

CRIME — SCORE: 20/RANK: 265

HAZARDS & ILLNESSES	AREA	U.S. AVG	HEALTHCARE	AREA	U.S. AVG	CRIME	AREA	U.S. AVG
Air-quality score	6	45	Physicians per capita	209.0	261.1	Violent crime rate	769.8	456.0
Water-quality score	6	33	Hospital beds per capita	292.5	432.2	Change in violent crime rate	-1.1%	-17.2%
Pollen/allergy score	77	61	No. teaching hospitals	0	4	Property crime rate	4,176.9	3,950.0
Stress score	88	50	Cost per doctor visit	$70	$67	Change in property crime rate	-15.3%	-16.8%
Cancer mortality per capita	177.8	169.0	Cost per dental visit	$79	$82			
Depression days per month	2.6	2.8	Cost per daily hospital room	$656	$733			

TRANSPORTATION — SCORE: 18/RANK: 268

COMMUTE	AREA	U.S. AVG	INTERCITY SERVICES	AREA	U.S. AVG	AUTOMOTIVE	AREA	U.S. AVG
Average commute time	24.5 min.	22.6 min.	Miles to nearest major airport	1	46	Insurance, annual premium	$1,036	$1,011
Commute by auto	93.1%	88.7%	Type of local airport	Small		Gas, cost per gallon	$1.47	$1.50
Commute by mass transit	.3%	1.8%	No. daily airline departures	12	294	Daily vehicle miles per capita	23.1	23.0
Work at home	2.4%	3.9%	Amtrak service	No				
Mass transit miles per capita	10.4	8.0	No. interstate highways	1	1			

LEISURE — SCORE: 74/RANK: 87

DINING & SHOPPING	AREA	U.S. AVG	ENTERTAINMENT	AREA	U.S. AVG	OUTDOOR ACTIVITIES	AREA	U.S. AVG
Restaurant rating	1	1	Professional sports rating	2	4	Golf-course rating	3	4
No. outlet malls	5	2	College sports rating	1	4	Ski-area rating	1	4
No. Starbucks	0	11	Zoo/aquarium rating	1	3	National Park rating	4	3
No. warehouse clubs	4	4	Amusement park rating	1	3	Sq. miles inland water	10.0	4.0
			Botanical garden/arboretum rating	1	3	Miles of coastline	70.9	11.4

ARTS & CULTURE — SCORE: 28/RANK: 237

MEDIA & LIBRARIES	AREA	U.S. AVG	PERFORMING ARTS	AREA	U.S. AVG	MUSEUMS	AREA	U.S. AVG
Arts radio rating	1	3	Classical music rating	4	4	Overall museum rating	3	6
No. public libraries	17	28	Ballet/dance rating	1	3	Art museum rating	4	5
Library volumes per capita	2.4	2.8	Professional theater rating	1	3	Science museum rating	6	4
			University arts programs rating	2	5	Children's museum rating	3	3

Memphis, TN

Score: 64.9   Rank: 109

Profile: Large-city complex
Location: Extreme southwest Tennessee along the Mississippi River and Arkansas and Mississippi border
Elevation: 284 feet
Time zone: Central Standard Time

PRO	CON
Entertainment	Crime rate
Cultural interest	Urban decay
Cost of living	Hot, humid summers

Sultry, soulful Memphis is an interesting and vivid place, located along the Mississippi River at the Arkansas border. The largest city in Tennessee, Memphis has a history of dramatic highs and lows: antebellum cotton-trading prosperity, Civil War destruction and reconstruction, yellow-fever epidemics, resurgence as a lumber and (again) cotton-trading center, and post–World War II decline. The low point was Martin Luther King's assassination in 1968. Today the city is on an upswing, thanks to recognition of its unique cultural assets and urban renewal. As the hometown of the blues and Elvis Presley (who was actually born in Tupelo, Mississippi), the city left its mark on the history of music, and a general resurgence in the popularity of blues has brought new life to Memphis as a tourist attraction. The historic Beale Street neighborhood provides music and entertainment opportunities for residents and tourists. The city is a patchwork of redevelopment, preservation, and decay, but downtown is generally becoming a more habitable place. Memphis recently acquired its first major-league sports team, the NBA Grizzlies, and it has several minor-league and collegiate sports attractions. The economic base is diverse—the city is headquarters for AutoZone (retail) and FedEx, and is known for its St. Jude Children's Research Hospital. Its status as hub for FedEx and Northwest Airlines says something of its central geographic location. The biggest downsides are a high crime rate and oppressive summers.

The city lies along the Mississippi River with a level landscape to the west in Arkansas and a level to slightly rolling landscape into Tennessee and northern Mississippi. The climate is a blend of continental and subtropical. Although not directly located on the Gulf and western Canada storm paths, it is still affected by both. Weather changes are frequent. Summers have periods of warm, steamy weather with thundershowers.

Winters are cool with a few periods of freezing temperatures. At 49.0 inches per year, Memphis is comparatively wet with precipitation spread evenly throughout the year. Extreme temperatures are rare.

POPULATION

DEMOGRAPHICS	AREA	U.S. AVG	ETHNIC COMPOSITION	AREA	U.S. AVG	RESIDENT PROFILE	AREA	U.S. AVG
Population	1,160,065		White	59.0%	75.1%	Single	49.8%	43.6%
Population density per sq. mile	385.7	447.3	Black	39.3%	12.3%	Married	50.2%	56.4%
Population growth	15.2%	16.1%	Asian	.9%	3.6%	Divorced	8.3%	8.4%
Median age	33.4	35.5	American Indian	.6%	.9%	Separated	5.5%	3.0%
Average family size	2.7	2.7	Hispanic	2.0%	12.5%	Married with children	26.3%	28.7%
			Diversity measure	54.1%	35.2%	Single with children	15.5%	10.1%

ECONOMY & JOBS — SCORE: 27/RANK: 239

INCOME	AREA	U.S. AVG	EMPLOYMENT	AREA	U.S. AVG	LARGEST EMPLOYING INDUSTRY
Per capita income	$23,876	$23,420	Unemployment rate	5.7%	6.1%	Food Manufacturing
Household income	$46,253	$46,060	Recent job growth	-.8%	.9%	
Household income < $25K	27.0%	26.4%	Projected future job growth	19.2%	15.1%	
Household income > $75K	27.2%	24.5%	White collar	56.7%	54.5%	
Household income growth	71.7%	57.3%	Blue collar	43.3%	45.5%	

COST OF LIVING — SCORE: 62/RANK: 126

INDEXES & TAXES	AREA	U.S. AVG	HOUSING	AREA	U.S. AVG	NECESSITIES	AREA	U.S. AVG
Cost of Living Index	89.2	100.0	Median home price	$130,900	$160,100	Food Index	98.3	100.0
Financial Progress Index	110.5	100.0	Home price appreciation	3.9%	7.1%	Housing Index	81.3	100.0
Income tax rate	0.000%	4.625%	Median rent	$626	$670	Utilities Index	82.8	100.0
Sales tax rate	9.250%	6.474%	Homes owned	63.8%	63.9%	Transportation Index	98.6	100.0
Property tax rate	$12.3	$15.6	Homes rented	27.3%	25.3%	Healthcare Index	88.0	100.0
			Housing affordability	54.0%	54.5%	Miscellaneous Cost Index	92.9	100.0

CLIMATE — SCORE: 47/RANK: 173

TEMPERATURE	AREA	U.S. AVG	PRECIPITATION	AREA	U.S. AVG	COMFORTS & HAZARDS	AREA	U.S. AVG
January low	31.6°F	26.4°F	Annual inches precipitation	49.0	35.9	July relative humidity	69.0%	68.8%
July high	91.6°F	86.7°F	Annual inches snowfall	6.0	24.2	Annual days mostly sunny	217	212
Annual days > 90°F	64	38	Annual days precipitation	106	111	Annual days with thunderstorms	53	39
Annual days < 32°F	59	88	Annual days rain > 0.5 inches	34	23	Tornado risk score	38	19
Annual days < 0°F	0	6	Annual days snow > 1.5 inches	2	6	Hurricane risk score	12	15

TEMPERATURE
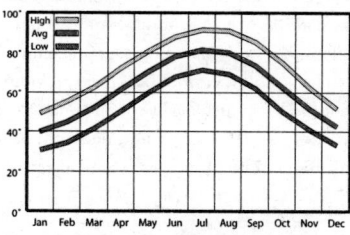

PRECIPITATION
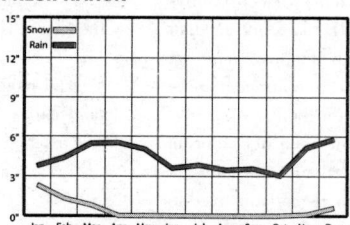

DAYS OF CLOUDS & PRECIPITATION
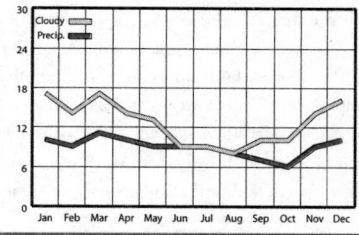

EDUCATION — SCORE: 29/RANK: 233

ACHIEVEMENT	AREA	U.S. AVG	PUBLIC SCHOOLS	AREA	U.S. AVG	HIGHER EDUCATION	AREA	U.S. AVG
High school degree	79.8%	80.2%	Expenditures per pupil	$4,874	$5,894	No. 2-year colleges	3	3
2-year college degree	4.7%	6.2%	Student/teacher ratio	14.2	16.7	No. 4-year colleges/universities	6	4
4-year college degree	14.9%	15.8%	Attending public school	86.3%	90.2%	No. highly ranked universities	0	1
Graduate/professional degree	7.7%	9.6%	State SAT score	1128	1020			
			State ACT score	20.4*	21.0			

HEALTH & HEALTHCARE — SCORE: 23/RANK: 254

HAZARDS & ILLNESSES	AREA	U.S. AVG	HEALTHCARE	AREA	U.S. AVG
Air-quality score	24	45	Physicians per capita	273.7	261.1
Water-quality score	12	33	Hospital beds per capita	501.9	432.2
Pollen/allergy score	66	61	No. teaching hospitals	7	4
Stress score	69	50	Cost per doctor visit	$69	$67
Cancer mortality per capita	181.1	169.0	Cost per dental visit	$86	$82
Depression days per month	2.5	2.8	Cost per daily hospital room	$470	$733

CRIME — SCORE: 0/RANK: 330

CRIME	AREA	U.S. AVG
Violent crime rate	1,104.4	456.0
Change in violent crime rate	-11.9%	-17.2%
Property crime rate	6,312.0	3,950.0
Change in property crime rate	-8.6%	-16.8%

TRANSPORTATION SCORE: 68/RANK: 104

COMMUTE	AREA	U.S. AVG	INTERCITY SERVICES	AREA	U.S. AVG	AUTOMOTIVE	AREA	U.S. AVG
Average commute time	24.5 min.	22.6 min.	Miles to nearest major airport	4	46	Insurance, annual premium	$1,263	$1,011
Commute by auto	90.8%	88.7%	Type of local airport	Medium		Gas, cost per gallon	$1.41	$1.50
Commute by mass transit	2.1%	1.8%	No. daily airline departures	500	294	Daily vehicle miles per capita	25.1	23.0
Work at home	1.6%	3.9%	Amtrak service	Yes				
Mass transit miles per capita	8.0	8.0	No. interstate highways	2	1			

LEISURE SCORE: 32/RANK: 225

DINING & SHOPPING	AREA	U.S. AVG	ENTERTAINMENT	AREA	U.S. AVG	OUTDOOR ACTIVITIES	AREA	U.S. AVG
Restaurant rating	1	1	Professional sports rating	6	4	Golf-course rating	5	4
No. outlet malls	1	2	College sports rating	4	4	Ski-area rating	1	4
No. Starbucks	13	11	Zoo/aquarium rating	6	3	National Park rating	2	3
No. warehouse clubs	4	4	Amusement park rating	3	3	Sq. miles inland water	6.0	4.0
			Botanical garden/arboretum rating	7	3	Miles of coastline	0.0	11.4

ARTS & CULTURE SCORE: 72/RANK: 91

MEDIA & LIBRARIES	AREA	U.S. AVG	PERFORMING ARTS	AREA	U.S. AVG	MUSEUMS	AREA	U.S. AVG
Arts radio rating	5	3	Classical music rating	5	4	Overall museum rating	8	6
No. public libraries	41	28	Ballet/dance rating	3	3	Art museum rating	6	5
Library volumes per capita	2.2	2.8	Professional theater rating	6	3	Science museum rating	7	4
			University arts programs rating	6	5	Children's museum rating	5	3

Merced, CA

Score: 12.4   Rank: 328

Profile: Small city
Location: Central California, mid-Central Valley, 80 miles south of Sacramento
Elevation: 22 feet
Time zone: Pacific Standard Time

PRO	CON
Nearby national parks	Economy
Recent job growth	Cost of living
Future college town	Low educational attainment

Merced is primarily an agricultural center and a travel gateway to Yosemite National Park. While it has some pleasant small-town character, it is plagued by an unusually high cost of living for the lifestyle and amenities offered. The COL Index and median home prices are well above national averages. Partly due to agriculture, unemployment is the third highest in the nation despite a recent spike in employment. The town does have an ace in the hole, however—recently it was chosen as the site for a major new University of California campus, securing a future as a mixed college and agricultural center not unlike Davis to the north. The school's opening was recently delayed to 2005 because of the lingering California budget crisis. When this facility is in place, the area's ranking should improve dramatically.

The immediate area is level and mainly agricultural. Just to the east, the Sierra Nevada foothills rise into an oak-studded grassland, giving way to the central Sierra, with mountains approaching 13,500 feet. Coastal mountains rise to the west to 4,000 feet, providing a dramatic landscape on all but the most dusty or hazy valley days. Climate is typical for the Central Valley—hot, dry summers and mild winters with frequent valley fog and about 90% of the year's annual rain.

POPULATION

DEMOGRAPHICS	AREA	U.S. AVG	ETHNIC COMPOSITION	AREA	U.S. AVG	RESIDENT PROFILE	AREA	U.S. AVG
Population	225,398		White	68.8%	75.1%	Single	41.6%	43.6%
Population density per sq. mile	116.9	447.3	Black	3.2%	12.3%	Married	58.4%	56.4%
Population growth	26.3%	16.1%	Asian	6.4%	3.6%	Divorced	7.3%	8.4%
Median age	29.1	35.5	American Indian	.8%	.9%	Separated	3.7%	3.0%
Average family size	3.4	2.7	Hispanic	43.4%	12.5%	Married with children	36.2%	28.7%
			Diversity measure	63.4%	35.2%	Single with children	12.5%	10.1%

ECONOMY & JOBS SCORE: 16/RANK: 276

INCOME	AREA	U.S. AVG	EMPLOYMENT	AREA	U.S. AVG	LARGEST EMPLOYING INDUSTRY
Per capita income	$13,713	$23,420	Unemployment rate	11.5%	6.1%	Fabricated Metal Product Manufacturing
Household income	$31,368	$46,060	Recent job growth	2.6%	.9%	
Household income < $25K	37.9%	26.4%	Projected future job growth	13.6%	15.1%	
Household income > $75K	10.9%	24.5%	White collar	39.6%	54.5%	
Household income growth	22.6%	57.3%	Blue collar	60.4%	45.5%	

COST OF LIVING — SCORE: 21/RANK: 261

INDEXES & TAXES	AREA	U.S. AVG	HOUSING	AREA	U.S. AVG	NECESSITIES	AREA	U.S. AVG
Cost of Living Index	111.7	100.0	Median home price	$174,260	$160,100	Food Index	114.7	100.0
Financial Progress Index	59.9	100.0	Home price appreciation	16.2%	7.1%	Housing Index	108.2	100.0
Income tax rate	6.000%	4.625%	Median rent	$630	$670	Utilities Index	119.4	100.0
Sales tax rate	7.250%	6.474%	Homes owned	54.2%	63.9%	Transportation Index	113.3	100.0
Property tax rate	$11.2	$15.6	Homes rented	38.5%	25.3%	Healthcare Index	130.6	100.0
			Housing affordability	52.0%	54.5%	Miscellaneous Cost Index	106.3	100.0

CLIMATE — SCORE: 92/RANK: 26

TEMPERATURE	AREA	U.S. AVG	PRECIPITATION	AREA	U.S. AVG	COMFORTS & HAZARDS	AREA	U.S. AVG
January low	36.3°F	26.4°F	Annual inches precipitation	14.2	35.9	July relative humidity	63.0%	68.8%
July high	94.7°F	86.7°F	Annual inches snowfall	0.0	24.2	Annual days mostly sunny	261	212
Annual days > 90°F	86	38	Annual days precipitation	52	111	Annual days with thunderstorms	3	39
Annual days < 32°F	24	88	Annual days rain > 0.5 inches	8	23	Tornado risk score	2	19
Annual days < 0°F	0	6	Annual days snow > 1.5 inches	0	6	Hurricane risk score	0	15

TEMPERATURE

PRECIPITATION

DAYS OF CLOUDS & PRECIPITATION

EDUCATION — SCORE: 1/RANK: 327

ACHIEVEMENT	AREA	U.S. AVG	PUBLIC SCHOOLS	AREA	U.S. AVG	HIGHER EDUCATION	AREA	U.S. AVG
High school degree	63.8%	80.2%	Expenditures per pupil	$5,139	$5,894	No. 2-year colleges	1	3
2-year college degree	8.2%	6.2%	Student/teacher ratio	21.1	16.7	No. 4-year colleges/universities	0	4
4-year college degree	7.6%	15.8%	Attending public school	96.1%	90.2%	No. highly ranked universities	0	1
Graduate/professional degree	3.4%	9.6%	State SAT score	1018*	1020			
			State ACT score	21.5	21.0			

HEALTH & HEALTHCARE — SCORE: 0/RANK: 329

HAZARDS & ILLNESSES	AREA	U.S. AVG	HEALTHCARE	AREA	U.S. AVG
Air-quality score	6	45	Physicians per capita	98.5	261.1
Water-quality score	11	33	Hospital beds per capita	186.7	432.2
Pollen/allergy score	65	61	No. teaching hospitals	1	4
Stress score	46	50	Cost per doctor visit	$65	$67
Cancer mortality per capita	173.7	169.0	Cost per dental visit	$90	$82
Depression days per month	2.7	2.8	Cost per daily hospital room	$1,427	$733

CRIME — SCORE: 38/RANK: 203

CRIME	AREA	U.S. AVG
Violent crime rate	617.3	456.0
Change in violent crime rate	-14.8%	-17.2%
Property crime rate	3,783.8	3,950.0
Change in property crime rate	-22.8%	-16.8%

TRANSPORTATION — SCORE: 4/RANK: 315

COMMUTE	AREA	U.S. AVG	INTERCITY SERVICES	AREA	U.S. AVG	AUTOMOTIVE	AREA	U.S. AVG
Average commute time	26.0 min.	22.6 min.	Miles to nearest major airport	56	46	Insurance, annual premium	$899	$1,011
Commute by auto	85.5%	88.7%	Type of local airport	Small		Gas, cost per gallon	$1.79	$1.50
Commute by mass transit	.3%	1.8%	No. daily airline departures	75	294	Daily vehicle miles per capita	14.4	23.0
Work at home	5.6%	3.9%	Amtrak service	Yes				
Mass transit miles per capita	5.5	8.0	No. interstate highways	0	1			

LEISURE — SCORE: 45/RANK: 182

DINING & SHOPPING	AREA	U.S. AVG	ENTERTAINMENT	AREA	U.S. AVG	OUTDOOR ACTIVITIES	AREA	U.S. AVG
Restaurant rating	1	1	Professional sports rating	2	4	Golf-course rating	1	4
No. outlet malls	0	2	College sports rating	1	4	Ski-area rating	8	4
No. Starbucks	3	11	Zoo/aquarium rating	2	3	National Park rating	3	3
No. warehouse clubs	3	4	Amusement park rating	1	3	Sq. miles inland water	3.0	4.0
			Botanical garden/arboretum rating	1	3	Miles of coastline	0.0	11.4

ARTS & CULTURE — SCORE: 3/RANK: 321

MEDIA & LIBRARIES	AREA	U.S. AVG	PERFORMING ARTS	AREA	U.S. AVG	MUSEUMS	AREA	U.S. AVG
Arts radio rating	1	3	Classical music rating	2	4	Overall museum rating	3	6
No. public libraries	16	28	Ballet/dance rating	1	3	Art museum rating	1	5
Library volumes per capita	1.5	2.8	Professional theater rating	1	3	Science museum rating	1	4
			University arts programs rating	1	5	Children's museum rating	1	3

Miami, FL

Profile: Regional center
Location: South Atlantic Coast near the southern tip of the Florida Peninsula
Elevation: 12 feet
Time zone: Eastern Standard Time

PRO	CON
Entertainment	Crime rate
Beaches and water recreation	Urban sprawl
Air service	Hurricane risk

Miami has always been the commercial and cultural center for Florida and the nearby Caribbean, but in the past 30 years it has emerged as a world-class international hub and a gateway for all of Latin America. In many ways it serves as the central logistical and cultural hub of the entire Western Hemisphere. The inevitable result is a diverse and invigorating Latin culture superimposed upon what was already a major commercial, resort, and retirement area dating back to the 1920s. Import/export and international financial trade with Latin countries make up a large part of the economy. The city is busy—in many ways stressful—and the mix of cultures, heat, and poverty has occasionally boiled over into ethnic and civil strife. But the city is fun and undeniably alive.

Downtown is fairly average with the usual glass skyscrapers. Wealthy retirees and others escaping the northeast winters have established themselves on Miami Beach, the high-rise-studded barrier island to the east, or Coral Gables just to the south. Inland, the area sprawls with low, mid-size buildings and housing for miles with a mix of neighborhoods, until ending abruptly at the Everglades. Inland areas are much warmer and uncomfortable. Covering almost all buildable land, vast residential areas sprawl 25 miles to the south to Homestead. Hurricane Andrew, one of the most devastating hurricanes on record, made a nearly successful attempt to reclaim the area for nature in 1992. To the north, residential and light-commercial developments merge with Fort Lauderdale.

There is no shortage of things to do in Miami—indoors or outdoors. The South Beach section of Miami Beach houses a historic district lined with pastel-colored, Art Deco buildings from the '20s and '30s, now filled with restaurants and clubs active throughout the day and evening. Water and beach recreation are superb, and Latin-accented nightlife goes on everywhere. Professional and college sports are a passion. There is a good assortment of museums and performing-arts amenities. Air service is excellent everywhere, particularly to international destinations. The employment picture is a bit bleak with 7% unemployment and recent job declines. The Cost of Living Index of 108.8 is high, but there is a great deal of variation in home prices depending on location. The crime rate is the second highest in the nation. Average commute times—over 30 minutes—are the worst in Florida and the 14th worst in the nation. Only Fort Lauderdale and West Palm Beach—both just to the north—have a higher hurricane risk. Taken together, the city offers world-class activities and an interesting cultural mix at a cost of crowding and a quality of life that depends on location.

Miami lies on a level coastal plain. The surrounding countryside is level and sparsely wooded with areas of water and swampland approaching the Everglades to the west. The climate is subtropical marine with long, warm, humid summers and abundant rainfall, followed by mild, dry winters. Sea breezes from the east and southeast may cause year-round temperature differences of 15°F or more from inland locations. Freezing conditions occur occasionally in the western suburbs. Strong thunderstorms with dangerous lightning can occur year-round and hurricanes are a risk in late summer and fall.

POPULATION

DEMOGRAPHICS	AREA	U.S. AVG	ETHNIC COMPOSITION	AREA	U.S. AVG	RESIDENT PROFILE	AREA	U.S. AVG
Population	2,332,599		White	76.7%	75.1%	Single	52.3%	43.6%
Population density per sq. mile	1,199.5	447.3	Black	17.4%	12.3%	Married	47.7%	56.4%
Population growth	20.4%	16.1%	Asian	1.6%	3.6%	Divorced	11.0%	8.4%
Median age	36.0	35.5	American Indian	.1%	.9%	Separated	5.0%	3.0%
Average family size	2.8	2.7	Hispanic	59.8%	12.5%	Married with children	22.9%	28.7%
			Diversity measure	68.2%	35.2%	Single with children	13.8%	10.1%

ECONOMY & JOBS — SCORE: 8/RANK: 304

INCOME	AREA	U.S. AVG	EMPLOYMENT	AREA	U.S. AVG	LARGEST EMPLOYING INDUSTRY
Per capita income	$19,850	$23,420	Unemployment rate	7.4%	6.1%	Healthcare and Social Assistance
Household income	$39,604	$46,060	Recent job growth	-2.1%	.9%	
Household income < $25K	32.2%	26.4%	Projected future job growth	13.1%	15.1%	
Household income > $75K	21.1%	24.5%	White collar	56.9%	54.5%	
Household income growth	47.1%	57.3%	Blue collar	43.1%	45.5%	

COST OF LIVING — SCORE: 41/RANK: 194

INDEXES & TAXES	AREA	U.S. AVG	HOUSING	AREA	U.S. AVG	NECESSITIES	AREA	U.S. AVG
Cost of Living Index	108.8	100.0	Median home price	$177,200	$160,100	Food Index	107.6	100.0
Financial Progress Index	77.6	100.0	Home price appreciation	12.6%	7.1%	Housing Index	110.1	100.0
Income tax rate	0.000%	4.625%	Median rent	$842	$670	Utilities Index	106.3	100.0
Sales tax rate	7.000%	6.474%	Homes owned	51.7%	63.9%	Transportation Index	109.5	100.0
Property tax rate	$18.6	$15.6	Homes rented	37.8%	25.3%	Healthcare Index	121.6	100.0
			Housing affordability	36.0%	54.5%	Miscellaneous Cost Index	104.6	100.0

CLIMATE — SCORE: 79/RANK: 68

TEMPERATURE	AREA	U.S. AVG	PRECIPITATION	AREA	U.S. AVG	COMFORTS & HAZARDS	AREA	U.S. AVG
January low	58.7°F	26.4°F	Annual inches precipitation	60.0	35.9	July relative humidity	75.0%	68.8%
July high	89.9°F	86.7°F	Annual inches snowfall	0.0	24.2	Annual days mostly sunny	248	212
Annual days > 90°F	30	38	Annual days precipitation	129	111	Annual days with thunderstorms	75	39
Annual days < 32°F	0	88	Annual days rain > 0.5 inches	33	23	Tornado risk score	52	19
Annual days < 0°F	0	6	Annual days snow > 1.5 inches	0	6	Hurricane risk score	98	15

TEMPERATURE

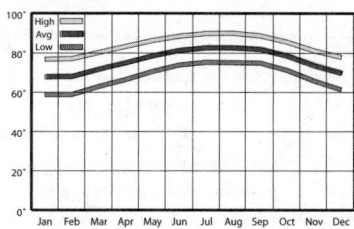

PRECIPITATION

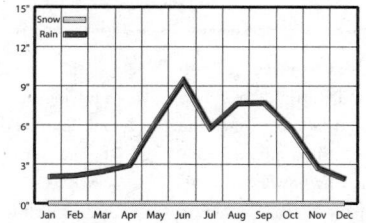

DAYS OF CLOUDS & PRECIPITATION

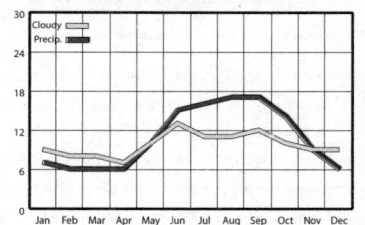

EDUCATION — SCORE: 8/RANK: 302

ACHIEVEMENT	AREA	U.S. AVG	PUBLIC SCHOOLS	AREA	U.S. AVG	HIGHER EDUCATION	AREA	U.S. AVG
High school degree	67.9%	80.2%	Expenditures per pupil	$5,952	$5,894	No. 2-year colleges	3	3
2-year college degree	6.1%	6.2%	Student/teacher ratio	20.3	16.7	No. 4-year colleges/universities	8	4
4-year college degree	12.3%	15.8%	Attending public school	86.2%	90.2%	No. highly ranked universities	1	1
Graduate/professional degree	9.4%	9.6%	State SAT score	996*	1020			
			State ACT score	20.5	21.0			

HEALTH & HEALTHCARE — SCORE: 65/RANK: 115

CRIME — SCORE: 2/RANK: 323

HAZARDS & ILLNESSES	AREA	U.S. AVG	HEALTHCARE	AREA	U.S. AVG	CRIME	AREA	U.S. AVG
Air-quality score	24	45	Physicians per capita	305.8	261.1	Violent crime rate	1,151.3	456.0
Water-quality score	38	33	Hospital beds per capita	455.1	432.2	Change in violent crime rate	-39.0%	-17.2%
Pollen/allergy score	49	61	No. teaching hospitals	16	4	Property crime rate	6,446.9	3,950.0
Stress score	93	50	Cost per doctor visit	$74	$67	Change in property crime rate	-38.2%	-16.8%
Cancer mortality per capita	162.6	169.0	Cost per dental visit	$95	$82			
Depression days per month	2.6	2.8	Cost per daily hospital room	$779	$733			

TRANSPORTATION — SCORE: 52/RANK: 159

COMMUTE	AREA	U.S. AVG	INTERCITY SERVICES	AREA	U.S. AVG	AUTOMOTIVE	AREA	U.S. AVG
Average commute time	30.1 min.	22.6 min.	Miles to nearest major airport	9	46	Insurance, annual premium	$1,707	$1,011
Commute by auto	86.4%	88.7%	Type of local airport	Large		Gas, cost per gallon	$1.54	$1.50
Commute by mass transit	6.4%	1.8%	No. daily airline departures	698	294	Daily vehicle miles per capita	19.3	23.0
Work at home	2.3%	3.9%	Amtrak service	Yes				
Mass transit miles per capita	21.5	8.0	No. interstate highways	1	1			

LEISURE — SCORE: 94/RANK: 19

DINING & SHOPPING	AREA	U.S. AVG	ENTERTAINMENT	AREA	U.S. AVG	OUTDOOR ACTIVITIES	AREA	U.S. AVG
Restaurant rating	4	1	Professional sports rating	9	4	Golf-course rating	7	4
No. outlet malls	3	2	College sports rating	6	4	Ski-area rating	1	4
No. Starbucks	31	11	Zoo/aquarium rating	8	3	National Park rating	10	3
No. warehouse clubs	8	4	Amusement park rating	9	3	Sq. miles inland water	5.0	4.0
			Botanical garden/arboretum rating	9	3	Miles of coastline	83.4	11.4

ARTS & CULTURE — SCORE: 85/RANK: 51

MEDIA & LIBRARIES	AREA	U.S. AVG	PERFORMING ARTS	AREA	U.S. AVG	MUSEUMS	AREA	U.S. AVG
Arts radio rating	5	3	Classical music rating	10	4	Overall museum rating	8	6
No. public libraries	40	28	Ballet/dance rating	7	3	Art museum rating	8	5
Library volumes per capita	2.0	2.8	Professional theater rating	8	3	Science museum rating	7	4
			University arts programs rating	9	5	Children's museum rating	4	3

Middlesex-Somerset-Hunterdon, NJ

Score: 71.9 **Rank:** 73

Profile: Mid-size-city complex
Location: East-central New Jersey, south of Newark and southwest of New York City
Elevation: 72 feet
Time zone: Eastern Standard Time

PRO
Strong and diverse economy
Proximity to New York City
Educated population

CON
Cost of living
Commute time
Urban sprawl

The three-county area contains such cities as New Brunswick, Perth Amboy, South Amboy, Edison, Piscataway, and Raritan River, and extends from the coastal "notch" below Staten Island west to the Pennsylvania border. Like many areas in the state, it is a mix of heavy industry, commercial and corporate activity, and a patchwork of residential towns and villages. Most of the heavy industry is near the mouth of the Raritan River, near Perth Amboy and South Amboy. The area has a strong corporate pedigree, with headquarters of such Fortune 500 companies as Merck & Co., Johnson & Johnson, Pharmacia/Upjohn, American Standard, Chubb, Foster Wheeler, Engelhard, and Supermarkets General.

The rest of the area is a livable balance of commercial, residential, and rural activity, and although urban sprawl is an issue, the state's rigorous efforts to contain development in the south and west portions of the region have paid off. The area is home to Rutgers University, the state's major public university, at New Brunswick. Educational attainment is high and the crime rate is the lowest in the state.

Coastal areas are flat and mainly built up. Inland sections are mainly level valleys among low rolling hills, with some wooded areas and open farmland. The climate is continental with distinct seasons and occasional marine influence. Summers are warm, hazy, and humid, with a few hot spells and frequent afternoon thundershowers, particularly inland. Winters are an East Coast mix, typically with clouds, rain, and snow, and varying temperatures frequently fluctuating above and below freezing. First freeze is mid-October, last is late April.

POPULATION

DEMOGRAPHICS	AREA	U.S. AVG	ETHNIC COMPOSITION	AREA	U.S. AVG	RESIDENT PROFILE	AREA	U.S. AVG
Population	1,211,230		White	85.6%	75.1%	Single	42.7%	43.6%
Population density per sq. mile	1,158.6	447.3	Black	6.1%	12.3%	Married	57.3%	56.4%
Population growth	18.8%	16.1%	Asian	6.5%	3.6%	Divorced	6.4%	8.4%
Median age	36.8	35.5	American Indian	.1%	.9%	Separated	2.4%	3.0%
Average family size	2.7	2.7	Hispanic	7.1%	12.5%	Married with children	28.6%	28.7%
			Diversity measure	48.8%	35.2%	Single with children	6.5%	10.1%

ECONOMY & JOBS
SCORE: 86/RANK: 43

INCOME	AREA	U.S. AVG	EMPLOYMENT	AREA	U.S. AVG	LARGEST EMPLOYING INDUSTRY
Per capita income	$35,698	$23,420	Unemployment rate	5.0%	6.1%	Computer Systems Design and Related Services
Household income	$79,975	$46,060	Recent job growth	.6%	.9%	
Household income < $25K	11.0%	26.4%	Projected future job growth	14.4%	15.1%	
Household income > $75K	53.1%	24.5%	White collar	68.2%	54.5%	
Household income growth	64.1%	57.3%	Blue collar	31.8%	45.5%	

COST OF LIVING
SCORE: 6/RANK: 308

INDEXES & TAXES	AREA	U.S. AVG	HOUSING	AREA	U.S. AVG	NECESSITIES	AREA	U.S. AVG
Cost of Living Index	137.0	100.0	Median home price	$284,300	$160,100	Food Index	111.0	100.0
Financial Progress Index	124.4	100.0	Home price appreciation	12.4%	7.1%	Housing Index	176.6	100.0
Income tax rate	2.450%	4.625%	Median rent	$1,164	$670	Utilities Index	124.5	100.0
Sales tax rate	6.000%	6.474%	Homes owned	72.0%	63.9%	Transportation Index	119.6	100.0
Property tax rate	$24.8	$15.6	Homes rented	23.4%	25.3%	Healthcare Index	116.8	100.0
			Housing affordability	54.0%	54.5%	Miscellaneous Cost Index	110.9	100.0

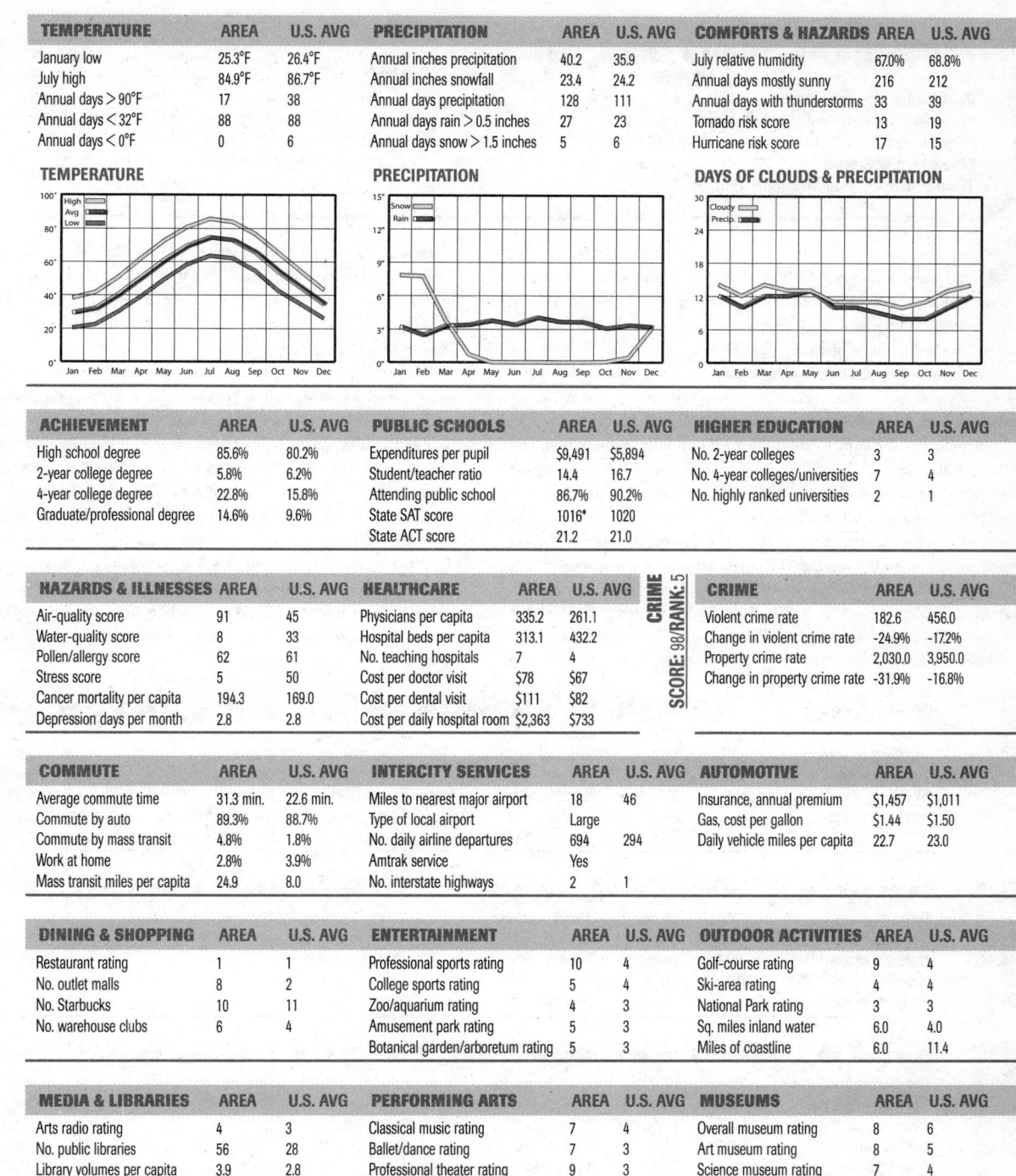

CLIMATE SCORE: 58/RANK: 137

TEMPERATURE	AREA	U.S. AVG	PRECIPITATION	AREA	U.S. AVG	COMFORTS & HAZARDS	AREA	U.S. AVG
January low	25.3°F	26.4°F	Annual inches precipitation	40.2	35.9	July relative humidity	67.0%	68.8%
July high	84.9°F	86.7°F	Annual inches snowfall	23.4	24.2	Annual days mostly sunny	216	212
Annual days > 90°F	17	38	Annual days precipitation	128	111	Annual days with thunderstorms	33	39
Annual days < 32°F	88	88	Annual days rain > 0.5 inches	27	23	Tornado risk score	13	19
Annual days < 0°F	0	6	Annual days snow > 1.5 inches	5	6	Hurricane risk score	17	15

TEMPERATURE

PRECIPITATION

DAYS OF CLOUDS & PRECIPITATION

EDUCATION SCORE: 92/RANK: 26

ACHIEVEMENT	AREA	U.S. AVG	PUBLIC SCHOOLS	AREA	U.S. AVG	HIGHER EDUCATION	AREA	U.S. AVG
High school degree	85.6%	80.2%	Expenditures per pupil	$9,491	$5,894	No. 2-year colleges	3	3
2-year college degree	5.8%	6.2%	Student/teacher ratio	14.4	16.7	No. 4-year colleges/universities	7	4
4-year college degree	22.8%	15.8%	Attending public school	86.7%	90.2%	No. highly ranked universities	2	1
Graduate/professional degree	14.6%	9.6%	State SAT score	1016*	1020			
			State ACT score	21.2	21.0			

HEALTH & HEALTHCARE SCORE: 17/RANK: 273

HAZARDS & ILLNESSES	AREA	U.S. AVG	HEALTHCARE	AREA	U.S. AVG
Air-quality score	91	45	Physicians per capita	335.2	261.1
Water-quality score	8	33	Hospital beds per capita	313.1	432.2
Pollen/allergy score	62	61	No. teaching hospitals	7	4
Stress score	5	50	Cost per doctor visit	$78	$67
Cancer mortality per capita	194.3	169.0	Cost per dental visit	$111	$82
Depression days per month	2.8	2.8	Cost per daily hospital room	$2,363	$733

CRIME SCORE: 98/RANK: 5

CRIME	AREA	U.S. AVG
Violent crime rate	182.6	456.0
Change in violent crime rate	-24.9%	-17.2%
Property crime rate	2,030.0	3,950.0
Change in property crime rate	-31.9%	-16.8%

TRANSPORTATION SCORE: 92/RANK: 24

COMMUTE	AREA	U.S. AVG	INTERCITY SERVICES	AREA	U.S. AVG	AUTOMOTIVE	AREA	U.S. AVG
Average commute time	31.3 min.	22.6 min.	Miles to nearest major airport	18	46	Insurance, annual premium	$1,457	$1,011
Commute by auto	89.3%	88.7%	Type of local airport	Large		Gas, cost per gallon	$1.44	$1.50
Commute by mass transit	4.8%	1.8%	No. daily airline departures	694	294	Daily vehicle miles per capita	22.7	23.0
Work at home	2.8%	3.9%	Amtrak service	Yes				
Mass transit miles per capita	24.9	8.0	No. interstate highways	2	1			

LEISURE SCORE: 92/RANK: 24

DINING & SHOPPING	AREA	U.S. AVG	ENTERTAINMENT	AREA	U.S. AVG	OUTDOOR ACTIVITIES	AREA	U.S. AVG
Restaurant rating	1	1	Professional sports rating	10	4	Golf-course rating	9	4
No. outlet malls	8	2	College sports rating	5	4	Ski-area rating	4	4
No. Starbucks	10	11	Zoo/aquarium rating	4	3	National Park rating	3	3
No. warehouse clubs	6	4	Amusement park rating	5	3	Sq. miles inland water	6.0	4.0
			Botanical garden/arboretum rating	5	3	Miles of coastline	6.0	11.4

ARTS & CULTURE SCORE: 95/RANK: 18

MEDIA & LIBRARIES	AREA	U.S. AVG	PERFORMING ARTS	AREA	U.S. AVG	MUSEUMS	AREA	U.S. AVG
Arts radio rating	4	3	Classical music rating	7	4	Overall museum rating	8	6
No. public libraries	56	28	Ballet/dance rating	7	3	Art museum rating	8	5
Library volumes per capita	3.9	2.8	Professional theater rating	9	3	Science museum rating	7	4
			University arts programs rating	10	5	Children's museum rating	3	3

Milwaukee-Waukesha, WI

Score: 53.6   Rank: 198

Profile: Large-city complex
Location: Extreme southeast Wisconsin along Lake Michigan, 40 miles north of Illinois border
Elevation: 693 feet
Time zone: Central Standard Time

PRO	CON
Downtown revitalization	Winter climate
Arts and culture	Economy
Proximity to Chicago	Cost of living

Somewhat in the economic and cultural shadow of Chicago, 90 miles south, Milwaukee is nevertheless a self-sufficient city, as well as a commercial and cultural center for Wisconsin. A melting pot for 19th-century immigrants from northern Europe, the city has kept up old-world traditions, most notably the brewing of beer. Following a period of industrial decline—including the brewing industry—the city has revitalized some areas, particularly downtown, and created an area of lakefront parks and museums, in modest imitation of Chicago. A repurposing project of the former Pabst brewery is currently in discussion. The business picture has changed to include more financial services and retailing companies along with the traditional base of metal products, electrical equipment, and machine tools. The town has a complement of cultural, performing arts, and recreational amenities, although Chicago is close enough to fill in the gaps. The city has good transportation services thanks to airlines choosing to avoid Chicago and good rail service arteries emanating from the Windy City. Suburbs have a true neighborhood character, many with European overtones. Waukesha, a few miles to the west, is a minor college town. A bit surprising considering proximity to Chicago is the city's full complement of major-league sports, including the NBA's Milwaukee Bucks and the MLB's Brewers. The economy has been affected by the slowdown in manufacturing, but this is gradually changing. The cost of living—particularly housing—is a negative on a Wisconsin scale.

The city is located on a shore plain where the Menomonee River flows into Lake Michigan. Terrain is generally flat near the lake, giving way to rolling hills inland with mixed farmland and woodland. The climate is continental with a wide temperature range and frequent storm systems from the west. Occasional severe winter storms can drop an excess of 10 inches of snow and deliver frigid Canadian air. Lakes Superior and Michigan moderate these arctic blasts somewhat, although winds from Lake Michigan can generate significant wind chills. Summer temperatures reach into the 80s and 90s with occasional warmer and humid spells. Winter precipitation is usually of long duration and low intensity and is snow or mixed rain and snow, while summer precipitation often comes as heavy showers and thunderstorms. First freeze is early October, last is early May.

POPULATION

DEMOGRAPHICS	AREA	U.S. AVG	ETHNIC COMPOSITION	AREA	U.S. AVG	RESIDENT PROFILE	AREA	U.S. AVG
Population	1,512,504		White	86.5%	75.1%	Single	45.2%	43.6%
Population density per sq. mile	1,036.0	447.3	Black	10.2%	12.3%	Married	54.8%	56.4%
Population growth	5.6%	16.1%	Asian	1.7%	3.6%	Divorced	7.8%	8.4%
Median age	35.8	35.5	American Indian	.5%	.9%	Separated	2.2%	3.0%
Average family size	2.6	2.7	Hispanic	3.1%	12.5%	Married with children	27.9%	28.7%
			Diversity measure	40.9%	35.2%	Single with children	9.8%	10.1%

ECONOMY & JOBS   SCORE: 50/RANK: 164

INCOME	AREA	U.S. AVG	EMPLOYMENT	AREA	U.S. AVG	LARGEST EMPLOYING INDUSTRY
Per capita income	$27,079	$23,420	Unemployment rate	6.5%	6.1%	Machinery Manufacturing
Household income	$53,304	$46,060	Recent job growth	.5%	.9%	
Household income < $25K	20.9%	26.4%	Projected future job growth	11.7%	15.1%	
Household income > $75K	31.1%	24.5%	White collar	57.9%	54.5%	
Household income growth	64.7%	57.3%	Blue collar	42.1%	45.5%	

COST OF LIVING   SCORE: 13/RANK: 287

INDEXES & TAXES	AREA	U.S. AVG	HOUSING	AREA	U.S. AVG	NECESSITIES	AREA	U.S. AVG
Cost of Living Index	106.8	100.0	Median home price	$181,300	$160,100	Food Index	100.5	100.0
Financial Progress Index	106.4	100.0	Home price appreciation	6.3%	7.1%	Housing Index	112.6	100.0
Income tax rate	6.930%	4.625%	Median rent	$688	$670	Utilities Index	125.2	100.0
Sales tax rate	5.600%	6.474%	Homes owned	65.3%	63.9%	Transportation Index	105.6	100.0
Property tax rate	$25.8	$15.6	Homes rented	30.2%	25.3%	Healthcare Index	99.0	100.0
			Housing affordability	57.0%	54.5%	Miscellaneous Cost Index	98.1	100.0

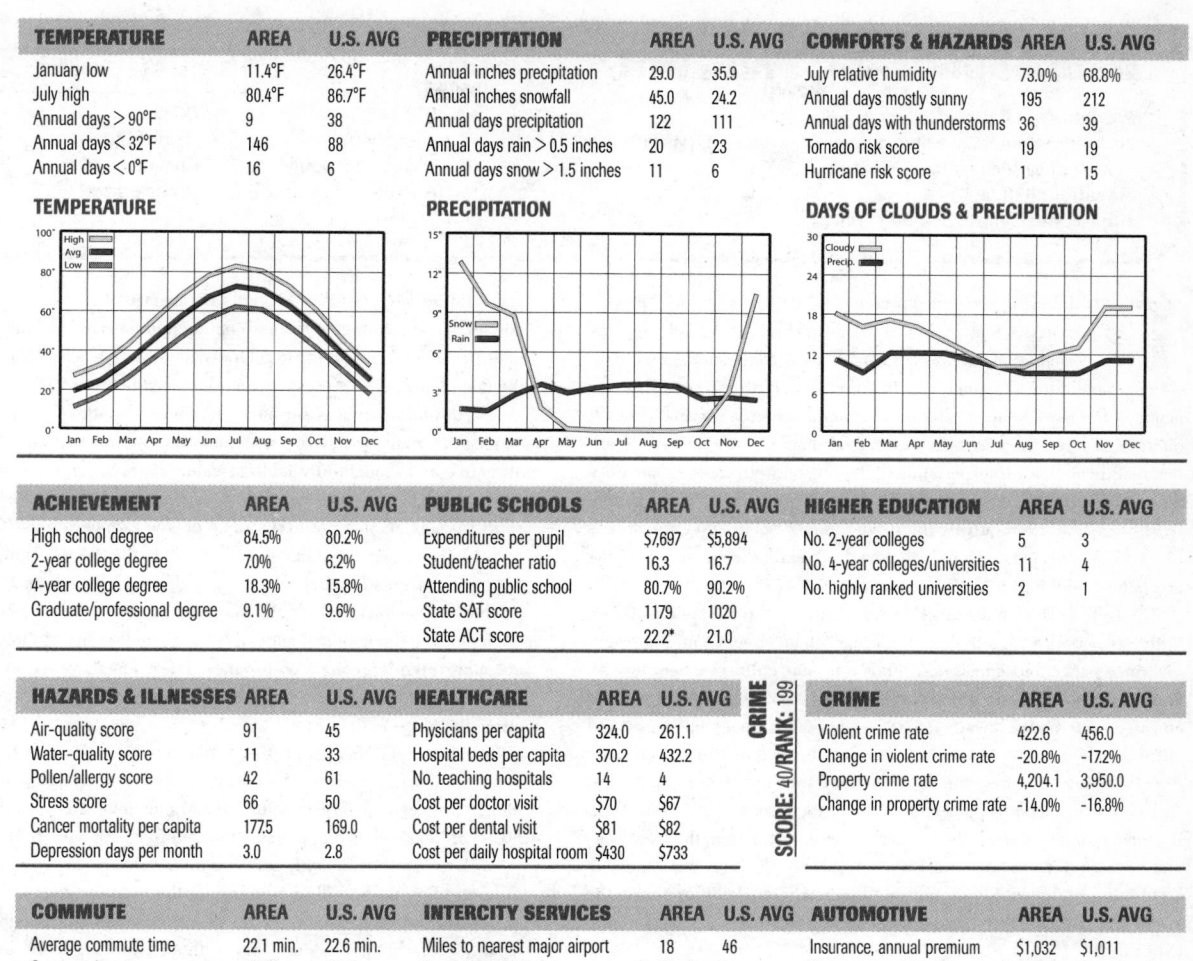

CLIMATE SCORE: 15/RANK: 279

TEMPERATURE	AREA	U.S. AVG	PRECIPITATION	AREA	U.S. AVG	COMFORTS & HAZARDS	AREA	U.S. AVG
January low	11.4°F	26.4°F	Annual inches precipitation	29.0	35.9	July relative humidity	73.0%	68.8%
July high	80.4°F	86.7°F	Annual inches snowfall	45.0	24.2	Annual days mostly sunny	195	212
Annual days > 90°F	9	38	Annual days precipitation	122	111	Annual days with thunderstorms	36	39
Annual days < 32°F	146	88	Annual days rain > 0.5 inches	20	23	Tornado risk score	19	19
Annual days < 0°F	16	6	Annual days snow > 1.5 inches	11	6	Hurricane risk score	1	15

TEMPERATURE

PRECIPITATION

DAYS OF CLOUDS & PRECIPITATION

EDUCATION SCORE: 63/RANK: 121

ACHIEVEMENT	AREA	U.S. AVG	PUBLIC SCHOOLS	AREA	U.S. AVG	HIGHER EDUCATION	AREA	U.S. AVG
High school degree	84.5%	80.2%	Expenditures per pupil	$7,697	$5,894	No. 2-year colleges	5	3
2-year college degree	7.0%	6.2%	Student/teacher ratio	16.3	16.7	No. 4-year colleges/universities	11	4
4-year college degree	18.3%	15.8%	Attending public school	80.7%	90.2%	No. highly ranked universities	2	1
Graduate/professional degree	9.1%	9.6%	State SAT score	1179	1020			
			State ACT score	22.2*	21.0			

HEALTH & HEALTHCARE SCORE: 47/RANK: 175

HAZARDS & ILLNESSES	AREA	U.S. AVG	HEALTHCARE	AREA	U.S. AVG	CRIME	AREA	U.S. AVG
Air-quality score	91	45	Physicians per capita	324.0	261.1	Violent crime rate	422.6	456.0
Water-quality score	11	33	Hospital beds per capita	370.2	432.2	Change in violent crime rate	-20.8%	-17.2%
Pollen/allergy score	42	61	No. teaching hospitals	14	4	Property crime rate	4,204.1	3,950.0
Stress score	66	50	Cost per doctor visit	$70	$67	Change in property crime rate	-14.0%	-16.8%
Cancer mortality per capita	177.5	169.0	Cost per dental visit	$81	$82			
Depression days per month	3.0	2.8	Cost per daily hospital room	$430	$733			

CRIME SCORE: 40/RANK: 199

TRANSPORTATION SCORE: 74/RANK: 84

COMMUTE	AREA	U.S. AVG	INTERCITY SERVICES	AREA	U.S. AVG	AUTOMOTIVE	AREA	U.S. AVG
Average commute time	22.1 min.	22.6 min.	Miles to nearest major airport	18	46	Insurance, annual premium	$1,032	$1,011
Commute by auto	88.0%	88.7%	Type of local airport	Medium		Gas, cost per gallon	$1.61	$1.50
Commute by mass transit	4.2%	1.8%	No. daily airline departures	285	294	Daily vehicle miles per capita	22.7	23.0
Work at home	2.8%	3.9%	Amtrak service	Yes				
Mass transit miles per capita	15.1	8.0	No. interstate highways	2	1			

LEISURE SCORE: 85/RANK: 47

DINING & SHOPPING	AREA	U.S. AVG	ENTERTAINMENT	AREA	U.S. AVG	OUTDOOR ACTIVITIES	AREA	U.S. AVG
Restaurant rating	4	1	Professional sports rating	6	4	Golf-course rating	7	4
No. outlet malls	5	2	College sports rating	3	4	Ski-area rating	3	4
No. Starbucks	21	11	Zoo/aquarium rating	7	3	National Park rating	1	3
No. warehouse clubs	5	4	Amusement park rating	1	3	Sq. miles inland water	4.0	4.0
			Botanical garden/arboretum rating	5	3	Miles of coastline	48.1	11.4

ARTS & CULTURE SCORE: 96/RANK: 10

MEDIA & LIBRARIES	AREA	U.S. AVG	PERFORMING ARTS	AREA	U.S. AVG	MUSEUMS	AREA	U.S. AVG
Arts radio rating	7	3	Classical music rating	9	4	Overall museum rating	9	6
No. public libraries	53	28	Ballet/dance rating	5	3	Art museum rating	9	5
Library volumes per capita	4.0	2.8	Professional theater rating	9	3	Science museum rating	7	4
			University arts programs rating	7	5	Children's museum rating	7	3

Minneapolis–St. Paul, MN

Score: 83.9   Rank: 24

Profile: Regional-center complex/Capital city
Location: Southeast Minnesota along upper Mississippi River, 20 miles west of Wisconsin border
Elevation: 838 feet
Time zone: Central Standard Time

PRO	CON
Education	Harsh winters
Diverse economy	Cost of living
Attractive downtown	Urban sprawl

The "twin cities" serve as a regional center for the upper Midwest and northern Great Plains as far as the Rocky Mountains. The fully cosmopolitan area is a balanced industrial, commercial, educational, and cultural center, and functions much as one city. The area is one of the most economically diverse in the country, serving as headquarters to large firms in agriculture, food, banking, technology, retailing, healthcare, and transportation. A few of the well-known companies include Best Buy, General Mills, 3M, US Bancorp, and United Healthcare. After a relatively flat period from 2002 to 2003, the area is likely to resume economic and job growth. Overall, the city has a strong, prosperous, and typically Midwestern feel.

The twin downtown areas sit on either side of the Mississippi River. Both are modern with attractive buildings, clean streets, entertainment, nightlife, parks, museums, and other arts and cultural amenities. St. Paul is the smaller and quieter of the two. In both cities, a network of elevated, interior walkways called "skyways" connect buildings and attractions—a feature necessitated by the harsh winter climate. According to one source, the area has more theaters, dance companies, and classical concerts per capita than any city outside of New York. Because Minneapolis–St. Paul is not a tourist destination, the local population enjoys these amenities almost exclusively. The population is highly educated, and there is an abundant intellectual energy among the area's citizens. The city ranked no. 1 in a 2002 study of Most Literate Cities (p. 117).

For those not interested in the arts and downtown scene, there is still plenty to do. Sports are a big attraction—the city has a full assortment of major- and minor-league sports teams. On the south side of Minneapolis, the Mall of America—with 400 stores—is the largest mall in the U.S. and is as much an amusement park as a mall. Such indoor facilities are particularly attractive given the winter climate. Summer recreation includes outdoor activities on the many surrounding lakes

and wildlife viewing. Winter-sports enthusiasts enjoy ice-skating and hockey, snowmobiling, and cross-country and downhill skiing at nearby facilities. For those wishing to get away, air service is excellent, although the dominance of Northwest Airlines can mean higher fares.

The downtown area is surrounded by a patchwork of residential and commercial neighborhoods. Some are attractive, others aren't. The more attractive and thoughtfully laid out suburbs are to the west near Eden Prairie and Orono, but these areas are experiencing congestion and sprawl issues, though not to the same degree as other cities. That said, the main downsides are climate and cost of living. Winters are long and hard, with several days below zero. Cost of living is high by national, and particularly regional, standards. The median home price of $189,900 is the highest in the nation outside of coastal regions, and Minnesota taxes are relatively high compared to other states. For those willing to wear warm clothes and sacrifice a little financially, the Twin Cities are an attractive place to live.

Terrain around the Twin Cities is flat or gently rolling, with a mix of open and densely wooded areas. Dotting the surrounding landscape are numerous lakes, the largest being Lake Minnetonka, 15 miles west. Most lakes are relatively small and shallow and freeze in winter. The climate is northern continental with seasonal temperatures varying from –30°F or lower to over 100°F. The area is near the northern edge of the influx of Gulf of Mexico moisture. Summers can be warm and humid, but are usually pleasant. Winters are cold, with days ranging from cloudy near freezing to clear, bitter cold, and windy. The area averages 34 nights per year below zero, far more than any other large American city. Severe storms, including blizzards, freezing rain, tornadoes, wind, and hailstorms occur. Most precipitation occurs during the summer period, and snow cover is persistent through the winter, averaging 6 to 8 inches in the city and 8 to 10 inches in the suburbs. First freeze is October 1, last is early May.

POPULATION

DEMOGRAPHICS	AREA	U.S. AVG	ETHNIC COMPOSITION	AREA	U.S. AVG	RESIDENT PROFILE	AREA	U.S. AVG
Population	3,054,637		White	92.5%	75.1%	Single	43.6%	43.6%
Population density per sq. mile	503.7	447.3	Black	3.4%	12.3%	Married	56.4%	56.4%
Population growth	20.3%	16.1%	Asian	2.9%	3.6%	Divorced	8.0%	8.4%
Median age	34.4	35.5	American Indian	.8%	.9%	Separated	1.9%	3.0%
Average family size	2.7	2.7	Hispanic	1.8%	12.5%	Married with children	30.6%	28.7%
			Diversity measure	27.3%	35.2%	Single with children	8.5%	10.1%

ECONOMY & JOBS SCORE: 42/RANK: 189

INCOME	AREA	U.S. AVG	EMPLOYMENT	AREA	U.S. AVG	LARGEST EMPLOYING INDUSTRY
Per capita income	$31,796	$23,420	Unemployment rate	4.1%	6.1%	Fabricated Metal Product Manufacturing
Household income	$65,330	$46,060	Recent job growth	-.5%	.9%	
Household income < $25K	15.0%	26.4%	Projected future job growth	19.4%	15.1%	
Household income > $75K	40.8%	24.5%	White collar	62.8%	54.5%	
Household income growth	79.0%	57.3%	Blue collar	37.2%	45.5%	

COST OF LIVING — SCORE: 10/RANK: 296

INDEXES & TAXES	AREA	U.S. AVG	HOUSING	AREA	U.S. AVG	NECESSITIES	AREA	U.S. AVG
Cost of Living Index	114.7	100.0	Median home price	$189,900	$160,100	Food Index	98.0	100.0
Financial Progress Index	121.4	100.0	Home price appreciation	12.2%	7.1%	Housing Index	118.0	100.0
Income tax rate	8.000%	4.625%	Median rent	$951	$670	Utilities Index	147.0	100.0
Sales tax rate	6.500%	6.474%	Homes owned	71.1%	63.9%	Transportation Index	113.8	100.0
Property tax rate	$19.5	$15.6	Homes rented	22.8%	25.3%	Healthcare Index	130.5	100.0
			Housing affordability	46.0%	54.5%	Miscellaneous Cost Index	106.4	100.0

CLIMATE — SCORE: 12/RANK: 289

TEMPERATURE	AREA	U.S. AVG	PRECIPITATION	AREA	U.S. AVG	COMFORTS & HAZARDS	AREA	U.S. AVG
January low	3.2°F	26.4°F	Annual inches precipitation	26.0	35.9	July relative humidity	69.0%	68.8%
July high	82.4°F	86.7°F	Annual inches snowfall	46.0	24.2	Annual days mostly sunny	200	212
Annual days > 90°F	15	38	Annual days precipitation	113	111	Annual days with thunderstorms	36	39
Annual days < 32°F	158	88	Annual days rain > 0.5 inches	16	23	Tornado risk score	20	19
Annual days < 0°F	34	6	Annual days snow > 1.5 inches	11	6	Hurricane risk score	0	15

TEMPERATURE

PRECIPITATION

DAYS OF CLOUDS & PRECIPITATION

EDUCATION — SCORE: 97/RANK: 8

ACHIEVEMENT	AREA	U.S. AVG	PUBLIC SCHOOLS	AREA	U.S. AVG	HIGHER EDUCATION	AREA	U.S. AVG
High school degree	90.6%	80.2%	Expenditures per pupil	$6,266	$5,894	No. 2-year colleges	19	3
2-year college degree	7.6%	6.2%	Student/teacher ratio	17.6	16.7	No. 4-year colleges/universities	16	4
4-year college degree	23.2%	15.8%	Attending public school	89.0%	90.2%	No. highly ranked universities	3	1
Graduate/professional degree	10.1%	9.6%	State SAT score	1173	1020			
			State ACT score	22.0*	21.0			

HEALTH & HEALTHCARE — SCORE: 42/RANK: 192

CRIME — SCORE: 69/RANK: 103

HAZARDS & ILLNESSES	AREA	U.S. AVG	HEALTHCARE	AREA	U.S. AVG	CRIME	AREA	U.S. AVG
Air-quality score	91	45	Physicians per capita	246.3	261.1	Violent crime rate	332.0	456.0
Water-quality score	30	33	Hospital beds per capita	280.8	432.2	Change in violent crime rate	-32.2%	-17.2%
Pollen/allergy score	47	61	No. teaching hospitals	16	4	Property crime rate	3,761.6	3,950.0
Stress score	35	50	Cost per doctor visit	$78	$67	Change in property crime rate	-21.6%	-16.8%
Cancer mortality per capita	163.2	169.0	Cost per dental visit	$97	$82			
Depression days per month	2.5	2.8	Cost per daily hospital room	$1,208	$733			

TRANSPORTATION — SCORE: 85/RANK: 47

COMMUTE	AREA	U.S. AVG	INTERCITY SERVICES	AREA	U.S. AVG	AUTOMOTIVE	AREA	U.S. AVG
Average commute time	23.7 min.	22.6 min.	Miles to nearest major airport	6	46	Insurance, annual premium	$1,144	$1,011
Commute by auto	85.9%	88.7%	Type of local airport	Large		Gas, cost per gallon	$1.52	$1.50
Commute by mass transit	3.7%	1.8%	No. daily airline departures	624	294	Daily vehicle miles per capita	25.5	23.0
Work at home	5.3%	3.9%	Amtrak service	Yes				
Mass transit miles per capita	10.9	8.0	No. interstate highways	2	1			

LEISURE — SCORE: 93/RANK: 21

DINING & SHOPPING	AREA	U.S. AVG	ENTERTAINMENT	AREA	U.S. AVG	OUTDOOR ACTIVITIES	AREA	U.S. AVG
Restaurant rating	1	1	Professional sports rating	7	4	Golf-course rating	9	4
No. outlet malls	3	2	College sports rating	8	4	Ski-area rating	5	4
No. Starbucks	41	11	Zoo/aquarium rating	9	3	National Park rating	3	3
No. warehouse clubs	7	4	Amusement park rating	10	3	Sq. miles inland water	10.0	4.0
			Botanical garden/arboretum rating	9	3	Miles of coastline	0.0	11.4

ARTS & CULTURE — SCORE: 98/RANK: 7

MEDIA & LIBRARIES	AREA	U.S. AVG	PERFORMING ARTS	AREA	U.S. AVG	MUSEUMS	AREA	U.S. AVG
Arts radio rating	10	3	Classical music rating	9	4	Overall museum rating	10	6
No. public libraries	132	28	Ballet/dance rating	7	3	Art museum rating	10	5
Library volumes per capita	3.5	2.8	Professional theater rating	10	3	Science museum rating	9	4
			University arts programs rating	10	5	Children's museum rating	8	3

Missoula, MT

Score: 67.0   **Rank:** 96

Profile: College town/Resort town
Location: Western Montana, 25 miles from Idaho border
Elevation: 3,361 feet
Time zone: Mountain Standard Time

PRO	CON
Attractive setting	Harsh winters
Outdoor recreation	Cost of living
College-town amenities	Isolation

Missoula, located in the extreme west-central part of the state, is a college town with an unusual mix of students, ranchers, "jet-setters," and nature lovers, set among a beautiful backdrop of mountains and scenic valleys. The city is home to the University of Montana, and the area is an outdoor paradise, with national forests, ski areas, raging rivers, and excellent fishing and bicycling. Missoula has become a sort of northerly Jackson Hole with a Boulder, Colorado, accent. Naturally, that brings high living costs and especially high housing costs.

The town is situated in the heart of the Montana Rockies in the extreme north portion of the Bitterroot Valley. The Bitterroot Range rises 5,000 feet to 7,000 feet above the valley floor just 20 miles to the southwest. The main ridge of the Rockies and Continental Divide rise to the east and northeast. The climate is continental semiarid. Mountains to the southwest block moisture while those to the northeast block some arctic air in winter. Summers are dry with moderate temperatures and cool nights. Some cold waves produce blizzard conditions as air funnels through the narrow valleys. This cold air can settle in the valley for long periods, especially in December and January, and bring cloudy conditions as well. Most precipitation occurs in May and early June as showers and thundershowers. First freeze is late September, last is mid-May.

POPULATION

DEMOGRAPHICS	AREA	U.S. AVG	ETHNIC COMPOSITION	AREA	U.S. AVG	RESIDENT PROFILE	AREA	U.S. AVG
Population	98,102		White	96.4%	75.1%	Single	41.4%	43.6%
Population density per sq. mile	37.8	447.3	Black	.2%	12.3%	Married	58.6%	56.4%
Population growth	24.7%	16.1%	Asian	1.2%	3.6%	Divorced	8.8%	8.4%
Median age	33.5	35.5	American Indian	2.0%	.9%	Separated	1.5%	3.0%
Average family size	2.7	2.7	Hispanic	1.3%	12.5%	Married with children	30.2%	28.7%
			Diversity measure	13.0%	35.2%	Single with children	8.4%	10.1%

ECONOMY & JOBS
SCORE: 81/RANK: 61

INCOME	AREA	U.S. AVG	EMPLOYMENT	AREA	U.S. AVG	LARGEST EMPLOYING INDUSTRY
Per capita income	$23,315	$23,420	Unemployment rate	3.1%	6.1%	Healthcare and Social Assistance
Household income	$40,912	$46,060	Recent job growth	13.6%	.9%	
Household income < $25K	29.9%	26.4%	Projected future job growth	13.5%	15.1%	
Household income > $75K	22.0%	24.5%	White collar	54.6%	54.5%	
Household income growth	75.3%	57.3%	Blue collar	45.4%	45.5%	

COST OF LIVING
SCORE: 30/RANK: 231

INDEXES & TAXES	AREA	U.S. AVG	HOUSING	AREA	U.S. AVG	NECESSITIES	AREA	U.S. AVG
Cost of Living Index	104.1	100.0	Median home price	$171,200	$160,100	Food Index	111.1	100.0
Financial Progress Index	83.7	100.0	Home price appreciation	7.8%	7.1%	Housing Index	106.3	100.0
Income tax rate	11.000%	4.625%	Median rent	$566	$670	Utilities Index	82.0	100.0
Sales tax rate	0.000%	6.474%	Homes owned	61.3%	63.9%	Transportation Index	98.8	100.0
Property tax rate	$16.0	$15.6	Homes rented	22.8%	25.3%	Healthcare Index	101.2	100.0
			Housing affordability	50.0%	54.5%	Miscellaneous Cost Index	106.7	100.0

CLIMATE
SCORE: 22/RANK: 256

TEMPERATURE	AREA	U.S. AVG	PRECIPITATION	AREA	U.S. AVG	COMFORTS & HAZARDS	AREA	U.S. AVG
January low	17.1°F	26.4°F	Annual inches precipitation	16.0	35.9	July relative humidity	56.0%	68.8%
July high	82.7°F	86.7°F	Annual inches snowfall	51.4	24.2	Annual days mostly sunny	158	212
Annual days > 90°F	19	38	Annual days precipitation	124	111	Annual days with thunderstorms	35	39
Annual days < 32°F	167	88	Annual days rain > 0.5 inches	5	23	Tornado risk score	9	19
Annual days < 0°F	24	6	Annual days snow > 1.5 inches	10	6	Hurricane risk score	0	15

TEMPERATURE

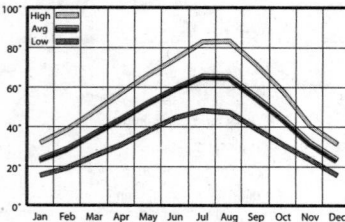

PRECIPITATION

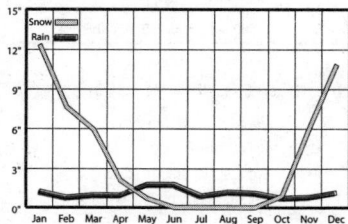

DAYS OF CLOUDS & PRECIPITATION

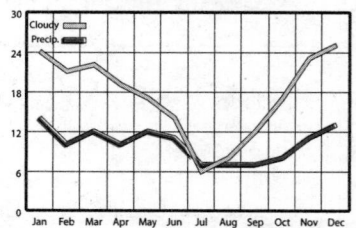

EDUCATION — SCORE: 78/RANK: 72

ACHIEVEMENT	AREA	U.S. AVG	PUBLIC SCHOOLS	AREA	U.S. AVG	HIGHER EDUCATION	AREA	U.S. AVG
High school degree	91.5%	80.2%	Expenditures per pupil	$5,377	$5,894	No. 2-year colleges	1	3
2-year college degree	5.0%	6.2%	Student/teacher ratio	16.2	16.7	No. 4-year colleges/universities	1	4
4-year college degree	22.1%	15.8%	Attending public school	91.2%	90.2%	No. highly ranked universities	0	1
Graduate/professional degree	10.7%	9.6%	State SAT score	1081	1020			
			State ACT score	21.7*	21.0			

HEALTH & HEALTHCARE — SCORE: 83/RANK: 54   CRIME — SCORE: 50/RANK: 166

HAZARDS & ILLNESSES	AREA	U.S. AVG	HEALTHCARE	AREA	U.S. AVG	CRIME	AREA	U.S. AVG
Air-quality score	86	45	Physicians per capita	330.3	261.1	Violent crime rate	324.2	456.0
Water-quality score	28	33	Hospital beds per capita	364.3	432.2	Change in violent crime rate	-17.2%	-17.2%
Pollen/allergy score	45	61	No. teaching hospitals	0	4	Property crime rate	4,265.8	3,950.0
Stress score	39	50	Cost per doctor visit	$53	$67	Change in property crime rate	-16.8%	-16.8%
Cancer mortality per capita	156.7	169.0	Cost per dental visit	$78	$82			
Depression days per month	2.4	2.8	Cost per daily hospital room	$562	$733			

TRANSPORTATION — SCORE: 83/RANK: 59

COMMUTE	AREA	U.S. AVG	INTERCITY SERVICES	AREA	U.S. AVG	AUTOMOTIVE	AREA	U.S. AVG
Average commute time	17.5 min.	22.6 min.	Miles to nearest major airport	174	46	Insurance, annual premium	$716	$1,011
Commute by auto	83.2%	88.7%	Type of local airport	Medium		Gas, cost per gallon	$1.53	$1.50
Commute by mass transit	.4%	1.8%	No. daily airline departures	115	294	Daily vehicle miles per capita	14.8	23.0
Work at home	5.4%	3.9%	Amtrak service	No				
Mass transit miles per capita	6.9	8.0	No. interstate highways	1	1			

LEISURE — SCORE: 43/RANK: 187

DINING & SHOPPING	AREA	U.S. AVG	ENTERTAINMENT	AREA	U.S. AVG	OUTDOOR ACTIVITIES	AREA	U.S. AVG
Restaurant rating	1	1	Professional sports rating	2	4	Golf-course rating	2	4
No. outlet malls	0	2	College sports rating	3	4	Ski-area rating	7	4
No. Starbucks	0	11	Zoo/aquarium rating	1	3	National Park rating	6	3
No. warehouse clubs	3	4	Amusement park rating	1	3	Sq. miles inland water	2.0	4.0
			Botanical garden/arboretum rating	2	3	Miles of coastline	0.0	11.4

ARTS & CULTURE — SCORE: 18/RANK: 271

MEDIA & LIBRARIES	AREA	U.S. AVG	PERFORMING ARTS	AREA	U.S. AVG	MUSEUMS	AREA	U.S. AVG
Arts radio rating	1	3	Classical music rating	2	4	Overall museum rating	4	6
No. public libraries	3	28	Ballet/dance rating	1	3	Art museum rating	4	5
Library volumes per capita	2.3	2.8	Professional theater rating	1	3	Science museum rating	2	4
			University arts programs rating	4	5	Children's museum rating	1	3

Mobile, AL

Score: 56.5   Rank: 174

Profile: Port and coastal city
Location: Southern tip of Alabama near the Gulf Coast
Elevation: 221 feet
Time zone: Central Standard Time

PRO	CON
Historic interest	Wet climate
Outdoor recreation	Crime rate
Arts and culture	Traffic congestion

Mobile is a major port and shipbuilding and commercial center at the head of Mobile Bay on the Gulf Coast. The area has a rich history as an antebellum seaport, and parts of the city reflect this heritage. A tourism industry is beginning to evolve in the area. For the region, Mobile has a relatively strong assortment of recreation, arts, and cultural assets. It is the wettest city in the United States with 67 inches of rain per year, although much arrives in short downpours as the city also rates as one of the sunniest in the state. There is a fairly high hurricane and tropical storm risk. Freezing occurs only 19 days per year, far lower than the rest of the state and much of the United States—an attraction for many.

Mobile is located 30 miles north of the Gulf of Mexico on a mainly level coastal plain. Coastal marshes and sandy beaches lie near the bay, while coniferous forests extend inland. The weather is humid subtropical with a strong marine influence from the Gulf. Summers are consistently warm, but temperatures are seldom as high as farther inland. Summer days are in the 90s but often cooled by an afternoon breeze, and evenings are warm and muggy. Winter is mild with one or two cooler snaps and an occasional frost. Summer thundershowers may occur every other day.

POPULATION

DEMOGRAPHICS	AREA	U.S. AVG	ETHNIC COMPOSITION	AREA	U.S. AVG	RESIDENT PROFILE	AREA	U.S. AVG
Population	548,095		White	72.1%	75.1%	Single	45.7%	43.6%
Population density per sq. mile	193.7	447.3	Black	25.2%	12.3%	Married	54.3%	56.4%
Population growth	14.9%	16.1%	Asian	1.4%	3.6%	Divorced	9.2%	8.4%
Median age	36.1	35.5	American Indian	1.1%	.9%	Separated	3.7%	3.0%
Average family size	2.6	2.7	Hispanic	1.2%	12.5%	Married with children	27.0%	28.7%
			Diversity measure	45.1%	35.2%	Single with children	12.9%	10.1%

ECONOMY & JOBS — SCORE: 36/RANK: 212

INCOME	AREA	U.S. AVG	EMPLOYMENT	AREA	U.S. AVG	LARGEST EMPLOYING INDUSTRY
Per capita income	$20,065	$23,420	Unemployment rate	6.3%	6.1%	Chemical Manufacturing
Household income	$37,313	$46,060	Recent job growth	2.7%	.9%	
Household income < $25K	32.7%	26.4%	Projected future job growth	18.0%	15.1%	
Household income > $75K	17.9%	24.5%	White collar	52.7%	54.5%	
Household income growth	57.8%	57.3%	Blue collar	47.3%	45.5%	

COST OF LIVING — SCORE: 53/RANK: 155

INDEXES & TAXES	AREA	U.S. AVG	HOUSING	AREA	U.S. AVG	NECESSITIES	AREA	U.S. AVG
Cost of Living Index	87.3	100.0	Median home price	$112,600	$160,100	Food Index	93.2	100.0
Financial Progress Index	91.1	100.0	Home price appreciation	4.6%	7.1%	Housing Index	69.9	100.0
Income tax rate	5.000%	4.625%	Median rent	$523	$670	Utilities Index	105.8	100.0
Sales tax rate	9.000%	6.474%	Homes owned	62.7%	63.9%	Transportation Index	98.5	100.0
Property tax rate	$4.1	$15.6	Homes rented	22.8%	25.3%	Healthcare Index	88.4	100.0
			Housing affordability	56.0%	54.5%	Miscellaneous Cost Index	98.5	100.0

CLIMATE — SCORE: 60/RANK: 132

TEMPERATURE	AREA	U.S. AVG	PRECIPITATION	AREA	U.S. AVG	COMFORTS & HAZARDS	AREA	U.S. AVG
January low	41.3°F	26.4°F	Annual inches precipitation	67.0	35.9	July relative humidity	73.0%	68.8%
July high	90.6°F	86.7°F	Annual inches snowfall	.4	24.2	Annual days mostly sunny	217	212
Annual days > 90°F	81	38	Annual days precipitation	124	111	Annual days with thunderstorms	80	39
Annual days < 32°F	19	88	Annual days rain > 0.5 inches	40	23	Tornado risk score	33	19
Annual days < 0°F	0	6	Annual days snow > 1.5 inches	1	6	Hurricane risk score	58	15

TEMPERATURE

PRECIPITATION

DAYS OF CLOUDS & PRECIPITATION

EDUCATION — SCORE: 8/RANK: 303

ACHIEVEMENT	AREA	U.S. AVG	PUBLIC SCHOOLS	AREA	U.S. AVG	HIGHER EDUCATION	AREA	U.S. AVG
High school degree	78.2%	80.2%	Expenditures per pupil	$4,542	$5,894	No. 2-year colleges	2	3
2-year college degree	5.7%	6.2%	Student/teacher ratio	16.1	16.7	No. 4-year colleges/universities	3	4
4-year college degree	12.9%	15.8%	Attending public school	83.8%	90.2%	No. highly ranked universities	0	1
Graduate/professional degree	7.0%	9.6%	State SAT score	1111	1020			
			State ACT score	20.1*	21.0			

HEALTH & HEALTHCARE — SCORE: 24/RANK: 251

HAZARDS & ILLNESSES	AREA	U.S. AVG	HEALTHCARE	AREA	U.S. AVG
Air-quality score	17	45	Physicians per capita	242.7	261.1
Water-quality score	57	33	Hospital beds per capita	479.4	432.2
Pollen/allergy score	70	61	No. teaching hospitals	5	4
Stress score	98	50	Cost per doctor visit	$51	$67
Cancer mortality per capita	186.0	169.0	Cost per dental visit	$76	$82
Depression days per month	3.7	2.8	Cost per daily hospital room	$301	$733

CRIME — SCORE: 10/RANK: 296

CRIME	AREA	U.S. AVG
Violent crime rate	535.8	456.0
Change in violent crime rate	-33.0%	-17.2%
Property crime rate	5,741.1	3,950.0
Change in property crime rate	6.6%	-16.8%

TRANSPORTATION — SCORE: 5/RANK: 314

COMMUTE	AREA	U.S. AVG	INTERCITY SERVICES	AREA	U.S. AVG	AUTOMOTIVE	AREA	U.S. AVG
Average commute time	25.4 min.	22.6 min.	Miles to nearest major airport	10	46	Insurance, annual premium	$833	$1,011
Commute by auto	92.5%	88.7%	Type of local airport	Small		Gas, cost per gallon	$1.41	$1.50
Commute by mass transit	1.1%	1.8%	No. daily airline departures	29	294	Daily vehicle miles per capita	27.3	23.0
Work at home	2.3%	3.9%	Amtrak service	Yes				
Mass transit miles per capita	3.0	8.0	No. interstate highways	2	1			

LEISURE
SCORE: 47/RANK: 173

DINING & SHOPPING	AREA	U.S. AVG	ENTERTAINMENT	AREA	U.S. AVG	OUTDOOR ACTIVITIES	AREA	U.S. AVG
Restaurant rating	1	1	Professional sports rating	2	4	Golf-course rating	3	4
No. outlet malls	2	2	College sports rating	4	4	Ski-area rating	1	4
No. Starbucks	1	11	Zoo/aquarium rating	1	3	National Park rating	2	3
No. warehouse clubs	3	4	Amusement park rating	1	3	Sq. miles inland water	8.0	4.0
			Botanical garden/arboretum rating	5	3	Miles of coastline	52.5	11.4

ARTS & CULTURE
SCORE: 45/RANK: 181

MEDIA & LIBRARIES	AREA	U.S. AVG	PERFORMING ARTS	AREA	U.S. AVG	MUSEUMS	AREA	U.S. AVG
Arts radio rating	1	3	Classical music rating	1	4	Overall museum rating	6	6
No. public libraries	24	28	Ballet/dance rating	1	3	Art museum rating	6	5
Library volumes per capita	1.6	2.8	Professional theater rating	1	3	Science museum rating	4	4
			University arts programs rating	8	5	Children's museum rating	3	3

Modesto, CA

Score: 25.0   Rank: 316

Profile: Small, agricultural town
Location: Central California, in the Central Valley, 80 miles southeast of Sacramento and 70 miles east of the Bay Area
Elevation: 22 feet
Time zone: Pacific Standard Time

PRO	CON
Winter climate	Lack of amenities
Small-town atmosphere	Violent crime
Nearby national parks	Unemployment

Mainly agricultural in character, Modesto is a "modest" Central Valley town—so named because the dignitary the town intended to name itself after refused the honor out of modesty. The unremarkable downtown has a typical, small-town feel enough to be the subject of the movie *American Graffiti* (although the actual filming was done in Marin County north of San Francisco). But there isn't much to do and unemployment is high. While the cost of living is fairly modest on a California scale, it is still high—and housing prices are high—for what's available. Incredibly, some people make the 2 to 3 hour commute into the San Francisco Bay Area. Yosemite National Park, 80 miles east, provides some recreational fulfillment.

Modesto is located in a completely flat area of agriculture and orchards along the Tuolumne River. Just 15 miles to the east, the Sierra foothills begin their persistent rise into the main Sierra Ridge. The climate is typical Central Valley Mediterranean with warm to hot, dry days and cool to warm nights in summer. Winter brings mild temperatures and valley fog. Almost all rain falls in winter.

POPULATION

DEMOGRAPHICS	AREA	U.S. AVG	ETHNIC COMPOSITION	AREA	U.S. AVG	RESIDENT PROFILE	AREA	U.S. AVG
Population	482,440		White	77.3%	75.1%	Single	42.9%	43.6%
Population density per sq. mile	322.8	447.3	Black	2.2%	12.3%	Married	57.1%	56.4%
Population growth	30.2%	16.1%	Asian	5.4%	3.6%	Divorced	9.9%	8.4%
Median age	31.9	35.5	American Indian	1.0%	.9%	Separated	3.7%	3.0%
Average family size	3.1	2.7	Hispanic	32.9%	12.5%	Married with children	32.6%	28.7%
			Diversity measure	55.7%	35.2%	Single with children	12.0%	10.1%

ECONOMY & JOBS
SCORE: 20/RANK: 264

INCOME	AREA	U.S. AVG	EMPLOYMENT	AREA	U.S. AVG	LARGEST EMPLOYING INDUSTRY
Per capita income	$18,962	$23,420	Unemployment rate	9.3%	6.1%	Food Manufacturing
Household income	$43,640	$46,060	Recent job growth	.7%	.9%	
Household income < $25K	26.9%	26.4%	Projected future job growth	11.4%	15.1%	
Household income > $75K	21.8%	24.5%	White collar	46.2%	54.5%	
Household income growth	46.1%	57.3%	Blue collar	53.8%	45.5%	

COST OF LIVING
SCORE: 17/RANK: 274

INDEXES & TAXES	AREA	U.S. AVG	HOUSING	AREA	U.S. AVG	NECESSITIES	AREA	U.S. AVG
Cost of Living Index	116.7	100.0	Median home price	$192,450	$160,100	Food Index	120.4	100.0
Financial Progress Index	79.7	100.0	Home price appreciation	15.4%	7.1%	Housing Index	119.5	100.0
Income tax rate	6.000%	4.625%	Median rent	$719	$670	Utilities Index	113.8	100.0
Sales tax rate	7.375%	6.474%	Homes owned	61.6%	63.9%	Transportation Index	114.0	100.0
Property tax rate	$11.1	$15.6	Homes rented	31.9%	25.3%	Healthcare Index	136.9	100.0
			Housing affordability	50.0%	54.5%	Miscellaneous Cost Index	106.3	100.0

CLIMATE SCORE: 92/RANK: 25

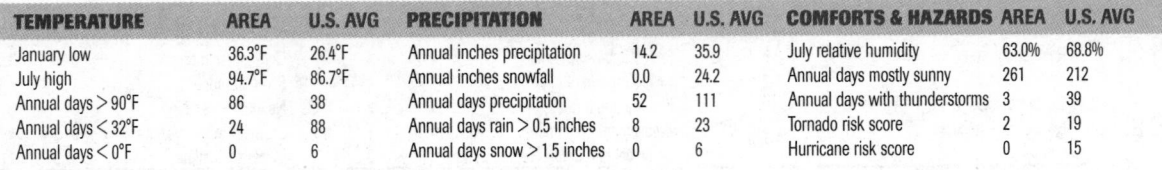

TEMPERATURE	AREA	U.S. AVG	PRECIPITATION	AREA	U.S. AVG	COMFORTS & HAZARDS	AREA	U.S. AVG
January low	36.3°F	26.4°F	Annual inches precipitation	14.2	35.9	July relative humidity	63.0%	68.8%
July high	94.7°F	86.7°F	Annual inches snowfall	0.0	24.2	Annual days mostly sunny	261	212
Annual days > 90°F	86	38	Annual days precipitation	52	111	Annual days with thunderstorms	3	39
Annual days < 32°F	24	88	Annual days rain > 0.5 inches	8	23	Tornado risk score	2	19
Annual days < 0°F	0	6	Annual days snow > 1.5 inches	0	6	Hurricane risk score	0	15

TEMPERATURE

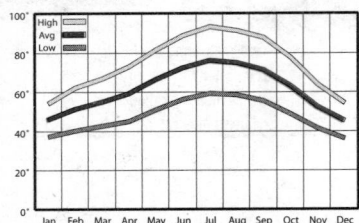

PRECIPITATION

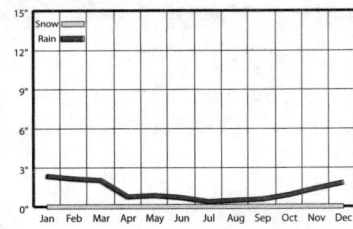

DAYS OF CLOUDS & PRECIPITATION

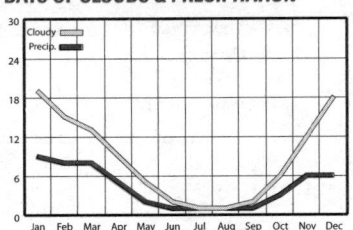

EDUCATION SCORE: 3/RANK: 320

ACHIEVEMENT	AREA	U.S. AVG	PUBLIC SCHOOLS	AREA	U.S. AVG	HIGHER EDUCATION	AREA	U.S. AVG
High school degree	70.4%	80.2%	Expenditures per pupil	$4,784	$5,894	No. 2-year colleges	1	3
2-year college degree	6.6%	6.2%	Student/teacher ratio	21.6	16.7	No. 4-year colleges/universities	1	4
4-year college degree	9.6%	15.8%	Attending public school	94.4%	90.2%	No. highly ranked universities	0	1
Graduate/professional degree	4.4%	9.6%	State SAT score	1018*	1020			
			State ACT score	21.5	21.0			

HEALTH & HEALTHCARE SCORE: 2/RANK: 323

CRIME SCORE: 27/RANK: 239

HAZARDS & ILLNESSES	AREA	U.S. AVG	HEALTHCARE	AREA	U.S. AVG	CRIME	AREA	U.S. AVG
Air-quality score	74	45	Physicians per capita	149.2	261.1	Violent crime rate	648.4	456.0
Water-quality score	13	33	Hospital beds per capita	333.6	432.2	Change in violent crime rate	-30.1%	-17.2%
Pollen/allergy score	74	61	No. teaching hospitals	3	4	Property crime rate	4,836.5	3,950.0
Stress score	96	50	Cost per doctor visit	$67	$67	Change in property crime rate	-27.4%	-16.8%
Cancer mortality per capita	164.0	169.0	Cost per dental visit	$94	$82			
Depression days per month	4.0	2.8	Cost per daily hospital room	$1,511	$733			

TRANSPORTATION SCORE: 2/RANK: 322

COMMUTE	AREA	U.S. AVG	INTERCITY SERVICES	AREA	U.S. AVG	AUTOMOTIVE	AREA	U.S. AVG
Average commute time	26.9 min.	22.6 min.	Miles to nearest major airport	55	46	Insurance, annual premium	$1,200	$1,011
Commute by auto	90.0%	88.7%	Type of local airport	Medium		Gas, cost per gallon	$1.72	$1.50
Commute by mass transit	.5%	1.8%	No. daily airline departures	250	294	Daily vehicle miles per capita	18.5	23.0
Work at home	4.7%	3.9%	Amtrak service	Yes				
Mass transit miles per capita	4.4	8.0	No. interstate highways	1	1			

LEISURE SCORE: 54/RANK: 149

DINING & SHOPPING	AREA	U.S. AVG	ENTERTAINMENT	AREA	U.S. AVG	OUTDOOR ACTIVITIES	AREA	U.S. AVG
Restaurant rating	1	1	Professional sports rating	4	4	Golf-course rating	2	4
No. outlet malls	4	2	College sports rating	4	4	Ski-area rating	9	4
No. Starbucks	11	11	Zoo/aquarium rating	1	3	National Park rating	1	3
No. warehouse clubs	3	4	Amusement park rating	1	3	Sq. miles inland water	2.0	4.0
			Botanical garden/arboretum rating	1	3	Miles of coastline	0.0	11.4

ARTS & CULTURE SCORE: 10/RANK: 298

MEDIA & LIBRARIES	AREA	U.S. AVG	PERFORMING ARTS	AREA	U.S. AVG	MUSEUMS	AREA	U.S. AVG
Arts radio rating	1	3	Classical music rating	4	4	Overall museum rating	3	6
No. public libraries	13	28	Ballet/dance rating	3	3	Art museum rating	2	5
Library volumes per capita	1.5	2.8	Professional theater rating	1	3	Science museum rating	2	4
			University arts programs rating	3	5	Children's museum rating	1	3

Monmouth-Ocean, NJ

Score: 52.8 **Rank:** 203

Profile: Commuter community
Location: Northern New Jersey shore area directly south of New York City
Elevation: 10 feet
Time zone: Eastern Standard Time

PRO	CON
Nearby beaches	Long commute
Entertainment	Cost of living
Proximity to New York City	Urban sprawl

Monmouth and Ocean counties make up a complex and diverse area along a 50-mile stretch of Jersey shore directly to the south of Staten Island and Manhattan. Monmouth County, the more northerly and populous of the two, contains over 50 towns and villages with only two having populations over 20,000. Ocean County spreads southward with beach towns and agricultural land. Fort Dix, a major military base, lies inland. The northern part of Monmouth County is mostly residential but with a healthy amount of commercial activity. The assortment of businesses includes major facilities of AT&T and Lucent Technologies. The population is well educated and fairly affluent. It is possible to commute to New York by rail or even by ferry, although many commute times are an hour or more. The area's average commute time of 33 minutes is the third longest in the United States. Cost of living is the third highest in the state. Some beach towns in Monmouth are a bit run-down, but they remain tourist attractions and offer live entertainment. Asbury Park, which experienced a heyday in the 1940s, was brought to national attention by Bruce Springsteen in the 1970s and Bon Jovi in the 1980s, and attempts to remain a center for live music today.

Most of the two-county area sits on a low coastal plain with partially wooded residential areas to the north and agricultural land inland. The climate is continental with a strong marine influence. Summer days vary between hot and muggy and fairly pleasant. Cool ocean breezes often bring comfortable weather along the coast and in the afternoon. Winters are cool, cloudy, and wet, although the marine influence diminishes the effect of many cold blasts, and below-zero temperatures are fairly uncommon. It may snow inland while giving rain or sleet near the shore. "Noreaster" storms moving up the coast from the south bring heavy rains and winter snows. The area is in a zone of active weather and frequent changes. First freeze is late October, last is mid-April.

POPULATION

DEMOGRAPHICS	AREA	U.S. AVG	ETHNIC COMPOSITION	AREA	U.S. AVG	RESIDENT PROFILE	AREA	U.S. AVG
Population	1,166,901		White	90.2%	75.1%	Single	43.2%	43.6%
Population density per sq. mile	1,053.0	447.3	Black	6.0%	12.3%	Married	56.8%	56.4%
Population growth	18.3%	16.1%	Asian	2.7%	3.6%	Divorced	6.7%	8.4%
Median age	39.5	35.5	American Indian	.2%	.9%	Separated	2.5%	3.0%
Average family size	2.6	2.7	Hispanic	4.7%	12.5%	Married with children	27.0%	28.7%
			Diversity measure	27.0%	35.2%	Single with children	7.0%	10.1%

ECONOMY & JOBS SCORE: 68/RANK: 106

INCOME	AREA	U.S. AVG	EMPLOYMENT	AREA	U.S. AVG	LARGEST EMPLOYING INDUSTRY
Per capita income	$30,380	$23,420	Unemployment rate	5.3%	6.1%	Healthcare and Social Assistance
Household income	$60,152	$46,060	Recent job growth	1.1%	.9%	
Household income < $25K	18.8%	26.4%	Projected future job growth	9.9%	15.1%	
Household income > $75K	37.9%	24.5%	White collar	62.3%	54.5%	
Household income growth	50.7%	57.3%	Blue collar	37.7%	45.5%	

COST OF LIVING SCORE: 6/RANK: 309

INDEXES & TAXES	AREA	U.S. AVG	HOUSING	AREA	U.S. AVG	NECESSITIES	AREA	U.S. AVG
Cost of Living Index	137.4	100.0	Median home price	$261,700	$160,100	Food Index	120.3	100.0
Financial Progress Index	93.3	100.0	Home price appreciation	14.7%	7.1%	Housing Index	162.5	100.0
Income tax rate	2.450%	4.625%	Median rent	$1,013	$670	Utilities Index	134.7	100.0
Sales tax rate	6.000%	6.474%	Homes owned	66.5%	63.9%	Transportation Index	117.2	100.0
Property tax rate	$26.4	$15.6	Homes rented	17.6%	25.3%	Healthcare Index	137.3	100.0
			Housing affordability	46.0%	54.5%	Miscellaneous Cost Index	120.8	100.0

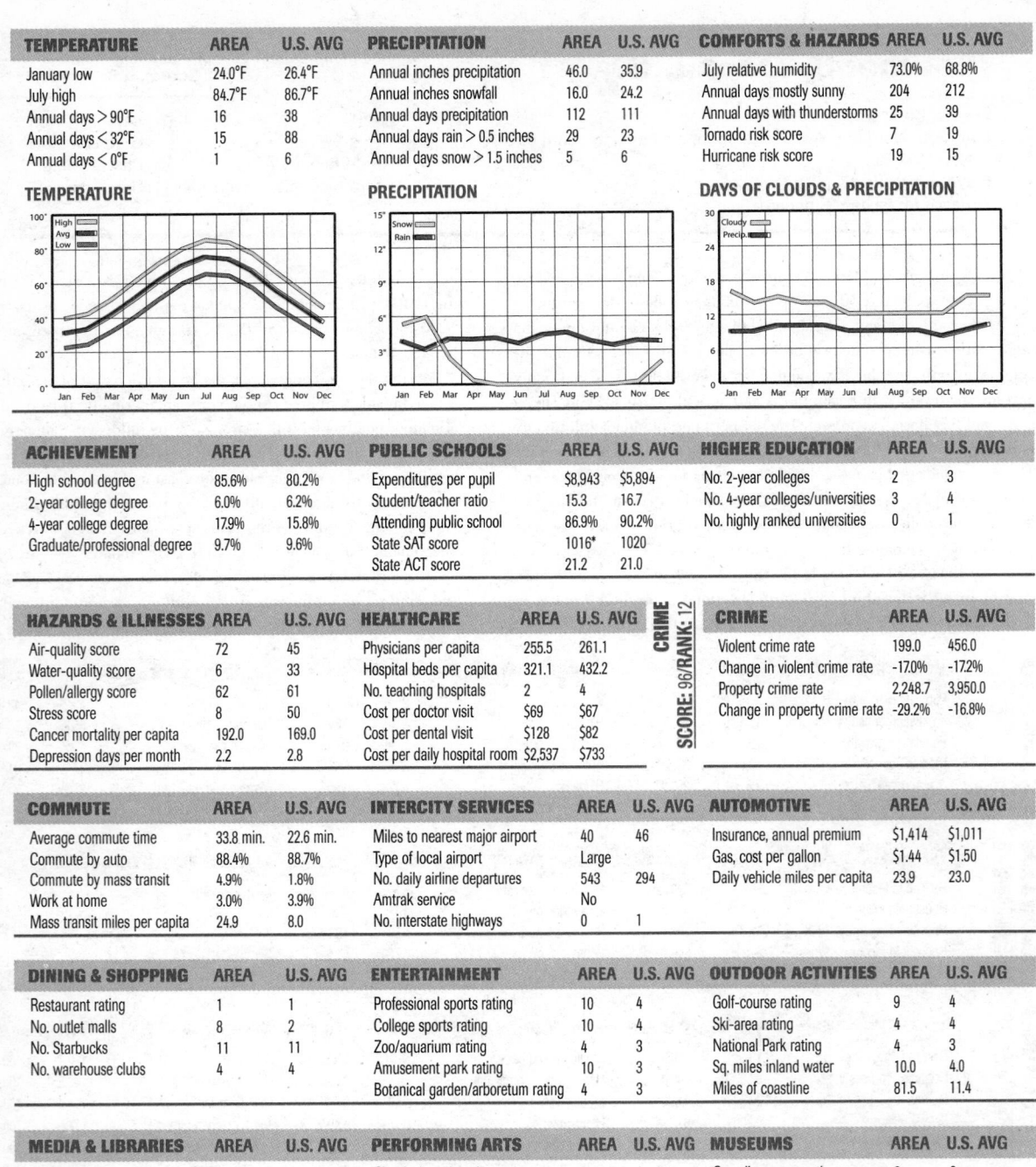

CLIMATE
SCORE: 83/RANK: 57

TEMPERATURE	AREA	U.S. AVG
January low	24.0°F	26.4°F
July high	84.7°F	86.7°F
Annual days > 90°F	16	38
Annual days < 32°F	15	88
Annual days < 0°F	1	6

PRECIPITATION	AREA	U.S. AVG
Annual inches precipitation	46.0	35.9
Annual inches snowfall	16.0	24.2
Annual days precipitation	112	111
Annual days rain > 0.5 inches	29	23
Annual days snow > 1.5 inches	5	6

COMFORTS & HAZARDS	AREA	U.S. AVG
July relative humidity	73.0%	68.8%
Annual days mostly sunny	204	212
Annual days with thunderstorms	25	39
Tornado risk score	7	19
Hurricane risk score	19	15

TEMPERATURE

PRECIPITATION

DAYS OF CLOUDS & PRECIPITATION

EDUCATION
SCORE: 61/RANK: 129

ACHIEVEMENT	AREA	U.S. AVG
High school degree	85.6%	80.2%
2-year college degree	6.0%	6.2%
4-year college degree	17.9%	15.8%
Graduate/professional degree	9.7%	9.6%

PUBLIC SCHOOLS	AREA	U.S. AVG
Expenditures per pupil	$8,943	$5,894
Student/teacher ratio	15.3	16.7
Attending public school	86.9%	90.2%
State SAT score	1016*	1020
State ACT score	21.2	21.0

HIGHER EDUCATION	AREA	U.S. AVG
No. 2-year colleges	2	3
No. 4-year colleges/universities	3	4
No. highly ranked universities	0	1

HEALTH & HEALTHCARE
SCORE: 6/RANK: 308

HAZARDS & ILLNESSES	AREA	U.S. AVG
Air-quality score	72	45
Water-quality score	6	33
Pollen/allergy score	62	61
Stress score	8	50
Cancer mortality per capita	192.0	169.0
Depression days per month	2.2	2.8

HEALTHCARE	AREA	U.S. AVG
Physicians per capita	255.5	261.1
Hospital beds per capita	321.1	432.2
No. teaching hospitals	2	4
Cost per doctor visit	$69	$67
Cost per dental visit	$128	$82
Cost per daily hospital room	$2,537	$733

CRIME
SCORE: 96/RANK: 12

CRIME	AREA	U.S. AVG
Violent crime rate	199.0	456.0
Change in violent crime rate	-17.0%	-17.2%
Property crime rate	2,248.7	3,950.0
Change in property crime rate	-29.2%	-16.8%

TRANSPORTATION
SCORE: 79/RANK: 68

COMMUTE	AREA	U.S. AVG
Average commute time	33.8 min.	22.6 min.
Commute by auto	88.4%	88.7%
Commute by mass transit	4.9%	1.8%
Work at home	3.0%	3.9%
Mass transit miles per capita	24.9	8.0

INTERCITY SERVICES	AREA	U.S. AVG
Miles to nearest major airport	40	46
Type of local airport	Large	
No. daily airline departures	543	294
Amtrak service	No	
No. interstate highways	0	1

AUTOMOTIVE	AREA	U.S. AVG
Insurance, annual premium	$1,414	$1,011
Gas, cost per gallon	$1.44	$1.50
Daily vehicle miles per capita	23.9	23.0

LEISURE
SCORE: 96/RANK: 11

DINING & SHOPPING	AREA	U.S. AVG
Restaurant rating	1	1
No. outlet malls	8	2
No. Starbucks	11	11
No. warehouse clubs	4	4

ENTERTAINMENT	AREA	U.S. AVG
Professional sports rating	10	4
College sports rating	10	4
Zoo/aquarium rating	4	3
Amusement park rating	10	3
Botanical garden/arboretum rating	4	3

OUTDOOR ACTIVITIES	AREA	U.S. AVG
Golf-course rating	9	4
Ski-area rating	4	4
National Park rating	4	3
Sq. miles inland water	10.0	4.0
Miles of coastline	81.5	11.4

ARTS & CULTURE
SCORE: 50/RANK: 163

MEDIA & LIBRARIES	AREA	U.S. AVG
Arts radio rating	4	3
No. public libraries	60	28
Library volumes per capita	3.1	2.8

PERFORMING ARTS	AREA	U.S. AVG
Classical music rating	7	4
Ballet/dance rating	6	3
Professional theater rating	8	3
University arts programs rating	2	5

MUSEUMS	AREA	U.S. AVG
Overall museum rating	8	6
Art museum rating	7	5
Science museum rating	7	4
Children's museum rating	7	3

Monroe, LA

Profile: Small city
Location: Northeast Louisiana along I-20
Elevation: 259 feet
Time zone: Central Standard Time

| **Score: 46.3** | **Rank: 247** |

PRO	CON
Nearby water recreation	Crime rate
Nature areas	Heat and humidity
Projected job growth	Isolation

Monroe along the Ouachita River is the commercial and cultural center for northeast Louisiana. An early-20th-century oil and gas boom has subsided but modestly sized commercial activities and papermaking remain. Employment and job-growth projections are reasonably healthy. The University of Louisiana at Monroe provides some college-town amenities, and water-recreation areas are plentiful. But the area has the highest crime rate in a high-crime state, and is fairly isolated from big-city amenities.

The terrain is level to gently rolling, with areas of agriculture and pine forest. Typical of inland portions of Gulf-bordering states, the climate is mainly humid subtropical with some continental influence from the north. Summers are consistently warm and humid with ample precipitation and thunderstorms, especially in early summer. Winters are mild but with occasional below-freezing temperatures, a few ice storms, and an infrequent light snow. First freeze is early November, last is late March.

POPULATION

DEMOGRAPHICS	AREA	U.S. AVG	ETHNIC COMPOSITION	AREA	U.S. AVG	RESIDENT PROFILE	AREA	U.S. AVG
Population	147,342		White	70.5%	75.1%	Single	46.3%	43.6%
Population density per sq. mile	241.2	447.3	Black	28.4%	12.3%	Married	53.7%	56.4%
Population growth	3.6%	16.1%	Asian	.7%	3.6%	Divorced	8.1%	8.4%
Median age	32.6	35.5	American Indian	.2%	.9%	Separated	5.0%	3.0%
Average family size	2.7	2.7	Hispanic	1.2%	12.5%	Married with children	27.5%	28.7%
			Diversity measure	47.8%	35.2%	Single with children	14.8%	10.1%

ECONOMY & JOBS SCORE: 30/RANK: 232

INCOME	AREA	U.S. AVG	EMPLOYMENT	AREA	U.S. AVG	LARGEST EMPLOYING INDUSTRY
Per capita income	$19,362	$23,420	Unemployment rate	6.8%	6.1%	Paper Manufacturing
Household income	$35,118	$46,060	Recent job growth	.9%	.9%	
Household income < $25K	35.7%	26.4%	Projected future job growth	18.4%	15.1%	
Household income > $75K	18.9%	24.5%	White collar	56.8%	54.5%	
Household income growth	65.2%	57.3%	Blue collar	43.2%	45.5%	

COST OF LIVING SCORE: 85/RANK: 50

INDEXES & TAXES	AREA	U.S. AVG	HOUSING	AREA	U.S. AVG	NECESSITIES	AREA	U.S. AVG
Cost of Living Index	85.6	100.0	Median home price	$98,010	$160,100	Food Index	90.5	100.0
Financial Progress Index	87.4	100.0	Home price appreciation	7.0%	7.1%	Housing Index	60.9	100.0
Income tax rate	4.000%	4.625%	Median rent	$487	$670	Utilities Index	115.6	100.0
Sales tax rate	9.500%	6.474%	Homes owned	63.9%	63.9%	Transportation Index	98.5	100.0
Property tax rate	$5.1	$15.6	Homes rented	24.9%	25.3%	Healthcare Index	91.2	100.0
			Housing affordability	56.0%	54.5%	Miscellaneous Cost Index	103.5	100.0

CLIMATE SCORE: 73/RANK: 89

TEMPERATURE	AREA	U.S. AVG	PRECIPITATION	AREA	U.S. AVG	COMFORTS & HAZARDS	AREA	U.S. AVG
January low	37.8°F	26.4°F	Annual inches precipitation	45.0	35.9	July relative humidity	71.0%	68.8%
July high	93.8°F	86.7°F	Annual inches snowfall	1.0	24.2	Annual days mostly sunny	217	212
Annual days > 90°F	87	38	Annual days precipitation	97	111	Annual days with thunderstorms	54	39
Annual days < 32°F	1	88	Annual days rain > 0.5 inches	29	23	Tornado risk score	26	19
Annual days < 0°F	0	6	Annual days snow > 1.5 inches	0	6	Hurricane risk score	15	15

TEMPERATURE

PRECIPITATION

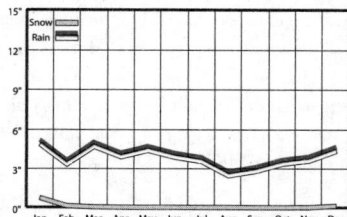

DAYS OF CLOUDS & PRECIPITATION

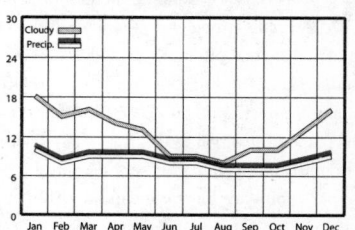

EDUCATION — SCORE: 19/RANK: 268

ACHIEVEMENT	AREA	U.S. AVG	PUBLIC SCHOOLS	AREA	U.S. AVG	HIGHER EDUCATION	AREA	U.S. AVG
High school degree	78.6%	80.2%	Expenditures per pupil	$4,720	$5,894	No. 2-year colleges	0	3
2-year college degree	3.0%	6.2%	Student/teacher ratio	15.6	16.7	No. 4-year colleges/universities	1	4
4-year college degree	14.8%	15.8%	Attending public school	91.9%	90.2%	No. highly ranked universities	0	1
Graduate/professional degree	7.9%	9.6%	State SAT score	1122	1020			
			State ACT score	19.6*	21.0			

HEALTH & HEALTHCARE — SCORE: 54/RANK: 151

CRIME — SCORE: 1/RANK: 325

HAZARDS & ILLNESSES	AREA	U.S. AVG	HEALTHCARE	AREA	U.S. AVG	CRIME	AREA	U.S. AVG
Air-quality score	3	45	Physicians per capita	269.4	261.1	Violent crime rate	887.0	456.0
Water-quality score	20	33	Hospital beds per capita	894.4	432.2	Change in violent crime rate	.2%	-17.2%
Pollen/allergy score	66	61	No. teaching hospitals	1	4	Property crime rate	6,126.4	3,950.0
Stress score	74	50	Cost per doctor visit	$61	$67	Change in property crime rate	-2.5%	-16.8%
Cancer mortality per capita	174.6	169.0	Cost per dental visit	$77	$82			
Depression days per month	2.7	2.8	Cost per daily hospital room	$386	$733			

TRANSPORTATION — SCORE: 48/RANK: 172

COMMUTE	AREA	U.S. AVG	INTERCITY SERVICES	AREA	U.S. AVG	AUTOMOTIVE	AREA	U.S. AVG
Average commute time	20.4 min.	22.6 min.	Miles to nearest major airport	101	46	Insurance, annual premium	$1,111	$1,011
Commute by auto	94.6%	88.7%	Type of local airport	Small		Gas, cost per gallon	$1.43	$1.50
Commute by mass transit	1.1%	1.8%	No. daily airline departures	66	294	Daily vehicle miles per capita	25.0	23.0
Work at home	1.8%	3.9%	Amtrak service	No				
Mass transit miles per capita	4.9	8.0	No. interstate highways	1	1			

LEISURE — SCORE: 9/RANK: 301

DINING & SHOPPING	AREA	U.S. AVG	ENTERTAINMENT	AREA	U.S. AVG	OUTDOOR ACTIVITIES	AREA	U.S. AVG
Restaurant rating	1	1	Professional sports rating	2	4	Golf-course rating	1	4
No. outlet malls	0	2	College sports rating	4	4	Ski-area rating	1	4
No. Starbucks	0	11	Zoo/aquarium rating	1	3	National Park rating	2	3
No. warehouse clubs	3	4	Amusement park rating	1	3	Sq. miles inland water	2.0	4.0
			Botanical garden/arboretum rating	3	3	Miles of coastline	0.0	11.4

ARTS & CULTURE — SCORE: 43/RANK: 188

MEDIA & LIBRARIES	AREA	U.S. AVG	PERFORMING ARTS	AREA	U.S. AVG	MUSEUMS	AREA	U.S. AVG
Arts radio rating	1	3	Classical music rating	3	4	Overall museum rating	2	6
No. public libraries	5	28	Ballet/dance rating	3	3	Art museum rating	3	5
Library volumes per capita	2.5	2.8	Professional theater rating	1	3	Science museum rating	1	4
			University arts programs rating	4	5	Children's museum rating	1	3

Montgomery, AL

Score: 44.6   Rank: 258

Profile: Capital city
Location: South-central Alabama
Elevation: 202 feet
Time zone: Central Standard Time

PRO	CON
Cost of living	Crime rate
Strong economy	Summer heat and humidity
Historic interest	Air service

Montgomery is a steamy old Southern town with a strong legacy as the first Confederate capital, and later, as a center of civil rights struggles in the mid–20th century. It remains the state capital today, but offers only modest amenities for a capital its size. Economy and employment have been relatively strong with a 3.3% annual job-growth rate into 2003. The few quality arts amenities include a Shakespeare festival and a fine arts museum. Crime rates are among the highest in the state. Air service, physicians per capita, and hospital beds per capita are low for a capital city.

This gently rolling area of Alabama has no significant topographic features and is a mix of open agricultural land and pine forest. The climate is humid subtropical with a strong influence from the Gulf of Mexico. Summers are warm, still, and humid with little change from day to day. Winter shifts between mild, moist, Gulf air and cool, continental, northern air cause clouds and rain. Temperature and precipitation are about average for the state.

POPULATION

DEMOGRAPHICS	AREA	U.S. AVG	ETHNIC COMPOSITION	AREA	U.S. AVG	RESIDENT PROFILE	AREA	U.S. AVG
Population	337,721		White	63.5%	75.1%	Single	46.6%	43.6%
Population density per sq. mile	168.2	447.3	Black	35.2%	12.3%	Married	53.4%	56.4%
Population growth	15.5%	16.1%	Asian	.8%	3.6%	Divorced	8.7%	8.4%
Median age	34.3	35.5	American Indian	.3%	.9%	Separated	3.5%	3.0%
Average family size	2.7	2.7	Hispanic	1.2%	12.5%	Married with children	29.4%	28.7%
			Diversity measure	51.1%	35.2%	Single with children	13.0%	10.1%

ECONOMY & JOBS SCORE: 82/RANK: 59

INCOME	AREA	U.S. AVG	EMPLOYMENT	AREA	U.S. AVG	LARGEST EMPLOYING INDUSTRY
Per capita income	$21,353	$23,420	Unemployment rate	5.5%	6.1%	Fabricated Metal Product Manufacturing
Household income	$41,426	$46,060	Recent job growth	3.3%	.9%	
Household income < $25K	29.1%	26.4%	Projected future job growth	15.5%	15.1%	
Household income > $75K	21.8%	24.5%	White collar	57.0%	54.5%	
Household income growth	54.7%	57.3%	Blue collar	43.0%	45.5%	

COST OF LIVING SCORE: 89/RANK: 37

INDEXES & TAXES	AREA	U.S. AVG	HOUSING	AREA	U.S. AVG	NECESSITIES	AREA	U.S. AVG
Cost of Living Index	84.8	100.0	Median home price	$99,530	$160,100	Food Index	95.2	100.0
Financial Progress Index	104.1	100.0	Home price appreciation	3.3%	7.1%	Housing Index	61.8	100.0
Income tax rate	5.000%	4.625%	Median rent	$537	$670	Utilities Index	107.0	100.0
Sales tax rate	9.000%	6.474%	Homes owned	66.0%	63.9%	Transportation Index	100.9	100.0
Property tax rate	$2.9	$15.6	Homes rented	23.7%	25.3%	Healthcare Index	93.0	100.0
			Housing affordability	59.0%	54.5%	Miscellaneous Cost Index	96.1	100.0

CLIMATE SCORE: 55/RANK: 149

TEMPERATURE	AREA	U.S. AVG	PRECIPITATION	AREA	U.S. AVG	COMFORTS & HAZARDS	AREA	U.S. AVG
January low	37.1°F	26.4°F	Annual inches precipitation	50.0	35.9	July relative humidity	73.0%	68.8%
July high	90.7°F	86.7°F	Annual inches snowfall	.2	24.2	Annual days mostly sunny	216	212
Annual days > 90°F	66	38	Annual days precipitation	109	111	Annual days with thunderstorms	62	39
Annual days < 32°F	39	88	Annual days rain > 0.5 inches	33	23	Tornado risk score	21	19
Annual days < 0°F	0	6	Annual days snow > 1.5 inches	1	6	Hurricane risk score	28	15

TEMPERATURE

PRECIPITATION

DAYS OF CLOUDS & PRECIPITATION

EDUCATION SCORE: 28/RANK: 238

ACHIEVEMENT	AREA	U.S. AVG	PUBLIC SCHOOLS	AREA	U.S. AVG	HIGHER EDUCATION	AREA	U.S. AVG
High school degree	80.7%	80.2%	Expenditures per pupil	$4,443	$5,894	No. 2-year colleges	4	3
2-year college degree	5.2%	6.2%	Student/teacher ratio	16.1	16.7	No. 4-year colleges/universities	5	4
4-year college degree	15.3%	15.8%	Attending public school	84.7%	90.2%	No. highly ranked universities	1	1
Graduate/professional degree	9.4%	9.6%	State SAT score	1111	1020			
			State ACT score	20.1*	21.0			

HEALTH & HEALTHCARE SCORE: 62/RANK: 124

HAZARDS & ILLNESSES	AREA	U.S. AVG	HEALTHCARE	AREA	U.S. AVG
Air-quality score	6	45	Physicians per capita	195.4	261.1
Water-quality score	30	33	Hospital beds per capita	359.4	432.2
Pollen/allergy score	57	61	No. teaching hospitals	1	4
Stress score	95	50	Cost per doctor visit	$53	$67
Cancer mortality per capita	174.2	169.0	Cost per dental visit	$63	$82
Depression days per month	3.7	2.8	Cost per daily hospital room	$745	$733

CRIME SCORE: 5/RANK: 314

CRIME	AREA	U.S. AVG
Violent crime rate	581.4	456.0
Change in violent crime rate	-5.2%	-17.2%
Property crime rate	5,638.5	3,950.0
Change in property crime rate	15.0%	-16.8%

TRANSPORTATION SCORE: 15/RANK: 281

COMMUTE	AREA	U.S. AVG	INTERCITY SERVICES	AREA	U.S. AVG	AUTOMOTIVE	AREA	U.S. AVG
Average commute time	22.7 min.	22.6 min.	Miles to nearest major airport	88	46	Insurance, annual premium	$827	$1,011
Commute by auto	93.9%	88.7%	Type of local airport	Small		Gas, cost per gallon	$1.42	$1.50
Commute by mass transit	.9%	1.8%	No. daily airline departures	111	294	Daily vehicle miles per capita	29.3	23.0
Work at home	2.2%	3.9%	Amtrak service	No				
Mass transit miles per capita	2.3	8.0	No. interstate highways	2	1			

LEISURE SCORE: 25/RANK: 246

DINING & SHOPPING	AREA	U.S. AVG	ENTERTAINMENT	AREA	U.S. AVG	OUTDOOR ACTIVITIES	AREA	U.S. AVG
Restaurant rating	1	1	Professional sports rating	2	4	Golf-course rating	3	4
No. outlet malls	0	2	College sports rating	4	4	Ski-area rating	1	4
No. Starbucks	0	11	Zoo/aquarium rating	4	3	National Park rating	1	3
No. warehouse clubs	3	4	Amusement park rating	1	3	Sq. miles inland water	4.0	4.0
			Botanical garden/arboretum rating	1	3	Miles of coastline	0.0	11.4

ARTS & CULTURE SCORE: 51/RANK: 161

MEDIA & LIBRARIES	AREA	U.S. AVG	PERFORMING ARTS	AREA	U.S. AVG	MUSEUMS	AREA	U.S. AVG
Arts radio rating	7	3	Classical music rating	3	4	Overall museum rating	5	6
No. public libraries	17	28	Ballet/dance rating	5	3	Art museum rating	6	5
Library volumes per capita	2.5	2.8	Professional theater rating	1	3	Science museum rating	3	4
			University arts programs rating	8	5	Children's museum rating	1	3

Muncie, IN

Score: 67.9   Rank: 90

Profile: Small town/College town
Location: Northeast Indiana, about 60 miles northeast of Indianapolis
Elevation: 700 feet
Time zone: Eastern Standard Time (no daylight savings time)

PRO	CON
College-town amenities	Winter climate
Small-town atmosphere	Employment
Cost of living	Low educational attainment

Muncie is an agricultural center with a college-town element and a variety of industry. In the 19th century the Ball family started manufacturing canning jars, and Ball jars are still the world standard. The family business endowed Ball State University, an attractive mid-size campus and good state school. The college-town influence includes healthcare and a few arts amenities. Other positives for the area include good air quality, a low crime rate, and a Cost of Living Index at 80.5, the lowest in the state and a good value for what's available. The city has served as a model "mid-America" town for sociological and marketing studies since the 1930s. The negatives include a harsh winter climate and slightly lower employment and educational attainment than would be expected in a college town.

The town is located in a mainly level agricultural plain with a few rolling hills to the south and areas of deciduous trees. Summers are warm and humid with thundershowers but extreme heat is rare. Winters are cold and variable with occasional blasts of cold polar air and snow. Snowfalls of 3 inches or more occur on average of two to three times each winter. First freeze is mid- to late October, the last is late April.

POPULATION

DEMOGRAPHICS	AREA	U.S. AVG	ETHNIC COMPOSITION	AREA	U.S. AVG	RESIDENT PROFILE	AREA	U.S. AVG
Population	118,197		White	94.2%	75.1%	Single	48.8%	43.6%
Population density per sq. mile	300.5	447.3	Black	4.6%	12.3%	Married	51.2%	56.4%
Population growth	-1.2%	16.1%	Asian	.7%	3.6%	Divorced	9.5%	8.4%
Median age	34.2	35.5	American Indian	.3%	.9%	Separated	1.8%	3.0%
Average family size	2.4	2.7	Hispanic	1.1%	12.5%	Married with children	24.5%	28.7%
			Diversity measure	18.1%	35.2%	Single with children	10.5%	10.1%

ECONOMY & JOBS SCORE: 52/RANK: 158

INCOME	AREA	U.S. AVG	EMPLOYMENT	AREA	U.S. AVG	LARGEST EMPLOYING INDUSTRY
Per capita income	$20,935	$23,420	Unemployment rate	5.3%	6.1%	Transportation Equipment Manufacturing
Household income	$37,248	$46,060	Recent job growth	3.0%	.9%	
Household income < $25K	34.1%	26.4%	Projected future job growth	11.7%	15.1%	
Household income > $75K	18.0%	24.5%	White collar	50.5%	54.5%	
Household income growth	52.2%	57.3%	Blue collar	49.5%	45.5%	

COST OF LIVING SCORE: 82/RANK: 58

INDEXES & TAXES	AREA	U.S. AVG	HOUSING	AREA	U.S. AVG	NECESSITIES	AREA	U.S. AVG
Cost of Living Index	80.5	100.0	Median home price	$86,500	$160,100	Food Index	95.6	100.0
Financial Progress Index	98.6	100.0	Home price appreciation	4.7%	7.1%	Housing Index	53.7	100.0
Income tax rate	3.400%	4.625%	Median rent	$570	$670	Utilities Index	93.5	100.0
Sales tax rate	6.000%	6.474%	Homes owned	63.1%	63.9%	Transportation Index	101.3	100.0
Property tax rate	$22.2	$15.6	Homes rented	28.9%	25.3%	Healthcare Index	94.4	100.0
			Housing affordability	50.0%	54.5%	Miscellaneous Cost Index	93.9	100.0

CLIMATE
SCORE: 50/RANK: 164

TEMPERATURE	AREA	U.S. AVG	PRECIPITATION	AREA	U.S. AVG	COMFORTS & HAZARDS	AREA	U.S. AVG
January low	19.7°F	26.4°F	Annual inches precipitation	39.0	35.9	July relative humidity	73.0%	68.8%
July high	85.4°F	86.7°F	Annual inches snowfall	21.0	24.2	Annual days mostly sunny	191	212
Annual days > 90°F	15	38	Annual days precipitation	122	111	Annual days with thunderstorms	45	39
Annual days < 32°F	122	88	Annual days rain > 0.5 inches	27	23	Tornado risk score	20	19
Annual days < 0°F	7	6	Annual days snow > 1.5 inches	7	6	Hurricane risk score	4	15

TEMPERATURE

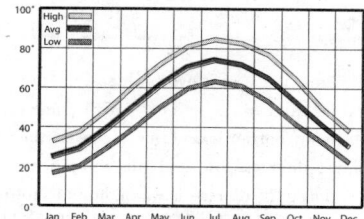

PRECIPITATION

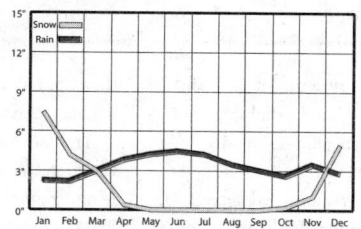

DAYS OF CLOUDS & PRECIPITATION

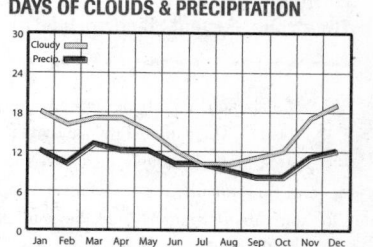

EDUCATION
SCORE: 39/RANK: 200

ACHIEVEMENT	AREA	U.S. AVG	PUBLIC SCHOOLS	AREA	U.S. AVG	HIGHER EDUCATION	AREA	U.S. AVG
High school degree	81.6%	80.2%	Expenditures per pupil	$6,591	$5,894	No. 2-year colleges	1	3
2-year college degree	4.4%	6.2%	Student/teacher ratio	16.3	16.7	No. 4-year colleges/universities	1	4
4-year college degree	10.8%	15.8%	Attending public school	94.5%	90.2%	No. highly ranked universities	0	1
Graduate/professional degree	9.6%	9.6%	State SAT score	1004*	1020			
			State ACT score	21.6	21.0			

HEALTH & HEALTHCARE
SCORE: 47/RANK: 174

CRIME
SCORE: 79/RANK: 67

HAZARDS & ILLNESSES	AREA	U.S. AVG	HEALTHCARE	AREA	U.S. AVG	CRIME	AREA	U.S. AVG
Air-quality score	24	45	Physicians per capita	258.9	261.1	Violent crime rate	289.7	456.0
Water-quality score	8	33	Hospital beds per capita	332.6	432.2	Change in violent crime rate	11.3%	-17.2%
Pollen/allergy score	65	61	No. teaching hospitals	1	4	Property crime rate	3,048.4	3,950.0
Stress score	23	50	Cost per doctor visit	$61	$67	Change in property crime rate	-34.0%	-16.8%
Cancer mortality per capita	166.9	169.0	Cost per dental visit	$70	$82			
Depression days per month	1.3	2.8	Cost per daily hospital room	$547	$733			

TRANSPORTATION
SCORE: 66/RANK: 111

COMMUTE	AREA	U.S. AVG	INTERCITY SERVICES	AREA	U.S. AVG	AUTOMOTIVE	AREA	U.S. AVG
Average commute time	19.8 min.	22.6 min.	Miles to nearest major airport	56	46	Insurance, annual premium	$770	$1,011
Commute by auto	84.4%	88.7%	Type of local airport	Small		Gas, cost per gallon	$1.44	$1.50
Commute by mass transit	1.2%	1.8%	No. daily airline departures	88	294	Daily vehicle miles per capita	18.6	23.0
Work at home	3.4%	3.9%	Amtrak service	No				
Mass transit miles per capita	9.2	8.0	No. interstate highways	1	1			

LEISURE
SCORE: 50/RANK: 166

DINING & SHOPPING	AREA	U.S. AVG	ENTERTAINMENT	AREA	U.S. AVG	OUTDOOR ACTIVITIES	AREA	U.S. AVG
Restaurant rating	1	1	Professional sports rating	2	4	Golf-course rating	2	4
No. outlet malls	0	2	College sports rating	3	4	Ski-area rating	2	4
No. Starbucks	0	11	Zoo/aquarium rating	1	3	National Park rating	1	3
No. warehouse clubs	1	4	Amusement park rating	1	3	Sq. miles inland water	2.0	4.0
			Botanical garden/arboretum rating	2	3	Miles of coastline	0.0	11.4

ARTS & CULTURE
SCORE: 78/RANK: 70

MEDIA & LIBRARIES	AREA	U.S. AVG	PERFORMING ARTS	AREA	U.S. AVG	MUSEUMS	AREA	U.S. AVG
Arts radio rating	1	3	Classical music rating	3	4	Overall museum rating	5	6
No. public libraries	5	28	Ballet/dance rating	1	3	Art museum rating	6	5
Library volumes per capita	3.6	2.8	Professional theater rating	1	3	Science museum rating	5	4
			University arts programs rating	7	5	Children's museum rating	4	3

Myrtle Beach, SC

Score: 42.1	Rank: 266

Profile: Beach city
Location: Northeast South Carolina on Atlantic Coast, 20 miles from North Carolina border
Elevation: 30 feet
Time zone: Eastern Standard Time

PRO	CON
Beaches and recreation	Crime rate
Entertainment	Arts and culture
Job growth	Tourist sprawl

Myrtle Beach might be called the "northernmost city in Florida." The wide, white, sandy beaches lined with high-rise hotels and residences look just like a beach resort city in Florida—and functionally, that is what Myrtle Beach is. The area is a center for tourism, particularly for the southeast region, and attracts travelers from the north during spring break. Serving this market are chain restaurants, amusement parks, miniature golf courses, and a variety of local events. Other amenities include over 100 golf courses and some country-and-western-themed museums and entertainment—making Myrtle Beach an emerging Branson. The springtime Canadian-American Days festival (or "Can-Am") draws thousands from north of the U.S. border. The area, much of it overbuilt and unattractive, has as a gaudy, commercial feel and an exceptionally high crime rate.

The city sits on a sandy barrier island in extreme northeastern South Carolina. Areas of level plain and low sand hills and pine trees cover the island and inland sections. The climate is warm, humid subtropical, typical of areas to the south. Summer days are warm and humid but moderated along the coast by sea breezes. Due to the warm marine influence and the Gulf Stream, winters are very mild, although temperatures do drop below freezing. Skies are sunny every 2 in 3 days, but plenty of rain falls year-round. The area is vulnerable to Atlantic hurricanes, although it's slightly north of the main hazard area.

POPULATION

DEMOGRAPHICS	AREA	U.S. AVG	ETHNIC COMPOSITION	AREA	U.S. AVG	RESIDENT PROFILE	AREA	U.S. AVG
Population	206,039		White	77.0%	75.1%	Single	43.0%	43.6%
Population density per sq. mile	181.7	447.3	Black	22.0%	12.3%	Married	57.0%	56.4%
Population growth	43.0%	16.1%	Asian	.6%	3.6%	Divorced	7.7%	8.4%
Median age	38.9	35.5	American Indian	.2%	.9%	Separated	4.7%	3.0%
Average family size	2.6	2.7	Hispanic	.8%	12.5%	Married with children	25.0%	28.7%
			Diversity measure	33.3%	35.2%	Single with children	11.9%	10.1%

ECONOMY & JOBS SCORE: 5/RANK: 312

INCOME	AREA	U.S. AVG	EMPLOYMENT	AREA	U.S. AVG	LARGEST EMPLOYING INDUSTRY
Per capita income	$24,768	$23,420	Unemployment rate	3.8%	6.1%	Accommodations and Food Services
Household income	$42,302	$46,060	Recent job growth	-5.5%	.9%	
Household income < $25K	26.8%	26.4%	Projected future job growth	28.4%	15.1%	
Household income > $75K	20.9%	24.5%	White collar	49.7%	54.5%	
Household income growth	69.1%	57.3%	Blue collar	50.3%	45.5%	

COST OF LIVING SCORE: 44/RANK: 185

INDEXES & TAXES	AREA	U.S. AVG	HOUSING	AREA	U.S. AVG	NECESSITIES	AREA	U.S. AVG
Cost of Living Index	94.9	100.0	Median home price	$141,020	$160,100	Food Index	105.7	100.0
Financial Progress Index	95.0	100.0	Home price appreciation	5.6%	7.1%	Housing Index	87.6	100.0
Income tax rate	7.000%	4.625%	Median rent	$594	$670	Utilities Index	89.7	100.0
Sales tax rate	5.000%	6.474%	Homes owned	57.9%	63.9%	Transportation Index	95.7	100.0
Property tax rate	$7.8	$15.6	Homes rented	19.3%	25.3%	Healthcare Index	97.7	100.0
			Housing affordability	63.0%	54.5%	Miscellaneous Cost Index	99.2	100.0

CLIMATE SCORE: 52/RANK: 158

TEMPERATURE	AREA	U.S. AVG	PRECIPITATION	AREA	U.S. AVG	COMFORTS & HAZARDS	AREA	U.S. AVG
January low	36.2°F	26.4°F	Annual inches precipitation	54.0	35.9	July relative humidity	75.0%	68.8%
July high	88.8°F	86.7°F	Annual inches snowfall	1.8	24.2	Annual days mostly sunny	219	212
Annual days > 90°F	45	38	Annual days precipitation	117	111	Annual days with thunderstorms	46	39
Annual days < 32°F	45	88	Annual days rain > 0.5 inches	31	23	Tornado risk score	15	19
Annual days < 0°F	0	6	Annual days snow > 1.5 inches	1	6	Hurricane risk score	65	15

TEMPERATURE

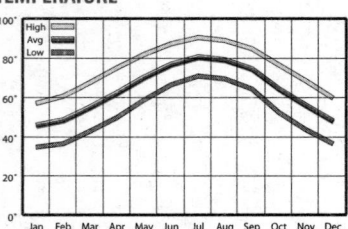

PRECIPITATION

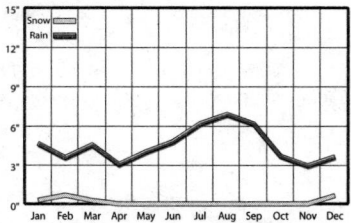

DAYS OF CLOUDS & PRECIPITATION

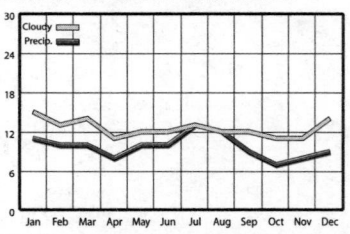

EDUCATION SCORE: 42/RANK: 191

ACHIEVEMENT	AREA	U.S. AVG	PUBLIC SCHOOLS	AREA	U.S. AVG	HIGHER EDUCATION	AREA	U.S. AVG
High school degree	81.2%	80.2%	Expenditures per pupil	$5,707	$5,894	No. 2-year colleges	1	3
2-year college degree	7.3%	6.2%	Student/teacher ratio	15.3	16.7	No. 4-year colleges/universities	1	4
4-year college degree	12.8%	15.8%	Attending public school	94.3%	90.2%	No. highly ranked universities	0	1
Graduate/professional degree	5.9%	9.6%	State SAT score	989*	1020			
			State ACT score	19.2	21.0			

HEALTH & HEALTHCARE SCORE: 70/RANK: 99

HAZARDS & ILLNESSES	AREA	U.S. AVG	HEALTHCARE	AREA	U.S. AVG
Air-quality score	24	45	Physicians per capita	183.5	261.1
Water-quality score	100	33	Hospital beds per capita	337.2	432.2
Pollen/allergy score	67	61	No. teaching hospitals	0	4
Stress score	85	50	Cost per doctor visit	$69	$67
Cancer mortality per capita	160.2	169.0	Cost per dental visit	$65	$82
Depression days per month	3.2	2.8	Cost per daily hospital room	$575	$733

CRIME SCORE: 3/RANK: 319

CRIME	AREA	U.S. AVG
Violent crime rate	789.2	456.0
Change in violent crime rate	-32.0%	-17.2%
Property crime rate	6,784.4	3,950.0
Change in property crime rate	-22.8%	-16.8%

TRANSPORTATION SCORE: 28/RANK: 238

COMMUTE	AREA	U.S. AVG	INTERCITY SERVICES	AREA	U.S. AVG	AUTOMOTIVE	AREA	U.S. AVG
Average commute time	23.7 min.	22.6 min.	Miles to nearest major airport	3	46	Insurance, annual premium	$1,062	$1,011
Commute by auto	93.4%	88.7%	Type of local airport	Small		Gas, cost per gallon	$1.39	$1.50
Commute by mass transit	.5%	1.8%	No. daily airline departures	51	294	Daily vehicle miles per capita	21.0	23.0
Work at home	2.3%	3.9%	Amtrak service	No				
Mass transit miles per capita	8.0	8.0	No. interstate highways	1	1			

LEISURE SCORE: 42/RANK: 191

DINING & SHOPPING	AREA	U.S. AVG	ENTERTAINMENT	AREA	U.S. AVG	OUTDOOR ACTIVITIES	AREA	U.S. AVG
Restaurant rating	1	1	Professional sports rating	2	4	Golf-course rating	2	4
No. outlet malls	3	2	College sports rating	3	4	Ski-area rating	1	4
No. Starbucks	0	11	Zoo/aquarium rating	1	3	National Park rating	1	3
No. warehouse clubs	3	4	Amusement park rating	6	3	Sq. miles inland water	3.0	4.0
			Botanical garden/arboretum rating	1	3	Miles of coastline	26.7	11.4

ARTS & CULTURE SCORE: 52/RANK: 159

MEDIA & LIBRARIES	AREA	U.S. AVG	PERFORMING ARTS	AREA	U.S. AVG	MUSEUMS	AREA	U.S. AVG
Arts radio rating	1	3	Classical music rating	4	4	Overall museum rating	4	6
No. public libraries	9	28	Ballet/dance rating	1	3	Art museum rating	3	5
Library volumes per capita	1.7	2.8	Professional theater rating	1	3	Science museum rating	3	4
			University arts programs rating	3	5	Children's museum rating	3	3

Naples, FL

Score: 76.1   Rank: 53

Profile: Beach resort town
Location: South Gulf coast, 40 miles south of Fort Myers, on the western edge of the Everglades
Elevation: 15 feet
Time zone: Eastern Standard Time

PRO	CON
Winter climate	Cost of living
Job growth	Air service
Attractive setting	Arts and culture

Naples, an upscale residential enclave with beaches and a variety of activities, serves more year-round and winter residents than vacationing tourists. There are many golf courses and golf-course developments with upscale housing and shopping areas. The area is generally attractive and has a relaxed, modern feel, not unlike Hilton Head Island, South Carolina. Job growth is by far the highest in the state and income levels are relatively high. There are plenty of parks, excellent beaches, and outstanding nature preserves to the east and south. With these attributes come the highest cost of living and median home prices of any metropolitan area in Florida. Commercial air service is still undeveloped, and air travel usually requires a 75-mile trip across the Everglades to Miami or Fort Lauderdale.

Naples is level and near the southernmost point of habitable land where the Everglades begin to drain into the ocean. Beaches give way to cypress and mangrove forests, and natural, undeveloped areas to the south. The Everglades marshes begin just to the east of town. The climate, distinctly subtropical with a strong marine influence, is similar to other southern Gulf locations. Summers are warm and humid with some sea breeze; winters are mild and relatively dry with temperatures mainly in the 70s and 80s. Afternoon thunderstorms are common in summer. Winter freezes, particularly near shore, are extremely rare.

POPULATION

DEMOGRAPHICS	AREA	U.S. AVG	ETHNIC COMPOSITION	AREA	U.S. AVG	RESIDENT PROFILE	AREA	U.S. AVG
Population	276,691		White	92.4%	75.1%	Single	37.4%	43.6%
Population density per sq. mile	136.6	447.3	Black	4.2%	12.3%	Married	62.6%	56.4%
Population growth	81.9%	16.1%	Asian	.6%	3.6%	Divorced	9.2%	8.4%
Median age	44.7	35.5	American Indian	.3%	.9%	Separated	2.4%	3.0%
Average family size	2.5	2.7	Hispanic	14.5%	12.5%	Married with children	20.7%	28.7%
			Diversity measure	40.6%	35.2%	Single with children	7.6%	10.1%

ECONOMY & JOBS
SCORE: 70/RANK: 97

INCOME	AREA	U.S. AVG	EMPLOYMENT	AREA	U.S. AVG	LARGEST EMPLOYING INDUSTRY
Per capita income	$39,668	$23,420	Unemployment rate	6.3%	6.1%	Healthcare and Social Assistance
Household income	$57,326	$46,060	Recent job growth	4.7%	.9%	
Household income < $25K	14.9%	26.4%	Projected future job growth	26.8%	15.1%	
Household income > $75K	35.1%	24.5%	White collar	53.0%	54.5%	
Household income growth	68.0%	57.3%	Blue collar	47.0%	45.5%	

COST OF LIVING
SCORE: 20/RANK: 263

INDEXES & TAXES	AREA	U.S. AVG	HOUSING	AREA	U.S. AVG	NECESSITIES	AREA	U.S. AVG
Cost of Living Index	123.0	100.0	Median home price	$252,090	$160,100	Food Index	104.2	100.0
Financial Progress Index	99.4	100.0	Home price appreciation	14.5%	7.1%	Housing Index	156.6	100.0
Income tax rate	0.000%	4.625%	Median rent	$793	$670	Utilities Index	100.2	100.0
Sales tax rate	6.000%	6.474%	Homes owned	55.4%	63.9%	Transportation Index	109.5	100.0
Property tax rate	$14.3	$15.6	Homes rented	19.2%	25.3%	Healthcare Index	108.4	100.0
			Housing affordability	59.0%	54.5%	Miscellaneous Cost Index	101.4	100.0

CLIMATE
SCORE: 83/RANK: 54

TEMPERATURE	AREA	U.S. AVG	PRECIPITATION	AREA	U.S. AVG	COMFORTS & HAZARDS	AREA	U.S. AVG
January low	52.3°F	26.4°F	Annual inches precipitation	54.0	35.9	July relative humidity	76.0%	68.8%
July high	91.5°F	86.7°F	Annual inches snowfall	0.0	24.2	Annual days mostly sunny	264	212
Annual days > 90°F	106	38	Annual days precipitation	112	111	Annual days with thunderstorms	93	39
Annual days < 32°F	1	88	Annual days rain > 0.5 inches	32	23	Tornado risk score	20	19
Annual days < 0°F	0	6	Annual days snow > 1.5 inches	0	6	Hurricane risk score	83	15

TEMPERATURE

PRECIPITATION

DAYS OF CLOUDS & PRECIPITATION

EDUCATION
SCORE: 64/RANK: 117

ACHIEVEMENT	AREA	U.S. AVG	PUBLIC SCHOOLS	AREA	U.S. AVG	HIGHER EDUCATION	AREA	U.S. AVG
High school degree	81.8%	80.2%	Expenditures per pupil	$5,984	$5,894	No. 2-year colleges	0	3
2-year college degree	6.8%	6.2%	Student/teacher ratio	18.6	16.7	No. 4-year colleges/universities	1	4
4-year college degree	18.2%	15.8%	Attending public school	97.6%	90.2%	No. highly ranked universities	0	1
Graduate/professional degree	9.7%	9.6%	State SAT score	996*	1020			
			State ACT score	20.5	21.0			

HEALTH & HEALTHCARE
SCORE: 74/RANK: 84

CRIME
SCORE: 66/RANK: 110

HAZARDS & ILLNESSES	AREA	U.S. AVG	HEALTHCARE	AREA	U.S. AVG	CRIME	AREA	U.S. AVG
Air-quality score	24	45	Physicians per capita	237.1	261.1	Violent crime rate	531.2	456.0
Water-quality score	23	33	Hospital beds per capita	219.6	432.2	Change in violent crime rate	-27.3%	-17.2%
Pollen/allergy score	65	61	No. teaching hospitals	0	4	Property crime rate	3,416.2	3,950.0
Stress score	38	50	Cost per doctor visit	$72	$67	Change in property crime rate	-30.9%	-16.8%
Cancer mortality per capita	156.4	169.0	Cost per dental visit	$84	$82			
Depression days per month	2.8	2.8	Cost per daily hospital room	$697	$733			

TRANSPORTATION
SCORE: 5/RANK: 313

COMMUTE	AREA	U.S. AVG	INTERCITY SERVICES	AREA	U.S. AVG	AUTOMOTIVE	AREA	U.S. AVG
Average commute time	24.0 min.	22.6 min.	Miles to nearest major airport	27	46	Insurance, annual premium	$1,023	$1,011
Commute by auto	90.0%	88.7%	Type of local airport	Small		Gas, cost per gallon	$1.51	$1.50
Commute by mass transit	1.3%	1.8%	No. daily airline departures	92	294	Daily vehicle miles per capita	17.7	23.0
Work at home	4.0%	3.9%	Amtrak service	No				
Mass transit miles per capita	0.0	8.0	No. interstate highways	1	1			

LEISURE SCORE: 62/RANK: 123

DINING & SHOPPING	AREA	U.S. AVG	ENTERTAINMENT	AREA	U.S. AVG	OUTDOOR ACTIVITIES	AREA	U.S. AVG
Restaurant rating	1	1	Professional sports rating	2	4	Golf-course rating	5	4
No. outlet malls	3	2	College sports rating	1	4	Ski-area rating	1	4
No. Starbucks	4	11	Zoo/aquarium rating	1	3	National Park rating	10	3
No. warehouse clubs	3	4	Amusement park rating	4	3	Sq. miles inland water	7.0	4.0
			Botanical garden/arboretum rating	3	3	Miles of coastline	66.6	11.4

ARTS & CULTURE SCORE: 13/RANK: 286

MEDIA & LIBRARIES	AREA	U.S. AVG	PERFORMING ARTS	AREA	U.S. AVG	MUSEUMS	AREA	U.S. AVG
Arts radio rating	1	3	Classical music rating	1	4	Overall museum rating	4	6
No. public libraries	8	28	Ballet/dance rating	1	3	Art museum rating	7	5
Library volumes per capita	1.5	2.8	Professional theater rating	1	3	Science museum rating	4	4
			University arts programs rating	2	5	Children's museum rating	1	3

Nashua, NH

Score: 59.6   Rank: 151

Profile: Small city/Commuter community
Location: Southern New Hampshire, 5 miles north of Massachusetts border
Elevation: 130 feet
Time zone: Eastern Standard Time

PRO	CON
Diverse economy	Harsh winters
Educated population	Urban sprawl
Proximity to Boston	Increasing home prices

Nashua, a small, self-sufficient city, has a robust economy dominated by manufacturing and high-tech industries. The local population is educated, and the crime rate low. It is close enough to Boston and its northern suburbs to serve as an attractive bedroom community for those preferring a more conservative political and tax environment. Cost of living, while no bargain on the national scale, is favorable compared to Boston. Access to the larger city's amenities and services is an asset. However, proximity comes at the cost of long, crowded commutes and rising home prices.

The town lies in the mostly-level valley of the Merrimack River surrounded by low, rolling, wooded hills. Most of the city lies on the west bank of the river and is growing toward the east. The climate is typically continental for areas of New England away from the coast. Summers are moderately warm and humid with occasional spells of hotter, stickier weather and thundershowers. Winters are cold with prevailing northwesterly winds bringing waves of cold, dry air. Snow is common and becomes heavy when "noreaster" storms move up the Atlantic Coast. Winter snow cover is prevalent but periods of thawing and bare ground regularly occur. First freeze is late September, last is late May.

POPULATION

DEMOGRAPHICS	AREA	U.S. AVG	ETHNIC COMPOSITION	AREA	U.S. AVG	RESIDENT PROFILE	AREA	U.S. AVG
Population	196,910		White	97.0%	75.1%	Single	38.3%	43.6%
Population density per sq. mile	607.7	447.3	Black	.8%	12.3%	Married	61.7%	56.4%
Population growth	17.0%	16.1%	Asian	1.6%	3.6%	Divorced	7.7%	8.4%
Median age	36.2	35.5	American Indian	.2%	.9%	Separated	2.2%	3.0%
Average family size	2.8	2.7	Hispanic	1.6%	12.5%	Married with children	35.2%	28.7%
			Diversity measure	14.6%	35.2%	Single with children	7.5%	10.1%

ECONOMY & JOBS SCORE: 70/RANK: 98

INCOME	AREA	U.S. AVG	EMPLOYMENT	AREA	U.S. AVG	LARGEST EMPLOYING INDUSTRY
Per capita income	$29,704	$23,420	Unemployment rate	5.8%	6.1%	Computer and Electronic Product Manufacturing
Household income	$63,653	$46,060	Recent job growth	-1.9%	.9%	
Household income < $25K	15.0%	26.4%	Projected future job growth	10.0%	15.1%	
Household income > $75K	39.3%	24.5%	White collar	64.0%	54.5%	
Household income growth	42.0%	57.3%	Blue collar	36.0%	45.5%	

COST OF LIVING SCORE: 46/RANK: 176

INDEXES & TAXES	AREA	U.S. AVG	HOUSING	AREA	U.S. AVG	NECESSITIES	AREA	U.S. AVG
Cost of Living Index	121.2	100.0	Median home price	$231,680	$160,100	Food Index	102.0	100.0
Financial Progress Index	111.9	100.0	Home price appreciation	14.9%	7.1%	Housing Index	143.9	100.0
Income tax rate	0.000%	4.625%	Median rent	$1,016	$670	Utilities Index	131.4	100.0
Sales tax rate	0.000%	6.474%	Homes owned	73.6%	63.9%	Transportation Index	104.4	100.0
Property tax rate	$21.7	$15.6	Homes rented	20.3%	25.3%	Healthcare Index	110.8	100.0
			Housing affordability	54.0%	54.5%	Miscellaneous Cost Index	106.6	100.0

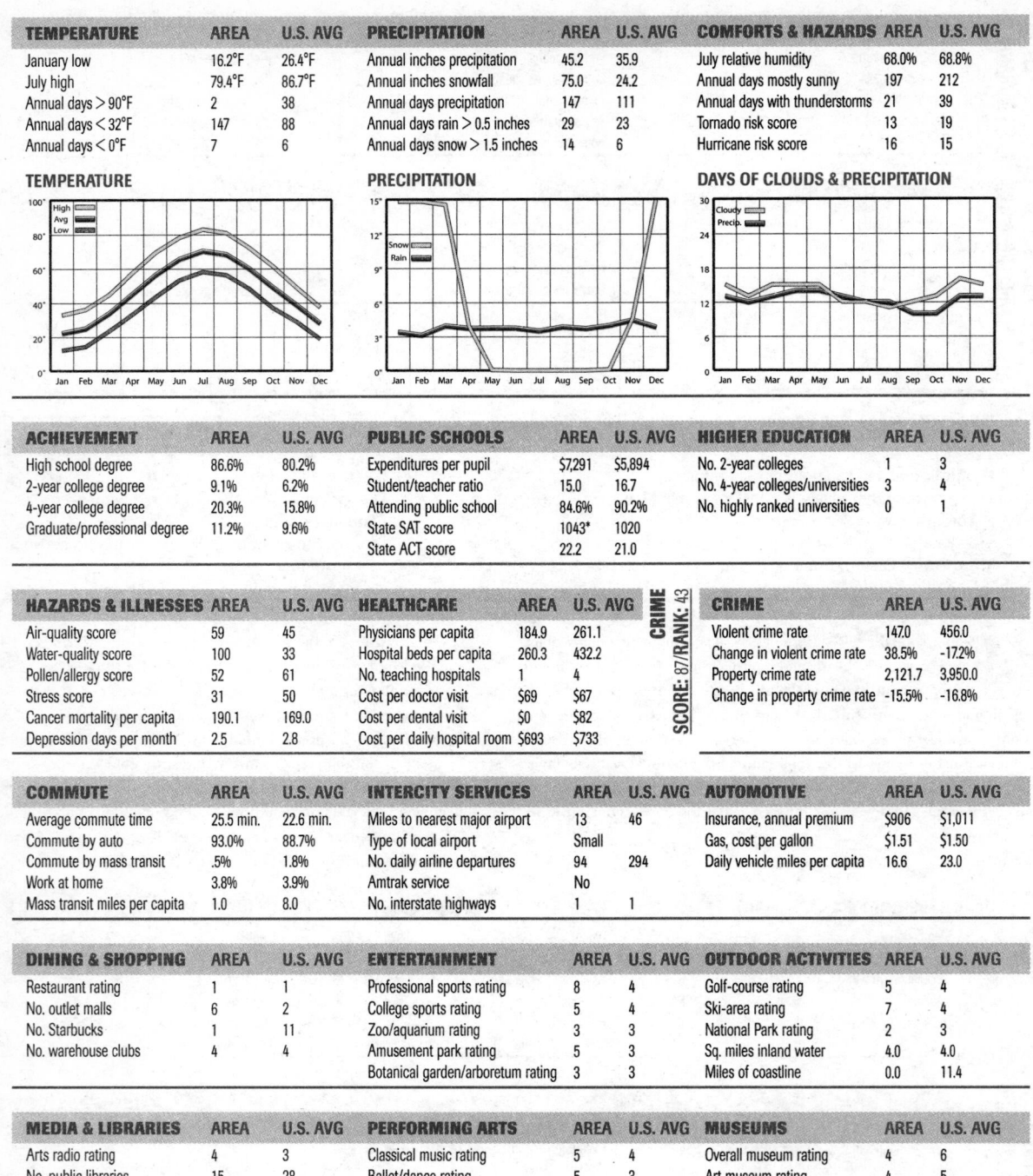

CLIMATE SCORE: 2/RANK: 322

TEMPERATURE	AREA	U.S. AVG	PRECIPITATION	AREA	U.S. AVG	COMFORTS & HAZARDS	AREA	U.S. AVG
January low	16.2°F	26.4°F	Annual inches precipitation	45.2	35.9	July relative humidity	68.0%	68.8%
July high	79.4°F	86.7°F	Annual inches snowfall	75.0	24.2	Annual days mostly sunny	197	212
Annual days > 90°F	2	38	Annual days precipitation	147	111	Annual days with thunderstorms	21	39
Annual days < 32°F	147	88	Annual days rain > 0.5 inches	29	23	Tornado risk score	13	19
Annual days < 0°F	7	6	Annual days snow > 1.5 inches	14	6	Hurricane risk score	16	15

TEMPERATURE

PRECIPITATION

DAYS OF CLOUDS & PRECIPITATION

EDUCATION SCORE: 76/RANK: 79

ACHIEVEMENT	AREA	U.S. AVG	PUBLIC SCHOOLS	AREA	U.S. AVG	HIGHER EDUCATION	AREA	U.S. AVG
High school degree	86.6%	80.2%	Expenditures per pupil	$7,291	$5,894	No. 2-year colleges	1	3
2-year college degree	9.1%	6.2%	Student/teacher ratio	15.0	16.7	No. 4-year colleges/universities	3	4
4-year college degree	20.3%	15.8%	Attending public school	84.6%	90.2%	No. highly ranked universities	0	1
Graduate/professional degree	11.2%	9.6%	State SAT score	1043*	1020			
			State ACT score	22.2	21.0			

HEALTH & HEALTHCARE SCORE: 30/RANK: 230

HAZARDS & ILLNESSES	AREA	U.S. AVG	HEALTHCARE	AREA	U.S. AVG	CRIME	AREA	U.S. AVG
Air-quality score	59	45	Physicians per capita	184.9	261.1	Violent crime rate	147.0	456.0
Water-quality score	100	33	Hospital beds per capita	260.3	432.2	Change in violent crime rate	38.5%	-17.2%
Pollen/allergy score	52	61	No. teaching hospitals	1	4	Property crime rate	2,121.7	3,950.0
Stress score	31	50	Cost per doctor visit	$69	$67	Change in property crime rate	-15.5%	-16.8%
Cancer mortality per capita	190.1	169.0	Cost per dental visit	$0	$82			
Depression days per month	2.5	2.8	Cost per daily hospital room	$693	$733			

CRIME SCORE: 87/RANK: 43

TRANSPORTATION SCORE: 56/RANK: 143

COMMUTE	AREA	U.S. AVG	INTERCITY SERVICES	AREA	U.S. AVG	AUTOMOTIVE	AREA	U.S. AVG
Average commute time	25.5 min.	22.6 min.	Miles to nearest major airport	13	46	Insurance, annual premium	$906	$1,011
Commute by auto	93.0%	88.7%	Type of local airport	Small		Gas, cost per gallon	$1.51	$1.50
Commute by mass transit	.5%	1.8%	No. daily airline departures	94	294	Daily vehicle miles per capita	16.6	23.0
Work at home	3.8%	3.9%	Amtrak service	No				
Mass transit miles per capita	1.0	8.0	No. interstate highways	1	1			

LEISURE SCORE: 59/RANK: 136

DINING & SHOPPING	AREA	U.S. AVG	ENTERTAINMENT	AREA	U.S. AVG	OUTDOOR ACTIVITIES	AREA	U.S. AVG
Restaurant rating	1	1	Professional sports rating	8	4	Golf-course rating	5	4
No. outlet malls	6	2	College sports rating	5	4	Ski-area rating	7	4
No. Starbucks	1	11	Zoo/aquarium rating	3	3	National Park rating	2	3
No. warehouse clubs	4	4	Amusement park rating	5	3	Sq. miles inland water	4.0	4.0
			Botanical garden/arboretum rating	3	3	Miles of coastline	0.0	11.4

ARTS & CULTURE SCORE: 24/RANK: 249

MEDIA & LIBRARIES	AREA	U.S. AVG	PERFORMING ARTS	AREA	U.S. AVG	MUSEUMS	AREA	U.S. AVG
Arts radio rating	4	3	Classical music rating	5	4	Overall museum rating	4	6
No. public libraries	15	28	Ballet/dance rating	5	3	Art museum rating	4	5
Library volumes per capita	3.5	2.8	Professional theater rating	8	3	Science museum rating	3	4
			University arts programs rating	8	5	Children's museum rating	3	3

Nashville, TN

Score: 52.6   **Rank:** 206

Profile: Capital city
Location: North-central Tennessee along the Cumberland River
Elevation: 605 feet
Time zone: Central Standard Time

PRO	CON
Entertainment	Crime rate
Expanding amenities	Urban sprawl
Future job growth	Hot, humid summers

Nashville is the capital and second largest city in Tennessee. Known worldwide as the center of country music, it has become a destination for music-related tourism. The city has been working for some time to renovate its downtown area and attract first-class amenities. Areas of downtown, notably the District, have stylish older buildings repurposed into shopping and nightlife areas. Nashville is a big sports town: The Tennessee Titans are the state's first NFL team and there are minor-league or secondary league teams in just about every sport. Vanderbilt University and Fisk University add a college-town dimension with the expected amenities. Beyond tourism and music, the economic base encompasses government, banking, finance, and insurance. A center of the Bible Belt, the city is sometimes called the

"Protestant Vatican." The city has a high growth rate and relatively low cost of living, but also some emerging problems with growth and sprawl.

Nashville is in a river valley along the edge of the Highland Rim, which rises 300 feet to 400 feet above the basin forming an amphitheater around the city from the southwest to the southeast. The climate is typical for the region with warm, humid summers and alternating periods of cool and cold in the winter. Topography generally does not affect the weather. Great extremes seldom occur but the location near major storm tracks brings frequent weather changes. Summer thunderstorms are sometimes severe. Periods of winter precipitation are common with an occasional stronger winter storm.

POPULATION

DEMOGRAPHICS	AREA	U.S. AVG	ETHNIC COMPOSITION	AREA	U.S. AVG	RESIDENT PROFILE	AREA	U.S. AVG
Population	1,270,520		White	83.2%	75.1%	Single	45.2%	43.6%
Population density per sq. mile	311.9	447.3	Black	15.2%	12.3%	Married	54.8%	56.4%
Population growth	29.0%	16.1%	Asian	1.1%	3.6%	Divorced	9.6%	8.4%
Median age	34.7	35.5	American Indian	.3%	.9%	Separated	3.0%	3.0%
Average family size	2.5	2.7	Hispanic	.9%	12.5%	Married with children	28.5%	28.7%
			Diversity measure	35.8%	35.2%	Single with children	10.2%	10.1%

ECONOMY & JOBS   SCORE: 40/RANK: 196

INCOME	AREA	U.S. AVG	EMPLOYMENT	AREA	U.S. AVG	LARGEST EMPLOYING INDUSTRY
Per capita income	$27,009	$23,420	Unemployment rate	3.9%	6.1%	Transportation Equipment Manufacturing
Household income	$51,379	$46,060	Recent job growth	-1.0%	.9%	
Household income < $25K	22.1%	26.4%	Projected future job growth	20.7%	15.1%	
Household income > $75K	30.1%	24.5%	White collar	59.3%	54.5%	
Household income growth	69.8%	57.3%	Blue collar	40.7%	45.5%	

COST OF LIVING   SCORE: 60/RANK: 133

INDEXES & TAXES	AREA	U.S. AVG	HOUSING	AREA	U.S. AVG	NECESSITIES	AREA	U.S. AVG
Cost of Living Index	92.3	100.0	Median home price	$140,670	$160,100	Food Index	99.5	100.0
Financial Progress Index	118.6	100.0	Home price appreciation	4.4%	7.1%	Housing Index	87.4	100.0
Income tax rate	0.000%	4.625%	Median rent	$678	$670	Utilities Index	86.6	100.0
Sales tax rate	9.250%	6.474%	Homes owned	65.9%	63.9%	Transportation Index	96.5	100.0
Property tax rate	$8.8	$15.6	Homes rented	25.7%	25.3%	Healthcare Index	80.9	100.0
			Housing affordability	56.0%	54.5%	Miscellaneous Cost Index	97.9	100.0

CLIMATE   SCORE: 21/RANK: 260

TEMPERATURE	AREA	U.S. AVG	PRECIPITATION	AREA	U.S. AVG	COMFORTS & HAZARDS	AREA	U.S. AVG
January low	29.0°F	26.4°F	Annual inches precipitation	46.0	35.9	July relative humidity	71.0%	68.8%
July high	90.2°F	86.7°F	Annual inches snowfall	10.7	24.2	Annual days mostly sunny	210	212
Annual days > 90°F	37	38	Annual days precipitation	119	111	Annual days with thunderstorms	55	39
Annual days < 32°F	75	88	Annual days rain > 0.5 inches	32	23	Tornado risk score	16	19
Annual days < 0°F	1	6	Annual days snow > 1.5 inches	3	6	Hurricane risk score	8	15

TEMPERATURE

PRECIPITATION

DAYS OF CLOUDS & PRECIPITATION

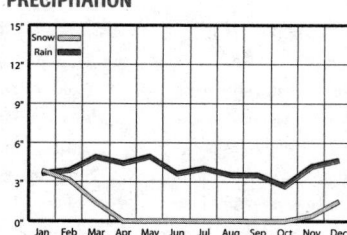

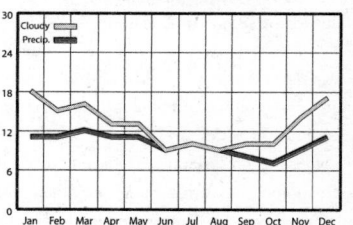

EDUCATION SCORE: 53/RANK: 155

ACHIEVEMENT	AREA	U.S. AVG	PUBLIC SCHOOLS	AREA	U.S. AVG	HIGHER EDUCATION	AREA	U.S. AVG
High school degree	81.1%	80.2%	Expenditures per pupil	$5,306	$5,894	No. 2-year colleges	4	3
2-year college degree	4.9%	6.2%	Student/teacher ratio	15.1	16.7	No. 4-year colleges/universities	12	4
4-year college degree	19.7%	15.8%	Attending public school	87.3%	90.2%	No. highly ranked universities	0	1
Graduate/professional degree	10.0%	9.6%	State SAT score	1128	1020			
			State ACT score	20.4*	21.0			

HEALTH & HEALTHCARE SCORE: 73/RANK: 87
CRIME SCORE: 7/RANK: 307

HAZARDS & ILLNESSES	AREA	U.S. AVG	HEALTHCARE	AREA	U.S. AVG	CRIME	AREA	U.S. AVG
Air-quality score	80	45	Physicians per capita	322.5	261.1	Violent crime rate	970.9	456.0
Water-quality score	39	33	Hospital beds per capita	452.5	432.2	Change in violent crime rate	-10.8%	-17.2%
Pollen/allergy score	68	61	No. teaching hospitals	5	4	Property crime rate	5,013.4	3,950.0
Stress score	82	50	Cost per doctor visit	$60	$67	Change in property crime rate	-18.8%	-16.8%
Cancer mortality per capita	162.8	169.0	Cost per dental visit	$69	$82			
Depression days per month	2.7	2.8	Cost per daily hospital room	$323	$733			

TRANSPORTATION SCORE: 19/RANK: 264

COMMUTE	AREA	U.S. AVG	INTERCITY SERVICES	AREA	U.S. AVG	AUTOMOTIVE	AREA	U.S. AVG
Average commute time	25.8 min.	22.6 min.	Miles to nearest major airport	7	46	Insurance, annual premium	$1,085	$1,011
Commute by auto	89.5%	88.7%	Type of local airport	Medium		Gas, cost per gallon	$1.43	$1.50
Commute by mass transit	2.2%	1.8%	No. daily airline departures	264	294	Daily vehicle miles per capita	34.3	23.0
Work at home	3.3%	3.9%	Amtrak service	No				
Mass transit miles per capita	5.4	8.0	No. interstate highways	3	1			

LEISURE SCORE: 65/RANK: 113

DINING & SHOPPING	AREA	U.S. AVG	ENTERTAINMENT	AREA	U.S. AVG	OUTDOOR ACTIVITIES	AREA	U.S. AVG
Restaurant rating	1	1	Professional sports rating	7	4	Golf-course rating	5	4
No. outlet malls	3	2	College sports rating	5	4	Ski-area rating	1	4
No. Starbucks	16	11	Zoo/aquarium rating	5	3	National Park rating	2	3
No. warehouse clubs	6	4	Amusement park rating	1	3	Sq. miles inland water	4.0	4.0
			Botanical garden/arboretum rating	5	3	Miles of coastline	0.0	11.4

ARTS & CULTURE SCORE: 73/RANK: 86

MEDIA & LIBRARIES	AREA	U.S. AVG	PERFORMING ARTS	AREA	U.S. AVG	MUSEUMS	AREA	U.S. AVG
Arts radio rating	8	3	Classical music rating	7	4	Overall museum rating	9	6
No. public libraries	44	28	Ballet/dance rating	3	3	Art museum rating	8	5
Library volumes per capita	1.8	2.8	Professional theater rating	1	3	Science museum rating	5	4
			University arts programs rating	9	5	Children's museum rating	1	3

Nassau-Suffolk, NY

Score: 85.5   Rank: 19

Profile: Commuter community
Location: Long Island
Elevation: 13 feet
Time zone: Eastern Standard Time

PRO	CON
Nearby water and beaches	Urban sprawl
Close to New York City	Cost of living
Low crime rate	Long commutes

Nassau and Suffolk counties occupy the western four-fifths of Long Island, east of New York City. The western two-thirds of the island, which stretches a total of 120 miles, consists of residential communities, shopping malls, and commercial districts that mainly support Manhattan commuters, although the area has a vibrant commercial, industrial, and service economy of its own. The built-up sections are a patchwork of small- and medium-size cities—which started as distinct towns separated by rural land and connected by the Long Island Rail Road—now connected by subdivisions. There are few recognizable names among these communities—Plainview, Hempstead, Brentwood, and Deer Park—most of which are fairly average in character. Exceptions are the Hamptons at the island's eastern end. Southhampton, East Hampton, Westhampton, and Bridgehampton, among others, have interesting histories as whaling communities and are known today for nice beaches, trendy restaurants, and wealthy enclaves. Closer to New York City, barrier-island, beach areas around Long Beach are nice but crowded on hot summer days. And Levittown, a famous subdivision from the 1940s, is a monument to early suburban architecture and planning.

Cost of living and particularly housing costs are high, although there is substantial variation across the island, with coastal areas being more expensive. Educational attainment is low related to public expenditures per pupil. New York City commutes are long, typically 45 minutes or more. Local amenities and entertainment include ample recreation, the New York Islanders hockey team, and low-cost air service to Islip by Southwest Airlines. In many ways Long Island provides the amenities and benefits of New York City without the big-city problems, hence the high ranking.

Long Island is the terminal moraine marking the southernmost advance of an ice sheet along the Atlantic Coast during the last ice age.

The terrain is generally flat with only a gradual rise in elevation toward the center from Long Island Sound on the northern shore and from the Atlantic Ocean on the southern shore. Most air masses affecting Long Island are continental in origin; however, the ocean has a pronounced influence on climate. Cool, summer sea breezes alleviate afternoon heat and moderate coastal temperatures. Tropical weather systems moving along the Atlantic Coast can produce episodes of heavy rain and strong winds in the late summer or fall. The winter season is relatively mild. Below-zero temperatures are only reported 1 or 2 days every other winter. Coastal low-pressure systems called "noreasters" are the principal source of snow, but snow totals are less than the rest of the state and rain is more likely. First freeze is mid-October, last is late April.

POPULATION

DEMOGRAPHICS	AREA	U.S. AVG	ETHNIC COMPOSITION	AREA	U.S. AVG	RESIDENT PROFILE	AREA	U.S. AVG
Population	2,803,547		White	87.6%	75.1%	Single	43.2%	43.6%
Population density per sq. mile	2,340.2	447.3	Black	7.2%	12.3%	Married	56.8%	56.4%
Population growth	7.4%	16.1%	Asian	3.8%	3.6%	Divorced	5.4%	8.4%
Median age	37.9	35.5	American Indian	.2%	.9%	Separated	2.8%	3.0%
Average family size	2.8	2.7	Hispanic	6.4%	12.5%	Married with children	29.8%	28.7%
			Diversity measure	38.8%	35.2%	Single with children	7.4%	10.1%

ECONOMY & JOBS — SCORE: 93/RANK: 24

INCOME	AREA	U.S. AVG	EMPLOYMENT	AREA	U.S. AVG	LARGEST EMPLOYING INDUSTRY
Per capita income	$33,841	$23,420	Unemployment rate	4.3%	6.1%	Healthcare and Social Assistance
Household income	$78,879	$46,060	Recent job growth	1.1%	.9%	
Household income < $25K	12.1%	26.4%	Projected future job growth	8.9%	15.1%	
Household income > $75K	53.2%	24.5%	White collar	65.2%	54.5%	
Household income growth	52.3%	57.3%	Blue collar	34.8%	45.5%	

COST OF LIVING — SCORE: 3/RANK: 318

INDEXES & TAXES	AREA	U.S. AVG	HOUSING	AREA	U.S. AVG	NECESSITIES	AREA	U.S. AVG
Cost of Living Index	159.6	100.0	Median home price	$333,600	$160,100	Food Index	129.6	100.0
Financial Progress Index	105.3	100.0	Home price appreciation	16.7%	7.1%	Housing Index	207.2	100.0
Income tax rate	7.125%	4.625%	Median rent	$1,324	$670	Utilities Index	150.4	100.0
Sales tax rate	8.500%	6.474%	Homes owned	72.6%	63.9%	Transportation Index	115.9	100.0
Property tax rate	$24.6	$15.6	Homes rented	15.7%	25.3%	Healthcare Index	165.7	100.0
			Housing affordability	42.0%	54.5%	Miscellaneous Cost Index	128.3	100.0

CLIMATE — SCORE: 75/RANK: 82

TEMPERATURE	AREA	U.S. AVG	PRECIPITATION	AREA	U.S. AVG	COMFORTS & HAZARDS	AREA	U.S. AVG
January low	24.8°F	26.4°F	Annual inches precipitation	41.5	35.9	July relative humidity	68.0%	68.8%
July high	83.2°F	86.7°F	Annual inches snowfall	24.9	24.2	Annual days mostly sunny	219	212
Annual days > 90°F	10	38	Annual days precipitation	125	111	Annual days with thunderstorms	22	39
Annual days < 32°F	85	88	Annual days rain > 0.5 inches	30	23	Tornado risk score	5	19
Annual days < 0°F	0	6	Annual days snow > 1.5 inches	4	6	Hurricane risk score	20	15

TEMPERATURE

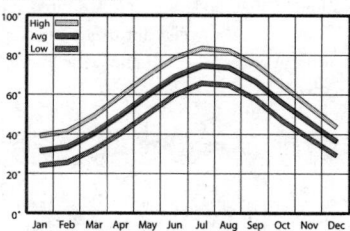

PRECIPITATION

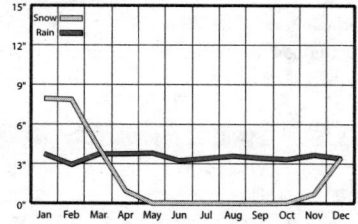

DAYS OF CLOUDS & PRECIPITATION

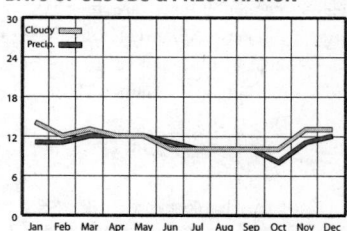

EDUCATION — SCORE: 96/RANK: 13

ACHIEVEMENT	AREA	U.S. AVG	PUBLIC SCHOOLS	AREA	U.S. AVG	HIGHER EDUCATION	AREA	U.S. AVG
High school degree	86.4%	80.2%	Expenditures per pupil	$11,562	$5,894	No. 2-year colleges	5	3
2-year college degree	7.5%	6.2%	Student/teacher ratio	14.5	16.7	No. 4-year colleges/universities	16	4
4-year college degree	17.7%	15.8%	Attending public school	87.9%	90.2%	No. highly ranked universities	2	1
Graduate/professional degree	13.7%	9.6%	State SAT score	1006*	1020			
			State ACT score	22.3	21.0			

HEALTH & HEALTHCARE — SCORE: 35/RANK: 211

HAZARDS & ILLNESSES	AREA	U.S. AVG	HEALTHCARE	AREA	U.S. AVG
Air-quality score	98	45	Physicians per capita	429.0	261.1
Water-quality score	20	33	Hospital beds per capita	483.8	432.2
Pollen/allergy score	62	61	No. teaching hospitals	20	4
Stress score	4	50	Cost per doctor visit	$91	$67
Cancer mortality per capita	190.4	169.0	Cost per dental visit	$107	$82
Depression days per month	2.9	2.8	Cost per daily hospital room	$1,370	$733

CRIME — SCORE: 99/RANK: 3

CRIME	AREA	U.S. AVG
Violent crime rate	136.2	456.0
Change in violent crime rate	-35.9%	-17.2%
Property crime rate	1,909.9	3,950.0
Change in property crime rate	-28.7%	-16.8%

TRANSPORTATION SCORE: 93/RANK: 21

COMMUTE	AREA	U.S. AVG	INTERCITY SERVICES	AREA	U.S. AVG	AUTOMOTIVE	AREA	U.S. AVG
Average commute time	33.0 min.	22.6 min.	Miles to nearest major airport	15	46	Insurance, annual premium	$1,558	$1,011
Commute by auto	83.0%	88.7%	Type of local airport	Large		Gas, cost per gallon	$1.64	$1.50
Commute by mass transit	9.6%	1.8%	No. daily airline departures	563	294	Daily vehicle miles per capita	26.3	23.0
Work at home	2.8%	3.9%	Amtrak service	No				
Mass transit miles per capita	32.4	8.0	No. interstate highways	0	1			

LEISURE SCORE: 99/RANK: 3

DINING & SHOPPING	AREA	U.S. AVG	ENTERTAINMENT	AREA	U.S. AVG	OUTDOOR ACTIVITIES	AREA	U.S. AVG
Restaurant rating	1	1	Professional sports rating	10	4	Golf-course rating	10	4
No. outlet malls	10	2	College sports rating	6	4	Ski-area rating	2	4
No. Starbucks	56	11	Zoo/aquarium rating	7	3	National Park rating	4	3
No. warehouse clubs	9	4	Amusement park rating	6	3	Sq. miles inland water	9.0	4.0
			Botanical garden/arboretum rating	10	3	Miles of coastline	172.5	11.4

ARTS & CULTURE SCORE: 86/RANK: 45

MEDIA & LIBRARIES	AREA	U.S. AVG	PERFORMING ARTS	AREA	U.S. AVG	MUSEUMS	AREA	U.S. AVG
Arts radio rating	4	3	Classical music rating	8	4	Overall museum rating	10	6
No. public libraries	126	28	Ballet/dance rating	8	3	Art museum rating	8	5
Library volumes per capita	6.3	2.8	Professional theater rating	9	3	Science museum rating	10	4
			University arts programs rating	10	5	Children's museum rating	7	3

New Bedford, MA

Score: 23.4   Rank: 319

Profile: Small coastal town
Location: Southern Massachusetts coast due west of Cape Cod
Elevation: 60 feet
Time zone: Eastern Standard Time

PRO	CON
Historic interest	Low educational attainment
Attractive setting	Economy
Proximity to Cape Cod	Cost of living

New Bedford is a former whaling port with the feel of an old New England coastal town, at least in the city center. One of the few historic attractions is the New Bedford National Whaling Historical Park. The main industry is fishing, but many residents travel to jobs in the surrounding region. Unemployment is the highest in the state and commute times are long. Other factors—low educational attainment, an extraordinarily low high-school graduation rate (the worst in the nation at 57.6%), and low higher education attainment—indicate the town's working-class nature. The Cost of Living Index of 124.8 is surprisingly high, although it may be related to proximity to Martha's Vineyard and Cape Cod. The high violent crime rate rounds out the negative picture.

The town sits in a coastal area at the head of Apponagansett Bay, facing southeast towards Martha's Vineyard. The climate is continental with a strong marine influence that moderates temperatures and reduces winter snow. Summers are mild with pleasant ocean breezes and an occasional thundershower. Winters are variable with frequent clouds and rain and occasional snow with stronger storms.

POPULATION

DEMOGRAPHICS	AREA	U.S. AVG	ETHNIC COMPOSITION	AREA	U.S. AVG	RESIDENT PROFILE	AREA	U.S. AVG
Population	177,035		White	95.1%	75.1%	Single	45.6%	43.6%
Population density per sq. mile	826.5	447.3	Black	2.6%	12.3%	Married	54.4%	56.4%
Population growth	.8%	16.1%	Asian	1.0%	3.6%	Divorced	7.2%	8.4%
Median age	37.1	35.5	American Indian	.2%	.9%	Separated	3.2%	3.0%
Average family size	2.6	2.7	Hispanic	4.1%	12.5%	Married with children	28.0%	28.7%
			Diversity measure	18.3%	35.2%	Single with children	10.2%	10.1%

ECONOMY & JOBS SCORE: 16/RANK: 277

INCOME	AREA	U.S. AVG	EMPLOYMENT	AREA	U.S. AVG	LARGEST EMPLOYING INDUSTRY
Per capita income	$24,073	$23,420	Unemployment rate	7.4%	6.1%	Fishing
Household income	$49,374	$46,060	Recent job growth	-2.4%	.9%	
Household income < $25K	26.3%	26.4%	Projected future job growth	10.0%	15.1%	
Household income > $75K	28.1%	24.5%	White collar	49.2%	54.5%	
Household income growth	78.4%	57.3%	Blue collar	50.8%	45.5%	

COST OF LIVING — SCORE: 14/RANK: 281

INDEXES & TAXES	AREA	U.S. AVG	HOUSING	AREA	U.S. AVG	NECESSITIES	AREA	U.S. AVG
Cost of Living Index	124.8	100.0	Median home price	$225,280	$160,100	Food Index	113.5	100.0
Financial Progress Index	84.3	100.0	Home price appreciation	14.9%	7.1%	Housing Index	139.9	100.0
Income tax rate	5.950%	4.625%	Median rent	$823	$670	Utilities Index	125.3	100.0
Sales tax rate	5.000%	6.474%	Homes owned	63.9%	63.9%	Transportation Index	116.1	100.0
Property tax rate	$13.0	$15.6	Homes rented	26.5%	25.3%	Healthcare Index	132.6	100.0
			Housing affordability	33.0%	54.5%	Miscellaneous Cost Index	110.9	100.0

CLIMATE — SCORE: 66/RANK: 113

TEMPERATURE	AREA	U.S. AVG	PRECIPITATION	AREA	U.S. AVG	COMFORTS & HAZARDS	AREA	U.S. AVG
January low	21.6°F	26.4°F	Annual inches precipitation	45.0	35.9	July relative humidity	76.0%	68.8%
July high	81.7°F	86.7°F	Annual inches snowfall	36.0	24.2	Annual days mostly sunny	211	212
Annual days > 90°F	5	38	Annual days precipitation	79	111	Annual days with thunderstorms	14	39
Annual days < 32°F	110	88	Annual days rain > 0.5 inches	27	23	Tornado risk score	5	19
Annual days < 0°F	0	6	Annual days snow > 1.5 inches	17	6	Hurricane risk score	21	15

TEMPERATURE

PRECIPITATION

DAYS OF CLOUDS & PRECIPITATION

EDUCATION — SCORE: 27/RANK: 241

ACHIEVEMENT	AREA	U.S. AVG	PUBLIC SCHOOLS	AREA	U.S. AVG	HIGHER EDUCATION	AREA	U.S. AVG
High school degree	74.5%	80.2%	Expenditures per pupil	$7,238	$5,894	No. 2-year colleges	0	3
2-year college degree	7.5%	6.2%	Student/teacher ratio	15.9	16.7	No. 4-year colleges/universities	1	4
4-year college degree	13.9%	15.8%	Attending public school	88.3%	90.2%	No. highly ranked universities	1	1
Graduate/professional degree	6.7%	9.6%	State SAT score	1038*	1020			
			State ACT score	22.3	21.0			

HEALTH & HEALTHCARE — SCORE: 14/RANK: 282 · CRIME — SCORE: 76/RANK: 78

HAZARDS & ILLNESSES	AREA	U.S. AVG	HEALTHCARE	AREA	U.S. AVG	CRIME	AREA	U.S. AVG
Air-quality score	17	45	Physicians per capita	141.2	261.1	Violent crime rate	599.9	456.0
Water-quality score	13	33	Hospital beds per capita	313.9	432.2	Change in violent crime rate	-41.7%	-17.2%
Pollen/allergy score	63	61	No. teaching hospitals	0	4	Property crime rate	2,698.9	3,950.0
Stress score	72	50	Cost per doctor visit	$73	$67	Change in property crime rate	-32.2%	-16.8%
Cancer mortality per capita	183.4	169.0	Cost per dental visit	$110	$82			
Depression days per month	3.4	2.8	Cost per daily hospital room	$746	$733			

TRANSPORTATION — SCORE: 6/RANK: 310

COMMUTE	AREA	U.S. AVG	INTERCITY SERVICES	AREA	U.S. AVG	AUTOMOTIVE	AREA	U.S. AVG
Average commute time	27.6 min.	22.6 min.	Miles to nearest major airport	26	46	Insurance, annual premium	$1,293	$1,011
Commute by auto	91.2%	88.7%	Type of local airport	Small		Gas, cost per gallon	$1.59	$1.50
Commute by mass transit	1.9%	1.8%	No. daily airline departures	156	294	Daily vehicle miles per capita	16.0	23.0
Work at home	2.5%	3.9%	Amtrak service	No				
Mass transit miles per capita	11.9	8.0	No. interstate highways	1	1			

LEISURE — SCORE: 77/RANK: 76

DINING & SHOPPING	AREA	U.S. AVG	ENTERTAINMENT	AREA	U.S. AVG	OUTDOOR ACTIVITIES	AREA	U.S. AVG
Restaurant rating	1	1	Professional sports rating	8	4	Golf-course rating	4	4
No. outlet malls	3	2	College sports rating	4	4	Ski-area rating	6	4
No. Starbucks	0	11	Zoo/aquarium rating	3	3	National Park rating	2	3
No. warehouse clubs	3	4	Amusement park rating	5	3	Sq. miles inland water	4.0	4.0
			Botanical garden/arboretum rating	3	3	Miles of coastline	25.4	11.4

ARTS & CULTURE — SCORE: 43/RANK: 189

MEDIA & LIBRARIES	AREA	U.S. AVG	PERFORMING ARTS	AREA	U.S. AVG	MUSEUMS	AREA	U.S. AVG
Arts radio rating	4	3	Classical music rating	5	4	Overall museum rating	7	6
No. public libraries	15	28	Ballet/dance rating	5	3	Art museum rating	5	5
Library volumes per capita	3.5	2.8	Professional theater rating	5	3	Science museum rating	3	4
			University arts programs rating	3	5	Children's museum rating	6	3

New Haven–Meriden, CT

| Score: 59.6 | Rank: 149 |

Profile: Large industrial city/College town
Location: South coast along Long Island Sound, 75 miles northeast of New York City
Elevation: 7 feet
Time zone: Eastern Standard Time

PRO	CON
Historic downtown core	Cost of living
College-town amenities	Air service
Healthcare	Areas of urban decay

A city of contrasts, New Haven is a mix of colonial history, Ivy League influences, run-down industrial sections, and blue-collar neighborhoods. Once an important manufacturing center, it is known today as the home of prestigious Yale University. The first planned city in the American Colonies, New Haven was laid out in 1638 in nine equal squares. The New Haven Green, a square reserved for the public, is now a pedestrian area surrounded by stately trees, the Yale campus, and an assortment of museums and architecturally significant homes and churches. Downtown has its own collection of interesting modern buildings. The university provides arts and culture and entertainment amenities. Healthcare resources are the best in the state. Although not bad on a state scale, cost of living is high and probably much higher than reported in nicer areas of town.

New Haven is located on a mostly level plain at the head of New Haven Harbor. Several creeks and small rivers enter the Long Island Sound through the New Haven area. Densely wooded hills and ridges rise to the north and northwest. The climate is a mix of continental New England and maritime weather with four seasons and frequent weather changes modified by the nearby water. Summers are warm and humid. Winters are cool with occasional cold blasts. The water and harbor create frequent clouds and fog, which further moderate temperatures but create gloomy periods. Summer thunderstorms are common, as is winter snow. Stronger storms are brought by coastal "noreasters" and late summer hurricane remnants. First freeze is mid-October, last is late April.

POPULATION

DEMOGRAPHICS	AREA	U.S. AVG	ETHNIC COMPOSITION	AREA	U.S. AVG	RESIDENT PROFILE	AREA	U.S. AVG
Population	549,333		White	84.3%	75.1%	Single	47.6%	43.6%
Population density per sq. mile	1,277.3	447.3	Black	10.7%	12.3%	Married	52.4%	56.4%
Population growth	3.6%	16.1%	Asian	2.4%	3.6%	Divorced	7.9%	8.4%
Median age	37.6	35.5	American Indian	.2%	.9%	Separated	2.5%	3.0%
Average family size	2.5	2.7	Hispanic	7.1%	12.5%	Married with children	24.7%	28.7%
			Diversity measure	38.0%	35.2%	Single with children	9.1%	10.1%

ECONOMY & JOBS SCORE: 90/RANK: 33

INCOME	AREA	U.S. AVG	EMPLOYMENT	AREA	U.S. AVG	LARGEST EMPLOYING INDUSTRY
Per capita income	$37,739	$23,420	Unemployment rate	5.0%	6.1%	Machinery Manufacturing
Household income	$68,472	$46,060	Recent job growth	.7%	.9%	
Household income < $25K	16.0%	26.4%	Projected future job growth	6.5%	15.1%	
Household income > $75K	45.4%	24.5%	White collar	62.5%	54.5%	
Household income growth	74.9%	57.3%	Blue collar	37.5%	45.5%	

COST OF LIVING SCORE: 12/RANK: 289

INDEXES & TAXES	AREA	U.S. AVG	HOUSING	AREA	U.S. AVG	NECESSITIES	AREA	U.S. AVG
Cost of Living Index	116.9	100.0	Median home price	$202,000	$160,100	Food Index	113.4	100.0
Financial Progress Index	124.8	100.0	Home price appreciation	10.6%	7.1%	Housing Index	125.5	100.0
Income tax rate	4.500%	4.625%	Median rent	$939	$670	Utilities Index	129.4	100.0
Sales tax rate	6.000%	6.474%	Homes owned	65.5%	63.9%	Transportation Index	105.5	100.0
Property tax rate	$22.6	$15.6	Homes rented	27.3%	25.3%	Healthcare Index	108.7	100.0
			Housing affordability	43.0%	54.5%	Miscellaneous Cost Index	108.9	100.0

CLIMATE   SCORE: 73/RANK: 88

TEMPERATURE	AREA	U.S. AVG	PRECIPITATION	AREA	U.S. AVG	COMFORTS & HAZARDS	AREA	U.S. AVG
January low	21.0°F	26.4°F	Annual inches precipitation	38.6	35.9	July relative humidity	70.0%	68.8%
July high	83.9°F	86.7°F	Annual inches snowfall	27.7	24.2	Annual days mostly sunny	208	212
Annual days > 90°F	6	38	Annual days precipitation	126	111	Annual days with thunderstorms	21	39
Annual days < 32°F	102	88	Annual days rain > 0.5 inches	24	23	Tornado risk score	9	19
Annual days < 0°F	1	6	Annual days snow > 1.5 inches	5	6	Hurricane risk score	19	15

TEMPERATURE

PRECIPITATION

DAYS OF CLOUDS & PRECIPITATION

EDUCATION   SCORE: 84/RANK: 53

ACHIEVEMENT	AREA	U.S. AVG	PUBLIC SCHOOLS	AREA	U.S. AVG	HIGHER EDUCATION	AREA	U.S. AVG
High school degree	83.7%	80.2%	Expenditures per pupil	$8,417	$5,894	No. 2-year colleges	1	3
2-year college degree	6.0%	6.2%	Student/teacher ratio	14.0	16.7	No. 4-year colleges/universities	6	4
4-year college degree	19.3%	15.8%	Attending public school	87.9%	90.2%	No. highly ranked universities	1	1
Graduate/professional degree	14.7%	9.6%	State SAT score	1026*	1020			
			State ACT score	22.1	21.0			

HEALTH & HEALTHCARE   SCORE: 53/RANK: 153

CRIME   SCORE: 64/RANK: 117

HAZARDS & ILLNESSES	AREA	U.S. AVG	HEALTHCARE	AREA	U.S. AVG	CRIME	AREA	U.S. AVG
Air-quality score	80	45	Physicians per capita	525.2	261.1	Violent crime rate	468.2	456.0
Water-quality score	23	33	Hospital beds per capita	415.9	432.2	Change in violent crime rate	-12.0%	-17.2%
Pollen/allergy score	54	61	No. teaching hospitals	5	4	Property crime rate	3,607.2	3,950.0
Stress score	25	50	Cost per doctor visit	$75	$67	Change in property crime rate	-32.7%	-16.8%
Cancer mortality per capita	182.1	169.0	Cost per dental visit	$123	$82			
Depression days per month	2.5	2.8	Cost per daily hospital room	$1,207	$733			

TRANSPORTATION   SCORE: 47/RANK: 174

COMMUTE	AREA	U.S. AVG	INTERCITY SERVICES	AREA	U.S. AVG	AUTOMOTIVE	AREA	U.S. AVG
Average commute time	23.2 min.	22.6 min.	Miles to nearest major airport	44	46	Insurance, annual premium	$1,248	$1,011
Commute by auto	88.5%	88.7%	Type of local airport	Small		Gas, cost per gallon	$1.61	$1.50
Commute by mass transit	2.9%	1.8%	No. daily airline departures	98	294	Daily vehicle miles per capita	22.6	23.0
Work at home	2.5%	3.9%	Amtrak service	No				
Mass transit miles per capita	9.8	8.0	No. interstate highways	1	1			

LEISURE   SCORE: 66/RANK: 110

DINING & SHOPPING	AREA	U.S. AVG	ENTERTAINMENT	AREA	U.S. AVG	OUTDOOR ACTIVITIES	AREA	U.S. AVG
Restaurant rating	1	1	Professional sports rating	10	4	Golf-course rating	9	4
No. outlet malls	5	2	College sports rating	3	4	Ski-area rating	5	4
No. Starbucks	5	11	Zoo/aquarium rating	4	3	National Park rating	3	3
No. warehouse clubs	4	4	Amusement park rating	5	3	Sq. miles inland water	6.0	4.0
			Botanical garden/arboretum rating	5	3	Miles of coastline	29.5	11.4

ARTS & CULTURE   SCORE: 95/RANK: 14

MEDIA & LIBRARIES	AREA	U.S. AVG	PERFORMING ARTS	AREA	U.S. AVG	MUSEUMS	AREA	U.S. AVG
Arts radio rating	4	3	Classical music rating	9	4	Overall museum rating	8	6
No. public libraries	28	28	Ballet/dance rating	5	3	Art museum rating	6	5
Library volumes per capita	3.9	2.8	Professional theater rating	9	3	Science museum rating	6	4
			University arts programs rating	8	5	Children's museum rating	3	3

New London–Norwich, CT-RI

Score: 73.3 **Rank:** 67

Profile: Small-city complex
Location: Eastern Connecticut along the Long Island Sound to 15 miles north along the Thames River
Elevation: 7 feet
Time zone: Eastern Standard Time

PRO	CON
Attractive setting	Cost of living
Historic interest	Transportation services
Strong economy	Low ethnic diversity

New London is located—not surprisingly—where the broad Thames River empties into the Long Island Sound. Norwich lies about 13 miles upriver. New London has a rich maritime history and is now home to the U.S. Coast Guard Academy. Norwich is an early industrial center, where the first paper and iron nails were made in the mid-1700s. Both cities remain industrial, with a substantial high-tech industry in New London, and have attractive downtown cores with areas of historic buildings. Employment is strong, with the highest projected employment growth in the state, albeit low on a national scale. Cost of living, while high, is moderate on a Connecticut scale.

Level terrain with marshes and beach at the coast give way to rolling and wooded terrain to the north. Hills around Norwich rise 500 feet. The climate is New England continental moderated by proximity to water. Summers are warm and humid but with refreshing sea breezes. The inland Norwich area is typically warmer in summer and colder in winter. Winters are cold and wet with occasional periods of more extreme cold. Since the area lies east of the main part of Long Island, coastal "noreaster" storms are strong and can produce significant rain and snow. First freeze is late October, last is late April.

POPULATION

DEMOGRAPHICS	AREA	U.S. AVG	ETHNIC COMPOSITION	AREA	U.S. AVG	RESIDENT PROFILE	AREA	U.S. AVG
Population	297,991		White	93.8%	75.1%	Single	43.1%	43.6%
Population density per sq. mile	449.9	447.3	Black	3.2%	12.3%	Married	56.9%	56.4%
Population growth	2.5%	16.1%	Asian	1.6%	3.6%	Divorced	8.3%	8.4%
Median age	37.4	35.5	American Indian	.6%	.9%	Separated	2.0%	3.0%
Average family size	2.6	2.7	Hispanic	2.9%	12.5%	Married with children	27.9%	28.7%
			Diversity measure	21.9%	35.2%	Single with children	7.9%	10.1%

ECONOMY & JOBS SCORE: 94/RANK: 18

INCOME	AREA	U.S. AVG	EMPLOYMENT	AREA	U.S. AVG	LARGEST EMPLOYING INDUSTRY
Per capita income	$28,075	$23,420	Unemployment rate	4.3%	6.1%	Chemical Manufacturing
Household income	$57,043	$46,060	Recent job growth	1.4%	.9%	
Household income < $25K	17.1%	26.4%	Projected future job growth	10.8%	15.1%	
Household income > $75K	34.0%	24.5%	White collar	54.5%	54.5%	
Household income growth	54.5%	57.3%	Blue collar	45.5%	45.5%	

COST OF LIVING SCORE: 16/RANK: 277

INDEXES & TAXES	AREA	U.S. AVG	HOUSING	AREA	U.S. AVG	NECESSITIES	AREA	U.S. AVG
Cost of Living Index	114.9	100.0	Median home price	$196,410	$160,100	Food Index	113.3	100.0
Financial Progress Index	105.8	100.0	Home price appreciation	11.4%	7.1%	Housing Index	122.0	100.0
Income tax rate	4.500%	4.625%	Median rent	$797	$670	Utilities Index	114.8	100.0
Sales tax rate	6.000%	6.474%	Homes owned	65.1%	63.9%	Transportation Index	111.3	100.0
Property tax rate	$18.0	$15.6	Homes rented	21.7%	25.3%	Healthcare Index	120.1	100.0
			Housing affordability	56.0%	54.5%	Miscellaneous Cost Index	105.0	100.0

CLIMATE SCORE: 74/RANK: 85

TEMPERATURE	AREA	U.S. AVG	PRECIPITATION	AREA	U.S. AVG	COMFORTS & HAZARDS	AREA	U.S. AVG
January low	18.8°F	26.4°F	Annual inches precipitation	38.6	35.9	July relative humidity	70.0%	68.8%
July high	81.5°F	86.7°F	Annual inches snowfall	27.7	24.2	Annual days mostly sunny	208	212
Annual days > 90°F	6	38	Annual days precipitation	126	111	Annual days with thunderstorms	21	39
Annual days < 32°F	102	88	Annual days rain > 0.5 inches	25	23	Tornado risk score	4	19
Annual days < 0°F	0	6	Annual days snow > 1.5 inches	5	6	Hurricane risk score	20	15

TEMPERATURE

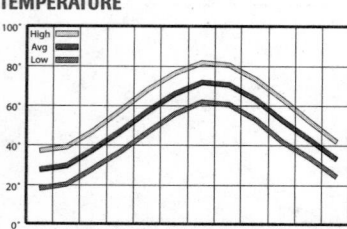

PRECIPITATION

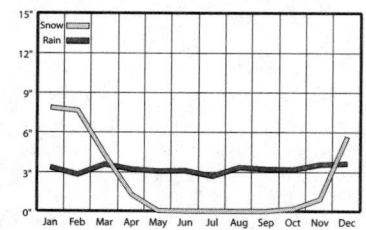

DAYS OF CLOUDS & PRECIPITATION

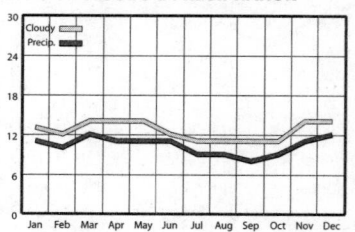

EDUCATION SCORE: 80/RANK: 65

ACHIEVEMENT	AREA	U.S. AVG	PUBLIC SCHOOLS	AREA	U.S. AVG	HIGHER EDUCATION	AREA	U.S. AVG
High school degree	86.0%	80.2%	Expenditures per pupil	$8,755	$5,894	No. 2-year colleges	2	3
2-year college degree	7.0%	6.2%	Student/teacher ratio	13.2	16.7	No. 4-year colleges/universities	2	4
4-year college degree	15.2%	15.8%	Attending public school	91.7%	90.2%	No. highly ranked universities	0	1
Graduate/professional degree	11.0%	9.6%	State SAT score	1026*	1020			
			State ACT score	22.1	21.0			

HEALTH & HEALTHCARE SCORE: 26/RANK: 242

CRIME SCORE: 73/RANK: 88

HAZARDS & ILLNESSES	AREA	U.S. AVG	HEALTHCARE	AREA	U.S. AVG	CRIME	AREA	U.S. AVG
Air-quality score	74	45	Physicians per capita	227.2	261.1	Violent crime rate	284.5	456.0
Water-quality score	43	33	Hospital beds per capita	197.9	432.2	Change in violent crime rate	.7%	-17.2%
Pollen/allergy score	58	61	No. teaching hospitals	1	4	Property crime rate	2,581.8	3,950.0
Stress score	23	50	Cost per doctor visit	$79	$67	Change in property crime rate	-5.2%	-16.8%
Cancer mortality per capita	178.3	169.0	Cost per dental visit	$107	$82			
Depression days per month	2.6	2.8	Cost per daily hospital room	$975	$733			

TRANSPORTATION SCORE: 28/RANK: 233

COMMUTE	AREA	U.S. AVG	INTERCITY SERVICES	AREA	U.S. AVG	AUTOMOTIVE	AREA	U.S. AVG
Average commute time	22.2 min.	22.6 min.	Miles to nearest major airport	32	46	Insurance, annual premium	$1,208	$1,011
Commute by auto	91.2%	88.7%	Type of local airport	Small		Gas, cost per gallon	$1.59	$1.50
Commute by mass transit	.6%	1.8%	No. daily airline departures	156	294	Daily vehicle miles per capita	29.8	23.0
Work at home	4.8%	3.9%	Amtrak service	Yes				
Mass transit miles per capita	0.0	8.0	No. interstate highways	1	1			

LEISURE SCORE: 79/RANK: 68

DINING & SHOPPING	AREA	U.S. AVG	ENTERTAINMENT	AREA	U.S. AVG	OUTDOOR ACTIVITIES	AREA	U.S. AVG
Restaurant rating	1	1	Professional sports rating	2	4	Golf-course rating	2	4
No. outlet malls	7	2	College sports rating	2	4	Ski-area rating	5	4
No. Starbucks	1	11	Zoo/aquarium rating	7	3	National Park rating	1	3
No. warehouse clubs	3	4	Amusement park rating	1	3	Sq. miles inland water	4.0	4.0
			Botanical garden/arboretum rating	2	3	Miles of coastline	34.9	11.4

ARTS & CULTURE SCORE: 81/RANK: 65

MEDIA & LIBRARIES	AREA	U.S. AVG	PERFORMING ARTS	AREA	U.S. AVG	MUSEUMS	AREA	U.S. AVG
Arts radio rating	1	3	Classical music rating	2	4	Overall museum rating	8	6
No. public libraries	25	28	Ballet/dance rating	1	3	Art museum rating	7	5
Library volumes per capita	3.4	2.8	Professional theater rating	1	3	Science museum rating	7	4
			University arts programs rating	1	5	Children's museum rating	7	3

New Orleans, LA

Score: 61.0   Rank: 139

Profile: Large city
Location: Southeast Louisiana on the Mississippi Delta south of Lake Pontchartrain
Elevation: 30 feet
Time zone: Central Standard Time

PRO	CON
Entertainment	Heat and humidity
Arts and culture	Crime rate
Historic interest	Congestion and traffic

New Orleans is a unique and diverse city. Originally a colonial settlement for the French, then the Spanish, and the French again, the city retains an extraordinarily rich legacy from both cultures. Famous examples include the French Quarter and Mardi Gras, which attracts large numbers of tourists and turns the functioning city into a carnival. Although local business is centered in the oil and gas and financial services industries, New Orleans is probably the most right-brained city in the country. Things get done, but at a relaxed, leisurely pace, generally with an element of artistic expression and fun. The local phrase "laissez les bon temps rouler," or "let the good times roll," sums it up.

Residents must have a laid-back attitude to prosper because the city can push an impatient person to the limit. Old infrastructures and geographic limitations have left the city with narrow streets and underdeveloped transportation routes. Traffic can be a major nuisance. Those using public transportation usually come out ahead. The summer climate is generally uncomfortable, and heavy downpours occur with almost no notice. Tourists are everywhere. The homeless population is high, particularly in the French Quarter. The crime rate is notoriously high, although recent years have shown improvement. Because of the surrounding water and swampland, residents can't easily escape the hustle and bustle. Available land has been developed into crowded, low, unattractive sprawl.

As in other large U.S. cities, strong negative attributes are balanced by positives. For arts, culture, entertainment, music, food, history, and architecture, there is hardly a better place to live. The area has a pleasant winter climate and a relatively low cost of living for the amenities and qualities available.

The New Orleans metro area is virtually surrounded by water. Lake Pontchartrain, some 610 square miles in area, borders the city on the north and the Mississippi River flows along the southern edge. In other directions, there are bayous, lakes, and marshlands. Elevations vary from a few feet *below* sea level (protected by massive levees) to a few feet above. Floods are a hazard, particularly when hurricanes and tropical storms are in the area. The climate is humid subtropical with an extra dose of humidity from nearby water and wetlands. That said, the water moderates temperatures. Summers are persistently warm and humid with almost daily showers and thundershowers. Winter is mild, with steady rains from December through March. Nearby water can produce dense fog. Late spring and late fall are the driest seasons.

POPULATION

DEMOGRAPHICS	AREA	U.S. AVG	ETHNIC COMPOSITION	AREA	U.S. AVG	RESIDENT PROFILE	AREA	U.S. AVG
Population	1,336,603		White	61.9%	75.1%	Single	50.7%	43.6%
Population density per sq. mile	393.2	447.3	Black	35.0%	12.3%	Married	49.3%	56.4%
Population growth	4.0%	16.1%	Asian	1.9%	3.6%	Divorced	8.4%	8.4%
Median age	35.1	35.5	American Indian	.5%	.9%	Separated	5.6%	3.0%
Average family size	2.7	2.7	Hispanic	3.6%	12.5%	Married with children	26.9%	28.7%
			Diversity measure	55.2%	35.2%	Single with children	16.2%	10.1%

ECONOMY & JOBS
SCORE: 56/RANK: 146

INCOME	AREA	U.S. AVG	EMPLOYMENT	AREA	U.S. AVG	LARGEST EMPLOYING INDUSTRY
Per capita income	$21,470	$23,420	Unemployment rate	6.6%	6.1%	Healthcare and Social Assistance
Household income	$40,672	$46,060	Recent job growth	2.2%	.9%	
Household income < $25K	30.8%	26.4%	Projected future job growth	13.1%	15.1%	
Household income > $75K	22.1%	24.5%	White collar	58.5%	54.5%	
Household income growth	66.4%	57.3%	Blue collar	41.5%	45.5%	

COST OF LIVING
SCORE: 36/RANK: 211

INDEXES & TAXES	AREA	U.S. AVG	HOUSING	AREA	U.S. AVG	NECESSITIES	AREA	U.S. AVG
Cost of Living Index	94.0	100.0	Median home price	$122,600	$160,100	Food Index	108.0	100.0
Financial Progress Index	92.2	100.0	Home price appreciation	6.0%	7.1%	Housing Index	76.1	100.0
Income tax rate	4.000%	4.625%	Median rent	$661	$670	Utilities Index	105.4	100.0
Sales tax rate	9.000%	6.474%	Homes owned	59.8%	63.9%	Transportation Index	105.8	100.0
Property tax rate	$6.0	$15.6	Homes rented	25.4%	25.3%	Healthcare Index	106.8	100.0
			Housing affordability	49.0%	54.5%	Miscellaneous Cost Index	99.1	100.0

CLIMATE
SCORE: 70/RANK: 97

TEMPERATURE	AREA	U.S. AVG	PRECIPITATION	AREA	U.S. AVG	COMFORTS & HAZARDS	AREA	U.S. AVG
January low	43.5°F	26.4°F	Annual inches precipitation	57.0	35.9	July relative humidity	77.0%	68.8%
July high	90.6°F	86.7°F	Annual inches snowfall	.2	24.2	Annual days mostly sunny	229	212
Annual days > 90°F	67	38	Annual days precipitation	113	111	Annual days with thunderstorms	68	39
Annual days < 32°F	13	88	Annual days rain > 0.5 inches	38	23	Tornado risk score	25	19
Annual days < 0°F	0	6	Annual days snow > 1.5 inches	1	6	Hurricane risk score	58	15

TEMPERATURE

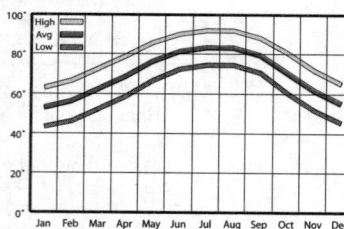

PRECIPITATION

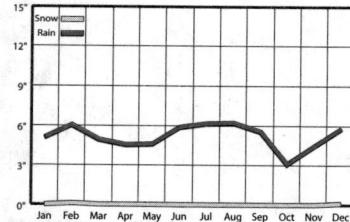

DAYS OF CLOUDS & PRECIPITATION

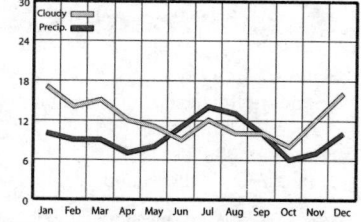

EDUCATION
SCORE: 3/RANK: 317

ACHIEVEMENT	AREA	U.S. AVG	PUBLIC SCHOOLS	AREA	U.S. AVG	HIGHER EDUCATION	AREA	U.S. AVG
High school degree	77.7%	80.2%	Expenditures per pupil	$5,346	$5,894	No. 2-year colleges	3	3
2-year college degree	3.6%	6.2%	Student/teacher ratio	16.3	16.7	No. 4-year colleges/universities	10	4
4-year college degree	15.0%	15.8%	Attending public school	75.4%	90.2%	No. highly ranked universities	0	1
Graduate/professional degree	8.1%	9.6%	State SAT score	1122	1020			
			State ACT score	19.6*	21.0			

HEALTH & HEALTHCARE
SCORE: 13/RANK: 286

CRIME
SCORE: 23/RANK: 252

HAZARDS & ILLNESSES	AREA	U.S. AVG	HEALTHCARE	AREA	U.S. AVG	CRIME	AREA	U.S. AVG
Air-quality score	24	45	Physicians per capita	390.8	261.1	Violent crime rate	786.7	456.0
Water-quality score	13	33	Hospital beds per capita	544.7	432.2	Change in violent crime rate	-41.0%	-17.2%
Pollen/allergy score	80	61	No. teaching hospitals	14	4	Property crime rate	4,961.4	3,950.0
Stress score	74	50	Cost per doctor visit	$58	$67	Change in property crime rate	-27.8%	-16.8%
Cancer mortality per capita	195.6	169.0	Cost per dental visit	$72	$82			
Depression days per month	2.3	2.8	Cost per daily hospital room	$557	$733			

TRANSPORTATION SCORE: 31/RANK: 226

COMMUTE	AREA	U.S. AVG	INTERCITY SERVICES	AREA	U.S. AVG	AUTOMOTIVE	AREA	U.S. AVG
Average commute time	26.7 min.	22.6 min.	Miles to nearest major airport	20	46	Insurance, annual premium	$1,733	$1,011
Commute by auto	86.7%	88.7%	Type of local airport	Medium		Gas, cost per gallon	$1.41	$1.50
Commute by mass transit	5.0%	1.8%	No. daily airline departures	218	294	Daily vehicle miles per capita	14.4	23.0
Work at home	1.8%	3.9%	Amtrak service	Yes				
Mass transit miles per capita	13.9	8.0	No. interstate highways	1	1			

LEISURE SCORE: 91/RANK: 30

DINING & SHOPPING	AREA	U.S. AVG	ENTERTAINMENT	AREA	U.S. AVG	OUTDOOR ACTIVITIES	AREA	U.S. AVG
Restaurant rating	7	1	Professional sports rating	6	4	Golf-course rating	5	4
No. outlet malls	2	2	College sports rating	4	4	Ski-area rating	1	4
No. Starbucks	12	11	Zoo/aquarium rating	8	3	National Park rating	4	3
No. warehouse clubs	5	4	Amusement park rating	1	3	Sq. miles inland water	10.0	4.0
			Botanical garden/arboretum rating	7	3	Miles of coastline	76.3	11.4

ARTS & CULTURE SCORE: 80/RANK: 62

MEDIA & LIBRARIES	AREA	U.S. AVG	PERFORMING ARTS	AREA	U.S. AVG	MUSEUMS	AREA	U.S. AVG
Arts radio rating	5	3	Classical music rating	7	4	Overall museum rating	8	6
No. public libraries	56	28	Ballet/dance rating	5	3	Art museum rating	7	5
Library volumes per capita	2.1	2.8	Professional theater rating	1	3	Science museum rating	7	4
			University arts programs rating	9	5	Children's museum rating	6	3

New York, NY

Score: 79.3   Rank: 40

Profile: National center
Location: Southeast corner of New York State, at mouth of Hudson River
Elevation: 87 feet
Time zone: Eastern Standard Time

PRO
Arts and culture
Commercial center
Ethnic diversity

CON
Cost of living
Crowding
Crime rate

As metropolitan areas are defined, New York is the second largest in the United States just behind Los Angeles–Long Beach, California. It includes the island of Manhattan, a seven-county area immediately north, western Long Island, and Staten Island. If the many nearby suburbs of New Jersey and Connecticut were also considered, New York would be the largest metro area in the country and the fourth largest in the world behind Tokyo, Mexico City, and Sao Paulo, Brazil. Regardless of how the area is defined, New York is among the richest and most complex places to live in America.

Boroughs, districts, and neighborhoods define the city. The borough of Manhattan, a 10-mile-long, 2-mile-wide island, is the financial, commercial, and entertainment core. Much of Lower Manhattan consists of narrow, haphazard streets, dating back to the city's earliest days as a Dutch colony. With the exception of older areas, such as Greenwich Village, the rest of the city follows an orderly grid pattern of avenues and streets laid out in 1811. (Broadway, another exception, moves at a gentle diagonal across the city.) Filling out the island are distinct districts. Lower Manhattan contains the Financial District. Midtown is the commercial center, with corporate headquarters, various media businesses, and world-class shopping along Fifth Avenue. Times Square and the Theater District, to the west, contain theaters and numerous restaurants. Surrounding Central Park, the Upper West and Upper East sides are predominantly residential, although both contain ample dining and shopping. The Upper East Side also contains posh enclaves unaffordable for most, outstanding museums, and the designer boutiques of Madison Avenue. Farther north above Central Park, neighborhoods start to decline, although Harlem is undergoing a rebirth.

The boroughs of Brooklyn, Queens, and the Bronx are a patchwork of residential and commercial areas and parks. They have a blue-collar

feel, and contain manufacturing and freight distribution centers for the area. Ethnic diversity is strong in all boroughs, while Queens is reputedly the most ethnically diverse area in the country. Staten Island, a mainly residential borough to the south, is connected to Manhattan by ferries and the Verrazano Narrows bridge.

New York offers a rich assortment of amenities, with world-class dining, shopping, and performing arts including theater, symphony, opera, and live music. Museums and architectural attractions, large and small, draw global audiences. Numerous major-league teams play in the area, including the MLB Yankees and Mets, NBA Knicks, NFL Giants and Jets, and NHL Islanders and Rangers. An extensive public transit system with subways and buses serves the urban core and links the boroughs. A suburban rail and ferry network services surrounding communities in Connecticut, Long Island, and New Jersey, while rail lines on the Northeast Corridor make such cities as Boston and Washington, D.C., easily accessible. Only 51% of New York commuters commute by auto—by far the lowest percentage in the nation. Three major airports—La Guardia, Kennedy, and nearby Newark—provide air service domestically and abroad. Surrounding the city are numerous recreation areas: Long Island beaches, the Poconos, the Hudson Valley, and the Jersey Shore, to name only a few.

The downsides are significant. The city is crowded and stressful, and some neighborhoods are run-down. The crime rate is high, although not as bad as expected when considered on a per capita basis. Cost of living is high in all categories, with a Cost of Living Index at 161. Median home prices of $320,300 don't buy much, especially in Manhattan, where prices can be five to six times higher than comparable properties in surrounding boroughs. Many residents don't own cars and choose to depend on public transit or an occasional car rental. On the good side, many public services, such as education, healthcare, and sanitation have rebounded since hitting a nadir in the 1970s. Civic pride has fluctuated over the years, but the events of September 11, 2001, have made many residents realize the significance of what they have.

The New York City area exceeds 300 square miles and is located mostly on islands, with elevations ranging from less than 50 feet over most of Manhattan, Brooklyn, and Queens to several hundred feet in northern Manhattan, the Bronx, and Staten Island. The area is close to storm tracks, and most weather approaches from the west producing higher summer and lower winter temperatures than would otherwise be expected in a coastal area. Summers are hot and humid with occasional long periods of discomfort. Sea breezes occasionally moderate summer heat and winter cold in Lower Manhattan. Manhattan and the inner boroughs are more likely to receive rain in winter while outlying areas get snow. Precipitation is distributed fairly evenly throughout the year. Summer rainfall is mainly from thunderstorms usually of brief duration. Late summer and fall rains associated with tropical storms may occur. Coastal "noreaster" storms can produce significant snow. First freeze is mid-November, last is early April.

POPULATION

DEMOGRAPHICS	AREA	U.S. AVG	ETHNIC COMPOSITION	AREA	U.S. AVG	RESIDENT PROFILE	AREA	U.S. AVG
Population	9,411,687		White	61.5%	75.1%	Single	54.2%	43.6%
Population density per sq. mile	8,201.2	447.3	Black	23.0%	12.3%	Married	45.8%	56.4%
Population growth	10.1%	16.1%	Asian	8.6%	3.6%	Divorced	6.6%	8.4%
Median age	34.9	35.5	American Indian	.4%	.9%	Separated	5.6%	3.0%
Average family size	2.6	2.7	Hispanic	20.0%	12.5%	Married with children	21.7%	28.7%
			Diversity measure	72.0%	35.2%	Single with children	11.8%	10.1%

ECONOMY & JOBS — SCORE: 13/RANK: 285

INCOME	AREA	U.S. AVG	EMPLOYMENT	AREA	U.S. AVG	LARGEST EMPLOYING INDUSTRY
Per capita income	$29,411	$23,420	Unemployment rate	7.4%	6.1%	Securities, Commodity Contracts, and Other
Household income	$52,380	$46,060	Recent job growth	-1.6%	.9%	Financial Investments and Related Activities
Household income < $25K	24.9%	26.4%	Projected future job growth	4.5%	15.1%	
Household income > $75K	33.9%	24.5%	White collar	61.6%	54.5%	
Household income growth	65.0%	57.3%	Blue collar	38.4%	45.5%	

COST OF LIVING — SCORE: 2/RANK: 323

INDEXES & TAXES	AREA	U.S. AVG	HOUSING	AREA	U.S. AVG	NECESSITIES	AREA	U.S. AVG
Cost of Living Index	161.0	100.0	Median home price	$320,300	$160,100	Food Index	139.1	100.0
Financial Progress Index	69.3	100.0	Home price appreciation	14.3%	7.1%	Housing Index	198.9	100.0
Income tax rate	10.525%	4.625%	Median rent	$1,073	$670	Utilities Index	154.3	100.0
Sales tax rate	8.250%	6.474%	Homes owned	46.3%	63.9%	Transportation Index	119.8	100.0
Property tax rate	$15.3	$15.6	Homes rented	47.5%	25.3%	Healthcare Index	174.7	100.0
			Housing affordability	40.0%	54.5%	Miscellaneous Cost Index	135.1	100.0

CLIMATE — SCORE: 77/RANK: 75

TEMPERATURE	AREA	U.S. AVG	PRECIPITATION	AREA	U.S. AVG	COMFORTS & HAZARDS	AREA	U.S. AVG
January low	25.9°F	26.4°F	Annual inches precipitation	40.0	35.9	July relative humidity	65.0%	68.8%
July high	85.2°F	86.7°F	Annual inches snowfall	29.0	24.2	Annual days mostly sunny	232	212
Annual days > 90°F	16	38	Annual days precipitation	121	111	Annual days with thunderstorms	20	39
Annual days < 32°F	81	88	Annual days rain > 0.5 inches	28	23	Tornado risk score	8	19
Annual days < 0°F	0	6	Annual days snow > 1.5 inches	6	6	Hurricane risk score	17	15

TEMPERATURE

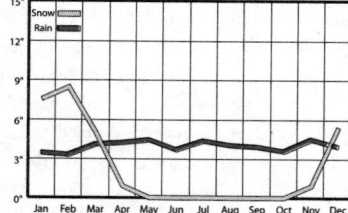

PRECIPITATION

DAYS OF CLOUDS & PRECIPITATION

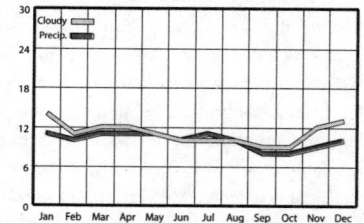

EDUCATION — SCORE: 99/RANK: 3

ACHIEVEMENT	AREA	U.S. AVG	PUBLIC SCHOOLS	AREA	U.S. AVG	HIGHER EDUCATION	AREA	U.S. AVG
High school degree	74.0%	80.2%	Expenditures per pupil	$8,640	$5,894	No. 2-year colleges	27	3
2-year college degree	5.2%	6.2%	Student/teacher ratio	17.3	16.7	No. 4-year colleges/universities	69	4
4-year college degree	16.6%	15.8%	Attending public school	80.3%	90.2%	No. highly ranked universities	8	1
Graduate/professional degree	12.6%	9.6%	State SAT score	1006*	1020			
			State ACT score	22.3	21.0			

HEALTH & HEALTHCARE SCORE: 25/RANK: 248

HAZARDS & ILLNESSES	AREA	U.S. AVG	HEALTHCARE	AREA	U.S. AVG
Air-quality score	47	45	Physicians per capita	406.8	261.1
Water-quality score	21	33	Hospital beds per capita	482.2	432.2
Pollen/allergy score	63	61	No. teaching hospitals	64	4
Stress score	50	50	Cost per doctor visit	$92	$67
Cancer mortality per capita	186.4	169.0	Cost per dental visit	$110	$82
Depression days per month	3.4	2.8	Cost per daily hospital room	$1,785	$733

CRIME SCORE: 77/RANK: 74

CRIME	AREA	U.S. AVG
Violent crime rate	773.7	456.0
Change in violent crime rate	-44.5%	-17.2%
Property crime rate	2,400.8	3,950.0
Change in property crime rate	-43.9%	-16.8%

TRANSPORTATION SCORE: 98/RANK: 7

COMMUTE	AREA	U.S. AVG	INTERCITY SERVICES	AREA	U.S. AVG	AUTOMOTIVE	AREA	U.S. AVG
Average commute time	38.9 min.	22.6 min.	Miles to nearest major airport	7	46	Insurance, annual premium	$2,279	$1,011
Commute by auto	51.2%	88.7%	Type of local airport	Large		Gas, cost per gallon	$1.70	$1.50
Commute by mass transit	36.7%	1.8%	No. daily airline departures	563	294	Daily vehicle miles per capita	15.7	23.0
Work at home	2.7%	3.9%	Amtrak service	Yes				
Mass transit miles per capita	62.9	8.0	No. interstate highways	3	1			

LEISURE SCORE: 100/RANK: 1

DINING & SHOPPING	AREA	U.S. AVG	ENTERTAINMENT	AREA	U.S. AVG	OUTDOOR ACTIVITIES	AREA	U.S. AVG
Restaurant rating	10	1	Professional sports rating	10	4	Golf-course rating	10	4
No. outlet malls	10	2	College sports rating	6	4	Ski-area rating	5	4
No. Starbucks	182	11	Zoo/aquarium rating	10	3	National Park rating	4	3
No. warehouse clubs	8	4	Amusement park rating	6	3	Sq. miles inland water	10.0	4.0
			Botanical garden/arboretum rating	10	3	Miles of coastline	26.5	11.4

ARTS & CULTURE SCORE: 100/RANK: 1

MEDIA & LIBRARIES	AREA	U.S. AVG	PERFORMING ARTS	AREA	U.S. AVG	MUSEUMS	AREA	U.S. AVG
Arts radio rating	9	3	Classical music rating	10	4	Overall museum rating	10	6
No. public libraries	279	28	Ballet/dance rating	10	3	Art museum rating	10	5
Library volumes per capita	5.1	2.8	Professional theater rating	10	3	Science museum rating	10	4
			University arts programs rating	10	5	Children's museum rating	10	3

Newark, NJ

Score: 43.5	**Rank: 261**

Profile: Large city/Commuter community
Location: Northern New Jersey near the lower Hudson River, west of New York City
Elevation: 10 feet
Time zone: Eastern Standard Time

PRO	CON
Proximity to New York City	Cost of living
Diverse economy	Urban decay
Transportation	Industrial setting

The Newark area is a diverse patchwork of communities including downtown Newark and a series of small cities, towns, and residential suburbs lying across the Hudson River from New York City. The five-county area includes such well-known cities as Parsippany, Morristown, and Livingston. Newark itself is a large and fairly run-down industrial center, although its geographic position near New York and the presence of transportation networks and various industries are helping to generate a rebound. Areas to the north and south of the downtown, such as Elizabeth and Jersey City, are some of the most industrial in the country with oil refineries, chemical plants, ports, and other monuments to heavy industry. The suburbs to the west have become major corporate centers, and headquarters to such giants as Lucent Technologies, American Home Products, Prudential, and drug giants Warner Lambert and Schering-Plough—in all, home to nine Fortune 500 companies and many of their research facilities. Areas farthest west, including Morristown and Basking Ridge, are pastoral and mainly upscale. The restored Newark Penn Station is a transportation hub for the state and the Northeast Corridor, and Newark Airport is a major hub for the New York area.

The employment picture is mixed, and projected employment growth is one-fifth the U.S. average. The Cost of Living Index is high at 140.5. Overall crime rates are lower than one might expect upon seeing parts of the area. Overall, reality is better than the statistics indicate but also worse—pockets of high crime and run-down housing exist everywhere.

The natural terrain—what little there is—is flat and marshy. To the northwest are wooded ridges oriented roughly in a southwest-to-northeast direction. The climate is predominantly continental with the usual variations in temperature, humidity, and precipitation with passing storms and air masses. The ridges to the northwest temper summer thunderstorms somewhat, and the city is close enough to the Atlantic to receive some moderating influence in summer and winter depending on wind direction. Summers are hot and muggy when winds are from the west or southwest but can be 15°F cooler when from the south or southeast. Winters are cool and wet. Passing "noreaster" storms typically produce 1 to 2 inches of precipitation as rain or snow. Snowfalls of 8 inches or more occur every other year. Snow is heavier to the west of the city. Cold polar air does invade, and below-zero temperatures occur one winter out of four. First freeze is late October, last is mid-April.

POPULATION

DEMOGRAPHICS	AREA	U.S. AVG	ETHNIC COMPOSITION	AREA	U.S. AVG	RESIDENT PROFILE	AREA	U.S. AVG
Population	2,064,011		White	79.1%	75.1%	Single	45.7%	43.6%
Population density per sq. mile	1,308.1	447.3	Black	14.2%	12.3%	Married	54.3%	56.4%
Population growth	7.7%	16.1%	Asian	4.4%	3.6%	Divorced	6.2%	8.4%
Median age	36.7	35.5	American Indian	.2%	.9%	Separated	3.6%	3.0%
Average family size	2.7	2.7	Hispanic	9.5%	12.5%	Married with children	28.4%	28.7%
			Diversity measure	56.6%	35.2%	Single with children	9.1%	10.1%

ECONOMY & JOBS SCORE: 89/RANK: 35

INCOME	AREA	U.S. AVG	EMPLOYMENT	AREA	U.S. AVG	LARGEST EMPLOYING INDUSTRY
Per capita income	$33,866	$23,420	Unemployment rate	6.1%	6.1%	Chemical Manufacturing
Household income	$68,961	$46,060	Recent job growth	1.9%	.9%	
Household income < $25K	16.9%	26.4%	Projected future job growth	3.8%	15.1%	
Household income > $75K	46.4%	24.5%	White collar	63.3%	54.5%	
Household income growth	63.3%	57.3%	Blue collar	36.7%	45.5%	

COST OF LIVING SCORE: 6/RANK: 310

INDEXES & TAXES	AREA	U.S. AVG	HOUSING	AREA	U.S. AVG	NECESSITIES	AREA	U.S. AVG
Cost of Living Index	140.5	100.0	Median home price	$301,900	$160,100	Food Index	110.2	100.0
Financial Progress Index	104.6	100.0	Home price appreciation	12.0%	7.1%	Housing Index	187.5	100.0
Income tax rate	2.450%	4.625%	Median rent	$987	$670	Utilities Index	119.3	100.0
Sales tax rate	6.000%	6.474%	Homes owned	67.5%	63.9%	Transportation Index	117.1	100.0
Property tax rate	$23.4	$15.6	Homes rented	26.0%	25.3%	Healthcare Index	118.5	100.0
			Housing affordability	49.0%	54.5%	Miscellaneous Cost Index	112.2	100.0

CLIMATE SCORE: 46/RANK: 178

TEMPERATURE	AREA	U.S. AVG	PRECIPITATION	AREA	U.S. AVG	COMFORTS & HAZARDS	AREA	U.S. AVG
January low	24.3°F	26.4°F	Annual inches precipitation	41.5	35.9	July relative humidity	65.0%	68.8%
July high	85.6°F	86.7°F	Annual inches snowfall	28.4	24.2	Annual days mostly sunny	207	212
Annual days > 90°F	20	38	Annual days precipitation	129	111	Annual days with thunderstorms	25	39
Annual days < 32°F	87	88	Annual days rain > 0.5 inches	29	23	Tornado risk score	15	19
Annual days < 0°F	0	6	Annual days snow > 1.5 inches	7	6	Hurricane risk score	16	15

TEMPERATURE

PRECIPITATION

DAYS OF CLOUDS & PRECIPITATION

EDUCATION SCORE: 88/RANK: 41

ACHIEVEMENT	AREA	U.S. AVG	PUBLIC SCHOOLS	AREA	U.S. AVG	HIGHER EDUCATION	AREA	U.S. AVG
High school degree	81.6%	80.2%	Expenditures per pupil	$10,159	$5,894	No. 2-year colleges	7	3
2-year college degree	4.9%	6.2%	Student/teacher ratio	14.5	16.7	No. 4-year colleges/universities	15	4
4-year college degree	19.5%	15.8%	Attending public school	85.4%	90.2%	No. highly ranked universities	3	1
Graduate/professional degree	12.1%	9.6%	State SAT score	1016*	1020			
			State ACT score	21.2	21.0			

HEALTH & HEALTHCARE SCORE: 21/RANK: 260

HAZARDS & ILLNESSES	AREA	U.S. AVG	HEALTHCARE	AREA	U.S. AVG
Air-quality score	80	45	Physicians per capita	326.0	261.1
Water-quality score	18	33	Hospital beds per capita	485.2	432.2
Pollen/allergy score	63	61	No. teaching hospitals	16	4
Stress score	42	50	Cost per doctor visit	$74	$67
Cancer mortality per capita	187.0	169.0	Cost per dental visit	$132	$82
Depression days per month	2.9	2.8	Cost per daily hospital room	$2,801	$733

CRIME SCORE: 75/RANK: 81

CRIME	AREA	U.S. AVG
Violent crime rate	540.8	456.0
Change in violent crime rate	-47.6%	-17.2%
Property crime rate	3,141.9	3,950.0
Change in property crime rate	-34.6%	-16.8%

TRANSPORTATION SCORE: 87/RANK: 41

COMMUTE	AREA	U.S. AVG	INTERCITY SERVICES	AREA	U.S. AVG	AUTOMOTIVE	AREA	U.S. AVG
Average commute time	30.8 min.	22.6 min.	Miles to nearest major airport	3	46	Insurance, annual premium	$1,633	$1,011
Commute by auto	86.6%	88.7%	Type of local airport	Large		Gas, cost per gallon	$1.45	$1.50
Commute by mass transit	7.1%	1.8%	No. daily airline departures	694	294	Daily vehicle miles per capita	23.1	23.0
Work at home	2.5%	3.9%	Amtrak service	Yes				
Mass transit miles per capita	24.9	8.0	No. interstate highways	1	1			

LEISURE SCORE: 93/RANK: 23

DINING & SHOPPING	AREA	U.S. AVG	ENTERTAINMENT	AREA	U.S. AVG	OUTDOOR ACTIVITIES	AREA	U.S. AVG
Restaurant rating	1	1	Professional sports rating	10	4	Golf-course rating	10	4
No. outlet malls	10	2	College sports rating	4	4	Ski-area rating	5	4
No. Starbucks	19	11	Zoo/aquarium rating	8	3	National Park rating	4	3
No. warehouse clubs	4	4	Amusement park rating	7	3	Sq. miles inland water	7.0	4.0
			Botanical garden/arboretum rating	4	3	Miles of coastline	0.0	11.4

ARTS & CULTURE SCORE: 94/RANK: 22

MEDIA & LIBRARIES	AREA	U.S. AVG	PERFORMING ARTS	AREA	U.S. AVG	MUSEUMS	AREA	U.S. AVG
Arts radio rating	4	3	Classical music rating	9	4	Overall museum rating	9	6
No. public libraries	114	28	Ballet/dance rating	8	3	Art museum rating	9	5
Library volumes per capita	3.8	2.8	Professional theater rating	10	3	Science museum rating	9	4
			University arts programs rating	10	5	Children's museum rating	9	3

Newburgh, NY-PA

Score: 9.9   Rank: 329

Profile: Small town/Commuter community
Location: Southern New York along the Hudson River, 50 miles north of New York City
Elevation: 292 feet
Time zone: Eastern Standard Time

PRO
Proximity to New York City
Attractive setting
Nearby recreation

CON
Cost of living
Long commute
Low educational attainment

This metropolitan area, extending from western Pennsylvania to east of the Hudson River, encompasses modestly sized Newburgh and numerous smaller towns in valleys and along both sides of the Hudson. Towns along the transportation corridors, particularly the Metra North rail line along the east side of the Hudson, have some small-town character while providing commuter access to New York City. The West Point Military Academy sits on a bluff overlooking the Hudson south of Newburgh. Educational attainment is low, and the 62.1% high school graduation rate is the lowest in the state. Cost of living and housing are high, and climate can be rough, particularly in winter. For those tolerant of the cost, commute, and winter, the ranking may understate the quality of life available.

The area is mainly hilly and wooded with deciduous trees. The east bank of the Hudson is a narrow, flat valley with hills rising to the east, while the west bank consists of high rocky bluffs, especially near West Point, with hills to the west. The climate is continental with a limited marine influence from the south. Summers are warm and frequently muggy, with evenings occasionally cooled by breezes from all directions. Summer showers and thundershowers are common. Winters are cold and fairly wet with snow common even as New York City receives rain. Periods of bitter cold with below-zero nighttime temperatures occur, although the Hudson Valley and hills shelter the area from the strongest winds and harshest cold. First freeze is late September, last is late April.

POPULATION

DEMOGRAPHICS	AREA	U.S. AVG	ETHNIC COMPOSITION	AREA	U.S. AVG	RESIDENT PROFILE	AREA	U.S. AVG
Population	406,868		White	92.7%	75.1%	Single	40.8%	43.6%
Population density per sq. mile	298.4	447.3	Black	4.4%	12.3%	Married	59.2%	56.4%
Population growth	21.2%	16.1%	Asian	1.6%	3.6%	Divorced	6.0%	8.4%
Median age	35.5	35.5	American Indian	.3%	.9%	Separated	3.2%	3.0%
Average family size	2.8	2.7	Hispanic	5.3%	12.5%	Married with children	33.3%	28.7%
			Diversity measure	35.8%	35.2%	Single with children	7.6%	10.1%

ECONOMY & JOBS SCORE: 79/RANK: 70

INCOME	AREA	U.S. AVG	EMPLOYMENT	AREA	U.S. AVG	LARGEST EMPLOYING INDUSTRY
Per capita income	$22,900	$23,420	Unemployment rate	4.6%	6.1%	Plastics and Rubber Products Manufacturing
Household income	$53,064	$46,060	Recent job growth	1.6%	.9%	
Household income < $25K	20.9%	26.4%	Projected future job growth	13.3%	15.1%	
Household income > $75K	31.1%	24.5%	White collar	54.2%	54.5%	
Household income growth	38.7%	57.3%	Blue collar	45.8%	45.5%	

COST OF LIVING SCORE: 11/RANK: 292

INDEXES & TAXES	AREA	U.S. AVG	HOUSING	AREA	U.S. AVG	NECESSITIES	AREA	U.S. AVG
Cost of Living Index	120.9	100.0	Median home price	$203,100	$160,100	Food Index	116.9	100.0
Financial Progress Index	93.6	100.0	Home price appreciation	13.1%	7.1%	Housing Index	126.1	100.0
Income tax rate	7.125%	4.625%	Median rent	$855	$670	Utilities Index	125.6	100.0
Sales tax rate	7.250%	6.474%	Homes owned	60.8%	63.9%	Transportation Index	117.6	100.0
Property tax rate	$21.5	$15.6	Homes rented	19.7%	25.3%	Healthcare Index	126.2	100.0
			Housing affordability	51.0%	54.5%	Miscellaneous Cost Index	113.9	100.0

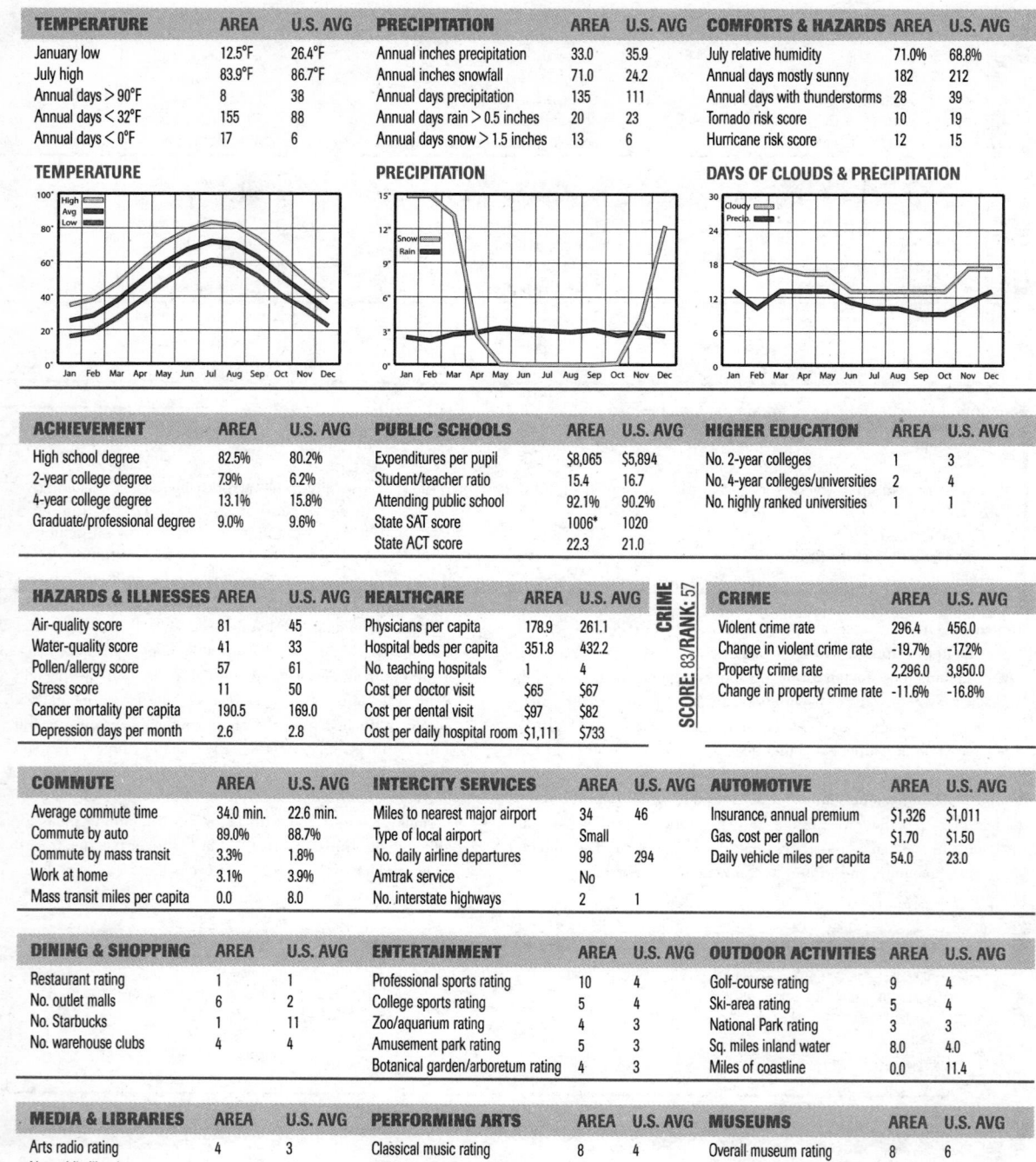

CLIMATE SCORE: 3/RANK: 321

TEMPERATURE	AREA	U.S. AVG	PRECIPITATION	AREA	U.S. AVG	COMFORTS & HAZARDS	AREA	U.S. AVG
January low	12.5°F	26.4°F	Annual inches precipitation	33.0	35.9	July relative humidity	71.0%	68.8%
July high	83.9°F	86.7°F	Annual inches snowfall	71.0	24.2	Annual days mostly sunny	182	212
Annual days > 90°F	8	38	Annual days precipitation	135	111	Annual days with thunderstorms	28	39
Annual days < 32°F	155	88	Annual days rain > 0.5 inches	20	23	Tornado risk score	10	19
Annual days < 0°F	17	6	Annual days snow > 1.5 inches	13	6	Hurricane risk score	12	15

TEMPERATURE

PRECIPITATION

DAYS OF CLOUDS & PRECIPITATION

EDUCATION SCORE: 88/RANK: 41

ACHIEVEMENT	AREA	U.S. AVG	PUBLIC SCHOOLS	AREA	U.S. AVG	HIGHER EDUCATION	AREA	U.S. AVG
High school degree	82.5%	80.2%	Expenditures per pupil	$8,065	$5,894	No. 2-year colleges	1	3
2-year college degree	7.9%	6.2%	Student/teacher ratio	15.4	16.7	No. 4-year colleges/universities	2	4
4-year college degree	13.1%	15.8%	Attending public school	92.1%	90.2%	No. highly ranked universities	1	1
Graduate/professional degree	9.0%	9.6%	State SAT score	1006*	1020			
			State ACT score	22.3	21.0			

HEALTH & HEALTHCARE SCORE: 9/RANK: 299

HAZARDS & ILLNESSES	AREA	U.S. AVG	HEALTHCARE	AREA	U.S. AVG	CRIME	AREA	U.S. AVG
Air-quality score	81	45	Physicians per capita	178.9	261.1	Violent crime rate	296.4	456.0
Water-quality score	41	33	Hospital beds per capita	351.8	432.2	Change in violent crime rate	-19.7%	-17.2%
Pollen/allergy score	57	61	No. teaching hospitals	1	4	Property crime rate	2,296.0	3,950.0
Stress score	11	50	Cost per doctor visit	$65	$67	Change in property crime rate	-11.6%	-16.8%
Cancer mortality per capita	190.5	169.0	Cost per dental visit	$97	$82			
Depression days per month	2.6	2.8	Cost per daily hospital room	$1,111	$733			

CRIME SCORE: 83/RANK: 57

TRANSPORTATION SCORE: 11/RANK: 293

COMMUTE	AREA	U.S. AVG	INTERCITY SERVICES	AREA	U.S. AVG	AUTOMOTIVE	AREA	U.S. AVG
Average commute time	34.0 min.	22.6 min.	Miles to nearest major airport	34	46	Insurance, annual premium	$1,326	$1,011
Commute by auto	89.0%	88.7%	Type of local airport	Small		Gas, cost per gallon	$1.70	$1.50
Commute by mass transit	3.3%	1.8%	No. daily airline departures	98	294	Daily vehicle miles per capita	54.0	23.0
Work at home	3.1%	3.9%	Amtrak service	No				
Mass transit miles per capita	0.0	8.0	No. interstate highways	2	1			

LEISURE SCORE: 48/RANK: 172

DINING & SHOPPING	AREA	U.S. AVG	ENTERTAINMENT	AREA	U.S. AVG	OUTDOOR ACTIVITIES	AREA	U.S. AVG
Restaurant rating	1	1	Professional sports rating	10	4	Golf-course rating	9	4
No. outlet malls	6	2	College sports rating	5	4	Ski-area rating	5	4
No. Starbucks	1	11	Zoo/aquarium rating	4	3	National Park rating	3	3
No. warehouse clubs	4	4	Amusement park rating	5	3	Sq. miles inland water	8.0	4.0
			Botanical garden/arboretum rating	4	3	Miles of coastline	0.0	11.4

ARTS & CULTURE SCORE: 11/RANK: 293

MEDIA & LIBRARIES	AREA	U.S. AVG	PERFORMING ARTS	AREA	U.S. AVG	MUSEUMS	AREA	U.S. AVG
Arts radio rating	4	3	Classical music rating	8	4	Overall museum rating	8	6
No. public libraries	27	28	Ballet/dance rating	5	3	Art museum rating	8	5
Library volumes per capita	3.3	2.8	Professional theater rating	8	3	Science museum rating	5	4
			University arts programs rating	8	5	Children's museum rating	3	3

Norfolk–Virginia Beach–Newport News, VA-NC

Score: 85.8   Rank: 17

Profile: Large-city complex
Location: Southeast Virginia coast
Elevation: 30 feet
Time zone: Eastern Standard Time

PRO
Nearby water recreation
Educated population
Stable economy

CON
Traffic congestion
Urban sprawl
Some unattractive areas

This complex area straddles the waterway known as Hampton Roads, a large estuarine bay that empties into the Chesapeake Bay and Atlantic Ocean. It is the largest metropolitan area in the state in terms of population. The cities of Norfolk, Chesapeake, and Portsmouth are on the south side of the waterway, with Virginia Beach a few miles to the east along the Atlantic Shore. Hampton and Newport News are on the north side. Long bridge-tunnel combinations connect the two areas. Norfolk is one of the best natural ports on the East Coast. The economy is mainly related to marine and military activities with shipbuilding, fishing, and seaport-related businesses among the largest. There are several large naval bases in the area. The area has an assortment of amenities, particularly related to its maritime history, and a good set of performing arts. Water and beach activities are excellent, although Virginia Beach can be crowded. For an area this size, there are relatively few sports teams and no major-league teams. Other downsides include some urban sprawl; frequent traffic problems, especially at bridges and tunnels; and extensive, unattractive naval and port areas. Cost of living is moderate for an East Coast area of this size. The marine climate is pleasant and there is plenty to do.

The city of Norfolk is almost surrounded by water, with the Chesapeake Bay immediately to the north, Hampton Roads and the James River to the west, and the Atlantic Ocean 18 miles to the east. Numerous rivers and waterways traverse the area. The land is low and level throughout the city. The climate is generally marine. The geographic location avoids the worst of northern and southern storm tracks. Cool Atlantic breezes frequently temper the long, warm summers. Extreme temperatures are infrequent. Winters are usually mild and may pass with no measurable snowfall.

POPULATION

DEMOGRAPHICS	AREA	U.S. AVG	ETHNIC COMPOSITION	AREA	U.S. AVG	RESIDENT PROFILE	AREA	U.S. AVG
Population	1,605,822		White	70.5%	75.1%	Single	47.2%	43.6%
Population density per sq. mile	683.7	447.3	Black	26.5%	12.3%	Married	52.8%	56.4%
Population growth	11.3%	16.1%	Asian	2.1%	3.6%	Divorced	7.1%	8.4%
Median age	33.8	35.5	American Indian	.3%	.9%	Separated	5.6%	3.0%
Average family size	2.7	2.7	Hispanic	2.8%	12.5%	Married with children	28.5%	28.7%
			Diversity measure	52.6%	35.2%	Single with children	11.3%	10.1%

ECONOMY & JOBS SCORE: 66/RANK: 110

INCOME	AREA	U.S. AVG	EMPLOYMENT	AREA	U.S. AVG	LARGEST EMPLOYING INDUSTRY
Per capita income	$21,424	$23,420	Unemployment rate	4.3%	6.1%	Transportation Equipment Manufacturing
Household income	$44,710	$46,060	Recent job growth	.6%	.9%	
Household income < $25K	23.0%	26.4%	Projected future job growth	15.9%	15.1%	
Household income > $75K	21.0%	24.5%	White collar	52.9%	54.5%	
Household income growth	45.2%	57.3%	Blue collar	47.1%	45.5%	

COST OF LIVING SCORE: 54/RANK: 151

INDEXES & TAXES	AREA	U.S. AVG	HOUSING	AREA	U.S. AVG	NECESSITIES	AREA	U.S. AVG
Cost of Living Index	95.0	100.0	Median home price	$134,610	$160,100	Food Index	94.0	100.0
Financial Progress Index	100.2	100.0	Home price appreciation	6.9%	7.1%	Housing Index	83.6	100.0
Income tax rate	5.750%	4.625%	Median rent	$748	$670	Utilities Index	137.8	100.0
Sales tax rate	4.500%	6.474%	Homes owned	55.3%	63.9%	Transportation Index	105.2	100.0
Property tax rate	$12.3	$15.6	Homes rented	32.5%	25.3%	Healthcare Index	94.5	100.0
			Housing affordability	52.0%	54.5%	Miscellaneous Cost Index	94.1	100.0

CLIMATE SCORE: 62/RANK: 124

TEMPERATURE	AREA	U.S. AVG	PRECIPITATION	AREA	U.S. AVG	COMFORTS & HAZARDS	AREA	U.S. AVG
January low	32.2°F	26.4°F	Annual inches precipitation	45.0	35.9	July relative humidity	71.0%	68.8%
July high	86.6°F	86.7°F	Annual inches snowfall	7.0	24.2	Annual days mostly sunny	212	212
Annual days > 90°F	30	38	Annual days precipitation	115	111	Annual days with thunderstorms	37	39
Annual days < 32°F	54	88	Annual days rain > 0.5 inches	27	23	Tornado risk score	14	19
Annual days < 0°F	0	6	Annual days snow > 1.5 inches	2	6	Hurricane risk score	41	15

TEMPERATURE

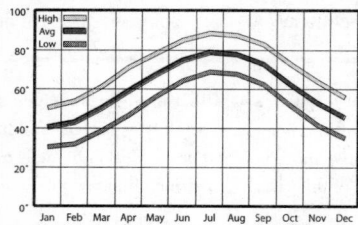

PRECIPITATION

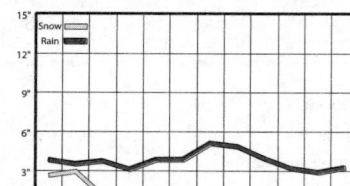

DAYS OF CLOUDS & PRECIPITATION

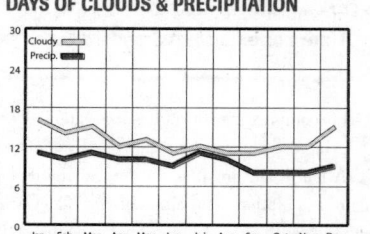

EDUCATION SCORE: 71/RANK: 95

ACHIEVEMENT	AREA	U.S. AVG	PUBLIC SCHOOLS	AREA	U.S. AVG	HIGHER EDUCATION	AREA	U.S. AVG
High school degree	84.7%	80.2%	Expenditures per pupil	$5,379	$5,894	No. 2-year colleges	4	3
2-year college degree	7.5%	6.2%	Student/teacher ratio	14.3	16.7	No. 4-year colleges/universities	6	4
4-year college degree	15.4%	15.8%	Attending public school	90.3%	90.2%	No. highly ranked universities	1	1
Graduate/professional degree	8.4%	9.6%	State SAT score	1024*	1020			
			State ACT score	20.6	21.0			

HEALTH & HEALTHCARE SCORE: 20/RANK: 263

CRIME SCORE: 46/RANK: 177

HAZARDS & ILLNESSES	AREA	U.S. AVG	HEALTHCARE	AREA	U.S. AVG	CRIME	AREA	U.S. AVG
Air-quality score	95	45	Physicians per capita	254.0	261.1	Violent crime rate	434.8	456.0
Water-quality score	43	33	Hospital beds per capita	344.4	432.2	Change in violent crime rate	-24.2%	-17.2%
Pollen/allergy score	69	61	No. teaching hospitals	11	4	Property crime rate	4,100.5	3,950.0
Stress score	39	50	Cost per doctor visit	$69	$67	Change in property crime rate	-17.7%	-16.8%
Cancer mortality per capita	185.9	169.0	Cost per dental visit	$87	$82			
Depression days per month	2.7	2.8	Cost per daily hospital room	$547	$733			

TRANSPORTATION SCORE: 35/RANK: 215

COMMUTE	AREA	U.S. AVG	INTERCITY SERVICES	AREA	U.S. AVG	AUTOMOTIVE	AREA	U.S. AVG
Average commute time	24.1 min.	22.6 min.	Miles to nearest major airport	14	46	Insurance, annual premium	$878	$1,011
Commute by auto	86.5%	88.7%	Type of local airport	Small		Gas, cost per gallon	$1.41	$1.50
Commute by mass transit	2.4%	1.8%	No. daily airline departures	141	294	Daily vehicle miles per capita	22.7	23.0
Work at home	3.9%	3.9%	Amtrak service	Yes				
Mass transit miles per capita	9.6	8.0	No. interstate highways	1	1			

LEISURE SCORE: 73/RANK: 86

DINING & SHOPPING	AREA	U.S. AVG	ENTERTAINMENT	AREA	U.S. AVG	OUTDOOR ACTIVITIES	AREA	U.S. AVG
Restaurant rating	1	1	Professional sports rating	3	4	Golf-course rating	5	4
No. outlet malls	2	2	College sports rating	5	4	Ski-area rating	1	4
No. Starbucks	16	11	Zoo/aquarium rating	8	3	National Park rating	5	3
No. warehouse clubs	7	4	Amusement park rating	9	3	Sq. miles inland water	8.0	4.0
			Botanical garden/arboretum rating	7	3	Miles of coastline	69.0	11.4

ARTS & CULTURE SCORE: 70/RANK: 100

MEDIA & LIBRARIES	AREA	U.S. AVG	PERFORMING ARTS	AREA	U.S. AVG	MUSEUMS	AREA	U.S. AVG
Arts radio rating	8	3	Classical music rating	6	4	Overall museum rating	9	6
No. public libraries	50	28	Ballet/dance rating	8	3	Art museum rating	9	5
Library volumes per capita	2.8	2.8	Professional theater rating	6	3	Science museum rating	10	4
			University arts programs rating	5	5	Children's museum rating	10	3

Oakland, CA

Score: 58.0   **Rank:** 165

Profile: Port city/Commuter community/Industrial center
Location: Northern California, on the east shore of San Francisco Bay
Elevation: 6 feet
Time zone: Pacific Standard Time

PRO	CON
Year-round climate	Cost of living
Recreation	Urban sprawl
Proximity to San Francisco	Violent crime

The Oakland area, encompassing Alameda and Contra Costa counties, covers most of the inhabitable land along the east shore of San Francisco Bay. The more level areas have been developed into a mix of industrial, commercial, and residential areas, including the cities of Berkeley, Hayward, Richmond, Concord, Walnut Creek, and Martinez, among others. Along the bay are the area's major port facilities and light and medium manufacturing. Large bedroom communities exist, especially in Contra Costa County to the east. While the Bay Area Rapid Transit system ("BART") makes commuting easier, trips to San Francisco are complex. The area's ethnicities, appearance, and amenities are characterized by diversity. Many outlying valleys contain unattractive commercial areas of urban sprawl, exemplified by Walnut Creek and Pleasanton. The city of Berkeley and the main campus of the University of California provide welcome relief in a less dense, college-town setting. The school adds a great deal of provocative but benign local culture and color.

Cost of living and commute times are the main negatives for the area. The Cost of Living Index of 179.3 is high by any standard, and median home prices are probably understated due to the abundance of low-end housing in industrial areas. The reported 32-minute commute time is the worst on the West Coast (with the exception of Bremerton, Washington, a ferry commute from Seattle). Crime is high, but has improved in recent years. Main attractions include an excellent Mediterranean climate, modified by the bay, and easy access to San Francisco and its amenities.

Oakland and many of the towns to the north and south are located on a mostly level coastal plain west of the 4,000-foot Diablo Range. Remaining natural vegetation is grassland with a few oak and coniferous trees. The marine air cools the area in summer and keeps it relatively mild in winter. Low stratus clouds, known locally as "fog," frequently blow in from the Pacific, particularly along the east shore of the bay, and may burn off or may linger all day. When the fog dissipates, expect sunny, mild weather in all seasons, except when winter rainstorms are present. Summer temperatures seldom reach the 90s along the bay, but can be warmer inland. Winter temperatures are seldom below freezing. Most rain occurs in winter.

POPULATION

DEMOGRAPHICS	AREA	U.S. AVG	ETHNIC COMPOSITION	AREA	U.S. AVG	RESIDENT PROFILE	AREA	U.S. AVG
Population	2,464,668		White	62.7%	75.1%	Single	50.6%	43.6%
Population density per sq. mile	1,690.7	447.3	Black	14.7%	12.3%	Married	49.4%	56.4%
Population growth	18.3%	16.1%	Asian	17.0%	3.6%	Divorced	10.3%	8.4%
Median age	35.5	35.5	American Indian	.6%	.9%	Separated	3.8%	3.0%
Average family size	2.6	2.7	Hispanic	17.0%	12.5%	Married with children	23.6%	28.7%
			Diversity measure	66.9%	35.2%	Single with children	11.2%	10.1%

ECONOMY & JOBS   SCORE: 23/RANK: 254

INCOME	AREA	U.S. AVG	EMPLOYMENT	AREA	U.S. AVG	LARGEST EMPLOYING INDUSTRY
Per capita income	$32,763	$23,420	Unemployment rate	6.2%	6.1%	Computer and Electronic Product Manufacturing
Household income	$71,689	$46,060	Recent job growth	1.2%	.9%	
Household income < $25K	14.9%	26.4%	Projected future job growth	14.3%	15.1%	
Household income > $75K	47.9%	24.5%	White collar	64.9%	54.5%	
Household income growth	76.3%	57.3%	Blue collar	35.1%	45.5%	

COST OF LIVING   SCORE: 0/RANK: 331

INDEXES & TAXES	AREA	U.S. AVG	HOUSING	AREA	U.S. AVG	NECESSITIES	AREA	U.S. AVG
Cost of Living Index	179.3	100.0	Median home price	$455,630	$160,100	Food Index	119.5	100.0
Financial Progress Index	85.2	100.0	Home price appreciation	16.4%	7.1%	Housing Index	283.0	100.0
Income tax rate	6.000%	4.625%	Median rent	$1,420	$670	Utilities Index	127.0	100.0
Sales tax rate	8.250%	6.474%	Homes owned	60.3%	63.9%	Transportation Index	123.2	100.0
Property tax rate	$11.3	$15.6	Homes rented	34.7%	25.3%	Healthcare Index	157.8	100.0
			Housing affordability	37.0%	54.5%	Miscellaneous Cost Index	108.7	100.0

CLIMATE SCORE: 99/RANK: 4

TEMPERATURE	AREA	U.S. AVG	PRECIPITATION	AREA	U.S. AVG	COMFORTS & HAZARDS	AREA	U.S. AVG
January low	42.7°F	26.4°F	Annual inches precipitation	18.7	35.9	July relative humidity	76.0%	68.8%
July high	69.7°F	86.7°F	Annual inches snowfall	0.0	24.2	Annual days mostly sunny	260	212
Annual days > 90°F	2	38	Annual days precipitation	63	111	Annual days with thunderstorms	2	39
Annual days < 32°F	1	88	Annual days rain > 0.5 inches	12	23	Tornado risk score	2	19
Annual days < 0°F	0	6	Annual days snow > 1.5 inches	0	6	Hurricane risk score	0	15

TEMPERATURE

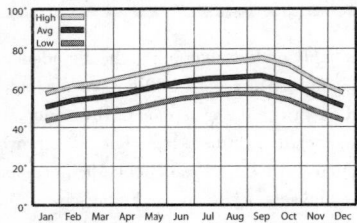

PRECIPITATION

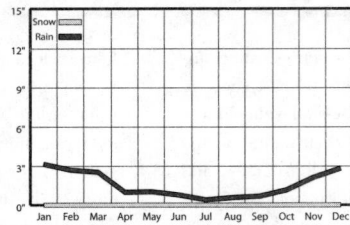

DAYS OF CLOUDS & PRECIPITATION

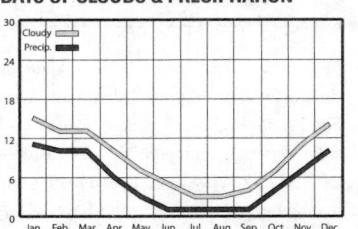

EDUCATION SCORE: 82/RANK: 61

ACHIEVEMENT	AREA	U.S. AVG	PUBLIC SCHOOLS	AREA	U.S. AVG	HIGHER EDUCATION	AREA	U.S. AVG
High school degree	84.2%	80.2%	Expenditures per pupil	$5,455	$5,894	No. 2-year colleges	15	3
2-year college degree	7.2%	6.2%	Student/teacher ratio	20.9	16.7	No. 4-year colleges/universities	9	4
4-year college degree	21.9%	15.8%	Attending public school	87.7%	90.2%	No. highly ranked universities	1	1
Graduate/professional degree	12.9%	9.6%	State SAT score	1018*	1020			
			State ACT score	21.5	21.0			

HEALTH & HEALTHCARE SCORE: 1/RANK: 325

CRIME SCORE: 45/RANK: 179

HAZARDS & ILLNESSES	AREA	U.S. AVG	HEALTHCARE	AREA	U.S. AVG	CRIME	AREA	U.S. AVG
Air-quality score	4	45	Physicians per capita	240.6	261.1	Violent crime rate	566.8	456.0
Water-quality score	10	33	Hospital beds per capita	240.5	432.2	Change in violent crime rate	-42.6%	-17.2%
Pollen/allergy score	97	61	No. teaching hospitals	8	4	Property crime rate	4,201.8	3,950.0
Stress score	93	50	Cost per doctor visit	$74	$67	Change in property crime rate	-26.4%	-16.8%
Cancer mortality per capita	174.3	169.0	Cost per dental visit	$98	$82			
Depression days per month	3.2	2.8	Cost per daily hospital room	$1,987	$733			

TRANSPORTATION SCORE: 0/RANK: 328

COMMUTE	AREA	U.S. AVG	INTERCITY SERVICES	AREA	U.S. AVG	AUTOMOTIVE	AREA	U.S. AVG
Average commute time	32.2 min.	22.6 min.	Miles to nearest major airport	14	46	Insurance, annual premium	$1,396	$1,011
Commute by auto	80.0%	88.7%	Type of local airport	Large		Gas, cost per gallon	$1.81	$1.50
Commute by mass transit	9.6%	1.8%	No. daily airline departures	546	294	Daily vehicle miles per capita	22.1	23.0
Work at home	4.0%	3.9%	Amtrak service	Yes				
Mass transit miles per capita	1.1	8.0	No. interstate highways	2	1			

LEISURE SCORE: 98/RANK: 5

DINING & SHOPPING	AREA	U.S. AVG	ENTERTAINMENT	AREA	U.S. AVG	OUTDOOR ACTIVITIES	AREA	U.S. AVG
Restaurant rating	1	1	Professional sports rating	10	4	Golf-course rating	7	4
No. outlet malls	5	2	College sports rating	9	4	Ski-area rating	9	4
No. Starbucks	84	11	Zoo/aquarium rating	5	3	National Park rating	4	3
No. warehouse clubs	8	4	Amusement park rating	5	3	Sq. miles inland water	10.0	4.0
			Botanical garden/arboretum rating	7	3	Miles of coastline	0.0	11.4

ARTS & CULTURE SCORE: 63/RANK: 124

MEDIA & LIBRARIES	AREA	U.S. AVG	PERFORMING ARTS	AREA	U.S. AVG	MUSEUMS	AREA	U.S. AVG
Arts radio rating	4	3	Classical music rating	8	4	Overall museum rating	9	6
No. public libraries	69	28	Ballet/dance rating	10	3	Art museum rating	9	5
Library volumes per capita	2.2	2.8	Professional theater rating	9	3	Science museum rating	10	4
			University arts programs rating	10	5	Children's museum rating	7	3

Ocala, FL

Score: 75.5 **Rank:** 58

Profile: Small city
Location: Central Florida, 60 miles east of Daytona Beach
Elevation: 75 feet
Time zone: Eastern Standard Time

PRO	CON
Cost of living	Hot, humid summers
Attractive downtown	Isolation
Nearby recreation	Violent crime

Ocala, an agricultural and manufacturing center, is about halfway between Gainesville to the north and Orlando to the southeast. With its attractive tree-lined streets and Old South–style homes, it resembles a typical Southern city rather than a Florida beach town. Ocala is the capital of Florida's thoroughbred industry, and ranching and horse-breeding are popular. Just east of town is the Ocala National Forest, a preserve of Florida pines, cypress, and hardwood trees with water and plenty of recreation. At 86.1, the Cost of Living Index is the lowest in the state and low by national standards. The location is a bit isolated from Orlando's services and amenities, 75 miles away.

The level area is characterized by a mix of open land and areas of medium-size trees, some tropical in nature. Summers are warm and humid with maximum temperatures averaging a little more than 90°F. Winters are mild with daytime temperatures in the 60s and 70s but with some occasional freezing. Rainfall is appreciable in every month but most comes from summer afternoon showers and thunderstorms. Ocala does not have a serious hurricane risk because of its inland location.

POPULATION

DEMOGRAPHICS	AREA	U.S. AVG	ETHNIC COMPOSITION	AREA	U.S. AVG	RESIDENT PROFILE	AREA	U.S. AVG
Population	272,553		White	84.5%	75.1%	Single	39.4%	43.6%
Population density per sq. mile	172.6	447.3	Black	13.8%	12.3%	Married	60.6%	56.4%
Population growth	39.9%	16.1%	Asian	.7%	3.6%	Divorced	9.7%	8.4%
Median age	44.6	35.5	American Indian	.4%	.9%	Separated	3.4%	3.0%
Average family size	2.4	2.7	Hispanic	4.8%	12.5%	Married with children	20.5%	28.7%
			Diversity measure	33.0%	35.2%	Single with children	10.1%	10.1%

ECONOMY & JOBS SCORE: 29/RANK: 234

INCOME	AREA	U.S. AVG	EMPLOYMENT	AREA	U.S. AVG	LARGEST EMPLOYING INDUSTRY
Per capita income	$18,517	$23,420	Unemployment rate	4.7%	6.1%	Transportation Equipment Manufacturing
Household income	$31,547	$46,060	Recent job growth	-1.1%	.9%	
Household income < $25K	37.3%	26.4%	Projected future job growth	15.0%	15.1%	
Household income > $75K	9.9%	24.5%	White collar	51.0%	54.5%	
Household income growth	40.6%	57.3%	Blue collar	49.0%	45.5%	

COST OF LIVING SCORE: 93/RANK: 22

INDEXES & TAXES	AREA	U.S. AVG	HOUSING	AREA	U.S. AVG	NECESSITIES	AREA	U.S. AVG
Cost of Living Index	86.1	100.0	Median home price	$101,610	$160,100	Food Index	101.7	100.0
Financial Progress Index	78.1	100.0	Home price appreciation	7.7%	7.1%	Housing Index	63.1	100.0
Income tax rate	0.000%	4.625%	Median rent	$542	$670	Utilities Index	93.9	100.0
Sales tax rate	7.000%	6.474%	Homes owned	67.7%	63.9%	Transportation Index	101.1	100.0
Property tax rate	$17.1	$15.6	Homes rented	17.5%	25.3%	Healthcare Index	98.4	100.0
			Housing affordability	57.0%	54.5%	Miscellaneous Cost Index	97.9	100.0

CLIMATE SCORE: 83/RANK: 56

TEMPERATURE	AREA	U.S. AVG	PRECIPITATION	AREA	U.S. AVG	COMFORTS & HAZARDS	AREA	U.S. AVG
January low	50.0°F	26.4°F	Annual inches precipitation	51.0	35.9	July relative humidity	74.0%	68.8%
July high	90.0°F	86.7°F	Annual inches snowfall	0.0	24.2	Annual days mostly sunny	242	212
Annual days > 90°F	104	38	Annual days precipitation	116	111	Annual days with thunderstorms	81	39
Annual days < 32°F	2	88	Annual days rain > 0.5 inches	31	23	Tornado risk score	25	19
Annual days < 0°F	0	6	Annual days snow > 1.5 inches	0	6	Hurricane risk score	69	15

TEMPERATURE

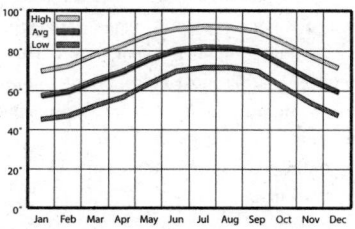

PRECIPITATION

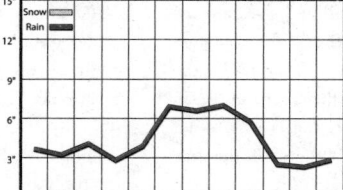

DAYS OF CLOUDS & PRECIPITATION

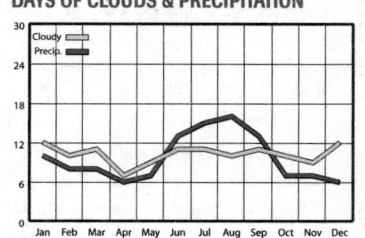

EDUCATION SCORE: 13/RANK: 285	ACHIEVEMENT	AREA	U.S. AVG	PUBLIC SCHOOLS	AREA	U.S. AVG	HIGHER EDUCATION	AREA	U.S. AVG
	High school degree	79.1%	80.2%	Expenditures per pupil	$5,050	$5,894	No. 2-year colleges	1	3
	2-year college degree	7.5%	6.2%	Student/teacher ratio	16.8	16.7	No. 4-year colleges/universities	0	4
	4-year college degree	8.6%	15.8%	Attending public school	92.0%	90.2%	No. highly ranked universities	0	1
	Graduate/professional degree	5.1%	9.6%	State SAT score	996*	1020			
				State ACT score	20.5	21.0			

HEALTH & HEALTHCARE SCORE: 35/RANK: 214	HAZARDS & ILLNESSES	AREA	U.S. AVG	HEALTHCARE	AREA	U.S. AVG	CRIME SCORE: 51/RANK: 160	CRIME	AREA	U.S. AVG
	Air-quality score	24	45	Physicians per capita	166.9	261.1		Violent crime rate	761.6	456.0
	Water-quality score	30	33	Hospital beds per capita	261.9	432.2		Change in violent crime rate	-29.7%	-17.2%
	Pollen/allergy score	76	61	No. teaching hospitals	1	4		Property crime rate	3,395.8	3,950.0
	Stress score	63	50	Cost per doctor visit	$64	$67		Change in property crime rate	-35.4%	-16.8%
	Cancer mortality per capita	176.0	169.0	Cost per dental visit	$76	$82				
	Depression days per month	2.8	2.8	Cost per daily hospital room	$635	$733				

TRANSPORTATION SCORE: 2/RANK: 323	COMMUTE	AREA	U.S. AVG	INTERCITY SERVICES	AREA	U.S. AVG	AUTOMOTIVE	AREA	U.S. AVG
	Average commute time	25.8 min.	22.6 min.	Miles to nearest major airport	65	46	Insurance, annual premium	$1,038	$1,011
	Commute by auto	93.4%	88.7%	Type of local airport	Small		Gas, cost per gallon	$1.53	$1.50
	Commute by mass transit	.2%	1.8%	No. daily airline departures	11	294	Daily vehicle miles per capita	29.7	23.0
	Work at home	2.7%	3.9%	Amtrak service	Yes				
	Mass transit miles per capita	0.0	8.0	No. interstate highways	1	1			

LEISURE SCORE: 32/RANK: 226	DINING & SHOPPING	AREA	U.S. AVG	ENTERTAINMENT	AREA	U.S. AVG	OUTDOOR ACTIVITIES	AREA	U.S. AVG
	Restaurant rating	1	1	Professional sports rating	2	4	Golf-course rating	2	4
	No. outlet malls	0	2	College sports rating	1	4	Ski-area rating	1	4
	No. Starbucks	0	11	Zoo/aquarium rating	1	3	National Park rating	9	3
	No. warehouse clubs	3	4	Amusement park rating	3	3	Sq. miles inland water	5.0	4.0
				Botanical garden/arboretum rating	1	3	Miles of coastline	0.0	11.4

ARTS & CULTURE SCORE: 31/RANK: 227	MEDIA & LIBRARIES	AREA	U.S. AVG	PERFORMING ARTS	AREA	U.S. AVG	MUSEUMS	AREA	U.S. AVG
	Arts radio rating	1	3	Classical music rating	4	4	Overall museum rating	5	6
	No. public libraries	9	28	Ballet/dance rating	1	3	Art museum rating	4	5
	Library volumes per capita	1.2	2.8	Professional theater rating	1	3	Science museum rating	4	4
				University arts programs rating	1	5	Children's museum rating	3	3

Odessa-Midland, TX

Score: 38.4   Rank: 283

Profile: Small towns
Location: West Texas high country near southeast corner of New Mexico
Elevation: 2,851 feet
Time zone: Central Standard Time

PRO	CON
Cost of living	Entertainment
Small-town atmosphere	Unattractive setting
Cost of housing	Economy

Midland was so named as the midpoint in an otherwise empty trip between Dallas and El Paso, while Odessa received its name from homesick Russian railroad laborers in the 1880s. The economic base is concentrated mainly in the oil and gas industry, and employment prospects are among the worst in Texas. The real story is cost of living and housing—the median home price of $66,550 is the fourth lowest in the nation. Diversions include the Permian Basin Petroleum Museum and the Confederate Air Force, the largest owner and operator of vintage aircraft from World War II. Otherwise, the area is hot, dry, dusty, and flat, with few amenities.

The Midland-Odessa region is on a relatively high southern extension of the Great Plains. The terrain is level with slight undulations. Vegetation consists mostly of native grasses and a few mesquite trees. The climate is semiarid. Summer daytime temperatures are hot but with a large diurnal range and most nights are comfortable. Humidity is low. Winters are characterized by frequent cold periods followed by rapid warming. Cloudiness is minimal. Summer showers are common and most of the annual precipitation comes from violent spring and early summer thunderstorms. Due to the flat nature of the countryside, local flooding and blowing dust may occur.

POPULATION

DEMOGRAPHICS	AREA	U.S. AVG	ETHNIC COMPOSITION	AREA	U.S. AVG	RESIDENT PROFILE	AREA	U.S. AVG
Population	239,981		White	78.0%	75.1%	Single	38.4%	43.6%
Population density per sq. mile	133.2	447.3	Black	7.1%	12.3%	Married	61.6%	56.4%
Population growth	6.4%	16.1%	Asian	1.4%	3.6%	Divorced	9.7%	8.4%
Median age	33.4	35.5	American Indian	.5%	.9%	Separated	3.7%	3.0%
Average family size	2.7	2.7	Hispanic	33.5%	12.5%	Married with children	34.2%	28.7%
			Diversity measure	54.5%	35.2%	Single with children	11.0%	10.1%

ECONOMY & JOBS   SCORE: 97/RANK: 9

INCOME	AREA	U.S. AVG	EMPLOYMENT	AREA	U.S. AVG	LARGEST EMPLOYING INDUSTRY
Per capita income	$20,640	$23,420	Unemployment rate	5.9%	6.1%	Mining
Household income	$39,029	$46,060	Recent job growth	2.6%	.9%	
Household income < $25K	31.2%	26.4%	Projected future job growth	7.3%	15.1%	
Household income > $75K	19.8%	24.5%	White collar	56.5%	54.5%	
Household income growth	45.3%	57.3%	Blue collar	43.5%	45.5%	

COST OF LIVING   SCORE: 90/RANK: 31

INDEXES & TAXES	AREA	U.S. AVG	HOUSING	AREA	U.S. AVG	NECESSITIES	AREA	U.S. AVG
Cost of Living Index	76.2	100.0	Median home price	$66,550	$160,100	Food Index	87.5	100.0
Financial Progress Index	109.2	100.0	Home price appreciation	4.0%	7.1%	Housing Index	41.3	100.0
Income tax rate	0.000%	4.625%	Median rent	$506	$670	Utilities Index	102.3	100.0
Sales tax rate	8.250%	6.474%	Homes owned	62.0%	63.9%	Transportation Index	96.6	100.0
Property tax rate	$21.3	$15.6	Homes rented	24.1%	25.3%	Healthcare Index	97.3	100.0
			Housing affordability	59.0%	54.5%	Miscellaneous Cost Index	99.0	100.0

CLIMATE   SCORE: 87/RANK: 43

TEMPERATURE	AREA	U.S. AVG	PRECIPITATION	AREA	U.S. AVG	COMFORTS & HAZARDS	AREA	U.S. AVG
January low	29.4°F	26.4°F	Annual inches precipitation	13.5	35.9	July relative humidity	53.0%	68.8%
July high	95.0°F	86.7°F	Annual inches snowfall	3.5	24.2	Annual days mostly sunny	263	212
Annual days > 90°F	92	38	Annual days precipitation	53	111	Annual days with thunderstorms	36	39
Annual days < 32°F	64	88	Annual days rain > 0.5 inches	7	23	Tornado risk score	26	19
Annual days < 0°F	0	6	Annual days snow > 1.5 inches	1	6	Hurricane risk score	1	15

TEMPERATURE

PRECIPITATION

DAYS OF CLOUDS & PRECIPITATION

EDUCATION   SCORE: 17/RANK: 273

ACHIEVEMENT	AREA	U.S. AVG	PUBLIC SCHOOLS	AREA	U.S. AVG	HIGHER EDUCATION	AREA	U.S. AVG
High school degree	73.6%	80.2%	Expenditures per pupil	$4,789	$5,894	No. 2-year colleges	2	3
2-year college degree	6.2%	6.2%	Student/teacher ratio	15.8	16.7	No. 4-year colleges/universities	1	4
4-year college degree	13.5%	15.8%	Attending public school	93.3%	90.2%	No. highly ranked universities	0	1
Graduate/professional degree	4.9%	9.6%	State SAT score	993*	1020			
			State ACT score	20.1	21.0			

HEALTH & HEALTHCARE   SCORE: 17/RANK: 272   **CRIME**   SCORE: 53/RANK: 153

HAZARDS & ILLNESSES	AREA	U.S. AVG	HEALTHCARE	AREA	U.S. AVG	CRIME	AREA	U.S. AVG
Air-quality score	24	45	Physicians per capita	179.2	261.1	Violent crime rate	460.6	456.0
Water-quality score	26	33	Hospital beds per capita	412.9	432.2	Change in violent crime rate	-34.2%	-17.2%
Pollen/allergy score	71	61	No. teaching hospitals	2	4	Property crime rate	3,937.5	3,950.0
Stress score	54	50	Cost per doctor visit	$65	$67	Change in property crime rate	-19.8%	-16.8%
Cancer mortality per capita	162.7	169.0	Cost per dental visit	$75	$82			
Depression days per month	1.6	2.8	Cost per daily hospital room	$374	$733			

TRANSPORTATION   SCORE: 56/RANK: 147

COMMUTE	AREA	U.S. AVG	INTERCITY SERVICES	AREA	U.S. AVG	AUTOMOTIVE	AREA	U.S. AVG
Average commute time	18.6 min.	22.6 min.	Miles to nearest major airport	7	46	Insurance, annual premium	$936	$1,011
Commute by auto	94.0%	88.7%	Type of local airport	Small		Gas, cost per gallon	$1.45	$1.50
Commute by mass transit	.1%	1.8%	No. daily airline departures	40	294	Daily vehicle miles per capita	21.2	23.0
Work at home	2.8%	3.9%	Amtrak service	No				
Mass transit miles per capita	0.0	8.0	No. interstate highways	1	1			

DINING & SHOPPING	AREA	U.S. AVG	ENTERTAINMENT	AREA	U.S. AVG	OUTDOOR ACTIVITIES	AREA	U.S. AVG
Restaurant rating	1	1	Professional sports rating	3	4	Golf-course rating	1	4
No. outlet malls	0	2	College sports rating	2	4	Ski-area rating	1	4
No. Starbucks	1	11	Zoo/aquarium rating	1	3	National Park rating	1	3
No. warehouse clubs	4	4	Amusement park rating	1	3	Sq. miles inland water	1.0	4.0
			Botanical garden/arboretum rating	1	3	Miles of coastline	0.0	11.4

MEDIA & LIBRARIES	AREA	U.S. AVG	PERFORMING ARTS	AREA	U.S. AVG	MUSEUMS	AREA	U.S. AVG
Arts radio rating	1	3	Classical music rating	3	4	Overall museum rating	5	6
No. public libraries	3	28	Ballet/dance rating	1	3	Art museum rating	5	5
Library volumes per capita	1.5	2.8	Professional theater rating	1	3	Science museum rating	6	4
			University arts programs rating	1	5	Children's museum rating	5	3

Oklahoma City, OK

Score: 58.5 Rank: 161

Profile: Capital city
Location: Center of Oklahoma
Elevation: 1,304 feet
Time zone: Central Standard Time

PRO	CON
Cost of living	Crime rate
Revitalizing economy	Arts and culture
Mild winters	Severe storms

Oklahoma City, the capital and largest city in the state, is a major center for the oil industry and related manufacturing. The city has a boomtown past reflected in its infrastructure. Resources spent to revitalize and modernize the downtown area have met with some success, although most of it is still fairly nondescript. There are a few interesting museums and some minor cultural amenities, but less than might be expected for a capital city of this size. More than 2,000 oil wells pump within the city limits—in fact, oil wells and derricks on the capitol lawn sum up the city's image. The main attractions are a Cost of Living Index of 84.3, one of the lowest among state capitals, a favorable economic situation, and a friendly, small-town atmosphere.

The area is located along the frequently dry North Canadian River. The surrounding country contains the gently rolling Arbuckle Mountains, 80 miles south. Although some Gulf influence exists, the climate is mainly continental. Summers are long and usually hot. Temperatures reach 100°F about 10 times a year, but can last 50 days or more. Breezes and relatively low humidity temper the heat somewhat. Winters are comparatively mild and short with one winter in three having temperatures below zero. Frequently located on the boundary of major air masses, spring and summer storms can be severe, spawning tornadoes and large hail, and winter "mixes" of sleet and freezing rain. First freeze is November 1, last is early April.

DEMOGRAPHICS	AREA	U.S. AVG	ETHNIC COMPOSITION	AREA	U.S. AVG	RESIDENT PROFILE	AREA	U.S. AVG
Population	1,109,083		White	76.8%	75.1%	Single	43.8%	43.6%
Population density per sq. mile	261.1	447.3	Black	13.8%	12.3%	Married	56.2%	56.4%
Population growth	15.7%	16.1%	Asian	2.0%	3.6%	Divorced	11.2%	8.4%
Median age	34.4	35.5	American Indian	6.0%	.9%	Separated	2.9%	3.0%
Average family size	2.6	2.7	Hispanic	4.5%	12.5%	Married with children	27.6%	28.7%
			Diversity measure	43.9%	35.2%	Single with children	11.1%	10.1%

INCOME	AREA	U.S. AVG	EMPLOYMENT	AREA	U.S. AVG	LARGEST EMPLOYING INDUSTRY
Per capita income	$21,406	$23,420	Unemployment rate	4.5%	6.1%	Fabricated Metal Product Manufacturing
Household income	$40,347	$46,060	Recent job growth	1.0%	.9%	
Household income < $25K	28.9%	26.4%	Projected future job growth	12.5%	15.1%	
Household income > $75K	19.1%	24.5%	White collar	58.1%	54.5%	
Household income growth	49.8%	57.3%	Blue collar	41.9%	45.5%	

INDEXES & TAXES	AREA	U.S. AVG	HOUSING	AREA	U.S. AVG	NECESSITIES	AREA	U.S. AVG
Cost of Living Index	84.3	100.0	Median home price	$96,400	$160,100	Food Index	92.1	100.0
Financial Progress Index	102.0	100.0	Home price appreciation	5.6%	7.1%	Housing Index	59.9	100.0
Income tax rate	7.000%	4.625%	Median rent	$561	$670	Utilities Index	109.1	100.0
Sales tax rate	8.375%	6.474%	Homes owned	61.5%	63.9%	Transportation Index	95.6	100.0
Property tax rate	$11.0	$15.6	Homes rented	23.9%	25.3%	Healthcare Index	92.4	100.0
			Housing affordability	57.0%	54.5%	Miscellaneous Cost Index	101.3	100.0

CLIMATE SCORE: 70/RANK: 98

TEMPERATURE	AREA	U.S. AVG	PRECIPITATION	AREA	U.S. AVG	COMFORTS & HAZARDS	AREA	U.S. AVG
January low	26.0°F	26.4°F	Annual inches precipitation	33.0	35.9	July relative humidity	65.0%	68.8%
July high	92.6°F	86.7°F	Annual inches snowfall	9.0	24.2	Annual days mostly sunny	237	212
Annual days > 90°F	64	38	Annual days precipitation	81	111	Annual days with thunderstorms	51	39
Annual days < 32°F	80	88	Annual days rain > 0.5 inches	23	23	Tornado risk score	62	19
Annual days < 0°F	0	6	Annual days snow > 1.5 inches	3	6	Hurricane risk score	2	15

TEMPERATURE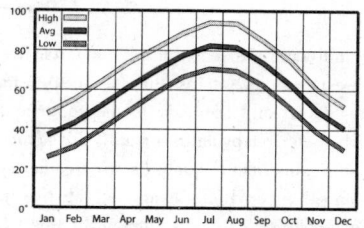

PRECIPITATION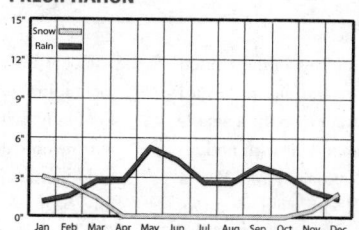

DAYS OF CLOUDS & PRECIPITATION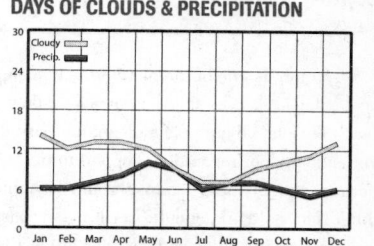

EDUCATION SCORE: 73/RANK: 90

ACHIEVEMENT	AREA	U.S. AVG	PUBLIC SCHOOLS	AREA	U.S. AVG	HIGHER EDUCATION	AREA	U.S. AVG
High school degree	81.3%	80.2%	Expenditures per pupil	$4,582	$5,894	No. 2-year colleges	4	3
2-year college degree	5.2%	6.2%	Student/teacher ratio	16.1	16.7	No. 4-year colleges/universities	10	4
4-year college degree	15.9%	15.8%	Attending public school	92.8%	90.2%	No. highly ranked universities	2	1
Graduate/professional degree	8.1%	9.6%	State SAT score	1131	1020			
			State ACT score	20.5*	21.0			

HEALTH & HEALTHCARE SCORE: 16/RANK: 275   **CRIME** SCORE: 23/RANK: 253

HAZARDS & ILLNESSES	AREA	U.S. AVG	HEALTHCARE	AREA	U.S. AVG	CRIME	AREA	U.S. AVG
Air-quality score	71	45	Physicians per capita	263.7	261.1	Violent crime rate	548.1	456.0
Water-quality score	41	33	Hospital beds per capita	474.6	432.2	Change in violent crime rate	-30.8%	-17.2%
Pollen/allergy score	92	61	No. teaching hospitals	8	4	Property crime rate	5,534.5	3,950.0
Stress score	57	50	Cost per doctor visit	$64	$67	Change in property crime rate	-22.0%	-16.8%
Cancer mortality per capita	165.4	169.0	Cost per dental visit	$86	$82			
Depression days per month	2.4	2.8	Cost per daily hospital room	$456	$733			

TRANSPORTATION SCORE: 41/RANK: 195

COMMUTE	AREA	U.S. AVG	INTERCITY SERVICES	AREA	U.S. AVG	AUTOMOTIVE	AREA	U.S. AVG
Average commute time	22.0 min.	22.6 min.	Miles to nearest major airport	7	46	Insurance, annual premium	$876	$1,011
Commute by auto	92.7%	88.7%	Type of local airport	Medium		Gas, cost per gallon	$1.39	$1.50
Commute by mass transit	.7%	1.8%	No. daily airline departures	102	294	Daily vehicle miles per capita	26.1	23.0
Work at home	3.3%	3.9%	Amtrak service	Yes				
Mass transit miles per capita	3.6	8.0	No. interstate highways	3	1			

LEISURE SCORE: 36/RANK: 210

DINING & SHOPPING	AREA	U.S. AVG	ENTERTAINMENT	AREA	U.S. AVG	OUTDOOR ACTIVITIES	AREA	U.S. AVG
Restaurant rating	1	1	Professional sports rating	3	4	Golf-course rating	5	4
No. outlet malls	0	2	College sports rating	8	4	Ski-area rating	1	4
No. Starbucks	6	11	Zoo/aquarium rating	6	3	National Park rating	1	3
No. warehouse clubs	4	4	Amusement park rating	4	3	Sq. miles inland water	4.0	4.0
			Botanical garden/arboretum rating	9	3	Miles of coastline	0.0	11.4

ARTS & CULTURE SCORE: 51/RANK: 160

MEDIA & LIBRARIES	AREA	U.S. AVG	PERFORMING ARTS	AREA	U.S. AVG	MUSEUMS	AREA	U.S. AVG
Arts radio rating	1	3	Classical music rating	4	4	Overall museum rating	8	6
No. public libraries	35	28	Ballet/dance rating	6	3	Art museum rating	7	5
Library volumes per capita	1.4	2.8	Professional theater rating	1	3	Science museum rating	5	4
			University arts programs rating	8	5	Children's museum rating	2	3

Olympia, WA

Score: 85.9 **Rank:** 16

Profile: Capital city
Location: West-central Washington at the south end of Puget Sound
Elevation: 100 feet
Time zone: Pacific Standard Time

PRO	CON
Attractive setting	Cloudy, wet winters
Nearby national parks	Cost of living
Educated population	Entertainment

Olympia is one of the more attractive capital cities in the United States. While there is heavy industry to the north toward Tacoma, Olympia is a clean, mid-size capital city with a small-town feel. Outdoor recreational opportunities are abundant with national forests, the Olympic Peninsula and Olympic National Park, Mount Rainier National Park, and the Washington coast all within a day's drive. Excellent city amenities and services are available in Seattle, 60 miles to the north, although traffic, particularly in the Tacoma area, can make the drive challenging. The population is highly educated and most of the area has a well-kept appearance. The area's lush greenery owes its existence to the marine climate, which brings a small downside—the area is the sixth cloudiest city in the nation and one of the rainiest, although rain is seasonal and seldom heavy. Nearby hydroelectric power results in the lowest utility costs in the country.

Local terrain is hilly and wooded with tall coniferous trees and low mountains to the west, high mountains (the Cascades) to the east, and gradually flattening forest and farmland to the south and east. The marine climate is characterized by mild, generally dry summers and wet, mild winters. Autumn rains from frequent Pacific weather systems usually begin about mid-October. Rains continue with few interruptions through spring. Pacific storms can be strong but the Coast Range moderates winds. Summer highs are a comfortable 70°F to 80°F with clear skies 2 out of every 3 days. Winter daytime temperatures are in the 40s and low 50s with nighttime temperatures in the 30s. Occasional blasts of Canadian air drop temperatures into the 10s and 20s. Snow accumulations sufficient to disrupt traffic occur infrequently. There is some fog mainly in spring and fall.

POPULATION

DEMOGRAPHICS	AREA	U.S. AVG	ETHNIC COMPOSITION	AREA	U.S. AVG	RESIDENT PROFILE	AREA	U.S. AVG
Population	217,641		White	91.3%	75.1%	Single	46.8%	43.6%
Population density per sq. mile	299.3	447.3	Black	1.8%	12.3%	Married	53.2%	56.4%
Population growth	35.0%	16.1%	Asian	4.4%	3.6%	Divorced	10.7%	8.4%
Median age	36.9	35.5	American Indian	1.6%	.9%	Separated	2.6%	3.0%
Average family size	2.7	2.7	Hispanic	5.0%	12.5%	Married with children	30.9%	28.7%
			Diversity measure	29.3%	35.2%	Single with children	11.0%	10.1%

ECONOMY & JOBS SCORE: 62/RANK: 124

INCOME	AREA	U.S. AVG	EMPLOYMENT	AREA	U.S. AVG	LARGEST EMPLOYING INDUSTRY
Per capita income	$22,804	$23,420	Unemployment rate	5.6%	6.1%	Healthcare and Social Assistance
Household income	$46,826	$46,060	Recent job growth	2.5%	.9%	
Household income < $25K	22.0%	26.4%	Projected future job growth	21.5%	15.1%	
Household income > $75K	22.0%	24.5%	White collar	60.2%	54.5%	
Household income growth	51.0%	57.3%	Blue collar	39.8%	45.5%	

COST OF LIVING SCORE: 45/RANK: 182

INDEXES & TAXES	AREA	U.S. AVG	HOUSING	AREA	U.S. AVG	NECESSITIES	AREA	U.S. AVG
Cost of Living Index	104.5	100.0	Median home price	$168,330	$160,100	Food Index	110.1	100.0
Financial Progress Index	95.5	100.0	Home price appreciation	5.1%	7.1%	Housing Index	104.6	100.0
Income tax rate	0.000%	4.625%	Median rent	$823	$670	Utilities Index	78.9	100.0
Sales tax rate	8.400%	6.474%	Homes owned	66.1%	63.9%	Transportation Index	106.0	100.0
Property tax rate	$14.7	$15.6	Homes rented	28.5%	25.3%	Healthcare Index	128.2	100.0
			Housing affordability	54.0%	54.5%	Miscellaneous Cost Index	102.2	100.0

CLIMATE SCORE: 45/RANK: 180

TEMPERATURE	AREA	U.S. AVG	PRECIPITATION	AREA	U.S. AVG	COMFORTS & HAZARDS	AREA	U.S. AVG
January low	30.4°F	26.4°F	Annual inches precipitation	51.0	35.9	July relative humidity	71.0%	68.8%
July high	78.4°F	86.7°F	Annual inches snowfall	19.0	24.2	Annual days mostly sunny	137	212
Annual days > 90°F	6	38	Annual days precipitation	163	111	Annual days with thunderstorms	5	39
Annual days < 32°F	89	88	Annual days rain > 0.5 inches	34	23	Tornado risk score	0	19
Annual days < 0°F	0	6	Annual days snow > 1.5 inches	5	6	Hurricane risk score	0	15

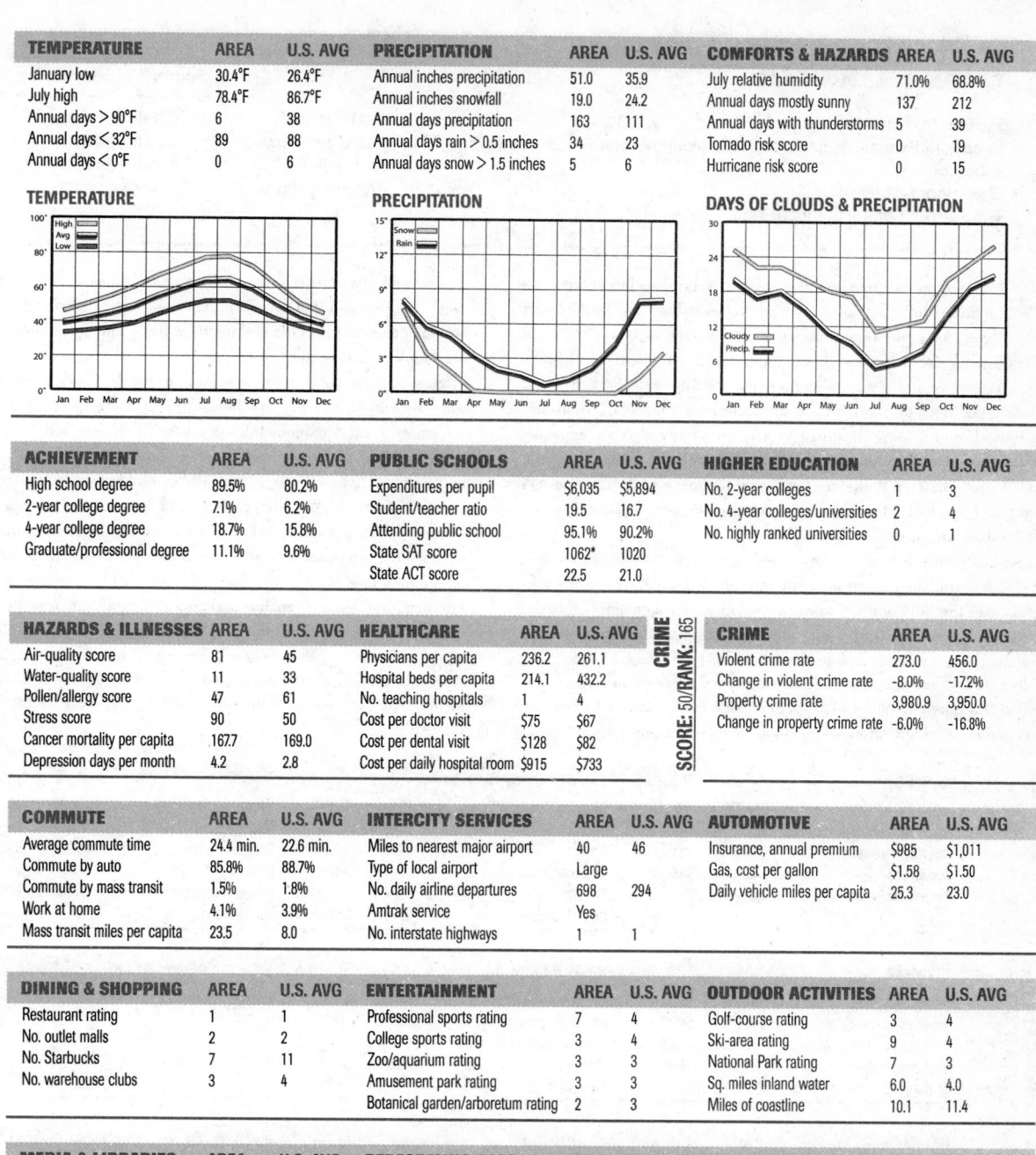

TEMPERATURE · PRECIPITATION · DAYS OF CLOUDS & PRECIPITATION

EDUCATION SCORE: 81/RANK: 62

ACHIEVEMENT	AREA	U.S. AVG	PUBLIC SCHOOLS	AREA	U.S. AVG	HIGHER EDUCATION	AREA	U.S. AVG
High school degree	89.5%	80.2%	Expenditures per pupil	$6,035	$5,894	No. 2-year colleges	1	3
2-year college degree	7.1%	6.2%	Student/teacher ratio	19.5	16.7	No. 4-year colleges/universities	2	4
4-year college degree	18.7%	15.8%	Attending public school	95.1%	90.2%	No. highly ranked universities	0	1
Graduate/professional degree	11.1%	9.6%	State SAT score	1062*	1020			
			State ACT score	22.5	21.0			

HEALTH & HEALTHCARE SCORE: 56/RANK: 143 — **CRIME** SCORE: 50/RANK: 165

HAZARDS & ILLNESSES	AREA	U.S. AVG	HEALTHCARE	AREA	U.S. AVG	CRIME	AREA	U.S. AVG
Air-quality score	81	45	Physicians per capita	236.2	261.1	Violent crime rate	273.0	456.0
Water-quality score	11	33	Hospital beds per capita	214.1	432.2	Change in violent crime rate	-8.0%	-17.2%
Pollen/allergy score	47	61	No. teaching hospitals	1	4	Property crime rate	3,980.9	3,950.0
Stress score	90	50	Cost per doctor visit	$75	$67	Change in property crime rate	-6.0%	-16.8%
Cancer mortality per capita	167.7	169.0	Cost per dental visit	$128	$82			
Depression days per month	4.2	2.8	Cost per daily hospital room	$915	$733			

TRANSPORTATION SCORE: 60/RANK: 131

COMMUTE	AREA	U.S. AVG	INTERCITY SERVICES	AREA	U.S. AVG	AUTOMOTIVE	AREA	U.S. AVG
Average commute time	24.4 min.	22.6 min.	Miles to nearest major airport	40	46	Insurance, annual premium	$985	$1,011
Commute by auto	85.8%	88.7%	Type of local airport	Large		Gas, cost per gallon	$1.58	$1.50
Commute by mass transit	1.5%	1.8%	No. daily airline departures	698	294	Daily vehicle miles per capita	25.3	23.0
Work at home	4.1%	3.9%	Amtrak service	Yes				
Mass transit miles per capita	23.5	8.0	No. interstate highways	1	1			

LEISURE SCORE: 84/RANK: 56

DINING & SHOPPING	AREA	U.S. AVG	ENTERTAINMENT	AREA	U.S. AVG	OUTDOOR ACTIVITIES	AREA	U.S. AVG
Restaurant rating	1	1	Professional sports rating	7	4	Golf-course rating	3	4
No. outlet malls	2	2	College sports rating	3	4	Ski-area rating	9	4
No. Starbucks	7	11	Zoo/aquarium rating	3	3	National Park rating	7	3
No. warehouse clubs	3	4	Amusement park rating	3	3	Sq. miles inland water	6.0	4.0
			Botanical garden/arboretum rating	2	3	Miles of coastline	10.1	11.4

ARTS & CULTURE SCORE: 27/RANK: 240

MEDIA & LIBRARIES	AREA	U.S. AVG	PERFORMING ARTS	AREA	U.S. AVG	MUSEUMS	AREA	U.S. AVG
Arts radio rating	3	3	Classical music rating	3	4	Overall museum rating	7	6
No. public libraries	27	28	Ballet/dance rating	4	3	Art museum rating	3	5
Library volumes per capita	2.7	2.8	Professional theater rating	3	3	Science museum rating	3	4
			University arts programs rating	5	5	Children's museum rating	5	3

Omaha, NE-IA

Score: 53.1   **Rank:** 201

Profile: Mid-size-city complex
Location: Extreme eastern Nebraska along Missouri River at Iowa border
Elevation: 982 feet
Time zone: Central Standard Time

PRO	CON
Stable economy	Harsh winters
Cost of living	Minor urban sprawl
Arts and culture	Property crime

This metropolitan area includes Omaha, Nebraska's largest city and Council Bluffs, an Iowa town on the east bank of the Missouri River. As a gateway to the Great Plains, Omaha is a world-class livestock, meatpacking, and grain-shipping city. The city has always been a gateway and transportation center, starting with the Lewis and Clark expedition and continuing as the eastern terminus of the transcontinental Union Pacific Railroad. Today the city's diverse economy includes food production and insurance. Mutual of Omaha, ConAgra, and Warren Buffett's Berkshire Hathaway Company have headquarters here. Led by Mr. Buffett, Omaha reportedly has more millionaires per capita than any other U.S. city.

Typically Midwestern, the city is well kept, generally clean, and not flashy or particularly creative in any way. Shaded streets and older suburbs cover the hills north of town, while newer development lies in the flatter areas to the west along I-80 and I-680. The Strategic Air Command headquarters and nearby Offutt Air Force Base provide a sizable military presence. On hand is a complex of entertainment venues called Ak-Sar-Ben (Nebraska spelled backwards) and a number of arts and cultural amenities, although some consider these to be local in quality and character. Creighton University brings a college-town element. The downsides of volatile climate and high property crime are just strong enough to effect the ranking negatively. The area is probably better than the ranking indicates.

Omaha is situated on the west bank of the Missouri River. The narrow river valley gives way to hills and ridges rising about 350 feet above the valley. Lush deciduous trees cover the hills, especially to the north, while the land to the west and south is more level and open as prairie and farmland. The climate is typically continental with relatively warm summers and cold, dry winters. It is situated midway between two distinctive climatic zones, the humid east and the dry west. Fluctuations between the two produce weather conditions characteristic of either zone or combinations of both. Omaha is also affected by most storm systems crossing the country causing periodic and rapid changes in weather, especially during winter months. Most precipitation falls during strong summer showers or thunderstorms mainly in the evening or nighttime. Although winters are relatively cold, precipitation is light. Wind can be significant, particularly to the west. First freeze is mid-October, last is late April.

POPULATION

DEMOGRAPHICS	AREA	U.S. AVG	ETHNIC COMPOSITION	AREA	U.S. AVG	RESIDENT PROFILE	AREA	U.S. AVG
Population	734,270		White	92.6%	75.1%	Single	39.7%	43.6%
Population density per sq. mile	296.6	447.3	Black	5.2%	12.3%	Married	60.3%	56.4%
Population growth	14.8%	16.1%	Asian	1.0%	3.6%	Divorced	7.6%	8.4%
Median age	34.0	35.5	American Indian	.5%	.9%	Separated	1.7%	3.0%
Average family size	2.6	2.7	Hispanic	3.5%	12.5%	Married with children	31.8%	28.7%
			Diversity measure	29.8%	35.2%	Single with children	8.7%	10.1%

ECONOMY & JOBS   SCORE: 81/RANK: 62

INCOME	AREA	U.S. AVG	EMPLOYMENT	AREA	U.S. AVG	LARGEST EMPLOYING INDUSTRY
Per capita income	$26,188	$23,420	Unemployment rate	4.0%	6.1%	Food Manufacturing
Household income	$52,174	$46,060	Recent job growth	1.8%	.9%	
Household income < $25K	19.8%	26.4%	Projected future job growth	18.2%	15.1%	
Household income > $75K	29.8%	24.5%	White collar	60.3%	54.5%	
Household income growth	72.1%	57.3%	Blue collar	39.7%	45.5%	

COST OF LIVING   SCORE: 28/RANK: 238

INDEXES & TAXES	AREA	U.S. AVG	HOUSING	AREA	U.S. AVG	NECESSITIES	AREA	U.S. AVG
Cost of Living Index	92.2	100.0	Median home price	$123,900	$160,100	Food Index	93.9	100.0
Financial Progress Index	120.6	100.0	Home price appreciation	4.5%	7.1%	Housing Index	77.0	100.0
Income tax rate	6.680%	4.625%	Median rent	$626	$670	Utilities Index	124.7	100.0
Sales tax rate	7.000%	6.474%	Homes owned	67.5%	63.9%	Transportation Index	101.4	100.0
Property tax rate	$22.6	$15.6	Homes rented	25.6%	25.3%	Healthcare Index	99.2	100.0
			Housing affordability	61.0%	54.5%	Miscellaneous Cost Index	97.5	100.0

CLIMATE — SCORE: 18/RANK: 269

TEMPERATURE	AREA	U.S. AVG	PRECIPITATION	AREA	U.S. AVG	COMFORTS & HAZARDS	AREA	U.S. AVG
January low	12.4°F	26.4°F	Annual inches precipitation	30.0	35.9	July relative humidity	68.0%	68.8%
July high	88.6°F	86.7°F	Annual inches snowfall	32.0	24.2	Annual days mostly sunny	220	212
Annual days > 90°F	38	38	Annual days precipitation	99	111	Annual days with thunderstorms	48	39
Annual days < 32°F	138	88	Annual days rain > 0.5 inches	18	23	Tornado risk score	23	19
Annual days < 0°F	13	6	Annual days snow > 1.5 inches	6	6	Hurricane risk score	1	15

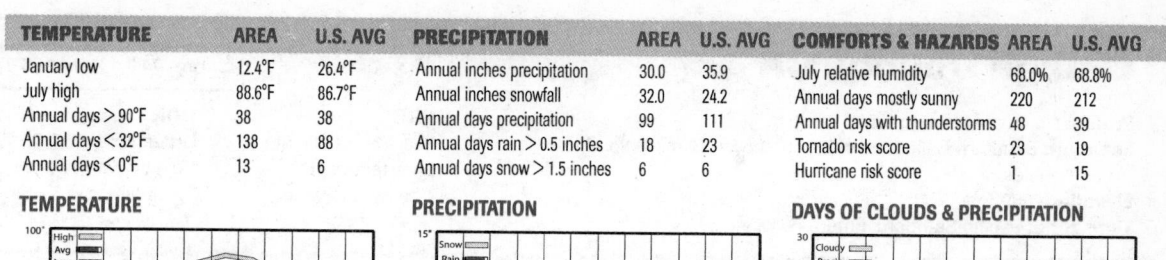

TEMPERATURE — PRECIPITATION — DAYS OF CLOUDS & PRECIPITATION

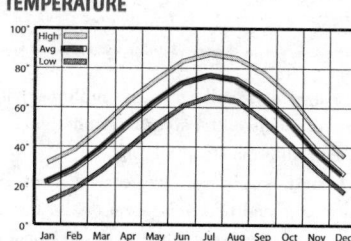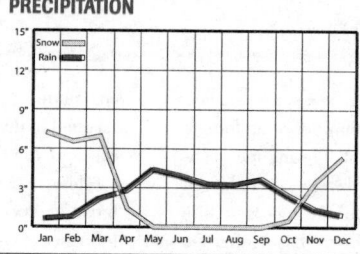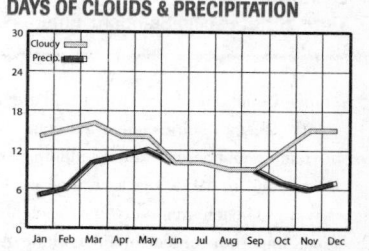

EDUCATION — SCORE: 69/RANK: 103

ACHIEVEMENT	AREA	U.S. AVG	PUBLIC SCHOOLS	AREA	U.S. AVG	HIGHER EDUCATION	AREA	U.S. AVG
High school degree	86.0%	80.2%	Expenditures per pupil	$5,382	$5,894	No. 2-year colleges	3	3
2-year college degree	5.8%	6.2%	Student/teacher ratio	15.7	16.7	No. 4-year colleges/universities	8	4
4-year college degree	19.7%	15.8%	Attending public school	85.0%	90.2%	No. highly ranked universities	1	1
Graduate/professional degree	9.0%	9.6%	State SAT score	1151	1020			
			State ACT score	21.7*	21.0			

HEALTH & HEALTHCARE — SCORE: 65/RANK: 113 — **CRIME** — SCORE: 16/RANK: 277

HAZARDS & ILLNESSES	AREA	U.S. AVG	HEALTHCARE	AREA	U.S. AVG	CRIME	AREA	U.S. AVG
Air-quality score	91	45	Physicians per capita	339.1	261.1	Violent crime rate	476.0	456.0
Water-quality score	13	33	Hospital beds per capita	523.4	432.2	Change in violent crime rate	-23.7%	-17.2%
Pollen/allergy score	50	61	No. teaching hospitals	7	4	Property crime rate	5,224.4	3,950.0
Stress score	29	50	Cost per doctor visit	$61	$67	Change in property crime rate	4.9%	-16.8%
Cancer mortality per capita	176.0	169.0	Cost per dental visit	$83	$82			
Depression days per month	2.7	2.8	Cost per daily hospital room	$505	$733			

TRANSPORTATION — SCORE: 74/RANK: 87

COMMUTE	AREA	U.S. AVG	INTERCITY SERVICES	AREA	U.S. AVG	AUTOMOTIVE	AREA	U.S. AVG
Average commute time	19.4 min.	22.6 min.	Miles to nearest major airport	6	46	Insurance, annual premium	$1,007	$1,011
Commute by auto	87.9%	88.7%	Type of local airport	Medium		Gas, cost per gallon	$1.50	$1.50
Commute by mass transit	1.3%	1.8%	No. daily airline departures	136	294	Daily vehicle miles per capita	19.9	23.0
Work at home	6.4%	3.9%	Amtrak service	Yes				
Mass transit miles per capita	6.1	8.0	No. interstate highways	1	1			

LEISURE — SCORE: 47/RANK: 175

DINING & SHOPPING	AREA	U.S. AVG	ENTERTAINMENT	AREA	U.S. AVG	OUTDOOR ACTIVITIES	AREA	U.S. AVG
Restaurant rating	1	1	Professional sports rating	3	4	Golf-course rating	5	4
No. outlet malls	1	2	College sports rating	5	4	Ski-area rating	4	4
No. Starbucks	6	11	Zoo/aquarium rating	8	3	National Park rating	2	3
No. warehouse clubs	4	4	Amusement park rating	1	3	Sq. miles inland water	4.0	4.0
			Botanical garden/arboretum rating	3	3	Miles of coastline	0.0	11.4

ARTS & CULTURE — SCORE: 84/RANK: 52

MEDIA & LIBRARIES	AREA	U.S. AVG	PERFORMING ARTS	AREA	U.S. AVG	MUSEUMS	AREA	U.S. AVG
Arts radio rating	5	3	Classical music rating	6	4	Overall museum rating	7	6
No. public libraries	33	28	Ballet/dance rating	1	3	Art museum rating	7	5
Library volumes per capita	2.8	2.8	Professional theater rating	8	3	Science museum rating	5	4
			University arts programs rating	8	5	Children's museum rating	7	3

Orange County, CA

Profile: Commuter community
Location: Southern California, along the coast 30 miles south of Los Angeles
Elevation: 850 feet
Time zone: Pacific Standard Time

PRO	CON
Year-round climate	Urban sprawl
Entertainment	Cost of living
Nearby beaches	Air quality

Orange County, once an agricultural area, is now a sprawling network of small cities and bedroom communities that form a dynamic commercial and residential area. Following the opening of Disneyland in 1955, the area was quickly developed. Today oil wells adjacent to beach areas serve as a metaphor for the general nature of the area. Important cities inland include Anaheim, Irvine, Garden Grove, and Costa Mesa and the wealthy coastal enclaves of Huntington Beach and Newport Beach. The area is socially and economically diverse, although to a lesser extent than Los Angeles to the north. Amenities include professional sports teams and a major airport. Although the area has increasingly developed its own economic base,

commuting to Los Angeles is still common. Building patterns have resulted in unattractive, cookie-cutter sprawl. Cost of living and housing costs are high even by California standards.

Most of Orange County is a broad, level coastal plain. Beaches are broad and oceans are calm and relatively warm due to the latitude and influence of Catalina Island to the west. The Santa Ana Mountains provide a dry mountainous backdrop to the east. The Mediterranean coastal climate is one of the best in North America. Sea breezes keep summers pleasant, with temperatures rarely above 90°F and cool evenings. Winters are mild and mainly dry with occasional mild Pacific storms. Inland weather is more variable. Smog is persistent in summer and inland.

POPULATION

DEMOGRAPHICS	AREA	U.S. AVG	ETHNIC COMPOSITION	AREA	U.S. AVG	RESIDENT PROFILE	AREA	U.S. AVG
Population	2,938,507		White	77.4%	75.1%	Single	48.3%	43.6%
Population density per sq. mile	3,721.1	447.3	Black	2.1%	12.3%	Married	51.7%	56.4%
Population growth	21.9%	16.1%	Asian	13.1%	3.6%	Divorced	10.0%	8.4%
Median age	33.6	35.5	American Indian	.5%	.9%	Separated	3.1%	3.0%
Average family size	2.9	2.7	Hispanic	26.2%	12.5%	Married with children	27.0%	28.7%
			Diversity measure	61.1%	35.2%	Single with children	9.1%	10.1%

ECONOMY & JOBS
SCORE: 39/RANK: 199

INCOME	AREA	U.S. AVG	EMPLOYMENT	AREA	U.S. AVG	LARGEST EMPLOYING INDUSTRY
Per capita income	$29,355	$23,420	Unemployment rate	3.8%	6.1%	Computer and Electronic Product Manufacturing
Household income	$68,923	$46,060	Recent job growth	1.2%	.9%	
Household income < $25K	13.1%	26.4%	Projected future job growth	19.5%	15.1%	
Household income > $75K	45.2%	24.5%	White collar	63.7%	54.5%	
Household income growth	50.0%	57.3%	Blue collar	36.3%	45.5%	

COST OF LIVING
SCORE: 1/RANK: 325

INDEXES & TAXES	AREA	U.S. AVG	HOUSING	AREA	U.S. AVG	NECESSITIES	AREA	U.S. AVG
Cost of Living Index	168.2	100.0	Median home price	$434,600	$160,100	Food Index	111.0	100.0
Financial Progress Index	87.3	100.0	Home price appreciation	13.3%	7.1%	Housing Index	269.9	100.0
Income tax rate	6.000%	4.625%	Median rent	$1,220	$670	Utilities Index	115.3	100.0
Sales tax rate	7.750%	6.474%	Homes owned	58.0%	63.9%	Transportation Index	110.7	100.0
Property tax rate	$10.8	$15.6	Homes rented	35.7%	25.3%	Healthcare Index	120.2	100.0
			Housing affordability	46.0%	54.5%	Miscellaneous Cost Index	107.2	100.0

CLIMATE
SCORE: 97/RANK: 9

TEMPERATURE	AREA	U.S. AVG	PRECIPITATION	AREA	U.S. AVG	COMFORTS & HAZARDS	AREA	U.S. AVG
January low	45.4°F	26.4°F	Annual inches precipitation	12.0	35.9	July relative humidity	71.0%	68.8%
July high	75.8°F	86.7°F	Annual inches snowfall	0.0	24.2	Annual days mostly sunny	258	212
Annual days > 90°F	5	38	Annual days precipitation	40	111	Annual days with thunderstorms	3	39
Annual days < 32°F	0	88	Annual days rain > 0.5 inches	8	23	Tornado risk score	16	19
Annual days < 0°F	0	6	Annual days snow > 1.5 inches	0	6	Hurricane risk score	2	15

TEMPERATURE

PRECIPITATION

DAYS OF CLOUDS & PRECIPITATION

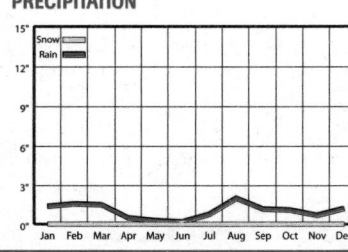

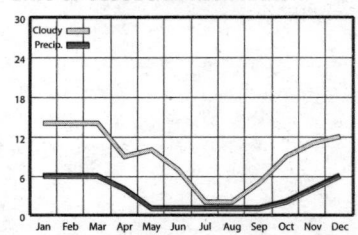

EDUCATION SCORE: 58/RANK: 139

ACHIEVEMENT	AREA	U.S. AVG	PUBLIC SCHOOLS	AREA	U.S. AVG	HIGHER EDUCATION	AREA	U.S. AVG
High school degree	79.5%	80.2%	Expenditures per pupil	$5,119	$5,894	No. 2-year colleges	8	3
2-year college degree	8.2%	6.2%	Student/teacher ratio	22.9	16.7	No. 4-year colleges/universities	8	4
4-year college degree	20.4%	15.8%	Attending public school	88.9%	90.2%	No. highly ranked universities	1	1
Graduate/professional degree	10.4%	9.6%	State SAT score	1018*	1020			
			State ACT score	21.5	21.0			

HEALTH & HEALTHCARE SCORE: 39/RANK: 200

CRIME SCORE: 96/RANK: 11

HAZARDS & ILLNESSES	AREA	U.S. AVG	HEALTHCARE	AREA	U.S. AVG	CRIME	AREA	U.S. AVG
Air-quality score	49	45	Physicians per capita	265.0	261.1	Violent crime rate	295.5	456.0
Water-quality score	16	33	Hospital beds per capita	277.4	432.2	Change in violent crime rate	-42.4%	-17.2%
Pollen/allergy score	45	61	No. teaching hospitals	7	4	Property crime rate	2,461.0	3,950.0
Stress score	31	50	Cost per doctor visit	$81	$67	Change in property crime rate	-40.8%	-16.8%
Cancer mortality per capita	166.3	169.0	Cost per dental visit	$76	$82			
Depression days per month	3.6	2.8	Cost per daily hospital room	$1,295	$733			

TRANSPORTATION SCORE: 10/RANK: 297

COMMUTE	AREA	U.S. AVG	INTERCITY SERVICES	AREA	U.S. AVG	AUTOMOTIVE	AREA	U.S. AVG
Average commute time	27.2 min.	22.6 min.	Miles to nearest major airport	4	46	Insurance, annual premium	$1,093	$1,011
Commute by auto	91.0%	88.7%	Type of local airport	Medium		Gas, cost per gallon	$1.73	$1.50
Commute by mass transit	1.9%	1.8%	No. daily airline departures	136	294	Daily vehicle miles per capita	23.0	23.0
Work at home	3.0%	3.9%	Amtrak service	Yes				
Mass transit miles per capita	8.2	8.0	No. interstate highways	1	1			

LEISURE SCORE: 96/RANK: 10

DINING & SHOPPING	AREA	U.S. AVG	ENTERTAINMENT	AREA	U.S. AVG	OUTDOOR ACTIVITIES	AREA	U.S. AVG
Restaurant rating	3	1	Professional sports rating	10	4	Golf-course rating	8	4
No. outlet malls	5	2	College sports rating	4	4	Ski-area rating	10	4
No. Starbucks	105	11	Zoo/aquarium rating	5	3	National Park rating	10	3
No. warehouse clubs	8	4	Amusement park rating	10	3	Sq. miles inland water	4.0	4.0
			Botanical garden/arboretum rating	8	3	Miles of coastline	39.8	11.4

ARTS & CULTURE SCORE: 53/RANK: 154

MEDIA & LIBRARIES	AREA	U.S. AVG	PERFORMING ARTS	AREA	U.S. AVG	MUSEUMS	AREA	U.S. AVG
Arts radio rating	5	3	Classical music rating	5	4	Overall museum rating	8	6
No. public libraries	53	28	Ballet/dance rating	7	3	Art museum rating	9	5
Library volumes per capita	1.9	2.8	Professional theater rating	5	3	Science museum rating	7	4
			University arts programs rating	8	5	Children's museum rating	5	3

Orlando, FL

Score: 61.9   Rank: 134

Profile: Diversified resort city
Location: East-central Florida, about 25 miles from the Atlantic Coast
Elevation: 106 feet
Time zone: Eastern Standard Time

PRO
Entertainment
Outdoor recreation
Cost of living

CON
Tourist impact
Hot, humid summers
Urban sprawl

Before Walt Disney World came to the area in the 1970s, Orlando was a sleepy town with an economy based on citrus and cattle. Not any more. The city has become a major tourist destination and entertainment center. A variety of activities and attractions have been built around the Disney complex. Golf and other outdoor recreational facilities are top quality. Most big-city amenities are present. Although entertainment is the largest industry, others of note include manufacturing, high-tech (which has softened recently), and some citrus-growing. Overall the employment base is becoming more diverse. The cost of living is reasonable for a place with so many amenities. The central location and transportation network make for excellent access to other areas in Florida.

Orlando has grown very rapidly since Disney arrived, resulting in urban sprawl and a homogeneous look to development. In 1998 the Sierra Club listed Orlando as the no. 1 sprawl-threatened city for a place its size. Traffic can be bad and commute times long. The crime rate is also one of the state's highest. For some residents, the continuous influx of tourists is intolerable. This attitude has led to development away from the main tourist attractions in places such as Winter Park and Maitland, which boast spacious homes and attractive residential landscapes.

The flat area is a mix of open land and mostly deciduous woods surrounded by lakes. The fertile terrain is suitable for orchards and citrus crops. The climate is subtropical with inland and marine influences. Summers are warm and humid but temperatures over 95°F are rare and breezes provide comfort. The rainy season extends from June through September, with scattered showers almost daily and thunderstorms. Winters are mild with light rainfall. Although not a great threat because of the inland location, hurricanes can create heavy rains.

POPULATION

DEMOGRAPHICS	AREA	U.S. AVG	ETHNIC COMPOSITION	AREA	U.S. AVG	RESIDENT PROFILE	AREA	U.S. AVG
Population	1,752,192		White	85.3%	75.1%	Single	42.2%	43.6%
Population density per sq. mile	501.9	447.3	Black	10.1%	12.3%	Married	57.8%	56.4%
Population growth	43.1%	16.1%	Asian	2.1%	3.6%	Divorced	9.9%	8.4%
Median age	35.5	35.5	American Indian	.4%	.9%	Separated	3.1%	3.0%
Average family size	2.6	2.7	Hispanic	10.0%	12.5%	Married with children	25.6%	28.7%
			Diversity measure	51.2%	35.2%	Single with children	10.0%	10.1%

ECONOMY & JOBS   SCORE: 14/RANK: 284

INCOME	AREA	U.S. AVG	EMPLOYMENT	AREA	U.S. AVG	LARGEST EMPLOYING INDUSTRY
Per capita income	$23,596	$23,420	Unemployment rate	5.0%	6.1%	Accommodations and Food Services
Household income	$45,146	$46,060	Recent job growth	-.5%	.9%	
Household income < $25K	23.1%	26.4%	Projected future job growth	26.4%	15.1%	
Household income > $75K	24.0%	24.5%	White collar	57.4%	54.5%	
Household income growth	49.3%	57.3%	Blue collar	42.6%	45.5%	

COST OF LIVING   SCORE: 77/RANK: 76

INDEXES & TAXES	AREA	U.S. AVG	HOUSING	AREA	U.S. AVG	NECESSITIES	AREA	U.S. AVG
Cost of Living Index	95.6	100.0	Median home price	$139,600	$160,100	Food Index	102.6	100.0
Financial Progress Index	100.6	100.0	Home price appreciation	9.3%	7.1%	Housing Index	86.7	100.0
Income tax rate	0.000%	4.625%	Median rent	$820	$670	Utilities Index	102.9	100.0
Sales tax rate	6.500%	6.474%	Homes owned	64.2%	63.9%	Transportation Index	97.1	100.0
Property tax rate	$15.4	$15.6	Homes rented	24.9%	25.3%	Healthcare Index	107.1	100.0
			Housing affordability	51.0%	54.5%	Miscellaneous Cost Index	98.3	100.0

CLIMATE   SCORE: 82/RANK: 60

TEMPERATURE	AREA	U.S. AVG	PRECIPITATION	AREA	U.S. AVG	COMFORTS & HAZARDS	AREA	U.S. AVG
January low	50.0°F	26.4°F	Annual inches precipitation	51.0	35.9	July relative humidity	74.0%	68.8%
July high	90.0°F	86.7°F	Annual inches snowfall	0.0	24.2	Annual days mostly sunny	242	212
Annual days > 90°F	104	38	Annual days precipitation	116	111	Annual days with thunderstorms	81	39
Annual days < 32°F	2	88	Annual days rain > 0.5 inches	31	23	Tornado risk score	42	19
Annual days < 0°F	0	6	Annual days snow > 1.5 inches	0	6	Hurricane risk score	75	15

TEMPERATURE

PRECIPITATION

DAYS OF CLOUDS & PRECIPITATION

EDUCATION   SCORE: 57/RANK: 141

ACHIEVEMENT	AREA	U.S. AVG	PUBLIC SCHOOLS	AREA	U.S. AVG	HIGHER EDUCATION	AREA	U.S. AVG
High school degree	82.8%	80.2%	Expenditures per pupil	$5,124	$5,894	No. 2-year colleges	4	3
2-year college degree	7.2%	6.2%	Student/teacher ratio	18.7	16.7	No. 4-year colleges/universities	4	4
4-year college degree	17.1%	15.8%	Attending public school	88.5%	90.2%	No. highly ranked universities	2	1
Graduate/professional degree	7.7%	9.6%	State SAT score	996*	1020			
			State ACT score	20.5	21.0			

HEALTH & HEALTHCARE   SCORE: 20/RANK: 265

HAZARDS & ILLNESSES	AREA	U.S. AVG	HEALTHCARE	AREA	U.S. AVG
Air-quality score	95	45	Physicians per capita	202.5	261.1
Water-quality score	25	33	Hospital beds per capita	313.5	432.2
Pollen/allergy score	78	61	No. teaching hospitals	2	4
Stress score	97	50	Cost per doctor visit	$62	$67
Cancer mortality per capita	167.1	169.0	Cost per dental visit	$78	$82
Depression days per month	4.1	2.8	Cost per daily hospital room	$760	$733

CRIME   SCORE: 8/RANK: 303

CRIME	AREA	U.S. AVG
Violent crime rate	878.1	456.0
Change in violent crime rate	-12.8%	-17.2%
Property crime rate	5,195.8	3,950.0
Change in property crime rate	-15.1%	-16.8%

TRANSPORTATION   SCORE: 47/RANK: 175

COMMUTE	AREA	U.S. AVG	INTERCITY SERVICES	AREA	U.S. AVG	AUTOMOTIVE	AREA	U.S. AVG
Average commute time	27.0 min.	22.6 min.	Miles to nearest major airport	11	46	Insurance, annual premium	$1,149	$1,011
Commute by auto	92.7%	88.7%	Type of local airport	Large		Gas, cost per gallon	$1.46	$1.50
Commute by mass transit	1.1%	1.8%	No. daily airline departures	529	294	Daily vehicle miles per capita	29.0	23.0
Work at home	2.2%	3.9%	Amtrak service	Yes				
Mass transit miles per capita	13.1	8.0	No. interstate highways	1	1			

LEISURE SCORE: 88/RANK: 38

DINING & SHOPPING	AREA	U.S. AVG	ENTERTAINMENT	AREA	U.S. AVG	OUTDOOR ACTIVITIES	AREA	U.S. AVG
Restaurant rating	3	1	Professional sports rating	4	4	Golf-course rating	7	4
No. outlet malls	4	2	College sports rating	4	4	Ski-area rating	1	4
No. Starbucks	22	11	Zoo/aquarium rating	4	3	National Park rating	1	3
No. warehouse clubs	8	4	Amusement park rating	10	3	Sq. miles inland water	10.0	4.0
			Botanical garden/arboretum rating	6	3	Miles of coastline	0.0	11.4

ARTS & CULTURE SCORE: 75/RANK: 81

MEDIA & LIBRARIES	AREA	U.S. AVG	PERFORMING ARTS	AREA	U.S. AVG	MUSEUMS	AREA	U.S. AVG
Arts radio rating	7	3	Classical music rating	4	4	Overall museum rating	7	6
No. public libraries	41	28	Ballet/dance rating	3	3	Art museum rating	8	5
Library volumes per capita	1.9	2.8	Professional theater rating	1	3	Science museum rating	5	4
			University arts programs rating	1	5	Children's museum rating	1	3

Owensboro, KY

| Score: 32.4 | Rank: 303 |

Profile: Small river town
Location: Northwestern Kentucky along the Ohio River, 100 miles west of Louisville
Elevation: 406 feet
Time zone: Eastern Standard Time

PRO	CON
Cost of living	Entertainment
Low crime rate	Arts and culture
Small-town atmosphere	Isolation

An industrial and agricultural center on the Ohio River, Owensboro is the third-largest city in Kentucky. It is known for a favorable small-business and manufacturing climate. Isolation is an issue, but a planned cross-river highway connection to I-64, a major east-west artery, will improve access to both Louisville and Evansville, Indiana. The city has a diverse industrial base, strong employment, and high income relative to the low cost of living. Despite some locally flavored amenities—a bluegrass music museum and an annual barbecue festival—there isn't much to do and little cultural stimulation.

Owensboro is located on a river plain of the Ohio River, with mostly level terrain of mixed agriculture and wooded areas. The climate is continental with effects from local storm tracks. Summers are hot and humid. Both summer and winter are highly variable, with alternations between cold northwesterly winds and warm southerly ones. Storms and weather transitions bring high winds in all seasons and strong thunderstorms in summer. Snow does occur, but large and lengthy accumulations are uncommon. First freeze is late October, last is early April.

POPULATION

DEMOGRAPHICS	AREA	U.S. AVG	ETHNIC COMPOSITION	AREA	U.S. AVG	RESIDENT PROFILE	AREA	U.S. AVG
Population	91,694		White	97.2%	75.1%	Single	37.4%	43.6%
Population density per sq. mile	198.3	447.3	Black	2.4%	12.3%	Married	62.6%	56.4%
Population growth	5.2%	16.1%	Asian	.3%	3.6%	Divorced	7.8%	8.4%
Median age	37.1	35.5	American Indian	.1%	.9%	Separated	1.7%	3.0%
Average family size	2.7	2.7	Hispanic	.4%	12.5%	Married with children	34.5%	28.7%
			Diversity measure	12.8%	35.2%	Single with children	8.2%	10.1%

ECONOMY & JOBS SCORE: 68/RANK: 105

INCOME	AREA	U.S. AVG	EMPLOYMENT	AREA	U.S. AVG	LARGEST EMPLOYING INDUSTRY
Per capita income	$19,804	$23,420	Unemployment rate	5.6%	6.1%	Fabricated Metal Product Manufacturing
Household income	$37,214	$46,060	Recent job growth	1.6%	.9%	
Household income < $25K	32.9%	26.4%	Projected future job growth	12.0%	15.1%	
Household income > $75K	16.0%	24.5%	White collar	48.5%	54.5%	
Household income growth	52.8%	57.3%	Blue collar	51.5%	45.5%	

COST OF LIVING SCORE: 72/RANK: 92

INDEXES & TAXES	AREA	U.S. AVG	HOUSING	AREA	U.S. AVG	NECESSITIES	AREA	U.S. AVG
Cost of Living Index	81.4	100.0	Median home price	$94,270	$160,100	Food Index	97.5	100.0
Financial Progress Index	97.5	100.0	Home price appreciation	4.8%	7.1%	Housing Index	58.6	100.0
Income tax rate	6.000%	4.625%	Median rent	$439	$670	Utilities Index	80.3	100.0
Sales tax rate	6.000%	6.474%	Homes owned	76.9%	63.9%	Transportation Index	96.7	100.0
Property tax rate	$9.8	$15.6	Homes rented	17.0%	25.3%	Healthcare Index	90.4	100.0
			Housing affordability	63.0%	54.5%	Miscellaneous Cost Index	96.4	100.0

CLIMATE SCORE: 40/RANK: 199

TEMPERATURE	AREA	U.S. AVG	PRECIPITATION	AREA	U.S. AVG	COMFORTS & HAZARDS	AREA	U.S. AVG
January low	18.0°F	26.4°F	Annual inches precipitation	40.0	35.9	July relative humidity	70.0%	68.8%
July high	85.0°F	86.7°F	Annual inches snowfall	25.0	24.2	Annual days mostly sunny	205	212
Annual days > 90°F	19	38	Annual days precipitation	127	111	Annual days with thunderstorms	43	39
Annual days < 32°F	119	88	Annual days rain > 0.5 inches	27	23	Tornado risk score	10	19
Annual days < 0°F	3	6	Annual days snow > 1.5 inches	4	6	Hurricane risk score	5	15

TEMPERATURE

PRECIPITATION

DAYS OF CLOUDS & PRECIPITATION

EDUCATION SCORE: 7/RANK: 307

ACHIEVEMENT	AREA	U.S. AVG	PUBLIC SCHOOLS	AREA	U.S. AVG	HIGHER EDUCATION	AREA	U.S. AVG
High school degree	80.7%	80.2%	Expenditures per pupil	$5,663	$5,894	No. 2-year colleges	2	3
2-year college degree	5.3%	6.2%	Student/teacher ratio	17.6	16.7	No. 4-year colleges/universities	2	4
4-year college degree	11.2%	15.8%	Attending public school	83.0%	90.2%	No. highly ranked universities	1	1
Graduate/professional degree	6.5%	9.6%	State SAT score	1106	1020			
			State ACT score	20.2*	21.0			

HEALTH & HEALTHCARE SCORE: 57/RANK: 141

HAZARDS & ILLNESSES	AREA	U.S. AVG	HEALTHCARE	AREA	U.S. AVG
Air-quality score	6	45	Physicians per capita	207.2	261.1
Water-quality score	49	33	Hospital beds per capita	604.1	432.2
Pollen/allergy score	72	61	No. teaching hospitals	0	4
Stress score	11	50	Cost per doctor visit	$63	$67
Cancer mortality per capita	172.6	169.0	Cost per dental visit	$71	$82
Depression days per month	2.5	2.8	Cost per daily hospital room	$513	$733

CRIME SCORE: 68/RANK: 104

CRIME	AREA	U.S. AVG
Violent crime rate	190.0	456.0
Change in violent crime rate	39.3%	-17.2%
Property crime rate	3,357.8	3,950.0
Change in property crime rate	-18.5%	-16.8%

TRANSPORTATION SCORE: 43/RANK: 187

COMMUTE	AREA	U.S. AVG	INTERCITY SERVICES	AREA	U.S. AVG	AUTOMOTIVE	AREA	U.S. AVG
Average commute time	19.5 min.	22.6 min.	Miles to nearest major airport	81	46	Insurance, annual premium	$847	$1,011
Commute by auto	93.5%	88.7%	Type of local airport	Medium		Gas, cost per gallon	$1.37	$1.50
Commute by mass transit	.5%	1.8%	No. daily airline departures	228	294	Daily vehicle miles per capita	20.1	23.0
Work at home	3.3%	3.9%	Amtrak service	No				
Mass transit miles per capita	0.0	8.0	No. interstate highways	0	1			

LEISURE SCORE: 0/RANK: 330

DINING & SHOPPING	AREA	U.S. AVG	ENTERTAINMENT	AREA	U.S. AVG	OUTDOOR ACTIVITIES	AREA	U.S. AVG
Restaurant rating	1	1	Professional sports rating	2	4	Golf-course rating	2	4
No. outlet malls	0	2	College sports rating	1	4	Ski-area rating	1	4
No. Starbucks	0	11	Zoo/aquarium rating	1	3	National Park rating	1	3
No. warehouse clubs	1	4	Amusement park rating	1	3	Sq. miles inland water	3.0	4.0
			Botanical garden/arboretum rating	1	3	Miles of coastline	0.0	11.4

ARTS & CULTURE SCORE: 7/RANK: 307

MEDIA & LIBRARIES	AREA	U.S. AVG	PERFORMING ARTS	AREA	U.S. AVG	MUSEUMS	AREA	U.S. AVG
Arts radio rating	1	3	Classical music rating	1	4	Overall museum rating	4	6
No. public libraries	1	28	Ballet/dance rating	1	3	Art museum rating	5	5
Library volumes per capita	1.9	2.8	Professional theater rating	1	3	Science museum rating	1	4
			University arts programs rating	2	5	Children's museum rating	1	3

Panama City, FL

Profile: Beach town/Military town
Location: Florida Panhandle on the Gulf Coast
Elevation: 112 feet
Time zone: Eastern Standard Time

Score: 45.9   **Rank:** 252

PRO	CON
Attractive beaches	Crime rate
Cost of living	Isolation
Water recreation	Tourist sprawl

Panama City is one of the more popular beach cities in the Florida Panhandle. The area has large, white, sandy beaches, particularly to the northwest in Panama City Beach, a separate city. While Panama City Beach is a spring-break destination with a substantial tourist-oriented infrastructure, including amusement parks, the older Panama City is relatively attractive. Nearby ocean currents support abundant marine life, and fishing and diving are popular. Aside from tourism, the largest employer is the Tyndall Air Force Base. Cost of living and especially housing are reasonable for a Florida beach town. High crime rates and isolation from cultural attributes and air service,

among other amenities, are the main downsides. There's little to do that isn't oriented to tourists.

Panama City sits in an area of beaches, coastal dunes, and wet lowland. The interior contains numerous creeks and bays, and forested swampland with a rich assortment of live oaks, magnolia, cypress, and pine. Climate is subtropical and mild but subject to occasional northern influences. The Gulf moderates summer heat. Average annual rainfall is high at 64.2 inches but monthly and yearly totals vary widely. Thunderstorms occur year-round, but most arrive in summer. Tropical storms occasionally affect the area.

POPULATION

DEMOGRAPHICS	AREA	U.S. AVG	ETHNIC COMPOSITION	AREA	U.S. AVG	RESIDENT PROFILE	AREA	U.S. AVG
Population	151,901		White	87.8%	75.1%	Single	39.6%	43.6%
Population density per sq. mile	198.9	447.3	Black	8.7%	12.3%	Married	60.4%	56.4%
Population growth	19.6%	16.1%	Asian	2.1%	3.6%	Divorced	10.5%	8.4%
Median age	37.8	35.5	American Indian	.9%	.9%	Separated	2.9%	3.0%
Average family size	2.6	2.7	Hispanic	3.5%	12.5%	Married with children	28.8%	28.7%
			Diversity measure	30.0%	35.2%	Single with children	10.4%	10.1%

ECONOMY & JOBS   SCORE: 15/RANK: 281

INCOME	AREA	U.S. AVG	EMPLOYMENT	AREA	U.S. AVG	LARGEST EMPLOYING INDUSTRY
Per capita income	$20,607	$23,420	Unemployment rate	4.8%	6.1%	Healthcare and Social Assistance
Household income	$36,595	$46,060	Recent job growth	.2%	.9%	
Household income < $25K	31.9%	26.4%	Projected future job growth	21.0%	15.1%	
Household income > $75K	15.0%	24.5%	White collar	53.1%	54.5%	
Household income growth	47.2%	57.3%	Blue collar	46.9%	45.5%	

COST OF LIVING   SCORE: 87/RANK: 43

INDEXES & TAXES	AREA	U.S. AVG	HOUSING	AREA	U.S. AVG	NECESSITIES	AREA	U.S. AVG
Cost of Living Index	88.7	100.0	Median home price	$113,120	$160,100	Food Index	103.7	100.0
Financial Progress Index	87.9	100.0	Home price appreciation	6.6%	7.1%	Housing Index	70.3	100.0
Income tax rate	0.000%	4.625%	Median rent	$542	$670	Utilities Index	86.0	100.0
Sales tax rate	7.000%	6.474%	Homes owned	53.8%	63.9%	Transportation Index	105.0	100.0
Property tax rate	$16.2	$15.6	Homes rented	21.3%	25.3%	Healthcare Index	103.6	100.0
			Housing affordability	59.0%	54.5%	Miscellaneous Cost Index	96.2	100.0

CLIMATE   SCORE: 68/RANK: 106

TEMPERATURE	AREA	U.S. AVG	PRECIPITATION	AREA	U.S. AVG	COMFORTS & HAZARDS	AREA	U.S. AVG
January low	43.0°F	26.4°F	Annual inches precipitation	64.2	35.9	July relative humidity	74.0%	68.8%
July high	89.7°F	86.7°F	Annual inches snowfall	.3	24.2	Annual days mostly sunny	220	212
Annual days > 90°F	55	38	Annual days precipitation	114	111	Annual days with thunderstorms	76	39
Annual days < 32°F	16	88	Annual days rain > 0.5 inches	37	23	Tornado risk score	28	19
Annual days < 0°F	0	6	Annual days snow > 1.5 inches	0	6	Hurricane risk score	60	15

TEMPERATURE

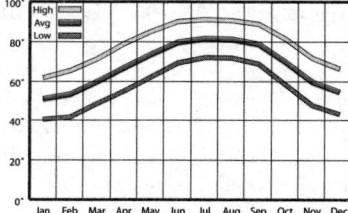

PRECIPITATION

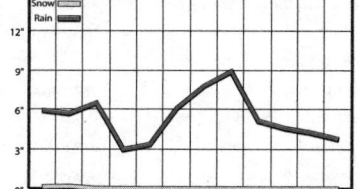

DAYS OF CLOUDS & PRECIPITATION

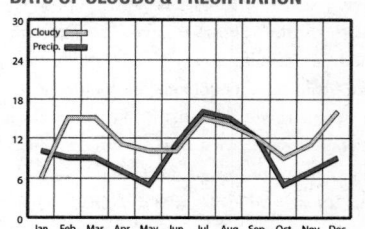

EDUCATION — SCORE: 35/RANK: 214

ACHIEVEMENT	AREA	U.S. AVG	PUBLIC SCHOOLS	AREA	U.S. AVG	HIGHER EDUCATION	AREA	U.S. AVG
High school degree	79.2%	80.2%	Expenditures per pupil	$5,109	$5,894	No. 2-year colleges	1	3
2-year college degree	7.4%	6.2%	Student/teacher ratio	17.7	16.7	No. 4-year colleges/universities	0	4
4-year college degree	11.5%	15.8%	Attending public school	94.9%	90.2%	No. highly ranked universities	0	1
Graduate/professional degree	6.6%	9.6%	State SAT score	996*	1020			
			State ACT score	20.5	21.0			

HEALTH & HEALTHCARE — SCORE: 56/RANK: 145 — CRIME SCORE: 8/RANK: 304

HAZARDS & ILLNESSES	AREA	U.S. AVG	HEALTHCARE	AREA	U.S. AVG	CRIME	AREA	U.S. AVG
Air-quality score	24	45	Physicians per capita	202.8	261.1	Violent crime rate	695.1	456.0
Water-quality score	82	33	Hospital beds per capita	409.5	432.2	Change in violent crime rate	9.2%	-17.2%
Pollen/allergy score	61	61	No. teaching hospitals	0	4	Property crime rate	5,284.2	3,950.0
Stress score	73	50	Cost per doctor visit	$58	$67	Change in property crime rate	-6.1%	-16.8%
Cancer mortality per capita	184.6	169.0	Cost per dental visit	$76	$82			
Depression days per month	1.0	2.8	Cost per daily hospital room	$661	$733			

TRANSPORTATION — SCORE: 40/RANK: 196

COMMUTE	AREA	U.S. AVG	INTERCITY SERVICES	AREA	U.S. AVG	AUTOMOTIVE	AREA	U.S. AVG
Average commute time	21.6 min.	22.6 min.	Miles to nearest major airport	79	46	Insurance, annual premium	$1,019	$1,011
Commute by auto	93.1%	88.7%	Type of local airport	Small		Gas, cost per gallon	$1.50	$1.50
Commute by mass transit	.2%	1.8%	No. daily airline departures	69	294	Daily vehicle miles per capita	28.6	23.0
Work at home	2.0%	3.9%	Amtrak service	No				
Mass transit miles per capita	6.3	8.0	No. interstate highways	0	1			

LEISURE — SCORE: 40/RANK: 196

DINING & SHOPPING	AREA	U.S. AVG	ENTERTAINMENT	AREA	U.S. AVG	OUTDOOR ACTIVITIES	AREA	U.S. AVG
Restaurant rating	1	1	Professional sports rating	2	4	Golf-course rating	2	4
No. outlet malls	2	2	College sports rating	1	4	Ski-area rating	1	4
No. Starbucks	0	11	Zoo/aquarium rating	1	3	National Park rating	1	3
No. warehouse clubs	3	4	Amusement park rating	5	3	Sq. miles inland water	7.0	4.0
			Botanical garden/arboretum rating	1	3	Miles of coastline	44.0	11.4

ARTS & CULTURE — SCORE: 27/RANK: 241

MEDIA & LIBRARIES	AREA	U.S. AVG	PERFORMING ARTS	AREA	U.S. AVG	MUSEUMS	AREA	U.S. AVG
Arts radio rating	1	3	Classical music rating	3	4	Overall museum rating	3	6
No. public libraries	8	28	Ballet/dance rating	1	3	Art museum rating	4	5
Library volumes per capita	1.2	2.8	Professional theater rating	1	3	Science museum rating	2	4
			University arts programs rating	1	5	Children's museum rating	6	3

Parkersburg-Marietta, WV-OH

Score: 54.5   Rank: 193

Profile: Small river towns/College town
Location: Northwestern West Virginia along the Ohio River
Elevation: 649 feet
Time zone: Eastern Standard Time

PRO	CON
College-town amenities	Heavy industry
Historic interest	Isolation
Water recreation	Low ethnic diversity

Parkersburg is a small town on the Ohio River with a primarily industrial heritage and a historic riverfront. Marietta, located across the river, is another industrial town with similar historic flavor. Nearby oil and gas fields supply resources to local chemical, plastics, and glass companies. DuPont, Borg-Warner, Ashland, Goodyear, Shell, and Union Carbide all produce plastics nearby. Significant numbers of smaller companies engage in glassmaking, both for commercial and artistic purposes. The cyclical economic base is diversifying somewhat with clothing and food distribution, as large companies begin to recognize the area's suitable location for access to the East Coast, Midwest, and South. Marshall University adds 13,000 students and a few college amenities, notably sports, although overall educational attainment is low.

Parkersburg is located at the confluence of the Little Kanawha and Ohio rivers. A series of wooded ridges parallel the rivers and rise as much as 150 feet above the valley floor. The climate is humid continental with frequent weather changes because of the location along major storm tracks. Summers are warm and humid; the ridges can block wind creating muggy conditions, but prolonged hot or cold weather is infrequent. Rain occurs year-round and snowfall varies greatly from year to year. The area is the farthest north where tender vegetation such as magnolias can survive most winters. First freeze is mid-October, last is late April.

POPULATION

DEMOGRAPHICS	AREA	U.S. AVG	ETHNIC COMPOSITION	AREA	U.S. AVG	RESIDENT PROFILE	AREA	U.S. AVG
Population	149,867		White	98.3%	75.1%	Single	36.9%	43.6%
Population density per sq. mile	149.5	447.3	Black	1.1%	12.3%	Married	63.1%	56.4%
Population growth	.5%	16.1%	Asian	.3%	3.6%	Divorced	7.5%	8.4%
Median age	39.8	35.5	American Indian	.2%	.9%	Separated	1.8%	3.0%
Average family size	2.6	2.7	Hispanic	.3%	12.5%	Married with children	31.6%	28.7%
			Diversity measure	6.0%	35.2%	Single with children	8.2%	10.1%

ECONOMY & JOBS   SCORE: 28/RANK: 238

INCOME	AREA	U.S. AVG	EMPLOYMENT	AREA	U.S. AVG	LARGEST EMPLOYING INDUSTRY
Per capita income	$19,666	$23,420	Unemployment rate	6.2%	6.1%	Chemical Manufacturing
Household income	$36,670	$46,060	Recent job growth	2.8%	.9%	
Household income < $25K	34.0%	26.4%	Projected future job growth	10.6%	15.1%	
Household income > $75K	14.9%	24.5%	White collar	52.5%	54.5%	
Household income growth	47.1%	57.3%	Blue collar	47.5%	45.5%	

COST OF LIVING   SCORE: 67/RANK: 107

INDEXES & TAXES	AREA	U.S. AVG	HOUSING	AREA	U.S. AVG	NECESSITIES	AREA	U.S. AVG
Cost of Living Index	86.8	100.0	Median home price	$91,450	$160,100	Food Index	104.4	100.0
Financial Progress Index	90.0	100.0	Home price appreciation	5.2%	7.1%	Housing Index	56.8	100.0
Income tax rate	6.000%	4.625%	Median rent	$452	$670	Utilities Index	120.3	100.0
Sales tax rate	6.500%	6.474%	Homes owned	73.3%	63.9%	Transportation Index	101.6	100.0
Property tax rate	$9.8	$15.6	Homes rented	16.3%	25.3%	Healthcare Index	91.7	100.0
			Housing affordability	59.0%	54.5%	Miscellaneous Cost Index	101.3	100.0

CLIMATE   SCORE: 46/RANK: 177

TEMPERATURE	AREA	U.S. AVG	PRECIPITATION	AREA	U.S. AVG	COMFORTS & HAZARDS	AREA	U.S. AVG
January low	24.4°F	26.4°F	Annual inches precipitation	38.4	35.9	July relative humidity	71.0%	68.8%
July high	85.6°F	86.7°F	Annual inches snowfall	24.2	24.2	Annual days mostly sunny	212	212
Annual days > 90°F	22	38	Annual days precipitation	150	111	Annual days with thunderstorms	44	39
Annual days < 32°F	98	88	Annual days rain > 0.5 inches	26	23	Tornado risk score	3	19
Annual days < 0°F	2	6	Annual days snow > 1.5 inches	7	6	Hurricane risk score	5	15

TEMPERATURE

PRECIPITATION

DAYS OF CLOUDS & PRECIPITATION

EDUCATION   SCORE: 34/RANK: 216

ACHIEVEMENT	AREA	U.S. AVG	PUBLIC SCHOOLS	AREA	U.S. AVG	HIGHER EDUCATION	AREA	U.S. AVG
High school degree	82.7%	80.2%	Expenditures per pupil	$5,810	$5,894	No. 2-year colleges	2	3
2-year college degree	5.9%	6.2%	Student/teacher ratio	16.1	16.7	No. 4-year colleges/universities	3	4
4-year college degree	9.5%	15.8%	Attending public school	93.9%	90.2%	No. highly ranked universities	0	1
Graduate/professional degree	5.6%	9.6%	State SAT score	1032	1020			
			State ACT score	20.3*	21.0			

HEALTH & HEALTHCARE   SCORE: 75/RANK: 80

HAZARDS & ILLNESSES	AREA	U.S. AVG	HEALTHCARE	AREA	U.S. AVG
Air-quality score	49	45	Physicians per capita	193.5	261.1
Water-quality score	16	33	Hospital beds per capita	589.8	432.2
Pollen/allergy score	60	61	No. teaching hospitals	1	4
Stress score	40	50	Cost per doctor visit	$68	$67
Cancer mortality per capita	165.4	169.0	Cost per dental visit	$71	$82
Depression days per month	4.6	2.8	Cost per daily hospital room	$437	$733

CRIME   SCORE: 79/RANK: 68

CRIME	AREA	U.S. AVG
Violent crime rate	303.6	456.0
Change in violent crime rate	46.8%	-17.2%
Property crime rate	2,036.3	3,950.0
Change in property crime rate	-17.9%	-16.8%

TRANSPORTATION   SCORE: 31/RANK: 228

COMMUTE	AREA	U.S. AVG	INTERCITY SERVICES	AREA	U.S. AVG	AUTOMOTIVE	AREA	U.S. AVG
Average commute time	20.9 min.	22.6 min.	Miles to nearest major airport	88	46	Insurance, annual premium	$930	$1,011
Commute by auto	94.1%	88.7%	Type of local airport	Medium		Gas, cost per gallon	$1.47	$1.50
Commute by mass transit	.6%	1.8%	No. daily airline departures	270	294	Daily vehicle miles per capita	18.8	23.0
Work at home	2.3%	3.9%	Amtrak service	No				
Mass transit miles per capita	0.0	8.0	No. interstate highways	1	1			

LEISURE SCORE: 9/RANK: 300

DINING & SHOPPING	AREA	U.S. AVG	ENTERTAINMENT	AREA	U.S. AVG	OUTDOOR ACTIVITIES	AREA	U.S. AVG
Restaurant rating	1	1	Professional sports rating	2	4	Golf-course rating	2	4
No. outlet malls	0	2	College sports rating	1	4	Ski-area rating	2	4
No. Starbucks	0	11	Zoo/aquarium rating	1	3	National Park rating	1	3
No. warehouse clubs	3	4	Amusement park rating	1	3	Sq. miles inland water	2.0	4.0
			Botanical garden/arboretum rating	1	3	Miles of coastline	0.0	11.4

ARTS & CULTURE SCORE: 75/RANK: 82

MEDIA & LIBRARIES	AREA	U.S. AVG	PERFORMING ARTS	AREA	U.S. AVG	MUSEUMS	AREA	U.S. AVG
Arts radio rating	1	3	Classical music rating	1	4	Overall museum rating	5	6
No. public libraries	10	28	Ballet/dance rating	3	3	Art museum rating	4	5
Library volumes per capita	3.1	2.8	Professional theater rating	1	3	Science museum rating	1	4
			University arts programs rating	6	5	Children's museum rating	1	3

Pensacola, FL

Score: 47.8   Rank: 239

Profile: Beach city/Military town
Location: Western tip of Florida Panhandle on Pensacola Bay along the Gulf Coast
Elevation: 112 feet
Time zone: Eastern Standard Time

PRO	CON
Nearby water	Urban sprawl
Historic interest	Arts and culture
Low cost of living	Air transport

Because of the strategic location and harbor protection, Pensacola has a rich and varied history, having "changed hands" among nations 13 times, with periods of French, British, and Spanish occupation. A lumber boom in the late 1800s also left its mark on architecture and historic sites. Today, the city has a strong military presence with the Pensacola Naval Air Station, headquarters of the Blue Angels. Santa Rosa Island, a barrier island with a white sand beach, is a major draw for watersports. Cost of living and home prices are among the lowest in the state. However, unattractive housing and commercial development are rampant. In 1998, Pensacola was no. 3 on the Sierra Club's list of small cities most threatened by urban sprawl. Except for museums, arts and culture is mainly absent, and there is little scheduled air service.

Pensacola is situated on a sandy slope bordering the Pensacola Bay breakwater. The Gulf of Mexico moderates the climate year-round. Summer temperatures are in the 80s and 90s, with an occasional 100°F day if sea breezes diminish. Winter highs are usually in the 50s. Freezing temperatures may occur December through February but extended cold waves are infrequent. Rainfall is usually well distributed through the year, but is heaviest in July and August. Fall is relatively dry. Summer rain comes as thunderstorms while winter rains are lighter but occur over longer periods. Snow is observed in 3 out of 10 winters but measurable amounts are rare. Gulf hurricanes are a risk from early July to mid-October.

POPULATION

DEMOGRAPHICS	AREA	U.S. AVG	ETHNIC COMPOSITION	AREA	U.S. AVG	RESIDENT PROFILE	AREA	U.S. AVG
Population	424,484		White	78.7%	75.1%	Single	45.0%	43.6%
Population density per sq. mile	252.8	447.3	Black	17.4%	12.3%	Married	55.0%	56.4%
Population growth	23.3%	16.1%	Asian	2.1%	3.6%	Divorced	10.1%	8.4%
Median age	36.2	35.5	American Indian	1.3%	.9%	Separated	3.8%	3.0%
Average family size	2.7	2.7	Hispanic	3.3%	12.5%	Married with children	27.8%	28.7%
			Diversity measure	38.8%	35.2%	Single with children	12.5%	10.1%

ECONOMY & JOBS SCORE: 8/RANK: 303

INCOME	AREA	U.S. AVG	EMPLOYMENT	AREA	U.S. AVG	LARGEST EMPLOYING INDUSTRY
Per capita income	$19,655	$23,420	Unemployment rate	3.9%	6.1%	Healthcare and Social Assistance
Household income	$36,969	$46,060	Recent job growth	-2.6%	.9%	
Household income < $25K	31.7%	26.4%	Projected future job growth	23.7%	15.1%	
Household income > $75K	15.8%	24.5%	White collar	53.0%	54.5%	
Household income growth	43.2%	57.3%	Blue collar	47.0%	45.5%	

COST OF LIVING SCORE: 88/RANK: 39

INDEXES & TAXES	AREA	U.S. AVG	HOUSING	AREA	U.S. AVG	NECESSITIES	AREA	U.S. AVG
Cost of Living Index	88.0	100.0	Median home price	$113,300	$160,100	Food Index	97.0	100.0
Financial Progress Index	89.6	100.0	Home price appreciation	5.2%	7.1%	Housing Index	70.4	100.0
Income tax rate	0.000%	4.625%	Median rent	$542	$670	Utilities Index	92.6	100.0
Sales tax rate	7.500%	6.474%	Homes owned	64.0%	63.9%	Transportation Index	98.9	100.0
Property tax rate	$14.3	$15.6	Homes rented	26.7%	25.3%	Healthcare Index	99.9	100.0
			Housing affordability	59.0%	54.5%	Miscellaneous Cost Index	99.3	100.0

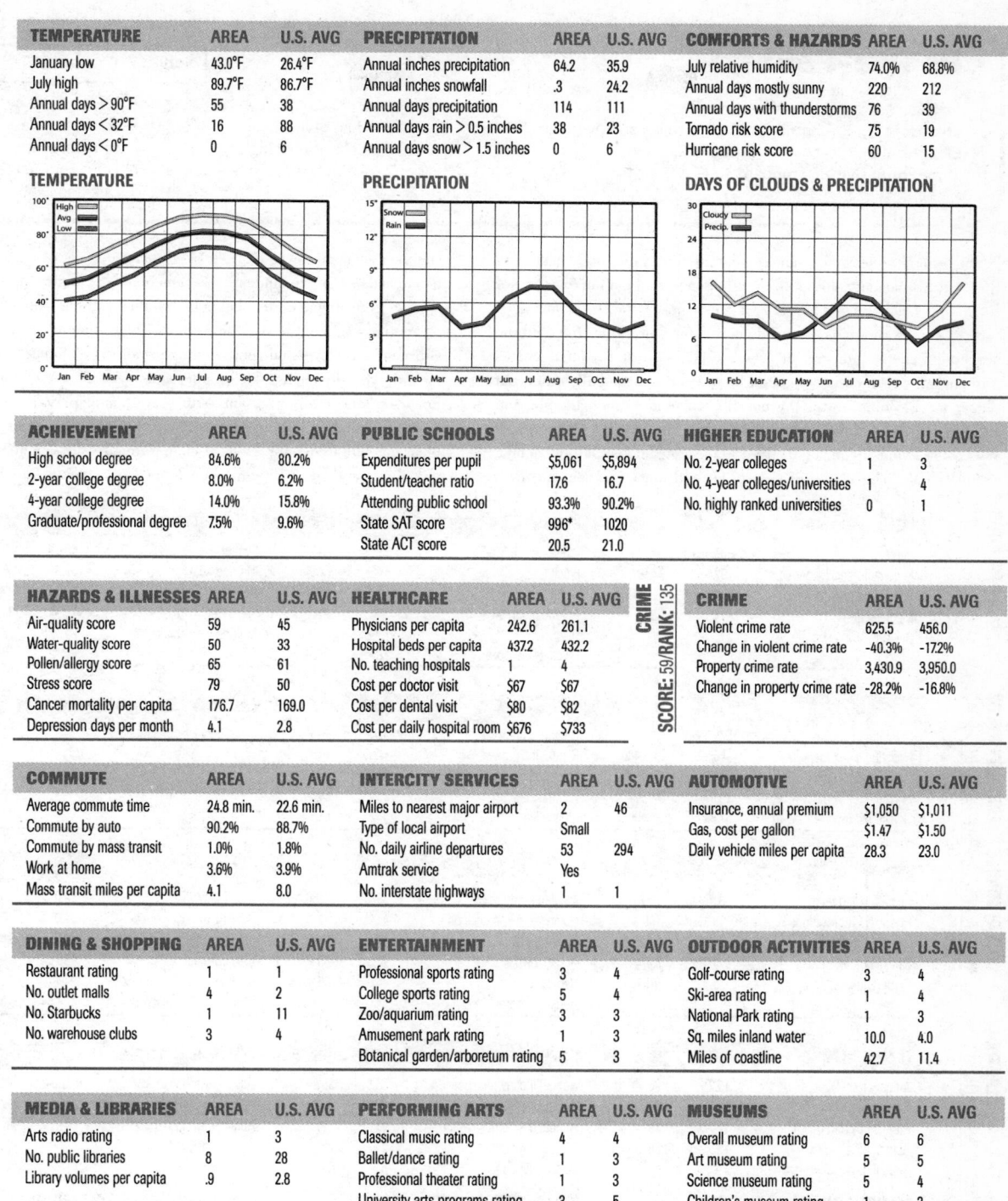

CLIMATE — SCORE: 68/RANK: 105

TEMPERATURE	AREA	U.S. AVG	PRECIPITATION	AREA	U.S. AVG	COMFORTS & HAZARDS	AREA	U.S. AVG
January low	43.0°F	26.4°F	Annual inches precipitation	64.2	35.9	July relative humidity	74.0%	68.8%
July high	89.7°F	86.7°F	Annual inches snowfall	.3	24.2	Annual days mostly sunny	220	212
Annual days > 90°F	55	38	Annual days precipitation	114	111	Annual days with thunderstorms	76	39
Annual days < 32°F	16	88	Annual days rain > 0.5 inches	38	23	Tornado risk score	75	19
Annual days < 0°F	0	6	Annual days snow > 1.5 inches	0	6	Hurricane risk score	60	15

TEMPERATURE

PRECIPITATION

DAYS OF CLOUDS & PRECIPITATION

EDUCATION — SCORE: 49/RANK: 169

ACHIEVEMENT	AREA	U.S. AVG	PUBLIC SCHOOLS	AREA	U.S. AVG	HIGHER EDUCATION	AREA	U.S. AVG
High school degree	84.6%	80.2%	Expenditures per pupil	$5,061	$5,894	No. 2-year colleges	1	3
2-year college degree	8.0%	6.2%	Student/teacher ratio	17.6	16.7	No. 4-year colleges/universities	1	4
4-year college degree	14.0%	15.8%	Attending public school	93.3%	90.2%	No. highly ranked universities	0	1
Graduate/professional degree	7.5%	9.6%	State SAT score	996*	1020			
			State ACT score	20.5	21.0			

HEALTH & HEALTHCARE — SCORE: 50/RANK: 166

CRIME — SCORE: 59/RANK: 135

HAZARDS & ILLNESSES	AREA	U.S. AVG	HEALTHCARE	AREA	U.S. AVG	CRIME	AREA	U.S. AVG
Air-quality score	59	45	Physicians per capita	242.6	261.1	Violent crime rate	625.5	456.0
Water-quality score	50	33	Hospital beds per capita	437.2	432.2	Change in violent crime rate	-40.3%	-17.2%
Pollen/allergy score	65	61	No. teaching hospitals	1	4	Property crime rate	3,430.9	3,950.0
Stress score	79	50	Cost per doctor visit	$67	$67	Change in property crime rate	-28.2%	-16.8%
Cancer mortality per capita	176.7	169.0	Cost per dental visit	$80	$82			
Depression days per month	4.1	2.8	Cost per daily hospital room	$676	$733			

TRANSPORTATION — SCORE: 8/RANK: 303

COMMUTE	AREA	U.S. AVG	INTERCITY SERVICES	AREA	U.S. AVG	AUTOMOTIVE	AREA	U.S. AVG
Average commute time	24.8 min.	22.6 min.	Miles to nearest major airport	2	46	Insurance, annual premium	$1,050	$1,011
Commute by auto	90.2%	88.7%	Type of local airport	Small		Gas, cost per gallon	$1.47	$1.50
Commute by mass transit	1.0%	1.8%	No. daily airline departures	53	294	Daily vehicle miles per capita	28.3	23.0
Work at home	3.6%	3.9%	Amtrak service	Yes				
Mass transit miles per capita	4.1	8.0	No. interstate highways	1	1			

LEISURE — SCORE: 52/RANK: 158

DINING & SHOPPING	AREA	U.S. AVG	ENTERTAINMENT	AREA	U.S. AVG	OUTDOOR ACTIVITIES	AREA	U.S. AVG
Restaurant rating	1	1	Professional sports rating	3	4	Golf-course rating	3	4
No. outlet malls	4	2	College sports rating	5	4	Ski-area rating	1	4
No. Starbucks	1	11	Zoo/aquarium rating	3	3	National Park rating	1	3
No. warehouse clubs	3	4	Amusement park rating	1	3	Sq. miles inland water	10.0	4.0
			Botanical garden/arboretum rating	5	3	Miles of coastline	42.7	11.4

ARTS & CULTURE — SCORE: 53/RANK: 156

MEDIA & LIBRARIES	AREA	U.S. AVG	PERFORMING ARTS	AREA	U.S. AVG	MUSEUMS	AREA	U.S. AVG
Arts radio rating	1	3	Classical music rating	4	4	Overall museum rating	6	6
No. public libraries	8	28	Ballet/dance rating	1	3	Art museum rating	5	5
Library volumes per capita	.9	2.8	Professional theater rating	1	3	Science museum rating	5	4
			University arts programs rating	3	5	Children's museum rating	1	3

Peoria-Pekin, IL

Score: 77.0 **Rank:** 51

Profile: Small-city complex
Location: North-central Illinois, 135 miles southwest of Chicago
Elevation: 662 feet
Time zone: Central Standard Time

PRO
Cost of living
Cost of housing
Attractive residential areas

CON
Economic cycles
Entertainment
No direct interstate to Chicago

Peoria is a pleasant, small community that, while not outstanding in any category, does well overall, hence the high ranking. One of the oldest cities in the state, it is a business, industrial, and agricultural center known as the headquarters for Caterpillar, Inc. and the heavy-equipment industry. It is also home to the United States Agricultural Research Laboratory. Life in Peoria is generally quiet, but Chicago is 135 miles away. Downtown is clean and unremarkable, and attractive residential areas surround the city in the hills. Home prices and cost of living are among the best in the state and are attractive on a national scale. The nature of Caterpillar and the equipment business

suggests economic cycles. There have been periods of extended economic malaise, but the industrial/commercial base is growing and diversifying. Educational attainment is high for a small non-college town.

Peoria is situated next to the Illinois River in a shallow river valley surrounded by level and gently rolling terrain. The climate is continental with typically changeable weather and a wide range of temperatures. Summer is generally pleasant, with some humid periods mid-season. Most precipitation falls in summer, mainly as thunderstorms. Falls are pleasant, with frequent periods of long, warm, dry days. Winter brings a mix of rain and snow. First freeze is late October, last is late April.

POPULATION

DEMOGRAPHICS	AREA	U.S. AVG	ETHNIC COMPOSITION	AREA	U.S. AVG	RESIDENT PROFILE	AREA	U.S. AVG
Population	346,569		White	93.0%	75.1%	Single	40.8%	43.6%
Population density per sq. mile	192.9	447.3	Black	5.3%	12.3%	Married	59.2%	56.4%
Population growth	2.2%	16.1%	Asian	1.0%	3.6%	Divorced	7.5%	8.4%
Median age	37.4	35.5	American Indian	.2%	.9%	Separated	1.7%	3.0%
Average family size	2.6	2.7	Hispanic	1.7%	12.5%	Married with children	29.9%	28.7%
			Diversity measure	22.9%	35.2%	Single with children	8.3%	10.1%

ECONOMY & JOBS — SCORE: 65/RANK: 115

INCOME	AREA	U.S. AVG	EMPLOYMENT	AREA	U.S. AVG	LARGEST EMPLOYING INDUSTRY
Per capita income	$23,956	$23,420	Unemployment rate	5.5%	6.1%	Machinery Manufacturing
Household income	$46,992	$46,060	Recent job growth	1.6%	.9%	
Household income < $25K	24.8%	26.4%	Projected future job growth	14.3%	15.1%	
Household income > $75K	25.9%	24.5%	White collar	55.4%	54.5%	
Household income growth	57.1%	57.3%	Blue collar	44.6%	45.5%	

COST OF LIVING — SCORE: 57/RANK: 140

INDEXES & TAXES	AREA	U.S. AVG	HOUSING	AREA	U.S. AVG	NECESSITIES	AREA	U.S. AVG
Cost of Living Index	83.9	100.0	Median home price	$87,000	$160,100	Food Index	99.0	100.0
Financial Progress Index	119.4	100.0	Home price appreciation	4.6%	7.1%	Housing Index	54.0	100.0
Income tax rate	3.000%	4.625%	Median rent	$600	$670	Utilities Index	93.5	100.0
Sales tax rate	8.000%	6.474%	Homes owned	70.3%	63.9%	Transportation Index	106.0	100.0
Property tax rate	$25.4	$15.6	Homes rented	24.0%	25.3%	Healthcare Index	91.7	100.0
			Housing affordability	54.0%	54.5%	Miscellaneous Cost Index	104.4	100.0

CLIMATE — SCORE: 39/RANK: 201

TEMPERATURE	AREA	U.S. AVG	PRECIPITATION	AREA	U.S. AVG	COMFORTS & HAZARDS	AREA	U.S. AVG
January low	15.7°F	26.4°F	Annual inches precipitation	35.0	35.9	July relative humidity	72.0%	68.8%
July high	85.5°F	86.7°F	Annual inches snowfall	23.0	24.2	Annual days mostly sunny	197	212
Annual days > 90°F	17	38	Annual days precipitation	111	111	Annual days with thunderstorms	49	39
Annual days < 32°F	132	88	Annual days rain > 0.5 inches	24	23	Tornado risk score	26	19
Annual days < 0°F	11	6	Annual days snow > 1.5 inches	5	6	Hurricane risk score	2	15

TEMPERATURE

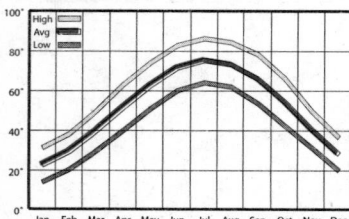

PRECIPITATION

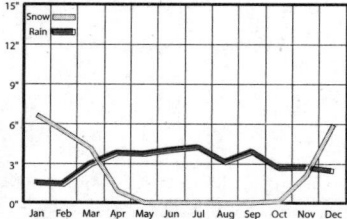

DAYS OF CLOUDS & PRECIPITATION

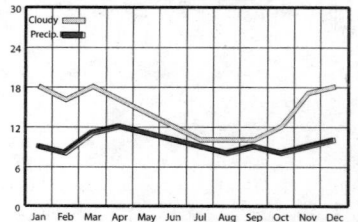

EDUCATION — SCORE: 37/RANK: 206

ACHIEVEMENT	AREA	U.S. AVG	PUBLIC SCHOOLS	AREA	U.S. AVG	HIGHER EDUCATION	AREA	U.S. AVG
High school degree	82.8%	80.2%	Expenditures per pupil	$5,338	$5,894	No. 2-year colleges	2	3
2-year college degree	6.8%	6.2%	Student/teacher ratio	15.6	16.7	No. 4-year colleges/universities	2	4
4-year college degree	14.2%	15.8%	Attending public school	87.2%	90.2%	No. highly ranked universities	0	1
Graduate/professional degree	6.9%	9.6%	State SAT score	1179	1020			
			State ACT score	20.2*	21.0			

HEALTH & HEALTHCARE — SCORE: 64/RANK: 116   CRIME — SCORE: 66/RANK: 112

HAZARDS & ILLNESSES	AREA	U.S. AVG	HEALTHCARE	AREA	U.S. AVG	CRIME	AREA	U.S. AVG
Air-quality score	49	45	Physicians per capita	267.8	261.1	Violent crime rate	496.3	456.0
Water-quality score	30	33	Hospital beds per capita	419.7	432.2	Change in violent crime rate	-30.7%	-17.2%
Pollen/allergy score	49	61	No. teaching hospitals	2	4	Property crime rate	3,269.2	3,950.0
Stress score	30	50	Cost per doctor visit	$66	$67	Change in property crime rate	-22.5%	-16.8%
Cancer mortality per capita	173.8	169.0	Cost per dental visit	$78	$82			
Depression days per month	3.0	2.8	Cost per daily hospital room	$478	$733			

TRANSPORTATION — SCORE: 61/RANK: 129

COMMUTE	AREA	U.S. AVG	INTERCITY SERVICES	AREA	U.S. AVG	AUTOMOTIVE	AREA	U.S. AVG
Average commute time	19.7 min.	22.6 min.	Miles to nearest major airport	120	46	Insurance, annual premium	$896	$1,011
Commute by auto	89.2%	88.7%	Type of local airport	Medium		Gas, cost per gallon	$1.47	$1.50
Commute by mass transit	1.0%	1.8%	No. daily airline departures	356	294	Daily vehicle miles per capita	21.4	23.0
Work at home	4.5%	3.9%	Amtrak service	No				
Mass transit miles per capita	5.5	8.0	No. interstate highways	1	1			

LEISURE — SCORE: 27/RANK: 240

DINING & SHOPPING	AREA	U.S. AVG	ENTERTAINMENT	AREA	U.S. AVG	OUTDOOR ACTIVITIES	AREA	U.S. AVG
Restaurant rating	1	1	Professional sports rating	3	4	Golf-course rating	4	4
No. outlet malls	0	2	College sports rating	2	4	Ski-area rating	2	4
No. Starbucks	0	11	Zoo/aquarium rating	4	3	National Park rating	1	3
No. warehouse clubs	3	4	Amusement park rating	1	3	Sq. miles inland water	4.0	4.0
			Botanical garden/arboretum rating	7	3	Miles of coastline	0.0	11.4

ARTS & CULTURE — SCORE: 76/RANK: 79

MEDIA & LIBRARIES	AREA	U.S. AVG	PERFORMING ARTS	AREA	U.S. AVG	MUSEUMS	AREA	U.S. AVG
Arts radio rating	1	3	Classical music rating	4	4	Overall museum rating	4	6
No. public libraries	35	28	Ballet/dance rating	3	3	Art museum rating	5	5
Library volumes per capita	6.0	2.8	Professional theater rating	1	3	Science museum rating	5	4
			University arts programs rating	3	5	Children's museum rating	1	3

Philadelphia, PA-NJ

Score: 70.6   Rank: 76

Profile: Large city
Location: Extreme southeastern Pennsylvania along Susquehanna River at New Jersey border
Elevation: 28 feet
Time zone: Eastern Standard Time

PRO
Arts and culture
Entertainment
Historic interest

CON
Economy
Some urban decay
Violent crime

The "City of Brotherly Love," a direct translation of its name from Greek, is the fifth largest metropolitan area in the United States. Philadelphia served as the nation's first capital and cultural center before being replaced in these roles by Washington, D.C., and New York City, respectively. Since the Industrial Revolution, the city has prospered as an important port and manufacturing center. Today, it's part of an economic corridor of large cities stretching down the East Coast from Boston to Washington, D.C. The metro area includes four counties across the Delaware River in New Jersey, including industrial Camden and the more upscale Cherry Hill.

"Philly" offers a full set of big-city amenities comparable to those of most major cities. In the late 17th century, William Penn laid out the city on a grid, one of the nation's first. Today, the modern downtown is adjacent to a large historic district anchored by Independence Hall and the waterfront. The majority of the land between the historic district and the Schuylkill River to the west resembles a typical large U.S. city with a mix of old and new structures. Large Fairmount Park contains many of the area's museums and historic buildings. Across the Schuylkill in University Park, a college town within the city, are the University of Pennsylvania and Drexel University. With these two schools and nearby Temple University and Villanova, the area offers more than its share of quality higher education. Some of the city's strong traditions, such as its major-league sports teams and Philly cheesesteaks, are nationally famous. Because of its history, museums, and performing arts, the city gets a top score for arts and culture.

Philadelphia is a city of neighborhoods. South Philadelphia has a mainly immigrant, working-class population, while North Philadelphia and areas west of University Park are rough and somewhat run-down.

Some of the best older suburbs lie along the old Pennsylvania Railroad lines running to the west. These have spacious, shady neighborhoods with historic homes situated around small-town cores and railroad stations. Most of the newer growth has occurred to the northwest in placid areas such as Valley Forge, resulting in some urban sprawl that's more-attractive than comparable rapid-growth areas in other cities.

The economy is diverse. Although not known for steel production like many of its Pennsylvania neighbors, the area is a center for the chemical industry, other specialty products, and financial services. Areas of New Jersey across the Susquehanna, particularly Camden, are highly industrial. While employment has been fairly steady, except for certain pockets of manufacturing that have declined nationally, future job-growth projections are low. However, the Cost of Living Index of 105.2, which is the highest in the state, is low by regional standards, especially for an East Coast city. The crime rate is high but probably lower than most would expect. Although location within the city is important, the outstanding amenities, cost of living, and central East Coast location make Philadelphia attractive overall.

The downtown area is in a broad, flat valley. Rolling, hilly countryside stretches to the north and west. The Appalachian Mountains to the west and the Atlantic Ocean to the east moderate the otherwise continental climate. Weather is variable and extreme temperatures seldom last for more than 3 or 4 days. In summer, high humidity can add discomfort to seasonably warm temperatures, while stagnant maritime air can engulf the area. Precipitation is fairly evenly distributed throughout the year, with maximum amounts in late summer as thunderstorms. Snowfall is more abundant in the northern suburbs, while precipitation may arrive as rain rather than snow within the city. Coastal storms produce heavy snowfalls every few years.

POPULATION

DEMOGRAPHICS	AREA	U.S. AVG	ETHNIC COMPOSITION	AREA	U.S. AVG	RESIDENT PROFILE	AREA	U.S. AVG
Population	5,149,098		White	81.4%	75.1%	Single	47.5%	43.6%
Population density per sq. mile	1,335.4	447.3	Black	14.0%	12.3%	Married	52.5%	56.4%
Population growth	4.6%	16.1%	Asian	2.8%	3.6%	Divorced	6.6%	8.4%
Median age	36.8	35.5	American Indian	.2%	.9%	Separated	4.1%	3.0%
Average family size	2.6	2.7	Hispanic	4.2%	12.5%	Married with children	26.9%	28.7%
			Diversity measure	45.8%	35.2%	Single with children	9.8%	10.1%

ECONOMY & JOBS SCORE: 62/RANK: 125

INCOME	AREA	U.S. AVG	EMPLOYMENT	AREA	U.S. AVG	LARGEST EMPLOYING INDUSTRY
Per capita income	$27,811	$23,420	Unemployment rate	5.4%	6.1%	Fabricated Metal Product Manufacturing
Household income	$55,192	$46,060	Recent job growth	-.6%	.9%	
Household income < $25K	20.9%	26.4%	Projected future job growth	7.7%	15.1%	
Household income > $75K	33.7%	24.5%	White collar	62.4%	54.5%	
Household income growth	55.6%	57.3%	Blue collar	37.6%	45.5%	

COST OF LIVING SCORE: 12/RANK: 290

INDEXES & TAXES	AREA	U.S. AVG	HOUSING	AREA	U.S. AVG	NECESSITIES	AREA	U.S. AVG
Cost of Living Index	105.2	100.0	Median home price	$152,000	$160,100	Food Index	107.5	100.0
Financial Progress Index	111.8	100.0	Home price appreciation	9.3%	7.1%	Housing Index	94.4	100.0
Income tax rate	7.760%	4.625%	Median rent	$892	$670	Utilities Index	125.5	100.0
Sales tax rate	6.000%	6.474%	Homes owned	70.2%	63.9%	Transportation Index	115.8	100.0
Property tax rate	$17.5	$15.6	Homes rented	23.6%	25.3%	Healthcare Index	106.8	100.0
			Housing affordability	48.0%	54.5%	Miscellaneous Cost Index	108.0	100.0

CLIMATE SCORE: 63/RANK: 121

TEMPERATURE	AREA	U.S. AVG	PRECIPITATION	AREA	U.S. AVG	COMFORTS & HAZARDS	AREA	U.S. AVG
January low	24.4°F	26.4°F	Annual inches precipitation	40.0	35.9	July relative humidity	67.0%	68.8%
July high	86.8°F	86.7°F	Annual inches snowfall	20.0	24.2	Annual days mostly sunny	205	212
Annual days > 90°F	19	38	Annual days precipitation	116	111	Annual days with thunderstorms	27	39
Annual days < 32°F	101	88	Annual days rain > 0.5 inches	28	23	Tornado risk score	20	19
Annual days < 0°F	0	6	Annual days snow > 1.5 inches	6	6	Hurricane risk score	16	15

TEMPERATURE

PRECIPITATION

DAYS OF CLOUDS & PRECIPITATION

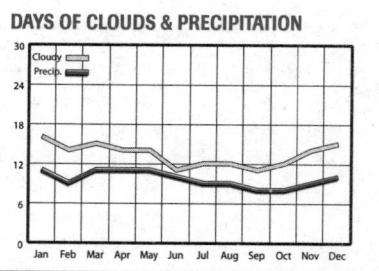

EDUCATION SCORE: 98/RANK: 6

ACHIEVEMENT	AREA	U.S. AVG	PUBLIC SCHOOLS	AREA	U.S. AVG	HIGHER EDUCATION	AREA	U.S. AVG
High school degree	82.2%	80.2%	Expenditures per pupil	$7,620	$5,894	No. 2-year colleges	21	3
2-year college degree	5.7%	6.2%	Student/teacher ratio	16.4	16.7	No. 4-year colleges/universities	41	4
4-year college degree	17.2%	15.8%	Attending public school	78.9%	90.2%	No. highly ranked universities	8	1
Graduate/professional degree	10.5%	9.6%	State SAT score	1002*	1020			
			State ACT score	21.5	21.0			

HEALTH & HEALTHCARE SCORE: 15/RANK: 279

HAZARDS & ILLNESSES	AREA	U.S. AVG	HEALTHCARE	AREA	U.S. AVG
Air-quality score	0	45	Physicians per capita	386.0	261.1
Water-quality score	13	33	Hospital beds per capita	420.4	432.2
Pollen/allergy score	66	61	No. teaching hospitals	51	4
Stress score	66	50	Cost per doctor visit	$73	$67
Cancer mortality per capita	188.6	169.0	Cost per dental visit	$77	$82
Depression days per month	3.2	2.8	Cost per daily hospital room	$1,493	$733

CRIME SCORE: 51/RANK: 162

CRIME	AREA	U.S. AVG
Violent crime rate	617.8	456.0
Change in violent crime rate	-11.3%	-17.2%
Property crime rate	3,120.9	3,950.0
Change in property crime rate	-18.3%	-16.8%

TRANSPORTATION SCORE: 93/RANK: 20

COMMUTE	AREA	U.S. AVG	INTERCITY SERVICES	AREA	U.S. AVG	AUTOMOTIVE	AREA	U.S. AVG
Average commute time	28.7 min.	22.6 min.	Miles to nearest major airport	10	46	Insurance, annual premium	$1,331	$1,011
Commute by auto	83.2%	88.7%	Type of local airport	Large		Gas, cost per gallon	$1.52	$1.50
Commute by mass transit	7.9%	1.8%	No. daily airline departures	669	294	Daily vehicle miles per capita	18.4	23.0
Work at home	2.8%	3.9%	Amtrak service	Yes				
Mass transit miles per capita	17.4	8.0	No. interstate highways	2	1			

LEISURE SCORE: 95/RANK: 14

DINING & SHOPPING	AREA	U.S. AVG	ENTERTAINMENT	AREA	U.S. AVG	OUTDOOR ACTIVITIES	AREA	U.S. AVG
Restaurant rating	8	1	Professional sports rating	10	4	Golf-course rating	10	4
No. outlet malls	7	2	College sports rating	6	4	Ski-area rating	4	4
No. Starbucks	52	11	Zoo/aquarium rating	8	3	National Park rating	3	3
No. warehouse clubs	9	4	Amusement park rating	6	3	Sq. miles inland water	5.0	4.0
			Botanical garden/arboretum rating	10	3	Miles of coastline	0.0	11.4

ARTS & CULTURE SCORE: 97/RANK: 12

MEDIA & LIBRARIES	AREA	U.S. AVG	PERFORMING ARTS	AREA	U.S. AVG	MUSEUMS	AREA	U.S. AVG
Arts radio rating	10	3	Classical music rating	10	4	Overall museum rating	10	6
No. public libraries	216	28	Ballet/dance rating	9	3	Art museum rating	10	5
Library volumes per capita	2.9	2.8	Professional theater rating	10	3	Science museum rating	9	4
			University arts programs rating	10	5	Children's museum rating	9	3

Phoenix-Mesa, AZ

Score: 40.8   Rank: 273

Profile: Regional center/Capital city
Location: South-central Arizona in a low desert valley
Elevation: 1,107 feet
Time zone: Mountain Standard Time (no daylight savings time)

PRO	CON
Pleasant winters	Intense summer heat
Entertainment	Urban sprawl
Air service	Economic cycles

Originally a resort city, Phoenix has grown phenomenally in the past 40 years into a full-scale urban center, made possible by air-conditioning. The Phoenix metropolitan area covers over 1,000 square miles. Downtown, which is fairly modest for a city its size, features a few skyscrapers, the capitol, government offices, and a few quality museums. Surrounding downtown are several large and fairly distinct suburb-cities, mostly built on a sprawling grid, in some cases separated by low hills. These include the middle-class suburbs of Peoria, Mesa, Chandler, and Glendale; upscale Scottsdale; and the college area of Tempe, home of Arizona State University.

As best exemplified by the temperature, Phoenix is a city of extremes. It has the highest average July temperature of any U.S. metropolitan area—almost 105°F. Many days are over 115°F, and temperatures exceeding 120°F occur occasionally. Even though this is "dry" heat, it is still oppressive. At 164, the area has the most days of any metropolitan

area over 90°F. In 2003, a record nighttime *low* temperature of 96°F was observed. Winters, on the other hand, are quite pleasant, with daytime highs in the 60s and 70s and only a few evenings below freezing, and no snow. It is little wonder that wealthy "snowbirds" from other parts of the country have used Phoenix as a winter hangout for years.

The low ranking is mainly the result of summer heat, the economy, air quality, and a relatively weak collection of arts and culture amenities for a city this size. The economy has been driven in part by high-tech companies relocating from California; in recent years the downturn in that industry has hurt the local economy, but this is likely to stabilize in the future. The area, trapped in a geographic bowl and dominated by long automobile trips, has the fifth poorest air quality in the United States. Agriculture and green spaces have actually elevated pollen counts to the point where Phoenix is in the worst 20% nationwide for the pollen/allergy score. Average commute times of 26 minutes are in the worst

20% nationwide and are probably worse than the data indicates due to the large number of retirees. For a large city, Phoenix has low ethnic diversity. On the plus side, Phoenix is the national hub for America West Airlines and a regional hub for Southwest, producing an abundance of air choices and reasonable fares. Major-league teams for football (Cardinals), baseball (Diamondbacks), basketball (Suns), and hockey (Coyotes) all play in the area.

Phoenix is located in the Salt River Valley, a broad, desert valley surrounded by low, desert mountains as high as the Superstition Mountains to the east at 5,000 feet. Natural vegetation is sparse to nonexistent; uncultivated freeway medians remain as plain dirt. Not surprisingly, the climate is considered arid. See above for a discussion of the area's extreme seasonal temperatures. Rain usually arrives in June as "monsoons"—tropical moisture flows from the south, which trigger large thunderstorms and raise humidity. Some Pacific storms get through mainly in March and April. Annual precipitation of 7 inches, annual rain days of 34, and annual cloud days of 70 are all among the lowest in the country.

POPULATION

DEMOGRAPHICS	AREA	U.S. AVG	ETHNIC COMPOSITION	AREA	U.S. AVG	RESIDENT PROFILE	AREA	U.S. AVG
Population	3,500,151		White	81.4%	75.1%	Single	44.8%	43.6%
Population density per sq. mile	240.2	447.3	Black	3.4%	12.3%	Married	55.2%	56.4%
Population growth	56.4%	16.1%	Asian	2.0%	3.6%	Divorced	10.3%	8.4%
Median age	33.5	35.5	American Indian	4.5%	.9%	Separated	3.1%	3.0%
Average family size	2.8	2.7	Hispanic	25.2%	12.5%	Married with children	26.6%	28.7%
			Diversity measure	49.3%	35.2%	Single with children	11.4%	10.1%

ECONOMY & JOBS — SCORE: 10/RANK: 296

INCOME	AREA	U.S. AVG	EMPLOYMENT	AREA	U.S. AVG	LARGEST EMPLOYING INDUSTRY
Per capita income	$24,777	$23,420	Unemployment rate	5.5%	6.1%	Computer and Electronic Product Manufacturing
Household income	$49,779	$46,060	Recent job growth	-.1%	.9%	
Household income < $25K	21.9%	26.4%	Projected future job growth	28.4%	15.1%	
Household income > $75K	27.8%	24.5%	White collar	60.3%	54.5%	
Household income growth	63.9%	57.3%	Blue collar	39.7%	45.5%	

COST OF LIVING — SCORE: 41/RANK: 193

INDEXES & TAXES	AREA	U.S. AVG	HOUSING	AREA	U.S. AVG	NECESSITIES	AREA	U.S. AVG
Cost of Living Index	98.7	100.0	Median home price	$145,800	$160,100	Food Index	104.3	100.0
Financial Progress Index	107.5	100.0	Home price appreciation	7.3%	7.1%	Housing Index	90.6	100.0
Income tax rate	3.900%	4.625%	Median rent	$835	$670	Utilities Index	104.5	100.0
Sales tax rate	8.100%	6.474%	Homes owned	60.2%	63.9%	Transportation Index	104.1	100.0
Property tax rate	$9.0	$15.6	Homes rented	26.3%	25.3%	Healthcare Index	117.5	100.0
			Housing affordability	51.0%	54.5%	Miscellaneous Cost Index	97.6	100.0

CLIMATE — SCORE: 90/RANK: 34

TEMPERATURE	AREA	U.S. AVG	PRECIPITATION	AREA	U.S. AVG	COMFORTS & HAZARDS	AREA	U.S. AVG
January low	37.6°F	26.4°F	Annual inches precipitation	7.0	35.9	July relative humidity	36.0%	68.8%
July high	104.8°F	86.7°F	Annual inches snowfall	0.0	24.2	Annual days mostly sunny	295	212
Annual days > 90°F	164	38	Annual days precipitation	34	111	Annual days with thunderstorms	23	39
Annual days < 32°F	32	88	Annual days rain > 0.5 inches	5	23	Tornado risk score	15	19
Annual days < 0°F	0	6	Annual days snow > 1.5 inches	0	6	Hurricane risk score	1	15

TEMPERATURE

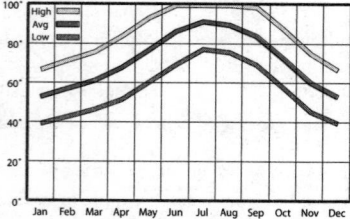

PRECIPITATION

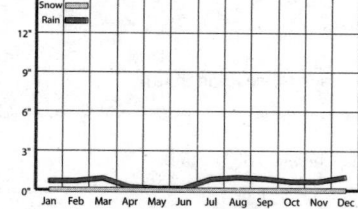

DAYS OF CLOUDS & PRECIPITATION

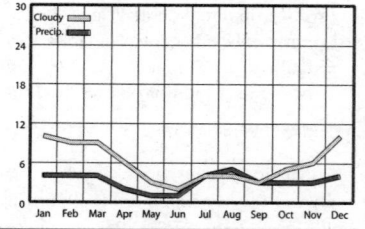

EDUCATION — SCORE: 75/RANK: 84

ACHIEVEMENT	AREA	U.S. AVG	PUBLIC SCHOOLS	AREA	U.S. AVG	HIGHER EDUCATION	AREA	U.S. AVG
High school degree	81.9%	80.2%	Expenditures per pupil	$4,500	$5,894	No. 2-year colleges	14	3
2-year college degree	7.7%	6.2%	Student/teacher ratio	19.6	16.7	No. 4-year colleges/universities	10	4
4-year college degree	16.6%	15.8%	Attending public school	94.4%	90.2%	No. highly ranked universities	1	1
Graduate/professional degree	8.5%	9.6%	State SAT score	1049*	1020			
			State ACT score	21.4	21.0			

HEALTH & HEALTHCARE — SCORE: 10/RANK: 298

HAZARDS & ILLNESSES	AREA	U.S. AVG	HEALTHCARE	AREA	U.S. AVG
Air-quality score	2	45	Physicians per capita	204.2	261.1
Water-quality score	21	33	Hospital beds per capita	242.5	432.2
Pollen/allergy score	71	61	No. teaching hospitals	13	4
Stress score	90	50	Cost per doctor visit	$67	$67
Cancer mortality per capita	161.0	169.0	Cost per dental visit	$96	$82
Depression days per month	2.6	2.8	Cost per daily hospital room	$763	$733

CRIME — SCORE: 19/RANK: 266

CRIME	AREA	U.S. AVG
Violent crime rate	566.5	456.0
Change in violent crime rate	-25.9%	-17.2%
Property crime rate	5,860.3	3,950.0
Change in property crime rate	-27.1%	-16.8%

TRANSPORTATION — SCORE: 60/RANK: 132

COMMUTE	AREA	U.S. AVG	INTERCITY SERVICES	AREA	U.S. AVG	AUTOMOTIVE	AREA	U.S. AVG
Average commute time	26.1 min.	22.6 min.	Miles to nearest major airport	16	46	Insurance, annual premium	$1,977	$1,011
Commute by auto	89.0%	88.7%	Type of local airport	Large		Gas, cost per gallon	$1.58	$1.50
Commute by mass transit	1.7%	1.8%	No. daily airline departures	691	294	Daily vehicle miles per capita	20.7	23.0
Work at home	3.6%	3.9%	Amtrak service	No				
Mass transit miles per capita	9.3	8.0	No. interstate highways	2	1			

LEISURE — SCORE: 94/RANK: 22

DINING & SHOPPING	AREA	U.S. AVG	ENTERTAINMENT	AREA	U.S. AVG	OUTDOOR ACTIVITIES	AREA	U.S. AVG
Restaurant rating	7	1	Professional sports rating	8	4	Golf-course rating	8	4
No. outlet malls	3	2	College sports rating	8	4	Ski-area rating	4	4
No. Starbucks	67	11	Zoo/aquarium rating	8	3	National Park rating	10	3
No. warehouse clubs	9	4	Amusement park rating	6	3	Sq. miles inland water	3.0	4.0
			Botanical garden/arboretum rating	7	3	Miles of coastline	0.0	11.4

ARTS & CULTURE — SCORE: 18/RANK: 269

MEDIA & LIBRARIES	AREA	U.S. AVG	PERFORMING ARTS	AREA	U.S. AVG	MUSEUMS	AREA	U.S. AVG
Arts radio rating	7	3	Classical music rating	6	4	Overall museum rating	9	6
No. public libraries	60	28	Ballet/dance rating	5	3	Art museum rating	9	5
Library volumes per capita	2.0	2.8	Professional theater rating	1	3	Science museum rating	9	4
			University arts programs rating	7	5	Children's museum rating	4	3

Pine Bluff, AR

	Score: 20.3 Rank: 325

Profile: Small industrial town
Location: Southeast, 40 miles from Little Rock, along the Arkansas River
Elevation: 219 feet
Time zone: Central Standard Time

PRO	CON
Home prices	Violent crime
Cost of living	Low educational attainment
Healthcare	High unemployment

Pine Bluff, the second oldest city in Arkansas, is a small, working-class, industrial and railroad town with some antebellum and Civil War history. Overshadowing any positive qualities is a horrendous violent crime rate, and the likely contributing factors of low educational attainment and high unemployment. The reported violent crime rate is the worst in the United States, hence the "zero" score in that category. Unemployment of 8.2% is in the worst 10% nationwide. On the positive side, housing costs are the third lowest in the country.

The area around Pine Bluff is mostly level, especially along the broad Arkansas Valley. As the name suggests, Pine Bluff is known for its large pine trees. Typical of the region, the climate is modified continental with exposure to all of North American climates. Summer has prolonged periods of warm and humid weather. Winters are mild with some cold spells. Most precipitation is in summer as thunderstorms with a dry period in late summer and fall. Snow is negligible, but the city is located in an area of relatively frequent ice storms.

POPULATION

DEMOGRAPHICS	AREA	U.S. AVG	ETHNIC COMPOSITION	AREA	U.S. AVG	RESIDENT PROFILE	AREA	U.S. AVG
Population	83,374		White	58.0%	75.1%	Single	44.2%	43.6%
Population density per sq. mile	94.2	447.3	Black	41.0%	12.3%	Married	55.8%	56.4%
Population growth	-2.5%	16.1%	Asian	.4%	3.6%	Divorced	7.6%	8.4%
Median age	35.2	35.5	American Indian	.3%	.9%	Separated	3.2%	3.0%
Average family size	2.6	2.7	Hispanic	1.8%	12.5%	Married with children	25.5%	28.7%
			Diversity measure	52.5%	35.2%	Single with children	11.7%	10.1%

ECONOMY & JOBS — SCORE: 34/RANK: 217

INCOME	AREA	U.S. AVG	EMPLOYMENT	AREA	U.S. AVG	LARGEST EMPLOYING INDUSTRY
Per capita income	$16,822	$23,420	Unemployment rate	8.2%	6.1%	Food Manufacturing
Household income	$33,714	$46,060	Recent job growth	1.1%	.9%	
Household income < $25K	39.0%	26.4%	Projected future job growth	9.3%	15.1%	
Household income > $75K	16.0%	24.5%	White collar	47.7%	54.5%	
Household income growth	57.5%	57.3%	Blue collar	52.3%	45.5%	

COST OF LIVING — SCORE: 84/RANK: 53

INDEXES & TAXES	AREA	U.S. AVG	HOUSING	AREA	U.S. AVG	NECESSITIES	AREA	U.S. AVG
Cost of Living Index	79.1	100.0	Median home price	$62,880	$160,100	Food Index	101.6	100.0
Financial Progress Index	90.8	100.0	Home price appreciation	3.0%	7.1%	Housing Index	39.1	100.0
Income tax rate	7.000%	4.625%	Median rent	$486	$670	Utilities Index	113.5	100.0
Sales tax rate	7.125%	6.474%	Homes owned	54.3%	63.9%	Transportation Index	99.2	100.0
Property tax rate	$10.2	$15.6	Homes rented	22.2%	25.3%	Healthcare Index	100.2	100.0
			Housing affordability	57.0%	54.5%	Miscellaneous Cost Index	98.9	100.0

CLIMATE — SCORE: 45/RANK: 182

TEMPERATURE	AREA	U.S. AVG	PRECIPITATION	AREA	U.S. AVG	COMFORTS & HAZARDS	AREA	U.S. AVG
January low	28.9°F	26.4°F	Annual inches precipitation	49.0	35.9	July relative humidity	70.0%	68.8%
July high	92.6°F	86.7°F	Annual inches snowfall	5.0	24.2	Annual days mostly sunny	220	212
Annual days > 90°F	70	38	Annual days precipitation	104	111	Annual days with thunderstorms	57	39
Annual days < 32°F	63	88	Annual days rain > 0.5 inches	31	23	Tornado risk score	11	19
Annual days < 0°F	0	6	Annual days snow > 1.5 inches	2	6	Hurricane risk score	10	15

TEMPERATURE

PRECIPITATION

DAYS OF CLOUDS & PRECIPITATION

EDUCATION — SCORE: 9/RANK: 301

ACHIEVEMENT	AREA	U.S. AVG	PUBLIC SCHOOLS	AREA	U.S. AVG	HIGHER EDUCATION	AREA	U.S. AVG
High school degree	73.3%	80.2%	Expenditures per pupil	$4,981	$5,894	No. 2-year colleges	0	3
2-year college degree	3.0%	6.2%	Student/teacher ratio	15.4	16.7	No. 4-year colleges/universities	1	4
4-year college degree	10.8%	15.8%	Attending public school	95.2%	90.2%	No. highly ranked universities	0	1
Graduate/professional degree	4.9%	9.6%	State SAT score	1118	1020			
			State ACT score	20.3*	21.0			

HEALTH & HEALTHCARE — SCORE: 54/RANK: 150

HAZARDS & ILLNESSES	AREA	U.S. AVG	HEALTHCARE	AREA	U.S. AVG
Air-quality score	6	45	Physicians per capita	181.1	261.1
Water-quality score	17	33	Hospital beds per capita	563.6	432.2
Pollen/allergy score	59	61	No. teaching hospitals	1	4
Stress score	60	50	Cost per doctor visit	$61	$67
Cancer mortality per capita	175.6	169.0	Cost per dental visit	$85	$82
Depression days per month	1.8	2.8	Cost per daily hospital room	$404	$733

CRIME — SCORE: 0/RANK: 331

CRIME	AREA	U.S. AVG
Violent crime rate	1,473.2	456.0
Change in violent crime rate	-11.2%	-17.2%
Property crime rate	6,725.8	3,950.0
Change in property crime rate	16.6%	-16.8%

TRANSPORTATION — SCORE: 25/RANK: 246

COMMUTE	AREA	U.S. AVG	INTERCITY SERVICES	AREA	U.S. AVG	AUTOMOTIVE	AREA	U.S. AVG
Average commute time	21.6 min.	22.6 min.	Miles to nearest major airport	38	46	Insurance, annual premium	$828	$1,011
Commute by auto	93.8%	88.7%	Type of local airport	Small		Gas, cost per gallon	$1.42	$1.50
Commute by mass transit	.3%	1.8%	No. daily airline departures	96	294	Daily vehicle miles per capita	22.3	23.0
Work at home	1.4%	3.9%	Amtrak service	No				
Mass transit miles per capita	2.9	8.0	No. interstate highways	0	1			

LEISURE — SCORE: 0/RANK: 331

DINING & SHOPPING	AREA	U.S. AVG	ENTERTAINMENT	AREA	U.S. AVG	OUTDOOR ACTIVITIES	AREA	U.S. AVG
Restaurant rating	1	1	Professional sports rating	2	4	Golf-course rating	1	4
No. outlet malls	0	2	College sports rating	1	4	Ski-area rating	1	4
No. Starbucks	0	11	Zoo/aquarium rating	1	3	National Park rating	1	3
No. warehouse clubs	1	4	Amusement park rating	1	3	Sq. miles inland water	4.0	4.0
			Botanical garden/arboretum rating	1	3	Miles of coastline	0.0	11.4

ARTS & CULTURE
SCORE: 1/RANK: 325

MEDIA & LIBRARIES	AREA	U.S. AVG	PERFORMING ARTS	AREA	U.S. AVG	MUSEUMS	AREA	U.S. AVG
Arts radio rating	1	3	Classical music rating	3	4	Overall museum rating	3	6
No. public libraries	4	28	Ballet/dance rating	1	3	Art museum rating	4	5
Library volumes per capita	1.9	2.8	Professional theater rating	1	3	Science museum rating	3	4
			University arts programs rating	3	5	Children's museum rating	1	3

Pittsburgh, PA

Score: 82.5   Rank: 28

Profile: Large city
Location: West-central Pennsylvania at the confluence of the Allegheny
  and Monongahela rivers into the Ohio River
Elevation: 760 feet
Time zone: Eastern Standard Time

PRO
Economic turnaround
Arts and culture
Cost of living

CON
Recent unemployment
Clouds and rain
Commute time

Once a rough and gritty center for the steel-making industry, Pittsburgh is now home to one lone blast furnace and a wide assortment of other industries. Remarkably, for a city of its size and location removed from major transportation routes and large cities, Pittsburgh is the headquarters of several Fortune 500 companies, including USX (once U.S. Steel, now more of an oil and gas company), Alcoa, HJ Heinz, PNC Bank, PPG Industries, Mellon Bank, Allegheny Teledyne, Consolidated Natural Gas, and Wesco. The former grime and smoke have largely blown away, leaving a livable city with historic and revitalized neighborhoods and plenty to do. Employment is shifting from blue-collar to professional jobs, although it is declining overall.

Pittsburgh is a city of neighborhoods. Steep hills rise on all sides of town; some neighborhoods can be reached by a 19th-century incline tram from the central city. The neighborhoods have unique identity and personality and the city's planning department recognizes 90 neighborhoods in all. The population is ethnically diverse. The downtown area is vibrant and active with nightlife along the river and active downtown shopping. Pittsburgh has major league teams in football (Steelers), hockey (Penguins), and baseball (Pirates). Fan support and interest, particularly for the Steelers football team, is legendary. The new Heinz Field and PNC Park are attractive, accessible sports venues.

Educational opportunities are excellent, particularly at the highest level with Duquesne and Carnegie-Mellon universities. The city has good public transportation facilities and a new light-rail system. As the major hub for US Airways, air service is good but this may change in the future. Early industrial wealth endowed the city with numerous cultural assets. The Carnegie-endowed museums, the Pittsburgh Symphony, and the zoo are all noted in their fields. At 90.0, the area has a lower Cost of Living Index than one might expect for what's available. Crime is also lower than expected given the area's gritty industrial history. It is noted as an excellent place to raise a family. The main downsides are weather and recent employment weakness.

Downtown Pittsburgh sits at the confluence of the "Three Rivers" (Allegheny, Monongahela, and Ohio), about 100 miles south of Lake Erie. Most of Pittsburgh lies in a narrow valley, with high, wooded bluffs surrounding the city. The climate is a humid continental type modified slightly by the Atlantic Seaboard and the Great Lakes. Summers are warm, still, and humid with periodic thunderstorms and occasional cooling from the northwest. Winters are cool and variable with intermittent periods of freezing and thawing. Precipitation is distributed evenly throughout the year. Cool northwest winds deliver moisture from the Great Lakes creating persistent cloudy conditions and showers, especially in winter. The area has the most cloudy days in the state, the 15th cloudiest in the country. Fog may persist in the valleys during colder months. First freeze is mid-October, last is end of April.

POPULATION

DEMOGRAPHICS	AREA	U.S. AVG	ETHNIC COMPOSITION	AREA	U.S. AVG	RESIDENT PROFILE	AREA	U.S. AVG
Population	2,346,525		White	93.8%	75.1%	Single	44.7%	43.6%
Population density per sq. mile	507.5	447.3	Black	5.3%	12.3%	Married	55.3%	56.4%
Population growth	-2.0%	16.1%	Asian	.7%	3.6%	Divorced	6.6%	8.4%
Median age	40.5	35.5	American Indian	.1%	.9%	Separated	3.1%	3.0%
Average family size	2.7	2.7	Hispanic	.7%	12.5%	Married with children	24.7%	28.7%
			Diversity measure	19.8%	35.2%	Single with children	8.3%	10.1%

ECONOMY & JOBS
SCORE: 21/RANK: 258

INCOME	AREA	U.S. AVG	EMPLOYMENT	AREA	U.S. AVG	LARGEST EMPLOYING INDUSTRY
Per capita income	$24,091	$23,420	Unemployment rate	4.9%	6.1%	Primary Metal Manufacturing
Household income	$41,809	$46,060	Recent job growth	-2.2%	.9%	
Household income < $25K	29.1%	26.4%	Projected future job growth	10.1%	15.1%	
Household income > $75K	22.2%	24.5%	White collar	57.8%	54.5%	
Household income growth	56.5%	57.3%	Blue collar	42.2%	45.5%	

COST OF LIVING SCORE: 54/RANK: 150

INDEXES & TAXES	AREA	U.S. AVG	HOUSING	AREA	U.S. AVG	NECESSITIES	AREA	U.S. AVG
Cost of Living Index	90.0	100.0	Median home price	$101,800	$160,100	Food Index	101.8	100.0
Financial Progress Index	99.0	100.0	Home price appreciation	6.3%	7.1%	Housing Index	63.2	100.0
Income tax rate	4.675%	4.625%	Median rent	$615	$670	Utilities Index	136.4	100.0
Sales tax rate	6.000%	6.474%	Homes owned	69.6%	63.9%	Transportation Index	100.4	100.0
Property tax rate	$19.9	$15.6	Homes rented	21.6%	25.3%	Healthcare Index	92.0	100.0
			Housing affordability	51.0%	54.5%	Miscellaneous Cost Index	102.0	100.0

CLIMATE SCORE: 29/RANK: 233

TEMPERATURE	AREA	U.S. AVG	PRECIPITATION	AREA	U.S. AVG	COMFORTS & HAZARDS	AREA	U.S. AVG
January low	20.8°F	26.4°F	Annual inches precipitation	36.0	35.9	July relative humidity	68.0%	68.8%
July high	82.5°F	86.7°F	Annual inches snowfall	45.0	24.2	Annual days mostly sunny	161	212
Annual days > 90°F	7	38	Annual days precipitation	152	111	Annual days with thunderstorms	36	39
Annual days < 32°F	124	88	Annual days rain > 0.5 inches	22	23	Tornado risk score	14	19
Annual days < 0°F	5	6	Annual days snow > 1.5 inches	9	6	Hurricane risk score	4	15

TEMPERATURE

PRECIPITATION

DAYS OF CLOUDS & PRECIPITATION

EDUCATION SCORE: 91/RANK: 28

ACHIEVEMENT	AREA	U.S. AVG	PUBLIC SCHOOLS	AREA	U.S. AVG	HIGHER EDUCATION	AREA	U.S. AVG
High school degree	85.1%	80.2%	Expenditures per pupil	$6,954	$5,894	No. 2-year colleges	26	3
2-year college degree	6.1%	6.2%	Student/teacher ratio	17.3	16.7	No. 4-year colleges/universities	15	4
4-year college degree	15.1%	15.8%	Attending public school	86.3%	90.2%	No. highly ranked universities	5	1
Graduate/professional degree	8.7%	9.6%	State SAT score	1002*	1020			
			State ACT score	21.5	21.0			

HEALTH & HEALTHCARE SCORE: 50/RANK: 165

CRIME SCORE: 78/RANK: 73

HAZARDS & ILLNESSES	AREA	U.S. AVG	HEALTHCARE	AREA	U.S. AVG	CRIME	AREA	U.S. AVG
Air-quality score	98	45	Physicians per capita	343.0	261.1	Violent crime rate	337.7	456.0
Water-quality score	23	33	Hospital beds per capita	530.6	432.2	Change in violent crime rate	-11.6%	-17.2%
Pollen/allergy score	73	61	No. teaching hospitals	18	4	Property crime rate	2,413.7	3,950.0
Stress score	61	50	Cost per doctor visit	$59	$67	Change in property crime rate	-10.5%	-16.8%
Cancer mortality per capita	185.2	169.0	Cost per dental visit	$60	$82			
Depression days per month	2.9	2.8	Cost per daily hospital room	$650	$733			

TRANSPORTATION SCORE: 93/RANK: 23

COMMUTE	AREA	U.S. AVG	INTERCITY SERVICES	AREA	U.S. AVG	AUTOMOTIVE	AREA	U.S. AVG
Average commute time	25.3 min.	22.6 min.	Miles to nearest major airport	13	46	Insurance, annual premium	$1,116	$1,011
Commute by auto	88.1%	88.7%	Type of local airport	Large		Gas, cost per gallon	$1.48	$1.50
Commute by mass transit	4.0%	1.8%	No. daily airline departures	663	294	Daily vehicle miles per capita	22.7	23.0
Work at home	2.5%	3.9%	Amtrak service	Yes				
Mass transit miles per capita	21.4	8.0	No. interstate highways	2	1			

LEISURE SCORE: 86/RANK: 46

DINING & SHOPPING	AREA	U.S. AVG	ENTERTAINMENT	AREA	U.S. AVG	OUTDOOR ACTIVITIES	AREA	U.S. AVG
Restaurant rating	1	1	Professional sports rating	7	4	Golf-course rating	9	4
No. outlet malls	2	2	College sports rating	6	4	Ski-area rating	5	4
No. Starbucks	29	11	Zoo/aquarium rating	8	3	National Park rating	2	3
No. warehouse clubs	4	4	Amusement park rating	6	3	Sq. miles inland water	4.0	4.0
			Botanical garden/arboretum rating	7	3	Miles of coastline	0.0	11.4

ARTS & CULTURE SCORE: 97/RANK: 9

MEDIA & LIBRARIES	AREA	U.S. AVG	PERFORMING ARTS	AREA	U.S. AVG	MUSEUMS	AREA	U.S. AVG
Arts radio rating	8	3	Classical music rating	9	4	Overall museum rating	9	6
No. public libraries	128	28	Ballet/dance rating	7	3	Art museum rating	10	5
Library volumes per capita	2.7	2.8	Professional theater rating	10	3	Science museum rating	9	4
			University arts programs rating	10	5	Children's museum rating	5	3

Pittsfield, MA

Score: 47.2   Rank: 243

Profile: Small town
Location: Extreme western Massachusetts in the Berkshires, 7 miles east of the New York border
Elevation: 1,158 feet
Time zone: Eastern Standard Time

PRO	CON
Nearby mountains	Harsh winters
Outdoor recreation	Isolation
Low crime rate	Economy

An old agricultural and minor industrial center, Pittsfield has evolved into a gateway to the Berkshires. Nearby ski resorts, particularly to the north, draw winter visitors. To the south, and not included in the area's statistics, are the Tanglewood performing arts center in Lenox and the Norman Rockwell Museum in Stockbridge. The town itself is quiet, nondescript, and fairly isolated from big-city amenities. Crime is the lowest in the state. But future projected job growth is the lowest in the state, and winters are more difficult than other Massachusetts locations.

The city is located in a relatively level section of a mostly hilly, wooded region. The surrounding mountains rise to 2,300 feet. Climate is continental with little Atlantic influence, but the area is far enough west to be affected by Lake Ontario. Summers are warm and humid with mostly pleasant evenings. Winters are variable with frequent cold snaps and heavy snows, although the mountains block some of the strongest weather. First freeze is late September, last is early May.

POPULATION

DEMOGRAPHICS	AREA	U.S. AVG	ETHNIC COMPOSITION	AREA	U.S. AVG	RESIDENT PROFILE	AREA	U.S. AVG
Population	83,584		White	97.3%	75.1%	Single	43.9%	43.6%
Population density per sq. mile	331.9	447.3	Black	1.3%	12.3%	Married	56.1%	56.4%
Population growth	-5.8%	16.1%	Asian	1.0%	3.6%	Divorced	8.1%	8.4%
Median age	41.1	35.5	American Indian	.2%	.9%	Separated	2.4%	3.0%
Average family size	2.4	2.7	Hispanic	1.3%	12.5%	Married with children	25.5%	28.7%
			Diversity measure	11.4%	35.2%	Single with children	7.9%	10.1%

ECONOMY & JOBS
SCORE: 75/RANK: 80

INCOME	AREA	U.S. AVG	EMPLOYMENT	AREA	U.S. AVG	LARGEST EMPLOYING INDUSTRY
Per capita income	$23,964	$23,420	Unemployment rate	4.9%	6.1%	Plastics and Rubber Products Manufacturing
Household income	$41,865	$46,060	Recent job growth	.3%	.9%	
Household income < $25K	29.3%	26.4%	Projected future job growth	5.4%	15.1%	
Household income > $75K	20.9%	24.5%	White collar	58.1%	54.5%	
Household income growth	34.4%	57.3%	Blue collar	41.9%	45.5%	

COST OF LIVING
SCORE: 25/RANK: 246

INDEXES & TAXES	AREA	U.S. AVG	HOUSING	AREA	U.S. AVG	NECESSITIES	AREA	U.S. AVG
Cost of Living Index	108.6	100.0	Median home price	$146,790	$160,100	Food Index	120.3	100.0
Financial Progress Index	82.1	100.0	Home price appreciation	7.9%	7.1%	Housing Index	91.2	100.0
Income tax rate	5.950%	4.625%	Median rent	$617	$670	Utilities Index	131.8	100.0
Sales tax rate	5.000%	6.474%	Homes owned	53.9%	63.9%	Transportation Index	110.0	100.0
Property tax rate	$13.4	$15.6	Homes rented	17.2%	25.3%	Healthcare Index	129.4	100.0
			Housing affordability	54.0%	54.5%	Miscellaneous Cost Index	113.3	100.0

CLIMATE
SCORE: 4/RANK: 316

TEMPERATURE	AREA	U.S. AVG	PRECIPITATION	AREA	U.S. AVG	COMFORTS & HAZARDS	AREA	U.S. AVG
January low	13.0°F	26.4°F	Annual inches precipitation	33.0	35.9	July relative humidity	70.0%	68.8%
July high	84.0°F	86.7°F	Annual inches snowfall	73.0	24.2	Annual days mostly sunny	184	212
Annual days > 90°F	10	38	Annual days precipitation	137	111	Annual days with thunderstorms	28	39
Annual days < 32°F	155	88	Annual days rain > 0.5 inches	27	23	Tornado risk score	7	19
Annual days < 0°F	16	6	Annual days snow > 1.5 inches	20	6	Hurricane risk score	13	15

TEMPERATURE

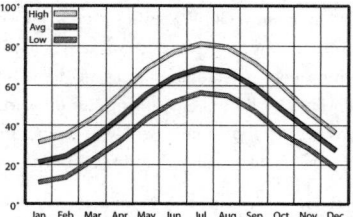

PRECIPITATION

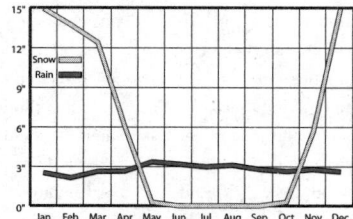

DAYS OF CLOUDS & PRECIPITATION

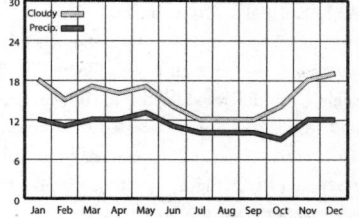

EDUCATION — SCORE: 69/RANK: 104

ACHIEVEMENT	AREA	U.S. AVG	PUBLIC SCHOOLS	AREA	U.S. AVG	HIGHER EDUCATION	AREA	U.S. AVG
High school degree	84.4%	80.2%	Expenditures per pupil	$7,600	$5,894	No. 2-year colleges	1	3
2-year college degree	8.0%	6.2%	Student/teacher ratio	16.2	16.7	No. 4-year colleges/universities	3	4
4-year college degree	15.0%	15.8%	Attending public school	86.6%	90.2%	No. highly ranked universities	2	1
Graduate/professional degree	11.0%	9.6%	State SAT score	1038*	1020			
			State ACT score	22.3	21.0			

HEALTH & HEALTHCARE — SCORE: 87/RANK: 41
CRIME — SCORE: 91/RANK: 29

HAZARDS & ILLNESSES	AREA	U.S. AVG	HEALTHCARE	AREA	U.S. AVG	CRIME	AREA	U.S. AVG
Air-quality score	6	45	Physicians per capita	524.0	261.1	Violent crime rate	231.0	456.0
Water-quality score	74	33	Hospital beds per capita	523.0	432.2	Change in violent crime rate	-26.8%	-17.2%
Pollen/allergy score	43	61	No. teaching hospitals	1	4	Property crime rate	1,909.4	3,950.0
Stress score	20	50	Cost per doctor visit	$85	$67	Change in property crime rate	-6.3%	-16.8%
Cancer mortality per capita	178.8	169.0	Cost per dental visit	$107	$82			
Depression days per month	2.4	2.8	Cost per daily hospital room	$729	$733			

TRANSPORTATION — SCORE: 72/RANK: 90

COMMUTE	AREA	U.S. AVG	INTERCITY SERVICES	AREA	U.S. AVG	AUTOMOTIVE	AREA	U.S. AVG
Average commute time	19.2 min.	22.6 min.	Miles to nearest major airport	34	46	Insurance, annual premium	$1,290	$1,011
Commute by auto	87.0%	88.7%	Type of local airport	Small		Gas, cost per gallon	$1.53	$1.50
Commute by mass transit	1.5%	1.8%	No. daily airline departures	131	294	Daily vehicle miles per capita	17.3	23.0
Work at home	5.5%	3.9%	Amtrak service	Yes				
Mass transit miles per capita	10.2	8.0	No. interstate highways	0	1			

LEISURE — SCORE: 70/RANK: 100

DINING & SHOPPING	AREA	U.S. AVG	ENTERTAINMENT	AREA	U.S. AVG	OUTDOOR ACTIVITIES	AREA	U.S. AVG
Restaurant rating	4	1	Professional sports rating	2	4	Golf-course rating	3	4
No. outlet malls	2	2	College sports rating	1	4	Ski-area rating	8	4
No. Starbucks	0	11	Zoo/aquarium rating	2	3	National Park rating	1	3
No. warehouse clubs	1	4	Amusement park rating	1	3	Sq. miles inland water	2.0	4.0
			Botanical garden/arboretum rating	3	3	Miles of coastline	0.0	11.4

ARTS & CULTURE — SCORE: 3/RANK: 319

MEDIA & LIBRARIES	AREA	U.S. AVG	PERFORMING ARTS	AREA	U.S. AVG	MUSEUMS	AREA	U.S. AVG
Arts radio rating	1	3	Classical music rating	1	4	Overall museum rating	7	6
No. public libraries	30	28	Ballet/dance rating	5	3	Art museum rating	8	5
Library volumes per capita	5.6	2.8	Professional theater rating	6	3	Science museum rating	4	4
			University arts programs rating	1	5	Children's museum rating	2	3

Pocatello, ID

Score: 39.1 Rank: 279

Profile: Small town/College town
Location: Southeastern Idaho at the upper end of the Snake River Valley
Elevation: 4,680 feet
Time zone: Mountain Standard Time

PRO	CON
Nearby outdoor recreation	Isolation
Attractive setting	Harsh climate
Low crime rate	Entertainment

Pocatello, a major transportation and education center for this part of the state, supports extensive agriculture, mainly by irrigation from the Snake River. Local Idaho State University provides some college-town flavor. But the main attractions are nearby fishing streams, the American Falls Reservoir, and Yellowstone National Park and the Grand Tetons less than 100 miles to the northeast. Unfortunately the latter two aren't close enough to be reflected in the statistics, and the rating might be understated for those willing to travel to outlying areas. By most standards, the area is isolated from urban services and amenities, but the town is self-contained enough to provide a reasonable lifestyle.

The Snake River Plain is a desert composed of sand, lava rock, and craters extending to the west. To the east the ground rises steadily toward the crests of the Continental Divide and the Grand Tetons. The climate is variable, invigorating, and by some standards harsh. Cloudy and unsettled weather prevails through the winter with measurable precipitation every 1 in 3 days, and occasional large snowfalls. Cold snaps drive temperatures below zero. Other Pacific-influenced winter periods can be mild. Spring is the wettest and windiest season. Summer evenings can be quite cool with temperatures in the 40s. Occasional summer thunderstorms and hail occur during the otherwise dry summer. Dry heat waves in July and August can drive temperatures into the 90s. Fall is the most pleasant season. First freeze is end of September, last is late May.

POPULATION

DEMOGRAPHICS	AREA	U.S. AVG	ETHNIC COMPOSITION	AREA	U.S. AVG	RESIDENT PROFILE	AREA	U.S. AVG
Population	75,804		White	94.0%	75.1%	Single	38.4%	43.6%
Population density per sq. mile	68.1	447.3	Black	.6%	12.3%	Married	61.6%	56.4%
Population growth	14.8%	16.1%	Asian	1.8%	3.6%	Divorced	7.8%	8.4%
Median age	30.0	35.5	American Indian	1.7%	.9%	Separated	1.8%	3.0%
Average family size	2.8	2.7	Hispanic	4.9%	12.5%	Married with children	32.9%	28.7%
			Diversity measure	19.7%	35.2%	Single with children	7.6%	10.1%

ECONOMY & JOBS SCORE: 93/RANK: 23

INCOME	AREA	U.S. AVG	EMPLOYMENT	AREA	U.S. AVG	LARGEST EMPLOYING INDUSTRY
Per capita income	$17,999	$23,420	Unemployment rate	5.4%	6.1%	Chemical Manufacturing
Household income	$39,862	$46,060	Recent job growth	2.1%	.9%	
Household income < $25K	30.7%	26.4%	Projected future job growth	22.1%	15.1%	
Household income > $75K	16.0%	24.5%	White collar	54.0%	54.5%	
Household income growth	51.1%	57.3%	Blue collar	46.0%	45.5%	

COST OF LIVING SCORE: 47/RANK: 172

INDEXES & TAXES	AREA	U.S. AVG	HOUSING	AREA	U.S. AVG	NECESSITIES	AREA	U.S. AVG
Cost of Living Index	85.1	100.0	Median home price	$99,830	$160,100	Food Index	98.2	100.0
Financial Progress Index	99.9	100.0	Home price appreciation	3.5%	7.1%	Housing Index	62.0	100.0
Income tax rate	8.200%	4.625%	Median rent	$499	$670	Utilities Index	87.6	100.0
Sales tax rate	5.000%	6.474%	Homes owned	60.6%	63.9%	Transportation Index	97.9	100.0
Property tax rate	$20.1	$15.6	Homes rented	24.6%	25.3%	Healthcare Index	99.9	100.0
			Housing affordability	52.0%	54.5%	Miscellaneous Cost Index	101.3	100.0

CLIMATE SCORE: 5/RANK: 314

TEMPERATURE	AREA	U.S. AVG	PRECIPITATION	AREA	U.S. AVG	COMFORTS & HAZARDS	AREA	U.S. AVG
January low	14.0°F	26.4°F	Annual inches precipitation	12.0	35.9	July relative humidity	62.0%	68.8%
July high	88.0°F	86.7°F	Annual inches snowfall	43.0	24.2	Annual days mostly sunny	205	212
Annual days > 90°F	33	38	Annual days precipitation	94	111	Annual days with thunderstorms	24	39
Annual days < 32°F	166	88	Annual days rain > 0.5 inches	4	23	Tornado risk score	6	19
Annual days < 0°F	15	6	Annual days snow > 1.5 inches	9	6	Hurricane risk score	0	15

TEMPERATURE

PRECIPITATION

DAYS OF CLOUDS & PRECIPITATION

EDUCATION SCORE: 63/RANK: 123

ACHIEVEMENT	AREA	U.S. AVG	PUBLIC SCHOOLS	AREA	U.S. AVG	HIGHER EDUCATION	AREA	U.S. AVG
High school degree	88.7%	80.2%	Expenditures per pupil	$4,588	$5,894	No. 2-year colleges	0	3
2-year college degree	7.3%	6.2%	Student/teacher ratio	19.0	16.7	No. 4-year colleges/universities	1	4
4-year college degree	16.4%	15.8%	Attending public school	95.4%	90.2%	No. highly ranked universities	0	1
Graduate/professional degree	8.5%	9.6%	State SAT score	1080	1020			
			State ACT score	21.2*	21.0			

HEALTH & HEALTHCARE SCORE: 60/RANK: 128

CRIME SCORE: 86/RANK: 46

HAZARDS & ILLNESSES	AREA	U.S. AVG	HEALTHCARE	AREA	U.S. AVG	CRIME	AREA	U.S. AVG
Air-quality score	24	45	Physicians per capita	212.4	261.1	Violent crime rate	328.0	456.0
Water-quality score	26	33	Hospital beds per capita	584.9	432.2	Change in violent crime rate	-30.1%	-17.2%
Pollen/allergy score	56	61	No. teaching hospitals	2	4	Property crime rate	3,004.7	3,950.0
Stress score	29	50	Cost per doctor visit	$49	$67	Change in property crime rate	-35.2%	-16.8%
Cancer mortality per capita	141.0	169.0	Cost per dental visit	$80	$82			
Depression days per month	3.0	2.8	Cost per daily hospital room	$478	$733			

TRANSPORTATION SCORE: 77/RANK: 76

COMMUTE	AREA	U.S. AVG	INTERCITY SERVICES	AREA	U.S. AVG	AUTOMOTIVE	AREA	U.S. AVG
Average commute time	17.2 min.	22.6 min.	Miles to nearest major airport	147	46	Insurance, annual premium	$682	$1,011
Commute by auto	86.4%	88.7%	Type of local airport	Large		Gas, cost per gallon	$1.53	$1.50
Commute by mass transit	.9%	1.8%	No. daily airline departures	452	294	Daily vehicle miles per capita	18.5	23.0
Work at home	4.2%	3.9%	Amtrak service	No				
Mass transit miles per capita	4.9	8.0	No. interstate highways	1	1			

LEISURE
SCORE: 0/RANK: 327

DINING & SHOPPING	AREA	U.S. AVG	ENTERTAINMENT	AREA	U.S. AVG	OUTDOOR ACTIVITIES	AREA	U.S. AVG
Restaurant rating	1	1	Professional sports rating	2	4	Golf-course rating	1	4
No. outlet malls	0	2	College sports rating	2	4	Ski-area rating	10	4
No. Starbucks	0	11	Zoo/aquarium rating	1	3	National Park rating	3	3
No. warehouse clubs	1	4	Amusement park rating	1	3	Sq. miles inland water	2.0	4.0
			Botanical garden/arboretum rating	1	3	Miles of coastline	0.0	11.4

ARTS & CULTURE
SCORE: 14/RANK: 282

MEDIA & LIBRARIES	AREA	U.S. AVG	PERFORMING ARTS	AREA	U.S. AVG	MUSEUMS	AREA	U.S. AVG
Arts radio rating	1	3	Classical music rating	1	4	Overall museum rating	3	6
No. public libraries	4	28	Ballet/dance rating	1	3	Art museum rating	1	5
Library volumes per capita	2.7	2.8	Professional theater rating	1	3	Science museum rating	3	4
			University arts programs rating	4	5	Children's museum rating	1	3

Portland, ME

Score: 48.7   Rank: 236

Profile: Small coastal city
Location: Southern Maine on the Atlantic Coast at Casco Bay
Elevation: 63 feet
Time zone: Eastern Standard Time

PRO
Attractive setting
Historic downtown
Educated population

CON
Harsh winters
Home prices
Low ethnic diversity

Portland is Maine's largest city and cultural center. It is a New England classic, with shipping, commercial fishing, and a quaint historic core know as the Old Port. Today that area is an active commercial and entertainment district, with some excellent seafood restaurants. The entire city has a slow pace and small-town, New England feel. The area has a highly educated population and professional workforce, with low unemployment and low crime. There are plenty of outdoor activities for all seasons. Portland would rate much higher if it weren't for the harsh New England winters and a high cost of living. The city is a good place to live for those tolerant of those issues.

The coastline around Portland is rugged and attractive. The surrounding country is mostly open and rolling. The 44-square-mile Sebago Lake is 15 miles to the northwest and the White Mountains are 45 miles beyond that. Portland has pleasant summers and falls, cold winters with frequent thaws, and disagreeable springs. Summer nights are cool and comfortable for sleeping. Autumn has the greatest number of sunny days and the least cloudiness. Winters are quite severe but begin late and then extend deep into the normal springtime. Temperatures well below zero are recorded frequently each winter. Cold waves sometimes come with strong winds, but extremely low temperatures generally come with light winds. The White Mountains block some snow and cold from the northwest. True blizzards are rare. Climate inland from the city is more extreme, as much as 10° to 15° cooler just a few miles inland. First freeze is late September, last is mid-May.

POPULATION

DEMOGRAPHICS	AREA	U.S. AVG	ETHNIC COMPOSITION	AREA	U.S. AVG	RESIDENT PROFILE	AREA	U.S. AVG
Population	247,395		White	98.4%	75.1%	Single	42.3%	43.6%
Population density per sq. mile	395.0	447.3	Black	.4%	12.3%	Married	57.7%	56.4%
Population growth	11.9%	16.1%	Asian	.8%	3.6%	Divorced	9.5%	8.4%
Median age	38.0	35.5	American Indian	.2%	.9%	Separated	1.9%	3.0%
Average family size	2.5	2.7	Hispanic	.5%	12.5%	Married with children	27.6%	28.7%
			Diversity measure	7.7%	35.2%	Single with children	8.7%	10.1%

ECONOMY & JOBS
SCORE: 66/RANK: 109

INCOME	AREA	U.S. AVG	EMPLOYMENT	AREA	U.S. AVG	LARGEST EMPLOYING INDUSTRY
Per capita income	$28,666	$23,420	Unemployment rate	2.5%	6.1%	Healthcare and Social Assistance
Household income	$52,418	$46,060	Recent job growth	-.0%	.9%	
Household income < $25K	20.0%	26.4%	Projected future job growth	14.0%	15.1%	
Household income > $75K	28.8%	24.5%	White collar	60.8%	54.5%	
Household income growth	60.3%	57.3%	Blue collar	39.2%	45.5%	

COST OF LIVING
SCORE: 13/RANK: 285

INDEXES & TAXES	AREA	U.S. AVG	HOUSING	AREA	U.S. AVG	NECESSITIES	AREA	U.S. AVG
Cost of Living Index	112.4	100.0	Median home price	$188,800	$160,100	Food Index	100.1	100.0
Financial Progress Index	99.4	100.0	Home price appreciation	11.8%	7.1%	Housing Index	117.3	100.0
Income tax rate	8.500%	4.625%	Median rent	$859	$670	Utilities Index	151.4	100.0
Sales tax rate	5.000%	6.474%	Homes owned	57.3%	63.9%	Transportation Index	107.6	100.0
Property tax rate	$20.4	$15.6	Homes rented	16.7%	25.3%	Healthcare Index	106.3	100.0
			Housing affordability	43.0%	54.5%	Miscellaneous Cost Index	103.8	100.0

CLIMATE SCORE: 0/RANK: 328

TEMPERATURE	AREA	U.S. AVG	PRECIPITATION	AREA	U.S. AVG	COMFORTS & HAZARDS	AREA	U.S. AVG
January low	11.7°F	26.4°F	Annual inches precipitation	41.0	35.9	July relative humidity	74.0%	68.8%
July high	79.1°F	86.7°F	Annual inches snowfall	74.0	24.2	Annual days mostly sunny	205	212
Annual days > 90°F	5	38	Annual days precipitation	127	111	Annual days with thunderstorms	18	39
Annual days < 32°F	160	88	Annual days rain > 0.5 inches	29	23	Tornado risk score	0	19
Annual days < 0°F	15	6	Annual days snow > 1.5 inches	15	6	Hurricane risk score	16	15

TEMPERATURE

PRECIPITATION

DAYS OF CLOUDS & PRECIPITATION

EDUCATION SCORE: 95/RANK: 16

ACHIEVEMENT	AREA	U.S. AVG	PUBLIC SCHOOLS	AREA	U.S. AVG	HIGHER EDUCATION	AREA	U.S. AVG
High school degree	90.1%	80.2%	Expenditures per pupil	$6,842	$5,894	No. 2-year colleges	3	3
2-year college degree	8.2%	6.2%	Student/teacher ratio	14.9	16.7	No. 4-year colleges/universities	4	4
4-year college degree	21.7%	15.8%	Attending public school	91.6%	90.2%	No. highly ranked universities	1	1
Graduate/professional degree	12.5%	9.6%	State SAT score	1004*	1020			
			State ACT score	22.5	21.0			

HEALTH & HEALTHCARE SCORE: 77/RANK: 73

CRIME SCORE: 97/RANK: 10

HAZARDS & ILLNESSES	AREA	U.S. AVG	HEALTHCARE	AREA	U.S. AVG	CRIME	AREA	U.S. AVG
Air-quality score	81	45	Physicians per capita	534.8	261.1	Violent crime rate	149.9	456.0
Water-quality score	100	33	Hospital beds per capita	368.7	432.2	Change in violent crime rate	-44.9%	-17.2%
Pollen/allergy score	51	61	No. teaching hospitals	3	4	Property crime rate	2,851.4	3,950.0
Stress score	21	50	Cost per doctor visit	$71	$67	Change in property crime rate	-37.5%	-16.8%
Cancer mortality per capita	185.3	169.0	Cost per dental visit	$0	$82			
Depression days per month	2.2	2.8	Cost per daily hospital room	$675	$733			

TRANSPORTATION SCORE: 41/RANK: 193

COMMUTE	AREA	U.S. AVG	INTERCITY SERVICES	AREA	U.S. AVG	AUTOMOTIVE	AREA	U.S. AVG
Average commute time	22.0 min.	22.6 min.	Miles to nearest major airport	6	46	Insurance, annual premium	$732	$1,011
Commute by auto	84.6%	88.7%	Type of local airport	Small		Gas, cost per gallon	$1.53	$1.50
Commute by mass transit	4.6%	1.8%	No. daily airline departures	73	294	Daily vehicle miles per capita	12.1	23.0
Work at home	4.4%	3.9%	Amtrak service	Yes				
Mass transit miles per capita	6.2	8.0	No. interstate highways	1	1			

LEISURE SCORE: 60/RANK: 132

DINING & SHOPPING	AREA	U.S. AVG	ENTERTAINMENT	AREA	U.S. AVG	OUTDOOR ACTIVITIES	AREA	U.S. AVG
Restaurant rating	1	1	Professional sports rating	3	4	Golf-course rating	3	4
No. outlet malls	4	2	College sports rating	4	4	Ski-area rating	7	4
No. Starbucks	6	11	Zoo/aquarium rating	1	3	National Park rating	2	3
No. warehouse clubs	4	4	Amusement park rating	4	3	Sq. miles inland water	7.0	4.0
			Botanical garden/arboretum rating	1	3	Miles of coastline	35.7	11.4

ARTS & CULTURE SCORE: 64/RANK: 117

MEDIA & LIBRARIES	AREA	U.S. AVG	PERFORMING ARTS	AREA	U.S. AVG	MUSEUMS	AREA	U.S. AVG
Arts radio rating	1	3	Classical music rating	4	4	Overall museum rating	7	6
No. public libraries	41	28	Ballet/dance rating	1	3	Art museum rating	6	5
Library volumes per capita	4.1	2.8	Professional theater rating	6	3	Science museum rating	2	4
			University arts programs rating	4	5	Children's museum rating	5	3

Portland-Vancouver, OR-WA

Score: 88.2   Rank: 12

Profile: Large-city complex
Location: Northwest Oregon along the Columbia River and
Oregon-Washington border
Elevation: 39 feet
Time zone: Pacific Standard Time

PRO	CON
Attractive downtown	Recent unemployment
Arts and culture	Cost of living
Nearby recreation	Clouds and rain

Founded in 1845 as a trading center at the junction of the Willamette and Columbia rivers, Portland grew during local gold rushes. The Greater Portland area includes Vancouver, Washington, and surrounding communities across the Columbia River. Once heavily dependent on the forest products industry, the economy has diversified and now includes a strong high-tech presence, earning Portland the nickname "Silicon Forest." Today the work force is slanted toward executive and professional positions. Job growth has slowed, as forest products and high-tech industries remain weak. However, Portland is a desirable place for business, and projected future job growth is high at 26.6%.

Although high on a national scale, cost of living is moderate among West Coast cities. The area has strong cultural amenities and a highly educated population for a big city. The downtown area is alive and full of restaurants, department stores, and museums, with noteworthy cleanliness and historic preservation. There are many neighborhoods with particularly well-preserved older housing. Although average commute times are long, the area has good public transit with a light-rail system among the nation's best. Excellent intercity rail service is also present.

With no Washington income tax and no Oregon sales tax, many residents choose to live in Vancouver and work and shop in Portland. Recreation and outdoor activities abound at the coast, 60 miles west, and the Oregon Cascades and Mount Hood ski area, 50 miles east. The Columbia River is well known for watersports, especially windsurfing. Aside from the short-term economy and wet weather, the city has a lot to offer for all lifestyles and interests.

Portland is situated midway between a low coastal range to the west and the higher Cascade range to the east, each starting their rise about 30 miles from the city. Both ranges are visible from the city. The natural landscape is heavily forested with large, coniferous trees. The climate is marine with a strong winter rainfall pattern. Almost 90% of annual precipitation occurs October through May. July and August are almost completely dry. There are only 5 days each year with measurable snow. The winter season is characterized by relatively mild temperatures, cloudy skies, and rain. Occasional cold spells with snow and freezing rain can occur when continental air invades. Summer produces pleasantly mild temperatures, northwesterly winds, and very little precipitation. First freeze is early November, last is early May.

POPULATION

DEMOGRAPHICS	AREA	U.S. AVG	ETHNIC COMPOSITION	AREA	U.S. AVG	RESIDENT PROFILE	AREA	U.S. AVG
Population	2,006,308		White	91.3%	75.1%	Single	44.3%	43.6%
Population density per sq. mile	399.1	447.3	Black	2.7%	12.3%	Married	55.7%	56.4%
Population growth	32.4%	16.1%	Asian	3.6%	3.6%	Divorced	11.2%	8.4%
Median age	35.0	35.5	American Indian	1.2%	.9%	Separated	2.9%	3.0%
Average family size	2.6	2.7	Hispanic	5.7%	12.5%	Married with children	27.1%	28.7%
			Diversity measure	31.5%	35.2%	Single with children	10.1%	10.1%

ECONOMY & JOBS   SCORE: 1/RANK: 325

INCOME	AREA	U.S. AVG	EMPLOYMENT	AREA	U.S. AVG	LARGEST EMPLOYING INDUSTRY
Per capita income	$27,307	$23,420	Unemployment rate	8.1%	6.1%	Computer and Electronic Product Manufacturing
Household income	$54,290	$46,060	Recent job growth	-1.4%	.9%	
Household income < $25K	19.0%	26.4%	Projected future job growth	26.6%	15.1%	
Household income > $75K	30.7%	24.5%	White collar	56.7%	54.5%	
Household income growth	74.8%	57.3%	Blue collar	43.3%	45.5%	

COST OF LIVING   SCORE: 20/RANK: 264

INDEXES & TAXES	AREA	U.S. AVG	HOUSING	AREA	U.S. AVG	NECESSITIES	AREA	U.S. AVG
Cost of Living Index	109.7	100.0	Median home price	$195,530	$160,100	Food Index	100.4	100.0
Financial Progress Index	105.5	100.0	Home price appreciation	4.8%	7.1%	Housing Index	121.4	100.0
Income tax rate	9.000%	4.625%	Median rent	$795	$670	Utilities Index	79.0	100.0
Sales tax rate	0.000%	6.474%	Homes owned	64.5%	63.9%	Transportation Index	110.7	100.0
Property tax rate	$14.8	$15.6	Homes rented	29.9%	25.3%	Healthcare Index	123.9	100.0
			Housing affordability	57.0%	54.5%	Miscellaneous Cost Index	104.5	100.0

CLIMATE   SCORE: 77/RANK: 74

TEMPERATURE	AREA	U.S. AVG	PRECIPITATION	AREA	U.S. AVG	COMFORTS & HAZARDS	AREA	U.S. AVG
January low	32.5°F	26.4°F	Annual inches precipitation	38.0	35.9	July relative humidity	74.0%	68.8%
July high	79.0°F	86.7°F	Annual inches snowfall	7.0	24.2	Annual days mostly sunny	137	212
Annual days > 90°F	8	38	Annual days precipitation	152	111	Annual days with thunderstorms	7	39
Annual days < 32°F	44	88	Annual days rain > 0.5 inches	23	23	Tornado risk score	3	19
Annual days < 0°F	0	6	Annual days snow > 1.5 inches	1	6	Hurricane risk score	0	15

TEMPERATURE   PRECIPITATION   DAYS OF CLOUDS & PRECIPITATION

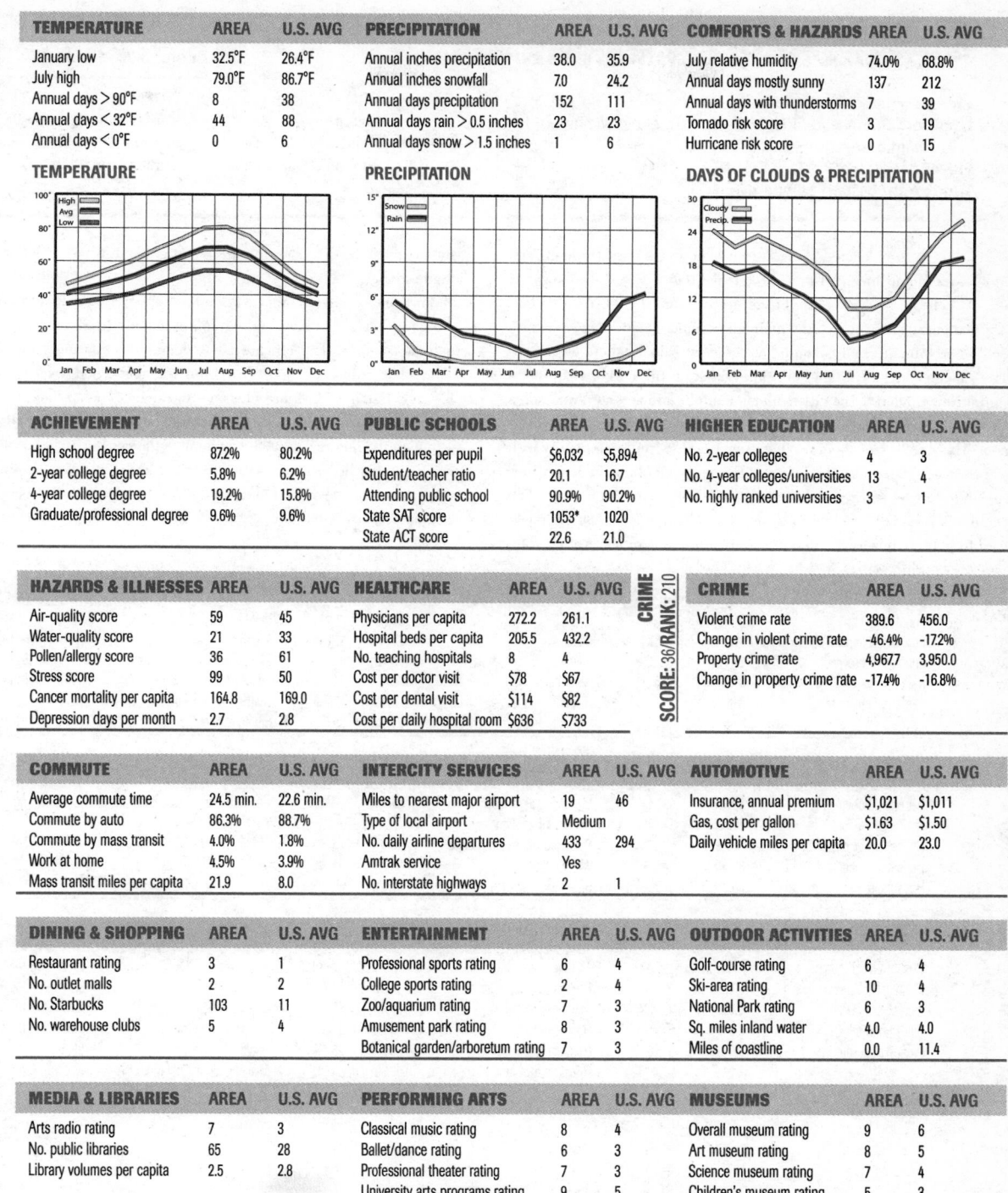

EDUCATION   SCORE: 85/RANK: 49

ACHIEVEMENT	AREA	U.S. AVG	PUBLIC SCHOOLS	AREA	U.S. AVG	HIGHER EDUCATION	AREA	U.S. AVG
High school degree	87.2%	80.2%	Expenditures per pupil	$6,032	$5,894	No. 2-year colleges	4	3
2-year college degree	5.8%	6.2%	Student/teacher ratio	20.1	16.7	No. 4-year colleges/universities	13	4
4-year college degree	19.2%	15.8%	Attending public school	90.9%	90.2%	No. highly ranked universities	3	1
Graduate/professional degree	9.6%	9.6%	State SAT score	1053*	1020			
			State ACT score	22.6	21.0			

HEALTH & HEALTHCARE   SCORE: 72/RANK: 92   **CRIME**   SCORE: 36/RANK: 210

HAZARDS & ILLNESSES	AREA	U.S. AVG	HEALTHCARE	AREA	U.S. AVG	CRIME	AREA	U.S. AVG
Air-quality score	59	45	Physicians per capita	272.2	261.1	Violent crime rate	389.6	456.0
Water-quality score	21	33	Hospital beds per capita	205.5	432.2	Change in violent crime rate	-46.4%	-17.2%
Pollen/allergy score	36	61	No. teaching hospitals	8	4	Property crime rate	4,967.7	3,950.0
Stress score	99	50	Cost per doctor visit	$78	$67	Change in property crime rate	-17.4%	-16.8%
Cancer mortality per capita	164.8	169.0	Cost per dental visit	$114	$82			
Depression days per month	2.7	2.8	Cost per daily hospital room	$636	$733			

TRANSPORTATION   SCORE: 84/RANK: 51

COMMUTE	AREA	U.S. AVG	INTERCITY SERVICES	AREA	U.S. AVG	AUTOMOTIVE	AREA	U.S. AVG
Average commute time	24.5 min.	22.6 min.	Miles to nearest major airport	19	46	Insurance, annual premium	$1,021	$1,011
Commute by auto	86.3%	88.7%	Type of local airport	Medium		Gas, cost per gallon	$1.63	$1.50
Commute by mass transit	4.0%	1.8%	No. daily airline departures	433	294	Daily vehicle miles per capita	20.0	23.0
Work at home	4.5%	3.9%	Amtrak service	Yes				
Mass transit miles per capita	21.9	8.0	No. interstate highways	2	1			

LEISURE   SCORE: 82/RANK: 57

DINING & SHOPPING	AREA	U.S. AVG	ENTERTAINMENT	AREA	U.S. AVG	OUTDOOR ACTIVITIES	AREA	U.S. AVG
Restaurant rating	3	1	Professional sports rating	6	4	Golf-course rating	6	4
No. outlet malls	2	2	College sports rating	2	4	Ski-area rating	10	4
No. Starbucks	103	11	Zoo/aquarium rating	7	3	National Park rating	6	3
No. warehouse clubs	5	4	Amusement park rating	8	3	Sq. miles inland water	4.0	4.0
			Botanical garden/arboretum rating	7	3	Miles of coastline	0.0	11.4

ARTS & CULTURE   SCORE: 89/RANK: 35

MEDIA & LIBRARIES	AREA	U.S. AVG	PERFORMING ARTS	AREA	U.S. AVG	MUSEUMS	AREA	U.S. AVG
Arts radio rating	7	3	Classical music rating	8	4	Overall museum rating	9	6
No. public libraries	65	28	Ballet/dance rating	6	3	Art museum rating	8	5
Library volumes per capita	2.5	2.8	Professional theater rating	7	3	Science museum rating	7	4
			University arts programs rating	9	5	Children's museum rating	5	3

Portsmouth-Rochester, NH-ME

Score: 37.8 **Rank:** 287

Profile: Small-city complex
Location: Southeastern New Hampshire along Maine border, adjacent to Atlantic Coast
Elevation: 63 feet
Time zone: Eastern Standard Time

PRO	CON
Historic interest	Winter climate
Nearby coastline	Isolation
Educated population	Entertainment

Portsmouth is located along the Piscataqua River just inland from New Hampshire's 13-mile stretch of Atlantic Coast. The towns of Rochester and Dover lie farther upriver and inland. With its history as a port center for wealthy merchant seamen, evident in some residential architecture, Portsmouth has the most New England feel of the state's major cities. The Market Square area on the harbor is quintessential New England. The city is a major shipbuilding center, with some additional economic diversity attracted by the favorable tax environment. The area boasts of being a tech savvy and "wired" community with over 85% of residents on the Internet. Downsides include the harsh New England climate, some run-down industrial areas, and little to do. The location is just far enough from Boston (70 miles) to be statistically isolated from big-city services and arts and culture amenities. All together,

the area may be better for those tolerant of harsh winters than the ranking indicates.

Portsmouth sits in a coastal tidewater area just inland from the Atlantic Coast. The surrounding area is mainly level and covered with deciduous trees. The climate is predominantly marine. Summers are rarely hot unless offshore flow from the north and west blocks sea breezes. Summer days are pleasant and nights cool. Winters are cold, cloudy, and wet, with occasional blasts of cold air from the north, although the marine influence moderates the coldest air. Coastal "noreaster" storms bring heavy snow in winter and periods of heavy rain at other times of the year. Fall is crisp and pleasant. First freeze is late September, last is late May.

POPULATION

DEMOGRAPHICS	AREA	U.S. AVG	ETHNIC COMPOSITION	AREA	U.S. AVG	RESIDENT PROFILE	AREA	U.S. AVG
Population	249,200		White	97.9%	75.1%	Single	40.6%	43.6%
Population density per sq. mile	397.0	447.3	Black	.6%	12.3%	Married	59.4%	56.4%
Population growth	11.6%	16.1%	Asian	1.1%	3.6%	Divorced	8.5%	8.4%
Median age	36.5	35.5	American Indian	.2%	.9%	Separated	2.1%	3.0%
Average family size	2.6	2.7	Hispanic	.9%	12.5%	Married with children	29.2%	28.7%
			Diversity measure	7.1%	35.2%	Single with children	7.5%	10.1%

ECONOMY & JOBS SCORE: 63/RANK: 120

INCOME	AREA	U.S. AVG	EMPLOYMENT	AREA	U.S. AVG	LARGEST EMPLOYING INDUSTRY
Per capita income	$26,650	$23,420	Unemployment rate	3.9%	6.1%	Computer and Electronic Product Manufacturing
Household income	$55,855	$46,060	Recent job growth	.5%	.9%	
Household income < $25K	17.9%	26.4%	Projected future job growth	18.2%	15.1%	
Household income > $75K	30.4%	24.5%	White collar	57.7%	54.5%	
Household income growth	58.3%	57.3%	Blue collar	42.3%	45.5%	

COST OF LIVING SCORE: 28/RANK: 236

INDEXES & TAXES	AREA	U.S. AVG	HOUSING	AREA	U.S. AVG	NECESSITIES	AREA	U.S. AVG
Cost of Living Index	127.5	100.0	Median home price	$254,130	$160,100	Food Index	101.1	100.0
Financial Progress Index	93.3	100.0	Home price appreciation	14.3%	7.1%	Housing Index	157.8	100.0
Income tax rate	0.000%	4.625%	Median rent	$930	$670	Utilities Index	149.3	100.0
Sales tax rate	0.000%	6.474%	Homes owned	63.7%	63.9%	Transportation Index	108.0	100.0
Property tax rate	$25.3	$15.6	Homes rented	20.2%	25.3%	Healthcare Index	109.7	100.0
			Housing affordability	50.0%	54.5%	Miscellaneous Cost Index	105.2	100.0

CLIMATE SCORE: 0/RANK: 329

TEMPERATURE	AREA	U.S. AVG	PRECIPITATION	AREA	U.S. AVG	COMFORTS & HAZARDS	AREA	U.S. AVG
January low	11.7°F	26.4°F	Annual inches precipitation	41.0	35.9	July relative humidity	74.0%	68.8%
July high	79.1°F	86.7°F	Annual inches snowfall	74.0	24.2	Annual days mostly sunny	205	212
Annual days > 90°F	5	38	Annual days precipitation	127	111	Annual days with thunderstorms	18	39
Annual days < 32°F	160	88	Annual days rain > 0.5 inches	26	23	Tornado risk score	3	19
Annual days < 0°F	15	6	Annual days snow > 1.5 inches	15	6	Hurricane risk score	16	15

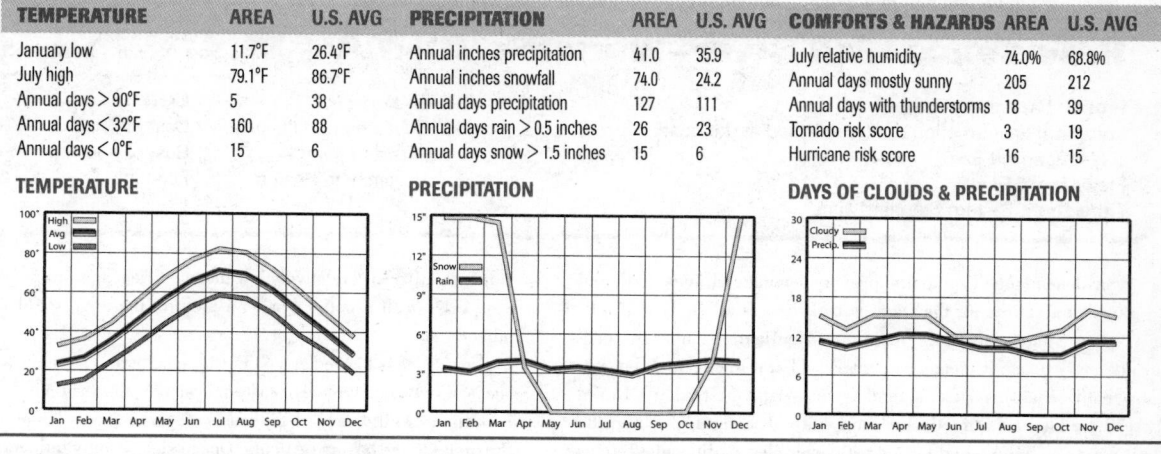

TEMPERATURE   PRECIPITATION   DAYS OF CLOUDS & PRECIPITATION

EDUCATION SCORE: 70/RANK: 101

ACHIEVEMENT	AREA	U.S. AVG	PUBLIC SCHOOLS	AREA	U.S. AVG	HIGHER EDUCATION	AREA	U.S. AVG
High school degree	88.1%	80.2%	Expenditures per pupil	$6,247	$5,894	No. 2-year colleges	2	3
2-year college degree	9.1%	6.2%	Student/teacher ratio	15.3	16.7	No. 4-year colleges/universities	1	4
4-year college degree	18.3%	15.8%	Attending public school	85.4%	90.2%	No. highly ranked universities	0	1
Graduate/professional degree	9.6%	9.6%	State SAT score	1043*	1020			
			State ACT score	22.2	21.0			

HEALTH & HEALTHCARE SCORE: 19/RANK: 267

HAZARDS & ILLNESSES	AREA	U.S. AVG	HEALTHCARE	AREA	U.S. AVG
Air-quality score	74	45	Physicians per capita	263.6	261.1
Water-quality score	63	33	Hospital beds per capita	243.9	432.2
Pollen/allergy score	53	61	No. teaching hospitals	0	4
Stress score	23	50	Cost per doctor visit	$68	$67
Cancer mortality per capita	186.1	169.0	Cost per dental visit	$0	$82
Depression days per month	2.9	2.8	Cost per daily hospital room	$694	$733

CRIME SCORE: 92/RANK: 27

CRIME	AREA	U.S. AVG
Violent crime rate	146.0	456.0
Change in violent crime rate	23.3%	-17.2%
Property crime rate	2,057.4	3,950.0
Change in property crime rate	-23.1%	-16.8%

TRANSPORTATION SCORE: 0/RANK: 331

COMMUTE	AREA	U.S. AVG	INTERCITY SERVICES	AREA	U.S. AVG	AUTOMOTIVE	AREA	U.S. AVG
Average commute time	26.8 min.	22.6 min.	Miles to nearest major airport	33	46	Insurance, annual premium	$908	$1,011
Commute by auto	89.2%	88.7%	Type of local airport	Small		Gas, cost per gallon	$1.48	$1.50
Commute by mass transit	.7%	1.8%	No. daily airline departures	94	294	Daily vehicle miles per capita	25.6	23.0
Work at home	5.5%	3.9%	Amtrak service	Yes				
Mass transit miles per capita	0.0	8.0	No. interstate highways	1	1			

LEISURE SCORE: 70/RANK: 98

DINING & SHOPPING	AREA	U.S. AVG	ENTERTAINMENT	AREA	U.S. AVG	OUTDOOR ACTIVITIES	AREA	U.S. AVG
Restaurant rating	1	1	Professional sports rating	8	4	Golf-course rating	4	4
No. outlet malls	5	2	College sports rating	4	4	Ski-area rating	7	4
No. Starbucks	2	11	Zoo/aquarium rating	4	3	National Park rating	2	3
No. warehouse clubs	3	4	Amusement park rating	5	3	Sq. miles inland water	5.0	4.0
			Botanical garden/arboretum rating	5	3	Miles of coastline	26.2	11.4

ARTS & CULTURE SCORE: 28/RANK: 236

MEDIA & LIBRARIES	AREA	U.S. AVG	PERFORMING ARTS	AREA	U.S. AVG	MUSEUMS	AREA	U.S. AVG
Arts radio rating	4	3	Classical music rating	5	4	Overall museum rating	8	6
No. public libraries	37	28	Ballet/dance rating	5	3	Art museum rating	5	5
Library volumes per capita	4.1	2.8	Professional theater rating	5	3	Science museum rating	4	4
			University arts programs rating	4	5	Children's museum rating	6	3

Providence–Fall River–Warwick, RI-MA

Score: 56.5 **Rank:** 173

Profile: Capital-city complex
Location: Eastern edge of Rhode Island at the head of Narragansett Bay
Elevation: 51 feet
Time zone: Eastern Standard Time

PRO
Educated population
Arts and culture
Proximity to Boston

CON
Cost of living
Cost of housing
Economy

Providence is the capital and primary commercial, industrial, and residential area for the state. Established as an enclave of religious tolerance and resident American rights in pre-Revolutionary times, it remains a center of liberal intellectual thought. It also retains a laid-back character despite its capital-city status. Brown University adds to the intellectual and cultural landscape. While the city is strong on culture and loaded with amenities, additional offerings and services are in Boston, 50 miles to the north. Warwick is a separate city to the south, while Fall River is an old textile town located just across the Massachusetts border. Both towns are closely tied to Providence. Water recreation is available in Narragansett Bay and Newport, a historic seaport and old-wealth enclave to the south. The area is conveniently located near other East Coast cities. Cost of living and particularly housing and real estate taxes are high, although residential areas are physically attractive and interesting. Statistically, the economy

is unattractive with relatively low income levels and future employment prospects. With a better financial picture, the area would rank much higher.

Providence is located at a point where numerous streams flow into the Narragansett Bay. Typical of eastern lowlands, the terrain is flat to slightly rolling, with heavy deciduous tree cover away from the water. Proximity to the bay and Atlantic Ocean significantly influences the climate, in part by moderating winter temperatures and snowfall. Snow cover does not remain for long periods. In summer, refreshing sea breezes often cool the otherwise uncomfortable days. At other times of year, fog occurs frequently. Measurable precipitation occurs about 1 day in 3 and is evenly distributed throughout the year. Most summer rainfall comes as thunderstorms. Late summer and fall tropical storms can hit, and the area is prone to coastal "noreaster" storms year-round. First freeze is late October, last is mid-April.

POPULATION

DEMOGRAPHICS	AREA	U.S. AVG	ETHNIC COMPOSITION	AREA	U.S. AVG	RESIDENT PROFILE	AREA	U.S. AVG
Population	1,213,264		White	92.0%	75.1%	Single	47.0%	43.6%
Population density per sq. mile	1,063.1	447.3	Black	3.2%	12.3%	Married	53.0%	56.4%
Population growth	7.0%	16.1%	Asian	2.7%	3.6%	Divorced	7.3%	8.4%
Median age	37.0	35.5	American Indian	.4%	.9%	Separated	2.3%	3.0%
Average family size	2.6	2.7	Hispanic	4.3%	12.5%	Married with children	27.0%	28.7%
			Diversity measure	27.0%	35.2%	Single with children	8.7%	10.1%

ECONOMY & JOBS SCORE: 91/RANK: 30

INCOME	AREA	U.S. AVG	EMPLOYMENT	AREA	U.S. AVG	LARGEST EMPLOYING INDUSTRY
Per capita income	$24,489	$23,420	Unemployment rate	5.5%	6.1%	Miscellaneous Manufacturing
Household income	$47,646	$46,060	Recent job growth	1.6%	.9%	
Household income < $25K	26.1%	26.4%	Projected future job growth	5.7%	15.1%	
Household income > $75K	26.0%	24.5%	White collar	54.8%	54.5%	
Household income growth	49.6%	57.3%	Blue collar	45.2%	45.5%	

COST OF LIVING SCORE: 9/RANK: 300

INDEXES & TAXES	AREA	U.S. AVG	HOUSING	AREA	U.S. AVG	NECESSITIES	AREA	U.S. AVG
Cost of Living Index	118.4	100.0	Median home price	$206,100	$160,100	Food Index	111.6	100.0
Financial Progress Index	85.8	100.0	Home price appreciation	14.6%	7.1%	Housing Index	128.0	100.0
Income tax rate	7.560%	4.625%	Median rent	$678	$670	Utilities Index	116.3	100.0
Sales tax rate	7.000%	6.474%	Homes owned	63.1%	63.9%	Transportation Index	115.0	100.0
Property tax rate	$27.3	$15.6	Homes rented	28.7%	25.3%	Healthcare Index	134.9	100.0
			Housing affordability	50.0%	54.5%	Miscellaneous Cost Index	105.8	100.0

CLIMATE — SCORE: 32/RANK: 224

TEMPERATURE	AREA	U.S. AVG	PRECIPITATION	AREA	U.S. AVG	COMFORTS & HAZARDS	AREA	U.S. AVG
January low	20.6°F	26.4°F	Annual inches precipitation	42.8	35.9	July relative humidity	68.0%	68.8%
July high	81.1°F	86.7°F	Annual inches snowfall	39.2	24.2	Annual days mostly sunny	205	212
Annual days > 90°F	8	38	Annual days precipitation	134	111	Annual days with thunderstorms	20	39
Annual days < 32°F	123	88	Annual days rain > 0.5 inches	29	23	Tornado risk score	3	19
Annual days < 0°F	2	6	Annual days snow > 1.5 inches	6	6	Hurricane risk score	22	15

TEMPERATURE

PRECIPITATION

DAYS OF CLOUDS & PRECIPITATION

EDUCATION — SCORE: 54/RANK: 152

ACHIEVEMENT	AREA	U.S. AVG	PUBLIC SCHOOLS	AREA	U.S. AVG	HIGHER EDUCATION	AREA	U.S. AVG
High school degree	77.0%	80.2%	Expenditures per pupil	$7,469	$5,894	No. 2-year colleges	2	3
2-year college degree	7.0%	6.2%	Student/teacher ratio	12.6	16.7	No. 4-year colleges/universities	10	4
4-year college degree	15.2%	15.8%	Attending public school	85.0%	90.2%	No. highly ranked universities	1	1
Graduate/professional degree	9.2%	9.6%	State SAT score	1006*	1020			
			State ACT score	21.7	21.0			

HEALTH & HEALTHCARE — SCORE: 19/RANK: 266

CRIME — SCORE: 66/RANK: 113

HAZARDS & ILLNESSES	AREA	U.S. AVG	HEALTHCARE	AREA	U.S. AVG	CRIME	AREA	U.S. AVG
Air-quality score	91	45	Physicians per capita	312.5	261.1	Violent crime rate	351.5	456.0
Water-quality score	40	33	Hospital beds per capita	345.2	432.2	Change in violent crime rate	-9.7%	-17.2%
Pollen/allergy score	61	61	No. teaching hospitals	9	4	Property crime rate	3,332.9	3,950.0
Stress score	38	50	Cost per doctor visit	$68	$67	Change in property crime rate	-16.3%	-16.8%
Cancer mortality per capita	188.0	169.0	Cost per dental visit	$0	$82			
Depression days per month	2.7	2.8	Cost per daily hospital room	$878	$733			

TRANSPORTATION — SCORE: 66/RANK: 110

COMMUTE	AREA	U.S. AVG	INTERCITY SERVICES	AREA	U.S. AVG	AUTOMOTIVE	AREA	U.S. AVG
Average commute time	22.6 min.	22.6 min.	Miles to nearest major airport	6	46	Insurance, annual premium	$1,213	$1,011
Commute by auto	89.4%	88.7%	Type of local airport	Small		Gas, cost per gallon	$1.61	$1.50
Commute by mass transit	2.0%	1.8%	No. daily airline departures	156	294	Daily vehicle miles per capita	22.9	23.0
Work at home	2.4%	3.9%	Amtrak service	Yes				
Mass transit miles per capita	12.2	8.0	No. interstate highways	2	1			

LEISURE — SCORE: 86/RANK: 43

DINING & SHOPPING	AREA	U.S. AVG	ENTERTAINMENT	AREA	U.S. AVG	OUTDOOR ACTIVITIES	AREA	U.S. AVG
Restaurant rating	1	1	Professional sports rating	5	4	Golf-course rating	5	4
No. outlet malls	3	2	College sports rating	6	4	Ski-area rating	7	4
No. Starbucks	9	11	Zoo/aquarium rating	6	3	National Park rating	1	3
No. warehouse clubs	4	4	Amusement park rating	3	3	Sq. miles inland water	7.0	4.0
			Botanical garden/arboretum rating	3	3	Miles of coastline	12.1	11.4

ARTS & CULTURE — SCORE: 78/RANK: 73

MEDIA & LIBRARIES	AREA	U.S. AVG	PERFORMING ARTS	AREA	U.S. AVG	MUSEUMS	AREA	U.S. AVG
Arts radio rating	1	3	Classical music rating	10	4	Overall museum rating	10	6
No. public libraries	80	28	Ballet/dance rating	8	3	Art museum rating	7	5
Library volumes per capita	3.3	2.8	Professional theater rating	10	3	Science museum rating	7	4
			University arts programs rating	10	5	Children's museum rating	5	3

Provo-Orem, UT

Score: 60.3 **Rank:** 146

Profile: Small city/College town
Location: North-central Utah at the south end of the greater Salt Lake City area
Elevation: 4,227 feet
Time zone: Mountain Standard Time

PRO	CON
Attractive setting	Urban sprawl
College-town amenities	Cost of living
Low crime rate	Low ethnic diversity

Provo is at the south end of a complex of cities extending north and south of Salt Lake City. Home to Brigham Young University, with 32,000 students, it has a strong college-town feel. There is some industry and commercial development in the area, including a large steel mill in nearby Geneva. Amenities and excellent outdoor recreation abound, with more options available in the cities along the Wasatch front to the north. The high population and job growth rate combined with a limited geography threaten the city's pleasant atmosphere. Robert Redford's Sundance resort to the east adds tourist traffic to the area. Quality of life in the future depends on how the city manages these pressures. Cost of living and especially housing are high by national and regional standards.

The area is located in a narrow plain between Lake Bonneville and the front range of the Wasatch. The immediate area is built up with grassland and a few trees to the west. Toward Heber City to the east is steep terrain and dense coniferous alpine forests. Similar to Salt Lake City to the north, the climate is a mountain-influenced semiarid continental type. Summers have hot, dry weather but low humidity and occasional cooling breezes from the mountains. Winters are mostly dry and cold with occasional light rain and infrequent but sometimes heavy snow. Because of the altitude and dry air, diurnal temperature changes are dramatic. Summer thunderstorms occur, but they're usually not severe. First freeze is mid-October, last is late April.

POPULATION

DEMOGRAPHICS	AREA	U.S. AVG	ETHNIC COMPOSITION	AREA	U.S. AVG	RESIDENT PROFILE	AREA	U.S. AVG
Population	387,817		White	96.1%	75.1%	Single	41.4%	43.6%
Population density per sq. mile	194.1	447.3	Black	.1%	12.3%	Married	58.6%	56.4%
Population growth	47.1%	16.1%	Asian	1.7%	3.6%	Divorced	4.8%	8.4%
Median age	23.4	35.5	American Indian	.6%	.9%	Separated	1.2%	3.0%
Average family size	3.9	2.7	Hispanic	5.1%	12.5%	Married with children	45.6%	28.7%
			Diversity measure	19.7%	35.2%	Single with children	7.1%	10.1%

ECONOMY & JOBS SCORE: 10/RANK: 295

INCOME	AREA	U.S. AVG	EMPLOYMENT	AREA	U.S. AVG	LARGEST EMPLOYING INDUSTRY
Per capita income	$18,385	$23,420	Unemployment rate	4.3%	6.1%	Food Manufacturing
Household income	$51,599	$46,060	Recent job growth	3.3%	.9%	
Household income < $25K	19.9%	26.4%	Projected future job growth	33.1%	15.1%	
Household income > $75K	28.1%	24.5%	White collar	57.7%	54.5%	
Household income growth	88.0%	57.3%	Blue collar	42.3%	45.5%	

COST OF LIVING SCORE: 21/RANK: 259

INDEXES & TAXES	AREA	U.S. AVG	HOUSING	AREA	U.S. AVG	NECESSITIES	AREA	U.S. AVG
Cost of Living Index	101.8	100.0	Median home price	$170,480	$160,100	Food Index	108.6	100.0
Financial Progress Index	108.0	100.0	Home price appreciation	2.9%	7.1%	Housing Index	105.9	100.0
Income tax rate	7.000%	4.625%	Median rent	$622	$670	Utilities Index	85.8	100.0
Sales tax rate	6.250%	6.474%	Homes owned	68.7%	63.9%	Transportation Index	101.4	100.0
Property tax rate	$7.1	$15.6	Homes rented	27.5%	25.3%	Healthcare Index	87.0	100.0
			Housing affordability	60.0%	54.5%	Miscellaneous Cost Index	100.0	100.0

CLIMATE SCORE: 55/RANK: 148

TEMPERATURE	AREA	U.S. AVG	PRECIPITATION	AREA	U.S. AVG	COMFORTS & HAZARDS	AREA	U.S. AVG
January low	18.5°F	26.4°F	Annual inches precipitation	15.0	35.9	July relative humidity	54.0%	68.8%
July high	82.8°F	86.7°F	Annual inches snowfall	58.0	24.2	Annual days mostly sunny	232	212
Annual days > 90°F	58	38	Annual days precipitation	88	111	Annual days with thunderstorms	35	39
Annual days < 32°F	134	88	Annual days rain > 0.5 inches	7	23	Tornado risk score	4	19
Annual days < 0°F	3	6	Annual days snow > 1.5 inches	13	6	Hurricane risk score	0	15

TEMPERATURE

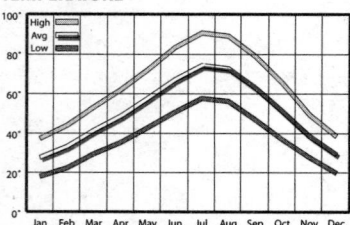

PRECIPITATION

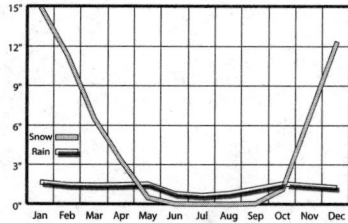

DAYS OF CLOUDS & PRECIPITATION

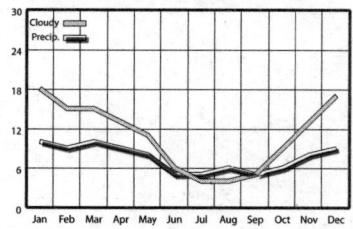

EDUCATION SCORE: 84/RANK: 52

ACHIEVEMENT	AREA	U.S. AVG	PUBLIC SCHOOLS	AREA	U.S. AVG	HIGHER EDUCATION	AREA	U.S. AVG
High school degree	89.4%	80.2%	Expenditures per pupil	$3,767	$5,894	No. 2-year colleges	2	3
2-year college degree	9.0%	6.2%	Student/teacher ratio	24.0	16.7	No. 4-year colleges/universities	1	4
4-year college degree	21.6%	15.8%	Attending public school	98.4%	90.2%	No. highly ranked universities	0	1
Graduate/professional degree	9.9%	9.6%	State SAT score	1125	1020			
			State ACT score	21.3*	21.0			

HEALTH & HEALTHCARE SCORE: 18/RANK: 271

CRIME SCORE: 89/RANK: 35

HAZARDS & ILLNESSES	AREA	U.S. AVG	HEALTHCARE	AREA	U.S. AVG	CRIME	AREA	U.S. AVG
Air-quality score	59	45	Physicians per capita	135.1	261.1	Violent crime rate	108.9	456.0
Water-quality score	30	33	Hospital beds per capita	284.9	432.2	Change in violent crime rate	-25.9%	-17.2%
Pollen/allergy score	60	61	No. teaching hospitals	1	4	Property crime rate	3,309.0	3,950.0
Stress score	0	50	Cost per doctor visit	$59	$67	Change in property crime rate	-24.9%	-16.8%
Cancer mortality per capita	114.1	169.0	Cost per dental visit	$75	$82			
Depression days per month	2.8	2.8	Cost per daily hospital room	$665	$733			

TRANSPORTATION SCORE: 53/RANK: 153

COMMUTE	AREA	U.S. AVG	INTERCITY SERVICES	AREA	U.S. AVG	AUTOMOTIVE	AREA	U.S. AVG
Average commute time	18.8 min.	22.6 min.	Miles to nearest major airport	41	46	Insurance, annual premium	$854	$1,011
Commute by auto	87.4%	88.7%	Type of local airport	Large		Gas, cost per gallon	$1.54	$1.50
Commute by mass transit	1.5%	1.8%	No. daily airline departures	452	294	Daily vehicle miles per capita	25.1	23.0
Work at home	4.4%	3.9%	Amtrak service	Yes				
Mass transit miles per capita	0.0	8.0	No. interstate highways	1	1			

LEISURE SCORE: 80/RANK: 62

DINING & SHOPPING	AREA	U.S. AVG	ENTERTAINMENT	AREA	U.S. AVG	OUTDOOR ACTIVITIES	AREA	U.S. AVG
Restaurant rating	1	1	Professional sports rating	2	4	Golf-course rating	2	4
No. outlet malls	1	2	College sports rating	9	4	Ski-area rating	10	4
No. Starbucks	0	11	Zoo/aquarium rating	1	3	National Park rating	10	3
No. warehouse clubs	3	4	Amusement park rating	1	3	Sq. miles inland water	8.0	4.0
			Botanical garden/arboretum rating	1	3	Miles of coastline	0.0	11.4

ARTS & CULTURE SCORE: 74/RANK: 87

MEDIA & LIBRARIES	AREA	U.S. AVG	PERFORMING ARTS	AREA	U.S. AVG	MUSEUMS	AREA	U.S. AVG
Arts radio rating	1	3	Classical music rating	4	4	Overall museum rating	5	6
No. public libraries	10	28	Ballet/dance rating	1	3	Art museum rating	7	5
Library volumes per capita	2.1	2.8	Professional theater rating	1	3	Science museum rating	6	4
			University arts programs rating	5	5	Children's museum rating	1	3

Pueblo, CO

	Score: 85.1 Rank: 20

Profile: Small town
Location: South-central Colorado along Arkansas River near the Front Range, 110 miles south of Denver
Elevation: 4,684 feet
Time zone: Pacific Standard Time

PRO	CON
Year-round climate	Urban sprawl
Cost of living	Unemployment
Health and healthcare	Isolation

Twenty-five years ago, the massive Colorado Fuel & Iron plant closed, changing Pueblo forever. Once a gritty steel town, Pueblo has been in transition ever since. Ranching and irrigated farming are economic mainstays. The real attractions now are the quiet, small-town life and a pleasant climate. The mountains and Royal Gorge area to the west provide outdoor recreation. The air quality is rated the best among cities on Colorado's Front Range. The city is a bit isolated, but many services and amenities are available in Colorado Springs, 25 miles north, which also provides jobs for some Pueblo residents who commute there. On the downside, there are some areas of unattractive growth outside of town. The area does not stand out in any category, but is consistently attractive across the board, thus the high ranking.

Lake Pueblo, the largest body of water in southern Colorado, is located 7 miles west of the city and provides a variety of watersports, fishing, and picnicking, and has a wildlife preserve. The surrounding countryside consists of rolling plains, broken by normally dry arroyos, and is covered mainly with sparse bunchgrass and occasional cacti. The climate is semiarid and marked by large diurnal temperature ranges. Summer days reach 90°F about half the time, but low humidity means reasonable comfort. Mountain breezes keep summer nights cool. Winter is comparatively mild due to abundant sunshine and mountain protection. Cold spells are usually broken by warm, dry, chinook winds coming down the mountains. Summer rains occur as sporadic afternoon thunderstorms. Winter precipitation is usually light.

POPULATION

DEMOGRAPHICS	AREA	U.S. AVG	ETHNIC COMPOSITION	AREA	U.S. AVG	RESIDENT PROFILE	AREA	U.S. AVG
Population	146,880		White	89.3%	75.1%	Single	43.2%	43.6%
Population density per sq. mile	61.5	447.3	Black	1.7%	12.3%	Married	56.8%	56.4%
Population growth	19.4%	16.1%	Asian	.8%	3.6%	Divorced	10.1%	8.4%
Median age	37.1	35.5	American Indian	.9%	.9%	Separated	3.0%	3.0%
Average family size	2.6	2.7	Hispanic	34.3%	12.5%	Married with children	25.4%	28.7%
			Diversity measure	53.4	35.2%	Single with children	11.8%	10.1%

ECONOMY & JOBS SCORE: 30/RANK: 231

INCOME	AREA	U.S. AVG	EMPLOYMENT	AREA	U.S. AVG	LARGEST EMPLOYING INDUSTRY
Per capita income	$17,714	$23,420	Unemployment rate	6.6%	6.1%	Healthcare and Social Assistance
Household income	$34,723	$46,060	Recent job growth	1.6%	.9%	
Household income < $25K	35.0%	26.4%	Projected future job growth	16.9%	15.1%	
Household income > $75K	13.9%	24.5%	White collar	51.7%	54.5%	
Household income growth	61.2%	57.3%	Blue collar	48.3%	45.5%	

COST OF LIVING SCORE: 58/RANK: 138

INDEXES & TAXES	AREA	U.S. AVG	HOUSING	AREA	U.S. AVG	NECESSITIES	AREA	U.S. AVG
Cost of Living Index	87.7	100.0	Median home price	$111,090	$160,100	Food Index	111.2	100.0
Financial Progress Index	84.4	100.0	Home price appreciation	5.3%	7.1%	Housing Index	69.0	100.0
Income tax rate	5.000%	4.625%	Median rent	$608	$670	Utilities Index	89.6	100.0
Sales tax rate	7.400%	6.474%	Homes owned	63.5%	63.9%	Transportation Index	94.0	100.0
Property tax rate	$9.9	$15.6	Homes rented	22.5%	25.3%	Healthcare Index	105.3	100.0
			Housing affordability	43.0%	54.5%	Miscellaneous Cost Index	91.5	100.0

CLIMATE SCORE: 66/RANK: 111

TEMPERATURE	AREA	U.S. AVG	PRECIPITATION	AREA	U.S. AVG	COMFORTS & HAZARDS	AREA	U.S. AVG
January low	14.7°F	26.4°F	Annual inches precipitation	11.9	35.9	July relative humidity	50.0%	68.8%
July high	91.1°F	86.7°F	Annual inches snowfall	30.8	24.2	Annual days mostly sunny	261	212
Annual days > 90°F	64	38	Annual days precipitation	78	111	Annual days with thunderstorms	40	39
Annual days < 32°F	153	88	Annual days rain > 0.5 inches	4	23	Tornado risk score	4	19
Annual days < 0°F	8	6	Annual days snow > 1.5 inches	6	6	Hurricane risk score	0	15

TEMPERATURE

PRECIPITATION

DAYS OF CLOUDS & PRECIPITATION

EDUCATION SCORE: 36/RANK: 209

ACHIEVEMENT	AREA	U.S. AVG	PUBLIC SCHOOLS	AREA	U.S. AVG	HIGHER EDUCATION	AREA	U.S. AVG
High school degree	81.3%	80.2%	Expenditures per pupil	$4,907	$5,894	No. 2-year colleges	1	3
2-year college degree	7.3%	6.2%	Student/teacher ratio	19.3	16.7	No. 4-year colleges/universities	1	4
4-year college degree	11.9%	15.8%	Attending public school	96.1%	90.2%	No. highly ranked universities	0	1
Graduate/professional degree	5.9%	9.6%	State SAT score	1104	1020			
			State ACT score	20.1*	21.0			

HEALTH & HEALTHCARE SCORE: 98/RANK: 6

HAZARDS & ILLNESSES	AREA	U.S. AVG	HEALTHCARE	AREA	U.S. AVG	CRIME	AREA	U.S. AVG
Air-quality score	49	45	Physicians per capita	245.8	261.1	Violent crime rate	580.9	456.0
Water-quality score	82	33	Hospital beds per capita	807.9	432.2	Change in violent crime rate	-45.8%	-17.2%
Pollen/allergy score	65	61	No. teaching hospitals	1	4	Property crime rate	4,621.4	3,950.0
Stress score	71	50	Cost per doctor visit	$67	$67	Change in property crime rate	-18.2%	-16.8%
Cancer mortality per capita	141.6	169.0	Cost per dental visit	$70	$82			
Depression days per month	4.6	2.8	Cost per daily hospital room	$577	$733			

CRIME SCORE: 32/RANK: 225

TRANSPORTATION SCORE: 45/RANK: 181

COMMUTE	AREA	U.S. AVG	INTERCITY SERVICES	AREA	U.S. AVG	AUTOMOTIVE	AREA	U.S. AVG
Average commute time	20.7 min.	22.6 min.	Miles to nearest major airport	38	46	Insurance, annual premium	$1,047	$1,011
Commute by auto	92.8%	88.7%	Type of local airport	Medium		Gas, cost per gallon	$1.52	$1.50
Commute by mass transit	.6%	1.8%	No. daily airline departures	75	294	Daily vehicle miles per capita	16.9	23.0
Work at home	3.2%	3.9%	Amtrak service	No				
Mass transit miles per capita	4.9	8.0	No. interstate highways	1	1			

LEISURE SCORE: 68/RANK: 105

DINING & SHOPPING	AREA	U.S. AVG	ENTERTAINMENT	AREA	U.S. AVG	OUTDOOR ACTIVITIES	AREA	U.S. AVG
Restaurant rating	1	1	Professional sports rating	2	4	Golf-course rating	1	4
No. outlet malls	0	2	College sports rating	2	4	Ski-area rating	10	4
No. Starbucks	2	11	Zoo/aquarium rating	2	3	National Park rating	1	3
No. warehouse clubs	3	4	Amusement park rating	1	3	Sq. miles inland water	2.0	4.0
			Botanical garden/arboretum rating	1	3	Miles of coastline	0.0	11.4

ARTS & CULTURE SCORE: 53/RANK: 150

MEDIA & LIBRARIES	AREA	U.S. AVG	PERFORMING ARTS	AREA	U.S. AVG	MUSEUMS	AREA	U.S. AVG
Arts radio rating	8	3	Classical music rating	3	4	Overall museum rating	4	6
No. public libraries	4	28	Ballet/dance rating	1	3	Art museum rating	6	5
Library volumes per capita	2.9	2.8	Professional theater rating	1	3	Science museum rating	1	4
			University arts programs rating	3	5	Children's museum rating	6	3

Punta Gorda, FL

Score: 77.4   Rank: 49

Profile: Small-town complex
Location: Gulf coast, 25 miles north of Fort Myers
Elevation: 15 feet
Time zone: Eastern Standard Time

PRO	CON
Pleasant winter climate	Arts and culture
Future job growth	Transportation services
Low crime rate	Low ethnic diversity

Punta Gorda is a mainly agricultural and residential area with a modest amount of light industry. Compared to other Gulf Coast cities, Punta Gorda is pleasant and quiet, not overrun by tourists. The area has the highest future job-growth expectations and the lowest crime rate in the state. While hospital services are better than average, the area is lacking in other services and arts and entertainment amenities.

Punta Gorda is located near the top of Charlotte Harbor, a large protected bay off the Gulf of Mexico. The terrain is level with residential areas close to water and agriculture mixed with cypress forests and swampland farther inland. The climate is subtropical with a strong Gulf influence. Summer temperatures are in the 80s or low 90s with humidity, some Gulf breezes, and frequent late afternoon thunderstorms. Winters are very pleasant, with bright, sunny, relatively dry days with temperatures in the 60s and 70s. Gulf hurricanes and tropical storms can bring heavy downpours, especially in late summer and fall.

POPULATION

DEMOGRAPHICS	AREA	U.S. AVG	ETHNIC COMPOSITION	AREA	U.S. AVG	RESIDENT PROFILE	AREA	U.S. AVG
Population	148,678		White	93.3%	75.1%	Single	33.2%	43.6%
Population density per sq. mile	214.3	447.3	Black	5.0%	12.3%	Married	66.8%	56.4%
Population growth	34.0%	16.1%	Asian	.9%	3.6%	Divorced	7.9%	8.4%
Median age	54.7	35.5	American Indian	.3%	.9%	Separated	2.0%	3.0%
Average family size	2.3	2.7	Hispanic	4.4%	12.5%	Married with children	15.5%	28.7%
			Diversity measure	17.9%	35.2%	Single with children	5.4%	10.1%

ECONOMY & JOBS SCORE: 24/RANK: 250

INCOME	AREA	U.S. AVG	EMPLOYMENT	AREA	U.S. AVG	LARGEST EMPLOYING INDUSTRY
Per capita income	$20,442	$23,420	Unemployment rate	3.9%	6.1%	Healthcare and Social Assistance
Household income	$32,633	$46,060	Recent job growth	3.3%	.9%	
Household income < $25K	32.8%	26.4%	Projected future job growth	34.7%	15.1%	
Household income > $75K	10.0%	24.5%	White collar	55.9%	54.5%	
Household income growth	26.7%	57.3%	Blue collar	44.1%	45.5%	

COST OF LIVING SCORE: 81/RANK: 61

INDEXES & TAXES	AREA	U.S. AVG	HOUSING	AREA	U.S. AVG	NECESSITIES	AREA	U.S. AVG
Cost of Living Index	95.2	100.0	Median home price	$131,710	$160,100	Food Index	103.3	100.0
Financial Progress Index	73.0	100.0	Home price appreciation	10.7%	7.1%	Housing Index	81.8	100.0
Income tax rate	0.000%	4.625%	Median rent	$668	$670	Utilities Index	103.2	100.0
Sales tax rate	7.000%	6.474%	Homes owned	61.0%	63.9%	Transportation Index	109.8	100.0
Property tax rate	$15.6	$15.6	Homes rented	13.5%	25.3%	Healthcare Index	99.5	100.0
			Housing affordability	56.0%	54.5%	Miscellaneous Cost Index	99.6	100.0

CLIMATE
SCORE: 82/RANK: 59

TEMPERATURE	AREA	U.S. AVG	PRECIPITATION	AREA	U.S. AVG	COMFORTS & HAZARDS	AREA	U.S. AVG
January low	52.3°F	26.4°F	Annual inches precipitation	54.0	35.9	July relative humidity	76.0%	68.8%
July high	91.5°F	86.7°F	Annual inches snowfall	0.0	24.2	Annual days mostly sunny	264	212
Annual days > 90°F	106	38	Annual days precipitation	112	111	Annual days with thunderstorms	93	39
Annual days < 32°F	1	88	Annual days rain > 0.5 inches	30	23	Tornado risk score	31	19
Annual days < 0°F	0	6	Annual days snow > 1.5 inches	0	6	Hurricane risk score	77	15

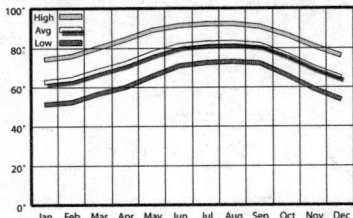

TEMPERATURE

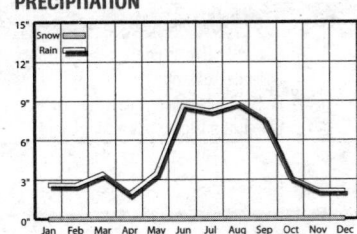

PRECIPITATION

DAYS OF CLOUDS & PRECIPITATION

EDUCATION
SCORE: 22/RANK: 256

ACHIEVEMENT	AREA	U.S. AVG	PUBLIC SCHOOLS	AREA	U.S. AVG	HIGHER EDUCATION	AREA	U.S. AVG
High school degree	82.2%	80.2%	Expenditures per pupil	$5,399	$5,894	No. 2-year colleges	0	3
2-year college degree	6.0%	6.2%	Student/teacher ratio	19.1	16.7	No. 4-year colleges/universities	0	4
4-year college degree	10.9%	15.8%	Attending public school	93.9%	90.2%	No. highly ranked universities	0	1
Graduate/professional degree	6.0%	9.6%	State SAT score	996*	1020			
			State ACT score	20.5	21.0			

HEALTH & HEALTHCARE
SCORE: 89/RANK: 34

CRIME
SCORE: 76/RANK: 77

HAZARDS & ILLNESSES	AREA	U.S. AVG	HEALTHCARE	AREA	U.S. AVG	CRIME	AREA	U.S. AVG
Air-quality score	24	45	Physicians per capita	221.3	261.1	Violent crime rate	232.6	456.0
Water-quality score	26	33	Hospital beds per capita	554.3	432.2	Change in violent crime rate	-15.4%	-17.2%
Pollen/allergy score	82	61	No. teaching hospitals	1	4	Property crime rate	2,757.1	3,950.0
Stress score	20	50	Cost per doctor visit	$66	$67	Change in property crime rate	-5.8%	-16.8%
Cancer mortality per capita	155.2	169.0	Cost per dental visit	$75	$82			
Depression days per month	3.2	2.8	Cost per daily hospital room	$692	$733			

TRANSPORTATION
SCORE: 10/RANK: 295

COMMUTE	AREA	U.S. AVG	INTERCITY SERVICES	AREA	U.S. AVG	AUTOMOTIVE	AREA	U.S. AVG
Average commute time	23.6 min.	22.6 min.	Miles to nearest major airport	38	46	Insurance, annual premium	$1,018	$1,011
Commute by auto	94.8%	88.7%	Type of local airport	Medium		Gas, cost per gallon	$1.50	$1.50
Commute by mass transit	.0%	1.8%	No. daily airline departures	92	294	Daily vehicle miles per capita	20.9	23.0
Work at home	2.3%	3.9%	Amtrak service	No				
Mass transit miles per capita	0.0	8.0	No. interstate highways	1	1			

LEISURE
SCORE: 61/RANK: 130

DINING & SHOPPING	AREA	U.S. AVG	ENTERTAINMENT	AREA	U.S. AVG	OUTDOOR ACTIVITIES	AREA	U.S. AVG
Restaurant rating	1	1	Professional sports rating	2	4	Golf-course rating	4	4
No. outlet malls	4	2	College sports rating	1	4	Ski-area rating	1	4
No. Starbucks	0	11	Zoo/aquarium rating	1	3	National Park rating	2	3
No. warehouse clubs	3	4	Amusement park rating	1	3	Sq. miles inland water	5.0	4.0
			Botanical garden/arboretum rating	1	3	Miles of coastline	37.3	11.4

ARTS & CULTURE
SCORE: 36/RANK: 209

MEDIA & LIBRARIES	AREA	U.S. AVG	PERFORMING ARTS	AREA	U.S. AVG	MUSEUMS	AREA	U.S. AVG
Arts radio rating	1	3	Classical music rating	3	4	Overall museum rating	1	6
No. public libraries	5	28	Ballet/dance rating	1	3	Art museum rating	1	5
Library volumes per capita	1.0	2.8	Professional theater rating	1	3	Science museum rating	2	4
			University arts programs rating	1	5	Children's museum rating	1	3

Racine, WI

Profile: Small industrial town
Location: Southeast Wisconsin along Lake Michigan between Milwaukee and Chicago
Elevation: 693 feet
Time zone: Central Standard Time

Score: 30.0   Rank: 307

PRO	CON
Diverse economy	Winter climate
Architectural interest	High unemployment
Waterfront park	Low educational attainment

Racine is an industrial center located 30 miles south of Milwaukee and 50 miles north of downtown Chicago. Local businesses include J.I. Case, a manufacturer of farm equipment, and the SC Johnson Co. of Johnson Wax fame. The Frank Lloyd Wright–designed Johnson's headquarters is one of the most famous commercial buildings in the country, and there are four other Wright buildings in town. However, the rest of the city has little of architectural or physical interest. There is a revitalized waterfront and a fair complement of parks and open areas. A few minor cultural amenities exist, with additional options in nearby Milwaukee and Chicago.

The Root River bisects Racine before entering Lake Michigan, providing settings for riverfront parks. The surrounding terrain is mainly level and built up or cleared for agriculture. The climate is mainly continental with some lake influence. Storm systems from the west cause frequent weather changes. Summers are warm and often humid, influenced both by the inflow of Gulf moisture from the south and the lake itself, although cooling afternoon breezes occur near shore. Winter brings storms, occasionally severe, dropping snow and temperature readings. Snow can remain on the ground for weeks. Winds off the lake moderate temperature but increase windchill factor. Summer precipitation is mainly thundershowers; spring and fall are variable with pleasant, dry days alternating with rainy periods.

POPULATION

DEMOGRAPHICS	AREA	U.S. AVG	ETHNIC COMPOSITION	AREA	U.S. AVG	RESIDENT PROFILE	AREA	U.S. AVG
Population	191,012		White	88.1%	75.1%	Single	42.5%	43.6%
Population density per sq. mile	573.4	447.3	Black	8.7%	12.3%	Married	57.5%	56.4%
Population growth	9.1%	16.1%	Asian	.9%	3.6%	Divorced	8.5%	8.4%
Median age	36.4	35.5	American Indian	.4%	.9%	Separated	1.9%	3.0%
Average family size	2.7	2.7	Hispanic	5.6%	12.5%	Married with children	29.3%	28.7%
			Diversity measure	34.3%	35.2%	Single with children	11.4%	10.1%

ECONOMY & JOBS
SCORE: 86/RANK: 45

INCOME	AREA	U.S. AVG	EMPLOYMENT	AREA	U.S. AVG	LARGEST EMPLOYING INDUSTRY
Per capita income	$24,781	$23,420	Unemployment rate	8.4%	6.1%	Chemical Manufacturing
Household income	$52,627	$46,060	Recent job growth	3.9%	.9%	
Household income < $25K	21.1%	26.4%	Projected future job growth	10.1%	15.1%	
Household income > $75K	28.9%	24.5%	White collar	50.0%	54.5%	
Household income growth	60.6%	57.3%	Blue collar	50.0%	45.5%	

COST OF LIVING
SCORE: 31/RANK: 227

INDEXES & TAXES	AREA	U.S. AVG	HOUSING	AREA	U.S. AVG	NECESSITIES	AREA	U.S. AVG
Cost of Living Index	95.6	100.0	Median home price	$130,220	$160,100	Food Index	101.5	100.0
Financial Progress Index	117.3	100.0	Home price appreciation	5.5%	7.1%	Housing Index	80.9	100.0
Income tax rate	6.930%	4.625%	Median rent	$609	$670	Utilities Index	128.6	100.0
Sales tax rate	5.100%	6.474%	Homes owned	69.7%	63.9%	Transportation Index	102.9	100.0
Property tax rate	$21.3	$15.6	Homes rented	24.6%	25.3%	Healthcare Index	98.4	100.0
			Housing affordability	57.0%	54.5%	Miscellaneous Cost Index	98.8	100.0

CLIMATE
SCORE: 16/RANK: 278

TEMPERATURE	AREA	U.S. AVG	PRECIPITATION	AREA	U.S. AVG	COMFORTS & HAZARDS	AREA	U.S. AVG
January low	11.4°F	26.4°F	Annual inches precipitation	29.0	35.9	July relative humidity	73.0%	68.8%
July high	80.4°F	86.7°F	Annual inches snowfall	45.0	24.2	Annual days mostly sunny	195	212
Annual days > 90°F	9	38	Annual days precipitation	122	111	Annual days with thunderstorms	36	39
Annual days < 32°F	146	88	Annual days rain > 0.5 inches	19	23	Tornado risk score	8	19
Annual days < 0°F	16	6	Annual days snow > 1.5 inches	11	6	Hurricane risk score	1	15

TEMPERATURE

PRECIPITATION

DAYS OF CLOUDS & PRECIPITATION

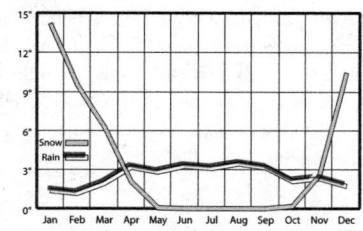

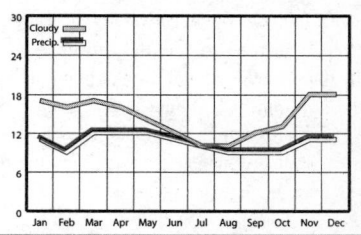

EDUCATION SCORE: 18/RANK: 271

ACHIEVEMENT	AREA	U.S. AVG	PUBLIC SCHOOLS	AREA	U.S. AVG	HIGHER EDUCATION	AREA	U.S. AVG
High school degree	82.9%	80.2%	Expenditures per pupil	$6,852	$5,894	No. 2-year colleges	0	3
2-year college degree	6.8%	6.2%	Student/teacher ratio	16.5	16.7	No. 4-year colleges/universities	0	4
4-year college degree	14.0%	15.8%	Attending public school	82.5%	90.2%	No. highly ranked universities	0	1
Graduate/professional degree	6.3%	9.6%	State SAT score	1179	1020			
			State ACT score	22.2*	21.0			

HEALTH & HEALTHCARE SCORE: 53/RANK: 154

CRIME SCORE: 46/RANK: 178

HAZARDS & ILLNESSES	AREA	U.S. AVG	HEALTHCARE	AREA	U.S. AVG	CRIME	AREA	U.S. AVG
Air-quality score	49	45	Physicians per capita	163.9	261.1	Violent crime rate	356.5	456.0
Water-quality score	10	33	Hospital beds per capita	314.0	432.2	Change in violent crime rate	-27.6%	-17.2%
Pollen/allergy score	43	61	No. teaching hospitals	2	4	Property crime rate	4,074.1	3,950.0
Stress score	68	50	Cost per doctor visit	$74	$67	Change in property crime rate	-7.2%	-16.8%
Cancer mortality per capita	168.8	169.0	Cost per dental visit	$78	$82			
Depression days per month	2.2	2.8	Cost per daily hospital room	$464	$733			

TRANSPORTATION SCORE: 63/RANK: 121

COMMUTE	AREA	U.S. AVG	INTERCITY SERVICES	AREA	U.S. AVG	AUTOMOTIVE	AREA	U.S. AVG
Average commute time	22.0 min.	22.6 min.	Miles to nearest major airport	16	46	Insurance, annual premium	$764	$1,011
Commute by auto	91.6%	88.7%	Type of local airport	Medium		Gas, cost per gallon	$1.58	$1.50
Commute by mass transit	1.4%	1.8%	No. daily airline departures	285	294	Daily vehicle miles per capita	12.6	23.0
Work at home	3.0%	3.9%	Amtrak service	Yes				
Mass transit miles per capita	9.9	8.0	No. interstate highways	1	1			

LEISURE SCORE: 66/RANK: 115

DINING & SHOPPING	AREA	U.S. AVG	ENTERTAINMENT	AREA	U.S. AVG	OUTDOOR ACTIVITIES	AREA	U.S. AVG
Restaurant rating	1	1	Professional sports rating	5	4	Golf-course rating	3	4
No. outlet malls	5	2	College sports rating	3	4	Ski-area rating	3	4
No. Starbucks	0	11	Zoo/aquarium rating	5	3	National Park rating	1	3
No. warehouse clubs	3	4	Amusement park rating	1	3	Sq. miles inland water	2.0	4.0
			Botanical garden/arboretum rating	2	3	Miles of coastline	11.8	11.4

ARTS & CULTURE SCORE: 4/RANK: 316

MEDIA & LIBRARIES	AREA	U.S. AVG	PERFORMING ARTS	AREA	U.S. AVG	MUSEUMS	AREA	U.S. AVG
Arts radio rating	3	3	Classical music rating	3	4	Overall museum rating	3	6
No. public libraries	5	28	Ballet/dance rating	3	3	Art museum rating	5	5
Library volumes per capita	2.2	2.8	Professional theater rating	3	3	Science museum rating	4	4
			University arts programs rating	6	5	Children's museum rating	2	3

Raleigh–Durham–Chapel Hill, NC

Score: 87.4 **Rank:** 13

Profile: Mid-size-city complex
Location: Northeast-central North Carolina, 40 miles south of Virginia border
Elevation: 441 feet
Time zone: Eastern Standard Time

PRO	CON
College-town amenities	Urban sprawl
Residential areas	Cost of living
Strong economy	Hot, humid summers

The Raleigh–Durham–Chapel Hill triad, sometimes referred to as the Research Triangle, is a multifaceted commercial center, capital city, and college town. It's also the educational, intellectual, and high-tech center of North Carolina and a large area of the South. Highlights include a solid, growing economic base; high degree of livability; and impressive amenities, many related to local universities. In addition to several smaller colleges, the area's nationally acclaimed schools include Duke University in Durham, North Carolina State University in Raleigh, and the University of North Carolina in Chapel Hill. Raleigh, the capital city, is plain and uninteresting with nondescript government buildings, a few historic sites, and nicer areas near the N.C. State campus to the southwest. Chapel Hill, the most attractive, has the strongest college-town feel and the best residential areas. The

Duke campus gives Durham a strong college flavor, but the rest of the town reflects its tobacco roots and the downtown area lacks interest. The immense 6,800-acre Research Triangle Park, the area's economic crown jewel, contains major corporate offices and extensive research facilities. Although the area is well kept and growth between the cities is well managed, sprawl may be an issue in the future—the triad is no. 1 on the Sierra Club's 1998 list of most sprawl-endangered cities. Cost of living, especially housing, is above national averages, rare for North Carolina.

Raleigh–Durham–Chapel Hill is located in a transitional zone between the Coastal Plain and the Piedmont Plateau. The surrounding terrain is rolling and heavily wooded. The central location between the mountains and coast means a favorable climate with the exception of some summer heat. The mountains form a partial barrier to cold-air masses, resulting in few winter days with temperatures below 20°F. During summer, tropical air is present over eastern and central sections of North Carolina, producing warm temperatures and high humidity. Rainfall is well distributed year-round with most occurring in summers as thunderstorms, some of which can be intense. The area is far enough inland to reduce the effects of coastal storms. While snow and sleet usually occur each year, excessive accumulations are rare.

POPULATION

DEMOGRAPHICS	AREA	U.S. AVG	ETHNIC COMPOSITION	AREA	U.S. AVG	RESIDENT PROFILE	AREA	U.S. AVG
Population	1,267,676		White	73.5%	75.1%	Single	48.4%	43.6%
Population density per sq. mile	363.1	447.3	Black	23.9%	12.3%	Married	51.6%	56.4%
Population growth	48.2%	16.1%	Asian	1.8%	3.6%	Divorced	7.4%	8.4%
Median age	33.3	35.5	American Indian	.3%	.9%	Separated	4.6%	3.0%
Average family size	2.5	2.7	Hispanic	2.3%	12.5%	Married with children	25.4%	28.7%
			Diversity measure	48.5%	35.2%	Single with children	10.2%	10.1%

ECONOMY & JOBS — SCORE: 30/RANK: 229

INCOME	AREA	U.S. AVG	EMPLOYMENT	AREA	U.S. AVG	LARGEST EMPLOYING INDUSTRY
Per capita income	$28,693	$23,420	Unemployment rate	4.6%	6.1%	Computer and Electronic Product Manufacturing
Household income	$56,436	$46,060	Recent job growth	-.4%	.9%	
Household income < $25K	20.0%	26.4%	Projected future job growth	24.8%	15.1%	
Household income > $75K	34.8%	24.5%	White collar	64.4%	54.5%	
Household income growth	75.8%	57.3%	Blue collar	35.6%	45.5%	

COST OF LIVING — SCORE: 23/RANK: 254

INDEXES & TAXES	AREA	U.S. AVG	HOUSING	AREA	U.S. AVG	NECESSITIES	AREA	U.S. AVG
Cost of Living Index	103.6	100.0	Median home price	$173,100	$160,100	Food Index	102.3	100.0
Financial Progress Index	116.0	100.0	Home price appreciation	4.3%	7.1%	Housing Index	107.5	100.0
Income tax rate	7.000%	4.625%	Median rent	$799	$670	Utilities Index	92.7	100.0
Sales tax rate	7.000%	6.474%	Homes owned	63.7%	63.9%	Transportation Index	99.9	100.0
Property tax rate	$11.0	$15.6	Homes rented	30.3%	25.3%	Healthcare Index	102.6	100.0
			Housing affordability	56.0%	54.5%	Miscellaneous Cost Index	104.5	100.0

CLIMATE — SCORE: 63/RANK: 120

TEMPERATURE	AREA	U.S. AVG	PRECIPITATION	AREA	U.S. AVG	COMFORTS & HAZARDS	AREA	U.S. AVG
January low	30.0°F	26.4°F	Annual inches precipitation	43.0	35.9	July relative humidity	71.0%	68.8%
July high	87.7°F	86.7°F	Annual inches snowfall	7.0	24.2	Annual days mostly sunny	220	212
Annual days > 90°F	25	38	Annual days precipitation	112	111	Annual days with thunderstorms	46	39
Annual days < 32°F	82	88	Annual days rain > 0.5 inches	29	23	Tornado risk score	13	19
Annual days < 0°F	0	6	Annual days snow > 1.5 inches	3	6	Hurricane risk score	29	15

TEMPERATURE
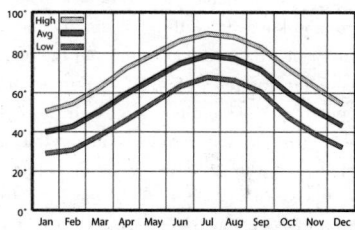

PRECIPITATION
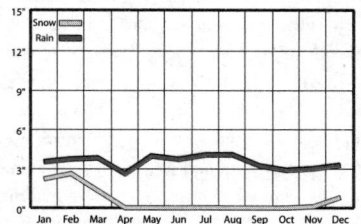

DAYS OF CLOUDS & PRECIPITATION
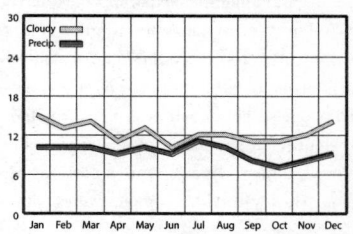

EDUCATION — SCORE: 96/RANK: 12

ACHIEVEMENT	AREA	U.S. AVG	PUBLIC SCHOOLS	AREA	U.S. AVG	HIGHER EDUCATION	AREA	U.S. AVG
High school degree	85.4%	80.2%	Expenditures per pupil	$5,390	$5,894	No. 2-year colleges	5	3
2-year college degree	6.9%	6.2%	Student/teacher ratio	15.5	16.7	No. 4-year colleges/universities	8	4
4-year college degree	24.6%	15.8%	Attending public school	91.6%	90.2%	No. highly ranked universities	2	1
Graduate/professional degree	14.4%	9.6%	State SAT score	1001*	1020			
			State ACT score	19.9	21.0			

HEALTH & HEALTHCARE — SCORE: 80/RANK: 65

HAZARDS & ILLNESSES	AREA	U.S. AVG	HEALTHCARE	AREA	U.S. AVG
Air-quality score	95	45	Physicians per capita	431.7	261.1
Water-quality score	52	33	Hospital beds per capita	384.8	432.2
Pollen/allergy score	65	61	No. teaching hospitals	6	4
Stress score	45	50	Cost per doctor visit	$76	$67
Cancer mortality per capita	161.2	169.0	Cost per dental visit	$80	$82
Depression days per month	1.7	2.8	Cost per daily hospital room	$536	$733

CRIME — SCORE: 29/RANK: 235

CRIME	AREA	U.S. AVG
Violent crime rate	497.7	456.0
Change in violent crime rate	-17.1%	-17.2%
Property crime rate	4,660.8	3,950.0
Change in property crime rate	-14.1%	-16.8%

TRANSPORTATION SCORE: 21/RANK: 258

COMMUTE	AREA	U.S. AVG	INTERCITY SERVICES	AREA	U.S. AVG	AUTOMOTIVE	AREA	U.S. AVG
Average commute time	24.9 min.	22.6 min.	Miles to nearest major airport	8	46	Insurance, annual premium	$834	$1,011
Commute by auto	90.8%	88.7%	Type of local airport	Medium		Gas, cost per gallon	$1.43	$1.50
Commute by mass transit	1.6%	1.8%	No. daily airline departures	352	294	Daily vehicle miles per capita	30.9	23.0
Work at home	2.6%	3.9%	Amtrak service	Yes				
Mass transit miles per capita	4.9	8.0	No. interstate highways	2	1			

LEISURE SCORE: 44/RANK: 184

DINING & SHOPPING	AREA	U.S. AVG	ENTERTAINMENT	AREA	U.S. AVG	OUTDOOR ACTIVITIES	AREA	U.S. AVG
Restaurant rating	3	1	Professional sports rating	5	4	Golf-course rating	6	4
No. outlet malls	2	2	College sports rating	10	4	Ski-area rating	1	4
No. Starbucks	17	11	Zoo/aquarium rating	4	3	National Park rating	1	3
No. warehouse clubs	5	4	Amusement park rating	1	3	Sq. miles inland water	2.0	4.0
			Botanical garden/arboretum rating	5	3	Miles of coastline	0.0	11.4

ARTS & CULTURE SCORE: 79/RANK: 68

MEDIA & LIBRARIES	AREA	U.S. AVG	PERFORMING ARTS	AREA	U.S. AVG	MUSEUMS	AREA	U.S. AVG
Arts radio rating	8	3	Classical music rating	7	4	Overall museum rating	8	6
No. public libraries	41	28	Ballet/dance rating	3	3	Art museum rating	8	5
Library volumes per capita	2.2	2.8	Professional theater rating	6	3	Science museum rating	7	4
			University arts programs rating	8	5	Children's museum rating	6	3

Rapid City, SD

Score: 38.4   Rank: 284

Profile: Small town
Location: Western South Dakota at the edge of the Black Hills
Elevation: 3,505 feet
Time zone: Eastern Standard Time

PRO	CON
Nearby mountains	Isolation
Cost of living	Tourist impact
Healthcare	Harsh climate

Rapid City is a gateway to the Black Hills of southwest South Dakota. Originally a center for the mining and timber industries, the town now relies on light industry and tourism. A few quality museums and amenities exist, but most have a tourist flavor. The Black Hills offer recreational opportunities and historic sites, but tourists crowd the area during the summer season. Like the rest of the state, the area is economically attractive with low costs and taxes and relatively high incomes. The location is very isolated—Denver, the nearest city with significant services and amenities, is 400 miles to the southwest. The rumble heard from 25 miles north every August comes from half a million Harley-Davidson motorcycles attending the annual Sturgis Rally.

Rapid City is located in an area of creek valleys and mostly coniferous wooded hills. To the west, the Black Hills rise to 3,000 feet into an alpine terrain. The climate is decidedly continental, with large swings in the weather and extreme conditions due to altitude and air-flow changes. Summers are warm and fairly dry with low humidity and cool, comfortable evenings. However, strong chinook winds off the mountains to the west can produce temperatures over 100°F. Winters are also quite changeable with polar-air masses alternating with warm southerly and chinook winds. Most precipitation comes as summer thunderstorms and winter snows, some heavy. The city averages 31 days a year with below-zero readings *and* 32 days a year above 90°F, the only city with such a climate profile. First freeze is late September, last is mid-May.

POPULATION

DEMOGRAPHICS	AREA	U.S. AVG	ETHNIC COMPOSITION	AREA	U.S. AVG	RESIDENT PROFILE	AREA	U.S. AVG
Population	90,856		White	94.7%	75.1%	Single	34.7%	43.6%
Population density per sq. mile	32.7	447.3	Black	.9%	12.3%	Married	65.3%	56.4%
Population growth	11.7%	16.1%	Asian	1.2%	3.6%	Divorced	7.8%	8.4%
Median age	35.4	35.5	American Indian	2.9%	.9%	Separated	1.6%	3.0%
Average family size	2.6	2.7	Hispanic	1.7%	12.5%	Married with children	31.1%	28.7%
			Diversity measure	26.5%	35.2%	Single with children	7.4%	10.1%

ECONOMY & JOBS SCORE: 48/RANK: 171

INCOME	AREA	U.S. AVG	EMPLOYMENT	AREA	U.S. AVG	LARGEST EMPLOYING INDUSTRY
Per capita income	$21,591	$23,420	Unemployment rate	2.6%	6.1%	Computer and Electronic Product Manufacturing
Household income	$40,540	$46,060	Recent job growth	-1.0%	.9%	
Household income < $25K	26.1%	26.4%	Projected future job growth	17.8%	15.1%	
Household income > $75K	18.0%	24.5%	White collar	50.5%	54.5%	
Household income growth	60.1%	57.3%	Blue collar	49.5%	45.5%	

COST OF LIVING — SCORE: 93/RANK: 23

INDEXES & TAXES	AREA	U.S. AVG	HOUSING	AREA	U.S. AVG	NECESSITIES	AREA	U.S. AVG
Cost of Living Index	90.0	100.0	Median home price	$113,680	$160,100	Food Index	105.8	100.0
Financial Progress Index	96.0	100.0	Home price appreciation	7.7%	7.1%	Housing Index	70.6	100.0
Income tax rate	0.000%	4.625%	Median rent	$622	$670	Utilities Index	103.8	100.0
Sales tax rate	6.000%	6.474%	Homes owned	57.0%	63.9%	Transportation Index	95.8	100.0
Property tax rate	$11.9	$15.6	Homes rented	19.8%	25.3%	Healthcare Index	92.5	100.0
			Housing affordability	51.0%	54.5%	Miscellaneous Cost Index	101.1	100.0

CLIMATE — SCORE: 7/RANK: 306

TEMPERATURE	AREA	U.S. AVG	PRECIPITATION	AREA	U.S. AVG	COMFORTS & HAZARDS	AREA	U.S. AVG
January low	10.0°F	26.4°F	Annual inches precipitation	16.0	35.9	July relative humidity	71.0%	68.8%
July high	87.0°F	86.7°F	Annual inches snowfall	40.0	24.2	Annual days mostly sunny	205	212
Annual days > 90°F	32	38	Annual days precipitation	96	111	Annual days with thunderstorms	40	39
Annual days < 32°F	169	88	Annual days rain > 0.5 inches	10	23	Tornado risk score	18	19
Annual days < 0°F	31	6	Annual days snow > 1.5 inches	9	6	Hurricane risk score	0	15

TEMPERATURE

PRECIPITATION

DAYS OF CLOUDS & PRECIPITATION

EDUCATION — SCORE: 70/RANK: 100

ACHIEVEMENT	AREA	U.S. AVG	PUBLIC SCHOOLS	AREA	U.S. AVG	HIGHER EDUCATION	AREA	U.S. AVG
High school degree	87.3%	80.2%	Expenditures per pupil	$4,715	$5,894	No. 2-year colleges	1	3
2-year college degree	7.7%	6.2%	Student/teacher ratio	16.2	16.7	No. 4-year colleges/universities	2	4
4-year college degree	17.9%	15.8%	Attending public school	92.6%	90.2%	No. highly ranked universities	0	1
Graduate/professional degree	8.8%	9.6%	State SAT score	1176	1020			
			State ACT score	21.4*	21.0			

HEALTH & HEALTHCARE — SCORE: 66/RANK: 111

CRIME — SCORE: 35/RANK: 215

HAZARDS & ILLNESSES	AREA	U.S. AVG	HEALTHCARE	AREA	U.S. AVG	CRIME	AREA	U.S. AVG
Air-quality score	6	45	Physicians per capita	320.3	261.1	Violent crime rate	339.1	456.0
Water-quality score	22	33	Hospital beds per capita	420.0	432.2	Change in violent crime rate	-12.9%	-17.2%
Pollen/allergy score	52	61	No. teaching hospitals	1	4	Property crime rate	4,633.3	3,950.0
Stress score	5	50	Cost per doctor visit	$65	$67	Change in property crime rate	-11.8%	-16.8%
Cancer mortality per capita	158.9	169.0	Cost per dental visit	$80	$82			
Depression days per month	2.0	2.8	Cost per daily hospital room	$621	$733			

TRANSPORTATION — SCORE: 76/RANK: 75

COMMUTE	AREA	U.S. AVG	INTERCITY SERVICES	AREA	U.S. AVG	AUTOMOTIVE	AREA	U.S. AVG
Average commute time	17.3 min.	22.6 min.	Miles to nearest major airport	285	46	Insurance, annual premium	$646	$1,011
Commute by auto	80.3%	88.7%	Type of local airport	Small		Gas, cost per gallon	$1.61	$1.50
Commute by mass transit	.2%	1.8%	No. daily airline departures	80	294	Daily vehicle miles per capita	21.5	23.0
Work at home	13.8%	3.9%	Amtrak service	No				
Mass transit miles per capita	3.9	8.0	No. interstate highways	1	1			

LEISURE — SCORE: 3/RANK: 320

DINING & SHOPPING	AREA	U.S. AVG	ENTERTAINMENT	AREA	U.S. AVG	OUTDOOR ACTIVITIES	AREA	U.S. AVG
Restaurant rating	1	1	Professional sports rating	2	4	Golf-course rating	2	4
No. outlet malls	0	2	College sports rating	1	4	Ski-area rating	2	4
No. Starbucks	0	11	Zoo/aquarium rating	5	3	National Park rating	10	3
No. warehouse clubs	3	4	Amusement park rating	1	3	Sq. miles inland water	2.0	4.0
			Botanical garden/arboretum rating	1	3	Miles of coastline	0.0	11.4

ARTS & CULTURE — SCORE: 2/RANK: 322

MEDIA & LIBRARIES	AREA	U.S. AVG	PERFORMING ARTS	AREA	U.S. AVG	MUSEUMS	AREA	U.S. AVG
Arts radio rating	1	3	Classical music rating	3	4	Overall museum rating	6	6
No. public libraries	4	28	Ballet/dance rating	1	3	Art museum rating	5	5
Library volumes per capita	1.7	2.8	Professional theater rating	1	3	Science museum rating	7	4
			University arts programs rating	2	5	Children's museum rating	1	3

Reading, PA

Profile: Small city
Location: East-central Pennsylvania, 60 miles northwest of Philadelphia
Elevation: 260 feet
Time zone: Eastern Standard Time

Score: 63.0   **Rank:** 122

PRO	CON
Historic interest	Economy
Attractive setting	Low educational attainment
Proximity to Philadelphia	Entertainment

Reading is an industrial center in southwest Pennsylvania with moderate economic adversity. Heavy industry and Victorian wealth have left an imprint on the town, which has done a good job preserving its historic heritage. It's also noted for its many outlet malls. Other highlights include a small-town feel, an attractive setting, a moderate cost of living, and proximity to Philadelphia and its amenities. On the downside, educational attainment, particularly high school graduation rates, are among the lowest in the state and nationwide.

The area is characterized by large, wooded hills surrounding flat mostly agricultural valleys. The continental-type climate is modified by ridges to the west and the ocean and its bays to the south and east. Summers are warm, still, and humid with occasional thunderstorms. Winters are fairly mild for the latitude. The mountains block some northwesterly cold air and moisture, creating more clear days than even Philadelphia to the southeast. The area may receive snow while Philadelphia is getting rain or a mix. Snow amounts are variable and freezing rain occurs occasionally. First freeze is mid-October, last is late April.

POPULATION

DEMOGRAPHICS	AREA	U.S. AVG	ETHNIC COMPOSITION	AREA	U.S. AVG	RESIDENT PROFILE	AREA	U.S. AVG
Population	382,108		White	93.8%	75.1%	Single	41.7%	43.6%
Population density per sq. mile	444.7	447.3	Black	2.6%	12.3%	Married	58.3%	56.4%
Population growth	13.5%	16.1%	Asian	1.3%	3.6%	Divorced	7.1%	8.4%
Median age	37.7	35.5	American Indian	.1%	.9%	Separated	2.8%	3.0%
Average family size	2.6	2.7	Hispanic	4.5%	12.5%	Married with children	27.7%	28.7%
			Diversity measure	27.8%	35.2%	Single with children	7.8%	10.1%

ECONOMY & JOBS   SCORE: 33/RANK: 222

INCOME	AREA	U.S. AVG	EMPLOYMENT	AREA	U.S. AVG	LARGEST EMPLOYING INDUSTRY
Per capita income	$22,811	$23,420	Unemployment rate	5.4%	6.1%	Primary Metal Manufacturing
Household income	$47,777	$46,060	Recent job growth	-2.2%	.9%	
Household income < $25K	23.0%	26.4%	Projected future job growth	7.7%	15.1%	
Household income > $75K	24.0%	24.5%	White collar	50.9%	54.5%	
Household income growth	49.1%	57.3%	Blue collar	49.1%	45.5%	

COST OF LIVING   SCORE: 50/RANK: 164

INDEXES & TAXES	AREA	U.S. AVG	HOUSING	AREA	U.S. AVG	NECESSITIES	AREA	U.S. AVG
Cost of Living Index	93.8	100.0	Median home price	$122,070	$160,100	Food Index	100.4	100.0
Financial Progress Index	108.5	100.0	Home price appreciation	5.2%	7.1%	Housing Index	75.8	100.0
Income tax rate	3.800%	4.625%	Median rent	$589	$670	Utilities Index	111.0	100.0
Sales tax rate	6.000%	6.474%	Homes owned	75.3%	63.9%	Transportation Index	105.6	100.0
Property tax rate	$21.5	$15.6	Homes rented	20.1%	25.3%	Healthcare Index	102.3	100.0
			Housing affordability	61.0%	54.5%	Miscellaneous Cost Index	103.9	100.0

CLIMATE   SCORE: 33/RANK: 220

TEMPERATURE	AREA	U.S. AVG	PRECIPITATION	AREA	U.S. AVG	COMFORTS & HAZARDS	AREA	U.S. AVG
January low	19.8°F	26.4°F	Annual inches precipitation	42.5	35.9	July relative humidity	71.0%	68.8%
July high	85.4°F	86.7°F	Annual inches snowfall	32.2	24.2	Annual days mostly sunny	206	212
Annual days > 90°F	16	38	Annual days precipitation	133	111	Annual days with thunderstorms	33	39
Annual days < 32°F	127	88	Annual days rain > 0.5 inches	26	23	Tornado risk score	7	19
Annual days < 0°F	2	6	Annual days snow > 1.5 inches	8	6	Hurricane risk score	11	15

TEMPERATURE

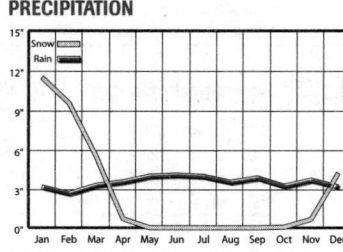

PRECIPITATION

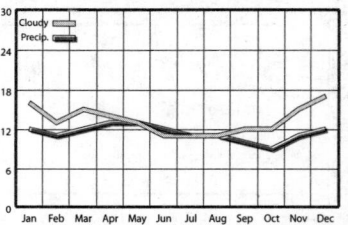

DAYS OF CLOUDS & PRECIPITATION

EDUCATION — SCORE: 14/RANK: 282

ACHIEVEMENT	AREA	U.S. AVG	PUBLIC SCHOOLS	AREA	U.S. AVG	HIGHER EDUCATION	AREA	U.S. AVG
High school degree	78.0%	80.2%	Expenditures per pupil	$6,476	$5,894	No. 2-year colleges	2	3
2-year college degree	5.7%	6.2%	Student/teacher ratio	17.6	16.7	No. 4-year colleges/universities	4	4
4-year college degree	12.0%	15.8%	Attending public school	88.1%	90.2%	No. highly ranked universities	0	1
Graduate/professional degree	6.4%	9.6%	State SAT score	1002*	1020			
			State ACT score	21.5	21.0			

HEALTH & HEALTHCARE — SCORE: 62/RANK: 125

HAZARDS & ILLNESSES	AREA	U.S. AVG	HEALTHCARE	AREA	U.S. AVG	CRIME — SCORE: 68/RANK: 105 / CRIME	AREA	U.S. AVG
Air-quality score	59	45	Physicians per capita	184.0	261.1	Violent crime rate	398.0	456.0
Water-quality score	63	33	Hospital beds per capita	394.2	432.2	Change in violent crime rate	15.0%	-17.2%
Pollen/allergy score	54	61	No. teaching hospitals	3	4	Property crime rate	2,690.0	3,950.0
Stress score	53	50	Cost per doctor visit	$57	$67	Change in property crime rate	-13.4%	-16.8%
Cancer mortality per capita	168.0	169.0	Cost per dental visit	$68	$82			
Depression days per month	4.0	2.8	Cost per daily hospital room	$781	$733			

TRANSPORTATION — SCORE: 26/RANK: 244

COMMUTE	AREA	U.S. AVG	INTERCITY SERVICES	AREA	U.S. AVG	AUTOMOTIVE	AREA	U.S. AVG
Average commute time	22.4 min.	22.6 min.	Miles to nearest major airport	34	46	Insurance, annual premium	$979	$1,011
Commute by auto	89.7%	88.7%	Type of local airport	Small		Gas, cost per gallon	$1.42	$1.50
Commute by mass transit	1.2%	1.8%	No. daily airline departures	63	294	Daily vehicle miles per capita	20.0	23.0
Work at home	3.7%	3.9%	Amtrak service	No				
Mass transit miles per capita	5.1	8.0	No. interstate highways	1	1			

LEISURE — SCORE: 57/RANK: 140

DINING & SHOPPING	AREA	U.S. AVG	ENTERTAINMENT	AREA	U.S. AVG	OUTDOOR ACTIVITIES	AREA	U.S. AVG
Restaurant rating	1	1	Professional sports rating	5	4	Golf-course rating	4	4
No. outlet malls	10	2	College sports rating	4	4	Ski-area rating	4	4
No. Starbucks	0	11	Zoo/aquarium rating	1	3	National Park rating	2	3
No. warehouse clubs	4	4	Amusement park rating	1	3	Sq. miles inland water	2.0	4.0
			Botanical garden/arboretum rating	1	3	Miles of coastline	0.0	11.4

ARTS & CULTURE — SCORE: 41/RANK: 191

MEDIA & LIBRARIES	AREA	U.S. AVG	PERFORMING ARTS	AREA	U.S. AVG	MUSEUMS	AREA	U.S. AVG
Arts radio rating	1	3	Classical music rating	4	4	Overall museum rating	6	6
No. public libraries	24	28	Ballet/dance rating	1	3	Art museum rating	6	5
Library volumes per capita	1.6	2.8	Professional theater rating	1	3	Science museum rating	6	4
			University arts programs rating	6	5	Children's museum rating	1	3

Redding, CA

Score: 56.3   Rank: 177

Profile: Small town
Location: Northern California, at the north end of the Central Valley
Elevation: 342 feet
Time zone: Pacific Standard Time

PRO	CON
Nearby outdoor recreation	Summer heat
Low property crime rate	High unemployment
Mild winters	Isolation

Redding is located along I-5 between the Central Valley and the mountainous region to the north into Oregon. The economy relies on forest products from the nearby mountains and some light manufacturing and food processing. The decline in the forest products industry and related mills has led to the unemployment rate of 7.1%, higher than the national average. Outdoor recreational opportunities are abundant around Lake Shasta to the north, in Trinity Alps to the northwest, and in the Sierra/Cascades to the east. In summer, trapped valley air and abundant sunshine lead to extreme heat with 98 days above 90°F, and readings of 105°F to 110°F not uncommon. The weather is pleasant the rest of the year. The city is a 3-hour drive from Sacramento, site of the nearest major air service and other amenities.

Low mountains surround Redding in three directions with higher mountains in the distance. Terrain is flat to slightly undulating with typical California valley vegetation—grasses and occasional trees. Summers are consistently hot and completely dry, while winters are cool and wet. The shape of the valley and latitude lead to more rainfall than most other valley locations.

POPULATION

DEMOGRAPHICS	AREA	U.S. AVG	ETHNIC COMPOSITION	AREA	U.S. AVG	RESIDENT PROFILE	AREA	U.S. AVG
Population	171,799		White	91.0%	75.1%	Single	38.2%	43.6%
Population density per sq. mile	45.4	447.3	Black	1.1%	12.3%	Married	61.8%	56.4%
Population growth	16.8%	16.1%	Asian	2.4%	3.6%	Divorced	10.0%	8.4%
Median age	39.4	35.5	American Indian	3.2%	.9%	Separated	3.4%	3.0%
Average family size	2.5	2.7	Hispanic	9.2%	12.5%	Married with children	25.3%	28.7%
			Diversity measure	24.7%	35.2%	Single with children	11.5%	10.1%

ECONOMY & JOBS — SCORE: 14/RANK: 283

INCOME	AREA	U.S. AVG	EMPLOYMENT	AREA	U.S. AVG	LARGEST EMPLOYING INDUSTRY
Per capita income	$18,151	$23,420	Unemployment rate	7.1%	6.1%	Healthcare and Social Assistance
Household income	$33,940	$46,060	Recent job growth	-.3%	.9%	
Household income < $25K	36.9%	26.4%	Projected future job growth	19.6%	15.1%	
Household income > $75K	13.9%	24.5%	White collar	51.6%	54.5%	
Household income growth	32.0%	57.3%	Blue collar	48.4%	45.5%	

COST OF LIVING — SCORE: 21/RANK: 260

INDEXES & TAXES	AREA	U.S. AVG	HOUSING	AREA	U.S. AVG	NECESSITIES	AREA	U.S. AVG
Cost of Living Index	105.3	100.0	Median home price	$166,760	$160,100	Food Index	114.4	100.0
Financial Progress Index	68.7	100.0	Home price appreciation	11.3%	7.1%	Housing Index	103.6	100.0
Income tax rate	6.000%	4.625%	Median rent	$608	$670	Utilities Index	87.5	100.0
Sales tax rate	7.250%	6.474%	Homes owned	61.2%	63.9%	Transportation Index	109.2	100.0
Property tax rate	$11.1	$15.6	Homes rented	20.6%	25.3%	Healthcare Index	120.3	100.0
			Housing affordability	50.0%	54.5%	Miscellaneous Cost Index	101.3	100.0

CLIMATE — SCORE: 96/RANK: 14

TEMPERATURE	AREA	U.S. AVG	PRECIPITATION	AREA	U.S. AVG	COMFORTS & HAZARDS	AREA	U.S. AVG
January low	36.7°F	26.4°F	Annual inches precipitation	22.1	35.9	July relative humidity	52.0%	68.8%
July high	98.0°F	86.7°F	Annual inches snowfall	2.4	24.2	Annual days mostly sunny	247	212
Annual days > 90°F	98	38	Annual days precipitation	71	111	Annual days with thunderstorms	10	39
Annual days < 32°F	22	88	Annual days rain > 0.5 inches	22	23	Tornado risk score	1	19
Annual days < 0°F	0	6	Annual days snow > 1.5 inches	1	6	Hurricane risk score	0	15

TEMPERATURE

PRECIPITATION

DAYS OF CLOUDS & PRECIPITATION

EDUCATION — SCORE: 27/RANK: 240

ACHIEVEMENT	AREA	U.S. AVG	PUBLIC SCHOOLS	AREA	U.S. AVG	HIGHER EDUCATION	AREA	U.S. AVG
High school degree	83.2%	80.2%	Expenditures per pupil	$5,277	$5,894	No. 2-year colleges	1	3
2-year college degree	9.8%	6.2%	Student/teacher ratio	21.4	16.7	No. 4-year colleges/universities	1	4
4-year college degree	11.3%	15.8%	Attending public school	92.4%	90.2%	No. highly ranked universities	0	1
Graduate/professional degree	5.3%	9.6%	State SAT score	1018*	1020			
			State ACT score	21.5	21.0			

HEALTH & HEALTHCARE — SCORE: 12/RANK: 291

HAZARDS & ILLNESSES	AREA	U.S. AVG	HEALTHCARE	AREA	U.S. AVG	CRIME	AREA	U.S. AVG
Air-quality score	59	45	Physicians per capita	255.5	261.1	Violent crime rate	491.9	456.0
Water-quality score	22	33	Hospital beds per capita	404.3	432.2	Change in violent crime rate	-22.4%	-17.2%
Pollen/allergy score	71	61	No. teaching hospitals	1	4	Property crime rate	2,861.3	3,950.0
Stress score	26	50	Cost per doctor visit	$61	$67	Change in property crime rate	-41.0%	-16.8%
Cancer mortality per capita	184.7	169.0	Cost per dental visit	$83	$82			
Depression days per month	1.7	2.8	Cost per daily hospital room	$1,327	$733			

CRIME — SCORE: 80/RANK: 64

TRANSPORTATION — SCORE: 49/RANK: 169

COMMUTE	AREA	U.S. AVG	INTERCITY SERVICES	AREA	U.S. AVG	AUTOMOTIVE	AREA	U.S. AVG
Average commute time	20.9 min.	22.6 min.	Miles to nearest major airport	136	46	Insurance, annual premium	$898	$1,011
Commute by auto	88.9%	88.7%	Type of local airport	Medium		Gas, cost per gallon	$1.77	$1.50
Commute by mass transit	.4%	1.8%	No. daily airline departures	144	294	Daily vehicle miles per capita	29.2	23.0
Work at home	5.9%	3.9%	Amtrak service	Yes				
Mass transit miles per capita	6.3	8.0	No. interstate highways	1	1			

LEISURE — SCORE: 74/RANK: 84

DINING & SHOPPING	AREA	U.S. AVG	ENTERTAINMENT	AREA	U.S. AVG	OUTDOOR ACTIVITIES	AREA	U.S. AVG
Restaurant rating	1	1	Professional sports rating	2	4	Golf-course rating	1	4
No. outlet malls	0	2	College sports rating	1	4	Ski-area rating	4	4
No. Starbucks	3	11	Zoo/aquarium rating	1	3	National Park rating	10	3
No. warehouse clubs	3	4	Amusement park rating	1	3	Sq. miles inland water	5.0	4.0
			Botanical garden/arboretum rating	4	3	Miles of coastline	0.0	11.4

ARTS & CULTURE — SCORE: 33/RANK: 220

MEDIA & LIBRARIES	AREA	U.S. AVG	PERFORMING ARTS	AREA	U.S. AVG	MUSEUMS	AREA	U.S. AVG
Arts radio rating	1	3	Classical music rating	3	4	Overall museum rating	5	6
No. public libraries	3	28	Ballet/dance rating	1	3	Art museum rating	6	5
Library volumes per capita	1.1	2.8	Professional theater rating	1	3	Science museum rating	4	4
			University arts programs rating	2	5	Children's museum rating	1	3

Reno, NV

Score: 89.3   Rank: 9

Profile: Small city
Location: Western Nevada, 15 miles east of the California border
Elevation: 4,400 feet
Time zone: Pacific Standard Time

PRO	CON
Nearby mountains	Urban sprawl
Attractive setting	Unattractive growth
Tax climate	Economic cycles

The self-described "Biggest Little City in the World," a former transportation, mining, and gambling center, has grown into a desirable place to live with an expanding variety of benefits and amenities. A favorable tax climate and strategic location as a distribution point to northern California have generated some commercial and industrial development. The city has a lively downtown with several casinos and some entertainment, but gambling and entertainment don't dominate the town as they do in Las Vegas to the south. The Sierra Nevada and Lake Tahoe areas to the west offer a wide range of recreational opportunities, with national forests and world-class ski areas. In recent years, a surge in incoming residents, particularly from California, has lead to sprawl, with some fairly unattractive subdivisions spreading haphazardly over the desert hills, especially to the north and west. Commercial zones close to downtown and the airport are also crowded and unattractive. The more appealing residential areas lie toward the Sierra Crest to the southwest. Cost of living, although rising, is still favorable for the region. The area ranks high in part because of consistency across all *Cities Ranked & Rated* categories.

Reno is located at the west edge of Truckee Meadows in a semiarid plateau lying in the lee of the Sierra Nevadas. To the immediate west, the Sierras rise to elevations of 9,000 feet to 11,000 feet. Desert hills to the east reach 6,000 feet to 7,000 feet. The Truckee River, flowing from the Sierras eastward through Reno, drains into Pyramid Lake, a remnant salt lake to the northeast. Landscape is primarily sagebrush desert with lush forests in the mountains to the west. The climate is high desert with daily temperature ranges often exceeding 45°F. While summer afternoon highs may exceed 90°F, a light jacket is often needed shortly after sunset. Nights with low temperatures over 60°F are rare. Summers are dry and mild with occasional hot spells. Winter afternoon temperatures are moderate. The rain shadow from the Sierras blocks the brunt of Pacific storms in winter. Most precipitation falls from December through March, mainly as mixed rain and snow. Brief late afternoon thunderstorms are common in summer. Sunshine is abundant in all seasons. First freeze is mid-September, last is early June.

POPULATION

DEMOGRAPHICS	AREA	U.S. AVG	ETHNIC COMPOSITION	AREA	U.S. AVG	RESIDENT PROFILE	AREA	U.S. AVG
Population	362,325		White	83.9%	75.1%	Single	47.0%	43.6%
Population density per sq. mile	57.1	447.3	Black	1.5%	12.3%	Married	53.0%	56.4%
Population growth	42.3%	16.1%	Asian	3.8%	3.6%	Divorced	14.7%	8.4%
Median age	35.8	35.5	American Indian	8.3%	.9%	Separated	3.0%	3.0%
Average family size	2.6	2.7	Hispanic	12.9%	12.5%	Married with children	23.9%	28.7%
			Diversity measure	42.5%	35.2%	Single with children	11.2%	10.1%

ECONOMY & JOBS — SCORE: 34/RANK: 216

INCOME	AREA	U.S. AVG	EMPLOYMENT	AREA	U.S. AVG	LARGEST EMPLOYING INDUSTRY
Per capita income	$27,602	$23,420	Unemployment rate	3.9%	6.1%	Accommodations and Food Services
Household income	$54,011	$46,060	Recent job growth	-1.7%	.9%	
Household income < $25K	18.0%	26.4%	Projected future job growth	13.6%	15.1%	
Household income > $75K	31.9%	24.5%	White collar	56.0%	54.5%	
Household income growth	68.9%	57.3%	Blue collar	44.0%	45.5%	

COST OF LIVING — SCORE: 33/RANK: 221

INDEXES & TAXES	AREA	U.S. AVG	HOUSING	AREA	U.S. AVG	NECESSITIES	AREA	U.S. AVG
Cost of Living Index	111.2	100.0	Median home price	$194,400	$160,100	Food Index	111.7	100.0
Financial Progress Index	103.5	100.0	Home price appreciation	6.8%	7.1%	Housing Index	120.7	100.0
Income tax rate	0.000%	4.625%	Median rent	$828	$670	Utilities Index	85.4	100.0
Sales tax rate	7.250%	6.474%	Homes owned	56.3%	63.9%	Transportation Index	112.7	100.0
Property tax rate	$10.9	$15.6	Homes rented	33.0%	25.3%	Healthcare Index	118.5	100.0
			Housing affordability	54.0%	54.5%	Miscellaneous Cost Index	102.0	100.0

CLIMATE — SCORE: 84/RANK: 51

TEMPERATURE	AREA	U.S. AVG	PRECIPITATION	AREA	U.S. AVG	COMFORTS & HAZARDS	AREA	U.S. AVG
January low	18.3°F	26.4°F	Annual inches precipitation	7.0	35.9	July relative humidity	50.0%	68.8%
July high	81.1°F	86.7°F	Annual inches snowfall	27.0	24.2	Annual days mostly sunny	255	212
Annual days > 90°F	52	38	Annual days precipitation	49	111	Annual days with thunderstorms	13	39
Annual days < 32°F	189	88	Annual days rain > 0.5 inches	1	23	Tornado risk score	1	19
Annual days < 0°F	3	6	Annual days snow > 1.5 inches	4	6	Hurricane risk score	0	15

TEMPERATURE

PRECIPITATION

DAYS OF CLOUDS & PRECIPITATION

EDUCATION — SCORE: 46/RANK: 176

ACHIEVEMENT	AREA	U.S. AVG	PUBLIC SCHOOLS	AREA	U.S. AVG	HIGHER EDUCATION	AREA	U.S. AVG
High school degree	82.4%	80.2%	Expenditures per pupil	$5,235	$5,894	No. 2-year colleges	1	3
2-year college degree	6.7%	6.2%	Student/teacher ratio	19.5	16.7	No. 4-year colleges/universities	3	4
4-year college degree	16.6%	15.8%	Attending public school	93.0%	90.2%	No. highly ranked universities	0	1
Graduate/professional degree	8.4%	9.6%	State SAT score	1027*	1020			
			State ACT score	21.3	21.0			

HEALTH & HEALTHCARE — SCORE: 27/RANK: 240

CRIME — SCORE: 39/RANK: 200

HAZARDS & ILLNESSES	AREA	U.S. AVG	HEALTHCARE	AREA	U.S. AVG	CRIME	AREA	U.S. AVG
Air-quality score	81	45	Physicians per capita	278.2	261.1	Violent crime rate	503.6	456.0
Water-quality score	4	33	Hospital beds per capita	334.6	432.2	Change in violent crime rate	-12.3%	-17.2%
Pollen/allergy score	63	61	No. teaching hospitals	1	4	Property crime rate	4,140.5	3,950.0
Stress score	72	50	Cost per doctor visit	$75	$67	Change in property crime rate	-22.6%	-16.8%
Cancer mortality per capita	180.7	169.0	Cost per dental visit	$80	$82			
Depression days per month	2.8	2.8	Cost per daily hospital room	$801	$733			

TRANSPORTATION — SCORE: 90/RANK: 32

COMMUTE	AREA	U.S. AVG	INTERCITY SERVICES	AREA	U.S. AVG	AUTOMOTIVE	AREA	U.S. AVG
Average commute time	19.2 min.	22.6 min.	Miles to nearest major airport	3	46	Insurance, annual premium	$1,140	$1,011
Commute by auto	85.1%	88.7%	Type of local airport	Medium		Gas, cost per gallon	$1.71	$1.50
Commute by mass transit	2.5%	1.8%	No. daily airline departures	123	294	Daily vehicle miles per capita	17.3	23.0
Work at home	3.5%	3.9%	Amtrak service	Yes				
Mass transit miles per capita	14.6	8.0	No. interstate highways	1	1			

LEISURE — SCORE: 74/RANK: 83

DINING & SHOPPING	AREA	U.S. AVG	ENTERTAINMENT	AREA	U.S. AVG	OUTDOOR ACTIVITIES	AREA	U.S. AVG
Restaurant rating	1	1	Professional sports rating	2	4	Golf-course rating	2	4
No. outlet malls	0	2	College sports rating	4	4	Ski-area rating	10	4
No. Starbucks	11	11	Zoo/aquarium rating	1	3	National Park rating	8	3
No. warehouse clubs	3	4	Amusement park rating	5	3	Sq. miles inland water	10.0	4.0
			Botanical garden/arboretum rating	3	3	Miles of coastline	0.0	11.4

ARTS & CULTURE — SCORE: 48/RANK: 172

MEDIA & LIBRARIES	AREA	U.S. AVG	PERFORMING ARTS	AREA	U.S. AVG	MUSEUMS	AREA	U.S. AVG
Arts radio rating	1	3	Classical music rating	6	4	Overall museum rating	5	6
No. public libraries	13	28	Ballet/dance rating	5	3	Art museum rating	5	5
Library volumes per capita	2.3	2.8	Professional theater rating	1	3	Science museum rating	5	4
			University arts programs rating	5	5	Children's museum rating	4	3

Richland-Kennewick-Pasco, WA

Score: 64.5   Rank: 114

Profile: Small-town complex
Location: Southeastern Washington at the confluence of the Snake and Columbia rivers
Elevation: 360 feet
Time zone: Pacific Standard Time

PRO	CON
Small-town atmosphere	Isolation
Cost of living	Entertainment
Water recreation	Harsh climate

This "tri-cities" area along the Snake-Columbia river confluence is agricultural, with irrigated vegetables, fruits, grains, seeds, and livestock dominating the physical and economic landscape. The towns, which are separated by a few miles, are clean, plain, and simple, with low crime and a lack of historic and cultural amenities. The area is isolated, although some amenities exist in the college town of Walla Walla, 40 miles east.

The area is in a broad, flat, agricultural valley. Dry, grassy hills rise to the south and east toward Walla Walla and the Blue Mountains of Washington and northeast Oregon. The climate is moderated somewhat by the prevailing flow of maritime air from the Pacific Ocean, although most moisture is blocked by the Cascade Range. The result is a semiarid landscape and climate featuring low rainfall, dry air, and large diurnal temperature ranges. Summer hot spells are common when the westerly airflow subsides; temperatures of 100°F are common. Cold spells occur when frigid Canadian air enters the valley. Strong winds can stir up dust. Occasional air stagnation may result from the valley location.

POPULATION

DEMOGRAPHICS	AREA	U.S. AVG	ETHNIC COMPOSITION	AREA	U.S. AVG	RESIDENT PROFILE	AREA	U.S. AVG
Population	203,111		White	86.6%	75.1%	Single	37.6%	43.6%
Population density per sq. mile	69.0	447.3	Black	1.0%	12.3%	Married	62.4%	56.4%
Population growth	35.4%	16.1%	Asian	2.6%	3.6%	Divorced	9.1%	8.4%
Median age	33.0	35.5	American Indian	.6%	.9%	Separated	2.4%	3.0%
Average family size	3.0	2.7	Hispanic	22.3%	12.5%	Married with children	36.8%	28.7%
			Diversity measure	41.4%	35.2%	Single with children	10.1%	10.1%

ECONOMY & JOBS SCORE: 40/RANK: 195

INCOME	AREA	U.S. AVG	EMPLOYMENT	AREA	U.S. AVG	LARGEST EMPLOYING INDUSTRY
Per capita income	$20,776	$23,420	Unemployment rate	6.7%	6.1%	Food Manufacturing
Household income	$47,437	$46,060	Recent job growth	2.4%	.9%	
Household income < $25K	24.1%	26.4%	Projected future job growth	21.4%	15.1%	
Household income > $75K	26.3%	24.5%	White collar	53.3%	54.5%	
Household income growth	54.2%	57.3%	Blue collar	46.7%	45.5%	

COST OF LIVING SCORE: 65/RANK: 114

INDEXES & TAXES	AREA	U.S. AVG	HOUSING	AREA	U.S. AVG	NECESSITIES	AREA	U.S. AVG
Cost of Living Index	96.2	100.0	Median home price	$140,220	$160,100	Food Index	103.5	100.0
Financial Progress Index	105.1	100.0	Home price appreciation	6.5%	7.1%	Housing Index	87.1	100.0
Income tax rate	0.000%	4.625%	Median rent	$740	$670	Utilities Index	75.5	100.0
Sales tax rate	8.300%	6.474%	Homes owned	61.4%	63.9%	Transportation Index	105.9	100.0
Property tax rate	$13.3	$15.6	Homes rented	27.9%	25.3%	Healthcare Index	124.3	100.0
			Housing affordability	52.0%	54.5%	Miscellaneous Cost Index	100.4	100.0

CLIMATE SCORE: 34/RANK: 217

TEMPERATURE	AREA	U.S. AVG	PRECIPITATION	AREA	U.S. AVG	COMFORTS & HAZARDS	AREA	U.S. AVG
January low	18.6°F	26.4°F	Annual inches precipitation	8.0	35.9	July relative humidity	60.0%	68.8%
July high	88.1°F	86.7°F	Annual inches snowfall	25.0	24.2	Annual days mostly sunny	202	212
Annual days > 90°F	33	38	Annual days precipitation	67	111	Annual days with thunderstorms	7	39
Annual days < 32°F	150	88	Annual days rain > 0.5 inches	5	23	Tornado risk score	0	19
Annual days < 0°F	4	6	Annual days snow > 1.5 inches	7	6	Hurricane risk score	0	15

TEMPERATURE

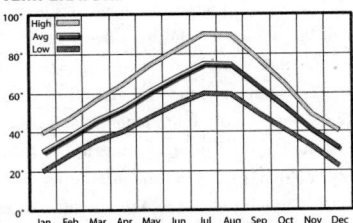

PRECIPITATION

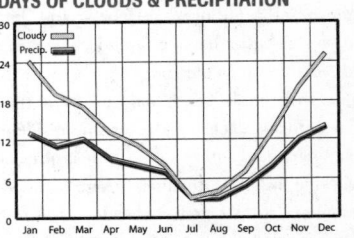

DAYS OF CLOUDS & PRECIPITATION

EDUCATION SCORE: 51/RANK: 160

ACHIEVEMENT	AREA	U.S. AVG	PUBLIC SCHOOLS	AREA	U.S. AVG	HIGHER EDUCATION	AREA	U.S. AVG
High school degree	80.1%	80.2%	Expenditures per pupil	$5,792	$5,894	No. 2-year colleges	1	3
2-year college degree	8.9%	6.2%	Student/teacher ratio	19.4	16.7	No. 4-year colleges/universities	0	4
4-year college degree	14.7%	15.8%	Attending public school	94.7%	90.2%	No. highly ranked universities	0	1
Graduate/professional degree	8.6%	9.6%	State SAT score	1062*	1020			
			State ACT score	22.5	21.0			

HEALTH & HEALTHCARE SCORE: 34/RANK: 218

HAZARDS & ILLNESSES	AREA	U.S. AVG	HEALTHCARE	AREA	U.S. AVG
Air-quality score	49	45	Physicians per capita	155.6	261.1
Water-quality score	11	33	Hospital beds per capita	233.0	432.2
Pollen/allergy score	46	61	No. teaching hospitals	0	4
Stress score	61	50	Cost per doctor visit	$71	$67
Cancer mortality per capita	160.8	169.0	Cost per dental visit	$123	$82
Depression days per month	4.3	2.8	Cost per daily hospital room	$777	$733

CRIME SCORE: 74/RANK: 86

CRIME	AREA	U.S. AVG
Violent crime rate	252.5	456.0
Change in violent crime rate	-32.8%	-17.2%
Property crime rate	3,822.4	3,950.0
Change in property crime rate	-26.5%	-16.8%

TRANSPORTATION SCORE: 96/RANK: 15

COMMUTE	AREA	U.S. AVG	INTERCITY SERVICES	AREA	U.S. AVG	AUTOMOTIVE	AREA	U.S. AVG
Average commute time	21.4 min.	22.6 min.	Miles to nearest major airport	125	46	Insurance, annual premium	$1,008	$1,011
Commute by auto	87.5%	88.7%	Type of local airport	Medium		Gas, cost per gallon	$1.60	$1.50
Commute by mass transit	1.5%	1.8%	No. daily airline departures	115	294	Daily vehicle miles per capita	20.1	23.0
Work at home	5.0%	3.9%	Amtrak service	Yes				
Mass transit miles per capita	33.2	8.0	No. interstate highways	0	1			

LEISURE SCORE: 40/RANK: 197

DINING & SHOPPING	AREA	U.S. AVG	ENTERTAINMENT	AREA	U.S. AVG	OUTDOOR ACTIVITIES	AREA	U.S. AVG
Restaurant rating	1	1	Professional sports rating	3	4	Golf-course rating	2	4
No. outlet malls	0	2	College sports rating	1	4	Ski-area rating	1	4
No. Starbucks	4	11	Zoo/aquarium rating	1	3	National Park rating	1	3
No. warehouse clubs	3	4	Amusement park rating	1	3	Sq. miles inland water	5.0	4.0
			Botanical garden/arboretum rating	1	3	Miles of coastline	0.0	11.4

ARTS & CULTURE SCORE: 22/RANK: 256

MEDIA & LIBRARIES	AREA	U.S. AVG	PERFORMING ARTS	AREA	U.S. AVG	MUSEUMS	AREA	U.S. AVG
Arts radio rating	5	3	Classical music rating	1	4	Overall museum rating	4	6
No. public libraries	12	28	Ballet/dance rating	3	3	Art museum rating	1	5
Library volumes per capita	3.3	2.8	Professional theater rating	1	3	Science museum rating	2	4
			University arts programs rating	1	5	Children's museum rating	1	3

Richmond-Petersburg, VA

Score: 75.9   Rank: 55

Profile: Capital-city complex
Location: East-central Virginia along the James River
Elevation: 177 feet
Time zone: Eastern Standard Time

PRO	CON
Historic interest	Urban sprawl
Capital-city amenities	Entertainment
Strong economy	Summer heat

The former capital of the Confederacy, Richmond is a modern capital city with a strong sense of history. Central areas are a mix of the old and new, with both historic and modern but unremarkable commercial buildings. Museums and historic sites are abundant. Outlying suburbs have sprawled concentrically, especially to the west and south toward Petersburg. Appealing residential areas lie across the James River to the south and in some of the western areas. Easy access to Washington, D.C., and pleasant residential settings have attracted businesses, and future job growth is projected at a robust 17.9%, the highest in the state. Retailers Circuit City and CarMax and financial services giant Capital One have headquarters in Richmond. Growth has generated considerable sprawl and some traffic problems, although most of the outlying areas are still attractive. The University of Richmond adds a few college-town amenities, including sports. Petersburg to the south has a notable historic center and is otherwise closely tied to Richmond. Any missing amenities are available in Washington, D.C., 100 miles north.

Richmond is located along the James River in a mostly wooded area at the border of the Coastal Plain and Piedmont Hills. The Blue Ridge Mountains lie about 90 miles west and the Chesapeake Bay is 60 miles east. Elevations range from a few feet above sea level along the river to over 300 feet in western sections of the city. The climate is modified continental. Summers are warm and humid, among the warmest in Virginia, and winters are generally mild. The mountains to the west act as a partial barrier to winter cold and storms. Precipitation is uniformly distributed through the year. Dry periods, especially in autumn, create periods of pleasant, mild weather. Snow usually remains on the ground only 1 to 2 days at a time and ice storms occur occasionally. Late summer and fall hurricanes along the coast can cause flooding.

POPULATION

DEMOGRAPHICS	AREA	U.S. AVG	ETHNIC COMPOSITION	AREA	U.S. AVG	RESIDENT PROFILE	AREA	U.S. AVG
Population	1,023,419		White	67.7%	75.1%	Single	47.4%	43.6%
Population density per sq. mile	347.5	447.3	Black	30.1%	12.3%	Married	52.6%	56.4%
Population growth	18.2%	16.1%	Asian	1.3%	3.6%	Divorced	7.5%	8.4%
Median age	36.2	35.5	American Indian	.5%	.9%	Separated	5.1%	3.0%
Average family size	2.5	2.7	Hispanic	1.5%	12.5%	Married with children	26.1%	28.7%
			Diversity measure	49.5%	35.2%	Single with children	10.5%	10.1%

ECONOMY & JOBS
SCORE: 70/RANK: 99

INCOME	AREA	U.S. AVG	EMPLOYMENT	AREA	U.S. AVG	LARGEST EMPLOYING INDUSTRY
Per capita income	$26,520	$23,420	Unemployment rate	4.2%	6.1%	Beverage and Tobacco Product Manufacturing
Household income	$52,306	$46,060	Recent job growth	1.6%	.9%	
Household income < $25K	20.2%	26.4%	Projected future job growth	17.9%	15.1%	
Household income > $75K	30.0%	24.5%	White collar	60.9%	54.5%	
Household income growth	55.9%	57.3%	Blue collar	39.1%	45.5%	

COST OF LIVING
SCORE: 49/RANK: 169

INDEXES & TAXES	AREA	U.S. AVG	HOUSING	AREA	U.S. AVG	NECESSITIES	AREA	U.S. AVG
Cost of Living Index	94.1	100.0	Median home price	$142,800	$160,100	Food Index	96.3	100.0
Financial Progress Index	118.4	100.0	Home price appreciation	6.9%	7.1%	Housing Index	88.7	100.0
Income tax rate	5.750%	4.625%	Median rent	$785	$670	Utilities Index	109.6	100.0
Sales tax rate	4.500%	6.474%	Homes owned	66.8%	63.9%	Transportation Index	101.0	100.0
Property tax rate	$12.0	$15.6	Homes rented	24.5%	25.3%	Healthcare Index	88.3	100.0
			Housing affordability	51.0%	54.5%	Miscellaneous Cost Index	93.9	100.0

CLIMATE
SCORE: 36/RANK: 209

TEMPERATURE	AREA	U.S. AVG	PRECIPITATION	AREA	U.S. AVG	COMFORTS & HAZARDS	AREA	U.S. AVG
January low	27.6°F	26.4°F	Annual inches precipitation	43.0	35.9	July relative humidity	72.0%	68.8%
July high	88.2°F	86.7°F	Annual inches snowfall	14.0	24.2	Annual days mostly sunny	210	212
Annual days > 90°F	41	38	Annual days precipitation	113	111	Annual days with thunderstorms	37	39
Annual days < 32°F	85	88	Annual days rain > 0.5 inches	27	23	Tornado risk score	21	19
Annual days < 0°F	0	6	Annual days snow > 1.5 inches	3	6	Hurricane risk score	21	15

TEMPERATURE

PRECIPITATION

DAYS OF CLOUDS & PRECIPITATION

EDUCATION
SCORE: 73/RANK: 89

ACHIEVEMENT	AREA	U.S. AVG	PUBLIC SCHOOLS	AREA	U.S. AVG	HIGHER EDUCATION	AREA	U.S. AVG
High school degree	82.6%	80.2%	Expenditures per pupil	$5,653	$5,894	No. 2-year colleges	4	3
2-year college degree	5.2%	6.2%	Student/teacher ratio	14.7	16.7	No. 4-year colleges/universities	5	4
4-year college degree	18.6%	15.8%	Attending public school	93.5%	90.2%	No. highly ranked universities	0	1
Graduate/professional degree	9.8%	9.6%	State SAT score	1024*	1020			
			State ACT score	20.6	21.0			

HEALTH & HEALTHCARE
SCORE: 78/RANK: 71

HAZARDS & ILLNESSES	AREA	U.S. AVG	HEALTHCARE	AREA	U.S. AVG
Air-quality score	95	45	Physicians per capita	318.2	261.1
Water-quality score	100	33	Hospital beds per capita	598.6	432.2
Pollen/allergy score	66	61	No. teaching hospitals	4	4
Stress score	50	50	Cost per doctor visit	$60	$67
Cancer mortality per capita	177.8	169.0	Cost per dental visit	$70	$82
Depression days per month	2.1	2.8	Cost per daily hospital room	$494	$733

CRIME
SCORE: 33/RANK: 222

CRIME	AREA	U.S. AVG
Violent crime rate	483.7	456.0
Change in violent crime rate	-19.8%	-17.2%
Property crime rate	4,244.9	3,950.0
Change in property crime rate	-10.5%	-16.8%

TRANSPORTATION
SCORE: 33/RANK: 219

COMMUTE	AREA	U.S. AVG	INTERCITY SERVICES	AREA	U.S. AVG	AUTOMOTIVE	AREA	U.S. AVG
Average commute time	24.3 min.	22.6 min.	Miles to nearest major airport	8	46	Insurance, annual premium	$848	$1,011
Commute by auto	87.0%	88.7%	Type of local airport	Small		Gas, cost per gallon	$1.42	$1.50
Commute by mass transit	2.4%	1.8%	No. daily airline departures	125	294	Daily vehicle miles per capita	28.5	23.0
Work at home	2.5%	3.9%	Amtrak service	Yes				
Mass transit miles per capita	7.5	8.0	No. interstate highways	3	1			

LEISURE SCORE: 53/RANK: 150

DINING & SHOPPING	AREA	U.S. AVG	ENTERTAINMENT	AREA	U.S. AVG	OUTDOOR ACTIVITIES	AREA	U.S. AVG
Restaurant rating	1	1	Professional sports rating	3	4	Golf-course rating	5	4
No. outlet malls	2	2	College sports rating	5	4	Ski-area rating	2	4
No. Starbucks	13	11	Zoo/aquarium rating	1	3	National Park rating	2	3
No. warehouse clubs	7	4	Amusement park rating	8	3	Sq. miles inland water	6.0	4.0
			Botanical garden/arboretum rating	8	3	Miles of coastline	0.0	11.4

ARTS & CULTURE SCORE: 90/RANK: 31

MEDIA & LIBRARIES	AREA	U.S. AVG	PERFORMING ARTS	AREA	U.S. AVG	MUSEUMS	AREA	U.S. AVG
Arts radio rating	5	3	Classical music rating	7	4	Overall museum rating	9	6
No. public libraries	51	28	Ballet/dance rating	3	3	Art museum rating	9	5
Library volumes per capita	3.1	2.8	Professional theater rating	8	3	Science museum rating	7	4
			University arts programs rating	8	5	Children's museum rating	7	3

Riverside–San Bernardino, CA

Score: 57.0   Rank: 170

Profile: Commuter community
Location: Southern California, 50 to 80 miles east of Los Angeles and Orange County
Elevation: 850 feet
Time zone: Pacific Standard Time

PRO	CON
Year-round climate	Urban sprawl
Recreation	Traffic
Projected job growth	Air quality

Riverside County and San Bernardino County to the north, like many metro area counties in the Southwest, extend into uninhabited desert areas, in this case east through the Mojave Desert to the Nevada/Arizona border. Cities in the western portion, including Riverside, San Bernardino, Ontario, and a patchwork of other communities, are developed suburbs of the Los Angeles area with a rapidly growing and increasingly self-sufficient economy. Old mansions, public buildings, and packing sheds serve as evidence of the orange-growing industry that once dominated the area. The resort communities of Palm Springs and Palm Desert lie to the east through a mountain gap. Today the main businesses are diversified light manufacturing, services, and retail, and the projected 10-year job-growth rate is the highest in the state. Cost of living and housing are relatively moderate for comparable areas in California. The area is now facing some of the same issues confronting Los Angeles—overcrowding, sprawl, poor air quality, and long freeway commutes. The average commute of 31 minutes is the second highest in the state.

The area is semiarid to arid with dry valleys surrounded by desert mountain ranges. Most of the valley floor to the west is built up. Moving east, coastal grasses and brush give way to desert foliage, including brush, creosote bush, and cactus. The climate varies by altitude and distance from the Pacific Ocean. Summers are warm in the western portion of the counties to extremely hot and dry eastward. Evenings, consistent with the desert climate and with some marine cooling, are comfortable. Winters are mild and mostly dry, but most annual precipitation, including rainy spells, occurs during this season. There are a few days each winter with below-freezing temperatures, but many winters are frost-free. Snow is rare but can occur.

POPULATION

DEMOGRAPHICS	AREA	U.S. AVG	ETHNIC COMPOSITION	AREA	U.S. AVG	RESIDENT PROFILE	AREA	U.S. AVG
Population	3,515,184		White	76.7%	75.1%	Single	44.0%	43.6%
Population density per sq. mile	128.9	447.3	Black	6.0%	12.3%	Married	56.0%	56.4%
Population growth	35.8%	16.1%	Asian	4.7%	3.6%	Divorced	9.8%	8.4%
Median age	31.8	35.5	American Indian	1.3%	.9%	Separated	4.0%	3.0%
Average family size	3.0	2.7	Hispanic	32.0%	12.5%	Married with children	28.9%	28.7%
			Diversity measure	62.6%	35.2%	Single with children	11.9%	10.1%

ECONOMY & JOBS SCORE: 28/RANK: 237

INCOME	AREA	U.S. AVG	EMPLOYMENT	AREA	U.S. AVG	LARGEST EMPLOYING INDUSTRY
Per capita income	$19,058	$23,420	Unemployment rate	6.3%	6.1%	Fabricated Metal Product Manufacturing
Household income	$45,837	$46,060	Recent job growth	2.7%	.9%	
Household income < $25K	25.2%	26.4%	Projected future job growth	25.3%	15.1%	
Household income > $75K	23.9%	24.5%	White collar	51.5%	54.5%	
Household income growth	37.5%	57.3%	Blue collar	48.5%	45.5%	

COST OF LIVING — SCORE: 14/RANK: 283

INDEXES & TAXES	AREA	U.S. AVG	HOUSING	AREA	U.S. AVG	NECESSITIES	AREA	U.S. AVG
Cost of Living Index	112.6	100.0	Median home price	$185,700	$160,100	Food Index	112.2	100.0
Financial Progress Index	86.8	100.0	Home price appreciation	12.1%	7.1%	Housing Index	115.3	100.0
Income tax rate	6.000%	4.625%	Median rent	$729	$670	Utilities Index	118.1	100.0
Sales tax rate	7.750%	6.474%	Homes owned	53.9%	63.9%	Transportation Index	106.4	100.0
Property tax rate	$11.3	$15.6	Homes rented	27.2%	25.3%	Healthcare Index	128.6	100.0
			Housing affordability	50.0%	54.5%	Miscellaneous Cost Index	105.1	100.0

CLIMATE — SCORE: 96/RANK: 13

TEMPERATURE	AREA	U.S. AVG	PRECIPITATION	AREA	U.S. AVG	COMFORTS & HAZARDS	AREA	U.S. AVG
January low	44.4°F	26.4°F	Annual inches precipitation	12.0	35.9	July relative humidity	69.0%	68.8%
July high	81.8°F	86.7°F	Annual inches snowfall	0.0	24.2	Annual days mostly sunny	268	212
Annual days > 90°F	20	38	Annual days precipitation	35	111	Annual days with thunderstorms	3	39
Annual days < 32°F	0	88	Annual days rain > 0.5 inches	2	23	Tornado risk score	2	19
Annual days < 0°F	0	6	Annual days snow > 1.5 inches	0	6	Hurricane risk score	2	15

TEMPERATURE

PRECIPITATION

DAYS OF CLOUDS & PRECIPITATION

EDUCATION — SCORE: 15/RANK: 279

ACHIEVEMENT	AREA	U.S. AVG	PUBLIC SCHOOLS	AREA	U.S. AVG	HIGHER EDUCATION	AREA	U.S. AVG
High school degree	74.9%	80.2%	Expenditures per pupil	$5,048	$5,894	No. 2-year colleges	9	3
2-year college degree	7.4%	6.2%	Student/teacher ratio	22.4	16.7	No. 4-year colleges/universities	5	4
4-year college degree	11.2%	15.8%	Attending public school	93.7%	90.2%	No. highly ranked universities	0	1
Graduate/professional degree	5.7%	9.6%	State SAT score	1018*	1020			
			State ACT score	21.5	21.0			

HEALTH & HEALTHCARE — SCORE: 5/RANK: 313   CRIME — SCORE: 63/RANK: 120

HAZARDS & ILLNESSES	AREA	U.S. AVG	HEALTHCARE	AREA	U.S. AVG	CRIME	AREA	U.S. AVG
Air-quality score	1	45	Physicians per capita	147.8	261.1	Violent crime rate	595.4	456.0
Water-quality score	19	33	Hospital beds per capita	217.4	432.2	Change in violent crime rate	-37.0%	-17.2%
Pollen/allergy score	51	61	No. teaching hospitals	8	4	Property crime rate	3,564.2	3,950.0
Stress score	68	50	Cost per doctor visit	$59	$67	Change in property crime rate	-34.8%	-16.8%
Cancer mortality per capita	164.2	169.0	Cost per dental visit	$106	$82			
Depression days per month	2.7	2.8	Cost per daily hospital room	$1,293	$733			

TRANSPORTATION — SCORE: 0/RANK: 330

COMMUTE	AREA	U.S. AVG	INTERCITY SERVICES	AREA	U.S. AVG	AUTOMOTIVE	AREA	U.S. AVG
Average commute time	31.1 min.	22.6 min.	Miles to nearest major airport	14	46	Insurance, annual premium	$1,378	$1,011
Commute by auto	89.4%	88.7%	Type of local airport	Medium		Gas, cost per gallon	$1.73	$1.50
Commute by mass transit	.6%	1.8%	No. daily airline departures	191	294	Daily vehicle miles per capita	23.8	23.0
Work at home	3.5%	3.9%	Amtrak service	Yes				
Mass transit miles per capita	6.7	8.0	No. interstate highways	1	1			

LEISURE — SCORE: 94/RANK: 17

DINING & SHOPPING	AREA	U.S. AVG	ENTERTAINMENT	AREA	U.S. AVG	OUTDOOR ACTIVITIES	AREA	U.S. AVG
Restaurant rating	1	1	Professional sports rating	9	4	Golf-course rating	10	4
No. outlet malls	8	2	College sports rating	2	4	Ski-area rating	10	4
No. Starbucks	59	11	Zoo/aquarium rating	5	3	National Park rating	10	3
No. warehouse clubs	9	4	Amusement park rating	7	3	Sq. miles inland water	7.0	4.0
			Botanical garden/arboretum rating	8	3	Miles of coastline	0.0	11.4

ARTS & CULTURE — SCORE: 69/RANK: 103

MEDIA & LIBRARIES	AREA	U.S. AVG	PERFORMING ARTS	AREA	U.S. AVG	MUSEUMS	AREA	U.S. AVG
Arts radio rating	9	3	Classical music rating	7	4	Overall museum rating	9	6
No. public libraries	78	28	Ballet/dance rating	6	3	Art museum rating	8	5
Library volumes per capita	1.3	2.8	Professional theater rating	5	3	Science museum rating	10	4
			University arts programs rating	8	5	Children's museum rating	8	3

Roanoke, VA

Score: 88.6   Rank: 11

Profile: Mid-size city
Location: Southwestern Virginia along the Blue Ridge Mountains
Elevation: 1,176 feet
Time zone: Eastern Standard Time

PRO	CON
Nearby mountains	Air service
Attractive downtown	Some industrial feel
Pleasant climate	Air quality

Roanoke is a mid-size commercial and transportation center located between the Blue Ridge and Appalachian mountains in the western part of the state. Transportation routes from tidewater Virginia and the Shenandoah Valley converge with routes over the mountains to the west. The city area is low and sprawling with mountains on the northwest and southeast horizons. The downtown area itself is compact and livable with a number of museums, performing-arts venues, and a famous farmer's market in the lively historic district. It is more "old" than "new" South, but with many modern amenities. The relatively diverse economy includes an industrial base ranging from heavy steel products to textiles and electronics. Cultural amenities are varied and abundant for the town's size, and nearby mountains offer recreational opportunities. Cost of living is reasonable, the climate attractive, and healthcare excellent, thanks to the Carilion medical complex. Poor air quality can result from the valley location, and the area still has a bit of an industrial feel from its days as a rail center; however, it is clean and well kept. Local residents complain about air service and often must drive to the D.C. area or south to Greensboro, North Carolina, to get favorable selection and prices.

Roanoke sits at the point where the Blue Ridge Mountains pinch against the main ridge of the Appalachians. The surrounding terrain is hilly to mountainous and generally wooded. Numerous mountain creeks and small streams empty into the headwaters of the Roanoke River. The climate is relatively mild. The mountains offer a natural barrier to winter cold and the destructive force of Atlantic hurricanes, which the inland location also helps to avoid. The elevation usually produces cool summer nights. Extreme temperatures are rare. Rainfall is well apportioned throughout the year. Snow usually falls each winter, occasionally producing significant accumulations. The mountain stream convergence can produce damaging floods. First freeze is late October, last is mid-April.

POPULATION

DEMOGRAPHICS	AREA	U.S. AVG	ETHNIC COMPOSITION	AREA	U.S. AVG	RESIDENT PROFILE	AREA	U.S. AVG
Population	235,918		White	86.6%	75.1%	Single	48.1%	43.6%
Population density per sq. mile	277.3	447.3	Black	12.1%	12.3%	Married	51.9%	56.4%
Population growth	5.1%	16.1%	Asian	.9%	3.6%	Divorced	8.9%	8.4%
Median age	40.1	35.5	American Indian	.1%	.9%	Separated	3.9%	3.0%
Average family size	2.4	2.7	Hispanic	1.3%	12.5%	Married with children	24.2%	28.7%
			Diversity measure	28.5%	35.2%	Single with children	9.1%	10.1%

ECONOMY & JOBS SCORE: 85/RANK: 50

INCOME	AREA	U.S. AVG	EMPLOYMENT	AREA	U.S. AVG	LARGEST EMPLOYING INDUSTRY
Per capita income	$25,422	$23,420	Unemployment rate	3.3%	6.1%	Fabricated Metal Product Manufacturing
Household income	$45,151	$46,060	Recent job growth	-.8%	.9%	
Household income < $25K	25.8%	26.4%	Projected future job growth	9.0%	15.1%	
Household income > $75K	24.0%	24.5%	White collar	59.3%	54.5%	
Household income growth	55.9%	57.3%	Blue collar	40.7%	45.5%	

COST OF LIVING SCORE: 74/RANK: 83

INDEXES & TAXES	AREA	U.S. AVG	HOUSING	AREA	U.S. AVG	NECESSITIES	AREA	U.S. AVG
Cost of Living Index	84.7	100.0	Median home price	$121,340	$160,100	Food Index	95.9	100.0
Financial Progress Index	113.6	100.0	Home price appreciation	5.9%	7.1%	Housing Index	75.4	100.0
Income tax rate	5.750%	4.625%	Median rent	$515	$670	Utilities Index	71.7	100.0
Sales tax rate	4.500%	6.474%	Homes owned	66.8%	63.9%	Transportation Index	86.5	100.0
Property tax rate	$11.7	$15.6	Homes rented	25.5%	25.3%	Healthcare Index	91.9	100.0
			Housing affordability	63.0%	54.5%	Miscellaneous Cost Index	93.2	100.0

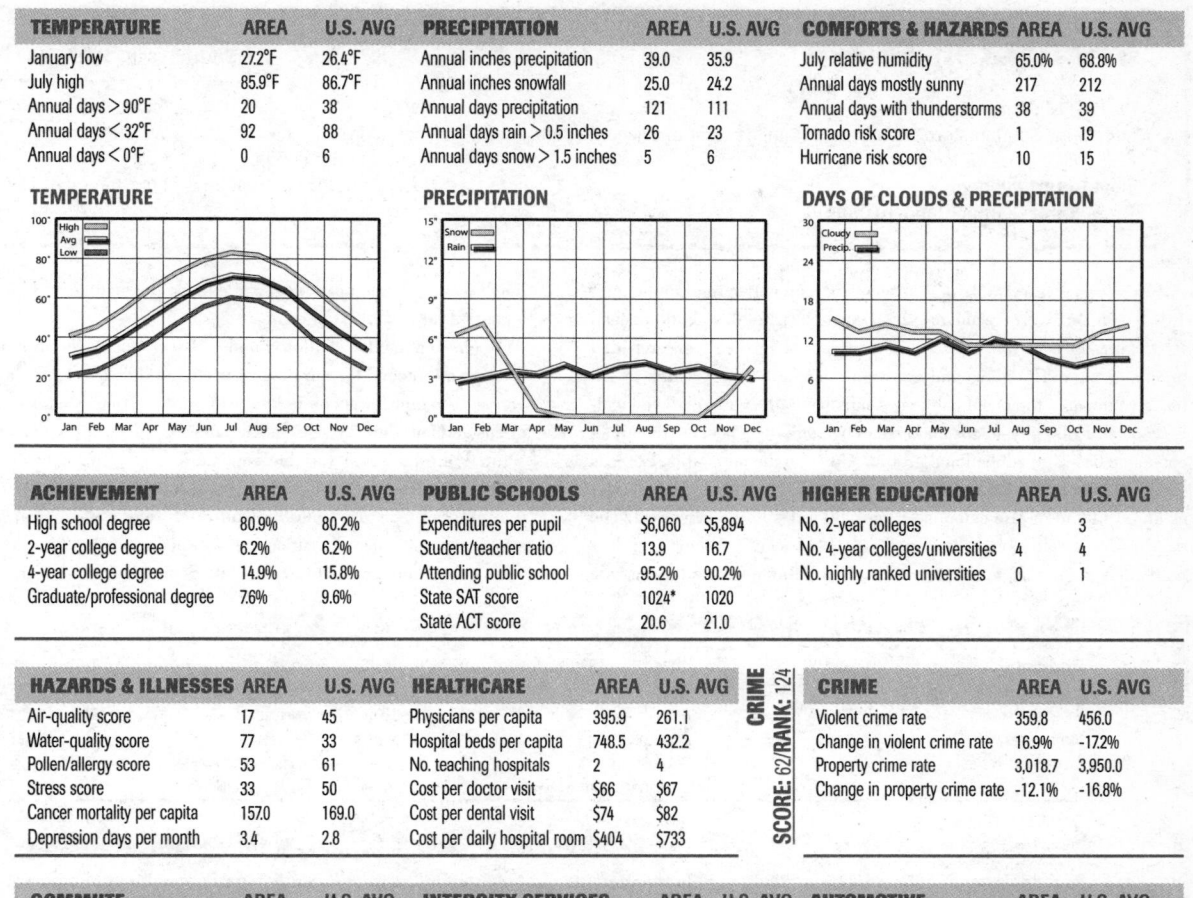

CLIMATE SCORE: 75/RANK: 81

TEMPERATURE	AREA	U.S. AVG
January low	27.2°F	26.4°F
July high	85.9°F	86.7°F
Annual days > 90°F	20	38
Annual days < 32°F	92	88
Annual days < 0°F	0	6

PRECIPITATION	AREA	U.S. AVG
Annual inches precipitation	39.0	35.9
Annual inches snowfall	25.0	24.2
Annual days precipitation	121	111
Annual days rain > 0.5 inches	26	23
Annual days snow > 1.5 inches	5	6

COMFORTS & HAZARDS	AREA	U.S. AVG
July relative humidity	65.0%	68.8%
Annual days mostly sunny	217	212
Annual days with thunderstorms	38	39
Tornado risk score	1	19
Hurricane risk score	10	15

TEMPERATURE

PRECIPITATION

DAYS OF CLOUDS & PRECIPITATION

EDUCATION SCORE: 66/RANK: 111

ACHIEVEMENT	AREA	U.S. AVG
High school degree	80.9%	80.2%
2-year college degree	6.2%	6.2%
4-year college degree	14.9%	15.8%
Graduate/professional degree	7.6%	9.6%

PUBLIC SCHOOLS	AREA	U.S. AVG
Expenditures per pupil	$6,060	$5,894
Student/teacher ratio	13.9	16.7
Attending public school	95.2%	90.2%
State SAT score	1024*	1020
State ACT score	20.6	21.0

HIGHER EDUCATION	AREA	U.S. AVG
No. 2-year colleges	1	3
No. 4-year colleges/universities	4	4
No. highly ranked universities	0	1

HEALTH & HEALTHCARE SCORE: 99/RANK: 2

HAZARDS & ILLNESSES	AREA	U.S. AVG
Air-quality score	17	45
Water-quality score	77	33
Pollen/allergy score	53	61
Stress score	33	50
Cancer mortality per capita	157.0	169.0
Depression days per month	3.4	2.8

HEALTHCARE	AREA	U.S. AVG
Physicians per capita	395.9	261.1
Hospital beds per capita	748.5	432.2
No. teaching hospitals	2	4
Cost per doctor visit	$66	$67
Cost per dental visit	$74	$82
Cost per daily hospital room	$404	$733

CRIME SCORE: 62/RANK: 124

CRIME	AREA	U.S. AVG
Violent crime rate	359.8	456.0
Change in violent crime rate	16.9%	-17.2%
Property crime rate	3,018.7	3,950.0
Change in property crime rate	-12.1%	-16.8%

TRANSPORTATION SCORE: 57/RANK: 141

COMMUTE	AREA	U.S. AVG
Average commute time	20.6 min.	22.6 min.
Commute by auto	89.1%	88.7%
Commute by mass transit	1.1%	1.8%
Work at home	2.2%	3.9%
Mass transit miles per capita	6.7	8.0

INTERCITY SERVICES	AREA	U.S. AVG
Miles to nearest major airport	3	46
Type of local airport	Small	
No. daily airline departures	64	294
Amtrak service	No	
No. interstate highways	1	1

AUTOMOTIVE	AREA	U.S. AVG
Insurance, annual premium	$800	$1,011
Gas, cost per gallon	$1.35	$1.50
Daily vehicle miles per capita	23.7	23.0

LEISURE SCORE: 29/RANK: 234

DINING & SHOPPING	AREA	U.S. AVG
Restaurant rating	1	1
No. outlet malls	0	2
No. Starbucks	0	11
No. warehouse clubs	1	4

ENTERTAINMENT	AREA	U.S. AVG
Professional sports rating	3	4
College sports rating	1	4
Zoo/aquarium rating	1	3
Amusement park rating	1	3
Botanical garden/arboretum rating	1	3

OUTDOOR ACTIVITIES	AREA	U.S. AVG
Golf-course rating	2	4
Ski-area rating	4	4
National Park rating	5	3
Sq. miles inland water	2.0	4.0
Miles of coastline	0.0	11.4

ARTS & CULTURE SCORE: 81/RANK: 61

MEDIA & LIBRARIES	AREA	U.S. AVG
Arts radio rating	1	3
No. public libraries	17	28
Library volumes per capita	4.0	2.8

PERFORMING ARTS	AREA	U.S. AVG
Classical music rating	3	4
Ballet/dance rating	1	3
Professional theater rating	1	3
University arts programs rating	6	5

MUSEUMS	AREA	U.S. AVG
Overall museum rating	5	6
Art museum rating	5	5
Science museum rating	5	4
Children's museum rating	1	3

Rochester, MN

Score: 60.6 **Rank:** 144

Profile: Mid-size city
Location: Southeastern Minnesota, 45 miles west of Wisconsin and 35 miles north of Iowa
Elevation: 1,006 feet
Time zone: Central Standard Time

PRO	CON
Healthcare	Winter climate
Educated population	Economy
Nearby outdoor recreation	Entertainment

Rochester is a livable mid-size commercial and agricultural center with a diverse economy. It's best known for the founding and presence of the Mayo Clinic, a leading medical research and practice center. The Mayo and its extensive health and research facilities give the area the best healthcare statistics in the nation. Mayo locally employs 1,600 physicians and researchers, giving a boost to the area's economic base and educational profile. Although the population exceeds 1 million, Rochester has a small-town feel. Missing amenities or services are available in Minneapolis-St Paul, 80 miles to the northwest. The nearby Dorer state forest, known for its hardwoods, provides outdoor recreation, such as camping, picnicking, and hiking. Downsides include harsh winters, some unemployment outside the healthcare industry, and a general lack of entertainment.

Rochester, in the shallow Zumbro River Valley, is surrounded by rolling and wooded terrain ranging from 1,000 feet to 1,300 feet in elevation. The climate is continental with large seasonal temperature variations and four definite seasons. Summers are pleasant but can be warm. Winters are cold and variable with periods of bitter cold and regular snow cover. Rochester lies near a storm track and the northern edge of the influx of moisture from the Gulf of Mexico, a position resulting in strong storms year-round. Flooding can occur on the Zumbro River in spring and summer. First freeze is late September, last is early May.

POPULATION

DEMOGRAPHICS	AREA	U.S. AVG	ETHNIC COMPOSITION	AREA	U.S. AVG	RESIDENT PROFILE	AREA	U.S. AVG
Population	128,961		White	95.7%	75.1%	Single	37.9%	43.6%
Population density per sq. mile	197.5	447.3	Black	.7%	12.3%	Married	62.1%	56.4%
Population growth	21.1%	16.1%	Asian	3.1%	3.6%	Divorced	6.8%	8.4%
Median age	35.3	35.5	American Indian	.3%	.9%	Separated	1.2%	3.0%
Average family size	2.7	2.7	Hispanic	1.1%	12.5%	Married with children	33.4%	28.7%
			Diversity measure	20.1%	35.2%	Single with children	7.4%	10.1%

ECONOMY & JOBS SCORE: 86/RANK: 41

INCOME	AREA	U.S. AVG	EMPLOYMENT	AREA	U.S. AVG	LARGEST EMPLOYING INDUSTRY
Per capita income	$30,215	$23,420	Unemployment rate	3.6%	6.1%	Computer and Electronic Product Manufacturing
Household income	$62,051	$46,060	Recent job growth	.7%	.9%	
Household income < $25K	17.1%	26.4%	Projected future job growth	13.2%	15.1%	
Household income > $75K	37.7%	24.5%	White collar	64.4%	54.5%	
Household income growth	73.4%	57.3%	Blue collar	35.6%	45.5%	

COST OF LIVING SCORE: 19/RANK: 267

INDEXES & TAXES	AREA	U.S. AVG	HOUSING	AREA	U.S. AVG	NECESSITIES	AREA	U.S. AVG
Cost of Living Index	102.7	100.0	Median home price	$150,750	$160,100	Food Index	94.8	100.0
Financial Progress Index	128.8	100.0	Home price appreciation	8.8%	7.1%	Housing Index	93.6	100.0
Income tax rate	8.000%	4.625%	Median rent	$714	$670	Utilities Index	135.6	100.0
Sales tax rate	7.000%	6.474%	Homes owned	74.9%	63.9%	Transportation Index	107.6	100.0
Property tax rate	$13.2	$15.6	Homes rented	20.9%	25.3%	Healthcare Index	114.2	100.0
			Housing affordability	54.0%	54.5%	Miscellaneous Cost Index	106.1	100.0

CLIMATE SCORE: 12/RANK: 291

TEMPERATURE	AREA	U.S. AVG	PRECIPITATION	AREA	U.S. AVG	COMFORTS & HAZARDS	AREA	U.S. AVG
January low	3.2°F	26.4°F	Annual inches precipitation	26.0	35.9	July relative humidity	69.0%	68.8%
July high	82.4°F	86.7°F	Annual inches snowfall	46.0	24.2	Annual days mostly sunny	200	212
Annual days > 90°F	15	38	Annual days precipitation	113	111	Annual days with thunderstorms	36	39
Annual days < 32°F	158	88	Annual days rain > 0.5 inches	18	23	Tornado risk score	20	19
Annual days < 0°F	34	6	Annual days snow > 1.5 inches	10	6	Hurricane risk score	0	15

TEMPERATURE

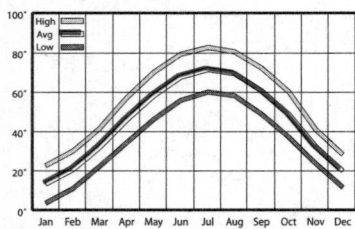

PRECIPITATION

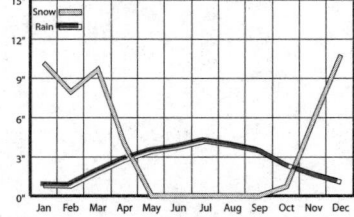

DAYS OF CLOUDS & PRECIPITATION

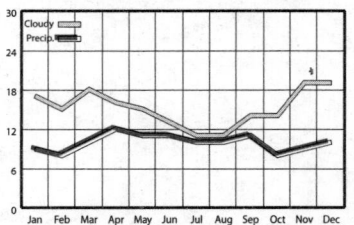

EDUCATION SCORE: 86/RANK: 47

ACHIEVEMENT	AREA	U.S. AVG	PUBLIC SCHOOLS	AREA	U.S. AVG	HIGHER EDUCATION	AREA	U.S. AVG
High school degree	91.0%	80.2%	Expenditures per pupil	$5,629	$5,894	No. 2-year colleges	1	3
2-year college degree	10.1%	6.2%	Student/teacher ratio	16.9	16.7	No. 4-year colleges/universities	1	4
4-year college degree	21.2%	15.8%	Attending public school	86.1%	90.2%	No. highly ranked universities	0	1
Graduate/professional degree	13.5%	9.6%	State SAT score	1173	1020			
			State ACT score	22.0*	21.0			

HEALTH & HEALTHCARE SCORE: 100/RANK: 1

HAZARDS & ILLNESSES	AREA	U.S. AVG	HEALTHCARE	AREA	U.S. AVG
Air-quality score	59	45	Physicians per capita	1814.5	261.1
Water-quality score	18	33	Hospital beds per capita	1016.3	432.2
Pollen/allergy score	46	61	No. teaching hospitals	2	4
Stress score	1	50	Cost per doctor visit	$90	$67
Cancer mortality per capita	151.5	169.0	Cost per dental visit	$90	$82
Depression days per month	1.3	2.8	Cost per daily hospital room	$829	$733

CRIME SCORE: 77/RANK: 75

CRIME	AREA	U.S. AVG
Violent crime rate	228.5	456.0
Change in violent crime rate	-9.9%	-17.2%
Property crime rate	2,951.2	3,950.0
Change in property crime rate	-14.0%	-16.8%

TRANSPORTATION SCORE: 98/RANK: 5

COMMUTE	AREA	U.S. AVG	INTERCITY SERVICES	AREA	U.S. AVG	AUTOMOTIVE	AREA	U.S. AVG
Average commute time	16.3 min.	22.6 min.	Miles to nearest major airport	70	46	Insurance, annual premium	$951	$1,011
Commute by auto	86.7%	88.7%	Type of local airport	Large		Gas, cost per gallon	$1.49	$1.50
Commute by mass transit	1.8%	1.8%	No. daily airline departures	624	294	Daily vehicle miles per capita	19.1	23.0
Work at home	5.9%	3.9%	Amtrak service	No				
Mass transit miles per capita	7.5	8.0	No. interstate highways	2	1			

LEISURE SCORE: 71/RANK: 95

DINING & SHOPPING	AREA	U.S. AVG	ENTERTAINMENT	AREA	U.S. AVG	OUTDOOR ACTIVITIES	AREA	U.S. AVG
Restaurant rating	1	1	Professional sports rating	2	4	Golf-course rating	9	4
No. outlet malls	1	2	College sports rating	9	4	Ski-area rating	5	4
No. Starbucks	0	11	Zoo/aquarium rating	1	3	National Park rating	3	3
No. warehouse clubs	3	4	Amusement park rating	1	3	Sq. miles inland water	2.0	4.0
			Botanical garden/arboretum rating	1	3	Miles of coastline	0.0	11.4

ARTS & CULTURE SCORE: 97/RANK: 8

MEDIA & LIBRARIES	AREA	U.S. AVG	PERFORMING ARTS	AREA	U.S. AVG	MUSEUMS	AREA	U.S. AVG
Arts radio rating	1	3	Classical music rating	4	4	Overall museum rating	3	6
No. public libraries	2	28	Ballet/dance rating	1	3	Art museum rating	4	5
Library volumes per capita	.7	2.8	Professional theater rating	1	3	Science museum rating	1	4
			University arts programs rating	2	5	Children's museum rating	1	3

Rochester, NY

Score: 51.2 Rank: 214

Profile: Mid-size city
Location: Northwestern New York on Lake Ontario
Elevation: 547 feet
Time zone: Eastern Standard Time

PRO	CON
Economy	Snow
Arts and culture	Rain
Nearby recreation	Cost of living

Rochester is a major industrial city and port of entry for Great Lakes shipping on the St. Lawrence Seaway. Commercial and industrial activity, led by the Eastman Kodak Company, includes chemicals, scientific instruments, food processing, and shipping. There are well-endowed arts and cultural assets and a strong university influence from the Rochester Institute of Technology and the University of Rochester. (Between local industry, higher education, and science museums, scientists and science buffs feel at home in the area.) Agriculture is also notable, as a combination of soil, moisture, and lake warmth create a long growing season for the latitude and a favorable environment for fruits, vegetables, and wineries. Climate is the main downside, with abundant clouds and rain and heavy lake-effect snows. The area is the fourth rainiest place in the country. Cost of living, while not bad on a state or national scale, is the highest in western New York.

The area is located on a broad plain defined by Lake Ontario and the Genesee River Valley. Twenty miles south, low rolling hills begin to rise to 1,000 feet. Vegetation is a mix of open farmland and deciduous woods. The climate is humid continental strongly modified by the Great Lakes. Precipitation is evenly distributed throughout the year in quantity, but frequency is much higher during winter. Snowfall is heavy, but highly variable over short distances. More snow falls to the east. Winters in general are cloudy, cold, and changeable with frequent thaws and rain. Snow covers the ground from Christmas into early March. The lake modifies extreme cold, and below-zero temperatures are infrequent but do occur more inland. Summers are warm and sunny with intermittent rain or thundershowers. Temperatures seldom exceed 90°F. Spring comes slowly and fall is brief. First freeze is mid-October, last is early May.

POPULATION

DEMOGRAPHICS	AREA	U.S. AVG	ETHNIC COMPOSITION	AREA	U.S. AVG	RESIDENT PROFILE	AREA	U.S. AVG
Population	1,102,581		White	89.0%	75.1%	Single	45.7%	43.6%
Population density per sq. mile	321.9	447.3	Black	7.4%	12.3%	Married	54.3%	56.4%
Population growth	3.8%	16.1%	Asian	1.9%	3.6%	Divorced	7.1%	8.4%
Median age	36.7	35.5	American Indian	.6%	.9%	Separated	4.1%	3.0%
Average family size	2.6	2.7	Hispanic	3.0%	12.5%	Married with children	27.8%	28.7%
			Diversity measure	31.2%	35.2%	Single with children	10.0%	10.1%

ECONOMY & JOBS — SCORE: 76/RANK: 78

INCOME	AREA	U.S. AVG	EMPLOYMENT	AREA	U.S. AVG	LARGEST EMPLOYING INDUSTRY
Per capita income	$24,016	$23,420	Unemployment rate	5.4%	6.1%	Chemical Manufacturing
Household income	$49,179	$46,060	Recent job growth	-.4%	.9%	
Household income < $25K	22.9%	26.4%	Projected future job growth	7.4%	15.1%	
Household income > $75K	27.1%	24.5%	White collar	57.2%	54.5%	
Household income growth	44.5%	57.3%	Blue collar	42.8%	45.5%	

COST OF LIVING — SCORE: 19/RANK: 266

INDEXES & TAXES	AREA	U.S. AVG	HOUSING	AREA	U.S. AVG	NECESSITIES	AREA	U.S. AVG
Cost of Living Index	90.5	100.0	Median home price	$95,300	$160,100	Food Index	112.6	100.0
Financial Progress Index	115.8	100.0	Home price appreciation	3.5%	7.1%	Housing Index	59.2	100.0
Income tax rate	7.125%	4.625%	Median rent	$639	$670	Utilities Index	133.8	100.0
Sales tax rate	8.000%	6.474%	Homes owned	67.7%	63.9%	Transportation Index	105.3	100.0
Property tax rate	$28.2	$15.6	Homes rented	23.8%	25.3%	Healthcare Index	104.2	100.0
			Housing affordability	50.0%	54.5%	Miscellaneous Cost Index	97.6	100.0

CLIMATE — SCORE: 13/RANK: 286

TEMPERATURE	AREA	U.S. AVG	PRECIPITATION	AREA	U.S. AVG	COMFORTS & HAZARDS	AREA	U.S. AVG
January low	16.7°F	26.4°F	Annual inches precipitation	31.3	35.9	July relative humidity	73.0%	68.8%
July high	82.2°F	86.7°F	Annual inches snowfall	88.4	24.2	Annual days mostly sunny	170	212
Annual days > 90°F	11	38	Annual days precipitation	182	111	Annual days with thunderstorms	29	39
Annual days < 32°F	135	88	Annual days rain > 0.5 inches	17	23	Tornado risk score	1	19
Annual days < 0°F	6	6	Annual days snow > 1.5 inches	19	6	Hurricane risk score	5	15

TEMPERATURE

PRECIPITATION

DAYS OF CLOUDS & PRECIPITATION

EDUCATION — SCORE: 93/RANK: 23

ACHIEVEMENT	AREA	U.S. AVG	PUBLIC SCHOOLS	AREA	U.S. AVG	HIGHER EDUCATION	AREA	U.S. AVG
High school degree	84.4%	80.2%	Expenditures per pupil	$8,436	$5,894	No. 2-year colleges	5	3
2-year college degree	10.0%	6.2%	Student/teacher ratio	13.7	16.7	No. 4-year colleges/universities	9	4
4-year college degree	16.2%	15.8%	Attending public school	90.2%	90.2%	No. highly ranked universities	2	1
Graduate/professional degree	11.0%	9.6%	State SAT score	1006*	1020			
			State ACT score	22.3	21.0			

HEALTH & HEALTHCARE — SCORE: 36/RANK: 209

HAZARDS & ILLNESSES	AREA	U.S. AVG	HEALTHCARE	AREA	U.S. AVG
Air-quality score	74	45	Physicians per capita	308.7	261.1
Water-quality score	25	33	Hospital beds per capita	471.6	432.2
Pollen/allergy score	67	61	No. teaching hospitals	7	4
Stress score	43	50	Cost per doctor visit	$63	$67
Cancer mortality per capita	171.5	169.0	Cost per dental visit	$81	$82
Depression days per month	3.5	2.8	Cost per daily hospital room	$917	$733

CRIME — SCORE: 81/RANK: 62

CRIME	AREA	U.S. AVG
Violent crime rate	236.1	456.0
Change in violent crime rate	-30.9%	-17.2%
Property crime rate	3,246.2	3,950.0
Change in property crime rate	-22.8%	-16.8%

TRANSPORTATION — SCORE: 66/RANK: 112

COMMUTE	AREA	U.S. AVG	INTERCITY SERVICES	AREA	U.S. AVG	AUTOMOTIVE	AREA	U.S. AVG
Average commute time	21.1 min.	22.6 min.	Miles to nearest major airport	4	46	Insurance, annual premium	$1,358	$1,011
Commute by auto	88.4%	88.7%	Type of local airport	Small		Gas, cost per gallon	$1.59	$1.50
Commute by mass transit	2.2%	1.8%	No. daily airline departures	142	294	Daily vehicle miles per capita	23.2	23.0
Work at home	3.1%	3.9%	Amtrak service	Yes				
Mass transit miles per capita	6.7	8.0	No. interstate highways	1	1			

LEISURE SCORE: 78/RANK: 72

DINING & SHOPPING	AREA	U.S. AVG	ENTERTAINMENT	AREA	U.S. AVG	OUTDOOR ACTIVITIES	AREA	U.S. AVG
Restaurant rating	1	1	Professional sports rating	3	4	Golf-course rating	7	4
No. outlet malls	1	2	College sports rating	8	4	Ski-area rating	4	4
No. Starbucks	9	11	Zoo/aquarium rating	5	3	National Park rating	1	3
No. warehouse clubs	8	4	Amusement park rating	6	3	Sq. miles inland water	4.0	4.0
			Botanical garden/arboretum rating	7	3	Miles of coastline	88.7	11.4

ARTS & CULTURE SCORE: 84/RANK: 56

MEDIA & LIBRARIES	AREA	U.S. AVG	PERFORMING ARTS	AREA	U.S. AVG	MUSEUMS	AREA	U.S. AVG
Arts radio rating	8	3	Classical music rating	4	4	Overall museum rating	9	6
No. public libraries	78	28	Ballet/dance rating	3	3	Art museum rating	8	5
Library volumes per capita	4.0	2.8	Professional theater rating	6	3	Science museum rating	7	4
			University arts programs rating	8	5	Children's museum rating	7	3

Rockford, IL

Score: 49.5   Rank: 231

Profile: Small town
Location: North-central Illinois near the Wisconsin border, 80 miles west of Chicago
Elevation: 743 feet
Time zone: Central Standard Time

PRO	CON
Small-town atmosphere	Harsh climate
Economic transition	High unemployment
Large water park	Isolation

Rockford is more of an industrial town and than a typical Illinois agricultural center. It has a diverse manufacturing base, which has partially transitioned away from its Rust Belt beginnings. Today local industries include aviation, aerospace, precision tools, and medicine along with the mainstays of agriculture and agricultural machinery. However, recent unemployment is 8.2% and property crime rates are the highest in the state. The downtown area has trees and a park along the Rock River. Nearby Magic Waters is acclaimed to be the world's largest water park. Some recreational opportunities are available in Wisconsin to the north, but residents must travel to Chicago for many amenities.

Rockford is located along the Rock River in an area of level to gently rolling terrain and open farmland. The climate is continental and variable. Summers are hot and sticky while winters are cold and blustery. Northeasterly winds from Lake Michigan cause cloudy periods in winter and some temperature moderation compared to areas farther west. Summers are hot but may also be cooled by lake winds. Precipitation is distributed evenly throughout the year, with slightly more arriving in summer, mainly as thunderstorms. Rockford is far enough north to have snow cover through the mid-winter months. First freeze is mid-October, last is late April.

POPULATION

DEMOGRAPHICS	AREA	U.S. AVG	ETHNIC COMPOSITION	AREA	U.S. AVG	RESIDENT PROFILE	AREA	U.S. AVG
Population	379,376		White	92.9%	75.1%	Single	39.0%	43.6%
Population density per sq. mile	244.1	447.3	Black	4.6%	12.3%	Married	61.0%	56.4%
Population growth	15.1%	16.1%	Asian	1.0%	3.6%	Divorced	8.4%	8.4%
Median age	36.2	35.5	American Indian	.2%	.9%	Separated	1.7%	3.0%
Average family size	2.6	2.7	Hispanic	3.8%	12.5%	Married with children	30.9%	28.7%
			Diversity measure	31.1%	35.2%	Single with children	8.8%	10.1%

ECONOMY & JOBS SCORE: 50/RANK: 166

INCOME	AREA	U.S. AVG	EMPLOYMENT	AREA	U.S. AVG	LARGEST EMPLOYING INDUSTRY
Per capita income	$23,144	$23,420	Unemployment rate	8.2%	6.1%	Machinery Manufacturing
Household income	$48,069	$46,060	Recent job growth	1.0%	.9%	
Household income < $25K	23.2%	26.4%	Projected future job growth	10.0%	15.1%	
Household income > $75K	24.0%	24.5%	White collar	50.5%	54.5%	
Household income growth	52.3%	57.3%	Blue collar	49.5%	45.5%	

COST OF LIVING SCORE: 31/RANK: 228

INDEXES & TAXES	AREA	U.S. AVG	HOUSING	AREA	U.S. AVG	NECESSITIES	AREA	U.S. AVG
Cost of Living Index	91.4	100.0	Median home price	$109,900	$160,100	Food Index	101.3	100.0
Financial Progress Index	112.0	100.0	Home price appreciation	3.5%	7.1%	Housing Index	68.3	100.0
Income tax rate	3.000%	4.625%	Median rent	$607	$670	Utilities Index	127.9	100.0
Sales tax rate	6.250%	6.474%	Homes owned	71.7%	63.9%	Transportation Index	104.4	100.0
Property tax rate	$36.2	$15.6	Homes rented	23.8%	25.3%	Healthcare Index	98.8	100.0
			Housing affordability	59.0%	54.5%	Miscellaneous Cost Index	99.9	100.0

CLIMATE SCORE: 22/RANK: 258

TEMPERATURE	AREA	U.S. AVG	PRECIPITATION	AREA	U.S. AVG	COMFORTS & HAZARDS	AREA	U.S. AVG
January low	11.5°F	26.4°F	Annual inches precipitation	37.0	35.9	July relative humidity	72.0%	68.8%
July high	84.2°F	86.7°F	Annual inches snowfall	33.0	24.2	Annual days mostly sunny	196	212
Annual days > 90°F	13	38	Annual days precipitation	114	111	Annual days with thunderstorms	42	39
Annual days < 32°F	142	88	Annual days rain > 0.5 inches	25	23	Tornado risk score	20	19
Annual days < 0°F	16	6	Annual days snow > 1.5 inches	10	6	Hurricane risk score	1	15

TEMPERATURE

PRECIPITATION

DAYS OF CLOUDS & PRECIPITATION

EDUCATION SCORE: 16/RANK: 276

ACHIEVEMENT	AREA	U.S. AVG	PUBLIC SCHOOLS	AREA	U.S. AVG	HIGHER EDUCATION	AREA	U.S. AVG
High school degree	81.6%	80.2%	Expenditures per pupil	$6,014	$5,894	No. 2-year colleges	2	3
2-year college degree	5.7%	6.2%	Student/teacher ratio	17.2	16.7	No. 4-year colleges/universities	1	4
4-year college degree	12.7%	15.8%	Attending public school	86.7%	90.2%	No. highly ranked universities	0	1
Graduate/professional degree	6.3%	9.6%	State SAT score	1179	1020			
			State ACT score	20.2*	21.0			

HEALTH & HEALTHCARE SCORE: 73/RANK: 86

HAZARDS & ILLNESSES	AREA	U.S. AVG	HEALTHCARE	AREA	U.S. AVG
Air-quality score	17	45	Physicians per capita	200.6	261.1
Water-quality score	35	33	Hospital beds per capita	343.4	432.2
Pollen/allergy score	39	61	No. teaching hospitals	1	4
Stress score	87	50	Cost per doctor visit	$64	$67
Cancer mortality per capita	166.8	169.0	Cost per dental visit	$77	$82
Depression days per month	3.6	2.8	Cost per daily hospital room	$661	$733

CRIME SCORE: 41/RANK: 195

CRIME	AREA	U.S. AVG
Violent crime rate	456.4	456.0
Change in violent crime rate	-31.4%	-17.2%
Property crime rate	4,444.6	3,950.0
Change in property crime rate	-22.7%	-16.8%

TRANSPORTATION SCORE: 26/RANK: 243

COMMUTE	AREA	U.S. AVG	INTERCITY SERVICES	AREA	U.S. AVG	AUTOMOTIVE	AREA	U.S. AVG
Average commute time	21.9 min.	22.6 min.	Miles to nearest major airport	61	46	Insurance, annual premium	$913	$1,011
Commute by auto	91.0%	88.7%	Type of local airport	Small		Gas, cost per gallon	$1.48	$1.50
Commute by mass transit	.5%	1.8%	No. daily airline departures	49	294	Daily vehicle miles per capita	23.5	23.0
Work at home	4.4%	3.9%	Amtrak service	No				
Mass transit miles per capita	4.0	8.0	No. interstate highways	1	1			

LEISURE SCORE: 24/RANK: 249

DINING & SHOPPING	AREA	U.S. AVG	ENTERTAINMENT	AREA	U.S. AVG	OUTDOOR ACTIVITIES	AREA	U.S. AVG
Restaurant rating	1	1	Professional sports rating	3	4	Golf-course rating	3	4
No. outlet malls	3	2	College sports rating	2	4	Ski-area rating	3	4
No. Starbucks	2	11	Zoo/aquarium rating	1	3	National Park rating	1	3
No. warehouse clubs	3	4	Amusement park rating	1	3	Sq. miles inland water	2.0	4.0
			Botanical garden/arboretum rating	1	3	Miles of coastline	0.0	11.4

ARTS & CULTURE SCORE: 39/RANK: 202

MEDIA & LIBRARIES	AREA	U.S. AVG	PERFORMING ARTS	AREA	U.S. AVG	MUSEUMS	AREA	U.S. AVG
Arts radio rating	1	3	Classical music rating	3	4	Overall museum rating	5	6
No. public libraries	23	28	Ballet/dance rating	1	3	Art museum rating	4	5
Library volumes per capita	4.4	2.8	Professional theater rating	6	3	Science museum rating	6	4
			University arts programs rating	1	5	Children's museum rating	6	3

Rocky Mount, NC

| Score: 34.0 | Rank: 301 |

Profile: Small town
Location: Northeastern North Carolina along I-95 corridor, 55 miles east of Raleigh-Durham
Elevation: 150 feet
Time zone: Eastern Standard Time

PRO
Small-town atmosphere
Historic interest
Proximity to Raleigh-Durham

CON
Declining industries
Economic cycles
Hot, humid summers

Rocky Mount is a typical small Southern town. Like many Carolina towns along transportation arteries, it started as an agricultural and tobacco center but has developed a strong manufacturing and economic base. Such diverse companies as Abbott Laboratories, Sprint, Sara Lee, and QVC Network have facilities here. That said, employment has slowed dramatically in recent years. The town has a well-kept downtown with several minor historic areas. Most cultural and recreational amenities exist in the Raleigh area to the west and the Outer Banks to the east.

Rocky Mount is located on the eastern Carolina coastal plain. The surrounding terrain is mainly level with agriculture and deciduous woodland. The climate is mainly humid subtropical with some moderated continental influence mainly in winter. Summers are warm and humid with frequent thundershowers. Winters are cool with occasional below-freezing temperatures, snow, and freezing rain.

POPULATION

DEMOGRAPHICS	AREA	U.S. AVG	ETHNIC COMPOSITION	AREA	U.S. AVG	RESIDENT PROFILE	AREA	U.S. AVG
Population	144,293		White	57.9%	75.1%	Single	48.2%	43.6%
Population density per sq. mile	138.0	447.3	Black	41.3%	12.3%	Married	51.8%	56.4%
Population growth	8.3%	16.1%	Asian	.2%	3.6%	Divorced	6.4%	8.4%
Median age	36.7	35.5	American Indian	.3%	.9%	Separated	6.3%	3.0%
Average family size	2.7	2.7	Hispanic	1.4%	12.5%	Married with children	26.4%	28.7%
			Diversity measure	53.6%	35.2%	Single with children	14.4%	10.1%

ECONOMY & JOBS
SCORE: 3/RANK: 321

INCOME	AREA	U.S. AVG	EMPLOYMENT	AREA	U.S. AVG	LARGEST EMPLOYING INDUSTRY
Per capita income	$16,830	$23,420	Unemployment rate	8.5%	6.1%	Fabricated Metal Product Manufacturing
Household income	$32,401	$46,060	Recent job growth	-1.3%	.9%	
Household income < $25K	37.3%	26.4%	Projected future job growth	11.2%	15.1%	
Household income > $75K	11.9%	24.5%	White collar	45.5%	54.5%	
Household income growth	34.1%	57.3%	Blue collar	54.5%	45.5%	

COST OF LIVING
SCORE: 70/RANK: 99

INDEXES & TAXES	AREA	U.S. AVG	HOUSING	AREA	U.S. AVG	NECESSITIES	AREA	U.S. AVG
Cost of Living Index	85.3	100.0	Median home price	$96,830	$160,100	Food Index	97.9	100.0
Financial Progress Index	81.0	100.0	Home price appreciation	3.8%	7.1%	Housing Index	60.1	100.0
Income tax rate	7.000%	4.625%	Median rent	$464	$670	Utilities Index	104.2	100.0
Sales tax rate	7.000%	6.474%	Homes owned	63.5%	63.9%	Transportation Index	97.0	100.0
Property tax rate	$9.7	$15.6	Homes rented	29.1%	25.3%	Healthcare Index	95.8	100.0
			Housing affordability	61.0%	54.5%	Miscellaneous Cost Index	101.0	100.0

CLIMATE
SCORE: 63/RANK: 123

TEMPERATURE	AREA	U.S. AVG	PRECIPITATION	AREA	U.S. AVG	COMFORTS & HAZARDS	AREA	U.S. AVG
January low	30.0°F	26.4°F	Annual inches precipitation	43.0	35.9	July relative humidity	71.0%	68.8%
July high	87.7°F	86.7°F	Annual inches snowfall	7.0	24.2	Annual days mostly sunny	220	212
Annual days > 90°F	25	38	Annual days precipitation	112	111	Annual days with thunderstorms	46	39
Annual days < 32°F	82	88	Annual days rain > 0.5 inches	28	23	Tornado risk score	12	19
Annual days < 0°F	0	6	Annual days snow > 1.5 inches	2	6	Hurricane risk score	37	15

TEMPERATURE

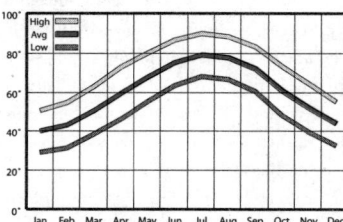

PRECIPITATION

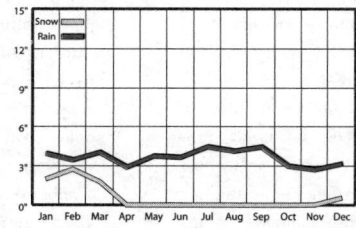

DAYS OF CLOUDS & PRECIPITATION

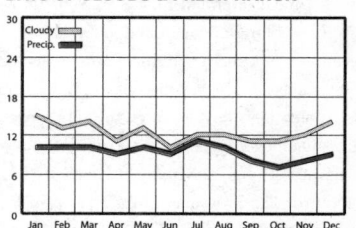

EDUCATION SCORE: 10/RANK: 297

ACHIEVEMENT	AREA	U.S. AVG	PUBLIC SCHOOLS	AREA	U.S. AVG	HIGHER EDUCATION	AREA	U.S. AVG
High school degree	71.8%	80.2%	Expenditures per pupil	$5,186	$5,894	No. 2-year colleges	2	3
2-year college degree	5.7%	6.2%	Student/teacher ratio	15.0	16.7	No. 4-year colleges/universities	1	4
4-year college degree	10.0%	15.8%	Attending public school	93.9%	90.2%	No. highly ranked universities	0	1
Graduate/professional degree	3.9%	9.6%	State SAT score	1001*	1020			
			State ACT score	19.9	21.0			

HEALTH & HEALTHCARE SCORE: 52/RANK: 159 | CRIME SCORE: 15/RANK: 279

HAZARDS & ILLNESSES	AREA	U.S. AVG	HEALTHCARE	AREA	U.S. AVG	CRIME	AREA	U.S. AVG
Air-quality score	24	45	Physicians per capita	138.6	261.1	Violent crime rate	599.5	456.0
Water-quality score	49	33	Hospital beds per capita	392.9	432.2	Change in violent crime rate	-15.0%	-17.2%
Pollen/allergy score	65	61	No. teaching hospitals	0	4	Property crime rate	5,119.7	3,950.0
Stress score	88	50	Cost per doctor visit	$69	$67	Change in property crime rate	-6.1%	-16.8%
Cancer mortality per capita	164.2	169.0	Cost per dental visit	$80	$82			
Depression days per month	4.3	2.8	Cost per daily hospital room	$421	$733			

TRANSPORTATION SCORE: 40/RANK: 197

COMMUTE	AREA	U.S. AVG	INTERCITY SERVICES	AREA	U.S. AVG	AUTOMOTIVE	AREA	U.S. AVG
Average commute time	22.1 min.	22.6 min.	Miles to nearest major airport	55	46	Insurance, annual premium	$766	$1,011
Commute by auto	94.0%	88.7%	Type of local airport	Medium		Gas, cost per gallon	$1.43	$1.50
Commute by mass transit	.5%	1.8%	No. daily airline departures	352	294	Daily vehicle miles per capita	23.0	23.0
Work at home	2.0%	3.9%	Amtrak service	Yes				
Mass transit miles per capita	0.0	8.0	No. interstate highways	2	1			

LEISURE SCORE: 15/RANK: 279

DINING & SHOPPING	AREA	U.S. AVG	ENTERTAINMENT	AREA	U.S. AVG	OUTDOOR ACTIVITIES	AREA	U.S. AVG
Restaurant rating	1	1	Professional sports rating	2	4	Golf-course rating	6	4
No. outlet malls	2	2	College sports rating	4	4	Ski-area rating	1	4
No. Starbucks	0	11	Zoo/aquarium rating	1	3	National Park rating	1	3
No. warehouse clubs	1	4	Amusement park rating	1	3	Sq. miles inland water	2.0	4.0
			Botanical garden/arboretum rating	1	3	Miles of coastline	0.0	11.4

ARTS & CULTURE SCORE: 62/RANK: 123

MEDIA & LIBRARIES	AREA	U.S. AVG	PERFORMING ARTS	AREA	U.S. AVG	MUSEUMS	AREA	U.S. AVG
Arts radio rating	1	3	Classical music rating	2	4	Overall museum rating	5	6
No. public libraries	4	28	Ballet/dance rating	1	3	Art museum rating	4	5
Library volumes per capita	1.6	2.8	Professional theater rating	1	3	Science museum rating	1	4
			University arts programs rating	2	5	Children's museum rating	4	3

Sacramento, CA

Score: 68.6   Rank: 85

Profile: Capital city
Location: Northern California, northern part of the Central Valley at the base of the Sierra Nevada
Elevation: 25 feet
Time zone: Pacific Standard Time

PRO	CON
Mild winters	Urban sprawl
Nearby recreation	Cost of living
Central location	Summer heat

Sacramento, the capital of California, has been a leading agricultural and transportation center for most of its history. In the past 10 years, as costs have escalated in California's coastal cities, thousands have migrated to the area for its reduced cost of living and proximity to San Francisco and Lake Tahoe. Downtown Sacramento is pleasant but lacking in activities. Most recent growth has occurred to the east, northeast, and south as typical California sprawl—freeways, strip malls, and endless developments of tightly packed, cookie-cutter homes. Traffic and smog are starting to become major problems. Job-growth projections are strong, although cutbacks in state government will affect this picture. The area has a broad variety of recreational opportunities including water and mountain sports. Excellent skiing is a moderate day trip away. Professional sports teams, such as the NBA Kings, add to recreation and the overall economy, and the arts and culture scene is respectable for a city of this size. The climate through most of the year is an advantage, although summers can be uncomfortably hot. At 123.4, the Cost of Living Index is high for what's available and is increasing.

At Sacramento, located along the banks of the Sacramento River, the valley is approximately 50 miles wide. The terrain is completely flat. To the east, rolling terrain rises gradually to the 8,000-foot to 10,000-foot Sierra Nevada crest. Local natural vegetation is grassland; deciduous trees have been planted in the inhabited area. The Mediterranean Central Valley climate is mild with abundant sunshine most of the year. Summer is dry with warm to hot afternoons and mostly mild nights. "Delta breezes" from the Bay Area cool the region. Most rain falls from November through March. Heavy snowfall and torrential winter rains fall on the western Sierra slopes and may produce flood conditions along the Sacramento River and its tributaries. Winter brings sometimes heavy and persistent ground fog.

POPULATION

DEMOGRAPHICS	AREA	U.S. AVG	ETHNIC COMPOSITION	AREA	U.S. AVG	RESIDENT PROFILE	AREA	U.S. AVG
Population	1,749,335		White	81.5%	75.1%	Single	43.8%	43.6%
Population density per sq. mile	428.6	447.3	Black	5.2%	12.3%	Married	56.2%	56.4%
Population growth	30.5%	16.1%	Asian	7.7%	3.6%	Divorced	11.1%	8.4%
Median age	35.3	35.5	American Indian	1.1%	.9%	Separated	3.5%	3.0%
Average family size	2.8	2.7	Hispanic	15.9%	12.5%	Married with children	26.8%	28.7%
			Diversity measure	53.3%	35.2%	Single with children	11.0%	10.1%

ECONOMY & JOBS
SCORE: 26/RANK: 242

INCOME	AREA	U.S. AVG	EMPLOYMENT	AREA	U.S. AVG	LARGEST EMPLOYING INDUSTRY
Per capita income	$25,059	$23,420	Unemployment rate	5.4%	6.1%	Healthcare and Social Assistance
Household income	$51,893	$46,060	Recent job growth	.8%	.9%	
Household income < $25K	20.8%	26.4%	Projected future job growth	22.3%	15.1%	
Household income > $75K	29.8%	24.5%	White collar	61.0%	54.5%	
Household income growth	56.2%	57.3%	Blue collar	39.0%	45.5%	

COST OF LIVING
SCORE: 10/RANK: 297

INDEXES & TAXES	AREA	U.S. AVG	HOUSING	AREA	U.S. AVG	NECESSITIES	AREA	U.S. AVG
Cost of Living Index	123.4	100.0	Median home price	$224,200	$160,100	Food Index	120.6	100.0
Financial Progress Index	89.7	100.0	Home price appreciation	15.3%	7.1%	Housing Index	139.3	100.0
Income tax rate	6.000%	4.625%	Median rent	$950	$670	Utilities Index	109.9	100.0
Sales tax rate	7.750%	6.474%	Homes owned	58.4%	63.9%	Transportation Index	112.5	100.0
Property tax rate	$11.1	$15.6	Homes rented	27.2%	25.3%	Healthcare Index	152.5	100.0
			Housing affordability	45.0%	54.5%	Miscellaneous Cost Index	101.8	100.0

CLIMATE
SCORE: 94/RANK: 19

TEMPERATURE	AREA	U.S. AVG	PRECIPITATION	AREA	U.S. AVG	COMFORTS & HAZARDS	AREA	U.S. AVG
January low	37.1°F	26.4°F	Annual inches precipitation	17.0	35.9	July relative humidity	66.0%	68.8%
July high	92.9°F	86.7°F	Annual inches snowfall	.1	24.2	Annual days mostly sunny	265	212
Annual days > 90°F	77	38	Annual days precipitation	57	111	Annual days with thunderstorms	5	39
Annual days < 32°F	17	88	Annual days rain > 0.5 inches	14	23	Tornado risk score	3	19
Annual days < 0°F	0	6	Annual days snow > 1.5 inches	0	6	Hurricane risk score	0	15

TEMPERATURE

PRECIPITATION

DAYS OF CLOUDS & PRECIPITATION

EDUCATION
SCORE: 57/RANK: 140

ACHIEVEMENT	AREA	U.S. AVG	PUBLIC SCHOOLS	AREA	U.S. AVG	HIGHER EDUCATION	AREA	U.S. AVG
High school degree	85.0%	80.2%	Expenditures per pupil	$5,233	$5,894	No. 2-year colleges	7	3
2-year college degree	8.1%	6.2%	Student/teacher ratio	21.6	16.7	No. 4-year colleges/universities	1	4
4-year college degree	17.5%	15.8%	Attending public school	91.8%	90.2%	No. highly ranked universities	0	1
Graduate/professional degree	8.4%	9.6%	State SAT score	1018*	1020			
			State ACT score	21.5	21.0			

HEALTH & HEALTHCARE
SCORE: 3/RANK: 319

HAZARDS & ILLNESSES	AREA	U.S. AVG	HEALTHCARE	AREA	U.S. AVG
Air-quality score	2	45	Physicians per capita	226.0	261.1
Water-quality score	8	33	Hospital beds per capita	232.3	432.2
Pollen/allergy score	74	61	No. teaching hospitals	7	4
Stress score	78	50	Cost per doctor visit	$67	$67
Cancer mortality per capita	179.4	169.0	Cost per dental visit	$104	$82
Depression days per month	1.9	2.8	Cost per daily hospital room	$1,874	$733

CRIME
SCORE: 59/RANK: 134

CRIME	AREA	U.S. AVG
Violent crime rate	499.8	456.0
Change in violent crime rate	-38.8%	-17.2%
Property crime rate	4,137.0	3,950.0
Change in property crime rate	-34.3%	-16.8%

TRANSPORTATION
SCORE: 21/RANK: 257

COMMUTE	AREA	U.S. AVG	INTERCITY SERVICES	AREA	U.S. AVG	AUTOMOTIVE	AREA	U.S. AVG
Average commute time	26.1 min.	22.6 min.	Miles to nearest major airport	11	46	Insurance, annual premium	$1,322	$1,011
Commute by auto	89.5%	88.7%	Type of local airport	Medium		Gas, cost per gallon	$1.73	$1.50
Commute by mass transit	1.5%	1.8%	No. daily airline departures	144	294	Daily vehicle miles per capita	21.7	23.0
Work at home	4.4%	3.9%	Amtrak service	Yes				
Mass transit miles per capita	9.5	8.0	No. interstate highways	2	1			

LEISURE SCORE: 90/RANK: 33

DINING & SHOPPING	AREA	U.S. AVG	ENTERTAINMENT	AREA	U.S. AVG	OUTDOOR ACTIVITIES	AREA	U.S. AVG
Restaurant rating	1	1	Professional sports rating	6	4	Golf-course rating	6	4
No. outlet malls	4	2	College sports rating	2	4	Ski-area rating	10	4
No. Starbucks	67	11	Zoo/aquarium rating	5	3	National Park rating	10	3
No. warehouse clubs	8	4	Amusement park rating	9	3	Sq. miles inland water	9.0	4.0
			Botanical garden/arboretum rating	5	3	Miles of coastline	0.0	11.4

ARTS & CULTURE SCORE: 67/RANK: 109

MEDIA & LIBRARIES	AREA	U.S. AVG	PERFORMING ARTS	AREA	U.S. AVG	MUSEUMS	AREA	U.S. AVG
Arts radio rating	9	3	Classical music rating	6	4	Overall museum rating	8	6
No. public libraries	42	28	Ballet/dance rating	4	3	Art museum rating	6	5
Library volumes per capita	1.6	2.8	Professional theater rating	9	3	Science museum rating	7	4
			University arts programs rating	5	5	Children's museum rating	2	3

Saginaw–Bay City–Midland, MI

Score: 50.9   Rank: 219

Profile: Small-industrial-city complex
Location: Eastern Michigan at the head of Saginaw Bay
Elevation: 662 feet
Time zone: Eastern Standard Time

PRO	CON
Nearby recreation	Industrial landscape
Historic areas	Economic cycles
Cost of living	Low educational attainment

This tri-city area sits on Saginaw Bay near the "thumb" of Michigan's "hand." The cities became a center for the chemical industry, notably Dow Chemical, because of local brine deposits and timber. The auto and forest products industries also have a strong presence. The cyclical nature of these businesses has clouded employment figures, which are steadier than one might expect. Rounding out the economic picture are agriculture, sugar-beet processing, and shipping. While the cities have a distinctly industrial character, they also serve as a gateway to outdoor recreational activities to the north. The extensive chemical plants have a good environmental record. Of the three cities, Midland probably has the most cultural amenities and interest, and Bay City won a 1999 National Trust for Historic Preservation Great American Main Street award.

The terrain is mainly level to gently rolling with a mix of agriculture and dense forests. The continental climate is heavily influenced by the Great Lakes. Summers are humid but moderate in temperature, seldom reaching 100°F. Winters are cold with frequent snow and rain/snow mixes. Cold air from the north and west are moderated somewhat by lake influences. However, lake moisture produces significant snows and snow cover is prevalent through winter. Most precipitation occurs in late spring, summer, and early fall. The lake effect generates clouds year-round making the area one of the cloudiest places in the nation. First freeze is early October, last is early May.

POPULATION

DEMOGRAPHICS	AREA	U.S. AVG	ETHNIC COMPOSITION	AREA	U.S. AVG	RESIDENT PROFILE	AREA	U.S. AVG
Population	403,878		White	90.0%	75.1%	Single	41.6%	43.6%
Population density per sq. mile	227.6	447.3	Black	7.3%	12.3%	Married	58.4%	56.4%
Population growth	1.1%	16.1%	Asian	.6%	3.6%	Divorced	7.6%	8.4%
Median age	37.3	35.5	American Indian	.6%	.9%	Separated	2.2%	3.0%
Average family size	2.7	2.7	Hispanic	3.6%	12.5%	Married with children	29.8%	28.7%
			Diversity measure	30.2%	35.2%	Single with children	10.7%	10.1%

ECONOMY & JOBS SCORE: 86/RANK: 46

INCOME	AREA	U.S. AVG	EMPLOYMENT	AREA	U.S. AVG	LARGEST EMPLOYING INDUSTRY
Per capita income	$22,368	$23,420	Unemployment rate	7.9%	6.1%	Transportation Equipment Manufacturing
Household income	$43,890	$46,060	Recent job growth	2.6%	.9%	
Household income < $25K	29.0%	26.4%	Projected future job growth	11.8%	15.1%	
Household income > $75K	24.2%	24.5%	White collar	51.6%	54.5%	
Household income growth	50.6%	57.3%	Blue collar	48.4%	45.5%	

COST OF LIVING SCORE: 68/RANK: 105

INDEXES & TAXES	AREA	U.S. AVG	HOUSING	AREA	U.S. AVG	NECESSITIES	AREA	U.S. AVG
Cost of Living Index	84.8	100.0	Median home price	$103,460	$160,100	Food Index	101.6	100.0
Financial Progress Index	110.3	100.0	Home price appreciation	5.5%	7.1%	Housing Index	64.3	100.0
Income tax rate	4.400%	4.625%	Median rent	$547	$670	Utilities Index	76.6	100.0
Sales tax rate	6.000%	6.474%	Homes owned	75.9%	63.9%	Transportation Index	97.5	100.0
Property tax rate	$13.6	$15.6	Homes rented	17.8%	25.3%	Healthcare Index	96.6	100.0
			Housing affordability	56.0%	54.5%	Miscellaneous Cost Index	98.6	100.0

CLIMATE SCORE: 18/RANK: 271

TEMPERATURE	AREA	U.S. AVG	PRECIPITATION	AREA	U.S. AVG	COMFORTS & HAZARDS	AREA	U.S. AVG
January low	16.5°F	26.4°F	Annual inches precipitation	29.0	35.9	July relative humidity	76.0%	68.8%
July high	83.8°F	86.7°F	Annual inches snowfall	47.0	24.2	Annual days mostly sunny	163	212
Annual days > 90°F	16	38	Annual days precipitation	181	111	Annual days with thunderstorms	38	39
Annual days < 32°F	147	88	Annual days rain > 0.5 inches	31	23	Tornado risk score	8	19
Annual days < 0°F	5	6	Annual days snow > 1.5 inches	10	6	Hurricane risk score	2	15

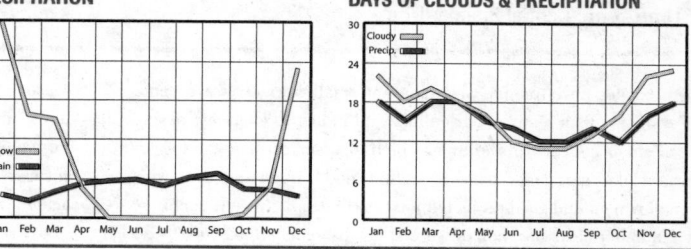

TEMPERATURE

PRECIPITATION

DAYS OF CLOUDS & PRECIPITATION

EDUCATION SCORE: 25/RANK: 247

ACHIEVEMENT	AREA	U.S. AVG	PUBLIC SCHOOLS	AREA	U.S. AVG	HIGHER EDUCATION	AREA	U.S. AVG
High school degree	83.3%	80.2%	Expenditures per pupil	$6,375	$5,894	No. 2-year colleges	2	3
2-year college degree	7.8%	6.2%	Student/teacher ratio	18.1	16.7	No. 4-year colleges/universities	2	4
4-year college degree	11.7%	15.8%	Attending public school	87.2%	90.2%	No. highly ranked universities	0	1
Graduate/professional degree	6.4%	9.6%	State SAT score	1140	1020			
			State ACT score	21.3*	21.0			

HEALTH & HEALTHCARE SCORE: 59/RANK: 133 — CRIME SCORE: 58/RANK: 139

HAZARDS & ILLNESSES	AREA	U.S. AVG	HEALTHCARE	AREA	U.S. AVG	CRIME	AREA	U.S. AVG
Air-quality score	81	45	Physicians per capita	223.1	261.1	Violent crime rate	543.7	456.0
Water-quality score	21	33	Hospital beds per capita	422.8	432.2	Change in violent crime rate	-27.5%	-17.2%
Pollen/allergy score	46	61	No. teaching hospitals	5	4	Property crime rate	3,254.0	3,950.0
Stress score	75	50	Cost per doctor visit	$59	$67	Change in property crime rate	-18.0%	-16.8%
Cancer mortality per capita	176.7	169.0	Cost per dental visit	$88	$82			
Depression days per month	3.0	2.8	Cost per daily hospital room	$610	$733			

TRANSPORTATION SCORE: 37/RANK: 208

COMMUTE	AREA	U.S. AVG	INTERCITY SERVICES	AREA	U.S. AVG	AUTOMOTIVE	AREA	U.S. AVG
Average commute time	21.5 min.	22.6 min.	Miles to nearest major airport	56	46	Insurance, annual premium	$966	$1,011
Commute by auto	92.9%	88.7%	Type of local airport	Small		Gas, cost per gallon	$1.55	$1.50
Commute by mass transit	.5%	1.8%	No. daily airline departures	65	294	Daily vehicle miles per capita	23.4	23.0
Work at home	3.2%	3.9%	Amtrak service	No				
Mass transit miles per capita	6.0	8.0	No. interstate highways	1	1			

LEISURE SCORE: 42/RANK: 190

DINING & SHOPPING	AREA	U.S. AVG	ENTERTAINMENT	AREA	U.S. AVG	OUTDOOR ACTIVITIES	AREA	U.S. AVG
Restaurant rating	1	1	Professional sports rating	2	4	Golf-course rating	5	4
No. outlet malls	3	2	College sports rating	4	4	Ski-area rating	4	4
No. Starbucks	0	11	Zoo/aquarium rating	2	3	National Park rating	2	3
No. warehouse clubs	3	4	Amusement park rating	1	3	Sq. miles inland water	2.0	4.0
			Botanical garden/arboretum rating	5	3	Miles of coastline	39.9	11.4

ARTS & CULTURE SCORE: 52/RANK: 158

MEDIA & LIBRARIES	AREA	U.S. AVG	PERFORMING ARTS	AREA	U.S. AVG	MUSEUMS	AREA	U.S. AVG
Arts radio rating	1	3	Classical music rating	4	4	Overall museum rating	6	6
No. public libraries	21	28	Ballet/dance rating	1	3	Art museum rating	6	5
Library volumes per capita	3.5	2.8	Professional theater rating	1	3	Science museum rating	3	4
			University arts programs rating	3	5	Children's museum rating	1	3

St. Cloud, MN

Score: 61.8 **Rank:** 136

Profile: Small town
Location: Central Minnesota, 60 miles northwest of Minneapolis–St. Paul along the upper Mississippi
Elevation: 1,028 feet
Time zone: Central Standard Time

PRO	CON
Nearby outdoor recreation	Winter climate
Low unemployment	Recent job declines
Small-town atmosphere	Low ethnic diversity

St. Cloud, an attractive and pleasant small town, has a diverse economy with a mix of agriculture and industry. There are several small colleges in the area, which also serves as a gateway to wilderness lakes and parks to the north. St. Cloud is quiet and clean with high employment and good projected job growth despite recent declines. It has a number of its own amenities and is close enough to share those of Minneapolis–St. Paul while being almost 20% lower on the cost of living scale.

The terrain is flat to gently rolling with numerous lakes and wooded areas. The continental climate is highly variable with four distinct seasons. Spring, summer, and fall are pleasant, with moderate temperatures and low humidity. Prolonged periods of hot, humid weather are infrequent. Thunderstorms are the principal source of rainfall and severe storms are common. Winters are cold with low humidity. On average in winter, 5 to 10 days reach temperatures between –20°F and –30°F. Heavy snowfalls occur, but the location north of most Gulf moisture and storm tracks means they are less frequent than in Minnesota cities to the south. Snow generally remains on the ground throughout winter. First freeze is late September, last is mid-May.

POPULATION

DEMOGRAPHICS	AREA	U.S. AVG	ETHNIC COMPOSITION	AREA	U.S. AVG	RESIDENT PROFILE	AREA	U.S. AVG
Population	172,183		White	98.5%	75.1%	Single	41.7%	43.6%
Population density per sq. mile	98.2	447.3	Black	.5%	12.3%	Married	58.3%	56.4%
Population growth	15.6%	16.1%	Asian	.7%	3.6%	Divorced	4.4%	8.4%
Median age	31.7	35.5	American Indian	.3%	.9%	Separated	1.2%	3.0%
Average family size	2.9	2.7	Hispanic	.6%	12.5%	Married with children	35.0%	28.7%
			Diversity measure	9.1%	35.2%	Single with children	6.3%	10.1%

ECONOMY & JOBS SCORE: 23/RANK: 253

INCOME	AREA	U.S. AVG	EMPLOYMENT	AREA	U.S. AVG	LARGEST EMPLOYING INDUSTRY
Per capita income	$20,748	$23,420	Unemployment rate	3.7%	6.1%	Printing and Related Support Activities
Household income	$43,220	$46,060	Recent job growth	-.6%	.9%	
Household income < $25K	25.0%	26.4%	Projected future job growth	16.7%	15.1%	
Household income > $75K	18.9%	24.5%	White collar	50.5%	54.5%	
Household income growth	58.0%	57.3%	Blue collar	49.5%	45.5%	

COST OF LIVING SCORE: 29/RANK: 233

INDEXES & TAXES	AREA	U.S. AVG	HOUSING	AREA	U.S. AVG	NECESSITIES	AREA	U.S. AVG
Cost of Living Index	98.2	100.0	Median home price	$132,630	$160,100	Food Index	98.2	100.0
Financial Progress Index	93.8	100.0	Home price appreciation	9.8%	7.1%	Housing Index	82.4	100.0
Income tax rate	8.000%	4.625%	Median rent	$535	$670	Utilities Index	135.2	100.0
Sales tax rate	6.500%	6.474%	Homes owned	72.2%	63.9%	Transportation Index	105.4	100.0
Property tax rate	$13.3	$15.6	Homes rented	17.7%	25.3%	Healthcare Index	109.7	100.0
			Housing affordability	63.0%	54.5%	Miscellaneous Cost Index	104.0	100.0

CLIMATE SCORE: 16/RANK: 277

TEMPERATURE	AREA	U.S. AVG	PRECIPITATION	AREA	U.S. AVG	COMFORTS & HAZARDS	AREA	U.S. AVG
January low	-1.4°F	26.4°F	Annual inches precipitation	26.8	35.9	July relative humidity	71.0%	68.8%
July high	81.8°F	86.7°F	Annual inches snowfall	43.1	24.2	Annual days mostly sunny	197	212
Annual days > 90°F	11	38	Annual days precipitation	122	111	Annual days with thunderstorms	36	39
Annual days < 32°F	178	88	Annual days rain > 0.5 inches	17	23	Tornado risk score	16	19
Annual days < 0°F	46	6	Annual days snow > 1.5 inches	9	6	Hurricane risk score	0	15

TEMPERATURE

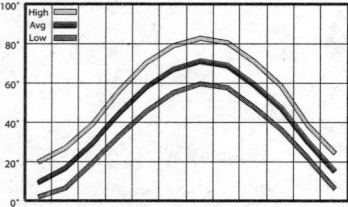

PRECIPITATION

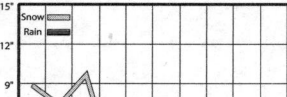
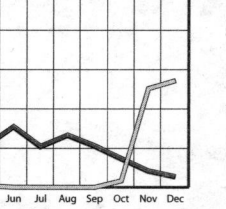

DAYS OF CLOUDS & PRECIPITATION

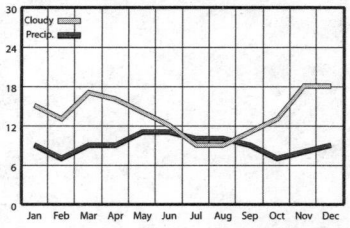

EDUCATION SCORE: 43/RANK: 118

ACHIEVEMENT	AREA	U.S. AVG	PUBLIC SCHOOLS	AREA	U.S. AVG	HIGHER EDUCATION	AREA	U.S. AVG
High school degree	86.0%	80.2%	Expenditures per pupil	$5,676	$5,894	No. 2-year colleges	1	3
2-year college degree	7.2%	6.2%	Student/teacher ratio	16.6	16.7	No. 4-year colleges/universities	3	4
4-year college degree	14.4%	15.8%	Attending public school	85.3%	90.2%	No. highly ranked universities	2	1
Graduate/professional degree	6.5%	9.6%	State SAT score	1173	1020			
			State ACT score	22.0*	21.0			

HEALTH & HEALTHCARE SCORE: 79/RANK: 69

CRIME SCORE: 72/RANK: 92

HAZARDS & ILLNESSES	AREA	U.S. AVG	HEALTHCARE	AREA	U.S. AVG	CRIME	AREA	U.S. AVG
Air-quality score	24	45	Physicians per capita	220.1	261.1	Violent crime rate	205.7	456.0
Water-quality score	26	33	Hospital beds per capita	566.9	432.2	Change in violent crime rate	28.8%	-17.2%
Pollen/allergy score	46	61	No. teaching hospitals	1	4	Property crime rate	2,804.6	3,950.0
Stress score	6	50	Cost per doctor visit	$73	$67	Change in property crime rate	-12.3%	-16.8%
Cancer mortality per capita	149.1	169.0	Cost per dental visit	$84	$82			
Depression days per month	2.3	2.8	Cost per daily hospital room	$680	$733			

TRANSPORTATION SCORE: 62/RANK: 123

COMMUTE	AREA	U.S. AVG	INTERCITY SERVICES	AREA	U.S. AVG	AUTOMOTIVE	AREA	U.S. AVG
Average commute time	19.7 min.	22.6 min.	Miles to nearest major airport	66	46	Insurance, annual premium	$957	$1,011
Commute by auto	78.7%	88.7%	Type of local airport	Large		Gas, cost per gallon	$1.50	$1.50
Commute by mass transit	.7%	1.8%	No. daily airline departures	624	294	Daily vehicle miles per capita	16.2	23.0
Work at home	12.2%	3.9%	Amtrak service	Yes				
Mass transit miles per capita	7.1	8.0	No. interstate highways	1	1			

LEISURE SCORE: 53/RANK: 156

DINING & SHOPPING	AREA	U.S. AVG	ENTERTAINMENT	AREA	U.S. AVG	OUTDOOR ACTIVITIES	AREA	U.S. AVG
Restaurant rating	1	1	Professional sports rating	2	4	Golf-course rating	2	4
No. outlet malls	1	2	College sports rating	5	4	Ski-area rating	4	4
No. Starbucks	0	11	Zoo/aquarium rating	1	3	National Park rating	4	3
No. warehouse clubs	3	4	Amusement park rating	1	3	Sq. miles inland water	5.0	4.0
			Botanical garden/arboretum rating	1	3	Miles of coastline	0.0	11.4

ARTS & CULTURE SCORE: 39/RANK: 197

MEDIA & LIBRARIES	AREA	U.S. AVG	PERFORMING ARTS	AREA	U.S. AVG	MUSEUMS	AREA	U.S. AVG
Arts radio rating	1	3	Classical music rating	3	4	Overall museum rating	4	6
No. public libraries	1	28	Ballet/dance rating	1	3	Art museum rating	2	5
Library volumes per capita	2.0	2.8	Professional theater rating	1	3	Science museum rating	2	4
			University arts programs rating	8	5	Children's museum rating	1	3

St. Joseph, MO

Score: 51.4   Rank: 213

Profile: Small city
Location: Northeast Missouri along the Missouri River at the Kansas border
Elevation: 894 feet
Time zone: Central Standard Time

PRO	CON
Historic interest	Future job growth
Cost of living	Entertainment
Proximity to Kansas City	Arts and culture

St. Joseph, once the eastern terminus of the Pony Express, is a former frontier town with agriculture and mixed industry. The diverse economy ranges from fence wire to Stetson hats to Sara Lee baked goods, but the economic outlook is uncertain. The future depends on the city's ability to attract businesses looking for an alternative to Kansas City. Current advantages include an attractive, historic downtown; low cost of living; and a short, 50-mile drive to the Kansas City area.

The city sits in the broad, flat Missouri Valley in a mainly agricultural area. The climate is continental with frequent alternations between moist Gulf air and cold continental air producing change and the occasional heavy storm. Summer brings warm days and mild nights with moderate humidity. Winters are not severely cold but have cold snaps. Falls are usually mild and pleasant. Spring is the stormiest season—in 2003, St. Joseph was the center of a tornado outbreak that devastated several nearby towns. First freeze is mid-October, last is mid-April.

POPULATION

DEMOGRAPHICS	AREA	U.S. AVG	ETHNIC COMPOSITION	AREA	U.S. AVG	RESIDENT PROFILE	AREA	U.S. AVG
Population	102,064		White	97.0%	75.1%	Single	38.0%	43.6%
Population density per sq. mile	120.8	447.3	Black	2.0%	12.3%	Married	62.0%	56.4%
Population growth	4.5%	16.1%	Asian	.4%	3.6%	Divorced	8.5%	8.4%
Median age	36.6	35.5	American Indian	.3%	.9%	Separated	2.0%	3.0%
Average family size	2.5	2.7	Hispanic	1.3%	12.5%	Married with children	29.4%	28.7%
			Diversity measure	14.6%	35.2%	Single with children	8.6%	10.1%

ECONOMY & JOBS — SCORE: 26/RANK: 243

INCOME	AREA	U.S. AVG	EMPLOYMENT	AREA	U.S. AVG	LARGEST EMPLOYING INDUSTRY
Per capita income	$19,382	$23,420	Unemployment rate	5.7%	6.1%	Food Manufacturing
Household income	$37,598	$46,060	Recent job growth	-2.0%	.9%	
Household income < $25K	33.0%	26.4%	Projected future job growth	5.8%	15.1%	
Household income > $75K	16.1%	24.5%	White collar	47.6%	54.5%	
Household income growth	59.4%	57.3%	Blue collar	52.4%	45.5%	

COST OF LIVING — SCORE: 85/RANK: 48

INDEXES & TAXES	AREA	U.S. AVG	HOUSING	AREA	U.S. AVG	NECESSITIES	AREA	U.S. AVG
Cost of Living Index	81.3	100.0	Median home price	$92,380	$160,100	Food Index	88.6	100.0
Financial Progress Index	98.6	100.0	Home price appreciation	7.0%	7.1%	Housing Index	57.4	100.0
Income tax rate	6.000%	4.625%	Median rent	$426	$670	Utilities Index	92.5	100.0
Sales tax rate	7.475%	6.474%	Homes owned	71.3%	63.9%	Transportation Index	94.5	100.0
Property tax rate	$6.0	$15.6	Homes rented	19.3%	25.3%	Healthcare Index	94.2	100.0
			Housing affordability	67.0%	54.5%	Miscellaneous Cost Index	100.4	100.0

CLIMATE — SCORE: 21/RANK: 261

TEMPERATURE	AREA	U.S. AVG	PRECIPITATION	AREA	U.S. AVG	COMFORTS & HAZARDS	AREA	U.S. AVG
January low	18.4°F	26.4°F	Annual inches precipitation	37.0	35.9	July relative humidity	69.0%	68.8%
July high	88.0°F	86.7°F	Annual inches snowfall	20.0	24.2	Annual days mostly sunny	213	212
Annual days > 90°F	40	38	Annual days precipitation	102	111	Annual days with thunderstorms	53	39
Annual days < 32°F	106	88	Annual days rain > 0.5 inches	25	23	Tornado risk score	25	19
Annual days < 0°F	9	6	Annual days snow > 1.5 inches	6	6	Hurricane risk score	1	15

TEMPERATURE

PRECIPITATION

DAYS OF CLOUDS & PRECIPITATION

EDUCATION — SCORE: 16/RANK: 275

ACHIEVEMENT	AREA	U.S. AVG	PUBLIC SCHOOLS	AREA	U.S. AVG	HIGHER EDUCATION	AREA	U.S. AVG
High school degree	80.9%	80.2%	Expenditures per pupil	$4,934	$5,894	No. 2-year colleges	0	3
2-year college degree	3.9%	6.2%	Student/teacher ratio	14.8	16.7	No. 4-year colleges/universities	1	4
4-year college degree	11.4%	15.8%	Attending public school	90.3%	90.2%	No. highly ranked universities	0	1
Graduate/professional degree	5.7%	9.6%	State SAT score	1165	1020			
			State ACT score	21.4*	21.0			

HEALTH & HEALTHCARE — SCORE: 56/RANK: 144

HAZARDS & ILLNESSES	AREA	U.S. AVG	HEALTHCARE	AREA	U.S. AVG
Air-quality score	49	45	Physicians per capita	167.5	261.1
Water-quality score	4	33	Hospital beds per capita	629.3	432.2
Pollen/allergy score	71	61	No. teaching hospitals	0	4
Stress score	45	50	Cost per doctor visit	$65	$67
Cancer mortality per capita	171.0	169.0	Cost per dental visit	$69	$82
Depression days per month	3.7	2.8	Cost per daily hospital room	$611	$733

CRIME — SCORE: 52/RANK: 159

CRIME	AREA	U.S. AVG
Violent crime rate	278.3	456.0
Change in violent crime rate	-27.4%	-17.2%
Property crime rate	4,460.7	3,950.0
Change in property crime rate	-15.6%	-16.8%

TRANSPORTATION — SCORE: 63/RANK: 124

COMMUTE	AREA	U.S. AVG	INTERCITY SERVICES	AREA	U.S. AVG	AUTOMOTIVE	AREA	U.S. AVG
Average commute time	19.5 min.	22.6 min.	Miles to nearest major airport	31	46	Insurance, annual premium	$837	$1,011
Commute by auto	90.5%	88.7%	Type of local airport	Medium		Gas, cost per gallon	$1.41	$1.50
Commute by mass transit	.3%	1.8%	No. daily airline departures	328	294	Daily vehicle miles per capita	20.3	23.0
Work at home	6.3%	3.9%	Amtrak service	No				
Mass transit miles per capita	7.0	8.0	No. interstate highways	1	1			

LEISURE SCORE: 6/RANK: 313

DINING & SHOPPING	AREA	U.S. AVG	ENTERTAINMENT	AREA	U.S. AVG	OUTDOOR ACTIVITIES	AREA	U.S. AVG
Restaurant rating	1	1	Professional sports rating	2	4	Golf-course rating	1	4
No. outlet malls	0	2	College sports rating	2	4	Ski-area rating	1	4
No. Starbucks	0	11	Zoo/aquarium rating	1	3	National Park rating	1	3
No. warehouse clubs	1	4	Amusement park rating	1	3	Sq. miles inland water	2.0	4.0
			Botanical garden/arboretum rating	1	3	Miles of coastline	0.0	11.4

ARTS & CULTURE SCORE: 3/RANK: 320

MEDIA & LIBRARIES	AREA	U.S. AVG	PERFORMING ARTS	AREA	U.S. AVG	MUSEUMS	AREA	U.S. AVG
Arts radio rating	1	3	Classical music rating	3	4	Overall museum rating	5	6
No. public libraries	5	28	Ballet/dance rating	1	3	Art museum rating	3	5
Library volumes per capita	4.1	2.8	Professional theater rating	1	3	Science museum rating	3	4
			University arts programs rating	3	5	Children's museum rating	1	3

St. Louis, MO-IL

Score: 67.0   Rank: 97

Profile: Large city
Location: Missouri-Illinois border along the Mississippi River
Elevation: 570 feet
Time zone: Central Standard Time

PRO	CON
Cost of living	Crime rate
Air service	Urban sprawl
Professional sports	Economy

Known since the early days as the "Gateway City" because of its access to transportation routes in all directions, St. Louis continues to be an important center of commerce and culture for the Mississippi River Basin. The area includes a number of mostly residential neighborhoods to the west and, on the Illinois side of the river, the more industrial East St. Louis and several agricultural counties. The downtown area has few highlights outside of the landmark Gateway Arch and the restored Union Station. Quality parks include Forest Park, the 1,300-acre site of the 1904 World's Fair, now the location of several major museums. To the west lies a patchwork of mostly quiet, shady neighborhoods. The Washington University and University City area is attractive. High commute times reflect problems with sprawl, but there is ample room and a variety of attractive choices among the neighborhoods.

The diverse economy is led by such companies as Anheuser-Busch and McDonnell-Douglas, now a part of Boeing. There are a number of manufacturing and distribution entities, some of which have slowed during the recent recession. The economy is stable if not rapidly growing, and cost of living is attractive for a large city. A number of amenities are directed at children, and St. Louis in general is considered a good place

to raise a family. Other advantages include a highly educated population for a large city, extensive air service, and popular professional sports teams—MLB Cardinals, NFL Rams, and NHL Blues—which are accessible and inexpensive by national standards. On the downside, violent crime is a persistent problem, and summer weather can be too hot and humid for some.

The city is located on a plain on the west bank of the Mississippi River with gently rolling hills and undulating plains rising to the west, and mostly level terrain to the east. Hilly areas are wooded and level areas are mainly farmland. The continental climate is affected by warm, moist air from the Gulf of Mexico and cold air masses from Canada, the mixing of which produces a variety of weather conditions and four distinct seasons. During summer, Gulf air tends to dominate, producing warm, humid conditions. Temperatures of 90°F or higher are common. Winters are brisk and stimulating, but prolonged periods of extreme cold are rare. Temperatures of zero or below are infrequent. Summer thunderstorms are common and sometimes severe. Spring is the wettest season. Snow is infrequent, with measurable snowfall on 5 to 10 days in most years. First freeze is mid-October, last is mid-April.

POPULATION

DEMOGRAPHICS	AREA	U.S. AVG	ETHNIC COMPOSITION	AREA	U.S. AVG	RESIDENT PROFILE	AREA	U.S. AVG
Population	2,633,925		White	83.7%	75.1%	Single	45.1%	43.6%
Population density per sq. mile	407.7	447.3	Black	14.7%	12.3%	Married	54.9%	56.4%
Population growth	5.7%	16.1%	Asian	1.1%	3.6%	Divorced	8.8%	8.4%
Median age	36.3	35.5	American Indian	.2%	.9%	Separated	3.1%	3.0%
Average family size	2.6	2.7	Hispanic	1.4%	12.5%	Married with children	28.0%	28.7%
			Diversity measure	36.3%	35.2%	Single with children	11.2%	10.1%

ECONOMY & JOBS SCORE: 71/RANK: 94

INCOME	AREA	U.S. AVG	EMPLOYMENT	AREA	U.S. AVG	LARGEST EMPLOYING INDUSTRY
Per capita income	$26,204	$23,420	Unemployment rate	6.1%	6.1%	Machinery Manufacturing
Household income	$51,803	$46,060	Recent job growth	1.3%	.9%	
Household income < $25K	22.2%	26.4%	Projected future job growth	11.4%	15.1%	
Household income > $75K	29.0%	24.5%	White collar	59.6%	54.5%	
Household income growth	63.2%	57.3%	Blue collar	40.4%	45.5%	

COST OF LIVING — SCORE: 50/RANK: 166

INDEXES & TAXES	AREA	U.S. AVG	HOUSING	AREA	U.S. AVG	NECESSITIES	AREA	U.S. AVG
Cost of Living Index	89.0	100.0	Median home price	$116,300	$160,100	Food Index	94.0	100.0
Financial Progress Index	124.0	100.0	Home price appreciation	7.2%	7.1%	Housing Index	72.2	100.0
Income tax rate	7.000%	4.625%	Median rent	$695	$670	Utilities Index	90.5	100.0
Sales tax rate	7.616%	6.474%	Homes owned	66.2%	63.9%	Transportation Index	106.8	100.0
Property tax rate	$15.1	$15.6	Homes rented	23.2%	25.3%	Healthcare Index	101.7	100.0
			Housing affordability	56.0%	54.5%	Miscellaneous Cost Index	99.9	100.0

CLIMATE — SCORE: 36/RANK: 211

TEMPERATURE	AREA	U.S. AVG	PRECIPITATION	AREA	U.S. AVG	COMFORTS & HAZARDS	AREA	U.S. AVG
January low	22.6°F	26.4°F	Annual inches precipitation	36.0	35.9	July relative humidity	70.0%	68.8%
July high	88.4°F	86.7°F	Annual inches snowfall	18.0	24.2	Annual days mostly sunny	206	212
Annual days > 90°F	37	38	Annual days precipitation	108	111	Annual days with thunderstorms	45	39
Annual days < 32°F	107	88	Annual days rain > 0.5 inches	22	23	Tornado risk score	44	19
Annual days < 0°F	3	6	Annual days snow > 1.5 inches	5	6	Hurricane risk score	4	15

TEMPERATURE

PRECIPITATION

DAYS OF CLOUDS & PRECIPITATION

EDUCATION — SCORE: 75/RANK: 82

ACHIEVEMENT	AREA	U.S. AVG	PUBLIC SCHOOLS	AREA	U.S. AVG	HIGHER EDUCATION	AREA	U.S. AVG
High school degree	83.4%	80.2%	Expenditures per pupil	$5,908	$5,894	No. 2-year colleges	12	3
2-year college degree	6.2%	6.2%	Student/teacher ratio	16.2	16.7	No. 4-year colleges/universities	15	4
4-year college degree	16.1%	15.8%	Attending public school	81.4%	90.2%	No. highly ranked universities	4	1
Graduate/professional degree	9.2%	9.6%	State SAT score	1165	1020			
			State ACT score	21.4*	21.0			

HEALTH & HEALTHCARE — SCORE: 22/RANK: 256

HAZARDS & ILLNESSES	AREA	U.S. AVG	HEALTHCARE	AREA	U.S. AVG
Air-quality score	72	45	Physicians per capita	297.0	261.1
Water-quality score	25	33	Hospital beds per capita	481.5	432.2
Pollen/allergy score	68	61	No. teaching hospitals	18	4
Stress score	92	50	Cost per doctor visit	$81	$67
Cancer mortality per capita	179.9	169.0	Cost per dental visit	$77	$82
Depression days per month	3.1	2.8	Cost per daily hospital room	$539	$733

CRIME — SCORE: 14/RANK: 284

CRIME	AREA	U.S. AVG
Violent crime rate	723.4	456.0
Change in violent crime rate	-19.4%	-17.2%
Property crime rate	4,778.4	3,950.0
Change in property crime rate	-4.8%	-16.8%

TRANSPORTATION — SCORE: 87/RANK: 44

COMMUTE	AREA	U.S. AVG	INTERCITY SERVICES	AREA	U.S. AVG	AUTOMOTIVE	AREA	U.S. AVG
Average commute time	25.5 min.	22.6 min.	Miles to nearest major airport	10	46	Insurance, annual premium	$1,213	$1,011
Commute by auto	89.7%	88.7%	Type of local airport	Large		Gas, cost per gallon	$1.44	$1.50
Commute by mass transit	2.7%	1.8%	No. daily airline departures	731	294	Daily vehicle miles per capita	28.8	23.0
Work at home	3.3%	3.9%	Amtrak service	Yes				
Mass transit miles per capita	13.2	8.0	No. interstate highways	4	1			

LEISURE — SCORE: 87/RANK: 40

DINING & SHOPPING	AREA	U.S. AVG	ENTERTAINMENT	AREA	U.S. AVG	OUTDOOR ACTIVITIES	AREA	U.S. AVG
Restaurant rating	3	1	Professional sports rating	8	4	Golf-course rating	7	4
No. outlet malls	1	2	College sports rating	4	4	Ski-area rating	1	4
No. Starbucks	21	11	Zoo/aquarium rating	9	3	National Park rating	2	3
No. warehouse clubs	7	4	Amusement park rating	10	3	Sq. miles inland water	6.0	4.0
			Botanical garden/arboretum rating	7	3	Miles of coastline	0.0	11.4

ARTS & CULTURE — SCORE: 89/RANK: 39

MEDIA & LIBRARIES	AREA	U.S. AVG	PERFORMING ARTS	AREA	U.S. AVG	MUSEUMS	AREA	U.S. AVG
Arts radio rating	7	3	Classical music rating	10	4	Overall museum rating	9	6
No. public libraries	116	28	Ballet/dance rating	5	3	Art museum rating	10	5
Library volumes per capita	4.5	2.8	Professional theater rating	8	3	Science museum rating	7	4
			University arts programs rating	10	5	Children's museum rating	10	3

Salem, OR

Score: 60.7 **Rank:** 141

Profile: Capital city
Location: North-central Oregon in Willamette Valley, 50 miles south of Portland
Elevation: 196 feet
Time zone: Pacific Standard Time

PRO	CON
Small-town atmosphere	Recent job declines
Nearby recreation	Clouds and rain
Proximity to Portland	Low educational attainment

Salem is the state capital and an agricultural center. State government buildings dominate a small but attractive downtown area; the surrounding built-up areas are unremarkable. Agriculture includes orchards, fruits, grapes, nursery stock, and vegetables. The area is close enough to Portland to enjoy some of its amenities and services while retaining a small-town environment. Some residents commute north, particularly to high-tech sectors south of Portland. While the state government lends some stability to the economy, the economic outlook is not encouraging, and the winter climate is gloomy.

Salem is located in the middle of Willamette Valley some 60 air miles east of the Pacific Ocean. The valley is approximately 50 miles wide with the city about equidistant from the Coast Range on the west and the Cascade Range on the east. Land is rolling with flat valleys and a mix of woods and farmland. The climate is marine, and some of the heaviest yearly rainfall in the country, up to 170 inches, occurs in the mountains surrounding the city. The valley floor receives about 40 annual inches of rainfall, most occurring during winter. In the immediate area, measurable amounts of snow fall only 3 or 4 days a year. Summer days are typically sunny to partly cloudy and pleasant, while winter days are cold, cloudy, and damp, with few extremes in either season. First freeze is late October, last is early May.

POPULATION

DEMOGRAPHICS	AREA	U.S. AVG	ETHNIC COMPOSITION	AREA	U.S. AVG	RESIDENT PROFILE	AREA	U.S. AVG
Population	357,812		White	91.8%	75.1%	Single	41.5%	43.6%
Population density per sq. mile	185.8	447.3	Black	.5%	12.3%	Married	58.5%	56.4%
Population growth	28.7%	16.1%	Asian	1.5%	3.6%	Divorced	9.4%	8.4%
Median age	34.5	35.5	American Indian	2.0%	.9%	Separated	2.9%	3.0%
Average family size	2.7	2.7	Hispanic	13.2%	12.5%	Married with children	27.8%	28.7%
			Diversity measure	35.7%	35.2%	Single with children	10.5%	10.1%

ECONOMY & JOBS
SCORE: 18/RANK: 267

INCOME	AREA	U.S. AVG	EMPLOYMENT	AREA	U.S. AVG	LARGEST EMPLOYING INDUSTRY
Per capita income	$21,307	$23,420	Unemployment rate	6.9%	6.1%	Wood Product Manufacturing
Household income	$45,688	$46,060	Recent job growth	1.3%	.9%	
Household income < $25K	23.2%	26.4%	Projected future job growth	18.6%	15.1%	
Household income > $75K	23.2%	24.5%	White collar	51.4%	54.5%	
Household income growth	70.5%	57.3%	Blue collar	48.6%	45.5%	

COST OF LIVING
SCORE: 41/RANK: 192

INDEXES & TAXES	AREA	U.S. AVG	HOUSING	AREA	U.S. AVG	NECESSITIES	AREA	U.S. AVG
Cost of Living Index	100.4	100.0	Median home price	$150,350	$160,100	Food Index	104.6	100.0
Financial Progress Index	97.0	100.0	Home price appreciation	3.8%	7.1%	Housing Index	93.4	100.0
Income tax rate	9.000%	4.625%	Median rent	$671	$670	Utilities Index	88.1	100.0
Sales tax rate	0.000%	6.474%	Homes owned	67.4%	63.9%	Transportation Index	103.3	100.0
Property tax rate	$16.2	$15.6	Homes rented	26.3%	25.3%	Healthcare Index	120.2	100.0
			Housing affordability	56.0%	54.5%	Miscellaneous Cost Index	106.1	100.0

CLIMATE
SCORE: 66/RANK: 112

TEMPERATURE	AREA	U.S. AVG	PRECIPITATION	AREA	U.S. AVG	COMFORTS & HAZARDS	AREA	U.S. AVG
January low	32.2°F	26.4°F	Annual inches precipitation	41.1	35.9	July relative humidity	74.0%	68.8%
July high	82.4°F	86.7°F	Annual inches snowfall	7.0	24.2	Annual days mostly sunny	159	212
Annual days > 90°F	7	38	Annual days precipitation	152	111	Annual days with thunderstorms	5	39
Annual days < 32°F	50	88	Annual days rain > 0.5 inches	25	23	Tornado risk score	1	19
Annual days < 0°F	0	6	Annual days snow > 1.5 inches	2	6	Hurricane risk score	0	15

TEMPERATURE

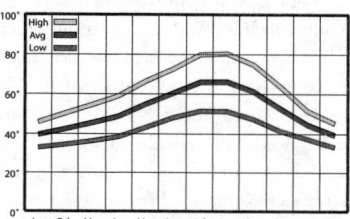

PRECIPITATION

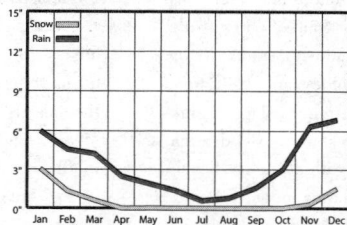

DAYS OF CLOUDS & PRECIPITATION

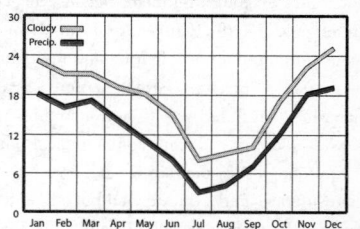

EDUCATION — SCORE: 36/RANK: 212

ACHIEVEMENT	AREA	U.S. AVG	PUBLIC SCHOOLS	AREA	U.S. AVG	HIGHER EDUCATION	AREA	U.S. AVG
High school degree	81.5%	80.2%	Expenditures per pupil	$5,744	$5,894	No. 2-year colleges	1	3
2-year college degree	6.5%	6.2%	Student/teacher ratio	19.1	16.7	No. 4-year colleges/universities	4	4
4-year college degree	13.6%	15.8%	Attending public school	91.9%	90.2%	No. highly ranked universities	1	1
Graduate/professional degree	7.2%	9.6%	State SAT score	1053*	1020			
			State ACT score	22.6	21.0			

HEALTH & HEALTHCARE — SCORE: 60/RANK: 132 | CRIME — SCORE: 30/RANK: 231

HAZARDS & ILLNESSES	AREA	U.S. AVG	HEALTHCARE	AREA	U.S. AVG	CRIME	AREA	U.S. AVG
Air-quality score	24	45	Physicians per capita	159.3	261.1	Violent crime rate	271.3	456.0
Water-quality score	30	33	Hospital beds per capita	220.6	432.2	Change in violent crime rate	-9.1%	-17.2%
Pollen/allergy score	51	61	No. teaching hospitals	0	4	Property crime rate	5,666.0	3,950.0
Stress score	81	50	Cost per doctor visit	$80	$67	Change in property crime rate	-23.4%	-16.8%
Cancer mortality per capita	151.1	169.0	Cost per dental visit	$111	$82			
Depression days per month	2.5	2.8	Cost per daily hospital room	$590	$733			

TRANSPORTATION — SCORE: 18/RANK: 271

COMMUTE	AREA	U.S. AVG	INTERCITY SERVICES	AREA	U.S. AVG	AUTOMOTIVE	AREA	U.S. AVG
Average commute time	23.5 min.	22.6 min.	Miles to nearest major airport	44	46	Insurance, annual premium	$877	$1,011
Commute by auto	87.6%	88.7%	Type of local airport	Medium		Gas, cost per gallon	$1.61	$1.50
Commute by mass transit	.7%	1.8%	No. daily airline departures	433	294	Daily vehicle miles per capita	15.7	23.0
Work at home	5.4%	3.9%	Amtrak service	Yes				
Mass transit miles per capita	6.7	8.0	No. interstate highways	1	1			

LEISURE — SCORE: 61/RANK: 126

DINING & SHOPPING	AREA	U.S. AVG	ENTERTAINMENT	AREA	U.S. AVG	OUTDOOR ACTIVITIES	AREA	U.S. AVG
Restaurant rating	1	1	Professional sports rating	3	4	Golf-course rating	3	4
No. outlet malls	3	2	College sports rating	3	4	Ski-area rating	8	4
No. Starbucks	6	11	Zoo/aquarium rating	2	3	National Park rating	8	3
No. warehouse clubs	3	4	Amusement park rating	3	3	Sq. miles inland water	3.0	4.0
			Botanical garden/arboretum rating	2	3	Miles of coastline	0.0	11.4

ARTS & CULTURE — SCORE: 45/RANK: 177

MEDIA & LIBRARIES	AREA	U.S. AVG	PERFORMING ARTS	AREA	U.S. AVG	MUSEUMS	AREA	U.S. AVG
Arts radio rating	3	3	Classical music rating	2	4	Overall museum rating	6	6
No. public libraries	10	28	Ballet/dance rating	3	3	Art museum rating	5	5
Library volumes per capita	2.2	2.8	Professional theater rating	3	3	Science museum rating	4	4
			University arts programs rating	3	5	Children's museum rating	5	3

Salinas, CA

Score: 59.3   Rank: 153

Profile: Beach town/Small city
Location: Northern California, on the south end of Monterey Bay, 110 miles south of San Francisco
Elevation: 267 feet
Time zone: Pacific Standard Time

PRO
Attractive setting
Year-round climate
Recreation and entertainment

CON
Cost of living
Isolation
Tourist impact

There's more to this diverse metropolitan area than the inland town of Salinas. Monterey County includes the famous ocean-side cities of Monterey, Carmel, and Pacific Grove. The area presents extreme contrasts. Agricultural Salinas was dubbed the "salad bowl of the nation" by John Steinbeck because of its lettuce crops. Monterey, Carmel, and Pacific Grove are located on the Monterey Peninsula, famous for golf, deep-sea fishing and the fishing industry, scuba diving, and dramatic scenery. Carmel, a noted artist colony and Hollywood refuge, has controlled growth and maintains a charming village character, while Monterey is more commercial. Both cities are tourist destinations, although they contain coastal communities with attractive beachside residences and a diminished but still active fishing industry. Pacific Grove, with its assortment of well-built Victorian and Craftsman-era homes, is probably the most livable city on the peninsula. As might be expected, cost of living is high, and one needs a large endowment to afford Carmel. Aside from that, the location is a bit isolated from big-city amenities and services, all of which are available to the north in San Francisco, which while not far is hard to get to.

Salinas sits in an agricultural valley. The peninsula cities are in an area of low hills with dense pine and cypress trees. Large sand dunes occur at the head of Monterey Bay. South of Carmel, hills grow larger and the coastline becomes rugged and elevated. The climate is coastal Mediterranean. Heavy, low stratus clouds, known locally as "fog," occur in all seasons. Summer days, when clear, are invariably sunny, cool, and breezy, but can be warmer to quite hot in Salinas and inland. Winters are moderate with periods of Pacific rain.

POPULATION

DEMOGRAPHICS	AREA	U.S. AVG	ETHNIC COMPOSITION	AREA	U.S. AVG	RESIDENT PROFILE	AREA	U.S. AVG
Population	413,408		White	67.3%	75.1%	Single	45.0%	43.6%
Population density per sq. mile	124.4	447.3	Black	4.5%	12.3%	Married	55.0%	56.4%
Population growth	16.2%	16.1%	Asian	8.0%	3.6%	Divorced	8.4%	8.4%
Median age	31.8	35.5	American Indian	.8%	.9%	Separated	3.2%	3.0%
Average family size	3.1	2.7	Hispanic	38.3%	12.5%	Married with children	31.7%	28.7%
			Diversity measure	63.4%	35.2%	Single with children	10.3%	10.1%

ECONOMY & JOBS SCORE: 4/RANK: 315

INCOME	AREA	U.S. AVG	EMPLOYMENT	AREA	U.S. AVG	LARGEST EMPLOYING INDUSTRY
Per capita income	$25,252	$23,420	Unemployment rate	6.9%	6.1%	Healthcare and Social Assistance
Household income	$59,292	$46,060	Recent job growth	-.4%	.9%	
Household income < $25K	14.9%	26.4%	Projected future job growth	13.6%	15.1%	
Household income > $75K	37.4%	24.5%	White collar	46.4%	54.5%	
Household income growth	76.3%	57.3%	Blue collar	53.6%	45.5%	

COST OF LIVING SCORE: 2/RANK: 324

INDEXES & TAXES	AREA	U.S. AVG	HOUSING	AREA	U.S. AVG	NECESSITIES	AREA	U.S. AVG
Cost of Living Index	169.5	100.0	Median home price	$431,880	$160,100	Food Index	115.7	100.0
Financial Progress Index	74.5	100.0	Home price appreciation	17.6%	7.1%	Housing Index	268.2	100.0
Income tax rate	6.000%	4.625%	Median rent	$1,014	$670	Utilities Index	121.3	100.0
Sales tax rate	7.250%	6.474%	Homes owned	48.6%	63.9%	Transportation Index	113.1	100.0
Property tax rate	$10.8	$15.6	Homes rented	40.3%	25.3%	Healthcare Index	130.8	100.0
			Housing affordability	49.0%	54.5%	Miscellaneous Cost Index	106.0	100.0

CLIMATE SCORE: 100/RANK: 1

TEMPERATURE	AREA	U.S. AVG	PRECIPITATION	AREA	U.S. AVG	COMFORTS & HAZARDS	AREA	U.S. AVG
January low	41.2°F	26.4°F	Annual inches precipitation	21.0	35.9	July relative humidity	75.0%	68.8%
July high	73.6°F	86.7°F	Annual inches snowfall	0.0	24.2	Annual days mostly sunny	265	212
Annual days > 90°F	1	38	Annual days precipitation	67	111	Annual days with thunderstorms	2	39
Annual days < 32°F	0	88	Annual days rain > 0.5 inches	13	23	Tornado risk score	3	19
Annual days < 0°F	0	6	Annual days snow > 1.5 inches	0	6	Hurricane risk score	0	15

TEMPERATURE

PRECIPITATION

DAYS OF CLOUDS & PRECIPITATION

EDUCATION SCORE: 10/RANK: 296

ACHIEVEMENT	AREA	U.S. AVG	PUBLIC SCHOOLS	AREA	U.S. AVG	HIGHER EDUCATION	AREA	U.S. AVG
High school degree	68.4%	80.2%	Expenditures per pupil	$5,264	$5,894	No. 2-year colleges	3	3
2-year college degree	6.5%	6.2%	Student/teacher ratio	21.4	16.7	No. 4-year colleges/universities	1	4
4-year college degree	13.8%	15.8%	Attending public school	92.9%	90.2%	No. highly ranked universities	0	1
Graduate/professional degree	8.7%	9.6%	State SAT score	1018*	1020			
			State ACT score	21.5	21.0			

HEALTH & HEALTHCARE SCORE: 0/RANK: 331

CRIME SCORE: 73/RANK: 87

HAZARDS & ILLNESSES	AREA	U.S. AVG	HEALTHCARE	AREA	U.S. AVG	CRIME	AREA	U.S. AVG
Air-quality score	17	45	Physicians per capita	168.1	261.1	Violent crime rate	558.1	456.0
Water-quality score	5	33	Hospital beds per capita	174.5	432.2	Change in violent crime rate	-31.4%	-17.2%
Pollen/allergy score	84	61	No. teaching hospitals	1	4	Property crime rate	2,913.8	3,950.0
Stress score	50	50	Cost per doctor visit	$68	$67	Change in property crime rate	-32.1%	-16.8%
Cancer mortality per capita	163.6	169.0	Cost per dental visit	$90	$82			
Depression days per month	2.1	2.8	Cost per daily hospital room	$1,439	$733			

TRANSPORTATION SCORE: 36/RANK: 209

COMMUTE	AREA	U.S. AVG	INTERCITY SERVICES	AREA	U.S. AVG	AUTOMOTIVE	AREA	U.S. AVG
Average commute time	23.2 min.	22.6 min.	Miles to nearest major airport	53	46	Insurance, annual premium	$915	$1,011
Commute by auto	82.6%	88.7%	Type of local airport	Medium		Gas, cost per gallon	$1.85	$1.50
Commute by mass transit	1.7%	1.8%	No. daily airline departures	250	294	Daily vehicle miles per capita	19.0	23.0
Work at home	4.7%	3.9%	Amtrak service	Yes				
Mass transit miles per capita	9.7	8.0	No. interstate highways	0	1			

LEISURE SCORE: 73/RANK: 92

DINING & SHOPPING	AREA	U.S. AVG	ENTERTAINMENT	AREA	U.S. AVG	OUTDOOR ACTIVITIES	AREA	U.S. AVG
Restaurant rating	1	1	Professional sports rating	4	4	Golf-course rating	4	4
No. outlet malls	4	2	College sports rating	1	4	Ski-area rating	8	4
No. Starbucks	9	11	Zoo/aquarium rating	7	3	National Park rating	9	3
No. warehouse clubs	1	4	Amusement park rating	1	3	Sq. miles inland water	2.0	4.0
			Botanical garden/arboretum rating	3	3	Miles of coastline	84.0	11.4

ARTS & CULTURE SCORE: 35/RANK: 213

MEDIA & LIBRARIES	AREA	U.S. AVG	PERFORMING ARTS	AREA	U.S. AVG	MUSEUMS	AREA	U.S. AVG
Arts radio rating	7	3	Classical music rating	3	4	Overall museum rating	6	6
No. public libraries	24	28	Ballet/dance rating	1	3	Art museum rating	4	5
Library volumes per capita	2.3	2.8	Professional theater rating	1	3	Science museum rating	3	4
			University arts programs rating	1	5	Children's museum rating	1	3

Salt Lake City–Ogden, UT

Score: 68.6   Rank: 84

Profile: Capital-city complex
Location: North-central Utah
Elevation: 4,260 feet
Time zone: Mountain Standard Time

PRO
Attractive setting
Attractive downtown
Nearby recreation

CON
Urban sprawl
Crowding
Nightlife

Salt Lake City, the cultural capital and headquarters for the Mormon community, is a self-contained, cosmopolitan city with global recognition since the 2002 Winter Olympics. Settlers originally chose the location for its isolation and favorable agricultural resources. Today, it serves as a major transportation hub and breakpoint for air, rail, and truck traffic bound for the Pacific Coast. A favorable business climate has led to the development of a wide range of industries, from manufactured goods to a more recent high-tech sector. Economic growth, combined with a favorable climate and local amenities, has attracted numerous new residents, many from California and other points west. Proximity to outstanding outdoor recreation, including skiing, rafting, and hiking in the Wasatch Mountains, is without parallel among metropolitan areas. By contrast, the desert areas to the west offer little recreation or economic interest.

Downtown Salt Lake is beautiful, with boulevards originally designed by Mormons to be wide enough for wagons to do a U-turn. The city itself preserves a clean, dignified character enhanced by the capitol and government buildings and the various landmarks and sites of the Mormon Church. Most unattractive sprawl, including commercial and industrial areas, is to the south. Areas to the north, toward Ogden, are more pleasant. Because of limited geography and high growth, the city is experiencing some crowding, traffic congestion, smog, and a rise in the cost of

living. A complete set of quality amenities is available, and entertainment is wholesome if a little subdued. The Mormon community maintains a strong influence on state government; conservative policies on alcohol and other matters are uncomfortable for some.

Salt Lake City is located in a dramatic valley surrounded by high mountains on three sides and the Great Salt Lake to the northwest. The city center is flat but the Wasatch Mountains to the east have peaks to 12,000 feet. The dry Oquirrh Mountains to the southwest of the city have peaks to above 10,000 feet. Heavily influenced by the mountains and the Great Salt Lake, the climate is semiarid continental with four distinct seasons. Summers have hot, dry weather, but high temperatures are generally tolerable because of low humidity and cool nights. Winters are cold but usually not severe. Mountains to the north block some cold air and the salt lake moderates cold from the northwest. Average annual snowfall is under 60 inches at the airport but much higher in the mountains. Heavy fog can develop under temperature inversions in the winter and persist for several days. In summer, the mountain ranges help to develop thunderstorms, which drift over the valley, particularly the eastern portion. The lake and mountains together create summer breezes and more precipitation than would otherwise occur in this high-desert environment. Heavy precipitation comes from Pacific storms in spring. First freeze is mid-October, last is late April.

POPULATION

DEMOGRAPHICS	AREA	U.S. AVG	ETHNIC COMPOSITION	AREA	U.S. AVG	RESIDENT PROFILE	AREA	U.S. AVG
Population	1,372,699		White	91.5%	75.1%	Single	43.7%	43.6%
Population density per sq. mile	848.7	447.3	Black	1.3%	12.3%	Married	56.3%	56.4%
Population growth	28.0%	16.1%	Asian	4.1%	3.6%	Divorced	9.4%	8.4%
Median age	28.6	35.5	American Indian	.9%	.9%	Separated	2.2%	3.0%
Average family size	3.1	2.7	Hispanic	8.9%	12.5%	Married with children	38.0%	28.7%
			Diversity measure	29.6%	35.2%	Single with children	10.0%	10.1%

ECONOMY & JOBS SCORE: 27/RANK: 240

INCOME	AREA	U.S. AVG	EMPLOYMENT	AREA	U.S. AVG	LARGEST EMPLOYING INDUSTRY
Per capita income	$22,998	$23,420	Unemployment rate	5.6%	6.1%	Miscellaneous Manufacturing
Household income	$56,636	$46,060	Recent job growth	2.8%	.9%	
Household income < $25K	16.9%	26.4%	Projected future job growth	28.5%	15.1%	
Household income > $75K	33.2%	24.5%	White collar	61.0%	54.5%	
Household income growth	83.2%	57.3%	Blue collar	39.0%	45.5%	

COST OF LIVING — SCORE: 26/RANK: 243

INDEXES & TAXES	AREA	U.S. AVG	HOUSING	AREA	U.S. AVG	NECESSITIES	AREA	U.S. AVG
Cost of Living Index	97.3	100.0	Median home price	$148,500	$160,100	Food Index	112.5	100.0
Financial Progress Index	124.1	100.0	Home price appreciation	3.0%	7.1%	Housing Index	92.2	100.0
Income tax rate	7.000%	4.625%	Median rent	$756	$670	Utilities Index	85.2	100.0
Sales tax rate	6.600%	6.474%	Homes owned	64.8%	63.9%	Transportation Index	100.1	100.0
Property tax rate	$8.0	$15.6	Homes rented	28.7%	25.3%	Healthcare Index	88.1	100.0
			Housing affordability	56.0%	54.5%	Miscellaneous Cost Index	99.4	100.0

CLIMATE — SCORE: 30/RANK: 229

TEMPERATURE	AREA	U.S. AVG	PRECIPITATION	AREA	U.S. AVG	COMFORTS & HAZARDS	AREA	U.S. AVG
January low	18.5°F	26.4°F	Annual inches precipitation	15.0	35.9	July relative humidity	54.0%	68.8%
July high	92.8°F	86.7°F	Annual inches snowfall	58.0	24.2	Annual days mostly sunny	232	212
Annual days > 90°F	58	38	Annual days precipitation	88	111	Annual days with thunderstorms	35	39
Annual days < 32°F	134	88	Annual days rain > 0.5 inches	7	23	Tornado risk score	6	19
Annual days < 0°F	3	6	Annual days snow > 1.5 inches	14	6	Hurricane risk score	0	15

TEMPERATURE

PRECIPITATION

DAYS OF CLOUDS & PRECIPITATION

EDUCATION — SCORE: 61/RANK: 128

ACHIEVEMENT	AREA	U.S. AVG	PUBLIC SCHOOLS	AREA	U.S. AVG	HIGHER EDUCATION	AREA	U.S. AVG
High school degree	87.5%	80.2%	Expenditures per pupil	$3,863	$5,894	No. 2-year colleges	3	3
2-year college degree	7.7%	6.2%	Student/teacher ratio	22.9	16.7	No. 4-year colleges/universities	3	4
4-year college degree	18.1%	15.8%	Attending public school	95.9%	90.2%	No. highly ranked universities	0	1
Graduate/professional degree	8.4%	9.6%	State SAT score	1125	1020			
			State ACT score	21.3*	21.0			

HEALTH & HEALTHCARE — SCORE: 40/RANK: 198

CRIME — SCORE: 53/RANK: 155

HAZARDS & ILLNESSES	AREA	U.S. AVG	HEALTHCARE	AREA	U.S. AVG	CRIME	AREA	U.S. AVG
Air-quality score	49	45	Physicians per capita	242.7	261.1	Violent crime rate	306.2	456.0
Water-quality score	37	33	Hospital beds per capita	271.1	432.2	Change in violent crime rate	-25.6%	-17.2%
Pollen/allergy score	60	61	No. teaching hospitals	8	4	Property crime rate	4,812.8	3,950.0
Stress score	64	50	Cost per doctor visit	$66	$67	Change in property crime rate	-29.1%	-16.8%
Cancer mortality per capita	132.5	169.0	Cost per dental visit	$76	$82			
Depression days per month	3.0	2.8	Cost per daily hospital room	$531	$733			

TRANSPORTATION — SCORE: 92/RANK: 26

COMMUTE	AREA	U.S. AVG	INTERCITY SERVICES	AREA	U.S. AVG	AUTOMOTIVE	AREA	U.S. AVG
Average commute time	22.4 min.	22.6 min.	Miles to nearest major airport	31	46	Insurance, annual premium	$930	$1,011
Commute by auto	88.3%	88.7%	Type of local airport	Large		Gas, cost per gallon	$1.57	$1.50
Commute by mass transit	3.2%	1.8%	No. daily airline departures	452	294	Daily vehicle miles per capita	25.5	23.0
Work at home	3.5%	3.9%	Amtrak service	Yes				
Mass transit miles per capita	19.5	8.0	No. interstate highways	2	1			

LEISURE — SCORE: 90/RANK: 31

DINING & SHOPPING	AREA	U.S. AVG	ENTERTAINMENT	AREA	U.S. AVG	OUTDOOR ACTIVITIES	AREA	U.S. AVG
Restaurant rating	1	1	Professional sports rating	6	4	Golf-course rating	5	4
No. outlet malls	1	2	College sports rating	6	4	Ski-area rating	10	4
No. Starbucks	11	11	Zoo/aquarium rating	7	3	National Park rating	8	3
No. warehouse clubs	7	4	Amusement park rating	3	3	Sq. miles inland water	10.0	4.0
			Botanical garden/arboretum rating	4	3	Miles of coastline	0.0	11.4

ARTS & CULTURE — SCORE: 83/RANK: 55

MEDIA & LIBRARIES	AREA	U.S. AVG	PERFORMING ARTS	AREA	U.S. AVG	MUSEUMS	AREA	U.S. AVG
Arts radio rating	9	3	Classical music rating	6	4	Overall museum rating	8	6
No. public libraries	34	28	Ballet/dance rating	5	3	Art museum rating	8	5
Library volumes per capita	2.6	2.8	Professional theater rating	9	3	Science museum rating	7	4
			University arts programs rating	4	5	Children's museum rating	7	3

San Angelo, TX

Score: 39.8   Rank: 277

Profile: Small city
Location: West-central Texas, about 200 miles northwest of San Antonio
Elevation: 1,953 feet
Time zone: Central Standard Time

PRO	CON
Cost of living	Isolation
Historic interest	Entertainment
Small-town atmosphere	Summer heat

San Angelo is a quiet, agricultural and light manufacturing center in west-central Texas. Originally a frontier fort, the city retains some outpost character along with a Spanish/Mexican influence. Industries include ranching, cotton, pecans, and light manufacturing with some oil and gas development. The city is also a commercial, health, and minor cultural center for a 13-county area. Goodfellow Air Force Base adds a military influence. Highlights include a few minor cultural amenities, minor-league sports, and Angelo State University with a population of 6,000 students. But the area is very isolated and there isn't much to do.

San Angelo is located near the center of Texas at the northern edge of the Edwards Plateau. The landscape is level to slightly rolling with hills up to 2,700 feet. The climate is semiarid or steppe but has some humid, temperate characteristics. Warm, dry weather predominates although changes may be rapid and frequent with the passage of northerly cold fronts. Summer high temperatures come with fair skies, southwest winds, and dry air. Rapid temperature drops occur after sunset, and most nights are pleasant with lows in the upper 60s and lower 70s. Temperatures can dip to zero or below. Rainfall is typical of the Great Plains region, much occurring as thunderstorms with wide variations in annual precipitation from year to year. Heavy rainfall occurs in spring and fall and may occur in late summer months with tropical storms. Winds can be high and persistent for several days, carrying dust if conditions are dry.

POPULATION

DEMOGRAPHICS	AREA	U.S. AVG	ETHNIC COMPOSITION	AREA	U.S. AVG	RESIDENT PROFILE	AREA	U.S. AVG
Population	103,018		White	82.7%	75.1%	Single	46.9%	43.6%
Population density per sq. mile	67.7	447.3	Black	5.5%	12.3%	Married	53.1%	56.4%
Population growth	4.6%	16.1%	Asian	1.6%	3.6%	Divorced	6.5%	8.4%
Median age	34.2	35.5	American Indian	.4%	.9%	Separated	2.2%	3.0%
Average family size	2.7	2.7	Hispanic	25.3%	12.5%	Married with children	36.9%	28.7%
			Diversity measure	50.4%	35.2%	Single with children	7.8%	10.1%

ECONOMY & JOBS
SCORE: 88/RANK: 39

INCOME	AREA	U.S. AVG	EMPLOYMENT	AREA	U.S. AVG	LARGEST EMPLOYING INDUSTRY
Per capita income	$19,675	$23,420	Unemployment rate	3.7%	6.1%	Healthcare and Social Assistance
Household income	$36,982	$46,060	Recent job growth	.8%	.9%	
Household income < $25K	32.1%	26.4%	Projected future job growth	9.3%	15.1%	
Household income > $75K	16.1%	24.5%	White collar	49.5%	54.5%	
Household income growth	51.8%	57.3%	Blue collar	50.5%	45.5%	

COST OF LIVING
SCORE: 95/RANK: 16

INDEXES & TAXES	AREA	U.S. AVG	HOUSING	AREA	U.S. AVG	NECESSITIES	AREA	U.S. AVG
Cost of Living Index	77.3	100.0	Median home price	$73,530	$160,100	Food Index	89.6	100.0
Financial Progress Index	102.0	100.0	Home price appreciation	5.0%	7.1%	Housing Index	45.7	100.0
Income tax rate	0.000%	4.625%	Median rent	$472	$670	Utilities Index	84.4	100.0
Sales tax rate	8.250%	6.474%	Homes owned	53.0%	63.9%	Transportation Index	98.1	100.0
Property tax rate	$23.9	$15.6	Homes rented	36.7%	25.3%	Healthcare Index	98.9	100.0
			Housing affordability	63.0%	54.5%	Miscellaneous Cost Index	100.6	100.0

CLIMATE
SCORE: 93/RANK: 23

TEMPERATURE	AREA	U.S. AVG	PRECIPITATION	AREA	U.S. AVG	COMFORTS & HAZARDS	AREA	U.S. AVG
January low	32.0°F	26.4°F	Annual inches precipitation	19.0	35.9	July relative humidity	57.0%	68.8%
July high	95.0°F	86.7°F	Annual inches snowfall	3.0	24.2	Annual days mostly sunny	254	212
Annual days > 90°F	109	38	Annual days precipitation	58	111	Annual days with thunderstorms	37	39
Annual days < 32°F	50	88	Annual days rain > 0.5 inches	12	23	Tornado risk score	20	19
Annual days < 0°F	0	6	Annual days snow > 1.5 inches	2	6	Hurricane risk score	2	15

TEMPERATURE

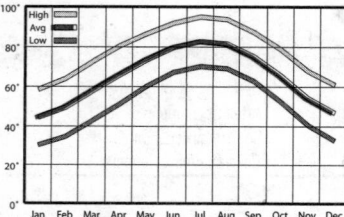

PRECIPITATION

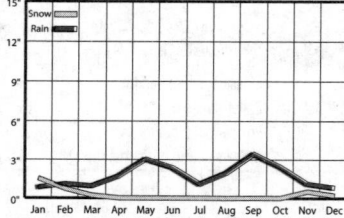

DAYS OF CLOUDS & PRECIPITATION

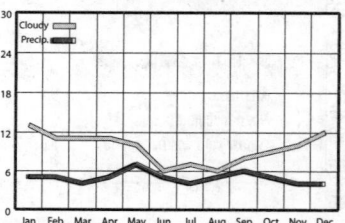

EDUCATION — SCORE: 31/RANK: 228

ACHIEVEMENT	AREA	U.S. AVG	PUBLIC SCHOOLS	AREA	U.S. AVG	HIGHER EDUCATION	AREA	U.S. AVG
High school degree	76.1%	80.2%	Expenditures per pupil	$5,568	$5,894	No. 2-year colleges	0	3
2-year college degree	5.1%	6.2%	Student/teacher ratio	14.4	16.7	No. 4-year colleges/universities	1	4
4-year college degree	14.5%	15.8%	Attending public school	96.3%	90.2%	No. highly ranked universities	0	1
Graduate/professional degree	5.5%	9.6%	State SAT score	993*	1020			
			State ACT score	20.1	21.0			

HEALTH & HEALTHCARE — SCORE: 69/RANK: 101   **CRIME — SCORE: 10/RANK: 295**

HAZARDS & ILLNESSES	AREA	U.S. AVG	HEALTHCARE	AREA	U.S. AVG	CRIME	AREA	U.S. AVG
Air-quality score	24	45	Physicians per capita	201.9	261.1	Violent crime rate	464.4	456.0
Water-quality score	26	33	Hospital beds per capita	799.9	432.2	Change in violent crime rate	-.4%	-17.2%
Pollen/allergy score	79	61	No. teaching hospitals	0	4	Property crime rate	5,328.6	3,950.0
Stress score	13	50	Cost per doctor visit	$77	$67	Change in property crime rate	15.7%	-16.8%
Cancer mortality per capita	158.2	169.0	Cost per dental visit	$66	$82			
Depression days per month	.5	2.8	Cost per daily hospital room	$492	$733			

TRANSPORTATION — SCORE: 72/RANK: 94

COMMUTE	AREA	U.S. AVG	INTERCITY SERVICES	AREA	U.S. AVG	AUTOMOTIVE	AREA	U.S. AVG
Average commute time	17.8 min.	22.6 min.	Miles to nearest major airport	108	46	Insurance, annual premium	$921	$1,011
Commute by auto	85.3%	88.7%	Type of local airport	Small		Gas, cost per gallon	$1.38	$1.50
Commute by mass transit	.4%	1.8%	No. daily airline departures	40	294	Daily vehicle miles per capita	18.3	23.0
Work at home	2.6%	3.9%	Amtrak service	No				
Mass transit miles per capita	4.1	8.0	No. interstate highways	0	1			

LEISURE — SCORE: 15/RANK: 283

DINING & SHOPPING	AREA	U.S. AVG	ENTERTAINMENT	AREA	U.S. AVG	OUTDOOR ACTIVITIES	AREA	U.S. AVG
Restaurant rating	1	1	Professional sports rating	3	4	Golf-course rating	1	4
No. outlet malls	0	2	College sports rating	4	4	Ski-area rating	1	4
No. Starbucks	0	11	Zoo/aquarium rating	1	3	National Park rating	1	3
No. warehouse clubs	1	4	Amusement park rating	1	3	Sq. miles inland water	3.0	4.0
			Botanical garden/arboretum rating	1	3	Miles of coastline	0.0	11.4

ARTS & CULTURE — SCORE: 6/RANK: 310

MEDIA & LIBRARIES	AREA	U.S. AVG	PERFORMING ARTS	AREA	U.S. AVG	MUSEUMS	AREA	U.S. AVG
Arts radio rating	1	3	Classical music rating	3	4	Overall museum rating	3	6
No. public libraries	3	28	Ballet/dance rating	1	3	Art museum rating	4	5
Library volumes per capita	2.8	2.8	Professional theater rating	1	3	Science museum rating	1	4
			University arts programs rating	3	5	Children's museum rating	2	3

San Antonio, TX

Score: 67.5   Rank: 93

Profile: Large city
Location: South-central Texas
Elevation: 794 feet
Time zone: Central Standard Time

PRO	CON
Strong economy	Urban sprawl
Attractive downtown	Crime rate
Entertainment	Summer heat

San Antonio, a modern city with a distinct Mexican influence, is the third largest city in Texas and the ninth largest in the United States. Modern skyscrapers in the downtown area attractively intermingle with the Alamo historic site and the Spanish Governors Palace. The Paseo del Rio, or River Walk, contains shops and sidewalk cafes along the San Antonio River—making downtown a popular destination. Other historic sites date back to the days of possession by Mexico. The winning of the Mexican War in the 19th century opened up large areas, such as New Braunfels and San Marcos, which were settled by European immigrants, particularly Germans.

Although the city has a laid-back character, there is a substantial business community that includes the headquarters of SBC Communications and Valero (oil and gas) and a number of smaller businesses. Four nearby air force facilities bring a strong military presence. The city has a full complement of museums and cultural assets, sports teams (notably the NBA's San Antonio Spurs), transportation facilities, and entertainment venues. These advantages are accompanied by a strong economy, low cost of living, and a favorable winter climate. Rapid growth has led to sprawl and a noticeable increase in crime. Better planning than most Texas cities has allowed San Antonio to avoid some growth-related issues, although the area is still at risk.

Located on the San Antonio River in a flat to gently rolling area, the city sits at the border of the coastal plain to the southeast and the hill country to the northwest. The climate is a mix of humid subtropical elements in summer and continental elements in winter. Temperatures are in the 50s in January, and above 90°F over 80% of the time in mid-summer. San Antonio is situated between a semiarid area to the west and a coastal area of heavy precipitation to the east. Precipitation is fairly well distributed throughout the year with the heaviest amounts occurring from May to September. Summer rain usually occurs as thunderstorms and most winter precipitation occurs as light rain or drizzle. Measurable snow occurs only once every 3 or 4 years. Tropical storms occasionally affect the city.

POPULATION

DEMOGRAPHICS	AREA	U.S. AVG	ETHNIC COMPOSITION	AREA	U.S. AVG	RESIDENT PROFILE	AREA	U.S. AVG
Population	1,660,205		White	78.0%	75.1%	Single	44.7%	43.6%
Population density per sq. mile	499.0	447.3	Black	7.5%	12.3%	Married	55.3%	56.4%
Population growth	25.3%	16.1%	Asian	1.7%	3.6%	Divorced	9.3%	8.4%
Median age	32.9	35.5	American Indian	.4%	.9%	Separated	3.8%	3.0%
Average family size	2.9	2.7	Hispanic	45.1%	12.5%	Married with children	32.3%	28.7%
			Diversity measure	59.9%	35.2%	Single with children	12.2%	10.1%

ECONOMY & JOBS SCORE: 52/RANK: 157

INCOME	AREA	U.S. AVG	EMPLOYMENT	AREA	U.S. AVG	LARGEST EMPLOYING INDUSTRY
Per capita income	$21,180	$23,420	Unemployment rate	5.6%	6.1%	Healthcare and Social Assistance
Household income	$43,228	$46,060	Recent job growth	4.0%	.9%	
Household income < $25K	27.0%	26.4%	Projected future job growth	24.6%	15.1%	
Household income > $75K	23.0%	24.5%	White collar	54.9%	54.5%	
Household income growth	66.0%	57.3%	Blue collar	45.1%	45.5%	

COST OF LIVING SCORE: 70/RANK: 100

INDEXES & TAXES	AREA	U.S. AVG	HOUSING	AREA	U.S. AVG	NECESSITIES	AREA	U.S. AVG
Cost of Living Index	82.8	100.0	Median home price	$110,700	$160,100	Food Index	84.4	100.0
Financial Progress Index	111.3	100.0	Home price appreciation	5.2%	7.1%	Housing Index	68.8	100.0
Income tax rate	0.000%	4.625%	Median rent	$635	$670	Utilities Index	80.5	100.0
Sales tax rate	7.875%	6.474%	Homes owned	60.6%	63.9%	Transportation Index	91.8	100.0
Property tax rate	$24.8	$15.6	Homes rented	29.3%	25.3%	Healthcare Index	89.4	100.0
			Housing affordability	59.0%	54.5%	Miscellaneous Cost Index	99.0	100.0

CLIMATE SCORE: 88/RANK: 39

TEMPERATURE	AREA	U.S. AVG	PRECIPITATION	AREA	U.S. AVG	COMFORTS & HAZARDS	AREA	U.S. AVG
January low	39.8°F	26.4°F	Annual inches precipitation	28.0	35.9	July relative humidity	67.0%	68.8%
July high	95.9°F	86.7°F	Annual inches snowfall	.5	24.2	Annual days mostly sunny	227	212
Annual days > 90°F	111	38	Annual days precipitation	81	111	Annual days with thunderstorms	36	39
Annual days < 32°F	22	88	Annual days rain > 0.5 inches	18	23	Tornado risk score	23	19
Annual days < 0°F	0	6	Annual days snow > 1.5 inches	0	6	Hurricane risk score	13	15

TEMPERATURE

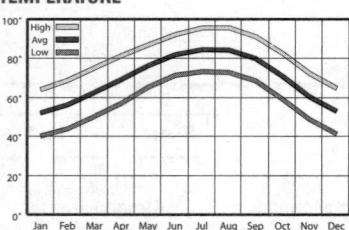

PRECIPITATION

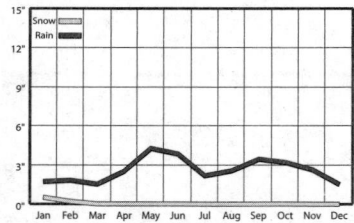

DAYS OF CLOUDS & PRECIPITATION

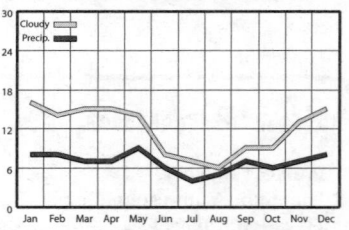

EDUCATION SCORE: 43/RANK: 187

ACHIEVEMENT	AREA	U.S. AVG	PUBLIC SCHOOLS	AREA	U.S. AVG	HIGHER EDUCATION	AREA	U.S. AVG
High school degree	77.3%	80.2%	Expenditures per pupil	$5,639	$5,894	No. 2-year colleges	5	3
2-year college degree	5.8%	6.2%	Student/teacher ratio	15.2	16.7	No. 4-year colleges/universities	6	4
4-year college degree	13.8%	15.8%	Attending public school	91.8%	90.2%	No. highly ranked universities	0	1
Graduate/professional degree	7.9%	9.6%	State SAT score	993*	1020			
			State ACT score	20.1	21.0			

HEALTH & HEALTHCARE SCORE: 7/RANK: 305

HAZARDS & ILLNESSES	AREA	U.S. AVG	HEALTHCARE	AREA	U.S. AVG
Air-quality score	94	45	Physicians per capita	308.2	261.1
Water-quality score	45	33	Hospital beds per capita	371.1	432.2
Pollen/allergy score	94	61	No. teaching hospitals	9	4
Stress score	79	50	Cost per doctor visit	$58	$67
Cancer mortality per capita	164.1	169.0	Cost per dental visit	$76	$82
Depression days per month	2.3	2.8	Cost per daily hospital room	$495	$733

CRIME SCORE: 0/RANK: 328

CRIME	AREA	U.S. AVG
Violent crime rate	676.3	456.0
Change in violent crime rate	39.6%	-17.2%
Property crime rate	6,358.0	3,950.0
Change in property crime rate	2.3%	-16.8%

TRANSPORTATION SCORE: 50/RANK: 165

COMMUTE	AREA	U.S. AVG	INTERCITY SERVICES	AREA	U.S. AVG	AUTOMOTIVE	AREA	U.S. AVG
Average commute time	24.5 min.	22.6 mins.	Miles to nearest major airport	6	46	Insurance, annual premium	$1,030	$1,011
Commute by auto	87.9%	88.7%	Type of local airport	Medium		Gas, cost per gallon	$1.37	$1.50
Commute by mass transit	3.3%	1.8%	No. daily airline departures	189	294	Daily vehicle miles per capita	26.6	23.0
Work at home	3.2%	3.9%	Amtrak service	Yes				
Mass transit miles per capita	20.9	8.0	No. interstate highways	3	1			

LEISURE SCORE: 62/RANK: 125

DINING & SHOPPING	AREA	U.S. AVG	ENTERTAINMENT	AREA	U.S. AVG	OUTDOOR ACTIVITIES	AREA	U.S. AVG
Restaurant rating	1	1	Professional sports rating	6	4	Golf-course rating	5	4
No. outlet malls	3	2	College sports rating	2	4	Ski-area rating	1	4
No. Starbucks	20	11	Zoo/aquarium rating	7	3	National Park rating	2	3
No. warehouse clubs	5	4	Amusement park rating	9	3	Sq. miles inland water	2.0	4.0
			Botanical garden/arboretum rating	4	3	Miles of coastline	0.0	11.4

ARTS & CULTURE SCORE: 50/RANK: 166

MEDIA & LIBRARIES	AREA	U.S. AVG	PERFORMING ARTS	AREA	U.S. AVG	MUSEUMS	AREA	U.S. AVG
Arts radio rating	3	3	Classical music rating	5	4	Overall museum rating	9	6
No. public libraries	32	28	Ballet/dance rating	3	3	Art museum rating	6	5
Library volumes per capita	1.4	2.8	Professional theater rating	1	3	Science museum rating	8	4
			University arts programs rating	9	5	Children's museum rating	6	3

San Diego, CA

Score: 71.5 Rank: 74

Profile: Large coastal city
Location: Southern California coast, 120 miles south of Los Angeles and 20 miles north of Mexican border
Elevation: 28 feet
Time zone: Pacific Standard Time

PRO	CON
Year-round climate	Cost of living
Recreation	Urban sprawl
Future job growth	Healthcare

If it weren't for cost of living and some urban sprawl, San Diego would likely be right at the top of the rankings. The climate is exceptional and the availability of activities and services is excellent. Downtown San Diego is modern but rather nondescript and features a nice waterfront area. Balboa Park just to the north is an urban treasure. San Diego Bay and Mission Bay to the north offer excellent boating and water recreation, and Sea World and the San Diego Zoo are nationally famous. Farther to the north along the coast, La Jolla is an attractive if expensive beach enclave. Residential areas have sprawled to the north along State Route 163 and I-15 in places like Poway and Rancho Bernardo. Areas to the south toward Mexico have a working-class character. Cost of living has jumped substantially in the past few years as new residents have flocked to the area. The Cost of Living Index of 157.7, up from 110 to 120 just a few years ago, is the 13th worst in the country. Growth and urban sprawl haven't *yet* produced problems to the same degree as other California communities, but the risk is present. The downtown commute is becoming more difficult, but jobs showing up in the suburban areas are lessening the impact. Travel downtown and to the airport is easy at all but the worst times, and suburban roadways are generally well planned and devoid of major traffic bottlenecks. Job growth overall is healthy because businesses are attracted to the area as an alternative to Los Angeles.

San Diego itself is located on a narrow coastal plain giving way to desert foothills to the east and north. Local vegetation is sparse coastal bush and grasses, with desert scrub inland. The Mediterranean climate is pleasant year-round. The strong Pacific influence creates cool summers and warm winters in comparison with other places at the same latitude. The climate varies according to proximity to the coast. Temperatures below freezing are rare while desert-influenced temperatures above 90°F or even 100°F do occur, generally inland. Desert winds bring the highest temperatures during early fall. Most precipitation falls in winter but there may be an occasional thunderstorm or tropical rain. Morning ocean-borne low clouds (called "fog" or "June gloom" locally) occur in summer but usually dissipate by afternoon. Humidity is low and sunshine is plentiful for a marine location.

POPULATION

DEMOGRAPHICS	AREA	U.S. AVG	ETHNIC COMPOSITION	AREA	U.S. AVG	RESIDENT PROFILE	AREA	U.S. AVG
Population	2,906,660		White	74.6%	75.1%	Single	50.3%	43.6%
Population density per sq. mile	691.3	447.3	Black	5.7%	12.3%	Married	49.7%	56.4%
Population growth	16.4%	16.1%	Asian	9.7%	3.6%	Divorced	10.3%	8.4%
Median age	33.4	35.5	American Indian	1.5%	.9%	Separated	3.5%	3.0%
Average family size	3.2	2.7	Hispanic	26.2%	12.5%	Married with children	26.5%	28.7%
			Diversity measure	59.7%	35.2%	Single with children	10.3%	10.1%

ECONOMY & JOBS SCORE: 15/RANK: 279

INCOME	AREA	U.S. AVG	EMPLOYMENT	AREA	U.S. AVG	LARGEST EMPLOYING INDUSTRY
Per capita income	$26,368	$23,420	Unemployment rate	4.3%	6.1%	Computer and Electronic Product Manufacturing
Household income	$54,972	$46,060	Recent job growth	1.4%	.9%	
Household income < $25K	18.8%	26.4%	Projected future job growth	23.1%	15.1%	
Household income > $75K	33.9%	24.5%	White collar	58.3%	54.5%	
Household income growth	56.9%	57.3%	Blue collar	41.7%	45.5%	

COST OF LIVING SCORE: 3/RANK: 320

INDEXES & TAXES	AREA	U.S. AVG	HOUSING	AREA	U.S. AVG	NECESSITIES	AREA	U.S. AVG
Cost of Living Index	157.7	100.0	Median home price	$379,300	$160,100	Food Index	113.3	100.0
Financial Progress Index	74.3	100.0	Home price appreciation	16.3%	7.1%	Housing Index	235.6	100.0
Income tax rate	6.000%	4.625%	Median rent	$1,175	$670	Utilities Index	125.1	100.0
Sales tax rate	7.750%	6.474%	Homes owned	51.9%	63.9%	Transportation Index	113.3	100.0
Property tax rate	$11.1	$15.6	Homes rented	39.1%	25.3%	Healthcare Index	127.5	100.0
			Housing affordability	37.0%	54.5%	Miscellaneous Cost Index	106.6	100.0

CLIMATE SCORE: 96/RANK: 11

TEMPERATURE	AREA	U.S. AVG	PRECIPITATION	AREA	U.S. AVG	COMFORTS & HAZARDS	AREA	U.S. AVG
January low	45.8°F	26.4°F	Annual inches precipitation	9.0	35.9	July relative humidity	68.0%	68.8%
July high	77.3°F	86.7°F	Annual inches snowfall	0.0	24.2	Annual days mostly sunny	267	212
Annual days > 90°F	3	38	Annual days precipitation	41	111	Annual days with thunderstorms	3	39
Annual days < 32°F	0	88	Annual days rain > 0.5 inches	5	23	Tornado risk score	5	19
Annual days < 0°F	0	6	Annual days snow > 1.5 inches	0	6	Hurricane risk score	3	15

TEMPERATURE

PRECIPITATION

DAYS OF CLOUDS & PRECIPITATION

EDUCATION SCORE: 79/RANK: 70

ACHIEVEMENT	AREA	U.S. AVG	PUBLIC SCHOOLS	AREA	U.S. AVG	HIGHER EDUCATION	AREA	U.S. AVG
High school degree	82.8%	80.2%	Expenditures per pupil	$5,457	$5,894	No. 2-year colleges	9	3
2-year college degree	7.5%	6.2%	Student/teacher ratio	21.4	16.7	No. 4-year colleges/universities	10	4
4-year college degree	18.7%	15.8%	Attending public school	91.1%	90.2%	No. highly ranked universities	2	1
Graduate/professional degree	10.9%	9.6%	State SAT score	1018*	1020			
			State ACT score	21.5	21.0			

HEALTH & HEALTHCARE SCORE: 9/RANK: 300

CRIME SCORE: 72/RANK: 91

HAZARDS & ILLNESSES	AREA	U.S. AVG	HEALTHCARE	AREA	U.S. AVG	CRIME	AREA	U.S. AVG
Air-quality score	72	45	Physicians per capita	269.5	261.1	Violent crime rate	509.1	456.4
Water-quality score	26	33	Hospital beds per capita	259.3	432.2	Change in violent crime rate	-35.9%	-17.2%
Pollen/allergy score	66	61	No. teaching hospitals	7	4	Property crime rate	3,051.7	3,950.0
Stress score	43	50	Cost per doctor visit	$75	$67	Change in property crime rate	-28.0%	-16.8%
Cancer mortality per capita	167.8	169.0	Cost per dental visit	$114	$82			
Depression days per month	2.0	2.8	Cost per daily hospital room	$1,399	$733			

TRANSPORTATION SCORE: 70/RANK: 97

COMMUTE	AREA	U.S. AVG	INTERCITY SERVICES	AREA	U.S. AVG	AUTOMOTIVE	AREA	U.S. AVG
Average commute time	25.3 min.	22.6 min.	Miles to nearest major airport	6	46	Insurance, annual premium	$1,357	$1,011
Commute by auto	82.2%	88.7%	Type of local airport	Large		Gas, cost per gallon	$1.78	$1.50
Commute by mass transit	2.6%	1.8%	No. daily airline departures	296	294	Daily vehicle miles per capita	24.3	23.0
Work at home	5.5%	3.9%	Amtrak service	Yes				
Mass transit miles per capita	17.2	8.0	No. interstate highways	3	1			

LEISURE SCORE: 96/RANK: 13

DINING & SHOPPING	AREA	U.S. AVG	ENTERTAINMENT	AREA	U.S. AVG	OUTDOOR ACTIVITIES	AREA	U.S. AVG
Restaurant rating	1	1	Professional sports rating	5	4	Golf-course rating	7	4
No. outlet malls	4	2	College sports rating	5	4	Ski-area rating	9	4
No. Starbucks	114	11	Zoo/aquarium rating	10	3	National Park rating	9	3
No. warehouse clubs	9	4	Amusement park rating	9	3	Sq. miles inland water	5.0	4.0
			Botanical garden/arboretum rating	10	3	Miles of coastline	54.1	11.4

ARTS & CULTURE
SCORE: 86/RANK: 48

MEDIA & LIBRARIES	AREA	U.S. AVG	PERFORMING ARTS	AREA	U.S. AVG	MUSEUMS	AREA	U.S. AVG
Arts radio rating	7	3	Classical music rating	6	4	Overall museum rating	9	6
No. public libraries	80	28	Ballet/dance rating	6	3	Art museum rating	9	5
Library volumes per capita	2.2	2.8	Professional theater rating	10	3	Science museum rating	9	4
			University arts programs rating	9	5	Children's museum rating	8	3

San Francisco, CA

Score: 65.3   Rank: 107

Profile: Regional center
Location: Northern California coast at the head of San Francisco Bay
Elevation: 155 feet
Time zone: Pacific Standard Time

PRO
Year-round climate
Arts and culture
Attractive setting

CON
Cost of living
Crowdedness
Recent economy

A world-class city, San Francisco has a lot going for it: exceptional arts and cultural activities, including performing arts and museums; a full-scale financial district; a commercial-industrial core; and all the education and services anyone could want. The climate is one of the most unusual in the world, and the area is among the most ethnically diverse in the country. In addition, such tourist attractions as Fisherman's Wharf, Chinatown, the cable car system, hilltop residential enclaves, and the wine country to the north make the city an interesting and fun place to live.

But downsides exist. The city's location on a peninsula poses a major problem: lack of space. There simply isn't enough room for all the people and activities. The downtown area is dense, as one may expect, but the residential areas to the south are as tightly packed as any city in the United States. The result is the second highest set of living costs and home prices in the country. At 196.4, the Cost of Living Index is almost *twice* the national average, and median home price of $516,400 is 3½ *times* the national median. Many residents live in outlying areas that are still expensive and require long, difficult commutes. Fortunately, the area's excellent public transit system (spearheaded by the Bay Area Rapid Transit, or BART) helps soften the blow. The nicer residential communities are north across the Golden Gate in Marin County and south along the peninsula in such places as San Mateo and Menlo Park. Attractive urban living has emerged in a formerly industrial area just south of the city near the new SBC Park, home of major league baseball's San Francisco Giants. The end of the dot.com era is reflected in a softening job market and a leveling off of real estate prices in these areas. If

it weren't for crowding and the high cost of living, San Francisco would likely be closer to the top of the *Cities Ranked & Rated* rankings.

The northern end of the peninsula containing downtown San Francisco is built up, giving way to lushly vegetated coastal mountains to the south. A long, narrow, mostly built-up plain extends along the east (bay) side of the peninsula toward San Jose. A similar topography extends north from the Golden Gate into Marin County. Geographic and strong marine influences result in the unusual climate. It is known as the "air-conditioned city" in summer, and heavy coats are worn frequently during summer in certain locations (hence the Mark Twain quip "I spent the coldest winter of my life one summer in San Francisco."). Reason: Differences between ocean and inland temperatures and the resulting pressure gradient bring heavy sea fogs and low, ocean-born stratus clouds inland with strong sea breezes. The area probably has greater variability in temperature, cloudiness, and sunshine than any other similarly sized urban area in the country. In certain locations, hills block the fog; in others, it pours in freely, at times covering the entire area including San Jose 50 miles south. Although there is almost no summer rain, fogs often produce a chilly drizzle. Maximum summer temperatures frequently reach only the 50s. Spring and fall are relatively fog free, and temperatures may rise into the 60s and 70s. Occasionally, early fall winds blowing from the deserts to the southeast block sea breezes and shoot temperatures into the 90s or even over 100°F. Winter temperatures are mild and consistent across the area. Eighty percent of precipitation occurs November through March. Snow may occur in the surrounding coastal mountains but melts quickly. Freezing temperatures in the city are rare.

POPULATION

DEMOGRAPHICS	AREA	U.S. AVG	ETHNIC COMPOSITION	AREA	U.S. AVG	RESIDENT PROFILE	AREA	U.S. AVG
Population	1,714,832		White	69.3%	75.1%	Single	52.8%	43.6%
Population density per sq. mile	1,688.5	447.3	Black	6.5%	12.3%	Married	47.2%	56.4%
Population growth	6.9%	16.1%	Asian	19.8%	3.6%	Divorced	10.9%	8.4%
Median age	37.9	35.5	American Indian	.4%	.9%	Separated	3.1%	3.0%
Average family size	2.4	2.7	Hispanic	16.5%	12.5%	Married with children	20.3%	28.7%
			Diversity measure	63.2%	35.2%	Single with children	7.8%	10.1%

ECONOMY & JOBS
SCORE: 4/RANK: 316

INCOME	AREA	U.S. AVG	EMPLOYMENT	AREA	U.S. AVG	LARGEST EMPLOYING INDUSTRY
Per capita income	$41,686	$23,420	Unemployment rate	5.6%	6.1%	Computer Systems Design and Related Services
Household income	$76,164	$46,060	Recent job growth	-.8%	.9%	
Household income < $25K	14.1%	26.4%	Projected future job growth	10.0%	15.1%	
Household income > $75K	51.2%	24.5%	White collar	66.3%	54.5%	
Household income growth	87.9%	57.3%	Blue collar	33.7%	45.5%	

COST OF LIVING — SCORE: 0/RANK: 330

INDEXES & TAXES	AREA	U.S. AVG	HOUSING	AREA	U.S. AVG	NECESSITIES	AREA	U.S. AVG
Cost of Living Index	196.4	100.0	Median home price	$516,400	$160,100	Food Index	120.8	100.0
Financial Progress Index	82.7	100.0	Home price appreciation	14.2%	7.1%	Housing Index	320.7	100.0
Income tax rate	6.000%	4.625%	Median rent	$1,775	$670	Utilities Index	144.4	100.0
Sales tax rate	8.500%	6.474%	Homes owned	49.0%	63.9%	Transportation Index	129.2	100.0
Property tax rate	$11.2	$15.6	Homes rented	41.8%	25.3%	Healthcare Index	170.5	100.0
			Housing affordability	40.0%	54.5%	Miscellaneous Cost Index	110.8	100.0

CLIMATE — SCORE: 99/RANK: 2

TEMPERATURE	AREA	U.S. AVG	PRECIPITATION	AREA	U.S. AVG	COMFORTS & HAZARDS	AREA	U.S. AVG
January low	41.2°F	26.4°F	Annual inches precipitation	21.0	35.9	July relative humidity	75.0%	68.8%
July high	73.6°F	86.7°F	Annual inches snowfall	0.0	24.2	Annual days mostly sunny	265	212
Annual days > 90°F	1	38	Annual days precipitation	67	111	Annual days with thunderstorms	2	39
Annual days < 32°F	0	88	Annual days rain > 0.5 inches	14	23	Tornado risk score	1	19
Annual days < 0°F	0	6	Annual days snow > 1.5 inches	0	6	Hurricane risk score	0	15

TEMPERATURE

PRECIPITATION

DAYS OF CLOUDS & PRECIPITATION

EDUCATION — SCORE: 81/RANK: 63

ACHIEVEMENT	AREA	U.S. AVG	PUBLIC SCHOOLS	AREA	U.S. AVG	HIGHER EDUCATION	AREA	U.S. AVG
High school degree	84.2%	80.2%	Expenditures per pupil	$5,786	$5,894	No. 2-year colleges	9	3
2-year college degree	5.6%	6.2%	Student/teacher ratio	19.9	16.7	No. 4-year colleges/universities	13	4
4-year college degree	28.6%	15.8%	Attending public school	77.2%	90.2%	No. highly ranked universities	2	1
Graduate/professional degree	16.4%	9.6%	State SAT score	1018*	1020			
			State ACT score	21.5	21.0			

HEALTH & HEALTHCARE — SCORE: 15/RANK: 281   CRIME — SCORE: 69/RANK: 101

HAZARDS & ILLNESSES	AREA	U.S. AVG	HEALTHCARE	AREA	U.S. AVG	CRIME	AREA	U.S. AVG
Air-quality score	95	45	Physicians per capita	482.1	261.1	Violent crime rate	533.8	456.0
Water-quality score	9	33	Hospital beds per capita	441.7	432.2	Change in violent crime rate	-39.6%	-17.2%
Pollen/allergy score	95	61	No. teaching hospitals	11	4	Property crime rate	3,392.6	3,950.0
Stress score	93	50	Cost per doctor visit	$77	$67	Change in property crime rate	-31.5%	-16.8%
Cancer mortality per capita	183.0	169.0	Cost per dental visit	$93	$82			
Depression days per month	4.5	2.8	Cost per daily hospital room	$2,576	$733			

TRANSPORTATION — SCORE: 100/RANK: 1

COMMUTE	AREA	U.S. AVG	INTERCITY SERVICES	AREA	U.S. AVG	AUTOMOTIVE	AREA	U.S. AVG
Average commute time	29.4 min.	22.6 min.	Miles to nearest major airport	15	46	Insurance, annual premium	$1,009	$1,011
Commute by auto	70.1%	88.7%	Type of local airport	Large		Gas, cost per gallon	$1.89	$1.50
Commute by mass transit	13.7%	1.8%	No. daily airline departures	546	294	Daily vehicle miles per capita	21.4	23.0
Work at home	6.0%	3.9%	Amtrak service	No				
Mass transit miles per capita	88.3	8.0	No. interstate highways	1	1			

LEISURE — SCORE: 98/RANK: 7

DINING & SHOPPING	AREA	U.S. AVG	ENTERTAINMENT	AREA	U.S. AVG	OUTDOOR ACTIVITIES	AREA	U.S. AVG
Restaurant rating	5	1	Professional sports rating	10	4	Golf-course rating	7	4
No. outlet malls	5	2	College sports rating	4	4	Ski-area rating	9	4
No. Starbucks	108	11	Zoo/aquarium rating	8	3	National Park rating	6	3
No. warehouse clubs	7	4	Amusement park rating	5	3	Sq. miles inland water	10.0	4.0
			Botanical garden/arboretum rating	9	3	Miles of coastline	76.1	11.4

ARTS & CULTURE — SCORE: 99/RANK: 3

MEDIA & LIBRARIES	AREA	U.S. AVG	PERFORMING ARTS	AREA	U.S. AVG	MUSEUMS	AREA	U.S. AVG
Arts radio rating	9	3	Classical music rating	10	4	Overall museum rating	10	6
No. public libraries	81	28	Ballet/dance rating	10	3	Art museum rating	10	5
Library volumes per capita	2.9	2.8	Professional theater rating	10	3	Science museum rating	10	4
			University arts programs rating	9	5	Children's museum rating	9	3

San Jose, CA

Score: 57.1 **Rank:** 168

Profile: Large city
Location: Northern California, on the south end of San Francisco Bay
Elevation: 67 feet
Time zone: Pacific Standard Time

PRO
Year-round climate
Entertainment
Proximity to San Francisco

CON
Cost of living
Economy
Crowding

San Jose is the principal city in the Santa Clara Valley, perhaps better known as the "Silicon Valley." Once the location of orchards and small towns, the valley now contains businesses and a vast, residential zone for those who work locally and in urban areas northward. Major high-tech manufacturers and a supporting array of small- and medium-size businesses fill the valley, known for the emergence of the electronics industry and perfection of the semiconductor, the integrated circuit, and the computer. Several defense technology suppliers are also present. During the late 1990's Internet boom, a high-tech culture with its own lingo and architectural style (long, low, glass-fronted buildings) emerged. An influx of educated workers from around the world, particularly Asia, created a highly diverse culture. Entertainment assets and cultural activities are abundant and varied, but some of the better activities, like the Paul Masson Winery concerts, are overcrowded, expensive, and hard to get into. The Technology Museum of Innovation in the revitalized San Jose downtown and surrounding activities are excellent. Like many recent-growth places in California, San Jose suffers from overcrowding and sprawl—in fact, neighborhoods cover buildable land in all directions and traffic along the main commute corridors is horrible. Many neighborhoods are dull and uninteresting, and the abundance of rental housing has led to poor maintenance and upkeep. That said, neighborhoods such as Los Gatos, Los Altos, and Palo Alto at the western edges adjacent to Coastal Range foothills feature exceptional housing and appealing, small downtowns, but homes under $1 million are rare. While the upward spiral of incomes drove prosperity in the late '90s, the tech-led economic contraction that followed has been severe, cutting into local jobs and incomes, although the Cost of Living Index at 184.1 is still the second highest in California and the third highest nationwide.

The broad, flat valley narrows considerably but continues south toward Gilroy, which is becoming increasingly built up. The sheltered, coastal, Mediterranean climate is ideal. Summers are clear, dry, and sunny, with normal daytime highs in the low 80s. In the evening, marine air often delivers low, stratus clouds, known locally as "fog," which typically burns off by mid-morning the next day. Light jackets are usually required in summer. The valley location and stable, summer air produce some hazy or smoggy days. Hot, desert winds sometimes blow in late summer and fall, but temperatures seldom reach 100°F. Winter is typically mild with days in the 60s and nights in the 40s, with occasional lows in the 30s or upper 20s. Winter is the rainy season; most precipitation falls when steady Pacific storms enter the area, but the coastal mountains reduce the impact.

POPULATION

DEMOGRAPHICS	AREA	U.S. AVG	ETHNIC COMPOSITION	AREA	U.S. AVG	RESIDENT PROFILE	AREA	U.S. AVG
Population	1,683,505		White	67.6%	75.1%	Single	51.3%	43.6%
Population density per sq. mile	1,303.8	447.3	Black	3.7%	12.3%	Married	48.7%	56.4%
Population growth	12.4%	16.1%	Asian	20.8%	3.6%	Divorced	10.1%	8.4%
Median age	34.2	35.5	American Indian	.5%	.9%	Separated	3.2%	3.0%
Average family size	2.8	2.7	Hispanic	25.5%	12.5%	Married with children	27.3%	28.7%
			Diversity measure	66.9%	35.2%	Single with children	9.7%	10.1%

ECONOMY & JOBS SCORE: 1/RANK: 326

INCOME	AREA	U.S. AVG	EMPLOYMENT	AREA	U.S. AVG	LARGEST EMPLOYING INDUSTRY
Per capita income	$39,175	$23,420	Unemployment rate	7.9%	6.1%	Computer and Electronic Product Manufacturing
Household income	$93,503	$46,060	Recent job growth	-4.2%	.9%	
Household income < $25K	9.0%	26.4%	Projected future job growth	12.3%	15.1%	
Household income > $75K	61.4%	24.5%	White collar	65.7%	54.5%	
Household income growth	94.1%	57.3%	Blue collar	34.3%	45.5%	

COST OF LIVING SCORE: 0/RANK: 329

INDEXES & TAXES	AREA	U.S. AVG	HOUSING	AREA	U.S. AVG	NECESSITIES	AREA	U.S. AVG
Cost of Living Index	184.1	100.0	Median home price	$478,000	$160,100	Food Index	118.2	100.0
Financial Progress Index	108.2	100.0	Home price appreciation	14.0%	7.1%	Housing Index	296.9	100.0
Income tax rate	6.000%	4.625%	Median rent	$1,821	$670	Utilities Index	128.3	100.0
Sales tax rate	8.250%	6.474%	Homes owned	57.5%	63.9%	Transportation Index	124.2	100.0
Property tax rate	$11.2	$15.6	Homes rented	38.0%	25.3%	Healthcare Index	152.7	100.0
			Housing affordability	48.0%	54.5%	Miscellaneous Cost Index	109.4	100.0

CLIMATE SCORE: 96/RANK: 12

TEMPERATURE	AREA	U.S. AVG	PRECIPITATION	AREA	U.S. AVG	COMFORTS & HAZARDS	AREA	U.S. AVG
January low	40.2°F	26.4°F	Annual inches precipitation	16.0	35.9	July relative humidity	70.0%	68.8%
July high	78.6°F	86.7°F	Annual inches snowfall	0.0	24.2	Annual days mostly sunny	257	212
Annual days > 90°F	20	38	Annual days precipitation	47	111	Annual days with thunderstorms	4	39
Annual days < 32°F	2	88	Annual days rain > 0.5 inches	6	23	Tornado risk score	1	19
Annual days < 0°F	0	6	Annual days snow > 1.5 inches	0	6	Hurricane risk score	0	15

TEMPERATURE

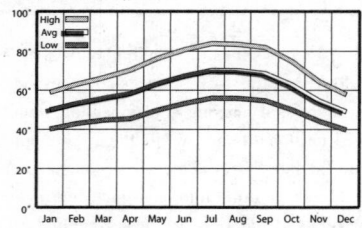

PRECIPITATION

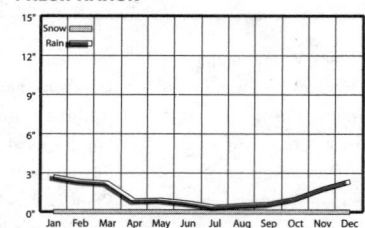

DAYS OF CLOUDS & PRECIPITATION

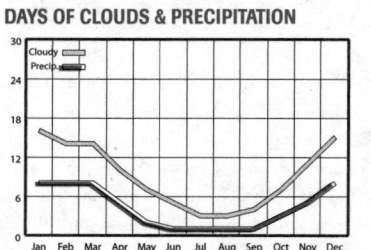

EDUCATION SCORE: 83/RANK: 57

ACHIEVEMENT	AREA	U.S. AVG	PUBLIC SCHOOLS	AREA	U.S. AVG	HIGHER EDUCATION	AREA	U.S. AVG
High school degree	83.4%	80.2%	Expenditures per pupil	$5,514	$5,894	No. 2-year colleges	9	3
2-year college degree	7.7%	6.2%	Student/teacher ratio	22.4	16.7	No. 4-year colleges/universities	6	4
4-year college degree	24.0%	15.8%	Attending public school	87.8%	90.2%	No. highly ranked universities	1	1
Graduate/professional degree	16.4%	9.6%	State SAT score	1018*	1020			
			State ACT score	21.5	21.0			

HEALTH & HEALTHCARE SCORE: 4/RANK: 317

CRIME SCORE: 90/RANK: 30

HAZARDS & ILLNESSES	AREA	U.S. AVG	HEALTHCARE	AREA	U.S. AVG	CRIME	AREA	U.S. AVG
Air-quality score	94	45	Physicians per capita	297.5	261.1	Violent crime rate	456.5	456.0
Water-quality score	11	33	Hospital beds per capita	278.5	432.2	Change in violent crime rate	-25.7%	-17.2%
Pollen/allergy score	89	61	No. teaching hospitals	5	4	Property crime rate	2,320.3	3,950.0
Stress score	35	50	Cost per doctor visit	$91	$67	Change in property crime rate	-36.1%	-16.8%
Cancer mortality per capita	163.9	169.0	Cost per dental visit	$116	$82			
Depression days per month	2.4	2.8	Cost per daily hospital room	$2,184	$733			

TRANSPORTATION SCORE: 38/RANK: 201

COMMUTE	AREA	U.S. AVG	INTERCITY SERVICES	AREA	U.S. AVG	AUTOMOTIVE	AREA	U.S. AVG
Average commute time	26.1 min.	22.6 min.	Miles to nearest major airport	6	46	Insurance, annual premium	$1,010	$1,011
Commute by auto	86.8%	88.7%	Type of local airport	Medium		Gas, cost per gallon	$1.78	$1.50
Commute by mass transit	3.2%	1.8%	No. daily airline departures	250	294	Daily vehicle miles per capita	23.6	23.0
Work at home	3.4%	3.9%	Amtrak service	Yes				
Mass transit miles per capita	16.3	8.0	No. interstate highways	1	1			

LEISURE SCORE: 95/RANK: 18

DINING & SHOPPING	AREA	U.S. AVG	ENTERTAINMENT	AREA	U.S. AVG	OUTDOOR ACTIVITIES	AREA	U.S. AVG
Restaurant rating	1	1	Professional sports rating	9	4	Golf-course rating	6	4
No. outlet malls	5	2	College sports rating	10	4	Ski-area rating	9	4
No. Starbucks	72	11	Zoo/aquarium rating	5	3	National Park rating	3	3
No. warehouse clubs	5	4	Amusement park rating	10	3	Sq. miles inland water	6.0	4.0
			Botanical garden/arboretum rating	6	3	Miles of coastline	0.0	11.4

ARTS & CULTURE SCORE: 75/RANK: 85

MEDIA & LIBRARIES	AREA	U.S. AVG	PERFORMING ARTS	AREA	U.S. AVG	MUSEUMS	AREA	U.S. AVG
Arts radio rating	4	3	Classical music rating	7	4	Overall museum rating	8	6
No. public libraries	33	28	Ballet/dance rating	9	3	Art museum rating	9	5
Library volumes per capita	2.4	2.8	Professional theater rating	9	3	Science museum rating	8	4
			University arts programs rating	8	5	Children's museum rating	9	3

San Luis Obispo–Atascadero–Paso Robles, CA

Score: 97.2   Rank: 3

Profile: College town
Location: Central California, half way between Los Angeles and San Francisco, 15 miles from the coast
Elevation: 238 feet
Time zone: Pacific Standard Time

PRO	CON
College-town atmosphere	Cost of living
Year-round climate	Isolation
Historic interest	Low job growth

San Luis Obispo is a charming college town, home to the California Polytechnic University. It has resisted the development seen in other parts of the state and preserves a pleasant, off-the-beaten-path character. The interesting downtown is accessible by foot and includes a 1772 Spanish mission. The university brings numerous arts and entertainment amenities. The central California coastal climate is ideal. Predictably, cost of living is high, although not as high as other places in the state. The absence of a strong commercial economy makes jobs difficult to find and future job-growth projections low. Location influences the rating positively and negatively—the town is isolated from big-city services and big-city problems.

San Luis Obispo is located in the center of the narrow Los Osos Valley, which opens to the northwest onto scenic Morro Bay. The town is far enough inland to be warmer and drier than many coastal locations. The climate is Mediterranean marine. The hills to the southwest tend to block some of the ocean-borne low, stratus clouds, resulting in mostly sunny and pleasant summer days. Very cold weather is unusual. Almost all precipitation falls in winter as rain.

POPULATION

DEMOGRAPHICS	AREA	U.S. AVG	ETHNIC COMPOSITION	AREA	U.S. AVG	RESIDENT PROFILE	AREA	U.S. AVG
Population	253,408		White	86.4%	75.1%	Single	46.8%	43.6%
Population density per sq. mile	76.7	447.3	Black	2.2%	12.3%	Married	53.2%	56.4%
Population growth	16.7%	16.1%	Asian	4.7%	3.6%	Divorced	9.8%	8.4%
Median age	37.6	35.5	American Indian	1.1%	.9%	Separated	2.7%	3.0%
Average family size	2.7	2.7	Hispanic	21.5%	12.5%	Married with children	23.6%	28.7%
			Diversity measure	38.6%	35.2%	Single with children	8.9%	10.1%

ECONOMY & JOBS
SCORE: 31/RANK: 226

INCOME	AREA	U.S. AVG	EMPLOYMENT	AREA	U.S. AVG	LARGEST EMPLOYING INDUSTRY
Per capita income	$25,332	$23,420	Unemployment rate	3.2%	6.1%	Healthcare and Social Assistance
Household income	$48,421	$46,060	Recent job growth	1.3%	.9%	
Household income < $25K	23.1%	26.4%	Projected future job growth	17.3%	15.1%	
Household income > $75K	27.2%	24.5%	White collar	53.8%	54.5%	
Household income growth	55.0%	57.3%	Blue collar	46.2%	45.5%	

COST OF LIVING
SCORE: 5/RANK: 312

INDEXES & TAXES	AREA	U.S. AVG	HOUSING	AREA	U.S. AVG	NECESSITIES	AREA	U.S. AVG
Cost of Living Index	155.1	100.0	Median home price	$380,130	$160,100	Food Index	112.4	100.0
Financial Progress Index	66.5	100.0	Home price appreciation	18.2%	7.1%	Housing Index	236.1	100.0
Income tax rate	6.000%	4.625%	Median rent	$917	$670	Utilities Index	116.6	100.0
Sales tax rate	7.250%	6.474%	Homes owned	52.9%	63.9%	Transportation Index	111.5	100.0
Property tax rate	$11.1	$15.6	Homes rented	33.3%	25.3%	Healthcare Index	112.0	100.0
			Housing affordability	42.0%	54.5%	Miscellaneous Cost Index	103.2	100.0

CLIMATE
SCORE: 98/RANK: 5

TEMPERATURE	AREA	U.S. AVG	PRECIPITATION	AREA	U.S. AVG	COMFORTS & HAZARDS	AREA	U.S. AVG
January low	38.3°F	26.4°F	Annual inches precipitation	12.0	35.9	July relative humidity	74.0%	68.8%
July high	73.9°F	86.7°F	Annual inches snowfall	0.0	24.2	Annual days mostly sunny	285	212
Annual days > 90°F	6	38	Annual days precipitation	45	111	Annual days with thunderstorms	2	39
Annual days < 32°F	24	88	Annual days rain > 0.5 inches	8	23	Tornado risk score	0	19
Annual days < 0°F	0	6	Annual days snow > 1.5 inches	0	6	Hurricane risk score	0	15

TEMPERATURE

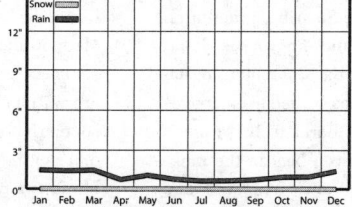

PRECIPITATION

DAYS OF CLOUDS & PRECIPITATION

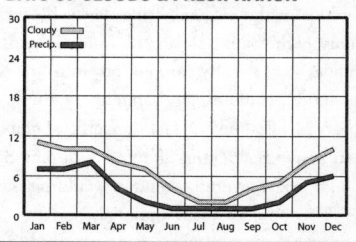

EDUCATION SCORE: 68/RANK: 105

ACHIEVEMENT	AREA	U.S. AVG	PUBLIC SCHOOLS	AREA	U.S. AVG	HIGHER EDUCATION	AREA	U.S. AVG
High school degree	85.6%	80.2%	Expenditures per pupil	$5,337	$5,894	No. 2-year colleges	1	3
2-year college degree	9.1%	6.2%	Student/teacher ratio	20.1	16.7	No. 4-year colleges/universities	1	4
4-year college degree	17.4%	15.8%	Attending public school	91.5%	90.2%	No. highly ranked universities	1	1
Graduate/professional degree	9.3%	9.6%	State SAT score	1018*	1020			
			State ACT score	21.5	21.0			

HEALTH & HEALTHCARE SCORE: 39/RANK: 201

HAZARDS & ILLNESSES	AREA	U.S. AVG	HEALTHCARE	AREA	U.S. AVG	CRIME SCORE: 93/RANK: 21 / CRIME	AREA	U.S. AVG
Air-quality score	59	45	Physicians per capita	244.7	261.1	Violent crime rate	295.7	456.0
Water-quality score	5	33	Hospital beds per capita	246.9	432.2	Change in violent crime rate	-57.0%	-17.2%
Pollen/allergy score	61	61	No. teaching hospitals	0	4	Property crime rate	2,484.2	3,950.0
Stress score	6	50	Cost per doctor visit	$83	$67	Change in property crime rate	-25.4%	-16.8%
Cancer mortality per capita	158.8	169.0	Cost per dental visit	$77	$82			
Depression days per month	1.7	2.8	Cost per daily hospital room	$1,239	$733			

TRANSPORTATION SCORE: 34/RANK: 217

COMMUTE	AREA	U.S. AVG	INTERCITY SERVICES	AREA	U.S. AVG	AUTOMOTIVE	AREA	U.S. AVG
Average commute time	21.2 min.	22.6 min.	Miles to nearest major airport	75	46	Insurance, annual premium	$917	$1,011
Commute by auto	86.4%	88.7%	Type of local airport	Small		Gas, cost per gallon	$1.84	$1.50
Commute by mass transit	.5%	1.8%	No. daily airline departures	49	294	Daily vehicle miles per capita	17.3	23.0
Work at home	5.4%	3.9%	Amtrak service	Yes				
Mass transit miles per capita	0.0	8.0	No. interstate highways	0	1			

LEISURE SCORE: 83/RANK: 54

DINING & SHOPPING	AREA	U.S. AVG	ENTERTAINMENT	AREA	U.S. AVG	OUTDOOR ACTIVITIES	AREA	U.S. AVG
Restaurant rating	1	1	Professional sports rating	2	4	Golf-course rating	3	4
No. outlet malls	1	2	College sports rating	4	4	Ski-area rating	10	4
No. Starbucks	8	11	Zoo/aquarium rating	2	3	National Park rating	10	3
No. warehouse clubs	1	4	Amusement park rating	1	3	Sq. miles inland water	2.0	4.0
			Botanical garden/arboretum rating	1	3	Miles of coastline	77.3	11.4

ARTS & CULTURE SCORE: 35/RANK: 214

MEDIA & LIBRARIES	AREA	U.S. AVG	PERFORMING ARTS	AREA	U.S. AVG	MUSEUMS	AREA	U.S. AVG
Arts radio rating	5	3	Classical music rating	3	4	Overall museum rating	6	6
No. public libraries	16	28	Ballet/dance rating	1	3	Art museum rating	9	5
Library volumes per capita	2.1	2.8	Professional theater rating	1	3	Science museum rating	3	4
			University arts programs rating	5	5	Children's museum rating	1	3

Santa Barbara–Santa Maria–Lompoc, CA

Score: 95.2 Rank: 4

Profile: Small-city complex/College town
Location: Central California coast, 90 miles northwest of Los Angeles
Elevation: 238 feet
Time zone: Pacific Standard Time

PRO	CON
Year-round climate	Cost of living
Coastline	Home prices
Small-town atmosphere	Economy

These three cities in Santa Barbara County offer highly contrasting places to live. Coastal Santa Barbara is the center of the "California Riviera"—an area of mild climate, coastline, Mediterranean architecture, laid-back ambience, and affluence. The University of California at Santa Barbara, about 10 miles north, brings amenities without dominating town life. Educational attainment is notably high. Santa Maria, 15 miles inland, is primarily agricultural. Lompoc, on a hilly projection into the Pacific known as Point Conception, contains the Vandenberg Air Force Base, a major coastal military installation and testing facility. Lompoc has started to emerge as an attractive residential alternative to tony Santa Barbara. If it weren't for high prices overall, the area would be difficult to beat in the rankings. The climate is exceptional, and the small-town ambience and attractiveness is well preserved compared to other California locations. The high Cost of Living Index of 173.6 and average home price of

$463,740 statistically represent the whole county, but Santa Barbara is assuredly more expensive. Because of this, the other towns, particularly Santa Maria, look attractive. The location is a bit isolated, but most residents love the area if they can afford it.

Santa Barbara is on a narrow coastal plain that spreads east-west, while Santa Maria and Lompoc are located inland and to the north, respectively. Oak-studded hills surround all three. The climate is Mediterranean marine. Temperatures are mild year-round, with those in summers tempered by sea breezes and cloudy mornings. Inland areas are warmer when breezes blow from the deserts to the southeast. The southerly orientation of Santa Barbara and the inland location of the other cities provide shelter from strong Pacific storms in winter. Santa Maria is far enough inland to experience temperatures of 32°F or lower several times in winter. Most precipitation occurs in winter.

POPULATION

DEMOGRAPHICS	AREA	U.S. AVG	ETHNIC COMPOSITION	AREA	U.S. AVG	RESIDENT PROFILE	AREA	U.S. AVG
Population	403,084		White	78.1%	75.1%	Single	47.9%	43.6%
Population density per sq. mile	147.2	447.3	Black	2.6%	12.3%	Married	52.1%	56.4%
Population growth	9.1%	16.1%	Asian	5.6%	3.6%	Divorced	9.1%	8.4%
Median age	33.7	35.5	American Indian	.9%	.9%	Separated	2.5%	3.0%
Average family size	2.8	2.7	Hispanic	31.1%	12.5%	Married with children	24.3%	28.7%
			Diversity measure	56.0%	35.2%	Single with children	8.9%	10.1%

ECONOMY & JOBS SCORE: 20/RANK: 262

INCOME	AREA	U.S. AVG	EMPLOYMENT	AREA	U.S. AVG	LARGEST EMPLOYING INDUSTRY
Per capita income	$25,258	$23,420	Unemployment rate	3.6%	6.1%	Computer and Electronic Product Manufacturing
Household income	$51,277	$46,060	Recent job growth	.8%	.9%	
Household income < $25K	20.8%	26.4%	Projected future job growth	14.3%	15.1%	
Household income > $75K	30.0%	24.5%	White collar	56.9%	54.5%	
Household income growth	43.4%	57.3%	Blue collar	43.1%	45.5%	

COST OF LIVING SCORE: 1/RANK: 326

INDEXES & TAXES	AREA	U.S. AVG	HOUSING	AREA	U.S. AVG	NECESSITIES	AREA	U.S. AVG
Cost of Living Index	173.6	100.0	Median home price	$463,740	$160,100	Food Index	116.0	100.0
Financial Progress Index	63.0	100.0	Home price appreciation	16.5%	7.1%	Housing Index	288.0	100.0
Income tax rate	6.000%	4.625%	Median rent	$1,015	$670	Utilities Index	111.9	100.0
Sales tax rate	7.750%	6.474%	Homes owned	48.8%	63.9%	Transportation Index	107.0	100.0
Property tax rate	$11.2	$15.6	Homes rented	38.7%	25.3%	Healthcare Index	114.8	100.0
			Housing affordability	46.0%	54.5%	Miscellaneous Cost Index	102.7	100.0

CLIMATE SCORE: 98/RANK: 6

TEMPERATURE	AREA	U.S. AVG	PRECIPITATION	AREA	U.S. AVG	COMFORTS & HAZARDS	AREA	U.S. AVG
January low	38.3°F	26.4°F	Annual inches precipitation	12.0	35.9	July relative humidity	74.0%	68.8%
July high	73.9°F	86.7°F	Annual inches snowfall	0.0	24.2	Annual days mostly sunny	285	212
Annual days > 90°F	6	38	Annual days precipitation	45	111	Annual days with thunderstorms	2	39
Annual days < 32°F	24	88	Annual days rain > 0.5 inches	8	23	Tornado risk score	1	19
Annual days < 0°F	0	6	Annual days snow > 1.5 inches	0	6	Hurricane risk score	0	15

TEMPERATURE

PRECIPITATION

DAYS OF CLOUDS & PRECIPITATION

EDUCATION SCORE: 54/RANK: 150

ACHIEVEMENT	AREA	U.S. AVG	PUBLIC SCHOOLS	AREA	U.S. AVG	HIGHER EDUCATION	AREA	U.S. AVG
High school degree	79.2%	80.2%	Expenditures per pupil	$5,246	$5,894	No. 2-year colleges	2	3
2-year college degree	6.8%	6.2%	Student/teacher ratio	20.9	16.7	No. 4-year colleges/universities	2	4
4-year college degree	18.0%	15.8%	Attending public school	90.8%	90.2%	No. highly ranked universities	1	1
Graduate/professional degree	11.4%	9.6%	State SAT score	1018*	1020			
			State ACT score	21.5	21.0			

HEALTH & HEALTHCARE SCORE: 43/RANK: 189

HAZARDS & ILLNESSES	AREA	U.S. AVG	HEALTHCARE	AREA	U.S. AVG
Air-quality score	59	45	Physicians per capita	246.4	261.1
Water-quality score	18	33	Hospital beds per capita	326.8	432.2
Pollen/allergy score	47	61	No. teaching hospitals	1	4
Stress score	2	50	Cost per doctor visit	$86	$67
Cancer mortality per capita	159.6	169.0	Cost per dental visit	$79	$82
Depression days per month	1.9	2.8	Cost per daily hospital room	$1,248	$733

CRIME SCORE: 94/RANK: 18

CRIME	AREA	U.S. AVG
Violent crime rate	343.7	456.0
Change in violent crime rate	-26.2%	-17.2%
Property crime rate	2,192.4	3,950.0
Change in property crime rate	-37.0%	-16.8%

TRANSPORTATION SCORE: 76/RANK: 79

COMMUTE	AREA	U.S. AVG	INTERCITY SERVICES	AREA	U.S. AVG	AUTOMOTIVE	AREA	U.S. AVG
Average commute time	19.3 min.	22.6 min.	Miles to nearest major airport	6	46	Insurance, annual premium	$926	$1,011
Commute by auto	83.4%	88.7%	Type of local airport	Small		Gas, cost per gallon	$1.85	$1.50
Commute by mass transit	1.4%	1.8%	No. daily airline departures	49	294	Daily vehicle miles per capita	5.9	23.0
Work at home	5.1%	3.9%	Amtrak service	Yes				
Mass transit miles per capita	8.1	8.0	No. interstate highways	0	1			

LEISURE SCORE: 85/RANK: 51

DINING & SHOPPING	AREA	U.S. AVG	ENTERTAINMENT	AREA	U.S. AVG	OUTDOOR ACTIVITIES	AREA	U.S. AVG
Restaurant rating	1	1	Professional sports rating	2	4	Golf-course rating	3	4
No. outlet malls	2	2	College sports rating	3	4	Ski-area rating	10	4
No. Starbucks	12	11	Zoo/aquarium rating	6	3	National Park rating	10	3
No. warehouse clubs	3	4	Amusement park rating	3	3	Sq. miles inland water	2.0	4.0
			Botanical garden/arboretum rating	4	3	Miles of coastline	77.6	11.4

ARTS & CULTURE SCORE: 34/RANK: 216

MEDIA & LIBRARIES	AREA	U.S. AVG	PERFORMING ARTS	AREA	U.S. AVG	MUSEUMS	AREA	U.S. AVG
Arts radio rating	5	3	Classical music rating	3	4	Overall museum rating	7	6
No. public libraries	15	28	Ballet/dance rating	5	3	Art museum rating	6	5
Library volumes per capita	1.8	2.8	Professional theater rating	5	3	Science museum rating	6	4
			University arts programs rating	7	5	Children's museum rating	1	3

Santa Cruz–Watsonville, CA

Score: 62.8   Rank: 124

Profile: Beach town/Small town
Location: Northern California on Pacific coast, 60 miles south of San Francisco
Elevation: 100 feet
Time zone: Pacific Standard Time

PRO
Beaches and outdoor recreation
Year-round climate
Educational attainment

CON
Economy
Healthcare
Cost of living

Santa Cruz, a colorful mix of college town, beach town, and cultural center, attracts hippies and yuppies alike. The city is famous for its wide, sandy beaches and beach amusements. Watsonville is an agricultural center inland, and Soquel and Capitola to the south are sedate beach towns. The University of California at Santa Cruz brings some college amenities. The population in general is highly educated. Outdoor recreation is available just to the north in the coastal forests and state parks of the Santa Cruz Mountains. The town of Santa Cruz itself offers plenty to do. However, the economy and cost of living are major downsides. Employment has been declining because of job losses at nearby high-tech companies. Some residents work in the San Jose area and the Santa Clara Valley, but the commute northward across the mountains is difficult. Cost of living and home prices are among the highest in the state. Healthcare resources are thin, but missing services are available to the north in San Jose and San Francisco.

The city lies on a narrow coastal plain at the foot of the Santa Cruz Mountains. The climate is coastal Mediterranean. Summers are cool and sunny when the area isn't blanketed by ocean-borne low, stratus clouds, known locally as "fog." The area is breezy at all times, and the fog may create a chill on summer days. Spring and fall are mild and experience less fog. Winters bring a mix of fog; clear, mild days; and Pacific storms, which can be heavy.

POPULATION

DEMOGRAPHICS	AREA	U.S. AVG	ETHNIC COMPOSITION	AREA	U.S. AVG	RESIDENT PROFILE	AREA	U.S. AVG
Population	253,814		White	83.3%	75.1%	Single	52.1%	43.6%
Population density per sq. mile	569.5	447.3	Black	1.8%	12.3%	Married	47.9%	56.4%
Population growth	10.5%	16.1%	Asian	6.1%	3.6%	Divorced	10.7%	8.4%
Median age	35.3	35.5	American Indian	.9%	.9%	Separated	2.9%	3.0%
Average family size	2.7	2.7	Hispanic	24.5%	12.5%	Married with children	24.8%	28.7%
			Diversity measure	49.0%	35.2%	Single with children	11.2%	10.1%

ECONOMY & JOBS SCORE: 6/RANK: 308

INCOME	AREA	U.S. AVG	EMPLOYMENT	AREA	U.S. AVG	LARGEST EMPLOYING INDUSTRY
Per capita income	$32,851	$23,420	Unemployment rate	6.1%	6.1%	Healthcare and Social Assistance
Household income	$69,148	$46,060	Recent job growth	.3%	.9%	
Household income < $25K	15.1%	26.4%	Projected future job growth	15.3%	15.1%	
Household income > $75K	45.7%	24.5%	White collar	58.2%	54.5%	
Household income growth	86.3%	57.3%	Blue collar	41.8%	45.5%	

COST OF LIVING SCORE: 1/RANK: 327

INDEXES & TAXES	AREA	U.S. AVG	HOUSING	AREA	U.S. AVG	NECESSITIES	AREA	U.S. AVG
Cost of Living Index	177.6	100.0	Median home price	$447,000	$160,100	Food Index	122.0	100.0
Financial Progress Index	83.0	100.0	Home price appreciation	16.2%	7.1%	Housing Index	277.6	100.0
Income tax rate	6.000%	4.625%	Median rent	$1,341	$670	Utilities Index	128.8	100.0
Sales tax rate	8.000%	6.474%	Homes owned	55.6%	63.9%	Transportation Index	123.8	100.0
Property tax rate	$10.7	$15.6	Homes rented	34.5%	25.3%	Healthcare Index	156.4	100.0
			Housing affordability	40.0%	54.5%	Miscellaneous Cost Index	107.3	100.0

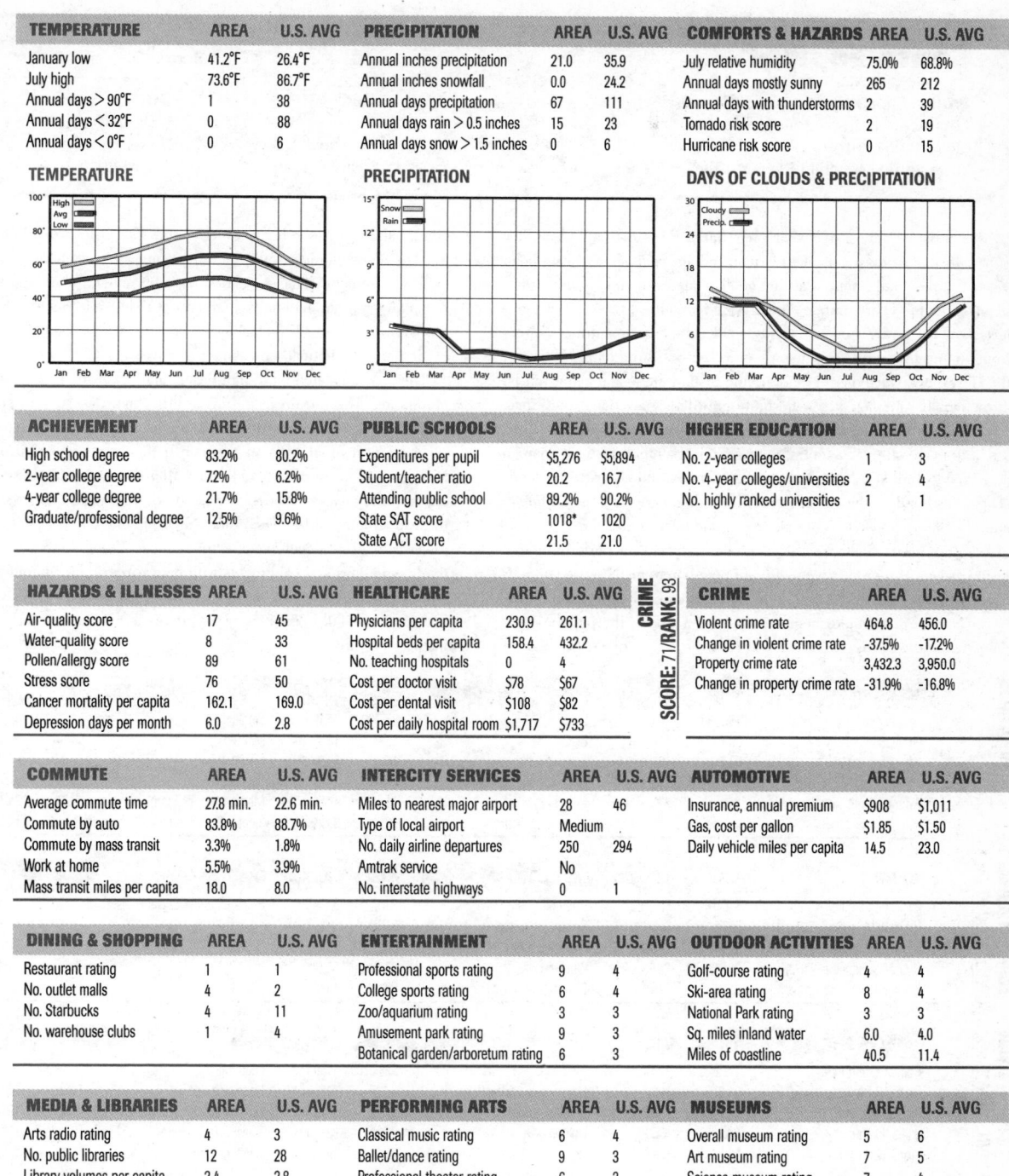

CLIMATE SCORE: 99/RANK: 3

TEMPERATURE	AREA	U.S. AVG	PRECIPITATION	AREA	U.S. AVG	COMFORTS & HAZARDS	AREA	U.S. AVG
January low	41.2°F	26.4°F	Annual inches precipitation	21.0	35.9	July relative humidity	75.0%	68.8%
July high	73.6°F	86.7°F	Annual inches snowfall	0.0	24.2	Annual days mostly sunny	265	212
Annual days > 90°F	1	38	Annual days precipitation	67	111	Annual days with thunderstorms	2	39
Annual days < 32°F	0	88	Annual days rain > 0.5 inches	15	23	Tornado risk score	2	19
Annual days < 0°F	0	6	Annual days snow > 1.5 inches	0	6	Hurricane risk score	0	15

TEMPERATURE

PRECIPITATION

DAYS OF CLOUDS & PRECIPITATION

EDUCATION SCORE: 70/RANK: 98

ACHIEVEMENT	AREA	U.S. AVG	PUBLIC SCHOOLS	AREA	U.S. AVG	HIGHER EDUCATION	AREA	U.S. AVG
High school degree	83.2%	80.2%	Expenditures per pupil	$5,276	$5,894	No. 2-year colleges	1	3
2-year college degree	7.2%	6.2%	Student/teacher ratio	20.2	16.7	No. 4-year colleges/universities	2	4
4-year college degree	21.7%	15.8%	Attending public school	89.2%	90.2%	No. highly ranked universities	1	1
Graduate/professional degree	12.5%	9.6%	State SAT score	1018*	1020			
			State ACT score	21.5	21.0			

HEALTH & HEALTHCARE SCORE: 2/RANK: 324 · **CRIME** SCORE: 71/RANK: 93

HAZARDS & ILLNESSES	AREA	U.S. AVG	HEALTHCARE	AREA	U.S. AVG	CRIME	AREA	U.S. AVG
Air-quality score	17	45	Physicians per capita	230.9	261.1	Violent crime rate	464.8	456.0
Water-quality score	8	33	Hospital beds per capita	158.4	432.2	Change in violent crime rate	-37.5%	-17.2%
Pollen/allergy score	89	61	No. teaching hospitals	0	4	Property crime rate	3,432.3	3,950.0
Stress score	76	50	Cost per doctor visit	$78	$67	Change in property crime rate	-31.9%	-16.8%
Cancer mortality per capita	162.1	169.0	Cost per dental visit	$108	$82			
Depression days per month	6.0	2.8	Cost per daily hospital room	$1,717	$733			

TRANSPORTATION SCORE: 82/RANK: 57

COMMUTE	AREA	U.S. AVG	INTERCITY SERVICES	AREA	U.S. AVG	AUTOMOTIVE	AREA	U.S. AVG
Average commute time	27.8 min.	22.6 min.	Miles to nearest major airport	28	46	Insurance, annual premium	$908	$1,011
Commute by auto	83.8%	88.7%	Type of local airport	Medium		Gas, cost per gallon	$1.85	$1.50
Commute by mass transit	3.3%	1.8%	No. daily airline departures	250	294	Daily vehicle miles per capita	14.5	23.0
Work at home	5.5%	3.9%	Amtrak service	No				
Mass transit miles per capita	18.0	8.0	No. interstate highways	0	1			

LEISURE SCORE: 67/RANK: 107

DINING & SHOPPING	AREA	U.S. AVG	ENTERTAINMENT	AREA	U.S. AVG	OUTDOOR ACTIVITIES	AREA	U.S. AVG
Restaurant rating	1	1	Professional sports rating	9	4	Golf-course rating	4	4
No. outlet malls	4	2	College sports rating	6	4	Ski-area rating	8	4
No. Starbucks	4	11	Zoo/aquarium rating	3	3	National Park rating	3	3
No. warehouse clubs	1	4	Amusement park rating	9	3	Sq. miles inland water	6.0	4.0
			Botanical garden/arboretum rating	6	3	Miles of coastline	40.5	11.4

ARTS & CULTURE SCORE: 41/RANK: 195

MEDIA & LIBRARIES	AREA	U.S. AVG	PERFORMING ARTS	AREA	U.S. AVG	MUSEUMS	AREA	U.S. AVG
Arts radio rating	4	3	Classical music rating	6	4	Overall museum rating	5	6
No. public libraries	12	28	Ballet/dance rating	9	3	Art museum rating	7	5
Library volumes per capita	2.4	2.8	Professional theater rating	6	3	Science museum rating	7	4
			University arts programs rating	5	5	Children's museum rating	3	3

Santa Fe, NM

Score: 99.3	**Rank: 2**

Profile: Capital city
Location: North-central New Mexico
Elevation: 7,710 feet
Time zone: Mountain Standard Time

PRO	**CON**
Climate and setting	Cost of living
Arts and culture	Urban sprawl
Historic interest	Tourist impact

Established almost 400 years ago, Santa Fe is the capital of New Mexico; a crossroads of American Indian, Spanish, and European cultures; and a tourist attraction. The area's distinct architecture, lifestyle, and food are unique among American cities. Over 250 art galleries and the recently opened Georgia O'Keeffe Museum attract visitors from around the world. The historic old town—with its plaza, Palace of the Governors, Navajo craft market, and restaurants—is a major tourist attraction. In summer, it can be quite crowded. Many local buildings, including homes in wealthier residential areas in the hills to the north, are built in a distinct "Santa Fe" style, which resembles historic Spanish and Pueblo Indian adobe structures and blends nicely with the landscape. Surrounding the city are over 1.5 million acres of national forest, stunning landscapes, downhill ski areas, and historic treasures, particularly to the north. Santa Fe has long been a haven for performing and visual artists. More recently an affluent population, many retired or self-employed, has been relocating to the area, although there is little industry or commercial employment thus far. As a whole, the population is educated and wealthy. At over 7,000 feet, the city is by far the highest capital and is also the highest metropolitan statistical area in the country. The elevation may cause health problems for some, and healthcare facilities are not extensive. Aside from a few other, minor downsides—a regionally, but not nationally, high cost of living; a few cold winter days; tourist impact; and a little tacky sprawl to the south—Santa Fe is a stimulating and aesthetically pleasing place to live.

The city is located on a high desert plateau at the foot of the Rocky Mountains. The terrain is rolling to hilly high desert, with scrub and sagebrush vegetation and dry creeks and washes. The landscape rises to scrub-pine covered hills in the north, then to the Sangre de Cristo Mountains to the northeast and Jemez Mountains to the northwest. To the south of the city, the land slopes gently down toward lower deserts and the Rio Grande Valley. The climate is arid continental with sunny, dry, pleasant days and cool evenings in summer. Winters are dry with relatively mild days and cold nights with below-freezing temperatures. Most winter precipitation falls as dry snow, which is seldom heavy. Much heavier snows fall in the nearby mountains. First freeze is early October, last is mid-May.

POPULATION

DEMOGRAPHICS	AREA	U.S. AVG	ETHNIC COMPOSITION	AREA	U.S. AVG	RESIDENT PROFILE	AREA	U.S. AVG
Population	152,830		White	87.5%	75.1%	Single	43.3%	43.6%
Population density per sq. mile	75.7	447.3	Black	1.0%	12.3%	Married	56.7%	56.4%
Population growth	30.6%	16.1%	Asian	1.2%	3.6%	Divorced	12.6%	8.4%
Median age	38.7	35.5	American Indian	2.1%	.9%	Separated	2.3%	3.0%
Average family size	2.6	2.7	Hispanic	41.1%	12.5%	Married with children	29.2%	28.7%
			Diversity measure	55.8%	35.2%	Single with children	11.1%	10.1%

ECONOMY & JOBS   SCORE: 36/RANK: 210

INCOME	AREA	U.S. AVG	EMPLOYMENT	AREA	U.S. AVG	LARGEST EMPLOYING INDUSTRY
Per capita income	$30,013	$23,420	Unemployment rate	3.4%	6.1%	Healthcare and Social Assistance
Household income	$52,824	$46,060	Recent job growth	3.2%	.9%	
Household income < $25K	19.9%	26.4%	Projected future job growth	30.6%	15.1%	
Household income > $75K	32.0%	24.5%	White collar	67.4%	54.5%	
Household income growth	63.4%	57.3%	Blue collar	32.6%	45.5%	

COST OF LIVING   SCORE: 11/RANK: 293

INDEXES & TAXES	AREA	U.S. AVG	HOUSING	AREA	U.S. AVG	NECESSITIES	AREA	U.S. AVG
Cost of Living Index	118.6	100.0	Median home price	$234,380	$160,100	Food Index	103.6	100.0
Financial Progress Index	94.9	100.0	Home price appreciation	6.1%	7.1%	Housing Index	145.6	100.0
Income tax rate	7.100%	4.625%	Median rent	$798	$670	Utilities Index	90.4	100.0
Sales tax rate	6.688%	6.474%	Homes owned	71.4%	63.9%	Transportation Index	107.2	100.0
Property tax rate	$5.1	$15.6	Homes rented	20.6%	25.3%	Healthcare Index	117.6	100.0
			Housing affordability	51.0%	54.5%	Miscellaneous Cost Index	102.2	100.0

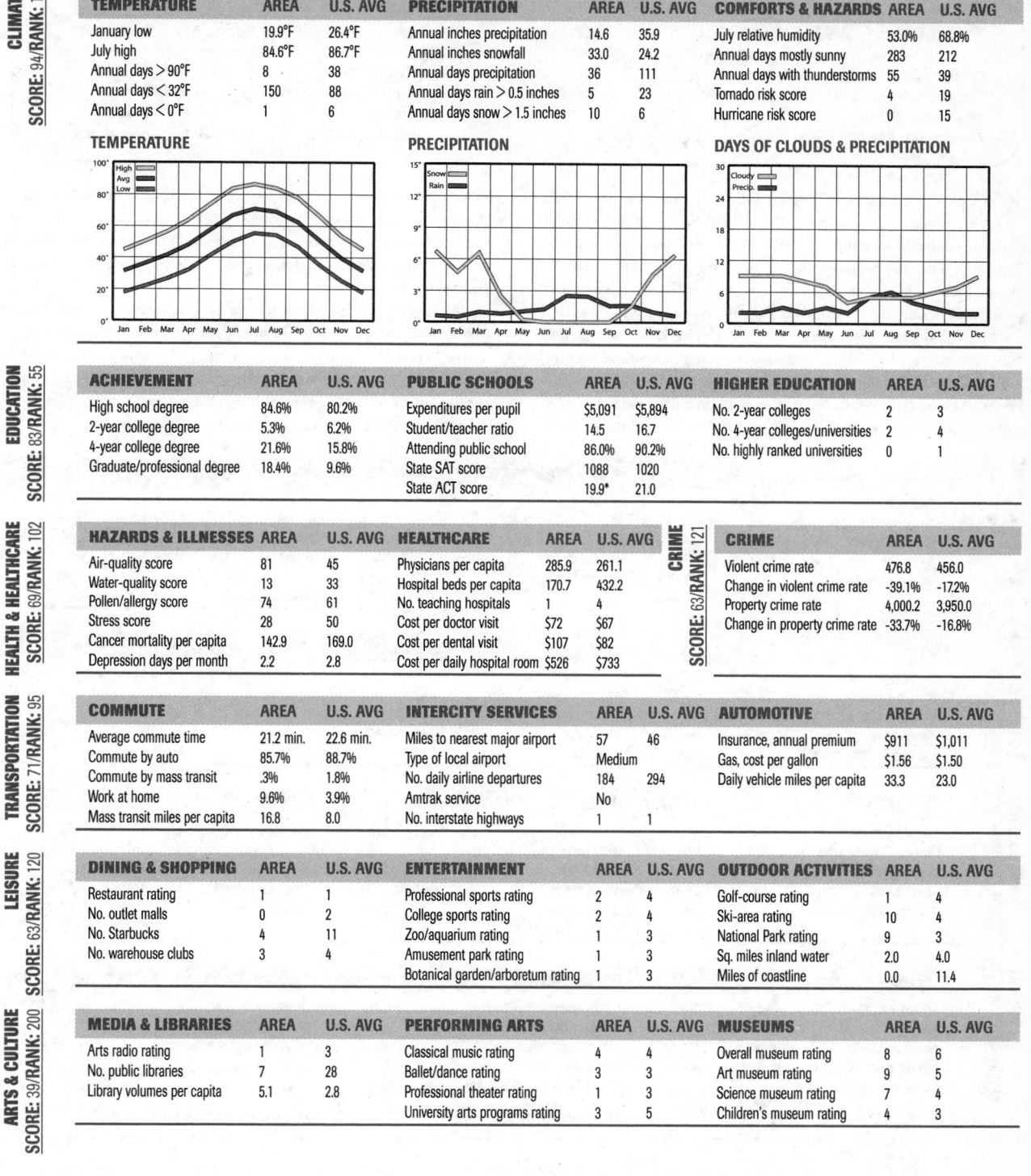

CLIMATE   SCORE: 94/RANK: 18

TEMPERATURE	AREA	U.S. AVG
January low	19.9°F	26.4°F
July high	84.6°F	86.7°F
Annual days > 90°F	8	38
Annual days < 32°F	150	88
Annual days < 0°F	1	6

PRECIPITATION	AREA	U.S. AVG
Annual inches precipitation	14.6	35.9
Annual inches snowfall	33.0	24.2
Annual days precipitation	36	111
Annual days rain > 0.5 inches	5	23
Annual days snow > 1.5 inches	10	6

COMFORTS & HAZARDS	AREA	U.S. AVG
July relative humidity	53.0%	68.8%
Annual days mostly sunny	283	212
Annual days with thunderstorms	55	39
Tornado risk score	4	19
Hurricane risk score	0	15

TEMPERATURE

PRECIPITATION

DAYS OF CLOUDS & PRECIPITATION

EDUCATION   SCORE: 83/RANK: 55

ACHIEVEMENT	AREA	U.S. AVG
High school degree	84.6%	80.2%
2-year college degree	5.3%	6.2%
4-year college degree	21.6%	15.8%
Graduate/professional degree	18.4%	9.6%

PUBLIC SCHOOLS	AREA	U.S. AVG
Expenditures per pupil	$5,091	$5,894
Student/teacher ratio	14.5	16.7
Attending public school	86.0%	90.2%
State SAT score	1088	1020
State ACT score	19.9*	21.0

HIGHER EDUCATION	AREA	U.S. AVG
No. 2-year colleges	2	3
No. 4-year colleges/universities	2	4
No. highly ranked universities	0	1

HEALTH & HEALTHCARE   SCORE: 69/RANK: 102

HAZARDS & ILLNESSES	AREA	U.S. AVG
Air-quality score	81	45
Water-quality score	13	33
Pollen/allergy score	74	61
Stress score	28	50
Cancer mortality per capita	142.9	169.0
Depression days per month	2.2	2.8

HEALTHCARE	AREA	U.S. AVG
Physicians per capita	285.9	261.1
Hospital beds per capita	170.7	432.2
No. teaching hospitals	1	4
Cost per doctor visit	$72	$67
Cost per dental visit	$107	$82
Cost per daily hospital room	$526	$733

CRIME   SCORE: 63/RANK: 121

CRIME	AREA	U.S. AVG
Violent crime rate	476.8	456.0
Change in violent crime rate	-39.1%	-17.2%
Property crime rate	4,000.2	3,950.0
Change in property crime rate	-33.7%	-16.8%

TRANSPORTATION   SCORE: 71/RANK: 95

COMMUTE	AREA	U.S. AVG
Average commute time	21.2 min.	22.6 min.
Commute by auto	85.7%	88.7%
Commute by mass transit	.3%	1.8%
Work at home	9.6%	3.9%
Mass transit miles per capita	16.8	8.0

INTERCITY SERVICES	AREA	U.S. AVG
Miles to nearest major airport	57	46
Type of local airport	Medium	
No. daily airline departures	184	294
Amtrak service	No	
No. interstate highways	1	1

AUTOMOTIVE	AREA	U.S. AVG
Insurance, annual premium	$911	$1,011
Gas, cost per gallon	$1.56	$1.50
Daily vehicle miles per capita	33.3	23.0

LEISURE   SCORE: 63/RANK: 120

DINING & SHOPPING	AREA	U.S. AVG
Restaurant rating	1	1
No. outlet malls	0	2
No. Starbucks	4	11
No. warehouse clubs	3	4

ENTERTAINMENT	AREA	U.S. AVG
Professional sports rating	2	4
College sports rating	2	4
Zoo/aquarium rating	1	3
Amusement park rating	1	3
Botanical garden/arboretum rating	1	3

OUTDOOR ACTIVITIES	AREA	U.S. AVG
Golf-course rating	1	4
Ski-area rating	10	4
National Park rating	9	3
Sq. miles inland water	2.0	4.0
Miles of coastline	0.0	11.4

ARTS & CULTURE   SCORE: 39/RANK: 200

MEDIA & LIBRARIES	AREA	U.S. AVG
Arts radio rating	1	3
No. public libraries	7	28
Library volumes per capita	5.1	2.8

PERFORMING ARTS	AREA	U.S. AVG
Classical music rating	4	4
Ballet/dance rating	3	3
Professional theater rating	1	3
University arts programs rating	3	5

MUSEUMS	AREA	U.S. AVG
Overall museum rating	8	6
Art museum rating	9	5
Science museum rating	7	4
Children's museum rating	4	3

Santa Rosa, CA

Score: 57.7   **Rank:** 166

Profile: Small city/Commuter community
Location: Northern California, 40 miles north of San Francisco
Elevation: 167 feet
Time zone: Pacific Standard Time

PRO	CON
Year-round climate	Cost of living
Nearby coastline	Cost of housing
Proximity to San Francisco	Difficult commutes

Santa Rosa, an area of rugged hills and valleys north of San Francisco, is the commercial center of Sonoma County. Santa Rosa itself lies along U.S. 101 with the communities of Rohnert Park, Petaluma, and Sonoma nearby. The metropolitan area extends to the rugged Pacific coastline. The area has a complex and mixed economy, partially self-sufficient and partially dependent on San Francisco and other Bay Area cities mainly to the south. Mostly residential Marin County to the south has access to San Francisco across the Golden Gate Bridge and to East Bay across the Richmond–San Rafael bridge. Abundant ferry service is also available. The combination of climate and proximity to the coast and San Francisco make the area attractive—particularly if one finds work locally rather than facing the challenging commute to "the City." While sprawl is an issue many areas east toward the Sonoma wine growing region and west toward the coast are still rural. High cost of living and housing are the major drawbacks.

Valleys are attractive and mainly flat, and surrounded by low, forested hills near the coast. The climate is Mediterranean marine with consistently comfortable summer temperatures and cool summer evenings. Winters vary from pleasant and sunny to chilly and wet. Most rain falls during winter and can be heavy, although the mountains reduce the force of Pacific storms. Freezing weather occurs occasionally.

POPULATION

DEMOGRAPHICS	AREA	U.S. AVG	ETHNIC COMPOSITION	AREA	U.S. AVG	RESIDENT PROFILE	AREA	U.S. AVG
Population	468,386		White	87.7%	75.1%	Single	45.3%	43.6%
Population density per sq. mile	297.2	447.3	Black	1.7%	12.3%	Married	54.7%	56.4%
Population growth	20.6%	16.1%	Asian	3.6%	3.6%	Divorced	11.4%	8.4%
Median age	37.9	35.5	American Indian	1.8%	.9%	Separated	3.2%	3.0%
Average family size	2.6	2.7	Hispanic	17.7%	12.5%	Married with children	23.4%	28.7%
			Diversity measure	40.6%	35.2%	Single with children	9.7%	10.1%

ECONOMY & JOBS
SCORE: 7/RANK: 305

INCOME	AREA	U.S. AVG	EMPLOYMENT	AREA	U.S. AVG	LARGEST EMPLOYING INDUSTRY
Per capita income	$29,835	$23,420	Unemployment rate	4.8%	6.1%	Computer and Electronic Product Manufacturing
Household income	$61,423	$46,060	Recent job growth	-.0%	.9%	
Household income < $25K	16.1%	26.4%	Projected future job growth	18.1%	15.1%	
Household income > $75K	38.3%	24.5%	White collar	58.3%	54.5%	
Household income growth	68.7%	57.3%	Blue collar	41.7%	45.5%	

COST OF LIVING
SCORE: 2/RANK: 322

INDEXES & TAXES	AREA	U.S. AVG	HOUSING	AREA	U.S. AVG	NECESSITIES	AREA	U.S. AVG
Cost of Living Index	177.3	100.0	Median home price	$432,390	$160,100	Food Index	120.6	100.0
Financial Progress Index	73.8	100.0	Home price appreciation	16.5%	7.1%	Housing Index	268.6	100.0
Income tax rate	6.000%	4.625%	Median rent	$1,163	$670	Utilities Index	143.1	100.0
Sales tax rate	7.500%	6.474%	Homes owned	56.0%	63.9%	Transportation Index	130.0	100.0
Property tax rate	$11.0	$15.6	Homes rented	27.6%	25.3%	Healthcare Index	165.6	100.0
			Housing affordability	47.0%	54.5%	Miscellaneous Cost Index	111.2	100.0

CLIMATE
SCORE: 95/RANK: 17

TEMPERATURE	AREA	U.S. AVG	PRECIPITATION	AREA	U.S. AVG	COMFORTS & HAZARDS	AREA	U.S. AVG
January low	35.7°F	26.4°F	Annual inches precipitation	30.0	35.9	July relative humidity	70.0%	68.8%
July high	83.6°F	86.7°F	Annual inches snowfall	0.0	24.2	Annual days mostly sunny	285	212
Annual days > 90°F	33	38	Annual days precipitation	47	111	Annual days with thunderstorms	4	39
Annual days < 32°F	43	88	Annual days rain > 0.5 inches	18	23	Tornado risk score	4	19
Annual days < 0°F	0	6	Annual days snow > 1.5 inches	0	6	Hurricane risk score	0	15

TEMPERATURE

PRECIPITATION

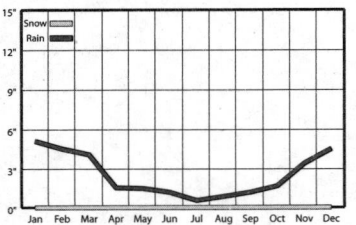

DAYS OF CLOUDS & PRECIPITATION

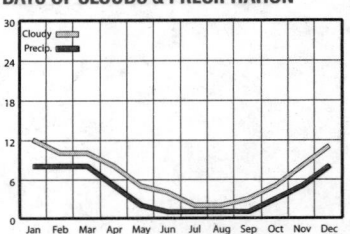

EDUCATION SCORE: 59/RANK: 135

ACHIEVEMENT	AREA	U.S. AVG	PUBLIC SCHOOLS	AREA	U.S. AVG	HIGHER EDUCATION	AREA	U.S. AVG
High school degree	84.2%	80.2%	Expenditures per pupil	$5,248	$5,894	No. 2-year colleges	3	3
2-year college degree	9.4%	6.2%	Student/teacher ratio	20.3	16.7	No. 4-year colleges/universities	1	4
4-year college degree	18.5%	15.8%	Attending public school	89.6%	90.2%	No. highly ranked universities	0	1
Graduate/professional degree	9.1%	9.6%	State SAT score	1018*	1020			
			State ACT score	21.5	21.0			

HEALTH & HEALTHCARE SCORE: 3/RANK: 320

HAZARDS & ILLNESSES	AREA	U.S. AVG	HEALTHCARE	AREA	U.S. AVG
Air-quality score	59	45	Physicians per capita	238.3	261.1
Water-quality score	6	33	Hospital beds per capita	524.0	432.2
Pollen/allergy score	91	61	No. teaching hospitals	2	4
Stress score	54	50	Cost per doctor visit	$75	$67
Cancer mortality per capita	173.7	169.0	Cost per dental visit	$114	$82
Depression days per month	2.2	2.8	Cost per daily hospital room	$1,821	$733

CRIME SCORE: 90/RANK: 31

CRIME	AREA	U.S. AVG
Violent crime rate	276.8	456.0
Change in violent crime rate	-41.6%	-17.2%
Property crime rate	2,964.7	3,950.0
Change in property crime rate	-30.3%	-16.8%

TRANSPORTATION SCORE: 64/RANK: 116

COMMUTE	AREA	U.S. AVG	INTERCITY SERVICES	AREA	U.S. AVG	AUTOMOTIVE	AREA	U.S. AVG
Average commute time	26.8 min.	22.6 min.	Miles to nearest major airport	56	46	Insurance, annual premium	$938	$1,011
Commute by auto	86.2%	88.7%	Type of local airport	Medium		Gas, cost per gallon	$1.84	$1.50
Commute by mass transit	1.7%	1.8%	No. daily airline departures	257	294	Daily vehicle miles per capita	19.4	23.0
Work at home	6.7%	3.9%	Amtrak service	No				
Mass transit miles per capita	7.4	8.0	No. interstate highways	0	1			

LEISURE SCORE: 92/RANK: 27

DINING & SHOPPING	AREA	U.S. AVG	ENTERTAINMENT	AREA	U.S. AVG	OUTDOOR ACTIVITIES	AREA	U.S. AVG
Restaurant rating	1	1	Professional sports rating	9	4	Golf-course rating	5	4
No. outlet malls	3	2	College sports rating	3	4	Ski-area rating	9	4
No. Starbucks	16	11	Zoo/aquarium rating	4	3	National Park rating	3	3
No. warehouse clubs	3	4	Amusement park rating	6	3	Sq. miles inland water	6.0	4.0
			Botanical garden/arboretum rating	6	3	Miles of coastline	45.0	11.4

ARTS & CULTURE SCORE: 45/RANK: 180

MEDIA & LIBRARIES	AREA	U.S. AVG	PERFORMING ARTS	AREA	U.S. AVG	MUSEUMS	AREA	U.S. AVG
Arts radio rating	4	3	Classical music rating	6	4	Overall museum rating	6	6
No. public libraries	13	28	Ballet/dance rating	6	3	Art museum rating	5	5
Library volumes per capita	1.5	2.8	Professional theater rating	6	3	Science museum rating	6	4
			University arts programs rating	3	5	Children's museum rating	6	3

Sarasota-Bradenton, FL

Score: 78.1   Rank: 43

Profile: Resort-city complex
Location: Central Florida Gulf Coast, just south of the Tampa–St. Petersburg area
Elevation: 11 feet
Time zone: Eastern Standard Time

PRO	CON
Leisure activities	Cost of living
Attractive setting	Cost of housing
Baseball spring training	Low ethnic diversity

Sarasota is an affluent resort community with some history to accompany the usual assortment of Florida beaches and watersports. In the late 1880s, golf was introduced to the area from Scotland. Today, there are more than 30 golf courses near downtown and the Scottish influence defines the appearance of many buildings. The area comes up short statistically in arts and culture amenities and some services, which are available in the Tampa Bay area, a reasonable drive to the northeast. Downsides include cost of living relative to income levels—the Financial Progress Index is the lowest in Florida—and high unemployment, although projected future job growth looks good. Like a few other places in Florida, Sarasota is statistically close to the highest rankings in many categories and is likely better than the numbers indicate.

Located on the shore of Sarasota Bay, Sarasota sits on level, sandy terrain across from a long, narrow barrier island. There are areas of banyan trees and other tropical plants. Inland sections contain agriculture and orchards. The climate is subtropical with a substantial Gulf influence. Summers are long, warm, and humid, with afternoon highs of 90°F or more and warm evenings in the 70s. Afternoon sea breezes and frequent thunderstorms moderate temperatures. Winters are quite mild with temperatures in the 60s and 70s and lows rarely below 50°F. Invasions of cold northern air produce an occasional light frost and a cold winter morning or two.

POPULATION

DEMOGRAPHICS	AREA	U.S. AVG	ETHNIC COMPOSITION	AREA	U.S. AVG	RESIDENT PROFILE	AREA	U.S. AVG
Population	620,136		White	92.9%	75.1%	Single	37.8%	43.6%
Population density per sq. mile	472.3	447.3	Black	5.3%	12.3%	Married	62.2%	56.4%
Population growth	26.7%	16.1%	Asian	.8%	3.6%	Divorced	9.4%	8.4%
Median age	48.0	35.5	American Indian	.2%	.9%	Separated	2.1%	3.0%
Average family size	2.2	2.7	Hispanic	4.9%	12.5%	Married with children	16.3%	28.7%
			Diversity measure	25.4%	35.2%	Single with children	6.3%	10.1%

ECONOMY & JOBS SCORE: 11/RANK: 293

INCOME	AREA	U.S. AVG	EMPLOYMENT	AREA	U.S. AVG	LARGEST EMPLOYING INDUSTRY
Per capita income	$27,702	$23,420	Unemployment rate	3.7%	6.1%	Food Manufacturing
Household income	$42,449	$46,060	Recent job growth	2.7%	.9%	
Household income < $25K	24.1%	26.4%	Projected future job growth	30.5%	15.1%	
Household income > $75K	21.0%	24.5%	White collar	55.6%	54.5%	
Household income growth	50.9%	57.3%	Blue collar	44.4%	45.5%	

COST OF LIVING SCORE: 78/RANK: 72

INDEXES & TAXES	AREA	U.S. AVG	HOUSING	AREA	U.S. AVG	NECESSITIES	AREA	U.S. AVG
Cost of Living Index	100.0	100.0	Median home price	$156,800	$160,100	Food Index	98.1	100.0
Financial Progress Index	90.4	100.0	Home price appreciation	11.4%	7.1%	Housing Index	97.4	100.0
Income tax rate	0.000%	4.625%	Median rent	$708	$670	Utilities Index	99.9	100.0
Sales tax rate	7.000%	6.474%	Homes owned	62.8%	63.9%	Transportation Index	109.8	100.0
Property tax rate	$9.8	$15.6	Homes rented	17.8%	25.3%	Healthcare Index	98.8	100.0
			Housing affordability	56.0%	54.5%	Miscellaneous Cost Index	101.4	100.0

CLIMATE SCORE: 82/RANK: 58

TEMPERATURE	AREA	U.S. AVG	PRECIPITATION	AREA	U.S. AVG	COMFORTS & HAZARDS	AREA	U.S. AVG
January low	50.1°F	26.4°F	Annual inches precipitation	49.0	35.9	July relative humidity	74.0%	68.8%
July high	90.4°F	86.7°F	Annual inches snowfall	0.0	24.2	Annual days mostly sunny	238	212
Annual days > 90°F	81	38	Annual days precipitation	107	111	Annual days with thunderstorms	88	39
Annual days < 32°F	4	88	Annual days rain > 0.5 inches	28	23	Tornado risk score	55	19
Annual days < 0°F	0	6	Annual days snow > 1.5 inches	0	6	Hurricane risk score	75	15

TEMPERATURE

PRECIPITATION

DAYS OF CLOUDS & PRECIPITATION

EDUCATION SCORE: 48/RANK: 170

ACHIEVEMENT	AREA	U.S. AVG	PUBLIC SCHOOLS	AREA	U.S. AVG	HIGHER EDUCATION	AREA	U.S. AVG
High school degree	84.7%	80.2%	Expenditures per pupil	$5,871	$5,894	No. 2-year colleges	1	3
2-year college degree	5.7%	6.2%	Student/teacher ratio	17.7	16.7	No. 4-year colleges/universities	2	4
4-year college degree	15.6%	15.8%	Attending public school	89.8%	90.2%	No. highly ranked universities	1	1
Graduate/professional degree	9.1%	9.6%	State SAT score	996*	1020			
			State ACT score	20.5	21.0			

HEALTH & HEALTHCARE SCORE: 52/RANK: 158

HAZARDS & ILLNESSES	AREA	U.S. AVG	HEALTHCARE	AREA	U.S. AVG
Air-quality score	6	45	Physicians per capita	261.6	261.1
Water-quality score	23	33	Hospital beds per capita	408.5	432.2
Pollen/allergy score	86	61	No. teaching hospitals	0	4
Stress score	60	50	Cost per doctor visit	$69	$67
Cancer mortality per capita	154.5	169.0	Cost per dental visit	$71	$82
Depression days per month	2.0	2.8	Cost per daily hospital room	$756	$733

CRIME SCORE: 30/RANK: 230

CRIME	AREA	U.S. AVG
Violent crime rate	665.2	456.0
Change in violent crime rate	-24.5%	-17.2%
Property crime rate	4,332.6	3,950.0
Change in property crime rate	-23.3%	-16.8%

TRANSPORTATION SCORE: 30/RANK: 229

COMMUTE	AREA	U.S. AVG	INTERCITY SERVICES	AREA	U.S. AVG	AUTOMOTIVE	AREA	U.S. AVG
Average commute time	22.5 min.	22.6 min.	Miles to nearest major airport	4	46	Insurance, annual premium	$1,063	$1,011
Commute by auto	91.8%	88.7%	Type of local airport	Small		Gas, cost per gallon	$1.46	$1.50
Commute by mass transit	.5%	1.8%	No. daily airline departures	33	294	Daily vehicle miles per capita	18.7	23.0
Work at home	4.0%	3.9%	Amtrak service	No				
Mass transit miles per capita	5.4	8.0	No. interstate highways	1	1			

LEISURE SCORE: 69/RANK: 103

DINING & SHOPPING	AREA	U.S. AVG	ENTERTAINMENT	AREA	U.S. AVG	OUTDOOR ACTIVITIES	AREA	U.S. AVG
Restaurant rating	1	1	Professional sports rating	2	4	Golf-course rating	5	4
No. outlet malls	2	2	College sports rating	1	4	Ski-area rating	1	4
No. Starbucks	3	11	Zoo/aquarium rating	6	3	National Park rating	1	3
No. warehouse clubs	3	4	Amusement park rating	1	3	Sq. miles inland water	4.0	4.0
			Botanical garden/arboretum rating	4	3	Miles of coastline	35.6	11.4

ARTS & CULTURE SCORE: 24/RANK: 251

MEDIA & LIBRARIES	AREA	U.S. AVG	PERFORMING ARTS	AREA	U.S. AVG	MUSEUMS	AREA	U.S. AVG
Arts radio rating	1	3	Classical music rating	3	4	Overall museum rating	7	6
No. public libraries	13	28	Ballet/dance rating	3	3	Art museum rating	7	5
Library volumes per capita	1.9	2.8	Professional theater rating	8	3	Science museum rating	7	4
			University arts programs rating	3	5	Children's museum rating	6	3

Savannah, GA

Score: 59.0   Rank: 156

Profile: Mid-size coastal city
Location: Southeast coast of Georgia at the mouth of the Savannah River along the South Carolina border
Elevation: 15 feet
Time zone: Eastern Standard Time

PRO
Historic preservation
Attractive downtown
Pleasant winters

CON
Summer heat
Performing arts
Air quality

Savannah is a beautiful, well-preserved historic city. Its appeal was so strong that Gen. William T. Sherman spared the city from Civil War destruction in 1864. Today, Southern charm radiates from old mansions; cobblestone, tree-shaded streets; and restored, historic areas, such as City Market with its nightlife and art galleries. However, the quality and appeal rapidly diminish away from the central area. Expenses—outside the historic district—are modest, giving a low, average Cost of Living Index of 91.0, but incomes are also low, resulting in the lowest Financial Progress Index in the state. The economy, arts, and education are getting a boost by the many northerners moving into the area. Coastal islands to the east, particularly Tybee Island, offer beaches, recreation, fine seafood restaurants, and local flavor. The overall quality of life, especially in the historic city center, is better than the statistics indicate.

Savannah is located on a coastal plain a few miles inland from the Atlantic along the Savannah River. Areas, particularly to the north and east, are flat with marshes. Land to the south and west is a mix of agriculture, woods, and swamps. The nearby Atlantic moderates the climate most of the time. Muggy conditions can occur in summer when sea breezes diminish. Most summer days are clear and pleasant. Winter temperatures are usually mild and snow is rare. Strong northwesterly blasts of cold air are usually blocked by the Appalachians. Most precipitation comes as summer thunderstorms. Severe tropical storms affect the area about once every 10 years.

POPULATION

DEMOGRAPHICS	AREA	U.S. AVG	ETHNIC COMPOSITION	AREA	U.S. AVG	RESIDENT PROFILE	AREA	U.S. AVG
Population	299,790		White	65.6%	75.1%	Single	45.9%	43.6%
Population density per sq. mile	220.2	447.3	Black	32.5%	12.3%	Married	54.1%	56.4%
Population growth	16.2%	16.1%	Asian	1.1%	3.6%	Divorced	9.3%	8.4%
Median age	34.5	35.5	American Indian	.2%	.9%	Separated	4.2%	3.0%
Average family size	2.8	2.7	Hispanic	2.5%	12.5%	Married with children	30.4%	28.7%
			Diversity measure	51.2%	35.2%	Single with children	13.5%	10.1%

ECONOMY & JOBS SCORE: 73/RANK: 88

INCOME	AREA	U.S. AVG	EMPLOYMENT	AREA	U.S. AVG	LARGEST EMPLOYING INDUSTRY
Per capita income	$21,565	$23,420	Unemployment rate	4.1%	6.1%	Healthcare and Social Assistance
Household income	$41,802	$46,060	Recent job growth	.5%	.9%	
Household income < $25K	28.8%	26.4%	Projected future job growth	16.2%	15.1%	
Household income > $75K	21.0%	24.5%	White collar	51.2%	54.5%	
Household income growth	54.5%	57.3%	Blue collar	48.8%	45.5%	

COST OF LIVING SCORE: 48/RANK: 171

INDEXES & TAXES	AREA	U.S. AVG	HOUSING	AREA	U.S. AVG	NECESSITIES	AREA	U.S. AVG
Cost of Living Index	91.0	100.0	Median home price	$122,550	$160,100	Food Index	104.0	100.0
Financial Progress Index	97.9	100.0	Home price appreciation	7.9%	7.1%	Housing Index	76.1	100.0
Income tax rate	6.000%	4.625%	Median rent	$568	$670	Utilities Index	92.9	100.0
Sales tax rate	6.000%	6.474%	Homes owned	61.1%	63.9%	Transportation Index	95.8	100.0
Property tax rate	$18.1	$15.6	Homes rented	28.5%	25.3%	Healthcare Index	97.6	100.0
			Housing affordability	59.0%	54.5%	Miscellaneous Cost Index	100.6	100.0

CLIMATE SCORE: 60/RANK: 131

TEMPERATURE	AREA	U.S. AVG	PRECIPITATION	AREA	U.S. AVG	COMFORTS & HAZARDS	AREA	U.S. AVG
January low	38.7°F	26.4°F	Annual inches precipitation	51.0	35.9	July relative humidity	74.0%	68.8%
July high	90.8°F	86.7°F	Annual inches snowfall	.3	24.2	Annual days mostly sunny	217	212
Annual days > 90°F	54	38	Annual days precipitation	112	111	Annual days with thunderstorms	64	39
Annual days < 32°F	35	88	Annual days rain > 0.5 inches	31	23	Tornado risk score	16	19
Annual days < 0°F	0	6	Annual days snow > 1.5 inches	1	6	Hurricane risk score	57	15

TEMPERATURE

PRECIPITATION

DAYS OF CLOUDS & PRECIPITATION

EDUCATION SCORE: 17/RANK: 272

ACHIEVEMENT	AREA	U.S. AVG	PUBLIC SCHOOLS	AREA	U.S. AVG	HIGHER EDUCATION	AREA	U.S. AVG
High school degree	79.9%	80.2%	Expenditures per pupil	$5,322	$5,894	No. 2-year colleges	1	3
2-year college degree	4.7%	6.2%	Student/teacher ratio	17.8	16.7	No. 4-year colleges/universities	4	4
4-year college degree	15.4%	15.8%	Attending public school	85.9%	90.2%	No. highly ranked universities	0	1
Graduate/professional degree	7.7%	9.6%	State SAT score	984*	1020			
			State ACT score	19.8	21.0			

HEALTH & HEALTHCARE SCORE: 30/RANK: 229

CRIME SCORE: 6/RANK: 310

HAZARDS & ILLNESSES	AREA	U.S. AVG	HEALTHCARE	AREA	U.S. AVG	CRIME	AREA	U.S. AVG
Air-quality score	6	45	Physicians per capita	274.2	261.1	Violent crime rate	734.8	456.0
Water-quality score	13	33	Hospital beds per capita	535.2	432.2	Change in violent crime rate	3.4%	-17.2%
Pollen/allergy score	64	61	No. teaching hospitals	1	4	Property crime rate	5,634.1	3,950.0
Stress score	85	50	Cost per doctor visit	$68	$67	Change in property crime rate	-8.8%	-16.8%
Cancer mortality per capita	181.8	169.0	Cost per dental visit	$74	$82			
Depression days per month	2.6	2.8	Cost per daily hospital room	$510	$733			

TRANSPORTATION SCORE: 33/RANK: 220

COMMUTE	AREA	U.S. AVG	INTERCITY SERVICES	AREA	U.S. AVG	AUTOMOTIVE	AREA	U.S. AVG
Average commute time	24.2 min.	22.6 min.	Miles to nearest major airport	8	46	Insurance, annual premium	$1,312	$1,011
Commute by auto	89.8%	88.7%	Type of local airport	Small		Gas, cost per gallon	$1.37	$1.50
Commute by mass transit	2.3%	1.8%	No. daily airline departures	49	294	Daily vehicle miles per capita	28.7	23.0
Work at home	2.0%	3.9%	Amtrak service	Yes				
Mass transit miles per capita	10.3	8.0	No. interstate highways	2	1			

LEISURE SCORE: 41/RANK: 193

DINING & SHOPPING	AREA	U.S. AVG	ENTERTAINMENT	AREA	U.S. AVG	OUTDOOR ACTIVITIES	AREA	U.S. AVG
Restaurant rating	3	1	Professional sports rating	3	4	Golf-course rating	2	4
No. outlet malls	2	2	College sports rating	4	4	Ski-area rating	1	4
No. Starbucks	3	11	Zoo/aquarium rating	2	3	National Park rating	3	3
No. warehouse clubs	3	4	Amusement park rating	3	3	Sq. miles inland water	5.0	4.0
			Botanical garden/arboretum rating	3	3	Miles of coastline	29.2	11.4

ARTS & CULTURE SCORE: 62/RANK: 126

MEDIA & LIBRARIES	AREA	U.S. AVG	PERFORMING ARTS	AREA	U.S. AVG	MUSEUMS	AREA	U.S. AVG
Arts radio rating	1	3	Classical music rating	4	4	Overall museum rating	7	6
No. public libraries	19	28	Ballet/dance rating	1	3	Art museum rating	5	5
Library volumes per capita	2.2	2.8	Professional theater rating	1	3	Science museum rating	5	4
			University arts programs rating	8	5	Children's museum rating	1	3

Scranton–Wilkes-Barre–Hazleton, PA

Score: 41.6   Rank: 271

Profile: Small-industrial-city complex
Location: Northeastern Pennsylvania, 40 miles from New York–
  New Jersey border
Elevation: 930 feet
Time zone: Eastern Standard Time

PRO	CON
Nearby recreation	Economy
Cost of living	Isolation
Historic interest	Low ethnic diversity

The cities of Scranton, Wilkes-Barre, and Hazleton are part of a declining coal mining and industrial center, now without its largest businesses. Some modest industrial development and urban renewal have taken place, but the economy and employment are still flat to declining. The area is gaining some ground as a gateway to the Pocono Mountains, a recreational area to the north and east with skiing and watersports. Local museums focusing on industrial heritage, such as the Anthracite Complex and the Steamtown National Historic Site, are excellent models of working historic preservation and education. The location is isolated from big-city amenities and services—New York City and Philadelphia to the southeast are not easily accessible.

The city complex lies at the southwest end of the crescent-shaped Lackawanna River Valley where that river empties into the Susquehanna River. Surrounding the valley to the northwest and east, mountains provide protection from winds and influence temperature and precipitation during both summer and winter. Summers are relatively cool with frequent shower and thunderstorm activity. Winter temperatures are not severe, and most precipitation occurs as rain. However, when warm moist air from the valleys to the southwest collides with cold air from the north, snow and blizzards can occur. The area is cloudier and rainier than most areas of the state. First freeze is mid-October, last is late April.

POPULATION

DEMOGRAPHICS	AREA	U.S. AVG	ETHNIC COMPOSITION	AREA	U.S. AVG	RESIDENT PROFILE	AREA	U.S. AVG
Population	617,289		White	97.6%	75.1%	Single	46.4%	43.6%
Population density per sq. mile	276.5	447.3	Black	1.6%	12.3%	Married	53.6%	56.4%
Population growth	-3.3%	16.1%	Asian	.7%	3.6%	Divorced	6.3%	8.4%
Median age	40.8	35.5	American Indian	.1%	.9%	Separated	2.8%	3.0%
Average family size	2.5	2.7	Hispanic	.7%	12.5%	Married with children	24.8%	28.7%
			Diversity measure	7.6%	35.2%	Single with children	7.5%	10.1%

ECONOMY & JOBS   SCORE: 17/RANK: 274

INCOME	AREA	U.S. AVG	EMPLOYMENT	AREA	U.S. AVG	LARGEST EMPLOYING INDUSTRY
Per capita income	$19,624	$23,420	Unemployment rate	5.3%	6.1%	Fabricated Metal Product Manufacturing
Household income	$34,708	$46,060	Recent job growth	-2.7%	.9%	
Household income < $25K	36.2%	26.4%	Projected future job growth	6.3%	15.1%	
Household income > $75K	14.0%	24.5%	White collar	49.5%	54.5%	
Household income growth	42.8%	57.3%	Blue collar	50.5%	45.5%	

COST OF LIVING   SCORE: 58/RANK: 135

INDEXES & TAXES	AREA	U.S. AVG	HOUSING	AREA	U.S. AVG	NECESSITIES	AREA	U.S. AVG
Cost of Living Index	86.4	100.0	Median home price	$102,450	$160,100	Food Index	95.7	100.0
Financial Progress Index	85.6	100.0	Home price appreciation	5.2%	7.1%	Housing Index	63.6	100.0
Income tax rate	5.000%	4.625%	Median rent	$550	$670	Utilities Index	112.4	100.0
Sales tax rate	6.000%	6.474%	Homes owned	66.3%	63.9%	Transportation Index	97.5	100.0
Property tax rate	$17.3	$15.6	Homes rented	22.6%	25.3%	Healthcare Index	90.9	100.0
			Housing affordability	56.0%	54.5%	Miscellaneous Cost Index	100.3	100.0

CLIMATE   SCORE: 19/RANK: 268

TEMPERATURE	AREA	U.S. AVG	PRECIPITATION	AREA	U.S. AVG	COMFORTS & HAZARDS	AREA	U.S. AVG
January low	18.4°F	26.4°F	Annual inches precipitation	34.8	35.9	July relative humidity	70.0%	68.8%
July high	83.0°F	86.7°F	Annual inches snowfall	51.3	24.2	Annual days mostly sunny	176	212
Annual days > 90°F	7	38	Annual days precipitation	153	111	Annual days with thunderstorms	31	39
Annual days < 32°F	132	88	Annual days rain > 0.5 inches	22	23	Tornado risk score	7	19
Annual days < 0°F	4	6	Annual days snow > 1.5 inches	11	6	Hurricane risk score	8	15

TEMPERATURE

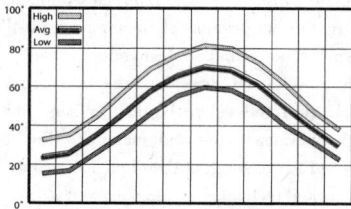

PRECIPITATION

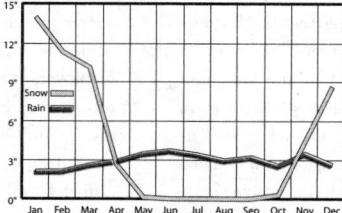

DAYS OF CLOUDS & PRECIPITATION

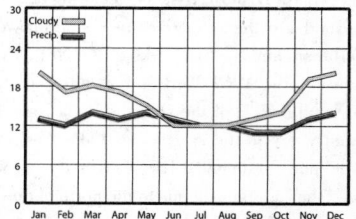

EDUCATION SCORE: 16/RANK: 278

ACHIEVEMENT	AREA	U.S. AVG	PUBLIC SCHOOLS	AREA	U.S. AVG	HIGHER EDUCATION	AREA	U.S. AVG
High school degree	81.4%	80.2%	Expenditures per pupil	$6,554	$5,894	No. 2-year colleges	8	3
2-year college degree	6.6%	6.2%	Student/teacher ratio	17.4	16.7	No. 4-year colleges/universities	8	4
4-year college degree	11.0%	15.8%	Attending public school	82.0%	90.2%	No. highly ranked universities	0	1
Graduate/professional degree	5.9%	9.6%	State SAT score	1002*	1020			
			State ACT score	21.5	21.0			

HEALTH & HEALTHCARE SCORE: 89/RANK: 35

CRIME SCORE: 94/RANK: 20

HAZARDS & ILLNESSES	AREA	U.S. AVG	HEALTHCARE	AREA	U.S. AVG	CRIME	AREA	U.S. AVG
Air-quality score	95	45	Physicians per capita	238.5	261.1	Violent crime rate	158.2	456.0
Water-quality score	82	33	Hospital beds per capita	563.7	432.2	Change in violent crime rate	-9.9%	-17.2%
Pollen/allergy score	55	61	No. teaching hospitals	6	4	Property crime rate	1,916.0	3,950.0
Stress score	55	50	Cost per doctor visit	$57	$67	Change in property crime rate	-15.3%	-16.8%
Cancer mortality per capita	176.9	169.0	Cost per dental visit	$61	$82			
Depression days per month	4.2	2.8	Cost per daily hospital room	$687	$733			

TRANSPORTATION SCORE: 39/RANK: 200

COMMUTE	AREA	U.S. AVG	INTERCITY SERVICES	AREA	U.S. AVG	AUTOMOTIVE	AREA	U.S. AVG
Average commute time	21.0 min.	22.6 min.	Miles to nearest major airport	54	46	Insurance, annual premium	$983	$1,011
Commute by auto	89.9%	88.7%	Type of local airport	Small		Gas, cost per gallon	$1.49	$1.50
Commute by mass transit	1.3%	1.8%	No. daily airline departures	63	294	Daily vehicle miles per capita	20.7	23.0
Work at home	2.8%	3.9%	Amtrak service	No				
Mass transit miles per capita	3.4	8.0	No. interstate highways	2	1			

LEISURE SCORE: 39/RANK: 201

DINING & SHOPPING	AREA	U.S. AVG	ENTERTAINMENT	AREA	U.S. AVG	OUTDOOR ACTIVITIES	AREA	U.S. AVG
Restaurant rating	1	1	Professional sports rating	3	4	Golf-course rating	7	4
No. outlet malls	2	2	College sports rating	5	4	Ski-area rating	5	4
No. Starbucks	0	11	Zoo/aquarium rating	1	3	National Park rating	2	3
No. warehouse clubs	3	4	Amusement park rating	1	3	Sq. miles inland water	4.0	4.0
			Botanical garden/arboretum rating	1	3	Miles of coastline	0.0	11.4

ARTS & CULTURE SCORE: 37/RANK: 207

MEDIA & LIBRARIES	AREA	U.S. AVG	PERFORMING ARTS	AREA	U.S. AVG	MUSEUMS	AREA	U.S. AVG
Arts radio rating	1	3	Classical music rating	4	4	Overall museum rating	6	6
No. public libraries	33	28	Ballet/dance rating	1	3	Art museum rating	4	5
Library volumes per capita	1.9	2.8	Professional theater rating	7	3	Science museum rating	6	4
			University arts programs rating	6	5	Children's museum rating	6	3

Seattle-Bellevue-Everett, WA

Score: 68.0   Rank: 88

Profile: Regional center
Location: East shore of Puget Sound in west-central Washington
Elevation: 125 feet
Time zone: Pacific Standard Time

PRO
Attractive setting and downtown
Arts and culture
Nearby recreation

CON
Sprawl and traffic
Clouds and rain
Cost of living

Seattle is a lively, attractive, and cosmopolitan city in a dramatic setting. The main downtown area sits on a narrow, hilly strip of land between Puget Sound to the west and Lake Washington to the east. Modern skyscrapers rise on high hills in the city center and apartments fill the lower areas along the water. To the south is the Pioneer Square Historic District, recalling late-19th-century commerce, and beyond are the attractive, new stadiums of the Seattle Mariners baseball team and the Seahawks of the NFL. To the immediate north of downtown is the 1962 World's Fair site punctuated by the landmark Space Needle. Most of the suburbs, some among the most attractive in the country, are to the east across Lake Washington in such places as Bellevue and Redmond. The University of Washington, nicknamed "U-Dub," has a large campus to the north of downtown and active sports and nightlife. The city has a full complement of cultural, recreational,

and transportation amenities. Local geography and policy have restrained growth, but there are significant traffic and congestion problems at Lake Washington crossings to the east and elsewhere.

From its origins as a center of the forest products industry and as a gateway to Alaska and the Yukon to the north, Seattle has become an important regional center with banking, high-tech companies, and consumer products. It retains its original character as a bustling seaport while also exuding intelligence and sophistication. Some of the largest employers include Microsoft (in Redmond to the northeast), Amazon.com (downtown), Starbucks (in a redeveloped industrial zone south of downtown), and Boeing's enormous labs and manufacturing facilities (in Everett to the north and to the south of the city). The economy is robust although the aerospace and technology sectors make it more cyclical than that of other large cities. Cost of living and particularly housing have risen substantially in recent years. And the long stretches of cloudy days and rainy periods can be a significant downside. In general, the area represents the usual big-city tradeoffs—abundant amenities in exchange for high costs and crowding—but with the additional elements of natural beauty and climate to consider.

Along the edge of Puget Sound, the area is hilly and heavily forested where not completely built up. The Cascade Range rises to the east (with 14,000-foot Mount Rainier to the southeast) and the Olympic Mountains rise across the Sound to the west. The climate is mild and moist, the result of prevailing westerly winds off the Pacific and the shielding effect of the Cascade Range. Steady marine air keeps winters comparatively warm and summers cool. Temperature extremes are moderate and usually of short duration. Normal summers have fewer than 3 days above 90°F. Summer nights are invariably cool. Daily winter highs are almost always above freezing. Winters are wet but as Seattle lies on the leeward side of the Olympic Mountains, the annual total of 39.0 inches makes Seattle drier than many cities in the East and Midwest. Long stretches of cloudy days and rainy periods tend to occur in all seasons except summer. Only 20% of rainfall occurs during the April to September dry season. Seattle is far enough north to get winter snow, about 15.0 inches per year, but it seldom remains more than 2 days. Thunderstorms and severe weather are rare.

POPULATION

DEMOGRAPHICS	AREA	U.S. AVG	ETHNIC COMPOSITION	AREA	U.S. AVG	RESIDENT PROFILE	AREA	U.S. AVG
Population	2,468,601		White	85.3%	75.1%	Single	47.2%	43.6%
Population density per sq. mile	557.9	447.3	Black	4.3%	12.3%	Married	52.8%	56.4%
Population growth	21.4%	16.1%	Asian	8.3%	3.6%	Divorced	11.6%	8.4%
Median age	35.8	35.5	American Indian	1.3%	.9%	Separated	2.7%	3.0%
Average family size	2.5	2.7	Hispanic	4.3%	12.5%	Married with children	23.9%	28.7%
			Diversity measure	39.2%	35.2%	Single with children	9.1%	10.1%

ECONOMY & JOBS — SCORE: 8/RANK: 302

INCOME	AREA	U.S. AVG	EMPLOYMENT	AREA	U.S. AVG	LARGEST EMPLOYING INDUSTRY
Per capita income	$36,187	$23,420	Unemployment rate	7.0%	6.1%	Transportation Equipment Manufacturing
Household income	$69,730	$46,060	Recent job growth	-.6%	.9%	
Household income < $25K	12.9%	26.4%	Projected future job growth	20.1%	15.1%	
Household income > $75K	46.2%	24.5%	White collar	62.4%	54.5%	
Household income growth	92.8%	57.3%	Blue collar	37.6%	45.5%	

COST OF LIVING — SCORE: 11/RANK: 294

INDEXES & TAXES	AREA	U.S. AVG	HOUSING	AREA	U.S. AVG	NECESSITIES	AREA	U.S. AVG
Cost of Living Index	123.0	100.0	Median home price	$258,300	$160,100	Food Index	106.7	100.0
Financial Progress Index	120.8	100.0	Home price appreciation	7.4%	7.1%	Housing Index	160.4	100.0
Income tax rate	0.000%	4.625%	Median rent	$923	$670	Utilities Index	74.2	100.0
Sales tax rate	8.800%	6.474%	Homes owned	60.4%	63.9%	Transportation Index	107.9	100.0
Property tax rate	$12.9	$15.6	Homes rented	32.2%	25.3%	Healthcare Index	123.7	100.0
			Housing affordability	54.0%	54.5%	Miscellaneous Cost Index	99.4	100.0

CLIMATE — SCORE: 80/RANK: 66

TEMPERATURE	AREA	U.S. AVG	PRECIPITATION	AREA	U.S. AVG	COMFORTS & HAZARDS	AREA	U.S. AVG
January low	33.0°F	26.4°F	Annual inches precipitation	39.0	35.9	July relative humidity	74.0%	68.8%
July high	75.1°F	86.7°F	Annual inches snowfall	15.0	24.2	Annual days mostly sunny	136	212
Annual days > 90°F	3	38	Annual days precipitation	160	111	Annual days with thunderstorms	7	39
Annual days < 32°F	32	88	Annual days rain > 0.5 inches	24	23	Tornado risk score	0	19
Annual days < 0°F	0	6	Annual days snow > 1.5 inches	2	6	Hurricane risk score	0	15

TEMPERATURE

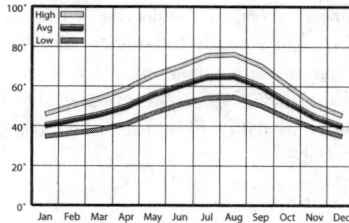

PRECIPITATION

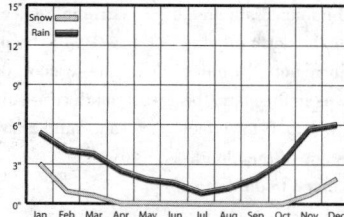

DAYS OF CLOUDS & PRECIPITATION

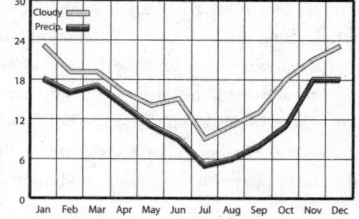

EDUCATION — SCORE: 94/RANK: 19

ACHIEVEMENT	AREA	U.S. AVG	PUBLIC SCHOOLS	AREA	U.S. AVG	HIGHER EDUCATION	AREA	U.S. AVG
High school degree	89.5%	80.2%	Expenditures per pupil	$5,838	$5,894	No. 2-year colleges	13	3
2-year college degree	6.4%	6.2%	Student/teacher ratio	20.4	16.7	No. 4-year colleges/universities	9	4
4-year college degree	24.2%	15.8%	Attending public school	89.1%	90.2%	No. highly ranked universities	2	1
Graduate/professional degree	11.6%	9.6%	State SAT score	1062*	1020			
			State ACT score	22.5	21.0			

HEALTH & HEALTHCARE SCORE: 51/RANK: 162

HAZARDS & ILLNESSES	AREA	U.S. AVG	HEALTHCARE	AREA	U.S. AVG
Air-quality score	89	45	Physicians per capita	315.4	261.1
Water-quality score	19	33	Hospital beds per capita	196.4	432.2
Pollen/allergy score	48	61	No. teaching hospitals	9	4
Stress score	98	50	Cost per doctor visit	$70	$67
Cancer mortality per capita	170.3	169.0	Cost per dental visit	$135	$82
Depression days per month	2.9	2.8	Cost per daily hospital room	$742	$733

CRIME SCORE: 37/RANK: 206

CRIME	AREA	U.S. AVG
Violent crime rate	371.1	456.0
Change in violent crime rate	-27.8%	-17.2%
Property crime rate	4,906.3	3,950.0
Change in property crime rate	-20.2%	-16.8%

TRANSPORTATION SCORE: 96/RANK: 13

COMMUTE	AREA	U.S. AVG	INTERCITY SERVICES	AREA	U.S. AVG	AUTOMOTIVE	AREA	U.S. AVG
Average commute time	27.3 min.	22.6 min.	Miles to nearest major airport	12	46	Insurance, annual premium	$1,615	$1,011
Commute by auto	83.4%	88.7%	Type of local airport	Large		Gas, cost per gallon	$1.60	$1.50
Commute by mass transit	6.7%	1.8%	No. daily airline departures	698	294	Daily vehicle miles per capita	24.8	23.0
Work at home	4.1%	3.9%	Amtrak service	Yes				
Mass transit miles per capita	39.4	8.0	No. interstate highways	2	1			

LEISURE SCORE: 98/RANK: 6

DINING & SHOPPING	AREA	U.S. AVG	ENTERTAINMENT	AREA	U.S. AVG	OUTDOOR ACTIVITIES	AREA	U.S. AVG
Restaurant rating	5	1	Professional sports rating	8	4	Golf-course rating	7	4
No. outlet malls	2	2	College sports rating	8	4	Ski-area rating	10	4
No. Starbucks	191	11	Zoo/aquarium rating	8	3	National Park rating	10	3
No. warehouse clubs	8	4	Amusement park rating	8	3	Sq. miles inland water	8.0	4.0
			Botanical garden/arboretum rating	8	3	Miles of coastline	69.8	11.4

ARTS & CULTURE SCORE: 92/RANK: 24

MEDIA & LIBRARIES	AREA	U.S. AVG	PERFORMING ARTS	AREA	U.S. AVG	MUSEUMS	AREA	U.S. AVG
Arts radio rating	5	3	Classical music rating	7	4	Overall museum rating	9	6
No. public libraries	89	28	Ballet/dance rating	8	3	Art museum rating	9	5
Library volumes per capita	2.9	2.8	Professional theater rating	10	3	Science museum rating	9	4
			University arts programs rating	9	5	Children's museum rating	10	3

Sharon, PA

Score: 29.6   Rank: 308

Profile: Small city
Location: Northwest Pennsylvania at Ohio border, 60 miles northwest of Pittsburgh
Elevation: 1,223 feet
Time zone: Eastern Standard Time

PRO
Nearby recreation
Proximity to Pittsburgh
Economy

CON
Clouds and rain
Entertainment
Arts and culture

Sharon is an old industrial town linked to the fortunes of the steel industry. With a relatively low unemployment rate and strong projected job growth, the economy fares better than most other Pennsylvania locations. There are few amenities in the immediate area, but what's lacking can be found in Pittsburgh. Lakes to the north provide recreational opportunities, and the Oil City–Franklin region, 40 miles east, is an attractive and historic area. As in many towns in the state, the appeal of cost of living and housing are bolstered by the small-town feel and proximity to Pittsburgh. On the downside, this is one of the cloudiest and rainiest places in the country and there isn't much to do.

Sharon is located in a high plateau where the mountains to the east start to level out toward Ohio. The landscape is rolling but level enough to support agriculture. The climate is humid continental with a Lake Erie influence. Summers are warm but seldom hot. Winters are cool and wet with frequent snow but normally little bitter cold. The mixing of air—a cool, damp, northwesterly airflow and warm, moist air from the southwest—and the surrounding geography results in abundant clouds and rain. Sharon ranks fifth in the nation in annual days of rain.

POPULATION

DEMOGRAPHICS	AREA	U.S. AVG	ETHNIC COMPOSITION	AREA	U.S. AVG	RESIDENT PROFILE	AREA	U.S. AVG
Population	119,514		White	94.9%	75.1%	Single	43.6%	43.6%
Population density per sq. mile	177.9	447.3	Black	4.5%	12.3%	Married	56.4%	56.4%
Population growth	-1.2%	16.1%	Asian	.5%	3.6%	Divorced	6.3%	8.4%
Median age	40.2	35.5	American Indian	.1%	.9%	Separated	2.8%	3.0%
Average family size	2.5	2.7	Hispanic	.5%	12.5%	Married with children	27.7%	28.7%
			Diversity measure	13.7%	35.2%	Single with children	8.0%	10.1%

ECONOMY & JOBS — SCORE: 22/RANK: 256

INCOME	AREA	U.S. AVG	EMPLOYMENT	AREA	U.S. AVG	LARGEST EMPLOYING INDUSTRY
Per capita income	$18,047	$23,420	Unemployment rate	4.7%	6.1%	Primary Metal Manufacturing
Household income	$35,425	$46,060	Recent job growth	-3.4%	.9%	
Household income < $25K	33.8%	26.4%	Projected future job growth	12.1%	15.1%	
Household income > $75K	12.0%	24.5%	White collar	46.3%	54.5%	
Household income growth	44.2%	57.3%	Blue collar	53.7%	45.5%	

COST OF LIVING — SCORE: 86/RANK: 44

INDEXES & TAXES	AREA	U.S. AVG	HOUSING	AREA	U.S. AVG	NECESSITIES	AREA	U.S. AVG
Cost of Living Index	83.7	100.0	Median home price	$94,690	$160,100	Food Index	100.6	100.0
Financial Progress Index	90.2	100.0	Home price appreciation	7.6%	7.1%	Housing Index	58.8	100.0
Income tax rate	2.800%	4.625%	Median rent	$474	$670	Utilities Index	126.0	100.0
Sales tax rate	6.000%	6.474%	Homes owned	69.8%	63.9%	Transportation Index	86.5	100.0
Property tax rate	$16.6	$15.6	Homes rented	19.2%	25.3%	Healthcare Index	87.7	100.0
			Housing affordability	59.0%	54.5%	Miscellaneous Cost Index	93.6	100.0

CLIMATE — SCORE: 8/RANK: 304

TEMPERATURE	AREA	U.S. AVG	PRECIPITATION	AREA	U.S. AVG	COMFORTS & HAZARDS	AREA	U.S. AVG
January low	18.3°F	26.4°F	Annual inches precipitation	38.0	35.9	July relative humidity	74.0%	68.8%
July high	81.8°F	86.7°F	Annual inches snowfall	57.6	24.2	Annual days mostly sunny	164	212
Annual days > 90°F	7	38	Annual days precipitation	181	111	Annual days with thunderstorms	36	39
Annual days < 32°F	136	88	Annual days rain > 0.5 inches	23	23	Tornado risk score	35	19
Annual days < 0°F	6	6	Annual days snow > 1.5 inches	13	6	Hurricane risk score	3	15

TEMPERATURE

PRECIPITATION

DAYS OF CLOUDS & PRECIPITATION

EDUCATION — SCORE: 35/RANK: 215

ACHIEVEMENT	AREA	U.S. AVG	PUBLIC SCHOOLS	AREA	U.S. AVG	HIGHER EDUCATION	AREA	U.S. AVG
High school degree	83.0%	80.2%	Expenditures per pupil	$6,075	$5,894	No. 2-year colleges	2	3
2-year college degree	4.9%	6.2%	Student/teacher ratio	16.1	16.7	No. 4-year colleges/universities	3	4
4-year college degree	11.3%	15.8%	Attending public school	91.6%	90.2%	No. highly ranked universities	1	1
Graduate/professional degree	6.0%	9.6%	State SAT score	1002*	1020			
			State ACT score	21.5	21.0			

HEALTH & HEALTHCARE — SCORE: 93/RANK: 23

HAZARDS & ILLNESSES	AREA	U.S. AVG	HEALTHCARE	AREA	U.S. AVG
Air-quality score	74	45	Physicians per capita	218.4	261.1
Water-quality score	30	33	Hospital beds per capita	554.5	432.2
Pollen/allergy score	54	61	No. teaching hospitals	1	4
Stress score	22	50	Cost per doctor visit	$55	$67
Cancer mortality per capita	165.7	169.0	Cost per dental visit	$59	$82
Depression days per month	3.8	2.8	Cost per daily hospital room	$670	$733

CRIME — SCORE: 93/RANK: 23

CRIME	AREA	U.S. AVG
Violent crime rate	174.0	456.0
Change in violent crime rate	-23.5%	-17.2%
Property crime rate	2,107.5	3,950.0
Change in property crime rate	-15.6%	-16.8%

TRANSPORTATION — SCORE: 43/RANK: 188

COMMUTE	AREA	U.S. AVG	INTERCITY SERVICES	AREA	U.S. AVG	AUTOMOTIVE	AREA	U.S. AVG
Average commute time	19.6 min.	22.6 min.	Miles to nearest major airport	52	46	Insurance, annual premium	$947	$1,011
Commute by auto	85.8%	88.7%	Type of local airport	Large		Gas, cost per gallon	$1.50	$1.50
Commute by mass transit	.2%	1.8%	No. daily airline departures	663	294	Daily vehicle miles per capita	17.9	23.0
Work at home	4.7%	3.9%	Amtrak service	No				
Mass transit miles per capita	0.0	8.0	No. interstate highways	1	1			

LEISURE — SCORE: 11/RANK: 294

DINING & SHOPPING	AREA	U.S. AVG	ENTERTAINMENT	AREA	U.S. AVG	OUTDOOR ACTIVITIES	AREA	U.S. AVG
Restaurant rating	1	1	Professional sports rating	3	4	Golf-course rating	3	4
No. outlet malls	3	2	College sports rating	1	4	Ski-area rating	3	4
No. Starbucks	0	11	Zoo/aquarium rating	1	3	National Park rating	1	3
No. warehouse clubs	1	4	Amusement park rating	1	3	Sq. miles inland water	1.0	4.0
			Botanical garden/arboretum rating	1	3	Miles of coastline	0.0	11.4

ARTS & CULTURE SCORE: 5/RANK: 313

MEDIA & LIBRARIES	AREA	U.S. AVG	PERFORMING ARTS	AREA	U.S. AVG	MUSEUMS	AREA	U.S. AVG
Arts radio rating	1	3	Classical music rating	3	4	Overall museum rating	1	6
No. public libraries	5	28	Ballet/dance rating	1	3	Art museum rating	1	5
Library volumes per capita	2.4	2.8	Professional theater rating	1	3	Science museum rating	1	4
			University arts programs rating	8	5	Children's museum rating	1	3

Sheboygan, WI

Score: 53.6   Rank: 199

Profile: Small town
Location: Eastern Wisconsin on the shore of Lake Michigan
Elevation: 693 feet
Time zone: Central Standard Time

PRO	CON
Small-town atmosphere	Winter climate
Low crime rate	Low educational attainment
Nearby recreation	Low ethnic diversity

Sheboygan, located about half way between Milwaukee and the Door Peninsula, or "thumb" of Wisconsin, is an industrial port town with a sense of humor. It's also a summer tourist and retirement destination for residents of the larger cities to the south. Major employers include plumbing products manufacturers Kohler and Bemis, both headquartered here, and food processing businesses specializing in cheese and sausage. Pluses include a nice downtown, an attractively developed riverfront, noted golf courses, and some arts assets endowed by the Kohler family. Additional amenities are available in Milwaukee, 60 miles south. The area has won some awards, including a 1995 National Trust for Historic Preservation Great American Main Street Award and *Money* magazine's "One of Best Places to Retire 2002." The crime rate is one of the lowest in the nation. On the downside, it is the only city in Wisconsin with job losses and educational attainment is the lowest in the state.

Sheboygan sits at the mouth of the Sheboygan River along a Lake Michigan coastal plain with mixed deciduous forest and clear areas. Land becomes rolling to hilly to the west. The climate is marine-influenced continental, although the "upwind" position relative to the lake diminishes lake effects in comparison with locations to the east and south. Summers are pleasant with periods of warm weather; cooling lake breezes and afternoon thundershowers are common. Winters are vigorous but milder than inland locations. Periods of cool, cloudy weather alternate with crisp, cold weather when air masses invade from the northwest. Snow is common and may linger although not in amounts seen to the east and south of the lake. The lake moderates the cold somewhat although winds can be strong. First freeze is early October, last is early May.

POPULATION

DEMOGRAPHICS	AREA	U.S. AVG	ETHNIC COMPOSITION	AREA	U.S. AVG	RESIDENT PROFILE	AREA	U.S. AVG
Population	112,480		White	94.5%	75.1%	Single	37.0%	43.6%
Population density per sq. mile	219.0	447.3	Black	3.1%	12.3%	Married	63.0%	56.4%
Population growth	8.3%	16.1%	Asian	1.5%	3.6%	Divorced	5.5%	8.4%
Median age	37.2	35.5	American Indian	.4%	.9%	Separated	1.5%	3.0%
Average family size	2.7	2.7	Hispanic	1.8%	12.5%	Married with children	34.9%	28.7%
			Diversity measure	16.6%	35.2%	Single with children	5.9%	10.1%

ECONOMY & JOBS SCORE: 98/RANK: 7

INCOME	AREA	U.S. AVG	EMPLOYMENT	AREA	U.S. AVG	LARGEST EMPLOYING INDUSTRY
Per capita income	$23,952	$23,420	Unemployment rate	4.6%	6.1%	Plastics and Rubber Products Manufacturing
Household income	$50,326	$46,060	Recent job growth	2.6%	.9%	
Household income < $25K	20.9%	26.4%	Projected future job growth	10.9%	15.1%	
Household income > $75K	23.9%	24.5%	White collar	45.1%	54.5%	
Household income growth	59.0%	57.3%	Blue collar	54.9%	45.5%	

COST OF LIVING SCORE: 32/RANK: 223

INDEXES & TAXES	AREA	U.S. AVG	HOUSING	AREA	U.S. AVG	NECESSITIES	AREA	U.S. AVG
Cost of Living Index	91.0	100.0	Median home price	$120,420	$160,100	Food Index	97.9	100.0
Financial Progress Index	117.8	100.0	Home price appreciation	4.1%	7.1%	Housing Index	74.8	100.0
Income tax rate	6.930%	4.625%	Median rent	$515	$670	Utilities Index	115.1	100.0
Sales tax rate	5.000%	6.474%	Homes owned	74.9%	63.9%	Transportation Index	107.2	100.0
Property tax rate	$23.1	$15.6	Homes rented	18.2%	25.3%	Healthcare Index	102.1	100.0
			Housing affordability	68.0%	54.5%	Miscellaneous Cost Index	92.3	100.0

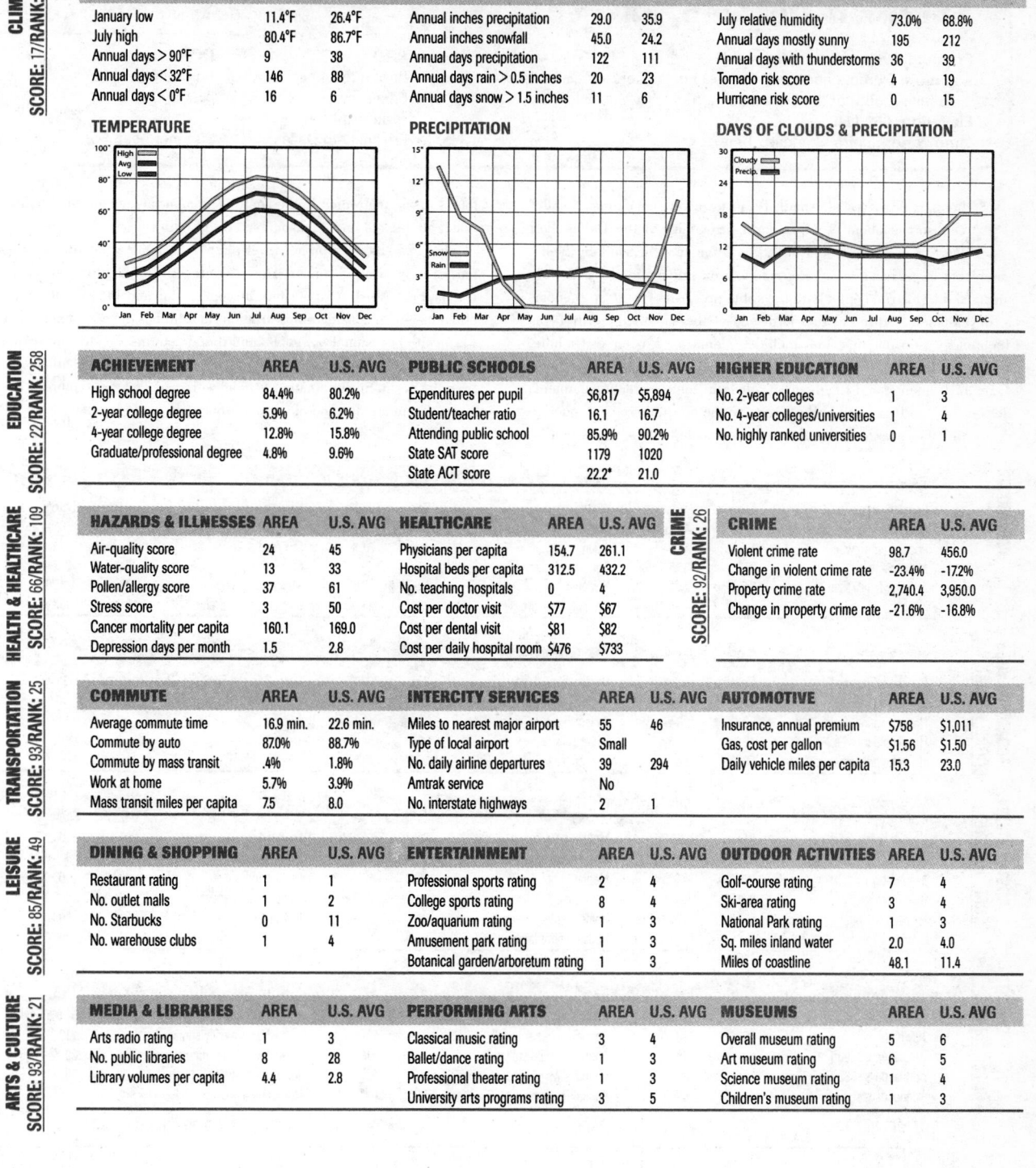

CLIMATE SCORE: 17/RANK: 273

TEMPERATURE	AREA	U.S. AVG	PRECIPITATION	AREA	U.S. AVG	COMFORTS & HAZARDS	AREA	U.S. AVG
January low	11.4°F	26.4°F	Annual inches precipitation	29.0	35.9	July relative humidity	73.0%	68.8%
July high	80.4°F	86.7°F	Annual inches snowfall	45.0	24.2	Annual days mostly sunny	195	212
Annual days > 90°F	9	38	Annual days precipitation	122	111	Annual days with thunderstorms	36	39
Annual days < 32°F	146	88	Annual days rain > 0.5 inches	20	23	Tornado risk score	4	19
Annual days < 0°F	16	6	Annual days snow > 1.5 inches	11	6	Hurricane risk score	0	15

TEMPERATURE

PRECIPITATION

DAYS OF CLOUDS & PRECIPITATION

EDUCATION SCORE: 22/RANK: 258

ACHIEVEMENT	AREA	U.S. AVG	PUBLIC SCHOOLS	AREA	U.S. AVG	HIGHER EDUCATION	AREA	U.S. AVG
High school degree	84.4%	80.2%	Expenditures per pupil	$6,817	$5,894	No. 2-year colleges	1	3
2-year college degree	5.9%	6.2%	Student/teacher ratio	16.1	16.7	No. 4-year colleges/universities	1	4
4-year college degree	12.8%	15.8%	Attending public school	85.9%	90.2%	No. highly ranked universities	0	1
Graduate/professional degree	4.8%	9.6%	State SAT score	1179	1020			
			State ACT score	22.2*	21.0			

HEALTH & HEALTHCARE SCORE: 66/RANK: 109

HAZARDS & ILLNESSES	AREA	U.S. AVG	HEALTHCARE	AREA	U.S. AVG	CRIME	AREA	U.S. AVG
Air-quality score	24	45	Physicians per capita	154.7	261.1	Violent crime rate	98.7	456.0
Water-quality score	13	33	Hospital beds per capita	312.5	432.2	Change in violent crime rate	-23.4%	-17.2%
Pollen/allergy score	37	61	No. teaching hospitals	0	4	Property crime rate	2,740.4	3,950.0
Stress score	3	50	Cost per doctor visit	$77	$67	Change in property crime rate	-21.6%	-16.8%
Cancer mortality per capita	160.1	169.0	Cost per dental visit	$81	$82			
Depression days per month	1.5	2.8	Cost per daily hospital room	$476	$733			

CRIME SCORE: 92/RANK: 26

TRANSPORTATION SCORE: 93/RANK: 25

COMMUTE	AREA	U.S. AVG	INTERCITY SERVICES	AREA	U.S. AVG	AUTOMOTIVE	AREA	U.S. AVG
Average commute time	16.9 min.	22.6 min.	Miles to nearest major airport	55	46	Insurance, annual premium	$758	$1,011
Commute by auto	87.0%	88.7%	Type of local airport	Small		Gas, cost per gallon	$1.56	$1.50
Commute by mass transit	.4%	1.8%	No. daily airline departures	39	294	Daily vehicle miles per capita	15.3	23.0
Work at home	5.7%	3.9%	Amtrak service	No				
Mass transit miles per capita	7.5	8.0	No. interstate highways	2	1			

LEISURE SCORE: 85/RANK: 49

DINING & SHOPPING	AREA	U.S. AVG	ENTERTAINMENT	AREA	U.S. AVG	OUTDOOR ACTIVITIES	AREA	U.S. AVG
Restaurant rating	1	1	Professional sports rating	2	4	Golf-course rating	7	4
No. outlet malls	1	2	College sports rating	8	4	Ski-area rating	3	4
No. Starbucks	0	11	Zoo/aquarium rating	1	3	National Park rating	1	3
No. warehouse clubs	1	4	Amusement park rating	1	3	Sq. miles inland water	2.0	4.0
			Botanical garden/arboretum rating	1	3	Miles of coastline	48.1	11.4

ARTS & CULTURE SCORE: 93/RANK: 21

MEDIA & LIBRARIES	AREA	U.S. AVG	PERFORMING ARTS	AREA	U.S. AVG	MUSEUMS	AREA	U.S. AVG
Arts radio rating	1	3	Classical music rating	3	4	Overall museum rating	5	6
No. public libraries	8	28	Ballet/dance rating	1	3	Art museum rating	6	5
Library volumes per capita	4.4	2.8	Professional theater rating	1	3	Science museum rating	1	4
			University arts programs rating	3	5	Children's museum rating	1	3

Sherman-Denison, TX

Score: 50.6	**Rank: 221**

Profile: Small-town complex
Location: Extreme northeast Texas, 90 miles north of Dallas and 15 miles south of the Oklahoma border
Elevation: 669 feet
Time zone: Central Standard Time

PRO	**CON**
Strong local economy	Entertainment
Small-town atmosphere	Arts and culture
Proximity to Dallas	Summer heat

Sherman is a typical, small Texas town on the plains. Smaller Denison is about 6 miles north. Proximity to the Dallas–Fort Worth metroplex, a central U.S. location, and the availability of a good labor force, has allowed Sherman to grow into a mid-size manufacturing and industrial center with favorable prospects for future economic development. Sitting at the north end of the so-called North Texas Technology Corridor, the area includes plants for Procter & Gamble, Johnson & Johnson Medical, Kaiser Aluminum, Consolidated Container, Texas Instruments, and Raytheon. Aside from some recreational amenities on the Red River and Lake Texoma to the north, there isn't much to do locally. However, additional amenities and big-city services can be found in the metroplex to the south. The area has notably high educational attainment and a reasonable cost of living.

The area sits on a broad, level plain with areas of deciduous trees, particularly around town. The climate is similar to that of the Dallas–Fort Worth area—a mix of continental and humid subtropical climates—with considerable variations at all times of year. Summers are warm with occasional hot spells and thunderstorms. Winters are generally mild but with occasional cold snaps and snow as polar air invades from the north. Spring weather is changeable and severe weather is possible; the area is located close to "tornado alley."

POPULATION

DEMOGRAPHICS	AREA	U.S. AVG	ETHNIC COMPOSITION	AREA	U.S. AVG	RESIDENT PROFILE	AREA	U.S. AVG
Population	113,860		White	87.3%	75.1%	Single	38.5%	43.6%
Population density per sq. mile	121.9	447.3	Black	6.5%	12.3%	Married	61.5%	56.4%
Population growth	19.8%	16.1%	Asian	.9%	3.6%	Divorced	9.1%	8.4%
Median age	37.7	35.5	American Indian	.9%	.9%	Separated	2.8%	3.0%
Average family size	2.5	2.7	Hispanic	12.3%	12.5%	Married with children	27.5%	28.7%
			Diversity measure	28.1%	35.2%	Single with children	8.9%	10.1%

ECONOMY & JOBS SCORE: 74/RANK: 86

INCOME	AREA	U.S. AVG	EMPLOYMENT	AREA	U.S. AVG	LARGEST EMPLOYING INDUSTRY
Per capita income	$20,456	$23,420	Unemployment rate	7.7%	6.1%	Computer and Electronic Product Manufacturing
Household income	$39,443	$46,060	Recent job growth	2.5%	.9%	
Household income < $25K	30.8%	26.4%	Projected future job growth	11.7%	15.1%	
Household income > $75K	18.1%	24.5%	White collar	48.8%	54.5%	
Household income growth	56.1%	57.3%	Blue collar	51.2%	45.5%	

COST OF LIVING SCORE: 92/RANK: 25

INDEXES & TAXES	AREA	U.S. AVG	HOUSING	AREA	U.S. AVG	NECESSITIES	AREA	U.S. AVG
Cost of Living Index	81.6	100.0	Median home price	$84,050	$160,100	Food Index	91.3	100.0
Financial Progress Index	103.0	100.0	Home price appreciation	6.7%	7.1%	Housing Index	52.2	100.0
Income tax rate	0.000%	4.625%	Median rent	$503	$670	Utilities Index	100.0	100.0
Sales tax rate	8.250%	6.474%	Homes owned	62.2%	63.9%	Transportation Index	104.9	100.0
Property tax rate	$22.6	$15.6	Homes rented	20.5%	25.3%	Healthcare Index	99.7	100.0
			Housing affordability	65.0%	54.5%	Miscellaneous Cost Index	99.0	100.0

CLIMATE SCORE: 87/RANK: 41

TEMPERATURE	AREA	U.S. AVG	PRECIPITATION	AREA	U.S. AVG	COMFORTS & HAZARDS	AREA	U.S. AVG
January low	33.9°F	26.4°F	Annual inches precipitation	32.0	35.9	July relative humidity	67.0%	68.8%
July high	96.1°F	86.7°F	Annual inches snowfall	3.0	24.2	Annual days mostly sunny	233	212
Annual days > 90°F	88	38	Annual days precipitation	79	111	Annual days with thunderstorms	46	39
Annual days < 32°F	39	88	Annual days rain > 0.5 inches	19	23	Tornado risk score	33	19
Annual days < 0°F	0	6	Annual days snow > 1.5 inches	1	6	Hurricane risk score	8	15

TEMPERATURE

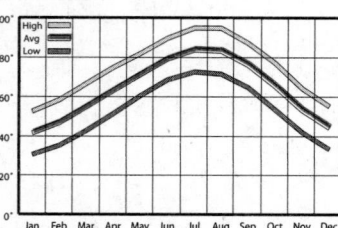

PRECIPITATION

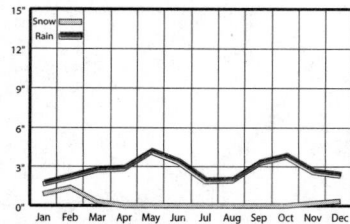

DAYS OF CLOUDS & PRECIPITATION

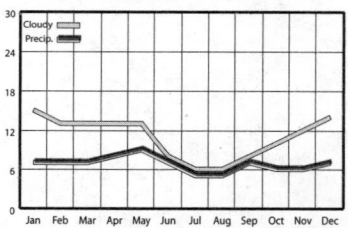

EDUCATION SCORE: 53/RANK: 156

ACHIEVEMENT	AREA	U.S. AVG	PUBLIC SCHOOLS	AREA	U.S. AVG	HIGHER EDUCATION	AREA	U.S. AVG
High school degree	78.5%	80.2%	Expenditures per pupil	$5,540	$5,894	No. 2-year colleges	1	3
2-year college degree	7.4%	6.2%	Student/teacher ratio	14.1	16.7	No. 4-year colleges/universities	1	4
4-year college degree	12.6%	15.8%	Attending public school	97.2%	90.2%	No. highly ranked universities	0	1
Graduate/professional degree	6.0%	9.6%	State SAT score	993*	1020			
			State ACT score	20.1	21.0			

HEALTH & HEALTHCARE SCORE: 57/RANK: 140 **CRIME SCORE: 50/RANK: 163**

HAZARDS & ILLNESSES	AREA	U.S. AVG	HEALTHCARE	AREA	U.S. AVG	CRIME	AREA	U.S. AVG
Air-quality score	24	45	Physicians per capita	181.8	261.1	Violent crime rate	342.2	456.0
Water-quality score	96	33	Hospital beds per capita	557.9	432.2	Change in violent crime rate	-29.8%	-17.2%
Pollen/allergy score	85	61	No. teaching hospitals	0	4	Property crime rate	4,190.8	3,950.0
Stress score	80	50	Cost per doctor visit	$67	$67	Change in property crime rate	-11.9%	-16.8%
Cancer mortality per capita	158.4	169.0	Cost per dental visit	$81	$82			
Depression days per month	5.9	2.8	Cost per daily hospital room	$563	$733			

TRANSPORTATION SCORE: 6/RANK: 311

COMMUTE	AREA	U.S. AVG	INTERCITY SERVICES	AREA	U.S. AVG	AUTOMOTIVE	AREA	U.S. AVG
Average commute time	24.9 min.	22.6 min.	Miles to nearest major airport	55	46	Insurance, annual premium	$925	$1,011
Commute by auto	93.1%	88.7%	Type of local airport	Medium		Gas, cost per gallon	$1.43	$1.50
Commute by mass transit	.2%	1.8%	No. daily airline departures	247	294	Daily vehicle miles per capita	37.8	23.0
Work at home	3.3%	3.9%	Amtrak service	No				
Mass transit miles per capita	4.4	8.0	No. interstate highways	1	1			

LEISURE SCORE: 18/RANK: 269

DINING & SHOPPING	AREA	U.S. AVG	ENTERTAINMENT	AREA	U.S. AVG	OUTDOOR ACTIVITIES	AREA	U.S. AVG
Restaurant rating	1	1	Professional sports rating	5	4	Golf-course rating	2	4
No. outlet malls	4	2	College sports rating	1	4	Ski-area rating	1	4
No. Starbucks	1	11	Zoo/aquarium rating	1	3	National Park rating	1	3
No. warehouse clubs	3	4	Amusement park rating	1	3	Sq. miles inland water	4.0	4.0
			Botanical garden/arboretum rating	1	3	Miles of coastline	0.0	11.4

ARTS & CULTURE SCORE: 25/RANK: 248

MEDIA & LIBRARIES	AREA	U.S. AVG	PERFORMING ARTS	AREA	U.S. AVG	MUSEUMS	AREA	U.S. AVG
Arts radio rating	1	3	Classical music rating	1	4	Overall museum rating	3	6
No. public libraries	8	28	Ballet/dance rating	1	3	Art museum rating	1	5
Library volumes per capita	3.3	2.8	Professional theater rating	1	3	Science museum rating	1	4
			University arts programs rating	2	5	Children's museum rating	1	3

Shreveport–Bossier City, LA

Score: 47.2   Rank: 242

Profile: Mid-size city
Location: Northwest corner of Louisiana near Texas border
Elevation: 30 feet
Time zone: Central Standard Time

PRO	CON
Downtown renewal	Heat and humidity
Cost of living	Economy
Cost of housing	Isolation

Shreveport is a commercial and cultural center for northwest Louisiana, northeast Texas, and southern Arkansas. In the early 20th century, the area experienced a major oil boom, which declined through the century. Recently a new riverfront entertainment district with nightlife and casinos has revitalized the downtown area. The city's museums and cultural amenities are among the state's best outside of New Orleans and Baton Rouge. There is plenty of outdoor and water recreation nearby. The crime rate and cost of living are by far the lowest in the state. Downsides include a soft economy and employment outlook, persistently hot summers, and a degree of isolation, although the area does have some commercial jet service.

The city sits on Red River bottomland with gently rolling terrain nearby especially to the west, with a mix of general agriculture, cotton plantations, and wooded areas throughout. At 209 feet, Shreveport is the highest city in the state. The climate is a mix of humid subtropical and continental types. Summer months are consistently still, warm, and humid, with temperatures frequently above 95°F. Winters are mild with cold spells of short duration. Below-freezing temperatures occur about 40 times per year, but temperatures drop below 15°F only 1 in 2 years. Rainfall is abundant with greater amounts in late spring and less in late summer. Measurable snowfall occurs 1 in 2 years.

POPULATION

DEMOGRAPHICS	AREA	U.S. AVG	ETHNIC COMPOSITION	AREA	U.S. AVG	RESIDENT PROFILE	AREA	U.S. AVG
Population	393,390		White	61.7%	75.1%	Single	47.9%	43.6%
Population density per sq. mile	169.8	447.3	Black	37.2%	12.3%	Married	52.1%	56.4%
Population growth	4.5%	16.1%	Asian	.6%	3.6%	Divorced	8.3%	8.4%
Median age	35.4	35.5	American Indian	.3%	.9%	Separated	6.2%	3.0%
Average family size	2.6	2.7	Hispanic	1.4%	12.5%	Married with children	26.0%	28.7%
			Diversity measure	51.3%	35.2%	Single with children	14.8%	10.1%

ECONOMY & JOBS — SCORE: 61/RANK: 127

INCOME	AREA	U.S. AVG	EMPLOYMENT	AREA	U.S. AVG	LARGEST EMPLOYING INDUSTRY
Per capita income	$20,652	$23,420	Unemployment rate	7.8%	6.1%	Healthcare and Social Assistance
Household income	$38,129	$46,060	Recent job growth	.8%	.9%	
Household income < $25K	34.0%	26.4%	Projected future job growth	10.2%	15.1%	
Household income > $75K	20.0%	24.5%	White collar	52.7%	54.5%	
Household income growth	66.8%	57.3%	Blue collar	47.3%	45.5%	

COST OF LIVING — SCORE: 70/RANK: 98

INDEXES & TAXES	AREA	U.S. AVG	HOUSING	AREA	U.S. AVG	NECESSITIES	AREA	U.S. AVG
Cost of Living Index	78.5	100.0	Median home price	$89,000	$160,100	Food Index	88.4	100.0
Financial Progress Index	103.5	100.0	Home price appreciation	5.0%	7.1%	Housing Index	55.3	100.0
Income tax rate	4.000%	4.625%	Median rent	$524	$670	Utilities Index	87.8	100.0
Sales tax rate	8.250%	6.474%	Homes owned	60.6%	63.9%	Transportation Index	94.7	100.0
Property tax rate	$11.0	$15.6	Homes rented	23.1%	25.3%	Healthcare Index	91.9	100.0
			Housing affordability	58.0%	54.5%	Miscellaneous Cost Index	93.6	100.0

CLIMATE — SCORE: 72/RANK: 93

TEMPERATURE	AREA	U.S. AVG	PRECIPITATION	AREA	U.S. AVG	COMFORTS & HAZARDS	AREA	U.S. AVG
January low	37.8°F	26.4°F	Annual inches precipitation	45.0	35.9	July relative humidity	71.0%	68.8%
July high	93.8°F	86.7°F	Annual inches snowfall	1.0	24.2	Annual days mostly sunny	217	212
Annual days > 90°F	87	38	Annual days precipitation	97	111	Annual days with thunderstorms	54	39
Annual days < 32°F	1	88	Annual days rain > 0.5 inches	29	23	Tornado risk score	45	19
Annual days < 0°F	0	6	Annual days snow > 1.5 inches	1	6	Hurricane risk score	15	15

TEMPERATURE

PRECIPITATION

DAYS OF CLOUDS & PRECIPITATION

EDUCATION — SCORE: 28/RANK: 237

ACHIEVEMENT	AREA	U.S. AVG	PUBLIC SCHOOLS	AREA	U.S. AVG	HIGHER EDUCATION	AREA	U.S. AVG
High school degree	79.0%	80.2%	Expenditures per pupil	$5,118	$5,894	No. 2-year colleges	2	3
2-year college degree	3.7%	6.2%	Student/teacher ratio	16.3	16.7	No. 4-year colleges/universities	2	4
4-year college degree	12.6%	15.8%	Attending public school	93.5%	90.2%	No. highly ranked universities	1	1
Graduate/professional degree	6.5%	9.6%	State SAT score	1122	1020			
			State ACT score	19.6*	21.0			

HEALTH & HEALTHCARE — SCORE: 49/RANK: 168   CRIME — SCORE: 18/RANK: 269

HAZARDS & ILLNESSES	AREA	U.S. AVG	HEALTHCARE	AREA	U.S. AVG	CRIME	AREA	U.S. AVG
Air-quality score	6	45	Physicians per capita	399.1	261.1	Violent crime rate	707.7	456.0
Water-quality score	30	33	Hospital beds per capita	664.5	432.2	Change in violent crime rate	-21.4%	-17.2%
Pollen/allergy score	62	61	No. teaching hospitals	3	4	Property crime rate	5,202.4	3,950.0
Stress score	73	50	Cost per doctor visit	$52	$67	Change in property crime rate	-23.7%	-16.8%
Cancer mortality per capita	183.5	169.0	Cost per dental visit	$63	$82			
Depression days per month	2.0	2.8	Cost per daily hospital room	$472	$733			

TRANSPORTATION — SCORE: 37/RANK: 206

COMMUTE	AREA	U.S. AVG	INTERCITY SERVICES	AREA	U.S. AVG	AUTOMOTIVE	AREA	U.S. AVG
Average commute time	21.9 min.	22.6 min.	Miles to nearest major airport	1	46	Insurance, annual premium	$1,126	$1,011
Commute by auto	92.8%	88.7%	Type of local airport	Small		Gas, cost per gallon	$1.44	$1.50
Commute by mass transit	1.8%	1.8%	No. daily airline departures	66	294	Daily vehicle miles per capita	25.8	23.0
Work at home	1.8%	3.9%	Amtrak service	No				
Mass transit miles per capita	6.1	8.0	No. interstate highways	2	1			

LEISURE SCORE: 17/RANK: 274

DINING & SHOPPING	AREA	U.S. AVG	ENTERTAINMENT	AREA	U.S. AVG	OUTDOOR ACTIVITIES	AREA	U.S. AVG
Restaurant rating	1	1	Professional sports rating	3	4	Golf-course rating	2	4
No. outlet malls	0	2	College sports rating	2	4	Ski-area rating	1	4
No. Starbucks	0	11	Zoo/aquarium rating	1	3	National Park rating	1	3
No. warehouse clubs	3	4	Amusement park rating	3	3	Sq. miles inland water	5.0	4.0
			Botanical garden/arboretum rating	4	3	Miles of coastline	0.0	11.4

ARTS & CULTURE SCORE: 43/RANK: 187

MEDIA & LIBRARIES	AREA	U.S. AVG	PERFORMING ARTS	AREA	U.S. AVG	MUSEUMS	AREA	U.S. AVG
Arts radio rating	1	3	Classical music rating	4	4	Overall museum rating	6	6
No. public libraries	33	28	Ballet/dance rating	5	3	Art museum rating	5	5
Library volumes per capita	2.3	2.8	Professional theater rating	1	3	Science museum rating	5	4
			University arts programs rating	5	5	Children's museum rating	1	3

Sioux City, IA-NE

Score: 41.8   Rank: 270

Profile: Small agricultural town
Location: Extreme western Iowa at the Missouri River and Nebraska border
Elevation: 1,103 feet
Time zone: Central Standard Time

PRO
Stable economy
Cost of living
Small-town atmosphere

CON
Harsh winters
Entertainment
Low educational attainment

Sioux City, an important agricultural processing and shipping center on the Missouri River, serves the "tri-state" area of northwest Iowa, northeast Nebraska, and South Dakota. The metro area includes Dakota County in northeastern Nebraska and no other major towns. This quiet but industrious city contains food-processing plants and a few notable museums, and has a strong small-town feel. Cost of living and home prices are among the lowest in the state, and the violent crime rate is the second lowest in the country. The stable economy is one of the healthiest in Iowa. However, there isn't much to do in the area. Omaha is about 80 miles to the south, making Sioux City relatively less isolated than other towns in the upper Midwest and Great Plains region.

The city is located along the Missouri River in an area of flat, river valleys and rolling, mostly agricultural land. The business district lies in the river valley and the residential sections, for the most part, spread over nearby hills, which rise 100 feet to 200 feet. Located in the center of the continent and in the northern half of the Great Plains, the climate of Sioux City is typically continental and subject to the movements of weather systems. Under normal conditions winters are cold and summers are warm and humid but not excessively hot. Most precipitation arrives from April to September. Temperature and precipitation fluctuate considerably by season and from year to year, as occurs elsewhere in the northern plains. First freeze is early October, last is late May.

POPULATION

DEMOGRAPHICS	AREA	U.S. AVG	ETHNIC COMPOSITION	AREA	U.S. AVG	RESIDENT PROFILE	AREA	U.S. AVG
Population	123,670		White	94.7%	75.1%	Single	39.9%	43.6%
Population density per sq. mile	108.8	447.3	Black	1.3%	12.3%	Married	60.1%	56.4%
Population growth	7.5%	16.1%	Asian	1.7%	3.6%	Divorced	7.9%	8.4%
Median age	33.9	35.5	American Indian	1.5%	.9%	Separated	2.0%	3.0%
Average family size	2.6	2.7	Hispanic	3.1%	12.5%	Married with children	30.1%	28.7%
			Diversity measure	31.8%	35.2%	Single with children	8.9%	10.1%

ECONOMY & JOBS SCORE: 18/RANK: 271

INCOME	AREA	U.S. AVG	EMPLOYMENT	AREA	U.S. AVG	LARGEST EMPLOYING INDUSTRY
Per capita income	$21,437	$23,420	Unemployment rate	5.0%	6.1%	Food Manufacturing
Household income	$42,492	$46,060	Recent job growth	-3.2%	.9%	
Household income < $25K	26.8%	26.4%	Projected future job growth	18.4%	15.1%	
Household income > $75K	20.8%	24.5%	White collar	51.3%	54.5%	
Household income growth	68.5%	57.3%	Blue collar	48.7%	45.5%	

COST OF LIVING SCORE: 44/RANK: 184

INDEXES & TAXES	AREA	U.S. AVG	HOUSING	AREA	U.S. AVG	NECESSITIES	AREA	U.S. AVG
Cost of Living Index	84.5	100.0	Median home price	$84,270	$160,100	Food Index	94.6	100.0
Financial Progress Index	107.2	100.0	Home price appreciation	3.0%	7.1%	Housing Index	52.3	100.0
Income tax rate	8.920%	4.625%	Median rent	$552	$670	Utilities Index	128.1	100.0
Sales tax rate	7.000%	6.474%	Homes owned	65.2%	63.9%	Transportation Index	102.5	100.0
Property tax rate	$19.7	$15.6	Homes rented	26.1%	25.3%	Healthcare Index	96.4	100.0
			Housing affordability	60.0%	54.5%	Miscellaneous Cost Index	101.1	100.0

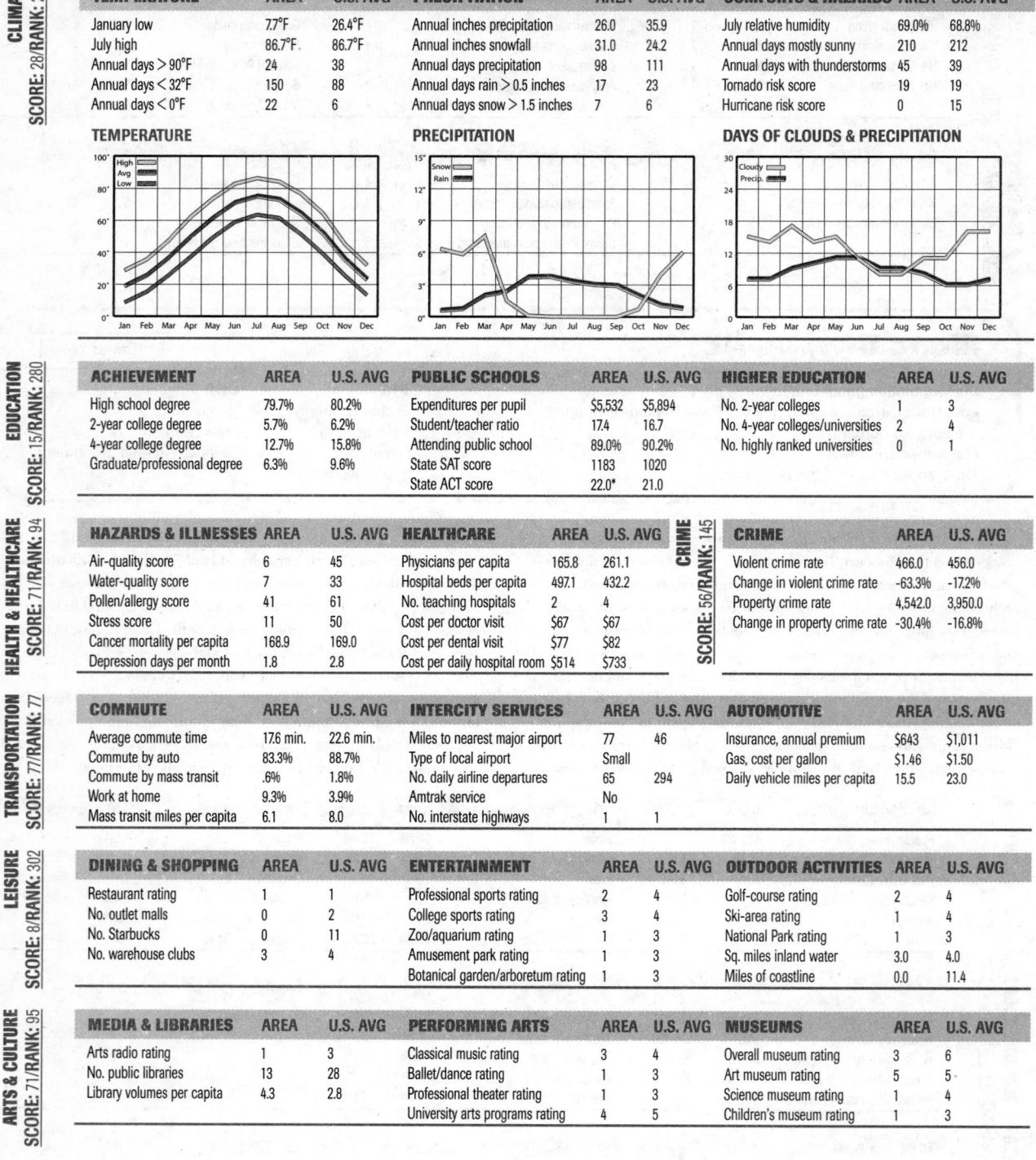

CLIMATE SCORE: 28/RANK: 237

TEMPERATURE	AREA	U.S. AVG	PRECIPITATION	AREA	U.S. AVG	COMFORTS & HAZARDS	AREA	U.S. AVG
January low	7.7°F	26.4°F	Annual inches precipitation	26.0	35.9	July relative humidity	69.0%	68.8%
July high	86.7°F	86.7°F	Annual inches snowfall	31.0	24.2	Annual days mostly sunny	210	212
Annual days > 90°F	24	38	Annual days precipitation	98	111	Annual days with thunderstorms	45	39
Annual days < 32°F	150	88	Annual days rain > 0.5 inches	17	23	Tornado risk score	19	19
Annual days < 0°F	22	6	Annual days snow > 1.5 inches	7	6	Hurricane risk score	0	15

TEMPERATURE

PRECIPITATION

DAYS OF CLOUDS & PRECIPITATION

EDUCATION SCORE: 15/RANK: 280

ACHIEVEMENT	AREA	U.S. AVG	PUBLIC SCHOOLS	AREA	U.S. AVG	HIGHER EDUCATION	AREA	U.S. AVG
High school degree	79.7%	80.2%	Expenditures per pupil	$5,532	$5,894	No. 2-year colleges	1	3
2-year college degree	5.7%	6.2%	Student/teacher ratio	17.4	16.7	No. 4-year colleges/universities	2	4
4-year college degree	12.7%	15.8%	Attending public school	89.0%	90.2%	No. highly ranked universities	0	1
Graduate/professional degree	6.3%	9.6%	State SAT score	1183	1020			
			State ACT score	22.0*	21.0			

HEALTH & HEALTHCARE SCORE: 71/RANK: 94

CRIME SCORE: 56/RANK: 145

HAZARDS & ILLNESSES	AREA	U.S. AVG	HEALTHCARE	AREA	U.S. AVG	CRIME	AREA	U.S. AVG
Air-quality score	6	45	Physicians per capita	165.8	261.1	Violent crime rate	466.0	456.0
Water-quality score	7	33	Hospital beds per capita	497.1	432.2	Change in violent crime rate	-63.3%	-17.2%
Pollen/allergy score	41	61	No. teaching hospitals	2	4	Property crime rate	4,542.0	3,950.0
Stress score	11	50	Cost per doctor visit	$67	$67	Change in property crime rate	-30.4%	-16.8%
Cancer mortality per capita	168.9	169.0	Cost per dental visit	$77	$82			
Depression days per month	1.8	2.8	Cost per daily hospital room	$514	$733			

TRANSPORTATION SCORE: 77/RANK: 77

COMMUTE	AREA	U.S. AVG	INTERCITY SERVICES	AREA	U.S. AVG	AUTOMOTIVE	AREA	U.S. AVG
Average commute time	17.6 min.	22.6 min.	Miles to nearest major airport	77	46	Insurance, annual premium	$643	$1,011
Commute by auto	83.3%	88.7%	Type of local airport	Small		Gas, cost per gallon	$1.46	$1.50
Commute by mass transit	.6%	1.8%	No. daily airline departures	65	294	Daily vehicle miles per capita	15.5	23.0
Work at home	9.3%	3.9%	Amtrak service	No				
Mass transit miles per capita	6.1	8.0	No. interstate highways	1	1			

LEISURE SCORE: 8/RANK: 302

DINING & SHOPPING	AREA	U.S. AVG	ENTERTAINMENT	AREA	U.S. AVG	OUTDOOR ACTIVITIES	AREA	U.S. AVG
Restaurant rating	1	1	Professional sports rating	2	4	Golf-course rating	2	4
No. outlet malls	0	2	College sports rating	3	4	Ski-area rating	1	4
No. Starbucks	0	11	Zoo/aquarium rating	1	3	National Park rating	1	3
No. warehouse clubs	3	4	Amusement park rating	1	3	Sq. miles inland water	3.0	4.0
			Botanical garden/arboretum rating	1	3	Miles of coastline	0.0	11.4

ARTS & CULTURE SCORE: 71/RANK: 95

MEDIA & LIBRARIES	AREA	U.S. AVG	PERFORMING ARTS	AREA	U.S. AVG	MUSEUMS	AREA	U.S. AVG
Arts radio rating	1	3	Classical music rating	3	4	Overall museum rating	3	6
No. public libraries	13	28	Ballet/dance rating	1	3	Art museum rating	5	5
Library volumes per capita	4.3	2.8	Professional theater rating	1	3	Science museum rating	1	4
			University arts programs rating	4	5	Children's museum rating	1	3

Sioux Falls, SD

Score: 66.3   **Rank:** 100

Profile: Small city
Location: Eastern South Dakota near the Iowa-Minnesota border at the junction of I-90 and I-29
Elevation: 1,427 feet
Time zone: Central Standard Time

PRO	CON
Small-town atmosphere	Cold winters
Strong economy	Isolation
Cost of living	Low ethnic diversity

Sioux Falls is the state's largest city and most important commercial and cultural center. This fairly typical Midwestern city has a strong and diverse economy. Business-friendly state laws have made it a center for the banking and credit-card industries with large operations for Wells Fargo, Citibank, and others. Although Gateway Computer moved its headquarters to San Diego, it still maintains a presence. Agricultural and meatpacking activities are also in the area. Aside from winter weather, the quality of life is high, with such attributes as low density, cleanliness, low crime rates, and an assortment of modest cultural amenities. For those seeking more, Minneapolis–St. Paul is 270 miles east. The combination of relatively high incomes and job growth with low cost of living, housing costs, and taxes creates one of the country's most favorable economic climates. A 2001 study of "Kid Friendly Cities" rated the area no. 3 out of 140 cities and a *Ladies Home Journal* 2002 study rated it as the no. 3 "least stressed" city.

Sioux Falls is located in the Big Sioux River Valley in southeast South Dakota. The surrounding terrain is gently rolling grassland with some wooded areas. The climate is Great Plains continental with frequent weather changes. In fall and winter, cold air masses can move in rapidly, bringing gusty winds and temperature drops of 20°F to 30°F in 1 day. There are one or two heavy snowfalls each winter. Severe cold spells usually last only a few days, but long stretches of below-freezing weather can occur. Summers are warm but not excessively hot; temperatures above 100°F occur only 1 in 3 years. Summer nights are pleasant. Rainfall is heaviest in spring and summer, and rain and melting snow can cause some flooding in the lower areas. Strong winds occur in all seasons. First freeze is early October, last is mid-May.

POPULATION

DEMOGRAPHICS	AREA	U.S. AVG	ETHNIC COMPOSITION	AREA	U.S. AVG	RESIDENT PROFILE	AREA	U.S. AVG
Population	180,200		White	98.2%	75.1%	Single	37.4%	43.6%
Population density per sq. mile	129.9	447.3	Black	.3%	12.3%	Married	62.6%	56.4%
Population growth	29.4%	16.1%	Asian	.6%	3.6%	Divorced	6.0%	8.4%
Median age	33.7	35.5	American Indian	.8%	.9%	Separated	.9%	3.0%
Average family size	2.7	2.7	Hispanic	.4%	12.5%	Married with children	34.2%	28.7%
			Diversity measure	13.5%	35.2%	Single with children	6.8%	10.1%

ECONOMY & JOBS   SCORE: 38/RANK: 204

INCOME	AREA	U.S. AVG	EMPLOYMENT	AREA	U.S. AVG	LARGEST EMPLOYING INDUSTRY
Per capita income	$26,977	$23,420	Unemployment rate	2.3%	6.1%	Healthcare and Social Assistance
Household income	$52,728	$46,060	Recent job growth	.6%	.9%	
Household income < $25K	19.1%	26.4%	Projected future job growth	22.5%	15.1%	
Household income > $75K	29.2%	24.5%	White collar	57.4%	54.5%	
Household income growth	88.9%	57.3%	Blue collar	42.6%	45.5%	

COST OF LIVING   SCORE: 79/RANK: 67

INDEXES & TAXES	AREA	U.S. AVG	HOUSING	AREA	U.S. AVG	NECESSITIES	AREA	U.S. AVG
Cost of Living Index	92.6	100.0	Median home price	$119,200	$160,100	Food Index	98.3	100.0
Financial Progress Index	121.3	100.0	Home price appreciation	5.2%	7.1%	Housing Index	74.0	100.0
Income tax rate	0.000%	4.625%	Median rent	$665	$670	Utilities Index	136.0	100.0
Sales tax rate	6.000%	6.474%	Homes owned	74.9%	63.9%	Transportation Index	98.6	100.0
Property tax rate	$18.3	$15.6	Homes rented	20.3%	25.3%	Healthcare Index	91.4	100.0
			Housing affordability	56.0%	54.5%	Miscellaneous Cost Index	100.3	100.0

CLIMATE SCORE: 19/RANK: 266

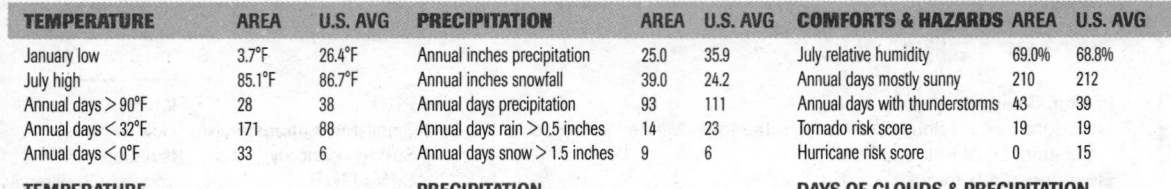

TEMPERATURE	AREA	U.S. AVG	PRECIPITATION	AREA	U.S. AVG	COMFORTS & HAZARDS	AREA	U.S. AVG
January low	3.7°F	26.4°F	Annual inches precipitation	25.0	35.9	July relative humidity	69.0%	68.8%
July high	85.1°F	86.7°F	Annual inches snowfall	39.0	24.2	Annual days mostly sunny	210	212
Annual days > 90°F	28	38	Annual days precipitation	93	111	Annual days with thunderstorms	43	39
Annual days < 32°F	171	88	Annual days rain > 0.5 inches	14	23	Tornado risk score	19	19
Annual days < 0°F	33	6	Annual days snow > 1.5 inches	9	6	Hurricane risk score	0	15

TEMPERATURE

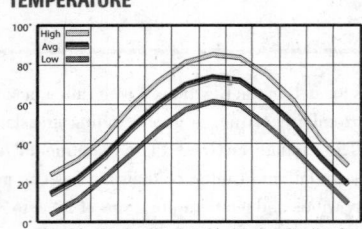

PRECIPITATION

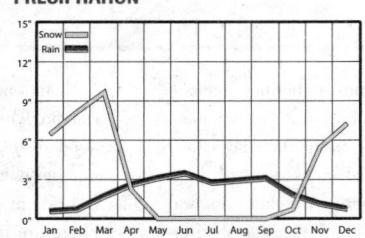

DAYS OF CLOUDS & PRECIPITATION

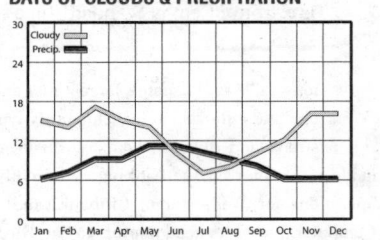

EDUCATION SCORE: 69/RANK: 102

ACHIEVEMENT	AREA	U.S. AVG	PUBLIC SCHOOLS	AREA	U.S. AVG	HIGHER EDUCATION	AREA	U.S. AVG
High school degree	88.5%	80.2%	Expenditures per pupil	$4,780	$5,894	No. 2-year colleges	2	3
2-year college degree	7.8%	6.2%	Student/teacher ratio	16.4	16.7	No. 4-year colleges/universities	2	4
4-year college degree	19.2%	15.8%	Attending public school	88.6%	90.2%	No. highly ranked universities	1	1
Graduate/professional degree	6.7%	9.6%	State SAT score	1176	1020			
			State ACT score	21.4*	21.0			

HEALTH & HEALTHCARE SCORE: 93/RANK: 21

CRIME SCORE: 95/RANK: 16

HAZARDS & ILLNESSES	AREA	U.S. AVG	HEALTHCARE	AREA	U.S. AVG	CRIME	AREA	U.S. AVG
Air-quality score	6	45	Physicians per capita	372.4	261.1	Violent crime rate	222.8	456.0
Water-quality score	4	33	Hospital beds per capita	664.7	432.2	Change in violent crime rate	-40.3%	-17.2%
Pollen/allergy score	37	61	No. teaching hospitals	2	4	Property crime rate	2,657.8	3,950.0
Stress score	1	50	Cost per doctor visit	$65	$67	Change in property crime rate	-32.7%	-16.8%
Cancer mortality per capita	163.5	169.0	Cost per dental visit	$79	$82			
Depression days per month	2.3	2.8	Cost per daily hospital room	$623	$733			

TRANSPORTATION SCORE: 84/RANK: 56

COMMUTE	AREA	U.S. AVG	INTERCITY SERVICES	AREA	U.S. AVG	AUTOMOTIVE	AREA	U.S. AVG
Average commute time	17.3 min.	22.6 min.	Miles to nearest major airport	3	46	Insurance, annual premium	$663	$1,011
Commute by auto	84.6%	88.7%	Type of local airport	Small		Gas, cost per gallon	$1.50	$1.50
Commute by mass transit	.2%	1.8%	No. daily airline departures	65	294	Daily vehicle miles per capita	17.9	23.0
Work at home	8.0%	3.9%	Amtrak service	No				
Mass transit miles per capita	7.0	8.0	No. interstate highways	2	1			

LEISURE SCORE: 20/RANK: 262

DINING & SHOPPING	AREA	U.S. AVG	ENTERTAINMENT	AREA	U.S. AVG	OUTDOOR ACTIVITIES	AREA	U.S. AVG
Restaurant rating	1	1	Professional sports rating	2	4	Golf-course rating	2	4
No. outlet malls	0	2	College sports rating	1	4	Ski-area rating	2	4
No. Starbucks	0	11	Zoo/aquarium rating	3	3	National Park rating	1	3
No. warehouse clubs	3	4	Amusement park rating	4	3	Sq. miles inland water	2.0	4.0
			Botanical garden/arboretum rating	1	3	Miles of coastline	0.0	11.4

ARTS & CULTURE SCORE: 21/RANK: 258

MEDIA & LIBRARIES	AREA	U.S. AVG	PERFORMING ARTS	AREA	U.S. AVG	MUSEUMS	AREA	U.S. AVG
Arts radio rating	1	3	Classical music rating	4	4	Overall museum rating	5	6
No. public libraries	15	28	Ballet/dance rating	1	3	Art museum rating	6	5
Library volumes per capita	3.0	2.8	Professional theater rating	1	3	Science museum rating	7	4
			University arts programs rating	4	5	Children's museum rating	5	3

South Bend, IN

Score: 62.2   Rank: 132

Profile: Diversified college town
Location: Extreme northern Indiana at Michigan border
Elevation: 700 feet
Time zone: Eastern Standard Time (no daylight savings time)

PRO	CON
College-town amenities	Harsh winters
Diverse economy	Crime rate
Nearby recreation	Unemployment

South Bend is located about 30 miles inland from where the Michigan-Indiana border intersects with the lower portion of Lake Michigan. The city has a well-balanced mix of industry, education, and cultural amenities. Once an automotive center and home to the Studebaker Motor Company, South Bend is still a manufacturing center for automotive and defense products. The 150-year-old Notre Dame University adds variety, college amenities, and a set of nationally followed sports programs, although the arts and culture influence is not as strong as in some large university towns. The College Football Hall of Fame is a special attraction. Good, local parks and the Lake Michigan shore provide recreation. Unemployment and crime have been problems recently and the area climate receives the full brunt of the Lake Michigan lake effect.

The area sits on a level, glacial, coastal plain with gently rolling terrain mainly to the south and east. The downwind location from Lake Michigan effects summer and winter weather. The lake moderates temperatures in all seasons but produces periods of high humidity and extended cloudiness year-round and heavy snows in winter. Precipitation is fairly well distributed, with most occurring in the summer as thundershowers. First freeze is early October, last is early May.

POPULATION

DEMOGRAPHICS	AREA	U.S. AVG	ETHNIC COMPOSITION	AREA	U.S. AVG	RESIDENT PROFILE	AREA	U.S. AVG
Population	267,120		White	85.8%	75.1%	Single	46.2%	43.6%
Population density per sq. mile	584.1	447.3	Black	11.4%	12.3%	Married	53.8%	56.4%
Population growth	8.1%	16.1%	Asian	1.4%	3.6%	Divorced	9.9%	8.4%
Median age	34.7	35.5	American Indian	.4%	.9%	Separated	2.6%	3.0%
Average family size	2.5	2.7	Hispanic	2.9%	12.5%	Married with children	24.6%	28.7%
			Diversity measure	32.8%	35.2%	Single with children	11.3%	10.1%

ECONOMY & JOBS SCORE: 60/RANK: 132

INCOME	AREA	U.S. AVG	EMPLOYMENT	AREA	U.S. AVG	LARGEST EMPLOYING INDUSTRY
Per capita income	$22,230	$23,420	Unemployment rate	5.1%	6.1%	Transportation Equipment Manufacturing
Household income	$43,880	$46,060	Recent job growth	-.1%	.9%	
Household income < $25K	24.9%	26.4%	Projected future job growth	16.2%	15.1%	
Household income > $75K	21.9%	24.5%	White collar	56.3%	54.5%	
Household income growth	54.8%	57.3%	Blue collar	43.7%	45.5%	

COST OF LIVING SCORE: 85/RANK: 49

INDEXES & TAXES	AREA	U.S. AVG	HOUSING	AREA	U.S. AVG	NECESSITIES	AREA	U.S. AVG
Cost of Living Index	82.4	100.0	Median home price	$92,500	$160,100	Food Index	92.4	100.0
Financial Progress Index	113.4	100.0	Home price appreciation	4.4%	7.1%	Housing Index	57.5	100.0
Income tax rate	3.400%	4.625%	Median rent	$603	$670	Utilities Index	108.0	100.0
Sales tax rate	6.000%	6.474%	Homes owned	69.3%	63.9%	Transportation Index	94.4	100.0
Property tax rate	$17.2	$15.6	Homes rented	22.8%	25.3%	Healthcare Index	97.0	100.0
			Housing affordability	57.0%	54.5%	Miscellaneous Cost Index	96.3	100.0

CLIMATE SCORE: 27/RANK: 239

TEMPERATURE	AREA	U.S. AVG	PRECIPITATION	AREA	U.S. AVG	COMFORTS & HAZARDS	AREA	U.S. AVG
January low	17.5°F	26.4°F	Annual inches precipitation	35.0	35.9	July relative humidity	72.0%	68.8%
July high	84.0°F	86.7°F	Annual inches snowfall	35.0	24.2	Annual days mostly sunny	182	212
Annual days > 90°F	14	38	Annual days precipitation	131	111	Annual days with thunderstorms	41	39
Annual days < 32°F	134	88	Annual days rain > 0.5 inches	23	23	Tornado risk score	74	19
Annual days < 0°F	10	6	Annual days snow > 1.5 inches	16	6	Hurricane risk score	2	15

TEMPERATURE

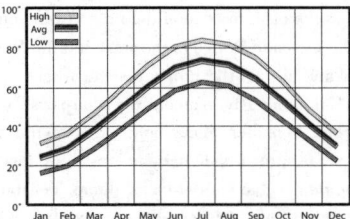

PRECIPITATION

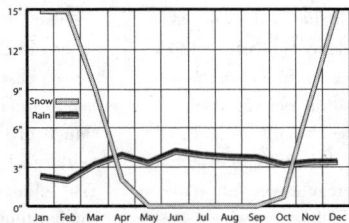

DAYS OF CLOUDS & PRECIPITATION

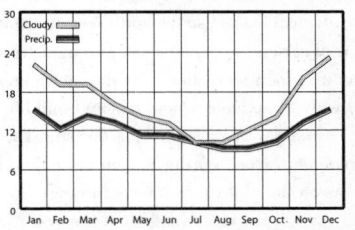

EDUCATION — SCORE: 37/RANK: 208

ACHIEVEMENT	AREA	U.S. AVG	PUBLIC SCHOOLS	AREA	U.S. AVG	HIGHER EDUCATION	AREA	U.S. AVG
High school degree	82.4%	80.2%	Expenditures per pupil	$6,439	$5,894	No. 2-year colleges	3	3
2-year college degree	5.4%	6.2%	Student/teacher ratio	17.2	16.7	No. 4-year colleges/universities	4	4
4-year college degree	14.4%	15.8%	Attending public school	84.0%	90.2%	No. highly ranked universities	2	1
Graduate/professional degree	9.2%	9.6%	State SAT score	1004*	1020			
			State ACT score	21.6	21.0			

HEALTH & HEALTHCARE — SCORE: 38/RANK: 203

HAZARDS & ILLNESSES	AREA	U.S. AVG	HEALTHCARE	AREA	U.S. AVG
Air-quality score	59	45	Physicians per capita	246.3	261.1
Water-quality score	13	33	Hospital beds per capita	333.3	432.2
Pollen/allergy score	56	61	No. teaching hospitals	4	4
Stress score	47	50	Cost per doctor visit	$56	$67
Cancer mortality per capita	181.4	169.0	Cost per dental visit	$78	$82
Depression days per month	2.0	2.8	Cost per daily hospital room	$816	$733

CRIME — SCORE: 10/RANK: 298

CRIME	AREA	U.S. AVG
Violent crime rate	459.1	456.0
Change in violent crime rate	-4.3%	-17.2%
Property crime rate	5,650.9	3,950.0
Change in property crime rate	7.5%	-16.8%

TRANSPORTATION — SCORE: 62/RANK: 126

COMMUTE	AREA	U.S. AVG	INTERCITY SERVICES	AREA	U.S. AVG	AUTOMOTIVE	AREA	U.S. AVG
Average commute time	20.2 min.	22.6 min.	Miles to nearest major airport	3	46	Insurance, annual premium	$793	$1,011
Commute by auto	89.3%	88.7%	Type of local airport	Small		Gas, cost per gallon	$1.45	$1.50
Commute by mass transit	2.1%	1.8%	No. daily airline departures	54	294	Daily vehicle miles per capita	21.4	23.0
Work at home	2.7%	3.9%	Amtrak service	Yes				
Mass transit miles per capita	7.1	8.0	No. interstate highways	1	1			

LEISURE — SCORE: 30/RANK: 231

DINING & SHOPPING	AREA	U.S. AVG	ENTERTAINMENT	AREA	U.S. AVG	OUTDOOR ACTIVITIES	AREA	U.S. AVG
Restaurant rating	1	1	Professional sports rating	3	4	Golf-course rating	3	4
No. outlet malls	2	2	College sports rating	6	4	Ski-area rating	3	4
No. Starbucks	0	11	Zoo/aquarium rating	3	3	National Park rating	1	3
No. warehouse clubs	3	4	Amusement park rating	1	3	Sq. miles inland water	2.0	4.0
			Botanical garden/arboretum rating	2	3	Miles of coastline	0.0	11.4

ARTS & CULTURE — SCORE: 72/RANK: 92

MEDIA & LIBRARIES	AREA	U.S. AVG	PERFORMING ARTS	AREA	U.S. AVG	MUSEUMS	AREA	U.S. AVG
Arts radio rating	1	3	Classical music rating	4	4	Overall museum rating	6	6
No. public libraries	13	28	Ballet/dance rating	1	3	Art museum rating	6	5
Library volumes per capita	3.8	2.8	Professional theater rating	1	3	Science museum rating	2	4
			University arts programs rating	8	5	Children's museum rating	6	3

Spokane, WA

Score: 54.8   **Rank:** 190

Profile: Mid-size city
Location: Extreme eastern Washington, 20 miles west of the Idaho border
Elevation: 1,880 feet
Time zone: Pacific Standard Time

PRO	CON
Attractive setting and downtown	Harsh winters
Arts and culture	Crime rate
Cost of living	Low ethnic diversity

Spokane, part of the "inland Northwest," is the financial, cultural, and retail center for a large area of Washington, Idaho, and western Montana. The dry climate and relatively plain infrastructure are atypical of the Pacific Northwest. Advantages include a diverse economy of agriculture, commerce, and industry and plenty of nearby outdoor and mountain recreation. The downtown area is clean, lively, and popular with attractive new and restored buildings, and the notable 100-acre Riverfront Park, once a world's fair site. The modest but diverse cultural amenities are noteworthy for a city with this size and location. Residential areas on the plateau to the south range from average to very attractive. The area to the east blends into Coeur d'Alene, Idaho, a growing recreation and retirement area. Southwest Airlines provides ample, inexpensive air service to other areas in the West. Overall the city is attractive, livable, and inexpensive. Except for rugged winters, recent job declines, and a relatively high crime rate for the region, Spokane is a nice place to live. It may be a little underrated in the rankings.

The city sits on the eastern edge of the broad Columbia Basin, which is bounded by the Cascade Range to the west and the Rocky Mountains to the east. Spokane sits on the upper plateau where the long gradual slope from the Columbia River meets the sharp rise of the Rockies. Much of the urban area lies along both sides of the Spokane River with residential areas spreading to plateau crests 500 feet above the city. The climate combines characteristics of damp, coastal weather with high-altitude, high-latitude, arid conditions. Rainfall is less than 50% of that directly west of the Cascades. However, the location receives more clouds and rain than most of eastern Washington. Continental air masses occasionally bring sub-zero winter temperatures. Summer weather is mild and arid while winter varies from coastal and wet to cold and dry. Like most of the Pacific Northwest, the majority of precipitation falls from October to April. Winter days are often cloudy or foggy with an occasional snowfall of several inches. First freeze is early October, last is early May.

POPULATION

DEMOGRAPHICS	AREA	U.S. AVG	ETHNIC COMPOSITION	AREA	U.S. AVG	RESIDENT PROFILE	AREA	U.S. AVG
Population	427,506		White	94.3%	75.1%	Single	43.1%	43.6%
Population density per sq. mile	242.4	447.3	Black	1.5%	12.3%	Married	56.9%	56.4%
Population growth	18.3%	16.1%	Asian	2.3%	3.6%	Divorced	10.5%	8.4%
Median age	35.8	35.5	American Indian	1.4%	.9%	Separated	2.4%	3.0%
Average family size	2.6	2.7	Hispanic	2.9%	12.5%	Married with children	29.0%	28.7%
			Diversity measure	18.7%	35.2%	Single with children	10.6%	10.1%

ECONOMY & JOBS — SCORE: 17/RANK: 273

INCOME	AREA	U.S. AVG	EMPLOYMENT	AREA	U.S. AVG	LARGEST EMPLOYING INDUSTRY
Per capita income	$22,438	$23,420	Unemployment rate	6.4%	6.1%	Primary Metal Manufacturing
Household income	$42,105	$46,060	Recent job growth	-.3%	.9%	
Household income < $25K	28.0%	26.4%	Projected future job growth	15.7%	15.1%	
Household income > $75K	21.0%	24.5%	White collar	55.7%	54.5%	
Household income growth	63.0%	57.3%	Blue collar	44.3%	45.5%	

COST OF LIVING — SCORE: 69/RANK: 103

INDEXES & TAXES	AREA	U.S. AVG	HOUSING	AREA	U.S. AVG	NECESSITIES	AREA	U.S. AVG
Cost of Living Index	89.4	100.0	Median home price	$108,500	$160,100	Food Index	105.3	100.0
Financial Progress Index	100.3	100.0	Home price appreciation	3.3%	7.1%	Housing Index	67.4	100.0
Income tax rate	0.000%	4.625%	Median rent	$569	$670	Utilities Index	75.9	100.0
Sales tax rate	8.100%	6.474%	Homes owned	66.6%	63.9%	Transportation Index	100.2	100.0
Property tax rate	$13.7	$15.6	Homes rented	27.1%	25.3%	Healthcare Index	117.8	100.0
			Housing affordability	57.0%	54.5%	Miscellaneous Cost Index	105.0	100.0

CLIMATE — SCORE: 30/RANK: 231

TEMPERATURE	AREA	U.S. AVG	PRECIPITATION	AREA	U.S. AVG	COMFORTS & HAZARDS	AREA	U.S. AVG
January low	19.6°F	26.4°F	Annual inches precipitation	17.0	35.9	July relative humidity	63.0%	68.8%
July high	84.3°F	86.7°F	Annual inches snowfall	53.0	24.2	Annual days mostly sunny	176	212
Annual days > 90°F	21	38	Annual days precipitation	114	111	Annual days with thunderstorms	11	39
Annual days < 32°F	141	88	Annual days rain > 0.5 inches	7	23	Tornado risk score	0	19
Annual days < 0°F	5	6	Annual days snow > 1.5 inches	13	6	Hurricane risk score	0	15

TEMPERATURE

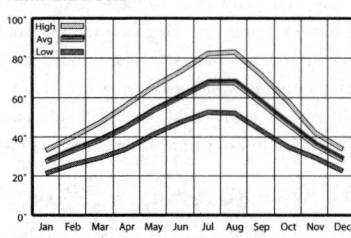

PRECIPITATION

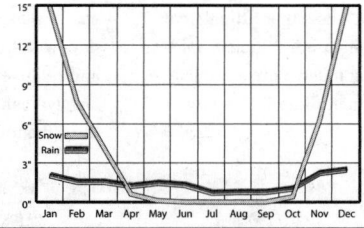

DAYS OF CLOUDS & PRECIPITATION

EDUCATION — SCORE: 77/RANK: 76

ACHIEVEMENT	AREA	U.S. AVG	PUBLIC SCHOOLS	AREA	U.S. AVG	HIGHER EDUCATION	AREA	U.S. AVG
High school degree	88.1%	80.2%	Expenditures per pupil	$5,879	$5,894	No. 2-year colleges	3	3
2-year college degree	9.7%	6.2%	Student/teacher ratio	20.3	16.7	No. 4-year colleges/universities	3	4
4-year college degree	16.2%	15.8%	Attending public school	90.8%	90.2%	No. highly ranked universities	1	1
Graduate/professional degree	9.2%	9.6%	State SAT score	1062*	1020			
			State ACT score	22.5	21.0			

HEALTH & HEALTHCARE — SCORE: 67/RANK: 107

HAZARDS & ILLNESSES	AREA	U.S. AVG	HEALTHCARE	AREA	U.S. AVG
Air-quality score	81	45	Physicians per capita	268.3	261.1
Water-quality score	5	33	Hospital beds per capita	388.1	432.2
Pollen/allergy score	42	61	No. teaching hospitals	3	4
Stress score	96	50	Cost per doctor visit	$67	$67
Cancer mortality per capita	163.8	169.0	Cost per dental visit	$112	$82
Depression days per month	3.2	2.8	Cost per daily hospital room	$609	$733

CRIME — SCORE: 13/RANK: 287

CRIME	AREA	U.S. AVG
Violent crime rate	457.6	456.0
Change in violent crime rate	-10.3%	-17.2%
Property crime rate	5,872.0	3,950.0
Change in property crime rate	-5.0%	-16.8%

TRANSPORTATION SCORE: 33/RANK: 221

COMMUTE	AREA	U.S. AVG	INTERCITY SERVICES	AREA	U.S. AVG	AUTOMOTIVE	AREA	U.S. AVG
Average commute time	21.2 min.	22.6 min.	Miles to nearest major airport	6	46	Insurance, annual premium	$1,230	$1,011
Commute by auto	87.6%	88.7%	Type of local airport	Medium		Gas, cost per gallon	$1.59	$1.50
Commute by mass transit	2.0%	1.8%	No. daily airline departures	115	294	Daily vehicle miles per capita	20.5	23.0
Work at home	4.8%	3.9%	Amtrak service	Yes				
Mass transit miles per capita	0.0	8.0	No. interstate highways	1	1			

LEISURE SCORE: 49/RANK: 168

DINING & SHOPPING	AREA	U.S. AVG	ENTERTAINMENT	AREA	U.S. AVG	OUTDOOR ACTIVITIES	AREA	U.S. AVG
Restaurant rating	1	1	Professional sports rating	3	4	Golf-course rating	2	4
No. outlet malls	0	2	College sports rating	3	4	Ski-area rating	9	4
No. Starbucks	12	11	Zoo/aquarium rating	1	3	National Park rating	3	3
No. warehouse clubs	4	4	Amusement park rating	1	3	Sq. miles inland water	3.0	4.0
			Botanical garden/arboretum rating	2	3	Miles of coastline	0.0	11.4

ARTS & CULTURE SCORE: 62/RANK: 125

MEDIA & LIBRARIES	AREA	U.S. AVG	PERFORMING ARTS	AREA	U.S. AVG	MUSEUMS	AREA	U.S. AVG
Arts radio rating	1	3	Classical music rating	4	4	Overall museum rating	5	6
No. public libraries	16	28	Ballet/dance rating	1	3	Art museum rating	5	5
Library volumes per capita	2.7	2.8	Professional theater rating	1	3	Science museum rating	1	4
			University arts programs rating	5	5	Children's museum rating	3	3

Springfield, IL

Score: 53.9   Rank: 196

Profile: Capital city
Location: Near the geographic center of Illinois
Elevation: 613 feet
Time zone: Central Standard Time

PRO	CON
Capital-city amenities	Recreation
Historic interest	Performing arts
Cost of living	Low ethnic diversity

Springfield, the state capital, is a major agricultural center with a strong government presence. This quiet town with a fairly well-educated population has a substantial heritage built around Abraham Lincoln's residence and activities. It is "altogether fitting" that the Lincoln memorabilia should be mixed into such a traditional, mid-American city. The low cost of living makes it that much more attractive. Aside from historic sites, however, there isn't much to do in the city or surrounding area.

Springfield is located in the middle of a vast agricultural plain with rolling terrain near the Sangamon River and Spring Creek. Numerous deciduous trees grow in the city itself. Climate is typical continental with sharp, seasonal changes. Summers bring sunny, clear, warm, and humid days with frequent afternoon thundershowers. Windy, changeable springs and relatively calm autumns with periods of warm, dry, Indian summers are typical. Winters are fairly cold. Precipitation is evenly spread throughout the year. First freeze is mid-October, last is mid-April.

POPULATION

DEMOGRAPHICS	AREA	U.S. AVG	ETHNIC COMPOSITION	AREA	U.S. AVG	RESIDENT PROFILE	AREA	U.S. AVG
Population	203,201		White	94.9%	75.1%	Single	39.4%	43.6%
Population density per sq. mile	171.8	447.3	Black	4.0%	12.3%	Married	60.6%	56.4%
Population growth	7.2%	16.1%	Asian	.6%	3.6%	Divorced	8.7%	8.4%
Median age	37.8	35.5	American Indian	.2%	.9%	Separated	1.6%	3.0%
Average family size	2.6	2.7	Hispanic	1.2%	12.5%	Married with children	30.1%	28.7%
			Diversity measure	22.4%	35.2%	Single with children	8.9%	10.1%

ECONOMY & JOBS SCORE: 68/RANK: 102

INCOME	AREA	U.S. AVG	EMPLOYMENT	AREA	U.S. AVG	LARGEST EMPLOYING INDUSTRY
Per capita income	$24,419	$23,420	Unemployment rate	5.4%	6.1%	Healthcare and Social Assistance
Household income	$45,936	$46,060	Recent job growth	-.4%	.9%	
Household income < $25K	24.1%	26.4%	Projected future job growth	9.8%	15.1%	
Household income > $75K	23.9%	24.5%	White collar	65.2%	54.5%	
Household income growth	51.3%	57.3%	Blue collar	34.8%	45.5%	

COST OF LIVING — SCORE: 59/RANK: 134

INDEXES & TAXES	AREA	U.S. AVG	HOUSING	AREA	U.S. AVG	NECESSITIES	AREA	U.S. AVG
Cost of Living Index	81.6	100.0	Median home price	$91,100	$160,100	Food Index	94.7	100.0
Financial Progress Index	120.0	100.0	Home price appreciation	2.1%	7.1%	Housing Index	56.6	100.0
Income tax rate	3.000%	4.625%	Median rent	$555	$670	Utilities Index	102.0	100.0
Sales tax rate	7.250%	6.474%	Homes owned	71.3%	63.9%	Transportation Index	97.5	100.0
Property tax rate	$22.3	$15.6	Homes rented	22.8%	25.3%	Healthcare Index	96.0	100.0
			Housing affordability	61.0%	54.5%	Miscellaneous Cost Index	92.9	100.0

CLIMATE — SCORE: 31/RANK: 227

TEMPERATURE	AREA	U.S. AVG	PRECIPITATION	AREA	U.S. AVG	COMFORTS & HAZARDS	AREA	U.S. AVG
January low	18.6°F	26.4°F	Annual inches precipitation	35.0	35.9	July relative humidity	71.0%	68.8%
July high	86.6°F	86.7°F	Annual inches snowfall	22.0	24.2	Annual days mostly sunny	200	212
Annual days > 90°F	28	38	Annual days precipitation	112	111	Annual days with thunderstorms	50	39
Annual days < 32°F	119	88	Annual days rain > 0.5 inches	20	23	Tornado risk score	34	19
Annual days < 0°F	8	6	Annual days snow > 1.5 inches	5	6	Hurricane risk score	2	15

TEMPERATURE

PRECIPITATION

DAYS OF CLOUDS & PRECIPITATION

EDUCATION — SCORE: 55/RANK: 149

ACHIEVEMENT	AREA	U.S. AVG	PUBLIC SCHOOLS	AREA	U.S. AVG	HIGHER EDUCATION	AREA	U.S. AVG
High school degree	87.4%	80.2%	Expenditures per pupil	$5,433	$5,894	No. 2-year colleges	2	3
2-year college degree	6.5%	6.2%	Student/teacher ratio	16.6	16.7	No. 4-year colleges/universities	0	4
4-year college degree	19.0%	15.8%	Attending public school	86.9%	90.2%	No. highly ranked universities	0	1
Graduate/professional degree	10.0%	9.6%	State SAT score	1179	1020			
			State ACT score	20.2*	21.0			

HEALTH & HEALTHCARE — SCORE: 70/RANK: 97

HAZARDS & ILLNESSES	AREA	U.S. AVG	HEALTHCARE	AREA	U.S. AVG
Air-quality score	49	45	Physicians per capita	432.1	261.1
Water-quality score	10	33	Hospital beds per capita	683.1	432.2
Pollen/allergy score	46	61	No. teaching hospitals	3	4
Stress score	42	50	Cost per doctor visit	$68	$67
Cancer mortality per capita	180.1	169.0	Cost per dental visit	$75	$82
Depression days per month	3.6	2.8	Cost per daily hospital room	$659	$733

CRIME — SCORE: 41/RANK: 194

CRIME	AREA	U.S. AVG
Violent crime rate	584.0	456.0
Change in violent crime rate	-31.2%	-17.2%
Property crime rate	3,959.8	3,950.0
Change in property crime rate	-22.8%	-16.8%

TRANSPORTATION — SCORE: 71/RANK: 96

COMMUTE	AREA	U.S. AVG	INTERCITY SERVICES	AREA	U.S. AVG	AUTOMOTIVE	AREA	U.S. AVG
Average commute time	19.5 min.	22.6 min.	Miles to nearest major airport	81	46	Insurance, annual premium	$895	$1,011
Commute by auto	91.1%	88.7%	Type of local airport	Large		Gas, cost per gallon	$1.48	$1.50
Commute by mass transit	.7%	1.8%	No. daily airline departures	731	294	Daily vehicle miles per capita	25.3	23.0
Work at home	4.1%	3.9%	Amtrak service	Yes				
Mass transit miles per capita	6.8	8.0	No. interstate highways	2	1			

LEISURE — SCORE: 16/RANK: 276

DINING & SHOPPING	AREA	U.S. AVG	ENTERTAINMENT	AREA	U.S. AVG	OUTDOOR ACTIVITIES	AREA	U.S. AVG
Restaurant rating	1	1	Professional sports rating	2	4	Golf-course rating	2	4
No. outlet malls	0	2	College sports rating	2	4	Ski-area rating	1	4
No. Starbucks	0	11	Zoo/aquarium rating	3	3	National Park rating	1	3
No. warehouse clubs	3	4	Amusement park rating	1	3	Sq. miles inland water	2.0	4.0
			Botanical garden/arboretum rating	7	3	Miles of coastline	0.0	11.4

ARTS & CULTURE — SCORE: 78/RANK: 72

MEDIA & LIBRARIES	AREA	U.S. AVG	PERFORMING ARTS	AREA	U.S. AVG	MUSEUMS	AREA	U.S. AVG
Arts radio rating	1	3	Classical music rating	3	4	Overall museum rating	7	6
No. public libraries	16	28	Ballet/dance rating	1	3	Art museum rating	7	5
Library volumes per capita	4.9	2.8	Professional theater rating	1	3	Science museum rating	5	4
			University arts programs rating	1	5	Children's museum rating	3	3

Springfield, MA

Score: 46.0 **Rank:** 251

Profile: Small city
Location: Southwest Massachusetts, on the Connecticut River, 6 miles north of the Connecticut border
Elevation: 179 feet
Time zone: Eastern Standard Time

PRO	CON
Nearby mountains	Future job growth
Central location	Winter climate
Cost of living	Violent crime

Springfield, the state's third-largest city, is a regional health, manufacturing, and finance center, and a center of innovation. Locals are credited with development of the Springfield Rifle, the 1895 Duryea motorcar, and basketball (thanks to Dr. James Naismith, in 1891), and maybe even the motorcycle. Today the modern downtown exhibits a sprinkling of history through its museums, buildings, and historic sites. The "five college" area to the north includes the University of Massachusetts in Amherst and Amherst, Holyoke, Smith, and Hampshire colleges. The Cost of Living Index at 104.5 is no bargain, but on a Massachusetts scale it is attractive, particularly scaled against local incomes and projected income growth. The employment picture is mixed, with low unemployment and job growth. Climate depresses the ranking, but even when included the area narrowly misses a higher rank.

The area sits in a broad valley in the western part of Massachusetts. Thickly wooded hills rise immediately to the east and west of the valley. The climate is continental with distinct seasons and highly variable weather. Bodies of water to the east and south have an effect. Summers are hot, humid, and calm with occasional thundershowers. The Berkshire Mountains to the west slow larger storm fronts. Winters bring frequent cold snaps and snow, particularly generated by moist mid-Atlantic storms colliding with cold, northerly air masses. First freeze is mid-October, last is late April.

POPULATION

DEMOGRAPHICS	AREA	U.S. AVG	ETHNIC COMPOSITION	AREA	U.S. AVG	RESIDENT PROFILE	AREA	U.S. AVG
Population	595,495		White	90.8%	75.1%	Single	48.0%	43.6%
Population density per sq. mile	183.0	447.3	Black	3.8%	12.3%	Married	52.0%	56.4%
Population growth	1.3%	16.1%	Asian	1.8%	3.6%	Divorced	8.1%	8.4%
Median age	36.3	35.5	American Indian	.3%	.9%	Separated	2.8%	3.0%
Average family size	2.5	2.7	Hispanic	5.3%	12.5%	Married with children	25.3%	28.7%
			Diversity measure	35.1%	35.2%	Single with children	9.8%	10.1%

ECONOMY & JOBS
SCORE: 72/RANK: 89

INCOME	AREA	U.S. AVG	EMPLOYMENT	AREA	U.S. AVG	LARGEST EMPLOYING INDUSTRY
Per capita income	$21,757	$23,420	Unemployment rate	5.7%	6.1%	Fabricated Metal Product Manufacturing
Household income	$43,948	$46,060	Recent job growth	-.4%	.9%	
Household income < $25K	28.0%	26.4%	Projected future job growth	5.8%	15.1%	
Household income > $75K	21.9%	24.5%	White collar	57.1%	54.5%	
Household income growth	39.0%	57.3%	Blue collar	42.9%	45.5%	

COST OF LIVING
SCORE: 25/RANK: 247

INDEXES & TAXES	AREA	U.S. AVG	HOUSING	AREA	U.S. AVG	NECESSITIES	AREA	U.S. AVG
Cost of Living Index	104.5	100.0	Median home price	$148,200	$160,100	Food Index	116.6	100.0
Financial Progress Index	89.6	100.0	Home price appreciation	9.3%	7.1%	Housing Index	92.0	100.0
Income tax rate	5.950%	4.625%	Median rent	$686	$670	Utilities Index	107.2	100.0
Sales tax rate	5.000%	6.474%	Homes owned	62.2%	63.9%	Transportation Index	111.5	100.0
Property tax rate	$17.8	$15.6	Homes rented	26.9%	25.3%	Healthcare Index	118.9	100.0
			Housing affordability	48.0%	54.5%	Miscellaneous Cost Index	107.4	100.0

CLIMATE
SCORE: 1/RANK: 327

TEMPERATURE	AREA	U.S. AVG	PRECIPITATION	AREA	U.S. AVG	COMFORTS & HAZARDS	AREA	U.S. AVG
January low	16.1°F	26.4°F	Annual inches precipitation	43.0	35.9	July relative humidity	68.0%	68.8%
July high	84.1°F	86.7°F	Annual inches snowfall	53.0	24.2	Annual days mostly sunny	188	212
Annual days > 90°F	20	38	Annual days precipitation	128	111	Annual days with thunderstorms	22	39
Annual days < 32°F	137	88	Annual days rain > 0.5 inches	26	23	Tornado risk score	19	19
Annual days < 0°F	6	6	Annual days snow > 1.5 inches	19	6	Hurricane risk score	16	15

TEMPERATURE

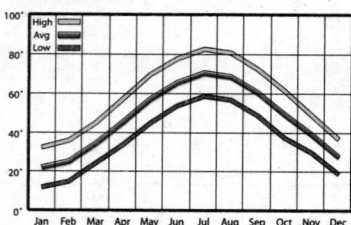

PRECIPITATION

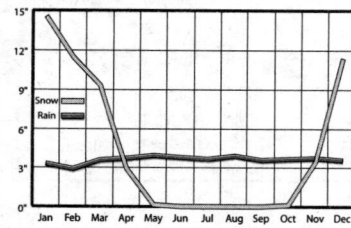

DAYS OF CLOUDS & PRECIPITATION

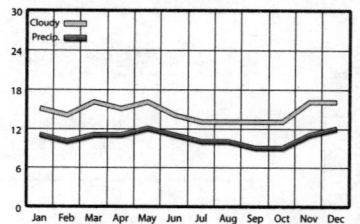

EDUCATION SCORE: 78/RANK: 73

ACHIEVEMENT	AREA	U.S. AVG	PUBLIC SCHOOLS	AREA	U.S. AVG	HIGHER EDUCATION	AREA	U.S. AVG
High school degree	81.6%	80.2%	Expenditures per pupil	$7,802	$5,894	No. 2-year colleges	4	3
2-year college degree	8.0%	6.2%	Student/teacher ratio	15.8	16.7	No. 4-year colleges/universities	11	4
4-year college degree	14.3%	15.8%	Attending public school	87.7%	90.2%	No. highly ranked universities	2	1
Graduate/professional degree	10.3%	9.6%	State SAT score	1038*	1020			
			State ACT score	22.3	21.0			

HEALTH & HEALTHCARE SCORE: 45/RANK: 181

CRIME SCORE: 15/RANK: 281

HAZARDS & ILLNESSES	AREA	U.S. AVG	HEALTHCARE	AREA	U.S. AVG	CRIME	AREA	U.S. AVG
Air-quality score	91	45	Physicians per capita	299.4	261.1	Violent crime rate	902.1	456.0
Water-quality score	72	33	Hospital beds per capita	349.2	432.2	Change in violent crime rate	20.0%	-17.2%
Pollen/allergy score	53	61	No. teaching hospitals	1	4	Property crime rate	3,643.1	3,950.0
Stress score	79	50	Cost per doctor visit	$81	$67	Change in property crime rate	-8.2%	-16.8%
Cancer mortality per capita	177.9	169.0	Cost per dental visit	$100	$82			
Depression days per month	3.3	2.8	Cost per daily hospital room	$672	$733			

TRANSPORTATION SCORE: 81/RANK: 61

COMMUTE	AREA	U.S. AVG	INTERCITY SERVICES	AREA	U.S. AVG	AUTOMOTIVE	AREA	U.S. AVG
Average commute time	21.8 min.	22.6 min.	Miles to nearest major airport	27	46	Insurance, annual premium	$1,335	$1,011
Commute by auto	87.5%	88.7%	Type of local airport	Medium		Gas, cost per gallon	$1.51	$1.50
Commute by mass transit	1.7%	1.8%	No. daily airline departures	209	294	Daily vehicle miles per capita	20.7	23.0
Work at home	4.2%	3.9%	Amtrak service	Yes				
Mass transit miles per capita	10.9	8.0	No. interstate highways	2	1			

LEISURE SCORE: 56/RANK: 143

DINING & SHOPPING	AREA	U.S. AVG	ENTERTAINMENT	AREA	U.S. AVG	OUTDOOR ACTIVITIES	AREA	U.S. AVG
Restaurant rating	1	1	Professional sports rating	3	4	Golf-course rating	5	4
No. outlet malls	1	2	College sports rating	4	4	Ski-area rating	7	4
No. Starbucks	3	11	Zoo/aquarium rating	2	3	National Park rating	1	3
No. warehouse clubs	4	4	Amusement park rating	3	3	Sq. miles inland water	3.0	4.0
			Botanical garden/arboretum rating	4	3	Miles of coastline	0.0	11.4

ARTS & CULTURE SCORE: 88/RANK: 37

MEDIA & LIBRARIES	AREA	U.S. AVG	PERFORMING ARTS	AREA	U.S. AVG	MUSEUMS	AREA	U.S. AVG
Arts radio rating	1	3	Classical music rating	4	4	Overall museum rating	9	6
No. public libraries	86	28	Ballet/dance rating	5	3	Art museum rating	7	5
Library volumes per capita	4.5	2.8	Professional theater rating	6	3	Science museum rating	5	4
			University arts programs rating	9	5	Children's museum rating	7	3

Springfield, MO

Score: 63.3   Rank: 119

Profile: Small city
Location: Southwest Missouri at the foot of the Ozark Mountains
Time zone: Central Standard Time
Elevation: 1,270 feet

PRO	CON
Nearby mountains	Economy
Nearby recreation	Property crime
Cost of living	Tourist sprawl

Springfield, the state's third largest city, serves as a gateway to the Ozark Mountains. The town is an important crossroads and agricultural center for livestock and poultry production. The Ozark Mountains provide recreation, scenic attractions, and relief from summer heat. There are a number of tourist attractions, some of which border on the tawdry. Branson, Missouri, a glittery entertainment and recreation center for country music fans, is 40 miles south. Branson's recent, rapid growth has helped the economy and put the area on the national map, but it has also created pockets of unattractive sprawl. The Cost of Living Index at 83.1 is attractive.

The flat to gently rolling terrain, located on an Ozark Mountain plateau, contains areas of mixed deciduous forest and farmland. The higher Ozarks and numerous, wooded creek valleys extend to the south and west into Arkansas. The climate is continental and "plateau," characterized by mild and changeable weather similar to other high places in southerly latitudes. Ozark winters are considerably milder and summers are appreciably cooler than conditions in nearby lower elevations. Hot, humid spells and cold can occur, but pockets of mountain air usually moderate them. First freeze is mid-October, last is mid-April.

POPULATION

DEMOGRAPHICS	AREA	U.S. AVG	ETHNIC COMPOSITION	AREA	U.S. AVG	RESIDENT PROFILE	AREA	U.S. AVG
Population	335,143		White	96.7%	75.1%	Single	37.2%	43.6%
Population density per sq. mile	809.5	447.3	Black	2.0%	12.3%	Married	62.8%	56.4%
Population growth	26.8%	16.1%	Asian	.5%	3.6%	Divorced	8.4%	8.4%
Median age	35.3	35.5	American Indian	.7%	.9%	Separated	2.1%	3.0%
Average family size	2.6	2.7	Hispanic	.8%	12.5%	Married with children	31.5%	28.7%
			Diversity measure	12.4%	35.2%	Single with children	8.0%	10.1%

ECONOMY & JOBS — SCORE: 43/RANK: 186

INCOME	AREA	U.S. AVG	EMPLOYMENT	AREA	U.S. AVG	LARGEST EMPLOYING INDUSTRY
Per capita income	$21,972	$23,420	Unemployment rate	4.0%	6.1%	Fabricated Metal Product Manufacturing
Household income	$40,086	$46,060	Recent job growth	3.5%	.9%	
Household income < $25K	30.3%	26.4%	Projected future job growth	21.1%	15.1%	
Household income > $75K	17.9%	24.5%	White collar	53.3%	54.5%	
Household income growth	65.4%	57.3%	Blue collar	46.7%	45.5%	

COST OF LIVING — SCORE: 65/RANK: 116

INDEXES & TAXES	AREA	U.S. AVG	HOUSING	AREA	U.S. AVG	NECESSITIES	AREA	U.S. AVG
Cost of Living Index	83.1	100.0	Median home price	$100,660	$160,100	Food Index	98.3	100.0
Financial Progress Index	102.8	100.0	Home price appreciation	4.1%	7.1%	Housing Index	62.5	100.0
Income tax rate	6.000%	4.625%	Median rent	$471	$670	Utilities Index	77.6	100.0
Sales tax rate	6.600%	6.474%	Homes owned	73.9%	63.9%	Transportation Index	94.9	100.0
Property tax rate	$8.9	$15.6	Homes rented	20.0%	25.3%	Healthcare Index	102.2	100.0
			Housing affordability	63.0%	54.5%	Miscellaneous Cost Index	95.9	100.0

CLIMATE — SCORE: 38/RANK: 205

TEMPERATURE	AREA	U.S. AVG	PRECIPITATION	AREA	U.S. AVG	COMFORTS & HAZARDS	AREA	U.S. AVG
January low	22.6°F	26.4°F	Annual inches precipitation	40.0	35.9	July relative humidity	70.0%	68.8%
July high	89.0°F	86.7°F	Annual inches snowfall	15.0	24.2	Annual days mostly sunny	216	212
Annual days > 90°F	40	38	Annual days precipitation	107	111	Annual days with thunderstorms	58	39
Annual days < 32°F	105	88	Annual days rain > 0.5 inches	27	23	Tornado risk score	30	19
Annual days < 0°F	3	6	Annual days snow > 1.5 inches	5	6	Hurricane risk score	3	15

TEMPERATURE

PRECIPITATION

DAYS OF CLOUDS & PRECIPITATION

EDUCATION — SCORE: 68/RANK: 106

ACHIEVEMENT	AREA	U.S. AVG	PUBLIC SCHOOLS	AREA	U.S. AVG	HIGHER EDUCATION	AREA	U.S. AVG
High school degree	82.8%	80.2%	Expenditures per pupil	$4,610	$5,894	No. 2-year colleges	2	3
2-year college degree	4.6%	6.2%	Student/teacher ratio	15.9	16.7	No. 4-year colleges/universities	6	4
4-year college degree	15.2%	15.8%	Attending public school	95.8%	90.2%	No. highly ranked universities	2	1
Graduate/professional degree	7.8%	9.6%	State SAT score	1165	1020			
			State ACT score	21.4*	21.0			

HEALTH & HEALTHCARE — SCORE: 96/RANK: 12

HAZARDS & ILLNESSES	AREA	U.S. AVG	HEALTHCARE	AREA	U.S. AVG
Air-quality score	17	45	Physicians per capita	262.0	261.1
Water-quality score	96	33	Hospital beds per capita	566.1	432.2
Pollen/allergy score	42	61	No. teaching hospitals	1	4
Stress score	58	50	Cost per doctor visit	$63	$67
Cancer mortality per capita	159.6	169.0	Cost per dental visit	$90	$82
Depression days per month	4.5	2.8	Cost per daily hospital room	$536	$733

CRIME — SCORE: 10/RANK: 297

CRIME	AREA	U.S. AVG
Violent crime rate	433.0	456.0
Change in violent crime rate	35.0%	-17.2%
Property crime rate	5,154.3	3,950.0
Change in property crime rate	10.3%	-16.8%

TRANSPORTATION — SCORE: 43/RANK: 186

COMMUTE	AREA	U.S. AVG	INTERCITY SERVICES	AREA	U.S. AVG	AUTOMOTIVE	AREA	U.S. AVG
Average commute time	21.0 min.	22.6 min.	Miles to nearest major airport	6	46	Insurance, annual premium	$841	$1,011
Commute by auto	91.1%	88.7%	Type of local airport	Small		Gas, cost per gallon	$1.40	$1.50
Commute by mass transit	.3%	1.8%	No. daily airline departures	56	294	Daily vehicle miles per capita	22.9	23.0
Work at home	6.1%	3.9%	Amtrak service	No				
Mass transit miles per capita	3.9	8.0	No. interstate highways	1	1			

LEISURE SCORE: 26/RANK: 245

DINING & SHOPPING	AREA	U.S. AVG	ENTERTAINMENT	AREA	U.S. AVG	OUTDOOR ACTIVITIES	AREA	U.S. AVG
Restaurant rating	1	1	Professional sports rating	2	4	Golf-course rating	2	4
No. outlet malls	3	2	College sports rating	3	4	Ski-area rating	1	4
No. Starbucks	0	11	Zoo/aquarium rating	3	3	National Park rating	4	3
No. warehouse clubs	4	4	Amusement park rating	1	3	Sq. miles inland water	2.0	4.0
			Botanical garden/arboretum rating	1	3	Miles of coastline	0.0	11.4

ARTS & CULTURE SCORE: 67/RANK: 106

MEDIA & LIBRARIES	AREA	U.S. AVG	PERFORMING ARTS	AREA	U.S. AVG	MUSEUMS	AREA	U.S. AVG
Arts radio rating	5	3	Classical music rating	4	4	Overall museum rating	5	6
No. public libraries	11	28	Ballet/dance rating	1	3	Art museum rating	4	5
Library volumes per capita	2.2	2.8	Professional theater rating	1	3	Science museum rating	1	4
			University arts programs rating	8	5	Children's museum rating	3	3

Stamford-Norwalk, CT

Score: 82.1   Rank: 30

Profile: Mid-size-city complex/Commuter community
Location: Southwestern tip of Connecticut along the Long Island Sound, 30 miles northeast of New York City
Elevation: 7 feet
Time zone: Eastern Standard Time

PRO	CON
Attractive setting	Cost of living
Proximity to New York City	Economy
Water recreation	Long commutes

Stamford is a manufacturing and commercial center containing the headquarters of over 20 Fortune 500 companies. Norwalk, 12 miles east, is primarily residential with a large population of New York City commuters. Both towns have a rich Revolutionary War–era history, and historic buildings and districts provide New England charm. The area features attractive residential areas with large wooded lots and high quality older and modern homes, some of the best in the region. A few unattractive areas of urban decay are also present, particularly in Stamford. Crime is low, and educational spending and attainment are relatively high. The natural setting and proximity to New York City's amenities and jobs make the area one of the most attractive in the state, but it comes at a price. At 202.9, Stamford-Norwalk has the highest Cost of Living Index in the country. Likewise, the median home price of $544,340 is also the nation's highest. Housing, property taxes, and transportation are major cost-of-living drivers but everything is expensive. The high overall ranking recognizes a broad assortment of amenities outside of cost of living.

Flat, marshy, coastal areas give way to hilly, densely forested terrain moving north from the Long Island Sound. Forests are mainly deciduous hardwoods, giving beautiful fall colors. The coastal climate features sea breezes, moderated temperatures both summer and winter, and reduced snow. Summers are warm and humid, but temperatures near the coast may be 5°F to 10°F cooler than inland. Winters are variable, with occasional cold snaps. Rain and snow mixes are common, and the area may receive snow while nearby New York City received rain. First freeze is mid-October, last is late April.

POPULATION

DEMOGRAPHICS	AREA	U.S. AVG	ETHNIC COMPOSITION	AREA	U.S. AVG	RESIDENT PROFILE	AREA	U.S. AVG
Population	359,642		White	84.9%	75.1%	Single	44.8%	43.6%
Population density per sq. mile	1,711.5	447.3	Black	8.9%	12.3%	Married	55.2%	56.4%
Population growth	9.0%	16.1%	Asian	4.0%	3.6%	Divorced	7.5%	8.4%
Median age	37.7	35.5	American Indian	.1%	.9%	Separated	2.2%	3.0%
Average family size	2.5	2.7	Hispanic	8.6%	12.5%	Married with children	24.4%	28.7%
			Diversity measure	42.4%	35.2%	Single with children	6.6%	10.1%

ECONOMY & JOBS SCORE: 57/RANK: 139

INCOME	AREA	U.S. AVG	EMPLOYMENT	AREA	U.S. AVG	LARGEST EMPLOYING INDUSTRY		
Per capita income	$46,951	$23,420	Unemployment rate	3.2%	6.1%	Machinery Manufacturing		
Household income	$86,410	$46,060	Recent job growth	-1.0%	.9%			
Household income < $25K	12.1%	26.4%	Projected future job growth	5.1%	15.1%			
Household income > $75K	56.3%	24.5%	White collar	73.5%	54.5%			
Household income growth	48.9%	57.3%	Blue collar	26.5%	45.5%			

COST OF LIVING SCORE: 0/RANK: 328

INDEXES & TAXES	AREA	U.S. AVG	HOUSING	AREA	U.S. AVG	NECESSITIES	AREA	U.S. AVG
Cost of Living Index	202.9	100.0	Median home price	$544,340	$160,100	Food Index	126.0	100.0
Financial Progress Index	90.7	100.0	Home price appreciation	12.3%	7.1%	Housing Index	338.1	100.0
Income tax rate	4.500%	4.625%	Median rent	$1,493	$670	Utilities Index	146.5	100.0
Sales tax rate	6.000%	6.474%	Homes owned	68.2%	63.9%	Transportation Index	109.5	100.0
Property tax rate	$15.2	$15.6	Homes rented	26.2%	25.3%	Healthcare Index	151.3	100.0
			Housing affordability	45.0%	54.5%	Miscellaneous Cost Index	122.5	100.0

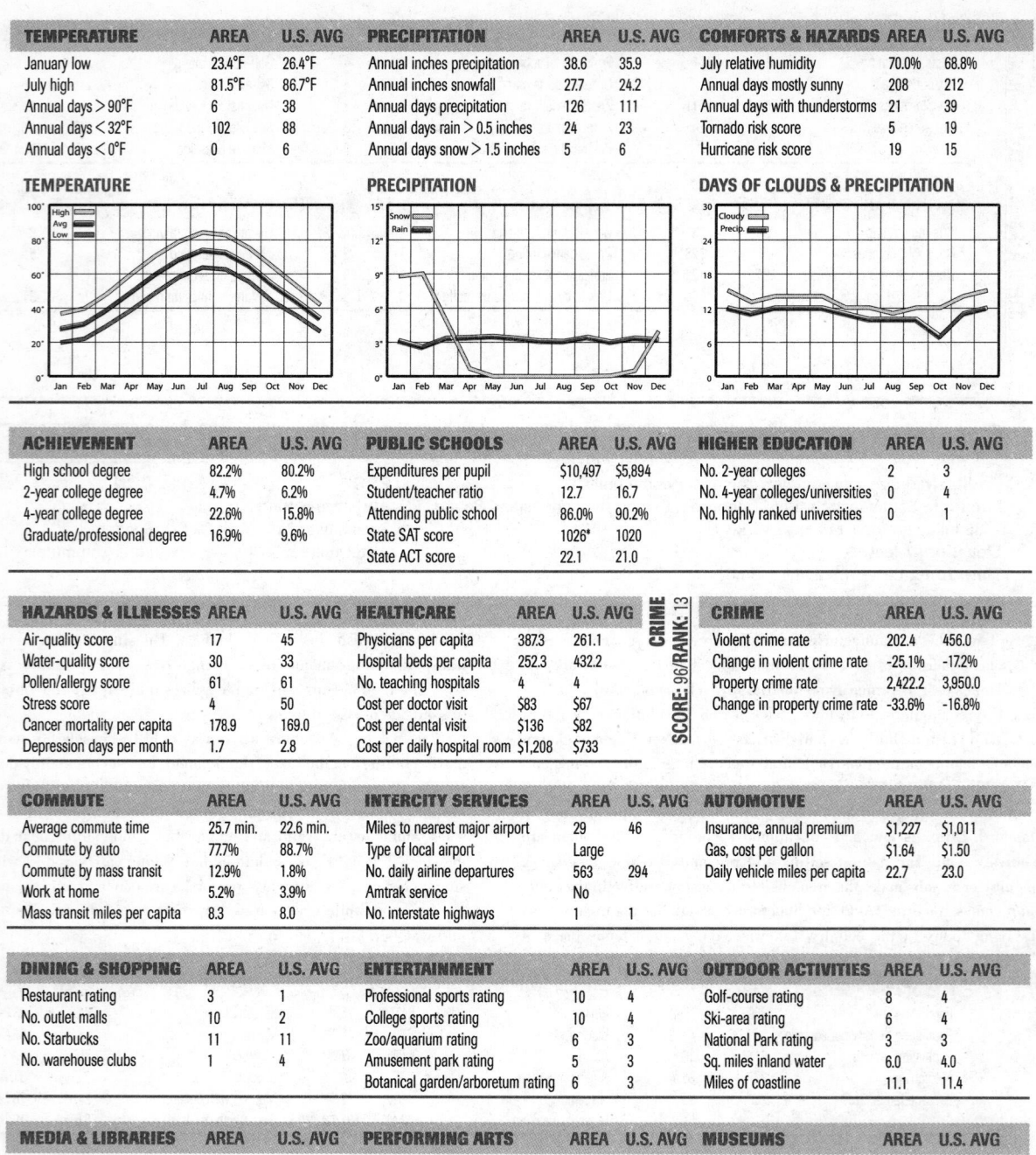

CLIMATE SCORE: 74/RANK: 84

TEMPERATURE	AREA	U.S. AVG	PRECIPITATION	AREA	U.S. AVG	COMFORTS & HAZARDS	AREA	U.S. AVG
January low	23.4°F	26.4°F	Annual inches precipitation	38.6	35.9	July relative humidity	70.0%	68.8%
July high	81.5°F	86.7°F	Annual inches snowfall	27.7	24.2	Annual days mostly sunny	208	212
Annual days > 90°F	6	38	Annual days precipitation	126	111	Annual days with thunderstorms	21	39
Annual days < 32°F	102	88	Annual days rain > 0.5 inches	24	23	Tornado risk score	5	19
Annual days < 0°F	0	6	Annual days snow > 1.5 inches	5	6	Hurricane risk score	19	15

TEMPERATURE — High / Avg / Low

PRECIPITATION — Snow / Rain

DAYS OF CLOUDS & PRECIPITATION — Cloudy / Precip.

EDUCATION SCORE: 88/RANK: 39

ACHIEVEMENT	AREA	U.S. AVG	PUBLIC SCHOOLS	AREA	U.S. AVG	HIGHER EDUCATION	AREA	U.S. AVG
High school degree	82.2%	80.2%	Expenditures per pupil	$10,497	$5,894	No. 2-year colleges	2	3
2-year college degree	4.7%	6.2%	Student/teacher ratio	12.7	16.7	No. 4-year colleges/universities	0	4
4-year college degree	22.6%	15.8%	Attending public school	86.0%	90.2%	No. highly ranked universities	0	1
Graduate/professional degree	16.9%	9.6%	State SAT score	1026*	1020			
			State ACT score	22.1	21.0			

HEALTH & HEALTHCARE SCORE: 24/RANK: 250

CRIME SCORE: 96/RANK: 13

HAZARDS & ILLNESSES	AREA	U.S. AVG	HEALTHCARE	AREA	U.S. AVG	CRIME	AREA	U.S. AVG
Air-quality score	17	45	Physicians per capita	387.3	261.1	Violent crime rate	202.4	456.0
Water-quality score	30	33	Hospital beds per capita	252.3	432.2	Change in violent crime rate	-25.1%	-17.2%
Pollen/allergy score	61	61	No. teaching hospitals	4	4	Property crime rate	2,422.2	3,950.0
Stress score	4	50	Cost per doctor visit	$83	$67	Change in property crime rate	-33.6%	-16.8%
Cancer mortality per capita	178.9	169.0	Cost per dental visit	$136	$82			
Depression days per month	1.7	2.8	Cost per daily hospital room	$1,208	$733			

TRANSPORTATION SCORE: 97/RANK: 12

COMMUTE	AREA	U.S. AVG	INTERCITY SERVICES	AREA	U.S. AVG	AUTOMOTIVE	AREA	U.S. AVG
Average commute time	25.7 min.	22.6 min.	Miles to nearest major airport	29	46	Insurance, annual premium	$1,227	$1,011
Commute by auto	77.7%	88.7%	Type of local airport	Large		Gas, cost per gallon	$1.64	$1.50
Commute by mass transit	12.9%	1.8%	No. daily airline departures	563	294	Daily vehicle miles per capita	22.7	23.0
Work at home	5.2%	3.9%	Amtrak service	No				
Mass transit miles per capita	8.3	8.0	No. interstate highways	1	1			

LEISURE SCORE: 87/RANK: 44

DINING & SHOPPING	AREA	U.S. AVG	ENTERTAINMENT	AREA	U.S. AVG	OUTDOOR ACTIVITIES	AREA	U.S. AVG
Restaurant rating	3	1	Professional sports rating	10	4	Golf-course rating	8	4
No. outlet malls	10	2	College sports rating	10	4	Ski-area rating	6	4
No. Starbucks	11	11	Zoo/aquarium rating	6	3	National Park rating	3	3
No. warehouse clubs	1	4	Amusement park rating	5	3	Sq. miles inland water	6.0	4.0
			Botanical garden/arboretum rating	6	3	Miles of coastline	11.1	11.4

ARTS & CULTURE SCORE: 82/RANK: 58

MEDIA & LIBRARIES	AREA	U.S. AVG	PERFORMING ARTS	AREA	U.S. AVG	MUSEUMS	AREA	U.S. AVG
Arts radio rating	4	3	Classical music rating	7	4	Overall museum rating	7	6
No. public libraries	17	28	Ballet/dance rating	7	3	Art museum rating	7	5
Library volumes per capita	4.2	2.8	Professional theater rating	8	3	Science museum rating	7	4
			University arts programs rating	5	5	Children's museum rating	8	3

State College, PA

		Score: 81.6 Rank: 31

Profile: College town
Location: Central Pennsylvania in the Nittany Valley at the central Allegheny ridge
Elevation: 1,200 feet
Time zone: Eastern Standard Time

PRO	CON
College-town amenities	Isolation
Educated population	Home prices
Attractive setting	Low ethnic diversity

The name State College says it all. The town is built around gigantic Penn State University, which provides the town with the usual college amenities and a strong sports program. At 75,000 in number, the student body outnumbers the town's non-student population, which is highly educated, 40% possessing graduate-level degrees. The area has the nation's second highest high school graduation rate, and crime rates are exceptionally low. The surrounding mountains provide some recreational opportunities. Although the area is centrally located, the orientation of mountains and highway thoroughfares makes it relatively isolated. Cost of living is modest for a college town, although median home prices are the third highest in the state.

The valley location, with its woods and rolling meadows, is green in summer and beautiful in fall. The Allegheny Plateau rises to the west. The climate is humid continental modified by the Great Lakes and the Allegheny ridges. Summers are typically sunny and warm but less humid than other areas of the state; readings over 90°F are rare. Winters are fairly cold with most daytime lows below freezing and an occasional subzero reading. There is plenty of precipitation but less than in areas west of the Alleghenies, closer to Lake Erie. The mountains block the heaviest snows and coldest arctic air but the area receives significant snow and cloud cover. First freeze is early October, last is mid-May.

POPULATION

DEMOGRAPHICS	AREA	U.S. AVG	ETHNIC COMPOSITION	AREA	U.S. AVG	RESIDENT PROFILE	AREA	U.S. AVG
Population	138,524		White	96.1%	75.1%	Single	44.0%	43.6%
Population density per sq. mile	125.1	447.3	Black	1.0%	12.3%	Married	56.0%	56.4%
Population growth	11.9%	16.1%	Asian	2.5%	3.6%	Divorced	5.4%	8.4%
Median age	28.7	35.5	American Indian	.1%	.9%	Separated	1.8%	3.0%
Average family size	2.6	2.7	Hispanic	.8%	12.5%	Married with children	30.7%	28.7%
			Diversity measure	17.3%	35.2%	Single with children	6.5%	10.1%

ECONOMY & JOBS   SCORE: 25/RANK: 246

INCOME	AREA	U.S. AVG	EMPLOYMENT	AREA	U.S. AVG	LARGEST EMPLOYING INDUSTRY
Per capita income	$19,594	$23,420	Unemployment rate	3.3%	6.1%	Computer and Electronic Product Manufacturing
Household income	$38,383	$46,060	Recent job growth	-1.8%	.9%	
Household income < $25K	31.1%	26.4%	Projected future job growth	17.0%	15.1%	
Household income > $75K	19.2%	24.5%	White collar	60.1%	54.5%	
Household income growth	46.8%	57.3%	Blue collar	39.9%	45.5%	

COST OF LIVING   SCORE: 63/RANK: 120

INDEXES & TAXES	AREA	U.S. AVG	HOUSING	AREA	U.S. AVG	NECESSITIES	AREA	U.S. AVG
Cost of Living Index	92.5	100.0	Median home price	$133,970	$160,100	Food Index	95.2	100.0
Financial Progress Index	88.4	100.0	Home price appreciation	5.3%	7.1%	Housing Index	83.2	100.0
Income tax rate	2.800%	4.625%	Median rent	$677	$670	Utilities Index	107.9	100.0
Sales tax rate	6.000%	6.474%	Homes owned	65.2%	63.9%	Transportation Index	89.4	100.0
Property tax rate	$13.8	$15.6	Homes rented	20.2%	25.3%	Healthcare Index	90.7	100.0
			Housing affordability	43.0%	54.5%	Miscellaneous Cost Index	102.0	100.0

CLIMATE   SCORE: 42/RANK: 190

TEMPERATURE	AREA	U.S. AVG	PRECIPITATION	AREA	U.S. AVG	COMFORTS & HAZARDS	AREA	U.S. AVG
January low	19.8°F	26.4°F	Annual inches precipitation	37.0	35.9	July relative humidity	67.0%	68.8%
July high	82.6°F	86.7°F	Annual inches snowfall	48.0	24.2	Annual days mostly sunny	180	212
Annual days > 90°F	8	38	Annual days precipitation	122	111	Annual days with thunderstorms	35	39
Annual days < 32°F	132	88	Annual days rain > 0.5 inches	20	23	Tornado risk score	4	19
Annual days < 0°F	4	6	Annual days snow > 1.5 inches	10	6	Hurricane risk score	6	15

TEMPERATURE

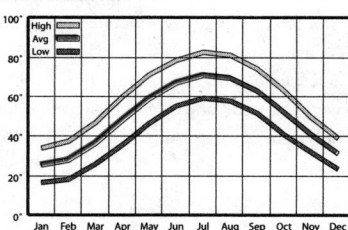

PRECIPITATION

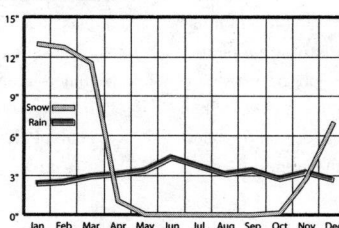

DAYS OF CLOUDS & PRECIPITATION

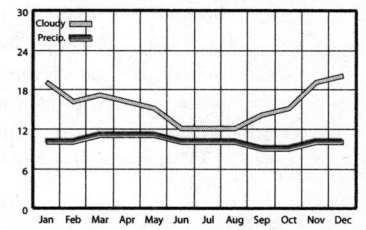

ACHIEVEMENT	AREA	U.S. AVG	PUBLIC SCHOOLS	AREA	U.S. AVG	HIGHER EDUCATION	AREA	U.S. AVG
High school degree	88.2%	80.2%	Expenditures per pupil	$6,953	$5,894	No. 2-year colleges	1	3
2-year college degree	4.8%	6.2%	Student/teacher ratio	15.4	16.7	No. 4-year colleges/universities	1	4
4-year college degree	18.8%	15.8%	Attending public school	91.5%	90.2%	No. highly ranked universities	0	1
Graduate/professional degree	17.5%	9.6%	State SAT score	1002*	1020			
			State ACT score	21.5	21.0			

HAZARDS & ILLNESSES	AREA	U.S. AVG	HEALTHCARE	AREA	U.S. AVG	CRIME	AREA	U.S. AVG
Air-quality score	6	45	Physicians per capita	192.0	261.1	Violent crime rate	120.0	456.0
Water-quality score	100	33	Hospital beds per capita	324.1	432.2	Change in violent crime rate	-21.2%	-17.2%
Pollen/allergy score	52	61	No. teaching hospitals	0	4	Property crime rate	2,242.6	3,950.0
Stress score	0	50	Cost per doctor visit	$60	$67	Change in property crime rate	-17.1%	-16.8%
Cancer mortality per capita	159.7	169.0	Cost per dental visit	$61	$82			
Depression days per month	.6	2.8	Cost per daily hospital room	$685	$733			

COMMUTE	AREA	U.S. AVG	INTERCITY SERVICES	AREA	U.S. AVG	AUTOMOTIVE	AREA	U.S. AVG
Average commute time	19.6 min.	22.6 min.	Miles to nearest major airport	70	46	Insurance, annual premium	$954	$1,011
Commute by auto	82.8%	88.7%	Type of local airport	Small		Gas, cost per gallon	$1.47	$1.50
Commute by mass transit	1.0%	1.8%	No. daily airline departures	81	294	Daily vehicle miles per capita	15.8	23.0
Work at home	5.8%	3.9%	Amtrak service	No				
Mass transit miles per capita	8.4	8.0	No. interstate highways	0	1			

DINING & SHOPPING	AREA	U.S. AVG	ENTERTAINMENT	AREA	U.S. AVG	OUTDOOR ACTIVITIES	AREA	U.S. AVG
Restaurant rating	1	1	Professional sports rating	2	4	Golf-course rating	2	4
No. outlet malls	0	2	College sports rating	9	4	Ski-area rating	3	4
No. Starbucks	1	11	Zoo/aquarium rating	1	3	National Park rating	1	3
No. warehouse clubs	3	4	Amusement park rating	1	3	Sq. miles inland water	1.0	4.0
			Botanical garden/arboretum rating	1	3	Miles of coastline	0.0	11.4

MEDIA & LIBRARIES	AREA	U.S. AVG	PERFORMING ARTS	AREA	U.S. AVG	MUSEUMS	AREA	U.S. AVG
Arts radio rating	1	3	Classical music rating	4	4	Overall museum rating	5	6
No. public libraries	5	28	Ballet/dance rating	3	3	Art museum rating	5	5
Library volumes per capita	2.0	2.8	Professional theater rating	1	3	Science museum rating	2	4
			University arts programs rating	5	5	Children's museum rating	1	3

Steubenville-Weirton, OH-WV

Score: 50.9 Rank: 217

Profile: Small-town complex
Location: Southeast Ohio along the Ohio River at the West Virginia border
Elevation: 1,223 feet
Time zone: Eastern Standard Time

PRO	CON
Cost of living	Declining downtown
Economic turnaround	Clouds and rain
Proximity to Pittsburgh	Entertainment

Steubenville is one of many towns in the region previously centered on steel production. The decline of steel and its related industries led to high unemployment and an over 7% drop in population from 1990 to 2000. But that trend has slowed and recent events position the area for a turnaround. A combination of low costs, local workforce, ground transport network, and strategic national location has convinced retailing giant Wal-Mart to locate a large distribution facility here. (This information is too recent to be included in job-growth statistics.) The facility will cover more space and employ more people than the existing central business district. An additional economic boost should come from large Wal-Mart suppliers drawn to the area. Pittsburgh and its amenities lie 50 miles to the east. There isn't much to do and the weather can be dreary, but economic promise and low cost of living, especially home prices, make the area attractive for those with patience.

Steubenville is located on a level floodplain extending west from the Ohio River. Areas to the north and south are hilly with dense deciduous forests. The climate is humid continental. The city is in a primary storm track located far enough north to receive a Lake Erie influence. Summers are warm and humid, while winters are fairly mild but subject to occasional cold snaps. Fall and spring are changeable. Long periods of cool, cloudy weather occur in all seasons. First freeze is late October, last is mid-April.

POPULATION

DEMOGRAPHICS	AREA	U.S. AVG	ETHNIC COMPOSITION	AREA	U.S. AVG	RESIDENT PROFILE	AREA	U.S. AVG
Population	129,663		White	97.0%	75.1%	Single	41.9%	43.6%
Population density per sq. mile	223.0	447.3	Black	2.4%	12.3%	Married	58.1%	56.4%
Population growth	-9.0%	16.1%	Asian	.4%	3.6%	Divorced	7.8%	8.4%
Median age	42.2	35.5	American Indian	.2%	.9%	Separated	1.6%	3.0%
Average family size	2.5	2.7	Hispanic	.4%	12.5%	Married with children	26.9%	28.7%
			Diversity measure	11.1%	35.2%	Single with children	8.4%	10.1%

ECONOMY & JOBS — SCORE: 76/RANK: 79

INCOME	AREA	U.S. AVG	EMPLOYMENT	AREA	U.S. AVG	LARGEST EMPLOYING INDUSTRY
Per capita income	$17,588	$23,420	Unemployment rate	6.8%	6.1%	Primary Metal Manufacturing
Household income	$31,625	$46,060	Recent job growth	.3%	.9%	
Household income < $25K	38.7%	26.4%	Projected future job growth	3.8%	15.1%	
Household income > $75K	10.9%	24.5%	White collar	42.8%	54.5%	
Household income growth	30.7%	57.3%	Blue collar	57.2%	45.5%	

COST OF LIVING — SCORE: 90/RANK: 34

INDEXES & TAXES	AREA	U.S. AVG	HOUSING	AREA	U.S. AVG	NECESSITIES	AREA	U.S. AVG
Cost of Living Index	83.8	100.0	Median home price	$79,360	$160,100	Food Index	102.4	100.0
Financial Progress Index	80.4	100.0	Home price appreciation	5.8%	7.1%	Housing Index	49.3	100.0
Income tax rate	4.993%	4.625%	Median rent	$457	$670	Utilities Index	134.4	100.0
Sales tax rate	6.500%	6.474%	Homes owned	73.2%	63.9%	Transportation Index	95.6	100.0
Property tax rate	$9.2	$15.6	Homes rented	18.1%	25.3%	Healthcare Index	89.0	100.0
			Housing affordability	59.0%	54.5%	Miscellaneous Cost Index	100.2	100.0

CLIMATE — SCORE: 29/RANK: 234

TEMPERATURE	AREA	U.S. AVG	PRECIPITATION	AREA	U.S. AVG	COMFORTS & HAZARDS	AREA	U.S. AVG
January low	20.8°F	26.4°F	Annual inches precipitation	36.0	35.9	July relative humidity	68.0%	68.8%
July high	82.5°F	86.7°F	Annual inches snowfall	45.0	24.2	Annual days mostly sunny	161	212
Annual days > 90°F	7	38	Annual days precipitation	152	111	Annual days with thunderstorms	36	39
Annual days < 32°F	124	88	Annual days rain > 0.5 inches	27	23	Tornado risk score	3	19
Annual days < 0°F	5	6	Annual days snow > 1.5 inches	9	6	Hurricane risk score	3	15

TEMPERATURE

PRECIPITATION

DAYS OF CLOUDS & PRECIPITATION

EDUCATION — SCORE: 18/RANK: 270

ACHIEVEMENT	AREA	U.S. AVG	PUBLIC SCHOOLS	AREA	U.S. AVG	HIGHER EDUCATION	AREA	U.S. AVG
High school degree	82.5%	80.2%	Expenditures per pupil	$6,043	$5,894	No. 2-year colleges	1	3
2-year college degree	7.0%	6.2%	Student/teacher ratio	14.5	16.7	No. 4-year colleges/universities	3	4
4-year college degree	8.0%	15.8%	Attending public school	90.5%	90.2%	No. highly ranked universities	0	1
Graduate/professional degree	4.7%	9.6%	State SAT score	1077	1020			
			State ACT score	21.4*	21.0			

HEALTH & HEALTHCARE — SCORE: 41/RANK: 193

HAZARDS & ILLNESSES	AREA	U.S. AVG	HEALTHCARE	AREA	U.S. AVG
Air-quality score	59	45	Physicians per capita	138.8	261.1
Water-quality score	13	33	Hospital beds per capita	684.0	432.2
Pollen/allergy score	71	61	No. teaching hospitals	0	4
Stress score	30	50	Cost per doctor visit	$61	$67
Cancer mortality per capita	187.2	169.0	Cost per dental visit	$69	$82
Depression days per month	2.1	2.8	Cost per daily hospital room	$569	$733

CRIME — SCORE: 24/RANK: 251

CRIME	AREA	U.S. AVG
Violent crime rate	218.4	456.0
Change in violent crime rate	-42.5%	-17.2%
Property crime rate	2,878.9	3,950.0
Change in property crime rate	86.4%	-16.8%

TRANSPORTATION — SCORE: 11/RANK: 294

COMMUTE	AREA	U.S. AVG	INTERCITY SERVICES	AREA	U.S. AVG	AUTOMOTIVE	AREA	U.S. AVG
Average commute time	22.4 min.	22.6 min.	Miles to nearest major airport	20	46	Insurance, annual premium	$787	$1,011
Commute by auto	90.2%	88.7%	Type of local airport	Large		Gas, cost per gallon	$1.48	$1.50
Commute by mass transit	.5%	1.8%	No. daily airline departures	663	294	Daily vehicle miles per capita	16.1	23.0
Work at home	1.9%	3.9%	Amtrak service	No				
Mass transit miles per capita	0.0	8.0	No. interstate highways	0	1			

LEISURE SCORE: 56/RANK: 144

DINING & SHOPPING	AREA	U.S. AVG	ENTERTAINMENT	AREA	U.S. AVG	OUTDOOR ACTIVITIES	AREA	U.S. AVG
Restaurant rating	1	1	Professional sports rating	3	4	Golf-course rating	2	4
No. outlet malls	2	2	College sports rating	1	4	Ski-area rating	1	4
No. Starbucks	0	11	Zoo/aquarium rating	1	3	National Park rating	1	3
No. warehouse clubs	1	4	Amusement park rating	1	3	Sq. miles inland water	2.0	4.0
			Botanical garden/arboretum rating	1	3	Miles of coastline	0.0	11.4

ARTS & CULTURE SCORE: 31/RANK: 226

MEDIA & LIBRARIES	AREA	U.S. AVG	PERFORMING ARTS	AREA	U.S. AVG	MUSEUMS	AREA	U.S. AVG
Arts radio rating	1	3	Classical music rating	1	4	Overall museum rating	4	6
No. public libraries	12	28	Ballet/dance rating	1	3	Art museum rating	1	5
Library volumes per capita	2.9	2.8	Professional theater rating	1	3	Science museum rating	1	4
			University arts programs rating	3	5	Children's museum rating	2	3

Stockton-Lodi, CA

Score: 0.0   Rank: 330

Profile: Small port/Industrial city
Location: Northern California, in Central Valley, 50 miles south of Sacramento
Elevation: 22 feet
Time zone: Pacific Standard Time

PRO	CON
Mild winters	Cost of living
Proximity to San Francisco	Unemployment
Relatively low home prices	Unattractive downtown

Stockton, an inland port at the end of a ship channel accessing the San Francisco Bay, is a gritty transportation and agricultural center. Lodi is a small, mostly agricultural town 12 miles north. Despite an attempted comeback with some downtown renewal and public relations efforts, and pleasant suburbs near the University of the Pacific campus, the area is generally unattractive and working class in character. Crime rates, particularly violent crime, are high, and unemployment hovers near 10%. There are few amenities and there isn't much to do. Winter climate and proximity to San Francisco (80 miles) are among the few positives. Ironically, the area may suffer from being a little too close to Sacramento and the Bay Area to develop its own amenities. While median home prices of $219,630 are relatively affordable by

California standards, the Cost of Living Index of 122.8 is extremely high considering what's available, hence the tie for the lowest rating.

Stockton is on the southeast corner of the broad delta formed by the confluence of the San Joaquin and Sacramento rivers. The surrounding terrain is flat, irrigated farm and orchard land, near sea level. The Sierra Nevada foothills rise about 25 miles to the east and northeast. The climate is Central Valley Mediterranean, with warm, dry days and relatively cool nights with clear skies and no rainfall. Winter brings mild temperatures with relatively light rain and frequent valley fog, which can last for 4 to 5 weeks. Most rain occurs in winter and snow is practically unknown.

POPULATION

DEMOGRAPHICS	AREA	U.S. AVG	ETHNIC COMPOSITION	AREA	U.S. AVG	RESIDENT PROFILE	AREA	U.S. AVG
Population	614,302		White	72.4%	75.1%	Single	47.9%	43.6%
Population density per sq. mile	439.0	447.3	Black	5.0%	12.3%	Married	52.1%	56.4%
Population growth	27.8%	16.1%	Asian	13.3%	3.6%	Divorced	9.2%	8.4%
Median age	32.1	35.5	American Indian	1.0%	.9%	Separated	3.9%	3.0%
Average family size	3.1	2.7	Hispanic	33.6%	12.5%	Married with children	29.1%	28.7%
			Diversity measure	65.5%	35.2%	Single with children	13.5%	10.1%

ECONOMY & JOBS SCORE: 13/RANK: 288

INCOME	AREA	U.S. AVG	EMPLOYMENT	AREA	U.S. AVG	LARGEST EMPLOYING INDUSTRY
Per capita income	$19,334	$23,420	Unemployment rate	9.2%	6.1%	Food Manufacturing
Household income	$44,975	$46,060	Recent job growth	1.5%	.9%	
Household income < $25K	25.8%	26.4%	Projected future job growth	12.9%	15.1%	
Household income > $75K	24.0%	24.5%	White collar	48.3%	54.5%	
Household income growth	46.7%	57.3%	Blue collar	51.7%	45.5%	

COST OF LIVING SCORE: 13/RANK: 288

INDEXES & TAXES	AREA	U.S. AVG	HOUSING	AREA	U.S. AVG	NECESSITIES	AREA	U.S. AVG
Cost of Living Index	122.8	100.0	Median home price	$219,630	$160,100	Food Index	117.7	100.0
Financial Progress Index	78.1	100.0	Home price appreciation	15.5%	7.1%	Housing Index	136.4	100.0
Income tax rate	6.000%	4.625%	Median rent	$757	$670	Utilities Index	112.3	100.0
Sales tax rate	7.750%	6.474%	Homes owned	57.8%	63.9%	Transportation Index	115.6	100.0
Property tax rate	$11.3	$15.6	Homes rented	36.9%	25.3%	Healthcare Index	144.4	100.0
			Housing affordability	47.0%	54.5%	Miscellaneous Cost Index	105.9	100.0

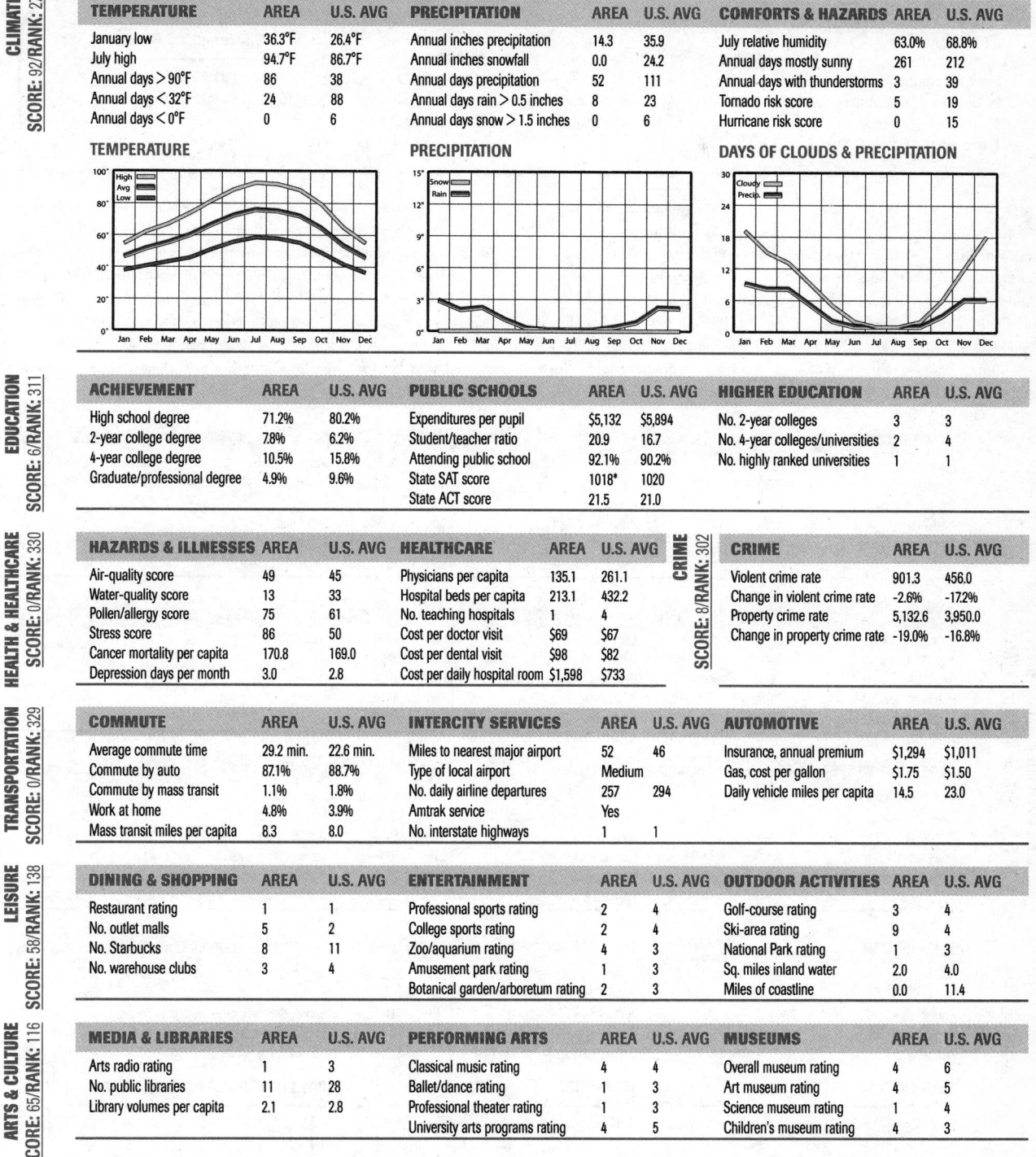

CLIMATE SCORE: 92/RANK: 27

TEMPERATURE	AREA	U.S. AVG
January low	36.3°F	26.4°F
July high	94.7°F	86.7°F
Annual days > 90°F	86	38
Annual days < 32°F	24	88
Annual days < 0°F	0	6

PRECIPITATION	AREA	U.S. AVG
Annual inches precipitation	14.3	35.9
Annual inches snowfall	0.0	24.2
Annual days precipitation	52	111
Annual days rain > 0.5 inches	8	23
Annual days snow > 1.5 inches	0	6

COMFORTS & HAZARDS	AREA	U.S. AVG
July relative humidity	63.0%	68.8%
Annual days mostly sunny	261	212
Annual days with thunderstorms	3	39
Tornado risk score	5	19
Hurricane risk score	0	15

TEMPERATURE

PRECIPITATION

DAYS OF CLOUDS & PRECIPITATION

EDUCATION SCORE: 6/RANK: 311

ACHIEVEMENT	AREA	U.S. AVG
High school degree	71.2%	80.2%
2-year college degree	7.8%	6.2%
4-year college degree	10.5%	15.8%
Graduate/professional degree	4.9%	9.6%

PUBLIC SCHOOLS	AREA	U.S. AVG
Expenditures per pupil	$5,132	$5,894
Student/teacher ratio	20.9	16.7
Attending public school	92.1%	90.2%
State SAT score	1018*	1020
State ACT score	21.5	21.0

HIGHER EDUCATION	AREA	U.S. AVG
No. 2-year colleges	3	3
No. 4-year colleges/universities	2	4
No. highly ranked universities	1	1

HEALTH & HEALTHCARE SCORE: 0/RANK: 330

HAZARDS & ILLNESSES	AREA	U.S. AVG
Air-quality score	49	45
Water-quality score	13	33
Pollen/allergy score	75	61
Stress score	86	50
Cancer mortality per capita	170.8	169.0
Depression days per month	3.0	2.8

HEALTHCARE	AREA	U.S. AVG
Physicians per capita	135.1	261.1
Hospital beds per capita	213.1	432.2
No. teaching hospitals	1	4
Cost per doctor visit	$69	$67
Cost per dental visit	$98	$82
Cost per daily hospital room	$1,598	$733

CRIME SCORE: 8/RANK: 302

CRIME	AREA	U.S. AVG
Violent crime rate	901.3	456.0
Change in violent crime rate	-2.6%	-17.2%
Property crime rate	5,132.6	3,950.0
Change in property crime rate	-19.0%	-16.8%

TRANSPORTATION SCORE: 0/RANK: 329

COMMUTE	AREA	U.S. AVG
Average commute time	29.2 min.	22.6 min.
Commute by auto	87.1%	88.7%
Commute by mass transit	1.1%	1.8%
Work at home	4.8%	3.9%
Mass transit miles per capita	8.3	8.0

INTERCITY SERVICES	AREA	U.S. AVG
Miles to nearest major airport	52	46
Type of local airport	Medium	
No. daily airline departures	257	294
Amtrak service	Yes	
No. interstate highways	1	1

AUTOMOTIVE	AREA	U.S. AVG
Insurance, annual premium	$1,294	$1,011
Gas, cost per gallon	$1.75	$1.50
Daily vehicle miles per capita	14.5	23.0

LEISURE SCORE: 58/RANK: 138

DINING & SHOPPING	AREA	U.S. AVG
Restaurant rating	1	1
No. outlet malls	5	2
No. Starbucks	8	11
No. warehouse clubs	3	4

ENTERTAINMENT	AREA	U.S. AVG
Professional sports rating	2	4
College sports rating	2	4
Zoo/aquarium rating	4	3
Amusement park rating	1	3
Botanical garden/arboretum rating	2	3

OUTDOOR ACTIVITIES	AREA	U.S. AVG
Golf-course rating	3	4
Ski-area rating	9	4
National Park rating	1	3
Sq. miles inland water	2.0	4.0
Miles of coastline	0.0	11.4

ARTS & CULTURE SCORE: 65/RANK: 116

MEDIA & LIBRARIES	AREA	U.S. AVG
Arts radio rating	1	3
No. public libraries	11	28
Library volumes per capita	2.1	2.8

PERFORMING ARTS	AREA	U.S. AVG
Classical music rating	4	4
Ballet/dance rating	1	3
Professional theater rating	1	3
University arts programs rating	4	5

MUSEUMS	AREA	U.S. AVG
Overall museum rating	4	6
Art museum rating	4	5
Science museum rating	1	4
Children's museum rating	4	3

Sumter, SC

Score: 40.7   **Rank:** 274

Profile: Military town
Location: East-central South Carolina, 45 miles east of Columbia
Elevation: 225 feet
Time zone: Eastern Standard Time

PRO	CON
Small-town atmosphere	Entertainment
Cost of living	Crime rate
Nearby recreation	Hot, humid summers

Sumter, in the center of the state, is a small, southern town and county seat. Shaw Air Force Base and agriculture are the economic mainstays. Downtown is nondescript and typically Southern with small areas of attractive housing mainly to the north. Outdoor recreation is available nearby, notably at large Marion Lake to the south. Additional amenities are modest, but the town is 45 miles from Columbia and 100 miles from Charleston and Myrtle Beach. The area offers a low cost of living, a slow pace of life, and quality healthcare facilities, but there is little to do in the immediate area.

Sumter is located along the banks of the Pocotaligo River in an area of level and gently rolling terrain with pine forests and agricultural land. The climate is humid temperate influenced by mountains to the northwest and water to the southeast. Summers are consistently warm and humid, and nearby swampy areas breed large insect populations. The mountains and prevailing wind patterns block cool air masses from the northwest, although local afternoon thundershowers do occur. Winters are mild with brief cold outbreaks and rain. Fall is the most pleasant season.

POPULATION

DEMOGRAPHICS	AREA	U.S. AVG	ETHNIC COMPOSITION	AREA	U.S. AVG	RESIDENT PROFILE	AREA	U.S. AVG
Population	105,198		White	44.4%	75.1%	Single	48.7%	43.6%
Population density per sq. mile	158.1	447.3	Black	54.0%	12.3%	Married	51.3%	56.4%
Population growth	2.5%	16.1%	Asian	1.1%	3.6%	Divorced	5.8%	8.4%
Median age	33.6	35.5	American Indian	.2%	.9%	Separated	6.8%	3.0%
Average family size	3.1	2.7	Hispanic	1.5%	12.5%	Married with children	32.3%	28.7%
			Diversity measure	53.8%	35.2%	Single with children	17.1%	10.1%

ECONOMY & JOBS SCORE: 28/RANK: 236

INCOME	AREA	U.S. AVG	EMPLOYMENT	AREA	U.S. AVG	LARGEST EMPLOYING INDUSTRY
Per capita income	$17,061	$23,420	Unemployment rate	7.5%	6.1%	Food Manufacturing
Household income	$34,456	$46,060	Recent job growth	1.9%	.9%	
Household income < $25K	34.0%	26.4%	Projected future job growth	11.5%	15.1%	
Household income > $75K	14.0%	24.5%	White collar	37.7%	54.5%	
Household income growth	53.0%	57.3%	Blue collar	62.3%	45.5%	

COST OF LIVING SCORE: 76/RANK: 80

INDEXES & TAXES	AREA	U.S. AVG	HOUSING	AREA	U.S. AVG	NECESSITIES	AREA	U.S. AVG
Cost of Living Index	82.4	100.0	Median home price	$90,640	$160,100	Food Index	100.8	100.0
Financial Progress Index	89.1	100.0	Home price appreciation	4.8%	7.1%	Housing Index	56.3	100.0
Income tax rate	7.000%	4.625%	Median rent	$468	$670	Utilities Index	93.9	100.0
Sales tax rate	6.000%	6.474%	Homes owned	66.1%	63.9%	Transportation Index	91.3	100.0
Property tax rate	$7.0	$15.6	Homes rented	26.6%	25.3%	Healthcare Index	93.2	100.0
			Housing affordability	65.0%	54.5%	Miscellaneous Cost Index	99.5	100.0

CLIMATE SCORE: 35/RANK: 215

TEMPERATURE	AREA	U.S. AVG	PRECIPITATION	AREA	U.S. AVG	COMFORTS & HAZARDS	AREA	U.S. AVG
January low	33.9°F	26.4°F	Annual inches precipitation	46.0	35.9	July relative humidity	73.0%	68.8%
July high	92.0°F	86.7°F	Annual inches snowfall	2.0	24.2	Annual days mostly sunny	223	212
Annual days > 90°F	64	38	Annual days precipitation	111	111	Annual days with thunderstorms	54	39
Annual days < 32°F	60	88	Annual days rain > 0.5 inches	31	23	Tornado risk score	9	19
Annual days < 0°F	0	6	Annual days snow > 1.5 inches	1	6	Hurricane risk score	40	15

TEMPERATURE

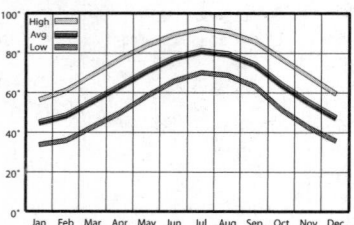

PRECIPITATION

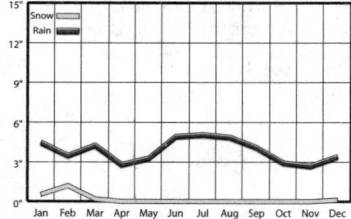

DAYS OF CLOUDS & PRECIPITATION

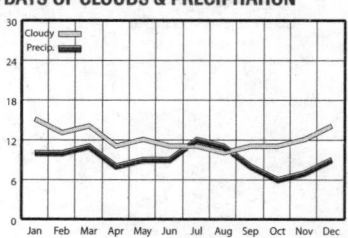

EDUCATION SCORE: 15/RANK: 281

ACHIEVEMENT	AREA	U.S. AVG	PUBLIC SCHOOLS	AREA	U.S. AVG	HIGHER EDUCATION	AREA	U.S. AVG
High school degree	74.3%	80.2%	Expenditures per pupil	$4,961	$5,894	No. 2-year colleges	2	3
2-year college degree	7.9%	6.2%	Student/teacher ratio	15.6	16.7	No. 4-year colleges/universities	1	4
4-year college degree	10.7%	15.8%	Attending public school	91.0%	90.2%	No. highly ranked universities	0	1
Graduate/professional degree	5.1%	9.6%	State SAT score	989*	1020			
			State ACT score	19.2	21.0			

HEALTH & HEALTHCARE SCORE: 35/RANK: 215

CRIME SCORE: 3/RANK: 320

HAZARDS & ILLNESSES	AREA	U.S. AVG	HEALTHCARE	AREA	U.S. AVG	CRIME	AREA	U.S. AVG
Air-quality score	24	45	Physicians per capita	138.8	261.1	Violent crime rate	914.4	456.0
Water-quality score	40	33	Hospital beds per capita	291.5	432.2	Change in violent crime rate	-16.2%	-17.2%
Pollen/allergy score	67	61	No. teaching hospitals	0	4	Property crime rate	5,397.4	3,950.0
Stress score	90	50	Cost per doctor visit	$60	$67	Change in property crime rate	4.4%	-16.8%
Cancer mortality per capita	168.7	169.0	Cost per dental visit	$75	$82			
Depression days per month	3.5	2.8	Cost per daily hospital room	$371	$733			

TRANSPORTATION SCORE: 91/RANK: 30

COMMUTE	AREA	U.S. AVG	INTERCITY SERVICES	AREA	U.S. AVG	AUTOMOTIVE	AREA	U.S. AVG
Average commute time	21.5 min.	22.6 min.	Miles to nearest major airport	42	46	Insurance, annual premium	$1,066	$1,011
Commute by auto	93.9%	88.7%	Type of local airport	Small		Gas, cost per gallon	$1.36	$1.50
Commute by mass transit	.8%	1.8%	No. daily airline departures	93	294	Daily vehicle miles per capita	17.6	23.0
Work at home	1.3%	3.9%	Amtrak service	No				
Mass transit miles per capita	26.2	8.0	No. interstate highways	3	1			

LEISURE SCORE: 4/RANK: 315

DINING & SHOPPING	AREA	U.S. AVG	ENTERTAINMENT	AREA	U.S. AVG	OUTDOOR ACTIVITIES	AREA	U.S. AVG
Restaurant rating	1	1	Professional sports rating	2	4	Golf-course rating	3	4
No. outlet malls	0	2	College sports rating	3	4	Ski-area rating	1	4
No. Starbucks	0	11	Zoo/aquarium rating	1	3	National Park rating	3	3
No. warehouse clubs	1	4	Amusement park rating	1	3	Sq. miles inland water	2.0	4.0
			Botanical garden/arboretum rating	1	3	Miles of coastline	0.0	11.4

ARTS & CULTURE SCORE: 60/RANK: 128

MEDIA & LIBRARIES	AREA	U.S. AVG	PERFORMING ARTS	AREA	U.S. AVG	MUSEUMS	AREA	U.S. AVG
Arts radio rating	1	3	Classical music rating	3	4	Overall museum rating	2	6
No. public libraries	3	28	Ballet/dance rating	1	3	Art museum rating	2	5
Library volumes per capita	1.5	2.8	Professional theater rating	1	3	Science museum rating	1	4
			University arts programs rating	2	5	Children's museum rating	1	3

Syracuse, NY

Score: 46.6   Rank: 246

Profile: Mid-size city
Location: North-central New York, 35 miles southeast of Lake Ontario's eastern shore
Elevation: 408 feet
Time zone: Eastern Standard Time

PRO
Nearby recreation
College-town amenities
Central location

CON
Winter snow
Winter gloom
Entertainment

Syracuse is located along the old Erie Canal, adjacent to the Finger Lakes region. It is a commercial and transportation center at the crossroads of major north-south and east-west routes. Local Anheuser-Busch and Bristol-Myers plants take advantage of the area's clean water and strategic location. However, the area's manufacturing industries are in trouble, and the recent closing of a Carrier (air-conditioning) plant has become a national symbol of troubles in that sector. Syracuse University adds a college-town element. Canal parks and a museum preserve the city's Erie Canal heritage. There are minor-league sports and the Syracuse basketball team is a local attraction. Oneida Lake nearby and Lake Ontario to the north provide recreational opportunities. Strong advantages include low cost of living and the state's highest recent job growth. However, Syracuse ties Utica to the east for the greatest annual snowfall in the country.

Gently rolling terrain stretches northward for about 30 miles to the eastern end of Lake Ontario. Hills rise to 1,500 feet about 5 miles south. To the west open land and woods cover rolling hills. The climate is continental with a lake influence. The location near the St. Lawrence storm track makes for dynamic weather. Summer temperatures rise quickly, occasionally exceeding 90°F, and fall rapidly after sunset. Hot, humid conditions happen only a few times a year. Winters are cold and somewhat severe. Temperatures average from the low 30s to the low teens. While Lake Ontario provides some moderation, below-zero temperatures do occur. Precipitation is evenly distributed year-round with thunderstorms in summer and frequent winter snow squalls fed by lake moisture. Winter days are cloudy. Over 100 inches of snow falls annually. First freeze is mid-October, last is late April.

POPULATION

DEMOGRAPHICS	AREA	U.S. AVG	ETHNIC COMPOSITION	AREA	U.S. AVG	RESIDENT PROFILE	AREA	U.S. AVG
Population	735,059		White	92.4%	75.1%	Single	45.2%	43.6%
Population density per sq. mile	238.4	447.3	Black	5.0%	12.3%	Married	54.8%	56.4%
Population growth	-1.0%	16.1%	Asian	1.4%	3.6%	Divorced	6.7%	8.4%
Median age	36.5	35.5	American Indian	.6%	.9%	Separated	3.9%	3.0%
Average family size	2.6	2.7	Hispanic	1.9%	12.5%	Married with children	29.3%	28.7%
			Diversity measure	22.3%	35.2%	Single with children	10.7%	10.1%

ECONOMY & JOBS SCORE: 95/RANK: 15

INCOME	AREA	U.S. AVG	EMPLOYMENT	AREA	U.S. AVG	LARGEST EMPLOYING INDUSTRY
Per capita income	$22,343	$23,420	Unemployment rate	5.2%	6.1%	Machinery Manufacturing
Household income	$44,748	$46,060	Recent job growth	2.6%	.9%	
Household income < $25K	25.9%	26.4%	Projected future job growth	8.1%	15.1%	
Household income > $75K	22.8%	24.5%	White collar	58.1%	54.5%	
Household income growth	45.4%	57.3%	Blue collar	41.9%	45.5%	

COST OF LIVING SCORE: 26/RANK: 242

INDEXES & TAXES	AREA	U.S. AVG	HOUSING	AREA	U.S. AVG	NECESSITIES	AREA	U.S. AVG
Cost of Living Index	88.4	100.0	Median home price	$86,200	$160,100	Food Index	109.4	100.0
Financial Progress Index	107.8	100.0	Home price appreciation	6.2%	7.1%	Housing Index	53.5	100.0
Income tax rate	7.125%	4.625%	Median rent	$600	$670	Utilities Index	144.1	100.0
Sales tax rate	7.000%	6.474%	Homes owned	65.3%	63.9%	Transportation Index	103.5	100.0
Property tax rate	$32.7	$15.6	Homes rented	20.4%	25.3%	Healthcare Index	101.6	100.0
			Housing affordability	50.0%	54.5%	Miscellaneous Cost Index	98.0	100.0

CLIMATE SCORE: 6/RANK: 309

TEMPERATURE	AREA	U.S. AVG	PRECIPITATION	AREA	U.S. AVG	COMFORTS & HAZARDS	AREA	U.S. AVG
January low	15.8°F	26.4°F	Annual inches precipitation	36.0	35.9	July relative humidity	73.0%	68.8%
July high	82.0°F	86.7°F	Annual inches snowfall	109.0	24.2	Annual days mostly sunny	164	212
Annual days > 90°F	6	38	Annual days precipitation	168	111	Annual days with thunderstorms	29	39
Annual days < 32°F	138	88	Annual days rain > 0.5 inches	21	23	Tornado risk score	6	19
Annual days < 0°F	9	6	Annual days snow > 1.5 inches	25	6	Hurricane risk score	4	15

TEMPERATURE

PRECIPITATION

DAYS OF CLOUDS & PRECIPITATION

EDUCATION SCORE: 93/RANK: 24

ACHIEVEMENT	AREA	U.S. AVG	PUBLIC SCHOOLS	AREA	U.S. AVG	HIGHER EDUCATION	AREA	U.S. AVG
High school degree	83.8%	80.2%	Expenditures per pupil	$8,011	$5,894	No. 2-year colleges	7	3
2-year college degree	9.8%	6.2%	Student/teacher ratio	14.4	16.7	No. 4-year colleges/universities	8	4
4-year college degree	14.2%	15.8%	Attending public school	92.5%	90.2%	No. highly ranked universities	3	1
Graduate/professional degree	9.9%	9.6%	State SAT score	1006*	1020			
			State ACT score	22.3	21.0			

HEALTH & HEALTHCARE SCORE: 46/RANK: 176

HAZARDS & ILLNESSES	AREA	U.S. AVG	HEALTHCARE	AREA	U.S. AVG
Air-quality score	100	45	Physicians per capita	317.0	261.1
Water-quality score	35	33	Hospital beds per capita	419.5	432.2
Pollen/allergy score	57	61	No. teaching hospitals	5	4
Stress score	51	50	Cost per doctor visit	$62	$67
Cancer mortality per capita	179.1	169.0	Cost per dental visit	$65	$82
Depression days per month	4.1	2.8	Cost per daily hospital room	$787	$733

CRIME SCORE: 70/RANK: 100

CRIME	AREA	U.S. AVG
Violent crime rate	329.0	456.0
Change in violent crime rate	9.0%	-17.2%
Property crime rate	2,878.4	3,950.0
Change in property crime rate	-14.6%	-16.8%

TRANSPORTATION SCORE: 73/RANK: 86

COMMUTE	AREA	U.S. AVG	INTERCITY SERVICES	AREA	U.S. AVG	AUTOMOTIVE	AREA	U.S. AVG
Average commute time	20.8 min.	22.6 min.	Miles to nearest major airport	5	46	Insurance, annual premium	$1,328	$1,011
Commute by auto	87.8%	88.7%	Type of local airport	Small		Gas, cost per gallon	$1.58	$1.50
Commute by mass transit	1.8%	1.8%	No. daily airline departures	129	294	Daily vehicle miles per capita	25.2	23.0
Work at home	3.8%	3.9%	Amtrak service	Yes				
Mass transit miles per capita	5.9	8.0	No. interstate highways	2	1			

LEISURE SCORE: 64/RANK: 117

DINING & SHOPPING	AREA	U.S. AVG	ENTERTAINMENT	AREA	U.S. AVG	OUTDOOR ACTIVITIES	AREA	U.S. AVG
Restaurant rating	1	1	Professional sports rating	3	4	Golf-course rating	7	4
No. outlet malls	1	2	College sports rating	5	4	Ski-area rating	4	4
No. Starbucks	2	11	Zoo/aquarium rating	5	3	National Park rating	1	3
No. warehouse clubs	4	4	Amusement park rating	1	3	Sq. miles inland water	6.0	4.0
			Botanical garden/arboretum rating	1	3	Miles of coastline	35.3	11.4

ARTS & CULTURE SCORE: 87/RANK: 41

MEDIA & LIBRARIES	AREA	U.S. AVG	PERFORMING ARTS	AREA	U.S. AVG	MUSEUMS	AREA	U.S. AVG
Arts radio rating	9	3	Classical music rating	9	4	Overall museum rating	9	6
No. public libraries	59	28	Ballet/dance rating	1	3	Art museum rating	6	5
Library volumes per capita	2.4	2.8	Professional theater rating	1	3	Science museum rating	6	4
			University arts programs rating	8	5	Children's museum rating	6	3

Tacoma, WA

Score: 75.3   Rank: 59

Profile: Mid-size port city
Location: West-central Washington at the south end of Puget Sound and the Seattle area
Elevation: 125 feet
Time zone: Pacific Standard Time

PRO	CON
Proximity to Seattle	Sprawl and traffic
Nearby recreation	Industrial setting
Downtown renewal	Clouds and rain

Tacoma is the working-class, industrial heart of the Puget Sound with shipping, paper and lumber mills, and other manufacturing. Its central location to Seattle (30 miles north), Olympia, and surrounding recreational opportunities along with a relatively low cost of living have led to a rebound. Following a recent clean up, the downtown is attractive. The area contains Pacific Lutheran University and a few amenities. However, traffic in the commercial section along I-5 can be horrendous. There is unattractive sprawl to the south mixed with attractive residential areas. For those with patience for congestion and tolerance of the marine climate, Tacoma might be a good bet.

Downtown Tacoma sits on a mostly built-up coastal plain rising to a hilly, wooded plateau immediately to the south. Hills rise into the Mount Rainier area to the southeast, and a series of Puget Sound fjords and inlets gives way to the Olympic Mountains and peninsula to the west. The climate is marine, with persistent cloudy, cool, and wet weather from October through May and drier, pleasant days most of the summer. At times in summer the marine influence can diminish, resulting in high temperatures and stagnant air conditions. Winter temperatures usually hover above freezing into the 50s with an occasional colder period.

POPULATION

DEMOGRAPHICS	AREA	U.S. AVG	ETHNIC COMPOSITION	AREA	U.S. AVG	RESIDENT PROFILE	AREA	U.S. AVG
Population	732,282		White	84.9%	75.1%	Single	45.3%	43.6%
Population density per sq. mile	437.0	447.3	Black	6.8%	12.3%	Married	54.7%	56.4%
Population growth	24.9%	16.1%	Asian	5.5%	3.6%	Divorced	11.2%	8.4%
Median age	34.3	35.5	American Indian	1.6%	.9%	Separated	3.4%	3.0%
Average family size	2.6	2.7	Hispanic	5.6%	12.5%	Married with children	27.4%	28.7%
			Diversity measure	40.3%	35.2%	Single with children	11.3%	10.1%

ECONOMY & JOBS SCORE: 12/RANK: 290

INCOME	AREA	U.S. AVG	EMPLOYMENT	AREA	U.S. AVG	LARGEST EMPLOYING INDUSTRY
Per capita income	$24,599	$23,420	Unemployment rate	7.7%	6.1%	Food Manufacturing
Household income	$52,137	$46,060	Recent job growth	.3%	.9%	
Household income < $25K	21.0%	26.4%	Projected future job growth	21.6%	15.1%	
Household income > $75K	29.2%	24.5%	White collar	50.5%	54.5%	
Household income growth	71.6%	57.3%	Blue collar	49.5%	45.5%	

COST OF LIVING SCORE: 28/RANK: 237

INDEXES & TAXES	AREA	U.S. AVG	HOUSING	AREA	U.S. AVG	NECESSITIES	AREA	U.S. AVG
Cost of Living Index	105.5	100.0	Median home price	$173,300	$160,100	Food Index	109.7	100.0
Financial Progress Index	105.3	100.0	Home price appreciation	6.7%	7.1%	Housing Index	107.6	100.0
Income tax rate	0.000%	4.625%	Median rent	$736	$670	Utilities Index	80.5	100.0
Sales tax rate	8.800%	6.474%	Homes owned	57.8%	63.9%	Transportation Index	104.3	100.0
Property tax rate	$14.7	$15.6	Homes rented	32.8%	25.3%	Healthcare Index	127.3	100.0
			Housing affordability	56.0%	54.5%	Miscellaneous Cost Index	102.7	100.0

CLIMATE SCORE: 80/RANK: 65

TEMPERATURE	AREA	U.S. AVG	PRECIPITATION	AREA	U.S. AVG	COMFORTS & HAZARDS	AREA	U.S. AVG
January low	33.0°F	26.4°F	Annual inches precipitation	38.8	35.9	July relative humidity	74.0%	68.8%
July high	75.1°F	86.7°F	Annual inches snowfall	14.3	24.2	Annual days mostly sunny	136	212
Annual days > 90°F	3	38	Annual days precipitation	164	111	Annual days with thunderstorms	7	39
Annual days < 32°F	31	88	Annual days rain > 0.5 inches	25	23	Tornado risk score	0	19
Annual days < 0°F	0	6	Annual days snow > 1.5 inches	1	6	Hurricane risk score	0	15

TEMPERATURE

PRECIPITATION

DAYS OF CLOUDS & PRECIPITATION

EDUCATION SCORE: 60/RANK: 131

ACHIEVEMENT	AREA	U.S. AVG	PUBLIC SCHOOLS	AREA	U.S. AVG	HIGHER EDUCATION	AREA	U.S. AVG
High school degree	83.6%	80.2%	Expenditures per pupil	$5,873	$5,894	No. 2-year colleges	2	3
2-year college degree	7.6%	6.2%	Student/teacher ratio	19.4	16.7	No. 4-year colleges/universities	2	4
4-year college degree	13.1%	15.8%	Attending public school	93.9%	90.2%	No. highly ranked universities	1	1
Graduate/professional degree	6.9%	9.6%	State SAT score	1062*	1020			
			State ACT score	22.5	21.0			

HEALTH & HEALTHCARE SCORE: 40/RANK: 199

CRIME SCORE: 21/RANK: 259

HAZARDS & ILLNESSES	AREA	U.S. AVG	HEALTHCARE	AREA	U.S. AVG	CRIME	AREA	U.S. AVG
Air-quality score	95	45	Physicians per capita	225.3	261.1	Violent crime rate	531.5	456.0
Water-quality score	17	33	Hospital beds per capita	259.7	432.2	Change in violent crime rate	-39.1%	-17.2%
Pollen/allergy score	48	61	No. teaching hospitals	3	4	Property crime rate	5,493.8	3,950.0
Stress score	99	50	Cost per doctor visit	$75	$67	Change in property crime rate	-13.7%	-16.8%
Cancer mortality per capita	171.5	169.0	Cost per dental visit	$137	$82			
Depression days per month	2.3	2.8	Cost per daily hospital room	$777	$733			

TRANSPORTATION SCORE: 69/RANK: 102

COMMUTE	AREA	U.S. AVG	INTERCITY SERVICES	AREA	U.S. AVG	AUTOMOTIVE	AREA	U.S. AVG
Average commute time	28.4 min.	22.6 min.	Miles to nearest major airport	16	46	Insurance, annual premium	$1,484	$1,011
Commute by auto	85.7%	88.7%	Type of local airport	Large		Gas, cost per gallon	$1.57	$1.50
Commute by mass transit	2.2%	1.8%	No. daily airline departures	698	294	Daily vehicle miles per capita	22.7	23.0
Work at home	4.8%	3.9%	Amtrak service	Yes				
Mass transit miles per capita	22.6	8.0	No. interstate highways	1	1			

LEISURE SCORE: 89/RANK: 39

DINING & SHOPPING	AREA	U.S. AVG	ENTERTAINMENT	AREA	U.S. AVG	OUTDOOR ACTIVITIES	AREA	U.S. AVG
Restaurant rating	1	1	Professional sports rating	7	4	Golf-course rating	5	4
No. outlet malls	3	2	College sports rating	3	4	Ski-area rating	10	4
No. Starbucks	24	11	Zoo/aquarium rating	6	3	National Park rating	10	3
No. warehouse clubs	4	4	Amusement park rating	3	3	Sq. miles inland water	8.0	4.0
			Botanical garden/arboretum rating	4	3	Miles of coastline	15.3	11.4

ARTS & CULTURE SCORE: 83/RANK: 53

MEDIA & LIBRARIES	AREA	U.S. AVG	PERFORMING ARTS	AREA	U.S. AVG	MUSEUMS	AREA	U.S. AVG
Arts radio rating	3	3	Classical music rating	5	4	Overall museum rating	8	6
No. public libraries	29	28	Ballet/dance rating	5	3	Art museum rating	8	5
Library volumes per capita	4.9	2.8	Professional theater rating	3	3	Science museum rating	7	4
			University arts programs rating	6	5	Children's museum rating	7	3

Tallahassee, FL

Score: 46.1   **Rank:** 249

Profile: Capital city/College town
Location: Middle of Florida Panhandle, 30 miles north of the Gulf of
Mexico and 20 miles from the Georgia border
Elevation: 68 feet
Time zone: Eastern Standard Time

PRO	CON
College-town amenities	Crime rate
Surrounding countryside	Air transport
Healthcare	Hot, humid summers

Tallahassee, more a Southern city than a Florida one, possesses a diverse character with no dominant image. Although the state capital, it doesn't come across as a typical capital city. Despite the presence of Florida State University and Florida A&M, it isn't a typical college town. Without tourist attractions, it isn't a tourist city either. Unfortunately, the reality of the place is not as attractive as one might expect for such a diverse profile. Bonuses include a few college-town amenities, particularly sports; nightlife; healthcare facilities; and high educational attainment. But crime, particularly violent crime, is among the state's highest, and air service is notably poor for a capital city (the three closest cities with major airports are 250 miles away). With 36 days below freezing, Tallahassee is by far the coldest place in Florida, although hardly cold by national standards.

Local terrain is rolling, with rich, red soil and forests of oak, live oak, pine, magnolia, and a variety of other subtropical vegetation. Numerous lakes surround the area, and the countryside is famous for its "canopy roads," long stretches of road completely sheltered by overhanging live oak trees. The climate is mild and moist with definite seasons. Winter brings considerable rain and cloudiness, with temperatures occasionally dropping into the teens. Summer is the least pleasant season: High temperatures and very high humidity cause considerable discomfort, plus thunderstorms occur every other day.

POPULATION

DEMOGRAPHICS	AREA	U.S. AVG	ETHNIC COMPOSITION	AREA	U.S. AVG	RESIDENT PROFILE	AREA	U.S. AVG
Population	289,274		White	57.3%	75.1%	Single	62.0%	43.6%
Population density per sq. mile	244.5	447.3	Black	39.9%	12.3%	Married	38.0%	56.4%
Population growth	23.8%	16.1%	Asian	1.5%	3.6%	Divorced	8.9%	8.4%
Median age	30.5	35.5	American Indian	.3%	.9%	Separated	3.3%	3.0%
Average family size	2.5	2.7	Hispanic	4.4%	12.5%	Married with children	19.7%	28.7%
			Diversity measure	52.5%	35.2%	Single with children	15.3%	10.1%

ECONOMY & JOBS   SCORE: 14/RANK: 282

INCOME	AREA	U.S. AVG	EMPLOYMENT	AREA	U.S. AVG	LARGEST EMPLOYING INDUSTRY
Per capita income	$24,303	$23,420	Unemployment rate	3.7%	6.1%	Healthcare and Social Assistance
Household income	$41,207	$46,060	Recent job growth	-2.4%	.9%	
Household income < $25K	30.2%	26.4%	Projected future job growth	20.3%	15.1%	
Household income > $75K	23.2%	24.5%	White collar	67.5%	54.5%	
Household income growth	56.8%	57.3%	Blue collar	32.5%	45.5%	

COST OF LIVING   SCORE: 67/RANK: 108

INDEXES & TAXES	AREA	U.S. AVG	HOUSING	AREA	U.S. AVG	NECESSITIES	AREA	U.S. AVG
Cost of Living Index	99.5	100.0	Median home price	$140,000	$160,100	Food Index	107.4	100.0
Financial Progress Index	88.2	100.0	Home price appreciation	6.0%	7.1%	Housing Index	87.0	100.0
Income tax rate	0.000%	4.625%	Median rent	$652	$670	Utilities Index	109.6	100.0
Sales tax rate	7.500%	6.474%	Homes owned	56.0%	63.9%	Transportation Index	102.7	100.0
Property tax rate	$15.6	$15.6	Homes rented	37.1%	25.3%	Healthcare Index	99.9	100.0
			Housing affordability	43.0%	54.5%	Miscellaneous Cost Index	108.6	100.0

CLIMATE   SCORE: 60/RANK: 133

TEMPERATURE	AREA	U.S. AVG	PRECIPITATION	AREA	U.S. AVG	COMFORTS & HAZARDS	AREA	U.S. AVG
January low	41.0°F	26.4°F	Annual inches precipitation	62.0	35.9	July relative humidity	76.0%	68.8%
July high	90.6°F	86.7°F	Annual inches snowfall	0.0	24.2	Annual days mostly sunny	233	212
Annual days > 90°F	87	38	Annual days precipitation	119	111	Annual days with thunderstorms	86	39
Annual days < 32°F	36	88	Annual days rain > 0.5 inches	38	23	Tornado risk score	14	19
Annual days < 0°F	0	6	Annual days snow > 1.5 inches	0	6	Hurricane risk score	50	15

TEMPERATURE

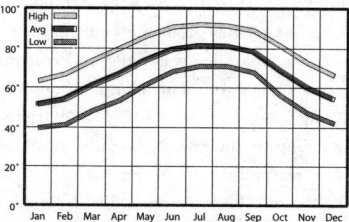

PRECIPITATION

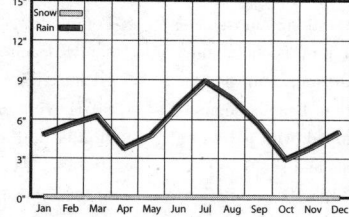

DAYS OF CLOUDS & PRECIPITATION

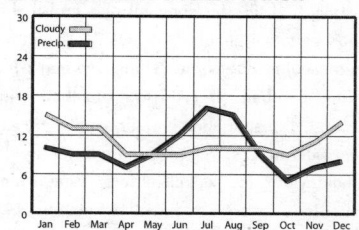

EDUCATION SCORE: 81/RANK: 64

ACHIEVEMENT	AREA	U.S. AVG	PUBLIC SCHOOLS	AREA	U.S. AVG	HIGHER EDUCATION	AREA	U.S. AVG
High school degree	85.9%	80.2%	Expenditures per pupil	$5,431	$5,894	No. 2-year colleges	1	3
2-year college degree	8.1%	6.2%	Student/teacher ratio	17.3	16.7	No. 4-year colleges/universities	2	4
4-year college degree	21.2%	15.8%	Attending public school	86.9%	90.2%	No. highly ranked universities	1	1
Graduate/professional degree	15.5%	9.6%	State SAT score	996*	1020			
			State ACT score	20.5	21.0			

HEALTH & HEALTHCARE SCORE: 89/RANK: 36

HAZARDS & ILLNESSES	AREA	U.S. AVG	HEALTHCARE	AREA	U.S. AVG
Air-quality score	24	45	Physicians per capita	218.1	261.1
Water-quality score	43	33	Hospital beds per capita	731.7	432.2
Pollen/allergy score	58	61	No. teaching hospitals	1	4
Stress score	78	50	Cost per doctor visit	$68	$67
Cancer mortality per capita	165.6	169.0	Cost per dental visit	$91	$82
Depression days per month	4.1	2.8	Cost per daily hospital room	$617	$733

CRIME SCORE: 9/RANK: 300

CRIME	AREA	U.S. AVG
Violent crime rate	989.0	456.0
Change in violent crime rate	-14.2%	-17.2%
Property crime rate	5,308.8	3,950.0
Change in property crime rate	-31.6%	-16.8%

TRANSPORTATION SCORE: 36/RANK: 211

COMMUTE	AREA	U.S. AVG	INTERCITY SERVICES	AREA	U.S. AVG	AUTOMOTIVE	AREA	U.S. AVG
Average commute time	22.7 min.	22.6 min.	Miles to nearest major airport	7	46	Insurance, annual premium	$1,026	$1,011
Commute by auto	86.5%	88.7%	Type of local airport	Small		Gas, cost per gallon	$1.50	$1.50
Commute by mass transit	2.1%	1.8%	No. daily airline departures	69	294	Daily vehicle miles per capita	24.8	23.0
Work at home	1.6%	3.9%	Amtrak service	Yes				
Mass transit miles per capita	8.2	8.0	No. interstate highways	1	1			

LEISURE SCORE: 15/RANK: 280

DINING & SHOPPING	AREA	U.S. AVG	ENTERTAINMENT	AREA	U.S. AVG	OUTDOOR ACTIVITIES	AREA	U.S. AVG
Restaurant rating	1	1	Professional sports rating	2	4	Golf-course rating	2	4
No. outlet malls	0	2	College sports rating	6	4	Ski-area rating	1	4
No. Starbucks	1	11	Zoo/aquarium rating	3	3	National Park rating	5	3
No. warehouse clubs	3	4	Amusement park rating	1	3	Sq. miles inland water	4.0	4.0
			Botanical garden/arboretum rating	4	3	Miles of coastline	0.0	11.4

ARTS & CULTURE SCORE: 50/RANK: 165

MEDIA & LIBRARIES	AREA	U.S. AVG	PERFORMING ARTS	AREA	U.S. AVG	MUSEUMS	AREA	U.S. AVG
Arts radio rating	7	3	Classical music rating	4	4	Overall museum rating	6	6
No. public libraries	8	28	Ballet/dance rating	3	3	Art museum rating	6	5
Library volumes per capita	2.2	2.8	Professional theater rating	1	3	Science museum rating	7	4
			University arts programs rating	8	5	Children's museum rating	1	3

Tampa–St. Petersburg–Clearwater, FL

Score: 77.4 Rank: 48

Profile: Large-city complex
Location: Central Florida Gulf Coast at Tampa Bay
Elevation: 57 feet
Time zone: Eastern Standard Time

PRO
Leisure activities
Winter climate
Cost of living

CON
Violent crime
Urban sprawl
Hot, humid summers

This metropolitan area includes Tampa, St. Petersburg, and Clearwater, all of which surround Tampa Bay. The area is varied and cosmopolitan with a pleasant climate and balanced local economy with less emphasis on tourism than many coastal Florida cities. A 1980s building boom created downtown skyscrapers, a major airport renovation, and the development of a cruise-ship terminal. Packing the area are activities popular with residents and tourists alike: amusement parks, museums, outdoor activities, and major-league professional sports, including baseball (Devil Rays), football (Buccaneers), and hockey (Lightning). Transportation and air service are excellent. Beachside areas in Clearwater and St. Petersburg are tastefully developed, with palm-tree lined boulevards and pockets of interesting restaurants and shops. A Cost of Living Index at 92.6 and median home prices at $128,100 are reasonable for the type of area. Downsides include the high violent crime rate, a mixed employment picture, and such sprawl-related issues as traffic and poor air quality. Tampa Bay just misses being one of the top rated areas.

The flat, coastal plain has coastal grasses, palm trees, and white sand, and much of it has an elevation of less than 15 feet. Most of the city area and coast is built up, with coastal plain forests of pine and laurel mixed with orchards and other agricultural uses inland. The Pinellas Peninsula, separating Tampa Bay from the Gulf, is an area of broad, sandy beaches and palm trees. Clearwater and St. Petersburg are located here. Summers are long, warm, and humid. Afternoon highs reach 90°F, with moderating afternoon sea breezes and frequent thunderstorms, and warm evenings in the 70s. Lightening occurs in abundance. (In fact, "Tampa" is a misspelling of a Native American term for "sticks of fire," meaning lightning.) Winters are mild with temperatures in the 60s and 70s, and lows rarely below 50°F.

POPULATION

DEMOGRAPHICS	AREA	U.S. AVG	ETHNIC COMPOSITION	AREA	U.S. AVG	RESIDENT PROFILE	AREA	U.S. AVG
Population	2,490,295		White	87.4%	75.1%	Single	44.7%	43.6%
Population density per sq. mile	974.9	447.3	Black	9.4%	12.3%	Married	55.3%	56.4%
Population growth	20.4%	16.1%	Asian	1.6%	3.6%	Divorced	10.8%	8.4%
Median age	40.6	35.5	American Indian	.3%	.9%	Separated	3.2%	3.0%
Average family size	2.3	2.7	Hispanic	9.7%	12.5%	Married with children	19.5%	28.7%
			Diversity measure	38.8%	35.2%	Single with children	9.4%	10.1%

ECONOMY & JOBS SCORE: 21/RANK: 259

INCOME	AREA	U.S. AVG	EMPLOYMENT	AREA	U.S. AVG	LARGEST EMPLOYING INDUSTRY
Per capita income	$24,630	$23,420	Unemployment rate	4.5%	6.1%	Computer and Electronic Product Manufacturing
Household income	$41,625	$46,060	Recent job growth	-.9%	.9%	
Household income < $25K	27.3%	26.4%	Projected future job growth	19.5%	15.1%	
Household income > $75K	21.0%	24.5%	White collar	58.8%	54.5%	
Household income growth	59.7%	57.3%	Blue collar	41.2%	45.5%	

COST OF LIVING SCORE: 87/RANK: 42

INDEXES & TAXES	AREA	U.S. AVG	HOUSING	AREA	U.S. AVG	NECESSITIES	AREA	U.S. AVG
Cost of Living Index	92.6	100.0	Median home price	$128,180	$160,100	Food Index	100.3	100.0
Financial Progress Index	95.7	100.0	Home price appreciation	11.0%	7.1%	Housing Index	79.6	100.0
Income tax rate	0.000%	4.625%	Median rent	$781	$670	Utilities Index	103.3	100.0
Sales tax rate	7.000%	6.474%	Homes owned	61.4%	63.9%	Transportation Index	100.6	100.0
Property tax rate	$14.9	$15.6	Homes rented	23.5%	25.3%	Healthcare Index	99.6	100.0
			Housing affordability	48.0%	54.5%	Miscellaneous Cost Index	98.3	100.0

CLIMATE SCORE: 81/RANK: 62

TEMPERATURE	AREA	U.S. AVG	PRECIPITATION	AREA	U.S. AVG	COMFORTS & HAZARDS	AREA	U.S. AVG
January low	50.1°F	26.4°F	Annual inches precipitation	49.0	35.9	July relative humidity	74.0%	68.8%
July high	90.4°F	86.7°F	Annual inches snowfall	0.0	24.2	Annual days mostly sunny	238	212
Annual days > 90°F	81	38	Annual days precipitation	107	111	Annual days with thunderstorms	88	39
Annual days < 32°F	4	88	Annual days rain > 0.5 inches	28	23	Tornado risk score	85	19
Annual days < 0°F	0	6	Annual days snow > 1.5 inches	0	6	Hurricane risk score	73	15

TEMPERATURE

PRECIPITATION

DAYS OF CLOUDS & PRECIPITATION

EDUCATION SCORE: 49/RANK: 166

ACHIEVEMENT	AREA	U.S. AVG	PUBLIC SCHOOLS	AREA	U.S. AVG	HIGHER EDUCATION	AREA	U.S. AVG
High school degree	81.9%	80.2%	Expenditures per pupil	$5,380	$5,894	No. 2-year colleges	3	3
2-year college degree	8.0%	6.2%	Student/teacher ratio	17.6	16.7	No. 4-year colleges/universities	9	4
4-year college degree	14.8%	15.8%	Attending public school	89.9%	90.2%	No. highly ranked universities	1	1
Graduate/professional degree	7.3%	9.6%	State SAT score	996*	1020			
			State ACT score	20.5	21.0			

HEALTH & HEALTHCARE SCORE: 26/RANK: 245

HAZARDS & ILLNESSES	AREA	U.S. AVG	HEALTHCARE	AREA	U.S. AVG
Air-quality score	94	45	Physicians per capita	255.3	261.1
Water-quality score	19	33	Hospital beds per capita	417.6	432.2
Pollen/allergy score	86	61	No. teaching hospitals	10	4
Stress score	91	50	Cost per doctor visit	$62	$67
Cancer mortality per capita	169.7	169.0	Cost per dental visit	$73	$82
Depression days per month	3.2	2.8	Cost per daily hospital room	$702	$733

CRIME SCORE: 11/RANK: 292

CRIME	AREA	U.S. AVG
Violent crime rate	904.1	456.0
Change in violent crime rate	-19.3%	-17.2%
Property crime rate	5,004.6	3,950.0
Change in property crime rate	-16.7%	-16.8%

TRANSPORTATION SCORE: 50/RANK: 160

COMMUTE	AREA	U.S. AVG	INTERCITY SERVICES	AREA	U.S. AVG	AUTOMOTIVE	AREA	U.S. AVG
Average commute time	25.6 min.	22.6 min.	Miles to nearest major airport	16	46	Insurance, annual premium	$1,308	$1,011
Commute by auto	92.1%	88.7%	Type of local airport	Large		Gas, cost per gallon	$1.45	$1.50
Commute by mass transit	1.3%	1.8%	No. daily airline departures	374	294	Daily vehicle miles per capita	23.7	23.0
Work at home	2.6%	3.9%	Amtrak service	Yes				
Mass transit miles per capita	8.7	8.0	No. interstate highways	2	1			

LEISURE SCORE: 90/RANK: 32

DINING & SHOPPING	AREA	U.S. AVG	ENTERTAINMENT	AREA	U.S. AVG	OUTDOOR ACTIVITIES	AREA	U.S. AVG
Restaurant rating	1	1	Professional sports rating	7	4	Golf-course rating	9	4
No. outlet malls	2	2	College sports rating	4	4	Ski-area rating	1	4
No. Starbucks	28	11	Zoo/aquarium rating	6	3	National Park rating	2	3
No. warehouse clubs	7	4	Amusement park rating	9	3	Sq. miles inland water	7.0	4.0
			Botanical garden/arboretum rating	1	3	Miles of coastline	76.5	11.4

ARTS & CULTURE SCORE: 83/RANK: 59

MEDIA & LIBRARIES	AREA	U.S. AVG	PERFORMING ARTS	AREA	U.S. AVG	MUSEUMS	AREA	U.S. AVG
Arts radio rating	1	3	Classical music rating	7	4	Overall museum rating	9	6
No. public libraries	62	28	Ballet/dance rating	6	3	Art museum rating	8	5
Library volumes per capita	2.2	2.8	Professional theater rating	8	3	Science museum rating	4	4
			University arts programs rating	2	5	Children's museum rating	7	3

Terre Haute, IN

Score: 55.3   Rank: 188

Profile: Small town
Location: Extreme west-central Indiana along the Wabash River, 10 miles from the Illinois border
Elevation: 808 feet
Time zone: Eastern Standard Time (no daylight savings time)

PRO	CON
Cost of living	Economy
Historic interest	Recreation
College-town amenities	Isolation

Terre Haute has a typically Midwestern mix of agriculture and industry, with an added college-town influence. The city is home to Indiana State University, the Rose-Hulman Institute of Technology, and the historic Saint-Mary-of-the-Woods College. None of these schools are particularly large, but they add variety to the area. Downtown, somewhat typical for the region, contains 800 historic buildings in an 80-block area. Overall cost of living is low and the median home price of $78,730 is the lowest in the state. There isn't much to do locally, but Indianapolis (80 miles northeast) and Bloomington (60 miles southeast) help compensate for what's missing.

The Wabash Valley is broad and flat at this location. To the west lie the mainly flat, agricultural prairies of Illinois. Terrain is gently rolling to the east. The climate is continental, with four distinct seasons, including warm, humid summers and variably cold winters. There is little in the local terrain to block the advance of storms and air masses from the north, west, or south. Weather changes are frequent, with wide temperature fluctuations and wet periods. Precipitation is evenly distributed throughout the year, with frequent spring and summer thunderstorms, some heavy. Collisions of southerly moisture and northerly cold air can produce periods of winter wind and snow. First freeze is mid-October, last is late April.

POPULATION

DEMOGRAPHICS	AREA	U.S. AVG	ETHNIC COMPOSITION	AREA	U.S. AVG	RESIDENT PROFILE	AREA	U.S. AVG
Population	147,934		White	97.0%	75.1%	Single	40.0%	43.6%
Population density per sq. mile	145.3	447.3	Black	2.0%	12.3%	Married	60.0%	56.4%
Population growth	.2%	16.1%	Asian	.7%	3.6%	Divorced	8.3%	8.4%
Median age	36.2	35.5	American Indian	.2%	.9%	Separated	1.4%	3.0%
Average family size	2.5	2.7	Hispanic	.6%	12.5%	Married with children	26.8%	28.7%
			Diversity measure	14.5%	35.2%	Single with children	7.8%	10.1%

ECONOMY & JOBS SCORE: 36/RANK: 211

INCOME	AREA	U.S. AVG	EMPLOYMENT	AREA	U.S. AVG	LARGEST EMPLOYING INDUSTRY
Per capita income	$19,323	$23,420	Unemployment rate	5.7%	6.1%	Chemical Manufacturing
Household income	$36,209	$46,060	Recent job growth	-.8%	.9%	
Household income < $25K	34.3%	26.4%	Projected future job growth	7.8%	15.1%	
Household income > $75K	15.1%	24.5%	White collar	51.1%	54.5%	
Household income growth	54.6%	57.3%	Blue collar	48.9%	45.5%	

COST OF LIVING SCORE: 87/RANK: 41

INDEXES & TAXES	AREA	U.S. AVG	HOUSING	AREA	U.S. AVG	NECESSITIES	AREA	U.S. AVG
Cost of Living Index	82.9	100.0	Median home price	$78,730	$160,100	Food Index	98.9	100.0
Financial Progress Index	93.1	100.0	Home price appreciation	3.6%	7.1%	Housing Index	48.9	100.0
Income tax rate	3.400%	4.625%	Median rent	$465	$670	Utilities Index	112.4	100.0
Sales tax rate	6.000%	6.474%	Homes owned	67.4%	63.9%	Transportation Index	106.2	100.0
Property tax rate	$15.1	$15.6	Homes rented	21.1%	25.3%	Healthcare Index	96.2	100.0
			Housing affordability	57.0%	54.5%	Miscellaneous Cost Index	100.0	100.0

CLIMATE SCORE: 50/RANK: 165

TEMPERATURE	AREA	U.S. AVG	PRECIPITATION	AREA	U.S. AVG	COMFORTS & HAZARDS	AREA	U.S. AVG
January low	19.7°F	26.4°F	Annual inches precipitation	39.0	35.9	July relative humidity	73.0%	68.8%
July high	85.4°F	86.7°F	Annual inches snowfall	21.0	24.2	Annual days mostly sunny	191	212
Annual days > 90°F	15	38	Annual days precipitation	122	111	Annual days with thunderstorms	45	39
Annual days < 32°F	122	88	Annual days rain > 0.5 inches	25	23	Tornado risk score	16	19
Annual days < 0°F	7	6	Annual days snow > 1.5 inches	6	6	Hurricane risk score	4	15

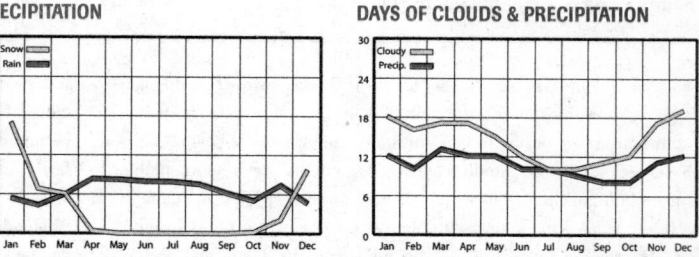

TEMPERATURE — High, Avg, Low (Jan–Dec)

PRECIPITATION — Snow, Rain (Jan–Dec)

DAYS OF CLOUDS & PRECIPITATION — Cloudy, Precip. (Jan–Dec)

EDUCATION SCORE: 33/RANK: 220

ACHIEVEMENT	AREA	U.S. AVG	PUBLIC SCHOOLS	AREA	U.S. AVG	HIGHER EDUCATION	AREA	U.S. AVG
High school degree	81.3%	80.2%	Expenditures per pupil	$5,482	$5,894	No. 2-year colleges	1	3
2-year college degree	5.3%	6.2%	Student/teacher ratio	16.7	16.7	No. 4-year colleges/universities	3	4
4-year college degree	10.4%	15.8%	Attending public school	94.1%	90.2%	No. highly ranked universities	0	1
Graduate/professional degree	8.2%	9.6%	State SAT score	1004*	1020			
			State ACT score	21.6	21.0			

HEALTH & HEALTHCARE SCORE: 38/RANK: 204

CRIME SCORE: 40/RANK: 197

HAZARDS & ILLNESSES	AREA	U.S. AVG	HEALTHCARE	AREA	U.S. AVG	CRIME	AREA	U.S. AVG
Air-quality score	17	45	Physicians per capita	213.6	261.1	Violent crime rate	343.1	456.0
Water-quality score	30	33	Hospital beds per capita	610.6	432.2	Change in violent crime rate	-30.6%	-17.2%
Pollen/allergy score	67	61	No. teaching hospitals	1	4	Property crime rate	4,670.9	3,950.0
Stress score	60	50	Cost per doctor visit	$59	$67	Change in property crime rate	-15.2%	-16.8%
Cancer mortality per capita	182.7	169.0	Cost per dental visit	$71	$82			
Depression days per month	1.7	2.8	Cost per daily hospital room	$439	$733			

TRANSPORTATION SCORE: 36/RANK: 212

COMMUTE	AREA	U.S. AVG	INTERCITY SERVICES	AREA	U.S. AVG	AUTOMOTIVE	AREA	U.S. AVG
Average commute time	20.5 min.	22.6 min.	Miles to nearest major airport	62	46	Insurance, annual premium	$773	$1,011
Commute by auto	87.1%	88.7%	Type of local airport	Medium		Gas, cost per gallon	$1.40	$1.50
Commute by mass transit	.6%	1.8%	No. daily airline departures	319	294	Daily vehicle miles per capita	31.3	23.0
Work at home	4.4%	3.9%	Amtrak service	No				
Mass transit miles per capita	1.9	8.0	No. interstate highways	1	1			

LEISURE SCORE: 19/RANK: 267

DINING & SHOPPING	AREA	U.S. AVG	ENTERTAINMENT	AREA	U.S. AVG	OUTDOOR ACTIVITIES	AREA	U.S. AVG
Restaurant rating	1	1	Professional sports rating	2	4	Golf-course rating	2	4
No. outlet malls	1	2	College sports rating	4	4	Ski-area rating	2	4
No. Starbucks	0	11	Zoo/aquarium rating	1	3	National Park rating	1	3
No. warehouse clubs	3	4	Amusement park rating	1	3	Sq. miles inland water	1.0	4.0
			Botanical garden/arboretum rating	1	3	Miles of coastline	0.0	11.4

ARTS & CULTURE SCORE: 41/RANK: 190

MEDIA & LIBRARIES	AREA	U.S. AVG	PERFORMING ARTS	AREA	U.S. AVG	MUSEUMS	AREA	U.S. AVG
Arts radio rating	1	3	Classical music rating	3	4	Overall museum rating	5	6
No. public libraries	14	28	Ballet/dance rating	1	3	Art museum rating	3	5
Library volumes per capita	3.0	2.8	Professional theater rating	1	3	Science museum rating	2	4
			University arts programs rating	8	5	Children's museum rating	1	3

Texarkana, TX-AR

Score: 35.6   **Rank:** 296

Profile: Small-town complex
Location: Extreme northeast Texas at the Texas-Arkansas border
Elevation: 259 feet
Time zone: Central Standard Time

PRO	CON
Cost of living	Crime rate
Nearby water recreation	Entertainment
Small-town atmosphere	Arts and culture

This area straddles the Texas-Arkansas border with Texarkana, Texas, to the west and Texarkana, Arkansas, to the east. The twin cities are inseparable. In fact, the state line bisects the post office, which serves them both simultaneously. Typical for the region, both cities are plain and quiet but with a diverse and fairly large manufacturing base. At 73.4 the area has the lowest Cost of Living Index in the country. Recreation opportunities abound in nearby lakes and state parks, but there isn't much to do in either town. The low rating is consistent with the notion that there is more to life than low living costs.

The city sits in an area of level to gently rolling land with mixed agricultural areas, cotton plantations, and pine forests. The climate is a mix of humid subtropical and continental types. Summer months are hot and fairly humid, but more pleasant than areas to the south near the Gulf. Winters are mild, with occasional, short periods of cold. Rainfall occurs as steady winter rains or as spring and summer thundershowers, which can be severe in spring.

POPULATION

DEMOGRAPHICS	AREA	U.S. AVG	ETHNIC COMPOSITION	AREA	U.S. AVG	RESIDENT PROFILE	AREA	U.S. AVG
Population	131,027		White	76.4%	75.1%	Single	42.3%	43.6%
Population density per sq. mile	86.7	447.3	Black	19.2%	12.3%	Married	57.7%	56.4%
Population growth	9.1%	16.1%	Asian	1.2%	3.6%	Divorced	9.4%	8.4%
Median age	36.0	35.5	American Indian	.5%	.9%	Separated	3.7%	3.0%
Average family size	2.6	2.7	Hispanic	6.3%	12.5%	Married with children	27.1%	28.7%
			Diversity measure	43.2%	35.2%	Single with children	11.8%	10.1%

ECONOMY & JOBS SCORE: 83/RANK: 56

INCOME	AREA	U.S. AVG	EMPLOYMENT	AREA	U.S. AVG	LARGEST EMPLOYING INDUSTRY
Per capita income	$18,590	$23,420	Unemployment rate	5.2%	6.1%	Fabricated Metal Product Manufacturing
Household income	$35,017	$46,060	Recent job growth	1.2%	.9%	
Household income < $25K	37.3%	26.4%	Projected future job growth	11.1%	15.1%	
Household income > $75K	16.1%	24.5%	White collar	50.0%	54.5%	
Household income growth	52.0%	57.3%	Blue collar	50.0%	45.5%	

COST OF LIVING SCORE: 98/RANK: 6

INDEXES & TAXES	AREA	U.S. AVG	HOUSING	AREA	U.S. AVG	NECESSITIES	AREA	U.S. AVG
Cost of Living Index	73.4	100.0	Median home price	$75,530	$160,100	Food Index	86.9	100.0
Financial Progress Index	101.6	100.0	Home price appreciation	4.8%	7.1%	Housing Index	46.9	100.0
Income tax rate	0.000%	4.625%	Median rent	$495	$670	Utilities Index	84.0	100.0
Sales tax rate	8.250%	6.474%	Homes owned	65.8%	63.9%	Transportation Index	95.2	100.0
Property tax rate	$22.3	$15.6	Homes rented	21.0%	25.3%	Healthcare Index	91.7	100.0
			Housing affordability	56.0%	54.5%	Miscellaneous Cost Index	86.7	100.0

CLIMATE SCORE: 73/RANK: 90

TEMPERATURE	AREA	U.S. AVG	PRECIPITATION	AREA	U.S. AVG	COMFORTS & HAZARDS	AREA	U.S. AVG
January low	37.8°F	26.4°F	Annual inches precipitation	45.0	35.9	July relative humidity	71.0%	68.8%
July high	93.8°F	86.7°F	Annual inches snowfall	1.0	24.2	Annual days mostly sunny	217	212
Annual days > 90°F	87	38	Annual days precipitation	97	111	Annual days with thunderstorms	54	39
Annual days < 32°F	1	88	Annual days rain > 0.5 inches	23	23	Tornado risk score	20	19
Annual days < 0°F	0	6	Annual days snow > 1.5 inches	1	6	Hurricane risk score	11	15

TEMPERATURE

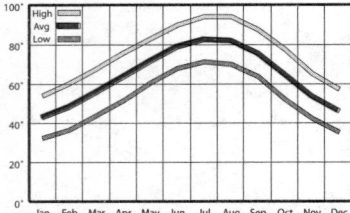

PRECIPITATION

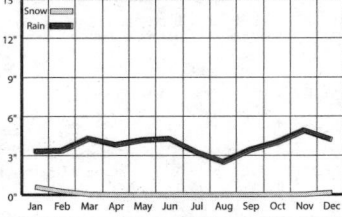

DAYS OF CLOUDS & PRECIPITATION

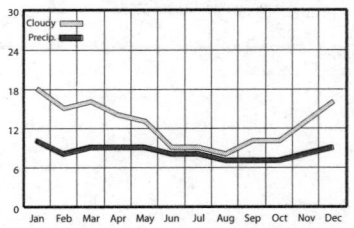

EDUCATION SCORE: 23/RANK: 255

ACHIEVEMENT	AREA	U.S. AVG	PUBLIC SCHOOLS	AREA	U.S. AVG	HIGHER EDUCATION	AREA	U.S. AVG
High school degree	76.4%	80.2%	Expenditures per pupil	$5,022	$5,894	No. 2-year colleges	1	3
2-year college degree	5.4%	6.2%	Student/teacher ratio	14.1	16.7	No. 4-year colleges/universities	0	4
4-year college degree	9.6%	15.8%	Attending public school	97.0%	90.2%	No. highly ranked universities	0	1
Graduate/professional degree	5.4%	9.6%	State SAT score	993*	1020			
			State ACT score	20.1	21.0			

HEALTH & HEALTHCARE SCORE: 79/RANK: 67

HAZARDS & ILLNESSES	AREA	U.S. AVG	HEALTHCARE	AREA	U.S. AVG
Air-quality score	3	45	Physicians per capita	229.0	261.1
Water-quality score	30	33	Hospital beds per capita	704.4	432.2
Pollen/allergy score	64	61	No. teaching hospitals	3	4
Stress score	63	50	Cost per doctor visit	$67	$67
Cancer mortality per capita	169.8	169.0	Cost per dental visit	$71	$82
Depression days per month	5.0	2.8	Cost per daily hospital room	$483	$733

CRIME SCORE: 17/RANK: 274

CRIME	AREA	U.S. AVG
Violent crime rate	599.0	456.0
Change in violent crime rate	2.3%	-17.2%
Property crime rate	4,569.2	3,950.0
Change in property crime rate	.5%	-16.8%

TRANSPORTATION SCORE: 32/RANK: 224

COMMUTE	AREA	U.S. AVG	INTERCITY SERVICES	AREA	U.S. AVG	AUTOMOTIVE	AREA	U.S. AVG
Average commute time	20.3 min.	22.6 min.	Miles to nearest major airport	69	46	Insurance, annual premium	$920	$1,011
Commute by auto	94.5%	88.7%	Type of local airport	Small		Gas, cost per gallon	$1.41	$1.50
Commute by mass transit	.3%	1.8%	No. daily airline departures	66	294	Daily vehicle miles per capita	28.4	23.0
Work at home	2.3%	3.9%	Amtrak service	Yes				
Mass transit miles per capita	0.0	8.0	No. interstate highways	1	1			

LEISURE SCORE: 7/RANK: 305

DINING & SHOPPING	AREA	U.S. AVG	ENTERTAINMENT	AREA	U.S. AVG	OUTDOOR ACTIVITIES	AREA	U.S. AVG
Restaurant rating	1	1	Professional sports rating	2	4	Golf-course rating	1	4
No. outlet malls	0	2	College sports rating	1	4	Ski-area rating	1	4
No. Starbucks	0	11	Zoo/aquarium rating	1	3	National Park rating	1	3
No. warehouse clubs	3	4	Amusement park rating	1	3	Sq. miles inland water	5.0	4.0
			Botanical garden/arboretum rating	1	3	Miles of coastline	0.0	11.4

ARTS & CULTURE SCORE: 7/RANK: 306

MEDIA & LIBRARIES	AREA	U.S. AVG	PERFORMING ARTS	AREA	U.S. AVG	MUSEUMS	AREA	U.S. AVG
Arts radio rating	1	3	Classical music rating	1	4	Overall museum rating	2	6
No. public libraries	5	28	Ballet/dance rating	1	3	Art museum rating	1	5
Library volumes per capita	3.8	2.8	Professional theater rating	1	3	Science museum rating	1	4
			University arts programs rating	1	5	Children's museum rating	3	3

Toledo, OH

Score: 41.9 Rank: 267

Profile: Mid-size city
Location: Northwest Ohio at the western corner of Lake Erie at the Michigan border
Elevation: 692 feet
Time zone: Eastern Standard Time

PRO	CON
Cost of living	Economy
Central location	Industrial feel
Nearby water recreation	Gloomy winters

Toledo is a hardworking city and a major Great Lakes port, transportation, and industrial center. Major industries include auto manufacturing and glassmaking. The city also serves a large agricultural region of the Maumee River and northwestern Ohio. Job losses in manufacturing have hit the area hard, and there are areas of economic decline. The city core is plain and unremarkable, but some nicer neighborhoods are to the west and south. There is not a lot to do, but a quality art museum and the venerable Toledo Mud Hens minor-league baseball team are part of an assortment of minor amenities. Civic pride among local residents is strong. Amenities and services missing locally are available in Detroit, 60 miles north, or Cleveland, 115 miles east. The location on Lake Erie's western shore means winters are not as severe as other parts of northern Ohio, but climate is hardly an attraction.

The city is located at the mouth of the Maumee River. Except for a 30-foot riverbank, the terrain is generally level with only a slight slope toward the river and Lake Erie. Climate is continental with some moderating effects from Lake Erie. Summers are warm and humid while winters are cool and humid with considerable cloudiness. Winter sun is only 30% of daylight hours, with December and January only clear 16% of the time. Snowfall, on the other hand, is generally light. A combination of flat terrain and occasionally high lake levels can result in flooding. First freeze is mid-October, last is late April.

POPULATION

DEMOGRAPHICS	AREA	U.S. AVG	ETHNIC COMPOSITION	AREA	U.S. AVG	RESIDENT PROFILE	AREA	U.S. AVG
Population	618,466		White	86.4%	75.1%	Single	47.1%	43.6%
Population density per sq. mile	453.2	447.3	Black	10.8%	12.3%	Married	52.9%	56.4%
Population growth	.7%	16.1%	Asian	1.0%	3.6%	Divorced	8.9%	8.4%
Median age	35.0	35.5	American Indian	.2%	.9%	Separated	2.3%	3.0%
Average family size	2.6	2.7	Hispanic	3.5%	12.5%	Married with children	27.7%	28.7%
			Diversity measure	33.3%	35.2%	Single with children	10.7%	10.1%

ECONOMY & JOBS SCORE: 24/RANK: 251

INCOME	AREA	U.S. AVG	EMPLOYMENT	AREA	U.S. AVG	LARGEST EMPLOYING INDUSTRY
Per capita income	$22,886	$23,420	Unemployment rate	6.5%	6.1%	Transportation Equipment Manufacturing
Household income	$43,082	$46,060	Recent job growth	-1.0%	.9%	
Household income < $25K	27.8%	26.4%	Projected future job growth	10.7%	15.1%	
Household income > $75K	22.1%	24.5%	White collar	52.7%	54.5%	
Household income growth	47.6%	57.3%	Blue collar	47.3%	45.5%	

COST OF LIVING SCORE: 39/RANK: 202

INDEXES & TAXES	AREA	U.S. AVG	HOUSING	AREA	U.S. AVG	NECESSITIES	AREA	U.S. AVG
Cost of Living Index	91.0	100.0	Median home price	$108,400	$160,100	Food Index	107.0	100.0
Financial Progress Index	100.9	100.0	Home price appreciation	5.5%	7.1%	Housing Index	67.3	100.0
Income tax rate	7.243%	4.625%	Median rent	$574	$670	Utilities Index	120.4	100.0
Sales tax rate	6.250%	6.474%	Homes owned	67.3%	63.9%	Transportation Index	100.3	100.0
Property tax rate	$16.7	$15.6	Homes rented	25.1%	25.3%	Healthcare Index	99.1	100.0
			Housing affordability	56.0%	54.5%	Miscellaneous Cost Index	100.0	100.0

CLIMATE SCORE: 40/RANK: 198

TEMPERATURE	AREA	U.S. AVG	PRECIPITATION	AREA	U.S. AVG	COMFORTS & HAZARDS	AREA	U.S. AVG
January low	17.2°F	26.4°F	Annual inches precipitation	32.0	35.9	July relative humidity	72.0%	68.8%
July high	83.8°F	86.7°F	Annual inches snowfall	37.0	24.2	Annual days mostly sunny	181	212
Annual days > 90°F	13	38	Annual days precipitation	136	111	Annual days with thunderstorms	40	39
Annual days < 32°F	145	88	Annual days rain > 0.5 inches	20	23	Tornado risk score	23	19
Annual days < 0°F	8	6	Annual days snow > 1.5 inches	9	6	Hurricane risk score	3	15

TEMPERATURE

PRECIPITATION

DAYS OF CLOUDS & PRECIPITATION

EDUCATION SCORE: 30/RANK: 230

ACHIEVEMENT	AREA	U.S. AVG	PUBLIC SCHOOLS	AREA	U.S. AVG	HIGHER EDUCATION	AREA	U.S. AVG
High school degree	84.1%	80.2%	Expenditures per pupil	$6,275	$5,894	No. 2-year colleges	4	3
2-year college degree	6.7%	6.2%	Student/teacher ratio	15.7	16.7	No. 4-year colleges/universities	3	4
4-year college degree	13.9%	15.8%	Attending public school	82.4%	90.2%	No. highly ranked universities	0	1
Graduate/professional degree	7.7%	9.6%	State SAT score	1077	1020			
			State ACT score	21.4*	21.0			

HEALTH & HEALTHCARE SCORE: 39/RANK: 202

CRIME SCORE: 11/RANK: 293

HAZARDS & ILLNESSES	AREA	U.S. AVG	HEALTHCARE	AREA	U.S. AVG	CRIME	AREA	U.S. AVG
Air-quality score	89	45	Physicians per capita	316.8	261.1	Violent crime rate	561.9	456.0
Water-quality score	12	33	Hospital beds per capita	528.1	432.2	Change in violent crime rate	1.2%	-17.2%
Pollen/allergy score	53	61	No. teaching hospitals	7	4	Property crime rate	5,467.5	3,950.0
Stress score	84	50	Cost per doctor visit	$70	$67	Change in property crime rate	-.8%	-16.8%
Cancer mortality per capita	179.8	169.0	Cost per dental visit	$80	$82			
Depression days per month	2.2	2.8	Cost per daily hospital room	$567	$733			

TRANSPORTATION SCORE: 60/RANK: 133

COMMUTE	AREA	U.S. AVG	INTERCITY SERVICES	AREA	U.S. AVG	AUTOMOTIVE	AREA	U.S. AVG
Average commute time	20.5 min.	22.6 min.	Miles to nearest major airport	41	46	Insurance, annual premium	$1,062	$1,011
Commute by auto	90.2%	88.7%	Type of local airport	Large		Gas, cost per gallon	$1.46	$1.50
Commute by mass transit	1.7%	1.8%	No. daily airline departures	781	294	Daily vehicle miles per capita	24.4	23.0
Work at home	2.6%	3.9%	Amtrak service	Yes				
Mass transit miles per capita	7.4	8.0	No. interstate highways	2	1			

LEISURE SCORE: 50/RANK: 165

DINING & SHOPPING	AREA	U.S. AVG	ENTERTAINMENT	AREA	U.S. AVG	OUTDOOR ACTIVITIES	AREA	U.S. AVG
Restaurant rating	1	1	Professional sports rating	6	4	Golf-course rating	5	4
No. outlet malls	0	2	College sports rating	5	4	Ski-area rating	2	4
No. Starbucks	0	11	Zoo/aquarium rating	7	3	National Park rating	2	3
No. warehouse clubs	1	4	Amusement park rating	1	3	Sq. miles inland water	2.0	4.0
			Botanical garden/arboretum rating	1	3	Miles of coastline	19.5	11.4

ARTS & CULTURE SCORE: 87/RANK: 40

MEDIA & LIBRARIES	AREA	U.S. AVG	PERFORMING ARTS	AREA	U.S. AVG	MUSEUMS	AREA	U.S. AVG
Arts radio rating	5	3	Classical music rating	5	4	Overall museum rating	6	6
No. public libraries	39	28	Ballet/dance rating	3	3	Art museum rating	8	5
Library volumes per capita	5.5	2.8	Professional theater rating	1	3	Science museum rating	5	4
			University arts programs rating	7	5	Children's museum rating	1	3

Topeka, KS

Score: 53.7	**Rank: 197**

Profile: Capital city
Location: Northeast Kansas, 60 miles west of Kansas City
Elevation: 877 feet
Time zone: Central Standard Time

PRO	CON
Capital-city amenities	Crime rate
Diverse economy	Job and income growth
Cost of living	Entertainment

Topeka, the capital of Kansas, is an industrial and transportation center with a diverse agricultural base and extensive dairy farming. Highlights in the traditionally laid-out downtown include the statehouse, Kansas Museum of History, Brown vs. Board of Education historic site, and Heartland Park, a state-of-the-art motorsports complex. Costs of living and housing are low, particularly for a capital city. But crime rates are high and projected job and income growth are relatively low. There isn't much to do. Some entertainment and cultural amenities are available in the university town of Lawrence, 20 miles east and in the Kansas City area.

The city straddles the Kansas River in a valley, 2 to 4 miles wide, bordered by rolling prairie. The climate is decidedly continental and highly variable. Summers are usually hot with low relative humidity and persistent southerly winds. Temperatures can exceed 100°F for 50 days or more, although 25% of summers have 2 or fewer days reaching 100°F. Frequent cold and snow characterize winter. Bitter cold spells are seldom prolonged. Spring is windy, while autumn brings warm days, cool nights, and relative dryness. Seventy percent of annual precipitation falls from April through September, the crop-growing months, predominantly as thunderstorms. Warm-season thunderstorms can deliver over 8 inches of rain in 24 hours. Tornadoes are a risk. First freeze is mid-October, last is late April.

POPULATION

DEMOGRAPHICS	AREA	U.S. AVG	ETHNIC COMPOSITION	AREA	U.S. AVG	RESIDENT PROFILE	AREA	U.S. AVG
Population	170,748		White	87.8%	75.1%	Single	42.8%	43.6%
Population density per sq. mile	310.5	447.3	Black	7.9%	12.3%	Married	57.2%	56.4%
Population growth	6.1%	16.1%	Asian	.9%	3.6%	Divorced	11.2%	8.4%
Median age	37.5	35.5	American Indian	1.4%	.9%	Separated	1.7%	3.0%
Average family size	2.6	2.7	Hispanic	6.9%	12.5%	Married with children	27.5%	28.7%
			Diversity measure	34.5%	35.2%	Single with children	10.3%	10.1%

ECONOMY & JOBS SCORE: 99/RANK: 3

INCOME	AREA	U.S. AVG	EMPLOYMENT	AREA	U.S. AVG	LARGEST EMPLOYING INDUSTRY
Per capita income	$22,508	$23,420	Unemployment rate	4.4%	6.1%	Healthcare and Social Assistance
Household income	$43,972	$46,060	Recent job growth	3.8%	.9%	
Household income < $25K	24.2%	26.4%	Projected future job growth	9.7%	15.1%	
Household income > $75K	21.2%	24.5%	White collar	60.4%	54.5%	
Household income growth	46.8%	57.3%	Blue collar	39.6%	45.5%	

COST OF LIVING SCORE: 56/RANK: 146

INDEXES & TAXES	AREA	U.S. AVG	HOUSING	AREA	U.S. AVG	NECESSITIES	AREA	U.S. AVG
Cost of Living Index	82.7	100.0	Median home price	$90,200	$160,100	Food Index	95.7	100.0
Financial Progress Index	113.3	100.0	Home price appreciation	5.1%	7.1%	Housing Index	56.0	100.0
Income tax rate	6.250%	4.625%	Median rent	$536	$670	Utilities Index	105.5	100.0
Sales tax rate	7.200%	6.474%	Homes owned	67.2%	63.9%	Transportation Index	98.8	100.0
Property tax rate	$18.4	$15.6	Homes rented	24.8%	25.3%	Healthcare Index	90.9	100.0
			Housing affordability	59.0%	54.5%	Miscellaneous Cost Index	97.8	100.0

CLIMATE — SCORE: 43/RANK: 189

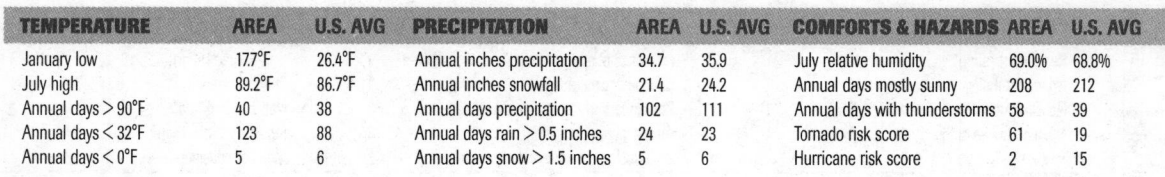

TEMPERATURE	AREA	U.S. AVG	PRECIPITATION	AREA	U.S. AVG	COMFORTS & HAZARDS	AREA	U.S. AVG
January low	17.7°F	26.4°F	Annual inches precipitation	34.7	35.9	July relative humidity	69.0%	68.8%
July high	89.2°F	86.7°F	Annual inches snowfall	21.4	24.2	Annual days mostly sunny	208	212
Annual days > 90°F	40	38	Annual days precipitation	102	111	Annual days with thunderstorms	58	39
Annual days < 32°F	123	88	Annual days rain > 0.5 inches	24	23	Tornado risk score	61	19
Annual days < 0°F	5	6	Annual days snow > 1.5 inches	5	6	Hurricane risk score	2	15

TEMPERATURE   **PRECIPITATION**   **DAYS OF CLOUDS & PRECIPITATION**

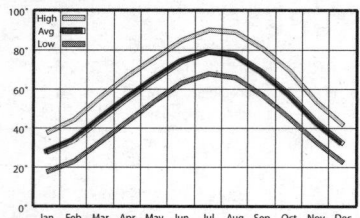 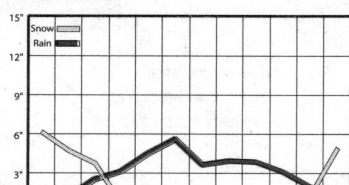 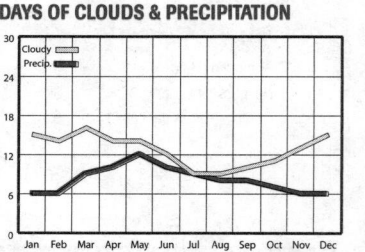

EDUCATION — SCORE: 43/RANK: 189

ACHIEVEMENT	AREA	U.S. AVG	PUBLIC SCHOOLS	AREA	U.S. AVG	HIGHER EDUCATION	AREA	U.S. AVG
High school degree	88.1%	80.2%	Expenditures per pupil	$5,971	$5,894	No. 2-year colleges	0	3
2-year college degree	4.0%	6.2%	Student/teacher ratio	14.9	16.7	No. 4-year colleges/universities	1	4
4-year college degree	16.5%	15.8%	Attending public school	87.8%	90.2%	No. highly ranked universities	0	1
Graduate/professional degree	8.8%	9.6%	State SAT score	1160	1020			
			State ACT score	21.5*	21.0			

HEALTH & HEALTHCARE — SCORE: 78/RANK: 70

CRIME — SCORE: 1/RANK: 326

HAZARDS & ILLNESSES	AREA	U.S. AVG	HEALTHCARE	AREA	U.S. AVG	CRIME	AREA	U.S. AVG
Air-quality score	17	45	Physicians per capita	251.8	261.1	Violent crime rate	706.5	456.0
Water-quality score	0	33	Hospital beds per capita	664.6	432.2	Change in violent crime rate	-17.8%	-17.2%
Pollen/allergy score	71	61	No. teaching hospitals	4	4	Property crime rate	6,780.6	3,950.0
Stress score	86	50	Cost per doctor visit	$61	$67	Change in property crime rate	3.0%	-16.8%
Cancer mortality per capita	154.5	169.0	Cost per dental visit	$81	$82			
Depression days per month	3.1	2.8	Cost per daily hospital room	$503	$733			

TRANSPORTATION — SCORE: 79/RANK: 67

COMMUTE	AREA	U.S. AVG	INTERCITY SERVICES	AREA	U.S. AVG	AUTOMOTIVE	AREA	U.S. AVG
Average commute time	18.0 min.	22.6 min.	Miles to nearest major airport	56	46	Insurance, annual premium	$761	$1,011
Commute by auto	92.1%	88.7%	Type of local airport	Medium		Gas, cost per gallon	$1.46	$1.50
Commute by mass transit	1.3%	1.8%	No. daily airline departures	328	294	Daily vehicle miles per capita	21.1	23.0
Work at home	3.1%	3.9%	Amtrak service	Yes				
Mass transit miles per capita	7.2	8.0	No. interstate highways	1	1			

LEISURE — SCORE: 52/RANK: 157

DINING & SHOPPING	AREA	U.S. AVG	ENTERTAINMENT	AREA	U.S. AVG	OUTDOOR ACTIVITIES	AREA	U.S. AVG
Restaurant rating	1	1	Professional sports rating	2	4	Golf-course rating	2	4
No. outlet malls	1	2	College sports rating	2	4	Ski-area rating	2	4
No. Starbucks	0	11	Zoo/aquarium rating	3	3	National Park rating	1	3
No. warehouse clubs	3	4	Amusement park rating	1	3	Sq. miles inland water	2.0	4.0
			Botanical garden/arboretum rating	4	3	Miles of coastline	0.0	11.4

ARTS & CULTURE — SCORE: 54/RANK: 151

MEDIA & LIBRARIES	AREA	U.S. AVG	PERFORMING ARTS	AREA	U.S. AVG	MUSEUMS	AREA	U.S. AVG
Arts radio rating	1	3	Classical music rating	1	4	Overall museum rating	5	6
No. public libraries	3	28	Ballet/dance rating	1	3	Art museum rating	2	5
Library volumes per capita	3.0	2.8	Professional theater rating	1	3	Science museum rating	3	4
			University arts programs rating	3	5	Children's museum rating	2	3

Trenton, NJ

Score: 57.0	**Rank:** 169

Profile: Capital city
Location: Western New Jersey along the Delaware River and Pennsylvania border, 40 miles north of Philadelphia
Elevation: 56 feet
Time zone: Eastern Standard Time

PRO	CON
Nearby college town	Economy
Historic interest	Industrial areas
Moderate cost of living	Long commute

Trenton, the capital of New Jersey, contains a mix of government and commercial activities. Like many places in the state, the area is characterized by contrasts. Numerous well-preserved historic districts date back to the Revolutionary War. Impoverished areas are also present and there's a strong working-class element. Princeton, a college town 15 miles northeast, contains Princeton University, arts and culture amenities, and a highly educated, mostly upper-middle-class population. Princeton also serves as a residence for commuters who endure a 1½-hour rail trip to New York City. Outside of Princeton, the economic outlook is mixed.

Trenton lies in the Delaware River Valley with level and gently rolling, mostly wooded and agricultural terrain to the east and more significant hills to the north and west. The climate is East Coast continental, with moderating effects from the Appalachian Mountains to the west and the Atlantic Ocean to the east. The climate is variable, with periods of extreme temperatures seldom lasting for more than a few days. The area is far enough inland to have periods of heat and relatively stagnant air, with humidity but little cooling from the marine zones. Precipitation is evenly distributed throughout the year with maximum amounts arriving in summer months. Winter is a mix of cool and colder periods, with rain or snow arriving from either the northwest leading continental air masses or the south as coastal Atlantic storms. First freeze is mid-October, last is late April.

POPULATION

DEMOGRAPHICS	AREA	U.S. AVG	ETHNIC COMPOSITION	AREA	U.S. AVG	RESIDENT PROFILE	AREA	U.S. AVG
Population	359,463		White	72.7%	75.1%	Single	52.7%	43.6%
Population density per sq. mile	1,590.8	447.3	Black	17.9%	12.3%	Married	47.3%	56.4%
Population growth	10.3%	16.1%	Asian	5.7%	3.6%	Divorced	6.9%	8.4%
Median age	36.4	35.5	American Indian	.2%	.9%	Separated	3.5%	3.0%
Average family size	2.6	2.7	Hispanic	9.8%	12.5%	Married with children	25.0%	28.7%
			Diversity measure	52.4%	35.2%	Single with children	10.3%	10.1%

ECONOMY & JOBS   SCORE: 86/RANK: 47

INCOME	AREA	U.S. AVG	EMPLOYMENT	AREA	U.S. AVG	LARGEST EMPLOYING INDUSTRY
Per capita income	$33,721	$23,420	Unemployment rate	5.0%	6.1%	Securities, Commodity Contracts, and Other
Household income	$69,514	$46,060	Recent job growth	1.8%	.9%	Financial Investments and Related Activities
Household income < $25K	14.9%	26.4%	Projected future job growth	9.2%	15.1%	
Household income > $75K	46.3%	24.5%	White collar	65.8%	54.5%	
Household income growth	68.1%	57.3%	Blue collar	34.2%	45.5%	

COST OF LIVING   SCORE: 17/RANK: 272

INDEXES & TAXES	AREA	U.S. AVG	HOUSING	AREA	U.S. AVG	NECESSITIES	AREA	U.S. AVG
Cost of Living Index	113.0	100.0	Median home price	$181,400	$160,100	Food Index	108.6	100.0
Financial Progress Index	131.1	100.0	Home price appreciation	12.4%	7.1%	Housing Index	112.7	100.0
Income tax rate	2.450%	4.625%	Median rent	$973	$670	Utilities Index	124.5	100.0
Sales tax rate	6.000%	6.474%	Homes owned	63.1%	63.9%	Transportation Index	115.7	100.0
Property tax rate	$22.7	$15.6	Homes rented	31.1%	25.3%	Healthcare Index	109.7	100.0
			Housing affordability	49.0%	54.5%	Miscellaneous Cost Index	112.4	100.0

CLIMATE — SCORE: 58/RANK: 139

TEMPERATURE	AREA	U.S. AVG	PRECIPITATION	AREA	U.S. AVG	COMFORTS & HAZARDS	AREA	U.S. AVG
January low	25.3°F	26.4°F	Annual inches precipitation	40.2	35.9	July relative humidity	67.0%	68.8%
July high	84.9°F	86.7°F	Annual inches snowfall	23.4	24.2	Annual days mostly sunny	216	212
Annual days > 90°F	17	38	Annual days precipitation	128	111	Annual days with thunderstorms	33	39
Annual days < 32°F	88	88	Annual days rain > 0.5 inches	28	23	Tornado risk score	17	19
Annual days < 0°F	0	6	Annual days snow > 1.5 inches	6	6	Hurricane risk score	15	15

TEMPERATURE

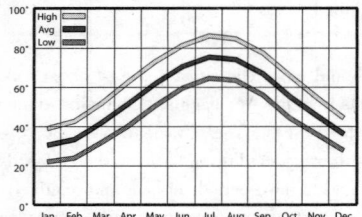

PRECIPITATION

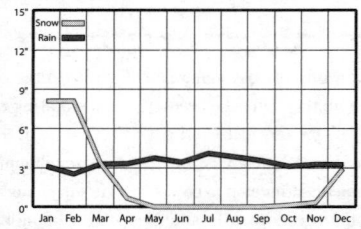

DAYS OF CLOUDS & PRECIPITATION

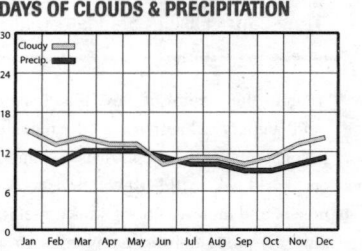

EDUCATION — SCORE: 73/RANK: 91

ACHIEVEMENT	AREA	U.S. AVG	PUBLIC SCHOOLS	AREA	U.S. AVG	HIGHER EDUCATION	AREA	U.S. AVG
High school degree	81.8%	80.2%	Expenditures per pupil	$9,802	$5,894	No. 2-year colleges	1	3
2-year college degree	5.4%	6.2%	Student/teacher ratio	14.4	16.7	No. 4-year colleges/universities	5	4
4-year college degree	18.5%	15.8%	Attending public school	83.6%	90.2%	No. highly ranked universities	1	1
Graduate/professional degree	15.5%	9.6%	State SAT score	1016*	1020			
			State ACT score	21.2	21.0			

HEALTH & HEALTHCARE — SCORE: 33/RANK: 219

HAZARDS & ILLNESSES	AREA	U.S. AVG	HEALTHCARE	AREA	U.S. AVG
Air-quality score	81	45	Physicians per capita	324.9	261.1
Water-quality score	6	33	Hospital beds per capita	558.2	432.2
Pollen/allergy score	64	61	No. teaching hospitals	4	4
Stress score	33	50	Cost per doctor visit	$77	$67
Cancer mortality per capita	186.4	169.0	Cost per dental visit	$109	$82
Depression days per month	2.6	2.8	Cost per daily hospital room	$3,152	$733

CRIME — SCORE: 33/RANK: 219

CRIME	AREA	U.S. AVG
Violent crime rate	564.9	456.0
Change in violent crime rate	5.6%	-17.2%
Property crime rate	3,654.1	3,950.0
Change in property crime rate	-7.9%	-16.8%

TRANSPORTATION — SCORE: 80/RANK: 64

COMMUTE	AREA	U.S. AVG	INTERCITY SERVICES	AREA	U.S. AVG	AUTOMOTIVE	AREA	U.S. AVG
Average commute time	27.1 min.	22.6 min.	Miles to nearest major airport	35	46	Insurance, annual premium	$1,186	$1,011
Commute by auto	79.8%	88.7%	Type of local airport	Large		Gas, cost per gallon	$1.43	$1.50
Commute by mass transit	6.1%	1.8%	No. daily airline departures	669	294	Daily vehicle miles per capita	25.1	23.0
Work at home	2.7%	3.9%	Amtrak service	Yes				
Mass transit miles per capita	24.9	8.0	No. interstate highways	1	1			

LEISURE — SCORE: 87/RANK: 41

DINING & SHOPPING	AREA	U.S. AVG	ENTERTAINMENT	AREA	U.S. AVG	OUTDOOR ACTIVITIES	AREA	U.S. AVG
Restaurant rating	1	1	Professional sports rating	10	4	Golf-course rating	8	4
No. outlet malls	8	2	College sports rating	6	4	Ski-area rating	4	4
No. Starbucks	3	11	Zoo/aquarium rating	4	3	National Park rating	3	3
No. warehouse clubs	3	4	Amusement park rating	5	3	Sq. miles inland water	6.0	4.0
			Botanical garden/arboretum rating	5	3	Miles of coastline	0.0	11.4

ARTS & CULTURE — SCORE: 92/RANK: 27

MEDIA & LIBRARIES	AREA	U.S. AVG	PERFORMING ARTS	AREA	U.S. AVG	MUSEUMS	AREA	U.S. AVG
Arts radio rating	6	3	Classical music rating	7	4	Overall museum rating	7	6
No. public libraries	18	28	Ballet/dance rating	6	3	Art museum rating	8	5
Library volumes per capita	4.2	2.8	Professional theater rating	9	3	Science museum rating	6	4
			University arts programs rating	8	5	Children's museum rating	5	3

Tucson, AZ

Profile: Mid-size city/College town
Location: South-central Arizona, 60 miles north of the Mexican border
Elevation: 2,555 feet
Time zone: Mountain Standard Time (no daylight savings time)

Score: 72.4   **Rank:** 70

PRO	CON
High desert climate	Crime rate
Arts and culture	Cyclical economy
Attractive setting	Long commutes

Tucson is a large and growing Sun Belt city known for its attractive setting, pleasant climate, and cosmopolitan nature. It attracts retirees and a younger crowd. The area consists of a modern downtown, with a historic district, surrounded by suburbs laid out in a grid. The University of Arizona, about a mile north of the downtown, gives the entire area a college-town feel. Tall, forested mountains surround the city up to an elevation of 9,000 feet. In the mountains are higher-priced homes, many of which were damaged by wildfires in 2003. The economy is mainly supported by the university, retirees, and high tech-industry; several large companies, such as IBM, have facilities in the area. The recent downturn in the tech sector has dampened the job picture, at least temporarily. However, cost of living is close to the U.S. average. The climate is close to ideal: The high altitude moderates the desert heat while the southerly location and dry surroundings moderate winter influences and create a generally pleasant atmosphere. The arts and culture scene is particularly strong for a city its size. On the downside, the crime rate is high, and some urban-sprawl issues—relatively long commutes and poor air quality—exist.

Located at the foot of the Catalina Mountains, Tucson lies in a broad, flat valley with many dry riverbeds and washes. The soil is sandy, and vegetation is mostly brush, cacti, and small trees. The climate is mid-altitude arid, characterized by a long hot season from April to October. Temperatures above 90°F prevail from May through September, with 100°F-plus temperatures an average of 41 days per year. Humidity is low and diurnal temperature ranges are high, often over 30°F. Summer thunderstorms, which can flood otherwise dry washes, produce 50% of annual precipitation. Pacific storms provide more steady rain from December through March. Snow may fall in higher mountains, but is infrequent in the city. Clear, sunny days are commonplace with some dust and haze at times. First freeze is late November, last is late February.

POPULATION

DEMOGRAPHICS	AREA	U.S. AVG	ETHNIC COMPOSITION	AREA	U.S. AVG	RESIDENT PROFILE	AREA	U.S. AVG
Population	881,221		White	81.3%	75.1%	Single	46.7%	43.6%
Population density per sq. mile	95.9	447.3	Black	2.8%	12.3%	Married	53.3%	56.4%
Population growth	32.1%	16.1%	Asian	2.2%	3.6%	Divorced	10.1%	8.4%
Median age	36.0	35.5	American Indian	4.7%	.9%	Separated	2.8%	3.0%
Average family size	2.6	2.7	Hispanic	27.3%	12.5%	Married with children	25.0%	28.7%
			Diversity measure	53.1%	35.2%	Single with children	10.5%	10.1%

ECONOMY & JOBS SCORE: 12/RANK: 291

INCOME	AREA	U.S. AVG	EMPLOYMENT	AREA	U.S. AVG	LARGEST EMPLOYING INDUSTRY
Per capita income	$22,341	$23,420	Unemployment rate	4.7%	6.1%	Transportation Equipment Manufacturing
Household income	$40,683	$46,060	Recent job growth	.6%	.9%	
Household income < $25K	29.2%	26.4%	Projected future job growth	22.6%	15.1%	
Household income > $75K	21.0%	24.5%	White collar	57.9%	54.5%	
Household income growth	59.9%	57.3%	Blue collar	42.1%	45.5%	

COST OF LIVING SCORE: 40/RANK: 199

INDEXES & TAXES	AREA	U.S. AVG	HOUSING	AREA	U.S. AVG	NECESSITIES	AREA	U.S. AVG
Cost of Living Index	98.0	100.0	Median home price	$149,400	$160,100	Food Index	103.8	100.0
Financial Progress Index	88.5	100.0	Home price appreciation	6.9%	7.1%	Housing Index	92.8	100.0
Income tax rate	3.900%	4.625%	Median rent	$707	$670	Utilities Index	105.8	100.0
Sales tax rate	7.600%	6.474%	Homes owned	58.8%	63.9%	Transportation Index	103.6	100.0
Property tax rate	$11.0	$15.6	Homes rented	28.4%	25.3%	Healthcare Index	109.8	100.0
			Housing affordability	47.0%	54.5%	Miscellaneous Cost Index	93.1	100.0

CLIMATE — SCORE: 95/RANK: 15

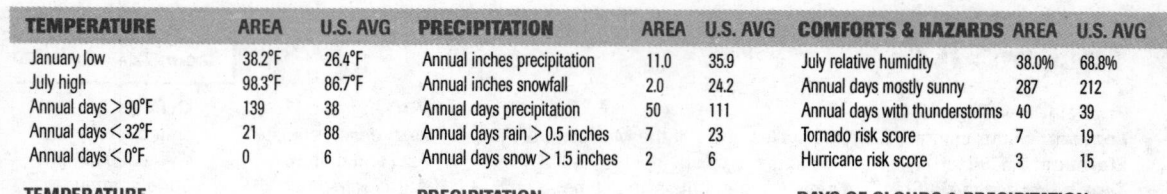

TEMPERATURE	AREA	U.S. AVG	PRECIPITATION	AREA	U.S. AVG	COMFORTS & HAZARDS	AREA	U.S. AVG
January low	38.2°F	26.4°F	Annual inches precipitation	11.0	35.9	July relative humidity	38.0%	68.8%
July high	98.3°F	86.7°F	Annual inches snowfall	2.0	24.2	Annual days mostly sunny	287	212
Annual days > 90°F	139	38	Annual days precipitation	50	111	Annual days with thunderstorms	40	39
Annual days < 32°F	21	88	Annual days rain > 0.5 inches	7	23	Tornado risk score	7	19
Annual days < 0°F	0	6	Annual days snow > 1.5 inches	2	6	Hurricane risk score	3	15

TEMPERATURE

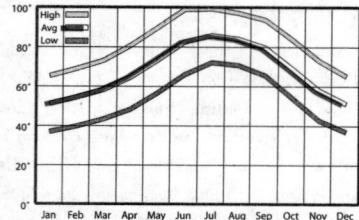

PRECIPITATION

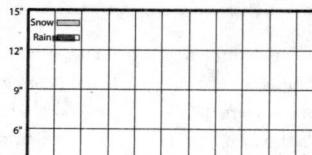

DAYS OF CLOUDS & PRECIPITATION

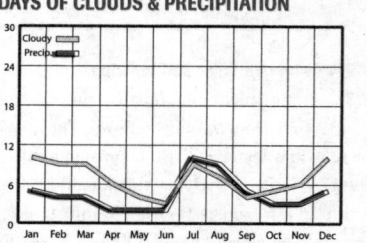

EDUCATION — SCORE: 55/RANK: 147

ACHIEVEMENT	AREA	U.S. AVG	PUBLIC SCHOOLS	AREA	U.S. AVG	HIGHER EDUCATION	AREA	U.S. AVG
High school degree	83.4%	80.2%	Expenditures per pupil	$4,632	$5,894	No. 2-year colleges	2	3
2-year college degree	6.6%	6.2%	Student/teacher ratio	18.4	16.7	No. 4-year colleges/universities	1	4
4-year college degree	15.9%	15.8%	Attending public school	90.9%	90.2%	No. highly ranked universities	1	1
Graduate/professional degree	10.9%	9.6%	State SAT score	1049*	1020			
			State ACT score	21.4	21.0			

HEALTH & HEALTHCARE — SCORE: 28/RANK: 238

CRIME — SCORE: 4/RANK: 315

HAZARDS & ILLNESSES	AREA	U.S. AVG	HEALTHCARE	AREA	U.S. AVG	CRIME	AREA	U.S. AVG
Air-quality score	99	45	Physicians per capita	303.7	261.1	Violent crime rate	671.6	456.0
Water-quality score	19	33	Hospital beds per capita	299.5	432.2	Change in violent crime rate	-23.4%	-17.2%
Pollen/allergy score	68	61	No. teaching hospitals	4	4	Property crime rate	6,927.4	3,950.0
Stress score	92	50	Cost per doctor visit	$64	$67	Change in property crime rate	-22.1%	-16.8%
Cancer mortality per capita	161.2	169.0	Cost per dental visit	$95	$82			
Depression days per month	2.9	2.8	Cost per daily hospital room	$882	$733			

TRANSPORTATION — SCORE: 42/RANK: 189

COMMUTE	AREA	U.S. AVG	INTERCITY SERVICES	AREA	U.S. AVG	AUTOMOTIVE	AREA	U.S. AVG
Average commute time	23.9 min.	22.6 min.	Miles to nearest major airport	6	46	Insurance, annual premium	$1,798	$1,011
Commute by auto	86.3%	88.7%	Type of local airport	Medium		Gas, cost per gallon	$1.51	$1.50
Commute by mass transit	2.3%	1.8%	No. daily airline departures	81	294	Daily vehicle miles per capita	20.3	23.0
Work at home	3.3%	3.9%	Amtrak service	Yes				
Mass transit miles per capita	12.8	8.0	No. interstate highways	2	1			

LEISURE — SCORE: 76/RANK: 78

DINING & SHOPPING	AREA	U.S. AVG	ENTERTAINMENT	AREA	U.S. AVG	OUTDOOR ACTIVITIES	AREA	U.S. AVG
Restaurant rating	5	1	Professional sports rating	3	4	Golf-course rating	4	4
No. outlet malls	1	2	College sports rating	9	4	Ski-area rating	4	4
No. Starbucks	11	11	Zoo/aquarium rating	5	3	National Park rating	10	3
No. warehouse clubs	4	4	Amusement park rating	2	3	Sq. miles inland water	2.0	4.0
			Botanical garden/arboretum rating	7	3	Miles of coastline	0.0	11.4

ARTS & CULTURE — SCORE: 83/RANK: 54

MEDIA & LIBRARIES	AREA	U.S. AVG	PERFORMING ARTS	AREA	U.S. AVG	MUSEUMS	AREA	U.S. AVG
Arts radio rating	7	3	Classical music rating	5	4	Overall museum rating	8	6
No. public libraries	19	28	Ballet/dance rating	1	3	Art museum rating	8	5
Library volumes per capita	1.4	2.8	Professional theater rating	7	3	Science museum rating	10	4
			University arts programs rating	5	5	Children's museum rating	4	3

Tulsa, OK

Score: 62.0   **Rank:** 133

Profile: Mid-size city
Location: Northeastern Oklahoma along the Arkansas River
Elevation: 676 feet
Time zone: Central Standard Time

PRO	CON
Cost of living	Recent unemployment
Attractive downtown	Violent crime
Arts and culture	Summer heat

Tulsa, located along the Arkansas River in the northeast part of the state, is a commercial, industrial, and cultural center. The major industry is oil, and several oil and gas companies make Tulsa their headquarters. An additional 1,000 companies have oil-related operations here. Recently the economic base has broadened into high-tech, telecommunications, banking, and financial services. There have been some setbacks in these industries, but the long-term economic picture is encouraging. Tulsa is also a transport center with an inland port. The downtown area is prosperous and modern with parks, gardens, and attractive older areas, such as the oil-boom era Art Deco district. Although not the largest city in the state, Tulsa has a full set of performing arts and museums and the highest educational attainment in the state. The Cost of Living Index of 86.8 makes the area a good value for what is available.

The city of Tulsa lies along the Arkansas River surrounded by gently rolling grassland and hardwood trees, mostly oaks. Tulsa is far enough north to escape long periods of heat in summer and far enough south to miss extreme winter cold. The influence of warm moist air from the Gulf of Mexico often brings high humidity but the climate is essentially continental. Summers are hot with frequent 100°F days, but low humidity and southerly breezes can moderate temperatures. Winters are generally mild with temperatures occasionally falling below zero but only for a short time. Falls are long with pleasant, sunny days and cool nights. Precipitation occurs evenly throughout the year with spring being the wettest. Thunderstorms are common and occasionally severe. Snow is light and remains only for brief periods. First freeze is early November, last is late March.

POPULATION

DEMOGRAPHICS	AREA	U.S. AVG	ETHNIC COMPOSITION	AREA	U.S. AVG	RESIDENT PROFILE	AREA	U.S. AVG
Population	821,256		White	78.8%	75.1%	Single	42.6%	43.6%
Population density per sq. mile	163.8	447.3	Black	9.3%	12.3%	Married	57.4%	56.4%
Population growth	15.8%	16.1%	Asian	1.1%	3.6%	Divorced	11.4%	8.4%
Median age	35.4	35.5	American Indian	10.1%	.9%	Separated	2.6%	3.0%
Average family size	2.5	2.7	Hispanic	3.0%	12.5%	Married with children	27.9%	28.7%
			Diversity measure	42.7%	35.2%	Single with children	10.2%	10.1%

ECONOMY & JOBS   SCORE: 15/RANK: 280

INCOME	AREA	U.S. AVG	EMPLOYMENT	AREA	U.S. AVG	LARGEST EMPLOYING INDUSTRY
Per capita income	$24,323	$23,420	Unemployment rate	5.9%	6.1%	Fabricated Metal Product Manufacturing
Household income	$44,811	$46,060	Recent job growth	.2%	.9%	
Household income < $25K	25.9%	26.4%	Projected future job growth	13.5%	15.1%	
Household income > $75K	24.2%	24.5%	White collar	57.8%	54.5%	
Household income growth	65.8%	57.3%	Blue collar	42.2%	45.5%	

COST OF LIVING   SCORE: 46/RANK: 179

INDEXES & TAXES	AREA	U.S. AVG	HOUSING	AREA	U.S. AVG	NECESSITIES	AREA	U.S. AVG
Cost of Living Index	86.8	100.0	Median home price	$111,300	$160,100	Food Index	99.7	100.0
Financial Progress Index	110.0	100.0	Home price appreciation	5.7%	7.1%	Housing Index	69.1	100.0
Income tax rate	7.000%	4.625%	Median rent	$595	$670	Utilities Index	96.7	100.0
Sales tax rate	7.917%	6.474%	Homes owned	62.6%	63.9%	Transportation Index	88.6	100.0
Property tax rate	$11.7	$15.6	Homes rented	24.1%	25.3%	Healthcare Index	96.8	100.0
			Housing affordability	57.0%	54.5%	Miscellaneous Cost Index	98.5	100.0

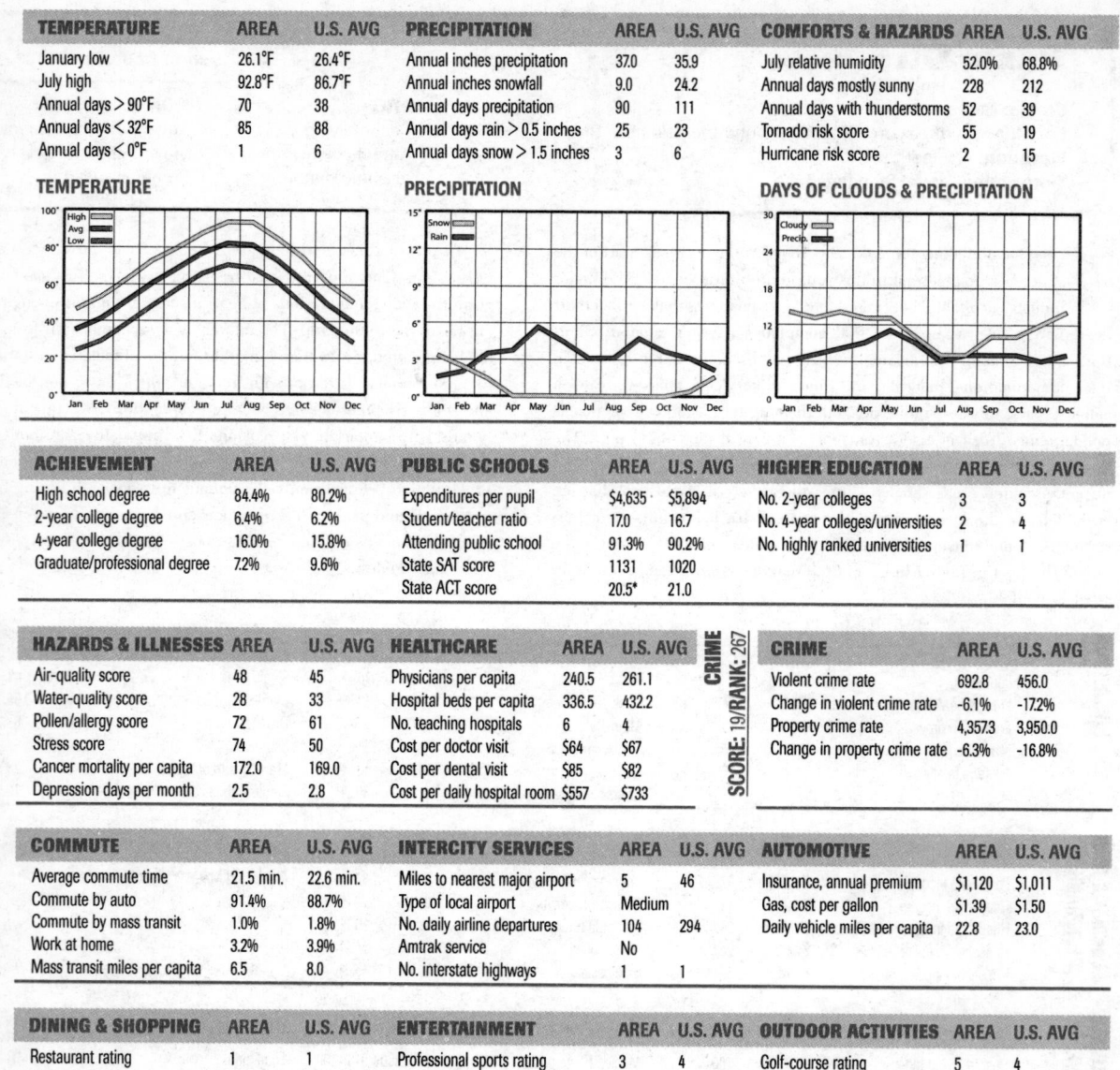

CLIMATE — SCORE: 78/RANK: 72

TEMPERATURE	AREA	U.S. AVG	PRECIPITATION	AREA	U.S. AVG	COMFORTS & HAZARDS	AREA	U.S. AVG
January low	26.1°F	26.4°F	Annual inches precipitation	37.0	35.9	July relative humidity	52.0%	68.8%
July high	92.8°F	86.7°F	Annual inches snowfall	9.0	24.2	Annual days mostly sunny	228	212
Annual days > 90°F	70	38	Annual days precipitation	90	111	Annual days with thunderstorms	52	39
Annual days < 32°F	85	88	Annual days rain > 0.5 inches	25	23	Tornado risk score	55	19
Annual days < 0°F	1	6	Annual days snow > 1.5 inches	3	6	Hurricane risk score	2	15

TEMPERATURE

PRECIPITATION

DAYS OF CLOUDS & PRECIPITATION

EDUCATION — SCORE: 52/RANK: 159

ACHIEVEMENT	AREA	U.S. AVG	PUBLIC SCHOOLS	AREA	U.S. AVG	HIGHER EDUCATION	AREA	U.S. AVG
High school degree	84.4%	80.2%	Expenditures per pupil	$4,635	$5,894	No. 2-year colleges	3	3
2-year college degree	6.4%	6.2%	Student/teacher ratio	17.0	16.7	No. 4-year colleges/universities	2	4
4-year college degree	16.0%	15.8%	Attending public school	91.3%	90.2%	No. highly ranked universities	1	1
Graduate/professional degree	7.2%	9.6%	State SAT score	1131	1020			
			State ACT score	20.5*	21.0			

HEALTH & HEALTHCARE — SCORE: 28/RANK: 237

CRIME — SCORE: 19/RANK: 267

HAZARDS & ILLNESSES	AREA	U.S. AVG	HEALTHCARE	AREA	U.S. AVG	CRIME	AREA	U.S. AVG
Air-quality score	48	45	Physicians per capita	240.5	261.1	Violent crime rate	692.8	456.0
Water-quality score	28	33	Hospital beds per capita	336.5	432.2	Change in violent crime rate	-6.1%	-17.2%
Pollen/allergy score	72	61	No. teaching hospitals	6	4	Property crime rate	4,357.3	3,950.0
Stress score	74	50	Cost per doctor visit	$64	$67	Change in property crime rate	-6.3%	-16.8%
Cancer mortality per capita	172.0	169.0	Cost per dental visit	$85	$82			
Depression days per month	2.5	2.8	Cost per daily hospital room	$557	$733			

TRANSPORTATION — SCORE: 52/RANK: 158

COMMUTE	AREA	U.S. AVG	INTERCITY SERVICES	AREA	U.S. AVG	AUTOMOTIVE	AREA	U.S. AVG
Average commute time	21.5 min.	22.6 min.	Miles to nearest major airport	5	46	Insurance, annual premium	$1,120	$1,011
Commute by auto	91.4%	88.7%	Type of local airport	Medium		Gas, cost per gallon	$1.39	$1.50
Commute by mass transit	1.0%	1.8%	No. daily airline departures	104	294	Daily vehicle miles per capita	22.8	23.0
Work at home	3.2%	3.9%	Amtrak service	No				
Mass transit miles per capita	6.5	8.0	No. interstate highways	1	1			

LEISURE — SCORE: 37/RANK: 208

DINING & SHOPPING	AREA	U.S. AVG	ENTERTAINMENT	AREA	U.S. AVG	OUTDOOR ACTIVITIES	AREA	U.S. AVG
Restaurant rating	1	1	Professional sports rating	3	4	Golf-course rating	5	4
No. outlet malls	0	2	College sports rating	5	4	Ski-area rating	1	4
No. Starbucks	4	11	Zoo/aquarium rating	6	3	National Park rating	1	3
No. warehouse clubs	4	4	Amusement park rating	1	3	Sq. miles inland water	7.0	4.0
			Botanical garden/arboretum rating	6	3	Miles of coastline	0.0	11.4

ARTS & CULTURE — SCORE: 74/RANK: 84

MEDIA & LIBRARIES	AREA	U.S. AVG	PERFORMING ARTS	AREA	U.S. AVG	MUSEUMS	AREA	U.S. AVG
Arts radio rating	1	3	Classical music rating	4	4	Overall museum rating	6	6
No. public libraries	40	28	Ballet/dance rating	3	3	Art museum rating	7	5
Library volumes per capita	2.6	2.8	Professional theater rating	5	3	Science museum rating	5	4
			University arts programs rating	6	5	Children's museum rating	7	3

Tuscaloosa, AL

Profile: College town
Location: West-central Alabama along the Black Warner River
Elevation: 160 feet
Time zone: Central Standard Time

Score: 64.7   Rank: 111

PRO	CON
College-town amenities	Summer heat and humidity
College sports	Crime rate
Healthcare	Isolation

Tuscaloosa is home to the University of Alabama, a large institution with nationally recognized sports programs, notably football's "Crimson Tide." The city has a strong college-town character with the usual entertainment and cultural amenities. The city scores well for cost of living (especially for a college town), healthcare, and overall quality of life, and relatively poorly for climate, crime, and transportation services. Mercedes-Benz builds its U.S. cars in the area. Tuscaloosa received a National Civic League All-America City Award in 2002.

The city is located in an area of level to low rolling hills on the banks of the Black Warner River. Dams just to the northeast contain Lake Tuscaloosa and Bankhead Lake. Land cover is mainly agricultural and southern pine forests. The climate is humid subtropical with long, hot summers in the 90s, persistent humidity, and frequent thunderstorms. Winters are mild with temperatures above freezing most days. Spring is variable, with strong storms. Fall is mild and pleasant with an occasional tropical downpour. First freeze is early November, last is late March.

POPULATION

DEMOGRAPHICS	AREA	U.S. AVG	ETHNIC COMPOSITION	AREA	U.S. AVG	RESIDENT PROFILE	AREA	U.S. AVG
Population	166,512		White	77.3%	75.1%	Single	45.4%	43.6%
Population density per sq. mile	125.6	447.3	Black	21.5%	12.3%	Married	54.6%	56.4%
Population growth	10.6%	16.1%	Asian	.8%	3.6%	Divorced	7.8%	8.4%
Median age	32.2	35.5	American Indian	.3%	.9%	Separated	2.4%	3.0%
Average family size	2.6	2.7	Hispanic	.7%	12.5%	Married with children	27.6%	28.7%
			Diversity measure	45.5%	35.2%	Single with children	10.1%	10.1%

ECONOMY & JOBS   SCORE: 63/RANK: 123

INCOME	AREA	U.S. AVG	EMPLOYMENT	AREA	U.S. AVG	LARGEST EMPLOYING INDUSTRY
Per capita income	$20,688	$23,420	Unemployment rate	3.8%	6.1%	Plastics and Rubber Products Manufacturing
Household income	$36,407	$46,060	Recent job growth	1.5%	.9%	
Household income < $25K	36.0%	26.4%	Projected future job growth	16.5%	15.1%	
Household income > $75K	19.9%	24.5%	White collar	53.4%	54.5%	
Household income growth	57.5%	57.3%	Blue collar	46.6%	45.5%	

COST OF LIVING   SCORE: 76/RANK: 79

INDEXES & TAXES	AREA	U.S. AVG	HOUSING	AREA	U.S. AVG	NECESSITIES	AREA	U.S. AVG
Cost of Living Index	90.9	100.0	Median home price	$121,770	$160,100	Food Index	94.7	100.0
Financial Progress Index	85.4	100.0	Home price appreciation	4.5%	7.1%	Housing Index	75.6	100.0
Income tax rate	5.000%	4.625%	Median rent	$523	$670	Utilities Index	100.7	100.0
Sales tax rate	9.000%	6.474%	Homes owned	68.9%	63.9%	Transportation Index	96.9	100.0
Property tax rate	$4.0	$15.6	Homes rented	24.5%	25.3%	Healthcare Index	94.5	100.0
			Housing affordability	47.0%	54.5%	Miscellaneous Cost Index	105.3	100.0

CLIMATE   SCORE: 22/RANK: 257

TEMPERATURE	AREA	U.S. AVG	PRECIPITATION	AREA	U.S. AVG	COMFORTS & HAZARDS	AREA	U.S. AVG
January low	35.1°F	26.4°F	Annual inches precipitation	53.0	35.9	July relative humidity	72.0%	68.8%
July high	92.3°F	86.7°F	Annual inches snowfall	1.0	24.2	Annual days mostly sunny	210	212
Annual days > 90°F	39	38	Annual days precipitation	118	111	Annual days with thunderstorms	58	39
Annual days < 32°F	60	88	Annual days rain > 0.5 inches	36	23	Tornado risk score	18	19
Annual days < 0°F	0	6	Annual days snow > 1.5 inches	1	6	Hurricane risk score	19	15

TEMPERATURE

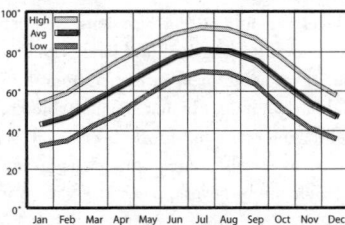

PRECIPITATION

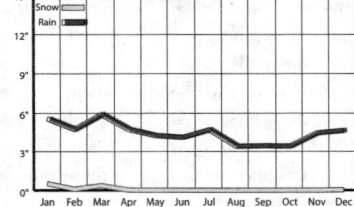

DAYS OF CLOUDS & PRECIPITATION

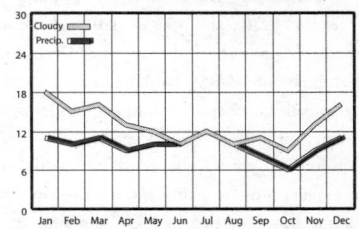

EDUCATION SCORE: 36/RANK: 211

ACHIEVEMENT	AREA	U.S. AVG	PUBLIC SCHOOLS	AREA	U.S. AVG	HIGHER EDUCATION	AREA	U.S. AVG
High school degree	78.8%	80.2%	Expenditures per pupil	$5,115	$5,894	No. 2-year colleges	1	3
2-year college degree	4.8%	6.2%	Student/teacher ratio	15.7	16.7	No. 4-year colleges/universities	2	4
4-year college degree	14.3%	15.8%	Attending public school	91.4%	90.2%	No. highly ranked universities	0	1
Graduate/professional degree	9.7%	9.6%	State SAT score	1111	1020			
			State ACT score	20.1*	21.0			

HEALTH & HEALTHCARE SCORE: 92/RANK: 24

CRIME SCORE: 16/RANK: 276

HAZARDS & ILLNESSES	AREA	U.S. AVG	HEALTHCARE	AREA	U.S. AVG	CRIME	AREA	U.S. AVG
Air-quality score	49	45	Physicians per capita	242.0	261.1	Violent crime rate	773.3	456.0
Water-quality score	63	33	Hospital beds per capita	479.2	432.2	Change in violent crime rate	8.5%	-17.2%
Pollen/allergy score	67	61	No. teaching hospitals	1	4	Property crime rate	5,201.9	3,950.0
Stress score	49	50	Cost per doctor visit	$52	$67	Change in property crime rate	-35.0%	-16.8%
Cancer mortality per capita	149.9	169.0	Cost per dental visit	$74	$82			
Depression days per month	1.8	2.8	Cost per daily hospital room	$596	$733			

TRANSPORTATION SCORE: 30/RANK: 230

COMMUTE	AREA	U.S. AVG	INTERCITY SERVICES	AREA	U.S. AVG	AUTOMOTIVE	AREA	U.S. AVG
Average commute time	21.2 min.	22.6 min.	Miles to nearest major airport	51	46	Insurance, annual premium	$818	$1,011
Commute by auto	91.9%	88.7%	Type of local airport	Small		Gas, cost per gallon	$1.42	$1.50
Commute by mass transit	.8%	1.8%	No. daily airline departures	111	294	Daily vehicle miles per capita	28.1	23.0
Work at home	2.2%	3.9%	Amtrak service	Yes				
Mass transit miles per capita	2.2	8.0	No. interstate highways	2	1			

LEISURE SCORE: 28/RANK: 239

DINING & SHOPPING	AREA	U.S. AVG	ENTERTAINMENT	AREA	U.S. AVG	OUTDOOR ACTIVITIES	AREA	U.S. AVG
Restaurant rating	1	1	Professional sports rating	2	4	Golf-course rating	2	4
No. outlet malls	1	2	College sports rating	6	4	Ski-area rating	1	4
No. Starbucks	0	11	Zoo/aquarium rating	1	3	National Park rating	2	3
No. warehouse clubs	3	4	Amusement park rating	1	3	Sq. miles inland water	2.0	4.0
			Botanical garden/arboretum rating	2	3	Miles of coastline	0.0	11.4

ARTS & CULTURE SCORE: 29/RANK: 235

MEDIA & LIBRARIES	AREA	U.S. AVG	PERFORMING ARTS	AREA	U.S. AVG	MUSEUMS	AREA	U.S. AVG
Arts radio rating	5	3	Classical music rating	3	4	Overall museum rating	5	6
No. public libraries	4	28	Ballet/dance rating	1	3	Art museum rating	4	5
Library volumes per capita	.6	2.8	Professional theater rating	1	3	Science museum rating	3	4
			University arts programs rating	6	5	Children's museum rating	4	3

Tyler, TX

Score: 61.1   Rank: 138

Profile: Small town
Location: Northeast Texas, 100 miles east of Dallas
Elevation: 259 feet
Time zone: Central Standard Time

PRO	CON
Diverse economy	Entertainment
Small-town atmosphere	Isolation
Cost of living	Summer heat

Tyler is the commercial and cultural capital of a region known as "east Texas." The area came to prominence with the huge oil boom of the 1920s and 1930s. Although petroleum and related industries are still important, the city has diversified both commercially and culturally. Businesses in food processing, cotton and cottonseed oil, furniture, machine shops, and forest products have developed, and the economy is strong. The well-kept downtown area has historic homes and is surrounded by mostly wooded, residential neighborhoods. Tyler does have some cultural amenities, but there isn't much to do. Outdoor recreation is available at nearby lakes and state parks. On a Texas scale, the Dallas–Fort Worth metroplex isn't too far away, but the drive is long for some service and amenities.

The terrain is level to gently rolling with dense southern pine forests predominately and intermittent agricultural land. The climate is mainly continental with a strong subtropical influence from the Gulf. Summer months are hot and fairly humid, but more comfortable than areas to the south near the Gulf. Winters are mild, with occasional, short periods of cold. Rainfall occurs as steady winter rains or as spring and summer thundershowers, which can be severe, particularly in spring.

POPULATION

DEMOGRAPHICS	AREA	U.S. AVG	ETHNIC COMPOSITION	AREA	U.S. AVG	RESIDENT PROFILE	AREA	U.S. AVG
Population	181,437		White	71.8%	75.1%	Single	43.2%	43.6%
Population density per sq. mile	195.4	447.3	Black	21.9%	12.3%	Married	56.8%	56.4%
Population growth	19.9%	16.1%	Asian	1.1%	3.6%	Divorced	8.2%	8.4%
Median age	35.9	35.5	American Indian	.4%	.9%	Separated	3.4%	3.0%
Average family size	2.6	2.7	Hispanic	12.8%	12.5%	Married with children	28.7%	28.7%
			Diversity measure	47.3%	35.2%	Single with children	10.2%	10.1%

ECONOMY & JOBS — SCORE: 94/RANK: 19

INCOME	AREA	U.S. AVG	EMPLOYMENT	AREA	U.S. AVG	LARGEST EMPLOYING INDUSTRY
Per capita income	$23,084	$23,420	Unemployment rate	4.8%	6.1%	Machinery Manufacturing
Household income	$43,361	$46,060	Recent job growth	1.6%	.9%	
Household income < $25K	27.9%	26.4%	Projected future job growth	14.5%	15.1%	
Household income > $75K	24.0%	24.5%	White collar	54.9%	54.5%	
Household income growth	68.1%	57.3%	Blue collar	45.1%	45.5%	

COST OF LIVING — SCORE: 90/RANK: 32

INDEXES & TAXES	AREA	U.S. AVG	HOUSING	AREA	U.S. AVG	NECESSITIES	AREA	U.S. AVG
Cost of Living Index	80.8	100.0	Median home price	$97,430	$160,100	Food Index	90.0	100.0
Financial Progress Index	114.3	100.0	Home price appreciation	5.7%	7.1%	Housing Index	60.5	100.0
Income tax rate	0.000%	4.625%	Median rent	$514	$670	Utilities Index	89.4	100.0
Sales tax rate	8.250%	6.474%	Homes owned	66.1%	63.9%	Transportation Index	88.8	100.0
Property tax rate	$19.8	$15.6	Homes rented	21.9%	25.3%	Healthcare Index	92.0	100.0
			Housing affordability	63.0%	54.5%	Miscellaneous Cost Index	96.9	100.0

CLIMATE — SCORE: 72/RANK: 92

TEMPERATURE	AREA	U.S. AVG	PRECIPITATION	AREA	U.S. AVG	COMFORTS & HAZARDS	AREA	U.S. AVG
January low	37.8°F	26.4°F	Annual inches precipitation	45.0	35.9	July relative humidity	71.0%	68.8%
July high	93.8°F	86.7°F	Annual inches snowfall	1.0	24.2	Annual days mostly sunny	217	212
Annual days > 90°F	87	38	Annual days precipitation	97	111	Annual days with thunderstorms	54	39
Annual days < 32°F	1	88	Annual days rain > 0.5 inches	24	23	Tornado risk score	41	19
Annual days < 0°F	0	6	Annual days snow > 1.5 inches	1	6	Hurricane risk score	16	15

TEMPERATURE

PRECIPITATION

DAYS OF CLOUDS & PRECIPITATION

EDUCATION — SCORE: 47/RANK: 175

ACHIEVEMENT	AREA	U.S. AVG	PUBLIC SCHOOLS	AREA	U.S. AVG	HIGHER EDUCATION	AREA	U.S. AVG
High school degree	78.8%	80.2%	Expenditures per pupil	$4,946	$5,894	No. 2-year colleges	1	3
2-year college degree	6.7%	6.2%	Student/teacher ratio	14.5	16.7	No. 4-year colleges/universities	1	4
4-year college degree	15.3%	15.8%	Attending public school	92.7%	90.2%	No. highly ranked universities	0	1
Graduate/professional degree	7.2%	9.6%	State SAT score	993*	1020			
			State ACT score	20.1	21.0			

HEALTH & HEALTHCARE — SCORE: 55/RANK: 146

HAZARDS & ILLNESSES	AREA	U.S. AVG	HEALTHCARE	AREA	U.S. AVG	CRIME (SCORE: 35/RANK: 213)	AREA	U.S. AVG
Air-quality score	24	45	Physicians per capita	335.7	261.1	Violent crime rate	492.9	456.0
Water-quality score	63	33	Hospital beds per capita	516.3	432.2	Change in violent crime rate	-23.7%	-17.2%
Pollen/allergy score	76	61	No. teaching hospitals	2	4	Property crime rate	4,539.6	3,950.0
Stress score	37	50	Cost per doctor visit	$66	$67	Change in property crime rate	-20.9%	-16.8%
Cancer mortality per capita	169.3	169.0	Cost per dental visit	$84	$82			
Depression days per month	2.6	2.8	Cost per daily hospital room	$805	$733			

TRANSPORTATION — SCORE: 13/RANK: 288

COMMUTE	AREA	U.S. AVG	INTERCITY SERVICES	AREA	U.S. AVG	AUTOMOTIVE	AREA	U.S. AVG
Average commute time	22.2 min.	22.6 min.	Miles to nearest major airport	87	46	Insurance, annual premium	$919	$1,011
Commute by auto	93.5%	88.7%	Type of local airport	Small		Gas, cost per gallon	$1.44	$1.50
Commute by mass transit	.3%	1.8%	No. daily airline departures	66	294	Daily vehicle miles per capita	31.7	23.0
Work at home	2.3%	3.9%	Amtrak service	No				
Mass transit miles per capita	0.0	8.0	No. interstate highways	1	1			

LEISURE SCORE: 21/RANK: 259

DINING & SHOPPING	AREA	U.S. AVG	ENTERTAINMENT	AREA	U.S. AVG	OUTDOOR ACTIVITIES	AREA	U.S. AVG
Restaurant rating	1	1	Professional sports rating	2	4	Golf-course rating	2	4
No. outlet malls	0	2	College sports rating	1	4	Ski-area rating	1	4
No. Starbucks	1	11	Zoo/aquarium rating	6	3	National Park rating	1	3
No. warehouse clubs	3	4	Amusement park rating	1	3	Sq. miles inland water	2.0	4.0
			Botanical garden/arboretum rating	3	3	Miles of coastline	0.0	11.4

ARTS & CULTURE SCORE: 10/RANK: 296

MEDIA & LIBRARIES	AREA	U.S. AVG	PERFORMING ARTS	AREA	U.S. AVG	MUSEUMS	AREA	U.S. AVG
Arts radio rating	1	3	Classical music rating	3	4	Overall museum rating	3	6
No. public libraries	6	28	Ballet/dance rating	1	3	Art museum rating	3	5
Library volumes per capita	2.7	2.8	Professional theater rating	1	3	Science museum rating	1	4
			University arts programs rating	2	5	Children's museum rating	1	3

Utica-Rome, NY

Score: 37.4   Rank: 289

Profile: Small-town complex
Location: Central New York, 50 miles east of Syracuse
Elevation: 706 feet
Time zone: Eastern Standard Time

PRO	CON
Nearby recreation	Winter snow
Low crime rate	Winter gloom
Cost of living	Entertainment

Utica and Rome, small towns separated by 16 miles, trace their origins to the Erie Canal. Both towns are hardworking and industrial in nature, but have little charm. However, nearby areas offer plentiful snow and winter sports, and the Adirondacks are a short distance to the northeast. Cooperstown, one of the most likeable small towns in the northeast and home to the National Baseball Hall of Fame, is on the shore of Lake Otsego, 40 miles southeast. Crime and cost of living are low, but there is little to do in the immediate area and winter weather is cloudy and snowy. Utica has the dubious distinction of being tied with Syracuse for receiving the nation's highest annual snowfall among metropolitan areas.

Utica and Rome sit in a broad, relatively level valley that opens onto Oneida Lake to the west. The landscape is mixed farmland and deciduous forest. The hilly Tug Hill Plateau rises to the north, and the mostly wooded Adirondack foothills rise to the northeast and east. The climate is humid continental with warm, sunny days and cool evenings and an occasional hot, sticky spell. Precipitation comes mainly in the form of afternoon thundershowers. Winters are harsh and snowy, as a rise in the terrain and the position with respect to storm tracks and Lake Ontario bring snow and snow squalls. Very heavy snows, as much as 200 inches per year, occur in some of the hills to the north.

POPULATION

DEMOGRAPHICS	AREA	U.S. AVG	ETHNIC COMPOSITION	AREA	U.S. AVG	RESIDENT PROFILE	AREA	U.S. AVG
Population	298,707		White	95.5%	75.1%	Single	43.0%	43.6%
Population density per sq. mile	113.8	447.3	Black	2.9%	12.3%	Married	57.0%	56.4%
Population growth	-5.7%	16.1%	Asian	.9%	3.6%	Divorced	6.6%	8.4%
Median age	38.9	35.5	American Indian	.2%	.9%	Separated	3.4%	3.0%
Average family size	2.6	2.7	Hispanic	1.6%	12.5%	Married with children	29.4%	28.7%
			Diversity measure	17.8%	35.2%	Single with children	8.9%	10.1%

ECONOMY & JOBS SCORE: 88/RANK: 38

INCOME	AREA	U.S. AVG	EMPLOYMENT	AREA	U.S. AVG	LARGEST EMPLOYING INDUSTRY
Per capita income	$18,851	$23,420	Unemployment rate	4.2%	6.1%	Fabricated Metal Product Manufacturing
Household income	$36,763	$46,060	Recent job growth	1.9%	.9%	
Household income < $25K	32.7%	26.4%	Projected future job growth	7.5%	15.1%	
Household income > $75K	15.0%	24.5%	White collar	52.1%	54.5%	
Household income growth	41.5%	57.3%	Blue collar	47.9%	45.5%	

COST OF LIVING SCORE: 35/RANK: 214

INDEXES & TAXES	AREA	U.S. AVG	HOUSING	AREA	U.S. AVG	NECESSITIES	AREA	U.S. AVG
Cost of Living Index	89.4	100.0	Median home price	$91,510	$160,100	Food Index	106.7	100.0
Financial Progress Index	87.7	100.0	Home price appreciation	7.0%	7.1%	Housing Index	56.8	100.0
Income tax rate	7.125%	4.625%	Median rent	$509	$670	Utilities Index	141.4	100.0
Sales tax rate	8.000%	6.474%	Homes owned	65.8%	63.9%	Transportation Index	105.1	100.0
Property tax rate	$31.6	$15.6	Homes rented	18.0%	25.3%	Healthcare Index	98.9	100.0
			Housing affordability	54.0%	54.5%	Miscellaneous Cost Index	99.8	100.0

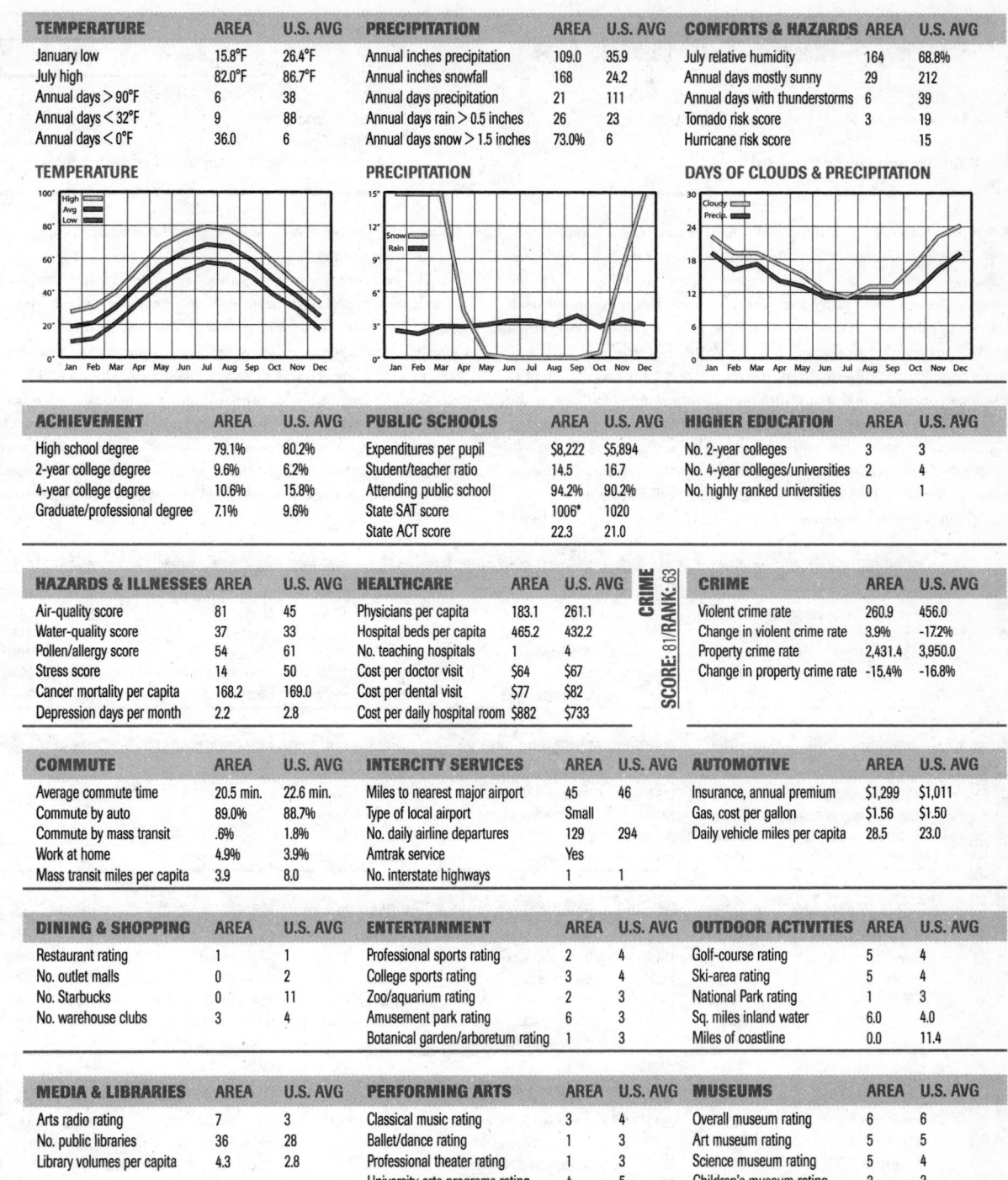

CLIMATE SCORE: 6/RANK: 310

TEMPERATURE	AREA	U.S. AVG	PRECIPITATION	AREA	U.S. AVG	COMFORTS & HAZARDS	AREA	U.S. AVG
January low	15.8°F	26.4°F	Annual inches precipitation	109.0	35.9	July relative humidity	164	68.8%
July high	82.0°F	86.7°F	Annual inches snowfall	168	24.2	Annual days mostly sunny	29	212
Annual days > 90°F	6	38	Annual days precipitation	21	111	Annual days with thunderstorms	6	39
Annual days < 32°F	9	88	Annual days rain > 0.5 inches	26	23	Tornado risk score	3	19
Annual days < 0°F	36.0	6	Annual days snow > 1.5 inches	73.0%	6	Hurricane risk score		15

TEMPERATURE

PRECIPITATION

DAYS OF CLOUDS & PRECIPITATION

EDUCATION SCORE: 62/RANK: 126

ACHIEVEMENT	AREA	U.S. AVG	PUBLIC SCHOOLS	AREA	U.S. AVG	HIGHER EDUCATION	AREA	U.S. AVG
High school degree	79.1%	80.2%	Expenditures per pupil	$8,222	$5,894	No. 2-year colleges	3	3
2-year college degree	9.6%	6.2%	Student/teacher ratio	14.5	16.7	No. 4-year colleges/universities	2	4
4-year college degree	10.6%	15.8%	Attending public school	94.2%	90.2%	No. highly ranked universities	0	1
Graduate/professional degree	7.1%	9.6%	State SAT score	1006*	1020			
			State ACT score	22.3	21.0			

HEALTH & HEALTHCARE SCORE: 74/RANK: 83

CRIME SCORE: 81/RANK: 63

HAZARDS & ILLNESSES	AREA	U.S. AVG	HEALTHCARE	AREA	U.S. AVG		CRIME	AREA	U.S. AVG
Air-quality score	81	45	Physicians per capita	183.1	261.1		Violent crime rate	260.9	456.0
Water-quality score	37	33	Hospital beds per capita	465.2	432.2		Change in violent crime rate	3.9%	-17.2%
Pollen/allergy score	54	61	No. teaching hospitals	1	4		Property crime rate	2,431.4	3,950.0
Stress score	14	50	Cost per doctor visit	$64	$67		Change in property crime rate	-15.4%	-16.8%
Cancer mortality per capita	168.2	169.0	Cost per dental visit	$77	$82				
Depression days per month	2.2	2.8	Cost per daily hospital room	$882	$733				

TRANSPORTATION SCORE: 56/RANK: 145

COMMUTE	AREA	U.S. AVG	INTERCITY SERVICES	AREA	U.S. AVG	AUTOMOTIVE	AREA	U.S. AVG
Average commute time	20.5 min.	22.6 min.	Miles to nearest major airport	45	46	Insurance, annual premium	$1,299	$1,011
Commute by auto	89.0%	88.7%	Type of local airport	Small		Gas, cost per gallon	$1.56	$1.50
Commute by mass transit	.6%	1.8%	No. daily airline departures	129	294	Daily vehicle miles per capita	28.5	23.0
Work at home	4.9%	3.9%	Amtrak service	Yes				
Mass transit miles per capita	3.9	8.0	No. interstate highways	1	1			

LEISURE SCORE: 46/RANK: 176

DINING & SHOPPING	AREA	U.S. AVG	ENTERTAINMENT	AREA	U.S. AVG	OUTDOOR ACTIVITIES	AREA	U.S. AVG
Restaurant rating	1	1	Professional sports rating	2	4	Golf-course rating	5	4
No. outlet malls	0	2	College sports rating	3	4	Ski-area rating	5	4
No. Starbucks	0	11	Zoo/aquarium rating	2	3	National Park rating	1	3
No. warehouse clubs	3	4	Amusement park rating	6	3	Sq. miles inland water	6.0	4.0
			Botanical garden/arboretum rating	1	3	Miles of coastline	0.0	11.4

ARTS & CULTURE SCORE: 17/RANK: 274

MEDIA & LIBRARIES	AREA	U.S. AVG	PERFORMING ARTS	AREA	U.S. AVG	MUSEUMS	AREA	U.S. AVG
Arts radio rating	7	3	Classical music rating	3	4	Overall museum rating	6	6
No. public libraries	36	28	Ballet/dance rating	1	3	Art museum rating	5	5
Library volumes per capita	4.3	2.8	Professional theater rating	1	3	Science museum rating	5	4
			University arts programs rating	4	5	Children's museum rating	3	3

Vallejo-Napa-Fairfield, CA

Score: 69.8   **Rank:** 78

Profile: Commuter community/Small-town complex
Location: Northern California, 30 to 50 miles northeast of San Francisco
Elevation: 267 feet
Time zone: Pacific Standard Time

PRO	CON
Year-round climate	Cost of living
Entertainment	Rising home prices
Proximity to San Francisco	Long commutes

This area containing Napa and Solano counties is a complex mix. Fairfield and Vacaville to the northeast serve mainly as residential communities along the I-80 corridor from San Francisco. To the south, Vallejo, once a gritty port and navy town, has transformed itself into a desirable commuter community. The world-famous Napa Valley, a Mediterranean-like wine-growing region, extends north from Vallejo to the city of Napa and beyond. The Travis Air Force Base is important to the local economy, and many firms are building new facilities in the open valleys to the east. Job growth is projected among the strongest in California. The strengthening economy has led to the second highest 3-year home-price appreciation in the nation. Cost of living and especially housing costs, while high and rising rapidly in the entire area, are out of sight in Napa. Attractions are the climate, relatively uncrowded living compared to the rest of the Bay Area, and recreational opportunities led by the wine country.

The two counties fill two valleys separated by low mountains. The low-lying sections have been built up or contain agriculture or marshland. The climate is Mediterranean marine, governed by the San Francisco Bay. Summer days are pleasantly warm; evenings are cool and incursions of low, stratus clouds are common. The area can be windy, particularly in Fairfield, when large temperature differences arise between the Bay and the inland Central Valley. In contrast, the Napa Valley experiences little wind because of its directional orientation. Most precipitation falls in winter as light to moderate rain, although some periods of persistent rain can cause flooding in Napa River.

POPULATION

DEMOGRAPHICS	AREA	U.S. AVG	ETHNIC COMPOSITION	AREA	U.S. AVG	RESIDENT PROFILE	AREA	U.S. AVG
Population	541,340		White	74.8%	75.1%	Single	45.3%	43.6%
Population density per sq. mile	342.2	447.3	Black	7.6%	12.3%	Married	54.7%	56.4%
Population growth	20.0%	16.1%	Asian	10.4%	3.6%	Divorced	9.7%	8.4%
Median age	35.2	35.5	American Indian	.8%	.9%	Separated	3.1%	3.0%
Average family size	2.9	2.7	Hispanic	20.5%	12.5%	Married with children	31.8%	28.7%
			Diversity measure	62.4%	35.2%	Single with children	10.3%	10.1%

ECONOMY & JOBS   SCORE: 22/RANK: 257

INCOME	AREA	U.S. AVG	EMPLOYMENT	AREA	U.S. AVG	LARGEST EMPLOYING INDUSTRY
Per capita income	$26,520	$23,420	Unemployment rate	5.3%	6.1%	Beverage Manufacturing
Household income	$63,508	$46,060	Recent job growth	2.1%	.9%	
Household income < $25K	14.9%	26.4%	Projected future job growth	25.9%	15.1%	
Household income > $75K	38.6%	24.5%	White collar	53.3%	54.5%	
Household income growth	65.2%	57.3%	Blue collar	46.7%	45.5%	

COST OF LIVING   SCORE: 6/RANK: 311

INDEXES & TAXES	AREA	U.S. AVG	HOUSING	AREA	U.S. AVG	NECESSITIES	AREA	U.S. AVG
Cost of Living Index	149.1	100.0	Median home price	$317,330	$160,100	Food Index	122.3	100.0
Financial Progress Index	90.8	100.0	Home price appreciation	18.4%	7.1%	Housing Index	197.1	100.0
Income tax rate	6.000%	4.625%	Median rent	$1,121	$670	Utilities Index	125.3	100.0
Sales tax rate	7.375%	6.474%	Homes owned	53.9%	63.9%	Transportation Index	125.4	100.0
Property tax rate	$10.7	$15.6	Homes rented	38.1%	25.3%	Healthcare Index	162.2	100.0
			Housing affordability	46.0%	54.5%	Miscellaneous Cost Index	108.2	100.0

CLIMATE   SCORE: 95/RANK: 16

TEMPERATURE	AREA	U.S. AVG	PRECIPITATION	AREA	U.S. AVG	COMFORTS & HAZARDS	AREA	U.S. AVG
January low	35.7°F	26.4°F	Annual inches precipitation	30.0	35.9	July relative humidity	70.0%	68.8%
July high	83.6°F	86.7°F	Annual inches snowfall	0.0	24.2	Annual days mostly sunny	285	212
Annual days > 90°F	33	38	Annual days precipitation	47	111	Annual days with thunderstorms	4	39
Annual days < 32°F	43	88	Annual days rain > 0.5 inches	20	23	Tornado risk score	1	19
Annual days < 0°F	0	6	Annual days snow > 1.5 inches	0	6	Hurricane risk score	0	15

TEMPERATURE

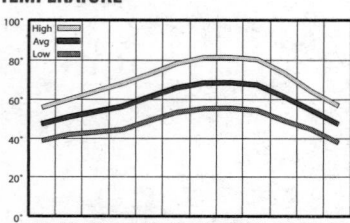

PRECIPITATION

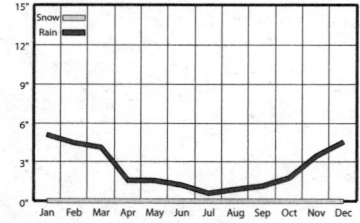

DAYS OF CLOUDS & PRECIPITATION

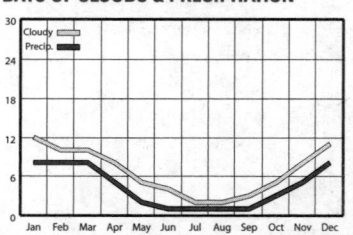

EDUCATION SCORE: 41/RANK: 193

ACHIEVEMENT	AREA	U.S. AVG	PUBLIC SCHOOLS	AREA	U.S. AVG	HIGHER EDUCATION	AREA	U.S. AVG
High school degree	81.7%	80.2%	Expenditures per pupil	$4,890	$5,894	No. 2-year colleges	2	3
2-year college degree	8.7%	6.2%	Student/teacher ratio	21.1	16.7	No. 4-year colleges/universities	2	4
4-year college degree	16.4%	15.8%	Attending public school	90.2%	90.2%	No. highly ranked universities	1	1
Graduate/professional degree	7.1%	9.6%	State SAT score	1018*	1020			
			State ACT score	21.5	21.0			

HEALTH & HEALTHCARE SCORE: 2/RANK: 322

HAZARDS & ILLNESSES	AREA	U.S. AVG	HEALTHCARE	AREA	U.S. AVG
Air-quality score	59	45	Physicians per capita	208.9	261.1
Water-quality score	4	33	Hospital beds per capita	735.7	432.2
Pollen/allergy score	94	61	No. teaching hospitals	1	4
Stress score	75	50	Cost per doctor visit	$68	$67
Cancer mortality per capita	179.1	169.0	Cost per dental visit	$110	$82
Depression days per month	3.4	2.8	Cost per daily hospital room	$1,762	$733

CRIME SCORE: 70/RANK: 97

CRIME	AREA	U.S. AVG
Violent crime rate	499.6	456.0
Change in violent crime rate	-35.5%	-17.2%
Property crime rate	3,273.1	3,950.0
Change in property crime rate	-29.5%	-16.8%

TRANSPORTATION SCORE: 39/RANK: 202

COMMUTE	AREA	U.S. AVG	INTERCITY SERVICES	AREA	U.S. AVG	AUTOMOTIVE	AREA	U.S. AVG
Average commute time	29.9 min.	22.6 min.	Miles to nearest major airport	26	46	Insurance, annual premium	$927	$1,011
Commute by auto	85.2%	88.7%	Type of local airport	Medium		Gas, cost per gallon	$1.77	$1.50
Commute by mass transit	1.2%	1.8%	No. daily airline departures	257	294	Daily vehicle miles per capita	26.5	23.0
Work at home	4.3%	3.9%	Amtrak service	No				
Mass transit miles per capita	9.3	8.0	No. interstate highways	1	1			

LEISURE SCORE: 96/RANK: 15

DINING & SHOPPING	AREA	U.S. AVG	ENTERTAINMENT	AREA	U.S. AVG	OUTDOOR ACTIVITIES	AREA	U.S. AVG
Restaurant rating	5	1	Professional sports rating	9	4	Golf-course rating	5	4
No. outlet malls	5	2	College sports rating	7	4	Ski-area rating	9	4
No. Starbucks	16	11	Zoo/aquarium rating	7	3	National Park rating	3	3
No. warehouse clubs	4	4	Amusement park rating	9	3	Sq. miles inland water	8.0	4.0
			Botanical garden/arboretum rating	3	3	Miles of coastline	0.0	11.4

ARTS & CULTURE SCORE: 38/RANK: 204

MEDIA & LIBRARIES	AREA	U.S. AVG	PERFORMING ARTS	AREA	U.S. AVG	MUSEUMS	AREA	U.S. AVG
Arts radio rating	4	3	Classical music rating	5	4	Overall museum rating	5	6
No. public libraries	13	28	Ballet/dance rating	5	3	Art museum rating	6	5
Library volumes per capita	1.8	2.8	Professional theater rating	6	3	Science museum rating	5	4
			University arts programs rating	2	5	Children's museum rating	3	3

Ventura, CA

Score: 60.0 Rank: 147

Profile: Beach town/Commuter community
Location: Southern California in the Santa Clara River coastal area
and inland valley northwest of Los Angeles
Elevation: 49 feet
Time zone: Pacific Standard Time

PRO	CON
Year-round climate	Urban sprawl
Recreation	Cost of living
High income levels	Transportation and
	air service

The inhabited portion of Ventura County consists of Ventura, a medium-size city at the coast and numerous towns, such as Oxnard, Simi Valley, and Santa Paula, spreading inland into the valley defined by the Santa Clara River. Ventura is a beach town along the original Pacific Coast Highway (U.S. 101). The area is a mix of agriculture, small industry, and residential areas. There is some high-tech industry and the recent employment trend is negative. The Cost of Living Index at 149.2 is high even by California standards, but the area has the lowest crime rate in the state and a fairly high educational attainment for a California noncollege town. The location is isolated by mountains and long freeway drives—Los Angeles is too far for a practical commute.

Public transportation facilities are lacking for an area its size. The coast and Channel Islands ("America's Galapagos") offer plenty of recreational opportunities.

The east-west running valley is flat to gently rolling with a gradual slope toward the coast. The inhabited area is bounded by two coastal ranges rising 4,000 feet. The mountains are dry and covered with oaks at lower elevations and some coniferous trees at higher ones. The climate is coastal Mediterranean with a winter rainy season and summer dry season. Clear, sunny days are the rule in summer, with occasional incursions of coastal low clouds called "fog" locally. Excessive heat is rare but may occur, especially inland.

POPULATION

DEMOGRAPHICS	AREA	U.S. AVG	ETHNIC COMPOSITION	AREA	U.S. AVG	RESIDENT PROFILE	AREA	U.S. AVG
Population	783,920		White	79.0%	75.1%	Single	44.5%	43.6%
Population density per sq. mile	424.7	447.3	Black	2.7%	12.3%	Married	55.5%	56.4%
Population growth	17.2%	16.1%	Asian	6.5%	3.6%	Divorced	9.3%	8.4%
Median age	34.4	35.5	American Indian	.7%	.9%	Separated	3.0%	3.0%
Average family size	3.1	2.7	Hispanic	33.2%	12.5%	Married with children	34.4%	28.7%
			Diversity measure	56.1%	35.2%	Single with children	10.0%	10.1%

ECONOMY & JOBS SCORE: 17/RANK: 272

INCOME	AREA	U.S. AVG	EMPLOYMENT	AREA	U.S. AVG	LARGEST EMPLOYING INDUSTRY
Per capita income	$27,463	$23,420	Unemployment rate	5.8%	6.1%	Computer and Electronic Product Manufacturing
Household income	$67,322	$46,060	Recent job growth	-1.0%	.9%	
Household income < $25K	14.0%	26.4%	Projected future job growth	20.2%	15.1%	
Household income > $75K	44.3%	24.5%	White collar	58.4%	54.5%	
Household income growth	47.6%	57.3%	Blue collar	41.6%	45.5%	

COST OF LIVING SCORE: 4/RANK: 316

INDEXES & TAXES	AREA	U.S. AVG	HOUSING	AREA	U.S. AVG	NECESSITIES	AREA	U.S. AVG
Cost of Living Index	149.2	100.0	Median home price	$357,850	$160,100	Food Index	110.3	100.0
Financial Progress Index	96.1	100.0	Home price appreciation	12.9%	7.1%	Housing Index	222.3	100.0
Income tax rate	6.000%	4.625%	Median rent	$1,142	$670	Utilities Index	112.4	100.0
Sales tax rate	7.250%	6.474%	Homes owned	61.4%	63.9%	Transportation Index	105.2	100.0
Property tax rate	$10.7	$15.6	Homes rented	33.5%	25.3%	Healthcare Index	116.2	100.0
			Housing affordability	49.0%	54.5%	Miscellaneous Cost Index	104.2	100.0

CLIMATE SCORE: 97/RANK: 10

TEMPERATURE	AREA	U.S. AVG	PRECIPITATION	AREA	U.S. AVG	COMFORTS & HAZARDS	AREA	U.S. AVG
January low	45.4°F	26.4°F	Annual inches precipitation	12.0	35.9	July relative humidity	71.0%	68.8%
July high	75.8°F	86.7°F	Annual inches snowfall	0.0	24.2	Annual days mostly sunny	258	212
Annual days > 90°F	5	38	Annual days precipitation	35	111	Annual days with thunderstorms	3	39
Annual days < 32°F	0	88	Annual days rain > 0.5 inches	7	23	Tornado risk score	1	19
Annual days < 0°F	0	6	Annual days snow > 1.5 inches	0	6	Hurricane risk score	1	15

TEMPERATURE

PRECIPITATION

DAYS OF CLOUDS & PRECIPITATION

EDUCATION SCORE: 40/RANK: 197

ACHIEVEMENT	AREA	U.S. AVG	PUBLIC SCHOOLS	AREA	U.S. AVG	HIGHER EDUCATION	AREA	U.S. AVG
High school degree	80.1%	80.2%	Expenditures per pupil	$5,071	$5,894	No. 2-year colleges	3	3
2-year college degree	7.9%	6.2%	Student/teacher ratio	22.4	16.7	No. 4-year colleges/universities	3	4
4-year college degree	17.4%	15.8%	Attending public school	89.5%	90.2%	No. highly ranked universities	1	1
Graduate/professional degree	9.5%	9.6%	State SAT score	1018*	1020			
			State ACT score	21.5	21.0			

HEALTH & HEALTHCARE SCORE: 32/RANK: 225

CRIME SCORE: 99/RANK: 2

HAZARDS & ILLNESSES	AREA	U.S. AVG	HEALTHCARE	AREA	U.S. AVG	CRIME	AREA	U.S. AVG
Air-quality score	2	45	Physicians per capita	190.6	261.1	Violent crime rate	261.7	456.0
Water-quality score	13	33	Hospital beds per capita	241.9	432.2	Change in violent crime rate	-39.4%	-17.2%
Pollen/allergy score	41	61	No. teaching hospitals	1	4	Property crime rate	1,957.4	3,950.0
Stress score	14	50	Cost per doctor visit	$70	$67	Change in property crime rate	-37.6%	-16.8%
Cancer mortality per capita	159.8	169.0	Cost per dental visit	$80	$82			
Depression days per month	3.3	2.8	Cost per daily hospital room	$1,267	$733			

TRANSPORTATION SCORE: 7/RANK: 306

COMMUTE	AREA	U.S. AVG	INTERCITY SERVICES	AREA	U.S. AVG	AUTOMOTIVE	AREA	U.S. AVG
Average commute time	25.4 min.	22.6 min.	Miles to nearest major airport	30	46	Insurance, annual premium	$945	$1,011
Commute by auto	91.6%	88.7%	Type of local airport	Medium		Gas, cost per gallon	$1.76	$1.50
Commute by mass transit	.6%	1.8%	No. daily airline departures	119	294	Daily vehicle miles per capita	23.4	23.0
Work at home	3.5%	3.9%	Amtrak service	Yes				
Mass transit miles per capita	4.5	8.0	No. interstate highways	0	1			

LEISURE SCORE: 81/RANK: 66

DINING & SHOPPING	AREA	U.S. AVG	ENTERTAINMENT	AREA	U.S. AVG	OUTDOOR ACTIVITIES	AREA	U.S. AVG
Restaurant rating	1	1	Professional sports rating	9	4	Golf-course rating	7	4
No. outlet malls	3	2	College sports rating	6	4	Ski-area rating	10	4
No. Starbucks	20	11	Zoo/aquarium rating	2	3	National Park rating	10	3
No. warehouse clubs	5	4	Amusement park rating	5	3	Sq. miles inland water	3.0	4.0
			Botanical garden/arboretum rating	4	3	Miles of coastline	35.9	11.4

ARTS & CULTURE SCORE: 20/RANK: 263

MEDIA & LIBRARIES	AREA	U.S. AVG	PERFORMING ARTS	AREA	U.S. AVG	MUSEUMS	AREA	U.S. AVG
Arts radio rating	5	3	Classical music rating	6	4	Overall museum rating	7	6
No. public libraries	22	28	Ballet/dance rating	6	3	Art museum rating	7	5
Library volumes per capita	2.1	2.8	Professional theater rating	5	3	Science museum rating	7	4
			University arts programs rating	3	5	Children's museum rating	3	3

Victoria, TX

Score: 37.4   Rank: 290

Profile: Small town
Location: Southeast Texas, 40 miles inland from the Gulf Coast
Elevation: 91 feet
Time zone: Central Standard Time

PRO	CON
Cost of living	Isolation
Small-town atmosphere	Entertainment
Nearby coastline	Hot, humid summers

Victoria, a small agricultural and industrial center, resides in the middle of a triangle formed by Houston, San Antonio, and Corpus Christi on the coastal plain of southeast Texas. Located on transportation routes about 30 miles inland from the Gulf, Victoria is home to several petrochemical and plastics companies, including large Dow Chemical and DuPont plants and an assortment of other manufacturers. Ranching and meatpacking round out the economic picture. While employment prospects are moderate, the town has healthy incomes in relation to cost of living. There is a historic downtown district. Victoria College and the University of Houston-Victoria provide some higher education but little in the way of college-town amenities or atmosphere. The city does have a few arts and cultural assets, including a small ballet and symphony, and residents pride themselves on *not* having to travel to Houston or San Antonio for these amenities. But there isn't much to do, and a 2-hour-plus drive is required for other services.

The city of Victoria is in the south-central Texas Coastal Plain on the Guadalupe River. The landscape is flat with numerous small creeks, waterways, and trees. The climate is humid subtropical. Summers are hot, usually in the 90s, with high humidity and occasional sea breezes. Winter conditions vary between clear, cold, dry periods and cloudy, mild, drizzly days as fronts move in from the north. The area gets fewer freezing days than most other Texas cities. Occasional summer and fall tropical disturbances may produce torrential rains.

POPULATION

DEMOGRAPHICS	AREA	U.S. AVG	ETHNIC COMPOSITION	AREA	U.S. AVG	RESIDENT PROFILE	AREA	U.S. AVG
Population	84,932		White	81.1%	75.1%	Single	37.5%	43.6%
Population density per sq. mile	96.2	447.3	Black	6.7%	12.3%	Married	62.5%	56.4%
Population growth	14.2%	16.1%	Asian	.8%	3.6%	Divorced	6.9%	8.4%
Median age	34.5	35.5	American Indian	.4%	.9%	Separated	2.6%	3.0%
Average family size	2.8	2.7	Hispanic	37.0%	12.5%	Married with children	36.6%	28.7%
			Diversity measure	56.2%	35.2%	Single with children	9.2%	10.1%

ECONOMY & JOBS SCORE: 88/RANK: 40

INCOME	AREA	U.S. AVG	EMPLOYMENT	AREA	U.S. AVG	LARGEST EMPLOYING INDUSTRY
Per capita income	$21,699	$23,420	Unemployment rate	5.1%	6.1%	Healthcare and Social Assistance
Household income	$43,566	$46,060	Recent job growth	.3%	.9%	
Household income < $25K	29.3%	26.4%	Projected future job growth	14.3%	15.1%	
Household income > $75K	24.0%	24.5%	White collar	51.7%	54.5%	
Household income growth	61.6%	57.3%	Blue collar	48.3%	45.5%	

COST OF LIVING SCORE: 95/RANK: 15

INDEXES & TAXES	AREA	U.S. AVG	HOUSING	AREA	U.S. AVG	NECESSITIES	AREA	U.S. AVG
Cost of Living Index	75.5	100.0	Median home price	$80,560	$160,100	Food Index	77.3	100.0
Financial Progress Index	123.0	100.0	Home price appreciation	3.2%	7.1%	Housing Index	50.0	100.0
Income tax rate	0.000%	4.625%	Median rent	$482	$670	Utilities Index	107.9	100.0
Sales tax rate	6.750%	6.474%	Homes owned	66.1%	63.9%	Transportation Index	97.0	100.0
Property tax rate	$21.1	$15.6	Homes rented	21.3%	25.3%	Healthcare Index	90.1	100.0
			Housing affordability	68.0%	54.5%	Miscellaneous Cost Index	89.2	100.0

CLIMATE SCORE: 85/RANK: 50

TEMPERATURE	AREA	U.S. AVG	PRECIPITATION	AREA	U.S. AVG	COMFORTS & HAZARDS	AREA	U.S. AVG
January low	43.0°F	26.4°F	Annual inches precipitation	36.0	35.9	July relative humidity	75.0%	68.8%
July high	94.0°F	86.7°F	Annual inches snowfall	.1	24.2	Annual days mostly sunny	222	212
Annual days > 90°F	105	38	Annual days precipitation	85	111	Annual days with thunderstorms	51	39
Annual days < 32°F	.11	88	Annual days rain > 0.5 inches	18	23	Tornado risk score	24	19
Annual days < 0°F	0	6	Annual days snow > 1.5 inches	0	6	Hurricane risk score	43	15

TEMPERATURE

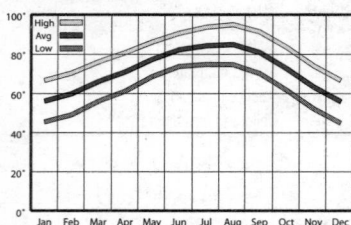

PRECIPITATION

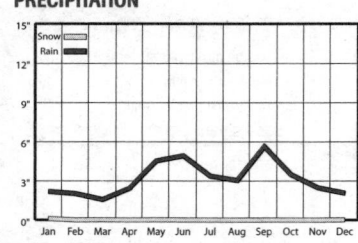

DAYS OF CLOUDS & PRECIPITATION

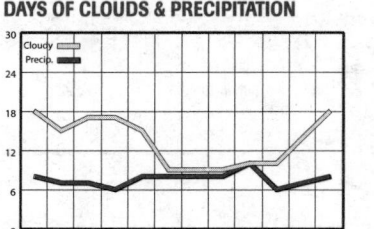

EDUCATION SCORE: 12/RANK: 290

ACHIEVEMENT	AREA	U.S. AVG	PUBLIC SCHOOLS	AREA	U.S. AVG	HIGHER EDUCATION	AREA	U.S. AVG
High school degree	75.6%	80.2%	Expenditures per pupil	$5,435	$5,894	No. 2-year colleges	1	3
2-year college degree	5.9%	6.2%	Student/teacher ratio	13.8	16.7	No. 4-year colleges/universities	0	4
4-year college degree	11.0%	15.8%	Attending public school	87.5%	90.2%	No. highly ranked universities	0	1
Graduate/professional degree	5.3%	9.6%	State SAT score	993*	1020			
			State ACT score	20.1	21.0			

HEALTH & HEALTHCARE SCORE: 34/RANK: 216

HAZARDS & ILLNESSES	AREA	U.S. AVG	HEALTHCARE	AREA	U.S. AVG
Air-quality score	24	45	Physicians per capita	253.1	261.1
Water-quality score	30	33	Hospital beds per capita	880.0	432.2
Pollen/allergy score	82	61	No. teaching hospitals	0	4
Stress score	40	50	Cost per doctor visit	$55	$67
Cancer mortality per capita	168.0	169.0	Cost per dental visit	$77	$82
Depression days per month	4.9	2.8	Cost per daily hospital room	$381	$733

CRIME SCORE: 36/RANK: 209

CRIME	AREA	U.S. AVG
Violent crime rate	573.3	456.0
Change in violent crime rate	-29.7%	-17.2%
Property crime rate	4,275.8	3,950.0
Change in property crime rate	-22.6%	-16.8%

TRANSPORTATION SCORE: 18/RANK: 269

COMMUTE	AREA	U.S. AVG	INTERCITY SERVICES	AREA	U.S. AVG	AUTOMOTIVE	AREA	U.S. AVG
Average commute time	21.4 min.	22.6 min.	Miles to nearest major airport	80	46	Insurance, annual premium	$928	$1,011
Commute by auto	94.6%	88.7%	Type of local airport	Small		Gas, cost per gallon	$1.37	$1.50
Commute by mass transit	.1%	1.8%	No. daily airline departures	42	294	Daily vehicle miles per capita	16.0	23.0
Work at home	2.8%	3.9%	Amtrak service	No				
Mass transit miles per capita	0.0	8.0	No. interstate highways	0	1			

LEISURE SCORE: 17/RANK: 272

DINING & SHOPPING	AREA	U.S. AVG	ENTERTAINMENT	AREA	U.S. AVG	OUTDOOR ACTIVITIES	AREA	U.S. AVG
Restaurant rating	1	1	Professional sports rating	2	4	Golf-course rating	1	4
No. outlet malls	0	2	College sports rating	1	4	Ski-area rating	1	4
No. Starbucks	0	11	Zoo/aquarium rating	2	3	National Park rating	1	3
No. warehouse clubs	3	4	Amusement park rating	1	3	Sq. miles inland water	2.0	4.0
			Botanical garden/arboretum rating	1	3	Miles of coastline	0.0	11.4

ARTS & CULTURE SCORE: 13/RANK: 288

MEDIA & LIBRARIES	AREA	U.S. AVG	PERFORMING ARTS	AREA	U.S. AVG	MUSEUMS	AREA	U.S. AVG
Arts radio rating	5	3	Classical music rating	3	4	Overall museum rating	2	6
No. public libraries	1	28	Ballet/dance rating	1	3	Art museum rating	2	5
Library volumes per capita	1.5	2.8	Professional theater rating	1	3	Science museum rating	1	4
			University arts programs rating	1	5	Children's museum rating	1	3

Vineland-Millville-Bridgeton, NJ

Score: 50.5   Rank: 222

Profile: Small-town complex
Location: Southern New Jersey, inland and 40 miles southeast of Philadelphia
Elevation: 10 feet
Time zone: Eastern Standard Time

PRO	CON
Small-town feel	Violent crime
Central location	Low future job growth
Cost of living	Healthcare

Cumberland County, in the southerly tidewater area of the state, has a mainly rural character with the towns of Vineland and Millville serving as its center. While the area is somewhat economically tied to Philadelphia and Wilmington, Delaware, to the north and northwest, it's primarily self-sufficient and most people work locally. Glassmaking is the primary industry, along with agriculture. The area has a rich and well-preserved history from the colonial era and Revolutionary War. Violent crime rates are notably high, but the cost of living is the lowest by far among New Jersey metropolitan areas. Services and amenities are sparse locally, but the area is strategically located between Philadelphia and Wilmington and beaches to the east.

The flat coastal plain contains marshes and tidewater creeks, with areas of agriculture and mixed pine and deciduous forests inland. The climate is continental with a strong marine influence. Summer days are usually pleasant because of breezes off the Delaware Bay and Atlantic Ocean, but hot, humid spells occur annually. Winters are cool, cloudy, and wet, with some moderation from nearby water and a little from the Appalachians to the northwest. Winter is a mix of rain and snow, with coastal "noreaster" storms moving up the coast from the south bringing heavy rains and winter snows. First freeze is late October, last is mid-April.

POPULATION

DEMOGRAPHICS	AREA	U.S. AVG	ETHNIC COMPOSITION	AREA	U.S. AVG	RESIDENT PROFILE	AREA	U.S. AVG
Population	147,768		White	81.2%	75.1%	Single	46.8%	43.6%
Population density per sq. mile	302.0	447.3	Black	12.9%	12.3%	Married	53.2%	56.4%
Population growth	7.0%	16.1%	Asian	.7%	3.6%	Divorced	7.1%	8.4%
Median age	35.8	35.5	American Indian	1.1%	.9%	Separated	4.3%	3.0%
Average family size	2.7	2.7	Hispanic	8.6%	12.5%	Married with children	26.3%	28.7%
			Diversity measure	57.9%	35.2%	Single with children	12.0%	10.1%

ECONOMY & JOBS   SCORE: 71/RANK: 96

INCOME	AREA	U.S. AVG	EMPLOYMENT	AREA	U.S. AVG	LARGEST EMPLOYING INDUSTRY
Per capita income	$18,407	$23,420	Unemployment rate	8.1%	6.1%	Nonmetallic Mineral Product Manufacturing
Household income	$40,867	$46,060	Recent job growth	2.7%	.9%	
Household income < $25K	29.9%	26.4%	Projected future job growth	6.0%	15.1%	
Household income > $75K	19.1%	24.5%	White collar	46.6%	54.5%	
Household income growth	35.6%	57.3%	Blue collar	53.4%	45.5%	

COST OF LIVING   SCORE: 39/RANK: 201

INDEXES & TAXES	AREA	U.S. AVG	HOUSING	AREA	U.S. AVG	NECESSITIES	AREA	U.S. AVG
Cost of Living Index	91.9	100.0	Median home price	$105,360	$160,100	Food Index	105.8	100.0
Financial Progress Index	94.7	100.0	Home price appreciation	4.9%	7.1%	Housing Index	65.4	100.0
Income tax rate	2.450%	4.625%	Median rent	$793	$670	Utilities Index	122.3	100.0
Sales tax rate	6.000%	6.474%	Homes owned	66.1%	63.9%	Transportation Index	103.6	100.0
Property tax rate	$24.0	$15.6	Homes rented	16.3%	25.3%	Healthcare Index	106.1	100.0
			Housing affordability	38.0%	54.5%	Miscellaneous Cost Index	103.9	100.0

CLIMATE   SCORE: 84/RANK: 53

TEMPERATURE	AREA	U.S. AVG	PRECIPITATION	AREA	U.S. AVG	COMFORTS & HAZARDS	AREA	U.S. AVG
January low	24.0°F	26.4°F	Annual inches precipitation	46.0	35.9	July relative humidity	73.0%	68.8%
July high	84.7°F	86.7°F	Annual inches snowfall	16.0	24.2	Annual days mostly sunny	204	212
Annual days > 90°F	16	38	Annual days precipitation	112	111	Annual days with thunderstorms	25	39
Annual days < 32°F	15	88	Annual days rain > 0.5 inches	29	23	Tornado risk score	10	19
Annual days < 0°F	1	6	Annual days snow > 1.5 inches	5	6	Hurricane risk score	21	15

TEMPERATURE

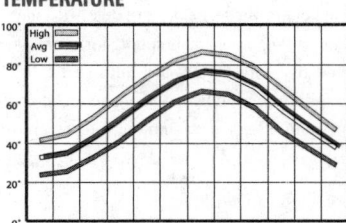

PRECIPITATION

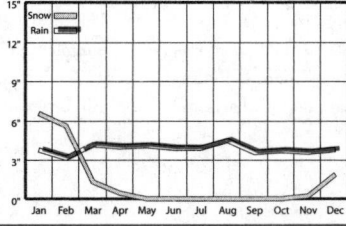

DAYS OF CLOUDS & PRECIPITATION

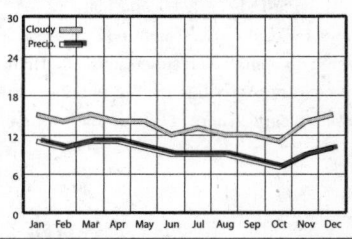

EDUCATION SCORE: 3/RANK: 318

ACHIEVEMENT	AREA	U.S. AVG	PUBLIC SCHOOLS	AREA	U.S. AVG	HIGHER EDUCATION	AREA	U.S. AVG
High school degree	67.8%	80.2%	Expenditures per pupil	$9,540	$5,894	No. 2-year colleges	1	3
2-year college degree	5.4%	6.2%	Student/teacher ratio	12.8	16.7	No. 4-year colleges/universities	0	4
4-year college degree	8.1%	15.8%	Attending public school	87.7%	90.2%	No. highly ranked universities	0	1
Graduate/professional degree	3.7%	9.6%	State SAT score	1016*	1020			
			State ACT score	21.2	21.0			

HEALTH & HEALTHCARE SCORE: 16/RANK: 277

HAZARDS & ILLNESSES	AREA	U.S. AVG	HEALTHCARE	AREA	U.S. AVG
Air-quality score	81	45	Physicians per capita	150.2	261.1
Water-quality score	4	33	Hospital beds per capita	372.2	432.2
Pollen/allergy score	56	61	No. teaching hospitals	0	4
Stress score	90	50	Cost per doctor visit	$73	$67
Cancer mortality per capita	178.4	169.0	Cost per dental visit	$105	$82
Depression days per month	3.9	2.8	Cost per daily hospital room	$2,392	$733

CRIME SCORE: 31/RANK: 227

CRIME	AREA	U.S. AVG
Violent crime rate	756.5	456.0
Change in violent crime rate	-21.1%	-17.2%
Property crime rate	4,011.3	3,950.0
Change in property crime rate	-27.7%	-16.8%

TRANSPORTATION SCORE: 77/RANK: 70

COMMUTE	AREA	U.S. AVG	INTERCITY SERVICES	AREA	U.S. AVG	AUTOMOTIVE	AREA	U.S. AVG
Average commute time	23.1 min.	22.6 min.	Miles to nearest major airport	32	46	Insurance, annual premium	$1,340	$1,011
Commute by auto	92.7%	88.7%	Type of local airport	Large		Gas, cost per gallon	$1.45	$1.50
Commute by mass transit	1.3%	1.8%	No. daily airline departures	669	294	Daily vehicle miles per capita	20.4	23.0
Work at home	2.1%	3.9%	Amtrak service	No				
Mass transit miles per capita	3.2	8.0	No. interstate highways	0	1			

LEISURE SCORE: 59/RANK: 134

DINING & SHOPPING	AREA	U.S. AVG	ENTERTAINMENT	AREA	U.S. AVG	OUTDOOR ACTIVITIES	AREA	U.S. AVG
Restaurant rating	1	1	Professional sports rating	8	4	Golf-course rating	5	4
No. outlet malls	5	2	College sports rating	3	4	Ski-area rating	3	4
No. Starbucks	0	11	Zoo/aquarium rating	2	3	National Park rating	2	3
No. warehouse clubs	1	4	Amusement park rating	4	3	Sq. miles inland water	4.0	4.0
			Botanical garden/arboretum rating	3	3	Miles of coastline	30.3	11.4

ARTS & CULTURE SCORE: 15/RANK: 280

MEDIA & LIBRARIES	AREA	U.S. AVG	PERFORMING ARTS	AREA	U.S. AVG	MUSEUMS	AREA	U.S. AVG
Arts radio rating	5	3	Classical music rating	4	4	Overall museum rating	7	6
No. public libraries	4	28	Ballet/dance rating	4	3	Art museum rating	6	5
Library volumes per capita	2.9	2.8	Professional theater rating	5	3	Science museum rating	3	4
			University arts programs rating	1	5	Children's museum rating	2	3

Visalia-Tulare-Porterville, CA

Score: 51.8   Rank: 211

Profile: Small-agricultural-town complex
Location: Central California, southeastern portion of the Central Valley at the foot of the Sierra Nevada
Elevation: 327 feet
Time zone: Pacific Standard Time

PRO	CON
Nearby national parks	High unemployment
Attractive landscape	Arts and culture
Cost of living	Isolation

This agricultural area, which includes the towns of Hanford, Tulare, and Porterville, is one of the largest producers of oranges and citrus fruits in the world. The land rises dramatically from flat, orchard land to Sequoia National Park, just 50 miles to the east. The Cost of Living Index at 94.1 and housing costs just under $113,600 are the lowest of California's metropolitan areas. On the downside, lack of economic diversity has resulted in the fourth highest unemployment rate in the country. Activities mainly include outdoor recreation, including some watersports. There is little in the way of entertainment and arts and culture nearby. Fresno is 40 miles northwest, but bigger cities are all more than 100 miles distant.

Just to the east, the Sierra Nevada rise dramatically, first as oak-studded foothills and then as a high ridge of granite, with peaks over 14,000 feet. Winter snow cover on these peaks creates a dramatic landscape. The climate is generally pleasant except for summer hot spells. Summers are hot and dry and winters are mild and relatively wet with 90% of annual precipitation. Summer evenings may be cooled by mountain breezes. Dense ground fogs are common, freezes are not.

POPULATION

DEMOGRAPHICS	AREA	U.S. AVG	ETHNIC COMPOSITION	AREA	U.S. AVG	RESIDENT PROFILE	AREA	U.S. AVG
Population	381,772		White	66.5%	75.1%	Single	43.3%	43.6%
Population density per sq. mile	79.1	447.3	Black	1.3%	12.3%	Married	56.8%	56.4%
Population growth	22.4%	16.1%	Asian	4.3%	3.6%	Divorced	8.1%	8.4%
Median age	29.3	35.5	American Indian	1.5%	.9%	Separated	3.6%	3.0%
Average family size	3.2	2.7	Hispanic	47.0%	12.5%	Married with children	31.8%	28.7%
			Diversity measure	58.5%	35.2%	Single with children	13.9%	10.1%

ECONOMY & JOBS — SCORE: 5/RANK: 313

INCOME	AREA	U.S. AVG	EMPLOYMENT	AREA	U.S. AVG	LARGEST EMPLOYING INDUSTRY
Per capita income	$15,413	$23,420	Unemployment rate	13.1%	6.1%	Food Manufacturing
Household income	$36,518	$46,060	Recent job growth	.9%	.9%	
Household income < $25K	33.3%	26.4%	Projected future job growth	12.3%	15.1%	
Household income > $75K	17.1%	24.5%	White collar	41.6%	54.5%	
Household income growth	49.3%	57.3%	Blue collar	58.4%	45.5%	

COST OF LIVING — SCORE: 38/RANK: 204

INDEXES & TAXES	AREA	U.S. AVG	HOUSING	AREA	U.S. AVG	NECESSITIES	AREA	U.S. AVG
Cost of Living Index	94.1	100.0	Median home price	$113,600	$160,100	Food Index	110.1	100.0
Financial Progress Index	82.7	100.0	Home price appreciation	5.1%	7.1%	Housing Index	70.6	100.0
Income tax rate	6.000%	4.625%	Median rent	$592	$670	Utilities Index	110.4	100.0
Sales tax rate	7.250%	6.474%	Homes owned	51.7%	63.9%	Transportation Index	106.6	100.0
Property tax rate	$10.8	$15.6	Homes rented	30.9%	25.3%	Healthcare Index	118.8	100.0
			Housing affordability	51.0%	54.5%	Miscellaneous Cost Index	101.5	100.0

CLIMATE — SCORE: 89/RANK: 36

TEMPERATURE	AREA	U.S. AVG	PRECIPITATION	AREA	U.S. AVG	COMFORTS & HAZARDS	AREA	U.S. AVG
January low	35.8°F	26.4°F	Annual inches precipitation	10.0	35.9	July relative humidity	61.0%	68.8%
July high	98.2°F	86.7°F	Annual inches snowfall	0.0	24.2	Annual days mostly sunny	271	212
Annual days > 90°F	107	38	Annual days precipitation	44	111	Annual days with thunderstorms	6	39
Annual days < 32°F	29	88	Annual days rain > 0.5 inches	6	23	Tornado risk score	3	19
Annual days < 0°F	0	6	Annual days snow > 1.5 inches	0	6	Hurricane risk score	0	15

TEMPERATURE

PRECIPITATION

DAYS OF CLOUDS & PRECIPITATION

EDUCATION — SCORE: 1/RANK: 325

ACHIEVEMENT	AREA	U.S. AVG	PUBLIC SCHOOLS	AREA	U.S. AVG	HIGHER EDUCATION	AREA	U.S. AVG
High school degree	61.7%	80.2%	Expenditures per pupil	$5,175	$5,894	No. 2-year colleges	3	3
2-year college degree	6.3%	6.2%	Student/teacher ratio	20.9	16.7	No. 4-year colleges/universities	0	4
4-year college degree	7.8%	15.8%	Attending public school	96.0%	90.2%	No. highly ranked universities	0	1
Graduate/professional degree	3.7%	9.6%	State SAT score	1018*	1020			
			State ACT score	21.5	21.0			

HEALTH & HEALTHCARE — SCORE: 6/RANK: 311

HAZARDS & ILLNESSES	AREA	U.S. AVG	HEALTHCARE	AREA	U.S. AVG
Air-quality score	59	45	Physicians per capita	111.3	261.1
Water-quality score	7	33	Hospital beds per capita	599.4	432.2
Pollen/allergy score	60	61	No. teaching hospitals	0	4
Stress score	23	50	Cost per doctor visit	$68	$67
Cancer mortality per capita	156.9	169.0	Cost per dental visit	$79	$82
Depression days per month	1.0	2.8	Cost per daily hospital room	$1,300	$733

CRIME — SCORE: 32/RANK: 223

CRIME	AREA	U.S. AVG
Violent crime rate	611.4	456.0
Change in violent crime rate	-11.9%	-17.2%
Property crime rate	4,063.1	3,950.0
Change in property crime rate	-17.7%	-16.8%

TRANSPORTATION — SCORE: 24/RANK: 251

COMMUTE	AREA	U.S. AVG	INTERCITY SERVICES	AREA	U.S. AVG	AUTOMOTIVE	AREA	U.S. AVG
Average commute time	21.9 min.	22.6 min.	Miles to nearest major airport	38	46	Insurance, annual premium	$1,025	$1,011
Commute by auto	87.2%	88.7%	Type of local airport	Small		Gas, cost per gallon	$1.70	$1.50
Commute by mass transit	.6%	1.8%	No. daily airline departures	75	294	Daily vehicle miles per capita	19.1	23.0
Work at home	4.9%	3.9%	Amtrak service	No				
Mass transit miles per capita	2.4	8.0	No. interstate highways	0	1			

DINING & SHOPPING	AREA	U.S. AVG	ENTERTAINMENT	AREA	U.S. AVG	OUTDOOR ACTIVITIES	AREA	U.S. AVG
Restaurant rating	1	1	Professional sports rating	2	4	Golf-course rating	2	4
No. outlet malls	0	2	College sports rating	1	4	Ski-area rating	5	4
No. Starbucks	5	11	Zoo/aquarium rating	1	3	National Park rating	10	3
No. warehouse clubs	3	4	Amusement park rating	1	3	Sq. miles inland water	2.0	4.0
			Botanical garden/arboretum rating	1	3	Miles of coastline	0.0	11.4

MEDIA & LIBRARIES	AREA	U.S. AVG	PERFORMING ARTS	AREA	U.S. AVG	MUSEUMS	AREA	U.S. AVG
Arts radio rating	1	3	Classical music rating	1	4	Overall museum rating	5	6
No. public libraries	18	28	Ballet/dance rating	1	3	Art museum rating	2	5
Library volumes per capita	4.1	2.8	Professional theater rating	1	3	Science museum rating	1	4
			University arts programs rating	1	5	Children's museum rating	1	3

Waco, TX

Score: 50.1   Rank: 227

Profile: Small city
Location: East-central Texas along I-35, 100 miles south of Dallas
Elevation: 501 feet
Time zone: Central Standard Time

PRO	CON
Cost of living	Arts and culture
College-town amenities	Crime rate
Historic interest	Summer heat

Waco is a commercial and transportation hub. The economic base consists of small to mid-size manufacturers in a variety of industries and a strong agricultural presence with ranching, poultry, and cotton. Another principle employer, Baylor University, which has 15,000 students, gives the area some college-town presence and amenities. There is a historic area, although some older buildings were destroyed in a 1953 tornado. The city prides itself as a good set for filmmaking because of its many neighborhood "looks" and varied terrain. Lakes within and outside the city provide watersports, but other outdoor recreation is lacking.

Waco is located in the rich agricultural region of the Brazos River Valley. The gently rolling, agricultural Blackland Prairies spread to the east and the rolling to hilly Grand Prairie with sagebrush and cactus starts to the west—the contrast between the two areas is one feature that attracts filmmakers. The climate is humid subtropical and continental with large temperature variations. Summer daytime temperatures are hot, especially in July and August. Highest temperatures are associated with fair skies, light winds, and comparatively low humidity. Winters are mild. Cold fronts moving down from the High Plains often bring strong, gusty, northerly winds and sharp temperature drops. Cold spells rarely last longer than 2 to 3 days. In an average year, April and May are the wettest months, while the July to August period is the driest. Most warm season rainfall occurs from thunderstorm activity. Winter precipitation is closely associated with frontal activity, and may arrive as rain, freezing rain, sleet, or snow. Most years have little snow.

DEMOGRAPHICS	AREA	U.S. AVG	ETHNIC COMPOSITION	AREA	U.S. AVG	RESIDENT PROFILE	AREA	U.S. AVG
Population	217,713		White	77.3%	75.1%	Single	43.9%	43.6%
Population density per sq. mile	209.0	447.3	Black	14.6%	12.3%	Married	56.1%	56.4%
Population growth	15.1%	16.1%	Asian	1.1%	3.6%	Divorced	8.9%	8.4%
Median age	32.2	35.5	American Indian	.4%	.9%	Separated	3.1%	3.0%
Average family size	2.6	2.7	Hispanic	17.3%	12.5%	Married with children	28.7%	28.7%
			Diversity measure	50.9%	35.2%	Single with children	10.7%	10.1%

INCOME	AREA	U.S. AVG	EMPLOYMENT	AREA	U.S. AVG	LARGEST EMPLOYING INDUSTRY
Per capita income	$20,393	$23,420	Unemployment rate	5.4%	6.1%	Food Manufacturing
Household income	$39,295	$46,060	Recent job growth	3.6%	.9%	
Household income < $25K	33.0%	26.4%	Projected future job growth	13.9%	15.1%	
Household income > $75K	21.1%	24.5%	White collar	53.5%	54.5%	
Household income growth	72.5%	57.3%	Blue collar	46.5%	45.5%	

INDEXES & TAXES	AREA	U.S. AVG	HOUSING	AREA	U.S. AVG	NECESSITIES	AREA	U.S. AVG
Cost of Living Index	78.3	100.0	Median home price	$77,290	$160,100	Food Index	88.4	100.0
Financial Progress Index	107.0	100.0	Home price appreciation	4.5%	7.1%	Housing Index	48.0	100.0
Income tax rate	0.000%	4.625%	Median rent	$535	$670	Utilities Index	96.0	100.0
Sales tax rate	8.250%	6.474%	Homes owned	62.6%	63.9%	Transportation Index	94.9	100.0
Property tax rate	$24.1	$15.6	Homes rented	26.3%	25.3%	Healthcare Index	96.7	100.0
			Housing affordability	54.0%	54.5%	Miscellaneous Cost Index	100.1	100.0

CLIMATE SCORE: 87/RANK: 42

TEMPERATURE	AREA	U.S. AVG	PRECIPITATION	AREA	U.S. AVG	COMFORTS & HAZARDS	AREA	U.S. AVG
January low	36.6°F	26.4°F	Annual inches precipitation	31.3	35.9	July relative humidity	67.0%	68.8%
July high	96.2°F	86.7°F	Annual inches snowfall	1.5	24.2	Annual days mostly sunny	231	212
Annual days > 90°F	105	38	Annual days precipitation	78	111	Annual days with thunderstorms	45	39
Annual days < 32°F	35	88	Annual days rain > 0.5 inches	18	23	Tornado risk score	28	19
Annual days < 0°F	0	6	Annual days snow > 1.5 inches	1	6	Hurricane risk score	18	15

TEMPERATURE

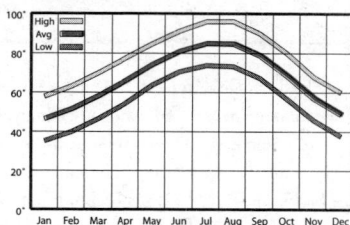

PRECIPITATION

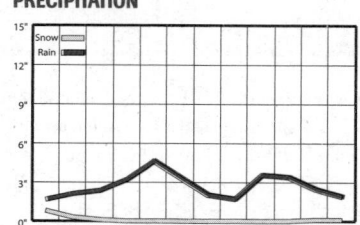

DAYS OF CLOUDS & PRECIPITATION

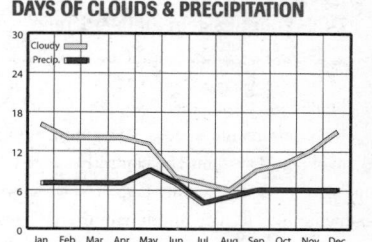

EDUCATION SCORE: 44/RANK: 185

ACHIEVEMENT	AREA	U.S. AVG	PUBLIC SCHOOLS	AREA	U.S. AVG	HIGHER EDUCATION	AREA	U.S. AVG
High school degree	76.6%	80.2%	Expenditures per pupil	$5,209	$5,894	No. 2-year colleges	2	3
2-year college degree	7.1%	6.2%	Student/teacher ratio	14.5	16.7	No. 4-year colleges/universities	1	4
4-year college degree	11.2%	15.8%	Attending public school	94.7%	90.2%	No. highly ranked universities	1	1
Graduate/professional degree	7.4%	9.6%	State SAT score	993*	1020			
			State ACT score	20.1	21.0			

HEALTH & HEALTHCARE SCORE: 24/RANK: 249

CRIME SCORE: 12/RANK: 289

HAZARDS & ILLNESSES	AREA	U.S. AVG	HEALTHCARE	AREA	U.S. AVG	CRIME	AREA	U.S. AVG
Air-quality score	24	45	Physicians per capita	203.5	261.1	Violent crime rate	536.7	456.0
Water-quality score	52	33	Hospital beds per capita	359.2	432.2	Change in violent crime rate	-42.4%	-17.2%
Pollen/allergy score	82	61	No. teaching hospitals	2	4	Property crime rate	5,963.9	3,950.0
Stress score	80	50	Cost per doctor visit	$71	$67	Change in property crime rate	1.1%	-16.8%
Cancer mortality per capita	161.6	169.0	Cost per dental visit	$65	$82			
Depression days per month	3.7	2.8	Cost per daily hospital room	$414	$733			

TRANSPORTATION SCORE: 50/RANK: 164

COMMUTE	AREA	U.S. AVG	INTERCITY SERVICES	AREA	U.S. AVG	AUTOMOTIVE	AREA	U.S. AVG
Average commute time	20.0 min.	22.6 min.	Miles to nearest major airport	91	46	Insurance, annual premium	$942	$1,011
Commute by auto	94.0%	88.7%	Type of local airport	Medium		Gas, cost per gallon	$1.43	$1.50
Commute by mass transit	.5%	1.8%	No. daily airline departures	247	294	Daily vehicle miles per capita	30.2	23.0
Work at home	2.4%	3.9%	Amtrak service	Yes				
Mass transit miles per capita	3.1	8.0	No. interstate highways	1	1			

LEISURE SCORE: 26/RANK: 243

DINING & SHOPPING	AREA	U.S. AVG	ENTERTAINMENT	AREA	U.S. AVG	OUTDOOR ACTIVITIES	AREA	U.S. AVG
Restaurant rating	1	1	Professional sports rating	2	4	Golf-course rating	2	4
No. outlet malls	1	2	College sports rating	5	4	Ski-area rating	1	4
No. Starbucks	2	11	Zoo/aquarium rating	3	3	National Park rating	1	3
No. warehouse clubs	1	4	Amusement park rating	1	3	Sq. miles inland water	2.0	4.0
			Botanical garden/arboretum rating	2	3	Miles of coastline	0.0	11.4

ARTS & CULTURE SCORE: 19/RANK: 267

MEDIA & LIBRARIES	AREA	U.S. AVG	PERFORMING ARTS	AREA	U.S. AVG	MUSEUMS	AREA	U.S. AVG
Arts radio rating	1	3	Classical music rating	3	4	Overall museum rating	6	6
No. public libraries	8	28	Ballet/dance rating	1	3	Art museum rating	5	5
Library volumes per capita	1.8	2.8	Professional theater rating	1	3	Science museum rating	3	4
			University arts programs rating	4	5	Children's museum rating	1	3

Washington, DC-MD-VA-WV

Score: 82.6   **Rank:** 26

Profile: National center
Location: Along the Potomac River between southern Maryland and northern Virginia, inland from Chesapeake Bay
Elevation: 26 feet
Time zone: Eastern Standard Time

PRO	CON
Uniquely attractive core	Cost of living
Arts and culture	Urban sprawl
Historic interest	Summer heat

The nation's capital is a unique place. The city was laid out in 1791 with ceremonial spaces and grand radial avenues superimposed over a grid system. The centrally located National Mall is an urban planning gem, with excellent open spaces, walking paths, and major monuments in a classic architectural style. The U.S. Capitol serves as the mall's eastern terminus opposite the Washington Monument to the west, just south of the White House. The Lincoln Memorial sits farther west beyond the Washington Monument on the banks of the Potomac River. Surrounding the area are numerous government offices. Lining the mall is the Smithsonian museum complex, probably the best set of museums in the world in a single location. To the northwest of the mall, but still within the city limits, is Georgetown, an upscale residential and commercial enclave, home to Georgetown University, George Washington Hospital, and a variety of entertainment and nightlife amenities. To the north and east lie socioeconomically mixed neighborhoods and areas of urban decay.

Residential communities surround the city on all sides. The largest, to the south and west in northern Virginia, include Arlington, Alexandria, McLean, and the more upscale Fairfax. Another major corridor runs along I-270 northwest through Bethesda, Silver Spring, Rockville, and Gaithersburg, all in Maryland. While public transit options are efficient in all directions, sprawl and traffic complications have led some to rely on "slug" commuting (see "Slugging It to Work" sidebar in chapter 3). In most areas, housing quality is excellent with large, often wooded, lots. However, parts of northern Virginia contain cookie-cutter housing along with fast-food chains and strip malls. Most of these outlying communities are self-contained. Several high-tech and Fortune 500 employers make their homes in Maryland and Virginia, particularly in Rockville-Gaithersburg and along the parkway to Dulles Airport in northern Virginia.

The dominance of the U.S. Government and its impact on the local economy and culture cannot be overstated. Not surprisingly, the area has a high percentage of well-educated citizens. But a significant number of educationally and economically disadvantaged people are also within its borders. The Cost of Living Index at 125.4 is high but not exorbitant for this type of area. Housing options and costs vary across the metropolitan area, and most can find an affordable situation. But urban sprawl is a concern. As development and business activity is flung farther out into the countryside, traffic and air quality, the former a big problem and the latter an emerging one, require attention. A recent attempt to turn part of the Civil War Manassas (Bull Run) battlefield into a commercial development illustrates the sprawl problem.

Washington, D.C., stands alone as a U.S. city with unique beauty, plenty to see and do, a relatively active and intellectually stimulating lifestyle, and a wide variety of employment and living options. It does have problems and isn't for everyone, but most who live there are glad they do.

Washington lies at the western edge of the mid-Atlantic Coastal Plain, about 50 miles east of the Blue Ridge Mountains and 35 miles west of Chesapeake Bay. The immediate area is flat with rolling hills starting just outside the city to the northwest and southwest. The climate is coastal continental with a subtropical influence. Summers are warm and humid with occasional hot, sticky spells and thunderstorms. Because of the inland location, summer heat and humidity aren't offset by sea breezes. Winters are cold but not severe. Precipitation is uniformly distributed throughout the year. Potomac floods can result from heavy rains, sometimes augmented by snowmelt and high tides. Normal winter snowfall is 16.0 inches, but occasional heavy snows of 25 inches or more do occur. First freeze is early November, last is April 1.

POPULATION

DEMOGRAPHICS	AREA	U.S. AVG	ETHNIC COMPOSITION	AREA	U.S. AVG	RESIDENT PROFILE	AREA	U.S. AVG
Population	5,162,029		White	73.1%	75.1%	Single	47.3%	43.6%
Population density per sq. mile	792.9	447.3	Black	20.4%	12.3%	Married	52.7%	56.4%
Population growth	22.2%	16.1%	Asian	4.6%	3.6%	Divorced	7.3%	8.4%
Median age	35.2	35.5	American Indian	.3%	.9%	Separated	4.5%	3.0%
Average family size	2.7	2.7	Hispanic	5.4%	12.5%	Married with children	29.0%	28.7%
			Diversity measure	58.8%	35.2%	Single with children	9.7%	10.1%

ECONOMY & JOBS   SCORE: 85/RANK: 48

INCOME	AREA	U.S. AVG	EMPLOYMENT	AREA	U.S. AVG	LARGEST EMPLOYING INDUSTRY
Per capita income	$35,242	$23,420	Unemployment rate	3.3%	6.1%	Computer Systems Design and Related Services
Household income	$72,781	$46,060	Recent job growth	1.2%	.9%	
Household income < $25K	10.9%	26.4%	Projected future job growth	16.5%	15.1%	
Household income > $75K	48.1%	24.5%	White collar	67.9%	54.5%	
Household income growth	58.6%	57.3%	Blue collar	32.1%	45.5%	

COST OF LIVING — SCORE: 5/RANK: 313

INDEXES & TAXES	AREA	U.S. AVG	HOUSING	AREA	U.S. AVG	NECESSITIES	AREA	U.S. AVG
Cost of Living Index	125.4	100.0	Median home price	$258,700	$160,100	Food Index	106.4	100.0
Financial Progress Index	123.7	100.0	Home price appreciation	12.6%	7.1%	Housing Index	160.7	100.0
Income tax rate	9.500%	4.625%	Median rent	$1,218	$670	Utilities Index	92.8	100.0
Sales tax rate	5.750%	6.474%	Homes owned	65.1%	63.9%	Transportation Index	112.7	100.0
Property tax rate	$11.7	$15.6	Homes rented	28.3%	25.3%	Healthcare Index	109.4	100.0
			Housing affordability	48.0%	54.5%	Miscellaneous Cost Index	105.0	100.0

CLIMATE — SCORE: 43/RANK: 186

TEMPERATURE	AREA	U.S. AVG	PRECIPITATION	AREA	U.S. AVG	COMFORTS & HAZARDS	AREA	U.S. AVG
January low	27.7°F	26.4°F	Annual inches precipitation	39.0	35.9	July relative humidity	64.0%	68.8%
July high	88.2°F	86.7°F	Annual inches snowfall	16.0	24.2	Annual days mostly sunny	207	212
Annual days > 90°F	37	38	Annual days precipitation	111	111	Annual days with thunderstorms	29	39
Annual days < 32°F	75	88	Annual days rain > 0.5 inches	27	23	Tornado risk score	12	19
Annual days < 0°F	0	6	Annual days snow > 1.5 inches	4	6	Hurricane risk score	13	15

TEMPERATURE

PRECIPITATION

DAYS OF CLOUDS & PRECIPITATION

EDUCATION — SCORE: 99/RANK: 2

ACHIEVEMENT	AREA	U.S. AVG	PUBLIC SCHOOLS	AREA	U.S. AVG	HIGHER EDUCATION	AREA	U.S. AVG
High school degree	87.8%	80.2%	Expenditures per pupil	$7,203	$5,894	No. 2-year colleges	9	3
2-year college degree	3.6%	6.2%	Student/teacher ratio	15.7	16.7	No. 4-year colleges/universities	25	4
4-year college degree	23.0%	15.8%	Attending public school	86.9%	90.2%	No. highly ranked universities	6	1
Graduate/professional degree	18.8%	9.6%	State SAT score	800*	1020			
			State ACT score	17.5	21.0			

HEALTH & HEALTHCARE — SCORE: 32/RANK: 223 / CRIME — SCORE: 67/RANK: 109

HAZARDS & ILLNESSES	AREA	U.S. AVG	HEALTHCARE	AREA	U.S. AVG	CRIME	AREA	U.S. AVG
Air-quality score	89	45	Physicians per capita	338.9	261.1	Violent crime rate	508.9	456.0
Water-quality score	54	33	Hospital beds per capita	258.1	432.2	Change in violent crime rate	-29.0%	-17.2%
Pollen/allergy score	69	61	No. teaching hospitals	20	4	Property crime rate	3,443.1	3,950.0
Stress score	43	50	Cost per doctor visit	$83	$67	Change in property crime rate	-29.4%	-16.8%
Cancer mortality per capita	176.8	169.0	Cost per dental visit	$102	$82			
Depression days per month	2.6	2.8	Cost per daily hospital room	$531	$733			

TRANSPORTATION — SCORE: 74/RANK: 83

COMMUTE	AREA	U.S. AVG	INTERCITY SERVICES	AREA	U.S. AVG	AUTOMOTIVE	AREA	U.S. AVG
Average commute time	32.8 min.	22.6 min.	Miles to nearest major airport	4	46	Insurance, annual premium	$1,140	$1,011
Commute by auto	82.9%	88.7%	Type of local airport	Large		Gas, cost per gallon	$1.52	$1.50
Commute by mass transit	8.2%	1.8%	No. daily airline departures	410	294	Daily vehicle miles per capita	22.5	23.0
Work at home	3.8%	3.9%	Amtrak service	Yes				
Mass transit miles per capita	24.4	8.0	No. interstate highways	2	1			

LEISURE — SCORE: 97/RANK: 8

DINING & SHOPPING	AREA	U.S. AVG	ENTERTAINMENT	AREA	U.S. AVG	OUTDOOR ACTIVITIES	AREA	U.S. AVG
Restaurant rating	3	1	Professional sports rating	9	4	Golf-course rating	10	4
No. outlet malls	4	2	College sports rating	9	4	Ski-area rating	2	4
No. Starbucks	155	11	Zoo/aquarium rating	10	3	National Park rating	4	3
No. warehouse clubs	10	4	Amusement park rating	2	3	Sq. miles inland water	8.0	4.0
			Botanical garden/arboretum rating	10	3	Miles of coastline	0.0	11.4

ARTS & CULTURE — SCORE: 99/RANK: 2

MEDIA & LIBRARIES	AREA	U.S. AVG	PERFORMING ARTS	AREA	U.S. AVG	MUSEUMS	AREA	U.S. AVG
Arts radio rating	9	3	Classical music rating	10	4	Overall museum rating	10	6
No. public libraries	153	28	Ballet/dance rating	9	3	Art museum rating	10	5
Library volumes per capita	3.0	2.8	Professional theater rating	10	3	Science museum rating	10	4
			University arts programs rating	10	5	Children's museum rating	10	3

Waterbury, CT

Score: 27.2	**Rank:** 312

Profile: Small city
Location: West-central Connecticut, 30 miles north of the Long Island Sound along the Naugatuck River
Elevation: 390 feet
Time zone: Eastern Standard Time

PRO	**CON**
Historic town center	Economy
Cost of living	Entertainment
Recent job declines	Arts and culture

Waterbury, settled in the late 1600s, is a typical New England town with a square surrounded by historic buildings. A major freeway crossroads, Waterbury is conveniently located close to the larger cities of Hartford, New Haven, and Bridgeport. Once an industrial center, known for the production of brass and brass products, the economy is in transition toward high-tech manufacturing and commercial banking. Recent employment trends have been negative, however, so the success of the transition remains to be seen. The area is just far enough from New York City and Hartford to be somewhat isolated from arts and culture and entertainment facilities. The cost of living, while high on a national scale, is relatively attractive for Connecticut.

Waterbury sits in a narrow river plain where several minor streams converge. Areas of deciduous wooded hills surround the city. Warm, humid summers with occasional thunderstorms are the rule. In winter, the location between colder, northern air masses and warm, moist air from the ocean and the south produces clouds, rain, rain/snow mixes, and a reasonable amount of snow. First freeze is early October, last is early May.

POPULATION

DEMOGRAPHICS	AREA	U.S. AVG	ETHNIC COMPOSITION	AREA	U.S. AVG	RESIDENT PROFILE	AREA	U.S. AVG
Population	232,519		White	87.7%	75.1%	Single	47.1%	43.6%
Population density per sq. mile	995.7	447.3	Black	7.4%	12.3%	Married	52.9%	56.4%
Population growth	4.9%	16.1%	Asian	1.2%	3.6%	Divorced	8.2%	8.4%
Median age	37.9	35.5	American Indian	.2%	.9%	Separated	2.7%	3.0%
Average family size	2.5	2.7	Hispanic	9.3%	12.5%	Married with children	24.6%	28.7%
			Diversity measure	36.3%	35.2%	Single with children	9.2%	10.1%

ECONOMY & JOBS SCORE: 56/RANK: 145

INCOME	AREA	U.S. AVG	EMPLOYMENT	AREA	U.S. AVG	LARGEST EMPLOYING INDUSTRY
Per capita income	$28,141	$23,420	Unemployment rate	6.3%	6.1%	Machinery Manufacturing
Household income	$56,423	$46,060	Recent job growth	-1.1%	.9%	
Household income < $25K	19.5%	26.4%	Projected future job growth	6.7%	15.1%	
Household income > $75K	34.1%	24.5%	White collar	55.3%	54.5%	
Household income growth	50.5%	57.3%	Blue collar	44.7%	45.5%	

COST OF LIVING SCORE: 16/RANK: 278

INDEXES & TAXES	AREA	U.S. AVG	HOUSING	AREA	U.S. AVG	NECESSITIES	AREA	U.S. AVG
Cost of Living Index	115.8	100.0	Median home price	$195,360	$160,100	Food Index	112.9	100.0
Financial Progress Index	103.8	100.0	Home price appreciation	9.3%	7.1%	Housing Index	121.3	100.0
Income tax rate	4.500%	4.625%	Median rent	$881	$670	Utilities Index	127.6	100.0
Sales tax rate	6.000%	6.474%	Homes owned	63.2%	63.9%	Transportation Index	104.0	100.0
Property tax rate	$13.1	$15.6	Homes rented	29.1%	25.3%	Healthcare Index	110.6	100.0
			Housing affordability	43.0%	54.5%	Miscellaneous Cost Index	112.1	100.0

CLIMATE SCORE: 2/RANK: 324

TEMPERATURE	AREA	U.S. AVG	PRECIPITATION	AREA	U.S. AVG	COMFORTS & HAZARDS	AREA	U.S. AVG
January low	16.1°F	26.4°F	Annual inches precipitation	43.0	35.9	July relative humidity	68.0%	68.8%
July high	84.1°F	86.7°F	Annual inches snowfall	53.0	24.2	Annual days mostly sunny	188	212
Annual days > 90°F	20	38	Annual days precipitation	128	111	Annual days with thunderstorms	7	39
Annual days < 32°F	137	88	Annual days rain > 0.5 inches	26	23	Tornado risk score	9	19
Annual days < 0°F	6	6	Annual days snow > 1.5 inches	8	6	Hurricane risk score	19	15

TEMPERATURE

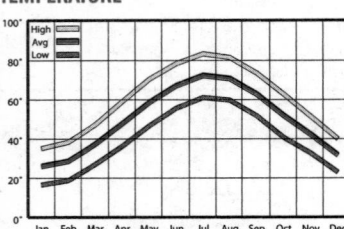

PRECIPITATION

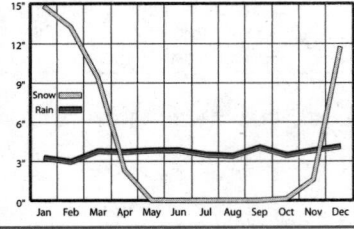

DAYS OF CLOUDS & PRECIPITATION

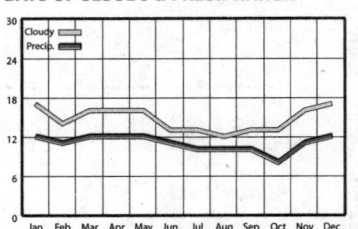

EDUCATION SCORE: 59/RANK: 136

ACHIEVEMENT	AREA	U.S. AVG	PUBLIC SCHOOLS	AREA	U.S. AVG	HIGHER EDUCATION	AREA	U.S. AVG
High school degree	83.5%	80.2%	Expenditures per pupil	$8,141	$5,894	No. 2-year colleges	1	3
2-year college degree	6.6%	6.2%	Student/teacher ratio	14.9	16.7	No. 4-year colleges/universities	1	4
4-year college degree	15.5%	15.8%	Attending public school	87.0%	90.2%	No. highly ranked universities	0	1
Graduate/professional degree	12.1%	9.6%	State SAT score	1026*	1020			
			State ACT score	22.1	21.0			

HEALTH & HEALTHCARE SCORE: 40/RANK: 196

HAZARDS & ILLNESSES	AREA	U.S. AVG	HEALTHCARE	AREA	U.S. AVG
Air-quality score	49	45	Physicians per capita	194.4	261.1
Water-quality score	38	33	Hospital beds per capita	210.1	432.2
Pollen/allergy score	53	61	No. teaching hospitals	2	4
Stress score	81	50	Cost per doctor visit	$80	$67
Cancer mortality per capita	181.8	169.0	Cost per dental visit	$98	$82
Depression days per month	3.6	2.8	Cost per daily hospital room	$889	$733

CRIME SCORE: 56/RANK: 146

CRIME	AREA	U.S. AVG
Violent crime rate	319.7	456.0
Change in violent crime rate	-2.6%	-17.2%
Property crime rate	4,177.2	3,950.0
Change in property crime rate	-26.3%	-16.8%

TRANSPORTATION SCORE: 17/RANK: 273

COMMUTE	AREA	U.S. AVG	INTERCITY SERVICES	AREA	U.S. AVG	AUTOMOTIVE	AREA	U.S. AVG
Average commute time	23.2 min.	22.6 min.	Miles to nearest major airport	32	46	Insurance, annual premium	$1,063	$1,011
Commute by auto	91.5%	88.7%	Type of local airport	Medium		Gas, cost per gallon	$1.60	$1.50
Commute by mass transit	2.2%	1.8%	No. daily airline departures	209	294	Daily vehicle miles per capita	17.8	23.0
Work at home	2.3%	3.9%	Amtrak service	No				
Mass transit miles per capita	6.5	8.0	No. interstate highways	1	1			

LEISURE SCORE: 56/RANK: 145

DINING & SHOPPING	AREA	U.S. AVG	ENTERTAINMENT	AREA	U.S. AVG	OUTDOOR ACTIVITIES	AREA	U.S. AVG
Restaurant rating	1	1	Professional sports rating	10	4	Golf-course rating	8	4
No. outlet malls	9	2	College sports rating	10	4	Ski-area rating	6	4
No. Starbucks	2	11	Zoo/aquarium rating	4	3	National Park rating	3	3
No. warehouse clubs	5	4	Amusement park rating	6	3	Sq. miles inland water	6.0	4.0
			Botanical garden/arboretum rating	4	3	Miles of coastline	0.0	11.4

ARTS & CULTURE SCORE: 57/RANK: 140

MEDIA & LIBRARIES	AREA	U.S. AVG	PERFORMING ARTS	AREA	U.S. AVG	MUSEUMS	AREA	U.S. AVG
Arts radio rating	4	3	Classical music rating	7	4	Overall museum rating	7	6
No. public libraries	12	28	Ballet/dance rating	5	3	Art museum rating	7	5
Library volumes per capita	3.4	2.8	Professional theater rating	8	3	Science museum rating	4	4
			University arts programs rating	4	5	Children's museum rating	3	3

Waterloo–Cedar Falls, IA

Score: 64.6   Rank: 113

Profile: Small-city complex
Location: Northeast Iowa along the Cedar River
Elevation: 868 feet
Time zone: Central Standard Time

PRO	CON
Attractive downtown	Harsh winters
Cost of living	Economic cycles
Outdoor recreation	Entertainment

Waterloo is a busy manufacturing and agricultural center, including a giant John Deere tractor works and other farm-implement makers. It is also a center for the cattle industry, with a 10-day National Cattle Congress each year. The town contains two notable science museums. Downtown is an attractive mix of old and new. While entertainment and nightlife are minimal, there are waterfront parks and a well-used bike trail running 52 miles to Cedar Rapids on an old railroad grade. The area is vulnerable to the economic cycles of the farm industry, but has attractive housing costs and overall cost of living. (The Cost of Living Index of 83.2 is the lowest in the state.) The third shortest commute time in the country makes it a stress-free place to live.

Cedar Falls, 5 miles west, won a 2002 National Trust for Historic Preservation Great American Main Street Award.

Waterloo is situated on the banks of the Cedar River in northeast Iowa. The terrain is flat to gently rolling, mainly farmland. The climate is humid continental with four distinct seasons and highly variable temperature and precipitation. Summer is warm and humid, and receives most of the year's rainfall as thunderstorms. Winter is cold and dry with occasional snow. Bitter cold occurs frequently—temperatures drop below zero an average of 31 days per year. First freeze is early October, last is late April.

POPULATION

DEMOGRAPHICS	AREA	U.S. AVG	ETHNIC COMPOSITION	AREA	U.S. AVG	RESIDENT PROFILE	AREA	U.S. AVG
Population	127,394		White	93.1%	75.1%	Single	39.2%	43.6%
Population density per sq. mile	224.5	447.3	Black	5.8%	12.3%	Married	60.8%	56.4%
Population growth	2.9%	16.1%	Asian	.8%	3.6%	Divorced	7.7%	8.4%
Median age	34.7	35.5	American Indian	.2%	.9%	Separated	2.0%	3.0%
Average family size	2.6	2.7	Hispanic	1.0%	12.5%	Married with children	28.5%	28.7%
			Diversity measure	21.8%	35.2%	Single with children	10.4%	10.1%

ECONOMY & JOBS SCORE: 53/RANK: 155

INCOME	AREA	U.S. AVG	EMPLOYMENT	AREA	U.S. AVG	LARGEST EMPLOYING INDUSTRY
Per capita income	$21,803	$23,420	Unemployment rate	5.1%	6.1%	Food Manufacturing
Household income	$41,213	$46,060	Recent job growth	-2.3%	.9%	
Household income < $25K	29.8%	26.4%	Projected future job growth	9.7%	15.1%	
Household income > $75K	22.1%	24.5%	White collar	51.6%	54.5%	
Household income growth	59.5%	57.3%	Blue collar	48.4%	45.5%	

COST OF LIVING SCORE: 45/RANK: 181

INDEXES & TAXES	AREA	U.S. AVG	HOUSING	AREA	U.S. AVG	NECESSITIES	AREA	U.S. AVG
Cost of Living Index	83.2	100.0	Median home price	$89,200	$160,100	Food Index	89.6	100.0
Financial Progress Index	105.6	100.0	Home price appreciation	7.2%	7.1%	Housing Index	55.4	100.0
Income tax rate	8.920%	4.625%	Median rent	$552	$670	Utilities Index	124.0	100.0
Sales tax rate	7.000%	6.474%	Homes owned	70.6%	63.9%	Transportation Index	99.6	100.0
Property tax rate	$24.5	$15.6	Homes rented	23.3%	25.3%	Healthcare Index	94.2	100.0
			Housing affordability	56.0%	54.5%	Miscellaneous Cost Index	97.5	100.0

CLIMATE SCORE: 30/RANK: 230

TEMPERATURE	AREA	U.S. AVG	PRECIPITATION	AREA	U.S. AVG	COMFORTS & HAZARDS	AREA	U.S. AVG
January low	6.9°F	26.4°F	Annual inches precipitation	34.0	35.9	July relative humidity	72.0%	68.8%
July high	83.6°F	86.7°F	Annual inches snowfall	31.0	24.2	Annual days mostly sunny	194	212
Annual days > 90°F	15	38	Annual days precipitation	99	111	Annual days with thunderstorms	43	39
Annual days < 32°F	159	88	Annual days rain > 0.5 inches	22	23	Tornado risk score	19	19
Annual days < 0°F	31	6	Annual days snow > 1.5 inches	6	6	Hurricane risk score	0	15

TEMPERATURE

PRECIPITATION

DAYS OF CLOUDS & PRECIPITATION

EDUCATION SCORE: 29/RANK: 234

ACHIEVEMENT	AREA	U.S. AVG	PUBLIC SCHOOLS	AREA	U.S. AVG	HIGHER EDUCATION	AREA	U.S. AVG
High school degree	86.4%	80.2%	Expenditures per pupil	$5,257	$5,894	No. 2-year colleges	1	3
2-year college degree	7.2%	6.2%	Student/teacher ratio	16.6	16.7	No. 4-year colleges/universities	1	4
4-year college degree	14.3%	15.8%	Attending public school	82.6%	90.2%	No. highly ranked universities	0	1
Graduate/professional degree	8.7%	9.6%	State SAT score	1183	1020			
			State ACT score	22.0*	21.0			

HEALTH & HEALTHCARE SCORE: 91/RANK: 27

HAZARDS & ILLNESSES	AREA	U.S. AVG	HEALTHCARE	AREA	U.S. AVG
Air-quality score	24	45	Physicians per capita	227.6	261.1
Water-quality score	54	33	Hospital beds per capita	471.8	432.2
Pollen/allergy score	43	61	No. teaching hospitals	2	4
Stress score	9	50	Cost per doctor visit	$68	$67
Cancer mortality per capita	165.4	169.0	Cost per dental visit	$73	$82
Depression days per month	1.8	2.8	Cost per daily hospital room	$532	$733

CRIME SCORE: 57/RANK: 142

CRIME	AREA	U.S. AVG
Violent crime rate	355.8	456.0
Change in violent crime rate	-23.6%	-17.2%
Property crime rate	4,212.0	3,950.0
Change in property crime rate	-24.3%	-16.8%

TRANSPORTATION SCORE: 90/RANK: 36

COMMUTE	AREA	U.S. AVG	INTERCITY SERVICES	AREA	U.S. AVG	AUTOMOTIVE	AREA	U.S. AVG
Average commute time	15.7 min.	22.6 min.	Miles to nearest major airport	54	46	Insurance, annual premium	$655	$1,011
Commute by auto	89.5%	88.7%	Type of local airport	Small		Gas, cost per gallon	$1.45	$1.50
Commute by mass transit	.6%	1.8%	No. daily airline departures	58	294	Daily vehicle miles per capita	20.8	23.0
Work at home	5.3%	3.9%	Amtrak service	No				
Mass transit miles per capita	6.4	8.0	No. interstate highways	0	1			

LEISURE SCORE: 13/RANK: 286

DINING & SHOPPING	AREA	U.S. AVG	ENTERTAINMENT	AREA	U.S. AVG	OUTDOOR ACTIVITIES	AREA	U.S. AVG
Restaurant rating	1	1	Professional sports rating	2	4	Golf-course rating	3	4
No. outlet malls	1	2	College sports rating	4	4	Ski-area rating	3	4
No. Starbucks	0	11	Zoo/aquarium rating	1	3	National Park rating	1	3
No. warehouse clubs	3	4	Amusement park rating	1	3	Sq. miles inland water	1.0	4.0
			Botanical garden/arboretum rating	1	3	Miles of coastline	0.0	11.4

ARTS & CULTURE SCORE: 85/RANK: 47

MEDIA & LIBRARIES	AREA	U.S. AVG	PERFORMING ARTS	AREA	U.S. AVG	MUSEUMS	AREA	U.S. AVG
Arts radio rating	1	3	Classical music rating	4	4	Overall museum rating	5	6
No. public libraries	6	28	Ballet/dance rating	1	3	Art museum rating	6	5
Library volumes per capita	2.7	2.8	Professional theater rating	1	3	Science museum rating	5	4
			University arts programs rating	4	5	Children's museum rating	3	3

Wausau, WI

Score: 52.1　**Rank:** 208

Profile: Small town
Location: North-central Wisconsin
Elevation: 1,196 feet
Time zone: Central Standard Time

PRO	CON
Small-town atmosphere	Cold winters
Outdoor recreation	Isolation
Low crime rate	Entertainment

Wausau is an agricultural center with diversified industry in forest products, paper, and food processing. The surrounding area is known for outdoor recreation, including watersports and hiking in summer and skiing and snowmobiling in winter. The town is small and pleasant, and the staid railroad station bearing the Wausau name is an insurance industry icon frequently seen in advertising for the namesake company.

The area is the coldest in Wisconsin and one of the coldest in the nation. Wausau sits in a shallow valley along the upper reaches of the Wisconsin River. Areas to the east are rolling and mixed with woods and farmland. Agricultural areas to the west are more level. Farther to the north lie several areas of national and state forest. The climate is decidedly continental with some influence from Lake Superior. Summers are pleasant with only 4 days per year over 90°F. Spring and fall are variable with periods of pleasant dry weather particularly in fall. Winters are harsh and cold as prevailing northwesterly winds deliver cold air. Lingering moisture from the south or Lake Superior produce snow, sometimes heavy. Snow cover persists through the winter. First freeze is early October, last is mid-May.

POPULATION

DEMOGRAPHICS	AREA	U.S. AVG	ETHNIC COMPOSITION	AREA	U.S. AVG	RESIDENT PROFILE	AREA	U.S. AVG
Population	126,728		White	97.0%	75.1%	Single	36.7%	43.6%
Population density per sq. mile	82.0	447.3	Black	.7%	12.3%	Married	63.3%	56.4%
Population growth	9.8%	16.1%	Asian	1.6%	3.6%	Divorced	5.2%	8.4%
Median age	36.6	35.5	American Indian	.5%	.9%	Separated	1.3%	3.0%
Average family size	2.8	2.7	Hispanic	.6%	12.5%	Married with children	35.7%	28.7%
			Diversity measure	12.5%	35.2%	Single with children	6.5%	10.1%

ECONOMY & JOBS SCORE: 83/RANK: 57

INCOME	AREA	U.S. AVG	EMPLOYMENT	AREA	U.S. AVG	LARGEST EMPLOYING INDUSTRY
Per capita income	$23,893	$23,420	Unemployment rate	4.3%	6.1%	Fabricated Metal Product Manufacturing
Household income	$49,498	$46,060	Recent job growth	2.4%	.9%	
Household income < $25K	22.2%	26.4%	Projected future job growth	15.3%	15.1%	
Household income > $75K	25.1%	24.5%	White collar	48.4%	54.5%	
Household income growth	63.8%	57.3%	Blue collar	51.6%	45.5%	

COST OF LIVING SCORE: 37/RANK: 207

INDEXES & TAXES	AREA	U.S. AVG	HOUSING	AREA	U.S. AVG	NECESSITIES	AREA	U.S. AVG
Cost of Living Index	89.8	100.0	Median home price	$111,720	$160,100	Food Index	95.7	100.0
Financial Progress Index	117.4	100.0	Home price appreciation	5.3%	7.1%	Housing Index	69.4	100.0
Income tax rate	6.930%	4.625%	Median rent	$520	$670	Utilities Index	118.3	100.0
Sales tax rate	5.500%	6.474%	Homes owned	75.9%	63.9%	Transportation Index	100.3	100.0
Property tax rate	$26.0	$15.6	Homes rented	17.2%	25.3%	Healthcare Index	106.4	100.0
			Housing affordability	66.0%	54.5%	Miscellaneous Cost Index	98.7	100.0

CLIMATE SCORE: 17/RANK: 274

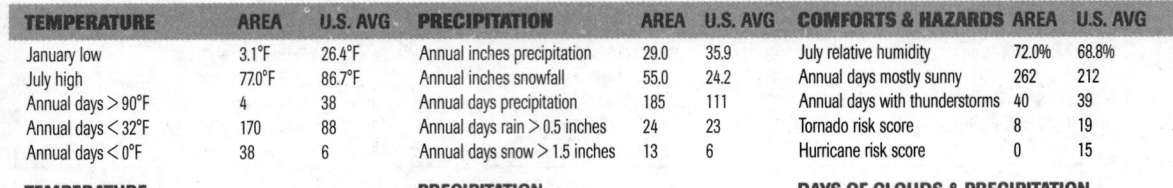

TEMPERATURE	AREA	U.S. AVG	PRECIPITATION	AREA	U.S. AVG	COMFORTS & HAZARDS	AREA	U.S. AVG
January low	3.1°F	26.4°F	Annual inches precipitation	29.0	35.9	July relative humidity	72.0%	68.8%
July high	77.0°F	86.7°F	Annual inches snowfall	55.0	24.2	Annual days mostly sunny	262	212
Annual days > 90°F	4	38	Annual days precipitation	185	111	Annual days with thunderstorms	40	39
Annual days < 32°F	170	88	Annual days rain > 0.5 inches	24	23	Tornado risk score	8	19
Annual days < 0°F	38	6	Annual days snow > 1.5 inches	13	6	Hurricane risk score	0	15

TEMPERATURE

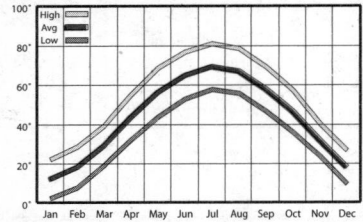

PRECIPITATION

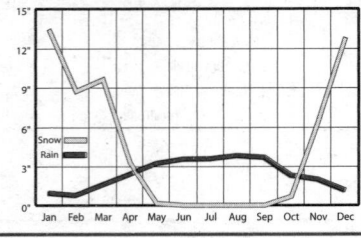

DAYS OF CLOUDS & PRECIPITATION

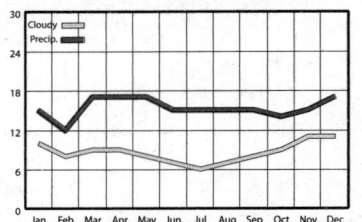

EDUCATION SCORE: 35/RANK: 213

ACHIEVEMENT	AREA	U.S. AVG	PUBLIC SCHOOLS	AREA	U.S. AVG	HIGHER EDUCATION	AREA	U.S. AVG
High school degree	83.8%	80.2%	Expenditures per pupil	$6,665	$5,894	No. 2-year colleges	2	3
2-year college degree	8.5%	6.2%	Student/teacher ratio	15.2	16.7	No. 4-year colleges/universities	0	4
4-year college degree	12.6%	15.8%	Attending public school	86.0%	90.2%	No. highly ranked universities	0	1
Graduate/professional degree	5.7%	9.6%	State SAT score	1179	1020			
			State ACT score	22.2*	21.0			

HEALTH & HEALTHCARE SCORE: 90/RANK: 31

CRIME SCORE: 82/RANK: 60

HAZARDS & ILLNESSES	AREA	U.S. AVG	HEALTHCARE	AREA	U.S. AVG	CRIME	AREA	U.S. AVG
Air-quality score	24	45	Physicians per capita	222.5	261.1	Violent crime rate	130.2	456.0
Water-quality score	43	33	Hospital beds per capita	495.9	432.2	Change in violent crime rate	48.8%	-17.2%
Pollen/allergy score	36	61	No. teaching hospitals	1	4	Property crime rate	2,185.7	3,950.0
Stress score	3	50	Cost per doctor visit	$88	$67	Change in property crime rate	-12.2%	-16.8%
Cancer mortality per capita	158.3	169.0	Cost per dental visit	$73	$82			
Depression days per month	3.3	2.8	Cost per daily hospital room	$440	$733			

TRANSPORTATION SCORE: 70/RANK: 100

COMMUTE	AREA	U.S. AVG	INTERCITY SERVICES	AREA	U.S. AVG	AUTOMOTIVE	AREA	U.S. AVG
Average commute time	18.4 min.	22.6 min.	Miles to nearest major airport	81	46	Insurance, annual premium	$750	$1,011
Commute by auto	81.2%	88.7%	Type of local airport	Small		Gas, cost per gallon	$1.55	$1.50
Commute by mass transit	.5%	1.8%	No. daily airline departures	39	294	Daily vehicle miles per capita	23.0	23.0
Work at home	11.9%	3.9%	Amtrak service	No				
Mass transit miles per capita	5.3	8.0	No. interstate highways	0	1			

LEISURE SCORE: 8/RANK: 304

DINING & SHOPPING	AREA	U.S. AVG	ENTERTAINMENT	AREA	U.S. AVG	OUTDOOR ACTIVITIES	AREA	U.S. AVG
Restaurant rating	1	1	Professional sports rating	2	4	Golf-course rating	1	4
No. outlet malls	0	2	College sports rating	1	4	Ski-area rating	2	4
No. Starbucks	1	11	Zoo/aquarium rating	1	3	National Park rating	1	3
No. warehouse clubs	1	4	Amusement park rating	1	3	Sq. miles inland water	3.0	4.0
			Botanical garden/arboretum rating	1	3	Miles of coastline	0.0	11.4

ARTS & CULTURE SCORE: 49/RANK: 168

MEDIA & LIBRARIES	AREA	U.S. AVG	PERFORMING ARTS	AREA	U.S. AVG	MUSEUMS	AREA	U.S. AVG
Arts radio rating	1	3	Classical music rating	3	4	Overall museum rating	2	6
No. public libraries	8	28	Ballet/dance rating	1	3	Art museum rating	4	5
Library volumes per capita	2.7	2.8	Professional theater rating	1	3	Science museum rating	1	4
			University arts programs rating	1	5	Children's museum rating	1	3

West Palm Beach–Boca Raton, FL

Score: 72.7 **Rank:** 69

Profile: Large-beach-city complex
Location: Easternmost point of Florida Peninsula along south Atlantic Coast
Elevation: 18 feet
Time zone: Eastern Standard Time

PRO	CON
Leisure activities	Urban sprawl
Arts and culture	Cost of living
Educational attainment	Crime rate

West Palm Beach is a complex area with a barrier island and inland communities. The barrier island of Palm Beach is an old money, retirement, and snowbird enclave. A string of communities along the inland coast, including Boca Raton, Delray Beach, and Boynton Beach, contain a socioeconomic mix. Boca Raton like Palm Beach and Miami Beach to the south is more upscale. The region consists of year-round residences and leisure activities typical of a tourist destination. The area features the largest museum in Florida, the Norton Museum of Art. Educational attainment is the highest in the state and among the highest nationwide outside of college towns. The economic picture is positive relative to most of the state. The area has its own scheduled, commercial jet service. Downsides include crowding and sprawl to the south and west, moderate crime, and cost of living and housing among the state's highest.

Palm Beach is on a long, narrow barrier island, separated by a narrow coastal waterway from the mainland. Inland, a narrow, sandy coastal plain includes land reclaimed from western swamps initially for agriculture and now for development. The Gulf Stream flows northward about 2 miles offshore, its nearest approach to the Florida coast, creating excellent ocean swimming and climate. Summers are warm and humid with sea breezes and afternoon showers. Winters are mild but can be quite warm.

POPULATION

DEMOGRAPHICS	AREA	U.S. AVG	ETHNIC COMPOSITION	AREA	U.S. AVG	RESIDENT PROFILE	AREA	U.S. AVG
Population	1,190,390		White	81.3%	75.1%	Single	43.6%	43.6%
Population density per sq. mile	603.0	447.3	Black	15.3%	12.3%	Married	56.4%	56.4%
Population growth	37.9%	16.1%	Asian	1.5%	3.6%	Divorced	9.4%	8.4%
Median age	42.4	35.5	American Indian	.2%	.9%	Separated	3.0%	3.0%
Average family size	2.4	2.7	Hispanic	11.5%	12.5%	Married with children	19.0%	28.7%
			Diversity measure	45.0%	35.2%	Single with children	9.5%	10.1%

ECONOMY & JOBS SCORE: 32/RANK: 223

INCOME	AREA	U.S. AVG	EMPLOYMENT	AREA	U.S. AVG	LARGEST EMPLOYING INDUSTRY
Per capita income	$32,873	$23,420	Unemployment rate	6.3%	6.1%	Healthcare and Social Assistance
Household income	$51,876	$46,060	Recent job growth	1.4%	.9%	
Household income < $25K	21.0%	26.4%	Projected future job growth	20.0%	15.1%	
Household income > $75K	30.9%	24.5%	White collar	60.2%	54.5%	
Household income growth	59.5%	57.3%	Blue collar	39.8%	45.5%	

COST OF LIVING SCORE: 43/RANK: 188

INDEXES & TAXES	AREA	U.S. AVG	HOUSING	AREA	U.S. AVG	NECESSITIES	AREA	U.S. AVG
Cost of Living Index	111.2	100.0	Median home price	$192,880	$160,100	Food Index	105.8	100.0
Financial Progress Index	99.4	100.0	Home price appreciation	12.6%	7.1%	Housing Index	119.8	100.0
Income tax rate	0.000%	4.625%	Median rent	$823	$670	Utilities Index	98.2	100.0
Sales tax rate	6.000%	6.474%	Homes owned	60.0%	63.9%	Transportation Index	109.4	100.0
Property tax rate	$17.1	$15.6	Homes rented	22.2%	25.3%	Healthcare Index	114.6	100.0
			Housing affordability	54.0%	54.5%	Miscellaneous Cost Index	105.9	100.0

CLIMATE SCORE: 64/RANK: 118

TEMPERATURE	AREA	U.S. AVG	PRECIPITATION	AREA	U.S. AVG	COMFORTS & HAZARDS	AREA	U.S. AVG
January low	55.9°F	26.4°F	Annual inches precipitation	62.1	35.9	July relative humidity	73.0%	68.8%
July high	89.6°F	86.7°F	Annual inches snowfall	0.0	24.2	Annual days mostly sunny	228	212
Annual days > 90°F	55	38	Annual days precipitation	131	111	Annual days with thunderstorms	79	39
Annual days < 32°F	1	88	Annual days rain > 0.5 inches	37	23	Tornado risk score	37	19
Annual days < 0°F	0	6	Annual days snow > 1.5 inches	0	6	Hurricane risk score	100	15

TEMPERATURE

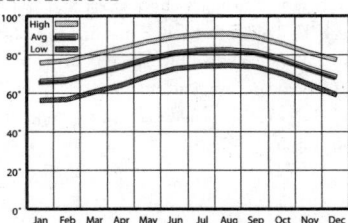

PRECIPITATION

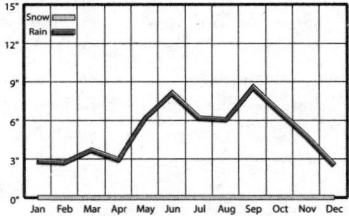

DAYS OF CLOUDS & PRECIPITATION

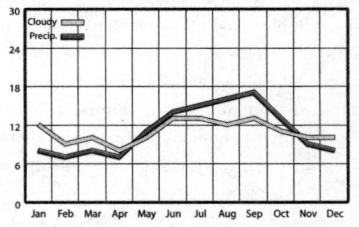

EDUCATION SCORE: 38/RANK: 202

ACHIEVEMENT	AREA	U.S. AVG	PUBLIC SCHOOLS	AREA	U.S. AVG	HIGHER EDUCATION	AREA	U.S. AVG
High school degree	83.6%	80.2%	Expenditures per pupil	$5,586	$5,894	No. 2-year colleges	3	3
2-year college degree	7.0%	6.2%	Student/teacher ratio	18.9	16.7	No. 4-year colleges/universities	4	4
4-year college degree	17.6%	15.8%	Attending public school	84.7%	90.2%	No. highly ranked universities	0	1
Graduate/professional degree	10.1%	9.6%	State SAT score	996*	1020			
			State ACT score	20.5	21.0			

HEALTH & HEALTHCARE SCORE: 61/RANK: 127

HAZARDS & ILLNESSES	AREA	U.S. AVG	HEALTHCARE	AREA	U.S. AVG		CRIME	AREA	U.S. AVG
Air-quality score	24	45	Physicians per capita	268.7	261.1		Violent crime rate	735.8	456.0
Water-quality score	20	33	Hospital beds per capita	334.0	432.2		Change in violent crime rate	-24.5%	-17.2%
Pollen/allergy score	50	61	No. teaching hospitals	2	4		Property crime rate	5,477.8	3,950.0
Stress score	88	50	Cost per doctor visit	$73	$67		Change in property crime rate	-27.9%	-16.8%
Cancer mortality per capita	159.7	169.0	Cost per dental visit	$81	$82				
Depression days per month	2.5	2.8	Cost per daily hospital room	$585	$733				

CRIME SCORE: 16/RANK: 275

TRANSPORTATION SCORE: 31/RANK: 227

COMMUTE	AREA	U.S. AVG	INTERCITY SERVICES	AREA	U.S. AVG	AUTOMOTIVE	AREA	U.S. AVG
Average commute time	25.7 min.	22.6 min.	Miles to nearest major airport	21	46	Insurance, annual premium	$1,225	$1,011
Commute by auto	91.3%	88.7%	Type of local airport	Medium		Gas, cost per gallon	$1.59	$1.50
Commute by mass transit	1.8%	1.8%	No. daily airline departures	326	294	Daily vehicle miles per capita	24.2	23.0
Work at home	3.1%	3.9%	Amtrak service	Yes				
Mass transit miles per capita	13.3	8.0	No. interstate highways	1	1			

LEISURE SCORE: 88/RANK: 42

DINING & SHOPPING	AREA	U.S. AVG	ENTERTAINMENT	AREA	U.S. AVG	OUTDOOR ACTIVITIES	AREA	U.S. AVG
Restaurant rating	5	1	Professional sports rating	3	4	Golf-course rating	10	4
No. outlet malls	2	2	College sports rating	3	4	Ski-area rating	1	4
No. Starbucks	20	11	Zoo/aquarium rating	5	3	National Park rating	2	3
No. warehouse clubs	8	4	Amusement park rating	1	3	Sq. miles inland water	10.0	4.0
			Botanical garden/arboretum rating	6	3	Miles of coastline	45.7	11.4

ARTS & CULTURE SCORE: 54/RANK: 149

MEDIA & LIBRARIES	AREA	U.S. AVG	PERFORMING ARTS	AREA	U.S. AVG	MUSEUMS	AREA	U.S. AVG
Arts radio rating	5	3	Classical music rating	5	4	Overall museum rating	7	6
No. public libraries	25	28	Ballet/dance rating	5	3	Art museum rating	8	5
Library volumes per capita	1.6	2.8	Professional theater rating	7	3	Science museum rating	6	4
			University arts programs rating	6	5	Children's museum rating	9	3

Wheeling, WV-OH

Score: 32.0   Rank: 305

Profile: Small river town
Location: Northern West Virginia Panhandle along the Ohio River
between the Ohio and Pennsylvania borders
Elevation: 645 feet
Time zone: Eastern Standard Time

PRO	CON
Attractive setting	Clouds and rain
Historic interest	Industrial feel
Proximity to Pittsburgh	Low ethnic diversity

Once a gateway for travelers coming west across the National Road, Wheeling remains a central point on transportation networks with good access to the Northeast and Midwest. The metro area includes Belmont County with Martins Ferry and a few other small towns in southeastern Ohio. The main industries are steel and metalworking. Wheeling-Pittsburgh Steel employs over 4,000 people. The city has a well-preserved older section downtown and a few arts and entertainment amenities. With Pittsburgh 60 miles to the northeast, big-city features aren't too far away. Downsides include recent unemployment and a cloudy, wet climate. But many predict that the strategic location, low overall costs, and proximity to Pittsburgh will attract new businesses.

These forces are already at work in nearby Steubenville, Ohio. Local prospects are probably better than the rankings indicate.

Wheeling sits on the east bank of the Ohio River in a narrow plain with steep, deciduous-wooded hills on all sides. The climate is humid continental. The city is in a primary storm track and resides far enough north to receive a Lake Erie influence. Summers are warm and humid, particularly in the bottom of the valley. Winters are fairly mild, but are subject to occasional cold snaps. Fall and spring are changeable, with periods of cool, cloudy weather—making the area one of the cloudiest and rainiest in the country.

POPULATION

DEMOGRAPHICS	AREA	U.S. AVG	ETHNIC COMPOSITION	AREA	U.S. AVG	RESIDENT PROFILE	AREA	U.S. AVG
Population	150,472		White	98.1%	75.1%	Single	40.9%	43.6%
Population density per sq. mile	158.3	447.3	Black	1.4%	12.3%	Married	59.1%	56.4%
Population growth	-5.5%	16.1%	Asian	.4%	3.6%	Divorced	7.6%	8.4%
Median age	41.2	35.5	American Indian	.1%	.9%	Separated	1.9%	3.0%
Average family size	2.5	2.7	Hispanic	.3%	12.5%	Married with children	27.5%	28.7%
			Diversity measure	9.0%	35.2%	Single with children	8.6%	10.1%

ECONOMY & JOBS
SCORE: 11/RANK: 294

INCOME	AREA	U.S. AVG	EMPLOYMENT	AREA	U.S. AVG	LARGEST EMPLOYING INDUSTRY
Per capita income	$18,438	$23,420	Unemployment rate	4.7%	6.1%	Healthcare and Social Assistance
Household income	$32,899	$46,060	Recent job growth	-.0%	.9%	
Household income < $25K	37.9%	26.4%	Projected future job growth	10.3%	15.1%	
Household income > $75K	13.9%	24.5%	White collar	48.4%	54.5%	
Household income growth	50.6%	57.3%	Blue collar	51.6%	45.5%	

COST OF LIVING
SCORE: 73/RANK: 86

INDEXES & TAXES	AREA	U.S. AVG	HOUSING	AREA	U.S. AVG	NECESSITIES	AREA	U.S. AVG
Cost of Living Index	84.8	100.0	Median home price	$75,120	$160,100	Food Index	104.9	100.0
Financial Progress Index	82.7	100.0	Home price appreciation	4.4%	7.1%	Housing Index	46.7	100.0
Income tax rate	6.000%	4.625%	Median rent	$457	$670	Utilities Index	139.5	100.0
Sales tax rate	6.500%	6.474%	Homes owned	68.6%	63.9%	Transportation Index	100.8	100.0
Property tax rate	$8.8	$15.6	Homes rented	18.0%	25.3%	Healthcare Index	94.6	100.0
			Housing affordability	51.0%	54.5%	Miscellaneous Cost Index	100.9	100.0

CLIMATE
SCORE: 30/RANK: 232

TEMPERATURE	AREA	U.S. AVG	PRECIPITATION	AREA	U.S. AVG	COMFORTS & HAZARDS	AREA	U.S. AVG
January low	20.8°F	26.4°F	Annual inches precipitation	152	35.9	July relative humidity	36	68.8%
July high	82.5°F	86.7°F	Annual inches snowfall	27	24.2	Annual days mostly sunny	1	212
Annual days > 90°F	7	38	Annual days precipitation	11	111	Annual days with thunderstorms	3	39
Annual days < 32°F	36.0	88	Annual days rain > 0.5 inches	68.0%	23	Tornado risk score		19
Annual days < 0°F	45.0	6	Annual days snow > 1.5 inches	161	6	Hurricane risk score		15

TEMPERATURE

PRECIPITATION

DAYS OF CLOUDS & PRECIPITATION

EDUCATION
SCORE: 6/RANK: 309

ACHIEVEMENT	AREA	U.S. AVG	PUBLIC SCHOOLS	AREA	U.S. AVG	HIGHER EDUCATION	AREA	U.S. AVG
High school degree	81.9%	80.2%	Expenditures per pupil	$6,121	$5,894	No. 2-year colleges	2	3
2-year college degree	4.5%	6.2%	Student/teacher ratio	15.5	16.7	No. 4-year colleges/universities	2	4
4-year college degree	8.9%	15.8%	Attending public school	83.6%	90.2%	No. highly ranked universities	0	1
Graduate/professional degree	5.7%	9.6%	State SAT score	1032	1020			
			State ACT score	20.3*	21.0			

HEALTH & HEALTHCARE
SCORE: 80/RANK: 66

HAZARDS & ILLNESSES	AREA	U.S. AVG	HEALTHCARE	AREA	U.S. AVG
Air-quality score	59	45	Physicians per capita	253.9	261.1
Water-quality score	20	33	Hospital beds per capita	1029.6	432.2
Pollen/allergy score	68	61	No. teaching hospitals	2	4
Stress score	58	50	Cost per doctor visit	$67	$67
Cancer mortality per capita	184.9	169.0	Cost per dental visit	$74	$82
Depression days per month	3.8	2.8	Cost per daily hospital room	$454	$733

CRIME
SCORE: 81/RANK: 61

CRIME	AREA	U.S. AVG
Violent crime rate	239.9	456.0
Change in violent crime rate	22.2%	-17.2%
Property crime rate	1,906.0	3,950.0
Change in property crime rate	-4.7%	-16.8%

TRANSPORTATION
SCORE: 18/RANK: 270

COMMUTE	AREA	U.S. AVG	INTERCITY SERVICES	AREA	U.S. AVG	AUTOMOTIVE	AREA	U.S. AVG
Average commute time	22.9 min.	22.6 min.	Miles to nearest major airport	39	46	Insurance, annual premium	$931	$1,011
Commute by auto	91.1%	88.7%	Type of local airport	Large		Gas, cost per gallon	$1.50	$1.50
Commute by mass transit	1.0%	1.8%	No. daily airline departures	663	294	Daily vehicle miles per capita	21.6	23.0
Work at home	3.4%	3.9%	Amtrak service	No				
Mass transit miles per capita	5.2	8.0	No. interstate highways	1	1			

LEISURE SCORE: 18/RANK: 271

DINING & SHOPPING	AREA	U.S. AVG	ENTERTAINMENT	AREA	U.S. AVG	OUTDOOR ACTIVITIES	AREA	U.S. AVG
Restaurant rating	1	1	Professional sports rating	5	4	Golf-course rating	2	4
No. outlet malls	0	2	College sports rating	1	4	Ski-area rating	2	4
No. Starbucks	0	11	Zoo/aquarium rating	3	3	National Park rating	1	3
No. warehouse clubs	3	4	Amusement park rating	1	3	Sq. miles inland water	3.0	4.0
			Botanical garden/arboretum rating	1	3	Miles of coastline	0.0	11.4

ARTS & CULTURE SCORE: 79/RANK: 67

MEDIA & LIBRARIES	AREA	U.S. AVG	PERFORMING ARTS	AREA	U.S. AVG	MUSEUMS	AREA	U.S. AVG
Arts radio rating	1	3	Classical music rating	4	4	Overall museum rating	5	6
No. public libraries	17	28	Ballet/dance rating	1	3	Art museum rating	6	5
Library volumes per capita	3.8	2.8	Professional theater rating	1	3	Science museum rating	5	4
			University arts programs rating	4	5	Children's museum rating	1	3

Wichita, KS

Score: 80.6   Rank: 35

Profile: Mid-size city
Location: South-central Kansas along the Arkansas River
Elevation: 1,340 feet
Time zone: Central Standard Time

PRO	CON
Strong economic base	Harsh climate
Cost of living	Economic cycles
Attractive downtown	Isolation

Wichita, the largest city in Kansas, features a diverse agricultural and industrial economy. Wheat fields and oil-industry facilities surround the city. Aviation pioneers brought aircraft production, particularly smaller aircraft, to the area. Beech, Cessna, Stearman, Lear, and Boeing all have plants nearby. That industry has slowed recently—as it often does—and the statistical impact has yet to be felt. The city center has been redeveloped with attractive parks along the Arkansas River, and there is a good collection of local amenities and things to do. The workforce is relatively well educated and paid, and the Cost of Living Index is reasonable at 85.8. With 170 miles to Tulsa and 190 miles to Kansas City, residents are mainly dependent on local features. The area ranks consistently well in most categories, thus the high ranking.

Wichita is flat with trees along the river and its tributaries. The climate is continental. Masses of warm, moist air from the Gulf of Mexico collide with cold, dry air from the Arctic to create a wide range of weather year-round. Summers are usually warm and humid, but can be extremely hot and dry. Winters are usually mild with brief periods of very cold weather and high windchill. Summer temperatures above 90°F are common, while winter below-zero highs occur about 2 days per year. Seventy percent of precipitation falls from April through September. The range of annual precipitation is notable, with over 50 inches in wet years and less than 15 in dry years. Thunderstorms occur mainly during spring and early summer with potential for damaging rain, hail, winds, and tornadoes.

POPULATION

DEMOGRAPHICS	AREA	U.S. AVG	ETHNIC COMPOSITION	AREA	U.S. AVG	RESIDENT PROFILE	AREA	U.S. AVG
Population	555,846		White	89.1%	75.1%	Single	40.1%	43.6%
Population density per sq. mile	187.3	447.3	Black	5.7%	12.3%	Married	59.9%	56.4%
Population growth	14.5%	16.1%	Asian	2.8%	3.6%	Divorced	8.9%	8.4%
Median age	34.4	35.5	American Indian	1.0%	.9%	Separated	1.8%	3.0%
Average family size	2.6	2.7	Hispanic	4.0%	12.5%	Married with children	31.7%	28.7%
			Diversity measure	35.5%	35.2%	Single with children	8.5%	10.1%

ECONOMY & JOBS SCORE: 94/RANK: 20

INCOME	AREA	U.S. AVG	EMPLOYMENT	AREA	U.S. AVG	LARGEST EMPLOYING INDUSTRY
Per capita income	$24,027	$23,420	Unemployment rate	6.3%	6.1%	Transportation Equipment Manufacturing
Household income	$47,797	$46,060	Recent job growth	2.0%	.9%	
Household income < $25K	23.1%	26.4%	Projected future job growth	12.3%	15.1%	
Household income > $75K	24.9%	24.5%	White collar	56.1%	54.5%	
Household income growth	58.3%	57.3%	Blue collar	43.9%	45.5%	

COST OF LIVING SCORE: 57/RANK: 142

INDEXES & TAXES	AREA	U.S. AVG	HOUSING	AREA	U.S. AVG	NECESSITIES	AREA	U.S. AVG
Cost of Living Index	85.8	100.0	Median home price	$100,600	$160,100	Food Index	95.2	100.0
Financial Progress Index	118.7	100.0	Home price appreciation	4.4%	7.1%	Housing Index	62.5	100.0
Income tax rate	6.250%	4.625%	Median rent	$599	$670	Utilities Index	105.8	100.0
Sales tax rate	6.300%	6.474%	Homes owned	68.9%	63.9%	Transportation Index	94.0	100.0
Property tax rate	$11.8	$15.6	Homes rented	23.8%	25.3%	Healthcare Index	99.5	100.0
			Housing affordability	57.0%	54.5%	Miscellaneous Cost Index	101.6	100.0

CLIMATE SCORE: 57/RANK: 140

TEMPERATURE	AREA	U.S. AVG	PRECIPITATION	AREA	U.S. AVG	COMFORTS & HAZARDS	AREA	U.S. AVG
January low	21.2°F	26.4°F	Annual inches precipitation	31.0	35.9	July relative humidity	66.0%	68.8%
July high	91.7°F	86.7°F	Annual inches snowfall	16.0	24.2	Annual days mostly sunny	224	212
Annual days > 90°F	62	38	Annual days precipitation	84	111	Annual days with thunderstorms	55	39
Annual days < 32°F	114	88	Annual days rain > 0.5 inches	18	23	Tornado risk score	88	19
Annual days < 0°F	2	6	Annual days snow > 1.5 inches	5	6	Hurricane risk score	1	15

TEMPERATURE

PRECIPITATION

DAYS OF CLOUDS & PRECIPITATION

EDUCATION SCORE: 44/RANK: 183

ACHIEVEMENT	AREA	U.S. AVG	PUBLIC SCHOOLS	AREA	U.S. AVG	HIGHER EDUCATION	AREA	U.S. AVG
High school degree	83.8%	80.2%	Expenditures per pupil	$5,477	$5,894	No. 2-year colleges	2	3
2-year college degree	5.0%	6.2%	Student/teacher ratio	16.1	16.7	No. 4-year colleges/universities	4	4
4-year college degree	17.2%	15.8%	Attending public school	89.0%	90.2%	No. highly ranked universities	0	1
Graduate/professional degree	8.1%	9.6%	State SAT score	1160	1020			
			State ACT score	21.5*	21.0			

HEALTH & HEALTHCARE SCORE: 43/RANK: 186

CRIME SCORE: 28/RANK: 237

HAZARDS & ILLNESSES	AREA	U.S. AVG	HEALTHCARE	AREA	U.S. AVG	CRIME	AREA	U.S. AVG
Air-quality score	4	45	Physicians per capita	244.1	261.1	Violent crime rate	520.8	456.0
Water-quality score	5	33	Hospital beds per capita	436.2	432.2	Change in violent crime rate	-4.9%	-17.2%
Pollen/allergy score	58	61	No. teaching hospitals	4	4	Property crime rate	4,691.8	3,950.0
Stress score	52	50	Cost per doctor visit	$62	$67	Change in property crime rate	-20.7%	-16.8%
Cancer mortality per capita	162.3	169.0	Cost per dental visit	$79	$82			
Depression days per month	2.9	2.8	Cost per daily hospital room	$702	$733			

TRANSPORTATION SCORE: 65/RANK: 114

COMMUTE	AREA	U.S. AVG	INTERCITY SERVICES	AREA	U.S. AVG	AUTOMOTIVE	AREA	U.S. AVG
Average commute time	19.1 min.	22.6 min.	Miles to nearest major airport	6	46	Insurance, annual premium	$787	$1,011
Commute by auto	91.1%	88.7%	Type of local airport	Large		Gas, cost per gallon	$1.50	$1.50
Commute by mass transit	.7%	1.8%	No. daily airline departures	74	294	Daily vehicle miles per capita	21.9	23.0
Work at home	4.3%	3.9%	Amtrak service	Yes				
Mass transit miles per capita	4.6	8.0	No. interstate highways	1	1			

LEISURE SCORE: 32/RANK: 224

DINING & SHOPPING	AREA	U.S. AVG	ENTERTAINMENT	AREA	U.S. AVG	OUTDOOR ACTIVITIES	AREA	U.S. AVG
Restaurant rating	1	1	Professional sports rating	3	4	Golf-course rating	3	4
No. outlet malls	0	2	College sports rating	2	4	Ski-area rating	1	4
No. Starbucks	2	11	Zoo/aquarium rating	5	3	National Park rating	1	3
No. warehouse clubs	4	4	Amusement park rating	4	3	Sq. miles inland water	2.0	4.0
			Botanical garden/arboretum rating	4	3	Miles of coastline	0.0	11.4

ARTS & CULTURE SCORE: 80/RANK: 64

MEDIA & LIBRARIES	AREA	U.S. AVG	PERFORMING ARTS	AREA	U.S. AVG	MUSEUMS	AREA	U.S. AVG
Arts radio rating	1	3	Classical music rating	6	4	Overall museum rating	8	6
No. public libraries	38	28	Ballet/dance rating	3	3	Art museum rating	6	5
Library volumes per capita	3.7	2.8	Professional theater rating	1	3	Science museum rating	8	4
			University arts programs rating	6	5	Children's museum rating	7	3

Wichita Falls, TX

Score: 36.0   **Rank:** 294

Profile: Small town
Location: Extreme north-central Texas, 15 miles south of the Oklahoma border
Elevation: 994 feet
Time zone: Central Standard Time

PRO	CON
Cost of living	Isolation
Small-town atmosphere	Entertainment
Nearby water recreation	Summer heat

Wichita Falls, named for a 5-foot waterfall considered significant in these flat parts, is an agricultural and ranching center that boomed during the 1930s with the discovery of oil. Agriculture and petroleum are still the economic mainstays. Like many small Texas towns, Wichita Falls is plain, clean, and quiet, and residents try to maintain such local amenities as a symphony, ballet, theater, and art museum. There are a number of lakes around the area, but on the whole, there isn't much to do. For big-city services and amenities, the Dallas–Fort Worth metroplex is 135 miles southeast.

The town is located in the North Central Plains of Texas, just south of the Red River separating Texas and Oklahoma. The topography is level to gently rolling agriculture and mesquite plain with few trees. The region lies between the humid subtropical climate of east Texas and the continental climate of the north and west. Climate is variable with rapid temperature changes, temperature extremes, and erratic rainfall. Summers are warm to hot with low humidity and lots of sun and wind. Temperatures frequently exceed 100°F. Polar air masses moving down from the north during winter can drop temperatures 20°F to 30°F within an hour. While variable, winters are on the whole relatively mild with few sub-zero readings. Snow accumulation occurs only once or twice a year. Most rainfall comes from brief showers, and prolonged dry periods are common.

POPULATION

DEMOGRAPHICS	AREA	U.S. AVG	ETHNIC COMPOSITION	AREA	U.S. AVG	RESIDENT PROFILE	AREA	U.S. AVG
Population	138,960		White	81.1%	75.1%	Single	41.4%	43.6%
Population density per sq. mile	90.4	447.3	Black	9.2%	12.3%	Married	58.6%	56.4%
Population growth	6.6%	16.1%	Asian	1.8%	3.6%	Divorced	9.2%	8.4%
Median age	33.7	35.5	American Indian	.7%	.9%	Separated	2.9%	3.0%
Average family size	2.6	2.7	Hispanic	17.6%	12.5%	Married with children	31.2%	28.7%
			Diversity measure	40.9%	35.2%	Single with children	9.6%	10.1%

ECONOMY & JOBS
SCORE: 66/RANK: 112

INCOME	AREA	U.S. AVG	EMPLOYMENT	AREA	U.S. AVG	LARGEST EMPLOYING INDUSTRY
Per capita income	$19,287	$23,420	Unemployment rate	5.5%	6.1%	Healthcare and Social Assistance
Household income	$36,732	$46,060	Recent job growth	2.0%	.9%	
Household income < $25K	32.7%	26.4%	Projected future job growth	10.6%	15.1%	
Household income > $75K	16.0%	24.5%	White collar	47.5%	54.5%	
Household income growth	52.7%	57.3%	Blue collar	52.5%	45.5%	

COST OF LIVING
SCORE: 96/RANK: 14

INDEXES & TAXES	AREA	U.S. AVG	HOUSING	AREA	U.S. AVG	NECESSITIES	AREA	U.S. AVG
Cost of Living Index	76.9	100.0	Median home price	$67,420	$160,100	Food Index	92.3	100.0
Financial Progress Index	101.8	100.0	Home price appreciation	3.1%	7.1%	Housing Index	41.9	100.0
Income tax rate	0.000%	4.625%	Median rent	$493	$670	Utilities Index	90.8	100.0
Sales tax rate	8.250%	6.474%	Homes owned	59.2%	63.9%	Transportation Index	99.6	100.0
Property tax rate	$22.7	$15.6	Homes rented	27.9%	25.3%	Healthcare Index	96.7	100.0
			Housing affordability	64.0%	54.5%	Miscellaneous Cost Index	100.4	100.0

CLIMATE
SCORE: 78/RANK: 73

TEMPERATURE	AREA	U.S. AVG	PRECIPITATION	AREA	U.S. AVG	COMFORTS & HAZARDS	AREA	U.S. AVG
January low	29.4°F	26.4°F	Annual inches precipitation	27.2	35.9	July relative humidity	66.0%	68.8%
July high	99.2°F	86.7°F	Annual inches snowfall	2.0	24.2	Annual days mostly sunny	248	212
Annual days > 90°F	106	38	Annual days precipitation	71	111	Annual days with thunderstorms	49	39
Annual days < 32°F	70	88	Annual days rain > 0.5 inches	18	23	Tornado risk score	71	19
Annual days < 0°F	0	6	Annual days snow > 1.5 inches	1	6	Hurricane risk score	4	15

TEMPERATURE

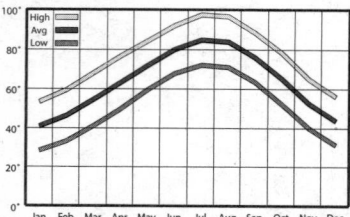

PRECIPITATION

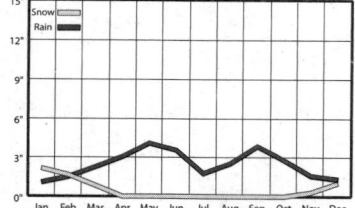

DAYS OF CLOUDS & PRECIPITATION

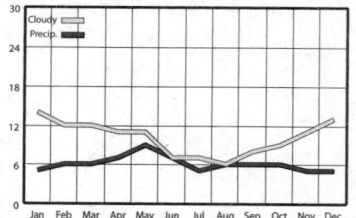

EDUCATION SCORE: 42/RANK: 192

ACHIEVEMENT	AREA	U.S. AVG	PUBLIC SCHOOLS	AREA	U.S. AVG	HIGHER EDUCATION	AREA	U.S. AVG
High school degree	79.7%	80.2%	Expenditures per pupil	$5,236	$5,894	No. 2-year colleges	0	3
2-year college degree	5.9%	6.2%	Student/teacher ratio	13.8	16.7	No. 4-year colleges/universities	1	4
4-year college degree	15.4%	15.8%	Attending public school	95.7%	90.2%	No. highly ranked universities	0	1
Graduate/professional degree	6.1%	9.6%	State SAT score	993*	1020			
			State ACT score	20.1	21.0			

HEALTH & HEALTHCARE SCORE: 58/RANK: 139

CRIME SCORE: 4/RANK: 316

HAZARDS & ILLNESSES	AREA	U.S. AVG	HEALTHCARE	AREA	U.S. AVG	CRIME	AREA	U.S. AVG
Air-quality score	49	45	Physicians per capita	230.3	261.1	Violent crime rate	663.2	456.0
Water-quality score	100	33	Hospital beds per capita	787.8	432.2	Change in violent crime rate	-.7%	-17.2%
Pollen/allergy score	84	61	No. teaching hospitals	2	4	Property crime rate	5,614.9	3,950.0
Stress score	29	50	Cost per doctor visit	$63	$67	Change in property crime rate	9.9%	-16.8%
Cancer mortality per capita	163.4	169.0	Cost per dental visit	$74	$82			
Depression days per month	2.5	2.8	Cost per daily hospital room	$538	$733			

TRANSPORTATION SCORE: 63/RANK: 120

COMMUTE	AREA	U.S. AVG	INTERCITY SERVICES	AREA	U.S. AVG	AUTOMOTIVE	AREA	U.S. AVG
Average commute time	17.4 min.	22.6 min.	Miles to nearest major airport	110	46	Insurance, annual premium	$924	$1,011
Commute by auto	88.2%	88.7%	Type of local airport	Small		Gas, cost per gallon	$1.41	$1.50
Commute by mass transit	.5%	1.8%	No. daily airline departures	1,310	294	Daily vehicle miles per capita	18.2	23.0
Work at home	4.0%	3.9%	Amtrak service	No				
Mass transit miles per capita	0.0	8.0	No. interstate highways	0	1			

LEISURE SCORE: 6/RANK: 311

DINING & SHOPPING	AREA	U.S. AVG	ENTERTAINMENT	AREA	U.S. AVG	OUTDOOR ACTIVITIES	AREA	U.S. AVG
Restaurant rating	1	1	Professional sports rating	2	4	Golf-course rating	2	4
No. outlet malls	0	2	College sports rating	3	4	Ski-area rating	1	4
No. Starbucks	1	11	Zoo/aquarium rating	1	3	National Park rating	1	3
No. warehouse clubs	3	4	Amusement park rating	1	3	Sq. miles inland water	2.0	4.0
			Botanical garden/arboretum rating	1	3	Miles of coastline	0.0	11.4

ARTS & CULTURE SCORE: 6/RANK: 309

MEDIA & LIBRARIES	AREA	U.S. AVG	PERFORMING ARTS	AREA	U.S. AVG	MUSEUMS	AREA	U.S. AVG
Arts radio rating	1	3	Classical music rating	3	4	Overall museum rating	3	6
No. public libraries	5	28	Ballet/dance rating	1	3	Art museum rating	4	5
Library volumes per capita	1.8	2.8	Professional theater rating	1	3	Science museum rating	3	4
			University arts programs rating	3	5	Children's museum rating	2	3

Williamsport, PA

Score: 51.0   Rank: 216

Profile: Small town
Location: North-central Pennsylvania along the upper Susquehanna River
Elevation: 524 feet
Time zone: Eastern Standard Time

PRO
Cost of living
Small-town atmosphere
Low crime rate

CON
Isolation
Economy
Low ethnic diversity

Williamsport is an old lumber town still noted for production of hardwood lumber, particularly furniture-grade cherry. It's better known as the birthplace of Little League Baseball and the location of the Little League World Series every August—the town attracts international attention at this time. The area has some well-preserved historic districts but is otherwise fairly plain. The economy lags with high unemployment and relatively low job growth. The area is isolated geographically from major transportation links, a fact that doesn't help the economy. Few amenities are available nearby and residents may have to travel to upstate New York to find what they need.

The town, in a narrow valley junction where the Lycoming River flows into the Susquehanna River, is surrounded by wooded hills and mountains on all sides. The climate is influenced by the lower elevation compared to the surrounding terrain. In the summer, warm, humid air can be trapped in the valley creating periods of discomfort. Winter extremes are moderated somewhat by the valley location and occasionally by warmer coastal weather, although deep fogs can occur. Snowfall varies and is much higher in the hills. First freeze is late October, last is late April.

POPULATION

DEMOGRAPHICS	AREA	U.S. AVG	ETHNIC COMPOSITION	AREA	U.S. AVG	RESIDENT PROFILE	AREA	U.S. AVG
Population	119,000		White	97.5%	75.1%	Single	39.7%	43.6%
Population density per sq. mile	96.4	447.3	Black	1.6%	12.3%	Married	60.3%	56.4%
Population growth	.2%	16.1%	Asian	.4%	3.6%	Divorced	7.8%	8.4%
Median age	38.8	35.5	American Indian	.2%	.9%	Separated	3.0%	3.0%
Average family size	2.6	2.7	Hispanic	.7%	12.5%	Married with children	28.0%	28.7%
			Diversity measure	12.2%	35.2%	Single with children	9.0%	10.1%

ECONOMY & JOBS SCORE: 47/RANK: 175

INCOME	AREA	U.S. AVG	EMPLOYMENT	AREA	U.S. AVG	LARGEST EMPLOYING INDUSTRY
Per capita income	$18,480	$23,420	Unemployment rate	5.7%	6.1%	Furniture and Related Product Manufacturing
Household income	$35,909	$46,060	Recent job growth	-2.4%	.9%	
Household income < $25K	32.8%	26.4%	Projected future job growth	5.8%	15.1%	
Household income > $75K	12.1%	24.5%	White collar	47.1%	54.5%	
Household income growth	40.3%	57.3%	Blue collar	52.9%	45.5%	

COST OF LIVING SCORE: 72/RANK: 91

INDEXES & TAXES	AREA	U.S. AVG	HOUSING	AREA	U.S. AVG	NECESSITIES	AREA	U.S. AVG
Cost of Living Index	82.9	100.0	Median home price	$98,630	$160,100	Food Index	94.1	100.0
Financial Progress Index	92.3	100.0	Home price appreciation	4.6%	7.1%	Housing Index	61.3	100.0
Income tax rate	2.800%	4.625%	Median rent	$477	$670	Utilities Index	99.9	100.0
Sales tax rate	6.000%	6.474%	Homes owned	62.3%	63.9%	Transportation Index	91.1	100.0
Property tax rate	$22.3	$15.6	Homes rented	15.8%	25.3%	Healthcare Index	87.5	100.0
			Housing affordability	61.0%	54.5%	Miscellaneous Cost Index	98.1	100.0

CLIMATE SCORE: 13/RANK: 287

TEMPERATURE	AREA	U.S. AVG	PRECIPITATION	AREA	U.S. AVG	COMFORTS & HAZARDS	AREA	U.S. AVG
January low	19.4°F	26.4°F	Annual inches precipitation	40.0	35.9	July relative humidity	72.0%	68.8%
July high	84.4°F	86.7°F	Annual inches snowfall	44.5	24.2	Annual days mostly sunny	181	212
Annual days > 90°F	13	38	Annual days precipitation	156	111	Annual days with thunderstorms	34	39
Annual days < 32°F	129	88	Annual days rain > 0.5 inches	26	23	Tornado risk score	11	19
Annual days < 0°F	4	6	Annual days snow > 1.5 inches	9	6	Hurricane risk score	7	15

TEMPERATURE

PRECIPITATION

DAYS OF CLOUDS & PRECIPITATION

EDUCATION SCORE: 31/RANK: 226

ACHIEVEMENT	AREA	U.S. AVG	PUBLIC SCHOOLS	AREA	U.S. AVG	HIGHER EDUCATION	AREA	U.S. AVG
High school degree	77.2%	80.2%	Expenditures per pupil	$6,351	$5,894	No. 2-year colleges	1	3
2-year college degree	7.1%	6.2%	Student/teacher ratio	16.3	16.7	No. 4-year colleges/universities	2	4
4-year college degree	10.3%	15.8%	Attending public school	92.4%	90.2%	No. highly ranked universities	0	1
Graduate/professional degree	5.9%	9.6%	State SAT score	1002*	1020			
			State ACT score	21.5	21.0			

HEALTH & HEALTHCARE SCORE: 91/RANK: 28

HAZARDS & ILLNESSES	AREA	U.S. AVG	HEALTHCARE	AREA	U.S. AVG
Air-quality score	6	45	Physicians per capita	196.6	261.1
Water-quality score	100	33	Hospital beds per capita	519.0	432.2
Pollen/allergy score	52	61	No. teaching hospitals	1	4
Stress score	26	50	Cost per doctor visit	$53	$67
Cancer mortality per capita	170.7	169.0	Cost per dental visit	$68	$82
Depression days per month	3.7	2.8	Cost per daily hospital room	$532	$733

CRIME SCORE: 93/RANK: 22

CRIME	AREA	U.S. AVG
Violent crime rate	188.4	456.0
Change in violent crime rate	-20.0%	-17.2%
Property crime rate	2,430.9	3,950.0
Change in property crime rate	-24.9%	-16.8%

TRANSPORTATION SCORE: 56/RANK: 144

COMMUTE	AREA	U.S. AVG	INTERCITY SERVICES	AREA	U.S. AVG	AUTOMOTIVE	AREA	U.S. AVG
Average commute time	19.6 min.	22.6 min.	Miles to nearest major airport	73	46	Insurance, annual premium	$942	$1,011
Commute by auto	91.1%	88.7%	Type of local airport	Small		Gas, cost per gallon	$1.46	$1.50
Commute by mass transit	.5%	1.8%	No. daily airline departures	81	294	Daily vehicle miles per capita	21.5	23.0
Work at home	4.0%	3.9%	Amtrak service	No				
Mass transit miles per capita	5.1	8.0	No. interstate highways	0	1			

LEISURE SCORE: 22/RANK: 260

DINING & SHOPPING	AREA	U.S. AVG	ENTERTAINMENT	AREA	U.S. AVG	OUTDOOR ACTIVITIES	AREA	U.S. AVG
Restaurant rating	1	1	Professional sports rating	2	4	Golf-course rating	1	4
No. outlet malls	0	2	College sports rating	5	4	Ski-area rating	4	4
No. Starbucks	0	11	Zoo/aquarium rating	1	3	National Park rating	1	3
No. warehouse clubs	3	4	Amusement park rating	1	3	Sq. miles inland water	2.0	4.0
			Botanical garden/arboretum rating	1	3	Miles of coastline	0.0	11.4

ARTS & CULTURE SCORE: 6/RANK: 308

MEDIA & LIBRARIES	AREA	U.S. AVG	PERFORMING ARTS	AREA	U.S. AVG	MUSEUMS	AREA	U.S. AVG
Arts radio rating	1	3	Classical music rating	3	4	Overall museum rating	2	6
No. public libraries	6	28	Ballet/dance rating	1	3	Art museum rating	1	5
Library volumes per capita	2.1	2.8	Professional theater rating	1	3	Science museum rating	1	4
			University arts programs rating	5	5	Children's museum rating	3	3

Wilmington, NC

Score: 56.5   Rank: 172

Profile: Mid-size port city
Location: Southern North Carolina coast
Time zone: Eastern Standard Time
Elevation: 30 feet

PRO	CON
Historic downtown	Cost of living
Nearby beaches	Cost of housing
Mild winters	Isolation

Wilmington is a shipping and agricultural center, particularly known for flowers, with origins as a port city. The historic town center and waterfront along the Cape Fear River are interesting and attractive. Because of the location on a peninsula formed by the Cape Fear River on the west and the Atlantic Intracoastal Waterway on the east, housing costs and cost of living tend to be higher than the rest of the state. The median home price of $150,060 is the second highest in North Carolina. The area is isolated from many big-city amenities and services, but climate is pleasant and residential sections are attractive.

Wilmington is located along the southern Atlantic Coast of North Carolina. Because of the curvature of the coastline, the ocean lies about 5 miles east and about 20 miles south. The surrounding terrain is typical of coastal Carolina, with low-lying, gently rolling land with rivers, creeks, and lakes with considerable swamp or marshland adjoining them. Large wooded areas alternate with cultivated fields. The maritime location makes the climate unusually mild for its latitude. Daily temperature variations are less than many nearby areas. Summers are warm and humid, usually with cool afternoon breezes but without excessive heat. High temperatures of 90°F or more are reached about 1 day in 3 but 100°F is rare. Cold air from the north invades in winter but doesn't last, and the season is short and mild. Rainfall is well distributed with most occurring during summer thunderstorms. The area is subject to coastal storms and hurricanes, with high winds, high tides, and heavy rain. Winter rain is more likely to be slow and steady and last 2 to 3 days. Snow accumulation is rare.

POPULATION

DEMOGRAPHICS	AREA	U.S. AVG	ETHNIC COMPOSITION	AREA	U.S. AVG	RESIDENT PROFILE	AREA	U.S. AVG
Population	244,279		White	80.2%	75.1%	Single	42.1%	43.6%
Population density per sq. mile	778.2	447.3	Black	18.8%	12.3%	Married	57.9%	56.4%
Population growth	42.6%	16.1%	Asian	.4%	3.6%	Divorced	7.9%	8.4%
Median age	38.6	35.5	American Indian	.4%	.9%	Separated	4.9%	3.0%
Average family size	2.5	2.7	Hispanic	1.3%	12.5%	Married with children	23.4%	28.7%
			Diversity measure	33.6%	35.2%	Single with children	10.6%	10.1%

ECONOMY & JOBS SCORE: 77/RANK: 76

INCOME	AREA	U.S. AVG	EMPLOYMENT	AREA	U.S. AVG	LARGEST EMPLOYING INDUSTRY
Per capita income	$24,100	$23,420	Unemployment rate	5.0%	6.1%	Nonmetallic Mineral Product Manufacturing
Household income	$40,224	$46,060	Recent job growth	.7%	.9%	
Household income < $25K	31.0%	26.4%	Projected future job growth	28.8%	15.1%	
Household income > $75K	21.1%	24.5%	White collar	51.7%	54.5%	
Household income growth	53.9%	57.3%	Blue collar	48.3%	45.5%	

COST OF LIVING SCORE: 52/RANK: 159

INDEXES & TAXES	AREA	U.S. AVG	HOUSING	AREA	U.S. AVG	NECESSITIES	AREA	U.S. AVG
Cost of Living Index	97.6	100.0	Median home price	$150,060	$160,100	Food Index	104.7	100.0
Financial Progress Index	87.9	100.0	Home price appreciation	4.1%	7.1%	Housing Index	93.2	100.0
Income tax rate	7.000%	4.625%	Median rent	$651	$670	Utilities Index	97.0	100.0
Sales tax rate	6.500%	6.474%	Homes owned	56.6%	63.9%	Transportation Index	89.5	100.0
Property tax rate	$9.9	$15.6	Homes rented	17.1%	25.3%	Healthcare Index	93.9	100.0
			Housing affordability	51.0%	54.5%	Miscellaneous Cost Index	104.4	100.0

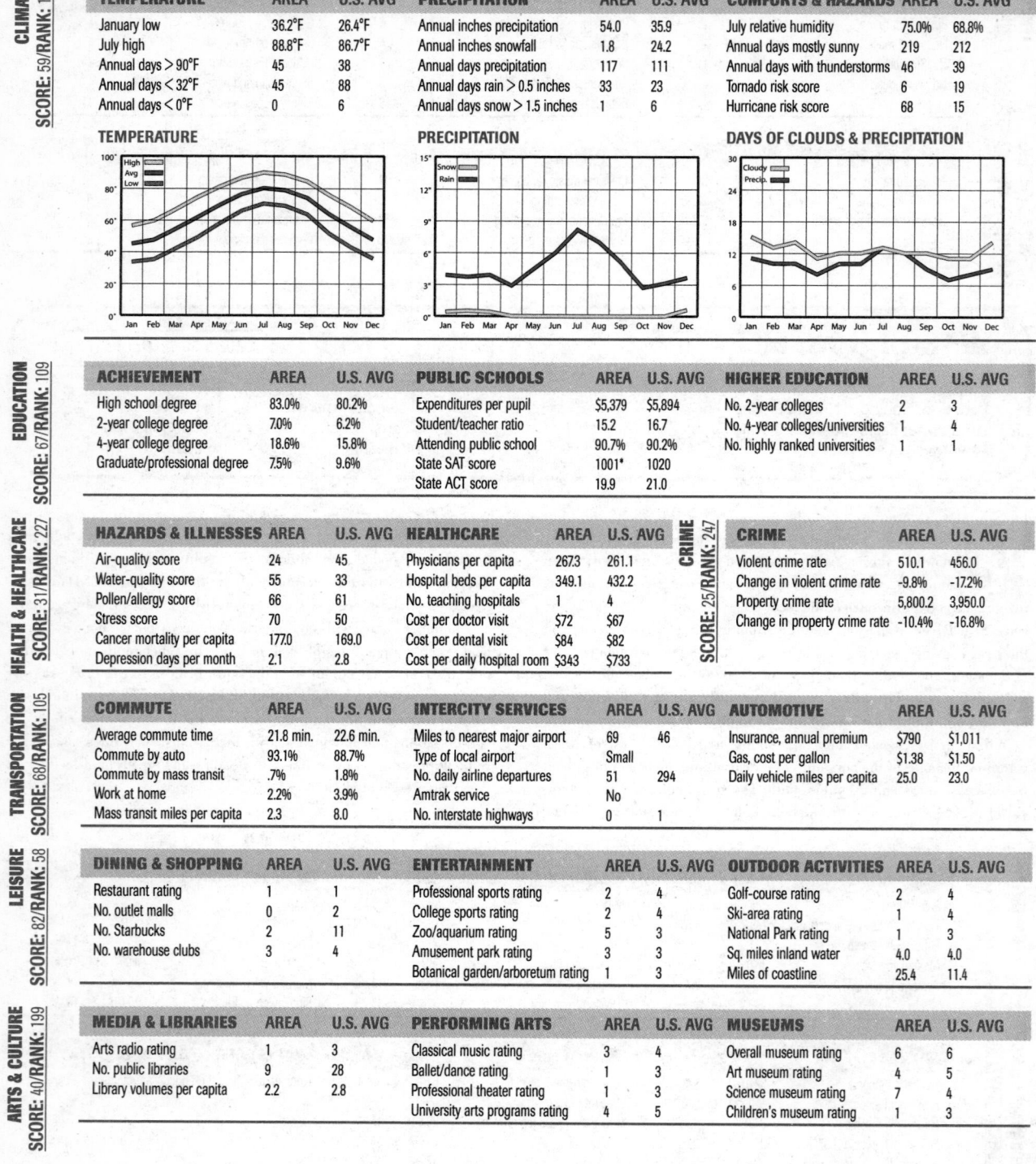

CLIMATE SCORE: 59/RANK: 134

TEMPERATURE	AREA	U.S. AVG	PRECIPITATION	AREA	U.S. AVG	COMFORTS & HAZARDS	AREA	U.S. AVG
January low	36.2°F	26.4°F	Annual inches precipitation	54.0	35.9	July relative humidity	75.0%	68.8%
July high	88.8°F	86.7°F	Annual inches snowfall	1.8	24.2	Annual days mostly sunny	219	212
Annual days > 90°F	45	38	Annual days precipitation	117	111	Annual days with thunderstorms	46	39
Annual days < 32°F	45	88	Annual days rain > 0.5 inches	33	23	Tornado risk score	6	19
Annual days < 0°F	0	6	Annual days snow > 1.5 inches	1	6	Hurricane risk score	68	15

TEMPERATURE

PRECIPITATION

DAYS OF CLOUDS & PRECIPITATION

EDUCATION SCORE: 67/RANK: 109

ACHIEVEMENT	AREA	U.S. AVG	PUBLIC SCHOOLS	AREA	U.S. AVG	HIGHER EDUCATION	AREA	U.S. AVG
High school degree	83.0%	80.2%	Expenditures per pupil	$5,379	$5,894	No. 2-year colleges	2	3
2-year college degree	7.0%	6.2%	Student/teacher ratio	15.2	16.7	No. 4-year colleges/universities	1	4
4-year college degree	18.6%	15.8%	Attending public school	90.7%	90.2%	No. highly ranked universities	1	1
Graduate/professional degree	7.5%	9.6%	State SAT score	1001*	1020			
			State ACT score	19.9	21.0			

HEALTH & HEALTHCARE SCORE: 31/RANK: 227

CRIME SCORE: 25/RANK: 247

HAZARDS & ILLNESSES	AREA	U.S. AVG	HEALTHCARE	AREA	U.S. AVG	CRIME	AREA	U.S. AVG
Air-quality score	24	45	Physicians per capita	267.3	261.1	Violent crime rate	510.1	456.0
Water-quality score	55	33	Hospital beds per capita	349.1	432.2	Change in violent crime rate	-9.8%	-17.2%
Pollen/allergy score	66	61	No. teaching hospitals	1	4	Property crime rate	5,800.2	3,950.0
Stress score	70	50	Cost per doctor visit	$72	$67	Change in property crime rate	-10.4%	-16.8%
Cancer mortality per capita	177.0	169.0	Cost per dental visit	$84	$82			
Depression days per month	2.1	2.8	Cost per daily hospital room	$343	$733			

TRANSPORTATION SCORE: 68/RANK: 105

COMMUTE	AREA	U.S. AVG	INTERCITY SERVICES	AREA	U.S. AVG	AUTOMOTIVE	AREA	U.S. AVG
Average commute time	21.8 min.	22.6 min.	Miles to nearest major airport	69	46	Insurance, annual premium	$790	$1,011
Commute by auto	93.1%	88.7%	Type of local airport	Small		Gas, cost per gallon	$1.38	$1.50
Commute by mass transit	.7%	1.8%	No. daily airline departures	51	294	Daily vehicle miles per capita	25.0	23.0
Work at home	2.2%	3.9%	Amtrak service	No				
Mass transit miles per capita	2.3	8.0	No. interstate highways	0	1			

LEISURE SCORE: 82/RANK: 58

DINING & SHOPPING	AREA	U.S. AVG	ENTERTAINMENT	AREA	U.S. AVG	OUTDOOR ACTIVITIES	AREA	U.S. AVG
Restaurant rating	1	1	Professional sports rating	2	4	Golf-course rating	2	4
No. outlet malls	0	2	College sports rating	2	4	Ski-area rating	1	4
No. Starbucks	2	11	Zoo/aquarium rating	5	3	National Park rating	1	3
No. warehouse clubs	3	4	Amusement park rating	3	3	Sq. miles inland water	4.0	4.0
			Botanical garden/arboretum rating	1	3	Miles of coastline	25.4	11.4

ARTS & CULTURE SCORE: 40/RANK: 199

MEDIA & LIBRARIES	AREA	U.S. AVG	PERFORMING ARTS	AREA	U.S. AVG	MUSEUMS	AREA	U.S. AVG
Arts radio rating	1	3	Classical music rating	3	4	Overall museum rating	6	6
No. public libraries	9	28	Ballet/dance rating	1	3	Art museum rating	4	5
Library volumes per capita	2.2	2.8	Professional theater rating	1	3	Science museum rating	7	4
			University arts programs rating	4	5	Children's museum rating	1	3

Wilmington-Newark, DE-MD

Score: 68.7	**Rank:** 83

Profile: Mid-size-city complex
Location: Extreme northern Delaware along the Delaware River
Elevation: 120 feet
Time zone: Eastern Standard Time

PRO	CON
Central location	Industrial setting
Cost of living	Future job growth
Educated population	Cancer rate

In 1802, a young Frenchman by the name of Henry Francis du Pont started a gunpowder factory where the Brandywine River meets the Delaware River near the top of Delaware Bay, site of present-day Wilmington. Led by the chemical industry, northern Delaware became a prosperous industrial center and remains so today with a healthy future job outlook. The downtown area is unremarkable, but by East Coast standards, Wilmington is manageably sized and has a number of big-city amenities. Its central location and access to large cities along the Northeast Corridor is a major advantage. Good rail service connects it to New York, Philadelphia, Baltimore, and Washington, D.C. Wilmington is also close to beach areas in southern Delaware and the tranquil Pennsylvania-Dutch country to the northwest. Cost of living is modest for a city in this region. Downsides include the heavy industrial feel, property crime, and the incidence of cancer—which while not alarming, may be connected with the industrial environment.

Wilmington is located on the flat and marshy Atlantic Coastal Plain. Low rolling hills extend to the north and northwest into Pennsylvania. The climate is influenced by the Atlantic and Chesapeake Bay. Summers are warm and humid and winters are usually mild. Maximum summer temperatures are usually in the 80s, with 100°F readings occurring only once every 6 years. Humidity and moist Delaware Bay winds can cause fog any month of the year. Zero-degree weather can be expected once every 4 years. Most winter precipitation occurs as rain or a rain/snow/sleet mix. Snow seldom remains on the ground for more than a few days. Summer thunderstorms are common, and occasional tropical downpours from Atlantic hurricanes may cause lowland flooding. First freeze is late October, last is mid-April.

POPULATION

DEMOGRAPHICS	AREA	U.S. AVG	ETHNIC COMPOSITION	AREA	U.S. AVG	RESIDENT PROFILE	AREA	U.S. AVG
Population	602,705		White	81.8%	75.1%	Single	46.0%	43.6%
Population density per sq. mile	231.8	447.3	Black	15.5%	12.3%	Married	54.0%	56.4%
Population growth	17.4%	16.1%	Asian	1.7%	3.6%	Divorced	8.1%	8.4%
Median age	35.3	35.5	American Indian	.2%	.9%	Separated	3.7%	3.0%
Average family size	2.6	2.7	Hispanic	2.7%	12.5%	Married with children	26.2%	28.7%
			Diversity measure	41.4%	35.2%	Single with children	10.7%	10.1%

ECONOMY & JOBS SCORE: 3/RANK: 320

INCOME	AREA	U.S. AVG	EMPLOYMENT	AREA	U.S. AVG	LARGEST EMPLOYING INDUSTRY
Per capita income	$29,338	$23,420	Unemployment rate	5.3%	6.1%	Credit Intermediation and Related Activities
Household income	$61,464	$46,060	Recent job growth	-.2%	.9%	
Household income < $25K	16.0%	26.4%	Projected future job growth	11.3%	15.1%	
Household income > $75K	38.3%	24.5%	White collar	61.5%	54.5%	
Household income growth	60.7%	57.3%	Blue collar	38.5%	45.5%	

COST OF LIVING SCORE: 37/RANK: 208

INDEXES & TAXES	AREA	U.S. AVG	HOUSING	AREA	U.S. AVG	NECESSITIES	AREA	U.S. AVG
Cost of Living Index	102.4	100.0	Median home price	$155,400	$160,100	Food Index	106.3	100.0
Financial Progress Index	127.9	100.0	Home price appreciation	8.1%	7.1%	Housing Index	96.5	100.0
Income tax rate	8.150%	4.625%	Median rent	$771	$670	Utilities Index	121.5	100.0
Sales tax rate	0.000%	6.474%	Homes owned	67.5%	63.9%	Transportation Index	98.1	100.0
Property tax rate	$9.1	$15.6	Homes rented	24.8%	25.3%	Healthcare Index	110.7	100.0
			Housing affordability	58.0%	54.5%	Miscellaneous Cost Index	102.0	100.0

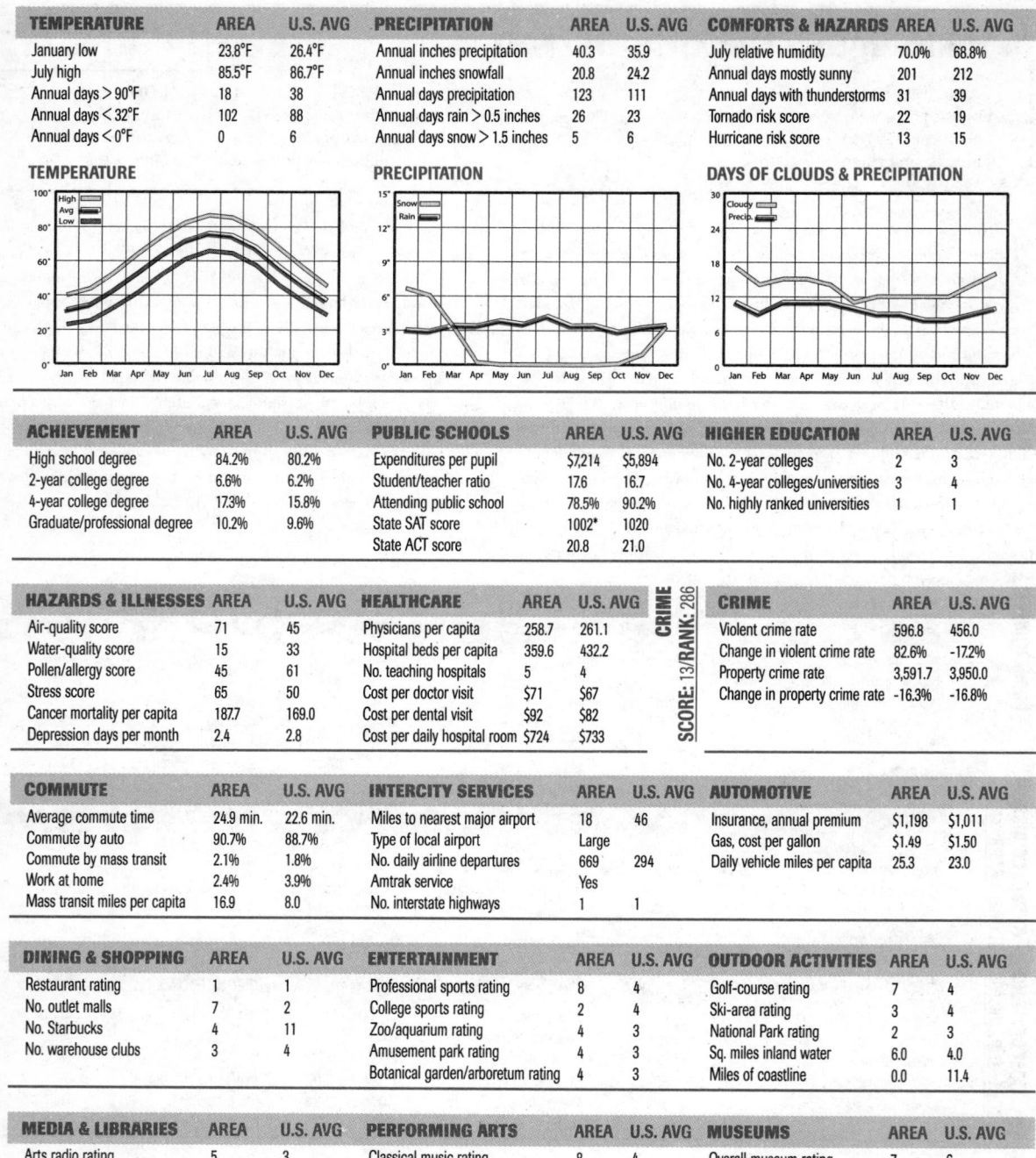

CLIMATE
SCORE: 52/RANK: 157

TEMPERATURE	AREA	U.S. AVG	PRECIPITATION	AREA	U.S. AVG	COMFORTS & HAZARDS	AREA	U.S. AVG
January low	23.8°F	26.4°F	Annual inches precipitation	40.3	35.9	July relative humidity	70.0%	68.8%
July high	85.5°F	86.7°F	Annual inches snowfall	20.8	24.2	Annual days mostly sunny	201	212
Annual days > 90°F	18	38	Annual days precipitation	123	111	Annual days with thunderstorms	31	39
Annual days < 32°F	102	88	Annual days rain > 0.5 inches	26	23	Tornado risk score	22	19
Annual days < 0°F	0	6	Annual days snow > 1.5 inches	5	6	Hurricane risk score	13	15

TEMPERATURE

PRECIPITATION

DAYS OF CLOUDS & PRECIPITATION

EDUCATION
SCORE: 32/RANK: 224

ACHIEVEMENT	AREA	U.S. AVG	PUBLIC SCHOOLS	AREA	U.S. AVG	HIGHER EDUCATION	AREA	U.S. AVG
High school degree	84.2%	80.2%	Expenditures per pupil	$7,214	$5,894	No. 2-year colleges	2	3
2-year college degree	6.6%	6.2%	Student/teacher ratio	17.6	16.7	No. 4-year colleges/universities	3	4
4-year college degree	17.3%	15.8%	Attending public school	78.5%	90.2%	No. highly ranked universities	1	1
Graduate/professional degree	10.2%	9.6%	State SAT score	1002*	1020			
			State ACT score	20.8	21.0			

HEALTH & HEALTHCARE
SCORE: 64/RANK: 118

CRIME
SCORE: 13/RANK: 286

HAZARDS & ILLNESSES	AREA	U.S. AVG	HEALTHCARE	AREA	U.S. AVG	CRIME	AREA	U.S. AVG
Air-quality score	71	45	Physicians per capita	258.7	261.1	Violent crime rate	596.8	456.0
Water-quality score	15	33	Hospital beds per capita	359.6	432.2	Change in violent crime rate	82.6%	-17.2%
Pollen/allergy score	45	61	No. teaching hospitals	5	4	Property crime rate	3,591.7	3,950.0
Stress score	65	50	Cost per doctor visit	$71	$67	Change in property crime rate	-16.3%	-16.8%
Cancer mortality per capita	187.7	169.0	Cost per dental visit	$92	$82			
Depression days per month	2.4	2.8	Cost per daily hospital room	$724	$733			

TRANSPORTATION
SCORE: 23/RANK: 252

COMMUTE	AREA	U.S. AVG	INTERCITY SERVICES	AREA	U.S. AVG	AUTOMOTIVE	AREA	U.S. AVG
Average commute time	24.9 min.	22.6 min.	Miles to nearest major airport	18	46	Insurance, annual premium	$1,198	$1,011
Commute by auto	90.7%	88.7%	Type of local airport	Large		Gas, cost per gallon	$1.49	$1.50
Commute by mass transit	2.1%	1.8%	No. daily airline departures	669	294	Daily vehicle miles per capita	25.3	23.0
Work at home	2.4%	3.9%	Amtrak service	Yes				
Mass transit miles per capita	16.9	8.0	No. interstate highways	1	1			

LEISURE
SCORE: 43/RANK: 183

DINING & SHOPPING	AREA	U.S. AVG	ENTERTAINMENT	AREA	U.S. AVG	OUTDOOR ACTIVITIES	AREA	U.S. AVG
Restaurant rating	1	1	Professional sports rating	8	4	Golf-course rating	7	4
No. outlet malls	7	2	College sports rating	2	4	Ski-area rating	3	4
No. Starbucks	4	11	Zoo/aquarium rating	4	3	National Park rating	2	3
No. warehouse clubs	3	4	Amusement park rating	4	3	Sq. miles inland water	6.0	4.0
			Botanical garden/arboretum rating	4	3	Miles of coastline	0.0	11.4

ARTS & CULTURE
SCORE: 43/RANK: 186

MEDIA & LIBRARIES	AREA	U.S. AVG	PERFORMING ARTS	AREA	U.S. AVG	MUSEUMS	AREA	U.S. AVG
Arts radio rating	5	3	Classical music rating	8	4	Overall museum rating	7	6
No. public libraries	23	28	Ballet/dance rating	6	3	Art museum rating	7	5
Library volumes per capita	2.3	2.8	Professional theater rating	8	3	Science museum rating	4	4
			University arts programs rating	10	5	Children's museum rating	2	3

Worcester, MA-CT

Score: 38.2   Rank: 286

Profile: Small city
Location: Center of Massachusetts dropping into northern Connecticut near the Rhode Island border
Elevation: 470 feet
Time zone: Eastern Standard Time

PRO
Nearby recreation
Local arts and culture
Proximity to larger cities

CON
Economy
Harsh winters
Air service

Worcester is the second largest city in Massachusetts. From its roots in the Industrial Revolution, it is evolving into a diverse research, manufacturing, and technology center, including biotechnology. The downtown is being restored and modernized, including the addition of a new 740,000-square-foot Medical City complex. Origins as a cultural center continue with the area's many small museums and colleges. The economy and employment picture is mixed and suggests transition, while cost of living is high for income levels available locally. The area did win a 2001 National Civic League All-America City Award.

Worcester is located in a valley surrounded by hills and ridges rising from 500 feet above the city to over 1,000 feet 15 miles north. There are long valleys, some with reservoirs, between the nearby hills. Proximity to the Atlantic Ocean, Long Island Sound, and the Berkshire Hills to the west plays an important part in weather and climate. Rapid weather changes occur when storms move up the East Coast from the Carolinas. The mountains provide some shelter from storm systems from the west. Summers are moderate. Winters are usually moderate for the latitude but have frequent cold snaps. Precipitation is spread evenly throughout the year, with summer thunderstorms developing over the mountains. First freeze is mid-October, last is late April.

POPULATION

DEMOGRAPHICS	AREA	U.S. AVG	ETHNIC COMPOSITION	AREA	U.S. AVG	RESIDENT PROFILE	AREA	U.S. AVG
Population	524,714		White	93.1%	75.1%	Single	44.6%	43.6%
Population density per sq. mile	609.7	447.3	Black	2.2%	12.3%	Married	55.4%	56.4%
Population growth	9.7%	16.1%	Asian	2.1%	3.6%	Divorced	7.8%	8.4%
Median age	36.7	35.5	American Indian	.2%	.9%	Separated	2.2%	3.0%
Average family size	2.6	2.7	Hispanic	4.3%	12.5%	Married with children	28.1%	28.7%
			Diversity measure	31.1%	35.2%	Single with children	9.4%	10.1%

ECONOMY & JOBS   SCORE: 39/RANK: 201

INCOME	AREA	U.S. AVG	EMPLOYMENT	AREA	U.S. AVG	LARGEST EMPLOYING INDUSTRY
Per capita income	$25,936	$23,420	Unemployment rate	6.4%	6.1%	Computer and Electronic Product Manufacturing
Household income	$54,294	$46,060	Recent job growth	-2.4%	.9%	
Household income < $25K	22.1%	26.4%	Projected future job growth	6.4%	15.1%	
Household income > $75K	31.7%	24.5%	White collar	59.9%	54.5%	
Household income growth	51.7%	57.3%	Blue collar	40.1%	45.5%	

COST OF LIVING   SCORE: 19/RANK: 265

INDEXES & TAXES	AREA	U.S. AVG	HOUSING	AREA	U.S. AVG	NECESSITIES	AREA	U.S. AVG
Cost of Living Index	114.3	100.0	Median home price	$192,500	$160,100	Food Index	112.1	100.0
Financial Progress Index	101.2	100.0	Home price appreciation	14.6%	7.1%	Housing Index	119.6	100.0
Income tax rate	5.950%	4.625%	Median rent	$827	$670	Utilities Index	110.5	100.0
Sales tax rate	5.000%	6.474%	Homes owned	64.3%	63.9%	Transportation Index	108.6	100.0
Property tax rate	$17.0	$15.6	Homes rented	27.3%	25.3%	Healthcare Index	127.7	100.0
			Housing affordability	50.0%	54.5%	Miscellaneous Cost Index	107.8	100.0

CLIMATE   SCORE: 3/RANK: 318

TEMPERATURE	AREA	U.S. AVG	PRECIPITATION	AREA	U.S. AVG	COMFORTS & HAZARDS	AREA	U.S. AVG
January low	16.2°F	26.4°F	Annual inches precipitation	45.2	35.9	July relative humidity	68.0%	68.8%
July high	79.4°F	86.7°F	Annual inches snowfall	75.0	24.2	Annual days mostly sunny	197	212
Annual days > 90°F	2	38	Annual days precipitation	147	111	Annual days with thunderstorms	21	39
Annual days < 32°F	147	88	Annual days rain > 0.5 inches	27	23	Tornado risk score	16	19
Annual days < 0°F	7	6	Annual days snow > 1.5 inches	21	6	Hurricane risk score	16	15

TEMPERATURE

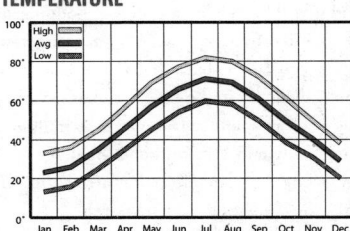

PRECIPITATION

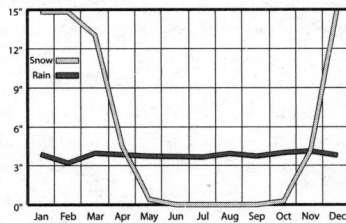

DAYS OF CLOUDS & PRECIPITATION

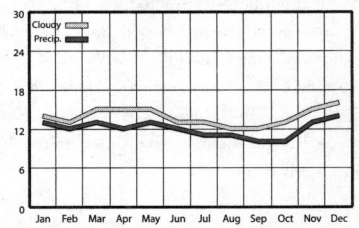

EDUCATION SCORE: 74/RANK: 87

ACHIEVEMENT	AREA	U.S. AVG	PUBLIC SCHOOLS	AREA	U.S. AVG	HIGHER EDUCATION	AREA	U.S. AVG
High school degree	83.4%	80.2%	Expenditures per pupil	$7,308	$5,894	No. 2-year colleges	1	3
2-year college degree	7.9%	6.2%	Student/teacher ratio	15.4	16.7	No. 4-year colleges/universities	10	4
4-year college degree	16.6%	15.8%	Attending public school	88.8%	90.2%	No. highly ranked universities	0	1
Graduate/professional degree	9.8%	9.6%	State SAT score	1038*	1020			
			State ACT score	22.3	21.0			

HEALTH & HEALTHCARE SCORE: 44/RANK: 185

CRIME SCORE: 88/RANK: 40

HAZARDS & ILLNESSES	AREA	U.S. AVG	HEALTHCARE	AREA	U.S. AVG	CRIME	AREA	U.S. AVG
Air-quality score	74	45	Physicians per capita	380.6	261.1	Violent crime rate	470.6	456.0
Water-quality score	72	33	Hospital beds per capita	406.5	432.2	Change in violent crime rate	-28.3%	-17.2%
Pollen/allergy score	58	61	No. teaching hospitals	4	4	Property crime rate	2,244.0	3,950.0
Stress score	54	50	Cost per doctor visit	$82	$67	Change in property crime rate	-30.7%	-16.8%
Cancer mortality per capita	177.4	169.0	Cost per dental visit	$107	$82			
Depression days per month	3.0	2.8	Cost per daily hospital room	$723	$733			

TRANSPORTATION SCORE: 16/RANK: 276

COMMUTE	AREA	U.S. AVG	INTERCITY SERVICES	AREA	U.S. AVG	AUTOMOTIVE	AREA	U.S. AVG
Average commute time	24.1 min.	22.6 min.	Miles to nearest major airport	40	46	Insurance, annual premium	$1,343	$1,011
Commute by auto	92.0%	88.7%	Type of local airport	Large		Gas, cost per gallon	$1.56	$1.50
Commute by mass transit	1.3%	1.8%	No. daily airline departures	746	294	Daily vehicle miles per capita	25.4	23.0
Work at home	2.5%	3.9%	Amtrak service	No				
Mass transit miles per capita	7.7	8.0	No. interstate highways	1	1			

LEISURE SCORE: 79/RANK: 67

DINING & SHOPPING	AREA	U.S. AVG	ENTERTAINMENT	AREA	U.S. AVG	OUTDOOR ACTIVITIES	AREA	U.S. AVG
Restaurant rating	1	1	Professional sports rating	8	4	Golf-course rating	5	4
No. outlet malls	3	2	College sports rating	6	4	Ski-area rating	6	4
No. Starbucks	3	11	Zoo/aquarium rating	4	3	National Park rating	2	3
No. warehouse clubs	5	4	Amusement park rating	5	3	Sq. miles inland water	5.0	4.0
			Botanical garden/arboretum rating	6	3	Miles of coastline	0.0	11.4

ARTS & CULTURE SCORE: 58/RANK: 139

MEDIA & LIBRARIES	AREA	U.S. AVG	PERFORMING ARTS	AREA	U.S. AVG	MUSEUMS	AREA	U.S. AVG
Arts radio rating	4	3	Classical music rating	5	4	Overall museum rating	7	6
No. public libraries	41	28	Ballet/dance rating	5	3	Art museum rating	7	5
Library volumes per capita	4.5	2.8	Professional theater rating	5	3	Science museum rating	6	4
			University arts programs rating	9	5	Children's museum rating	3	3

Yakima, WA

Score: 42.3 Rank: 265

Profile: Small agricultural city
Location: South-central Washington east of the Cascade Range
Elevation: 1,066 feet
Time zone: Pacific Standard Time

PRO	CON
Small-town atmosphere	Economy
Dry climate	Arts and culture
Nearby mountains	Air quality

Yakima, at the eastern base of the Cascade Range, is a small city with a mainly agricultural economy. Good soil, sunny days, and irrigation from the Yakima River support the area's many orchards, which produce apples, pears, peaches, and other fruits for the U.S. market. The city has a plain, small-town character, although a large Hispanic population attracted by farm labor adds a hint of cultural diversity. The city is highly dependent on agriculture and currently has high unemployment, and there isn't much to do. Yakima is an excellent illustration of the "rain shadow" effect: The city is one of the 10 driest in the nation with 8.0 inches of rain annually, while Seattle, west of the Cascade Range, receives five times as much rain with three times as many cloudy days.

Yakima, located in a small east-west valley, resides in an area of complex topography with a number of minor valleys and ridges rising as much as 1,000 feet. There are marked variations in temperature and winds within short distances. The valley is mostly farm and orchard land while surrounding hills are dry and grass covered. The valley climate is relatively mild and dry. It has characteristics of both maritime and continental climates modified by nearby mountains. Summers are dry and hot; afternoons can reach 100°F, but the dry air reduces the impact and leads to cool evenings usually in the 50s. Summer inversions trap air in the valley creating poor air quality. The maritime influence is strongest in winter, which is cloudy and cool with only light snowfall. Below-zero temperatures may occur. Most precipitation arrives in fall and winter. First freeze is early November, last is late March.

POPULATION

DEMOGRAPHICS	AREA	U.S. AVG	ETHNIC COMPOSITION	AREA	U.S. AVG	RESIDENT PROFILE	AREA	U.S. AVG
Population	224,823		White	68.0%	75.1%	Single	42.8%	43.6%
Population density per sq. mile	52.3	447.3	Black	.7%	12.3%	Married	57.2%	56.4%
Population growth	19.1%	16.1%	Asian	1.3%	3.6%	Divorced	8.0%	8.4%
Median age	31.5	35.5	American Indian	7.5%	.9%	Separated	3.1%	3.0%
Average family size	3.1	2.7	Hispanic	35.9%	12.5%	Married with children	30.4%	28.7%
			Diversity measure	55.0%	35.2%	Single with children	13.5%	10.1%

ECONOMY & JOBS SCORE: 4/RANK: 317

INCOME	AREA	U.S. AVG	EMPLOYMENT	AREA	U.S. AVG	LARGEST EMPLOYING INDUSTRY
Per capita income	$16,518	$23,420	Unemployment rate	9.3%	6.1%	Food Manufacturing
Household income	$37,597	$46,060	Recent job growth	1.7%	.9%	
Household income < $25K	30.8%	26.4%	Projected future job growth	13.8%	15.1%	
Household income > $75K	16.8%	24.5%	White collar	42.9%	54.5%	
Household income growth	58.8%	57.3%	Blue collar	57.1%	45.5%	

COST OF LIVING SCORE: 69/RANK: 101

INDEXES & TAXES	AREA	U.S. AVG	HOUSING	AREA	U.S. AVG	NECESSITIES	AREA	U.S. AVG
Cost of Living Index	92.8	100.0	Median home price	$125,550	$160,100	Food Index	107.8	100.0
Financial Progress Index	86.3	100.0	Home price appreciation	3.3%	7.1%	Housing Index	78.0	100.0
Income tax rate	0.000%	4.625%	Median rent	$596	$670	Utilities Index	74.7	100.0
Sales tax rate	7.600%	6.474%	Homes owned	61.6%	63.9%	Transportation Index	101.8	100.0
Property tax rate	$13.0	$15.6	Homes rented	30.3%	25.3%	Healthcare Index	125.0	100.0
			Housing affordability	54.0%	54.5%	Miscellaneous Cost Index	98.9	100.0

CLIMATE SCORE: 34/RANK: 218

TEMPERATURE	AREA	U.S. AVG	PRECIPITATION	AREA	U.S. AVG	COMFORTS & HAZARDS	AREA	U.S. AVG
January low	18.6°F	26.4°F	Annual inches precipitation	8.0	35.9	July relative humidity	60.0%	68.8%
July high	88.1°F	86.7°F	Annual inches snowfall	25.0	24.2	Annual days mostly sunny	202	212
Annual days > 90°F	33	38	Annual days precipitation	67	111	Annual days with thunderstorms	7	39
Annual days < 32°F	150	88	Annual days rain > 0.5 inches	4	23	Tornado risk score	0	19
Annual days < 0°F	4	6	Annual days snow > 1.5 inches	7	6	Hurricane risk score	0	15

TEMPERATURE

PRECIPITATION

DAYS OF CLOUDS & PRECIPITATION

EDUCATION SCORE: 4/RANK: 316

ACHIEVEMENT	AREA	U.S. AVG	PUBLIC SCHOOLS	AREA	U.S. AVG	HIGHER EDUCATION	AREA	U.S. AVG
High school degree	69.4%	80.2%	Expenditures per pupil	$5,709	$5,894	No. 2-year colleges	1	3
2-year college degree	5.3%	6.2%	Student/teacher ratio	19.9	16.7	No. 4-year colleges/universities	1	4
4-year college degree	10.1%	15.8%	Attending public school	96.1%	90.2%	No. highly ranked universities	0	1
Graduate/professional degree	5.9%	9.6%	State SAT score	1062*	1020			
			State ACT score	22.5	21.0			

HEALTH & HEALTHCARE SCORE: 37/RANK: 208

CRIME SCORE: 43/RANK: 189

HAZARDS & ILLNESSES	AREA	U.S. AVG	HEALTHCARE	AREA	U.S. AVG	CRIME	AREA	U.S. AVG
Air-quality score	17	45	Physicians per capita	171.7	261.1	Violent crime rate	266.2	456.0
Water-quality score	20	33	Hospital beds per capita	237.7	432.2	Change in violent crime rate	-54.1%	-17.2%
Pollen/allergy score	46	61	No. teaching hospitals	2	4	Property crime rate	5,558.9	3,950.0
Stress score	80	50	Cost per doctor visit	$59	$67	Change in property crime rate	-26.1%	-16.8%
Cancer mortality per capita	159.0	169.0	Cost per dental visit	$117	$82			
Depression days per month	4.1	2.8	Cost per daily hospital room	$889	$733			

TRANSPORTATION SCORE: 58/RANK: 137

COMMUTE	AREA	U.S. AVG	INTERCITY SERVICES	AREA	U.S. AVG	AUTOMOTIVE	AREA	U.S. AVG
Average commute time	19.4 min.	22.6 min.	Miles to nearest major airport	102	46	Insurance, annual premium	$987	$1,011
Commute by auto	87.2%	88.7%	Type of local airport	Large		Gas, cost per gallon	$1.62	$1.50
Commute by mass transit	.4%	1.8%	No. daily airline departures	698	294	Daily vehicle miles per capita	18.0	23.0
Work at home	5.5%	3.9%	Amtrak service	No				
Mass transit miles per capita	4.3	8.0	No. interstate highways	1	1			

LEISURE SCORE: 49/RANK: 169

DINING & SHOPPING	AREA	U.S. AVG	ENTERTAINMENT	AREA	U.S. AVG	OUTDOOR ACTIVITIES	AREA	U.S. AVG
Restaurant rating	1	1	Professional sports rating	2	4	Golf-course rating	2	4
No. outlet malls	0	2	College sports rating	5	4	Ski-area rating	7	4
No. Starbucks	4	11	Zoo/aquarium rating	1	3	National Park rating	10	3
No. warehouse clubs	3	4	Amusement park rating	1	3	Sq. miles inland water	3.0	4.0
			Botanical garden/arboretum rating	1	3	Miles of coastline	0.0	11.4

ARTS & CULTURE SCORE: 46/RANK: 176

MEDIA & LIBRARIES	AREA	U.S. AVG	PERFORMING ARTS	AREA	U.S. AVG	MUSEUMS	AREA	U.S. AVG
Arts radio rating	7	3	Classical music rating	3	4	Overall museum rating	6	6
No. public libraries	20	28	Ballet/dance rating	1	3	Art museum rating	2	5
Library volumes per capita	2.7	2.8	Professional theater rating	1	3	Science museum rating	1	4
			University arts programs rating	1	5	Children's museum rating	3	3

Yolo, CA

Score: 53.2   Rank: 200

Profile: Small town/College town
Location: Northern California, northern part of the Central Valley, 20 miles west of Sacramento
Elevation: 25 feet
Time zone: Pacific Standard Time

PRO	CON
Mild winters	Cost of living
Educational attainment	Home prices
College-town amenities	Local healthcare

Yolo County is a mainly agricultural area with two small cities, Davis and Woodland. The former, home to the University of California at Davis, has a college-town character, with broad tree-lined streets and numerous shops and small businesses. Woodland, just 10 miles north, is an agricultural and industrial center that has recently emerged as a warehousing and distribution center with easy access to the San Francisco Bay Area. Dixon, to the south, is becoming a bedroom community for Sacramento. Many services, apparently lacking locally, are available in nearby Sacramento or the Bay Area to the southwest. Davis, as a college town, lifts the educational attainment and climate of the whole county. On the downside, cost of living and particularly housing in Davis are higher than reflected in the aggregate Yolo numbers, in part due to local restrictions on development. (Those restrictions help control sprawl and increase quality of life.) Someone living in the county may experience something better or worse than the average numbers indicate depending on location.

The landscape is level and agricultural, consistent with most of the Central Valley. Coastal ranges rise to the west to 3,000 feet. The Mediterranean Central Valley climate is mild with abundant sunshine most of the year. Summers are warm, dry, and usually cloud-free, and some days experience cooling bay breezes. Winters are cool and moist with few freezes. Most rain falls from November through March. Winter brings periods of persistent ground fog.

POPULATION

DEMOGRAPHICS	AREA	U.S. AVG	ETHNIC COMPOSITION	AREA	U.S. AVG	RESIDENT PROFILE	AREA	U.S. AVG
Population	180,856		White	72.2%	75.1%	Single	44.8%	43.6%
Population density per sq. mile	178.6	447.3	Black	4.4%	12.3%	Married	55.2%	56.4%
Population growth	28.2%	16.1%	Asian	5.7%	3.6%	Divorced	8.7%	8.4%
Median age	29.7	35.5	American Indian	1.9%	.9%	Separated	3.8%	3.0%
Average family size	2.8	2.7	Hispanic	33.6%	12.5%	Married with children	27.9%	28.7%
			Diversity measure	56.8%	35.2%	Single with children	9.6%	10.1%

ECONOMY & JOBS SCORE: 9/RANK: 299

INCOME	AREA	U.S. AVG	EMPLOYMENT	AREA	U.S. AVG	LARGEST EMPLOYING INDUSTRY
Per capita income	$22,508	$23,420	Unemployment rate	4.5%	6.1%	Food Manufacturing
Household income	$45,881	$46,060	Recent job growth	.9%	.9%	
Household income < $25K	26.2%	26.4%	Projected future job growth	24.3%	15.1%	
Household income > $75K	27.3%	24.5%	White collar	58.5%	54.5%	
Household income growth	58.4%	57.3%	Blue collar	41.5%	45.5%	

COST OF LIVING SCORE: 9/RANK: 299

INDEXES & TAXES	AREA	U.S. AVG	HOUSING	AREA	U.S. AVG	NECESSITIES	AREA	U.S. AVG
Cost of Living Index	136.9	100.0	Median home price	$275,690	$160,100	Food Index	121.9	100.0
Financial Progress Index	71.4	100.0	Home price appreciation	17.5%	7.1%	Housing Index	171.2	100.0
Income tax rate	6.000%	4.625%	Median rent	$779	$670	Utilities Index	115.9	100.0
Sales tax rate	7.250%	6.474%	Homes owned	57.8%	63.9%	Transportation Index	118.0	100.0
Property tax rate	$10.9	$15.6	Homes rented	32.5%	25.3%	Healthcare Index	155.3	100.0
			Housing affordability	43.0%	54.5%	Miscellaneous Cost Index	104.6	100.0

CLIMATE — SCORE: 93/RANK: 22

TEMPERATURE	AREA	U.S. AVG	PRECIPITATION	AREA	U.S. AVG	COMFORTS & HAZARDS	AREA	U.S. AVG
January low	36.0°F	26.4°F	Annual inches precipitation	30.0	35.9	July relative humidity	67.0%	68.8%
July high	94.0°F	86.7°F	Annual inches snowfall	.5	24.2	Annual days mostly sunny	276	212
Annual days > 90°F	82	38	Annual days precipitation	60	111	Annual days with thunderstorms	6	39
Annual days < 32°F	25	88	Annual days rain > 0.5 inches	21	23	Tornado risk score	2	19
Annual days < 0°F	0	6	Annual days snow > 1.5 inches	0	6	Hurricane risk score	0	15

TEMPERATURE **PRECIPITATION** **DAYS OF CLOUDS & PRECIPITATION**

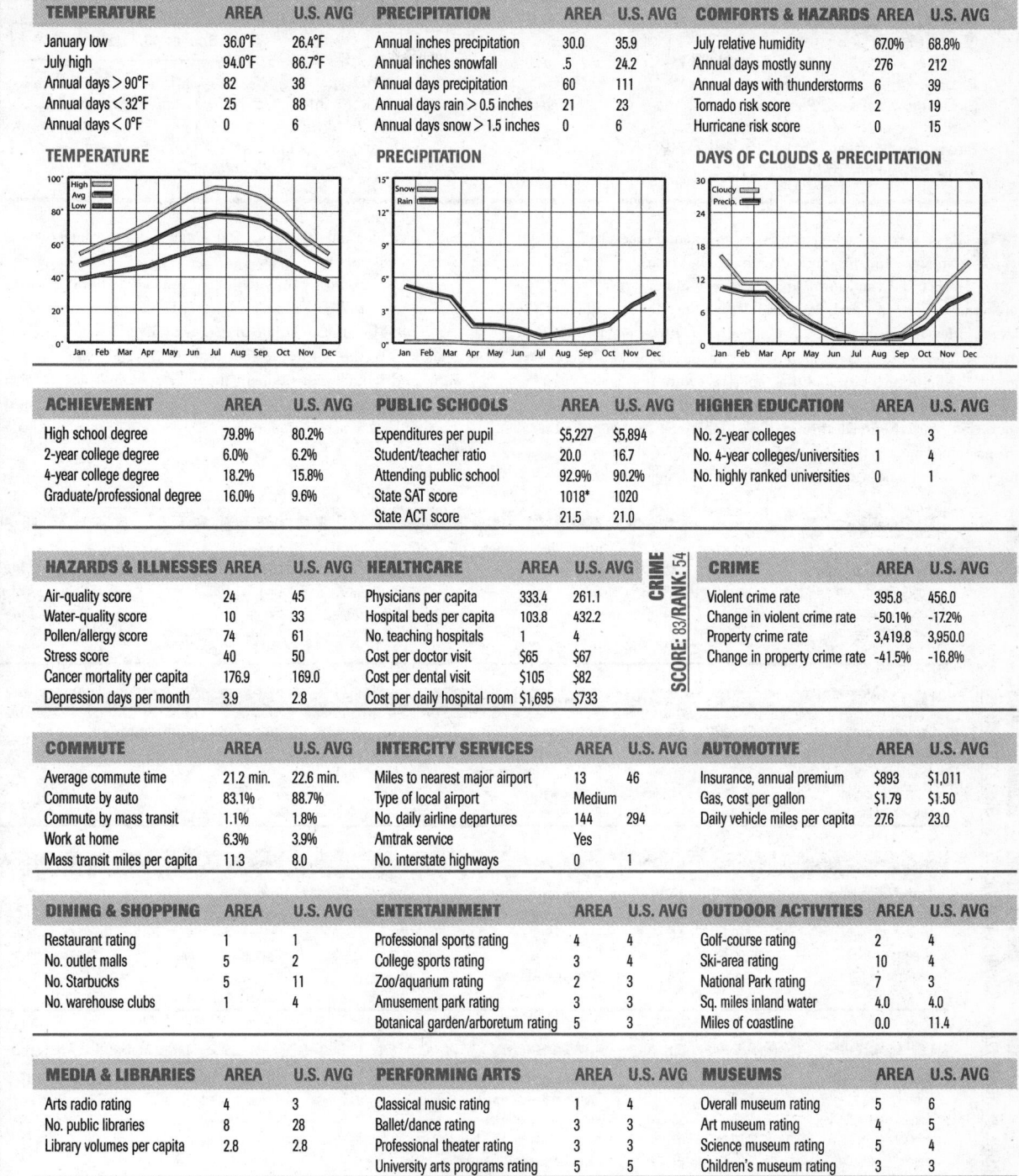

EDUCATION — SCORE: 63/RANK: 122

ACHIEVEMENT	AREA	U.S. AVG	PUBLIC SCHOOLS	AREA	U.S. AVG	HIGHER EDUCATION	AREA	U.S. AVG
High school degree	79.8%	80.2%	Expenditures per pupil	$5,227	$5,894	No. 2-year colleges	1	3
2-year college degree	6.0%	6.2%	Student/teacher ratio	20.0	16.7	No. 4-year colleges/universities	1	4
4-year college degree	18.2%	15.8%	Attending public school	92.9%	90.2%	No. highly ranked universities	0	1
Graduate/professional degree	16.0%	9.6%	State SAT score	1018*	1020			
			State ACT score	21.5	21.0			

HEALTH & HEALTHCARE — SCORE: 4/RANK: 315

HAZARDS & ILLNESSES	AREA	U.S. AVG	HEALTHCARE	AREA	U.S. AVG
Air-quality score	24	45	Physicians per capita	333.4	261.1
Water-quality score	10	33	Hospital beds per capita	103.8	432.2
Pollen/allergy score	74	61	No. teaching hospitals	1	4
Stress score	40	50	Cost per doctor visit	$65	$67
Cancer mortality per capita	176.9	169.0	Cost per dental visit	$105	$82
Depression days per month	3.9	2.8	Cost per daily hospital room	$1,695	$733

CRIME — SCORE: 83/RANK: 54

CRIME	AREA	U.S. AVG
Violent crime rate	395.8	456.0
Change in violent crime rate	-50.1%	-17.2%
Property crime rate	3,419.8	3,950.0
Change in property crime rate	-41.5%	-16.8%

TRANSPORTATION — SCORE: 55/RANK: 148

COMMUTE	AREA	U.S. AVG	INTERCITY SERVICES	AREA	U.S. AVG	AUTOMOTIVE	AREA	U.S. AVG
Average commute time	21.2 min.	22.6 min.	Miles to nearest major airport	13	46	Insurance, annual premium	$893	$1,011
Commute by auto	83.1%	88.7%	Type of local airport	Medium		Gas, cost per gallon	$1.79	$1.50
Commute by mass transit	1.1%	1.8%	No. daily airline departures	144	294	Daily vehicle miles per capita	27.6	23.0
Work at home	6.3%	3.9%	Amtrak service	Yes				
Mass transit miles per capita	11.3	8.0	No. interstate highways	0	1			

LEISURE — SCORE: 60/RANK: 128

DINING & SHOPPING	AREA	U.S. AVG	ENTERTAINMENT	AREA	U.S. AVG	OUTDOOR ACTIVITIES	AREA	U.S. AVG
Restaurant rating	1	1	Professional sports rating	4	4	Golf-course rating	2	4
No. outlet malls	5	2	College sports rating	3	4	Ski-area rating	10	4
No. Starbucks	5	11	Zoo/aquarium rating	2	3	National Park rating	7	3
No. warehouse clubs	1	4	Amusement park rating	3	3	Sq. miles inland water	4.0	4.0
			Botanical garden/arboretum rating	5	3	Miles of coastline	0.0	11.4

ARTS & CULTURE — SCORE: 31/RANK: 228

MEDIA & LIBRARIES	AREA	U.S. AVG	PERFORMING ARTS	AREA	U.S. AVG	MUSEUMS	AREA	U.S. AVG
Arts radio rating	4	3	Classical music rating	1	4	Overall museum rating	5	6
No. public libraries	8	28	Ballet/dance rating	3	3	Art museum rating	4	5
Library volumes per capita	2.8	2.8	Professional theater rating	3	3	Science museum rating	5	4
			University arts programs rating	5	5	Children's museum rating	3	3

York, PA

Score: 43.7   Rank: 260

Profile: Small city
Location: Southeast Pennsylvania, 110 miles west of Philadelphia and 20 miles north of the Maryland border
Elevation: 351 feet
Time zone: Eastern Standard Time

PRO	CON
Historic interest	Economy
Cost of living	Educational attainment
Central location	Entertainment

Parts of York look much as they did in colonial times, with a downtown area of historic brick buildings and nearby factories, farmers markets, and town squares. The buildings reveal the city's importance during the early Industrial Revolution. Today, aside from the large Harley-Davidson plant, the area has a diverse base of mostly small manufacturers, but recent employment trends are weak. There isn't much to do in the city, but the area is centrally located between Harrisburg and Baltimore to the north and south, respectively; the historic Gettysburg National Military Park to the west; and larger cities to the east. Baltimore is the closest big city at 60 miles. For those not seeking employment and willing to travel for certain amenities and services,

York has a pleasant small-town feel with a slow pace and is more attractive than the ranking indicates.

The area has mostly rolling hills given to agricultural use with intermittent creek valleys and wooded areas. The hills become larger toward the south. The climate is humid continental, with some influence from mountains to the northwest and water to the southeast. Summers are warm and humid with frequent thunderstorms and an occasional hot spell. While most bitter cold weather avoids the area in winter, there is snow and snow accumulation. First freeze is mid-October, last is late April.

POPULATION

DEMOGRAPHICS	AREA	U.S. AVG	ETHNIC COMPOSITION	AREA	U.S. AVG	RESIDENT PROFILE	AREA	U.S. AVG
Population	389,209		White	95.6%	75.1%	Single	39.0%	43.6%
Population density per sq. mile	430.2	447.3	Black	2.7%	12.3%	Married	61.0%	56.4%
Population growth	14.6%	16.1%	Asian	.9%	3.6%	Divorced	7.5%	8.4%
Median age	38.2	35.5	American Indian	.2%	.9%	Separated	2.7%	3.0%
Average family size	2.6	2.7	Hispanic	1.5%	12.5%	Married with children	31.0%	28.7%
			Diversity measure	16.3%	35.2%	Single with children	8.2%	10.1%

ECONOMY & JOBS   SCORE: 37/RANK: 208

INCOME	AREA	U.S. AVG	EMPLOYMENT	AREA	U.S. AVG	LARGEST EMPLOYING INDUSTRY
Per capita income	$23,287	$23,420	Unemployment rate	4.6%	6.1%	Transportation Equipment Manufacturing
Household income	$47,924	$46,060	Recent job growth	-1.5%	.9%	
Household income < $25K	20.9%	26.4%	Projected future job growth	12.4%	15.1%	
Household income > $75K	21.8%	24.5%	White collar	50.1%	54.5%	
Household income growth	46.8%	57.3%	Blue collar	49.9%	45.5%	

COST OF LIVING   SCORE: 64/RANK: 117

INDEXES & TAXES	AREA	U.S. AVG	HOUSING	AREA	U.S. AVG	NECESSITIES	AREA	U.S. AVG
Cost of Living Index	91.3	100.0	Median home price	$123,900	$160,100	Food Index	90.2	100.0
Financial Progress Index	111.9	100.0	Home price appreciation	3.9%	7.1%	Housing Index	77.0	100.0
Income tax rate	2.800%	4.625%	Median rent	$589	$670	Utilities Index	112.9	100.0
Sales tax rate	6.000%	6.474%	Homes owned	76.3%	63.9%	Transportation Index	104.0	100.0
Property tax rate	$14.4	$15.6	Homes rented	19.1%	25.3%	Healthcare Index	89.2	100.0
			Housing affordability	63.0%	54.5%	Miscellaneous Cost Index	101.7	100.0

CLIMATE   SCORE: 33/RANK: 222

TEMPERATURE	AREA	U.S. AVG	PRECIPITATION	AREA	U.S. AVG	COMFORTS & HAZARDS	AREA	U.S. AVG
January low	22.5°F	26.4°F	Annual inches precipitation	36.0	35.9	July relative humidity	67.0%	68.8%
July high	86.8°F	86.7°F	Annual inches snowfall	35.0	24.2	Annual days mostly sunny	193	212
Annual days > 90°F	24	38	Annual days precipitation	125	111	Annual days with thunderstorms	33	39
Annual days < 32°F	107	88	Annual days rain > 0.5 inches	25	23	Tornado risk score	14	19
Annual days < 0°F	1	6	Annual days snow > 1.5 inches	8	6	Hurricane risk score	12	15

TEMPERATURE

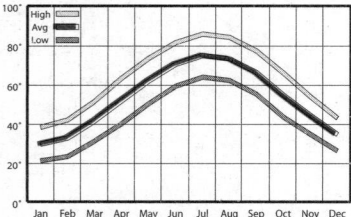

PRECIPITATION

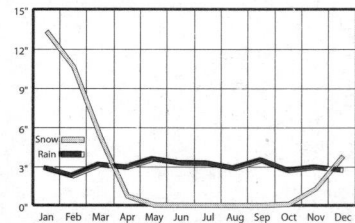

DAYS OF CLOUDS & PRECIPITATION

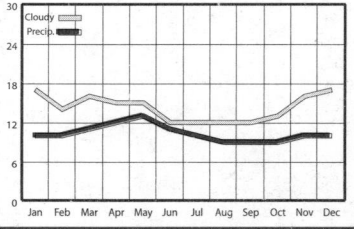

EDUCATION SCORE: 38/RANK: 204

ACHIEVEMENT	AREA	U.S. AVG	PUBLIC SCHOOLS	AREA	U.S. AVG	HIGHER EDUCATION	AREA	U.S. AVG
High school degree	80.7%	80.2%	Expenditures per pupil	$5,753	$5,894	No. 2-year colleges	4	3
2-year college degree	5.7%	6.2%	Student/teacher ratio	17.0	16.7	No. 4-year colleges/universities	1	4
4-year college degree	12.5%	15.8%	Attending public school	92.2%	90.2%	No. highly ranked universities	2	1
Graduate/professional degree	5.9%	9.6%	State SAT score	1002*	1020			
			State ACT score	21.5	21.0			

HEALTH & HEALTHCARE SCORE: 55/RANK: 148   **CRIME** SCORE: 88/RANK: 39

HAZARDS & ILLNESSES	AREA	U.S. AVG	HEALTHCARE	AREA	U.S. AVG	CRIME	AREA	U.S. AVG
Air-quality score	17	45	Physicians per capita	191.7	261.1	Violent crime rate	202.9	456.0
Water-quality score	43	33	Hospital beds per capita	223.7	432.2	Change in violent crime rate	2.0%	-17.2%
Pollen/allergy score	47	61	No. teaching hospitals	2	4	Property crime rate	2,396.5	3,950.0
Stress score	31	50	Cost per doctor visit	$56	$67	Change in property crime rate	-18.5%	-16.8%
Cancer mortality per capita	168.6	169.0	Cost per dental visit	$55	$82			
Depression days per month	5.2	2.8	Cost per daily hospital room	$370	$733			

TRANSPORTATION SCORE: 9/RANK: 300

COMMUTE	AREA	U.S. AVG	INTERCITY SERVICES	AREA	U.S. AVG	AUTOMOTIVE	AREA	U.S. AVG
Average commute time	24.0 min.	22.6 min.	Miles to nearest major airport	16	46	Insurance, annual premium	$972	$1,011
Commute by auto	93.1%	88.7%	Type of local airport	Small		Gas, cost per gallon	$1.46	$1.50
Commute by mass transit	.5%	1.8%	No. daily airline departures	81	294	Daily vehicle miles per capita	21.8	23.0
Work at home	3.1%	3.9%	Amtrak service	No				
Mass transit miles per capita	4.1	8.0	No. interstate highways	1	1			

LEISURE SCORE: 27/RANK: 244

DINING & SHOPPING	AREA	U.S. AVG	ENTERTAINMENT	AREA	U.S. AVG	OUTDOOR ACTIVITIES	AREA	U.S. AVG
Restaurant rating	1	1	Professional sports rating	4	4	Golf-course rating	3	4
No. outlet malls	8	2	College sports rating	2	4	Ski-area rating	5	4
No. Starbucks	1	11	Zoo/aquarium rating	1	3	National Park rating	2	3
No. warehouse clubs	3	4	Amusement park rating	1	3	Sq. miles inland water	2.0	4.0
			Botanical garden/arboretum rating	2	3	Miles of coastline	0.0	11.4

ARTS & CULTURE SCORE: 17/RANK: 272

MEDIA & LIBRARIES	AREA	U.S. AVG	PERFORMING ARTS	AREA	U.S. AVG	MUSEUMS	AREA	U.S. AVG
Arts radio rating	1	3	Classical music rating	3	4	Overall museum rating	4	6
No. public libraries	15	28	Ballet/dance rating	5	3	Art museum rating	1	5
Library volumes per capita	1.1	2.8	Professional theater rating	1	3	Science museum rating	1	4
			University arts programs rating	3	5	Children's museum rating	1	3

Youngstown-Warren, OH

Score: 37.0   Rank: 291

Profile: Mid-size-industrial-town complex
Location: Northeastern Ohio near the Pennsylvania border halfway between Cleveland and Pittsburgh, Pennsylvania
Elevation: 1,178 feet
Time zone: Eastern Standard Time

PRO
Small-town atmosphere
Cost of living

Proximity to larger cities

CON
Economic decline
Low educational attainment
Rugged winters

Youngstown's early prosperity and character emerged from the steel industry. Few places have seen a more pronounced decline in that industry than Youngstown, although steel and steel products manufacturing remain important to the local economy. Today the city struggles with some success to diversify into automobile assembly, other manufacturing, and a wide range of small businesses. Warren, to the north, also has an industrial character but with a bit of historical charm. Youngstown's location midway between Cleveland and Pittsburgh, 80 miles from the center of each, is attractive for business and for those seeking a smaller-town lifestyle with access to big-city services and amenities. There are some attractive recreational areas in the nearby Appalachian foothills and in Pennsylvania to the east.

The area mainly lies in a river valley surrounded by low wooded hills and ridges. The region has numerous streams and lakes, both natural and man-made. The climate is modified continental with a moderating influence from Lake Erie, 50 miles to the northwest. Cold air invasions from Canada are frequent but are modified by passage over the lake. The lake effect produces persistent cloudiness, snow flurries, and occasional heavier snows. The area has the highest cloudiness, days of precipitation, and total annual snowfall in the state. Summer is typically warm and humid with thundershowers and few temperature extremes. First freeze is mid-October, last is early May.

POPULATION

DEMOGRAPHICS	AREA	U.S. AVG	ETHNIC COMPOSITION	AREA	U.S. AVG	RESIDENT PROFILE	AREA	U.S. AVG
Population	588,632		White	88.7%	75.1%	Single	44.5%	43.6%
Population density per sq. mile	376.5	447.3	Black	10.0%	12.3%	Married	55.5%	56.4%
Population growth	-2.0%	16.1%	Asian	.6%	3.6%	Divorced	8.8%	8.4%
Median age	39.7	35.5	American Indian	.2%	.9%	Separated	2.5%	3.0%
Average family size	2.6	2.7	Hispanic	1.6%	12.5%	Married with children	27.2%	28.7%
			Diversity measure	24.1%	35.2%	Single with children	10.6%	10.1%

ECONOMY & JOBS
SCORE: 46/RANK: 179

INCOME	AREA	U.S. AVG	EMPLOYMENT	AREA	U.S. AVG	LARGEST EMPLOYING INDUSTRY
Per capita income	$19,436	$23,420	Unemployment rate	6.4%	6.1%	Transportation Equipment Manufacturing
Household income	$36,916	$46,060	Recent job growth	.9%	.9%	
Household income < $25K	32.7%	26.4%	Projected future job growth	11.6%	15.1%	
Household income > $75K	15.8%	24.5%	White collar	46.9%	54.5%	
Household income growth	44.7%	57.3%	Blue collar	53.1%	45.5%	

COST OF LIVING
SCORE: 54/RANK: 152

INDEXES & TAXES	AREA	U.S. AVG	HOUSING	AREA	U.S. AVG	NECESSITIES	AREA	U.S. AVG
Cost of Living Index	82.9	100.0	Median home price	$93,600	$160,100	Food Index	98.2	100.0
Financial Progress Index	94.9	100.0	Home price appreciation	4.4%	7.1%	Housing Index	58.1	100.0
Income tax rate	6.993%	4.625%	Median rent	$535	$670	Utilities Index	124.3	100.0
Sales tax rate	6.000%	6.474%	Homes owned	71.1%	63.9%	Transportation Index	85.1	100.0
Property tax rate	$19.7	$15.6	Homes rented	20.9%	25.3%	Healthcare Index	90.5	100.0
			Housing affordability	56.0%	54.5%	Miscellaneous Cost Index	93.4	100.0

CLIMATE
SCORE: 8/RANK: 303

TEMPERATURE	AREA	U.S. AVG	PRECIPITATION	AREA	U.S. AVG	COMFORTS & HAZARDS	AREA	U.S. AVG
January low	18.3°F	26.4°F	Annual inches precipitation	38.0	35.9	July relative humidity	74.0%	68.8%
July high	81.8°F	86.7°F	Annual inches snowfall	57.6	24.2	Annual days mostly sunny	164	212
Annual days > 90°F	7	38	Annual days precipitation	181	111	Annual days with thunderstorms	36	39
Annual days < 32°F	136	88	Annual days rain > 0.5 inches	22	23	Tornado risk score	26	19
Annual days < 0°F	6	6	Annual days snow > 1.5 inches	12	6	Hurricane risk score	2	15

TEMPERATURE

PRECIPITATION

DAYS OF CLOUDS & PRECIPITATION

EDUCATION
SCORE: 14/RANK: 284

ACHIEVEMENT	AREA	U.S. AVG	PUBLIC SCHOOLS	AREA	U.S. AVG	HIGHER EDUCATION	AREA	U.S. AVG
High school degree	82.1%	80.2%	Expenditures per pupil	$5,925	$5,894	No. 2-year colleges	5	3
2-year college degree	5.0%	6.2%	Student/teacher ratio	16.8	16.7	No. 4-year colleges/universities	1	4
4-year college degree	10.3%	15.8%	Attending public school	89.5%	90.2%	No. highly ranked universities	0	1
Graduate/professional degree	4.8%	9.6%	State SAT score	1077	1020			
			State ACT score	21.4*	21.0			

HEALTH & HEALTHCARE
SCORE: 48/RANK: 170

CRIME
SCORE: 39/RANK: 202

HAZARDS & ILLNESSES	AREA	U.S. AVG	HEALTHCARE	AREA	U.S. AVG	CRIME	AREA	U.S. AVG
Air-quality score	95	45	Physicians per capita	207.1	261.1	Violent crime rate	400.2	456.0
Water-quality score	7	33	Hospital beds per capita	500.0	432.2	Change in violent crime rate	-27.4%	-17.2%
Pollen/allergy score	61	61	No. teaching hospitals	5	4	Property crime rate	4,052.0	3,950.0
Stress score	64	50	Cost per doctor visit	$50	$67	Change in property crime rate	-4.4%	-16.8%
Cancer mortality per capita	180.9	169.0	Cost per dental visit	$66	$82			
Depression days per month	1.8	2.8	Cost per daily hospital room	$408	$733			

TRANSPORTATION
SCORE: 24/RANK: 249

COMMUTE	AREA	U.S. AVG	INTERCITY SERVICES	AREA	U.S. AVG	AUTOMOTIVE	AREA	U.S. AVG
Average commute time	21.5 min.	22.6 min.	Miles to nearest major airport	47	46	Insurance, annual premium	$821	$1,011
Commute by auto	91.4%	88.7%	Type of local airport	Large		Gas, cost per gallon	$1.43	$1.50
Commute by mass transit	1.2%	1.8%	No. daily airline departures	663	294	Daily vehicle miles per capita	19.5	23.0
Work at home	2.7%	3.9%	Amtrak service	Yes				
Mass transit miles per capita	1.8	8.0	No. interstate highways	2	1			

LEISURE SCORE: 63/RANK: 121

DINING & SHOPPING	AREA	U.S. AVG	ENTERTAINMENT	AREA	U.S. AVG	OUTDOOR ACTIVITIES	AREA	U.S. AVG
Restaurant rating	1	1	Professional sports rating	3	4	Golf-course rating	5	4
No. outlet malls	3	2	College sports rating	4	4	Ski-area rating	3	4
No. Starbucks	1	11	Zoo/aquarium rating	1	3	National Park rating	1	3
No. warehouse clubs	4	4	Amusement park rating	1	3	Sq. miles inland water	3.0	4.0
			Botanical garden/arboretum rating	1	3	Miles of coastline	0.0	11.4

ARTS & CULTURE SCORE: 65/RANK: 114

MEDIA & LIBRARIES	AREA	U.S. AVG	PERFORMING ARTS	AREA	U.S. AVG	MUSEUMS	AREA	U.S. AVG
Arts radio rating	1	3	Classical music rating	6	4	Overall museum rating	6	6
No. public libraries	38	28	Ballet/dance rating	1	3	Art museum rating	6	5
Library volumes per capita	3.1	2.8	Professional theater rating	1	3	Science museum rating	1	4
			University arts programs rating	4	5	Children's museum rating	1	3

Yuba City–Marysville, CA

Score: 25.2   Rank: 315

Profile: Small-town complex
Location: Northern California, northern part of Central Valley, 30 miles north of Sacramento
Elevation: 100 feet
Time zone: Pacific Standard Time

PRO	CON
Mild winters	Economy
Nearby recreation	Cost of living
Proximity to Sacramento	Entertainment

Yuba City and Marysville are Central Valley cities separated by the Sacramento River at the junction of the Feather River. The local economy is largely agricultural and working class in character. Local amenities are noticeably lacking and there is little in the way of attractive small-town flavor. Proximity to Sacramento and the Lake Tahoe Region add to the list of available amenities, and for that reason the statistical rating probably underestimates reality—for those willing to drive 30 miles or more. The climate is pleasant particularly in winter, and there is plenty of nearby recreation with water and wildlife viewing areas. The area has one of the highest unemployment rates in the state at 11.0%, and cost of living, while low on the California scale, is high relative to what is available in the region.

The immediate area is level with a mix of general agriculture and orchards. Both rivers are broad and slow moving. The Sierra Nevada rises to the east and northeast, with oak-studded foothills beginning just a few miles east of town. In summer, the Mediterranean valley climate produces hot, dry, clear days, with spells of oppressive 100°F-plus heat. Winters are mild and occasionally foggy, with a few freezing days but little chance for snow. Most of the year's rain arrives in winter.

POPULATION

DEMOGRAPHICS	AREA	U.S. AVG	ETHNIC COMPOSITION	AREA	U.S. AVG	RESIDENT PROFILE	AREA	U.S. AVG
Population	144,919		White	83.6%	75.1%	Single	38.7%	43.6%
Population density per sq. mile	117.5	447.3	Black	2.2%	12.3%	Married	61.3%	56.4%
Population growth	18.2%	16.1%	Asian	5.9%	3.6%	Divorced	9.7%	8.4%
Median age	33.1	35.5	American Indian	2.3%	.9%	Separated	3.8%	3.0%
Average family size	2.7	2.7	Hispanic	15.4%	12.5%	Married with children	27.6%	28.7%
			Diversity measure	54.0%	35.2%	Single with children	10.3%	10.1%

ECONOMY & JOBS SCORE: 0/RANK: 330

INCOME	AREA	U.S. AVG	EMPLOYMENT	AREA	U.S. AVG	LARGEST EMPLOYING INDUSTRY
Per capita income	$17,081	$23,420	Unemployment rate	11.0%	6.1%	Food Manufacturing
Household income	$34,857	$46,060	Recent job growth	.3%	.9%	
Household income < $25K	35.1%	26.4%	Projected future job growth	20.8%	15.1%	
Household income > $75K	17.0%	24.5%	White collar	45.7%	54.5%	
Household income growth	43.8%	57.3%	Blue collar	54.3%	45.5%	

COST OF LIVING SCORE: 22/RANK: 258

INDEXES & TAXES	AREA	U.S. AVG	HOUSING	AREA	U.S. AVG	NECESSITIES	AREA	U.S. AVG
Cost of Living Index	109.4	100.0	Median home price	$158,490	$160,100	Food Index	119.1	100.0
Financial Progress Index	67.9	100.0	Home price appreciation	12.8%	7.1%	Housing Index	98.4	100.0
Income tax rate	6.000%	4.625%	Median rent	$571	$670	Utilities Index	110.7	100.0
Sales tax rate	7.250%	6.474%	Homes owned	58.6%	63.9%	Transportation Index	118.0	100.0
Property tax rate	$11.2	$15.6	Homes rented	28.4%	25.3%	Healthcare Index	155.2	100.0
			Housing affordability	56.0%	54.5%	Miscellaneous Cost Index	102.7	100.0

CLIMATE SCORE: 94/RANK: 20

TEMPERATURE	AREA	U.S. AVG	PRECIPITATION	AREA	U.S. AVG	COMFORTS & HAZARDS	AREA	U.S. AVG
January low	36.0°F	26.4°F	Annual inches precipitation	30.0	35.9	July relative humidity	67.0%	68.8%
July high	94.0°F	86.7°F	Annual inches snowfall	.5	24.2	Annual days mostly sunny	276	212
Annual days > 90°F	82	38	Annual days precipitation	60	111	Annual days with thunderstorms	6	39
Annual days < 32°F	25	88	Annual days rain > 0.5 inches	19	23	Tornado risk score	2	19
Annual days < 0°F	0	6	Annual days snow > 1.5 inches	0	6	Hurricane risk score	0	15

TEMPERATURE

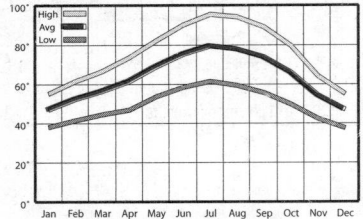

PRECIPITATION

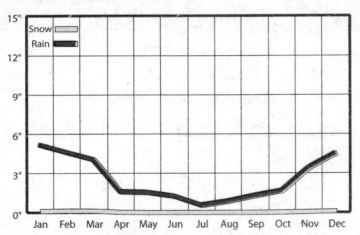

DAYS OF CLOUDS & PRECIPITATION

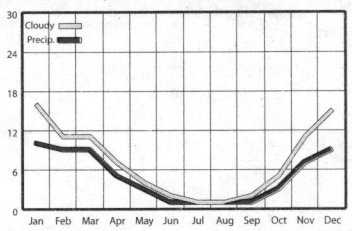

EDUCATION SCORE: 9/RANK: 300

ACHIEVEMENT	AREA	U.S. AVG	PUBLIC SCHOOLS	AREA	U.S. AVG	HIGHER EDUCATION	AREA	U.S. AVG
High school degree	72.6%	80.2%	Expenditures per pupil	$5,176	$5,894	No. 2-year colleges	1	3
2-year college degree	8.8%	6.2%	Student/teacher ratio	20.6	16.7	No. 4-year colleges/universities	0	4
4-year college degree	10.0%	15.8%	Attending public school	95.0%	90.2%	No. highly ranked universities	0	1
Graduate/professional degree	4.4%	9.6%	State SAT score	1018*	1020			
			State ACT score	21.5	21.0			

HEALTH & HEALTHCARE SCORE: 1/RANK: 327

HAZARDS & ILLNESSES	AREA	U.S. AVG	HEALTHCARE	AREA	U.S. AVG
Air-quality score	17	45	Physicians per capita	171.1	261.1
Water-quality score	15	33	Hospital beds per capita	234.3	432.2
Pollen/allergy score	74	61	No. teaching hospitals	0	4
Stress score	96	50	Cost per doctor visit	$61	$67
Cancer mortality per capita	183.7	169.0	Cost per dental visit	$106	$82
Depression days per month	4.3	2.8	Cost per daily hospital room	$1,710	$733

CRIME SCORE: 71/RANK: 94

CRIME	AREA	U.S. AVG
Violent crime rate	463.5	456.0
Change in violent crime rate	-62.7%	-17.2%
Property crime rate	3,635.0	3,950.0
Change in property crime rate	-28.6%	-16.8%

TRANSPORTATION SCORE: 3/RANK: 318

COMMUTE	AREA	U.S. AVG	INTERCITY SERVICES	AREA	U.S. AVG	AUTOMOTIVE	AREA	U.S. AVG
Average commute time	25.7 min.	22.6 min.	Miles to nearest major airport	30	46	Insurance, annual premium	$1,067	$1,011
Commute by auto	85.8%	88.7%	Type of local airport	Medium		Gas, cost per gallon	$1.68	$1.50
Commute by mass transit	.3%	1.8%	No. daily airline departures	144	294	Daily vehicle miles per capita	15.1	23.0
Work at home	7.0%	3.9%	Amtrak service	No				
Mass transit miles per capita	4.7	8.0	No. interstate highways	0	1			

LEISURE SCORE: 57/RANK: 141

DINING & SHOPPING	AREA	U.S. AVG	ENTERTAINMENT	AREA	U.S. AVG	OUTDOOR ACTIVITIES	AREA	U.S. AVG
Restaurant rating	1	1	Professional sports rating	2	4	Golf-course rating	1	4
No. outlet malls	3	2	College sports rating	1	4	Ski-area rating	10	4
No. Starbucks	2	11	Zoo/aquarium rating	1	3	National Park rating	4	3
No. warehouse clubs	3	4	Amusement park rating	1	3	Sq. miles inland water	2.0	4.0
			Botanical garden/arboretum rating	1	3	Miles of coastline	0.0	11.4

ARTS & CULTURE SCORE: 5/RANK: 314

MEDIA & LIBRARIES	AREA	U.S. AVG	PERFORMING ARTS	AREA	U.S. AVG	MUSEUMS	AREA	U.S. AVG
Arts radio rating	1	3	Classical music rating	1	4	Overall museum rating	1	6
No. public libraries	6	28	Ballet/dance rating	1	3	Art museum rating	1	5
Library volumes per capita	1.8	2.8	Professional theater rating	1	3	Science museum rating	1	4
			University arts programs rating	1	5	Children's museum rating	1	3

Yuma, AZ

Score: 52.7   Rank: 204

Profile: Small desert town
Location: Southwest corner of Arizona along the Colorado River and California border, 25 miles north of the Mexican border
Elevation: 138
Time zone: Mountain Standard Time (no daylight savings time)

PRO
Desert climate
Low crime rate
Cost of living

CON
Economy
Summer heat
Educational attainment

Yuma is located at the extreme southwest corner of Arizona where the state borders California just north of the Mexican border. A true oasis in the desert, Yuma was originally settled as a crossing point at the Colorado River for California settlers. Today, the dry, desert climate is the main attraction. Yuma, one of the driest and sunniest places in the country, averages almost 300 days of sunshine each year. Retirees are attracted to the climate, access to California, and low cost of living and crime rate by regional standards. On the downside, physicians per capita is the fourth lowest in the nation. Proximity to the Mexican border gives a slight border-town flavor with increased unemployment and lower educational attainment.

Yuma is located in the Colorado River Valley, which narrows at this point with rugged, hilly, desert terrain on all sides. Green vegetation only grows at the river. The rest of the terrain has scant vegetation, mostly sagebrush, scrub, and short grasses. The climate is true desert. Summers bring dry and sometimes oppressive desert heat during the day followed by relatively cool evenings. *Average* high temperatures from June to September are over 100°F. During the short winter, daytime temperatures are mild, usually in the 70s, but nights can drop below freezing. Precipitation is minimal, with just over 3 inches usually occurring on 10 or fewer days each year. First freeze is mid-December, last is early February.

POPULATION

DEMOGRAPHICS	AREA	U.S. AVG	ETHNIC COMPOSITION	AREA	U.S. AVG	RESIDENT PROFILE	AREA	U.S. AVG
Population	167,407		White	69.6%	75.1%	Single	38.0%	43.6%
Population density per sq. mile	30.4	447.3	Black	2.3%	12.3%	Married	62.0%	56.4%
Population growth	56.6%	16.1%	Asian	2.6%	3.6%	Divorced	6.3%	8.4%
Median age	34.2	35.5	American Indian	2.0%	.9%	Separated	2.8%	3.0%
Average family size	3.1	2.7	Hispanic	52.8%	12.5%	Married with children	32.9%	28.7%
			Diversity measure	56.4%	35.2%	Single with children	12.5%	10.1%

ECONOMY & JOBS   SCORE: 0/RANK: 331

INCOME	AREA	U.S. AVG	EMPLOYMENT	AREA	U.S. AVG	LARGEST EMPLOYING INDUSTRY
Per capita income	$15,271	$23,420	Unemployment rate	34.0%	6.1%	Healthcare and Social Assistance
Household income	$31,911	$46,060	Recent job growth	-4.0%	.9%	
Household income < $25K	36.9%	26.4%	Projected future job growth	23.4%	15.1%	
Household income > $75K	11.9%	24.5%	White collar	44.6%	54.5%	
Household income growth	34.7%	57.3%	Blue collar	55.4%	45.5%	

COST OF LIVING   SCORE: 68/RANK: 104

INDEXES & TAXES	AREA	U.S. AVG	HOUSING	AREA	U.S. AVG	NECESSITIES	AREA	U.S. AVG
Cost of Living Index	88.5	100.0	Median home price	$99,920	$160,100	Food Index	102.8	100.0
Financial Progress Index	76.8	100.0	Home price appreciation	5.5%	7.1%	Housing Index	62.1	100.0
Income tax rate	3.900%	4.625%	Median rent	$659	$670	Utilities Index	123.4	100.0
Sales tax rate	8.800%	6.474%	Homes owned	48.5%	63.9%	Transportation Index	104.1	100.0
Property tax rate	$8.9	$15.6	Homes rented	29.4%	25.3%	Healthcare Index	106.5	100.0
			Housing affordability	50.0%	54.5%	Miscellaneous Cost Index	95.2	100.0

CLIMATE   SCORE: 90/RANK: 33

TEMPERATURE	AREA	U.S. AVG	PRECIPITATION	AREA	U.S. AVG	COMFORTS & HAZARDS	AREA	U.S. AVG
January low	37.6°F	26.4°F	Annual inches precipitation	7.0	35.9	July relative humidity	36.0%	68.8%
July high	104.8°F	86.7°F	Annual inches snowfall	0.0	24.2	Annual days mostly sunny	295	212
Annual days > 90°F	164	38	Annual days precipitation	34	111	Annual days with thunderstorms	23	39
Annual days < 32°F	32	88	Annual days rain > 0.5 inches	2	23	Tornado risk score	4	19
Annual days < 0°F	0	6	Annual days snow > 1.5 inches	0	6	Hurricane risk score	3	15

TEMPERATURE

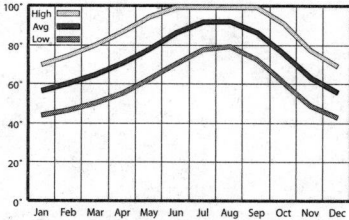

PRECIPITATION

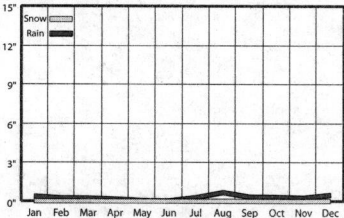

DAYS OF CLOUDS & PRECIPITATION

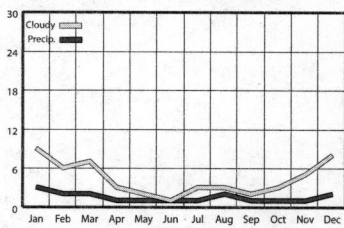

EDUCATION — SCORE: 2/RANK: 322

ACHIEVEMENT	AREA	U.S. AVG	PUBLIC SCHOOLS	AREA	U.S. AVG	HIGHER EDUCATION	AREA	U.S. AVG
High school degree	65.8%	80.2%	Expenditures per pupil	$4,595	$5,894	No. 2-year colleges	1	3
2-year college degree	4.9%	6.2%	Student/teacher ratio	20.8	16.7	No. 4-year colleges/universities	0	4
4-year college degree	7.2%	15.8%	Attending public school	97.6%	90.2%	No. highly ranked universities	0	1
Graduate/professional degree	4.7%	9.6%	State SAT score	1049*	1020			
			State ACT score	21.4	21.0			

HEALTH & HEALTHCARE — SCORE: 9/RANK: 301

HAZARDS & ILLNESSES	AREA	U.S. AVG	HEALTHCARE	AREA	U.S. AVG
Air-quality score	24	45	Physicians per capita	106.3	261.1
Water-quality score	18	33	Hospital beds per capita	191.8	432.2
Pollen/allergy score	66	61	No. teaching hospitals	0	4
Stress score	16	50	Cost per doctor visit	$74	$67
Cancer mortality per capita	150.1	169.0	Cost per dental visit	$100	$82
Depression days per month	2.1	2.8	Cost per daily hospital room	$552	$733

CRIME — SCORE: 94/RANK: 19

CRIME	AREA	U.S. AVG
Violent crime rate	389.0	456.0
Change in violent crime rate	-49.4%	-17.2%
Property crime rate	3,234.3	3,950.0
Change in property crime rate	-59.9%	-16.8%

TRANSPORTATION — SCORE: 94/RANK: 22

COMMUTE	AREA	U.S. AVG	INTERCITY SERVICES	AREA	U.S. AVG	AUTOMOTIVE	AREA	U.S. AVG
Average commute time	18.6 min.	22.6 min.	Miles to nearest major airport	135	46	Insurance, annual premium	$1,079	$1,011
Commute by auto	80.4%	88.7%	Type of local airport	Small		Gas, cost per gallon	$1.59	$1.50
Commute by mass transit	6.0%	1.8%	No. daily airline departures	54	294	Daily vehicle miles per capita	11.9	23.0
Work at home	1.6%	3.9%	Amtrak service	Yes				
Mass transit miles per capita	0.0	8.0	No. interstate highways	2	1			

LEISURE — SCORE: 61/RANK: 129

DINING & SHOPPING	AREA	U.S. AVG	ENTERTAINMENT	AREA	U.S. AVG	OUTDOOR ACTIVITIES	AREA	U.S. AVG
Restaurant rating	1	1	Professional sports rating	2	4	Golf-course rating	8	4
No. outlet malls	0	2	College sports rating	3	4	Ski-area rating	4	4
No. Starbucks	0	11	Zoo/aquarium rating	1	3	National Park rating	10	3
No. warehouse clubs	3	4	Amusement park rating	1	3	Sq. miles inland water	3.0	4.0
			Botanical garden/arboretum rating	1	3	Miles of coastline	0.0	11.4

ARTS & CULTURE — SCORE: 41/RANK: 193

MEDIA & LIBRARIES	AREA	U.S. AVG	PERFORMING ARTS	AREA	U.S. AVG	MUSEUMS	AREA	U.S. AVG
Arts radio rating	1	3	Classical music rating	3	4	Overall museum rating	4	6
No. public libraries	7	28	Ballet/dance rating	1	3	Art museum rating	3	5
Library volumes per capita	2.1	2.8	Professional theater rating	1	3	Science museum rating	1	4
			University arts programs rating	1	5	Children's museum rating	1	3

Canada Metropolitan Areas

As the world's second largest country in land area, Canada offers spectacular geography, rich cultures, and a fascinating assortment of cities. While just larger than the U.S. in land area, Canada had a population of 31.4 million in 2001, a figure outnumbered by its southern neighbor by a factor of nine to one. That fact only begins the comparisons between U.S. and Canadian cities. With respect to their U.S. counterparts, Canadian cities are cleaner, generally more livable, and distinctly more international with pockets of strong European influence.

There is more to know about Canada and Canadian history than can possibly be presented here. The historic rivalry between the French and British, largely eliminated in the United States by the Louisiana Purchase, remains alive in Canada. French language and culture dominate Québec and influence other eastern provinces. In fact, upon arriving blindfolded in Québec City, one would insist they were in France—at least until the arrival of winter. Most of the rest of the country exhibits an attenuated British influence in custom, infrastructure, and style of government. This becomes slightly more obvious in the Maritime provinces of the Atlantic and in British Columbia, most particularly in its English-style capital of Victoria.

Canada is a British-style constitutional monarchy with 10 self-governing provinces and 3 territories. That in itself doesn't influence its cities, but like much of Europe, Canada takes a more socialistic approach than the United States. The healthcare system is nationalized, and governments at all levels exert greater influence on social issues and city infrastructure. As a result, Canadian cities have a more planned look and feel, and are resistant to the anything-goes urban sprawl found in many U.S. equivalents. They are cleaner and generally lack the high crime rates and areas of urban blight found to the south. That isn't to say that Canadian cities don't have problems, but most people comparing the two countries notice these differences right away.

Immigration has been an important recent influence on Canadian cities, much as it was in U.S. cities in the late 19th century. Canada has generally more relaxed immigration policies than the United States. In the 1990s, immigration experienced a big surge, almost doubling the numbers entering the country. Because of the British influence, the country is particularly attractive to wealthy Hong Kong residents, and immigrants from Asia now comprise 60% of the quarter of a million immigrants arriving each year. The cities of Toronto and Vancouver in particular have large and growing Asian communities, which add strong international flavor but also aggravate growth-related problems already evident in those cities.

Ranking & Rating Canadian Cities

In this chapter, *Cities Ranked & Rated* sets out to (1) compare Canadian cities with each other and (2) to compare them with U.S. counterparts. As with the 331 U.S. government–defined Metropolitan Statistical Areas (MSAs) in chapter 5, the Canada government has identified 27 Census Metropolitan Areas (CMAs) using a definition largely modeled after that of the United States. (See chapter 1 for more on these definitions.) This chapter presents statistics for each CMA, along with a brief description of its character, topography, and climate.

Due to space and the unavailability of certain comparable data with respect to the U.S. MSAs, the tables are abbreviated but retain important comparative statistics

Canadian Metropolitan Area	Canada Rank	Comparable U.S. Rank	2001 Population	1996 - 2001 Population Growth	Unemployment Rate	Cost of Living Index	Annual Precipitation (mm/inches)	Annual Snowfall (cm/inches)	Days Below -20°C / -4°F	University Degree	Museum Rating
Vancouver, British Columbia	1	20	1,986,965	8.5%	7.2%	108.5	1,474.9 / 58.1	43.6 / 17.2	0.0	28.7%	9
Montréal, Québec	2	30	3,426,350	3.0%	7.5%	95.6	1,062.6 / 41.8	226.2 / 89.1	7.7	25.9%	10
Victoria, British Columbia	3	35	311,902	2.5%	6.6%	94.2	686.1 / 27.0	12.5 / 4.9	0.0	26.6%	9
Ottawa-Hull, Ontario-Québec	4	35	1,063,664	6.5%	5.6%	123.2	914.2 / 36.0	202.7 / 79.8	18.9	33.0%	10
Toronto, Ontario	5	40	4,682,897	9.8%	5.9%	137.2	834.0 / 32.8	133.1 / 52.4	1.4	30.8%	10
Calgary, Alberta	6	60	951,395	15.8%	4.9%	121.6	412.6 / 16.2	126.7 / 49.9	26.0	27.4%	7
Québec City, Québec	7	65	682,757	1.6%	6.9%	75.7	504.0 / 19.8	114.8 / 45.2	31.1	24.9%	9
Edmonton, Alberta	8	70	937,845	8.7%	5.5%	118.9	476.9 / 18.8	123.5 / 48.6	28.1	21.3%	5
Winnipeg, Manitoba	9	75	671,274	0.6%	5.6%	94.7	504.0 / 19.8	114.8 / 45.2	57.5	22.7%	7
Abbotsford, British Columbia	10	90	147,370	8.0%	8.2%	101.7	1,573.2 / 61.9	63.5 / 25.0	0.0	15.2%	3
St. Catharines-Niagara, Ontario	11	120	377,099	1.2%	6%	103.6	871.6 / 34.3	136.6 / 53.8	0.9	15.6%	5
Saskatoon, Saskatchewan	12	130	225,927	3.1%	6.7%	96.2	350.0 / 13.8	97.2 / 38.3	52.1	23.8%	4
Halifax, Nova Scotia	13	150	359,183	4.7%	7.2%	102.1	1,508.0 / 59.4	151.8 / 59.8	0.9	27.9%	6
St. John's, Newfoundland and Labrador	14	160	172,918	-0.7%	11.3%	92.0	1,513.7 / 59.6	322.3 / 126.9	1.0	22.7%	6
London, Ontario	15	165	432,451	3.8%	6.7%	101.9	987.1 / 38.9	202.4 / 79.7	5.0	21.1%	8
Kingston, Ontario	16	180	146,838	1.6%	6.9%	101.0	968.2 / 38.1	180.9 / 71.2	11.3	23.7%	7
Thunder Bay, Ontario	17	190	121,986	-3.7%	8.8%	97.6	711.6 / 28.0	187.6 / 73.9	49.1	18.3%	3
Regina, Saskatchewan	18	195	192,800	-0.4%	6%	111.5	388.1 / 15.3	105.9 / 41.7	47.7	23.0%	5
Trois-Rivières, Québec	19	200	137,507	-1.7%	9.2%	75.7	1,099.8 / 43.3	241.3 / 95.0	30.1	19.2%	7
Hamilton, Ontario	20	230	662,401	6.1%	5.7%	101.9	910.0 / 35.8	151.8 / 59.8	3.4	20.0%	5
Oshawa, Ontario	21	235	296,298	10.2%	6%	116.5	877.9 / 34.6	118.4 / 46.6	3.4	15.3%	5
Sherbrooke, Québec	22	245	153,811	2.8%	6.9%	102.8	1,144.1 / 45.0	294.3 / 115.9	35.7	21.8%	4
Windsor, Ontario	23	265	307,877	7.3%	6.3%	101.0	805.2 / 31.7	126.6 / 49.8	1.6	20.6%	5
Kitchener-Waterloo, Ontario	24	270	414,284	8.2%	5.5%	104.5	907.9 / 35.7	159.5 / 62.8	7.6	20.4%	2
Saint John, New Brunswick	25	290	122,678	-2.4%	9.2%	95.8	1,390.3 / 54.7	256.9 / 101.1	15.2	17.6%	3
Chicoutimi-Jonquière, Québec	26	310	154,938	-3.4%	12.4%	77.1	1,002.1 / 39.5	301.5 / 118.7	37.1	16.9%	2
Sudbury, Ontario	27	320	155,219	-6.1%	9.1%	99.3	899.3 / 35.4	274.4 / 108.0	36.4	14.9%	3

Table 6.1: Canada Metropolitan Areas: Rankings & Selected Statistics

Source: Statistics Canada, Environment Canada, Canadian Global Almanac 2003

such as cost of living and climate. Eight categories—Economy & Jobs, Cost of Living, Climate, Education, Crime, Transportation, Leisure, and Arts & Culture—are blended with a "quality of life" rating to achieve the Canada ranking on a scale from 1 to 27, 1 being the top city. Because of the smaller data sample and because each of the eight categories does not have a score calculated into the ranking, the approach is more qualitative than that of chapter 5.

Each city is then compared with a U.S. counterpart. Where possible, equivalent U.S. cities are identified based on physical nature, function, or specific data attributes. These equivalencies may be close, as in the case of many U.S. Great Lakes and Canadian Prairie cities, or they may be hard to identify, as in the heavily French- and European-influenced cities of Québec and the east. Regardless, from facts and these equivalencies, *Cities Ranked & Rated* offers a comparable U.S. rank showing where the Canadian city might fall if the places in chapters 5 and 6 were ranked together.

For the Canada city rankings with comparable U.S. rankings and key data, see Table 6.1.

Data Sources

Sources for Canadian data are patterned after those collected for U.S. equivalents. However, subtle differences in collection and aggregation underlie certain items, including marketbaskets used for cost of living, averaging approaches used for home prices, and the calculation of tax rates. While these items are close enough for reasonable comparison, this qualifier should be kept in mind.

Most data comes from the Canada national government statistics and analysis agency, Statistics Canada (www.statcan.ca). Data for population and population trends, economy and jobs, education, crime, and transportation comes from this source, most of which is updated through 2001. Climate data comes from Environment Canada Climate Normals (www.climate.weatheroffice.ec. gc.ca/climate_normals). Data relevant to the descriptive text comes from Transport Canada, Citizenship and Immigration Canada, Natural Resources Canada, and other agencies. The Canadian Global Almanac 2003 (John Wiley & Sons Canada, 2002) organizes certain Canadian government data for easy interpretation and provides broad, fact-based insight. A few local websites, notably the financial planning site Taxtips.ca, also provided valuable information. Canadian city and provincial sites were used, as were a number of travel guides and publications. Finally, the authors used a network of Canadian contacts and local travel experience as a guide.

What follows is a discussion of the major data categories and their contents and insights.

Population

Ninety percent of Canada's population lies within 161 kilometers (100 miles) of the U.S. border, a fact driven not only by economic ties to the United States, but the obvious influence of climate. Two-thirds of the population live in Ontario or Québec, and about 60% live in Census Metropolitan Areas. This latter figure is lower than in the United States, where more than 80% live in Metropolitan Statistical Areas. (But note that Canada defines CMAs as having 100,000 or more people in the core city or cities while a U.S. MSA requires 50,000.) A full 15% of Canada's population live in the Toronto CMA, a far greater dominance than the New York area in the U.S., which with all nearby metropolitan areas included represents only about 7% of the U.S. population.

Population statistics show total population, density, growth, and demographics. Similar to the United States, average growth in all of Canada is about 1% per year. Calgary is the fastest growing at 15.3% per year, while Sudbury and other natural resource–based towns such as Chicoutimi-Jonquière are losing population. The *visible minorities* is a self-explanatory and uniquely Canadian statistic, as are the numbers delineating the percentage using French or English as a primary language and those who are bilingual with both. All population statistics are sourced from Statistics Canada.

Economy & Jobs / Cost of Living

The Canadian economy is a mix of agriculture, natural resources, manufacturing, and general commerce. Vast areas of natural resources, particularly timber, petroleum, and mining products, have had strong influences on the economy. In fact, the country's economy in general and that of many cities are tied to these primary industries. This has led to strong boom and bust cycles, particularly in Alberta and the northern areas of Ontario and Québec. Canada's unemployment has historically been higher than that of the United States, ranging from 7.2% to 10.7% during the past 20 years and currently at a relative low of 7.5%. Unemployment has been a chronic problem in natural resource areas, but it is also emerging as an issue in major cities because of job losses in the high-tech sector and immigration.

The Cost of Living Index is calculated in a manner similar to that of the United States, and is basically comparable. That is to say, Toronto, with the nation's highest COL Index at 137, is 37% higher than the Canadian average and also 37% higher than the U.S. average. Housing is generally less expensive at a average just over C$171,000 (US$121,277) in 2001 versus US$147,000 in the U.S. for the same period. However, there are some differences in the way data is collected for Canadian home prices: The Canadian number is an average, not a mean, and is based on value, not price. Regardless of these differences, Canadian housing prices are slightly higher than the number indicates because of higher interest rates and the non-deductability of mortgage interest. As in the United States, housing prices vary greatly depending on geographic location—home prices average C$84,300 (US$59,787) in Chicoutimi-Jonquière, Québec, and C$237,000 (US$168,085) in Toronto.

A comparison between the personal tax climates of Canada and the United States points to some important differences. As all Canadians will quickly tell you, taxes *are* higher in Canada, but government services are also broader and deeper, most notably in the provision of national health insurance. But when all is added up, Canadian taxes are not *that much* higher than those of the United States. For income tax, Canadian citizens are taxed at the national and provincial level, with important differences from the United States, such as the non-deductability of mortgage interest mentioned above. Combined national and provincial tax burden is 29% to 35% depending on the province for a family income of C$100,000 (US$70,922). In the United States, this figure might run from 18% to 25% depending on the state. But factoring in 7.15% for U.S. FICA payroll tax (including Social Security, Medicare, and other benefits), which rises to 15.3% for the self-employed, brings combined final income tax rates much closer. The data tables show the highest *marginal* income tax rate for each province.

Sales taxes raise a distinct difference between the U.S. and Canada. Like most U.S. states, provinces collect a sales tax ranging in effect from zero (Alberta and the northern territories) to 8% (Ontario) and 10% (Prince Edward Island). But, additionally, with no comparable concept on the immediate U.S. horizon, there is a national 7% Goods and Services Tax (GST), essentially a national sales tax. Unlike U.S. state sales taxes, this tax is collected not only on goods but services, such as auto repair and hair styling. In some provinces, notably Québec, the provincial sales tax (PST) is levied not only on the price of the item but the price plus the GST, creating in essence a tax on a tax. Three provinces—Nova Scotia, Newfoundland

and Labrador, and New Brunswick—have combined GST and PST into a Harmonized Sales Tax (HST), but this doesn't affect the resulting tax burden. Bottom line: Sales/consumption taxes in Canada are decidedly higher. Property taxes vary by locality, but are generally lower than in the United States.

According to a Statistics Canada study, Canadians pay a tax on property values that ranges from 0.7% to 1.9%—generally on the higher side in Ontario and Québec. When the lower property values are factored in, the burden is truly less than in the United States—but remember the mortgage interest subsidy on income taxes doesn't exist in this country. So the system may favor property owners at the expense of lower income residents who pay proportionately more GST/PST; however, when the extra government health services are factored in, tax payments in Canada and the United States start to look fairly even. For more detail on Canadian taxes, see Taxtips.ca (www.taxtips.ca).

Climate

That climate is a major player in the quality of life and livability of Canadian cities is no surprise to anyone. The country has one of the most interesting and dynamic climate profiles in the world, and climate patterns can produce weather ranging from exceptionally pleasant to literally dangerous. The mainly inhabited areas of Canada can be loosely divided into four climate zones:

- Pacific region has a marine climate typical of the U.S. Pacific Northwest west of the Cascade Range. The marine influence moderates temperatures to give few extremes in summer or winter. Most of the abundant precipitation falls as rain, with almost continuous clouds and drizzle particularly in winter and little snow at lower elevations. This climate persists primarily west of the Rockies in British Columbia.

- The Prairie region is characterized by a strong continental climate with extreme seasonal and even daily variation, warm pleasant summers, and bitterly cold, windy winters. The region is the driest in Canada with intermittent summer rain as thundershowers and relatively light snow except in the strongest storms. The area gets the most sunshine in Canada. Alberta east of the Rockies, Saskatchewan, and Manitoba are in this region.

- The Great Lakes region is made up of the areas in Ontario surrounding (or surrounded by) lakes Superior, Huron, Erie, and Ontario and moves east into parts of Québec. As in the United States, the region is a highly seasonal, continental climate with a marine influence determined by location of water and prevailing winds. The area is far enough south and east to receive warm, moist Gulf of Mexico air in the summer creating hot, sticky conditions with thundershowers and occasional severe weather interchanged with cooler, milder air from the north. Winter, likewise, is a mix with relatively mild air and some rain along with blasts of northerly cold and snow. The position of most Canadian cities to the north and west of water means they receive less snow than their U.S. equivalents to the south and east of the lakes. Nevertheless, temperatures below −20°C (−4°F) are recorded nearly everywhere in winter and heavy snowfalls are common.

- The Maritime region is principally the provinces bordering the Atlantic and spreading into eastern Québec. Here alternating continental and marine influences produce a mix of weather with mostly pleasant summers and highly variable winters ranging from deep cold and heavy snow to mild periods with clouds and rain. Clouds, fog, and rain are almost constant in cities on the Atlantic, with St. John's, Newfoundland, receiving precipitation 2 in 3 days each year. The so-called St. Lawrence storm track brings heavy weather, particularly in winter with heavy snows followed by intense cold as the storms pass.

The climate statistics in the tables represent average data collected by Environment Canada over a 30-year period.

Education, Crime & Transportation

This section represents a sampling of key data related mainly to the condition of public services in Canadian cities. For education, the level of attainment is shown with the double purpose of indicating systematic educational achievement and the level of education of the local population. U.S. readers need to understand the "college" and "university" terminology: "College," called "Cégeps" in Québec, is basic post high-school education, usually 1 to 3 years in duration. Curriculum is often geared to specific trades in arts, business, science, technology, or health, but may also include basic university-level requirements. Certificates are awarded upon completion, and many continue at the "university" level, another 1 to 4 years with higher level academic, professional, and post-graduate training. The "college" system is somewhat comparable to the U.S. junior-college system, particularly in states like

California where many students complete basic requirements in a junior college before transferring to a state university. But a Canadian college certificate usually carries more weight than a U.S. junior college or "associate" degree. University graduation rates in Canada are comparable to U.S. 4-year college graduation rates.

Crime rates shown are provincial averages from the 2000 Uniform Crime Reporting Survey. The figure represents the number of reported crimes per 100,000 residents. Data on public transportation in Canada varies considerably among cities. Public transportation is generally considered excellent, especially in the larger cities, with a coordinated mix of bus and light- and heavy-rail systems. It has a well-deserved reputation for being clean, efficient, and timely. Although there have been cutbacks in recent years, intercity rail, as managed by the VIA system (comparable to Amtrak in the U.S.), is good and still serves such distant destinations as Chicoutimi-Jonquière, Québec; Prince Rupert, British Columbia; and even Churchill in remote northern Manitoba. Commercial air service is predictably good in the larger cities and is available in smaller CMAs. The statistic showing the number of passengers departing each day through the local airport is sourced from the Airports Council International 2002 North America Passenger Traffic Report (www.aci-na.org).

Leisure / Arts & Culture

This section includes an abbreviated selection of leisure and arts and culture attributes. *Cities Ranked & Rated* assigns a 1 to 10 rating based on availability, quality, and access. Features with national or international renown get the highest scores. Canada is a nation rich in recreational assets, particularly outdoor recreation with vast expanses of mountains, water, forests, parks, and coastline and ample snow for winter sports. Entertainment is plentiful and quite multicultural in the big cities, while somewhat lacking in the mid-size cities and smaller towns. Spectator sports are big, with hockey and Canadian football (CFL) adding to the usual mix of baseball and basketball. Ice-skating, skiing, snowmobiling, and most watersports are abundant in Canada. Some of the country's arts and culture assets, particularly classical music and ballet, are world-renowned. Canada has always had a strong influence on the pop culture and music scene, bringing such diverse acts as Gordon Lightfoot, Billy Idol, and Celine Dion, among others.

Cities Ranked & Rated assigns a "quality of life" rating to each city. This number takes into consideration not only leisure and arts and culture assets, but also economic opportunity, climate, appearance, heritage, and ease of living.

Abbotsford, British Columbia

Canada Rank: 10

Profile: Small city
Location: Along Fraser River and Highway 1, 56 kilometers (35 miles) southeast of Vancouver
Elevation: 58 meters/190 feet

PRO
Strong economy
Attractive setting

CON
High home prices
Wet climate

Abbotsford is a rapidly growing small city and residential area on the outskirts of Vancouver, 8 kilometers (5 miles) north of the U.S. border. Once largely driven by agriculture and the nearby U.S. border crossing, the economic base is growing and diversifying. Manufacturing has become the largest source of employment and aerospace and high-tech industries are important contributors. The town area is attractive and mostly modern with airport facilities nearby. Most residents work in the area but 20% commute to Vancouver or, more likely, its outskirt cities of Surrey and Langley.

The area lies in the broad flat valley of the Fraser River surrounded by low, fir-forested mountains and several lakes. The climate is decidedly marine with cool pleasant summers and relatively mild winters. The annual precipitation total is among the highest in Canada.

Abbotsford compares to Everett, Washington, part of the Seattle-Bellevue-Everett metropolitan area (no. 88) and gets a comparable U.S. rank of 90.

POPULATION

Population	147,370	Median age	35.4	Visible minorities	17.8%
Population density	653.9 sq. km / 252.5 sq. mile	Average family size	3.2	English-speaking	–
Population growth	8.0%	Single	27.9%	French-speaking	–
		Married	55.7%	Bilingual	–

ECONOMY & JOBS

Household income	C$48,721 / US$34,554
Unemployment rate	8.2%
White collar	66.0%
Blue collar	34.0%

COST OF LIVING

Cost of Living Index	101.7	Average home price	C$195,437 / US$138,608
Provincial income tax	14.7%	Average rent	C$706 / US$501
Provincial sales tax	7.5%	Homes owned	71%
		Homes rented	29%

CLIMATE

January low	0.6°C / 33.1 °F	Annual days > 30°C / 86°F	0.44	Annual days precipitation	177.2
July high	23.4°C / 74.1°F	Annual days < 0°C / 32°F	19.6	Annual days snowfall	13.8
Annual precipitation	1,573.2mm / 61.9 in.	Annual days < -20°C / -4°F	0	Annual sun hours	–
Annual snowfall	63.5cm / 25.0 in.				

TEMPERATURE

PRECIPITATION

EDUCATION

High school degree	75%
Completed trade school	14%
College degree	17%
University degree	15.2%

CRIME

Violent crime rate	1,217
Change in violent crime rate	-2.8%
Property crime rate	3,762
Change in property crime rate	2.9%

TRANSPORTATION

Commute by auto	75.7%
Commute by mass transit	1.4%
Work at home	9.9%
Air service (passengers a day)	< 500

LEISURE

Restaurant rating	8	Spectator-sports rating	3
Golf-course rating	5	Inland water rating	9
Ski-area rating	8	Park rating	7
		Quality of life rating	7

ARTS & CULTURE

Library rating	8
Classical music rating	2
Ballet/dance rating	7
Museum rating	3

Calgary, Alberta

Canada Rank: 6

Profile: Large city
Location: Southern Alberta along Highway 1 at the foot of the Rocky Mountains
Elevation: 1,084 meters/3,556 feet

PRO	CON
Nearby mountains	Cost of living
Strong economy	Cold winters

By a sizable margin, Calgary is the fastest growing city in Canada. Located within sight of the Rocky Mountains, the city is modern and clean with a favorable business climate, no provincial sales taxes, and a strong oil industry. The economy has diversified, particularly with tourism, but the area has a boom-town feel and the lowest unemployment rate in Canada at 4.9%. There is plenty to do, both day and night, with mountain recreation opportunities and an active nightlife scene. While not as strong or renowned as larger Canadian cities, the local assortment of arts amenities is complete. The growth and boom-town climate have brought a notably high Cost of Living Index at 121.6, particularly considering lower taxes and land availability.

The climate is northern Great Plains with some mountain influence, including warming chinook winds in winter, but there is no shelter from advancing northerly cold and bitter cold temperatures are common.

Although a bit smaller, Calgary is similar to Denver, Colorado (no. 60), and gets that comparable U.S. rank.

POPULATION

Population	951,395	Median age	34.9	Visible minorities	17.5%
Population density	520 sq. km / 200.8 sq. mile	Average family size	3.2	English-speaking	90.7%
Population growth	15.8%	Single	34.1%	French-speaking	0.1%
		Married	50.9%	Bilingual	7.3%

ECONOMY & JOBS

Household income	C$58,861 / US$41,745
Unemployment rate	4.9%
White collar	80.0%
Blue collar	20.0%

COST OF LIVING

Cost of Living Index	121.6	Average home price	C$201,750 / US$143,085
Provincial income tax	10.0%	Average rent	C$766 / US$543
Provincial sales tax	0.0%	Homes owned	71%
		Homes rented	29%

CLIMATE

January low	-15.1°C / 4.8 °F	Annual days > 30°C / 86°F	4.5	Annual days precipitation	113.6
July high	22.9°C / 73.2°F	Annual days < 0°C / 32°F	196	Annual days snowfall	56.8
Annual precipitation	412.6mm / 16.2 in.	Annual days < -20°C / -4°F	26	Annual sun hours	2,395
Annual snowfall	126.7cm / 49.9 in.				

TEMPERATURE

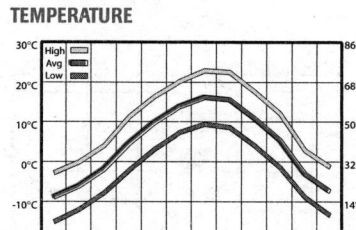

PRECIPITATION

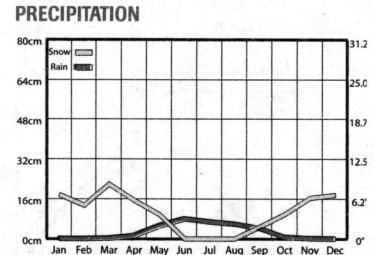

EDUCATION

High school degree	83%
Completed trade school	12%
College degree	19%
University degree	27.4%

CRIME

Violent crime rate	719
Change in violent crime rate	30.0%
Property crime rate	1,639
Change in property crime rate	-1.1%

TRANSPORTATION

Commute by auto	66.3%
Commute by mass transit	12.2%
Work at home	7.1%
Air service (passengers a day)	21,597

LEISURE

Restaurant rating	5	Spectator-sports rating	7
Golf-course rating	7	Inland water rating	4
Ski-area rating	9	Park rating	10
		Quality of life rating	8

ARTS & CULTURE

Library rating	8
Classical music rating	7
Ballet/dance rating	5
Museum rating	7

Chicoutimi-Jonquière, Québec

Canada Rank: 26

Profile: Small-town complex
Location: Northeastern Québec along the Saguenay River, 129 kilometers (80 miles) west of the St. Lawrence Seaway
Elevation: 6.4 meters/21 feet

PRO	CON
Attractive setting	Economy
Cost of living	Isolation

The cities of Chicoutimi and Jonquière lie in the center of a large, forested wilderness in northeastern Québec. Thanks to location, they developed economically as a major center for the pulp and paper industry. Because of greater efficiencies in that industry, employment levels have declined, leaving the area with a 12.4% unemployment rate, the highest in Canada. The attractive fjord setting and nearby recreation have attracted some tourist trade, but there isn't much to do in these towns overall. Chicoutimi is the more interesting of the two; Jonquière has retained more of an industrial character. The area is separated from Québec City by 209 kilometers (130 miles) of wilderness, making access to most big-city amenities and services a challenge.

The area is located in a dramatic river valley setting surrounded by heavily wooded hills. The wet, northern climate, partly influenced by the Atlantic Ocean and St. Lawrence River, produces plenty of cold and the second highest snowfall in the country.

A comparable U.S. city might be Lewiston-Auburn, Maine, (no. 313), giving the area a comparable U.S. rank of 310.

POPULATION

Population	154,938	Median age	39.8	Visible minorities	0.6%
Population density	245.6 sq. km / 94.8 sq. mile	Average family size	3.1	English-speaking	0.1%
Population growth	-3.4%	Single	38.3%	French-speaking	82.5%
		Married	42.9%	Bilingual	17.4%

ECONOMY & JOBS

Household income	C$41,854 / US$29,684
Unemployment rate	12.4%
White collar	73.0%
Blue collar	27.0%

COST OF LIVING

Cost of Living Index	77.1	Average home price	C$84,377 / US$59,482
Provincial income tax	24.0%	Average rent	C$458 / US$325
Provincial sales tax	7.5%	Homes owned	62%
		Homes rented	38%

CLIMATE

January low	-19.5°C / -3.1°F	Annual days > 30°C / 86°F	3.4	Annual days precipitation	150.3
July high	23.4°C / 74.1°F	Annual days < 0°C / 32°F	197.5	Annual days snowfall	50.9
Annual precipitation	1,002.1mm / 39.5 in.	Annual days < -20°C / -4°F	37.1	Annual sun hours	1,676
Annual snowfall	301.5cm / 118.7 in.				

TEMPERATURE

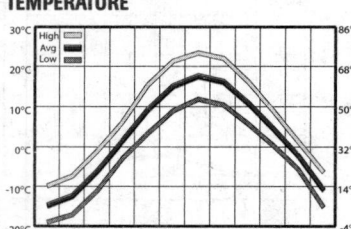

PRECIPITATION

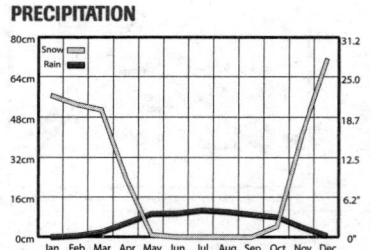

EDUCATION

High school degree	81%
Completed trade school	20%
College degree	20%
University degree	16.9%

CRIME

Violent crime rate	719
Change in violent crime rate	30.0%
Property crime rate	1,639
Change in property crime rate	-1.1%

TRANSPORTATION

Commute by auto	81.5%
Commute by mass transit	2.4%
Work at home	4.1%
Air service (passengers a day)	< 500

LEISURE

Restaurant rating	3	Spectator-sports rating	1
Golf-course rating	3	Inland water rating	9
Ski-area rating	3	Park rating	8
		Quality of life rating	2

ARTS & CULTURE

Library rating	2
Classical music rating	1
Ballet/dance rating	1
Museum rating	2

Edmonton, Alberta

Profile: Large capital city
Location: Center of Alberta along Saskatchewan River
Elevation: 671 meters/2,201 feet

Canada Rank: 8

PRO	CON
Strong economy	Cost of living
Capital-city amenities	Cold winters

Edmonton, Alberta's capital, is Canada's sixth largest city recently outgrown by Calgary, its southern neighbor. Along with Vancouver, Edmonton serves as the major economic and cultural center of western Canada. The area has a long history as an agricultural and transportation gateway between the Prairie provinces and the west. The oil industry has brought cyclical economic boosts during the last 60 years with explosive growth in the 1970s. More recently the city has diversified economically. The tax and business climate are among the best in Canada. The city is laid out in a grid with a mix of old and modern buildings. There are some run-down areas, particularly to the east, and a concentration of industrial areas to the north. Nicer residential sections lie to the west, the location of the West Edmonton Mall, the world's largest and more of an amusement park than a mall. The Cost of Living Index at 118.9 is high but typical of an area with a strong economy. The city has a complete set of leisure and arts amenities.

Edmonton has a strong northern interior climate. The main ridge of the Rocky Mountains is visible to the west across the generally flat to gently rolling, treeless landscape.

Like Calgary, Edmonton compares to Denver, Colorado (no. 60) economically and geographically, but with the harsher climate gets a comparable U.S. rank of 70.

POPULATION

Population	937,845	Median age	36.6	Visible minorities	14.6%
Population density	181.7 sq. km / 70.2 sq. mile	Average family size	3.2	English-speaking	90.9%
Population growth	8.7%	Single	33.7%	French-speaking	0.1%
		Married	50.2%	Bilingual	7.5%

ECONOMY & JOBS

Household income	C$51,685 / US$36,656		
Unemployment rate	5.5%		
White collar	76.0%		
Blue collar	24.0%		

COST OF LIVING

Cost of Living Index	118.9	Average home price	C$146,529 / US$103,921
Provincial income tax	10.0%	Average rent	C$628 / US$445
Provincial sales tax	0.0%	Homes owned	66%
		Homes rented	34%

CLIMATE

January low	-16.0°C / 3.2°F	Annual days > 30°C / 86°F	3.2	Annual days precipitation	125.8
July high	22.8°C / 73.0°F	Annual days < 0°C / 32°F	178.6	Annual days snowfall	54.5
Annual precipitation	476.9mm / 18.8 in.	Annual days < -20°C / -4°F	28.1	Annual sun hours	2,303
Annual snowfall	123.5cm / 48.6 in.				

TEMPERATURE

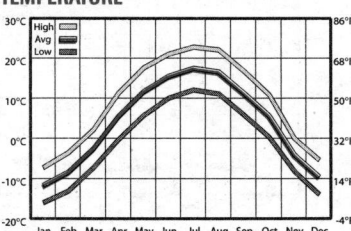

PRECIPITATION

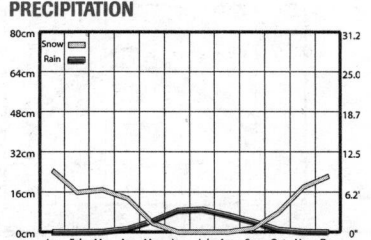

EDUCATION

High school degree	80%
Completed trade school	14%
College degree	19%
University degree	21.3%

CRIME

Violent crime rate	1,099
Change in violent crime rate	3.8%
Property crime rate	3,546
Change in property crime rate	10.3%

TRANSPORTATION

Commute by auto	72.4%
Commute by mass transit	8.1%
Work at home	6.4%
Air service (passengers a day)	10,330

LEISURE

Restaurant rating	7	Spectator-sports rating	8
Golf-course rating	6	Inland water rating	7
Ski-area rating	5	Park rating	8
		Quality of life rating	7

ARTS & CULTURE

Library rating	7
Classical music rating	3
Ballet/dance rating	5
Museum rating	5

Halifax, Nova Scotia

Profile: Large port city
Location: Central Nova Scotia on the Atlantic Coast
Elevation: 70 meters/230 feet

Canada Rank: 13

PRO	CON
Attractive setting	Cloudy, wet climate
Historic interest	Tourist impact

Halifax, a major port city on a natural harbor, is the only Canadian Atlantic city normally operational year-round. The area grew up as a shipping hub and a regional, naval, and governmental center, but has also become a tourist destination. Its crowded waterfront, which has elements of Boston and San Francisco, contains a mix of modern and preserved, historic buildings; entertainment; and tourist activity. This popular area can become crowded, particularly when cruise ships arrive. Most of the residential areas lie inland and to the southwest. The tight geography and water barriers have made public transportation by necessity an important way to get around. In fact, at 9.3%

the area has one of the higher rates of public transport utilization in the country.

The terrain is rocky, hilly, and wooded, typical of the Atlantic Coast. The strong Maritime climate brings heavy clouds, fog, and rain year-round. Annual rainfall is just exceeded by Saint John, New Brunswick, to the northeast and by a handful of U.S. cities. The surrounding terrain is mostly hilly and heavily wooded.

Halifax compares with Portland, Maine (no. 236), although bitter cold is less common, and with Boston, Massachusetts (no. 71), earning a comparable U.S. rank of 150.

POPULATION

Population	359,183	Median age	36.6	Visible minorities	7.0%
Population density	65.4 sq. km / 40.6 sq. mi	Average family size	3.1	English-speaking	88.9%
Population growth	4.7%	Single	34.5%	French-speaking	0.1%
		Married	49.3%	Bilingual	10.7%

ECONOMY & JOBS

Household income	C$46,491 / US$32,972
Unemployment rate	7.2%
White collar	84.0%
Blue collar	16.0%

COST OF LIVING

Cost of Living Index	102.1	Average home price	C$134,286 / US$95,238
Provincial income tax	16.7%	Average rent	C$657 / US$466
Provincial sales tax	7.5%	Homes owned	62%
		Homes rented	38%

CLIMATE

January low	-8.6°C / 16.5°F	Annual days > 30°C / 86°F	0.9	Annual days precipitation	151.6
July high	22.9°C / 73.2°F	Annual days < 0°C / 32°F	136.4	Annual days snowfall	24
Annual precipitation	1,508mm / 59.4 in.	Annual days < -20°C / -4°F	0.9	Annual sun hours	1,949
Annual snowfall	151.8cm / 59.8 in.				

TEMPERATURE

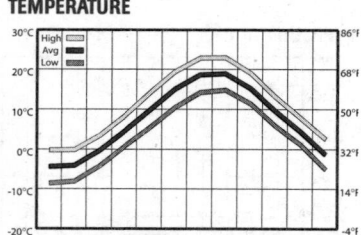

PRECIPITATION

EDUCATION

High school degree	83%
Completed trade school	14%
College degree	19%
University degree	27.9%

CRIME

Violent crime rate	1,046
Change in violent crime rate	5.8%
Property crime rate	3,141
Change in property crime rate	4.8%

TRANSPORTATION

Commute by auto	63.5%
Commute by mass transit	9.3%
Work at home	5.9%
Air service (passengers a day)	8,393

LEISURE

Restaurant rating	5	Spectator-sports rating	2
Golf-course rating	2	Inland water rating	8
Ski-area rating	3	Park rating	6
		Quality of life rating	7

ARTS & CULTURE

Library rating	7
Classical music rating	3
Ballet/dance rating	3
Museum rating	6

Hamilton, Ontario

Profile: Mid-size industrial city
Location: Southwestern Ontario at the western corner of Lake Ontario, 81 kilometers (50 miles) west of Toronto
Elevation: 93 meters/305 feet

Canada Rank: 20

PRO	CON
Revitalizing downtown	Industrial feel
Close to Toronto	Clouds and rain

Hamilton sits in the strategic center of the "Golden Horseshoe" stretching from Toronto to the Niagara/Buffalo area along Lake Ontario. A center to the steel industry, Hamilton is known to many Canadians as "Steeltown." Despite the presence of that industry's infrastructure, the town has modernized and, to some extent, capitalized on its location and ability to offer a relatively attractive lifestyle for a reasonable price. Outside of professional sports, McMaster University, and a handful of museums, there are few local amenities, but the area is close enough to Toronto and Buffalo (97 kilometers/60 miles) to take advantage of their offerings. Cost of living and home prices are 30% lower than Toronto.

Physically Hamilton surrounds the western corner of Lake Ontario. Much of the city is elevated on the Niagara Escarpment, which sits above lowlands containing the major industry and highways. Although the city is on the west (windward) side of Lake Ontario, it is close enough to Lake Huron to the northwest to pick up a wet and sometimes snowy climate.

Geographically and historically, the area is like Toledo, Ohio (no. 267), although recent modernization reminds some of nearby Buffalo (no. 205). The comparable U.S. rank is 230.

POPULATION

Population	662,401	Median age	37.8	Visible minorities	9.8%
Population density	1,341.4 sq. km / 517.9 sq. mile	Average family size	3.2	English-speaking	91.7%
Population growth	6.1%	Single	29.4%	French-speaking	0.1%
		Married	53.5%	Bilingual	6.8%

ECONOMY & JOBS

Household income	C$52,786 / US$37,437
Unemployment rate	5.7%
White collar	74.0%
Blue collar	26.0%

COST OF LIVING

Cost of Living Index	101.9	Average home price	C$183,113 / US$129,867
Provincial income tax	11.2%	Average rent	C$670 / US$475
Provincial sales tax	8.0%	Homes owned	68%
		Homes rented	32%

CLIMATE

January low	-9.7°C / 14.5°F	Annual days > 30°C / 86°F	9.1	Annual days precipitation	157.7
July high	26.3°C / 79.3°F	Annual days < 0°C / 32°F	142.1	Annual days snowfall	55.7
Annual precipitation	910.0mm / 35.8 in.	Annual days < -20°C / -4°F	3.4	Annual sun hours	2,079
Annual snowfall	151.8cm / 59.8 in.				

TEMPERATURE

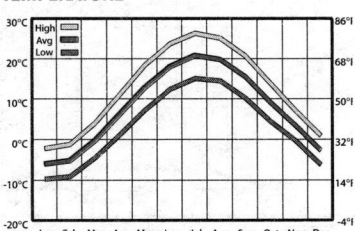

PRECIPITATION

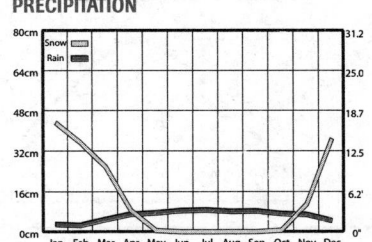

EDUCATION

High school degree	80%
Completed trade school	11%
College degree	21%
University degree	20%

CRIME

Violent crime rate	903
Change in violent crime rate	1.8%
Property crime rate	6,509
Change in property crime rate	1.6%

TRANSPORTATION

Commute by auto	73.2%
Commute by mass transit	7.5%
Work at home	6.0%
Air service (passengers a day)	2,318

LEISURE

Restaurant rating	5	Spectator-sports rating	7
Golf-course rating	5	Inland water rating	7
Ski-area rating	3	Park rating	5
		Quality of life rating	5

ARTS & CULTURE

Library rating	5
Classical music rating	5
Ballet/dance rating	4
Museum rating	5

Kingston, Ontario

Profile: Small city/University town
Location: Eastern Ontario along the St. Lawrence River, half way between Toronto and Montréal
Elevation: 93 meters/305 feet

PRO	**CON**
Historic interest	Arts and culture
Attractive downtown	Entertainment

Canada Rank: 16

Kingston, at one time the provincial capital of Canada under British rule, serves as an economic and cultural hub in the Toronto-Montréal corridor. The location makes it a popular stopover on the Toronto-Montréal trip, and several businesses are located in the area to take advantage of this. The city has an attractive and historic downtown and many preserved older buildings and military installations. The well-recognized Queens University adds a university-town element. Overall, Kingston has more of a European flair than most cities in the province. Beyond downtown are quiet areas of shaded streets and parks. The nearby Thousand Islands provide some recreational

opportunities. However, the downtown core only has a few restaurants, and the area is generally quiet with relatively little to do compared to other cities in the region.

The city sits on the north shore of the St. Lawrence River where it originates from Lake Ontario. Typical of the region, the climate is continental with a marine influence. Winters are fairly cold and wet.

Physically, Kingston is uniquely Canadian and comparable U.S. cities are hard to identify, but like its geography, it is statistically in the middle in many categories. The comparable U.S. rank is 180.

POPULATION

Population	146,838	Median age	38.1	Visible minorities	4.2%
Population density	213.9 sq. km / 82.6 sq. mile	Average family size	3	English-speaking	87.6%
Population growth	1.6%	Single	32.0%	French-speaking	0.8%
		Married	49.9%	Bilingual	8.0%

ECONOMY & JOBS

Household income	C$47,979 / US$34,028	Cost of Living Index	101	Average home price	C$156,445 / US$110,954
Unemployment rate	6.9%	Provincial income tax	11.2%	Average rent	C$672 / US$477
White collar	82.0%	Provincial sales tax	8.0%	Homes owned	64%
Blue collar	18.0%			Homes rented	36%

COST OF LIVING

CLIMATE

January low	-12.2°C / 10.0°F	Annual days > 30°C / 86°F	2.4	Annual days precipitation	157.4
July high	24.8°C / 76.6°F	Annual days < 0°C / 32°F	145.7	Annual days snowfall	52.3
Annual precipitation	968.2mm / 38.1 in.	Annual days < -20°C / -4°F	11.3	Annual sun hours	2,012
Annual snowfall	180.9cm / 71.2 in.				

TEMPERATURE

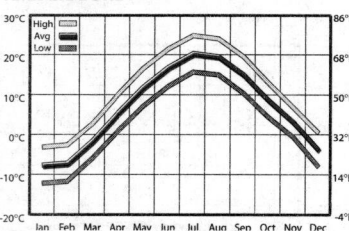

PRECIPITATION

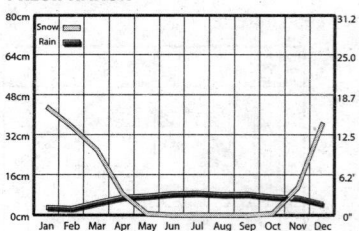

EDUCATION

High school degree	84%
Completed trade school	11%
College degree	22%
University degree	23.7%

CRIME

Violent crime rate	903
Change in violent crime rate	1.8%
Property crime rate	6,509
Change in property crime rate	1.6%

TRANSPORTATION

Commute by auto	68.3%
Commute by mass transit	3.3%
Work at home	7.5%
Air service (passengers a day)	< 500

LEISURE

Restaurant rating	7	Spectator-sports rating	2
Golf-course rating	5	Inland water rating	9
Ski-area rating	6	Park rating	7
		Quality of life rating	6

ARTS & CULTURE

Library rating	4
Classical music rating	3
Ballet/dance rating	3
Museum rating	7

Kitchener-Waterloo, Ontario

Canada Rank: 24

Profile: Mid-size city/University town
Location: Southwestern Ontario, 121 kilometers (75 miles) west of Toronto
Elevation: 371 meters/1,217 feet

PRO	CON
Low unemployment	Home prices
Proximity to Toronto	Entertainment

Kitchener and Waterloo are fairly nondescript cities in a nondescript region of western Ontario. Both support a modest assortment of industry and agriculture in the nearby region, and Waterloo is home to the respected University of Waterloo and Wilfrid Laurier University. While providing some university-town feel, these schools don't add many activities to Waterloo. In general, the area is quiet and light in outdoor recreation and most forms of entertainment. Adding character is a Mennonite community. A strong German influence also exists; this community holds an annual Oktoberfest. A growing number of residents seeking a quiet, smaller-town lifestyle and big-city opportunities commute to the "GTA" (Greater Toronto Area), the fringes of which begin about 45 miles east.

The area, which sits on mostly level terrain, is more exposed to Lake Huron than most cities in Ontario. This results in colder winters and more rain and snow.

Considering the Mennonite influence and other features, Kitchener-Waterloo might compare to Elkhart-Goshen, Indiana (no. 272), with some of the university feel of nearby South Bend, Indiana, mixed in. The comparable U.S. rank is 270.

POPULATION

Population	414,284	Median age	35.3	Visible minorities	10.7%
Population density	1,391.7 sq. km / 537.3 sq. mile	Average family size	3.2	English-speaking	91.4%
Population growth	8.2%	Single	30.4%	French-speaking	0.1%
		Married	53.9%	Bilingual	6.9%

ECONOMY & JOBS

Household income	C$55,528 / US$39,382
Unemployment rate	5.5%
White collar	69.5%
Blue collar	30.5%

COST OF LIVING

Cost of Living Index	104.5	Average home price	C$172,550 / US$122,376
Provincial income tax	11.2%	Average rent	C$695 / US$493
Provincial sales tax	8.0%	Homes owned	67%
		Homes rented	33%

CLIMATE

January low	-11°C / 12.2°F	Annual days > 30°C / 86°F	6.9	Annual days precipitation	164.4
July high	25.9°C / 78.6°F	Annual days < 0°C / 32°F	160.4	Annual days snowfall	96.6
Annual precipitation	907.9mm / 35.7 in.	Annual days < -20°C / -4°F	7.6	Annual sun hours	1,969
Annual snowfall	159.5cm / 62.8 in.				

TEMPERATURE

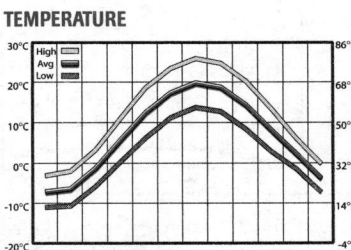

PRECIPITATION

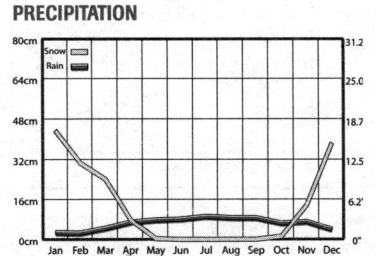

EDUCATION

High school degree	79%
Completed trade school	11%
College degree	19%
University degree	20.4%

CRIME

Violent crime rate	903
Change in violent crime rate	1.8%
Property crime rate	6,509
Change in property crime rate	1.6%

TRANSPORTATION

Commute by auto	76.4%
Commute by mass transit	3.7%
Work at home	5.7%
Air service (passengers a day)	< 500

LEISURE

Restaurant rating	7	Spectator-sports rating	2
Golf-course rating	6	Inland water rating	3
Ski-area rating	6	Park rating	4
		Quality of life rating	5

ARTS & CULTURE

Library rating	4
Classical music rating	3
Ballet/dance rating	1
Museum rating	2

London, Ontario

Canada Rank: 15

Profile: Mid-size city/University town
Location: Southwestern Ontario, 201 kilometers (125 miles) west of Toronto
Elevation: 278 meters/912 feet

PRO	CON
University-town amenities	Entertainment
Small-town feel	Winter climate

London is a middle-of-the-road industrial and agricultural town known for its auto assembly plants, insurance company head offices, and the University of Western Ontario. It is fairly clean and quiet, with a few historic buildings downtown and modest areas of local entertainment. The university brings some university-town amenities, most notably a good collection of museums. The location is a bit isolated from major-city amenities and air service.

The terrain is fairly nondescript. The climate is continental with a strong marine influence particularly from Lake Huron to the north, giving wetter and snowier winters than many other Ontario locations.

The city could be compared to Lansing–East Lansing, Michigan (no. 162), and gets a comparable U.S. rank of 165.

POPULATION

Population	432,451	Median age	36.9	Visible minorities	9.0%
Population density	514.7 sq. km / 198.7 sq. mile	Average family size	3.1	English-speaking	92.2%
Population growth	3.8%	Single	31.4%	French-speaking	0.0%
		Married	50.8%	Bilingual	6.6%

ECONOMY & JOBS

Household income	C$48,026 / US$34,061	Cost of Living Index	101.9	Average home price	C$157,597 / US$111,771
Unemployment rate	6.7%	Provincial income tax	11.2%	Average rent	C$648 / US$460
White collar	75.0%	Provincial sales tax	8.0%	Homes owned	63%
Blue collar	25.0%			Homes rented	37%

COST OF LIVING

CLIMATE

January low	-10.1°C / 13.8°F	Annual days > 30°C / 86°F	8.1	Annual days precipitation	170.4
July high	25.2°C / 77.4°F	Annual days < 0°C / 32°F	148	Annual days snowfall	65.6
Annual precipitation	987.1mm / 38.9 in.	Annual days < -20°C / -4°F	5	Annual sun hours	1,858
Annual snowfall	202.4cm / 79.7 in.				

TEMPERATURE

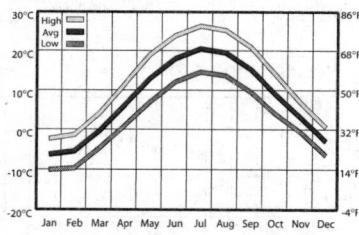

PRECIPITATION

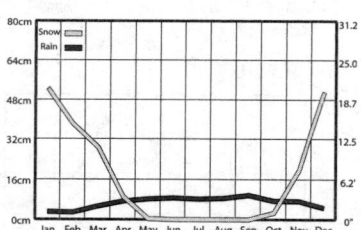

EDUCATION

High school degree	82%
Completed trade school	11%
College degree	22%
University degree	21.1%

CRIME

Violent crime rate	903
Change in violent crime rate	1.8%
Property crime rate	6,509
Change in property crime rate	1.6%

TRANSPORTATION

Commute by auto	72.3%
Commute by mass transit	5.6%
Work at home	6.8%
Air service (passengers a day)	< 500

LEISURE

Restaurant rating	5
Golf-course rating	6
Ski-area rating	5

Spectator-sports rating	2
Inland water rating	7
Park rating	4
Quality of life rating	6

ARTS & CULTURE

Library rating	6
Classical music rating	6
Ballet/dance rating	4
Museum rating	8

Montréal, Québec

Profile: Regional center
Location: South-central Québec along the St. Lawrence River
Elevation: 371 meters/1,217 feet

Canada Rank: 2

PRO	CON
Arts and culture	Economic cycles
Attractive downtown	Political uncertainty

Montréal, a cosmopolitan city with a European accent, is the cultural and economic center of eastern Canada. Its diverse economic base includes manufacturing, service, financial, and government activities. The attractive downtown contains an extraordinary collection of old and modern buildings with a variety of urban settings. The suburbs are also appealing. The excellent public transportation system includes a modern subway. While French language and culture dominate the city, many residents are bilingual and the primary language depends on the neighborhood. The city is packed with cultural and entertainment amenities, including museums, restaurants, theater, and other performing arts. McGill University and the University of Montréal add to the educational and cultural mix. While hurt by the tax structure and political uncertainty caused by the separatist movement in the last decade, the economy has rebounded. At 95.6, the Cost of Living Index is exceptionally low for a city that offers so much.

The area along the St. Lawrence River has rocky and somewhat hilly, wooded terrain. Climate is mainly continental with generally pleasant summers and brisk winters with considerable snow.

Montréal is truly unique against a U.S. background, but might compare to New Orleans (no. 139) culturally and geographically. However, in comparison to that U.S. city, Montréal's crime rate is much lower and the level of intellectual stimulation is much higher. Montréal gets a comparable U.S. rank of 30 and would be higher with a more attractive climate.

POPULATION

Population	3,426,350	Median age	37.9	Visible minorities	13.6%
Population density	2,351.7 sq. km / 908.0 sq. mile	Average family size	3.1	English-speaking	8.5%
Population growth	3.0%	Single	40.9%	French-speaking	39.8%
		Married	40.0%	Bilingual	49.7%

ECONOMY & JOBS

Household income	C$42,123 / US$29,874
Unemployment rate	7.5%
White collar	79.0%
Blue collar	21.0%

COST OF LIVING

Cost of Living Index	95.6	Average home price	C$142,206 / US$100,855
Provincial income tax	24.0%	Average rent	C$568 / US$403
Provincial sales tax	7.5%	Homes owned	50%
		Homes rented	50%

CLIMATE

January low	-12.4°C / 9.7°F	Annual days > 30°C / 86°F	8.2	Annual days precipitation	163.9
July high	26.6°C / 79.9°F	Annual days < 0°C / 32°F	132.2	Annual days snowfall	53.9
Annual precipitation	1,062.6mm / 41.8 in.	Annual days < -20°C / -4°F	7.7	Annual sun hours	2,015
Annual snowfall	226.2cm / 89.1 in.				

TEMPERATURE

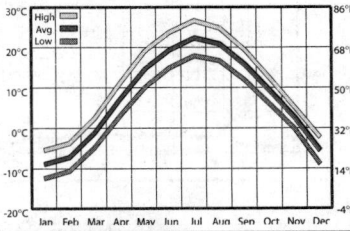

PRECIPITATION

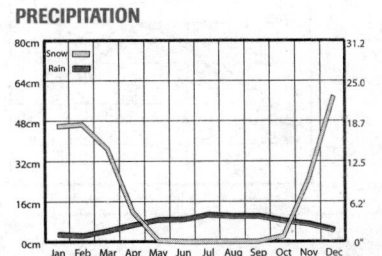

EDUCATION

High school degree	80%
Completed trade school	11%
College degree	18%
University degree	25.9%

CRIME

Violent crime rate	719
Change in violent crime rate	30.0%
Property crime rate	1,639
Change in property crime rate	-1.1%

TRANSPORTATION

Commute by auto	61.7%
Commute by mass transit	20.5%
Work at home	5.5%
Air service (passengers a day)	24,126

LEISURE

Restaurant rating	10	Spectator-sports rating	10
Golf-course rating	8	Inland water rating	5
Ski-area rating	9	Park rating	7
		Quality of life rating	9

ARTS & CULTURE

Library rating	10
Classical music rating	10
Ballet/dance rating	10
Museum rating	10

Oshawa, Ontario

Profile: Small industrial city
Location: Along Lake Ontario, 81 kilometers (50 miles) east of Toronto
Elevation: 84 meters/276 feet

Canada Rank: 21

PRO	CON
Proximity to Toronto	Industrial setting
Nearby water	Economic cycles

Oshawa, an outlying eastern suburb in the "GTA" (Greater Toronto Area), is known mostly as a center for automobile manufacturing and assembly. The area contains several auto plants and mostly middle-class neighborhoods but little else. Economically, Oshawa is dependent on Toronto, but the center city is too far for a regular commute given normal traffic conditions. The many smaller suburbs between Oshawa and Toronto along Highway 401 connect the area to the larger city, and many commute to other suburbs along this route. The economy has experienced large swings in the past, but has recently been strengthening. Most amenities and services are located in Toronto, and

the arts and culture and leisure ratings reflect the proximity. Cost of living also gets a Toronto "halo" and is higher than might be expected for the city type.

The setting on a flat, coastal plain to the northwest of Lake Ontario receives relatively less harsh winters than its U.S. counterparts to the south in New York.

Oshawa compares to Flint, Michigan (no. 234), geographically and economically, although that U.S. city is more complete. Proximity to Toronto is an advantage, so the comparable U.S. rank is 235.

POPULATION

Population	296,298	Median age	35.8	Visible minorities	7.0%
Population density	911.1 sq. km / 351.8 sq. mile	Average family size	3.3	English-speaking	92.8%
Population growth	10.2%	Single	28.8%	French-speaking	0.1%
		Married	54.5	Bilingual	6.7%

ECONOMY & JOBS / COST OF LIVING

Household income	C$62,956 / US$44,650	Cost of Living Index	116.5	Average home price	C$182,790 / US$129,638
Unemployment rate	6%	Provincial income tax	11.2%	Average rent	C$740 / US$525
White collar	72.0%	Provincial sales tax	8.0%	Homes owned	76%
Blue collar	28.0%			Homes rented	24%

CLIMATE

January low	-9.2°C / 15.4°F	Annual days > 30°C / 86°F	2.8	Annual days precipitation	142.1
July high	21.9°C / 71.4°F	Annual days < 0°C / 32°F	131.8	Annual days snowfall	28.5
Annual precipitation	877.9mm / 34.6 in.	Annual days < -20°C / -4°F	3.4	Annual sun hours	2,025
Annual snowfall	118.4cm / 46.6 in.				

TEMPERATURE

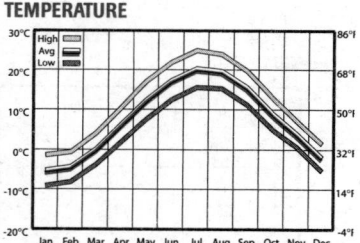

PRECIPITATION

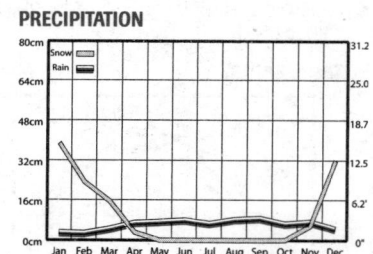

EDUCATION

High school degree	80%
Completed trade school	12%
College degree	23%
University degree	15.3%

CRIME

Violent crime rate	903
Change in violent crime rate	1.8%
Property crime rate	6,509
Change in property crime rate	1.6%

TRANSPORTATION

Commute by auto	75.8%
Commute by mass transit	6.7%
Work at home	5.2%
Air service (passengers a day)	< 500

LEISURE

Restaurant rating	5	Spectator-sports rating	5
Golf-course rating	3	Inland water rating	8
Ski-area rating	4	Park rating	4
		Quality of life rating	5

ARTS & CULTURE

Library rating	4
Classical music rating	5
Ballet/dance rating	5
Museum rating	5

Ottawa-Hull, Ontario-Québec

Profile: Capital-city complex
Location: Along Ottawa River at the Ontario-Québec border
Elevation: 79 meters/259 feet

Canada Rank: 4

PRO	CON
Strong economic base	Cost of living
Attractive downtown	Cold winters

Ottawa is the capital of Canada and its downtown appearance reflects it in every way. The city has avoided tall buildings and skyscrapers in favor of a uniform and dignified, historic appearance. Majestic Gothic government buildings dominate the downtown core, and the area as a whole is clean and inviting. The shady suburbs and parks surrounding the city are also appealing. Hull is a quiet, French-speaking suburb across the Ottawa River. The economy gets a boost from telecommunications research and manufacturing by the likes of Northern Telecom and Bell Canada (whose joint Bell Northern

Research labs are among the world's most advanced). The government provides a stable base behind the technology component, and Carleton University adds a university element. Not surprisingly, the cost of living is high, with a COL Index of 123.2.

The terrain is rolling with mostly deciduous trees that yield spectacular fall seasons. The great distance from large bodies of water makes the winter climate more severe than most places in eastern Canada.

Although much is different, Ottawa compares to Washington, D.C. (no. 26), and gets a comparable U.S. rank of 35.

POPULATION

Population	1,063,664	Median age	36.6	Visible minorities	14.1%
Population density	555.6 sq. km / 214.5 sq. mile	Average family size	3.2	English-speaking	45.8%
Population growth	6.5%	Single	35.4%	French-speaking	9.0%
		Married	48.1	Bilingual	44.0%

ECONOMY & JOBS

Household income	C$59,009 / US$41,850
Unemployment rate	5.6%
White collar	87.0%
Blue collar	13.0%

COST OF LIVING

Cost of Living Index	123.2	Average home price	C$173,610 / US$123,128
Provincial income tax	11.2%	Average rent	C$719 / US$510
Provincial sales tax	8.0%	Homes owned	62%
		Homes rented	38%

CLIMATE

January low	-14.8°C / 5.4°F	Annual days > 30°C / 86°F	10.3	Annual days precipitation	163.4
July high	26.4°C / 79.5°F	Annual days < 0°C / 32°F	153.4	Annual days snowfall	56.6
Annual precipitation	914.2mm / 36.0 in.	Annual days < -20°C / -4°F	18.9	Annual sun hours	2,054
Annual snowfall	202.7cm / 79.8 in.				

TEMPERATURE

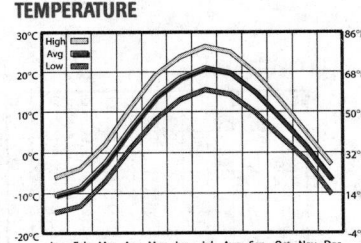

PRECIPITATION

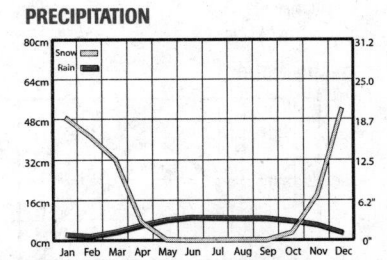

EDUCATION

High school degree	86%
Completed trade school	8%
College degree	19%
University degree	33%

CRIME

Violent crime rate	903
Change in violent crime rate	1.8%
Property crime rate	6,509
Change in property crime rate	1.6%

TRANSPORTATION

Commute by auto	60.4%
Commute by mass transit	17.3%
Work at home	6.1%
Air service (passengers a day)	8,811

LEISURE

Restaurant rating	9	Spectator-sports rating	6
Golf-course rating	8	Inland water rating	6
Ski-area rating	8	Park rating	8
		Quality of life rating	8

ARTS & CULTURE

Library rating	6
Classical music rating	7
Ballet/dance rating	7
Museum rating	10

Québec City, Québec

Canada Rank: 7

Profile: Capital city
Location: East-central Québec along the St. Lawrence River, 242 kilometers (150 miles) northeast of Montréal
Elevation: 74 meters/243 feet

PRO
Attractive setting and downtown
Historic interest

CON
Tourist impact
Cold winters

Québec City, the capital of the province of Québec, is one of the oldest and most interesting cities in North America. The irregular cobblestone streets and stone buildings surrounded by a perimeter wall add to the city's distinct European flavor. The economy is mainly supported by the Québec government and tourism. The city's atmosphere and amenities attract millions of visitors each year. Some of the country's better museums, arts, and entertainment are located there. The largest ski area in eastern Canada is 16 kilometers (10 miles) north. The old city is crowded and tight. Most residents live in the relatively nondescript suburbs outside the old city walls to the west. Cost of living (with a COL Index of 75.7) and housing are surprisingly low for what's available, but household incomes are among the lowest in Canada.

The city is located in the St. Lawrence Valley with hilly to mountainous, wooded terrain, particularly to the north. The climate is continental with relatively severe winters due to latitude and distance from major bodies of water.

A comparable U.S. city is almost impossible to identify, although the historic roots and preservation recall Charlottesville, Virginia (no. 1), but the climate is harsh and the economy is weaker. The comparable U.S. rank is 65.

POPULATION

Population	682,757	Median age	39.5	Visible minorities	1.6%
Population density	601.1 sq. km / 232.1 sq. mile	Average family size	3	English-speaking	0.2%
Population growth	1.6%	Single	44.3%	French-speaking	69.6%
		Married	36.9	Bilingual	30.0%

ECONOMY & JOBS

Household income	C$41,864 / US$29,691
Unemployment rate	6.9%
White collar	83.0%
Blue collar	17.0%

COST OF LIVING

Cost of Living Index	75.7	Average home price	C$101,520 / US$72,000
Provincial income tax	24.0%	Average rent	C$523 / US$371
Provincial sales tax	7.5%	Homes owned	55.5%
		Homes rented	44.5%

CLIMATE

January low	-23.6°C / -10.5°F	Annual days > 30°C / 86°F	4.6	Annual days precipitation	181.9
July high	26.1°C / 79.0°F	Annual days < 0°C / 32°F	175.9	Annual days snowfall	76.4
Annual precipitation	504.0mm / 19.8 in.	Annual days < -20°C / -4°F	31.1	Annual sun hours	1,910
Annual snowfall	114.8cm / 45.2 in.				

TEMPERATURE

PRECIPITATION

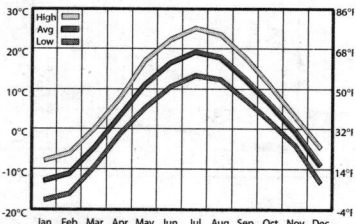

EDUCATION

High school degree	85%
Completed trade school	13%
College degree	22%
University degree	24.9%

CRIME

Violent crime rate	719
Change in violent crime rate	30.0%
Property crime rate	1,639
Change in property crime rate	-1.1%

TRANSPORTATION

Commute by auto	71.8%
Commute by mass transit	9.3%
Work at home	5.2%
Air service (passengers a day)	1,665

LEISURE

Restaurant rating	8	Spectator-sports rating	2
Golf-course rating	5	Inland water rating	4
Ski-area rating	9	Park rating	6
		Quality of life rating	7

ARTS & CULTURE

Library rating	3
Classical music rating	7
Ballet/dance rating	5
Museum rating	9

Regina, Saskatchewan

Profile: Capital city
Location: Southeastern Saskatchewan along Highway 1
Elevation: 79 meters/259 feet

Canada Rank: 18

PRO	CON
Small-town feel	Entertainment
Attractive downtown	Cold winters

Regina, a small city rising above the seemingly endless prairie, is the capital of the province and a regional agricultural, commercial, and financial center. The city is clean, quiet, and traditional, but there isn't a whole lot to do. The few highlights include some worthwhile museums mostly of a local character, a few parks, a CFL team, and good air service to the rest of Canada.

Regina sits in a shallow creek valley on a treeless prairie. The continental climate is harsh and changeable with little to block northerly bitter cold and wind. There are 47.7 days each year with temperatures below –20°C (–4°F). On the positive side, the area is far enough north and away from water to be relatively dry and sunny compared to most Canadian cities.

Bismarck, North Dakota (no. 195), might be a good U.S. comparison, although that American city is in a more lush and protected river valley setting. Nonetheless, the comparable U.S. rank is 195.

POPULATION

Population	192,800	Median age	35.9	Visible minorities	5.2%
Population density	157.2 sq. km / 60.7 sq. mile	Average family size	3.1	English-speaking	93.9%
Population growth	-0.4%	Single	34.6%	French-speaking	0.1%
		Married	49.2%	Bilingual	5.6%

ECONOMY & JOBS

Household income	C$47,757 / US$33,870
Unemployment rate	6%
White collar	82.0%
Blue collar	18.0%

COST OF LIVING

Cost of Living Index	111.5	Average home price	C$107,706 / US$76,387
Provincial income tax	15.5%	Average rent	C$567 / US$402
Provincial sales tax	6.0%	Homes owned	68%
		Homes rented	32%

CLIMATE

January low	-21.6°C / -6.9°F	Annual days > 30°C / 86°F	15.7	Annual days precipitation	114.5
July high	25.7°C / 78.3°F	Annual days < 0°C / 32°F	199.6	Annual days snowfall	57.2
Annual precipitation	388.1mm / 15.3 in.	Annual days < -20°C / -4°F	47.7	Annual sun hours	2,365
Annual snowfall	105.9cm / 41.7 in.				

TEMPERATURE

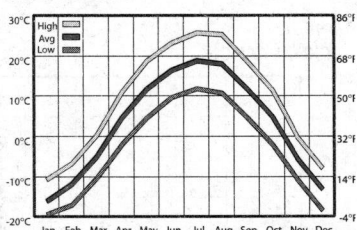

PRECIPITATION

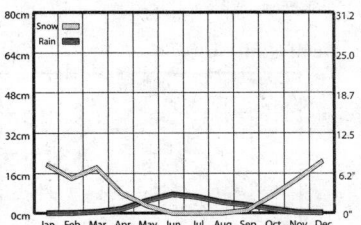

EDUCATION

High school degree	80%
Completed trade school	13%
College degree	16%
University degree	23%

CRIME

Violent crime rate	1,802
Change in violent crime rate	8.0%
Property crime rate	5,793
Change in property crime rate	11.0%

TRANSPORTATION

Commute by auto	75.2%
Commute by mass transit	4.1%
Work at home	5.9%
Air service (passengers a day)	1,942

LEISURE

Restaurant rating	3
Golf-course rating	2
Ski-area rating	2

Spectator-sports rating	3
Inland water rating	5
Park rating	4
Quality of life rating	4

ARTS & CULTURE

Library rating	7
Classical music rating	5
Ballet/dance rating	1
Museum rating	5

St. Catharines–Niagara, Ontario

Profile: Small-city complex
Location: Along the Ottawa River at the Ontario-Québec border
Elevation: 79 meters/259 feet

Canada Rank: 11

PRO	CON
Small-town feel	Arts and culture
Relatively mild climate	Tourist impact

The St. Catharines–Niagara metropolitan area includes the small cities of St. Catharines and Niagara Falls, the more historic and upscale enclave of Niagara-on-the-Lake, and a few other small towns. The area is well known for agriculture and as the gateway to Niagara Falls and Buffalo, New York, to the east. The local towns have a clean and attractive small-town feel. Only Niagara Falls itself suffers a bit from tourism and tourist sprawl; the impact is mainly felt in summer. There isn't much to do in the immediate area, but activities and amenities are available in Buffalo across the border and in Toronto, 145 kilometers (90 miles) away by road.

The influence from Lake Ontario brings extended warmth to the area, particularly in fall. However, the cities are far enough west to avoid the brunt of the lake-effect snows observed in upstate New York to the east. The resulting climate is excellent for fruit orchards and wine grapes—in fact, the area has some of the best wineries in Canada.

A direct U.S. comparison is not easy to make. St. Catharines–Niagara may compare most closely to Green Bay, Wisconsin (no. 108), and has a comparable U.S. rank of 120.

POPULATION

Population	377,009	Median age	40.2	Visible minorities	4.5%
Population density	744.7 sq. km / 287.5 sq. mile	Average family size	3	English-speaking	90.8%
Population growth	1.2%	Single	27.1%	French-speaking	0.2%
		Married	53.3%	Bilingual	8.3%

ECONOMY & JOBS

Household income	C$45,881 / US$32,540
Unemployment rate	6%
White collar	71.5%
Blue collar	28.5%

COST OF LIVING

Cost of Living Index	103.6	Average home price	C$145,432 / US$103,143
Provincial income tax	11.2%	Average rent	C$630 / US$447
Provincial sales tax	8.0%	Homes owned	73%
		Homes rented	27%

CLIMATE

January low	-7.7°C / 18.1°F	Annual days > 30°C / 86°F	13.7	Annual days precipitation	151
July high	27.1°C / 80.8°F	Annual days < 0°C / 32°F	129.2	Annual days snowfall	44.6
Annual precipitation	871.6mm / 34.3 in.	Annual days < -20°C / -4°F	0.9	Annual sun hours	2,079
Annual snowfall	136.6cm / 53.8 in.				

TEMPERATURE

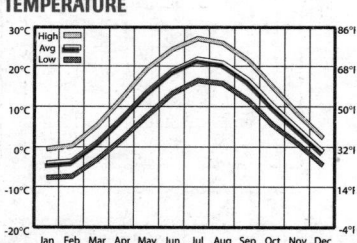

PRECIPITATION

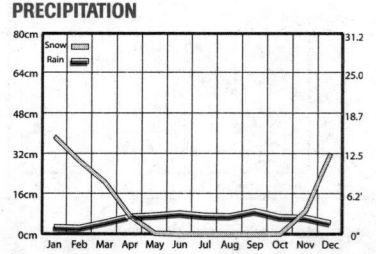

EDUCATION

High school degree	79%
Completed trade school	12%
College degree	20%
University degree	15.6%

CRIME

Violent crime rate	903
Change in violent crime rate	1.8%
Property crime rate	6,509
Change in property crime rate	1.6%

TRANSPORTATION

Commute by auto	78.0%
Commute by mass transit	1.9%
Work at home	5.7%
Air service (passengers a day)	< 500

LEISURE

Restaurant rating	4	Spectator-sports rating	3
Golf-course rating	5	Inland water rating	8
Ski-area rating	3	Park rating	8
		Quality of life rating	7

ARTS & CULTURE

Library rating	5
Classical music rating	3
Ballet/dance rating	3
Museum rating	5

Saint John, New Brunswick

Profile: Small port town
Location: Along southeast coast of New Brunswick, 97 kilometers (60 miles) northeast of the U.S. border at Maine
Elevation: 109 meters/358 feet

Canada Rank: 25

PRO	CON
Historic interest	Economic cycles
Nearby water recreation	Industrial feel

Saint John, originally a Loyalist colony, is a major shipping and industrial gateway for eastern Canada. Industries include shipbuilding, oil refining, pulp and paper, and shipping for a variety of bulk commodities. Economic cycles in a number of these industries have affected the city, parts of which have a gritty industrial feel. Current unemployment is 9.2%, but cost of living and particularly housing are low on a Canadian scale. The downtown area has been revitalized and contains a number of historic buildings with interesting Victorian-era architectural ornamentation. However, the area isn't as interesting as Halifax to the east, and doesn't offer much to do.

The terrain is mostly low, wooded hills. The climate is a rigorous mix of marine and continental. While the area gets a distinct marine influence with frequent Bay of Fundy fogs and precipitation, cold air still invades from the northwest dropping temperatures below −20°C (−4°F) 15.2 times a year.

The area compares to Portsmouth, New Hampshire (no. 287), and gets a comparable U.S. rank of 290.

POPULATION

Population	122,678	Median age	37.9	Visible minorities	2.6%
Population density	101.4 sq. km / 39.2 sq. mile	Average family size	3.1	English-speaking	87.5%
Population growth	-2.4%	Single	30.8%	French-speaking	0.1%
		Married	51.4%	Bilingual	12.3%

ECONOMY & JOBS

Household income	C$41,596 / US$29,501
Unemployment rate	9.2%
White collar	78.0%
Blue collar	22.0%

COST OF LIVING

Cost of Living Index	95.8	Average home price	C$99,483 / US$70,555
Provincial income tax	17.8%	Average rent	C$481 / US$341
Provincial sales tax	7.5%	Homes owned	67%
		Homes rented	33%

CLIMATE

January low	-11.6°C / 11.1°F	Annual days > 30°C / 86°F	0.8	Annual days precipitation	162.3
July high	22.4°C / 72.3°F	Annual days < 0°C / 32°F	168.6	Annual days snowfall	55.7
Annual precipitation	1,390.3mm / 54.7 in.	Annual days < -20°C / -4°F	15.2	Annual sun hours	1,894
Annual snowfall	256.9cm / 101.1 in.				

TEMPERATURE

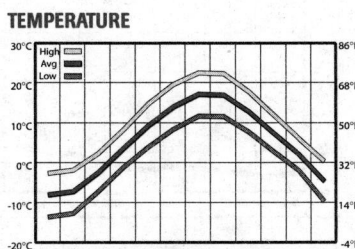

PRECIPITATION

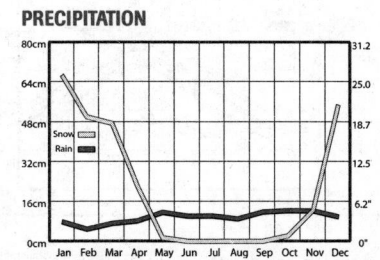

EDUCATION

High school degree	79%
Completed trade school	14%
College degree	18%
University degree	17.6%

CRIME

Violent crime rate	988
Change in violent crime rate	4.8%
Property crime rate	2,664
Change in property crime rate	-0.7%

TRANSPORTATION

Commute by auto	72.6%
Commute by mass transit	4.1%
Work at home	4.7%
Air service (passengers a day)	552

LEISURE

Restaurant rating	3	Spectator-sports rating	2
Golf-course rating	2	Inland water rating	9
Ski-area rating	1	Park rating	5
		Quality of life rating	3

ARTS & CULTURE

Library rating	5
Classical music rating	3
Ballet/dance rating	1
Museum rating	3

St. John's, Newfoundland and Labrador

Canada Rank: 14

Profile: Small port city
Location: Southwestern tip of Newfoundland
Elevation: 141 meters/462 feet

PRO	CON
Attractive setting	Cloudy, wet climate
Cost of living	Isolation

St. John's, the capital of Newfoundland and Labrador, is an old port city reputed to be the oldest city in North America. The natural harbor and central location for Atlantic shipping virtually guarantee its prominence as a shipping center and refueling stop, and as a hub for the fishing industry. Although recent oil discoveries have added to the economy, unemployment is still high. The downtown area on the waterfront is fairly nondescript. The oil industry is financing some new construction, but not without controversy. Because of fires early in the city's history, many of the more interesting historic buildings are in the hills away from downtown. Many modest amenities are available in the area, but it's 940 miles by air or ferry to Halifax for any that are missing.

Downsides include an unpleasant, Maritime climate with rain almost 2 in 3 days year-round and an inhospitable, rocky, hilly, mostly treeless landscape away from town.

Although economic statistics differ, Anchorage, Alaska (no. 160), is the most similar U.S. city. The comparable U.S. rank is the same at 160.

POPULATION

Population	172,918	Median age	36.3	Visible minorities	1.4%
Population density	596.9 sq. km / 230.5 sq. mile	Average family size	3.2	English-speaking	94.5%
Population growth	-0.7%	Single	35.1%	French-speaking	0.0%
		Married	51.0%	Bilingual	5.4%

ECONOMY & JOBS

Household income	C$45,675 / US$32,394
Unemployment rate	11.3%
White collar	84.0%
Blue collar	16.0%

COST OF LIVING

Cost of Living Index	92	Average home price	C$114,086 / US$80,912
Provincial income tax	18.0%	Average rent	C$550 / US$390
Provincial sales tax	7.5%	Homes owned	69.5%
		Homes rented	30.5%

CLIMATE

January low	-8.6°C / 16.5°F	Annual days > 30°C / 86°F	0.2	Annual days precipitation	215.8
July high	20.3°C / 68.5°F	Annual days < 0°C / 32°F	174	Annual days snowfall	84.2
Annual precipitation	1,513.7mm / 59.6 in.	Annual days < -20°C / -4°F	1	Annual sun hours	1,527
Annual snowfall	322.3cm / 126.9 in.				

TEMPERATURE

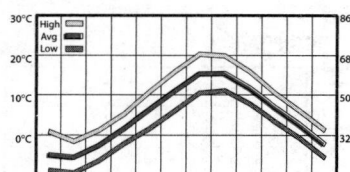

PRECIPITATION

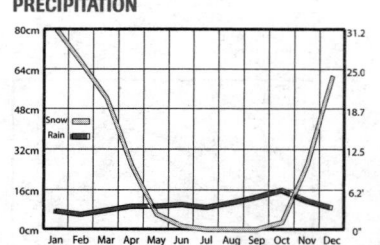

EDUCATION

High school degree	80%
Completed trade school	20%
College degree	17%
University degree	22.7%

CRIME

Violent crime rate	892
Change in violent crime rate	-1.4%
Property crime rate	2,459
Change in property crime rate	1.8%

TRANSPORTATION

Commute by auto	73.1%
Commute by mass transit	2.6%
Work at home	5.0%
Air service (passengers a day)	< 500

LEISURE

Restaurant rating	6	Spectator-sports rating	2
Golf-course rating	2	Inland water rating	8
Ski-area rating	2	Park rating	7
		Quality of life rating	5

ARTS & CULTURE

Library rating	3
Classical music rating	3
Ballet/dance rating	1
Museum rating	6

Saskatoon, Saskatchewan

Profile: Mid-size city
Location: Southwestern Saskatchewan along the South Saskatchewan River
Elevation: 504 meters/1,653 feet

Canada Rank: 12

PRO	CON
Attractive downtown	Isolation
Small-town feel	Cold winters

Regina may be the provincial capital, but Saskatoon is stronger economically and culturally. Of the two Saskatchewan Prairie cities, Saskatoon is larger, more modern and progressive, and offers more to do. However, it's still fairly plain and quiet. Saskatoon is home to the University of Saskatchewan and serves as center to a large agricultural area and potash industry. There are some modest cultural and entertainment amenities, but the real highlight is the vast outdoors and its recreational opportunities.

Although the city sits in more of a river valley than Regina or Winnipeg, the downtown is visible for miles across the prairie. The northern plains climate is pleasant in summer, but quite rugged the rest of the year. Saskatoon's winter cold is second only to Winnipeg in intensity.

Saskatoon compares to Fargo-Morehead, North Dakota (no. 87), but the university presence and cost-of-living profile aren't as strong. The comparable U.S. rank is 130.

POPULATION

Population	225,927	Median age	34.4	Visible minorities	5.6%
Population density	120.8 sq. km / 46.6 sq. mile	Average family size	3.3	English-speaking	92.9%
Population growth	3.1%	Single	34.8%	French-speaking	0.0%
		Married	49.5%	Bilingual	6.5%

ECONOMY & JOBS

Household income	C$43,392 / US$30,774
Unemployment rate	6.7%
White collar	76.5%
Blue collar	23.5%

COST OF LIVING

Cost of Living Index	96.2
Provincial income tax	15.5%
Provincial sales tax	6.0%

Average home price	C$128,335 / US$91,018
Average rent	C$578 / US$410
Homes owned	65%
Homes rented	35%

CLIMATE

January low	-22.3°C / -8.1°F	Annual days > 30°C / 86°F	11.3	Annual days precipitation	111.9
July high	24.9°C / 76.8°F	Annual days < 0°C / 32°F	198.9	Annual days snowfall	56.8
Annual precipitation	350mm / 13.8 in.	Annual days < -20°C / -4°F	52.1	Annual sun hours	2,381
Annual snowfall	97.2cm / 38.3 in.				

TEMPERATURE

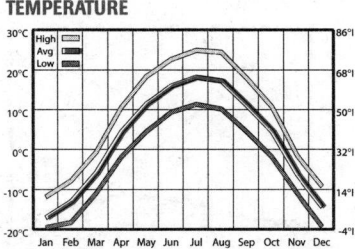

PRECIPITATION

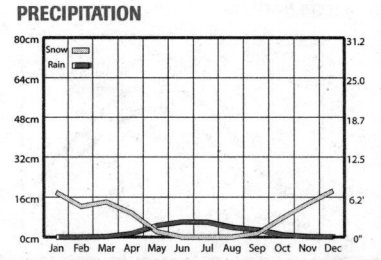

EDUCATION

High school degree	80%
Completed trade school	14%
College degree	17%
University degree	23.8%

CRIME

Violent crime rate	1,802
Change in violent crime rate	8.0%
Property crime rate	5,793
Change in property crime rate	11.0%

TRANSPORTATION

Commute by auto	73.7%
Commute by mass transit	3.8%
Work at home	7.2%
Air service (passengers a day)	2,089

LEISURE

Restaurant rating	2
Golf-course rating	3
Ski-area rating	2

Spectator-sports rating	1
Inland water rating	7
Park rating	7
Quality of life rating	5

ARTS & CULTURE

Library rating	7
Classical music rating	4
Ballet/dance rating	1
Museum rating	4

Sherbrooke, Québec

Canada Rank: 22

Profile: Small city
Location: Southeastern Québec, 56 kilometers (35 miles) north of the U.S. border at Vermont
Elevation: 241 meters/790 feet

PRO	CON
Attractive setting	Entertainment
Nearby outdoor recreation	Arts and culture

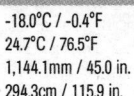herbrooke is a bicultural industrial center located at the edge of the mountainous area extending southward across the U.S. border into Vermont and New York. The city is fairly nondescript and run-down in some areas with a few interesting examples of Victorian-era architecture. There isn't much to do in town, but the nearby mountains and lakes afford a number of quality recreational opportunities. The pace of life is slow and home prices are reasonable.

The surrounding terrain is mainly hilly and wooded. The area is far enough away from major bodies of water to experience harsh winters, but summers are quite pleasant.

The area might compare to Pittsfield, Massachusetts (no. 243), and the comparable U.S. rank is 245.

POPULATION

Population	153,811	Median age	38.1	Visible minorities	2.6%
Population density	385.6 sq. km / 148.9 sq. mile	Average family size	3	English-speaking	1.9%
Population growth	2.8%	Single	42.8%	French-speaking	58.8%
		Married	36.4%	Bilingual	39.1%

ECONOMY & JOBS

Household income	C$36,744 / US$26,060
Unemployment rate	6.9%
White collar	74.0%
Blue collar	26.0%

COST OF LIVING

Cost of Living Index	102.8
Provincial income tax	24.0%
Provincial sales tax	7.5%

Average home price	C$99,458 / US$70,538
Average rent	C$484 / US$343
Homes owned	52%
Homes rented	48%

CLIMATE

January low	-18.0°C / -0.4°F	Annual days > 30°C / 86°F	3.4	Annual days precipitation	192.2
July high	24.7°C / 76.5°F	Annual days < 0°C / 32°F	189	Annual days snowfall	79.4
Annual precipitation	1,144.1mm / 45.0 in.	Annual days < -20°C / -4°F	35.7	Annual sun hours	1,901
Annual snowfall	294.3cm / 115.9 in.				

TEMPERATURE

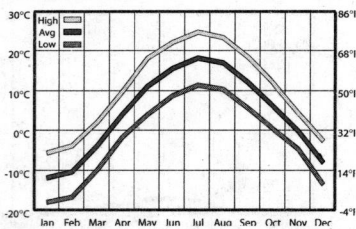

PRECIPITATION

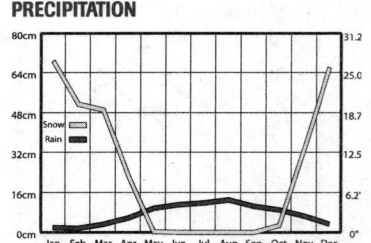

EDUCATION

High school degree	81%
Completed trade school	14%
College degree	20%
University degree	21.8%

CRIME

Violent crime rate	719
Change in violent crime rate	30.0%
Property crime rate	1,639
Change in property crime rate	-1.1%

TRANSPORTATION

Commute by auto	75.1%
Commute by mass transit	5.2%
Work at home	5.9%
Air service (passengers a day)	< 500

LEISURE

Restaurant rating	4
Golf-course rating	3
Ski-area rating	7

Spectator-sports rating	2
Inland water rating	8
Park rating	7
Quality of life rating	4

ARTS & CULTURE

Library rating	3
Classical music rating	3
Ballet/dance rating	1
Museum rating	4

Sudbury, Ontario

Canada Rank: 27

Profile: Small mining city
Location: Northern Ontario, north of Lake Huron, 403 kilometers (250 miles) northwest of Toronto
Elevation: 347 meters/1,138 feet

PRO	CON
Nearby recreation	Isolation
Pleasant summers	Entertainment

Sudbury is a major mining center located in a unique geologic area known as the Precambrian or Canadian Shield. Enormous mines supplying most of the world's nickel have been the economic mainstay for years; other metals are mined as well. The area was once an environmental disaster with so much impact from mining and smelting that the astronauts used it for training in lunar exploration. Public and private sectors have worked together on a cleanup with some success. The town itself lacks interest and there isn't much to do outside a well-known science museum. The area is extremely isolated from larger cities. Outdoor recreational opportunities are available, particularly in the Killarney Provincial Park to the south.

The terrain is rocky and rough—early railroad builders had a particularly difficult time cutting through it. The climate can bring protracted periods of deep winter cold and wind.

Sudbury compares with some differences to Butte, Montana, which is not a U.S. metropolitan area. The equivalent U.S. ranking is 320.

POPULATION

Population	155,219	Median age	38.9	Visible minorities	2.0%
Population density	128.6 sq. km / 49.7 sq. mile	Average family size	3	English-speaking	58.0%
Population growth	-6.1%	Single	29.5%	French-speaking	1.5%
		Married	52.1%	Bilingual	40.1%

ECONOMY & JOBS

Household income	C$45,255 / US$32,096
Unemployment rate	9.1%
White collar	76.0%
Blue collar	24.0%

COST OF LIVING

Cost of Living Index	99.3	Average home price	C$121,671 / US$86,291
Provincial income tax	11.2%	Average rent	C$569 / US$404
Provincial sales tax	8.0%	Homes owned	66%
		Homes rented	34%

CLIMATE

January low	-18.6°C / -1.5°F	Annual days > 30°C / 86°F	5.4	Annual days precipitation	163.9
July high	24.8°C / 76.6°F	Annual days < 0°C / 32°F	182.3	Annual days snowfall	78.4
Annual precipitation	899.3mm / 35.4 in.	Annual days < -20°C / -4°F	36.4	Annual sun hours	1,960
Annual snowfall	274.4cm / 108.0 in.				

TEMPERATURE

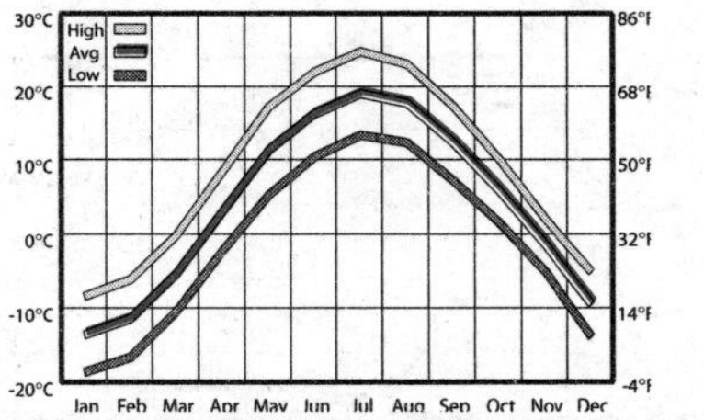

PRECIPITATION

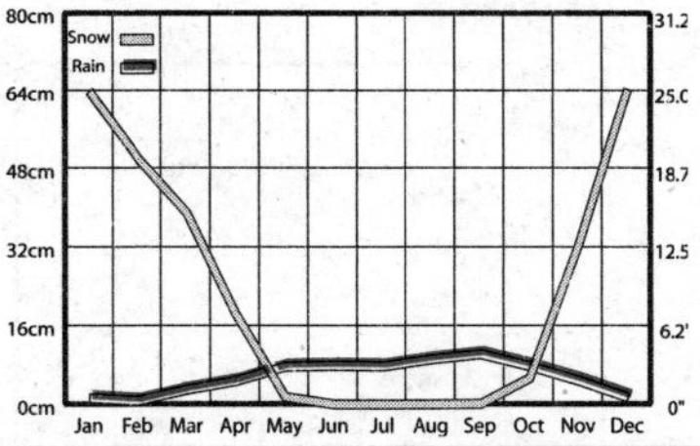

EDUCATION

High school degree	79%
Completed trade school	15%
College degree	21%
University degree	14.9%

CRIME

Violent crime rate	903
Change in violent crime rate	1.8%
Property crime rate	6,509
Change in property crime rate	1.6%

TRANSPORTATION

Commute by auto	74.7%
Commute by mass transit	4.7%
Work at home	4.3%
Air service (passengers a day)	< 500

LEISURE

Restaurant rating	2	Spectator-sports rating	1
Golf-course rating	2	Inland water rating	9
Ski-area rating	4	Park rating	7
		Quality of life rating	2

ARTS & CULTURE

Library rating	5
Classical music rating	1
Ballet/dance rating	1
Museum rating	3

Thunder Bay, Ontario

Profile: Small port city
Location: Northern Ontario on the shore of Lake Superior, 48 kilometers (30 miles) from the U.S. border at Minnesota
Elevation: 199 meters/653 feet

PRO	CON
Nearby outdoor recreation	Economic cycles
Pleasant summers	Entertainment

Thunder Bay, a major Great Lakes inland port, is mainly supported by the shipping of grain and agricultural products and, to a smaller extent, by mining products and manufactured goods. The waterfront is crowded with grain and other shipping terminals. The small, nondescript downtown areas show wear and tear from past economic cycles, although some renewal efforts are underway. Although there is little in the way of in-town entertainment and culture, Thunder Bay is the gateway to world-class lakes, parks, and fishing, making the city a popular summer destination.

The terrain is rocky, moderately hilly, and wooded with numerous lakes and streams. The climate is decidedly continental. Summers are pleasant and moderated by Lake Superior. Winters are bleak and cold with the third highest number of −20°C (−4°F) days in Canada.

The area compares to Duluth, Minnesota (no. 148), but has a less attractive downtown than that city to the south and lacks some of its entertainment. Thunder Bay gets a U.S. equivalent ranking of 190.

POPULATION

Population	121,986	Median age	39.1	Visible minorities	2.2%
Population density	133.1 sq. km / 51.4 sq. mile	Average family size	3.1	English-speaking	91.7%
Population growth	-3.7%	Single	31.0%	French-speaking	0.1%
		Married	50.3%	Bilingual	7.4%

ECONOMY & JOBS

Household income	C$47,489 / US$33,680
Unemployment rate	8.8%
White collar	74.0%
Blue collar	26.0%

COST OF LIVING

Cost of Living Index	97.6	Average home price	C$129,161 / US$91,604
Provincial income tax	11.2%	Average rent	C$570 / US$404
Provincial sales tax	8.0%	Homes owned	72%
		Homes rented	28%

CLIMATE

January low	-21.1°C / -6.0°F	Annual days > 30°C / 86°F	5.8	Annual days precipitation	139.5
July high	24.2°C / 75.6°F	Annual days < 0°C / 32°F	203.3	Annual days snowfall	61.3
Annual precipitation	711.6mm / 28.0 in.	Annual days < -20°C / -4°F	49.1	Annual sun hours	2,183
Annual snowfall	187.6cm / 73.9 in.				

TEMPERATURE

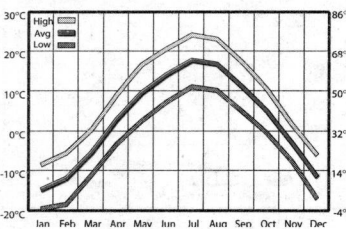

PRECIPITATION

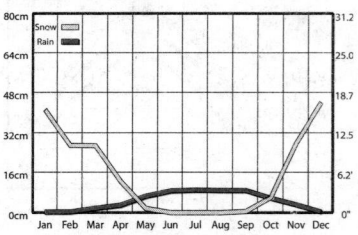

EDUCATION

High school degree	80%
Completed trade school	14%
College degree	21%
University degree	18.3%

CRIME

Violent crime rate	903
Change in violent crime rate	1.8%
Property crime rate	6,509
Change in property crime rate	1.6%

TRANSPORTATION

Commute by auto	78.5%
Commute by mass transit	2.9%
Work at home	4.5%
Air service (passengers a day)	1,542

LEISURE

Restaurant rating	2	Spectator-sports rating	2
Golf-course rating	3	Inland water rating	10
Ski-area rating	5	Park rating	9
		Quality of life rating	5

ARTS & CULTURE

Library rating	5
Classical music rating	3
Ballet/dance rating	1
Museum rating	3

Toronto, Ontario

Canada Rank: 5	

Profile: National center
Location: Northwest shore of Lake Ontario
Elevation: 113 meters/371 feet

PRO	CON
Attractive downtown	Cost of living
Entertainment, arts, and culture	Crowding and sprawl

Toronto, a world-class city and cosmopolitan center, is the largest city in Canada with almost 15% of the country's population. Set in a mostly flat plain north of Lake Ontario, the city has a modern and attractive downtown with a number of unique waterfront features including the CN Tower and the Skydome. A mix of neighborhoods spreads in all directions. Recent immigration and a strong world presence give the city an international flavor that's reflected in most neighborhoods, restaurants, and the arts. There is no shortage of intellectual stimulation or things to do. Toronto has a strong, diverse economy as the transport, commercial, and financial hub for the country and the provincial capital for Ontario. It is also home to York University and the University of Ontario. On the downside, the city has some urban sprawl, traffic, and crowding—problems not commonly found in Canada. At 137.2, the Cost of Living Index is the highest in the country.

The climate is continental with a lake influence. Summers are warm and humid, while winters are cold but not extreme. The north shore location often means Toronto receives little to no snow while New York, south of Lake Ontario, can get 60 centimeters (23.4 inches) from the same storm system.

New York, New York (no. 40), is the functional U.S. equivalent, but Toronto is cleaner and looks more like Chicago. The equivalent U.S. ranking of 40 would be higher with a lower cost of living and fewer traffic problems.

POPULATION

Population	4,682,897	Median age	36.2	Visible minorities	36.8%
Population density	2,203.6 sq. km / 850.8 sq. mile	Average family size	3.3	English-speaking	87.4%
Population growth	9.8%	Single	32.5%	French-speaking	0.1%
		Married	52.9%	Bilingual	8.0%

ECONOMY & JOBS

Household income	C$35,969 / US$25,510
Unemployment rate	5.9%
White collar	80.0%
Blue collar	20.0%

COST OF LIVING

Cost of Living Index	137.2	Average home price	C$273,397 / US$193,899
Provincial income tax	11.2%	Average rent	C$870 / US$617
Provincial sales tax	8.0%	Homes owned	63%
		Homes rented	37%

CLIMATE

January low	-7.3°C / 18.9°F	Annual days > 30°C / 86°F	9.5	Annual days precipitation	145
July high	26.4°C / 79.5°F	Annual days < 0°C / 32°F	106.6	Annual days snowfall	42
Annual precipitation	834.0mm / 32.8 in.	Annual days < -20°C / -4°F	1.4	Annual sun hours	2,038
Annual snowfall	133.1mm / 52.4 in.				

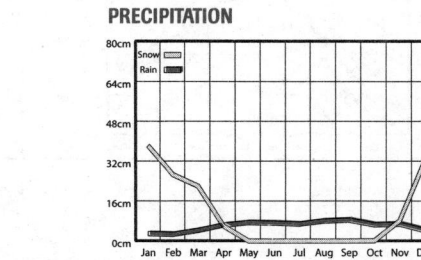

TEMPERATURE

PRECIPITATION

EDUCATION

High school degree	82%
Completed trade school	8%
College degree	17%
University degree	30.8%

CRIME

Violent crime rate	903
Change in violent crime rate	1.8%
Property crime rate	6,509
Change in property crime rate	1.6%

TRANSPORTATION

Commute by auto	60.3%
Commute by mass transit	20.9%
Work at home	6.3%
Air service (passengers a day)	71,402

LEISURE

Restaurant rating	10	Spectator-sports rating	10
Golf-course rating	8	Inland water rating	6
Ski-area rating	6	Park rating	8
		Quality of life rating	8

ARTS & CULTURE

Library rating	10
Classical music rating	10
Ballet/dance rating	10
Museum rating	10

Trois-Rivières, Québec

Canada Rank: 19

Profile: Small industrial town
Location: East-central Québec, along the St. Lawrence River
Elevation: 55 meters/180 feet

PRO
Historic interest
Cost of living

CON
Economy
Industrial feel

Trois-Rivières is an old industrial town mainly supported by pulp and paper manufacturing. It's also one of the oldest towns in North America. Although the forest products industry dominates the town's economy and appearance, there is also a historical presence with some interesting sites and museums. The historic areas downtown offer some local entertainment and color, but overall other Québec cities offer more. Considerable outdoor recreation is available, particularly to the north. The decline in employment in the forest products industry has left its mark, but the cost of living is among the lowest in Canada.

Physically the area sits in the mostly level St. Lawrence Valley with wooded areas and hills, particularly to the north. The climate is typical for the region with pleasant summers and relatively cold winters. The area is far enough from large bodies of water to be drier and colder than many other places in eastern Canada.

Trois-Rivières compares somewhat to the Appleton-Neenah-Oshkosh metropolitan area of Wisconsin (no. 117), but has a weaker economy and a less attractive setting. The equivalent U.S. ranking is 200.

POPULATION

Population	137,507	Median age	41.2	Visible minorities	0.9%
Population density	433.9 sq. km / 167.5 sq. mile	Average family size	2.9	English-speaking	0.1%
Population growth	-1.7%	Single	41.2%	French-speaking	75.4%
		Married	37.6%	Bilingual	24.4%

ECONOMY & JOBS

Household income	C$35,969 / US$25,510
Unemployment rate	9.2%
White collar	73.0%
Blue collar	27.0%

COST OF LIVING

Cost of Living Index	75.7	Average home price	C$82,942 / US$58,824
Provincial income tax	24.0%	Average rent	C$458 / US$325
Provincial sales tax	7.5%	Homes owned	57%
		Homes rented	43%

CLIMATE

January low	-17.6°C / 0.3°F	Annual days > 30°C / 86°F	4.8	Annual days precipitation	116.6
July high	25.5°C / 77.9°F	Annual days < 0°C / 32°F	172.3	Annual days snowfall	48.7
Annual precipitation	1,099.8mm / 43.3 in.	Annual days < -20°C / -4°F	30.1	Annual sun hours	1,910
Annual snowfall	241.3cm / 95.0 in.				

TEMPERATURE

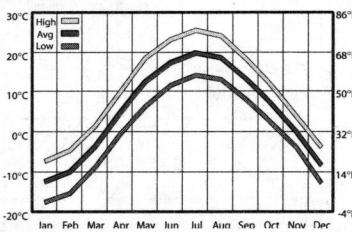

PRECIPITATION

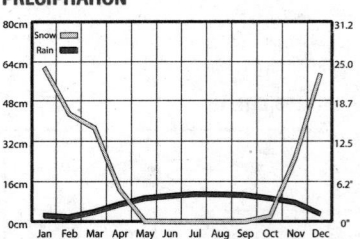

EDUCATION

High school degree	81%
Completed trade school	15%
College degree	19%
University degree	19.2%

CRIME

Violent crime rate	719
Change in violent crime rate	30.0%
Property crime rate	1,639
Change in property crime rate	-1.1%

TRANSPORTATION

Commute by auto	79.7%
Commute by mass transit	2.8%
Work at home	5.2%
Air service (passengers a day)	< 500

LEISURE

Restaurant rating	7	Spectator-sports rating	1
Golf-course rating	3	Inland water rating	6
Ski-area rating	7	Park rating	6
		Quality of life rating	4

ARTS & CULTURE

Library rating	3
Classical music rating	1
Ballet/dance rating	1
Museum rating	7

Vancouver, British Columbia

Canada Rank: 1

Profile: Regional center
Location: Southwest corner of British Columbia along the Straits of Georgia
Elevation: 86 meters/282 feet

PRO	CON
Attractive setting	Crowding and sprawl
Year-round climate	Cost of living

Vancouver, a rapidly growing cosmopolitan city, is the commercial, financial, industrial, and shipping center for the western half of Canada. It's also a busy gateway to the world, particularly the Pacific Rim. Downtown is set on a beautiful natural harbor with forested mountains to the north. The core is attractive and modern with a number of historic districts and waterfront parks and beaches. Neighborhoods vary with some typical big-city suburbs spreading mainly east. The area has seen a large influx of Asian immigration, which, while adding a cultural dimension, has exacerbated some crowding and traffic problems already brought on by the constrained geography. The area has a full set of arts and entertainment amenities, the usual big-city services, and is home to Simon Fraser University. Recreational facilities are varied and excellent.

The climate is marine and considerably milder than most Canada cities, with persistent clouds and rain but few heavy rains, little snow, and no violent weather. Temperatures are comfortable with only 19.6 days per year below freezing and no bitter cold. The climate, a major draw for Canadians, is generally regarded as the most pleasant in the country.

Vancouver compares closely to Seattle, Washington (no. 88), to the south, but with less crowding (so far) and a more stable economy. Still a bit congested, wet, and expensive, the area gets a comparable U.S. ranking of 20.

POPULATION

Population	1,986,965	Median age	37.4	Visible minorities	36.9%
Population density	1,917.5 sq. km / 740.4 sq. mile	Average family size	3.2	English-speaking	87.9%
Population growth	8.5%	Single	33.9%	French-speaking	0.1%
		Married	50.1%	Bilingual	7.4%

ECONOMY & JOBS

Household income	C$49,940 / US$35,418
Unemployment rate	7.2%
White collar	81.5%
Blue collar	18.5%

COST OF LIVING

Cost of Living Index	108.5	Average home price	C$294,847 / US$209,111
Provincial income tax	14.7%	Average rent	C$814 / US$577
Provincial sales tax	7.5%	Homes owned	61.5%
		Homes rented	38.5%

CLIMATE

January low	2.7°C / 36.9°F	Annual days > 30°C / 86°F	0.44	Annual days precipitation	169.1
July high	22°C / 71.6°F	Annual days < 0°C / 32°F	19.6	Annual days snowfall	9.6
Annual precipitation	1,474.9mm / 58.1 in.	Annual days < -20°C / -4°F	0	Annual sun hours	1,919
Annual snowfall	43.6cm / 17.2 in.				

TEMPERATURE

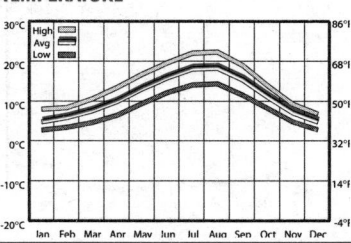

PRECIPITATION

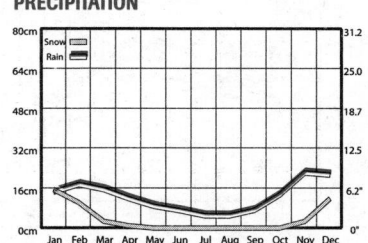

EDUCATION

High school degree	84%
Completed trade school	11%
College degree	18%
University degree	28.7%

CRIME

Violent crime rate	1,217
Change in violent crime rate	-2.8%
Property crime rate	3,762
Change in property crime rate	2.9%

TRANSPORTATION

Commute by auto	72.2%
Commute by mass transit	10.5%
Work at home	8.1%
Air service (passengers a day)	41,307

LEISURE

Restaurant rating	10	Spectator-sports rating	7
Golf-course rating	9	Inland water rating	9
Ski-area rating	10	Park rating	10
		Quality of life rating	10

ARTS & CULTURE

Library rating	10
Classical music rating	9
Ballet/dance rating	9
Museum rating	9

Victoria, British Columbia

Profile: Capital city
Location: Southern end of Vancouver Island
Elevation: 347 meters/1,138 feet

Canada Rank: 3

PRO	CON
Attractive downtown	High home prices
Year-round climate	Tourist impact

Victoria is a provincial capital and the cultural capital of "British" British Columbia. The city was once an important commercial center and port for distributing the natural resources of Vancouver Island and, to a lesser extent, for serving the mainland, but that role has diminished with the depletion of those resources and the emergence of Vancouver to the east. Today the area has turned its history, pleasant downtown, and strong British influence into a tourist attraction. Tourism is now the dominant industry, and the city is particularly crowded in summer. Nonetheless, Victoria is quiet and pleasant. The downtown, harbor area, and suburbs are particularly clean and attractive

with a European flavor. The cultural and entertainment amenities are mainly of interest to tourists, but are of sufficient quality to benefit residents. Some services and amenities require a trip to Vancouver, usually a full-day excursion.

The area is surrounded by saltwater channels and islands. Wooded hills and mountains rise to the northwest. The Pacific marine climate is mild but wet with few temperature extremes. Summers are very pleasant.

A U.S. counterpart doesn't really exist, but there are similarities to Olympia, Washington (no. 16). Victoria gets a comparable U.S. rank of 35.

POPULATION

Population	311,902	Median age	41	Visible minorities	8.9%
Population density	1,246.1 sq. km / 481.1 sq. mile	Average family size	2.9	English-speaking	90.6%
Population growth	2.5%	Single	31.7%	French-speaking	0.0%
		Married	47.6%	Bilingual	8.6%

ECONOMY & JOBS

Household income	C$46,387 / US$32,899
Unemployment rate	6.6%
White collar	85.0%
Blue collar	15.0%

COST OF LIVING

Cost of Living Index	94.2	Average home price	C$243,970 / US$173,028
Provincial income tax	14.7%	Average rent	C$728 / US$516
Provincial sales tax	7.5%	Homes owned	72%
		Homes rented	28%

CLIMATE

January low	7.2°C / 45.0°F	Annual days > 30°C / 86°F	0.05	Annual days precipitation	149.3
July high	20.1°C / 68.2°F	Annual days < 0°C / 32°F	10.3	Annual days snowfall	3.4
Annual precipitation	686.1mm / 27.0 in.	Annual days < -20°C / -4°F	0	Annual sun hours	2,082
Annual snowfall	12.5cm / 4.9 in.				

TEMPERATURE

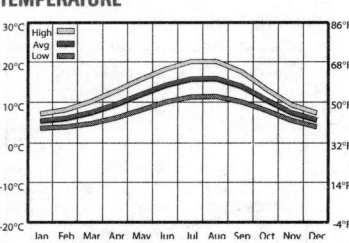

PRECIPITATION

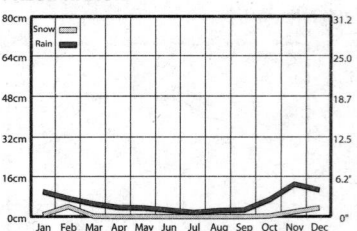

EDUCATION

High school degree	86%
Completed trade school	12%
College degree	20%
University degree	26.6%

CRIME

Violent crime rate	1,217
Change in violent crime rate	-2.8%
Property crime rate	3,762
Change in property crime rate	2.9%

TRANSPORTATION

Commute by auto	60.9%
Commute by mass transit	8.8%
Work at home	9.2%
Air service (passengers a day)	3,020

LEISURE

Restaurant rating	9	Spectator-sports rating	2
Golf-course rating	8	Inland water rating	5
Ski-area rating	5	Park rating	9
		Quality of life rating	9

ARTS & CULTURE

Library rating	8
Classical music rating	6
Ballet/dance rating	5
Museum rating	9

Windsor, Ontario

Canada Rank: 23

Profile: Mid-size city
Location: Southwestern Ontario across the Detroit River from Detroit, Michigan
Elevation: 176 meters/577 feet

PRO	CON
Entertainment	Industrial feel
Proximity to Detroit	Unattractive areas

Windsor, essentially a border town with strong ties to Detroit, Michigan, is linked physically and metaphorically to the United States by the Ambassador Bridge. Like Detroit, the area's economy is driven by the auto industry and related manufacturing, but it also benefits from trade with the United States. The revitalized downtown and attractive waterfront areas provide entertainment for Canadians and Americans alike. While entertainment is a plus, most arts, cultural activities, sports, and services are found in Detroit. There are many areas of the city that reflect its heavy industrial character. Unlike many Canadian cities, Windsor offers little historic interest and no European flavor.

The terrain is mostly level coastal plain. The climate is Great Lakes marine, a continental type with relatively few extremes due to water moderation. Still, winters are cold and damp.

The area might compare to Toledo, Ohio (no. 267), or Detroit (no. 263) without its size and big-city amenities. The comparable U.S. rank is 265.

POPULATION

Population	307,877	Median age	39	Visible minorities	12.9%
Population density	836.4 sq. km / 322.9 sq. mile	Average family size	3.2	English-speaking	87.8%
Population growth	7.3%	Single	30.8%	French-speaking	0.2%
		Married	49.3%	Bilingual	10.5%

ECONOMY & JOBS

Household income	C$54,542 / US$38,682
Unemployment rate	6.3%
White collar	67.0%
Blue collar	33.0%

COST OF LIVING

Cost of Living Index	101	Average home price	C$160,656 / US$113,940
Provincial income tax	11.2%	Average rent	C$658 / US$467
Provincial sales tax	8.0%	Homes owned	72%
		Homes rented	28%

CLIMATE

January low	-4.5°C / 23.9°F	Annual days > 30°C / 86°F	20.7	Annual days precipitation	115.7
July high	27.9°C / 82.2°F	Annual days < 0°C / 32°F	122.8	Annual days snowfall	45
Annual precipitation	805.2mm / 31.7 in.	Annual days < -20°C / -4°F	1.6	Annual sun hours	2,045
Annual snowfall	126.6cm / 49.8 in.				

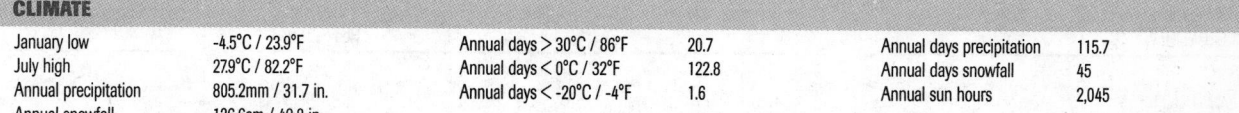

TEMPERATURE

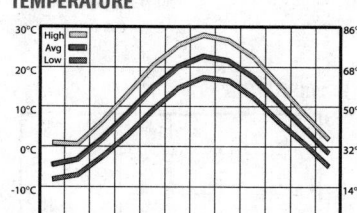

PRECIPITATION

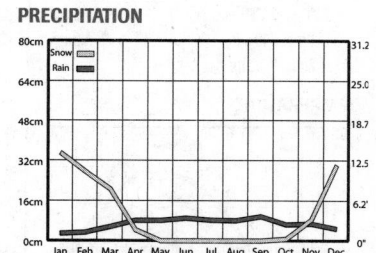

EDUCATION

High school degree	82%
Completed trade school	11%
College degree	17%
University degree	20.6%

CRIME

Violent crime rate	903
Change in violent crime rate	1.8%
Property crime rate	6,509
Change in property crime rate	1.6%

TRANSPORTATION

Commute by auto	77.0%
Commute by mass transit	2.8%
Work at home	3.5%
Air service (passengers a day)	< 500

LEISURE

Restaurant rating	7	Spectator-sports rating	5
Golf-course rating	5	Inland water rating	8
Ski-area rating	4	Park rating	7
		Quality of life rating	5

ARTS & CULTURE

Library rating	5
Classical music rating	5
Ballet/dance rating	3
Museum rating	5

Winnipeg, Manitoba

Profile: Mid-size capital city
Location: Southeastern Manitoba at the confluence of Red and Assiniboine rivers
Elevation: 239 meters/784 feet

Canada Rank: 9

PRO	CON
Attractive downtown	Severe winters
Arts and culture	Unattractive landscape

If it weren't for the climate, Winnipeg would be among the top cities in Canada and in North America. Similar to Chicago or St. Louis in the United States, the city serves as a transportation gateway and commercial center for a vast agricultural region, mainly to the west. The city itself is clean, well planned, and modern with attractive buildings and parks and never a feeling of crowding. The economic base is diverse and secure, and the surprising arts and culture establishment is among the best in Canada. The Royal Winnipeg Ballet has a global reputation, and the other performing arts and museums complement it. The downside is climate, which is so severe that the city is the object of ridicule from most Canadians ("Winterpeg, Mani-snowba").

Winnipeg sits in the path of arctic air flow with no topographic protection. Winter cold extends beyond unpleasant to plainly dangerous. Summers, in contrast, are pleasant to quite warm and dry. The city may be the coldest but is also the sunniest in Canada.

The area is similar to Chicago, Illinois (no. 155), but not as big; Minneapolis–St. Paul, Minnesota (no. 24), but not as expensive; and St. Louis, Missouri (no. 97), but culturally stronger. The comparable U.S. rank is 75.

POPULATION

Population	671,274	Median age	37.3	Visible minorities	12.5%
Population density	161.7 sq. km / 62.4 sq. mile	Average family size	3.1	English-speaking	87.9%
Population growth	0.6%	Single	33.1%	French-speaking	0.1%
		Married	49.3%	Bilingual	10.9%

ECONOMY & JOBS

Household income	C$44,562 / US$31,604
Unemployment rate	5.6%
White collar	78.0%
Blue collar	22.0%

COST OF LIVING

Cost of Living Index	94.7	Average home price	C$104,331 / US$73,994
Provincial income tax	17.4%	Average rent	C$540 / US$383
Provincial sales tax	7.0%	Homes owned	65.5%
		Homes rented	34.5%

CLIMATE

January low	-23.6°C / -10.5°F	Annual days > 30°C / 86°F	13.5	Annual days precipitation	123.5
July high	26.1°C / 79.0°F	Annual days < 0°C / 32°F	194	Annual days snowfall	54.7
Annual precipitation	504.0mm / 19.8 in.	Annual days < -20°C / -4°F	57.5	Annual sun hours	2,577
Annual snowfall	114.8cm / 45.2 in.				

TEMPERATURE

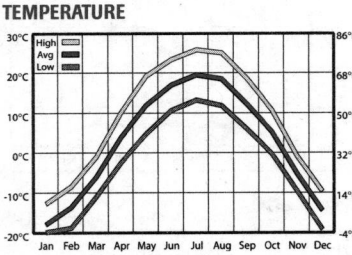

PRECIPITATION

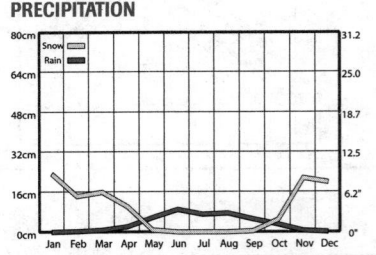

EDUCATION

High school degree	78%
Completed trade school	12%
College degree	17%
University degree	22.7%

CRIME

Violent crime rate	1,620
Change in violent crime rate	-1.5%
Property crime rate	5,136
Change in property crime rate	11.5%

TRANSPORTATION

Commute by auto	70.0%
Commute by mass transit	14.3%
Work at home	5.6%
Air service (passengers a day)	7,351

LEISURE

Restaurant rating	8	Spectator-sports rating	5
Golf-course rating	6	Inland water rating	8
Ski-area rating	3	Park rating	5
		Quality of life rating	7

ARTS & CULTURE

Library rating	8
Classical music rating	8
Ballet/dance rating	10
Museum rating	7

chapter 7

Emerging U.S. Metropolitan Areas

In June 2003 the U.S. Office of Management and Budget (OMB) redefined U.S. statistical geography as explained earlier in chapter 1. One outcome was the creation of 45 new Metropolitan Statistical Areas (MSAs). Since most of these cities are, by definition, growing rapidly, *Cities Ranked & Rated* considers it important to evaluate them. Since the OMB determination was too recent to do a full analysis and treatment, this chapter presents an abbreviated assessment.

Ranking & Rating Emerging Cities

The evaluation of emerging cities includes an abbreviated statistical table similar to that presented for the 331 principal U.S. areas in chapter 5. The source and use of these attributes are explained in chapter 3 and summarized in Table 5.1. The main difference between the data collected for chapter 5 and the abbreviated data shown here is that detailed leisure and arts and culture ratings have been consolidated into two single ratings presented on a 1–10 scale.

Rankings are determined within the set of emerging cities on a 1–45 scale, 1 being the best and 45 the worst. Because the data set is so abbreviated, there is no attempt to feather these cities into the principal metropolitan area rankings in chapter 5.

Table 7.1 shows the rankings and selected statistics for these areas. For an alphabetical listing of the emerging cities refer to Table 1.3.

Table 7.1: Emerging U.S. Metropolitan Areas: Rankings & Selected Statistics

Emerging U.S. Metropolitan Area	Emerging MSA Rank	2002 Population	1990 - 2002 Population Growth	Unemployment Rate	Cost of Living Index	Annual Precipitation (inches)	Annual Snowfall (inches)	Days Above 90°F	Days Below 32°F	4-Year College Degree	Leisure Rating	Arts & Culture Rating
Ithaca, NY	1	96,493	2.5%	2.9%	96.2	38.5	107	9	136	20.8%	7	6
Bend, OR	2	121,506	62.1%	7.3%	106.5	47.3	7	15	54	17.1%	7	3
Mount Vernon–Anacortes, WA	3	105,822	33.0%	7.6%	104.6	32.6	3.8	1	56	13.8%	4	2
Logan, UT	4	105,391	32.7%	3.2%	92.1	17.6	57.5	23	145	19.8%	5	2
Coeur d'Alene, ID	5	114,415	63.9%	6.5%	96.8	17	51	18	140	13.1%	6	3
Prescott, AZ	6	179,030	66.2%	3.2%	101.2	21.6	21	3	210	13.1%	3	3
Vero Beach, FL	7	120,519	33.6%	7.5%	103.9	49.8	0	34	1	15.2%	5	3
Blacksburg-Christiansburg-Radford, VA	8	154,456	9.8%	3.4%	85.4	40.6	24	31	90	14.2%	3	2
Brunswick, GA	9	94,902	15.4%	3.8%	134.6	52	0	83	16	12.1%	5	2
Idaho Falls, ID	10	103,498	16.6%	2.9%	86.0	11.3	43	33	166	16.2%	5	1
Lewiston, ID	11	57,987	12.9%	4.1%	91.6	12.6	15	40	89	12.7%	3	2
Ames, IA	12	80,910	9.0%	2.6%	88.2	31.8	33	26	137	24.9%	3	3
Bowling Green, KY	13	106,256	20.6%	5.0%	86.7	47.4	11	51	76	13.3%	4	2
Columbus, IN	14	71,906	13.0%	4.2%	87.4	40.2	25	19	119	13.6%	3	2
Ocean City, NJ	15	102,842	8.2%	6.1%	129.1	40.7	18	16	15	15.5%	6	1
Wenatchee, WA	16	101,967	30.0%	9.1%	101.4	8.9	27.2	33	115	13.5%	2	1
Winchester, VA-WV	17	106,276	26.3%	3.5%	88.2	40.4	23	28	116	11.6%	2	2
Harrisonburg, VA	18	113,079	28.2%	2.3%	95.1	44.5	71	2	145	14.3%	2	2
Hot Springs, AR	19	89,640	22.1%	5.5%	84.9	51.3	7	62	51	11.7%	2	2
Farmington, NM	20	116,673	27.4%	7.3%	90.2	8.2	13.6	58	152	8.8%	3	2
Gainesville, GA	21	148,913	56.0%	3.4%	94.8	49.7	3	50	54	11.9%	2	3
Morgantown, WV	22	111,857	7.0%	3.8%	88.0	37.1	43	8	121	12.7%	2	2
Salisbury, MD	23	112,202	14.8%	4.9%	90.6	41.9	14	21	67	12.3%	1	2
Sandusky, OH	24	79,432	3.5%	4.9%	97.8	32.6	37	14	141	11.0%	5	2
Michigan City–LaPorte, IN	25	109,669	2.4%	6.0%	89.1	35.4	39	17	132	9.0%	1	2
Lebanon, PA	26	121,328	6.7%	4.0%	89.5	36	35	24	107	9.5%	2	2
Kingston, NY	27	178,649	8.1%	3.5%	112.4	35.8	63	11	150	13.8%	2	1
Elizabethtown, KY	28	108,254	7.3%	5.1%	81.5	43.9	17	35	90	8.5%	2	1
St. George, UT	29	94,677	95.0%	4.1%	102.0	8.4	3.5	113	90	13.9%	4	3
Fond du Lac, WI	30	98,082	8.9%	4.9%	91.6	28.3	36	7	163	12.0%	4	1
Fairbanks, AK	31	83,233	7.1%	5.8%	113.7	10.8	67.8	0	225	16.4%	2	2
Dalton, GA	32	123,862	25.6%	3.5%	88.4	53.3	4	48	73	7.0%	1	2
Cleveland, TN	33	105,857	21.2%	4.5%	86.1	53.3	4	48	73	9.5%	2	2
Monroe, MI	34	148,326	11.0%	6.1%	102.3	32	39	11	139	9.6%	1	2
Morristown, TN	35	125,882	25.1%	4.9%	82.1	53.2	10	27	91	7.8%	2	2
Danville, IL	36	82,529	-6.5%	7.1%	81.8	40.2	25	15	122	8.3%	1	1
Jefferson City, MO	37	142,368	17.9%	3.0%	85.4	39.9	27	37	108	14.1%	2	3
Valdosta, GA	38	122,650	23.6%	3.1%	84.1	63.3	0.1	86	31	11.1%	1	2
Rome, GA	39	92,136	13.4%	4.8%	85.2	53.3	4	48	73	10.0%	2	2
Carson City, NV	40	55,155	36.4%	6.0%	113.2	10.5	21.2	50	178	11.9%	3	2
Hinesville–Fort Stewart, GA	41	74,225	25.9%	4.9%	87.7	49.2	0.1	69	31	8.7%	2	1
Madera, CA	42	128,657	46.1%	12.8%	116.0	10.6	0	107	29	8.2%	2	1
Longview-Kelso, WA	43	94,680	15.3%	9.8%	101.3	48.1	5	6	57	8.4%	2	1
Hanford-Corcoran, CA	44	136,303	34.3%	14.1%	98.3	7.4	0.1	111	30	7.6%	2	1
El Centro, CA	45	146,356	33.9%	17.1%	100.7	3	0.1	179	2	6.6%	2	1

Source: U.S. Census Bureau, Department of Labor, National Climatic Data Center, Center for Education Statistics, Sperling's BestPlaces

Ames, IA

Emerging City Rank: 12

Profile: College town
Location: Central Iowa, north of Des Moines
Elevation: 921 feet

PRO
College-town amenities
Cost of living

CON
Outdoor recreation
Harsh winters

Home to Iowa State University, Ames is a pleasant college town 25 miles north of Des Moines along I-35. The economic base is steady, educational attainment is high, and the cost of living at 88.2 is reasonable for the profile. It has a solid Midwestern feel, but some may not find enough to do in the area nor in Des Moines to the south. The terrain is mainly slightly rolling and agricultural; the climate is continental with strong seasonal variations.

POPULATION
Population	80,910
Population growth	9.0%
Diversity measure	13.7%

ECONOMY & JOBS
Household income	$48,074
Unemployment rate	3.0%
Recent job growth	-9.0%

COST OF LIVING
Cost of Living Index	88.2
Median home price	$113,100
Home price appreciation	4.8%

CLIMATE
January low	11.0°F
July high	86.0°F
July relative humidity	60.0%

Annual days > 90°F	26
Annual days < 32°F	137
Annual days < 0°F	16

Annual inches precipitation	31.8
Annual inches snowfall	33.0
Annual days precipitation	106

EDUCATION
High school degree	93.5%
4-year college degree	24.9%
Graduate/professional degree	19.6%

HEALTH & HEALTHCARE
Air-quality score	5
Physicians per capita	194.0
Hospital beds per capita	344.8

AMENITIES
Miles to nearest major airport	34
Leisure rating	2
Arts & Culture rating	2

Bend, OR

Emerging City Rank: 2

Profile: Resort town
Location: Central Oregon, just east of the Cascade Range
Elevation: 3,623 feet

PRO
Nearby mountains
Outdoor recreation

CON
Cost of living
Isolation

Bend is an artsy resort community in the high Oregon desert just east of the Cascade Range and the Mount Bachelor ski area. It is Oregon's Aspen with a fairly upscale clientele, several resort communities, and an attractive small downtown. Downsides include a high cost of living, especially housing, and a difficult (particularly in winter), 160-mile drive to Portland for services. Climate is typical high desert: dry with sagebrush, pleasant summers, and variable winters.

POPULATION
Population	121,506
Population growth	62.1%
Diversity measure	10.9%

ECONOMY & JOBS
Household income	$41,042
Unemployment rate	6.2%
Recent job growth	-.1%

COST OF LIVING
Cost of Living Index	106.5
Median home price	$181,700
Home price appreciation	5.0%

CLIMATE
January low	33.0°F
July high	82.0°F
July relative humidity	25.0%

Annual days > 90°F	15
Annual days < 32°F	54
Annual days < 0°F	4

Annual inches precipitation	47.3
Annual inches snowfall	7.0
Annual days precipitation	136

EDUCATION
High school degree	88.4%
4-year college degree	17.1%
Graduate/professional degree	7.9%

HEALTH & HEALTHCARE
Air-quality score	3
Physicians per capita	246.1
Hospital beds per capita	190.1

AMENITIES
Miles to nearest major airport	103
Leisure rating	4
Arts & Culture rating	3

Blacksburg-Christiansburg-Radford, VA

Emerging City Rank: 8

Profile: Small-town complex/College-town complex
Location: Southwestern Virginia, southwest of Roanoke
Elevation: 2,080 feet

PRO	CON
Attractive setting	Low incomes
Cost of living	Arts and culture

This tri-city area, home to Virginia Polytechnic Institute (better known as Virginia Tech), combines small-town feel and college-town amenities with a mountain setting, outdoor recreation, and proximity to Roanoke (30 miles to the northeast). While some big-city services and amenities are missing, the blend of available features and cost of living are attractive. The location along the Appalachian and Blue Ridge mountains experiences a relatively pleasant climate in all seasons.

POPULATION		ECONOMY & JOBS		COST OF LIVING	
Population	154,456	Household income	$33,526	Cost of Living Index	85.4
Population growth	9.8%	Unemployment rate	3.2%	Median home price	$123,000
Diversity measure	14.1%	Recent job growth	3.1%	Home price appreciation	9.3%

CLIMATE					
January low	25.0°F	Annual days > 90°F	31	Annual inches precipitation	40.6
July high	86.4°F	Annual days < 32°F	90	Annual inches snowfall	24.0
July relative humidity	54.0%	Annual days < 0°F	0	Annual days precipitation	120

EDUCATION		HEALTH & HEALTHCARE		AMENITIES	
High school degree	80.1%	Air-quality score	6	Miles to nearest major airport	26
4-year college degree	14.2%	Physicians per capita	165.7	Leisure rating	3
Graduate/professional degree	13.6%	Hospital beds per capita	311.4	Arts & Culture rating	2

Bowling Green, KY

Emerging City Rank: 13

Profile: Small town/College town
Location: Western Kentucky, south of Louisville
Elevation: 496 feet

PRO	CON
Small-town feel	Isolation
Nearby national park	Hot, humid summers

Bowling Green, located 120 miles south of Louisville and 20 miles north of the Tennessee border, has a diverse economic and agricultural base. Best known as the city where the Chevrolet Corvette is built, this pleasant, small town is also home to the 15,000 students of Western Kentucky University. Mammoth Cave National Park is located just to the north. The area is a gently rolling mix of deciduous woods and agricultural land. The climate is continental with a strong subtropical influence in summer.

POPULATION		ECONOMY & JOBS		COST OF LIVING	
Population	106,256	Household income	$38,659	Cost of Living Index	86.7
Population growth	20.6%	Unemployment rate	4.6%	Median home price	$108,200
Diversity measure	13.8%	Recent job growth	1.1%	Home price appreciation	4.9%

CLIMATE					
January low	28.0°F	Annual days > 90°F	51	Annual inches precipitation	47.4
July high	90.0°F	Annual days < 32°F	76	Annual inches snowfall	11.0
July relative humidity	59.0%	Annual days < 0°F	1	Annual days precipitation	119

EDUCATION		HEALTH & HEALTHCARE		AMENITIES	
High school degree	78.2%	Air-quality score	6	Miles to nearest major airport	61
4-year college degree	13.3%	Physicians per capita	231.5	Leisure rating	4
Graduate/professional degree	9.2%	Hospital beds per capita	879.0	Arts & Culture rating	2

Brunswick, GA

Profile: Historic port town
Location: Southeast Georgia, along the Atlantic Coast
Elevation: 10 feet

Emerging City Rank: 9

PRO	CON
Nearby coastal areas	Cost of living
Attractive/historic downtown	Summer heat

Brunswick, a historic port town located half way between Savannah and Jacksonville, Florida, serves as a gateway to the resort islands of Jekyll and St. Simons. The attractive location and ambience has made the area a retirement favorite, but at 134.6 the Cost of Living Index is by far the highest among emerging metropolitan areas. Downtown is quaint and full of historic interest and coastal areas offer excellent recreation. Bigger city services are 50 miles away in Savannah to the north and Jacksonville, Florida, to the south. Summers can be very hot and humid when sea breezes fail.

POPULATION		ECONOMY & JOBS		COST OF LIVING	
Population	94,902	Household income	$40,104	Cost of Living Index	134.6
Population growth	15.4%	Unemployment rate	3.9%	Median home price	$155,000
Diversity measure	34.8%	Recent job growth	1.3%	Home price appreciation	6.9%

CLIMATE					
January low	43.0°F	Annual days > 90°F	83	Annual inches precipitation	52.0
July high	92.0°F	Annual days < 32°F	16	Annual inches snowfall	0.0
July relative humidity	59.0%	Annual days < 0°F	0	Annual days precipitation	114

EDUCATION		HEALTH & HEALTHCARE		AMENITIES	
High school degree	79.3%	Air-quality score	5	Miles to nearest major airport	62
4-year college degree	12.1%	Physicians per capita	186.5	Leisure rating	2
Graduate/professional degree	7.3%	Hospital beds per capita	491.0	Arts & Culture rating	2

Carson City, NV

Profile: Capital city
Location: Extreme western Nevada, south of Reno
Elevation: 4,687 feet

Emerging City Rank: 40

PRO	CON
Nearby mountains	Unattractive sprawl
Year-round climate	Home prices

Carson City is located in a beautiful mountain setting just east of the main Sierra Nevada rise and Lake Tahoe and to the south of attractive Carson Valley. Reno, one of the top-ranked *Cities Ranked & Rated* cities at no. 9, lies 30 miles to the north. Surprising for a capital city, Carson City is an ugly mix of second-tier casinos and urban sprawl, especially south and east. Most residents avoid the city. There are attractive residential areas in the mountains and valleys farther south and west into the Carson Valley, but they are becoming expensive as more Californians move in.

POPULATION		ECONOMY & JOBS		COST OF LIVING	
Population	55,155	Household income	$54,577	Cost of Living Index	113.2
Population growth	36.4%	Unemployment rate	5.5%	Median home price	$195,200
Diversity measure	32.9%	Recent job growth	-.1%	Home price appreciation	6.5%

CLIMATE					
January low	20.9°F	Annual days > 90°F	50	Annual inches precipitation	10.5
July high	88.9°F	Annual days < 32°F	178	Annual inches snowfall	21.2
July relative humidity	20.0%	Annual days < 0°F	2	Annual days precipitation	50

EDUCATION		HEALTH & HEALTHCARE		AMENITIES	
High school degree	82.5%	Air-quality score	8	Miles to nearest major airport	24
4-year college degree	11.9%	Physicians per capita	257.5	Leisure rating	3
Graduate/professional degree	6.6%	Hospital beds per capita	232.1	Arts & Culture rating	2

Cleveland, TN

Profile: Small town
Location: Eastern Tennessee, northeast of Chattanooga
Elevation: 864 feet

Emerging City Rank: 33

PRO	CON
Nearby recreation and national park	Low educational attainment
Small-town feel	Entertainment

Cleveland is a nondescript, Southern town located along I-75 west of the Appalachian mountains. Plenty of outdoor recreation is available, but there isn't much else to do. The closest larger city, Chattanooga, 25 miles to the southwest, provides amenities and some services not present in the immediate area. The terrain is attractive with wooded mountains, and the climate is continental with a strong subtropical influence, particularly in summer.

POPULATION		ECONOMY & JOBS		COST OF LIVING	
Population	105,857	Household income	$38,960	Cost of Living Index	86.1
Population growth	21.2%	Unemployment rate	4.9%	Median home price	$107,200
Diversity measure	12.3%	Recent job growth	-1.7%	Home price appreciation	4.3%

CLIMATE					
January low	29.0°F	Annual days > 90°F	48	Annual inches precipitation	53.3
July high	90.0°F	Annual days < 32°F	73	Annual inches snowfall	4.0
July relative humidity	56.0%	Annual days < 0°F	0	Annual days precipitation	120

EDUCATION		HEALTH & HEALTHCARE		AMENITIES	
High school degree	71.6%	Air-quality score	6	Miles to nearest major airport	67
4-year college degree	9.5%	Physicians per capita	138.9	Leisure rating	2
Graduate/professional degree	5.2%	Hospital beds per capita	299.5	Arts & Culture rating	2

Coeur d'Alene, ID

Profile: Small resort town
Location: Northern Idaho, east of Spokane, Washington
Elevation: 2,181 feet

Emerging City Rank: 5

PRO	CON
Attractive setting	Crowding and sprawl
Nearby recreation	Cold winters

Coeur d'Alene, located in a beautiful mountain setting on a lake, is becoming a favorite destination for retirees and others. There is plenty to do and the summer climate is particularly pleasant and fresh. Spokane, 20 miles to the west, is close enough to provide most amenities and services. The 12-year growth rate of 63.9% should raise eyebrows—growth and crowding are having an impact on the area. The latitude and exposure to northerly air masses create harsh winter conditions at times.

POPULATION		ECONOMY & JOBS		COST OF LIVING	
Population	114,415	Household income	$40,525	Cost of Living Index	96.8
Population growth	63.9%	Unemployment rate	5.9%	Median home price	$140,400
Diversity measure	10.6%	Recent job growth	1.2%	Home price appreciation	4.1%

CLIMATE					
January low	20.0°F	Annual days > 90°F	18	Annual inches precipitation	17.0
July high	83.0°F	Annual days < 32°F	140	Annual inches snowfall	51.0
July relative humidity	31.0%	Annual days < 0°F	10	Annual days precipitation	113

EDUCATION		HEALTH & HEALTHCARE		AMENITIES	
High school degree	87.3%	Air-quality score	3	Miles to nearest major airport	35
4-year college degree	13.1%	Physicians per capita	187.9	Leisure rating	3
Graduate/professional degree	6.0%	Hospital beds per capita	260.5	Arts & Culture rating	3

Columbus, IN

Profile: Small town
Location: Southern Indiana, south of Indianapolis
Elevation: 628 feet

PRO
Architectural interest
Nearby recreation

CON
Entertainment
Economic cycles

Columbus is a typical Midwestern town with a unique element: An endowment in the 1950s made possible the virtual museum of modern and postmodern architecture in the downtown area. Buildings by Eliel and Eero Saarinen, I. M. Pei, and others surround restored older buildings in an attractive setting. Brown County State Park to the west provides recreation and Cummins Engine powers the economy. Otherwise there isn't much to do, but Indianapolis is only 40 miles to the north. The climate is typical transition-zone continental with warm, humid summers and highly variable winters.

POPULATION		ECONOMY & JOBS		COST OF LIVING	
Population	71,906	Household income	$51,396	Cost of Living Index	87.4
Population growth	13.0%	Unemployment rate	3.6%	Median home price	$109,500
Diversity measure	6.4%	Recent job growth	2.7%	Home price appreciation	4.3%

CLIMATE					
January low	18.0°F	Annual days > 90°F	19	Annual inches precipitation	40.2
July high	85.0°F	Annual days < 32°F	119	Annual inches snowfall	25.0
July relative humidity	59.0%	Annual days < 0°F	8	Annual days precipitation	127

EDUCATION		HEALTH & HEALTHCARE		AMENITIES	
High school degree	83.8%	Air-quality score	6	Miles to nearest major airport	41
4-year college degree	13.6%	Physicians per capita	242.0	Leisure rating	1
Graduate/professional degree	8.4%	Hospital beds per capita	420.0	Arts & Culture rating	1

Dalton, GA

Profile: Small Southern town
Location: Northern Georgia, near the Tennessee border
Elevation: 767 feet

PRO
Economy
Nearby recreation

CON
Educational attainment
Arts and culture

Dalton, a typical Southern town along I-75, is noted for its carpet industry. The area ships more than half of the world's tufted carpets, and everywhere are carpet mills and outlet stores, the latter a tourist attraction. Downtown is older with a few historic buildings. There isn't a lot to do locally, but Chattanooga, Tennessee, is 20 miles north and Atlanta is 75 miles south. Terrain is hilly and wooded. The climate is mostly subtropical with a continental winter influence.

POPULATION		ECONOMY & JOBS		COST OF LIVING	
Population	123,862	Household income	$44,467	Cost of Living Index	88.4
Population growth	25.6%	Unemployment rate	3.2%	Median home price	$116,500
Diversity measure	15.5%	Recent job growth	1.0%	Home price appreciation	7.0%

CLIMATE					
January low	29.0°F	Annual days > 90°F	48	Annual inches precipitation	53.3
July high	90.0°F	Annual days < 32°F	73	Annual inches snowfall	4.0
July relative humidity	56.0%	Annual days < 0°F	0	Annual days precipitation	120

EDUCATION		HEALTH & HEALTHCARE		AMENITIES	
High school degree	62.4%	Air-quality score	6	Miles to nearest major airport	84
4-year college degree	7.0%	Physicians per capita	145.3	Leisure rating	1
Graduate/professional degree	4.1%	Hospital beds per capita	285.0	Arts & Culture rating	2

Danville, IL

Emerging City Rank: 36

Profile: Small town
Location: East-central Illinois, at the Indiana border
Elevation: 602 feet

PRO	CON
Cost of living	Entertainment
Small-town feel	Arts and culture

Danville is a quiet, typically Midwestern community about 35 miles east of Champaign-Urbana along I-74. The economy, once tied to coal and clay mining and agriculture, has diversified but still shows high unemployment. There isn't much to do; however, the University of Illinois to the west provides some amenities. At 81.8, the Cost of Living Index is low among emerging metro areas, but oddly this "emerging" area is losing population. Terrain is mostly flat and the climate is continental.

POPULATION		ECONOMY & JOBS		COST OF LIVING	
Population	82,529	Household income	$32,394	Cost of Living Index	81.8
Population growth	-6.5%	Unemployment rate	8.3%	Median home price	$71,900
Diversity measure	11.0%	Recent job growth	1.2%	Home price appreciation	6.9%

CLIMATE					
January low	18.0°F	Annual days > 90°F	15	Annual inches precipitation	40.2
July high	85.0°F	Annual days < 32°F	122	Annual inches snowfall	25.0
July relative humidity	59.0%	Annual days < 0°F	7	Annual days precipitation	127

EDUCATION		HEALTH & HEALTHCARE		AMENITIES	
High school degree	78.7%	Air-quality score	4	Miles to nearest major airport	77
4-year college degree	8.3%	Physicians per capita	152.7	Leisure rating	1
Graduate/professional degree	4.2%	Hospital beds per capita	501.6	Arts & Culture rating	1

El Centro, CA

Emerging City Rank: 45

Profile: Small agricultural town
Location: Southern California, near the Mexican border
Elevation: -45 feet

PRO	CON
Pleasant winters	Economy
Cost of living	Summer heat

El Centro is a dry, dusty, agricultural center in the vast Imperial Valley, which is irrigated by the Colorado River. The winter climate is mild, cost of living is low on a California scale, and the location is 115 miles east of San Diego and only 12 miles north of the Mexican border. There have been mostly unsuccessful attempts to establish retirement communities in the area, but the valley is physically unattractive, has extreme unemployment, and experiences deep-valley desert heat—half the days each year are over 90°F.

POPULATION		ECONOMY & JOBS		COST OF LIVING	
Population	146,356	Household income	$28,638	Cost of Living Index	100.7
Population growth	33.9%	Unemployment rate	22.9%	Median home price	$128,200
Diversity measure	62.5%	Recent job growth	-1.2%	Home price appreciation	14.0%

CLIMATE					
January low	44.0°F	Annual days > 90°F	179	Annual inches precipitation	3.0
July high	107.0°F	Annual days < 32°F	2	Annual inches snowfall	.1
July relative humidity	20.0%	Annual days < 0°F	0	Annual days precipitation	16

EDUCATION		HEALTH & HEALTHCARE		AMENITIES	
High school degree	59.0%	Air-quality score	3	Miles to nearest major airport	94
4-year college degree	6.6%	Physicians per capita	75.2	Leisure rating	2
Graduate/professional degree	3.7%	Hospital beds per capita	146.9	Arts & Culture rating	1

Elizabethtown, KY

Profile: Small town
Location: West-central Kentucky, south of Louisville
Elevation: 708 feet

Emerging City Rank: 28

PRO	CON
Cost of living	Entertainment
Central location	Arts and culture

Elizabethtown, a transportation center, is located at the junction of the north-south I-65 and east-west Western Kentucky Parkway, 35 miles south of Louisville. The central location makes diverse industry possible, and there is some historic interest in the small, nondescript downtown. Besides Louisville, the area is close to Fort Knox to the north, Mammoth Cave to the south, and Bardstown to the east. Terrain is flat to gently rolling with mixed uses. The climate is variable.

POPULATION		ECONOMY & JOBS		COST OF LIVING	
Population	108,254	Household income	$33,853	Cost of Living Index	81.5
Population growth	7.3%	Unemployment rate	4.9%	Median home price	$82,900
Diversity measure	21.1%	Recent job growth	.4%	Home price appreciation	5.0%

CLIMATE					
January low	25.0°F	Annual days > 90°F	35	Annual inches precipitation	43.9
July high	88.0°F	Annual days < 32°F	90	Annual inches snowfall	17.0
July relative humidity	58.0%	Annual days < 0°F	2	Annual days precipitation	125

EDUCATION		HEALTH & HEALTHCARE		AMENITIES	
High school degree	80.9%	Air-quality score	6	Miles to nearest major airport	34
4-year college degree	8.5%	Physicians per capita	192.1	Leisure rating	2
Graduate/professional degree	6.4%	Hospital beds per capita	400.0	Arts & Culture rating	1

Fairbanks, AK

Profile: Frontier town
Location: East-central Alaska, north of the Alaska Range
Elevation: 418 feet

Emerging City Rank: 31

PRO	CON
Attractive setting	Bitter winters
Nearby recreation	Isolation

Fairbanks, a low, sprawling frontier town along the Chena River, supports a huge land area. Mining, forest products, the Alaska Pipeline, and tourism drive the economy and recent job growth has been healthy. The area has a strong sense of community and an educated population. As with all of Alaska, cost of living is high. The summer climate and nearby recreation are exceptional, but winters are equally extraordinary with depressing darkness and below-zero temperatures almost daily.

POPULATION		ECONOMY & JOBS		COST OF LIVING	
Population	83,233	Household income	$54,432	Cost of Living Index	113.7
Population growth	7.1%	Unemployment rate	5.6%	Median home price	$137,700
Diversity measure	39.8%	Recent job growth	5.8%	Home price appreciation	4.1%

CLIMATE					
January low	-19.3°F	Annual days > 90°F	0	Annual inches precipitation	10.8
July high	72.4°F	Annual days < 32°F	225	Annual inches snowfall	67.8
July relative humidity	49.0%	Annual days < 0°F	116	Annual days precipitation	108

EDUCATION		HEALTH & HEALTHCARE		AMENITIES	
High school degree	91.8%	Air-quality score	3	Miles to nearest major airport	7
4-year college degree	16.4%	Physicians per capita	217.5	Leisure rating	2
Graduate/professional degree	10.7%	Hospital beds per capita	257.1	Arts & Culture rating	2

Farmington, NM

Emerging City Rank: 20

Profile: Small town
Location: Northwest corner of New Mexico
Elevation: 5,590 feet

PRO	CON
Nearby mountains	Entertainment
Cost of living	Arts and culture

Farmington is located in the high San Juan Plateau near the Four Corners at the edge of the large Navajo reservation that spreads west into Arizona. The town itself is fairly plain, but areas to the north and east into Durango, the Colorado San Juan Mountains, and the Santa Fe National Forest offer excellent mountain recreation. The reservation and a moderate oil and gas industry support the local economy, and cost of living is reasonable for the region. Climate and terrain are typical of the high-desert location.

POPULATION

Population	116,673
Population growth	27.4%
Diversity measure	65.5%

ECONOMY & JOBS

Household income	$35,676
Unemployment rate	7.9%
Recent job growth	.7%

COST OF LIVING

Cost of Living Index	90.2
Median home price	$106,600
Home price appreciation	3.7%

CLIMATE

January low	16.8°F	Annual days > 90°F	58	Annual inches precipitation	8.2
July high	91.7°F	Annual days < 32°F	152	Annual inches snowfall	13.6
July relative humidity	29.0%	Annual days < 0°F	8	Annual days precipitation	73

EDUCATION

High school degree	76.8%
4-year college degree	8.8%
Graduate/professional degree	4.8%

HEALTH & HEALTHCARE

Air-quality score	2
Physicians per capita	147.4
Hospital beds per capita	148.3

AMENITIES

Miles to nearest major airport	147
Leisure rating	1
Arts & Culture rating	2

Fond du Lac, WI

Emerging City Rank: 30

Profile: Small industrial town
Location: East-central Wisconsin, on Lake Oshkosh
Elevation: 750 feet

PRO	CON
Nearby recreation	Entertainment
Small-town feel	Low ethnic diversity

Along with its agricultural and recreational base, Fond du Lac is an industrial town specializing in forest products, machine tools, and boat motors. The town reflects a strong 19th-century heritage with a few historic neighborhoods displaying early wealth. Nearby areas offer abundant summer and winter recreation. The terrain is mostly flat with mixed woods and agriculture. The higher-latitude continental climate gives cool, pleasant summers and winters with periods of bitter cold.

POPULATION

Population	98,082
Population growth	8.9%
Diversity measure	4.4%

ECONOMY & JOBS

Household income	$44,933
Unemployment rate	5.1%
Recent job growth	3.6%

COST OF LIVING

Cost of Living Index	91.6
Median home price	$128,800
Home price appreciation	5.7%

CLIMATE

January low	7.9°F	Annual days > 90°F	7	Annual inches precipitation	28.3
July high	82.0°F	Annual days < 32°F	163	Annual inches snowfall	36.0
July relative humidity	62.0%	Annual days < 0°F	25	Annual days precipitation	120

EDUCATION

High school degree	84.2%
4-year college degree	12.0%
Graduate/professional degree	4.9%

HEALTH & HEALTHCARE

Air-quality score	5
Physicians per capita	157.0
Hospital beds per capita	271.2

AMENITIES

Miles to nearest major airport	51
Leisure rating	2
Arts & Culture rating	1

Gainesville, GA

Profile: Small city
Location: Northeast Georgia, northeast of Atlanta
Elevation: 1,249 feet

Emerging City Rank: 21

PRO	CON
Nearby recreation	Entertainment
Diverse economy	Cost of living

Gainesville is a prosperous industrial and recreational center located along Lake Lanier. The area combines a Southern small-town feel with such advantages as excellent water recreation, proximity to Atlanta (50 miles to the southwest), and a relatively pleasant climate. The high growth rate attests to the area's emerging popularity.

Cost of living and particularly housing have escalated in recent years. The gently rolling terrain is mainly covered with pine forests and becomes hillier to the north and northeast. The mixed continental and subtropical climate is moderated by elevation in summer.

POPULATION		ECONOMY & JOBS		COST OF LIVING	
Population	148,913	Household income	$52,458	Cost of Living Index	94.8
Population growth	56.0%	Unemployment rate	3.4%	Median home price	$140,300
Diversity measure	31.8%	Recent job growth	1.7%	Home price appreciation	6.9%

CLIMATE					
January low	32.0°F	Annual days > 90°F	50	Annual inches precipitation	49.7
July high	90.0°F	Annual days < 32°F	54	Annual inches snowfall	3.0
July relative humidity	58.0%	Annual days < 0°F	0	Annual days precipitation	111

EDUCATION		HEALTH & HEALTHCARE		AMENITIES	
High school degree	70.5%	Air-quality score	4	Miles to nearest major airport	56
4-year college degree	11.9%	Physicians per capita	192.1	Leisure rating	2
Graduate/professional degree	6.8%	Hospital beds per capita	498.9	Arts & Culture rating	3

Hanford-Corcoran, CA

Profile: Small-agricultural-town complex
Location: Central California, southeast of Fresno
Elevation: 248 feet

Emerging City Rank: 44

PRO	CON
Nearby mountains	Economy
Mild winters	Entertainment

Located in the southern San Joaquin Valley 35 miles of Fresno, Hanford is a rather dull town supporting a wide variety of agriculture, while Corcoran is a similar but smaller town farther into the flatlands to the west. Areas to the east produce citrus crops. The Sierra Nevada and its national parks begin their rise 20 miles east. But there is little to do and little cultural interest except for some interesting Chinese heritage; distance from the mountains and haze reduce the appeal of the setting. Climate is typical California Central Valley, with dry and sometimes unbearably hot summers and cool, moist, and occasionally foggy winters.

POPULATION		ECONOMY & JOBS		COST OF LIVING	
Population	136,303	Household income	$31,072	Cost of Living Index	98.3
Population growth	34.3%	Unemployment rate	11.5%	Median home price	$123,000
Diversity measure	79.1%	Recent job growth	2.5%	Home price appreciation	13.6%

CLIMATE					
January low	36.0°F	Annual days > 90°F	111	Annual inches precipitation	7.4
July high	98.0°F	Annual days < 32°F	30	Annual inches snowfall	.1
July relative humidity	24.0%	Annual days < 0°F	0	Annual days precipitation	43

EDUCATION		HEALTH & HEALTHCARE		AMENITIES	
High school degree	68.8%	Air-quality score	4	Miles to nearest major airport	31
4-year college degree	7.6%	Physicians per capita	82.9	Leisure rating	2
Graduate/professional degree	2.7%	Hospital beds per capita	122.5	Arts & Culture rating	1

Harrisonburg, VA

Emerging City Rank: 18

Profile: Small town/College town
Location: Western Virginia, center of the Shenandoah Valley
Elevation: 1,352 feet

PRO	CON
Nearby recreation	Entertainment
Small-town feel	Air service

Harrisonburg is a small, diverse town in the heart of the Shenandoah region. The downtown area is attractive and historic, particularly in the core area near James Madison University. The university brings some minor local arts amenities, and the nearby Blue Ridge and Appalachian mountains offer plenty of recreation and outdoor interest. In addition to the university, agriculture, agricultural processing, and other light industries are the economy's main supports. Partly due to the mountain alignment, larger cities to the east are somewhat difficult to access for big-city services, but the area has a pleasant atmosphere and relatively cool summers for the region.

POPULATION		ECONOMY & JOBS		COST OF LIVING	
Population	113,079	Household income	$41,784	Cost of Living Index	95.1
Population growth	28.2%	Unemployment rate	2.4%	Median home price	$142,400
Diversity measure	14.2%	Recent job growth	2.3%	Home price appreciation	9.4%

CLIMATE					
January low	18.0°F	Annual days > 90°F	2	Annual inches precipitation	44.5
July high	81.0°F	Annual days < 32°F	145	Annual inches snowfall	71.0
July relative humidity	59.0%	Annual days < 0°F	0	Annual days precipitation	174

EDUCATION		HEALTH & HEALTHCARE		AMENITIES	
High school degree	74.0%	Air-quality score	7	Miles to nearest major airport	85
4-year college degree	14.3%	Physicians per capita	167.1	Leisure rating	2
Graduate/professional degree	8.4%	Hospital beds per capita	260.0	Arts & Culture rating	2

Hinesville–Fort Stewart, GA

Emerging City Rank: 41

Profile: Military town
Location: Southeastern Georgia, southwest of Savannah
Elevation: 48 feet

PRO	CON
Proximity to Savannah	Low educational attainment
Mild winters	Entertainment

This small town supports large Fort Stewart, home to the U.S. Third Infantry. There is little of interest in the immediate area, but coastal areas 30 miles to the east offer some recreation while Savannah, 40 miles to the northeast, makes a more complete offering. Educational attainment is low. Cost of living is also low but not as low as might be expected. The area sits in a mainly level coastal plain. The climate is predominantly humid subtropical with hot, sticky summers.

POPULATION		ECONOMY & JOBS		COST OF LIVING	
Population	74,225	Household income	$37,616	Cost of Living Index	87.7
Population growth	25.9%	Unemployment rate	4.8%	Median home price	$109,200
Diversity measure	57.0%	Recent job growth	-.1%	Home price appreciation	7.1%

CLIMATE					
January low	38.0°F	Annual days > 90°F	69	Annual inches precipitation	49.2
July high	91.0°F	Annual days < 32°F	31	Annual inches snowfall	.1
July relative humidity	57.0%	Annual days < 0°F	0	Annual days precipitation	111

EDUCATION		HEALTH & HEALTHCARE		AMENITIES	
High school degree	84.9%	Air-quality score	6	Miles to nearest major airport	31
4-year college degree	8.7%	Physicians per capita	51.2	Leisure rating	2
Graduate/professional degree	4.5%	Hospital beds per capita	66.0	Arts & Culture rating	1

Hot Springs, AR

Emerging City Rank: 19

Profile: Small resort town
Location: West-central Arkansas, southwest of Little Rock
Elevation: 632 feet

PRO	CON
Nearby outdoor recreation	Tourist impact
Cost of living	Arts and culture

Hot Springs is a spa and resort town at the base of the Ouachita Mountains, 50 miles southwest of Little Rock. The area boasts natural hot springs as well as the boyhood home of Bill Clinton. Surrounding unusual Hot Springs National Park are several resorts, some tacky tourist sprawl, and a few historic sites. The setting is attractive and known for beautiful spring and autumn seasons, but summers are hot and sticky and there isn't much to do beyond the tourist attractions.

POPULATION		ECONOMY & JOBS		COST OF LIVING	
Population	89,640	Household income	$33,627	Cost of Living Index	84.9
Population growth	22.1%	Unemployment rate	5.5%	Median home price	$97,700
Diversity measure	18.8%	Recent job growth	1.7%	Home price appreciation	4.5%

CLIMATE					
January low	30.0°F	Annual days > 90°F	62	Annual inches precipitation	51.3
July high	92.0°F	Annual days < 32°F	51	Annual inches snowfall	7.0
July relative humidity	56.0%	Annual days < 0°F	0	Annual days precipitation	111

EDUCATION		HEALTH & HEALTHCARE		AMENITIES	
High school degree	78.3%	Air-quality score	5	Miles to nearest major airport	49
4-year college degree	11.7%	Physicians per capita	265.5	Leisure rating	2
Graduate/professional degree	6.3%	Hospital beds per capita	693.9	Arts & Culture rating	2

Idaho Falls, ID

Emerging City Rank: 10

Profile: Agricultural town
Location: Eastern Idaho, northeast of Pocatello
Elevation: 4,710 feet

PRO	CON
Nearby national parks	Entertainment
Nearby recreation	Arts and culture

Idaho Falls is situated on the northeast portion of the Snake River Plain, at the edge of a large agricultural area. It serves as a gateway to Yellowstone National Park and the Grand Tetons to the northeast and east, respectively. The town itself is nondescript and doesn't have much to do, but the setting is attractive and the summer climate is pleasant. Educational attainment is high while cost of living is low. The town is attractive for outdoors-oriented residents.

POPULATION		ECONOMY & JOBS		COST OF LIVING	
Population	103,498	Household income	$39,713	Cost of Living Index	86.0
Population growth	16.6%	Unemployment rate	3.4%	Median home price	$103,300
Diversity measure	18.9%	Recent job growth	-1.3%	Home price appreciation	4.2%

CLIMATE					
January low	14.0°F	Annual days > 90°F	33	Annual inches precipitation	11.3
July high	88.0°F	Annual days < 32°F	166	Annual inches snowfall	43.0
July relative humidity	26.0%	Annual days < 0°F	15	Annual days precipitation	94

EDUCATION		HEALTH & HEALTHCARE		AMENITIES	
High school degree	87.2%	Air-quality score	5	Miles to nearest major airport	187
4-year college degree	16.2%	Physicians per capita	183.6	Leisure rating	2
Graduate/professional degree	7.9%	Hospital beds per capita	301.5	Arts & Culture rating	1

Ithaca, NY

Profile: College town
Location: Central upstate New York, southwest of Syracuse
Elevation: 836 feet

Emerging City Rank: 1

PRO	CON
Attractive downtown	Wet climate
College-town amenities	Isolation

Ithaca is most noted as home to Ivy League Cornell University. As might be expected, the town is attractive, activities are plentiful, and educational attainment is high. Additionally the location, at the south end of Cayuga Lake in the Finger Lakes region, affords access to nearby outdoor recreation, interesting landscapes, and a number of wineries. Cost of living is reasonable for the region. Larger cities, such as Syracuse 60 miles northeast, are hard to get to and the Lake Ontario–influenced, humid continental climate produces lots of snow and precipitation—almost 1 day in 2 on average year-round.

POPULATION

Population	96,493
Population growth	2.5%
Diversity measure	16.7%

ECONOMY & JOBS

Household income	$36,790
Unemployment rate	2.1%
Recent job growth	1.1%

COST OF LIVING

Cost of Living Index	96.2
Median home price	$130,100
Home price appreciation	11.6%

CLIMATE

January low	15.0°F	Annual days > 90°F	9	Annual inches precipitation	38.5
July high	82.0°F	Annual days < 32°F	136	Annual inches snowfall	107.0
July relative humidity	59.0%	Annual days < 0°F	8	Annual days precipitation	170

EDUCATION

High school degree	91.4%
4-year college degree	20.8%
Graduate/professional degree	26.7%

HEALTH & HEALTHCARE

Air-quality score	6
Physicians per capita	218.7
Hospital beds per capita	234.2

AMENITIES

Miles to nearest major airport	51
Leisure rating	4
Arts & Culture rating	3

Jefferson City, MO

Profile: Capital city
Location: East-central Missouri, south of Columbia
Elevation: 600 feet

Emerging City Rank: 37

PRO	CON
Cost of living	Entertainment
Capital-city amenities	Isolation

Jefferson City, along the Missouri River near the center of the state, is an uninspiring capital somewhat off the beaten path. There are some capital-city amenities and minor historical sites, but there is little to do overall. The state had to pass a law requiring state officials to live there. Most culture and entertainment is found in Columbia, home of the University of Missouri, 30 miles to the north. The town is isolated from air service, found mainly in St. Louis, 100 miles east.

POPULATION

Population	142,368
Population growth	17.9%
Diversity measure	8.6%

ECONOMY & JOBS

Household income	$46,061
Unemployment rate	3.8%
Recent job growth	-1.8%

COST OF LIVING

Cost of Living Index	85.4
Median home price	$100,700
Home price appreciation	6.4%

CLIMATE

January low	18.0°F	Annual days > 90°F	37	Annual inches precipitation	39.9
July high	89.0°F	Annual days < 32°F	108	Annual inches snowfall	27.0
July relative humidity	62.0%	Annual days < 0°F	7	Annual days precipitation	110

EDUCATION

High school degree	81.7%
4-year college degree	14.1%
Graduate/professional degree	7.0%

HEALTH & HEALTHCARE

Air-quality score	6
Physicians per capita	163.7
Hospital beds per capita	610.4

AMENITIES

Miles to nearest major airport	99
Leisure rating	2
Arts & Culture rating	3

Kingston, NY

Profile: Small town
Location: Hudson River Valley, south of Albany
Elevation: 295 feet

Emerging City Rank: 27

PRO	CON
Historic interest	Cost of living
Nearby recreation	Arts and culture

Kingston is a pleasant but nondescript town in the Hudson River Valley, 60 miles south of Albany and 100 miles north of New York City. As the first capital of New York, the town contains some sites of historic interest enhanced by the nearby mansions of 19th-century tycoons such as the Vanderbilt family. The setting is attractive and nearby ski areas and the Ashokan Reservoir provide some recreation, but the Cost of Living Index at 112.4 is high and winters can be severe.

POPULATION	
Population	178,649
Population growth	8.1%
Diversity measure	22.0%

ECONOMY & JOBS	
Household income	$44,687
Unemployment rate	4.3%
Recent job growth	1.6%

COST OF LIVING	
Cost of Living Index	112.4
Median home price	$156,100
Home price appreciation	11.3%

CLIMATE					
January low	13.0°F	Annual days > 90°F	11	Annual inches precipitation	35.8
July high	83.0°F	Annual days < 32°F	150	Annual inches snowfall	63.0
July relative humidity	57.0%	Annual days < 0°F	15	Annual days precipitation	133

EDUCATION		HEALTH & HEALTHCARE		AMENITIES	
High school degree	81.7%	Air-quality score	5	Miles to nearest major airport	58
4-year college degree	13.8%	Physicians per capita	180.2	Leisure rating	2
Graduate/professional degree	11.2%	Hospital beds per capita	260.8	Arts & Culture rating	1

Lebanon, PA

Profile: Small town
Location: East-central Pennsylvania, east of Harrisburg
Elevation: 460 feet

Emerging City Rank: 26

PRO	CON
Small-town feel	Low educational attainment
Cost of living	Low ethnic diversity

Lebanon is an old transportation and minor industrial center located on the route of the original canal through the region. Bypassed by modern transport routes I-78 and the Pennsylvania Turnpike, this quiet town with a typical core is centrally located between Harrisburg, Hershey, Lancaster, and Reading. Annville, a minor college town 5 miles west, is attractive but areas of Lebanon itself have a somewhat gritty, working-class feel. Sheltered by the main Allegheny Ridge to the northwest, the climate is pleasant for the region, with warm, humid summers and variable winters with relatively less snow and bitter cold than other areas in the northeast.

POPULATION	
Population	121,328
Population growth	6.7%
Diversity measure	9.4%

ECONOMY & JOBS	
Household income	$43,242
Unemployment rate	3.2%
Recent job growth	-.2%

COST OF LIVING	
Cost of Living Index	89.5
Median home price	$116,100
Home price appreciation	4.1%

CLIMATE					
January low	22.5°F	Annual days > 90°F	24	Annual inches precipitation	36.0
July high	86.8°F	Annual days < 32°F	107	Annual inches snowfall	35.0
July relative humidity	53.0%	Annual days < 0°F	1	Annual days precipitation	125

EDUCATION		HEALTH & HEALTHCARE		AMENITIES	
High school degree	78.6%	Air-quality score	5	Miles to nearest major airport	21
4-year college degree	9.5%	Physicians per capita	212.6	Leisure rating	2
Graduate/professional degree	5.9%	Hospital beds per capita	230.8	Arts & Culture rating	2

Lewiston, ID-WA

Emerging City Rank: 11

Profile: Small town/College town
Location: Northwestern Idaho, along the Snake River
Elevation: 738 feet

PRO	CON
Nearby outdoor recreation	Isolation
Mild winters	Economic cycles

Lewiston, in a deep canyon at the confluence of the Snake and Clearwater rivers, has a distinctly Old West feel. Forest-products mills and a few other industries are the economic mainstays. Moscow, 20 miles northwest, is home to the University of Idaho. The nearby terrain is varied and offers plenty of outdoor and water recreation. The area is isolated; Boise to the south and Spokane to the northwest are both difficult trips. The area has a mild and mainly dry year-round climate.

POPULATION		ECONOMY & JOBS		COST OF LIVING	
Population	57,987	Household income	$38,404	Cost of Living Index	91.6
Population growth	12.9%	Unemployment rate	4.2%	Median home price	$116,900
Diversity measure	26.0%	Recent job growth	2.4%	Home price appreciation	4.9%

CLIMATE					
January low	26.0°F	Annual days > 90°F	40	Annual inches precipitation	12.6
July high	89.0°F	Annual days < 32°F	89	Annual inches snowfall	15.0
July relative humidity	29.0%	Annual days < 0°F	0	Annual days precipitation	101

EDUCATION		HEALTH & HEALTHCARE		AMENITIES	
High school degree	85.6%	Air-quality score	6	Miles to nearest major airport	89
4-year college degree	12.7%	Physicians per capita	206.9	Leisure rating	3
Graduate/professional degree	5.8%	Hospital beds per capita	362.2	Arts & Culture rating	2

Logan, UT-ID

Emerging City Rank: 4

Profile: College town
Location: Extreme northern Utah, near Idaho border
Elevation: 4,507 feet

PRO	CON
Attractive setting	Isolation
Nearby recreation	Entertainment

Logan, located at the south end of the Cache Valley against the Wasatch Range and the dramatic Wellsville Mountains to the west, is an attractive college town, well known for its scenic beauty and recreation. It is home to Utah State University and a center of Mormon culture and history. Cost of living is reasonable for the type of area, but geography makes Ogden and especially Salt Lake City to the south a fairly long trip at 75 miles. The climate is generally dry and pleasant with a few blasts of rigorous winter weather each year.

POPULATION		ECONOMY & JOBS		COST OF LIVING	
Population	105,391	Household income	$43,303	Cost of Living Index	92.1
Population growth	32.7%	Unemployment rate	3.7%	Median home price	$137,400
Diversity measure	13.7%	Recent job growth	4.1%	Home price appreciation	3.0%

CLIMATE					
January low	15.9°F	Annual days > 90°F	23	Annual inches precipitation	17.6
July high	87.0°F	Annual days < 32°F	145	Annual inches snowfall	57.5
July relative humidity	24.0%	Annual days < 0°F	7	Annual days precipitation	94

EDUCATION		HEALTH & HEALTHCARE		AMENITIES	
High school degree	90.2%	Air-quality score	5	Miles to nearest major airport	67
4-year college degree	19.8%	Physicians per capita	137.6	Leisure rating	2
Graduate/professional degree	10.1%	Hospital beds per capita	238.2	Arts & Culture rating	2

Longview-Kelso, WA

Emerging City Rank: 43

Profile: Industrial town/Port town
Location: Southwest Washington, north of Portland, Oregon
Elevation: 26 feet

PRO	CON
Nearby mountains	Unattractive downtown
Proximity to Portland	Economy

Longview-Kelso is a grain-loading and forest-products center serving ocean traffic coming up the Columbia River. The area contains a complex of grain elevators and mills, and unattractive urban sprawl far worse than that of most Pacific Northwest towns. The area is close to Portland, 40 miles to the south, and is a western gateway to the Mount St. Helens area. Cost of living is high. The terrain is generally hilly with wooded hilltops and broad, flat, mostly agricultural valleys away from industrial areas. The climate is Pacific Northwest with a marine influence that brings relatively dry summers and cool, wet periods most of the rest of the year. The industrial feel and sprawl dominate. Those expecting a lush, stimulating, and attractive Pacific Northwest city won't find it here.

POPULATION

Population	94,680
Population growth	15.3%
Diversity measure	11.5%

ECONOMY & JOBS

Household income	$40,400
Unemployment rate	9.5%
Recent job growth	-3.5%

COST OF LIVING

Cost of Living Index	101.3
Median home price	$159,600
Home price appreciation	6.0%

CLIMATE

January low	33.7°F	Annual days > 90°F	6	Annual inches precipitation	48.1
July high	77.7°F	Annual days < 32°F	57	Annual inches snowfall	5.0
July relative humidity	47.0%	Annual days < 0°F	0	Annual days precipitation	174

EDUCATION

High school degree	83.2%
4-year college degree	8.4%
Graduate/professional degree	4.9%

HEALTH & HEALTHCARE

Air-quality score	4
Physicians per capita	190.1
Hospital beds per capita	209.1

AMENITIES

Miles to nearest major airport	62
Leisure rating	2
Arts & Culture rating	1

Madera, CA

Emerging City Rank: 42

Profile: Small agricultural town
Location: California San Joaquin Valley, northwest of Fresno
Elevation: 272 feet

PRO	CON
Nearby mountains	Cost of living
Mild winters	Economy

Madera, along State Route 99, is one of many small, agricultural towns in California's Central Valley. Like its neighbors, Madera is dull overall and offers few amenities. However, the high cost of living exceeds many other valley towns. Minor services and amenities are available in Fresno, 20 miles to the southeast. The terrain is flat with mountains to the east that are usually not visible through the valley haze. The Mediterranean climate is hot and dry in summer, with normally pleasant evenings, and mild in winter.

POPULATION

Population	128,657
Population growth	46.1%
Diversity measure	51.4%

ECONOMY & JOBS

Household income	$36,176
Unemployment rate	10.3%
Recent job growth	1.9%

COST OF LIVING

Cost of Living Index	116.0
Median home price	$196,600
Home price appreciation	9.7%

CLIMATE

January low	37.0°F	Annual days > 90°F	107	Annual inches precipitation	10.6
July high	98.0°F	Annual days < 32°F	29	Annual inches snowfall	0.0
July relative humidity	24.0%	Annual days < 0°F	0	Annual days precipitation	45

EDUCATION

High school degree	65.4%
4-year college degree	8.2%
Graduate/professional degree	3.8%

HEALTH & HEALTHCARE

Air-quality score	4
Physicians per capita	93.3
Hospital beds per capita	260.4

AMENITIES

Miles to nearest major airport	24
Leisure rating	2
Arts & Culture rating	1

Michigan City–LaPorte, IN

Emerging City Rank: 25

Profile: Small-town complex
Location: Extreme northern Indiana, at the Michigan border
Elevation: 608 feet

PRO	CON
Nearby recreation	Harsh winters
Proximity to Chicago	Low educational attainment

Michigan City and LaPorte have a strong industrial heritage. Both towns have been rediscovered lately for their recreational opportunities along the southeastern Lake Michigan shore. There are some minor arts and culture amenities, cost of living is low, and Chicago, 60 miles to the west, is relatively close. The continental climate is pleasant in summer, but proximity to the lake causes high winter winds and substantial precipitation, while also moderating extreme cold.

POPULATION

Population	109,669
Population growth	2.4%
Diversity measure	14.4%

ECONOMY & JOBS

Household income	$42,305
Unemployment rate	6.5%
Recent job growth	1.3%

COST OF LIVING

Cost of Living Index	89.1
Median home price	$113,400
Home price appreciation	4.3%

CLIMATE

January low	13.0°F	Annual days > 90°F	17	Annual inches precipitation	35.4
July high	84.0°F	Annual days < 32°F	132	Annual inches snowfall	39.0
July relative humidity	57.0%	Annual days < 0°F	12	Annual days precipitation	125

EDUCATION

			HEALTH & HEALTHCARE			AMENITIES	
High school degree	80.6%		Air-quality score	4		Miles to nearest major airport	29
4-year college degree	9.0%		Physicians per capita	164.1		Leisure rating	1
Graduate/professional degree	5.0%		Hospital beds per capita	617.3		Arts & Culture rating	2

Monroe, MI

Emerging City Rank: 34

Profile: Small port town
Location: Southeastern Michigan, just north of Ohio border
Elevation: 593 feet

PRO	CON
Small-town feel	Entertainment
Historic interest	Cost of living

Monroe is an old manufacturing and port city along the western shore of Lake Erie between Detroit and Toledo, Ohio. The setting is flat and uninteresting. However, this typically Midwestern town contains numerous early-20th-century homes on shaded streets and some historic attractions related to earlier French settlement. It is quiet with plenty of water recreation but not much else to do. Cost of living, which is a bit high for what is offered, may reflect the value of the historic homes. The area is mainly level with areas of deciduous woods. The climate is continental with some lake influence, although its west shore location diminishes winter snows compared to other lake locations.

POPULATION

Population	148,326
Population growth	11.0%
Diversity measure	13.3%

ECONOMY & JOBS

Household income	$55,802
Unemployment rate	7.5%
Recent job growth	3.7%

COST OF LIVING

Cost of Living Index	102.3
Median home price	$160,600
Home price appreciation	6.9%

CLIMATE

January low	17.3°F	Annual days > 90°F	11	Annual inches precipitation	32.0
July high	83.4°F	Annual days < 32°F	139	Annual inches snowfall	39.0
July relative humidity	55.0%	Annual days < 0°F	7	Annual days precipitation	133

EDUCATION

			HEALTH & HEALTHCARE			AMENITIES	
High school degree	83.1%		Air-quality score	2		Miles to nearest major airport	22
4-year college degree	9.6%		Physicians per capita	87.0		Leisure rating	1
Graduate/professional degree	4.7%		Hospital beds per capita	130.1		Arts & Culture rating	2

Morgantown, WV

Emerging City Rank: 22

Profile: College town
Location: Extreme northern West Virginia
Elevation: 823 feet

PRO	CON
College-town amenities	Low incomes
Cost of living	Low ethnic diversity

Morgantown, along the Monongahela River, is home to West Virginia University and a selection of typical West Virginia businesses including chemicals and forest products. There is plenty of recreation in the nearby mountains and rivers, and Pittsburgh is 70 miles to the north. The downtown area is interesting and livable with a few minor cultural amenities. The cost of living is low. The climate is mostly pleasant in summer, but can be hot and humid, while major storm tracks bring cloudy, wet, winter weather.

POPULATION		ECONOMY & JOBS		COST OF LIVING	
Population	111,857	Household income	$33,647	Cost of Living Index	88.0
Population growth	7.0%	Unemployment rate	4.1%	Median home price	$88,700
Diversity measure	7.8%	Recent job growth	2.2%	Home price appreciation	4.7%

CLIMATE					
January low	20.8°F	Annual days > 90°F	8	Annual inches precipitation	37.1
July high	83.0°F	Annual days < 32°F	121	Annual inches snowfall	43.0
July relative humidity	60.0%	Annual days < 0°F	5	Annual days precipitation	154

EDUCATION		HEALTH & HEALTHCARE		AMENITIES	
High school degree	81.1%	Air-quality score	5	Miles to nearest major airport	61
4-year college degree	12.7%	Physicians per capita	672.3	Leisure rating	2
Graduate/professional degree	14.0%	Hospital beds per capita	778.7	Arts & Culture rating	2

Morristown, TN

Emerging City Rank: 35

Profile: Small town
Location: Eastern Tennessee, east of Knoxville
Elevation: 1,283 feet

PRO	CON
Cost of living	Economy
Nearby recreation	Low educational attainment

Morristown is a nondescript town located along I-81, a major transportation route, at the northwestern base of the Great Smoky Mountains, 50 miles east of Knoxville. Those mountains and nearby water provide plenty of recreation. Owing to a low-cost workforce and a central location relative to U.S. markets, the town has a diverse industrial base of auto parts, furniture, and other manufacturing. Costs of living and housing are attractive, although there are signs of economic strain in the employment figures. The climate is mainly continental with some subtropical influence, giving variable weather with periods of summer heat and humidity and winter cold.

POPULATION		ECONOMY & JOBS		COST OF LIVING	
Population	125,882	Household income	$35,492	Cost of Living Index	82.1
Population growth	25.1%	Unemployment rate	5.5%	Median home price	$95,600
Diversity measure	8.7%	Recent job growth	-2.0%	Home price appreciation	4.4%

CLIMATE					
January low	26.0°F	Annual days > 90°F	27	Annual inches precipitation	53.2
July high	87.0°F	Annual days < 32°F	91	Annual inches snowfall	10.0
July relative humidity	60.0%	Annual days < 0°F	0	Annual days precipitation	128

EDUCATION		HEALTH & HEALTHCARE		AMENITIES	
High school degree	68.4%	Air-quality score	6	Miles to nearest major airport	47
4-year college degree	7.8%	Physicians per capita	139.0	Leisure rating	2
Graduate/professional degree	4.4%	Hospital beds per capita	272.5	Arts & Culture rating	2

Mount Vernon–Anacortes, WA

| Emerging City Rank: 3 |

Profile: Small-town complex
Location: Northwest Washington, along Puget Sound
Elevation: 23 feet

PRO	CON
Attractive setting	Economy
Mild year-round climate	Cost of housing

An area of uncommon scenic beauty, Mount Vernon is adjacent to a vast river delta that stretches west to the Puget Sound but is otherwise surrounded by mountains. Anacortes is a main port gateway to the San Juan Islands and an oil terminal and refining center. The economy, currently weak, is a mix of farming, forest products, fishing, tourism, and some industry. The area is located centrally between Seattle, Bellingham, and Vancouver, British Columbia, with easy access to all three. The marine climate gives very pleasant and mostly dry summers, while winters are cool, wet, and variable, but not as wet as the latitude might suggest due to the shadowing effects of the Olympic Mountains to the southwest. That said, occasional snows and strong windy Pacific storms can occur.

POPULATION	
Population	105,822
Population growth	33.0%
Diversity measure	23.7%

ECONOMY & JOBS	
Household income	$44,529
Unemployment rate	7.0%
Recent job growth	-.1%

COST OF LIVING	
Cost of Living Index	104.6
Median home price	$176,300
Home price appreciation	6.0%

CLIMATE					
January low	33.6°F	Annual days > 90°F	1	Annual inches precipitation	32.6
July high	73.7°F	Annual days < 32°F	56	Annual inches snowfall	3.8
July relative humidity	51.0%	Annual days < 0°F	0	Annual days precipitation	155

EDUCATION			HEALTH & HEALTHCARE			AMENITIES	
High school degree	84.0%		Air-quality score	4		Miles to nearest major airport	67
4-year college degree	13.8%		Physicians per capita	241.0		Leisure rating	2
Graduate/professional degree	7.0%		Hospital beds per capita	267.4		Arts & Culture rating	2

Ocean City, NJ

| Emerging City Rank: 15 |

Profile: Beach resort town
Location: Southeastern New Jersey, south of Atlantic City
Elevation: 19 feet

PRO	CON
Beach areas	Cost of living
Nearby recreation	Economy

Ocean City, on a barrier island 15 miles south of Atlantic City, is primarily a middle-class, beach resort town. It has the infrastructure and flavor typical of nearby beach towns, but it has resisted the development of ugly sprawl and high-rise buildings. Cost of living and especially housing are high among emerging metropolitan areas. For the region, the year-round climate is quite pleasant, with Atlantic waters moderating both summer heat and winter cold.

POPULATION	
Population	102,842
Population growth	8.2%
Diversity measure	19.7%

ECONOMY & JOBS	
Household income	$42,651
Unemployment rate	4.8%
Recent job growth	2.7%

COST OF LIVING	
Cost of Living Index	129.1
Median home price	$275,900
Home price appreciation	11.4%

CLIMATE					
January low	22.0°F	Annual days > 90°F	16	Annual inches precipitation	40.7
July high	84.0°F	Annual days < 32°F	15	Annual inches snowfall	18.0
July relative humidity	57.0%	Annual days < 0°F	1	Annual days precipitation	111

EDUCATION			HEALTH & HEALTHCARE			AMENITIES	
High school degree	81.9%		Air-quality score	5		Miles to nearest major airport	55
4-year college degree	15.5%		Physicians per capita	174.1		Leisure rating	2
Graduate/professional degree	6.5%		Hospital beds per capita	250.9		Arts & Culture rating	1

Prescott, AZ

Profile: Small city
Location: Northwest Arizona, south end of Chino Valley
Elevation: 5,354 feet

Emerging City Rank: 6

PRO	CON
Attractive downtown	Home prices
Historic interest	Entertainment

Prescott is a historic, desert mountain city located about 90 miles northwest of Phoenix, 100 miles south of Flagstaff, and 60 miles south of Sedona, a popular arts and retirement community. Prescott picks up some character from all three places, but is primarily a clean, quiet city with an Old West feel. There are some minor arts and cultural assets. The year-round, high-desert climate is pleasant and dry, although given to frequent below-freezing nights.

POPULATION		ECONOMY & JOBS		COST OF LIVING	
Population	179,030	Household income	$32,709	Cost of Living Index	101.2
Population growth	66.2%	Unemployment rate	3.3%	Median home price	$154,900
Diversity measure	35.2%	Recent job growth	2.2%	Home price appreciation	6.9%

CLIMATE					
January low	15.0°F	Annual days > 90°F	3	Annual inches precipitation	21.6
July high	82.0°F	Annual days < 32°F	210	Annual inches snowfall	21.0
July relative humidity	33.0%	Annual days < 0°F	0	Annual days precipitation	82

EDUCATION		HEALTH & HEALTHCARE		AMENITIES	
High school degree	84.7%	Air-quality score	4	Miles to nearest major airport	83
4-year college degree	13.1%	Physicians per capita	174.8	Leisure rating	2
Graduate/professional degree	8.1%	Hospital beds per capita	118.4	Arts & Culture rating	3

Rome, GA

Profile: Small Southern town
Location: Northwest Georgia, northwest of Atlanta
Elevation: 2,181 feet

Emerging City Rank: 39

PRO	CON
Nearby recreation	Low educational attainment
Cost of living	Arts and culture

Rome, a typical Southern town, is located near an area of mountains, rivers, and lakes in northwest Georgia. The city is plain and unremarkable with some areas of unattractive sprawl. The economy is healthy and cost of living low. There are a few items of historic interest, but the town offers little entertainment or intellectual stimulation. Atlanta is 70 miles southeast. The terrain is hilly and wooded. The climate is subtropical with a continental influence mostly in winter.

POPULATION		ECONOMY & JOBS		COST OF LIVING	
Population	92,136	Household income	$41,778	Cost of Living Index	85.2
Population growth	13.4%	Unemployment rate	4.4%	Median home price	$104,700
Diversity measure	25.6%	Recent job growth	1.4%	Home price appreciation	7.1%

CLIMATE					
January low	29.0°F	Annual days > 90°F	48	Annual inches precipitation	53.3
July high	90.0°F	Annual days < 32°F	73	Annual inches snowfall	4.0
July relative humidity	57.0%	Annual days < 0°F	0	Annual days precipitation	120

EDUCATION		HEALTH & HEALTHCARE		AMENITIES	
High school degree	71.5%	Air-quality score	4	Miles to nearest major airport	61
4-year college degree	10.0%	Physicians per capita	309.3	Leisure rating	2
Graduate/professional degree	5.8%	Hospital beds per capita	1002.9	Arts & Culture rating	2

St. George, UT

Emerging City Rank: 29

Profile: Small resort town
Location: Extreme southwest Utah, near Arizona border
Elevation: 2,880 feet

PRO	CON
Nearby national parks	Rapid growth and sprawl
Dry climate	Cost of housing

St. George, 8 miles from the Arizona border along I-15, is a retirement community near some of the most attractive mountain and recreational areas in the country. The surrounding red-rock terrain is stunning and Zion National Park is 30 miles to the northeast.

The town itself is uninteresting and the rapid 95% growth rate has produced some unattractive sprawl. Climate is dry, mid-altitude desert and features pleasant winters but hot and often uncomfortable summers. The area is 115 miles northeast of Las Vegas.

POPULATION		ECONOMY & JOBS		COST OF LIVING	
Population	94,677	Household income	$41,285	Cost of Living Index	102.0
Population growth	95.0%	Unemployment rate	4.0%	Median home price	$169,500
Diversity measure	10.2%	Recent job growth	7.6%	Home price appreciation	2.8%

CLIMATE					
January low	25.8°F	Annual days > 90°F	113	Annual inches precipitation	8.4
July high	101.6°F	Annual days < 32°F	90	Annual inches snowfall	3.5
July relative humidity	19.0%	Annual days < 0°F	0	Annual days precipitation	65

EDUCATION		HEALTH & HEALTHCARE		AMENITIES	
High school degree	87.6%	Air-quality score	6	Miles to nearest major airport	112
4-year college degree	13.9%	Physicians per capita	163.7	Leisure rating	4
Graduate/professional degree	7.0%	Hospital beds per capita	161.6	Arts & Culture rating	3

Salisbury, MD

Emerging City Rank: 23

Profile: Small resort town
Location: Delmarva Peninsula, near Delaware border
Elevation: 33 feet

PRO	CON
Small-town feel	Entertainment
Nearby outdoor recreation	Isolation

Salisbury, a quiet, small town along the Wicomico River, has a history as a port and transportation center serving eastern Maryland, Delaware, and the Delmarva portion of Virginia, a mainly agricultural area. The area is pleasant with few extremes because of the

nearby waters of the Chesapeake Bay and Atlantic Ocean. Cost of living is reasonable for the region. Major cities are near enough to provide the cultural amenities and services missing locally, but they take effort to access.

POPULATION		ECONOMY & JOBS		COST OF LIVING	
Population	112,202	Household income	$40,322	Cost of Living Index	90.6
Population growth	14.8%	Unemployment rate	4.8%	Median home price	$113,700
Diversity measure	43.4%	Recent job growth	-3.3%	Home price appreciation	9.9%

CLIMATE					
January low	29.0°F	Annual days > 90°F	21	Annual inches precipitation	41.9
July high	86.0°F	Annual days < 32°F	67	Annual inches snowfall	14.0
July relative humidity	54.0%	Annual days < 0°F	0	Annual days precipitation	113

EDUCATION		HEALTH & HEALTHCARE		AMENITIES	
High school degree	78.2%	Air-quality score	6	Miles to nearest major airport	81
4-year college degree	12.3%	Physicians per capita	267.4	Leisure rating	1
Graduate/professional degree	7.3%	Hospital beds per capita	512.5	Arts & Culture rating	2

Sandusky, OH

Profile: Port town
Location: Northern Ohio, along Lake Erie
Elevation: 597 feet

PRO
Recreational amenities
Central location

CON
Industrial areas
Low ethnic diversity

Emerging City Rank: 24

Sandusky is an old port town on Lake Erie with strong ties to the steel industry. The area has evolved into a major recreation and entertainment area with offshore islands and bays and the famed Cedar Point amusement park. While there is still plenty of industry, the area has become more livable. Easy access to Cleveland to the east and Toledo to the west is available. Lake effects moderate the continental climate, but produce snow, clouds, and precipitation.

POPULATION		ECONOMY & JOBS		COST OF LIVING	
Population	79,432	Household income	$45,935	Cost of Living Index	97.8
Population growth	3.5%	Unemployment rate	4.5%	Median home price	$142,200
Diversity measure	11.2%	Recent job growth	.1%	Home price appreciation	4.8%

CLIMATE					
January low	18.1°F	Annual days > 90°F	14	Annual inches precipitation	32.6
July high	81.3°F	Annual days < 32°F	141	Annual inches snowfall	37.0
July relative humidity	59.0%	Annual days < 0°F	6	Annual days precipitation	135

EDUCATION		HEALTH & HEALTHCARE		AMENITIES	
High school degree	84.0%	Air-quality score	5	Miles to nearest major airport	44
4-year college degree	11.0%	Physicians per capita	232.9	Leisure rating	2
Graduate/professional degree	5.6%	Hospital beds per capita	616.9	Arts & Culture rating	2

Valdosta, GA

Profile: Small town
Location: Extreme southern Georgia, near the Florida border
Elevation: 215 feet

PRO
Cost of living
Mild winters

CON
Arts and culture
Hot, humid summers

Emerging City Rank: 38

Valdosta is an agricultural shipping point and a stop on the major I-75 artery south into Florida. The area lacks interest in general, but does have some history and a few performing arts and cultural amenities. The cost of living is low. The surrounding terrain is flat and uninteresting. The inland subtropical climate brings mild winters with rainy periods and warm, sticky summers with occasional downpours. Total rainfall is among the highest of all U.S. metro areas.

POPULATION		ECONOMY & JOBS		COST OF LIVING	
Population	122,650	Household income	$35,329	Cost of Living Index	84.1
Population growth	23.6%	Unemployment rate	3.0%	Median home price	$101,100
Diversity measure	47.3%	Recent job growth	1.9%	Home price appreciation	7.1%

CLIMATE					
January low	40.0°F	Annual days > 90°F	86	Annual inches precipitation	63.3
July high	91.0°F	Annual days < 32°F	31	Annual inches snowfall	.1
July relative humidity	59.0%	Annual days < 0°F	0	Annual days precipitation	114

EDUCATION		HEALTH & HEALTHCARE		AMENITIES	
High school degree	75.1%	Air-quality score	5	Miles to nearest major airport	72
4-year college degree	11.1%	Physicians per capita	163.1	Leisure rating	1
Graduate/professional degree	6.4%	Hospital beds per capita	552.0	Arts & Culture rating	2

Vero Beach, FL

Emerging City Rank: 7

Profile: Beach town
Location: Central Florida, north of Fort Pierce
Elevation: 17 feet

PRO	CON
Beaches	Cost of living
Small-town atmosphere	High unemployment

Vero Beach is an attractive, quiet, and somewhat upscale beach community along the central Florida coast. Tourists, retirees, agriculture, and fishing mainly support the area economy, but unemployment is fairly high. The cost of living is high by Florida standards. The area comes with the traditional leisure amenities of a Florida coastal city. The subtropical coastal climate is pleasant year-round. Summer temperatures are tempered by ocean breezes and by the frequent formation of afternoon cumulus clouds and showers.

POPULATION		ECONOMY & JOBS		COST OF LIVING	
Population	120,519	Household income	$44,541	Cost of Living Index	103.9
Population growth	33.6%	Unemployment rate	11.1%	Median home price	$167,300
Diversity measure	38.6%	Recent job growth	-.4%	Home price appreciation	10.3%

CLIMATE					
January low	54.0°F	Annual days > 90°F	34	Annual inches precipitation	49.8
July high	90.0°F	Annual days < 32°F	1	Annual inches snowfall	0.0
July relative humidity	63.0%	Annual days < 0°F	0	Annual days precipitation	120

EDUCATION		HEALTH & HEALTHCARE		AMENITIES	
High school degree	81.6%	Air-quality score	6	Miles to nearest major airport	35
4-year college degree	15.2%	Physicians per capita	260.5	Leisure rating	3
Graduate/professional degree	7.9%	Hospital beds per capita	539.3	Arts & Culture rating	3

Wenatchee, WA

Emerging City Rank: 16

Profile: Small town
Location: Central Washington, east slope of Cascade Range
Elevation: 645 feet

PRO	CON
Nearby mountains	Unemployment
Year-round climate	Cost of housing

Wenatchee is a mountain gateway between western Washington and the agricultural areas of the Columbia Plateau to the east. The economy is supported by agriculture and forest products, but current unemployment is high. The physical setting is attractive and the original downtown area is pleasant (winning a National Trust for Historic Preservation 2003 Great American Main Street Award), but the geography doesn't support recent growth and ugly sprawl has emerged to the north of town. The mountain rain shadow and marine influence create a pleasant year-round climate.

POPULATION		ECONOMY & JOBS		COST OF LIVING	
Population	101,967	Household income	$41,066	Cost of Living Index	101.4
Population growth	30.0%	Unemployment rate	8.7%	Median home price	$166,400
Diversity measure	36.8%	Recent job growth	-3.2%	Home price appreciation	5.9%

CLIMATE					
January low	24.3°F	Annual days > 90°F	33	Annual inches precipitation	8.9
July high	87.9°F	Annual days < 32°F	115	Annual inches snowfall	27.2
July relative humidity	28.0%	Annual days < 0°F	2	Annual days precipitation	70

EDUCATION		HEALTH & HEALTHCARE		AMENITIES	
High school degree	78.9%	Air-quality score	6	Miles to nearest major airport	92
4-year college degree	13.5%	Physicians per capita	205.0	Leisure rating	2
Graduate/professional degree	6.6%	Hospital beds per capita	267.7	Arts & Culture rating	1

Winchester, VA–WV

Profile: Small town
Location: Northern Virginia, north end of Shenandoah Valley
Elevation: 717 feet

Emerging City Rank: 17

PRO	CON
Historic interest	Local entertainment
Central location	Urban sprawl

Winchester is a small town with a diverse base of agriculture and light to moderate industry. Having changed hands 72 times during the Civil War, the town sits in the middle of an area of considerable historic interest. The downtown core with its historic buildings is attractive and interesting, but some unattractive sprawl exists outside of town, particularly to the south. Residents enjoy a blend of small-town life and a low cost of living with convenience to Washington, D.C, to the east, mountains to the west, and countryside on all sides. The mountains produce a mild climate for the region.

POPULATION

Population	106,276
Population growth	26.3%
Diversity measure	11.5%

ECONOMY & JOBS

Household income	$43,382
Unemployment rate	3.2%
Recent job growth	1.8%

COST OF LIVING

Cost of Living Index	88.2
Median home price	$135,500
Home price appreciation	8.5%

CLIMATE

January low	21.0°F	Annual days > 90°F	28
July high	87.0°F	Annual days < 32°F	116
July relative humidity	55.0%	Annual days < 0°F	0

Annual inches precipitation	40.4
Annual inches snowfall	23.0
Annual days precipitation	116

EDUCATION

High school degree	76.4%
4-year college degree	11.6%
Graduate/professional degree	6.7%

HEALTH & HEALTHCARE

Air-quality score	7
Physicians per capita	271.0
Hospital beds per capita	452.6

AMENITIES

Miles to nearest major airport	42
Leisure rating	2
Arts & Culture rating	2

Category Rankings of Principal U.S. Metropolitan Areas

Economy & Jobs

Scoring and ranking for Economy & Jobs is built around personal income and employment figures. The scoring and ranking process looks at income and employment levels and into recent and projected *trends* and *growth* in those areas. Category scoring gives current unemployment rate (2003) and recent job growth figures (mid-2002 to mid-2003) the highest weighting.

Metro Areas, Strongest to Weakest Economy

RANK		SCORE	RANK		SCORE
1.	Billings, MT	100	22.	Pocatello, ID	93
2.	Elkhart-Goshen, IN	99	23.	Ann Arbor, MI	93
3.	Anchorage, AK	99	24.	Nassau-Suffolk, NY	93
4.	Topeka, KS	99	25.	Kokomo, IN	92
5.	Lubbock, TX	98	26.	Fort Wayne, IN	92
6.	Sheboygan, WI	98	27.	Bryan-College Station, TX	92
7.	Madison, WI	98	28.	Abilene, TX	91
8.	Odessa-Midland, TX	97	29.	Appleton-Oshkosh-Neenah, WI	91
9.	Danbury, CT	97	30.	Providence-Fall River-Warwick, RI-MA	91
10.	Bloomington, IN	96	31.	Oklahoma City, OK	90
11.	Lansing-East Lansing, MI	96	32.	New Haven-Meriden, CT	90
12.	Charlottesville, VA	96	33.	Dutchess County, NY	90
13.	Glens Falls, NY	96	34.	Jackson, MS	89
14.	Honolulu, HI	96	35.	Newark, NJ	89
15.	Decatur, AL	95	36.	Bergen-Passaic, NJ	89
16.	Enid, OK	95	37.	San Angelo, TX	88
17.	Syracuse, NY	95	38.	Victoria, TX	88
18.	Tyler, TX	94	39.	Utica-Rome, NY	88
19.	Wichita, KS	94	40.	Lincoln, NE	88
20.	New London-Norwich, CT-RI	94	41.	Amarillo, TX	86
21.	Manchester, NH	93	42.	Saginaw-Bay City-Midland, MI	86

continued

Metro Areas, Strongest to Weakest Economy *(continued)*

RANK		SCORE	RANK		SCORE
43.	Huntsville, AL	86	99.	Nashua, NH	70
44.	Racine, WI	86	100.	Naples, FL	70
45.	Rochester, MN	86	101.	Gadsden, AL	68
46.	Trenton, NJ	86	102.	Owensboro, KY	68
47.	Middlesex-Somerset-Hunterdon, NJ	86	103.	Springfield, IL	68
48.	Roanoke, VA	85	104.	La Crosse, WI-MN	68
49.	Auburn-Opelika, AL	85	105.	Brockton, MA	68
50.	Washington, DC-MD-VA-WV	85	106.	Monmouth-Ocean, NJ	68
51.	Corpus Christi, TX	84	107.	Hamilton-Middletown, OH	67
52.	Jamestown, NY	84	108.	Wichita Falls, TX	66
53.	Bridgeport, CT	84	109.	Norfolk-Virginia Beach-Newport News, VA-NC	66
54.	Casper, WY	83	110.	Janesville-Beloit, WI	66
55.	Texarkana, TX-AR	83	111.	Lawrence, KS	66
56.	Cheyenne, WY	83	112.	Portland, ME	66
57.	Wausau, WI	83	113.	Lake Charles, LA	65
58.	Montgomery, AL	82	114.	Great Falls, MT	65
59.	Hagerstown, MD	82	115.	Peoria-Pekin, IL	65
60.	Benton Harbor, MI	82	116.	Greenville-Spartanburg-Anderson, SC	65
61.	Houma, LA	81	117.	Killeen-Temple, TX	64
62.	Missoula, MT	81	118.	Evansville-Henderson, IN-KY	64
63.	Omaha, NE-IA	81	119.	Charleston-North Charleston, SC	64
64.	Dothan, AL	80	120.	Beaumont-Port Arthur, TX	63
65.	Brazoria, TX	80	121.	Tuscaloosa, AL	63
66.	Bangor, ME	80	122.	Portsmouth-Rochester, NH-ME	63
67.	Baltimore, MD	80	123.	Los Angeles-Long Beach, CA	63
68.	Anniston, AL	79	124.	Alexandria, LA	62
69.	Macon, GA	79	125.	Olympia, WA	62
70.	Newburgh, NY-PA	79	126.	Philadelphia, PA-NJ	62
71.	Green Bay, WI	78	127.	Shreveport-Bossier City, LA	61
72.	Buffalo-Niagara Falls, NY	78	128.	Akron, OH	61
73.	Hartford, CT	78	129.	Birmingham, AL	61
74.	Jonesboro, AR	77	130.	Longview-Marshall, TX	60
75.	Wilmington-Newark, DE-MD	77	131.	South Bend, IN	60
76.	Detroit, MI	77	132.	Albany, GA	60
77.	Steubenville-Weirton, OH-WV	76	133.	Atlanta, GA	60
78.	Kalamazoo-Battle Creek, MI	76	134.	Grand Junction, CO	59
79.	Rochester, NY	76	135.	Kansas City, MO-KS	59
80.	Waco, TX	75	136.	Atlantic City-Cape May, NJ	59
81.	Florence, SC	75	137.	Houston, TX	58
82.	Lancaster, PA	75	138.	Fort Walton Beach, FL	57
83.	Pittsfield, MA	75	139.	Goldsboro, NC	57
84.	Sherman-Denison, TX	74	140.	Grand Rapids-Muskegon-Holland, MI	57
85.	Columbia, SC	74	141.	Burlington, VT	57
86.	Albany-Schenectady-Troy, NY	74	142.	Stamford-Norwalk, CT	57
87.	Augusta-Aiken, GA-SC	73	143.	Dayton-Springfield, OH	56
88.	Savannah, GA	73	144.	New Orleans, LA	56
89.	Lima, OH	72	145.	Columbus, OH	56
90.	Springfield, MA	72	146.	Waterbury, CT	56
91.	Fitchburg-Leominster, MA	72	147.	Little Rock-North Little Rock, AR	55
92.	St. Louis, MO-IL	71	148.	Binghamton, NY	55
93.	Champaign-Urbana, IL	71	149.	Albuquerque, NM	55
94.	Vineland-Millville-Bridgeton, NJ	71	150.	Cleveland-Lorain-Elyria, OH	54
95.	Bloomington-Normal, IL	71	151.	Lafayette, LA	53
96.	Cincinnati, OH-KY-IN	71	152.	Fayetteville-Springdale-Rogers, AR	53
97.	Decatur, IL	70	153.	Elmira, NY	53
98.	Richmond-Petersburg, VA	70	154.	Bellingham, WA	53

RANK		SCORE
155.	Waterloo–Cedar Falls, IA	53
156.	Duluth-Superior, MN-WI	53
157.	Muncie, IN	52
158.	San Antonio, TX	52
159.	Jackson, MI	52
160.	Fort Smith, AR-OK	51
161.	Cumberland, MD-WV	51
162.	Dover, DE	51
163.	Rockford, IL	50
164.	Kenosha, WI	50
165.	Corvallis, OR	50
166.	Milwaukee-Waukesha, WI	50
167.	Lawton, OK	49
168.	Lafayette, IN	49
169.	Allentown-Bethlehem-Easton, PA	49
170.	Rapid City, SD	48
171.	Huntington-Ashland, WV-KY-OH	48
172.	Lexington, KY	48
173.	Williamsport, PA	47
174.	Indianapolis, IN	47
175.	Davenport-Moline-Rock Island, IA-IL	47
176.	Chattanooga, TN-GA	46
177.	Galveston-Texas City, TX	46
178.	Harrisburg-Lebanon-Carlisle, PA	46
179.	Youngstown-Warren, OH	46
180.	Louisville, KY-IN	45
181.	Iowa City, IA	45
182.	Chicago, IL	45
183.	Fort Worth–Arlington, TX	44
184.	Melbourne-Titusville-Palm Bay, FL	43
185.	Springfield, MO	43
186.	Fargo-Moorhead, ND-MN	43
187.	Dubuque, IA	43
188.	Denver, CO	43
189.	Danville, VA	42
190.	Grand Forks, ND-MN	42
191.	Greensboro-Winston-Salem-High Point, NC	42
192.	Minneapolis–St. Paul, MN-WI	42
193.	Mansfield, OH	41
194.	Bismarck, ND	41
195.	Richland-Kennewick-Pasco, WA	40
196.	Nashville, TN	40
197.	Gary, IN	40
198.	Lewiston-Auburn, ME	40
199.	Hattiesburg, MS	39
200.	Worcester, MA-CT	39
201.	Orange County, CA	39
202.	Sioux Falls, SD	38
203.	Jacksonville, FL	38
204.	Athens, GA	38
205.	Charlotte-Gastonia-Rock Hill, NC-SC	38
206.	York, PA	37
207.	Eau Claire, WI	37
208.	Dallas, TX	37
209.	Johnson City-Kingsport-Bristol, TN-VA	36
210.	Terre Haute, IN	36
211.	Mobile, AL	36
212.	Santa Fe, NM	36

RANK		SCORE
213.	Canton-Massillon, OH	35
214.	Des Moines, IA	35
215.	Pine Bluff, AR	34
216.	Baton Rouge, LA	34
217.	Reno, NV	34
218.	Cedar Rapids, IA	34
219.	Lakeland-Winter Haven, FL	33
220.	Knoxville, TN	33
221.	Lynchburg, VA	33
222.	Reading, PA	33
223.	Daytona Beach, FL	32
224.	Fayetteville, NC	32
225.	West Palm Beach–Boca Raton, FL	32
226.	Columbus, GA-AL	31
227.	Greeley, CO	31
228.	San Luis Obispo-Atascadero-Paso Robles, CA	31
229.	Monroe, LA	30
230.	Pueblo, CO	30
231.	Asheville, NC	30
232.	Raleigh-Durham-Chapel Hill, NC	30
233.	Ocala, FL	29
234.	Barnstable-Yarmouth, MA	29
235.	Sumter, SC	28
236.	Parkersburg-Marietta, WV-OH	28
237.	Riverside-San Bernardino, CA	28
238.	Boston, MA-NH	28
239.	Memphis, TN-AR-MS	27
240.	Salt Lake City-Ogden, UT	27
241.	St. Joseph, MO	26
242.	El Paso, TX	26
243.	Bremerton, WA	26
244.	Sacramento, CA	26
245.	Jersey City, NJ	26
246.	Clarksville-Hopkinsville, TN-KY	25
247.	Brownsville–Harlingen-San Benito, TX	25
248.	State College, PA	25
249.	Punta Gorda, FL	24
250.	Las Cruces, NM	24
251.	Toledo, OH	24
252.	Flint, MI	23
253.	Eugene-Springfield, OR	23
254.	St. Cloud, MN	23
255.	Oakland, CA	23
256.	Sharon, PA	22
257.	Vallejo-Fairfield-Napa, CA	22
258.	Tampa–St. Petersburg-Clearwater, FL	21
259.	Fort Pierce-Port St. Lucie, FL	21
260.	Pittsburgh, PA	21
261.	Kankakee, IL	21
262.	Altoona, PA	20
263.	Modesto, CA	20
264.	Lowell, MA-NH	20
265.	Santa Barbara-Santa Maria-Lompoc, CA	20
266.	Charleston, WV	19
267.	Jacksonville, NC	18
268.	Fort Myers–Cape Coral, FL	18
269.	Sioux City, IA-NE	18
270.	Salem, OR	18

continued

Metro Areas, Strongest to Weakest Economy (continued)

RANK		SCORE
271.	Fort Lauderdale, FL	18
272.	Spokane, WA	17
273.	Scranton–Wilkes-Barre–Hazleton, PA	17
274.	Ventura, CA	17
275.	Merced, CA	16
276.	Fort Collins–Loveland, CO	16
277.	New Bedford, MA	16
278.	Lawrence, MA-NH	16
279.	Panama City, FL	15
280.	Tulsa, OK	15
281.	San Diego, CA	15
282.	Orlando, FL	14
283.	Tallahassee, FL	14
284.	Redding, CA	14
285.	Austin–San Marcos, TX	13
286.	Chico-Paradise, CA	13
287.	Stockton-Lodi, CA	13
288.	New York, NY	13
289.	Tucson, AZ	12
290.	Tacoma, WA	12
291.	Colorado Springs, CO	12
292.	Sarasota-Bradenton, FL	11
293.	Wheeling, WV-OH	11
294.	Columbia, MO	11
295.	Jackson, TN	10
296.	Johnstown, PA	10
297.	Phoenix-Mesa, AZ	10
298.	Provo-Orem, UT	10
299.	Erie, PA	9
300.	Medford-Ashland, OR	9

RANK		SCORE
301.	Yolo, CA	9
302.	Pensacola, FL	8
303.	Miami, FL	8
304.	Seattle-Bellevue-Everett, WA	8
305.	Joplin, MO	7
306.	Santa Rosa, CA	7
307.	Laredo, TX	6
308.	Gainesville, FL	6
309.	Biloxi-Gulfport-Pascagoula, MS	6
310.	Hickory-Morganton-Lenoir, NC	6
311.	Santa Cruz–Watsonville, CA	6
312.	Myrtle Beach, SC	5
313.	Bakersfield, CA	5
314.	Visalia-Tulare-Porterville, CA	5
315.	Yakima, WA	4
316.	Salinas, CA	4
317.	San Francisco, CA	4
318.	Rocky Mount, NC	3
319.	Greenville, NC	3
320.	Boise, ID	3
321.	Wilmington, NC	3
322.	McAllen-Edinburg-Mission, TX	2
323.	Florence, AL	2
324.	Fresno, CA	2
325.	Las Vegas, NV-AZ	1
326.	Portland-Vancouver, OR-WA	1
327.	San Jose, CA	1
328.	Yuma, AZ	0
329.	Yuba City–Marysville, CA	0
330.	Flagstaff, AZ-UT	0
331.	Boulder-Longmont, CO	0

Cost of Living

The Cost of Living score incorporates the U.S. Bureau of Labor Statistics Cost of Living Index, a composite measure of the normal expenses for daily living necessities like food, utilities, transportation, and miscellaneous costs. In addition, costs of housing and income and sales taxes are included and receive high weighting. Included with lower weighting are home price appreciation, property taxes, and the cost of auto insurance.

Metro Areas, Least to Most Expensive

RANK		SCORE
1.	Casper, WY	100
2.	Dothan, AL	99
3.	Clarksville-Hopkinsville, TN-KY	99
4.	McAllen-Edinburg-Mission, TX	99
5.	Texarkana, TX-AR	98
6.	Alexandria, LA	98
7.	Longview-Marshall, TX	98
8.	Johnson City–Kingsport–Bristol, TN-VA	97

RANK		SCORE
9.	Joplin, MO	97
10.	Florence, AL	97
11.	Anniston, AL	96
12.	Gadsden, AL	96
13.	Wichita Falls, TX	96
14.	Brownsville-Harlingen-San Benito, TX	96
15.	San Angelo, TX	95
16.	Victoria, TX	95

RANK		SCORE
17.	Cheyenne, WY	94
18.	Houma, LA	94
19.	Killeen-Temple, TX	94
20.	Jackson, TN	94
21.	Rapid City, SD	93
22.	Ocala, FL	93
23.	Johnstown, PA	93
24.	Laredo, TX	93
25.	Sherman-Denison, TX	92
26.	Decatur, AL	91
27.	Amarillo, TX	91
28.	Waco, TX	91
29.	Beaumont–Port Arthur, TX	91
30.	Melbourne–Titusville–Palm Bay, FL	91
31.	Odessa-Midland, TX	90
32.	Tyler, TX	90
33.	Steubenville-Weirton, OH-WV	90
34.	Daytona Beach, FL	90
35.	Montgomery, AL	89
36.	Danville, VA	89
37.	Lakeland–Winter Haven, FL	89
38.	Enid, OK	88
39.	Abilene, TX	88
40.	Pensacola, FL	88
41.	Terre Haute, IN	87
42.	Tampa–St. Petersburg–Clearwater, FL	87
43.	Panama City, FL	87
44.	Evansville-Henderson, IN-KY	86
45.	Sharon, PA	86
46.	Jacksonville, NC	86
47.	South Bend, IN	85
48.	Fort Walton Beach, FL	85
49.	Monroe, LA	85
50.	St. Joseph, MO	85
51.	Lubbock, TX	84
52.	Kokomo, IN	84
53.	Pine Bluff, AR	84
54.	Fort Wayne, IN	83
55.	Albany, GA	83
56.	Altoona, PA	83
57.	Fort Myers–Cape Coral, FL	83
58.	Lima, OH	82
59.	Decatur, IL	82
60.	Muncie, IN	82
61.	Lafayette, LA	81
62.	Fort Smith, AR-OK	81
63.	Punta Gorda, FL	81
64.	Lake Charles, LA	80
65.	Chattanooga, TN-GA	80
66.	Knoxville, TN	80
67.	Bryan–College Station, TX	79
68.	Jonesboro, AR	79
69.	Sioux Falls, SD	79
70.	Lynchburg, VA	79
71.	Corpus Christi, TX	78
72.	Lawton, OK	78
73.	Sarasota-Bradenton, FL	78
74.	Lafayette, IN	77

RANK		SCORE
75.	Orlando, FL	77
76.	Gainesville, FL	77
77.	Tuscaloosa, AL	76
78.	Mansfield, OH	76
79.	Hattiesburg, MS	76
80.	Sumter, SC	76
81.	Fayetteville-Springdale-Rogers, AR	75
82.	Grand Forks, ND-MN	75
83.	Roanoke, VA	74
84.	Auburn-Opelika, AL	74
85.	Huntington-Ashland, WV-KY-OH	74
86.	Brazoria, TX	73
87.	Cumberland, MD-WV	73
88.	Columbus, GA-AL	73
89.	El Paso, TX	73
90.	Wheeling, WV-OH	73
91.	Owensboro, KY	72
92.	Williamsport, PA	72
93.	Fort Pierce–Port St. Lucie, FL	72
94.	Jacksonville, FL	71
95.	Augusta-Aiken, GA-SC	70
96.	Shreveport–Bossier City, LA	70
97.	San Antonio, TX	70
98.	Galveston–Texas City, TX	70
99.	Erie, PA	70
100.	Rocky Mount, NC	70
101.	Goldsboro, NC	69
102.	Spokane, WA	69
103.	Yakima, WA	69
104.	Jackson, MS	68
105.	Saginaw–Bay City–Midland, MI	68
106.	Yuma, AZ	68
107.	Florence, SC	67
108.	Parkersburg-Marietta, WV-OH	67
109.	Tallahassee, FL	67
110.	Bangor, ME	66
111.	Indianapolis, IN	66
112.	Harrisburg-Lebanon-Carlisle, PA	66
113.	Biloxi-Gulfport-Pascagoula, MS	66
114.	Springfield, MO	65
115.	Richland-Kennewick-Pasco, WA	65
116.	Columbia, MO	65
117.	Dover, DE	64
118.	York, PA	64
119.	Elkhart-Goshen, IN	63
120.	Great Falls, MT	63
121.	Bismarck, ND	63
122.	State College, PA	63
123.	Hickory-Morganton-Lenoir, NC	63
124.	Fargo-Moorhead, ND-MN	62
125.	Memphis, TN-AR-MS	62
126.	Greenville, NC	62
127.	Little Rock–North Little Rock, AR	61
128.	Fayetteville, NC	61
129.	Las Cruces, NM	61
130.	Macon, GA	60
131.	Jackson, MI	60
132.	Fort Worth–Arlington, TX	60

continued

Metro Areas, Least to Most Expensive *(continued)*

RANK		SCORE	RANK		SCORE
133.	Nashville, TN	60	189.	Charlottesville, VA	42
134.	Springfield, IL	59	190.	Dallas, TX	42
135.	Billings, MT	58	191.	Boise, ID	42
136.	Huntsville, AL	58	192.	Salem, OR	41
137.	Pueblo, CO	58	193.	Phoenix-Mesa, AZ	41
138.	Charleston, WV	58	194.	Miami, FL	41
139.	Scranton-Wilkes-Barre-Hazleton, PA	58	195.	La Crosse, WI-MN	40
140.	Wichita, KS	57	196.	Akron, OH	40
141.	Peoria-Pekin, IL	57	197.	Lexington, KY	40
142.	Canton-Massillon, OH	57	198.	Dubuque, IA	40
143.	Anchorage, AK	56	199.	Tucson, AZ	40
144.	Topeka, KS	56	200.	Vineland-Millville-Bridgeton, NJ	39
145.	Kalamazoo-Battle Creek, MI	56	201.	Toledo, OH	39
146.	Gary, IN	56	202.	Fort Lauderdale, FL	39
147.	Bloomington, IN	55	203.	Louisville, KY-IN	38
148.	Manchester, NH	55	204.	Visalia-Tulare-Porterville, CA	38
149.	Hamilton-Middletown, OH	55	205.	Appleton-Oshkosh-Neenah, WI	37
150.	Norfolk-Virginia Beach-Newport News, VA-NC	54	206.	Wausau, WI	37
151.	Youngstown-Warren, OH	54	207.	Binghamton, NY	37
152.	Pittsburgh, PA	54	208.	Wilmington, NC	37
153.	Oklahoma City, OK	53	209.	Birmingham, AL	36
154.	Mobile, AL	53	210.	Dayton-Springfield, OH	36
155.	Baton Rouge, LA	53	211.	New Orleans, LA	36
156.	Kankakee, IL	53	212.	Utica-Rome, NY	35
157.	Wilmington-Newark, DE-MD	52	213.	Jamestown, NY	35
158.	Columbia, SC	52	214.	Davenport-Moline-Rock Island, IA-IL	35
159.	Greenville-Spartanburg-Anderson, SC	52	215.	Medford-Ashland, OR	35
160.	Athens, GA	51	216.	Glens Falls, NY	34
161.	Flint, MI	51	217.	Bloomington-Normal, IL	34
162.	Las Vegas, NV-AZ	51	218.	Grand Junction, CO	34
163.	St. Louis, MO-IL	50	219.	Benton Harbor, MI	33
164.	Elmira, NY	50	220.	Duluth-Superior, MN-WI	33
165.	Reading, PA	50	221.	Reno, NV	33
166.	Austin-San Marcos, TX	50	222.	Bremerton, WA	33
167.	Richmond-Petersburg, VA	49	223.	Sheboygan, WI	32
168.	Grand Rapids-Muskegon-Holland, MI	49	224.	Cincinnati, OH-KY-IN	32
169.	Eugene-Springfield, OR	49	225.	Janesville-Beloit, WI	32
170.	Savannah, GA	48	226.	Racine, WI	31
171.	Champaign-Urbana, IL	48	227.	Green Bay, WI	31
172.	Lansing-East Lansing, MI	47	228.	Rockford, IL	31
173.	Pocatello, ID	47	229.	Missoula, MT	30
174.	Houston, TX	47	230.	Lawrence, KS	30
175.	Bellingham, WA	47	231.	Charleston-North Charleston, SC	30
176.	Hagerstown, MD	46	232.	Allentown-Bethlehem-Easton, PA	30
177.	Nashua, NH	46	233.	Lewiston-Auburn, ME	29
178.	Greensboro-Winston-Salem-High Point, NC	46	234.	Asheville, NC	29
179.	Tulsa, OK	46	235.	St. Cloud, MN	29
180.	Lancaster, PA	45	236.	Omaha, NE-IA	28
181.	Olympia, WA	45	237.	Portsmouth-Rochester, NH-ME	28
182.	Waterloo-Cedar Falls, IA	45	238.	Tacoma, WA	28
183.	Eau Claire, WI	44	239.	Kansas City, MO-KS	27
184.	Sioux City, IA-NE	44	240.	Columbus, OH	27
185.	Myrtle Beach, SC	44	241.	Cedar Rapids, IA	27
186.	West Palm Beach-Boca Raton, FL	43	242.	Syracuse, NY	26
187.	Greeley, CO	43	243.	Salt Lake City-Ogden, UT	26
188.	Bakersfield, CA	43	244.	Colorado Springs, CO	26

RANK		SCORE
245.	Fresno, CA	26
246.	Pittsfield, MA	25
247.	Springfield, MA	25
248.	Charlotte-Gastonia-Rock Hill, NC-SC	25
249.	Albuquerque, NM	24
250.	Lincoln, NE	23
251.	Atlanta, GA	23
252.	Atlantic City-Cape May, NJ	23
253.	Kenosha, WI	23
254.	Des Moines, IA	23
255.	Raleigh-Durham-Chapel Hill, NC	23
256.	Corvallis, OR	22
257.	Iowa City, IA	22
258.	Yuba City-Marysville, CA	22
259.	Merced, CA	21
260.	Redding, CA	21
261.	Provo-Orem, UT	21
262.	Fitchburg-Leominster, MA	20
263.	Naples, FL	20
264.	Portland-Vancouver, OR-WA	20
265.	Rochester, MN	19
266.	Rochester, NY	19
267.	Cleveland-Lorain-Elyria, OH	19
268.	Worcester, MA-CT	19
269.	Buffalo-Niagara Falls, NY	18
270.	Burlington, VT	18
271.	Flagstaff, AZ-UT	18
272.	Trenton, NJ	17
273.	Detroit, MI	17
274.	Modesto, CA	17
275.	New London-Norwich, CT-RI	16
276.	Waterbury, CT	16
277.	Fort Collins-Loveland, CO	16
278.	Chico-Paradise, CA	16
279.	Madison, WI	15
280.	Albany-Schenectady-Troy, NY	15
281.	Hartford, CT	14
282.	Denver, CO	14
283.	Riverside-San Bernardino, CA	14
284.	New Bedford, MA	14
285.	Ann Arbor, MI	13
286.	Portland, ME	13
287.	Milwaukee-Waukesha, WI	13

RANK		SCORE
288.	Stockton-Lodi, CA	13
289.	New Haven-Meriden, CT	12
290.	Baltimore, MD	12
291.	Philadelphia, PA-NJ	12
292.	Newburgh, NY-PA	11
293.	Santa Fe, NM	11
294.	Seattle-Bellevue-Everett, WA	11
295.	Dutchess County, NY	10
296.	Chicago, IL	10
297.	Minneapolis-St. Paul, MN-WI	10
298.	Sacramento, CA	10
299.	Providence-Fall River-Warwick, RI-MA	9
300.	Brockton, MA	9
301.	Yolo, CA	9
302.	Jersey City, NJ	8
303.	Boulder-Longmont, CO	8
304.	Bridgeport, CT	7
305.	Barnstable-Yarmouth, MA	7
306.	Lowell, MA-NH	7
307.	Lawrence, MA-NH	7
308.	Newark, NJ	6
309.	Middlesex-Somerset-Hunterdon, NJ	6
310.	Monmouth-Ocean, NJ	6
311.	Vallejo-Fairfield-Napa, CA	6
312.	Washington, DC-MD-VA-WV	5
313.	Los Angeles-Long Beach, CA	5
314.	San Luis Obispo-Atascadero-Paso Robles, CA	5
315.	Danbury, CT	4
316.	Boston, MA-NH	4
317.	Ventura, CA	4
318.	Honolulu, HI	3
319.	Nassau-Suffolk, NY	3
320.	Bergen-Passaic, NJ	3
321.	San Diego, CA	3
322.	New York, NY	2
323.	Santa Rosa, CA	2
324.	Salinas, CA	2
325.	Orange County, CA	1
326.	Santa Barbara-Santa Maria-Lompoc, CA	1
327.	Santa Cruz-Watsonville, CA	1
328.	Stamford-Norwalk, CT	0
329.	Oakland, CA	0
330.	San Francisco, CA	0
331.	San Jose, CA	0

Climate

Climate rankings include an assortment of temperature, precipitation, sky cover, and hazard features outlined in chapter 3. The highest weightings are given to temperature extremes (above 90°F, below 32°F, below 0°F), days of rain, and snowfall. Average temperatures, humidity, and total rainfall get slightly less weight, and climate hazards receive the lowest weighting.

Metro Areas, Most to Least Favorable Climate

RANK		SCORE
1.	Salinas, CA	100
2.	Oakland, CA	99
3.	Santa Cruz–Watsonville, CA	99
4.	San Francisco, CA	99
5.	Honolulu, HI	98
6.	San Luis Obispo–Atascadero–Paso Robles, CA	98
7.	Santa Barbara–Santa Maria–Lompoc, CA	98
8.	Los Angeles–Long Beach, CA	97
9.	Orange County, CA	97
10.	Ventura, CA	97
11.	Riverside–San Bernardino, CA	96
12.	San Diego, CA	96
13.	Redding, CA	96
14.	San Jose, CA	96
15.	Vallejo–Fairfield–Napa, CA	95
16.	Tucson, AZ	95
17.	Santa Rosa, CA	95
18.	Santa Fe, NM	94
19.	Sacramento, CA	94
20.	Yuba City–Marysville, CA	94
21.	San Angelo, TX	93
22.	Galveston–Texas City, TX	93
23.	Yolo, CA	93
24.	Bakersfield, CA	93
25.	Modesto, CA	92
26.	Merced, CA	92
27.	Stockton–Lodi, CA	92
28.	Brownsville–Harlingen–San Benito, TX	91
29.	Las Cruces, NM	91
30.	Chico–Paradise, CA	91
31.	Abilene, TX	90
32.	Colorado Springs, CO	90
33.	Phoenix–Mesa, AZ	90
34.	Yuma, AZ	90
35.	Laredo, TX	89
36.	Visalia–Tulare–Porterville, CA	89
37.	Fresno, CA	89
38.	San Antonio, TX	88
39.	El Paso, TX	88
40.	Austin–San Marcos, TX	88
41.	Odessa–Midland, TX	87
42.	Waco, TX	87
43.	Sherman–Denison, TX	87
44.	Amarillo, TX	86
45.	Corpus Christi, TX	86
46.	Fort Worth–Arlington, TX	86
47.	Dallas, TX	86
48.	Lubbock, TX	85
49.	Victoria, TX	85
50.	Albuquerque, NM	85
51.	Vineland–Millville–Bridgeton, NJ	84
52.	Atlantic City–Cape May, NJ	84
53.	Reno, NV	84
54.	Naples, FL	83
55.	Monmouth–Ocean, NJ	83
56.	Ocala, FL	83

RANK		SCORE
57.	Gainesville, FL	83
58.	Punta Gorda, FL	82
59.	Orlando, FL	82
60.	Sarasota–Bradenton, FL	82
61.	Bellingham, WA	81
62.	Tampa–St. Petersburg–Clearwater, FL	81
63.	Fort Myers–Cape Coral, FL	81
64.	Bremerton, WA	80
65.	Charleston, WV	80
66.	Tacoma, WA	80
67.	Seattle–Bellevue–Everett, WA	80
68.	Huntington–Ashland, WV–KY–OH	79
69.	Miami, FL	79
70.	Las Vegas, NV–AZ	79
71.	Wichita Falls, TX	78
72.	Fort Lauderdale, FL	78
73.	Tulsa, OK	78
74.	Lakeland–Winter Haven, FL	77
75.	New York, NY	77
76.	Portland–Vancouver, OR–WA	77
77.	Melbourne–Titusville–Palm Bay, FL	76
78.	Daytona Beach, FL	76
79.	Biloxi–Gulfport–Pascagoula, MS	76
80.	McAllen–Edinburg–Mission, TX	76
81.	Nassau–Suffolk, NY	75
82.	Roanoke, VA	75
83.	Lawton, OK	75
84.	New London–Norwich, CT–RI	74
85.	Stamford–Norwalk, CT	74
86.	New Haven–Meriden, CT	73
87.	Bridgeport, CT	73
88.	Texarkana, TX–AR	73
89.	Longview–Marshall, TX	73
90.	Monroe, LA	73
91.	Tyler, TX	72
92.	Shreveport–Bossier City, LA	72
93.	Atlanta, GA	72
94.	Lafayette, LA	71
95.	Baton Rouge, LA	71
96.	Jacksonville, NC	71
97.	Enid, OK	70
98.	Oklahoma City, OK	70
99.	Houma, LA	70
100.	New Orleans, LA	70
101.	Charlottesville, VA	69
102.	Grand Junction, CO	69
103.	Lynchburg, VA	69
104.	Fort Walton Beach, FL	68
105.	Panama City, FL	68
106.	Pensacola, FL	68
107.	Bryan–College Station, TX	67
108.	Killeen–Temple, TX	67
109.	Beaumont–Port Arthur, TX	67
110.	Corvallis, OR	66
111.	Pueblo, CO	66
112.	Salem, OR	66

RANK	SCORE
113. New Bedford, MA	66
114. Lake Charles, LA	65
115. Asheville, NC	65
116. Barnstable-Yarmouth, MA	65
117. West Palm Beach–Boca Raton, FL	64
118. Eugene-Springfield, OR	64
119. Fort Pierce–Port St. Lucie, FL	64
120. Philadelphia, PA-NJ	63
121. Raleigh–Durham–Chapel Hill, NC	63
122. Rocky Mount, NC	63
123. Flagstaff, AZ-UT	63
124. Norfolk–Virginia Beach–Newport News, VA-NC	62
125. Alexandria, LA	62
126. Fayetteville, NC	62
127. Albany, GA	61
128. Goldsboro, NC	61
129. Hattiesburg, MS	61
130. Savannah, GA	60
131. Dover, DE	60
132. Mobile, AL	60
133. Tallahassee, FL	60
134. Wilmington-Newark, DE-MD	59
135. Danville, VA	59
136. Hickory-Morganton-Lenoir, NC	59
137. Trenton, NJ	58
138. Middlesex-Somerset-Hunterdon, NJ	58
139. Greensboro–Winston-Salem–High Point, NC	58
140. Wichita, KS	57
141. Medford-Ashland, OR	57
142. Boise, ID	57
143. Brazoria, TX	56
144. Charleston–North Charleston, SC	56
145. Houston, TX	56
146. Johnson City–Kingsport–Bristol, TN-VA	56
147. Montgomery, AL	55
148. Provo-Orem, UT	55
149. Boulder-Longmont, CO	55
150. Denver, CO	54
151. Greeley, CO	54
152. Fort Collins–Loveland, CO	54
153. Augusta-Aiken, GA-SC	53
154. Fayetteville-Springdale-Rogers, AR	53
155. Athens, GA	53
156. Greenville, NC	53
157. Jacksonville, FL	52
158. Myrtle Beach, SC	52
159. Wilmington, NC	52
160. Jackson, MS	51
161. Greenville-Spartanburg-Anderson, SC	51
162. Cumberland, MD-WV	51
163. Bloomington, IN	50
164. Macon, GA	50
165. Muncie, IN	50
166. Terre Haute, IN	50
167. Kokomo, IN	49
168. Lafayette, IN	49
169. Indianapolis, IN	49
170. Jonesboro, AR	48

RANK	SCORE
171. Fort Smith, AR-OK	48
172. Columbus, GA-AL	48
173. Bergen-Passaic, NJ	47
174. Dothan, AL	47
175. Memphis, TN-AR-MS	47
176. Newark, NJ	46
177. Dayton-Springfield, OH	46
178. Parkersburg-Marietta, WV-OH	46
179. Jersey City, NJ	46
180. Olympia, WA	45
181. Louisville, KY-IN	45
182. Pine Bluff, AR	45
183. Hagerstown, MD	44
184. Little Rock–North Little Rock, AR	44
185. Charlotte–Gastonia–Rock Hill, NC-SC	44
186. Topeka, KS	43
187. Washington, DC-MD-VA-WV	43
188. Baltimore, MD	43
189. Columbus, OH	43
190. Fort Wayne, IN	42
191. State College, PA	42
192. Altoona, PA	42
193. Casper, WY	41
194. Cheyenne, WY	41
195. Johnstown, PA	41
196. Ann Arbor, MI	40
197. Detroit, MI	40
198. Owensboro, KY	40
199. Toledo, OH	40
200. Champaign-Urbana, IL	39
201. Peoria-Pekin, IL	39
202. Lexington, KY	39
203. Decatur, IL	38
204. Springfield, IL	38
205. Evansville-Henderson, IN-KY	38
206. Bloomington-Normal, IL	37
207. Knoxville, TN	37
208. Jackson, TN	37
209. St. Louis, MO-IL	36
210. Richmond-Petersburg, VA	36
211. Fargo-Moorhead, ND-MN	36
212. Grand Forks, ND-MN	36
213. Florence, SC	35
214. Columbia, SC	35
215. Sumter, SC	35
216. Harrisburg-Lebanon-Carlisle, PA	34
217. Richland-Kennewick-Pasco, WA	34
218. Yakima, WA	34
219. Lancaster, PA	33
220. Hamilton-Middletown, OH	33
221. York, PA	33
222. Reading, PA	33
223. Providence–Fall River–Warwick, RI-MA	32
224. Cincinnati, OH-KY-IN	32
225. Allentown-Bethlehem-Easton, PA	32
226. Lawrence, KS	31
227. Springfield, MO	31
228. Boston, MA-NH	31

continued

Metro Areas, Most to Least Favorable Climate *(continued)*

RANK		SCORE
229.	Waterloo–Cedar Falls, IA	30
230.	Salt Lake City–Ogden, UT	30
231.	Spokane, WA	30
232.	Wheeling, WV–OH	30
233.	Steubenville–Weirton, OH–WV	29
234.	Pittsburgh, PA	29
235.	Joplin, MO	29
236.	Bangor, ME	28
237.	Gary, IN	28
238.	Sioux City, IA–NE	28
239.	Elkhart–Goshen, IN	27
240.	South Bend, IN	27
241.	Chicago, IL	27
242.	Anniston, AL	26
243.	Gadsden, AL	26
244.	Iowa City, IA	26
245.	Flint, MI	26
246.	Auburn–Opelika, AL	25
247.	Birmingham, AL	25
248.	Des Moines, IA	25
249.	Janesville–Beloit, WI	24
250.	Chattanooga, TN–GA	24
251.	Bismarck, ND	24
252.	Madison, WI	23
253.	Lima, OH	23
254.	Mansfield, OH	23
255.	Columbia, MO	23
256.	Missoula, MT	22
257.	Tuscaloosa, AL	22
258.	Rockford, IL	22
259.	Kansas City, MO–KS	21
260.	Nashville, TN	21
261.	St. Joseph, MO	21
262.	Decatur, AL	20
263.	Huntsville, AL	20
264.	Clarksville–Hopkinsville, TN–KY	20
265.	Florence, AL	20
266.	Akron, OH	19
267.	Sioux Falls, SD	19
268.	Scranton–Wilkes-Barre–Hazleton, PA	19
269.	Saginaw–Bay City–Midland, MI	18
270.	Omaha, NE–IA	18
271.	Cedar Rapids, IA	18
272.	Sheboygan, WI	17
273.	Wausau, WI	17
274.	Davenport–Moline–Rock Island, IA–IL	17
275.	Appleton–Oshkosh–Neenah, WI	16
276.	Racine, WI	16
277.	Green Bay, WI	16
278.	St. Cloud, MN	16
279.	Cleveland–Lorain–Elyria, OH	15

RANK		SCORE
280.	Kenosha, WI	15
281.	Milwaukee–Waukesha, WI	15
282.	Buffalo–Niagara Falls, NY	14
283.	Great Falls, MT	14
284.	Canton–Massillon, OH	14
285.	Lincoln, NE	13
286.	Rochester, NY	13
287.	La Crosse, WI–MN	13
288.	Williamsport, PA	13
289.	Rochester, MN	12
290.	Minneapolis–St. Paul, MN–WI	12
291.	Eau Claire, WI	12
292.	Jamestown, NY	11
293.	Kalamazoo–Battle Creek, MI	11
294.	Erie, PA	11
295.	Billings, MT	10
296.	Brockton, MA	10
297.	Grand Rapids–Muskegon–Holland, MI	10
298.	Lawrence, MA–NH	10
299.	Jackson, MI	9
300.	Kankakee, IL	9
301.	Lowell, MA–NH	9
302.	Lansing–East Lansing, MI	8
303.	Youngstown–Warren, OH	8
304.	Sharon, PA	8
305.	Binghamton, NY	7
306.	Elmira, NY	7
307.	Rapid City, SD	7
308.	Anchorage, AK	6
309.	Syracuse, NY	6
310.	Utica–Rome, NY	6
311.	Dubuque, IA	6
312.	Manchester, NH	5
313.	Pocatello, ID	5
314.	Duluth–Superior, MN–WI	5
315.	Glens Falls, NY	4
316.	Pittsfield, MA	4
317.	Albany–Schenectady–Troy, NY	4
318.	Dutchess County, NY	3
319.	Newburgh, NY–PA	3
320.	Fitchburg–Leominster, MA	3
321.	Worcester, MA–CT	3
322.	Hartford, CT	2
323.	Nashua, NH	2
324.	Waterbury, CT	2
325.	Danbury, CT	1
326.	Springfield, MA	1
327.	Burlington, VT	1
328.	Benton Harbor, MI	0
329.	Portland, ME	0
330.	Portsmouth–Rochester, NH–ME	0
331.	Lewiston–Auburn, ME	0

Education

Education rankings represent a cross section of attainment, investment, preference, and resources. The highest weighting is given to high school, 4-year college, and graduate school graduation rates; ratio of public to private school attendance for primary/secondary schools; and number of 4-year and highly rated universities in the area. Less weight is given to student-teacher ratios, investment per pupil, and 2-year college availability and attainment.

Metro Areas, Strongest to Weakest Education

RANK		SCORE	RANK		SCORE
1.	Boston, MA-NH	100	45.	Charlottesville, VA	87
2.	Washington, DC-MD-VA-WV	99	46.	Bryan-College Station, TX	87
3.	New York, NY	99	47.	Rochester, MN	86
4.	Chicago, IL	99	48.	Danbury, CT	86
5.	Madison, WI	98	49.	Portland-Vancouver, OR-WA	85
6.	Philadelphia, PA-NJ	98	50.	State College, PA	85
7.	Iowa City, IA	98	51.	Kansas City, MO-KS	85
8.	Minneapolis-St. Paul, MN-WI	97	52.	Provo-Orem, UT	84
9.	Boulder-Longmont, CO	97	53.	New Haven-Meriden, CT	84
10.	Lawrence, KS	97	54.	Cedar Rapids, IA	84
11.	Atlanta, GA	96	55.	Santa Fe, NM	84
12.	Raleigh-Durham-Chapel Hill, NC	96	56.	Des Moines, IA	84
13.	Nassau-Suffolk, NY	96	57.	San Jose, CA	83
14.	Burlington, VT	96	58.	Lincoln, NE	83
15.	Columbia, MO	95	59.	Bloomington, IN	82
16.	Portland, ME	95	60.	Bridgeport, CT	82
17.	Albany-Schenectady-Troy, NY	95	61.	Oakland, CA	82
18.	Barnstable-Yarmouth, MA	94	62.	Olympia, WA	81
19.	Seattle-Bellevue-Everett, WA	94	63.	San Francisco, CA	81
20.	Hartford, CT	94	64.	Tallahassee, FL	81
21.	Los Angeles-Long Beach, CA	93	65.	New London-Norwich, CT-RI	80
22.	Fort Collins-Loveland, CO	93	66.	Lansing-East Lansing, MI	80
23.	Rochester, NY	93	67.	Cheyenne, WY	80
24.	Syracuse, NY	93	68.	Manchester, NH	80
25.	Colorado Springs, CO	92	69.	Columbia, SC	79
26.	Middlesex-Somerset-Hunterdon, NJ	92	70.	San Diego, CA	79
27.	Lowell, MA-NH	92	71.	Binghamton, NY	79
28.	Pittsburgh, PA	91	72.	Missoula, MT	78
29.	Champaign-Urbana, IL	91	73.	Springfield, MA	78
30.	Gainesville, FL	91	74.	Grand Forks, ND-MN	78
31.	Corvallis, OR	90	75.	Bremerton, WA	77
32.	Austin-San Marcos, TX	90	76.	Spokane, WA	77
33.	Denver, CO	90	77.	Flagstaff, AZ-UT	77
34.	Baltimore, MD	90	78.	Jamestown, NY	76
35.	Ann Arbor, MI	89	79.	Nashua, NH	76
36.	Bloomington-Normal, IL	89	80.	Caspar, WY	76
37.	Boise, ID	89	81.	Buffalo-Niagara Falls, NY	76
38.	Dallas, TX	89	82.	St. Louis, MO-IL	75
39.	Stamford-Norwalk, CT	88	83.	Fort Walton Beach, FL	75
40.	Fargo-Moorhead, ND-MN	88	84.	Phoenix-Mesa, AZ	75
41.	Newark, NJ	88	85.	Lexington, KY	74
42.	Columbus, OH	87	86.	Duluth-Superior, MN-WI	74
43.	Brockton, MA	87	87.	Worcester, MA-CT	74
44.	Dutchess County, NY	87	88.	Asheville, NC	73

continued

Metro Areas, Strongest to Weakest Education *(continued)*

RANK		SCORE		RANK		SCORE
89.	Richmond-Petersburg, VA	73		145.	Great Falls, MT	56
90.	Oklahoma City, OK	73		146.	Fitchburg-Leominster, MA	56
91.	Trenton, NY	73		147.	Tucson, AZ	55
92.	Bismarck, ND	72		148.	Greenville-Spartanburg-Anderson, SC	55
93.	Kalamazoo–Battle Creek, MI	72		149.	Springfield, IL	55
94.	Lawrence, MA-NH	72		150.	Santa Barbara–Santa Maria–Lompoc, CA	54
95.	Norfolk-Virginia Beach–Newport News, VA-NC	71		151.	Honolulu, HI	54
96.	Anchorage, AK	71		152.	Providence–Fall River–Warwick, RI-MA	54
97.	Auburn-Opelika, AL	71		153.	Galveston–Texas City, TX	53
98.	Santa Cruz-Watsonville, CA	71		154.	Jackson, MS	53
99.	Huntsville, AL	70		155.	Nashville, TN	53
100.	Rapid City, SD	70		156.	Sherman-Denison, TX	53
101.	Portsmouth-Rochester, NH-ME	70		157.	Knoxville, TN	52
102.	Sioux Falls, SD	69		158.	Lubbock, TX	52
103.	Omaha, NE-IA	69		159.	Tulsa, OK	52
104.	Pittsfield, MA	69		160.	Richland-Kennewick-Pasco, WA	51
105.	San Luis Obispo–Atascadero–Paso Robles, CA	68		161.	Fayetteville, NC	51
106.	Springfield, MO	68		162.	Elmira, NY	51
107.	Newburgh, NY-PA	68		163.	Indianapolis, IN	50
108.	Greensboro–Winston-Salem–High Point, NC	67		164.	Greeley, CO	50
109.	Wilmington, NC	67		165.	Little Rock–North Little Rock, AR	50
110.	Glens Falls, NY	67		166.	Tampa–St. Petersburg–Clearwater, FL	49
111.	Roanoke, VA	66		167.	Davenport–Moline–Rock Island, IA-IL	49
112.	Dayton-Springfield, OH	66		168.	Greenville, NC	49
113.	La Crosse, WI-MN	66		169.	Pensacola, FL	49
114.	Charlotte–Gastonia–Rock Hill, NC-SC	65		170.	Sarasota-Bradenton, FL	48
115.	Bangor, ME	65		171.	Grand Rapids–Muskegon–Holland, MI	48
116.	Houston, TX	65		172.	Birmingham, AL	48
117.	Naples, FL	64		173.	Grand Junction, CO	47
118.	Killeen-Temple, TX	64		174.	Charleston–North Charleston, SC	47
119.	Bergen-Passaic, NJ	64		175.	Tyler, TX	47
120.	Eau Claire, WI	63		176.	Reno, NV	47
121.	Milwaukee-Waukesha, WI	63		177.	Green Bay, WI	46
122.	Yolo, CA	63		178.	Brazoria, TX	46
123.	Pocatello, ID	63		179.	Jacksonville, NC	46
124.	Eugene-Springfield, OR	62		180.	Lawton, OK	45
125.	Abilene, TX	62		181.	Cleveland-Lorain-Elyria, OH	45
126.	Utica-Rome, NY	62		182.	Hattiesburg, MS	45
127.	Fort Worth–Arlington, TX	61		183.	Wichita, KS	44
128.	Salt Lake City–Ogden, UT	61		184.	Appleton-Oshkosh-Neenah, WI	44
129.	Monmouth-Ocean, NJ	61		185.	Waco, TX	44
130.	Athens, GA	60		186.	Jacksonville, FL	43
131.	Tacoma, WA	60		187.	San Antonio, TX	43
132.	Billings, MT	60		188.	St. Cloud, MN	43
133.	Detroit, MI	60		189.	Topeka, KS	43
134.	Albuquerque, NM	59		190.	Longview-Marshall, TX	42
135.	Santa Rosa, CA	59		191.	Myrtle Beach, SC	42
136.	Waterbury, CT	59		192.	Wichita Falls, TX	42
137.	Bellingham, WA	58		193.	Vallejo-Fairfield-Napa, CA	41
138.	Harrisburg–New Lebanon–Carlisle, PA	58		194.	Hamilton-Middletown, OH	41
139.	Orange County, CA	58		195.	Amarillo, TX	41
140.	Sacramento, CA	57		196.	Lynchburg, VA	40
141.	Orlando, FL	57		197.	Ventura, CA	40
142.	Akron, OH	57		198.	Allentown-Bethlehem-Easton, PA	40
143.	Lafayette, IN	56		199.	Clarksville-Hopkinsville, TN-KY	40
144.	Melbourne–Titusville–Palm Bay, FL	56		200.	Muncie, IN	39

RANK		SCORE
201.	Atlantic City–Cape May, NJ	39
202.	West Palm Beach–Boca Raton, FL	38
203.	Janesville-Beloit, WI	38
204.	York, PA	38
205.	Chico-Paradise, CA	38
206.	Peoria-Pekin, IL	37
207.	Johnson City–Kingsport-Bristol, TN	37
208.	South Bend, IN	37
209.	Pueblo, CO	36
210.	Daytona Beach, FL	36
211.	Tuscaloosa, AL	36
212.	Salem, OR	36
213.	Wausau, WI	36
214.	Panama City, FL	35
215.	Sharon, PA	35
216.	Parkersburg-Marietta, WV-OH	34
217.	Kenosha, WI	34
218.	Fayetteville-Springfield-Rogers, AR	33
219.	Cincinnati, OH-KY-IN	33
220.	Terre Haute, IN	33
221.	Charleston, WV	33
222.	Jackson, TN	33
223.	Medford-Ashland, OR	32
224.	Wilmington-Newark, DE-MD	32
225.	Augusta-Aiken, GA-SC	32
226.	Williamsport, PA	31
227.	Flint, MI	31
228.	San Angelo, TX	31
229.	Kokomo, IN	30
230.	Toledo, OH	30
231.	Benton Harbor, MI	30
232.	Lewiston-Auburn, ME	30
233.	Memphis, TN-AR-MS	29
234.	Waterloo–Cedar Falls, IA	29
235.	Dover, DE	28
236.	Las Cruces, NM	28
237.	Shreveport–Bossier City, LA	28
238.	Montgomery, AL	28
239.	Fort Lauderdale, FL	27
240.	Redding, CA	27
241.	New Bedford, MA	26
242.	Fort Wayne, IN	26
243.	Louisville, KY-IN	26
244.	Enid, OK	26
245.	Jonesboro, AR	26
246.	Fort Pierce–Port St. Lucie, FL	25
247.	Saginaw–Bay City-Midland, MI	25
248.	Fort Myers–Cape Coral, FL	25
249.	Evansville-Henderson, KY-IN	24
250.	Jackson, MI	24
251.	Biloxi-Gulfport-Pascagoula, MS	24
252.	Goldsboro, NC	23
253.	Decatur, AL	23
254.	Gary, IN	23
255.	Texarkana, TX-AR	23
256.	Punta Gorda, FL	23
257.	Columbus, GA-AL	22
258.	Sheboygan, WI	22
259.	Beaumont–Port Arthur, TX	21
260.	Joplin, MO	21
261.	Erie, PA	21
262.	Corpus Christi, TX	20
263.	Cumberland, MD-WV	20
264.	Lima, OH	20
265.	Canton-Massillon, OH	20
266.	Chattanooga, TN-GA	19
267.	Huntington-Ashland, WV-KY-OH	19
268.	Monroe, LA	19
269.	Las Vegas, NV-AZ	18
270.	Steubenville-Weirton, OH-WV	18
271.	Racine, WI	18
272.	Savannah, GA	17
273.	Odessa-Midland, TX	17
274.	Macon, GA	17
275.	St. Joseph, MO	16
276.	Rockford, IL	16
277.	Hickory-Morganton-Lenoir, NC	16
278.	Scranton–Wilkes-Barre–Hazleton, PA	16
279.	Riverside–San Bernardino, CA	15
280.	Sioux City, IA-NE	15
281.	Sumter, SC	15
282.	Reading, PA	14
283.	Dothan, AL	14
284.	Youngstown-Warren, OH	14
285.	Ocala, FL	13
286.	Mansfield, OH	13
287.	Decatur, IL	13
288.	Florence, AL	13
289.	Fresno, CA	12
290.	Victoria, TX	12
291.	Gadsden, AL	12
292.	Baton Rouge, LA	11
293.	Fort Smith, AR-OK	11
294.	Altoona, PA	10
295.	Lakeland–Winter Haven, FL	10
296.	Salinas, CA	10
297.	Rocky Mount, NC	10
298.	Anniston, AL	10
299.	Albany, GA	9
300.	Yuba City-Marysville, CA	9
301.	Pine Bluff, AR	9
302.	Miami, FL	8
303.	Mobile, AL	8
304.	Johnstown, PA	8
305.	Hagerstown, MD	7
306.	Jersey City, NJ	7
307.	Owensboro, KY	7
308.	Florence, SC	6
309.	Wheeling, WV-OH	6
310.	Kankakee, IL	6
311.	Stockton-Lodi, CA	6
312.	El Paso, TX	5
313.	Lake Charles, LA	5
314.	Elkhart-Goshen, IN	5
315.	Lancaster, PA	4
316.	Yakima, WA	4

continued

Metro Areas, Strongest to Weakest Education *(continued)*

RANK		SCORE
317.	New Orleans, LA	3
318.	Vineland-Millville-Bridgeton, NJ	3
319.	Bakersfield, CA	3
320.	Modesto, CA	3
321.	Alexandria, LA	3
322.	Yuma, AZ	2
323.	Danville, VA	2
324.	Dubuque, IA	2

RANK		SCORE
325.	Visalia-Tulare-Porterville, CA	1
326.	Brownsville–Harlingen–San Benito, TX	1
327.	Merced, CA	1
328.	Lafayette, LA	0
329.	McAllen-Edinburg-Mission, TX	0
330.	Houma, LA	0
331.	Laredo, TX	0

Health & Healthcare

These rankings are derived from a mix of health hazard and healthcare attributes. Highly weighted hazard attributes include air quality, allergy and pollen index, and cancer rate. Highly rated healthcare attributes include doctors and hospital beds per capita. Less weight is given to water quality, teaching hospitals, and healthcare costs.

Metro Areas, Healthiest to Least Healthy

RANK		SCORE
1.	Rochester, MN	100
2.	Iowa City, IA	99
3.	Lynchburg, VA	99
4.	Roanoke, VA	99
5.	Columbia, MO	98
6.	Bismarck, ND	98
7.	Pueblo, CO	98
8.	Grand Forks, ND-MN	97
9.	Charlottesville, VA	97
10.	Johnson City-Kingsport-Bristol, TN-VA	96
11.	Springfield, MO	96
12.	Great Falls, MT	96
13.	Grand Junction, CO	96
14.	Madison, WI	95
15.	Billings, MT	95
16.	Dothan, AL	95
17.	Fargo-Moorhead, ND-MN	94
18.	Asheville, NC	94
19.	La Crosse, WI-MN	94
20.	State College, PA	93
21.	Sioux Falls, SD	93
22.	Sharon, PA	93
23.	Jonesboro, AR	93
24.	Burlington, VT	92
25.	Hickory-Morganton-Lenoir, NC	92
26.	Tuscaloosa, AL	92
27.	Florence, AL	91
28.	Williamsport, PA	91
29.	Waterloo–Cedar Falls, IA	91
30.	Lubbock, TX	90
31.	Jackson, TN	90
32.	Wausau, WI	90

RANK		SCORE
33.	Tallahassee, FL	89
34.	Goldsboro, NC	89
35.	Punta Gorda, FL	89
36.	Scranton–Wilkes-Barre–Hazleton, PA	89
37.	Little Rock–North Little Rock, AR	88
38.	Janesville-Beloit, WI	88
39.	Erie, PA	88
40.	Pittsfield, MA	87
41.	Enid, OK	87
42.	Cumberland, MD-WV	87
43.	Cedar Rapids, IA	86
44.	Jamestown, NY	86
45.	Harrisburg-Lebanon-Carlisle, PA	86
46.	Danville, VA	86
47.	Auburn-Opelika, AL	85
48.	Eau Claire, WI	85
49.	Johnstown, PA	85
50.	Duluth-Superior, MN-WI	84
51.	Charleston, WV	84
52.	Gadsden, AL	84
53.	Lexington, KY	83
54.	Missoula, MT	83
55.	Appleton-Oshkosh-Neenah, WI	83
56.	Huntington-Ashland, WV-KY-OH	83
57.	Knoxville, TN	82
58.	Green Bay, WI	82
59.	Alexandria, LA	82
60.	Altoona, PA	81
61.	Raleigh–Durham–Chapel Hill, NC	80
62.	Greensboro–Winston-Salem–High Point, NC	80
63.	Fayetteville-Springdale-Rogers, AR	80
64.	Des Moines, IA	80

RANK		SCORE
65.	Lansing–East Lansing, MI	80
66.	Wheeling, WV-OH	80
67.	St. Cloud, MN	79
68.	Texarkana, TX-AR	79
69.	Lewiston-Auburn, ME	79
70.	Athens, GA	78
71.	Richmond-Petersburg, VA	78
72.	Topeka, KS	78
73.	Portland, ME	77
74.	Binghamton, NY	77
75.	Corvallis, OR	76
76.	Kalamazoo–Battle Creek, MI	76
77.	Chattanooga, TN-GA	76
78.	Anniston, AL	76
79.	Dubuque, IA	76
80.	Boulder-Longmont, CO	75
81.	Fort Myers-Cape Coral, FL	75
82.	Parkersburg-Marietta, WV-OH	75
83.	Naples, FL	74
84.	Greenville-Spartanburg-Anderson, SC	74
85.	Utica-Rome, NY	74
86.	Fort Collins–Loveland, CO	73
87.	Nashville, TN	73
88.	Joplin, MO	73
89.	Rockford, IL	73
90.	Portland-Vancouver, OR-WA	72
91.	Casper, WY	72
92.	Florence, SC	72
93.	Greenville, NC	71
94.	Fort Lauderdale, FL	71
95.	Sioux City, IA-NE	71
96.	Ann Arbor, MI	70
97.	Myrtle Beach, SC	70
98.	Springfield, IL	70
99.	Elmira, NY	70
100.	Lincoln, NE	69
101.	Santa Fe, NM	69
102.	San Angelo, TX	69
103.	Bellingham, WA	68
104.	Jackson, MI	68
105.	Hagerstown, MD	68
106.	Gainesville, FL	67
107.	Columbia, SC	67
108.	Spokane, WA	67
109.	Colorado Springs, CO	66
110.	Bloomington-Normal, IL	66
111.	Rapid City, SD	66
112.	Sheboygan, WI	66
113.	Omaha, NE-IA	65
114.	Miami, FL	65
115.	Birmingham, AL	65
116.	Wilmington, NC	64
117.	Peoria-Pekin, IL	64
118.	Fort Pierce–Port St. Lucie, FL	64
119.	Bryan–College Station, TX	63
120.	Fort Walton Beach, FL	63
121.	Fort Smith, AR-OK	63
122.	Medford-Ashland, OR	63

RANK		SCORE
123.	Manchester, NH	62
124.	Montgomery, AL	62
125.	Reading, PA	62
126.	Albany-Schenectady-Troy, NY	61
127.	West Palm Beach–Boca Raton, FL	61
128.	Pocatello, ID	60
129.	Salem, OR	60
130.	Mansfield, OH	60
131.	Hartford, CT	60
132.	Allentown-Bethlehem-Easton, PA	60
133.	Benton Harbor, MI	59
134.	Augusta-Aiken, GA-SC	59
135.	Saginaw–Bay City–Midland, MI	59
136.	Bangor, ME	59
137.	Glens Falls, NY	58
138.	Wichita Falls, TX	58
139.	Amarillo, TX	58
140.	Sherman-Denison, TX	57
141.	Davenport–Moline–Rock Island, IA-IL	57
142.	Owensboro, KY	57
143.	Olympia, WA	56
144.	Panama City, FL	56
145.	St. Joseph, MO	56
146.	Abilene, TX	55
147.	Tyler, TX	55
148.	York, PA	55
149.	Boise, ID	54
150.	Monroe, LA	54
151.	Pine Bluff, AR	54
152.	Macon, GA	54
153.	Lowell, MA-NH	53
154.	New Haven–Meriden, CT	53
155.	Racine, WI	53
156.	Canton-Massillon, OH	53
157.	Sarasota-Bradenton, FL	52
158.	Rocky Mount, NC	52
159.	Decatur, IL	52
160.	Seattle-Bellevue-Everett, WA	51
161.	Decatur, AL	51
162.	Kokomo, IN	51
163.	Pittsburgh, PA	50
164.	Pensacola, FL	50
165.	Dutchess County, NY	50
166.	Buffalo–Niagara Falls, NY	50
167.	Cheyenne, WY	49
168.	Clarksville-Hopkinsville, TN-KY	49
169.	Shreveport–Bossier City, LA	49
170.	Eugene-Springfield, OR	48
171.	Youngstown-Warren, OH	48
172.	Kankakee, IL	48
173.	Champaign-Urbana, IL	47
174.	Milwaukee-Waukesha, WI	47
175.	Muncie, IN	47
176.	Syracuse, NY	46
177.	Denver, CO	46
178.	Jackson, MS	46
179.	Dayton-Springfield, OH	46
180.	Springfield, MA	45

continued

Metro Areas, Healthiest to Least Healthy *(continued)*

RANK		SCORE	RANK		SCORE
181.	Columbus, GA-AL	45	237.	Tulsa, OK	28
182.	Elkhart-Goshen, IN	45	238.	Tucson, AZ	28
183.	Lawrence, KS	44	239.	Reno, NV	27
184.	Worcester, MA-CT	44	240.	Daytona Beach, FL	27
185.	Lafayette, IN	44	241.	Fort Wayne, IN	27
186.	Charlotte-Gastonia-Rock Hill, NC-SC	43	242.	Atlanta, GA	26
187.	Santa Barbara-Santa Maria-Lompoc, CA	43	243.	New London-Norwich, CT-RI	26
188.	Wichita, KS	43	244.	Tampa-St. Petersburg-Clearwater, FL	26
189.	Lima, OH	43	245.	Lancaster, PA	26
190.	Minneapolis-St. Paul, MN-WI	42	246.	New York, NY	25
191.	Huntsville, AL	42	247.	Danbury, CT	25
192.	Evansville-Henderson, IN-KY	42	248.	Bergen-Passaic, NJ	25
193.	Steubenville-Weirton, OH-WV	41	249.	Stamford-Norwalk, CT	24
194.	Albany, GA	41	250.	Waco, TX	24
195.	Bloomington, IN	40	251.	Mobile, AL	24
196.	Tacoma, WA	40	252.	Austin-San Marcos, TX	23
197.	Hattiesburg, MS	40	253.	Memphis, TN-AR-MS	23
198.	Salt Lake City-Ogden, UT	40	254.	Cleveland-Lorain-Elyria, OH	23
199.	Waterbury, CT	40	255.	Bridgeport, CT	23
200.	Orange County, CA	39	256.	Flagstaff, AZ-UT	22
201.	San Luis Obispo-Atascadero-Paso Robles, CA	39	257.	Charleston-North Charleston, SC	22
202.	Toledo, OH	39	258.	St. Louis, MO-IL	22
203.	Greeley, CO	38	259.	Anchorage, AK	21
204.	Terre Haute, IN	38	260.	Newark, NJ	21
205.	South Bend, IN	38	261.	Hamilton-Middletown, OH	21
206.	Grand Rapids-Muskegon-Holland, MI	37	262.	Norfolk-Virginia Beach-Newport News, VA-NC	20
207.	Fitchburg-Leominster, MA	37	263.	Orlando, FL	20
208.	Yakima, WA	37	264.	Detroit, MI	20
209.	Barnstable-Yarmouth, MA	36	265.	Lake Charles, LA	20
210.	Rochester, NY	36	266.	Portsmouth-Rochester, NH-ME	19
211.	Melbourne-Titusville-Palm Bay, FL	35	267.	Providence-Fall River-Warwick, RI-MA	19
212.	Baltimore, MD	35	268.	Atlantic City-Cape May, NJ	19
213.	Sumter, SC	35	269.	Provo-Orem, UT	18
214.	Nassau-Suffolk, NY	35	270.	Galveston-Texas City, TX	18
215.	Ocala, FL	35	271.	Gary, IN	18
216.	Columbus, OH	34	272.	Middlesex-Somerset-Hunterdon, NJ	17
217.	Richland-Kennewick-Pasco, WA	34	273.	Odessa-Midland, TX	17
218.	Victoria, TX	34	274.	Biloxi-Gulfport-Pascagoula, MS	17
219.	Albuquerque, NM	33	275.	Oklahoma City, OK	16
220.	Kenosha, WI	33	276.	Corpus Christi, TX	16
221.	Akron, OH	33	277.	Las Vegas, NV-AZ	16
222.	Trenton, NJ	33	278.	Vineland-Millville-Bridgeton, NJ	16
223.	Washington, DC-MD-VA-WV	32	279.	Philadelphia, PA-NJ	15
224.	Ventura, CA	32	280.	San Francisco, CA	15
225.	Bremerton, WA	32	281.	Lakeland-Winter Haven, FL	15
226.	Dover, DE	31	282.	Chico-Paradise, CA	14
227.	Honolulu, HI	31	283.	New Bedford, MA	14
228.	Wilmington-Newark, DE-MD	31	284.	Lawrence, MA-NH	14
229.	Nashua, NH	30	285.	Jacksonville, FL	13
230.	Beaumont-Port Arthur, TX	30	286.	Cincinnati, OH-KY-IN	13
231.	Flint, MI	30	287.	El Paso, TX	13
232.	Savannah, GA	30	288.	New Orleans, LA	13
233.	Boston, MA-NH	29	289.	Fayetteville, NC	12
234.	Kansas City, MO-KS	29	290.	Redding, CA	12
235.	Longview-Marshall, TX	29	291.	Indianapolis, IN	12
236.	Killeen-Temple, TX	28	292.	Las Cruces, NM	11

RANK		SCORE
293.	Jacksonville, NC	11
294.	Louisville, KY-IN	11
295.	Brazoria, TX	10
296.	Phoenix-Mesa, AZ	10
297.	Lawton, OK	10
298.	Fort Worth-Arlington, TX	10
299.	San Diego, CA	9
300.	Yuma, AZ	9
301.	Newburgh, NY-PA	9
302.	Chicago, IL	8
303.	Brownsville-Harlingen-San Benito, TX	8
304.	Houma, LA	8
305.	Dallas, TX	7
306.	San Antonio, TX	7
307.	Baton Rouge, LA	7
308.	Visalia-Tulare-Porterville, CA	6
309.	Lafayette, LA	6
310.	Jersey City, NJ	6
311.	Monmouth-Ocean, NJ	6

RANK		SCORE
312.	Brockton, MA	5
313.	Riverside-San Bernardino, CA	5
314.	McAllen-Edinburg-Mission, TX	5
315.	Yolo, CA	4
316.	San Jose, CA	4
317.	Laredo, TX	4
318.	Los Angeles-Long Beach, CA	3
319.	Santa Rosa, CA	3
320.	Sacramento, CA	3
321.	Bakersfield, CA	3
322.	Santa Cruz-Watsonville, CA	2
323.	Vallejo-Fairfield-Napa, CA	2
324.	Modesto, CA	2
325.	Fresno, CA	1
326.	Oakland, CA	1
327.	Yuba City-Marysville, CA	1
328.	Salinas, CA	0
329.	Houston, TX	0
330.	Merced, CA	0
331.	Stockton-Lodi, CA	0

Crime

The crime ranking includes violent and property crime rates, as explained in chapter 3, and the 5-year *change* in these rates. All of this data is weighted equally.

Metro Areas, Lowest to Highest Crime

RANK		SCORE
1.	Danbury, CT	100
2.	Bismarck, ND	99
3.	Nassau-Suffolk, NY	99
4.	Ventura, CA	99
5.	Jamestown, NY	98
6.	Lowell, MA-NH	98
7.	Middlesex-Somerset-Hunterdon, NJ	98
8.	Portland, ME	97
9.	Glens Falls, NY	97
10.	Lawrence, MA-NH	97
11.	Dutchess County, NY	96
12.	Orange County, CA	96
13.	Stamford-Norwalk, CT	96
14.	Monmouth-Ocean, NJ	96
15.	State College, PA	95
16.	Sioux Falls, SD	95
17.	Green Bay, WI	95
18.	Scranton-Wilkes-Barre-Hazleton, PA	94
19.	Santa Barbara-Santa Maria-Lompoc, CA	94
20.	Yuma, AZ	94
21.	Sharon, PA	93
22.	Williamsport, PA	93
23.	Manchester, NH	93

RANK		SCORE
24.	San Luis Obispo-Atascadero-Paso Robles, CA	93
25.	Lynchburg, VA	92
26.	Sheboygan, WI	92
27.	Portsmouth-Rochester, NH-ME	92
28.	Pittsfield, MA	91
29.	Bergen-Passaic, NJ	91
30.	La Crosse, WI-MN	90
31.	Appleton-Oshkosh-Neenah, WI	90
32.	Barnstable-Yarmouth, MA	90
33.	San Jose, CA	90
34.	Santa Rosa, CA	90
35.	Harrisburg-Lebanon-Carlisle, PA	89
36.	Lafayette, IN	89
37.	Provo-Orem, UT	89
38.	Ann Arbor, MI	88
39.	York, PA	88
40.	Worcester, MA-CT	88
41.	Binghamton, NY	87
42.	Nashua, NH	87
43.	Boston, MA-NH	87
44.	Erie, PA	86
45.	Albany-Schenectady-Troy, NY	86
46.	Pocatello, ID	86

continued

Metro Areas, Lowest to Highest Crime *(continued)*

RANK		SCORE	RANK		SCORE
47.	Lancaster, PA	86	103.	San Francisco, CA	69
48.	Fort Collins–Loveland, CO	85	104.	Cedar Rapids, IA	68
49.	Hattiesburg, MS	85	105.	Reading, PA	68
50.	Fitchburg-Leominster, MA	85	106.	Owensboro, KY	68
51.	Fargo-Moorhead, ND-MN	84	107.	Boise, ID	67
52.	Bloomington-Normal, IL	84	108.	Washington, DC-MD-VA-WV	67
53.	Medford-Ashland, OR	84	109.	Bakersfield, CA	67
54.	Billings, MT	83	110.	Asheville, NC	66
55.	Corvallis, OR	83	111.	Naples, FL	66
56.	Newburgh, NY-PA	83	112.	Peoria-Pekin, IL	66
57.	Yolo, CA	83	113.	Providence–Fall River–Warwick, RI-MA	66
58.	Florence, AL	82	114.	Hickory-Morganton-Lenoir, NC	65
59.	Wausau, WI	82	115.	Casper, WY	65
60.	Bloomington, IN	82	116.	Grand Rapids–Muskegon–Holland, MI	65
61.	Wheeling, WV-OH	81	117.	New Haven–Meriden, CT	64
62.	Utica-Rome, NY	81	118.	Cheyenne, WY	64
63.	Rochester, NY	81	119.	Champaign-Urbana, IL	64
64.	Grand Forks, ND-MN	80	120.	Des Moines, IA	63
65.	Eau Claire, WI	80	121.	Santa Fe, NM	63
66.	Redding, CA	80	122.	Jersey City, NJ	63
67.	Burlington, VT	79	123.	Riverside–San Bernardino, CA	63
68.	Parkersburg-Marietta, WV-OH	79	124.	Roanoke, VA	62
69.	Elmira, NY	79	125.	Grand Junction, CO	62
70.	Muncie, IN	79	126.	Fort Wayne, IN	62
71.	Johnstown, PA	78	127.	Lexington, KY	61
72.	Fayetteville-Springdale-Rogers, AR	78	128.	Allentown-Bethlehem-Easton, PA	61
73.	Pittsburgh, PA	78	129.	Bangor, ME	61
74.	Rochester, MN	77	130.	Columbia, MO	60
75.	New York, NY	77	131.	Greeley, CO	60
76.	Iowa City, IA	76	132.	Bridgeport, CT	60
77.	Punta Gorda, FL	76	133.	Las Vegas, NV-AZ	60
78.	Hartford, CT	76	134.	Pensacola, FL	59
79.	Chico-Paradise, CA	76	135.	Indianapolis, IN	59
80.	New Bedford, MA	76	136.	Sacramento, CA	59
81.	Mansfield, OH	75	137.	Janesville-Beloit, WI	58
82.	Evansville-Henderson, IN-KY	75	138.	Saginaw–Bay City–Midland, MI	58
83.	Newark, NJ	75	139.	Lawrence, KS	58
84.	Danville, VA	74	140.	Waterloo–Cedar Falls, IA	57
85.	Richland-Kennewick-Pasco, WA	74	141.	Fort Walton Beach, FL	57
86.	Brazoria, TX	74	142.	Decatur, IL	57
87.	Madison, WI	73	143.	Cumberland, MD-WV	56
88.	Buffalo–Niagara Falls, NY	73	144.	Fort Lauderdale, FL	56
89.	New London–Norwich, CT-RI	73	145.	Sioux City, IA-NE	56
90.	Salinas, CA	73	146.	Waterbury, CT	56
91.	St. Cloud, MN	72	147.	Dothan, AL	55
92.	San Diego, CA	72	148.	Cleveland-Lorain-Elyria, OH	55
93.	Lewiston-Auburn, ME	71	149.	Lansing–East Lansing, MI	54
94.	Decatur, AL	71	150.	Augusta-Aiken, GA-SC	54
95.	Santa Cruz-Watsonville, CA	71	151.	Lima, OH	54
96.	Yuba City–Marysville, CA	71	152.	Bremerton, WA	54
97.	Charlottesville, VA	70	153.	Jonesboro, AR	53
98.	Abilene, TX	70	154.	Salt Lake City-Ogden, UT	53
99.	Syracuse, NY	70	155.	Odessa-Midland, TX	53
100.	Vallejo-Fairfield-Napa, CA	70	156.	Brockton, MA	53
101.	Hagerstown, MD	69	157.	Boulder-Longmont, CO	52
102.	Minneapolis-St. Paul, MN-WI	69	158.	Fort Pierce–Port St. Lucie, FL	52

RANK		SCORE	RANK		SCORE
159.	St. Joseph, MO	52	217.	Flagstaff, AZ-UT	34
160.	Ocala, FL	51	218.	Anchorage, AK	34
161.	Killeen-Temple, TX	51	219.	Athens, GA	33
162.	Philadelphia, PA-NJ	51	220.	Richmond-Petersburg, VA	33
163.	Missoula, MT	50	221.	Trenton, NJ	33
164.	Greenville-Spartanburg-Anderson, SC	50	222.	Detroit, MI	33
165.	Sherman-Denison, TX	50	223.	Pueblo, CO	32
166.	Olympia, WA	50	224.	Lakeland–Winter Haven, FL	32
167.	Altoona, PA	49	225.	Visalia-Tulare-Porterville, CA	32
168.	Kenosha, WI	49	226.	Kankakee, IL	31
169.	Duluth-Superior, MN-WI	48	227.	Vineland-Millville-Bridgeton, NJ	31
170.	Dover, DE	48	228.	El Paso, TX	31
171.	Gary, IN	48	229.	Greensboro–Winston-Salem–High Point, NC	30
172.	Lawton, OK	48	230.	Salem, OR	30
173.	Colorado Springs, CO	47	231.	Sarasota-Bradenton, FL	30
174.	Eugene-Springfield, OR	47	232.	Las Cruces, NM	30
175.	Austin–San Marcos, TX	47	233.	Raleigh–Durham–Chapel Hill, NC	29
176.	Racine, WI	46	234.	Daytona Beach, FL	29
177.	Atlanta, GA	46	235.	Lafayette, LA	29
178.	Norfolk–Virginia Beach–Newport News, VA-NC	46	236.	Goldsboro, NC	28
179.	Columbia, SC	45	237.	Wichita, KS	28
180.	Kokomo, IN	45	238.	Hamilton-Middletown, OH	28
181.	Albany, GA	45	239.	Cincinnati, OH-KY-IN	27
182.	Oakland, CA	45	240.	Fayetteville, NC	27
183.	Huntington-Ashland, WV-KY-OH	44	241.	Modesto, CA	27
184.	Huntsville, AL	44	242.	Johnson City–Kingsport–Bristol, TN-VA	26
185.	Atlantic City–Cape May, NJ	44	243.	Fort Myers–Cape Coral, FL	26
186.	Enid, OK	43	244.	Benton Harbor, MI	26
187.	Knoxville, TN	43	245.	Chicago, IL	26
188.	Denver, CO	43	246.	Charleston, WV	25
189.	Yakima, WA	43	247.	Columbus, GA-AL	25
190.	Akron, OH	42	248.	Wilmington-Newark, DE-MD	25
191.	Los Angeles–Long Beach, CA	42	249.	Steubenville-Weirton, OH-WV	24
192.	Rockford, IL	41	250.	Lake Charles, LA	24
193.	Springfield, IL	41	251.	Fort Worth–Arlington, TX	24
194.	Honolulu, HI	41	252.	Dubuque, IA	23
195.	Jacksonville, FL	41	253.	Flint, MI	23
196.	Bryan–College Station, TX	40	254.	Oklahoma City, OK	23
197.	Milwaukee-Waukesha, WI	40	255.	New Orleans, LA	23
198.	Terre Haute, IN	40	256.	Jackson, MI	22
199.	Louisville, KY-IN	40	257.	Clarksville-Hopkinsville, TN-KY	22
200.	Birmingham, AL	39	258.	Houma, LA	22
201.	Youngstown-Warren, OH	39	259.	Gadsden, AL	21
202.	Reno, NV	39	260.	Tacoma, WA	21
203.	Bellingham, WA	38	261.	Longview-Marshall, TX	21
204.	Elkhart-Goshen, IN	38	262.	Gainesville, FL	20
205.	Merced, CA	38	263.	Melbourne–Titusville–Palm Bay, FL	20
206.	Great Falls, MT	37	264.	Galveston–Texas City, TX	20
207.	Canton-Massillon, OH	37	265.	Fresno, CA	20
208.	Seattle-Bellevue-Everett, WA	37	266.	Jackson, MS	19
209.	Portland-Vancouver, OR-WA	36	267.	Tulsa, OK	19
210.	Davenport–Moline–Rock Island, IA-IL	36	268.	Phoenix-Mesa, AZ	19
211.	Victoria, TX	36	269.	Jackson, TN	18
212.	Charleston–North Charleston, SC	36	270.	Little Rock–North Little Rock, AR	18
213.	Rapid City, SD	35	271.	Shreveport-Bossier City, LA	18
214.	Tyler, TX	35	272.	Texarkana, TX-AR	17
215.	Dayton-Springfield, OH	35	273.	Biloxi-Gulfport-Pascagoula, MS	17
216.	Beaumont–Port Arthur, TX	34	274.	McAllen-Edinburg-Mission, TX	17

continued

Metro Areas, Lowest to Highest Crime *(continued)*

RANK		SCORE
275.	Tuscaloosa, AL	16
276.	Kalamazoo–Battle Creek, MI	16
277.	Omaha, NE-IA	16
278.	West Palm Beach–Boca Raton, FL	16
279.	Rocky Mount, NC	15
280.	Springfield, MA	15
281.	Baltimore, MD	15
282.	St. Louis, MO-IL	14
283.	Jacksonville, NC	14
284.	Houston, TX	14
285.	Joplin, MO	13
286.	Spokane, WA	13
287.	Wilmington, NC	13
288.	Dallas, TX	13
289.	Fort Smith, AR-OK	12
290.	Macon, GA	12
291.	Waco, TX	12
292.	Lincoln, NE	11
293.	Toledo, OH	11
294.	Tampa–St. Petersburg–Clearwater, FL	11
295.	Springfield, MO	10
296.	San Angelo, TX	10
297.	South Bend, IN	10
298.	Mobile, AL	10
299.	Tallahassee, FL	9
300.	Columbus, OH	9
301.	Baton Rouge, LA	9
302.	Panama City, FL	8

RANK		SCORE
303.	Orlando, FL	8
304.	Stockton-Lodi, CA	8
305.	Auburn-Opelika, AL	7
306.	Nashville, TN	7
307.	Charlotte-Gastonia-Rock Hill, NC-SC	7
308.	Alexandria, LA	6
309.	Anniston, AL	6
310.	Amarillo, TX	6
311.	Savannah, GA	6
312.	Montgomery, AL	5
313.	Corpus Christi, TX	5
314.	Brownsville-Harlingen-San Benito, TX	5
315.	Greenville, NC	4
316.	Wichita Falls, TX	4
317.	Tucson, AZ	4
318.	Myrtle Beach, SC	3
319.	Sumter, SC	3
320.	Kansas City, MO-KS	3
321.	Laredo, TX	3
322.	Lubbock, TX	2
323.	Chattanooga, TN-GA	2
324.	Miami, FL	2
325.	Topeka, KS	1
326.	Florence, SC	1
327.	Monroe, LA	1
328.	Pine Bluff, AR	0
329.	Albuquerque, NM	0
330.	Memphis, TN-AR-MS	0
331.	San Antonio, TX	0

Transportation

Transportation rankings measure local and intercity transport services. Commute times and availability of mass-transit service are weighted the highest, followed closely by the availability of intercity air service. Amtrak service is also factored but with a lower weight.

Metro Areas, Best to Poorest Transportation

RANK		SCORE
1.	San Francisco, CA	100
2.	Kenosha, WI	99
3.	Chicago, IL	99
4.	Florence, SC	99
5.	Rochester, MN	98
6.	New York, NY	98
7.	Gary, IN	98
8.	Stamford-Norwalk, CT	97
9.	Bergen-Passaic, NJ	97
10.	Los Angeles–Long Beach, CA	97
11.	Richland-Kennewick-Pasco, WA	96

RANK		SCORE
12.	Denver, CO	96
13.	Seattle-Bellevue-Everett, WA	96
14.	Dallas, TX	96
15.	Boston, MA-NH	95
16.	Champaign-Urbana, IL	95
17.	Atlanta, GA	95
18.	Danbury, CT	94
19.	Yuma, AZ	94
20.	Fort Worth–Arlington, TX	94
21.	Nassau-Suffolk, NY	93
22.	Sheboygan, WI	93

RANK		SCORE
23.	Pittsburgh, PA	93
24.	Philadelphia, PA-NJ	93
25.	Middlesex-Somerset-Hunterdon, NJ	92
26.	Bloomington-Normal, IL	92
27.	Salt Lake City–Ogden, UT	92
28.	Honolulu, HI	91
29.	Anchorage, AK	91
30.	Sumter, SC	91
31.	Waterloo–Cedar Falls, IA	90
32.	Boulder-Longmont, CO	90
33.	Reno, NV	90
34.	Great Falls, MT	90
35.	Grand Forks, ND-MN	89
36.	Iowa City, IA	89
37.	Dubuque, IA	89
38.	Green Bay, WI	88
39.	Fargo-Moorhead, ND-MN	88
40.	Brockton, MA	88
41.	Newark, NJ	87
42.	Jersey City, NJ	87
43.	St. Louis, MO-IL	87
44.	Abilene, TX	86
45.	Cheyenne, WY	86
46.	Las Vegas, NV-AZ	86
47.	Lubbock, TX	86
48.	Madison, WI	85
49.	Minneapolis–St. Paul, MN-WI	85
50.	Sioux Falls, SD	84
51.	Ann Arbor, MI	84
52.	Eugene-Springfield, OR	84
53.	Portland-Vancouver, OR-WA	84
54.	Elmira, NY	83
55.	Missoula, MT	83
56.	Bryan–College Station, TX	83
57.	Dayton-Springfield, OH	83
58.	Appleton-Oshkosh-Neenah, WI	82
59.	Santa Cruz-Watsonville, CA	82
60.	Cedar Rapids, IA	82
61.	Billings, MT	81
62.	Springfield, MA	81
63.	Lincoln, NE	81
64.	Lafayette, IN	80
65.	Bloomington, IN	80
66.	Hartford, CT	80
67.	Trenton, NJ	80
68.	Jamestown, NY	79
69.	Monmouth-Ocean, NJ	79
70.	Topeka, KS	79
71.	La Crosse, WI-MN	78
72.	Pocatello, ID	77
73.	Des Moines, IA	77
74.	Decatur, IL	77
75.	Sioux City, IA-NE	77
76.	Vineland-Millville-Bridgeton, NJ	77
77.	Bismarck, ND	76
78.	Santa Barbara–Santa Maria–Lompoc, CA	76
79.	Rapid City, SD	76
80.	Detroit, MI	76

RANK		SCORE
81.	Erie, PA	75
82.	Buffalo–Niagara Falls, NY	75
83.	Davenport–Moline–Rock Island, IA-IL	75
84.	Washington, DC-MD-VA-WV	74
85.	Milwaukee-Waukesha, WI	74
86.	Omaha, NE-IA	74
87.	Syracuse, NY	73
88.	Casper, WY	73
89.	Columbia, MO	73
90.	Cleveland-Lorain-Elyria, OH	73
91.	Pittsfield, MA	72
92.	Galveston–Texas City, TX	72
93.	San Angelo, TX	72
94.	Santa Fe, NM	71
95.	Atlantic City–Cape May, NJ	71
96.	Springfield, IL	71
97.	Wausau, WI	70
98.	Eau Claire, WI	70
99.	San Diego, CA	70
100.	Lawton, OK	70
101.	Binghamton, NY	69
102.	Tacoma, WA	69
103.	Kansas City, MO-KS	69
104.	Wilmington-Newark, DE-MD	68
105.	Amarillo, TX	68
106.	Memphis, TN-AR-MS	68
107.	Medford-Ashland, OR	67
108.	Duluth-Superior, MN-WI	67
109.	Bellingham, WA	67
110.	Rochester, NY	66
111.	Muncie, IN	66
112.	Providence–Fall River–Warwick, RI-MA	66
113.	Corpus Christi, TX	66
114.	Louisville, KY-IN	65
115.	Wichita, KS	65
116.	State College, PA	64
117.	Santa Rosa, CA	64
118.	Kokomo, IN	64
119.	Elkhart-Goshen, IN	64
120.	St. Joseph, MO	63
121.	Racine, WI	63
122.	Cincinnati, OH-KY-IN	63
123.	Wichita Falls, TX	63
124.	St. Cloud, MN	62
125.	Baltimore, MD	62
126.	South Bend, IN	62
127.	Peoria-Pekin, IL	61
128.	Enid, OK	61
129.	Houston, TX	61
130.	Albany-Schenectady-Troy, NY	60
131.	Olympia, WA	60
132.	Phoenix-Mesa, AZ	60
133.	Toledo, OH	60
134.	Corvallis, OR	59
135.	Lansing–East Lansing, MI	59
136.	Albany, GA	59
137.	Lima, OH	58
138.	Yakima, WA	58

continued

Metro Areas, Best to Poorest Transportation *(continued)*

RANK		SCORE
139.	Kalamazoo–Battle Creek, MI	58
140.	Roanoke, VA	57
141.	Grand Junction, CO	57
142.	Albuquerque, NM	57
143.	Williamsport, PA	56
144.	Nashua, NH	56
145.	Utica–Rome, NY	56
146.	Odessa–Midland, TX	56
147.	Lancaster, PA	55
148.	Yolo, CA	55
149.	Fayetteville–Springdale–Rogers, AR	54
150.	Boise, ID	54
151.	Jonesboro, AR	54
152.	Canton–Massillon, OH	54
153.	Provo–Orem, UT	53
154.	Altoona, PA	53
155.	Flagstaff, AZ–UT	53
156.	El Paso, TX	53
157.	Lowell, MA–NH	52
158.	Tulsa, OK	52
159.	Miami, FL	52
160.	Grand Rapids–Muskegon–Holland, MI	51
161.	Gainesville, FL	51
162.	Evansville–Henderson, IN–KY	50
163.	Jackson, TN	50
164.	Waco, TX	50
165.	Tampa–St. Petersburg–Clearwater, FL	50
166.	San Antonio, TX	50
167.	Lawrence, MA–NH	49
168.	Redding, CA	49
169.	Columbus, OH	49
170.	Hamilton–Middletown, OH	48
171.	Benton Harbor, MI	48
172.	Monroe, LA	48
173.	New Haven–Meriden, CT	47
174.	Orlando, FL	47
175.	Laredo, TX	47
176.	Burlington, VT	46
177.	Fort Wayne, IN	46
178.	Janesville–Beloit, WI	46
179.	Goldsboro, NC	46
180.	Dover, DE	45
181.	Pueblo, CO	45
182.	Joplin, MO	45
183.	Barnstable–Yarmouth, MA	44
184.	Bangor, ME	44
185.	Austin–San Marcos, TX	44
186.	Sharon, PA	43
187.	Owensboro, KY	43
188.	Springfield, MO	43
189.	Lexington, KY	42
190.	Lawrence, KS	42
191.	Tucson, AZ	42
192.	Portland, ME	41
193.	Indianapolis, IN	41
194.	Colorado Springs, CO	41

RANK		SCORE
195.	Oklahoma City, OK	41
196.	Harrisburg–Lebanon–Carlisle, PA	40
197.	Fresno, CA	40
198.	Rocky Mount, NC	40
199.	Panama City, FL	40
200.	Scranton–Wilkes-Barre–Hazleton, PA	39
201.	Vallejo–Fairfield–Napa, CA	39
202.	San Jose, CA	38
203.	Mansfield, OH	38
204.	Akron, OH	38
205.	Charleston, WV	38
206.	Saginaw–Bay City–Midland, MI	37
207.	Athens, GA	37
208.	Shreveport–Bossier City, LA	37
209.	Salinas, CA	36
210.	Terre Haute, IN	36
211.	Tallahassee, FL	36
212.	Brownsville–Harlingen–San Benito, TX	36
213.	Norfolk–Virginia Beach–Newport News, VA–NC	35
214.	Auburn–Opelika, AL	35
215.	Charlotte–Gastonia–Rock Hill, NC–SC	35
216.	San Luis Obispo–Atascadero–Paso Robles, CA	34
217.	Chico–Paradise, CA	34
218.	Dothan, AL	34
219.	Richmond–Petersburg, VA	33
220.	Spokane, WA	33
221.	Savannah, GA	33
222.	Fort Collins–Loveland, CO	32
223.	Columbus, GA–AL	32
224.	Lake Charles, LA	32
225.	Texarkana, TX–AR	32
226.	Parkersburg–Marietta, WV–OH	31
227.	New Orleans, LA	31
228.	West Palm Beach–Boca Raton, FL	31
229.	Fort Lauderdale, FL	30
230.	Greensboro–Winston-Salem–High Point, NC	30
231.	Sarasota–Bradenton, FL	30
232.	Tuscaloosa, AL	30
233.	Asheville, NC	29
234.	Las Cruces, NM	29
235.	New London–Norwich, CT–RI	28
236.	Charlottesville, VA	28
237.	Huntsville, AL	28
238.	Myrtle Beach, SC	28
239.	Brazoria, TX	27
240.	Fayetteville, NC	27
241.	Greenville, NC	27
242.	Reading, PA	26
243.	Fort Walton Beach, FL	26
244.	Rockford, IL	26
245.	Little Rock–North Little Rock, AR	26
246.	Flint, MI	25
247.	McAllen–Edinburg–Mission, TX	25
248.	Pine Bluff, AR	25
249.	Allentown–Bethlehem–Easton, PA	24
250.	Youngstown–Warren, OH	24

RANK		SCORE
251.	Visalia-Tulare-Porterville, CA	24
252.	Johnstown, PA	23
253.	Killeen-Temple, TX	23
254.	Beaumont–Port Arthur, TX	23
255.	Wilmington, NC	23
256.	Bakersfield, CA	21
257.	Hickory-Morganton-Lenoir, NC	21
258.	Bridgeport, CT	21
259.	Sacramento, CA	21
260.	Columbia, SC	21
261.	Raleigh–Durham–Chapel Hill, NC	21
262.	Lynchburg, VA	20
263.	Jacksonville, FL	20
264.	Jackson, MI	20
265.	Greenville-Spartanburg-Anderson, SC	19
266.	Knoxville, TN	19
267.	Nashville, TN	19
268.	Wheeling, WV-OH	18
269.	Victoria, TX	18
270.	Salem, OR	18
271.	Melbourne–Titusville–Palm Bay, FL	18
272.	Waterbury, CT	17
273.	Jackson, MS	17
274.	Fort Smith, AR-OK	17
275.	Worcester, MA-CT	16
276.	Lewiston-Auburn, ME	16
277.	Johnson City–Kingsport–Bristol, TN-VA	16
278.	Fort Myers–Cape Coral, FL	16
279.	Danville, VA	15
280.	Longview-Marshall, TX	15
281.	Montgomery, AL	15
282.	Charleston–North Charleston, SC	14
283.	Daytona Beach, FL	14
284.	Chattanooga, TN-GA	14
285.	Glens Falls, NY	13
286.	Tyler, TX	13
287.	Clarksville-Hopkinsville, TN-KY	13
288.	Macon, GA	13
289.	Fitchburg-Leominster, MA	12
290.	Biloxi-Gulfport-Pascagoula, MS	12

RANK		SCORE
291.	Alexandria, LA	12
292.	Newburgh, NY-PA	11
293.	Steubenville-Weirton, OH-WV	11
294.	Jacksonville, NC	11
295.	Orange County, CA	10
296.	Hattiesburg, MS	10
297.	Punta Gorda, FL	10
298.	Greeley, CO	10
299.	York, PA	9
300.	Florence, AL	9
301.	Huntington-Ashland, WV-KY-OH	9
302.	Pensacola, FL	8
303.	Augusta-Aiken, GA-SC	8
304.	Anniston, AL	8
305.	Ventura, CA	7
306.	Kankakee, IL	7
307.	Baton Rouge, LA	7
308.	New Bedford, MA	6
309.	Decatur, AL	6
310.	Sherman-Denison, TX	6
311.	Lakeland–Winter Haven, FL	6
312.	Hagerstown, MD	5
313.	Naples, FL	5
314.	Mobile, AL	5
315.	Cumberland, MD-WV	4
316.	Birmingham, AL	4
317.	Merced, CA	4
318.	Yuba City-Marysville, CA	3
319.	Fort Pierce–Port St. Lucie, FL	3
320.	Lafayette, LA	3
321.	Gadsden, AL	3
322.	Manchester, NH	2
323.	Ocala, FL	2
324.	Modesto, CA	2
325.	Dutchess County, NY	1
326.	Bremerton, WA	1
327.	Houma, LA	1
328.	Portsmouth-Rochester, NH-ME	0
329.	Riverside–San Bernardino, CA	0
330.	Oakland, CA	0
331.	Stockton-Lodi, CA	0

Leisure

Leisure rankings are determined by an assortment of recreational amenities and opportunities, including outdoor sports such as skiing, golf, and water recreation; amusements such as zoos, aquariums, and amusement parks; national parks and coastline; professional and college-level spectator sports; and shopping. Weightings are slightly higher for professional sports, national parks, coastline, inland water, and fine restaurants.

Metro Areas, Best to Poorest Leisure

RANK		SCORE		RANK		SCORE
1.	New York, NY	100		57.	Fort Lauderdale, FL	83
2.	Chicago, IL	99		58.	Portland-Vancouver, OR-WA	82
3.	Los Angeles–Long Beach, CA	99		59.	Wilmington-Newark, DE-MD	82
4.	Nassau-Suffolk, NY	99		60.	Houma, LA	82
5.	San Francisco, CA	98		61.	Fort Worth–Arlington, TX	81
6.	Seattle-Bellevue-Everett, WA	98		62.	Jacksonville, NC	81
7.	Oakland, CA	98		63.	Ventura, CA	81
8.	Bergen-Passaic, NJ	97		64.	Eugene-Springfield, OR	80
9.	Boston, MA-NH	97		65.	Kansas City, MO-KS	80
10.	Washington, DC-MD-VA-WV	97		66.	Cincinnati, OH-KY-IN	80
11.	Monmouth-Ocean, NJ	96		67.	Provo-Orem, UT	80
12.	San Diego, CA	96		68.	New London-Norwich, CT-RI	79
13.	Vallejo-Fairfield-Napa, CA	96		69.	Worcester, MA-CT	79
14.	Orange County, CA	96		70.	Lakeland–Winter Haven, FL	79
15.	Philadelphia, PA-NJ	95		71.	Brockton, MA	78
16.	Detroit, MI	95		72.	Rochester, NY	78
17.	San Jose, CA	95		73.	Lawrence, MA-NH	78
18.	Phoenix-Mesa, AZ	94		74.	Honolulu, HI	77
19.	Miami, FL	94		75.	Lowell, MA-NH	77
20.	Riverside–San Bernardino, CA	94		76.	New Bedford, MA	77
21.	Newark, NJ	93		77.	Duluth-Superior, MN-WI	76
22.	Minneapolis–St. Paul, MN-WI	93		78.	Tucson, AZ	76
23.	Baltimore, MD	93		79.	Akron, OH	76
24.	Bridgeport, CT	93		80.	Fitchburg-Leominster, MA	76
25.	Middlesex-Somerset-Hunterdon, NJ	92		81.	Danbury, CT	75
26.	Cleveland-Lorain-Elyria, OH	92		82.	Indianapolis, IN	75
27.	Santa Rosa, CA	92		83.	Allentown-Bethlehem-Easton, PA	75
28.	Denver, CO	91		84.	Reno, NV	74
29.	Atlanta, GA	91		85.	Redding, CA	74
30.	New Orleans, LA	91		86.	Melbourne–Titusville–Palm Bay, FL	74
31.	Salt Lake City–Ogden, UT	90		87.	Dayton-Springfield, OH	73
32.	Jersey City, NJ	90		88.	Colorado Springs, CO	73
33.	Tampa–St. Petersburg–Clearwater, FL	90		89.	Salinas, CA	73
34.	Sacramento, CA	90		90.	Norfolk–Virginia Beach–Newport News, VA-NC	73
35.	Dallas, TX	89		91.	Galveston–Texas City, TX	72
36.	Tacoma, WA	89		92.	Flint, MI	72
37.	Houston, TX	89		93.	Dutchess County, NY	72
38.	Orlando, FL	88		94.	Rochester, MN	71
39.	Fort Collins-Loveland, CO	88		95.	Ann Arbor, MI	71
40.	West Palm Beach–Boca Raton, FL	88		96.	Hartford, CT	71
41.	Stamford-Norwalk, CT	87		97.	Pittsfield, MA	70
42.	St. Louis, MO-IL	87		98.	Canton-Massillon, OH	70
43.	Trenton, NJ	87		99.	Fresno, CA	70
44.	Pittsburgh, PA	86		100.	Portsmouth-Rochester, NH-ME	70
45.	Boulder-Longmont, CO	86		101.	Anchorage, AK	69
46.	Providence–Fall River–Warwick, RI-MA	86		102.	Sarasota-Bradenton, FL	69
47.	Bremerton, WA	86		103.	Daytona Beach, FL	69
48.	Sheboygan, WI	85		104.	Grand Junction, CO	68
49.	Santa Barbara–Santa Maria–Lompoc, CA	85		105.	Pueblo, CO	68
50.	Milwaukee-Waukesha, WI	85		106.	Manchester, NH	68
51.	Las Vegas, NV-AZ	84		107.	Kenosha, WI	67
52.	Olympia, WA	84		108.	Santa Cruz–Watsonville, CA	67
53.	Greeley, CO	84		109.	Bloomington, IN	67
54.	Gary, IN	83		110.	Racine, WI	66
55.	Buffalo–Niagara Falls, NY	83		111.	Albuquerque, NM	66
56.	San Luis Obispo–Atascadero–Paso Robles, CA	83		112.	New Haven–Meriden, CT	66

RANK	SCORE
113. Charleston–North Charleston, SC	66
114. Charlotte–Gastonia–Rock Hill, NC-SC	65
115. Nashville, TN	65
116. Syracuse, NY	64
117. Albany–Schenectady–Troy, NY	64
118. Hamilton–Middletown, OH	64
119. Visalia–Tulare–Porterville, CA	64
120. Santa Fe, NM	63
121. Bellingham, WA	63
122. Grand Rapids–Muskegon–Holland, MI	63
123. Youngstown–Warren, OH	63
124. San Antonio, TX	62
125. Naples, FL	62
126. Yuma, AZ	61
127. Barnstable–Yarmouth, MA	61
128. Salem, OR	61
129. Punta Gorda, FL	61
130. Yolo, CA	60
131. Portland, ME	60
132. Athens, GA	60
133. Chico–Paradise, CA	60
134. Vineland–Millville–Bridgeton, NJ	59
135. Nashua, NH	59
136. Boise, ID	59
137. Atlantic City–Cape May, NJ	58
138. Lancaster, PA	58
139. Stockton–Lodi, CA	58
140. Reading, PA	57
141. Knoxville, TN	57
142. Yuba City–Marysville, CA	57
143. Springfield, MA	56
144. Brazoria, TX	56
145. Waterbury, CT	56
146. Steubenville–Weirton, OH-WV	56
147. Lafayette, IN	55
148. Greenville–Spartanburg–Anderson, SC	55
149. Glens Falls, NY	55
150. Johnstown, PA	54
151. Modesto, CA	54
152. Appleton–Oshkosh–Neenah, WI	53
153. St. Cloud, MN	53
154. Richmond–Petersburg, VA	53
155. Fort Myers–Cape Coral, FL	53
156. Hagerstown, MD	53
157. Topeka, KS	52
158. Kalamazoo–Battle Creek, MI	52
159. Pensacola, FL	52
160. Corvallis, OR	51
161. Cumberland, MD-WV	51
162. Fort Pierce–Port St. Lucie, FL	51
163. Muncie, IN	50
164. Toledo, OH	50
165. Austin–San Marcos, TX	50
166. Harrisburg–Lebanon–Carlisle, PA	50
167. Yakima, WA	49
168. Spokane, WA	49
169. Clarksville–Hopkinsville, TN-KY	49
170. Elmira, NY	48

RANK	SCORE
171. Burlington, VT	48
172. Newburgh, NY-PA	48
173. Green Bay, WI	47
174. Omaha, NE-IA	47
175. Mobile, AL	47
176. Great Falls, MT	46
177. Corpus Christi, TX	46
178. Utica–Rome, NY	46
179. Columbus, OH	46
180. Bryan–College Station, TX	45
181. Beaumont–Port Arthur, TX	45
182. Merced, CA	45
183. Lansing–East Lansing, MI	44
184. Raleigh–Durham–Chapel Hill, NC	44
185. Missoula, MT	43
186. Benton Harbor, MI	43
187. Bangor, ME	43
188. Brownsville–Harlingen–San Benito, TX	43
189. Wilmington, NC	43
190. Lafayette, LA	43
191. Saginaw–Bay City–Midland, MI	42
192. Myrtle Beach, SC	42
193. Bakersfield, CA	42
194. Billings, MT	41
195. Savannah, GA	41
196. Richland–Kennewick–Pasco, WA	40
197. Madison, WI	40
198. Louisville, KY-IN	40
199. Flagstaff, AZ-UT	40
200. Panama City, FL	40
201. Scranton–Wilkes-Barre–Hazleton, PA	39
202. Baton Rouge, LA	39
203. Lincoln, NE	38
204. Binghamton, NY	38
205. Medford–Ashland, OR	38
206. Kokomo, IN	38
207. El Paso, TX	37
208. Tulsa, OK	37
209. Little Rock–North Little Rock, AR	37
210. Oklahoma City, OK	36
211. Greenville, NC	36
212. Jackson, MI	36
213. Johnson City–Kingsport–Bristol, TN-VA	36
214. Jamestown, NY	35
215. Lynchburg, VA	35
216. Chattanooga, TN-GA	35
217. Charlottesville, VA	34
218. Fort Walton Beach, FL	34
219. Jacksonville, FL	34
220. Gainesville, FL	33
221. Greensboro–Winston-Salem–High Point, NC	33
222. Columbia, SC	33
223. Biloxi–Gulfport–Pascagoula, MS	33
224. Memphis, TN-AR-MS	32
225. Wichita, KS	32
226. Ocala, FL	32
227. Fort Wayne, IN	31
228. Mansfield, OH	31

continued

Metro Areas, Best to Poorest Leisure *(continued)*

RANK		SCORE
229.	Birmingham, AL	31
230.	Bloomington-Normal, IL	30
231.	Erie, PA	30
232.	South Bend, IN	30
233.	Fayetteville-Springdale-Rogers, AR	30
234.	Des Moines, IA	29
235.	Roanoke, VA	29
236.	Jackson, MS	29
237.	Abilene, TX	28
238.	Tuscaloosa, AL	28
239.	Asheville, NC	28
240.	Peoria-Pekin, IL	27
241.	Altoona, PA	27
242.	York, PA	27
243.	Waco, TX	26
244.	Dover, DE	26
245.	Springfield, MO	26
246.	Kankakee, IL	26
247.	Champaign-Urbana, IL	25
248.	Eau Claire, WI	25
249.	Montgomery, AL	25
250.	La Crosse, WI-MN	24
251.	Rockford, IL	24
252.	Davenport-Moline-Rock Island, IA-IL	23
253.	Lawton, OK	23
254.	Goldsboro, NC	23
255.	Las Cruces, NM	23
256.	Hickory-Morganton-Lenoir, NC	23
257.	Lubbock, TX	22
258.	Williamsport, PA	22
259.	Evansville-Henderson, IN-KY	22
260.	Decatur, IL	21
261.	Tyler, TX	21
262.	Sioux Falls, SD	20
263.	Janesville-Beloit, WI	20
264.	McAllen-Edinburg-Mission, TX	20
265.	Decatur, AL	20
266.	Enid, OK	19
267.	Terre Haute, IN	19
268.	Huntington-Ashland, WV-KY-OH	19
269.	Lexington, KY	18
270.	Wheeling, WV-OH	18
271.	Sherman-Denison, TX	18
272.	Charleston, WV	17
273.	Shreveport-Bossier City, LA	17
274.	Victoria, TX	17
275.	Fargo-Moorhead, ND-MN	16
276.	Cedar Rapids, IA	16
277.	Springfield, IL	16
278.	Longview-Marshall, TX	16
279.	Florence, AL	16

RANK		SCORE
280.	San Angelo, TX	15
281.	Rocky Mount, NC	15
282.	Tallahassee, FL	15
283.	State College, PA	14
284.	Odessa-Midland, TX	14
285.	Alexandria, LA	14
286.	Waterloo-Cedar Falls, IA	13
287.	Fort Smith, AR-OK	13
288.	Danville, VA	13
289.	Anniston, AL	13
290.	Columbia, MO	12
291.	Lima, OH	12
292.	Gadsden, AL	12
293.	Sharon, PA	11
294.	Florence, SC	10
295.	Huntsville, AL	10
296.	Killeen-Temple, TX	10
297.	Macon, GA	10
298.	Augusta-Aiken, GA-SC	10
299.	Monroe, LA	9
300.	Lake Charles, LA	9
301.	Parkersburg-Marietta, WV-OH	9
302.	Fayetteville, NC	9
303.	Dubuque, IA	8
304.	Sioux City, IA-NE	8
305.	Wausau, WI	8
306.	Iowa City, IA	7
307.	Texarkana, TX-AR	7
308.	Amarillo, TX	6
309.	St. Joseph, MO	6
310.	Wichita Falls, TX	6
311.	Joplin, MO	6
312.	Auburn-Opelika, AL	6
313.	Albany, GA	5
314.	Columbus, GA-AL	5
315.	Hattiesburg, MS	5
316.	Sumter, SC	4
317.	Elkhart-Goshen, IN	4
318.	Dothan, AL	4
319.	Grand Forks, ND-MN	3
320.	Rapid City, SD	3
321.	Cheyenne, WY	2
322.	Casper, WY	2
323.	Laredo, TX	2
324.	Lewiston-Auburn, ME	2
325.	Jonesboro, AR	1
326.	Jackson, TN	1
327.	Pocatello, ID	0
328.	Bismarck, ND	0
329.	Owensboro, KY	0
330.	Lawrence, KS	0
331.	Pine Bluff, AR	0

Arts & Culture

Arts & Culture rankings include museums, performing arts, arts media, and libraries. The highest weighting is given to the museum rating, professional performing arts such as classical music and theater, and library facilities. Somewhat lower weight is given to university arts programs and arts media.

Metro Areas, Best to Most Limited Arts & Cultural Amenities

RANK		SCORE	RANK		SCORE
1.	New York, NY	100	46.	Ann Arbor, MI	86
2.	San Francisco, CA	99	47.	Lansing–East Lansing, MI	86
3.	Boston, MA-NH	99	48.	Miami, FL	85
4.	Washington, DC-MD-VA-WV	99	49.	Lincoln, NE	85
5.	Chicago, IL	98	50.	Waterloo–Cedar Falls, IA	85
6.	Los Angeles–Long Beach, CA	98	51.	Rochester, NY	84
7.	Minneapolis–St. Paul, MN-WI	98	52.	Bloomington, IN	84
8.	Philadelphia, PA-NJ	97	53.	Omaha, NE-IA	84
9.	Pittsburgh, PA	97	54.	Salt Lake City–Ogden, UT	83
10.	Rochester, MN	97	55.	Tampa–St. Petersburg–Clearwater, FL	83
11.	Milwaukee-Waukesha, WI	96	56.	Tacoma, WA	83
12.	Buffalo–Niagara Falls, NY	96	57.	Tucson, AZ	83
13.	Kansas City, MO-KS	96	58.	Stamford-Norwalk, CT	82
14.	Cincinnati, OH-KY-IN	96	59.	Austin–San Marcos, TX	82
15.	Middlesex-Somerset-Hunterdon, NJ	95	60.	Gainesville, FL	82
16.	Denver, CO	95	61.	Bridgeport, CT	81
17.	New Haven–Meriden, CT	95	62.	New London–Norwich, CT-RI	81
18.	Newark, NJ	94	63.	Roanoke, VA	81
19.	Baltimore, MD	94	64.	New Orleans, LA	80
20.	Cleveland-Lorain-Elyria, OH	94	65.	Albuquerque, NM	80
21.	Dallas, TX	93	66.	Baton Rouge, LA	80
22.	Houston, TX	93	67.	Wichita, KS	80
23.	Sheboygan, WI	93	68.	Greenville-Spartanburg-Anderson, SC	79
24.	Albany-Schenectady-Troy, NY	93	69.	Raleigh–Durham–Chapel Hill, NC	79
25.	Seattle-Bellevue-Everett, WA	92	70.	Wheeling, WV-OH	79
26.	Trenton, NJ	92	71.	Providence–Fall River–Warwick, RI-MA	78
27.	Columbus, OH	92	72.	Muncie, IN	78
28.	Detroit, MI	91	73.	Springfield, IL	78
29.	Atlanta, GA	91	74.	Jacksonville, NC	77
30.	Madison, WI	91	75.	Flint, MI	77
31.	Honolulu, HI	90	76.	Erie, PA	77
32.	Dayton-Springfield, OH	90	77.	Akron, OH	76
33.	Richmond-Petersburg, VA	90	78.	Hamilton-Middletown, OH	76
34.	Louisville, KY-IN	90	79.	Peoria-Pekin, IL	76
35.	St. Louis, MO-IL	89	80.	Lexington, KY	76
36.	Portland-Vancouver, OR-WA	89	81.	San Jose, CA	75
37.	Hartford, CT	89	82.	Orlando, FL	75
38.	Indianapolis, IN	88	83.	Parkersburg-Marietta, WV-OH	75
39.	Springfield, MA	88	84.	Provo-Orem, UT	74
40.	Huntington-Ashland, WV-KY-OH	88	85.	Corvallis, OR	74
41.	Syracuse, NY	87	86.	Tulsa, OK	74
42.	Toledo, OH	87	87.	Anchorage, AK	73
43.	Fort Wayne, IN	87	88.	Nashville, TN	73
44.	Nassau-Suffolk, NY	86	89.	Columbia, MO	73
45.	San Diego, CA	86	90.	Charleston–North Charleston, SC	72

continued

Metro Areas, Best to Most Limited Arts & Cultural Amenities
(continued)

RANK		SCORE	RANK		SCORE
91.	Memphis, TN-AR-MS	72	145.	Binghamton, NY	56
92.	South Bend, IN	72	146.	Evansville-Henderson, IN-KY	56
93.	Duluth-Superior, MN-WI	71	147.	Beaumont-Port Arthur, TX	55
94.	Fresno, CA	71	148.	Bloomington-Normal, IL	55
95.	Las Cruces, NM	71	149.	Jackson, MS	55
96.	Sioux City, IA-NE	71	150.	West Palm Beach-Boca Raton, FL	54
97.	Norfolk-Virginia Beach-Newport News, VA-NC	70	151.	Topeka, KS	54
98.	Charlotte-Gastonia-Rock Hill, NC-SC	70	152.	Orange County, CA	53
99.	Knoxville, TN	70	153.	Pueblo, CO	53
100.	State College, PA	70	154.	Lafayette, IN	53
101.	Riverside-San Bernardino, CA	69	155.	Pensacola, FL	53
102.	Grand Rapids-Muskegon-Holland, MI	69	156.	Cedar Rapids, IA	53
103.	Corpus Christi, TX	69	157.	Hagerstown, MD	52
104.	Bergen-Passaic, NJ	68	158.	Saginaw-Bay City-Midland, MI	52
105.	Lawrence, MA-NH	68	159.	Myrtle Beach, SC	52
106.	Charleston, WV	68	160.	Oklahoma City, OK	51
107.	Sacramento, CA	67	161.	Asheville, NC	51
108.	El Paso, TX	67	162.	Montgomery, AL	51
109.	Springfield, MO	67	163.	Monmouth-Ocean, NJ	50
110.	Gary, IN	66	164.	Greeley, CO	50
111.	Boise, ID	66	165.	San Antonio, TX	50
112.	Medford-Ashland, OR	66	166.	Tallahassee, FL	50
113.	Champaign-Urbana, IL	66	167.	Jersey City, NJ	49
114.	Youngstown-Warren, OH	65	168.	Jamestown, NY	49
115.	Stockton-Lodi, CA	65	169.	Wausau, WI	49
116.	Columbia, SC	65	170.	Reno, NV	48
117.	Danbury, CT	64	171.	Green Bay, WI	48
118.	Portland, ME	64	172.	Huntsville, AL	48
119.	Killeen-Temple, TX	64	173.	Fort Pierce-Port St. Lucie, FL	47
120.	Oakland, CA	63	174.	La Crosse, WI-MN	47
121.	Allentown-Bethlehem-Easton, PA	63	175.	Yakima, WA	46
122.	Charlottesville, VA	63	176.	Bryan-College Station, TX	46
123.	Des Moines, IA	63	177.	Eau Claire, WI	46
124.	Spokane, WA	62	178.	Amarillo, TX	46
125.	Savannah, GA	62	179.	Santa Rosa, CA	45
126.	Rocky Mount, NC	62	180.	Salem, OR	45
127.	Athens, GA	61	181.	Mobile, AL	45
128.	Fargo-Moorhead, ND-MN	61	182.	Brockton, MA	44
129.	Boulder-Longmont, CO	60	183.	Fitchburg-Leominster, MA	44
130.	Las Vegas, NV-AZ	60	184.	Burlington, VT	44
131.	Goldsboro, NC	60	185.	New Bedford, MA	43
132.	Lubbock, TX	60	186.	Wilmington, NC	43
133.	Sumter, SC	60	187.	Shreveport-Bossier City, LA	43
134.	Fort Worth-Arlington, TX	59	188.	Monroe, LA	43
135.	Lowell, MA-NH	59	189.	Auburn-Opelika, AL	43
136.	Abilene, TX	59	190.	Elkhart-Goshen, IN	42
137.	Worcester, MA-CT	58	191.	Santa Cruz-Watsonville, CA	41
138.	Harrisburg-Lebanon-Carlisle, PA	58	192.	Yuma, AZ	41
139.	Birmingham, AL	58	193.	Barnstable-Yarmouth, MA	41
140.	Waterbury, CT	57	194.	Reading, PA	41
141.	Greensboro-Winston-Salem-High Point, NC	57	195.	Terre Haute, IN	41
142.	Fort Collins-Loveland, CO	56	196.	Wilmington-Newark, DE-MD	40
143.	Eugene-Springfield, OR	56	197.	Johnstown, PA	40
144.	Kalamazoo-Battle Creek, MI	56	198.	Lafayette, LA	40

RANK		SCORE
199.	Santa Fe, NM	39
200.	St. Cloud, MN	39
201.	Rockford, IL	39
202.	Columbus, GA-AL	39
203.	Vallejo-Fairfield-Napa, CA	38
204.	Altoona, PA	38
205.	Lake Charles, LA	38
206.	Colorado Springs, CO	37
207.	Daytona Beach, FL	37
208.	Scranton–Wilkes-Barre–Hazleton, PA	37
209.	Canton-Massillon, OH	36
210.	Punta Gorda, FL	36
211.	Decatur, IL	36
212.	Lima, OH	36
213.	San Luis Obispo-Atascadero-Paso Robles, CA	35
214.	Salinas, CA	35
215.	Chattanooga, TN-GA	35
216.	Santa Barbara-Santa Maria-Lompoc, CA	34
217.	Billings, MT	34
218.	Florence, AL	34
219.	Redding, CA	33
220.	Little Rock–North Little Rock, AR	33
221.	Johnson City-Kingsport-Bristol, TN-VA	33
222.	Lawton, OK	33
223.	Galveston–Texas City, TX	32
224.	Biloxi-Gulfport-Pascagoula, MS	32
225.	Albany, GA	32
226.	Yolo, CA	31
227.	Steubenville-Weirton, OH-WV	31
228.	Ocala, FL	31
229.	Lakeland–Winter Haven, FL	30
230.	Kenosha, WI	30
231.	Chico-Paradise, CA	30
232.	Bangor, ME	30
233.	Mansfield, OH	29
234.	Tuscaloosa, AL	29
235.	Dover, DE	29
236.	Melbourne-Titusville-Palm Bay, FL	28
237.	Portsmouth-Rochester, NH-ME	28
238.	Davenport–Moline–Rock Island, IA-IL	28
239.	Olympia, WA	27
240.	Manchester, NH	27
241.	Panama City, FL	27
242.	Greenville, NC	26
243.	Fayetteville-Springdale-Rogers, AR	26
244.	Longview-Marshall, TX	26
245.	Kokomo, IN	25
246.	Lynchburg, VA	25
247.	Sherman-Denison, TX	25
248.	Macon, GA	25
249.	Sarasota-Bradenton, FL	24
250.	Nashua, NH	24
251.	Alexandria, LA	24
252.	Jacksonville, FL	23
253.	Florence, SC	23
254.	Augusta-Aiken, GA-SC	23
255.	Joplin, MO	23
256.	Brazoria, TX	22

RANK		SCORE
257.	Richland-Kennewick-Pasco, WA	22
258.	Fort Lauderdale, FL	21
259.	Appleton-Oshkosh-Neenah, WI	21
260.	Sioux Falls, SD	21
261.	Jackson, TN	21
262.	Bremerton, WA	20
263.	Ventura, CA	20
264.	Atlantic City–Cape May, NJ	20
265.	Jackson, MI	20
266.	Bellingham, WA	19
267.	Waco, TX	19
268.	Fayetteville, NC	19
269.	Phoenix-Mesa, AZ	18
270.	Elmira, NY	18
271.	Missoula, MT	18
272.	Utica-Rome, NY	17
273.	York, PA	17
274.	Danville, VA	17
275.	Houma, LA	16
276.	Great Falls, MT	16
277.	Janesville-Beloit, WI	16
278.	Casper, WY	16
279.	Vineland-Millville-Bridgeton, NJ	15
280.	Dubuque, IA	15
281.	Lewiston-Auburn, ME	15
282.	Bakersfield, CA	14
283.	Anniston, AL	14
284.	Pocatello, ID	14
285.	Naples, FL	13
286.	Fort Myers–Cape Coral, FL	13
287.	Victoria, TX	13
288.	Dutchess County, NY	12
289.	Visalia-Tulare-Porterville, CA	12
290.	Gadsden, AL	12
291.	Bismarck, ND	12
292.	Clarksville-Hopkinsville, TN-KY	11
293.	Newburgh, NY-PA	11
294.	Odessa-Midland, TX	11
295.	Glens Falls, NY	10
296.	Modesto, CA	10
297.	Tyler, TX	10
298.	Decatur, AL	10
299.	Kankakee, IL	9
300.	McAllen-Edinburg-Mission, TX	9
301.	Jonesboro, AR	9
302.	Benton Harbor, MI	8
303.	Dothan, AL	8
304.	Brownsville–Harlingen–San Benito, TX	7
305.	Iowa City, IA	7
306.	Texarkana, TX-AR	7
307.	Owensboro, KY	7
308.	Williamsport, PA	6
309.	San Angelo, TX	6
310.	Wichita Falls, TX	6
311.	Cheyenne, WY	6
312.	Yuba City-Marysville, CA	5
313.	Cumberland, MD-WV	5
314.	Sharon, PA	5

continued

Metro Areas, Best to Most Limited Arts & Cultural Amenities (continued)

RANK		SCORE
315.	Grand Junction, CO	4
316.	Racine, WI	4
317.	Hickory-Morganton-Lenoir, NC	4
318.	Pittsfield, MA	3
319.	Merced, CA	3
320.	St. Joseph, MO	3
321.	Grand Forks, ND-MN	3
322.	Flagstaff, AZ-UT	2

RANK		SCORE
323.	Enid, OK	2
324.	Rapid City, SD	2
325.	Fort Smith, AR-OK	1
326.	Lawrence, KS	1
327.	Pine Bluff, AR	1
328.	Lancaster, PA	0
329.	Fort Walton Beach, FL	0
330.	Hattiesburg, MS	0
331.	Laredo, TX	0

Quality of Life

The Quality of Life rating comes from a subjective assessment determined by the authors according to their personal experience and that of selected sources. Physical attractiveness, heritage, stimulation and interest, friendliness of residents, and overall ease of living (lack of stress) figure equally into this ranking.

Metro Areas, Highest to Lowest Quality of Life

RANK		SCORE
1.	Madison, WI	99
2.	Ann Arbor, MI	99
3.	San Luis Obispo-Atascadero-Paso Robles, CA	99
4.	Santa Barbara-Santa Maria-Lompoc, CA	99
5.	Asheville, NC	98
6.	Olympia, WA	98
7.	Washington, DC-MD-VA-WV	97
8.	Boulder-Longmont, CO	97
9.	Santa Fe, NM	97
10.	Minneapolis-St. Paul, MN-WI	95
11.	Denver, CO	95
12.	San Diego, CA	95
13.	Charleston-North Charleston, SC	95
14.	Santa Rosa, CA	95
15.	Santa Cruz-Watsonville, CA	95
16.	Colorado Springs, CO	95
17.	San Francisco, CA	94
18.	Fort Collins-Loveland, CO	94
19.	Boston, MA-NH	93
20.	Seattle-Bellevue-Everett, WA	93
21.	Portland-Vancouver, OR-WA	93
22.	State College, PA	93
23.	Naples, FL	93
24.	New York, NY	92
25.	Chicago, IL	92
26.	Austin-San Marcos, TX	92
27.	Raleigh-Durham-Chapel Hill, NC	92
28.	Middlesex-Somerset-Hunterdon, NJ	91
29.	Charlottesville, VA	91

RANK		SCORE
30.	San Antonio, TX	90
31.	Burlington, VT	90
32.	Billings, MT	90
33.	Bellingham, WA	90
34.	Missoula, MT	90
35.	Albuquerque, NM	89
36.	Providence-Fall River-Warwick, RI-MA	89
37.	Monmouth-Ocean, NJ	89
38.	Salt Lake City-Ogden, UT	88
39.	Portland, ME	88
40.	Pittsburgh, PA	87
41.	Tucson, AZ	87
42.	Danbury, CT	87
43.	Corvallis, OR	86
44.	Duluth-Superior, MN-WI	86
45.	Boise, ID	86
46.	Nashua, NH	86
47.	Bremerton, WA	86
48.	Cincinnati, OH-KY-IN	84
49.	Atlanta, GA	84
50.	Provo-Orem, UT	84
51.	Savannah, GA	84
52.	Sarasota-Bradenton, FL	84
53.	Louisville, KY-IN	81
54.	Stamford-Norwalk, CT	81
55.	Des Moines, IA	81
56.	Fort Worth-Arlington, TX	81
57.	Lafayette, IN	81
58.	La Crosse, WI-MN	81

RANK		SCORE
59.	Tuscaloosa, AL	81
60.	Portsmouth-Rochester, NH-ME	81
61.	Ventura, CA	81
62.	Philadelphia, PA-NJ	79
63.	Milwaukee-Waukesha, WI	79
64.	Cleveland-Lorain-Elyria, OH	79
65.	Dallas, TX	79
66.	Honolulu, HI	79
67.	Nassau-Suffolk, NY	79
68.	Omaha, NE-IA	79
69.	Norfolk-Virginia Beach-Newport News, VA-NC	79
70.	Phoenix-Mesa, AZ	79
71.	West Palm Beach-Boca Raton, FL	78
72.	Spokane, WA	76
73.	Green Bay, WI	76
74.	Salem, OR	76
75.	Sioux Falls, SD	76
76.	Flagstaff, AZ-UT	76
77.	Lancaster, PA	76
78.	Houston, TX	75
79.	Nashville, TN	75
80.	Sacramento, CA	75
81.	Medford-Ashland, OR	75
82.	Champaign-Urbana, IL	75
83.	Auburn-Opelika, AL	75
84.	Baltimore, MD	73
85.	Tampa-St. Petersburg-Clearwater, FL	73
86.	Lexington, KY	73
87.	Bergen-Passaic, NJ	73
88.	Brockton, MA	72
89.	Chattanooga, TN-GA	72
90.	Lakeland-Winter Haven, FL	72
91.	Pocatello, ID	72
92.	Grand Junction, CO	72
93.	Buffalo-Niagara Falls, NY	68
94.	St. Louis, MO-IL	68
95.	Indianapolis, IN	68
96.	Miami, FL	68
97.	New Orleans, LA	68
98.	Anchorage, AK	68
99.	Charlotte-Gastonia-Rock Hill, NC-SC	68
100.	Lowell, MA-NH	68
101.	Worcester, MA-CT	68
102.	Eugene-Springfield, OR	68
103.	Wilmington, NC	68
104.	Vallejo-Fairfield-Napa, CA	68
105.	Mansfield, OH	68
106.	Augusta-Aiken, GA-SC	68
107.	Columbia, MO	67
108.	Manchester, NH	67
109.	Benton Harbor, MI	67
110.	Baton Rouge, LA	64
111.	Athens, GA	64
112.	Eau Claire, WI	64
113.	Columbus, GA-AL	64
114.	Dover, DE	64
115.	Melbourne-Titusville-Palm Bay, FL	64
116.	Jacksonville, FL	64

RANK		SCORE
117.	Appleton-Oshkosh-Neenah, WI	64
118.	Fort Myers-Cape Coral, FL	64
119.	Dutchess County, NY	64
120.	Kansas City, MO-KS	60
121.	Bridgeport, CT	60
122.	Tulsa, OK	60
123.	Riverside-San Bernardino, CA	60
124.	Cedar Rapids, IA	60
125.	Hagerstown, MD	60
126.	Punta Gorda, FL	60
127.	Fort Lauderdale, FL	60
128.	Atlantic City-Cape May, NJ	60
129.	Vineland-Millville-Bridgeton, NJ	60
130.	Dubuque, IA	60
131.	Lincoln, NE	58
132.	Greenville-Spartanburg-Anderson, SC	58
133.	San Jose, CA	58
134.	Columbia, SC	58
135.	Oakland, CA	58
136.	Orange County, CA	58
137.	Pueblo, CO	58
138.	Fayetteville-Springdale-Rogers, AR	58
139.	Los Angeles-Long Beach, CA	57
140.	Greenville, NC	57
141.	Sheboygan, WI	55
142.	Bloomington, IN	55
143.	Harrisburg-Lebanon-Carlisle, PA	55
144.	York, PA	55
145.	Newburgh, NY-PA	55
146.	Glens Falls, NY	55
147.	Iowa City, IA	55
148.	Lawrence, KS	55
149.	Springfield, MA	50
150.	Rochester, NY	50
151.	Roanoke, VA	50
152.	Lawrence, MA-NH	50
153.	Waterbury, CT	50
154.	Jackson, MS	50
155.	Wausau, WI	50
156.	New Bedford, MA	50
157.	Johnstown, PA	50
158.	St. Cloud, MN	50
159.	Daytona Beach, FL	50
160.	Salinas, CA	50
161.	Little Rock-North Little Rock, AR	50
162.	Johnson City-Kingsport-Bristol, TN-VA	50
163.	Biloxi-Gulfport-Pascagoula, MS	50
164.	Dayton-Springfield, OH	47
165.	Tacoma, WA	47
166.	Memphis, TN-AR-MS	47
167.	Fargo-Moorhead, ND-MN	47
168.	Evansville-Henderson, IN-KY	47
169.	Reno, NV	47
170.	Mobile, AL	47
171.	Ocala, FL	47
172.	Fayetteville, NC	47
173.	Lewiston-Auburn, ME	47
174.	Rochester, MN	46

continued

Metro Areas, Highest to Lowest Quality of Life *(continued)*

RANK		SCORE	RANK		SCORE
175.	Las Cruces, NM	46	231.	Springfield, MO	28
176.	Las Vegas, NV-AZ	46	232.	Kalamazoo-Battle Creek, MI	28
177.	Visalia-Tulare-Porterville, CA	46	233.	Fitchburg-Leominster, MA	28
178.	Albany-Schenectady-Troy, NY	42	234.	Reading, PA	28
179.	Hartford, CT	42	235.	Altoona, PA	28
180.	Jersey City, NJ	42	236.	Davenport-Moline-Rock Island, IA-IL	28
181.	Yuma, AZ	42	237.	Lynchburg, VA	28
182.	Barnstable-Yarmouth, MA	42	238.	Casper, WY	28
183.	Longview-Marshall, TX	42	239.	Detroit, MI	18
184.	Great Falls, MT	42	240.	Huntington-Ashland, WV-KY-OH	18
185.	Janesville-Beloit, WI	42	241.	Fort Wayne, IN	18
186.	Bismarck, ND	42	242.	Wheeling, WV-OH	18
187.	Tyler, TX	42	243.	Muncie, IN	18
188.	Cumberland, MD-WV	42	244.	Sioux City, IA-NE	18
189.	Pittsfield, MA	42	245.	Charleston, WV	18
190.	Rapid City, SD	42	246.	Allentown-Bethlehem-Easton, PA	18
191.	Columbus, OH	33	247.	Rocky Mount, NC	18
192.	Lansing-East Lansing, MI	33	248.	Abilene, TX	18
193.	Waterloo-Cedar Falls, IA	33	249.	Birmingham, AL	18
194.	Gainesville, FL	33	250.	Greensboro-Winston-Salem-High Point, NC	18
195.	New London-Norwich, CT-RI	33	251.	Binghamton, NY	18
196.	Hamilton-Middletown, OH	33	252.	Topeka, KS	18
197.	Peoria-Pekin, IL	33	253.	Pensacola, FL	18
198.	South Bend, IN	33	254.	Montgomery, AL	18
199.	Knoxville, TN	33	255.	Yakima, WA	18
200.	Grand Rapids-Muskegon-Holland, MI	33	256.	Terre Haute, IN	18
201.	Beaumont-Port Arthur, TX	33	257.	Lafayette, LA	18
202.	Bloomington-Normal, IL	33	258.	Lake Charles, LA	18
203.	Greeley, CO	33	259.	Canton-Massillon, OH	18
204.	Tallahassee, FL	33	260.	Kenosha, WI	18
205.	Jamestown, NY	33	261.	Jackson, TN	18
206.	Fort Pierce-Port St. Lucie, FL	33	262.	Anniston, AL	18
207.	Bryan-College Station, TX	33	263.	Jonesboro, AR	18
208.	Wilmington-Newark, DE-MD	33	264.	Dothan, AL	18
209.	Scranton-Wilkes-Barre-Hazleton, PA	33	265.	Brownsville-Harlingen-San Benito, TX	18
210.	Florence, AL	33	266.	Owensboro, KY	18
211.	Bangor, ME	33	267.	San Angelo, TX	18
212.	Macon, GA	33	268.	Sharon, PA	18
213.	Jackson, MI	33	269.	Racine, WI	18
214.	Danville, VA	33	270.	Grand Forks, ND-MN	18
215.	Clarksville-Hopkinsville, TN-KY	33	271.	Enid, OK	18
216.	Decatur, AL	33	272.	Toledo, OH	17
217.	McAllen-Edinburg-Mission, TX	33	273.	Lubbock, TX	17
218.	Williamsport, PA	33	274.	Chico-Paradise, CA	17
219.	Cheyenne, WY	33	275.	New Haven-Meriden, CT	10
220.	St. Joseph, MO	33	276.	Newark, NJ	10
221.	Richmond-Petersburg, VA	32	277.	Springfield, IL	10
222.	Orlando, FL	32	278.	Jacksonville, NC	10
223.	Fresno, CA	32	279.	Goldsboro, NC	10
224.	Saginaw-Bay City-Midland, MI	32	280.	Huntsville, AL	10
225.	Decatur, IL	32	281.	Shreveport-Bossier City, LA	10
226.	Akron, OH	31	282.	Elkhart-Goshen, IN	10
227.	Yolo, CA	31	283.	Rockford, IL	10
228.	Trenton, NJ	28	284.	Galveston-Texas City, TX	10
229.	Wichita, KS	28	285.	Kokomo, IN	10
230.	Corpus Christi, TX	28	286.	Alexandria, LA	10

RANK		SCORE
287.	Florence, SC	10
288.	Joplin, MO	10
289.	Waco, TX	10
290.	Elmira, NY	10
291.	Utica-Rome, NY	10
292.	Victoria, TX	10
293.	Kankakee, IL	10
294.	Hickory-Morganton-Lenoir, NC	10
295.	Fort Smith, AR-OK	10
296.	Fort Walton Beach, FL	10
297.	Hattiesburg, MS	10
298.	Laredo, TX	10
299.	Youngstown-Warren, OH	7
300.	Stockton-Lodi, CA	7
301.	Oklahoma City, OK	7
302.	Monroe, LA	7
303.	Brazoria, TX	7
304.	Richland-Kennewick-Pasco, WA	7
305.	Houma, LA	7
306.	Modesto, CA	7
307.	Syracuse, NY	6
308.	El Paso, TX	6

RANK		SCORE
309.	Erie, PA	2
310.	Parkersburg-Marietta, WV-OH	2
311.	Killeen-Temple, TX	2
312.	Amarillo, TX	2
313.	Lima, OH	2
314.	Redding, CA	2
315.	Albany, GA	2
316.	Steubenville-Weirton, OH-WV	2
317.	Panama City, FL	2
318.	Sherman-Denison, TX	2
319.	Bakersfield, CA	2
320.	Gadsden, AL	2
321.	Odessa-Midland, TX	2
322.	Texarkana, TX-AR	2
323.	Wichita Falls, TX	2
324.	Merced, CA	2
325.	Flint, MI	0
326.	Gary, IN	0
327.	Sumter, SC	0
328.	Myrtle Beach, SC	0
329.	Lawton, OK	0
330.	Yuba City–Marysville, CA	0
331.	Pine Bluff, AR	0

index

U.S. & Canadian Cities